France

THE ROUGH GUIDE

There are more than one hundred Rough Guide titles
covering destinations from Amsterdam to Zimbabwe

Forthcoming titles include
Dominican Republic • Jerusalem • Laos • Melbourne • Sydney

Rough Guide Reference Series
Classical Music • European Football • The Internet • Jazz
Opera • Reggae • Rock Music • World Music

Rough Guide Phrasebooks
Czech • French • German • Greek • Hindi & Urdu • Hungarian • Indonesian
Italian • Japanese • Mandarin Chinese • Mexican Spanish • Polish
Portuguese • Russian • Spanish • Thai • Turkish • Vietnamese

Rough Guides on the Internet
www.roughguides.com

ROUGH GUIDE CREDITS

Text editor: Sue Jackson
Series editor: Mark Ellingham
Editorial: Martin Dunford, Jonathan Buckley, Jo Mead, Kate Berens, Amanda Tomlin, Ann-Marie Shaw, Paul Gray, Chris Schüler, Helena Smith, Judith Bamber, Kieran Falconer, Orla Duane, Olivia Eccleshall, Ruth Blackmore, Sophie Martin, Jennifer Dempsey, Geoff Howard, Claire Saunders, Anna Sutton, Gavin Thomas, Alexander Mark Rogers (UK); Andrew Rosenberg, Andrew Taber (US)
Production: Susanne Hillen, Andy Hilliard, Link Hall, Helen Ostick, James Morris, Julia Bovis, Michelle Draycott, Cathy McElhinney

Cartography: Melissa Flack, Maxine Burke, Nichola Goodliffe, Ed Wright
Picture research: Eleanor Hill, Louise Boulton
Online editors: Alan Spicer, Kate Hands (UK); Geronimo Madrid (US)
Finance: John Fisher, Neeta Mistry, Katy Miesiaczek
Marketing & Publicity: Richard Trillo, Simon Carloss, Niki Smith, David Wearn (UK); Jean-Marie Kelly, SoRelle Braun (US)
Administration: Tania Hummel, Charlotte Marriot

ACKNOWLEDGEMENTS

The authors would like to express their gratitude for the support and assistance given by William and Stephanie Knight, Michael and Joy Alder, Rory Fox Challands, Kala and Nikki Hickman-Robertson, Dominique, Francis and Michael Taulelle, M. Jean-Claude Soum, Bernard Hartmann, Elisabeth Mielecki, Jennifer Stubbings, Laurent-Sartori, Pascal Belmas and Pascal Saint-Père. Thanks also to Cathy McElhinney for typesetting, Eleanor Hill for picture research, Maxine Burke and The Map Studio for mapping, Gillian Armstrong for proofreading, Hanry Barrkman and Andrew Rosenberg for additional research, and Lucy Leveugle for art updates.

PUBLISHING INFORMATION

This sixth edition published April 1999 by
  Rough Guides Ltd, 62–70 Shorts Gardens, London, WC2H 9AB.
Distributed by the Penguin Group:
Penguin Books Ltd, 27 Wrights Lane, London W8 5TZ
Penguin Books USA Inc., 375 Hudson Street, New York 10014, USA
Penguin Books Australia Ltd, 487 Maroondah Highway, PO Box 257, Ringwood, Victoria 3134, Australia
Penguin Books Canada Ltd, 10 Alcorn Avenue, Toronto, Ontario, Canada M4V 1E4
Penguin Books (NZ) Ltd, 182–190 Wairau Road, Auckland 10, New Zealand
Typeset in Linotron Univers and Century Old Style to an original design by Andrew Oliver.
Printed in England by Clays Ltd, St Ives PLC.
Illustrations in Part One and Part Three by Edward Briant.

Illustration on p.1 by Henry Iles; p.1053 by Jane Strother
© Rough Guides Ltd
No part of this book may be reproduced in any form without permission from the publisher except for the quotation of brief passages in reviews.
1152pp – Includes index
A catalogue record for this book is available from the British Library
ISBN 1-85828-415-5

The publishers and authors have done their best to ensure the accuracy and currency of all the information in *The Rough Guide to France*, however, they can accept no responsibility for any loss, injury, or inconvenience sustained by any traveller as a result of information or advice contained in the guide.

France

THE ROUGH GUIDE

written and researched by

Kate Baillie, Tim Salmon, Margo Daly,
Rachel Kaberry, Sheridan Humphreys,
Greg Ward, Jan Beart Albrecht,
Jan Dodd, Sarah Knight,
Claire Alder, Dave Abram and Danny Aeberhard

THE ROUGH GUIDES

We set out to do something different when the first Rough Guide was published in 1982. Mark Ellingham, just out of university, was travelling in Greece. He brought along the popular guides of the day, but found they were all lacking in some way. They were either strong on ruins and museums but went on for pages without mentioning a beach or taverna. Or they were so conscious of the need to save money that they lost sight of Greece's cultural and historical significance. Also, none of the books told him anything about Greece's contemporary life – its politics, its culture, its people, and how they lived.

So with no job in prospect, Mark decided to write his own guidebook, one which aimed to provide practical information that was second to none, detailing the best beaches and the hottest clubs and restaurants, while also giving hard-hitting accounts of every sight, both famous and obscure, and providing up-to-the-minute information on contemporary culture. It was a guide that encouraged independent travellers to find the best of Greece, and was a great success, getting shortlisted for the Thomas Cook travel guide award,

and encouraging Mark, along with three friends, to expand the series.

The Rough Guide list grew rapidly and the letters flooded in, indicating a much broader readership than had been anticipated, but one which uniformly appreciated the Rough Guide mix of practical detail and humour, irreverence and enthusiasm. Things haven't changed. The same four friends who began the series are still the caretakers of the Rough Guide mission today: to provide the most reliable, up-to-date and entertaining information to independent-minded travellers of all ages, on all budgets.

We now publish more than 100 titles and have offices in London and New York. The travel guides are written and researched by a dedicated team of more than 100 authors, based in Britain, Europe, the USA and Australia. We have also created a unique series of phrasebooks to accompany the travel series, along with an acclaimed series of music guides, and a best-selling pocket guide to the Internet and World Wide Web. We also publish comprehensive travel information on our web site:

www.roughguides.com

READERS' LETTERS

The following people wrote in with useful comments and contributions to the last edition. Thanks to you all and please keep writing!

Tim Whelan, Yaron Sheffer, Cliff Dalzell, Tony Ward, Les Holloway, Daniel Mee, Nick Makepeace, Peter Goldsmith, Charles Sulochi, Simon Tombs, Clare West, Nick Turner, Edna Patterden, Sally and David Turner, Helen and Roger Barber, Derek Reid, John Law, J. Le Breton, Alex Engleman, Mrs D.E. Honey, Janet Lyke, Emma and Paul Dry, Phil Rippon, Mrs K Williams, Richard Flint, James Conquil, Mike Gerrard, Katharine Cowan, Joel Anderson, T. Simpkins, Maria Corden, Philip Rush, Claire Post, Linda Pinc, Ann Christian, Mrs A. Brain, K. Butterfield, Eric Carlson, Soonjung Hahn, Bernadette Fallon, Mark Johnson, Paul Mousley, Ben Norland, BC Stroude, D. Palme, E. Werenowska, Stephen Miller, Edward Green, Madeleine Simon, Paul Hardy, John Shakespeare, Demond and Sheila Parkes, Julie Harper, Andrew Park, George New, Richard Smith, Molly Rowe, Pam Williams, Claudia Alexander, Lorraine Osborne, Roz Bond, H. Clarke, Dave Fairhurst, Jane Hebden, Robert Tresidden, Mrs Corrine Beighton, Trevor Hales, Kate Collison, Trevor Brockway, Judith Rivers, Mrs and Mrs P. Frankish, P. Hitch, Neal McCall, John Lewis, Susan Morris, Malcolm and Judy Bridges, Garry and Michelle Ayres, Paul Bristow, Zoë Bremer, Amanda Grubb.

HELP US UPDATE

We've gone to a lot of effort to ensure that this new edition of *The Rough Guide to France* is accurate and up-to-date. However, things change – places get "discovered", opening hours are notoriously fickle, restaurants and rooms raise prices or lower standards. If you feel we've got it wrong or left something out, we'd like to know, and if you can remember the address, the price, the time, the phone number, so much the better.

We'll credit all contributions, and send a copy of the next edition (or any other Rough Guide if you prefer) for the best letters. Please mark letters: "Rough Guide France Update" and send to:
Rough Guides, 62–70 Shorts Gardens, London WC2H 9AB, or Rough Guides, 375 Hudson St, 9th floor, New York NY 10014.
Or send email to: mail@roughguides.co.uk
Online updates about this book can be found on Rough Guides' Web site at www.roughguides.com

CONTENTS

• CHAPTER 14: THE RHÔNE VALLEY AND PROVENCE 849–925

• CHAPTER 15: THE CÔTE D'AZUR 926–996

• CHAPTER 16: CORSICA 997–1051

PART THREE CONTEXTS 1053

LIST OF MAPS

MAP SYMBOLS

----	Chapter division boundary	✕	Airport
▬▬▪▬▪▬	International boundary	◉	Youth Hostel
▪▪ ▬▬	Regional boundary	△	Campground
═══	Road	⌂	Refuge
▬▬▬	Pedestrianised streets	—	Fortified wall
⊞⊞⊞⊞	Steps	♯	Fort
▬▪▬	Railway	⌒	Cave
▬▬▬	River	∴	Ruin
⌣⌣⌣⌣	Canal	⌂	Monastery
— —	Ferry route	🏛	Château
------	Footpath	(*i*)	Information office
⌇	Lighthouse	⊠	Post office
⌂	Rock outcrop	⊞	Hospital
▲	Mountain peak	♦	Museum
⌂⌂	Mountain range	▮	Building
⋀⋀⋀	Cutting	✚	Church
⌒	View point	▨	Park
◆	Point of interest	▨	National Park
P	Parking	⊹	Cemetery
ⓡ	RER station	▨	Beach
Ⓜ	Metro station		

INTRODUCTION

T he sheer physical diversity of France would be hard to exhaust in a lifetime of visits. The landscapes range from the fretted coasts of Brittany to the limestone hills of Provence, the canyons of the Pyrenees and the half-moon bays of Corsica, from the lushly wooded valleys of the Dordogne to the glaciated peaks of the Alps. Each **region** looks and feels different, has its own style of architecture, its characteristic food, and often its own patois or dialect. Though the French word *pays* is the term for a whole country, local people frequently refer to their own immediate vicinity as *mon pays* – my country – and to a person from another town as a foreigner. This strong sense of regional identity, often expressed in the form of active separatist movements as in Brittany and Corsica, has persisted over centuries in the teeth of centralized administrative control from Paris.

Perhaps the most striking feature of the French **countryside** is the sense of space. There are huge tracts of woodland and undeveloped land without a house in sight. Industrialization came relatively late, and the country remains very rural. Away from the main urban centres, hundreds of towns and villages have changed only slowly and organically, their old houses and streets intact, as much a part of the natural landscape as the rivers, hills and fields.

The nation's legacy of history and culture is so widely dispersed across the land that even if you were to confine your travelling to one particular region you would still have a powerful sense of the past without having to seek out major sights. With its wealth of local detail, France is an ideal country for dawdling; there is always something to catch the eye and gratify the senses, whether you're meandering down a lane, picnicking by a slow, green river, or sipping Pernod in a village café. There is also endless scope for all kinds of **outdoor activities**, from walking, canoeing and cycling to the more expensive pleasures of skiing and sailing.

If you need more urban stimuli to activate the pleasure buds – clubs, shops, fashion, movies, music, hanging out with the beautiful and famous – then the great **cities** provide them in abundance. Paris, of course, is an outstanding cultural centre, with its stunning contemporary buildings and atmospheric back streets, its art and its ethnic diversity. And the great provincial cities like Lille and Lyon, Bordeaux, Toulouse, Marseille and Nice vie with the capital and each other, like the city states of old, for prestige in the arts, ascendancy in sport and innovation in urban transport.

For a thousand years and more, France has been at the cutting edge of **European development**, and the legacy of this wealth, energy and experience is everywhere evident in the astonishing variety of things to see: from the Gothic cathedrals of the north to the Romanesque churches of the centre and west, the châteaux of the Loire, the Roman monuments of the south, the ruined castles of the English and the Cathars and

---

THE EURO

France is one of eleven countries who have opted to join the European Monetary Union and, from January 1, 1999, is beginning to phase in the single European currency, the euro. Initially, however, it will only be possible to make paper transactions in the new currency (if you have, for example, a euro bank or credit-card account), and the franc will remain the normal unit of currency. Euro notes and coins are scheduled to be issued at the beginning of 2002, and to replace the franc entirely by the end of that year.

the Dordogne's prehistoric cave-paintings. If not all the legacy is so tangible – the literature, music and ideas of the 1789 Revolution, for example – much has been recuperated and illustrated in museums and galleries across the nation, from colonial history to fishing techniques, aeroplane design to textiles, migrant shepherds to manicure, battlefields and coalmines.

Many of the **museums** are models of clarity and modern design. Among those that the French do best are museums devoted to local arts, crafts and customs like the Musée des Arts et Traditions Populaires in Paris and the Musée Dauphinois in Grenoble. But inevitably first place must go to the fabulous collections of fine art, many of which are in **Paris**, for the simple reason that the city has nurtured so many of the finest creative artists of the last hundred years, both French, Monet and Matisse for example, and foreign, such as Picasso and Van Gogh.

If you are quite untroubled by a need to improve your mind in the contemplation of old stones and works of art, France is equally well endowed to satisfy the grosser appetites. The French have made a high art of daily life: eating, drinking, dressing, moving and simply being. The **pleasures of the palate** run from the simplest picnic of crusty baguette, ham and cheese washed down by an inexpensive red wine through what must be the most elaborate take-away food in the world, available from practically every *charcuterie*; such basic regional dishes as *cassoulet*; the liver-destroying riches of Périgord and Burgundy cuisine; the fruits of the sea; extravagant pastries and ice cream cakes; to the trance-inducing refinements – and prices – of the great chefs. And there are wines to match, at all prices, and not just from the renowned vineyards of Bordeaux, Burgundy and Champagne. If you feel inadequate in the face of all this choice, never be afraid to ask advice, for most French people are true devotees, ever ready to explain the arcane mysteries to the uninitiated.

The people
Visual appearance is important to the French. No effort is too great to make things look good: witness the food shops in even the poorest neighbourhoods of a city, always sparkling clean and beautifully displayed. The people too take pride in looking neat and sharp; they inspect others and expect to be looked at. Life is theatre, lived much more in the public eye – especially in the warm Mediterranean south – than in Anglo-Saxon societies. And for the visitor it's a free and entertaining spectacle.

The French are extremely courteous with each other – it's not unusual for someone entering a restaurant to say "Good evening" to the entire company – and rather formal in their manners. At the same time, if they want something, they may be quite direct in ways that are disconcerting for Anglo-Saxons brought up in the belief that it's improper to state clearly what you mean or feel. If you are feeling self-conscious about coping with the language, this can seem like rudeness: it isn't. If you observe the formalities and make an effort to communicate, you'll find the French as friendly and interested as anyone else.

As for their reputed arrogance, the French are certainly proud of their culture, something that is reinforced by the education system. Artists and thinkers are held in high esteem in France and their opinions are listened to. Even prime ministers tend to be literate, and are often accomplished authors. But in a world dominated by commercial values and, in addition, the English language, the French (not unnaturally, for their language was once the *lingua franca* of the educated) feel this culture is under threat.

Where to go and when
France is easy to travel around. Restaurants and hotels proliferate, and the lower-budget ones are much cheaper than in most other developed western European countries. Train services are admirably efficient, as is the road network, especially the (toll-paying) autoroutes, and cyclists are much admired and encouraged. Information is highly

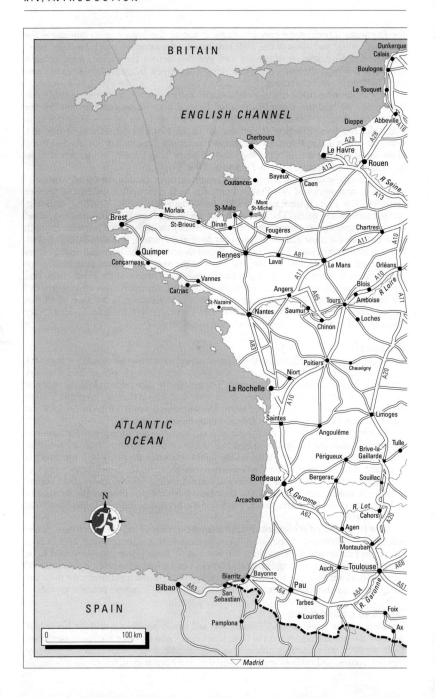

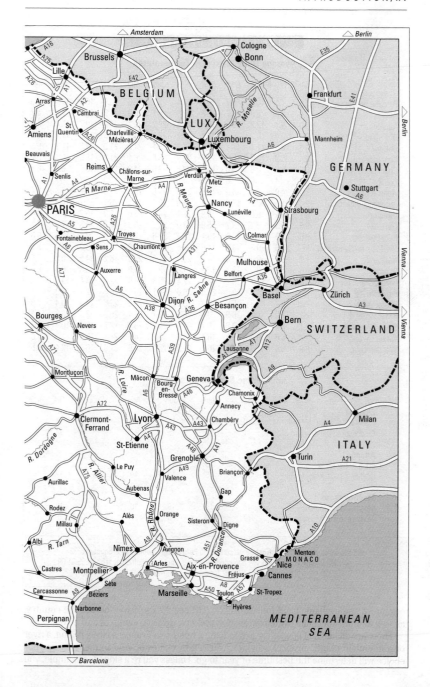

THE CLIMATE OF FRANCE

Average Daily Maximum Temperatures

	Jan	Feb	March	April	May	June	July	Aug	Sept	Oct	Nov	Dec
Paris/Île de France	7.5	7.1	10.2	15.7	16.6	23.4	25.1	25.6	20.9	16.5	11.7	7.8
Alsace	5.5	5.3	9.3	13.7	15.8	23.0	24.1	26.3	21.2	14.9	7.6	4.7
Aquitaine	10.0	9.4	12.2	19.5	18.0	23.7	27.2	25.7	24.2	19.7	15.4	11.0
Auvergne	8.0	6.4	10.1	15.9	17.1	24.2	27.0	24.5	23.3	17.0	11.0	8.3
Brittany	9.3	8.6	11.1	17.1	16.0	22.7	25.1	24.2	21.2	16.5	12.1	9.3
Burgundy	6.1	5.9	10.3	15.3	15.8	23.8	25.8	26.1	21.2	15.5	9.1	6.2
Champagne-Ardenne	6.2	5.6	8.9	13.8	15.1	22.5	23.8	24.9	19.3	15.0	9.6	6.2
Corsica	13	14	16	18	21	25	27	28	26	22	17	14
Franche-Comté	5.4	4.8	9.8	14.6	15.5	23.0	25.0	26.5	21.8	15.2	9.6	5.8
Languedoc-Roussillon	12.4	11.5	12.5	17.6	20.1	26.5	28.4	28.1	26.1	21.0	15.8	13.5
Limousin	6.1	6.1	9.6	16.1	14.9	22.1	24.8	23.6	21.0	16.2	12.8	8.5
Lorraine	5.5	5.3	9.3	13.7	15.8	23.0	24.1	26.3	21.2	14.9	7.6	4.7
Midi-Pyrénées	10.0	9.0	12.3	18.3	19.1	26.4	27.6	27.2	25.0	19.3	15.5	9.8
Nord/Pas de Calais	6.6	5.6	8.3	13.7	14.9	21.5	22.7	24.0	19.3	15.3	8.3	6.9
Normandy	7.6	6.4	8.4	13.0	14.0	20.0	21.6	22.0	18.2	14.5	10.8	7.9
Picardy	6.6	5.6	8.3	13.7	14.9	21.5	22.7	24.0	19.3	15.3	8.3	6.9
Poitou-Charentes	10.0	8.7	11.7	18.2	16.4	22.4	25.3	24.6	22.0	18.4	14.0	9.8
Provence	12.2	11.9	14.2	18.5	20.8	26.6	28.1	28.4	25.2	22.1	16.8	14.1
Rhône Valley	7.4	6.7	10.8	15.8	17.3	25.6	27.6	27.6	23.5	16.5	10.4	7.8
Riviera/Côte d'Azur	12.2	11.9	14.2	18.5	20.8	26.6	28.1	28.4	25.2	22.2	16.8	14.1
Savoy/ Dauphiny Alps	3.1	3.7	7.9	13.8	15.7	22.4	26.8	25.7	22.7	15.9	10.7	6.3
Val de Loire	7.8	6.8	10.3	16.1	16.4	23.6	25.8	24.5	21.1	16.2	11.2	7.0
Western Loire	9.9	8.6	11.3	17.7	16.7	23.3	25.7	24.6	21.8	16.9	12.4	9.5

Average Sea Temperatures

	May	June	July	Aug	Sept	Oct
Channel						
Calais to Le Havre	10	13	16	17	16	14
Cherbourg to Brest	11	13	15	17	16	14
Atlantic						
Brest to Bordeaux	13	15	17	18	17	15
Bordeaux to St-Jean-de-Luz	14	15	18	19	19	17
Mediterranean						
Montpellier to Toulon	15	19	19	20	20	17
Île de Levant to Menton	17	19	20	22	22	19

All temperatures are in **Centigrade**: to convert to **Fahrenheit** multiply by 9/5 and add 32.
For a recorded **weather forecast** you can phone the Paris forecasting office at ☎01.45.55.91.09
(☎01.45.55.95.02 for specific inquiries).

organized and available from tourist offices (Offices de Tourisme) across the country, as well as from specialist organizations for walkers, cyclists, campers and so on.

There are all kinds of pegs on which to hang a holiday in France: a city, a region, a river or a mountain range, physical activities, cathedrals, châteaux. And in many cases your choice will determine the best time of year to go. Unless you're a skier, for example, you wouldn't choose the mountains between November and May; nor at this time would you head for the seaside – except for the Mediterranean coast which is at its most attractive in spring. Climate, otherwise, need not be a major consideration in planning when to go. Northern France, like nearby Britain, is wet and unpredictable. Paris perhaps has a marginally better climate than New York, rarely reaching the extremes of heat and cold of that city, but only south of the Loire does the weather become significantly warmer. West coast weather, even in the south, is tempered by the proximity of the Atlantic, subject to violent storms and close thundery days even in summer. The centre and east, as you leave the coasts behind, have a more continental climate, with colder winters and hotter summers. The most reliable weather is along and behind the Mediterranean and on Corsica, where winter is short and summer long and hot.

The single most important factor in deciding when to visit France is tourism itself. As most French people take their holidays in their own country, it's as well to avoid the main French holiday periods – mid-July to the end of August, with August being particularly bad. Almost the entire country closes down, except for the tourist industry itself. You can easily walk half a mile and more in Paris, for example, in search of an open boulangerie, and the city seems deserted by all except fellow tourists. Prices in the resorts rise to take full advantage and you can't find a room for love nor money, and not even a space in the campsites on the Côte d'Azur. The seaside is the worst, but the mountains and popular regions like the Dordogne are not far behind. Easter, too, is a bad time for Paris; half Europe's schoolchildren seem to descend on the city. For the same reasons, ski buffs should keep in mind the February school ski break. And no one who values life, limb, and sanity should ever be caught on the roads the last weekend of July or August, and least of all on the weekend of August 15.

PART ONE

THE
BASICS

GETTING THERE FROM BRITAIN

The quickest way of reaching France from Britain is, of course, by air, though it is now rivalled closely by the Channel Tunnel London–Paris rail link, which makes the 340-kilometre journey in just three hours. The standard rail- or road-and-sea routes are significantly more affordable, but can be uncomfortable and tiring – and if you're just going for a short break, the journey time can significantly eat into your holiday.

BY AIR

If your destination is other than Paris, where the entire journey takes about the same time as by Eurostar, flying can represent a considerable saving in time compared to other methods of getting there. Nice, Toulouse and Lyon, for example, are just ninety minutes from London. As often as not, if you live outside London, you'll find it pays to go to the capital and fly on to France from there. The cheapest fares are generally on the London–Paris route. Prices are highly competitive with those of Eurostar and can cost as little as £75 even with the big airlines; you should add on at least £85 to fly to a regional airport such as Nice, and another £125 to fly into Corsica. Direct flights from British regional airports do exist, and are detailed below: prices are not unfavourable compared with London fares. To find the best deals you should shop around, ideally a month or so before you plan to leave.

Air France, British Airways, Britair and British Midland are the main carriers to France from Britain, offering **scheduled flights** and APEX (Advance Purchase Excursion) fares which must be reserved one or two weeks in advance (depending on the route taken), and must include one Saturday night. Your return date must be fixed when purchasing, and no subsequent changes are allowed. The new low-cost no-frills airlines which also offer scheduled flights to France are Debonair, EasyJet, Ryanair and KLM UK; there are no advance purchase conditions with these airlines but obviously the earlier you book your seat the greater chance you have of taking advantage of special offers and availability. Alternatively, you can take the London–Paris leg of a long-haul flight to more distant destinations with airlines such as MAS (Malaysian) or PIA (Pakistan International) – STA Travel (see below) are specialists in this. The snapshot fare prices we have quoted below include airport taxes of between £12 to £20.

Air France fly to Paris Charles de Gaulle (abbreviated as Paris CDG) five to nine times daily from Heathrow, four flights daily Monday–Friday from London City airport, and daily from Manchester, Birmingham, Edinburgh and Glasgow. From Heathrow there is at least one flight a day direct to Lyon, Nice and Toulouse. Flights to Corsica with Air France – into Ajaccio, Bastia or Calvi – involve a change in Paris, including a swop from Paris CDG to Paris Orly. **British Airways** fly to Paris CDG five times daily from Gatwick; from Heathrow seven times daily to Paris CDG and six times daily to Orly. BA also fly directly to Paris CDG from Newcastle (2 daily), Birmingham (3–5 daily), Manchester (2-5 daily), Glasgow (Mon–Sat 1–2 daily), Aberdeen (2–3 daily) and Edinburgh (2–3 daily). To regional destinations in France, BA offer three flights daily from Gatwick to Bordeaux, Lyon, Marseille and Toulouse, one flight daily from Gatwick to Montpellier, one flight weekly from Gatwick to Perpignan and one flight daily from Birmingham to Lyon. From Heathrow, BA schedule four flights daily to Nice. **Britair** focuses on destinations in Brittany and Normandy, flying from Gatwick to Brest, Nantes and Rennes, Caen (except Aug), Le Havre and Deauville (Aug only) with prices from around £135; they also have a service to Paris from Southampton (2 daily; cheapest APEX ticket from £115). **British Midland** fly to Paris CDG from Heathrow (6-7 daily; £155) and directly from Leeds-Bradford (1–3 daily; fares from £99) and East Midlands (1–4 daily), and to Nice twice daily from Heathrow and twice weekly from East Midlands (£199).

The trend for low-cost airlines with scheduled flights offering direct sales means even cheaper flights are available, though not generally from Gatwick or Heathrow, and don't expect things like meals either. **Debonair** and **EasyJet** both fly from London Luton airport to Nice, (respectively 2 daily and 3–4 daily) for around £130 return while **Ryanair** fly from Stansted to St Etienne (2 daily)

and Carcasonne (1 daily). **KLM UK** fly from Stansted to Paris four times daily (from £75); as the airline operates from virtually all British airports to a variety of destinations, regional passengers can get through flights via Amsterdam or Stansted to Paris; a flight from Edinburgh to Paris, for example (with a 1hr 45min wait in Amsterdam and 2hr 30min flying time), costs around £152.

If you shop around, you can often come up with a cheaper flight. A good place to look for **discount fares** from London to France is the classified travel sections of papers like the Saturday

AIRLINES AND AGENTS

AIRLINES

Air France, 10 Warwick St, 1st Floor, London W1R 5RA (☎0181/742 6600; www.airfrance.fr).

Britair, 239 Longbridge House, Gatwick Airport, West Sussex, Crawley RH6 (reservations via Air France ☎0181/742 6600).

British Airways, 156 Regent St, London W1R 5TA (☎0345/222 111; www.britishairways.com).

British Midland, Donington Hall, Castle Donington, Derby DE74 2SB (☎0345/554 554; www.iflybritishmidland.com).

Debonair, 146 Prospect Way, London Luton Airport, Luton, Beds LU2 9BA (direct sales ☎01582/634300; www.debonair-airways.com).

EasyJet, London Luton Airport, Luton, Beds LU2 9LS (direct sales ☎01582/702 900; www.easyjet.com).

KLM UK (direct sales ☎0990/074 074; www.airuk.co.uk).

Ryanair (direct sales ☎0541/569 569, bookings through any branch of Going Places, or via e-mail on info@ryanair.ie).

TRAVEL AGENTS

Campus Travel, 52 Grosvenor Gardens, London SW1W 0AG (☎0171/730 3402); and branches in Birmingham (☎0121/414 1848); Brighton (☎01273/570 226); Bristol (☎0117/929 2494; Cambridge (☎01223/324 283); Edinburgh (☎0131/668 3303); Glasgow (☎0141/5531818); Manchester (☎0161/833 2046); Oxford (☎01865/242 067). Student/youth travel specialists, with branches also in YHA shops and on university campuses all over Britain. www.campustravel.co.uk.

Thomas Cook, Head office: 45 Berkeley St, London W1X 5AE and high streets across London and the UK (nationwide ☎0990/666 222; Flights Direct ☎0990/101 520). Long established one-stop travel agency for package holidays or scheduled flights, with bureau de change (issuing Thomas Cook travellers cheques), own travel insurance and car rental. www.tch.thomascook.com.

Council Travel, 28a Poland St, London W1V 3DB (☎0171/437 7767). Flights and student discounts. Specialize in student/youth travel. www.ciee.org.

Masterfare, 19–21 Connaught St, London W2 (☎0171/262 0599). Discount agent with competitive deals.

Nouvelles Frontières, 2–3 Woodstock St, London W1R 1HE (☎0171/629 7772). French agency. Most charters go via Paris.www.nouvelles-frontieres.com.

STA Travel, 86 Old Brompton Rd, London SW7 3LH, 117 Euston Rd, London NW1 2SX, 38 Store St, London WC1E 7BZ and 11 Goodge St, London W1P 2SX (☎0171/361 6161). There are also branches in Manchester (☎0161/834 0668); Leeds (☎0113/244 9212); Bristol (☎0117/929 4399); Cambridge (☎01223/366 966); Newcastle-upon-Tyne (☎0191/233 2111); Oxford (☎01865/792 800); Glasgow (☎0141/338 6000), and on university campuses throughout Britain. Worldwide specialists in low-cost flights and tours for students and under-26s. Also offices abroad. www.statravel.co.uk.

Trailfinders, 215 Kensington High St, London W6 6BD (☎0171/937 5400); and in Birmingham (☎0121/236 1234); Bristol (☎0117/929 9000); Manchester M3 (☎0161/839 6969); Glasgow (☎0141/353 2224). One of the best-informed and most efficient agents for independent travellers. www.trailfinders.com

FRENCH PACKAGE TOUR OPERATORS & VILLA AGENCIES

Allez France (☎01903/742345). Self-drive and fly-drive accommodation packages (cottages, villas, hotels and caravans) to various French destinations.

Bike Tours (☎01225/310859; www.biketours. co.uk). Biking trips to France.

Brittany Ferries (☎0990/360 360; www.brittany-ferries.com). Emphasis on self-catering, ferry-drive holidays: mobile homes, gîtes, holiday homes and hotels.

British Airways Holidays (☎0870/2424245). Good for city-break flights from regional airports.

Corsican Affair (☎0171/385 8438). Fly-drive, hotel packages and self-catering.

Dominique's Villas (☎0171/738 8772). Small, upmarket agency with a diverse and tempting range of mostly older properties (some quite historic) in the Loire, Dordogne, Provence and on the Côte d'Azur. Most are for large groups, sleeping six to eight or more.

Gîtes de France Ltd (Chambres d'Hôte). The UK operations of this French Government letting service was taken over in 1997 by Brittany Ferries (enquiries in Britain ☎0990/360 360; in Ireland ☎021/277 801) although you can still deal directly with Gîtes de France, 59 rue St-Lazare, Paris 75009 (Mon–Sat 10am–6.30pm; ☎01.48.70.75.75). Houses, cottages and chalets all over France from as little as £126 for one week; ferry crossing extra.

Keycamp Holidays (☎0181/395 4000). Mobile homes and tents. Twelve days in the south of France from £669 for two adults and up to four children in high season, including ferry or Eurotunnel.

Martin Randall Travel, 10 Barley Mow Passage, London W4 4PH (☎0181/742 3355; info@martin-randall.co.uk). Small-group cultural tours led by experts on art, architecture, archeology or music. Tours range from opera in Paris and Lyon (£1190 seven-day tour includes four operas, transport, accommodation and some meals) to Romanesque Burgundy (eight days costs £1040).

Paris Travel Service (☎01992/456 000). Good for regional flights and rail deals via London. Wide range of packages; eg £187 Eurostar and three nights' basic accommodation, or £173 with flight from Manchester.

Plas y Brenin National Mountain Centre (☎01690/720 214; www.pyb.co.uk). Springtime ski-mountaineering courses in the Alps, including parts of the High Level Route. A six-day course, not including accommodation or food (though these are organised), or transport from the UK, costs £425.

Sally Short Break Holidays (☎0181/427 4445). Ferry for car and two adults plus two-star hotel in central Paris from £142 per person for 5 nights' accommodation.

Susie Madron's Cycling for Softies (☎0161/248 8282). An easy-going cycle holiday operator to most regions, including Provence. Seven-day tours (excluding flights), with accommodation in family-owned hotels, breakfast and dinner, bike, panniers and emergency backup (not luggage transfer) for around £598 per person.

Time Off (☎0990/846363 or 0345/336622). Short breaks to Paris by air or Eurostar (and Orient Express packages) in comfortable central accommodation. Two nights in a one-star hotel, travelling by Eurostar, from £151. Flight and accommodation packages to Nice from £345 for seven nights.

Travelscene Ltd (☎0181/427 4445). Short breaks to Disneyland Paris or Northern France, travelling by air or Eurostar or self-drive via Eurotunnel or ferry.

Vacances en Campagne (☎01798/869 411). Self-catering accommodation all over France and Corsica – from apartments and cottages to large manor houses. High standards, careful information and not cheap, but good value for money.

VFB Holidays (☎01242/240 300). Good-value self-catering, ferry and road holidays, plus alpine resorts in the Midi, Alsace and Burgundy and fly-drive holidays to Corsica and city-breaks in Nice, Paris and Lille. Their brochure has a huge range of well-detailed cottages, farmhouses and villas to choose from.

Voyages Ilena (☎0171/924 4440). Classy hotels and self-catering accommodation all over Corsica; flights and fly-drives, too.

editions of the *Independent* and the *Daily Telegraph*, and Sundays like the *Observer*, *Sunday Times* and *Independent on Sunday*, where agents advertise special deals; if you're in London, check the back pages of the listings magazine *Time Out*, the *Evening Standard* or the free travel mag *TNT*, found outside main-line train stations. Independent travel specialists STA Travel and Campus Travel do deals for students and anyone under 26, or can simply sell a scheduled ticket at a discount price – as can Nouvelles Frontières. All these are worth contacting to see what deals they currently have on offer, whether these involve seats on their own or a tour operator's **charter flight** – in theory this is supposed to be sold in conjunction with accommodation, but it is sometimes possible just to buy the air ticket at a discount through your travel agent. Bear in mind that any travel agent can sell you a **package deal** with a tour operator (see below) and these can often offer exceptional bargain travel.

STUDENT/YOUTH FLIGHTS

STA Travel offers flights to various cities for which any person under 26 is eligible; the various airlines all have different policies on discounts for full-time students who are over 26 – British Airways, for example, allows discounts for students under 34. Current return price to Paris (Charles de Gaulle) is £80. Campus Travel student/youth charter returns to Paris start at £78 with British Midland, but you need to arrive and depart mid-week. Both organizations also offer limited special offers. Air France do a special-deal flight pass within Europe for students called the European Hip Hop Skytrekker Airpass which can be used solely to hop about France (32 destinations); you must purchase a miniumum of four fare sectors which cost between £52 and £77 (maximum of eight allowed). A sample route, costing £260 would be London–Toulouse–Lyon–Brest–Paris–London.

PACKAGE TOURS

Any travel agent will be able to provide details of the many operators running **package tours** to France (see box above), which can work out to be a competitively priced way of travelling. Some are straightforward travel-plus-beach-hotel affairs, which provide a fixed base, whereas others offer city breaks, tandem touring, air-and-rail packages or stays in country cottages. If your trip is geared around specific interests – like cycling or self-catering in the countryside – packages can work out much cheaper than the same arrangements made on arrival. A package will also include flights and accommodation plus often transfers to and from your hotel or a rental car, which can leave you more time to enjoy your holiday if you're on a tight schedule.

In addition to the addresses in the box, bear in mind that most of the ferry companies (see p.7 for telephone numbers) also offer their own travel and accommodation deals. The **French Holiday Service** at the French Travel Centre, 178 Piccadilly, London W1V 0AL (☎0171/355 4747) can book the largest range of package holidays in France, including most of those listed in the box below. More complete lists of package operators are available from the **French Government Tourist Office**, also at 178 Piccadilly, London W1V 0AL (☎0891/244 123).

BY TRAIN

The **Channel Tunnel** has slashed travelling time by train from London to Lille and Paris and has also led to a multitude of cut-rate deals on regular train and ferry or hovercraft fares via Calais, Boulogne or Dieppe.

EUROSTAR

Eurostar operate high-speed passenger trains daily from London Waterloo to the continent via Ashford in Kent (itself 1 hr from London) and the Channel Tunnel. There are at least fifteen services daily to Paris Gare du Nord (3hr) with extra services on weekdays, at least three stopping daily at Calais-Fréthun (1hr 30min) and one daily at Lille (2hr), and a separate direct train to Disneyland Paris (one daily summer and school holidays, one daily weekends only in winter; 3hr). The service to Brussels (at least 8 daily) also stops in Lille. There is also a ski-season only direct service from Waterloo/Ashford to the French Alps (Moutiers-Salins and Bourg-St-Maurice; one weekly, outbound and inbound Sat am Dec–April; 7hr); skis are carried free.

Expensive first-class **fares**, aimed at business travellers, include meals. Standard Class return fares to Paris range from £79 (weekend day-trip) to £220, but frequently advertised special offers can go as low as £59. Besides such offers, and day-trips, the cheapest ticket to Paris is the 'Excursion', a return ticket which can be purchased up to 30min before departure and must include a Saturday night, with fixed outward and return dates and no refunds; it's usually less than £99. However, excursion tickets are limited, and you'll have a greater chance of getting one if you book at least a week or more in advance. A more realistic average price for a high-season ticket with changeable departure and return times, bought close to your departure date, is £115. Return fares to Disneyland Paris range from £89 to £149 for adults, and your kids

FERRY ROUTES AND PRICES

Route	Operator	Crossing Time	Frequency	One-Way Fares Small car 2 adults	Foot passengers
BRITTANY					
Portsmouth–St-Malo	*Brittany Ferries*	9hr	March-Nov 2 daily	£81–157	£18–32
Plymouth–Roscoff	*Brittany Ferries*	6hr	1–12 weekly	£74–141	£31–57
Weymouth–St-Malo	*Condor Ferries*	4hr 20min	May to mid-Oct 1 daily	£155–170	£25
NORMANDY					
Newhaven-Dieppe	*P&O Stena Line*	4hr	2 daily	£59–£135	£24
Newhaven-Dieppe	*P&O Stena Line*	2hr 15min	2–3 daily	£59–£135	£24
CHERBOURG					
Portsmouth–Cherbourg	*P&O European Ferries*	5hr–7hr15min	1–3 daily	£77–137	£15–30
Portsmouth–Cherbourg	*P&O European Ferries*	2hr 45min	mid-May to Oct 2–3 daily	£77–137	£15–30
Poole–Cherbourg	*Brittany Ferries*	4hr 30min	1–2 daily	£70–135	£16–28
Portsmouth–Caen	*Brittany Ferries*	6hr	1–3 daily	£70–135	£16–28
Portsmouth–Le Havre	*P&O European Ferries*	5hr 45min– 7hr 45min	2–3 daily	£77–137	£15–30
PAS-DE-CALAIS					
Folkestone–Boulogne	*Hoverspeed‡*	55min	4 daily	£70–94	£25
Dover–Calais	*P&O Stena Line*	1hr 30min	30 daily	£62–110	£24
Dover–Calais	*Sea France*	1hr 30min	15 daily	£73–95	£11
Dover–Calais	*Hoverspeed‡‡*	35–50min	11–17 daily	£77–105	£25
BELGIUM					
Hull–Zeebrugge	*P&O North Sea Ferries*	14hr	1 daily	£94–115	£36–45

Relevant ferry companies in Britain

Brittany Ferries	☎0990/360360.	*Ship
Condor Ferries	☎01305/761551.	*Elite Fastcraft
Hoverspeed ☎0990/240241 or 0990/595522.		*Superstar Express
‡*Seacat high-speed catamaran.*	**P&O North Sea Ferries**	☎01482/377177.
‡‡*Hovercraft and Seacat.*	**P&O Stena Line**	☎0990/980980.
P&O European Ferries ☎0990/980555.	**Sea France**	☎0990/711711.

will set you back each £54 if they're aged 4–11, and £79 if they're any older. There are concessions for those under 26 (student discounted tickets are only available from STA, Campus Travel and Wasteels, not directly from Eurostar), over 60, or for holders of an international rail pass. A standard return on the Eurostar Ski train is £199 (with a less flexible Ski Saver tickets for £149 return). Tickets to

Lille are generally at least £10 cheaper than those to Paris in the same category.

Tickets can be bought directly over the phone from Eurostar (see number overleaf), from most travel agents, from all main rail stations in Britain or through **SNCF** (Société Nationale des Chemins de Fer – the French railway) in London, from the Waterloo International and Ashford ticket office, and the new Eurostar shop. You can get through-ticketing – including the tube journey to Waterloo International – if you travel on GNER or Virgin train services from Manchester and Edinburgh, or on the Alphaline Rail Service from South Wales, Avon and West Wiltshire for around an extra £30. There is still no sign of the promised direct high-speed Eurostar services from the north of England, Scotland and the Midlands.

The Eurostar can be used to make fast and affordable train connections to other parts of France, particularly from Lille where you can connect at the same station with the high-speed TGV network to Lyon, Bordeaux, Nice and Cannes. For example, you can travel from London to Lille (2hr) and change for the TGV to Bordeaux (5hr).

RAIL AND SEA

Crossing the Channel **by sea** works out slightly cheaper than using the Channel Tunnel, but takes considerably longer and is obviously less convenient unless you live down south. You can catch one of the many trains from London Victoria which connect with cross-Channel ferries or hovercrafts, with an onward train service on the other side. However, the **Hoverspeed SeaTrain Express** is now the only packaged-up combined train/sea ticket to Paris available. Trains depart once daily from London Charing Cross at 8.55am for Folkestone, connecting with a highspeed Seacat to Boulogne, with another train connection to Paris Gare du Nord, arriving at 5.17pm. Tickets cost £44 one way or £59 return (no youth price available); return tickets last up to two months.

TRAIN PASSES

If you plan to use the rail network to get around France, there are several **train passes** you might consider buying.

The **Eurodomino Freedom pass**, available from the International Rail Centre at London Victoria, or from Rail Europe (SNCF), Wasteels or Eurotrain offers unlimited rail travel through France for any three (£105), five (£145) or ten (£220) days within a calendar month; passengers under 26 pay £85, £115 and £185 respectively. A child (4–11 yrs) fare is half the adult price. The pass also entitles you to reductions on rail/ferry links to France.

InterRail passes cover eight European "zones" and are available for either 22-day or one-month periods; you must have been resident in Europe for at least six months before you can buy the pass. The passes for those over 26 have now been extended to cover the same territory as for those under 26 and the only difference now is the price. France is in the zone including Belgium, the Netherlands and Luxembourg. A 22-day pass to travel this area is £159/229, a two-zone pass valid for a month is £209/279, a three-zone, £229/309 and an all-zones £259/349. The pass is available from the same outlets as the Eurodomino (see above) and STA Travel. InterRail passes do not include travel between Britain and the continent, although InterRail Pass holders are eligible for discounts on rail travel in Britain and Northern Ireland and cross-Channel ferries.

The InterRail pass and the Eurodomino Freedom Pass give a discount on the London–Paris Eurostar service.

USEFUL TRAIN AND BUS ADDRESSES

Eurotrain, Campus Travel, 52 Grosvenor Gardens, London SW1W 0AG (☎0171/730 3402).

Eurolines, 52 Grosvenor Gardens, London SW1 (bookings and enquiries ☎0990/143219 or Luton ☎01582/404511; www.eurolines.co.uk). Tickets can also be purchased from any National Express agent (☎0990/808080).

Eurostar, Waterloo International Station, London SE1 8SE; Ashford International Terminal, Kent; Eurostar ticket office, 102–104 Victoria St, London SW1 (Mon–Fri 9am–5.30pm, Sat 9am–3.45pm; reservations ☎0990/186 186).

Eurotunnel, Customer Services Centre (☎0990/353535).

Hoverspeed SeaTrain Express (bookings ☎0990/240 241).

International Rail Centre, Victoria Station, London SW1V 1JY (European information line ☎0990/848 848).

NIR Travel, 28–30 Great Victoria Street Station, Belfast 2 (☎01232/230 671). InterRail agents.

Rail Europe, 179 Piccadilly, London W1V (☎0990/848 848).

Wasteels, Platform 2, Victoria Station, London SW1V 1JY (☎0171/834 7066).

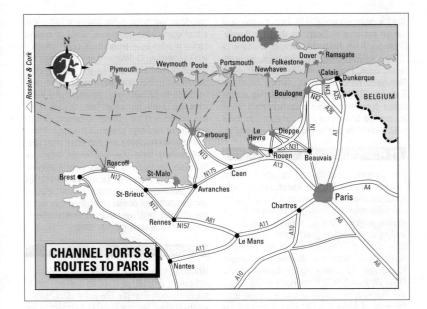

CHANNEL PORTS & ROUTES TO PARIS

Rosslare & Cork

BY BUS

Eurolines run regular bus/ferry services from Victoria to over sixty French cities. Prices are very much lower than for the same journey by train, with adult return fares in July and August and around Christmas currently at £49 for Paris, £45 for Lille, £98 for Lyon, £109 for Bordeaux, and £126 for Toulouse; off-peak fares are around £5 to £10 cheaper. Reginal return fares from England and Wales are available as are student and youth discounts. Prices are very much lower than for the same journey by train. As well as ordinary tickets on its scheduled coach services to an extensive list of European cities, Eurolines offers a pass for Europe-wide travel, for either 30 days (over 26 £199; youth pass £159) or 60 days (over 26 £249; youth pass £199). **Tickets** are available from the company direct, from National Express agents or from most high-street travel agents.

BY CAR AND TRAIN

The most convenient way of taking your car across to France is to drive down to the **Channel Tunnel**, load your car on the train shuttle, and be whisked under the Channel in 35 minutes, emerging at Sangatte on the French side, just outside Calais.

The Channel Tunnel entrance is off the M20 at junction 11A, just outside Folkestone, and the sole operator, **Eurotunnel**, offers a continuous service with with up to four departures per hour (only 1 per hour midnight–6am; 24hr recorded departure info ☎0891/555566, 50p per min). Because of the frequency of the service, you don't have to buy a ticket in advance (though this might be advisable in mid-summer or during school holidays; in any case you must arrive at least 25 minutes before departure); the target loading time is just ten minutes. Inside the carriages, you can get out of your car to stretch your legs during the crossing. Tickets are available through Eurotunnel's Customer Service Centre or from your local travel agent. Fares are calculated per car, regardless of the number of passengers. Rates depend on the time of year, time of day and length of stay (the cheapest ticket is for a day-trip, followed by a five-day return); it's cheaper to travel between 10pm and 6am, while the highest fares are reserved for weekend departures and returns in July and August. As an example, a five-day trip at an off-peak time starts at £95 (passengers included) in the low season and goes up to £135 in the peak period.

If you don't want to drive far when you've reached France, you can take advantage of

SNCF's motorail (☎0990/848 848), putting your car on the train in Calais for Avignon, Biarritz, Bordeaux, Brive, Narbonne, Nice, or Toulouse, or in Paris for Avignon, Biarritz, Bordeaux, Briancon, Brive, Evian, Frejus, Lyon, Marseille, Moutiers, Narbonne, Nice, St-Gervais, Tarbes, Toulon or Toulouse. This is a relatively expensive option: Calais–Nice, for example, costs from £546 return for car and driver, plus £102 for each additional adult and £51 for children aged between 4 and 11.

BY FERRY/HOVERCRAFT

The cheapest cross-Channel options for most travellers are the **ferry** or **hovercraft** (or high-speed catamaran) links between Dover and Calais and Folkestone and Boulogne. However, if your starting point is further west than London, it may well be worth heading direct to one of the south-coast ports and catching one of the ferries to Normandy or Brittany – Newhaven to Dieppe, Portsmouth to Cherbourg/Le Havre/Caen/St Malo; Weymouth to St Malo; Poole to Cherbourg; and Plymouth to Roscoff. If you're coming from the north of England or Scotland, opting for the Hull–Zeebrugge (Belgium) crossing overnight with North Sea Ferries makes a lot of sense.

Ferry prices are seasonal and, for **motorists**, depend on the size of your vehicle. The popular Dover–Calais routing costs just over £62 one-way for a car and two adults in low season, but cheaper deals are regularly available. Return prices are substantially cheaper than one-way fares, but generally need to be booked in advance – details of routes, companies and cur-

rent fares are given in the box on p.7. You can either contact the companies direct to reserve space in advance – essential in peak season if you're intending to drive – or any travel agent in the UK or France will do it for you. All ferry companies also offer **foot passenger** fares only, from £15 to £25 one-way; accompanying **bicycles** can usually be carried free, at least in the low season, and for a charge of around £5 one-way in mid- and high seasons.

The ferry companies will also often offer **special deals** on three-, five- and ten-day returns, or discounts for regular users who own a property abroad. The tour operator **Eurodrive** (☎0181/324 4000) can also arrange discounts on ferry crossings and the shuttle for people taking their cars across the Channel, and can book accommodation in northern France at competitive rates.

HITCHING

Hitching from Calais or Boulogne to Paris is notoriously difficult, so you'd be well advised to accept through-lifts only. The worst black holes – where hitchers become invisible to drivers – are Abbeville and Beauvais, and if you can possibly afford one of the cheaper bus or train tickets, you'll save yourself a lot of trouble. If not, get friendly with drivers on the boat over and try to get a promise of a lift before docking. Dieppe is not that much easier to hitch from. From Caen's port – Ouistreham – you can get a cheap local bus to the city if your thumb fails you. It may well be worth contacting the **ride-share organization** Allostop Provoya; see p.37 for information.

GETTING THERE FROM IRELAND

If you want to fly directly to France from Dublin or Belfast you'll be limited by the choice available, and will have to fly into Paris or catch a routing through London or Amsterdam. There are no direct flights from Ireland to Corsica.

In the **Irish Republic**, Aer Lingus fly direct from **Cork and Dublin** to Paris CDG (respectively once and five times daily) with a few seats at £129 return and a standard fare of £199. Ryanair offer three flights daily from Dublin to Beauvais Tillé airport outside Paris for £97.50. Budget Travel organizes charter flights from Dublin to

Nice for £199 (May to mid-Oct), while Go Holidays arranges them (April to Sept) from Shannon, Cork and Dublin to Nantes, Toulouse, Montpelier, Marseille, Lyon, Paris and Nice, from £179 return. Alternatives via Britain are unlikely to be attractive considering the additional time factor and the cost of a flight from Dublin to Britain. For up-to-date details, contact USIT, specialists in student/youth travel, or Trailfinders (see box on p.12).

In **Northern Ireland**, British Airways fly directly from Belfast City Airport to Paris CDG. Otherwise, a routing through London or Amsterdam is the best option. The Paris Travel Service (☎01992/456 000), based just outside London, has package deals including flights from Belfast.

BY CAR AND FERRY

The cheapest way of getting to France – though far from the quickest – is by **ferry** from Cork or Rosslare outside Wexford to the various ports in Normandy or Brittany.

Ferry **prices** vary according to season and, for motorists, the size of their car; note that return prices are substantially cheaper but generally need to be booked in advance. Brittany Ferries prices vary from around £95 to £260 for a small

FERRY ROUTES AND PRICES					
Route	**Operator**	**Crossing Time**	**Frequency**	**One-Way Fares** Small car 2 adults (IR£)	Foot passenger (IR£)
Cork–Roscoff	Brittany Ferries	14hr	April–Oct	£95–260 1 weekly	£30–60
Rosslare–Cherbourg	Irish Ferries	17.5hr	all year 1–2 weekly	£99–275	£75
Rosslare–Roscoff	Irish Ferries	15hr	May–Sept every 2nd day	£99–275	£75

Addresses in Ireland

Brittany Ferries, 42 Grand Parade, Cork (☎021/277 801).

Irish Ferries, 2–4 Merrion Row, Dublin (☎01/661 0511); Cork (☎021/551 995).

car and two adults one-way; foot passengers will pay between £30 and £60. With Irish Ferries, the corresponding rates are £99–275 and £75. Often ferry companies will offer special deals on return fares for a specified period, so check first.

You can either contact the companies direct to reserve space in advance (essential at peak season if you're driving), or any competent travel agent at home can do it for you. Details of routes, companies and fares are given in the box above.

USEFUL ADDRESSES IN IRELAND

AIRLINES

Aer Lingus, 40 O'Connell St, Dublin (☎01/844 4777); 46 Castle St, Belfast BT1 (☎0645/737 747); 2 Academy St, Cork (☎021/327 155); 136 O'Connell St, Limerick (☎061/474 239). *www.aerlingus.ie*

British Airways, 60 Dawson St, Dublin (☎1800/626 747); 9 Fountain Centre, College St, Belfast (☎0345/222 111). *www.british-airways.com*

Ryanair, Phoenix House, Conyngham Rd, Dublin 8 (☎01/609 7800, flight information ☎1550/200 200 – 58p per min).

DISCOUNT FLIGHT AGENTS

Budget Travel, 134 Lower Baggot St, Dublin (☎01/661 1866).

Joe Walsh Tours, 8–11 Baggot St, Dublin (☎01/876 3053); 31 Castle St, Belfast (☎01232/241 144). Discounted flight agent.

Thomas Cook, 11 Donegall Place, Belfast (☎01232/554 455); 118 Grafton St, Dublin (☎01/677 1721). Package holiday and flight agent who can also arrange travellers cheques, insurance and car hire.

Trailfinders, 4 Dawson St, Dublin 2 (☎01/677 7888). Comprehensive flight and travel agent with deals on hotels, insurance, tours and car rental.

USIT, Aston Quay, O'Connell Bridge, Dublin (☎01/679 8833); Fountain Centre, College St, Belfast (☎01232/324 073); 33 Ferryquay St, Derry (☎01504/371 888); 10–11 Market Parade, Patrick St, Cork (☎021/270 900); Victoria Place, Eyre Square, Galway (☎091/565177); 36–37 George St, Waterford (☎051/872601); also branches in Athlone, Coleraine, Jordanstown and Maynoth. Student and youth specialists. *www.usit.ie*

TOUR OPERATORS

Go Holidays, 28 North Great George St, Dublin 1 (☎01/874 4126). French holiday specialists City breaks to Paris - a special five-night deal from £199 including flight and B&B in a central hotel; tours and transfers can be added on. Also Disneyland Paris packages, charter flights to regional destinations and Paris, fly-drive packages, resorts and apartments.

Irish Ferries, 2–4 Merrion Row, Dublin (☎01/661 0511). Self-drive self-catering package holidays –

camping, mobile homes, apartments – to all coastal regions of France. A typical six-night package, including taking your car on the ferry and an apartment, costs IR £450–550 for two people.

Neenan Travel, 12 South Leinster St, Dublin 2 (☎01/676 5181; email *con@neenantrav.ie*). Their Breakaway Tours department offers packages to Paris and Disneyland Paris; a five-day flight and accommodation package to Paris from £249 per person.

GETTING THERE FROM NORTH AMERICA

Getting to France from North America is straightforward; there are direct flights from over thirty major cities to Paris (the only transatlantic gateway in France), with connections from all over the continent. Nearly a dozen different scheduled airlines operate flights, making Paris one of the cheapest destinations in Europe. If France is part of a longer European trip, a Eurail train pass may be a useful option (see box on p.16).

SHOPPING FOR TICKETS

Barring special offers, the cheapest fare is usually an **Apex** ticket, although this will carry certain restrictions: you have to book – and pay – at least 21 days before departure, spend at least seven days abroad (maximum stay three months), and you tend to get penalized if you change your schedule. On transatlantic routes there are also winter **Super Apex** tickets, sometimes known as "Eurosavers" – slightly cheaper than an ordinary Apex, but limiting your stay to between 7 and 21 days. Some airlines also issue **Special Apex** tickets to people younger than 24, often extending the maximum stay to a year. Many airlines offer youth or student fares to **under-25s**; a passport or driving licence are sufficient proof of age, though these tickets are subject to availability and can have eccentric booking conditions. It's worth remembering that most cheap return fares involve spending at least one Saturday night away and that many will only give a percentage refund if you need to cancel or alter your journey, so make sure you check the restrictions carefully before buying a ticket.

You can normally cut costs further by going through a specialist flight agent – either a **consolidator**, who buys up blocks of tickets from the airlines and sells them at a discount, or a **discount agent**, who deals in blocks of tickets offloaded by the airlines, and often offers special student and youth fares and a range of other travel-related services such as travel insurance, rail passes, car rental, tours and the like. Bear in mind, though, that penalties for changing your plans can be stiff, and that these companies make their money by dealing in bulk – don't expect them to answer lots of questions. Some agents specialize in **charter flights**, which may be cheaper than anything available on a scheduled flight, but again departure dates are fixed and withdrawal penalties are high (check the refund policy). If you travel a lot, **discount travel clubs** are another option – the annual membership fee may be worth it for benefits such as cut-price air tickets and car rental.

A further possibility is to see if you can arrange a **courier flight**, although the hit-or-miss nature of these makes them most suitable for a single traveller who travels light and has a very flexible schedule. In return for shepherding a parcel through customs and possibly giving up your baggage allowance, you can expect to get a deeply discounted ticket. For more options, consult *Courier Bargains: How to Travel Worldwide for Next to Nothing* by Kelly Monaghan ($17.50 postpaid from The Intrepid Traveler, PO Box 438, New York, NY 10034). Flights are issued on a first-come, first-served basis, and there's no guarantee that the Paris route will be available at the time you want. Round-trip fares cost from around $350 round trip, with last-minute specials as low as $150 for flights booked within three days of departure.

Don't automatically assume that tickets purchased through a travel specialist will be cheapest – once you get a quote, check with the airlines and you may turn up an even better deal. Be advised also that the pool of travel companies is swimming with sharks – exercise caution and never deal with a company that demands cash up front or refuses to accept payment by credit card.

Note that fares are heavily dependent on **season**, and are highest from around early June to the end of August; they drop during the "shoulder" seasons, September–October and

AGENTS AND TOUR OPERATORS IN NORTH AMERICA

AIRLINES

Air Canada (☎1-800/776 3000; in Canada ☎1-800/555-1212 for information).
Air France (☎1-800/237 2747; in Canada ☎1-800/667 2747).
American Airlines (☎1-800/433 7300).
AOM French Airlines (☎1-310/338 9613).
British Airways (☎1-800/247 9297).
Canadian Airlines (☎1-800/426-7000; in Canada (☎1-800/665-1177).

Continental Airlines (☎1-800/231 0856).
Delta Airlines (☎1-800/241 4141).
Iceland Air (☎1-800/223-5500).
Northwest Airlines (☎1-800/225 2525).
Tower Air (☎1-800/221 2500).
TWA (☎1-800/982 4141).
United Airlines (☎1-800-538 2929).
US Air (☎1-800/622 1015).
Virgin Atlantic Airways (☎1-800/862 8621).

DISCOUNT TRAVEL COMPANIES

Air Brokers International (☎1-800/883 3273). Consolidator.
Air Courier Association (☎303/279 3600). Courier-flight broker.
Airhitch (☎212/864 2000). Standby-seat broker: For a set price, they guarantee to get you on a flight as close to your preferred destination as possible, within a week.
American Airlines Fly Away Vacations (☎1-800/321-2121). Package tours, fly-drive programmes.
Back Door Travel (☎425/771 8303). Off-the-beaten path, small-group travel with budget travel guru Rick Steves and his enthusiastic guides. Twenty-one-day "Slow Dance through France Tour", $3100; 14-day tours of East or West France, $2150.
British Airways Holidays (☎1-800/359 8722). Package tours.
Cosmos Tourama (☎1-800/221-0090). Travel club.
Council Travel (☎1-800/226 8624). Nationwide US student travel organization with branches (among others) in New York, San Francisco, Washington DC, Boston, Austin, Seattle, Chicago, Minneapolis.
Delta Dream Vacations (☎1-800/872 7786). Packages, escorted tours, fly-drive programmes.
Educational Travel Center (☎1-800/747 5551). Student/youth discount agent.
Flight Centre (☎1-604/739 9539). Discount air fares from Canadian cities.
France Vacations (☎1-800/332 5332). Air/hotel packages through AOM French Airlines.
High Adventure Travel Inc (☎1-800/428 8735). Travel company with a highly recommended Web site: *http://www.highadv.com*.
Holidaze Ski Tours (☎1-800/526 2827). Ski specialist.
Interworld Travel (☎305/443 4929). Consolidator.
Last Minute Travel Club (☎1-800/LAST MIN). Travel club specializing in standby deals.

Lifelong Learning Inc (☎1-800/854 4080). Small adventure cruises with stops in Corsica.
New Frontiers/Nouvelles Frontières (☎1-800/366 6387 or ☎514/526 8444). French discount-travel firm; also markets charters to Paris and Lyon. Branches in New York, Montréal, Los Angeles, San Francisco and Québec City.
Now Voyager (☎212/431 1616). Agent specializing in courier flights.
REI Adventures (☎1-800/622 2236). Hiking trips in France. Nine-day hiking trip in Provence, $1395. Nine-day hiking trip in Dordogne, $1395.
Saga International Holidays (☎1-800/432 1432). Specialist in group travel for 50s plus.
STA Travel (☎1-800/777 0112). Worldwide specialist in independent travel with branches in the Los Angeles, San Francisco and Boston areas. STA also has French branches in Paris and Grenoble.
TFI Tours International (☎1-800/745 8000). Consolidator; offices in New York, Las Vegas, San Francisco, Los Angeles.
Travac (☎1-800/872 8800). Consolidator and charter broker; branches in New York and Orlando.
Travel Avenue (☎1-800/333 3335). Discount travel agent.
Travel Cuts (☎416/979 2406). Canadian specialist student travel organization with branches all over the country.
Travel Savings Club (☎1-800/444 9800). Discount travel club.
Travelers Advantage (☎1-800/548 1116). Discount travel club.
Unitravel (☎1-800/325 2222). Consolidator.
Vantage Travel (☎1-800/322 6677). Specialist in group travel for seniors.
Worldtek Travel (☎1-800/243 1723). Discount travel agency.
Worldwide Adventures (☎1-800/387 1483). Adventure holidays.

April–May, and you'll get the best deals during the low season, November through March (excluding Christmas). Note that Friday, Saturday and Sunday travel tends to carry a premium, and that one-way fares are generally slightly more than half the round-trip.

If you have a specific destination in mind in France outside Paris and you're in a hurry – and if you're prepared to pay extra – it's possible to be ticketed straight through to any of more than a dozen **regional airports**. Most of these entail connecting flights on Air Inter, Air France's domestic arm, and require a change of planes in Paris (check to make sure there's no inconvenient transfer between Charles de Gaulle and Orly). Some sample round-trip add-on fares from Paris are: Bordeaux $110; Brest $125; Grenoble $125; Lyon $110; Marseille $160; Nice $160; Strasbourg $110; Toulouse $140.

FLIGHTS FROM THE USA

Transatlantic fares to France from the USA are very reasonable, thanks to intense competition. Any local travel agent should be able to access airlines' up-to-the-minute fares, although they may not have time to research all the possibilities, and you could call the airlines direct. The lowest discounted scheduled fares you're likely to get in low and high season flying midweek to Paris are $473/900 from Chicago, $500/814 from Houston, $575/947 from Los Angeles, $395/757 from New York and $490/767 from Washington DC.

Most airlines use Paris as the transatlantic gateway to France. Some charter carriers offer non-stop flights to Nice, Marseille and Lyon in late spring to early autumn. In addition, Air France has regular scheduled non-stop services into Nice from New York. Nearly a dozen different scheduled

TOUR OPERATORS IN NORTH AMERICA

Abercrombie & Kent (☎1-800/323 7308). Walking tours, barge and canal trips all over France. A walking tour in Burgundy with barge accommodation is $1990.

Adventure Center (☎1-800/227 8747). Small-group hiking or cycling tours in France and Corsica. Thirteen-day "Cycling in the Loire Valley" costs $1000; fifteen-day Hiking in Provence, $670.

Adventures on Skis (☎1-800/628 9655). Skiing and sport packages from $745.

AESU Travel (☎1-800/638 7640). Riviera packages, tours, independent city stays and discount air fares for under-35s.

Backroads (☎1-800/462 2848). Trendy hiking tours. A six-day trip in Bourgogne, Dordogne or the Basque country is $2600.

Butterfield & Robinson (☎1-800/678 1147). Biking and walking trips all over France. An eight-day bike tour of Alsace wine villages costs $3950.

CBT Bicycle Tours (☎1-800/736 BIKE). Bike tours throughout France from $110 to $125 per day, some starting or ending in Paris.

Contiki Tours (☎1-800/CONTIKI). Budget tours to Europe for under-35s. A fourteen-day tour of France costs $1800 including airfare from NY.

Cosmos Tourama/Globus (☎1-800/221 0090). Group tours and city breaks; Cosmos has the budget trips.

EC Tours (☎1-800/388 0877). City tours and tours of regions like Normandy, the Loire and the French Riviera.

ETT Tours (☎1-800/551 2085). Independent travel with some possibilities for group tours.

Euro-Bike Tours (☎1-800/321 6060). Luxury bike tours in Provence, Brittany, Normandy and the Loire. $2095 for a seven-day tour of Burgundy. $3095 for a fourteen-day tour of Brittany, Normandy and the Loire valley.

The French Experience (☎1-800/28 FRANCE). Self-drive tours, apartment and cottage rentals, air-fare arrangements. A three-day Château Country tour in Brittany or the Loire Valley, including car costs $419.

Himalayan Travel (☎1-800/225 2380). Trekking and cycling in the French and Corsican interior. $1150 for an seven-day self-guided bike trip around Alsace.

International Study Tours (☎1-800/833 2111). Theme tours such as "Collectibles for the Inquisitive Mind" cost between $3000 and $4000. Nine to ten night river cruises on the Rhone and barge trips for $2000-$3000. Land only.

Mountain Travel-Sobek (☎1-800/227 2384). Hiking in Haute Savoie and Provence. A nine-day hiking trip in Provence is $2390. The "Mont Blanc" circuit, a thirteen day hike through France, Italy and Switzerland around Mont Blanc is $2390.

Vacances en Campagne (☎1-800/327 6097). Short-term rentals of châteaux and country houses in France and Corsica.

NORTH AMERICAN AND AUSTRALASIAN EUROPEAN RAIL PASSES

There are a number of European rail passes that can only be purchased before leaving home, though consider carefully how much travelling you are going to be doing: these all-encompassing passes only really begin to pay for themselves if you intend to see a fair bit of France and the rest of the Europe.

The best-known and most flexible is the **Eurail Youthpass** (for under-26s), which costs US$376 for fifteen days, and there are also one-month and two-month versions; if you're 26 or over you'll have to buy a first-class **Eurail** pass, which costs US$538 for the fifteen-day option. You stand a better chance of getting your money's worth out of a **Eurail Flexipass**, which is good for a certain number of travel days in a two-month period. This, too, comes in under-26/first-class versions: ten days for under-26s costs US$444, for over-26s US$634; and for fifteen days US$585 and US$836.

A scaled-down version of the Flexipass, the **Europass** allows travel in France, Germany, Italy, Switzerland and Spain for US$366 and US$580 for ten days in two months, on up to $516 and $746 for fifteen days in two months; there are also cheaper three- and four-country combinations, as well as the option of adding adjacent "associate" countries. A further alternative is to attempt to buy an **InterRail Pass** in Europe (see "Getting there from Britain", p.8) – most agents don't check residential qualifications, but once you're in Europe it'll be too late to buy a Eurail pass if you have problems. You can purchase Eurail passes from one of the agents listed below.

North Americans and Australasians are also eligible to purchase **more specific passes** valid for travel in France only (see "Getting around", p.31, for details).

Rail contacts in North America

CIT Tours, 342 Madison Ave, Suite 207, New York, NY 10173 (☎1-800/223 7987). Eurail passes only.

Rail Europe, 226 Westchester Ave, White Plains, NY 10604 (☎1-800/438 7245). Official Eurail pass agent in North America; also sells the widest

range of European regional and individual country passes.

ScanTours, 1535 6th St, Suite 205, Santa Monica, CA 90401 (☎1-800/223 7226). Eurail and other European country passes.

---

airlines operate flights to Paris. **Air France** has the most frequent and convenient service, but fares tend to be on the expensive side. Other airlines offering non-stop services to Paris from a variety of US cities are United, daily from Chicago, San Francisco and Washington DC; Delta, daily from Cincinnati, Atlanta and New York; TWA daily from New York and three times a week from St Louis. AOM French Airlines offers non-stop service to Paris from Los Angeles three to five times a week, depending on the season. For the best fares, check the ads in Sunday newspaper travel sections and book with a discount agent or consolidator. It's also worth considering charter flights, which operate from late spring to early autumn. New Frontiers, a Canadian discount travel agency, has summer non-stop charters from Los Angeles to Paris on Corsair from $800 round-trip.

FLIGHTS FROM CANADA

The strong links between France and Québec's Francophone community ensure regular air services from **Canada to Paris**. The main route is

Vancouver–Toronto–Montréal–Paris Charles de Gaulle, although most departures originate in Toronto.

Air France and Air Canada offer non-stop services to Paris from the major Canadian cities. There are also some excellent charter deals. Canada 3000/Fiesta West is a good source of information. The lowest discounted scheduled fares for midweek travel to Paris will be around CDN$825/1249 from Montréal, CDN$825/1249 from Toronto, and CDN$1115/1639 from Vancouver and CDN$1003/1353 from Halifax on Iceland Air.

PACKAGE TOURS

Hundreds of tour operators specialize in travel to France, and many can put together very **flexible deals**, sometimes amounting to no more than a flight plus car or train pass and accommodation. If you're planning to travel in moderate or luxury style, and especially if your trip is geared around special interests, such packages can work out cheaper than the same arrangements made on arrival. A tour is inevitably more confining than independent travel, but it can help you make the most of time if you're on a tight schedule; a tour can also ensure a worry-free first few days of a trip, and time to find your feet.

Of greater interest are the package tour operators that help you explore the country's unique points: many organize walking or cycling trips through the countryside, boat trips along canals, and any number of theme tours based around history, art, wine and so on. The box on p.15 mentions a few of the possibilities, and a travel agent will be able to point out others. (Remember: bookings made through a travel agent cost no more than going through the tour operator.)

Many **airlines** have reasonably priced packages including round-trip air fare, hotel, some sightseeing tours and, in the case of fly-drive

packages, a rental car. Delta offers a seven-day fly-drive package to Paris starting at $628 for New York departures. British Airways has a seven-day Paris tour starting at $772, including transatlantic air fare via London, hotels and sightseeing. American offers a seven-day England–France fly-drive package, including Channel Tunnel crossing, from $800. A seven-day eastern France fly-drive programme via Paris Orly starts at $478. American also has a variety of hotel/sightseeing packages (air fare from the US not included), such as a seven-day Nice/Paris package for $673 and a seven-day Nice/French Riviera package for $452, with optional extensions for Monaco and Cannes. American also offers "Paris stopovers", starting at $52 per person for one night's hotel and breakfast.

GETTING THERE FROM AUSTRALIA & NEW ZEALAND

Many people travelling to France from Australia and New Zealand will choose to travel via London, although there are direct flights to Paris. There are also alternative stopover points in Europe, often available at economical fares. Fares to France vary according to the season and the carrier. In general, low season lasts from mid- January to the end of February, and from October 1 to the middle of November; high season is the second half of May, from the beginning of June to the end of August, and from the beginning of December to mid-January. Seasonal fare increases are A/NZ$200–400.

FROM AUSTRALIA

The only direct flights to France from **Australia** are to Paris, but internal add-on flights are "common rated" to the same price. **Discount** agents should be able to get you at least ten percent off the following low-season published fares to Paris. Conditions may apply to the following, such as booking three months in advance: Alitalia/Qantas (Milan) $1395, KLM (Amsterdam), JAL (Tokyo), Lufthansa (Frankfurt), Olympic (Athens) $1530, Thai International (Bangkok), Singapore Airlines, Qantas $1670, Thai $1792 (2 stops), British Airways (via London) $1885, Air France (on to 87 destinations within France) $1903, Qantas/Air France $1980 (3 stops).

Airpasses, coupons and discounts on further flights within Europe vary with airlines, but the basic rules are that they must be pre-booked with the main ticket, are valid for three months, and are available only with a return fare with the one airline – for example, you have to fly to France with British Airways alone to be eligible for their airpass deals. Air France offer a **Euroflyer** for use in France and Europe at A$190 each flight (min 3, max 9). KLM's **Passport to Europe** uses coupons for single flights within Europe: three coupons for A$476, up to six for

AGENTS & TOUR OPERATORS IN AUSTRALIA AND NZ

AIRLINES

Aeroflot (☎02/ 9262-2233).

Air France (☎9244 2100; in New Zealand ☎09/303 3521).

Air New Zealand (☎13/2476; in New Zealand ☎09/366 2803).

Alitalia (☎1300 653 757; in New Zealand ☎09/379 4457).

British Airways (☎02/9258 3300; in New Zealand ☎09/356 8690).

Cathay Pacific (☎02/9931 5500; in New Zealand ☎09/379 0861).

Garuda (☎02/9334 9944; in New Zealand ☎09/366 1855).

JAL (☎02/92721111; in New Zealand ☎09/379 9906).

KLM (☎02/9231 6333 or 1-800/505 747).

Lauda Air (☎02/9251 6155 or ☎1-800/642 438; in New Zealand (☎09/303 1529).

Lufthansa (☎1300 655 727).

Malaysia Airlines (Sydney local-call rate ☎13/2627; in New Zealand (☎09/373 2741).

Qantas (☎13/1211).

Singapore Airlines (Sydney local-call rate ☎13/1011; in New Zealand ☎9350 0129).

Thai Airways (☎1300 651 960; in New Zealand ☎09/377 3886).

United Airlines (☎13 1777; in New Zealand ☎09/307 9500).

TRAVEL AGENTS

Brisbane Flight Centre, 260 Queen St, Brisbane (☎07/3229 9211).

Budget Travel, 16 Fort St, Auckland; other branches around the city (☎09/366 0061 or ☎0-800/808 040).

Destinations Unlimited, 3 Milford Rd, Milford, Auckland (☎09/373 4033).

Flight Centres Australia: Level 11, 33 Berry St, North Sydney (☎131 600, 02/9460 0555); 19 Bourke St, Melbourne (☎03/9650 2899); plus other branches nationwide. New Zealand: National Bank Towers, 205–225 Queen St, Auckland (☎09/209 6171); Shop 1M, National Mutual Arcade, 152 Hereford St, Christchurch (☎03/379 7145); 50–52 Willis St, Wellington (☎04/472 8101).

Passport Travel, Kings Cross Plaza, Ste 11/401 St Kilda Rd, Melbourne (☎03 9867 3888).

STA Travel Australia: 855 George St, Sydney (☎02/9212 1255 or ☎1300 360 960); 256 Flinders St, Melbourne (☎03/9654 7266); other offices in state capitals and major universities. New Zealand: Travellers' Centre, 10 High St, Auckland (☎09/309 0458); 233 Cuba St, Wellington (☎04/385 0561); 90 Cashel St, Christchurch (☎03/379 9098); other offices in Dunedin, Palmerston North, Hamilton and major universities.

Thomas Cook, Australia: 321 Kent St, Sydney (☎02/9248 6100); 257 Collins St, Melbourne (☎03/9282 0222); branches in other state capitals. New Zealand: Shop 250a, St Luke's Square, Auckland (☎09/849 2071).

Topdeck Travel, 65 Glenfell St, Adelaide (☎08/8232 7222).

Tymtro Travel, Sydney (☎02/9223 2211).

SPECIALIST OPERATORS

Adventure Travel Shop, 50 High St, Auckland (☎09/303 1805). A range of outdoor active tours in Normandy, Brittany and the rest of France.

Adventure World (☎02/9956 7766) 73 Walker St Nth Sydney; level 3, 333 Adelaide St, Brisbane (☎07/3229 0599); 8 Victoria Ave, Perth (☎08/9221 2300); 101 Great South Rd, Remuera, Auckland (☎09/524 5118). A wide selection of city ministays and active holidays throughout France.

Alpine World, Inski, 343 Pacific Hwy, Crows Nest (☎02/9955 3744, 1800 063 063). Tailored skiing holidays in France.

CIT, 2/263 Clarence St, Sydney (☎02 9267 1255) offices in Melbourne, Brisbane, Adelaide and

Perth. Accommodation packages, rail passes and art and architecture tours.

Destinations Adventure, 2nd Floor, Premier Building, cnr Queen and Durham streets, East Auckland (☎09/309 0464). Agents for "The Imaginative Traveller" trekking holidays in France.

Eurolynx, 3rd Floor, 20 Fort St, Auckland (☎09/379 9716). Go-as-you-please accommodation and car rental.

European Travel Office, 122 Rosslyn St, West Melbourne (☎03/9329 8844); Level 20, 133 Castlereagh St, Sydney (☎02/9267 7727); 407 Great South Rd, Penrose, Auckland (☎09/525 3074).

SPECIALIST OPERATORS cont

French Travel Connection, Level 6/33 Chandler St, St Leonards (☎02/9966 8600, 1800 505150).

French Cottages and Travel, 674 High St, East Kew, Melbourne (☎03/9859 4944).

France Unlimited, 16 Goldsmith St, Elwood, Melbourne (☎03/9531 8787). Walking and cycling holidays throughout France.

French Bike Tours, 16 Goldsmith St, Elwood, Melbourne (☎03/9531 4135). A varied selection of cycling holidays in France to suit your budget.

Peregrine Adventures (wholesaler), 258 Lonsdale St, Melbourne (☎03/9663 8611); offices in Brisbane, Sydney, Adelaide, Perth and Hobart. Graded walking holidays in France for all fitness levels.

Thor Travel, 228 Rundle St, Adelaide (☎08/8232 3155). A wide selection of walking holidays in France.

Top Deck Travel (wholesaler), Level 1/ 62 Clarence, Sydney (☎02/9299 8844). Overland expeditions through France.

Trafalgar Tours, Trafalgar Tours House, 27 Belgrave St, Manly, NSW (☎02/9657 3333, 1300 787 878).

Travel Notions, 136 Bridge Rd, Glebe, Sydney (☎02/9552 2852). "Cycling for Softies"Seven–fifteen- day centre-based and go-where-you-please cycling holidays throughout rural France.

Ya'lla Tours, 1st Floor, West Tower, 608 St Kilda Rd, Melbourne (☎03/9510 2844, 1300 362 844). Wide range of accommodation and transport packages.

YHA Travel, 422 Kent St, Sydney (☎02/9261 1111); 205 King St, Melbourne (☎03/9670 9611); 38 Stuart St, Adelaide (☎08/8231 5583); 154 Roma St, Brisbane (☎07/3236 1680); 236 William St, Northbridge, Perth (☎08/9227 5122); 69a Mitchell St, Darwin (☎08/8981 2560); 28 Criterion St, Hobart (☎03/6234 9617). Accommodation and adventure tours throughout France.

A$816 in the low season, A$537 and 961 in the shoulder period, A$635 and A$1157 in the peak period; Lufthansa start at A$611 for three coupons plus A$171 for any additional coupons (max 9) during the low seasons up to A$684 plus A$203 for any additional coupons. British Airways have a zone system: around A$135 for each flight within France, A$200 each for single flights to and around Germany, Italy and Belgium, although you may have to travel via London which will cost A$165 (min 3, max 12).

FROM NEW ZEALAND

From New Zealand, the best discounted deals to Paris from Auckland are: Japanese Airlines (NZ$2200, with an overnight stop in Tokyo), Thai International (NZ$2265), Malaysian Airlines (NZ$2295) and Garuda (NZ$2249). For **stopovers** in Europe, British Airways charge NZ$2399 via London, and Qantas/Alitalia are slightly less at NZ$2295 via Rome and London. For **side-trips** within Europe, Qantas/Lufthansa have a four-coupon deal on a six-month fare for NZ$2600.

RED TAPE AND VISAS

Citizens of EU (European Union) countries, and thirty other countries, including Australia, Canada, the United States, New Zealand, Malaysia and Singapore do not need any sort of visa to enter France, and can stay for up to ninety days. All other passport holders (including British Travel Document holders) must obtain a visa before arrival in France. Obtaining a visa from your nearest French consulate is fairly automatic, but check their hours before turning up, and leave plenty of time, since there are often queues (particularly in London in summer). Australians can obtain a visa on the spot in London. Note that the British Visitor's Passport is no longer valid.

Three types of **visa** are currently issued: a transit visa, valid for two months; a short-stay (*court séjour*) visa, valid for ninety days after the date of issue and good for multiple entries; and a long-stay (*long séjour*) visa, which allows for multiple stays of ninety days over three years, but which is issued only after an examination of an individual's circumstances. EU citizens (or other non-visa citizens) who **stay longer than three months** are officially supposed to apply for a **Carte de Séjour**, for which you'll have to show proof of income at least equal to the minimum wage (at least 6700F per month). However, EU passports are rarely stamped, so there is no evidence of how

FRENCH EMBASSIES AND CONSULATES OVERSEAS

UK
Consulate (Visas Section): 6a Cromwell Place, London SW7 (visa applications Mon–Fri 9am–10am & 1.30–2.30pm; ☎0171/838 2051 or premium rate ☎0891/887733); 11 Randolph Crescent, Edinburgh (visa applications Mon–Fri 9.30am–1pm; ☎0131/220 6324 or premium rate ☎0891/600215).

Ireland
36 Ailesbury Road, Dublin 4 (☎01/260 1666).

USA
Embassy: 4101/Reservoir Rd NW, Washington DC 20007 (☎202/944 6000); **Consulates**: 285 Peachtree Center, Avenue Suite 2800, Marquis two (☎(404) 522-4226); Park Square Building, Suite 75031 St James Avenue, Boston, MA 02116 (☎617/542 7374737); North Michigan Ave, Olympia Centre Suite 2020, Chicago, IL 60611-2819 (☎312/787 53602727); Allen Parkway Suite 976 Houston, Texas 77019 (☎713/528-2181); 10990 Wilshire Boulevard, Suite 300, Los Angeles, CA 90024 (☎310/235 3200); 934 Fifth Ave, New York, NY 10021 (☎212/606 3689); 2 South Biscayne Boulevard, One Biscayne Tower, Suite 1710 Miami, Florida 331311 (☎305/372-9799); 340 Poydras Street Amoco Building, Suite 1710, New Orleans, Louisiana (☎504/523 5772); 540 Bush St, San Francisco CA 94108 (☎415/397 4330); 4101 Reservoir Road NW, Washington DC 20007 (☎202/944-6000).

Canada
Embassy: 42 Promenade Ottawa, ON K1M 2C9 (☎613/789 1795). **Consulates**: 1 place Ville Marie Bureau 22601, Montréal, Québec H3B 4S3 (☎514/878 4385); 25 rue St-Louis, Québec QC G1R 3Y8 (☎418/694-2294); 130 Bloor Street West, Suite 400 Toronto, ON M5S 1N5 (☎416/925 8044); 1201–736 Granville St, Vancouver BC V6Z 1H9 (☎604/681 4345); 250 Lutz Street, PO BOX 1109, Moncton, New Brunswick EIC 8B6 (☎506/857 4191).

Australia
492 St Kilda Road, Melbourne, VIC 3001 (☎03/9820 0921); 31 Market St, Sydney, NSW 2000 (☎02/9261 5779).

New Zealand
1 Williston St, PO Box 1695, Wellington (☎04/472 0200).

long you've been in the country. If your passport does get stamped, you can cross the border – to Belgium or Germany, for example – and re-enter for another ninety days legitimately.

CUSTOMS

With the Single European Market you can bring in and take out most things as long as you have paid tax on them in an **EU country** and they are for personal consumption. Customs may be suspicious if they think you are going to resell goods (or break the chassis of your car). Limits still apply to drink and tobacco bought in duty-free shops: 200 cigarettes, 250g tobacco or 50 cigars; one litre of spirits or two litres of fortified wine, or two litres of sparkling wine; two litres of table wine; 50gm of perfume and 250ml of toilet water.

Americans can bring home up to $400 worth of goods purchased overseas duty-free, including a litre of alcohol or wine, 200 cigarettes and 100 cigars. If you carry back between $400 and $1000 worth of stuff you'll have to go through the red lane and pay ten percent of the value in duty; above $1000 and the duty depends on the items. For the full rundown on customs niceties, request a copy of the pamphlet *Know Before You Go* from the US Customs Service, PO Box 7407, Washington DC 20044. Their information line (☎202/927 6724) lists other publications for travellers, but they must be requested by mail.

Canadians are exempt from paying duty on up to $300 worth of goods after spending seven days out of the country (or $100 worth after a trip lasting two to six days). Those goods may include up to 1 litres of spirits or wine, 24 355ml bottles of beer and 200 cigarettes. For more details, call ☎1-800/461 9999 and request a copy of the government's *I Declare* brochure.

Travellers returning to **Australia** can bring in $400 worth of "gifts" duty-free (for under-18s this is reduced to $200), not including personal purchases such as clothing which don't incur duty, plus 250 cigarettes or 250g of tobacco and one bottle of alcohol (beer, wine or spirits). **New Zealand** permits $700 worth of "gifts", plus six 750ml bottles of wine or beer (45 litres in all), 1125ml of spirits; 200 cigarettes, or 250g tobacco, or 50 cigars, or a mixture of these not exceeding 250g. In both countries, certain goods must be declared for inspection and may be prohibited: these include cordless phones purchased overseas, artefacts containing wood or other plant material, and foodstuffs.

COSTS, MONEY AND BANKS

From January 1, 1999, it will be possible for commercial transactions to be paid for by cheque in euros, and prices will often be given in both francs and euros. By the end of 2002, the euro will have replaced the currencies of all member countries, such as France, who have opted to join the European monetary union. However, until then the franc remains the normal unit of currency in France.

Because of the relatively low cost of accommodation and eating out, at least by northern European standards, France may not seem an outrageously expensive place to visit but this will depend on the relative strength of your own country's currency. When and where you go also makes a difference: in main resorts hotel prices can go up by a third during July and August, and Paris is considerably more expensive than the rest of the country. For a reasonably comfortable existence, including a hotel room for two, a light restaurant lunch and a proper restaurant dinner plus moving around, café stops and museum visits, you need to allow at least 600F a day per person. But by counting the pennies, staying at a cheap hostel (100F for bed and breakfast) or camping (from 30F) and being strong-willed about extra cups of coffee and doses of culture, you could manage on 250F a day, to include a cheap restaurant meal; less if your eating is limited to street snacks or market food.

For two or more people, **hotel accommodation** is nearly always cheaper and better value than hostels, which are only worth staying at if you're by yourself and want to meet other travellers. A sensible average estimate for a double room would be around 250F, though perfectly adequate but simple doubles can be had from 160F. Single-rated and -sized rooms are often available, beginning from 140F in a cheap hotel. Breakfast at hotels is normally an extra 30F, for coffee, croissant and orange juice, about the same as you'd pay in a bar (where you'll normally find the coffee and ambience more agreeable). As for other **food**, you can spend as much or as little as you like. There are large numbers of reasonable **restaurants** with three- or four-course menus for between 65F and 120F; the lunchtime or *midi* menu is nearly always cheaper. **Picnic fare**, obviously, is much less costly, especially when you buy in the markets and cheap supermarket chains; take-away baguette sandwiches from cafés are not extortionate. **Wine** and **beer** are both very cheap in supermarkets; buying wine from the barrel at village co-op cellars will give you the best value for money. The mark-up on wine in restaurants is high, though the house wine in cheaper establishments is still very good value. **Drinks** in cafés and bars are what really make a hole in your pocket: black coffee, wine and draught lager are the cheapest drinks to order; glasses of tap water are free; and remember that it's cheaper to be at the bar than at a table.

Transport will inevitably be a large item of expenditure if you move around a lot, which makes some kind of train-pass a good idea, although French trains are in any case good value, with many discounts available (some sample one-way fares: Paris to Marseille 528F, Paris to Bordeaux 298F). Buses are cheaper, though prices vary enormously from one operator to another. Bicycles cost about 80F per day to rent. Petrol prices are around 6.59F a litre for unleaded (*sans plomb*), around 6.79F a litre for Super, and around 4.79F a litre for diesel; there are 3.8 litres to the US gallon. Most motorways have tolls: rates vary, but to give you an idea, Calais to Montpellier would cost you around 397F just to use the autoroutes.

Museums and monuments can prove one of the biggest wallet-eroders. **Reduced admission** is often available for those over 60 and under 18, for which you'll need your passport as proof of age, and for students under 26 for which you'll need the ISIC (International Student Identity Card). Many museums and monuments are free for children under twelve, and nearly always for kids under four. Under-26s can also get a free Youth Card or *Carte Jeune*, available in France from youth travel agencies like USIT and from main tourist offices (120F, valid for a year) which entitles you to reductions in France and throughout Europe. Several towns operate a global ticket for their museums and monuments (detailed in the *Guide*).

CURRENCY AND THE EXCHANGE RATE

French currency is the **franc** (abbreviated as F or sometimes FF), divided into 100 centimes. Francs come in notes of 500, 100, 50 and 20F, and there are coins of 20, 10, 5, 2 and 1F, and 50, 20, 10 and 5 centimes. During most of 1998, the exchange rate hovered around 9.6F to the pound, 5.6F to the US dollar, 3.6F to the Canadian dollar, 3.5F for the Australian dollar, and 2.9F for the New Zealand dollar. For the most up to date exchange rates, consult the useful Currency Converter Internet site: *www.oanda.com*.

CHANGING MONEY

Standard **banking hours** are Monday to Friday 9am to 4pm or 5pm. Some close at midday (noon/12.30pm–2/2.30pm); some are open on Saturday 9am to noon. All are closed on Sunday and public holidays. They will have a notice on the door if they do currency exchange, and **rates and commission** vary from bank to bank so shop around. The usual procedure is a 1–2 percent commission on travellers' cheques and a flat rate charge on cash (a 30F charge for changing 200F is not uncommon). Be wary of banks claiming to charge no commission at all; often they are merely adjusting the exchange rate to their own advantage.

There are **money-exchange counters** (*bureaux de change*) at all the French airports and train stations of big cities, with usually one or two in town centres as well, often keeping much longer hours than the high-street banks. You'll also find **automatic exchange machines** at airports and train stations and outside many money exchange bureaux. They accept £10 and £20 notes as well as dollars and other European currency notes, but offer a very poor rate of exchange.

TRAVELLERS' CHEQUES AND EUROCHEQUES

Travellers' cheques are one of the safest ways of carrying your money. Worldwide, they're available from almost any major bank (in most cases whether you have an account there or not), and from special American Express or Thomas Cook offices, usually for a service charge of 1 percent on the amount purchased. The Bank of Ireland has the lowest rate of 1.5 percent; the highest rate is 2 percent and some banks have a minimum charge (eg in Britain NatWest charges £4). Check with your own bank first as they may offer cheques free of charge provided you meet certain conditions. The most widely recognized brands are Visa, Thomas Cook and American Express, which most banks will change, and there are American Express and Thomas Cook offices in France; American Express travellers' cheques can also be cashed at post offices.

French franc travellers' cheques can be worthwhile: they may often be used as cash, and you should get the face value of the cheques when you change them, so commission is only paid on purchase. Banks being banks, however, this is not always the case.

Eurocheques, available to Europeans with an annual charge of between £4 and £8 and commission of between 1.6 and 2 percent (with a minimum charge of around £1.75 from a cash dispenser and £2 to write a cheque, with a maximum charge of £5), are no longer such a good idea for France as most banks and post offices now refuse to cash them. You can still use the card, however, in Automatic Teller Machines (ATMs) and as a debit card, and write out cheques in francs to hotels and restaurants, etc.

The latest way of carrying your money abroad is with a **Visa TravelMoney Card**, a sort of electronic travellers' cheque. The temporary disposable debit card is "loaded up" with an amount between £100 and £5000 and can then be used (in conjunction with a PIN number) in any ATM carrying the Visa sign in France (and 112 other countries). When your funds are depleted, you simply throw the card away. It's recommended you buy at least a second card as back up in case your first is lost or stolen, though like travellers' cheques the cards can be replaced if such mishaps occur. Up to nine cards can be bought to access the same funds – useful for couples/families travelling together. Charges are 2 percent commission with a minimum charge

of £3. In Britain, the cards are sold by Thomas Cook; you can go into any office or order the card by telephone (call ☎01733/318900) using a debit or credit card and your card will be sent out the next day by registered post. In the US it is called Visa Travel Money (VTM and is a prepaid card which functions at any ATM machine where there is a Visa sign, with a PIN number. For more information call ☎1.800.444.1244/ 1.800.543.8227 or consult the Visa Web site (*www.visa.com*).

CREDIT AND DEBIT CARDS

Credit cards are widely accepted; just watch for the window stickers. Visa – known as the *Carte Bleue* in France – is almost universally recognized; Access, Mastercard – sometimes called Eurocard – and American Express rank a bit lower. It's always worth checking, however, that restaurants and hotels will accept your card; some smaller ones don't. Be aware, also, that French cards have a smart chip and machines may reject the magnetic strip of British, American or Australasian cards, even if they are valid. If your card is refused because of this, we suggest you say "Les cartes britanniques/américaines/canadiennes/de Nouvelle Zealand ne sont pas cartes à puce, mais à piste magnétique. Ma carte est valable et je vous serais très reconnaissant(e) de demander la confirmation auprès de votre banque ou de votre centre de traitement."

You can also use credit cards for **cash advances** at banks and in ATMs. The charge tends to be higher– for example 4.1 percent instead of the 1.5 percent at home for Visa cards. The PIN number should be the same as you use at home but check with your credit card company before you leave. Also, because French credit cards are smart cards, some ATMs balk at foreign plastic and tell you that your request for money has been denied. If that happens, just try another machine. All ATMs give you the choice of instructions in French or English. Post offices will give cash advances on Visa credit cards if you are having a problem using them in ATMs.

Debit cards can also be used in ATMs or to pay for goods and services if they carry the appropriate Visa symbol or there's an "edc" (European acceptance) sign. You will be charged around one percent or a minimum of £1.50 to use your debit card in an ATM, so don't constantly take small sums out. You would not want the use of ATMs to be your sole source of money on a long trip far from home as a lost, stolen or malfunctioning card would leave you with nothing, so always have some spare currency or travellers' cheques as a backup.

HEALTH AND INSURANCE

Citizens of all EU and Scandinavian countries are entitled to take advantage of French health services under the same terms as residents, if they have the correct documentation. British citizens need form E111, available from post offices. North American and other non-EU citizens have to pay for most medical attention and are strongly advised to take out some form of travel insurance.

Under the French Social Security system, every hospital visit, doctor's consultation and prescribed medicine incurs a charge. Although all employed French people are entitled to a refund of 70–75 percent of their medical and dental expenses, this can still leave a hefty shortfall, especially after a stay in hospital (accident victims even have to pay for the ambulance that takes them there).

To find a **doctor**, stop at any *pharmacie* and ask for an address, or look under "Médecins qualifiés" in the Yellow Pages of the phone directory. To qualify for Social Security refunds, make sure the doctor is a *médecin conventionné*. An average consultation fee would be between 110F and 150F. You will be given a *Feuille de Soins* (Statement of Treatment) for later documentation of insurance claims. Prescriptions should be taken to a *pharmacie* where they must be paid for; the medicines will have little stickers (*vignettes*) attached to them, which you must remove and stick to your *Feuille de Soins*, together with the prescription itself. In serious emergencies you will always be admitted to the nearest **hospital** (*hôpital*), either under your own power or by ambulance, which even French citizens must pay for; many people instead call the *pompiers* (fire brigade), who are equipped to deal with medical emergencies, when there is a medical emergency.

As getting a refund entails a complicated bureaucratic procedure and in any case does not cover the full cost of treatment, it's always a better idea to take out ordinary **travel insurance**, which generally allows full reimbursement, less the first few pounds or dollars of every claim, and also covers the cost of repatriation. If you're travelling in your own car, you may want to have breakdown cover which includes personal insurance.

TRAVEL INSURANCE

Having medical care is the most important reason for taking out **medical insurance**. The let-out clauses on the cover of money and possessions

EMERGENCY NUMBERS

Fire brigade (*pompiers*), the most reliable emergency service: ☎18.

Emergency medical advice; private ambulance service; information on nearest hospital, doctor, pharmacy: ☎15.

The phone numbers and addresses of hospitals and the phone numbers for SOS Médecins (for emergency doctor call-out) are given in the *Guide* for all the main cities. You will also find the number for the local police station, which can provide addresses of doctors on call, and for pharmacies

Rape crisis (*SOS Viol*): ☎0800.05.95.95.

AIDS information (SIDA Info Service): ☎0800.84.08.00.

All these numbers are free.

open after hours. All pharmacies, signalled by an illuminated green cross, are equipped, and obliged, to give first-aid on request – though they will make a charge. When closed, they all display the address of the nearest open pharmacy, day or night.

---

are getting more and more restrictive; make sure you know exactly what the terms and conditions are. If you're going to ski, rock-climb or engage in any other high-risk activities, the premiums will be higher, but definitely worth it – the cost of a mountain rescue can run into F100,000s.

When considering any insurance policy, check carefully that it will cover you in case of an accident. Note also that very few insurers will arrange on-the-spot payments in the event of a major expense or loss; you will usually be reimbursed only after going home. In all case of loss or theft of goods, claims can only be dealt with if a report is made to the local police within 24 hours and a copy of the report (*constat de vol*) sent with the claim; addresses of the Commissariat de Police are given in the main towns and cities.

Most policies in Britain and Ireland are broadly similar, but before signing up you should always read the small print to see what is covered; often money and credit cards are covered only if stolen from your person.

Bank and **credit cards** often have certain levels of medical or other insurance included, especially if you use them to pay for your trip. This can be quite comprehensive, anticipating anything from lost or stolen baggage and missed connections to charter companies going bankrupt. For example, Barclaycard automatically insures anything you've purchased with the card for 100 days, gives travel insurance for up to £50,000 if you pay for your holiday with the card and has a free International Rescue Service of legal advice, translation assistance, money transfer, contacting relatives and accompanying children home. If you have a good "all risks" **home insurance** policy it may well cover your possessions against loss or theft even when

overseas, and many **private medical schemes** also cover you when abroad – make sure you know the procedure and the helpline number.

Nearly all travel agents and tour operators will offer you insurance when you book your flight or holiday, and some will insist you take it. However, there are moves to ban packages which compel you to take out travel agents' own policies – often more expensive than if you shopped around with banks or **specialist insurance companies**. The best-value **travel insurance schemes**, such as those offered by the Columbus Travel Insurance, cost from around £26.50 a month in Europe. ISIS policies, from STA Travel or branches of Endsleigh Insurance, are also usually good value. If you are going on an **extended trip**, Columbus does a special "Globetrotter" policy offering basic coverage (it doesn't cover baggage, money or missed departures) for £109 for six months or £185 for a year. Full cover for an entire year can cost as much as £411. While rates for annual **multi-trip** policies are enticing, they don't provide cover for extended trips: with each separate trip usually limited to a month, they are handy for frequent travel and can usually incorporate married couples at a saving on individual rates. The annual multi-trip policy offered by Worldwide is the least discriminatory, good for any couple, whether gay, straight, relatives or just flatmates, as long as they live at the same address, with unlimited trips of either 31 or 62 days' duration (single £69/£79, couples £89/£109). Columbus does an annual multi-trip policy with as many trips of up to 60 days as you like for £48 (Europe) or £89 (worldwide); American Express has an annual travel insurance policy open to non-card holders for an unlimited number of trips in Europe up to 31 or 62

TRAVEL INSURANCE COMPANIES

BRITAIN AND IRELAND
Age Concern (☎01883/346964).
American Express (☎0800/700 737).
Campus Travel or **STA** in Britain (see p.4 for addresses) and **USIT** in Ireland (see p.12).
Columbus Travel Insurance (☎0171/375 0011).
Endsleigh Insurance (☎0171/436 4451).
Frizzell Insurance (☎01202/292 333).
Marcus Hearne & Co (☎0171/739 3444).
Snowcard Insurance Services (☎01327/262 805).
Worldwide (☎01892/833 338).

USA AND CANADA
Access America (☎1-800/284-8300).
Carefree Travel Insurance (☎1-800/323 3149).

International Student Insurance Service
(ISIS) – sold by STA Travel (☎1-800/777-0112).
Travel Assistance International (☎1-800/821-2828).
Travel Guard (☎1-800/826-1300).
Travel Insurance Services (☎1-800/937-1387).

AUSTRALIA AND NEW ZEALAND
Australian Federation of Travel Agents (☎02 9264 3299).
Cover More (☎02 9202 8000).
Ready Plan (1300 555 017).
United Travel Agents Group (13 1398, 9956 8399).

days' duration (31-day European £59.95, 62-day £79.95), or worldwide cover for trips of up to 91 days (£94.95).

You may want to contact an even more specialized travel insurance firm to cover all your needs, like Snowcard Insurance Services who specialize in mountaineering and activity holiday travel insurance, or Age Concern who cover travellers over 65 (no upper age limit).

US AND CANADIAN COVER

Before buying an insurance policy, check that you're not already covered. Canadian provincial **health plans** typically provide some overseas medical coverage, though they are unlikely to pick up the full tab in the event of a mishap. Holders of official **student and youth cards** (see p.22) are entitled to accident coverage and hospital inpatient benefits – the annual membership is far less than the cost of comparable insurance. Students may also find that their student health coverage extends during the vacations and for one term beyond the date of last enrolment. Bank and **credit cards** (particularly American Express) often provide certain levels of medical or other insurance, and travel insurance may also be included if you use a major credit or charge card to pay for your trip. **Homeowners' or renters' insurance** often covers theft or loss of documents, money and valuables while overseas.

After exhausting the possibilities above, you might want to contact a specialist **travel insurance** company; your travel agent can usually recommend one (or see the box above). Policies vary: some are comprehensive while others cover only certain risks (accidents, illnesses, delayed or lost luggage, cancelled flights, etc). In particular, ask whether the policy pays medical costs up front or reimburses you later, and whether it provides for medical evacuation to your home country. For policies that include lost or stolen luggage, check exactly what is and isn't covered, and make sure the per-article limit will cover your most valuable possession.

The best premiums are usually to be had through student/**youth travel agencies** – ISIS policies, for example, cost $48–69 for fifteen days (depending on level of coverage), $80–105 for a month, $149–207 for two months, $510–700 for a year. If you're planning to do any "dangerous sports", such as skiiing or mountaineering, figure on a surcharge of 20–50 percent.

Most North American travel policies apply only to items lost, stolen or damaged while in the custody of an identifiable, responsible third party – hotel porter, airline, luggage consignment, etc. Even in these cases you will have to contact the local police within a certain time limit to have a complete report made out so that your insurer can process the claim.

AUSTRALASIAN COVER

Travel insurance in **Australia** and **New Zealand** is put together by the airlines and travel agent groups such as UTAG, AFTA, Cover

More and Ready Plan in conjunction with insurance companies. They are all similar in premium and coverage, however Ready Plan give the best value for money coverage. A typical policy will cost A$196/NZ$220 for one month, A$271/NZ$320 for two months and A$335/NZ$400 for three months. As with all policies, make sure that you are covered for any activities you might be planning, especially if you are hiking or skiing.

DISABLED VISITORS

France has no special reputation for providing facilities for disabled travellers. For people in wheelchairs, the haphazard parking habits and stepped village streets are serious obstacles, and public toilets with disabled access are rare. In the major cities and coastal resorts, however, ramps or other forms of access are gradually being added to hotels, museums and some theatres and concert halls. APF, the French paraplegic organization (see below), which has an office in each département, will be the most reliable source of information on accommodation with disabled access and other facilities.

Public **transport** is certainly not wheelchair-friendly, and although many train stations now have ramps to enable wheelchair-users to board and descend from carriages, at others it is still up to the guards to carry the chair. The high-speed **TGVs** (including Eurostar) all have places for wheelchairs in the First Class saloon coach for which you must book in advance, though no higher fee is charged; on other trains, a wheelchair symbol within the timetable denotes whether that service offers special features and you and your companion are again upgraded to first class with no extra charge. The *Guide du Voyageur à Mobilité Réduite*, available free at main train stations, details all facilities. **Taxis** are obliged by law to carry you and to help you into the vehicle, also to carry your guide dog if you are blind. Specialist taxi services are available in some towns: these are detailed in the Ministry of Transport and Tourism's pamphlet *Guide des Transports à l'Usage des Personnes à Mobilité Réduite*, available at airports, main train stations and some tourist offices. The guide also gives some indication of the accessibilty of urban public transport systems, and the availability of cars for hire with hand controls. Hertz has a fleet at the airports of Paris, Lyon, Marseille and Nice which can be booked 48 hours in advance (in France ☎0800.05.33.11).

Up-to-date information is best obtained from organizations at home before you leave or from the French disability organizations. The publication *Touristes Quand Même!*, produced by the CNRH (see box on p.28), lists facilities throughout France but is not updated regularly. Some tourist offices have information but, again, it is not always very reliable. For Paris, *Access in Paris* by Gordon Couch and Ben Roberts, published in Britain by Quiller Press and available from RADAR (£6.95), is a thorough guide to accommodation, monuments, museums, restaurants and travel to the city. The Holiday Care Service has an information sheet on accessible **accommodation** in France.

Most of the cross-Channel **ferry companies** offer good facilities, though up-to-date information about access is difficult to get hold of. Eurostar, having been established in the 1990s, offers an excellent deal for wheelchair users. There are two special spaces in the first class carriages for wheelchairs, with an accompanying seat for a companion. Fares are a flat-rate £72 return from Paris and London (with fully flexible dates) for both wheelchair-bound person and companion and, though it's not absolutely guaranteed, you will normally get the First Class meal as well. No advance bookings are necessary, though the limited spaces might make it wise to reserve ahead of time and also to arrange the special assistance which Eurostar offers at either end. As far as **airlines** go, British Airways has a better-than-average record for treatment of disabled passengers, and from North America, Virgin and Air Canada come out tops in terms of disability awareness (and seating arrangements) and might be worth contacting first for any information they can provide.

CONTACTS FOR TRAVELLERS WITH DISABILITIES

FRANCE

APF (Association des Paralysés de France), 17 bd Auguste-Blanqui, 75013 Paris (☎01.40.78.69.00). A national organization providing useful information and lists of new and accessible accommodation. Their guide *Où Ferons-Nous Étape* is available at the office or by post to a French address.

CNRH (Comité National Français de Liaison pour la Réadaptation des Handicapés), 236bis rue de Tolbiac, 75013 Paris (☎01.53.80.66.66). Information service whose various useful guides include a *Guide Touristique pour les Personnes à Mobilitée Réduite*, available in English for 60F.

BRITAIN AND IRELAND

Access Travel, 16 Haweswater Ave, Astley, Lancashire M29 7BL (☎01942/888844, fax 891811). Tour operator that can arrange flights, transfer and accommodation. This is a small business, personally checking out places before recommendation. They can guarantee accommodation standards in several regions of France: Pas de Calais, Loire Valley, Normandy and Puy de Dôme. Established 1991; ATOL bonded.

GDBA (Guide Dogs for the Blind Association) Holidays, Shap Rd, Kendal, Cumbria LA9 6NZ (☎01539/735080). Specialists in activity holidays for the visually impaired and unsighted. A week's tandem touring in Normandy for £360 per person with half-board, and walking tours in the Pyrenees for £480 per person for a week (includes half-board and flight).

Holiday Care Service, 2nd floor, Imperial Building, Victoria Rd, Horley, Surrey RH6 7PZ (☎01293/774535, fax 784647; Minicom ☎01293/776943).

Provides free lists of accessible accommodation abroad. Information on financial help for holidays available.

RADAR (Royal Association for Disability and Rehabilitation), 12 City Forum, 250 City Rd, London EC1V 8AF (☎0171/250 3222, fax 0171/250 0212; Minicom ☎0171/250 4119). A good source of advice on holidays and travel abroad. They produce a guide for European holidays (£5 inc. p&p) alternate years and the useful publication *Access in Paris* (see p.27) is available through them.

TRIPSCOPE, The Courtyard, Evelyn Rd, London W4 (☎0181/994 9294). This registered charity provides a phone-in travel information service offering free advice on UK and international transport for those with a mobility problem.

CANADA

Twin Peaks Press, Box 129, Vancouver, WA 98666; ☎360/694 2462 or 1-800/637 2256. Publishes excellent travel guides including the *Directory of Travel Agencies for the Disabled* ($19.95).

AUSTRALIA AND NEW ZEALAND

ACROD (Australian Council for Rehabilitation of the Disabled), PO Box 60, Curtin ACT 2605 (☎ 02 6282 4333); 24 Cabarita Road, Cabarita NSW 2137 (☎02 9743 2699). A body that will provide lists of travel agencies and tour operators for people with disabilities.

Disabled Persons Assembly, PO Box 10, 138 The Terrace, Wellington (☎04/472 2626). Organization that will provide details of tour operators and travel agencies for people with disabilities.

INFORMATION AND MAPS

The French Government Tourist Office gives away large quantities of maps and glossy brochures for every region of France, including lists of hotels and campsites. Some of these – like the maps of the inland waterways or footpaths, lists of festivals and so on – can be useful; others are just so much dead wood.

TOURIST OFFICES

In France itself you'll find a **tourist office** – usually an Office du Tourisme (OT) but sometimes a Syndicat d'Initiative (SI) – in practically every town and many villages (addresses, phone, fax and opening hours are detailed in the *Guide*). For the practical purposes of visitors, there is little difference between them: SIs have wider responsibilities for encouraging business, while Offices du Tourisme deal exclusively with tourism; sometimes they share premises and call themselves an OTSI. In small villages where there is no OT or SI, the mairie, or town hall, will offer a similar service.

From all these offices you can get specific local information, including listings of hotels and restaurants, leisure activities, car and bike rental, bus timetables, laundries and countless other things. And always ask for the free town plan (though some places, like Paris, now charge a nominal 5F). They also usually have maps and local walking guides on sale. In mountain regions they display daily meteorological information and

often share premises with the local hiking and climbing organizers. In the big cities you can usually also pick up free *What's On* guides. The regional or departmental tourist offices also offer useful practical information.

In Paris, many of the French regions have tourist offices; for example, Alsace's is on the Champs Élysées and Lorraine's is across from the Louvre. They are good places to plan excursions prior to setting out, as you can pick up useful maps and other ephemera, and get seasonal advice.

MAPS

In addition to the various free leaflets – and the maps in this guide – the one extra map you'll probably want is a reasonable **road map** of France. The Michelin map no. 989 (1:1,000,000) is the best for the whole country. A useful free map for car drivers, obtainable from filling stations and traffic information kiosks in France, is the Bison Futé map, showing alternative back routes to the congested main roads, clearly signposted on the ground by special green Bison Futé road signs.

For more **regional detail**, the Michelin yellow series (1:200,000) is best for the motorist. You can get the whole series in one large spiral-bound *Atlas Routier*.

If you're planning to **walk or cycle,** check the IGN (Institut Géographique National) maps – either green (1:100,000 and 1:50,000), or the more detailed blue (1:25,000) series. The IGN 1:100,000 series is the smallest scale available that has the contours marked – essential for cyclists, who tend to cycle off 1:25,000 maps in a couple of hours. Didier Richard maps (1:50,000) show walking paths in Corsica, the Alps, Provence and the Southern Rhone while routes in the French Pyrenees are well-covered by the twelve maps in the *Randonnées Pyrénées* series (1:50,000).

For those wanting to plan a visit to the **battlefields of northern France**, the two maps of Major and Mrs Holt's *Battle Map Series* are available direct from its English authors (T. & V. Holt, Oak Housem, Woodnesborough, Sandwich CT13 0NJ, England; ☎ & fax 01304/614123).

MAP OUTLETS

BRITAIN AND IRELAND

Blackwell's Map and Travel Shop, 53 Broad St, Oxford OX1 (☎01865/792792; *bookshop.blackwell.co.uk*).

Daunt Books, 83 Marylebone High St, London W1M 3DE (☎0171/224 2295); 193 Haverstock Hill, London NW3 4QL (☎0171/794 4006).

Easons Bookshop, 40 O'Connell St, Dublin 1 (☎01/873 3811; mail order available).

Fred Hanna's Bookshop, 27–29 Nassau St, Dublin 2 (☎01/677 1255).

Heffers Map Shop, 3rd Floor, in Heffers Stationery Department, 19 Sidney St, Cambridge, CB2 (☎01223/568467; mail order available; *www.heffers.co.uk*).

Hodges Figgis Bookshop, 56–58 Dawson St, Dublin 2 (☎01/677 4754; mail order available).

National Map Centre, 22–24 Caxton St, London SW1 (☎0171/222 2466; *www.mapsworld.com*).

Newcastle Map Centre, 55 Grey St, Newcastle upon Tyne, NE1 (☎0191/261 5622).

James Thin Melven's Bookshop, 29 Union St, Inverness, (☎01463/233500; mail order available; *www.jthin.co.uk*).

John Smith and Sons, 57–61 St Vincent St, Glasgow, G2 (☎0141/221 7472; mail order available; *www.johnsmith.co.uk*).

Stanfords, 12–14 Long Acre, WC2E (☎0171/836 1321); maps by mail or phone order are available on this number and via email: *sales@stanfords.co.uk*. Also in Campus Travel at 52 Grosvenor Gardens, SW1W (☎0171/730 1314); in British Airways offices at 156 Regent St, W1R (☎0171/434 4744); and outside London at 29 Corn Street, Bristol BS1 (☎0117/929 9966).

The Travel Bookshop, 13–15 Blenheim Crescent, London W11 (☎0171/229 5260; *www.thetravelbookshop.co.uk*).

Waterstone's, Queens Bldg, 8 Royal Ave, Belfast BT1 (☎01232/247355); 7 Dawson St, Dublin 2 (☎01/679 1415); 69 Patrick St, Cork (☎021/276 522).

USA

Adventurous Traveler Bookstore, PO Box 1468, Williston, VT 05495 (1-800/282-3963).

The Complete Traveler Bookstore, 199 Madison Ave, New York, NY 10016 (☎212/685-9007); 3207 Fillmore St, San Francisco, CA 92123 (☎415/923-1511).

Map Link Inc, 30 S La Petera Lane, Unit #5, Santa Barbara, CA 93117 (☎805/692-6777).

Phileas Fogg's Books & Maps, #87 Stanford Shopping Center, Palo Alto, CA 94304 (1-800/533-FOGG in California; ☎1-800/533-FOGG elsewhere in US).

Rand McNally,* 444 N Michigan Ave, Chicago, IL 60611 (☎312/321-1751); 150 E 52nd St, New York, NY 10022 (☎212/758-7488); 595 Market St, San Francisco, CA 94105 ☎415/777-3131); 1201 Connecticut Ave NW, Washington, DC 20003 (☎202/223-6751).

*For other locations, or for maps by **mail order**, call☎1-800/333-0136 (ext 2111).

Sierra Club Bookstore, 6014 College Avenue, Oakland, CA 94618 (☎510/658-7470).

Travel Books & Language Center, 4931 Cordell Ave, Bethesda, MD 20814 (☎1-800/220-2665).

Traveler's Bookstore, 22 W 52nd St, New York, NY 10019 (☎212/664-0995).

CANADA

Open Air Books and Maps, 25 Toronto St, Toronto, ON M5R 2C1 (☎416/363-0719).

Ulysses Travel Bookshop, 4176 St-Denis, Montréal (☎514/843-9447).

World Wide Books and Maps, 736 Granville St, Vancouver, BC V6Z 1E4 (☎604/687-3320).

Australia and New Zealand

Map Land, 372 Little Burke St, Melbourne (☎03/9670 4383).

The Map Shop, 16a Peel St, Adelaide (☎08/8231 2033).

Perth Map Centre, 884 Hay St, Perth (☎08/9322 5733).

Specialty Maps, 58 Albert St, Auckland (☎09/307 2217).

Travel Bookshop Shop 3/ 175 Liverpool St, Sydney 2000 (☎02 92618200).

GETTING AROUND

With the most extensive train network in western Europe, France is a country in which to travel by rail. The nationally owned French train company, the SNCF (Société Nationale des Chemins de Fer), runs fast, modern trains. In rural areas where branch lines have been closed, routes are covered by buses operated by the SNCF. It's an integrated service, with buses timetabled to meet trains and the same ticket covering both.

The private bus services are confusing and unco-ordinated. Approximate journey times and frequencies can be found in the "Travel details" at the end of each chapter, and local peculiarities

are also pointed out in the text of the *Guide*. For a more private kind of independent transport, by car or bicycle, you'll need to be aware of a number of French road rules and peculiarities. Hitching is less and less popular, but walking, on the extensive network of "GR" footpaths (see p.38), is recommended, as are the more specialist realms of inland boating and cross-country skiing, both of which have a high profile in France.

TRAINS

The **SNCF** has pioneered one of the most efficient, comfortable and user-friendly railway systems in the world. Its staff are, with a few exceptions, courteous and helpful; and its trains – for the most part, fast, clean and frequent – continue, in spite of the closure of some rural lines, to serve a vast part of the country.

Pride and joy of the system are the high-speed **TGVs** (*trains à grande vitesse*), capable of 300kph, and their offspring **Eurostar**. At present, the main shape of the network resembles an upside-down "Y", with the stem stretching from Lille in the north to Paris, where the arms begin, one reaching down the east side of the country to Marseille and the Mediterranean, the other down the west to Bordeaux and the Spanish frontier, with tentacles reaching into Brittany and Normandy, the Alps, Pyrenees and Jura. Although

FRENCH GOVERNMENT TOURIST OFFICES

Australia
Lev 22/25 Bligh St
Sydney NSW 2000 ☎612/9231 5244
fax 612/9221 8682

Canada
1981 av McGill College, Suite 490
Montréal, QUE H3A 2W9 ☎514/288 4264
fax 514/845 4868

Ireland
10 Suffolk St,
Dublin 2 ☎01/679 0813 fax 01/679 0814

UK
178 Piccadilly
London W1V 0AL ☎0891/244123 (50p/min)
fax 0171 493 6594

USA
444, Madison Ave, 16th floor
New York, NY 10022 ☎212/838 7800
fax 212/838 7855

676 North Michigan Ave
Chicago, IL 60611-2819 ☎312/751 7800
fax 312/337 6339

9454 Wilshire Blvd, Suite 715
Beverly Hills CA 90212-2967 ☎310/271 6665
☎310/272 2661
fax 310/276 2835

Note that New Zealand does not have a French Government Tourist Office.

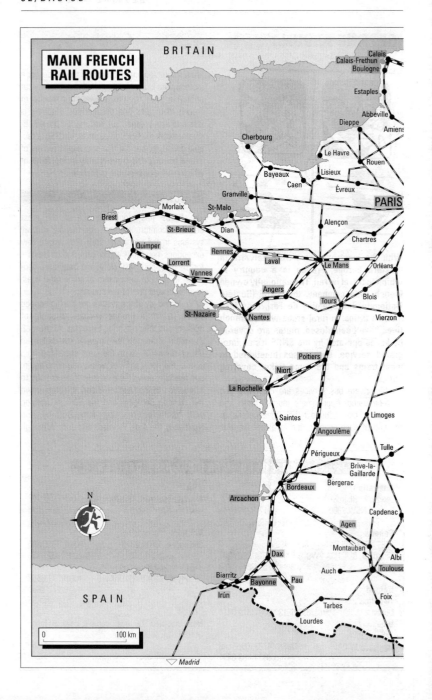

MAIN FRENCH
RAIL ROUTES

BRITAIN

Calais
Calais-Frethun
Boulogne
Estaples
Abbeville
Dieppe
Amiens
Cherbourg
Le Havre
Rouen
Bayeaux
Lisieux
Caen
Évreux
Granville
PARIS
Brest
Morlaix
St-Malo
Alençon
St-Brieuc
Dian
Chartres
Quimper
Rennes
Lorrent
Laval
Le Mans
Orléans
Vannes
Angers
Tours
Blois
St-Nazaire
Nantes
Vierzon
Poitiers
Niort
La Rochelle
Saintes
Limoges
Angoulême
Périgueux
Tulle
Brive-la-
Gaillarde
Bordeaux
Bergerac
Arcachon
Capdenac
Agen
Montauban
Albi
Dax
Auch
Toulouse
Biarritz
Pau
Bayonne
Foix
Irún
Tarbes
SPAIN
Lourdes

N

0   100 km

▽ Madrid

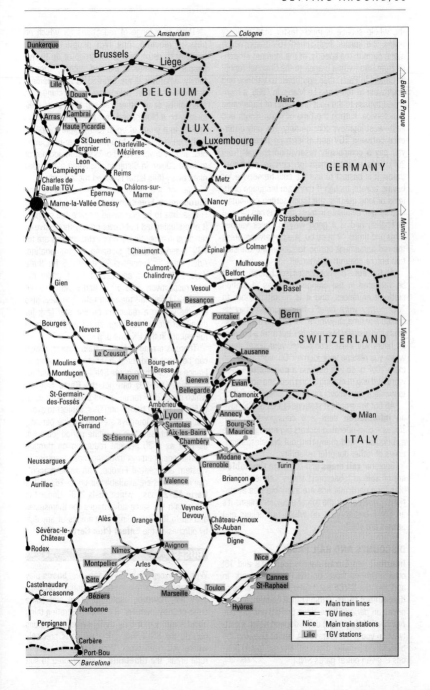

the whole service is much faster than ordinary trains, the special high-speed TGV track, which alone permits top speeds, at the moment stretches from Lille (with a branch to the Channel Tunnel at Calais) to Paris, then southeast to Valence and southwest to Tours and Le Mans. In 1996, a high-speed bypass to the east and south of Paris came into service, cutting the time of north–south and east–west journeys considerably. The only difference between TGV and other train **fares** is that you pay a compulsory reservation charge (from 20F), plus a supplement on certain peak-hour trains. It is easiest to use the counter service for buying tickets, though if there are language problems or long queues, the touch-screen computerized system available in most stations can be read in English and is a good way to check various fares and times - if need be, you can always press the red annulment button to cancel the transaction before committing yourself.

All **tickets** – but not passes (see below) – must be validated in the orange machines at station platform entrances, and it is an offence not to "*Compostez votre billet*". Train journeys may be broken any time, anywhere, for as long as the ticket is valid (usually two months), but after a break of 24 hours you must "*composte*" your ticket again when you resume your journey. On night trains an extra 100F or so will buy you a **couchette** – well worth it if you're making a long haul and don't want to waste a day recovering from a sleepless night.

All but the smallest stations (gares SNCF) have an **information** desk and *consignes automatiques* – coin-operated lockers big enough to take a rucksack – and many rent out bicycles, sometimes of rather doubtful reliability.

Regional **rail maps** and complete **timetables** are on sale at tobacconist shops. Leaflet timetables for a particular line are available free at stations. "*Autocar*" at the top of a column means it's an SNCF bus service, on which rail tickets and passes are valid.

DISCOUNTS AND RAIL PASSES

InterRail and **Eurail** passes (see pp.8 and 16) offer unlimited travel on the French network. In addition, the **SNCF** itself offers a whole range of **discounted fares** within France on standard rail prices on *période bleue* (blue period) and *période blanche* (white period) days, depending on exactly when you want to travel. A leaflet showing the blue, white (smaller discount) and red (peak) periods is given out at gares SNCF.

There is a range of reductions for which no pass is required. Any two people travelling together (*à deux*), or a small group of up to five people – whether a married couple, friends, family, whatever – are entitled to a 25 percent discount on return tickets on TGVs, subject to availability, or on other trains if they start their journey on a blue period day; the same reduction applies to a group of up to four people travelling with a child under 12, to under 26-year-olds, over-60s, and for anyone who books a return journey of at least 200km in distance, including a Saturday night away (this latter is called the *séjour*).

One of the most valuable passes is the **Eurodomino Freedom pass**, which, for use in France, has to be purchased outside the country. It offers unlimited rail travel on any three, five or ten days in a month; the only extra charges are for TGV reservation and sleeping accommodation. Adult rates in second class are £105 for three days, £145 for five and £220 for ten; under-26s pay, respectively, £85, £115 and £185. Children aged 4–11 pay half the adult rate. The pass also entitles you to a reduction on Eurostar (ask for details at time of booking), and is available from rail agents in the UK (see p.8).

There is a range of other train passes, which can be purchased through most travel agents in France or from main gares SNCF and are valid for one year. Over-60s can get the **Carte Senior**, which costs 285F for unlimited travel. It offers up to 50 percent off tickets on TGVs, subject to availability, or other journeys starting in blue periods, a 25 percent reduction on white period journeys, as well as a 30 percent reduction on through international journeys involving most countries in western and central Europe. The same percentage reductions are available for under-26s with a **Carte 12–25** pass, which costs 270F. Under-12s can obtain the same advantages for themselves and up to four travelling companions of any age by purchasing the **Enfant Plus Carte** (350F).

BUSES

With the exception of SNCF services, **buses** play a generally minor role in France's public transport. They are, however, useful for local and some cross-country journeys. The most frustrating thing about them is that they rarely serve the regions outside the SNCF network – which is precisely where you need them. Where they do exist in rural areas, the **timetable** is constructed to suit working, market and school hours – all often dauntingly early. They are, generally speaking, cheaper and slower than trains.

Larger towns usually have a **gare routière** (bus station), often next to the gare SNCF. However, the private bus companies don't always work together and you'll frequently find them leaving from an array of different points (the local tourist office will usually help locate them). The most convenient lines are those run as an extension of rail links by SNCF, which always run to/from the SNCF station and will also access areas not easily reached by rail.

DRIVING

Driving in France can be a real pleasure. The network of autoroutes is magnificent and often provides huge, sweeping views of countryside. Congestion, because of the size and shape of the country, is much less than in Britain. This is equally true of the older main roads of *routes nationales* (marked N6 or RN117, for example, on signs and maps) and the smaller *départementales* (marked with a D). Do not shun these latter: you can often travel for kilometres across country, seeing few other cars, on a road as broad and well-maintained as a major road in Britain.

Of course, there are times when it is wiser not to drive: most obviously in big urban agglomerations, around major seaside resorts in high season, and at peak holiday migrations like the beginning and end of the month-long August holiday and the notoriously congested weekends nearest July 14 and August 15. Cost can also be a discouraging factor. **Fuel** costs 6.59F a litre for unleaded (*sans plomb*), around 6.79F for Super and around 4.79F for diesel, but there is considerable variation, from expensive on the autoroutes to cheapest at supermarket chains like Intermarché.

In addition, there is a charge for the use of the autoroutes themselves (payable at the frequent **toll gates** or *péages*). To give you an idea of the costs involved: the toll from Calais to Reims is 99F and 105F from Calais to Paris, while Paris direct to Marseille or Nice is 267F and 349.5F respectively. A journey from Calais to Montpellier, for example, taking in three different toll gates, would cost you around 397F. If, for whatever reason, you are allergic to autoroutes, the best way to avoid them is to use the Bison Futé map, free from petrol stations, which gives all manner of **alternative routes** (often signed as *itinéraire bis*) across the country.

The costs can, however, be amortized if your car carries a full complement of passengers, and the extra mobility and carrying capacity make it much easier to camp. But, practical considerations

---

CAR RENTAL AGENCIES

BRITAIN AND IRELAND

Avis (☎0990/900 500; Irish Republic ☎01/874 5844).

Budget (☎0800/181 181; Irish Republic ☎0800/973 159).

Europcar (☎0345/222 525; Irish Republic ☎01/874 5844).

Hertz (☎0990/996 699; Irish Republic ☎01/676 7476).

Holiday Autos (☎0990/300 400; Irish Republic ☎01/872 9366).

National Car Rental (☎0990/365365)

Thrifty (☎0990/168238)

USA AND CANADA

Alamo (international ☎1-800/522-9696).

Auto Europe (☎1-800/223-5555).

Avis (☎1-800/331-1084).

Budget (☎1-800/527-0700).

Dollar (☎1-800/421-6868).

Europe by Car (☎1-800/223-1516).

Hertz (☎1-800/654-3001; in Canada ☎1-800/263-0600).

Holiday Autos (☎1-800/422-7737)

National (☎1-800/CAR-RENT).

Thrifty (☎1-800/367-2277).

AUSTRALIA AND NEW ZEALAND

Avis (☎1-800/225 533; in New Zealand ☎09/525 1982).

Budget (local-call rate ☎13 2848; in New Zealand ☎09/275 2222).

Citroën Peugeot Euro Lease 02 9949 1711.

Fly and Drive Holidays (in New Zealand ☎09/529 3790).

Hertz (local-call rate ☎13 1918; in New Zealand ☎09/309 0989).

Renault Eurodrive (☎02/9299 3344).

Remember that you have to be eighteen years of age to drive in France, regardless of whether you hold a licence. Most rental companies will only deal with people over 25 unless an extra insurance premium, typically around 130F–150F per day, is paid (but you still must be over 21 and have driven for at least one year). OTU Voyage (Paris office ☎01.40.29.12.12), the student travel agency, can arrange car hire for young drivers, with prices beginning from 459F for three days, insurance extra.

aside, the great gain is the freedom to explore places that would otherwise remain inaccessible, in particular the sparsely populated upland areas like the Massif Central and the mountain ranges of the Alps and Pyrenees. Here, too, many roads have been constructed with the motorist in mind, to provide spectacular views of otherwise unviewable places: roads like the Corniche des Cévennes, the Route Napoléon in the western Alps, and the high Alpine and Pyrenean passes, although you need to remember that many of the latter are snowbound through winter and spring (you get plenty of notice from information boards on the approach roads).

If you run into **mechanical difficulties**, all the major car manufacturers have garages and service stations in France. You can find them in the Yellow Pages (*Pages Jaunes*) of the phone book under *Garages d'automobiles*. For breakdowns, look under *Dépannages*. If you have an accident or break-in, you should make a report to the local police (and keep a copy) in order to make an insurance claim. Many car insurance policies cover taking your car to Europe; check with your insurer while planning your trip. However, you're advised to take out extra cover for motoring assistance in case your car breaks down, costing around £37 for eight days. Look into the RAC's European Motoring Assistance (☎0800/550055; *www.rac.co.uk*), the AA's Five-Star Europe cover (☎0800/444500; *www.theaa.co.uk*), or Europ Assistance (☎0645/947000).

Car rental in France costs upwards of 2000F a week (from around 290F–520F a day), but can be cheaper if arranged before you leave home – in the UK, Holidays Autos offer competitive deals on car rental in France. You'll find the big firms – Hertz, Avis, Europcar and Budget – at airports and in most big cities, with addresses detailed throughout the *Guide*. Rental from airports normally includes a surcharge. Local firms can be cheaper but you need to check the small print and

be sure of where the car can be returned to. It's normal to pay an indemnity of around 1000F against any damage to the car – they will take your credit card number rather than cash. You should return the car with a full tank of fuel. Extras are often pressed on you, like medical cover, which you may already have from travel insurance. The cost of car rental includes the basic legally necessary car insurance. North Americans and Australians in particular should be forewarned that it is very difficult to arrange the hire of a car with **automatic transmission** – not popular in France; if you can't drive a manual you should try to book an automatic well in advance, possibly before you leave home, and be prepared to pay a much higher price for it.

RULES OF THE ROAD

British, EU and US **driving licences** are valid in France, though an International Driver's Licence makes life easier if you get a police officer unwilling to peruse a document in English. GB stickers are, by law, meant to be displayed, and a Green Card, though not a legal requirement, might save some hassle. If the vehicle is rented, its registration document (*carte grise*) and the insurance papers must be carried. If your car is right-hand drive, you must have your headlight dip adjusted to the right before you go – it's a legal requirement – and as a courtesy change or paint them to yellow or stick on black glare deflectors.

The law of *priorité à droite* – **giving way** to traffic coming from your right, even when it is coming from a minor road – is being phased out as it is a major cause of accidents. It still applies in built-up areas, so you still have to be vigilant in towns, keeping a lookout along the roadside for the yellow diamond on a white background that gives you right of way – until you see the same sign with an oblique black slash, which indicates vehicles emerging from the right have right of way. At roundabouts the *priorité à droite* law no longer applies. "Stop" signs mean stop completely: "*Cédez le passage*" means "Give way". Other signs warning of potential dangers are *déviation* (diversion), *gravillons* (loose chippings), *nids de poules* (potholes) and *chaussée déformée* (uneven surface).

Fines of up to 2,500F for driving violations are exacted on the spot, and only cash is accepted. The fines for exceeding the speed limit by 1–30kph range from 900F to 5000F. Speed limits are: 130kph (80mph) on the tolled autoroutes;

110kph (68mph) on dual carriageways; 90kph (56mph) on other roads; and 50kph (37mph) in towns. For all drivers in wet weather and for drivers with less than two-years' experience, at all times these limits are 110kph, 100kph, and 80kph respectively. Random breath tests are common, and the legal blood alcohol limit (0.05 percent alcohol) is lower than in the UK; fines range from 900F to 30,000F.

Autoroute driving, though fast, is very boring when it's not hair-raising, and tolls are expensive. Nevertheless, it is the only realistic way of covering large distances in a single day. For information on road conditions, call Inter-services Route (☎08.36.68.20.00; 24hour).

HITCHING

If you're intent on **hitching**, you'll have to rely almost exclusively on car drivers, as lorries very rarely give lifts. Even so, it won't be easy. Looking as clean, ordinary and respectable as possible makes a very big difference, as conversations with French drivers soon make clear. Experience also suggests that hitching the less-frequented D roads is much quicker. In mountain areas a rucksack and hiking gear will help procure a lift from fellow aficionados.

Autoroutes are a special case. Hitching on the autoroute itself is strictly illegal, but you can make excellent time going from one service station to another. (If you get stuck, at least there's food, drink, shelter and washing facilities at most service stations. It helps to have the *Guide des Autoroutes*, published by Michelin, which shows all the rest stops, service stations, tollbooths (*péages*), exits, etc. Remember to get out at the service station before your driver leaves the autoroute. The tollbooths are a second best (and legal); ordinary approach roads can be disastrous.

For major long-distance rides, and for a greater sense of safety, you might consider using the national **hitching organization**, Allostop Provoya, 8 rue Rochambeau (on square Montholon), 17009 Paris (Mon–Fri 9am–7.30pm, Sat 9am–1pm & 2–6pm; Mº Cadet/Poissonnière; ☎01.53.20.42.42, fax 53.20.42.44). The cost comprises a registration fee (30F for a journey less

For information on traffic and road conditions throughout France, ring the multilingual service, Autoroutel (☎08.36.68.10.77) or consult their Web site: *www.autoroutes.fr*.

than 200km, 50F if less than 400km, 60F if less than 500km and a maximum of 70F if more than, or you can buy a 180F membership card which is good for eight trips over two years), plus a charge of 22 centimes for every kilometre of the journey. Allostop Provoya can be emailed on *allostop@ecritel.fr*.

BICYCLES AND MOPEDS

Bicycles (*vélos*) have high status in France. All the car ferries carry them for nothing; the SNCF makes minimal charges; and the French (Parisians excepted) respect cyclists – both as traffic and, when you stop off at a restaurant or hotel, as customers. These days more and more cyclists are using **mountain bikes**, which the French call VTTs (*vélos tout terrain*), even for touring holidays, although if you've ever made a direct comparison you'll soon realize that it's much less effort, and much quicker, to cycle long distances and carry luggage on a traditionally styled touring or racing bike.

Restaurants and hotels along the way are nearly always obliging about looking after your bike, even to the point of allowing it into your room. Most large towns have well-stocked retail and **repair shops**, where parts are normally cheaper than in Britain or the US. However, if you're using a foreign-made bike with non-standard metric wheels, it's a good idea to carry spare tyres. Inner tubes are not a problem, as they adapt to either size, though make sure you get the right valves.

The **train network** runs various schemes for cyclists, all of them covered by the free leaflet *Guide du Train et du Vélo*, available from most stations. Trains marked with a bicycle in the timetable allow you to take a bike as free accompanied luggage. Otherwise, you have to send your bike parcelled up as registered luggage for a fee of 150F. Although it may well arrive in less time, the SNCF won't guarantee delivery in under five days; and you do hear stories of bicycles disappearing altogether.

You can normally load your bike straight onto the train at the **ferry** port – as on the boat train at Dieppe – but remember that you must first go to the ticket office of the station to register it (there is time). Don't just try to climb on the train with it, as both you and your bike will end up left behind. Ferries either take bikes free or charge a maximum of £5 one way. British Airways and Air France both take bikes free. You may have to box them though, and you should contact the airlines first. Eurostar

A CYCLING VOCABULARY

to adjust	régler	loose	déserré
axle	l'axe	to lower	baisser
ball-bearing	le roulement à billes	mudguard	le garde-boue
battery	la pile	pannier	le pannier
bent	tordu	pedal	le pédale
bicycle	le vélo	pump	la pompe
bottom bracket	le logement du pédalier	puncture	la crevaison
brake cable	le cable	rack	le porte-bagages
brakes	les freins	to raise	remonter
broken	cassé	to repair	réparer
bulb	l'ampoule	saddle	la selle
chain	la chaîne	to screw	visser/serrer
cotter pin	la clavette	spanner	la clef
to deflate	dégonfler	spoke	le rayon
derailleur	le dérailleur	to straighten	redresser
frame	le cadre	stuck	coincé
gears	les vitesses	tight	serré
grease	la graisse	toe clips	les cale-pieds
handlebars	le guidon	tyre	le pneu
to inflate	gonfler	wheel	la roue
inner tube	la chambre à air		

allow you to take your bicycle as part of your baggage allowance provided it is dismantled and stored in a special bike bag, and the dimensions don't exceed 120cm by 90cm. Otherwise it needs to be sent on unaccompanied, with a guaranteed arrival of 24 hours (you can register it up to ten days in advance; book through Esprit Europe ☎0800/186 186); the fee is £20 one way.

Bikes – usually mountain bikes – are often available **to rent** from campsites, youth hostels and gîtes d'étapes, as well as from specialist cycle shops and some tourist offices for around 80F per day; these machines are likely to be more reliable, though more expensive, than those of the SNCF. The bikes are often not insured, however, and you will be presented with the bill for its replacement if it's stolen or damaged. Check whether your travel insurance policy covers you for this if you intend to rent a bike.

As for **maps**, a minimum requirement is the IGN 1:100,000 series – the smallest scale that carries contours. In the UK, the **Cyclists' Touring Club**, Cotterell House, 68 Meadrow, Godalming, Surrey GU7 3HS (☎01483/417 217, fax 01483/426 994; email cycling@ctc.org.uk), will suggest routes and supply advice for members (£25 p.a. or £12.50 for unemployed). They run a particularly good insurance scheme. Companies running specialist bike touring holidays are listed on pp.5 and 15.

MOPEDS AND SCOOTERS

Mopeds and **scooters** are relatively easy to find: everyone in France, from young kids to grandmas, rides one of these, and although they're not built for any kind of long-distance travel, they're ideal for shooting around town and nearby. Places that rent out bicycles will often also rent out mopeds; you can expect to pay 160F a day for a 50cc Suzuki, for example, or 200F for an 80cc motorbike, 295F for a 125cc. Crash helmets are now compulsory on all mopeds.

WALKWAYS

Long-distance walkers are well served in France by a network of over 30,000km of long-distance marked **footpaths**, known as sentiers de grande randonnée or, more commonly, simply as **GRs**. They're fully signposted and equipped with campsites and rest huts along the way. Some are real marathons, like the GR5 from the coast of Holland to Nice, the trans-Pyrenean GR10 or the Grande Traversée des Alpes (the GRX). The Chemin de St-Jacques – GR65 – follows the ancient pilgrim route from Le Puy in the Auvergne to the Spanish border above St-Jean-Pied-de-Port and on to the shrine of Santiago de Compostela, while GR3 traces the Loire from source to sea. There are many more.

Each path is described in a **Topoguide** (available in Britain from Stanfords, see p.30), which gives a detailed account of the route (in French), including maps, campsites, refuge huts, sources of provisions, etc. In addition, many tourist offices can provide guides to their local footpaths, especially in popular hiking areas, where they often share premises with professional mountain guides and hike leaders. The latter organize climbing and walking expeditions for all levels of experience. *Topoguides* are produced by the principal French walkers' organization, the Fédération Française de la Randonnée Pédestre, 14 rue Riquet, 75019 Paris (☎01.44.89.93.93, fax 01.40.35.85.67). The main climbing organization is the Club Alpin Français, 24 ave de Laumière, 75019 Paris (☎01.53.72.87.00, fax 01.42.03.55.60). In Corsica, you can find out details about rambling and climbing from the Parc Naturel Régional de la Corse, 2 rue Major Lambroschini, off Cours Napoléon in Ajaccio (☎04.95.51.79.10, fax 95.21.88.17).

Maps are listed under the "Information and maps" section on p.30; you might also like to look at the specialized walking sheets produced by Didier et Richard of Grenoble for the Alps. **Guidebooks** worth looking out for are listed on p.1097.

INLAND WATERWAYS

With some 7500km of navigable rivers and canals, **boating** can be one of the best and most relaxed ways of exploring France. Except on parts of the Moselle, there is no charge for use of the waterways, and you can travel without a permit for up to six months in a year. For information on maximum dimensions, documentation, regulations and so forth, ask at a French Government Tourist Office for their booklet *Boating on the Waterways*. They also have brochures on boating in particular regions of France, and lists of French and British firms that rent out boats. British companies organizing **boating holidays** include Hoseasons (☎01502/500 555), Crown Blue Line

(☎01603/630513), Abercrombie & Kent (☎0171/730 9600) and Just France (☎0181/780 0303). The most attractive boats, based on a scaled-down version of real commercial barges, are run by French Country Cruises (☎01572/821 330, fax 01572/821 072). A week's hire of one of their boats, capable of sleeping five people, costs from £525 in low season to £910 in peak. For a full list, write to the Syndicat National des Loueurs de Bateaux de Plaisance, Port de la Bourdonnais, 75007 Paris (☎01.44.37.04.00, fax 01.45.77.21.88).

The principal **areas** for boating are Brittany, Burgundy, Picardy-Flanders, Alsace and Champagne. Brittany's canals join up with the Loire, but this is only navigable as far as Angers, with no links eastwards. Other waterways permit numerous permutations, including joining up via the Rhône and Saône with the Canal du Midi in Languedoc and then northwestwards to Bordeaux and the Atlantic. The eighteenth-century Canal de Bourgogne and 300-year-old Canal du Midi are fascinating examples of early canal engineering. The latter completely transformed the fortunes of coastal Languedoc, and in particular Sète, whose attractive harbour dates from that period. Together with its continuation, the Canal du Sète à Rhône, it passes within easy reach of several interesting areas.

The through-journey from the **Channel to the Mediterranean** requires some planning. The Canal de Bourgogne has an inordinate number of locks, while other waterways demand considerable skill and experience – the Rhône and Saône rivers, for example, have tricky currents. The most direct route is from Le Havre to just beyond Paris, then south either on Canal du Loing et de Briare or Canal du Nivernais to the Canal Latéral de la Loire, which you follow as far as Digoin in southern Burgundy, where it crosses the River Loire and meets the Canal du Centre. You follow the latter as far as Châlon, where you continue south on the Saône and Rhône until you reach the Mediterranean at Port St-Louis in the Camargue.

ACCOMMODATION

At most times of the year, you can turn up in any French town and find a room, or a place in a campsite. Booking a couple of nights in advance can be reassuring, however, as it saves you the effort of trudging round and ensures that you know what you'll be paying. In most towns, you'll be able to get a double for around 160–220F, or a single for around 130–160F. We've detailed a selection of hotels in most of the destinations listed in the *Guide*, and given a price range for each (see box); as a general rule the areas around train stations have the highest density of cheap hotels. Phone numbers as well as addresses are given in the *Guide*, and the "Language" section at the back (see pp.1098–1103) should help you make a reservation call, though many hoteliers and campsite managers – and almost all youth hostel managers – speak some English. We've also included fax numbers if you want to fax through booking requests before you leave home.

Problems arise mainly between July 15 and August 31, when the French take their own vacations en masse. The first weekend of August is the busiest time of all. During this period, hotel and hostel accommodation can be hard to come by, particularly in the coastal resorts, and you may find yourself falling back on local tourist offices for help and ideas. Some tourist offices offer a **booking service** – these are detailed in the *Guide* – but they cannot guarantee rooms at a particular price. All tourist offices can provide lists of hotels, the various hostels or the organizations such as CROUS (see p.42) to contact, details of campsites, and bed and breakfast possibilities (chambres d'hôte and fermes auberges).

With **campsites**, you can be more relaxed, unless you're touring with a caravan or camper van or looking for a place on the Côte d'Azur. Big cities can be difficult throughout the year: we've

ACCOMMODATION PRICE CATEGORIES

All the hotels listed in this book have been price-graded according to the following scale, and though costs will rise slightly overall with the life of this edition, the relative comparisons should remain valid. Paris is far more expensive than the rest of the country. Other big cities have a good variety of cheap establishments; in small towns or villages where the choice is limited, you may not be so lucky. Swanky resorts, particularly those on the Côte d'Azur, have very high July and August prices, but are still less expensive than Paris. If you are staying more than three days it's often possible to negotiate a lower price, particularly out of season. The prices quoted are for the cheapest available double room in high season, although remember that many of the cheap places will have more expensive rooms with en-suite facilities.

What you get for your money varies enormously between establishments. For under 180F, the bed is likely to be old and floppy. There won't be soundproofing and showers will be communal, though you may have your own toilet, bidet and washbasin. Over 250F, the decor may not be anything to write home about, but rooms will have their own bath or shower though not necessarily a toilet, and comfortable furniture. A more comfortable room will be had for around 300F with its own complete bathroom and perhaps a TV. At more than 450F, you should expect a higher standard of fittings and something approaching luxury. Breakfast is not normally included but is generally available at about 30F.

① Under 160F	④ 300–400F	⑦ 600–700F
② 160–220F	⑤ 400–500F	⑧ Over 700F
③ 220–300F	⑥ 500–600F	

given a greater range of possibilities for them in the *Guide* and very detailed accommodation listings for Paris, the worst case of all.

HOTELS

Hotel recommendations are given in the text of the *Guide* for almost every town or village mentioned. Full **accommodation lists** for each province are available from any French Government Tourist Office (see p.31) or from local tourist offices, and are especially handy during peak season. All French hotels are **graded** from zero to five stars. The price more or less corresponds to the number of stars, though the system is a little haphazard, having more to do with ratios of bathrooms-per-guest than genuine quality; and ungraded and single-star hotels are often very good. At the cheapest level, what makes a difference in **cost** is whether a room contains a shower: if it does, the bill will be around 30–50F more. **Breakfast**, too, can add 20–35F per person to a bill – though there is no obligation to take it and you will nearly always do better at a café. The cost of eating **dinner** in a hotel's restaurant can be a more important factor to bear in mind when picking a place to stay. Officially, it is illegal for hotels to insist on your taking meals, but they often do in places heavily dependent on seasonal tourism. But this is not always such a bad thing, especially in times of economic recession; you can get a real bargain. **Single rooms** are only marginally cheaper than doubles, so sharing always slashes costs. Most hotels willingly provide rooms with **extra beds**, for three or more people, at good discounts.

The cheapest rooms in a hotel will always have a wash-basin (*lavabo*) and sometimes a bidet; this area is often partitioned off from the rest of the room (referred to as a *cabinet de toilette*) which allows some privacy if you're travelling with a friend and means that you can wash in the sink to save money: the shared showers down the hall are not usually free – they cost between 15F to 20F per shower (*douche*). If you plan to shower everyday and there is more than one of you, it's worth adding up what the ultimate cost will be – you might be better off moving to a more expensive room with its own shower. Rooms will often have a shower cabinet but no toilet (*WC*); if wandering dark halls late at night in search of a toilet is not your idea of fun, ask for a bathroom (*salle de bain*) which will get you both a toilet and

a shower in a separate room; these do occasionally have bath tubs (*bain*) too. Hotels with at least one star or above have a telephone in the rooms, though some phones can only receive calls.

Note that many family-run hotels are closed every year for two or three weeks some time between May and September – where possible we've detailed this in the text. In addition, some hotels in smaller towns and villages close for one or two nights a week, usually Sunday or Monday – if in doubt, ring first to check.

In country areas, in addition to standard hotels, you will also come across **chambres d'hôte** and **fermes auberges**, bed-and-breakfast accommodation in someone's house or farm. These vary in standard and are rarely a cheap option, usually costing the equivalent of a two-star hotel. However, if you're lucky, they may be good sources of traditional home-cooking and French company. The brown leaflets available in tourist offices list most of them.

A very useful option, especially if it's late at night, are the **motel chains**. In contrast to the downtown hotels which often offer doubtful value (worn-out mattresses, dust, noise, etc) you can count on a decent and reliable standard in the chains even if they are without much charm. Among the cheapest is the one-star **Formule 1** chain, well signposted on the outskirts of most big towns. They are characterless, but provide rooms for up to three people from 120F. With a Visa, Mastercard, Eurocard or American Express credit card, you can let yourself into a room at any hour of the day or night. Addresses are most easily available on Minitel – 3615 or 3616 Formule 1 – but the hotels are not difficult to find as long as you're travelling by car, and a brochure with full details can be picked up at any one of them. Other cheap chains include 1re Classe, Etap Hôtel and Balladins; they tend to be grouped together near autoroute exits. More comfortable but still affordable **chain hotels** are Campanile, Ibis, Climat de France and Clarine which all have en-suite rooms with cable TV and direct dial phones from 270F–320F. The **Campanile** chain of motels is reachable on the World Wide Web at *www.campanile.fr* and will not only accept reservations by computer message, but will send a written confirmation within 3 to 5 days. They will also send a complete list of their locations in France by email request within a few days. **Ibis** provide a very affordable, dependable level of comfort which make them highly suitable for frazzled families for whom the concept of nightlife does not exist; prices start from about 300F per en-suite double and include cable TV. In the UK, call ☎0181/746 3233 and request a detailed location booklet.

YOUTH HOSTELS, FOYERS AND STUDENT ACCOMMODATION

At between 60F and 120F per night for a dormitory bed, and generally breakfast thrown in, **youth hostels** – *auberges de jeunesse* – are invaluable for single travellers on a budget. Many of the modern ones now offer rooms for couples, with en-suite showers, but they don't necessarily work out cheaper than hotels – particularly if you've had to pay a bus fare out to the edge of town to reach them. However, many hostels are beautifully sited, and they allow you to cut costs by preparing your own food in their kitchens (not often possible), or eating in their cheap canteens. To stay at FUAJ or LFAJ hostels (see below) you must be a member of Hostelling International (HI)/the International Youth Hostel Federation (IYHF). Head offices and membership fees, which differ from country to country, are listed in the box opposite. If you don't join up before you leave home, a membership card can be purchased in relevant French hostels for 100F.

Slightly confusingly, there are three rival French youth hostel associations (see box below): the main two being the Fédération Unie des Auberges de Jeunesse (FUAJ; 180 hostels), which has its hostels detailed in the *International Handbook*, and the Ligue Française pour les Auberges de Jeunesse (LFAJ; 100 hostels). HI membership covers both organizations, and you'll find all their hostels detailed in the text. The third organisation is the Union des Centres de Recontres Internationales de France (UCRIF) with 60 hostels in France; membership is not required. There are now also several **independent hostels**, particularly in Paris, where dorm beds cost from 95F to120F with breakfast thrown in, though these tend to be party places with an emphasis on good times rather than sleep. The best of the Parisian hostels are the Maisons Internationales de la Jeunesse et des Etudiants (MIJE), in beautiful old mansions int he Marais district.

A few large towns provide a more luxurious standard of hostel accommodation in **Foyers des Jeunes Travailleurs/euses**, residential hostels for young workers and students, where you can usually get a private room for around 60F. They normally have a good cafeteria or canteen.

At the height of summer (usually July & Aug only), there's also the possibility of staying in **student accommodation** in university towns and cities. The main organization for this is CROUS, Académie de Paris, 39 av Georges-Bernanos, Paris 75005 (☎01.40.51.36.00; *www.cnous.fr*). Prices are similar to the official hostels, from around 70F per person, and you don't need membership.

GÎTES AND REFUGES

In the countryside, a third hostel-style alternative exists. **Gîtes d'étape** are less formal than the youth hostels, often run by the local village or municipality (whose mayor will probably be in charge of the key), and they provide bunk beds and primitive kitchen and washing facilities from around 40F. They are marked on the large-scale IGN walkers' maps and listed in the individual GR *Topoguides*. Mountain areas are well supplied with **refuge huts**, mostly run by the Club Alpin Français (CAF) and mostly only open in summer. They are the only available shelter once you are above the villages. Costs are from around 60F for the night, less if you're a member of a climbing organization affiliated to the CAF. Meals – invariably four courses – cost around 80F, which is not unreasonable when you consider that all supplies have to be brought up by mule or helicopter.

A guide, *Gîtes d'Étape et Refuges*, is published by Guides La Cadole; it's available in French book shops for 110F.

RENTED ACCOMMODATION: GÎTES DE FRANCE

If you are planning to stay a week or more in any one place it might be worth considering **renting a house**. You can do this by checking adverts from the innumerable private and foreign owners in British Sunday newspapers (*Observer* and *Sunday Times*, mainly), or trying one of the numerous holiday firms that market accommodation/travel packages (see the boxes on pp.5 or 14 for a brief selection of these).

The French Government letting service, the **Gîtes de France**, is represented by Brittany Ferries in the UK (enquiries ☎0990/360360; ☎021/277801 in the Irish Republic), although you can still deal directly with Gîtes de France, 59 rue St-Lazare, Paris 75009 (Mon–Sat 10am–6.30pm; ☎01.49.70.75.75).

CAMPING

Practically every village and town in the country has at least one **campsite** to cater for the thousands of people who spend their holiday under canvas – camping is a very big deal in France. The cheapest – at around 22F–30F per person per night – is usually the **camping municipal**, run by the local municipality. In season or whenever they're officially open, they are always clean and

have plenty of hot water; often they are situated in prime local positions. Out of season, those that stay open often don't bother to collect the overnight charge.

If you're planning to do a lot of camping, an **international camping carnet** is a good investment, available in the UK from the AA or the RAC or the Carefree Travel Service (☎01203/422024), who also book inspected camping sites in Europe and arrange ferry crossings. The carnet serves as useful identification, covers you for third party insurance when camping, and helps you get 10 percent reductions camp sites listed in the CCI information booklet which comes with your carnet. It is available in the US from Family Campers and RVers (FCRV), 4804 Transit Rd, Building 2, Depew, NY 14043 (☎1-800/245 9755); and in Canada from 51 W 22nd St, Hamilton, ON LC9 4N5 (☎1-800/245 9755). The carnet is good for discounts at member sites and serves as useful identification. FCRV annual membership costs $20, and the carnet an additional $10.

On the coast especially, there are **superior categories** of campsite where you'll pay prices similar to those of a hotel for the facilities – bars, restaurants and sometimes swimming pools. These have rather more permanent status than the *campings municipaux*, with people often spending a whole holiday in the one base. If you plan to do the same, and particularly if you have a caravan, camper or a big tent, it's wise to book ahead – reckon on paying at least 35F a head with a tent, 40F with a camper van. Inland, **camping à la ferme** – on somebody's farm – is another possibility (generally without facilities). Lists of sites are detailed in the Tourist Board's *Accueil à la Campagne* booklet.

A number of companies also specialize in selling **camping holidays**, including Allez France (☎01903/748 166), Canvas Holidays (☎01383/644000 or ☎01992/553535), Eurocamp (☎01565/626 262), Keycamp (☎0181/395 4000), Eurosites (☎01706/830739), Haven Holidays (☎01442/233111) and Sunsites (☎01565/625 555). Twelve nights' camping at Argelès, near Perpignan, with Sunsites, for example, costs from £862 for two adults, with up to four children under 18 free, which includes the price of the Channel ferry.

Lastly, **a word of caution**: never camp rough (*camping sauvage*, as the French call it) on anyone's land without first asking permission. If the dogs don't get you, the guns might

– farmers have been known to shoot before asking questions. In many parts of France, *camping sauvage* on public land isn't tolerated – Brittany being a notable exception. On beaches, it's best to camp out only where other people are doing so.

EATING AND DRINKING

French cuisine has taken a bit of a knocking in recent years. The wonderful ingredients are still there, as every town and village market testifies. But those little family restaurants serving classic peasant dishes that celebrate the region's produce in each exquisite mouthful – and where the bill is less than 100F – are few and far between. The processed, boil-in-the-bag and ready-to-microwave productions of the global food industry, all so inimical to the basic culinary arts of France, are making serious inroads. That's not to say you can't eat well in France – far from it – but be prepared for disappointments at run-of-the-mill establishments.

In the rarefied world of **haute cuisine**, where the top chefs are national celebrities, a battle is currently raging between traditionalists, determined to preserve the purity of French cuisine, and those who experiment with different flavours from around the world to create novel combinations, for example seafood and cinnamon. At this level, French food is still brilliant – in both camps – and the good news is that prices are continuing to come down. Many gourmet palaces offer weekday lunchtime menus where you can sample culinary genius for around 290F.

France is also a great place for **foreign cuisine**, in particular North African, Caribbean (known as Antillais) and Asiatic. Moroccan, Thai or Vietnamese restaurants are not necessarily cheap options but they are usually good value for money.

On the whole, **vegetarians** can expect a somewhat lean time in France. A few cities have specifically vegetarian restaurants (detailed in the text), but elsewhere you'll have to hope you find a sympathetic restaurant (crêperies and pizzerias can be good standbys). Sometimes they're willing to replace a meat dish on the *menu fixe* with an omelette; other times you'll have to pick your way through the *carte*. Remember the phrase "Je suis végétarien(ne); il y a quelques plats sans viande?" (I'm a vegetarian; are there any non-meat dishes?). Many vegetarians swallow a few principles and start eating fish and shellfish on holiday. **Vegans**, however, should probably forget all about eating in French restaurants and stick to self-catering.

BREAKFAST AND SNACKS

A croissant, *pain au chocolat* (a square-shaped chocolate-filled light pastry) or a sandwich in a bar or café, with hot chocolate or coffee, is generally the best way to eat **breakfast** – at a fraction of the cost charged by most hotels. (The days when hotels gave you mounds of croissants or brioches for breakfast seem to be long gone; now it's usually always bread, jam and a jug of coffee or tea for about 30F.) Croissants and sometimes hard-boiled eggs are displayed on bar counters until around 9.30am or 10am. If you stand – cheaper than sitting down – you just help yourself to these with your coffee, the waiter keeps an eye on how many you've eaten and bills you accordingly.

At **lunchtime**, and sometimes in the evening, you may find cafés offering *a plat du jour* (chef's daily special) at between 40F and 75F, or *formules*, a limited or no-choice menu. *Croques-monsieur* or *croques-madame* (variations on the toasted-cheese sandwich) are on sale at cafés, brasseries and many street stands, along with *frites* (potato fries), crêpes, *galettes* (wholewheat pancakes), *gauffres* (waffles), *glaces* (ice creams) and all kinds of fresh-filled baguettes (these very filling sandwiches usually cost between 18F to 28F to take away). For variety, there are Tunisian snacks like *brik à l'œuf* (a fried pastry with an egg inside), *merguez* (spicy North African sausage), Greek souvlaki (kebabs) and Middle Eastern falafel (deep-fried chickpea balls in flat bread with salad). Wine bars are good for French regional sausages and cheese, usually served with brown bread (*pain de campagne*).

Crêpes, or pancakes with fillings, served up at ubiquitous crêperies, are popular lunchtime food. The savoury buckwheat variety (often called *galettes*) provide the main course; the sweet white-flour ones are dessert. They taste nice enough, but are usually poor value in comparison with a restaurant meal; you need at least three, normally at over 30F each, to feel full. **Pizzerias**, usually *au feu du bois* (wood-fire-baked), are also very common. They are somewhat better value than crêperies, but quality and quantity vary greatly – look before you leap into the nearest empty seats.

For **picnics**, the local outdoor market or supermarket will provide you with almost everything you need from tomatoes and avocados to cheese and pâté. Cooked meat, prepared snacks, ready-made dishes and assorted salads can be bought at *charcuteries* (delicatessens), which you'll find everywhere – even in small villages, though the same things are cheaper at supermarket counters. You purchase by weight, or you can ask for *une tranche* (a slice), *une barquette* (a carton) or *une part* (a portion).

Salons de thé, which open from mid-morning to late evening, serve brunches, salads, quiches, and the like, as well as gateaux, ice cream and a wide selection of teas. They tend to be a good deal pricier than cafés or brasseries – you're paying for the posh surroundings. As bars are to men in France, *salons de thé* are to women, and they generally have a more female ambience and clientele. For cakes and pastries to take away, you'll find impressive arrays at every boulangerie-pâtisserie.

FULL-SCALE MEALS

There's no difference between **restaurants** (or auberges or *relais* as they sometimes call themselves) and **brasseries** in terms of quality or price range. The distinction is that brasseries, which resemble cafés, serve quicker meals at most hours of the day, while restaurants tend to stick to the traditional meal times of noon to 2pm, and 7pm to 9.30pm. After 9pm or so, restaurants often serve only à la carte meals (single dishes chosen from the menu) – invariably more expensive than eating the set *menu fixe*. In touristy areas in high season, and for all the more upmarket places, it's wise to make reservations – easily done on the same day. In small towns it may be impossible to get anything other than a bar sandwich after 10pm or even earlier; in major cities, town centre brasseries will serve until 11pm or midnight and one or two may stay open all night.

When hunting, avoid places that are half empty at peak time, use your nose and regard long menus with suspicion. Don't forget that **hotel restaurants** are open to non-residents, and often very good value. In many small towns and villages, you'll find the only restaurants are in hotels. Since restaurants change hands frequently and have their ups and downs, it's also worth asking people you meet (locals, not fellow tourists) for recommendations. This is the conversational equivalent of commenting on the weather in Britain and will usually elicit strong views and sound advice.

Prices, and what you get for them, are posted outside. Normally there's a choice between one or more *menus fixes*, where the number of courses has been already determined and the choice is limited, and choosing individually from the *carte* (menu). **Menus fixes** are normally the cheapest option. At the bottom end of the price range, they revolve around standard dishes such as steak and chips (*steak frites*), chicken and chips (*poulet frites*) and various concoctions involving innards. But further up the scale they can be much the best-value way of sampling regional specialities, sometimes running to five or more courses. If you're simply not that hungry, just go for the *plat du jour*.

Going **à la carte** offers greater choice and, in the better restaurants, unlimited access to the chef's specialities – though you'll pay for the privilege. A simple and perfectly legitimate tactic is to have just one course instead of the expected three or four. You can share dishes or go for several starters – a useful strategy for vegetarians. There's no minimum charge.

In the French **sequence of courses**, any salad (sometimes vegetables, too) comes separate from the main dish, and cheese precedes a dessert. You will be offered coffee, which is always extra, to finish off the meal.

Service compris or *s.c.* means the **service charge** is included. *Service non compris, s.n.c.* or *servis en sus* means that it isn't and you need to calculate an additional fifteen percent. **Wine** (*vin*) or a **drink** (*boisson*) is occasionally included in the cost of a *menu fixe*. When ordering house wine, the cheapest option, ask for *un quart* (0.25 litre), *un demi-litre* (0.5 litre) or *une carafe* (1 litre). If you're worried about the cost ask for *vin ordinaire* or the *vin de table*. In the *Guide* the lowest price menu or the range of menus is given; where average à la carte prices are given it assumes you'll have three courses and half a bottle of wine.

The French are much better disposed towards **children** in restaurants than other nationalities, not simply by offering reduced-price children's menus but in creating an atmosphere – even in otherwise fairly snooty establishments – that positively welcomes kids; some even have in-house games and toys for them to occupy themselves with. It is regarded as self-evident that large family groups should be able to eat out together.

A rather murkier area is that of **dogs** in the dining room; it can be quite a shock in a provincial hotel to realize that the majority of your fellow diners are attempting to keep dogs concealed beneath their tables.

CHEESE

Charles de Gaulle once commented that "You can unite the French only through fear. You cannot simply bring together a country that has over 265 kinds of cheese." For serious **cheese**-lovers, France is the ultimate paradise. Other countries may produce individual cheeses which are as good as, or even better than, the best of the French, but no country

---

REGIONAL CUISINE

The **geography of France** explains much of the pride of place the country holds in European cuisines. The French can fish and breed seafood in the Channel waters, the Atlantic Ocean and the Mediterranean as well as catch freshwater fish in a thousand lakes and rivers. Mountains, forests, deltas and plains with climates ranging from the aridly sun-soaked to northern cold and wetness allow an extraordinary variety of produce. Added to this is the historical and social factor of a class of *paysans* – smallholders – who have passed down traditional methods from generation to generation. Though it is true that in recent years industrialization has standardized and sanitized production methods, food imports have greatly increased, and pollution has taken its toll, there remains a strong connection between the countryside and the table, reflected in the different regional cuisines. The gastronomic map of France features certain regions – Alsace, Provence, Brittany and the Pays Basque – in which the preservation of a distinctive cuisine owes much to historical separation. Burgundy, the Auvergne, Normandy and the Dordogne have absorbed classic French cooking from different corners of the country.

Dishes from **Alsace** and **Lorraine** are based on game, pork, beef and lamb, pickled cabbage, and flans with pizza-like pastries. Mussels and chips, accompanied by beer, are a staple of **northern France**. Butter and cream are the rich basis of many **Normandy** specialities, which include famous cheeses, apple and pear dishes, and seafood. **Brittany** has oysters, lobsters and other produce from the sea; crêpes and *galettes* with sweet and savoury fillings; and buttery cakes and flans. Seafood again features prominently on menus all along the **Atlantic Coast**. The famous Charolais beef of **Burgundy**, combined with the local wines and mustard, produces mouthwatering variations; snails too are a speciality. Duck and goose in their myriad forms belong to the **Dordogne**, marinated and served with prunes, preserves and truffles. In the **Auvergne**, cabbage, pork and bean stew is a favourite, along with cheeses, sausages and garlic soups. **Languedoc** has the celebrated Rocquefort cheese as a basis for many dishes, and serves snails in appetizing ways, along with the rum-flambéed crêpes *languedociennes*. **Lyon** has a special position as the meeting place of north and south, combining sausages and smoked meats with the famous Bresse chicken, dumplings, southern salads and the tasty *tarte Lyonnais*. The **Pays Basque** specializes in wild pigeon and Bayonne ham, white tuna and the delicious ewe's milk cheese, *brébis*, as well as the rich cherry and chocolate gâteau Basque. **Provence**, with its Mediterranean climate, yields olives, garlic, lavender honey and delicious fruit and vegetables, all used to perfection in pasta dishes, fish soups, stews and grills, mixed salads and flans. In **Corsica** wild herbs give the cuisine its unique flavour, with specialities like smoked pork, game, shellfish, eel and trout, and a range of dishes made from the local chestnuts.

You'll find regional specialities detailed within each chapter.

WINES

French **wines** are unrivalled in the world for their range, sophistication, diversity and status. Individual wines from other countries may be able to compete with the best of French wines, but however hard foreign producers try, the French market is uncrackable. The French simply see no reason to try any wines but their own. Sipping a Nuits St-Georges, Sancerre, Chablis, Châteauneuf-du-Pape or one of the top champagnes – assuming you can afford them – it's hard to disagree.

With the exception of the northwest of the country and the mountains, wine is produced just about everywhere. The **great wine-producing regions** are Champagne, Bordeaux and Burgundy, closely followed by the Loire and Rhône valleys. Alsace also has some great wines, and there are some beautiful wines to be had in the lesser wine regions of Bergerac, Languedoc, Roussillon and Provence.

The quality of the *vins de pays*, though very variable, is still exceptional for the price. Quality wines are denoted by the *appellation d'origine contrôlée* (AOC), which strictly controls the amount of wine that a particular area, whether several hundred square kilometres or just two, may produce. Within each appellation there is enormous diversity generated by the different types of soil, the lie of the land, the type of grape grown – there are over sixty varieties – the ability of the wine to age, and the individual skills of the wine-grower.

It's an extremely complex business and it's not difficult to feel intimidated by the seemingly innate expertise of all French people. Many individual wines and *appellations* are mentioned in the text, but trusting your own taste response is the most important thing. Knowing the grape types that you particularly like (or dislike), whether you like wines very fruity, dry, light or heavy, is all useful when you are discussing your choice with a waiter, wine-grower or wine merchant. The more interest you show, the more helpful advice you are likely to receive. The only thing the French cannot tolerate is people ordering Coke to accompany a gourmet meal. We've detailed the main wine-growing regions – and their produce – throughout the *Guide*.

offers a range that comes anywhere near them in terms of sheer inventiveness. In fact, there are officially over 400 types of French cheese (with new ones being created every year), whose recipes are jealously guarded secrets. Many cheese-makers have successfully protected their products by AC (*appellation d'origine controlée*) laws similar to those for wines, which means that the subtle differences between French local cheeses have not been overwhelmed by the industrialized uniformity that has plagued other countries.

Most restaurants keep a well-stocked *plateau de fromages* (cheeseboard), kept at room temperature and served with bread, but not butter. Apart from the ubiquitous Brie, Camembert and numerous varieties of goat's cheese (*chèvre*), there will usually be one or two local cheeses on offer – these are the ones to go for. Your best bet for local produce is a *fromagerie*, which often has 200 varieties or more to choose from. We've indicated the best national and regionally available cheeses in the text.

DRINKING

Wherever you can eat you can invariably **drink**, and vice versa. Drinking is done at a leisurely pace whether it's a prelude to food (*apéritif*), a

sequel (*digestif*), or the accompaniment, and **cafés** are the standard places to do it. Every bar or café has to display its full **price list**, usually without the fifteen percent service charge added, with the cheapest drinks at the bar (*au comptoir*), and progressively increasing prices for sitting at a table inside (*la salle*), or outside (*la terrasse*). You pay when you leave, and it's perfectly acceptable to sit for hours over just one cup of coffee.

Wine (*vin*) is drunk at just about every meal or social occasion. Red is *rouge*, white *blanc*, or there's *rosé*. *Vin de table* or *vin ordinaire* – table wine – is generally drinkable and always cheap, although it may be disguised and priced-up as the house wine, or *cuvée*. The price of AOC (*appellation d'origine contrôlée*) wines can vary from 10F to 100F and over, and that's the vineyard price. You can buy a very decent bottle of wine for 20F or 30F, and 60F and over will buy you something really nice. By the time restaurants have added their considerable mark-up, wine can constitute an alarming proportion of the bill.

The basic **wine terms** are: *brut*, very dry; *sec*, dry; *demi-sec*, sweet; *doux*, very sweet; *mousseux*, sparkling; *méthode champenoise*, mature and sparkling. There are grape varieties as well, but the complexities of the subject take up volumes. A glass of wine is simply *un rouge*, *un rosé* or *un*

FOOD AND DISHES

Basic Terms

l'addition	bill/check	*fourchette*	fork	*offert*	free	*table*	table
beurre	butter	*huile*	oil	*pain*	bread	*verre*	glass
bouteille	bottle	*lait*	milk	*poivre*	pepper	*vinaigre*	vinegar
couteau	knife	*moutarde*	mustard	*sel*	salt		
cuillère	spoon	*œuf*	egg	*sucre*	sugar		

Snacks

un sandwich/	**a sandwich**	**œufs**	**eggs**
une baguette		*au plat*	fried
au jambon	with ham	*à la coque*	boiled
au fromage	with cheese	*durs*	hard-boiled
au saucisson	with sausage	*brouillés*	scrambled
à l'ail	with garlic		
au poivre	with pepper	**omelette**	**omelette**
au pâté (de campagne)	with pâté (country-style)	*nature*	plain
		aux fines herbes	with herbs
croque-monsieur	grilled cheese & ham sandwich	*au fromage*	with cheese
croque-madame	grilled cheese & bacon, sausage, chicken or an egg	**some terms**	
		chauffé	heated
		cuit	cooked
pain bagnat	bread roll with egg, olives, salad, tuna, anchovies & olive oil	*cru*	raw
		emballé	wrapped
		à emporter	take-away
panini	toasted Italian sandwich	*fumé*	smoked
tartine	buttered bread or open sandwich	*salé*	salted/spicy
		sucré	sweet

Pasta (pâtes), Pancakes (crêpes) and Flans (tartes)

nouilles	noodles	*socca*	thin chickpea flour pancake
pâtes fraîches	fresh pasta	*panisse*	thick chickpea flour pancake
raviolis	pasta parcels of meat or chard, a Provençal, not Italian invention	*pissaladière*	tart of fried onions with anchovies & black olives
		tarte flambée	thin pizza-like pastry topped with onion, cream & bacon or other combinations
crêpe au sucre/ aux œufs	pancake with sugar/eggs		
galette	buckwheat pancake		

Soups (soupes) and Starters (hors d'œuvres)

baudroie	fish soup with vegetables, garlic & herbs	*rouille*	red pepper, garlic & saffron mayonnaise served with fish soup
bisque	shellfish soup		
bouillabaisse	soup with five fish & other bits to dip	*soupe à l'oignon*	onion soup with rich cheese topping
bouillon	broth or stock	*velouté*	thick soup, usually fish or poultry
bourride	thick fish soup		
consommé	clear soup		
garbure	potato, cabbage & meat soup	**starters**	
pistou	parmesan, basil & garlic paste added to soup	*assiette anglaise*	plate of cold meats
		crudités	raw vegetables with dressings
potée auvergnate	cabbage & meat soup	*hors d'œuvres*	combination of the above
potage	thick vegetable soup	*variés*	plus smoked or marinated fish

Fish (poisson), Seafood (fruits de mer) and Shellfish (crustaces or coquillages)

aiglefin	small haddock or fresh cod	crabe	crab	loup de mer	sea bass
anchois	anchovies	crevettes grises	shrimp	maquereau	mackerel
anguilles	eels	crevettes roses	prawns	merlan	whiting
barbue	brill	daurade	sea bream	moules	mussels (with
baudroie	monkfish or anglerfish	éperlan	smelt or whitebait	(marinière)	shallots in white wine sauce)
		escargots	snails		
bigourneau	periwinkle	favou(ille)	tiny crab	oursin	sea urchin
brème	bream	flétan	halibut	palourdes	clams
bulot	whelk	friture	assorted fried fish	poissons de roche	fish from shore-line rocks
cabillaud	cod				
calmar	squid	gambas	king prawns	praires	small clams
carrelet	plaice	hareng	herring	raie	skate
claire	type of oyster	homard	lobster	rouget	red mullet
colin	hake	huîtres	oysters	saumon	salmon
congre	conger eel	langouste	spiny lobster	sole	sole
coques	cockles	langoustines	saltwater cray-fish (scampi)	thon	tuna
coquilles St-Jacques	scallops			truite	trout
		limande	lemon sole	turbot	turbot
		lotte de mer	monkfish	violet	sea squirt

fish dishes and terms

aïoli	garlic mayonnaise served with salt cod & other fish	la douzaine	a dozen	mousse/ mousseline	mousse
		frit	fried		
		friture	deep-fried small fish	pané	breaded
anchoïade	anchovy paste or sauce			poutargue	mullet roe paste
		fumé	smoked	raïto	red wine, olive, caper, garlic & shallot sauce
arête	fish bone	fumet	fish stock		
assiette de pêcheur	assorted fish	gigot de mer	large fish baked whole		
				quenelles	light dumplings
béarnaise	sauce of egg yolks, white wine, shallots & vinegar	grillé	grilled	thermidor	lobster grilled in its shell with cream sauce
		hollandaise	butter & vinegar sauce		
beignet	fritter	à la meunière	in a butter, lemon & parsley sauce		
darne	fillet or steak				

Meat (viande) and Poultry (volaille)

agneau (de pré-salé)	lamb (grazed on salt marshes)	gigot (d'agneau)	leg (of lamb)	os	bone
		grenouilles (cuisses de)	frogs (legs)	poitrine	breast
andouille, andouillette	tripe sausage			porc	pork
		grillade	grilled meat	poulet	chicken
bifteck	steak	hâchis	chopped meat or mince hamburger	poussin	baby chicken
bœuf	beef			ris	sweetbreads
boudin blanc	sausage of white meats			rognons	kidneys
		langue	tongue	rognons blancs	testicles
boudin noir	black pudding	lapin, lapereau	rabbit, young rabbit	sanglier	wild boar
caille	quail			steak	steak
canard	duck	lard, lardons	bacon, diced bacon	tête de veau	calf's head (in jelly)
caneton	duckling				
contrefilet	sirloin roast	lièvre	hare	tournedos	thick slices of fillet
coquelet	cockerel	merguez	spicy, red sausage		
dinde, dindon	turkey				
entrecôte	rib steak	mouton	mutton	tripes	tripe
faux filet	sirloin steak	museau de veau	calf's muzzle	tripoux	mutton tripe
foie	liver	oie	goose	veau	veal
foie gras	(duck/goose) liver	onglet	cut of beef	venaison	venison

Meat and poultry dishes and terms

aïado	roast shoulder of lamb stuffed with garlic & other ingredients	sauté	lightly cooked in butter
aile	wing	steak au poivre (vert/rouge)	steak in a black (green/red) peppercorn sauce
au feu de bois	cooked over wood fire	steak tartare	raw chopped beef, topped with a raw egg yolk
au four	baked		
baeckoffe	Alsatian hotpot of pork, mutton & beef baked with potato layers	tagine	North African casserole
		tournedos rossini	beef fillet with foie gras & truffles
blanquette, daube, estouffade, hochepôt, navarin, ragoût	types of stew	viennoise	fried in egg & breadcrumbs
blanquette de veau	veal in cream & mushroom sauce	**terms for steaks**	
		bleu	almost raw
bœuf bourguignon	beef stew with Burgundy, onions & mushrooms	saignant	rare
		à point	medium
canard à l'orange	roast duck with an orange & wine sauce	bien cuit	well done
		très bien cuit	very well done
canard périgourdin	roast duck with prunes, pâté de foie gras & truffles	brochette	kebab
carré	best end of neck, chop or cutlet	**garnishes and sauces**	
cassoulet	a casserole of beans & meat	américaine	white wine, cognac & tomato
choucroute	pickled cabbage with peppercorns, sausages, bacon & salami	arlésienne	with tomatoes, onions, aubergines, potatoes & rice
		au porto	in port
civit	game stew	auvergnat	with cabbage, sausage & bacon
confit	meat preserve	beurre blanc	sauce of white wine & shallots, with butter
côte	chop, cutlet or rib		
cou	neck	bonne femme	with mushroom, bacon, potato & onions
coq au vin	chicken cooked until it falls off the bone with wine, onions & mushrooms	bordelaise	in a red wine, shallot and bone-marrow sauce
cuisse	thigh or leg		
épaule	shoulder	boulangère	baked with potatoes & onions
en croûte	in pastry	bourgeoise	with carrots, onions, bacon, celery & braised lettuce
farci	stuffed		
gigot (d'agneau)	leg (of lamb)	chasseur	white wine, mushrooms and shallots
grillade	grilled meat		
garni	with vegetables	châtelaine	with artichoke hearts & chestnut purée
gésier	gizzard		
grillé	grilled	diable	strong mustard seasoning
hâchis	chopped meat or mince hamburger	forestière	with bacon & mushroom
		fricassée	rich, creamy sauce
magret de canard	duck breast	mornay	cheese sauce
marmite	casserole	pays d'auge	cream & cider
médaillon	round piece	périgourdine	with foie gras & possibly truffles
mijoté	stewed		
pavé	thick slice	piquante	gherkins or capers, vinegar & shallots
pieds et paques	mutton or pork tripe & trotters		
poêlé	pan-fried	provençale	tomatoes, garlic, olive oil & herbs
poulet de Bresse	chicken from Bresse – the best		
râble	saddle	savoyarde	with gruyère cheese
rôti	roast	véronique	grapes, wine & cream

Vegetables (légumes), Herbs (herbes) and Spices (é...)

ail	garlic	echalotes	shallots	pâte	
anis	aniseed	endive	chicory	persil	
artichaut	artichoke	épinard	spinach	petits p...	
asperge	asparagus	estragon	tarragon	piment	
avocat	avocado	fenouil	fennel	pois chic...	
basilic	basil	férigoule	thyme (in	pois	
betterave	beetroot		Provençal)	mange-tou...	snow peas
blette/bette	Swiss chard	fèves	broad beans	pignons	pine nuts
cannelle	cinnamon	flageolets	white beans	poireau	leek
capre	caper	gingembre	ginger	poivron (vert,	sweet pepper
cardon	cardoon, a beet	haricots (verts,	beans (French/	rouge)	(green, red)
	related to	rouges,	string, kidney,	pommes de	
	artichoke	beurres)	butter)	terre	potatoes
carotte	carrot	laurier	bay leaf	primeurs	spring vegetables
céleri	celery	lentilles	lentils	radis	radish
champignon,	types of	maïs	corn	riz	rice
cèpe,	mushrooms	menthe	mint	safran	saffron
chanterelle		moutarde	mustard	salade verte	green salad
chou (rouge)	(red) cabbage	oignon	onion	sarrasin	buckwheat
choufleur	cauliflower	panais	parsnip	tomate	tomato
concombre	cucumber	pélandron	type of string	truffes	truffles
cornichon	gherkin		bean		

vegetable dishes and terms

alicot	puréed potato	gratiné	browned with	petits farcis	stuffed tomatoes,
	with cheese		cheese or butter		aubergines,
allumettes	very thin chips	à la grecque	cooked in oil &		courgettes &
à l'anglaise	boiled		lemon		peppers
beignet	fritter	jardinière	with mixed diced	pimenté	peppery hot
biologique	organic		vegetables	piquant	spicy
duxelles	fried mushrooms	mousseline	mashed potato	pistou	ground basil, olive
	& shallots with		with cream &		oil, garlic &
	cream		eggs		parmesan
farci	stuffed	à la parisienne	sautéed in butter	râpée	grated or shredded
feuille	leaf		(potatoes); with	sauté	lightly fried in butter
fines herbes	mixture of		white wine	à la vapeur	steamed
	tarragon, parsley		sauce & shallots	en verdure	garnished with
	& chives	parmentier	with potatoes		green vegetables

Fruit (fruit) and Nuts (noix)

abricot	apricot	figue	fig	noisette	hazelnut
acajou	cashew nut	fraise (de bois)	strawberry	noix	nuts
amande	almond		(wild)	orange	orange
ananas	pineaple	framboise	raspberry	pamplemousse	grapefruit
banane	banana	fruit de la passion	passion fruit	pastèque	watermelon
brugnon, nectarine	nectarine	grenade	pomegranate	pêche	peach
cacahouète	peanut	groseille	redcurrant	pistache	pistachio
cassis	blackcurrant	mangue	mango	poire	pear
cérise	cherry	marron	chestnut	pomme	apple
citron	lemon	melon	melon	prune	plum
citron vert	lime	mirabelle	small yellow	pruneau	prune
datte	date		plum	raisin	grape
		myrtille	bilberry	reine-claude	greengage

fruit dishes and terms

agrumes	citrus fruits	flambé	set aflame in alcohol
beignet	fritter	fougasse	bread flavoured with orange-
compôte	stewed fruit		flower water or almonds
coulis	sauce of puréed fruit		(can be savoury)
crème de marrons	chestnut purée	frappé	iced

Desserts (desserts or entremets) and Pastries (pâtisserie)

bombe	moulded ice-cream dessert	marrons Mont Banc	chestnut purée &
brioche	sweet, high yeast breakfast		cream on a rum-soaked
	roll		sponge cake
calisson	almond sweet	mousse au chocolat	chocolate mousse
charlotte	custard & fruit in lining of	omelette norvégienne	baked alaska
	almond fingers	palmier	caramelized puff pastry
chichi	doughnut shaped in a stick	parfait	frozen mousse, sometimes
clafoutis	heavy custard & fruit tart		ice cream
crème Chantilly	vanilla-flavoured &	petit-suisse	a smooth mixture of cream
	sweetened whipped cream		& curds
crème fraîche	sour cream	petits fours	bite-sized cakes/pastries
crème pâtissière	thick, eggy pastry-filling	poires belle hélène	pears & ice cream in
crêpe suzette	thin pancake with orange		chocolate sauce
	juice & liqueur	tarte tatin	upside-down apple tart
fromage blanc	cream cheese	tarte tropezienne	sponge cake filled with
gaufre	waffle		custard cream topped
glace	ice cream		with nuts
île flottante/	soft meringues floating on	tiramisu	mascarpone cheese,
œufs à la neige	custard		chocolate & cream
macaron	macaroon	yaourt, yogourt	yoghurt
madeleine	small sponge cake		

dessert dishes and terms

barquette	small boat-shaped flan	gênoise	rich sponge cake
bavarois	refers to the mould, could be a	pâte	pastry or dough
	mousse or custard	sablé	shortbread biscuit
coupe	a serving of ice cream	savarin	a filled, ring-shaped cake
crêpe	pancake	tarte	tart
galettes	buckwheat pancake	tartelette	small tart

And one final note: always call the waiter or waitress *Monsieur* or *Madame* (*Mademoiselle* if a young woman), never *Garçon*, no matter what you've been taught in school.

---

blanc. You may have the choice of *un ballon* (round glass) or a smaller glass (*un verre*). *Un pichet* (a pitcher) is normally a quarter-litre. A glass of wine a bar will cost around 30F.

The best way to **buy bottles** of wine is directly from the producers (*vignerons*), either at vineyards, at Maisons or Syndicats du Vin (representing a group of wine-producers), or at Coopératifs Vinicoles (wine-producer co-ops). At all these places you can sample the wines first. It's best to make clear at the start how much you want to buy (if it's only one or two bottles) and you will not be popular if you drink several glass-es and then leave without making a purchase. The most economical option is to buy *en vrac*, which you can also do at some wine shops (*caves*), taking an easily obtainable plastic five- or ten-litre container (usually sold on the premises) and getting it filled straight from the barrel. In cities supermarkets are the best places to buy your wine.

Familiar light Belgian and German brands, plus French brands from Alsace, account for most of the **beer** you'll find. Draught beer (*à la pression*, usually Kronenbourg) is the cheapest drink you can have next to coffee and wine – ask for *un pression* or *un demi* (0.33 litre). A *demi* costs around 17F. For a wider choice of draught and bottled beer you need to go to the special beer-drinking establishments or English-style pubs found in most city centres and resorts. A small bottle at one of these places will cost at least twice as much as a *demi* in a café. In supermarkets, however, bottled or canned beer is exceptionally cheap.

Strong alcohol is consumed from as early as 5am as a pre-work fortifier, and then at any time through the day according to circumstance, though the national reputation for drunkenness has lost much of its truth. Brandies and the dozens of *eaux de vie* (spirits) and liqueurs are always available. Among less familiar names, try Poire William (pear brandy), Marc (a spirit distilled from grape pulp), or just point to the bottle with the most attractive colour. Measures are generous, but they don't come cheap: the same applies for imported spirits like whisky (Scotch). *Pastis* – the generic name of aniseed drinks such as Pernod or Ricard – is served diluted with water and ice (*glaçons*). It's very refreshing and not expensive. Two drinks designed to stimulate the appetite – *un apéritif* – are Pineau (cognac and grape juice) and Kir (white wine with a dash of Cassis – blackcurrant liquor, or with champagne instead of wine for a Kir Royal). Cocktails are served at most late-night bars, discos and music places, as well as at upmarket hotel bars and at every seaside promenade café; they usually cost at least 45F.

On the **soft drink** front, you can buy cartons of unsweetened fruit juice in supermarkets, although in the cafés the bottled (sweetened) nectars such as apricot (*jus d'abricot*) and blackcurrant (*cassis*) still hold sway. You can also get fresh orange or lemon juice (*orange/citron pressé*), at a price. A *citron pressé* is a refreshing choice for the extremely thirsty on a hot day – the lemon juice is served in the bottom of a long ice-filled glass, with a jug of water and a sugar bowl to sweeten it to your taste. Other drinks to try are syrups (*sirops*) of mint, grenadine or other flavours mixed with water. The standard fizzy drinks of lemonade (*limonade*), Coke (*coca*) and so forth are all available. Bottles of **mineral water** (*eau minérale*) and spring water (*eau de source*) – either sparkling (*gazeuse*) or still (*eau plate*) – abound, from the big brand names to the most obscure spa product. But there's not much wrong with the tap water (*l'eau de robinet*) which will always be brought free to your table if you ask for it.

Coffee is invariably espresso – small, black and very strong. *Un café* or *un express* is the regular; *un crème* is with milk; *un grand café* or *un grand crème* are large cups. In the morning you could also ask for *un café au lait* – espresso in a large cup or bowl filled up with hot milk. *Un déca* is decaffeinated, now widely available. Ordinary **tea** (*thé*) is Lipton's nine times out of ten and is normally served black and you can usually have a slice of lemon (*limon*) with it if you want; to have milk with it, ask for *un peu de lait frais* (some fresh milk). *Chocolat chaud* – **hot chocolate** – unlike tea, lives up to the high standards of French food and drink and can be had in any café.

After overeating, **herb teas** (*infusions* or *tisanes*), served in every *salon de thé*, can be soothing. The more common ones are *verveine* (verbena), *tilleul* (lime blossom), *menthe* (mint) and *camomille* (camomile).

COMMUNICATIONS: POST, PHONES AND THE MEDIA

French post offices (bureaux de poste or PTTs) – look for bright yellow La Poste signs – are generally open 9am to 7pm Monday to Friday, and 9am to noon on Saturday. However, don't depend on these hours: in smaller towns and villages offices may close earlier and for lunch, while in Paris the main post office is open 24 hours.

You can receive mail at the central post offices of most towns. It should be addressed (preferably with the surname first and in capitals) "**Poste Restante**, Poste Centrale", followed by the name of the town and its postcode, detailed in the *Guide* for all the main cities. To collect your mail you need a passport or other convincing ID and there may be a charge of around a couple of francs. You should ask for all your names to be checked, as filing systems are not brilliant.

For sending letters, remember that you can buy **stamps** (*timbres*) with less queueing from tabacs. Standard letters (20g or less) and postcards within France and to European Union countries cost 3F, to North America 4.40F and to the Antipodes 5.20F. Inside many post offices you will find a row of yellow-coloured *guichet automatiques* – automatic ticket machines with instructions available in English with which you can weigh packages and buy the appropriate stamps; sticky labels and tape are also dispensed. A machine can change notes into change, so there is no need to queue for counter service. If you're sending parcels abroad, you can try to check prices on the *guichet* if available or in various leaflets available: small post offices don't often send foreign mail and may

need reminding, for example, of the reductions for printed papers and books. Faxes can be sent from all main post offices: the official French word is *télécopie*, but people use fax. You can also use Minitel (see below) at post offices, change money, make photocopies and phone calls. To post your letter on the street, look for the bright yellow postboxes.

PHONES

You can make domestic and international **phone calls** from any telephone box (*cabine*) and can receive calls where there's a blue logo of a ringing bell. A 50-unit (40.60F) and 120-unit (97.50F) **phone card** (called a *télécarte*) is essential, since coin boxes are being phased out. Phone cards are available from tabacs and newsagents as well as post offices, tourist offices and some train station ticket offices. You can also use credit cards in many call boxes. Coin-only boxes still exist in cafés, bars, hotel foyers and rural areas; they take 50 centimes, 1F, 5F or 10F pieces; put the money in after lifting up the receiver and before dialling. You can keep adding more coins once you are connected. Local calls are timed in France, at 0.813F for 3 minutes (1F minimum); long-distance calls within France cost up to 2.44F for 3 minutes depending on the distance. Off-peak charges apply for both on weekdays between 7pm and 8am and after noon on Saturday until 8am Monday.

For **calls** within France – local or long-distance – simply dial all ten digits of the number. Numbers beginning with ☎08.00. are free numbers; those beginning with ☎08.36 are premium-rate (from 2.23F per minute), and those beginning with 06 are mobile and therefore also expensive to call. The major **international calling codes**, are given in the box opposite; remember to omit the initial 0 of the local area code from the subscriber's number.

Cheap rates operate between 7pm and 8am Monday to Friday, from midnight to 8am and noon to midnight on Saturday, and all day Sunday. From a private phone, a call to the UK (*Royaume-Unis*) will cost between 1.64F to 2.47F/minute, from a public phone 2.17F to 2.57F; to Ireland 1.95F to 2.97F/minute or 2.85F to 3.52F; to US (*États-Unis*) and Canada 1.95–2.97F/minute or 2.85F to 3.52F; to Australia and New Zealand 4.31–6.55F/ minute

TELEPHONES

IDD CODES
From France dial ☎00 + IDD code + area code minus first 0 + subscriber number
Britain ☎44   Ireland ☎353   USA and Canada ☎1   Australia ☎61   New Zealand ☎64
From Britain to France: dial ☎00 33 + nine digit number (leaving out the first 0)
From the USA and Canada to France: dial ☎011 33 + nine digit number (leaving out the first 0)
From Australia to France: dial ☎011 33 + nine digit number (leaving out the first 0)
From New Zealand to France: dial ☎0044 33 + nine digit number (leaving out the first 0)
Within France: telephone numbers have **ten digits**; the first eight digits are preceded by by 01 for the Parisian and Île de France area, 02 for the north west, 03 for the north east, 04 for the south east, and 05 for the south west. Even when you are within the same area, you must dial all ten digits.

TIME
France and Corsica are one hour ahead of GMT, It is six hours ahead of Eastern Standard Time, and nine hours ahead of Pacific Standard Time. This also applies during daylight savings seasons from the end of March to the end of September.

USEFUL NUMBERS WITHIN FRANCE

Weather (☎ 01.45.56.71.71).

Telegrams (by phone: internal (☎36.55); external (☎08.00.33.44.11) – all languages.

Time ☎36.99.

International operator For Canada and the US (☎00.33.11); for all other countries (☎00.33) followed by the country code – ie, for the UK (☎00.33.44), and for Australia (00.33.61).

International directory assistance
For Canada and the US (☎00.33.12.11); for all other countries (☎00.33.12) followed by the country code.

French operator (☎13) to signal a fault.

French directory assistance (☎12).

Traffic and road conditions
Paris & Île de France (☎01.48.99.33.33).
Rest of France (☎08.36.68.20.00).

---

or 7.99F to 10.16F. By far the most convenient way of making international calls is to use a **calling card**, opening an account before you leave home; calls will be billed monthly to your credit card, to your phone bill if you are already a customer or to your home address. However, the convenience aspect must be stressed because the rates per minute of these cards are many times higher than the cost of calling from a public phone in France, with flat rates only. The best value is offered by Interglobe (☎0171/9720800; 50p min to the UK), followed by AT&T (☎0500/626262; $US1.50/min to the UK), then Cable and Wireless Calling Card (☎0500/100505; 68p/min to the UK), and Swiftcall Global Card (☎0800/7691444; 70p/min to the UK). British Telecom's BT Charge Card (☎0800/345600 or 0800/345144) offers the worst value with calls from France to the UK charged at 90p per minute. But since all of these cards are free to obtain, it's certainly worth getting one at least for emergencies. You dial a free number (make sure you have with you the relevant number for France), your account number and then the number you wish to

call. The drawback is that the free number is often engaged and you have to dial a great many digits. If you need to make many foreign calls from France, several companies offer cheap-rated phone cards, such as the bargain-basement store Tati who sell a 50F or 100F **Intercall Carte Téléphone** (0800.51.79.43) for calling overseas which you can use in a public or private telephone; a 50F card gives you, for example, 15 minutes to Australia, 32 minutes to Canada or the US and 29 minutes to the UK. These rates work out much cheaper than using France Telecom from a public phone.

To avoid payment altogether, you can, of course, make a reverse charge or **collect call** – known in French as *téléphoner en PCV* by contacting the international operator (see box above). You can also do this through the operator in the UK, by dialling the Home Direct number ☎0800.89.00.33; to get an English-speaking operator for North America, dial ☎00.00.11.

Some British **mobile phones**, as long as they're digital, will work in France.

MINITEL

Many French phone subscribers have **Minitel**, a dinosaurial online computer that's been around since the early 1980s, which allows access through the phone lines to directories, databases, chat lines, etc. You will also find it in post offices. Most organizations, from sports federations to government institutions to gay groups, have a code consisting of numbers and letters to call up information, leave messages, make reservations, etc. You dial the number on the phone, wait for a fax-type tone, then type the letters on the keyboard, and finally, press *Connexion Fin* (the same key ends the connection). If you're at all computer-literate and can understand basic keyboard terms in French (*retour* – return, *envoi* – enter, etc), you shouldn't find them hard to use. Be warned that most services cost more than phone rates. Directory enquiries (☎12) are free.

THE INTERNET

The appearance of the first cyber cafés here in 1996 created a wave of media excitement, but France has actually been relatively slow to take up **Internet** connections. This is due in part to its familiarity with Minitel, which is far too slow to link up to even the slowest normal modem, and the fact that ownership of personal computers is very low. An additional problem is the dominance of the English language on the Net.

France Telecom launched its own online service in 1996 and has been busy selling a Minitel programme for PCs, and many French towns (and top Paris museums) now have sites on the World Wide Web. You can get into a list of all French servers via the Centre National de Research Scientifique on *http://www.urec.fr/* or visit the Ministry of Culture's site on *http://web.culture.fr/*.

It is, however, still considered pretty cool to have an email address as part of your *coordonnées* (contact details), and most analysts believe France will have to junk the Minitel box altogether if it's going to take part in the Internet revolution.

Some interesting/useful sites you might like to browse are detailed in the box below. We have tried to list details of cyber cafés and other places such as libraries which offer Internet access so you can stay on line while travelling. It's easy to open a free Internet account to use while you're away with Hotmail or Yahoo: head for *www.hotmail.com* or *www.yahoo.com* to find out how.

NEWSPAPERS AND MAGAZINES

English-language newspapers, such as the *European*, the *Washington Post*, *New York Times* and the *International Herald Tribune*, are on sale the same day in Paris, and in most large cities and resorts the day after publication. Of the **French daily papers**, *Le Monde* is the most intellectual; it is widely respected, but somewhat austere, making no concessions to such frivolities as photographs. *Libération*, founded by Jean-Paul Sartre in the 1960s, is moderately left-wing, independent, and more colloquial, with good, if choosy, coverage, while rigorous left-wing criticism of the French government comes from *L'Humanité*, the Communist Party paper. The other nationals are all firmly right-wing in their politics: *Le Figaro* is the most respected. The top-selling national is *L'Équipe*, which is dedicated to sports coverage, while *Paris-Turf* focuses on horse-racing. The widest circulations are enjoyed by the **regional dailies**. The most important of these is the Rennes-based *Ouest-France* – though for travellers, this, like the rest of the regionals, is mainly of interest for its listings.

USEFUL WEBSITES

Many useful websites have been listed in "The Basics" as an alternative to receiving brochures. Below are some more general, fun or interesting sites; they are in English unless stated otherwise.

www.fr-holidaystore.co.uk
France Holiday Store 98 is a useful site for plannning with tour operators – everything from cycling to canal cruising, fly-drive and short breaks and skiing. Property search with over 1000 places

listed with photos-plus-brochure searches and regional and tourist info.

www.jazzfrance.com
Brilliant bi-lingual site for jazz fans with everything from venues and festivals covered,and an up-to-date diary. Links to music stores.

www.lemonde.fr
In French only; a version of the highbrow daily newspaper, *Le Monde*.

Weeklies of the *Newsweek/Time* model include the wide-ranging and socialist-inclined *Le Nouvel Observateur*, its right-wing counterpoint *L'Express* and the boringly centrist *L'Événement de Jeudi* and the newcomer with a bite, *Marianne*. The best investigative journalism is in the weekly satirical paper *Le Canard Enchaîné*. *Charlie Hebdo* is a sort of *Private Eye* or *Spy Magazine* equivalent. There is also *Paris-Match* for gossip about stars and the royal families. **Monthlies** include the young and trendy – and cheap – *Nova*, which has excellent listings of cultural events, and *Actuel*, which is good for current events. There are, of course, the French versions of *Vogue*, *Elle* (weekly) and *Marie-Claire*, and the relentlessly urban *Biba*, for women's fashion and lifestyle,

Moral **censorship** of the press is rare. On the newsstands you'll find pornography of every shade, as well as covers featuring drugs, sex, blasphemy and bizarre forms of grossness alongside knitting patterns and DIY. You'll also find French **comics** (*bandes dessinées*), which often indulge such adult interests: wildly and wonderfully illustrated, they are considered to be quite an artform and whole museums are devoted to them.

Some of the huge numbers of homeless people in France (*les sans-logement*) make a bit of money by selling magazines on the streets which combine culture, humour and self-help with social and political issues. Costing 10F, the most well-known of these is *L'Itinerant*.

TV AND RADIO

French TV has six channels: three public – France 2, Arte/La Cinquième and FR3; one subscription – Canal Plus (with some unencrypted programmes); and two commercial open broadcasts – TF1 and M6. In addition there are the **cable** networks, which include France Infos (French news), CNN, the BBC World Service, BBC Prime (*Eastenders* etc), MTV, Planète, which specialises in documentaries, Paris Première (lots of *VO* (voice-over) films), and Canal Jimmy (*Friends* and the like in *VO*). There are two music channels: the American MTV and the French-run MCM, where you can get a real education on French rap.

Arte/La Cinquième is a joint Franco-German cultural venture that transmits simultaneously in French and German: offerings include highbrow programmes, daily documentaries, art criticism, serious French and German movies and complete operas. During the day (6am–7pm), La Cinquième uses the frequency to broadcast educational programmes. **Canal Plus** is the main **movie channel** (and funder of the French film industry), with repeats of foreign films usually shown at least once in the original language. **FR3** screens a fair selection of serious movies, with its *Cinéma de Minuit* slot late on Sunday nights good for foreign, undubbed films. The main French **news broadcasts** are at 8.30pm on Arte and at 8pm on F2 and at TF1.

If you've got a **radio**, you can tune into English-language news on the BBC World Service on 648kHz AM or 198kHz long wave from midnight to 5am (and Radio 4 during the day). The Voice of America transmits on 90.5, 98.8 and 102.4 FM. If you're in the Paris area, you can listen to the **news in English** on Radio France International (RFI) for an hour (3–4pm) on 738 kHz AM. For radio **news in French**, there's the state-run France Inter (87.8 FM), Europe 1 (104.7 FM) or round-the-clock news on France Infos (105.5 FM).

BUSINESS HOURS AND PUBLIC HOLIDAYS

Basic hours of business are 8am or 9am to noon or 1pm, and 2pm or 3pm to 6.30pm or 7.30pm. In big city centres shops and other businesses stay open throughout the day, and in July and August most tourist offices and museums are open without interruption. Otherwise almost everything closes for a couple of hours at midday, or even longer in the south. Small food shops often don't re-open till halfway through the afternoon, closing around 7.30pm or 8pm just before the evening meal.

The standard **closing days** are Sunday and/or Monday, with shops taking turns to close with their neighbours; many food shops such as boulangeries (bakeries) that open on Sunday will do so in the morning only. In small towns you'll find everything except the odd boulangerie (bakery) shut on both days. This includes **banks** (which in cities are usually open Mon–Fri 9am–4/5pm), making it all too easy to find yourself dependent on hotels for money-changing at poor rates and high commission. Restaurants and cafés also often close on a Sunday or Monday.

Museums tend to open between 9am and 10am, close for lunch at noon until 2pm or 3pm, and then run through to 5pm or 6pm, although in the big cities they will stay open all day. **Closing days** are usually Tuesday or Monday, sometimes both. **Admission charges** can be very off-putting, though many state-owned museums have one day of the week (often Sun) when they're free or half-price, and you can often get

reductions if you're under 26 or over 60. **Cathedrals** are almost always open all day every day, with charges only for the crypt, treasuries or cloister and little fuss about how you're dressed. **Church** opening hours are often more restricted; you may have to attend Mass on Sunday morning (or at other times which you'll see posted up on the door) to take a look. In small towns and villages, however, getting the key is not difficult – ask anyone nearby or seek out the priest, whose house is known as the *presbytère*.

PUBLIC HOLIDAYS

There are thirteen national holidays (*jours fériés*), when most shops and businesses (though not necessarily restaurants), and some museums, are closed. **May** in particular is a big month for holidays, as Ascension Day normally falls then, as sometimes does Pentecost as well as May Day and Victory Day.

January 1 New Year's Day
Easter Sunday
Easter Monday
Ascension Day (forty days after Easter)
Pentecost or Whitsun (seventh Sunday after Easter, plus the Monday)
May 1 May Day/Labour Day
May 8 Victory in Europe Day
July 14 Bastille Day
August 15 Assumption of the Virgin Mary
November 1 All Saints' Day
November 11 1918 Armistice Day
December 25 Christmas Day

FESTIVALS AND ANNUAL EVENTS

It's hard to beat the experience of arriving in some small French village, expecting no more than a bed for the night, to discover the streets decked out with flags and streamers, a band playing in the square and the entire population out celebrating the feast of their patron saint. Apart from Bastille Day (July 14) and the Assumption of the Virgin Mary (August 15), there are traditional folk festivals still thriving in Brittany and the remote rural regions of the south, as well as a full calendar of festivals devoted to films and to music from jazz and folk to rock and classical. In addition, the Tour de France (first three weeks of July), the Paris Marathon and the Formula I Grand Prix in Monte Carlo never fail to draw the crowds.

FESTIVALS

Catholicism is deeply ingrained in the culture of French rural areas, and as a result **religious feast days** still bring people out in all their finery, ready to indulge once Mass has been said. Most of these occasions, along with the celebrations around wine and food production, are usually very genuine affairs. Other festivals, based for example on historical events, folklore or literature, are often obviously money-spinners and shows for municipal prestige – not something to go out of your way for.

One **folk festival** that is definitely worth attending is the **Inter-Celtic** event held at **Lorient** in Brittany every August. Another annual event with deep historical roots is the great gypsy gathering at **Les-Saintes-Maries-de-la-Mer** in the Camargue. Though exploited for every last centime and, in recent years, given a heavy police presence, it is a unique and exhilarating spectacle to be part of.

Bonfires are lit and fireworks set off for **Bastille Day,** for the **Fête de St-Jean** on June 24, three days from the summer solstice, and for the **Assumption of the Virgin Mary** on August 15. **Mardi Gras** – the last blowout before Lent – is far less of an occasion than in other Catholic countries, although the towns on the Côte d'Azur put on a show at great expense and in questionable taste.

FESTIVALS CALENDAR

AIX Aix en Musique mid-June to early July

AIX International Dance Festival mid-July

ALÈS: Festival du Jeune Théâtre second-third week July

ANNECY Festival de la Vieille Ville second week July

ARLES Gypsy & World Music Festival mid-July

AURILLAC International Street Theatre Festival last week Aug

AVIGNON Dance and Drama Festival last two weeks July

BASTIA Corsica Mediterranean Film Festival Oct

BELFORT Eurockénnes Rock Festival first week July

BORDEAUX Doc Martens Rock Festival last week July

CALVI Corsica Jazz Festival third week June

CANNES International Film Festival May

CHALON-SUR-SAÔNE National Festival of Street Artists third week July

CHARLEVILLE-MÉZIÈRES Triennial World Festival of Puppet Theatre last ten days Sept

CLERMONT-FERRAND Festival of short films end Jan to early Feb

COLMAR Colmar International Festival/Classical music end-Aug to early Sept

CRÉTEIL (outside Paris) International festival of women's films end March/early April

FESTIVALS (cont)

DIJON International Folk and Wine Festival first week Sept

DINARD Chamber Music late July to early Aug

DOUAI International Festival of the French Language/drama, dance, music, cinema from Francophone countries May

FORT-LOUIS (nr Strasbourg) Rock Festival end Aug

GANNAT (nr Vichy) World Folk Festival last ten days July

GRENOBLE Festival of European Theatre first week July

JUAN-LES-PINS International Jazz Festival last two weeks July

LA ROCHELLE Contemporary Arts Festival June & July

LA ROCHELLE International Film Festival end June/1st week July

LE MANS 24-hour car rally mid-June

LES ARCS Chamber Music late July to early Aug

LES-SAINTES-MARIES-DE-LA-MER Gypsy Festival May 24

LIMOGES International Festival of French-Speaking Communities end Sept to mid-Oct

LOCRONAN Breton Troménie Pardon second Sun July

LORIENT Inter-Celtic Festival first full week Aug

MARCIAC Jazz in Marciac second-third week Aug

MENTON Chamber Music Festival Aug

METZ International Contemporary Music Festival mid-Nov

MOND-DE-MARSAN Flamenco Festival mid-July

MONTE CARLO Formula 1 Grand Prix May, Ascension Day to following Sun

MONTPELLIER International Dance Festival end June to mid-July

MONTPELLIER Festival de Radion France et Montpellier/Classical music, early music and jazz mid-July to early Aug

MURAT International Folklore Festival first full week Aug

NICE Mardi Gras Feb, week before Lent

NICE Festival of Contemporary Music (electro-acoustic) Nov

NÎMES La Féria du Carnaval Feb, week before Lent

ORCIVAL Pilgrimage to Notre-Dame d'Orcival May 24

PARIS Marathon mid-April

PARIS Roland Garros tennis tournament last week May to first week June

PARIS Gay Pride June 21

PARIS New Morning All Stars Jazz Festival July

PARIS La Villette Jazz Festival first week July

PARIS Fête de l'Humanité/Cultural festival sponsored by the Communist Party early Sept

PARIS Festival d'Automne/International theatre, dance and music mid-Sept to Dec

PARIS JVC Jazz Festival Oct

PARIS Montmartre Vintage Festival early Oct

PARTHENAY Jazz Festival first-second week July

PARTHENAY Festival of Traditional Music Aug

PÉRIGUEUX International Mime Festival first full week Aug

PRADES Festival Pablo Casals/Classical music late July to early Aug

PUY-EN-VELAY Festival of the Roi de l'Oiseau mid-Sept

QUIMPER Semaines Musicales/Classical music Aug

RENNES Tombées de la Nuit/Theatre and music festival first ten days July

RENNES Les Transmusicales/International rock festival second week Dec

ROQUE D'ANTHÉRO International Piano Festival first three weeks Aug

ST-LIZIER Chamber Music late July to early Aug

ST-MALO La Route du Rock/Rock festival third week Aug

STRASBOURG Film Festival March

STRASBOURG International Mime and Clown Festival Nov

UZÈS Festival de la Nouvelle Danse mid-June

VAISON-LA-ROMAINE L'Été de Vaison Dance Festival mid-July to early Aug

VIENNE Jazz à Vienne first fortnight July

MUSIC, FILM AND THEATRE

The best contemporary popular music in France is distinctly un-French, combining sounds from West, Central and North Africa, the Caribbean and Latin America, though the old chanson tradition is undergoing something of a revival, and rap has taken strides. Meanwhile jazz and classical music continues to thrive. In theatre, the French have developed their own heavyweight brand of intellectual drama in which directors (not playwrights) dominate. Innovative dance can't compete with the United States, but there are several excellent regional companies and festivals that bring in the best international talent. The French have treated film as an art form, deserving of state subsidy, ever since its origination with the Lumière brothers in 1895.

MUSIC

Standard **French rock** largely deserves its miserable reputation. Sixties rocker Johnny Halliday is still France's biggest music star; Patrick Bruel, idol of love-lorn adolescents, appeals equally across the generations, and Seventies disco music, epitomized by Claude François, remains depressingly popular. This said, half of all albums bought in France are recorded by British and American bands, and the dominance of Anglo-Saxon music on the radio prompted a new law insisting that radio stations' output must be at least forty percent French.

However, France is in the forefront of the **World Music** (*sono mondial*) scene. **Algerian raï** flourishes, with singers like Cheb Khaled and Zahouania enjoying megastar status. Daddy Yod from Guadeloupe sings **ragga**; Angélique Kidjo, from Benin, is a brilliant vocalist as is the Senegalese singer Youssou N'Dour; and the best **"alternative" rock** band, until their recent demise, was the Franco-Spanish **Mano Negra**, whose music, heavily influenced by Latin American tours, combined rap, reggae, rock and salsa sounds. The **"ethnically French"** have produced their own rewarding hybrids, best exemplified in the Pogue-like chaos of Les Négresses Vertes. Other names to look out for producing eclectic sounds are Louise Attaque, Mano Solo, Gabriel Yacoub and Thomas Ferson, and groups like Paris Combo, Pigalle and Castafiore Bazooka. French "country music", known as **Astérix rock**, with accordions as the main instruments, has a raucous energy going for it. The culture of the dispossessed suburbs has found musical expression in **rap and hip-hop**. France is the second biggest producer of rap music after the US, and names to look out for include the internationally known MC Solaar and names like NTM, IAM, Doc Gynéco and Alliance Ethnik.

Electronic music has long been a French obsession, with the world-famous **Jean Michel Jarre** at the fore. With such a tradition, it's not surprising that **house and techno** are popular in France. DJs to look out for are the internationally known Laurent Garnier plus Manu le Malin, Sex Toy, DJ Cam, Chris the French Kiss, and the techno twosome Daft Punk. The best **trance/jungle** DJ is Gilb-R, while **Etienne Daho**, who found fame as a pop star in the 1980s, has gained another following with the trance/jungle feel of his 1998 album.

But the French are probably right not to abandon **chansons**, epitomized by Edith Piaf and developed by Georges Brassens and the Belgian Jacques Brel in the Fifties and Sixties, and reaching their sly, sexy best with the legendary Serge Gainsbourg, who died in 1991. Today, the elderly Charles Aznavour and younger singer-composers like Arlette Denis and Dominique A continue the tradition, while Juliette has added a postmodern flavour.

Jazz has long enjoyed an appreciative audience in France: Charlie Parker, Dizzy Gillespie, Bud Powell and Miles Davis were being listened to in the Fifties, when elsewhere in Europe their names were known only to a tiny coterie of fans. Gypsy guitarist Django Reinhardt and his partner, violinist Stéphane Grappelli, whose work represents the distinctive and undisputed French contribution to the jazz canon, had much to do with the music's popularity. But it was also greatly enhanced by the presence of many front-rank black American musicians, for whom Paris was a haven of freedom and culture after the racial prejudice and philistinism of the States. Among them were the soprano sax player Sidney Bechet, who set up in legendary partnership with French clarinettist Claude Luter, and Bud Powell, whose turbulent exile partly inspired the tenor man played by Dexter Gordon (himself a veteran of the Montana club) in the film *Round Midnight*. In Paris you can listen to a different band every night for weeks, from trad, through bebop and free jazz, to highly contemporary experimental. And there are many excellent festivals, particularly in the south (see p.59).

If your taste is for **classical music** and its development, you're also in for a treat. Paris has two **opera** houses and in the provinces there are no less than twelve companies, of which Strasbourg and Toulouse are said to be the best, and a further dozen orchestras. Monaco's opera house is renowned for drawing the top international stars. The places to check out for **concerts** are the Maisons de la Culture (in all the larger cities), churches (where chamber music is as much performed as sacred music, often without charge), and festivals – of which there are hundreds, the most famous being at Aix in July.

Contemporary and experimental computer-based work flourishes: leading exponents are Paul Mefano and Pierre Boulez, founder of the IRCAM centre in Paris and himself one of the first pupils of Olivier Messiaen, the grand old man of modern French music who died in 1992.

CINEMA

While it's true that over sixty percent of films shown in **French cinemas** are from the United States, there are ciné-clubs in almost every city, censorship is very slight, students get discounts, and foreign films are usually shown in their **original language** with subtitles (look for v*ersion originale* or *v.o.* in the listings). Investment in film production in France is nearly twice the level of that in the UK, and the number of films made annually is three times as great – though, of course, nowhere near the output of the United States. The Paris Archives du Film possess the largest collection of silent and early talkie movies in the world, and have embarked on a 15-year, 17-million-franc programme to transfer all the pre-1960 stock onto acetate to avoid disintegration.

While the old is treasured and preserved, the new in French cinema for a while revolved around the Nureyev of moviedom, the actor **Gérard Départieu** whose cinema career began in 1965 and whose most memorable roles have been in *The Last Woman* (1975), *The Return of Martin Guerre* (1981), *Danton* (1983), *Jean de Florette* (1985) and *Camille Claudel* (1987). Jean-Paul

Rappeneau's 1989 screening of the late nineteenth-century play *Cyrano de Bergerac*, starring Départieu and with rhyming couplets throughout, was, at the time, the most expensive French film ever made and exceeded all box office expectations in America and Britain. Départieu went on to act in English in the American film *Green Card* (1990), then played Columbus in the American-French co-production *1492: Conquest of Paradise* (1991), before returning to French cinema as the collier Maheu in the movie version of Zola's *Germinal* (1992). He hasn't done anything interesting since the adaptation of the Balzac novel *Le Colonel Chabrot* in 1993. Nowadays it's women who have taken over the reins as France's most talented actors: most regal is Isabelle Adjani who seems to have been young and beautiful forever, beginning her career in 1975 at just 16. Top of the list for talent though is **Juliette Binoche** who won an Oscar in 1998 for her role portraying a French-Canadian nurse in *The English Patient*, and other younger names to look out for are Charlotte Gainsbourg (Serge Gainsbourg's daughter), Sophie Marceau and Romane Bohringer.

Contemporary politics and cinematographic innovation made a dramatic comeback in French cinema with the 1996 winner of the French Césars award for best film, *La Haine*, by **Mathieu Kassovitz**. A brilliant and strikingly original portrayal of exclusion and racism in the Paris banlieue, *La Haine* is worlds away from the early 1980s-style movies that used Paris as a backdrop, such as *Diva* and *Subway*. But *La Haine* would seem to be a one-off, with glossy star-vehicle "heritage" movies like *Beaumarchais L'Insolent* (a French equivalent of *The Madness of King George*) and *Le Hussard sur le Toit*, which broke budget records and flopped, lapping up funds. There is still no current force in French movie-making to touch on the prolific New Wave period of the Sixties, pioneered by **Jean-Luc Godard** and others. His 1960 film *Au Bout de Souffle* (*Breathless*) made Jean-Paul Belmondo and Jean Seberg pinups around the world. **Luc Besson**, born a year before *Breathless*, was first noticed for his film *Subway* (1984) starring Christopher Lambert, and his other big successes have been *The Big Blue* (1995), *Nikita* (1990) and *Léon* (1994). Other stalwart directors, some of whom have crossed over to America include Léos Carax (*Boy Meets Girl*, 1983), Claude Berri (*Jean de Florette*, 1986), Jean-Jacques Beineix (*Diva*, 1981; *Betty Blue*, 1986) Agnès Varda, Bertrand Tavernier (*Mississippi*

Blues, 1994), Patrice Leconte (*Ridicule* 1996) and Patrice Chereau whose film *La Reine Margot* starring Isabelle Adjani won the Prix du Jury at Cannes in 1994. Many foreign directors – notably Polanski, Kurosawa, Wajda, and the late **Kieslowski**, director of the *Three Colours* trilogy – work or have worked in France, benefiting from public subsidies.

The director to watch out for at the moment is **Cédric Klapisch** whose popular 1996 film *Chacun Cherche Son Chat* (When the Cat's Away) about day-to-day life in the Bastille area of Paris was followed by *Un Air de Famille*, a black comedy about a dysfunctional family set in a local bar. Recent French films have included *Ponette*, directed by Jacques Dillon, about a four-year-old girl who refuses to accept the death of her mother, *Love Etc* by Marion Vernoux and starring Charlotte Gainsbourg, and *Ma Vie Sexuelle* directed by d'Arnaud Desplechin.

The **Cannes Film Festival**, where the prized Palme d'Or is handed out, is not, in any public sense, a festival; it's more a screening of what's new for those in the industry. Filmfests where anyone can go along include those at **La Rochelle** (Rencontres Internationales d'Art Contemporain; June–July); **Créteil**, in the Paris suburbs (festival of women's films; March/April); **La Ciotat** (silent films; July); **Reims** (thrillers; Oct–Nov); and **Strasbourg** (general films; March).

THEATRE

The earlier **theatre** generation of **Genet**, **Anouilh** and **Camus**, joined by **Beckett** and **Ionesco**, hasn't really had successors. In the 1950s, **Roger Planchon** set up a company in a suburb of Lyon, determined to play to working-class audiences. It became the Théâtre Nationale Populaire, the number-two state theatre after the Comédie Française, and now does the classics with all due decorum. Bourgeois farces, postwar classics, Shakespeare, Racine and Cyrano de Bergerac make up the staple fare in most theatres. But certain directors in France do extraordinary things with the medium. Classic texts are

BUYING TICKETS

The FNAC shops in all big towns and Virgin Megastores in the main cities have copious listings of what's on and are the best booking agencies for gigs, ballet or theatre. Booking details for festivals are given in the *Guide*.

shuffled to produce theatrical moments where spectacular and dazzling sensation takes precedence over speech. Their shows are overwhelming: huge casts, vast sets – sometimes in real buildings never before used for theatre – exotic lighting effects, original music scores. A unique experience, even if you haven't understood a word. Directors' names to look out for are **Peter Brook** (the English director who has been in Paris for decades; he is based at the Centre Internationale de Création), **Ariane Mnouchkine**, **Patrice Chereau** (also a film director; see above) and **Jérôme Savary**.

Café-théâtre, literally a revue, monologue or mini-play performed in a place where you can drink and sometimes eat, is probably less accessible than a Racine tragedy at the Comédie Française. The humour or puerile dirty jokes, wordplay, and allusions to current fads, phobias and politicians can leave even a fluent French speaker in the dark.

For details of **Paris theatres**, see Chapter One. In other cities, the theatres are often part of the Maisons de la Culture or Centres d'Animation Culturelle; local tourist offices usually have schedules and tickets are not expensive. The two major theatre festivals are the **Festival Mondial du Théâtre** in Nancy (June) and the **Festival d'Avignon** (July).

DANCE AND MIME

The French regional **contemporary dance companies** – including Régine Chopinot's troupe from La Rochelle, Jean-Claude Gallotta's from Grenoble, Mathilde Monnier's from Montpellier, Karine Saporta's from Caen, and Joëlle Bouvier and Régis Obadia's from Angers – easily rival the Paris-based troupes, though the exciting choreographers Jean-François Duroure and the Californian Carolyn Carlson are both based in or around the capital. Other names to watch for are Maguy Marin in Créteil and François Verret in Aubervilliers.

Humour, everyday actions and obsessions, social problems and the darker shades of life find expression in the myriad current dance forms. A multidimensional performing art is created by combinations of movement, mime, ballet, music from the medieval to contemporary jazz-rock, speech, noise and theatrical effects. Philippe Genty's company in Paris combines dance, drama and marionettes to astonishing effect while the Gallotta-choreographed film *Rei-Dom* opened up a whole new range of possibilities. Many of the traits of the modern epic theatre are shared with dance, including crossing international frontiers.

Though the famous Lecoq School of Mime and Improvisation in Paris still turns out excellent artists, pure **mime** – as practised by the incomparable Marcel Marceau – hardly exists, except on the streets and at Périgueux's international festival of mime.

For **classical ballet** (again well represented in festivals), the two most renowned companies are the Ballet de l'Opéra National de Paris at the Opéra-Garnier and the Opéra-Bastille, whose dance director is Brigitte Lefèvre, and the Ballet National de Marseille, whose artistic director is Roland Petit. Other classical ballet companies are based in Avignon, Bordeaux, Lyon, Toulouse and St Etienne.

SPORTS

More than any of the cultural jamborees, it is sporting events that really excite the French – cycling, football, tennis and skiing. At the local level, the gentle sobriety of boules is the most obvious manifestation of sporting life.

SPECTATOR SPORTS

The sport the French are truly mad about is **cycling**: first and foremost in their sporting calendar is the **Tour de France** race in July. It was, after all, in Paris's Palais Royale gardens in 1791 that the precursor of the modern bicycle, the *célerifière*, was presented, and seventy years later the Parisian father and son team of Pierre and Ernest Michaux constructed the *vélocipede* (hence the modern French term *vélo* for bicycle), the first really efficient bicycle. The French can also legitimately claim the sport of cycle racing as their own, with the first event, a 1200-metre sprint, held in Paris's Parc St Cloud in 1868 – sadly denting national pride, however, the first champion was an Englishman.

That most French of sporting events, and the the world's premier cycling race, the Tour de France, was inaugurated in 1903; France, though, hasn't had a victory since Bernard Hinault in 1985. Covering 4000-odd-kilometres, the 25-stage three-week course changes every year but some truly arduous mountain stages and some time trials are always part of the action, and sometimes foreign countries are included in the itinerary (for example, it began in Ireland in 1998). An aggregate of each rider's times is made daily, the winner of the preceding stage wearing the coveted yellow jersey (*maillot jaune*). Huge crowds turn

out to cheer on the cyclists at the finishing line of the ultimate stage on the Champs-Élysées in late July when the French president himself presents the jersey to the overall winner. Requiring what seems like inhuman endurance, around 200 riders usually start the race but sometimes less than 150 finish, and in fact in 1998 the event was rocked by drug scandals. Nicholas Chaine, of the Crédit Lyonnais bank, which sponsored the race supplied this unusually honest quotable quote: "Let's not be hypocrites. You just don't do that on fizzy mineral water and salads."

Other classic long-distance bike races include the 600-km **Bordeaux–Paris**, the world's longest single stage race, first held in 1891; the **Paris–Roubaix**, instigated in 1896, which is reputed to be the most exacting one-day race in the world; the **Paris–Brussels** held since 1893; and the rugged six-day **Paris–Nice** event, covering over 1100km. The **Grand Prix des Nations**, always held somewhere in France, with locations changing every year, is the world's foremost **time trial**; the Palais Omnisport de Bercy in Paris (see p.171) holds other time trials and cycling events.

Here, as everywhere, **football** (*le foot*) has quasi-religious standing and, although France has never made it to the finals before, it is particularly fitting that they should both host and win the **1998 World Cup** here in France, as it was, after all, a Frenchman, Jules Rimet, who invented the tournament. France's victory, beating the favourites, Brazil, three-nil just two days before Bastille Day, was at the magnificent new Stade de France on the edge of Paris. The captain of the team was Didier Deschamps, but the hero of the match was **Zinedine "Zizou" Zidane** who

FOOTBALL UNITES FRANCE

For the abandoned section of the population, the World Cup may have been an ephemeral opening, an illusion of fraternity. But such illusions are useful; they can alter people's minds.
Laurent Joffrin, *Libération*, July 1998

France's hosting of the **1998 World Cup** in July 1998 was marred in its early stages by ticket scandals that left many foreign fans without seats, and widespread English and German football hooliganism, but finished with France's biggest street party since the end of World War II as it celebrated its victory over Brazil, and a feeling of unprecendented racial unity flooded the country.

Of the 32 teams which make it to the World Cup, France's was the most **diverse ethnically**. Half of the squad's 22 players were of foreign extraction, yet only two were really born outside France: some came from overseas *départements* make France truly a global nation - the others mainly from ex-French colonies. For the first time, the national team really reflected how France looks in the 1990s.

On the evening of July 12, 1998 France frenziedly celebrated its multi-ethnic team's three-nil win against Brazil. Just two days before Bastille Day, the traditional celebration of French nationalism, the *rouge-blanc-bleu* flags were already out in force, but for the first time those carrying them along the Champs Elysées were just as likely to be the marginalized young blacks and "*beurs*" (French-born North Africans) from the *quartiers difficiles* on the edge of Paris. The hero of the match, despite **Jean-Marie Le Pen**'s racist right-wing **Front National (NF)** party's calls to ban players of foreign extraction from the national team, was **Zinedine "Zizou" Zidane**, the Marseille-born son of Algerian parents. The wild scenes all over the country, with black, white and *beurs* embracing in the streets, were a revelation in a country which had published survey only a fortnight before declared itself as having the most racist attitudes in Europe (producing fifteen percent of Front National votes in the last parliamentary elections), and leading Le Pen, conscious of popularity polls, to backtrack, declaring that he had always understood that France could be "composed of different races and religions" if they were prepared to be patriotic. Even so, he downplayed the sociopolitical importance of the situation, shrugging it off as a historical "detail". Of course, the jubilation and Le Pen's backtracking, may also have a lot to do with the fact that the economic woes of France from the early 1990s are ending, and conservative and right-wing attitudes always soften during good times.

The French President, **Jacques Chirac**, had been an enthusiastic supporter of the team through the competition, gaining media attention and popularity in the opinion polls as the cameras cut to him happily waving his *Allez les Bleus* scarf and chanting the team players' names as they made their victory jog. He used the Bastille Day press conference as a political platform to warn the right wing to drop support for the Front National's policies of racial discrimination, and to praise France's "tricolour and multi-colour" World Cup win. He stated that suspicion of immigrants went against French principles of democracy, humanism and republicanism. Chirac bestowed the Légion d'Honneur on **Aimé Jacquet**, the French coach, and applauded his strength against Front National demands for exclusion of immigrants from the team.

scored two powerful headers in the first half, his first goals of the tournament. In the last minute, **Emmanuel Petit** scored an amazing third goal. The win came even though they were down to ten men. The Brazilian star, Ronaldo, with ankle injuries, was cleared to play only 45 minutes before kick-off but after the match the Brazilian coach Mario Zagallo confirmed that Ronaldo really had not been fit to play and that it had been a "major psychological blow" for the other players, who were depending on his skill. At the start of the second half, Ronaldo's near goal was blocked by the acrobatic French goalkeeper **Fabien Barthez**, who received a hero's reception after the match for his efforts.

Within France, current champions are **Lens**, a small ex-coal-mining city in the north, with a high unemployment rate and the most vocal supporters in France: in the Stade de Lens they say the Lens supporters are just like the English – they never stop singing. Their coach, the white-haired and expressionless Daniel Leclercq, has been dubbed *Le Sorcier* for both his achievement in turning a so-so team into champions in just one year and his inscrutable air. There were no Lens players in the World Cup team.

The three most rich and powerful clubs are Paris St-Germain, Olympique Marseille and Monaco. **Paris St-Germain** is owned by Canal Plus, the French cable TV station, but hardly enjoys a local following. **Olympique Marseille**, still popular with the home crowd, is back in the First Division after its fall from grace with its previous owner, corrupt politician and businessman Bernard Tapie, although its game is not very edifying. Its new owner is Robert Louis Dreyfus, the boss of Adidas, who has been spending lots of money trying to buy the best new players including **Robert Pirés** (World Cup 1998 player). Pirés, who cost 70 million francs, nearly went to Juventus, currently Europe's best team. The most famous Olympique Marseille player is **Laurent Blanc**, who also played in the 1998 World Cup. **Monaco** has the only black coach in France, **Jean Tigana**, a cultured man, good with young players. Monaco beat one of England's most successful teams, Manchester United, in the quarter finals of the European League and went on to be beaten by Juventus in the 97/98 season. Monaco's most famous player is the shaven-headed **Fabien Barthez**, the skilful goalkeeper who played for the French team in the World Cup in 1998.

Yet, with relatively meagre funds by European standards, French football continues to lose a lot of its best players to clubs in Italy and Britain, and to a lesser extent in Germany and Spain. Over half the champion World Cup team play in **Italy** including the current football hero **Zinadine Zidane** and the French captain **Didier Deschamps** at Juventus, and **Youri Djorkaeff** at Inter Milan. In **Britain**, the French influence is most obvious at Arsenal, with its coach Arsène Wenger, and players **Emmanuel Petit**, **Patrick Vieira** (both World Cup 1998 champions) and teenage **Nicolas Anelka** (the French Ronaldo). Chelsea has **Franck Lebœuf** and defender **Marcel Desailly** (both world champions). Newcastle United had the handsome, long-haired **David Ginola** (now at Spurs), for several seasons; and **Stephane Guivarc'h** has recently moved from Newcastle to Rangers. At Liverpool, Gérard Houillier is now sole manager.

The legendary footballer/ philosopher **Eric Cantona** was perhaps France's most famous football export, playing for Manchester United for several seasons; he now drinks *pastis* in Marseille's bars and has begun an acting career. In Germany **Bixente Lizarazu**, who also played for the national team in 1998, plays for Bayern Munich, and in Spain, World Cup 1998 champion **Christian Karembeu** is with Real Madrid.

Although confined mainly to the south and southwest of the country, the sport that arouses most passion in France is **rugby**, currently in the final throes of transformation from amateur to professional status. With their dedication to élan in all things, the French game is stylish and open, and in very good health as far as skill is concerned. The forwards are tough and the three-quarters fast. Sides to watch for are Toulouse and Brive (past winners of the European Heineken Cup), Dax and Agen, and the Basque teams of Bayonne and Biarritz still have their reputation as keepers of the game's soul. But, as with soccer, the French game does not have the funds and has to watch its stars tempted away by Anglo-Saxon money, with players like Philippe Saint-André at Gloucester, Thierry Lacroix at Harlequins and Alain Penaud at Saracens.

Crowds gather in the Basque country for the national ball game of **pelota**, which is like a lethally (sometimes literally) fast variety of team squash played in a walled court with a ball of solid wood and wicker slings strapped to the players' arms.

Lastly, in and around the Camargue, the number-one sport is **bullfighting**. Though not to everyone's taste, it is at least a considerably less gruesome variety than that practised by the Spanish – usually bloodless and involving variations on the theme of removing cockades from the base of the bull's horns. It's generally the "fighters", rather than the bulls, who get hurt. The big event of the year is the Whitsun Féria de Pentecôte in Nîmes.

PARTICIPATORY SPORTS

In every town or village square, particularly in the south, you'll see the older generation playing **boules** or **pétanque**. The principle is the same as British bowls but the terrain is always rough (never grass) and the area much smaller. The metal ball is usually thrown upwards from a distance of about 10m, to land and skid towards the wooden marker (*cochonnet*). It's very male-dominated, and socially the equivalent of darts or perhaps pool: there are café or village teams and endless championships.

SKIING

One sport that millions of visitors come to France to practise rather than watch is **skiing**. And whether downhill, cross-country, or mountaineering, it's also enthusiastically pursued by the French. It can be an expensive sport to practise independently, however, and the best deals are often to be had from package operators (see pp.5, 14 and 18). These can be arranged in France or before you leave (most travel agents sell all-in packages). In France, the umbrella organization to contact is the Fédération Française de Ski, 50 rue des Marquisats, 74000 Annecy (☎04.50.51.40.34, fax 04.50.51.75.90).

The best skiing is generally to be had in the **Alps**. The higher the resort the longer the season, and the fewer the anxieties you'll have about there being enough snow. These resorts are almost all modern, with the very latest in lift technology. They're terrific for full-time skiing, but they lack the cachet, charm or the nightlife of the older resorts such as Megève and Courchevel. The foothills of the Alps in Provence have the same mix of old and new on a smaller scale. The clientele are Riviera residents and prices are not

cheap, though at least you can nip down to the coast for a quick swim when you're bored with snow. The **Pyrenees** are a friendlier range of mountains, less developed (though that can be a drawback if you want to get in as many different runs as possible per day) and warmer, which means more problems with the snow.

Cross-country skiing (*ski de fond*) is being promoted hard, especially in the smaller ranges of the Jura and Massif Central. It's easier on the joints, but don't be fooled into thinking it's any less athletic a sport. For the really experienced and fit, though, it can be a good means of transport, using snowbound GR routes to discover villages still relatively uncommercialized. Several independent operators organize ski-mountaineering courses in the French mountains (see pp.5, 14 and 17).

TROUBLE AND THE POLICE

Petty theft is endemic in all the major cities and along the Côte d'Azur. Drivers, particularly with foreign number plates or in hire cars with Parisian registration, face a high risk of break-ins. Vehicles are rarely stolen, but car radios and luggage make tempting targets.

It obviously makes sense to take the normal **precautions**: not flashing wads of notes or travellers' cheques around; carrying your bag or wallet securely; never letting cameras and other valuables out of your sight; and parking your car

overnight in an attended garage or within sight of a police station. But the best security is having a good insurance policy, keeping a separate record of cheque numbers, credit card numbers and the phone numbers for cancelling them (see p.23), and the relevant details of all your valuables.

If you need to **report a theft**, go along to the *commissariat de police* (addresses are given in the *Guide* for the major cities), where they will fill out a *constat de vol*. The first thing they'll ask for is your passport, and vehicle documents if relevant. Although the police are not always as co-operative as they might be, it is their duty to assist you if you've lost your passport or all your money.

If you have an **accident** while driving, you have officially to fill in and sign a *constat à l'aimable* (jointly agreed statement); car insurers are supposed to give you this with the policy, though in practice few seem to have heard of it. For **non-criminal driving offences** such as speeding, the police can impose an on-the-spot fine.

People caught smuggling or possessing **drugs**, even a few grams of marijuana, are

The emergency number to call for police is ☎17

liable to find themselves in jail, and consulates will not be sympathetic. This is not to say that hard-drug consumption isn't a visible activity: there are scores of kids dealing in *poudre* (heroin) in the big French cities and the authorities seem unable to do much about it. As a rule, people are no more nor less paranoid about cannabis busts than they are in the UK or North America.

Should you be **arrested** on any charge, you have the right to contact your consulate (addresses are given on p.20).

THE POLICE

The **two main types of police** – the Police Nationale and the Gendarmerie Nationale – are for all practical purposes indistinguishable. The CRS (Compagnies Républicaines de Sécurité), on the other hand, are an entirely different proposition. They are a mobile force of paramilitary heavies, used to guard sensitive embassies, "control" demonstrations, and generally intimidate the populace on those occasions when the public authorities judge that it is stepping out of line. Armed with guns, CS gas and truncheons, they have earned themselves a reputation for brutality over the years, particularly at those moments when the tensions inherent in the long civil war of French politics have reached boiling point. Not quite in the same league, but with an ugly recent history, is the separate **Paris police force**. This bunch are prone to pulling up "nonconformists" – often just ordinary teenagers and black people – for identity checks. You can be stopped anywhere in France and asked to produce ID. If it happens to you, it's not worth being difficult or facetious. The police can also be rather sensitive on political issues: a group of Danish students wearing "Chirac Non!" T-shirts against the French nuclear tests in the Pacific were surrounded on their arrival, accompanied in force to their hotel and made to change.

Lastly, in the Alps or Pyrenees, you may come across specialized **mountaineering sections** of the police force. They are unfailingly helpful, friendly and approachable, providing rescue services and guidance.

RACISM

Racist attitudes in the populace and the police are rife. A survey on French attitudes to race, commissioned by the French government and published in June 1998, resulted in 38 percent of the population declaring themselves racist, double the figures for similar surveys in Britain and Germany. Percentage votes for the **Front National** were fifteen percent in the last parliamentary elections, and support for this neo-fascist, racist party, headed by **Jean-Marie Le Pen**, is growing. Its heartland is in Provence and the Cote d'Azur, where by 1997 four cities had Front National Mayors. The alliance with conservatives has led to changes in educational, cultural and sporting and programmes to suit Front National policies; their fundamental priority is the withdrawal of benefits to immigrants who have not yet been granted French citizenship. The mood in France after the 1998 World Cup victory of its multi-cultural team (see box p.65) has already forced the Le Pen to modify some of his racist statements.

It will take a long time for the warm glow created by the World Cup to transform France into a racially tolerant country, and for the moment being black, particularly if you are Arab or look as if you might be, makes your chances of avoiding unpleasantness very low. Hotels claiming to be booked up, police demanding your papers, and abuse from ordinary people is horribly frequent. In addition, even entering the country can be difficult. Changes in passport regulations have put an end to outright refusal to let some British holidaymakers in, but customs and immigration officers can still be obstructive and malicious. In North African-dominated areas of cities, identity checks by the police are very common and not pleasant. The clampdown on illegal immigration (and much tougher laws) have resulted in a significant increase in police stop-and-search operations. Carrying your passport at all times is a good idea.

If you suffer a **racial assault**, you're likely to get a much more sympathetic hearing from your consulate than from the police. There are many anti-racism organizations which will offer support (though they may not have English-speakers): Mouvement contre le Racisme et pour l'Amitié entre les Peuples (MRAP) and SOS Racism have offices in most big cities.

GAY AND LESBIAN FRANCE

France is more liberal on homosexuality than most other European countries. The legal age of consent is sixteen. Gay communities thrive especially in Paris, Toulouse and Nice and many of the southern towns, though lesbian life is rather less upfront. Addresses are listed in the Guide, and you'll find details of groups and publications for the whole country in the box below.

In general, the French consider sexuality to be a private matter and homophobic assaults are very rare. On the whole, gays tend to be discreet outside specific gay venues, parades and the prime gay areas of Paris and the coastal resorts. Lesbians tend to be extremely discreet.

Hedonistic lifestyles have changed, here as elsewhere, since the advent of AIDS (SIDA in French). The resulting homophobia, though not as extreme as in Britain or parts of America, has nevertheless increased the suffering among gay men. The Pasteur Institute in Paris is at the forefront of research into the virus, though its gay patients have complained of being treated like cattle. A group of gay doctors and the association AIDES

GAY AND LESBIAN CONTACTS AND INFORMATION

ARCL (Les Archives, Recherches et Cultures Lesbiennes), based at the Maison des Femmes, below (☎01.46.28.54.94). ARCL publish a biannual directory of lesbian, gay and feminist addresses in France, **L'Annuaire** (70F), and organize frequent meetings around campaigning, artistic and intellectual issues.

ARIS, 16 rue Polycarpe, Lyon (☎04.78.27.10.10). Gay and lesbian centre organizing various activities and producing a bimonthly bulletin.

Centre Gai et Lesbienne, 3 rue Keller, 17011 Paris (☎01.43.57.21.47, fax 01.43.57.27.93; Mº Ledru-Rollin; Mon–Sat 2–8pm, Sun 2–7pm; www.cglparis.org). The main information centre for the gay, lesbian, bisexual and transexual community in the capital. The centre publishes a free map/guide to gay and lesbian Paris and a monthly magazine *3 Keller*, and is the meeting place for numerous campaigning, identity, health, arts and intellectual groups.

Centre Gai et Lesbienne Toulouse, 4 rue de Belfort (☎05.61.62.30.62). Open for phone calls and visits Mon–Fri 5–8pm, Sat 3–8pm, and on Sunday the Café Positif is open from 3 to 7pm.

Collectif Gai et Lesbien Marseille et Provence, Maison des Associations, 93 La Canebière, Marseille (☎04.91.42.07.48; Mon, Wed & Fri 4–7pm) or at Le Local, 9 rue Barbaroux, Marseille (☎04.91.92.38.48). Publishes the bimonthly bulletin.

Collectif Homosexuel d'Aide et d'Information de Loire-Atlantique, Maison des Associations, 42 rue Hauts Pavés, Nantes (☎02/40.93.38.24). Brings together different gay and lesbian groups, ranging from Christian organizations to rambling enthusiasts.

Les Flamands Roses, Centre Culturel Libertaire, 1–2 rue Denis-du-Péage, Lille (☎03.20.47.62.65). Gay and lesbian social and campaigning group; publishes a monthly bulletin, *Les Flamands Roses*.

Gai Amitié Initiative Lorraine, postal address PO Box 258, Nancy Cedex 54005 (☎03.83.32.63.14). Gay and lesbian social and information network; publishes trimonthly bulletin, *Le Chardon Rose*.

Maison des Femmes, 163 rue de Charenton, 17012 Paris (☎01.43.43.41.13, fax 01.43.43.42.13; Mº Faidherbe-Chaligny; Mon 5–8pm, Wed 3–8pm, Fri 5–10pm; café Fri 8pm–midnight). The main women's centre in the capital and home to ARCL and other lesbian groups.

Minitel. 36.15 GAY the Minitel number to dial for information on groups, contacts, messages, etc.

Gay and Lesbian Media

Fréquence Gaie (FG), 98.2 FM. 24-hour gay and lesbian radio station with music, news, chats, information on groups and events, etc.

Guide Gai Pied is the most comprehensive gay guide to France, published annually and carrying a good selection of lesbian and gay addresses, with an English section (79F; available in newsagents and bookshops in France). You can look at the site Gai Pied on the Internet: www.gaipied.fr.

Lesbia. The most widely available lesbian publication, available from most newsagents. Each monthly issue features a wide range of articles, listings, reviews, lonely hearts and contacts.

Spartacus International Gay Guide. Guidebook in English focusing mainly on gay travel in Europe with an extensive section on France.

(Association pour l'Entraide et l'Information SIDA), however, have consistently provided sympathetic counselling and treatment, and the gay press has done a great deal to disseminate the facts about AIDS and to provide hope and encouragement. Lesbian organizations fight alongside gays on the general issue of anti-homosexuality, while campaigning separately on the far more numerous and varied repressions to which women are subject.

WORK AND STUDY

Specialists aside, most Britons, North Americans and Australasians who manage to survive for long periods of time in France do it on luck, brazenness and willingness to live in pretty basic conditions. The current unemployment rate in France is running at a high twelve percent. In the cities, bar work, club work, freelance translating or teaching English, software fixing, data processing and typing or working as an au pair are some of the ways people scrape by; in the countryside, the options come down to seasonal fruit- or grape-picking, teaching English, busking or DIY oddjobbing. Remember that unemployment in France is very high.

Anyone staying in France for over three months must have a *carte de séjour*, or residency permit – citizens of the EU are entitled to one automatically. France has a **minimum wage** (the SMIC – Salaire Minimum Interprofessional de Croissance), indexed to the cost of living; it's currently around 40F an hour (for a maximum 169-hour month). Employers, however, are likely to pay lower wages to temporary foreign workers who don't have easy legal resources, and make them work longer hours. By law, however, all EU nationals are entitled to exactly the same pay, conditions and trade union rights as French nationals. It's worth noting that if you're a full-time non-EU student in France (see p.72), you can get a non-EU **work permit** for the following summer so long as your visa is still valid.

If you're looking for something secure, it's important to plan well in advance. A few books which might be worth consulting are *Work Your Way Around the World* by Susan Griffiths (Vacation Work), *A Year Between* and *Working Holidays* (both Central Bureau) and *Living and Working in France* by Victoria Pybus, published by Vacation Work 1998. **In France**, check out the "Offres d'Emploi" (Job Offers) in *Le Monde, Le Figaro* and the *International Herald Tribune*; keep an eye on the notice boards at English and North American bookshops and churches; and try the youth information agency CIDJ (Centre d'Information et de Documentation Jeunesse), 101 quai Branly, 17015 Paris, or CIJ (Centre d'Information Jeunesse) offices in other main cities, which sometimes have temporary jobs for foreigners. The national employment agency, ANPE (Agence Nationale pour l'Emploi), with offices all over France, advertises temporary jobs in all fields and, in theory, offers a whole range of services to job seekers open to all EU citizens, but is not renowned for its helpfulness to foreigners. Non-EU citizens will have to show a work permit to apply for any of their jobs. Vac-Job, 46 av Réné-Coty, 17014 Paris (☎01.43.20.70.51) publishes the annual *Emplois d'Été en France* (*Summer Jobs in France*), which may be useful.

Finding a job in a **French language school** is also best done in advance. In Britain, jobs are often advertised in the *Guardian's* "Education" section (every Tues), or in the weekly *Times Educational Supplement*. Late summer is usually the best time. You don't need fluent French to get a post, but a degree and a TEFL (Teaching English as a Foreign Language) qualification are normally required. The month-long TEFL course currently costs £944. The annual *ELT Guide* (£12.95) gives a thorough breakdown of TEFL courses available; the booklet is produced by EFL Ltd, 1 Malet St, London WC1E 7JA (☎0171/255 1969, fax 255 1972), and the same company publishes the monthly *ELT Gazette* which is filled with job advertisements (subscription for 12 issues £25.50). Vacation Work, 9 Park End St, Oxford OX1 1HJ (☎01865/241978, fax 790885) publishes the useful *Teaching English Abroad* (£10.99 plus £1.50 post and packaging) while the British Council's Web site (*www.britcoun.org /english/ engvacs.htm*) has a list of English-teaching vacancies.If you apply for jobs from home, most schools will fix up the necessary papers for you. It's just feasible to find a teaching job when you're in France, but you may have to accept semi-official status and no job security. For the addresses of schools, look under Écoles de Langues in the Professions directory of the local phone book. Offering **private lessons** (via university notice boards or classified ads), you'll have lots of competition, and it's hard to reach the people who can afford it, but it's always worth a try.

Some people find jobs **selling magazines** on the street and **leafleting** by asking people already doing it for the agency address. The American/Irish/British **bars and restaurants** in the main cities and resorts sometimes have vacancies. You'll need to speak French, look smart and be prepared to work very long hours. Obviously, the better your French, the better your chances are of finding work.

Au pair work is usually arranged through one of a dozen agencies, listed in Vacation Work's guide (see p.70). In Britain, the *Lady* is the magazine for classified adverts for such jobs, arranged privately. As initial numbers to ring, try Avalon Au Pairs (☎01344/778 246) in Britain, the American

Institute for Foreign Study (☎203/869 9090) in the US, or Accueil Familial des Jeunes Étrangers (☎01.42.22.50.34; 690F joining fee) in Paris. These have positions for female au pairs only and will fill you in on the general terms and conditions (never very generous); you shouldn't get paid less than 1650F a month (on top of board and lodging and some sort of travel pass). It is wise to have an escape route (like a ticket home) in case you find the conditions intolerable and your employers insufferable. It may be better to apply once in France, where you can at least meet the family first and check things out.

Temporary jobs in the **travel industry** revolve around courier work – supervising and working on bus tours or summer campsites. You'll need good French (and maybe even another language) and should write to as many tour operators as you can, preferably in early spring. In Britain, ads occasionally appear in the *Guardian's* "Media" section (every Mon) while travel magazines like the very reliable *Wanderlust* (every two months; £2.80) have a Job Shop section which often advertises job opportunities with tour companies. Getting work as a courier on a campsite is slightly easier. It usually involves putting up tents at the beginning of the season, taking them down again at the end, and general maintenance and troubleshooting work in the months between; Canvas Holidays (☎01383/644 018) are worth approaching. The British company PGL Young Adventure Ltd, Alton Court, Penyard Lane, Ross-on-Wye HR9 (☎01989/764 211; *www.pgl.co.uk*) runs several children's activity centres in France, employing people proficient in watersports or with youth-work experience, and offers general catering, domestic and driving work, between May and September every year; you should apply before April.

An offbeat possibility if you want to discover rural life is being a **working guest** on an organic farm. The period can be anything from a week to a couple of months and the work may involve cheese-making, market gardening, beekeeping,

FRENCH BUREAUCRACY: A WARNING

French officialdom and bureaucracy can damage your health. That Gallic shrug and "Ce n'est pas possible" is not the result of training programmes in making life difficult for foreigners: it drives most French citizens mad as well. Sorting out social security, long-stay visas, job contracts, bank accounts, tenancy agreements, university enrolment or any other financial, legal or state matter, requires serious commitment. Your reserves of patience, diligence, energy (both physical and mental) and equanimity in the face of bloody-mindedness and Catch-22s, will be tested to the full. Expect to spend days repeatedly visiting the same office and considerable sums on official translations of every imaginable document.

wine-producing and building. For details of the scheme and a list of French addresses, you can write to Willing Workers on Organic Farms (WWOOF), 19 Bradford Road, Lewes BN7 1RB, in the UK, WWOOF W Tree, Buchan, VIC 3885 in Australia or WWOOF RR2, Carlson Rd, S18 C9, Nelson, British Columbia VIL 5P5 in Canada, enclosing an SAE.

CLAIMING BENEFIT

Any British or EU citizen who has been signing on for **jobseeker's allowance** for a minimum period of four to six weeks at home, and intends to continue doing so in France, needs a letter of introduction from their own Social Security office, plus an E303 certificate of authorization (be sure to give them plenty of warning to prepare this). You must register within seven days with the ANPE (Agence Nationale pour l'Emploi), whose offices are listed under "Administration du Travail et de l'Emploi" in the Yellow Pages or ANPE in the White Pages.

It's possible to claim benefit for up to three months while you look for work, but it can often take that amount of time for the paperwork to be processed (also see warning on p.71).

Pensioners can arrange for their **pensions** to be paid in France, but not, unfortunately, to receive French state pensions.

STUDYING IN FRANCE

It's relatively easy to be a **student** in France. Foreigners pay no more than French nationals to enrol for a course, and the only problem then is to support yourself. Your *carte de séjour* and – if you're an EU citizen – social security will be assured, and you'll be eligible for subsidized accommodation, meals and all the student reductions. In general, French universities are much less formal than British ones and many people perfect their fluency in the language while studying. There are strict entry requirements, including an exam in French, for undergraduate degrees, but not for postgraduate courses. For full **details and prospectuses**, contact the Cultural Service of any French embassy or consulate (see p.20). In Britain, the embassy will refer you to the French Institute, 17 Queensbury Place, London SW7 2DT (☎0171/838 2148), a cultural centre which has a cinema and a library where you can come to pick up a list of language courses in France (library hours Tues–Fri noon–7pm & Sat noon–6pm); otherwise send a letter requesting the list accompanied by a self-addressed envelope. The embassies and consulates can also give details of **language courses** at French universities and colleges, which are often combined with lectures on French "civilization" and usually very costly. You'll find ads for lesser language courses advertised all over the place.

DIRECTORY

BEACHES Beaches are public property within 5m of the high-tide mark, so you can kick sand past private villas. Under a different law, however, you can't camp.

CAMERAS AND FILM Film is considerably cheaper in North America than France or Britain, so stock up if you're coming from there. If you're bringing a video camcorder, make sure any tapes you purchase in France will be compatible. Again, American videotape prices are way below French prices.

CHILDREN AND BABIES Kids are generally welcome everywhere, and in most bars and restaurants, though French children seem to be much more well-trained at a younger age in restaurant etiquette. Hotels charge by the room, with a small supplement for an additional bed or cot, and family-run places will usually babysit or offer a listening service while you eat or go out. Especially in the seaside towns, most restaurants have children's menus or will cook simpler food on request. You'll have no difficulty finding disposable nappies (*couches à jeter*), but nearly all baby foods have added sugar and salt, and French milk powders are very rich indeed. SNCF charge nothing on trains and buses for under-4s, and half-fare for 4–11s (see p.34 for other reductions). In most museums children under 4 are free and it's usually half price for under-18s while entry to many monuments is free for under-12s. Most local tourist offices have details of specific activities for children – in particular, many resorts supervise "clubs" for children on the beach. And almost every town down to small ones has a children's playground with a good selection of activities. Most parks, even in Paris, have a children's play area; unfortunately the majority of parks are gravelled rather than grassed and when there are lawns they are often out of bounds (*pelouse interdite*), so sprawling horizontally with toddlers and napping babies is usually not an option. Something to beware of – not that you can do much about it – is the difficulty of negotiating a child's buggy over the large cobbles that cover many of the older streets in town centres.

CONTRACEPTIVES Contraception was only legalized in 1967 but condoms (*préservatifs* or *capotes*) have been available at all pharmacies ever since, as well as (now) from many clubs and street dispensers (10F for 3–4 condoms) in larger cities. You can also get spermicidal cream and jelly (*dose contraceptive*), plus the suppositories (*ovules, suppositoires*) and (with a prescription) the Pill (*la pillule*), a diaphragm (*le diaphragme*) or IUD (*le sterilet*). Test sticks (*tests réactifs*) for the Persona monitor (only available in Europe) are readily available in pharmacies for 95F per packet.

ELECTRICITY This is almost always 220V, using plugs with two round pins. If you haven't bought the appropriate transformer before leaving home, the best place in France to find the right one is the electrical section of a department store, where someone is also more likely to speak English; cost is around 60F.

FISHING You get fishing rights by becoming a member of an authorized fishing club – tourist offices have details.

LAUNDRY Laundries are common in French towns, and some are listed in the *Guide* – elsewhere look in the phone book under "Laveries Automatiques". They are often unattended, so come pre-armed with small change. Machines are normally graded into 5kg, 8kg or 10kg wash sizes, and the smallest costs around 12F for a load, though some laundries only have bigger machines and charge around 20F. The alternative *blanchisserie* or pressing services are likely to be expensive, and hotels in particular charge very high rates. If you're doing your own washing in hotels, keep quantities small as most forbid doing any laundry in your room.

LEFT LUGGAGE Luggage lockers of various sizes are available at most SNCF stations (terrorist attacks have meant the closure of several left luggage facilities at Paris stations as they constitute a security threat), in addition to *consigne* (left luggage) for larger items or longer periods.

PEDESTRIANS French drivers pay no heed to pedestrian/zebra crossings marked with horizontal white stripes on roads. It is very dangerous to step out onto one and assume drivers will stop as in Australasia and Britain. Take just as great care as you would crossing at any other point. Also be careful at traffic lights: check cars are not still speeding towards you even when the green man is showing.

PETROL The cheapest gas (*essence*) or diesel fuel (*gasoil*) can be bought at out-of-town superstores.

Four-star is *super*; unleaded is *sans plomb*. See p.35 for average prices.

SAFE SEX Paris has the highest number of people suffering from AIDS of any city in Europe, and studies show that there are almost equal numbers of heterosexual and homosexual people who are HIV-positive. Among heterosexuals (excluding drug users) the number of women who are HIV-positive has overtaken men. See "Contraceptives" above.

SWIMMING POOLS Swimming pools (*piscines*) are well signposted in most French towns and reasonably priced, usually around 16F for a swim. Tourist offices have their addresses. You may be requested to wear a bathing cap, whether you are male or female, so come prepared.

TIME France is one hour ahead of GMT (Greenwich Mean Time) throughout the year. It is six hours ahead of Eastern Standard Time, and nine hours ahead of Pacific Standard Time. This also applies during daylight savings seasons, which are observed in France (as in most of Europe) from the end of March through to the end of September.

TOILETS Ask for *les toilettes* or look for signs for the WC (pronounced 'vay say'); when reading the details of facilities outside hotels, don't confuse *lavabo*, which means wash-basin, with lavatory. Usually found downstairs along with the phone, French toilets in bars are still often of the hole-in-the-ground squatting variety, and tend to lack toilet paper. Standard of cleanliness are often not high, and men shouldn't expect much privacy in the urinal, which often won't have a door. Both bar and restaurant toilets are usually free, as are toilets in museums, though toilets in railway stations and department stores are commonly staffed by attendants who will expect a bit of spare change. Some have coin-operated locks, so always keep 50 centimes and one and two franc pieces handy for these and for the frequent Tardis-like public toilets found on the streets. These beige-coloured boxes have automatic doors which open when you insert coins to the value of two francs, and are cleaned automatically once you exit. Children under ten aren't allowed in on their own.

WEATHER Paris and Île de France ☎08.36.68.02.75; rest of France ☎01.36.68.01.01.

PART TWO

THE

GUIDE

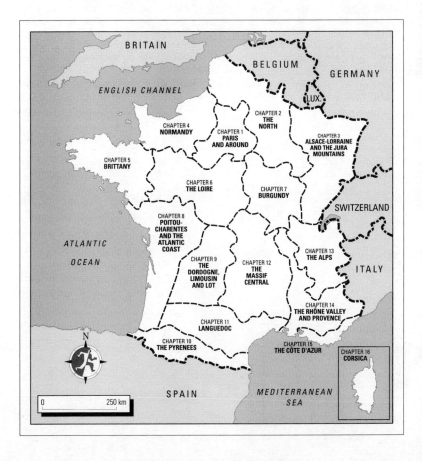

CHAPTER ONE

PARIS AND AROUND

PARIS is the paragon of style – perhaps the most glamorous and superbly high-tech city in Europe. And yet it is also deeply traditional, a village-like and in parts dilapidated metropolis whose appeal to outsiders is tempered by the notorious disdain of its inhabitants. Large immigrant populations, particularly from Algeria and West and Central Africa, add another current to the city. While such contradictions and contrasts may be the reality of any city, they are the makings of Paris. Consider the tiny lanes and alleyways of the Latin Quarter, Montmartre or Ménilmontant against the monumental vistas from the Louvre to La Défense or from Les Invalides to Trocadéro; the multiplicity of markets, old-fashioned pedestrian arcades and small shops against the giant underground commercial complexes of Montparnasse, the Louvre and Les Halles; or the obsession with refashioning old buildings and museums and creating ground-breaking architecture, building new bridges and métro lines – while old ladies still iron sheets by hand in the laundries of Auteil.

Paris has long created its own myth. Famous names and events are invested with a peculiar glamour that elevates the city and its people to a legendary realm. It is only in recent decades that Paris has let slip its status as the centre of Western intellectual, artistic and literary movements and as the natural place of European asylum for dissidents and the disillusioned, for those who have been censored, oppressed or forced into exile from every corner of the globe.

Perhaps it is not surprising that, having found themselves for so long at the supposed navel of the world, Parisians feel superior to ordinary mortals. The most tangible and immediate pleasures of Paris are to be found in its streetlife and along the leisurely banks and bridges of the river Seine. Few cities can compete with the thousand-and-one cafés, bars and restaurants that line every street and boulevard, and the city's compactness makes it possible to experience the individual feel of the different quartiers. You can move easily, even on foot, from the calm, almost small-town atmosphere of **Montmartre** and parts of the **Latin Quarter** to the busy commercial centres of the **Bourse** and **Opéra-Garnier** or to the aristocratic mansions of the **Marais**. Every district has its mouth-watering **street market**, and in the **13ᵉ arrondissement** you can discover strange edibles and fiery spirits in the Chinese supermarkets.

The city's lack of open space is redeemed by unexpected havens like the **Mosque**, **Arènes de Lutèce** and the **Place des Vosges**, and courtyards of grand mansions like the **Hôtel de Sully**. The garden of **Les Halles** has at long last provided greenery in the centre, while the gravelled paths and formal beauty of the **Tuileries** create the backdrop for the ultimate Parisian Sunday promenade. The quaysides of the Left and Right Banks of the **River Seine** and the islands make for a wonderful wander, and the Latin Quarter's two splendid parks, the **Luxembourg** and the **Jardin des Plantes** afford further outdoor pleasure.

A grand and imposing backdrop to the streetlife is provided by the monumental architecture of the **Arc de Triomphe**, **Louvre**, **Eiffel Tower**, **Hôtel de Ville**, bridges and state institutions. The habit of breaking architectural moulds has continued from the **Pompidou Centre** (Centre Georges Pompidou) through La Villette, the Louvre Pyramid, the Grande Arche de La Défense to the new Bibliothèque Nationale, as well

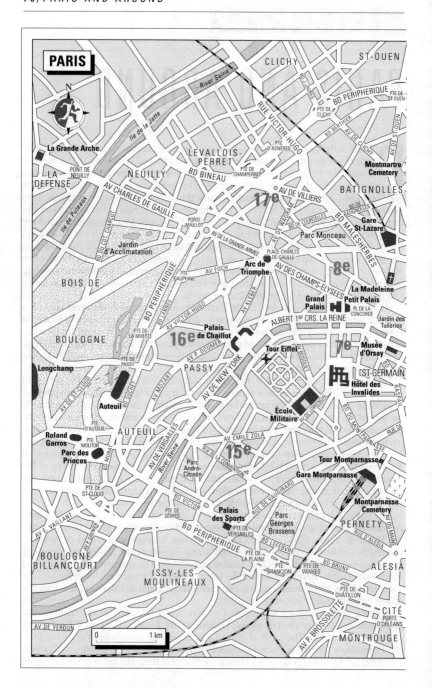

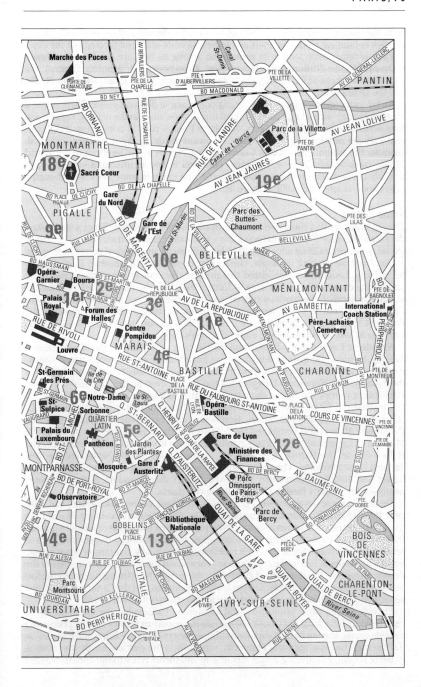

as in the stunning smaller-scale examples of postmodernist and deconstructivist tendencies in housing blocks, schools and industrial units scattered throughout the city.

Paris is remarkable too for its **museums**: among its best are the **Louvre, Musée d'Orsay, Musée National du Moyen-Age, Beaubourg (Pompidou Centre)**, the **Cité des Sciences** at La Villette, the **Palais de Tokyo, Marmottan, Picasso, Rodin** and the **Orangerie**.

As for **entertainment**, the city's strong points are in film and music. Paris is a real **cinema** capital, with a large percentage of the films on show in the original version and thus accessible to English-speakers. Although French rock is notoriously awful, current Parisian **music** ranges from **jazz** and **avant-garde** to **West African** and **Arab sounds**: the vibrant cultural mix has meant that Paris is in the forefront of the **World Music** (*sono mondial*) scene. **Classical concerts** in fine architectural settings – particularly chapels and churches – are frequent, and entry is sometimes free, though a ticket price of upwards of 80F is more likely.

Some history

The city's history has conspired to create this sense of being apart. From a shaky start the kings of France – whose seat was Paris – gradually extended their control over their feudal rivals, centralizing administrative, legal, financial and political power as they did so, until anyone seeking influence, publicity or credibility – in whatever field – had to be in Paris. Louis XIV consolidated this process. Supremely autocratic, considering himself the embodiment of the state – "L'état, c'est moi" – he inaugurated the tradition of Paris as symbol: the glorious reflection of the pre-eminence of the state. The Cour Carrée of the Louvre, the Observatoire and Invalides, and the triumphal arches of the Portes St-Martin and St-Denis are his. It is a tradition his successors have been only too happy to follow, whether as king, emperor or president.

Napoléon I added to the Louvre and built the Arc de Triomphe, the Madeleine and Arc du Carrousel. He instituted the Grandes Écoles, those super-universities for supercompetent administrators, engineers and teachers – and totally reorganized the rest of the country, too. **Napoléon III** extended the Louvre even further and had his Baron Haussmann redraw the rest of the city. The **Third Republic** had its World Fairs and bequeathed the Eiffel Tower. Recent presidents have initiated the skyscrapers at La Défense, the Tour Montparnasse, Beaubourg and Les Halles shopping precinct. **President Mitterrand** completed the high-tech Parc de la Villette complex and the Musée d'Orsay and added the glass pyramid entrance to the Louvre, the Grande Arche at La Défense, the Bastille opera house, the Institut du Monde Arabe and the new national library building. The scale of all this publicly financed construction is extraordinary – so, too, the architecture. The new buildings should, and do, feature as prominently on any visitor's itinerary as the classic city sights.

Yet despite these developments Paris remains compact and remarkably uniform, basically the city that Haussmann remodelled in the mid-nineteenth century. He laid out those long geometrical boulevards lined with rows of grey bourgeois residences that are the hallmark of Paris. In doing so, he cut great swathes through the stinking wen of medieval slums that housed the city's rebellious poor, already veterans of three revolutionary uprisings in half a century. If urban renewal and modernization were part of the design, so too was the intention of controlling the masses by opening up more effective fields of fire for artillery and facilitating troop movements. Not that it succeeded in preventing the 1871 Commune, the most determined insurrection since 1789.

Though riotous street protests are still a feature of Parisian life, the traditional barricade-builders have long since been booted into the suburban factory-land or depressing satellite towns, leaving behind ever-increasing numbers of people living and begging on the streets. The decaying parts of the city, especially in the east and north, are gradually being rebuilt, introducing a new mix of arty and media types to the underprivileged communities who continue to live in the dank, unsanitary housing of areas like Belleville and the Goutte d'Or.

A large proportion of these downtrodden communities are made up of immigrants and their descendants, each ethnic group bringing its own styles and traditions. However, while most Parisians appreciate the diversity of restaurants and the music, racist tensions are undeniable.

Points of arrival and departure

Nowadays most British travellers to Paris will find themselves arriving by Eurostar at the very central Gare du Nord train station while flights to the two main airports, Charles de Gaulle and Orly, continue to be the main entry point for more far-flung visitors. Those arriving from other parts of France or continental Europe by train arrive at one of the six central mainline train stations. Those taking **buses** end up at the eastern edge of the city: **Eurolines** (☎01.49.72.51.51) and almost all the buses coming into Paris – whether international or domestic – arrive and depart from the **main gare routière** at 28 av du Général-de-Gaulle, Bagnolet; Métro Gallieni (line 3) links it to the centre. If you're **driving** in yourself, don't try to go straight across the city to your destination. Use the ring road – the **boulevard périphérique** – to get around to the nearest *porte*: it's much quicker, except at rush hour, and easier to find your way.

Disneyland Paris is linked by bus from both Charles de Gaulle and Orly airports: for details of these services, plus train links from the centre to the purpose built Marne La Vallée TGV, see p.195..

By air

Roissy-Charles de Gaulle Airport (24hr information in English ☎01.48.62.22.80), often also referred to as Charles de Gaulle and abbreviated to CDG or Paris CDG, is 23km northeast of the city. The airport has two main terminals referred to as CDG 1 and CDG 2. Make sure you know which terminal your flight is departing from when it's time to leave Paris, so you take the correct bus or get off at the right train station. A TGV (high-speed train) station links the airport with Bordeaux, Brussels, Lille, Lyon, Nantes, Marseille and Rennes. CDG is connected with the centre by various forms and combinations of transport. **Roissyrail** runs on RER line B every fifteen minutes from 5am until midnight, from both CDG 1 and 2 (TGV) stations to Gare du Nord, Châtelet les Halles, St-Michel and Denfert Rochereau where you can transfer to the ordinary métro. For those arriving at CDG 1 airport terminal take the free airport shuttle to the first station; from terminal CDG 2 there is direct access to the second station. Taking about thirty minutes to Gare du Nord, this is the quickest route and costs 47F one-way (second class). Leaving Paris: all but the first train of the day depart from platform 43 of Gare du Nord where there is an English-speaking information desk indicated by a large question mark (staffed daily 7am–7pm); confirm here which station you should get off at by checking the airline code on your ticket against the information board, or ask the staff to help you. **Air France bus** (information in English ☎01.41.56.89.00) offers three services with differing routes, times and prices. The green-coded line 2 (60F one way, 105F return) leaves from CDG 2 every twelve minutes from 5.40am to 11pm terminating at Porte Maillot (métro) on the northwest edge of the city, stopping at av Carnot, outside Charles-de-Gaulle-Étoile RER/métro between the Arc de Triomphe and rue Tilsitt. The orange-coded line 5 leaves from CDG 1 but takes the same route as line 2 and costs the same (every 20min 6am–11pm). The yellow-coded line 4 (70F one-way, 120F return) departs from both CDG 1 and CDG 2 every thirty minutes from 7am to 9.30pm, terminating near Gare

Montparnasse and stopping at Gare de Lyon; journey times vary from 25 minutes to over an hour in rush hour. Leaving Paris, the green-coded line 2 (for CDG 2) and orange-coded route 5 (CDG 1). buses departs from av Carnot, right outside the RER exit of Charles-de-Gaulle-Étoile, and from Porte Maillot. The yellow-coded line 4 (for both CDG 1 and CDG 2) leaves from 2bis bd Diderot outside Gare de Lyon and near Gare Montparnasse at rue du Commandant-René-Mouchotte in front of the Méridien Hotel. **Roissybus** connects CDG 2 with the Opéra-Garnier (corner of rues Auber and Scribe; RER Auber/Métro Opéra) every fifteen minutes from 5.45am to 11pm. At 45F this is the cheapest route and takes around 45 minutes. The **Airport Shuttle** is a mini-bus door-to-door airport service, with no extra charge for luggage, can work out to be more reasonable than a taxi (89F per head if there are more than two people, 120F for a single person; advance bookings – English-speaking – on ☎01.45.38.55.72, fax 01.43.21.35.67). **Taxis** into central Paris from CDG cost at least 205F, plus a small luggage supplement (6F per piece of luggage), and should take between fifty minutes and one hour.

Orly Airport (information in English daily 6am–11.30pm ☎01.49.75.15.15), 14km south of Paris, has two terminals, Orly Sud and Orly Ouest, linked by shuttle bus but easily walkable; Ouest (West) is used for domestic flights while Sud (South) handles international flights. The airport is connected with the centre by various means of transport. **Orlyrail** is a bus–rail link; the shuttle bus goes to RER line C station Pont de Rungis where the Orlyrail train leaves every fifteen minutes (every half hour after until 9pm) from 5.45am to 11.10pm for the Gare d'Austerlitz and other métro connection stops (30F; train 35min, total journey around 50min). Leaving Paris: from Gare d'Austerlitz the train runs from 5.50am to 11.50pm. **Orlyval** is a fast **Val** train shuttle link to RER line B station Antony thence métro connection stops to Denfert-Rochereau, St-Michel and Châtelet les Halles; runs every five to seven minutes from 6am to 10.30pm, from 7am Sundays and holidays (57F; 30min). An **Air France bus** (information in English ☎01.41.56.89.00) to the Invalides Air France Terminal via Montparnasse (stopping at Porte d'Orléans and Duroc if requested in advance) leaves every twelve minutes from 5.50am to 11pm (45F one-way, 75F return; about 35min). Leaving Paris, the bus can be caught from the Invalides Air France Terminal and from Montparnasse on rue du Commandant-René-Mouchotte in front of the Méridien Hotel. The **Orlybus** runs to Denfert-Rochereau RER/métro station in the 14ᵉ (every 12min 6.30am–11.30pm; 30F one way; around 30min); leaving Paris the bus departs from place Denfert Rochereau (6am–11.30pm). Finally, the **Jetbus** to métro Villejuif Louis Aragon (métro line 7), runs every twelve to fifteen minutes between 6am and 10.15pm (24F; 15min). The same **Aiport Shuttle** service (see above) as for Charles de Gaulle is offered to and from Orly, while **taxis** take about 35 minutes to the centre of Paris and cost at least 130F.

By Eurostar

One of the most common ways of arriving in Paris is now by **Eurostar** to **Gare du Nord** – a bustling convergence of international, long distance and suburban trains, the métro and several bus routes. There are two bureaux de change at the station (daily 6.15am to 11pm), and a small **tourist office** (Mon–Sat 8am-8pm) which can book accommodation for a small fee (see p.162). Coming off the train, turn left for tourist information, the métro and the RER, and right for taxis (a sample price would be 46F to a hotel in the 17ᵉ) and the heavy-security **left luggage** (Mon–Fri 6.15am-11.15pm, Sat & Sun 6.45am-11.15pm; lockers come in small, medium or large sizes for 15F, 20F or 30F and storage is for up to 48 hours with an excess charge of 30F per day), both down the escalators opposite the Avis car rental desk. You can even get a shower (21F for 20min) in the public toilets (daily 6am-9pm; toilets 2.80F) at the bottom of the métro escalators.

By ordinary train

Arriving by train Paris's six **mainline stations** are equipped with cafés, restaurants, tabacs, banks, bureaux de change (long waits in season), and are all connected with the métro system; Gare du Nord and Gare de Lyon have tourist offices which book same-day accommodation (see p.89). The central number for **information** in English is ☎01.45.82.08.41 (for information on suburban lines call ☎01.40.52.75.75); for reservations call ☎08.36.35.35.35 (national) or ☎01.53.90.20.20 (Île de France). The **Gare du Nord** (rue Dunkerque: 10ᵉ) (trains from Boulogne, Calais, the UK, including high-speed Eurostar, and other north-European countries, and **Gare de l'Est** (place du 11-Novembre-1918, 10ᵉ); serving eastern France, central and eastern Europe, are side by side in the northeast of the city. The **Gare St-Lazare** (place du Havre, 8ᵉ); serving the Normandy coast, Dieppe and connections with boats from the UK, is the most central, close to the Madeleine and the Opéra-Garnier. Still on the Right Bank but towards the southwest corner is the **Gare de Lyon** (place Louis-Armand, 12ᵉ) for trains from Italy and Switzerland and TGV lines to southeast France). South of the river, **Gare Montparnasse** (bd de Vaugirard, 15ᵉ) is the terminus for Chartres, Brittany, the Atlantic coast and TGV lines to southwest France. **Gare d'Austerlitz** (bd de l'Hôpital, 13ᵉ) is for ordinary trains to southwest France, the Loire Valley, Spain and Portugal. The motorail station, **Gare de Paris-Bercy**, is down the tracks from the Gare de Lyon on bd de Bercy, 12ᵉ.

At the time of writing, other **left luggage** options are limited at train stations as a security measure; if you find there are no facilities at the station you arrive at, you'll just have to make your way to Gare du Nord where this service is definitely offered (see above).

Information

The main Paris **tourist office** is at 127 av des Champs-Élysées, 8ᵉ (May–Sept daily 9am–8pm; Oct–March Mon–Sat 9am–8pm, Sun 11am–6pm; ☎01.49.52.53.54, fax 01.49.52.53.00; métro Charles-de-Gaulle–Étoile). The Web site of the tourist office, *www.paris.org*, has impressive detail on Paris and France, recent essays on Paris to read, and links to other sites – unfortunately not all as up-to-date as they could be. There are **branch offices** at two of the mainline train stations, Gare de Lyon (Mon–Sat 8am–8pm; ☎01.43.43.33.24) and Gare du Nord (same hours; ☎01.45.26.94.82), and also at the Eiffel Tower (daily April–Sept 11am–6pm; ☎01.45.51.22.15). Most of the printed information is behind the counter and not all of it is free: the useful *Paris Map* costs 5F; the monthly *Paris Le Journal*, detailing what's on, is free and also available at the *Bureau d'Accueil* (see below) or in museums and shops. Within the new Carrousel du Louvre, underground below the triumphal arch at the east end of the Tuileries is the **Espace du Tourism d'Île de France** (10am–7pm; closed Tues; ☎01.44.50.19.98) with stylishly presented information on attractions and activities in Paris and the surrounding area.

Alternative sources of information are the **Hôtel de Ville information office** – *Bureau d'Accueil* – at 29 rue de Rivoli, 4ᵉ (Mon–Sat 9am–6pm; ☎01.42.76.43.43; métro Hôtel-de-Ville) and electronic **billboards** in the streets. Also good for the latest special exhibitions at museums and other cultural information are Paris's two listings magazines: *Pariscope* (*www.pariscope.fr*) and *L'Officiel des Spectacles* (see p.162). For recorded **tourist information in English**, phone ☎01.49.52.53.56.

City transport

Finding your way around is remarkably easy. Paris proper, without its suburbs (*banlieues*), is relatively small, with an integrated **public transport system** of bus, métro and trains – the **RATP** (*Régie Autonome des Transports Parisiens*) – that is cheap, fast and meticulously signposted. To help you get your bearings above ground, think of the Louvre as the centre. The Seine flows east to west, cutting the city in two. The area north of the river is known as the Right Bank or *rive droite*; to the south is the Left Bank or *rive gauche*. Roughly speaking, west is smart and east is scruffy. The landmarks you most often catch glimpses of as you move about are the Eiffel Tower, to the west, and the white domes of the Sacré-Cœur on top of the hill of Montmartre, to the north.

The métro and RER

The **métro**, combined with the **RER** (*Réseau Express Régional*) suburban express lines, is the simplest way of moving around. It runs from 5.30am to 12.30am; RER trains from 5am to midnight. Stations (abbreviated: Mº Concorde, RER Luxembourg etc) are frequent, though the interchanges can involve a lot of legwork including many stairs. Free **maps** of varying sizes and detail are available at most stations (in descending scale, ask for either a *Grand Plan de Paris*, a *Petit Plan de Paris* or a *Paris Plan de Poche*) and every station has a big plan of the network outside the entrance and several inside. A new and state-of-the-art line, the Météor (#14), now runs from Madeleine to Tolbiac-Massena, and is worth a visit just for its innovative and stylistic design. The lines are colour-coded and designated by numbers for the métro and by letters for the RER, although they are signposted within the system with the names of the terminus stations: for example, travelling from Montparnasse to Châtelet, you follow the sign "Direction Porte-de-Clignancourt"; from Gare d'Austerlitz to Grenelle you follow "Direction Boulogne–Pont-de-St-Cloud". The numerous interchanges (*correspondances*) make it possible to travel all over the city in a more or less straight line. For RER journeys beyond the city, make sure that the station you want is illuminated on the platform display board.

Buses

Don't use the métro to the exclusion of the city's **buses**. They are not difficult to use and you do see much more. There are free **route maps** available at métro stations, bus terminals and the tourist office; the best bus map, showing the métro and RER as well, is the *Grand Plan de Paris*. Every bus stop displays the numbers of the buses that stop there, a map showing all the stops on the route and the times of the first and last buses. You can buy a single ticket (8F) from the driver, or use a pre-purchased carnet ticket or pass. A red button should be pressed to request a stop and an *arrêt demandé* sign will then light up. Only the #20 bus route (see p.88) is designed to be easily accessible for wheelchairs and prams. Generally speaking, buses run from 6.30am to 8.30pm with some services continuing to 12.30am. Around half the lines don't operate on Sundays and holidays.

From mid–April to mid-September, a special **Balabus** service (not to be confused with batobus, below) passes all the major tourist sights between La Défense Grande Arche and Gare de Lyon, on Sundays and holidays between noon and 9pm. Bus stops are marked "Balabus". Standard bus fares apply.

Night buses (*Noctambus*) run on eighteen routes every hour from 1am to 5.30am between place du Châtelet near the Hôtel de Ville and the suburbs, stopping en route. Again, there is a reduced service on Sunday.

Tickets and passes

For a short stay in the city, **carnets** of ten tickets can be bought from any station or tabac – currently 48F, as opposed to 8F for an individual ticket. The integrated system is divided into five **zones**, though the entire métro system itself fits into zones 1 and 2. The same **tickets** are valid for bus, métro and, within the city limits and immediate suburbs (zones 1 and 2) the RER express rail lines, which also extend far out into the Île de France. Only one ticket is ever needed on the métro system, and within zones 1 and 2 for any RER or bus journey, but you cannot switch between buses or between bus and métro/RER on the same ticket. Night buses require separate tickets costing 30F each, unless you have a weekly or monthly travel pass (see below). For RER journeys beyond zones 1 and 2 you must buy a RER ticket; visitors often get caught out, for instance, when they take the RER to La Défense instead of the métro. Children under four travel free and from four to ten at half price. Don't buy from the touts who hang round the main stations; you'll pay well over the odds, quite often for a used ticket, and be sure to keep your ticket until the end of the journey; you'll be fined on the spot if you can't produce one.

A *mobilis* **day pass** is also available (from 30F for the city, 70F to include the outer suburbs and airports).

If you've arrived early in the week and are staying more than three days, it's more economical to have a **Carte Orange** with a weekly coupon (*coupon hebdomadaire*). It costs 75F for zones 1 and 2, is valid for an unlimited number of journeys from Monday morning to Sunday evening, and is on sale at all métro stations and tabacs (you'll need a passport photo). You can only buy a coupon for the current week until Wednesday; from Thursday you can buy a coupon to begin the following Monday. There is also a monthly coupon (*mensuel*) for 255F for zones 1 and 2. You need to write your *Carte Orange* number on the coupon.

Other possibilities are the **Paris Visites**, 1-, 2-, 3- and 5-day visitors' passes at 50F, 80F, 120F and 170F for Paris and close suburbs, or 100F, 175F, 245F and 300F to include the airports, Versailles and Disneyland Paris (make sure you buy this one when you arrive at Roissy-Charles de Gaulle or Orly to get maximum value). A half-price child's version is available for 1, 2 or 3 days. You can buy them from métro and RER stations as well as tourist offices. *Paris Visites* passes can begin on any day; they also allow you discounts at certain monuments and museums. Both the *Carte Orange* and the *Paris Visites* entitle you to **unlimited travel** (in the zones you have chosen) on bus, métro, RER, SNCF and the Montmartre funicular. On the métro you put the *Carte Orange* coupon through the turnstile slot, but make sure to return it to its plastic folder; it is reusable throughout the period of its validity. On a bus you show the whole *carte* to the driver as you board – don't put it into the punching machine.

The RATP also runs numerous **excursions**, some to quite far-flung places, which are far less expensive than those offered by commercial operators. Details are available from the RATP's Bureau de Tourisme, place de la Madeleine, 1^e (☎01.40.06.71.45; M^o Madeleine). For 24-hour recorded information in English on all RATP services call ☎08.36.68.41.14 (premium rate).

Taxis

If it's late at night or you feel like treating yourself, don't hesitate to use the taxis. Their **charges** are fairly reasonable: between 40F and 70F for a central daytime journey but considerably more if you call one out. Before you get into the taxi you can tell which rate is operating from the three small indicator lights on its roof: "A" (passenger side) indicates the daytime rate (7am–7pm) for Paris and the *boulevard périphérique* (around 3.45F/km); "B" is the rate for Paris at night, on Sunday and on public holidays, and for the suburbs during the day (around 5.45F/km); "C" (driver's side) is the night rate for the suburbs (around 7F/km). In addition there's a pick-up charge of around 13F, a time charge of around 120F an hour for when the car is stationary, an extra charge of 5F if you're picked up from a mainline train station, and a 6F charge for each piece of luggage carried. Tipping is not mandatory, but ten percent will be expected. Taxi drivers do not have to take more than **three passengers** (they don't like people sitting in the front); if a fourth passenger is accepted, an extra charge of 9F will be added. Waiting at a **taxi rank** (*arrêt taxi* – there are around 470 of them) is usually more effective than hailing from the street. The large white light

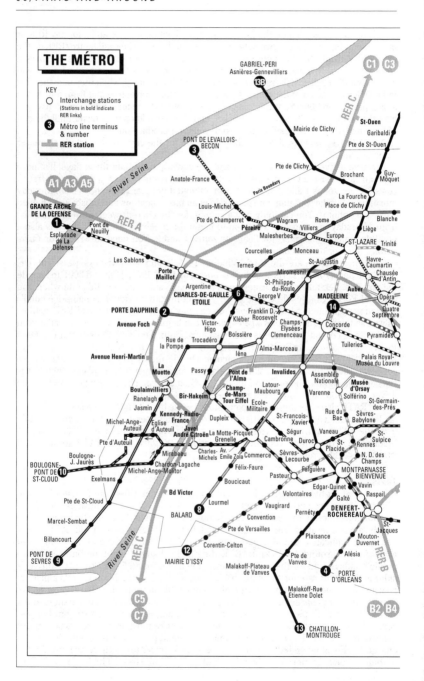

THE MÉTRO

KEY

○ Interchange stations
(Stations in bold indicate RER links)

❸ Métro line terminus & number

▨ RER station

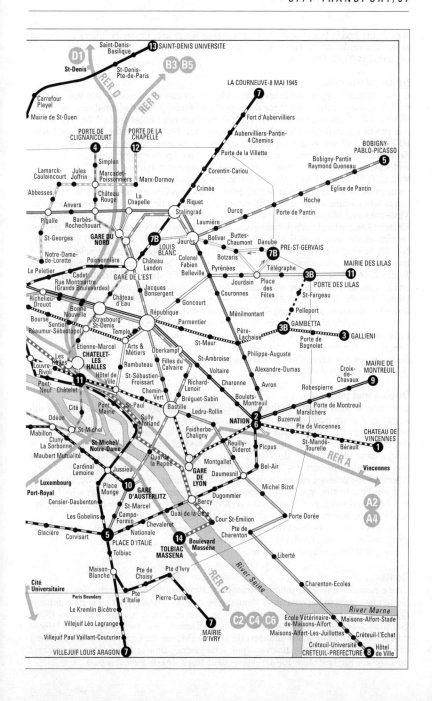

signals the taxi is free; the orange light means it's in use. Phone numbers are shown at the taxi ranks or try Taxis Bleus (☎01.49.36.10.10), Alpha Taxis (☎01.45.85.85.85) or Artaxi (☎01.42.41.50.50).

Disabled travellers

If you are handicapped, **taxis** are obliged by law to carry you and to help you into the vehicle – also to carry your guide dog if you are blind. Specially adapted taxis are available on ☎01.41.83.15.15 or ☎01.47.08.93.50, but they need to be notified the day before and can be contacted weekday business hours only. For travel on the **buses**, **métro** or **RER**, the RATP offers accompanied journeys for disabled people not in wheelchairs – *Service d'Accompagnement* – which is available Monday to Friday from 8am until 6pm and costs over 60F an hour. You have to book your minder on ☎01.45.83.67.77, ☎01.42.71.20.53, or 01.48.93.06.23 a day in advance. Blind passengers can request a free companion from the volunteer organisation Auxiliaires des Aveugles (☎01.43.06.39.38).

For **wheelchair** users some RER stations are accessible, though only a very few like Vincennes and Marne-la-Vallée (for Disneyland) autonomously, while others, including Châtelet-Les-Halles, Denfert-Rochereau, Gare de Lyon and Grande Arche de la Défense require an official to work the lift. The new Météor line is easily accessible. One bus line, No. 20, linking Gare de Lyon and Gare St-Lazare, via Opéra, has specially designed lower floors for wheelchair users. A leaflet giving details, *Handicaps et Déplacements en Région Ile-de-France*, is available free at main métro/RER stations. A **Braille métro map** and a separate bus map are obtainable from L'Association Valentin Haüy (AVH), 5 rue Duroc, 7e (☎01.44.49.27.27). Aihrop (Mon–Fri 8am–noon & 1.30–6pm; ☎01.40.24.34.76) arranges transport to and from the airports and within the city.

A useful publication, *Access in Paris* by Gordon Couch and Ben Roberts, published in Britain by Quiller Press, is available from the London-based organisation RADAR (see p.28). The French tourist office publish a comprehensive guide in English, *Paris Ile-de-France For Every One* [sic]: *a guide for people with reduced mobility*, which costs 60F but it was last updated in 1995.

Driving and parking

Travelling around by **car** – in the daytime at least – is hardly worth it because of the difficulty of finding parking spaces. Really, you're better off finding a motel-style place with parking on the edge of the city and using the public transport system. But if you're determined to use the pay-and-display parking system you must first buy a *Paris Carte* from a tabac, then look for the blue 'P' signs alongside grey parking meters. Introduce the card into the meter – costs are 10F an hour, for a maximum of two hours. Alternatively, covered car parks cost up to 15F per hour. Whatever you do, don't park in a bus lane or the Axe Rouge **express routes** (marked with a red square). Should you be towed away, you'll find your car in the pound (*fourrière*) belonging to that particular arrondissement – check with the local mairie for the address.

In the event of a **breakdown**, call SOS Dépannage (☎01.47.07.99.99) for round-the-clock assistance. Alternatively, ask the police.

See p.180 for details of car and bike rental.

Boats

There remains one final mode of transport, **Batobus**, which operates from May to September, stopping at six points along the Seine in this order: port de la Bourdonnais (Eiffel Tower–Trocadéro), quai de Solférino (Musée d'Orsay), quai Malaquais (Saint Germain-des-Prés), quai de Montebello (Notre-Dame), quai de l'Hôtel de Ville (Hôtel-de-Ville–Centre-Pompidou) and quai du Louvre (Musée du Louvre). Boats run every thirty minutes or so from 10am to 7pm: total journey time is 20 minutes, and tickets cost 20F for the first stop, 10F for subsequent stops, or 60F for a day pass.

BOAT TRIPS, BALLOONS AND HELI-RIDES

Bateaux-Mouches **boat trips** start from the Embarcadère du Pont de l'Alma on the Right Bank in the 8ᵉ (reservations ☎01.42.25.96.10, information ☎01.40.76.99.99; Mᵒ Alma-Marceau). The rides, lasting one hour and costing 40F, depart at 11am, 11.30am, 12.15pm, 1pm and every half-hour from 2pm to 10pm; winter departures are fewer. The night-time cruises use such bright lights to illuminate the streetscapes they almost blind passers-by – much more fun on-board than off, and at all times a narration in six languages blares out. Make sure you avoid the outrageously priced lunch and dinner trips, for which "correct" dress is mandatory. *Bateaux-Mouches* has many competitors, all much of a muchness and detailed in *Pariscope* under "Croisières" in the "Visites-Promenades" section.

Less blatantly tourist fodder are the **canal boat trips** run by *Canauxrama* (reservations ☎01.42.39.15.00) between the Port de l'Arsenal, opposite 50 bd de la Bastille, 12ᵉ (Mᵒ Bastille), and the Bassin de la Villette, 13 quai de la Loire, 19ᵉ (Mᵒ Jaurès), on the Canal St-Martin. Departing daily at 9.45am and 2.45pm from La Villette and at 9.45am and 2.30pm from the Bastille, the ride lasts three hours – not a bad bargain for 75F. A more stylish vessel for exploring the canal is the catamaran of Paris-Canal with 3-hour trips between the Musée d'Orsay, quai Anatole-France, 7ᵉ (Mᵒ Solférino), and the Parc de la Villette (La Folie des Visites Guidées; Mᵒ Porte-de-Pantin); boats operate in both directions daily, leaving the museum at 9.30am, and the park at 2.30pm (95F; reservations on ☎01.42.40.96.97).

A **helicopter tour** above all the city's sights is somewhat prohibitively priced, but if whirligig rides turn you on more than a four-star meal or a stalls seat at the theatre, then a quick loop around La Défense is on. Contact *Héli-France* at the *Héliport de Paris*, 4 av de la Porte-de-Sèvres, 15ᵉ (Mon–Fri 8am–8pm, Sat & Sun 9am–6pm; ☎01.45.54.95.11; Mᵒ Balard). A thirty-minute trip will set you back an astronomical 850F for each passenger, and a minimum of five is required.

Even classier, and far more extravagant, are the **balloon trips** organized by Air Atmosphère, 87bis bd de la République, 92100 Boulogne (☎01.46.09.44.22) or France Montgolfière, 16 passage de la Main d'Or, 75011 Paris (☎01.47.00.66.44).

Accommodation

Not surprisingly, Paris hotels are the most expensive in France, though compared with other European capitals, **accommodation** prices are not exorbitant. It's possible to find somewhere decent and centrally located for 220F for a double with a shower, as long as you've booked in advance or it's out of season and you're prepared to hunt around – there are lots of bargains in the 11ᵉ on the edge of the Marais. Further out, in the 17ᵉ or 20ᵉ you could go as low as 170F for a small room with just a washbasin and perhaps a bidet. For average comfort and location you'd be looking at least 300F. If you're stuck, the main **tourist office** at Champs Elysées and the branches at Gare du Nord, Gare de Lyon and the Eiffel Tower will endeavour to find you a room: all book accommodation for that day only (20F–55F commission for a hotel room depending on how many stars it has, 8F for a hostel). The **Accueil des Jeunes en France** (AJF) at the Banlieue section of the Gare du Nord (June–Sept 10am–6.30pm; ☎01.42.85.86.19) and within the travel agency OTU Voyages Beauborg, 119 rue St-Martin, opposite the Pompidou Centre, 4ᵉ (Mon–Fri 10am–6.45pm, Sat 10am–5.30pm; ☎01.40.29.12.12; Mᵒ Châtelet-Les Halles), guarantee to find young people a room, though not necessarily a cheap one, for a fee of 10F.

Our recommendations (given below) are divided by arrondissement (see map overleaf) and listed in ascending price order. (Where there are only very few rooms in a hotel in the lower price categories, we show the complete price range on offer).

ACCOMMODATION PRICE CATEGORIES

Each hotel in this chapter has a symbol which corresponds to one of eight price categories. The prices quoted are for the cheapest available double room in high season, though remember that many of the cheap places will have more expensive rooms with en-suite facilities.

① Under 160F	③ 220–300F	⑤ 400–500F	⑦ 600–700F
② 160–220F	④ 300–400F	⑥ 500–600F	⑧ Over 700F

1er hotels

Henri IV, 25 place Dauphine; ☎01.43.54.44.53 (M° Pont-Neuf/Cité). An ancient and well-known bargain in a beautiful and dead central location on the Île de la Cité. Nothing more luxurious than a *cabinet de toilette* and now very run-down. Essential to book. ②

Vauvilliers, 6 rue Vauvilliers; ☎01.42.36.89.08 (M° Châtelet-Les Halles/Louvre). Book far in advance for this well-established cheapie. ②.

du Palais, 2 Quai de la Mégisserie; ☎01.42.36.98.25, fax 01.42.21.41.67 (M° Châtelet). The rooms at the top are basic and cheap; alternatively pay 100F more for a view over the Seine and a shower in your room. Location and views at this price are hard to beat. ③.

Lion d'Or, 5 rue de la Sourdière; ☎01.42.60.79.04, fax 01.42.60.09.14 (M° Tuileries). Spartan, but clean, friendly and very central. ④.

Agora, 7 rue Cossonerie; ☎01.42.33.46.02, fax 01.42.33.80.99 (M° Châtelet–Les Halles). Charming and peaceful with individually styled rooms. ⑤.

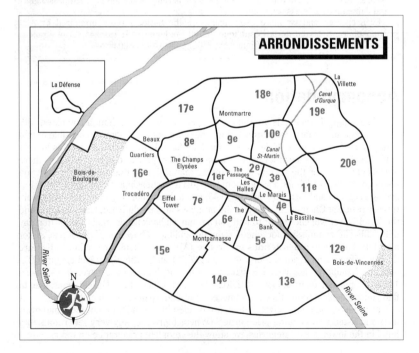

ARRONDISSEMENTS

Ducs d'Anjou, 1 rue Ste-Opportune; ☎01.42.36.92.24, fax 01.42.36.16.63 (M° Châtelet). A carefully renovated old building overlooking the endlessly crowded place Ste-Opportune in the middle of Les Halles. ⑦.

Hôtel Brighton, 218 rue de Rivoli;☎ 01.47.03.61.61, fax 01.42.60.41.78 (M° Tuileries). The charm of faded splendour and magnificent views over the Tuileries from the rooms with balconies. Doubles start at 650F with more spacious rooms up to 900F. ⑦.

Costes, 239 rue St-Honoré;☎01.42.44.50.00, fax 01.42.44.50.01 (M° Tuileries). The recent redesign, marrying Second Empire style with the amenities required for a luxurious and technologically-connected stay, is highly stylish and has proved an instant success. Mingle with media and fashion celebrities. Doubles start at 2000F. ⑦.

2ᵉ hotels

Tiquetonne, 6 rue Tiquetonne; ☎01.42.36.94.58 (M° Etienne-Marcel). Old-fashioned, well-maintained cheapie on a pedestrian street, but close to the red-light stretch of St-Denis. ②.

Les Noailles, 9 rue Michodière; ☎01.47.42.92.90, fax 01.49.24.92.71 (M° Opéra/4-Septembre). Contemporary styling with traditional pleasures of garden and *terrasse*. ⑧

Vivienne, 40 rue Vivienne; ☎01.42.33.13.26, fax 01.40.41.98.19 (M° rue-Montmartre).Traditional comfort and wooden floors. Ideal location for Opéra Garnier, *grands boulevards* and nightlife. ④–⑤.

3ᵉ hotels

du Marais, 16 rue de Beauce; ☎01.42.72.30.26 (M° Arts-et-Métiers/Filles-du-Calvaire/Temple). The genuine article: a prewar Paris cheapie, untouched, with brown spiral stairs, tiled floors, Turkish loos and an old-fashioned bar on the ground floor. Primitive, certainly, but clean, quiet and with pleasant service. ②.

Picard, 26 rue de Picardie; ☎01.48.87.53.82, fax 01.48.87.02.56 (M° Temple/République). Clean and comfortable hotel on the edge of the Marais and next door to Paris's best Internet café. Now popular with young American backpackers. Run by a charming and very accommodating Pole. ③.

de Saintonge, 16 rue de Saintonge; ☎01.42.77.91.13, fax 01.48.87.76.41 (M° Filles-du-Calvaire). In a sixteenth-century house on the edge of the Marais, near the Picasso Museum, though only the stone-vaulted cellar, where breakfast is taken, retains much character. Very relaxing, with all mod cons, including cable TV and safes in the rooms; all the bathrooms have baths to soak in. ⑥.

Pavilion de la Reine, 28 pl des Vosges, 3ᵉ; ☎01.40.29.19.19, fax 01.40.29.19.20 (M° Bastille). A good honeymoon or romantic weekend hotel choice for those prepared to splurge, in one of the *place's* much admired seventeenth-century mansions. The decor is atmospherically antique, right down to the four-poster beds, but all modern comforts come with the deal, from air-conditioning to 24-hour room service. ⑧.

4ᵉ hotels

Moderne, 3 rue Caron; ☎01.48.87.97.05 (M° St-Paul/Bastille). Much better than the first impression of the staircase would suggest, and the price is amazing for this area. ②.

Grand Hôtel du Loiret, 8 rue des Mauvais-Garçons; ☎01.48.87.77.00, fax 01.48.04.96.56 (M° Hôtel-de-Ville). Simple, but very good value for the price. ②

Grand Hôtel Jeanne d'Arc, 3 rue de Jarente; ☎01.48.87.62.11, fax 01.48.87.37.31 (M° St-Paul). Clean, quiet and attractive; rooms have all mod cons including cable TV. Booking essential. ④.

du Septième Art, 20 rue St-Paul; ☎01.42.77.04.03, fax 01.42.77.69.10 (M° St-Paul/Sully Morland). Pleasant, comfortable place decorated with posters and photos from old movies, and a similarly themed *salon de thé* downstairs. The stairs and bathrooms live up to the black-and-white-movie style. Every room equipped with a safe. ⑤.

Grand Hôtel Mahler, 5 rue Mahler; ☎01.42.72.60.92, fax 01.42.72.25.37 (M° St-Paul). Right in the heart of the Marais; breakfast is served in a renovated seventeenth-century vaulted wine cellar. ⑥.

St-Louis Marais, 1 rue Charles-V; ☎01.48.87.87.04, fax 01.48.87.33.26 (M° Sully-Morland). A very comfortable restored seventeenth-century mansion. ⑦.

de Lutèce, 65 rue St-Louis-en-l'Île, 4ᵉ; ☎01.43.26.23.52, fax 01.43.29.60.25 (Mº Pont-Marie). Small but exquisite rooms on the most desirable island in France. ⑧.

5ᵉ hotels

du Commerce, 14 rue de la Montagne-Ste-Geneviève; ☎01.43.54.89.69 (Mº Maubert-Mutualité). Only to be considered by those on the tightest of budgets, this somewhat gloomy hotel is extremely economical for the heart of the Latin Quarter. No reservations and lots of competition, so arrive before 10am, and be brave – the management are notoriously surly. Communal washing and toilets. ①.

Médicis, 214 rue St-Jacques; ☎01.43.54.14.66 (RER Luxembourg). Very primitive, but the prices are cut-price making it very popular with hard-up backpackers, and unlike *du Commerce*, the owners are charming. ①–②.

le Central, 6 rue Descartes; ☎01.46.33.57.93 (Mº Maubert-Mutualité/Cardinal-Lemoine). Clean, decent but dowdy rooms in a typically Parisian house atop the Montagne Ste-Geneviève, overlooking the gates of the former École Polytechnique and surrounded by popular brasseries; all rooms come with a shower. One of a dying breed. ③.

Marignan, 13 rue du Sommerard; ☎01.43.54.63.81 (Mº Maubert-Mutualité). One of the best bargains in town, with a free breakfast thrown in. Totally sympathetic to the needs of rucksack-toting foreigners, with free laundry and ironing facilities, plus a room to eat your own food in – plates, fridge, microwave and kettle provided. Even the maid speaks English. Rooms for 2, 3 and 4–5 people; no reservations for single rooms though you need to turn up early. ③.

des Alliés, 20 rue Berthollet; ☎01.43.31.47.52, fax 01.45.35.13.92 (Mº Censier-Daubenton). Simple, clean and well run; bargain prices. Rooms with bathroom are very spacious. No lift. ③–④.

Esmeralda, 4 rue St-Julien-le-Pauvre; ☎01.43.54.19.20, fax 01.40.51.00.68 (Mº St-Michel/Maubert-Mutualité). A discreet and ancient house on square Viviani, with a superb view of Notre-Dame; most rooms are doubles with shower and toilet but there are some much cheaper singles with wash-basin only for 160F. ④–⑤.

de la Sorbonne, 6 rue Victor-Cousin; ☎01.43.54.58.08, fax 01.40.51.05.18 (RER Luxembourg/Mº Maubert-Mutualité). An attractive old building, quiet, comfortable and close to the Luxembourg gardens. ⑤.

des Grandes Écoles, 75 rue du Cardinal-Lemoine; ☎01.43.26.79.23, fax 01.43.25.28.15 (Mº Cardinal-Lemoine). Refurbished, and comfortable, in the heart of the Latin Quarter, enclosing a beautiful courtyard garden. ⑤–⑦.

des Trois Collèges, 16 rue Cujas; ☎01.43.54.67.30, fax 01.46.34.02.99 (RER Luxembourg). Light, airy rooms and young, helpful staff in this classy modernised hotel; breakfast is served in the attached *salon de thé*. ⑦.

Agora St-Germain, 42 rue des Bernardins; ☎01.46.34.13.00, fax 01.46.34.75.05 (Mº Maubert-Mutualité). Very pleasant, and all the comfort you'd expect for the price. ⑦.

Libertal Quartier Latin, 9 rue des Écoles; ☎01.44.27.06.45, fax 01.43.25.36.70 (Mº Cardinal-Lemoine/Maubert-Mutualité). Part of the Libertal group focusing on small charming hotels in Paris. The individual rooms come straight from a style mag, with air-conditioning, double glazing and a kettle to ensure you're entirely comfortable, plus luxuriously spacious white bathrooms. ⑧.

6ᵉ hotels

St-Michel, 17 rue Gît-le-Cœur; ☎01.43.26.98.70, fax 01.40.46.95. 69 (Mº St-Michel). Simple, but perfectly acceptable and friendly. Great location in a very attractive old street close to the river and opposite a little arthouse cinema. Breakfast is included in the price. ③.

de Nesle, 7 rue de Nesle; ☎01.43.54.62.41 (Mº St-Michel). Characterful erstwhile hippy haven, small and friendly. No reservations – arrive before 10am. ③–④.

Récamier, 3bis place St-Sulpice; ☎01.43.26.04.89, fax 01.46.33.27.73 (Mº St-Sulpice/St-Germain-des-Prés). Comfortable, old-fashioned and solidly bourgeois hotel offers few concessions to modernity or fashion; superbly situated. ④–⑦.

Grand Hôtel des Balcons, 3 rue Casimir-Delavigne; ☎01.46.34.78.50, fax 01.46.34.07.27 (Mº Odéon). An attractive and comfortable hotel, complete with Art Deco entrance, in a lovely location near the Odéon and Luxembourg gardens. ⑤.

des Marronniers, 21 rue Jacob; ☎01.43.25.30.60, fax 01.40.46.83.56 (Mº St-Germain-des-Prés). Relatively pricey, but a delightful place with a dining room overlooking a secret garden. Good for a special occasion. ⑦.

de l'Angleterre, 44 rue Jacob; ☎01.42.60.34.72, fax 01.42.60.16.93 (Mº St-Germain-des-Prés). Classy and elegant, this was once the British Embassy. Later, Hemingway lived in room 14, athough in those days he only paid three francs a night, not 980F. ⑧.

7e hotels

du Palais Bourbon, 49 rue de Bourgogne; ☎01.45.51.63.32, fax 01.45.55.20.21 (Mº Varenne). A handsome old building in a sunny street by the Musée Rodin. Rooms are spacious and light. ③– ⑥.

de la Paix, 19 rue du Gros-Caillou; ☎01.45.51.86.17 (Mº École-Militaire). Recent renovations have inflated prices but this is still the best bargain within proximity of the Eiffel Tower. ④.

Grand Hôtel Lévèque, 29 rue Cler; ☎01.47.05.49.15, fax 01.45.50.49.36 (Mº École-Militaire/Latour-Maubourg). Clean and decent; nice people, who speak some English. Good location smack in the middle of the rue Cler market. Book a month ahead. ④

Le Pavillon, 54 rue St-Dominique; ☎01.45.51.42.87, fax 01.45.51.32.79 (Mº Invalides/Latour-Maubourg). A tiny former convent set back from the tempting shops of the rue St-Dominique in a leafy courtyard. A lovely setting, but the rooms are a little pokey for the price. ⑤.

Solférino, 91 rue de Lille; ☎01.47.05.85.54, fax 01.45.55.51.16 (Mº Solférino/RER Musée-d'Orsay). Attractive place featuring an old-fashioned cage-lift, with a few bargain rooms. ⑤.

du Palais Bourbon, 49 rue de Bourgogne; ☎01.45.51.63.32, fax 01.45.55.20.21 (Mº Varenne). A handsome old building in a sunny street by the Musée Rodin. Rooms are spacious and light. ③–⑥.

de la Tulipe, 33 rue Malar; ☎01.45.51.67.21, fax 01.47.53.96.37 (Mº Latour-Maubourg). Cottage-like place with a patio for summer breakfast and drinks. But, as with all hotels in this area, you pay for the location rather than great luxury. ⑥.

Bersoly's St-Germain, 28 rue de Lille; ☎01.42.60.73.79, fax 01.49.27.05.55 (Mº Bac). Small but exquisite rooms each named after an artist. Impeccable service. ⑦.

8e hotels

d'Artois, 94 rue la Boétie; ☎01.43.59.84.12, fax 01.43.59.50.70 (Mº St-Philippe-du-Roule). One of the cheapest in this smartest part of town, with unusually spacious rooms. ③.

de la Paix, 22 rue Roquépine; ☎01.42.65.14.36, fax 01.42.65.14.36 (Mº St-Augustin). A bit gloomy, but in a very Parisian fashion. ④.

de L'Élysée, 12 rue des Saussaies; ☎01.42.65.29.25, fax 01.42.65.64.28 (Mº St-Philippe-du-Roule). Chandeliers and four-posters – classic luxury. ⑦.

Le Bristol, 112 rue du Faubourg St-Honoré; ☎01.53.43.43.00, fax 01.53.43.43.01 (Mº Miromesnil). Paris's most luxurious and spacious hotel manages to remain discreet and warm. Gobelins tapestries, private roof gardens with some of the rooms and a large colonnaded interior garden, as well as the expected swimming-pool, health club and gourmet restaurant. Doubles start at 3250F, but you could always plump for the 300m2 presidential suite at 34,000F per night. ⑦.

9e hotels

Perfect Hotel, 39 Rue Rodier; ☎01.42.81.18.86, fax 01.42.85.01.38 (Mº Anvers). Popular hotel on a lively street populated with restaurants. Simple, clean rooms and a warm welcome. ②.

de Beauharnais, 51 rue de la Victoire; ☎01.48.74.71.13 (Mº Le Peletier/Havre-Caumartin). Louis Quinze; First Empire. . . every room decorated in a different period style. At the cheaper end of this price bracket with reasonable discounts outside high season. ⑤.

des Croisés, 63 rue St-Lazare; ☎01.48.74.78.24, fax 01.49.95.04.43 (Mº Trinité). Low on mod cons but great on style: a hotch-potch of different periods. Good value. ⑤.

Chopin, 46 passage Jouffroy; ☎01.47.70.58.10, fax 01.42.47.00.70 (Mº Rue-Montmartre). Splendid period building in an old passage. Entrance on bd Montmartre, near rue du Faubourg-Montmartre. ⑤.

10e hotels

Palace, 9 rue Bouchardon; ☎01.40.40.09.45 or 01.42.06.59.32, fax 01.42.06.16.90 (M° Strasbourg-St-Denis). Gloomy corridors but acceptable rooms in a busy, colourful and central district near the Porte St-Martin. Popular with backpackers. Nice, helpful owners. ①.

Moderne du Temple, 3 rue d'Aix; ☎01.42.08.09.04, fax 01.42.41.72.17 (M° République/Goncourt). Bargain cheapie run by Czechs. ①–②.

du Jura, 6 rue de Jarry; ☎01.47.70.06.66 (M° Gare-de-l'Est/Château-d'Eau). A bit basic, but friendly and decent. ②.

Résidence Magenta, 35 rue Yves-Toudic; ☎01.42.40.17.72, fax 01.42.02.59.66 (M° République/Jacques-Bonsergent). Friendly, clean, attractive hotel with patio breakfast area. The top rooms, 61 and 62, are particularly nice. ④.

Belta Hôtel Résidence, 46 rue Lucien-Sampaix; ☎01.46.07.23.87, fax 01.42.09.87.27 (M° Gare-de-l'Est). Good location on the St-Martin canal bank. Totally renovated, in bland airport style, but comfortable. ⑤.

11e hotels

de Vienne, 43 rue de Malte; ☎01.48.05.44.42 (M° République/Oberkampf). Very pleasant, clean, good-value cheapie, with nicely decorated rooms (none with toilet, some have showers), run by a charming old couple. No lift. Closed Aug. No credit cards. ②.

Mary's, 15 rue de Malte; ☎01.47.00.81.70, fax 01.47.00.58.06 (M° République/Oberkampf). Comfortable and clean hotel on the edge of the Marais, run by courteous people; cheaper rooms are good value for money but en-suite rooms suffer from money-saving gadgets such as hand-held showers and lack of direct phones. ②.

de Nevers, 53 rue de Malte; ☎01.47.00.56.18, fax 01.43.57.77.39 (M° République/Oberkampf). Clean and decent accommodation with a sympathetic proprietor. Excellent breakfasts. ②.

des Arts, 2 rue Godefroy-Cavaignac; ☎01.43.79.72.57 (M° Voltaire). Pretty foyer and rooms that are well-furnished, but overall not much charm, and a tad fusty. However, hospitable and acceptable at the price. No lift. ③.

Pax, 12 rue de Charonne; ☎01.47.00.40.98, fax 01.42.28.57.81 (M° Ledru-Rollin/Bastille). A reasonable establishment if you want to be in the centre of the Bastille's nightlife. No lift. ③.

Grand Hôtel Amelot, 54 rue Amelot, 11e; ☎01.48.06.15.19, fax 01.48.06.69.77 (M° St-Sébastien-Froissart). Recently renovated, well-run establishment in a good location on the edge of the Marais and close to the Cirque d'Hiver where there are several amiable bars. Rooms are spacious and pleasantly decorated with attractive modern bathrooms – some with baths. Except for a few bargain 150F single rooms, all have bathroom and cable TV. Excellent value. ③–⑤.

St-Martin, 12 rue Léon-Frot; ☎01.43.71.09.14, fax 01.43.71.88.44 (M° Boulets-Montreuil). Dull neighbourhood, but a nice, friendly hotel with all mod cons. ④.

du Nord et de l'Est, 49 rue de Malte; ☎01.47.00.71.70, fax 01.43.57.51.16 (M° République/Oberkampf). Clean and comfortable, all rooms en suite with direct phone, TV and bathroom; popular with business people. ④.

Beaumarchais, 3 rue Oberkampf; ☎01.43.38.16.16, fax 01.43.38.32.86 (M° Filles-du-Calvaire/Oberkampf). Fashionable, gay-friendly hotel with personal service and colourful Fifties-inspired decor; all rooms en suite with air-conditioning, individual safes and cable TV. ⑤.

Hôtel-Résidence Trousseau, 13 rue Trousseau; ☎01.48.05.55.55, fax 01.01.48.05.83.97 (M° Bastille/Ledru-Rollin). Modern serviced studio apartments which can sleep from two to six people, coming with fully equipped kitchens – perfectly positioned for food shopping in the nearby place d'Aligre market – and satellite TV. Car parking available for 80F per day. ⑤.

Méridional, 36 bd Richard-Lenoir; ☎01.48.05.75.00, fax 01.43.57.42.85 (M° Bréguet-Sabin/Bastille). Attractive, with light rooms and a decorative garden. ⑥.

12e hotels

de Reims, 26 rue Hector-Malot; ☎01.43.07.46.18 (M° Gare-de-Lyon/Ledru-Rollin). Old-fashioned hotel on a quiet street with access to the Promenade Plantée, and close to the place d'Aligre market. Closed Aug. ②.

du Midi, 31 rue Traversière; ☎01.43.07.88.68, fax 01.43.07.37.77 (M⁰ Ledru-Rollin). Clean pleasant accommodation close to the Gare de Lyon and the Viaduct des Arts; most rooms have shower, toilet and TV. ③–④.

des Pyrénées, 204 rue du Faubourg-St-Antoine; ☎01.43.72.07.46, fax 01.43.72.98.45 (M⁰ Faidherbe-Chaligny). Comfortable and quiet behind its posh reception area. ④.

Saphir, 35 rue de Citeaux; ☎01.43.07.77.28, fax 01.43.46.67.45 (M⁰ Faidherbe-Chaligny). On a quiet street off the Faubourg St-Antoine. No special charms, but comfortable. ⑤.

13ᵉ hotels

Tolbiac, 122 rue de Tolbiac; ☎01.44.24.25.54, fax 01.45.85.43.47 (M⁰ Tolbiac). On a noisy junction, but all rooms are very pleasant, with loos and showers; breakfast is only 15F. In July & Aug you can rent small studios by the week. ③.

Résidence Les Gobelins, 9 rue des Gobelins; ☎01.47.07.26.90, fax 01.43.31.44.05 (M⁰ Les Gobelins). Delightful establishment that's well known, so book far in advance. ④.

Le Vert-Galant, 41 rue Croulebarbe; ☎01.44.08.83.50, fax 01.44.08.83.69 (M⁰ Les Gobelins). In a quiet, verdant backwater, above a renowned Basque restaurant. Cosy rooms, some with kitchenette, and a vine climbing up the wall from the garden. ⑤.

14ᵉ hotels

Ouest, 27 rue de Gergovie; ☎01.45.42.64.99, fax 01.45.42.46.65 (M⁰ Pernety). Basic but perfectly acceptable, in a very pleasant part of town. ②.

Le Lionceau, 22 rue Daguerre; ☎01.43.22.53.53, fax 01.43.21.08.21 (M⁰ Denfert-Rochereau). Decent-sized rooms and decorated with murals throughout. On the pedestrianized market street. ③.

de la Loire, 39bis rue du Moulin-Vert; ☎01.45.40.66.88, fax 01.45.40.89.07 (M⁰ Alésia/Plaisance). Attractive hotel on a very quiet street, with breakfast served in a little garden. ④.

15ᵉ hotels

Mondial, 136 bd de Grenelle; ☎01.45.79.73.57, fax 01.45.79.58.65 (M⁰ La Motte-Picquet). Friendly and decent, with large rooms and good views in spite of a rather grim appearance. Right opposite the raised métro. ③.

Pasteur, 33 rue du Docteur-Roux; ☎01.47.83.53.17, fax 01.45.66.62.39 (M⁰ Pasteur). A small garden, and rooms that are comfortable and well-equipped for the price. ④

Tour Eiffel Dupleix, 11 rue Juge; ☎01.45.78.29.29, fax 01.45.78,60.00 (M⁰ Dupleix). Recently renovated, with tasteful rooms and a tiny garden in which to breakfast. ⑤.

Wallace, 89 rue Fondary; ☎01.45.78.83.30, fax 01.40.58.19.43 (M⁰ Émile-Zola). Unpretentious, charming place with a pretty garden in the courtyard. ⑦.

16ᵉ hotels

Keppler, 12 rue Keppler; ☎01.47.20.65.05, fax 01.47.23.02.29 (M⁰ George-V/Kléber). Rooms a little small, but spotless, quite comfortable, and just a few steps from the Champs-Élysées. ⑤.

Hameau de Passy, 48 rue Passy; ☎01.42.88.47.55, fax 01.42.30.83.72 (M⁰ Muette). Tucked away in a mews – utterly peaceful and with faultless service. ⑥.

17ᵉ hotels

Avenir-Jonquière, 23 rue de la Jonquière; ☎01.46.27.83.41 (M⁰ Guy-Môquet/Brochant). Clean, friendly establishment offering bargain accommodation and particularly reasonable single rates. Close to the tempting food stores on Ave de St Ouen. ②.

des Batignolles, 26–28 rue des Batignolles; ☎01.43.87.70.40,fax 01.44.70.01.04 (M⁰ Rome/Place-de-Clichy). Quiet and very reasonable, in a neighbourhood that prides itself on its village character. ②.

Jouffroy, 28 passage Cardinet; ☎01.47.54.06.00, fax 01.47.63.83.12 (M⁰ Malesherbes). Charming owners and pastel-coloured flowery wallpaper in a quiet passage between rue Jouffroy and rue Cardinet. ④.

du Roi René, 72 place Félix-Lobligeois; ☎01.42.26.72.73, fax 01.42.63.74.99 (M° Rome/Villiers). Very nice location by a mini-Greek temple and public garden. ⑤.

18e hotels

Versigny, 31 rue Letort; ☎01.42.59.20.90, fax 01.42.59.32.66 (M° Jules-Joffrin). Unmodernized and basic – fine if you're tough and want a cheap sleep. ②.

Idéal, 3 rue des Trois-Frères; ☎01.46.06.63.63, fax 01.42.64.97.01 (M° Abbesses). Marvellous location on the slopes of Montmartre. Basic, but clean, friendly and used to backpackers. ②.

André Gill, 4 rue André-Gill; ☎01.42.62.48.48, fax 01.42.62.77.92 (M° Pigalle/Abbesses). Very adequate, quiet rooms in a great location on the slopes of Montmartre, in a dead-end alley off rue des Martyrs. ③.

des Arts, 5 rue Tholozé; ☎01.46.06.30.52, fax 01.46.06.10.83 (M° Abbesses). All mod cons in the thick of Montmartre. ⑤.

Ermitage, 24 rue Lamarck; ☎01.42.64.79.22 (M° Lamarck-Caulaincourt/Château-Rouge). Discreet hotel only a stone's throw from Sacré Coeur yet completely undisturbed by the throngs of tourists. Approach via M° Anvers and the *funiculaire* to avoid the steep climb. ⑤.

Terrass, 12 rue Joseph de Maistre; ☎01.46.06.72.85, fax 01.42.52.29.11 (M° Blanche). On the southwest side of the butte, with magnificent views from the terrace-garden. Spacious rooms done out in antiques and warm colours. Doubles starting at 1290F going up to 1730F. ⑦.

19e hotels

Ibis Paris La Villette, 31 Quai de L'Oise; ☎01.40.38.04.04, fax 01.40.38.90 (M° Corentin Cariou/Ourcq). Situated right on the canal facing the Parc de la Villette, this good-value modern chain hotel is a great spot to stay if you want to spend a few days exploring the park or attending concerts at the Cité de la Musique. It is also a wise choice for people with their own cars, easily reached from the *boulevard périphérique* exiting at the Porte de la Villette, with free parking included. ③.

Rhin et Danube, 3 place Rhin-et-Danube; ☎01.42.45.10.13, fax 01.42.06.88.82 (M° Danube. Away from the centre on the airy heights of Belleville and geared to self-catering. Good value. ④.

20e hotels

Ermitage, 42bis rue de l'Ermitage; ☎01.46.36.23.44 (M° Jourdain). A clean and decent cheapie, close to the leafy rue des Pyrénées with its provincial feel. ②.

Tamaris, 14 rue des Maraîchers, ☎01.43.72.85.48, fax 01.43.56.81.75 (M° Porte de Vincennes). Simple, clean, attractive, and run by pleasant people. Extremely good value. Close to métro and the terminus of #26 bus route from Gare du Nord. ②.

Pyrénées-Gambetta, 12 av du Père-Lachaise; ☎01.47.97.76.57, fax 01.47.97.17.61 (M° Gambetta). Perfect for anyone passionate about the Père-Lachaise cemetery. Very pleasant. All rooms with cable TV. ④.

Hostels, student accommodation and campsites

There are numerous places offering **hostel** accommodation. The cheapest accommodation is to be had in the hostels run by the **French Youth Hostel Association**, for which you need Hostelling International (HI) membership (no age limit), and those connected with the **MIJE** (*Maison Internationale de la Jeunesse et des Étudiants*) and **UCRIF** (*Union des Centres de Rencontres Internationaux de France*). There is also a handful of privately run hostels.

Current costs for dorm bed and breakfast are: youth hostels from 120F, MIJE hostels from 125F and UCRIF hostels 120–130F. Single or double rooms are more expensive. There is no age limit and no advance bookings. MIJE hostels, mostly centrally situated in historic buildings, have a seven-day stay limit; for the other hostels it varies but is normally less. Bear in mind, too, that there is occasionally a curfew of around 11pm, though some hostels will loan you a key. We've detailed only the most central of the UCRIF hostels: for a full list contact their main office at 27 rue de Turbigo, 2ᵉ (Mon–Fri 10am–6pm; ☎01.40.26.57.24; fax 01.40.26.58.20; Mᵒ Étienne-Marcel). Independent hostels are even cheaper, around 98F for a dorm room off-season, rising to about 110F in summer.

HI hostels

D'Artagnan, 80 rue Vitruve, 20ᵉ; ☎01.40.32.34.53, fax 01.42.32.34.55 (Mᵒ Porte-de-Bagnolet). Colourful funky modern hostel, with a fun atmosphere and lots of facilities including a video cinema, restaurant and bar, and a local swimming pool nearby. On the eastern edge of the city near the village-like Charonne with some good bars, and handy for the Père-Lachaise cemetery. Very popular so try to get here early – reservations by fax or from other HI hostels only. Dorms 120F, doubles 129F per person; both include sheets and breakfast.

Jules Ferry, 8 bd Jules-Ferry, 11ᵉ; ☎01.43.57.55.60, fax 01.40.21.79.92 (Mᵒ République). Smaller and more central than D'Artagnan, in a lively area at the foot of the Belleville hill. Very difficult to get a place but when full, they will help you find a bed elsewhere.

MIJE hostels

Le Fauconnier, 11 rue du Fauconnier, 4ᵉ; ☎01.42.74.23.45 (Mᵒ St-Paul/Pont-Marie). A superbly renovated seventeenth-century building with a courtyard. Dorms sleep 4–8. Breakfast included.

Le Fourcy, 6 rue de Fourcy, 4ᵉ; ☎01.42.74.23.45 (Mᵒ St-Paul). Another beautiful mansion, this one has a small garden and a restaurant with menus from 50F. Dorms only, sleeping 4–8.

François Miron, 6 rue François-Miron; 4ᵉ (Mᵒ Hôtel-de-Ville). Annexe of above.

Maubuisson, 12 rue des Barres, 4ᵉ; ☎01.42.74.23.45 (Mᵒ Pont-Marie/Hôtel-de-Ville). Magnificent medieval building in a quiet street. Restaurant has menus from 32F. Dorms only, sleeping 4. Breakfast included.

UCRIF hostels

Centre International de Paris/Louvre, 20 rue Jean-Jacques-Rousseau, 1ᵉʳ; ☎01.53.00.90.90, fax 01.53.00.90.91 (Mᵒ Louvre/Châtelet-Les Halles).

Independent hostels

Auberge International des Jeunes Ste-Marguerite, 10 rue Trousseau, 11ᵉ; ☎01.47.00.62.00, fax 01.47.00.33.16 (Mᵒ Bastille/Ledru-Rollin). Despite the official-sounding name, a laid-back independent (but very noisy) hostel in a great location 5min walk from the Bastille. Clean and professionally run with 24hr reception, generous breakfast and free luggage storage. Under 100F.

Foyer International d'Accueil de Paris Jean Monnet, 30 rue Cabanis, 14ᵉ; ☎01.45.89.89.15, fax 01.45.81.63.91 (Mᵒ Glacière). A huge, efficiently run hostel in a fairly sedate area. Facilities include meeting–rooms and a disco; ideal for groups. 281F for a single, 131F in a dormitory.

Maison Internationale des Jeunes, 4 rue Titon, 11ᵉ; ☎01.43.71.99.21, fax 01.43.71.78.58 (Mᵒ Faidherbe-Chaligny). For 18- to 30-year-olds. Operates like a youth hostel, but does not require YHA membership. Dorms and doubles both 110F per person. Breakfast included.

Three Ducks Hostel, 6 place Étienne-Pernet, 15ᵉ; ☎01.48.42.04.05, fax 01.48.42.99.99 (Mᵒ Commerce/Félix Faure). A private youth hostel with no age limit; kitchen facilities as well as a bar with the cheapest beer in town. Essential to book ahead between May & Oct: send the price of the first night. Lock-out 11am–5pm, curfew at 2am. June–Sept 127F: Oct–May 87F; some rooms for couples at 147F per person.

Woodstock Hostel, 48 rue Rodier, 9ᵉ; ☎01.48.78.87.76 (Mᵒ Anvers/St-Georges). Another hostel in the Three Ducks stable, with its own bar. A great location in a pretty untouristy street near Montmartre: dorm 97F; double 107F per person. Price includes breakfast.

Young and Happy Hostel, 80 rue Mouffetard, 5ᵉ; ☎01.45.35.09.53, fax 01.47.07.22.24 (Mᵒ Monge/Censier-Daubenton). Noisy, basic and studenty in a lively, if a tad touristy, position. Dorms, with shower, sleep 4–8 and there are a few doubles (127F each). You can book in adavance but you have to turn up early, between 8am and 11am to keep the room. Dorms 107F, cheaper in winter.

Student accommodation

Student accommodation is let out during vacation time. The organization to contact is CROUS, Académie de Paris, 39 av Georges-Bernanos, 5e; ☎01.40.51.36.00 (Mº Port-Royal).

Campsites

Camping du Bois de Boulogne, Allée du Bord-de-l'Eau, 16e; ☎01.45.24.30.00, fax 01.42.24.42.95 (Mº Porte-Maillot then bus #244 to Route des Moulins 6am–8.30pm). Open all year. Much the most central campsite, next to the River Seine in the Bois de Boulogne, and usually booked out in summer. The ground is pebbly, but the site is well-equipped and has a useful information office. 70–95F for a tent with two people; and there are also mobile homes from 250F per night. A camping shuttle bus runs April–Oct from 8.30am to 1am.

Camping du Parc de la Colline, Route de Lagny, 77200 Torcy; ☎01.60.05.42.32 (RER line A4 to Torcy, then phone from the station and they will come and collect you or take bus #421 to stop Le Clos). Open all year. To the east of the city near Disneyland.

Camping du Parc-Étang, Base de Loisirs, 78180 Montigny-le-Bretonneux; ☎01.30.58.56.20 (RER line C St-Quentin-en-Yvelines; métro connections for RER line C at Invalides/St-Michel/Gare-d'Austerlitz). Open all year; southwest of Paris.

The city

Paris is an extremely compact city of twenty **arrondissements** that are strictly confined within the 78-square-kilometre limits of its ring road, the **boulevard périphérique**, built over the nineteenth-century city defences. The **Seine** flows in an arc through the middle from east to west, with its two islands, the **Île de la Cité** – where Notre-Dame sits at the historic heart of the capital – and the **Île St-Louis**. In the centre, north of the river on the **Right Bank**, or *rive droite,* is the Louvre; the banking, media and commercial quarter contained within the *grands boulevards*; **Les Halles**, the nightlife and daytime shopping quarter around the site of the city's former main food market (now the Forum des Halles); and the aristocratic **Marais**. South of the islands is the **Latin Quarter** (*quartier Latin*), so called because it was the language of the university founded here in the thirteenth century; and **St-Germain-des-Prés**, the quartier that evolved around an abbey, established on the site of a church of the same name in the sixth century.

East of St-Germain is the **7e**, with the **Eiffel Tower**, Invalides, the parliament and embassies. Across the river the **8e** has the **Champs-Élysées**, **Arc de Triomphe** and the most expensive shops; while to the east, the Marais borders on the trendy **Bastille** quarter. The outer arrondissements, continuing the clockwise spiral centred on the Île de la Cité, were mostly incorporated into the city in the nineteenth century. Those to the east accommodated the poor and working class, while the west were, and still are, the addresses for the aristocracy and new rich.

There are any number of **ways of exploring Paris** – you certainly don't have to start with the Louvre or Notre-Dame. Our account is structured in chunks of territory that share a common identity even though they do not always correspond exactly with the boundaries of the twenty arrondissements. We start with the Île de la Cité, then move to the Right Bank and the Voie Triomphale, the city's greatest vista. This leads from the Louvre right out to the northwest perimeter, from which we move east to the Marais and the Bastille. We continue with the inner arrondissements on the Left Bank, followed by the southern arrondissements, the rich Beaux Quartiers to the west, and beyond them, outside the city, the modern business district of La Défense, then Montmartre and the northern arrondissements and, finally, the east of the city with the old villages of Belleville and Ménilmontant, including the Père-Lachaise cemetery and out to Vincennes.

Île de la Cité

The **Île de la Cité** is where Paris began. The earliest settlements were here, as was the small Gallic town of Lutetia, overrun by Julius Cæsar's troops in 52 BC. A natural defensive site commanding a major east–west river trade route, it was an obvious candidate for a bright future. The Romans garrisoned it and laid out one of their standard military town plans, overlapping onto the Left Bank. While it never achieved any great political importance, they endowed it with an administrative centre that became the palace of the Merovingian kings in 508, then of the counts of Paris, who in 987 became kings of France.

Today the lure of the island lies in its tail-end **square du Vert-Galant** and, at the opposite end, the **cathedral of Notre-Dame**. The central section has been dulled by heavy-handed nineteenth-century demolition that displaced 25,000 people and replaced them by four vast edifices largely given over to housing the law. The space in front of the cathedral was a by-product, allowing a full-frontal view.

Pont-Neuf and the quais, Sainte-Chapelle and the Conciergerie

Arriving on the island by the **Pont-Neuf**, the city's oldest bridge, you will find steps behind the **statue of Henri IV** (who commissioned the bridge) leading down to the **quais** and the **square du Vert-Galant**, a small tree-lined green enclosed within the triangular stern of the island. The prime spot to occupy is the extreme point beneath a weeping willow – haunt of lovers, sparrows and sunbathers.

On the other side of the bridge, across the street from the king's statue, seventeenth-century houses flank the entrance to the sanded, chestnut-shaded **place Dauphine**, one of the city's most secluded and exclusive squares. The further end is blocked by the dull mass of the **Palais de Justice**, which swallowed up the palace that was home to the French kings until Étienne Marcel's bloody revolt in 1358 frightened them off to the greater security of the Louvre.

The only part of the older complex that remains in its entirety is Louis IX's **Sainte-Chapelle** (daily: April–Sept 9.30am–6.30pm; Oct–March 10am–5pm; 32F, or 50F combined admission to the Conciergerie; Mᵒ Cité), built to house a collection of holy relics he had bought at extortionate rates from the bankrupt empire of Byzantium. Though much restored, the chapel remains one of the finest achievements of French High Gothic (consecrated in 1248). Very tall in relation to its length, it looks like a cathedral choir lopped off and transformed into an independent building. Its most radical feature is its fragility: created by reducing the structural masonry to a minimum to make way for a huge expanse of exquisite glass (mostly original with some nineteenth-century restorations) in the upper chapel, which is reached via a spiral staircase. The impression inside is of being enclosed within the wings of myriad brilliant butterflies.

It pays to get to Sainte-Chapelle as early as possible to avoid the worst of the crowds that flock here and to the **Conciergerie** (daily: April–Sept 9.30am–6.30pm; Oct–March 10am–5pm; 32F, combined ticket with Ste-Chapelle 50F; Mᵒ Cité), Paris's oldest prison, where Marie-Antoinette – and, in their turn, the leading figures of the Revolution – were incarcerated before execution. The entrance is around the corner from Sainte-Chapelle, facing the river on Quai de l'Horloge; outside is the Tour de l'Horloge built in 1370, Paris's first public clock. Inside, the enormous vaulted late-Gothic *Salle des Gens d'Arme*, canteen and recreation room of the royal household staff, is architecturally impressive, but the chief interest of the Conciergerie is Marie-Antoinette's cell and various macabre mementos of the guillotine's victims.

If you keep along the north side of the island from the Conciergerie you come to **place Lépine**, named after the police boss who gave Paris's coppers their white truncheons and whistles. There is an exuberant **flower market** here six days a week, with birds and pets – cruelly caged – on Sunday. The police headquarters is right behind.

MUSEUMS & GALLERIES

1 Atelier de Henri Bouchard
2 Centre Georges Pompidou
3 Centre Nationale de la Photographie
4 Cité des Sciences
5 Espace Montmartre-Salvador Dali
6 Fondation Le Corbusier
7 Forum des Halles (M. Grévin II,
   M. de l'Holographie, Centre Culturelle
   des Halles, Espace Photographique de Paris)
8 Grand Palais (Palais de la Découverte)
9 Institut du Monde Arabe
10 Jeu de Paume
11 Maison de Balzac
12 Maison Européenne de la Photographie
13 Maison Victor Hugo
14 Manufacture des Gobelins
15 M. de l'Argenterie
16 M. de l'Armée
17 M. Arménien et M. d'Ennery
18 M. Art Juif
19 M. d'Art Naïf Max Fourny
20 M. Arts Africans et Océaniens
21 M. Assistance Publique
22 M. Atelier Adzak
23 M. Bourdelle
24 M. Branly
25 M. Carnavalet
26 M. Cernushi
27 M. Cognacq-Jay
28 M. des Contrefaçons
29 M. des Costumes
30 M. du Cristal
31 M. de la Curiosité
32 M. Delacroix
33 M. Edith Piaf
34 M. Fondation Dapper
35 M. Grévin
36 M. Gustave Moreau
37 M. de l'Histoire de France
38 M. d'Histoire Naturelle
39 M. Jacquemart-André
40 M. Jean-Moulin
41 M. Kwok-On
42 M. du Louvre (M. des Arts de la Mode,
   M. des Arts Décoratifs, M. de la Publicité)
43 M. des Lunettes
44 M. Maillol
45 M. Marmottan
46 M. de Montmartre
47 M. de la Musique
48 M. National des Arts et Traditions Populaires
49 M. National du Moyen Age (Cluny)
50 M. National des Techniques
51 M. Nissim de Camondo
52 M. d'Orsay
53 M. du Panthéon Bouddhique
54 M. Pasteur
55 M. de la Perfumerie
56 M. Picasso
57 M. de la Poste
58 M. de la Poupée
59 M. de la Préfecture de Police
60 M. de Radio-France
61 M. Renan-Scheffer
62 M. Rodin
63 M. de la S.E.I.T.A
64 M. de la Serrure Bricard
65 M. Valentin-Haüy
66 M. Zadkine
67 Orangerie
68 Palais Chaillot (M. du Cinéma,
   M. des Monuments Français et
   M. de l'Homme, M. de la Marine)
69 Palais de Tokyo (M. d'Art Moderne
   de la Ville de Paris)
70 Pavillon de l'Arsenal

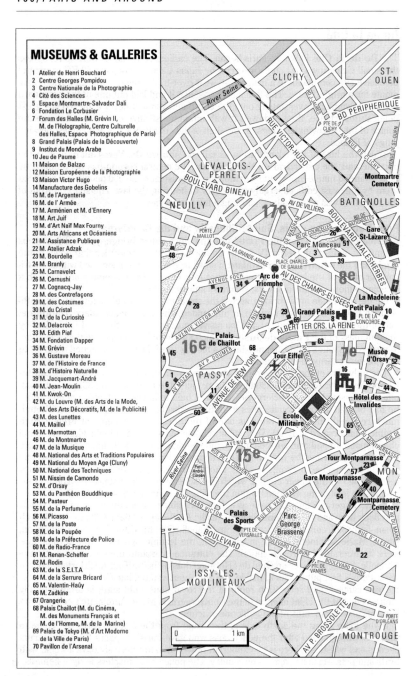

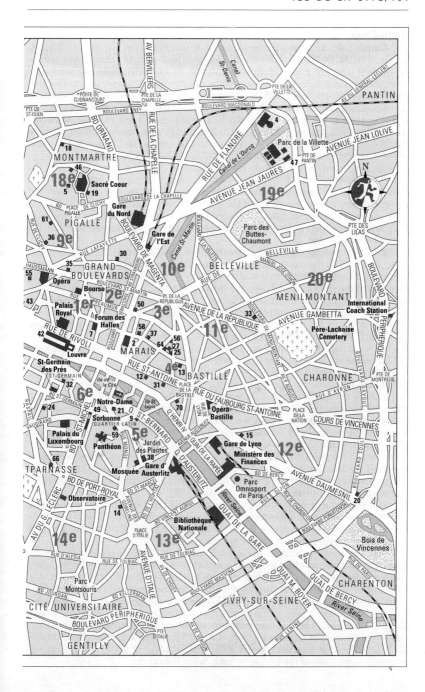

Notre-Dame

The **Cathédrale de Notre-Dame** (Mon–Fri & Sun 8am–7pm, Sat 8am–12.30pm & 2–7pm; free; M° St-Michel/Cité) itself is so much photographed that, seeing it even for the first time, the edge of your response may be somewhat dulled by familiarity. Described as the greatest masterpiece of the Middle Ages, it is truly impressive: that great H-shaped west front, with its strong vertical divisions counterbalanced by the horizontal emphasis of gallery and frieze, all centred on the rose window. It demands to be seen as a whole, though that can scarcely have been possible when the medieval houses clustered close about it. It is a solid, no-nonsense design, confessing its Romanesque ancestry. For more fantastical Gothic, look rather at the north transept facade with its crocketed gables and huge fretted window space.

Getting in to see the **Cathédrale de Notre-Dame** (Mon–Fri & Sun 8am–7pm, Sat 8am–12.30pm & 2–7pm; M° St-Michel/Cité) is at times so popular (weekends, summer) that there are long queues out onto the square. This is the real tourist heart and can get uncomfortably crowded, and the immediate area is crammed with tacky souvenir shops. On the fun side, there is always a bunch of spectators jostling for a view of the young rollerbladers going through their gymnastic stunts just outside the cathedral on the Pont au Double.

Notre-Dame was begun in 1160 under the auspices of Bishop de Sully and completed around 1345. In the nineteenth century, Viollet-le-Duc carried out extensive renovation work, including remaking most of the statuary – the entire frieze of Old Testament kings, for instance, damaged during the Revolution by enthusiasts who took them for the kings of France (the originals can be seen in the Musée National du Moyen Age; see p.121) – and adding the steeple and baleful-looking gargoyles, which you can see close-up if you brave the ascent of the **towers** (daily: April–Sept 9.30am–7.30pm; Oct–March 10am–5pm; 32F, or 50F combined admission to the *crypte archéologique* – see below). Ravaged by weather and pollution, its beauty may still be partially masked by scaffolding put up for further restoration work.

Inside, the immediately striking feature is the dramatic contrast between the darkness of the nave and the light falling on the first great clustered pillars of the choir, emphasizing the special nature of the sanctuary. It is the end walls of the transepts that admit all this light, nearly two-thirds glass, including two magnificent rose windows coloured in imperial purple. These, the vaulting and the soaring shafts reaching to the springs of the vaults are all definite Gothic elements and there remains a strong sense of Romanesque in the stout round pillars of the nave and the general sense of four-squareness. Free **guided tours** (1–1hr 30min) take place in French every weekday at noon and on Saturday at 2pm, and in English on Wednesday at noon. There are free organ **concerts** every Sunday at 5pm or 5.30pm, plus four **masses** on Sunday morning and one at 6.30pm. The **trésor** (daily 9.30am–6pm; 15F) is not really worth the entry fee.

On the pavement by the west door of the cathedral is a spot known as **kilomètre zéro**, from which all main road distances in France are calculated. For the Île de la Cité is the symbolic heart of the country, or at least of the France that in the schoolbooks fights wars, undergoes revolutions and launches space rockets.

Before you leave, walk round to the public garden at the east end for a view of the flying buttresses supporting the choir, and then along the riverside under the south transept, where you can sit in springtime with the cherry blossom drifting down. And say a prayer of gratitude that the city authorities had the sense to throw out Presidnet "Paris-must-adapt-itself-to-the-automobile" Pompidou's scheme for extending the quayside expressway along here. Out in front of the cathedral, in the plaza separating it from Haussmann's police HQ, is the entrance to the **crypte archéologique** (daily: April–Sept 10am–6pm; Oct–March 10am–4.30pm; 32F, combined entry with the towers 50F), an interesting museum containing the remains of the original cathedral, as well as streets and houses of the Cité as far back as the Roman era.

Le Mémorial de la Déportation

At the eastern tip of the island is the symbolic tomb of the 200,000 French who died in Nazi concentration camps during World War II – Resistance fighters, Jews and forced labourers among them. The **Mémorial de la Déportation** is scarcely visible above ground; stairs hardly shoulder-wide descend into a space like a prison yard (gates to crypt open daily 10am–noon & 2–5pm; free). Within the crypt, thousands of points of light represent the dead. Floor and ceiling are black, and it ends in a black, raw hole, with a single naked bulb hanging in the middle. Either side are empty barred cells. Above the exit are the words "Forgive. Do not forget." In contrast, the little green park surrounding the memorial is not grim in the least, and is a popular hang-out on a fine evening.

The Voie Triomphale

La Voie Triomphale, or Triumphal Way, stretches in a dead straight line from the **Louvre** palace to the modern complex of corporate skyscrapers at **La Défense**, 9km away. Incorporating some of the city's most famous landmarks – the **Tuileries** gardens, **Champs-Élysées** avenue and the **Arc de Triomphe** – its monumental constructions have been erected over the centuries by kings and emperors, presidents and corporations, to promulgate French power and prestige.

The tradition dies hard. Further self-aggrandizement has been given expression in an enormous, marble-clad cubic arch at the head of La Défense, and in a **glass pyramid** entrance in the central courtyard of the much-expanded Louvre.

The Arc de Triomphe and Champs-Élysées

The best view of this grandiose but simple geometry is from the top of the **Arc de Triomphe**, Napoléon's homage to the armies of France and himself (daily April–Sept 9.30am–11pm; Oct–March 10am–10.30pm; 35F; M° Charles-de-Gaulle–Étoile, access from stairs on north corner of av des Champs-Élysées). Your attention, however, is most likely to be caught not by the view but by the mesmerizing traffic directly below you, around the massive **place Charles-de-Gaulle** (still better known as place de l'Étoile) – the world's first organized roundabout. Twelve wide avenues make up the star (*étoile*), of which the busiest is the **Champs-Élysées**. At Christmas this is where the fairy lights are draped, and where cars converge on December 31 to hoot in the New Year. Bastille Day's procession of president, tanks and guns is less appealing. The avenue's pavements have recently been widened and new trees planted, but there are still too many airline offices, car showrooms, fast-food outlets and over-bright shopping arcades to recuperate the old glamour represented by the *Lido* cabaret, *Fouquet's* bar and restaurant, the perfumier Guerlain's shop and the former *Claridges* hotel.

North of the Champs-Élysées is the **Musée Jacquemart-André**, 158 bd Haussmann, 8e (Wed–Sun 10am–6pm; 47F; M° Miromesnil/St-Philippe-du-Roule) with a collection of Rembrandts and fifteenth- and sixteenth-century Italian genius represented by Botticelli, Titian, Tintoretto, Tiepolo and Donatello. A short way west in the magnificent *Hôtel Salomon de Rothschild*, 11 rue Berryer, 8e (M° George-V), the **Centre National de la Photographie** hosts important temporary exhibitions of photography (daily except Tues noon–7pm; 30F).

The stretch of the Champs-Elysées between the Rond-Point roundabout, whose Lalique glass fountains disappeared during the German occupation, and place de la Concorde is bordered by chestnut trees and municipal flower beds, pleasant enough to stroll among but not sufficiently dense to muffle the squeal of accelerating tyres. The gigantic building with overloaded Neoclassical exteriors, glass roofs and exuberant flying statuary rising above the greenery to the south is the

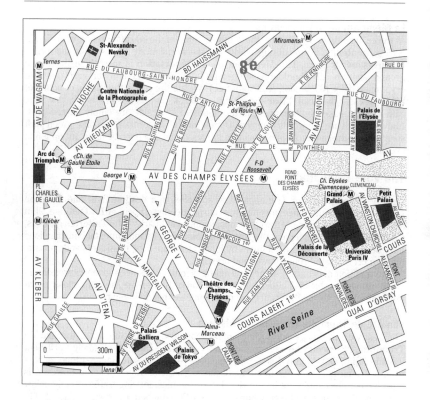

Grand Palais, created with its neighbour, the **Petit Palais**, for the 1900
Exposition Universelle. Major temporary art exhibitions are held in the Grand
Palais, and one wing is given over to the **Palais de la Découverte**, av Franklin-
D-Roosevelt, 8ᵉ; (Tues–Sat 9.30am–6pm, Sun & hols 10am–7pm; 27F or 40F including the planetarium; Mᵒ Champs-Élysées-Clemenceau/Franklin-D-Roosevelt), a
science museum with plenty of interactive exhibits, some very good temporary
exhibitions and an excellent planetarium. The Petit Palais houses the **Musée des
Beaux-Arts** (Tues–Sun 10am–5.40pm; 27F), with the odd Impressionist gem, lots
of Art Nouveau furniture and jewellery, and vast canvases recording Paris street
battles during the 1830 and 1848 revolutions. At the Seine end of the av Winston-
Churchill, the road running between the Grand Palais and the Petit Palais, the
English World War II leader himself is honoured by a statue, which was unveiled
on November 11, 1998, the eightieth anniversary of Armistice Day by Queen
Elizabeth II. Georges Clemenceau, French Prime Minister at the end of World War
I is commemorated by a statue at the other end of the avenue, in place
Clemenceau.

On the north side of the avenue, combat police guard the high walls round the presidential **Palais de l'Élysée** and the line of ministries and embassies ending with the
US in prime position on the corner of place de la Concorde. On Thursdays and at weekends you can see a different manifestation of the self-images of states in the **postage-
stamp market** at the corner of avs Gabriel and Marigny.

Place de la Concorde and the Tuileries

The Champs-Élysées descends to **place de la Concorde**, where more crazed traffic makes crossing over to the middle a death-defying task. As it happens, some 1300 people did die here between 1793 and 1795, beneath the Revolutionary guillotine: Louis XVI, Marie-Antoinette, Danton and Robespierre among them. The centrepiece of the *place* is an **obelisk** from the temple of Luxor, offered as a favour-currying gesture by the viceroy of Egypt in 1829. It serves merely to pivot more geometry: the alignment of the French parliament, the Assemblée Nationale, on the far side of the Seine with the church of the Madeleine to the north (see p.110).

The symmetry continues beyond place de la Concorde in the formal layout of the **Tuileries gardens**, disrupted only by the bodies lounging on the grass, kids chasing their boats round the ponds, and gay men cruising the terrace overlooking the river. A major project of replanting and tree surgery, recasting statues and relandscaping took place between 1991 and 1997 as part of the Grand Louvre Project, and the revamped Tuileries (with 3000 new trees) adds new perspectives to the Louvre whilst retaining features from Le Nôtre's original garden. The final part of the project is the reconstruction of the pedestrian Solférino bridge which will pass from the Quai des Tuileries to the Musée d'Orsay. The two buildings flanking the garden at the Concorde end are the Orangerie by the river and the **Jeu de Paume** by rue de Rivoli (Tues noon–9.30pm, Wed–Fri noon–7pm, Sat & Sun 10am–7pm; 38F; Mº Concorde). This ex-royal tennis court and ex-Impressionists museum has had huge windows cut into its classical temple walls to light the city's best exhibition space for contemporary art.

Also affected by the Grand Louvre project is the **Orangerie**, a private art collection, inherited by the state with the stipulation that it should always stay together. The plan is to enlarge, restructure and convert many of the existing exterior walls to glass, in line with Monet's request that as much natural light as possible reach his masterpieces and the museum should reopen in autumn 2001. After all the upheaval the Orangerie's centrepiece, comprising two oval rooms arranged by Monet as panoramas for his largest waterlily paintings, will go back to their original position as stipulated by Monet. The rest of the collection, containing works by artists such as Renoir, Sisley, Matisse, Cézanne, Utrillo, Modigliani and Soutine will be re-arranged and possibly added to from the collection's reserves.

The Louvre

Paris's largest monument, at the start of the Voie Triomphale, is the **Louvre**, for centuries the site of the French court, and renowned today as one of the world's greatest art galleries. It was begun by Philippe-Auguste in 1200 as a fortress to store his scrolls, jewels and swords while he himself lived on the Île de la Cité. Charles V was the first French king to make the castle his residence, but not until François I in the mid-sixteenth century were the beginnings of the palace laid and the fortress demolished. From then on, almost every sovereign added to it, with Catherine de Médicis, Henri II's widow, contributing the Palais des Tuileries extension, burnt to the ground during the Paris Commune (1871), across what is now the underpass avenue du Gal-Lemonnier. The whole lot was nearly demolished under both Louis XIV and Louis XV but the Louvre survived to be given further additions by Napoléons I and III, and finally by Mitterrand in the 1980s. It was during the French Revolution that the palace was first opened to the public to display the former kings' art treasures, a collection greatly expanded by Napoléon I's requisitions in his foreign campaigns.

Every alteration and addition up to 1988 created a surprisingly homogeneous building, with a grandeur, symmetry, and Frenchness entirely suited to this most historic of Parisian edifices. Then came the pyramid, bang in the centre of the Cour Napoléon. It was an extraordinary leap of daring and imagination. Conceived by the Chinese-born architect Ieoh Ming Pei, it has no connection to its surroundings, save as a symbol of symmetry. Mitterrand also managed to persuade the Finance Ministry to move out of the northern Richelieu wing, which now, with its two courtyards roofed over in glass, houses the French sculpture collection of the museum. A public passageway, the **passage Richelieu**, linking the Cour Napoléon with rue de Rivoli, allows you to look down into these courtyards – a

---

THE MUSEUM PASS

If you're planning to visit a great many museums in a short time, it is worth buying the *Carte Musées et Monuments* **pass** (80F 1-day, 160F 3-day, 240F 5-day; available from the tourist office, RER/métro stations and museums) – valid for 70 museums and monuments in and around Paris, and allowing you to bypass ticket queues (though the pass doesn't provide entry to special exhibitions). Many museums offer **reductions** on admission fees to certain age groups and students: the latter should show an ISIC or Youth Card (though students obviously over 25 may be refused), while under-25s and under-18s will need to show their passports; cheaper admission for over-60s has been cut back at many places but come armed with your passport just in case. Under 12s are usually free. Some museums have free or half-price admission on Sunday; many are closed on Monday and Tuesday.

better view of the Chevaux de Marly (which once graced Place de la Concorde) and Puget's monumental sculptures than you get from within the museum.

Mitterrand's project also dramatically extended the Louvre underground, with the **Hall Napoléon** beneath the pyramid leading into a series of galleries known as the **Carrousel du Louvre**. Very smart shops, cheap and expensive restaurants, exhibition and conference spaces fill the vast spaces, and an inverted glass pyramid lets in light from place du Carrousel.

Napoléon's pink marble **Arc du Carrousel**, just east of place du Carrousel, which originally formed a gateway for the former Tuileries Palace, has always looked a bit out of place (though it sits precisely on the Voie Triomphale axis); now it is definitively and forlornly upstaged by the Pyramide.

ACCESS AND OPENING HOURS

The pyramid is the **main entrance** to the Louvre, although alternative access directly from the métro, the porte des lions, the Pont du Carrousel or from rue de Rivoli via passage Richelieu allows you to avoid the queue for the pyramid. The *Café Marly*, overlooking the pyramid from the north wing, is the classiest place to eat here.

Lifts and escalators lead from the Hall Napoléon beneath the pyramid into the three wings of the **Louvre.** The permanent collection is open on Monday, and Wednesday to Sunday from 9am to 6pm, staying open until 9.45pm on Monday (selected rooms only) and Wednesdays. Opening hours of the Histoire du Louvre rooms and Medieval are Monday and Wednesday from 9am to 9.45pm; Thursday to Sunday 10am–8.30pm. Everything is closed on Tuesday. The usual entry charge is 45F but after 3pm and on Sunday this is reduced to 26F. Under-18s get in free at all times, and on the first Sunday of each month admission is free for everyone else; same-day re-admission allowed. Tickets can be bought in advance (advisable because of the queues in the Hall Napoléon for the ticket office) by telephoning ☎01.49.87.54.54; from branches of FNAC or over the Internet. Each of the three wings – Sully, around the Cour Carrée; Denon, the southern wings; and Richelieu, to the north, has four floors: the *entresol* (the level reached from the escalators in the Hall Napoléon), the *rez-de-chaussée* (ground floor), then the first and second floors. These are then divided into numbered rooms and colour-coded for the main categories of the collection (see below). At first overwhelming and seemingly nonsensical, the layout of the museum is a delight to discover and following the collections through their arrangements is absorbing and rewarding. The indispensable floorplan, available from the information desk in the Hall Napoléon, highlights some of the more famous masterpieces, such as the *Mona Lisa*, for those wishing to do a whistle-stop tour, although don't expect to be able to contemplate them peacefully without being jostled by other visitors wishing to take a look. If the crowds get too much and you can't take anything else in, your ticket allows you to leave and re-enter as many times as you like throughout the day.

THE MUSEUMS

The **seven basic categories** of the museum's collections: Oriental antiquities; Egyptian antiquities; Greek, Etruscan and Roman antiquities; sculpture; decorative arts; painting; and graphic arts. Each category spreads over more than one wing and several floors. An added bonus from all the building works has been the opportunity to excavate the remains of the **medieval Louvre** – Philippe-Auguste's twelfth-century fortress and Charles V's fourteenth-century palace conversion – under the Cour Carrée. The foundations and archeological findings are now on show along with a permanent exhibition on the **history of the Louvre**, from the Middle Ages up to the current transformations. The medieval Louvre is all in the *entresol* floor in the Sully wing, and easy to find.

Oriental Antiquities – including the newly presented Islamic Art collection – covers the Sumerian, Babylonian, Assyrian and Phoenician civilizations, plus the art of ancient Persia. **Egyptian Antiquities** contains jewellery, domestic objects, sandals, sarcophagi and dozens of examples of the delicate naturalism of Egyptian decorative technique, such as the wall tiles depicting a piebald calf galloping through fields of papyrus, and a duck taking off from a marsh. Among the major exhibits are: the pink granite *Mastaba Sphinx*, the *Kneeling Scribe* statue (Sully ground floor 2 & 5), a wooden statue of Chancellor Nakhti, the god Amon, protector of Tutankhamun, a bust of Amenophis IV, Sethi I and the goddess Hathor. The **Greek and Roman Antiquities** include the *Winged Victory of Samothrace* (Denon first floor, at the top of the great staircase) and the *Venus de Milo* (Sully ground floor 9), biggest crowd-pullers in the museum after the *Mona Lisa*. *Venus*, striking a classic model's pose dates from the late second-century BC. Her antecedents are all on display, too, from the delightful *Dame d'Auxerre* (seventh-century BC) and the fifth-century BC bronze *Apollo of Piombino*, still looking straight ahead in the archaic manner, to the classical perfection of the *Athlete of Benevento*. In the Roman section are some very attractive mosaics from Asia Minor and luminous frescoes from Pompeii and Herculaneum, which already seem to foreshadow the decorative lightness of touch of a Botticelli still a thousand years and more away.

The **Applied Arts** collection is heavily weighted on the side of vulgar imperial opulence and, to twentieth-century eyes, ecological abuses such as the entire doors of tortoiseshell in the work of the renowned cabinet-maker Boulle (active around 1700). There is also a great deal of tapestry – of the very first quality and workmanship, but perhaps the smaller, less public items, such as Marie-Antoinette's travelling case, the carved Parisian ivories of the thirteenth century, and the Limoges enamels and Byzantine ivories are more immediately attractive.

The **Sculpture section** covers the entire development of the art in France from Romanesque to Rodin, all in the new Richelieu wing, and Italian and northern European sculpture in Denon, including Michelangelo's *Slaves*, designed for the tomb of Pope Julius II (Denon ground floor 10). The huge glass-covered courtyards of the Richelieu wing – the Cour Marly with the Marly Horses which once graced place de la Concorde, and the Cour Puget with Puget's *Milon de Crotone* as the centrepiece – are very impressive, if a bit overwhelming. Upstairs, on the second floor, Napoléon III's apartments, long used by the Finance Ministry, of flock wallpaper, matching upholstery and vast chandeliers, are now open to view.

The largest section by far is the **paintings:** French from the year dot to mid-nineteenth century, along with Italians, Dutch, Germans, Flemish and Spanish. Some are so familiar from reproduction in advertisements and on chocolate boxes that it is a surprise to see them on a wall in a frame. At the time of writing, the definitive arangement is not yet completed so it is advisable to ask at the **information desk** in the Hall Napoléon for the precise location of particular works. The early Italians (Denon first floor 5 & 7) are perhaps the most interesting part of the collection. All the big names are represented – Giotto, Fra Angelico, Botticelli, Filippo Lippi, Raphael; works to look out for include Uccello's *Battle of San Romano*, a *Crucifixion* by Mantegna, and Paolo Veronese's *Marriage at Cana*, a huge work painted in 1563. If you want to get near the *Mona Lisa* (Denon, first floor 5), go first or last thing in the day. No one, incidentally, pays the slightest bit of attention to the other Leonardos right alongside, including the *Virgin of the Rocks*. Non-Italian works worth lingering over include Quentin Matsy's moralistic *Moneychanger and his Wife,* Rembrandt's superb *Supper at Emmaus*, and a number of paintings by Poussin. There are also famous canvases by French nineteenth-century artists (Denon, first floor): David's *Coronation of Napoléon*, Ingres' *The Turkish Bath*, Géricault's intensely dramatic *Raft of the Medusa* and the icon of nineteenth-century revolution, Delacroix's *Liberty Leading the People*. Look out, too, for

Courbet's later *Funeral at Ornans*, perhaps the best-known Realist painting of all, its events rendered with dour, passive precision.

The other museums housed in the Louvre palace (entrance at 107 rue de Rivoli), have all been undergoing reorganization – work which should be finished by mid-2001. Already up and running is the **Musée de la Mode et du Textile** (Tues, Thurs & Fri 11am–6pm, Wed 11am–9pm, Sat & Sun 10am–6pm; 30F), a museum of fashion whose exquisite collection is too large to be shown all at once and too fragile to be exposed for long periods, resulting in a yearly rotation of the garments and textiles based on changing themes. The **Musée des Arts Décoratifs** (same hours and ticket as above) starts on the third floor with the Middle Ages to the Renaissance section. The collection of religious art and everyday objects from the bourgeoisie seems rather humble in comparison with the high art next door but the craftsmanship and devotion is nonetheless apparent, and the thematic arrangement with two period mock-ups (a late-fourteenth-century castle bedroom and a fifteenth-century reception room) brings it to life. In the meantime, the rest of the permanent collection may be closed but comprises furnishings, fittings and objects of French interiors such as beds, blankets, cupboards, tools, stained glass and lampshades – almost anything illustrating decorative skills from the Renaissance to the present day. The **contemporary** section includes works by French, Italian and Japanese designers, including some great examples of Philippe Starck. The rest of the twentieth-century collection is fascinating – a bedroom by Guimard, Jeanne Lanvin's Art Deco apartments, and a salon created by Georges Hoentschel for the 1900 Exposition Universelle.

The **Musée de la Publicité** also forms part of the complex of the above museums and is due to open by the year 2000. It deals with the art of advertising from nineteenth-century poster art to contemporary electronic publicity. Check *Pariscope* for opening hours and prices.

Opéra district

In the narrow streets of the 1er and 2e arrondissements, between the Louvre and **boulevards Haussmann**, **Montmartre**, **Poissonnière** and **Bonne-Nouvelle**, the grandiose financial, cultural and political state institutions are surrounded by well-established **commerce** – the rag trade, media, sex and well-heeled shopping. In contrast to the hulks of the Bourse, Banque de France and the Bibliothèque Nationale are the once crumbling and secretive **passages** – shopping arcades long predating the concept of pedestrian precincts, with glass roofs, tiled floors and unobtrusive entrances. Most have now been rendered as chic and immaculate as they originally were in the nineteenth century, with mega-premiums on their leases. Many are closed at night and on Sundays.

The passages

Foremost among the *passages* is the **Galerie Vivienne**, between rue Vivienne and rue des Petits-Champs, with its flamboyant decor of Grecian and marine motifs enticing you to buy Jean-Paul Gaultier or Yuki Torri gear. The neighbouring **Galerie Colbert**, gorgeously lit by bunches of bulbous lamps, has become a showcase extension for the Bibliothèque Nationale. But the best stylistically are the dilapidated three-storey **passage du Grand-Cerf**, between rue St-Denis and rue Dussouds, and **Galerie Véro-Dodat**, between rue Croix-des-Petits-Champs and rue Jean-Jacques Rousseau, named after the two pork butchers who set it up in 1824. This last is the most homogeneous and aristocratic *passage*, though a little dilapidated, with painted ceilings and panelled shop fronts divided by black marble columns. At no. 26, Monsieur Capia keeps a collection of antique dolls in a shop piled high with miscellaneous curios.

North of rue St-Marc the grid of arcades round the **passage des Panoramas** is still a touch rough, with no fancy mosaics for your feet. An old brasserie with carved wood panelling has been restored, and there are still bric-a-brac shops, bars, stamp dealers, and an upper-crust printshop with its original 1867 fittings. In **passage Jouffroy**, across boulevard Montmartre, a Monsieur Segas sells walking canes and theatrical antiques opposite a shop for dolls house fittings and furnishings, while Paul Vulin spreads his second-hand books further down along the passageway, and *Ciné-Doc* serves cinephiles. Crossing rue de la Grange-Batelière, you enter **passage Verdeau**, where a few of the old postcard and camera dealers still trade alongside smart new art galleries.

The garment business

Mass-produced clothes is the business of **place du Caire**, the centre of the **rag trade** district. The frenetic trading and deliveries of cloth, the food market on rue des Petits-Carreaux, and general toing and froing make a lively change from the office-bound quarters further west. Beneath an extraordinary pseudo-Egyptian facade of grotesque Pharaonic heads (a celebration of Napoléon's conquest of Egypt), an archway opens on to a series of arcades, the **passage du Caire**. These, contrary to any visible evidence, are the oldest of all the *passages* and entirely monopolized by wholesale clothes shops.

The garment business gets progressively more upmarket west of the trade area. The upper end of **rue Étienne-Marcel**, and Louis XIV's **place des Victoires**, adjoined to the north by the appealingly asymmetrical **place des Petits-Pères**, are the centre for new-name designer clothes, displayed to deter all those without the necessary funds. The boutiques on **rue St-Honoré** and its Faubourg extension have the established names, paralleled across the Champs-Élysées by **rue François-1er**, where Dior has at least four blocks on the corner with avenue Montaigne. Pierre Marly, the optician's at 380 rue St-Honoré, exhibits a collection of visual aides, from the first medieval corrective lenses to specs worn by contemporary celebrities, and Hermès, at 24 rue du Faubourg-St-Honoré, displays a small collection of its original saddlery items. The aristocratic **place Vendôme**, with Napoléon high on a column clad with recycled Austro-Russian cannons, has all the fashionable accessories for haute couture, plus the original Ritz, various banks and the Law and Order ministry.

Place Madeleine and the Opéra-Garnier

Another obese Napoleonic structure on the classical temple model is the church of **La Madeleine**, which serves for society weddings and for the perspective across place de la Concorde. There's a **flower market** every day except Sunday along the east side of the church, and a luxurious **Art Nouveau loo** by the métro at the junction of place and bd Madeleine. But the square holds greatest appeal for window-gazing gourmets. In the northeast corner – at Fauchon – are two blocks of the best **food display** in Paris, with a snack bar for epicurean treats.

Boulevard de la Madeleine, becoming boulevard des Capucines, leads to the most preposterous building in Paris, the **Opéra-Garnier**, whose architect, Charles Garnier, looks suitably foolish in a golden statue on the rue Auber side of his edifice. Excessively ornate and covering three acres in extent, this provided ample space for aristocratic preening, ceremonial pomp and the social intercourse of opera-goers, for whom the performance itself was a very secondary matter. You can see round the **interior** (daily 10am–5pm; 30F), including the auditorium – rehearsals permitting – whose ceiling is the work of Chagall. The visit includes the **Bibliothèque-Musée de l'Opéra**, dedicated to the artists connected with the Opéra throughout history, and containing model sets, dreadful nineteenth-century paintings, and rather better temporary exhibitions on operatic themes.

Palais Royal

The **avenue de l'Opéra** was built at the same time as its namesake – and left deliberately bereft of trees lest they mask the vista of the Opéra. It leads down to the **Palais Royal**, originally Richelieu's residence, which now houses various government and constitutional bodies, and the **Comédie Française,** where the classics of French theatre are performed. The palace **gardens** to the north were once a gastronomic, gambling and amusement hot spot overlooked by apartments that were occupied by Cocteau and Colette, amongst others. New shops and cafés have opened in the arcades, and the flower beds are sumptuous. Folly has returned in the form of Daniel Buren's black-and-white pillars in different sizes, which stand above flowing water in the main courtyard of the palace. Kids use these monochrome Brighton-rock lookalikes as an adventure playground, but for most people the palace grounds are just a useful short cut from the Louvre to rue des Petits-Champs. Beyond this street, just to the left, is the forbidding wall of the old **Bibliothèque Nationale**; you can enter free of charge and peer into the atmospheric reading rooms or pay to enter the various exhibitions (closed Mon).

Les Halles to Beaubourg

In 1969 the main **Les Halles** market was moved to the suburbs after more than eight hundred years in the heart of the city. There was widespread opposition to the destruction of Victor Baltard's nineteenth-century pavilions, and considerable disquiet at what renovation of the area would mean. The authorities' excuse was the RER and métro interchange they had to install below. Digging began in 1971, and the hole was only finally filled at the end of the 1980s. Hardly any trace remains of the working-class quarter, with its night bars and bistros serving market traders; rents now rival the 16e, and the all-night places serve and profit from salaried and speed-popping types.

The Forum des Halles

From the RER station at Châtelet-Les Halles you surface only after ascending levels -4 to 0 of the **Forum des Halles** centre, which stretches underground from the Bourse du Commerce rotunda to rue Pierre-Lescot. The overground section comprises aquarium-like arcades of shops enclosed by glass buttocks with white steel creases sliding down to an imprisoned patio. To cover up for all this, commerce, poetry, arts and crafts pavilions top two sides in a simple construction – save for the mirrors – that just manages to be out of sync with the curves and hollows below.

The **gardens** above the extensive underground complex do, however, provide much-needed greenery and open space, as well as fountains and a tropical greenhouse housed in a glass pyramid.

Beneath the garden, amidst the uninspiring shops, there's scope for various diversions such as swimming, billiards, discovering Paris through videos, movie-going, and photography exhibitions. After a spate of air-conditioning and artificial light, you can seek relief in the water cascading down the perfect Renaissance proportions of the **Fontaine des Innocents**, or in the high Gothic and Renaissance **church of St-Eustache**, where a woman preached the abolition of marriage from the pulpit during the Commune.

There are always hundreds of people around the Forum filling in time, hustling or just loafing about. Pickpocketing is pretty routine; the law plus canine arm is often in evidence, and at night the atmosphere can be quite tense, although the labyrinth of tiny streets southeastwards to **place du Châtelet** teems with jazz bars, nightclubs and restaurants, and is far more crowded at 2am than 2pm.

To the north, rues Montmartre, Montorgueil and Turbigo concentrate on food – strictly not for vegetarians – with shops featuring the cadavers of wild boar, deer and feathered friends, alongside *pâté de foie gras* and caviar. On the riverfront due south, the three blocks of the **Samaritaine department store** (Mon–Sat 9.30am–7pm, Thurs till 10pm) recall the days when art rather than marketing psychology determined the decoration of a store. Built in 1903 in pure Art Nouveau style, its gold, green and glass exteriors, interior ceramic tiles and wrought-iron staircases and balconies have all been restored, though best of all is the view from the roof – the most central high location in the city.

Centre Georges Pompidou

In the daytime, the main flow of feet is still from Les Halles to the **Centre Georges Pompidou** (more familarly known as the **Beaubourg**; Mº Rambuteau/Hôtel-de-Ville), though three-quarters of it is closed for major repair work until a planned grand re-opening as part of the Millennium celebrations on New Year's Eve 1999. Whether it will be ready in time remains to be seen, but it's certainly an inspirational deadline. This famous building by Renzo Piano and Richard Rogers, now one of the most popular Parisian buildings, was considered outrageous when it opened in 1977 for its external-ized infrastructure, brightly-coloured pipes and ducts, lack of a monumental entrance, and an escalator rising up within a glass tube on the outside. But the overload of visitors and corrosion have taken their toll. The centre was designed for 5000 visitors a day but ended up attracting a figure five times that amount. It was closed in October 1997, to provide time for necessary maintenance, and to create more space for the ever-growing modern art collection and the highly popular multimedia library. It is planned to re-open during the life of this book, on December 31, 1999 – times and prices will have changed (and there may be a charge for the ride up the escalator) so consult the Paris tourist office for exact details, but, to give a rough idea, the centre was open afternoons and evenings except Tuesdays and up to 10pm at weekends. Admission to the centre was free with an extra charge of 35F for the **Musée National d'Art Moderne** (see below)and temporary exhibitions of 27–45F; a day pass cost 70F.

The sloping piazza is not totally deserted – a few portrait artists still harass passers-by, and the drug-dealers who became another symptom of its success still hang about on its corners, but it no longer has the shifting spectacle of buskers performing mime, magic and music, and the backpackers and other young people who used to enjoy the free show. It's now dominated by another extraordinary architectural sight, a gigantic teepee, the **Tipi** (Mon, Wed–Fri & Sun noon–6pm, Sat 2–6pm; free), inside which the latest information about the centre is relayed in a suitably high-tech way via individual interactive computer screens. You can also access images and details of some of the vast collection of the Musée National d'Art. During the closure, a selection of pieces are on show at the Musée d'Art Moderne de la Ville de Paris at the Palais de Tokyo (see p.128) until September 1999, and other exhibitions from the collection will be set up in Paris at the Grand Palais and the Jeu de Paume, as well as in other French cities and overseas. A ground-floor exhibition area, the **Galerie Sud**, has been given over to major temporary exhibitions until the end of April 1999, which have included works by Max Ernst and David Hockney.

On the northern edge of the centre, down some steps off the piazza, a small separate one-level building, the **Atelier Brancusi**, is open as usual (Mon & Wed–Fri noon–8pm, Sat, Sun & hols 10am–8pm; closed Tues & May 1; 20F). When he died in 1956, the sculptor **Constantin Brancusi** bequeathed the contents of his 15e arrondissement studio to the state: the condition was that it had to be reconstructed exactly as it was found. The artist had become obsessed with the spatial relationship of the sculptures in his studio, going so far as to supplant a sold work with a plaster copy, and the four inter-linked rooms of the studio faithfully adhere to his arrangements. Studios one and two are crowded with fluid sculptures of highly polished brass and marble, his trademark abstract bird and column shapes, stylised busts and poised objects that look as though they want to take off into space. Unfortunately the rooms are behind glass creating a feeling of sterility and distance. Perhaps the most satisfying rooms are studios three and four, his private quarters, where you really get an idea of how the artist lived and worked.

The surrounding cafés, like the Café Beauborg (see p.114), are still popular – there's the view of the brilliant building after all, and the **Stravinsky fountain** (see below) still provides a colourfully kinetic focus.

MUSÉE NATIONAL D'ART MODERNE

The **Musée National d'Art Moderne** is second-to-none, with a constantly expanding collection of exclusively twentieth-century art. Contemporary movements and works dated as recently as a couple of years ago find their place here along with the late-Impressionists, Fauvists, Cubists, Figuratives, Abstractionists and the rest of this century's Western art trends. The lighting and hanging are superb, although only a sixth of the whole collection is exhibited at any one time.

A huge cut-out by Matisse, *La Tristesse du Roi*, greets you on entry. In a different world, Picasso's *Femme Assise* of 1909 brings in the reduced colours and double dimensions of **Cubism**, presented in its fuller development by Braque's *L'Homme à la Guitare* (1914), and, later, in Léger's solid balancing act, *Les Acrobates en Gris* (1942–44). Marcel Duchamp's games with the status of art objects (the bearded Mona Lisa, bottle-racks, etc) are some of the most enjoyable of the **Dada** School. Among **Abstracts**, there's the sensuous rhythm of colour in Sonia Delaunay's *Prismes Électriques* (1914), and a good number of Kandinskys at his most harmonious and playful. Dali disturbs, amuses or infuriates with *Six Apparitions de Lénine sur un Piano* (1931), and there are more Surrealist images from Magritte and de Chirico. Moving to the Expressionists, one of the most compelling pictures – of 1920s female emancipation as viewed by a male contemporary – is the portrait of the journalist Sylvia von Harden by Otto Dix. In contrast, the gender of the sleeping woman in *Le Rêve* by Matisse has no importance – it is simply a painting of the human body at its most relaxed. Jumping forward to Francis Bacon you find the tension and the torment of the human body and mind in the portraits, and – no matter that the figure is minute – in *Van Gogh in Landscape* (1957). Squashed-up cars, lines and squares, wrapped-up grand pianos and Warhol's *Electric Chair* (1966) may be on show, while for a reminder that **contemporary** art can still hold onto its roots, there's the classic subject of *Le Peintre et son Modèle* by Balthus, painted in 1980–81. Installation art is also included in the contemporary section on the third floor along with a huge collection of videos to consult.

Quartier Beaubourg and the Hôtel de Ville

Visual entertainments around Beaubourg include the clanking gold *Défenseur du Temps* clock in the Quartier de l'Horloge; a *trompe-l'œil* as you look west along rue Aubry-le-Boucher from Beaubourg; a nine-digit timepiece counting down the milliseconds to the year 2000 on the south side of the building; and colourful moving sculptures and fountains by Jean Tinguely and Niki de St-Phalle in the pool in front of **Église St-Merri** on place Igor Stravinsky. This squirting waterworks pays homage to Stravinsky and shows scant respect for passers-by; beneath it lies IRCAM, founded by the composer Pierre Boulez, a research centre for contemporary music, with an overground extension by Renzo Piano.

Small commercial art galleries where you can browse to your heart's content for free are concentrated north of rue Aubrey-le-Boucher on **rue Quincampoix**, including Zabriskie at no. 37 (Tues–Sat 2–7pm) showing classic and cutting-edge contemporary photography.

Rue Renard runs down to **place de l'Hôtel de Ville**, where the oppressively vertical, gleaming and gargantuan mansion is the seat of the city's government. Those opposed to the establishments of kings and emperors created their alternative municipal governments at this building in 1789, 1848 and 1870. But with the defeat of the Commune in 1871, the conservatives concluded that the Parisian municipal authority had to go if order, property, morality and the suppression of the working class were to be maintained. For a hundred years Paris was ruled directly by the ministry of the interior. The next head of an independent municipality was Jacques Chirac, elected in 1977. Amazingly he even held the position whilst prime minister, eventually relinquishing it in 1995 when he became president. Chirac virtually nominated his successor: the current mayor of Paris, **Jean Tiberi**.

The Marais, the Île St-Louis and the Bastille

Jack Kerouac translated **rue des Francs-Bourgeois**, the Marais' main east–west axis along with rue Rivoli/rue St-Antoine, as "street of the outspoken middle classes". The original owners of the mansions lining its length would not have taken kindly to such a slight on their blue-bloodedness. The name's origin is medieval, and it was not until the sixteenth and seventeenth centuries that the **Marais**, as the area between Beaubourg and the Bastille is known, became a fashionable aristocratic district. After the Revolution it was abandoned to the masses who, up until some thirty years ago, were living ten to a room on unserviced, squalid streets. Since then, gentrification has proceeded apace and the middle classes are finally ensconced – mostly media, arty or gay, and definitely outspoken.

The renovated mansions, their grandeur concealed by the narrow streets, have become museums, libraries, offices and chic apartments, flanked by shops selling designer clothes, house and garden accoutrements, works of art and one-off trinkets. Though cornered by Haussmann's boulevards, the Marais itself was spared the baron's heavy touch, and very little has been pulled down in the recent gentrification. This is Paris at its most seductive – old, secluded, as unthreatening by night as it is by day, and with as many alluring shops, bars and places to eat as you could wish for.

Rue des Francs-Bourgeois, the Picasso museum and the place des Vosges

Rue des Francs-Bourgeois begins with the eighteenth-century magnificence of the **Palais Soubise** which houses the Archives Nationales de France and the Musée de l'Histoire de France. Opposite, at the back of a driveway for the Crédit Municipal bank, stands a pepperpot tower which formed part of Philippe-Auguste's twelfth-century **city walls**. Further down the street are two of the grandest Marais hôtels, **Carnavalet** and

Lamoignon, housing respectively the Musée Carnavalet and the Bibliothèque Historique de la Ville de Paris.

The **Musée de l'Histoire de France** (Mon & Wed–Fri noon–5.45pm, Sat & Sun 1.45–5.45pm; closed Tues and hols; 20F) within the Palais Soubise, at no. 60 rue des Francs-Bourgeois, shows permanent and temporary exhibitions of historical documents from the national archives; more interestingly the museum provides an opportunity to enter perhaps Marais' most splendid mansion, with some fine Rococo interiors, and paintings by the likes of Boucher.

The **Musée Carnavalet**, whose entrance is off rue des Francs-Bourgeois at 23 rue de Sévigné (Tues–Sun 10am–5.40pm; 27F, 35F with special exhibitions; M° St-Paul), presents the history of Paris from its origins until the Belle Époque in an extensive and beautifully presented collection filling two adjoining converted Renaissance mansions which in themselves repay a visit. Paris's history is presented as viewed and lived by its people: working class, bourgeoisie, aristocrats and royalty. The collection begins with nineteeth- and early twentieth-century shop and inn signs (beautiful objects in themselves) and fascinating models of Paris through the ages, along with maps and plans. The stairwell to the first floor boasts a glorious *trompe-l'oeil*; and decorative arts feature strongly, with numerous recreated salons and boudoirs from the time of Louis XII to Louis XVI from buildings which had to be destroyed for Haussmann's boulevards. The second floor has rooms full of mementos of the French Revolution: models of the Bastille, original *Declarations of the Rights of Man and the Citizen*, tricolors and liberty caps, sculpted allegories of Reason, crockery with Revolutionary slogans, models of the guillotine and execution orders to make you shed a tear for the royalists as well. Not all the rooms are open at the same time: the Second Empire to the twentieth century section is only open 10–11.50am; and the section on the sixteenth to the eighteenth century from 1.10–5.40pm, so to see everything you should arrive at 10am. However, the ticket lasts all day so you can return. After an exhausting trawl of the collection, you can rest in the peaceful, formally laid-out garden courtyards.

One block south of the Musée Carnavalet, the area around narrow **rue des Rosiers** is traditionally the **Jewish quarter** of the city, and remains so, despite incursions by trendy clothes shops. It has a distinctly Mediterranean flavour, testimony to the influence of the North African Sephardim, who replenished Paris's Jewish population, depleted when its Ashkenazim were rounded up by the Nazis and the French police and transported to the concentration camps. A **Museum of Jewish Art and History** is due to open to the public at the end of 1998 in a nearby Marais mansion, the Hôtel de Saint-Aignan; contact the tourist office for details.

To the north of the Musée Carnavalet, at 5 rue de Thorigny, the magnificent seventeenth-century Hôtel Salé houses the **Musée Picasso** (9.30am–6pm; closed Tues; 30F, reduced Sun to 20F; disabled access; M° Chemin Vert/St-Paul), opened in 1986 and representing the largest collection of the Paris-based Spanish artist anywhere. A large proportion of the works from the collection were personally owned by Picasso at the time of his death in 1973, and the state had first option on them in lieu of taxes owed. They include examples of all the different media he used, paintings he bought or was given by his contemporaries, his African masks and sculptures, photographs, letters and other personal memorabilia. The works themselves are not Picasso's most enjoyable – the museums of the Côte d'Azur and the Picasso gallery in Barcelona are more exciting. But the collection does leave you with a definite sense of the man and his life, partly because these were the works he wanted to keep, and many are accompanied by photographs. The paintings of his wives, lovers and families are some of the gentlest and most endearing: the portraits of Marie-Thérèse and Claude Dessinant Françoise and Paloma, for example. The portrait of Dora Maar, like that of Marie-Thérèse, was painted in 1937, during the Spanish Civil War when Picasso was going through his worst personal and political crises. This is the period when emotion and passion play

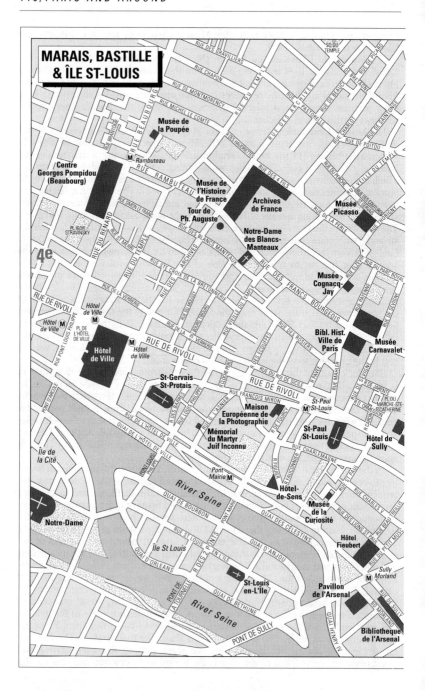

MARAIS, BASTILLE & ÎLE ST-LOUIS

SQ. DU TEMPLE

RUE DES GRAVILLIERS

RUE CHAPON

RUE DE MONTMORENCY

RUE MICHEL LE COMTE

Musée de la Poupée

Rambuteau

Centre Georges Pompidou (Beaubourg)

RUE RAMBUTEAU

Musée de l'Histoire de France

Tour de Ph. Auguste

Archives de France

Musée Picasso

PL. IGOR / STRAVINSKY

Notre-Dame des Blancs-Manteaux

4e

Musée Cognacq-Jay

RUE DE RIVOLI

Hôtel de Ville

Hôtel de Ville

Bibl. Hist. Ville de Paris

Musée Carnavalet

Hôtel de Ville

Hôtel de Ville

RUE DE RIVOLI

St-Gervais St-Protais

St-Paul St-Louis

Maison Européenne de la Photographie

Mémorial du Martyr Juif Inconnu

St-Paul St-Louis

Hôtel de Sully

Île de la Cité

Pont Marie

Hôtel-de-Sens

River Seine

QUAI DE BOURBON

Musée de la Curiosité

Notre-Dame

Île St Louis

Hôtel Fieubert

QUAI D'ORLEANS

Sully Morland

St-Louis en-L'Île

Pavillon de l'Arsenal

River Seine

PONT DE SULLY

Bibliothèque de l'Arsenal

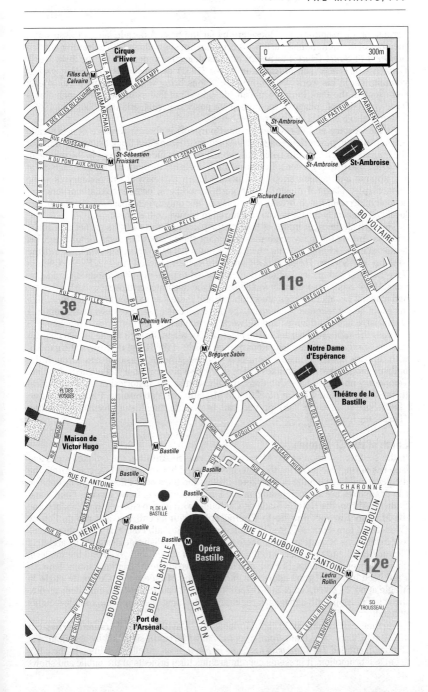

hardest on his paintings, and these are by far the best. A decade later, Picasso was a member of the Communist Party – his cards are on show along with a drawing entitled *Staline à la Santé* (Here's to Stalin) and his delegate credentials for the 1948 World Congress of Peace. The *Massacre in Korea* (1951) demonstrates the lasting pacifist commitment in his work. Temporary exhibitions bring works from the periods least represented: the Pink Period, Cubism (despite some fine examples here, including a large collection of collages), the immediate postwar period, and the 1950s and 1960s. There is also a cinema and reference library.

At the western end of rue des Francs-Bourgeois is the masterpiece of aristocratic urban planning, **place des Vosges**, a vast square of stone and brick symmetry built for the majesty of Henri IV and Louis XIII, whose statue is hidden by trees in the middle of the grass and gravel gardens. Expensive high-heels tap through the arcades pausing at art, antique and fashion shops, and people lunch al fresco at the restaurants while buskers play classical music. In the garden, toddlers, octogenarians, workers and schoolchildren on lunch breaks sit or play in the only green space of any size in the locality – unusually for Paris, you're allowed to sprawl on the grass.

Through all the vicissitudes of history, the *place* has never lost its cachet as a smart address. Among the many celebrities who made their homes here was Victor Hugo; his house, at no. 6, where he wrote much of his novel *Les Misérables*, is now a museum, the **Maison de Victor Hugo** (Tues–Sun 10am–5.40pm; closed hols; 27F; M° Chemin Vert/Bastille) and in fact a whole room is devoted to posters of its various stage adaptations. Hugo was extraordinarily multi-talented: he decorated and drew, as well as wrote, and many of his ink drawings are exhibited, and there's an extraordinary Japanese dining room he put together. That apart, the usual portraits, manuscripts and memorabilia shed sparse light on the man and his work, particularly if you don't read French.

From the southwest corner of the *place*, a door leads through to the formal château garden, *orangerie* and exquisite Renaissance facade of the **Hôtel de Sully**. The garden, with its park benches, makes for a peaceful rest-stop, or you can pass through the building, nodding at the sphinxes on the stairs, as a pleasing shortcut to rue St-Antoine. Temporary photographic exhibitions, usually with social, historical or anthropological themes, are mounted in the hôtel by the **Mission du Patrimoine Photographique** (Tues–Sun 10am–6.30; 25F) or you can browse in the history-focused bookshop (Tues–Sun 10am–7pm).

South of rue St-Antoine

In the southern section of the Marais, **below rue St-Antoine**, the crooked steps and lanterns of rue Cloche-Perce, the tottering timbered houses of rue François-Miron, the medieval buildings behind St-Gervais-et-Protais and the smell of flowers and incense on rue des Barres are all good indulgence in Paris picturesque. Between rues Fourcy and François-Miron, the Hôtel Hénault de Cantoube, with its two-storey *crypte*, has become the **Maison Européenne de la Photographie** with its entrance at 4 rue du Fourcy (Wed–Sun 11am–8pm; 30F, free Wed after 5pm; M° St-Paul/Pont Marie), hosting excellent exhibitions of contemporary photography, with a stylish café designed by architect Nestor Perkal. Shift eastwards to the next tangle of streets and you'll find the modern, chi-chi flats of the "Village St-Paul" and its expensive clusters of antique shops. **Rue St-Paul** itself has some good addresses, including the **Musée de la Curiosité et de la Magie** at no. 11 (Wed, Sat & Sun 2–7pm; 45F; M° St-Paul/Sully-Morland), dedicated to the art of illusion, with a magician regularly performing seemingly impossible sleights of hand.

Further east again, at 21 bd Morland, the **Pavillon de l'Arsenal** (Tues–Sat 10.30am–6.30pm, Sun 11am–7pm; free; M° Sully-Morland), signalled by a sculpture of Rimbaud, entitled *The Man with his Souls in Front*, is an excellent addition to the city's art of self-promotion. It presents current architectural projects to the public and shows how past and present developments have evolved as part and parcel of Parisian history. To this end they have a permanent exhibition of photographs, plans and models, including a model of the whole city linked to a touch-screen choice of 30,000 images.

The Île St-Louis

Often considered to be the most romantic part of Paris, the peaceful **Île St-Louis** is prime strolling territory. Unlike its larger neighbour, the Île de la Cité, the Île St-Louis has no monuments or museums, just high houses on single-lane streets, tree-lined quais, a school, church, restaurants, cafés, interesting little shops, and the best sorbets in the world at *Berthillon*, 31 rue St-Louis-en-l'Île (see p.148). It's also where the likes of the Aga Khan and the pretender to the throne of France have their Parisian residences, and the island is indeed the most covetable of the city's addresses. A popular approach to bring you right to *Berthillon* is to cross Pont Louis-Philippe just east of the Hôtel de Ville; you're then positioned to join the throngs strolling with their ice-creams down rue St-Louis-en-l'Île for a spot of window shopping. Alternatively, you can find seclusion on the **southern quais**, tightly clutching your triple-sorbet cornet as you descend the various steps or climb over the low gate on the right of the garden across boulevard Henri-IV to reach the best sunbathing spot in Paris. The island is particularly atmospheric in the evening, and dinner here (see p.148 for restaurant recommendations), followed by an arm-in-arm wander along the quais is a must in any lovers' itinerary.

The Bastille

The landmark column topped with the gilded "Spirit of Liberty" on **place de la Bastille** was erected not to commemorate the surrender in 1789 of the prison – whose only visible remains have been transported to square Henri-Galli at the end of boulevard Henri-IV – but the July Revolution of 1830 that replaced the autocratic Charles X with the "Citizen King" Louis-Philippe. When Louis-Philippe fled in the more significant 1848 Revolution, his throne was burnt beside the column and a new inscription added. Four months later, the workers again took to the streets. All of eastern Paris was barricaded, with the fiercest fighting on rue du Faubourg-St-Antoine. The rebellion was quelled with the usual massacres and deportation of survivors, and it is of course the 1789 Bastille Day, symbol of the end of feudalism in Europe, that France celebrates every year on July 14.

The Bicentennial in 1989 was marked by the inauguration of the **Opéra-Bastille** (see p.166), Mitterrand's pet project and subject of the most virulent sequence of rows and resignations. Filling almost the entire block between rues de Lyon, Charenton and Moreau, it has shifted the focus of place de la Bastille, so that the column is no longer the pivotal point; in fact, it's easy to miss it altogether when dazzled by the night-time glare of lights emanating from this "hippopotamus in a bathtub", as one critic dubbed it.

The Opéra's construction destroyed no mean amount of low-rent housing, and the **quartier de la Bastille** has long been trendier than Les Halles. But, as with most speculative developments, the pace of change is uneven: cobblers and ironmongers still survive alongside cocktail haunts and sushi bars. **Place and rue d'Aligre** still have their raucous daily market and, on **rue de Lappe**, Balajo is one remnant of a very Parisian tradition: the *bals musettes*, or music halls of 1930s *"gai Paris"*, frequented between the wars by Piaf, Jean Gabin and Rita Hayworth. It was founded by one Jo de France, who introduced glitter and spectacle into what were then seedy gangster dives, and brought Parisians from the other side of the city to the rue de Lappe lowlife. Now the street is full of fun, trendy bars, full to bursting on the weekends. You'll find art galleries clustered around **rue Keller** and the adjoining stretch of **rue de Charonne**; and indie music shops and gay, lesbian and hippy outfits on rues Keller and **des Taillandiers**.

Quartier Latin

On the Left Bank of the river, the pivotal point of the **quartier Latin** is **place St-Michel**, where the tree-lined **boulevard St-Michel** begins. It has lost its radical penniless chic now, preferring harder commercial values. The cafés and shops are jammed with people, mainly young and – in summer – largely foreign.

Rue de la Huchette, the Mecca of beats and bums in the post-World War II years, with its Théatre de la Huchette still showing Ionesco's *La Cantatrice Chauve* ("The Bald Prima Donna") over fifty years on, is now mostly given over to indifferent Greek restaurants, as is the adjoining rue Xavier-Privas, with the odd couscous joint thrown in. Connecting it to the riverside is the city's narrowest street, the **Chat-qui-Pêche**, evocative of what Paris must have looked like at its medieval worst.

Rue St-Jacques

Things improve as you move away from the boulevard St-Michel. At the end of rue de la Huchette, **rue St-Jacques** is aligned on the main street of Roman Paris, and was in medieval times the road up which millions of pilgrims trudged at the start of their long march to St-Jacques-de-Compostelle in Spain. One block south of rue de la Huchette, and west of rue St Jacques, is the mainly fifteenth-century church of **St-Séverin** with its entrance on rue des Prêtres St-Séverin (Mon–Fri 11am–7.30pm, Sat 11am–8pm, Sun 9am–9pm; M° St-Michel/Cluny-La Sorbonne). It is one of the city's most elegant churches, with splendidly virtuoso chiselwork in the pillars of the Flamboyant choir, as well as stained glass by the modern French painter Jean Bazaine.

East of rue St Jacques, and back towards the river, **square Viviani** – with a welcome patch of grass and trees – provides the most flattering of all views of Notre-Dame. The mutilated and disfigured church is **St-Julien-le-Pauvre** (daily 10am–7.30pm; M° St-Michel/Maubert Mutualité). The same age as Notre-Dame, it used to be the venue for university assemblies until rumbustious students tore it apart in the 1500s. Across rue Lagrange from the square, rue de la Bûcherie is the home of the American-run English-language bookshop **Shakespeare and Co** (see p.175), haunted by the shades of James Joyce and other great expatriate literati – though Sylvia Beach, publisher of *Ulysses*, had her original shop on rue de l'Odéon.

The river bank and Institut du Monde Arabe

Books, postcards, prints, and assorted goods are on sale from the **bouquinistes**, who display their wares in green padlocked boxes hooked onto the parapet of the **riverside quais**. Continuing upstream, you come to the **Pont de Sully** – with a dramatic view of the apse and steeple of Notre-Dame – and the beginning of a riverside garden dotted with pieces of modern sculpture, known as the **Musée de Sculpture en Plein Air** (Tues–Sun 10am–5pm; free; M° Jussieu/Gare de l'Austerlitz).

At the end of the Pont de Sully, in the angle between quai St-Bernard and rue des Fossés-St-Bernard, is the **Institut du Monde Arabe** (Tues–Sun 10am–6pm; 25F for the museum, special exhibitions extra; disabled access; M° Jussieu/Cardinal-Lemoine), a cultural centre built to further understanding of the Arab world. Designed principally by Jean Nouvel, its elegant glass and aluminium mass is cleft in two, the riverfront half-bowed and tapering to a knife-like prow, while the broad southern facade, comprising thousands of tiny light-sensitive shutters, employs high-tech ingenuity to mimic the *moucharabiyah* – the traditional Arab latticework balcony. Inside, there's a permanent exhibition of glass, rugs, ceramics, illuminated manuscripts, woodcarving, metalwork and scientific instruments from the Islamic world. On the ground floor, diverse and brilliant contemporary Arab paintings and sculptures are exhibited, while in the basement the audiovisual centre, Espace Image et Son (Tues–Sat 10am–6pm; free), allows you to access thousands of slides, photographs, films and recordings; there is also a specialist library (Tues–Sat 1–8pm; free). When you need a rest, take the fastest lifts in Paris up to the café-restaurant on the ninth floor, which has a brilliant view over the Seine, or drink mint tea and nibble cakes at the outdoor café downstairs, marvelling at the aperture action of the windows; both can be frequented without paying for the museum.

Montagne Ste-Geneviève and the Sorbonne

The nearby area around the slopes of the **Montagne Ste-Geneviève**, the hill on which the Panthéon stands, is good for a stroll. The best approach is from **place Maubert** (good **market** Tues, Thurs & Sat mornings) or from the St-Michel/St-Germain crossroads, where the walls of the third-century **Roman baths** are visible in the garden of the Hôtel de Cluny, a sixteenth-century mansion built by the abbots of the powerful Cluny monastery as their Paris pied-à-terre. It now houses the **Musée National du Moyen-Age**, 6 place Paul-Painlevé, off rue des Écoles (9.15am–5.45pm; closed Tues; 30F, reduced Sun to 20F; M° Cluny-La Sorbonne/St-Michel), a treasure house of medieval art and tapestries. The numerous beauties here include a marvellous depiction of the grape harvest; a Resurrection embroidered in gold and silver thread, with sleeping guards in medieval armour; and a whole room of sixteenth-century Dutch tapestries full of flowers and birds; there's a woman embroidering while her servant patiently holds the threads for her, a lover making advances, and a woman in her bath which is overflowing into a duck pond. But the greatest wonder of all is the late fifteenth-century *La Dame à la Licorne* (The Lady with the Unicorn), perhaps made in Brussels, consisting of six richly-coloured and detailed allegoric scenes, featuring a beautiful woman flanked by a lion and a unicorn. Quite simply, it is the most stunning piece of tapestry – and indeed art – you are likely to see in many a long day. A vast array of medieval sculptures include fascinating fragments such as the heads of the kings of Judea from the cathedral of Notre Dame (see p.102), lopped off during the French Revolution.

The grim-looking buildings on the other side of rue des Écoles are the **Sorbonne**, **Collège de France**, and **Lycée Louis-le-Grand**, which numbers Molière, Robespierre, Pompidou and Victor Hugo among its graduates and Sartre among its teachers. All these institutions are major constituents of the brilliant world of French intellectual activity; you can put your nose in the Sorbonne courtyard without anyone objecting. Nearby, the traffic-free **place de la Sorbonne**, with its lime trees, cafés and student habitués, is a lovely place to sit.

The Panthéon and St-Étienne-du-Mont

Further up the hill, the broad rue Soufflot provides an appropriately grand perspective on the domed and porticoed **Panthéon** (daily: April–Sept 9.30am–6.30pm; Oct–March 10am–5.30pm; 32F; RER Luxembourg/M° Cardinal Lemoine), Louis XV's grateful response to St-Geneviève, patron saint of Paris, for curing him of illness. The Revolution transformed it into a mausoleum for the great, with the ashes of Voltaire, Rousseau, Hugo, Zola in the vast – and creepy – barrel-vaulted crypt below. The interior is worth a visit for sheer understanding of the French "grand design" – and to see a working model of **Foucault's Pendulum** swinging from the dome. The French physicist Léon Foucault devised the experiment, conducted at the Panthéon in 1851, to vividly demonstate the rotation of the earth: while the pendulum appeared to rotate over a 24-hour period, it was in fact the earth beneath it turning. The demonstration wowed the scientific establishment and the public alike, with huge crowds turning up to watch the ground move beneath their feet. A video with headphones in English tells the whole story.

More interesting than the Panthéon is the mainly sixteenth-century church of **St-Étienne-du-Mont** (daily 8am–noon & 2–7.30pm; RER Luxembourg/M° Cardinal Lemoine), on the corner of rue Clovis, whose beautifully carved facade combines

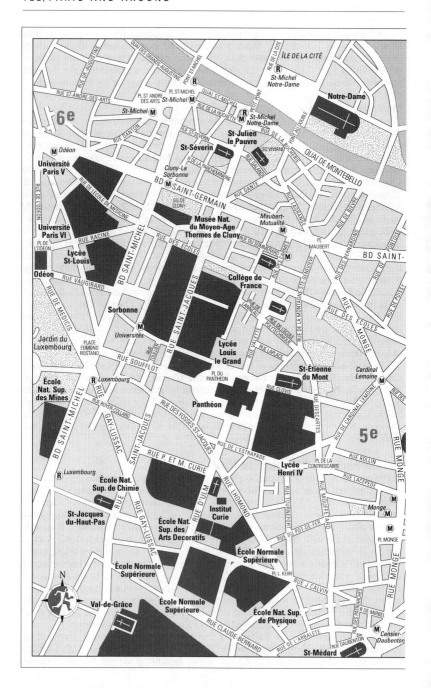

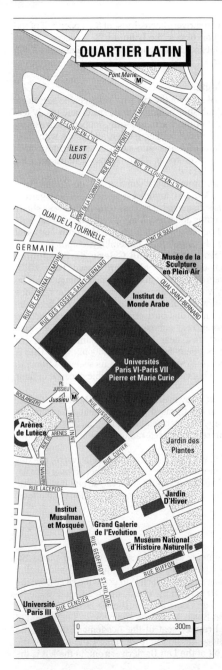

QUARTIER LATIN

Pont Marie

RUE ST-LOUIS-EN-L'ILE

ÎLE ST
LOUIS

RUE DES DEUX PONTS

RUE ST-LOUIS-EN-L'ILE

QUAI DE LA TOURNELLE

RUE DE LA TOURNELLE

PONT DE SULLY

GERMAIN

**Musée de la
Sculpture
en Plein Air**

RUE DE CARDINAL LEMOINE

RUE DES FOSSÉS-SAINT-BERNARD

QUAI SAINT-BERNARD

**Institut du
Monde Arabe**

**Universités
Paris VI-Paris VII
Pierre et Marie Curie**

PL
JUSSIEU
Jussieu

BOULANGERS

RUE JUSSIEU

**Arènes
de Lutèce**

ARENES

RUE LINNE

R DE NAVARRE

**Jardin des
Plantes**

RUE CUVIER

RUE LACEPEDE

**Jardin
D'Hiver**

**Institut
Musulman
et Mosquée**

**Grand Galerie
de l'Evolution**

RUE GEOFFROY ST-HILAIRE

**Muséum National
d'Histoire Naturelle**

RUE BUFFON

**Université
Paris III**

RUE CENSIER

0   300m

Renaissance Gothic and Baroque elements. The interior, if not exactly beautiful, is highly unexpected. The space is divided into three aisles by free-standing pillars connected by a narrow catwalk, and flooded with light by an exceptionally tall clerestory. Again, unusually – for they mainly fell victim to the destructive anticlericalism of the Revolution – the church still possesses its rood screen, a broad low arch supporting a gallery reached by twining spiral stairs. There is also some good seventeenth-century glass in the cloister. Further down rue Clovis, a huge piece of Philippe-Auguste's twelfth-century **city walls** emerges from among the houses.

There is not much point in going further south on rue St-Jacques: the area is dull and lifeless once you are over the Gay-Lussac intersection, though Baroque enthusiasts might like to take a look at the seventeenth-century church of **Val-de-Grâce** on place Alphonse-Laveran (daily 9am–5pm; RER Port Royal), with its pedimented front and ornate cupola copied from St Peter's in Rome, while around the corner on **boulevard de Port-Royal** are another big market and several brasseries.

East of the Panthéon

More enticing wandering is to be had in the villagey streets east of the Panthéon. **Rue de la Montagne-Ste-Geneviève** climbs up from place Maubert across rue des Écoles to the gates of the Ministry of Research and Technology. There's a sunny little café outside and several restaurants in rue de l'École-Polytechnique. Rue Descartes runs into the tiny and attractive **place de la Contrescarpe**. Once an arty hang-out where Hemingway wrote – in the café *La Chope* – and Georges Brassens sang, it is now extremely touristy.

The medieval **rue Mouffetard** begins here, a cobbled lane winding downhill to the church of **St-Médard**, once a country parish beside the now-covered river Bièvre. Most of the upper half of the street is given over to rather touristy eating places; the bottom half, however, with its sumptuous fruit and veg stalls – among lots of clothes and shoe shops and cafés – still maintains an authentic neighbourhood air.

The Paris mosque and Jardin des Plantes

A little further east, across rue Monge, are some of the city's most agreeable surprises. Down rue Daubenton, past a delightful Arab shop selling sweets, spices and gaudy tea-glasses, you come to the crenellated walls of the **Paris mosque**, topped by greenery and a great square minaret. You can walk in the sunken garden and patios with their polychrome tiles and carved ceilings (guided tours 9am–noon & 2–6pm; tour 15F; closed Fri & Muslim hols), but not the prayer room. There is also a **tearoom** (see p.150), open to all, and a **hammam** (see p.171).

Opposite the mosque is the **Jardin des Plantes** (daily: summer 7.30am–7.45pm; winter 8am–dusk; free; M° Austerlitz/Jussieu/Monge), founded as a medicinal herb garden in 1626 and gradually evolving as Paris's botanical gardens, with hothouses, shady avenues of trees, lawns to sprawl on, museums and a zoo. Magnificent, varied floral beds make a fine approach to the collection of buildings which form the **Muséum National d'Histoire Naturelle**. Musty museums of paleontology, mineralogy, entomology and paleobotany should be sidestepped in favour of the **Grand Galerie de l'Évolution**, with its entrance off rue Buffon (10am–6pm, Thurs till 10pm; closed Tues; 40F), housed in a dramatically restored nineteenth-century glass-domed building. You'll be wowed by the sheer scale of the interior, where the story of evolution and the relations between human beings and nature is told with stuffed animals that look real, a combination of clever lighting effects, ambient music and birdsong, videos and touch-screen databases. In a contrastingly small space, real animals can be seen in the small **ménagerie** across the park to the northeast near rue Cuvier (summer Mon–Sat 9am–6pm, Sun till 6.30pm; winter Mon–Sat 9am–5pm, Sun till 6.30pm; 30F). This is France's oldest zoo, operating here since the Revolution. Despite its scale, it's home to a surprising assortment of creatures, from big cats to snakes, possible because of their unacceptably cramped conditions.

The gardens are a pleasant space to while away the middle of a day. By the rue Cuvier exit is a fine Cedar of Lebanon planted in 1734, raised from seed sent over from the Oxford Botanical Gardens, and a slice of an American sequoia more than 2000 years old. In the nearby physics labs, Henri Becquerel discovered radioactivity in 1896, and two years later the Curies discovered radium.

A short distance away to the northwest, with an entrance in rue de Navarre, rue des Arènes and another through a passage on rue Monge, is Paris's other Roman remain, the **Arènes de Lutèce**, an unexpected backwater hidden from the street. It is a partly restored amphitheatre, with a boules pitch in the centre, benches, gardens and a kids' playground behind.

St-Germain

The northern half of the 6e arrondissement, asymmetrically centred on **place St-Germain-des-Prés**, is one of the most physically attractive, lively and stimulating square kilometres in the city. The most dramatic approach is to cross the river from the Louvre by the footbridge, the **Pont des Arts**, with the classic upstream view of the Île de la Cité, with barges moored at the quai de Conti, and the Tour St-Jacques and Hôtel de Ville breaking the skyline of the Right Bank. The dome and pediment at the end of the bridge belong to the **Institut de France**, seat of the Académie Française, an august body of writers and scholars whose mission is to safeguard the purity of the French language. This is the grandiose bit of the Left Bank riverfront; to the left is the

Hôtel des Monnaies, redesigned as the Mint in the late eighteenth century; to the right is the **Beaux-Arts**, the School of Fine Art, whose students throng the quais on sunny days, sketchpads on knees.

The riverside

The riverside part of the 6e arrondissement is cut lengthwise by **rue St-André-des-Arts** and **rue Jacob**. It is full of bookshops, commercial art galleries, antique shops, cafés and restaurants, but poke your nose into courtyards and side streets. The houses are four- to six-storeys high, seventeenth and eighteenth century, some noble, some stiff, some bulging and skew, all painted in infinite gradations of grey, pearl and off-white. Broadly speaking, the further west the posher.

Historical associations are legion: Picasso painted *Guernica* in rue des Grands-Augustins; Molière started his career in rue Mazarine; Robespierre and co split ideological hairs at the *Café Procope* in rue de l'Ancienne-Comédie. In rue Visconti, Racine died, Delacroix painted, and Balzac's printing business went bust. In the parallel rue des Beaux-Arts, Oscar Wilde died, Corot and Ampère (father of amps) lived, and the crazy poet Gérard de Nerval went walking with a lobster on a lead.

If you're looking for lunch, **place and rue St-André-des-Arts** offer numerous places to snack, but more tempting is the brilliant food market in **rue Buci** up towards boulevard St-Germain. Before you get to Buci, there is an intriguing little passage on the left, **Cour du Commerce St André**, where Marat had a printing press and Dr Guillotin perfected his notorious machine by lopping off sheep's heads in the loft next door. A couple of smaller courtyards open off it, revealing another stretch of Philippe-Auguste's twelfth-century city wall.

An alternative corner for midday food or quiet is around rue de l'Abbaye and rue du Furstemberg, with a tiny square where Delacroix's old studio overlooks a secret garden and is now the **Musée Delacroix**, at no. 6 rue du Furstemberg (9.30am–6pm; closed Tues; 30F), with a small collection of the artist's personal belongings as well as temporary exhibitons of his work. This is also the beginning of some very upmarket shopping territory, in rue Jacob, rue de Seine and rue Bonaparte in particular.

Place St-Germain-des-Prés

Place St-Germain-des-Prés, the hub of the quartier, is only a stone's throw away, with the *Deux Magots* café (see p.151) on the corner and *Flore* (see p.151) just down the street – both renowned for the number of philosophico-politico-poetico-literary backsides that have shined their seats, although nowadays you're more likely to be dragged into some street-clown's act than engaged in high-flown debate.

The tower opposite the *Deux Magots* belongs to the **church of St-Germain**, all that remains of an enormous Benedictine monastery. The interior is its best aspect, with the pure Romanesque lines still clear under the deforming paint of nineteenth-century frescoes.

St-Sulpice and the Palais du Luxembourg

South of boulevard St-Germain, the streets round St-Sulpice are calm and classy. **Rue Mabillon** is pretty, with a row of old houses set back below the level of the modern street. On the left are the **halles St-Germain**, on the site of a fifteenth-century market. **Rue St-Sulpice** – with excellent shops for edibles – leads through to the front of the enormous **church of St-Sulpice** (daily 7.30am–7.30pm), an austerely classical church, erected either side of 1700, with a Doric colonnade surmounted by an Ionic, and Corinthian pilasters in the towers, only one of which is finished. For many, however, the main attraction of **place St-Sulpice** is Yves Saint Laurent Rive Gauche, the most elegant fashion boutique on the Left Bank. The least posh bit of the quartier is the eastern edge,

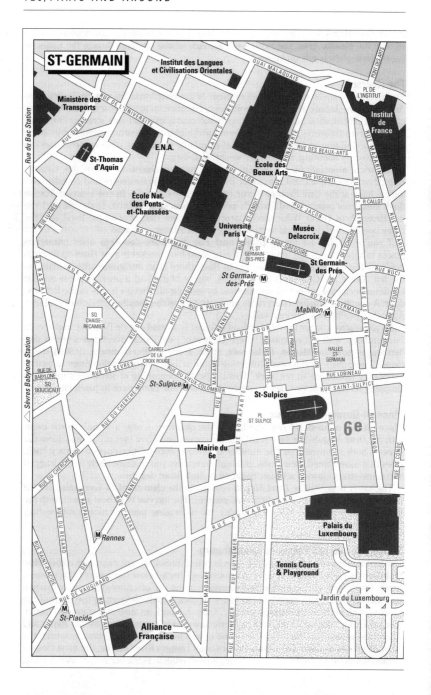

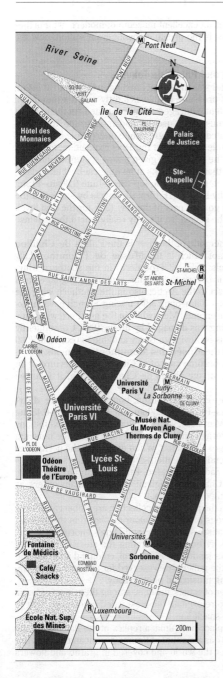

along boulevard St-Michel, where the university is firmly implanted. Scientific and medical bookshops display skeletons and instruments of torture and there are a couple of weird and wonderful shops in rue Racine, but really all is elegance round here.

To the south, rue Férou, where a gentleman called Pottier composed the Revolutionary anthem – the *Internationale* – in 1776, connects with **rue de Vaugirard**, Paris's longest street, and the **Palais du Luxembourg**, constructed for Marie de Médicis, Henri IV's widow, to remind her of the Palazzo Pitti and Giardino di Boboli of her native Florence. Today it is the seat of the French Senate and its **gardens** the chief recreation ground of the Left Bank, with tennis courts, pony rides, children's playground, boules pitch, yachts to rent on the pond and, in the wilder southeast corner, a miniature orchard of elaborately espaliered pear trees. With its strollers and mooners and garish parterres it has a distinctly Mediterranean air on summer days, when the most contested spot is the shady **Fontaine de Médicis** in the northeast corner.

Trocadéro, Eiffel Tower and Les Invalides

The vistas across the river between the 7e arrondissement south of the river and the 8e and 16e on the north are impressive – particularly at night. Look from the terrace of the **Palais de Chaillot**, on place du Trocadéro, across the river to the **Tour Eiffel** and **École Militaire**, from the ornate 1900 Pont Alexandre III along the grassy Esplanade to the **Hôtel des Invalides**. But the scale and the style are despotic. The Palais de Chaillot, like a latterday Pharaoh's mausoleum (1937), is home to a theatre for diverse but usually radical productions and also contains several interesting museums, and its smaller neighbour, the **Palais de Tokyo**, houses an excellent museum of modern art. Further upstream on the south bank of the river is the ornate erstwhile train station, now the **Musée d'Orsay**.

The Eiffel Tower, Palais de Chaillot and Palais de Tokyo

When completed in 1889, the **Tour Eiffel** was the tallest building in the world at 300m, and its 7000 tonnes of steel, in terms of pressure, still sit as lightly on the ground as a child in a chair. Reactions to it were violent. Outraged critics protested "in the name of menaced French art and history" against this "useless and monstrous" tower. "Is Paris", they asked, "going to be associated with the grotesque, mercantile imaginings of a constructor of machines?" But it stole the show at the 1889 Exposition, for which it had been constructed. In the 1980s the tower was given a new system of illumination from within its superstructure, so that it now looks at its magical best after dark, as light and fanciful as a filigree minaret. Going to the top (Sept–June 9.30am–11pm; July & Aug 9am–midnight) costs 59F (by lift) or 31F (first two levels by stairs and the final level by lift), or you can choose to go only part of the way (20F for the first level, 42F for the second, or 14F if you take the stairs), so it's only really worth the expense on an absolutely clear day.

Facing the Eiffel Tower from the other side of the river is the **Palais de Chaillot**, containing four museums, the biggest of which is the **Musée de l'Homme** (daily except Tues 9.45am–5.15pm; closed hols; 30F; Mº Trocadéro) in the southern wing. Full of high-tech interactive displays, it covers the origins, cultures, languages and genetics of human beings from Polynesia to the Arctic; also in the southern wing the **Musée de la Marine** (daily except Tues 10am–6pm; 38F) tracing French naval history with models of ships and their accoutrements. Meanwhile in the northern wing only the theatre is open as the rest of the wing was damaged by fire in 1996. Consequently the **Musée du Cinéma Henri-Langlois** is moving to Bercy and due to reopen in 2000 as part of the Maison du Cinéma, whilst the **Musée des Monuments Français** is benefiting from the upset through plans to become part of a "Cité de l'Architecture et du Patrimoine" set in the northern wing of the Palais de Chaillot which, if followed through, won't open until 2001.

The **Palais de Tokyo**, on avenue du Président-Wilson, houses the **Musée d'Art Moderne de la Ville de Paris** (Tues–Fri 10am–5.30pm, Sat & Sun 10am–6.45pm; closed public hols; 30F; Mº Iéna/Alma-Marceau), with excellent temporary exhibitions but whose permanent collection is in storage until the end of 1999 whilst the museum hosts a selection from the Centre Georges Pompidou. When displayed, the permanent collection illustrates the schools and trends of twentieth-century art always richly represented by artists such as Vlaminck, Zadkine, Picasso, Braque, Juan Gris, Valadon, Matisse, Dufy, Utrillo, both Delaunays, Chagall, Modigliani, Léger and many others, as well as sculpture and painting by contemporary artists.

Among the most spectacular works in the permanent collection are Robert and Sonia Delaunay's huge whirling wheels and cogs of rainbow colour displayed in the ground-floor corridor; the leaping figures of Matisse's *La Danse*; and Dufy's enormous mural, *La Fée Électricité* (done for the electricity board), illustrating the story of electricity from Aristotle to the then-modern power station, in 250 lyrical, colourful panels filling three entire walls. The upper floors of the gallery are reserved for all sorts of contemporary and experimental work, including music and photography.

On sale in the bookshop are a number of artists' designs, among them a set of Sonia Delaunay's playing cards, guaranteed to rejuvenate the most jaded cardsharp. Next to it is an excellent and reasonably priced snack bar.

Just beyond the Palais de Tokyo, in place de l'Alma, a replica of the flame from the Statue of Liberty given to France in 1987 as a symbol of Franco-American relations has been adopted by mourners from all over the world and covered in graffiti and flowers since Princess Diana's fatal car crash in the underpass here. Messages from angry Parisians state that this misappropriation is not always welcome.

Around the École Militaire

Stretching back from the legs of the Eiffel Tower, the long rectangular gardens of the **Champs de Mars** lead to the eighteenth-century buildings of the **École Militaire**, originally founded in 1751 by Louis XV for the training of aristocratic army officers, and attended by Napoléon, among other fledgling leaders. The surrounding quartier may be expensive and sought after as an address, but physically it's uninspiring. Witness the **UNESCO building** at the back of the École Militaire which was controversial at the time of its construction in 1958, but looks somewhat pedestrian and badly weathered today. It can be visited (Mon–Fri 9.30am–5.39pm; free), and there are a number of art-works inside, of which the most noticeable are an enormous mobile by Alexander Calder and a quiet Japanese garden. One unexpected corner of this rather austere quartier is the wedge of early nineteenth-century streets between avenue Bosquet and Les Invalides. Chief among them is the market street of **rue Cler** and its cross-streets rue de Grenelle and rue St-Dominique, full of classy little shops, some with their original painted glass panels.

Out on the river bank at quai d'Orsay is the **American Church** which, together with the American College nearby at 31 av Bosquet, is a nodal point in the well-organized life of the large American community. The noticeboard is usually plastered with job and accommodation offers and demands. The other quayside attraction is the **sewers**, or *les égouts,* whose entrance is 50m east of the Pont de l'Alma and quai d'Orsay junction (May–Oct 11am–5pm; Nov–April 11am–4pm; closed Thurs & Fri; 25F). Guidebooks always bill this as an outing for kids, though it's doubtful that they'll be terribly inspired by the unilluminating film, small museum and very brief look at some tunnels with a lot of smelly water swirling about.

Les Invalides

The **Esplanade des Invalides**, striking due south from **Pont Alexandre III**, is a more attractive and uncluttered vista than Chaillot-École Militaire. The wide facade of the **Hôtel des Invalides** – topped by its distinctive dome and resplendent gilding – fills the whole of the further end of the Esplanade. It was built as a home for invalided soldiers on the orders of Louis XIV. Under the dome are two churches, one for the soldiers, the other intended as a mausoleum for the king but now containing the mortal remains of Napoléon. Les Invalides today houses the vast **Musée de l'Armée** (daily: Oct–March 10am–5pm; April–Sept 10am–5.45pm; 37F ticket also valid for Napoléon's tomb, see below), an enormous national war museum whose largest part is devoted to the uniforms and weaponry of Napoléon's armies with numerous personal items of the emperor, including his campaign tent and bed, and even his dog – stuffed. Later French wars are illustrated, too, through paintings, maps and engravings. Sections on the two world wars are good, with coverage of deportation and resistance as well as specific battles. Some of the oddest exhibits are Secret Service sabotage devices, such as a rat and a lump of coal stuffed with explosives.

Both of the Invalides churches are cold and dreary inside. The **Église du Dôme** (same hours and ticket as Musée de l'Armée above), in particular, is a supreme example of architectural pomposity, with Corinthian columns and pilasters, and grandiose frescoes in abundance. Napoléon lies in a hole in the floor in a cold, smooth sarcophagus of red porphyry, enclosed within a gallery decorated with friezes of execrable taste and grovelling piety, captioned with quotations of awesome conceit from the great man: "Co-operate with the plans I have laid for the welfare of peoples"; "By its simplicity my code of law has done more good in France than all the laws which have preceded me"; "Wherever the shadow of my rule has fallen, it has left lasting traces of its value."

Musée Rodin and around

Immediately east of Les Invalides is the **Musée Rodin,** on the corner of rue de Varenne (Tues–Sun 9.30am–5/5.45pm; 28F, Sun 18F; garden only 5F; M° Varenne), housed in a beautiful eighteenth-century mansion which the sculptor leased from the state in return for the gift of all his work at his death. Major projects like *The Burghers of Calais, The Thinker, The Gate of Hell* and *Ugolini and Son* are exhibited in the garden – the latter forming the centrepiece of the ornamental pond. Indoors (very crowded) are works in marble like *The Kiss, The Hand of God, The Cathedral* – those two perfectly poised, almost sentient, hands. There is something particularly fascinating about the works, like *Romeo and Juliet* and *La Centauresse (The Centaur),* which are only half-created, not totally liberated from the raw block of stone.

The rest of rue de Varenne and the parallel rue de Grenelle are full of aristocratic mansions, including the **Hôtel Matignon,** the prime minister's residence. At 61 rue de Grenelle, an elegant eighteenth-century house has been turned into the **Musée Maillol** (daily except Tues 11am–6pm; 40F; M° Rue-du-Bac), showing overbearing numbers of Aristide Maillol's painted and sculpted female nudes, minor works by Matisse, Dufy, Bonnard, Picasso, Degas, Gauguin and Kandinsky, a few Duchamps, and Soviet installation art of the 1970s.

From here, **rue du Bac** leads south into rue de Sèvres, cutting across **rue de Babylone,** another of the quartier's livelier streets, with the crazy, rich man's folly, **La Pagode,** at 57bis, brought over from Japan at the turn of the century. Used as a cinema until recently, its future is uncertain.

Musée d'Orsay

Close to the Musée Maillol on the riverfront, in a former railway station whose stone facade disguises a huge vault of steel and glass, is the **Musée d'Orsay,** at 1 rue de Bellechasse (Tues, Wed, Fri & Sat 9/10am–6pm, Thurs 9/10am–9.45pm, Sun 9am–6pm; 40F; M° Solférino/RER Musée d'Orsay). Housing the painting and sculpture of the immediately pre-modern period, 1848–1914, and thus bridging the gap between the Louvre and Beaubourg, its highlights are the electrifying works of the **Impressionists** and, scarcely less impressive, of the **Post-Impressionists**.

The design of the Musée d'Orsay is very clever, in fact some find the space overdesigned and the collection overwhelmingly large. But don't let that put you off; the collection itself remains unsurpassed, even if you visit the top floor only, and artworks have been given the best lighting you could wish for, making a visit to the Musée d'Orsay essential to a trip to Paris.

On the **ground floor,** the mid-nineteenth-century sculptors, including Barye, caster of super-naturalistic bronze animals, occupy the centre gallery. To their right, rooms dedicated to Ingres and Delacroix (the bulk of whose work is in the Louvre) serve to illustrate the academies of the early nineteenth century. Puvis de Chavannes, Gustave Moreau, the Symbolists and early Degas follow, while in the galleries to the left Daumier, Corot, Millet and the Realist school depart from the academic parameters of subject matter and idealization of the past, and lead on to Manet's *Olympia* (1863) controversial for the colour contrasts and sensual surfaces, as for its portrayal of Olympia as nothing more than a high-class whore.

To get the chronological continuation you have to go straight up to the top level where you will pass firstly through the private collection donated by Moreau-Nélaton, room 29. An assiduous collector and art historian, his collection contains some of the most famous Impressionist images, Monet's *Poppies,* as well as Manet's more controversial *Déjeuner sur l'Herbe,* which sent the critics into apoplexies of rage and disgust when it appeared in 1863, and was refused for that year's Salon. The next few rooms are full of the well-known masterpieces which typify Impressionism; Degas' ballet-dancers, demonstrating his principal interest in movement and line as opposed to the more common Impressionist concern with light; and numerous landscapes and outdoor scenes by **Renoir, Sisley, Pissarro** and **Monet**, owing much of their brilliance to the novel practice of setting up easels in the open to capture the light. *Le Berceau* 1872, by Berthe Morisot, the first woman to join the early Impressionists, is one of the few to have a complex human emotion as its subject – perfectly synthesized within the classic techniques of the movement. A very different touch, all shimmering light and wide brush strokes, is to be seen in Renoir's depiction of a good time being had by all in *Le bal du Moulin de la Galette* – a favourite Sunday afternoon out on the Butte Montmartre.

The development of Monet's obsession with light continues with five of his Rouen cathedral series, each painted in different light conditions, along with one from his waterlilies series painted around fifteen years later; whilst room 35 is full of the blinding colours and disturbing rhythms of **Van Gogh**. **Cézanne**, a step removed from the preoccupations of the mainstream Impressionists, is wonderfully represented in room 36. One of the canvases most revealing of his art is *Still Life with Apples and Oranges* (1895–1900), in which the background abandons perspective while the fruit has an extraordinary solidity.

The rest of this level is given over to the various offspring of Impressionism. Among a number of pointillist works by Seurat (the famous *Cirque*), Signac and various other artists is the dreamlike precursor of the moderns, Rousseau's *La Charmeuse de Serpent*, of 1907. There's Gauguin, post- and pre-Tahiti, as well as lots of Toulouse-Lautrec at his caricaturial nightclubbing best. Take the opportunity for a break on the top level in the Café des Hauteurs, the outside terrace offers Seine views, whilst inside you can sit in the light filtering through the huge clock-face.The **middle level** takes in Rodin and other late nineteenth-century sculptors, several rooms of superb Art Nouveau furniture and *objets*, and the sumptuous reception room (room 51) of the station hotel. Vuillard and Bonnard are tucked away here (rooms 71 & 72), while Klimt and Munch feature in the rooms overlooking the Seine.

Montparnasse and southern Paris

Montparnasse divides the lands of the well-heeled opinion-formers and power-brokers of St-Germain and the 7ᵉ from the amorphous populations of the three southern arrondissements which have been subjected to large-scale developments, most notably along the riverfronts both east and west. There are lively areas: **rue du Commerce** in the 15ᵉ, **Pernety** in the 14ᵉ, and the **Buttes-aux-Cailles** in the 13ᵉ, plus three good parks – **André Citroën, Georges-Brassens** and **Montsouris**.

Like other Left Bank quartiers, Montparnasse still trades on its association with the wild characters of the interwar artistic and literary boom. Many were habitués of the cafés *Select, Coupole, Dôme, Rotonde* and *Closerie des Lilas*, all still going strong on **boulevard du Montparnasse**. Another major subcommunity in the quartier in the early years of the century consisted of outlawed Russian revolutionaries. They were so many that the Tsarist police ran a special Paris section to keep tabs on them. Trotsky lived in rue de la Gaîté near the cemetery – a fascinating street of old theatres and cafés – and Lenin lodged further south in the 14ᵉ arrondissement.

Most of the life of the quarter is concentrated between the junction with boulevard Raspail, where Rodin's *Balzac* broods over the traffic, and at the station end of boulevard du Montparnasse, where the colossal **Tour du Montparnasse** has become one of the city's principal, if unloved, landmarks. You can go up to the top for less than the Eiffel Tower (daily: summer 9.30am–11.30pm; winter 9.30am–10.30pm; 48F; entrance on the north side), or you could spend the same amount on a drink in the 56th-storey bar.

One block northwest of the tower, on rue Antoine-Bourdelle, a garden of sculptures invites you into the **Bourdelle museum**, the artist's old atelier (Tues–Sun 10am–5.40pm; 18F, or 27F if there's a temporary exhibition).

Montparnasse cemetery, the catacombs and the Observatoire

Just south of boulevard Edgar-Quinet (with a good **street market** and cafés full of traders) is the main entrance to the **Montparnasse cemetery** (April–Oct Mon–Fri 8am–6pm, Sat 8.30am–6pm, Sun 9am–6pm; Nov–March closes at 5.30pm), a gloomy city of the dead, with ranks of miniature temples, dreary and bizarre, and plenty of illustrious names, from Baudelaire to Sartre and André Citroën to Saint-Saëns. In the southwest corner is an old windmill, one of the seventeenth-century taverns frequented by the carousing, versifying students who gave the district its name of Mount Parnassus.

If you are determined to spend your time among the dear departed, you can also get down into the **catacombs** (daily except Mon 2–4pm, Sat & Sun 9–11am & 2–4pm; 27F) in nearby **place Denfert-Rochereau**, formerly place d'Enfer (Hell Square). These are abandoned quarries stacked with millions of bones cleared from the old charnel houses in 1785, claustrophobic in the extreme, and cold.

Rue Schoelcher and boulevard Raspail on the east side of the cemetery have some interesting examples of twentieth-century architecture, from Art Nouveau to contemporary facades of glass in the **Cartier Foundation** at 259 bd Raspail (daily except Mon noon–8pm; 30F). Designed by Jean Nouvel in 1994, this presents all kinds of contemporary art – installations, videos, multi-media – in temporary exhibitions. For a more classical style, there's the **Observatoire de Paris**, on av de l'Observatoire, just east of Montparnasse cemetery. From the 1660s, when it was constructed, until 1884, all French maps had the zero meridian through the middle of this building. After that date, they reluctantly agreed that 0° longitude should pass through a small village in Normandy that happens to be due south of Greenwich. The Paris meridian line is visible in the garden behind on boulevard Arago.

The 15ᵉ arrondissement

The western edge of the 15ᵉ arrondissement fronts the Seine from the **Porte de Javel** to the Eiffel Tower. From Pont Mirabeau northwards, the river bank is marred by a sort of mini-Défense development of half-cocked futuristic towers with pretentious galactic names, rising out of a litter-blown pedestrian platform some 10m above street level. Far pleasanter riverside strolling is to be had on the narrow midstream island, the **Allée des Cygnes**, which you can reach from the Pont de Grenelle. A scaled-down version of the **Statue of Liberty** stands at the downstream end. South of Pont Mirabeau, between rue Balard and the river, is the city's newest park, the **Parc Citroën** (Mº Balard), so named because the site used to be the Citroën motor works. Its best features are the glasshouses full of exotic-smelling shrubs and the fountain display, which on a hot day tempts park-goers to run through. The gardens are less successful, with more concrete than greenery.

It was in the **rue du Commerce**, running down the middle of the arrondissement from Mº La Motte Piquet-Grenelle, that George Orwell worked as a dishwasher, described in his *Down and Out in Paris and London*. These days it is a lively, old-fashioned high street full of small shops and peeling, shuttered houses. Towards the end of the street is place du Commerce, with a bandstand in the middle, a model of old-fashioned petit-bourgeois respectability – it might be a frozen frame from a 1930s movie. Cafés and pâtisseries proliferate as rue du Commerce ends at place Étienne-Pernet, where cottagey houses still survive.

The other park in the 15ᵉ arrondissement, the **Parc Georges-Brassens**, lies in the southeast corner (Mº Convention/Porte-de-Vanves). It's a delight, with a garden of scented herbs and shrubs designed principally for the blind (best in late spring), puppets and rocks and merry-go-rounds for kids, a mountain stream with pine and birch trees, beehives, and a tiny terraced vineyard. The corrugated pyramid with a helter-skelter-like spiral is the Silvia-Montfort theatre.

On the west side of the park, in a secluded garden in passage Dantzig, off rue Dantzig, stands an unusual polygonal building known as **La Ruche**. Home to Fernand Léger, Modigliani, Chagall, Soutine and many other artists at the start of the century, it is still used by creative types. In the sheds of the old horse market between the park and rue Brançion, a **book market** is held every Saturday and Sunday morning.

The 14ᵉ below Montparnasse

The gargantuan development around place de Catalogne gives way to a walkway along the old rue Vercingétorix and to the changing but still cosy atmosphere, long lived in by artists, of **Pernety**. Wandering acound Cité Bauer, rue des Thermopyles and rue Didot reveals adorable houses, secluded courtyards and quiet mews, and on the corner of rue du Moulin Vert and rue Hippolyte-Maindron you'll find Giacometti's old ramshackle studio and home. At the end of Impasse Floriment, behind a petrol station on rue d'Alésia, a bronze relief of Georges Brassens smoking his pipe adorns the tiny house where he lived and wrote his songs from 1944 to 1966.

Rue d'Alésia, the main east–west route through the 14ᵉ, is best known for its good-value clothes shops, many selling discounted couturier creations. There are more artistic associations south of rue d'Alésia near the junction with av Réné-Coty: Dali, Lurcat, Miller and Durrell lived in the tiny cobbled street of **Villa Seurat** off rue de la Tombe-Issoire; Lenin and his wife, Krupskaya, lodged across the street at 4 rue Marie-Rose; Le Corbusier built the studio at no. 53 av Reille, close to the secretive and verdant square du Montsouris which links with rue Nansouty; and Georges Braque's home was in the cul-de-sac now named after him off this street. All these characters would have taken strolls in **Parc Montsouris** (RER Cité-Universitaire). Along with a lake and waterfall, its more surprising features include a meteorological office, a marker of the old meridian line, near boulevard Jourdan, and, by the southwest entrance, a kiosk run by the French Astronomy Association. The strange array of buildings across the boulevard from the park form the **Cité Universitaire**, home to several thousand students from over one hundred different countries.

The 13ᵉ arrondissement

The 13ᵉ is one of the most disparate areas of the city, with its eastern edge in the throes of mammoth development. **Place d'Italie** with the ornate mairie and vast new Gaumont cinema is the hub, with each of the major roads radiating out into very different quartiers.

Northeast of place d'Italie, between boulevards de l'Hôpital and Vincent-Auriol, is the immense **Hôpital de la Salpêtrière**, built under Louis XIV to dispose of the dispossessed. It later became a psychiatric hospital, fulfilling much the same function. Jean Charcot, who believed that susceptibility to hypnosis was proof of hysteria, staged his theatrical demonstrations on poor, troubled women here, with Freud a captive member of his audiences. For a more positive statement about women, take a look at the building at 5 rue Jules-Breton, which declares in large letters on its facade, "In humanity, woman has the same duties as man. She must have the same rights in the family and in society."

Avenue des Gobelins, leading north, has the **Gobelins tapestry workshops** at no. 42, which have operated here for some four hundred years. Tapestries are still being made by the same, painfully slow methods, but now feature cartoons by contemporary painters (guided visits Tues–Thurs 2pm & 2.45pm; 45F; Mᵒ Gobelins). Hidden away just to the north, visible from rue des Gobelins or the courtyard at 4 rue Gustave-Geffroy, is an exquisite fairytale octagonal tower and gateway, all that remains of the **Château de la Reine Blanche**, where the young Charles VI of France supposedly went mad after a riotous party.

Between boulevard Auguste-Blanqui and rue Bobillot is a hill (*butte*) where quails (*cailles*) must once have nested. **Rue de la Butte-aux-Cailles** and its side streets have the fabric of pre-1960s Paris and still a glut of bars, restaurants and little shops, even if rents now are pretty high. To the south, below rue Tolbiac, small houses with fancy brickwork, decorative tiles and timbers, crazy-paving walls and near vertical roofs have remained intact: between rues Boussingault and Brillat-Savarin and on place de l'Abbé-G-Henocque, rue Dieulafoy and rue Henri-Pape.

Over to the east, amongst all the 1960s high-rise, is the main **Chinese quarter** of Paris. Avenues de Choisy and d'Ivry are full of Chinese, Thai, Cambodian, Vietnamese and Laotian restaurants and food shops, as is "Les Olympiades", a raised pedestrian area between tower blocks with one entrance at 66 av d'Ivry, next door to a Buddhist temple off the submerged rue du Disque.

Following rue Tolbiac or boulevard Vincent-Auriol to the river, you reach a vast building site which, French economy permitting, is to become an entirely new district called **Seine Rive Gauche**, stretching from the Gare d'Austerlitz to the perimeter. Its star attraction, which Mitterrand managed to inaugurate though not open just before his death, is the new **Bibliothèque Nationale de France**. Accessible from quai de la Gare (M° Quai-de-la-Gare), it has four enormous L-shaped towers forming the corners of a huge platform surrounding a sunken pine copse with glass walls that allow light to filter through to the underground library spaces. It's an extraordinary building, designed by unknown architect Dominique Perrault. Unfortunately shutters had to be added to the towers to protect the books and manuscripts from sunlight; as a result the view from outside is a bit disappointing. The reading rooms are open to everyone over 18 (Tues–Sat 10am–7pm, Sun noon–6pm; 20F for a day pass), but the garden level is reserved for accredited researchers only.

The Beaux Quartiers and Bois de Boulogne

The **Beaux Quartiers** are the 16e and 17e arrondissements. The 16e is aristocratic and rich; and the 17e – or at least the southern part of it – middle-class and rich, embodying the cautious values of the nineteenth-century manufacturing and trading classes. The northern half of the 16e, towards place Victor-Hugo and place de l'Étoile, is leafy and distinctly metropolitan in feel. The southern part, around the old villages of **Auteuil** and **Passy**, has an almost provincial feel and is full of pleasant surprises for the walker. There are several interesting pieces of early twentieth-century architecture scattered through the district, especially those by Hector Guimard (designer of the swirly green Art Nouveau métro stations) and by Le Corbusier and Mallet-Stevens, architects of the first "Cubist" buildings. Also in the area is the wonderful **Musée Marmottan**.

Auteuil

A good place to start an architectural exploration is the **Église-d'Auteuil** métro station, with several Guimard buildings in the vicinity: at 34 rue Boileau, 8 av de la Villa-de-la-Réunion, 41 rue Chardon-Lagache, 142 av de Versailles and 39 bd Exelmans. From the métro exit, **rue d'Auteuil**, with a lingering village high-street air, leads to **place Lorrain**, which has a Saturday market. There are more Guimard houses at the further end of rue La Fontaine, which begins here: no. 14 is perhaps the best in the city. On rue Poussin, just off the *place*, is the entrance to **Villa Montmorency**, a typical 16e *villa* (mews), a sort of private village of leafy lanes and English-style gardens. Gide and the Goncourt brothers of *Prix* fame lived in this one.

Behind it is rue du Dr-Blanche where, in a cul-de-sac on the right, are **Le Corbusier**'s first private houses (1923), looked after by the Fondation Le Corbusier. You can visit one of the houses, the **Villa Roche** (Mon–Fri 10am–12.30pm & 1.30–6.30pm; closed Aug; 15F). Built in strictly Cubist style, very plain, with windows in bands, the only extravagance is the raising of one wing on piers and a curved frontage. They look commonplace enough now from the outside, but what a contrast to anything that had gone before, and once you're inside, the spatial play still seems groundbreaking. Further along rue du Dr-Blanche, the tiny **rue Mallet-Stevens** was built entirely by Mallet-Stevens, also in Cubist style.

After taking a left at the northern end of rue du Dr-Blanche, then right on boulevard Beauséjour, use the shortcut immediately opposite rue du Ranelagh across the disused *Petite Ceinture* train line to reach avenue Raphaël followed by a pleasant walk along the shady trees of pretty green-lawned Jardin du Ranelagh to the **Musée Marmottan**, 2 rue Louis-Boilly, 16e (daily except Mon 10am–5pm; 40F; M^o Muette). Among its collection of Monet paintings, bequeathed by the artist's son, is the canvas entitled *Impression, Soleil Levant* (Impression, Sunrise), an 1872 rendering of a misty sunrise over Le Havre, whose title the critics usurped to give the Impressionist movement its name. There's a dazzling collection of canvases from Monet's last years at Giverny, including several *Nymphéas* (water lilies), *Le Pont Japonais*, *L'Allée des Rosiers*, *La Saule Pleureur*, where rich colours are laid on in thick, excited whorls and lines. To all intents and purposes, these are abstractions, much more "advanced" than the work of, say, **Renoir**, Monet's exact contemporary, some of whose paintings are on display, as are those of other Impressionists, including **Berthe Morisot**.

Passy

Passy, too, offers scope for a good meandering walk. From La Muette métro, head east along the old high street, **rue de Passy**, past an eye-catching parade of boutiques, until you reach **place de Passy** and the crowded but leisurely terrace of *Le Paris Passy* café. From the *place*, stroll southeast along cobbled, pedestrianized **rue de l'Annonciation**, a pleasant mixture of down-to-earth and well-heeled which gives more of the flavour of old Passy. You may not want your Bechstein repaired or your furniture lacquered, but as you approach the end of the street, past several food shops with delectable displays, there'll be no holding back the salivary glands. When you hit rue Raynouard, cross the road and veer to your right, where at no. 47 you'll discover a delightful, summery little house with pale green-shutters and a decorative iron entrance porch, tucked away down some steps amongst a tree-filled garden. Here Balzac moved in the 1840s to outrun his creditors. In fact the deceptively tiny place extends down the hillside for three storeys, which made it easy for Balzac to slip out of the back door and into town unnoticed. The **Maison de Balzac** (Tues–Sun 10am–5.40pm; 17.5F) repays a visit even if you've never read the writer. Memorabilia includes a room devoted to the development of ideas for the creation of a monument to Balzac, resulting in the the famously blobby Rodin sculpture of the writer that was caricatured by contemporary cartoonists (see p. 131).

Behind the house, reached via some steps descending from rue Raynouard, **rue Berton** is a cobbled path with gas lights still in place, blocked off by the heavy security of the Turkish embassy. On the other side, arrived at by heading down avenue de Lamballe and then right into avenue du Général Mangin to cobbled **rue d'Ankara**, you can see the embassy building, an eighteenth-century château half hidden by greenery and screened by a high wall and guards. This was once a clinic where the pioneering Dr Blanche tried to treat the mad Maupassant and Gérard de Nerval, amongst others. It's a short walk from here down to the river which is crossed at this point by the **Pont Bir Hakeim**, a bridge famously featured in *Last Tango in Paris*. You're well placed now to cross the bridge and head north along the water to the Eiffel Tower about 500m along.

Bois de Boulogne

The **Bois de Boulogne**, running all down the west side of the 16ᵉ, is supposedly modelled on London's Hyde Park, though it is a very French interpretation. It offers all sorts of facilities: the **Jardin d'Acclimatation** has lots of attractions for kids (see p.174); the **Parc de Bagatelle** (Mᵒ Port de Neuilly, then bus #43 or Mᵒ Porte Maillot, then bus #244) features beautiful displays of tulips, hyacinths and daffodils in the first half of April, irises in May, water lilies and roses at the end of June; a riding school; **bike rental** at the entrance to the Jardin d'Acclimation; **boating** on the Lac Inférieur; and **race courses** at Longchamp and Auteuil. The best, and wildest, part for walking is towards the southwest corner. When it was opened to the public in the eighteenth century, people said of it, "Les mariages du bois de Boulogne ne se font pas devant Monsieur le Curé" ("Unions cemented in the Bois de Boulogne do not take place in the presence of a priest"). Today's after-dark unions are no less disreputable.

If you have any interest in the beautiful and highly specialized skills, techniques and artefacts developed in the long ages that preceded industrialization, standardization and mass production, you should visit the fascinating **Musée National des Arts et Traditions Populaires**, 6 av du Mahatma Gandhi, Bois de Boulogne (daily except Tues 9.45am–5.15pm; 25F, 32F with exhibitions; Mᵒ Les Sablons/Porte-Maillot), beside the main entrance to the Jardin d'Acclimatation. Boat-building, shepherding, farming, weaving, blacksmithing, pottery, stone-cutting, games and clairvoyance are all beautifully illustrated and displayed.

La Défense

La Défense (Mᵒ/RER Grande-Arche-de-la-Défense), has been elevated to one of the top places of pilgrimage for visitors to Paris by **La Grande Arche**, a beautiful and astounding 112-metre hollow cube clad in white marble, standing 6km out from the Arc de Triomphe at the far end of the Voie Triomphale, from which it stands at a slight angle. Suspended within its hollow – which could enclose Notre-Dame with ease – are open lift shafts and a "cloud" canopy. The roof section belongs to the Fondation Internationale des Droits de l'Homme, who stage exhibitions and conferences on issues related to human rights. You can ride up to the roof (daily 10am–7pm; 40F) to see these, admire the "Map of the Heavens" marble patios and, on a clear day, scan to the Louvre and beyond.

Between the Grande Arche and the river is the **business complex** of La Défense, a perfect monument to late-twentieth-century capitalism. There is no formal pattern to the arrangements of towers. Token apartment blocks, offices of ELF, Esso, IBM, banks and other businesses compete for size, dazzle of surface and ability to make you dizzy. Mercifully, bizarre **artworks** transform the nightmare into comic entertainment, like **Joan Miró**'s giant wobbly creatures despairing at their misfit status beneath the biting edges and curveless heights of the buildings and Alexander **Calder**'s red-iron offering, a *stabile* rather than a mobile. A statue commemorating the defence of Paris in 1870 (for which the district is named) perches on a concrete plinth in front of a coloured plastic waterfall and fountain pool, while nearer the river disembodied people clutch each other round endlessly repeated concrete flower beds. You'll find details of all the sculptures in the **Art Défense** exhibition space beside the waterfall. A good way to approach the Grande Arche, see the sculptures and watch the main attraction loom is to get out of the métro a stop before at Esplanade-de-la-Défense.

If you're desperate to hand over money to the firms surrounding you, there's the enormous Quatre-Temps shopping centre to the left of the Grande Arche as you face it, and a FNAC bookshop in the CNIT building oppposite. Fun but expensive is **Le Dôme-Imax**, a 180° projection cinema between Quatre Temps and the Grande Arche (daily 12.15–8pm; 60F; programme details in *Pariscope*).

The 17ᵉ arrondissement

The 17ᵉ arrondissement is most interesting in its eastern half. The classier western end is cold and soulless, cut by too many wide and uniform boulevards. A route that takes in the best of it would be from **place des Ternes**, with its cafés and flower market, through the stately wrought-iron gates of place de la République Dominicaine into the small and formal **Parc Monceau**, surrounded by pompous residences. **Rue de Lévis** (a few blocks up rue Berger from Mᵒ Monceau) has one of the city's most strident, colourful and appetizing markets every day of the week except Monday, and is also a good restaurant area, particularly up around rue des Dames and rue Cheroy.

Further north still, across the St-Lazare train tracks, **rue des Batignolles** is the heart of Batignolles "village", now sufficiently self-conscious to have formed an association for the preservation of its "*caractère villageois*". At the north end of the street, the attractive semicircular place du Dr-Lobligeois frames a small colonnaded church whose entrance was modelled on the Madeleine. Behind it is the tired and trampled greenery of square Batignolles, with the marshalling yards beyond. The long **rue des Moines** leads northeast towards Guy-Môquet. This is the working-class Paris of the movies, all small, animated, friendly shops, four- or five-storey houses in shades of peeling grey, and brown-stained bars where men drink standing at the *zinc*.

Montmartre and northern Paris

Montmartre lies in the middle of the largely petit bourgeois and working-class 18ᵉ arrondissement, respectable round the slopes of the butte, distinctly less so towards the **Gare du Nord** and **Gare de l'Est**, where depressing slums crowd along the train tracks. The butte itself has a relaxed, sunny, countrified air; **Pigalle**, at the foot of the hill, is full of sex shops and peep shows interspersed with tired-looking women in shop doorways. On its northern edge lies the extensive St-Ouen flea market.

Place des Abbesses and up to the Butte

In spite of being one of the city's chief tourist attractions, the **Butte Montmartre** manages to retain the quiet, almost secretive, air of its rural origins. The most popular access route is via the rue de Steinkerque and the steps below the Sacré-Cœur (the funicular railway from place Suzanne-Valadon is covered by the *Carte Orange*). For a quieter approach, go up via place des Abbesses or rue Lepic.

Place des Abbesses is postcard-pretty, with one of the few complete surviving Guimard métro entrances. East, at the Chapelle des Auxiliatrices in rue Yvonne-Le-Tac, Ignatius Loyola founded the Jesuit movement in 1534. It is also supposed to be the place where St Denis, the first bishop of Paris, had his head chopped off by the Romans around 250 AD. He is said to have carried it until he dropped, where the cathedral of St-Denis now stands north of the city.

To continue from place des Abbesses to the top of the Butte, two quiet and attractive routes are up rue de la Vieuville and the stairs in rue Drevet to the minuscule **place du Calvaire**,with a lovely view back over the city, or up rue Tholozé, then right below the **Moulin de la Galette** – the last survivor of Montmartre's forty-odd windmills, immortalized by Renoir – into rue des Norvins.

Artistic associations abound hereabouts. Zola, Berlioz, Turgenev, Seurat, Degas and Van Gogh lived in the area. Picasso, Braque and Juan Gris invented Cubism in an old piano factory in place Émile-Goudeau, known as the **Bateau-Lavoir**, still serving as artists' studios, though the original building burnt down some years ago. And Toulouse-Lautrec's inspiration, the **Moulin Rouge**, survives also, albeit a mere shadow of its former self, on the corner of bd de Clichy and place Blanche.

The **Musée de Montmartre**, at 12 rue Cortot (daily except Mon 11am–6pm; 25F), just over the brow of the hill, tries to recapture something of the feel of those pioneering days, but it's a bit of a disappointment, except for the occasionally excellent temporary exhibition. The house itself, rented at various times by Renoir, Dufy, Suzanne Valadon, and her alcoholic son Utrillo, is worth visiting for the view over the neat terraces of the tiny **Montmartre vineyard** and the north side of the Butte. The entrance to the vineyard is on the steep rue de Saules.

Place du Tertre and Sacré-Cœur

The **place du Tertre** is the heart of tourist Montmartre, photogenic but totally bogus, jammed with tourists, overpriced restaurants and "artists" doing quick portraits while you wait. Between place du Tertre and the Sacré-Cœur, the old church of **St-Pierre** is all that remains of the Benedictine abbey that occupied the Butte Montmartre from the twelfth century on. Though much altered, it still retains its Romanesque and early Gothic feel. In it are four ancient columns, two by the door, two in the choir, leftovers from a Roman shrine that stood on the hill – *mons mercurii* (Mercury's Hill), the Romans called it. As for the **Sacré-Cœur** itself, graceless and vulgar pastiche though it is, its white pimply domes are an essential part of the Paris skyline. The best thing about it is the view from the **tower** (daily: summer 9am–7pm; winter 9am–6pm; 15F), almost as high as the Eiffel Tower and showing the layout of the whole city. Construction was started in the 1870s on the initiative of the Catholic Church to atone for the "crimes" of the Commune. **Square Willette**, the space at the foot of the monumental staircase, is named after the local artist who turned out on inauguration day to shout "Long live the devil!"

Montmartre cemetery

West of the Butte, near the beginning of rue Caulaincourt in place Clichy, lies the Montmartre cemetry. Ramshackle and peeling, on a tiny courtyard full of plants, it epitomizes the kind-hearted, instinctively arty, sepia Paris that every romantic visitor secretly cherishes. Most of the guests have been there years. The cemetery is tucked down below street level in the hollow of an old quarry with its entrance on av Rachel under rue Caulaincourt. A tangle of trees and funereal pomposity, it holds the graves of Zola, Stendhal, Berlioz, Degas, Feydeau, Offenbach and Truffaut, among others.

St-Ouen flea market

Officially open Sunday to Monday 7.30am to 7pm – unofficially, from 5am – the **puces de St-Ouen** (Mᵒ Porte-de-Clignancourt) claims to be the largest flea market in the world, the name "flea" deriving from the state of the second-hand mattresses, clothes and other junk sold here when the market first operated outside the city walls. Nowadays it is predominantly a proper – and expensive – antiques market (mainly furniture, but including old café bar counters, telephones, traffic lights, posters, jukeboxes and petrol pumps), with what is left of the rag-and-bone element confined to the further reaches of rues Fabre and Lécuyer.

Pigalle

From place Clichy in the west to Barbès-Rochechouart in the east, the hill of Montmartre is underlined by the sleazy **boulevards of Clichy and Rochechouart**, the centre of the roadway often occupied by bumper-car pistes and other funfair sideshows. At the Barbès end, where the métro clatters by on iron trestles, the crowds teem round the Tati department stores, the city's cheapest, while the pavements are lined with West and North African street vendors offering cloth, watches and trinkets. At the place Clichy end, tour buses from all over Europe feed their contents into massive hotels. In the middle, between place Blanche and place Pigalle, sex shows, sex shops, tiny bars where hostesses lurk in complicated tackle, and street prostitutes (both male and female) coexist with one of Paris' most elegant private villas on avenue Frochot. In the adjacent streets are the city's best specialist music shops.

Perfectly placed amongst all the sex shops and shows is the new **Musée de l'Erotisme** (daily 10am–2am; 40F), exploring different cultures' approaches to sex. The ground floor and first floor are dedicated to sacred and ethnographic art, where proud phalluses and well-practised positions in the art from Asia, Africa and pre-Colombian Latin America reveal a strong link between the spiritual and the erotic. European art (apart from the copies of Ancient Greek vases, where there's no beating about the bush), on the other hand uses sex to satirize and ridicule religion with lots of naughty nuns and priests caught in compromising situations. Humour is the main theme in the basement. Have a go on the metal outline of a naked women with a metal ring and baton attached. The aim is to get the ring from one end to the other without it touching the filament – the longer you succeed the more she moans. Beware, it's quite loud! The rest of the floors upstairs are devoted to temporary exhibitions which change every three months.

The Goutte d'Or

Along the north side of boulevard de la Chapelle, between boulevard Barbès and the Gare du Nord rail lines, stretches the poetically named quarter of the **Goutte d'Or** (Drop of Gold), a name that derives from the medieval vineyard that occupied this site. It has gradually become an immigrant ghetto since World War I, when large numbers of North Africans were first imported to replenish the ranks of Frenchmen dying in the trenches. It's currently in the throes of redevelopment, but old men still talk for hours over tea in the numerous tiny cafés, restaurants serve Tunisian delicacies for next to nothing, tiny shops sell snazzy cloth and jewellery and Raï music resonates from the upper balconies. Much of rue de la Goutte d'Or itself is new, but remains, with its tributary lanes, distinctly North African and poor. On Wednesday and Saturday the **boulevard de la Chapelle market** attracts large crowds and has excellent deals.

Canal St-Martin and La Villette

The **Bassin de la Villette** and the **canals** at the northeastern gate of the city were for generations the centre of a densely populated working-class district. The jobs were in the main meat market and abattoirs of Paris or in the many interlinked industries that spread around the waterways. The amusements were skating or swimming, betting on cockfights or eating at the numerous restaurants famed for their fresh meat. Now La Villette is the wonderworld of laser-guided culture and postmodernist architecture, and the recipient of public spending worth over a billion pounds.

The whole Villette complex stands at the junction of the **Ourcq** and **St-Denis canals**. The first was built by Napoléon to bring fresh water into the city; the second is an extension of the Canal St-Martin built as a short cut to the great western loop of the Seine around Paris.

Canal St-Martin and Place de Stalingrad

The **Canal St-Martin** runs underground at the Bastille to surface again in boulevard Jules-Ferry by rue du Faubourg-du-Temple, another key point in the annals of revolutionary street fighting. The southern section of the canal is the most attractive. Plane trees line the cobbled quais and elegant high, arched footbridges punctuate the spaces between locks. A few mementos of the area's old identity remain, such as the facade of the **Hôtel du Nord** of Marcel Carné's film, at 102 quai de Jemappes. But grossly bland and strident apartment blocks have elbowed in among the traditional, solid, mid-nineteenth-century residences, and north of rue des Récollets redevelopment has totally transformed both banks.

At **place de Stalingrad**, the beautifully restored Rotonde de la Villette was one of Ledoux's tollhouses in Louis XVI's tax wall, where taxes were levied on all goods coming into the city – a major bone of contention in the lead-up to the 1789 Revolution.

Beyond the *place* is the **Bassin de la Villette** dock, now used for Sunday strolls, fishing and canoeing. Recobbled, and with its dockside buildings converted into offices for canal boat trips, and a cinema with an attached waterfront brasserie, the Bassin has lost all vestiges of its former status as France's premier port. At rue de Crimée a unique hydraulic bridge marks the end of the dock and the beginning of the Canal de l'Ourcq. If you keep to the south bank on quai de la Marne, you can cross directly into the Parc de la Villette.

The Parc de la Villette

The **Parc de la Villette** (daily 6am–1am; free) music, art and science complex between av Corentin-Cariou and av Jean-Jaurès, has so many disparate and disconnected elements, and such a clash of architectural styles, that it's hard to know where to start. To help you get your bearings, there are **information** centres at the entrances by M° Porte-de-la-Villette, to the north, and M° Porte-de-Pantin, to the south, plus another by the canal bridge; all the different films and exhibitions are detailed in *Pariscope*.

The main attraction has to be the enormous **Cité des Sciences et de l'Industrie** (Tues–Sat 10am–6pm, Sun 10am–7pm; 50F day M° Porte-de-la-Villette; good disabled facilities and access). This high-tech museum devoted to science and all its applications is built into the concrete hulk of the abandoned abattoirs on the north side of the canal de l'Ourcq. Four times the size of Beaubourg, its giant walls of glass hang beneath a dark-blue lattice of steel, with white rod walkways accelerating out towards the Géode across a moat. Inside are crow's-nests and cantilevered platforms, bridges and suspended walkways, the different levels linked by lifts and escalators around a huge central space open to the full 40m height of the roof. It may be colossal, but you are more likely to lose yourself mentally rather than physically and come out after several hours reeling with images and ideas, while none the wiser in actual fact about DNA, quasars, bacteria reproduction, rocket launching or whatever.

The **permanent exhibition**, called Explora, covers different subjects such as sounds, robotics, expression and behaviour, oceans, energy, light, ecology, maths, medicine, space, language, etc. The emphasis is on exploring, and the means used are interactive computers, videos, holograms, animated models and games. In *Expressions et comportements* you can intervene in stories acted out on videos, changing the behaviour of the characters to engineer a different outcome. Hydroponic plants grow for real in a green bridge across the central space. You can steer robots through mazes; make music by your own movements; experiment with motion in an "inertia carousel"; watch computer-guided puppet shows; and see holograms of different periods' visions of the universe.

When all this interrogation and stimulation becomes too much, you can relax in cafés within Explora, before joining the queue for the **planetarium**. Back on the ground floor the **Louis-Lumière Cinema** shows 3-D films (entry with day pass) and the **Salle Jean-Bertin** shows documentaries in French (screenings 10.15am, 2.15pm & 4.15pm; closed Mon; free); the **Cité des Enfants** and **Techno Cité** for children and teenagers (see p.173); and a whole programme of **temporary exhibitions**. Below ground is the multimedia library, the **mediatheque** (daily noon–8pm; free), **restaurants** and an **aquarium** (free).

In front of the complex balances the **Géode** (hourly shows 10am–9pm; closed Mon; 57F), a bubble of reflecting steel dropped from an intergalactic boules game into a pool of water that ripples the mirrored image of the Cité. Inside the bubble, half the sphere is a screen for Omnimax 180° films, not noted for their plots but a great visual experience. Or there's the **Cinaxe**, between the Cité and the Canal St-Denis (screenings every 15 min 11am–6pm; closed Mon; 34F or 29F with day pass) combining 70mm film shot at thirty frames a second with seats that move. Beside the Géode is a real 1957 French **submarine**, the **Argonaute** (Tues–Fri 10.30am–5.30pm, Sat & Sun 10.30am–6pm; 25F or free entry with day pass), and towards the bridge over the canal de l'Ourcq, a **dragon slide**. South of the canal are bizarrely landscaped **themed gardens** of "mirrors", "mists", "winds and dunes" and "islands"; over to the east is the **Zenith** inflatable rock music venue, with jazz at **Hot Brass** in one of the park's bright-red "follies". To the south, the largest of the old **market halls** – an iron-frame structure designed by Baltard, the engineer of the vanished Les Halles pavilions – is now a vast and brilliant exhibition space, the **Grande Salle**.

South of the Grande Salle is the brand-new **Cité de la Musique**, in two complexes to either side of the Porte-de-Pantin entrance. To the west is the national music academy; while to the east lies a concert hall, the very chic *Café de la Musique*, a music and dance information centre, and the **Musée de la Musique** (Tues–Thurs noon–6pm, Fri & Sat noon–7.30pm, Sun 10am–6pm; 35F) presenting the history of music from the end of the Renaissance to the present day, both visually – a collection of 4500 instruments – and aurally, with headsets and interactive displays. Designed by Christian de Portzamparc, the buildings make abstract artistic statements with their wedge, wavy and funnelling shapes, musical patterns, and varied colours and textures. Around the concert hall, a glass-roofed arcade with pale blue sloping walls even gives out deep relaxation sounds.

Belleville, Ménilmontant, Père-Lachaise and the Bois de Vincennes

The **eastern districts** of Paris are no longer the revolutionary hotbeds they were in the nineteenth century, and the predominantly working-class identity of the area is changing as a slow process of rebuilding takes place. **Belleville** and **Ménilmontant** have long had large immigrant populations of Slavs, Greeks, Portuguese, Chinese, Vietnamese, Jews, Arabs, Armenians, Senegalese, Malians – still very much in evidence against a backdrop of some much more pleasing architectural additions than the old high-rise shelving-unit housing. Exploring the old villagey streets and admiring the best of the new constructions are the main pleasures of this part of town, which also offers wonderful views down onto the city; and for a focus to your wandering, there's **Père-Lachaise cemetery**.

Parc des Buttes-Chaumont

At the northern end of the Belleville heights, a short walk from La Villette, is the **parc des Buttes-Chaumont** (Mº Buttes-Chaumont/Botzaris), constructed by Haussmann in the 1860s to camouflage what until then had been a desolate warren of disused quarries and miserable shacks. The sculpted beak-shaped park stays open all night and, equally rarely for Paris, you're not cautioned off the grass. At its centre is a huge rock upholding a delicate Corinthian temple and surrounded by a lake which you cross via a suspension bridge or the shorter Pont des Suicides. Louis Aragon, the literary grand old man of the French Communist Party, wrote of this bridge that it claimed victims among passers-by who had no intention of dying but found themselves suddenly tempted by the abyss. Feeble metal grills erected along its sides have put an end to such impulses.

Belleville and Ménilmontant

The route from Buttes-Chaumont to Père-Lachaise will take you through the one-time villages of **Belleville** and **Ménilmontant**. Many of the old village lanes disappeared in the tower-block mania of the 1960s and 1970s, but others have now been opened up, and many of the newest buildings are imaginative infill, following the height and curves of their older neighbours. Dozens of cobbled and gardened *villas* remain intact: east of Buttes-Chaumont towards place Rhin-et-Danube, between rue Boyer (with a 1920s Soviet-style building at no. 25) and rue des Pyrénées just north of Père-Lachaise, and out to the east by Porte de Bagnolet, up the very picturesque steps from place Octave-Chanute.

The first main street you cross coming down from Buttes-Chaumont, **rue de Belleville**, has become the new Chinatown of Paris. Vietnamese and Chinese shops and restaurants have proliferated over the last few years, adding considerable visual and gastronomic cheer to the area. African and oriental fruits, spices, music and fabrics can be bought at the **boulevard de Belleville market** on Tuesdays and Fridays. Edith Piaf was abandoned just a few hours old on the steps of no. 72 rue de Belleville, and there's a small **museum** dedicated to her at 5 rue Créspin-du-Gast (Mon–Thurs 1–6pm; closed Sept; by appointment on ☎01.43.55.52.72; donation; Mº Ménilmontant/St-Maur). Rue Ramponneau, just southeast of the crossroads with bd de Belleville and now entirely rebuilt, was where the last Communard on the last barricade held out alone for a final fifteen minutes.

You get fantastic views down onto the city centre from the higher reaches of Belleville and Ménilmontant: the best place to watch the sunset is the **Parc de Belleville** (Mº Couronnes/Pyrénées), which descends in a series of terraces and waterfalls from rue Piat. And from **rue de Ménilmontant**, by rues de l'Ermitage and Boyer, you can look straight down to Beaubourg.

Père-Lachaise cemetery

Père-Lachaise cemetery (daily 7.30am–6pm; Mº Gambetta/Père-Lachaise/Alexandre-Dumas) is like a miniature city devastated by a neutron bomb: a great number of dead, seemingly empty houses and temples of every size and style, and exhausted survivors, some congregating aimlessly, some searching persistently. The cemetery was opened in 1804 after an urgent stop had been put on further burials in the overflowing city cemeteries and churchyards, and to be interred in Père-Lachaise quickly became the ultimate symbol of riches and success. A free **map** of the cemetery is available at the entrance on rue des Rondeaux by Av du Père Lachaise, or you can buy a more detailed souvenir one for 10F at newsagents near here and the Boulevard de Ménilmontant entrance.

Swarms flock to the now-sanitized tomb of ex-Doors lead singer Jim Morrison (division 6), cleansed of all its graffiti and watched vigilantly by security guards. Colette's tomb (division 4), close to the main Ménilmontant entrance, is very plain though always covered in flowers. The same is true of Sarah Bernhardt's (division 44) and the great chanteuse Edith Piaf's (division 97). Marcel Proust lies in his family's conventional tomb (division 85), which honours the medical fame of his father. In division 92, nineteenth-century journalist Victor Noir – shot for daring to criticize a relative of Napoléon III – lies flat on his back, fully clothed, his top hat fallen by his feet.

Corot (division 24) and Balzac (division 48) both have superb busts, Balzac looking particularly satisfied with his life. Géricault reclines on cushions of stone (division 12), paint palette in hand; Chopin (division 11) has a willowy muse weeping for his loss. The most impressive of the individual tombs is that of Oscar Wilde (division 89), adorned with a strange Pharaonic winged messenger (sadly robbed almost immediately of its prominent penis by a scandalised cemetery employee, who, so the story goes, used it as a paperweight) sculpted by Jacob Epstein and a grim verse from *The Ballad of Reading Gaol* behind. Nearby, in division 96, is the grave of Modigliani and his lover Jeanne Herbuterne, who killed herself in crazed grief a few days after he died in agony from meningitis.

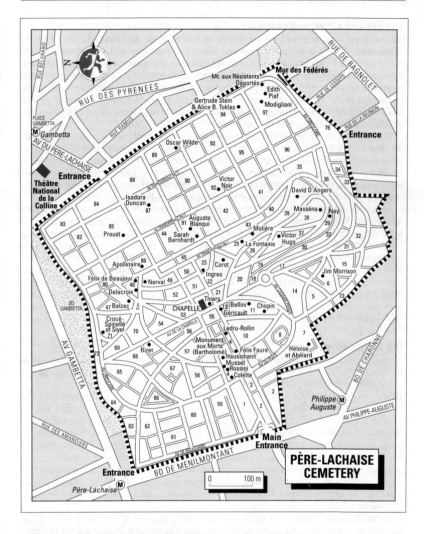

But it is the monuments to the collective, violent deaths that have the power to change a sunny outing to Père-Lachaise into a much more sombre experience. In division 97, you'll find the memorials to those who died in the Nazi concentration camps, to executed Resistance fighters and to those who were never accounted for in the genocide of the last world war. The sculptures are relentless in their images of inhumanity, of people forced to collaborate in their own degradation and death. Finally, there is the *Mur des Fedérés* (division 76), the wall where the last troops of the Paris Commune were lined up and shot in the final days of the battle in 1871. The man who ordered their execution, Adolphe Thiers, lies in the centre of the cemetery in division 55.

The 11e and 12e arrondissements

To the south and west of Père-Lachaise, around **rue de la Roquette** and **rue de Charonne**, there's nothing very special about the passages and ragged streets that make up the **11e arrondissement**, except that they are utterly Parisian, with the odd detail of a building, the display of veg in a simple greengrocer's, sunlight on a café table or graffiti on a Second Empire street fountain to charm the aimless wanderer. The closer you get to the Bastille, the more chunks are missing – demolition areas of several blocks at a time. It's depressing, but so too is the northeast corner of the 11e, where the buildings are crumbling and the poverty very much in evidence.

There are quiet havens from the mania of the Bastille traffic in the courtyards of **rue du Faubourg-St-Antoine**. Since the fifteenth century, this has been the principal artisan and working-class quartier of Paris, the cradle of revolutions and mother of street-fighters. From its beginnings the principal trade associated with it has been **furniture-making**, and the maze of interconnecting yards and passages are still full of the workshops of the related trades: marquetry, stainers, polishers and inlayers.

Alongside **avenue Daumesnil**, the main artery of the **12e arrondissement**, an old railway line has been converted into the **Promenade Plantée**, a "green corridor" for walkers and cyclists running all the way from the junction with rue Ledru-Rollin to the Jardin de Reuilly and on out to Vincennes (see below). Below, the railway arches have been transformed into a string of art workshops and galleries, the **Viaduc des Arts**, running from nos. 15 to 121. South of the avenue is the gorgeous nineteenth-century extravaganza of the Gare de Lyon, a high-rise business area, the Stalinesque 400-metre-long **Ministère des Finances** building, and, facing the national library across the river, the very welcome new green space of the **Parc de Bercy** (M° Bercy) replacing the warehouses where for centuries the capital's wine supplies were unloaded from river barges.

Out to Vincennes

Across the *boulevard périphérique* at the end of av Daumesnil, on the edge of the Bois de Vincennes, is the **Musée des Arts Africains et Océaniens**, 293 av Daumesnil, 12e (Mon, Wed–Fri & hols 10am–5.30pm, Sat & Sun till 6pm; 30F; M° Porte-Dorée), with a 1930s colonial facade of jungles, hard-working natives and the place names of the French empire. This strange museum – one of the least crowded in the city – has an African gold brooch of curled-up sleeping crocodiles on one floor and, in the basement, five live crocodiles in a tiny pit surrounded by tanks of tropical fish. Imperialism is much in evidence in a gathering of culture and creatures from the old French colonies: hardly any of the black African artefacts are dated – the collection predates European acknowledgement of history on that continent, and the captions are a bit suspicious too. These masks and statues, furniture, adornments and tools should be exhibited with paintings by Expressionists, Cubists and Surrealists to show the influence they had. Picasso and friends certainly came here often.

In the **Bois de Vincennes** itself, the city's only extensive green space besides the Bois de Boulogne, you can spend an afternoon boating on Lac Daumesnil (by the zoo) or rent a bike from the same place and feed the ducks on Lac des Minimes on the other side of the wood (or bus #112 from Vincennes métro). The fenced enclave on the southern side of Lac Daumesnil is a **Buddhist centre** with a Tibetan temple, Vietnamese chapel and international pagoda, all occasionally visitable. As far as real woods go, the *bois* opens out once you're east of avenue de St-Maurice, but the area is so overrun with roads that countryside sensations don't stand much chance. To the north is the **Parc Floral** (summer 9.30am–8pm; winter 9.30am–5/6pm; 10F; bus #112 or short walk from M° Château-de-Vincennes), one of the best gardens in Paris. Flowers are always in bloom in the "Jardin des Quatres Saisons"; you can picnic beneath pines while the kids play, then wander through concentrations of camellias, cacti, ferns, irises and bonsaï

trees. Abutting the Parc Floral is the **Cartoucherie de Vincennes**, an old ammunitions factory, now home to four theatre companies including the radical Théâtre du Soleil.

On the northern edge of the *bois*, the **Château de Vincennes** (daily 10am–5/6pm; choice of guided visits 32F or 22F; Mº Château-de-Vincennes), royal medieval residence, then state prison, porcelain factory, weapons dump and military training school, is still undergoing restoration work started by Napoléon III. Visits include the Flamboyant Gothic **Chapelle Royale**, completed in the mid-sixteenth century and decorated with superb Renaissance stained-glass windows around the choir.

Eating and drinking

Eating and drinking are among the chief delights of Paris, as they are in the country as a whole. There is a tremendous variety of foods, from Senegalese to Caribbean, from Thai to eastern European and North African, as well as regional French cuisines, notably from the southwest. There's also the diversity of eating and drinking establishments: luxurious **restaurants** in the traditional style or elbow-to-elbow bench- and trestle-table jobs; spacious **brasseries** and **cafés** where you can watch the world go by while nibbling on a baguette sandwich; or dark, cavernous **beer cellars** and tiny **wine bars** with sawdust on the floor offering wines by the glass from every region of France. You could take coffee and cakes in a chintzy **salon de thé**, in a bookshop or gallery, or even in the confines of a mosque. **Bars** can be medieval vaults, minimalist or postmodern design units, London-style pubs or period pieces in styles ranging from the Naughty Nineties to the Swinging Sixties. The variety is endless and the distinctions between bars, cafés, pubs, ice-cream parlours, sandwich bars, brasseries and wine bars can't always be clearly drawn. **Gay** establishments proliferate in the Marais and around the Bastille quartier; the only **lesbian** bar in town is *La Champmeslé*, in the 2e.

It's true that the old-time cheap neighbourhood cafés and bistros are a dying breed, while fast-food chains have burgeoned at an alarming speed. Quality is also in decline at the lower end of the restaurant market, particularly in tourist hot spots. Yet, however much Parisians bemoan the changing times, you'll find you're still spoiled for choice even on a modest budget. There are numerous **fixed price menus** (*prix fixe*) for under 80F, particularly at lunchtime, providing staple dishes; for 150F you'll have the choice of more interesting dishes; and for 200F, you should be getting some gourmet satisfaction.

The big **boulevard cafés and brasseries** are always more expensive than those a little further removed, and addresses in the smarter or more touristy arrondissements set prices soaring. A snack or drink on the Champs-Élysées, place St-Germain-des-Prés or rue de Rivoli, for instance, will be double or triple the price of Belleville, Batignolles or the southern 14e. Many bars have **happy hours**, but prices can double after 10pm, and any clearly trendy, glitzy or stylish place is bound to be expensive.

STUDENT RESTAURANTS

Students of any age are eligible to apply for tickets for the university restaurants under the direction of CROUS de Paris. A list of addresses, which includes numerous cafés and brasseries, is available from their offices at 39 av Georges-Bernanos, 5e (☎01.40.51.36.00; Mon–Fri 9am–5pm; RER Port-Royal). The tickets, however, have to be obtained from the particular restaurant of your choice (opening hours generally 11.30am–2pm & 6–8pm). Not all serve both midday and evening meals, and times change with each term. Though the food is not wonderful, it is certainly filling, and you can't complain about the price. They will cost you 13.70F if you're studying at a French university, 23F if you can produce an International Student Card; 28.20F otherwise.

PARIS FOR VEGETARIANS

The chances of finding vegetarian main dishes on the menus of regular French restaurants are not good. Though you can choose a selection of non-meat starters or order an omelette or a salad, you'll be much better off going to an ethnic restaurant – Middle Eastern or Indian make a good choice – or a proper **vegetarian restaurant**. There are not many of the latter, but the numbers are slowly increasing as awareness of health and a vegetarian diet catch on (the moral/ecological motive is very rare amongst Parisians). All the establishments listed below are reviewed in the pages that follow.

Aquarius 1, 54 rue Ste-Croix-de-la-Bretonnerie, 4^e. p.149.
Aquarius 2, 40 rue Gergovie, 14e. p.157.
Country Life, 6 rue Daunou, 2e. p.147.
Au Grain de Folie, 24 rue de la Vieuville, 18e. p.160.
Grand Appetit, 9 rue de la Cerisaie, 4e. p.149.
Le Grenier de Notre-Dame, 18 rue de la Bûcherie, 5e. p.150.
Joy in Food, 2 rue Truffaut, 17e. p.160.
La Petite Légume, 36 rue Boulangers, 5e. p.151.
Les Quatre et Une Saveurs, 72 rue du Cardinal-Lemoine, 5e. p.151.
La Ville de Jagannath, 10 rue St Maur, 11e. p.155.

The different eating and drinking establishments are listed here under arrondissement. They are divided into **restaurants**, including some brasseries, and **bars and cafés**, incorporating snack bars, ice-cream parlours and *salons de thé*. You'll also find lists of **vegetarian** (not Paris's strongest suit) and **late-night** possibilities.

1er arrondissement

Bars and cafés

Angélina, 226 rue de Rivoli (M^o Tuileries). Daily 9am–7pm; closed Tues in July & Aug. A long-established gilded cage, where the well-coiffed sip the best hot chocolate in town. Pâtisseries and other desserts of the same high quality. Not cheap.

Aux Bons Crus, 7 rue des Petits-Champs (M^o Palais-Royal). Mon–Sat 11am–midnight; closed Mon evening. A relaxed workaday place that has been serving good wines and cheese, sausage and ham for over eighty years. Wine from 10F a glass; plate of cold meats from 55F.

Café Marly, Cour Napoléon du Louvre, 93 rue de Rivoli (M^o Palais-Royale–Musée-du-Louvre). Daily till 2am. Inside the Louvre, with tables beneath the colonnade overlooking the Pyramide in summer; very chic, very classy and very expensive.

Restorama, Le Carrousel du Louvre (M^o Louvre). Daily 9am–9pm. One vast underground fast-food eating hall served by over a dozen different outlets: rôtisseries, hamburgers, pizzas, Tex-Mex, Chinese, Lebanese, Japanese, crêperies, salad bars – easy to eat for under 40F. Access from place du Carrousel or the Louvre Pyramide.

Le Rubis, 10 rue du Marché-St-Honoré (M^o Pyramides). Mon–Fri 7am–10pm, Sat 8am–4pm; closed mid-Aug. One of the oldest wine bars, with a reputation for excellent wines, snacks and plats du jour. Very small and very crowded. Glasses of wine from 5.50F.

Le Sous-Bock, 49 rue St-Honoré (M^o Châtelet-Les Halles). Daily 11am–5am. Hundreds of bottled beers (around 40F a pint) and whiskies to sample, plus simple, inexpensive food. Mussels a speciality (60–75F). Frequented by night owls. Happy hour 3–7pm.

Taverne Henri IV, 13 place du Pont-Neuf (M^o Pont-Neuf). Mon–Fri noon–10pm, Sat noon–4pm; closed Aug. Yves Montand used to come here when Simone Signoret lived in the adjacent place Dauphine. Good food but a bit pricey for a full meal. Plates of meats and cheeses around 70F, sandwiches 30F, wine from 20F a glass.

Restaurants

Le Dauphin, 167 rue St-Honoré; ☎01.42.60.40.11 (M° Palais-Royal–Musée-du-Louvre). Nov–May daily noon–2.30pm & 7–11.30pm; June–Oct till 12.30am. A genuine bistrot with menus at 95F & 150F. Seafood platter during oyster season for 167F. Excellent *lapereau* (young rabbit) *à la grand-mère* and *magret de canard*.

Foujita, 41 rue St-Roch; ☎01.42.61.42.93 (M° Tuileries/Pyramides). Mon–Sat noon–2.15pm & 7.30–10pm; closed mid-Aug. One of the cheaper but best Japanese restaurants, as proven by the numbers of Japanese eating here. Quick and crowded; soup, sushis, rice and tea for 72F at lunchtime; plate of sushis or sushamis for under 110F.

Le Gros Minet, 1 rue des Prouvaires; ☎01.42.33.02.62 (M° Châtelet-Les Halles). Mon–Sat noon–2pm & 7.30–11.30pm. Relaxed, small and charming restaurant, specializing in duck recipes.

Higuma, 32bis rue Sainte Anne; ☎01.47.03.38.59 (M° Pyramides). Daily 11.30am–10pm. Authentic Japanese canteen with cheap filling ramen dishes and a variety of set menus starting at 63F.

L'Incroyable, 26 rue de Richelieu; ☎01.42.96.24.64 (M° Palais-Royal). Tues–Thurs lunch & 6.30–9pm, Mon & Sat lunch only. Hidden in a tiny passage, a very pleasant restaurant serving decent meals for 80F lunch; 110F eves.

Au Pied de Cochon, 6 rue Coquillière; ☎01.42.36.11.75 (M° Châtelet-Les Halles). Daily 24 hours. For extravagant middle-of-the-night pork chops and oysters. Seafood platter 198F. *Carte* up to 300F.

Au Rendez-vous des Camionneurs, 72 quai des Orfèvres; ☎01.43.54.88.74 (M° St-Michel). Daily noon–2pm & 7–11.30pm. Crowded, traditional establishment serving snails, steaks and scallops. Midday menus under 100F; evening menu 130F, à la carte around 175F.

La Tour de Montlhéry (Chez Denise), 5 rue des Prouvaires; ☎01.42.36.21.82 (M° Louvre-Rivoli/Châtelet). Mon–Fri till midnight, Sat lunch only. An old-style Les Halles bistrot serving substantial food; always crowded and smoky; *carte* from 200F.

2ᵉ arrondissement

Bars and cafés

L'Arbre à Cannelle, 57 passage des Panoramas (M° Rue-Montmartre). Mon–Sat till 6.30pm. Exquisite wooden panelling, frescoes and painted ceilings; puddings, flans and *assiettes gourmandes* for 60–75F.

Le Café, 62 rue Tiquetonne (M° Les Halles/Étienne-Marcel). Daily 10am–2am. On the junction with rue Étienne-Marcel; quiet and secluded, with people playing chess and old maps adorning the walls. *Plats du jour* 45–55F.

La Champmeslé, 4 rue Chabanais (M° Pyramides). Mon–Wed 7pm–2am, Thurs–Sat 7pm–4am. Lesbian bar, with the back room reserved for women and the front rooms for mixed company. Cocktails (from 45F), picture/photo exhibitions, and Thurs night cabaret.

Juveniles, 47 rue de Richelieu (M° Palais-Royal). Mon–Sat noon–midnight. Very popular tiny wine bar run by a Brit. Wine from 68F a bottle; *plats du jour* around 68F.

Kitty O'Shea's, 10 rue des Capucines (M° Opéra). Daily noon–1.30am. An Irish pub with excellent Guinness and Smithwicks. A favourite haunt of Irish expats. The *John Jameson* restaurant upstairs serves high-quality, pricey, Gaelic food, including seafood flown in from Galway.

Restaurants

Country Life, 6 rue Daunou; ☎01.42.97.48.51 (M° Opéra). Mon–Thurs 11.30am–2.30pm & 6.30–10pm, Fri 11.30am–2.30pm. Vegetarian soup, hors d'œuvres, lasagne and salad for under 70F. Menu details gluten and soya contents. No alcohol, no smoking.

Dilan, 13 rue Mandar; ☎01.42.21.14.88 (M° Les Halles/Sentier). Mon–Sat noon–2pm & 7.30–11.30pm; closed Sun. An excellent-value Kurdish restaurant, offering beautiful starters, stuffed aubergines (*babaqunuc*), fish with yoghurt and courgettes (*kanarya*). Midday menu 62F.

Drouot, 103 rue de Richelieu; ☎01.42.96.68.23 (M° Richelieu-Drouot). Daily noon–3pm & 6.30–10pm. Admirably cheap food, served at a frantic pace, in Art Deco surroundings. Menu around 80F.

La Taverne du Nil, 9 rue du Nil; ☎01.42.33.51.82 (M° Sentier). Mon–Fri till 11pm, closed Sun midday & Aug. Very good Lebanese food; delicious lamb kebabs and meze. Menus from 60F to 182F.

3e arrondissement

Bars and cafés

L'Apparemment Café, 18 rue des Coutures-St-Servais (Mº St-Sébastien-Froissart). Mon–Fri noon–2am, Sat 4pm–2am, Sun 12.30pm–midnight. Chic but cosy café resembling a series of comfortable sitting rooms, with quiet corners and deep sofas. Popular Sunday brunch until 4pm costs 90F.

Web Bar, 32 rue de Picardie (Mº Filles-du-Calvaire). Mon–Sat 8.30am–2am, Sun noon–midnight. Paris's best cyber café, on three levels in a converted industrial space, with 15 terminals on a gallery level. A real culture zone: pick up a printed programme of the art exhibitions, short film screenings and other arty events or consult their Web site: *www.webbar.fr*. Comfy couches to loll on and a resident DJ make it a good place to chill, and simple healthy food comes in generous portions (37F for a delicious quiche with loads of salad; lunch menu 51F or 61F).

Restaurants

Chez Nénesse, 17 rue Saintonge; ☎01.42.78.48.49 (Mº Arts-et-Métiers). Mon–Fri noon–2pm & 7.45–10pm; closed Aug. Steak in bilberry sauce, figs stuffed with cream of almonds, and homemade chips Thurs lunchtimes are some of the unique delights at this restaurant. À la carte around 160F.

Le Marais-Cage, 8 rue de Beauce; ☎01.48.87.44.51 (Mº Arts-et-Métiers/Filles-du-Calvaire). Mon–Fri noon–2.15pm & 7–10.30pm, Sat evenings only; closed Aug. Friendly, popular West Indian restaurant; good food, especially seafood. 130F menu midday, 160F and 199F evening, wine included with all.

Le Quincampe, 78 rue Quincampoix; ☎01.40.27.01.45 (Mº Étienne-Marcel/Rambuteau/RER Châtelet). Noon–11pm; closed Mon pm, Sat lunch & Sun. Moroccan restaurant and *salon de thé* where you can eat around a real fire in the room at the back, or take a delicious mint tea; pleasant atmosphere and high-quality food; tagines, *pastilla* and *plat du jour* 80F.

4e arrondissement

Bars and cafés

Bar Central, 33 rue Vieille-du-Temple, cnr rue Ste-Croix-de-la-Bretonnerie (Mº St-Paul). Mon–Thurs 4pm–1am, Fri–Sun 2pm–2am. One of the most enduring gay bars in the Marais attracting a quieter, non-sceney clientele.

Bar de Jarente, 5 rue de Jarente (Mº St-Paul). A lovely old-fashioned café-bar off the pretty place du Marché Ste-Catherine remains nonchalantly indifferent to the shifting trends arround it.

Berthillon, 31 rue St-Louis-en-l'Île (Mº Pont-Marie). Wed–Sun 10am–8pm. Long queues for these excellent ice creams and sorbets (22F a triple) with a big choice of fruity flavours – like rhubarb – you've probably never tasted before. Also available at *Lady Jane* and *Le Flore-en-l'Île*, both on quai d'Orléans, as well as at four other island sites listed on the door.

Bofinger, 7 rue de la Bastille; ☎01.42.72.87.82 (Mº Bastille). Daily until 1am. A popular turn-of-the-century brasserie with its original decor, serving sauerkraut and seafood. Weekday lunchtime menu at 119F, evening 169F, both including wine, otherwise over 200F.

Ma Bourgogne, 19 place des Vosges (Mº St-Paul). Daily until 12.30am, till 1am in summer. A quiet and pleasant arty cafe with tables under the arcades on the northwest corner of the square. Best in the morning when the sun hits this side of the square. Serves somewhat pricey meals too – lunch and dinner menu 195F.

Café Beaubourg, 43 rue St-Merri (Mº Rambuteau/Hôtel de Ville). Mon–Thurs & Sun 8am–1am, Sat 8am–2am. An intellectuals' haunt designed by Christian de Partzamparc and overlooking Beaubourg's piazza; expensive, rather sour service, and very stylish loos.

Café des Phares, 7 place de la Bastille, west side (Mº Bastille). Daily 7am–4am. Every Sun at 11am a public philosophy debate is held in the back room here, run by Nietzsche specialist Marc Sautet, who also offers private philosophical consultations.

Dame Tartine, 2 rue Brisemiche (Mº Rambuteau/Hôtel-de-Ville). Daily noon–11.30pm. Overlooking the Stravinsky pool, serving particularly delicious open toasted sandwiches (from 30F). Inside the relaxed atmosphere matches the mellow yellow walls.

L'Ébouillanté, 6 rue des Barres (M° Hôtel-de-Ville). Tues–Sun noon–10pm, till 9pm in winter. Tiny *salon de thé* in a picturesque cobbled pedestrian-only street behind the church of St-Gervais, serving chocolate cakes and pâtisseries as well as savoury dishes. *Plats du jour* for 67F, Tunisian crêpes for 45F and generous salads.

Épices et Délices, 53 rue Vieille-du-Temple (M° St-Paul). Daily till midnight. Restaurant and *salon de thé* with very pleasant service and food; salads from 60F, 70F evening menu.

Grand Appetit, 9 rue de la Cerisaie (M° Bastille). Mon–Thurs noon–7pm, Fri & Sun noon–2pm. Vegetarian meals served by dedicated eco-veggies at the back of a shop.

Le Petit Fer à Cheval, 30 rue Vieille-du-Temple (M° St-Paul). Mon–Fri 9am–2am, Sat & Sun 11am–2am; food noon–midnight. Very attractive small bistrot/bar with trad decor including a huge zinc bar, a popular drinking spot with tables outside. Agreeable wine and good-value *plats*, and sandwiches from 35F.

Le Petit Marcel, 63 rue Rambuteau (M° Rambuteau). Mon–Sat till 2am. Speckled tabletops, mirrors and Art Nouveau tiles, cracked and faded ceiling and about eight square metres of drinking space. Friendly barstaff and "local" atmosphere.

Le Quetzal, 10 rue de la Verrerie, cnr rue Moussy (M° St-Paul). Mon–Thurs 2pm–4am, Fri–Sun 5pm–5am. A fashionable and stylish gay bar, with space for dancing.

Le Rouge Gorge, 8 rue St-Paul (M° St-Paul). Mon–Sat 11am–2am, Sun 11am–8pm. The young, enthusiastic clientele sip familiar wines and snack on *chèvre chaud* and smoked salmon salad, or tuck into more substantial fare (*plats du jour* around 60F) while listening to jazz or classical music.

Sacha Finkelsztajn, 27 rue des Rosiers (M° St-Paul). Wed–Sun 10am–2pm & 3–7pm; closed Aug; and 24 rue des Écouffes (M° St-Paul); 10am–1pm & 3–7pm; closed Wed. Marvellous for takeaway goodies: gorgeous east European breads, cakes, *gefilte* fish, aubergine purée, tarama, *blinis* and *borscht*.

La Tartine, 24 rue de Rivoli (M° St-Paul). Mon & Wed–Sun until 10pm; closed Aug. The genuine 1900s article, which still cuts across class boundaries in its clientele. A good selection of affordable wines, plus excellent cheese and *saucisson* with *pain de campagne*.

Le Temps des Cerises, 31 rue de la Cerisaie (M° Bastille). Mon–Fri until 8pm; food at midday only. Closed Aug. It is hard to say what is so appealing about this café, with its dirty yellow decor, old posters and prints of *vieux Paris*, save that the *patronne* knows most of the clientele, who are young, relaxed and not the dreaded *branchés*. 68F menu.

Au Volcan de Sicile, 62 rue du Roi-de-Sicile (M° Hôtel-de-Ville). Flooded with sunshine at midday, this is a good café to sit and sip on the corner of the exquisite and minuscule place Tibourg.

Restaurants

Aquarius 1, 54 rue Ste-Croix-de-la-Bretonnerie; ☎01.48.87.48.71 (M° St-Paul/Rambuteau). Mon–Sat noon–10pm; closed last fortnight in Aug. Vegetarian restaurant established in 1974: not the austere and penitential place it once was though. Alcohol is now served ("'hard drinks") but there's still no smoking. Also health food store and New Age bookshop. Lunch menu at 62F, evening 62F and 92F. Hot dishes from 22–64F.

Auberge de Jarente, 7 rue Jarente; ☎01.42.77.49.35 (M° St-Paul). Tues–Sat noon–2.30pm & 7.30–10.30pm; closed Aug. A hospitable and friendly Basque restaurant, serving first-class food: *cassoulet*, hare stew, *magret de canard*, and *piperade* – the Basque omelette. Menus at 117F and 132F, and 185F with wine.

La Canaille, 4 rue Crillon; ☎01.42.78.09.71 (M° Sully-Morland/Bastille). Daily to midnight; closed Sat & Sun lunch. Bar in front, restaurant behind. Simple, traditional and well-cooked food in a friendly atmosphere. There are 79F and 89F lunch menus – 130F in the evening – and à la carte at 140F.

Les Fous d'en Face, 3 rue du Bourg-Tibourg; ☎01.48.87.03.75 (M° Hôtel-de-Ville). Daily 11.30am–3pm & 7pm–midnight. Delightful little restaurant and wine bar serving wonderful marinated salmon and scallops. Midday menu under 90F, otherwise *carte* 140F upwards.

Goldenberg's, 7 rue des Rosiers; ☎01.48.87.20.16 (M° St-Paul). Daily until 2am. The best-known Jewish restaurant in the capital but success has made service pretty surly; its *borscht*, *blinis*, potato strudels, *zakouski* and other central European dishes are a treat. Daily changing *plat du jour* 80F, *carte* around 200F.

Le Grizli, 7 rue St-Martin; ☎01.48.87.77.56 (M° Châtelet). Mon–Sat till 11pm. Turn-of-the-century bistrot serving superb food with specialities from the Pyrenees. 115F midday menu; 155F evening.

Pitchi-Poï, 7 rue Caron; (cnr place du Marché-Ste-Catherine; ☎01.42.77.46.15 (M⁰ St-Paul). Daily noon–3pm & 7.30–11pm. Excellent Polish/Jewish cuisine in a lovely location with sympathetic ambience and 150F lunch and dinner menu, kids' menu 73F, choice of delicious hors d'œuvres from 43F.

5ᵉ arrondissement

Bars and cafés

Café de la Mosquée, 39 rue Geoffroy-St-Hilaire (M⁰ Monge). Daily 8am–midnight. You can drink mint tea and eat sweet cakes beside a fountain and assorted fig trees in the courtyard of this Paris mosque – a delightful haven of calm. The interior of the salon is beautifully Arabic. Meals served in the adjoining restaurant: *couscous* from 55F, *tagines* from 70F.

Cyber Café Latino, 13 rue de l'École-Polytechnique (M⁰ Maubert-Mutualité). Mon–Sat 11.30am–2am. Small friendly bar with a Venezuelan owner, Latino sounds on the stereo and fruit smoothies and tapas on the menu; six computers out the back to surf the Net.

La Fourmi Ailée, 8 rue du Fouarre (M⁰ Maubert-Mutualité). Daily noon–midnight. Simple, light fare – including weekend brunch – in this former feminist bookshop which has been transformed into a *salon de thé* with a rarified atmosphere; a high ceiling painted with a lovely mural and a bookfilled wall. Around 69F for a *plat*.

Le Piano Vache, 8 rue Laplace (M⁰ Cardinal-Lemoine). Daily noon–2am. Venerable student bar with canned music and relaxed atmosphere.

Les Pipos, 2 rue de l'École-Polytechnique (M⁰ Maubert-Mutualité/Cardinal-Lemoine). Mon–Sat 8am–2am; closed three weeks in Aug. Old, carved, wooden bar, and its own wines at 14–25F a glass; *plats*, which change every day, from 50F to 75F.

Polly Magoo, 11 rue St-Jacques (M⁰ St-Michel/Maubert-Mutualité). Mon–Thurs & Sun noon–4am, Fri & Sat noon–6am. A scruffy all-nighter frequented by chess addicts.

Le Violon Dingue, 46 rue de la Montagne-Ste-Geneviève (M⁰ Maubert-Mutualité). Daily 6pm–1.30am. Happy hour 6–10pm. A long, dark, student pub that's also popular with young travellers; noisy and friendly. English-speaking bar staff and cheap drinks.

Restaurants

Bistro de la Sorbonne, 4 rue Toullier; ☎01.43.54.41.49 (RER Luxembourg). Closed Sun. Traditional French and delicious North African food is served here in large portions at reasonable prices. Crowded and attractive student/local ambience. 69F lunch menu; 95F and 140F eves.

Brasserie Balzar, 49 rue des Écoles; ☎01.43.54.13.67 (M⁰ Maubert-Mutualité). Daily until 1am; closed Aug. A traditional literary-bourgeois brasserie frequented by the intelligentsia of the Latin Quarter. *À la carte* about 180F.

au Buisson Ardent, 25 rue Jussieu; ☎.01.43.54.93.02 (M⁰ Jussieu). Mon–Fri; closed two weeks Aug. Copious helpings of first-class traditional cooking: mussels, duck, warm goat cheese salad, lamb, etc. 70F menu lunch, 145F eves. Reservations recommended.

Chez Léna et Mimile, 32 rue Tournefort; ☎01.47.07.72.47 (M⁰ Censier-Daubenton). Mon–Fri until 11pm, Sat evening only. The high south-facing high *terrasse* is the main attraction, overlooking a shady little square, and the 185F menu with wine and coffee included is excellent. 98F menu at lunchtime on weekdays.

Chieng-Maï, 12 rue Frédéric-Sauton; ☎01.43.25.45.45 (M⁰ Maubert-Mutualité). Closed Sun. Excellent Thai dishes; 69F menu at lunchtime; otherwise 122F and 173F menus.

Foyer du Vietnam, 80 rue Monge; ☎01.45.35.32.54 (M⁰ Monge). Mon–Sat until 10pm. Casual authentic Vietnamese with dishes from 30F and menus for 56F and 67F.

Le Grenier de Notre-Dame, 18 rue de la Bûcherie (M⁰ Maubert-Mutualité). Daily noon–11.30pm. Some veggies love this tiny place, which has been operating since 1978. Others hate it and its posh candle-lit atmosphere, cramped tables and cheesy music. Substantial fare, including couscous, fried tofu, cauliflower cheese. Menus at 75F and 105F.

Kootchi, 40 rue du Cardinal-Lemoine; ☎01.44.07.20.56 (M⁰ Cardinal-Lemoine). Closed Sun. A well-regarded Afghan restaurant, with pretty good prices: 55F menu at lunchtime, 98F in the evening.

Mavrommatis, 42 rue Daubenton; ☎01.43.31.17.17 (M⁰ Censier-Daubenton). Closed Mon. A sophisticated Greek restaurant, quite expensive (lunchtime menu 120F), but you are definitely tasting Greek food at its best.

La Petite Légume, 36 rue Boulangers (M° Jussieu). Mon–Sat noon–2.30pm & 7.30–10pm. This is a health-food grocery that doubles as a vegetarian restaurant, serving quality ingredients in a variety of *plats* for around 58F.

Les Quatre et Une Saveurs, 72 rue du Cardinal-Lemoine; ☎01.43.26.88.80 (M° Cardinal-Lemoine). Tues–Sat till 10pm. Inventive high-class macrobiotic vegetarian food. 120F or 130F menu includes coffee.

Student restaurants at 8bis rue Cuvier (M° Jussieu), 31 av Georges-Bernanos (M° Port-Royal); rue de Santeuil (M° Censier-Daubenton) & 12 place du Panthéon (M° Cardinal-Lemoine).

Tashi Delek, 4 rue des Fossés-St-Jacques; ☎01.43.26.55.55 (RER Luxembourg). Mon–Sat noon & eve until 10.30pm; closed Aug. An enjoyable Tibetan restaurant run by refugees, where you can eat for as little as 52F at lunchtime and 64F in the evening.

6ᵉ arrondissement

Bars and cafés

L'Alsace à Paris, 9 place St-André-des-Arts; ☎01.43.26.21.48 (M° St-Michel). A very busy and well-worn brasserie, with menus at 119F and 169F – but also delicious and cheap *tartes flambées* like thin pizzas that you can take away.

L'Assignat, 7 rue Guénégaud (M° Pont-Neuf). Mon–Sat 7.30am–8.30pm, food noon–3.30pm; closed July. Zinc counter, bar stools, bar football and young regulars from the nearby art school in an untouristy café close to quai des Augustins. 27F for a sandwich and a glass of wine.

Chez Georges, 11 rue des Canettes (M° Mabillon). Tues–Sat noon–2am; closed July 14–Aug 15. Situated in a narrow street off place St-Sulpice, this is an attractive wine bar in the spit-on-the-floor mode, with its old shop front still intact.

La Closerie des Lilas, 171 bd du Montparnasse (M° Port-Royal). Daily noon–1.30am. The smartest, artiest, classiest Montparnasse café, with excellent cocktails for around 60F. The tables are name-plated after celebrated former habitués (Verlaine, Mallarmé, Lenin, Modigliani, Léger, Strindberg). Very expensive restaurant; brasserie meals for under 140F; resident pianist.

Les Deux Magots, 170 bd St-Germain (M° St-Germain-des-Prés). Daily 6.30am–1.30am; closed one week in Jan. Right on the cnr of place St-Germain-des-Prés, it too owes its reputation to the intellos of the Left Bank, past and present. In summertime it picks up a lot of foreigners seeking the exact location of the spirit of French culture, and buskers galore play to the packed terrace. Come early for an expensive but satisfying 75F breakfast.

Le 10, 10 rue de l'Odéon (M° Odéon). Daily 6.30pm–2am. The beer here is very cheap, which is why it attracts youth, particularly foreigners. Small dark bar with old posters, a jukebox, and a lot of chatting-up.

Le Flore, 172 bd St-Germain (M° St-Germain-des-Prés). Daily 7am–1.30am. The great rival and immediate neighbour of *Les Deux Magots*, with a very similar clientele. Sarte, De Beauvoir, Camus and Marcel Carné used to hang out here.

Le Mazet, 60 rue St-André-des-Arts (M° Odéon). Mon–Thurs 10am–2am, Fri & Sat till 3.30am; closed Sun; happy hour 5–8pm A well-known hang-out for buskers (with a lock-up for their instruments) and heavy drinkers. For an evil concoction, try a *bière brûlée* – it's flambéed with gin. Small glass beer 20F, cocktails 49F.

La Paillote, 45 rue Monsieur-le-Prince (RER Luxembourg/M° Odéon). Mon–Sat 9pm–dawn; closed Aug. *The* late-night bar for jazz fans, with one of the best collections of recorded jazz in the city. Soft drinks start from 30F.

La Palette, 43 rue de Seine (M° Odéon). Mon–Sat 8am–2am. Once-famous Beaux-Arts student hang-out, now more for art dealers and their customers. The service can be uncivil, but the murals and every detail of the decor are superb, including, of course, a large selection of colourful, used palettes.

Pub Saint-Germain, 17 rue de l'Ancienne-Comédie (M° Odéon). Open 24hr. 26 draught beers and hundreds of bottles. Huge, crowded and expensive. Hot food at mealtimes, otherwise cold snacks. For a taste of "real" French beer, try *ch'ti* (patois for "northerner"), a *bière de garde* from the Pas-de-Calais. Live music nightly from 10pm.

La Taverne de Nesle, 32 rue Dauphine (M° Odéon). Mon–Thurs & Sun 9pm–4am, Fri & Sat till 5am. Vast selection of beers. Full of local night birds. Cocktails from 45F.

Restaurants

aux Charpentiers, 10 rue Mabillon; ☎01.43.26.30.05 (M⁰ Mabillon). Daily until 11pm; closed hols. A friendly, old-fashioned place belonging to the *Compagnons des Charpentiers* (Carpenters' Guild), with appropriate decor of roof-trees and tie beams. Traditional *plats du jour* are their forte, for about 75F. Around 200F à la carte; lunch menu at 120F.

Lipp, 151 bd St-Germain (M⁰ St-Germain-des-Prés). Daily until 12.30am; closed mid-July to mid-Aug. A 1900s brasserie, and one of the best-known establishments on the Left Bank; haunt of the very successful and very famous. *Plat du jour* 100–115F; no reservations, so be prepared to wait.

Le Muniche, 7 rue St-Benoît; ☎01.42.61.12.70 (M⁰ St-Germain-des-Prés). Daily noon–2am. A crowded old-style brasserie with an oyster bar, mirrors and theatre posters on the walls, serving classic French brasserie fare: seafood, *choucroute*, leg of lamb. Menus at 98F and 149F; *carte* 180F.

Orestias, 4 rue Grégoire-de-Tours; ☎01.43.54.62.01 (M⁰ Odéon). Mon–Sat lunch & eve until 11.30pm. A mixture of Greek and French cuisine. Good helpings and very cheap – with a menu at 46F (weekdays only until 8pm).

Le Petit Saint-Benoît, 4 rue St-Benoît; ☎01.42.60.27.92 (M⁰ St-Germain-des-Prés). Mon–Fri noon–2.30pm & 7–10.30pm. A simple, genuine and very appealing local for the neighbourhood's chattering classes. Serves solid, traditional fare in a brown-stained, aproned atmosphere. Menu at 130F.

Le Petit Zinc, 11 rue St-Benoit; ☎01.42.61.20.60 (M⁰ St-Germain-des-Prés). Daily noon–2am. Excellent traditional dishes, especially seafood, in stunning Art-Nouveau style premises (built thirty years ago). Not cheap – menu 169F, seafood platter 450F for two.

Polidor, 41 rue Monsieur-le-Prince; ☎01.43.26.95.34 (M⁰ Odéon). Mon–Sat until 12.30am, Sun until 11pm. A traditional bistrot, open since 1845, whose visitors' book, they say, boasts more of history's big names than all the glittering palaces put together. Not as cheap as it was in James Joyce's day, but good food and great atmosphere. Lunches at 55F during the week, and an excellent 100F evening menu.

Le Procope, 13 rue de l'Ancienne-Comédie; ☎01.40.46.79.00 (M⁰ Odéon). Daily noon–1am. The first establishment to serve coffee in Paris. Since it opened in 1686 it has retained its reputation as the place for powerful intellectuals. Good 109F menu (up to 8pm) and 123F with wine included after 11pm. At other times you won't see any change out of 200F.

Restaurant des Beaux-Arts, 11 rue Bonaparte; ☎01.43.26.92.64 (M⁰ St-Germain-des-Prés). Daily lunch & eve until 10.45pm. The traditional hang-out of Beaux Arts students. The choice is wide, portions are generous and queues are long in high season. The atmosphere is generally good, though the waitresses can get pretty tetchy. Menu at 79F including wine.

Student restaurants at 8bis rue de l'Eperon (M⁰ Odéon); 46 rue de Vaugirard (RER Luxembourg/M⁰ Mabillon) and 21 rue d'Assas (M⁰ Port-Royal/Notre-Dame-des-Champs).

7e arrondissement

Bars and cafés

Café du Museé d'Orsay, 1 rue Bellechasse (RER Musée-d'Orsay/M⁰ Solférino). Tues–Sun 11am–5pm. Superb views over the Seine in the museum's magnificent rooftop café. Snacks and drinks. Quick and friendly service.

Le Poch'tron, 25 rue de Bellechasse (M⁰ Solférino). Mon–Fri 9am–10.30pm. With a fine selection of wines by the glass, this is an excellent place to revive yourself after visiting the museums in the arrondissement. Also serves lunch and dinner, main dishes at around 70F.

Restaurants

au Babylone, 13 rue de Babylone; ☎01.45.48.72.13 (M⁰ Sèvres-Babylone). Mon–Sat lunch only; closed Aug. Lots of old-fashioned charm and culinary basics like *rôti de veau* and steak, plus wine on the 90F menu.

Le Bourdonnais, 113 av La Bourdonnais; ☎01.47.05.47.06 (M⁰ École-Militaire). Daily noon–2.30pm & 8–11pm. A gem of a restaurant and a high-class one at that. À la carte costs upwards of 400F, but there's a superb midday menu including wine for 240F, and an evening menu at 320F.

Chez Germaine, 30 rue Pierre-Leroux; ☎01.42.73.28.34 (M⁰ Duroc/Vaneau). Closed Sun, Sat pm & Aug. A simple, tiny and unbelievably cheap restaurant, with a midday 49F menu and evening 65F menu, including wine; the *carte* costs up to about 90F.

8ᵉ arrondissement
Bars and cafés

Barry's, 9 rue Duras (Mᵒ Champs-Élysées-Clemenceau). Mon–Sat 11am–3pm. Salads, snacks and sandwiches for under 30F in a tiny street behind the Élysée palace.

Le Fouquet's, 99 av des Champs-Élysées (Mᵒ George-V). Daily till 1.30am. Such a well-established watering hole for stars of the stage and screen, politicians, newspaper editors and advertising barons, that it's now been classified as a "Monument Historique". You pay dearly to sit in the deep leather armchairs, and as for the restaurant don't expect any change from 300F.

Musée Jacquemart-André, 158 bd Haussmann; ☎01.45.62.11.59 (Mᵒ St-Philippe-du-Roule/Miromesnil). Daily 11am–6pm. A sumptuously appointed *salon de thé* in a nineteenth-century palazzo, with salads at 57–85F, a lunch *formule* at 86F and a popular weekend brunch for 130F; museum ticket not needed.

Restaurants

aux Amis du Beaujolais, 28 rue d'Artois; ☎01.45.63.92.21 (Mᵒ George-V/St-Philippe-du-Roule). Mon–Sat noon–3pm & 6.30–9pm; closed middle two weeks of July. If you can fathom the hand-written menu, you'll find good traditional French stews and sautéed steaks, and Beaujolais. Around 150F.

Dragons Élysées, 11 rue de Berri; ☎01.42.89.85.10 (Mᵒ George-V). Daily 11am–3pm & 7–11pm. The Chinese-Thai cuisine encompasses dim sum, curried seafood and baked mussels, but the overriding attraction is the extraordinary decor. Beneath a floor of glass tiles water runs from pool to pool inhabited by exotic fish. 80F menu, 200F Thai seafood menu, carte 250F.

Yvan, 1bis rue J-Mermoz; ☎01.43.59.18.40 (Mᵒ Franklin-D-Roosevelt). Mon–Sat noon–2.30pm & 7pm–midnight; closed Sat lunch & Sun. Fish specialities and pigeon with polenta attract a stylish clientele. Extremely good food and menus from 168F.

9ᵉ arrondissement
Bars and cafés

Le Dépanneur, 27 rue Fontaine; ☎01.40.16.40.20 (Mᵒ Pigalle). Relaxed and fashionable all-night bar.

au Général Lafayette, 52 rue Lafayette (Mᵒ Le-Peletier/Cadet). Daily noon–4am. Old-time brasserie where all sorts rub shoulders trying the large variety of beers and wines on offer.

Le Grand Café Capucines, 4 bd des Capucines (Mᵒ Opéra). A favourite all-nighter with over-the-top Belle Époque decor and excellent seafood. Boulevard prices mean 20F for an espresso.

Restaurants

Chartier, 7 rue du Faubourg-Montmartre; ☎01.47.70.86.29 (Mᵒ Montmartre). Daily 11.30am–3pm & 6–10pm. Dark-stained woodwork, brass hat-racks, mirrors, waiters in long aprons – the original decor of a turn-of-the-century soup kitchen. Though crowded and rushed, it's worth a visit, and the food's not bad at all. Under 100F.

aux Deux-Théâtres, 18 rue Blanche, cnr rue Pigalle; ☎01.45.26.41.43 (Mᵒ Trinité). Daily 11.30am–2.30pm & 7–11pm. A distinctly bourgeois but welcoming and friendly place, whose 169F menu includes coffee and wine. The entrées and desserts are particularly good.

Le Relais Savoyard, 13 rue Rodier, cnr rue Agent-Bailly; ☎01.45.26.17.18 (Mᵒ Notre-Dame-de-Lorette/Anver/Cadet). Mon–Sat until 10pm; closed Aug. At the back of a very ordinary local bar; very good three-course meal for 72F, with a more sophisticated menu at 115F.

La Table d'Anvers, 2 place d'Anvers; ☎01.48.78.35.21 (Mᵒ Anvers). Noon–2.30pm & 7.30–11.30pm; closed Sat lunchtime and Sun. This is one of the city's best restaurants, whose chef is renowned for his original combinations. Lunch menus at 190F and 450F give a good taste of his skills. Evening menus at 250F and 550F; à la carte over 600F.

10ᵉ arrondissement
Bars and cafés

L'Atmosphère, 49 rue Lucien-Sampaix (Mᵒ Gare-de-l'Est). Tues–Fri 11am–2am, Sat & Sun 5.30pm–2am. Lively bar with food and occasional live music next to the canal St-Martin. The Hotel du Nord on the opposite bank was the setting for the eponymous film of 1938, and the name of this bar comes from a quote in the film.

China Express Nord, 3 bd Denain (M⁰ Gare du Nord). Daily 11am–10pm, closed Sun in winter. A good place to fill up on chicken and noodles, near the Gare du Nord. Dish of the day and Cantonese rice 30F.

Quasre Shireen, 14 rue Faubourg-St-Denis (M⁰ Strasbourg-St-Denis). Daily until midnight. Fast-food Indian cheapie, with rice and curry for 25F.

Le Réveil du Dixième, 35 rue du Château-d'Eau; ☎01.42.41.77.59 (M⁰ Château-d'Eau). Mon–Sat 7.15am–9pm. A welcoming, unpretentious wine bar serving glasses of wine and regional *plats* or a menu at 150F including wine.

Restaurants

de Bourgogne, 26 rue des Vinaigriers; ☎01.46.07.07.91 (M⁰ Jacques-Bonsergent). Mon–Fri lunch & eve until 10pm, Sat lunch only; closed Aug. Homely, old-fashioned restaurant; dinner around 80F.

Flo, 7 cours des Petites-Écuries; ☎01.47.70.13.59 (M⁰ Château-d'Eau). Daily until 1.30am. Handsome old-time brasserie where you eat elbow to elbow at long tables, served by waiters in ankle-length aprons. Excellent food and atmosphere; good-value menus, including wine, at 123F midday, and 169F eve with a 128F *formule* after 10pm.

Julien, 16 rue du Faubourg-St-Denis; ☎01.47.70.12.06 (M⁰ Strasbourg-St-Denis). Daily until 1.30am. Part of the same enterprise as *Flo* (above), with an even more splendid decor. Same good Alsatian cuisine at the same prices, and it's just as crowded.

Pooja, 91 passage Brady; ☎01.48.24.00.83 (M⁰ Strasbourg-St-Denis/ Château-d'Eau). Daily noon–2.30pm & 5–11pm; closed Mon lunchtime. Located in a passage that is Paris's own slice of the Indian subcontinent, authentic, good-value Indian cuisine. *Formules* at 45F lunch and 85F evening.

Terminus Nord, 23 rue de Dunkerque; ☎01.42.85.05.15 (M⁰ Gare du Nord). Daily until 1am. A magnificent 1920s brasserie where a full meal costs around 250F, but where you could easily satisfy your hunger with just a main course and still enjoy the decor for considerably less. 128F menu after 10pm.

11e arrondissement

Bars and cafés

Bar des Ferrailleurs, 18 rue de Lappe, 11ᵉ (M⁰ Bastille). Daily 5pm–2am. Dark and stylishly sinister, with rusting metal decor, an eccentric owner and fun wig-wearing bar staff. Relaxed friendly crowd.

Boca Chica, 58 rue de Charonne (M⁰ Ledu-Rollin). Daily 8am–2am. Popular tapas bar/bodega. Heaving by night and restful in the morning when you can get coffee and croissant for 10F, and a newspaper for an extra 5F. Colourful arty decor.

Café Charbon, 109 rue Oberkampf (M⁰ St-Maur/Parmentier). Daily 9am–2am. A very successful and attractive resuscitation of a turn-of-the-century café, drawing a young and trendy clientele. Nice *plats du jour* for 50–60F at lunchtime: lots of salads and vegetarian dishes. DJ Thurs, Fri & Sat 10pm–2am and live music on Sun from 8.30pm.

Café de l'Industrie, 16 rue St-Sabin (M⁰ Bastille). Noon–2am; closed Sat. Rugs on the floor around solid old wooden tables, miscellaneous objects on the walls, and a young, unpretentious crowd enjoying the comfortable lack of minimalism. One of the best Bastille addresses. *Plats du jour* from 48F.

Cithea, 114 rue Oberkampf, (M⁰ Parmentier). Daily 5pm–2am. Bar and venue next door to the *Café Charbon* for Afro funk, funk reggae, world beat, jazz fusion, etc on Thurs, Fri & Sat nights. Cocktails 45F. No admission charge for the music, but busy.

Fouquet's, 130 rue de Lyon (M⁰ Bastille). Mon–Fri till midnight; closed Sat & Sun midday. A smart, expensive café-restaurant underneath the new Opéra, sister establishment to the Champs-Elysées *Fouquet's*. But with perfect French courtesy they will leave you undisturbed for hours with a 15F coffee. Menu, including wine, at 170F.

Havanita Café, 11 rue de Lappe (M° Bastille). Daily 5pm–2am. Large, comfortable, Cuban-style bar with battered old leather sofa. Cocktails from 48F; happy hour 5–8pm.

Iguana, 15 rue de la Roquette; cnr rue Daval (M° Bastille). Daily 10am–2am. A place to be seen in. Decor of trellises, colonial fans, and a brushed bronze bar. The clientele studies *récherché* art reviews, and the coffee is excellent.

Jacques-Mélac, 42 rue Léon-Frot (M° Charonne). Mon–Fri 9am–10.30pm; closed weekends & Aug. Some way off the beaten track (between Père-Lachaise and place Léon-Blum) but a highly respected and very popular bistrot *à vins*, whose patron even makes his own wine – the solitary vine winds round the front of the shop. The food (*plats* around 70F, menu 130F), wines and atmosphere are great; no bookings.

SanZSanS, 49 rue du Faubourg-St-Antoine (M° Bastille). Daily 9am–2am. Gothic decor of red velvet, oil paintings and chandeliers, with a young clientele in the evening. Drinks reasonably priced; main courses for around 48F–65F, and there's always a vegetarian dish on offer.

Restaurants

Les Amognes, 243 rue du Faubourg-St-Antoine; ☎01.43.72.73.05 (M° Faidherbe-Chaligny). Noon–2.30pm & 7.30–10.30pm; closed Mon lunch, Sun & two weeks in Aug. Excellent, interesting food in a very popular place. Need to book. Menu at 190F, otherwise well over 250F.

Astier, 44 rue Jean-Pierre-Timbaud; ☎01.43.57.16.35 (M° Parmentier). Mon–Fri until 10pm; closed Aug, fortnight in May & fortnight at Christmas. Very successful and popular. Simple decor, unstuffy atmosphere, and fresh, refined food. Essential to book. Menu at 135F.

Bistrot du Peintre, 116 av Ledru-Rollin; ☎01.47.00.34.39 (M° Faidherbe-Chaligny). Mon–Sat 7am–2am, Sun 10am–8pm. Small tables jammed together beneath Art Nouveau frescoes and wood panelling. Traditional Parisian bistrot food with *plats du jour* from 62F.

Chez Omar, 47 Rue De Bretagne (M° Arts-et-Metiers). Closed Sun. Very popular North African resto in a nice old brasserie set with mirrors. Attracts a young crowd. Couscous 60–98F.

Les Cinq Points Cardinaux, 14 rue Jean-Macé; ☎01.43.71.47.22 (M° Faidherbe-Chaligny/ Charonne). Mon–Fri noon–2pm & 7–10pm; closed Aug. An excellent, simple, old-time bistrot, still mainly frequented by locals. Prices under 60F for lunch, and under 100F in the evening.

L'Homme Bleu, 57 rue Jean-Pierre-Timbaud (M° Parmentier). Mon–Sat evenings only till 10pm. Very affordable and pleasant Berber restaurant. Popular with students.

La Mansouria, 11 rue Faidherbe; ☎01.43.71.00.16 (M° Faidherbe-Chaligny). Tues–Sat lunchtime & evening until 11.30pm; closed 2 weeks in Aug. An excellent, elegant Moroccan restaurant. Superb couscous and tagines. Menu at 170F.

Thai Elephant, 43–45 rue de la Roquette; ☎01.47.00.42.00 (M° Bastille/Richard-Lenoir). Daily except Sat lunchtime till midnight. Superb Thai restaurant in tropical forest decor. Worth every centime. 150F midday menu, otherwise over 270F.

au Trou Normand, 9 rue Jean-Pierre-Timbaud; ☎01.48.05.80.23 (M° Filles-du-Calvaire/ Oberkampf/République). Mon–Fri lunch & eve until 9.30pm, Sat eve only; closed Aug. A small, totally unpretentious and very attractive local bistrot, serving good traditional food at knock-down prices. *Plat du jour* from 30F.

La Ville de Jagannath, 10 rue St Maur, 11 (M° St-Maur). Closed Mon lunch and Sun. Authentic vegetarian Indian food served in thalis. Lunch menu 50F. For a small corkage fee you can bring your own wine.

12ᵉ arrondissement

Bars and cafés

Le Baron Rouge, 1 rue Théophile-Roussel, cnr place d'Aligre market (M° Ledru-Rollin). Tues–Sat 10am–2pm & 5–9.30pm, Sun 10am–2pm only. Another popular and local bar. As well as the wines – around 16F per litre from the barrel to take away – it serves a few snacks of cheese, *foie gras,* and *charcuterie*.

Le Penty Bar, cnr place d'Aligre & rue Emilio-Castellar. Small, old-fashioned café making no concessions to 1990s sanitation, and still charging only 7F for a sit-down cup of coffee.

Restaurants

L'Ébauchoir, 43–45 rue de Cîteaux; ☎01.43.42.49.31 (M° Faidherbe-Chaligny). Mon–Sat until 11pm. Good bistrot fare in a sympathetic atmosphere; midday menu for 66F; *carte* 150F upwards. Best to book for the evening.

Le Gourmandise, 271 av Daumesnil; ☎01.43.43.94.41 (M° Porte-Dorée). Till 10.30pm; closed Mon lunch, Sun and first two weeks Aug. Superb and original food with a good menu at 165F.

ETHNIC RESTAURANTS IN PARIS

AFGHAN
Kootchi, 40 rue du Cardinal-Lemoine, 5e. See p.150.

AFRICAN AND NORTH AFRICAN
Le Berbère, 50 rue de Gergovie, 14e. North African. p.157.
Chez Omar, 47 Rue de Bretagne, 11e. p.155.
Fouta Toro, 3 rue du Nord, 18e. Senegalese. p.160.
L'Homme Bleu, 57 rue Jean-Pierre-Timbaud, 11e. Berber. p.155.
La Mansouria, 11 rue Faidherbe-Chaligny, 11e. Moroccan. p.155.
N'Zadette M'Foua, 152 rue du Château, 14e. Congolese. p.158.
au Port de Pidjiguiti, 28 rue Étex, 18e. Guinea-Bissau. p.160
Le Quincampe, 78 rue Quincampoix, 3e. Moroccan. p.148.

GREEK
Mavrommatis, 42 rue Daubenton, 5e. p.150.
Orestias, 4 rue Grégoire-de-Tours, 6e. p.152.

INDIAN
La Ville de Jagannath, 10 rue St Maur, 11e. p.155.

INDO-CHINESE
Blue Elephant, 43–45 rue de la Roquette, 11e. p.155.
Chieng-Maï, 12 rue Frédéric-Sauton, 5e. Thai. p.150.
Dragons Élysées, 11 rue de Berri, 8e. Chinese and Thai. p.153.
Foyer du Vietnam, 80 rue Monge, 5e. Vietnamese. p.150.
Lao Siam, 49 rue de Belleville, 20e. Thai and Laotian. p.161.
Lao-Thai, 128 rue de Tolbiac; 13e. Thai and Laotian. p.157.

Le Pacifique, 35 rue de Belleville, 20e. Chinese. p.161.
Pho-Dong-Huong, 14 rue Louis-Bonnet, 20e. Vietnamese. p.161.
Phuong Hoang, Terrasse des Olympiades, 52 rue du Javelot, 13e. Vietnamese, Thai and Singaporean. p.157.
Taï Yen, 5 rue de Belleville, 20e. Chinese. p.162.
Thai Elephant, 43–45 rue de la Roquette, 11e. p.155.
Thuy Huon and Tricotin, Kiosque de Choisy, 15 av de Choisy, 13e. Thai, Chinese and Cambodian. p.157.

ITALIAN
Da Attilio, 21 rue Cronstadt, 15e. p.158.
Rittal et Courts, 1 rue des Envierges; 20e. p.161.

JAPANESE
Foujita, 41 rue St-Roch, 1er. p.147.

JEWISH
Goldenberg's, 7 rue des Rosiers, 4e. p.149.

KURDISH
Dilan, 13 rue Mandar, 2e. p.147.

LEBANESE
aux Saveurs du Liban, 11 rue Eugène-Jumin, 19 e, p. 161.
La Taverne du Nil, 9 rue du Nil, 2e· p.147.

POLISH
Pitchi-Poï, 7 rue Caron, 4e. p.150.

TIBETAN
Tashi Delek, 4 rue des Fossés-St-Jacques, 5e. p.151.

WEST INDIAN
Le Marais-Cage, 8 rue de Beauce, 3e. p.148.

13ᵉ arrondissement

Bars and cafés

La Folie en Tête, 33 rue Butte-aux-Cailles (Mᵒ Place-d'Italie/Corvisart). Mon–Sat 5pm–2am. Cheap beer, sandwiches and midday *plat du jour*. Occasional concerts and solidarity events. A very warm and laid-back address.

Le Merle Moqueur, 11 rue Butte-aux-Cailles (Mᵒ Place-d'Italie/Corvisart). Daily 9pm–1am. Old-time co-op still going strong and still popular, with live rock some nights.

Restaurants

Auberge Etchegorry, 41 rue Croulebarbe; ☎01.44.08.83.51 (Mᵒ Gobelins). Mon–Sat till 10.30pm. A former *guinguette* on the banks of the Biévre, this Basque restaurant has preserved an old-fashioned atmosphere of relaxed conviviality, and the food's good too. Menus from 130F.

Chez Gladines, 30 rue des Cinq-Diamants; ☎01.45.80.70.10 (Mᵒ Corvisart). Daily 9am–2am. This small corner bistrot is always welcoming. Excellent wines and dishes from the southwest; the mashed/fried potato is a must and goes best with *magret de canard*. 60F lunch menu, around 120F à la carte.

Lao-Thai, 128 rue de Tolbiac; ☎01.44.24.28.10 (Mᵒ Tolbiac). Daily except Wed 11.30am–2.30pm & 7–11pm. Big glass-fronted resto on a busy interchange. Finely spiced Thai and Laotian food, with coconut, ginger and lemongrass flavours. Around 120F.

Phuong Hoang, Terrasse des Olympiades, 52 rue du Javelot; ☎01.45.84.75.07 (Mᵒ Tolbiac; take the escalator up from rue Tolbiac). Mon–Fri noon–3pm & 7–11.30pm. Vietnamese, Thai and Singapore specialities on lunch menus at 50F and 70F; *carte* 100–150F. If it's full or doesn't take your fancy, try *Le Le Lai* or *New Chinatown* nearby.

Student restaurant at 105 bd de l'Hôpital (Mᵒ St-Marcel).

Le Temps des Cerises, 18–20 rue Butte-aux-Cailles; ☎01.45.89.69.48 (Mᵒ Place-d'Italie/Corvisart). Mon–Fri noon–2pm & 7.30–11pm, Sat 7.30–11pm. A well-established workers' co-op with elbow-to-elbow seating and a different daily choice of imaginative dishes. 58F lunch menu and evening menus starting at 78F.

Thuy Huong & Tricotin, Kiosque de Choisy, 15 av de Choisy; ☎01.45.86.87.07 or 01.45.84.74.44 (Mᵒ Porte-de-Choisy). Daily except Thurs noon–2.30pm & 7–10.30pm. *Thuy Huong* is in the inner courtyard of this Chinese shopping centre and is more of a café. *Tricotin* has two restaurants, visible from the avenue; no. 1 specializes in Thai dishes, no. 2 in the other Asiatic cuisines. Not easy to work out what's on the menu (*méduse*, by the way, is jellyfish), but you can depend on the dim sum, the duck dishes and the Vietnamese rice pancakes. Around 100F, or 80F at *Thuy Huong*.

14ᵉ arrondissement

Bars and cafés

L'Entrepôt, 7–9 rue Francis-de-Pressensé (Mᵒ Pernety). Mon–Sat noon–midnight. Cinema with a spacious café; 77F midday menu, 150F à la carte in the evening.

Mustangs, 84 bd du Montparnasse (Mᵒ Montparnasse-Bienvenue). Daily 9am–5am. Young crowd and happy atmosphere. A good place to finish up the evening after nightclubbing in St-Germain. Tex-Mex food, cocktails and beers.

La Pause Gourmande, 27 rue Campagne-Première (Mᵒ Raspail). Mon–Fri 8.30am–7pm, Sat 8.30am–3pm. Delicious salads and savoury and sweet *tartes* from 28F.

Le Rallye, 6 rue Daguerre (Mᵒ Denfert-Rochereau). Tues–Sat until 8pm; closed Aug. A good place to recover from the Catacombs or Montparnasse cemetery. The patron offers a bottle for tasting; gulping the lot would be considered bad form. Good cheese and *saucisson*.

Restaurants

Aquarius 2, 40 rue Gergovie; ☎01.45.41.36.88 (Mᵒ Pernety). Mon–Sat noon–2.15pm & 7–10.30pm. Imaginative vegetarian meals served with proper Parisian bustle. 60F menu midday.

Le Berbère, 50 rue de Gergovie; ☎01.45.42.10.29 (Mᵒ Pernety). Daily lunchtime & evening until 10pm. Very unprepossessing decor-wise, but serves wholesome, unfussy and cheap North African food. Couscous from 60F.

Bergamote, 1 rue Nièpce; ☎01.43.22.79.47 (Mᵒ Pernety). Tues–Sat lunchtime & evening until 11pm; closed Aug. A small, sympathetic bistrot in a quiet, ungentrified street off rue de l'Ouest. Only about 10 tables; book at weekends. 98F *formule* at lunchtime, 125F in the evening; *carte* around 160F.

La Coupole, 102 bd du Montparnasse; ☎01.43.20.14.20 (Mᵒ Vavin). Daily 7.30–10.30am & noon–2am. The largest and perhaps most famous and enduring arty-chic Parisian hang-out for dining, dancing and debate. After 11pm, menu at 119F including wine, or *carte* from 170F. Dancing 3–7pm weekends (Sat 60F, Sun 80F), Fri & Sat 9.30pm–4am (90F).

N'Zadette M'Foua, 152 rue du Château; ☎01.43.22.00.16 (Mᵒ Pernety). Daily 7pm–2am. A small Congolese restaurant, with tasty dishes such as *maboké* (meat or fish baked in banana leaves). Reservations required at weekends. Menu at 85F, à la carte around 120F.

au Rendez-Vous des Camionneurs, 34 rue des Plantes; ☎01.45.40.43.36 (Mᵒ Alésia). Mon–Fri lunchtime & 6–9.30pm; closed Aug. No lorry drivers any more, but good food for under 100F; menu at 72F and a quarter of wine for under 15F. Wise to book.

La Route du Château, 123 rue du Château; ☎01.43.20.09.59 (Mᵒ Pernety). Tues–Sat lunchtime & evening until 12.30am, Mon lunchtime only; closed Aug. An old-fashioned bistrot atmosphere, with linen tablecloths and a rose on your table. The food is beautifully prepared and cooked. Menus at 85F and 148F.

Student restaurants at 13/17 rue Dareau (Mᵒ St-Jacques) and in the Cité Universitaire (RER Cité Universitaire).

15ᵉ arrondissement

Bars and cafés

au Roi du Café, 59 rue Lecourbe (Mᵒ Volontaires/Sèvres-Lecourbe). Daily till 2am. An oasis in the midst of the 15ᵉ. Traditional café with a decor that hasn't changed much this century and a pleasant terrace albeit on a busy road.

Restaurants

Le Café du Commerce, 51 rue du Commerce; ☎01.45.75.03.27 (Mᵒ Émile-Zola). Daily noon–midnight. A two-storey restaurant that's been catering for *le petit peuple* for over a hundred years. Still varied, nourishing and cheap fare. *Plats du jour* 55–65F; *formules* 82F and 117F; *carte* around 145F.

Da Attilio, 21 rue Cronstadt; ☎01.40.43.91.90 (Mᵒ Convention/Porte-de-Vanves). Mon–Sat till 9.30pm. Close to the Parc Georges Brassens. Unprepossessing decor and run-of-the-mill food, but very friendly service and a great atmosphere. Different Italian specialities each day; *plats du jour* 50F.

L'Ostréade, 11 bd Vaugirard; ☎01.43.21.87.41 (Mᵒ Montparnasse). Daily 11.30am–5pm & 7–11pm. A seafood brasserie with tapas on a 89F *formule*, and excellent oysters. Around 175F for a full whack.

Sampieru Corsu, 12 rue de l'Amiral-Roussin (Mᵒ Cambronne). Mon–Fri lunchtimes & 7–9.30pm. Decorated with the posters and passionate declarations of international socialism, this restaurant has as its purpose the provision of meals for the homeless, unemployed and low-paid. The principle is that you pay what you can and it is left to your conscience how you settle the bill. The minimum requested is 45F for a three-course meal with wine. However poor you might feel, as a tourist in Paris you should be able to pay more. The restaurant only survives on the generosity of its supporters, and it's a wonderful place.

Student restaurant at 156 rue Vaugirard (Mᵒ Pasteur).

16ᵉ arrondissement

Bars and cafés

Totem, southern wing of the Palais de Chaillot, place du Trocadéro (Mᵒ Trocadéro). Daily noon–2am. Native American themed-restaurant but with some French traditional dishes thrown in; the 129F lunch menu isn't bad, but the views from the terrace are magnificent.

17ᵉ arrondissement

Bars and cafés

Bar Belge, 75 av de St-Ouen (Mᵒ Guy-Môquet). Mon–Sat 3.30pm–1am. Belgian beers and *moules frites* for 65F, *coq au vin* 70F and *poulet aux cèpes* 65F.

LATE NIGHT PARIS

For bars and brasseries in Paris to stay open after midnight is not at all unusual; the list below is of cafés and bars that remain open after 2am, and restaurants that are open beyond midnight. Note that the three **Drugstores**, at 133 av des Champs-Élysées and 1 av Matignon in the 8e, and 149 bd St-Germain in the 6e, stay open till 2am, with bars, restaurants, shops and tabacs.

BARS AND CAFÉS

Café des Phares, 7 place de la Bastille, west side, 4e. Daily 7am–4am. p.148.

La Champmeslé, 4 rue Chabanais, 2e. Till 4am Thurs–Sun. p.147

Le Dépanneur, 27 rue Fontaine, 9e. All-nighter. p.153.

au Général Lafayette, 52 rue Lafayette, 9e. Daily till 4am. p.153.

Le Grand Café Capucines, 4 bd des Capucines, 9e. All-nighter. p.153.

Le Mazet, 60 rue St-André-des-Arts, 6e. Mon–Thurs till 2am; Fri & Sat till 3.30am. p.151.

Mustangs, 84 Boulevard de Montparnasse 14e. Till 5am. p. 157

La Paillote, 45 rue Monsieur-le-Prince, 6e. Mon–Sat 9pm–dawn.p.151.

Polly Magoo, 11 rue St-Jacques, 5e. All-nighter, closing 4–5am. p.150.

Pub Saint-Germain, 17 rue de l'Ancienne-Comédie, 6e. 24hr. p.151.

Le Quetzal, 10 rue de la Verrerie, 4e. Mon–Thurs 2pm–4am, Fri–Sun 5pm–5am. p.149.

Le Sous-Bock, 49 rue St-Honoré, 1er. Till 5am. p.146.

La Taverne de Nesle, 32 rue Dauphine, 6e. Mon–Thurs & Sun 9pm–4am, Fri & Sat till 5am. p.151.

RESTAURANTS

Bofinger, 3–7 rue de la Bastille, 4e. Daily until 1am. p.148.

Brasserie Balzar, 49 rue des Écoles, 5e. Till 1am. p.150.

Chez Ginette, 101 rue Caulaincourt, 18e. Till 2am. p.160.

Chez Gladines, 30 rue des Cinq-Diamants, 13e. Till 2.00am. p.157.

La Coupole, 102 bd du Montparnasse, 14e. Till 2am. p.158.

Le Dauphin, 167 rue St-Honoré, 1er. June–Oct till 12.30am. p.147.

Flo, 7 cours des Petites-Écuries, 10e. Till 1.30am. p.154.

Fouta Toro, 3 rue du Nord, 18e. Till 1am. p.160.

Goldenberg's, 7 rue des Rosiers, 4e. Daily until 2am. p.149

Julien, 16 rue du Faubourg-St-Denis, 10e. Till 1.30am. p.154.

Lipp, 151 bd St-Germain, 6e. Daily till 12.30am. p.152.

Le Muniche, 7 rue St-Benôit, 6e. Daily till 2am. p.152.

N'Zadette, M'Foua, 152 rue due Château, 14e. Till 2am. p.158.

Le Pacifique, 35 rue de Belleville, 20e. Daily till 1am. p.161.

Le Petit Zinc, 11 rue St-Benôit, 6e. Daily till 2am. p.152.

Au Pied de Cochon, 6 rue Coquillière, 1er. 24hr. p.147.

Polidor, 41 rue Monsieur-le-Prince, 6e. Mon–Sat till 12.30am. p.152.

Le Procope, 13 rue de l'Ancienne-Comédie, 6e. Daily till 1am. p.152.

La Route du Château, 123 rue du Château, 14e. Till 12.30am. p.158.

Taï Yen, 5 rue de Belleville, 20e. Till 2am. p.162.

Terminus Nord, 23 rue de Dunkerque, 10e. Till 1.00am. p.154.

Au Virage Lepic, 61 rue Lepic, 18e. Till 2am. p.160.

Chamignon, 64 rue Batignolles (Mo Rome/Place-de-Clichy). Daily except Weds till 8pm. A local boulangerie on one side and an old habitués café on the other where you can sit and snack on quiche, sandwiches and pastries. Tables on the street in the summer.

Restaurants

Joy in Food, 2 rue Truffaut; ☎01.43.87.96.79 (M° Place-Clichy). Mon–Sat noon–2.30pm. Minuscule veggie place, with its mind on higher things: meditation sessions at 8pm Mon–Sat. Good, inexpensive food in an attractive atmosphere; 71–100F.

La P'tite Lili, 8 rue des Batignolles; %01.45.22.54.22 (M° Place-Clichy). Noon–2.30pm & 7–9.30pm. Simple and small menu but carefully prepared and delicious home-made traditional desserts.

Sangria, 13bis rue Vernier; ☎01.45.74.78.74 (M° Porte-de-Champerret). For 80F at midday and 99F in the evening you can help yourself to starters and wine in addition to enjoying three other courses. Very popular and crowded.

18ᵉ arrondissement

Bars and cafés

La Petite Charlotte, 24 rue des Abbesses (M° Abbesses). Tues–Sun till 8pm. Crêpes, pâtisseries and 58F *formule* on sunny tables.

Le Refuge, cnr rue Lamarck & the steps of rue de la Fontaine-du-But (M° Lamarck-Caulaincourt). Mon–Sat till 8.30pm. A gentle café stop with a long view west down rue Lamarck to the country beyond.

Le Sancerre, 35 rue des Abbesses (M° Abbesses). Daily 7am–2am. A fashionable hang-out for the young and trendy of all nationalities on the southern slopes of Montmartre.

Restaurants

L'Assiette, 78 rue Labat; ☎01.42.59.06.63 (M° Château-Rouge). Closed Wed eve & Sun. A bit out of the way, but very friendly, with delicious *champignons forestières, chocolate charlotte*, and a surprising beetroot sorbet starter. An extraordinarily good-value 98F menu.

Chez Ginette, 101 rue Caulaincourt; ☎01.46.06.01.49 (M° Lamarck-Caulaincourt). Mon–Sat lunchtime & evening till 2am; closed Aug. Good, uncomplicated food (*blanquette de veau, boeufgros sel*, etc) in a traditional "Parisian" environment, with live piano and dancing. Noisy and fun. *Carte* around 130F. Wise to book, especially at weekends.

Fouta Toro, 3 rue du Nord; ☎01.42.55.42.73 (M° Marcadet-Poissonniers). Daily except Tues 7.30pm–1am. A tiny, crowded, welcoming Senegalese diner in a very scruffy alley northeast of Montmartre. No more than 70F all-in. Be prepared for a wait unless you come at 8pm or after 10.30pm.

au Grain de Folie, 24 rue La Vieuville; ☎01.42.58.15.57 (M° Abbesses). Daily 12.30–2.30pm & 7–11.30pm. Tiny, simple, cheap and friendly, with just the sort of traditional atmosphere that you would hope for from Montmartre. Vegetarian. Soup and tart 60F, menu 100F.

Marie-Louise, 52 rue Championnet; ☎01.46.06.86.55 (M° Simplon). Tues–Sat lunchtime & evening until 10pm; closed Aug. A bit of a trek north, but the excellent traditional French cuisine at this renowned restaurant is definitely worth the journey. Menu at 130F, otherwise around 180F.

au Port de Pidjiguiti, 28 rue Étex; ☎01.42.26.71.77 (M° Guy-Môquet). Tues–Sun lunchtime & eve until 11pm; closed Jan. Very pleasant atmosphere and excellent food. It is run by a village in Guinea-Bissau, whose inhabitants take turns in staffing the restaurant; the proceeds go to the village. Good-value wine list. Menu 100F; à la carte around 120F.

au Virage Lepic, 61 rue Lepic; ☎01.42.52.46.79 (M° Blanche/Abbesses). Daily except Tues 7pm–2am. Simple, traditional fare in a noisy, friendly atmosphere created by the singers – in the French/Parisian idiom. Small, smoky and very enjoyable. Around 100F.

19ᵉ arrondissement

Restaurants

Café de la Musique, 213 av Jean-Jaures (M° Porte-de-Pantin). Daily till 2am. Part of the Cité de la Musique, this café with a popular terrace, was designed by the Cité architect Portzamparc and exudes sophistication, discretion and comfort, but be prepared to pay over the odds for a coffee.

Le Rendez-vous des Quais, 10 Quai de la Seine (M° Jaurès/Stalingrad). Daily 11.30am–12.30am. Attached to the MK2 art-house cinema, the outside tables of this café/brasserie sit right on the banks of the Bassin de la Villette providing a relaxing spot for a refreshment before or after the canal cruises which depart opposite.

GOURMET RESTAURANTS OF PARIS

If you're feeling flush, have something to celebrate or simply fancy a superb meal out, there are, of course, some really spectacular Parisian restaurants. The relentlessly creative **Pierre Gagnaire**, currently considered the most exciting chef in Paris, has a restaurant that bears his name at 6 rue Balzac, 8ᵉ (☎01.44.35.18.25). The other greats include: *Lucas Carton* (9 place de la Madeleine, 8ᵉ; ☎01.42.65.22.90) with splendid Art Noveau decor and chef Alain Senderens; *Taillevent* (15 rue Lamennais, 8ᵉ; ☎01.45.61.12.90); *Les Ambassadeurs* (in the *Hôtel Crillon*, 10 place de la Concorde, 8ᵉ; ☎01.44.71.16.16); *Ledoyen* (1 av Dutuit, 8ᵉ; ☎01.47.42.35.98), headed by a Flemish woman chef, Ghislaine Arabian; *L'Ambroisie* (9 place des Vosges, 4ᵉ; ☎01.42.78.51.45) and *Guy Savoy* (18 rue Troyon, 17ᵉ; ☎01.43.80.40.61). At midday during the week you may find menus of around 300F–395F; *prixe fixe* menus ranges from 480F to 1500F; and there's no limit on the amount you can pay for beautiful wines.

aux Saveurs du Liban, 11 rue Eugène-Jumin (Mᵒ Porte-de Pantin). Mon–Sat 11am–11pm. Excellent authentic Lebanese food at this tiny restaurant in a lively local street not far from the Parc de la Villette. Very good value with *plats* for 30F and wine for 9F a glass; sandwiches from 18F to take away; 40F lunch-time formula.

20ᵉ arrondissement

Bars and cafés

Le Baratin, 3 rue Jouye-Rouve (Mᵒ Pyrénées). Tues–Fri 11am–1am, Sat 6pm–1am. Friendly, unpretentious bistrot à vins in a run-down area with a good mix of people. Fine selection of lesser-known wines and whiskies. Midday menu 65F.

Bistrot Cave des Envierges, 11 rue des Envierges (Mᵒ Pyrénées). Wed–Fri noon–midnight, Sat & Sun noon–8pm. Another bistrot à vins purveying good-quality, lesser-known wines to connoisseurs. An attractive bar – though more a place to taste and buy wine than eat – in a great location above the Parc de Belleville.

La Flèche d'Or, 102bis rue de Bagnolet, cnr rue des Pyrénées (Mᵒ Alexandre-Dumas). Daily 10am–2am. A large, lively café attracting the biker, arty, post-punkish Parisian young. The decor is *très destroy*, ie railway sleepers and a sawn-off bus front hanging from the ceiling, and the building itself is the old Bagnolet station on the *petite ceinture* railway that encircled the city until around thirty years ago. It's a nightly venue for live World Music, pop, punk, ska, fusion and chanson, and the reasonably priced food also has a multicultural slant.

Rittal et Courts, 1 rue des Envierges; ☎01.46.36.51.59 (Mᵒ Pyrénées). Tues–Sat noon–2am, Sun noon-7pm. Mellow bar/café/trattoria which specializes in showing "Courts Metrages" - short films – Tues–Sun 3.30–7pm, Sat midnight–2am. It's in an unbeatable situation overlooking the Parc de Belleville: get a pavement table on a summer evening and you'll have the best restaurant view in Paris. The Italian food is tasty and affordable, with a large pasta selection, including loads of vegetarian options; 50–90F.

Restaurants

La Fontaine aux Roses, 27 av Gambetta; ☎01.46.36.74.75 (Mᵒ Père-Lachaise). Tues–Sat till 10pm; closed Sun evening, Mon & Aug. Small, beautiful restaurant with first-rate menus: midday 120F and evenings 170F, both including kir royale, wine and coffee.

Lao Siam, 49 rue de Belleville; ☎01.40.40.09.68 (Mᵒ Belleville). Daily till 11pm. Extremely good Thai and Laotian food, popular with locals. Dishes 42F–60F.

Le Pacifique, 35 rue de Belleville; ☎01.42.49.66.80 (Mᵒ Belleville). Daily 11am–1am. A huge Chinese eating house with variable culinary standards but low prices. Main courses from 50F, 85F or 100F menu

Pho-Dong-Huong, 14 rue Louis-Bonnet; ☎01.43.57.42.81 (Mᵒ Belleville). Daily except Tues noon–10.30pm. Spotlessly clean Vietnamese resto, where all dishes are under 50F and come with piles of fresh green leaves. Spicy soups, crispy pancakes, but slow service.

aux **Rendez-Vous des Amis**, 10 av Père-Lachaise; ☎01.47.97.72.16 (Mº Gambetta). Mon–Sat noon–2.30pm; closed last week July to mid-Aug. Unprepossessing surroundings for very good, simple and satisfying family cooking. Main courses 45–78F; menu at 65F.

Taï Yen, 5 rue de Belleville; ☎01.42.41.44.16 (Mº Belleville). Daily 10am–2am. Admire the koi carps like embroidered satin cushions idling round their aquarium while you wait for the generous soups and steamed specialities of this Chinese restaurant. 65F menu, dishes from 49F.

Le Zéphyr, 1 rue Jourdain; ☎01.46.36.65.81 (Mº Jourdain). Mon–Sat till 11.30pm. A rather trendy but relaxed 1930s-style bistrot with menus at 69F and 130F.

Music and nightlife

The strength of the Paris **music scene** is its diversity – a reputation gained mainly from its absorption of immigrant and exile populations. The city has no rivals in Europe for the variety of **world music** to be discovered: Algerian, West and Central African, Caribbean and Latin American sounds are represented in force. **Rap** and **hip-hop** are fashionable both imported and home-grown, whilst the recent success in French **dance music** and DJs, although popular in France, has a bigger following abroad. Commercial French **popular music** is, on the whole, to be avoided; two bands worth listening to for their fascinating mix of styles are Mano Negra and Les Négresses Vertes. Recent success in the world of French dance music with groups such as Daft Punk and Air has been taken more seriously abroad than in France.

Jazz fans are in for a treat, with all styles from New Orleans to current experimental to be heard, although in most clubs expense is a real drawback to enjoyment. Admission charges are generally high, and when they're not levied there's usually a whacking charge for your first drink, and subsequent drinks don't come cheap.

Then there is the tradition of **chansons**, epitomized by the sublime Edith Piaf and developed to its greatest heights by Georges Brassens and the Belgian Jacques Brel. This music survives with Charles Aznavour still singing and younger singer-composers like Arlette Denis rejuvenating the tradition.

Nightlife recommendations – for **dance clubs and discos** – are to some extent incorporated with those for rock, world music and jazz, with which they merge. Separate sections, however, detail places that are mainly for dancing or which cater for a primarily gay or lesbian clientele. Bear in mind that some clubs operate very snooty door policies.

Classical music, as you might expect in this Neoclassical city, is alive and well and takes up twice the space of "jazz-pop-folk-rock" in the listings magazines. The **Paris Opéra**, with its two homes – the Opéra-Garnier and Opéra-Bastille – puts on a fine selection of opera and ballet. The need for advance reservations (except sometimes for the concerts held in churches) rather than the price is the major inhibiting factor here. If you're interested in the **contemporary** scene of Systems composition and the like, check out the Cité de la Musique auditorium at La Villette. At the end of the section are details of all the **stadium venues** for major events from heavy metal to opera.

On June 21 the Fête de la Musique sees live bands and free concerts of every kind of music throughout the city.

Information and tickets

For exhaustive listings of **what's on** in the city, there are the weekly guides, published on a Wednesday: (Web site: *www.pariscope.fr*), and *L'Officiel des Spectacles. Pariscope* is probably the easiest to find your way around, but since both are just listings, mainly in French with a bit of English and a minimum of comment, there is not much difference between them (*L'Officiel* is cheaper). The best places to get **tickets** for concerts, whether rock, jazz, chansons or classical, are: FNAC Forum des Halles, 1–5 rue Pierre-Lescot, 1ᵉʳ, ☎01.40.41.40.00; (Mº Chatelet-Les Halles); the FNAC Musique branches at

4 place de la Bastille, 12ᵉ (Mon, Tues, Thurs & Sat 10am–8pm, Wed & Fri 10am–10pm; Mᵒ Bastille), and 24 bd des Italiens, 9ᵉ (Mon–Sat 10am–midnight; Mᵒ Richelieu-Drouot/4-Septembre/Chaussée-d'Antin); or Virgin Megastore at 56–60 av des Champs-Élysées, 8ᵉ (Mᵒ Franklin-D-Roosevelt), and in the Carrousel du Louvre, beneath the Louvre, 1ᵉʳ (Mon–Thurs 10am–midnight, Fri & Sat 10am–1am, Sun 2pm–midnight; Mᵒ Palais-Royal/Musée-du-Louvre).

Music venues

Most of the **music venues** listed below are clubs. A few of them will have live music all week, but the majority host bands on just a couple of nights, usually Friday and Saturday, when admission prices are also hiked up. *La Locomotive, La Guinguette Pirate* and *Le Saint* are your best bets for a not-too-expensive good night out.

Mainly rock

La Cigale, 120 bd de Rochechouart, 18ᵉ; ☎01.42.23.15.15 (Mᵒ Pigalle). Music from 8.30pm. Rita Mitsouko, punk, indie, etc. An eclectic programming policy in an old-fashioned converted theatre, long a fixture on the Pigalle scene.

Le Divan du Monde, 75 rue des Martyrs, 18ᵉ; ☎01.44.92.77.66 (Mᵒ Notre-Dame-de-Lorette). Daily 7pm–5am. A new, youthful venue in a café whose regulars once included Toulouse-Lautrec. An eclectic, exciting programming policy. 50–80F for concerts.

Élysée Montmartre, 72 bd de Rochechouart, 18ᵉ; ☎01.44.92.45.45 (Mᵒ Anvers). An historic Montmartre nightspot, now dedicated to rock. Inexpensive and fun, it pulls in a young, excitable crowd. Around 80F. Mainly rock.

La Guinguette Pirate, Bateau quai de la Gare, 13ᵉ; ☎01.44..24.89.89 (Mᵒ Quai-de-la-Gare).Tues–Sat 9pm–2am. Beautiful barge, moored alongside the quay in front of the Bibliothèque Nationale, hosting funk, reggae, rock and folk concerts; 30F.

La Locomotive, 90 bd de Clichy, 18ᵉ; ☎01.53.41.88.88 (Mᵒ Blanche). Daily; Concerts start at 1am. Enormous high-tech nightclub with three dance floors: one for Techno; one for rock, heavy metal and concerts; and one for rap and funk. One of the most crowded and popular in the city. 60F week-days, 100F weekends, including one drink.

New Riverside, 7 rue Grégoire-de-Tours, 6ᵉ; ☎01.43.54.46.33 (Mᵒ Odéon). Daily 11pm–dawn. Good, friendly club playing rock and pop music in a sixteenth-century cellar. At weekends, break-fast included in admission price; and free admission for women weekdays and before midnight Fri & Sat. Otherwise, Mon–Thurs 70F, Fri, Sat & Sun 100F.

Rex Club, 5 bd Poissonnière, 2ᵉ; ☎01.42.36.83.98 (Mᵒ Montmartre). Tues–Sun 11pm–6am; some-times closed Sun & Mon. Separate rooms for the club (drum'n'bass and house) and the live music venue – rock, funk, soul, raï, rap. Concerts start around 8pm; 60–100F. Club from 11pm; 60–90F

Le Saint, 7 rue St-Séverin, 5ᵉ; ☎01.43.25.50.04 (Mᵒ St-Michel). Tues–Sun 11am–dawn. Good value, varied music played in an ancient cellar; popular with students. 50F including one drink Tues–Thurs, 80F weekends.

Mainly Latin and Caribbean

L'Escale, 15 rue Monsieur-le-Prince, 6ᵉ; ☎01.43.54.63.47 (Mᵒ Odéon). 11pm–4am. More Latin-American musicians must have passed through here than any other club. The dancing sounds, salsa mostly, are in the basement (disco on Wed), while on the ground floor every variety of South American music is given an outlet. Drinks 80F.

Mambo Club, 20 rue Cujas, 5ᵉ; ☎01.43.54.89.21 (Mᵒ St-Michel/Odéon). Wed–Sat 11pm–dawn, Sun 4pm–dawn for "themed *soirées*". Afro-Cuban and Antillais music in a seedy dive with people of all ages and nationalities. 110F admission in the evening, 80F during the day.

Bals musettes

Balajo, 9 rue de Lappe, 11ᵉ; ☎01.47.00.07.87 (Mᵒ Bastille). Mon, Fri & Sat 10pm–4.30am. The old-style music hall of *gai* but straight *Paris* – extravagant 1930s decor and vast dance floor. The music encompasses everything from mazurka to tango, cha-cha, twist, and the slurpy chansons of between the wars. Admission price is around 100F; free for women Mon 11.30pm–1am.

Chapelle des Lombards, 19 rue de Lappe, 11ᵉ; ☎01.43.57.24.24 (Mᵒ Bastille). Tues–Sat 10.30pm–dawn. This erstwhile *bal musette* still plays the occasional waltz and tango, but for the most part the music is salsa, reggae, steel drums, gwo-kâ, zouk, raï and the blues. The doormen are not too friendly and its renown as a pick-up joint means unabashed advances. Tues–Thurs 100F entry and first drink, Fri & Sat 120F.

Le Tango, 13 rue au Maire, 3ᵉ; ☎01.42.72.17.78 (Mᵒ Arts-et-Métiers). Fri, Sat & the eve of public hols only 11pm–dawn. The music is *musette* and jazzy Latin American: salsa, calypso and reggae. There's no vetting here and people dance with abandon to please themselves, not the adjudicators of style; it's also a prime pick-up joint. Admission Fri 40F, Sat 60F; drinks from 30F; obligatory cloakroom fee.

Mainly jazz

Le Baiser Salé, 58 rue des Lombards, 1ᵉʳ; ☎01.42.33.37.71 (Mᵒ Châtelet). 8am–5am. A bar downstairs and a small, crowded upstairs room with live music every night from 10pm – usually jazz, rhythm & blues, Latino-rock, reggae or Brazilian. 123F first drink includes charge for music.

Le Bilboquet, 13 rue St-Benoît, 6ᵉ; ☎01.45.48.81.84 (Mᵒ St-Germain). Mon–Sat 9pm–dawn. A rather smart, comfortable bar/restaurant with live jazz every night – local and international stars. Food served until 1am. The music starts at 10.45pm. No admission, but pricey drinks: 120F.

L'Eustache, 37 rue Berger, 1ᵉʳ; ☎01.40.26.23.20 (Mᵒ Châtelet-Les Halles). 11am–4am; Thurs, Fri & Sat live jazz 10.30pm–2am and cheap beer in this young and friendly Les Halles café – in fact, the cheapest good jazz in the capital.

Instants Chavirés, 7 rue Richard-Lenoir, Montreuil; ☎01.42.87.25.91 (Mᵒ Robespierre). Tues–Sat 8pm–1am; concerts at 9.30pm. Avant-garde jazz joint – no comforts – on the eastern edge of the city where musicians go to hear each other play. Admission 35–80F, depending on the celebrity of the band; drinks from 15F.

New Morning, 7–9 rue des Petites-Écuries, 10ᵉ; ☎01.45.23.51.41 (Mᵒ Château-d'Eau). 9pm–1.30am (concerts start around 10pm). This is the place where the big international names in jazz come to play. Blues and Latin, too. Admission around 110F.

Le Petit Journal, 71 bd St-Michel, 5ᵉ; ☎01.43.26.28.59 (RER Luxembourg). Mon–Sat 10pm–2am; closed Aug. A small, smoky bar with good, mainly French, traditional and mainstream sounds. First drink 100–150F.

Le Petit Journal Montparnasse, 13 rue du Commandant-Mouchotte, 14ᵉ; ☎01.43.21.56.70 (Mᵒ Montparnasse). Mon–Sat 9pm–2am. Under the *Hôtel Montparnasse*, and sister establishment to the above, with bigger visiting names, both French and international. First drink 100F.

Le Petit Opportun, 15 rue des Lavandières-Ste-Opportune, 1ᵉʳ; ☎01.42.36.01.36 (Mᵒ Châtelet-Les Halles). Tues–Sat 9pm–3am. Music from 11pm. Arrive early to get a seat for the live music in the dungeon-like cellar where the acoustics play strange tricks and you can't always see the musicians. Fairly eclectic policy and a crowd of genuine connoisseurs. First drink 100F.

Le Sunset, 60 rue des Lombards, 1ᵉʳ; ☎01.40.26.46.60 (Mᵒ Châtelet-Les Halles). Mon–Sat 8pm–4am. Restaurant upstairs, jazz club in the basement, featuring the best musicians – the likes of Alain Jeanmarie and Turk Mauró – and frequented by musicians in the wee small hours. Admission and first drink 50F–100F.

Théâtre Dunois, 108 rue du Chevaleret, 13ᵉ; ☎01.45.70.81.16 (Mᵒ Chevaleret). Daily from 7pm; closed July & Aug. Concerts Mon–Fri & Sun 8.30–11.30pm. Out of the way, but a very pleasant venue giving consistent support to free and experimental jazz. One of the few places in Paris to hear improvised music, as opposed to free jazz. Admission 70F, students 50F.

Utopia, 79 rue de l'Ouest, 14ᵉ; ☎01.43.22.79.66 (Mᵒ Pernety). Mon–Sat 10.30pm–dawn; closed Aug. No genius here, but good French blues singers interspersed with jazz and blues tapes, with a mainly young and studenty audience. Generally very pleasant atmosphere. Drinks from 50F.

Mainly chansons

Caveau des Oubliettes, 11 rue St-Julien-le-Pauvre, 5ᵉ; ☎01.43.54.94.97 (Mᵒ St-Michel). Fri & Sat 9pm–2am. French popular music of bygone times – Piaf and earlier – sung with exquisite nostalgia in the ancient prisons of Châtelet. Admission 70F, drinks from 20F.

Le Lapin Agile, 22 rue des Saules, 18e; ☎01.46.06.85.87 (Mº Lamarck-Caulaincourt). Tues–Sun 9pm–2am. Old haunt of Apollinaire, Utrillo and other Montmartre artists, some of whose pictures adorn the walls. Cabaret, poetry and chansons; you may be lucky enough to catch singer-composer Arlette Denis, who carries Jacques Brel's flame. Admission 130F including drink, students 90F.

Nightclubs and discos

Les Bains, 7 rue du Bourg-l'Abbé, 3e; ☎01.48.87.01.80 (Mº Étienne-Marcel). Daily midnight–dawn (Sun rock; Mon "disturbance of the peace"; Wed "disco inferno"). This is as posey as they come – an old Turkish bathhouse with plunge pool. The music is house, rap and funk, with occasional live (usually dross) bands. Admission 100F, fussy bouncers and expensive drinks.

La Casbah, 18–20 rue de la Forge-Royale, 11e; ☎01.43.71.04.39 (Mº Bastille). Daily 9pm–5am. Bar upstairs, dancing down. The outstanding feature of this rather fancy and exclusive place is the decor: beautiful, authentic stuff from Morocco – doors, furniture, plasterwork – matched by the *zouave* costumes of the waiters and waitresses. Around 100F, or 150F for a table.

El Globo, 8 bd Strasbourg, 10e; ☎01.42.41.55.70 (Mº Strasbourg-St-Denis). Sat, Sun & public hols 10pm–dawn. Currently very popular with Beaux Quartiers rebels, 10e arrondissement punks and all sorts. Lots of room to dance to international hits past and present. 1970s disco on Sat night. Admission 100F, drinks 50F, or 25F 11pm–midnight.

Flash Back, 37 rue Grégoire-de-Tours, 6e; ☎01.43.25.56.10 (Mº Mabillon). Tues–Sun 11am–dawn. Techno and commercial rock in a futuristic decor. Admission 70F.

Le Moloko, 26 rue Fontaine, 9e; ☎01.48.74.50.26 (Mº Blanche). Daily 9pm–6am. A new, fashionable and successful addition to the night scene, frequented by the young and gorgeous, the trendy and posey, all sorts. Jukebox instead of DJs, occasionally live music in the early evening. Drinks from 50F. Admission on Wed & Sat only 20F/40F.

Le Palace, 8 rue du Faubourg-Montmartre, 9e; ☎01.47.70.75.02 (Mº Montmartre). Daily 11pm–dawn. Packed every night with revellers in their best party gear. Some nights it's thematic fancy dress, some nights the music is all African, other times the place is booked for TV dance shows. It's big, the bopping is good, and the clientele are an exuberant spectacle in themselves. Mon–Thurs admission 100F, weekends 120F, drinks from 50F.

Le Shéhérazade, 3 rue de Liège, 9e; ☎01.40.16.17.18 (Mº Liège). Mon–Thurs 11pm–dawn, Fri–Sun midnight–dawn. Popular with the youthful, mixed, dancing crowd. House music, with occasional variant evenings. Exotic decor in a former Russian cabaret. 100F admission plus drink; vodka 80–90F a shot.

Zed Club, 2 rue des Anglais, 5e; ☎01.43.54.93.78 (Mº Maubert-Mutualité). Wed–Sat 10.30pm–3.30am. *The* rock 'n' roll club. 50F entry Wed, 50F entry plus drink Thurs, 100F entry plus drink Fri & Sat.

Classical and contemporary music

Paris is a stimulating environment for **classical music,** both established and contemporary. The former is well represented in performances within churches – sometimes free or very cheap – and in an enormous choice of commercially promoted concerts held every day of the week. Contemporary and experimental computer-based work flourishes.

Concert venues

The **Cité de la Musique** at La Villette has given Paris two new, major concert venues: the **Conservatoire** (the national music academy) at 209 av Jean-Jaurès, 19e (☎01.40.40.46.46; Mº Porte-de-Pantin); and the **Salle des Concerts** at 221 av Jean-Jaurès, 19e (☎01.44.84.44.84; Mº Porte-de Pantin). Ancient music, contemporary works, jazz, chansons and music from all over the world are featured.

These apart, the top **auditoriums** are: Salle Pleyel, 252 rue du Faubourg-St-Honoré, 8e (☎01.45.61.06.30; Mº Ternes); Salle Gaveau, 45 rue de la Boétie, 8e (☎01.45.62.09.71; Mº Miromesnil); Théâtre des Champs-Élysées, 15 av Montaigne, 8e (☎01.49.52.50.50;

M° Alma-Marceau); and the Théâtre Musical de Paris, 1 place du Châtelet, 1er (☎01.40.28.28.40; M° Châtelet). **Tickets** are best bought at the box offices, though for big names you may find overnight queues, and a large number of seats are always booked by subscribers. The price range is very reasonable. **Churches** and **museums** are also good places to hear classical music. The Église St-Séverin, 1 rue des Prêtres st-Séverin, 5e(M° St-Michel); the Église St-Julien le Pauvre, 23 quai de Montebello, 5e (☎01.42.08.49.00; M° St-Michel); and the Sainte Chapelle, 4 bd du Palais, 1er (☎01.42.77.65.65; M° Cité) all host regular concerts. The Musée du Louvre, palais du Louvre, 1er (☎01.40.20.84.00; M° Louvre-Rivoli/ Palais-Royal-Musée-du-Louvre) and the Musée d'Orsay, 1 rue de Bellechasse, 7e (☎01.40.49.47.17; M° Solférino/RER Musée d'Orsay) both host chamber music recitals in their auditoriums.

Classical concerts also take place for **free** at Radio France, 166 av du Président-Kennedy, 16e (☎01.42.30.15.16; M° Passy).

Opera

The first performance at the **Opéra-Bastille** – the six-hour-long *Les Troyens* by Berlioz – cast something of a shadow on the project's proclaimed commitment to popularizing its art. Since then it has been plagued by rows and resignations, and opinions differ on the quality of the acoustics and productions, bickering which doesn't stop it being packed at every performance. To judge the place for yourself, tickets (60–590F) can be booked Monday to Saturday 11am to 6pm on ☎08.36.69.78.68 or at the ticket office (Mon–Sat 11am–6.30pm). The cheapest seats are only available to personal callers; unfilled seats are sold at discount to students five minutes before the curtain goes up. For programme details, phone ☎01.43.43.96.96.

More big-scale opera productions are staged at the **Théâtre Musical de Paris** (see above). Rather less grand opera is also performed at the **Opéra-Comique** (Salle Favard, 5 rue Favart, 2e; (☎01.42.86.88.83; M° Richelieu-Drouot), and smaller productions still take place at the old **Opéra-Garnier**, place de l'Opéra, 9e (☎08.36.69.78.68; M° Opéra). Both opera and recitals are also put on at the multipurpose performance halls (see below).

Contemporary music

Pierre Boulez' post-serialist experiments received massive public funding for many years in the form of a vast laboratory of acoustics and "digital signal processing" – a complex known as **IRCAM** – housed underneath the Beaubourg arts centre. Boulez' Ensemble Intercontemporain is now based in the Cité de la Musique, but IRCAM occasionally has concerts.

Other Paris-based practitioners of contemporary and experimental music include Laurent Bayle, Jean-Claude Eloy, Pascal Dusapin, Luc Ferrarie, and the English composer George Benjamin.

Festivals

Festivals are plentiful in all the diverse fields that come under the far too general term of "classical". The **Festival d'Art Sacré** involves concerts and recitals of church music (end of March/beginning of April; also Nov/Dec); concerts feature in the general arts **Festival d'Automne** (end of Sept–end Dec); and a summer **festival of classical chamber** music is held at the Château de Sceaux to the south of the city (mid-July to third week in Sept).

For details of these and more, pick up the current year's **festival schedule** from one of the tourist offices or from the Hôtel de Ville, 29 rue du Rivoli, 4e (M° Hôtel-de-Ville). During January the Hôtel de Ville sponsors a week of two concert tickets for the price of one.

The big performance halls

Events at any of the performance spaces listed below will be well-advertised on bill-boards and posters throughout the city. Tickets can be obtained at the halls them-selves, though it's easier to get them through agents like FNAC or Virgin Megastore.

Le Bataclan, 50 bd Voltaire, 11e; ☎01.47.00.30.12 (M^o Oberkampf). One of the best places for visiting and native rock bands.

Forum des Halles, Niveau 3, Porte Rambuteau, 15 rue de l'Équerre-d'Argent, 1er; ☎01.42.03.11.11 (M^o Châtelet). Varied functions – theatre, performance art, rock, etc – often hosting foreign touring groups.

Maison des Cultures du Monde, 101 bd Raspail, 6e; ☎01.45.44.72.30 (M^o Rennes). All the arts from all over the world, for once not dominated by Europeans.

Olympia, 28 bd des Capucines, 9e; ☎01.47.42.25.49 (M^o Madeleine/Opéra). A recently renovated old-style music hall hosting occasional well-known rock groups and large, popular concert performers.

Palais des Congrès, place de la Porte-Maillot, 17e; ☎01.40.68.22.22 (M^o Porte-Maillot). Opera, ballet, orchestral music, trade fairs, and the superstars of US and British rock.

Palais Omnisports de Bercy, 8 bd de Bercy, 12e; ☎01.43.46.12.21 (M^o Bercy). Opera, cycle racing, Bruce Springsteen, ice hockey, and Citroën launches – the newest multipurpose stadium, with seats to give vertigo to the most level-headed, but an excellent space when used in the round.

Palais des Sports, Porte de Versailles, 15e; ☎01.48.28.40.48 or 01.44.68.44.68 (M^o Porte-de-Versailles). Another vast-scale auditorium, ideal if you want to see your favourite rock star in miniature 1km away.

Zenith, Parc de la Villette, 211 av Jean-Jaurès, 20e; ☎01.42.08.60.00 or 01.42.40.60.00 (M^o Porte-de-Pantin). Seating for 6500 people in an inflatable stadium designed exclusively for rock and pop concerts. Head for the concrete column with a descending red aeroplane.

Film, theatre and dance

Cinema addicts have a choice of around three hundred films showing in Paris in any one week, which puts moving visuals on an equal footing with the still visuals of the art museums and galleries. **Théâtre**, on the other hand, is less accessible to non-natives, especially the cabaret and comics of the *café-théâtres*. However, there is stimulation in the cult of the director; Paris is home to Peter Brook, Ariane Mnouchkine and other exiles, as well as French talent, including excellent touring companies from the provinces. Suburban theatres rival the city proper for bold experimental theatre. Also, transcending language barriers, there are exciting developments in **dance**, much of it incorporating **mime**. **Circus**, too, has a seasonal home at the Cirque d'Hiver Bouglione (see p.175) with an international festival every January.

The main **festivals** include the Festival International: Films des Femmes (end March/beginning of April; see overleaf); the Festival Exit (April), featuring international contemporary dance, performance and theatre at Créteil's Maison des Arts; Paris Quartier d'Été (July), with music, theatre and cinema events around the city; the Festival d'Automne (between Sept & Dec), with traditional and experimental theatrical, musical, dance and multimedia productions from all over the world; and the Nouveau Festival International de Danse de Paris (end Sept–beginning Oct) based at the Théâtre du Châtelet, with state-of-the-art international dance; the Festival du Cinéma en Plein Air (mid July–end Aug) at Parc de la Villette, showing free films in the park.

Information and tickets

The most comprehensive **film listings** are given in *Pariscope*. You rarely need to book in advance; programmes (*séances*) often start around midday and continue through to the early hours. The average price is 40–45F, with lower rates often on Monday or

Wednesday and for earlier *séances*, plus student reductions are available from Monday to Thursday. UGC and Gaumont sell multi-tickets, which work out at around 30F a seat, and some independents offer a *carte de fidélité*, giving you a free sixth entry. Almost all of the huge selection of foreign films will be shown at some cinemas in the original – *version originale* or *v.o.* in the listings. Dubbed films will be listed as *v.f.* and English versions of co-productions as *version anglaise* or *v.a.*

Stage productions are detailed in *Pariscope* and *L'Official des Spectacles* with brief résumés or reviews. Prices vary between 30F and 170F for state theatres (around 115F for the suburbs), and 60F and 260F for commercial theatres (most closed Sun & Mon). Half-price previews are advertised in *Pariscope*, etc, and there are weekday student discounts. Prices are high for epic productions by top directors which may be seven hours long or even carry over several days; these always need booking in advance. Tickets can be bought directly from the theatres, from FNAC shops and Virgin Megastores (see pp.178), or at the **ticket kiosks** on place de la Madeleine, 8ᵉ, opposite no. 15 and on the parvis of the Gare du Montparnasse, 14ᵉ (Tues–Sat 12.30–8pm, Sun 12.30–4pm). They sell half-price same-day tickets and charge a 16F commission, but be prepared to queue. Tickets for **café-théatres** average around 80F, and it's best to book in advance for Friday and Saturday performances, directly from the venues.

In May the mairie sponsors a week of two theatre tickets for the price of one; in June, three days of 10F cinema tickets if you buy one normal entry; and in February, a week of "18hr–18F" – 18F cinema tickets for 6pm screenings.

Many cinemas and theatres have unwaged ushers who will expect a 5F **tip**.

Film and video

Even though many of the smaller movie houses in obscure corners of the city have closed in recent years, and the big chains, UGC and Gaumont, keep opening new multi-screen cinemas, you still have a fantastic choice of **films**, covering every place and period, with new works (excepting British movies) arriving long before London and New York. If your French is good enough for subtitles, go and see a Senegalese, Taiwanese, Brazilian or Finnish film that would never be seen in Britain or the US. Or choose your own **video** clips at the Vidéothèque de Paris (see below). The **International Festival of Women's Films** is organized by the Maison des Arts, place Salvador-Allende, 94000 Créteil (☎01.43.99.22.11; Mº Créteil-Préfecture); programme details are available from mid-March. For the biggest screens of all, check-out the 180° Omnimax projection system at La Villette and La Défense (see pp 140 and 136).

Venues

Cinémathèques at Salle Garance, Centre Beaubourg, 4ᵉ (Mº Rambuteau); Musée du Cinéma, Palais de Chaillot, cnr avs Président-Wilson & Albert-de-Mun, 16ᵉ (Mº Trocadéro); Salle Grands Boulevards, 42 bd Bonne Nouvelle, 10ᵉ (Mº Bonne-Nouvelle) ☎01.56.26.01.01. For seriously committed film freaks, the three *cinémathèques* offer a choice of over fifty films a week, many of which would never be shown commercially. Tickets are 28F; 17F for students. The Cinémathèque Française which was in the Palais de Chaillot is moving to the Maison du Cinéma, a grand project in Bercy with will also house a museum and library.

L'Arlequin, 76 rue des Rennes, 6ᵉ (Mº St-Suplice). The Latin Quarter's best cinephile's palace, offering special screenings of classics every Sun at 11pm followed by debates in the café opposite.

L'Entrepôt, 7–9 rue Francis-de-Pressensé, 14ᵉ (Mº Pernety). One of the best alternative Paris movie houses, which has been keeping ciné-addicts happy for years with its three screens dedicated to the obscure, the subversive and the brilliant. It also shows videos, satellite and cable TV, and has a bookshop (Mon–Sat 2–8pm) and a restaurant (daily noon–midnight).

Grand Action and Action Écoles, 5 & 23 rue des Écoles, 5ᵉ (Mᵒ Cardinal-Lemoine/Maubert-Mutualité); Action Christine Odéon, 4 rue Christine, 6ᵉ (Mᵒ Odéon/St-Michel). The Action chain specializes in new prints of ancient classics and screens contemporary films from different countries.

Le Grand Rex, 1 bd Poissonnière, 2ᵉ (Mᵒ Bonne-Nouvelle). Just as outrageous as La Pagode (see below), but in the kitsch line, with a *Metropolis*-style tower blazing its neon name, 2750 seats, and a ceiling of stars and Moorish city skyline; foreign films always dubbed.

Max Linder Panorama, 24 bd Poissonnière, 9ᵉ (Mᵒ Bonne-Nouvelle). Opposite Le Grand Rex, and with almost as big a screen, this always shows films in the original and has state-of-the-art sound and Art Deco decor.

MK2 Quai de la Seine, 14 quai de la Seine, 19ᵉ (Mᵒ Jaurès/Stalingrad). Part of the MK2 chain but distinctive in style – covered in famous cinematic quotes and on the banks of the Bassin de la Villette – and with a varied art-house repertoire.

La Pagode, 57bis rue de Babylone, 7ᵉ (Mᵒ François-Xavier). The most beautiful of the city's cinemas, transplanted from Japan at the turn of the century to be a rich Parisienne's party place. The wall panels of the Grande Salle auditorium are embroidered in silk; golden dragons and elephants hold up the candelabra; and a battle between Japanese and Chinese warriors rages on the ceiling. Unfortunately, recent financial problems could mean that this unique cinema is closed; check *Pariscope* for details.

Le Studio 28, 10 rue de Tholozé, 18ᵉ (Mᵒ Blanche/Abbesses). In its early days, after one of the first showings of Buñuel's *L'Age d'Or*, this was done over by extreme right-wing Catholics who destroyed the screen and the paintings by Dali and Ernst in the foyer. The cinema still hosts avant-garde premières, followed occasionally by discussions with the director, as well as regular festivals.

Vidéothèque de Paris, 2 Grande Gallerie, Porte St-Eustache, Forum des Halles, 1ᵉʳ (RER Châtelet-Les Halles). Tues–Sun 1–8.30pm, Thurs till 10pm; entry 30F/25F. This screens four films or videos daily, but also has a library of 4000 videos of newsreel footage, film clips, ads, documentaries, etc – all connected with Paris – that you can access yourself from a computer terminal. You can make your choice via a Paris place-name, an actor, a director, a date, and so on; there are instructions in English at the desk, and a friendly "librarian" to help you out. Internet connection also available.

Drama

Bourgeois farces, postwar classics, Shakespeare, Racine and *Cyrano de Bergerac* – all are staged with the same range of talent or lack of it that you'd find in London or New York. What is rare are home-grown, socially concerned and realist **dramas**, though touring foreign companies make up for that. Exciting contemporary work is provided by the superstar breed of directors such as Peter Brook, Ariane Mnouchkine and Patrice Chereau; spectacular and dazzling sensation tends to take precedence over speech in their productions, which feature huge casts, extraordinary sets and overwhelming sound and light effects – an experience, even if you haven't understood a word.

Venues

Bouffes du Nord, 37bis bd de la Chapelle, 10ᵉ; ☎01.46.07.34.50 (Mᵒ Chapelle). Peter Brook's permanent base in Paris; the occasional concert is also performed.

Cartoucherie, route du Champ-de-Manoeuvre, 12ᵉ (Mᵒ Château-de-Vincennes). Home to several interesting theatre companies including Ariane Mnouchkine's workers' co-op, Théâtre du Soleil (☎01.43.28.97.04), whose 1996 interpretation of Molière's *Tartuffe*, with the protagonist as a mullah in a North African city, dazzled French and foreign critics.

Comédie Française, 2 rue Richelieu, 1ᵉʳ; ☎01.44.58.15.15 (Mᵒ Palais-Royal). The national theatre for the classics plus contemporary work.

Maison de la Culture de Bobigny, 1 bd Lénine, Bobigny; ☎01.41.60.72.72 (Mᵒ Pablo-Picasso). The resident company, MC93, stages highly challenging productions; also dance by François Verret.

Odéon Théâtre de l'Europe, 1 place Paul-Claudel, 6ᵉ; ☎01.44.41.36.36 (Mᵒ Odéon). Contemporary plays and foreign-language productions in the theatre that became an open parliament during May 1968.

Théâtre des Amandiers, 7 av Pablo-Picasso, Nanterre, 92; ☎01.46.14.70.00 (RER Nanterre-Université & theatre bus). The suburban base for Jean-Paul Vincent's exciting productions; also excellent dance.

Théâtre de la Bastille, 79 rue de la Roquette, 11ᵉ; ☎01.43.57.42.14 (Mᵒ Bastille). One of the best places for new work and fringe productions.

Théâtre de la Colline, 15 rue Malte-Brun, 20ᵉ; ☎01.44.62.52.52 (Mᵒ Gambetta). A national theatre putting on works by both epic directors and less well-established innovators.

Théâtre de la Main-d'Or, 15 passage de la Main-d'Or, 11ᵉ; ☎01.48.05.67.89 (Mᵒ Bastille). An interesting experimental space, with occasional classics and English productions including a festival of English theatre in the spring.

Théâtre National de Chaillot, Palais de Chaillot, place du Trocadéro, 16ᵉ; ☎01.53.65.30.00 (Mᵒ Trocadéro). A national theatre where Jérôme Savary, artistic director, stages his outrageous productions.

Dance and mime

The French **regional dance companies** from La Rochelle, Marseille, Grenoble, Angers and Montpellier easily rival the Paris-based troupes, but Paris-based choreographers Maguy Marin, Karine Saporta and François Verret are worth looking out for. The current trend is in multidimensional performing art combining movement, mime, ballet, speech, noise, theatrical effects and music from medieval to jazz-rock. Though the famous mime schools of Marcel Marceau and Lecoq still turn out excellent artists, pure mime hardly exists except on the streets; Beaubourg's piazza is one of the best place to catch performances.

Many of the theatres listed above under "Drama" include these new forms in their programmes. Plenty of space and critical attention is also given to **tap**, **tango**, **folk** and **jazz dancing**, and to visiting traditional dance troupes from all over the world. As for **ballet**, the principal stage is at the old opera house, the Opéra-Garnier; other major productions are at the Théâtre de la Ville and the Théâtre Musical de Paris.

Venues

Centre Beaubourg, rue Beaubourg, 4ᵉ; ☎01.44.78.13.15 (Mᵒ Rambuteau/RER Châtelet-Les Halles). The Grande Salle in the basement is used for dance performances by visiting companies.

Centre Mandapa, 6 rue Wurtz, 13ᵉ; ☎01.45.89.01.60 (Mᵒ Glacière). The one theatre dedicated to traditional dances from around the world.

L'Espace Kiron, 10 rue la Vacquerie, 11ᵉ; ☎01.44.64.11.50 (Mᵒ Voltaire). Venue for experimental dance and performance art.

Maison des Arts de Créteil, place Salvador-Allende, Créteil; ☎01.45.13.19.19 (Mᵒ Créteil-Préfecture). Maguy Marin's company's home base and venue for the Festival Exit (see above).

Opéra-Garnier, place de l'Opéra, 9ᵉ; ☎01.44.73.13.00 (Mᵒ Opéra). Main home of the Ballet de l'Opéra National de Paris.

Théâtre Musical de Paris, place du Châtelet, 4ᵉ; ☎01.40.28.28.40 (Mᵒ Châtelet). A major ballet venue where, in 1910, Diaghilev put on the first season of Russian ballet. Today it still hosts ballet companies from abroad. Closed for renovation until July 1999.

Théâtre de la Ville, 2 place du Châtelet, 4ᵉ; ☎01.42.74.22.77 (Mᵒ Châtelet). The height of success for dance productions is to end up here. Works by Karine Saporta, Maguy Marin and Pina Bausch are regularly featured, along with modern theatre classics, comedy and concerts.

Café-théâtre

Café-théâtre, with its word-play and allusions to current fads, phobias and politicians, can be incomprehensible even to a fluent French-speaker. Puerile, dirty jokes are also its stock in trade. But the atmosphere can be fun, and every so often an original talent will appear.

The Marais has a high concentration of **venues**: you could try the tiny Blancs-Manteaux, 15 rue des Blancs-Manteaux, 4ᵉ (☎01.48.87.15.84; Mᵒ Hôtel-de-Ville/Rambuteau); or the *Café de la Gare*, 41 rue du Temple, 4ᵉ (☎01.42.78.52.51; Mᵒ Hôtel-de-Ville/Rambuteau), which has a reputation for novelty.

Daytime amusements and sports

When it's cold and wet and you've had your fill of café vistas and peering at museums, monuments and the dripping panes of shopfronts, don't despair or retreat back to your hotel. As well as movies, Paris offers a whole host of pleasant ways to pass the time indoors – **skating, bowling, billiards, swimming, hammams** – or outdoors, with all the **popular sports** to watch or participate in.

Information

L'Officiel des Spectacles has the best listings of **sports facilities** (under "Activités sportives"). Information on municipal facilities is also available from Allo Sports (Mon–Fri 10.30am–5pm; ☎01.42.76.54.54) or Direction Jeunesse et Sports, 25 bd Bourdon, 4ᵉ (Mon–Fri noon–7pm; ☎01.42.76.22.60; Mᵒ Bastille), while the Mairie de Paris gives away a weighty free book, *Le Guide du Sport à Paris* (ask for it at the tourist office, town halls or the Direction Jeunesse et Sports), which provides an arrondissement-by-arrondissement list of sporting facilities. For current **sporting events** there's the daily sports paper *L'Équipe*. A major venue for all sports, including athletics, cycling, show jumping, ice hockey, ballroom dancing, judo and motorcross, is the Palais des Omnisports Paris-Bercy (POPB) at 8 bd Bercy, 12ᵉ (☎01.40.02.60.60, Mᵒ Bercy).

Participatory activities

Billiards and bowling You can do both at Le Stadium, 66 av d'Ivry, 13ᵉ (daily 10am–2am; ☎01.45.86.55.52; Mᵒ Porte-d'Ivry) and at Bowling Mouffetard, Centre-Commercial Mouffetard-Monge, 73 rue Mouffetard, 5ᵉ (daily 11am–2am; ☎01.43.31.09.35; Mᵒ Monge). Bowling costs 15F–33F a session – more in the evenings and at weekends; shoe hire is 8F–10F. Billiards will set you back around 60F an hour plus an average 100F deposit.

Boules The classic French game involving balls, boules (or pétanque*)*, is best performed (if you have your own set or are prepared to make some new French friends) or watched at the Arènes de Lutèce (p.124) and the Bois de Vincennes (p.144). On balmy summer evenings it's a common sight in the city's parks and gardens.

Cycling Since 1996 the Mairie de Paris has made great efforts to introduce dedicated cycle lanes in Paris, which now add up to 100km. You can pick up a free leaflet, *Paris à Vélo*, outlining the routes, from town halls, the tourist office, or bike hire outlets (p.180). If you prefer cycling in a more natural environment, the Bois de Boulogne and the Bois de Vincennes have extensive bike tracks. On Sundays cycling by the Seine is popular, when its central quais (and along the Canal St-Martin) are closed to cars between 10am and 4pm. Excellent half-day bicycle tours (170F, under-26 150F) are offered by Paris à Vélo C'est Sympa, 37 bd Bourdon, 4ᵉ (☎01.48.87.60.01; Mᵒ Bastille) including a "Paris by night" excursion (190F, under-26 170F).

Hammams Luxurious, laid-back and very Parisian, the best hammam or Turkish baths is the Hammam de la Mosquée, 39 rue Geoffroy-St-Hilaire, 5ᵉ (☎01.43.31.18.14; Turkish bath 85F, massage extra; Mᵒ Censier-Daubenton); times may change, so check first, but generally women on Mon & Wed–Sat 10am–9pm, men Tues 2–9pm & Sun 10am–9pm.

Ice skating The city's only permanent rink is the Patinoire des Buttes-Chaumont, 30 rue Edouard-Pailleron, 19ᵉ (☎01.42.39.08.72; Mᵒ Bolivar). Mon, Tues & Thurs 3–9pm, Wed 10am–9pm, Fri 3pm–midnight, Sat 10am–midnight, Sun 10am–6pm; entry including skate rental around 50F. From Nov to March a small rink is set up in the Orangerie corner of the Tuileries gardens.

In-line skating Roller-blading has become so popular in Paris that it takes over the streets every Friday night from 9.45pm, when between 5000 and 10,000 rollerskaters meet on Place d'Italie in the

13ᵉ (Mᵒ Place d'Italie) for a 40km circuit of the city, accompanied by roller-blading police officers and tag-along cyclists. If you want to join in the fun, the best place to find more information and to hire roller-skates and -blades is Nomades, 37 bd Bourdon, 4ᵉ (Mon–Fri 11am–7pm, Sat & Sun 10am–7pm; ☎01.44.54.07.44; Mᵒ Bastille), with its own bar out back where you can meet other bladers. Hire is a reasonable 50F per day on a weekday and 60F at the weekend (half-day 30F/40F) but the deposit is 1000F and hiring the recommended protective pads will cost another 30F. Bike N'Roller, 6 rue St-Julien-Le-Paure, 5ᵉ (Wed–Sat 10am–7.30pm, Sun 9am–8pm; ☎01.44.07.35.89) also hires rollers and blades from 25F per hour, 75F per day. The main outdoor in-line skating and skate-boarding arena is the concourse of the Palais de Chaillot (Mᵒ Trocadéro). Les Halles (around the Fontaine des Innocents), the Beaubourg piazza and place du Palais-Royal are also very popular. On Sundays, the central quays of the Seine and the stretch of road along the Canal St-Martin are car-free between 10am and 4pm, making way for a stream of rollerbladers and cyclists.

Swimming *L'Officiel des Spectacles* lists all the municipal pools (usually 16F), of which the unchlorinated student hang-out Jean Taris, 16 rue de Thouin, 5ᵉ (Mᵒ Cardinal-Lemoine), the Art Deco Butte aux Cailles, 5 place Verlaine, 13ᵉ (Mᵒ Place-d'Italie) and the 50m-long Piscine Susanne Berlioux/Les Halles, 10 place de la Rotonde, niveau 3, Porte du Jour, Forum des Halles, 1ᵉʳ (RER Châtelet-Les Halles) are among the best.

Tennis and squash One of the nicest places to play tennis is on one of the six asphalt courts at the Jardins du Luxembourg (daily 8am–9pm; hourly rates are 37F by day, 53F by night; reservations only on Minitel 3615; Mᵒ Notre-Dame-des-Champs). However, to play on municipal courts such as these, you need first to apply for a Carte Paris-Tennis from the mairie, while private clubs demand steep membership fees. It's much easier to play squash, with several dedicated centres, including Squash Montmartre (14 rue Achille-Martinet, 18ᵉ; 01.42.55.38.30; Mᵒ Lamarck-Caulaincourt), who charge 30F for your novice first half-hour, while the Club Quartier Latin (19 rue de Pontoise, 5e; ☎01.43.25.31.99; Mᵒ Maubert-Mutualité) has some squash courts which cost 60F–75F for 40min to an hour.

Spectator sports

Cycling The biggest event of the French sporting year is the grand finale of the Tour de France on the Champs-Élysées in late July. Huge crowds turn out to cheer on the cyclists at the finishing line of the ultimate stage in the gruelling three-week 4000km-odd event and the French president presents the yellow jersey (*maillot jaune*) to the overall winner. Another classic bike event ending in Paris is the 600-km Bordeaux–Paris, the world's longest single stage race, first held in 1891. Races commencing in Paris include the Paris–Roubaix, instigated in 1896, which is reputed to be the most exacting one-day race in the world, and the rugged six-day Paris–Nice event, covering over 1100km. The Palais Omnisport de Bercy (see p.17) holds other bike races and cycling events. For more information on the Tour de France and other cycling events, see "Basics", p.64.

Football and rugby The Parc des Princes, 24 rue du Commandant-Guilbaud, 16ᵉ (☎01.42.88.02.76; Mᵒ Porte-de-St-Cloud) is the capital's main stadium for both rugby union and domestic football events, and home ground to the first-division Paris football team Paris-SG (St-Germain) plus the rugby team Le Racing. In 1998 France hosted the World Cup and the action in Paris centred around the specially built Stade de France, on rue Francis de Pressensé in St-Denis (☎01.55.93.00.00; RER Stade-de-France-St-Denis), which is now the venue for international football matches and rugby Five Nations' Cup Matches.

Horse-racing The biggest races are the Prix de la République and the Grand Prix de L'Arc de Triomphe on the first and last Sun in Oct at Auteuil and Longchamp, both in the Bois de Boulogne. Trotting races, with the jockeys in chariots, run from Aug to Sept on the Route de la Ferme in the Bois de Vincennes. *L'Humanité* and *Paris-Turf* carry details of all races; admission charges are under 30F. If you want to place a bet, any bar or café with the letters "PMU" will take your money on a three-horse bet, known as *le tiercé*.

Running The Paris Marathon is held in May over a route from place de la Concorde to Vincennes. Up-to-date information is available from the runners' shop, Marathon, 26 rue de Lyon, 12ᵉ (☎01.42.27.48.18; Mᵒ Gare de Lyon).

Tennis The French Tennis Open takes place in the last week of May and first week of June at Roland-Garros, 2 av Gordon-Bennett, 16ᵉ (☎01.47.43.48.00; Mᵒ Porte d'Auteuil). A few tickets are sold each day, but only for unseeded matches.

Kids' stuff

The biggest attraction for **kids** to have hit the Paris area is, of course, **Disneyland Paris** (see p.194), though within the city there are plenty of other, far less expensive possibilities for keeping them entertained. Wednesday afternoons, when primary school children have free time, and Saturdays, are the big times for children's activities and entertainment; Wednesdays continue to be child-centred even during the school holidays. The tours around the **sewers** and the **catacombs** will delight some children; while smaller ones can enjoy performances of **Guignol** (the equivalent of Punch and Judy) in the city's parks. Many of the **museums** and **amusements** already detailed will appeal, particularly the Musée de la Curiosité (see p.118) and the Grande Galerie d'Evolution (see p.193); the best treat for children of every age from three upwards is the **Cité des Sciences** in the Parc de la Villette. A number of museums have special children's activities on Wednesdays and Saturdays, details of which are carried in the booklet *Objectif Musée*, available from the museums or from the Direction des Musées de France, 34 quai du Louvre, 1er (closed Tues; ☎01.40.15.73.00); the Musée du Moyen Age, Musée d'Art Moderne de la Ville de Paris, Carnavalet, the Louvre, the Institut du Monde Arabe and the Musée d'Orsay have regular or special programmes but they will of course be conducted in French. Otherwise, the most useful **sources of information** for current shows, exhibitions and events are the special sections in the listings magazines ("Enfants" in *Pariscope*, and "Jeunes" in *L'Officiel des Spectacles*) and the Kiosque Paris-Jeunes at the Direction Jeunesse et Sports, 25 bd Bourdon, 4^e (Mon–Fri noon–7pm; ☎01.42.76.22.60; M° Bastille), and at the CIDJ, 101 quai Branly, 15e (Mon–Fri 9.30am–6pm & Sat 9.30am–1pm; ☎01.43.06.15.38; M° Bir-Hakeim). The tourist office also publish a free booklet in French, *Paris-Ile-de-France Avec Des Yeux Enfants* with lots of ideas and contacts.

Cité des Sciences

The **Cité des Enfants** (for kids aged 3–12) is a totally engaging special section of the Cité des Sciences et de l'Industrie – detailed on p.140 – in the Parc de la Villette, in the 19e (Tues–Sat 10am–6pm, Sun 10am–7pm; adults 50F, under-7s free, children over-7 35F; Cité des Enfants 25F, children under-3 free; children must be accompanied by at least one adult, combined ticket with Cité des Sciences 55F, children 45F; Géode Tues–Sun 10am–8pm: adult or child 50F, combined ticket with Cité, adult 92F, child 79F; M° Porte-de-la-Villette). The kids can touch, smell and feel inside things, play about with water, construct buildings on a miniature construction site, experiment with sound and light, manipulate robots, put together their own television news, and race their own shadows. It's beautifully organized and managed, and if you haven't got a child it's worth borrowing one to get in here. Sessions run for ninety minutes from 9am, 10am, between 10.30am and 3.30pm, at 4.30pm and 5pm – booking is recommended.

A new space on the ground floor, **Techno Cité** (90min sessions; Tues & Sat 2pm & 4pm; during summer hols Tues–Sat 10.30am, 12.30pm, 2.30pm & 4.30pm; over-11s only; extra 25F) offers hands-on application of technology to industry. You can write a program for a robotic videotape selector, for example, or design a prototype racing bike.

The rest of the museum is also pretty good for kids, particularly the planetarium, the various film shows, the Argonaute submarine, children's *médiathèque* (noon–8pm) and the frequent temporary exhibitions designed for the young. In the park, there's lots of wide open green space, the dragon slide and seven themed gardens featuring mirrors, trampolines, water jets and spooky music.

Jardin d'Acclimatation

This **garden** in the Bois de Boulogne by Porte des Sablons (Oct–May daily 10am–6pm; June–Sept 10am–7.30pm; adult 12F, child 6F, under-3s free, rides from 10F; special attractions Wed, Sat, Sun & all week during school hols, including a mini train from Mº Porte-Maillot, behind *L'Orée du Bois* restaurant, every 10min from 1.30–6pm: 5F one way, 10F return)Mº Les Sablons/Porte-Maillot; is a cross between a funfair, zoo and amusement park. Temptations range from bumper cars, go-karts, pony and camel rides, to sea lions, birds, bears and monkeys; plus there's a magical mini-canal ride (*la rivière enchantée*; 11F), distorting mirrors, scaled-down farm buildings, and a puppet theatre. Astérix and friends may be explaining life in their **Gaulish village**, or Babar the world of the elephants in the **Musée en Herbe**. The **Théâtre du Jardin pour l'Enfance et la Jeunesse** puts on musicals and ballets.

Outside the *jardin*, in the Bois de Boulogne, older children can amuse themselves with **minigolf** and **bowling**, or **boating** on the Lac Inférieur. By the entrance to the *jardin* there's **bike rental** for roaming the wood's cycle trails.

Parc Floral

Fun and games are always to be had at the **Parc Floral**, in the Bois de Vincennes, route de la Pyramide (daily March–Sept 9.30am–8pm, Oct–Feb 9.30am–5pm; admission 10F, 6–10s 5F plus supplements for some activities, under-6s free, over-60s 5F; Mº Château-de-Vincennes, then a 7-min walk past the Chateau Vincennes or bus #112). The excellent playground has slides, swings, ping-pong (raquet 25F, ball 5F), pedal carts (42F–60F per half-hour), minigolf modelled on Paris monuments (from 1.45pm; 30F, children under 12 15F), an electric car circuit, and a little train touring all the gardens (April–Oct daily 10.30am–5pm; 6F). Tickets for the activities are sold at the playground between 1.45pm and 5.30pm weekdays and until 7pm on weekends; activities stop 15 minutes afterwards. On Wednesdays at 2.30pm (May–Sept) there are free performances by clowns, puppets and magicians. Also in the park is a children's theatre, the **Théâtre Astral**, which has mime, clowns or other not-too-verbal shows for small children aged 3 to 8 (Wed 3pm, Sun & public hols 4.30pm & during school hols Mon–Fri 3pm; 33F; ☎01.42.41.88.33). There are also a series of pavilions with child-friendly educational exhibitions (free entry) which look at nature in Paris; the best is the **butterfly garden** (mid-May to mid-Oct Mon–Fri 1.30–5.15pm, Sat & Sun 1.30pm–6pm).

Parc Zoologique

The top Paris **zoo** is in the Bois de Vincennes at 53 av de St-Maurice, 12ᵉ (April–Sept Mon–Sat 9am–6pm, Sun & hols 9am–6.30pm; Oct–March Mon–Sat 9am–5pm, Sun & hols 9am–5.30pm; 40F/30F, under-4s free; Mº Porte-Dorée). This was one of the first in the world to get rid of cages and use landscaping to give the animals more room to exercise.

Jardin des Enfants aux Halles

Right in the centre of town, just west of the Forum, the **Jardin des Enfants aux Halles** is great if you want to lose your charges for the odd hour (summer Tues–Thurs & Sat 10am–7pm, Fri 2–5pm, Sun 1–7pm; winter till 4pm; closed Mon & during bad weather; 2.50F for a one-hour slot; Mº/RER Châtelet-Les Halles; 7–11s only except Sat am). You may have to reserve a place an hour or so in advance for this small but cleverly designed space filled with a whole series of fantasy landscapes. On Wednesday, animators organize adventure games; and at all times the children are supervised by professional child-carers, who speak several languages, including English. On Saturday mornings (10am–2pm), adults too can go in and play while they take charge of their under-seven-year-olds.

Grande Arche, La Défense, Paris

Pompidou Centre fountains

PETER WILSON

Flower shop, Ile St-Louis, Paris

S. THOMPSON, TRAVEL INK

Reims cathedral

A. COWIN, TRAVEL INK

House nr Mulhouse, Alsace

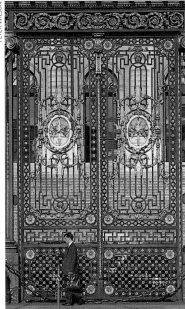

Palais de Justice, Paris

Louvre pyramid, Paris

Monet's garden, Giverny, Normandy

NEIL SETCHFIELD

Strasbourg

CHRIS COE, AXIOM

Scenery near Epernay, Champagne

J. DEGRANGE, GREG EVANS INT'L

Carnac, Brittany

Funfairs and the circus

The Tuileries gardens normally have a **funfair** in July, and there's usually a **merry-go-round** at the Forum des Halles and beneath Tour St-Jacques at Châtelet, with carousels for smaller children on place de la République and at the Rond-Point des Champs-Elysées, by av Matignon; the going rate for a ride is 10F. The *Cirque d'Hiver Bouglione*, 110 rue Amelot, 11ᵉ (Mº Filles-du-Calvaire; details in *Pariscope*, etc) is open from October to January, or you can spend an entire day at the **circus** courtesy of the Cirque de Paris in RER Villeneuve-La Garenne in the Parc des Chanteraines, 115 bd Charles-de-Gaulle (Oct–June Wed, Sun & school hols 10am–5pm; 295F/under-12s 230F including a meal; ☎01.47.99.40.40; RER Gennevilliers/St-Denis); lessons in juggling, tightrope-walking, clowning and make-up are followed by lunch in the ring then by the show. You can, if you prefer, just attend the show at 3pm (70–155F).

Shopping

Even if you don't plan – or can't afford – to buy, Parisian **shops and markets** are one of the chief delights of the city. Flair for style and design is as evident here as it is in other aspects of the city's life. Parisians' fierce attachment to their small local traders, especially when it comes to food, has kept alive a wonderful variety of shops, despite the pressures to concentrate consumption in gargantuan underground and multi-storey complexes. Among specific areas, the square kilometre around **place St-Germain-des-Prés** is hard to beat, packed with books, antiques, gorgeous garments, art works and playthings. But in every quartier you'll find enticing displays of all manner of consumables.

Bookshops

Books are not cheap in France – foreign books least of all – but don't let that stop you browsing. The best areas are the narrow streets of the *quartier Latin* and along the Seine where rows of **stalls** are perched against the river parapet. Here we've listed a few specialists and favourites.

Books in English

Abbey Bookshop/La Librairie Canadienne, 29 rue de la Parcheminerie, 5ᵉ (Mº St-Michel). Mon–Sat 10am–7pm. A Canadian bookshop round the corner from Shakespeare & Co (see below), with lots of second-hand British and North American fiction; good social science sections; knowledgeable and helpful staff – and free coffee.

Shakespeare & Co, 37 rue de la Bûcherie, 5ᵉ (Mº Maubert-Mutualité). Daily noon–midnight. A cosy, famous literary haunt, American-run, with the biggest selection of second-hand English books in town. Also poetry readings and such.

W H Smith, 248 rue de Rivoli, 1ᵉʳ(Mº Concorde). Mon–Sat 9.30am–7pm. Paris outlet of the British chain. Wide range of new books and newspapers.

Books in French

Artcurial, 9 av Matignon, 8ᵉ; ☎01.42.99.16.16 (Mº Franklin-D-Roosevelt). Tues-Sun 10am–7.15pm; closed two weeks in Aug. The art bookshop in Paris.

FNAC, at the Forum des Halles, niveau 2, Porte Pierre-Lescot, 1ᵉʳ(Mº/RER Châtelet-Les Halles); 136 rue de Rennes, 6ᵉ (Mº Montparnasse); 74 av des Champs-Élysées, 8ᵉ (Mº George-V); 24 bd des Italiens, 9ᵉ (Mº Richelieu Drouot); and 26–30 av des Termes, 17ᵉ (Mº Termes). Mon–Sat 10am–7.30pm with the bd des Italiens store open until midnight. Not the most congenial of bookshops, but it's the biggest and covers everything.

Galerie Maeght, 42 rue du Bac 16e (M^o Rue du Bac). Tues–Sat 9.30am–7pm. Famous art gallery which makes its own beautifully printed art books.

Présence Africaine, 25bis rue des Écoles, 5e (M^o Maubert-Mutualité). Mon–Sat 10am–7pm. Specialist black African bookshop, with titles ranging from literature to economics and philosophy by Caribbean and North American as well as African writers.

Parallèles, 47 rue St-Honoré, 1^er(M^o Châtelet-Les Halles). Mon–Sat 10am–7pm. An alternative bookshop with everything from anarchism to New Age. Good for info on current events and gigs.

Clothes

The haute couture shows may be well out-of-bounds, but there's nothing to prevent you trying on fabulously expensive creations by famous **couturiers** in rue du Faubourg-St-Honoré, av François-1er and av Victor-Hugo – apart from the intimidating air of the assistants and the awesome chill of the marble portals. Likewise, you can treat the **younger designers** round place des Victoires and in the Marais and St-Germain areas as stops on your sightseeing itinerary. The long-time darlings of the glitterati are Jean-Paul Gaultier and Azzedine Alaïa who, in 1991, were prevailed upon to design some gear for the city's **cheapest department store** – Tati (whose main branch is at 13 place de la République, 11e (M^o République)). Three new star designers are British – John Galliano at Dior, Beatle's daughter Stella McCartney at Chloé and the controversial Alexander McQueen at Givenchy. For smart **clothes** without the fancy labels the best areas are rue St-Placide and rue St-Dominique in the 6e and 7e. The **department stores** Galeries Lafayette and Au Printemps have good selections of designer prêt-à-porter; and the **Forum des Halles** is chock-a-block with clothes shops at less competitive prices. The **sales** take place in January and July, with reductions of up to forty percent on designer clothes. Ends of lines and old stock of the couturiers are sold year round in **discount shops** concentrated in rue d'Alésia in the 14e and rue St-Placide in the 6e. For **shoes**, take a wander down rue Meslay in the 3e.

Designer fashion

The addresses below are those of the main or most conveniently located shops.

Agnès B, 6 rue du Jour, 1er (M^o Châtelet-Les Halles).

Azzedine Alaïa, 7 rue de Moussy, 4e (M^o Hôtel-de-Ville).

Chanel, 31 rue Cambon, 1er (M^o Madeleine).

Christian Lacroix, 73 rue du Faubourg-St-Honoré, 8e (M^o Concorde).

Gianni Versace, 62 rue du Faubourg-St-Honoré, 8e (M^o Concorde).

Giorgio Armani, 25 place Vendôme, 1er (M^o Opéra).

Inès de la Fressange, 14 av Montaigne, 8e (M^o Alma-Marceau).

Issey Miyake, 3 place des Vosges, 4e (M^o St-Paul).

Jean-Paul Gaultier, 30 rue du Faubourg St-Antoine, 12e (M^o Bastille).

Jil Sander, 52 av Montaigne, 8e (M^o Franklin-D-Roosevelt).

Junko Shimada, 54 rue Étienne-Marcel, 2e (M^o Châtelet-Les Halles).

Kenzo, 3 place des Victoires, 1er (M^o Bourse).

Sonia Rykiel, 175 bd St-Germain, 6e (M^o St-Germain-des-Prés).

Thierry Mugler, 49 av Montaigne, 8e (M^o Alma-Marceau).

Yves Saint-Laurent, 6 place St-Sulpice, 6e (M^o St-Sulpice/Mabillon).

Department stores

Au Bon Marché, 38 rue de Sèvres, 7e (M^o Sèvres-Babylone). Mon–Sat 9.30am–7pm. Paris's oldest department store, founded in 1852. Prices are lower on average than at the chicer Galeries Lafayette and Printemps. Excellent kids' department and an alluring food hall.

Au Printemps, 64 bd Haussmann, 9ᵉ (Mº Havre-Caumartin). Books, records, a *parfumerie* even bigger than that of rival Galeries Lafayette, excellent fashion for women – less so for men.

Galeries Lafayette, 40 bd Haussmann, 9ᵉ (Mº Havre-Caumartin). Mon–Sat 9.30am–6.45pm, Thurs till 9pm. The store's forte is, above all, high fashion. Two complete floors are given over to the latest creations by leading designers for men, women and children. Then there's household stuff, tableware, furniture, a huge *parfumerie*, etc – all under a superb 1900 dome.

La Samaritaine, 75 rue de Rivoli, Iᵉʳ (Mº Louvre-Rivoli/Châtelet). Mon–Sat 9.30am–7pm, Thurs till 10pm. The largest of the department stores, spread over three buildings, whose boast is to provide anything anyone could possibly want. It aims downmarket of the previous two. You get a superb view of Paris from the eleventh-floor rooftop, and from the inexpensive tenth-floor terrace café (closed Oct–March).

Food

You can, of course, find sumptuous food stores all over Paris: the listings below are for the **specialist places**, palaces of gluttony many of them, with prices to match. Economical food shopping is invariably best done at the **street markets or supermarkets**, though save your bread buying at least for the local boulangerie. The cheapest supermarket chain is Ed Discount. Food markets are detailed at the end of this section.

Bread

Poilâne, 8 rue du Cherche-Midi, 6ᵉ (Mº Sèvres-Babylone). Mon–Sat 7.15am–8.15pm. Bakes to ancient and secret family recipes; there is always a queue.

Charcuterie

Divay, 4 rue Bayen, 17ᵉ (Mº Ternes). 8am–1.30pm & 3.30–7.30pm; closed Wed & Sun afternoon, Mon & Aug. *Foie gras, choucroute, saucisson* and suchlike.

Goldenberg's, 7 rue des Rosiers, 4ᵉ (Mº St-Paul). Daily 9am–2am. Superlative Jewish deli and restaurant.

Cheese

Barthélémy, 51 rue de Grenelle, 7ᵉ (Mº Bac). Tues–Sat 8.30am–1pm & 4–7.30pm; closed Aug. Purveyors of cheeses to the rich and powerful.

Carmès et Fils, 24 rue de Lévis, 17ᵉ (Mº Villiers). Tues–Sat 8.30am–1pm & 4–7.30pm, Sun am only; closed Aug. A family of experts who mature many of the cheeses in their own cellars.

Chocolates and pâtisseries

À la Mère de Famille, 35 rue du Faubourg-Montmartre, 9ᵉ (Mº Le Peletier). Tues–Sat 8.30am–1.30pm & 3–7pm. An eighteenth-century *confiserie* serving *marrons glacés*, prunes from Agen, dried fruit, sweets, chocolates and even some wines.

Debauve and Gallais, 30 rue des Sts-Pères, 6ᵉ (Mº St-Germain-des-Prés). Mon–Sat 9am–7pm; closed Aug. A beautiful, ancient shop specializing in chocolate and elaborate sweets.

Gourmet groceries

Fauchon, 26 place de la Madeleine, 8ᵉ (Mº Madeleine). Mon–Sat 9.40am–7pm. Carries an amazing range of super-plus groceries and wine, all at exorbitant prices; there's a self-service counter for pâtisseries and *plats du jour*, and a *traiteur* which stays open a little later, until 8.30pm.

Hédiard, 21 place de la Madeleine, 8ᵉ (Mº Madeleine). Mon–Sat 8am–10pm. Since 1850 the aristocrat's grocer. Several other branches throughout the city.

Health food

Diététique DJ Fayer, 45 rue St-Paul, 4ᵉ (Mº St-Paul). Mon–Sat 9.30am–1.30pm & 2.30–8.45pm. Tiny shop, one of the city's oldest specialists in dietary, macrobiotic and vegetarian fare.

Salmon, seafood and caviar

Comptoir du Saumon, 60 rue François-Miron, 4e (Mº St-Paul). Mon–Sat 10am–10pm. Salmon especially, but eels, trout and all things fishy as well, plus a delightful little restaurant in which to taste the fare. Three other branches.

Snails

La Maison de l'Escargot, 79 rue Fondary, 15e (Mº Dupleix). Tues–Sat 9am–7.30pm, Sun 9am–1pm; closed mid-July to Sept. They even sauce them and re-shell them while you wait.

Wine

Le Baron Rouge, 1 rue Théophile-Roussel, 12e (Mº Ledru-Rollin). Tues–Fri 10am–2pm & 5–9.30pm, Sat 10am–9.30pm, Sun 10.30am–1pm. A good selection of dependable lower-range French wines; 7F for a small tasting glass. Very drinkable Merlot at 16F a litre, if you bring your own containers.

Caves Michel Renaud, 12 place de la Nation, 12e (Mº Nation). 9.30am–1pm & 2–8.30pm; closed Sun pm and Mon am. Established in 1870 and purveying superb-value French and Spanish wines, champagnes and Armagnac.

Music

New **cassettes and CDs** are not particularly cheap in Paris, but there are plenty of second-hand bargains, and you may come across selections that are novel enough to tempt you. Like the live music scene, there are albums of Brazilian, Caribbean, Antillais, African and Arab sounds that would be specialist rarities in London or the States, and there's every kind of jazz.

Afric' Music, 3 rue des Plantes, 14e (Mº Mouton-Duvernet). Mon–Sat 10am–7pm. A small shop with an original selection of African, Caribbean and reggae discs.

BPM Records, 1 rue Keller, 11e (Mº Bastille). Mon–Sat noon–8pm. Specialists in house, including acid, hip-hop, rap, techno and dub. A good place to pick up club flyers.

Camara, 45 rue Marcadet, 18e (Mº Marcadet-Poissonnière). Mon–Sat noon–8pm. The best selection of West African music on cassette and video in town.

Crocodisc, 40–42 rue des Écoles, 5e (Mº Maubert-Mutualité). Tues–Sat 11am–7pm. Folk, Oriental, Afro-Antillais, funk, reggae, salsa, rap, soul, country, new and second-hand. Some of the best prices in town.

Crocojazz, 64 rue de la Montagne-Ste-Geneviève 5e; 40; & 42 rue des Ecoles, 5e (all Mº Maubert-Mutualité). Tues–Sat 11am–1pm & 2–7pm. Mainly new imports: jazz, blues, gospel and country.

Dream Store, 4 place St-Michel, 6e (Mº St-Michel). Mon 1.30pm–7.15pm, Tues–Sat 9.30am–7.15pm. Good discounts on jazz and classical in particular but also rock and folk.

FNAC Musique, 4 place de la Bastille, 12e, next to opera house (Mº Bastille). Mon–Sat 10am–8pm, Wed till 10pm. Extremely stylish shop in black, grey and chrome, with computerized catalogues, books, every variety of music, and a concert booking agency. The other FNAC shops (see above under "Bookshops") also sell music and hi-fi; the branch at 24 bd des Italiens, 9e, has a greater emphasis on rock and popular music, and stays open till midnight.

Paul Beuscher, 15–29 bd Beaumarchais, 4e; ☎01.44.54.36.00 (Mº Bastille). Mon–Fri 9.45am–12.30pm & 2–7pm, Sat 9.45am–7pm. A music department store that's been going strong for over 100 years. Instruments, scores, books, recording equipment, etc.

Virgin Megastore, 56–60 av des Champs-Élysées, 8e (Mº Franklin-D-Roosevelt); and Carrousel du Louvre, 1er (Mº Louvre–Rivoli). Mon–Sat 10am–midnight, Sun noon–midnight. The biggest and trendiest of all Paris's music shops. Concert booking agency and expensive Internet connection.

Sport and outdoor pursuits

Au Vieux Campeur, 48 rue des Écoles, 5e (Mº Maubert-Mutualité). Mon 2–7pm, Tues–Fri 9.30am–8.30pm, Sat 9.30am–8pm. Maps, guides, climbing, hiking, camping, ski gear, plus a kids' climbing wall.

Le Ciel Est à Tout le Monde, 10 rue Gay-Lussac, 5ᵉ (RER Luxembourg). Mon–Sat 10am–7pm; closed Mon in Aug. The best kite shop in Europe. It also sells frisbees, boomerangs, etc, plus books and traditional toys.

Nomades, 37 bd Bourdon, 4ᵉ (☎01.44.54.07.44; Mᵒ Bastille). Mon–Fri 11am–7pm, Sat & Sun 10am–7pm. The place to buy and hire roller-blades and equipment, with its own bar out back where you can find out about the scene. See also "In-line skating" p.171.

Markets

Markets, like shops, are grand spectacles. Mouthwatering arrays of **food** from half the countries of the globe, intoxicating in colour, shape and smell, assail the senses in even the drabbest parts of town. Though the food is perhaps the best offering of the Paris markets, there are also street markets dedicated to **second-hand goods** (the *marchés aux puces*), **clothes** and **textiles, flowers, birds, books** and **stamps**. Note that several of the markets listed below are described in more detail in the *Guide*.

Flea markets (marchés aux puces)

Porte de Montreuil, 20ᵉ (Mᵒ Porte-de-Montreuil). Sat, Sun & Mon 7am–7pm. Best of the flea markets for second-hand clothes – cheapest on Mon when leftovers from the weekend are sold off. Also old furniture, household goods and assorted junk.

Porte de Vanves, av Georges-Lafenestre/av Marc-Sangnier, 14ᵉ (Mᵒ Porte-de-Vanves). Sat & Sun 7am–7pm. The obvious choice for bric-a-brac.

St-Ouen/Porte de Clignancourt, 18ᵉ (Mᵒ Porte-de-Clignancourt). Sat, Sun & Mon 7.30am–7pm. The biggest and most touristy flea market, with stalls selling new and secondhand clothes, shoes, records, books and junk of all sorts, as well as expensive antiques.

Books and stamps

Marché aux Livres, Pavillon Baltard, Parc Georges-Brassens, rue Brancion, 15ᵉ (Mᵒ Porte-de-Vanves). Sat & Sun 9am–6pm. Second-hand and antiquarian books.

Marché aux Timbres, junction of avs Marigny and Gabriel, 8ᵉ (Mᵒ Champs-Élysées–Clemenceau). Thurs, Sat, Sun & hols 10am–dusk. *The* stamp market.

Food markets

Markets usually start between 7am and 8am and tail off around 1pm. The covered markets have specific opening hours, which are given below along with details of locations and days of operation.

Belleville, bd de Belleville, 20ᵉ (Mᵒ Belleville/Ménilmontant). Tues & Fri.

Buci, rue de Buci & rue de Seine, 6ᵉ (Mᵒ Mabillon). Tues–Sun.

Carmes, place Maubert, 5ᵉ (Mᵒ Maubert-Mutualité). Tues, Thurs & Sat.

Convention, rue de la Convention, 15ᵉ (Mᵒ Convention). Tues, Thurs & Sun.

Dejean, place du Château-Rouge, 18ᵉ (Mᵒ Château-Rouge). Tues–Sun.

Edgar-Quinet, bd Edgar-Quinet, 14ᵉ (Mᵒ Edgar-Quinet). Wed & Sat.

Enfants-Rouges, 39 rue de Bretagne, 3ᵉ (Mᵒ Filles-du-Calvaire). Tues–Sat 8am–1pm & 4–7pm, Sun 9am–1pm.

Monge, place Monge, 5ᵉ (Mᵒ Monge). Wed, Fri & Sun.

Montorgueil, rue Montorgueil & rue Montmartre, 1ᵉʳ (Mᵒ Châtelet-Les Halles/Sentier). Tues–Sat 8am–1pm & 4pm–7pm, Sun 9am–1pm.

Mouffetard, rue Mouffetard, 5ᵉ (Mᵒ Censier-Daubenton). Tues–Sun.

Place d'Aligre, 12ᵉ (Mᵒ Ledru-Rollin). Tues–Sun until 1pm.

Port-Royal, bd Port-Royal, nr Val-de-Grâce, 5ᵉ (RER Port-Royal). Tues, Thurs & Sat.

Porte-St-Martin, rue du Château-d'Eau, 10ᵉ (Mᵒ Château-d'Eau). Tues–Sat 8am–1pm & 4–7.30pm, Sun 8am–1pm.

Raspail, bd Raspail, between rue du Cherche-Midi & rue de Rennes, 6ᵉ (Mᵒ Rennes). Tues & Fri. Organic on Sun.

Rue Cler, 7ᵉ (Mᵒ École-Militaire). Tues–Sat.

Rue de Lévis, 17ᵉ (Mᵒ Villiers). Tues–Sun.

Rue du Poteau, 18ᵉ (Mᵒ Jules-Joffrin). Tues–Sat.

Secrétan, av Secrétan/rue Riquet, 19ᵉ (Mᵒ Bolivar). Tues–Sat 8am–1pm & 4–7.30pm, Sun 8am–1pm.

Saint-Germain, rue Mabillon, 6ᵉ (Mᵒ Mabillon). Tues–Sat 8am–1pm & 4–7.30pm, Sun 8am–1pm.

Tang Frères, 48 av d'Ivry, 13ᵉ (Mᵒ Porte-d'Ivry). Tues–Sun 9am–7.30pm. Not really a market, but a vast emporium of all things Oriental, where speaking French will not help you discover the nature and uses of what you see before you. In the same yard there is also a Far Eastern flower shop.

Ternes, rue Lemercier, 17ᵉ (Mᵒ Ternes). Tues–Sat 8am–1pm & 4–7.30pm, Sun 8am–1pm.

Listings

Airlines Air France, 119 av des Champs-Élysées, 8ᵉ (☎08.02.80.28.02); British Airways, 12 rue Castiglione, 1ᵉʳ (☎08.02.80.29.02); British Midland, 4 pl de Londres, Roissy-en-France 95700 (☎01.48.62.55.52); Aer Lingus. 47 av de l'Opéra, 2ᵉ (☎01.47.42.12.50); Qantas, 7 rue Scribe, 9ᵉ (☎01.44.55.52.05); Air Canada, 31 rue Falguière 15ᵉ (☎01.44.50.20.20); Delta, 4 rue Scribe, 9ᵉ (☎01.47.68.92.92).

American Express, 11 rue Scribe, 9ᵉ; ☎01.47.77.79.79 (Mon–Fri 9am–6.30pm, Sat 9am–5pm, Sun 10am–5pm; Mᵒ Opéra).

Babysitting Two main agencies: Ababa, with English speakers (☎01.45.49.46.46), and Kid Services (☎01.47.66.00.52). Apart from these, you could scan the notices at the American Church, 65 quai d'Orsay, 6ᵉ (Mᵒ Invalides), or at the Alliance Française, 101 bd Raspail, 6ᵉ (Mᵒ St-Placide).

Banks and change Money-exchange bureaux are at the airports (Charles de Gaulle 6.30am–11.30pm; Orly 6.30am–11pm); train stations (latest at Gare de Lyon: 6.30am–11pm); and CCF, 115 av Champs-Élysées, 8ᵉ (8.30am–8pm; Mᵒ Georges-V). There are also automatic exchange machines at the airports, train stations and outside many money-exchange bureaux. Credit and debit cards can be used in many cash machines. Also see American Express, above.

Bike rental Charges start from about 80F a day with a caution (deposit) of 1000F–2500F. If you want a bike for Sunday, when all of Paris takes to the quais, you'll need to book in advance. Try Paris-Vélo, 2 rue du Fer-à-Moulin, 5ᵉ (☎01.43.37.59.22; Mᵒ Censier-Daubenton), 21-speed and mountain bikes; Paris À Vélo C'est Sympa, 37 bd Bourdon, 4ᵉ (01.48.87.60.01; Mᵒ Bastille), who also offer commendable bicycle tours; Bike N'Roller, 6 rue St-Julien-Le-Pauvre; 5ᵉ (☎01.44.07.35.89); or the Maison du Vélo, 11 rue Fénélon, 10ᵉ (Mᵒ Gare du Nord or Poissonniere), with summer outlets at the Gare-de-L'est and Gare-du-Montparnasse.

Buses For national and international buses, including Eurolines (☎01.49.72.51.51), you can get information and tickets at the main terminus, 28 av du Général-de-Gaulle, Bagnolet (Mᵒ Gallieni).

Car rental Local firms include Acar, 99 bd Auguste-Blanqui, 13ᵉ (☎01.45.88.28.38); Dergi, 133bis rue de Paris, 20ᵉ (☎01.43.68.55.55; Mᵒ Liberté); Locabest, 3 rue Abel, 12ᵉ (☎01.43.46.05.05; Mᵒ Gare-de-Lyon), and 104 bd Magenta, 10ᵉ (☎01.44.72.08.05; Mᵒ Gare du Nord). Look up 'location' in the Yellow Pages for others.

Dental treatment Emergency service: SOS Dentaire, 87 bd Port-Royal, 5ᵉ; ☎01.43.37.51.00 (Mᵒ Port-Royal).

Embassies/Consulates Australia, 4 rue Jean-Rey, 15ᵉ (☎01.40.59.33.00; Mᵒ Bir-Hakeim); Britain, 35 rue du Faubourg-St-Honoré, 8ᵉ (☎01.44.51.31.00; Mᵒ Concorde); Canada, 35 av Montaigne, 8ᵉ (☎01.44.43.29.00; Mᵒ Franklin-D-Roosevelt); Ireland, 4 rue Rude, 16ᵉ (☎01.44.17.67.00; Mᵒ Charles-de-Gaulle–Étoile); New Zealand, 7ter rue Léonardo-de-Vinci, 16ᵉ (☎01.45.00.24.11; Mᵒ Victor-Hugo); South Africa, 59 quai d'Orsay, 7ᵉ (☎01.53.59.23.23; Mᵒ Invalides); USA, rue St-Florentin, 1ᵉʳ (☎01.43.12.22.22; Mᵒ Concorde).

Emergencies Call ☎18 or SOS-Médecins (☎01.47.07.77.77) for 24-hr medical help; ☎15 for 24-hr ambulance (SAMU) service.

Feminism Best place to make contact is the Maison des Femmes, 163 rue de Charenton, 12ᵉ (Wed & Fri 4–7pm, Fri café 7–10pm; ☎01.43.43.41.13; Mᵒ Reuilly-Diderot/Gare de Lyon). A women's meeting place used by a variety of lesbian and feminist groups.

Festivals There's not much in the carnival line, though kids armed with bags of flour aiming to make a total fool of you appear on the streets during Mardi Gras (in Feb). There are free concerts and street performers all over Paris for the Fête de la Musique which coinicides with the summer solstice (June 21), with Gay Pride around this date. July 14 (Bastille Day) is celebrated with official pomp in parades of tanks down the Champs-Élysées, firework displays and concerts. The French Communist Party, with the left-wing newspaper *L'Humanité*, hosts an annual Fête de l'Humanité in September at La Courneuve, just north of Paris, with representatives of just about every CP or ex-CP in the world, bands and eats that bring in Parisians of most political persuasions. See Basics for other music and religious festivals.

Gay and lesbian life A few bars and clubs are listed in the "Nightlife" and "Eating and drinking" sections. There are numerous gay organizations (far fewer lesbian ones): best place for information is the Centre Gai et Lesbienne, 3 rue Keller, 11ᵉ; ☎01.43.57.21.47 (Mᵒ Ledru-Rollin). The Gay Switchboard equivalent is SOS Écoute Gai (daily 6–10pm; ☎01.44.93.01.02). Lots of free mags with the latest listings can be picked up at the gay bookshop Les Mots à la Bouche, 6 rue Ste-Croix-de-la-Bretonnerie, 4ᵉ (☎01.42.78.88.30; Mᵒ St-Paul) in the heart of the very gay Marais district.

Helpline SOS Helpline in English: any problems, call ☎01.47.23.80.80 (daily 3–11pm). The American Church offers help and counselling on ☎01.45.50.26.49 (Mon–Sat 9.30am–1pm).

Hitching Allostop-Provoya, 8 rue Rochambeau, square Montholon, 9ᵉ (Mon–Fri 9am–7.30pm, Sat 9am–1pm & 2–6pm; ☎01.53.20.42.42; Mᵒ Cadet/Poissonnière) is the national hitching organisation. See Basics, for more details.

Hospitals English-speaking hospitals include the American Hospital, 63 bd Victor-Hugo, Neuilly-sur-Seine (☎01.46.41.25.25; Mᵒ Porte Maillot then bus #82 to terminus); and the Hertford British Hospital, 3 rue Barbès, Levallois-Perret (☎01.46.39.22.22; Mᵒ Anatole-France).

Internet access At Vidéothèque de Paris (see p.169); Virgin Megastore (p.178); British Council Library; *Web Bar* (p.148); and *Cyber Café Latino* (p.150).

Language schools French lessons from the Alliance Française, 101 bd Raspail, 6ᵉ (☎01.45.44.38.28), and numerous other establishments. A full list is obtainable from embassy cultural sections.

Laundries Self-service places have multiplied in Paris over the last few years, and you'll probably find one near where you're staying.

Left luggage As a security measure only the left-luggage lockers, with heavy security, at the Gare du Nord are definitely operating.

Libraries The British Council, 9 rue de Constantine, 7ᵉ, has a paying library, with daily newspapers (Mon–Fri 11am–6pm; ☎01.49.55.73.23; Mᵒ Invalides); the American Library in Paris, 10 rue du Général-Camou, 7ᵉ (Tues–Sat 10am–7pm; ☎01.53.59.12.60; Mᵒ École-Militaire), with American papers and a vast range of books, also charges readers. The library of the Canadian Council, next door to the British, is free. Interesting French collections include the BPI–Brantôme at 11 rue Brantôme, 3ᵉ (Mon & Wed–Fri noon–10pm, Sat, Sun & pub hols 10am–10pm; closed Tues & May 1; Mᵒ Rambuteau) the smaller temporary home of the nearby Pompidou Centre's library with a vast collection, including all the foreign press, videos and a language lab; Bibliothèque Forney at the Hôtel de Sens, with books being a good excuse if you want to visit this medieval bishop's palace at 1 rue du Figuier in the 4ᵉ; (Tues–Sat 1.30–8pm; 20F; Mᵒ Pont-Marie); and the Historique de la Ville de Paris, in the Hôtel Lamoignon, a sixteenth-century mansion housing centuries of texts and picture books on the city at 24 rue Pavée, 4ᵉ; (Mon–Sat 9.30am–6pm; Mᵒ St-Paul).

Lost property Bureau des Objets Trouvés, 36 rue des Morillons, 15ᵉ (Mᵒ Convention; Mon, Thurs & Fri 8.30am–5pm, Tues & Thurs till 8pm; ☎01.55.76.20.00).

Petrol There are 24-hr filling stations at all the *portes* of the city and in every arrondissement.

Pharmacies 24-hr service at Dhery, 84 av des Champs-Élysées, 8ᵉ (☎01.45.62.02.41; Mᵒ George-V).

Police ☎17 for emergencies. To report a theft, go to the *commissariat de police* of the arrondissement in which the theft took place.

Post office Main office at 52 rue du Louvre, Paris 75001 (Mᵒ Châtelet-Les Halles). Open daily 24hr for letters, poste restante, faxes, telegrams. and phone calls; currency exchange Mon–Fri 8am–7pm, Sat 8am–noon.

Train information For the bulk of information, see "City transport" (see p.83). Eurostar (☎08.36.35.35.39); Hoverspeed SeaTrain Express (☎08.00.90.17.77).

Travel firms Council Travel, 16 rue de Vaugirard, 6ᵉ (☎08.00.14.81.48; Mᵒ Odéon), is a dependable student/youth agency as is OTU Voyages, 119 rue St-Martin, 4ᵉ, opposite the Pompidou Centre

(☎01.40.29.12.12), Access Voyages, 6 rue Pierre-Lescot, 1er (☎01.44.76.84.50; M° Châtelet-Les Halles) has cheap transatlantic and train fares.

Out from the city

The region around the capital – the Île de France – and the borders of the neighbouring provinces are studded with large-scale **châteaux**. Many were royal or noble retreats for hunting and other leisured pursuits; some – like **Versailles** – were for more serious state show but they are all undoubtedly impressive: Vaux-le-Vicomte for its homogeneity and Chantilly for its masterpiece-studded art collection. If you have even the slightest curiosity about church buildings, make sure you visit the **cathedral** of **Chartres**, which is all it is cracked up to be – and more. Closer in, on the edge of the city itself, **St-Denis** boasts a cathedral second only to Notre-Dame among Paris churches – a visit to which can be combined with a wander back along the banks of the St-Denis canal. Other **waterside walks** include **Chatou** and the Marne-side towns with

---

ARTISTIC HAUNTS

For painters in search of visual inspiration, the countryside around Paris began to take a primary role in the late nineteenth-century and attracted many a Parisian-based artist, either on a day jaunt or on a more permanent basis. The towns along the banks of the Seine read like a roll-call of Musée d'Orsay paintings, and pockets of unchanged towns and scenery remain. Local museums, set up to record these pioneering artistic days, are well worth a visit.

Auvers-Sur-Oise
On the banks of the River Oise, about 35km northwest of Paris, **AUVERS** makes an attractive rural excursion. It is the place where Van Gogh spent the last two months of his life, in a frenzy of painting activity, producing more canvases than the days of his stay. The church at Auvers, the portrait of Dr Gachet, black crows flapping across a wheat field – many of Van Gogh's best-known works belong to this period. He died, in his brother's arms, after an incompetent attempt to shoot himself, in the tiny attic room he rented in the *Auberge Ravoux*. The **auberge** still stands, repaired and renovated, on the main street. A visit to Van Gogh's room (Tues–Sun 10am–6pm; 30F) is surprisingly moving. There is a short video about his time in Auvers.

At the entrance to the village is the **Château d'Auvers** which offers a fascinating tour (infra-red helmet on head) of the world the Impressionists inhabited (May–Oct Tues–Sun 10am–8pm; Nov–April 10am–6.30pm; 50F; ☎05.34.48.48.48). Most evocative of all is a walk through the old part of the village, past the church and the red lane into the famous wheat field and up the hill to the cemetery where, against the far left wall in a humble ivy-covered grave, the Van Gogh brothers lie side by side.

Auvers boasts a further artistic connection in Van Gogh's predecessor, Daubigny – contemporary of Corot and Daumier. A small museum (Weds–Sun: April–Oct 2.30–6.30pm; Nov–March 2–5.30pm; 20F), dedicated to him and his art and can be visited above the tourist office. His studio-house (Tues–Sun: April–Oct 2–6pm; 20F), built to his own requirements, can also be visited at 61 rue Daubigny. From here, Daubigny would go off for weeks at a time, in his boat, to paint. This is represented by a boat sitting in the garden which is, in fact, a replica of a smaller boat once owned by Monet.

To reach Auvers you can take trains from Gare du Nord or Gare St-Lazare, changing at Pontoise.

their memories of carousing, carefree painters and musicians in the early 1900s, when these places were open countryside or small villages. **Auvers-Sur-Oise** has a museum that transports you back to Impressionist days and landscapes, as well as laying claim to Van Gogh's final inspiration and resting-place. Whether the various suburban museums deserve your attention will depend on your degree of interest in the subjects they represent – china at **Sèvres**, French prehistory at **St-Germain-en-Laye**, Napoléon at **Malmaison**, or horses at **Chantilly**. The biggest pull for kids is without question **Disneyland Paris**, out beyond the bizarre satellite town of **Marne-la-Vallée**, but they might also like the air and space museum at **Le Bourget**.

Cathedrals

You'd have to go a very long way indeed to find any edifice to beat that of **Chartres** and it is well worth an excursion from Paris. The cathedral of **St-Denis**, right on the edge of Paris, predates Chartres and represents the first breakthroughs in Gothic art. It is also the burial place of almost all the French kings.

Chatou

A long narrow island in the Seine, the **Île de Chatou** was once a rustic spot to which Parisians came on the newly opened rail line to row on the river, and to dine and flirt at the *guinguettes*. A favourite haunt of many artists was the **Maison Fournaise**, just below the Pont de Chatou road bridge, which is now once again a restaurant (summer daily; winter Mon–Sat: lunch & eve until 10pm; menu 150F, *carte* 200–250F; ☎01.30.71.41.91), with a small **museum** of memorabilia (Wed–Sun 11am–5pm; permanent exhibition 15F, temporary exhibition 25F). One of Renoir's best-known canvases, *Le Déjeuner des Canotiers*, shows his friends lunching on the balcony, which is still shaded by a magnificent riverside plane tree. As well as many Impressionists, Vlaminck, Derain, other Fauves, and Matisse, were also habitués.

Access to the island is from the Rueil-Malmaison RER stop. Take the exit av Albert-1er, go left out of the station and right along the dual carriageway onto the bridge – a ten-minute walk. Bizarrely, the island hosts a twice-yearly **ham and antiques fair** (March & Sept), which is fun to check out.

Barbizon

The landscape and country living around **Barbizon**, southeast of Paris, inspired painters such as Rousseau and Millet to set up camp here, initiating an artistic movement, the Barbizon group. More painters followed as well as writers and musicians, all attracted by the lifestyle and community. The *Auberge du Père Ganne*, on the main road, became the place to stay, not unrelated to the fact that the generous owner accepted the artists' decorations of his inn and furniture as payment. Now home to a **museum** (Mon & Wed–Fri 10am–12.30pm & 2–5/6pm, Sat & Sun 10am–5/6pm; 25F), the inn still contains the original painted furniture as well as many Barbizon paintings.

Meudon

The tranquil suburb of **Meudon**, to the southwest of Paris, was where **Rodin** spent the last years of his life. In 1895, he acquired the **Villa des Brillants** (19 av Rodin, Meudon; ☎01.45.34.13.09; May–Oct Fri–Sun 1–6pm; 10F; RER line C to Meudon-Val Fleury, then a 15-minute walk along avs Barbusse & Rodin), and installed his studio in the first room you encounter as you enter through the veranda. It was in this room that he used to dine with his companion, Rose Beuret, on summer evenings, and here that he married her, after fifty years together, just a fortnight before her death in February 1917. His own death followed in November, and they are buried together on the terrace below the house, beneath a version of *The Thinker*. The classical facade behind them masks an enormous pavilion containing plaster casts of many of the most famous works.

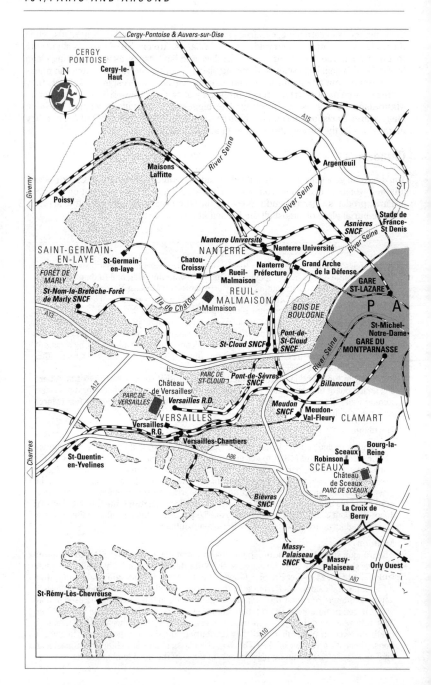

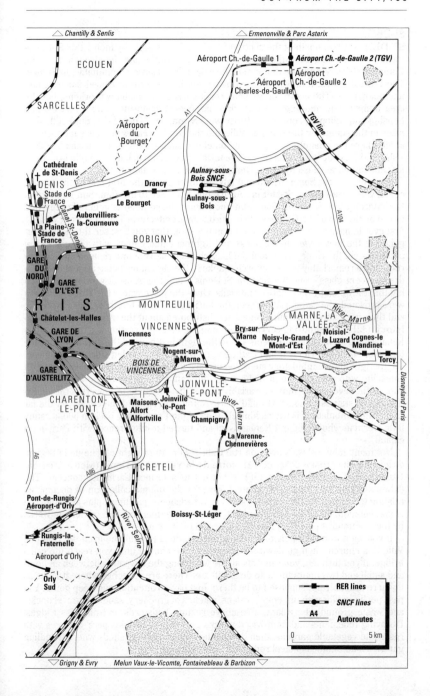

△ *Chantilly & Senlis*   △ *Ermenonville & Parc Asterix*

ECOUEN

Aéroport Ch.-de-Gaulle 1   **Aéroport Ch.-de-Gaulle 2 (TGV)**

Aéroport
Ch.-de-Gaulle 2

SARCELLES

Aéroport
Charles-de-Gaulle

TGV line

A1

Aéroport
du
Bourget

A104

+ Cathédrale
de St-Denis

Drancy

**Aulnay-sous-
Bois SNCF**

DENIS
Stade de
France

Le Bourget

**Aulnay-sous-
Bois**

Aubervilliers-
la-Courneuve

**La Plaine-
Stade de
France**

BOBIGNY

Canal St-Denis

**GARE
DU
NORD**   **GARE
D'L'EST**

River Marne

**MARNE-LA-
VALLÉE**

R I S

MONTREUIL

A3

Châtelet-les-Halles

VINCENNES

Vincennes

Bry-sur-
Marne

Noisy-le-Grand
Mont-d'Est

Noisiel-
le Luzard

Cognes-le
Mandinet

**GARE DE
LYON**

Nogent-sur-
Marne

**BOIS DE
VINCENNES**

Torcy

A4

△ *Disneyland Paris*

**GARE
D'AUSTERLITZ**

CHARENTON-
LE-PONT

**JOINVILLE-
LE-PONT**

Maisons
Alfort
Alfortville

Joinville-
le-Pont

River Marne

Champigny

**La Varenne-
Chennevières**

A6

A86

CRETEIL

River Seine

**Pont-de-Rungis
Aéroport-d'Orly**

**Rungis-la-
Fraternelle**

Boissy-St-Léger

Aéroport d'Orly

**Orly
Sud**

	RER lines
	SNCF lines
A4	Autoroutes

0   5 km

▽ *Grigny & Evry*   *Melun Vaux-le-Vicomte, Fontainebleau & Barbizon* ▽

St-Denis

ST-DENIS, 10km north of the centre of Paris and accessible by métro (M° St-Denis-Basilique), has long been the bastion of the Red suburbs and the stronghold of the Communist Party, and one of the most heavily industrialized communities in France. The recession has, however, taken a heavy toll in the form of closed factories and unemployment. The centre of St-Denis retains traces of small-town origins, but the area immediately abutting the cathedral has been transformed into a fortress-like housing and shopping complex. A thrice-weekly **market** (Tues, Fri & Sun) still takes place in the square by the Hôtel de Ville and the covered *halles* nearby, a multi-ethnic affair where the quantity of offal on the butchers' stalls – ears, feet, tails and bladders – shows this is not wealthy territory. The town's chief claim to fame, though, is its magnificent cathedral, close by the St-Denis Basilique métro station.

Begun by Abbot Suger, friend and adviser to kings, in the first half of the twelfth century, the **Basilique St-Denis** (April–Sept Mon–Sat 10am–7pm, Sun noon–7pm; Oct–March Mon–Sat 10am–5pm, Sun noon–5pm; closed hols) is generally regarded as the birthplace of the Gothic style in European architecture. The west front was the first ever to have a rose window, but it is in the choir that you best see the clear emergence of the new style: the slimness and lightness that comes with the use of the pointed arch, the ribbed vault and the long shafts of half-column rising from pillar to roof. It is a remarkably well-lit church thanks to the clerestory being almost one hundred percent glass – another first for St-Denis – and the transept windows being so big that they occupy their entire end walls. Once the place where the kings of France were crowned, the cathedral has been the burial place of all but three since 1000 AD, and their very fine tombs and effigies are distributed about the transepts and **ambulatory** (32F; closed during services). Among the most interesting are the enormous Renaissance memorial to François 1er on the right just beyond the entrance, and the tombs of Louis XII, Henri II and Catherine de Médicis on the left side of the church. To the right of the ambulatory steps you can see the stocky little general Bertrand du Guesclin, who gave the English the runaround after the death of the Black Prince, and on the level above him – invariably graced by bouquets of flowers – the undistinguished statues of Louis XVI and Marie-Antoinette. Around the corner on the far side of the ambulatory is Clovis himself, king of the Franks way back in 500, a canny little German who wiped out Roman Gaul and turned it into France, with Paris for a capital.

Not many minutes' walk away on rue Gabriel-Péri, third right off rue de la Légion-d'Honneur, the **Musée d'Art et d'Histoire de la Ville de St-Denis** (Mon & Wed–Sat 10am–5.30pm, Sun 2–6.30pm; 15F) is housed in a former Carmelite convent. The exhibits are not of spectacular interest, save for the unique collection of documents relating to the Commune: posters, cartoons, broadsheets, paintings, plus an audiovisual presentation. There is also an exhibition of manuscripts and rare editions of works by the Communist poet Paul Éluard, native son of St-Denis.

If you want to **walk back to Paris,** follow rue de la République from the Hôtel de Ville to a church, then go down the left side of the church until you reach the canal bridge. If you turn left, you can walk all the way along the towpath – between an hour-and-a-half and two hours to Porte de la Villette. There are stretches where it looks as if you're probably not supposed to be there. Just pay no attention and keep going. You pass peeling *villas* with unkempt gardens, patches of greenery, sand and gravel docks, and waste ground where larks rise above rusting bedsteads and doorless fridges. Decaying tenements and improvised shacks give way to lock-keepers' cottages with roses and vegetable gardens, then derelict factories and huge sheds where trundling gantries load bundles of steel rods onto Belgian barges.

Chartres

About 80km southwest of Paris, **CHARTRES** is a small and relatively undistinguished town. However, its **Cathédrale Notre-Dame** (Mon–Sat 7.30am–7.15pm, Sun 8.30am–7.15pm) is one of the finest examples of Gothic architecture in Europe and, built between 1194 and 1260, perhaps the quickest ever to be constructed. It is best experienced on a cloud-free winter's day when the low sun transmits the stained-glass colours to the interior stone, the quiet scattering of people leaves the acoustics unconfused, and the exterior is unmasked for miles around. For a medieval pilgrim, however, the cathedral would have been a glistening, fabulous jewel with all the exterior sculptures brightly painted and the walls inside whitewashed and covered with a myriad of refractions from the stained-glass windows. These, too, in their original pristine state would have been so bright they would have glittered from the outside along with the gold of the crowns and halos of the statuary.

For the contemporary visitor, however, there are more than enough wonders to enthral: the geometry of the building, unique in being almost unaltered since its consecration; the details of the stonework, the Renaissance choir screen and hosts of sculpted figures above each transept door; and the shining circular symmetries of the transept windows, virtually all of which are original, dating from the twelfth and thirteenth centuries. On the floor of the nave, hidden by chairs except on special occasions, is an original thirteenth-century labyrinth comprising a path over 200m long enclosed within a 13-metre diameter, the same size as the rose window above the main doors. It's a great rarity, since the authorities at other cathedrals had them pulled up as distracting frivolities.

Among paying extras, the crypt and treasures can wait for another time but, crowds permitting, it's worth climbing the **north tower** for its bird's eye view of the sculptures and structure of the cathedral (times vary, check in the cathedral; 25F). There are gardens at the back from where you can contemplate at ease the complexity of stress factors balanced by the flying buttresses. And if you hear a passionate and erudite Englishman giving **guided tours** as you're wandering around, it is probably Malcolm Miller, almost an institution in himself and a world expert on Chartres Cathedral. He does two tours daily from April to November (in the winter he may be away on a lecture tour, telephone for details ☎02.37.21.75.02) at noon and 2.45pm (40F), starting just inside the West Door.

Though the cathedral is the focus of a visit to Chartres, there are a few other attractions. The **Musée des Beaux Arts** (daily except Sun am & Tues May–Oct 10am–noon & 2–6pm; Nov–April 10am–noon & 2–5pm; 10F), in the former episcopal palace just north of the cathedral, has some beautiful tapestries, a room full of Vlaminck, and Zurbaran's *Sainte Lucie*, as well as good temporary exhibitions. Behind it, rue Chantault leads past old town houses to the river Eure and Pont du Massacre. You can follow this reedy river lined with ancient wash houses upstream via rue du Massacre on the right bank. The cathedral appears from time to time through the trees and, closer at hand, on the left bank, is the Romanesque church of **St-André**, now used for art exhibitions, jazz concerts and so on. Crossing back over at the end of rue de la Tannerie into rue du Bourg takes you back to the cathedral through the medieval town, decorated with details such as the carved salmon on a house on place de la Poissonnerie.

The **memorial** on the corner of rue Collin d'Arleville and boulevard de la Résistance is to Jean Moulin, Prefect of Chartres until he was sacked by the Vichy government in 1942. When the Germans occupied Chartres in 1940, he refused under torture to sign a document to the effect that black soldiers in the French army were responsible for Nazi atrocities. He later became de Gaulle's number one man on the ground, co-ordinating the Resistance, and died at the hands of Klaus Barbie in 1943.

PRACTICALITIES
From the **gare SNCF** (trains roughly every two hours from Gare du Montparnasse; 1hr), avenue J-de-Beauce leads straight up to place Châtelet. Diagonally opposite is rue Ste-Même, which leads to place Jean-Moulin; turn left here and you'll find the cathedral and the **tourist office** (April–Sept Mon–Sat 9am–7pm, Sun 9.30am–5.30pm; Oct–March Mon–Sat 10am–6pm, Sun 10am–1pm & 2.30–4.30pm; ☎02.37.21.50.00). They can supply **free maps** and help with **rooms** if you want to stay. Cloître-Notre-Dame, along the south side of the cathedral, has plenty of **eating** places, the one cheap one being *Café Serpente*, at no. 2. The best meals to be had in Chartres are at *La Truie qui File*, place de la Poissonnerie (closed Sun eve, Mon & Aug; ☎02.37.21.53.90).

Châteaux

The mansions and palaces around the capital are all very impressive at first sight, and most have played an integral part in French history. None more so than **Versailles** which epitomizes Louis XIV and his reign but whose size and splendour may over-whelm.

That said, **Vaux-le-Vicomte**'s classical magnificence and **Fontainebleau**'s Italianate decoration are easy to appreciate; **Chantilly** has a gorgeous Book of Hours and a bizarre horse collection; and **Malmaison** is interesting for its former occupants. You can also enjoy the country air by taking a stroll in the gardens, parks and forests that surround the châteaux, and you can get comfortably back to Paris in a day. Some châteaux, whose principal function these days is to house museums, are described later in this chapter, while the tourist office in Paris can provide full lists of others.

Versailles

The **Palace of Versailles** (May–Sept Tues–Sun 9am–6.30pm; Oct–April Tues–Sun 9am–5.30pm; closed hols; 45F, 35F after 3.30pm, or 70F for longer tours) is one of the three most-visited monuments in France. Apart from a few areas you can visit on your own, most of the palace can only be viewed in guided groups, whose various itineraries can be booked in the morning at entrance D. Long queues are common, though by hiring an audioguide (25F from entrance C) you avoid the queues and have access to many more rooms. Don't set out to see all the palace in one day – it is not possible.

To **get there**, take the RER line C5 to Versailles-Rive Gauche (40min), turn right out of the station and immediately left to approach the palace. You can get maps of the park from the **tourist office** on rue des Réservoirs, to the right of the palace (☎01.39.50.36.22; daily: May–Oct 9am–7pm; Nov–April 9am–noon & 2–6pm) or from their summer-only office in front of the palace gates.

THE PALACE
The **palace** was inspired by the young Louis XIV's envy of his finance minister's château at Vaux-le-Vicomte (see below), which he was determined to outdo. He recruited the design team of Vaux-le-Vicomte architect Le Vau, painter Le Brun and gardener Le Nôtre, and ordered something a hundred times the size. Versailles is the apotheosis of French regal indulgence and even if its extravagant decor and blatant self-propaganda of the Sun King are not to your liking, it will certainly leave an impression.

Construction began in 1664 and lasted virtually until Louis XIV's death in 1715. It was never meant to be a home; kings were not homely people. Second only to God, and the head of an immensely powerful state, Louis XIV was an institution rather than a private individual. His risings and sittings, comings and goings, were minutely regulated and rigidly encased in ceremony, attendance at which was an honour much sought after by courtiers. Versailles was the headquarters of every arm of the state. More than 20,000 people – nobles, administrative staff, merchants, soldiers and servants – lived in the palace in a state of unhygienic squalor, according to contemporary accounts.

Following Louis XIV's death, the château was abandoned for a few years before being reoccupied by Louis XV in 1722. It remained the residence of the royal family until the Revolution of 1789, when the furniture was sold and the pictures dispatched to the Louvre. Thereafter it fell into ruin and was nearly demolished by Louis-Philippe. In 1871, during the Paris Commune, it became the seat of the nationalist government, and the French parliament continued to meet in Louis XV's opera building until 1879. Restoration only began in earnest between the two world wars.

Of the rooms you can visit without a guide, the most stunning is the dazzling **Galerie des Glaces** – or Hall of Mirrors – where the Treaty of Versailles was signed to end World War I. Overdoses of gilding await you in the **grands appartements**, the state apartments of the king and queen, and the royal **chapel**, a grand structure that ranks among France's finest Baroque creations.

THE PARK AND GRAND AND PETIT TRIANONS

If you just feel like taking a look and a walk, the **park** (daily 7am–dusk; fountains play May–Sept Sun 11.15–11.45am & 3.30–5pm) is free except on Sundays (21F), and the scenery better the further you go from the palace. There are even informal groups of trees near the lesser outcrops of royal mania: the Italianate **Grand Trianon**, designed by Hardouin-Mansart in 1687 as a "country retreat" for Louis XIV; and the more modest Greek **Petit Trianon**, built by Gabriel in the 1760s for Louis XV's mistress, Mme de Pompadour (summer Tues–Sun 10am–6.30pm; winter Tues–Fri 10am–12.30pm & 2–5.30pm, Sat & Sun 10am–5.30pm; Grand Trianon 25F, Petit Trianon 15F, combined ticket 30F). More charming than either of these is **Le hameau de Marie-Antoinette**, a play village and farm built in 1783 for Louis XVI's queen to indulge the fashionable Rousseau-inspired fantasy of returning to the natural life.

Distances in the park are considerable. If you can't manage them on foot, a *petit train* shuttles between the terrace in front of the château and the Trianons (32F). There are **bikes** for hire at the Grille de la Reine, Porte St-Antoine and by the Grande Canal. **Boats** are for hire on the Grande Canal, within the Park.

Near the park entrance at the end of boulevard de la Reine is the **Hôtel Palais Trianon**, where the final negotiations for the Treaty of Versailles took place in 1919; the hotel has a wonderfully posh **tearoom**. The style of the *Trianon* is very much that of the town in general. The dominant population is aristocratic, with the pre-revolutionary titles disdainful of those dating merely from Napoléon. On Bastille Day both lots show their colours with black ribbons and ties.

Vaux-le-Vicomte

Of all the great mansions within reach of a day's outing from Paris, the classical **château of Vaux-le-Vicomte** (April–Oct daily 10am–6pm; Nov–March group bookings only – essential to phone ☎01.64.14.41.90; 56F), 46km southeast of Paris, is the most architecturally harmonious, the most aesthetically pleasing and the most human in scale.

To get there, take a train from Gare de Lyon to Melun (40min), then a taxi for the seven-kilometre ride to the château (approximately 100–120F).

THE CHÂTEAU

Louis XIV's finance superintendent, Nicholas Fouquet, had the **château** built at colossal expense, using the top designers of the day – architect Le Vau, painter Le Brun and landscape gardener Le Nôtre. The result was magnificence and precision in perfect proportion, and a bill that could only be paid by someone who occasionally confused the state's account with his own. The house-warming party, to which the king was invited, was more extravagant than any royal event – a comparison which other finance ministers ensured that Louis took to heart. Within three weeks Fouquet was jailed for life on trumped-up charges, and the design team carted off to build the king's own gaudy piece of one-upmanship at Versailles.

Seen from the entrance, the château is a rather austere grey pile surrounded by an artificial moat, and it's only when you go through to the south side – where clipped box and yew, fountains and statuary stand in formal gardens – that you can look back and appreciate the very harmonious and very French qualities of the building: the combination of steep, tall roof and central dome with classical pediment and pilasters.

As to the interior, the main artistic interest lies in the work of Le Brun, who was responsible for the two fine **tapestries** in the entrance, made in the local workshops set up by Fouquet specifically to adorn his house (and subsequently removed by Louis XIV to become the famous Gobelins works in Paris), as well as numerous **painted ceilings**, notably in Fouquet's Bedroom, the Salon des Muses, his *Sleep* in the Cabinet des Jeux, and the so-called King's Bedroom, whose decor is the first example of the style that became known as "Louis Quatorze".

Other points of interest are the **kitchens**, which have not been altered since construction, and – if you read French – a room displaying letters in the hand of Fouquet, Louis XIV and other notables. One, dated November 1794 (mid-Revolution), addresses the incumbent Duc de Choiseul-Praslin as *tu*. "Citizen," it says, "you've got a week to hand over one hundred thousand pounds . . .", and signs off with "Cheers and brotherhood". You can imagine the shock to the aristocratic system.

Every Saturday evening from May to mid-October, between 8pm and midnight (75F entrance), the **state rooms** are illuminated with a thousand candles, as they probably were on the occasion of Fouquet's fateful party. The **fountains** and other waterworks can be seen in action on the second and last Saturdays of each month between April and October, from 3pm until 6pm. In the stables, the **Musée des Équipages** comprises a collection of horse-drawn vehicles, including those used by Charles X fleeing Paris and the Duc de Rohan retreating from Moscow.

Fontainebleau

From the Gare de Lyon it's just a fifty-minute train ride to **FONTAINEBLEAU** (25min from Melun), famous for its vast, rambling **château** (daily except Tues: May–Oct 9.30am–5pm; Nov–April 9.30am–12.30pm & 2–5pm; 35F; Musée Chinois open when there's enough staff; Musée Napoléon guided tours morning only; Petits Appartements guided tours afternoon only although both prone to change, ring for details ☎01.60.71.50.70). Bus #AB from Fontainebleau-Avon station will take you to the château gates in a few minutes.

THE CHÂTEAU

The **château** owes its existence to its situation in the middle of a magnificent forest, which made it the perfect base for royal hunting expeditions. A hunting lodge was built here as early as the twelfth century, but only began its transformation into a luxurious palace during the sixteenth on the initiative of François 1er, who imported a colony of Italian artists – most notably Rosso il Fiorentino and Niccolò dell'Abate – to carry out the decoration. They were responsible for the celebrated **Galerie François-1er** – which had a seminal influence on the subsequent development of French aristocratic art and design – the Salle de Bal, the Salon Louis XIII, and the Salle du Conseil with its eighteenth-century decoration. The palace continued to enjoy royal favour well into the nineteenth century; Napoléon spent huge amounts of money on it, as did Louis-Philippe.

The **gardens** are equally luscious, but if you want to escape to the relative wilds, the surrounding **forest** of Fontainebleau is full of walking and cycling trails, all marked on Michelin map #196 (*Environs de Paris*).

Chantilly

CHANTILLY, a small town 40km north of Paris, is associated mainly with horses. Some 3000 thoroughbreds prance the forest rides of a morning, and two of the season's classiest flat races are held here. The stables in the château are given over to a museum of the horse.

Trains take about thirty minutes from Paris's Gare du Nord to Chantilly. Occasional free buses pass from the station to the château, though it's an easy walk away. **Footpaths** GR11 and 12 pass through the château park and its surrounding forest, if you want a peaceful and leisurely way of exploring this bit of country.

THE CHÂTEAU AND THE MUSÉE VIVANT DU CHEVAL

The Chantilly estate used to belong to two of the most powerful clans in France: first to the Montmorencys, then, through marriage, to the Condés. The present **château** (March–Oct daily except Tues 10am–6pm; Nov–Feb Mon & Wed–Fri 10.30am–12.45pm & 2–5pm, Sat & Sun 10.30am–5pm; 39F; park open daily, 17F) was put up in the late nineteenth century. It's an imposing rather than beautiful structure, surrounded by water and looking out over a formal arrangement of pools and pathways designed by the busy Le Nôtre.

The entrance is across a moat, past two realistic bronzes of hunting hounds. The visitable parts are mainly made up of an enormous collection of paintings and drawings of which only the *galeries de peinture* on the first floor are accessible without a guided tour. Stipulated to remain as organized by Henri d'Orléans (the donor of the château), the paintings are not well displayed, and you quickly get visual indigestion from the massed ranks of good, bad and indifferent, deployed as if of equal value. Some highlights, however, are in the Rotunda of the picture gallery; Piero di Cosimo's *Simonetta Vespucci* and Raphael's *Madone de Lorette*. Raphael is also well represented in the so-called Sanctuary, with his *Three Graces* displayed alongside Filippo Lippi's *Esther et Assuerius* and forty miniatures from a fifteenth-century Book of Hours attributed to the French artist Jean Fouquet. Pass through the Galerie de Psyche with its series of sepia stained glass illustrating Apuleius' *Golden Ass*, to the room known as the Tribune, where Italian art, including Botticelli's *Autumn*, takes up two walls, and Ingres and Delacroix have a wall each.

A free guided tour will take you round the main apartments. The first port of call is the well-stocked **library**, where the museum's single greatest treasure is kept, *Les Très Riches Heures du Duc de Berry*, the most celebrated of all the Books of Hours. The illuminated pages illustrating the months of the year with representative scenes from contemporary (early 1400s) rural life – like harvesting and ploughing, sheep-shearing and pruning – are richly coloured and drawn with a delicate naturalism. Only facsimiles are on view, but these give an excellent idea of the original. Thousands of other fine books are also displayed here. The rest of the tour is less interesting but if it leaves you with a hunger for more then you can pay for a guided visit to the small apartments on the ground floor.

A rather unique view of the château can be experienced by going up in a hot-air balloon (daily: March–Oct 10am–7pm; departure every 10 mins, duration of flight 10 mins; 45F), the *aérophile*, which is moored in the park. If the weather's not suitable or if you just don't fancy the hot-air balloon, you can take a 25min commentated boat trip (Feb 15–Nov 15 daily 10am–7pm; 45F, or 65F for both the boat and the balloon) all the way round the château and be dropped off at the entrance to the museum.

Five minutes' walk along the château drive, the colossal stable block has been transformed into a museum of the horse, the **Musée Vivant du Cheval** (April–Oct Mon & Weds–Fri 10.30am–5.30pm, Sat & Sun 10.30am–6pm; May & Jun also open Tues 10.30am–5.30pm; July & Aug also open Tues 2–5.30pm; Nov–March Mon–Fri 2–5pm, Sat & Sun 10.30am–5pm; 50F). The building was erected at the beginning of the eighteenth century by the incumbent Condé prince, who believed he would be reincarnated as a horse and wished to provide fitting accommodation for 240 of his future relatives. In the main hall, horses of different breeds from around the world are stalled, with a ring for demonstrations (April–Oct 11.30am, 3.30pm & 5.15pm; Nov–March weekends & public hols 11.30am, 3.30pm & 5.15pm, weekdays 3.30pm only), followed by a series of life-size models illustrating the various activities horses are used for. In the rooms off here are collections of paintings, horseshoes, veterinary equipment, bridles and saddles, a mock-up of a blacksmith's, children's horse toys (including a chain-driven number, with handles in its ears, which belonged to Napoléon III), and a fanciful Sicilian cart painted with scenes of Crusader battles.

Malmaison

The **château of Malmaison** (Mon & Weds–Fri 10am–noon & 1.30–5/6pm, Sat & Sun 10am–5/6pm; combined ticket with Bois-Préau museum 30F), set in the beautiful grounds of the **Bois-Préau**, about 15km west of central Paris, is a relatively small and surprisingly enjoyable place to visit.

This was the home of the Empress Josephine, and – during the 1800–1804 Consulate – of Napoléon, too. According to his secretary, "it was the only place next to the battlefield where he was truly himself". After their divorce, Josephine stayed on here, occasionally receiving visits from the emperor until her death in 1814.

Tours of the château include the private and official apartments, in part with original furnishings, as well as Josephine's clothes, china, glass and personal possessions. There are other Napoleonic bits in the **Bois-Préau museum** (Thurs–Sun same hours as château).

To get to **Malmaison** take the métro to Grande-Arche-de-la-Défense, then bus #258 to Malmaison-Château. Alternatively, if you'd like a walk, take the RER to Rueil-Malmaison and follow the GR11 footpath from the Pont de Chatou along the left bank of the Seine and into the château park.

Museums

The assortment of **museums** in the general vicinity of Paris are of specialist interest: **ceramics** at Sèvres, **prehistory** at St-Germain-en-Laye, and **aviation** at Le Bourget. All are excellent and shouldn't be missed if any of the subjects arouse interest. Some of the museums also provide a good excuse for walks.

Musée de l'Air et d'Espace

The French were always adventurous, pioneering aviators, and the name of **LE BOUR-GET** is intimately connected with their earliest exploits. Lindbergh landed here after his epic first flight across the Atlantic. From World War I to the development of Orly in the 1950s, this was Paris's principal airport, though nowadays it sees only internal flights. Some of the older buildings have been turned into a fascinating museum of flying machines.

To get there, take RER line B from Gare du Nord to Gare du Bourget, then bus #152 to Le Bourget/Musée de l'Air. Alternatively, take bus #350 from Gare du Nord, Gare de l'Est and Porte de la Chapelle, or #152 from Porte de la Villette.

The **museum** (Tues–Sun 10am–5/6pm; 30F) occupies the old airport buildings, and consists of five adjacent hangars and the Grande Galerie taking you from the earliest attempts to fly through to the latest spacecrafts. The Montgolfier brothers are the first on the scene with their invention of the hot air balloon. The room dedicated to them shows society going balloon-crazy before real aeroplane madness begins in the Grande Galerie; the first contraption to fly 1km, the first cross-channel flight, the first aerobatics. . . successes and failures are all on display here. Post-1918 continues in the hangars; however, the majority of the world-war I & II planes are indefinitely closed to the public. Highlights of world-war 11 planes are on display with the first Concorde prototype in the Hall Concorde whilst **Hangars C and D** cover the years from 1945 to the present day. Having lost eighty percent of its capacity in 1945, the French aviation industry has recovered to the extent that it now occupies a pre-eminent position in the world. Its high-tech achievement is represented here by the super-sophisticated best-selling Mirage fighters and two Ariane space-launchers, Ariane I and the latest, Ariane V (both parked on the tarmac outside). **Hangar E** contains light and sporty aircraft and **Hangar F**, nearest to the entrance, is devoted to **space**, with rockets, satellites, space capsules, etc. Some are mock-ups, some the real thing. Among the latter are a Lunar Roving Vehicle, the Soyuz craft in which a French astronaut flew, and France's own first successful space rocket. Everything is accompanied by extremely good explanatory panels – though in French only.

Musée des Antiquités Nationales

ST-GERMAIN is not specially interesting as a town, but if you've been to the prehistoric caves of the Dordogne, or plan to go, the **Musée des Antiquités Nationales** (daily except Tues 9am–5.15pm; 25F) is worth a visit. It is housed in the unattractively renovated château opposite St-Germain-en-Laye RER station, and was one of the main residences of the French court before Versailles was built.

The presentation and lighting make the visit a real pleasure. The extensive Stone Age section includes a mock-up of the Lascaux caves, a beautiful collection of decorative objects, tools and so forth, and a profile of Abbé Breuil, the priest who first published studies on paleolithic art and its meanings. All ages of prehistory are covered, right down into historical times with Celts, Romans and Franks: abundant evidence that the French have been a talented, arty lot for a very long time. The end-piece is a room of comparative archeology, with objects from cultures across the globe.

From right outside the château, a **terrace** – Le Nôtre arranging the landscape again – stretches for more than 2km above the Seine, with a view over the whole of Paris. Behind it is the **forest** of St-Germain, a sizeable expanse of woodland that's nowadays crisscrossed by too many roads to make this a convincing wilderness.

Musée de l'Île-de-France

The **Musée de l'Île-de-France** is housed in the **château of Sceaux**, a nineteenth-century replacement of the original – demolished post-Revolution – which matched the now-restored Le Nôtre grounds. The park is the usual classical geometry of terraces, water and woods, but if you fancy a stroll you can get off the RER at La-Croix-de-Berny at the southern end. Otherwise it's a five- to ten-minute walk from Parc-de-Sceaux station (15min from Denfert-Rochereau): turn left on av de la Duchesse-du-Maine, right into av Rose-de-Launay, and right again on av Le-Nôtre: the château gates are on your left.

The recently restored château was a country residence and the **museum** itself (April–Sept Mon, Wed–Sun 10am–6pm; Oct–March till 5pm; 23F; disabled access) evokes the Paris countryside of the *ancien régime* with its aristocratic and royal domains many of which no longer exist; and of the nineteenth century, with its riverside scenes and eating and dancing places, the *guinguettes*, that inspired so many artists. The collection consists of paintings, prints, and ceramics from various bygone Ile de France manufacturers.

Temporary exhibitions and a summer **festival of classical chamber music** (mid-July to third week in Sept) are held in the Orangerie, which, along with the Pavillon de l'Aurore (in the northeast corner of the park), survives from the original residence. For details of the concerts, call ☎01.46.60.07.79. In the summer you can get snacks and drinks in the park.

Musée National de la Céramique

The **Musée National de la Céramique** (daily except Tues 10am–5pm; 22F) in Sèvres is in easy reach of Paris: take the métro to the Pont-de-Sèvres terminus; cross the bridge and spaghetti junction; the museum is the massive building facing the river bank on your right. If you're interested in ceramics you will find much to savour here – not just French pottery and china, but Islamic, Chinese, Italian, German, Dutch and English. There is also, inevitably, a comprehensive collection of Sèvres ware, as the stuff is made right here. Close by, overlooking the river, the **Parc de St-Cloud** is good for fresh air and visual order, with a geometrical sequence of pools and fountains delineating a route down to the river and across to the city.

Disneyland Paris

Children will love **Disneyland Paris**, 32km east of the capital – there are no two ways about it. What their minders will think of it is another matter. For a start, there has to be the question of whether it's worth the money. Quite why American parents might bring their charges here is hard to fathom: even British parents might well decide that it would be easier, and cheaper, to buy a family package to Florida, where sunshine is assured and where the conflict between enchanted kingdom and enchanting city does not arise. In fact, foul north European weather does have its advantages. On an off-season wet and windy weekday (Mon & Thurs are the best) you can probably get round every ride you want. Otherwise, one-hour waits for the big rides are common.

The resort

With the opening of Space Mountain, Disneyland Paris does now provide a variety of good fear-and-thrill rides, though the majority of attractions remain very safe and staid. It takes its inspiration from film sets, not funfairs or big tops, which is why it's so wonderful for children. These sets are "real" – you can go into them and round them and the characters talk to you. All the structures are incredibly detailed, and their shades and textures worked out with the precision of a brain surgeon. But if you're not a child, solid buildings masquerading as flimsy film sets and constantly being filmed by swarming hordes of camcorder operators can well fail to fulfil any kind of escapist fantasy.

The **Magic Kingdom** is divided into four "lands" radiating out from **Main Street USA. Fantasyland** appeals to the youngest kids, with Sleeping Beauty's Castle, Peter Pan's Flight, Dumbo the Flying Elephant, the Mad Hatter's Teacups and Alice in Wonderland's Maze among its attractions. **Adventureland** has the most outlandish sets and two of the best rides – Pirates of the Caribbean and Indiana Jones and the Temple of Doom. **Frontierland** has the *Psycho*-inspired but insipid Phantom Manor and the hair-raising roller coaster Big Thunder Mountain, modelled on a runaway mine train. In **Discoveryland** there's a high-tech 3-D Michael Jackson film, a 360-degree

Parisian exposé in Le Visionarium, the Nautilus submarine of *20,000 Leagues Under the Sea* and the startling Space Mountain (see above). The grand **parade** of floats representing all the top box-office Disney movies sallies down Main Street USA at 3pm sharp every day (a good time to try for the more popular rides). Night-time Electrical Parades and **firework displays** take place several times a week.

Besides the theme park, the complex includes **Festival Disney**, the evening entertainments complex where you can splash out 325F for Buffalo Bill's Wild West Show, with real guns, horses, bulls and bison (nightly 6.30pm & 9.30pm; children 3–11 195F); and **grounds** beyond which you can play golf, do workouts, jog, ride bikes or ponies, skate, sail and take part in team sports. Festival Disney and the six themed **hotels** are a mixed bag of hideous eyesores and over-ambitious kitsch designed by some of the world's leading architectural names – Michael Graves, Antoine Predock, Robert Stern and Frank Gehry. According to Disney executives, Europeans needed something special: though they actually *invented* fairy-tales and castles, they have since run out of good ideas!

Practicalities

To reach Disneyland from Paris, take RER line A to Marne-la-Vallée Chessy/Disneyland (about 35–40 min; 76F return, child 38F; for prices of 1-, 2- and 3-day Paris Visite transport card including EuroDisney see p.85). If you're coming straight from the airport, there is a shuttle bus from both Charles de Gaulle and Orly (times and frequencies change seasonally, but roughly every 45min 8.30am–8pm; for recorded information call ☎01.64.30.66.56; adults 85F one-way, children 65F, under-3s free). Marne-la-Vallée Chessy also has its own TGV train station, linked to Lille, Lyon, and London (see p.82 for details of the direct Eurostar from London Waterloo and Ashford in Kent). If you're **driving**, the park is 32km east from Paris along the A4 (Exit 13 for Ranch Davy Crockett and Exit 14 for the park and the hotels); from Calais follow the A26 changing to the A1, the A104 and finally the A4.

Admission charges for the "passports" are: January to March excluding Christmas hols one-day pass 160F (child aged 3-11 130F), two-day pass 305F (250F), three-day pass 415F (335F); April to September and third week December to first week January one-day pass 200F (155F), two-day pass 385F (300F), three-day pass 545F (420F). Children under three are free. Opening hours vary greatly depending on the season and whether it is a weekend, and should be checked when you buy your ticket (or via the Internet on *www.disneylandparis.com*) but they are roughly low season daily 10am to 6pm, Saturday and Sunday till 8pm; high season daily 9am to 11pm.

Special packages are available in advance (for details call ☎01.60.30.60.53 in France, ☎1/407 W. DISNEY in the US and ☎0990/030303 in the UK) or you can buy admission passes and train tickets in Paris at all RER line A and B stations and in major métro stations.

The **accommodation** will be out of many people's price range, the least expensive hotel room – the two-star *Hotel Santa Fé* – off season being 435F a night (2 adults, 2 children), rising to around 2500F peak season for a room in the *Disneyland Hotel* inside the Magic Kingdom on Main Street. The cheapest alternative if you have a car is the park's *Davey Crockett Ranch*, a 15-minute drive away, with self-catering log cabins (sleeping 4–6) from 300F to 800F. To really economize, you could camp at the nearby *Camping du Parc de la Colline*, Route de Lagny, 77200 Torcy (☎01.60.05.42.32) which is open all year.

travel details

Trains

Gare d'Austerlitz to: Tours (hourly; 1hr).

Gare de l'Est to: Metz (9 daily; 2hr 30min); Nancy (11 daily; 2–3hr); Reims (8 daily; 1hr 30min); Strasbourg (every 2 hours; 4hr).

Gare de Lyon to: Avignon (6 daily; 4 hr); Besançon (6 daily; 2hr 30min); Dijon (8 daily; 1hr 40min); Grenoble (6 daily; 3hr 20min); Lyon (hourly; 2hr–2hr 30min); Marseille (every 2 hrs; 4hr 40min); Nice (6 daily; 7hr).

Gare Montparnasse to: Bayonne (6 daily; 4hr 30min); Bordeaux (hourly; 3hr); Brest (hourly until 7pm; 5hr 30min–6hr); Carcassonne (4 daily; 8hr); Nantes (frequent; 3hr 30min); Pau (8 daily; 5hr 30min); Poitiers (every 2 hr; 1hr 40min); Rennes (hourly; 2hr 30min); Toulouse (6 daily; 6hr–6hr 30min).

Gare du Nord to: Amiens (at least hourly; 1hr 45min); Arras (roughly every 2 hrs; 50min); Boulogne (at least hourly; 2hr 30min); Lille (hourly; 1hr).

Gare St-Lazare to: Caen (hourly; 2hr–2hr 30min); Cherbourg (roughly every 2 hrs; 3–3hr 30min); Dieppe (2 daily; 2hr 15min); Le Havre (every 2–3 hrs; 2–2hr 30min); Rouen (hourly; 1hr 15min).

Hitching

Hitching out of Paris isn't easy, especially in high summer when you are likely to face long delays. It's much better to spend a few extra francs taking a train or bus 50km clear of the city. Alternatively, for a small fee, you can register with the hitching organization Allostop-Provoya; they will find you a ride and require you only to make a small contribution towards petrol (see "Listings" for details).

CHAPTER TWO

THE NORTH

W hen conjuring up exotic holiday locations, you're unlikely to light upon the **north** of France. Even among the French, the most enthusiastic tourists of their own country, it has few adherents. Artois and Flanders include the most heavily industrialized parts of the country, while across the wheat fields of the more sparsely populated regions of Picardy and Champagne a few drops of rain are all that is required for total gloom to descend. It is likely, however, that you'll arrive and leave France via this region, and there are reasons to stop within easy reach of the channel ports – of which **Boulogne** is by far the most appealing.

The north of France has been on the path of various invaders into the country, from northern Europe as well as from Britain, and the events that have taken place in Flanders, Artois and Picardy have shaped French history. The bloodiest battles were those of World War I, above all the **Battle of the Somme**, which took place north of Amiens, and **Vimy Ridge**, near Arras, where the trenches have been preserved in perpetuity. Throughout the north, but particularly around the villages of the Somme, monuments and cemeteries are powerful reminders of the devastating human wastage of those years.

Picardy boasts two of France's finest cathedrals, at **Amiens** and **Laon**. Further south, the *maisons*, vineyards and produce of the **Champagne** region are the main draw, for which the best bases are **Épernay** and **Reims**, the latter with another fine cathedral. Other attractions include the bird sanctuary of **Marquenterre**; the wooded wilderness of the **Ardennes**; industrial archeology in the coalfields around Douai where Zola's *Germinal* was set; the great medieval castle of **Coucy-le-Château**; and the battle sites of the Middle Ages – **Agincourt** and **Crécy** – whose names are so familiar in the history of Anglo-French rivalry.

Though the past is not forgotten, the present life of the region does not feed on it. In city centres from **Lille** to **Troyes**, you'll find your fill of food, culture and entertainment in the company of locals similarly intent on having a good time; and in addition to the more obvious pleasures of the Champagne region, there's the possibility of finding relatively lucrative employment during the harvest season towards the end of September.

ACCOMMODATION PRICE CATEGORIES

Each hotel in this chapter has a symbol which corresponds to one of eight price categories.

① Under 160F	④ 300–400F	⑦ 600–700F
② 160–220F	⑤ 400–500F	⑧ Over 700F
③ 220–300F	⑥ 500–600F	

The prices quoted are for the cheapest available double room in high season, though remember that many of the cheap places will have more expensive rooms with en-suite facilities.

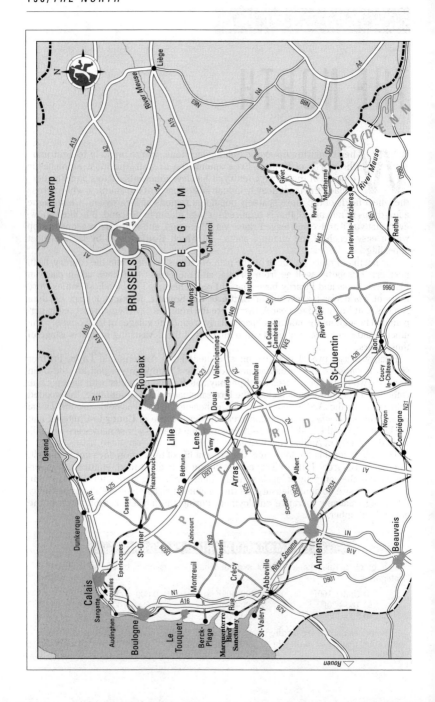

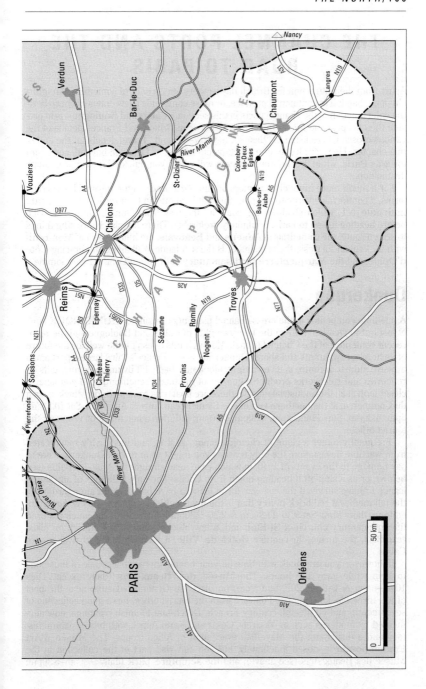

THE CHANNEL PORTS AND THE ROAD TO PARIS

Apart from their attraction for British day-trippers after a sniff of something foreign, a shopping bag full of continental produce, or more commonly a few crates of cheap beer, the chief function of the channel ports in this section – **Calais** and **Boulogne** – is to provide the cheapest and most efficient route between Britain and France. Details of the various crossings are listed in "Basics"; (see p.7–10) and "Travel details" at the end of this chapter. There are frequent train connections east to **Lille** and beyond, and south towards **Paris**, while the autoroute system will whisk you quickly off to your ultimate destination.

For a much more immediate immersion into *La France* – little towns, idiosyncratic farms, a comfortable verge to sleep off the first baguette and *vin rouge* – the old **route nationale N1**, which shadows the coast all the way from Dunkerque to Abbeville before heading inland to Paris, is infinitely preferable. There are also interesting things to see en route: the cathedrals at **Amiens** and **Beauvais**, the hilltop town of **Montreuil** with its Vauban fortress, the remains of Hitler's Atlantic Wall along the bracing **Côte d'Opale**, and the **Marquenterre bird sanctuary** at the mouth of the River Somme.

Dunkerque

A one-time competitor in the cross-channel passenger business, **DUNKERQUE** finally lost out in October 1997 to the heavyweights of Calais and Boulogne and the more recent contender of the Channel tunnel. Although this doesn't bode well for the future of its hotels, restaurants and shops, Dunkerque is still France's third largest port and a massive industrial centre in its own right, albeit now badly hit by unemployment; its oil refineries and steelworks produce a quarter of the total French output. If you fancy a closer look at all this industrial muscle, there are boat trips from place du Minck, bassin du Commerce, at the northern end of rue Clemenceau (July & Aug Mon–Sat 10.30am, 3pm, 4.30pm, Sun 11am, 3pm, 4.30pm, 5.30pm; 39F; for other times of year, ask the tourist office).

Frequently under a cloud of chemical smog, as it is, and unstylishly resurrected from wartime devastation, the only reasons you might want to visit Dunkerque are to pay homage to the events of 1940, in which case head straight for Malo-les-Bains (see below), or as a stop-off if heading north from Calais. The only buildings of any significance to have survived the last war (or at least to have been rebuilt afterwards) are the tall medieval red-brick **belfry** that is the town's chief landmark (July & Aug guided tours daily Mon–Sat 9.30–11.30am & 2.30–5.30pm hourly; 20F); the much-restored fifteenth-century church of **St-Éloi**; and, a few blocks south of the church on place Jean-Bart, the turn-of-the-century **Hôtel de Ville**, a Flemish fancy to rival that of Calais.

If, however, you are stuck with time on your hands, there are a couple of museums to help while away the hours. The **Musée des Beaux-Arts** (daily except Tues 10am–noon & 2–6pm; 20F, Sun free), on place du Général-de-Gaulle near the post office, three blocks along rue Poincaré from the tourist office, has a good collection of seventeenth- and eighteenth-century French, Dutch and Flemish paintings, now augmented by moderns such as Vasarely, César and Karel Appel, with bits of natural history and a display on the May 1940 evacuation of Allied troops. The **Musée d'Art Contemporain** is closed indefinitely, but you can visit part of the collection in the Musée des Beaux Arts (see above), and the **sculpture park** (daily 9.30am–5.30pm;

DUNKERQUE 1940

The evacuation of 350,000 Allied troops from the beaches of Dunkerque from May 27 to June 4, 1940, has become one of those heroic wartime legends which conveniently conceals the fact that the Allies, through their own incompetence, almost lost their entire armed forces in the first few weeks of the war.

The German army had taken just ten days to reach the English Channel and could very easily have finished off the job. Unable to believe the ease with which he had overcome a numerically superior enemy, Hitler ordered his generals to halt their lightning advance, giving Allied forces trapped in the Pas-de-Calais enough time to organize Operation Dynamo, the largest wartime evacuation ever undertaken. Initially it was hoped that around 10,000 men would be saved, though thanks to low-lying cloud and the assistance of over 1750 vessels – among them pleasure cruisers, fishing boats and river ferries – 140,000 French and over 200,000 British soldiers were successfully shipped back to England.

In France, the ratio of Brits to French evacuees caused bitter resentment since Churchill had promised that the two sides would go *bras dessus, bras dessous* ("arm in arm"). Meanwhile, the British media played up the "remarkable discipline" of the troops as they waited to embark, the "victory" of the RAF over the Luftwaffe, and the "disintegration" of the French army all around. In fact, there was widespread indiscipline in the early stages as men fought for places on board; the battle for the skies was evenly matched; and the French fought long and hard to cover the whole operation, some 150,000 of them remaining behind to become prisoners of war. In addition, the Allies lost 7 destroyers and 177 fighter planes and were forced to abandon over 60,000 vehicles.

July & Aug 9am–8pm; free), beside the canal on avenue des Bains, is still open to the public. More interesting, especially for children, is the **Musée Portuaire** (daily except Tues 10am–12.45pm & 1.30–6pm; July &Aug 10am–6pm; 25F), at 9 quai de la Citadelle on the Bassin du Commerce, illustrating the history of Dunkerque the port, from its beginnings as a fishing hamlet (models of boats, tools of the different trades, etc).

Practicalities

The **tourist office** (May–Sept Mon–Sat 9am–6.30pm, Sun 10am–noon & 3–5pm; Oct–April Mon–Fri 9am–noon & 1.30–5.30pm, Sat 9am–5.30pm, Sun 10am–noon & 3–5pm; ☎03.28.66.79.21, fax 03.28.26.27.28), a short walk from the **gare SNCF**, is on the ground floor of the town belfry on rue de l'Amiral Ronarc'h. If you're looking to **rent a car**, Europcar, 1 rue du Chemin-de-Fer (Mon–Fri 8am–7pm, Sat 8am–noon & 2–6pm; ☎03.28.66.45.61), provides affordable rates.

Two cheap **accommodation** options by the station on place de la Gare are *Terminus Nord* (☎03.28.66.54.26; ①) and the comfortable two-star *Le Select* (☎03.28.66.64.47, fax 03.28.66.03.47; ②). More salubrious hotels away from the station include the *Borel*, overlooking the fishing boats of the Bassin du Commerce on rue Hermitte (☎03.28.66.51.80, fax 03.28.59.33.82; ④), a modern three-star with well set-up rooms; and the equally well-equipped but more old-fashioned *Europ* (close by at 13 rue Leughenaer (☎03.28.66.29.07, fax 03.28.63.67.87; ④). Alternatively, try the centrally placed *Welcome*, at 37 rue Poincaré (☎03.28.59.20.70, fax 03.28.21.03.49; ④). There's also a seafront HI **youth hostel** on place Paul-Asseman, 2km east of the centre, practically at Malo-les-Bains (☎03.28.63.36.34, fax 03.28.63.24.54; take blue bus #3 to Piscine, direction "Malo-les-Bains".

You could do a lot worse than **eat** at the station buffet, the *Richelieu*, though it's not especially cheap. Other possibilities include *Aux Halles*, on rue de l'Amiral-Ronarc'h, near the tourist office, a pleasant bar/brasserie with a decent *menu complet* for 50F; or the *Taverne le Tormore*, 11 place Charles-Valentin, near the town hall, a brasserie/grill with Flemish dishes. At 37 rue Poincaré, the Alsatian-Flemish *Relais d'Alsace* is a reliable standby, with menus from 69F. For more enjoyable eating options, head for Malo-les-Bains (see below).

Malo-les-Bains and around

A more attractive place to stop off is **MALO-LES-BAINS**, a surprisingly pleasant nine-teenth-century seaside suburb on the east side of town (bus #3 & #9), from whose vast sandy beach the Allied troops embarked in 1940 (see box above). Digue des Alliés is the dirtier end of an extensive **beachfront** promenade lined with cafés and restaurants; at the cleaner Digue des Mers end, the beach can almost seem pleasant when the sun comes out – that is, if you avert your eyes from the industrial inferno to the west. The suburb actually reveals its turn-of-the-century charm away from the seafront, a few parallel blocks inland along avenue Faidherbe and its continuation avenue Kléber, with the pretty green place Turenne sandwiched in between; around here you'll find some excellent pâtisseries, boulangeries and charcuteries.

Places to **stay** include the *Hirondelle*, 48 av Faidherbe (☎03.28.63.17.65, fax 03.28.66.15.43; ③), a modern two-star in a great position; and the unassuming, less expensive *Au Bon Coin*, 49 av Kléber (☎03.28.69.12.63, fax 03.28.69.64.03; ②), whose cosy bar is good for a drink. Both have well-regarded restaurants specializing in seafood: menus from 65F at the *Hirondelle*, and from 80F at the more intimate and relaxed *Au Bon Coin*. Also on avenue Kléber are a few ethnic eateries, including a Vietnamese and a North African restaurant. For a quiet coffee or **snack** in light airy surrounds, try *Le Central* on place Turenne, a welcoming corner bar facing the park. Two popular beachfront brasseries, again specializing in seafood, are *L'Iguane*, 15 Digue des Alliés, a down-to-earth establishment offering generous servings (couscous too), and the stylish but more expensive *Le Pavois*, at the nicer end of the beach.

Moving on from Dunkerque by car, you'll be shepherded quickly (unless you take pains to avoid it) onto the autoroute system, with links to Belgium, Germany and Paris. Heading west along the coast, on the other hand, brings you to Vauban-walled **GRAV-ELINES**, 16km from Dunkerque, site of one of France's many nuclear reactors.

Calais

CALAIS is less than 40km from England – the Channel's narrowest crossing – and by far the busiest French passenger port. The port (and its accompanying petrochemical works) dominates the town; in fact, there's not much else here. In the last war the British destroyed it to impede its use, fearing a German invasion, but the French still refer to it as "the most English town in France", an influence that began after the battle of Crécy in 1346, when Edward III seized it for use as a beachhead in the Hundred Years' War. It remained in English hands until 1558, when its loss caused Mary Tudor famously to say: "When I am dead and opened, you shall find Calais lying in my heart." The association has been maintained by various Brits across the centuries: Lady Emma Hamilton, Lord Nelson's mistress; Oscar Wilde on his uppers; Nottingham lacemakers who set up business in the early nineteenth century; and, nowadays, nine million British travellers per year, plus another million-odd day-trippers.

Arrival, information and accommodation

Don't bother walking into town from the ferry terminal (Calais-Maritime train station). There's a free daytime **bus** service to place d'Armes and the central Calais-Ville train station in Calais-Sud. The **gare routière** is at the southern end of boulevard Jacquard,

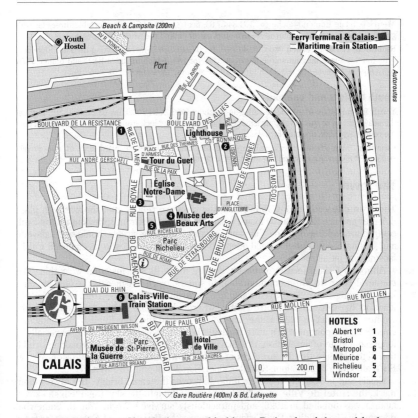

△ Beach & Campsite (200m)
Youth Hostel
AV R. POINCARE
Port
RUE DE L.P. AYRON
Ferry Terminal & Calais-Maritime Train Station
▷ Autoroutes
BOULEVARD DE LA RESISTANCE
BOULEVARD DES ALLIES
RUE DE LA MER
RUE DES ALLIES
❶ Lighthouse
PLACE D'ARMES
RUE DES THERMES
CDT BONNINQUE
❷
RUE DE LISBONNE
QUAI DE LA LOIRE
RUE ANDRE GERSCHELL
Tour du Guet
RUE DE LA PAIX
RUE DE LONDRES
RUE DE MOSCOU
RUE ROYALE
Église Notre-Dame
❸
PLACE D'ANGLETERRE
❹ Musée des Beaux Arts
❺
RUE RICHELIEU
RUE DE STRASBOURG
Parc Richelieu
RUE DE ROME
RUE DE BRUXELLES
BD CLEMENCEAU
ⓘ
N
QUAI DU RHIN
❻ Calais-Ville Train Station
RUE MOLLIEN
RUE MOLLIEN
AVENUE DU PRESIDENT WILSON
BD JACQUARD
RUE PAUL BERT
RUE DESCARTES
CALAIS
Parc St-Pierre
Musée de la Guerre
Hôtel de Ville
RUE JEAN JAURES
RUE ARISTIDE BRIAND
0   200 m

HOTELS
Albert 1er	1
Bristol	3
Metropol	6
Meurice	4
Richelieu	5
Windsor	2

▽ Gare Routiére (400m) & Bd. Lafayette

by the municipal theatre. If you're intent on **hitching** to Paris, take a left out of the ferry terminal – the new autoroute bypass begins almost immediately, leading to both the A26 and the old N1. If you plan to **rent a car**, Avis (☎03.21.34.66.50) and Budget (☎03.21.96.42.20) are located in place d'Armes; cheaper options include EuroRent, 1 rue des Thermes (☎03.21.34.41.99) and Citer at the ferry terminal (☎03.21.34.58.45). For ferry crossings, see p.7–10.

Should you need to stay, there's plenty of cheap **accommodation** available, though it can be tricky finding a room late in the day in high season. If you're going to miss the boat home, phone before you arrive to book a room. Alternatively, you could use the **tourist office accommodation service** at 12 bd Clemenceau, the continuation of rue Royale (Mon–Sat 9am–7pm, Sun 10am–1pm; ☎03.21.96.62.40, fax 03.21.96.01.92), for which there is a small charge.

Hotels

Albert 1er, 51–53 rue de la Mer (☎03.21.34.36.08, fax 03.21.34.14.05). Only hotel with seafront views, albeit a little worn and noisy. ③.

Bristol, 13 rue du Duc-de Guise, off rue Royale (☎03.21.34.53.24). A clean, simple and pleasant place to stay. ②.

Metropol, 43 quai du Rhin (☎03.21.97.54.00, fax 03.21.96.69.70). On the canal between the tourist office and town hall. Comfortable, modern and nondescript. ④.

Meurice, 5 rue Edmond-Roche (☎03.21.34.57.03, fax 03.21.34.14.71). Comfortable three-star with grand entrance and antique furniture in a quiet street behind the Musée des Beaux-Arts. ④.

Richelieu, 17 rue Richelieu (☎03.21.34.61.60, fax 03.21.85.89.28). Overlooking the Parc Richelieu. This hotel offers a bargain soirée étape, at 350F for two, which includes B&B and dinner at *La Brasérade* just across rue Royale. All rooms have shower, TV and toilet. ③.

Youth hostels and campsites

Youth hostel, av du Maréchal-de-Lattre-de-Tassigny (☎03.21.34.70.20, fax 03.21.96.87.80). Right at the seaward end of rue Royale, ultra-modern hostel just one block from the beach. Single and double rooms available; disabled facilities.

Camping municipal, 26 av Poincaré, on the beach at the seaward end of rue Royale (☎03.21.97.89.79). An exposed site close to the beach.

The town

The town divides in two: **Calais-Nord**, the old town rebuilt after the war with place d'Armes and rue Royale as its focus, is separated by canals from sprawling **Calais-Sud**, centred around the Hôtel de Ville and the main shopping streets, boulevard Lafayette and Jacquard – the latter named after the inventor of looms, who mechanized Calais' lacemaking industry.

Although Calais-Nord is nominally the old town, its charms soon wear thin. The medieval **Tour du Guet** on the drab main square, place d'Armes, is the only building in the quarter to have survived wartime bombardment. From the Tour, rue de la Paix leads to the **church of Notre-Dame**, where Charles de Gaulle married local girl Yvonne Vendroux in 1921. Rather spuriously dubbed the only English Perpendicular church on the continent, it's not a particularly good example of the style, especially in its present state of dereliction. Frill-fanciers can enjoy the unusual lacemaking exhibition in the **Musée des Beaux-Arts et de la Dentelle** on rue Richelieu (Mon, Wed & Fri 10am–noon & 2–5.30pm, Sat till 6.30pm, Sun 2–6.30pm; 10F, Wed free).

Calais-Sud is scarcely more exciting. Just over the canal bridge, the town's landmark, the **Hôtel de Ville**, raises its belfry over 60m into the sky; this Flemish extravaganza was finished in 1926, and miraculously survived World War II. Somewhat dwarfed by the building, Rodin's famous bronze, the **Burghers of Calais**, records for ever the self-sacrifice of these local dignitaries, who offered their lives to assuage the brutal lust of the victor at Crécy, Edward III – only to be spared at the last minute by the intervention of the Queen. For a record of Calais' wartime travails you can consult the fascinating **Musée de la Guerre** (April–Sept daily 10am–6pm; Oct–Nov & Feb–March daily except Tues 11am–5pm; 15F), installed in a former German *Blockhaus* in the Parc St-Pierre across the street.

Eating and drinking

Calais is full of **eateries**, mostly mediocre, catering for its day-tripper trade: place d'Armes is full of such examples, with rue Royale offering your best bet. There are plenty of self-service and fast-food outlets at the beach.

Café de Paris, 72 rue Royale. Popular with locals and tourists alike for its cheap fare; *plats du jour* from 55F, menu at 62F.

Channel, 3 bd de la Résistance, overlooking the yacht basin. Generous menus and stylish decor; the popular 98F menu – the lowest – is not available on Sun, though a wide range of delicious desserts always is. Closed Sun eve & Tues.

Le Grand Bleu, 8 rue J-P-Avron (☎03.21.97.97.98; wise to book). A smart, modern, seafood restaurant on the waterfront, with menus from 130F.

SHOPPING

Place d'Armes and **rue Royale** are the main shopping areas in Calais-Nord, with everything from clothes and chocolate to leather and dolls, try Le Vignoble on rue Royale for a good selection of wine. Generally, however, the streets of Calais-Sud – particularly **boulevards Jacquard** and **Lafayette** – are a better bet. Prisunic department store is on bd Jacquard with an acceptable food and wine department. For establishments with a more individual character, try the Comtesse du Barry for *foie gras* and other such luxury comestibles, or the Charcuterie Lablanche, which sells takeaway *plats* and salads. More colourful still are the **markets** around place d'Armes (Wed & Sat) and bd Lafayette; Thurs & Sat). For **seafood**, try Huitrière Calaisienne, in bd Lafayette, or Sole Berckoise, in bd Jacquard. The best of the **hypermarkets** or *grands surfaces* is the Auchan complex on the Boulogne road, the old N1 (Mon–Sat 9am–9pm; bus #5), which gives change in sterling should you wish it; this is closely followed by Le Continent, on the east side of town in avenue Georges-Guynenier (daily 9am–9pm; bus #4). Cité Europe, a vast new shopping complex by the channel tunnel terminal and just off the A16 in the direction of Boulogne, offers you a large Carrefour as well as high-street clothes shops and food shops all under one roof (Mon–Fri 9am–10pm, Sat 8.30am–10pm; bus #7).

Histoire Ancienne, 20 rue Royale. Greek-run brasserie with a charming interior, particularly its old bar; the good, mainly French menu includes the occasional Greek dish plus inexpensive, interesting salads that will delight vegetarians. Menus from 61F at lunchtime; otherwise from 98F.

Le Touquet, 57 rue Royale. This large old brasserie is a local institution, with lots of seafood; menus from 69F and 119F. Closed Mon.

Le Troubador, quai du Rhin. Hidden away in a quiet street near the station and tourist office, this bar is a popular hang-out for local music-heads: lots of long hair around the games tables by day and bands by night.

Around Calais

Understandably, most tourists travel non-stop through the **Pas-de-Calais** – France's northernmost *département* – en route to warmer climes and more varied scenery. However, if you're on a short break to one of the channel ports, it's worth making the effort to venture inland; **Cassel** in particular is a minor gem for this part of France.

St-Omer

The first stop inland for many visitors to France is **ST-OMER**, a quiet and unassuming but distinctly foreign little town. The landscape seems to expand and the town itself has flights of Flemish magnificence, especially in the **Hôtel de Ville** and some of the recently restored mansions on rue Gambetta. The Gothic **Basilique Notre-Dame** contains some noteworthy statuary, and there are some handsome exhibits in the eighteenth-century **Hôtel Sandelin** museum on rue Carnot (Wed–Sun 10am–noon & 2–6pm, Thurs & Fri till 5pm; 15F) – in particular, a glorious piece of medieval goldsmithing known as the *Pied de Croix de St-Bertin*.

Aside from the pleasant **public gardens** to the west of town, there's the possibility of exploring the nearby **marais**, a network of Flemish waterways cut between plots of land on reclaimed marshes east of town along the river. You can join a *bâteau-promenade* leaving from the quai du Haut-Pont, north from the gare SNCF along the Canal de l'Aa (July–Aug daily 3pm, 4pm & 5pm; 42F; tickets from the Café du Haut-Pont), or from the bridge on the D209, 2km west of the gare SNCF (daily July & Aug; April–June

& Sept Sat & Sun only; 40F per person) from where you can also hire boats. Round trips on the *bâteaux-promenades* take roughly two hours, the longer one including a ride down the unique vertical boat-lift at Arques. For further information, including times, visit the **tourist office** by the **gare routière** on place P-Painlevé.

To get to the centre of town from the exuberant 1903 **gare SNCF**, cross over the canal and walk ten minutes down rue F-Ringot, past the PTT and into rue Carnot. The **tourist office** is on place P-Painlevé (Mon–Fri 9am–noon & 2–5pm; May–Sept also Sat 9.30am–12.30pm & 2–6pm, Sun 9.30am–12.30pm; ☎03.21.98.08.51, fax 03.21.98.22.82). For **accommodation**, try the pretty, old *Hôtel St-Louis* at 25 rue d'Arras (☎03.21.38.35.21, fax 03.21.38.57.26; ②; restaurant from 75F); the *Bretagne*, 2 place du Vainquai, near the train station (☎03.21.38.25.78, fax 03.21.93.51.22; ④; restaurant from 90F; closed Sat noon, Sun eve and Jan 2–16); or the *Ibis*, 2 rue Henri-Dupuis, near the cathedral (☎03.21.93.11.11, fax 03.21.88.80.20; ④; restaurant 97F including wine). The nearest **campsite** is near the *Forêt de Clairmarais*, 4.5km east of St-Omer (☎03.21.38.34.80; April–Oct), although there's no transport out there.

For other **places to eat**, try establishments around place Maréchal-Foch or the *Auberge du Bachelin*, 12 bd de Strasbourg, on the north side of the town centre (menus from 65F).

The Blockhaus at Eperlecques

In the **Forêt d'Eperlecques,** 12km north of St-Omer (several trains daily from Calais to Watten station, on the eastern edge of the forest, about 4km from the site), is the largest ever **Blockhaus** or concrete bunker, built in 1943–44 by the Germans – or rather 6000 half-starved slave labourers (March Sun 2.15–6pm; April, Oct & Nov daily 2.15–6pm; May Mon–Sat 10am–noon & 2.15–6pm & Sun 10am–7pm; June & Sept Mon–Sat 10am–noon & 2.15–7pm, Sun 10am–7pm; July & Aug daily 10am–7pm; 39F; ☎03.21.88.44.22). It was designed to launch V2 rockets against London, but fortunately the RAF and French Resistance prevented its ever being ready for use.

La Coupole

Of all the World War II converted bunker museums **La Coupole** (daily April–Oct 9am–7pm; Nov–March 10am–6pm; 55F; ☎03.21.93.07.07)is the most modern and stimulating. As you walk around the site of an intended V2 rocket launchpad, you can listen on multilingual infra-red headsets to a discussion of the occupation of northern France by the Nazis, the use of prisoners as slave labour and the technology and ethics of the first liquid-fuelled rocket – advanced through Hitler and taken at the end of the war by the Soviets, the French and the Americans and developed in the space race. Films, models and photographs, all with accompanying text in four different languages help to develop each theme. Getting there by car is easy: it's 5km south-west of St-Omer, just off the D928 (A26 junctions 3 & 4), but there are only a few buses running from St-Omer train station (ring La Coupole or St-Omer tourist office for times).

Cassel

Twenty-three kilometres east of St-Omer is the tiny hilltop town of **CASSEL**. Hills are rare in Flanders, and Cassel was much fought over from Roman times onwards. Marshall Foch spent "some of the most distressing hours" of his life here during World War I, and it was up to the top of Cassel's hill that the "Grand Old Duke of York" marched his 10,000 men in 1793, though, as hinted in the nursery rhyme, he failed to take the town.

Cassel's train station, 3km west of town, is linked only to Dunkerque, so you really need your own transport to make the trip worthwhile. Once here, however, your efforts will be rewarded with the very Flemish **Grande-Place**, lined with some magnificent mansions, from which narrow cobbled streets fan out. From the **public gardens** you have an unrivalled view over Flanders, with Belgium just 10km away. Here among the trees is Cassel's only remaining wooden **windmill** – there used to be 29 pounding their oil mills day and night – which revolves on its axis every Sunday. The nearby nineteenth-century mansion is the headquarters of the frequently banned Flemish radio station, Ulyenspiegel.

There are two good *places* to eat on the central Grand-Place: *La Taverne Flamande* (closed Tues eve & Wed; from 89F), specializing in Flemish cuisine; and the simpler *À l'Hôtel de Ville*, with a filling, tasty menu at 70F.

The Côte d'Opale

The **Côte d'Opale** is the stretch of Channel coast between Calais and the mouth of the River Somme, with huge, wild and windswept sandy beaches. In the northern part, as far as Boulogne, these are fringed, as on the English side of the Channel, by white chalk cliffs. It is here, between the prominent headlands of **Cap Blanc-Nez** and **Cap Gris-Nez**, where the D940 coast road winds high above the sea, that you can best appreciate the "opal" in the name: the sea and sky merge in an opalescent, oyster-grey continuum in the prevailing weather conditions. The southern part of the coast is flatter, and the beach, uninterrupted for 40km, is backed by a landscape of pine-anchored dunes and brackish tarns, punctuated every few hundred metres by solid German pillboxes now toppled on their noses by the shifting sand foundations. An organization called Eden 62 publishes ten leaflets detailing walks around the area (Eden 62, B.P.65–62930 Wimereux; ☎03.21.32.13.74, fax 03.21.87.33.07).

Eurotunnel and the "Site des Deux Caps"
Right on the outskirts of Calais, **BLÉRIOT-PLAGE** commemorates Louis Blériot's epic first cross-Channel flight in 1909. Six kilometres further along the foreshore of well-conserved dunes, by the dreary village of **SANGATTE**, the Channel tunnel comes ashore; the actual terminal is 5km to the east outside the village of **COQUELLES**. Thereafter, the road winds up onto the grassy windswept heights of **Cap Blanc-Nez**, topped by an obelisk commemorating the Dover Patrol who kept the Channel free from U-boats during World War I. For an overall history of "Chunnel" exploits go to the **Musée du Transmanche** (April–June & Sept Tues–Sun 10am–6pm; July & Aug also open Mon; 20F), housed in the basement of *Le Thomé du Gamond*, a rather pricey restaurant with panoramic views situated just off the D940 opposite the turn-off to the Cap Blanc-Nez obelisk (open all year round from noon only; menus from 80F, plus snacks). From here, 130m above sea level, you can spot the Channel craft plying the water to the north, while to the south you look down on **WISSANT** and its enormous beach between the capes from which Julius Cæsar set sail in 55 BC for a first look at Britain.

Modern Wissant remains a small and quietly attractive place, popular out of season with windsurfers and weekending Britons only. But it has some good places **to stay** and **to eat**. First and foremost is the old red-timbered *Hôtel de la Plage*, 1 Place Edouard Houssen, whose rooms are arranged around a wide courtyard (☎03.21.35.91.87, fax 03.21.85.48.10; ③–④), with buffet breakfast for the modern more expensive rooms). It also offers a *soirée étape*, which comprises bed and dinner at 250F per adult in its restaurant, whose good family cuisine otherwise costs from 85F. A decent alternative is the much smaller *Le Vivier*, in the village centre (☎03.21.35.93.61, fax 03.21.82.10.99; ②; closed mid-Jan to mid-Feb), with a good restaurant offering similar prices; or the clean and modern *Escale*, on the crossroads in neighbouring **ESCALLES** (☎03.21.85.25.00, fax 03.21.35.44.22; ③; restaurant from 75F). The Wissant **campsite**, though a *municipal*, costs more than 50F.

To Cap Gris-Nez and the Blockhaus at Audinghen

The GR du Littoral footpath follows all a the clifftops here, passing through Wissant and continuing up to **Cap Gris-Nez**, just 28km from the English coast. Otherwise, the turn-off to the second cape is 1km outside **AUDINGHEN**, followed by a 3km walk, drive or cycle.

The entire Côte d'Opale is studded with massive concrete bunkers, or *Blockhäuser* (see also p.206), that were part of the German World War II defences known as the Atlantic Wall. One of them is just after the Cap Gris-Nez turn-off beside the D940. Equipped with a gun that could hit the English coast, it has been converted into a rather rough-and-ready **museum** (daily June–Sept 9am–7pm; Oct–May 9am–noon & 2–6pm; closed Dec & Jan; 25F) of the paraphernalia of war. Burrowing two or three floors below ground level, it has curiosity value rather than any great attractions. The best exhibits are British propaganda material and a poster cautioning troops against the dangers of VD, in which a portly officer, buttons popping with excitement, is propositioned by a German Fräulein ("Komm' mit mi'!").

Audinghen itself is a drab little place. If you're stuck for somewhere to stay, you'd do better in the charming though faded seaside villages of **AUDRESELLES** and **AMBLETEUSE** further on.

Wimereux

Just 4km north of Boulogne, **WIMEREUX** is a traditional, turn-of-the-century seaside resort. Once favoured by the vacationing miners of the north of France, it still preserves a certain faded charm, only really enlivened in the summer months, when it buzzes to the sound of Dutch, Belgian, English and German voices.

The **tourist office** is on quai Alfred-Giard, near the river (daily April–Sept 9am–7pm; Oct–March Mon–Sat 9am–1pm & 3–7pm, Sun 10am–noon & 2–5pm; ☎03.21.83.27.17, fax 03.21.32.76.91). Opposite is a small market on Tuesday and Friday mornings, good for picnic material. The town itself is easily reached by local **bus** from Boulogne (line 1 goes via the coast, line 2 via Wimille, the village just inland from Wimereux) or by **train** (to Wimille) about every two hours.

The main street, rue Carnot, has three reasonable **hotels**: the attractive, modernized *Hôtel du Centre*, at no. 78 (☎03.21.32.41.08, fax 03.21.33.82.48; ③; restaurant from 99F), the simple, old-fashioned *des Arts*, with a popular bar and restaurant, at no. 143 (☎03.21.32.43.13; ①; closed Sun eve), and the *Auberge de Maître Hans*, at no. 12 (☎03.21.32.41.04; ②). You can **camp** at *L'Olympic*, on avenue de la Libération. For a sit-down meal, try *Le Charolais*, 25 rue Napoléon, the narrow road heading for Boulogne; smart but relaxed, it has a set menu from 75F; closed Wed evening & Sun. For a real gourmet treat, try the *Atlantic*, on the front at Wimereux (☎03.21.32.41.01; cheapest menu 115F, *carte* around 300F), or *La Brocante*, by the church in neighbouring Wimille (☎03.21.83.19.31; menu from 140F, *carte* 400F).

Boulogne-sur-Mer

BOULOGNE is quite different from Dunkerque and Calais – recommendation in itself. It has long been an important harbour and claims to be the largest fishing base in Europe. Rising above the port is an attractive medieval quarter, the **ville haute**, contained within the old town walls and dominated by a grand, domed cathedral. Below, amid the newer shopping streets of the *ville basse*, are some of the best charcuteries and pâtisseries in the north, along with an impressive array of fish restaurants. Alone among the northeast channel ports, this is a place that might actually tempt you to stay.

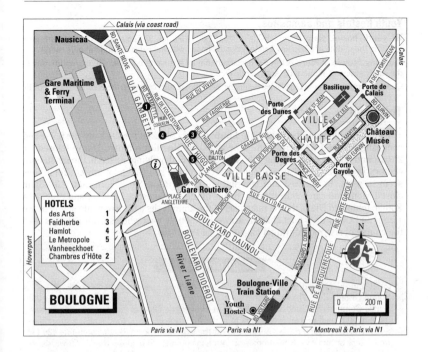

Arrival, information and accommodation

Ferries dock within a few minutes' walk of the town centre. If you arrive by hovercraft, a little further out, you'll be met by a free shuttle **bus** (Hoverspeed ☎03.21.30.27.26). If you intend to stay, the **tourist office** (summer Mon–Sat 9am–7pm, Sun 10am–1pm & 2–5pm; winter Mon–Sat 9am–6pm; ☎03.21.31.68.38, fax 03.21.33.81.09), housed in a small Art Deco pavilion across the bridge from the ferry terminal, can supply a mass of information and advise on availability of rooms – which, in summer, get taken early.

There's plenty of inexpensive **accommodation** in Boulogne if you've missed your boat and need somewhere basic to stay; most of the cheap hotels are close to the port area. There are also some upmarket places around the centre, but rates are competitive.

Hotels

des Arts, 102–112 quai Gambetta (☎03.21.31.53.31, fax 03.21.33.69.05). Very reasonable hotel right opposite the port; rooms are clean, light and well set up; many with balcony. No lift: be prepared for a long climb. ①.

Faidherbe, 12 rue Faidherbe (☎03.21.31.60.93, fax 03.21.87.01.14). Respectable, well-tended and slightly worn central two-star; all rooms have bathroom and TV. ①–③.

Hamiot, cnr rue Faidherbe &bd Gambetta (☎03.21.31.44.20). Cheap hotel on the main road above a popular bistrot. ①.

Le Metropole, 51 rue Thiers (☎03.21.31.54.30, fax 03.21.30.45.72). A plush three-star with spacious rooms in the midst of a fashionable street; central but not noisy. ④.

Vanheeckhoet Chambres d'Hôte, 24-26 rue de Lille (☎03.21.80.41.50). A pleasant B&B in the centre of the old town. ②.

Youth hostels and campsites

HI youth hostel, place Rouget-de-l'Îsle (☎03.21.80.14.50, fax 03.21.80.45.62) opposite the gare SNCF in the middle of a housing estate. Friendly hostel with individual en-suite double rooms.

Camping Moulin Wibert. A three-star place 10min by bus along bd Sainte-Beuve, on the way to the sandy strand of Wimereux. April to mid-Oct.

Camping municipal at la Capelle-lès-Boulogne, near the Auchan centre on the N42. April 15–Sept 15.

The town

The quiet cobbled streets of the **ville haute** make a pleasant respite from the noise and congestion of the *ville basse*. Within the walls, the **Basilique Notre-Dame** (closed for 2hr around noon, except during July & Aug) is an odd building, raised in the nineteenth century by the town's vicar, without any architectural knowledge or advice. Yet it does seem to work. In the vast and labyrinthine **crypt** (Mon–Sat 2–5pm, Sun 2.30–5pm; closed Mon) you can see frescoed remains of the Romanesque building and relics of a Roman temple to Diana. In the main part of the church sits a bizarre white statue of the Virgin and Child on a boat-chariot, drawn here on its own wheels from Lourdes over the course of six years during a pilgrimage in the 1940s.

SHOPPING

You'll find everything in the consumer line – clothes, furniture, sheets, hats, plates – around Grande-Rue, Thiers, Faidherbe and Nationale. For general shopping, head for the Centre Commercial Liane, on the corner of boulevards Diderot and Danou, a downmarket shopping mall on two levels; lots of neon, milling teenagers, food stalls, a supermarket and a cheap cafeteria. If you want to hit the serious hypermarkets, catch bus #20 for the Leclerc or bus #8 for the monstrous Auchan complex, 8km along the N42 towards St-Omer – certainly the most convenient place for large-scale food and wine shopping.

More fastidious foodies should cross the Pont de l'Entente-Cordiale into Grande-Rue. For **charcuterie**, try Bourgeois, on the corner of Grande-Rue and Victor-Hugo; for **chocolates** and other goodies, head for De Marchez, on the corner of Thiers and Faidherbe. Check out the **fish** selection at Aux Pêcheurs d'Étaples, a large poissonnerie on the Grande-Rue, opposite place Dalton. Next door, the Comtesse du Barry specializes in *foie gras* and other gastronomic luxuries. One other shop that should not be missed is Philippe Olivier's famous **fromagerie**, just around the corner in rue Thiers, which has a selection of over two hundred cheeses – in various states of maturation.

As far as **department stores** go, there's a Nouvelles Galeries on rue Thiers, where you'll also find plenty of fashion boutiques. For Parisian women's clothes, try Cloë, on rue Nationale. A wide selection of **hats** are on sale at Monteil, on the corner of rues Faidherbe and Hugo; and you can choose from over 600 **handbags** at Maroquinerie Florence, on rue Faidherbe between rues Thiers and Victor-Hugo. Roger, at 67 rue Thiers, has a beautiful selection of **shoes**; while Divine, on place Charpentier, by the town theatre, sells exquisite French **lingerie**. At Leclercq, 15 Grande-Rue, you'll find beautiful **homeware**, including glass, cutlery and plates.

French **fabrics** are highly regarded, and Opale Tissus, on rue Nationale, has rolls of the stuff; for interesting, albeit expensive, **children's clothes**, pop down to Clafoutis further down, while a range of fantastic French **linen goods** (including some amusing Babar pillowcases and duvet covers) are found at Texti Linge on narrow rue Félix-Adam.

The best **bookshop** is Le Furet du Nord, 14 Grande-Rue, with a wide selection of maps and an excellent *papeterie* downstairs. If you're looking to **cycle** or **bike** from Boulogne, Motul is a large motorbike/cycle shop at 106 rue Thiers; it also sells mountain-bike supplies. From place Lorraine and place Charpentier, rue Faidherbe heads uphill (but downmarket) with lots of **bargain shops, hi-fi and electronics**. And don't miss the Wednesday and Saturday **markets** on place Dalton.

Nearby, the **Château Musée** (Mon & Wed–Sat 9.30am–12.30pm & 2–5pm, Sun 10am–12.30pm & 2.30–5.30pm; 5.30pm; 20F) has Egyptian funerary objects donated by a local-born Egyptologist and a good collection of Greek pots. Alternatively – and free – you can climb up the most ancient monument in the old town, the twelfth-century **Beffroi** (Mon–Fri 8am–6pm, Sat 8am–noon; access via the Hôtel de Ville), or stroll round along the **medieval walls**, decked out with rosebeds, gravel paths and benches for picnicking, with impressive views over the town and port.

Outside the *ville haute* the place to head for is the town's smart new aquarium at the Centre National de la Mer or **Nausiccá**, on boulevard Sainte-Beuve (daily July–Aug 9.30am–8pm; Sept–May 9.30am–6.30pm; closed 2 weeks in Jan; 65F). Ultraviolet lighting and New Age music create a suitably weird ambience, while hammerhead sharks circle overhead and giant conger eels conceal themselves in rusty pipes – definitely not for piscophobes. There's plenty of educational stuff, too (in French and English throughout), and a half-hour film show, though only a passing nod towards environmental issues.

Three kilometres north of Boulogne on the N1 stands the **Colonne de la Grande Armée**, where, in 1803, Napoléon is said to have changed his mind about invading Britain and turned his troops east towards Austria. The column was originally topped by a bronze figure of Napoléon symbolically clad in Roman garb – though his head, equally symbolically, was shot off by the British navy in the last war. It is now displayed in the château museum (see above).

Eating and drinking

A large fishing port, Boulogne is a good spot to **eat** fresh fish and seafood. There are dozens of possibilities for eating around place Dalton and the *ville haute*, but bear in mind the day-tripper trade and be selective. If you're after a **drink**, there is a concentration of bars in the place opposite the Hôtel de Ville, and several lively bars in place Dalton, with *au Bureau*, *Le Saint Germain* and the *Pub JF Kennedy* being most popular.

Bar Hamiot, 1 rue Faidherbe. The brasserie remains as popular as ever with locals and tourists alike offering a large range of dishes from 30F omelettes and 55–90F fish dishes to 65F and 95F menus. The special on Sat is couscous.

Chez Jules, 8 place Dalton. A large establishment in a lively square specializing in seafood with excellent 120F or 150F menus; simple fish and chips for around 70F.

Un Cornet d'Amour, 91 rue Thiers. An excellent pâtisserie with a comfortable *salon de thé*, reasonably priced, with lots of local ladies taking tea.

Le Doyen, 11 rue Doyen, off place Dalton (☎03.21.30.13.08). The most affordable of the better restaurants, with a menu at 100F. Closed Wed eve & Sun.

Estaminet du Château, 2 rue du Château, off rue de Lille by the *basilique* (☎03.21.91.49.66). Closed Thurs. Opposite Notre-Dame in the *ville haute*, this restaurant has an excellent menu from 60F and inexpensive à la carte dishes (quarter roast chicken 30F). Plain food in a nice old stone building, prettily decorated.

L'Étoile de Marrakech, 228 rue Nationale. A friendly Moroccan restaurant where the chef comes out and shakes your hand; olives, bread and spicy sausage come as complimentary starters, and the servings of couscous (from 79F) are incredibly generous. Closed Wed.

La Houblonnière, rue Monsigny. A good brasserie with menus from 68F and plats from 40–60F.

L'Huitrière, 11 place Lorraine. The freshest fish and seafood in a small, unpretentious restaurant hidden behind a blue- and white-awninged poissonnerie front. Menus at 80–90F.

Le Marivaux, facing *La Houblonnière* (see above) in rue Monsigny. A brasserie with prices and quality that match its opposite number.

La Matelote, 80 bd Ste-Beuve (☎03.21.30.17.97). Opposite the *Nausicc6*, a very smart restaurant featuring a *dégustation* menu at 350F; less well-heeled diners can go for the 160F menu; à la carte fish from 120F. Loving care taken over the food and service, but it's rather snooty. Closed Sun eve.

Pizzeria Milano, 16 rue Coquelin. Excellent pizzas from 30F to 50F, with takeaway available.

Sucré Salé, 13 rue Monsigny. Smart, modern eatery combining the roles of restaurant, café, bar, *salon de thé* and pâtisserie; its speciality is gourmet salads, making it a good choice for vegetarians. Light, airy and sparse, with a wonderful range of teas and coffees. Daily 8am–8pm except Sun afternoon.

From Boulogne to Amiens

South of **Boulogne** the coast is even wilder and more magnificent, but without your own transport it's hard to get down to the beach. A band of unstable dunes forces the D940 coast road and the Calais–Paris railway to keep 3 or 4km inland. With the exception of **Étaples**, the seaside towns are artificial resorts of twentieth-century creation. They are only of interest inasmuch as they provide access to the beach. But that really is worth getting to, and its eerie beauty is best experienced by walking the coastal GR path or any one of the several marked paths which the local tourist offices promote, or by visiting the bird sanctuary at **Marquenterre**. For car-drivers, a lane at Dannes leads directly into the dunes.

The quickest route south is the **A16**, recently extended from Boulogne to **Abbeville** and meaning non-stop motorway all the way to Paris. More interesting, if you have time and want to take in the battlefeld of **Agincourt**, would be a winding cross-country route exploring some of the English-looking side valleys on the north side of the River Canche, like the Crequoise, Planquette and Ternoise, whose farms and hamlets have been largely bypassed by the onward march of French modernity.

Le Touquet and Étaples

Situated among dunes and wind-flattened tamarisks and pines, **LE TOUQUET** is a kind of French Hollywood on the sea, with ambitious villas freed from the discipline of architectural fashion hidden away behind its trees. Now dully suburban, this was the height of fashion in the 1920s and 1930s and for a spell after World War II, ranking alongside places on the Côte d'Azur. At one time flights arrived from Britain every ten minutes, but the opening up of long-distance air travel put an end to this era. Nowadays, air traffic consists of private aircraft much of it piloted by Brits benefiting from the short hop over the channel.

It is an extraordinary set-up really and not one where many vistors will feel at home. With strict sociological intent, however, take a glimpse at the *Le Manoir* hotel on avenue du Golf (☎03.21.06.28.28, fax 03.21.06.28.29; ⑦), the most palatial of the town's bunch, which includes *Le Westminster*, avenue du Verger (☎03.21.05.48.48, fax 03.21.05.45.45; ⑧), and *Le Bristol*, 17 rue Jean-Monnet (☎03.21.05.49.95, fax 03.21.05.90.93; ⑤). And if you've got kids, an expensive treat worth indulging in is Le Touquet's **swimming complex** right on the front, which boasts no fewer than three giant water slides (55F upwards); there's also the vast Bagatelle amusement park, 10km south of Le Touquet, on the D940 (daily April to mid-Sept 10am–7pm).

To get to Le Touquet, take the train from Boulogne to **ÉTAPLES**, a much more down-to-earth fishing village near the mouth of the River Canche, from where a local bus covers the last 4km; alternatively, you can take one of the four daily buses directly from Boulogne (☎03.21.31.77.48 for times) from outside the *Café de la Station* on boulevard Daunou; the bus heads down the coast to Berck. The **tourist office** in the Palais de l'Europe on place de l'Hermitage (☎03.21.06.72.00, fax 03.21.06.72.01; daily 9am–7pm) can furnish you with a free map of the town, and if you're looking for somewhere reasonable to **stay** the night, try the **youth hostel** *Riva Bella*, 12 rue Léon Garet (☎03.21.05.08.22), or the Armide, 56 rue Léon-Garet (☎03.21.05.21.76; half-board; ③). There's also a campsite, on the waterfront of the Canche estuary, but this requires three-nights' minimum stay.

Places to **eat** are generally expensive here. For a treat, visit *Le Café des Arts*, 80 rue de Paris (☎03.21.05.21.55; closed Mon), or *Auberge de la Dune aux Loups*, on the avenue of the same name (☎03.21.05.42.54; closed Tues & Wed), where you can eat their speciality fish on the terrace. Also good for seafood is the *Pêcheurs d'Étaples* (from 100F), on the riverside just up the road in Étaples, quai de la Canche (☎03.21.94.06.90). More affordable than these is *Les Sports*, 22 rue St-Jean, a classic brasserie with a menu at 75F.

Montreuil-sur-Mer

Once a port, **MONTREUIL-SUR-MER** is now stranded 13km inland from the sea at Étaples. Perched on a sharp little hilltop above the River Canche and surrounded by its ancient walls, this is an immediately appealing place. Laurence Sterne spent a night here on his *Sentimental Journey*, and it was the scene of much of the action in Victor Hugo's *Les Misérables*, perhaps best evoked by the steep cobbled street of pavée St-Firmin, first left after the Porte de Boulogne, a short climb from the gare SNCF.

Two heavily damaged Gothic churches grace the main square: the **church of St-Saulve** and a tiny wood-panelled **chapelle** tucked into the side of the red-brick *Hôtel-Dieu*. To the south there are numerous cobbled lanes to wander down, all lined with half-timbered artisan houses. In the northwestern corner of the walls lies Vauban's **citadelle** (daily except Tues 9am–noon & 2–6pm; closed Oct; 10F) – ruined, overgrown and, after dark, pretty atmospheric, with subterranean gun emplacements and a fourteenth-century tower that records the coats of arms of the French noblemen killed at Agincourt. A path following the top of the walls provides views out across the Canche estuary.

For **accommodation**, there's the classy and expensive *Château de Montreuil* (☎03.21.81.53.04, fax 03.21.81.36.43; ⑨; closed Dec 15–Jan), overlooking the citadel and much loved by the English. It also contains a top-class restaurant (closed Thurs noon & Mon out of season), whose lunchtime menu is good value at 270F with wine. For delightful **food** and accommodation at more manageable prices, there's no beating *Le Darnétal*, in place Darnétal (☎03.21.06.04.87, fax 03.21.86.64.67; ③; closed Mon evening & Tues; also Jan 15–30 & July 1–7); restaurant from 95F. Another good bet is the *Clos des Capucins* on the wide place de Gaulle, the shopping centre of the town (☎03.21.06.08.65, fax 03.21.81.20.45; ③; menu from 98F). There's also an HI **youth hostel** (☎03.21.06.10.83), housed in one of the citadel's outbuildings and giving access to the place long after the gates have been closed to the public. The municipal **campsite** is by the River Canche, below the walls.

In the second half of August, Montreuil puts on a surprisingly lively mini-arts **festival** of opera, theatre and dance, *Les Malins Plaisirs*. For information on this and other aspects of the town, visit the **tourist office** by the citadel at 21 rue Carnot (May–Oct Mon–Sat 9.30am–12.30pm & 2–6.30pm, Sun 10am–12.30pm & 3–6pm; Nov–April Mon–Sat 10am–12.30pm & 2–6.30pm, Sun 10am–12.30pm; ☎03.21.06.04.27).

Agincourt and Crécy

Two of the bloodiest Anglo-French battles of the Middle Ages took place near the attractive little town of **HESDIN** on the River Canche (a town familiar to Simenon fans from the TV series *Inspector Maigret*). Getting to either site is really only feasible with your own transport.

Twenty kilometres southwest of Hesdin, at the **Battle of Crécy**, Edward III inflicted his first of many defeats on the French in 1346, thus beginning the Hundred Years' War. This was the first appearance on the continent of the new English weapon – the six-foot longbow – and the first use in European history of gunpowder. There's not a lot to see today, just the **Moulin Édouard III** (now a watchtower), 1km northeast of the little town of **CRÉCY-EN-PONTHIEU** on the D111 to **WADICOURT**, site of the windmill from which Edward watched the hurly-burly of battle. Further south, on the D56 to Fontaine, the battered **croix de Bohème** marks the place where King John of Bohemia died, having insisted on leading his men into the fight, in spite of his blindness.

Ten thousand more died in the heaviest defeat ever of France's feudal knighthood at the **Battle of Agincourt** on October 25, 1415. Forced by muddy conditions to fight on foot in their heavy armour, the French, though three times as strong in number, were sitting ducks to the lighter, mobile English archers. The rout took place near present-day **AZINCOURT**, about 12km northeast of Hesdin off the D928, and a **museum** in the village (April–Oct daily 11am–5pm; Nov–March afternoons only; 10F) includes a short film about the battle, with noticeboards placed at strategic points on the battlefield to indicate the sequence of fighting. Just east of the village, by the crossroads of the D104 and the road to Maisoncelle, a **cross** marks the position of the original grave pits.

The Marquenterre bird sanctuary

Ornithologists will need no persuasion, but if you know nothing of birds, the **Parc ornithologique du Marquenterre** (April–daily 9.30am–7pm; Oct daily 10am–5pm; Nov–March Sat & Sun only 10am–5pm; 45F; ☎03.22.25.03.06) will be a revelation. In terms of landscape, it is beautiful and strange: all dunes, tamarisks and pine forest, full of salty meres and ponds thick with water plants. This is "new" land formed by the erosion of the Normandy coast and the silting of the Somme estuary, where thousands of cattle are grazed today to give their meat the much-prized flavour of the "salt meadows".

One of only two bird sanctuaries in the whole of France, Marquenterre is a tiny reserve in an area that gives new meaning to the word "sanctuary". From the opening of the waterfowl season – July 14, Bastille Day, ironically – gunshots can be heard, day and night, all around. No species, however rare, is spared.

You'll need to rent binoculars unless you carry your own, and there's no point in trying to manage without. Once inside, there's a choice of two itineraries, the longer being the more interesting. It takes you from resting area to resting area whence you can train your glasses on dozens of species – ducks, geese, oyster-catchers, terns, egrets, redshanks, greenshanks, spoonbills, herons, storks, godwits – some of them fat-cat residents, most taking a breather from their epic migratory flights to and from the ends of the earth. In April and May they head north, and they return from the end of August to October, so these are the best times to visit.

The nearest town of any size is **RUE**, one of a number of attractive former fishing villages in the area now stranded inland by the silting up of the Somme. It's worth a halt for the splendid Gothic vaulting and facade of the **Chapelle du St-Esprit** (April–Oct daily 9.30am–5.30pm).

The Somme estuary

After Marquenterre, the road meanders through yet more dry fishing hamlets, whose crouching cottages are reminders of their former poverty. Some, like **LE CROTOY**, with enough sea still to attract the yachties, are enjoying the inevitable holiday- and second-home boom. Its south-facing beach has attracted numerous writers and painters over the years: Jules Verne wrote *Twenty Thousand Leagues Under the Sea* here; Colette, Toulouse-Lautrec and Seurat were also frequent visitors. If you're planning to stay, bed and breakfast **accommodation** is provided by Mme Larsonnier at 26 quai Courbet on the harbour (☎03.22.24.50.87; ③).

On the other side of the bay lies **ST-VALÉRY-SUR-SOMME**, accessible in summer by resuscitated **steam train** (July & Aug Tues–Sun; June & Sept Wed, Sat & Sun only; 56F) from Le Crotoy, and by two buses a day from Abbeville or Noyelles during July and August. This is the place from which William, Duke of Normandy set sail to conquer

England in 1066. With its walled and gated medieval citadel still intact and its brightly painted quays, free of modern development, looking out over mudflats and tilting boats, this really is the jewel of the coast. Apart from the **Écomusée Picarvie** (mid-Feb to mid-Nov Mon & Wed–Sun 2–7pm; June & Aug also open Tues; 20F) with its interesting collection of tools and artefacts relating to vanished trades and ways of life, there is little to do but enjoy the quiet. People walk and dig for shellfish, but you have to be extremely careful about the tide. At high tide it is up to the quays, but withdraws 14km at low tide, creating a dangerous current; equally, it returns very suddenly, cutting off the unwary. The town's **tourist office** (July & Aug daily 10am–7pm; Sept–June 10am–noon & 2.30–5pm; closed Mon; ☎03.22.60.93.50, fax 03.22.60.80.34) is situated on the quayside.

There are two very attractive **hotels**, both with deservedly popular restaurants: the *Hoteldu Port et des Bains* (☎03.22.60.80.09; ②; restaurant from 81F), right on the quayside after the tourist office (see above) as you drive in from Rue; and the grander *Relais Guillaume de Normandy* (☎03.22.60.82.36, fax 03.22.60.81.82; ③; restaurant from 85F), on the waterside promenade at the foot of the old town.

About 9km to the east of St-Valéry, and 2km from the station in Noyelles-sur-Mer (served by the steam train) lies the hamlet of **NOLETTE**. This is home to one of the most unusual war graves in France, a **Chinese cemetery**, where 887 members of the Chinese Labour Corps are buried. Employed by the British army in World War I, most of them died of disease. Their neat headstones, sharing two or three rather perfunctory and patronizing epitaphs – "A good reputation endures for ever", "A noble duty bravely done" – lie in a field just outside the village.

Abbeville

ABBEVILLE lies about halfway from Calais to Paris and makes a convenient stop-off on the N1. Until hit by a German air raid in May 1940, it was also a very beautiful town. Nowadays, all that remains of its former glories is a superbly ornate Flemish-style **gare SNCF**; reputedly the oldest **belfry** in France; and the Gothic **church of St-Vulfran**, on a par with the cathedrals at Amiens and Beauvais. Badly scarred during the war, restoration work only finished in 1993. The western facade still bears superficial scars but the interior pillars have been replaced with exact copies and the keystones painted with their original colours. Abbeville also has the eighteenth-century **château of Bagatelle**, 2km south of town – not to be confused with the nearby amusement park of the same name – set in ten hectares of parkland (guided visits July & Aug only daily except Tues 2–6pm; 30F).

The **tourist office** is at 1 place de l'Amiral-Courbet (☎03.22.24.27.92, fax 03.22.31.08.26) and organizes guided visits to the cathedral. If you are looking for somewhere to **stay**, a cheap option is the *Grand-Hôtel de la Gare*, 21 av de la Gare (☎03.22.24.04.09; ①). A more comfortable alternative is the *Hôtel de France*, in place du Pilori in the town centre (☎03.22.24.00.42, fax 03.22.24.26.15; ④; with a nice restaurant; menus from 98F).

Amiens

Were it not for the cathedral, few travellers would stop at **AMIENS**. Badly scarred during both world wars, and with heavy traffic pounding along the ring road built over its old city walls, it's not an immediately likable place. Yet there is more to the town than first meets the eye. St-Leu, the medieval quarter north of the cathedral with its network of canals, has recently been renovated; the town's university makes its presence felt; and within a few minutes' walk from the train station the *hortillonnages* (see below) transport you into a peaceful rural landscape.

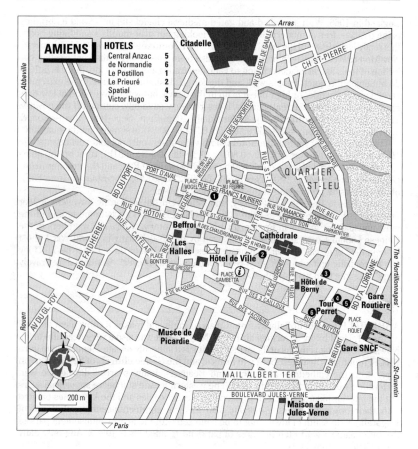

Arrival, information and accommodation

The main **gare SNCF** (Amiens-Nord) and **gare routière** are both situated on the rectangular place A-Fiquet. Connected to the train station is a new two-storey shopping complex, Amiens 2, where you'll find most things you need – including a supermarket and public toilets. The **tourist office**, where you can book accommodation, is south of the cathedral, just off place Gambetta at 6bis rue Dusevel (summer daily 9am–6.30pm; winter Mon–Sat 9am–6.30pm, Sun 9am–5pm; ☎03.22.71.60.50, fax 03.22.71.60.51).

Economical **accommodation** can be found on rue Alexandre-Fatton, a quiet street opposite the station: at no. 15, the *Hôtel Spatial* (☎03.22.91.53.23, fax 03.22.92.27.87; ①) has free parking and simple doubles; and at no. 17, the *Central Anzac* (☎03.22.91.34.08, fax 03.22.91.36.02; ①) has cheaper rooms still. A good alternative is the newly renovated *Hôtel de Normandie*, in the adjacent rue Lamartine (☎03.22.91.74.99, fax 03.22.92.06.56; ①). The upgraded *Victor Hugo*, 2 rue de l'Oratoire (☎03.22.91.57.91, fax 03.22.92.74.02; ①), is right in sight of the cathedral; *Le Prieuré*, 17 rue Porion (☎03.22.92.27.67, fax 03.22.92.46.16; ③), has rooms with shower, TV, telephone and toilet; and the more upmarket *Le Postillon*, 17 place au Feurre (☎03.22.22.00.20, fax 03.22.91.86.57; ④), boasts a view of the cathedral.

The city

The **Cathédrale Notre-Dame** (daily:April–Nov 8.30am–7pm; Oct–March 8.30am–noon & 2–5pm; closed during services) provides the city's very obvious focus. First of all, it dominates all else by its sheer size – it's the biggest Gothic building in France – but its appeal lies mainly in its unusual uniformity of style. Begun in 1220 under the architect Robert de Luzarches, only the tops of the towers were unfinished in 1269, and so the building escaped the influence of succeeding architectural fads that marred the "purity" of some of its slower sisters.

A miraculous laser scrub, currently being used on the west front, has revealed traces of the original polychrome exterior adding excitement to the question as to whether these colours should adorn the sculptures. Until the cleaning is finished in 2000, the best time to appreciate the detail of some of the many pieces of sculpture adorning the three main porches, is when the early afternoon sun falls obliquely across it. By way of contrast, the interior is all vertical lines and no fuss: a light, calm and unaffected space. Ruskin thought the apse "not only the best, but the very first thing done perfectly in its manner by northern Christendom". The later embellishments, like the sixteenth-century choir stalls (guided tours only, daily 3pm), are works of breathtaking virtuosity. The same goes for the sculpted panels depicting the life of St Firmin, Amiens' first bishop, on the right side of the choir screen. The figures in the crowd scenes are shown in fifteenth-century costume, the men talking serious business, while their wives listen more credulously to the preacher's words. One of the most atmospheric ways of seeing the cathedral is during a Sunday morning mass (10.15am), when you will be uplifted by sublime Gregorian chanting.

Just north of the cathedral is the **quartier St-Leu**, a very Flemish-looking network of canals and cottages that was once the centre of Amiens' thriving textile industry. The town still produces much of the country's velvet, but the factories moved out to the suburbs long ago, leaving St-Leu to rot away in peace – until, that is, the local property developers moved in. The slums have been tastefully transformed into neat brick cottages on cobbled streets, and the waterfront has been colonized by restaurants and clubs.

On the edge of town, the canals still provide a useful function as waterways for the **hortillonnages** – a series of incredibly fertile market gardens, reclaimed from the marshes created by the very slow-flowing Somme. Farmers travel about them in black, high-prowed punts and a few still take their produce into the city by boat for the Saturday morning **market**, the *marché sur l'eau*, on the river bank of place Parmentier. If you want to look around the *hortillonnages*, turn right as you come out of the station and continue straight ahead for about five minutes until you reach the river and the *chemin de halage* or towpath, which you can wander down. A map here shows pedestrian routes and viewpoints. If you walk further up boulevard de Beauvillé to no. 54, you will find the Association des Hortillonnages and the embarkation point for their inexpensive, one-hour **boat trips** (daily April–Oct; regular departures (normally depends on a minimum of 12 people); 2–6pm; 28F).

If you're interested in Picardy culture, you might take a look at Amiens' two regional museums. Five minutes' walk south of central place Gambetta, a nineteenth-century mansion houses the **Musée de Picardie** (daily except Mon 10am–12.30pm & 2–6pm; 20F), whose star exhibit is a collection of rare sixteenth-century paintings on wood donated to the cathedral by a local literary society, some of the pictures still in their original frames carved by the same craftsmen who worked the choir stalls. Close by the cathedral, in the seventeenth-century **Hôtel de Berny** (Thurs–Sun 2–6pm; 10F), is an annexe to the main museum, with local-history collections, including a portrait of Choderlos de Laclos, author of *Les Liaisons Dangereuses*, who was born in Amiens. A third museum or documentation centre, at 2 rue Dubois, was the **house of Jules Verne**, who spent most of his life in Amiens and died here (Mon–Fri 9am–noon & 2–6pm, Sat 2–6pm; 15F).

Just to the west of the city, at Tirancourt off the N1 to Abbeville, a large new muse-um/park, **Samara**, recreates the life of prehistoric man in northern Europe with recon-structions of dwellings and displays illustrating the way of life, trades and so on (daily: mid-March to mid-Nov 9.30am–6pm; 60F).

Eating, drinking and entertainment

There are plenty of cheap brasseries and **restaurants** around the station, but by far the most attractive area to look is **St-Leu**, both for appearance and general ambience. Two favourite places are in the pretty, cobbled place du Don directly below the cathedral, with room to sit outside in good weather. The *Soupe à Cailloux* (closed Mon in winter) serves delicious family cuisine, including regional dishes, for a reasonable price (week-day lunch menu at 68F, other times from 90F), and is consequently very popular. The equally attractive *As du Don*, across the square, does a *formule* for 89F, while just over the canal is Amiens' best gourmet restaurant, *Les Marissons* (☎03.22.92.96.66; closed Sat noon & Sun; menus from 110F, *carte* from 300F). There are also several **bars** and pubs in the area.

For eating **in town**, one of the nicest places to go is the handsome *T'chiot Zinc* (closed Sun & Mon noon; menu at 89F, *plats* for 48F), at 18 rue Noyon opposite the sta-tion, serving traditional country fare. A total contrast is the hip Tex-Mex *Steak-Easy*, with an aeroplane hanging from the ceiling, at 18 rue Metz-l'Évêque (guacamole, spare ribs and other un-Gaelic fare; around 90F for a meal).

For one week in May Amiens bursts into life for its annual international **jazz festval**. On the third weekend in June, the local costumes come out for the **Fête d'Amiens**; and in November there's a **cinema festival**. In August, traditional Picardy **marionettes** give performances (mostly evenings) at the Maison du Théâtre, 8 rue des Majots, in the quartier St-Leu: call Théâtre d'Animation Picard (☎03.22.92.42.06) for reservations – tickets are around 50F. To purchase or take a look at hand-made marionettes, you should visit the workshop of Jean-Pierre Facquier at 67 rue du Don.

Beauvais

As you head south from Amiens towards Paris, the countryside becomes broad and flat – agricultural, though not rustic. **BEAUVAIS** seems to fit into this landscape. Rebuilt, like Amiens, after the last world war, it's a drab, neutral place redeemed only by its radi-ating Gothic cathedral.

The **Cathédrale St-Pierre** rises above the town, its roof, unadorned by tower or spire, seeming squat for all its height. This is a building that perhaps more than any other in northern France demonstrates the religious materialism of the Middle Ages – its main intention to be taller and larger than its rivals. The choir, completed in 1272, was once 5m higher than that of Amiens; though only briefly, as it collapsed in 1284. Its replacement, only completed three centuries later, was raised by the sale of indulgences – a right granted to the local bishops by Pope Leo X. This, too, fell within a few years and, the authorities having overreached themselves financially, the church remained unfinished, forlorn and mutilated. The appeal of the building, and its real beauty, lies in its glass, its sculpted doorways and the remnants of the so-called Basse-Oeuvre, a ninth-century Carolingian church incorporated into the structure. It also contains a couple of remarkable clocks, including one 12m high that displays the night sky over Beauvais and features the Archangel Michael helping to weigh souls at the Last Judgement.

Stopping at Beauvais to break your journey, you'll probably want to give the rest of the town no more than a passing look. The **church of St-Étienne**, a few blocks to the south of the cathedral on rue de Malherbe, houses yet more spectacular Renaissance stained-glass windows. There's also the **Galerie Nationale de Tapisserie** behind the cathedral (Tues–Sun 9.30–11.30am & 2–4.30/6pm; 25F), a museum of the tapestry for which Beauvais was once renowned, and the **Musée Départemental** (Mon & Wed–Sun 10am–noon & 2–6pm; 10F), devoted to painting, local history and archeology, in the sharp, black-towered building opposite. The rousing **statue** in the central square is of local heroine Jeanne Hachette, a fighter and inspiration in the defence of the town in 1472 against Charles the Bold, Duke of Burgundy.

Practicalities

Beauvais is an hour by train from Paris, and the **gare SNCF** is a short walk from the centre of town – take avenue de la République, then turn right up rue de Malherbe. Opposite the Galerie Nationale de la Tapisserie, at 1 rue Beauregard, the **tourist office** can provide exhaustive information. If you want to stay, three inexpensive choices are the *Normandie*, 20 rue de la Taillerie (☎03.44.45.07.61; ①), *Le Brazza*, 22 rue de la Madeleine (☎03.44.45.03.86; ①) between the station and the centre of town, and *Hôtel du Palais*, within sight of the cathedral, 9 rue St-Nicolas (☎03.44.45.12.58, fax 03.44.45.66.23; ①). There's a *camping municipale* (☎03.44.02.00.22; mid-May to mid–Sept) just out of town on the Paris road.

For fine **food** on the square, call in at *Le Marignan*, 1 rue de Malherbe (☎03.44.48.15.15), with menus from 62F in the brasserie downstairs, and from 98F in the very good restaurant upstairs.

THE INDUSTRIAL NORTH AND THE BATTLEFIELDS

Picardy, Artois and Flanders are littered with the monuments, battlefields and cemeteries of the two world wars, but nowhere as intensely as the region northeast of Amiens, between **Albert** and **Arras**. It was here, among the fields and villages of the Somme, that the main battle lines of World War I were drawn. They can be visited most spectacularly at **Vimy Ridge**, just off the A26 north of Arras, where the trenches have been left *in situ*. Lesser sites, often more poignant, are dotted over the countryside around Albert and along the **Circuit de Souvenir**.

A more enduring and more domestic presence in the life of northern France has been that of the **coalfields** and all their related heavy industrial works. At their peak of production they formed a continuous stretch from Béthune in the west to Valenciennes in the east, though the industry is now in terminal decline. At **Lewarde** you can visit one of the pits, while at the big industrial city of **Lille**, or the pleasant town of **Douai**, you can see what the masters did with takings from the muck.

Lille

LILLE, by far the largest city in the north, is the very symbol of French industry and working-class politics. Its mayor, Pierre Mauroy, was the first Socialist prime minister appointed by Mitterrand in 1981. In every direction the city spreads far into the countryside, a mass of suburbs and heavy industrial plants. Lille exhibits most of the problems and assets of contemporary France – some of the worst poverty and racial conflict in the country, a crime rate rivalled only by Paris and Marseille, and a certain regionalism; *Lillois* sprinkle their speech with a French-Flemish patois and to some extent assert a Flemish identity. But there is also classic French affluence. The city has a

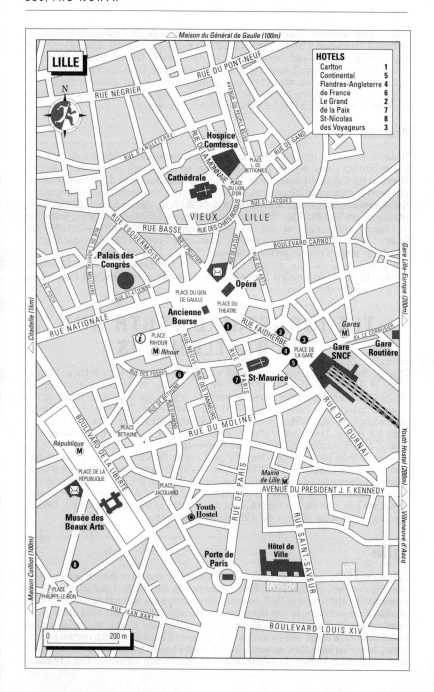

△ Maison du Général de Gaulle (100m)

LILLE

N

RUE NEGRIER

RUE DU PONT-NEUF

RUE D'ANGLETERRE

AVENUE DU PEUPLE BELGE

RUE DE GAND

HOTELS

Carlton	1
Continental	5
Flandres-Angleterre	4
de France	6
Le Grand	2
de la Paix	7
St-Nicolas	8
des Voyageurs	3

Hospice Comtesse

RUE DE LA MONNAIE

PLACE L. DE BETTIGNIES

Cathédrale

PLACE DU LION D'OR

RUE ST-JACQUES

VIEUX LILLE

RUE ESQUERMOISE

RUE BASSE

RUE DES CHATS BOSSUS

RUE DE LA CLEF

RUE DU PELLETIER

BOULEVARD CARNOT

RUE DE L'HOPITAL MILITAIRE

Palais des Congrès

RUE ST-ETIENNE

RUE DES ARTS

Gare Lille-Europe (200m) ▷

△ Citadelle (1km)

AV. FOCH

RUE NATIONALE

PLACE DU GEN. DE GAULLE

Opéra

PLACE DU THEATRE

Ancienne Bourse

RUE FAIDHERBE

Gares Ⓜ

AV. LE CORBUSIER

RUE NEUVE

RUE DE PARIS

RUE DE LA GARE

② ③

④

PLACE DE LA GARE

Gare SNCF

Gare Routière

ⓘ PLACE RIHOUR

Ⓜ Rihour

①

RUE DES FOSSES

RUE DE BETHUNE

RUE DES TANNEURS

RUE AMIENS

⑥

⑦

⑤

St-Maurice

Youth Hostel (200m) ▷

△ Maison Coilliot (100m)

République Ⓜ

PLACE BETHUNE

BOULEVARD DE LA LIBERTE

RUE DU MOLINET

▷ Villeneuve d'Ascq

PLACE DE LA RÉPUBLIQUE

PLACE JACQUARD

RUE DE PARIS

Mairie de Lille Ⓜ

AVENUE DU PRESIDENT J. F. KENNEDY

RUE SAINT-SAUVEUR

RUE DE TOURNAI

Youth Hostel ◉

Musée des Beaux Arts

⑧

PLACE PHILIPPE-LE-BON

Porte de Paris

Hôtel de Ville

RUE JEAN BART

BOULEVARD LOUIS XIV

0 ⟶ 200 m

lovely central heart, Vieux Lille, some vibrant and obviously prosperous commercial areas, modern residential squares, a large university, a brand-new métro system, and a very serious attitude to its culture and restaurants. Although you may not consider Lille a prime destination, if you're travelling through this region it's worth at least a day and a night.

Arrival, information and accommodation

The central Grande-Place is just a few minutes' walk from the **gare routière** and adjacent **gare SNCF** (originally Paris's Gare du Nord, but brought here brick by brick in 1865). Despite being the fifth-largest city in France, the centre of Lille is small enough to walk round and, unless you choose to visit Villeneuve-d'Ascq on the outskirts, you won't even need to use the city's efficient métro system.

The **tourist office** is in place Rihour (Mon 1–6pm, Tues–Sat 10am–6pm, Sun & hols 10am–noon & 2–5pm; ☎03.20.21.94.21, fax 03.20.21.94.20), ten minutes' walk from the station along rue Faidherbe and through place du Théâtre and place du Général-de-Gaulle. They operate a free accommodation booking service for Lille (30F for the rest of France). There should be few problems finding a cheap place to **stay** if you don't mind the slightly seedy station area.

Hotels

Carlton, 3 rue de Paris (☎03.20.13.33.13, fax 03.20.51.48.17). Posh four-star with all the frills, right down to a red carpet outside. ⑧.

Continental, 11 place de la Gare (☎03.20.06.22.24, fax 03.20.51.85.57). More upmarket version of *des Voyageurs*, complete with satellite TV. ①–④.

Flandres-Angleterre, 13 place de la Gare (☎03.20.06.04.12, fax 03.20.06.37.76). Much the classiest of the train station lot: all rooms with bath or shower and toilet. ③.

de France, 10 rue de Béthune (☎03.20.57.14.78, fax 03.20.57.06.01). Fantastic location right in the centre of the pedestrianized area. Big, clean, comfortable rooms, some with balcony. ①.

Le Grand, 51 rue Faidherbe (☎03.20.06.31.57, fax 03.20.06.24.44). Comfortable two-star, all rooms with shower, toilet and TV. ②.

La Paix, 46bis rue de Paris (☎03.20.54.63.93, fax 03.20.63.98.97). Classy two-star with leather lounges and a gleaming wooden staircase. Great position, all rooms with shower, toilet and TV. ④.

St-Nicolas, 11bis rue Nicolas-Leblanc, off place Lebon (☎03.20.57.73.26). Available cheapie not far from place de la République. ①.

des Voyageurs, 10 place de la Gare (☎03.20.06.43.14). Slip of a building directly opposite the station, offering basic, cheap rooms – worth it just for the wrought-iron lift. ①.

Youth hostels and campsites

Youth hostel, 12 rue Malpart, off rue de Paris (☎03.20.57.08.94, fax 03.20.63.98.93).

Camping Les Ramiers, Bondues (☎03.20.23.13.42). Lille's nearest site is actually in the village of Bondues, about 10km north of the city and linked by bus. Closed Nov–April.

The city

The point to make for is the **Grande-Place** (otherwise known as place du Général-de-Gaulle), which marks the southern boundary of the old quarter, **Vieux Lille**. To the south is the central pedestrianized shopping area which extends along rue de Béthune as far as the adjacent squares of place Béthune and place de la République. On Saturdays, especially, the area is so jammed with shoppers that you can hardly move, and crowded outdoor cafés add to the street life. The major **festival** of the year, the Grande Braderie, takes place over the first weekend of September, when a big street parade and vast flea-market fill the streets of the old town by day, and the evenings see a *moules frites* frenzy in all the restaurants, with empty mussel shells piled up in the streets.

Vieux Lille

One side of the Grande-Place is dominated by the old exchange building, the lavishly ornate **Ancienne Bourse**, as perfect a representative of its age as could be imagined. To the merchants of seventeenth-century Lille, all things Flemish were the epitome of wealth and taste; they were not men to stint on detail, neither here nor on the impos-ing surrounding mansions. Recently cleaned up, the courtyard is now an organized flea-market, with stalls selling books, junk and flowers. Lounging around the fountain at the centre of the *place* is a favourite *Lillois* pastime. In the middle is a **column** com-memorating the city's resistance to the Austrian siege of 1792, topped by *La Déesse* (the goddess), modelled on the wife of the mayor at the time.

In the adjacent square of **place du Théâtre**, you can see how Flemish Renaissance architecture became assimilated and Frenchified in grand flights of Baroque extrav-agance. The superlative example of this style is the **Opéra**, whose facade sports sculptures symbolizing music and tragedy, with Apollo among the muses. It was built at the turn of this century by Louis Cordonnier, who also designed the extravagant **belfry** of the neighbouring Nouvelle Bourse and Chamber of Commerce, now the city's main PTT.

From the north side of these two squares, the smart shopping streets, rues Esquermoise and Lepelletier, lead towards the heart of old Lille, a warren of red-brick terraces on cobbled lanes and passages. It is an area of great character and charm suc-cessfully reclaimed and reintegrated into the mainstream of the city's life, having been for years a dilapidated North African ghetto. Head up towards rue d'Angleterre, rue du Pont-Neuf and the Porte de Gand, rue de la Monnaie and place du Lion-d'Or. Places to eat and drink are everywhere.

There are no particular sights apart from the **Hospice Comtesse** on rue de la Monnaie. Twelfth-century in origin – though much reconstructed in the eighteenth cen-tury – it served as a hospital until as recently as 1945. Its old ward, the **Salle des Malades**, and the chapel can be visited (daily except Tues 10am–12.30pm & 2–6pm; 15F).

Charles de Gaulle was born in this part of the town, at 9 rue Princesse, in 1890. The house is now a **museum** (Wed–Sun 10am–noon & 2–5pm; 15F); among the exhibits is the bullet-riddled Citroën in which he was driving when the OAS attempted to assassi-nate him in 1962. Another must for military buffs is the nearby **citadelle** that overlooks the old town to the northwest, constructed in familiar star-shaped fashion by Vauban in the seventeenth century. Still in military hands, it too can be visited, though only on Sundays and by guided tour (35F; details from tourist office).

Amid all the city's secular pomp, Lille's ecclesiastical architecture seems rather sub-dued. Its cathedral, the nineteenth-century **Notre-Dame-de-la-Treille**, just off rue de la Monnaie, is undistinguished and still unfinished. More impressive is the cathedral-esque **church of St-Maurice**, close to the station off place de la Gare, a classic red-brick Flemish Hallekerke, with the characteristic five aisles of the style.

South of the Grande-Place

Just south of the Grande-Place is **place Rihour**, a largely modern square with an old palace that now houses the tourist office, hidden behind an ugly war monument of gigan-tic proportions. Close by the busiest shopping street, **rue de Béthune**, leads into place de Béthune, with some excellent cafés, and beyond to the **Musée des Beaux-Arts** on place de la République (Mon 2–6pm, Wed–Thurs & Sat–Sun 10am–6pm, Fri 10am–7pm; 30F). Like so many French art museums, it studiously covers each genre: paintings, ceramics, tapestries and so on. Here, though, the emphasis is very much on the Flemish painters, from "primitives" like Dieric Bouts, through the northern Renaissance to Ruisdael, de Hooch and the seventeenth-century schools. It's an instructive display, helped by a small library of art books provided for browsing through in the entrance hall. There's an additional scattering of Impressionists, including Monet, and also works by Corot.

A couple of blocks to the south of the museum, on rue de Fleurus, is **Maison Coilliot**, a ceramics shop and one of the few houses built by Hector Guimard, who made his name designing the Art Nouveau entrances to the Paris métro. Built at the height of the Art Nouveau movement, it's as striking today as it obviously was to the conservative burghers of Lille (there are no other such buildings in Lille), but it also displays the somewhat muddled eclecticism of the style, coming over as half brick-faced mansion, half timber-framed cottage. East of the museum, near the triumphal arch of **Porte de Paris**, the city's **Hôtel de Ville** is also worth a quick look, executed in a bizarre, Flemish Art Deco style, with a tall belfry and viewing platform (April–Sept Sun only).

Villeneuve d'Ascq: Musée d'Art Moderne

Thanks to Eurostar and the international extension of the TGV network Lille has become the transport hub of northern Europe, a position it is trying to exploit to turn itself into an international business centre, with the appropriate space-age facilities. Hence, **Euralille**, the burgeoning complex of buildings behind the old gare SNCF.

One definite success is the new **Lille-Europe TGV and Eurostar station**: lots of props and struts and glass and sunscreens, but it's lean, elegant and functional, a fitting setting for the magnificent trains that use it. The other developments smack of a new totalitarianism; manipulation of the consuming masses by the distant powers of international finance. Literally treading on the roof of the new station is an anonymous boot-shaped tower reminiscent of nothing so much as the home of the old woman in the nursery rhyme who lived in a shoe. And opposite is an enormous shopping centre with galvanized walkways, marbled malls and relentless muzak. This controlled environment is traceable to the utopian dreams of Le Corbusier, whose paternity is acknowledged in the **avenue Le Corbusier**, which sweeps over the soon-to-opened plaza to the Lille-Europe station. There are other ironies, too, such as the fashion for "factory" architecture now that there are no more factories – there's more than thirteen percent unemployment in Lille, more than sixteen percent in neighbouring Roubaix, and more than twenty percent among the immigrant community.

As a mark of Lille's cultural ambition, there's the suburb of **Villeneuve-d'Ascq**, where acres of parkland, an old windmill or two, and a whole series of mini-lakes form the backdrop for the **Musée d'Art Moderne** (daily except Tues 10am–6pm; 25F), housing an unusually good collection in its uninviting red-brick buildings. To get there, take the métro to Pont-de-Bois, then bus #41.

The ground floor of the museum is generally given over to temporary exhibitions of varying quality by contemporary French artists. The permanent collection starts on the first floor with canvases by Picasso, Braque, Modigliani, Miró and a whole room devoted to Fernand Léger and Georges Rouault. On the top floor, a small room – easy to miss but worth the search – contains graphics by many of the above. Meanwhile, outside on the grass, Giacometti and Calder provide some playful picnic backdrops.

Eating

A Flemish flavour and taste for mussels (*moules*) characterize Lille's cuisine. The main area for **cafés**, **brasseries** and **restaurants** is around place Rihour and along rue de Béthune. Rue Royale has a selection of fairly pricey ethnic eateries from Cambodian to

Japanese. The best general area for cheap restaurants is the student quarter along the Solférino and rue Masséna.

Bar de la Cloche, 13 place du Théâtre. Excellent small brasserie serving twenty different wines by the glass. Inexpensive *plats* 40–60F, *tartines* and cheeses 20–25F. Relaxed, casual and popular with the older set.

Brasserie Jean, 2 rue Faidherbe, cnr place du Théâtre. Large, bright brasserie specializing in Flemish-style dishes and taking up nearly a whole corner under the *Hôtel Carlton*. There's an excellent 78F menu.

Coq Hardi, 44 place Général-de-Gaulle. In a prime position on the main square, you can people-watch whilst eating one of the salads at 30–40F or specialities of the region from the 88F menu. Also open for drinks outside of mealtimes.

L'Endroit, 18 rue Masséna (☎03.20.30.18.92). Old bar and bistrot offering charming French dishes in a very attractive atmosphere. Closed Sat lunch & Sun. Menus at 68F.

Flandre Liban, 125 rue des Postes. Excellent Lebanese restaurant in a mainly North African and Middle Eastern quarter. Go for the mezze menu at 95F.

La Galetière, 4 place Louise-de-Bettignies (☎03.20.54.89.92). Good-value crêperie in the old town. If full or closed, try the equally good *Beaurepaire II* round the corner on place Lione d'Or. Closed Sun & Mon.

La Huîtrière, 3 rue des Chats-Bossus (☎03.20.55.43.41). A wonderful, colourful shop tiled with mosaics of seaside and rural working scenes, which sells everything from fish, seafood, chicken, meats, wine, with huge lobsters alive in their tanks. An expensive, chandelier-hung restaurant at the back specializes in fish and seafood at 150–178F a dish; a staggering 480F menu, 260F for lunch. Closed Sun eve, hols & July 22–Aug 23.

Lino, 1 rue des Trois-Couronnes. Top-quality, moderately priced, authentic Italian – no pizza here. Cosy, rustic decor. Around 120F. Closed Sun.

aux Moules, 34 rue de Béthune (☎03.20.12.90.92). The place to eat mussels; it's been serving them since 1930 in its Art Deco-style interior; nothing much over 60F, including other brasserie fare. Daily noon–midnight.

Paul, place du Théâtre, cnr rue Faidherbe (☎03.20.78.20.78). *Paul* is an institution in Lille and here the boulangerie, pâtisserie, *salon de thé* and restaurant all under one roof. The 126F three-course menu in the restaurant is a good deal, but the main reason to come here is to taste the delights of the pâtisserie in the *salon de thé*. Daily 6.30am–midnight.

Piccolo Mondo, 2 rue des Molfonds, off rue de Béthune. Lille's best pizza place also serves pasta and offers several vegetarian alternatives.

Les Trois Brasseurs, 22 place de la Gare. Dark, smoke-stained dining stalls surround copper cauldrons in this genuine brasserie that brews its own beer and serves real brasserie fare such as marrow bone and *tarte à la bière* – with a pint of Blanche de Lille, that would cost you 100F.

Drinking and nightlife

The **cafés** around the Grande-Place and place Rihour are always buzzing with life. Rue de Paris has lots of tacky, loud, crushed **bars** raging at all hours, while rue Basse and nearby place Louise-de-Bettignies have some trendier spots. Bars are thick on the ground in rues Solférino and Masséna, attracting a young crowd. Art and music events are always worth checking up on – there's a particularly lively jazz scene. Pick up a copy of the free weekly **listings magazine**, *Sortir*, from the tourist office, or look in the local paper, *La Voix du Nord*.

L'Angle Saxo, 36 rue d'Angleterre (☎03.20.06.15.06). Relaxed bar with good jazz – and you can hear yourself speak. Drinks are pricier than the pubs. Daily 9pm–2am.

Bar Jazz, 55 rue Basse. More jazz here in a slick, modern interior. Daily 10am–2am, Sun from 6pm.

Le Basse, 57 rue Basse. Groovy bar, an intimate atmosphere and lots of plants. Tues–Sat 10am–2am, Sun & Mon from 5pm.

Café au Bureau, rue de Béthune. Done out with plenty of brass and dark woodwork, and offering a hundred kinds of beer. Tables outside are crowded with young things watching the parade.

Father Moustache, 19 rue Masséna. In a street lined with bars, this is as good a place as any to join a mainly student crowd. Daily 9pm–2am.

L'Imaginaire, place Louise-de-Bettignies, next door to the *Hôtel Treille*. Arty young bar with paintings adorning the walls. Mon–Sat 10pm–2am.

Listings

Banks All the banks have big branches on rue Nationale and you can guarantee to find one open until 4pm on Saturday. There's a branch of Barclays here too.

Books Le Furet du Nord, 11 place Général-de-Gaulle, is a huge bookstore with a wide selection of books in English.

Cinema There are several cinemas in Lille with a concentration on rue de Béthune. Le Métropole on rue des Ponts-de-Comines shows original-language versions with normally a couple in English. Gaumont at no. 25 rue des Alpes and UGC on rue de Béthune will usually have one of their screens in English.

Doctors SOS Médecins (☎03.20.30.97.97).

Hitch-hiking Auto Pass, 21 rue Patou (☎03.20.14.31.91), is an organization that puts hitch-hikers and drivers in touch with each other.

Laundry There are four outlets of Lavorama: at 72 rue Pierre-LeGrand, 148 rue de la Louvière, 148 rue des Stations and 4 rue Ovigneur.

Markets The loud and colourful Wazemmes market takes centres around place de la Nouvelle Aventure. Main day Sunday but also open Tues and Thurs (7am–2pm). A smaller food market takes place in *vieux Lille* on place du Concert (Wed, Fri & Sun 7am–2pm).

Post office place du Théâtre, cnr bd Carnot or 7 place de la République. Mon–Fri 8am–5pm, Sat 8am–noon.

Taxi Gare (☎03.20.06.64.00), Ray (☎03.20.55.55.20), Radio Taxi Union (☎03.20.06.06.06).

Douai and around

Right at the heart of mining country, 35km south of Lille, and badly damaged in both world wars, **DOUAI** is a surprisingly attractive and lively town, its streets of eighteenth-century houses cut through by both river and canal. Once a haven for English Catholics fleeing Protestant oppression in Tudor England, Douai later became the seat of Flemish local government under Louis XIV, an aristocratic past evoked in the novels of Balzac.

Centre of activity is the **place d'Armes**, overlooked by the massive Gothic belfry on rue de la Mairie of the **Hôtel de Ville**, popularized by Victor Hugo and renowned for its carillon of 62 bells – the largest single collection of bells in Europe – which plays a great variety of tunes. It rings every quarter-hour, and there are hour-long concerts every Saturday at 10.45am, on public holidays at 11am, and in summer on Monday at 9pm (guided tours July & Aug daily at 10am & 11am, plus on-the-hour 2–5pm; rest of year Mon–Sat on the hour 2–5pm, also Sun 10am, 11am, 3pm & 5pm; 15F).

One block north of the town hall, on **rue Bellegambe**, is an outrageous Art Nouveau shop front serving a very ordinary haberdashery store. Rising above the old town, at the end of the street, are the Baroque dome and tower of the **church of St-Pierre**, an immense, mainly eighteenth-century church with – among other treasures – a spectacular carved Baroque organ case. East of the place d'Armes, Douai's oldest church, the twelfth-century **church of Notre-Dame**, suffered badly in the last war but has been refreshingly modernized inside. Beyond the church is the better of the town's two surviving medieval gateways, the **Porte Valenciennes,** now the centre of a triumphal roundabout.

With the exception of the 1970s extension to the old Flemish Parliament building, the riverfront west of the town hall is pleasant to wander along. Between the river and the canal to the west, on rue de Chartreux, the **Ancienne Chartreuse** is now a museum (Mon & Wed–Sat 10am–noon & 2–5pm, Sun 3–6pm; 12F with a good collection of paintings by Flemish, Dutch and French masters, including Van Dyck, Rubens, Rodin and Douai's own Jean Bellegambe.

Practicalities
The **gare SNCF** is a five-minute walk from place d'Armes – left down boulevard Faidherbe, then right down rue de Valenciennes. **The tourist office** (July & Aug daily 9am–noon & 2–6pm; rest of year closed Sun; ☎03.27.88.26.79, fax 03.27.96.42.29) is within the fifteenth-century *Hôtel du Dauphin*, on the *place*. For **accommodation** there's the *Hôtel de Paris*, across the square from the tourist office (☎03.27.88.95.63; ②), or the better *Grand Cerf*, 46 rue St-Jacques (☎03.27.88.79.60, fax 03.27.98.05.74; ④). A far classier option is *La Terrasse*, a swanky four-star in the narrow terrasse St-Pierre (☎03.27.88.70.04, fax 03.27.88.36.05; ④–⑦), to one side of the church of St-Pierre; its restaurant is well regarded, with menus from 145F. Just northeast of the place d'Armes is the PTT, whence buses leave for Lewarde (Line 1 orange).

Lewarde

A visit to the colliery at **LEWARDE**, 7km east of Douai, is a must for admirers of Zola's *Germinal*, perhaps the most electrifying "naturalistic" novel ever written. The bus from Douai heads east across the flat and featureless beet fields, down a road lined with poor brick dwellings that recall the company-owned housing of *Germinal*, intersected by streets named after Pablo Neruda, Jean-Jacques Rousseau, Georges Brassens and other luminaries of the French and international Left. This is the traditional heart of France's coal-mining country, always dispiriting and now depressed by closures and recession. Even the distinctive landmarks of slag heap and winding gear are fast disappearing with demolition and landscaping.

The bus puts you down at the main square in Lewarde, leaving a fifteen-minute walk down the D132 towards Erchin. The **Centre Historique Minier** (March–Oct daily 9am–5.30pm; Nov–Feb Mon–Sat 1–5pm, Sun 10am–5pm; guided visits 1hr 30min: March–Oct 62F; Nov–Feb; 54F) is on the left in the old Fosse Delloye, sited, like so many pits, amid woods and fields. Visits are guided by retired miners, many of whom are not French, but Polish, Italian or North African – Polish labour was introduced in the 1920s, other nationalities successively after World War II. One Polish guide went down the pit at 14 and was brought up at 38 with silicosis, which had also killed his father at 52. "Ce n'est pas un métier," he said – "It's not what you'd call a career."

The main part of the tour – in addition to film shows and visits to the surface installations of winding gear, machine shops, cages, sorting areas and the rest – is the exploration of the pit-bottom roadways and faces, equipped to show the evolution of mining from the earliest times to today. These French pits were extremely deep and hot, with steeply inclined narrow seams that forced the miners to work on slopes of 55° and more, just as Étienne and the Maheu family do in Zola's story.

Accidents were a regular occurrence in the old days: the northern French pits had a particularly bad record in the last years of the nineteenth century. The worst mining disaster occurred at Courrières in 1906, when 1100 men were killed. Incredibly, despite the fact that the owners made little effort to search for survivors, thirteen men suddenly emerged after twenty days of wandering in the gas-filled tunnels without food, water or light. The first person they met thought that they were ghosts and fainted in fright. More incredible still, a fourteenth man surfaced alone after another four days.

Cambrai and Le Cateau

CAMBRAI, like Douai 26km to the north, has kept enough of its character to repay a passing visit, despite the tank battle of November 1917 (see box below) and the fact that the heavily defended Hindenburg Line ran through the town centre for most of World War I.

The huge, cobbled main square, **place Aristide-Briand**, is dominated by the Neoclassical Hôtel de Ville, and still suggests the town's former wealth, based on the textile and agricultural industries. Cambrai's chief treasure for once is not its cathedral but the **church of St-Géry**, off rue St-Aubert west of the main square, which contains a celebrated *Mise au Tombeau* by Rubens. The **Musée Municipal** (Wed–Sun 10am–noon & 2-6pm; 20F) on rue de l'Épée, south of the town square, is also worth a visit. The paintings of Velázquez feature prominently alongside various Flemish masters, works by Utrillo, and by Matisse, a native of Le Cateau (see below).

Cambrai's **tourist office** is housed in the Maison Espagnole on the corner of avenue de la Victoire, at 48 rue de Noyon (Mon–Fri 9am–noon & 2–6pm, Sat 10am–noon & 2–6pm, Sun 2–6pm; ☎03.27.78.36.15, fax 03.27.74.82.82). Central **accommodation** comprises *Le Mouton Blanc*, 33 rue d'Alsace-Lorraine (☎03.27.81.30.16, fax 03.27.81.83.54; ③; restaurant from 98F; closed Sun eve & Mon, plus the eve of public hols & Aug 1–15), which is a convenient and moderately priced hotel close to the station with a posh restaurant inside and an inexpensive half-service one around the corner. The cheaper hotels are way out on the other side of town on the highway, while the nearest **campsite** is 10km away and is signposted off the D939 to Arras.

Le Cateau

Twenty-two kilometres east of Cambrai along an old Roman road, the small town of **LE CATEAU-CAMBRÉSIS** is the birthplace of Henri Matisse (1869–1954). As a gift to his home town, Matisse bequeathed it a collection of his works. Some of them are now displayed in the **Musée Matisse** (Mon & Wed–Sat 10am–noon & 2–6pm, Sun 10am–12.30pm & 2.30–6pm; 16F), housed in the local château in the centre of town, and in order to display more the museum will be closed from early summer 1999 for

---

CAMBRAI 1917

At dawn on November 20, 1917, the first full-scale tank battle in history began at **Cambrai**, when over 400 British tanks poured over the Hindenburg Line. In just 24 hours, the Royal Tank Corps and British Third Army made an advance that was further than any undertaken by either side since the trenches had first been dug in 1914. A fortnight later, however, casualties on both sides had reached 50,000, and the armies were back where they'd started.

Although in some respects the tanks were ahead of their time, they still relied on cavalry and plodding infantry as their back-up and runners for their lines of communication. And, before they even reached the "green fields beyond", most of them had broken down. World War I tanks were primitive machines, operated by a crew of eight who endured almost intolerable conditions: with no ventilation system, the temperature inside could rise to 48°C. The steering alone required three men, each on separate gearboxes, communicating by hand signals through the din of the tank's internal noise. Maximum speed (6km/ph) dropped to almost 1km/ph over rough terrain, and refuelling was necessary every 55km. Consequently, of the 179 tanks lost in the battle at Cambrai, very few had been destroyed by the enemy; the majority broke down and were abandoned by their crews.

two to three years to double its floor-space. Although there are no major works here, it still deserves a visit, being the third-largest collection of his work in France. Matisse's work occupies the first floor and includes several studies for the chapel in Vence plus a whole series of his characteristically simple pen-and-ink sketches. Also worth looking at is the work of local Cubist Auguste Herbin on the ground floor, particularly his psychedelic upright piano.

Arras, Albert and the Somme battlefields

Around **Arras** and **Albert**, some of the fiercest and most futile battles of World War I took place, and at one time the trenches even cut through the grandiose main square in Arras, now restored to its former glory. At nearby **Vimy Ridge**, the Canadians fell in their thousands; at **Notre-Dame de Lorette**, the French suffered the same fate. Albert is not a place to linger, but makes a convenient base for exploring the many war cemeteries in the area.

Arras

ARRAS, with its fine old centre, is one of the prettiest towns in northern France. It was renowned for its tapestries in the Middle Ages, giving its name to the hangings behind which Shakespeare's Hamlet killed Polonius. Subsequently the town fell under Spanish control, and many of its citizens today claim that Spanish blood runs in their veins. Only in 1654 was Arras returned to the kingdom of France.

Although almost destroyed in World War I, the town bears few obvious battle scars. Reconstruction here, particularly after the last war, has been careful and stylish, and two grand arcaded squares in the centre – **Grand' Place** and the smaller **place des Héros** – preserve their historic, harmonious character. On every side are restored seventeenth-and eighteenth-century mansions, built in relatively restrained Flemish style, and, on place des Héros, there's a grandly ornate **Hôtel de Ville**, its entrance hall housing a permanent photographic display documenting the wartime destruction of the town and sheltering a pair of *géants* (festival giants) awaiting the city's next fête.

Also inside the town hall is the entrance to the **belfry viewing platform** (Mon–Sat 10am–noon & 2–6pm, Sun 10am–noon & 2.30–6.30pm; 14F) and **les souterrains** (or *les boves*), cold, dark passageways and spacious vaults tunnelled beneath the centre of the city (Mon–Sat 10am–noon & 2–6pm, Sun 10am–noon & 3–6.30pm; 20F). Once down, you're escorted around an impressive area and given an interesting survey of local history. During World War I, the rooms – many of which have fine, tiled floors and lovely pillars and stairways – were used as a British barracks and hospital.

Arras's other main sight is its cathedral, next to the former Benedictine **Abbaye St-Vaast**, an enormous grey-stone classical building, still pockmarked by shrapnel, that was erected in the eighteenth century by Cardinal Rohen. now houses the **Musée des Beaux-Arts**, entrance at 22 rue Paul-Donnier (April–Sept Mon & Wed–Sat 10am–noon & 2–6pm, Sun 10am–noon & 3–6pm; Oct–March Mon &Wed–Fri closes 5pm; 20F), with a mediocre collection of paintings, including a couple of Jordaens and Brueghels, fragments of sculpture, local ceramics and some of the tapestries or *arras* (the final "s" is pronounced) that made the town famous in medieval times.

On the western edge of town, next to the Vauban barracks, is a **war cemetery** and **memorial** by the British architect Sir Edwin Lutyens, a movingly elegiac, classical colonnade of ivy-covered brick and stone, commemorating 35,928 missing soldiers, the endless columns of their names inscribed on the walls.

It is a mournful corner of town. Around the back of the old brick Vauban fortress, in an overgrown moat, is the **Mur des Fusillés**, where some two hundred Resistance fighters were shot by firing squad in the last war– most of them of Polish descent, most of them miners, and most of them Communists.

Practicalities

The **tourist office** is in the *Hôtel de Ville* on place des Héros (June–Sept Mon–Sat 9am–6.30pm, Sun 10am–noon & 2.30–6.30pm; Oct–May Mon–Sat 9am–noon & 2–6pm, Sun 10am–noon & 3–6.30pm; ☎03.21.51.26.95, fax 03.21.71.07.34). It's worth consulting for details of transport and tours of local battlefields (see "Vimy Ridge and around", below). To reach the Vimy memorial, you can also **rent a car** from Hertz, bd Carnot (☎03.21.23.11.14), or Euroto, 15 av Paul-Michonneau (☎03.21.55.05.05), for a slightly cheaper deal.

If you are **staying** the night, there are two good, inexpensive hotels in the town centre: the *Ibis*, 11 rue de Justice, off place des Héros (☎03.21.23.61.61, fax 03.21.71.31.31; ③), a comfortable, reliable two-star, fully accessible for the disabled; and *Hôtel des Trois Luppars*, 47 Grand' Place (☎03.21.07.41.41, fax 03.21.24.24.80; ③), a friendly family-run place with modern facilities in a characterful old building. For a more luxurious night, go to the *Univers*, a lovely classical building round a courtyard in place de la Croix-Rouge, near the Abbaye St-Vaast (☎03.21.71.34.01, fax 03.21.71.41.42; ④; restaurant 99F–195F). The newly modernized, well-positioned **youth hostel** is at 59 Grand' Place (☎03.21.22.70.02, fax 03.21.07.46.15; closed Nov–Jan). A **campsite** (April–Oct) lies 1km out of town on the Bapaume road.

Restaurants worth trying include *La Rapière*, 44 Grand' Place, with excellent regional food and menus at 85F or 115F; and, for a splurge, the gourmet *La Faisanderie*, a few doors away (from 135F). Pizzerias abound, and two particularly good ones are on rue Petit-Viéziers, *Le Petit Théâtre* and *Aux Petits-Viéziers*, while *Le Palerme* at 50 Grand' Place also serves pasta. For something different, an excellent *shwarma* place (eat in or take away) is tucked away in rue des Trois-Visages, just around the corner from the *Hôtel de Ville*, with a luscious range of Middle Eastern sweets.

Les Grandes Arcades, the hotel on Grand' Place, also serves good and not wildly expensive **regional food** (including the local speciality *andouillette*, or tripe sausage – an acquired taste); and you'll find a good **fromagerie**, *Jean-Claude Leclercq*, at 39 place des Héros. Saturdays are a good day for food and wine, when the squares are taken up with a morning **market**, and Esto Cave, an extensive sixteenth-century wine cellar run by the delightfully large and quirky proprietor of *Les Trois Luppars*, is open for the sale of fine wines (10am–1pm & 3–8pm).

Vimy Ridge and around

Eight kilometres north of Arras on the D49, **Vimy Ridge**, or Hill 145, was the scene of some of the direst trench warfare of World War I: almost two full years of battle, culminating in its capture by the crack Canadian Corps in April 1917. It is a vast site, given in perpetuity to the Canadian people out of respect for their sacrifices, and has been preserved, in part, as it was during the conflict. There's an **information centre** (April–Nov daily 10am–6pm; free) supervised by bilingual Canadian students, who run free guided tours and can fill you in on all the horrific details. You really need your own transport to get here, otherwise the nearest bus-stop is forty-five minutes' walk away (the tourist office in Arras (see above) has details).

Near the information centre, long worms of neat, sanitized trenches meander over the now grassy ground, still heavily pitted and churned by shell bursts beneath the planted pines. There are examples of dugouts – hideous places where men used to shelter during heavy bombardments and where makeshift hospitals were set up. Beneath the ground lie some 11,000 bodies still unaccounted for and countless rounds of unexploded ammunition. Signs are still required to warn against straying from the directed paths.

On the brow of the ridge, 1500m north of the information centre, overlooking the slag-heap-dotted plain of Artois, a great white **monument** towers, like a giant funerary stele, rent down the middle by elemental force, with allegorical figures half-emerging from the stone towards the top, and inscribed with the names of 60,000 Canadians and Newfoundlanders who lost their lives during the war. An unenviable task to design a fitting memorial to such slaughter, but this one, aided by its setting, succeeds with great drama.

Back from the ridge, there's a subdued **memorial** to the Moroccan Division who also fought at Vimy, and in the woods behind, on the headstones of another exquisitely maintained **cemetery**, you can read the names of half the counties of rural England.

La Targette, Neuville-St-Vaast and Notre-Dame de Lorette

At the crossroads (D937/D49) of **LA TARGETTE**, 8km north from the centre of Arras and accessible from there by bus, the **Musée de la Targette** (daily 9am–8pm; 20F) contains an interesting collection of World War I and II *objets de guerre*. It is the private collection of one David Bardiaux, assembled with passion and meticulous attention to detail, under the inspiration of tales told by his grandfather, a veteran of Verdun. Its interest lies in the absolute precision with which the thirty-odd mannequins of British, French, Canadian and German soldiers are dressed and equipped, down to their sweet and tobacco tins and such rarities as a 1915 British-issue cap with earflaps, very comfortable for the troops but withdrawn because the top brass thought it made their men look like yokels. All the exhibits have been under fire; some belonged to known individuals and are complete with stitched-up tears of old wounds. When you're finished, the *Café Flambeau* serves well-priced food.

More **cemeteries** lie a little to the south of La Targette, nominally at **NEUVILLE-ST-VAAST**, though the village is actually 1km away to the east. There is a small British cemetery, a huge French one, and an equally large German cemetery containing the remains of 44,833 Germans. If you haven't been to a German war cemetery before, the macabre, skeletal black crosses – each one represents four soldiers – come as quite a shock. So, too, do the handful of individual Jewish headstones that stand out from the rest. The Polish sculptor Henri Gaudier-Brzeska died in action here in 1915 – a Polish **memorial** and Czech **cemetery** face each other across the main street of the village itself.

On a bleak hill a few kilometres to the northwest of Vimy Ridge (and 5km north of Neuville-St-Vaast) is the church of **Notre-Dame de Lorette**, scene of a costly French offensive in May 1915. The original church was blasted to bits during the war and rebuilt in grim Neo-Byzantine style in the 1920s, grey and dour on the outside but rich and bejewelled inside. It now stands at the centre of a vast graveyard with over 20,000 crosses laid out in pairs, back to back, each one separated by a cluster of blood-red roses. There are 20,000 more buried in the ossuary, and there's the small **Musée Vivant 1914–1918** (daily 9am–8pm; 20F) behind the church, displaying photographs, uniforms and other military paraphernalia. You can reach Notre-Dame de Lorette by bus from Arras, direction "Lens".

Albert and around

The church at **ALBERT** – now, with the rest of the town, completely rebuilt – was one of the minor landmarks of World War I. Its tall tower was hit by German bombing early on in the campaign, leaving the statue of the Madonna on top leaning at a precarious angle. The British, entrenched over three years in the region, came to know it as the "Leaning Virgin". Army superstition had it that when she fell the war would end, a myth inspiring frequent hopeful pot shots by disgruntled troops. Before embarking on a visit of the region's battle sites and war cemeteries, otherwise known as the *circuit de* *souvenir* (see below), you might want to stop in at the **Musée des Abris** (daily: March–June & Sept–Nov 9.30am–noon & 2–6pm; July & Aug 9.30am–6pm; 20F), a museum which has re-enactments of fifteen different scenes from life in the trenches of the Somme in 1916. The mannequins look slightly too jolly and eager but it does go some way to bringing the props to life. Otherwise, unless you have a really strong battlefield interest – in which case you could spend weeks here roaming the region – modern Albert does not invite much of a stay.

As you arrive (trains from Amiens or Arras), the town's new tower, capped now by an equally improbably posed statue, is the first thing that catches the eye. The **tourist office** is close by on rue Gambetta (April–Sept Mon–Sat 10am–noon & 2–6.30pm, Sun 9.30am–noon; Oct–March Mon–Sat 10am–noon & 3–5pm; ☎03.22.75.16.42, fax 03.22.75.11.72) together with a couple of good **hotels**: the moderately priced *Basilique*, 3–5 rue Gambetta (☎03.22.75.04.71, fax 03.22.75.10.47; ③; restaurant 65–190F); and the cheaper *La Paix*, 43 rue Victor-Hugo (☎03.22.75.01.64, fax 03.22.75.44.17; ①), whose restaurant has simpler menus from 79F.

The Circuit de Souvenir

Was it for this the clay grew tall?
O what made fatuous sunbeams toil
To break earth's sleep at all?

Wilfred Owen, *Futility*

The **Circuit de Souvenir** conducts you from graveyard to mine crater, trench to memorial. There's not a lot to see; nothing, at least, that is going to satisfy any appetite for shocking atrocities or scenes of destruction. Neither do you get much sense of movement or even of battle tactics. But you will find that, even if you start out with the feeling that your interest in war is somehow puerile or mawkish, you have in fact embarked on a sort of pilgrimage, in which each successive step becomes more harrowing and oppressive.

The **cemeteries** are the most moving aspect of the region – beautiful, the grass perfectly mown, an individual bed of flowers at the foot of every gravestone. And there are tens of thousands of them, all identical, with a man's name, if it is known (nearly half the British dead have never been found), and his rank and regiment. Just reading the names of the regiments evokes a world of experience quite different from today's: locally recruited regiments, young men from Welsh border farms, mill towns, and villages, who had never been abroad, wiped out in a morning, men from all corners of the Empire. In the lanes between Albert and Bapaume you'll see the cemeteries everywhere: at the angle of copses, halfway across a wheat field, in the middle of a bluebell wood, moving and terrible in their simple beauty. What follows is necessarily just a selected handful of some of the better-known sites.

A good place to start is the station at **HAMEL** (7km by train north of Albert), where the 51st Highland Division walked abreast to their deaths with their pipes playing. Just across the river, towards the village of **THIÉPVAL**, the 5000 Ulstermen who died in the Battle of the Somme are commemorated by the incongruously Celtic **Ulster Memorial**, a replica of the Helen's Tower at Clandeboyne near Belfast (**information bureau** open Mon–Sat 11am–5pm; closed Dec &Jan). Probably the most famous of Edwin Lutyens' many memorials is south of Thiépval: the colossal **Memorial to the Missing**, in memory of the 73,357 British troops whose bodies were never recovered at the Somme. A half-hour hike west of Hamel station is the Newfoundlanders' memorial at **BEAUMONT-HAMEL**. Here, on the hilltop where most of them died, a series of trenches has been preserved, now grassed over and eroding, where German faced Canadian a few paces apart. It all seems so small-scale now and almost more appropriate to the antics of

THE BATTLE OF THE SOMME

On July 1, 1916, the British and French launched the **Battle of the Somme** to relieve pressure on the French army defending Verdun. The front ran roughly northwest–south-east, 6km east of Albert across the valley of the Ancre and over the almost treeless high ground north of the Somme – huge hedgeless wheat fields now, their monotony relieved by an undulation as slow as the rhythm of a long sea swell. These windy open hills had no intrinsic value, nor was there any long-term strategic objective – the region around Albert was chosen simply because it was where the two Allied armies met.

There were 57,000 British casualties on the first day alone, approximately 20,000 of them dead, making it the costliest defeat the British army has ever suffered. Sir Douglas Haig is the usual scapegoat for the Somme, yet he was only following the military think-ing of the day, which is where the real problem lay. As AJP Taylor put it, "Defence was mechanized: attack was not." Machine guns were far more efficient, barbed wire more effective, and, most important of all, the rail lines could move defensive reserves far faster than the attacking army could march. The often ineffective heavy preliminary bom-bardment favoured by both sides only made matters worse, since the shells forewarned the enemy of an offensive and churned the trenches into a giant muddy quagmire.

Despite the bloody disaster of the first day, the battle wore on until bad weather in November made further attacks impossible. The cost of this futile struggle was 415,000 British, 195,000 French, and around 600,000 German casualties.

the party of schoolchildren witnessed running around here shooting each other with their fingers than to anything as obscene as what took place.

Five kilometres east at **POZIÈRES**, on the Albert–Bapaume road, *Le Tommy* café has a World War I permanent **exhibition** (daily 9.30am–6pm) in its back garden con-sisting mainly of a reconstructed section of and "equipped" with genuine battlefield relics. It's a bit amateurish, but quite interesting if you're passing through. The guide had first collected objects from the battlefield as a boy to sell for pocket money. Farmers apparently still turn up about 75 tonnes of shells every year – not really sur-prising when you think the British alone fired one-and-a-half million in the last week of June 1916.

Another fine Lutyens memorial stands near **VILLERS-BRETONNEUX**, some 18km southwest of Albert near the River Somme itself. As at Vimy, the landscaping of the **Australian Memorial** is dramatic – for the full effect, climb up to the view-ing platform of the stark white central tower. The monument was one of the last to be inaugurated in July 1938, when the prospects for peace were already looking bleak.

In recognition of the importance of these horrific events, a fascinating museum has been set up in **PÉRONNE**, on the River Somme, some 40km south of Arras: the **Historial de la Grande Guerre** (May–Sept daily 10am–6pm; Jan 17–April & Oct–Dec 19 daily except Mon 10am–5.30pm; 39F). All kinds of exhibits – such as newsreel and film footage, newspapers, posters, commemorative plates, Otto Dix drawings, artificial limbs – combine with displays of hardware to provide a broad view of the whole cata-strophe. There's a **TGV station** about 15km away from Péronne – the Gare Haute Picardie – which is thirty minutes from the Eurostar stop at Lille-Europe; for a **taxi** to or from the station, call Mouret (☎03.22.84.15.83), Fouque (☎03.22.84.52.49), Carlier (☎03.22.84.40.80) or Huzgan (☎03.22.84.30.13).

There is not, however, much else to keep you in Péronne, although it is pleasant enough. The **tourist office** is on rue Louis XI, opposite the museum (June–Sept Mon–Sat 9am–noon & 3–6.30pm, Sun 10am–noon & 2–6pm; winter closed Sun; ☎03.22.84.42.38, fax 03.22.84.51.25), and if you want to **stay** the night, the *Hostellerie des Remparts* is on the opposite side of the main square at 23 rue Beaubois (☎03.22.84.01.22, fax 03.22.84.38.96; ②; restaurant from 95F). Alternatively, there's a *Campanile* (☎03.22.84.22.22, fax 03.22.84.16.86; ③) just out of town on the N17 to Roye and Paris.

AISNE AND OISE

To the southeast, away from the coast and the main Paris through-routes, the often rainwashed and dull province of Picardy becomes considerably more inviting. Particularly in the *départements* of **Aisne** and **Oise**, where the region merges with neighbouring Champagne, there are some real attractions set amid lush, wooded hills. **Laon**, **Soissons** and **Noyon** all centre around handsome Gothic cathedrals; while at **Compiègne**, Napoléon Bonaparte and Napoléon III enjoyed the luxury of the magnificent château and embellished it to their hearts' content.

Transport is good for once, too, with a network of bus connections from Amiens and good train and bus links with Paris.

St-Quentin

A pleasant and prosperous industrial centre, **ST-QUENTIN** is a convenient place to pause en route to somewhere else, but makes no great demands on your time.

Thanks to St-Quentin's Communist mayor, the central **place de l'Hôtel de Ville** is now completely closed to traffic. One side of it is dominated by a particularly good-looking, arcaded, late-Gothic **Hôtel de Ville**, whose bells ring protracted, syncopated changes every quarter-hour. To the right, rue St-André leads to the town's skyscrapingly massive but outwardly rather uninspiring Gothic **Basilique**. Inside, its main virtue is its sheer size. In fact, it's a miracle that it is still standing at all, since the retreating Germans mined all 300 pillars in 1918 and were only prevented from setting them off by lack of time – you can still see the marks left by the mines. Another curiosity is the maze in the paving of the nave designed for penitents to figure out on their knees.

Of much greater interest is the **Musée Antoine-Lécuyer** on rue Lécuyer, at the end of rue Raspail (Mon & Wed–Sat 10am–noon & 2–5pm, Sun 2–6pm; closed Tues and public hols; 15F, Wed free), which contains a big collection of pastel portraits of the leading politicians, nobles, artists and socialites of eighteenth-century France by locally born **Maurice-Quentin de Latour**. The other interesting collection, said to be one of the largest in the world, is that of more than half-a-million butterflies and other insects, housed in the **Musée d'Entomologie**, at 14 rue de la Sellerie, just off the main square (Mon & Wed–Sat 2–6pm, Sun 3–5.30pm; 15F).

Practicalities

To get to the centre of town from the **gare SNCF**, follow rue Général-Leclerc over the Somme, and up rue d'Isle. The **tourist office** is at 27 rue V. Basch, just off the main square (Mon–Sat 8am–noon & 1.30–6.30pm, Sun 11am–12.30pm & 3–5.30pm; Nov–March closed Sun morning; ☎03.23.67.05.00, fax 03.23.67.78.71), and will recommend **accommodation**. Try the basic *Hôtel du Départ*, place du Monument-aux-Morts (☎03.23.62.31.69; ①), just to the right as you come out of the station. Two clean, decent hotels off the main square in the centre of town are *Le Florence*, 42 rue Zola (☎03.23.64.22.22, fax 03.23.62.52.85; ①; restaurant from 95F; closed Mon lunch & Sun), and the *Hôtel de la Paix et Albert I*, 3 place du 8-Octobre (☎03.23.62.77.62; ②), on the road between the train station and the town centre. The town's **campsite** and **youth hostel** are on bd Jean-Bouin (both ☎03.23.62.68.66; March–Nov), 2km from the station by the river – take any bus to the *basilique* then bus #4 to rue H-Dunant.

Laon and around

Looking out over the plains of Champagne and Picardy from the spine of a high narrow ridge, girt still by its gated medieval walls, **LAON**, 36km southeast of St-Quentin, is one of the gems of the region. Dominating it all and visible for miles around are the five great towers of one of the earliest and finest Gothic cathedrals in the country. Of all the cathedral towns in the Aisne, Laon is the one to head for.

Arrival, information and accommodation

Arriving by train or road, you find yourself in the disappointingly shabby and characterless lower town, or **ville basse**. To get to the upper town, or **ville haute**, you can either walk – a stiff climb up the steps at the end of avenue Carnot – or take the **Poma 2000** (Mon–Sat 7am–8pm; July & Aug Sun also 2.30–6pm; one-way 6.40F, round-trip 8.50F), a fully automated, diminutive, rubber-tyred, overland métro, Laon's pride and joy. You board next to the train station and get out by the town hall on place Général-Leclerc; from there a left turn down rue Serrurier brings you nose to nose with the cathedral.

The **tourist office** is right by the cathedral (March–June & Sept–Oct Mon–Sat 9am–12.30pm & 2–6.30pm, Sun 11am–1pm & 2–6pm; July & Aug Mon–Sat 9am–1pm & 2–7pm, Sun 11am–1pm & 2–5pm; Nov–Feb Mon–Sat 9am–12.30pm & 2–6pm, Sun 11am–1pm & 2–5pm; ☎03.23.20.28.62, fax 03.23.20.68.11), housed within the impressive Gothic Hôtel-Dieu, built in 1209. Budget **accommodation** is mostly in the *ville basse*. Try the avenue Carnot, straight in front of the gare SNCF, where you'll find *Le Welcome* (☎03.23.23.06.11; ①) and the perfectly decent *Le Carnot* (☎03.23.23.02.08, fax 03.23.23.71.67; ①), which has a good, no-frills restaurant. For rooms in the *ville haute*, the cheapest solution is the hostel *Maison des Jeunes*, 20 rue du Cloître, by the cathedral (☎03.23.20.27.64). As for hotels, *La Paix*, 52 rue St-Jean (☎03.23.79.06.34; ①; restaurant from 60F) is a good bet, as is the charming and characterful old *Hôtel des Chevaliers*, at 3 rue Serrurier, near the Poma stop (☎03.23.27.17.50, fax 03.23.23.40.71; ①; closed July). On the eastern edge of the town, along avenue de Gaulle, there's a concentration of motel-type places: try the *Campanile* (☎03.23.23.15.05, fax 03.23.23.04.25, ②; restaurant from 84F) or the adjacent *Première Classe* (☎03.23.23.44.55, fax 03.23.23.21.01; ①). The **camping municipal** is on the south side of the *ville basse*, near the *stade municipal*, just off the N44. Alternatively, there's *Camping La Chenaie*, on allée de la Chenaie, on the northwest side of the town (April–Oct).

The town

Laon's number-one attraction is its magnificent **Cathédrale Notre-Dame** (daily 8am–6.30pm; summer till 7pm; guided tours all year Sat, Sun & public hols 3pm and daily July & Aug from tourist office). Built in the second half of the twelfth century, this was a trendsetter in its day, elements of its design – the gabled porches, the imposing towers, and the gallery of arcades above the west front – being repeated at Chartres, Reims and Notre-Dame in Paris. When wrapped in thick mist, the towers seem otherworldly. The creatures craning from the uppermost ledges appear to be reckless mountain goats borrowed from some medieval bestiary and are reputed to have been carved in memory of the valiant horned steers who lugged the cathedral's masonry up from the plains below. Inside, the effects are no less dramatic – the high white nave lit by the dense ruby, sapphire and emerald tones of the stained glass, which at close range reveals the appealing scratchy, smoky quality of medieval glass.

Crowding in the cathedral's lee are a web of quiet, grey, eighteenth-century streets. One – rue Pourier – leads past the PTT and onto the thirteenth-century **Porte d'Ardon** which looks out over the southern part of the *ville basse*. A left turn at the post office along rue Ermant leads to the little twelfth-century octagonal **Chapelle des Templiers** – the Knights Templar – set in a secluded garden by the **Musée de Laon**, 32 rue Georges-Ermant (daily except Tues 10am–noon & 2am–6pm; winter 2–5pm; 16F), with a collection of classical antiquities.

The rest of the *ville haute*, which rambles along the ridge to the west of the cathedral into the Le Bourg quarter around the early Gothic **church of St-Martin**, is good to wander in, with grand views from the **ramparts**.

Eating, drinking and entertainment

Rue Châtelaine, in the *ville haute*, has a good range of **boulangeries** and **fromageries** for assembling picnics. Simple **snacks** can be had at the *Le Parvis* overlooking the west front of the cathedral; *Crêperie Agora*, an inexpensive Breton place near the cathedral at 16 rue des Cordeliers (open until 1am; closed Sat lunch & Mon); or you could try the *Brasserie Chenizelles*, at 1 rue du Bourg, the continuation of rue Chatelaine. *Le Welcome*, next door to the arts complex on place Aubrey, is an Irish-style bar and is a good place for just a drink. **Restaurants** in Laon tend to be expensive: *La Petite Auberge*, the gourmets' favourite, at 45 bd Pierre-Brossolette in the *ville basse* near the station, falls into this category, but serves traditional French cuisine using the freshest ingredients (menus at 150F & 210F). Next door, the *Saint-Amour* is more economical and still very good (menus at 75F & 89F).

There's usually something going on at the *Maison des Arts* on place Aubrey – including the annual ten-day international **film festival** in early April – and a concentration of events during the Heures Médiévales festival in the second and third weeks of September.

Coucy-le-Château and the Forêt St-Gobain

About 30km west of Laon, in hilly countryside on the far side of the forest of St-Gobain (a worthwhile cycling trip in itself), lie the straggling ruins of one of the greatest castles of the Middle Ages, **Coucy-le-Château** (May–Aug Mon–Fri 10am–12.30pm & 2–6.30pm, Sat closes 7pm, Sun 10am–7pm; Sept–Oct & March–April closes Mon–Fri 6pm, Sat & Sun 6.30pm; Nov–Feb closes Mon–Fri 4.30pm, Sat & Sun 5pm). The power of its lords, the Sires de Coucy, rivalled and often even exceeded that of the king – "King I am not, neither Prince, Duke nor Count. I am the Sire of Coucy" was Enguerrand III's proud boast. The retreating Germans capped the destruction of World War I battles by blowing up the castle's keep as they left in 1917, but enough remains, crowning a wooded spur, to be extremely evocative. A small **museum** (May–Sept 2.30–6.30pm; Oct–April 2.30–6pm; free) in the tower at the Porte de Soissons, on the south side of the walled part of town, has a display of photographs showing how it looked pre-1917 which can be compared with today's remains from the vantage point of the roof.

The entire modern village of **COUCY-LE-CHÂTEAU-AUFFRIQUE** is contained within the vast ring of walls, entered through the original gates, squeezed between powerful, round flanking towers. There is a footpath all around the outside, and the *Hôtel Bellevue* within (☎03.23.52.69.70, fax 03.34.52.69.79; ②; closed Feb), should you need a place to **stay**. **Bicycles** can be rented from the **tourist** office, in the central square (daily 10am–12.30pm & 2–6pm; ☎03.23.52.44.55) near the Porte de Soissons.

It's hard to get to Coucy-le-Château without a car, though several Laon–Soissons trains stop at **ANIZY-PINON**, which, if you're otherwise hitching, cuts the distance by about half – and there is an infrequent bus onto Soissons. If you continue into the nearby **Forêt**

St-Gobain, include **ST-GOBAIN** itself, 13km north of Coucy, in your itinerary. The original eighteenth-century **glassworks** – the firm is now a vast conglomerate – hides behind a classical facade, pretending it's nothing so vulgar as a factory.

Soissons

Half-an-hour by train southwest of Laon or 30km down the N2, **SOISSONS** can lay claim to a long and highly strategic history. Before the Romans arrived it was already a town, and in 486 AD it was here that the Romans suffered one of their most decisive defeats at the hands of Clovis the Frank, making Soissons one of the first real centres of the Frankish kingdom. Napoléon, too, considered it a crucial military base, a judgement borne out this century in extensive war damage.

The town boasts the fine, if little-sung, **Cathédrale Notre-Dame** – thirteenth century for the most part with majestic glass and vaulting – at the west end of the main square, place F-Marquigny. More impressive still is the ruined **Abbaye de St-Jean-des-Vignes**, to the south of the cathedral down rue Panleu and right down rue St Jean. The facade of this tremendous Gothic building rises sheer and grand, impervious to the now empty space behind it. The **monastery** (Mon–Fri 9am–6pm, Sat 9am–7pm, Sun 10am–7pm; free), save for remnants of a cloister and refectory, was dismantled in 1804. Near the *abbaye* is the impressive eighteenth-century **Hôtel de Ville** with its grand stone gate.

Practicalities

Soissons is relatively compact. From the **gare SNCF** (with good services to Laon and Paris) the main square is a fifteen-minute walk away along avenue du Général-de-Gaulle and then rue St-Martin. The **gare routière** is closer to the centre by the river on Le Mail: infrequent buses leave for Compiègne and Laon. The **tourist office** is on place F-Marquigny by the cathedral (summer Mon–Sat 9.30am–6.30pm, Sun 9.30am–12.30pm & 2–6.30pm; winter daily 9.30am–12.30pm & 2–6.30pm; ☎03.23.53.17.37, fax 03.23.59.67.72).

The town is a useful and attractive place to stay if you're exploring this part of the country, and there are a couple of moderately priced **hotels**: the *Terminus* by the station (☎03.23.53.33.59; ①; closed Mon & Aug) and the *Pot d' Étain*, 7 rue St-Quentin (☎03.23.53.27.39; ①), makes a more central alternative and also has a decent restaurant (from 75F). Alternatively there's a **campsite**, 1km from the station on avenue du Mail.

An excellent place for **crêpes** and *galettes* is *La Galettière* (closed Sun lunch and Mon) at 1 rue du Beffroi by the cathedral, and there's a good Tunisian **restaurant**, the *Sidi Bou*, on rue de la Bannière, down towards the river.

Compiègne and around

Thirty-eight kilometres west of Soissons lies **COMPIÈGNE**, whose reputation as a tourist centre rests on the presence of a vast royal palace, built at the edge of the Forêt de Compiègne in order that generations of French kings could play at "being peasants", in Louis XIV's words. Although the town itself is a bit of a one-horse place with a bland, Sunday-afternoon feel, it's worth a visit for the opulent palace interiors and the car and Second Empire museums.

Arrival, information and accommodation

The **gares routière** and SNCF are adjacent to each other, just a few minutes' walk away from the centre of town: cross the wide River Oise and go up rue Solférino to place de l'Hôtel-de-Ville. The **tourist office** (Mon–Sat 9.15am–12.15pm & 1.45–6.30pm, Sun 9.30am–12.30pm & 2.30–5pm; ☎03.44.40.01.00, fax 03.44.40.23.28) takes up part of the ornate Hôtel de Ville and, for a couple of francs, will provide you with a plan of the town, on which is conveniently marked an exhaustive visitors' route, including the forest paths (see below).

As for **accommodation**, there are cheapish rooms at the *Hôtel St-Antoine*, 17 rue de Paris (☎03.44.23.22.27; ①), concealed above a Thai restaurant; and the *Lion d'Or*, 4 rue du Général-Leclerc (☎03.44.23.32.17; ①). More comfortable is the *Hôtel de Flandre*, an enormous, recently redecorated place on the riverside at 16 quai de la République (☎03.44.83.24.40, fax 03.44.90.02.75; ②). Much the best place to stay, however, is the *Hôtel de France*, 17 rue E-Floquet, centrally located right next to the Hôtel de Ville (☎03.44.40.02.74, fax 03.44.40.48.37; ②; good restaurant from 145F), a charming old place with very reasonable rates. The **campsite** is along avenue Royale, into the forest beyond the palace.

The town

Compiègne itself is plain disappointing, though that shouldn't come as a surprise, as a platoon of German soldiers burnt it down in 1942 to provide their commander with evidence of a subjugated community. Several half-timbered buildings remain on the pedestrianized rue Napoléon and rue des Lombards, south of the main place de l'Hôtel-de-Ville. The most striking building, as so often in these parts, is the **Hôtel de Ville** – Louis XII-Gothic – its ebullient nineteenth-century statuary including the image of Joan of Arc, who was captured in this town by the Burgundians before being handed to the English.

But Compiègne's star attraction is two blocks east of the town hall down rue des Minimes. For all its pompous excess, there is a certain fascination about the seventeenth- and eighteenth-century **Palais National** particularly its interior (daily except Tues April–Sept 9.15am–6.15pm; Oct–March closes at 4.30pm; guided tours only, last tour leaves 45min before closing; 23F, 17F on Sun, all-inclusive). The lavishness of Marie-Antoinette's rooms, the sheer, vulgar sumptuousness of the First and Second Empire, and the evidence of the unseemly haste with which Napoléon I moved in, scarcely a dozen years after the Revolution is impressive. The palace also houses the **Musée du Second Empire** and the **Musée de la Voiture**, the latter containing a wonderful array of antique bicycles, tricycles and fancy aristocratic carriages, as well as the world's first steam coach. The **Théâtre Impérial**, planned (but never finished) by Napoléon III, has recently been completed at a cost of some thirty million francs. Originally designed with just two seats for Napoléon and his wife, it now seats 900 and is regularly used for concerts.

If you don't want to take the guided tour, a visit to the palace gardens or **petit parc** (daily summer/winter 7.30/8am–6.30/8pm) is a pleasant alternative. Serene and formal, they include a long, straight avenue extending far into the **Forêt de Compiègne**, which touches the edge of town. Very ancient, and cut by a succession of hills, streams and valleys, this is grand rambling country for walkers or cyclists – the GR12 goes through it. East of Compiègne, some 6km into the forest and not far from the banks of the Aisne, is a green and sandy clearing guarded by cypress trees, known as the **Clairière de l'Armistice**. Here, in what was then a rail siding for rail-mounted artillery, World War I was brought to an end on November 11, 1918. A plaque commemorates the deed: "Here the criminal pride of the German empire was brought low, vanquished by the free peoples whom it had sought to enslave." To avenge this humiliation, Hitler had the French sign their capitulation on June 22, 1940, on the same spot, in the very same rail carriage. The original car was taken immediately to Berlin, then destroyed by fire in the last days of the war. Its replacement,housed in a small **museum** (daily except Tues 9am–noon & 1.30/2–5.30/6.30pm; 3F), is similar, and the objects inside are the originals.

If you have an interest in Greek vases, the **Musée Vivenel**, on rue d'Austerlitz (Tues–Sat 9am–noon & 2–6pm; closed Sun & Mon; closes at 5pm in winter; 12F), has one of the best collections around, especially a series illustrating the Panathenaic Games from Italy – a welcome dose of classical restraint and good taste compared with the palace. There is also a section on the forest's flora and fauna, which includes a wild boar the size of an armoured car. Also of specialist interest is the **Musée des Figurines**, by the side of the town hall (same hours and price), with reputedly the world's largest collection of wafer-thin military figurines in mock-up battles from ancient Greece to World War II.

VIEUX-MOULIN and **ST-JEAN-AUX-BOIS** are a couple of villages worth heading for right in the heart of the forest; while 13km southeast of Compiègne at **PIERRE-FONDS** there's a classic medieval **château** (May–Aug daily 10am–6pm; March, April, Sept & Oct Mon–Sat 10am–12.30pm & 2–6pm, Sun 10am–6pm; Jan, Feb, Nov & Dec Mon–Sat 10am–12.30pm & 2–5pm, Sun 10am–5.30pm; 32F), built in the twelfth century and heavily restored since to make the model fairy-tale affair of turrets, towers and moat. The inside displays a varied range of medieval artefacts. Pierrefonds is served by three buses daily from the train station in Compiègne.

Eating, drinking and entertainment

Compiègne has no shortage of cheap **eateries** like *À la Dernière Minute* on place de la Gare and the crêperie *La Bolée* on rue St Martin. More rewarding **restaurants** are the *Bistrot de Flandre*, 2 rue d'Amiens, and an excellent Vietnamese place, *Le Phnom Penh*, 13 rue des Lombards, which manages to combine French and Thai flavours in a dish of frogs' legs. *Le Bouchon* at 5 rue St-Martin (noon–3.30pm & 8–11pm; ☎03.44.40.05.32) is a wine bar offering a lunch menu at 69F and *plats du jour* for 48F; a glass of wine costs about 25F. *Le Lombard*, a contemporary-style bar/brasserie on rue des Lombards, has a good range of gourmet salads which should please vegetarians.

For just a pastry and coffee, try *Les Muscadines*, 1 rue Solférino, just by the bridge, with a relaxing atmosphere and magazines to browse through. Lastly, on Saturdays, there's a big all-day **market** in the square by place de l'Hôtel-de-Ville.

Noyon

Further up the Oise, and a possible day-trip from Compiègne, is **NOYON**, another of Picardy's cathedral towns. Its quiet provinciality belies a long, illustrious history, first as a Roman prefecture, then as seat of a bishopric from 531. Here, in 768, Charlemagne was crowned king of Neustria, largest of the Frankish kingdoms; in 987, Hugues Capet was crowned king of France; and, to cap it all, John Calvin was born here in 1509.

Rowing along the Oise on his *Inland Journey of 1876*, Robert Louis Stevenson stopped briefly at Noyon, which he described as "a stack of brown roofs at the best, where I believe people live very respectably in a quiet way". It is a bit like that, though the **cathedral**, to which Stevenson warmed – "my favourite kind of mountain scenery" – is impressive, at least in passing. Spacious and a little stark, it successfully blends Romanesque and Gothic, and is flanked by the ruins of thirteenth-century cloisters and a strange, exquisitely shaped **Renaissance library** that contains a ninth-century illuminated bible (only open to the public on the two days of the year, normally the third weekend of September, known as *journées du patrimoine*). On the south side of the cathedral, the old episcopal palace now houses the **Musée du Noyonnais** (April–Oct daily except Tues 10am–noon & 2–6pm; winter closes 5pm; 20F price also includes Musée Calvin, see below)a small, well-presented collection of local archaeological findings and cathedral treasure. Close by, signs direct you to the **Musée Calvin** (same hours and ticket as Musée du Noyonnais), ostensibly on the site of the Reformer's birthplace. The respectable citizens of Noyon were never among their local boy's adherents and tore down the original long before its tourist potential was appreciated.

If you intend to **stay**, *Le St Eloi*, at 81 bd Carnot (☎03.44.44.01.49, fax 03.44.09.20.90; ③; restaurant from 130F), is the best option and is just off the roundabout between the train station and the cathedral. The local **campsite** is 4km out of town along the N32 to Compiègne. **Buses**, mainly for Compiègne, leave from outside the **gare SNCF**. Big days in Noyon are Saturday morning, when a colourful **market** spills out across place de l'Hôtel-de-Ville, and the first Tuesday of the month, when a livestock market takes over virtually the entire town centre.

CHAMPAGNE AND THE ARDENNES

Bubbly is the reason most people visit **Champagne**. The cultivation of vines was already well-established in Roman times, when Reims was the capital of the Roman province of Belgae (Belgium), and by the seventeenth century, still wines from the

---

CHAMPAGNE: THE FACTS

Nowhere else in France, let alone the rest of the world, are you allowed to make **champagne**. You can blend wines from chalk-soil vineyards, double-ferment them, turn and tilt the bottles little by little to clear the sediment, add some vintage liqueur, store the result for years at the requisite constant temperature and high humidity in sweating underground *caves* carved from chalk soil, and finally produce a bubbling golden liquid; but you cannot call it champagne. It's perhaps an outrageous monopoly in order to keep the region's sparkling wines in the luxury class, although the locals will tell you the difference comes from the squid fossils in the chalk, the lie of the land and its critical climate, the evolution of the grapes, the regulated pruning methods, the legally enforced quantity of juice pressed.

Three authorized **grape varieties** are used in champagne: Chardonnay, the only white grape, growing best on the Côte des Blancs and contributing a light and elegant element; Pinot Noir, grown mainly on the Montagne de Reims slopes, giving body and long life; and Pinot Meunier, cultivated primarily in the Marne valley, adding flowery aromas.

The vineyards are owned either by *maisons*, who produce the *grande marque* champagne, or by small cultivators called *vignerons*, who sell the grapes to the *maisons*. The *vignerons* also make their own champagne and will happily offer you a glass and sell you a bottle at half the price of a *grande marque* (ask at any tourist information office in the Champagne region or at the CIVC in Epernay for a list of addresses – see below). The difference between the two comes down to capital. The *maisons* can afford to blend grapes from anything up to sixty different vineyards and to tie up their investment while their champagne matures for several years longer than the legal minimum (one year for non-vintage, three years vintage). So the wine they produce is undoubtedly superior – and not a lot cheaper here than in a good discount off-licence in Britain or the US.

If you could visit the head offices of Cartier or Dior, the atmosphere would probably be similar to that in the champagne *maisons* whose palaces are divided between Epernay and Reims. Visits to the handful of *maisons* that organize regular **guided tours** are no longer free, and some require appointments, but don't be put off – they all speak English and a generous *dégustation* is nearly always thrown in. Their audiovisuals and (cold) cellar tours are on the whole very informative, and do more than merely plug brand names. Local tourist offices can provide full lists of addresses and times of visits.

If you want to work on the **harvest**, contact either the *maisons* direct; the *Agence Nationale pour l'Emploi*, 11 rue Jean-Moët, Epernay (☎03.26.89.52.60), or 40 rue de Talleyrand, Reims (☎03.26.51.01.33); or try the youth hostel in Verzy, at 14 rue du Bassin (☎03.26.97.90.10), where casual workers are often recruited or work is advertised.

region had gained a considerable reputation. Contrary to popular myth, however, it was not Dom Pérignon, cellar master of the Abbaye de Hautvillers near Epernay, who then "invented" champagne. He was probably responsible for the innovation of mixing grapes from different vineyards, but the wine's well-known tendency to re-ferment within the bottle was not controllable until eighteenth-century glass-moulding techniques (developed in Britain) produced sufficiently strong vessels to contain the natural effervescence.

Away from the vineyards with their serried ranks of vines, the region's rolling plains are an uninspiring sight, growing more wheat and cabbages per hectare than any other region of France, though it seems to bring the villages no great benefit. Some places look so run-down you feel the shutters would fall off if you so much as popped a paper bag – and few are much more than hamlets, with grocery vans doing the rounds once a week, and not a boulangerie in sight.

At least the official capital of Champagne, the cathedral city of **Reims**, is worth a visit in its own right, and it has a reasonably full cultural calendar. For champagne-worshippers, however, **Epernay** is the place to head for, where you can sample vintages to your heart's content and go on several underground visits to the *caves* of the different *maisons*. Across the plains, neither **Châlons-en-Champagne** nor the smaller, further-flung towns like **Chaumont** or **Langres** dotted along the Marne towards its source are much of an incentive to break your journey. The only real attraction in the rest of the region is the town of **Troyes**, some way off to the southwest, which is easily Champagne's most beautiful city.

Reims

Laid flat by the bombs of World War I, **REIMS** (pronounced like a nasal "Rance") doesn't give an attractive first impression if you arrive by car – a seemingly large industrial centre with little to redeem it. However, the town is not as large as it looks, and there are other reasons for visiting here – apart from its world champagne status, Reims possesses one of the most impressive Gothic cathedrals in France, formerly the coronation church of dynasties of French monarchs going back to Clovis, first king of the Franks, whose 1500th anniversary celebrations in 1996 provoked fierce controversy between Catholics and secularists.

Arrival, information and accommodation

The cathedral is less than ten minutes' walk from the **gare SNCF** and **gare routière**, and the **tourist office** (Easter–June & Sept Mon–Sat 9am–7.30pm, Sun 9.30am–6.30pm; July & Aug Mon–Sat 9am–8pm, Sun 9.30am–7pm; Oct–Easter Mon–Sat 9am–6.30pm, Sun & hols 9.30am–5.30pm; ☎03.26.77.45.25, fax 03.26.77.45.27) is conveniently located next door in a picturesque ruin. They can book **accommodation** for no charge. Rooms are generally affordable and easy to come by in Reims, with plenty of central hotels, many on place Drouet-d'Erlon.

Hotels

au Bon Accueil, 31 rue de Thillois (☎03.26.88.55.74). A small, old hotel in an excellent central location with the cheapest single rates in town – just a little more than the youth hostel. Basic rooms have toilet and shower. ①.

Continental, 93 place Drouet-d'Erlon (☎03.26.40.39.35, fax 03.26.47.51.12). Well situated, and all rooms are quiet, with bathroom and TV. ④.

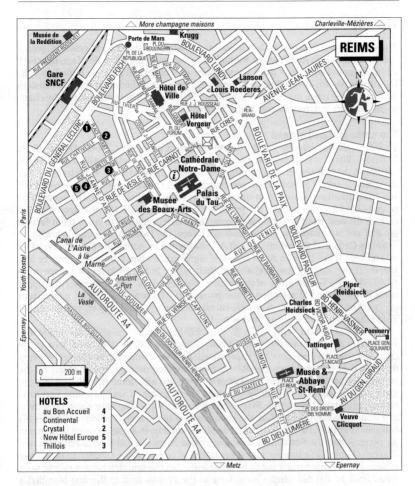

Crystal, 86 place Drouet-d'Erlon (☎03.26.88.44.44, fax 03.26.47.49.28). The small courtyard blocks out much of the traffic noise; small but respectable rooms and pleasant service. ③.

New Hôtel Europe, 29 rue Buirette (☎03.26.47.39.39, fax 03.26.40.14.37). Quiet turn-of-the-century four-storey three-star. ④.

Thillois, 17 rue de Thillois (☎03.26.40.65.65). Basic, with shared washing facilities for the cheaper rooms, but well located. Closed Sun. ①.

Youth hostels

Centre International de Séjour, 1 chaussée Bocquaine, Parc Léo Lagrange (☎03.26.40.52.60, fax 03.26.47.35.70). A large, well-run HI youth hostel with single or double rooms, and self-catering, though breakfast is available. It's a 15-min walk from the station on the other side of the canal: cross over the big roundabout in front of the station, turn right down bd du Général-Leclerc to Pont de Vesle; chaussée Bocquaine is the first left after the bridge. There's a curfew of 11pm, but no day-time lockout and a late key available for a deposit; no HI card required.

The city

The old centre of Reims stretches from the cathedral and its adjacent episcopal palace north to place de la République's triumphal Roman arch, the Porte de Mars, punctuated by the grand squares of place Royale, place du Forum and place de l'Hôtel-de-Ville. Over to the south, about fifteen minutes' walk from the cathedral, is the other historical focus of the town, the Abbaye de St-Remi. To the east of here are most of the champagne *maisons* and, further east still, a museum of cars.

The cathedral and around

The lure of the interior of thirteenth-century **Cathédrale Notre-Dame** (daily 7.30am–7.30pm) is the kaleidoscopic patterns in the stained glass, with Marc Chagall designs in the east chapel and champagne processes glorified in the south transept. But the greatest appeal is outside: an inexplicable joke, running around the restored but still badly mutilated statuary on the west front – the giggling angels who seem to be responsible for disseminating the prank are a rare delight. Not all the figures on the cathedral's west front are originals – some have been removed to spare them further erosion and are now at the former bishop's palace, the Palais du Tau (see below).

Reims Cathedral was where Joan of Arc succeeded in getting the Dauphin crowned as Charles VII in 1429 – an act of immense significance when France was more or less wiped off the map by the English and their allies. In all, 26 kings of France were crowned in the Gothic glory of this edifice. Between June and September the upper parts of the cathedral are open to the public (10–11.30am & 2–5.30pm; guided tour every 30min; 25F), as well as a walk round the transepts and chevet, you get to see inside the framework of the cathedral roof.

At the **Palais du Tau** (July & Aug 9.30am–6.30pm; mid-Nov to mid-March 10am–noon & 2–5pm; rest of year 9.30am–12.30pm & 2–6pm; 32F), next door to the cathedral, you can appreciate the expressiveness of the statuary from close up – a view that would never have been possible in their intended monumental positions on the cathedral. Apart from the grinning angels, there are also some friendly-looking gargoyles and a superb Eve, shiftily clutching the monster of sin. As added narrative, embroidered tapestries of the *Song of Songs* line the walls. The palace also preserves, in a state of unlikely veneration, the paraphernalia of the arch-reactionary Charles X's coronation in 1824, right down to the Dauphin's hat box. In being anointed here in purple pomp – after the Revolution, Robespierre and Napoléon had tried to achieve a new France – Louis XVI's brother stated his intention to return the country to the *ancien régime*. His attempt turned out to be short-lived, but the tradition he was calling upon dated back to 496 AD when Clovis, king of the Franks (and of the first identifiably French post-Roman entity), was baptized in Reims.

Just west of the cathedral on rue Chanzy, the **Musée des Beaux-Arts** (daily except Tues & hols 10.30am–noon & 2–6pm; 10F) is the city's principal art museum, which, though ill-suited to its ancient building and very diverse, does effectively cover French art from the Renaissance to the present. Few of the works are among the particular artists' best, but the collection does contain one of David's replicas of his famous Marat death scene, a set of 27 Corots, two great Gauguin still lifes, some beautifully observed sixteenth-century German portraits, and various interesting odds and ends, including an old tabac sign from nineteenth-century Reims. As long as you don't feel compelled to look at everything, an hour or so could be happily spent here.

The same cannot be said for the museum five minutes away in the **Hôtel de Vergeur**, 36 place du Forum (Tues–Sun 2–6pm; 20F). This is a stuffed treasure house of all kinds of beautiful objects, including two sets of Dürer engravings – an *Apocalypse* and *Passion of Christ*, but you have to go through a long guided tour of the whole works.

By the museum there's access to sections of the partly submerged arcades of the **crypto portique Gallo-Romain** (mid-June to mid-Sept Tues–Sun 2–6pm; free), which date back to 200 AD. Reims' other Roman monument, the quadruple-arched **Porte de Mars**, on place de la République, belongs to the same era.

The Abbaye St-Remi, the Automobile Museum and Musée de la Reddition

Most of the early French kings were buried in Reims' oldest building, the eleventh-century **Basilique St-Remi**, fifteen minutes' walk from the cathedral on rue Simon (Mon–Wed, Fri & Sun 8am–dusk, Thurs & Sat 9am–dusk; closed during services; music & light show July–Sept Sat 9.30pm; free), part of a former Benedictine abbey named after the 22-year-old bishop who baptized Clovis and 3000 of his warriors. An immensely spacious building, with aisles wide enough to drive a bus along, it preserves its Romanesque transept walls and ambulatory chapels, some of them with modern stained glass that works beautifully. The spectacular abbey buildings alongside the church house the **Musée St-Remi** (Mon–Fri 2–6.30pm, Sat & Sun 2–7pm; 10F), the city's archeological and historical museum, whose eclectic collection includes some fine tapestries on St-Remi's life, plus sixteenth-century weapons and armour.

If you have even a passing interest in old cars you should make for the **Centre de l'Automobile**, 84 av Georges-Clemenceau (April–Oct daily except Tues 10am–noon & 2–6pm; Nov–March Sat & Sun 10am–noon & 2–5pm; 30F), fifteen minutes' walk southeast of the cathedral. All the vehicles are part of the private collection of Philippe Charbonneaux, designer of a number of the postwar classics on display. In addition to the full-scale cars, there's an impressive selection of models, antique toys and period posters.

On the opposite side of town, behind the station in rue Franklin-Roosevelt, is the rather less interesting **Musée de la Reddition**, "Museum of Surrender" (April–Nov daily except Tues & hols 10am–noon & 2–6pm; 10F), based around an old schoolroom that served as Eisenhower's HQ from February 1945. In the early hours of May 7, 1945, General Jodl agreed to the unconditional surrender of the German army, thus ending World War II in Europe. The room has been left exactly as it was (minus the ashtrays and carpet), with the Allies' battle maps on the walls. The visit includes a good documentary film and numerous photographs and press cuttings.

Champagne tasting

For the serious business of Reims, head to place des Droits-de-l'Homme and place St-Niçaise, near the Abbaye St-Remi. These are both within striking distance of the majority of the Reims **maisons**, most of which charge a small entrance fee for their tours but include a *dégustation* and have English guides. Only four can be visited without an appointment: the houses of Mumm, Taittinger, Piper-Heidsieck and, for part of the year, Pommery.

The best of the regular guided tours is **Mumm** at 34 rue du Champ-de-Mars (March–Oct daily 9–11am & 2–5pm; Nov–Feb Mon–Fri same hours, Sat & Sun afternoons only; 20F; 45min). Established in 1827, Mumm is familiar for its red-slashed Cordon Rouge label – its un-French-sounding name being the legacy of its founders, affluent German wine-makers from the Rhine Valley. The tour is fairly informal – you can wander freely about its cellar museum and throw questions at the approachable guides – though you pick up the basics from a pre-tour video. There's not a lot of walking despite 25km of cellars and a reported 35 million bottles of wine; some of the vintage bottles date from 1911. It all ends with a generous glass of either Cordon Rosé, the populist choice; the more unusual and expensive Mumm de Cramant, made entirely of the cru of the Cramant village; or their standard Cordon Rouge.

At **Taittinger**, 9 place St-Niçaise (Mon–Fri 9.30am–noon & 2–4.30pm, Sat & Sun 9–11am & 2–5pm; Dec–Feb Mon–Fri only; 25F; 1hr), there are still more ancient *caves*, with doodles and carvings added by more recent workers, and statues of St Vincent and St Jean, patron saints respectively of *vignerons* and cellar hands.

Although founded in 1785, **Piper-Heidsieck**, at 51 bd Henry-Vasnier (March–Nov daily 9–11.45am & 2–5.15pm; Dec–Feb closed Tues & Wed; 35F), is better known in the New World than the Old, having been the champagne of the American movie industry since first appearing – with Laurel and Hardy – in the 1934 classic *Sons of the Desert*. The champagne of the Oscars gives a fair whack of sponsorship for film prizes and festivals too, and really the only folk who'll get anything out of the tour – which ends up at a gallery of celebrity snaps – are confirmed film buffs and lovers of tackiness: the antique *caves* are toured by automatic five-seater car shuttle resembling a ghost train. Out of the darkness and timed to a cliché-ridden narration loom giant fibreglass grapes and vast hands armed with secateurs, or life-size badly proportioned lumpy figures positioned as cellar masters. You emerge to a glittering photo-studded foyer and a snooty atmosphere and a much-needed drink.

Top of the list of appointment-only houses is the **Maison Veuve Clicquot-Ponsardin**, 1 place des Droits-de-l'Homme (☎03.26.89.54.41). In the early days of capitalism, the widowed Mme Clicquot not only took over her husband's business, but later bequeathed it to her business manager rather than to her children – both radical breaks with tradition. In keeping with this past, the *maison* is one of the least pompous and its video the best. The *caves*, with their horror-movie fungi, are old Gallo-Roman quarries. The **House of Pommery**, 5 place du Général-Gouraud (April–Oct daily 11am–5.30pm; Nov–March Mon–Fri by appointment only; 20F; ☎03.26.61.62.55), has also excavated Roman quarries for their cellars; they claim – in good champagne one-upmanship – to have been the first to do so. Other appointment-only *maisons* are **Ruinart**, 4 rue des Crayères (☎03.26.77.51.51), **Charles Heidsieck**, 4 bd Henry-Vasnier (☎03.26.84.43.50), and **Lanson**, 12 bd Lundy (☎03.26.78.50.50).

Finally, to get an overview of the various champagnes available (plus wines from all over France), it's worth visiting La Vino Cave, 43 place Drouet-d'Erlon (9.30am–1pm & 2.30–7.30pm, closed Mon am & Sun), where you can also buy all the paraphernalia of the bubbly business from champagne flutes to snazzy servers.

Eating and drinking

Place Drouet-d'Erlon, a wide pedestrianized boulevard lined with **bars** and **restaurants**, is also where you'll find most of the city's **nightlife**, such as it is. For self-catering, there's a big Wednesday and Saturday **market** in place du Boulingrin (6am–lpm), while vegetarians can top up supplies at La Vie Claire, 25 place Drouet-d'Erlon.

Le Bangkok, 24 rue de Tambour. Excellent, well-priced Thai place. Closed Mon & Sat lunch & all day Sun.

aux Bons Amis, 13 rue Gosset (☎03.26.07.73.06). Excellent value traditional French cooking. Lunchtime set menus at 55F and 67F. Closed Sat & Sun.

Boyer, 64 bd Henry-Vasnier (☎03.26.82.80.80). Reputed to be one of France's finest gastronomic restaurants – with prices and style to match– *Boyer* is set in a restored eighteenth-century château and equipped with a helipad. Closed Mon & Tues lunch.

Chèvre et Menthe, 63 rue de Barbatre. A very good-value, plain establishment with an interesting range of gourmet salads from 19F; recommended for vegetarians. Daily *carte* dishes might include moussaka (45F) as well as more traditional choices.

Le Colbert, 64 place Drouet-d'Erlon (☎03.26.47.55.79). Traditional cuisine – including an excellent regional Champagne–Ardenne menu (157F) – in a daintily set up and popular restaurant. Menus from 79F, and affordable champagne by the glass.

aux Côteaux, 86 place Drouet-d'Erlon. Bustling friendly place serving unusual pizzas (around 45F) and an equally interesting range of salads. Open till midnight; closed Sun.

au Coup de Fourchette, 58 rue du Dr-Thomas (☎03.26.40.25.81). *Choucroute* and other specialities from Alsace at very reasonable prices. 80F menu.

La Grappa, 49 rue du Colonel-Fabien. Handy for the youth hostel, this Italian is popular – particularly with families – and serves inexpensive pasta and pizza dishes.

Le Paysan, 16 rue de Fismes (☎03.26.40.25.51). Genuine peasant dishes, copious and delicious, in suitably rustic surroundings with genuinely warm service. It's some way northwest of the station: follow rue de Courcelles, and rue de Fismes will be on your left. Menus under 100F during the week. Closed Sat midday & Sun evening.

au Petit Bacchus, 11 rue de l'Université (☎03.26.47.10.05). Reasonably priced traditional cooking in an interior of sparse brick floor, bare tables. Around 100F. Closed Sun.

au Petit Comptoir, 17 rue de Mars (☎03.26.40.58.58). Close to the Marché du Boulingrin, with traditional dishes from 95F (no menus) served in a solid provincial middle-class milieu. Champagne by the glass too. Closed Sat lunch & Sun.

Entertainment

For drinking into the early hours there are plenty of large terrace **cafés** on place Drouet-d'Erlon, including *Café Leffe*, at no. 85, which has a wide selection of beers; and *Le Gaulois*, at nos. 2–4, with excellent cocktails and ice-creams. If you want to dance, try *Le Curtayn Club* at 7 bd Général-Leclere (daily 10pm–4am). *L'Usine*, 115 rue Lesage (☎03.26.04.56.38), hosts a **rock festival** in October, with concerts throughout the year. The *Opéra Cinema*, 3 rue T-Dubois (☎03.26.47.29.36), shows undubbed **films**. In the summer, over 120 **classical concerts** – many of them free – take place as part of Les Flâneries Musicales d'Été; pick up a leaflet at the tourist office.

Epernay and around

EPERNAY, 26km south of Reims, is *the* Champagne town to head for, beautifully situated below rolling, vine-covered hills, with wealth-impregnated tree-lined streets. In addition to some of the most famous *maisons*, there are also several smaller houses to tour, and the town makes a good base for exploring the surrounding villages and vineyards.

Information and accommodation

The information-packed **tourist office** is at 7 av de Champagne (Mon–Sat 9.30am–12.30pm & 1.30–7pm, Sun 11am–4pm; mid-Oct to Easter closes 5.30pm and Sun; ☎03.26.53.33.00, fax 03.26.51.95.22). If you feel like roaming around the *vignerons*, **bikes** can be rented from Rover Cycles, 10 place Hugues-Plomb (Tues–Sat 9am–noon & 2–7pm; ☎03.26.55.29.61), not far from place de la République at the other end of rue Général-Leclerc.

The cheapest **hotels** in Epernay are *St-Pierre*, 1 rue Jeanne-d'Arc (☎03.26.54.40.80; ①), in a quiet street away from the centre, and *Le Chapon Fin*, 2 place Mendès-France (☎03.26.55.40.03; ②), by the train station. Classier rooms are to be had at the *Hôtel de Champagne*, 30 rue E-Mercier (☎03.26.53.10.60, fax 03.26.51.94.63; ④). The *Foyer des Jeunes Travailleurs* **hostel**, in easy walking distance of the station at 2 rue Pupin (☎03.26.51.62.51; Mon–Fri 9am–8pm, Sat 10am–2pm; 16–25s only), has dorm-style accommodation and a cheap cafeteria. The **campsite** is 1.5km to the north on route de Cumières in the Parc des Sports, on the south bank of the Marne (☎03.26.55.32.14; April–Sept).

The town

The loveliest of Epernay's streets is **avenue de Champagne**, running east from the central place de la République, which is worth a stroll for its eighteenth- and nineteenth-century mansions and champagne *maisons*.

The largest, and probably the most famous *maison* of all, is **Moët et Chandon**, 18 av de Champagne (daily 9.30–11.30am/noon & 2–4.30pm; mid-Nov to March Mon–Fri only; 25F on weekdays, 30F Sat & Sun, includes *dégustation*), who own Mercier, Ruinart and a variety of other concerns, including Dior perfumes. By its own reckoning, a Moët champagne cork pops somewhere in the world every two seconds. The cellars are adorned with mementos of Napoléon, a good friend of the original M. Moët. True to tradition, the bottles are still turned by hand, a process of *remuage* (riddling) explained in detail by the guide; by the time you reach the generous *dégustation* you appreciate why the stuff costs so much.

Of the other maison visits, one of the most rewarding is **Mercier**, 70 av de Champagne (Mon–Sat 9.30–11.30am & 2–4.30pm, Sun 9.30–11.30am & 2–5.30pm; Dec–Feb closed Tues & Wed; 25F includes *dégustation*), whose glamour relic is a giant barrel that held 200,000 bottles' worth when M. Mercier took it to the 1889 Paris Exposition, with the help of 24 oxen – only to be upstaged by the Eiffel Tower. Visits round the cellars are by electric train and are great fun, climaxing in *dégustation*.

Castellane, by the station at 57 rue de Verdun (daily May–Oct 10am–noon & 2–6pm; April Mon–Fri 2–6pm, Sat & Sun 10am–noon & 2–6pm; 20F includes *dégustation*), provides Epernay with its chief landmark: a tower looking like a kind of Neoclassical signal box. As well as the inevitable cellars – and a *dégustation* – the visit includes a rather good museum with bottles and their labels, publicity posters, old tools and tableaux of champagne-making and related processes. Best of all, you get to climb to the top of the tower, which allows unsurpassed views of the town and surrounding vineyards.

Epernay has many other *grand maisons* that can be visited by appointment, but perhaps more worthwhile are the many smaller houses. Two which offer tours with *dégustation* are located on rue Chaude-Ruelle, west of av de Champagne, with views over the town: **Janisson-Baradon**, at no. 65 (☎03.26.54.45.85; 20F), and **Leclerc-Briant**, at no. 67 (☎03.26.54.45.33; 20F).

Esterlin, at 25 av de Champagne (daily 10am–12.30pm & 1.30–6pm; Sept–May closes at 5pm) don't offer guided tours of their cellars, but if you want to see their ten-minute video on the painstaking process of making champagne then you'll get a free *dégustation* to sip throughout.

Die-hard champagne lovers might wander into the **Musée du Champagne** at 13 av de Champagne (March–Nov Weds–Sun 10am–noon & 2–6pm; 10F). The exhibits themselves are humdrum, but the building is worth a peek, housed as it is in Château Perrier, an impressive example of a nineteenth-century champagne mansion, with a Louis XIII exterior and a flamboyant marble interior featuring a rather grand staircase.

Eating and drinking

Decent **restaurants** in Epernay are not cheap, but good food is assured at *La Table Kobus*, 3 rue du Dr-Rousseau (☎03.26.58.42.68; from 200F; closed Sun eve & Mon), and at *Les Berceaux*, 13 rue des Berceaux (☎03.26.55.28.84; menus from 135F; closed Sun eve & Mon), which also has a wine bar. Several cheaper, culturally varied places are on rue Gambetta, between the gare and place de la République: *Le Bel Azur*, at no. 33, has Tunisian specialities; while *Le Messina*, at no. 17, has pizza and inexpensive pasta. For a major blowout, head 5km north on the N2051 to Champillon and the *Royal Champagne* (☎03.26.52.87.11; weekday lunchtime menus from 195F, otherwise from 265F).

Around Epernay

The villages in the vineyards of the Montagne de Reims, Côte des Blancs and Vallée de la Marne which surround Epernay, promote a range of "attractions": the world's largest champagne bottle and cork in Mardeuil; the world's largest champagne glass and an artisan chocolate producer in Pierry; a snail farm in Olizy-Violaine, a museum of marriage in Oger, and a traditional *vigneron*'s house and turn-of-the-century school room at Oeuilly. Full details of these are available from Epernay's tourist office, along with lists of all the champagne producers. But the best reason for taking yourself out into the countryside is to view the vines. Many of the villages have conserved their sleepy old stone charm: **VERTUS**, 16km south, is particularly pretty, so too is **HAUTVILLERS**, 6km north, where the abbey of Dom Pérignon fame is only visitable by appointment in advance from its owners, Moët et Chandon (☎03.26.51.20.00). Various "champagne excursions" by minibus, horse-drawn carriage or hot air balloon are touted, but there are regular local **buses** (the gare routière is on the corner of rues Dr-Verron and Dr-Rousseau one block northeast from place de la République).

Troyes

TROYES, ancient capital of Champagne, is a gem. Its high narrow streets of restored, half-timbered houses protect an elegant Gothic cathedral, half-a-dozen superb lesser churches, a fistful of Renaissance mansions, and several exceptionally good museums.

Arrival, information and accommodation

The **gare SNCF** and **gare routière** are side by side off bd Carnot (part of the ring road). Not all buses use the main station, though, and if you're heading for the countryside it's best to check first with the regional tourist office at 16 bd Carnot (June to mid-Sept Mon–Sat 9am–12.30pm & 2–6.30pm; mid-Sept to May 10am–noon & 2–6.30pm; ☎03.25.82.62.70, fax 03.25.73.06.81). Information on the town of Troyes can also be obtained from the **tourist office** on rue Mignard, opposite the church of St Jean (July–Aug Mon–Sat 9.30am–8.30pm, Sun 10–noon & 2–5pm; Sept 1–mid-Sept Mon–Fri closes at 6.30pm, Sun as above; mid-Sept–June Mon–Sat 10am–12.30pm & 2–6.30pm, Sun 10am–noon & 2–5pm; ☎03.25.73.36.88). Smaller tourist information offices can be found in all the churches mentioned below, with the same opening hours as the churches.

Places to **stay** around the station are plentiful, though for not much more you can find accommodation right in the centre of the old town. Outside term time there may be room in the city's foyers – the tourist office has details.

Hotels

de la Gare, 8 bd Carnot (☎03.25.78.22.84, fax 03.25.74.16.26). A simple but comfortable two-star near the station. ②.

Grand Hôtel, 4 av Mal-Joffre (☎03.25.79.90.90, fax 03.25.78.48.93). Right opposite the station, a big three-star hotel with swimming pool and garden. ②

Patiote, next door to the Grand Hôtel and managed by the same people, it has less competitive rates. ③.

Le Relais St-Jean, 51 rue Paillot-de-Montabert (☎03.25.73.89.90, fax 03.25.73.88.60). Posh hotel in a half-timbered building in a narrow street right in the centre. ⑤.

Select, 1 rue de Vauluisant (☎03.25.73.36.16). In the old part of town right next to the museum. Run-down and basic, but friendly, and with very economical deals for family rooms. ①.

Splendid, 44 bd Carnot (☎03.25.73.08.52, fax 03.25.93.41.04). Near the station on a very busy road. Rooms have shower and TV. ②.

du Théâtre, 35 rue Jules-Lebocey (☎03.25.73.18.47, fax 03.25.73.85.73) In a quiet location virtually opposite the Théâtre Madeleine, with friendly management and a good-value, old-fashioned brasserie downstairs. ②.

Youth hostels and campsites

HI youth hostel, Chemin Ste Scholastique, Rosières (☎03.25.82.00.65, fax 03.25.72.93.78). 5km out of town on the Dijon road; take bus #8 direction "Rosières", stop "Liberté". Opposite the sign saying "Vielaines", a path leads down to this former fourteenth-century priory. Open year round; HI card required.

Campsite, 7, rue Roger-Salengro, Pont Ste-Marie (☎03.25.81.02.64), 5km out on the N60 to Châlons, on the left. May to mid-Oct.

The town

As tourist pamphlets are at pains to point out, the ring of boulevards round the town is shaped like a champagne cork. In fact it's just as much like a sock – a shape that's just as suitable, since hosiery and woollens have been Troyes' most important industry since the end of the Middle Ages, when Louis XIII decreed that charitable houses had to be self-supporting and the orphanage of the Hôpital de la Trinité set their charges to knitting stockings.

Some of the old machines and products used for creating garments can be seen in a **Musée de la Bonneterie** (July & Aug daily except Tues 10am–6pm; Sept–June daily except Tues 10am–noon & 2–6pm; 30F), in the sixteenth-century *Hôtel de Vauluisant*, opposite the church of St-Pantaléon at 4 rue de Vauluisant. Beautifully restored and visually appealing, it sets an example for all crafts museums with its respect for the traditions and lack of sentimentality. The building also houses the **Musée Historique de Troyes** (same hours and ticket), a small collection of unsophisticated religious art from the Troyes school. Just one block east is **La Maison de l'Outil**, 7 rue de la Trinité (Mon–Fri 9am–1pm & 2–6.30pm, Sat & Sun 10am–1pm & 2–6pm; 30F), in the beautiful sixteenth-century *Hôtel de Mauroy*, a surprisingly fascinating museum of tools, with seventeenth- and eighteenth-century exhibits providing a window into the world of the workers who used them and the people who crafted them.

Despite being raked by numerous fires in the Middle Ages, Troyes has retained many of its timber-framed buildings south of the central main shopping street, in **rue Émile-Zola**, around the cathedral and particularly in the streets and alleyways of the **old town** off the pedestrianized rue Champeaux. The church of **St-Jean au Marché**, between rues Émile-Zola and Champeaux (July & Aug daily 10am–12.30pm & 1.30–7pm; Sept–June daily 10am–noon & 2–4pm), is where Henry V married Catherine of France after being recognized as heir to the French throne in the 1420 Treaty of Troyes. Other churches worth seeking out are the church of **Ste-Madeleine**, on the road of the same name (same hours as St-Jean), whose delicate stonework rood screen – used to keep the priest separate from the congregation – is one of the few left in France; the sumptuous church of **St-Pantaléon** (daily: July–Aug 10am–12.30pm & 2–6pm; Sept–June 10am–12.30pm & 2–5.30pm), southwest of church of St-Jean, on rue Vauluisant; and the Gothic **Basilique St-Urbain**, place Vernier (same hours as church of St-Jean), its exterior dramatizing the Day of Judgment with the damned and the devils providing a wicked variety of gargoyles.

Heading east from St-Urbain across the covered canal, you come to **La Cité quartier**, full of more museums and ancient buildings, and centred on the **Cathédrale St-Pierre-et-St-Paul** (July to mid-Sept 9am–1pm & 2–7pm; mid-Sept to June 9am–1pm & 2–6pm), whose pale Gothic nave is stroked with reflections from the wonderful stained-glass windows.

Next door to the cathedral, housed in the old bishops' palace on place St-Pierre, is the **Musée d'Art Moderne** (daily except Tues 11am–6pm; 30F), an outstanding museum displaying part of an extraordinary private collection of art, particularly rich in Fauvist paintings by the likes of Vlaminck and Derain – along with other, first-class works by Degas, Courbet, Gauguin, Matisse (a tapestry and three canvases), Bonnard, Braque, Modigliani, Rodin, Robert Delaunay and Ernst. On the other side of the cathedral, the **Abbaye St-Loup** (daily except Tues 10am–noon & 2–6pm; 30F, Wed free) houses collections of paintings, natural history and archeology and has a showcase window onto an ornate Baroque library. In similar vein, the **Hôtel-Dieu**, back down rue de la Cité, has a richly decorated sixteenth-century apothecary (July & Aug same days and hours as Abbaye St-Loup; Sept–June Weds, Sat & Sun hours as above; 20F, Wed free; entrance on quai des Comtes de Champagne).

Quite different from the rash of Christian churches in Troyes is the **synagogue** on rue Brunneval, inaugurated in memory of the Jewish scholar Rachi (1040–1105) in 1987. He was a member of the small Jewish community which flourished for a time during the eleventh and twelfth centuries under the protection of the Counts of Champagne. His commentaries on both the Old Testament and the Talmud are still important to academics today: the Rachi University Institute opposite is devoted to studying his work.

Clothes shopping

Today the garment business still accounts for more than half the town's employment, and buying **clothes from the factory** is one of the town's chief attractions. Designer-label clothes can be bought at half the normal shop price. Espace Belgrand in rue Belgrand, off bd du 14-Juillet, and William de Faye opposite have quite a number (both open Mon 2–7pm, Tues–Fri 10am–7pm, Sat 9.30am–7pm); rues Émile-Zola and des Bas Trévois are also worth a wander. Or you can go out to the manufacturers on the outskirts, where dozens of factory shops sell clothes, shoes and leather goods designed for everyone from Nike to Laura Ashley and Yves St-Laurent to Jean-Paul Gaultier. The best array is in the four giant sheds of Marques Avenue, 114 bd de Dijon, St-Julien-les-Villas (hours as above), south of the city on the N71 to Dijon. Or, at Pont-Ste-Marie, to the northeast of Troyes along the D960 to Nancy, there's Le Centre des Marques (rue Marc-Verdier) and McArthur Glen (rue Danton), both with the same hours as Espace Belgrand. Buses for the outlets on the outskirts of town depart from the bus station by Marché les Halles.

Eating and drinking

Rue Champeaux is packed with places to **eat**: crêpes are on offer at *Crêperie la Tourelle*, the half-timbered building at no. 9, with its own tiny tower and views of the church of St-Jean; while at the end of the street, on place Alexandre-Israël, the popular bar/brasserie *L'Odyssée* serves inexpensive snacks and *plats du jour*. A good place to try the regional speciality of *andouillette* is the *Cheval de 3* (☎03.25.80.58.23; closed in the evening on Tues, Weds and Sun). *Les Gourmets*, 3 rue Raymonde-Poincaré (☎03.25.73.80.78; menus from 130F) serves excellent fishy foods. For brasserie food try *Le Bistroquet*, place Langevin (closed Sun eve; menus from 89F), the *Hôtel du Théâtre*'s brasserie (see above; closed Sun evening; menus from 70F), or the *Café de la Gare*, 14 bd Carnot, where you can eat as many starters and desserts as you want from the buffet for 59F. Troyes' top restaurant is *Le Valentino*, 11 cour de la Rencontre (☎03.03.25.73.14.14; closed Sat lunch, Mon & 3 weeks in Aug & Sept; menus from 110F), whose inventive chef is keen on Thai elements. *Le Café du Musée*, 59 rue de la Cité, near the cathedral, has a decent upstairs restaurant (closed Sun & Mon eve) and a cool contemporary bar downstairs (Mon–Sat until 3am), with a wide range of beers. *Le Tricasse*, 2 rue Charbonnet, is perennially popular, with tables and the occasional live band, while nearby narrow rue Paillot-de-Montabert has a few good bars, including the tiny and consistently packed out *Bar des Bougnets des Pouilles*.

Self-caterers should head for the Marché les Halles, a daily covered **market** on the corner of rue Général-de-Gaulle and rue de la République, close to the Hôtel de Ville. Vegetarians and the health-conscious will think they're in heaven at Coopérative Hermes, 39 rue Général-Saussier, a surprisingly good – for France – wholesale/health-food store.

The Plateau de Langres

The Seine, Marne, Aube and several other lesser rivers rise in the **Plateau de Langres** between Troyes and Dijon. Hunting for sources is a thankless task – there are no bubbling springs – and you're more likely to be conscious of undifferentiated water everywhere. Main routes from Troyes to the Burgundian capital of Dijon skirt this area; to the east, the N19 (which the train follows) takes in **Chaumont** and **Langres**, two towns that could briefly slow your progress if you're in no hurry, and the home village of General de Gaulle, **Colombey-Les-Deux-Églises**.

Chaumont

Situated on a steep ridge between the Marne and Suize valleys, **CHAUMONT**, 93km east of Troyes, is best approached by train, which enables you to cross the town's stupendous mid-nineteenth-century viaduct.

The **tourist office** is on Place de la Gare (summer Mon–Sat 9am–7pm, Sun 10am–noon & 2–5pm; winter Mon–Sat 9.30am–12.30pm & 2.30–6pm; ☎03.25.03.80.80) and will be able to provide plans and help with accommodation. The main ancient building to look at is the **Basilique St-Jean-Baptiste**. Built with the same dour, grey stone of most Champagne churches, it has, nevertheless, a wonderful Renaissance addition to the Gothic transept of balconies and turreted stairway. The decoration includes a fifteenth-century polychrome *Mise en Tombeau* with muddy tears but expressive faces, and an *Arbre de Jessé* of the early sixteenth-century Troyes school, in which all the characters are sitting in the tree, properly dressed in the style of the day.

As for the rest of the old town, there's not much to do except admire the strange, bulging towers of the houses, through which the shapes of wide spiral staircases are visible. You shouldn't leave, however, without taking a look at **Le Silo**, 7–9 av Foch, near the gare SNCF (July & Aug Tues–Fri 2–6.30pm, Sat 9am–1pm; Sept–June Tues, Thurs & Fri 2–6pm, Wed & Sat 10–7pm; free), a former agricultural co-op transformed into a graphic arts centre and *médiathèque*. As well as hosting temporary exhibitions, it's the main venue for Chaumont's international **poster festival**, held every year in the first fortnight of June.

If you decide to **stay**, *Le Terminus Reine*, on place Général-de-Gaulle (☎03.25.03.66.66, fax 03.25.03.28.95; ③), is an old-fashioned hotel with great charm. Its restaurant, *La Chaufferie*, is the best place to eat. For a cheap room, there's a **youth hostel** at 1 rue Carcassonne (☎03.25.03.22.77; bus #2 from the gare SNCF to Suize).

Colombey-Les-Deux-Églises

Twenty-seven kilometres northwest of Chaumont, on the N19 to Troyes, is **COLOMBEY-LES-DEUX EGLISES**, the village where Gaullist leaders come to pay homage at the grave of **General de Gaulle**. De Gaulle's family home, "La Boiserie", is open to the public (daily except Tues 10am–noon & 2–5pm; Sept until 5.30pm; closed Jan; 18F), but the most impressive memorial is the pink granite Cross of Lorraine, symbol of the French Resistance movement, standing over 40m high on a hill just west of the village, signposted off the N19.

The best place to **stay** here is *Les Dhuits*, a hotel with restaurant, on the main road (☎03.25.01.50.10, fax 03.25.01.56.22; ③; menu around 100F).

Langres

LANGRES, 35km south of Chaumont and just as spectacularly situated above the Marne, suffered far less war damage and retains its encirclement of gateways, towers and ramparts. Walking this circuit, which gives views east to the hills of Alsace and southwest across the Plateau de Langres, is the best thing to do if you're just stopping for an hour or so. Don't miss the St-Ferjeux tower with its beautiful metal sculpture *Air and Dreams*. Wandering inside the walls is also rewarding – Renaissance houses and narrow streets give the feel of a place time has left behind, swathed in the mists of south Champagne. Langres was home to the eighteenth-century Enlightenment philosopher Diderot for the first sixteen years of his life, and people like to make the point that, if he were to return to Langres today, he'd have no trouble finding his way around.

The **Musée du Breuil de St-Germain**, in one of the best of the town's sixteenth-century mansions, at 2 rue Chambrûlard is unfortunately closed as the building is no longer safe and is awaiting funds before restoration work can begin. However, part of the museum's collection can be visited in the **Musée de Langres** (daily: April–Sept 10am–noon & 2–6pm; Oct–March 10am–noon & 2–5pm; 20F) on place du Centenaire, near the cathedral. Head to level 1 of the new wing for the section devoted to Diderot, normally displayed in the Musée du Breuil St-Germain, with his encyclopedias and various other first editions of his works, plus a portrait by Van Loos. Of the museum's own collection, the first part is devoted mainly to local archeology, with a rich Gallo-Roman section, but the highlight is the superbly restored Romanesque **chapel of St Didier**, incorporated into the old wing of the museum and containing a fourteenth-century painted ivory Annunciation. Nearby, sets of dining knives, a craft for which this area was famous for several centuries, are on display along with other local decorative arts. Local *faïence* – glazed terracotta – is featured, though these nicely crafted pieces are upstaged by the sixteenth-century tiles from Rouen in one of the nave chapels of the **Cathédrale St-Mammès**. This grey-stone edifice has not been improved by the eighteenth-century addition of a new facade, but there's an amusing sixteenth-century relief of the *Raising of Lazarus*, in which the apostles watch, totally blasé, while the locals look like kids at a good horror movie.

Practicalities

The **tourist office** is just inside the town's main gate, the Porte des Moulins (May–June & Sept Mon–Sat 9.30am–noon & 1.30–6.30pm, Sun 10.30am–12.30pm & 2–6pm; July & Aug Mon–Sat 9am–12.30pm & 1.30–7pm, Sun 10.30am–12.30pm & 2–6pm; Oct–April as May–June but Mon–Sat only and closing at 6pm; ☎03.25.87.67.67, fax 03.25.88.99.07), on the other side of town from the **gare SNCF** (infrequent connections to Troyes and Dijon); they can give you a useful map with a walking route that takes in the main sights. The bus timetable from the train station to the Porte des Moulins is loosely based on the train timetable; however, the last **bus** leaves at 7pm Monday to Friday, 4pm on Saturday and there is no connection on Sunday.

For **accommodation**, there's a **youth hostel** close by the Porte des Moulins on place des États-Unis (☎03.25.87.09.69, fax 03.25.88.83.25; closed Sat & Sun eve), and the reasonable *Auberge Jeanne d'Arc*, 26 rue Gambetta (☎03.25.87.03.18, fax

03.25.88.82.85; ②; closed Mon, and Tues out of season), in the centre of town. More comfortable rooms can be had at the characterful *Hôtel le Cheval Blanc*, in a converted church on rue de l'Estrés (☎03.25.87.07.00, fax 03.25.87.23.13; ④); or in the seventeenth-century *Grand Hôtel de L'Europe*, 23–25 rue Diderot (☎03.25.87.10.88, fax 03.25.87.60.65; ②–③). For good but expensive food, try *Restaurant Diderot* at the *Cheval Blanc* (see above; closed Tues eve & Wed lunch). Better value is to be had at the *Lion d'Or*, just outside the town on the route de Vesoul (☎03.25.87.03.30; closed Mon & Sun eve). Langres has its own excellent bright-orange cheese which you can buy at the Friday **market** on place Jenson.

The Ardennes

To the north of Reims, the scenery of the **Ardennes** region along the Meuse valley knocks spots off any landscape in Champagne. Most of the hills lie over the border in Belgium, but there's enough of interest on the French side to make it well worth exploring.

In war after war, the people of the Ardennes have been engaged in protracted last-ditch battles down the valley of the Meuse which, once lost, gave invading armies a clear path to Paris. The rugged, hilly terrain and deep forests (frightening even to Julius Caesar's legionnaires) gave some advantage to World War II's Resistance fighters when the Ardennes was annexed to Germany, but even peacetime living has never been easy. The land is unsuitable for crops, and the slateworks and ironworks, which were the main source of employment during the last century, were closed down during the 1980s. The only major investment in the region has been a nuclear power station in the loop of the Meuse at Chooz, to which locals responded by etching "Nuke the Élysée!" high on a half-cut cliff of slate just downstream.

Tourism, the main growth industry, is developing apace – there are walking and boating possibilities, plus good train and bus connections – though the eerie isolated atmosphere of this region remains.

Charleville-Mézières

The twin towns of **CHARLEVILLE** and **MÉZIÈRES** provide a good starting point for exploring the northern part of the region, which spreads across the meandering Meuse before the valley closes in and the forests take over. Of the two, Charleville is the one to head for; aside from its main square, its major virtue is as a base for the Ardennes countryside.

Arrival, information and accommodation
From the **gare SNCF**, the main square – place Ducale – is a five-minute ride away on bus #1, #3 or #5; the **gare routière** is a couple of blocks northeast of place Ducale, between rues du Daga and Noël. The **regional tourist office** for the Ardennes is at 22 place Ducale (☎03.24.56.06.08, fax 03.24.59.20.10), with Charleville-Mézières' tourist office at no. 4 (Tues–Sat 9.30am–noon & 1.30–6pm; ☎03.24.32.44.80).

Three fairly central that are worth trying are the *Hôtel de Paris*, 24 av G-Corneau (☎03.24.33.34.38, fax 03.24.59.11.21; ③); the *Central*, 23 av du Maréchal Leclerc (☎03.24.33.33.69, fax 03.24.59.38.25; ②); and *Le Relais du Square*, 3 place de la Gare (☎03.24.33.38.76, fax 03.24.33.56.66; ③), a smart three-star hotel in a tree-filled square near the station. The town **campsite** (☎03.24.30.00.11) is north of place Ducale, over the river and left along rue des Paquis.

The town

Charleville's main sight is the beautifully arcaded central **place Ducale**, the result of the seventeenth-century local duke's envy of the contemporary place des Vosges in Paris. Despite the posh setting, the shops in the arcades remain very down-to-earth – poissonnières amongst them – and the cafés charge reasonable prices to sit outside, a very good position on Tuesdays, Thursdays and Saturdays, when the **market** is held here.

From 31 place Ducale you can reach the complex of old and new buildings housing the **Musée de l'Ardenne** (Tues–Sun 10am–noon & 2–6pm; 25F; or 35F combined ticket with Musée Arthur Rimbaud, see below) covering the different economic activities of the region over the ages: local paintings, prehistoric artefacts, legends, puppetry, weapons and coins. You need to keep up a good pace to get round all the rooms, but it's fun and informative.

The most famous person to emerge from the town was Arthur Rimbaud (1854–91), who ran away from Charleville four times before he was 17, so desperate was he to escape from quiet provincialism. He is honoured in the **Musée Arthur Rimbaud**, housed in a very grand stone windmill – a contemporary of the place Ducale – on quai Arthur-Rimbaud, two blocks north of the main square (Tues–Sun 10am–noon & 2–6pm; 20F; or 35F ticket with Musée de l'Ardenne). It contains a host of pictures of him and those he hung out with, as well as facsimiles of his writings and related documents. A few steps down the quayside is the spot where he composed *Le Bateau Ivre*. After penning poetry in Paris, journeying to the Far East and trading in Ethiopia and Yemen, Rimbaud died in a Marseille hospital, and his body was brought back to his home town – probably the last place he would have wanted to be buried. True Rimbaud fanatics can also visit his **tomb** in the cemetery west of the place Ducale at the end of avenue Charles Boutet.

Charleville is also a major international **puppetry centre** (its school is justly famous), and every three years it hosts one of the largest puppet festivals in the world, the **Festival Mondial des Théâtres de Marionnettes** (the next one is in 2000). As many as 150 professional troupes – some from as far away as Mali and Burma – put on something like fifty shows a day on the streets and in every available space in town. Tickets are cheap, and there are shows for adults as well as the usual stuff aimed at kids. If you miss the festival you can still catch one of the puppet performances in the summer months every year (☎03.24.33.72.50 for booking and information), or if you're passing by the Institut de la Marionnette between 10am and 9pm you can see one of the automated episodes of the *Four Sons of Aymon* enacted on the facade's clock every hour, or all twelve scenes on Saturday at 9.15am.

Eating and drinking

There are plenty of places to **eat** and **drink** in Charleville. For something a bit special, *La Côte à l'Os*, at 11 cours Aristide-Briand (☎03.24.59.20.16), specializes in *fruits de mer* and local *Ardennais* cuisine; daily chalkboard menus from 79F. *La Cigogne*, at 40 rue Dubois-Crancé (☎03.24.33.25.39; closed Mon & first week Aug), also serves very good regional dishes, with menus from 88F. Worth checking out for a drink or a coffee is the *Ideal Bar* on rue de la République – a characterful, down-to-earth local despite its chandelier-style lights and dark wood interior; or you could sit under the arcades on place Ducale at *Au Caveau*.

North of Charleville

George Sand wrote, of the stretch of the Meuse that winds through the Ardennes, that "its high wooded cliffs, strangely solid and compact, are like some inexorable destiny that encloses, pushes and twists the river without permitting it a single whim or any escape". What all the tourist literature writes about, however, are the legends of medieval struggles between Good and Evil whose characters have given names to some of the curious rocks and crests. The grandest of these, where the schist formations have taken the most peculiar turns, is the **Roc de la Tour**, also known as the Devil's Castle, up a path off the D31, 3.5km out of **MONTHERMÉ**, a slate-roofed little town with nothing of great interest except a twelfth-century **church** with late medieval frescoes.

The journey through this frontier country should ideally be done on foot or skis, or **by boat**. The alternatives for the latter are good old bateau-mouche-type cruises (Loisirs-Accueil en Ardennes, 5 rue du Moulin, Charleville-Mézières; ☎03.24.56.06.08) or live-in pleasure boats – not wildly expensive if you can split the cost four or six ways. These are hired out, with bikes on board, by Ardennes Plaisance in Charleville-Mézières, 76 rue des Forges-St-Charles (☎03.24.56.47.61) or Ardennes Nautisme in Sedan, 16 rue du Château (☎03.24.27.05.15), the next town downstream from Charleville. The latter moor their boats just east of Dom-Le-Mesnil on the D764 at the junction of the Meuse and the Canal des Ardennes. Loisirs-Accueil shares an office with the local walking organization which can provide footpath maps; for details of canoeing, biking or riding, contact the **regional tourist office** at Charleville (see above). For **public transport** from Charleville, trains follow the Meuse into Belgium, and a few buses run up to Monthermé and **LES HAUTES-RIVIÈRES**, the latter on the River Semoy.

The **GR12** is a good walking route, circling the **Lac des Vieilles Forges** (17km northwest of Charleville – and with canoe hire), then meeting the Meuse at Bogny and crossing over to Hautes-Rivières in the even more sinuous **Semoy Valley**. There are plenty of other tracks, too, though beware of *chasse* signs – French hunters tend to hack through the undergrowth with their safety catches off and are notoriously trigger-happy. Wild boar are the main quarry being hunted, and nowhere near as dangerous as their pursuers: the bristly beasts would seem to be more intelligent, too, rooting about near the crosses of the Resistance memorial near **REVIN**, while hunters stalk the forest at a respectful distance. The abundance of wild boar is partly explained when you rootle around on the forest floor yourself and discover, between the trees to either side of the river, an astonishing variety of mushrooms, and, in late summer, wild strawberries and bilberries. For a quaint insight into life in the forest stop in at the **Musée de la Forêt**, situated right on the edge of the Ardennes forest, 2km north of Renwez on the D40 (daily: April & May 2–5pm; June & mid-Sept to Oct 9am–noon & 2–7pm; July to mid-Sept 9am–7pm; 25F). All manner of wood-cutting, gathering and transporting is enacted by log dummies along with displays of utensils and flora and fauna of the forest; it's also a tranquil spot for a picnic.

A good place to **stay**, overlooking the river at Revin, is the *Hôtel Francois-1er*, 46 quai Camille-Desmoulins (☎03.24.40.15.88, fax 03.24.40.32.93; ③), which rents out bikes and canoes and gives good advice on walks. There's a youth hostel in **GIVET**, route des Chaumières (☎03.24.42.09.60, fax 03.24.42.02.44).

travel details

Buses

Amiens to: Albert (2 daily; 40min); Beauvais (4 daily; 1hr 15min); St-Quentin (2 daily; 2hr 30min).

Boulogne to: Calais (4 daily; 1hr); Le Touquet (4 daily; 1hr).

Calais to: Boulogne (5 daily; 1hr); Le Touquet (5 daily; 2hr).

Dunkerque to: Calais (8 daily; 30min).

Reims to: Troyes (3 daily; 2hr 30min).

Trains

Amiens to: Compiègne (6 daily; 1hr 15min); Laon (several daily; 2hr); Paris (very frequently; 1hr 45min–2hr).

Beauvais to: Paris (6 daily; 1hr 10min).

Boulogne-Ville to: Amiens (8 daily; 1hr 15min); Arras (4 daily; 2hr); Calais-Ville (9 daily; 30min); Étaples-Le Touquet (9 daily; 20min), Montreuil (7 daily; 30min); Paris (8 daily; 3hr).

Calais-Ville to: Amiens (6 daily; 1hr 45min); Boulogne-Ville (frequent; 30min); Étaples-Le Touquet (9 daily; 1hr); Lille (frequent; 1hr–1hr 30min); Paris (6 daily; 3hr 30min).

Charleville-Mézières to: Givet (10 daily; 1hr).

Dunkerque to: Arras (7 daily; 1hr 20min); Calais-Ville (3 Mon–Fri; 1hr); Paris (6 daily; 3hr 10min).

Laon to: Paris (4 daily; 2hr); Soissons (4 daily; 1hr 40min).

Lille to: Arras (very frequent; 30/40min); Brussels (frequently; 2hr); Lyon (TGV 7 daily; 3hr); Paris (very frequently; 2–2hr 30min).

Reims to: Charleville-Mézières (8 daily; 55min); Epernay (frequently; 25min); Paris (frequently; 2hr).

St-Quentin to: Compiègne (12 daily; 30/40min); Paris (frequently; 1hr 45min).

Troyes to: Chaumont (6 daily; 45min); Langres (4 daily; 1hr 10min); Paris (frequently; 1hr 30min).

Ferries See "Basics", p.7–10.

CHAPTER THREE

ALSACE-LORRAINE AND THE JURA MOUNTAINS

F rance's eastern frontier provinces, **Alsace**, **Lorraine** and **Franche-Comté**, where the Jura mountains lie, have had a complex and tumultuous history. For a thousand years they have been a battleground, disputed through the Middle Ages by independent dukes and bishops whose allegiance was endlessly contested by the kings of France and the princes of the Holy Roman Empire, and the scene, this century, of some of the worst fighting of both world wars.

The democratically minded burghers of **Alsace** had already created a plethora of well-heeled, semi-autonomous towns for themselves centuries before their seventeenth-century incorporation into the French state. Sharing the Germans' taste for Hansel-and-Gretel-type decoration, they adorned their buildings with all manner of frills and fancies – oriel windows, carved timberwork and Toytown gables – and with Teutonic orderliness they still maintain them, festooned with flowers and in pristine condition. Not that you should ever call an Alsatian German. Their mother tongue, Elsassisch, is a Germanic dialect, but their neighbours across the Rhine have behaved in decidedly unneighbourly fashion twice in the last 130 years, annexing them along with much of Lorraine from 1870 to 1918 and again from 1940 to 1944 under Hitler's Third Reich. They remain fiercely and proudly Alsatian and French – in that order.

The combination of influences makes for a culture and atmosphere as distinctive as any in France. It is seen at its most vivid in the numerous little wine towns that punctuate the **Route du Vin** along the eastern margin of the wet and woody Vosges mountains; at **Colmar**; and in the great cathedral city of **Strasbourg**, now one of the capitals of the European Union. But the province is not just a quaint setting for coach tours: it's also an industrial powerhouse, making cars, railway engines, textiles, machine tools and telephones, as well as half the beer in France.

By comparison, **Lorraine**, a large region taking in the northern border shared with Luxembourg, Germany and Belgium, is rather colourless although it has suffered much the same vicissitudes as Alsace. However, the elegant eighteenth-century town of **Nancy**, the cathedral city and provincial capital **Metz**, and the depressing and unforgettable WorldWar I battlefield of **Verdun**, are well worth visiting.

More impressive are the wooded plateaux, pastures and valleys of the **Jura mountains** abutting the German and Swiss frontiers further south, rural and poor, but partly rejuvenated by the attentions of the leisure industry. *Ski de fond* – cross-country skiing – is the speciality, and it's ideal terrain. It's good walking country, too, without the grinding ascents of the neighbouring Alps. The Jura has its own **Route du Vin**, without the hordes of tourists. The mountains and lakes here are also much less tourist-congested than the Vosges in summer; if it's peace and quiet you are looking for, it's here you will find it.

LORRAINE

During World War II, when de Gaulle and the Free French chose **Lorraine**'s double-barred cross as their emblem, they were making a powerful point. For it is this region, above all others, that the French associate with war. Its name derives from the Latin, *Lotharii regnum*, "the kingdom of Lothar", who was one of the three grandsons of Charlemagne, among whom his empire was divided by the Treaty of Verdun in 843 AD.

Lorraine has been the principal route of invasion from the German lands across the Rhine ever since, even though the trench-like valleys of the rivers **Meuse** and **Moselle** form a main line of defence. Joan of Arc was born here in 1412, at **Domrémy-la-Pucelle** on the Meuse, when the land was disputed by the dukes of Burgundy and the kings of France, and it only finally became part of the kingdom of France in 1766. In 1792 a mixed army of Prussians and other alarmed royalist enemies of the French Revolution was stopped by Revolutionary forces at the battle of Valmy to the west of Verdun. 1870 saw a humiliating defeat of Napoléon III's armies at the hands of the Prussians on the heights above Metz. Then, this century, the two world wars saw terrible fighting in the area, both ultimately involving American as well as French armies.

Of all the killing fields the bloodiest was **Verdun**, where the French army fought one of the most costly and protracted battles of all time from 1916 to 1918. The battlefield is a site of national pilgrimage. The SNCF still lays on extra trains here for the celebration of Armistice Day, though there are now few left alive who knew and mourn the 750,000 dead. For a fascinating and detailed history of all the various battlefields there is no better account than Richard Holmes' *Fatal Avenue*.

The rest of Lorraine – a rolling, windswept plateau of farmland to the south, moribund coalfields and heavy industry along the Belgian and German frontiers north of **Metz** – seems to stand in the shadows. General Patton, who commanded the US troops which liberated the area in 1944, said he could imagine "no greater burden than to be the owner of this nasty country where it rains every day and the whole wealth of the people consists in assorted manure piles". That is an unnecessarily harsh judgement. The landscape may not be the prettiest in France, but if this is your first stop out of Paris, you will notice that the people seem far friendlier.

Metz and around

METZ (pronounced "Mess"), the capital of Lorraine, lies on the east bank of the River Moselle, close to the Autoroute de l'Est linking Paris and Strasbourg and the main train line. Its origins go back at least to Roman times, when, as now, it stood astride major trade routes. On the death of Charlemagne it became the capital of Lothar's portion of his empire, managing to maintain its prosperity in spite of the dynastic wars that

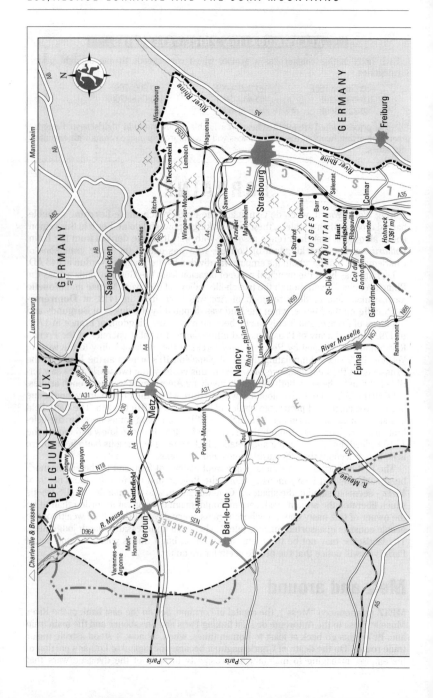

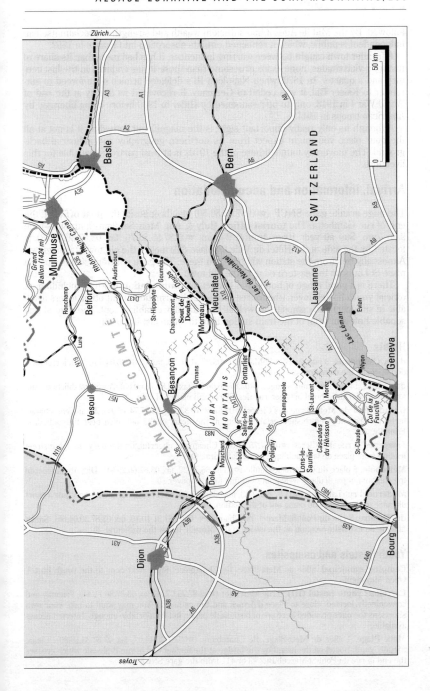

followed. By the Middle Ages it had sufficient wealth and strength to proclaim itself an independent republic, which it remained until its absorption into France in 1552.

A frontier town caught between warring influences, it has had more than its share of history's vicissitudes, none more gruesome than those it has endured in the last century and a quarter. In 1870, when Napoléon III's defeated armies were forced to surrender to Kaiser Bill, it was ceded to Germany. It recovered its liberty at the end of World War I in 1918, only to be re-annexed by Hitler in 1940 before being liberated by American troops in 1944.

Although its only really important sight is the magnificent cathedral, it is not at all the dour place you might expect from its northern geography and industrial background. The university founded here in the 1970s is at least partly responsible for this liveliness.

Arrival, information and accommodation

The huge granite **gare SNCF** (☎03.87.63.50.50) stands opposite the **post office** at the end of rue Gambetta. The **tourist office** (July & Aug Mon–Sat 9am–9pm; Sept–June 9am–7pm, Sun all year 10am–1pm & 3–5pm; ☎03.87.55.53.76, fax 03.87.36.59.43) is located by the side of the Hôtel de Ville on place d'Armes in the old town (see below). Almost any bus from the station will take you there. The **gare routière** stands close to place St-Louis on the eastern edge of the old town.

There is a good range of hotels and budget **accommodation** in Metz, including an official youth hostel, foyer (the tourist office has information about other foyers available in summer) and campsite, as well as the odd ritzy establishment. The several reasonable hotels in front of the train station tend to fill up fast in season.

Hotels

de la Cathedrale, 3 rue du Pont-St-Marcel (☎03.87.31.10.10, fax 03.87.30.04.66). Wonderful location opposite the cathedral. ⑤.

du Centre, 14 rue Dupont-des-Loges (☎03.87.36.06.93, fax 03.87.75.60.66). A well-established comfortably modernized hotel between rue des Clercs and place St-Louis. ③.

Grand-Hôtel de Metz, 3 rue des Clercs (☎03.87.36.16.33, fax 03.87.74.17.04). An ancient, characterful and recently refurbished establishment in the heart of the old town near the cathedral. Friendly. ③.

Lafayette, 24 rue des Clercs (☎03.87.75.21.09). Cheap and cheerful, on the busy shopping street leading from place de la République to the cathedral. ①.

Métropole, 5 place du Général-de-Gaulle (☎03.87.66.26.22, fax 03.87.66.29.91). Directly in front of the station; not particularly welcoming but fine for a stopover. ③.

Moderne, 1 rue Lafayette (☎03.87.66.57.33, fax 03.87.55.98.59). Functional and friendly, just a short distance to the left as you come out of the station. ③.

du Théâtre, 3 rue du Pont-St-Marcel, Île Chambière (☎03.87.31.10.10, fax 03.87.30.04.66). Smart hotel in an exquisite location on the island in the Moselle below the cathedral. ⑤.

Youth hostels and campsites

Camping municipal, allée de Metz-Plage, Île Chambière. Right next door to the youth hostel. Open May–Sept.

Carrefour youth hostel (HI), 6 rue Marchant (☎03.87.75.07.26, fax 03.87.36.71.44). Friendly and conveniently located, close to Place d'Armes and the cathedral. You may want to take your own sheets, as the ones provided here are of disposable paper, but comfortable enough. Internet access available.

Metx Plage, 1 allée de Metz-Plage, Île Chambière (☎03.87.30.44.02, fax 03.87.33.19.80). Clean, friendly youth hostel on the island by the bridge at the further end of rue Belle-Isle which crosses the end of rue du Pont-St-Marcel. Bus #3 or #11 from the gare SNCF.

The city

Metz in effect is two towns: the original French quarters gathered round the cathedral and the **Ville allemande**, undertaken as part of a once-and-for-all process of Germanification after the Prussian occupation in 1871. The latter, although unmistakably Teutonic in style, has considerable elegance and grandeur. The **gare SNCF** sets the tone, a vast and splendid granite structure of 1870 in Rhenish Romanesque, which looks like a bizarre cross between a Scottish laird's hunting lodge and a dungeon. Its gigantic dimensions reflect the Germans' long-term strategic intention to use it as the fulcrum of their military transport system in subsequent wars of conquest against the French. It is matched by the **post office** opposite as well as by some imposing bourgeois apartment buildings in the surrounding streets. The whole quarter was meant to serve as a model of superior town planning in contrast to the squalid Latin hugger-mugger of the old French neighbourhoods, which begin five minutes' walk to the north in place de la République.

The *place* is a main parking area, bounded to one side by shops and cafés, with army barracks to the south and the formal gardens of the **Esplanade**, overlooking the Moselle, to the west. To the right, as you look down the esplanade, is the handsome classical **Palais de Justice** in yellow stone. To the left, a gravel drive leads past the old arsenal, now converted into a prestigious concert hall by the postmodernist architect Riccardo Bofill. It continues to the **church of St-Pièrre-aux-Nonnains**, not much to look at but claiming to be one of the oldest churches in France, with elements from the fourth century – with, nearby, the octagonal thirteenth-century **Chapelle des Templiers**.

From the north side of place de la République, **rue des Clercs** cuts through the attractive, bustling and largely pedestrianized heart of the old city, where most of the shops are located. Past the **place St-Jacques**, with its numerous outdoor cafés, you come to the eighteenth-century **place d'Armes**, where the lofty Gothic **cathedral of St-Étienne** towers above the pedimented and colonnaded classical facade of the **Hôtel de Ville**. It boasts the tallest nave in France after Beauvais and Amiens cathedrals, but its best feature is without doubt the stained glass, both medieval and modern, including windows by Chagall in the north transept and ambulatory.

From here a short walk up rue des Jardins brings you to the city's best museum, the **Musée d'Art et d'Histoire**, 2 rue du Haut-Poirier (daily except Tues 10am–noon & 2–5/6pm; 20F), a treasure-house of Gallo-Roman sculpture, but equally strong on mock-ups of vernacular architecture from the medieval and Renaissance periods. The art section is less impressive, although it includes works by Corot and Delacroix. When the museum was extended in the 1930s, the remains of Roman baths were discovered which are now one of the most interesting things about the museum.

For the city's most compelling townscape, as well as the most dramatic view of the cathedral, you have only to go down to the river bank and cross to the tiny **Île de la Comédie**, dominated by its classical eighteenth-century square and theatre (the oldest in France) and a rather striking Protestant church erected under the German occupation. An older and equally beautiful square is the **place St-Louis** with its Gothic arcades some ten minutes' walk to the east of the cathedral along the curiously named rue En-Fournirue. On the way, wander up into the Italianate streets climbing the **hill of Ste-Croix** to your left, the legacy of the Lombard bankers who came to run the city's finances in the thirteenth century.

The **Porte des Allemands**, at the end of rue des Allemands is definitely worth a look: a massive, fortified double gate that once barred the eastern entrances to the medieval city.

After a long day, you'll have no trouble finding a nice café or bar to relax in. **Rue des Jardins** has some interesting shops - clothes, records and antiques/junk; and at night, the cathedral and other significant buildings are lit up making a pleasant late stroll.

Eating and drinking

Eating is easy in Metz, with plenty of **cafés** on place St-Jacques that are popular with locals and tourists. For night-time **drinking**, there are plenty of bars, clubs and music venues.

Restaurants

Café de l'Abreuvoir, 8 rue de l'Abreuvoir, near place St-Louis. Cosy, noisy and fashionable, with a very French atmosphere and simple, good wine-bar fare (*andouillette* and *quiche Lorraine* at around 50F per *plat*). Till midnight.

Octobre Rouge, Rue de Palais, between En Nexirue and rue Blondel. (☎87.36.44.17) Russian/French pizza restaurant, with an unusual, interesting and reasonably priced menu from 40F. Shiny metallic decor. Open noon-2.30pm, 7-11pm. Closed Sun lunch.

Restaurant du Pont-St-Marcel, 1 rue du Pont-St-Marcel, Île Chambière (☎03.87.30.12.29). A seventeenth-century establishment on the island, distinctive for its excellent regional cuisine and staff dressed in regional costume. Menus at 98F and 165F, including eel and suckling pig, and wines from the French Moselle. Closed Sun evening & Mon.

Le Relais des Tanneurs, 2bis rue des Tanneurs, off the end of rue En-Fournirue (☎03.87.75.49.09). Unpretentious, with traditional French cooking. Lots of specialities, including mussels, scallops and *ris de veau*; menus from 65–160F, *carte* around 120F, *plats du jour* 40–60F. Closed Sun & Aug 1–15.

à la Ville de Lyon, 7 rue Piques (☎03.87.36.07.01). Just below the cathedral, this specializes in the best traditional cooking. Atmosphere is quite formal (you'll wish you weren't wearing jeans). From 200F. Closed Sun evening, all day Mon & Aug.

Cafés and bars

Comédie Café, Quai Vautris, just across the Pont-Des-Roches from the theatre. Stylish and cosy bar/café. Open noon-2pm and 5pm-2am.

Irish Pub, 3 place de Chambre. Crowded and smoky. Till 1am.

Café Jehanne d'Arc, place Jeanne-d'Arc. Fifteen-minute walk northeast of place d'Armes, with medieval beams and frescoes, and occasional music. Free jazz concerts in the square, every Thurs evening in summer. Till 2 or 3am.

Café Mathis, 72 rue En-Fournirue. A minute old-time place spilling over into the garden of the former chapel of St-Genest in summertime, opposite a house where Rabelais once lived. Closed Sun.

L'Oscar, 1 rue Paul-Bezançon. Live music on Thurs. Till 2.30am.

Les Trinitaires, 10–12 rue des Trinitaires, north of place Ste-Croix, opposite *Café Jehanne d'Arc*. For serious jazz, rock, folk and chansons fans who like the extra enhancement of Gothic cellars, this is the place to go. It's hosted such eminent musicians as Dexter Gordon, Max Roach and Archie Shepp. Live music at 9pm. Closed Sun & Mon.

Le Tunnel, 27 place du Quarteau at the south end of place St-Louis. Loud rock music with your drink. Till 2.30/3.30am weekends.

The battlefields of 1870

Just north of Metz, beyond the Moselle, the land rises to a bleak windswept plateau across which the conquering might of German armies has rolled three times in the last hundred years or so. Stone memorials stand among the fields marking the site of individual, particularly German, regiments' actions.

The N3 and the D903, christened the Voie de la Liberté on the milestones, cross the southern half of the **August 1870 battlefield**, passing the farms of Malmaison and Moscou, whose buildings, disposed in easily fortified squares, became strongpoints of defence in the battles. Moscou was named by one of his veterans, in oddly nostalgic memory of Napoléon I's disastrous Russian campaign.

To the north among the now-dying mining communities around **ST-PRIVAT**, you can see a plethora of **memorials** to the Prussian Guards' regiments. If you want to arrive in Verdun in appropriately sombre mood, then there is no better approach than this.

Verdun and the battlefield

At Verdun even the pretence of rationality failed. The slaughter was so hideous that even a trench system could not survive . . . In the town, tourists inspect the memorials. One monument shows French soldiers forming a human wall of comradeship against the enemy. In another, France is personified as a medieval knight; resting on a sword, he dominates a steep flight of steps built into the old ramparts. There is another view of reality. Near the railway station, Rodin's statue shows a winged Victory as neither calm nor triumphant, but demented by rage and horror. Her legs are tangled in a dead soldier and she shrieks for survival.

Donald Horne, *The Great Museum*

The small country town of **VERDUN** lies in a bend of the River Meuse, 68km west of Metz. Of no great interest in itself, what makes it remarkable is its association with the ghastly battle that took place on the bleak uplands to the north between 1916 and 1918.

Long a frontier town, in the aftermath of German victory in the 1870–71 war Verdun and its environs became the most heavily fortified military region in France, the linchpin of its northeastern defences. For this reason, and in order to break the stalemate of trench warfare, the German General Erich von Falkenhayn chose it as the target for an offensive that, in 1916, was the most devastating ever launched in the annals of war. His intention was "to bleed the French army to death and strike a devastating blow at the morale of the French people". He advanced to within 5km of the town, but never succeeded in taking it. Gradually the French clawed back the lost ground, but final victory came only in the last months of the war in 1918 and then only with the aid of US troops under the command of General Pershing.

The best part of a million men died in the battle, both French and German, to say nothing of the numbers scarred for life by their experiences. But it was particularly devastating for the French: the battle was fought on their native soil against the enemy who had humiliated them so badly in 1870, and it decimated the country's young male population. Most of the names inscribed on the thousands of sad memorials that stand in every village, hamlet and town of France belong to men who died at Verdun. It was also the battle that made the reputation of Philippe Pétain, the general who organized the defence of Verdun. Without it, it is arguable whether he would have become head of the collaborationist Vichy régime in 1940.

The town

Given the pounding it received in World War I and the bomb damage of World War II, Verdun is not as grim as you might expect. The liveliest part lies between the river and the steep little hill dominated by the **cathedral of Notre-Dame**, along rues St-Paul and Mazel. The **Rodin memorial** stands beside a handsome eighteenth-century gateway at the northern end of rue St-Paul, where it joins avenue Garibaldi. Nearby, and as striking as the Rodin memorial, is the simple engraving listing all the years between 450 and 1916 that Verdun has been involved in bloody conflict. Another fine gate, the fourteenth-century **Porte Chaussée** guards the river-crossing in the middle of town. Beyond it, further along rue Mazel, a flight of steps climbs up to the **Monument de la Victoire**, where a helmeted warrior leans on his sword in commemoration of the 1916 battle, while in the crypt below a roll is kept of all the soldiers, French and American, who took part. At the end of the street, a crooked lane and steps lead to the cathedral, whose outward characteristics are Gothic. Ironically, its earlier Romanesque origins were only uncovered by shell damage in 1916. The crypt was subsequently dug out, revealing some of the original carved capitals; the new replacements show scenes from the World War I fighting. The rather beautiful **Bishop's Palace** behind it has been converted into a Centre Mondial de la Paix, hosting exhibitions and conferences.

Rue du Rû, the continuation of rue Mazel, takes you to the underground galleries of the **Citadelle** (daily: April 4–Dec 9.30am–noon & 2–5.30pm; July & Aug 9.30am–8pm; 17F), used as shelter and hospital for thousands of soldiers during the battle. The Unknown Soldier, whose remains now lie under the Arc de Triomphe in Paris, was chosen from among the dead who lie here.

To discover Verdun's ancient and religious history, visit the **Musée de la Princerie** on rue de la Belle Vierge (9.30am–noon, 2–6pm; closed Tues and 31 Oct – 1 April).

Practicalities

The **tourist office** (May–Sept 9 Mon–Sat 9am–7pm, Sun 9am–5pm; Oct–April Mon–Sat 9am–noon & 2–5pm, Sun 10am–1pm; ☎03.29.86.14.18, fax 03.29.84.22.42) lies just across the River Meuse from the Porte Chaussée opposite the end of the bridge. From May 1 to September 15, staff at the tourist office run daily minibus four-hour **tours of the battlefield** (in English, French or German: May to mid-Sept 2pm; 145F) – not exactly cheap, but the guides are interesting and the experience is not one that you're likely to repeat. The **gare SNCF** and the **bus station** are both on avenue Garibaldi.

As for **accommodation**, there is much more to choose from in Metz or Nancy. However, if you do need to spend the night in Verdun, the most attractive place to stay is the very friendly *Hôtel St-Paul*, 12 place St-Paul (☎/fax 03.29.86.02.16; ①; closed Dec 7–Jan 7), close to the Rodin memorial. Decent and inexpensive alternatives are *Hôtel Montaulbain*, 4 rue de la Vieille-Prison (☎03.29.86.00.47; ①), and the youth hostel, located between the cathedral and **Centre Mondial de la Paix,** with a fantastic view over the town and its surroundings; good-value accommodation; some rooms with TV and bath.

You shouldn't have trouble finding somewhere to **eat**; there are plenty of brasseries and crêperies along the river. The *Hôtel St-Paul* (see above) has a good traditional restaurant with menus from 90F, and *The Cotton Club*, housed in an old cinema on the waterfront, serves light meals; coffee anytime (with magazines to read during the afternoon) and drinks until 3am. It also has bands and theme nights. Open 11am–3am. For a gourmet take-out, try the delicatessen Charcuterie Bolzan in rue Chaussée.

The battlefield

The **Battle of Verdun** opened on the morning of February 21, 1916, with a German artillery barrage that lasted ten hours and expended two million shells. It concentrated on the forts of Vaux and Douaumont, which the French had built after the 1870 Franco-Prussian War. By the time the main battle ended ten months later, nine villages had been pounded to nothing. Not even their sites are detectable in aerial photos of the time. The heavy artillery shells ploughed the ground to a depth of 8m and, although much of it is now reforested, there are parts even today that steadfastly refuse anchorage to any but the coarsest vegetation.

The most visited part of the battlefield extends along the hills north of Verdun, but the fighting also spread well to the west of the Meuse, to the hills of Mort-Homme and Hill 304, to Vauquois and the Argonne, and south along the Meuse to St-Mihiel, where the Germans held an important salient until dislodged by US forces in 1918.

The only really effective way to explore the area is by car. The main sights are reached via the D913 or by a minor road, the D112, that leaves the main N3 to Metz opposite the Cimetière du Faubourg-Pavé on the outskirts of Verdun and is soon

THE MAGINOT LINE

Like the Séré de Rivières forts constructed along the line of the rivers Meuse and Moselle after the 1870–71 war (such as Génicourt, Paroches and Troyon on the Meuse – not open to the public), the **Maginot Line** was designed to keep the Germans out. Constructed between 1930 and 1940, it was the brainchild of the French Minister of War (1929–31), André Maginot. Spanning the entire length of the French–German border, it comprised a complete system of defence in depth. There were advance posts equipped with anti-tank weapons and machine guns. There were fortified police stations close to the frontier. But the main line consisted of a continuous chain of underground strongpoints linked by anti-tank obstacles and equipped with state-of-the-art machinery. It was of course hugely expensive and, when put to the test in 1940, proved to be worse than useless: the Germans simply violated Belgian neutrality and drove round the other end of the Line.

One of the largest forts, the **Fort de Fermont**, situated about 50km north of Verdun near the small town of Longuyon, is open to the public (☎03.82.39.35.35; May–Aug daily 1.30–5pm; April–Sept weekends only 2pm & 3.30pm; but times are irregular so check in advance; 30F). Armed with nine fire points, it was served by 6km of underground tunnels and a garrison of 600. The entrance is hidden in woodland. Nothing shows above ground but the scarcely noticeable cupolas of the gun turrets. Below, the tunnels are equipped with power plants, electric trains, monorails, elevators and all the other technological paraphernalia necessary to support such a lunatic enterprise. The place has the feel of a nuclear bunker.

Getting there without your own transport is not easy. There are trains to Longuyon from Metz and Verdun (change at Conflans), but you'll have to hitch or walk the last 5km to the fort. Alternatively, there are sections of the Maginot Line in Alsace that are closer to transport links. The **Four à Chaux** fortress dating from 1930 and 1935 at Lembach has been restored, and now houses a museum of World War II (three guided tours per day (phone for details, ☎03.88.94.48.62).

enclosed by appropriately gloomy conifer plantations. On the right you pass a **monument** to André Maginot, who was himself wounded in the battle and under whose later stewardship at the Ministry of War the famous Maginot Line (see box below) was built. Shortly afterwards a sign points out a forest ride to the **Fort de Souville**, the furthest point of the German advance in 1916.

The site is not on the main tourist beat and it is a very moving, if rather frightening twenty-minute walk over ground absolutely shattered by artillery fire, with pools of black water standing in the now grassy shell-holes, as if the players in some malevolent game had been abruptly and mysteriously removed. The fort itself lies half-hidden among the scrub, the armoured gun turrets still lowering in their pits, the tunnels to their control rooms dank and dangerous with collapse. A little way beyond the fort, where the D112 meets the D913, a stone lion marks the precise spot at which the German advance was checked. To the left the road continues to Fleury and Douaumont.

Fleury and the Fort de Vaux

The horrifying story of the battle is graphically documented in the **Musée-Memorial de Fleury** (daily mid-March to Sept 9am–6pm; Sept to mid-March 9am–noon & 2–5pm; closed Dec 19–Jan 22; 20F), which is included in the tourist office's guided tour. Contemporary newsreels and photos present the stark truth; and in the well of the museum, a section of the shell-torn terrain that was once the village of Fleury has been reconstructed as the battle left it.

Also included in the tour is the **Fort de Vaux**, 4km east of Fleury (daily 9am–6.30pm; 20F), where, after six days' hand-to-hand combat in the confined, gas-filled tunnels, the

French garrison, reduced to drinking their own urine, were left with no alternative but surrender. On the exterior wall of the fort a plaque commemorates the last messenger pigeon sent to the command post in Verdun vainly asking for reinforcements. Having safely delivered its message, the pigeon expired as a result of flying through the gas-filled air above the battlefield. It was posthumously awarded the *Légion d'Honneur*.

Douaumont

The principal memorial to the carnage stands in the middle of the battlefield a short distance along the D913 beyond Fleury. It is the **Ossuaire de Douaumont** (daily: April–Sept 9am–5.30pm; March, Oct & Nov 9am–noon & 2–5pm), a vast and surreal structure with the stark simplicity of a Romanesque crypt or a Carolingian sarcophagus, from which rises a central tower shaped like a projectile aimed at the heavens. Its vaults contain the bones of thousands upon thousands of unidentified soldiers, French and German, some of them visible through windows set in the base of the building. When the battle ended in 1918, the ground was covered in fragments of corpses; 120,000 French bodies were identified, just a third of the total killed.

Across the road, a cemetery contains the graves of 15,000 men who died more or less whole: Christians commemorated by rows of identical crosses, Muslims of the French colonial regiments by gravestones aligned in the direction of Mecca. Nearby, a wall commemorates the Jewish dead, beneath a treeless ridge-top on whose tortured, pitted ground around the remains of the Fort de Thiaumont some of them must have died.

The **Fort de Douaumont** (mid-March to Sept daily 9.30am–6pm; Oct to mid-March Tues–Sun 10am–noon & 2–4/6pm; closed Jan; 20F) is 900m further on. Completed in 1912 and commanding the highest point of land, it was the strongest of the 38 forts built to defend Verdun. But, in one of those inexplicable aberrations of military top brass, the armament of these forts was greatly reduced in 1915. When the Germans attacked in 1916, twenty men were enough to overrun the garrison of 57 French territorials. The fort is on three levels, two of them underground. Its claustrophobic, dungeon-like galleries are hung with stalactites. The Germans, who held it for eight months, had 3000 men housed in its cramped quarters with no toilets, continuously under siege, its ventilation ducts blocked for protection against gas, infested with fleas and lice and plagued by rats that attacked the sleeping and the dead indiscriminately. In one night, when their ammunition exploded, 1300 men died in the blast. When the French retook the fort, it was with Moroccan troops in the vanguard. General Mangin, revered by officialdom as the heroic victor of the battle, was known to his troops as "the butcher" for his practice of shoving colonial troops into the front line as cannon fodder.

Last stop on the guided tour is the so-called **Tranchée des Baïonnettes** (Trench of the Bayonets), where, legend has it, two entire infantry platoons are thought to have been buried alive in an upright position with fixed bayonets during a German bombardment on June 11, 1916. A concrete memorial has been built around the area. Though not particularly interesting to look at, it still makes for a very moving experience. Sadly, the bayonets have been stolen.

Mort-Homme, Vauquois and the Argonne

West of the Meuse there are a number of equally evocative, though much less visited, battle sites. The **hill of Mort-Homme**, above the farming village of **Chattancourt**, was furiously contested in 1916 as the Germans sought to outflank the main French positions above Verdun. The access road comes to an end at the memorial on top of the hill, where the ground is still a chaos of shell-holes. On the way up you get a chillingly clear picture of how exposed these low hills were before the conifer plantations.

A dozen kilometres further west this exposed country gives way to the friendlier contours of the **Argonne**. Just off the D38, above the prettily rustic hamlet of **VAUQUOIS**,

ST-MIHIEL AND THE VOIE SACRÉE

In an attempt to cut Verdun off as early as 1914, the Germans captured the town of **St-Mihiel** on the River Meuse to the south of it, which gave them control of the main supply route into Verdun. The only route left open to the French – and that far from safe – was the N35, winding north from Bar-le-Duc over the open hills and wheatfields. In memory of all those who kept the supplies going, the road is called **La Voie Sacrée** (The Sacred Way) and marked with milestones capped with the helmet of the *poilu* (the slang term for the French infantryman).

Just behind the town of St-Mihiel to the east, on the Butte de Montsec, is a memorial to the Americans who died here in 1918 and a US cemetery at **Thiancourt** on the main road.

is the steep wooded hill known as the **Butte de Vauquois**. Steps lead to the top, where an astonishing sight awaits you. The whole of the hilltop has been blown away by mine explosions, both French and German. The largest, a German sixty-tonner, killed over a hundred French soldiers on May 14, 1916. Of the village of Vauquois, which once stood here, not a trace survives. Extensive networks of trenches and rusting wire entanglements are visible in the woods round about. Below the hill lies the village of **VARENNES-EN-ARGONNE**, where Louis XVI and the royal family were recognized and arrested on the night of June 21, 1791, as they tried to escape from Revolutionary France. A plaque marks the spot opposite the Hôtel de Ville and the post office. Just uphill is a memorial to American soldiers from Pennsylvania, and the entire area is riddled with tunnels and bunkers from World War I. One that was known as the **Abri du Kronprinz**, off the D38 4km from Varennes, was used by the German Crown Prince during the battle for Verdun.

Nancy and around

NANCY lies on the banks of the River Meurthe. It was spared the Prussian occupation that afflicted the rest of the region from 1870 to 1918, and its centre, largely unaffected by the undistinguished modern sprawl that blights the valley sides, remains a model of eighteenth-century classicism. For this, it has the last of the independent dukes of Lorraine to thank, the dethroned King of Poland and father-in-law of Louis XV, Stanislas Leszczynski. During the twenty-odd years of his office in the mid-eighteenth century, he ordered some of the most successful urban renewal of the period in all France.

Arrival, information and accommodation

The part of Nancy that you are likely to want to see extends no more than a ten- to fifteen-minute walk either side of **rue Stanislas**, the main axis and shopping street connecting the **gare SNCF** (☎03.83.56.50.50) and the principal **place Stanislas**, itself a leisurely twenty minutes away on foot. The **tourist office**, on the south side of place Stanislas in the Hôtel de Ville (Mon–Sat 9am–7pm, Sun & hols 10am–noon & 2–5pm; Oct–May 10am–1pm only; ☎03.83.35.22.41, fax 03.83.37.63.07), is well-stocked with information about both city and region, and organises *le petit train touristique,* a frequent 45-minute guided tour of the town (July–Aug day and night; 35F). The **gare routière** is just five minutes' walk behind the Hôtel de Ville on the south side of the square, close to the cathedral.

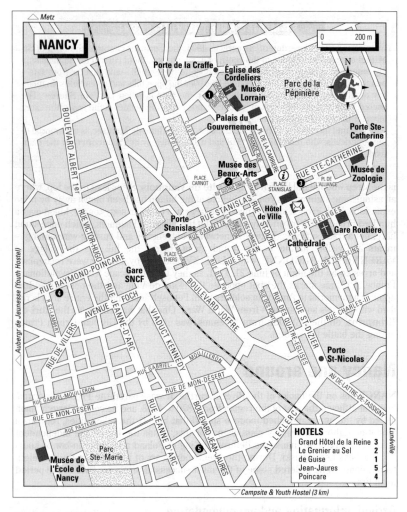

HOTELS

Grand Hôtel de la Reine **3**
Le Grenier au Sel **2**
de Guise **1**
Jean-Jaures **5**
Poincare **4**

▽ *Campsite & Youth Hostel (3 km)*

Accommodation

Reasonable **accommodation** is not hard to find in Nancy. There are plenty of hotels visible from the station, and signs directing you to most of the others. All are within ten to fifteen minutes' walk of the station; the nicest are listed below.

HOTELS

Le Grenier à Sel, 28 rue Gustave Simon (☎03.83.31.98, fax 03.83.35.32). New owners have completely renovated this beautiful 1714 building. Seven rooms all different in appearance. Also a restaurant. Excellent value. ②.

de Guise, rue de Guise just off Grande-Rue (☎03.83.32.24.68, fax 03.83.35.75.63). In the old part of Nancy, and former residence of the countess of Bressy. Friendly and atmospheric. Closed Aug 9–24 & Dec 20–Jan 2). ①.

Jean-Jaurès, south of the station at 14 bd Jean-Jaurès (☎03.83.27.74.14, fax 03.83.90.20.94). Slightly weary and worn, but friendly and in a pretty location. ①.

Poincaré, 81 rue Raymond-Poincaré, turn left out of the station (☎03.83.40.25.99, fax 03.83.27.22.43). Friendly and clean, with a special bargain at weekends: if you stay Friday and Saturday night, you get Sunday night thrown in free. ①.

Grand Hôtel de la Reine, 2 place Stanislas (☎03.83.35..03.01, fax 03.83.32.86.04). The grandest hotel in town, for location and luxury. ⑦.

YOUTH HOSTEL AND CAMPSITE

Château de Rémicourt, 149 rue de Vandoevre (☎03.83.27.73.67, fax 03.83.41.41.35). Spacious and pretty **youth hostel**, but a fair distance from the centre in the suburb of Villers-lès-Nancy to the southwest off the N74 Dijon road/av Général-Leclerc, near the Rond-Point du Vélodrome. To get there, take bus #6 on rue des Carmes, direction "Vandœuvre", stop Mangin; walk back to the main road, turn left, then right at the first major intersection. Leaving the École d'Architecture at the edge of a park on your left, take the next left, a small road running uphill beside the park, and a gate on the left leads to the château. Close to the botanical gardens.

Camping de Brabois campsite (April–Oct), is near the youth hostel (follow signs above).

The town

Pride of place must go to the beautiful **place Stanislas**, the middle of which belongs to the solitary statue of its inspirer, the portly Stanislas himself, who was responsible for laying out the square in the 1750s. On the south side stands the imposing **Hôtel de Ville**, its roof-line topped by a balustrade ornamented with florid urns and amorini, while along its walls lozenge-shaped lanterns dangle from the beaks of gilded cocks; similar motifs adorn the other buildings bordering the square. Its entrances are closed by magnificent wrought-iron gates, with the best work of all in the railings of the north-eastern and northwestern corners, which frame gloriously extravagant fountains dominated by lead statues of Neptune and Amphitrite.

In the corner where rue Stanislas joins the square, the **Musée des Beaux-Arts** (currently under renovation but still open daily except Mon am & Tues 10.30am–6pm; 30F joint ticket with **Musée de l'École de Nancy** (see below);Wed free for students) boasts work by Dufy and Matisse, but nothing outstanding. Both buildings are due to be completed early in 1999. Time is better spent at the **Aquarium Tropical Musée de Zoologie**, 34 rue Ste-Cathérine (daily 10am–noon & 2–6pm; 30F, students 20F). Upstairs is a colossal jumble of stuffed animals and birds, woefully displayed and labelled, while downstairs is a startling aquarium of exotic fish whose colours surpass even the daring of Matisse.

On its north side, place Stanislas opens into the long, tree-lined **place de la Carrière**, a fine eighteenth-century transformation of what was originally a jousting ground. Its further end is closed by the classical colonnades of the **Palais du Gouvernement**, former residence of the governor of Lorraine. Behind it, in the old fifteenth-century Palais Ducal and entered through a handsome doorway surmounted by an equestrian statue of one of the dukes is the **Musée Lorrain**, 64 Grande-Rue (daily except Tues: May–Sept 10am–6pm; Oct–April 10am–noon & 2–5pm; closed public hols; 15F). Dedicated to the history and traditions of Lorraine it contains, among other treasures, a room full of superb etchings by the Nancy-born seventeenth-century artist, Jacques Callot, whose concern with social issues, evident in series such as *The Miseries of War* and *Les Gueux,* presaged much nineteenth- and twentieth-century art. The ticket is also valid for the next-door **Musée Régional des Arts et Traditions Populaires** (same hours as Musée Lorrain; 15F) housed in the Église des Cordeliers et Chapelle

ART NOUVEAU NANCY

A traditional handicraft and metal-working town, at the turn of this century Nancy became a centre of **Art Nouveau** to rival Paris, the most illustrious exponent of the "School of Nancy" being the manufacturer of glass and ceramics, Émile Gallé. The town's moment of glory was short-lived, however, and all that now remains are a handful of buildings and, best of all, the Musée de l'École de Nancy, housed in a turn-of-the-century villa. For a post-museum coffee in the same kind of atmosphere, try the Art Nouveau café-restaurant of the former hotel *L'Excelsior*, opposite the train station, built in 1910 and preserved virtually intact to this day. Keep your eyes open as you walk around Nancy as there are many other expressions of small Art Nouveau.

Ducale,where rural life in the region in days gone by is illustrated. On the other side of the Palais du Gouvernement, you can play crazy golf, admire the deer or just collapse with exhaustion on the green grass of the **Parc de la Pépinière**, a sort of cross between a formal French garden and an English park. There is also a free zoo. At the end of Grande-Rue the medieval city gate, **Porte de la Craffe**, is now an annexe of the museum (daily except Tues: mid-June to mid-Sept 10am–noon & 2–6pm; 5F), containing medieval sculpture.

A half-hour walk southwest of the train station, the **Musée de l'École de Nancy**, 36 rue Sergent-Blandan (daily except Tues 10am–noon & 2–5/6pm; 15F), is housed in a 1909 villa built for the Corbin family, founders of the Magasins Réunis chain of department stores. Even if you are not into Art Nouveau, this collection is exciting. Although not all of it belonged to the Corbins, the museum is arranged as if it were a private house. The furniture is outstanding – all swirling curvilinear forms, whether the object is mantelpiece or sofa, buffet or piano – and the standards of workmanship are superlative, with a fair sprinkling of Gallé's work on display, too. Another quirky sight is the **Musée du Téléphone,** 11 rue Maurice Barres, just off Place Stanislas (Wed–Fri 10am–noon & 2–6pm; 15F, 10F students).

Eating and drinking

There are plenty of places to **eat** and **drink** in Nancy. Good streets for restaurants include Grande-Rue, rue Maréchaux and rue des Ponts. The place Stanislas has several cafés, making good vantage points to watch Nancy go by.

Restaurants

L'Aiglon, 5 rue Stanislas, near the square (☎03.83.32.21.43). An interesting and well-prepared meal here would cost you 110–120F, including wine and coffee. For more sophisticated traditional and local cuisine, with dishes like *choucroute, tourte lorraine, baeckeoffe, poule-au-pot,* you can't go wrong. Closed Tues.

Chez Bagot, 45 Grande-Rue (☎03.83.37.42.43). Set menus from 75F. Menu includes Breton fish specialities. Closed Sun evenings and Mondays.

L'Excelsior, 50 rue Henri-Poincaré, cnr rue Mazagran in front of the train station (☎03.83.35.24.57). A turn-of-the-century Art Nouveau brasserie, frequented by everyone who aspires to being anyone in Nancy. Superb interior, and good food. Menus at 97F and 140F. It's also the best daytime stop for coffee. Till 12.30am.

Le Faitout, 7 rue Gustave-Simon (☎03.83.35.36.52) Delicious, organic food which is also beautifully presented. Don't let the decor put you off. There is a vegetarian set meal for 85F, local specialities also available. Open 11.45am-2.15pm & 7.30-10.30pm..

Pissenlits, 25 rue des Ponts (☎03.83.37.43.97). Real old-fashioned bistrot fare at 45–75F a *plat*, in an attractive atmosphere. Closed Sun & Mon lunchtime. Poor man's version of *La Table de Mengin*. Same kitchen, lower prices.

La Table de Mengin, 27 rue des Ponts (☎03.83.35.17.25). One of the best restaurants in the region. 160F menu is a bargain; à la carte 400F and more. Closed Sun & Mon.

Le Wagon, 75 rue des Chaligny (☎03.83.32.32.16). Original dining car from 1927, the Orient Express permanently ready to depart from Nancy. Menus 85-250F.

Cafés and bars

Place Stanislas is perfect for a coffee, day or night. Start your evening here, and continue along the Grande-Rue and its offshoots, where you will certainly find a late night bar (Mexican, English, French or just plain groovy!)

Bar des Carmes, corner rue du Lycée and rue des Carmes. Straight stand-up shot at a tiny and delightful old-fashioned bar.

El'Lips, 3 Rue Lafayette. Techno night spot. Loud music, loud decor. Open 6pm–2am; weekends until 5am.

Le Glacier, place Stanislas. A popular place to watch the world go by till 4am; closed Sun.

Grand Café du Commerce, place Stanislas, corner of rue Stanislas. Elegant place to be seen. Till 2am.

Grand Café Foy, place Stanislas, next door to the *Café du Commerce* and equally grand.

Planète Café, rue St Michel, just off Grande-Rue. Hip little café-bar with club-like interior and outdoor tables. Open 5pm–2am.

Queens Pub, place Stanislas next to the Musée. English theme pub/café with the usual French café fare.

Théâtre le Vertgo, 29 rue de la Visitation (☎03.83.36.51.40). Postmodern gargoyles contribute to the interesting theatrical atmosphere. Bands and other performances regularly. Mon–Sat until 2am; 5am if there's a show.

Lunéville

LUNÉVILLE, a twenty-minute train ride east of Nancy or a half-hour drive along the banks of the River Meurthe. If you are travelling by train from Nancy, plan ahead because there are not many trains outside peak hours. Everything in this town is closed from noon–2pm, except the cafés.

Lunéville was renowned for the **faïence** (ceramic tile) works set up by Stanislas. There is now a small collection of it – not worth a detour unless you're a specialist – in a museum in the immense eighteenth-century **château** (daily except Tues 10am–noon & 2–5/6pm; 9F), dubbed *Le Petit Versailles,* which dominates the town. The rest of the museum is occupied by cavalry uniforms and weaponry, Lunéville being a garrison town; the formal château gardens, host to an extensive rookery, are good for picnicking.

While you're in town, the only thing worth a visit is M. Chapleur's private motorcycle museum, the **Musée de la Moto et du Vélo** (Tues–Sun 9am–noon & 2–6pm; closed Nov 15–Feb 28; 20F), directly opposite the gates of the château. Monsieur Chapleur started collecting in the 1930s when he was a mechanic at Citroën. The museum has over 200 models of different origins on display, all overhauled and in working order. And they are beauties – works of art in copper, brass, chrome and steel. Some of the bicycles go back to 1865, and the motorbikes date mostly from 1900 to 1940. Several of the older bikes are probably unique; one certainly is – a 1906 René Gillet 4.5hp belt-driven tandem. Many look like flying bombs and must have been incredibly dangerous to ride: bits of Meccano with a couple of hefty cylinders welded on, and capable of 100km/ph in 1900.

Between the gare SNCF and the château run the small-scale cottagey streets of the old town, where the newly restored, splendidly Baroque **church of St-Jacques**, Stanislas' gift to the town, raises its enormous twin towers.

From the **gare SNCF**, the rue Carnot north will bring you to the back of the old theatre which adjoins the château, where the **tourist office** is housed (daily 9am–noon & 2–6pm; ☎03.83.74.06.55, fax 03.83.73.57.95): following the signs, you'll find it right at the front of the château on the Place de la 2eme Division du Cavalerie. Should you wish to **stay**, *Hôtel des Pages*, 5 quai des Petits-Bosquets (☎03. 83.73.46.63; ③) is close to the château and very peaceful. For something very special, the place to go is the *Château d'Adoménil*, a couple of kilometres out of town across the River Meurthe (☎03.83.74.04.81, fax 03.83.74.21.78; ⑤; closed Sun out of season). Its seven beautifully furnished and luxuriously equipped rooms overlook water, orchards and a home farm, and its **restaurant** belongs in the top category (closed Sun evening out of season, Tues lunchtime, Mon & Feb; cheapest menu 210F, *carte* upwards of 400F). **Camping** is at 69 Quai des Beitis Bosquets (☎03.83.73.37.58), near the château. As for eating, perhaps try something a bit different while you're here: *New Vien Tong*, 29 rue de Lorrain (☎03.83.73.33.96) has freshly prepared Chinese, Vietnamese and Thai food; meals from 40F. The decor is very French Indo-China and the atmosphere is friendly and calm.

ALSACE

There's no denying **Alsace**'s attractiveness, with its old stone and half-timbered towns set amid the thickly wooded hills of the Vosges, but it's a quaintness that has become

THE FOOD AND WINE OF ALSACE

The cuisine of Alsace is quite distinct from that of other regions of France, because of its German origins, albeit tempered by French refinement. The classic dish is the chopped pickled cabbage of **sauerkraut**, or *choucroute*, which includes the use of juniper berries in the pickling stage and is cooked with goose grease or lard and smoked pork, with ham and a variety of sausages added. The qualification *à l'alsacienne* after the name of a dish usually means "with *choucroute*".

Strasbourg **sausages** and boiled **potatoes** are another common ingredient in Alsatian cooking. One of the best culinary incarnations of the spud is the three-meat hotpot, **baeckoffe**, which consists of pork, mutton and beef marinated in wine and cooked between layers of potato for a couple of hours in a baker's oven.

Onions, too, are a favourite dish, either in the form of an onion tart, which is made with a béchamel sauce, or *flammeküche* (*tarte flambée* in French), made with a mixture of onion, cream and pieces of chopped smoked pork breast baked on a base of thin pizza-like pastry. **Noodles** are also a common feature, and don't miss the chance to sample a *matelote* or stew of river fish cooked in Riesling or Vosges trout cooked *au bleu*, briefly boiled in Riesling with a dash of vinegar.

Like the Germans, Alsatians are fond of their **pastries**. The dessert fruit tarts made with cherries or yellow *mirabelle* plums – *tarte alsacienne* – are delicious. Cake-lovers should try *kugelhopf*, a moulded dome-shaped cake with a hollow in the middle, made with raisins and almonds, and *birewecks*, made with dried fruit marinated in Kirsch.

All of these delights can be washed down with the region's **white wines**, renowned for their dry, clean-tasting fruitiness and compatibility with any kind of food. The best-known of them are Riesling, Gewürztraminer, Sylvaner and Tokay, named after the type of grape from which they are made – unlike other wine-growing regions in the country, the taste of Alsatian wines does not vary from locality to locality. There are, incidentally, a few reds – from Ottrott, Marlenheim and Cleebourg – but it is the whites which make the region's reputation. The term *Edelzwicker* on a label means the wine is a high-quality blend.

Alsace also shares the German predilection for **beer** and has long been the heartland of French hop-growing and brewing. Its fruit brandies are honoured too, especially Kirsch which is made from cherries, and *quetsche* and *mirabelle* from different varieties of plum.

a commodity. **Strasbourg**, the Alsatian capital and, along with Brussels, one of the main centres of the European Union, escapes the tweeness of some of the smaller towns of the foothills. **Saverne** and **Wissembourg**, to the north, also avoid the worst of the tourist-brochure image, giving access to some spectacular ruined castles in the **northern Vosges**.

South of Strasbourg, along the **Route du Vin**, there are countless picturesque medieval villages and yet more ruined castles which suffer to varying degrees from the attention of the tour buses. A very different, sobering experience is the concentration camp of **Le Struthof**, hidden away in the Vosges forest. **Colmar** is almost excessively twee, yet still worth a visit for Grünewald's amazing Issenheim altarpiece. By contrast, **Mulhouse** is thoroughly industrial but boasts some unusually good museums devoted to cars, trains, electricity and printed fabrics.

Every town has a **tourist office**, which in smaller places is usually in the mairie or Hotel de Ville (town hall). Special tourist maps cost around 3F, but free maps containing as much information are always available.

Strasbourg

STRASBOURG owes both its name – "the city of the roads" – and its wealth to its position on the west bank of the Rhine, long one of the great natural transport arteries of Europe. Its medieval commercial pre-eminence was damaged by too close involvement in the religious struggles of the sixteenth and seventeenth centuries, but recovered with the city's absorption into France in 1681. Along with the rest of Alsace, it suffered annexation by Germany from 1871 to the end of World War I and again from 1940 to 1944.

Today those animosities have been submerged in the togetherness of the European Union, of which, as the seat of the Council of Europe, the European Court of Human Rights and the European Parliament, it is one of the capitals. Prosperous, beautiful and modern, with an orderliness that is Germanic rather than Latin, Strasbourg is big enough – with a population of over a quarter of a million people – to have a metropolitan air without being overwhelming. It has one of the loveliest cathedrals in France and one of the oldest and most active universities: this is the one city in eastern France that is definitely worth a special detour.

Arrival, information and accommodation

The **gare SNCF** (SNCF information ☎08.36.35.35.35) lies on the west side of the city centre, barely fifteen minutes' walk from the cathedral along rue du Maire-Kuss and rue du 22-Novembre. The main **tourist office** is at 17 place de la Cathédrale (June–Sept Mon–Sat 8.30am–7pm, Sun 9am–6pm; Oct–May Mon–Sat 9am–6pm, Sun 9am–12.30pm & 2–5pm; ☎03.88.52.28.28), with the regional office for the Bas-Rhin nearby at 9 rue du Dôme (same hours, ☎03.88.22.01.02). There is also a tourist office at the train station, in the new shopping complex.

The **airport shuttle** (*navette*), departing every 15 minutes, drops-off at Baggersee, (connection point for the very convenient and futuristic tram); and all stops in central Strasbourg.

Most of the city centre is now pedestrian-only, but several car parks around Strasbourg cater for those who are **driving** into town. At Parking Rotonde, to the north, and at Parking Étoile to the south, a 12F fee gives you unlimited parking and tram tickets for the journey into the town centre; further south, Parking Baggersee is free and has easy access to the tram, which takes you to the town centre in fifteen minutes.

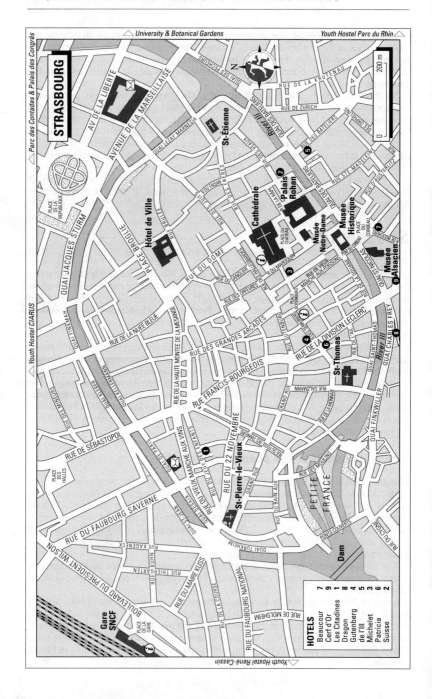

△ University & Botanical Gardens

Youth Hostel Parc du Rhin △

STRASBOURG

△ Parc des Contades & Palais des Congrés

◁ Youth Hostel CIARUS

▽ Youth Hostel René-Cassin

200 m

St-Étienne

Cathédrale

Palais Rohan

Musée Notre-Dame

Musée Historique

Musée Alsacien

Hôtel de Ville

St-Thomas

St-Pierre-le-Vieux

PETITE FRANCE

Dam

Gare SNCF

AV DE LA LIBERTÉ
AVENUE DE LA MARSEILLAISE
QUAI JACQUES STURM
PLACE DE LA RÉPUBLIQUE
QUAI LEZAY MARNESIA
RUE DES PÊCHEURS
RUE DE LA KRUTENAU
RUE DE ZURICH
QUAI DES BATELIERS
QUAI DES PÊCHEURS
RUE DES BATELIERS
QUAI SAINT-NICOLAS
QUAI DES BATELIERS
RUE STE-MADELEINE
RUE D'AUSTERLITZ
PLACE DU CORBEAU
RUE DE BOUXWILLER
QUAI FINKMATT
RUE DE LA NUÉE BLEUE
PLACE BROGLIE
RUE BRÛLÉE
RUE DU DÔME
RUE DES FRÈRES
RUE DU SANGLIER
RUE DU MAROQUIN
PLACE DU CHÂTEAU
RUE DES ORFÈVRES
RUE DES GRANDES ARCADES
RUE DU VIEUX MARCHÉ AUX POISSONS
RUE GUTENBERG
RUE DE LA DIVISION LECLERC
QUAI TELLEMANN
QUAI CHARLES FREY
QUAI SAINT-THOMAS
River Ill
RUE FRANCIS-BOURGEOIS
RUE DE LA HAUTE MONTÉE DE LA MÉSANGE
QUAI FINKWILLER
RUE SALZMANN
GRAND'RUE
RUE DE LA LAMPE
RUE DE LA MÉSANGE
RUE DES MINEURS
QUAI LIBERTÉ
RUE DE SÉBASTOPOL
PLACE DES HALLES
RUE DU 22 NOVEMBRE
RUE DU VIEUX MARCHÉ AUX VINS
RUE DU FAUBOURG SAVERNE
RUE KAGENECK
RUE THIERGARTEN
QUAI TURCKHEIM
RUE DES MOULINS
PONTS COUVERTS
RUE DU BAIN AUX PLANTES
GRAND'RUE
RUE DE LA COURSE
BOULEVARD DU PRÉSIDENT WILSON
RUE DU FAUBOURG NATIONAL
RUE DU MAIRE KUSS
PLACE DE LA GARE
RUE DE MOLSHEIM
RUE DU DÔME

HOTELS	
Beaucour	7
Cerf d'Or	9
Les Citadines	1
Dragon	8
Gutenberg	4
de l'Ill	5
Michelet	3
Patricia	6
Suisse	2

Accommodation

When you are looking for a place to **stay**, bear in mind that once a month the European Parliament is in session for three or four days, bringing its hundreds of MPs and their entourages into town, which puts all the city's facilities under pressure, especially hotel accommodation. The youth hostels, at least, are less affected, though it is said that even they play host to one or two Euro-deputies. The station area has the usual clutch of hotels.

HOTELS

Beaucour, 5 rue des Bouchers (☎03.88.76.72.00, fax 03.88.76.72.60). Very central, just off place du Corbeau, in a handsome old house with its own courtyard. ⑧.

Cerf d'Or, 6 place de l'Hôpital (☎03.88.36.20.05, fax 03.88.36.68.67). Sixteenth-century hotel with its own bar and restaurant (menu from 95F) on the south side of the River Ill. Closed Dec 24–Jan 2. ④.

Les Citadines, 50–54 rue du Jeu des Enfants (☎03.88.75.34.34, fax 03.88.32.47.49) Good possibility in lively part of town. Close to Place Kleber. ⑤-⑥.

Dragon, 2 rue de l'Écarlate and 12 rue de Dragon (☎03.88.35.79.80, fax 03.88.25.78.95). Fully modernized luxury hotel south of the River Ill. Closed Dec 23–27. ⑥.

Gutenberg, 31 rue des Serruriers (☎03.88.32.17.15, fax 03.88.75.76.67). An old house in central location, with period furniture in some rooms. Closed Jan 1–11. ③-⑤.

de l'Ill, 8 rue des Bateliers (☎03.88.36.20.01, fax 03.88.35.30.03). The best bargain in Strasbourg; a quiet, comfortable, family-run place just 50m from the river, in sight of the cathedral. Closed Dec 21–Jan 5. ③.

Michelet, 48 rue du Vieux-Marché-aux-Poissons, off place Gutenberg (☎03.88.32.47.38). An outwardly unprepossessing but perfectly acceptable old hotel. ②-③.

Patricia, 1a rue du Puits (☎03.88.32.14.60, fax 03.88.32.19.08). Great location in the back streets of the old town not far from place Gutenberg. ②-③.

Suisse, 2–4 rue de la Râpe (☎03.88.35.22.11, fax 03.88.25.74.23). A good possibility directly underneath the cathedral's east end. ⑤.

YOUTH HOSTELS AND CAMPSITES

CIARUS, 7 rue Finkmatt (☎03.88.15.27.88/90, fax 03.88.15.27.89). A Protestant hostel near the Palais de Justice, just north of the centre; bus #10 or #20 from the station to place Pierre.

La Montagne-Verte campsite, 2 rue Robert-Forrer (☎03.88.30.25.46). A well-equipped site behind the *René-Cassin* youth hostel. Closed Nov–Feb.

Parc du Rhin, rue des Cavaliers (☎03.88.45.54.20, fax 03.88.45.54.21). HI youth hostel close to the Pont de l'Europe over the Rhine to Germany; bus #2 from Homme de Fer, or #21 near the tourist office, direction "Kehl", stop Parc du Rhin.

René-Cassin, 9 rue de l'Auberge-de-Jeunesse (☎03.88.30.26.46, fax 03.88.30.35.16). HI youth hostel 3km southwest of the city centre. Bus #3, #23 from Homme de Fers, stop Auberge de Jeunesse, and bus #0 from the gare SNCF, stop Nid de Cigognes.

The city

It isn't difficult to find your way around Strasbourg on foot, as the city centre is concentrated on a small island encircled by the **River Ill**. If you want a map, the tourist office has them (3F for the the one with all the museums and sights marked on it; free otherwise), but be warned – hardly any street names are marked. However, it's a nice town to lose yourself in.

Visible throughout the city is the magnificent filigree spire of the pink **cathedral** that dominates not just the city but most of Alsace; it is to the south of this building that you'll find the cream of the museums. To the north of here, **place Kléber** is the heart of the commercial district, and **place Gutenberg** is nominally the main square. About a fifteen-minute walk west on the tip of the island is **Petite France**, where timber-framed houses and gently flowing canals hark back to the city's medieval trades of tanning and dyeing.

Place Gutenberg and the cathedral

Right at the heart of medieval Strasbourg, with its steep-pitched roofs and brightly painted facades, **place Gutenberg** was named after the printer and pioneer of moveable type, whose statue occupies the middle of the square; he lived in the city in the early fifteenth century. On the west side stands the sixteenth-century **Hôtel de Commerce**, where the writer Arthur Young watched the night-time destruction of the magistrates' records during the Revolution. And on the corner of rue du Vieux-Marché-aux-Poissons, the sculptor Jean Arp was born.

From wherever you are in the city centre, the one landmark you can see is the **Cathédrale de Notre-Dame** (daily 7–11.30am & 12.40–7pm; closed during services; free entrance to the cathedral), soaring out of the close huddle of medieval houses at its feet, with a single spire of such delicate, flaky lightness it seems the work of confectioners rather than masons. It's worth slogging up the 332 steps to the spire's **viewing platform** (daily: April–Sept 9am–6.30pm; July & Aug 8.30am–7pm; March & Oct 9am–5.30pm; Nov–Feb 9am–4.30pm; 20F) for the superb view of the old town, and, in the distance, the Vosges to the west and the Black Forest to the east.

The interior, too, is magnificent, the high nave a model of proportion and enhanced by a glorious sequence of stained-glass windows. The finest are those in the south aisle next to the door, depicting the life of Christ and the Creation, but all are beautiful, including, in the apse, the modern glass designed in 1956 by Max Ingrand to commemorate the first European institutions in the city. On the left of the nave, the cathedral's organ perches precariously above one of the arches, like a giant gilded eagle, while further down on the same side is the late fifteenth-century pulpit, a masterpiece of intricacy in stone by the appropriately named Hans Hammer.

In the south transept are the cathedral's two most popular sights. One is the slender triple-tiered central column known as the **Pilier des Anges**, decorated with some of the most graceful and expressive statuary of the thirteenth century. The other is the huge and enormously complicated **astrological clock** built by Schwilgué of Strasbourg in 1842: a favourite with the tour-group operators, whose customers roll up in droves to witness the clock's crowning performance of the day, striking the hour of noon, which it does with unerring accuracy, at 12.30pm – that being 12 o'clock Strasbourg time. Death strikes the chimes; the apostles parade in front of Christ, who occupies the highest storey of the clock; and as each one passes he receives Christ's blessing.

Strasbourg's museums

Most of Strasbourg's **museums** are to be found to the south of the cathedral, between the tree-lined place du Château and the river. Check with the tourist office for museum passses/discounts if you are planning to visit them all.

Right next to the cathedral, place du Château is enclosed to the east and south by the Lycée Fustel and the **Palais Rohan** (Mon & Wed–Sat 10am–noon & 1.30–6pm, Sun 10am–5pm; closed Tues & public hols; 20F), both eighteenth-century buildings, the latter designed for the immensely powerful Rohan family, who, for several generations in a row, cornered the market in cardinals' hats. There are three museums in the Palais Rohan itself (all same times and prices as above): the **Musée des Arts Décoratifs**, **Musée des Beaux-Arts** and **Musée Archéologique**. The rooms of the château are vast, opulent and ostentatious but not especially interesting. Of the three collections, only the Arts Décoratifs stands out – and that's of slightly specialist interest – with its eighteenth-century faïence tiles crafted in the city by Paul Hannong.

THE ALSATIAN LANGUAGE

Travelling through the province, it's easy to mistake the language being spoken in the shops and streets for German. In fact, it is *Elsässisch* , or Alsatian, a High German dialect, known to philologists as Alemannic. To confuse matters further, there are two versions, High and Low Alemannic, as well as an obscure Frankish dialect spoken in the Wissembourg region and a Romance one called *Welche* from the valleys around Orbey. You will hear a different version spoken in almost every town.

Most daily transactions are conducted in French, and *Elsässisch* has still not made it onto the school curriculum. Yet it remains a living language, with a rich medieval literary legacy, and is still spoken by young and old throughout Alsace and even parts of Lorraine. A recent upsurge in nationalist feeling has meant that *Elsässisch* is beginning to reappear on menus and shop signs.

In many ways, it's a miracle that it has survived at all, since both French and German rule have tended to discourage the Alsatian language. During the French Revolution, the language was suppressed in favour of French for nationalistic reasons, only to be ousted by German when the Prussians annexed the region in 1870. On its return to French rule, all things Germanic were disdained, and many Alsatians began to speak French once more . . . until the Nazi occupation brought in laws that made the speaking of French and even the wearing of berets imprisonable offences. To top off the linguistic confusion, a proposal by Strasbourg's Socialist mayor in 1991 that street signs should be bilingual has now been passed, so that signs bearing both *Strasse* and *rue* are now in evidence around the town.

Next door, in the mansion lived in by the cathedral architects, the **Musée de l'Oeuvre Notre-Dame** (Tues–Sat 10am–noon & 1.30–6pm, Sun 10am–5pm; 20F) houses the original sculptures from the cathedral exterior, damaged in the Revolution and replaced today by copies; both sets are worth seeing. And there are other treasures here: glass from the city's original Romanesque cathedral; the eleventh-century Wissembourg Christ, said to be the oldest representation of a human figure in stained glass; and the architect's original parchment drawings for the statuary (not on display at the time of writing), done in fascinating detail down to the different expressions on each figure's face.

The **Musée d'Art Moderne et Contemporain** is due to reopen in November 1998 in rue de Molsheim. It features an impressive permanent collection of works by such artists as Monet, Picasso, Klimt, Ernst, Klee and the Alsatian Dadaist Hans Arp and his wife, the Swiss Surrealist, Sophie Täuber.

The **Musée Historique**, 3 place de la Grande Boucherie by **Place du Marché-aux-Cochons-de-Lait** (Sucking-Pig Market), closed for renovation until 1999, is mainly concerned with the city, though it also has an oddball collection of mechanical toys upstairs. Last, but by no means least, in a typically Alsatian house on the other side of the river on quai St-Nicolas across the Pont du Corbeau, there's the **Musée Alsacien,** 23 quai St-Nicholas (Mon & Wed–Sat 10am–noon & 1.30–6pm, Sun 10am–5pm; 20F), containing painted furniture and other local artefacts.

Other interesting museums are the **Centre Tomi Ungerer,** 4 rue de la Haute-Montée (☎03.88.32.31.54) which houses the private collections and works of this Strasbourg-born artist. Check the opening hours before you visit; currently Thurs 9am–noon, 2–6pm by appointment; and **CEEAC** (Centre Européen d'Actions Artistiques – slightly pretentious name for a rather good gallery), 7 rue de l'Abreuvoir (Wed–Sat 2–6pm, ☎03.88.25.69.70; free), has travelling exhibitions by contemporary foreign artists.

The rest of the old town

On the far side of the Pont du Corbeau, the medieval **Cour du Corbeau** still looks much as it must have done in the fourteenth century. Downstream, the **quai des Bateliers** was part of the old business quarter, and the streets leading off it – rue Ste-Madeleine, rue de la Krutenau and rue de Zurich – are still worth a wander. Two bridges upstream, the Pont St-Thomas leads to the **church of St-Thomas** (April–Nov 10am–noon & 2–6pm; Dec–March 10am–noon & 2–5pm; closed Sun am for services), with a Romanesque facade and Gothic towers. Since 1549 it has been the city's principal Protestant church. Strasbourg was a bastion of the Reformation, and one of its leaders, Martin Bucer, preached in this church. The amazing piece of sculpture behind the altar is Jean-Baptiste Pigalle's **tomb of the Maréchal de Saxe**, a very capable French military commander active against the Duke of Cumberland in the campaigns of the War of Austrian Succession in the middle of the eighteenth century.

From here, it's a short walk upstream to the **Pont St-Martin**, which marks the beginning of the district known as **La Petite France**, where the city's millers, tanners and fishermen used to live. At the far end of a series of canals are the so-called **Ponts Couverts** (they are in fact no longer covered), built as part of the fourteenth-century city fortifications and still punctuated by watchtowers. Just beyond is a **dam** built by Vauban (daily mid-Oct to mid-March 9am–7pm; mid-March to mid-Oct till 8pm; free) to protect the city from waterborne assault. The whole area is extremely picturesque, with winding streets – most notably rue du Bain-aux-Plantes – bordered by sixteenth- and seventeenth-century houses adorned with flowers and elaborately carved woodwork. Predictably, it's a top-of-the-bill tourist hot spot.

The area east of the cathedral is good for a stroll, too, where rue des Frères leads to place St-Étienne. **Place du Marché-Gayot**, off rue des Frères behind the cathedral, is very lively, with a couple of studenty cafés on one side. From the north side of the cathedral, rue du Dôme leads to the eighteenth-century **place Broglie**, with the Hôtel de Ville, the *préfet*'s residence and some imposing eighteenth-century mansions. It was at 4 place Broglie in 1792 that Rouget de l'Isle first sang what later became known as the *Marseillaise* for the mayor of Strasbourg, who had challenged him to compose a rousing song for the troops of the army of the Rhine.

The German quarter and the Palais de l'Europe

Across the river here, **place de la République** is surrounded by vast German neo-Gothic edifices erected during the post-1870 Imperial Prussian occupation, a good example being the main **post office** on avenue de la Liberté. At the centre of the square is a war memorial showing a mother holding two dead sons in her arms, one German and one French, testifying to the split personality of this frontier city whose inhabitants found themselves fighting, not always willingly, in both Allied and German armies during the war. At the other end of avenue de la Liberté, across the confluence of the Ill and Aar, is the city's **university**, where Goethe studied. Adjacent, at the beginning of boulevard de la Victoire, are the splendidly Teutonic municipal baths, the **Grand Établissement Municipal de Bains**, where you can take a sauna or Turkish bath or just swim.

From in front of the university, the wide, straight alleé de la Robertsau, flanked by confident turn-of-the-century bourgeois residences, leads to the **Palais de l'Europe**, home of the Council of Europe and, for the moment, the European Parliament until its new home across the river opens in 1998/99. The buildings are surprisingly disappointing, with the one exception of Richard Rogers' contribution for the European Court of Human Rights, with its curving glass entrance and silver towers rising to a boat-like superstructure overlooking a sweep of canal. To visit the European Parliament you have to book (☎03.88.17.20.07; no charge).

Opposite the Palais, the **Orangerie** is Strasbourg's best bit of greenery, and hosts a variety of exhibitions and free concerts. Here the *cicognes* (storks) that perch on top of most buildings in the town. have their nests. There is also a zoo with small animals such as monkeys, and exotic birds.

Eating, drinking and entertainment

For the classic Strasbourg **eating** experience, you have to go to a **winstub**, usually translated as a "wine bar", a cosy establishment with bare beams, panels and benches, and a noisy, convivial atmosphere. In the classic version there is a special table set aside for the *patron's* buddies and regulars. The food tends towards *choucroute, tarte à l'oignon*, knuckle of pork and horseradish, ham *en croûte*: the Alsatian classics, washed down with local wines. Place du Marché-Gayot behind the cathedral is full of **cafés**, most open until late, and there is a good selection of **restaurants** in rue du Faubourg Saverne.

Restaurants

La Bourse, place de Lattre-de-Tassigny (☎03.88.36.40.53). Quite a sedate brasserie, in agreeable, spacious surroundings across the river in the direction of place de l'Étoile. 50–200F (50F lunchtime menu). Till 11pm. Closed Mon & Wed lunchtime.

Les 3 Brasseurs, 22 rue des Veaux. Wonderful *winstub*, where they brew their own beer: the enormous copper brewing equipment is part of the decor. *Tarte flambée* and beer menus from 79F. Other Alsatian specialities available. Open daily 24 hr.

La Choucrouterie, 20 rue St-Louis, by the church of St-Louis just across Pont St-Thomas (☎03.88.36.52.87). *Choucroute* specialist with menus at 150–220F, *plats* from about 70F. Cabaret acts. Mon–Sat 7pm–1am; closed first 2 weeks Aug.

Flam's, 1 rue de l'Epine and others at rues des Frères & du Faisan (☎03.88.75.77.44). *Tarte flambée* restaurant, very popular with locals. A good place to sample the local speciality with the 67F all-you-can-eat *tarte flambée* menu (plus dessert). Meals from 31F. Daily noon–10.30pm.

Gurtlerhoft, 13 Place de la Cathédrale (☎03.88.75.00.75). Downstairs, away from the crowds and very seductive. Not as expensive as it looks. Menus from 135F.

Poêles de Carottes, 18 rue de la Krutenau (☎03.88.35.74.74). Vegetarian restaurant close to the unversity. Lunch 59F, dinner 98F. Mon–Sat noon–2.30pm & 7–10pm.

La Robe des Champs, 4 rue de l'Écurie (☎03.88.22.36.82). Potato-fanciers will enjoy the variety of things they can do – inexpensively – with the spud here. Menu 39–90F. Closed lunchtimes Sat & Sun; last week in July & first week in Aug.

Le Saint-Sépulcre, 15 rue des Orfèvres, off rue des Hallesbardes (☎03.88.32.39.97). Traditional *winstub*. Menu 90–160F. Closed Sun & Mon & first fortnight in July.

La Victoire, 24 quai des Pêcheurs (☎03.88.35.39.35). A *winstub*, worth experiencing for its lively student ambience rather than the food. Menu from 100F, *plats* 44F. Closed Sat evening, Sun & first 3 weeks in Aug.

Winstub Strissel, 5 place de la Grande-Boucherie (☎03.88.32.14.73). *Winstub* with Alsatian fare and a menu at 60–125F (otherwise, 70F or more per *plat*). Closed Sun, Mon & 1 week in Feb & July.

Zür Zehnerglock, 4 rue du Vieil-Hôpital, near the cathedral (☎03.88.32.87.09). Quality food and a little live music to sweeten the digestion on Fri. Menu 90–120F, *plats* around 75F. Closed Sun & Mon.

Cafés and bars

Académie de la Bière, 17 rue Adolphe-Seyboth, near the church of St-Pierre. This is Strasbourg's most famous *bierstub*. Mon–Fri 8am–4am, Sat 9am–4am, Sun 10am–4am.

Café des Anges, 5 rue Ste-Cathérine (☎03.88.37.12.67). Easy-going place run by a collective, catering for a slightly older clientele than many bars, with rock or jazz concerts most evenings on the ground floor. Till 3am; usually closed Sun.

Café Brant, place Sebastian-Brant. Atmospheric café close to the University. Outdoor tables make it perfect for summer meals. Till 10pm.

Jamaïque, Grand' Rue. Jamaican theme bar with bands. Till late.

Montmartre, 6 rue du Vieux-Marché-aux-Poissons (☎03.88.32.40.58). Shiny Parisian-style café near the cathedral.

Monte-Carlo, quai Turkheim. Hip gay bar, with performances and club nights.

Opéra Café, place Broglie. Stylish and friendly café next door to the theatre. Outdoor tables (no plastic chairs in sight). Open even when the theatre season is over.

Rive Gauche, corner rue Marie Kuss and quai St-Jean. Parisian-style ambience.

La Salamandre, 3 rue Paul-Janet (☎03.88.25.79.42). A popular bar (free entrance) famous for its rock concerts (tickets 50–120F) and theme nights (20–30F); 9pm–1.30am.

Tapas Café, South of Petit France, cross the Pont des Moulins and you'll see it next to the fire station. Cool Spanish bar, with wonderful, affordable tapas. Till late.

Entertainment

Strasbourg usually has lots going on. In summer, pick up the *Saison d'Été* **listings leaflet** from the tourist office or *Strasbourg Actualités*, with entertainment info and practical listings. If you're here during university term-time, you might want to check the notice boards at the university as well. **Free concerts** are held regularly in the Parc des Contades and Parc de l'Orangerie, which also boasts a 24-lane bowling alley. The best of the annual **festivals** starts with music from around the world in mid-June, followed by jazz in July, and contemporary world music in mid-September and early October. In addition, there's Les Nuits de Strasbourg, a firework, light and music display at the Ponts Couverts during July and August; and, on July 14, a fireworks display and street entertainment. At the Marché de Noël (end-Nov to Dec 24), an annual event for over 400 years, you can buy tree decorations, gifts, crafts, sweets and Alsatian Christmas cookies, *bredele*.

Listings

Ambulance (SAMU) Anti-poison (☎03.88.37.37.37).

Bikes Bicycles can be rented from the gare SNCF, Parking Ste-Aurélie, place du Château and place de l'Étoile for 30F a day.

Boat trips For information on River Ill boat trips, ask at the tourist office (see p.273).

Books Librairie International Kléber, 1 rue des Francs-Bourgeois, sells new books, French and English; La Librocase, 2 quai des Pêcheurs, sells second-hand books. The Quai des Brumes, 35 quai des Bateliers, although small, also has a very good range. The Bookworm, 4 rue de Pâques, is a small English bookshop with new and used books, audio books, children's books and greetings cards.

Buses Eurolines have an office at 5 rue des Frères (☎03.88.22.73.74). Some out-of-town buses leave from place des Halles.

Car rental Europcar, at the airport (☎03.88.68.95.55) and 15 place de la Gare (☎03.88.15.55.66); Avis, Galérie Marchande, place de la Gare (☎03.88.32.30.44); Hertz, at the airport (☎03.88.68.93.11) and 6 bd de Metz by the gare SNCF (☎03.88.32.57.62).

Cinemas Le Club, 32 rue du Vieux-Marché-aux-Vins (☎03.36.68.20.22) and Le Star, 27 rue du Jeu-des-Enfants, the parallel street (☎03.88.32.44.97. L'Odyssée, 3 rue des Francs-Bourgeois (☎03.88.75.10.47), show a combination of classic and contemporary films.

Markets The city's biggest fruit and vegetable market takes place every Tues and Sat am on bd de la Marne; Marché aux Puces (flea market) is on rue du Vieul-Hôpital (near the cathedral); Wed & Sat.

Post office, 4 av de la Liberté (☎03.88.52.31.00).

Rape crisis SOS Viol (☎0800.05.95.95); SOS Femmes Solidarité (Rape/battered women support line) (☎03.88.24.06.06).

Taxis Station Centrale (☎03.88.36.13.13); Novotaxi (☎03.88.75.19.19).

The northern Vosges

The **northern Vosges** begin at the Saverne gap northwest of Strasbourg and run up to the German border where they continue as the Pfälzerwald. They don't reach the same heights as the southern Vosges, nor do they boast any famous vineyards. As a result, they are spared the mass tourism of the southern range. Much of the region is designated a

HIKING, CYCLING AND DRIVING IN THE NORTHERN VOSGES

Numerous **cycling** and **motoring** routes designed to bring you into contact with the most interesting sights, villages and landscapes are detailed in the pamphlet *Panorama Nord*, published by the Office Départemental du Tourisme du Bas-Rhin, 9 rue du Dôme, 67000 Strasbourg (☎03.88.15.45.80, fax 03.88.75.67.64). Independent hikers and cyclists will find further routes marked on the Club Vosgien 1:50,000 and 1:25,000 maps (on sale in bookshops and tourist offices) in addition to the three **GRs** (Sentiers de Grande Randonnée), which cross the Parc Naturel Régional des Vosges du Nord: GR53–55, GR531 and GR532. Don't get too excited when you see a road sign for picnic area: in the Vosges: this usually means a cleared parking area with some concrete tables. It's a good idea to do some research before you set off, even if you are just planning a short drive and lunch, so that you end up far from campervan traffic.

One easy cycle route in the region is along the Rhon-Rhin canal. It's flat all the way from Strasbourg down past Mulhouse, with bars and cafés along the way for regular pit-stops, and places to pitch tents. Again, be wary of the official picnic areas. The *Carte des Parcours Cyclables* is a free map, with descriptions, of cycle routes in the region from Wissembourg to Colmar. Cycling routes in this region are continually being developed and improved: possible routes include:

Canal de la Marne au Rhin: 50km Strasbourg to Saverne, and further into the Moselle if you wish.

Haguenau–Woerth–Lembach: 24km circuit through forests and 1870-battlefields.

Geispolsheim-Barr/Geispolsheim-Obernai: 25km each section, through vineyards with beautiful views of the Rhine valley.

If you want your **accommodation** and **baggage transport** taken care of, there are organisations in each town that can arrange this for you (usually around 2500F for 6 days, including meals), details from tourist offices. For large hiking groups you will need to book in advance, for one or two people, only one day's notice is usually needed.

For further information, the regional tourist office (see above) has the most up-to-date books and maps for about 50F, or contact the Club Vosgien, 71 ave des Vosges, 67000 Strasbourg (☎03.88.35.30.76). Alternatively, you will find that every tourist office in the Bas-Rhin region has plenty of information and maps, and will be able to give you all the necessary advice about the routes. Some of them even organise cycling and hiking trips with a guide, but with the amount of information available, you should be able to manage on your own quite easily. If you want to stay in a gîte d'étape, contact the Gîtes de France Bas-Rhin, 7 place des Meuniers, 67000 Strasbourg (☎03.88.75.56.60, fax 03.88.23.00.97). The Club Alpin Français, Section Strasbourg Bas-Rhin, 2 rue des Ecrivains (☎03.88.35.27.62) also arranges various mountain activities.

Parc Naturel, and there are numerous hiking possibilities, as well as a couple of attractive towns – **Saverne** and **Wissembourg** – built in the characteristic red sandstone of the Vosges.

Transport here is patchy, as elsewhere in Alsace, though not hopeless. SNCF buses wind their way through the villages and apple orchards around Hagenau, and the Strasbourg–Sarreguemines and Hagenau–Bitche train lines cut across the range. Saverne and Wissembourg are also linked to Strasbourg by rail. Even so, the easiest way to explore the region is with your own transport – hilly work, if it's a bike.

Saverne and around

SAVERNE, seat of the exiled Catholic prince-bishops of Strasbourg during the Reformation, commands the only easy route across the Vosges into Alsace, at a point where the hills are pinched to a narrow waist. It is a small and friendly town, not as picturesque as some of its neighbours, but it has the region's characteristic steep-pitched roofs, dormer windows and window boxes full of geraniums. It's also the best launch pad from which to explore the northern Vosges.

The town has a couple of sights worth visiting, not least its vast red sandstone **Château des Rohan**, on place de Gaulle, built in rather austere classical style by one of the Rohans who was Prince-Bishop at the time, and now housing the **Musée Rohan** (March–June & Sept–Nov 2–5pm; closed Tues; July–Aug 10am–noon & 2–6pm; Dec–March Sundays only 2–5pm; 25F) and youth hostel. A feature of the museum is the collection of local resistance journalist, Louise Weiss. The River Zorn and the Marne–Rhine canal both weave their way through the town, the latter framing the château's formal gardens in a graceful right-angle bend. Alongside the château, the **church of Notre-Dame-de-la-Nativité** contains another finely carved pulpit by Hans Hammer. Horticultural distraction can be found in the town's famed rose garden, **La Roseraie** (☎03.88.71.83.33, daily 9am–7pm; 15F), to the west of the centre by the river, which boasts over four hundred varieties; and the **botanical gardens** 3km out of town off the N4 Metz/Nancy road.

There are several relatively easy **walks** around Saverne (the tourist office can give details), the most popular being the one to the ruined **Château du Haut-Barr** (2hr return). Follow rue du Haut-Barr southeast along the canal past the leafy suburban villas until you reach the woods, where a signboard indicates the various walks possible. Take the path marked "Haut-Barr" through woods of chestnut, beech and larch, and you'll see the castle standing dramatically on a narrow sandstone ridge with fearsome drops on both sides and views across the wooded hills and eastward over the plain towards Strasbourg. Approaching by road you'll pass an early **telegraph station**, part of the Paris–Strasbourg line dating from around 1800 (daily noon–6pm except Mon in July & Aug).

If you're driving, there are several beautiful small towns and villages within easy reach of Saverne, in particular Bouxwiller, Neuwiller, Pfaffenhoffen and Ingwiller, from where an alternative road to Bitche (see p.285) leads through the densely wooded heart of the northern Vosges. A focus to your explorations could be the **Château of Lichtenburg** (April–Oct Mon 1.30–6pm, Tues–Sat 10am–6pm, Sun & hols 10am–7pm; closed noon–1.30pm out of season), dating back to the thirteenth century and much restored, situated just a short way outside Ingwiller.

Practicalities

The **tourist office** is at 37 Grand' Rue (May–Sept Mon–Fri 9am–noon & 2–6pm, Sat, Sun & hols 10am–noon & 3–6pm; Oct–April Mon–Fri 10am–noon & 2–4pm, Sat 10am–noon & 3–5pm; closed Sun; ☎03.88.91.80.47, fax 03.88.71.02.90). They will be able to provide you with a map of walks in the area published by the Saverne Centre de Randonnées Pedestres (part of the Club Vosgien).

For **accommodation** in town, there's the *Europe*, at 7 rue de la Gare (☎03.88.71.12.07, fax 03.88.71.11.43; ④), with bright, modern rooms. About 1km out of town on the way to the Château du Haut-Barr is the *Maison Familiale OPCV*, 88 route du Haut-Barr (☎03.88.91.10.82, ①): a friendly and comfortable hotel, it's easy to find – follow the signs for the château. The *Hotel/Restaurant Chez Jean*, 3 rue de la Gare (☎03.88.91.10.19, fax 03.88.91.27.45; ④) also has a restaurant with good Alsatian food such as *choucroute* and *preskopf de bœuf au Raifort*; menus 80–300F. The friendly HI **youth hostel** is in the Château Rohan, on place de Gaulle (☎03.88.91.14.84, fax 03.88.71.15.97; reception open 8–10am & 5–10pm) and there's also a **campsite** about 1km from town below the Château du Haut-Barr, on rue du Père Liebermann (☎03.88.91.35.65; closed Oct–March). As for **food**, gourmets will appreciate the *Taverne Katz* on the main street, 80 Grand' Rue (☎03.88.71.16.56; closed Tues eve & Wed; menu 55–185F). Not only is it a beautiful old house with an ornately carved facade and plush decor within, but the food is excellent, traditional Alsatian cuisine, with very good *baeckoffe* and divine sorbets. More modest, but with a genuinely local ambience, there's the *Restaurant de la Marne,* 5 rue du Griffon (☎03.88.91.19.18, fax 03.88.91.01.24; closed Sun pm in summer, and one-and-a-half days a week in winter depending on weather; menu from 65F, 40F at lunch) overlooking the Marne–Rhine canal in the centre of town. There is also a restaurant at the Château du Haut-Barr (see above).

Wissembourg

WISSEMBOURG, 60km north of Strasbourg and right on the German border, is a small town of cobbled and higgledy-piggledy prettiness, largely given over to catering for moneyed German weekenders. The townspeople have a curious linguistic anomaly; they speak an ancient dialect derived from Frankish, unlike their fellow Alsatians whose language is closer to modern German.

At the end of rue Nationale, the town's main commercial street, stands the imposing Gothic **church of St-Paul-et-St-Pierre**, with a Romanesque belfry and some fine twelfth- and thirteenth-century stained glass, once attached to the town's abbey. Beneath the apse, the meandering River Lauter flows under the Pont du Sel beside the town's most striking secular building and first hospital, the **Maison du Sel** (1450). A few minutes' walk away, on the northern edge of the town, another fine old building, with beautifully carved woodwork round its windows, contains the town's folk museum, the **Musée Westercamp**, 3 rue du Musée (April–Sept Mon–Thurs 2–6pm, Fri–Sat 9am–noon & 2–6pm, Sun & hols 10am–noon & 2–6pm; closed January; by appointment only other times; 15F). Along the southern edge of town, following the riverbank from the Tour des Husgenossen in the western corner, a long section of the **medieval walls** survives intact, built – like the houses – in the local red sandstone.

The **tourist office** is at 9 place de la République (June–Sept Mon–Fri 9am–noon & 2–6pm, Sat & Sun 10am–noon & 2–5pm; Oct–May Mon 2–5pm, Tues–Fri 9am–noon & 2–5pm, Sat 10am–noon & 2–5pm; ☎03.88.94.10.11, fax 03.88.94.18.82). From the train station the "Office du Tourisme" signs are for cars – if you are on foot the quickest route is to turn left out of the station and walk to the roundabout, where you'll see signs of café life. Turn right and you're in town.

Should you want to stay, much the most attractive **hotel** is the *Hôtel du Cygne*, 3 rue du Sel, next to the town hall on the central place de la République (☎03.88.94.00.16, fax 03.88.54.38.28; ④; closed Feb 1–Mar 2 & July 1–17; restaurant 120–350F). Otherwise, try the *Hôtel Restaurant au Moulin de la Walk*, 2 rue de la Walk, by the hospital just outside the old town (☎03.88.94.06.44, fax 03.88.54.38.03; ③; closed Sun eve, Mon, Jan 8–30 & June 15–30): it has a very good but rather pricey restaurant, with the cheapest menu at 180F, easy listening music included. Friendly and less expensive is the *Hôtel de la Gare*, opposite the gare SNCF (☎03.88.94.13.67, fax 03.88.94.06.88; ③), whose restaurant is also cheaper (menu at 55–145F; closed Sun). In the main street, the hotel/restaurant *L'Escargot,* 40 rue Nationale (☎03.88.94.90.29, fax 03.88.94.90.29; ③; closed Jan 1–14; restaurant closed Sun; menu at 55–130F – both places serve Alsatian cuisine.

In addition to the hotel **restaurants** above there are a couple of reasonable places to eat on the main rue Nationale: *Au Petit Dominicains*, 36 rue Nationale (☎03.88.94.90.87; closed Mon eve, Tues & Jan 21–31; menu at 45–120F) serves traditional Alsatian food. A much fancier establishment, with a chef who rings his own inventive changes on the traditional regional cuisine, is *À l'Ange*, 2 rue de la République (☎03.88.94.12.11; closed Tues eve, Wed, Feb 26–Mar 15; menu at 165–330F), in a beautiful old house by the stream next to place du Marché-aux-Choux. The prices reflect the excellent cooking, influenced by the proximity of

Germany: the cheapest menu is the lunchtime 165F, otherwise you'll be looking at twice that. For simple *tarte flambées*, *Au Saumon*, by little Venice, behind the Maison du Sel (☎03.88.94.17.60) has a nice garden and outdoor oven, from 30F. *La Mirabelle*, 3 rue Générale Leclerc (☎03.88.54.82.14) is a nice outdoor café for summer meals, also from 30F.

Nearby **Woerth**, 25km southwest along the D27, has a **museum** dedicated to an important engagement in the 1870 Franco-Prussian War, reconstructed here with the aid of 4000 lead soldiers (April–Oct 2–5pm; July & Aug closes 6pm; Nov–Mar Sat & Sun 2–5pm; closed Jan; ☎03.88.09.30.31). Those with a sweet tooth can indulge at the *Bindier Restaurant* (☎03.88.09.30.79), noted for its desserts and ice-creams. It's moderately priced, with a menu at 45–85F, and the quality of cooking compensates for the ban on tobacco and alcohol. The nearest HI **youth hostel** to Wissembourg, and the closest hostel to the Maginot Line, *La Maison des Soeurs,* is at 10 rue du Moulin (☎03.88.54.03.30, fax 03.88.09.58.32; mid-March to Nov; bus from Haguenau); there is a kitchen for members plus camping facilities and a friendly English manager.

The Route des Châteaux

Scattered among the wooded hills to the west of Wissembourg are a host of ruined castles that once stood guard over the frontier with Germany, and the winding D3 and its smaller tributaries that cross the now untenanted frontier take you close to most of them. The ruins of the **Château du Fleckenstein** (daily mid-March to Sept 9.30am–6pm; Oct to mid-Nov 9.30am–5pm; 15F), 7km north of Lembach (see below), are perhaps the most spectacular, rising above the forest on a narrow sand-stone outcrop, just a stone's throw from the German border. Six kilometres further on at Obersteinbach, the **Maison des Châteaux-Forts**, at 42 rue Principal (March–April Sundays; May–June Sat & Sun; July–Oct Wed, Sat & Sun; 15F; call in advance because opening hours vary; ☎03.88.09.56.34), is an information centre, with displays and maps on the other castles in the area. A rather more modern fortress, just outside Lembach, is the **Four à Chaux**, part of the Maginot Line (guided tours mid-March to April 10am, 2pm & 3pm; May–June 10am, 2pm, 3pm & 4pm; July–Sept 10am & 11am, 2pm, 3pm, 4pm & 5pm; Oct to mid-Nov 10am, 2pm & 3pm; ☎03.88.94.48.62).

THE POLES OF WISSEMBOURG

Stanislas Leszczynski, born in the Polish-Ukrainian city of Lemberg (now Lvóv) in 1677, lasted just five years as the elected king of Poland before being forced into exile by the Russian Tsar Peter the Great. For the next twenty-odd years he lived on a French pension in Wissembourg, along with a motley entourage of Polish expats. After fifteen years of relatively humdrum existence in the town's Ancien Hôpital south of the main church, Stanislas' luck changed when he managed, against all odds, to get his daughter, Marie, betrothed to the 15-year-old king of France, Louis XV. Marie was not quite so fortunate: married by proxy in Strasbourg Cathedral, and having never even set eyes on the groom, she subsequently had a total of ten children, only to be ultimately rejected by Louis, who preferred hunting and the company of his two more powerful mistresses, Madame de Pompadour and Madame du Barry. Bolstered by his daughter's marriage, Stanislas had another brief spell on the Polish throne from 1733 to 1736, but eventually gave it up in favour of the comfortable dukedom of Barr and Lorraine. He lived out his final years in true aristocratic style in the capital, Nancy, which he transformed into one of France's most beautiful towns.

An agreeable base for exploring this area is the village of **LEMBACH**, where the homely and unpretentious *Hôtel au Heimbach*, 15 rue de Wissembourg (☎03.88.94.43.46, fax 03.88.94.20.85; ③), is a pleasant place to stay. Directly opposite, the *Auberge du Cheval Blanc* (☎03.88.94.41.86; closed Mon & Tues Feb & July; menu at 185–440F) serves exquisite but expensive cuisine.

The road continues westwards through wet, sparsely populated country to the big French army camp at **Bitche** (in Lorraine) around 32km from Lembach. This garrison town, dominated by a squat dark Vauban **fort** atop its commanding bluff, has nothing to detain you, but if you need a **bed**, the *Hôtel de la Gare*, 2 av Trumelet-Faber (☎/fax 03.87.96.00.14; ①; closed Sat, Sun & hols), is friendly and clean; its restaurant is acceptable, too, with a menu at 48F.

The southern Vosges

The **southern Vosges** cover a much greater area than the northern range, stretching as far south as Belfort in Franche-Comté. The major tourist attractions are along the **Route du Vin**, which follows the foot of the mountains along the western edge of the wide flat valley of the Rhine; every turn in the road reveals yet another exquisitely preserved medieval village. Many of these, such as **Colmar**, the main centre for the route, suffer from an overdose of visitors. To escape from the crowds, you'll need to head for the hills proper, along the **Route des Crêtes**, which traces the central ridge of the Vosges to the west. The **Route Romane d'Alsace** which stretches from Wissembourg to Feldbach, past Mulhouse is less travelled, with some wonderful examples of early Romanic and Gothic architecture.

The Route du Vin

Alsace is a region both blessed and cursed by tourism, and no more so than along the so-called **Route du Vin**, which stretches from Marlenheim, west of Strasbourg, to Thann, near Mulhouse. The problem with Alsace is that, left to its own devices, it stays on the right side of Disneyland but, under the impact of tourism and the desire to make money, it comes close to caricaturing itself.

Set against the "blue line of the Vosges", the route winds north–south through endless terraced vineyards which produce the region's famous fruity white wines. Opportunities for tasting the local produce are plentiful, with free *dégustations* along the roadside, in the *caveaux* of most villages, and at the region's countless wine festivals. For a closer look at the vines themselves you can follow various *sentiers vinicoles* (vineyard paths); local tourist offices have details. In the midst of this sea of vines are dozens of flowery and typically picturesque Alsatian villages, dominated from the heights above by an extraordinary number of ancient ruined castles, testimony to the province's turbulent past.

The Route du Vin is deceptively hilly work on a bike, but **getting around** is definitely easier with your own transport. Otherwise you're dependent either on the train, which narrowly misses some of the best villages; or the region's poor bus service. In summer there's a wine festival each weekend in a different town, with *dégustations*, bargains, *tarte flambée*, and traditional Alsatian music.

Obernai and around

Picturesque little **OBERNAI**, on the D422, is the first place most people head for when travelling south along the route. The **tourist office,** Place du Beffroi (8am–noon & 2–6pm; ☎03.88.95.64.13) has lots of useful information about wine and easy to follow routes for exploring the region. Miraculously unscathed during the last two world wars,

Obernai has retained almost its entire **rampart system**, including no fewer than fifteen towers, as well as street after street of carefully maintained medieval houses. Not surprisingly, it also gets more than its fair share of visitors, though this shouldn't put you off as the town is just about big enough to absorb the crowds. If you're thinking of staying the night, the only reasonably priced **hotels** are the *Maison du Vin*, 18 rue du Général-Gouraud (☎03.88.95.55.80, fax 03.88.95.54.00; ①), whose pretty rooms are above a wine shop; and *La Diligence*, 23 place de la Mairie (☎03.88.95.55.69, fax 03.88.95.42.46; ③), with a charming and reasonably priced *salon de thé* serving *petits plats* all day. *La Halle au Blé* café is a good place for a hot chocolate after a hard day's hiking in the Vosges.

ROSHEIM, 7km north of Obernai and up in the hills a little to the west of the D422, is relatively off the beaten track. Its two main sights are the Romanesque **church of St-Pierre-et-St-Paul**, whose roof is peppered with comical sculptured figures contemporary with the building, and the twelfth-century **Heidenhüs**, at 24 rue de la Principale, thought to be the oldest building in Alsace. The simple, clean, friendly family-run *Hôtel Alpina*, 39 rue du Lion (☎03.88.50.49.30, fax 03.88.49.25.75; ①), with an attractive terrace and breakfast room, makes a very nice place to stay. **Rosenwiller**, a couple of kilometres up the hill among the vineyards, has a prettily sited and atmospherically overgrown **Jewish cemetery** at the edge of the woods, testimony to Alsace's once numerous Jewish community.

From Rosheim's gare SNCF, 1.5km northeast of the village, a **steam train** runs up the valley on Sundays and holidays to **Ottrott**, which produces one of the few red wines of Alsace. An elegantly restored and modernized village house at 11 rue des Châteaux has been transformed into a rather luxurious **hotel**, the *Hostellerie des Châteaux* (☎03.88.48.14.14, fax 03.88.95.95; ⑦), with a sauna, swimming pool and overpriced restaurant. Just out of town is the Aquarium d'Ottrot, **Les Naïdes** (daily 9.30am–6.30pm), with sharks and crocodiles: follow the signs.

Ottrott brings you within hiking distance – 6km – of **Mont Ste-Odile** (763m), whose summit is surrounded by a mysterious Celtic wall, originally built in the seventh century BC. It is almost 10km in length and in parts reaches a height of 3.5m. Ste Odilia herself is buried in the small **chapel** on top of the hill, a pilgrimage site even today. According to tradition, she was cast out by her father at birth on account of her blindness, but miraculously regained her sight during childhood and returned to found the convent on Mont Ste-Odile, where she cured thousands of blindness and leprosy. Accommodation is available here at *Le Mont Ste-Odile,* (☎03.88.95.80.53, fax 03.88.95.82.98; ①). Bookings advisable.

Barr

For some reason, **BARR**, west of the main road, is bypassed by many coach groups. Every bit as charming as Obernai, it's easy to while away a couple of hours wandering its twisting cobbled streets, at their busiest during the mid-July **wine festival** and on Sundays when the vintners come to ply their wines. The town has just one specific sight, **La Folie Marco**, at 30 rue du Docteur-Sultzer (July–Sept daily except Tues 10am–noon & 2–6pm; June & Oct Sat & Sun 10am–noon & 2–6pm; ☎03.88.08.94.72), an unusually large eighteenth-century house on the outskirts of town along the road to Obernai, which has displays of period French and Alsatian furniture. There are regular *dégustations* in the garden cellar, and a festival of dance and waltz at the end of May. There is also a restaurant serving Alsatian specialities; menus 95–130F, *tarte flambée* 35F. Some interesting walks begin behind the Hôtel de Ville, including one to Mont Ste-Odile (13.9km, 3–4 hours).

The nearest **gare SNCF** is in the neighbouring village of Gertwiller, 1km to the east. The nicest place to **stay** in Barr is the superb *Hôtel Le Manoir*, 11 rue St-Marc (☎03.88.08.03.40, fax 03.88.08.53.71; ①–③ on the edge of town, with light, spacious

ALSACE AND HITLER'S REICH

When Hitler conquered France in 1940, he not only occupied Alsace, but also incorporated it into the German state, making it subject to German laws and outlawing all manifestations of French and Alsatian culture. Worst of all, he conscripted 140,000 young Alsatian men, citizens of France, into the German armies, on pain of terrible reprisals against their families if they attempted to escape. They are known as the **"malgré-nous"**: soldiers against their will.

Most of the *malgré-nous* were sent to the Russian front, where, as one survivor related, they were used as human minesweepers: sent into attack first across the Russian minefields. Forty thousand died and forty thousand have never been accounted for. Some deserted, and were hidden by their families, and others mutilated themselves. Many were taken prisoner and ended up in the Soviet Gulag, in the notorious camp at Tambov, in particular, northeast of Odessa, where they either died or were eventually repatriated in broken health. Having experienced the fascist Legion of French Volunteers against Bolshevism, the Russians were understandably not very sympathetic to Frenchmen fighting in German uniform, and dragged their feet over sending them back. The last *malgré-nous* to be released came home in 1955, after ten years in a Siberian camp.

Yet the most bitter experience for these soldiers was finding themselves, after so much suffering, treated as traitors by their fellow Frenchmen. A friend, recounting her father's experience as a *malgré-nous*, said: "The Germans took our children as if they were their own and after all that we were treated by France as the bloody Germans of the east."

For fifty years the veterans' association has fought for recognition of these unwilling soldiers of the Reich and for compensation in the form of pensions and invalidity benefits. And still the painful ambiguity endures. Thirteen Alsatian *malgré-nous* fought with the infamous Waffen SS Das Reich division, which was responsible, on its march to join battle with the Allies in Normandy in 1944, for the terrible massacres in Tulle and Oradour-sur-Glane (see p.627). Put on trial in the 1950s, they were granted amnesty for domestic political reasons. But the request in 1996 for a war veteran's pension by one of these old soldiers has caused outrage amongst the survivors of Oradour.

rooms and a superb buffet breakfast for 40F. Alternatively, there are two **campsites**: the *Camping St-Martin*, at Rue de l'Ill, near the Catholic church (☎03.88.08.00.45; June to mid-Oct), and *Camping Municipal Ste-Odile "Wepfermatt"*, 3km out of town at 137 rue de la Vallée (☎03.88.08.02.38; March–Oct). St-Pierre, 3km south of Barr, also has a campsite – *Beau Séjour* (☎03.88.08.52.24 or 03.88.08.90.79; mid-May to Sept). For a really good *tarte flambée* in a restaurant with great atmosphere, *Les Caveau des Tanneurs*, 32 rue Neuve (☎03.88.08.91.50; lunch & dinner every day: try the *munster* (a kind of cheese) and cumin version: from 35F. *Winstub S'Barrer Stubbel*, 5 place de l'Hôtel de Ville (☎03.88.57.44) has good local specialities at reasonable prices.

Le Struthof concentration camp

Deep in the forests and hills of the Vosges, over 20km west of Barr, **Le Struthof-Natzwiller** (daily: March to mid-June 9am–noon & 2–5.30pm; mid-June to mid-Sept 10am–6pm; mid-Sept to Dec 10am–noon & 2–6pm; closed Jan–Feb; 8F; ☎03.88.97.04.49) was the only Nazi concentration camp to be built on French soil (though at the time, of course, it was part of the Greater German Reich). The site is almost perversely beautiful, its stepped terraces cut into steep hillside, giving fantastic views across the Bruche valley. Set up shortly after Hitler's occupation of Alsace-Lorraine in 1940, it is thought that over 10,000 people died here. When the Allies liberated the camp on November 23, 1944, they found it empty – the remaining prisoners having already been transported to Dachau.

The barbed wire and watchtowers are as they were, though only two of the prisoners' barracks remain, one of which is now a **museum** on the deportations. Captions are in French only, but the pictures suffice to tell the story. An arson attack by neo-Nazis in 1976 only served to underline the need for such displays. At the foot of the camp is the crematorium with its ovens still intact. A couple of kilometres down the road to the west, towards Schirmeck, the Germans built a gas chamber – proof that Le Struthof was a fully integrated part of the Nazi killing machine. To the east, the two main granite quarries worked by the internees still survive, clearly signposted from the main road.

Sélestat

Back on the Route du Vin, **SÉLESTAT**, midway between Strasbourg and Colmar, is a delightful, relatively cosmopolitan old town, which makes a good base for exploring the central and most popular section of the route. The choice of reasonable accommodation is better than average, and the town itself contains a couple of interesting churches and a great museum for bibliophiles.

The oldest and finest of the two churches is the **church of Ste-Foy**. Built by the monks of Conques and much restored since, though its clean, austerely Romanesque lines have not been entirely wiped out. Close by, to the north, the much larger Gothic **church of St-Georges** sports spectacularly multi-coloured roof tiles and some very fine stained glass. For a brief period in the late fifteenth and early sixteenth centuries, Sélestat was the intellectual centre of Alsace, due mainly to its Latin School, which attracted a group of Humanists led by Beatus Rhenanus, whose personal library was one of the most impressive collections of its time. At the **Bibliothèque Humaniste**, housed in the town's former corn exchange just by St-Georges (July & Aug Mon–Fri 9am–noon & 2–6pm, Sat & Sun 9am–5pm; rest of the year Sat 9am–noon; 20F), Rhenanus' collection is now on display along with some unusual and very rare books and manuscripts from as far back as the seventh century.

Sélestat is comparatively well served transport-wise, with frequent train connections to Strasbourg and Colmar, as well as a branch line that heads north to Strasbourg via Molsheim; the **gare SNCF** is west of the town centre down avenue de la Liberté. For a place to **stay**, there's none better than the comfortable, friendly *Auberge des Alliés*, 39 rue des Chevaliers, in the middle of town (☎03.88.92.09.34, fax 03.88.92.12.88; ③; closed Sun pm & Mon and first 2 weeks July and 2 weeks over Christmas); its restaurant (menus 98–240F) is good value and worth a look for its splendid tiled stove. A funky modern alternative is the *Vaillant* on place de la République (☎03.88.92.09.46; ③; restaurant 90–150F) – the groovy lifesize statue in the foyer is called Tom. There's a **campsite**, *Les Cigones* (☎03.88.92.03.98; May to mid-Oct), south of the centre behind Vauban's remaining ramparts. Further information is available from the **tourist office** by the ring road on boulevard du Général-Leclerc (☎03.88.58.87.20, fax 03.88.92.88.63).

Castles around Sélestat

Within easy range of Sélestat are a whole host of **ruined castles**. Seven kilometres north, and accessible by train, the village of **DAMBACH-LA-VILLE**, with its walls and three fortified gates all intact, is one of the highlights of the route. There's a cheap **campsite**, *Camping Municipal* (☎03.88.92.48.60; mid-May to Sept), 1km east on the D210, as well as the small but most attractive and inexpensive *Hôtel à la Couronne*, 13 place du Marché (☎03.88.92.40.85, fax 03.88.92.63.63; ②; closed Thurs, Feb 12–March 1 & Nov 15–30). A thirty-minute climb west of the village is the formidable **castle of Bernstein**. In the Middle Ages, Alsace was culturally more German than French, and this is a typically German mountain keep, tall and narrow with few openings and little use for everyday living. Around it are residential buildings enclosed within an outer wall, the masonry cut into protruding knobs, which gives it a curious pimpled texture. There is a mini-train tour of the town and vineyards, (Mon, Thurs & Sat 5pm; 30F) leaving from the main town square.

From **SCHIRWILLER**, another attractive village just 3km northwest of Sélestat, you can climb a steep, marked path to the **castle of Ortenbourg**. Like Bernstein, it has a lofty refuge-tower with courtyards outside, very well-preserved and protected by a rock-cut ditch. A few hundred metres southwest of here is **Ramstein castle**, built in 1293 to protect the besiegers of Ortenbourg.

The best cluster of castles, however, is southwest of Sélestat. Four kilometres away, **KINTZHEIM** boasts a small but wonderful ruined castle built around a cylindrical refuge-tower. Today it's an aviary, the **Volerie des Aigles**, for birds of prey, with magnificent displays of aerial prowess by eagles and vultures (☎03.88.92.84.33 for details of afternoon demonstrations April–Nov). If you have a yen to watch Barbary apes at play in the Vosgian jungle, you can do just that a couple of kilometres further west at the **Montagne des Singes** (daily: April–Oct 10am–noon & 1–5/6pm; July & Aug no lunchtime closure; 40F; ☎03.88.82.11.05). Also on the way to Kintzheim from Sélestat is the rather tacky bird-based amusement park, the **Parc des Cigognes et Loisirs** (April–Sept 10am–7pm; Oct, Nov & Mar Wed, Sat & Sun; ☎03.88.92.05.94).

Another 5km on, the ruins of **Oudenbourg castle**, its sizeable hall preserved among the trees, is dwarfed by the massive **Haut-Koenigsbourg** (daily 9am–noon & 1–4/5/6pm, no lunchtime closure June–Sept; closed Jan 5–Feb 5 & Nov 11; 36F; ☎03.88.92.11.46 or 03.88.82.50.60 in winter), one of the biggest, most popular castles in Alsace, and – astride its 757-metre bluff – by far the highest. Ruined after an assault in 1633, it was heavily restored in the early years of this century for Kaiser Wilhelm II. It's easy to criticize some of the detail of the restoration, but it's an enjoyable experience and a remarkably convincing re-creation of a castle-palace of the age of Dürer. There are guided tours, but it's best explored on your own. The views all around are fantastic. There's a winding road down to Bergheim from here (see below), if you'd rather not retrace your tracks to Sélestat.

Ribeauvillé and around

RIBEAUVILLÉ is the largest town between Sélestat and Colmar – not as pretty as some of its immediate neighbours, but right at the foot of the mountains and well placed for exploring the many castles and villages that surround it.

If you wish to **stay** here, there's the rather fancy and friendly little *Hôtel de la Tour*, in a converted winery at 1 rue de la Mairie (☎03.89.73.72.73, fax 03.89.73.38.74; ⑤; closed Jan 1–March 15), with a Turkish bath and a *winstub*. Two local **campsites** are *Camping des Trois Châteaux* (☎03.89.73.20.00; July & Aug), to the north of Ribeauvillé, and the much plusher *Pierre-de-Courbertin* site (☎03.89.73.66.71; March–Nov) to the south.

In the vicinity of the town is a threesome of fortresses built by the counts of Ribeaupierre: **St-Ulrich castle**, an hour's haul up a marked path; just north of it the smaller **Girsberg castle**, balanced on a pinnacle which somehow provides room for a bailey, two towers and other buildings; and, further on, the ruins of **Haut-Ribeaupierre**.

BERGHEIM, 3.5km northeast of Ribeauvillé, retains a good part of its old fortifications, with three towers still surviving; despite being one of the most beautiful Alsatian villages, it rarely attracts the attentions of the tour groups. Also within easy walking range of Ribeauvillé, this time to the south, the village of **HUNAWIHR** is another beguiling hamlet, with a fourteenth-century walled **church** standing out amid the green vines. Hunawihr is at the forefront of the Alsatian ecological movement aimed at reintroducing the stork – the *cigogne* – to the region, and there's a **reserve** to the east of the village, **Centre Cigognes et Loutres** (April–Oct daily 10am–noon & 2–6pm; Nov

1–11 Wed, Sat & Sun 10am–noon & 2–5pm; shows at 3pm & 4pm, plus 5pm & 6pm in July & Aug; 45F; but call to check show times ☎03.89.73.72.62). There is also an otter breeding reserve and a butterfly glasshouse, **Jardin des papillons exotiques vivants** (April to mid-Nov 10am–6/7pm; 30F), with a good collection of orchids.

Last, nearer to the hub of Colmar, there are a couple of tourist targets you may want to avoid, or at least for which you should time your visits carefully. A couple of kilometres south of Hunawihr, the walled village of **RIQUEWIHR** is exceptionally well-preserved, with plenty of medieval houses and a château containing a **postal museum**, the Musée d'Histoire des PTT d'Alsace (April to mid-Nov daily except Tues 10am–noon & 2–6pm); consequently it suffers more visitors per annum than any other village along the route.

KAYSERSBERG, still further southwest, also plays host to more than its fair share of tour buses. It boasts a fortified **bridge** and a handsome sixteenth-century wooden altarpiece in the main **church**. But the town's principal renown is as the birthplace of Nobel Peace Prize winner Albert Schweitzer, who spent most of his extremely active, and not always peaceful, life at the leprosy hospital he founded at Lambaréné in French Equatorial Africa, now Gabon. During World War I he was interned by the French authorities as an "enemy alien", but nowadays he is suitably honoured with the **Centre Culturel Albert Schweitzer**, 126 rue du Général-de-Gaulle (Easter & May 2–Oct daily 9am–noon & 2–6pm).

Two kilometres from Kaysersberg in the village of **KIENTZHEIM**, the very comfortable *Hostellerie de l'Abbaye d'Alspach*, 2–4 rue Foch (☎03.89.47.16.00, fax 03.89.78.29.73; ③; closed Jan 9–March 10), in a former abbey as the name suggests, makes a good base for visiting Colmar, 10km away. Try some of the homemade wine.

Colmar

COLMAR, a fifty-minute train ride south of Strasbourg, has sprawled unattractively on both sides of the train tracks, but the old centre remains typically and whimsically Alsatian, with crooked houses, half-timbered and painted, on crooked lanes – all extremely pretty and very touristy. Colmar's attractions don't stop at its buildings; it is also the proud possessor of one of the last and most extraordinary of all Gothic paintings – the altarpiece for St Anthony's monastery at Issenheim, painted by Mathias Grünewald.

Arrival, information and accommodation

From the **gare SNCF**, on rue de la République, it's a ten-minute walk down avenue de la République to the **tourist office** on place d'Unterlinden (Mon–Sat 9am–6/7pm, Sun & hols 9.30am–2pm; ☎03.89.20.68.92, fax 03.89.41.34.13). Besides selling Club Vosgien hiking maps and a booklet of day walks in the hills behind the town, they'll also give you details of the **buses** to the towns and villages of the Route du Vin, which leave from outside the gare SNCF. **Bikes** can be rented from La Cyclothéque, 31 route d'Ingersheim (Mon 2–6pm, Tues–Sat 8am–noon & 2–6.30pm; ☎03.89.79.14.18), Cycles Geiswiller, 6 bd du Champ de Mars (Tues–Fri 8.30am–noon & 2–6.30pm, Sat 8.30–noon & 2–6pm; ☎03.89.41.30.59), and Cycles Mayer, 6 rue du Pont-Rouge (Tues–Sat 8.30am–noon & 2–6.30pm; ☎03.89.79.12.47).

Accommodation is not as overpriced as you might expect, with a number of reasonable hotels very close to the gare SNCF. There's the quiet and comfortable *Hôtel Colbert,* 2 rue des Trois-Épis, parallel to rue de la République, (☎03.89.41.31.05, fax 03.89.23.66.75; ③), and *La Chaumière*, 74 rue de la République, (☎03.89.41.08.99; ②). For more luxury, there's the *Grand Hôtel Bristol*, 7 place de la Gare, directly opposite the station exit (☎03.89.23.59.59, fax 03.89.23.92.26; ⑤).a relic of the grand old prewar days of tourism, now comfortably refurbished and part of a chain. There are also two **hostels**: the central *Maison des Jeunes et de la Culture,* 17 rue Camille-Schlumberger (☎03.89.41.26.87, fax 03.89.23.20.16), two streets over from av de la République; and the the HI youth hostel, *Auberge de Jeunesse Mittelhardt* at 2 rue Pasteur (☎03.89.80.57.39, fax 03.89.80.76.16) – take bus #4 from the station or rue d'Unterlinden, stop Pont Rouge off the route d'Ingersheim or N415 going west (look out for the cyber café and bicycle rental shop). This place gets very busy in summer with lots of teenagers – unfortunately the rooms are not insulated as in some of the other hostels in France. The nearest **campsite,** *Camping Colmar-Horbourg-Wihr* is 2km from the centre of town on Route de Neuf-Brisach (☎03.89.41.15.94; closed Dec & Jan). Take bus #1 from the station, direction "Wihr", stop Plage de l'Ill.

The town

The *pièce de résistance* of the **Musée d'Unterlinden,** housed in a former Dominican convent, 1 rue d'Unterlinden (April–Oct daily 9am–6pm; Nov–March daily except Tues 9am–noon & 2–5pm; closed public hols; 32F) is the **Issenheim altarpiece,** originally designed as a single piece. On the front was the Crucifixion, almost luridly expressive: a tortured Christ with stretched ribcage and outsize hands turned upwards, fingers splayed in pain, flanked by his pale, fainting mother, saints John and Mary Magdalene. Then it unfolded, relative to its function on feast days, Sundays and weekdays, to reveal an Annunciation, Resurrection, Virgin and Child, and finally a sculpted panel depicting saints Anthony, Augustine and Jerome. Completed in 1515, the painting is affected by Renaissance innovations in light and perspective while still rooted in the medieval spirit, with an intense mysticism and shifts of mood in its subject matter. Also worth a look is the collection of modern paintings in the basement, which includes works by Picasso, Léger and Vasarely.

A short walk into the old town, the **Dominican church** on rue des Serruriers (mid-March to Dec Mon–Sat 10am–6pm, Sun 10am–1pm & 3–6pm; 5F) has some fine glass and, above all, a radiantly beautiful altarpiece known as *The Virgin in a Bower of Roses*, painted in 1473 by Martin Schongauer, who is also represented in the Musée d'Unterlinden. At the other end of rue des Serruriers you come to the **Collégiale St-Martin** on a café-lined square. Known locally as "the cathedral", it's worth a quick peek for its stonework and stained glass, as is the sixteenth-century **Maison Pfister,** on the south side of the church, for its painted panels. Frédéric Auguste Bartholdi, the nineteenth-century sculptor responsible for New York's Statue of Liberty, was born at 30 rue des Marchands. This has been turned into the **Musée Bartholdi** (March–Dec daily except Tues 10am–noon & 2–6pm; closed public hols; 15F), containing Bartholdi's personal effects, plus the original designs for the statue, along with sundry Colmarabilia.

Rue des Marchands continues south to the Ancienne Douane or **Koïfhus,** its gaily painted roof tiles loudly proclaiming the city's medieval prosperity. This is the heart of Colmar's old town, a short step away from the archly picturesque quarter down the Grand' Rue, cut through by the River Lauch and known as **La Petite Venise.** The dolly-mixture colours of the old fishing cottages on quai de la Poissonnerie are more touristy even than Strasbourg's Petite France. Twice as tall, but similarly over-restored, are the black-and-white half-timbered tanners' houses on **quai des Tanneurs,** which leads off from the Koïfhus, with open verandahs on the top floor originally designed for drying hides.

There are two other museums that you will see if you take a stroll through the old town, **Musée Animé Jouet et des Petitis Trains,** 40 rue Vauban, (10am–noon & 2–6pm; closed Tues & Jan) which has a collection of toy trains; and the **Museum** d'Histoire Naturelle, 11 rue Turenne (Mar–Dec 10am–noon & 2–6pm; closed Tues & Sun 2–6pm).

Eating and drinking

Restaurants in Colmar are generally overpriced, particularly Alsatian ones. *Winstub Brenner*, 1 rue de Turenne (☎03.89.41.42.43; closed Tues evenings and Wed, second fortnight Jan, third week June & third week Nov; from 50F) serves delicious, generous meals and has a lovely terrace by little Venice – ask for a side order of *pommes sautées* if you're really hungry. A fun establishment for both food and atmosphere is *S'Parisser Stewwele*, 4 place Jeanne-d'Arc (☎03.89.41.42.33; closed Tues, second half of Feb, third week June & third week Nov; main course 60–70F, or from 160F à la carte). *Le Petit Bouchon* is at 11 rue Alspach (☎03.89.23.45.57; menus at 89–210F). Otherwise, you could amass a sumptuous picnic from the town's numerous pâtisseries and charcuteries. There's a fruit and veg **market** every Thursday around the Koïfhus at place de l'Ancienne-Douane, and every Saturday on place St-Joseph.

Munster and the Route des Crêtes

MUNSTER owes its existence and its name to a band of Irish monks who founded a monastery here in the seventh century, some 19km west of Colmar up the narrowing valley of the River Fecht, overlooked by Le Petit Ballon (1267m) and Le Hohneck (1362m), among the highest peaks of the Vosges. Its name today is particularly associated with a rich, creamy and exceedingly smelly cheese, the crowning glory of many an Alsatian meal. Although of no special interest in itself, the town makes a peaceful and verdant base either for exploring further into the mountain range or for visiting Colmar and other places along the Route du Vin.

It is accessible by **train** from Colmar (gare SNCF ☎03.89.77.34.17). The **tourist office**, 1 rue du Couvnet (Mon–Fri 9.30am–12.30pm & 2–6pm, Sat 10am–noon & 2–6pm; closed Sun; ☎03.89.77.31.80, fax 03.89.77.07.17) has lots of information about hiking in the Munster valley and the Parc National Regional des Ballons des Vosges. The Maison du Parc, 1 cour de l'Abbaye, (May–Sept 9.30am–12.30pm & 2–6.30pm; closed Mon am; Oct–April Mon–Fri 10am–noon & 2–6pm, ☎03.89.77.90.20) is the place to get all the information you need about the Parc.

If you want to **stay**, the large, modern *Hôtel Verte-Vallée*, 10 rue Alfred-Hartmann (☎03.89.77.15.15, fax 03.89.77.17.40; ④), in the depths of the wooded valley, with its squeaky-clean and pastel atmosphere, makes a perfect haven for a day or two. It has a good restaurant specializing in traditional French dishes, with a terrace overlooking the stream (closed Jan 3–27; menu at 82–250F, *carte* 180F or more). Less well-appointed but blessed with stupendous views are two hotels perched high on the north side of the valley in the hamlet of Hohrodberg: *Hôtel Panorama*, 3 route du Linge (☎03.89.77.36.53, fax 03.89.77.03.93; ③), and, with rather awful decor, *Hôtel Roess* (☎03.89.77.36.00; ③), 100m higher up. Both have restaurants. There is a **youth hostel**, *Luttenbach/Munster* at 13 rue de la Gare (☎03.89.77.34.20). **Campsite**, *Camping Municipale du Parc de la Fecht* is on the route de Gunsbach (☎03.88.77.21.08).

The Route des Crêtes

Above Munster the main road to Gérardmer crosses the mountains by the principal pass, the Col de la Schlucht, where it intersects the so-called Route des Crêtes. Built for strategic purposes during World War I, it's a spectacular trail traversing thick forest and open pasture where the herds of cows that produce the Munster cheese graze in summer; in winter this becomes one long cross-country ski route. Starting in **Cernay**, 15km west of Mulhouse, it follows the main ridge of the Vosges, including the highest peak of the range, the Grand Ballon (1424m), north as far as **Ste-Marie-aux-Mines**,

---

HIKING IN THE SOUTHERN VOSGES

There is no shortage of waymarked paths in the **southern Vosges**. Six **GRs** – *Sentiers de Grande Randonnée* or "long-distance footpaths" – cross the Vosges. It's a good way to see the less tourist-congested castles.

GR7: Ballon d'Alsace to Remiremont.
GR53: Wissembourg to Belfort (part of the route coincides with GR5).
GR59: Ballon d'Alsace to Besançon.
GR531: Wissembourg to the Ballon d'Alsace.
GR532: Soultz-sous-Forêts to Belfort.
GR533: Sarrebourg to Belfort, along the west flank of the Vosges.

There are five treks of between five and eleven days' duration described in *Les Grandes Traversées des Vosges*, published by the Office Départemental du Tourisme du Bas-Rhin, 9 rue du Dôme, 67000 Strasbourg (☎03.88.15.45.80), with details of accommodation, access and so on. They are structured to show different aspects of the Vosges in landscapes, history and traditional culture. Another useful contact for information is the Haut-Rhin regional tourist office, Association Départementale du Tourisme du Haut-Rhin, 1 rue Schlumberger, 68006 Colmar (☎03.89.20.10.68, fax 03.89.23.33.91).

Organized walks, involving guides or luggage transport or both, are arranged by various companies and tourist offices. For example, Horizons d'Alsace, 7 Grand` Rue, Kientzheim (☎03.89.78.20.30, fax 03.89.78.12.22), organises the walk, accommodation and meals, baggage transport. It is essential to book in advance. A six-day trip will cost around 2500F.

Belfort in Franche-Comté is another good place to base a hiking trip in the Southern Vosges. The Ballon d'Alsace, in the centre of the Parc Regional des Ballons des Vosges is the meeting point of the GR5, GR7 and GR59, and a discovery trail has been marked out around the summit. A number of PR trails (rambles) begin from here. The Malsaucy lake along the GR5 trail is another popular hiking area. Contact the Belfort tourist office (see below) for maps and information.

20km west of Sélestat, once at the heart of a silver-mining district. From Munster it is also accessible by a twisting minor road through Hohrodberg (see above), which takes you past the beautiful glacial lakes, the Lac Blanc and the Lac Noir, as well as the eerie World War I battlefield of Linge, where the French and German trenches, once separated literally by a few metres, are still clearly visible.

Mulhouse and around

Thirty-five kilometres south of Colmar, **MULHOUSE** is a large sprawling industrial city. It was Swiss until 1798 when, at the peak of its prosperity, based on printed cotton fabrics and allied trades, it voted to become part of France, but many people who live here work in Basle in Switzerland. It is also the home town of Alfred Dreyfus, the unfortunate Jewish army officer who was wrongly convicted of espionage in 1894 (see 'Contexts', p.1063). Not having much of an old town, it is no city for strollers, but there are four or five unusually good – and rather unusual – museums in the town and its vicinity that delve into the region's manufacturing past. Wallpaper, firemen, railway, automobiles and fabrics are all given their platform. There is also a jazz festival in August, which is a good time to be out partying in this town, with concerts in the museums, the schools, the streets, as well as in the cafés and bars.

Closest to the gare SNCF, just along the canal to the right, is the excellent **Musée de l'Impression sur Étoffes**, 3 rue des Bonnes-Gens (daily: May–Sept 9am–6pm; rest of the year 10am–6pm; 36F). It contains a vast collection of the most beautiful fabrics imaginable – eighteenth-century Indian and Persian imports that revolutionized the European ready-to-wear market in their time; silks from Turkestan; batiks from Java, Senegalese materials, some superb kimonos from Japan, and a unique display of scarves from France, Britain and the US.

Again out of the centre of Mulhouse, near the northwestern suburb of **DORNACH**, in the direction of the A36 autoroute, is the **Musée Français du Chemin de Fer**, 2 rue Alfred-de-Glehn (April–Sept daily 9am–6pm; Oct–March Tues–Sun 9am–5pm plus Mon during school & public hols); take bus #17 from *Porte-Jeune Place* to stop *Musée du Chemin de Fer*. Railway rolling stock on display includes Napoléon III's ADCs' drawing room, decorated by Viollet-le-Duc in 1856, and a luxuriously appointed 1926 diner from the *Golden Arrow*. There are cranes, stations, signals and related artefacts, but the stars of the show are the big locomotive engines with brightly painted boilers, gleaming wheels and pistons, and tangles of brass and copper piping – real works of art. In the same complex is the **Musée des Sapeurs-Pompiers** (times as above), its antique fire engines and other memorabilia the personal collection of a retired local firefighter. These museums have now been joined by a third: **Electropolis – Musée de l'Énergie Électrique**, 55 rue du Pâturage (daily except Mon 10am–6pm), devoted to the production and uses of electricity.

A couple of kilometres north of the city centre, the **Musée National de l'Automobile**, 192 av de Colmar (daily: May–Sept 10am–6pm; Oct–April closed Tues; 57F; bus #1, #4 or #17 from Porte-Jeune Schuman or Porte-Jeune Place to stop Musée de l'Histoire), has a collection of over six hundred cars, originally the private collection of local business sharks, the Schlumpf brothers. The vehicles range from the industry's earliest attempts, like the extraordinary wooden-wheeled Jacquot steam "car" of 1878, to 1968 Porsche racing vehicles and contemporary factory prototypes. The largest group is that of racing made Bugatti models: dozens of glorious racing cars, coupés and limousines, the pride of them the two Bugatti Royales, out of only seven that were constructed – one of them Ettore Bugatti's own, with bodywork designed by his son.

Practicalities

Place de la Réunion, nominally the centre of town, is five minutes' walk north of the **gare SNCF** (☎03.89.46.50.50). The **tourist office** is on the way at 9 av Foch (July–Sept Mon–Sat 9am–8pm, Sun 10am–1pm; Oct–June Mon–Sat 9am–7pm; closed Sun; ☎03.89.45.68.31, fax 03.89.45.66.16). As for **accommodation**, overpriced rooms and oversized dogs sums up the hotel situation in Mulhouse. The following are comfortable and affordable and have a big dog in the foyer: *Hôtel Saint-Bernard*, 3 rue des Fleurs (☎03.89.45.82.32, fax 03.39.45.26.32; ②) with Internet access in the "library" in the foyer; *Hôtel de Paris*, 5 passage de l'Hôtel-de-Ville (☎03.89.45.21.41, fax 03.89.36.08.31; ①) *Hôtel Schoenberg*, 14 rue Schoenberg, behind the station (☎03.89.44.19.41, fax 03.89.44.49.80; ②), and *Hôtel Central,* 15–17 Passage Central (☎03.89.46.18.84, fax 03.89.56.31.66, ①–③) has rooms priced to suit most budgets. The HI **youth hostel** is at 37 rue de l'Illberg (☎03.89.42.63.28, fax 03.89.59.74.94; bus #1, #2 or #8, stop Salle des Sports), and also has facilities for camping. There is a pleasant **campsite,** *Camping de l'Ill*, on rue Pierre-de-Coubertin, near the suburb of Dornach, 4km from the city centre on the banks of the River Ill (☎03.89.06.20.66; closed Oct–March); take bus #7 from Porte Jeune Place.

As at Colmar and Strasbourg, Mulhouse's Alsatian **restaurants** are none too cheap, but there are plenty of them – look for the outdoor terraces full of tourists. The *Crêperie Crampous Mad*, 14 rue des Tondeurs (☎03.89.45.79.43; closed Sun; menu 50–100F), is a good standby. For a really good seafood meal, *Le Bistrot à Huitres*, 2 rue Moenschberg (☎03.89.64.01.60; menus from 125F). You can drown your sorrows at *Gambrinus,* 5 rue des Franciscains, north of place de la Réunion (☎03.89.66.18.65; menu 45–150F), which boasts over thirty **beers** on tap and offers simple dishes to wash them down with.

In late August, Mulhouse hosts the region's hottest **jazz festival** (festival dates and information: ☎03.89.45.63.95, *www.alsacom.com/jazz-a-mulhouse*). To find out what's going on at other times of the year, get hold of a copy of *Mulhouse Poche*, the free listings quarterly, or *Mulhouse Echo*. The tourist office should be well-stocked with both of these.

Rixheim and Pulversheim

In the village of **RIXHEIM**, 6km east of Mulhouse, the **Musée du Papier-Peint**, 28 rue Zuber (June–Sept daily 9am–noon & 2–6pm; winter daily except Tues 10am–noon & 2–6pm; 30F; train to Rixheim or bus #10 from Mulhouse, stop Centre Europe), a subsidiary of the printed fabrics museum, is housed in the former headquarters of the Teutonic Knights. A museum of wallpaper may not be everyone's idea of a fun afternoon out, but this contains a stunning cornucopia of antique painted wallpaper, and there are demonstrations of printing the stuff.

Just past **PULVERSHEIM**, 10km northwest off the D430 at Ungersheim, Mulhouse attempts to confront environmental issues in the **Écomusée d'Alsace** (daily: July & Aug 9am–7pm; April–June & Sept 9.30am–6pm; March & Oct 10am–5pm; Nov–Feb 10.30am–4.30pm; ☎03.89.74.44.54); a regional bus runs frequent services Monday to Saturday from the gare SNCF, direction "Guebwiller" (April–Nov 65F return; Dec–March 26F return). "Éco" may be a somewhat misleading prefix for this open-air museum, but it's certainly plenty of fun for adults and kids, with over fifty traditional Alsatian buildings spanning the centuries, as well as on-site craft workers doing their various things. It's a vast complex already, and there are plans to enlarge it further to incorporate the nearby potassium mine which recently ceased production.

FRANCHE-COMTÉ AND THE JURA MOUNTAINS

The **Jura mountains** – gentle in the west, precipitous in the east, with wide, high forested plateaux in between – cover most of the old county of **Franche-Comté**, once part of the realms of the Grand Dukes of Burgundy, but properly French only since the late 1600s. The towns, especially the capital **Besançon,** are beautiful tranquil with the River Doubs flowing through, and here you will find some of the prettiest villages in France, such as **Baume-Les-Messiuers** and **Château Chalon**. Otherwise, what there is to see is countryside – hundreds of square kilometres of woodland, lake and pasture that is hard to get around without a car, and is best explored on foot or by bicycle. There are several **GR footpaths** in the area, including the marathon GR5 from the Netherlands to the Med, and the GR9, which snakes its way through the Parc Régional du Haut-Jura. One of the best things about this part of France in summer is that you will barely notice other tourists. **Franche-Comté** is divided into four départments: the Territoire de Belfort, the Haute-Saône, the Doubs (around Besançon), and largest of all, the Jura.

Belfort and around

Nestled in the gap between the southern reaches of the Vosges and the northern outliers of the Jura mountains – the one natural chink in France's eastern geological armour and the obvious route for invaders – **BELFORT** is assured of a place in French

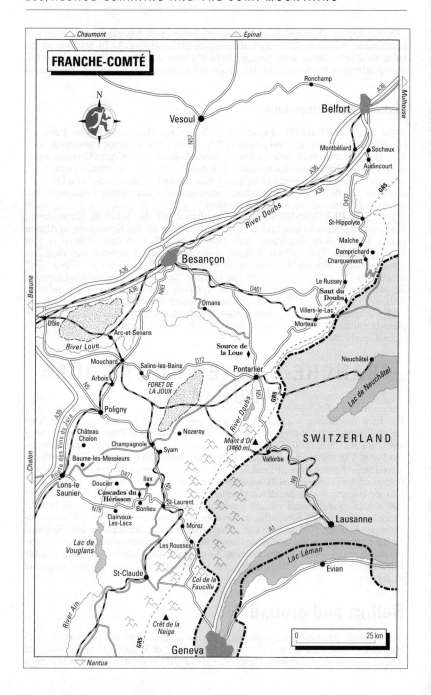

hearts for its deeds of military daring. Its name is particularly linked with the 1870 Prussian War, when its long resistance to siege spared it the humiliating annexation to Germany suffered by much of neighbouring Alsace-Lorraine. The commanding officer at the time, Colonel Denfert-Rochereau, earned himself the honour of numerous street names as well as that of a Parisian métro station. These days it is an interesting town with a mixed population.

Finding your way around Belfort is easy enough. The town is sliced in two by the River Savoureuse: the **new town** to the west is the commercial hub; to the east lies the quieter **old town**, laid out below the massive red **château**. Built by the ubiquitous fortress-architect Vauban on the site of a medieval fort, it now houses the **Museum of Art and History** (May–Sept 10am–7pm; Oct–April 10am–2pm & 2–5pm; closed Tues; ☎03.84.54.25.51/52). The museum contains works by Dürer, Doré and Rodin. The other collections include military objects from Belfort's centuries of conflicts, and artefacts from Bronze and Iron Ages found in the funeral cave at Cravanche in 1876. Vauban is also responsible for the fortifications surrounding Belfort, creating a five-sided old town whose street plan is still largely unchanged.

The most famous and photographed phenomenon in town is the eleven-metre-high red sandstone **lion** applied to the rock-face that you pass on the way up to the castle, fashioned by Bartholdi to commemorate the 1870 siege. From the **viewing platform** (Nov–March Mon–Fri 10am–noon and 2–5pm, weekends and hols 8am–noon and 2–5pm; April–Oct daily 8am–noon and 2–5pm; July–Sept daily 8am–7pm) at the front paw of the lion, you get some stunning views over the town and surrounding countryside.

Belfort is a good base for exploring the north-eastern corner of the **River Doubs**. After that, it's either follow the autoroute directly to Besançon which is a lively town with lots of good restaurants, or take your time and lose yourself in the hills and forests and pretty towns along the scenic route.

Practicalities

The **gare routière** and **gare SNCF** are at the end of Faubourg-de-France, the main pedestrianized shopping drag in the new town. The **tourist office** is on place de la Commune, just off Faubourg-de-France (mid–June to mid–Sept Mon–Sat 9.30am–6.30pm; mid–Sept to mid–June daily except Sun 9am–12.30pm & 1.30–6pm; ☎03.84.28.12.23, fax 03.84.21.03.99).

There is an excellent choice of hotels: the *Au Relais d'Alsace,* 5 av de la Laurencie (☎03.84.22.15.55, fax 03.84.28.70.48;②) will be happy to advise you about what's happening in the region, and it's also where out-of-town musicians stay when they perform in Belfort. There's also the *Hôtel Vauban,* 4 rue du Magasin (☎03.84.21.59.37, fax 03.84.21.41.67; ③) where the owners are also artists. For grandeur there is *Le Tonneau d'Or,* 1 rue Reiset (☎03.84.58.57.56, fax 03.84.58.57.50; ⑤).

The **youth hostel**, *Résidence Madrid,* is west of the railway line at 6 rue de Madrid (☎03.84.21.39.16, fax 03.84.28.58.95). Belfort's **campsite,** *Les Promenades d'Essert,* is on ave du Général Leclerc, just before the foyer, in the Parc des Loisirs (☎03.84.21.03.30; mid–May to mid–Sept).

Inexpensive places to **eat** – and **cafés** can be found in the place d'Armes and place de la Republique, in between antique shops and old-fashioned grocery stores such as Épicerie de Lion, rue de la Porte de France. *Aux Crêpes d'Antan,* 13 rue du Quai (☎03.84.22.82.54) has delicious crêpes, starting from 30F. *Bistrot Boeuf-Carottes,* 14 rue Lecourbe (☎03.84.21.15.40) is another good place to eat, with *plats* from 60F and menus from 69F. *Café Théâtre* (9am–1am) behind the theatre on Place Corbis has outdoor tables by the river and is a pleasant place for a coffee. *La Poudrière,* place de l'Arsenal (closed late July–Aug) is the best place for live music.

Ronchamp

Before you take to the hills, there is one day-trip from Belfort worth undertaking – the mining town of **RONCHAMP**, 20km west (train or bus), where the architect Le Corbusier built one of his most enduring and atypical masterpieces in the 1950s, the **Chapelle de Notre-Dame-du-Haut** (daily 9am–7pm; 10F). It stands, all in concrete, above the town on the top of a wooded hill, white and reflective, visible from miles away, with its aerodynamic tower and wave-curved roof cutting into the sky beyond. Inside, the rough-textured walls are pierced with unequal embrasures, several closed by patterns of primary glass, whose reds, blues and yellows stain the dipping floor. Simplicity itself, with pared-down crucifix and steel altar rail, it's highly atmospheric.

The **tourist office** is on rue le Corbusier (May–Sept Mon–Fri 9am–noon & 2–6pm, Sat 9.30am–noon & 2–6pm; Oct–April Tues–Fri 9am–noon & 2–5pm). If it's getting late and you're worried about a place to **stay**, there are rooms at *La Pomme d'Or*, 19 rue le Corbusier, alongside the train line (☎03.84.20.62.12, fax 03.84.63.59.45; ①; restaurant from 55F).

Youth hostellers can take another twenty-minute train ride west to Vesoul, where the HI **youth hostel** is by the Lac de Vaivre–Vesoul (☎03.84.76.48.55; bus #1 to stop Camping), but check the train timetables. There are not many trains to/from either Belfort or Vesoul.

Montbéliard

MONTBÉLIARD is not far from Belfort and, because of the Peugeot factory (the second car production plant to be created in Europe) is another thriving industrial town in this region. There are some unexpected pleasures in Montbéliard: the town has been part of France only since 1793, so the architecture of the old town has a strong Germanic look. The imposing **Château des Ducs de Wurtemburg** (May–Sept 10am–noon & 1.30–6.30pm; closed Tues; 30F) constructed during the fifteenth and sixteenth centuries, has been restored to house various exhibitions: there is always a specialist international exhibition as well as the permanent display of the collection of famous French zoologist **Georges Cuvier** who was born in Montbéliard and whose work paved the way for Darwin; there is also a display of the Gallo-Roman objects found nearby at the remains of the huge **Roman theatre** at Mandeure (rue du Theatre, Mandeure; daily 24hr; free). The old houses around the château are being repainted in their original colours. Note the circular stairwells, always at the back of the house – an architectural curiosity developed in the days when space was taxed, as part of an elaborate tax-avoidance scheme. The **Bourg des Halles** covered market was built in the sixteenth century, and is another fine Germanic building. The industry/mechanical theme infects everything around here. Every two years in December there is a fabulous **festival**, "Les Machinent Rient et le Révillon de Boulons" when crazy mechanical vehicles/moveable sculptures and their creators fill the streets like surrealist Peugeots. There is an outdoor Christmas market 'Lumières de Noële' every year around the St-Martin church, and also a three-kilometre labyrinth at the **Parc du Près-la-Rose**.

The choice of hotels and restaurants is slightly better in Belfort, but don't ignore Montbéliard and the museums in the nearby villages. The **tourist office** is at 1 rue Henri Mouat (May–Sept Mon–Fri 9am–noon 1.30–7pm Sat–Sun 9am–noon 1.30–6pm;Oct–April Mon–Fri 9am–noon Sat 10am–1pm ☎03.81.94.45.60, fax 03.81.32.12.07). For local events, which may influence whether you stay in Montbéliard or Belfort which both have some good music and art festivals, get the free cultural magazine *Atmosphere,* or *Montbéliard Magazine*, available in tourist offices. For **accommodation**, the *Hôtel-Restaurant l'Auberge Mon Repos*, 8 rue des Grands-Jardins (☎03.81.94.52.67; ①) is very peaceful with a large garden, or the *Hôtel de la Balance*, 40

CROSS-COUNTRY SKIING & MOUNTAIN BIKING IN THE JURA

The nature of the Jura's terrain – high plateaux guaranteeing winter snow but without excessively steep gradients – has made it France's most popular **cross-country skiing** destination. Known as *ski du fond*, the goal of any superfit *fondeur* is the 210-kilometre Grande Traversée du Jura (GTJ), which roughly follows the long-distance GR5 footpath across the high plateau from Villiers-le-Lac to Hauteville-Lompnes.

The same gentle topography and established infrastructure which enable cross-country skiing have made this region an ideal high-summer venue for **mountain biking**, currently enjoying an upsurge in popularity in the eastern Jura, with hundreds of waymarked cross-country skiing pistes used in season doubling as trails for adventuresome mountain bikers. The 300-kilometre **GTJ–VTT**, starting near Montbéliard, has become the greatest long-distance challenge in the area. Many people cycle on the roads in the area; there aren't that many cars, and if you can handle the hills, go for it.

Cycling in the Doubs region is flatter and very scenic, with proper cycling paths. The 65-kilometre **Tour des Lacs** takes in some caves and waterfalls. There are 21 routes listed in the *Guide de Cyclotourisme du Doubs*; 35F published by ADED, Hôtel du Départment, 25031 Besançon, and also available from the Besançon tourist office.

The headquarters of the regional tourist board, the **Comité Departemental du Tourisme**, BP 652, 39021, Lons-le-Saunier (☎03.84.85.89.82), can supply plenty of information, maps and literature – in English – on outdoor leisure opportunities of all kinds in the Jura.

---

rue de Belfort (☎03.81.96.77.41, fax 03.81.91.47.16; ③) in the old town, which also has a restaurant from 100F. There are plenty of outdoor *cafés* in the old town area: *Café de la Paix,* 12 Rue des Febvres, near Les Halles, is a nice place to relax. There is also a *cyber café* (few and far between in this part of France): *Cybercentre,* 2 cour des Halles (☎03.81.91.10.85; Mon–Sat 2–8pm; call in advance or ask at the tourist office because they are planning to relocate mid-99; Internet access 10F per hour).

The Doubs Valley

The River Doubs runs a course like a hairpin, doubling back on itself repeatedly, with its most dramatic change of course at **AUDINCOURT**, a short way south of Belfort and the place where Peugeots are made. The town's chief sight is the modern **church of Sacré-Cœur**, which has windows and a tapestry by Fernand Léger. Just north of Audincourt, **Sochaux** is home to the **Musée Peugeot** (daily 10am–6pm; 35F), which displays the products of over a century of automotive manufacturing, from the Bey of Tunis' one-off quadricycle to contemporary rally winners and concept cars.

From Audincourt, southwards and upstream, the D437 follows the valley of the Doubs, winding and climbing steadily between steep, wooded banks to the bridging point at **ST-HIPPOLYTE**, where you'll find the riverside *Hôtel Bellevue* (☎03.81.96.51.53, fax 03.81.96.52.40; ①) and a **campsite** (May–Oct). Seven kilometres west along the D39, the *Auberge de Moricemaison*, in Valoreille (☎03.81.64.01.72; ①), offers rustic simplicity and wholesome evening meals from 55F.

A less congested scenic route from **Besançon** follows the D464 south of the river, but without a car you'd have to hitch all this – manageable but slow. Beyond St-Hippolyte the road climbs onto a wide plateau at an altitude of around 850m, with grassy cattle pastures encompassed by fir-clad ridges and dotted with broad-roofed farms and barns. Once up here, cycling is easy enough. Alternatively, it's a lovely but long hike of well over 50km along the **GR5 footpath** from St-Hippolyte across the plateau and up the Doubs valley to the plunging waterfall of the **Saut du Doubs** outside **Villers-le-Lac** – the beginning of the **GTJ** marathon cross-country ski piste. To reach the fall, it's a four-kilometre walk from the last houses above the north end of the lake in **Villers** along a track through the woods.

By road, Villiers is 47km south of St-Hippolyte along the D437, turning east at **MORTEAU**, a village with nothing more than a much-altered, thirteenth-century priory church to recommend it. The D437 is part of the *Route du Comté*, so if you like cheese, it's worth the detour. There is accommodation here in the form of a **gîte** on rue des Moulinots (☎03.81.67.48.72) and, up on the plateau, the *Hôtel des Montagnards* also offers a warm welcome (☎03.81.67.08.86, fax 03.81.67.14.57; ②; closed Sun out of season).

Besançon

The capital of Franche-Comté, **BESANÇON**, is an ancient and attractive grey-stone town at the northern edge of the Jura mountains, enclosed in a loop of the River Doubs, whose lugubrious meanders define the layout of the old town. The tongue of land it sits on has been protected since Roman times, when it lay on a major trading route; the indefatigable Vauban added the still-extant fortifications and a citadelle to guard the natural breach in the river. Once a major centre of French clock-making (until the Far East became important in the manufacturing industry), Besançon was also the birthplace of artificial silk – or rayon – in 1890. It counts among its native sons both the pioneering Lumière brothers and epic novelist Victor Hugo.

The **River Doubs** rises on the high plateau 100km to the south of here, making a diversion far to the northwest of the town, gathering tributaries and broadening as it briefly crosses the Swiss border before entering Besançon. A lazy journey upstream to **PONTARLIER** can make a rewarding excursion over a couple of days. From Pontarlier a direct return north to Besançon can be made by following the **River Loue's** steep descent through its heavily wooded valley past the pretty mill town of **Ornans**.

Arrival, information and accommodation

The **gare SNCF** is at the end of avenue Maréchal-Foch (☎03.81.53.50.50 for information), while the **gare routière** is on rue Proudhon off rue de la République; **buses** for Pontarlier and Salins-les-Bains leave from here. The **tourist office**, by the second bridge on rue de l'Armée-Française (April–Sept Mon–Sat 9am–7pm, Sun 10am–noon, plus mid–June to mid–Sept Sun 3–5pm; Oct–March Mon–Sat 9am–6pm; ☎03.81.80.92.55, fax 03.81.80.58.30), provides a free accommodation service.

Hotels include the comfortable and friendly family-run *Granvelle*, 13 rue Lecourbe, close to the **Citadelle** (☎03.81.81.33.92, fax 03.81.81.31.77, ②); *Florel*, 6 rue de la Viotte opposite the station (☎03.81.80.41.08, fax 03.81.50.44.40; ①); the dead central *Regina*, 91 Grande-Rue (☎03.81.81.50.22, fax 03.81.81.60.20; ②); the *Hôtel de Paris*, 33 rue des Granges (☎03.81.81.36.56, fax 03.81.61.94.90; ②), with free parking for guests; and the *Hôtel du Nord*, at 8–10 rue de Moncey in the centre (☎03.81.81.34.56; fax 03.81.81.85.96; ②). There is no official **youth hostel**, but the *Centre International de Séjour* at 19 rue Martin-du-Gard, 4km northwest of the centre (☎81.50.07.54; bus #8, stop *L'Épitaphe*), fulfils the same function, though at slightly greater expense. Alternatively, there's the *Foyer des Jeunes Filles*, 18 rue de la Cassotte (☎03.81.80.90.01; women only), and CROUS, whose main office is at 38 av de l'Observatoire (☎03.81.50.26.88); though to get a room you must head for the university itself (open July & Aug; bus #7 direction "Campus", stop Université). **Camping** is at Plage de Chalezeule, 5km out on the Belfort road (May–Oct; bus #1 towards Palente).

The town

Once you're in the old town, getting around is simple and some of the most interesting things to see are outdoors and free – such as the beautiful bluish stone walls of most buildings, and the signs of Roman life that still remain. Rue de la République leads from the river to the central **place du 8-Septembre** and the sixteenth-century **Hôtel de Ville**. The principal street, **Grande-Rue**, cuts across the square along the line of an old Roman road. At its northwestern end – the livelier part of town with shops and cafés – there is the excellent **Musée des Beaux-Arts** (daily except Tues 9.30am–noon & 2–6pm; 21F), with some good nineteenth- and twentieth-century works, two magnificent Bonnards, and a wonderful clock collection. Midway down the street, the fine sixteenth-century **Palais Granvelle** houses a not very illuminating local-history museum. Continuing up the street, you pass place Victor-Hugo (he was born at no. 140) and arrive at the **Porte Noire**, a second-century Roman triumphal arch spanning the street and partially embedded in the adjoining houses. Beside it, in the shady little **square Archéologique A-Castan**, are the remains of a *nymphaeum*, a small reservoir of water fed by an aqueduct. Beyond the arch is the pompous eighteenth-century **Cathédrale St-Jean** (April–Sept daily; Feb, March & Oct–Dec daily except Tues & Wed; closed Jan. Guided visits at hourly intervals 9.50–11.50am & 2.50–5.50pm; 14F), which houses the nineteenth-century **Horloge Astronomique**, detailing over a hundred terrestrial and celestial positions and containing some 30,000 parts.

The spectacular **citadelle** (July–Aug 9am–7pm; Sept–June 10am–5pm; closed hols; 40F) is a steep, fifteen-minute climb from here, with a crow's-nest view of the town and the noose-like bend in the river that contains it. It houses many worthwhile museums (times as above): for animal lovers there's the **Musée d'Histoire Naturelle** (a **noctarium, aquarium, insectarium** and **zoo**); the **Musée Comtois**, with pottery, furniture, a good collection of nineteenth-century marionettes, as well as some marvellous old farming implements; the **Espace Vauban**, devoted to the military architect; and – possibly best of all – the **Musée de la Résistance et de la Déportation**, a superb aid to understanding postwar France's political consciousness (English audio commentary available). The first rooms document the rise of Nazism and French Fascism through photographs and exhibits, including a bar of soap stamped *RIF* – "Pure Jew Fat". In the section on the Vichy government, there's a telegram of encouragement sent by Marshall Pétain to the French troops of the "legion of volunteers against Bolshevism", who were fighting alongside the Germans on the eastern front. Finally, as counterbalance, much is made of General Leclerc's vow at Koufra in the Libyan desert, whose capture in January 1941 was the first, entirely French, victory of the war – "We will not stop until the French flag flies once more over Metz and Strasbourg" – a vow which he kept when he entered the latter city at the head of a division in November 1944.

Eating, drinking and entertainment

There are plenty of lively and inexpensive restaurants, cafés and bars along the river near Place Battant, particularly along the little street running parallel to the river. *Brasserie du Commerce*, 5 rue des Granges, has rather grand decor and ambience, and *Brasserie du Palais Granvelle*, in a lovely shady park next door to the Palais Granvelle, is the best place for breakfast and other daily coffee hits.

Two good places for a substantial **meal** are the century-old *Restaurant au Petit Polonais*, 81 rue des Granges (closed Sat eve & Sun; ☎03.81.81.23.67), and for lunch try the superb *Le Café-Café*, 5bis rue Luc Breton (Mon–Sat lunch only; ☎03.81.81.15.24; *plats* from 65F).

The two biggest **cultural events** of the year in Besançon are **Jazz en Franche-Comté**, which takes place in June and July, and an international young conductors' competition in the first two weeks of September.

Pontarlier and around

Thirty kilometres southwest of Morteau by train lies **PONTARLIER**, one of the bigger Jura towns, and not very interesting in itself except as a transit point and recreational base. If you need **accommodation** here, try the *Hôtel de Morteau*, 26 rue Jeanne-d'Arc, near the river (☎03.81.39.14.83, fax 03.81.39.75.07; ②), with an excellent restaurant, from 70F. There's also an HI **youth hostel** at 2 rue Jouffroy, near the station (☎/fax 03.81.39.06.57); two **gîtes** – *Le Gounefay*, route du Grand-Taureau (☎03.81.39.05.99), and the *Chalet-Refuge du Larmont* (☎03.81.39.11.25); plus a **camping municipal** in rue de Toulourbief. For a couple of places to **eat**, try the *Le Petit Vannolles*, 8 rue de Vannolles, for a snack; or the *Brasserie de la Poste*, 55 rue de la République, for a meal. Good-quality **mountain bikes** can be rented from Vélos Pernet, 23 rue de la Republique (☎03.81.46.48.00), for 80F per day; and Sports et Neige, at no. 4 (☎03.81.39.04.69), has cross-country **ski gear**. The **tourist office,** 14 bis rue de la Gare (9am–noon & 2–6pm; closed Sun; ☎3.81.46.48.33, fax 03.81.46.83.32) has some good hiking maps for 12F and 58F – this is a good base for hiking.

Just south of town, past a divinely aromatic chocolate factory that will have chocoholics drooling, a steep road to the left ascends for 11km to **Le Grand Taureau**, whose 1328-metre summit is just a short walk from the road's end and offers a view over the whole Jura Massif and across Switzerland to the Alps. A couple of kilometres further south of Pontarlier, the **Château de Joux** (daily: Easter–June 10am–noon & 2–4.30pm; July & Aug 9am–6pm; Sept & Oct 10–11.30am & 2–4.30pm; 32F) stands over the defile known as La Cluse et Mijoux, the ancient Franco-Swiss frontier. It was originally constructed in the eleventh century, and Vauban had a hand in remodelling and modernizing it, but most of what you see today is less than a century old. The fort's history and impressive appearance are of more interest than its collection of military uniforms.

Moving on, there are **trains** and **buses** to Besançon; trains to Frasne, where you can catch the TGV to Dijon and Paris; and local buses to the six-kilometre-long **Lac de St-Point**, where you can pick up the GR5 again to make the ascent of **Mont d'Or** (1463m) overlooking Lake Geneva and the Alps, and to Mouthe, where the River Doubs emerges from an underground cavern.

Ornans and the Valley of the Loue

Some 17km north of Pontarlier, the D67 splits west off the N57 and plunges precipitously into the **Valley of the Loue**. A couple of kilometres above the village of Ouhans lies the source of the river, issuing from an enormous rock beneath a tiered cliff, in winter entirely fringed with icicles. From this point you can continue on foot along the **GR595 footpath** down the valley bounded by densely wooded limestone cliffs, a descent no less dramatic by road as it passes through a string of pretty villages.

Roughly halfway between Pontarlier and Besançon, **ORNANS** is the prettiest of all, an archetypal Franche-Comté town that has become the touristic focal point of the valley. The Loue here is an abrupt trench with the river washing the foundations of ancient balconied houses. The town is easily appreciated from the numerous footbridges spanning the river. Pierre Vernier, inventor of the eponymous gauge, and the painter **Gustave Courbet** were both born here: the latter's house is now the **Musée de la Maison Natale de Gustave Courbet** (daily except Tues 10am–noon & 2–6pm) displaying some of his drawings, sculpture and locally painted scenes. The **tourist office** is at 7 rue Pierre Vernier, Mon–Sat 9.30am–noon & 2–6pm (☎/fax03.81.62.21.50). There's **accommodation** in the form of the riverside *Hôtel Le Progrès*, 11 rue Jacques

Gervais (☎03.81.62.16.79, fax 03.81.62.19.10; ②), and the pricier but better-placed *Hôtel de la Cascade* (☎03.81.60.95.30, fax 03.81.60.95.30; ③) in the centre of **MOUTHIER**, further down the D67. There are **campsites** and **gîtes d'étapes** in Ornans, Vuillifans and Mouthier Haute-Pierre (both up in the valley).

Arc-et-Senans and Salins-les-Bains

At the southeastern edge of the Forest of Chaux, some 7km north of Mouchard, is the unfinished eighteenth-century "salt city" of the **Saline Royale d'ARC-ET-SENANS** (April–June 9am–noon & 2–6pm; July & Aug 9am–7pm; Sept & Oct 9am–noon & 2–6pm; 38F), commissioned by royal decree in 1773 to replace the ageing works at Salins-les-Bains (see below). The complex, dreamed up by the Revolutionary architect Claude-Nicolas Ledoux, was to have become a model utopian city. His grandiose project reflected the egalitarian social concerns of the pre-Revolutionary era: the settlement was to have radiated along the primary axes of a clock-face from a nucleus housing the administrative offices, distillation plants, public baths and other municipal utilities.

Sadly, the socio-aesthetic ideals could not overcome the works' functional deficiencies: the pipeworks linking the new plant with Salins deteriorated rapidly and only half of the central arc was ever completed. Salt production continued until the end of the nineteenth century, but all that remains today is the impressively restored semi-circle of eleven buildings, a monumental epitaph to Ledoux's unconsummated vision. The beautiful complex now houses two musuems, usually with exhibitions about architecture.

If you've developed a taste for saltworks, **SALINS-LES-BAINS**, 8km east of Mouchard, is worth a further detour (back along the tree-lined country road that leads to the entrance to the Saline Royale). Once you're in the town you will notice loudspeakers along the mainstreet, for music during the summer. Confined at the bottom of a narrow valley piercing the flank of the Jura's central plateau, the recuperative spa town of Salins has been producing salt for around a thousand years. The Chalon family moved in on the town in the thirteenth century and the wealth they accrued from the control and sale of the "white gold" essential for the preservation of food enabled them to become among the most influential of the Comté's medieval overlords. This prominence, as well as the town's key position on the route to Switzerland, accounts for the two lofty forts overlooking the town. The **Salines de Salins**, or brine-wells (1-hr guided tours daily: Feb–Easter & mid–Sept to Dec 10.30am, 2.30pm & 4pm; Easter to mid–Sept hourly 9–11am & 2.30–5.30pm; 24F), are inevitably the town's main attraction: once inside the vaulted underground galleries, you are shown the pumps which drew up the brine solution from the rock salt that was too deep to mine, while other salt-related activities are also innovatively depicted. There are two forts perched on the hills above the town, which make good walking destinations.

For further information, visit the **tourist office** in Place des Salines (May–Sept 9am–noon & 2–6pm; Oct–April closed Sun & Mon; ☎03.84.73.01.34, fax 03.84.37.92.85). Having styled itself as a spa town since the 1840s (and still doing so), Salins has some grand **hotels** that once accommodated the fashionably ailing gentry. The *Grand Hôtel des Bains*, in place des Alliés (☎03.84.37.90.50, fax 03.84.37.96.80; ③), offers comfortable accommodation; or try the old-fashioned *Hôtel des Deux Forts*, in place du Vigneron (☎03.84.37.93.75; ②). The *Hôtel Bon Accueil*, on 50 rue de la Liberté, north of the central square (☎03.84.37.94.31; ②), is slightly less expensive, and has a café/restaurant from 60F. There is a **campsite** (May–Sept, ☎03.84.37.92.70) on avenue Général-de-Gaulle.

Dôle and the Jura lowlands

Halfway between Besançon and Dijon on the edge of the flat and fertile valley of the Saône, **DÔLE** is quiet and provincial. The medieval capital of the Comté region until Louis XI ordered its destruction in 1479, it's a place to stay overnight, or rest, and attractive enough in a subdued way. Grey-stone houses with barred ground-floor windows stand on narrow streets around the vast, stolid **collegiate of Notre-Dame**, with its lofty belfry – you can climb it, the view is well worth it. Inside the church, there is a wonderful Rococo organ, and beautiful windows by the same hand as those in Notre-Dame de Paris and Strasbourg Cathedral. The Rhône–Rhine canal washes the feet of the town, and along its bank below the church runs the narrow rue Pasteur, birthplace of the French biologist and chemist **Louis Pasteur** who discovered the rabies virus (and its cure), and whose name is commemorated in the process of "pasteurization", another of his discoveries. He was the son of a tanner, and his house, like those of his father's workmates, backs onto a pretty waterside walkway leading to an island. The newly renovated house is now a **museum** (April–Oct daily except Tues 10am–noon & 2–6pm; no lunchtime closure July & Aug; 15F).

Whatever happens in Dôle happens between the Grande-Rue – leading up from the bridge – and place Grévy, with the **tourist office**, 6 place Grévy (July & Aug daily except Sun 9am–6.30pm; Sept–June Mon 2–6pm, Tues–Fri 9am–noon & 2–6pm, Sat 9am–noon; ☎03.84.72.11.22, fax 03.84.82.49.27) on one side and cafés on the other. At the top of Grande-Rue is the delightful place aux Fleurs, with its fountain and amusing bronze sculpture of *Les Trois Commères* ("The Three Gossips"). There are some reasonable **hotels** here, including *Le Grand Cerf*, 6 rue Arney, near place Grévy (☎03.84.72.11.68; closed 27 Jul–16 Aug, ①); and *La Chaumière*, across the river on avenue Maréchal-Juin (☎03.84.70.72.40, fax 03.84.79.25.60; ③). But the cheapest rooms, as usual, are at the HI **youth hostel** *St-Jean,* place Jean XXIII (☎03.84.82.36.74, fax 03.84.79.17.69). To get there, take bus #1, direction "Mesnils-Poiset", stop Les Paters. There's a **campsite**, *Camping du Pasquier*, by the river (☎03.84.72.02.61; mid-March to Oct). For **food**, there are various pizzerias and crêperies, like the canalside *La Demi-Lune*, 39 rue Pasteur (closed Mon out of season), and *Le Bec Fin,* 67 rue Pasteur (☎03.84.82.43.43) is for the gourmands; menus from 105F. The **gare routière** is next to the train station.

The Forêt de Chaux

To the east of Dôle lie the 200 square kilometres of the ancient **Forêt de Chaux**, France's third-largest forest and site of some of the country's earliest industrial endeavours. Set in a clearing in the southern central part of the forest are the ancient settlements of **La Vieille-Loye** and **Turot**, since early Christian times centres of charcoal burning – once essential in the production of metals – and, until very recently, glass manufacture, at one time producing up to one million bottles a year.

Access to the forest – which makes an agreeable alternative to the main roads to Salins-les-Bains or Besançon – is easiest from the N5/N72 Salins road to the south and west. In this part of the forest you'll find many waymarked walking trails wending their way beneath the overhead canopy of oak, chestnut and beech.

Lons-le-Saunier to Arbois

At the base of the central plateau's west-facing rim, set picturesquely astride rivers and in the midst of fertile soils, are a number of towns that have supported centuries of agriculture, recently accommodating the small, specialist industries so typical of the Jura. The spa town and departmental capital of **Lons-le-Saunier** is a tranquil town, with fireworks on July 14, and on July 31 for St-Désiré, and outdoor music concerts in summer. South of the town a string of vineyards traces the plateau's edge to just beyond **Arbois**, the Jura's wine-making capital. This is the eighty-kilometre **Route des Vins du Jura**, where the region's distinctive wines are cultivated and manufactured from a variety of vines.

Between Lons and Arbois, a scenic detour can be made into the hills to visit the ancient, time-locked villages of **Baume-Les-Messieurs** and **Château Chalon**. And at **Poligny** more wines and the long-refined flavour of Comté cheese, produced in the Jura since the thirteenth century, are available for sampling at the Maison du Comté.

Lons-le-Saunier

Once the site of a neolithic settlement, **LONS-LE-SAUNIER** was all but destroyed by a fire in the early seventeenth century. Most buildings you'll see today date from this era, and a wander around some of the older examples is an agreeable way to fill half a day.

The central **place de la Liberté**, a ten-minute walk north of the train station, is a good place to start. Should you happen to be in the square on the hour, the **theatre clock** at the eastern end of the *place* will chime a familiar half-dozen notes from *La Marseillaise* to honour Lons' most famous son, Rouget de Lisle, the anthem's composer (see p.928). Just north of the *place* is the attractive, colonnaded thoroughfare of **rue du Commerce**, where some of Lons' oldest buildings line the street in which de Lisle was born. Continuing north through the place de la Comédie and past the ancient **salt well**, Le Puits Salé, you arrive at the **Musée Municipal d'Archéologie**, 25 rue Richebourg (Mon & Wed–Fri 10am–noon & 2–6pm, Sat & Sun 2–5pm; closed Tues; free entry Wed). It presents some absorbing prehistoric displays, including a touching Neolithic family scene circa 4000 BC, a dug-out canoe found locally, and a life-size replica of a 210-million-year-old plateosaurus, France's oldest-known dinosaur. The museum, which also mounts various temporary exhibitions, is housed in the old Bel cheese factory, whose enduringly popular *La Vache Qui Rit* cheese spread is now produced in larger premises near the station (you might see a big lorry with the familiar cow on it). Returning south along rue Richebourg to avenue Jean-Moulin, you come to the inevitable **statue** of Rouget de Lisle, designed by Frédéric Bartholdi, the sculptor who went on to refine de Lisle's stirring pose on a much grander scale in the Statue of Liberty. A left turn here leads to the pleasant **Parc Edouard Guenon** containing the **Salines** (☎03.84.24.20.34 for admission details) with their ornate *fin-de-siècle* exterior. Lavishly equipped with a sauna, Turkish bath and jacuzzi, its saline immersions not only soothe the usual aches and pains, but are also renowned for their ability to cure juvenile bed-wetting.

Practicalities

Lons' **tourist office** is close to the theatre clock at 1 rue Pasteur (Mon–Sat 8.30–noon & 2–6pm; ☎03.84.24.65.01, fax 03.84.43.22.59). For information about the Jura region, the **Comité Général du Tourisme** is at 8 rue Louis Rousseau (☎03.84.87.08.77). If you want to **stay**, two good hotels are the *Hôtel des Sports*, 21 rue St-Désiré, south of the place de la Liberté (☎03.84.24.04.42, fax 03.84.24.02.20; ①), easygoing and clean (rugby is the favourite sport here) or the cosy *Nouvel Hôtel*, 50 rue Lecourbe (☎03.84.47.20.67, fax 03.84.43.27.49; ②), just west of the *place*. There's a rather pricey **campsite**, *Camping de la Marjorie* (☎03.84.24.26.94), on the northeast edge of town. To **eat** really cheaply, try the restaurant/*pension* of the *famille* Ferrard in 7 rue Tamisier, parallel to rue du Commerce, where just 50F will ensure a filling meal. For a truly inspired meal in a charming setting, pay a visit to the *Bistrot des Marronniers*, 22 rue de Vallière, west off rue St-Désiré (closed Sun; menu from 60F). For a coffee or drink, the *Grand Café de Strasbourg* next to the theatre has a beautiful interior.

Baume-Les-Messieurs and Château Chalon

Twenty kilometres east of Lons is the tiny village of **BAUME-LES-MESSIEURS**, tucked in a cliff-bound valley festooned with foliage on all but the steepest faces. From Lons, the quickest – as well as most interesting – way to get there is to take the N471 Champagnole road and turn down the narrow and steep lanes descending into the valley from the north; the **Belvédère des Roches de Baume**, signposted off the N471, gives stunning views of the village and the verdant Seille valley out as far as the Château Chalon and beyond if the weather is up to it.

In the village, the main attraction is the **abbey** (guided tours mid–June to mid–Sept 10–6pm; 25F). Monks were active in the area in the fourth century, and it is thought that the Irish St Columba was here in the sixth century, along with other monks, before leaving for Cluny (see p.538). In spite of visitors clacking over the ancient stone floors, an atmosphere of monastic tranquillity still pervades the place. Consecrated in 909 by Benedictines, it was disbanded by the newly formed Republic in 1792, and today the interior and its twelfth-century **church**, in whose crypt rest three members of the once-dominant Chalon family, remain open to the public. **Accommodation** is available at the abbey at the *Gothique Café* (☎03.84.44.64.47, ④); there are three beautiful rooms that will make you feel as though you're back in the Middle Ages, and the café itself has lovely meals using local produce: from 45F.

Two kilometres south of the village, at the very end of the valley, are the **Grottes de Baume** (April–Sept several 40-min guided tours daily 9am–6pm; 25F), one of the many limestone stalactite cave systems throughout the region. Those who are particularly energetic may wish to ascend the stairway cut into the rock on the valley's eastern face; at times exposed and best avoided if conditions are wet, it leads to the clifftop and the Belvédère des Roches de Baume viewpoint described above. Others may opt for a meal at the *Restaurant des Grottes* (☎03.84.44.61.59, lunchtimes only; 80–140F) near the beautiful, fern-draped **waterfall** with a stunning view back down the valley.

As you head north out of Baume, you'll see the limestone cliffs recede as the valley opens out, revealing miles of vineyards that yield the distinctive yellow wine of Château Chalon, produced from the Sauvignon grape. The fortified hilltop village of **CHÂTEAU CHALON** overlooks the vines and was built around a castle (not open to the public) of the once-influential Comtoise family who give the village its name. A short wander will lead you past promising baskets of Chalon (expect to pay around 160F a bottle) to the fortified **church**. Dating from the eleventh century and possessing some impressive stained glass and early examples of vaulting, an archway outside by the porch leads to the **Belvédère de la Rochette**, looking out across the valley back towards Baume. The views from the village are indescribably beautiful, and free.

Poligny and Arbois

Back on the Route des Vins du Jura, the attractive medieval town of **POLIGNY**, at the south of the Culée de Vaux Valley, is noteworthy for its well-preserved, early Romanesque buildings, including the **church of St-Hippolyte**, with the characteristic, bell-like tower seen all over Franche-Comté. But the town's principal attraction is the hallowed **Maison du Comté** in avenue de la Résistance, which leads south from the central place des Deportés (July & Aug daily 1-hr guided tours; ☎03.84.37.23.51), an old fromagerie that now forms the headquarters of the Comité Interprofessional du Gruyère du Comté. Displays show the process of cheese-making from extracting milk to producing the finished article, alongside audiovisual presentations exalting the industry. Gruyère officers, an institution of tax collectors founded by Charlemagne, once collected the 60-centimetre-wide *meules* of cheese as payment – each the product of 500 litres of milk; now, with over 800 years' experience of production, Comté cheese has earned the distinguished *Appellation d'Origine Contrôlée* (AOC) label more commonly reserved for vintage wines.

The attractive medieval houses and other sites of interest in Poligny are indicated on the blue *Walking Through the Old Town* leaflet available from the friendly **tourist office** in rue Victor–Hugo (May–Sept Mon–Fri 9am–noon & 2–6pm, Sat & Sun 9.30am–noon & 2–6pm; Oct–April Tues–Fri 9am– noon & 2–6pm, Sat 9am–noon & 2–5pm; ☎ 03.84.37.24.21).

There's no mistaking that **ARBOIS**, 10km to the north, is the capital of this region's viticulture. Glittering wine emporia line the central place de la Liberté, entreating you to sample the unusual local wines, of which the sweet *vin de paille* is rarest – so called because its grapes are dried on beds of straw, giving the wine a strong aftertaste equal to that of the better-known Château Chalon. Chocolatier M. Hirsinger has developed chocolates to eat with wines, especially the Jura's own *vin jaune*, a wine flavoured with walnuts. A visit to the Hirsinger chocolate shop on place de la Liberté is a must: try the delicious ice cream.

Louis Pasteur lived in the town after his family moved from Dôle, and his boyhood home, the **Maison de Louis Pasteur** on avenue Pasteur (mid–May to mid–Sept 9.45am–5.15pm; mid–Sept to mid–Nov Dec 11–22 & mid–Feb to mid-May 10am–4pm; closed Tues; 32F). The **tourist office** is in rue de l'Hôtel de Ville (May–Sept Mon–Sat 9.15am–12.30pm & 2.30–6.30pm, Sun 10am–noon & 3–5pm; Oct–April Mon 3–6pm, Wed–Fri 9am–noon & 2–6pm, closed Tues; ☎03.84.37.47.37), and in the basement is the **Musée de la Vigne et du Vin** (Jul–Aug 10am–6pm; otherwise 10am–noon & 2–6pm; closed Tues; 15F), which details the development and production of wine in the Jura.

If you're **staying** overnight in town, try the cheap and friendly *Hôtel Mephisto*, 33 place Faramand, just over the river (☎03.84.66.06.49; ①), or the more luxurious *Hôtel Les Messageries* (☎03.84.66.15.45, fax 03.84.37.41.09; ②–④), up from the Maison Pasteur. There's a **campsite**, *Camping Les Vignes*, on avenue Général-Leclerc (☎/fax 03.84.66.14.12; April–Sept), 1km east of the centre. For a **meal**, try the *Restaurant La Cuisance*, with lunchtime menus around 50F and evening menus from 70F to 100F; or there's a good pizzeria, *Au Jardin Venitien*, 1 rue Mercière (☎03.84.37.49.22; pizzas from 35F).

The Central Plateau and the Jura mountains

On the broad upland plateau, the Jura landscape unrolls, stretches and rises in increasingly abrupt steps to the mountains bordering the Swiss frontier. With its lakes and pine forests, small farming communities and – at the higher altitudes – huge ski resorts enveloping tiny villages, semi-deserted in summer, this is the most beautiful area of the Jura and, as you might expect – despite trains linking **Champagnole**, **Morez** and **St-Claude** with Arbois and Pontarlier – best appreciated with your own transport.

Champagnole and the Forêt de la Joux

Although at a major crossroads on the plateau, **CHAMPAGNOLE**, an industrial town largely rebuilt after a major fire in 1798, holds little intrinsic interest for the passing visitor, with the exception of an **archeological museum**, 26 rue Baronne-Delfort (July–Aug 2–6pm; closed Tues; 15F) above the tourist office, which displays an interesting array of Gallic and Roman artefacts found in the vicinity. However, the town does serve as a useful base for exploring the surrounding countryside, in particular the Forêt de la Joux, to the northeast.

For central **accommodation**, try the *Hôtel de la Londaine*, 31 rue du Général–Leclerc (☎03.84.52.06.69; ①), and for old-style grandeur, the *Grand Hotel Ripotot*, 54 rue

Maréchal Foch (☎03.84.52.15.45, fax 03.84.52.09.11; ③) which is definitely the nicest hotel in town. The **campsite** *Camping de Boyse,* is on rue Georges-Vallery (June to mid–Sept). The **tourist office** is in an annexe of the mairie at 26 rue Baronne-Delort (☎03.84.52.43.67), and provides lots of information about exploring the surrounding forests and lakes, including a hiking kit for 30F. If you are planning a walk in the region, this is the place to get information.

Out of Champagnole, things start to get remote and beautiful. To the southeast, the D279 passes the **château at SYAM**, built in 1818 (summer Sat & Sun only), and continues to the **Gorges de la Langouette**, 17km away. Here, a half-hour walk leads down to the narrow 47-metre-deep gorge sliced through the cretaceous escarpment by the River Saine. Other riverine curiosities in the area include the **Perte de l'Ain**, near the village of Bourg-de-Sirod, where a half-hour walk from an electricity station leads through the woods, past a waterfall and lesser cascades, to a boulder-strewn chasm where the Ain takes a brief subterranean detour. Another pleasant ten-minute walk a few kilometres northeast – just past the village of Conte – leads to a natural amphitheatre from whose base rises the **source of the Ain**.

A couple of kilometres north of the source, spread over a small hill surrounded by pastures, is the old walled village of **NOZEROY**, ancestral home of the Chalon family, who dominated regional politics in feudal times. The town preserves much of its medieval charm today with the **Porte de l'Horloge** – once part of the town's fortifications – framing the beginning of the Grande-Rue. This thoroughfare, lined with many ancient houses, ends at the place des Annonciades and the ruins of the thirteenth-century **castle**.

North of Nozeroy, on the other side of the D471 Champagnole–Pontarlier road, the **Forêt de la Joux** is considered one of the most beautiful of France's native pine forests. It is crisscrossed by a net of narrow fire roads, but if you don't have a car the Gare de la Joux, in the heart of the forest on the Champagnole–Pontarlier rail line, is accessible on foot or by bicycle. There are many well-marked walking trails through the forest: the most popular area is the **Sapins de la Glacière**. The **Route des Sapins** is the approved tourist drive, signposted for 50km from the D471 to the village of Levier, passing lookouts and the 45-metre-high **Sapin Président** along the way. But the less regimented can just as easily enjoy getting mildly disorientated by following any number of lesser, unmarked roads and discovering the wonder of the forest for themselves.

The Lake District

South of Champagnole, the flattened plateau, unable to shed the Haute Jura's winter run-off, collects the meltwaters in a series of natural and not-so-natural lakes: the **Region des Lacs**, loosely strung along the valley of the River Ain. Where the ground begins to crumple upward to the eastern summits, gorges and waterfalls highlight each successive step, and lookouts survey the tiny villages, each with its characteristic domed belfry beaten from metal or composed from a mosaic of tiles and slates. Some of the lakes charge parking fees during the day, but after 6pm, when the crowds and swimming supervisors go home, the lakes are deserted and peaceful, perfect for an evening picnic watching the sun set.

Clairvaux-les-Lacs and the Cascades du Hérisson

The region's main resort town is **CLAIRVAUX-LES-LACS**. It is here that the northern tip of the serpentine **Lac de Vouglans**, dammed 25km downstream, reverts to the River Ain which feeds it. The **Grand Lac**, just south of town, is the focus of summer resort activity, with a beach area and watersports facilities. It's calm and scenic, in spite of all the camping activity going on around it. The **Office du Tourisme du Pays des Lacs**, 36 Grande-Rue (Mon–Sat 9am–noon & 2–6pm; Jul–Aug Sun 10am–noon;

☎03.84.25.27.47, fax 03.84.25.23.00) is the place to find information about the region and outdoor activities such as boat hire and bike hire. For hiking, the *63 Circuits de Petite Randonnée* (45F from the tourist office) has all you need to know.

Simple, inexpensive **accommodation** can be found at the *Hôtel Raillette*, 50 rue Neuve (☎03.84.25.82.21; ①). On the Grand Lac, providing more comfortable lodgings, there's the *Chaumière du Lac* (☎03.84.25.81.52, fax 0383.25.24.54; ②; closed Nov–March) and the *Hôtel Bellevue* (☎03.84.25.82.37; ①; closed Oct–May) – the latter offering a view worthy of its name.

Surrounded by hills, **Lac Chalain**, 16km north of Clairvaux and near the village of Doucier, has a much more impressive setting. It's also a very popular spot for **camping**. There are five campsites in town: *Fayolan*, on the lake (☎03.84.25.26.19); *La Ferme du Villaret*, on a farm, route des Moirans (☎03.84.25.26); *Le Grand Lac*, on the lake (☎03.84.25.26.19); *La Grisière et Europe Vacances*, near the lake with mobile homes for hire (☎03.84.25.80.48); and *Les Tilleuls*, 6 chemin des Tilleuls (☎03.84.25.81.45), also with mobile homes for hire.

By far the most interesting sight around here – and one of the Jura's best-known natural spectacles – is the **Cascades du Hérisson**, a septet of waterfalls descending nearly 300m in just 3km: worth considering if you plan to undertake a return walk to all the falls. Well-marked from either end of the gorge, the easiest walk, accessible by road via Val-Dessous southeast of Doucier, leads to the best-known and prettiest of the falls, the **Éventail**. A ten-minute stroll from the car park leads to the cascade, which spreads out in ever-widening tiers, giving it the fan-like appearance after which it is named. Continuing upstream, you'll shake off most casual spectators and pass through the woods of wild oak and springtime daffodils to the dramatic **Grand Saut**, with its clear drop of 60m; the pathway passes behind the waterfall – an alarmingly windy spot to shower in. A steep climb leads to smaller *sauts* feeding the odd swimming-hole, past a kiosk (with access south to the village of Bonlieu) to the uppermost **Saut Girard**, 4km up from the Éventail and close to the village of **ILAY**. There's a choice of restaurants here, but only one **hotel**, the *Auberge du Hérisson*, 5 rue des Lacs (☎03.84.25.58.18, fax 03.84.25.51.11; ③; closed mid–Oct to March; restaurant from 69F), they'll also be able to provide some tourist information.

A short drive up the N78 east of Ilay leads to a lookout atop **Pic de l'Aigle**: at nearly 1000m high, this is one of the best spots from which to view the Jura's topography. On fine days, the views are said to extend as far as Mont Blanc to the east, and west to the plain of the Saône.

The Haute Jura

As you climb from the plateau through the pine forests to the scrawny higher pastures, the temperatures dip and the landscape takes a bleaker turn towards the summits of the **Haute Jura**. The main roads struggle up the valleys towards the Swiss border, but less demanding routes run along the mountains' narrow folds linking Pontarlier to **Morez** and **St-Claude**; when they're not passing through woodland or low cloud, these can provide memorable motoring. While the main towns in the area are valley-bound and claustrophobic, the resort towns tend to be expensive or rather soulless out of season, but most people come up here for the views across Lac Léman (Lake Geneva) in Switzerland towards the perennial snowscapes of the Alps.

Up to Morez and Les Rousses

The main **trans-Jura route** into Switzerland is the N5, which begins its ascent to the frontier around St-Laurent-en-Grandvaux, great for skiing but unmemorable apart from the picturesque **Lac de l'Abbaye**, 4km south of town on the D437. Also on the Arbois–St-Claude rail line is **MOREZ**, 12km up the road, a town squeezed along the narrow valley floor and noted for the manufacture of watches and spectacles. The **tourist office** is in the central place Jaurès (May–Sept Mon–Sat 9am–noon & 2–6pm, Sun 9am–noon; Oct–April Mon 10am–noon & 2–5pm, Tues–Fri 9am–noon & 2–6pm; ☎03.84.33.08.73) along with the **gare routière**, from which buses depart for La Cure on the Franco-Swiss border. Once on the Swiss side, you can catch trains down to Nyon on Lac Léman and to Geneva itself.

A couple of kilometres before the frontier, **LES ROUSSES** exists purely for skiing – downhill and especially cross-country – but just before it a lane leads down to a very attractive HI **youth hostel** in an old, red-shuttered farmhouse by a stream, 2km away at Bief-de-la-Chaille (☎03.84.60.02.80, fax 03.84.60.04.63; closed mid–April to mid–May & Oct to mid–Dec). There's also a **gîte d'étape** at Prémanon on the D25 (☎03.84.60.54.82; closed May, June & Sept to mid-Dec). From the youth hostel you can see the eerie spheres of the satellite-tracking station on the summit of **La Dôle** (1677m), the Jura's highest peak, just over the Swiss border. The **GR9 footpath** passes through here, beginning a magnificent hiking section all along the crest of the ridge to the Col de la Faucille and beyond (see below).

There are plenty of **hotels** in Les Rousses itself: the *Hôtel de France*, 323 rue Pasteur (☎03.84.60.01.45, fax 03.84.60.04.63; ④), is the town's best, but less extravagant lodgings can be found at the *Hôtel du Gai Pinson*, 1465 route Blanche (☎03.84.60.02.15; ③), or the *El Patio*, 344 rue Pasteur (☎03.84.60.02.01; ②). For a **meal**, try the restaurant at the *Hôtel Restaurant Les Gentianes*, or the *Restaurant Les P'Losses* (from 85F) in the winter sports centre on the Geneva road southwest of town. There are plenty of cafés and pizzerias.

St-Claude

From Morez, the train line leaves the N5 and heads along the Gorges de la Bienne to the industrial town of **ST-CLAUDE**, to the southwest, hemmed in claustrophobically by even higher mountains than Morez. It's famous for pipes (the smokers' kind) and diamonds, and there's a **museum**, the Musée des Pipiers, Diamantiers et Lapidaires, (July–Aug daily 9.30am–6.30pm though worth checking as opening hours sometimes vary; ☎03.84.45.54.45) dedicated to both of these opposite the fortified cathedral of St-Pierre on rue du Marché. The **tourist office**, 6 rue du Marché 24 (Mon–Fri 8.30am–noon & 2–6pm, Sat 9am–noon & 2–5.30pm; Jul–Aug 9am–noon & 2–5.30pm; ☎03.84.45.34) stocks the English-language guide *Discovery*, which gives a florid description of a two-hour walk around the town.

Should you wish to **stay** here, the *Hôtel Le Média*, 7 rue de la Poyat (☎03.84.45.63.31, fax 03.84.41.07.38; ①), off the main rue du Pré, is marginally better than the *Hôtel de la Poste*, on rue Reybert (☎03.84.45.52.34; ①), opposite the tourist office. Plusher accommodation can be found at the *Jura Hôtel*, 40 av de la Gare (☎03.84.45.24.04, fax 03.84.45.58.10; ②), or the *Hôtel Le Joly* in Le Martinet, 3km southwest of town on the Col de la Faucille road, right next to a campsite (☎03.84.45.12.36). Wholesome, inexpensive food is served at the restaurant of *Hôtel Le Média* and at *Le Bayard*, in the central place du Pré.

What gives purpose to the rest of the onward route from either St-Claude or Les Rousses are the superb views from the crest of the great fir-clad ridge that overlooks Lac Léman to the east. The N5 crosses the ridge at the **Col de la Faucille** (1323m). If it's clear, the view is unbelievably dramatic from the Col or the GR footpath; the whole range of the western Alps stretches out before you, dominated by Mont Blanc, with the steely cusp of Lac Léman at your feet. There's an even better view from the top of nearby **Mont Rond** (1534m), accessible by chair lift. Of course, if it's not clear, the journey will have been in vain, but if you're carrying on south of Geneva, 30km away, it's downhill all the way – with the thought of some revitalizing bars of Swiss chocolate at the day's end.

travel details

Buses

Belfort to: Ronchamp (1 daily; 45min).

Besançon to: Ornans (4 daily; 30min); Pontarlier (4 daily; 1hr); Salins-les-Bains (3 weekly; 1hr).

Colmar to: Mulhouse (up to hourly; 1hr); Sélestat (hourly; 1hr).

Haguenau to: Neuwillen (4 daily; 1hr 10min); Pfaffenhoffen (4 daily; 30min); Saverne (4 daily; 1hr 40min).

Morez to: Lons (1 most days; 1hr 45min); St-Claude (3 weekly; 1hr).

St-Claude to: Lyon (daily; 3hr 40min).

Saverne to: Molsheim (2 daily; 1hr).

Sélestat to: St-Dié (5–6 daily; 1hr 10min).

Verdun to: Metz (5 daily Mon–Sat; 2hrs).

Trains

Belfort to: Besançon (10 daily; 1hr–1hr 15min); Dôle (5 daily; 1hr 30min); Paris-Est (2 daily; 5hr); Ronchamp (12 daily; 5 min); Montbéliard (hourly, 20min).

Besançon to: Bourg-en-Bresse (4–5 daily; 2hr 30min); Dijon (10 daily; 1hr); Dôle (10 daily; 30min); Lons (several daily; 1–1hr 30min); Morez (4 daily; 2hr 10min–2hr 30min); Morteau (4 daily; 1hr–1hr 45min); Paris-Lyon direct (up to 6 daily; 2hr 30min); St-Claude (4 daily; 2hr 30min–3hr); St-Laurent (4 daily; 1hr 40min–2hr).

Dôle to: Dijon (10 daily; 30min); Paris-Lyon (10 daily; 4hr); Pontarlier (3 daily; 1hr 20min).

Metz to: Longuyon (2 daily; 1hr 30min); Mulhouse (7 daily; 2hr 30min); Nancy (hourly; 1hr); Paris-Est (4 daily; 3hr); Strasbourg (every 2hr; 1hr 30min).

Mulhouse to: Belfort (up to 5 daily; 30–45 min); Colmar (every 30min; 20 min).

Nancy to: Lunéville (hourly during peak hours, then every 3 hours; 30min); Paris-Est (hourly; 3hr); Saverne (3 daily; 1hr); Strasbourg (2 daily; 1hr 20 min).

St-Claude to: Bourg (4–5 daily; 1hr 40min–2hr), connecting with TGV to Paris; Champagnole (5 daily; 1hr).

Strasbourg to: Barr (9 daily; 55min); Basel (hourly; 1hr 30min–2hr); Besançon (8 daily; 2hr 15min); Colmar (hourly; 50min); Dambach (9 daily; 1hr); Dôle (10 daily; 3hr 30min); Ingwillen (6 daily; 30min); Molsheim (9 daily; 20min); Mulhouse (hourly; 1hr 20min); Obernai (9 daily; 40min); Paris-Est (every 2hr; 4hr 30min); Rosheim (9 daily; 25min); Sarreguemines (6 daily; 1hr 20min); St-Dié (3 daily; 1hr 50min); Sélestat (hourly; 20min); Wingen-Moden (6 daily; 40min); Wissembourg (up to 5 daily; 1hr).

Verdun to: Metz, direct and/or changing at Conflans (4 daily; 1hr–1hr 15min); Nancy (2 daily; 1hr 40min); Paris-Est (up to 5 daily; 3hr).

CHAPTER FOUR

NORMANDY

Though now firmly incorporated into the French mainstream, the seaboard province of Normandy has a history of prosperous independence as one of the crucial powers of medieval Europe. Colonized by Scandinavian Vikings (or Norsemen) from the ninth century onwards, it began to colonize in turn during the eleventh and twelfth centuries, with military expeditions conquering not only England but as far afield as Sicily and parts of the Near East. Later, as part of France, it was instrumental in the settlement of Canada.

Normandy has always had large ports: **Rouen**, on the Seine, is the nearest navigable point to Paris; **Dieppe**, **Le Havre** and **Cherbourg** have important transatlantic trade. Inland, it is overwhelmingly agricultural – a fertile belt of tranquil pastureland, where the chief interest for most visitors will be the groaning restaurant tables of regions such as the **Pays d'Auge**. Much of the seaside is a little overdeveloped; the last French emperor created, towards the end of the nineteenth century, a "Norman Riviera" around **Trouville** and **Deauville**, and an air of pretension still hangs about their elegant promenades. But more ancient harbours such as **Honfleur** and **Barfleur** remain visually irresistible, and there are numerous seaside villages with few crowds or affectations. The banks of the Seine, too, hold several delightful little communities.

Normandy also boasts extraordinary Romanesque and Gothic architectural treasures, although only the much-restored capital, Rouen, has a complete medieval centre. The attractions are more often single buildings than entire towns. Most famous of all is the spectacular *merveille* on the island of **Mont St-Michel**, but there are also the monasteries at **Jumièges** and **Caen**; the cathedrals of **Bayeux** and **Coutances**; and Richard the Lionheart's castle above the Seine at **Les Andelys**. **Bayeux** has, in addition, its vivid and astonishing tapestry, while among more recent creations are Monet's garden at **Giverny** and, at Le Havre, a fabulous collection of paintings by Dufy, Boudin, as well as other Impressionists. Furthermore, Normandy's vernacular architecture makes it well worth exploring inland – the back roads through the countryside are lined with splendid centuries-old half-timbered manor houses. It is remarkable how much has survived or been restored since the Allied landings in 1944 and the subsequent **Battle of Normandy**, which has its own legacy in a series of war museums, memorials and cemeteries.

ACCOMMODATION PRICE CATEGORIES

Each hotel in this chapter has a symbol which corresponds to one of eight price categories.

① Under 160F	④ 300–400F	⑦ 600–700F
② 160–220F	⑤ 400–500F	⑧ Over 700F
③ 220–300F	⑥ 500–600F	

The prices quoted are for the cheapest available double room in high season, though remember that many of the cheap places will have more expensive rooms with en-suite facilities.

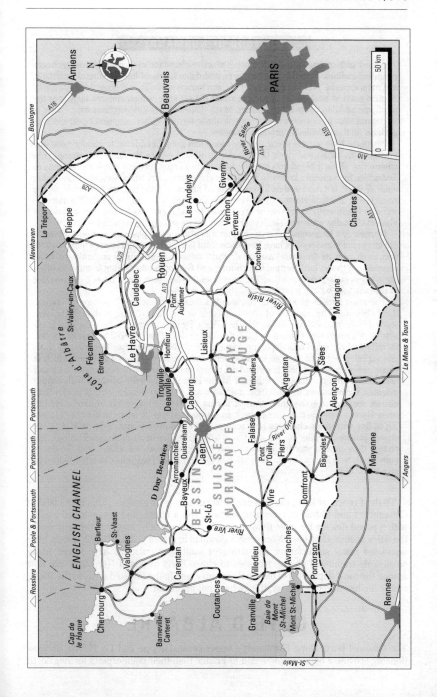

THE FOOD OF NORMANDY

The **food of Normandy** owes its most distinctive characteristic – its gut-bursting, heart-pounding richness – to the lush orchards and dairy herds of its agricultural heartland, and most especially the area southeast of Caen known as the Pays d'Auge. Menus abound in meat such as veal (*veau*) cooked in *vallée d'Auge* style, which consists largely of the profligate addition of cream and butter. Many dishes also feature orchard fruit, either in its natural state or in successively more alcoholic forms – either as apple or pear cider, or perhaps further distilled to produce brandies.

Normans have a great propensity for blood and guts. In addition to gamier meat and fowl such as rabbit and duck (a speciality in Rouen, where the birds are strangled to ensure that all their blood gets into the sauce), they enjoy such intestinal preparations as *andouilles*, the sausages known in English as chitterlings, and *tripes*, stewed for hours *à la mode de Caen*, but rendered no less palatable. A full blow-out at country restaurants in the small towns of inland Normandy – places like Conches, Vire and the Suisse Normande – will also traditionally entail one or two pauses between courses for the *trou normand*: a glass of Calvados while you catch your breath before struggling on with the feast.

Normandy's long coastline ensures that it is also a great place for **seafood**. Many of the larger ports and resorts have long waterfront lines of restaurants competing for attention, each with its *"copieuse" assiette de fruits de mer*. **Honfleur** is probably the most enjoyable of these, but **Dieppe**, **Cherbourg** and **Granville** also spring to mind as offering endless eating opportunities. The menus tend to be much the same as those on offer in Brittany (see p.371), if perhaps slightly more expensive.

The most famous products of Normandy's meadow-munching cows are, of course, their **cheeses**. The tradition of cheese-making in the Pays d'Auge is thought to have started in the monasteries during the Dark Ages. By the eleventh century the local products were already well defined; in 1236, the *Roman de la Rose* referred to *Angelot* cheese, identified with a small coin depicting a young angel killing a dragon. The principal modern varieties began to emerge in the seventeenth century – **Pont l'Evêque**, which is square with a washed crust, is soft but not runny, and **Livarot**, which is round, thick and firm, has a stronger flavour. Although Marie Herel is generally credited with having invented **Camembert** in the 1790s, a smaller and stodgier version of that cheese had already existed for some time. A priest fleeing the Revolution seems to have stayed in Mme Herel's farmhouse at Camembert, and suggested modifications in her cheese-making in line with the techniques he'd seen employed to manufacture Brie de Meaux – a slower process, gentler on the curd and with more thorough drainage. The rich full cheese thus created was an instant success in the market at Vimoutiers, and the development of the railways (and the invention of the chipboard cheesebox in 1880) helped to give it a worldwide popularity.

To the French, at least, the essence of Normandy is its produce. This is the land of Camembert and Calvados, cider and seafood, and a butter- and cream-based cuisine with a proud disdain for most things *nouvelle*. Economically, however, the richness of the dairy pastures has been Normandy's downfall in recent years. EU milk quotas have liquidated many small farms, and stringent sanitary regulations have forced many small-scale traditional cheese factories to close. Parts of inland Normandy are now among the most depressed of the whole country, and in the forested areas to the south, where life has never been easy, things have not improved.

CÔTE D'ALBÂTRE

The Channel ports along Normandy's upper coast, **Dieppe** and **Le Havre**, unquestionably provide a better introduction to France than their counterparts further north in Picardy, though things get livelier and warmer to the west, and it's only a short train or bus ride to Rouen. An impressive display of white cliffs has earned this stretch of seashore the epithet of "Alabaster Coast", and occasional surprises can be found beyond the windswept and tide-chased walks, such as a wonderful Lutyens fantasy at **Varengeville** and the Hammer Horror Benedictine distillery at **Fécamp**.

Dieppe and around

Crowded between high cliff headlands, **DIEPPE** is an enjoyably small-scale port that used to be more of a resort. During the nineteenth century, Parisians came here by train to take the sea air, promenading along the front while the English colony indulged in the peculiar pastime of swimming. These days, it's not a place many travellers go out of their way to visit, but it's one of the nicer ferry ports in northern France, and you're unlikely to regret to spending an afternoon or evening here before or after a Channel crossing. With kids in tow, the aquariums of the **Cité de la Mer** are the obvious attraction; otherwise, you could settle for admiring the cliffs and the castle as you stroll the extravagant seafront lawns. Meanwhile, the business of the port goes on as ever, with Dieppe's commercial docks unloading half the bananas of the Antilles and forty percent of all shellfish destined to slither down French throats. The markets sell fish right off the boats, displayed with the usual Gallic flair, and the sole, scallops and turbot available in profusion at the restaurants may well tempt you to stay.

Arrival, information and accommodation

Dieppe's **tourist office** is on the pont Ango, which separates the ferry harbour from the pleasure port; you can't miss it if you're arriving by ferry (July & Aug Mon–Sat 9am–1pm & 2–8pm, Sun 10am–1pm & 3–6pm; Easter–June & Sept Mon–Sat 9am–1pm & 2–7pm, Sun 10am–1pm & 3–6pm; Oct–Easter Mon–Sat 9am–noon & 2–6pm; ☎02.35.84.11.77). A beach annexe where quai Duquesne reaches the oceanfront is open in summer only (mid-June to mid-Sept Sun–Thurs 10am–7.30pm, Fri & Sat 10am–8pm). The main **post office** is at 2 bd Maréchal-Joffre (Mon–Fri 8.30am–6pm, Sat 8.30am–noon; ☎02.35.04.70.14).

Between four and five P&O Stena Line **ferries** sail daily, all year round, between Newhaven in England and Dieppe's **gare maritime**; for information, call ☎02.35.06.39.03. Connecting trains for the ferries draw up on the quay, but the main **gare SNCF** (☎02.35.98.50.50) is 500m away on boulevard Clemenceau, 1km from the beach. Trains are much the quickest way to get to Rouen or Paris, but buses along the coast leave from the **gare routière** (☎02.35.84.21.97) alongside.

Hotels

Dieppe has plenty of **hotels**; on the whole, prices get progressively cheaper as you head further inland from the seafront, which is actually among the quietest areas of town, especially near the castle end away from the car ferry traffic.

Les Arcades, 1–3 Arcades de la Bourse (☎02.35.84.14.12). Long-established hotel, under the eponymous arcades facing the port; particularly suitable for tired passengers not wanting to walk more than 175m to find a bed. Restaurant with full, good-value menus from 95F. ④.

Grand Duquesne, 15 place Saint Jacques (☎02.35.84.21.51). Small, well-refurbished *pension*, just off place du Puits Salé in view of the main door of the Cathedral, where every room has bath and phone, and menus start at 72F. ②.

de la Jetée, 5 rue de l'Asile Thomas (☎02.35.84.89.98). Simple but very welcoming place overlooking the sea, near the Cité de la Mer, with ten plain but spacious rooms. ①.

La Plage, 20 bd de Verdun (☎02.35.84.18.28). Slightly upmarket rooms, all with English (satellite) TV, facing the sea but set back somewhat from the street, alongside the *Windsor*. No restaurant. ③.

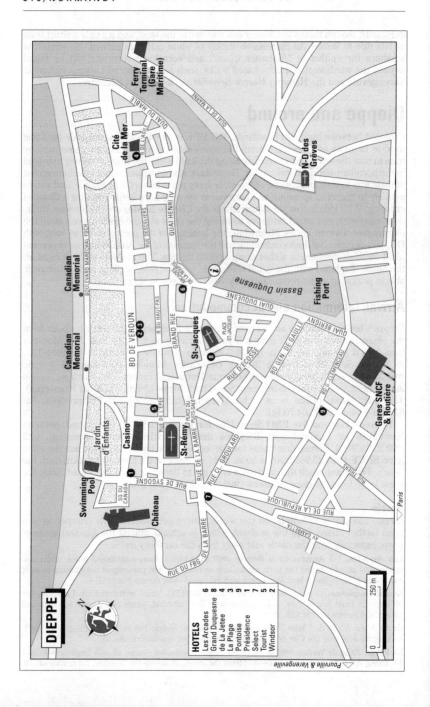

DIEPPE

N

Ferry Terminal (Gare Maritime)

Cité de la Mer 4

N-D des Grèves

QUAI DU HÂBLE

R. DE L'ASILE

QUAI DE LA MARNE

RUE DESCELIERS

QUAI HENRI IV

Canadian Memorial

Canadian Memorial

BOULEVARD MARÉCHAL FOCH

BD DE VERDUN

RUE DE CHASTES

i

6

Bassin Duquesne

QUAI DUQUESNE

Fishing Port

2/3

R DU HAUT-PAS

GRAND RUE

QUAI BÉRIGNY

St-Jacques

PLACE ST-JACQUES

8

RUE DE L'ÉPÉE

5

RUE D'ÉCOSSE

BD GEN DE GAULLE

Jardin d'Enfants

Casino

1

SQ DU CANADA

St-Rémy

PLACE DU PUITS-SALÉ

RUE DE LA BARRE

RUE CL. GROULARD

9

BD G. CLEMENCEAU

Gares SNCF & Routière

Swimming Pool

Château

7

RUE DE SYGOGNE

RUE DE LA RÉPUBLIQUE

RUE FRÈRES

RUE DU FBG DE LA BARRE

AV. GAMBETTA

Paris

Pourville & Varengeville

HOTELS
Les Arcades	6
Grand Duquesne	8
de La Jetee	4
La Plage	3
Pontoise	9
Présidence	1
Select	7
Tourist	5
Windsor	2

0   250 m

Hôtel-Restaurant Pontoise, 10 rue Thiers (☎02.35.84.14.57). A basic, inexpensive option, not far from the gare SNCF and well away from the beach. ②.

Présidence, bd de Verdun (☎02.35.84.31.31). This ugly grey modern block, below the château at the far west end of the seafront, holds 89 spacious and well-equipped rooms, while menus at the *Panoramic* restaurant start at 85F. ④.

Select, 1 rue Toustain (☎02.35.84.14.66). Rather faded red-brick building at the western end of rue de la Baine, opposite the steps up to the château. There's a terrace bar serving afternoon teas, and live jazz on Fridays, but no restaurant. ③.

Tourist, 16 rue de la Halle au Blé (☎02.35.06.10.10). Plain rooms in converted town-house, one block from the beach behind the Casino; an en-suite shower or toilet costs an additional 60F. No restaurant. ②.

Windsor, 18 bd de Verdun (☎02.35.84.15.23). You pay premium rates for sea-facing rooms in this *logis*, where the glass-fronted first-floor dining room has menus from 105F. The rooms themselves can be shabby, but they do have satellite TV. ④.

Youth hostels and campsites

HI youth hostel, 48 rue Louis Fromager (☎02.35.84.85.73). Inconveniently located hostel, 2km southwest of the gare SNCF in the quartier Janval which offers beds for 67F in two-, four- and six-bed dorms only. Served by bus route #2 from the tourist office (direction "Val Druel", Stop Château Michel). Mid-Feb to mid–Nov only.

Camping Vitamin, Chemin des Vertus (☎02.35.82.11.11). Three-star place on the #2 bus route. April–Oct.

The town

Modern Dieppe is still laid out along the three axes dictated by its eighteenth-century town planners, though these central streets have become a little run-down, and are in any case left in continual shadow. The **boulevard de Verdun** runs for over a kilometre along the seafront, from the fifteenth-century castle in the west to the port entrance, and passes the Casino, along with the grandest and oldest hotels. A short way inland, parallel to the seafront, is the **rue de la Barre** and its pedestrianized continuation, the **Grande Rue**. Along the harbour's edge, an extension of the Grande Rue, **quai Henry IV** has a colourful backdrop of cafés, brasseries and restaurants.

The **place du Puits Salé**, dominated by the huge **Café des Tribunaux**, is at the centre of the old town. Currently looking very spruce following a lavish restoration, the café was built as an inn towards the end of the seventeenth century, and briefly became Dieppe's town hall after the previous one was bombarded by the British in 1694. In the late nineteenth century, it was favoured by painters and writers such as Renoir, Monet, Sickert, Whistler and Pissarro. It's now a cavernous café, the haunt of college students and open until after midnight. For English visitors, its most evocative association is that the exiled and unhappy Oscar Wilde drank here regularly.

As for monuments, the obvious place to start is the medieval **castle** overlooking the seafront from the west, home of the **Musée de Dieppe** and two showpiece collections (June–Sept daily 10am–noon & 2–6pm; Oct–May Mon & Wed–Sun 10am–noon & 2–5pm; 15F). The first is a group of carved ivories – virtuoso pieces of sawing, filing and chipping of the plundered riches of Africa, shipped back to the town by early Dieppe "explorers". The other permanent exhibition is made up of a hundred or so prints by the co-founder of Cubism, Georges Braque, who went to school in Le Havre, spent summers in Dieppe and is buried just west of the town at Varangeville-sur-Mer (see overleaf).

An exit from the western side of the castle takes you out onto a path up to the **cliffs**. On the other side, a flight of steps leads down to the **square du Canada**, originally a commemoration of the role played by Dieppe sailors in the colonization of Canada. Now a small plaque is dedicated to the Canadian soldiers who died in the suicidal 1942 raid on Dieppe, justified later as a trial run for the 1944 Normandy landings.

The **Cité de la Mer**, at 37 rue de l'Asile-Thomas, just back from the harbour, sets out simultaneously to entertain children and to serve as a centre for scientific research, and succeeds in both without being all that interesting for the casual adult visitor (daily: May–Aug 10am–7pm; Sept–April 10am–noon & 2–6pm; 25F). Kids are certain to enjoy learning the principles of navigation by operating radio-controlled boats (5F for 3min). Thereafter, the museum traces the history of sea-going vessels, featuring a Viking *drakkar* under construction, following methods depicted in the Bayeux Tapestry. Next comes a very detailed geological exhibition covering the formation of the local cliffs, in which we learn how to convert shingle into sandpaper. Visits culminate with large **aquariums** filled with the marine life of the Channel: flat fish with bulbous eyes and twisted faces, retiring octopuses, battling lobsters and hermaphrodite scallops (the white part is male, the orange, female). Thanks to a typical lack of sentimentality, jars of fish soup, whose exact provenance is not made explicit, are on sale at the exit.

Eating and drinking

The most promising area to look for **restaurants** in Dieppe is along the quai Henri IV, which makes a lovely place to stroll and compare menus of a summer's evening. The beach itself holds no formal restaurants, but it does have a couple of open-air **cafés** selling mussels, salads, and so on, and plenty of crêpe stands.

As well as the daily spectacle of the fish on sale in the **port de pêche**, there's an all-day open-air **market** in the place Nationale and Grande Rue on Saturday. The largest of several hypermarkets in the area is Mammouth (Mon–Sat 9am–9pm), out of town at the Centre Commercial du Belvédère on the route de Rouen (RN 27), and reached by free courtesy buses from the tourist office.

Les Écamias, 129 quai Henri IV (☎02.35.84.67.67). Small, friendly traditional French restaurant, at the quieter, seaward end of the main quay not far from the Cité de la Mer. Each of the two separate dining rooms (hence the plural) in neighbouring buildings serves the same menu, with a 70F option that includes *moules marinières* and stuffed shellfish; they also offer skate with capers. Closed Mon (except in Aug), and Sun pm in winter.

La Marmite Dieppoise, 8 rue Saint-Jean (☎02.35.84.24.26). Rustic, busy little restaurant, between St-Jacques church and the arcades de la Bourse. Lunch menu from 86F, dinners at 145F or 215F, with the latter featuring the local speciality *marmite Dieppoise* (seafood pot, with shellfish and white fish). Closed Sun pm and Mon, and also Thurs pm out of season.

Le Newhaven, 53 quai Henri IV (☎02.35.84.89.72). Reliable seafood specialist, at the slightly quieter end of the quayside, and serving good menus from 64F. The 100F menu of Dieppe specialities is fine if you hanker after fish livers and squid, while the 119F one offers the safer option of mussels followed by skate, and there are wonderful baked oysters on the 145F one. Closed Sun pm in winter.

Le St Jacques, 12 rue de l'Oranger (☎02.35.84.52.04). Busy, not to say peremptory bistrot, in town near the St-Jacques church, with menus from 65F that offer considerably more meat dishes than is normal in Dieppe, while still preparing the usual fishy delights. Closed Mon, and Thurs pm.

Le Tréport

Thirty kilometres east of Dieppe, on the border with Picardy, **LE TRÉPORT** is a seaside resort that has clearly seen better days. It was already something of a bathing station when the railways arrived in 1873, and promoted this as "the prettiest beach in Europe, just three hours from Paris". It remained the capital's favoured resort until the 1950s – and is still served by around five trains daily – but it can't ever have been that pretty, and these days its charms are definitely fading.

Le Tréport divides into three sections: the flat wedge-shaped **seafront** area, bounded on one side by the Channel, on another by the harbour at the mouth of the river Bresle, and on the third by imposing 100-metre-high white chalk cliffs; the **old town**, higher up the slopes on safer ground; and the **modern town** further inland. The seafront itself is entirely taken up by a hideous pink-and-orange concrete apartment block, with one or two snack bars but no other sign of life, facing the Casino and a drab grey shingle beach. The more sheltered harbourside Quai Francois-1er around the corner holds most of the action, lined with restaurants, souvenir shops and cafés. The assorted stone jetties and wooden piers around the harbour make an enjoyable stroll, watching the comings and goings of the fishing boats.

Climbing up from the Quai, you come to the heavily nautical **Église St-Jacques**, built in the fifteenth century to replace an eleventh-century original that crumbled into the sea, along with the cliff on which it stood. Nearby, next to the fortified former town hall that is now the local library, successive flights of steps, 365 of them in all, climb to the top of the cliffs.

Practicalities

Trains and **buses** arrive in Le Tréport on the far side of the harbour, a short walk from the main quai. Turning left as you hit the main drag will bring you to the **tourist office**, on quai Sadi-Carnot (Easter–Sept daily 10am–noon & 2–6pm; Oct–Easter Mon–Sat 10am–noon & 2–5pm; ☎02.35.86.05.69).

Of the **hotels**, the best in terms of a sea view and good-quality food is the *Riche-Lieu* at 50 quai Francois-1er (☎02.35.86.26.55; ②), which has modernized rooms with showers on four floors and a wide range of menus starting at 85F for a "bistrot" meal. The *Matelote*, 34 quai Francois-1er (☎02.35.86.01.13), is a quayside seafood **restaurant** with a high gourmet reputation.

West along the coast

From Dieppe to Le Havre the coast is eroding at a ferocious rate, and it's conceivable that the small resorts here, tucked in among the cliffs at the ends of a succession of valleys, may not last more than another century or so. For the moment, however, they are quietly prospering, with casinos, sports centres and yacht marinas ensuring a modest but steady summer trade.

Varengeville

If the museum in Dieppe (see p.317) has awakened your interest in Georges Braque, you may be interested in visiting his **grave** in the clifftop church some way north of **VARENGEVILLE**, 8km west of town (25min ride on bus #311 or #312, pm only). Braque's marble tomb is topped by a sadly decaying mosaic of a white dove in flight. More impressive is his vivid blue Tree of Jesse stained-glass window inside the church, through which the sun rises in summer.

Back along the road towards town from the church, the house at the **Bois des Moutiers**, built for Guillaume Mallet from 1898 onwards and un-French in almost every respect, was one of architect **Edwin Lutyens'** first commissions. Lutyens, then aged just 29, was at the start of a career that was to culminate during the 1920s when he laid out most of the city of New Delhi. The real reason to visit, however, is to enjoy the magnificent **gardens**, designed by Mallet in conjunction with Gertrude Jekyll, and at their most spectacular in the second half of May (mid-March to mid-Nov only, Sun–Fri 10am–noon & 2pm–sunset, Sat 2pm–sunset; admission 40F during May and June, otherwise 35F). Enthusiastic guides lead you through the highly innovative engineering of the house and grounds, replete with quirks and games. The colours of the

Burne-Jones tapestry hanging in the stairwell were copied from Renaissance cloth in William Morris's studio; the rhododendrons were chosen from similar samples. Paths lead through vistas based on paintings by Poussin, Lorrain and other seventeenth-century artists; no modern roses, with their anachronistic colours, are allowed to spoil the effect.

St-Valéry-en-Caux

The first sizeable community west of Dieppe is **ST-VALÉRY-EN-CAUX**, a rebuilt town which is the clearest reminder of the fighting – and massive destruction – of the Allied retreat of 1940. A monument on the western cliffs pays tribute to the French cavalry division who faced Rommel's tanks on horseback, brandishing their sabres with hopeless heroism, while beside the ruins of a German artillery emplacement on the opposite cliffs another commemorates a Scottish division, rounded up while fighting their way back to Le Havre and the boats home.

Much the most attractive house to survive in St-Valéry, the Renaissance Maison Henri-IV on the quai d'Aval, serves as the **tourist office** (May to mid-Sept daily 10am–12.30pm & 3–7pm; mid-Sept to April Wed–Sat 10am–12.30pm & 3–7pm, Sun 10am–12.30pm; ☎02.35.97.00.63).

The *Terrasses*, 22 rue le Perrey (☎02.35.97.11.22; closed Xmas & Jan; ④), is the only **hotel-restaurant** actually facing the sea; another, much cheaper, *logis*, the seven-room *La Marine*, 113 rue St-Léger (☎02.35.97.05.09; mid-Feb to mid-Nov; ②), is tucked away in a backstreet on the west side of the harbour. There are also two year-round **campsites**, the 2-star *Falaise d'Amont* (☎02.35.97.05.07) on the eastern cliffs, and the larger 4-star *d'Etennemare* (☎02.35.97.15.79), set back from the sea southwest of the harbour. The *Restaurant du Port*, overlooking the harbour at 18 quai d'Amont (☎02.35.97.08.93; closed Sun pm & Mon in low season), has a delicious 118F seafood menu.

Fécamp

FÉCAMP, roughly halfway between Dieppe and Le Havre, is a serious fishing port with an attractive seafront promenade. One compelling reason to pay a brief visit is to see the **Benedictine Distillery** on rue Alexandre-le-Grand, in the narrow strip of streets running parallel to the ports towards the town centre. A taste for nineteenth-century operatic horror sets is more important than a liking for the liqueur in question. Tours lasting ninety minutes (daily June to mid-Sept 10am–6pm; mid-March to May & mid-Sept to mid-Nov 10am–noon & 2–5.30pm; tours mid-Nov to mid-March 10.30am & 3.30pm; 27F) start with a small **museum**, set firmly in the Middle Ages with props of manuscripts, locks, testaments, lamps and religious paintings beneath a nightmarish mock-Gothic roof. The first whiff of Benedictine comes in the grim rust-and-grey-coloured Salle des Abbés, and at this point the script abruptly changes – from mysterious monks to PR for an exclusive product. The boxes of ingredients are a rare treat for the nose (take it easy with the myrrh), and there's further theatricality in the old distillery where boxes of herbs are flung with gusto into copper vats and alembics. (Commercial production has long since moved to an out-of-town site.) Finally you are offered a *dégustation* in their bar across the road – neat, in a cocktail, or on crêpes; make sure you hold onto your ticket to qualify.

If your aesthetic sensibilities need soothing after this, the soaring medieval nave and Renaissance carved screens of the **church of the Trinité**, up in the town centre, may do the trick. Alternatively, Fécamp is now also home to the modern **Musée des Terres-Neuvas et de la Pêche**, on the seafront at 27 bd Albert 1er (July & Aug daily 10am–noon & 2–6.30pm; Sept–June daily except Tues 10am–noon & 2–5.30pm; 20F). Spreading across two floors, with lots of miniature model boats and amateur paintings, it focuses on the long tradition whereby the fishermen of Fécamp decamp en masse each year to catch cod in the cold, foggy waters off Newfoundland. Sailing vessels continued to make the trek from the sixteenth century right up until 1931; today vast refrigerated container ships have taken their place.

Fécamp's main **tourist office** is opposite the distillery at 113 rue Alexandre-le-Grand (July & Aug Mon–Fri 10am–6pm; Sept–June Mon–Sat 9am–12.15pm & 1.45–6pm; ☎02.35.28.51.01); the peculiar hours are because there's another summer-only office alongside the museum on the seafront (July & Aug daily 11am–1pm & 3–8pm; ☎02.35.29.16.34).

Hotels tend to be set back away from the sea on odd side streets. It's a popular place; you need to reserve a room at the *Hôtel de l'Univers*, facing St-Étienne church at 5 place St-Étienne (☎02.35.28.05.88; ②), or the *Angleterre*, 93 rue de la Plage (☎02.35.28.01.60; ③). Good-value **fish restaurants** include *La Marée*, 75 quai Bérigny (closed Sun eve & Mon; ☎02.35.29.39.15), which is attached to a fish shop and offers menus from 100F, and the *Martin*, 18 place St-Étienne (closed Sun eve & Mon; ☎02.35.28.23.82, where the cooking is rooted in the finest Norman tradition of adding strong alcohol to just about everything, whether it's gin with your scallops or brandy on your sole.

The **youth hostel** (☎02.35.29.75.79, reservations ☎02.35.29.36.35; July to mid-Sept) stands up near the lighthouse on the Côte de la Vierge east of the port, along the route du Commandant-Roquigny. A superb **campsite**, the *Camping de Renneville* (☎02.35.28.20.97; March–Dec), is a short walk out of town on the western cliffs.

Étretat

ÉTRETAT, another 20km west towards Le Havre, is a very different kettle of fish to Fécamp. Here the alabaster cliffs are at their most spectacular – their arches, tunnels and the solitary "needle" out to sea will doubtless be familiar from tourist brochures – and the town itself has grown up simply as a pleasure resort. There isn't even a port of any kind: the seafront consists of a sweeping unbroken curve of concrete above the shingle beach.

Étretat is a very pretty little place, centring on the **place Foch** just back from the sea, where the old wooden market *halles* still stand, the ground floor now converted into souvenir shops, but the beams of the balcony and roof bare and ancient. As soon as you step onto the beach you see the cliff formations to either side. To the west, on the **Falaise d'Aval**, a straightforward if precarious walk leads up the crumbling side of the cliff, with lush lawns and pastures to the inland side and German fortifications on the shore side extending to the point where the turf abruptly stops, occasionally ripped by the latest fall of cliff. From the windswept top you can see further rock formations and possibly even glimpse Le Havre, but the views back to the village sheltered in the valley, and the **Falaise d'Amont** on its eastern side – which Maupassant compared to an elephant dipping its trunk into the ocean – are what stick in the memory. The cliff itself presents an idyllic rural scene, with a gentle footpath winding up the green hillside to the little chapel of Notre-Dame.

Étretat's **tourist office** is alongside the main road through the centre of town, on place M-Guillard (mid-June to mid-Sept daily 10am–7pm; mid-March to mid-June & mid-Sept to mid-Oct daily 10am–noon & 2–6pm; mid-Oct to mid-March Fri 2–6pm, Sat 10am–noon & 2–6pm, Sun 10am–noon; ☎02.35.27.05.21). Four **hotels** crowd onto the corners of place Foch, all significantly cheaper than the grand sea-view places. Much the most picturesque is the *Hôtel la Résidence*, 4 bd René-Coty (☎02.35.27.02.87; ②–④), a dramatic half-timbered old mansion that has beautiful wooden carvings decorating its every nook and cranny. The quality of rooms however is variable, and few are as elegant as the facade. More dependable, and also without a restaurant, is the *Hôtel des Falaises*, opposite at 1 bd René-Coty (☎02.35.27.02.77; ②) – in fact from its modernized rooms you get a better view of the *Résidence* than if you're actually staying there. *L'Escale*, on place Foch itself (closed Dec & Jan; ☎02.35.27.03.69; ③), has simple but pleasant rooms, and a snack restaurant downstairs specializing in *moules-frites* and crêpes. **Campers** will find the *Camping Municipal* (April to mid-Oct; ☎02.35.27.07.67) 1km out on rue Guy-de-Maupassant.

Much the best **restaurant** is the *Galion*, distinct from the adjoining *Résidence* at 4 bd René-Coty (closed Wed & mid-Dec to mid-Jan; ☎02.35.29.48.74), where the 115F menu makes a definitive introduction to all that's best in Norman cuisine.

Le Havre

Most ferry passengers head straight out of the port of **LE HAVRE** as quickly as the traffic will allow to escape a city that most guidebooks dismiss as dismal, disastrous and gargantuan. While it is not the most picturesque or tranquil place in Normandy, it is not the soulless urban sprawl the warnings suggest, even if the port – the second-largest in France after Marseille – does take up half the Seine estuary, extending way beyond the town. The city was originally built on the orders of François I in 1517 to replace the ancient ports of Harfleur and Honfleur, then silting up, and its name was soon changed from the mouth-challenging Franciscopolis to Le Havre – "The Harbour". It became the principal trading post of France's northern coast, prospering especially during the American War of Independence and thereafter, importing cotton, sugar and tobacco. In the years before the outbreak of war in 1939, it was the European home of the great luxury liners like the *Normandie*, *Île de France* and *France*.

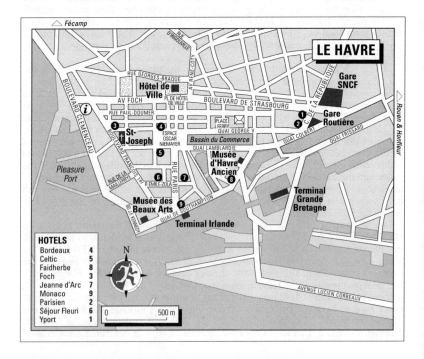

Le Havre suffered heavier damage than any other port in Europe during World War II. Following its near-total destruction, it was rebuilt to the specifications of a single architect, Auguste Perret, between 1946 and 1964 – which makes it a rare entity, and one visibly circumscribed by constraints of time and money. The sheer sense of space can be exhilarating, as the showpiece monuments have a dramatic and winning self-confidence and the few surviving churches and other relics of the old city have been sensitively integrated into the whole. The skyline has been kept deliberately low, but the endless mundane residential blocks, which were thrown up as economically and swiftly as possible after the war, get dispiriting after a while. However, with the sea visible at the end of almost every street and open public space and expanses of water at every turn, even those visitors who ultimately fail to agree with Perret's famous dictum that "concrete is beautiful" should enjoy a stroll around his city.

Arrival, information and accommodation

Le Havre's rather inconspicuous and not very central **tourist office** is on the main oceanfront drag, at 186 bd Clémenceau, near its intersection with av Foch (May–Sept Mon–Sat 8.45am–7pm, Sun 10am–12.30pm & 2.30–6pm; Oct–April Mon–Sat 8.45am–6.30pm, Sun 10am–1pm; ☎02.35.74.04.04).

Cross-Channel **ferries** from Britain and Ireland to Le Havre dock in two separate harbours. The **Terminal de Grande Bretagne**, not far from the rail and bus stations in the Bassin de la Citadelle (☎02.35.19.78.78), is served by three daily P&O sailings from Portsmouth, while the **Terminal Irlande**, further west on boulevard Kennedy, a little nearer the town centre (☎02.35.53.28.83), is the point of arrival for Irish Continental boats from Rosslare and, in summer, Cork. Both have small tourist information kiosks, open in summer.

The **gare SNCF** (☎02.35.98.50.50) is 1.5km west of the Hôtel de Ville, on Cours de la République, right alongside the **gare routière** (☎02.35.26.67.23) across boulevard de Strasbourg. Shuttle buses from the gare SNCF run to both ferry terminals.

Hotels

Le Havre holds two main concentrations of **hotels**: one group faces the gare SNCF, and most of the rest lie within walking distance of the ferry terminal. The nearest **campsite** is *Forêt de Montgeon* (☎02.35.46.52.39; mid-April to Sept), north of the town centre in a 700-acre forest, on bus #1 from the Hôtel de Ville or gare SNCF, direction "Jacques-Monod".

de Bordeaux, 147 rue Louis Brindeau (☎02.35.22.69.44). Smart, comfortable hotel, affiliated to the "Best Western" chain, on the north side of the Espace Oscar Niemeyer, facing the Volcano (see below). ④.

Celtic, 106 rue Voltaire (☎02.35.42.39.77). Friendly and comfortable option, in the long buildings that flank the Espace Oscar Niemeyer, overlooking the Volcano. No restaurant. ②.

Faidherbe, 21 rue Général Faidherbe (☎02.35.42.20.27). Simple rooms, some with sea views, in welcoming family hotel very near the ferry port in the old town. ①.

Foch, 4 rue de Caligny (☎02.35.42.50.69). Plain cream-coloured cement building, beside the main entrance to the St-Joseph church. All rooms have TV plus bath or shower. ④.

Grand Hôtel Parisien, 1 cours de la République (☎02.35.25.23.83). A well-appointed place, with congenial management, facing the gare SNCF on a busy corner. All rooms have shower and TV. Twenty-five percent reductions on Fri & Sat from Dec to March. ②.

Jeanne d'Arc, 91 rue Emile-Zola (☎02.35.21.67.27). Tiny little hotel, where the old-fashioned but clean rooms are given a personal touch by the owner's needlework. ①.

Le Monaco, 16 rue de Paris (☎02.35.42.21.01). Bright hotel on a busy corner overlooking the quay, handy for the ferries and with a good-value brasserie downstairs. Closed second fortnight in Feb, and Mon from July to Oct. ②.

Séjour Fleuri, 71 rue Emile-Zola (☎02.35.41.33.81). On a side road off rue de Paris, close to the ferry terminal; not exactly "fleuri", but cheered up by some bright red shutters and a couple of windowboxes. Two hotels knocked into one make for uneven corridors. No restaurant. ①.

Yport, 27 cours de la République (☎02.35.25.21.08). Another option opposite the SNCF station, this time slightly quieter, being set just back from the street, and unusually hospitable. Guests in the cheaper rooms are charged 25F to have a shower, so you might as well have en-suite facilities. No restaurant. ①–③.

The town

One reason visitors tend to dismiss Le Havre out of hand is that it's easy – whether by train, bus or your own vehicle – to get to and from the city without ever seeing its downtown area, giving the impression that it's merely an endless industrial sprawl.

The Perret-designed central **Hôtel de Ville**, a logical first port of call as it houses the tourist office (see above), is a low flat-roofed building that stretches for over a hundred metres, topped by a seventeen-storey concrete tower. Surrounded by pergola walkways, flower beds, and flowing water from strata of fountains, it's an attractive, lively place with a high-tech feel, and is often the venue for imaginative civic-minded exhibitions.

Perret's other major creation, clearly visible northwest of the town hall, was the **church of St-Joseph**. Instead of the traditional elongated cross shape, the church is built on a cross of which all four arms are equally short. From the outside it's a plain mass of speckled concrete, the main doors thrown open to hint at dark interior spaces within resembling an underground car park. In fact, when you get inside it all makes sense: the altar is right in the centre, with the hundred-metre bell tower rising directly above it. Very simple patterns of stained glass, all around the church and right the way up the tower, create a bright interplay of coloured light, focusing on the altar. A tight spiral concrete staircase winds its way up one corner of the shaft of the tower – not that visitors can climb it, or indeed would want to.

Le Havre's boldest specimen of modern architecture is even newer – the cultural centre known as the **Volcano** (or less reverentially as the "yoghurt pot"), standing at the end of the Bassin du Commerce dominating the **Espace Oscar Niemeyer**. The Brazilian architect for which it is named designed this slightly asymmetrical, smooth, gleaming white cone, cut off abruptly just above the level of the surrounding buildings, so that its curving planes were undisturbed by doors or windows; the entrance is concealed beneath a white walkway in the open plaza below.

The **Bassin du Commerce**, which stretches away from the complex, is of minimal commercial significance. Kayaks and rowing boats can be rented to explore its regular contours, and a couple of larger boats are moored permanently to serve as clubs or restaurants – it's all disconcertingly quiet, serving mainly as an appropriate stretch of water for the graceful white footbridge of the Passarelle du Commerce to cross.

Until recently, the modern **Musée des Beaux-Arts** (daily except Tues 10am–noon & 2–6pm; 10F; all details currently subject to change), overlooking the harbour entrance, was renowned as one of the best-designed art galleries in France, using natural light to its full advantage to display an enjoyable assortment of nineteenth- and twentieth-century French paintings. However, at the time this book went to press the museum was closed for a thorough overhaul, to enable it to show a much greater proportion of its permanent collection than before, and it remains to be seen whether the ambience will remain the same. The highlights will presumably still be over two hundred canvases by **Eugène Boudin**, including greyish landscapes produced all along the Norman coastline, with views of Trouville, Honfleur and Étretat, and a lovely set of works by **Raoul Dufy** (1877–1953), which make Le Havre seem positively radiant, whatever the weather outside.

If you have the time to spare, you might like to see what old Le Havre looked like in the prewar days when Jean-Paul Sartre wrote *La Nausée* here. He taught philosophy for five years during the 1930s in a local school, and his almost transcendent disgust with the place cannot obscure the fascination he felt in exploring the seedy dockside quarter of St-François, in those spare moments when he wasn't visiting Simone de Beauvoir in Rouen. Little survives of the city Sartre knew, but pictures and bits gathered from the rubble are on display in one of the very few buildings that escaped, the **Musée de l'Ancien Havre** at 1 rue Jérôme-Bellarmato, just south of the Bassin du Commerce (Wed–Sun 10am–noon & 2–6pm; 12F).

The once-great port of **Harfleur** is now no more than a suburb of Le Havre, 6km upstream from the centre. While no longer sufficiently distinctive to be worth visiting, it earned an undying place in history, however, as the landing place of Henry V's English army in 1415, en route to victory at Agincourt. Laid to siege, Harfleur surrendered in late September, following a final English onslaught spurred on – according to Shakespeare – by Henry's cry of "Once more unto the breach, dear friends . . ."

Eating

Few of the **restaurants** in Le Havre are worth making a fuss about, except perhaps for some in the suburb of **Sainte-Adresse**. There are, however, lots of bars, cafés and brasseries around the gare SNCF, and all sorts of crêperies and ethnic alternatives – couscous, South American, Caribbean – in the backstreets of the St-François district.

If you're **shopping** for food to take home, possibilities include the central **market**, just west of place Gambetta and ideal for fresh produce, and two hypermarkets: Mammouth at Montivilliers (signposted from the Tancarville road) or the larger Auchan at the Mont Gaillard Centre Commercial (follow cours de la République beyond the gare SNCF, through the tunnel, then look for signs).

L'Huitrière, 12 quai Michel Féré (☎02.35.21.24.16). Seafood specialists in the St-Francis quarter, facing the rotating bridge between the English and French ferry ports. Even the simplest 91F *assiette* includes clams, shrimps and langoustines; the four-person 1112F *Abondance* has to be seen to be believed. They also have branches in Étretat and Dieppe.

Palissandre, 33 rue de Bretagne (☎02.35.21.69.00). Old-fashioned wood-panelled bistrot in the historic St-François district, where the conventional menus from 85F feature dishes such as fish stewed in cider, and an express menu guarantees service within twenty minutes. Closed Wed pm, Sat am & Sun.

Le Petit Bedon, 37–39 rue Louis Brindeau (☎02.35.41.36.81). A relatively formal option near the Volcano, where menus from 120F include dishes such as monkfish cooked in squid ink. On the whole, the starters are more exciting than the main courses. Closed Sat am, Sun & first fortnight in Aug.

La Petite Brocante, 75 rue Louis Brindeau (☎02.35.21.42.20). Lively central bistrot, where the set menus are a little pricey at 125F and up but there's always a good-value *plat du jour*, as often as not fresh fish. Closed Sun & first three weeks in Aug.

Tilbury, 39 rue Jean-de-la-Fontaine (☎02.35.21.23.50). Attractive, unusual place in the old town – individual tables are kitted out like horse-drawn carriages – where the emphasis is on baked dishes (they even bake snail *brioches*) and low-priced lunches. Closed Sat am, Sun pm & Mon.

THE SEINE VALLEY

The days of the **Seine**'s tidal bore and treacherous sandbanks are over. Heavy ships now serenely make their way up the looping river to the provincial capital of **Rouen**, the largest city of Normandy and the only one to merit a long stay. Further upstream, Monet's wonderful house and garden at **Giverny** and the medieval English frontier stronghold of **Château Gaillard** at **Les Andelys** also justify taking a slow route into Paris.

An enormous new bridge across the mouth of the Seine opened in 1995: the **Pont de Normandie** links Le Havre with Honfleur, and makes access between the coasts of Upper and Lower Normandy much more direct. Further inland, the immense **Tancarville** suspension bridge offers another choice of banks and routes, while just upstream from **Caudebec** the yellow stays of the magnificent **Pont de Brotonne** refract into strange optical effects as you cross. Scenically, the best way to go is along the north (right) bank – fortunately the route taken by Le Havre–Rouen buses (#191 & #192).

Along the Right Bank

The first town of any size on the right bank of the Seine is **CAUDEBEC-EN-CAUX**. Most traces of its long past were destroyed by fire in the last war, after which it was rebuilt. The damage – and previous local history – is recorded in the thirteenth-century **Maison des Templiers**, one of the few buildings to be spared. You can **rent bicycles** from M. Jaubert on rue de la Vicomte. A **market** has been held every Saturday since 1390 in the main square.

Two absolutely indistinguishable *logis de France* face the river side by side from quai Guilbaud, with all but identical prices – the *Normotel La Marine* at no. 18 (☎02.35.96.20.11; ③; closed Jan), and the *Normandie* at no. 19 (☎02.35.96.25.11; ②; closed Feb), and there's a riverside **campsite** to the north, the *Barre Y Va* (☎02.35.96.26.38; April–Sept).

Just beyond the Pont de Brotonne as you continue towards Rouen, the medieval **abbey** in **ST-WANDRILLE** was founded – so legend has it – by a seventh-century count who, with his wife, renounced all earthly pleasures on the day of their wedding. The abbey's buildings are an attractive if curious collection: part ruin, part restoration and, in the case of the main buildings, part transplant – a fifteenth-century barn brought here just a few years ago from another Normandy village miles away. Benedictine monks are on hand to show visitors around the abbey every afternoon at 3pm and 4pm, and also at 11.30am on Sunday (20F); you can hear their Gregorian chanting in their new church at morning (Mon–Sat 9.30am, Sun 10am) and evening (Mon–Wed, Fri & Sat 5.30pm, Thurs 6.45pm, Sun & hols 5pm) services.

There's a crêperie opposite the abbey, and the more upmarket *Deux Coronnes* restaurant in the place de l'Église (☎02.35.96.11.44; closed Sun eve, Mon & Sept) is a seventeenth-century inn where delicious menus start at 130F.

In the next loop of the Seine, 12km on from St-Wandrille, comes the highlight of the Seine valley: the majestic **abbey** in **JUMIÈGES** (mid-June to mid-Sept daily 9am–6.30pm; mid-Sept to Oct & April to mid-June Mon–Fri 9am–noon & 2–5pm, Sat & Sun 9am–noon & 2–6pm; Nov–March Mon–Fri 10am–noon & 2–4pm, Sat & Sun 10am–noon & 2–5pm; 25F). Destroyed as a deliberate act of policy during the Revolution, the main outline of today's haunting ruin dates from the eleventh century; William the Conqueror himself attended its consecration in 1067. The towers, nearly 60m high, still stand, along with part of the nave, roofless now and even more impressive because of it.

DUCLAIR, not far beyond Jumièges, holds a couple of nice **hotels**, with the *Hôtel de la Poste* opposite the landing stage for the town's little *bac*, at 286 quai de la Libération (☎02.35.37.50.04; ③), and *Le Tartarin* further up at 125 place du Général-de-Gaulle (☎02.35.37.50.38; ①).

Rouen

ROUEN, the capital of Upper Normandy, is one of France's most ancient and historic cities. Standing on the site of Roman Rotomagus, the lowest point on the river then

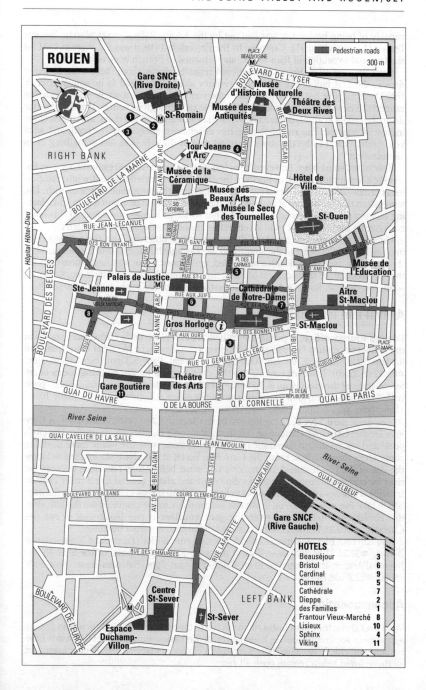

ROUEN

Pedestrian roads

0   300 m

PLACE
BEAUVOISINE

BOULEVARD DE L'YSER

**Gare SNCF
(Rive Droite)**

**Musée
d'Histoire Naturelle**

St-Romain

**Musée des
Antiquités**

**Théâtre des
Deux Rives**

RUE LOUIS RICARD

RUE BEAUVOISINE

RIGHT BANK

**Tour Jeanne
d'Arc** ④

**Musée de la
Céramique**

RUE JEANNE D'ARC

BOULEVARD DE LA MARNE

**Musée des
Beaux Arts**

**Hôtel de
Ville**

**Musée le Secq
des Tournelles**

St-Ouen

SQ
VERDREL

RUE JEAN-LECANUET

RUE DES FAULX

RUE DES BON ENFANTS

R DES
BASNAGE

RUE GANTERIE

RUE DE L'HÔPITAL

RUE DE L'HÔPITAL

RUE ORBEC

Hôpital Hôtel-Dieu ◁

BOULEVARD DES BELGES

R DE LA
FÈVRE

RUE ST-LO

RUE DE JOYEUSE

PL DES
CARMES
⑤

RUE D'AMIENS

**Musée de
l'Éducation**

Palais de Justice

Ste-Jeanne

PLACE DU
VIEUX MARCHÉ

⑧

VIEILLE TOUR

RUE JEANNE D'ARC

RUE AUX JUIFS

RUE DU BEC

**Cathédrale
de Notre-Dame** ⑦

**Aître
St-Maclou**

Gros Horloge ⑥

BONNETIERS

RUE ST-ROMAIN

⑥

St-Maclou

RUE AUX OURS

RUE DES BONNETIERS

RUE DE LA RÉPUBLIQUE

ℹ ⑨

PLACE
ST-MARC

RUE DU GENERAL LECLERC

**Théâtre
des Arts**

RUE DES AUGUSTINES

Gare Routière ⑪

RUE GRAND PONT

⑩

PL DE LA
RÉPUBLIQUE

QUAI DU HAVRE

Q DE LA BOURSE

Q P. CORNEILLE

QUAI DE PARIS

River Seine

QUAI CAVELIER DE LA SALLE

QUAI JEAN MOULIN

River Seine

AV DE BRETAGNE

RUE ST-SEVER

CHAMPLAIN

QUAI D'ELBEUF

BOULEVARD D'ORLEANS

COURS CLEMENCEAU

**Gare SNCF
(Rive Gauche)**

RUE DES EMMURÉES

RUE LAFAYETTE

HOTELS

Beauséjour	3
Bristol	6
Cardinal	9
Carmes	5
Cathédrale	7
Dieppe	2
des Familles	1
Frantour Vieux-Marché	8
Lisieux	10
Sphinx	4
Viking	11

**Centre
St-Sever**

✝ **St-Sever**

LEFT BANK

BOULEVARD DE L'EUROPE

**Espace
Duchamp-
Villon**

capable of being bridged, it was laid out by the Viking Rollo shortly after he became Duke of Normandy in 911. Captured by the English in 1419, it was the stage in 1431 for the trial and execution of Joan of Arc, and returned to French control in 1449.

Over the centuries, Rouen has suffered repeated devastation; there were 45 major fires in the first half of the thirteenth century alone. It has had to be almost entirely rebuilt during the last fifty years, and now you could spend a whole day wandering around the city without realizing that the Seine ran through its centre. War-time bombs destroyed all its bridges, the area between the cathedral and the quais, and much of the industrial quarter. The riverside area has never been adequately restored, and what you might expect to be the most beautiful part of the city is in fact something of an abomination.

Enormous sums have, however, been lavished on an upmarket restoration job on the streets a few hundred metres north of the river, which turned the centre into the closest approximation to a medieval city that modern imaginations could come up with. The suggestion that for historical authenticity the houses should be painted in bright, clashing colours was not deemed appropriate, but so far as it goes, the whole of this inner core can be very seductive, and its churches are impressive by any standards.

Outside the renovated quarters, things are rather different. The city spreads deep into the loop of the Seine to the south, and increasingly into the hills to the north, while the riverbank itself is lined with a fume-filled, multi-laned motorway. As the nearest point that large container ships can get to Paris, the port remains the country's fourth largest – albeit in decline. Rouen's docks and industries stretch endlessly away to the south.

Arrival and information

Rouen's **tourist office**, opposite the cathedral at 25 place de la Cathédrale, stands in the sixteenth-century "House of the Exchequer" (May–Sept Mon–Sat 9am–7pm, Sun 9.30am–12.30pm & 2.30–6pm; Oct–April Mon–Sat 9am–6.30pm, Sun 10am–1pm; ☎02.32.08.32.40). It serves each day as the starting point for 2hr **walking tours** of different areas of the city (10am & 3pm; 35F). For more sedate visitors, a motorized "**petit train**" makes a 40min loop tour from the tourist office at regular intervals (daily 10am, 11am, 2pm, 4pm & 5pm; 30F).

The main **gare SNCF**, at the top end of rue Jeanne-d'Arc (☎02.35.98.50.50), is Gare Rive Droite; Gare Rive Gauche on the south bank only handles goods traffic. The city's pride and joy, its multibillion-franc new **Métro** system, is on the whole more useful to commuters than tourists. From the Gare Rue Verte, at the SNCF station, trains follow the line of the rue Jeanne-d'Arc, making two stops before they resurface to cross the river by bridge; thereafter the tracks dip below and above ground like a roller coaster. Individual journeys cost 8F, a book of tickets is 59F. All **buses** except #2A from the gare SNCF take five minutes to run down rue Jeanne-d'Arc to the centre. From the fifth stop, the Théâtre des Arts by the river, the **gare routière** is one block west in rue des Charettes (☎02.35.71.81.71), tucked away behind the riverfront buildings.

You can rent **bicycles** from Rouen Cycles, 45 rue St-Éloi (Tues–Sat 8.30am–noon & 2–7pm; ☎02.35.71.34.30), as well as at the gare SNCF. The **post office** is at 45 rue Jeanne-d'Arc, in the centre of town (Mon–Fri 8am–7pm, Sat 8am–noon; post code 76000; ☎02.35.08.73.73).

Accommodation

With over three thousand **hotel** rooms in town, there should be no difficulty in finding appropriate accommodation in Rouen, even at the busiest times. Few of the hotels have restaurants, chiefly because there's so wide a choice of places to eat all over town, and all those listed below remain open all year.

Hotels

Beauséjour, 9 rue Pouchet (☎02.35.71.93.47). Good value place near the station (turn right as you come out), though once you're past the attractive orange facade with its windowboxes, and the nice garden courtyard, the rooms themselves are on the plain side, even if they do all have shower and TV. ②.

Bristol, 45 rue aux Juifs (☎02.35.71.54.21) Clean, pretty little nine-room hotel, in a half-timbered house overlooking the Palais de Justice. All rooms are en suite, and have TV. ②.

Le Cardinal, 1 place de la Cathédrale (☎02.35.70.24.42). Very good value hotel in a stunning location facing the cathedral; the rooms have excellent en-suite facilities. No restaurant. ③.

des Carmes, 33 place des Carmes (☎02.35.71.92.31). Twelve-room hotel in a beautifully decorated nineteenth-century house in quiet central square, complete with blue shutters, a short walk north from the cathedral. Guests are not given keys to stay out late. No restaurant, but buffet breakfasts for 34F. ②.

de la Cathédrale, 12 rue St-Romain (☎02.35.71.57.95). One of the very nicest hotels in Rouen. Quiet, central rooms alongside the cathedral and archbishop's palace, with a quaint old courtyard with flowers. Set in a pedestrianized street – so parking is a problem – that's lined with fourteenth-century timber-framed houses. No restaurant. ④.

de Dieppe, place Bernard Tissot (☎02.35.71.96.00). Grand traditional hotel, immediately opposite the station, which is affiliated to the Best Western chain. Prices for the very clean and well-equipped rooms are greatly discounted at weekends. ⑤.

Hôtel des Familles, 4 rue Pouchet (☎02.35.71.88.51). Very friendly and characterful place, set back beyond a small gravel yard and a short walk to the right as you come out from the Gare Rive Droite. Incorporates the old *Hôtel de la Paix*; hence the two entrances. No restaurant. ②.

Frantour Vieux Marché, 15 rue de la Pie (☎02.35.71.00.88). Very modern place, set around a venerable old courtyard, just a toss of a match from the place du Vieux-Marché. A high standard of comfort has quickly made this the most popular upmarket hotel in town. ⑤.

de Lisieux, 4 rue de la Savonnerie (☎02.35.71.87.73). At the junction of rue de la Savonnerie and rue du Bec, between cathedral and river. Bishop Cauchon, who prosecuted Joan of Arc in 1431, is said to have stayed – and died – here in 1442. If so, it has been modernized since – every room now has en-suite facilities – losing much of the original character in the process. No restaurant. ③.

Sphinx, 130 rue Beauvoisine (☎02.35.71.35.86). Very basic accommodation, at the north end of the street near the Musée des Antiquités. Some of the rooms has its own shower; there's a charge of 10F per shower; and an extra bed in the room costs 60F. No restaurant. ①.

Viking, 21 quai du Havre (☎02.35.70.34.95). Just in front of the gare routière, to the right at the bottom of rue Jeanne-d'Arc. Overlooking not only the river, but also the main roads, the noise of which is only partly dampened by the double glazing. No restaurant. ③.

Youth hostels and campsites

HI youth hostel, 118 bd de l'Europe (☎02.35.72.06.45). From the gare SNCF on the north bank, take bus #12, direction "Parc des Expositions", as far as the Diderot stop. Dorm beds 59F, 11pm curfew.

Camping L'Aubette, 23 Vert Buisson in St-Léger du Bourg-Denis (☎02.35.08.47.69). Significantly less accessible than the *Camping Municipal*, and 5km east of town.

Camping Municipal, rue Jules-Ferry in Déville-lès-Rouen (☎02.35.74.07.59). Surprisingly small site, 4km northwest of town – bus #2 from the Théâtre des Arts – that's geared towards caravans rather than tents.

The town

Rouen spends a bigger slice of its budget on monuments than any other provincial town – which annoys many a Rouennais – and, as a tourist, your one complaint may be the lack of time to visit them all.

The place du Vieux-Marché to the cathedral

The obvious place to start sightseeing is the **place du Vieux-Marché**, where a small plaque and a huge cross (nearly 20m high) mark the spot on which Joan of Arc was burnt to death on May 30, 1431. A new memorial **church** to the saint has been built in the square (Mon–Thurs & Sat 10am–12.30pm & 2–6pm, Fri & Sun 2–6pm). It's a wacky, spiky-looking thing, said to represent either an upturned boat or the flames that consumed Joan, but indisputably an architectural triumph, part of an ensemble of buildings that manages to incorporate in similar style a covered food market. The theme of the church's fish-shaped windows is continued in the scaly tiles that adorn its roof, which is elongated to form a walkway across the square. The outline of that vanished church's foundations is visible on the adjacent lawns, which also mark the precise spot of Joan's martyrdom. The square itself is surrounded by fine old brown-and-white half-timbered houses; many of those on the south side now serve as restaurants. The private **Musée Jeanne d'Arc**, tucked in among them in an ancient cellar in the back of a gift shop, draws large crowds to its collection of tawdry waxworks and facsimile manuscripts (daily except Mon; May to mid-Sept 9.30am–6.30pm; mid-Sept to April 10am–noon & 2–6.30pm; 24F).

From place du Vieux-Marché, **rue du Gros-Horloge** leads east towards the cathedral. Just across rue Jeanne-d'Arc you come to the **Gros Horloge** itself. A colourful one-handed clock, it used to be on the adjacent Gothic **belfry** until it was moved down by popular demand in 1529, so that people could see it better. When the restoration work in progress when this book went to press is complete you should be able to pay a small fee to climb up rather too many steps to see its workings and, if the sponginess of the lead roofing agrees with your nerves, totter around the top for a marvellous view of the old city.

The **Cathédrale de-Notre-Dame** somehow remains at heart the Gothic masterpiece that was built in the twelfth and thirteenth centuries, although all kinds of vertical extensions have since been added. The west facade – intricately sculpted like the rest of the exterior – was Monet's subject for a series of studies of changing light, which now hang in the Musée d'Orsay in Paris (see p.130). Inside, the carvings of the misericords in the choir provide a study of fifteenth-century life – in secular scenes of work and habits along with the usual mythical beasts. The **ambulatory** and **crypt** – closed on Sundays and during services – hold the assorted tombs of various recumbent royalty, stretching back as far as Duke Rollo, who died "enfeebled by toil" in 933 AD, and the eponymous heart of Richard the Lionheart.

St-Ouen and around

The **church of St-Ouen**, next to the Hôtel de Ville (which itself occupies buildings that were once part of the abbey), is larger than the cathedral and has far less decoration, so that the Gothic proportions have that instant impact rivalled by nothing built since the Middle Ages (mid-March to Oct daily except Tues 10am–12.30pm & 2–6pm; Nov to mid-Dec and mid-Jan to mid-March Wed, Sat & Sun 10am–12.30pm & 2–4.30pm). The world that produced it – and, nearer the end of the era, the light and grace of the **church of St-Maclou** not far to the south – was one of mass death from the Plague; the **Aître St-Maclou** (daily 8am–8pm; entrance between 184 & 186 rue Martainville) was a cemetery for the victims. It's now the tranquil garden courtyard of the Fine Arts school, but if you examine the one open lower storey of the surrounding buildings you'll discover the original deathly decorations and a mummified cat. In the square outside are several good antique bookshops, and a few art shops.

Just past the Hôtel de Ville, the **Musée des Antiquités** occupies a seventeenth-century convent on rue Beauvoisine (Mon & Wed–Sat 10am–5.30pm, Sun 10am–noon & 2–6pm; 10F); its tapestries and Middle Ages collection are particularly good.

The **rue Eau de Robec**, which runs east from rue Damiette just south of Saint-Ouen, was described by one of Flaubert's characters in an earlier age as a "degraded little Venice". It's now a textbook example of how Rouen has been restored. Where once a shallow stream flowed beneath the raised doorsteps of venerable half-timbered houses, a thin trickle now makes its way along a stylized cement bed crossed by concrete walkways. It remains an attractive ensemble, if a rather ersatz one, and the houses themselves are now predominantly inhabited by antique dealers, interspersed with the odd café.

The Musée des Beaux-Arts and around

Rouen's imposing **Musée des Beaux-Arts** commands the square Verdrel from just east of the central rue Jeanne d'Arc (daily except Tues 10am–6pm; 20F). Even this grand edifice is not quite large enough to display some of its medieval tapestries, which trail inelegantly along the floor, but the collection as a whole is consistently absorbing. Unexpected highlights include dazzling Russian icons from the sixteenth century onwards, and an entertaining three-dimensional eighteenth-century Nativity from Naples. Many of the biggest names among the painters – Caravaggio, Velázquez, Rubens – tend to be represented by a single minor work, but there are several Monets, including a *Rouen Cathedral* from 1894, and a recently acquired *Vue Générale de Rouen*. The central sculpture court, roofed over but very light, is dominated by a wonderful three-part mural of the course of the Seine from Paris to Le Havre, prepared by Raoul Dufy in 1937 for the Palais de Chaillot in Paris.

Rouen's history as a centre for *faïencerie*, or earthenware pottery, is recorded in the **Musée de la Céramique**, facing the Beaux-Arts from the north (daily except Tues 10am–1pm & 2–6pm; 13F). A series of beautiful rooms, some of which incorporate sixteenth-century wood panelling rescued from a demolished nunnery of St-Amand, display specimens from the seventeenth century onwards. Assorted tiles and plates reflect the eighteenth-century craze for Chinoiserie, although the genuine Chinese and Japanese pieces nearby possess a sophistication contemporary French craftsmen could only dream of emulating. The mood changes abruptly in the Revolutionary era, as witnessed by plates bearing slogans from both sides of the political fence.

Behind the Beaux-Arts, housed in the old and barely altered church of St-Laurent on rue Jacques-Villon, the **Musée Le Secq des Tournelles** consists of a brilliant collection of wrought-iron objects of all dates and descriptions, among them nutcrackers and door knockers, spiral staircases that lead nowhere and hideous implements of torture (daily except Tues 10am–1pm & 2–6pm; 13F).

The Tour Jeanne d'Arc

The pencil-thin **Tour Jeanne d'Arc** (daily except Tues 10am–noon & 2–5.30pm; 10F), a short way southeast of the gare SNCF at the junction of rue du Donjon and rue du Cordier, is all that remains of the castle of Philippe-Auguste, built in 1205 for the imprisonment and trial of Joan of Arc. It served as the castle's keep and entranceway, and was itself fully surrounded by a moat. It was not however Joan's actual prison – that was the Tour de la Pucelle, demolished in 1809 – while the trial took place first of all in the castle's St-Romain chapel, and then later in its great central hall, both of which were destroyed in 1590.

The tall, sharp-pointed tower was bought by public subscription in 1860, and restored to its present state. After seeing a small collection of Joan-related memorabilia, visitors climb the steep spiral staircase to the very top, but you can't see out over the city, let alone step outside into the open air.

Eating and drinking

Unlike the hotels, which sometimes have cheaper weekend rates, Rouen's upmarket **restaurants** tend to charge more over weekends, when families eat out. The greatest concentration of restaurants is in place du Vieux-Marché, where there's a daily **food market**, while the area just north is full of Tunisian **takeaways**, **crêperies** and so forth.

Restaurants

Auberge St-Maclou, 224–226 rue Martainville (☎02.35.71.06.67). Half-timbered building in the shadow of St-Maclou church, with tables on the street outside and an old-style ambience inside. The pedestrian street gets crowded in summer, but the menus are far from over-priced – the 67F set lunch includes cocktail, wine and coffee. Prices to suit all budgets, and dishes including mussels and duck, as well as excellent desserts. Closed Sun pm and Mon.

des Beaux-Arts, 34 rue Damiette (☎02.35.70.17.15). On pretty pedestrianized street north of Saint-Maclou church. Very good-value Algerian cuisine: *couscous* from 50F or *tajine* from 68F, with all kinds of sausages and assorted meats. Closed Wed in winter.

Brasserie Paul, 1 place de la Cathédrale (☎02.35.71.86.07). The definitive address for Rouen's definitive bistrot, an attractive Belle Époque place with seating both indoors and on a terrace in full view of the cathedral. Daily lunch specials such as the goats' cheese and smoked duck salad that was Simone de Beauvoir's regular favourite in 1937, cost around 60F.

Flunch, 60 rue des Carmes (☎02.35.71.81.81). Large and good self-service, with many fresh dishes and a 35F daily *formule*. On street running north from the cathedral. Daily 11am–10pm.

Gill, 9 quai de la Bourse (☎02.35.71.16.14). Absolutely classic French restaurant, voted the best in the province by a local magazine on account of such Gilles Tournadre specialities as lobster grilled with asparagus and pigeon baked in puff pastry. The cheapest menu will set you back 199F. Closed Sun & Mon June–Sept; otherwise Sun pm & Mon.

Gill, Le Bistrot du Chef . . . en Gare, 1st floor, Gare Rive Droite (☎02.35.71.48.66). The name may seem convoluted to outsiders, but to Rouennais it signals a true marvel; the bistrot in the main railway station is now run under the auspices of the city's top chef. There's an excellent self-service cafeteria downstairs, while the more formal dining room upstairs is open for lunch only, with set menus from 75F. Closed Mon pm, Sat am, Sun & Aug.

Jumbo, 11 rue Guillaume le Conquerant (☎02.35.70.35.88). Another good self-service, off the northeast corner of place du Vieux-Marché. Put together your own large salad for under 25F, or choose from a variety of cooked dishes. Daily 11.15am–2.30 pm & 6.30–9.30pm.

Les Maraichers – Le Bistrot d'Adrien, 37 place du Vieux Marché (☎02.35.71.57.73). Deservedly the most popular of the Vieux-Marché's many restaurants, with a streetside terrace right in front of the St-Jeanne church. Styled to resemble a *fin-de-siècle* Parisian bistrot, serving varied set menus until 11pm nightly and à la carte until midnight. Menus start at 78F, with lots of *andouillettes*, snails and tongues, but plenty of wholesome possibilities too, and great desserts.

Pascaline, 5 rue de la Poterne (☎02.35.89.67.44). North of Palais de Justice, near the flower market; classic bistrot with a green wooden enclosure attached to the front of a half-timbered house. They do great value buffets of salads (32F), main courses (45F) and desserts (37F) – you can have all three for 79F – as well as more formal set menus from 99F that provide a good opportunity to sample Rouennais *caneton* (duckling).

Le P'tit Bec, 182 rue Eau de Robec (☎02.35.07.63.33). Friendly brasserie-cum-tearoom that has become Rouen's most popular lunch spot, with a simple 75F menu holding such joys as salmon tagliatelle and chocolate fondants, with plenty of vegetarian options; also serves afternoon tea. There's seating both indoors and outside, on the pedestrianized street, beside the running water and in view of the gorgeous blue half-timbered mansion next door. The only evening it's open is Friday; closed all day Sun.

au Temps des Cerises, 4–6 rue des Basnages (☎02.35.89.98.00). If you've come to Normandy for the cheeses, this is the place to get it all out of your system. Turkey breast in Camembert, goats' cheese crêpes, and above all fondues of every description. Lunch menus from 60F, from 88F in the evening. Trendy if slightly over-styled. Closed Mon am & Sun.

Bars

Some of Rouen's most agreeable **bars** are in the maze of streets between rue Thiers and place du Vieux-Marché. Incoming sailors used to head straight for this area of the city, and the small bars are still there even if the sailors aren't.

Le Bateau Ivre, 17 rue des Sapins (☎02.35.70.09.05). Low-key but atmospheric hang-out, with wooden tables, which puts on a mostly rock-oriented programme of music and performance, with an open night on Thursdays that seems to attract lovers of traditional French chansons. Open until 2am Tues & Wed, 4am Thurs–Sat. Closed Sun, Mon & all Aug.

Big Ben Pub, 95 rue du Gros-Horloge (☎02.35.88.44.50). Right under the big clock – hence the name. A Mexican-themed restaurant which incorporates an always-packed bar, strictly speaking entered from a side street – 30 rue des Vergetiers. Usually as crowded inside as the street outside. Open noon to 2am; closed Sun.

Exo 7, 13 place des Chartreux (☎02.35.03.32.30). Traditionally the centre of Rouen's heavy rock scene, a long way south of the centre, the *Exo 7* (note the pun) is these days becoming a bit more eclectic, with the odd techno dance night as well. Open Wed–Sat 10.30pm–4am.

Scottish Pub, 21 rue Verte (☎02.35.71.46.22). Bar and restaurant right next to the station, open until 2am, which puts on jazz groups from time to time. Closed Sat lunchtime and Sun all day.

La Taverne Saint Amand, 11 rue Saint-Amand (☎02.35.88.51.34). Popular bar with draught Guinness, off rue de la République above the cathedral.

Nightlife and entertainment

As you would expect in a conurbation of 400,000, there's always plenty going on in Rouen, from classical concerts in churches to alternative events in community and commercial centres. An annual handbook, *Le P'tit Normand*, available in all newsagents, is helpful with addresses and telephone numbers. For current events, pick up the free *Cette Semaine à Rouen* from the tourist office.

Rouen has several **theatres**, which mainly work to winter seasons. The most highbrow and big-spectacle is the **Théâtre des Arts**, 22 place des Arts (☎02.35.98.50.98), which puts on opera, ballet and concerts. The more adventurous repertory company of the **Théâtre des Deux Rives** (☎02.35.70.22.82), based opposite the Musee des Antiquités at the top end of rue Louis Ricard (no. 48; happily at the junction with rue de Joyeuse), presents work by playwrights such as Beaumarchais, Shakespeare, Beckett and Gorky.

Major **concerts** often take place in the **Théâtre Duchamp-Villon** in the Saint-Sever complex (☎02.35.62.31.31). Also south of the river, but a long way further out, are **Théâtre Charles Dullin**, allée des Arcades, Grand Quévilly (☎02.35.68.48.91), and **Théâtre Maxime Gorki**, rue François Mitterand, Petit Quévilly (☎02.35.72.67.55), which specializes in contemporary and traditional music from around Europe.

Upstream from Rouen

Upstream from Rouen towards Paris, high cliffs on the north bank of the Seine imitate the coast, looking down on waves of green and scattered river islands. By the time you reach **Les Andelys**, 25km out of Rouen, you're within 100km of the capital, meaning that accommodation and eating prices tend to be geared towards affluent weekend and day-trippers. Large country estates abound in this agreeable countryside, and public transport is minimal – it's assumed any visitor has, if not a residence, then at least a car. However, infrequent buses run from Rouen to Les Andelys, and trains from Rouen call at **Vernon**. This area also boasts one of Normandy's most-visited tourist attractions in the village of **Giverny**.

Les Andelys

The most dramatic sight anywhere along the Seine has to be Richard the Lionheart's **Château Gaillard**, perched high above **LES ANDELYS**. Constructed in a position of impregnable power, it looked down over any movement on the river at the frontier of the English king's domains. It was built in less than a year (1196–97) and might have survived intact had Henry IV not ordered its destruction in 1603. As it is, the dominant outline remains. Visits to the château are permitted between mid-March and mid-November only (Mon & Thurs–Sun 10am–noon & 2–6pm, Wed 2–6pm; 18F). On foot, you can make the steep climb up via a path that leads off rue Richard Coeur-de-Lion in Petit Andely. The only route for motorists is extraordinarily convoluted, following a long-winded one-way system that starts opposite the church in Grand Andely.

The **tourist office** for Les Andelys is at 24 rue Philippe-Auguste in Petit Andely (June–Sept Mon–Sat 9.30am–noon & 2–6pm, Sun 9.30am–noon & 2–5.30pm; Oct–May daily 2–5.30pm; ☎02.32.54.41.93). The nicest places to **stay** have to be the two Seine-side hotels; the eighteenth-century *Chaîne d'Or*, opposite the thirteenth-century St-Sauveur church at 27 rue Grande (☎02.32.54.00.31; ⑤; closed Jan, Sun pm & Mon), and the *Normandie* at 1 rue Grande (☎02.32.54.10.52; ③; closed Dec; restaurant closed Wed pm & Thurs). There's also a lovely riverside **campground**, far below the château, the *L'Île des Trois Rois* (April–Oct; ☎02.32.54.23.79).

Giverny

Roughly 15km south of the ancient fortifications of Les Andelys, on the north bank of the river, you come to **Monet's gardens** – complete with water-lily pond – at **GIVERNY** (gardens and house April–Oct daily except Mon 10am–6pm, last ticket sold 5.30pm, no advance sales; 35F, 25F gardens only). Monet lived here from 1883 till his death in 1926, and the gardens that he laid out were considered by many of his friends to be his masterpiece. In fact art lovers who make the pilgrimage here tend to be outnumbered by garden enthusiasts. None of Monet's original paintings are on display – most are in the Orangerie and Musée d'Orsay in Paris – whereas the gardens are still lovingly tended in all their glory.

Visits start in the huge studio, built in 1915, where Monet painted his last and largest water-lily canvases; it now serves as a well-stocked book and gift store, albeit disappointingly short of good-quality reproductions of the famous works. A gravel footpath leads from there to the house proper. Apart from the bedroom, hung with family photos and paintings by friends and family, and the salon with its washed-out reproductions, all the main rooms are crammed almost floor-to-ceiling with Monet's collection of Japanese prints. Most of the original furnishings are gone, but you do get a real sense of how the kitchen used to be, with all its walls and fittings painted a glorious bright yellow; Monet designed his own yellow crockery to harmonize with the surroundings. By contrast, the stairs and upstairs rooms are a pale blue.

Colourful flower gardens, with trellised walkways and shady bowers, stretch down from the house. At the bottom, a dank underpass beneath the road leads to the *jardin d'eau*, focused around the narrow **water-lily pond**. Footpaths around the perimeter, as well of course as arching Japanese footbridges, offer differing views of the water lilies themselves, cherished by gardeners in rowing boats. May and June, when the rhododendrons flower around the pond, and the wisteria that winds over the Japanese bridge is in bloom, are the best times to visit. Whenever you come, however, you'll have to contend with camera-happy crowds jostling to capture their own impressions of the water lilies.

A few minutes' walk up Giverny's village street stands the new **Musée d'Art Américain** (April–Oct daily except Mon 10am–6pm; 35F), an unattractive edifice that hides a spacious and well-lit gallery devoted to American artists resident in France between 1865 and 1915. Some took their admiration of Monet to a point that now seems embarrassing, painting many of the same scenes, but there are some interesting works by John Singer Sargent, Winslow Homer and, especially, Mary Cassatt.

Giverny's one **hotel**, the *Musardière*, stands not far beyond Monet's house at 123 rue Claude-Monet (☎02.32.21.03.18; ④); dinner menus in its restaurant start at 145F, and there's a pleasant little tea-room and restaurant, *Les Nymphéas* (☎02.32.21.20.31), is opposite the house itself. The nearest inexpensive accommodation is the *Hôtel d'Évreux*, 11 place d'Évreux (☎02.32.21.16.12; ③), a fine seventeenth-century town house offering good food and comfortable accommodation in the heart of **VERNON**, across the river.

To reach the gardens from the gare SNCF in Vernon, either rent a bike or catch the bus that leaves from the station at 1.15pm and returns from the car park opposite the gardens at 3.15pm and 5.15pm (15F return).

BASSE NORMANDIE

As you head west along the coast of Lower Normandy, a succession of somewhat smug and exclusive resorts – of which only **Honfleur** is especially memorable – is followed first by the beaches where the Allied armies landed in 1944, and then by the wilder, and in some places deserted, shore around the **Cotentin Peninsula**. There are two absolutely unmissable sights – the glorious island abbey of **Mont St-Michel**, and the **Bayeux Tapestry**.

The Norman Riviera

The only section of the Norman coast to have any serious delusions of grandeur is the stretch that lies immediately east of the mouth of the Seine. The new **Pont de Normandie** across from Le Havre is starting to make such places as **Trouville** and **Deauville** too hectic for comfort, though only **Honfleur** could be said to have all that much to lose.

Honfleur

HONFLEUR, the best preserved of the old ports of Normandy and the first you come to on the eastern Calvados coast, is a near-perfect seaside town that lacks only a beach. It used to have one, but with the accumulation of silt from the Seine the sea has steadily withdrawn, leaving the eighteenth-century waterfront houses of **boulevard Charles-V** stranded and a little surreal. The ancient port, however, still functions – the channel to the beautiful *Vieux Bassin* is kept open by regular dredging – and though only pleasure craft now use the moorings in the harbour basin, fishing boats tie up alongside the pier nearby, and you can usually buy fish either directly from the boats or from stands on the pier, still by right run by fishermen's wives.

Honfleur is highly picturesque, and has been moving upmarket at an ever greater rate since the vast **Pont de Normandie** spanned the mouth of the Seine in 1995. Despite now being just a few minutes' drive from the giant metropolis of Le Havre, however, the old port still feels not so very different to the town that was the subject of artists' brush strokes in the second half of the nineteenth century.

Arrival and information

Honfleur's **tourist office** is across from the town hall on place Arthur-Boudin (July & Aug Mon–Sat 9.30am–7pm, Sun 10am–1pm; Easter to mid-July & Sept Mon–Sat 9.30am–12.30pm & 2–6.30pm, Sun 10am–1pm; Oct–Easter Mon–Sat 9am–noon & 2–5.30pm; ☎02.31.89.23.30). For much of the year, it organizes two-hour **guided walking tours** of the town (mid-July to mid-Sept Tues & Thurs 10pm, Sat 3pm; mid-April to mid-July and last fortnight of Sept, Sat 3pm only; 28F).

The **gare routière**, on place de la Porte-du-Rouen, is served by over a dozen direct daily **buses** from Caen (#20), and up to eight express services from Le Havre (Bus

Verts; ☎02.31.89.28.41). However, the nearest **train station** is at Pont l'Evêque, connected by the Lisieux bus, #50 (a 20min ride).

Accommodation

If finding budget **accommodation** is one of your main priorities, it probably makes sense for you not to stay in Honfleur at all, and simply to visit for the day. Especially on summer weekends, so many visitors turn up that even the most ordinary hotel can get away with charging rates well above the average for Normandy. No hotels overlook the harbour itself.

HOTELS

Belvédère, 36 route Émile-Renouf (☎02.31.89.08.13). Small, central nine-room hotel, with tranquil and tasteful rooms, an exquisite little garden, and a restaurant where dinner menus start at 98F. ④.

des Cascades, 17 place Thiers (☎02.31.89.05.83). Large hotel/restaurant open onto both place Thiers and the cobbled rue de la Ville behind. Slightly noisy rooms upstairs, and a good value if not all that exciting restaurant with outdoor seating on both sides; menus climb from 80F towards the expensive *fruits de mer*. Closed Mon pm, all Tues out of season, and Dec–Feb. ②.

du Dauphin, 10 place Berthelot (☎02.31.89.15.53). Grey slate town house just around the corner from Ste-Catherine church, with a wide assortment of rooms. Closed Jan. ④–⑨.

Le Hamelin, 16 place Hamelin (☎02.31.89.16.25). Five basic rooms, some with showers, in plain building very near the Lieutenance in the liveliest part of town. The restaurant downstairs has standard seafood menus from 88F, and manages to squeeze a few tables onto the street. ②–④.

des Loges, 18 rue Brulée (☎02.31.89.38.26). Brightly refurbished hotel on a quiet side street just 100m inland from Ste-Catherine church, decked out with flowers and with a good standard of rooms. ④.

Tilbury, 30 place Hamelin (☎02.31.98.83.33). Absolutely central, a stone's throw from the Lieutenance. Well-equipped and comfortable rooms above a crêperie. ③.

CAMPSITE

Camping du Phare, place Jean-de-Vienne, at the western end of bd Charles-V (☎02.31.89.10.26). Mid-March to Sept only.

The town

Visitors to Honfleur inevitably gravitate towards the old centre, around the **Vieux Bassin**. At the *bassin*, slate-fronted houses, each of them one or two storeys higher than seems possible, harmonize despite their tottering and ill-matched forms into a backdrop that is only excelled by the **Lieutenance** at the harbour entrance. This latter was the dwelling of the King's Lieutenant, and has been the gateway to the inner town ever since Samuel Champlain sailed from Honfleur to found Québec in 1608. The church of **St-Étienne** nearby is now the **Musée de la Marine**, which combines a collection of model ships with several rooms of antique Norman furnishings (July & Aug daily 10am–1pm & 2–6.30pm; April–June & Sept daily except Mon 10am–noon & 2–6pm; mid-Feb to March & Oct to mid-Nov Tues–Fri 2–5.30pm, Sat & Sun 10am–noon & 2–5.30pm; 15F). Just behind it, two seventeenth-century **salt stores**, used to contain the precious commodity during the days of the much-hated *gabelle*, or salt tax, now serve as **the Musée d'Ethnographie et d'Art Populaire Normand** (same hours; 15F, or combined ticket 25F), filled with everyday artefacts from old Honfleur.

Honfleur's artistic past – and its present concentration of galleries and painters – owes most to Eugène Boudin, forerunner of Impressionism. He was born and worked in the town, trained the 15-year-old Monet, and was joined for various periods by Pissarro, Renoir and Cézanne. At the same time, Baudelaire paid visits to the town, which was also home to the composer Erik Satie. There's a fair selection of Boudin's works in the **Musée Eugène Boudin**, west of the port on place Erik-Satie (July & Aug daily except Tues 10am–noon & 2–6.30pm; Oct–Dec and mid-Feb to mid-March Mon & Wed–Fri 2.30–5pm, Sat & Sun 10am–noon & 2.30–5pm; rest of year daily except Tues 10am–noon & 2-6pm; 16F), and his crayon seascapes in particular are quite appealing here in context, though the Dufys, Marquets, Frieszes and, above all, the Monets are the most impressive paintings on show.

Admission also gives you access to one of Monet's subjects featured in the museum, the detached belfry of the **church of Ste-Catherine** (daily 9am–noon & 2–6pm). The church and belfry are built almost entirely of wood – supposedly due to economic restraints after the Hundred Years' War. It's a change from the great stone Norman churches and has the added peculiarity of being divided into twin naves, with one balcony running around both. From **rue de l'Homme-de-Bois** behind you can see yacht masts through the houses overlooking the *bassin* and, in the distance, the huge industrial panorama of Le Havre's docks.

Eating

With its abundance of day-trippers and hotel guests, Honfleur supports an astonishing number of **restaurants**, most specializing in seafood. Surprisingly few face onto the harbour itself; the narrow buildings around the edge seem to be better suited to being snack bars, crêperies, cafés and ice-cream parlours.

L'Absinthe, 10 quai de la Quarantaine (☎02.31.89.39.00). This lovely eighteenth-century mansion houses the most imaginative of the row of five restaurants that stand just around the corner from the *bassin*, with such dishes as scallop *carpaccio* or *foie gras* in ginger nestling on menus that range from 169F to 350F. Closed mid-Nov to to end of Dec.

L'Assiette Gourmand, 2 quai des Passagers (☎02.31.89.24.88). One of the very finest restaurants in Normandy, in the heart of old Honfleur. It's possible to spend an absolute fortune, but the 165F menu, with its salmon *tartare* and irresistible desserts, gives you a pretty good idea of what chef Gérard Bonnefoy can achieve. Closed Sun pm & Mon out of season.

Auberge de la Lieutenance, 12 place Ste-Catherine (☎02.31.89.07.52). Not in fact by the Lieutenance, despite the name. Plenty of outdoor seating on the cobbled pedestrian square, facing both church and belfry and overshadowed for no obvious reason by a giant thumb. Gourmet dining with a heavy emphasis on oysters; menus start at 98F. Closed Sun pm & mid-Nov to Dec.

au P'tit Mareyeur, 4 rue Haute (☎02.31.98.84.23). No distance from the centre, but all the seating is indoors and there are no views. Very good fish dishes – red crab soup with garlic – plus plenty of creamy *pays d'Auge* sauces and superb desserts. The main menu, at 120F, includes warm oysters. Closed Mon pm & Tues.

Taverne de la Mer, 35 rue Haute (☎02.31.89.57.77). Small converted bar not far from place Hamelin, with no outdoor seating, but a magnificent selection of fresh seafood, including specialities grilled on an open wood fire. The only set menu, at 119F, consists entirely of fish, with main courses such as Basque-style tuna steaks; you can also get a large *assiettes de fruits de mer* for a similar price. Closed Mon & Tues am.

Le Vieux Honfleur, 13 quai St-Etienne (☎02.31.89.15.31). The best of the restaurants around the harbour itself, with spacious alfresco dining – in shade at lunchtime – on the pedestrianized eastern side of the harbour. Very simple menus, but the seafood is very good, as befits prices starting at 160F. Closed Jan.

Trouville and Deauville

Heading west along the corniche from Honfleur, green fields and fruit trees lull the land's edge, and cliffs rise from sandy beaches all the way to Trouville, 15km away. The resorts aren't exactly cheap but they're relatively undeveloped, and if you want to stop along the coast this is the place to do it. The next stretch, from Trouville to Cabourg, is what you might call the Riviera of Normandy with Trouville as "Nice" and Deauville as "Cannes", within a stone's throw of each other.

TROUVILLE retains some semblance of a real town, with a constant population and industries other than tourism. But it is still a resort – and has been ever since the imperial jackass Napoléon III started bringing his court here every summer in the 1860s. One of his dukes, looking across the river, saw, instead of marshlands, money – and lots of it, in the form of a racetrack. His vision materialized and villas appeared between the racetrack and the sea to become **DEAUVILLE**. Now you can lose money on the horses, cross five streets and lose more in the casino, then lose yourself across 200m of sports and "cure" facilities and private swimming huts before reaching the *planches*, 500m of boardwalk, beyond which rows of primary-coloured parasols obscure the view of the sea. French exclusiveness and self-esteem ooze from every suntanned pore.

Practicalities

Visits to the **tourist office** on place de la Mairie in Deauville (Mon–Sat 9am–12.30pm & 2–6.30pm, Sun 11am–4pm; ☎02.31.14.40.00), or the one at 32 quai F-Moureaux in Trouville (July & Aug Mon–Sat 9.30am–12.30pm & 2–7pm, Sun 10am–4pm; April–June, Sept & Oct Mon–Sat 9.30am–noon & 2–6.30pm, Sun 10.30am–12.30pm; Nov–March Mon–Sat 9.30am–noon & 2–6pm, Sun 10.30am–12.30pm; ☎02.31.14.60.70), are repaid with some spectacularly revolting brochures (in English).

Trouville and Deauville share their **gare SNCF** and **gare routière** (☎02.31.88.95.36), in between the two just south of the marina. Each day, a dozen of the hourly buses from Caen continue along the coast to Honfleur.

As you might imagine, **hotels** tend to be either luxurious or overpriced. The *Café-Hôtel des Sports*, 27 rue Gambetta (☎02.31.88.22.67; closed Sun in winter; ③), behind Deauville's fish market is the least expensive, while the *Charmettes*, 22 rue de la Chapelle (☎02.31.88.11.67; closed Jan; ③), and *Le Trouville*, 1 rue Thiers (☎02.31.98.45.48; closed Jan; ③), are Trouville's closest equivalents. Trouville also has a couple of **campsites**, *Le Hamel* (April to mid-Sept; ☎02.31.88.15.56) and *Le Chant des Oiseaux* (April–Sept; ☎02.31.88.06.42).

Chez Henri at 44 rue Mirabeau in Deauville (☎02.31.87.18.17) is a top-quality **bistrot** with prices that are high but not outrageous; good **fish restaurants** in Trouville include *Les Vapeurs* at 160 bd F-Moureaux (☎02.31.88.15.24), and *La Petite Auberge*, 7 rue Carnot (closed Tues & Wed in winter; ☎02.31.88.11.07), though both get very crowded at weekends.

Deauville's **American Film Festival**, held in the first week of September, is the antithesis of Cannes, with public admission to a wide selection of previews.

Houlgate

A hundred years ago, **HOULGATE**, 15km west of Deauville, was every bit as glamorous and sophisticated a destination as its neighbours. What makes it different today is that it has barely changed since then. Its long straight beach remains lined by a stately procession of Victorian villas, with the town's handful of commercial enterprises confined to the narrow parallel street, the **rue des Bains**, fifty metres inland. As a result, Houlgate is the most relaxed of the local resorts, ideal if you're looking for a peaceful family break where the only stress is deciding whether to paddle or play mini-golf.

Houlgate's **tourist office** is well back from the sea on boulevard des Belges (mid-June to mid-Sept Mon–Sat 9am–7pm, Sun 9am–12.30pm & 2–7pm; mid-Sept to mid-June Mon–Sat 9am–12.30pm &2–6.30pm; ☎02.31.24.34.79) The *Hostellerie Normandie*, just off the rue des Bains at 11 rue E-Deschanel (☎02.31.28.77.77; ③; closed Oct–Feb, plus Mon pm & Tues in low season), is a pretty little **hotel** covered with ivy and creeping flowers, with a 65F lunch menu on which you can follow half a dozen oysters with a plate of *moules frites*. Above the **Vaches Noires** ("black cows") cliffs on the corniche road east of town, *La Ferme Auberge des Aulnettes* (☎02.31.28.00.28; closed Jan, plus

Tues pm & Wed in low season; ③), is a lovely country house set in pleasant gardens, with a good restaurant and room to sit outside in the evening. The best **campsite** in the area, *Les Falaises* (April–Oct; ☎02.31.24.81.09), is close at hand.

Dives and Cabourg

DIVES, the port from which William the Conqueror sailed for Hastings, is another 3km west from Houlgate, though like Honfleur it's now pushed well back from the sea. A lively Saturday **market** focuses around the ancient oak *halles*, whose steep tiled roof must be five times the height of its walls; on market days, it's crammed with mouthwatering delicacies and Norman specialities. Dives has a reasonable **hotel**, the *Hôtel de la Gare* (☎02.31.91.24.52; ②; closed Dec & Jan), and there's a **campsite** on the way to Cabourg (and two more off the Cabourg–Lisieux road).

At the much newer town of **CABOURG**, across the mouth of the Dives river, the *fin-de-siècle* streets of the town centre fan out in perfect symmetry from what must be the straightest promenade in France, with semi-circular avenues linking them together. The resort, contemporary with Deauville, seems to be stuck in the nineteenth century – immobilized by Proust perhaps, who wrote for a while in the **Grand Hôtel**, one of an outrageous ensemble of buildings around the **Jardins du Casino**. The **tourist office** here has full details on hotels (July & Aug daily 9.30am–7pm; Sept–June Mon–Sat 9.30am–12.30pm & 2–6.30pm, Sun 10am–12.30pm & 2.30–6pm; ☎02.31.91.01.09). *L'Oie qui Fume*, 18 av de la Brèche-Buhot (☎02.31.91.27.79; closed Sun pm, Mon, & mid-Nov to mid-Feb), is 100m back from the sea on a quiet road half a dozen streets west of the centre; menus at 134F and 190F – both feature goose (*oie*).

Caen

CAEN, capital and largest city of Basse Normandie, is not a place where you'll want to spend much time; in the months of fighting in 1944, it was devastated. The central feature is a ring of ramparts that no longer have a castle to protect, and, though there are the scattered spires and buttresses of two abbeys and eight old churches, roads and roundabouts fill the wide spaces where prewar houses stood. Approaches are along thunderous dual carriageways through industrial suburbs – once an economic success story, currently hammered by unemployment. Even so, the city that nine hundred years ago was the favoured residence of William the Conqueror remains – in parts – highly impressive.

Arrival and information

Caen's **tourist office** is across the street from the church of St-Pierre in the beautiful sixteenth-century *Hôtel d'Escoville* at 14 place St-Pierre (July & Aug Mon–Sat 10am–7pm, Sun 10am–1pm & 2–5pm; Sept–June Mon–Sat 10am–1pm & 2–6pm, Sun 10am–1pm; ☎02.31.27.14.14). The main **post office** is on place Gambetta (Mon–Fri 8am–7pm, Sat 8am–noon).

The **gare SNCF** (☎02.31.83.50.50) is 1km south of the town centre, with the **gare routière** so close that you can walk directly to it from platform 1. The Brittany Ferries service from Portsmouth, promoted as sailing to Caen, in fact docks at Ouistreham, 15km north (see p.345). Buses from the gare routière connect with each sailing.

CTAC, the extensive local **bus** service (☎02.31.85.42.76), makes a one-way circuit between the Tour le Roi stop, north of the pleasure port, and the gare SNCF, heading north up avenue du 6-Juin and south down rue St-Jean.

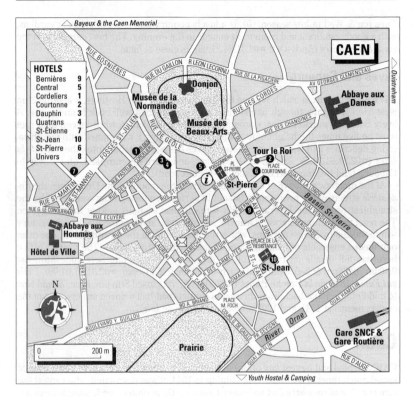

△ *Bayeux & the Caen Memorial*

CAEN

HOTELS

Bernières	9
Central	5
Cordeliers	1
Courtonne	2
Dauphin	3
Quatrans	4
St-Étienne	7
St-Jean	10
St-Pierre	6
Univers	8

▽ *Youth Hostel & Camping*

Accommodation

Caen has a great number of **hotels**; though, as ever in the bomb-damaged cities of Normandy, few could be called attractive. The main concentrations are near the gare SNCF, around the pleasure port, and just west of the castle and tourist office. With plenty of dedicated restaurants in town, few hotels other than those specifically mentioned below bother to provide food.

Hotels

Bernières, 50 rue de Bernières (☎02.31.86.01.26). Bright, central and very good-value hotel, halfway between the churches of St-Pierre and St-Jean. ①–③.

Central Hôtel, 23 place J-Letellier (☎02.31.86.18.52). By Caen standards a budget hotel; not as quiet as it used to be, but very central. Good views of the château from the balconies of the higher rooms (but no lift to get up to them). ②.

des Cordeliers, 4 rue des Cordeliers (☎02.31.86.37.14). Smart, friendly hotel with a wide range of rooms, in small pedestrian street near the castle; bar but no restaurant. ②–④.

Courtonne, place Courtonne (☎02.31.93.47.83). Friendly, modernized hotel overlooking the pleasure port; all rooms have bath or shower, phone and TV. ③.

Hôtel-Restaurant le Dauphin, 29 rue Gémare (☎02.31.86.22.26). Rather ugly but very central hotel, tucked away behind the tourist office. Part of it was a priory during the eighteenth century – not that you'd ever guess; the rooms are comfortable without being exciting in any way. Grand restaurant, with a 100F weekday menu; weekend menus 165F and 250F. Closed Sat, and mid-July to early Aug. ④–⑦.

le Quatrans, 17 rue Gémare (☎02.31.86.25.57). A little way behind the tourist office, but unmissable thanks to its garish neon-lit exterior. The pastel theme of the facade continues inside; some might find it all a bit cloying, but the service is friendly, and at least everything works. Cheaper rooms are without showers. ②.

St-Étienne, 2 rue de l'Académie (☎02.31.86.35.82). Friendly budget hotel in an old stone house in the characterful St-Martin district, not far from the Abbaye des Hommes. The cheapest rooms do not have showers. ①.

St-Jean, 20 rue des Martyrs (☎02.31.86.23.35). Simple but well-equipped rooms – all have shower or bath – facing St-Jean church near the *Petite Auberge*. No restaurant. ①.

St-Pierre, 40 bd des Alliés (☎02.31.86.28.20). In town, immediately opposite the Tour le Roi, alongside the eponymous bus stop and place Courtonne. Cheaper rooms do not have showers. No restaurant. ②.

Univers, 12 quai Vendeuvre (☎02.31.85.46.14). In town, near the port de Plaisance. All rooms have shower or bath. No restaurant. ②.

Youth hostels and campsites

HI youth hostel Robert-Remé, 68 bis rue E-Restout, Grâce-de-Dieu (☎02.31.52.19.96). About 500m southwest of the gare SNCF. Beds in both four-bed dorms, or two-bed private rooms cost 62F per person. Take bus #17 from the town centre (Tour le Roi) or gare SNCF, direction "Grace de Dieu", stop Lycée Fresnil. June–Sept.

Camping OMJ, route de Louvigny (☎02.31.72.60.92). The municipal campsite is near the foyer, beside the River Orne, (bus #13, direction "Louvigny", stop Camping). Mid-May to Sept only.

The town

A virtue has been made of the necessity of clearing away the rubble of Caen's medieval houses, which formerly pressed up against its ancient **château ramparts**. The resulting open green space means that those walls are now fully visible for the first time in centuries. In turn, walking the circuit of the ramparts gives a good overview of the city, with a particularly fine prospect of the reconstructed fourteenth-century facade of the nearby church of **St-Pierre**. Some magnificent Renaissance stonework has survived intact at the church's east end.

Within the castle walls, it's possible to visit the former **Exchequer**, which dates from shortly after the Norman Conquest of England, and to inspect a garden that has been re-planted with the kind of herbs and medicinal plants that would have been cultivated here during the Middle Ages. Also inside the precinct, though not in original structures, are two **museums**. Much the best is the **Beaux Arts**, housed in a 1960s stone building (daily except Tues 10am–6pm; 20F, free on Wed). Its comprehensive displays – from fifteenth-century Italian and Flemish primitives to contemporary French artists – include masterpieces by Poussin, Géricault, Monet and Bonnard, as well as an exceptional collection of engravings by Dürer and Rembrandt. The other museum, the **Musée de Normandie** (April–Sept Wed–Fri 10am–12.30pm & 1.30–6pm, Sat–Mon 9.30am–12.30pm & 2–6pm; Oct–March daily except Tues 9.30am–12.30pm & 2–6pm; 10F, free on Wed), is devoted to Norman history, and ranges from archeological finds dating from Roman Rouen to the impact of the Industrial Revolution.

The **Abbaye aux Hommes**, at the west end of rue St-Pierre, was founded by William the Conqueror and designed to hold his tomb within the huge, austere Romanesque **church of St-Étienne**. However, his burial here, in 1087, was hopelessly undignified. The funeral procession first caught fire and was then held to ransom, as various factions squabbled over his rotting corpse for any spoils they could grab. A further interruption came when a man halted the service to object that the grave had been constructed without compensation on the site of his family house, and the assembled nobles had to pay him off before William could be laid to rest. During the Revolution the tomb was again ransacked, and it now holds a solitary thigh-bone rescued from the river. Still, the building itself is a wonderful Romanesque monument. Guided tours take place daily at 9.30am, 11am, 2.30pm and 4pm. Adjoining the church are the abbey buildings, designed during the eighteenth century and now housing the Hôtel de Ville (visitable during office hours); there are some splendid rooms inside, and the carving is especially notable.

At the other end of the town centre, at the end of rue des Chanoines, is the **Abbaye aux Dames**, commissioned by William's wife Matilda in the hope of saving her soul after committing the godless sin of marrying her cousin. Her monument – the church of **La Trinité** – is even more starkly impressive than her husband's, with a gloomy pillared crypt, wonderful stained glass behind the altar, and odd sculptural details like the fish curled up in the holy-water stoup. The convent buildings today house the regional council but are open to the public for free guided tours (daily 2.30pm & 4pm).

Most of the centre of Caen is taken up with busy new shopping developments and pedestrian precincts, where the cafés are distinguished by names such as *Fast Food Glamour Vault*. Outlets of the big Parisian stores – and of the aristocrats' grocers, Hédiard, in the cours des Halles – are here, along with good local rivals. The main city **market** takes place on Friday, spreading along both sides of Fosse St-Julien, and there's also a Sunday market in place Courtonne. The **pleasure port,** at the end of the canal which links Caen to the sea, is where most life goes on, at least in summer.

Just north of Caen, at the end of avenue Marshal-Montgomery in the Folie Couvrechef area, the relatively new **Caen Memorial** – "a museum for peace" – stands on a plateau named after General Eisenhower (July & Aug daily 9am–9pm, last entry 8.15pm; Sept, Oct & mid-Feb to June daily 9am–7pm, last entry 5.45pm; Nov, Dec & mid-Jan to mid-Feb Mon–Sat 9am–6pm, Sun 9am–7pm; closed first fortnight of Jan; 69F), on a clifftop beneath which the Germans had their HQ in June and July 1944. Funds and material for it came from the US, Britain, Canada, Germany, Poland, the former Czechoslovakia, the USSR and France. One section in this typically French high-tech, novel-architecture conception deals with the rise of fascism in Germany, another with resistance and collaboration in France. A third charts all the major battles of World War II, and finally there's a film documentary on all the conflicts since 1945. Though a touch naive in its historical analysis, it is a great improvement on the older war-glorifying museums of Normandy. The memorial is on bus routes #12 (Mon–Fri) and #14 (Sat & Sun) from the Tour le Roi stop in the centre of town.

Eating

Caen's town centre offers two major areas for **eating**: cosmopolitan restaurants in the pedestrianized **quartier Vaugueux** and the streets off **rue de Geôle**, near the western ramparts, particularly rue des Croisiers and rue Gémare, with more traditional French restaurants.

L'Alcide, 1 place Courtonne (☎02.31.44.18.06). Very conspicuous but rather anonymous-looking bistrot-style place, which turns out to be surprisingly good, serving classic French dishes cooked with great attention to detail. Menus from 78F up to 139F. Closed Sat.

Le Bouchon du Vaugueux, 12 rue du Graindorge (☎02.31.44.26.26). Intimate little brasserie in the Vaugueux quarter, offering a daily lunch menu at 69F, good-value salads from around 45F, and dinner menus from 89F. Closed Mon pm & Sun, also the first 3 weeks of Aug.

Restaurant Maître Corbeau, 94 rue du Geôle (☎02.31.86.33.97). Fondue is the specialty in this eccentric little place, and they won't let you forget it, festooning the whole place with cheesy iconography. A typical fondue costs around 80F, while set menus start from 88F. Closed Sat am and Sun.

La Petite Auberge, 17 rue des Equipes-d'Urgence (☎02.31.86.43.30). Plain and simple restaurant, with a nice view of the St-Jean church. Very good-value Norman specialities – a daily 68F menu that doesn't force you to eat tripe. Closed Sun pm, Mon & Sept.

Tongasoa, 7 rue du Vaugueux (☎02.31.43.87.15). Midday menu 55F; evening menus from 85F. Dishes from Madagascar, Réunion and the Seychelles – especially fish, curried, cooked with ginger and tropical fruits, or just plain. Cocktails galore, in lurid colours. Closed Sun lunchtime.

The D-Day beaches

Despite the best efforts of Stephen Spielberg, it is all but impossible now to picture the scene at dawn on **D-Day**, June 6, 1944, when Allied troops landed along the Norman coast between the mouth of the Orne and Les Dunes de Varneville on the Cotentin Peninsula. For the most part, these are innocuous beaches backed by gentle dunes, and yet this foothold in Europe was won at the cost of 100,000 soldiers' lives. That the invasion happened here, and not nearer to Germany, was partly due to the failure of the Canadian raid on Dieppe in 1942. The ensuing **Battle of Normandy** killed thousands of civilians and reduced nearly six hundred towns and villages to rubble but, within a week of its eventual conclusion, Paris was liberated.

The **beaches** are still often referred to by their wartime code names: Sword, Juno, Gold, Omaha and Utah. Substantial traces of the fighting are rare, the most remarkable being the remains of the astounding **Mulberry Harbour** at **Arromanches**, 10km northeast of Bayeux. Further west, at **Pointe du Hoc** on Omaha Beach, the cliff heights are still deeply pitted with German bunkers and shell holes, while the church at **Ste-Mère-Église**, from which the US paratrooper who became entangled in the steeple, dangled during heavy fighting throughout *The Longest Day*, still stands, and now has a model parachute permanently fastened to the roof.

Just about every coastal town has its **war museum**. These tend as a rule to shy away from the unbearable reality of war in favour of *Boy's Own*-style heroics, but the wealth of incidental human detail can nonetheless be overpowering. Veterans and their descendants apart, visitors these days come to this stretch of coast for its **seaside**: sand and seafood (the best oysters are at Courseulles), plenty of campsites and no Deauville chic.

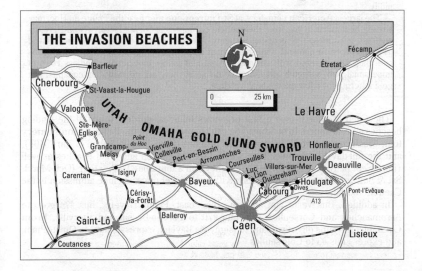

THE WAR CEMETERIES

The **World War II cemeteries** that dot the Norman countryside are filled with foreigners; most of the French dead are buried in the churchyards of their home towns. After the war, some felt that the soldiers should remain buried in the original makeshift graves that were dug where they fell. Instead, commissions gathered the remains into purpose-built cemeteries devoted to the separate warring nations.

The **British** and **Commonwealth** cemeteries are magnificently maintained, and open in every sense. They tend not to be screened off with hedges or walls, or to be forbidding expanses of manicured lawn, but are instead intimate, punctuated with bright flowers. The family of each soldier was invited to suggest an inscription for his tomb, making each grave very personal, and yet part of a common attempt to bring meaning to the carnage. Some epitaphs are questioning – "One day we will understand"; some are accepting – "Our lad at rest"; some matter-of-fact, simply giving the home address; some patriotic, quoting the "corner of a foreign field that is forever England". And interspersed among them all is the chilling refrain of the anonymous "A soldier . . . known unto God". Thus the cemetery at **Ryes**, where so many of the graves bear the date of D-Day, and so many of the victims are under 20, remains immediate and accessible – each grave clearly contains a unique individual. Even the monumental sculpture is subdued, a very British sort of fumbling for the decent thing to say. The understatement of the memorial at **Bayeux**, with its painfully contrived Latin epigram commemorating the return as liberators of "those whom William conquered", conveys an entirely appropriate humility and deep sadness.

An even more eloquent testimony to the futility of war is afforded by the **German** cemeteries, filled with soldiers who served a cause so despicable as to render any talk of "nobility" or "sacrifice" simply obscene. What such cemeteries might have been like had the Nazis won doesn't bear contemplation. As it is, they are sombre places, inconspicuous to minimize the bitterness they still arouse. At **Orglandes** ten thousand are buried, three to each of the plain headstones set in the long flat lawn, almost hidden behind an anonymous wall. There are no noble slogans and the plain entrance is without a dedicatory monument. At the superb site of **Mont d'Huisnes** near Mont St-Michel, the circular mausoleum holds another ten thousand, filed away in cold concrete tiers. There is no attempt to defend the indefensible, and yet one feels an overpowering sense of sorrow – that there is nothing to be said in such a place bitterly underlines the sheer waste and stupidity.

The largest **American** cemetery, at **St-Laurent-sur-mer** near the Pointe du Hoc, may already be familiar to you from the opening sequences of *Saving Private Ryan*. Here, by contrast, the atmosphere is one of certainty. The rows of crosses are as neat and clinical as graph paper. At one end, a muscular giant dominates a huge array of battlefield plans and diagrams, covered with surging arrows and pincer movements. Endless rows of impersonal graves stretch away into the distance; there are no individual epitaphs, just gold lettering for a few exceptional warriors.

The Caen Memorial (see p.342) organizes bilingual **guided tours** of the landing beaches all year round. In summer, you can choose between the half-day **Montgomery** tour, which covers Sword, Juno and Gold beaches (June–Sept daily 9am & 2pm; 340F), and the full-day **Eisenhower** tour, which takes in Omaha and Utah beaches as well (June–Sept daily 9am; 480F). In winter, they run a four-hour **D-Day** tour (Oct–March Sat & Sun 1pm; April–May daily 1pm; 340F). All ticket prices include admission to the Caen Memorial.

In addition, Bus Verts run all along this coast. **From Bayeux**, bus #74 goes to Arromanches and Corseulles, and bus #70 to Port-en-Bessin and Vierville. **From Caen**, bus #30 runs directly inland to Isigny via Bayeux, express bus #1 to Ouistreham, and express bus #3 to Courseulles.

Ouistreham

The small community of **OUISTREHAM**, on the coast 15km north of Caen and connected to it by a fast dual carriageway, gives the impression that it can barely believe its luck at having become a major ferry port. Since Brittany Ferries started their service here in 1986, the easternmost of the D-Day resorts has developed an extensive array of reasonable hotels and restaurants.

Several cafés and brasseries in the place Courbonne, immediately outside the gare maritime, are eager to liberate passengers from their spare change, while *Le Channel*, around the corner at 79 av Michel-Cabieu (☎02.31.96.51.69; ①–③), is just about the best value for both **eating and sleeping**. Menus start with the 55F *menu pêcheur*, which includes mussels, while the 88F and 144F options increase in splendour; the guest rooms are in a separate building across the street. Good value hotels near the beach include the *Hôtel de la Plage* at 39–41 av Pasteur (☎02.31.96.85.16; closed Nov–Feb; ②), and the *St-Georges* at 51 av Andry (☎02.31.97.18.79; ④), while *Le Britania* [sic], immediately across from the ferry terminal at 63 rue des Dunes (closed Jan; ☎02.31.96.88.26), is a convenient top-quality restaurant.

Arromanches

At **ARROMANCHES**, 10km northeast of Bayeux, an artificial **Mulberry harbour**, "Port Winston", protected the landings of 2,500,000 men and 500,000 vehicles during the invasion. Two of these prefab concrete constructions were built in Britain, while "doodlebugs" blitzed overhead; they were then submerged in rivers away from the prying eyes of German aircraft, and finally towed across the Channel at 6kph as the invasion began. The seafront **Musée du Débarquement**, in Arromanches' main square (May–Aug daily 9am–6.30pm; Sept–April daily 9am–11.30am & 2–5.30pm; closed first three weeks of Jan; 35F), recounts the whole story by means of models, machinery and movies – and the evidence of your own eyes. A huge picture window runs the length of the museum, enabling you to look straight out to where the bulky remains of the harbour, whose sheer scale is impossible to appreciate at this distance, make a strange intrusion on the beach and shallow sea bed (the other one, slightly further west on Omaha Beach, was destroyed by a ferocious storm within a few weeks). There are war memorials throughout Arromanches, with Jesus and Mary high up on the cliffs above the invasion site and helicopter trips available to overlook the area.

Nonetheless, Arromanches somehow manages to be quite a cheerful place to stay, with a lively pedestrian street of bars and brasseries, and a long expanse of sand where you can rent windsurf boards. *La Marine* at 2 quai Canada (mid-Feb to mid-Nov; ☎02.31.22.34.19; ③), is a slightly expensive **hotel**, with an excellent sea-view restaurant that serves fishy menus from 95F. Across the main square stands the *Arromanches*, 2 rue du Colonel-Michel (closed Jan, plus Tues pm & Wed in winter; ☎02.31.22.36.26; ③), which has menus from 72F up to 160F, while the cheaper *Normandie* is nearby at 5 place du 6-Juin (Feb to mid-Dec; ☎02.31.22.34.32; ②).

Bayeux and around

BAYEUX's perfectly preserved medieval ensemble, magnificent cathedral and world-famous tapestry make it one of the high points of this part of Normandy. Set back from the coast west of Caen, and just fifteen minutes away by train, it's a much smaller city, whose charms can pall somewhat with the influx of summer tourists.

Arrival, information and accommodation

Bayeux's **tourist office** stands in the centre of town, on the arched pont St-Jean (Mon–Fri 9am–6pm, Sat 9am–noon & 2–6pm, Sun 9.30am–noon & 2.30–6pm; ☎02.31.51.28.28).The **gare SNCF** (☎02.31.92.80.50) is fifteen minutes' walk away to the west, just outside the "ring road", while the **gare routière** is on the other side of town on rue du Manche, alongside place St-Patrice. For information on **local buses**, call Bus Verts du Calvados (☎02.31.92.02.92), whose services stop at both the gare SNCF and the gare routière.

Hotels

As one of Normandy's most important tourist destinations, Bayeux is well-equipped with accommodation. On the whole, however, the hotels are more expensive than usual; even the "unofficial youth hostel" listed below is far from cheap. There's a large **campsite** on boulevard d'Eindhoven (mid-March to mid-Nov; ☎02.31.92.08.43), on the northern ring road (RN13) near the river.

d'Argouges, 21 rue St-Patrice (☎02.31.92.88.86). Very stylish eighteenth-century building, with an imposing courtyard entered via an archway on the west side of place St-Patrice, and a well-kept garden around the back. A quiet but expensive place to stay. No restaurant. ③–⑤.

Family Home, 39 rue Général-Dais (☎02.31.92.15.22). Central seventeenth-century house which describes itself variously as a maison d'hôtes (guesthouse) and an auberge de jeunesse (youth hostel). Its prices are over the usual odds (hostel accommodation is 105F per person) and it's a bit self-consciously jolly – but it has its advocates, and people return again and again. Room prices include breakfasts. Meals are taken communally, Madame Lefèvre presiding at the head of a long table in an old oak-beamed dining room. ①–③.

de la Gare, 26 place de la Gare (☎02.31.92.10.70). Old but perfectly adequate basic hotel, beside the station, on the ring road 15 minutes' walk from the cathedral. Tours of D-Day beaches arranged. No restaurant. ①.

Hôtel-Restaurant Lion d'Or, 71 rue St-Jean (☎02.31.92.06.90). Grand old coaching inn set back behind a courtyard, just beyond the pedestrianized section of the rue St-Jean, outside Les Halles des Grains (now the assembly rooms). The rooms themselves are brighter and newer than the exterior might lead you to expect. Closed mid-Dec to mid-Jan. Menus from 150F. ⑤.

Hôtel-Restaurant Notre Dame, 44 rue des Cuisiniers (☎02.31.92.87.24). Friendly and very pleasant *logis*, virtually in front of the cathedral, with a magnificent view. Menus from 90F, with a special Norman one at 125F. Closed mid-Nov to mid-Dec, plus Sun pm & Mon in winter. ②–③.

Reine Mathilde, 23 rue Larcher (☎02.31.92.08.13). Simple but well-equipped rooms – all have showers and TV – backing onto the canal, between the tapestry and the cathedral. No restaurant as such, but there's a really nice open-air brasserie downstairs that serves dinner between May and Sept, with the cheapest menu at 50F and a good four-course meal for 99F. ③.

Le Relais des Cèdres, 1 bd Sadi-Carnot (☎02.31.21.98.07). Pretty guesthouse, not far from the station but within sight of the cathedral. The rooms are fine, and good value, although the atmosphere is not all that welcoming. ①–③.

Sports, 19 rue St-Martin (☎02.31.92.28.53). Basic rooms not far from the river in the heart of town, with a brasserie downstairs. The management are very reluctant to turn the heating on, so this can be an icebox in winter. ②.

The town

The seventeenth-century building called the Centre Guillaume-le-Conquérant served as a seminary before the hype surrounding the world-famous **Bayeux Tapestry** began to resound in its stone chambers (May–Aug daily 9am–7pm; mid-March to April & Sept to mid-Oct daily 9am–6.30pm; mid-Oct to mid-March daily 9.30am–12.30pm & 2–6pm; 38F). But visits to the world-famous Romanesque cartoon are well-planned and highly atmospheric, if somewhat exhausting: you start off with a projection of slides on swathes of canvas hung as sails, before moving onto an almost full-length reproduction of the original, complete with photographic extracts and detailed commentary. Upstairs in the plush theatre, there's a film (French and English versions alternate) on the general context and craft of the piece – which you can skip if you feel you know the 1066 story well enough by now. Beyond this – and the souvenirs table – you finally approach the real thing, a seventy-metre strip of linen recounting the story of the Norman Conquest of England with an explanatory subtext in Latin. Although embroidered nine centuries ago – and used as a wagon cover during Napoleonic times – the brilliance of its coloured wools has barely faded, and the tale is enlivened throughout with scenes of medieval life, popular fables and mythical beasts. The quality of the draughtsmanship, and the sheer vigour and detail, are stunning. The work is thought to have been done by nuns in England, working under commission from Bishop Odo, William's half-brother, for the inauguration of Bayeux Cathedral in 1077.

The **Cathédrale Notre-Dame** (July & Aug daily 9am–7pm; Sept–June daily 9am–6pm) was the first home of the tapestry and is just a short walk away from its latest resting-place. Despite such eighteenth-century vandalism as the monstrous fungoid baldachin that flanks the pulpit, the original Romanesque plan of the building is still intact, although only the crypt and towers date from the original work of 1077. The crypt is a beauty, its columns graced with frescoes of angels playing trumpets and bagpipes, looking exhausted by their performance for eternity. Next to the cathedral, in the shadow of the 200-year-old Liberty Tree, the former palace of the archbishops of Bayeux has over the centuries received a considerable quantity of porcelain and lace donated by local families. Named the **Musée Baron Gerard** in honour of its most generous patron, it has recently been renovated to display its collection to far better advantage (June to mid-Sept daily 9am–7pm; mid-Sept to May daily 10am–12.30pm & 2–6pm; 38F).

Set behind massive guns, next to the ring road on the southwest side of town, Bayeux's **Musée de la Bataille de Normandie** (May to mid-Sept daily 9.30am–6.30pm; mid-Sept to April daily 10am–12.30pm & 2–6pm; 31F) is one of the old school of war museums, with its emphasis firmly on hardware rather than humans. By way of contrast, the understated and touching **British War Cemetery** stands immediately across the road (see box on p.344).

Although Bayeux's newest museum, the **General de Gaulle Memorial** at 10 rue de Bourbesneur, near place de Gaulle (daily mid-March to mid-Nov 9.30am–12.30pm & 2–6.30pm; 20F), is aimed squarely at French devotees of the great man, it does make an interesting detour for foreign visitors. The sheer obsessiveness of the displays, which focus on the three separate day-trips De Gaulle made to Bayeux during the course of his long life, somehow illuminates the extent to which he came to epitomize the very essence of a certain kind of Frenchness – which to foreigners seems scarcely removed from self-parody.

Eating

Several of the hotels have good **restaurants**, while the *Family Home* serves a filling and good-value dinner at 8pm each evening for around 65F. Otherwise, most of Bayeux's restaurants are in the rue St-Jean leading east from the river, or near the main door of the cathedral. Watch out for Sundays: virtually everywhere is shut.

Le Petit Normand, 35 rue Larcher (☎02.31.22.88.66). Sixteenth-century house by the cathedral, offering good traditional cooking, with seafood specialities and local cider. Lunch menus from 60F, dinner from 95F. Closed Sun pm between Sept & June.

Le Printanier, 2 rue des Bouchers (☎02.31.92.03.01). Good-value if garishly decorated bistrot, slightly off the beaten track though very central, which serves inexpensive menus continuously from lunchtime until around 9pm. Closed Sun, & Mon am.

La Rapière, 53 rue St-Jean (☎02.31.92.94.79). Probably the most popular traditional choice, housed in the fifteenth-century Hôtel du Croissant, down a clearly signed side alley. The cheapest menu is 79F; the next, at 145F, features oysters and skate. Closed mid-Dec to Jan, as well as Tues pm & Wed out of season.

La Table du Terroir, 42 rue St-Jean (☎02.31.92.05.53). A rendezvous for closet meat freaks, tucked away behind a butcher's shop and serving the freshest, bloodiest flesh on a well-judged trio of menus, at 55F, 95F and 135F. Closed Sun pm, & mid-Oct to mid-Nov.

Cerisy and Balleroy

Heading southwest from Bayeux towards St-Lô, you pass close to the remarkable Romanesque **Abbaye de Cerisy-la-Forêt** (Easter to mid-Nov daily 9am–6.30pm, free; guided tours Easter–Sept Tues–Sun 10.30am–12.30pm & 2.30–6.30pm, Oct to mid-Nov Sat & Sun 10.30am–noon & 2–6pm; 8F), halfway along the D572 and 5km to the north of it. With its triple tiers of windows and arches, the delicate workmanship of the nave and choir lap the sunlight into the cream Caen stone and make you sigh in wonder at the skills of medieval Norman masons.

No less notable is the **Château de Balleroy** (mid-March to mid-Oct only, daily except Wed 9am–noon & 2–6pm; 50F), 3km southeast of the same junction, where you switch to an era when architects ruled over craftsmen. The main street of the village leads straight to the brick-and-stone château, a masterpiece of the celebrated seven-teenth-century architect, François Mansart, and standing like a faultlessly reasoned and dogmatic argument for the power of its owners and their class. Until his recent death, it belonged to the flamboyant American press magnate Malcolm Forbes, pal of Nixon, Ford and Nancy Reagan. His is the enlarged colour photograph sharing the stairwell with Dutch still lifes, and he left his mark on most other aspects of the house, too – only the salon remains in its original state of glory, with brilliant portraits of the (then) royal family by Mignard. The expensive admission also includes a **hot air balloon museum**, which was one of Mr Forbes' hobbies.

The Cotentin Peninsula

Until Brittany Ferries inaugurated its direct services to Brittany, the **Cotentin Peninsula**, in the far west of Normandy hard against the frontier with Brittany, provided many visitors with their first taste of western France. Now that Caen, too, has direct sailings, the port of **Cherbourg** sees only a fraction of the traffic it had twenty years ago, but the peninsula itself remains worth exploring.

Cherbourg

If the murky metropolis of **CHERBOURG** is your port of arrival, best to head straight out and on; the town itself is almost devoid of interest, and there are some really nice places within a very few kilometres to either side. Napoléon inaugurated the transformation of what had been a rather poor, but perfectly situated, natural harbour into a major transatlantic port, by means of massive artificial breakwaters. An equestrian statue commemorates his boast that in Cherbourg he would "recreate the wonders of Egypt", though there are as yet no pyramids nearer than the Louvre.

Arrival, information and accommodation

Several cross-Channel ferry companies still sail into Cherbourg's **gare maritime**, just east of the town centre (daily 5.30am–11.30pm; ☎02.33.44.20.13). Services from **Portsmouth**, including the new Superstar Express, which takes a mere 2hr 45min for the crossing, are operated by P&O (5–6 daily; ☎02.33.85.65.70), and from **Poole** by Brittany Ferries (1–2 daily; ☎02.33.88.44.88). Irish Ferries also sail to Cherbourg, from Rosslare (2–4 weekly; ☎02.33.44.28.96).

Cherbourg's **tourist office** is at 2 quai Alexandre III (June–Aug, Mon–Sat 9am–6.30pm; Sept–May Mon 1.30–6pm, Tues–Fri 9am–noon & 1.30–6pm, Sat 9am–noon; ☎02.33.93.52.02). The **gare SNCF** (☎02.33.57.50.50), on avenue François-Miller/place Jean-Jaurès, is served by regular trains to Paris, Bayeux and Caen. Buses to Coutances (☎02.33.98.13.38) and St-Lô, Valognes and Barfleur (☎02.33.44.32.22) run from the **gare routière** opposite, which is hidden from view by a building on avenue François-Miller.

By usual Norman standards, **room rates** are very reasonable. The local youth hostel has been closed for refurbishment for several years, but the *Foyer des Jeunes Travailleurs*, 33 rue de Maréchal-Leclerc (☎02.33.53.32.47; 70F), just over a kilometre east of the gare SNCF on bus #8, offers a reasonable equivalent.The closest **campsite** is the *Camping de Collignon*, 3km east towards Barfleur at Tourlaville (☎02.33.20.16.88; May-Sept).

Croix de Malte, 5 rue des Halles (☎02.33.43.19.16; fax 02.33.43.65.66). Simple hotel without restaurant on three upstairs floors, one block back from the harbour and around the corner from the theatre. Clean and recently renovated rooms – all 24 have TV and at least a shower – with the cheapest rates being for the perfectly acceptable ones in the attic. ②.

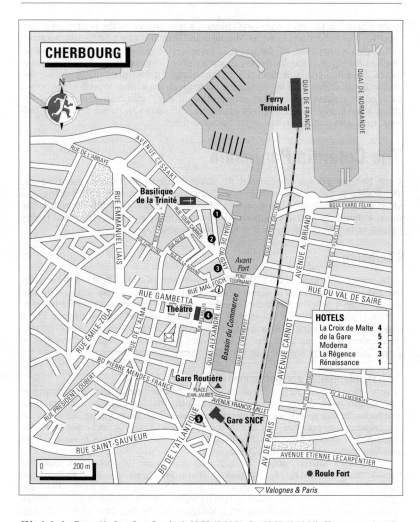

Hôtel de la Gare, 10 place Jean-Jaurès (☎02.33.43.06.81; fax 02.33.43.12.20). Very convenient for the gares SNCF and routière, if not exactly stunning in itself. ①.

Moderna, 28 rue de la Marine (☎02.33.43.05.30; fax 02.33.43.97.37). Rooms ranging from basic to lavish, slightly back from the harbour and tourist office; most have phones, showers and British TV. ①–③.

La Régence, 42 quai de Caligny (☎02.33.43.05.16; fax 02.33.43.98.37). Small neat rooms with balconies overlooking the harbour, just around the corner from the tourist office. The restaurant downstairs kicks off with a reasonable 70F menu; it's not the best along the quai, but there's something to be said for eating where you sleep. ③.

Hôtel de la Renaissance, 4 rue de l'Église (☎02.33.43.23.90; fax 02.33.43.96.10). Rooms of all kinds, some with sea views, in friendly hotel, facing the port in the most appealing quarter of town – the "Église" of the address is the attractive Trinité. ①.

The town

If you are waiting for a boat, the best way of filling time is to settle into a café or restaurant or do some last-minute shopping. Don't, however, leave your food shopping for the town. Unless you hit the Thursday **market**, held around rue des Halles, the standard fallback is Le Continent hypermarket, a real monster opposite the ferry quay.

As for walking off lunch, the only area which really encourages a ramble is over by the mainly fifteenth-century but much altered **Basilique de la Trinité** and the town **beach** – an unexpected pleasure, even if you wouldn't dream of swimming from it. Over to the south, you could alternatively climb up to the **Fort du Roule** for a view of the whole port; the fort itself contains a **museum of the war and liberation** (April–Sept daily 10am–6pm; Oct–March daily except Mon 9.30am–noon & 2–5.30pm; 15F).

Eating

Restaurants in Cherbourg divide readily into the glass-fronted seafood places along the quai de Caligny, each with its "copious" *assiette de fruits de mer*, and the more varied, more adventurous and less expensive little places tucked away in the pedestrianized streets and alleyways of the old town.

Café de Paris, 40 quai de Caligny (☎02.33.43.12.36). Work your up through the ranks of *assiettes de fruits de mer*, from the 75F *Matelot* to the *Amiral* at 500F for two; there's also a quick 98F menu if you're in a hurry. Here it's the live lobsters in the fish tanks set into the windows that get the sea views, not you, but the food is excellent.

Café du Théâtre, 8 place de Gaulle (☎02.33.43.01.49). Attractive set-up adjoining the theatre, with a café behind plate-glass windows on the ground floor and a full-scale brasserie upstairs, arranged on three sides of the central opening. Very varied menus – not just seafood – from 79F, and much more of a sense than usual of participating in the life of the town.

Le Faitout, 25 rue Tour-Carrée (☎02.33.04.25.04). Basement restaurant in the shopping district that offers traditional French cuisine at very reasonable prices; a bowl of mussels can be had for under 40F, and there's a daily special for 55F. Closed Sun, & Mon lunchtime.

Le Grandgousier, 21 rue de l'Abbaye (☎02.33.53.19.43). The definitive French fish restaurant; the rosy glow starts, but does not end, with the decor. Menus start at 99F, but this is a place to expect to spend a lot and dine well. The waiters share that expectation too – it's amiable enough but they know their worth. Imagine any combination of fish, throw in a bit of caviar and a few crab claws, and you'll find it somewhere on the menu. Closed Sat lunchtime, Sun pm, and Mon lunchtime in winter.

La Moulerie, 73 rue au Blé (☎02.33.01.11.90). A restaurant solely devoted to the adoration of mussels, served in colossal ceramic bowls with a choice of a dozen wine-based sauces varying from sauerkraut through mustard to cumin, plus chips galore. Prices range 45–60F, and there are set menus at 80F and 120F. You could if you want have a mussel salad to start, a *quiche aux moules*, or even snails for a change, but if you do you'll never finish the main course. Blue-checked tablecloths, sailors' costumes, fishing nets . . . an absolute delight. Closed Sun, & Mon lunchtime.

Around the Cotentin

Once you get away from Cherbourg, the largely rural Cotentin Peninsula is geographically an area of transition. Little ports such as **Barfleur** on the indented northern headland presage the rocky Breton coast, while inland the meadows resemble the farmlands of the Bocage and the Bessin. The long western flank with its flat beaches serves as a prelude to Mont St-Michel (see p.354), and hill towns such as **Coutances** and **Avranches** contain architectural and historical relics associated with the abbey.

Travelling by bus is not easy in northern Cotentin. Nor is hitching: the local patois has a special pejorative word for "stranger" used for foreigners, Parisians and southern Cotentins alike.

Barfleur

The pleasant little harbour village of **BARFLEUR**, 25km east of Cherbourg, was the biggest port in Normandy seven centuries ago. The population has since dwindled from nine thousand to six hundred, and fortunes have diminished alongside – most recently through the invasion of a strain of plankton that poisoned all the mussels. It's now a surprisingly low-key place, where the sweeping crescent of the grey granite quayside sees little tourist activity.

Near the town, about a thirty-minute walk, is the **Gatteville lighthouse**, the tallest in France. It guards the rocks on which William, son and heir of Henry I of England (and recently "outed" by historians as being gay), was drowned in 1120, together with three hundred of his nobles.

Barfleur has a fine selection of **hotels**. *Le Conquérant* stands a short distance back from the sea at 16–18 rue St-Thomas-Becket (☎02.33.54.00.82; ②; closed mid-Nov to mid-March); its nicest rooms face onto a lovely garden courtyard, and there's a summer-only crêperie. *Le Moderne* is tucked away south of the main road at 1 place de Gaulle (☎02.33.23.12.44; ①–③; closed mid-Sept to mid-March, plus Tues & Wed from Oct to mid-Feb). Some of the rooms are very inexpensive, while the restaurant is quite superb.

St-Vaast

Pretty **ST-VAAST-LA-HOUGUE**, 11 km south of Barfleur, is more of a resort, with lots of tiny Channel-crossing yachts moored in the bay where Edward III landed on his way to Crécy and a string of fortifications from Vauban's time. The *Hôtel de France et des Fuchsias*, just back from the sea at 18 rue du Maréchal-Foch (☎02.33.54.42.26; ②–⑥; closed Mon in winter & Jan to mid-Feb), with its splendid gardens and excellent restaurant, is an ideal stopover for ferry passengers – in fact both it and the annexe at the end of the garden are packed throughout the season with British visitors.

La Hague and the Nez de Jobourg

If you go west from Cherbourg to **LA HAGUE**, the northern tip of the peninsula, you'll find wild and isolated countryside where you can lean against the wind, watch waves smashing against rocks or sunbathe in a spring profusion of wild flowers. But the discharges of "low-level" radioactive wastes from the **Cap Hague nuclear reprocessing plant** may discourage you from swimming. In 1980, the Greenpeace vessel, *Rainbow Warrior*, chased a ship bringing spent Japanese fuel into Cherbourg harbour. The *Rainbow Warrior's* crew were arrested, but all charges were dropped when 3000 Cherbourg dockers threatened to strike in their support.

The main road, the D901, continues a couple of kilometres beyond the nuclear plant to **GOURY**, where the fields finally roll down to a craggy pebble coastline. Almost the only building here, the *Auberge de Goury* (☎02.33.52.77.01; closed for dinner on Sun & Mon), is a really excellent **restaurant**, facing the octagonal lifeboat station and looking out towards a slate-grey lighthouse. It specializes in charcoal-grilled fish and meat, with a wide-ranging cheeseboard that includes the extraordinary *voluptueuse*, and is very popular at lunchtimes.

South of La Hague a great curve of sand – some of it military training ground – takes the land's edge to **FLAMANVILLE** and another nuclear installation. But the next two sweeps of beach down to **CARTARET**, with sand dunes like mini-mountain ranges, are probably the best beaches in Normandy if you've got transport and a desire for solitude. There are no resorts, no hotels and just two **campsites** – at Le Rozel and Surtainville.

Château de Pirou

Turn off the main coastal road, the D650, roughly 30km south of Cartaret, for a few hundred metres to reach the **Château de Pirou** (July & Aug daily 9am–noon & 2–7pm; April–June daily & Sept 10am–noon & 2–6pm; Oct–March daily except Tues

10am–noon & 2–6pm; 20F). Although you see nothing from the road, once you've passed through its three successive fortified gateways you find yourself confronted by a ravishing little castle. Some historians have suggested that this is the oldest castle in Normandy, dating back to the earliest Viking raids; it's thought to have taken its current form around the twelfth century.

Coutances

The old hill town of **COUTANCES**, 65km south of Cherbourg, confined by its site to just one main street, has on its summit a landmark for all the surrounding countryside: the **Cathédrale de Notre-Dame**. Essentially Gothic, it is still very Norman in its unconventional blending of architectural traditions, and the octagonal lantern crowning the crossing in the nave is nothing short of divinely inspired. The son et lumière on Sunday evenings and throughout the summer is for once a true complement to the light stone building. Also illuminated on summer nights (and left open) are the formal fountained **public gardens**.

Coutances' **gare SNCF** (☎02.33.07.50.77), about a mile southeast of the town centre (at the bottom of the hill), also serves as the stop for buses heading north and south. The local **tourist office** is housed behind the Hôtel de Ville in place Georges-Léclerc (July & Aug Mon–Sat 10am–1pm & 2–7pm, Sun 3–7pm; Sept–June Mon–Fri 10am–12.30pm & 2–6pm; ☎02.33.45.17.79). The cream-coloured *Hôtel du Normandie*, behind and below the cathedral at 2 place du Gaulle (☎02.33.45.01.40; ③; closed Sun eve, Mon eve & Fri eve between Sept and mid-May), has the usual assortment of rooms, and menus that range from the good-value 53F option (not Sun) to an excellent 95F spread. A better alternative for motorists is the hotel *Relais du Viaduc* (☎02.33.45.02.68; ②; closed second fortnight of Feb, plus Fri eve & Sat in low season), at the junction of the D7 and D971, south of town, which serves fine food.

Granville

From Coutances, the D971 runs down to the coast at **GRANVILLE**, the Norman equivalent of Brittany's St-Malo (see p.374), with a history of piracy and the severe citadel of the **haute ville** guarding the approaches to the bay of Mont St-Michel. Though the most lively town and popular resort in the area, it simply doesn't match the appeal of its Breton rival, with its nightmarish traffic and hordes of tourists milling around in summer in the vain hope of finding some way of amusing themselves. The great difference between Granville and St-Malo is that here the fortified citadel contains virtually nothing of interest, just three or four long, narrow, parallel streets of forbidding grey-granite eighteenth-century houses. The views up and down the coast, across to Mont St-Michel and out to the Îles Chausey, are dramatic, but not unusually so. However, if you want to get to the Channel Islands or the Îles Chausey, whose granite was quarried for the Mont St-Michel, this is where you embark.

Granville's **tourist office** is below the citadel at 4 cours Jonville (July & Aug Mon–Sat 9am–7.30pm, Sun 10.30am–12.30pm & 4–6pm; Sept–June Mon–Sat 9am–12.30pm & 2–7pm; ☎02.33.91.30.03). Trains between Paris and Cherbourg arrive well to the east at the **gare SNCF** (☎02.33.57.50.50) on avenue Maréchal-Leclerc, which also serves as the **gare routière**.

With so many visitors in summer, it's well worth booking **accommodation** in advance. There are no hotels in old Granville; most are concentrated in the new town, either beneath the walls on the seaward side, or near the station. The *Michelet*, 5 rue Jules-Michelet (☎02.33.50.06.55; ③), which has no restaurant, is well-equipped but characterless; the *Normandy Chaumière*, 20 rue Paul-Poirier not far from the tourist office (☎02.33.50.01.71; ③; closed Tues eve & Wed out of season), has a reasonable restaurant. Options nearer the station include the *Terminus* at 5 place de la Gare (☎02.33.50.02.05;

②). The modern, oceanfront *Centre Regional de Nautisme* (☎02.33.50.18.95; closed Sun in low season), a kilometre south of the station in the town centre, serves as Granville's **youth hostel**. Dorm beds cost 57F, while a private double is 98F; sailing lessons are easy to arrange.

Where Granville really does excel is in its waterfront **restaurants**, hard below the citadel walls. The best must be a couple facing the small-boat harbour, towards the end of the peninsula; the *Restaurant du Port*, 19 rue du Port (☎02.33.50.00.55), has a mouthwatering assortment of very fishy menus, while the *Phare*, nearby at no. 11 (☎02.33.50.12.94; closed Tues eve & Wed Sept–June), has the standard mussels and *panaché de poissons* on its 86F menu, and an extraordinarily copious *assiette des fruits de mer* on the 138F one. Up in the old town, *L'Échauguette*, 24 rue St-Jean (☎02.33.50.51.87), serves good simple meals, grilled over an open fire.

St-Jean-Le-Thomas

South of Granville the crowded towns and small resorts all compete for views and proximity to Mont St-Michel. **ST-JEAN-LE-THOMAS** is the first point from which you can walk at low tide across the bay to the abbey, although it's not a walk to take on a drunken – or any other – impulse. The tide, as they like to tell you, comes up faster than galloping horses. A special phone line (☎02.33.50.02.67) gives advice on timing.

Avranches

AVRANCHES is the nearest large town to Mont St-Michel, and it has always had close connections with the abbey. The Mont's original church was founded by a bishop of Avranches, spurred on by the Archangel Michael, who supposedly became so impatient with the lack of progress that he prodded a hole in the bishop's skull – still to be seen in Avranches' **St-Gervais basilica**. Robert of Torigny, a subsequent abbot of St-Michel, played host in the town on several occasions to Henry II of England, the most memorable being when Henry was obliged, barefoot and bareheaded, to do public penance for the murder of Thomas à Becket, on May 22, 1172. The arena for this act of contrition was Avranches Cathedral, designed, most inexpertly, by de Torigny himself: it swiftly "crumbled and fell for want of proper support", and all that marks the site today is a fenced-off platform – the *plate-forme*. A more vivid evocation of the area's medieval splendours comes from the illuminated manuscripts from the Mont, on display in the town **museum** (July & Aug daily 9.30am–noon & 2–6pm; April–June & Sept daily except Tues 9.30am–noon & 2–6pm; 15F).

In high summer, one bus per day runs to Mont St-Michel from the **tourist office** on place Géneral-de-Gaulle (July & Aug daily 9am–8pm; Sept–June Mon–Fri 10am–12.30pm & 2–7pm; ☎02.33.58.00.22). **Market** day is Thursday, and piped disco music on the streets goes on all summer. The **gare SNCF** is far below the town centre.

Though still some distance from the Mont, Avranches is not a bad place to base yourself. Reasonable **hotels** include *Hôtel du Jardins des Plantes*, 10 place Carnot (☎02.33.58.03.68; ③), which has a good-value basic restaurant, and the gloriously oldfashioned *Le Croix d'Or*, 83 rue de la Constitution (☎02.33.58.04.88; ②; March–Nov), with its gardens and topnotch restaurant.

Mont St-Michel

The island of **MONT ST-MICHEL** was once known as the Mount in Peril from the Sea, as many pilgrims in medieval times drowned or were sucked under by quicksand while trying to cross the bay to the eighty-metre-high rocky outcrop. The Archangel Michael was its vigorous protector, the most militant spirit of the Church Militant, with a marked tendency to leap from rock to rock in titanic struggles against Paganism and

VISITING MONT ST-MICHEL

Access to the **island** of Mont St-Michel is free and unrestricted, although there's a 15F fee to **park** on either the causeway or the sands below it (which are submerged by the tides). It pays to **get there early**, before the tour parties arrive.

Between May and September, the **abbey** is open daily from 9am to 5.30pm; from October to April, it's open daily from 9.30am until 4.30pm. It's **closed** on Jan 1, May 1, Nov 1, Nov 11, and Dec 25. Paying the standard 40F **admission fee** – ages 12–25 25F, under-12s free – entitles you to wander the generally accessible areas, and to join an expert-led **guided tour** in the language of your choice. Tours last 45min between mid-June and mid-Sept, and a full hour the rest of the year; the daily schedule for each language is displayed at the entrance. More detailed **two-hour tours**, in French only, take you both higher and deeper and cost 65F (ages 12–25 45F). **Mass** is said at 12.15pm every day, with a nursery provided below for children under eight years old.

In summer, the Mont re-opens to visitors at **night** (mid-April to May Fri & Sat 10pm–1am; June–Aug daily except Mon 10pm–1am, last admission midnight; Sept daily except Mon 9.30pm–midnight, last admission 11pm; 60F, ages 12–25 50F). This experience is promoted as **Les Imaginaires**. Visitors are free to wander at their own pace through 24 rooms, each of which is illuminated and has music playing.

Evil. The abbey dates back to the eighth century, when the Archangel supposedly appeared to a bishop of Avranches, Aubert, who duly founded a monastery on the island poking out of the Baie du Mont St-Michel. Since the eleventh century – when work on the sturdy church at the peak commenced – new buildings have been grafted onto the island to produce a fortified hotch-potch of Romanesque and Gothic buildings clambering to the pinnacle of the graceful church, forming probably the most recognizable silhouette in France after the Eiffel Tower.

The Mont is barely an island any more – the causeway (*digue*) that now leads to it is never submerged, and is silting up on both sides; couple this with the ever-constant array of tour buses and cars that use it as a car park, and the distant vision of a once remote and isolated little haven is a million miles away. It was once a large religious community, and there were never more than forty monks resident until it was converted into a prison at the time of the Revolution. On its thousandth anniversary in 1966, the Benedictines were invited to return; today, three nuns and three monks maintain a presence.

The abbey

The **abbey**, an architectural ensemble that incorporates the high-spired Archangel-topped church and the magnificent Gothic buildings known since 1228 as the **Merveille** ("The Marvel") – incorporating the entire north face, with the cloister, Knights' Hall, Refectory, Guest Hall and cellars – is visible from all around the bay, but it becomes if anything more awe-inspiring the closer you approach. In Maupassant's words:

I reached the huge pile of rocks which bears the little city dominated by the great church. Climbing the steep narrow street, I entered the most wonderful Gothic dwelling ever made for God on this earth, a building as vast as a town, full of low rooms under oppressive ceilings and lofty galleries supported by frail pillars. I entered that gigantic granite jewel, which is as delicate as a piece of lacework, thronged with towers and slender belfries which thrust into the blue sky of day and the black sky of night their strange heads bristling with chimeras, devils, fantastic beasts and monstrous flowers, and which are linked together by carved arches of intricate design.

The Mont's rock comes to a sharp point just below what is now the transept of the **church**, a building where the transition from Romanesque to Gothic is only too evident in the vaulting of the nave. In order to lay out the church's ground plan in the traditional shape of the cross, supporting crypts had to be built up from the surrounding hillside, and in all construction work the Chausey granite has had to be sculpted to match the exact contours of the hill. Space was always limited, and yet the building has grown through the centuries, with an architectural ingenuity that constantly surprises in its geometry – witness the shock of emerging into the light of the cloisters from the sombre Great Hall.

Not surprisingly, the building of the monastery was no smooth progression: the original church, choir, nave and tower all had to be replaced after collapsing. The style of decoration has varied, too, along with the architecture. That you now walk through halls of plain grey stones is a reflection of modern taste, specifically that of the director of the French Department of Antiquities. In the Middle Ages, the walls of public areas such as the refectory would have been festooned with tapestries and frescoes, while the original coloured tiles of the cloisters have long since been stripped away to reveal bare walls.

To get a clearer sense of the abbey's historical development, be sure to take a look at the intriguing scale models in the reception area, which depict it during four different epochs.

The rest of the island

The base of Mont St-Michel rests on a primeval slime of sand and mud. Just above that, you pass through the heavily fortified **Porte du Roi** onto the narrow **Grande Rue**, climbing steadily around the base of the rock and lined with medieval gabled houses and a jumble of overpriced postcard and souvenir shops, maintaining the ancient tradition of prising pilgrims from their money. A plaque near the main staircase records that Jacques Cartier was presented to King François I here on May 8, 1532 and charged with exploring the shores of Canada.

The rather dry **Musée Maritime** offers an insight into the island's ties with the sea, while the Archangel Michael manages in just fifteen minutes to lead visitors on a voyage through space and time in the **Archéoscope**, with the full majestic panoply of multimedia mumbo jumbo. Further along the Grande Rue and up the steps towards the abbey church, next door to the eleventh-century **church of St-Pierre**, the absurd **Musée Grévin** contains such edifying specimens as a wax model of a woman drowning in a sea of mud. (All open Feb to mid-Nov daily 9am–6pm; 75F for all, or 45F each one.)

Large crowds gather each day at the **North Tower**, to watch the tide sweep in across the bay. During the high tides of the equinoxes (March and Sept), the waters are alleged to rush in like a foaming galloping horse. Seagulls wheel away in alarm, and those foolish enough to be wandering too late on the sands toward Tombelaine have to sprint to safety.

Practicalities

Mont St-Michel has its own **tourist office**, in the lowest gateway (mid-June to mid-Sept Mon–Sat 9am–7pm, Sun 9am–noon & 2–6pm; mid-Sept to mid-June Mon, Tues & Thurs–Sat 9am–noon & 2–6pm; ☎02.33.60.14.30). Regular buses run from the nearest gare SNCF at Pontorson (see below).

The island holds a surprising number of **hotels** and **restaurants**, if nothing like enough to cope with the sheer number of visitors. Most are predictably expensive, though virtually all the hotels seem to keep a few cheaper rooms. The most famous hotel, *La Mère Poulard* (☎02.33.60.14.01; ④–⑨), uses the time-honoured legend of its fluffy omelettes, as enjoyed by Leon Trotsky and Margaret Thatcher (not simultaneously), to justify extortionate charges. Higher up the Mont, however, prices fall to more realistic levels. The very cheapest rooms are at the *Crêperie la Sirène* (☎02.33.60.08.60; ②), and the *Hôtel Du Guesclin* (☎02.33.60.14.10; ③; closed mid-Nov to mid-March), though the *Hôtel La Croix Blanche* (☎02.33.60.14.04; ⑤; closed mid-Nov to mid-Dec) and the *Mouton Blanc* (☎02.33.60.14.08; ④; closed Jan) serve much better food.

In addition, the main approach road to the island, the D976, is lined shortly before the causeway by around a dozen large and virtually indistinguishable hotels and motels, each with its own brasserie or restaurant. Typical among these are the *Motel Vert* (☎02.33.60.09.33; closed mid-Nov to mid-Feb; ③); the *Hôtel Formule Verte* (☎02.33.60.14.13; closed mid-Nov to mid-Feb; ③); and the *Hôtel de la Digue* (☎02.33.60.14.02; closed mid-Nov to mid-March; ④). The 350-pitch *Camping du Mont-St-Michel* (mid-Feb to mid-Nov; ☎02.33.60.09.33) is also on the mainland just short of the causeway.

Most visitors to Mont St-Michel find themselves lodging either at Avranches or **PONTORSON**, 6km inland. The latter has the nearest gare SNCF, connected to the Mont by an overpriced bus service (30F return), but, as ever, renting out cycles, too. Nothing much about Pontorson itself is worth staying for, although the café attached to the station isn't bad.

The **hotels** are not especially interesting, but both the *Montgomery*, 13 rue du Couesnon (☎02.33.60.00.09; ③; closed Nov–March), and the *Le Bretagne*, 59 rue du Couesnon (☎02.33.60.10.55; ③; closed Mon & mid-Jan to mid-Feb), along the main road, have very distinguished restaurants. An HI **youth hostel** stands near the cathedral, a kilometre west of the station, in the *Centre Duguesclin* on rue Général-Patton (☎02.33.60.00.18; Easter to mid-Sept; dorm beds cost 43F per night).

INLAND NORMANDY

It's hard to pin down specific highlights in **inland Normandy**. The pleasures lie in the feel of particular landscapes – the lush meadows and orchards, the classic half-timbered houses and farm buildings, and the rivers and forests of the Norman countryside. **Gastronomy** is, of course, another major motivation – the cheeses, creams, apple and pear brandies and ciders for which the region is famous. The **Pays d'Auge** country south of Lisieux and the **Vire Valley** to the west are the best for this. The **Suisse Normande** is canoeing and rock-climbing country, and there are endless good walks in the stretch along the southern border of the province designated as the **Parc Naturel Régional de Normandie-Maine**. Of the towns, **Conches** is the most charming, **Falaise** has William the Conqueror as a constant fall-back attraction, and **Lisieux** has religious myths, and a spectacularly revolting basilica to back them up.

South of the Seine

Heading south from the Seine you can follow the River Risle from the estuary just east of Honfleur, or the Eure and its tributaries from upstream of Rouen. Between the two stretches the long featureless **Neubourg Plain**. The lowest major crossing point over the Risle is at **PONT-AUDEMER**, where medieval houses lean out at alarming angles over the crisscrossing roads, rivers and canals. From here, perfect cycling roads lined with timbered farmhouses follow the river south.

Le Bec-Hellouin

The size and tranquil ethos of the **Abbaye de Bec-Hellouin**, upstream from Pont-Audemer just before Brionne, give a monastic feel to the whole valley (June–Sept tours Mon & Wed–Fri at 10am, 11am, 3pm, 4pm & 5pm; Sat at 10am, 11am, 3pm & 4pm; Sun & hols at noon, 3pm, 3.30pm, 4pm & 6pm; Oct–May tours Mon & Wed–Sat at 11am, 3.15pm & 4.30pm; Sun & hols at noon, 3pm, & 4pm; 25F.) Bells echo across the water and white-robed monks go soberly about their business. From the eleventh century onwards, the abbey was one of the most important centres of intellectual learning in the Christian world; the philosopher Anselm was abbot here before becoming Archbishop of Canterbury in 1093. Due to the Revolution, most of the monastery buildings are recent – the monks only returned in 1948 – but there are some survivals and appealing clusters of stone ruins, including the fifteenth-century **bell tower of St-Nicholas** and the cloister. Recent archbishops of Canterbury have maintained tradition by coming here on retreat.

In the rather twee adjacent town of **Bec-Hellouin** is a **vintage car museum** (mid-June to mid-Sept daily 9am–noon & 2–7pm; mid-Sept to mid-June Fri–Tues 9am–noon & 2–7pm; 25F), and a distinctly un-ascetic **restaurant**, the wonderful *Auberge de l'Abbaye* (☎02.32.44.86.02; closed Mon eve, all day Tues in winter, and all Jan; ⑤), which also has half a dozen expensive rooms. The *Restaurant de la Tour* on place Guillaume-le-Conquérant nearby (closed Dec, plus Tues pm & Wed in low season; ☎02.32.44.86.15) is a more affordable place to eat, with some outdoor tables.

Brionne and Beaumont-le-Roger

BRIONNE, on the Rouen–Lisieux rail line, is a small town with large regional **markets** on Thursday and Sunday. The fish hall is on the left bank, the rest by the church on the right bank. Above them both, with panoramic views, is an excellent example of a Norman **donjon**. If you decide to **stay**, the *Auberge du Vieux Donjon* (☎02.32.44.80.62; ⑤) on the marketplace is good, though pricey.

The River Charentonne joins the Risle near Serquigny. The town is also the meeting point of rail lines and main roads and the banks are clogged with fuming industrial conglomerations. But 7km upstream, at **BEAUMONT-LE-ROGER**, you are back in pastoral tranquillity. The ruins of a thirteenth-century **priory church** slowly crumble to the ground, the slow restoration of one or two arches unable to keep pace. In the village, little happens beyond the hammering of the church bell next door to the abbey by a nodding musketeer. Just across the Risle from here, on the D25 near Le Val-St-Martin, huge stables are spread across an absurdly sylvan setting, and **horses** are available for riding.

The next riverside village, **LA FERRIÈRE-SUR-RISLE**, has an especially beautiful **church**, with some interesting sculpture, and a fourteenth-century covered **market hall**. Paddocks and meadows lead down to the river and a small and inviting **hotel**, the *Vieux-Marché* (☎02.32.30.70.69; ②).

Conches-en-Ouche

Fourteen kilometres east of La Ferrière across the wild and open woodland of the **Forêt de Conches**, **CONCHES-EN-OUCHE** is many a Norman's favourite heartland town, standing above the River Rouloir on an abrupt and narrow spur. At the highest point, in the middle of a row of medieval houses, is the **church of Ste-Foy**, its windows a stunning sequence of Renaissance stained glass. Behind are the gardens of the **Hôtel de Ville**, where a robust, if anatomically odd, stone boar gazes proudly out over a spectacular view. Next to that, you can scramble up the slippery steps of the ruined twelfth-century **castle**. Conches is given a certain edge over other towns with equal lists of historic relics, by the pieces of modern sculpture that seem to lie around every other corner.

Across the main street from the castle is a long **park**, with parallel avenues of trees, a large ornamental lake and fountain. The **hotel** *Grand'Mare*, alongside at 13 av Croix de Fer (☎02.32.30.23.30; ①), serves up enjoyable dinners in its restaurant, including a good 98F menu with oxtail braised in sherry and some fruit desserts; the *Bistrot* in the same building is a less formal place to have lunch. There's also a **municipal campsite**, *La Forêt* (April–Sept; ☎02.32.30.22.49), and on Thursday the whole town is taken up by a **market**.

Évreux

If you're heading south to Conches from Rouen, you follow first the River Eure, and then its tributary the Iton, passing through ÉVREUX, capital of the Eure *département*. It's hardly an exciting place, but an afternoon's wander in the vicinity of the **cathedral** – a minor classic with its Flamboyant exterior decoration and original fourteenth-century windows – and the **ramparts** alongside the Iton river bank is pleasant.

The old *Biche*, at 9 rue St-Joséphine on place St-Taurin at the edge of town (☎02.32.38.66.00; ①), is a strange but splendid Belle Époque hotel, with a lurid pink interior, a triangular dining room and even some triangular bedrooms. In its restaurant (closed Sun pm), 135F buys you a magnificent meal of oysters braised in cider and a garlicky seafood *pot au feu*, to the musical accompaniment of an unlikely assortment of funk and disco classics.

Lisieux and the Pays d'Auge

The rolling hills and green twisting valleys of the **Pays d'Auge**, which stretches south of the cathedral town of **Lisieux**, are scattered with magnificent half-timbered manor houses. The pastures here are the lushest in the province, their produce the world-famous cheeses of Camembert, Livarot and Pont L'Évêque. And beside them are hectares of orchards, yielding the best of Norman ciders, both apple and pear (*poiré*), as well as Calvados apple brandy.

Lisieux

LISIEUX, 35 minutes by train from Caen, is the main town of the Pays d'Auge, and a good place to get to know its cheeses and ciders is at the large street **market** on Wednesday and Saturday. Most people, however, come to Lisieux as a place of pilgrimage based around the cult of St Thérèse, the most popular French spiritual figure of the last hundred years. Passivity, self-effacement and masochism were her trademarks, and she is honoured by the grotesquely gaudy and gigantic **Basilique de Ste-Thérèse**, completed in 1954 on a slope to the southwest of the town centre. Huge mosaics of her face decorate the nave, and every night except Sunday between June and September, at 9.45pm, as part of a stunningly tasteless (and expensive) laser show, her beatific smile is simultaneously projected onto every column in the church. The faithful can ride on a white, flag-bedecked fairground train around the holiest sites, which include the infinitely restrained and sober **Cathédrale St-Pierre**.

Lisieux's **tourist office**, 11 rue d'Alençon, is the best place to gather information on the rural areas further inland (June–Sept Mon–Sat 8.30am–6.30pm, Sun 10.30am–12.30pm & 2.30–5pm; Oct–May Mon–Sat 8.30am–noon & 1.30–6pm; ☎02.31.62.08.41). The quantity of pilgrims means that Lisieux is full of good-value places to stay – among its **hotels** are *Hôtel de la Terrasse*, up on the hill near the Basilica at 25 av Ste-Thérèse (☎02.31.62.17.65; closed Jan, & Mon in winter; ②), *Hôtel de Lourdes*, 4 rue au Char near the cathedral (☎02.31.31.19.48; ②), and the *Hôtel des Arts*, backing onto the Bishop's Gardens at 26 rue Condorcet (☎02.31.62.00.02; ①). There is also a large **campsite**, *de la Vallée* (April to mid-Oct; ☎02.31.62.00.40), but campers would probably be better off somewhere more rural, such as Livarot or Orbec. If Thérèse isn't your prime motivation, Saturday is the best day to visit, for the large street market – stacked with Pays d'Auge cheeses.

Into the Pays d'Auge

Though the tourist authorities responsible for the Pays d'Auge have laid out a **Route du Fromage** and a **Route du Cidre**, you won't be missing out if you don't follow these itineraries. For really good solid Norman cooking this is the perfect area to look out for *fermes auberges*, working farms which welcome paying visitors to share their meals. Local tourist information offices can provide copious lists of these and of local producers from whom you can buy your cheese and booze.

Beuvron-en-Auge

By far the prettiest of the Pays d'Auge villages is **BEUVRON-EN-AUGE**, 7km north of the N13 halfway between Lisieux and Caen. It consists of an oval central *place*, ringed by a glorious ensemble of multicoloured half-timbered houses including the yellow and brown sixteenth-century **Vieux Manoir**. Immediately alongside, the eighteenth-century *Auberge de la Boule d'Or* (☎02.31.79.78.78; closed Jan, plus Sun pm & Mon; ③), offers three attractive bedrooms. The very centre of the *place* is taken up by the *Pavé d'Auge* **restaurant** (☎02.31.79.26.71; closed Mon May–Aug), where menus featuring chicken and *andouille* in cider or salmon start at 136F.

Orbec

The larger town of **ORBEC**, 19km southeast of Lisieux, also epitomizes the simple pleasures of the region. Along the Rue Grande, you'll see several houses in which the gaps between the timbers are filled with intricate patterns of coloured tiles and bricks. Debussy composed *Jardin sous la Pluie* in one of these, and the oldest and prettiest of the lot – a tanner's house dating back to 1568, and once again called the **Vieux Manoir** – holds a museum of local history. On the whole, though, it's more fun just to walk down behind the church to the river, and its watermill and paddocks. The *Hôtel de France*, 152 rue Grande (☎02.31.32.74.02; ②; closed mid-Dec to mid-Jan) serves good meals for 90F and upwards.

Livarot

The centre of the cheese country is the old town of **LIVAROT**, with the rather faded **hotel** and restaurant *du Vivier* (☎02.31.63.50.29; ①) in its heart. Set in a grand house near the Vie river on its western outskirts, the **Musée du Fromage** illustrates the history and manufacture of Livarot's eponymous cheese, and doles out free samples (April–Oct Mon–Fri 10am–noon & 2–6pm; 15F).

Vimoutiers and Camembert

VIMOUTIERS, due south of Livarot, contains yet another **cheese museum**, at 10 av Général-de-Gaulle (May–Oct Mon 2–6pm, Tues–Sat 9am–noon & 2–6pm, Sun 10am–noon & 2.30–6pm; Nov, Dec, March & April Mon 2–6pm, Tues–Fri 9am–noon & 2–6pm, Sat 9am–noon; 25F). This one specializes in labels – the cheeses underneath are mostly polystyrene.

A statue in the town's main square honours Marie Harel, who, at the nearby village of **CAMEMBERT** (tiny, hilly and very rural), developed the original cheese early in the nineteenth century, promoting it with a skilful campaign that included sending free samples to Napoléon. Marie is confronted across the main street by what might be called the statue of the Unknown Cow.

Vimoutiers is the venue of a **market** on Monday afternoons and Fridays. Its **tourist office** (same hours; ☎02.33.39.30.29), in the cheese museum, has piles of information on local cheese-related attractions. Of its **hotels**, the very central but far from welcoming *Soleil d'Or*, 15 place Mackau (☎02.33.39.07.15; closed Feb; ①), has a good 65F menu and an even better 100F one, and there is also a superbly clean and very cheap year-round **campsite** – *La Campière*, 9 rue du 8-Mai (☎02.33.39.18.86) – near the **Escale du Vitou**, a lake just outside the village.

Vegetarian travellers in particular – though not exclusively – should make a beeline for the village of **Ticheville**, 5km southeast on the D12. An unobtrusive house tucked away just north of the main street has been converted by its British owners into *La Maison du Vert* (☎02.33.36.95.84; ②), a friendly hotel that serves excellent vegetarian and vegan meals – dinner costs around 105F – and is set in lovely rolling gardens.

Falaise

William the Conqueror, or William the Bastard as he is more commonly known over here, was born in **FALAISE**, 40km southwest of Lisieux. His mother, Arlette, a laundrywoman, was spotted by his father, Duke Robert of Normandy, at the washing place below the château. She was a shrewd woman, scorning secrecy in her eventual assignation by riding publicly through the main entrance to meet him. During her pregnancy, she is said to have dreamed of bearing a mighty tree that cast its shade over Normandy and England.

Both the keep of the **castle**, and the **Fontaine d'Arlette** on the riverside beneath it, still exist, though so heavily restored as to be scarcely worth the ten-minute tour. The town itself was devastated in the war. The struggle to close the "Falaise Gap" in August 1944 was the climax of the Battle of Normandy, as the Allied armies sought to encircle the Germans and cut off their retreat. By the time the Canadians entered the town on August 17, they could no longer tell where the roads had been and had to bulldoze a new four-metre strip straight through the middle.

The **tourist office** can be found at 32 rue Georges-Clemenceau (May–Sept Mon–Sat 10am–6pm, Sun 10am–4pm; Oct–April Mon–Sat 10am–6pm; ☎02.31.90.17.26). As the main Caen–Argentan road, this is also the (rather noisy) location of most of Falaise's few **hotels**, such as the *Poste* at no. 38 (☎02.31.90.13.14; ③). The **campsite**, *Camping du Château* (☎02.31.90.16.55; Easter–Sept), next to Arlette's fountain and the municipal swimming pool, is in a much better location.

The Suisse Normande

The area known as the **Suisse Normande** lies roughly 25km south of Caen, along the gorge of the River Orne, between Thury-Harcourt and Putanges. The name is a little far-fetched – there are certainly no mountains – but it is quite distinctive, with cliffs and crags and wooded hills at every turn. The energetic race along the Orne in canoes and kayaks, while the less hearty are content with pedalos or a bizarre species of inflatable rubber tractor, and high above climbers dangling from thin ropes claw at the sheer rock face. For mere walkers the Orne can be frustrating: footpaths along the river are few and far between, and often entirely overgrown.

The Suisse Normande is usually approached from Caen or Falaise and contrasts dramatically with the prairie-like expanse of wheat fields en route. On wheels, the best access is via the D235 from Caen (signed to Falaise then right through Ifs). The Bus Verts #34 will take you to **Thury-Harcourt** or **Clécy** on its way to Flers, and there are occasional special summer train excursions from Caen.

Thury-Harcourt and Clécy

At **THURY-HARCOURT**, the **tourist office** on place St-Sauveur can suggest walks, rides and gîtes d'étape throughout the Suisse Normande; SIVOM at 15 rue de Condé rents out canoes. **Hotels** are for the most part quite expensive, though the flowery *Hôtel du Val d'Orne*, down by the river at 9 route d'Aunay (☎02.31.79.70.81; closed Sat lunch in summer, Fri pm & all Sat in low season; ②), keeps its room rates low, and has a decent **restaurant**. There's also an attractive four-star **campsite**, the *Vallée du Traspy* (mid-April to mid-Sept; ☎02.31.79.61.80).

CLÉCY, 10km to the south, is a slightly better bet for finding a room, although its visitors outnumber its residents in peak season. The **hotel** facing the church in the village centre, *Au Site Normand*, 1 rue des Châtelets (☎02.31.69.71.05; ②; closed Tues eve & Wed out of season), consists of an old-fashioned and good-value dining room in the main timber-framed building, and a cluster of newer units around the back. The river is a kilometre away, down the hill. En route, in the Parc des Loisirs, is a **Musée du Chemin de Fer Miniature** (July & Aug daily 10am–noon & 2–6.30pm; Easter–June & Sept daily 10am–noon & 2–6pm; Oct–Nov Sun 2–5pm; March–Easter Sun 2–5.30pm; 25F), featuring a gigantic model railway layout certain to appeal to children. The *Moulin du Vey* (☎02.31.69.71.08; ⑤; closed Dec & Jan), set in spacious grounds on the far bank of the river, is a luxury hotel that takes its name from the restored watermill right by the bridge, which is itself, confusingly, now a restaurant. The western river bank continues in a brief splurge of restaurants, takeaways and snack bars as far as the municipal **campsite** (☎02.31.69.70.36; April–Sept).

Pont d'Ouilly

If you're planning on walking, or cycling, one good central spot in which to base yourself is **PONT D'OUILLY**, at the point where the main road from Vire to Falaise crosses the river. It's a small town, with a few basic shops, an old covered market hall and a promenade (with bar) slightly upstream alongside the weir; you can walk along the riverside down to Le Mesnil Villement.

As well as its **campsite**, overlooking the river (☎02.31.69.46.12; Easter–Sept), Pont d'Ouilly can offer an attractive **hotel**, the *du Commerce* (☎02.31.69.80.16; ②; closed Sun pm & Mon Oct–May, plus all Jan). This is the quintessential French village hotel, with a friendly welcome and attentive service. Its restaurant is very popular with local families, serving superb, definitive Norman cooking, with plenty of creamy Pays d'Auge sauces, on menus that start at 65F. About a kilometre north, the more upmarket *Auberge St-Christophe* (☎02.31.69.81.23; ③; closed Sun pm, Mon & mid-Feb to mid-March) stands in a beautiful setting on the right bank of the Orne, covered with ivy and geraniums and opposite a roofless and now overgrown Art Deco factory.

.   A short distance south of Pont-d'Ouilly is the **Roche d'Oëtre**, a high rock with a tremendous view into the deep and totally wooded gorge of the Rouvre. The river widens soon afterwards into the **Lac du Rabodanges**, formed by the many-arched Rabodanges Dam. It's a popular spot where people practise every watersport, and with a **campsite**, *Les Retours*, perfectly situated between the dam and the bridge on D121.

Southern Normandy

In addition to the more northerly routes across Normandy described elsewhere in this chapter, motorists heading west from Paris towards Brittany may choose to get just a brief taste of the province by following the line of the N12 through **Alençon** and **Domfront**.

Alençon

ALENÇON, a fair-sized and busy town, is known for its traditional – and now pretty much defunct – lacemaking industry. The **Musée des Beaux-Arts et de la Dentelle** (daily except Mon 10am–noon & 2–6pm; 20F) is housed in a former Jesuit school and has all the best trappings of a modern museum. The highly informative history of lacemaking upstairs, with examples of numerous different techniques, can, however, be tedious for anyone not already riveted by the subject. It also contains an unexpected collection of gruesome Cambodian artefacts like spears and lances, tiger skulls and elephants' feet, gathered by a "militant socialist" French governor at the turn of the century. The paintings in the adjoining Beaux-Arts section are nondescript, except for a few works by Courbet and Géricault. Wandering around the town might take you to Ste-Thérèse's birthplace on rue St-Blaise, just in front of the gare routière – if, that is, you haven't had a surfeit of the saint at Lisieux. The **Château des Ducs**, the old town castle close by the museum, looks impressive but doesn't encourage visitors. It is a prison, and people in Alençon have nightmarish memories of its use by the Gestapo during the war.

If you want to **stay**, Alençon has good shops and cafés in a few well-pedestrianized streets at the heart of its abysmal one-way traffic system. The **tourist office** is housed in the fifteenth-century Maison d'Ozé on place La Magdelaine (July & Aug Mon & Sat 9.30am–noon & 2–6.30pm, Tues–Fri 9.30am–6.30pm, Sun 10am–12.30pm & 2.30–5.30pm; Sept–June Mon–Sat 9.30am–noon & 2–6.30pm; ☎02.33.26.11.36).

The **gare routière** and the **gare SNCF** are both northeast of the centre, in an area that holds Alençon's prime concentration of **hotels**. The two *logis*, *l'Industrie*, 20 place Général-de-Gaulle (☎02.33.27.19.30; closed Sun pm & Mon; ②), and the *Grand Hôtel de la Gare*, 50 av Wilson (☎02.33.29.03.93; ①), are decent and have fixed-price menus for around 70F. Back in the town centre, the *Jardin Gourmand*, 14 rue de Sarthe (☎02.33.32.22.56; closed Mon & Tues pm), is a romantic little restaurant with menus from 70F. The local **youth hostel**, 3km northwest of town on the D204 towards Colombiers at 1 rue de la Paix, Damigny (☎02.33.29.00.48; 40F), is not attractive in itself, but organizes lots of activities in the woods and on the river.

The **Forêt d'Écouves**, north of Alençon and inaccessible by public transport, is a dense mixture of spruce, pine, oak and beech, unfortunately a favoured spot of the military – and, in autumn, deer hunters, too. You can usually ramble along the cool paths, happening on wild mushrooms and even the odd wild boar.

Carrouges

One alternative base at the western end of the Forêt d'Écouves is the hill town of **CARROUGES**, with its fine old-style **château** set in spacious grounds at the foot of the hill (mid-June to Aug daily 9.30–11.30am & 2–6.30pm; April to mid-June & Sept daily 10–11.30am & 2–6pm; Oct–March daily 10–11.30am & 2–4.30pm; 25F). Its two highlights are a superb restored brick staircase and a room in which hang portraits of fourteen successive generations of the Le Veneur family, an extraordinary illustration of the processes of heredity. The town also offers two appealing, very similar and almost adjacent small **hotels**. The *Hôtel du Nord* (☎02.33.27.20.14; ①; closed mid-Dec to mid-Jan, plus Fri Sept–June) offers well-prepared local cuisine on menus that start at 57F; all rooms at the tiny *St-Pierre* (☎02.33.27.20.02; ②) have showers, and the cheapest menu is 70F.

Bagnoles-de-l'Orne

West of Carrouges, the spa town of **BAGNOLES-DE-L'ORNE** is quite unlike anywhere else in this part of the world. The monied sick and convalescent come from all over France to its thermal baths, and business is so good they maintain a reservations office next to the Pompidou Centre in Paris. The layout is formal and spacious, centring on a lake with gardens where horse-drawn *calèches* take the clients to an enormous casino, and with so many visitors to keep entertained, and spending money, there are innumerable cultural events of a restrained and stressless nature.

Whether you'd actually want to spend time in Bagnoles depends on your disposable income as well as your health. Furthermore, the town as a whole operates to a season that lasts roughly from early April to the end of October; arrive in winter, and you may find everything shut. The numerous hotels are expensive and sedate places, in which it's possible to be too late for dinner at seven o'clock and locked out altogether at nine, and the **campsite**, *de la Vée* (☎02.33.37.87.45; April–Oct), south of town, is rather forlorn.

Contact the **tourist office** on place du Marché (April–Oct daily 10am–noon & 2–6.30pm; Nov–March Mon–Fri 10am–noon & 2–6pm; ☎02.33.37.85.66) for details on accommodation in Bagnoles and its less exclusive sister town of **TESSE-MADELEINE**. Among the cheaper options in Bagnoles proper – all near the central roundabout – are the *Albert 1er* at 7 av Dr-Poulain (☎02.33.37.80.97; ②; closed Nov–Jan), which has excellent menus from 98F, and the *Grand Veneur* at 6 place République (☎02.33.37.86.79; ②; closed Nov–March). **Restaurants**, in both towns, tend to be better value; the *de la Terrasse* (☎02.33.30.80.96) in Bagnoles is well-tried and popular, with a traditional dining room offering six menus from 75F upwards, and a cheaper crêperie.

Domfront

The road through the forest from Bagnoles, the D335 and then the D908, climbs above the lush woodlands and progressively narrows to a hog's back before entering **DOM-FRONT**. Less happens here than at Bagnoles, but it has the edge on countryside.

A public park, near the long-abandoned former railway station, leads up to some redoubtable **castle** ruins perched on an isolated rock. Eleanor of Aquitaine was born in this castle in October 1162, and Thomas à Becket came to stay for Christmas 1166, saying mass in the **Notre-Dame-sur-l'Eau** church down by the river, which has sadly been ruined by vandals. The views from the flower-filled gardens that surround the mangled keep are spectacular, including a very graphic panorama of the ascent you've made to get up.

A slender footbridge connects the castle with the narrow little village itself, which boasts an abundance of half-timbered houses. Near its sweet little central square, the modern **St-Julien church**, constructed out of concrete segments during the 1920s, is bursting with exciting mosaics.

On summer afternoons (July & Aug, Mon–Sat 3pm), free **guided tours** of old Domfront leave from the **tourist office**, 21 rue St-Julien (Mon–Sat 10am–noon & 2.30–6.30pm; ☎02.33.38.53.97). Domfront's **hotels**, clustered together at the foot of the hill below the old town, make useful and very pleasant stopovers. Two *logis de France* stand side by side; the *Relais St-Michel* (☎02.33.38.64.99; ②) has widely varied menus at under 100F, while the *Hôtel de France* (☎02.33.38.51.44; ①) is a little cheaper, and has a nice little bar and garden. Campers should take note that the local **campsite**, *du Champs Passais* (April to mid-Oct; ☎02.33.37.37.66), is exceptionally small.

The Bocage

The region centring on **St-Lô**, just south of the Cotentin, is known as the **Bocage**, from a word that refers to a type of cultivated countryside common in the west of France, where fields are cut by tight hedgerows rooted into walls of earth well over a metre high. An effective form of smallhold farming – at least in pre-industrial days – it also proved to be a perfect system of anti-tank barricades. When the Allied troops tried to advance through the region in 1944, it was almost impenetrable – certainly bearing no resemblance to the East Anglian plains where they had trained. The war here was hand-to-hand slaughter, and the destruction of villages was often wholesale.

St-Lô

The city of **ST-LÔ**, 60km south of Cherbourg and 36km southwest of Bayeux, is still known as the "Capital of the Ruins". Memorial sites are everywhere and what is new speaks as tellingly of the destruction as the ruins that have been preserved. In the main square, the gate of the old prison commemorates Resistance members executed by the Nazis, people deported east to the concentration camps and soldiers killed in action. When the bombardment of St-Lô was at its fiercest, the Germans refused to take any measures to protect the prisoners and the gate was all that survived. Samuel Beckett was here during the battle and after, working for the Irish Red Cross as interpreter, driver and provision-seeker – for such things as rat poison for the maternity hospitals. He said he took away with him a "time-honoured conception of humanity in ruins".

All the trees in the city are the same height, all planted to replace the battle's mutilated stumps. But the most visible – and brilliant – reconstruction is the **Cathédrale de Notre-Dame**. Its main body, with a strange southward-veering nave, has been conventionally repaired and rebuilt. But the shattered west front and the base of the collapsed north tower have been joined by a startling sheer wall of icy green stone that makes no attempt to mask the destruction.

By way of contrast to such memories, a lighthouse-like 1950s folly spirals to nowhere on the main square. Should you feel the urge to climb its staircase, make your way into the brand-new and even more pointless labyrinth of glass at its feet, which now houses St-Lô's **tourist office** (Mon–Sat 9am–noon & 2–6pm; ☎02.33.05.02.09), and pay the 10F admission fee. More compelling, around behind the mairie, is a **Musée des Beaux-Arts** (April–Oct daily except Tues 10am–noon & 2–6pm; Nov–March daily except Tues 2–6pm; 10F). This is full of treasures: a Boudin sunset; a Lurçat tapestry of his dog, *Nadir and the Pirates*; works by Corot, van Loo, Moreau; a Léger watercolour; a fine series of unfaded sixteenth-century Flemish tapestries on the lives of two peasants; and sad bombardment relics of the town.

St-Lô makes an interesting pause but it's virtually abandoned at **night**. Most of the hotels, restaurants and bars, however, are just across the river, near the **gare SNCF**. Overlooking the river from the brow of a ridge beside the station, the upmarket *logis Hôtel des Voyageurs*, 5–7 av Briovère (☎02.33.05.08.63; ③), is home to the *Tocqueville* restaurant, which serves a delicious trout soufflé on its 96F menu. If you'd rather be up in town, try *La Cremaillère*, 27 rue Belle (☎02.33.57.14.68; closed Sat am & Sun; ②).

The Vire Valley

Once St-Lô was taken in the Battle of Normandy, the armies speedily moved on for their next confrontation. The **Vire Valley**, trailing south from St-Lô, saw little action – and its towns and villages seem to have been rarely touched by any historic or cultural mainstream. The motivation in coming to this landscape of rolling hills and occasional gorges is essentially to consume the region's cider, Calvados (much of it bootleg), its fruit pastries, and its sausages made from pigs' intestines.

From St-Lô to Tessy

The best section of the valley is south of St-Lô through the Roches de Ham to Tessy-sur-Vire. The **Roches de Ham** are a pair of sheer rocky promontories high above the river. Though promoted as "viewing tables", the pleasure lies as much in the walk up, through lanes lined with blackberries, hazelnuts and rich orchards. Downstream from the Roches, and a good place to stop for the night, is **LA CHAPELLE-SUR-VIRE**. Its **church**, towering majestically above the river, has been an object of pilgrimage since the twelfth century. Next to the bridge on the lower road is the *Auberge de la Chapelle* (☎02.33.56.32.83; ①), a good but rather expensive restaurant with a few cheap **rooms**.

An alternative base for the Roches, over to the east, is **TORIGNI-SUR-VIRE**, which was the base of the Grimaldi family before they attained princeliness in Monaco. A spacious country town, it boasts a few grand buildings, the scant remains of a sixteenth-century castle and an attractive **campsite**, *Camping du Lac* (☎02.33.56.91.74). At **TESSY-SUR-VIRE** there's little to see other than the river itself, though the town has a luxurious **campsite**, along with a couple of **hotels** and Wednesday **market**.

Vire

VIRE itself is worth visiting specifically for the **food**; in fact the one problem is what to do when you're not eating. The town is best known for its dreaded *andouille* sausages, but you can gorge yourself instead on salmon trout fresh from the river, accompanied by local *poiré*. Choosing a **hotel**, it makes sense to go for one with a good dining room. At the central *Hôtel de France*, 4 rue d'Aignaux (☎02.31.68.00.35; ②), the 98F menu is packed with local specialities, including *andouille* for both starter and main course, but no one's going to make you eat it if you don't want to – there's always *tripes a là mode de Caen* instead. *Au Vrai Normand*, 14 rue Armand-Gasté (☎02.31.67.90.99), is the best dedicated **restaurant**.

For some exercise (and you'll need it), head 6km south along D76 to **Lac de la Dathée**. Set in open country, the lake is circled by footpaths or can be crossed by rented sailing boat or windsurfer – contact the *Maison des Jeunes et de la Culture*, 1 rue des Halles (☎02.31.68.08.04).

Villedieu-les-Poêles

VILLEDIEU-LES-POÊLES – literally "City of God the Frying Pans" – is a lively though touristy place, 28km west of Vire. Copper souvenirs and kitchen utensils gleam from its rows of shops, and the tourist office has lists of dozens of local *ateliers* for more direct purchases, plus details of the copperwork museum.

All of this can seem a bit obsessive, though there is more authentic interest at the **Fonderie de Cloches** at 13 rue du Pont-Chignon, one of the twelve remaining bell foundries in Europe. Work here is only part-time due to limited demand, but it's open to visits all year round, and you may find the forge lit (July & Aug daily 8am–6pm; Sept–June Tues–Sat 8am–noon & 2–5.30pm; 16F). Expert craftsmen will show you the moulds, composed of an unpleasant-looking combination of clay, goat's hair and horse shit.

The local **tourist office** is on place des Costils (June–Sept only; ☎02.33.61.05.69). If you're charmed into staying, the dining room of the comfortable *Fruitier* on place Gostils (☎02.33.90.51.00; closed Sat in winter; ③) has plate-glass windows to watch the goings-on in the square, there's a reasonable 69F menu, and the 115F menu is packed with regional delights. In the heart of the main street, the very welcoming *logis Hôtel St-Pierre et St-Michel*, 12 place de la République (☎02.33.61.00.11; closed Jan, plus Fri in low season; ③), houses another stylishly refurbished restaurant. There's also a **campsite** by the river, *Le Pré de la Rose* (Easter–Oct; ☎02.33.61.02.44).

travel details

Buses

Alençon to: Bagnoles (5 daily; 30min); Évreux (1 daily; 2hr); Vimoutiers (1–3 daily; 1hr 30min).

Caen to: Bayeux (4 daily; 50min); Cabourg (3 daily; 40min); Clécy (5 daily, 2 on Sun; 50min) via Thury-Harcourt (36min); Deauville (3 daily; 1hr); Falaise (3 daily; 45min); Honfleur (3 daily; 1hr 30min); Le Havre (2 daily; 1hr 30min) via Honfleur (55min); Lisieux (5 daily; 45min); Vire (2–5 daily; 1hr 30min).

Dieppe to: Paris (5 daily; 2hr 15min); Le Tréport (3 daily; 30min); Fécamp (4 daily; 2hr 20min) via St-Valéry (1hr).

Le Havre to: Honfleur (8 daily; 30 min); 2 daily express services continue to Caen (1hr 25min); Fécamp (7 daily; 1hr 30min) via Étretat (50min).

Rouen to: Dieppe (2 daily; 1hr 45min); Fécamp (2 daily; 2hr 30min); Le Havre (hourly; 2hr 45min) via Jumièges and Caudebec; Lisieux (2 daily; 2hr 30min).

Trains

Through services to Paris connect with all ferries at Dieppe, Le Havre and Cherbourg: if you're doing this it's easiest to buy a combined rail–ferry–rail ticket at your point of departure.

Caen to: Cherbourg (hourly; 1hr 15min) via Bayeux (20min) and Valognes (1hr); Le Mans (9 daily; 2hr) and Tours (2hr 30min) via Argentan (50min) and Alençon (1hr 15min); Lisieux (hourly; 30min); Paris-St-Lazare (20 daily; 2hr); Rennes (5 daily; 3hr) via Bayeux (20min), St-Lô (1hr), Coutances (1hr 15min) and Pontorson (2hr).

Cherbourg to: Paris (10 daily; 3hr 10min) via Valognes (20min) and Caen (1hr 15min).

Dieppe to: Paris-St-Lazare (8 daily; 2hr 15min); Rouen (8 daily; 1hr).

Granville to: Coutances (8 daily; 30min); Paris (6 daily; 3hr 30min).

Le Havre to: Paris (12 daily; 2hr 15min) via Rouen (1hr).

Rouen to: Caen (8 daily; 2hr 15min); Fécamp (hourly; 1hr); Paris-St-Lazare (12 daily; 1hr 15min).

Ferries

Caen (Ouistreham) to: Portsmouth (1 or 2 daily; 6hr) with Brittany Ferries (☎02.31.36.36.36).

Cherbourg to: Poole (4hr 30min) with Brittany Ferries (☎02.33.88.44.68); Portsmouth (5–6 daily; 2hr 45min to 4hr 45min) with P&O (☎02.33. 85.65.70); Rosslare (2–4 weekly; 17hr) with Irish Continental (☎02.33.44.28.96).

Dieppe to: Newhaven (4–5 daily; 2hr 15min–4hr) with P&O Stena Line (☎02.35.06.39.03).

Granville to: Jersey, Guernsey and the Îles Chausey with Émeraude Lines (☎02.33.50.16.36), Jolie France (☎02.33.50.31.81) and Channiland (☎02.33.51.77.45).

Le Havre to: Portsmouth (3 daily; 5hr 30min) with P&O (☎02.35.19.78.78); Rosslare (3 weekly; 21hr) and Cork (June–Aug, 1 weekly; 21hr) with Irish Continental (☎02.35.53.28.83).

CHAPTER FIVE

BRITTANY

No one area – and certainly no one city or town – in **Brittany** encapsulates the character of the province; that lies in its people and in its geographical unity. For generations Bretons risked their lives fishing and trading on the violent seas, or struggled with the arid soil of the interior. This toughness and resilience is tinged with Celtic culture: mystical, musical, sometimes morbid and defeatist, sometimes vital and inspired.

Though archeologically Brittany is one of the richest sites in the world – the alignments at Carnac rival Stonehenge – its first appearance in recorded history is as the quasi-mythical "Little Britain" of Arthurian legend. In the days when to travel by sea was safer and easier than by land, it was intimately connected with "Great Britain" across the water, and settlements such as St-Malo, St-Pol and Quimper were founded by Welsh and Irish missionary "saints" whose names are not to be found in any official breviary. Brittany remained independent until the sixteenth century, its last ruler, Duchess Anne, only managing to protect the province's autonomy through marriage to two consecutive French monarchs. After her death, in 1532, François I took her daughter and lands, and sealed the union with an act supposedly enshrining certain privileges. These included a veto over taxes by the local *parlement* and the people's right to be tried, or conscripted to fight, only in their province. The successive violations of this treaty by Paris, and subsequent revolts, form the core of Breton history since the Middle Ages.

Bretons have seen their language steadily eradicated and the interior severely depopulated. But people still tend to treat France as a separate country, even if few actively support Breton nationalism (which it's a criminal offence to advocate) much beyond putting *Breizh* (Breton for "Brittany") stickers on their cars. But there have been many successes in reviving the language, and the recent economic resurgence, helped partly by summer tourism, has largely been due to local initiatives, like Brittany Ferries re-establishing an old trading link, carrying produce and passengers across to Britain and Ireland. At the same time a Celtic artistic identity has consciously been revived, and local festivals – above all August's **Inter-Celtic Festival** at Lorient – celebrate traditional Breton music, poetry and dance, with fellow Celts treated as comrades.

For most visitors, it is the Breton **coast** that is the dominant feature. After the Côte d'Azur, this is now the most popular summer resort area in France – for both French and foreign tourists. The attractions are obvious: warm white-sand beaches, towering cliffs,

---

ACCOMMODATION PRICE CATEGORIES

Each hotel in this chapter has a symbol which corresponds to one of eight price categories.

① Under 160F	④ 300–400F	⑦ 600–700F
② 160–220F	⑤ 400–500F	⑧ Over 700F
③ 220–300F	⑥ 500–600F	

The prices quoted are for the cheapest available double room in high season, though remember that many of the cheap places will have more expensive rooms with en-suite facilities.

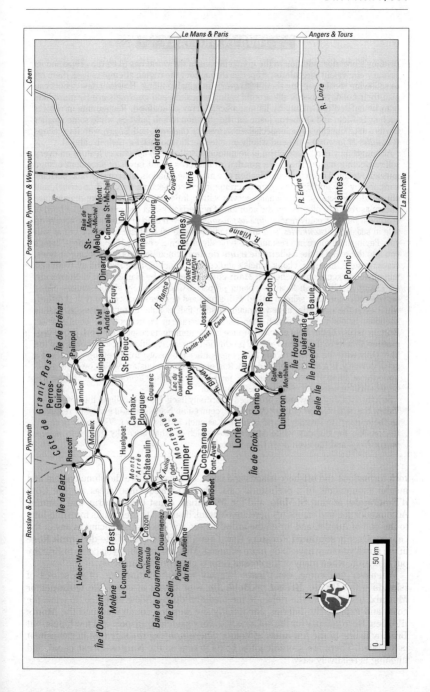

FOOD IN BRITTANY

Brittany's proudest addition to the great cuisines of the world has to be the **crêpe** and its savoury equivalent the **galette**; crêperies throughout the region attempt to pass them off as satisfying meals, serving them with every imaginable filling. However, few people can plan their holidays specifically around eating pancakes, and gourmets are far more likely to be enticed to Brittany by its magnificent array of **seafood**. Restaurants in resorts such as St-Malo and Quiberon jostle for the attention of fish fanatics, while some smaller towns – like Cancale, which specializes in oysters (*huîtres*), and Erquy, with its scallops (*Coquilles St-Jacques*) – depend wholly on one specific mollusc for their livelihood.

Although they can't quite claim to be uniquely Breton, two appetizers feature on every self-respecting menu. These are **moules marinières**, giant bowls of succulent orange mussels steamed open in a combination of white wine, shallots and parsley (and perhaps enriched by the addition of cream or crème fraiche to become *moules à la crème*), and **soupe de poissons**, traditionally served with a little pot of the garlicky mayonnaise known as *rouille* (coloured by the addition of pulverized sweet red pepper) and a bowl of croutons. Jars of freshly made *soupe de poissons* – or even crab or lobster – are always on sale in seaside *poissonneries*, and make an ideal way to take a taste of France home with you. Paying a bit more in a restaurant – typically on menus costing 150F or more – brings you into the realm of the **assiette de fruits de mer**, a mountainous heap of langoustines, crabs, oysters, mussels, clams, whelks and cockles, most of them raw and all (with certain obvious exceptions) delicious. **Main courses** tend to be plainer than in Normandy, for example, with fresh local fish being prepared with relatively simple sauces. Skate served with capers, or salmon baked with a mustard or cheese sauce, are typical dishes, while even the **cotriade**, a stew containing such fish as sole, turbot or bass, as well as shellfish, is distinctly less rich than its Mediterranean equivalent, the bouillabaisse. Brittany is also better than much of France in maintaining its respect for fresh green **vegetables**, thanks to the extensive local production of peas, cauliflowers, artichokes and the like. Only with the **desserts** can things get rather too heavy; **far Breton**, considered a great delicacy, is a stodgy baked concoction of sponge and custard which owes its gravitas to the addition of such ingredients as pig's blood, while *îles flottantes* are meringue icebergs adrift in a sea of crème brulée or custard.

Strictly speaking, no **wine** is produced in Brittany itself. However, along the lower Loire Valley, the *département* of Loire-Atlantique, centred on Nantes, is still generally regarded as "belonging" to Brittany – and is treated as such in this chapter. Vineyards here are responsible for the dry white Muscadet – which is what normally goes into *moules marinières* – and the even drier Gros-Plant.

rock formations and offshore islands and islets, and everywhere the stone dolmen and menhir monuments of a prehistoric past. The most frequented areas are the **Côte d'Émeraude**, around **St-Malo**, and the **Morbihan coast** below **Auray** and **Vannes**. Accommodation and campsites here are plentiful, if pushed to their limits from mid-June to the end of August, and for all the crowds there are resorts as enticing as any in the country. Over in **southern Finistère** ("land's end") and along the **Côte de Granit Rose** in the north you may have to do more planning. This is true, too, if you come to Brittany out of season, when many of the coastal resorts close down completely.

Whenever you come, don't leave Brittany without visiting one of its scores of **islands** – the **Île de Bréhat** or **Belle Île** – or taking in cities like **Quimper** or **Morlaix**, testimony to the riches of the medieval duchy. Allow time, too, to leave the coast and explore the interior, particularly the western country around the **Monts d'Arées**. Here you pay for the solitude with very sketchy transport and few hotels, but Brittany is one of the few areas of France where *camping sauvage* (not in campsites) is tolerated. There are sporadic gîtes, boats to rent on the **Nantes–Brest canal**, and hitching is relatively easy.

Finally, a note on the **pardons**, pilgrimage festivals commemorating local saints, which guidebooks (and tourist offices) tend to promote as spectacles. These are not, unlike most French festivals, phoney affairs kept alive for tourists, but deeply serious and rather gloomy religious occasions. If you're looking for traditional Breton fun, and you can't make the Lorient festival (or the smaller *Quinzaine Celtique* at Nantes in June/July), look out for gatherings organized by **Celtic folklore groups** – *Circles* or *Bagadou*.

THE NORTH COAST AND RENNES

Medieval Brittany was obliged vigorously to defend its independence against potential incursors, and today its eastern approaches remain guarded by the heavily fortified citadels of **Fougères** and **Vitré**. Along the coast from Mont St-Michel, only just across the border in Normandy, are some of Brittany's finest old towns. One of the most spectacular introductions to the province is that which greets ferry passengers from Portsmouth; the **River Rance**, guarded by magnificently preserved **St-Malo** on its estuary, and beautiful medieval **Dinan** 20km upstream. To the west stretches a varied coastline culminating in one of the most seductive of the islands, the **Île de Bréhat**, and the colourful chaos of the **Côte de Granit Rose**. Inland all roads curl eventually to **Rennes**, the Breton capital, which lies a short way north of the legendary forest of **Brocéliande** (Paimpont), the location of the Arthurian tales.

The frontier towns

If you're entering Brittany by road from Normandy, Maine or Le Mans, you're likely to pass through **Dol-de-Bretagne**, **Fougères**, or close to **Vitré**. All of these were, at one time or another, heavily fortified strategic sites.

Dol-de-Bretagne

During the Middle Ages, **DOL-DE-BRETAGNE**, 30km west of Mont St-Michel, was an important bishopric. It no longer has a bishop, though its huge granite **cathedral** endures, with its strange, squat, tiled towers. Alongside is the **Musée Historique de Dol** (Easter–Sept daily 2.30–6pm), bloated by the usual array of posed waxworks but with two rooms of astonishing wooden bits and pieces rescued in assorted states of decay from churches, often equally rotting, all over Brittany. These carvings and statues, some still brightly polychromed with their crust of eggy paint, range from the thirteenth to the nineteenth centuries.

Dol still has a few streets packed with venerable buildings, most notably the pretty **Grande-Rue**, where one Romanesque edifice dates back as far as the eleventh century, alongside an assortment of 500-year-old half-timbered houses that look down on the bustle of shoppers below.

All approaches to Dol from the bay are guarded by the former island of **Mont Dol**, now eight rather marshy kilometres in from the sea. This abrupt granite outcrop, looking mountainous beyond its size on such a flat plain, was the legendary site of a battle between the Archangel Michael and the Devil. Various fancifully named indentations in the rock, such as the "Devil's Claw", testify to the savagery of their encounter, which as usual the Devil lost. The site has been occupied since prehistoric times – flint implements have been unearthed alongside the bones of mammoths, sabre-toothed tigers, and even rhinoceroses. Later on, it appears to have been used for worship by the Druids, before becoming, like Mont St-Michel, an island monastery, all traces of which

A BRETON GLOSSARY

Estimates of the number of Breton-speakers range from 400,000 to 800,000. You may well encounter it spoken as a first, day-to-day language by the very old and the young in parts of Finistère and the Morbihan. Learning Breton is not really a viable prospect for visitors without a grounding in Welsh, Gaelic or some other Celtic language. However, as you travel through the province, it's interesting to note the roots of Breton place names, many of which have a simple meaning in the language. Below are some of the most common:

aber	estuary	*hen*	old	*nevez*	sea
bihan	little	*hir*	long	*parc*	new
bran	hill	*inis*	island	*mor*	field
braz	big	*ker*	town or house	*penn*	end, head
creach	height	*koz*	old	*plou*	parish
cromlech	stone circle	*lan*	church	*pors*	port, farmyard
dol	table	*lann*	heath	*roch*	stone
dolmen	stone table	*lech*	flat stone	*ster*	river
du	black	*mario*	dead	*stivel*	fountain, spring
gavre	goat	*men*	stone	*trez*	sand, beach
goat	forest	*menez*	mountain	*trou*	valley
goaz	stream	*menhir*	long stone	*ty*	house
guen	white	*meur*	big	*wrach*	witch

have long vanished. A plaque proclaims that visiting the small chapel on top earns a Papal Indulgence. The climb is pleasant, too, a steep footpath winding up among the chestnuts and beeches to a solitary bar.

There is not a great deal to keep casual visitors in Dol for very long. However, the **tourist office**, at 3 Grande-Rue (July & Aug daily 9.30am–12.30pm & 2.30–7.30pm; Easter–June & Sept daily 10.30am–noon & 3.30–7pm; Oct–Easter Thurs 2–4pm; ☎02.99.48.15.37), can direct you eastwards to a very reasonable **hotel**, the *Bretagne*, next to the market at 17 place Chateaubriand (☎02.99.48.02.03; ②; closed Oct). Rooms at the back look out across a small vestige of ramparts towards Mont Dol. The best **campsite** nearby is the *Vieux Chêne* (April–Sept; ☎02.99.48.09.55), 3km east towards Baguer-Pican on RN176.

A couple of nice **fish restaurants** can be found in the ancient houses on rue Ceinte, as it winds its way from Grande-Rue to the Cathedral: *Le Porche au Pain* at no. 1, and *La Grabotais* at no. 4 (closed Mon; ☎02.99.48.19.89).

Cancale

Along the coast north of Dol, the pinnacle of Mont St-Michel is clearly visible from every vantage point, of which the most spectacular is the **Pointe du Grouin**, a perilous and windy height which also overlooks the bird sanctuary of the **Îles des Landes** to the east. Just south of the *pointe,* and less than 15km from St-Malo across the peninsula, **CANCALE** should not be missed by those who attribute magical properties to **oysters**. In the old church of **St-Méen** at the top of the hill, the town's obsession is documented with meticulous precision by the small **Musée des Arts et Traditions Populaires** (July & Aug Mon 2.30–6.30pm, Tues–Sun 10am–noon & 2.30–6.30pm; June & Sept Thurs–Sun 2.30–6.30pm, and groups by appointment; ☎02.99.89.79.32; 15F). Cancale oysters were found in the camps of Julius Cæsar, taken daily to Versailles for Louis XIV, and even accompanied Napoléon on the march to Moscow.

From the rue des Parcs next to the jetty of the port, you can see the *parcs* where the oysters are grown at low tide. The rocks of the cliff behind are streaked and shiny like mother-of-pearl; underfoot the beach is littered with countless generations of empty shells. The port area is very pretty and very smart, with a long line of upmarket glass-fronted hotels and restaurants. Cancale's **hotels** mostly insist that you eat if you want to stay; among the best value are *Le Phare* (☎02.99.89.60.24; ③) and the *Émeraude* (☎02.99.89.61.76; ④) – both set above their own restaurants, at numbers 6 and 7 respectively on quai Thomas – and *La Houle*, 18 quai Gambetta (☎02.99.89.62.38; ②). *Au Pied de Cheval*, 10 quai Gambetta (☎02.99.89.76.95), is an informal place to sample a few oysters, with great baskets of them spread across its wooden quayside tables. A dozen raw oysters on a bed of seaweed cost from 26F.

Fougères

FOUGÈRES lies on the main Caen–Rennes road, a town that has a topography impossible to grasp from a map; streets that look a few metres long turn out to be precipitous plunges down the escarpments of its split-levelled site, and lanes collapse into flights of steps. The most dominant feature of Fougères is its robust **castle**, built well below the level of the main part of town, on a low spit of land that separates, and is towered over by, two mighty rock faces. Its massive and seemingly impregnable bulk is protected by great curtain walls growing out of the rock, and encircled by a hacked-out moat full of weirs and waterfalls – none of which prevented its repeated capture by such medieval adventurers as du Guesclin. It is, however, eighteenth-century Fougères that is always featured in the summer-night theatrical performances at the château, based on the book that immortalized the town, Balzac's *The Chouans*. It tells, in rampant best-seller vein, the story of the counter-revolutionary Chouan rebellion in Brittany during the early 1790s, and makes great play of the strange layout of the town. Within the castle, the focus is more prosaic, and footwear – the main industry of the town – is presented in a **museum** included in the hourly château tours (castle open mid-June to mid-Sept daily 9am–7pm, no tours noon or 1pm; April to mid-June & second fortnight of Sept daily 9.30am–noon & 2–6pm; Oct–March daily 10am–noon & 2–5pm; 30F).

The best approach to the castle is from **place des Arbres** beside St-Léonard's church off the main street of the old fortified town. The formal terraces give way to the water meadows of the River Nançon, which you can cross beside a little cluster of medieval houses still standing on the river bank. Alternatively, on the longer route down rue Nationale, you'll pass the **Musée de La Villéon** at no. 51, which commemorates an Impressionist who painted numerous memorable Breton landscapes (mid-June to Aug Wed–Sun 10.30am–12.30pm & 2.30–6.30pm; Easter to mid-June & first fortnight of Sept Sat & Sun 11am–12.30pm & 2.30–5pm; free).

The **Forêt de Fougères**, a short way out on the D177 towards Vire (see p.365), is one of the most enjoyable in the province. The beech woods are spacious and light, with various megaliths and trails of old stones scattered in among the chestnut and spruce. It's quite a contrast to their normal bleak and windswept haunts to see dolmens sporting themselves in such verdant surroundings.

Practicalities

Fougères's **tourist office**, at 1 place Aristide-Briand, provides copious information on all aspects of the town and local countryside (July & Aug Mon–Sat 9am–7pm, Sun 10am–noon & 2–4pm; Sept–June Mon–Sat 9.30am–12.30pm & 2–6pm, Sun 10am–noon & 2–4pm; ☎02.99.94.12.20). The *Grand Hôtel des Voyageurs*, nearby at 10 place Gambetta (☎02.99.99.08.20; ②; closed second fortnight of Aug) is a particularly nice place to stay, with an excellent restaurant downstairs (closed Sat). There are no hotels in the immediate vicinity of the château, but the squares on all sides are crammed with an abundance of appealing bars and crêperies. At *La Table du Roy* (☎02.99.99.77.37), which has lots of outdoor seating beside the moat, 50F buys a plate of *moules frites* and a glass of wine, and there are dinner menus at 82F and 98F.

Vitré

VITRÉ, just north of the Le Mans–Rennes motorway, rivals Dinan as the best-preserved medieval town in Brittany. Its walls are not quite complete, but the thickets of medieval stone cottages that lie outside them have hardly changed. The towers of the **castle** itself have pointed slate-grey roofs in best fairy-tale fashion, looking like freshly sharpened pencils, though, unfortunately, the municipal offices and **museum** of shells, birds, bugs and local history inside are not exactly thrilling (July–Sept daily 10am–12.30pm & 2–6.15pm; April–June daily 10am–noon & 2–5.30pm; Oct–March Wed–Fri 10am–noon & 2–5.30pm, Sat–Mon 2–5.30pm; 26F).

Vitré is a market town rather than an industrial centre, with its principal **market** held on Mondays in the square in front of **Notre-Dame church**. The old city is full of twisting streets of half-timbered houses, a good proportion of which are bars; **rue Beaudrairie** in particular has a fine selection.

Vitré's **gare SNCF** is a little way south of the centre, where the ramparts have disappeared and the town blends into its newer sectors. Nearby is the **tourist office** (July & Aug daily 10am–7pm; Sept–June Mon–Fri 10am–noon & 1.30–6pm, Sat 10am–noon; ☎02.99.75.04.46), and most of the **hotels** too. Both the *Petit-Billot*, 5 place du Général-Leclerc (☎02.99.75.02.10; ②), and *Chêne-Vert*, 2 place de Gaulle (☎02.99.75.00.58; ①; closed late Sept to late Oct), are good value, while rooms on the higher floors of the *Hôtel du Château*, 5 rue Rallon (☎02.99.74.58.59; ②; closed Sun out of season), on a quiet road just below the castle, have views of the ramparts.

Of the **restaurants**, *Le St-Yves*, immediately below the castle at 1 place St-Yves (☎02.99.74.68.78), serves menus from 55F to 175F; the 75F one should suit most requirements. *La Soupe aux Choux*, at the top of rue de la Baudrairie at 32 rue Notre-Dame (☎02.99.75.10.86; closed Tues), prepares simple but classic French food, with 45F lunches.

St-Malo

ST-MALO, walled and built with the same grey granite stone as Mont St-Michel, 45km east, presents its best face to the sea; if you are not planning to arrive by ferry, consider the ten-minute shuttle across the River Rance from Dinard as an alternative to get a perspective on the town. The city was originally a fortified island at the mouth of the Rance, controlling not only the estuary but the open sea beyond. For centuries its pirate-mariners forced English ships passing up the Channel to pay tribute. They brought wealth from further afield, too. Jacques Cartier, who colonized Canada, lived in and sailed from St-Malo, and the Argentinian name for the Falklands, *las Malvinas*, derives from the islands' first French colonists, *les Malouins*.

These days, St-Malo is more visited than anywhere in Brittany – and not just for the use of its ferry terminal. The *intra-muros* streets of the **old citadelle** are a unique experience: at times they can be sombre and grim (particularly beneath grey skies), but in high summer or at sunset they become light and almost unreal. Much of what you see today has been lovingly and precisely rebuilt stone by stone, as eighty percent of the city was destroyed in August 1944.

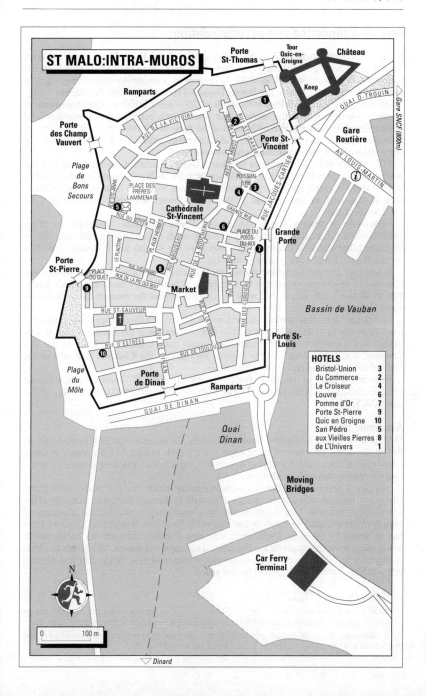

ST MALO:INTRA-MUROS

Porte St-Thomas

Tour Quic-en-Groigne

Château

Keep

Ramparts

QUAI D-TROUIN

▷ Gare SNCF (800m)

Porte des Champ Vauvert

RUE DE LA VICTOIRE

Porte St-Vincent

Gare Routière

AV LOUIS MARTIN

Plage de Bons Secours

PLACE DES FRÈRES-LAMMENAIS

POISSON-ERIE

Cathédrale St-Vincent

GRANDE RUE

RUE JACQUES-CARTIER

RUE DU BOYER

RUE STE-ANNE

PLACE DU POIDS-DU-ROI

Grande Porte

PL. AUX HERBES

RUE BROUSSAIS

RUE DE LA BOUCHERIE

Porte St-Pierre

LE PLAOTRE

RUE THÉVENARD

RUE DE LA PIE QUI BOIT

PLACE DU GUET

RUE DE LA HERS

Market

RUE DES CORDIERS

Bassin de Vauban

RUE ST-SAUVEUR

RUE DE DINAN

RUE DE TOULOUSE

RUE D'ESTRÉES

Porte St-Louis

Plage du Môle

Porte de Dinan

Ramparts

QUAI DE DINAN

Quai Dinan

HOTELS

Bristol-Union	3
du Commerce	2
Le Croiseur	4
Louvre	6
Pomme d'Or	7
Porte St-Pierre	9
Quic en Groigne	10
San Pédro	5
aux Vieilles Pierres	8
de L'Univers	1

Moving Bridges

Car Ferry Terminal

N

0   100 m

▽ Dinard

Arrival, information and accommodation

St-Malo's helpful **tourist office** (July & Aug Mon–Sat 8.30am–8pm, Sun 10am–7pm; April–June & Sept Mon–Sat 9am–7pm, Sun 10am–noon & 2–6pm; Oct–March Mon–Sat 9am–noon & 2–6pm; ☎02.99.56.64.48) is housed in a single-storey building, right in front of the city walls, beside the Bassin Duguay-Trouin in the Port des Yachts.

Officially, the **gare routière** (☎02.99.40.83.33) – not a building, just an expanse of concrete – is right next to the tourist office (see above), but most buses, whether local or long-distance, coincide also with trains at the **gare SNCF**(☎02.99.40.70.20), 2km out from the citadelle on place Hermine, and convenient neither for the old town nor the ferry (take care if you're planning a tight connection).

TIV (☎02.99.40.83.33) run buses to Dinard, Dinan, Cancale, Combourg and Rennes, while Les Courriers Bretons, 13 rue d'Alsace (☎02.99.56.79.09), go to Cancale, Mont St-Michel and Fougères, and also run day-trips to Mont St-Michel (summer daily 9.30am; Wed & Sat only in low season; 108F). Dinan buses are also operated by CAT (☎02.96.39.21.05).

Saint-Malo is always busy with **boats**. From the Gare Maritime du Naye (☎02.99.40.64.41), Brittany Ferries sail to Portsmouth (mid-March to mid-Nov, daily at 10.45am; otherwise less frequently; journey time 8hr 45min) and Plymouth (mid-Nov to mid-March, Fri at noon; journey time 8hr).

In summer, regular passenger **ferries to Dinard** operate from the **quai Dinan**, just outside the westernmost point of the ramparts in front of the port (Émeraude Lines; ☎02.99.40.48.40; 20F single, 30F return). The trip across the estuary takes an all-too-short ten minutes.

Émeraude Lines also conduct excursions up the river to Dinan (see p.380), day-trips from Granville in Normandy (see p.353), and cruises along the Brittany coast to Cap Fréhel and Cézembre, to the Pointe du Grouin near Cancale, and out to the Îles Chausey. You'll find details of the various services to the **Channel Islands** in the "Travel details" at the end of this chapter.

Bicycles can be rented from Cycles Diazo, 47 quai Duguay-Trouin (☎02.99.40.31.63), Cycles Nicole, 11 rue Robert-Schumann (☎02.99.56.11.06), or the gare SNCF, as usual.

Accommodation

St-Malo boasts over a hundred **hotels**, including the seaside boarding houses just off the beach, along with several **campsites** and a **youth hostel**. In high season it needs every one of them, and if you plan to stay the night before catching a summer ferry, make a reservation well in advance.

You pay a premium for the privilege of staying within the city walls, since that's where any nightlife takes place, and it's a fair walk in through the docks from any of the surrounding suburbs. Unfortunately, the *intra-muros* hotels tend to take advantage of high summer demand by insisting that you eat in their own restaurants. Cheaper rates can be found by the gare SNCF, or in suburban Paramé, although it's hardly worth being away from the citadelle for the sake of saving a few francs. The youth hostel is notoriously busy. The four municipal campsites also tend to be full in July and August, and you may have to travel inland to find space.

HOTELS IN THE CITADELLE

Bristol-Union, 4 place de la Poissonerie (☎02.99.40.83.36). Very correct rooms, in a nice little square facing the former fish market, just off the Grande Rue. Closed mid-Nov to Jan, no restaurant. ③.

du Commerce, 11 rue St-Thomas (☎02.99.56.18.00). Very cheap, very plain, but if you're on a tight budget you can't do better within the walls. Closed Jan to mid-Feb. ②.

Le Croiseur, 2 place de la Poissonerie (☎02.99.40.80.40). Clean and relatively modern place, near the Grande Porte. Open all year, no restaurant. ②.

Hôtel-Restaurant Pomme d'Or, 4 place du Poids-du-Roi (☎02.99.40.90.24). Seventeen modernized rooms in a venerable building, just inside the citadelle near the ramparts – take a sharp left after entering through the Grande Porte. Conventional menus start around 90F. Closed Jan to mid-Feb. ③.

Hôtel-Restaurant Porte St-Pierre, 2 place du Guet (☎02.99.40.91.27). Comfortable *logis*, peeping out to sea over the walls of the citadelle, near the small Porte St-Pierre and handy for the plage de Bon Secours. Menus from 85F upwards. Closed Dec & Jan. ④.

Hôtel-Restaurant de l'Univers, 10 place Chateaubriand (☎02.99.40.89.52). One of the grand hotels that face you immediately upon entering the porte St-Vincent. Some good-value rooms, and an excellent 75F menu in the restaurant downstairs, with tables out on the square opposite the château. Restaurant closed Wed. ③.

Hôtel-Restaurant Aux Vieilles Pierres, 9 rue Thévenard (☎02.99.56.46.80). Bargain-priced six-room hotel, near place aux Herbes. Menus at 88F with fish soup and steak, or 125F for the full spread. ②.

du Louvre, 2 rue des Marins (☎02.99.40.86.62). Pleasant family-run place just off Grande Rue, between the Grande Porte and Cathédrale St-Vincent. Closed Dec to mid-Feb, except Christmas and New Year. ③.

Quic en Groigne, 8 rue d'Estrées (☎02.99.20.22.20). Friendly little hotel at the far end of the citadelle, with nicely styled en-suite rooms. ④.

San Pédro, 1 rue Ste-Anne (☎02.99.40.88.57). Small, 12-room refurbished hotel in a nice quiet setting, just inside the walls in the north of the citadelle, near the porte des Bés. Rooms on the higher floors enjoy sea views. ③.

HOTELS OUTSIDE THE WALLS

Arrivée, 52 bd de la République (☎02.99.56.30.78). Budget hotel on a corner very near the gare SNCF. Open all year, no restaurant. ②.

Le Beaufort, 25 Chaussée du Sillon, Paramé (☎02.99.40.99.99). Sea view hotel, unfortunately half an hour's walk from the citadelle, with modernized rooms – some with lovely balconies – and a good restaurant. ④.

Les Charmettes, 64 bd Hébert, Paramé (☎02.99.56.07.31). One of Paramé's cheaper options, not on the front itself, though a few rooms have sea views, but very near the beach and the imposing *Grand Hôtel*. Closed Jan, no restaurant. ②.

de l'Europe, 44 bd de la République (☎02.99.56.13.42). Year-round cheap but clean rooms in a genuinely friendly (if noisy) hotel, near the gare SNCF. ②.

La Rance, 15 quai Sebastopol, St-Servan (☎02.99.81.78.63). Small, tasteful option in sight of the Tour Solidro, with 11 spacious rooms and no restaurant. ④.

HOSTEL AND CAMPSITES

Centre Patrick Varangot, 37 rue du Père-Umbricht, Paramé (☎02.99.40.29.80). Also known as the *Centre des Rencontres Internationals*, this is one of the busiest hostels in France, though not formally part of the national network; 2km northeast of the gare SNCF on Paramé's main street, a short way back from the beach (bus #1, #2 or #5). Dorm beds 69F, private doubles 164F; no curfew.

La Cité d'Aleth, Saint-Servan (☎02.99.81.60.91). Much the nearest campsite to the citadelle, on the headland southwest of Saint-Malo. Open all year. Reachable in summer on bus #1.

Les Ilôts, av de la Guimorais, Rothéneuf (☎02.99.56.98.72). July & Aug only. Inland, to the northeast.

Le Nicet, av de la Varde, Rothéneuf (☎02.99.40.26.32). June–Aug only. On the coast by Pointe de Nicet. Reservations essential.

Les Nielles, av John Kennedy, Paramé (☎02.99.40.26.35). Mid-June to Aug only. On the beach at the plage du Minhic.

The citadelle and suburbs

The **citadelle** of St-Malo, very much the prime destination for visitors, was for many years joined to the mainland only by a long, single causeway, before the original line of the coast was hidden forever by the construction of the harbour basin. Although its streets of restored seventeenth- and eighteenth-century houses can be crowded to the point of absurdity in summer, away from the more popular thoroughfares random exploration is fun. You can surface to the sunlight on the ramparts to enjoy wonderful views all round, especially to the west as the sun sets over the sea.

Besides the prominent **Grande Porte**, the main gate of the citadelle is the **Porte St-Vincent**. The town **Musée de la Ville** in the castle to the right (Easter–Sept daily 10am–noon & 2–6pm; Oct–Easter daily except Mon 10am–noon & 2–6pm; 25F) is something of a hymn of praise to the "prodigious prosperity" enjoyed by St-Malo during its days of piracy, colonialism and slave trading. Climbing the 169 steps of the castle keep, you pass a fascinating mixture of maps, diagrams and exhibits – chilling handbills from the Nazi occupation, accounts of the "infernal machine" used by the English to blow up the port in 1693, and savage four-pronged *chausse-trappes*, thrown by pirates onto the decks of ships being boarded to immobilize their crews.

You can pass under the ramparts at a couple of points and onto the open shore, where a huge **beach** stretches away beyond the rather featureless resort-suburb of **Paramé**. When the tide is low, the most popular walk is out to the small island of **Grand-Bé** – sometimes you even need to queue to get onto the short causeway. Solemn warnings are posted of the dangers of attempting to return from the island when the tide has risen too far – if you're caught there, there you have to stay. The island "sight" is the tomb of the nineteenth-century writer-politician **Chateaubriand** (1768–1848), who was described by Marx as "the most classic incarnation of French *vanité* . . . the false profundity, Byzantine exaggeration, emotional coquetry . . . a never-before-seen mishmash of lies". Suitably enough he features heavily on all the tourist brochures, which – with no apparent irony – extol his "modesty" in choosing so "isolated" a burial spot.

St-Servan, within walking distance along the corniche south of the citadelle, was the city's original settlement, converted to Christianity by St-Malou (or Maclou) in the sixth century; later, in the twelfth century, they moved to the impregnable island we now call St-Malo. The town curves round several small inlets and beaches to face the river. It's dominated by the distinctive **Tour Solidor**, which consists of three linked towers built in 1382, and in cross-section looks just like the ace of clubs. Originally known in Breton as the *Steir Dor*, or "gate of the river", it now holds a museum of Cape Horn clipper ships, open all year for ninety-minute guided visits (Easter–Sept daily 10am–noon & 2–6pm; Oct–Easter daily except Mon 10am–noon & 2–6pm; 20F). Most of the great European explorers of the Pacific are covered, from Magellan onwards, but naturally the emphasis is on French heroes such as Bougainville, who was responsible for spreading the brightly-coloured bougainvillea plant around the globe. Tours culminate with a superb view from the topmost ramparts.

Follow the main road due south from St-Servan, ignoring signs for the Barrage de la Rance – or take bus #5 from the gare SNCF – and at a roundabout high above town you'll come to the new **Grand Aquarium** (mid-June to mid-Sept, daily 9am–9pm, 50F; mid-Sept to mid-June, daily 9.30am–6pm; 44F). This postmodern structure can be a bit bewildering at first, but once you get the hang of it it's an entertaining place, where you can either learn interesting facts about slimy monsters of the deep or simply pull faces back at them. Its eight distinct fish tanks include one shaped like a Polo mint, where dizzy visitors stand in the hole in the middle as myriad fish whirl around them. There's actually another aquarium, logically enough named the **Petit Aquarium**, set into the walls of the old city, but this is far superior.

For last-minute **shopping**, St-Malo's citadelle contains a few specialists, but buying in any quantity is best done in Le Continent **hypermarket** on the southwest outskirts of the town. There are **markets** in both St-Malo (*intramuros*) and St-Servan on Tuesdays and Fridays, and in Paramé on Wednesdays and Saturdays.

Eating

Intramuros St-Malo boasts even more **restaurants** than hotels, with a long crescent lining the inside of the ramparts between the Porte St-Vincent and the Grande Porte. Prices are probably higher than anywhere else in Brittany, however, especially on the open café terraces – the demand is inflated by day-trippers and ferry-passengers having last-night blowouts. Bear in mind that most of the crêperies also serve *moules* and similar quasi-snacks. All the restaurants listed below are in the citadelle.

Astrolabe, 8 rue des Cordiers (☎02.99.40.36.82). Quality cuisine, down a few steps just south of the Grande Porte. Lunch costs 80F, while in the evening you can compose your own menu from the extensive *carte*. 135F can buy a superb spread, with, for example, some sensational grilled langoustines and a *gratin du Granny-Smith* from the wide range of lush desserts. Serves until late, open all year, but closed all day Mon & Tues lunchtime.

Le Chalut, 8 rue de la Corne du Cerf (☎02.99.56.71.58). Exclusive dining room, in a stylish blue-painted bistrot a short way in from the porte St-Vincent. A small 95F menu offers the catch of the day, otherwise you pay 175F or 300F for gourmet fish dinners. Closed Mon, plus Sun pm between Sept and June.

Le Chasse Marée, 4 rue Grout de St-Georges (☎02.99.40.85.10). Nautical decor and haute cuisine, just round the corner from the post office, with a few tables out on the quiet street and more upstairs. The 87F menu, served until 9pm, has oysters followed by red mullet or coley; the 145F features a scallop and duck salad to start, and a mixed fish grill or fish couscous; for 190F you can pick at will from the à la carte menu, so half a lobster is a possibility. Closed Sun, plus Sat pm in low season.

Crêperie la Brigantine, 13 rue de Dinan (☎02.99.56.82.82). Sweet and savoury pancakes at very reasonable prices – the seafood fillings are exceptional. An individual crêpe can cost under 10F, and there's a 58F full menu. Closed Tues pm, Wed in low season, and mid-Jan to mid-Feb.

Delauney, 6 rue Ste-Barbe (☎02.99.40.92.46). Between Porte St-Vincent and Cathédrale St-Vincent. Formerly owned by Jean-Paul Delauney, it has changed hands (albeit within the family) to Brigette and Didier Delauney, but the traditional French cooking remains to the same high standard. The cheapest menu is 125F, served at lunchtime and 7–8pm only; otherwise menus start at 138F. Closed Sun.

Duchesse Anne, 5–7 place Guy-la-Chambre (☎02.99.40.85.33). Right next to the Porte St-Vincent. The best known of St-Malo's upmarket restaurants, which continues to work hard to keep up its reputation – and its prices. There are no set menus; you might manage to get a lunch for under 100F, but dinner will be well over 200F. Whole baked fish is the main speciality. Closed Wed, plus Sun pm in low season, and all Dec & Jan.

Dinard

The former fishing village of **DINARD** sprawls around the western approaches to the Rance estuary, just across from St-Malo but a good twenty minutes away by road. While it might not feel out of place on the Côte d'Azur, with its casino, spacious villas and social calendar of regattas and ballet, here in Brittany it's a little incongruous. Its nineteenth-century metamorphosis was largely thanks to the tastes of the affluent English and Americans, though these days age rather than nationality seems to be the common factor uniting most of its summer influx of tourists. Although Dinard is a hilly town, undulating over a succession of pretty little coastal inlets, it attracts great numbers of older visitors; as a result, prices tend to be high, and pleasures sedate.

Central Dinard faces north to the open sea, across the curving bay that holds the attractive **plage de l'Écluse**. As so often, the buildings that line the waterfront are, with the exception of the casino in the middle, venerable Victorian villas rather than hotels or shops, and so the beach itself has a low-key atmosphere, despite the summer crowds. An unexpected **statue of Alfred Hitchcock** dominates its main access point; standing on a giant egg, with a ferocious-looking bird perched on each shoulder, he was placed here to commemorate the town's annual festival of English-language films.

Enjoyable **coastal footpaths** lead off in either direction from the principal beach, enlivened by notice boards holding reproductions of paintings produced at points along the way. It may well come as a surprise to see that Pablo Picasso's *Deux Femmes Courants sur la Plage* and *Baigneuses sur la Plage*, both of which look quintessentially Mediterranean with their blue skies and golden sands, were in fact painted here in Dinard during his annual summer visits throughout the 1920s. The path that heads east leads up to the Pointe du Moulinet for views over to St-Malo, and then as the **Promenade du Clair de Lune** continues past the tiny and now-exclusive port, and down to the estuary beach, the plage du Prieuré.

Practicalities

Full information on Dinard can be picked up from the **tourist office**, in the centre at 2 bd Féart (July & Aug daily 9.30am–7.30pm; Easter–June & Sept Mon–Sat 9am–12.15pm & 2–7pm; Oct–Easter Mon–Sat 9am–12.15pm & 2–6pm; ☎02.99.46.94.12). Many visitors simply come over for the day on one of the regular Émeraude Lines **boats** from St-Malo; tickets can be bought in Dinard a couple of hundred metres east of the tourist office at 27 av George-V, above the pleasure port.

Dinard tends to be an expensive place to stay, but it does have a wide selection of **hotels** to choose from, including the central and very English *Hôtel-Restaurant Altair*, 18 bd Féart (☎02.99.46.13.58; ③), a little way inland from the tourist office, and two nice places near the pleasure port. The *Hôtel-Restaurant Printania*, 5 av George-V (☎02.99.46.13.07; ②; closed mid-Nov to mid-March), on the quiet street as it drops to the port, has a magnificent terrace restaurant, looking over towards St-Malo; the *Hôtel-Restaurant de la Vallée*, 6 av George-V (☎02.99.46.13.58; ③), unfortunately faces the wrong way for views of St-Malo, and its most basic rooms look straight onto a bare cliff. **Campsites** include the municipal *Port Blanc*, also near the plage du Port-Blanc on rue du Sergent-Boulanger (☎02.99.46.10.74; April–Sept), and *La Ville Mauny* (☎02.99.46.94.73; mid-April toSept), in the woods southwest of the centre.

Dinan

The wonderful citadel of **DINAN** has preserved almost intact its three-kilometre encirclement of protective masonry, with street upon colourful street of late medieval houses within. Like St-Malo, it's best seen when arriving by boat up the River Rance, where you can see its castle and fortifications to their best advantage. Behind the houses on the left bank quay where the boats tie up, a steep and cobbled street with fields and bramble thickets on either side climbs up to the thirteenth-century ramparts, partly hidden by trees.

Arrival, information and accommodation

Both the Art Deco **gare SNCF** (☎02.96.39.22.39) and the **gare routière** (☎02.96.39.21.05) are in the rather gloomy modern quarter, on place du 11-Novembre, ten minutes' walk west of the walled town. Dinan's **tourist office** is very central, in the sixteenth-century *Hôtel Kératry* at 6 rue de l'Horloge (mid-June to Sept Mon–Sat 9am–7pm, Sun 10am–12.30pm & 3–5.30pm; Oct to mid-June Mon–Sat 9am–12.30pm & 2–6pm; ☎02.96.39.75.40).

In summer, **boats** along the Rance take two and a half hours to sail between the port downstream and Dinard and St-Malo, with the exact schedule varying according to the tides (adults 95F; under-13s 60F). It's only possible to do a day return by boat (adults 130F; under-13s 75F) if you start from St-Malo or Dinard; starting from Dinan, you'd have to come back by bus or train. For details, contact Émeraude Lines in Dinan, on the quai de la Rance (☎02.96.39.18.04), Dinard (☎02.99.46.10.45) or St-Malo (☎02.99.40.48.40).

HOTELS AND B&BS

Arvor, 5 rue Pavie (☎02.96.39.21.22). Renovated eighteenth-century town house, facing the tourist office, with some surviving flourishes of the convent that previously occupied the site. Smart, well-equipped rooms, and free parking. No restaurant. ③.

Bed & Breakfast, 55 rue de Coëtquen (☎02.96.85.23.49). Very friendly English-run B&B just southwest of the city walls, with one en-suite double bedroom. ③.

Café-Hôtel du Théâtre, 2 rue Ste-Claire (☎02.96.39.06.91). Very simple rooms above a bar, right by the tourist office and Théâtre des Jacobins, and under the same efficient management as the nearby *Restaurant Cantorbery* (see below). ①.

Hôtel-Restaurant Duchesse Anne, 10 place du Guesclin (☎02.96.39.09.43). Comfortable if not luxurious rooms on the quieter side of the square, above a basic restaurant where set menus start at 62F. ②.

Logis de Jerzual, 25 rue du Petit Fort (☎02.96.85.46.54). Chambres d'hôte on the exquisite little lane that leads up from the port, halfway up to the porte du Jerzual. Garden terrace looking down on the street. Inaccessible by car, so deathly quiet in the mornings. ③.

de l'Océan, 9 place du 11-Novembre (☎02.96.39.21.51). Extremely convenient and well-run (if rather basic) hotel, outside the walls opposite the gare SNCF. No restaurant. ①.

de la Porte Saint-Malo, 35 rue St-Malo (☎02.96.39.19.76). Very comfortable rooms in a tasteful small hotel just outside the walls, beyond the porte St-Malo. No restaurant. ②.

du Vieux St-Sauveur, 19 place St-Sauveur (☎02.96.85.30.20). Ancient edifice facing the St-Sauveur church, with a slightly noisy bar downstairs, but four nicely equipped and very good value en-suite rooms upstairs. No restaurant. ②.

YOUTH HOSTEL AND CAMPSITE

HI youth hostel, Moulin de Méen, Vallée de la Fontaine-des-Eaux (☎02.96.39.10.83). 2km from the gare SNCF and unfortunately not on any bus route; to walk there, follow the quay downstream from the port on the town side. Dorm bed 49F.

Camping Municipal, 103 rue Châteaubriand (☎02.96.39.11.96). Just outside the western ramparts. June–Sept.

The town

For all its slightly unreal perfection, Dinan is not excessively overrun with tourists. There are no very vital museums; the monument is the town itself, and time is best spent wandering from crêperie to café, admiring overhanging houses along the way. Unfortunately, you can only walk along one small stretch of the ramparts, from the Jardin Anglais behind St-Sauveur church to a point just short of Tour Sillon overlooking the river. You can get a good general overview from the **Tour de l'Horloge** (April–Sept, daily 10am–7pm; 14F), dating from the end of the fifteenth century.

As you might guess from its blending of two separate towers, the fourteenth-century **keep** that once protected the town's southern approach was built by Estienne Le Tour, architect of St-Malo's Tour Solidor (see p.378). It's now known as the **Château de Duchesse Anne**, with a small **local history museum** housed in the ancient Tour Coëtquen (June to mid-Oct daily 10am–6.30pm mid-Oct to May daily except Tues 1.30–5.30pm; 20F). On the lower floor, a group of stone fifteenth-century notables looks for all the world like a medieval time capsule, about to de-petrify at any moment.

St-Sauveur church, very much the town's focus, is a real mixture of ages, with a Romanesque porch and an eighteenth-century steeple. Even its nine Gothic chapels feature five different patterns of vaulting in no symmetrical order, and the most complex pair, in the centre, would make any spider proud. A cenotaph contains the heart of Bertrand du Guesclin, the fourteenth-century Breton warrior (and later Constable of France) who fought and won a single combat with the English knight Thomas of Canterbury, in what is now place du Guesclin, to settle the outcome of the siege of Dinan in 1364. Relics of his life and battles are scattered all over Brittany and Normandy; in death, he spread himself between four separate burial places for four different parts of his body (the French kings restricted themselves to three burial sites). North of the church, rue du Jerzual leads down to the gate of the same name and on down (as rue du Petit-Fort) to the port and a majestic old bridge over the Rance, lined with artisans' shops and restaurants.

On the last weekend in September or the first weekend in October – check with the tourist office – the **Fête des Remparts** is celebrated with medieval-style jousting, banquets, fairs and processions, culminating in an immense fireworks display. There's a **market** every Thursday in the places du Champ and du Guesclin (the original medieval fairground).

Eating and drinking

All sorts of specialist **restaurants**, including several ethnic alternatives, are tucked away in the old streets of Dinan. Stroll of an evening through the town and down to the port, and you'll pass at least twenty places. For **bars**, explore the series of tiny parallel alleyways between the place des Merciers and the rue de la Ferronnerie. Along rue de la Cordonnerie, the busiest of the lot, the various hang-outs define themselves by their taste in music: *À la Truye qui File* at no. 14 is a sort of contemporary folky Breton dive, while *Morgan's Tavern*, next door at no. 12, is considerably more raucous.

Le Cantorbery, 6 rue Ste-Claire (☎02.96.39.02.52). Reasonable food served in an old stone house, with rafters, a spiral staircase and a real wood fire. Open every day in season. Lunch from 70F, traditional dinner menus from 98F, with a good 135F option. Closed Sun pm & Mon, plus all Feb.

Chez La Mère Pourcel, 3 place des Merciers (☎02.96.39.03.80). Beautiful half-timbered fifteenth-century house in the central square. The lunch menu, at 97F, is pretty minimal, but for 135F you can get stuffed clams and red mullet in olive cream, and you're up to gourmet class with the exquisitely simple fish on the 162F one. Closed Sun pm, and Mon in low season, and all Feb.

Crêperie Connetable, 1 rue de l'Apport (☎02.96.39.02.52). Magnificent old house opposite the *Mère Pourcel* beside the place des Merciers. Sit if you dare at the pavement tables, where all that prevents the upper storeys from crashing down around your ears are a couple of misshapen pillars. Crêpes and snacks in the perfect spot for people-watching.

Le Relais des Corsaires, 7 rue du Quai, port du Dinan (☎02.96.39.40.17). Just across the road from the waterfront. Restaurant menu from 98F, offering cockles and mussels followed by scallops or monkfish. The good-value grill menu, in theory served in the adjacent *Petit Corsaire* but in low season served in the same building, costs 88F and is "grill" in name only, featuring dishes like leek soufflé and *îles flottantes*. Closed Sun pm & Wed in low season.

Le Saint Louis, 9–11 rue de Léhon (☎02.96.39.89.50). Very good value restaurant just inside the porte St-Louis, specialising in buffets; a 75F menu entitles you to choose at will from extensive buffets of hors d'oeuvres and desserts, while the 89F option offers the same deal plus a conventional main course.

Rennes

For a city that has been the capital and power centre of Brittany since the 1532 union with France, Rennes is – outwardly at least – uncharacteristic of the province, with its Neoclassical layout and pompous major buildings. What potential it had to be a

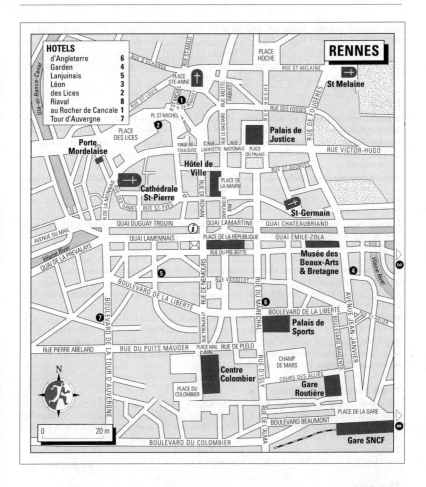

HOTELS

d'Angleterre	6
Garden	4
Lanjuinais	5
Léon	3
des Lices	2
Riaval	8
au Rocher de Cancale	1
Tour d'Auvergne	7

picturesque tourist spot was destroyed in 1720, when a drunken carpenter managed to set light to virtually the whole city. Only the area known as **Les Lices**, at the junction of the canalized Ille and the River Vilaine, was undamaged. The remodelling of the rest of the city was handed over to Parisian architects, not in deference to the capital but in an attempt to rival it.

Arrival, information and accommodation

Rennes' modern **gare SNCF** (☎02.99.65.50.50), on the express TGV line between Paris and Brest, is well south of the Vilaine, fifteen minutes' walk from the central **tourist office** on the Pont de Nemours (Mon 1–6pm, Tues–Sat 9am–6pm; ☎02.99.79.01.98). Just east of the gare SNCF stands the new **gare routière** on bd Solferino, but most local buses start and finish on or near place de la République, alongside the tourist office. Rennes is a busy junction, with direct services to St-Malo (TIV; ☎02.99.79.23.44), Dinan and Dinard (Armor Express; ☎02.99.50.64.17), Mont St-Michel (Courriers Bretons; ☎02.99.56.79.09) and Nantes (Societé Transports Tourisme de l'Ouest; ☎02.40.20.45.20).

Unfortunately, there are very few **hotels** in the old part of Rennes – and those that there are can be very hard to find. If you've arrived by train or bus, it's easier to settle for staying near the gares SNCF and routière.

Hotels

d'Angleterre, 19 rue du Maréchal-Joffre (☎02.99.79.38.61). Not brilliant, but scrupulously maintained and relatively cheap, a short way south of the river towards the station. No restaurant. ①.

Garden Hôtel, 3 rue Duhamel (☎02.99.65.45.06). Comfortably, nicely decorated and very personal hotel, north of the gare SNCF not far from the river, with a pleasant little garden café but no restaurant. ④.

Hôtel-Restaurant Au Rocher de Cancale, 10 rue St-Michel (☎02.99.79.20.83). Four-room hôtel on a lively pedestrian street, between place Ste-Anne and place St-Michel, in the heart of medieval Rennes. Beautifully restored ground floor, modern facilities upstairs. The restaurant (closed Sat & Sun), has menus from 62F at lunchtime and 90F in the evening. ②.

Lanjuinais, 11 rue Lanjuinais (☎02.99.79.02.03). Standard refurbished upmarket hotel, on a quiet little street just around the corner from the tourist office, less than 50 metres south of the river. No restaurant. ③.

de Léon, 15 rue de Léon (☎02.99.30.55.28). Quiet little 11-room hotel, off the beaten track northeast of the gare SNCF, offering old-fashioned but adequate rooms at knockdown rates. ①.

des Lices, 7 place des Lices (☎02.99.79.14.81). Forty rooms, all with TV, in a very comfortable and friendly modern hotel on the edge of the prettiest part of old Rennes, very convenient for the place des Lices parking. No restaurant. ③.

Riaval, 9 rue de Riaval (☎02.99.50.65.58). Friendly hotel with neat budget rooms, well away from the centre, but only a few minutes walk east of the gare SNCF, on a quiet street. No restaurant. ①.

Tour d'Auvergne, 20 bd de la Tour-d'Auvergne (☎02.99.30.84.16). Simple but welcoming option, above a little brasserie ten minutes' walk from the tourist office. Some low-priced rooms have ensuite shower facilities. No restaurant. ①.

Youth hostel and campsite

HI youth hostel: Centre International de Séjour, 10–12 Canal St-Martin (☎02.99.33.22.33). With a cafeteria and a laundry; 3km out from the centre, next to the Canal d'Ille et Rance. Buses #20 and #22 run weekdays only from the gare SNCF, direction "St-Gregoire", stop Coëtlogon; at weekends catch bus #2. Year-round.

Camping municipal des Gayeulles, rue de Professeur-Maurice-Audin (☎02.99.36.91.22). 1km east of central Rennes; take bus #3. April to mid-Oct.

The city

Rennes' surviving **medieval quarter**, bordered by the canal to the west and the river to the south, radiates from **Porte Mordelaise**, the old ceremonial entrance to the city, now more prominently exposed following building work in 1990. A few streets from the porte, the **place des Lices** is dominated by two empty market halls, but originally it was the venue for tournaments – that is, jousting "lists". It was here, in 1337, that the hitherto unknown Bertrand du Guesclin, then aged 17, fought and defeated several older opponents. This set him on his career as a soldier, during which he was to save Rennes when it was under siege by the English. However, after the Bretons were defeated at Auray in 1364, he fought for the French, and twice invaded Brittany.

The one central building to escape the 1720 fire was the **Palais de Justice** on rue Hoche downtown. Ironically, however, the Palais was all but ruined by a major conflagration in 1994; the exact circumstances remain somewhat mysterious, but it's thought the blaze was sparked by a stray flare set off during a demonstration by Breton fishermen.

The entire structure has been concealed ever since behind plastic screens, and reconstruction is not expected to finish any time soon.

The **south bank** of the river is every bit as busy, if not busier, than the north – should you feel upon arriving that Rennes feels oddly empty, the chances are that everyone's in the giant **Colombier Centre**, just west of the gare SNCF. This vast new mall is Rennes at its most modern, packed with shops of all kinds, plus cafés and snack bars, and featuring an amazing crystal model of itself in its main entrance hall. Slightly nearer the river, **rue Vasselot** has its own array of half-timbered old houses.

Two major museums are housed in former university buildings at 20 quai Émile-Zola, on the south bank of the Vilaine (both open daily except Tues 10am–noon & 2–6pm; 25F combined ticket). The **Musée de Bretagne** (15F) introduces visitors to the history and culture of Brittany, with an emphasis on ancient times. Its prehistoric section kicks off with the bones of a woolly rhinoceros found at Dol, then ranges via stone axes and bronze swords to a model of the Cairn du Barnenez (see p.393) and an extraordinary bronze Goddess of Ménéz-Hom dated to the first century AD. Later displays include the marriage contract drawn up for Duchess Anne and Charles VIII of France, and nineteenth-century costumes from all over Brittany, but, disappointingly, there's no attempt to cover the last hundred years.

The **Musée des Beaux-Arts** (20F), entered via the same lobby, also reaches back a few millennia, featuring Egyptian, Greek, Etruscan and Roman artefacts. However, many of its finest art works, which include drawings by Leonardo da Vinci and Botticelli, are not usually on public display. Instead you'll find indifferent Impressionist views of Brittany by the likes of Boudin and Sisley, interspersed with the odd treasure such as Pieter Boel's startlingly modern-looking seventeenth-century animal studies, Pierre-Paul Ruben's *Tiger Hunt*, and Picasso's *Baigneuse à Dinard*.

Eating and drinking

Most of Rennes' more interesting **bars**, **restaurants** and **nightlife** in general are to be found in the streets just south of place Ste-Anne and St-Aubin church. Rues St-Michel and Penhoët, each with a fine assemblage of ancient wooden buildings, are the epicentre at the moment, while ethnic alternatives can be found along rue St-Malo just to the north. While you're exploring, look around the back of the excellent crêperie at 5 place Ste-Anne, through an archway off rue Motte-Fablet, to get an extraordinary glimpse of medieval high-rise housing.

Rue Vasselot is the nearest equivalent south of the river, though if you're just looking for a quick snack, don't forget the various outlets in the Centre Colombier.

L'Auberge St-Sauveur, 6 rue St-Sauveur (☎02.99.79.32.56). Classy romantic restaurant, in an attractive medieval house near the cathedral, with rich, meaty dinner menus at 110F and 165F and lighter lunches for 60F. Closed Sat lunchtime & Sun.

La Chope, 3 rue de la Chalotais (☎02.99.79.34.54). A little way below place de la République on the south side of the river. Classic, busy brasserie open until midnight every day except Sunday, serving meals from 85F upwards.

Le Chouin, 12 rue d'Isly (☎02.99.30.87.86). A fine fish restaurant, not far from the gare SNCF. Menu 99F midday, à la carte in the evening. Closed Sun and Mon.

Le Khalifa, 20 haut de la place des Lices (☎02.99.30.87.30). Assorted Moroccan dishes, served outside or in an atmospheric dining room. Couscous and brochettes 59F and up, tajine 69F, as well as various set menus. Closed Sat lunchtime & Sun.

Le Parc à Moules, 8 rue George-Dattin (☎02.99.31.44.28). On a small street leading north from the river halfway between the tourist office and the place des Lices. Mussels from Mont-St-Michel Bay cooked in twelve different delicious ways for around 45F, and a weekday lunch menu offering *moules frites* for 49F, plus more expensive fishy dishes. Closed Sat lunch & Sun.

La Tourniole, 37 rue Vasselot (☎02.99.79.05.91). Lovely, very traditional small restaurant halfway between the gare SNCF and the river, offering a hearty 65F set lunch and dinner menus that start at 85F. Fish, meat and even vegetarian specialities prepared to perfection. Closed Sun and Mon.

Entertainment and nightlife

Rennes is seen at its best in the first ten days of July, when the **Festival des Tombées de la Nuit** takes over the whole city to celebrate Breton culture with music, theatre, film, mime and poetry in joyful rejection of the influences of both Paris and Hollywood (information from 8 place du Maréchal-Juin, 35000 Rennes; ☎02.99.30.38.01). In the first week of December, the **Transmusicales** rock festival attracts big-name acts from all over France and the world at large, though still with a Breton emphasis (☎02.99.31.12.10).

The varied season of the Théâtre National de Bretagne, 1 rue St-Helier (☎02.99.31.55.33), runs from mid-October to mid-June. All year round, in a different auditorium on the same premises, *Club Ubu* (☎02.99.30.31.68) puts on large-scale gigs. Live **jazz** gigs take place daily except Sundays at *Déjazey Jazz Club*, 54 rue Saint-Malo (☎02.99.38.70.72). The *Barantic*, 4 rue St-Michel, is one of the city's favourite **bars**, putting on occasional live music for a mixed crowd of Breton nationalists and boisterous students; if you don't like the look of it, or it's too full, there are half a dozen similar alternatives within spitting distance.

The friendly bookshop Co-op Breizh at 17 rue Penhöet (☎02.99.79.01.87) has cassettes of Breton and Celtic music along with books and posters, while L'Arvor cinema at 29 rue d'Antrain (☎02.99.38.72.40) shows *v.o.* (original language) films.

The Forêt de Paimpont

Thirty kilometres to the west of Rennes, the **Forêt de Paimpont**, known also by its ancient name of Brocéliande, is – according to song and legend – the forest of the wizard Merlin. Medieval Breton minstrels, like their Welsh counterparts from whom or with whom the stories originated, set the tales of King Arthur and the Holy Grail both in Grande Bretagne and here in Petite Bretagne. For all the magic of these shared legends, however, and a succession of likely sites, few people come out here. If you like the idea of roaming around for a day it isn't difficult. The bus from Rennes to Guer runs twice a day past the southern edge of the forest, stopping at Forges-les-Paimpont, and another bus runs, around the north corner, to **MAURON**.

Mauron is a good point to start. From the hamlet of **FOLLE-PENSÉE**, just south of the village, it's a circuitous but enjoyable twenty-minute walk to **La Fontaine de Barenton** – Merlin's spring. The path leads off from the end of the road at Folle-Pensée, turning to the right, running through pines and gorse to a junction of forest tracks: here, take the track straight ahead for about 100m, where an unobvious path to the left goes into the woods and turns back north to the spring – walled, and filled by the most delicious water imaginable, as you might expect from the elixir of eternal youth. After drinking, stroke the great stone slab beside the spring to call up a storm, roaring lions and a horseman in black armour. Here Merlin first set eyes on Vivianne, who bound him willingly in a prison of air.

The Fountain of Eternal Youth is hidden nearby and accessible only to the pure in heart. Another forest walk, more scenic but without a goal, is the **Val sans Retour** (the Valley of No Return), off the GR37 from Tréhorenteuc to La Guette. The path to follow leads out from the D141 just south of Tréhorenteuc to a steep valley from which exits are barred by thickets of gorse and giant furze on the rocks above; at one point it skirts an overgrown table of rock, the **Rocher des Faux Amants**, from which the seductress Morgane le Fay supposedly enticed unwary boys.

Accommodation in the forest

The little market village of **PAIMPONT** is the most obvious and enjoyable base for exploring the forest. It's right at the centre of the woods, backs onto a marshy lake whose shores are thick with wild mushrooms (*cèpes*), and has some excellent **accommodation**. At the *Relais de Brocéliande* in town (☎02.99.07.81.07; ②), a real flower-bedecked delight, you can stuff yourself for 120F in the restaurant under the gaze of stuffed animal heads. There are also a couple of **campsites** in the heart of the forest, including the municipal one on the edge of the village (☎02.97.07.89.16; May–Sept), a gîte d'étape-cum-chambre d'hôte in tiny Trudeau on the D40 (☎02.99.07.81.40; dorm beds 49; B&B ③), and a lovely **youth hostel**, at Le Choucan-en-Brocéliande, a couple of kilometres out on the Concoret road (April to mid-Oct; ☎02.97.22.76.75; 49F). Information on them all can be picked from the summer-only **tourist office** next to the lakeside abbey (June–Sept Mon–Fri 10am–1pm & 2.30–6pm; ☎02.99.07.24.83).

The north coast from Dinard to Lannion

The coast that stretches from St-Malo to Finistère at the far western end of Brittany is divided into two distinct regions either side of the bay of **St-Brieuc**. First come the exposed green headlands of the **Côte d'Émeraude**; beyond St-Brieuc itself the shore is more extravagantly indented, with a succession of secluded little bays and an increasing proliferation of huge pink granite boulders seen at their best on the **Côte de Granit Rose** near Perros-Guirec.

The Côte d'Émeraude

To the west of the Rance, beyond Dinard, begins the green of the **Côte d'Émeraude**. Though composed mainly of developed family resorts, it also offers wonderful camping, at its best around the heather-backed beaches near **Cap Fréhel**. Camping is forbidden within 5km of the headland itself, a high, warm expanse of heath and cliffs with views extending on good days as far as Jersey and the Île de Bréhat. The **Fort la Latte**, to the east, is used regularly as a film set. Its tower, containing a cannonball factory, is accessible only over two drawbridges (guided tours: June–Sept daily 10am–12.30pm & 2.30–6.30pm; Oct–May Sun & hols 2.30–5.30pm; 15F).

The nearest places to stay are the ideal, isolated **campsite** at Pléherel, the *Camping du Pont L'Étang* (☎02.96.41.40.45; May–Sept), and a basic summer-only **youth hostel** on the D16 just outside Plévenon en route towards the Cap – full address Kérivet-en-Frehel, La Ville Hardrieux (☎02.96.41.48.98; mid-April to mid-Sept).

Erquy

Further round the headland, the perfect crescent of beach at **ERQUY** curves through more than 180 degrees. At low tide, the sea disappears way beyond the harbour entrance, leaving gentle ripples of paddling sand. Adventurers equipped with suitable boots could walk right across its mouth, from the grassy wooded headland on the left side over to the picturesque little lighthouse at the end of the jetty on the right.

Erquy's **tourist office** on the boulevard de la Mer (mid-June to mid-Sept daily 9.30am–12.30pm & 2–7pm, mid-Sept to mid-June daily except Mon 9.30am–12.30pm & 2–5pm; ☎02.96.72.30.12) co-ordinates information for the surrounding area. The *Hôtel Beauséjour*, 21 rue de la Corniche (☎02.96.72.30.39; closed Sun pm & Mon in winter; ③), has a good view of the bay, and excellent fish dinners from 78F, while the more upmarket **restaurant** *L'Escurial* (closed Sun pm & Mon; ☎02.96.72.31.56) by the seafront serves a five-course menu (for 200F) that consists entirely of **scallops**, the town's speciality. There are several **campsites** on the promontory (dotted with tiny coves) that leads to the Cap d'Erquy north of town, including the *St-Pabu* (☎02.96.72.24.65; April–Oct) right beside the sea.

Le Val-André

The huge beach in the broader bay of **LE VAL-ANDRÉ** is of finer, sweeter-smelling sand, and the endless pedestrian promenade that stretches along the seafront feels oddly Victorian, consisting solely of huge old houses undisturbed by shops or bars. However, Le Val-André is definitely more of a town than Erquy, and rue A-Charner, running parallel to the sea one street back, is busy with holiday-makers in summer.

Le Val-André's helpful **tourist office** (July & Aug Mon–Sat 9am–12.30pm & 2.30–6pm; Sept–June Mon–Fri 9am–noon & 2.30–5pm; ☎02.96.72.20.55) is located in the modern casino at the very centre of the waterfront. Of its **hotels**, the tastefully refurbished *Hôtel de la Mer*, 63 rue A-Charner (☎02.96.72.20.44; ①; closed Jan), uses a fine muscadet to transport *moules marinières* onto a hitherto undreamed-of plane. However, with the success of the business many guests find themselves having to sleep in the characterless *Nuit et Jour* motel, run by the same management. The similar-looking but slightly more imposing *Hôtel Regina*, slightly nearer the centre at 45 rue A-Charner (☎02.96.72.22.63; ②), is a more dependable if perhaps less exciting choice.

St-Brieuc

The major city on the Côte d'Émeraude, **ST-BRIEUC** is far too busy being the industrial centre of the north to concern itself with entertaining tourists. It's an odd-looking city, with two very deep wooded valleys spanned by viaducts at its core, and it's almost impossible to bypass. The streets are hectic, with the town centre cut in two by a virtual motorway and unrelieved by any public. Motorists and cyclists, unfortunately, have little choice but to plough straight through rather than attempting to negotiate the backroads and steep hills around. Apart from the sturdy-looking **St-Stephen's cathedral**, the fine views of the valley from **Tertre Aubé** and a handful of half-timbered houses in the streets around place au Lin, there's nothing to keep you here.

If you decide to use the city as a base, the best place to **stay** is the central *Champ du Mars*, 13 rue du Général-Leclerc (☎02.96.33.60.99; ③), which offers mussels as well as fish soup for around 40F in the old-fashioned, green-painted brasserie downstairs. St-Brieuc also has a **youth hostel**, 2km out, in the magnificent fifteenth-century Manoir de la Ville-Guyomard (☎02.96.78.70.70), on bus route #1 from the station. Some of the nicest **eating** options in town are in the old quarter, behind the cathedral. The traditional French cooking at *Le Madure*, 14 rue Quinquaine (☎02.96.51.20.17; closed Sun & Mon), is served à la carte, with steaks around 87F and salads half that; the fondues at *Le Chaudron*, 19 rue Fardel (☎02.96.33.01.72; closed Sun & Wed lunchtime) start at 80F per person.

North from St-Brieuc

Moving northwest towards Paimpol, the coast becomes wilder and harsher and the seaside towns tend to be crammed into narrow rocky inlets or set well back in river estuaries. **BINIC** is a narrow port surrounded by meadows, with a thin strip of beach and the decent (if relatively pricey) *Hôtel Benhuyc*, 1 quai Jean-Bart (☎02.96.73.39.00; ④), while at the sedate family resort of **ST-QUAY-PORTRIEUX**, a little further on, the *Gerbot d'Avoine* (☎02.96.70.40.09; ③; closed Jan), beside the beach, is the best place to stay, despite the hideous decor of its rooms.

After St-Quay, the coastal road shifts inland, through **PLOUHA**, the traditional boundary between French-speaking and Breton-speaking Brittany. It's a viable proposition to hitch from here to **KERMARIA-AN-ISQUIT**, signposted off the D21 from Plouha, to see the extraordinary medieval frescoes of a *Danse Macabre* in the thirteenth-century **chapel** of the village. They show Ankou, who is death or death's assistant, leading representatives of every social class in a Dance of Death. An encounter between three living nobles out hunting and three philosophical corpses is also depicted, and there's a statue of the infant Jesus refusing milk from Mary's proffered breast. In summer, the caretaker, Mme Hervé Droniou, usually keeps the church open (daily 9am–noon & 2–6pm; donation); at other times, you have to find her in the house just up the road on the left to let you in.

Paimpol

Back on the north coast, **PAIMPOL** is still an attractive town with a tangle of cobbled alleyways and fine grey-granite houses, but has lost something in its transition from working fishing port to pleasure harbour. It was once the centre of a cod and whaling fleet that sailed to Iceland each February, sent off with a ceremony marked by a famous *pardon*. From then until September the town would be empty of its young men. The whole area was commemorated in Pierre Loti's book, *Pêcheur d'Islande*; the author, and his heroine, lived in the **place du Martray** in the centre of town.

Thanks to naval shipyards and the like, the open sea is not visible from Paimpol; a maze of waterways leads to its two separate harbours. Both are usually filled with the high masts of yachts, but are still also used by the fishing vessels that keep a fish market and a plethora of *poissonneries* busy. This is doubtless a very pleasant place to arrive by boat, threading through the rocks, but from close quarters the tiny port area is a little disappointing, very much rebuilt and quite plain. Even so, it is always lively in summer.

A couple of kilometres short of town, the D786 passes the substantial ruins of the **Abbaye de Beauport** (mid-June to mid-Sept daily 10am–7pm, with regular 90-min guided tours; mid-Sept to mid-June daily except Tues 10am–noon & 2–5pm; 25F), established in 1202 by Count Alain de Goëlo. The abbey is currently being restored, but the main appeal for visitors is the sheer romance of its setting. Its stone walls are covered with wild flowers and ivy, the central cloisters are engulfed by a huge tree, and birds fly everywhere. The Norman Gothic chapterhouse is the most noteworthy building to survive, but wandering through and over the roofless halls you may spot architectural relics from all periods of its history. Footpaths lead down through the salt meadows where the monks raised their sheep to the sea, offering the same superb views of the hilltop abbey that must have been appreciated by generations of arriving pilgrims.

Possible places to **stay** in Paimpol include the luxurious *Repaire de Kerroc'h*, overlooking the small-boat harbour from quai Morand (☎02.96.20.50.13; ④), which serves gourmet meals from 85F up to 350F; the very hospitable *Hôtel Berthelot* at 1 rue du Port (☎02.96.20.88.66; ②); and the plainer *Hôtel Origano*, just back from the front at 7bis rue du Quai (☎02.96.22.05.49; ③). A year-round HI **youth hostel** in the grand old *Château de Kerraoul* (☎02.96.20.83.60) offers dorm beds for around 65F and has facilities for **camping**.

As for **restaurants**, *La Cotriade*, on the far side of the harbour on the quai Armand-Dayot (☎02.96.20.81.08; closed Wed eve & Thurs) is the best bet for authentic fish dishes, with a simple 88F menu, including a *véritable Cassoulet Paimpolais* and a 150F menu that features a delicious crab mousse.

The Île de Bréhat

Two kilometres off the coast at Pointe de l'Arcouest, 6km northwest of Paimpol, the **ÎLE DE BRÉHAT** – in reality two islands joined by a tiny bridge – gives the appearance of spanning great latitudes. On the north side are windswept meadows of hemlock and yarrow, sloping down to chaotic erosions of rock; on the south, you're in the midst of palm trees, mimosa and eucalyptus. All around is a multitude of little islets – some accessible at low tide, others *propriété privée*, most just pink-orange rocks. All in all, this has to be one of the most beautiful places in Brittany.

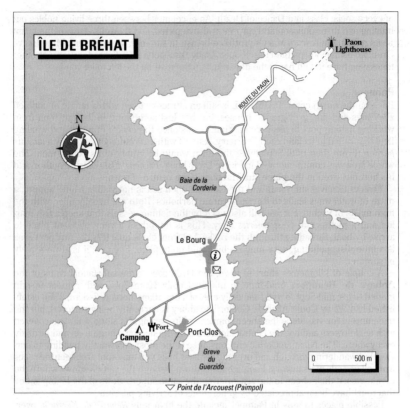

ÎLE DE BRÉHAT

Paon Lighthouse

ROUTE DU PAON

N

Baie de la Corderie

D 104

Le Bourg (i) ⊠

⚑ 🏰 Fort
Camping   Port-Clos

Greve du Guerzido

0   500 m

▽ Point de l'Arcouest (Paimpol)

As you might expect, this island paradise has attracted Parisians and the like looking for holiday homes. Over half the houses now have temporary residents, and young Bréhatins leave in ever-increasing numbers for lack of a place of their own, let alone a job. In winter the remaining 300 or so natives have the place to themselves, without even a *gendarme*; the summer sees two imported from the mainland, along with upwards of 3000 tourists. As a visitor, though, you should find the Bréhatins friendly enough – it's the holiday-home owners that they really resent.

The beach to swim from at low tide is the **Grève de Guerzido,** on the east side facing the mainland. Near **LE BOURG**, or Bréhat village, which is the centre of all activity on the island, the sea tends to be a bit murky, and the east coast generally is less accessible because of private property. But in the north, even when Le Bourg is blocked up with visitors, you can walk and laze about in near solitude. Bréhat no longer has a castle (blown up twice by the English), but it does have a **lighthouse** and a nineteenth-century **fort**, in the woods near the campsite (see below).

Practicalities

Bréhat is connected regularly by **ferry** from the Pointe de l'Arcouest, 6km northwest of Paimpol and served by buses in summer from the gare SNCF there. Sailings, with Vedettes de Bréhat (☎02.96.55.86.99), are roughly hourly in high summer, and every two hours for the rest of the year, with the first boat out to Bréhat at 8.30am in summer, and last boat back at 7.45pm; the round-trip costs 40F. The same company also operates boats in summer from Binic and St-Quay-Portrieux (see p.388), and Erquy (see p.387). In addition, up to three daily 45-minute guided **boat tours** circle the island (April–Sept; 70F).

No cars are permitted on the island, and there's barely a road wide enough for its few light farm vehicles. You can rent **bikes** by the day at the ferry port (or take one with you for 50F; to do so in summer you have to catch a ferry before 10am), but it's easy to walk from one end to the other in half an hour.

The **tourist office** is in the old mairie in the main square in Le Bourg (Mon–Sat 10am–1pm & 3–6pm; ☎02.96.20.04.15). The three **hotels** are expensive and tend to be permanently booked through the summer, while all close for at least part of the winter. Both the *Vieille Auberge* in Le Bourg (☎02.96.20.00.24; ④; closed Nov–March) and the *Bellevue* in Port-Clos (☎02.96.20.00.05; ⑤; closed Jan to mid-Feb) insist on demi-pension in high season. There's also a wonderful **campsite** in the woods high above the sea west of the port (☎02.96.20.00.36; mid-June to mid-Sept); when that's closed you can pitch your tent almost anywhere.

Restaurants are neither numerous nor cheap – though *La Potinière* on the beach at Guerzido (☎02.96.20.00.29) serves inexpensive *moules frites* – so many visitors prefer to buy picnic food at the small market that's held most days in Le Bourg.

The Côte de Granit Rose

The whole of the northernmost stretch of the Breton coast, from Bréhat to **Trégastel**, has loosely come to be known as the **Côte de Granit Rose**. There are indeed great granite boulders scattered in the sea around the island of Bréhat, and at the various headlands to the west, but the most memorable stretch of coast lies around **Perros-Guirec**, where the pink granite rocks are eroded into fantastic shapes.

Tréguier

The D786 turns west from Paimpol, passing over a green ria on the bridge outside Lézardrieux before arriving at **TRÉGUIER**, one of the very few hill-towns in Brittany. Its central feature is the **Cathédrale de St-Tugdual**, which contains the tomb of St Yves, a native of the town who died in 1303 and – for his incorruptibility – became the patron saint of lawyers. Attempts to bribe him continue to this day; his tomb is surrounded by marble plaques and an inferno of candles invoking his aid.

The *Hôtel-Restaurant d'Estuaire* on the waterfront (☎02.96.92.30.25; ①) is a nice place to **stay** – the sea views are great – with reasonable menus from 70F; *La Poissonnerie du Trégor*, up in town at 2 rue Renan (☎02.96.92.30.27), is an excellent fish **restaurant** that's no more expensive. During the **market** each Wednesday, clothes and so on are spread out in the square by the cathedral, and food and fresh fish down by the port.

Château de la Roche-Jagu

About 10km inland from Tréguier, on a heavily wooded slope above the Trieux river, stands the fifteenth-century **Château de la Roche-Jagu** (July & Aug daily 10am–7pm; Easter–June & Sept–Oct daily 10.30am–noon & 2–6pm; 35F). It's a gorgeous building, a harmonious combination of fortress and home, that plays host to lavish annual exhibitions, usually on some sort of Celtic theme. The rooms within are bare, but climb right up to the top to admire the beautiful woodwork of the restored eaves, and walk the two long indoor galleries, offering tremendous views over the river.

Perros-Guirec and Ploumanac'h

PERROS-GUIREC is the most popular resort along this coast, though not perhaps the most exciting, consisting largely of a network of tree-lined avenues of suburban villas.

It does stand, however, at one end of the long **Sentier des Douaniers** pathway, which winds round the clifftops to the tiny resort of **PLOUMANAC'H** past an astonishing succession of deformed and water-sculpted rocks. Birds wheel overhead towards the offshore bird sanctuary of Sept-Îles, and battered boats shelter in the narrow inlets or bob uncontrollably out on the waves. There are patches and brief causeways of grass, clumps of purple heather and yellow gorse. Occasionally the rocks have crumbled into a sort of granite grit to make up a tiny beach; one boulder is strapped down by bands of ivy that prevent it rolling into the sea.

Hotels in Perros-Guirec itself include the old-fashioned *Les Violettes*, 19 rue du Calvaire (☎02.96.23.21.33; ②), which has a seriously cheap restaurant, and two with sea views, the *Gulf Stream*, high on the hillside at 26 rue des Sept-Îles (☎02.96.23.21.86; closed mid-Nov to March; ②), and the *Bon Accueil*, 11 rue de Landerval (☎02.96.23.25.77; ④), which has a gourmet restaurant. Ploumanac'h offers the *Hôtel du Parc* (☎02.96.91.40.80; ③; closed mid-Jan to mid-Feb) and the luxurious *Les Rochers* (☎02.96.91.44.49; ④; closed Oct–Easter). The nicest place to **camp** has to be *Le Ranolien* (☎02.96.91.43.58; March to mid-Nov), backing onto the Sentier des Douaniers near a little beach about halfway around, but directly accessible on the other side by road.

Trégastel and Trébeurden

Of the smaller villages further round the coast to the west, **TRÉGASTEL**, with a couple of campsites, including the *Tourony* by the beach (☎02.96.23.86.61; Easter–Sept), and **TRÉBEURDEN**, with the *Le Toëno* **youth hostel** (☎02.96.23.52.22; open all year), are functional stopovers. Trégastel has managed to squeeze in an **aquarium** under a massive pile of boulders, and has a couple of huge lumps of pink granite slap in the middle of its fine beach.

The strangest sight along this coast, however, outdoing anything the erosions can manage, is just south of Trégastel on the **route de Calvaire**, where an old stone saint halfway up a high calvary raises his arm to bless or harangue the gleaming white discs and puffball dome of the **Pleumier-Bodou Telecommunications Centre**. A new pink granite "dolmen" commemorates its opening by De Gaulle in 1962, when it was the first receiving station to pick up signals from the American Telstar satellite. The centre is no longer operational, and has been re-modelled as a **Museum of Telecommunications** that's also known as **Cosmopolis** (July & Aug daily 10am–7pm; May & June daily 10am–6pm; April daily except Sat 10am–6pm; Sept Sun–Fri 10am–6pm, Sat 2–6pm; otherwise peculiar hours which include being closed Sat Oct–March, & closed Sun in most of Nov & Jan; 43F). Inside the golf-ball itself, the **Radôme**, frequent spectacular *son et lumière* shows explain the history of the whole ensemble, and there's also a smaller **planetarium** alongside. One final incongruous note is struck by the reconstructed **Gaulish village** nearby (same hours; additional donation 15F), which is designed to raise money for a French charity working in Africa, and thus incorporates some traditional huts from Togo.

The Bay of Lannion

Despite being significantly back from the sea on the estuary of the River Léguer, **Lannion** gives its name to the next bay west along the Breton coast – and it's the bay rather than the town that is most likely to impress visitors. One enormous beach stretches from **St-Michel-en-Grève**, which is little more than a bend in the road, as far as **Locquirec**; at low tide you can walk hundreds of metres out on the sands.

Lannion

LANNION, set amid plummeting hills and stairways, is a historic city with streets of medieval housing and a couple of interesting old churches – but it's also a centre for a burgeoning and extremely high-tech telecommunications industry, and one of modern

Brittany's real success stories, hence its rather self-satisfied nickname, *ville heureuse* or "happy town". In addition to admiring the half-timbered houses around the **place de Général-Leclerc** and along **rue des Chapeliers**, it's well worth climbing from the town up the 142 granite steps which lead to the twelfth-century Templar **Église de Brélévenez**. This church was remodelled three hundred years later to incorporate a granite bell tower, and the views from its terrace are quite stupendous.

The *Hôtel Bretagne* at 32 av de Général-de-Gaulle (☎02.96.37.00.33; ③; closed Sat & Sun eve out of season), opposite the station, is a *logis* with a good restaurant; the *Porte de France*, an eighteenth-century coaching inn at 5 rue Jean-Savidan (☎02.96.46.54.81; ③), is a more luxurious option with no restaurant. There's also a year-round **youth hostel**, *Les Korrigans*, conveniently positioned very near the station and the town centre at 6 rue du 73e-Territorial (☎02.96.37.91.28).

Locquirec

LOCQUIREC, across the bay from Lannion, manages to have beaches on both sides, without ever quite being thin enough to be a real peninsula. Around the main port, smart houses stand in sloping gardens, looking very southern English with their whitewashed stone panels, grey slate roofs and jutting turreted windows. On the last Sunday in July, Locquirec holds a combined *pardon de St-Jacques* and Festival of the Sea.

Locquirec veers dangerously close to being over-twee, and none of its **hotels** is all that cheap either – although the *Grand Hôtel des Bains*, 15 rue de l'Église (☎02.98.67.41.02; ⑦) has so gorgeous a setting that perhaps it doesn't matter. Nearby, the *Hôtel du Port* (☎02.98.67.42.10; ②; closed Dec–Easter) also enjoys a sea view, and the municipal **campsite**, a kilometre south along the corniche (mid-April to mid-Sept; ☎02.98.67.40.85), is beautifully positioned, too.

The Cairn du Barnenez

At the mouth of the Morlaix estuary, 6km north of Plouézoch, the prehistoric stone **Cairn du Barnenez** surveys the waters from the summit of a hill (July & Aug daily 10am–1pm & 2–6.30pm; April–June & Sept daily 10am–12.30pm & 2–6.30pm; Oct–March daily 10am–noon & 2–5pm; 25F). As on the island of Gavrinis in the Morbihan (see p.430), its ancient masonry has been laid bare by recent excavations, and provides a stunning sense of the architectural prowess of the megalith builders. Radiocarbon testing has shown the work here to date back to around 4500 BC, which makes this one of the oldest large monuments in the world.

The ensemble consists of two distinct stepped pyramids. Each rises in successive tiers, built of large flat stones chinked with pebbles; the second was added onto the side of the first, and the two are encircled by a series of terraces and ramps. The whole thing measures roughly 70m long by 15–25m wide and 6m high. Both pyramids were long buried under the same eighty-metre-long earthen mound. While the actual cairns are completely exposed to view, most of the passages and chambers that lie within them are sealed off. The two minor corridors that are open simply cut through the edifice from one side to the other, and were exposed by quarrying activities around thirty years ago – which inadvertently provided a good insight into the construction methods. Local tradition has it that one tunnel runs right through this "home of the fairies", and continues out deep under the sea.

FINISTÈRE – LAND'S END

It's hard to resist the appeal of the **Finistère coast**, with its ocean-fronting cliffs and headlands. Summer crowds may detract from the best parts of the **Crozon peninsula** and the **Pointe de Raz**, but there are many kilometres of coast where you can enjoy near solitude. If you've transport, explore the semi-wilderness of the **northern stretches** beyond Brest and the little fishing village of **Le Conquet**, or the misty offshore islands of **Ouessant and Molène**. From the top of **Ménez-Hom** you can admire the anarchic limits of western France, and in the two cities of **Morlaix** and **Quimper**, you'll witness distinctly Breton modern life as well as ancient splendours. Of these, the **parish closes** south of Morlaix reveal much of the mythology of the medieval past.

Roscoff

The opening of the deep-water port at **ROSCOFF** in 1973 was part of a general attempt to revitalize the Breton economy. The ferry services to Plymouth and to Cork are intended not just to bring tourists, but also to revive the traditional trading links between the Celtic nations of Brittany, Ireland and southwest England – links which were suppressed for centuries as an act of French state policy after the union of Brittany with France in 1532. In fact, Roscoff has long been a major port. It was here that Mary Queen of Scots landed in 1548 on her way to Paris to be engaged to François, the son and heir of Henri II of France. And it was here that Bonnie Prince Charlie, the Young Pretender, landed in 1746 after his defeat at Culloden.

Roscoff itself has, however, remained a small resort, where almost all activity is confined to **rue Gambetta** and to the **old port** – the rest of the roads are residential backstreets full of retirement homes and institutions. One factor in preserving its old character is that both the ferry port and the gare SNCF are some way from the centre.

The town's main church, **Notre-Dame-de-Croas-Batz** at the far end of rue Gambetta (which becomes rue Amiral-Réveillère), was built in the sixteenth century. Bretons take a particular pride in ornate Renaissance belfries such as the one which embellishes this church, with its sculptured ships and protruding stone cannon. From the side, rows of bells can be seen hanging in galleries, one above the other like a tall, but narrow, wedding cake created by an early Walt Disney. Some way beyond is the grand **Thalassotherapy Institute** of Rock Roum, and a kilometre further on is Roscoff's best **beach**, at Laber, surrounded by expensive hotels and apartments.

The old **harbour** is livelier, mixing an economy based on fishing with relatively low-key pleasure trips to the Île de Batz (see below). The island looks almost walkable; a narrow pier stretches over 300m or 400m towards it before abruptly plunging into deep rocky waters. The Pointe de Bloscon and the white fisherman's chapel, the **Chapelle Ste-Barbe**, make a good vantage point, particularly when the tide is in; the tide goes out a long way (and dictates the embarkation point for the boat trips). Below the headland are the *viviers*, where you can see trout, salmon, lobsters and crabs being reared for the pot.

In 1828, Henri Olivier took onions to England from Roscoff, thereby founding a trade which flourished until the 1930s. In the bar of the *Hôtel du Centre*, you can see old photographs of "Johnnies": men in black berets with strings of onions hanging over the handlebars of their bicycles. Older people of the town travelled as children with their fathers as far afield as Glasgow.

Practicalities

Brittany Ferries **boats** from Plymouth (6hr) or Cork (19hr) dock at the Port de Bloscon (☎02.98.29.28.28), to the east (and just out of sight) of Roscoff. The helpful **tourist office** is at 46 rue Gambetta in town (July & Aug Mon–Sat 9am–12.30pm & 1.30–7pm, Sun 10am–12.30pm; April–June & Sept Mon–Sat 9am–noon & 2–6pm; Oct–March Mon–Fri 10am–noon & 2–5pm, Sat 10am–noon; ☎02.98.61.12.13). Regular trains run to Morlaix, with connections beyond, from the **gare SNCF** (☎02.98.69.70.20), a few hundred metres south of the town proper. Most buses also go from here, including a direct service to Brest run by Les Cars du Kreisker (☎02.98.69.00.93). **Bikes** can be rented from Desbordes François, 13 rue Brizeux (☎02.98.69.72.44), as well as from the gare SNCF.

For a small town, Roscoff is well-equipped with **hotels**, which are well accustomed to late-night arrivals from the ferries. Be warned, however, that most of them close in winter. Very much the obvious places to **eat** are the dining rooms of the hotels themselves, though it's not easy to get a meal much after 9pm.

Hotels

du Centre, 5 rue Gambetta (☎02.98.61.24.25). *Logis de France*, entered via the main street but looking out on the port. Very much a family hotel, also known as *Chez Janie*. Menus from 90F, with a squid salad to start. Closed Jan to mid-Feb. ③.

Les Chardons Bleus, 4 rue Amiral-Réveillère (☎02.98.69.72.03; fax 02.98.61.27.86). Very friendly and helpful hotel with a good restaurant (menus from 90F; closed Thurs Sept–June, plus Sun in winter) but no sea views. Closed Feb. ③.

Hôtel-Restaurant des Arcades, 15 rue Amiral-Réveillère (☎02.98.69.70.45). Sixteenth-century building with superb views from some of its modernized rooms and from the restaurant; menus 58F and upwards. Closed Oct–Easter. ②.

Hôtel-Restaurant le Bellevue, rue Jeanne d'Arc (☎02.98.61.23.38). Seafront *Logis de France*, on the opposite side of the pleasure harbour to the town centre and thus somewhat nearer the ferry terminal. It would in theory be quieter, were it not for the lively downstairs bar. Pleasant rooms, and fine views from the dining room, where the 110F menu offers salmon baked in cheese with mustard. Closed Dec to mid-March. ④.

Les Tamaris, 49 rue É-Corbière (☎02.98.61.22.99; fax 02.98.69.74.36). Renovated, comfortably furnished rooms looking out towards the Île de Batz. No restaurant. Closed Oct–March. ③.

Youth hostel and campsites

HI youth hostel, on the Île de Batz (see below).

Camping municipal de Perharidy, 2km west of town (☎02.98.69.70.86). Just off the route de Santec. May–Sept.

Camping du Manoir de Kerestat, 2km south towards St-Pol (☎02.98.69.71.92). July & Aug only.

The Île de Batz

The **ÎLE DE BATZ** (pronounced *Ba*), just off the coast at Roscoff and inhabited by just under a thousand hardy farmers and fishers, is a somewhat windswept spot, but well endowed with sandy beaches. For **campers** looking to have a stretch of coastline to themselves, it could be ideal.

The island's first recorded inhabitant was a "laidly worm", a dragon that infested the place in the sixth century. Such dragons normally symbolize pre-Christian religions, in this case perhaps a Druidic serpent cult. Allegorical or not, when St Pol arrived to found a monastery he wrapped a Byzantine stole around the unfortunate creature's neck and cast it into the sea. These days, there are no dragons; there aren't even any trees, just an awful lot of seaweed which is collected and sold for fertilizer.

Practicalities

Two separate companies sail very regularly to the Île de Batz from Roscoff all year, for around 30F return; Armein Excursions (☎02.98.61.77.75) and Vedettes de l'Île de Batz (☎02.98.61.78.87). The port is home to the basic *Hôtel-Restaurant Roch Ar Mor* (☎02.98.61.78.28; ②; closed Oct–March), but the **youth hostel**, at the evocatively-named Creach ar Bolloc'h, provides a picturesque alternative (April–Sept; ☎02.98.61.77.69; 65F), and also runs sailing classes.

St-Pol-de-Léon

The main road south from Roscoff passes by fields of the famous Breton artichokes before arriving after 6km at **ST-POL-DE-LÉON**. It's not an exciting place but – assuming you've got your own transport – it has two churches that at least merit a pause. The **Cathédrale**, in the main town square, was rebuilt towards the end of the thirteenth century along the lines of Coutances (see p.353) – a quiet classic of unified Norman architecture. The remains of St Pol are inside, alongside a large bell, rung over the heads of pilgrims during his *pardon* on March 12 in the unlikely hope of curing headaches and ear diseases. Just downhill is the original **Kreisker Chapel**, with access to the top of its sharp-pointed soaring granite belfry (now coated in yellow moss).

Morlaix

MORLAIX, one of the great old Breton ports, thrived off trade with England in between wars during the "Golden Period" of the late Middle Ages. Built up the slopes of a steep valley with sober stone houses, the town was originally protected by an eleventh-century castle and a circuit of walls. Little is left of either, but the old centre remains in part medieval – cobbled streets and half-timbered houses. Its present grandeur comes from the pink-granite viaduct carrying trains from Paris to Brest way above the town centre. Coming by road from the north, the opening view is of shiny yacht masts paralleling the pillars of the viaduct.

Arrival, information and accommodation

The **tourist office** in Morlaix is in a central one-storey building, almost under the viaduct in place des Otages (mid-June to mid-Sept Mon–Sat 9.30am–12.30pm & 1.30–7pm, Sun 10am–12.30pm; mid-Sept to mid-June Tues–Sat 9am–noon & 2–6pm; ☎02.98.62.14.94). All **buses** conveniently depart from place Cornic, right under the viaduct, but the **gare SNCF** (☎02.98.63.56.24) is on rue Armand-Rousseau, high above the town at the western end of the viaduct. To reach it on foot, you have to climb the steep steps of Venelle de la Roche. **Bikes** can be rented from Henri Le Gall, 1 rue de Callac (☎02.98.88.60.47).

In addition to the many (fairly uninspiring) **hotels** in old Morlaix, there's an HI **youth hostel**, 1km from the town centre at 3 route de Paris (☎02.98.88.13.63; year round); take the Kernégues bus to rue de Paris or place Traoulan, and it's just off to the left.

Hotels

de l'Europe, 1 rue d'Aiguillon (☎02.98.62.11.99). Slightly eccentric but very central old place, near the Jacobin convent. While the rooms are modern and well-equipped but not all that characterful, the public spaces, furnished in a variety of styles, are more flamboyant – and the restaurant is superb, with menus from 79F. ②.

Hôtel-Restaurant les Halles, 23 rue du Mur (☎02.98.88.03.86). Friendly little hotel facing the attractive place des Halles, with a garage for motor bikes and bicycles. Closed Sun. Slightly shabby rooms, but they're clean enough, and there's a very good cheap restaurant with menus at 55F and 75F. ②.

du Port, 3 quai de Léon (☎02.98.88.07.54). Bright, modern option, overlooking the port from the left bank. It doesn't have a restaurant, but each room has its own kitchenette – presumably for yacht owners who fancy a night on shore. ②.

Le Roy d'Ys, 8 place des Jacobins (☎02.98.63.30.55). Small central hotel, across the square from the town museum. The cheapest rooms do not have their own showers; guests have to pay 15F extra to use shared showers. No restaurant, but a downstairs bar. Closed Nov. ②.

The town

On her way from Roscoff to Paris, Mary Queen of Scots passed through Morlaix in 1548 and stayed at the **Jacobin convent** that fronts place des Jacobins. She was at the time just five years old, and a contemporary account records that the crush to catch a glimpse of the infant was so great that the inner town's "gates were thrown off their hinges and the chains from all the bridges were broken down". The **Musée des Jacobins** in the convent church contains a reasonably entertaining assortment of Roman wine jars, bits that have fallen off medieval churches, cannon and kitchen utensils, and a few modern paintings (July & Aug Sun, Mon, & Wed–Fri 10am–12.30pm & 2–6.30pm, Sat 2–6.30pm; Easter–June & Sept–Oct Sun, Mon, & Wed–Fri 10am–noon & 2–6pm, Sat 2–6pm; Nov–Easter Sun, Mon, & Wed–Fri 10am–noon & 2–5pm, Sat 2–5pm; 25F).

The **church of St-Mathieu**, off rue de Paris, contains a sombre and curious statue of the Madonna and Child; Mary's breast was apparently lopped off by a prudish former priest, to leave the babe suckling at nothing. The whole statue opens down the middle to reveal a separate figure of God the Father, clutching a crucifix. In April 1993, the figure of Christ was stolen, but the thief, who preferred to pray at home, repented in October 1994 and returned it anonymously.

Duchess Anne of Brittany, who had by then become Queen of France, visited Morlaix in 1506. She is reputed to have stayed at the **Maison de la Reine Anne**, 33 rue du Mur, which, although much restored, does indeed date from the sixteenth century. Its intricate external carvings, and the lantern roof and splendid Renaissance staircase inside, make it the most beautiful of the town's ancient houses, each of its storeys overhanging the square below by a few more centimetres. The house is open to the public in summer (April–Sept Mon–Sat 10.30am–6.30pm), and at other times by arrangement (☎02.98.88.23.26).

Eating

The best hunting ground for **restaurants** in Morlaix is to be found between St-Melaine church and place des Jacobins.

Les Bains Douches, 45 allée du Poan Ben (☎02.98.63.83.83). Small bistrot that doesn't quite live up to its unusual location – set in the former public baths, and reached via a little footbridge across a canal – but makes an attractive spot for a light 59F lunch. Closed lunchtime on Sat & Sun.

Brocéliande, 5 rue des Bouchers (☎02.98.88.73.78). In the southeast of town, beyond the place des Halles and St-Mathieu church. Elegant evening-only dining in a *fin-de-siècle* atmosphere; a typical main course from the choice à la carte menu costs around 75F, as does the cheapest set meal. Closed Tues.

La Dolce Vita, 3 rue Ange-de-Guernisac (☎02.98.63.37.67). Italian place in a pretty central alley, with pizzas mostly priced at 40–50F, plus pasta, salads, and a few conventional seafood and meat dishes. Closed Mon, plus 3 wks in Feb and 2 wks in Oct.

La Marée Bleue, 3 rampe Ste-Mélaine (☎02.98.63.24.21). Well-respected seafood restaurant, a minute's walk up from the tourist office. The 78F menu is a bit limited, but 160F ensures you a superb *assiette de fruits de mer*, and 230F buys a five-course feast. Closed Sun pm & Mon Sept–June.

Nightlife and drinking

Morlaix has recently acquired its own small **brewery**, set up to produce real ale similar to that its owners had enjoyed on visiting Britain. You should be able to find the resultant brew, *Coreff* – it means "beer" – in local **bars**, or you can visit the brewery itself at 1 place de la Madeleine (tours Mon–Wed at 10.30am, 2pm & 3.30pm; ☎98.63.41.92).

Among bars to look out for while you're in Morlaix are *Ty Coz*, at 10 Venelle au Beurre (closed Thurs), near the youth hostel, which has boisterous Bretons playing darts, and draught *Coreff* beer, and the lively *Tempo Piano Bar*, facing the port on quai de Tréguier (☎02.98.63.29.11), where there are regular jazz and blues concerts.

The parish closes

Morlaix makes an excellent base for visiting the countryside towards Brest, where **enclos paroissiaux** (walled churchyards incorporating cemetery, calvary and ossuary) celebrate the distinctive character of Breton Catholicism – closer to the Celtic past than to Rome – in elaborately sculpted scenes. Stone calvaries are covered in detailed scenes of the Crucifixion above a crowd of saints, gospel stories and legends; in richer parishes, a high stone arch leads into the churchyard, adjoining an equally majestic ossuary, where bones would be taken when the tiny cemeteries filled up. Most of the parish closes date from the two centuries either side of the union with France in 1532 – Brittany's wealthiest period – and nothing is more telling of the decline in the province's fortunes. The interiors of the churches are often decorated as richly as the architectural ensemble without, while their villages can be battling against poverty.

The most famous *enclos* are in three neighbouring parishes off the N12 between Morlaix and Landivisiau on a clearly signposted route that's served by an SNCF bus. At **ST-THÉGONNEC**, the entire east wall of the church is a carved and painted retable, with saints in niches and a hundred scenes depicted, but the pulpit and the painted oak entombment in the crypt beneath the ossuary are acknowledged masterpieces. At **LAMPAUL-GUIMILIAU**, the painted wooden baptistry, the dragons on the beams and the suitably wicked faces of the robbers on the calvary are the key components. Poor Katel Gollet (Katherine the Damned) is depicted as being tormented in hell at **GUIM-ILIAU** – for the crime of hedonism rather than manslaughter. In the legend she danced all her suitors to death until the reaper-figure Ankou stepped in to whirl her to eternal damnation. Further on at **LA ROCHE** (15km or so on towards Brest), where the ruined castle above the Elhorn estuary is said to have been her home, it is Ankou who appears on the ossuary with the inscription "I kill you all". If you've got transport, a five-kilometre detour southeast of La Roche brings further variations at **LA MARTYRE** (where Ankou clutches his disembodied head) and its adjoining parish **PLOUDIRY**, the sculpting of its ossuary affirming the equality of social classes – in the eyes of Ankou.

St-Thégonnec makes the best base for a tour of the parish closes. The *Auberge de St-Thégonnec*, 6 place de la Mairie (☎02.98.79.61.18; ④; closed Jan & Feb, Sun eve & Mon), has a superb restaurant, while the *Moulin de Kerlaviou* (☎02.98.79.60.57; ③), is a ravishing farmhouse **B&B** in almost absurdly pastoral riverside setting 2km west of St-Thégonnec.

The abers and the western islands

The coast west of Roscoff is some of the most dramatic in Brittany, a jagged series of **abers** – deep, narrow estuaries – in the midst of which are clustered small, isolated resorts. It's a little on the bracing side, especially if you're making use of the numerous **campsites**, but that just has to be counted as part of the appeal. In summer, at least, the temperatures are mild enough, and things get progressively more sheltered as you move around towards **Le Conquet** and Brest.

Around the abers

If you're dependent on public transport, the only stop on the Roscoff–Brest bus before it turns inland is **PLOUESCAT**. It is not quite on the sea itself, but there are campsites nearby on each of three adjacent beaches; of the hotels, best value is the *Roc'h-Ar-Mor*, right on the beach at Porsmeur (☎02.98.69.63.01; ①; closed Oct–Easter).

BRIGNOGAN-PLAGE, on the next *aber*, has a small natural harbour, once the lair of wreckers, with beaches and weather-beaten rocks to either side, as well as its own menhir. The two high-season **campsites** are the central municipal site at Kéravezan

(☎02.98.83.41.65; June–Sept) and the *du Phare*, east of town (☎02.98.83.45.06; May–Sept), while the hotel *Castel Regis* (☎02.98.83.40.22; ③; closed Oct–March) is expensive but beautifully sited among the rocks, right at the headland. There are also schools of sailing and riding.

The *aber* between Plouguerneau and **L'ABER-WRAC'H** has a stepping-stone crossing just upstream from the bridge at Llanellis, built in Gallo-Roman times, and its long cut stones still cross the three channels of water (access off the D28 signposted "Rascoll"), and continue past farm buildings to the right to "Pont du Diable". L'Aber-Wrac'h itself is a promising place to spend a little time. It's an attractive, modest-sized resort, within easy reach of a whole range of sandy beaches and a couple of worthwhile excursions. Beyond the tiny fishing port, the Baie des Anges stretches away towards the Atlantic, with the only sound the cry of seagulls feasting on the oyster beds. The recently renovated *Hôtel la Baie des Anges* (☎02.98.04.90.04; ④; closed Nov–Easter), commands stunning views out to sea from the start of its vast curve; walk its full length to reach *Le Brennig* at the far end (☎02.98.04.81.12), a lovely restaurant with menus from 90F. A municipal **campsite**, *de Penn Enez* (☎02.98.04.99.82; mid-June to mid-Sept), nestles among the dunes at the very tip of the headland.

For drivers and cyclists there's a beautiful corniche road west of **TRÉMAZAN**, whose ruined castle was the point of arrival in Brittany for Tristan and Iseult. Odd little chapels dot the route, and the views of sea and rocks are unhindered before turning inland just before Le Conquet.

Le Conquet

LE CONQUET, at the far western tip of Brittany, 24km beyond Brest, is a wonderful place, scarcely developed, with a long beach of clean white sand, protected from the winds by the narrow spit of the Kermorvan peninsula. It is very much a working fishing village, with grey-stone houses leading down to the stone jetties of a cramped harbour. It occasionally floods, by the way, causing great amusement to locals who watch the waves wash over cars left there by tourists taking the ferry out to Ouessant and Molène. A good walk 5km south brings you to the lighthouse at **Pointe St-Mathieu**, looking out to the islands from its site among the ruins of a Benedictine abbey. A small exhibition explains the abbey's history, including the legend that it holds the skull of St Matthew, brought here from Ethiopia by local seafarers (July & Aug daily 11am–7pm; June & Sept daily 2.30–6.30pm; April & May Wed, Sat & Sun 2.30–6.30pm; Oct & Nov Wed, Sat & Sun 2–6pm; 10F).

The *Relais du Vieux Port*, quai Drellac (☎02.98.89.15.91; ②), offers three attractive but inexpensive **rooms** right by the jetty in Le Conquet, and has a simple crêperie downstairs. Nearby, the larger *Pointe Ste Barbe* (☎02.98.89.00.26; ②–⑦; closed Mon out of season & mid-Nov to mid-Dec), offers amazing sea views to guests in its more expensive rooms, and has a great restaurant, where menus start at 100F. There are also two well-equipped **campsites**, *Le Théven* (☎02.98.89.06.90; April–Sept) and *Quère* (☎02.98.89.11.71; mid-June to mid-Sept).

The Île d'Ouessant and Île de Molène

The **Île d'Ouessant**, ("Ushant" in English), lies 30km northwest of Le Conquet, and its lighthouse at **Creac'h** (said to be the strongest in the world) is regarded as the entrance to the English Channel. It's at the end of a chain of smaller islands and half-submerged granite rocks. Most are uninhabited, or like **Beniguet** the preserve only of rabbits, but the **Île de Molène**, midway, has a village and can be visited. Both Molène and Ouessant are served by at least one ferry each day from Le Conquet and Brest; however, it is not practicable to visit more than one in a single day.

GETTING TO OUESSANT AND MOLÈNE

Penn Ar Bed (☎02.98.80.24.68) sail to **Ouessant** and **Molène** all year, with up to five daily departures from **Le Conquet** (first sailing at 8am daily in summer; return fare 152F adult, 90F under-17s), and one daily at 8.30am from **Brest** (return fare 180F adult, 108F under-17s). They also depart from **Camaret** at 9am on Wed and Sat from May until mid-July, and daily at 9am from mid-July until the end of August (return fare 164F adult, 98F under-17s).

Finist'Mer operate high-speed ferries to **Ouessant** in summer only, from **Camaret** (☎02.98.27.88.44; return fare 152F adult, 83F under-17s), **Le Conquet** (☎02.98.89.16.61; 140F adult, 72F under-17s) and **Lanildut**, 25km northwest of Brest (☎02.98.04.40.72; 145F adult, 77F under-17s). Bikes cost 65–70F extra. Between mid-May and early July, and in the first week of September, they offer a daily departure from **Camaret** at 8.30am, calling at **Le Conquet** at 9.30am, and another departure from **Le Conquet** at 11.15am. From early July until the end of August, they offer the same morning departure from **Camaret** plus up to seven ferries from **Le Conquet**. Certain summer sailings call in at **Molène** as well. Between mid-July and late August they run an additional service from **Lanildut**, departing at 9.30am daily and taking just half an hour to reach **Ouessant**.

In addition, you can **fly** to Ouessant with **Finist'Air** (☎02.98.84.64.87). The fifteen-minute flights leave **Brest** daily at 8.30am and 5pm in summer, 8.30am and 4.45pm in winter. The adult fare is 350F, under-13s travel half-price, and groups of three or more adults go for 275F each.

Île d'Ouessant

You arrive on the **Île d'Ouessant** at the new **harbour** in the ominous-sounding Baie du Stiff. There is a scattering of houses here and dotted around the island, but the single town – with the only hotels and restaurants – is 4km away at **LAMPAUL**. Everybody from the boat heads there, either by the bus that meets each ferry or on bicycles rented from one of the many waiting entrepreneurs – a good idea, as the island is a bit too big to explore on foot.

Lampaul has not a lot to it and quickly becomes very familiar. The best beaches are sprawled around its bay, and, in case you should forget the perils of the sea, the town cemetery's **war memorial** lists all the ships in which townsfolk were lost, alongside graves of unknown sailors washed ashore and a chapel of wax "*proëlla* crosses" symbolizing the many islanders who never returned.

At nearby **NIOU**, the **Maison du Niou** is actually two houses, one of which is a museum of island history, and the other is a reconstruction of a traditional island house, complete with two massive "box beds", one for the parents and the other for the children (June–Sept daily 10.30am–6.30pm; April & May daily except Mon 2–6.30pm; Oct–March daily except Mon 2–4pm; 15F). Officially, it forms half of the **Eco-Musée d'Ouessant**, in combination with the **Creac'h lighthouse** (May–Sept daily 10.30am–6.30pm; April daily except Mon 2–6.30pm; Oct–March daily except Mon 2–4pm). This contains a small museum about lighthouses, and makes a good point from which to set out along the barren and exposed rocks of the north coast. Particularly in September and other times of migration, this is a remarkable spot for birdwatching. The star-shaped formations of crumbling walls are not extra-terrestrial relics, but built so that the sheep – peculiarly tame here – can shelter from the strong winds.

Ouessant's **tourist office** is in the main square in Lampaul (April–Aug Mon–Sat 9.30am–12.30pm & 1.30–5pm, Sun 9.30am–12.30pm; Sept–March Mon–Sat 9.45am–noon & 2–4pm, Sun 10am–noon; ☎02.98.48.85.83). In Lampaul, the adjacent **hotels** *Océan* (☎02.98.48.80.03; ②) and *Fromveur* (☎02.98.48.81.30; ②) both offer basic accommodation; the *Fromveur* specializes in traditional island cooking, which consists of attempting to render seaweed and mutton as palatable as possible. The *Roch Ar Mor*, just down the street (☎02.98.48.80.19; ②; closed Jan–March), is a marginally more attractive alternative. There is a small official **campsite**, the *Penn ar Bed* (☎02.98.48.84.65; March–Nov). You could, in fact, camp almost anywhere on the island, making arrangements with the nearest farmhouse (which may well let out rooms, too).

All the hotel **restaurants** serve menus for under 100F, but if you just come for a day, it's a good idea to buy a picnic before you set out – the Lampaul shops have limited and rather pricey supplies.

Île de Molène

The **Île de Molène** is quite well populated for a sparse strip of sand. Its inhabitants make their money from seaweed collecting and drying – and to an extent from crabbing and from crayfish, which they gather on foot, canoe and even tractor at low tide. The tides here are more than usually dramatic, halving or doubling the island's territory at a stroke. It's not called "the bald isle" for nothing. Few people do more than look at Molène as an afternoon's excursion from Le Conquet, but it's quite possible to stay here and to enjoy it, too. There are **rooms** – very chilly in winter – at *Kastell An Doal* (☎02.98.07.39.11; ②), one of the old buildings by the port.

Brest

BREST is set in a magnificent natural harbour, known as the Rade de Brest, and sheltered from the ocean storms by the Crozon peninsula to its south. It has always played an important role in war, and in trade whenever peace allowed. Today it is the base of the French Atlantic Fleet with a dry dock that can accommodate ships of up to 500,000 tonnes; the town, as a ship repair centre, ranks sixth in the world.

During World War II, Brest was continually bombed to prevent the Germans from using it as a submarine base. When the Americans liberated it on September 18, 1944, after a six-week siege, they found the town devastated beyond recognition. The architecture of the postwar town is raw and bleak. There have been attempts, as in Caen, to green the city, but despite the heaviest rainfall in France the site has proved too windswept to respond.

Arrival, information and accommodation

The **gare SNCF** (☎02.98.80.50.50) and **gare routière** (☎02.98.44.46.73) are together in place du 19ème-RI at the bottom of avenue Clémenceau. **Bus** services include those to Plouescat and Roscoff (Les Cars du Kreisker; ☎02.98.69.00.93); to the Crozon peninsula via Land'vennec (☎02.98.27.02.02); and to Le Conquet (Sarl St Mathieu Transports; ☎02.98.98.12.02). Brest's **tourist office** on avenue Clémenceau faces place de la Liberté (July & Aug Mon–Sat 9.30am–6.30pm, Sun 10am–noon & 2–4pm; Sept–June Mon–Sat 10am–12.30pm & 2–6pm; ☎02.98.44.24.96).

As well as the sailings to Ouessant, detailed on p.400, in summer three boats per day make the 45-minute crossing from Brest's Port de Commerce to Le Fret on the Crozon peninsula (May–Sept; Vedettes Armoricaines; ☎02.98.44.44.04), to be met by buses for Crozon (15min), Morgat (30min) and Camaret (40min). Vedettes Armoricaines, and other operators, also run excursions around the harbour and the Rade de Brest (1hr 30min).

The vast majority of Brest's **hotels** remain open throughout the year; only a few, however, bother to maintain their own restaurants. Several lie within easy walking distance of the stations, in the vicinity of the central place de la Liberté. The year-round

youth hostel is on rue de Kerbriant, Port de Plaisance du Moulin-Blanc (☎02.98.41.90.41; 69F including breakfast), 3km east of gares SNCF and routière in a wooded setting near Océanopolis, on bus route #7 or the Bus Albatros.

Hotels

Astoria, 9 rue Traverse (☎02.98.80.19.10). Peaceful central hotel with a cheerful ambience and decor, not far up from the port. ③.

Bellevue, 53 bd Victor-Hugo (☎02.98.80.51.78). Six-storey sound-proofed building, equipped with a lift. Not easy to find, but not far from the gare SNCF and well on the way to the lively St-Martin area; look for St-Michel church. No restaurant. ②.

de la Gare, 4 bd Gambetta (☎02.98.44.47.01). Simple option opposite the stations, where you pay a little extra for an uninterrupted view of the Rade de Brest, from the upper stories. No restaurant. ②.

Hôtel-Restaurant Le Vauban, 17 av Clémenceau (☎02.98.46.06.88). Very near the centre, between the gare SNCF and the Hôtel de Ville. Grand curving white edifice, with a surprisingly homely atmosphere. A simple restaurant serves couscous and so on from around 50F (closed Sun eve & Mon). ①.

Océania, 82 rue de Siam (☎02.98.80.66.66). Brest's finest upmarket hotel, offering large, attractively fitted rooms on the town's principal thoroughfare, plus a classy restaurant. ⑥.

Pasteur, 29 rue Louis Pasteur (☎02.98.46.08.73). Clean, good value budget hotel near the St-Louis church. No restaurant. ②.

St-Louis, 6 rue d'Algésiras (☎02.98.44.23.91). Friendly, reasonably comfortable option, just off the main square near the tourist office. No restaurant. ①.

The town

As a tourist centre, Brest has little to offer. Few relics of the past remain. The fifteenth-century **castle** looks impressive on its headland and offers a superb panorama of the city, but once inside it is not especially interesting. Three of its towers house the **National Maritime Museum** (daily except Tues 9am–noon & 2–6pm; 30F). The fourteenth-century **Tour Tanguy** on the opposite bank of the River Penfeld, with its conical slate roof, serves as the **Museum of Old Brest** (June–Sept daily 10am–noon & 2–7pm; Oct–May Wed & Thurs 2–5pm, Sat & Sun 2–6pm; free). Dioramas convey a vivid impression of just how attractive the city used to be.

Brest's newest and largest attraction is **Océanopolis**, a couple of kilometres east of the city centre beside the Port de Plaisance du Moulin-Blanc (June–Sept daily 9.30am–7pm; Oct–May Mon 2–6pm, Tues–Fri 9.30am–6pm, Sat, Sun & school hols 9.30am–7pm; 50F summer, 47F winter). Beneath its futuristic white dome lies the largest aquarium in Europe, containing half a million gallons of water and all kinds of fish, seals, molluscs, seaweed and sea anemones. The top floor of the complex is obsessively high-tech, but some of it is quite playful – there's a bizarre kitchen in which the microwave, the fridge and each place-setting on the table hold TV screens, all extolling the virtues of fish – while other parts seem to be purely aesthetic, such as a transparent cylinder filled with circling mackerel. For the moment, Océanopolis is not quite the fun palace you might expect from the advertisements on display all over Brittany, and it's not really worth going far out of your way to see it. However, shortly before this book went to press plans were announced to develop the complex into a "marine science theme park", with the addition of a 3-D cinema and two new pavilions, covering marine life in the polar and tropical regions. Watch this space.

Eating and drinking

Most of Brest's restaurants are to be found in the immediate area of the stations. There are a lot of lively **bars** in town.

Bar Écossais, rue Jean-Jaurès. Positively festooned with Scottish memorabilia, this bar attracts a lively Celtic crowd.

Café de la Plage, place Guerin. A favourite haunt of students at the top end of rue Jean-Jaurès, near the St-Martin church.

La Maison de l'Océan, 2 quai de la Douane (☎02.98.80.44.84). Blue-hued fish restaurant down by the port, open every day and serving wonderful assortments of seafood from 80F.

Ma Petite Folie, plage du Moulin Blanc (☎02.98.42.44.42). Converted fishing boat, moored in the pleasure port, which serves a wonderfully fishy 110F set menu and also offers a wide range of à la carte dishes and daily specials. Closed Sun & 2 weeks in mid-Aug.

Le Ruffé, 1 rue Yves-Collet (☎02.98.46.07.70). An attractive place between the gare SNCF and the tourist office that prides itself on good, traditional French seafood dishes, served on menus costing 75F and upwards. Daily except Sun until 11.30pm.

La Taverne St-Martin, 92 rue Jean-Jaurès (☎02.98.80.48.17). A few hundred metres east (and up) from the tourist office. Warm and friendly brasserie/restaurant behind a wooden half-timbered facade, open from 8am until 1am daily. Lunch from 60F, dinner from 85F, plus lots of à la carte snacks. Steak tartare is the house speciality.

The Crozon peninsula

The **Crozon peninsula**, a craggy outcrop of land shaped like a long-robed giant, arms outstretched to defend bay and roadstead, is the central feature of Finistère's torn chaos of estuaries and promontories. Much the easiest way for cyclists, and travellers relying on public transport, to reach the peninsula from Brest is via the ferries to Le Fret (see opposite).

Motorists heading for Crozon have to follow a circuitous route skirting this complex coast through **Plougastel-Daoulas**. At the church here, the calvary shows more torment for Katel Gollet (Katherine the Damned), in this case being raped by devils, but with a more sympathetic sculpting of Katel herself than at Guimiliau (see p.398).

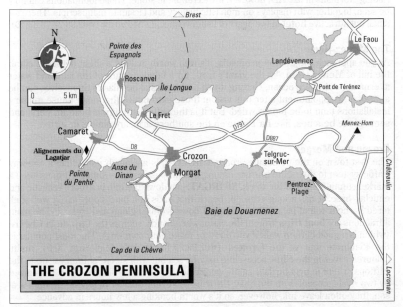

THE CROZON PENINSULA

Daoulas and Le Faou

Ten kilometres beyond Plougastel-Daoulas, the abbey at **DAOULAS** holds Brittany's only Romanesque cloister. It now stands beautiful and isolated at the edge of cool monastery gardens, since its surrounding buildings were destroyed during the Revolution. Since 1984 it has been used as a cultural centre for Finistère, which stages ambitious historical exhibitions lasting for around six months at a time (current information on ☎02.98.25.84.39).

From Daoulas the motorway and railway cut down to Châteaulin (see p.415) and Quimper. For Crozon, you'll need to veer west at **LE FAOU**, a tiny medieval port, still with some of its sixteenth-century gabled houses and set on its own individual estuary. From beside the pretty little village church – whose porch holds some intriguing carved apostles – a sheltered corniche follows the river to the sea, where there are sailing and windsurfing facilities.

Le Faou holds two good and very similar **hotels**, each equipped with a top-class restaurant; the *Relais de la Place* (☎02.98.81.91.19; ③) and the *La Vieille Renommée* (☎02.98.81.90.31; ④; closed Mon Sept–June, & all Nov). The one snag is that they're not in the most attractive part of town, near the river, but a few hundred metres south in the newer and much noisier main square.

Landévennec

Nine kilometres west of Le Faou, by way of a beautiful shoreline road, the **Pont de Térénez** spans the Aulne – outlet for the Nantes–Brest canal – to the Crozon peninsula. Doubling back to the right as soon as you cross the bridge brings you after a further 5km to **LANDÉVENNEC**, where archeologists are uncovering the outline of what may be Brittany's oldest abbey (June–Sept Mon–Sat 10am–7pm, Sun 2–7pm; Oct–May daily 2–6pm; 25F). Nothing survives above ground of the original thatched hut, constructed in a forest clearing by St Gwennolé around 485 AD. After the abbey had been pillaged by raiding Normans in 913 AD, however, it was rebuilt in stone. Those foundations can now be seen, together with displays on monastic history and facsimile manuscripts. There's a small but attractive **hotel** in the heart of Landévennec, *Le St-Patrick* (☎02.98.27.70.83; ②).

The Menez-Hom

As you approach the Crozon peninsula, it's well worth making a slight detour to climb the hill of **Menez-Hom**, "at the giant's feet", for a fabulous view of the land and water alternating out to the ocean. Getting down to the coastal headlands themselves can be a bit of a disappointment after this vision: those extremities that don't house military installations tend to be too crowded. But it is the cliffs that tourists head for here, and some of the **beaches**, like **La Palue** on the southern arm, are almost deserted.

Crozon and Morgat

The first town on the peninsula proper, **CROZON**, is not much more than a one-way traffic system to distribute tourists among the various resorts – though it does keep a market running most of the week. **MORGAT**, just down the hill, is a more realistic and enticing base. It has a long crescent beach that ends in a pine slope, and a well-sheltered harbour full of pleasure boats raced down from England and Ireland. The main attractions are **boat trips** around the various headlands, such as the **Cap de la Chèvre** (which is a good clifftop walk if you'd rather make your own way). The most popular is the 45-minute tour of the **Grottes** (☎02.98.27.10.71; daily May–Sept, 45F), multi-coloured caves in the cliffs, accessible only by sea but with steep "chimneys" up to the clifftops, where in bygone days saints would lurk to rescue the shipwrecked. Organized by two rival companies on the quay, the trips run every quarter of an hour in high season; they often leave full, however, so it's worth booking a few hours in advance.

The **tourist office** for the whole peninsula is in what used to be the gare SNCF at Crozon (☎02.98.26.17.18); an information office for the Crozon–Morgat area stands at the start of Morgat's beach crescent on the boulevard du France (July & Aug Mon–Sat 9.30am–7pm, Sun 10am–1pm; May, June & Sept Mon–Sat 9.15am–noon & 2–6.30pm; ☎02.98.27.07.92).

All the **hotels** in Morgat are quite expensive. Appealing options include the grand *Hôtel-Restaurant de la Ville d'Ys*, which enjoys fabulous views just above the port (☎02.98.27.06.49; ③; closed Oct–March), and has a good dinner-only restaurant, and the quieter *Julia*, 400 metres from the beach at 43 rue de Tréflez (☎02.98.27.05.89; ②; closed Nov to mid-Feb). Immediately below the *Ville d'Ys* at the far end of the beach, *Les Échoppes*, 24 quai du Kador (☎02.98.26.12.63; closed Oct–Easter), a flowery stone cottage with tiny little windows, is Morgat's best **restaurant**, serving good menus from 100F.

With a total of 865 pitches available, **campers** are spoilt for choice; best are the three-star sites at *Plage de Goulien* (mid-June to mid-Sept; ☎02.98.27.17.10) and *Les Pins*, towards the pointe de Dinan (mid-June to mid-Sept; ☎02.98.27.21.95).

Camaret

CAMARET is another sheltered port, at the very tip of the peninsula. Its most distinguishing feature is the pink-orange **château de Vauban**, standing four-square at the end of the long jetty that runs back parallel to the main town waterfront. Walled, moated, and accessible via a little gatehouse reached by means of a drawbridge, it was built in 1689 to guard the approaches to Brest; these days it guards no more than a motley assortment of decaying half-submerged fishing boats, abandoned to rot beside the jetty. There are two beaches nearby – a small one to the north and another, larger and more attractive, in the low-lying (and rather marshy) Anse de Dinan. In high season, *Penn Ar Bed* (☎02.98.70.02.37) operate an irregular ferry service from Camaret to the island of **Sein** (see p.407; 168F return), and also to **Ouessant** (see p.400; 168F return).

A little walk away from the centre, around the port towards the protective jetty, the quai du Styvel contains a row of excellent **hotels**. Both the *Vauban* (☎02.98.27.91.36; ②) and *du Styvel* (☎02.98.27.92.74; ②) are exceptionally hospitable, with rooms that look right out across the bay, but only the *Styvel* has a restaurant. There are also various **campsites** to fall back on, such as the four-star *Lambézen* (April to mid-Sept; ☎02.98.27.91.41) and the municipal *Lannic* (mid-June to mid-Sept; ☎02.98.27.91.31). Back along the quayside in the centre of town, *La Voilerie*, 7 quai Toudouze (☎02.98.27.99.55), is an excellent **fish restaurant**.

South towards Quimper

Moving south of the Crozon peninsula, you soon enter the ancient kingdom of **Cornouaille**. Its capital, **Quimper**, is a city as enticing as any in France, and along the south coast Bénodet, Loctudy and Pont-Aven (made famous by Gauguin) are thriving resorts. Roads radiate from Quimper in all directions, but the **western tip** of Finistère, if you follow the line of the Bay of Douarnenez, still feels isolated. With a few exceptions – most notably its "land's end" capes – it has kept out of the tourist mainstream.

Locronan

LOCRONAN, a short way from the sea on the minor road that leads down from the Crozon peninsula, is a prime example of a Breton town that has remained frozen in its ancient form by more recent economic decline. From 1469 through to the seventeenth century, it was a successful centre for woven linen, supplying sails to the French,

English and Spanish navies. It was first rivalled by Vitré and Rennes, before suffering the "agony and ruin" so graphically described in its small **museum** (daily 10am–7pm; 15F). As a result, the rich medieval houses of the town centre have never been super-seded or surrounded by modern development. Film directors love its authenticity, even if Roman Polanski, filming *Tess*, deemed it necessary to change all the porches, put new windows on the Renaissance houses, and bury the main square in mud to make it all look a bit more English.

Today Locronan is once more prosperous, with its main source of income the tourists who buy wooden statues carved by local artisans, pottery brought up from the Midi, and leather jackets of less specified provenance. This commercialization shouldn't, however, put you off making at least a passing visit, for the town itself is genuinely remarkable, centred around the focal **Église Saint-Ronan**. Be sure to take the time to walk down the hill of the **rue Moal**, where there's a lovely little stone chapel, with surprising modern stained glass, and a wooden statue of a depressed-look-ing Jesus, sitting alone cross-legged.

Practicalities

Staying in Locronan can be an expensive business; contact the **tourist office**, in the main square, for details (July & Aug daily 10am–7pm; Sept–June daily 10am–noon & 2–6pm; ☎02.98.91.70.14). The *Hôtel du Prieuré*, 11 rue du Prieuré (☎02.98.91.70.89; closed mid-Nov to mid-March; ③), has a good restaurant with menus from 70F, but is normally reserved well in advance.

Douarnenez

Sufficient quantities of tuna, sardines and assorted crustaceans are still landed at the port of **DOUARNENEZ**, in the superbly sheltered Baie du Douarnenez, south of the Crozon peninsula, to keep the largest fish canneries in Europe busy. However, the catch has been declining ever since 1923, when eight hundred fishing boats brought in 100 million sardines during the six-month season. Over the last fifteen years or so, Douarnenez has therefore set out – at phenomenal expense, the subject of considerable local controversy – to redefine itself as a living museum of all matters maritime.

The whole area of **Port-Rhu**, on the west side of town, now constitutes the remark-able **Port-Musée** (daily mid-June to Sept 10am–7pm; Oct to mid-June 10am–noon & 2–6pm; tickets sold in the Boat Museum, June–Sept 60F, Oct–May 48F). The entire waterfront is taken up with fishing and other vessels gathered from all over Europe, which visitors are invited to roam in and out of, up and down ladders and all over the decks, through oily metallic-smelling engine rooms and sleeping quarters divided into wooden compartments. Sail-makers and net-menders work on the jetties, and children can operate a scaled-down eighteenth-century crane by walking inside a wooden treadmill. Across the street, the associated **boat museum** (same times) doubles as a working boatyard, where visitors can join in the construction of seagoing vessels, using techniques from all over the world. Once again, the emphasis is on fishing, and the craft on show include a *moliceiro* from Portugal and coracles from Wales and Ireland. With cafés and snack bars on site, there is easily enough here to spend a whole day without seeing it all, though even the most boat-hungry appetite may well be fully slaked after a couple of hours.

Of the three separate harbour areas in Douarnenez, much the most appealing is the rough-and-ready **port de Rosmeur**, on the east side, which is nominally the fishing port used by the smaller local craft. Its quayside – far from totally commercialized, but holding a reasonable number of cafés and restaurants – curves between a pristine wooded promontory to the right and the fish canneries to the left, which continue around the north of the headland. You can buy fresh fish at the waterfront, or go on a sea-fishing excursion yourself. The various **beaches** around town look pretty enough, but they are dangerous for swimming.

Practicalities

The **tourist office** in Douarnenez is at 2 rue du Dr-Mével (July & Aug Mon–Sat 9am–7pm; Sun 10am–1pm & 4–7pm; Sept–June Mon–Sat 9am–noon & 2–6pm; ☎02.98.92.13.35), a short walk up from the Port-Musée. Among good-value **hotels** are *de la Rade*, 31 quai du Grand-Port (☎02.98.92.01.81; ②; closed Nov–Easter), with a bar downstairs and a restaurant on the first floor looking out on the port de Rosmeur, and *des Halles*, higher up alongside the busy market *halles* (☎02.98.92.02.75; ②; closed Sun & all Jan).

Close by on the bay, there's a **campsite**, *Croas Men* (April to mid-Sept; ☎02.98.74.00.18), at Tréboul/Les Sables Blancs. Good seafood **restaurants** include *Le Tristan*, 25 rue du Rosmeur (☎02.98.92.20.17), just above the port de Rosmeur, and the *Pourquoi Pas*, 15 quai de Port-Rhû (☎02.98.92.76.13), beside the museum, which does fine fishy lunches.

The Baie des Trépassés and the Pointe du Raz

The **Baie des Trépassés** (Bay of the Dead), 30km west of Douarnenez, gets its grim name from the shipwrecked bodies that are washed up there, and is a possible site of sunken Ys (see p.408). However, it's a very attractive spot; green meadows, too exposed to support trees, end abruptly on the low cliffs to either side, there's a huge expanse of flat sand (in fact little else at low tide), and out in the crashing waves surfers and windsurfers get thrashed to within an inch of their lives. Beyond them, you can usually make out the white-painted houses along the harbour on the Île de Sein, while the various uninhabited rocks in between hold a veritable forest of lighthouses.

In total, less than half a dozen scattered buildings intrude upon the emptiness, including two **hotels**, both with tremendous views. Right in the middle is the pink *Hôtel de la Baie des Trépassés* (☎02.98.70.61.34; ②–④; closed Jan to mid-Feb), which has menus from 102F. The larger *Relais de la Pointe du Van* is slightly higher up, to the right (☎02.98.70.62.79; ③; closed Oct–March).

The **Pointe du Raz** – the Land's End of both Finistère and France – has recently been designated as a "Grande Site Nationale", and with its former military installations now thankfully cleared away it makes a dramatic spectacle. You can walk out to the plummeting fissures of the *pointe*, filling and draining with a deafening surf-roar, and beyond, high above on precarious paths.

Audierne

Though on the whole the exposed southwestern extremities of Brittany are not areas you'd immediately associate with a classic summer sun-and-sand holiday, **AUDIERNE**, 25km west of Douarnenez on the Bay of Audierne, is an exception. An active fishing port, specializing in prawns and crayfish, it spreads along the northern shore of the Goyen estuary a short way back from the sea. From the town centre, the road continues just over 1km to the long, curving and surprisingly sheltered **beach** of Ste-Evette.

The **hotel** *Au Roi Gradlon*, in a superb position at the very mouth of the estuary (☎02.98.70.04.51; ④; closed Sun pm, Mon Oct–May, & Jan to mid-Feb), consists of several floors that drop down to the beach.

The Île de Sein

Just 8km out to sea, off the end of the Pointe du Raz, the little **Île de Sein** was made famous during World War II when the entire male population answered General de Gaulle's call to join him in exile in England. It was reputed also to have been the very last refuge of the Druids in Brittany, a misty and inaccessible spot where they held out long after the rest of the country was Christianized. Roman sources tell of a shrine served by nine virgin priestesses. The island is featureless enough to have been completely submerged by the sea on occasion, but a few hundred people still live on it, gathering rainwater and fishing for scallops, lobster and crayfish.

The principal departure point for **boats** to Sein is Ste-Evette beach, just outside **Audierne** (see above). Services are operated by Vedette-Biniou (June to early July, and first half of Sept, daily at 10am; early July to end of Aug daily at 10am, 1.30pm & 5pm; 125F return, under-17s 65F; ☎02.98.70.21.15), and Penn Ar Bed (April–Aug, 1–3 departures daily, first at 9.30am; Sept–March daily except Wed 9.30am; return fare 128F, under-17s 65F; ☎02.98.70.02.37). Between mid-July and mid-August, Penn Ar Bed also run trips to Sein from **Brest** via **Camaret** on Saturdays and Sundays.

Sein is hardly bursting with facilities for tourists, but can offer a hotel-cum-crêperie, the *Trois Dauphins* (☎02.98.70.92.09; ②; closed Oct–May), and a handful of more formal restaurants.

Quimper

QUIMPER, capital of the ancient diocese, kingdom and later duchy of **Cornouaille**, is the oldest Breton city. According to legend, the first bishop of Quimper, St Corentin, came with the first Bretons across the Channel some time between the fourth and seventh centuries to the place they named Little Britain. He lived by eating a regenerating and immortal fish all his life, and was made bishop by one King Gradlon, whose life he later saved when the sea-bed city of **Ys** was destroyed. According to one version, Gradlon built Ys in the Baie de Douarnenez, protected from the water by gates and locks to which only he and his daughter had keys. But St Corentin suspected her of evil doings, and was proven right: the princess's keys unlocked the gates, the city flooded and Gradlon escaped only by obeying Corentin and throwing his daughter into the sea. Back on dry land and in need of a new capital, Gradlon founded Quimper.

Modern Quimper is very relaxed, active enough to have the bars – and the atmosphere – to make it worth going out café-crawling. Still "the charming little place" known to Flaubert, it takes at most half an hour to cross it on foot. The word "kemper" denotes the junction of the two rivers, the Steir and the Odet, around which are the cobbled streets (now mainly pedestrianized) of the medieval quarter, dominated by the cathedral towering nearby. As the Odet curves from east to southwest, it is crossed by numerous low, flat bridges, bedecked with geraniums, and chrysanthemums in the autumn. You can stroll along the boulevards on both banks of the river, where several ultramodern edifices blend in a surprisingly harmonious way with their ancient – and attractive – surroundings. Overlooking all are the wooded slopes of **Mont Frugy**. There is no great pressure in Quimper to rush around monuments or museums, and the most enjoyable option may be to take a boat and drift down "the prettiest river in France" to the open sea at Bénodet.

Arrival, information and accommodation

Quimper's **tourist office** is on the south bank of the Odet at 7 rue de la Déesse, place de la Résistance (July & Aug Mon–Sat 9am–7pm, Sun 10am–1pm; April–June & Sept Mon–Sat 9am–12.30pm & 1.30–6.30pm, Sun 10am–1pm; Oct–March Mon–Sat 9am–noon & 1.30–6pm, Sun 10am–1pm; ☎02.98.53.04.05).

The **gare SNCF** (☎02.98.98.31.26) and **gare routière** (☎02.98.90.88.89) are next to each other on avenue de la Gare, 1km east of the centre. **Bus services** include those to Bénodet, which leave from place de la Résistance (Compagnie Armoricaine de Transport,

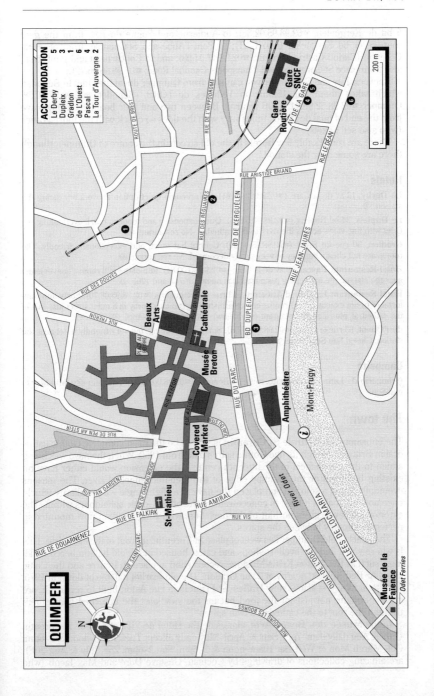

5 bd de Kérguelen, ☎02.98.95.02.36); to Audierne and Pointe du Raz, from the gare routière or bd Kérguelen (also CAT); to Pont l'Abbé and St-Guenolé, from place St-Corentin (Cariou Castric Lecoeur; ☎02.98.47.04.08); and to Concarneau and Pont-Aven, also from place St-Corentin (Sarl Transports Caoudal Réné; ☎02.98.56.96.72).

Between July and September you can **sail** from Quimper down the Odet to Bénodet, which takes about 1hr 15min, on Vedettes de l'Odet (Bénodet ☎02.98.57.00.58, Quimper ☎02.98.52.98.41; 110F return). Between two and four boats each day leave from the end of quai de l'Odet; times vary with the tides so check with the tourist office (who also sell tickets).

There are remarkably few **hotels** in the old streets in the centre of Quimper, though there are some near the station.

Hotels

Le Derby, 13 av de la Gare (☎02.98.52.06.91). Surprisingly quiet option above a bar facing the station. ②.

Le Dupleix, 34 bd Dupleix (☎02.98.90.53.35). Quite expensive and modern hotel, overlooking the Odet with fine views across the river to the cathedral. No restaurant. ④.

Gradlon, 30 rue du Brest (☎02.98.95.04.39). Central but quiet, and exceptionally friendly. The rooms are not cheap, but they're very nicely decorated. No restaurant. ④.

Hôtel-Restaurant Pascal, 19 av de la Gare (☎02.98.90.00.81). Run-of-the-mill rooms, conveniently near the station; the unexciting restaurant has menus at 74F and 120F. ②.

Hôtel-Restaurant La Tour d'Auvergne, 13 rue des Réguaires (☎02.98.95.08.70). Forty-one comfortable (if not exactly fancy) rooms in a refurbished *logis* tucked away in a quiet street just east of the cathedral, plus a good restaurant (see below). Closed Sun Oct–April. ③.

de l'Ouest, 63 rue le Déan (☎02.98.90.28.35). Small, unassuming, but very friendly hotel near the station. Closed Sun Sept–June. ①.

Campsite

Orangerie de Lannion campsite, route de Bénodet (☎02.98.90.62.02). Four-star site. Mid-May to mid-Sept.

The town

The enormous **Cathédrale St-Corentin** is said to be the most complete Gothic cathedral in Brittany, though its neo-Gothic spires date from 1856. When the nave was being added to the old chancel in the fifteenth century, the extension would either have hit existing buildings or the swampy edge of the then-unchannelled river. The masons eventually found a solution and placed the nave at a slight angle – a peculiarity which, once noticed, makes it hard to concentrate on the other Gothic splendours within. The exterior, however, gives no hint of the deviation, with King Gradlon now mounted in perfect symmetry between the spires.

The heart of old Quimper lies west of place St-Corentin, in front of the cathedral. This is where you'll find the liveliest shops and cafés, housed in the old half-timbered buildings, such as the Breton Keltia-Musique record shop in place au Beurre and the Celtic shop, Ar Bed Keltiek, nearby at 2 rue Grallon. The old market hall burnt down in 1976, but the light and spacious new **Halles St-Francis** in rue Astor, built to replace it, are quite a delight, not just for the food but for the view past the upturned boat rafters through the roof to the cathedral's twin spires.

In the **Musée des Beaux-Arts**, alongside the Hôtel de Ville at 4 place St-Corentin (July & Aug daily 9am–7pm; Sept & April–May daily except Tues 10am–noon & 2–6pm; Oct–March Mon & Wed–Sat 10am–noon & 2–6pm, Sun 2–6pm; 25F, July & Aug 30F), are amazing collections of drawings by Cocteau, Gustave Doré and Max Jacob (who was born in Quimper), paintings of the Pont-Aven school, and Breton scenes by the likes of Eugène Boudin. Only the old Dutch oils upstairs let the collection down.

Faïence – tin-glazed earthenware – has been made in and around Quimper since 1690, a story told by the excellent **Musée de la Faïence Jules Verlinque**, on the south bank of the Odet at 14 rue Jean-Baptiste-Bosquet (May–Oct Mon–Sat 10am–6pm; 26F). The museum demonstrates that little has changed in the Breton pottery business since some unknown artisan hit on the idea of painting ceramic ware with naive "folk" designs. That was in around 1875, as the coming of the railways brought the first influx of tourists. Highlights of the collection include pieces commemorating such events as the Great War, the first automobile accident, and the death of Zola, but there are also some fascinating specimens produced by fine artists in the 1920s.

As you walk through the town, it is impossible to ignore *faïence* – you are invited to look and to buy on every corner. On weekdays, it's also possible to visit the major *atelier* **H-B Henriot**, in the allées de Locmarion just behind the museum (Mon–Fri 9–11.30am & 1.30–4pm; 16F; ☎02.98.90.09.36). H-B Henriot maintain a bright, modern **gift shop** alongside; the prices, even for the seconds, are similar to those on offer everywhere else, but the selection is superb (Mon–Thurs 9.30am–7pm, Fri & Sat 9.30am–6pm).

Eating and drinking

Though the pedestrian streets west of the cathedral are unexpectedly short on places to eat, there are quite a few **restaurants** further east on the north side of the river, en route to the gare SNCF. Rue Aristide-Briand here is a particularly promising area, with some lively bars. Place au Beurre, north of the cathedral, is a good bet for crêperies.

L'Assiette, 5bis rue Jean-Jaurès (☎02.98.53.03.65). Relaxed and inexpensive red-painted bistrot, south of the river, with imaginative menus that start at 60F. Closed Sun & Mon.

Le Capucin Gourmand, 29 rue des Réguaires (☎02.98.95.43.12). Gourmet French cooking, not far east of the cathedral. Menus start at 80F and zoom on up to over 300F; most offer very little choice, though all those costing more than 100F feature at least some meat dishes. Closed Sun pm & Mon.

La Krampouzerie, 9 rue du Sallé on the place au Beurre (☎02.98.95.13.08). One of the best of Quimper's many crêperies. Most crêpes cost under 20F, though you can get a wholewheat galette with scallops for 40F, or with seaweed for 28F. Closed Sun, & Mon in winter.

La Tour d'Auvergne, 13 rue des Réguaires (☎02.98.95.08.70). Formal hotel dining room that offers high-quality menus from 125F up to 270F, with an emphasis on fresh local seafood: the mussels and monkfish are recommended, the baked strawberries divine. Closed Sun Oct–April.

Trattoria Mario, 35 rue des Réguaires (☎02.98.95.42.15). Italian meals of pizza (from 33F) and fresh pasta, behind the post office. Closed Sun lunch and all day Mon.

Entertainment

Quimper's **Festival de Cornouaille** started in 1923 and has gone from strength to strength since. This great jamboree of Breton music, costumes, theatre and dance is held in the week before the fourth Sunday in July, attracting guest performers from the other Celtic countries and a scattering of other, sometimes highly unusual, ethnic-cultural ensembles. The whole thing culminates in an incredible Sunday parade through the town. The official programme does not appear until July, but you can get provisional details in advance from the tourist office. Accommodation is at a premium in Quimper while the festival is on.

Not so widely known are the **Semaines Musicales** which breathe life into the rather stuffy nineteenth-century theatre on boulevard Dupleix during the first three weeks of August. The music is predominantly classical and tends to favour French composers such as Berlioz, Debussy, Bizet and Poulenc.

Bénodet

Once out of its city channel, the Odet takes on the shape of most Breton inlets, spreading out to lake proportions then turning narrow corners between gorges. The family resort of **BÉNODET** at the mouth of the river (reachable by boat from Quimper – see p.408) has a long sheltered beach on the ocean side, with amusements for children and beachside nurseries. Among the nicest **hotels in** Bénodet are the *Hôtel-Restaurant Le Minaret*, an odd-looking building in a superb seafront position on the corniche de l'Estuaire (☎02.98.57.03.13; ③; closed Nov–March), and the *Bains de Mer*, 11 rue du Kérguelen (☎02.98.57.03.41; ③; closed mid-Nov to mid-March). Bénodet also has several large **campsites** – if anything, rather too many of them – such as the enormous four-star *du Letty*, southeast of the village by plage du Letty on rue du Canvez (☎02.98.57.04.69; mid-June to mid-Sept).

Along the south coast

The coast that continues east of Bénodet is rocky and repeatedly cut by deep valleys. It suffered heavily in the hurricane of 1987, but the small resort of **BEGMEIL** survives, albeit with fewer trees to protect its vast expanse of dunes. These are ideal for **campers**, with several official sites, and just back from the seafront there's also the hotel *Thalamot* (☎02.98.94.97.38; ③; closed Oct–April).

Around **la Forêt-Fouesnant** in particular, the hills are much too steep for cyclists to climb, and forbidden to heavy vehicles such as caravans. The Forêt-Fouesnant minor road may look good, but there are few beaches or places to stop. Motorists would do best to take the more direct D44, a few kilometres inland, followed by the D783, which leads close to the major towns along the route.

Concarneau

The first sizeable town you come to east of Bénodet is **CONCARNEAU**, where the third most important fishing port in France does a reasonable job of passing itself off as a holiday resort. Its greatest asset is its **Ville Close**, the small and very well fortified old city located a few metres offshore on an irregular rocky island in the bay. This can get too crowded for comfort in high summer, but otherwise it's a real delight. Like those of the citadelle at Le Palais on Belle-Île, its ramparts were completed by Vauban in the seventeenth century. The island itself, however, had been inhabited for at least a thousand years before that, and is first recorded as the site of a priory founded by King Gradlon of Quimper.

Concarneau boasts that it is a *ville fleurie*, and the flowers are most in evidence inside the walls, where climbing roses and clematis swarm all over the various gift shops, restaurants and crêperies. Walk the central pedestrianized street to the far end, and you can pass through a gateway to the shoreline to watch the fishing boats go by. In summer, however, the best views of all come from the promenade on top of the ramparts (July & Aug daily 9am–7pm; May–June & Sept daily 10am–6pm; 5F).

The **Musée de la Pêche**, immediately inside the Ville Close (mid-June to mid-Sept daily 9.30am–7pm; mid-Sept to mid-June daily 9.30am–12.30pm & 2–6pm; 30F), provides an insight into the traditional life Concarneau shared with so many other Breton ports, illuminating the history and practice of catching whales, tuna – with dragnets the size of central Paris – herring and sardines.

Arrival, information and accommodation

There's no rail service to Concarneau, but SNCF **buses** connect the town with Quimper and Rosporden. The **tourist office** (July & Aug daily 9am–8pm; May & June

Mon–Sat 9am–noon & 2–6.30pm, Sun 9.30am–12.30pm; Sept–April Mon–Sat 9am–noon & 2–6.30pm; ☎02.98.97.01.44) is on the quai d'Aiguillon, not far from the long-distance bus stop.

The Ville Close is almost completely devoid of hotels, so most of those that Concarneau has to offer skulk in the backstreets of the mainland, and tend to be full most of the time. Probably the best bet of all is the **youth hostel** (☎02.98.97.03.47; open all year), for once very near the city centre but also enjoying magnificent ocean views. It's just around the tip of the headland on the quai de la Croix, with a good crêperie opposite and a windsurfing shop a little further along.

de France et d'Europe, 9 av de la Gare (☎02.98.97.00.64). Bright, modernized and very central hotel near the main bus stop. No restaurant. Closed Sat mid-Nov to mid-March. ④.

Le Galion, 15 rue St-Guénolé (☎02.98.97.30.16). Upmarket restaurant at the far end of the Ville Close that offers a few expensive rooms, and is otherwise noteworthy only for the meagreness of the portions on its nouvelle menus, starting at 135F. Closed Sun pm, Mon, & all Feb. ④.

Hôtel-Restaurant les Océanides, 3 rue du Lin (☎02.98.97.08.61). *Logis de France*, a couple of streets up from the sea above the fishing port, with a highly recommended and far from expensive restaurant. Closed Sun pm in May & June, all Sun Oct–April. ②.

Hôtel des Voyageurs, 9 place Jean-Jaurès (☎02.98.97.08.06). Cheap basic accommodation, right opposite the entrance to the Ville Close. ②.

Eating and drinking

For an atmospheric meal in Concarneau, choose from any of the restaurants along the main street that runs through the Ville Close, or explore the lanes that lead off it. There are, however, plenty of cheaper places back in town.

L'Assiette de Pêcheur, 12 rue St-Guénolé (☎02.98.70.75.84). Smart seafood restaurant at the far end of the Ville Close, in the same square as *Le Galion*, with a good 92F menu. Closed Oct–Easter, plus Sun pm & Mon except July & Aug.

Chez Armande, 15 av du Dr-Nicholas (☎02.98.97.00.76). Excellent seafood not far south of the market on the mainland, on menus starting at 95F. Closed Wed, & Tues pm in winter.

L'Écume, 3 place St-Guenolé (☎02.98.97.33.27). One of several good-value crêperies in the heart of the Ville Close. A great spot to watch the world go by, and menus to suit all tastes from 60F. Closed Wed, plus Nov–March.

L'Escale, 19 quai Carnot (☎02.98.97.03.31). Waterfront restaurant on the main road in town that's a favourite with local fishermen, with lunch menus for around 50F. Closed Sun.

Pont-Aven

PONT-AVEN, 14km east of Concarneau and just inland from the tip of the Aven estuary, is a small port packed with tourists and art galleries. This was where Gauguin came to paint in the 1880s, before he left for Tahiti in search of a South Seas idyll. He produced some of his finest work in Pont-Aven, and his influence was such that the **Pont-Aven School** of fellow artists – the best known of whom was Émile Bernard – developed here; but for all the local hype, the town has no permanent collection of Gauguin's work. The **Musée Municipal** (mid-June to mid-Sept daily 10am–7pm; mid-Feb to mid-June & mid-Sept to Dec daily 10am–12.30pm & 2–6pm; 25F) in the mairie holds changing exhibitions of the school and other artists active during the same period, but you can't count on paintings by the man himself.

Gauguin aside, Pont-Aven is pleasant in its own right. Just upstream of the little granite bridge at the heart of town, the **promenade Xavier-Grall** crisscrosses the tiny river itself on landscaped walkways, offering glimpses of the backs of venerable mansions, dripping with red ivy, and a little "chaos" of rocks in the stream itself. A longer walk – allow an hour – leads into the **Bois d'Amour**, wooded gardens which have long provided inspiration to painters, poets and musicians.

Practicalities

Pont-Aven's **tourist office**, 5 place de l'Hôtel de Ville (July & Aug daily 9.30am–7.30pm; April–June & Sept–Oct daily 9.15am–12.30pm & 2–7pm; Nov–March Mon–Sat 10am–12.30pm & 2–6pm; ☎02.98.06.04.70), sells an excellent English-language guide booklet to the town, plus route maps of local walks, for a mere 2F. Much the best of its three relatively expensive **hotels** is the central *Hôtel des Ajoncs d'Or*, 1 place de l'Hôtel de Ville (☎02.98.06.02.06; ④; closed Jan), where gourmet menus start at 100F. The nicest of the local **campsites** is *Le Spinnaker* (May–Sept; ☎02.98.06.01.77), set in a large wooded park.

Riec-sur-Bélon

From the unremarkable village of **RIEC-SUR-BÉLON**, 5km southeast of Pont-Aven, back roads snake down for another 4km to reach a dead end at the **port du Bélon**, on the sinuous estuary of the Bélon river. The coastal footpath that leads from here along the thickly wooded shoreline is clearly signposted to offer optional loop trails of 3km, 6km and 8km.

Many of the oysterbeds visible at low tide in the sands off the port belong to *Chez Jacky* (☎02.98.06.90.32), a popular seafood **restaurant**. Once past the well-stocked vivarium at its entrance, you'll find bare wooden benches and tables inside, and beyond that a lovely seafront terrace. The ambience is informal, but both the food, and the prices, are to be taken seriously. Local oysters are 80F a dozen, while a huge platter of mostly raw shellfish costs 200F per person.

Quimperlé and Le Pouldu

The final town of any size in Finistère, **QUIMPERLÉ** straddles a hill and two rivers, the Isole and the Elle, cut by a sequence of bridges. It's an atmospheric place, particularly in the medieval muddle of streets around **Ste-Croix church**. This was copied in plan from schema brought back by crusaders of the Church of the Holy Sepulchre in Jerusalem and is notable for its original Romanesque apse. There are some good **bars** nearby and, on Fridays, a **market** on the square higher up on the hill. Both the **hotels** – *L'Europe* (☎02.98.96.00.02; ②) and *Auberge de Toulföen* (☎02.98.96.00.29; ④; closed Oct) – have reasonable rooms.

At the mouth of the River Laïta, which constitutes the eastern limit of Finistère, the community of **LE POULDU** was another of Paul Gauguin's favourite haunts. It is divided into two distinct sections. The tiny **port**, on one bank of the narrow wooded estuary, is shielded from the open sea by a curving spit of sand. The **beach**, more developed than in Gauguin's day but still very picturesque, is a couple of kilometres away, and the headland separating the two is indented with delightful little sandy coves.

The *Hôtel des Bains* (☎02.98.39.90.11; ③; closed Sept–April) drops down to the beach from the main road, with its large glass-fronted rooms commanding superb views, and menus starting at 85F, while the appealingly weather-beaten white *Hôtel du Pouldu* (☎02.98.39.90.66; ②; closed Oct–March) stands next to the port. Le Pouldu would also make an ideal spot to **camp** for a few days; among sites near the beach is the *Vieux Four* (June–Sept; ☎02.98.39.94.34).

INLAND BRITTANY: THE NANTES–BREST CANAL

The **Nantes–Brest canal** is a meandering chain of waterways from Finistère to the Loire, linking rivers with stretches of canal built at Napoléon's instigation to bypass the belligerent English fleets off the coast. Finally completed in 1836, it came into its own at the end of the century as a coal, slate and fertilizer route. The building of the dam at Lac Guerlédan in the 1920s chopped the canal in two, leaving a whole section unnavigable by barge. Road transport had already superseded water haulage; now tourism is breathing life back into the canal.

En route it passes through riverside towns, such as **Josselin** and **Malestroit**, that long predate its construction; commercial ports and junctions – **Pontivy**, most notably – that developed in the nineteenth century because of it; the old port of **Redon**, a patchwork of water, where the canal crosses the River Vilaine; and a sequence of scenic splendours, including the string of lakes around the **Barrage de Guerlédan**, near Mur-de-Bretagne. As a focus for exploring **inland Brittany**, whether by barge, bike, foot or all three, the canal is ideal. Not every stretch is accessible, but there are detours to be made away from it, such as the wild and desolate **Monts d'Arrée** to the north of the canal in Finistère.

The Finistère stretch

As late as the 1920s, steamers would make their way across the Rade de Brest and down the Aulne River to **Châteaulin**, the first real town on the canal route. If you're walking the canal seriously, **Pont-Coblant** and **Pleyben** are just 10km further away on the map, but be warned that the meanders make it a several-hour hike. Pick your side of the water, too; there are no bridges between Châteaulin and Pont-Coblant.

Châteaulin

CHÂTEAULIN is a quiet place, where the main reason to stay is the canal itself – or river as it is here. Most bars sell permits for its salmon and trout fishing (as do fishing shops, some of which rent out tackle). You should have little difficulty finding a room at the **hotel** *Le Christmas* on rue des Écoles (☎02.98.86.01.24; ②), which climbs from the town centre towards Pleyben. Within a couple of minutes' walk upstream from the statue to Jean Moulin (the Resistance leader who was *sous-préfet* here from 1930 to 1933) and the town centre, you're on towpaths full of rabbits and squirrels and overhung by trees full of birds.

Huelgoat and its forest

HUELGOAT is the halfway point between Morlaix and Carhaix on the minor road D769, making a pleasant overnight stop, next to its own small **lake**. Spreading north and east from the village is the **Forêt de Huelgoat**, a landscape of trees, giant boulders and waterfalls tangled together in primeval chaos – or at least up until 1987; just how fragile it really was, just how miraculous had been its long survival, was demonstrated by the hurricane of that October, which smashed it to smithereens in the space of fifteen minutes. After several years of cleaning up, the forest has now returned to a fairly close approximation of its former glories, and it is once again possible to walk for several kilometres along the various paths that lead into the depths of the woods.

One or two of the village's **hotels** were too hard hit by the post-hurricane decline in tourism to survive, but the *Hôtel du Lac*, beside the lake at 12 rue du Général-de-Gaulle (☎02.98.99.71.14; ③; closed mid-Nov to mid-Dec), is still there, offering well-refurbished **rooms** and good food. Also beside the lake, on the road towards Brest, the *Camping du Lac* (☎02.98.99.78.80; mid-June to mid-Sept), is complete with swimming pool.

Le Faouët, St-Fiacre and Kernascléden

Thirty kilometres south of Carhaix on the D769, the secluded town of **LE FAOUËT** is served neither by buses nor trains, and distinguished mainly by its large old **market**

hall. Above a floor of mud and straw, still used by local traders, rises an intricate latticework of ancient wood, propped on granite pillars and topped by a little clock tower.

The church at **ST-FIACRE**, just over 2km south, is notable for its rood screen, brightly polychromed and carved as intricately as lace. The original purpose of a rood screen was to separate the chancel from the congregation – the decorations of this 1480 masterpiece go rather further than that. They depict scenes from the Old and New Testaments as well as a dramatic series on the wages of sin. Drunkenness is demonstrated by a man somehow vomiting a fox; theft by a peasant stealing apples; and so on. The **hotel** *Croix d'Or*, opposite the old market in the heart of Le Faouët at 9 place Bellanger (☎02.97.23.07.33; closed mid-Dec to mid-Jan, plus Sun pm & Mon in low season; ③), has a 125F menu that features snail ravioli and skate's wing with thyme.

At the ornate and gargoyle-coated church at **KERNASCLÉDEN**, 15km southeast of Le Faouët along the D782, the focus turns from carving to frescoes. The themes, however, contemporary with St-Fiacre, are equally gruesome. On the damp-infested wall of a side chapel, horned devils stoke the fires beneath a vast cauldron filled with the souls of the damned, and you may be able to discern the outlines of a Dance of Death, a faded cousin to that at Kermaria (see p.388).

The central stretch: Gouarec to Redon

Although the canal is limited to canoeists between Carhaix and Pontivy, it's worth some effort to follow on land, particularly for the scenery from **Gouarec** to **Mur-de-Bretagne**. At the centre is the trailing **Lac de Guerlédan**, created by the construction of a barrage near Mur, and backed, to the south, by the enticing **Forêt de Quénécan**. Approaching by road, the canal path is most easily joined at Gouarec, covered by the five daily buses between Carhaix and Loudéac.

Gouarec

At **GOUAREC**, the River Blavet and the canal meet in a confusing swirl of water that shoots off, edged by footpaths, in the most unlikely directions. The old schist houses of the town are barely disturbed by traffic or development, nor are there great numbers of tourists. For a comfortable overnight stop, the *Hôtel du Blavet* (☎02.96.24.90.03; ②), is in an ideal waterside position. Don't be put off by its extravagant menus – they have affordable meals as well. There's also a well-positioned municipal **campsite**, the *Tost Aven* (☎02.96.24.85.42; April–Sept), next to the canal and away from the main road.

Quénécan Forest

For the 15km between Gouarec and Mur-de-Bretagne, the N164 skirts the edge of **Quénécan Forest**, within which is the series of artificial lakes created when the **Barrage of Guerlédan** was completed in 1928. Though sadly once again damaged by the hurricane, it's a beautiful stretch of river, a little overrun by campers and caravans, but peaceful enough nonetheless.

The best places to stay are just off the road, past the villages of **ST-GELVEN** and Caurel. At the former, the ravishing *Hôtellerie de l'Abbaye Bon-Repos* (☎02.96.24.98.38; closed Tues pm & Wed in low season; ③) is an absolutely irresistible, inexpensive **hotel-restaurant**, nestling beside the water at the end of a venerable avenue of ancient trees, and housed in the intact outbuildings of a twelfth-century Cistercian abbey. Porthole-like windows pierce the thick slate walls of its five cosy guest rooms, to look out across extensive riverfront grounds to the dramatic wooded slopes beyond.

From just before **CAUREL**, the brief loop of the D111 leads to tiny sandy beaches – a bit too tiny in season – with **campsites** *Les Pins* (☎02.96.28.52.22) and *Les Pommiers* (☎02.96.28.52.35). At the spot known, justifiably, as **BEAU RIVAGE** is a complex containing a campsite, hotel, restaurant, snack bar and 140-seat glass-topped cruise boat.

Pontivy

You can again take **barges** all the way to the Loire from **PONTIVY**, the central junction of the Nantes–Brest canal, where the course of the canal breaks off once more from the Blavet. When the waterway opened, the small medieval centre of the town was expanded, redesigned and given broad avenues to fit its new role. It was even briefly renamed Napoléonville, in honour of the man responsible for its new prosperity.

These days, Pontivy is a bright market town, its twisting old streets contrasting with the stately riverside promenades. At its northern end, occupying a commanding hillside site, is the **Château de Rohan**, built by the lord of Josselin in the fifteenth century (mid-June to Sept daily 10am–noon & 2–6pm; Oct to mid-June Wed–Sun closes 5pm; 15F). Used in summer for low-key cultural events and temporary exhibitions, the castle still belongs to the Josselin family, who are slowly restoring it. At the moment, one impressive facade, complete with deep moat and two forbidding towers, looks out over the river – behind that, the structure rather peters out.

Pontivy's helpful **tourist office** is just below the castle, on place de Gaulle (☎02.97.25.04.10). Among local **hotels** are the low-priced *Robic*, 2 rue Jean-Jaurès (☎02.97.25.11.80; ②; closed Sun pm in winter), which has a good restaurant with menus from 55F, and the smarter *Porhoët*, near the tourist office at 41 rue du Général-de-Gaulle (☎02.97.25.34.88; ③). In addition, the local **youth hostel**, 2km from the gare SNCF on the Île des Recollets (☎02.97.25.58.27; 49F), has undergone a long overdue renovation, and is looking great.

Josselin

A short way south from Timadeuc, you come to the three Rapunzel towers embedded in a vast sheet of stone of the **château** in **JOSSELIN** (July–Aug daily 10am–6pm; June & Sept daily 2–6pm; Feb–May & Oct to mid-Nov, Wed, Sun and hols 2–6pm; closed mid-Nov to Jan; 20F). The Rohan family used to own a third of Brittany, but the present duke contents himself with the position of local mayor. The pompous apartments of his residence are not very interesting, even if they do contain the table on which the Edict of Nantes was signed in 1598. But the Duchess's collection of dolls, housed in the **Musée des Poupées**, behind the castle, is something special (same hours as castle; June & Sept also open daily 10am–noon).

The town is full of medieval splendours, from the gargoyles of the **basilica** to the castle **ramparts**, and the half-timbered houses in between. **Notre-Dame-du-Roncier** is built on the spot where, in the ninth century, a peasant supposedly found a statue of the Virgin under a bramble bush. The statue was burnt during the Revolution, but an important *pardon* is held each year on September 8.

Josselin's **tourist office** is in a superb old house on the place de la Congrégation, up in town next to the castle entrance (☎02.97.22.36.43). Just across from the Basilica, the *Hôtel de France*, 6 place Notre Dame(☎02.97.22.23.06; ③; closed Sun pm & Mon between Oct and March), is an ivy-covered *logis* which is amazingly quiet considering its central location, where you can choose on the 81F menu between duck in cider or trout with almonds. The *Hôtel du Chateau*, 1 rue du Général-de-Gaulle (☎02.97.22.20.11; closed Feb; ③), is also a treat – it's a lovely medieval building by the river, facing the castle, with a gorgeous antique-filled banqueting hall. The nearest good **campsite** is at Bas de la Lande, half an hour's walk from the castle, south of the river and west of town (May–Sept; ☎02.97.22.22.20).

Guéhenno and Lizio

One of the largest and best Breton calvaries is at **GUÉHENNO**, south of Josselin on the D123. Sculpted in 1550, the figures include the cock that crowed after Peter's denials, Mary Magdalene with the shroud and a recumbent Christ in the crypt. Its appeal is enhanced by the naivety of its amateur restoration. After damage caused by Revolutionary soldiers in 1794 – who amused themselves by playing boules with the heads of the statues – all the sculptors approached for the work demanded exorbitant fees, so the parish priest and his assistant decided to undertake the task themselves.

Over to the east, off the D151, **LIZIO** has also set itself up as a centre for arts and crafts, with ceramic and weaving workshops its speciality. A **Festival Artisanal** is held on the second Sunday in August, along with street theatre (and pancakes). There are several **gîtes** in the town and a **campsite**, *Le Val Jouin* (☎02.97.74.84.76; mid-May to mid-Oct).

Malestroit and around

Not a lot happens in **MALESTROIT**, which celebrated its thousand-year anniversary in 1987. But the town is full of unexpected and enjoyable corners. As you come into the main square, the **place du Bouffay** in front of the church, the houses are covered with unlikely carvings – an anxious bagpipe-playing hare looking over its shoulder at a dragon's head on one beam, while an oblivious sow in a blue buckled belt threads her distaff on another. The **church** itself is decorated with drunkards and acrobats outside, torturing demons and erupting towers within. Beside the grey canal, the matching grey slate tiles on the turreted rooftops bulge and dip, while on its central island overgrown houses stand next to the stern walls of an old mill.

Two kilometres west of Malestroit (and with no bus connection), the village of **ST-MARCEL** hosts a **Musée de la Résistance Bretonne** (mid-June to mid-Sept daily 10am–7pm; mid-Sept to mid-June daily except Tues 10am–noon & 2–6pm; 25F). The museum stands on the site of a June 1944 battle in which the Breton *maquis*, joined by Free French forces parachuted in from England, successfully diverted the local German troops from the main Normandy invasion movements.

The museum's strongest feature is its presentation of the pressures that made many French collaborate: the reconstructed street corner from which all life has been jerked out by the occupiers; the big colourful propaganda posters offering work in Germany, announcing executions of *maquis*, equating resistance with aiding US and British big business; and against these the low-budget, flimsily printed Resistance pamphlets. All the labelling is in French, which non-speakers may find rather frustrating.

PRACTICALITIES

If you arrive in Malestroit by barge (this is a good stretch to travel), you'll moor very near the town centre. The helpful **tourist office** stands on the boulevard du Pont-Neuf, next to the main bridge over the river (daily 10am–noon & 2–6pm; ☎02.97.75.14.57); they can provide details of **boat rental**. Nearby on the same road is the **gare routière**, served by buses from Vannes and Rennes, while across the river there's a **campsite**, *La Daufresne* (☎02.97.75.13.33; May–Oct), down below the bridge next to the swimming pool. However, the only **hotel** is a few hundred metres away on the far side of the old centre. The unexciting *Hôtel St-Michel*, at 1 Faubourg St-Michel (☎02.97.75.13.01; ①), is at the start of the D10 towards Serent; it has a bar but no restaurant.

Redon

Thirty-four kilometres east of Malestroit, at the junction not only of the rivers Oust and Vilaine and the canal, but also of the train lines to Rennes, Vannes and Nantes and of six major roads, **REDON** is not easy to avoid. And you shouldn't try to, either. A wonderful grouping of water and locks, it's a town with history, charm and life.

Until World War I, Redon was the seaport for Rennes. Its industrial docks – or what remains of them – are therefore on the Vilaine, while the canal, even in the very centre of town, is almost totally rural, its towpaths shaded avenues. Shipowners' houses from the seventeenth and eighteenth centuries can be seen along quai Jean-Bart by the *bassin* and quai Duguay-Truin next to the river. A rusted wrought-iron workbridge, equipped with a gantry, still crosses the river, but the main users of the port now are cruise ships heading down the Vilaine to La Roche-Bernard.

Redon was once also a religious centre, its first abbey founded in 832 by St Conwoion. The most prominent church today is **St-Sauveur**. Its unique four-storeyed Romanesque belfry is squat, almost obscured by later roofs and the high choir, and is best seen from the adjacent cloisters; the Gothic tower is entirely separated from the main building by a fire. Inside the church, you'll find the tomb of the judge who tried the legendary Bluebeard – Joan of Arc's friend, Gilles de Rais.

PRACTICALITIES

Redon's **tourist office** (July & Aug Mon–Sat 9am–7pm, Sun 10am–noon & 4–7pm; Sept–June Mon–Sat 9.30am–12.30pm & 3–6pm; ☎02.99.71.06.04) is in the place du Parlement, next to the modern *halles* (scene of a Monday **market**), while the **gare SNCF** (☎02.99.71.74.10) is five minutes' walk west of the town centre. What long-distance buses serve the town – it takes less than an hour to get to Rennes, Nantes or Vannes – also operate from here. **Bicycles** can be rented from Cycles Gicquel in place St-Sauveur (☎02.99.71.02.82), and **canoes** and **barges** from the Comptoir Nautique, 2 quai Surcouf (☎02.99.71.46.03).

Most of the **hotels** are concentrated in town and near the gare SNCF rather than in the port area. The large white *Hôtel le France* looks down on the canal from 30 rue Duguesclin, on the corner of quai de Brest (☎02.99.71.06.11; ①); its recently renovated rooms offer a considerable degree of comfort for the price, but it has no restaurant. Nearer the station, the *Hôtel Chandouineau*, 1 rue Thiers (02.99.71.02.04; ⑤), is luxurious, with just seven bedrooms, and its restaurant serves gourmet menus from 95F.

THE SOUTHERN COAST

Brittany's **southern coast** takes in the province's – and indeed Europe's – most famous prehistoric site, the alignments of **Carnac**, with the associated megaliths of the beautiful, island-studded **Golfe de Morbihan**. The beaches are not as spectacular as in Finistère, but there are more safe places to swim and the water is warmer. Of the cities, **Lorient** has Brittany's most compelling **festival** and **Vannes** has one of the liveliest medieval town centres. Further east, **La Baule** does a good impression of a Breton St-Tropez, and you can escape to the islands of **Belle-Île**, **Hoëdic** and **Houat**. Inevitably it's popular, and in summer you can be hard pressed to find a room, but if you're prepared to make reservations, or you're camping, there shouldn't be much problem.

Lorient and around

LORIENT, Brittany's fourth-largest city, lies on an immense natural harbour protected from the ocean by the Île de Groix and strategically located at the junction of the rivers

Scorff, Ter and Blavet. A functional, rather depressing port today, it was once a key base for French and English colonialism, and was founded in the mid-seventeenth century for trading operations by the Compagnie des Indes, an equivalent of the Dutch and English East India Companies. Apart from the name, little else remains to suggest the plundered wealth that once arrived here. During the last war, Lorient was a major target for the Allies; the Germans held out until May 1945, by which time the city was almost completely destroyed. The only substantial remains were the U-boat pens – subsequently greatly expanded by the French for their nuclear submarines.

Across the estuary in Port-Louis there's a **museum of the Compagnie des Indes**, a pretty dismal temple to imperialism (June–Sept daily except Tues 10am–7pm; Oct & mid-Dec to May daily except Tues 1.30–6pm; closed Nov to mid-Dec; 30F). Time would be more enjoyably spent on a boat trip, either up the estuary towards Hennebont or out to the Île de Groix. This 8km-long steep-sided rock is a short way out to sea and has no permanent population, though there is an HI **youth hostel** (☎02.97.86.81.38; April–Oct), with a **campsite** alongside (☎02.97.86.53.08). The coast around Lorient itself is unenticing and plagued with thick drifts of seaweed.

The Inter-Celtic Festival

The overriding reason people come to Lorient is for the **Inter-Celtic Festival**, held for ten days from the first Friday to the second Sunday in August. The biggest Celtic event in Brittany, or anywhere else for that matter, attracts representatives from all seven Celtic countries. In a popular celebration of cultural solidarity, with up to 250,000 people in attendance at over 150 different shows, five languages mingle and Scotch and Guinness flow with French and Spanish wines and ciders. There is a certain competitive element, with championships in various categories, but the feeling of mutual enthusiasm and conviviality is paramount. Most of the activities – embracing music, dance and literature – take place around the central place Jules-Ferry, and this is where most people end up sleeping, too, as accommodation is pushed to the limit.

For schedules of the festival, and further details of temporary accommodation, contact the Office du Tourisme de Pays de Lorient, 2 rue Paul-Bart, 56100 Lorient (☎02.97.21.24.29), bearing in mind that the festival programme is not finalized before May. For certain specific events, you need to reserve tickets well in advance.

Practicalities

Lorient's **tourist office**, beside the pleasure port on the quai de Rohan (July & Aug Mon–Sat 9am–12.30pm & 2–6pm, Sun 10am–noon & 2–5pm; Sept–June Mon–Sat 9am–12.30pm & 2–6pm; ☎02.97.21.07.84), can provide full details on local boat trips, and organizes some excursions itself.

Unless you arrive during the festival, there's a huge choice of **hotels**. Among reasonable, fairly central options are two on rue Lazare-Carnot as it curves away south of the tourist office: all the rooms in the *Victor Hugo Hôtel* at no. 36 (☎02.97.21.16.24; ②) have TV, and there's an action-packed 99F menu offering langoustines, wild pheasant pâté and duck à l'orange, while the *Hôtel d'Arvor*, at no. 104 (☎02.97.21.07.55; ①), also has a good-value restaurant. There's also an HI **youth hostel**, next to the River Ter at 41 rue Victor-Schoelcher, 3km out on bus line C from the gare SNCF (☎02.97.37.11.65; closed mid-Dec to Jan). *Le Pic*, just south of the gare SNCF, at 2 bd Maréchal-Franchet-d'Esperey (☎02.97.21.18.29; closed Sat pm & Sun), is an imaginative little **restaurant**, with varied menus from 70F.

St-Cado

Twelve kilometres east of Port-Louis, a large bridge spans the broad estuary of the Etel river. A short detour north of the village of Belz on the eastern shore brings you to the delightful islet of **ST-CADO**, a speck on the water dotted with perhaps twenty white-painted houses.

From the mainland, you walk across a spindly little bridge to reach the island itself. Its main feature is a twelfth-century chapel that stands on the site of a Romanesque predecessor built by St Cado around the sixth century. Cado, who was a prince of "Glamorgant", returned in due course to his native Wales and was martyred, but Welsh pilgrims still make their way to this pretty little spot. As Cado is a patron saint of the deaf, it's said that hearing problems can be cured by lying on his stone "bed" inside the chapel. A little fountain behind the chapel only emerges from the sea at low tide.

The Presqu'île de Quiberon

The **Quiberon peninsula**, south of Carnac (see p.424), is well worth visiting on its own merits; **Quiberon** is quite a lively port, and you can get boats out to the islands or walk the shores of this narrow peninsula. The ocean-facing shore, known as the **Côte Sauvage**, is a wild and highly unswimmable stretch, where the stormy seas look like flashing scenes of snowy mountain tops. The sheltered eastern side has safe and calm sandy beaches, and plenty of campsites.

Quiberon

The town of **QUIBERON** itself centres on a miniature golf course surrounded by bars, pizzerias and some surprisingly good clothes and antique shops. The cafés by the long bathing beach are the most enjoyable, along with the old-fashioned *Café du Marché* next to the PTT.

Port-Maria, the fishing harbour and **gare maritime** for the islands of Belle-Île, Houat and Hoëdic (see pp.423), is the most active part of town and has the best concentration of **hotels** and **fish restaurants**. Port-Maria was once famous for its sardines, canned locally, but those days are long gone.

Arrival, information and accommodation

Between July and September, the special Tire Bouchon train links Quiberon's **gare SNCF**, which is a short way above the town proper, with Auray. There are also **buses** right to the **gare maritime** from Vannes (#23 & #24) and Auray (#24) via Carnac.

The **tourist office** at 14 rue de Verdun (July & Aug, Mon–Sat 9am–8pm, Sun 9.30am–noon & 3–7pm; Sept–June Mon–Sat 9am–12.30pm & 2–6.30pm; ☎02.97.50.07.84), downhill and left from the gare SNCF, has an illuminated map outside that purports to monitor exactly which hotels are full, hour by hour.

For most of the year, it's hard to get **accommodation** in Quiberon. In July and August, the whole peninsula is packed, while in winter it gets very quiet indeed. The nicest area in which to stay is along the seafront in Port-Maria.

HOTELS

Hôtel-Restaurant Au Bon Accueil, 6 quai de Houat (☎02.97.50.07.92). One of the best value of Port-Maria's seafront hotels. The rooms are basic but inexpensive, and the friendly dining room downstairs, with something of the atmosphere and decor of a village bar, serves good fish soup and seafood specialities on menus that start at 76F. Closed Jan. ②.

Hôtel-Restaurant de Kermorvan, 45 rue de Kermorvan (☎02.97.30.44.74). A good fall-back in the busier seasons, away from the seafront up near Quiberon's gare SNCF. Reasonable meals, and an attractive garden. April–Oct only. ②.

Le Neptune, 4 quai de Houat (☎02.97.50.09.62). Alongside *Au Bon Accueil* in Port-Maria, and offering a bit more luxury. Some rooms enjoy seafront balconies, and there are the usual seafood menus ranging from 89F to 195F. Closed Jan, & Mon in low season. ④.

L'Océan, 7 quai de l'Océan (☎02.97.50.07.58). Seems to have given up the unequal struggle to keep a restaurant going, but still has reasonably priced rooms. Closed Oct–March. ②.

YOUTH HOSTEL AND CAMPSITES

Les Filets Bleus, 45 rue du Roc'h-Priol (☎02.97.50.15.54). An HI youth hostel 1.5km southeast of the gare SNCF. May–Sept.

Do-Mi-Si-La-Mi campsite, St-Julien (☎02.97.50.22.52). On the sheltered east coast north of Quiberon town. April–Oct.

Camping municipal, Kerne (☎02.97.50.05.07). One of the few sites on the Côte Sauvage, above the cliffs, 1km northwest of Port-Maria. July & Aug.

EATING

Once again, the most appealing area in which to browse the menus is along the water-front in Port-Maria, with its seafood **restaurants** competing to attract ferry passengers. Hotel-owners are very insistent on persuading guests to pay for half-board – at the *Bon Accueil*, for example, that's no great hardship – but there are plenty of alternatives to choose from if you do manage to escape their clutches.

Ancienne Forge, 20 rue Verdun (☎02.97.50.18.64). Set back from the road that leads down to the port from the gare SNCF, with slightly unadventurous but good-value seafood-heavy menus from 82F. Closed Jan, Wed in low season.

La Belle Époque, 42 rue de Port-Maria (☎02.97.50.17.68). Intimate little place as you come to the seafront in Port-Maria, with an adequate fishy menu at 80F, a better one at 90F, and an excellent one at 140F.

de la Criée, 11 quai de l'Océan (☎02.97.30.53.09). Changing fish specialities served every day, fresh from the morning's catch at the quayside. The 89F menu includes stuffed mussels, and fish smoked on the premises. Closed Jan, Sun pm, & Mon in low season.

Belle-Île

BELLE-ÎLE, 45 minutes by ferry from Quiberon, has its own Côte Sauvage on its Atlantic coast, while the landward side is fertile, cultivated ground, interrupted by deep estuaries with tiny ports. To appreciate the island's contrasts, some form of transport is advisable – you can **rent bikes** at the port and main town of **LE PALAIS**, and if you're in a small car the ferry fare is relatively low.

The island once belonged to the monks of Redon; then to the ambitious Nicholas Fouquet, Louis XIV's minister; later to the English, who in 1761 swapped it for Menorca in an unrepeatable bargain deal. Docking at Le Palais, the abrupt star-shaped fortifications of the **citadelle** are the first thing you see (July & Aug daily 9am–7pm; April–June daily 9am–6pm; Sept & Aug daily 9.30am–6pm; Nov–March daily 9.30am–noon & 2–5pm; 20F). Built along stylish and ordered lines by the great fortress builder, Vauban, it is startling in size – filled with doorways leading to mysterious cellars and underground passages, endless sequences of rooms, dungeons and deserted cells. It only ceased being a prison in 1961, having numbered a succession of state enemies and revolutionaries among its inmates, including Ben Bella of Algeria. Less involuntarily, painters such as Monet and Matisse, the writers Flaubert and Proust, and the actress Sarah Bernhardt all spent time on the island. And presumably Alexandre Dumas, too, as Porthos's death, in *The Three Musketeers*, takes place here. A **museum** documents the island's history, in fiction as much as in fact.

For exploring the island, a coastal footpath runs on bare soil the length of the **Côte Sauvage**. At the Sauzon end you'll find the **Grotte de l'Apothicairerie**, so called because it was once full of cormorants' nests, arranged like the jars on a pharmacist's shelves. It's reached by descending a slippery flight of steps cut into the rock. Be careful: most years someone falls and drowns. Inland, on the D25 back towards Le Palais, you pass the two **menhirs**, Jean and Jeanne, said to be lovers petrified as punishment for wanting to meet before their marriage. Another larger menhir used to lie near these two; it was broken up to help construct the road that separates them.

Belle-Île's second town, **SAUZON**, is set at the mouth of a long estuary, 6km to the west of Le Palais. If you're staying any length of time, and you've got transport, it's probably a better place to base yourself.

Getting to Belle-Île

Throughout the year, at least five **ferries** each day (up to seven in high summer) sail from Port-Maria, at the southernmost tip of the Quiberon peninsula, to Belle-Île. They are operated by the Compagnie Morbihannaise et Nantaise de Navigation (adults 105F return, under-13s 64F, under-26s 64F on certain sailings only; small car 404F return; Le Palais ☎02.97.31.80.01; Port-Maria ☎02.97.50.06.90); the crossing takes 45 minutes. The usual port of call in Belle-Île is **Le Palais**, but in July and August the same company sends a few boats direct to **Sauzon**, which takes about half an hour, and also runs a limited service between Sauzon and **Lorient** (1hr 30min; ☎02.97.21.03.97).

Between July and September, and occasionally out of season as well, day trips to the island, organized by Navix (165F; ☎02.97.46.60.00) set out regularly from Vannes, Port-Navalo and La Trinité, and slightly less frequently from Locmariaquer, Auray and Le Bono.

Practicalities

The island's **tourist office** is next to the **gare maritime** as you arrive in Le Palais (July to mid-Sept Mon–Sat 9am–7.30pm, Sun 9am–1pm; mid-Sept to June Mon–Sat 9.30am–6.30pm, Sun 10am–noon; ☎02.97.31.81.93).

Accommodation in Le Palais includes the reasonably priced *Hôtel du Commerce*, place Hôtel-de-Ville (☎02.97.31.81.71; ③), and the simple *Frégate* at the quayside (☎02.97.31.54.16; closed Nov–March; ①). The recently refitted *Hôtel-Restaurant de Bretagne* on quai Macé (☎02.97.31.80.14; ⑤) is a little more expensive and has an excellent sea-view restaurant. There are also three **campsites**, including the year-round *Camping de l'Océan* (☎02.97.31.83.86), and a wildly over-subscribed **youth hostel** (☎02.97.31.81.33; closed Oct; 49F), a short way out of town along the clifftops from the citadelle, at Haute-Boulogne.

Sauzon has one good hotel in a magnificent setting, the *du Phare* (☎02.97.31.60.36; ③; closed Nov–Easter) – where guests must eat its delicious 85F fish dinners – and two **campsites**, *Pen Prad* (☎02.97.31.64.82; April–Sept) and *La Source* (☎02.97.31.60.95; April–Sept).

Houat and Hoëdic

The islands of **Houat** and **Hoëdic** can also be reached by ferry from Quiberon-Port Maria (Compagnie Morbihannaise et Nantaise de Navigation; ☎02.97.50.06.90; 100F return). There is at least one sailing every day of the year, except for the first Thursday of each month in winter; the crossing to Houat takes forty minutes, and to Hoëdic another 25. Navix run day-trips to Houat only from Vannes and Port-Navalo on Thursdays in June and Sept, and daily in July and August (115F; ☎02.97.46.60.00).

You can't take your car to these two very much smaller versions of Belle-Île. Both have a feeling of being left behind by the passing centuries, although the younger fishermen of Houat have revived the island's fortunes by establishing a successful fishing co-operative. Houat in particular has excellent **beaches** – as ever on its sheltered (eastern) side – that fill up with campers in the summer even though camping is not strictly legal. Hoëdic on the other hand has a large municipal **campsite** (☎02.97.30.63.32).

There is a small and not particularly cheap **hotel** on each island; on Houat it's the *Hôtel-Restaurant des Îles* (☎02.97.30.68.02; ③; closed Oct–March) and on Hoëdic *Les Cardinaux* (☎02.97.52.37.27; ③; closed Sun in winter).

Carnac

The **alignments** at **CARNAC** – rows of 2000 or so menhirs, or standing stones, stretching for over 4km to the north of the village – constitute the most important prehistoric site in Europe, long predating Knossos, the Pyramids, Stonehenge or the great Egyptian temples of the same name at Karnak. Mercifully, they now stand a few kilometres in from the sea, meaning you can combine a reasonably tranquil visit to the stones with a stay in the popular, modern seaside resort, pretty hectic by Brittany's mild standards.

The alignments

According to local legend, the standing stones at Carnac are Roman soldiers turned to stone by Pope St-Cornély. Another theory, with a certain amount of mathematical backing, says the giant menhir of Locmariaquer and the Carnac stones were an observatory for the motions of the moon – a sort of three-dimensional Neolithic graph paper for plotting the movements of heavenly bodies. But history has seen them used as ready-quarried stone, and dug up and removed by peasants to protect their precious crops from academic visitors when prehistoric archeology became fashionable. It's impossible to say how many have disappeared, nor really to prove anything from what's left; and in any case their actual arrangement may never have been particularly important, with their significance lying in some great annual ceremony as each one was erected.

Thanks to increasing numbers of visitors, the principal *alignements* have recently been fenced off, and you are no longer free to wander at will among them. The area will be allowed to re-vegetate at a natural pace, but there's no predicting how long that process will take, and even when it's complete the chances are that access will still be restricted. For the moment, a temporary **visitor centre** at the Alignements de Kermario (daily 9am–6pm) sells books and maps of the site, and holds an interesting scale model; a much larger facility is due to be constructed in the near future. The stones themselves are clearly visible on the far side of the fence, though from this or indeed almost any distance they tend to look like no more than stumps in the heather.

The grandly named **Archéoscope**, across the road from the Alignements de Menec, is presumably intended as some sort of substitute for a close-up inspection of the actual megaliths (mid-Feb to mid-Nov daily 10am–noon & 2–6.30pm; 45F; call for the times of English-language performances ☎02.97.52.07.49). In fact, it's a terribly designed and uncomfortable building, containing a small theatre that puts on over-priced half-hour audio-visual presentations. Some of the effects are quite spectacular, but basically it takes a lot of portentous booming to manage to inform you that no one knows very much.

Carnac's **Musée de Préhistoire**, at 10 place de la Chapelle in town (July & Aug Mon–Fri 10am–6.30pm, Sat & Sun 10am–noon & 2–6.30pm; June & Sept daily except Tues 10am–noon & 2–6pm; Oct–May daily except Tues 10am–noon & 2–5pm; April–Sept 30F, Oct–March 25F), is a disappointingly dry museum of archeology that's likely to leave anyone whose command of French is less than perfect almost completely in the dark as to what all the fuss is about. It traces the history of the area from earliest times, starting with 450,000-year-old chipping tools and leading by way of the Neanderthals to the meglaith builders and beyond. As well as authentic physical relics, it holds reproductions and casts of the carvings at Locmariaquer, a scale model of the Alignements de Menec, and diagrams of how the stones may have been moved into place.

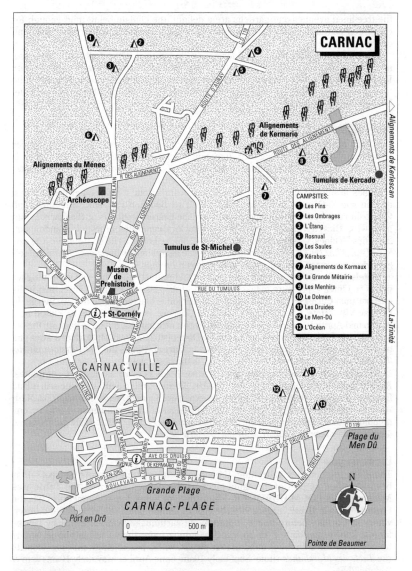

CARNAC

Alignements de Kermario

Alignements du Ménec

Archéoscope

Tumulus de Kercado

Tumulus de St-Michel

Musée de Prehistoire

St-Cornély

CARNAC-VILLE

CAMPSITES:
1. Les Pins
2. Les Ombrages
3. L'Étang
4. Rosnual
5. Les Saules
6. Kérabus
7. Alignements de Kermaux
8. La Grande Métairie
9. Les Menhirs
10. Le Dolmen
11. Les Druides
12. Le Men-Dû
13. L'Océan

Plage du Men Dû

Grande Plage

CARNAC-PLAGE

Port en Drô

0   500 m

Alignements de Kerlescan

La Trinité

Pointe de Beaumer

The town

Carnac itself, divided between the original **Carnac-Ville** and the seaside resort of **Carnac-Plage**, is extremely popular and swarming with holiday-makers in July and August. For most of the year, the alignments are, if anything, only a sideshow. But, as a holiday centre, it has its special charm, especially in late spring and early autumn when it is less crowded – and cheaper. The town and seafront remain well wooded, and the tree-lined avenues and gardens are a delight, the climate being mild enough for evergreen oak and Mediterranean mimosa to grow alongside native stone pine and cypress.

The town's five **beaches** extend for nearly 3km in total. The small plage Légenèse, nearest the yacht club, is reputed to be the beach on which the ill-fated *Chouan* Royalists landed in 1795. The two most attractive beaches, usually counted as one of the five, are **plages Men Dû** and **Beaumer**, which lie to the east towards La Trinité beyond Pointe Churchill.

Practicalities

The main **tourist office** for Carnac is slightly back from the main beach at 74 av des Druides (July & Aug Mon–Sat 9am–7pm, Sun 3–7pm; Sept–June Mon–Sat 9am–noon & 2–6pm; ☎02.97.52.13.52). An annexe in the place de l'Église in town is open between Easter and September (Tues–Sat 9.30am–12.30pm & 2–6pm).

Buses to Auray, Quiberon and Vannes stop near the tourist office on av des Druides, and on rue St-Cornély in Carnac-Ville. The Tire Bouchon **rail** link with Auray and Quiberon runs between July and September; the nearest station is at Plouharnel, 4km northwest. **Bicycles** can be rented from several local campsites, or from Le Randonneur, 20 av des Druides, Carnac-Plage (☎02.97.52.02.55), or Lorcy, 6 rue de Courdiec, Carnac-Ville (☎02.97.52.09.73). The Grande Metairie site also arranges horseback tours. There's a **market** in Carnac on Wednesday and Sunday mornings.

Hotels in Carnac are at a premium in July and August, when you can expect higher prices and intense pressure to take half-board (*demi-pension*). Carnac-Ville is marginally cheaper than Carnac-Plage, although the distinction is blurred where the two merge. In **Carnac-Ville**, *Hôtel Chez Nous*, 5 place de la Chapelle (☎02.97.52.07.28; ③; closed mid-Nov to mid-April), is central and convenient, with a nice garden, but no restaurant; the old stone, ivy-clad *Hôtel le Ratelier*, 4 Chemin de Douët (☎02.97.52.05.04; ③; closed Tues pm, plus Wed Oct–March), has menus from 90F. In **Carnac-Plage**, the *Hôtel-Restaurant Ho-Ty*, 15 av de Kermario (☎02.97.52.11.12; ②), is the best value.

As befits such a family-oriented place, Carnac holds as many as eighteen **campsites**. Among the best are the *Men Dû* (☎02.97.52.04.23; mid-April to Sept) near the sea, inland from the plage du Men Dû, and the more expensive *Grande Metairie* (☎02.97.52.24.01; April to mid-Sept) near the Kercado tumulus. Most of the **restaurants** worth recommending are in hotels, such as the cheerful *Bistrot du Pêcheur* in the *Hôtel La Marine* at 4 place de la Chapelle (☎02.97.52.07.33; ④; April–Sept).

Locmariaquer

Thanks to the complex patterning, the stone of the roof on Gavrinis (see p.431) has been identified as part of the same piece as the dolmen known as the **Table des Marchands** at **LOCMARIAQUER**, 12km south of Auray. Locmariaquer also has the **Grand Menhir Brisé**, supposedly the crucial central point of the megalithic observatory of Carnac. Before being floored by an earthquake in 1722, it was by far the largest known menhir – 22m high and weighing more than a full jumbo jet at 347 tonnes. It now lies on the ground in four pieces, with a possible fifth missing, close to the *Table des Marchands* (June–Sept daily 10am–6pm; April & May daily 10am–1pm & 2–6pm; 25F).

There are a couple of reasonable small **hotels** in Locmariaquer, both with good restaurants. *L'Escale* (☎02.97.57.32.51; ③; closed Oct–March), is right on the waterfront, with a great view from its terrace, while the *Lautram* is set slightly back from the sea, facing the church (☎02.97.57.31.32; ②; closed Oct–March). **Campsites** include the excellent *La Ferme Fleurie* (mid-Feb to Nov; ☎02.97.57.34.06), one kilometre towards Kerinis and open all year, and the summer-only *Lann Brick* (June to mid-Sept; ☎02.97.57.32.79), 1.5km further on, nearer the beach.

Auray

Some people find **AURAY**, with its over-restored ancient quarter, slightly dull – but it is a lot less crowded than Vannes, a lot cheaper than Quiberon town, and usefully placed for exploring Carnac, the Quiberon peninsula and the Gulf of Morbihan.

The centre of the town today is **place de la République**, with its eighteenth-century Hôtel de Ville. In a neighbouring square, linked to the place de la République by rue du Lait, is the seventeenth-century **church of St-Gildas**, with its fine Renaissance porch. A **covered market** adjoins the Hôtel de Ville, but on Mondays an open-air market fills the surrounding streets with colour – and stops all traffic for a considerable radius.

However, Auray's showpiece is undoubtedly the ancient quarter of **St-Goustan**, with its delightful fifteenth- and sixteenth-century houses. The bend in the River Loch, an early defended site, was a natural setting for a town – and, with its easy access to the gulf, it soon became one of the busiest ports of Brittany. Today, as you look at it from the Promenade du Loch on the opposite bank, with the small seventeenth-century stone bridge still spanning the river, it is not difficult to imagine it in its heyday. In 1776, Benjamin Franklin landed here on his way to seek the help of Louis XVI in the American War of Independence.

Practicalities

Auray's **tourist office** is up in town at 20 rue du Lait, very near the Hôtel de Ville on place de la République (Mon–Sat 9.30am–noon & 2–6pm; ☎02.97.24.09.75). A small annex is maintained in July and August at the **gare SNCF**, twenty minutes' walk from the centre, from where buses run through the centre of Auray and on to La Trinité, Carnac and the gare SNCF at Quiberon.

The most appealing place to **stay** is down by the port in the St-Goustan quarter, where the *Hôtel du Marin*, 1 place du Rolland (☎02.97.24.14.58; ②), offers simple accommodation over a bar. Up in town, *Hôtel de la Mairie*, place de la Mairie (☎02.97.24.04.65; ②), is also pleasant, and the *Olympic Bar*, 19 rue Clémenceau (☎02.97.24.06.69), is a friendly restaurant-cum-bar with menus at 47F and 75F.

Ste-Anne-d'Auray

Perhaps the largest of the Breton **pardons** takes place at **STE-ANNE-D'AURAY** on July 26. Some 25,000 pilgrims gather for the occasion to hear Mass in the church, mount the *scala sancta* on their knees, and buy trinkets from the street stalls. The origin of this *pardon* lies in the discovery in 1623 of a statue of Ste Anne by a local peasant, one Nicolazic. He claimed to have been directed to the spot by visionary appearances of the saint (the Virgin's mother) and to have been instructed by her to build a church. Illiterate, speaking only Breton, and with no more than a subsistence livelihood, he managed to raise the necessary funds and construct his church (since destroyed, along with the statue during the Revolution). On his deathbed, twenty years later, the church authorities were still accusing him of making up his story, and the debate continues today with the ongoing campaign to have Nicolazic canonized.

Ste-Anne's status as a pilgrimage centre led to its being chosen as the site for the vast **Monument aux Morts** erected to the memory of the 250,000 Breton dead of the Great War. Even the 200m of closely inscribed wall that surrounds the monument is insufficient to list all the victims by name. All in all, Ste-Anne is a sad and solemn place, not really somewhere to stop, despite its abundant hotels.

Vannes

It was from **VANNES** that the great Breton hero, Nominöe, set out to unify Brittany –
giving the Franks a terrible pasting and pushing the borders past Nantes and Rennes,
where they remained up until the French Revolution nearly a millennium later. Here,
too, the Breton *États* assembled to ratify the Act of Union in the building known as *La
Cohue*. **Vieux Vannes**, the old centre of chaotic streets crammed around the cathedral
and enclosed by ramparts, gardens and a tiny stream, has every reason to vaunt its historic charms.

Arrival, information and accommodation

Vannes' **tourist office** is at 1 rue Thiers (July & Aug Mon–Sat 9am–7pm, Sun
10am–1pm & 3–7pm; Sept–June Mon–Sat 9am–noon & 2–6pm; ☎02.97.47.24.34), on the
corner of rue du Drézen, near place Gambetta. The **gare SNCF** (☎02.97.42.50.50) is 25
minutes' walk north of the town centre. Buses to Auray, Carnac, Quiberon and other
destinations leave from the **gare routière** alongside. **Boats** around the gulf are operated from the **gare maritime**, a little way south of the centre on the parc du Golfe, by
Navix (☎02.97.46.60.00) and Compagnies des Îles (☎02.97.46.18.19).
   In peak season, Vannes can get claustrophobic, but it offers a better choice of **hotels**
than anywhere else around the gulf. The town has also finally acquired its own **youth
hostel**, 4km southeast of the town centre in Séné (☎02.97.66.94.25), on bus route #4
from Place de la République. The nearest **campsite** is *Camping Conleau* at the far end
of avenue du Maréchal-Juin, beyond the Aquarium, and alongside the gulf (April–Sept;
☎02.97.63.13.88).

Hotels

Le Bretagne, 36 rue du Méné (☎02.97.47.20.21). Just outside the walls, around the corner from
the Porte-Prison. Simple rooms – one is utterly basic, several have showers or bath – above the
Taverne de Maître brasserie, which specializes in *choucroute* and has a wide assortment of draught
lagers. ①/②.

Hôtel-Restaurant la Voile d'Or, 1 place Gambetta (☎02.97.42.71.81). Extremely central, taking up
half of the grand crescent at the head of the port, but the actual rooms are neither especially grand
nor expensive. Standard menus in the restaurant that spreads out into the square below start at
either 105F indoors, or 120F on the terrace, with the usual *soupe de poissons* and *steack frites*. ②.

Le Marina, 4 place Gambetta (☎02.97.47.22.81). Fourteen pleasantly refurbished rooms, right in
the thick of the things by the port, with sea views and bright sun in the morning. Downstairs there's
a bar rather than a restaurant. ②.

au Relais du Golfe, 10 place du Général-du-Gaulle (☎02.97.47.14.74). Small cheap rooms, rather
crudely converted, above a bar near the post office. ①.

The town

The new town centre of Vannes is **place de la République**; the focus was shifted outside the medieval city in the nineteenth-century craze for urbanization. The grandest of
the public buildings here, guarded by a pair of sleek and dignified bronze lions, is the
Hôtel de Ville at the top of rue Thiers. By day, however, the streets of the old city, with
their overhanging, witch-hatted houses and busy commercial life, are the chief source
of pleasure. **Place Henri-IV** in particular is stunning, as are the views from it down the
narrow side streets.
   La Cohue, which fills a block between rue des Halles and place du Cathédrale, has
recently become the **Musée de Vannes** (June–Sept daily 10am–6pm; Oct–May Mon &

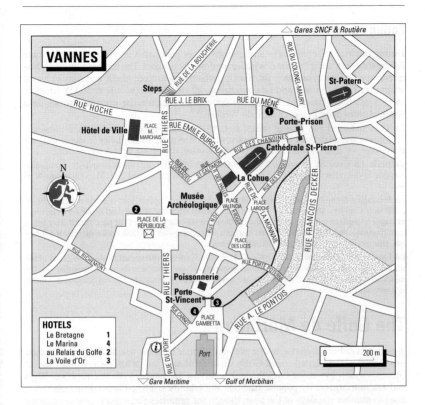

Wed–Sat 10am–noon & 2–6pm, Sun 2–6pm; 25F), having served at various times over the past 750 years as high court and assembly room, prison, revolutionary tribunal, theatre and marketplace. Upstairs it still houses the collection of what was the local Beaux-Arts museum, while the main gallery downstairs is the venue for different temporary exhibitions.

The **Cathédrale St-Pierre** is a rather forbidding place, with its stern main altar almost imprisoned by four solemn grey pillars. The light – purple through new stained glass – illuminates the desiccated finger of the Blessed Pierre Rogue, who was guillotined on the main square in 1796. For a small fee, in summer you can examine the assorted treasures, in the chapterhouse, which include a twelfth-century wedding chest, brightly decorated with enigmatic scenes of romantic chivalry.

Housed in the sombre fifteenth-century Château Gaillard on rue Noé, the **Musée Archéologique** is said to have one of the world's finest collections of prehistoric artefacts (July & Aug Mon–Sat 9.30am–6pm; Sept–June Mon–Sat 2–6pm; 20F). But much like the displays at Carnac, it's all pretty lifeless – some elegant stone axes, more recent Oceanic exhibits by way of context, but nothing very illuminating.

The huge **Aquarium**, in the parc du Golfe on the right bank of the port from place Gambetta, claims the best collection of tropical fish in Europe, 400-odd electric eels and a crocodile "discovered in the Paris sewers" (June–Aug daily 9am–7pm; Sept–May daily 9am–noon & 1.30–6.30pm; 50F).

Eating and drinking

Dining out in old Vannes can be an expensive experience, whether you eat in the intimate little restaurants along the rue des Halles, or down by the port. The leading venues for **live music** are *Le Studio*, on place Bir-Hakeim, which puts on jazz, blues, and African bands when they come to town, and *Le Contretemps*, 22 rue Hoche (☎02.97.42.40.11), which is more a jazz buffs' hang-out. During the first week of August, the open-air **Vannes Jazz Festival** takes place in the Théâtre de Verdure.

Le Commodore, 3 rue Pasteur (☎02.97.46.42.62). Unassuming marine-themed local restaurant, tucked away around the back of the post office, which offers plenty of fishy treats on menus that start at little over 50F at lunchtime, more like 70F in the evening. Closed Sun, & Mon lunchtime.

Crêperie La Cave St Gwenaël, 23 rue St-Gwenaël (☎02.97.47.47.94). Atmospheric, good-value crêperie in the cellar of a lovely old house, facing the cathedral. Closed Sun, Mon lunchtime & all Jan.

La Jonquière, 9 rue des Halles (☎02.97.54.08.34). Very central option, part of a popular Brest-based chain with a modern approach and efficient multi-lingual staff. Despite the road being very narrow, it manages to squeeze a few tables onto the cobbles. For 66F you can take your pick from the buffets of hors d'oeuvres and desserts; set menus start at a little more, with the 138F option offering a full *assiette*, plus, perhaps, pan-fried angler fish with scallops.

Le Lys, 51 rue Maréchal-Leclerc (☎02.97.42.29.30). Gourmet restaurant, a short way east of the walled city. The *nouvelle*-tinged seafood concoctions get progressivly more inventive as the menus rise from 120F, but the portions are never less than reasonable. Closed Sun pm, & Mon in low season.

The Golfe de Morbihan

It comes as rather a surprise to discover that Vannes is on the sea. Its harbour is a channelled inlet of the ragged-edged **Golfe de Morbihan** – *mor bihan* means "little sea" in Breton – which lets in the tides through a narrow gap between the peninsulas of **Rhys** and **Locmariaquer.** By popular tradition the **islands** scattered around this enclosure used to number the days of the year, though for centuries the waters have been rising and there are now fewer than one for each week. Of these, thirty are owned by film stars and the like, while two – the **Île-aux-Moines** and **Île d'Arz** – have regular populations

---

GULF TOURS

In season, dozens of boats leave for **gulf tours** each day from Vannes, Port Navalo, La Trinité, Locmariaquer, Auray and Larmor-Baden. These are among the options:

Navix (☎02.97.46.60.00), who are based in Vannes, run deluxe *vedettes* around the gulf, including half-day (95F) and full-day (115F) tours, excursions to the Île-aux-Moines and the Île d'Arz, and gastronomic cruises for lunch (July & Aug, daily except Mon, departs noon) and dinner (July & Aug, Tues, Fri & Sat, departs 8pm). Other Navix sailings depart from Port Navalo and Locmariaquer (95–150F, plus expensive dinner cruises), and, to no fixed schedule, from Auray, Le Bono and La Trinité. In July and August, they also go to Belle-Île (140F) and **Houat** (130F) from Vannes and Port Navalo.

Compagnie des Îles (☎02.97.46.18.19) run gulf tours (95–150F) and excursions to the Île-aux-Moines (75F) from Vannes. They also operate a more limited programme of similar cruises from **Port Navalo** (115F) and Port Haliguen in Quiberon (115–135F).

Izenah Croisières (☎02.97.57.23.24 or 02.97.26.31.45) run gulf tours in summer (60–85F) and a year-round ferry service, with departures every half-hour, to the Île des Moines (20F return) from Port Blanc at Baden.

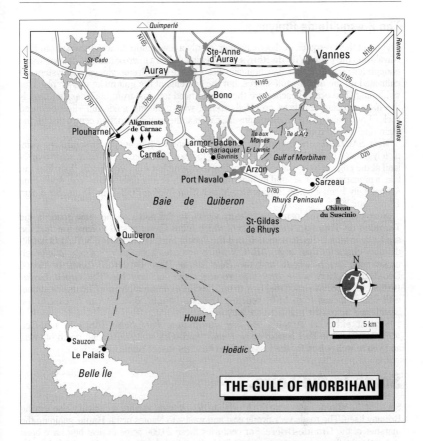

THE GULF OF MORBIHAN

and ferry services and end up in summer being like Safeway on a Saturday morning. The rest are the best, and a **boat tour** around them, or at least a trip out to Gavrinis near the mouth of the gulf, is a fairly compelling attraction. As the boats thread their way through the baffling muddle of channels, you lose track of what is island and what is mainland; and everywhere there are megalithic ruins, stone circles disappearing beneath the water, and solitary menhirs on small hillocks.

Er Lannic and Gavrinis islands

A dramatic group of menhirs, arranged in a figure of eight, is to be seen on the tiny barren island of **Er Lannic** – though only at low tide when the water gives these smaller islets the appearance of stranded hovercraft skirted with mud. The best island for megalithic monuments is, however, **Gavrinis**. It contains (almost consists of) a tumulus that has been partially uncovered to reveal a chamber in which all the slabs of stone are carved with curving lines like fingerprints, axeheads and spirals – purely decorative according to archeologists. The island is a fifteen-minute **ferry** ride from Larmor-Baden; in summer, the boat trips include guided tours of the cairn (April–Oct daily, every half-hour 9.30–11.30am & 1.30–5pm; ☎02.97.42.63.44; 55F).

The Presqu'île de Rhuys

The tip of the Presqu'île de Locmariaquer is only a few hundred metres away from Port Navalo and the **Presqu'île de Rhuys**. This peninsula has a micro-climate of its own, warm enough for pomegranates, figs, bougainvillea and the only Breton vineyards. Oysters are cultivated on the muddy gulf shores, but the currents of the gulf make this no place for swimming. The ocean beaches are the ones to head for: east from St-Gildas-de-Rhuys is the most enticing and least crowded stretch, with glittering gold- and silver-coloured rocks. For details on the whole peninsula, call in at the new information centre just off the main road as you come into Sarzeau.

Near **SARZEAU**, the impressive fourteenth-century **Château de Suscinio** is a completely moated castle that was once a hunting lodge of the Dukes of Brittany, set in marshland at the edge of a tiny village and holding a sagging but still vivid mosaic floor. You can take a precarious stroll around its high ramparts (July & Aug daily 10am–7pm; April–June & Sept daily 10am–noon & 2–7pm; Oct–March Mon–Wed & Fri 2–5pm, Thurs, Sat & Sun 10am–5pm; 20F).

Near the tip of the peninsula, clearly visible to the north of the main road, is the **Tumulus de Thumiac**, from the top of which Julius Cæsar is said to have watched the sea battle in which the Romans defeated the Veneti. Further on, **PORT NAVALO** has little more character than larger **ARZON** which precedes it, but there's a cute little beach tucked into the headland, and the *Hôtel de la Plage* (☎02.97.53.75.92; ②; closed Dec–March) offers some cosy little **rooms** above its busy bar. The *Grand Largue* (☎02.97.53.71.58; ④; closed mid-Nov to mid-Dec) is a considerably more luxurious option, with dinner menus from 140F. Vedettes Thalassa (☎02.97.53.70.25) run **ferries** to the islands and across the gulf from the jetty nearby.

Stay at either of Arzon's two big **campsites**, *Port Sable* (April to mid-Oct; ☎02.97.53.71.98) in Port Navalo or *Le Tindio* (April–Oct; ☎02.97.53.75.59) north of town, and you're well-poised for the less crowded beaches east of Saint-Gildas.

South to the Loire

South of the **Vilaine**, in leaving the Morbihan *département* you are technically also leaving Brittany itself. The roads veer firmly east and west – to Nantes or **La Baule**, avoiding the marshes of the **Grande-Brière**. For centuries these 20,000 acres of peat bog have been deemed to be the common property of all who lived in them. The scattered population, the *Brièrois*, made and make their living by fishing for eels in the streams, gathering reeds and – on the nine days permitted each year – cutting the peat. Tourism has arrived only recently, and is resented. The touted attraction is renting a punt to get yourself lost for a few hours with your pole tangled in the rushes.

Guérande

On the edge of the marshes of the Grande-Brière, just before you come to the sea, is the tiny, absolutely gorgeous walled town of **GUÉRANDE**. Guérande gave its name to this peninsula, and derived its fortune from controlling the salt pans that form a chequerboard across the surrounding inlets. This "white country" is composed of bizarre-looking *oeillets*, each 70 to 80 square metres in extent, in which sea water, since Roman times, has been collected and evaporated.

Guérande today is still entirely enclosed by its stout fifteenth-century ramparts. Although you can't walk along them, a spacious promenade leads right the way around the outside, passing four fortified gateways; for half its length the broad old moat remains filled with water. The main entrance, the **Porte St-Michel** on the east side of town, now holds a small museum of local history (April–Sept daily 10am–12.30pm & 2.30–7pm, Oct daily 10am–noon & 2–6pm; 10F).

Guérande's **tourist office** is just outside the Porte St-Michel at 1 place du Marché au Bois (July & Aug Mon–Sat 9.30am–7pm, Sun 10am–1pm; Sept–June Mon–Sat 9.30am–12.30pm & 1.30–6pm; ☎02.40.24.96.71). Tucked out of sight behind the market, the pretty *Roc-Maria*, 1 rue des Halles (☎02.40.24.90.51; ③; closed mid-Nov to mid-Dec, plus Wed & Thurs in low season), offers cosy **rooms** above a crêperie in a fifteenth-century town house. Opposite the porte Vannetoise and the most impressive stretch of ramparts, to the north, the *Hôtel des Voyageurs*, 1 place du 8 Mai 1945 ((☎02.40.24.90.13; ③; hotel closed Sun pm & Mon in low season, restaurant closed Oct–March), is a *logis* serving good menus from 90F.

La Baule

There is something very surreal about emerging from the Brière to the coast at **LA BAULE** – an imposing, moneyed landscape where the dunes are no longer bonded together with scrub and pines, but with massive apartment buildings and luxury hotels. Sited on the long stretch of dunes that link the former island of Le Croisic to the mainland, it owes its existence to a storm in 1779 that engulfed the old town of Escoublac in silt from the Loire, and thereby created a wonderful crescent of sandy beach.

Neither La Baule's permanence nor its affluence seems in any doubt these days; it's hard to imagine the England football team staying anywhere else in homely Brittany than La Baule, which was their base during the ill-fated World Cup campaign of 1998. This is a resort that very firmly imagines itself in the south of France: around the crab-shaped bay, bronzed nymphettes and would-be Clint Eastwoods ride across the sands into the sunset against a backdrop of cruising lifeguards, horse-dung removers and fantastically priced cocktails. It can be fun if you feel like a break from the more subdued Breton attractions – and the beach is undeniably impressive. It's not a place to imagine you're going to enjoy strolling around in search of hidden charms; the back streets have an oddly rural feel, but hold nothing of any interest.

Full details on staying in La Baule can be had from the **tourist office**, away from the seafront at 8 place de la Victoire (mid-May to mid-Sept daily 9am–7.30pm, mid-Sept to mid-May Mon–Sat 9.30am–noon & 2–6pm; ☎02.40.24.34.44). La Baule has two **gare SNCFs**, the barely used La-Baule-les-Pins, and the main La-Baule-Escoublac near the tourist office on place Rhin-et-Danube (☎02.40.66.50.50), where the TGVs from Paris arrive. The **gare routière** is at 4 place de la Victoire (☎02.40.60.25.58).

Few of the **hotels** are cheap, particularly in high season, and in low season more than half are closed. The cheapest options are near the main gare SNCF, less than 1km from the beach; these include the *Hôtel-Restaurant la Coquille*, 10 av Clemenceau (☎02.40.60.38.47; ①), and the classier *Marini*, 22 av Clemenceau (☎02.40.60.23.29; ③; closed mid-Nov to mid-March). The best of the many local **campsites**, 2km back from the beach, is *La Roseraie*, 20 av Sohier (April–Sept; ☎02.40.60.46.66).

Le Croisic

The small port of **LE CROISIC**, sheltering from the ocean around the corner of the headland, is a more realistic and more attractive place to stay than La Baule. These days it's basically a pleasure port, but fishing boats do still sail from its harbour, near the very slender mouth of the bay, and there's a modern **fish market** near the long Tréhic jetty, where you can go to see the day's catch auctioned. The hills on either side of the harbour, Mont Lenigo and Mont Esprit, are not natural; they are formed from the ballast left by the ships of the salt trade. If you are staying, choose between the **hotels** *Les*

Nids, 83 bd Général-Leclerc (☎02.40.23.00.63; ③; closed Jan–March), or the purple-and-white *Estacade*, near the end of the port at 4 quai de Lénigo (☎02.40.23.03.77; ③), where the 85F menu includes *soupe de poissons* and fish of the day.

Close by, all around the rocky sea coast known as the **Grande Côte**, are a whole range of **campsites**, including the *Océan* (☎02.40.23.07.69; April–Sept). For equally good beaches and a chance of cheaper **hotel** accommodation, you could go east from La Baule to **Pornichet** (though preferably keeping away from the plush marina) or to the tiny **St-Marc**, where in 1953 Jacques Tati filmed *Monsieur Hulot's Holiday*.

St-Nazaire

The best sandy coves in the region are to be found on the western outskirts of **ST-NAZAIRE**, linked by wooded paths and almost deserted. But it's a gloomy city. It was bombed to extinction in World War II, and its shipyards, in more or less continuous operation since constructing Julius Cæsar's fleet, are now closing. The one reason you might want to stay is the relative ease of finding inexpensive **hotel** space – so elusive in this area in summer. Options include the *St Louis*, 48 rue des Halles (☎02.40.22.40.34; ③), and the new *Korali*, opposite the station on place de la Gare (☎02.40.01.89.89; ③). There's also a **hostel**, the *Foyer du Jeune Travailleur*, at 30 rue Soleil-Levant (☎02.40.00.94.10). Even if St-Nazaire is a familiarly depressing town in total industrial decline, it has one inspiring piece of engineering – the **Pont St-Nazaire**, a great elongated S-curved suspension bridge over the mouth of the Loire. Driving across it incurs a heavy toll, but bikes go over for free.

Nantes

NANTES, the former capital of Brittany, is no longer officially part of the province: it was transferred to the Pays de la Loire in 1962 when the modern administrative regions were established. Nonetheless, such bureaucracy is not taken too seriously in the city, and its history is closely bound up with Breton fortunes. A considerable medieval centre, it later achieved great wealth from colonial expeditions, the slave trade and shipbuilding – activities in turn surpassed by more recent industrial growth. Despite the tower blocks masking the Loire and motorways tearing past the city, it remains to its inhabitants an integral part of Brittany.

Arrival, information and accommodation

Nantes' **tourist office**, housed in a shack outside the colonnaded Palais de la Bourse, in place du Commerce (Mon–Fri 9am–7pm, Sat 10am–6pm, Sun 10am–1pm & 1.30–6pm; ☎02.40.47.04.51), provides a free book-size guide, including an excellent town map, and runs various guided tours of the city. There's a subsidiary office alongside the château at 1 rue de la Château (Wed–Sun 10am–1pm & 1.30–6pm).

The **gare SNCF** (☎02.40.08.50.50), a little way east of the château, is served by three or more TGVs daily from Paris (just 2hr away). It has two exits; for most facilities (tramway, buses, hotels) use Accès Nord. There are two central **bus** stations. Local buses use the Gare des Bus on cours Franklin, alongside place du Commerce, while the long-distance **gare routière** (☎02.40.47.62.70) is 400m away on allée Baco, near place Ricordeau. Modern rubber-wheeled **trams** run along the old riverfront, past the gare SNCF and the two bus stations. Flat-fare tickets are valid for one hour, rather than just a single journey, though one-day tickets are also available. **Bicycles** can be rented from Seguir Bernard, 38 rue des Alouettes (☎02.40.46.56.32), as well as the gare SNCF.

Although it holds plenty of **hotels** to suit all budgets, Nantes is one of those cities where you won't necessarily stumble upon a suitable place just by walking or driving

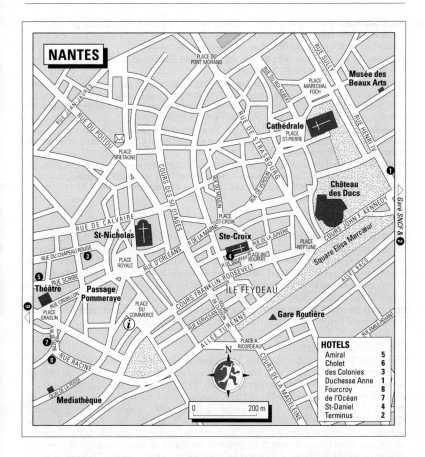

around at whim. Instead, there are two main concentrations: one, as ever, in the immediate vicinity of the gare SNCF, and one in the narrow streets around the place Greslin. The HI **youth hostel**, *Cité Universitaire Internationale*, in a postmodern former tobacco factory at 2 place de la Manu (☎02.40.20.57.25), is open from July to mid-September only; within 100m of the gare SNCF, it's accessible by taking tramway #1 towards Malachère and getting off at Manufacture.

Hotels

Amiral, 26bis rue Scribe (☎02.40.69.20.21). Well-maintained little hotel – even if it is above a porn cinema – on lively pedestrianized street just north of place Graslin, and perfect for young night owls. Room rates for Saturday and Sunday nights drop by up to 70F. ④.

Cholet, 10 rue Gresset (☎02.40.73.31.04). Quiet, friendly option very close to place Graslin, where all the wide assortment of rooms have en-suite facilities. Rates drop at weekends. ③.

des Colonies, 5 rue du Chapeau Rouge (☎02.40.48.79.76). Neat, good-value little hotel a couple of blocks up from place Graslin, and in walking distance of everything. Discounts on weekends. No restaurant. ③.

Duchesse Anne, 3–4 place de la Duchesse Anne (☎02.40.74.3029). Large and very grand hotel in a slightly noisy location, alongside the Château des Ducs less than 500m from the gare SNCF, with castle views from the most opulent of its consistently palatial rooms. ④.

Fourcroy, 11 rue Fourcroy (☎02.40.44.68.00). Basic and economical rooms in a backstreet just below place Graslin, near the Médiathèque. ②.

l'Océan, 11 rue Maréchal-de-Lattre-de-Tassigny (☎02.40.69.73.51). A pleasant hotel, with helpful management, just below place Graslin near the Médiathèque. Parking space is available around the back. No restaurant, though there is a restaurant of the same name on the quai de la Fosse a few metres away at the bottom of the street. Closed last two weeks of Dec. ①.

St-Daniel, 4 rue du Bouffay (☎02.40.47.41.25). These simple but pleasant and well-lit rooms, on a cobbled street just off the place du Bouffay in the very heart of the old city, are much in demand in summer. Paying 20F extra gets you a TV in your room. ①.

Terminus, 3 allée du Commandant-Charcot (☎02.40.74.24.51). Very near the gare SNCF, on the way towards the château. All rooms have double beds and TV. A reasonable restaurant, so long as you skip the very limited 50F menu and head for those at 80F and upwards. ②.

The city

The Loire, the source of Nantes' riches, has dwindled from the centre. As recently as the 1930s the river crossed the city in seven separate channels, but German labour as part of reparations for World War I filled in five. What are still called "islands" in the centre are now surrounded and isolated, not by water, but by hectic dual carriageways. These are not easy to cross, but they do at least mean that Nantes is separated into a series of discernible districts: the older medieval city is concentrated around the cathedral, with the château prominent in its southeast corner, and the elegant nineteenth-century town lies to the west, across the cours des 50-Otages.

The Château des Ducs

Though no longer on the waterfront, and subjected to a certain amount of damage over the centuries, the **Château des Ducs** still preserves the form in which it was built by two of the last rulers of independent Brittany, François II, and his daughter Duchess Anne, born here in 1477. The list of famous people who have been guests or prisoners, defenders or belligerents, of the castle is impressive. It includes Gilles de Rais (Bluebeard), publicly executed in 1440; Machiavelli, in 1498; John Knox as a galley-slave in 1547–49; and Bonnie Prince Charlie preparing for Culloden in 1745. The most significant act in the castle was the signing of the **Edict of Nantes** in 1598 by Henri IV. The edict ended the Wars of Religion by granting a certain degree of toleration to the Protestants, but had far more crucial consequences when it was revoked, by Louis XIV in 1685.

The stout ramparts of the château remain pretty much intact, and most of the encircling moat is filled with water, surrounded by well-tended lawns which make a popular spot for lunchtime picnics. Within the walls stand a rather incongruous pot-pourri of buildings added in differing styles over the years. Until recently, these housed a number of museums, but all are currently closed while their contents are rationalized into one much larger mega-museum, which is unlikely to open much before 2005. Until then, visits will probably to continue to consist of a brief walk into the courtyard and up onto the walls (July & Aug daily 10am–noon & 2–6pm; Sept–June daily except Tues 10am–noon & 2–6pm; 10F).

The cathedral

In 1800 the Spaniards Tower, the castle's arsenal, exploded, shattering the stained glass of the **Cathédrale de St-Pierre-et-St-Paul** over 200m away. This was just one of many disasters that have befallen the church. It was used as a barn during the Revolution;

bombed during World War II; and damaged by a fire in 1971, just when things seemed in order again. Restored and finally re-opened, its soaring height and lightness are emphasized by the clean white stone. It contains the tomb of François II and his wife Margaret, the parents of Duchess Anne – with somewhat grating symbols of Power, Strength and Justice for him and Fidelity, Prudence and Temperance for her.

The Musée des Beaux Arts

Nantes' **Musée des Beaux Arts**, east of the cathedral on rue Clemenceau, has a respectable collection of paintings displayed in excellent modern galleries, and plays host to a high standard of temporary exhibitions (Mon, Wed, Thurs & Sat 10am–6pm; Fri 10am–9pm, Sun 11am–6pm; 30F). Not all its Renaissance and contemporary works are on display at any one time, but you should be able to take in canvases ranging from a gorgeous *David Triumphant* by Delaunay to Chagall's *Le Cheval Rouge* and Monet's *Nymphéas*.

The nineteenth-century town

The financier Graslin took charge of the development of the western part of the city in the 1780s, when Nantes' prosperity was at a high due to the sugar and slave trades. **Place Royale**, with its distinctive fountain, was first laid out in the closing years of the eighteenth century, and has been rebuilt since it was bombed in 1943; the 1780s also produced the nearby **place Graslin**, named after its creator, with the elaborately styled **Grand Théâtre**, whose Corinthian portico contrasts with the 1895 Art Nouveau of *La Cigale* brasserie on the corner.

West of the place Royale on rue Crebillon, a spectacular nineteenth-century multi-level shopping centre, the **Passage Pommeraye**, drops down three flights of stairs towards the river. The attention to detail lavished upon it is on a scale undreamt of in modern malls, giving a glimpse of early consumerism; each of the gas lamps that light the central area is held by an individually crafted marble cherub.

Just south of here is the elongated former **Île Feydeau**, a typical victim of the modern "development" of Nantes. Its eighteenth-century houses, seen at their best in rue Kervegan, retain some of their Baroque charm – but the road is bisected by cours Olivier-de-Clisson and its horrendous traffic jams. The one thing of interest here today is the **Musée Jules-Verne**, 3 rue de l'Hermitage (Mon & Wed–Sat 10am–noon & 2–5pm, Sun 2–5pm; 10F), commemorating the birthplace of the first serious writer of science fiction.

Rue Voltaire runs west of the place Graslin, leading to the **Musée d'Histoire Naturelle** at no. 12 (Tues–Sat 10am–noon & 2–6pm, Sun 2–5pm; 30F), centring on a vivarium, whose miserable animals are not for the squeamish (the soft-shelled turtle in particular tugs at the heartstrings). But don't let this put you off the eccentric assortment of oddities of its museum collection: rhinoceros toenails, a coelecanth and an aepyornis egg, and slightly tatty stuffed specimens of virtually every bird and animal imaginable. There is an Egyptian mummy, too, as well as a shrunken Maori head and a complete tanned human skin – taken in 1793 from the body of a soldier whose dying wish was to be made into a drum.

Further along is Viollet-le-Duc's **Palais Dobrée** (daily except Mon 10am–noon & 1.30–5.30pm; 20F), a nineteenth-century mansion given over to two museums, one of which claims to feature Duchess Anne's heart in a box.

Eating

Unlike hotels, **restaurants** fill the winding lanes of the old city; it shouldn't take long to come up with something if you wander the pedestrian streets in the centre. Nantes is big enough to have all sorts of ethnic alternatives as well, with Algerian, Italian, Chinese, Vietnamese and Indian places in addition to those listed here.

Brasserie Côté Rive, 5 square Fleuriot de l'Angle (☎02.40.20.35.20). Bright, brisk brasserie a short walk west of the cours des 50-Ôtages and just east of place Royale. All-you-can-eat *moules frites* for 49F, seafood couscous at 82F, and a good fishy menu for 98F. Open daily until after midnight.

Le Carnivore, 7 allée des Tanneurs (☎02.40.47.87.00). The rendezvous of choice for incorrigible meat-eaters, offering not just the steaks you might expect, but even rarefied pleasures such as ostrich and buffalo. Menus start at 65F.

La Cigale, 4 place Graslin (☎02.51.84.94.94). Famous late nineteenth-century brasserie, offering fine meals in opulent surroundings. Fish is a speciality. Menus 75F and 135F, served until midnight in keeping with the tradition of providing post-performance refreshments for patrons of the adjacent theatre.

La Mangeoire, 16 rue des Petites-Écuries (☎02.40.48.70.83). Very good country food. The 58F lunch menu in particular is a real bargain, there's a solid 82F dinner menu, and the "Gourmet" for 142F is a delight; even if you can't stomach the dozen snails, there's a mixed fish grill to sate any appetite. Closed Sun & Mon.

Le Pescadou, 8 allée Baco (☎02.40.35.29.50). Despite being somewhat off the beaten track, near the gare routière, this is Nantes' most fashionable venue for fresh fish, with menus from 90F. Closed Sat lunch & Sun.

Le Petit Bacchus, 5 rue Beauregard (☎02.40.47.50.46). Red-painted half-timbered house, with the atmosphere and decor of a World War I *estaminet*, just off rue des 50-Ôtages in a little alley leading down to the cours F-Roosevelt. Lovely 80F menu featuring duck à l'orange or fish of the day. Closed Sun, plus first 3 weeks in Aug.

travel details

Buses

Brest to: Le Conquet (4 daily; 30min); Quimper (6 daily; 1hr 30min); Roscoff (5 daily; 1hr 30min).

Quimper to: Camaret (5 daily; 1hr 30min) via Locronan & Crozon (1hr 20min); Pointe du Raz (3 daily; 1hr 15min) via Audierne (1hr); Quimperlé (6 daily; 1hr 30min) via Concarneau (30min);

Rennes to: Dinan (6 daily, 1hr 20min); Dinard (8 daily; 1hr 40min); Fougères (7 daily; 1hr); Vannes (8 daily; 2hr).

Roscoff to: Morlaix (3–6 daily; 50min); Vannes via Quimper (1 only Mon, Thurs & Sat; 4hr).

St-Brieuc to: Dinan (4 daily; 1hr); Lannion via Guingamp (4 daily; 1hr 40min); St-Cast, via Lamballe, Le Val-André, Erquy & Cap Fréhel (4 daily; 1hr 50min); Paimpol (8 daily; 1hr 30min).

St-Malo to: Cancale (4 daily; 35min); Combourg (2 daily; 1hr); Dinan (4 daily; 45min); Dinard (8 daily, 30min); Fougères via Pontorson (3 daily; 2hr); Mont St-Michel (4 daily; 1hr 30min); Rennes (5 daily; 1hr 30min); St-Cast via St-Jacut (3 daily; 1hr).

Vannes to: Malestroit (4 daily; 45 min); Ploërmel (4 daily; 1hr 25min); Rennes (8 daily; 2hr) via Josselin (1hr).

Trains

Brest to: Paris-Montparnasse (7 daily; 4hr), via Landerneau (12min), Landivisiau (20min), Morlaix (35min) & Rennes (2hr 10min); Quimper (6 daily, 1hr 30min).

Guingamp to: Paimpol (June–Sept only, 4–5 daily; 45min).

Quimper to: Lorient (4 daily; 30min); Redon (2 daily; 1hr 40min); Vannes (4 daily; 1hr).

Rennes to: Brest (8 daily; 2hr 10min) via St Brieuc (45min) & Morlaix (1hr 40min); Caen (4 daily; 3hr) via Dol & Pontorson; Nantes (4 daily; 1hr 30min); Paris-Montparnasse (8 daily; 2hr 10min); Quimper (4 daily; 2hr 30min) via Vannes (1hr).

Roscoff to: Morlaix (6 daily; 30min).

St-Brieuc to: Lannion to via Plouaret & Guingamp (June–Sept. only, 1–4 daily; 1hr).

St-Malo to: Caen (8 daily; 3hr 30min); Dinan (8 daily; 1hr); Dol (12 daily; 25min); Rennes (12 daily; 1hr; connections for Paris on TGV).

Ferries

St-Malo: Brittany Ferries to Portsmouth (1 daily mid-March to mid-Nov, otherwise less frequently; 9hr daytime crossing) and Plymouth (1 weekly mid-Nov to mid-March; 8hr). Émeraude Lines (☎02.99.40.48.40) to Dinard, Dinan up the River Rance, along the Brittany coast to Cap Fréhel, Cézembre and Dinard (May–Sept), Jersey (mid-March to mid-Nov), Guernsey & Sark (April–Sept), & Îles Chausey in Normandy. Condor Ferries (☎02.99.20.03.00) run services to Jersey (4 daily April–Sept, 2 daily Oct, 1 daily second half of March and first half of Nov), Guernsey (2 daily April–Oct, 1 daily second half of March and first half of Nov) and Sark (daily April–Oct). Channiland (☎02.99.40.40.90) go to Jersey (1–4 daily mid-March to mid-Nov), slightly less frequently to Guernsey and Sark.

Roscoff: Brittany Ferries to Plymouth (6hr) & Cork (13–17hr).

For details of ferries to Ouessant & Molène see p.400; to Bréhat, see p.390; to Batz, see p.395; to Groix, see p.420; to Sein, see p.408; to Belle-Île, see p.423; & for tours of the Gulf of Morbihan see p.430.

For general information on renting barges for use on the inland waterways, contact the Comité de Promotion Touristique des Canaux Bretons, Office du Tourisme, place du Parlement, 35600 Rennes (☎02.99.71.06.04).

CHAPTER SIX

THE LOIRE

The density of châteaux and all their great Renaissance intrigues and associations can prove quite intimidating, but if you pick your castles selectively, rid yourself of a sense of duty to guided tours, and spend days on riverbanks with supplies of cheese, fruit and white Loire wines, the Loire can be one of the most enjoyable of all French regions.

The Loire's central region of **Touraine**, known as "the heart of France", has the best wines, the most scented flowers and delicious fruit, two of the best châteaux in **Chenonceau** and **Azay-le-Rideau**, and, it's argued, the purest French accent in the land. It also takes in three of the Loire's most pleasurable tributaries: the **Cher**, **Indre** and **Vienne**, each with its own individual attractions. If you have just a week to spare for the region, then these are the parts to spend it in. The most imposing palaces and hunting lodges are upstream around **Blois** – including the Renaissance turreted fantasy of **Chambord** – with the wild and watery region of the **Sologne** to the east, good for long walks and rides, as well as the fascinating troglodyte dwellings carved out of the rockfaces around **Saumur**.

As well as the select handful of châteaux, the region has a few unexpected sights, most unmissable of which are the gardens at **Villandry**, outside Tours; the Romanesque abbey at **St-Benoît-sur-Loire**; and the stunning tapestries in **Angers**, capital of the ancient wine-producing county of **Anjou**. Of the cities, **Tours** and Angers provide the best urban bases, **Orléans** has charm, and **Le Mans**, though some way north of the Loire valley in the topographically uninspiring *département* of **Sarthe**, is the least touristy and most authentically lively, even outside race times. Further upstream, and quite some distance south of the Loire itself, the marshy farming land of **Berry** contains few sights, in addition to the magnificent cathedral and medieval town of **Bourges**, lying between the Loire and the Cher.

The lowest – and best – stretch of the **Loire** flows through Touraine, languidly floating by long islands of reed and willows before it reaches its estuary. But the Loire is still the wild river of whirlpools, quicksands, shifting banks and channels, with vicious currents and a propensity to flood. Plans to control the water levels of the central stretch with dams have been dropped, thanks to hard campaigning by conservationists,

ACCOMMODATION PRICE CATEGORIES

Each hotel in this chapter has a symbol which corresponds to one of eight price categories.

① Under 160F	④ 300–400F	⑦ 600–700F
② 160–220F	⑤ 400–500F	⑧ Over 700F
③ 220–300F	⑥ 500–600F	

The prices quoted are for the cheapest available double room in high season, though remember that many of the cheap places will have more expensive rooms with en-suite facilities.

despite strong interest from various businesses including the four nuclear power stations that use the river water for their cooling. The longest river in France, the Loire is for the most part too unpredictable for swimming or boating, and no goods are carried along it.

In general, this is a prime tourism region, where air-conditioned cars and bus tours are the norm. Train lines run along the river towards Nantes and Brittany and up through Tours to Paris, but if you're exploring on your own, it's a good idea to rent some means of transport, at least for occasional forays. Buses can be sparse, their schedules not geared to outsiders, and trains are too limiting. But this is wonderful and easy cycling country, best of all on the floodbanks, or *levées*, of the river itself.

Which châteaux?

The Loire **châteaux** are very much part of the landscape, but the choice of which to visit is vast and bewildering, and trying to pack in the maximum can quickly dent your appreciation of their architecture, settings and historical significance.

Of the most famous, **Azay-le-Rideau** (p.479) and **Chenonceaux** (p.475) both belong exclusively to the Renaissance period and are undoubtedly the most beautiful, rivalled only by the gardens of **Villandry** (p.473). **Blois** (p.462), with its four wings representing four distinct periods, is extremely impressive, followed by the monstrously huge **Chambord** (p.465). For an evocation of medieval times, the citadel of **Loches** (p.460) is hard to beat; other feudal fortresses include the lesser-known **Fougères-sur-Bièvre** (p.464), the ruined **Chinon** (p.481), **Langeais** (p.474), still furnished in fifteenth-century style, **Meung-sur-Loire** (p.449), with its vile dungeons, and **Amboise** (p.472).

Many châteaux that started life as serious military defences were turned into luxurious residences by their regal or ducal owners: good examples are **Brissac** (p.493), **Chaumont** (p.463), with its nineteenth-century stables, **Ussé** (see p.479) and **Sully** (p.451). At Ussé and Sully it is the setting and exterior appearance that are most striking, so you can admire them without forking out for admission. **Le Plessis-Bourré** (p.493) is a fine example of late fifteenth-century elegant residence and strong defences combined. At **Valençay** (p.478), the interior of the Renaissance château is Napoleonic; **Cheverny** (see p.464) is the prime example of seventeenth-century magnificence; its neighbour **Beauregard** (p.465) encloses a sixteenth-century core with seventeenth-century additions but is most famous for its portrait gallery. Other châteaux are more compelling for their contents than for their architecture: **Argent-sur-Sauldre** (p.454), with a brilliant ceramics collection; **St-Brisson** (p.452), with art exhibitions and medieval weaponry demonstrations; cadillacs at the château in **St-Michel-sur-Loire** (p.474); a museum of living donkeys at **Gizeux** (p.474); and **La Bussière** (p.452), celebrating fish and fishing in a fine lake setting with Le Nôtre gardens. At **Saumur** (p.483), a museum of the horse rivals the attraction of the castle itself, while at **Angers** (p.488) the extremely impressive medieval castle pales into insignificance when set against the tapestry of the Apocalypse it houses, the greatest work of art in the Loire valley.

Entry prices can be pretty steep, particularly for the privately owned châteaux. There is no consistency in the concessions offered: if you're over 65, under 25, a student or still at school, check for any reductions and make sure you've got proof of age or a student card with you.

Orléans and around

ORLÉANS is the northernmost city on the Loire, sitting at the apex of a huge arc in the river as it switches direction and starts to flow southwest. The proximity to Paris, just over 100km away, is a problem for this ancient city. Not only do many Orléanais go

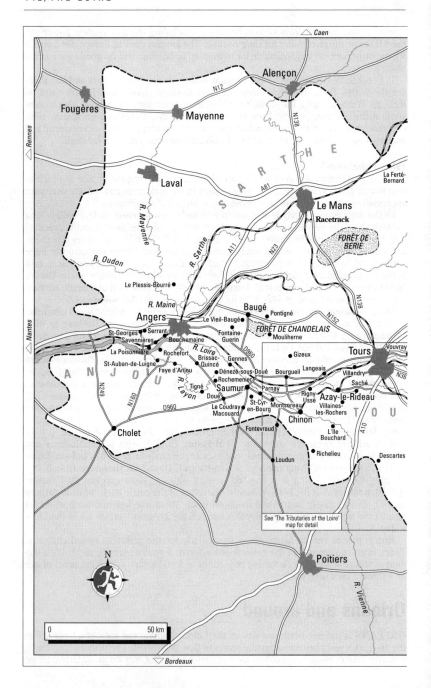

△ Caen

Alençon

N12

Fougères

Mayenne

N138

Laval

La Ferté-
Bernard

R. Mayenne

S A R T H E

△ Rennes

R. Oudon

A81

Le Mans

Racetrack

R. Sarthe

A11

N23

FORÊT DE
BERIE

Le Plessis-Bourré ●

R. Maine

Baugé

Pontigné

N152

N138

Angers

Le Vieil-Baugé ●

FORÊT DE CHANDELAIS

△ Nantes

St-Georges

Serrant

Fontaine-
Guerin

● Mouliherne

Savennières

Bouchemaine

R. Loire

D960

Gizeux

Tours

Vouvray

La Poissonnière

Rochefort

Brissac-
Quincé

Gennes

Bourgueil

Langeais

Villandry

N36

St-Auban-de-Luigne

Faye d'Anjou

Dénezé-sous-Doué

Saché

A N J O U

R. Layon

Rochemenier

Saumur

Parnay

Rigny

Azay-le-Rideau

N249

N160

Tigné

Doué

Le Coudray
Macouard

Montsoreau

Ussé

Villaines-
les-Rochers

T O U

D960

St-Cyr-
en-Bourg

Chinon

Cholet

Fontevraud

L'Ile
Bouchard

A10

Loudun

Richelieu

Descartes

See 'The Tributaries of the Loire'
map for detail

N

Poitiers

R. Vienne

0   50 km

▽ Bordeaux

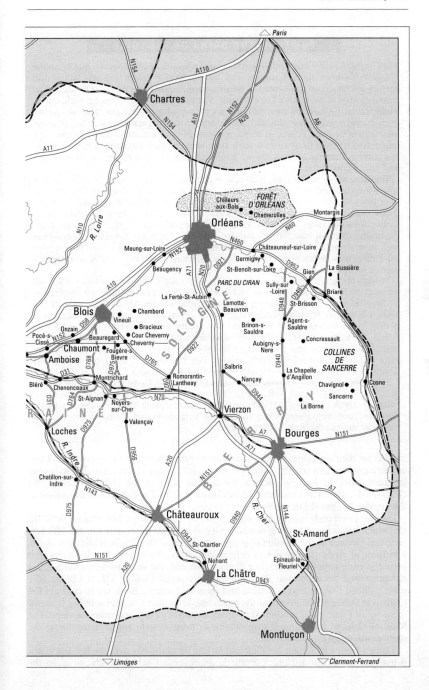

THE FOOD AND DRINK OF THE LOIRE

Fish from the river features on most restaurant menus. Favourites are *filet de sandre* (pickerel), salmon (often flavoured with sorrel), stuffed bream and eels softened in mature red wine, and little smelt-like fishes served deep-fried (*la friture de la Loire*). The favoured meat of the eastern Loire is **game**. Pheasant, guinea fowl, pigeon, duck, quails, young rabbit, venison and even wild boar are all hunted in the Sologne. They are served in rich sauces made from the wild mushrooms of the region's forests or the common *champignon de Paris*, cultivated on a huge scale in caves cut out of the limestone rock along the Loire and its tributaries. Both Tours and Le Mans specialize in *rillettes* or potted pork; in Touraine *charcuteries* you'll also find *pâté au biquion*, made from pork, veal and young goat's meat.

The Loire valley is also great **fruit-** and **vegetable**-growing country. There are greengages from orchards in Anjou, called *Reine Claudes* after François I's queen. Market stalls overflow with summer fruits, and old varieties of apples and pears can still be found. *Tarte Tatin*, an upside-down apple tart, is said to have originated from Lamotte-Beuvron in the Sologne. Tours is famous for its French beans, and Saumur for its potatoes. Asparagus (the best from Vineuil) appears in soufflés, omelettes and other egg dishes as well as on its own, accompanied by vinaigrette made (if you're lucky) with local walnut oil. Finally, from Berry, comes the humble lentil, whose green variety often accompanies salmon or trout.

Though not as famous as the produce of Bordeaux and Burgundy, the Loire valley has some of the finest **wines** in France, and there are well over twenty different *appellations* to discover. Sancerre, halfway along the river, produces some well-known flinty, very dry white wines made from the Sauvignon grape, as well as some good reds and a rosé (see p.453). There are the mellow whites and rosés of the Anjou vineyards in the west (see p.493), the fruity sparkling *méthode champenoise* wines around Saumur, and the sweet, still wines of Vouvray (see p.471). The Cabernet grape is used to produce the rich, ruby reds of Chinon (see p.480) and Bourgueil (see p.474); these are some of the best Touraine wines, and many are capable of maturing over decades.

To go with the wine, Touraine has some of the best soft goat's **cheese**: Ste-Maure, shaped into a long cylinder with a piece of straw running through the middle; the small, round *crottin de Chavignol* goat's cheese from Sancerre, eaten fresh or matured, when it becomes hard with a very sharp flavour; the pyramid-shaped Pouligny-St-Pierre and Valençay; and the flat, round Selles-sur-Cher.

to Paris for their evenings out, they commute to work there as well. To counter its subordinate position as a country suburb to the capital, Orléans feels compelled to recoup its faded glory by harking back to the turning point in the Hundred Years' War (1339–1453), when Paris was infested by disease and the English, and Orléans itself as the key city to central France, was under siege.

Despite a rich early history of being a centre of revolt against Julius Cæsar in 52 BC (for which it was burnt to the ground), besieged by Attila the Hun in the mid-fifth century, and elevated to the position of temporary capital of the Frankish kingdom in 498, it is **Joan of Arc**'s (Jeanne d'Arc) deliverance of the city in 1429 that the town feels bound to commemorate. Crazed or divinely inspired, the seventeen-year-old peasant girl presented herself to the Dauphin, the uncrowned Charles VII, at Chinon (see p.481), rallied French troops at Blois and then led them up the Loire to confront the English at Orléans. She informed the encircling army that God had sent her to throw them out of France, and proceeded to break all military rules and raise the siege. The Maid of Orléans is honoured everywhere in town despite people questioning the story's authenticity.

There's been a lot of new building and tarting up of the city over the last few years. It may not have provided much aesthetic improvement, which is difficult given the beauty of Orléans's ancient buildings, but it's been a valiant and not entirely vain attempt to bring back some pride to the place.

Arrival, information and accommodation

The **Centre d'Arc**, a large modern shopping centre on place d'Arc, is the first thing you'll see as you step out of the **gare SNCF** (☎08.36.35.35.35). The **tourist office** is in the Centre d'Arc on the south side overlooking place Albert-1er (April–Sept Tues–Sat 9am–7pm, Mon opens at 10am, Sun 10am–noon; Oct–March Tues–Sat 9am–6.30pm; ☎02.38.24.05.05, fax 02.38.54.49.84), where you can pick up *Orléans Poche*, a free **listings magazine** telling what's going on around the town. The **gare routière**, on rue Marcel-Proust (☎02.38.53.94.75), is a short way northeast off rue Prince-Albert-1er.

Accommodation in Orléans is good, with a few cheap hotels near the unusually appealing station area, and a youth hostel and campsites not too far out.

Hotels

de Blois, 1 av de Paris (☎02.38.62.61.61). Conveniently placed opposite the station above an interesting, typically French bar. The rooms are a little dingy, but good value. ①.

Charles Sanglier, 8 rue Charles-Sanglier (☎02.38.53.38.50, fax 02.38.68.01.85). Comfortable enough and very central. ③.

Jackotel, 18 Cloître-St-Aignan (☎02.38.54.48.48, fax 02.38.77.17.59). Charming hotel with a small garden and views onto the cloisters of St-Aignan. ④.

Marguerite, 14 place du Vieux-Marché (☎02.38.53.74.32, fax 02.38.53.31.56). Not particularly special, except for its location on the market square. ②.

de Paris, 29 Faubourg-Bannier (☎02.38.53.39.98, fax 02.38.81.03.97). Small, very cheap and pleasant rooms above a brasserie, just across place Gambetta from the gare SNCF. ①.

St-Aignan, 3 place Gambetta (☎02.38.53.15.35, fax 02.38.77.02.36). Good value, with pleasant service. ③.

Youth hostel and campsites

Youth hostel, 14 rue du Faubourg-Madeleine (☎02.38.62.45.75). On the continuation of rue Porte-Madeleine to the west of town; bus #B, direction "Paul-Bert", from the gares SNCF and routière. Reception 7.15–9.30am & 5.30–10/10.30pm, curfew 10/10.30pm. Daily mid-Feb to Nov; daily except Sat mid-Feb to March.

Olivet campsite, rue du Pont-Bouchet in Olivet (☎02.38.63.53.94). 6km south of Orléans between the River Loiret and the Loire; bus #S to Aumône. April–Oct.

St-Jean-de-la-Ruelle campsite, rue de la Roche, St-Jean-de-la-Ruelle (☎02.38.88.39.39). The closest campsite to Orléans is 3km away out on the Blois road; bus #D, stop "Roche aux Fées". April to mid–Oct.

The city

Saint Joan turns up all over town. In pride of place in the large, central **place du Martroi**, at the end of rue de la République, rises a bulky mid-nineteenth-century likeness of her on horseback, with a series of copper-green friezes around the base, depicting scenes from her action-filled life. To the east, the **Cathédrale Ste-Croix** (daily 9am–noon & 2–6pm), battered for the best part of 600 years by various wars, is full of Joan of Arc, who celebrated her victory over the English here. In the north transept, her pedestal is supported by two jagged and golden leopards, representing the English, on an altar carved with the battle scene. In the nave, the late-nineteenth-century stained-glass windows tell the story of her life, starting from the north transept, with caricatures of the loutish English and snooty French nobles. Across place d'Étape from

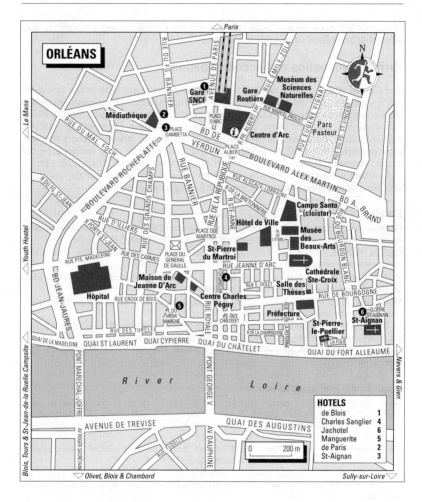

the cathedral, outside the red-brick Renaissance **Hôtel de Ville**, Joan appears again, in pensive mood, her skirt now shredded by twentieth-century bullets.

You are spared the Maid in the **Musée des Beaux-Arts**, opposite the Hôtel de Ville (Tues & Sun 11am–6pm, Wed 10am–10pm & Thurs–Sat 10am–6pm; 20F), where the main collections are of fourteenth- to sixteenth-century Italian, Dutch and Flemish works on the second floor and eighteenth-century French portraits on the first floor. If you'd rather escape to more recent times, head down to the modern art collection in the basement, which houses canvases by Picasso, Miró, Braque, Dufy, Renoir and Monet, as well as Auguste Rodin's studies of Gauguin, and photographs of Picasso by Man Ray. The museum regularly stages good temporary exhibitions; the tourist information office has details.

If you follow rue Jeanne d'Arc east from the cathedral and turn left down rue Charles-Sanglier, you'll find the ornate sixteenth-century **Hôtel Cabu** (May, June &

Sept Tues–Sun 2–6pm; July & Aug Tues–Sat 10am–6pm; Oct–April Wed, Sat & Sun 2–6pm; 15F), a historical and archeological museum containing a collection of rather beautiful bronze animals from the Gallo-Roman period, along with medieval ivories and more Joan of Arc mementos. The entrance is on square Abbé-Desnoyers.

At the end of rue Jeanne-d'Arc, on place Général-de-Gaulle, is the semi-timbered **Maison de Jeanne d'Arc** (May–Oct Tues–Sun 10am–noon & 2–6pm; Nov–April afternoons only; 13F) – a 1960s reconstruction of the house where Joan stayed. Its contents are fun, most of all for children, with good models and displays of the breaking of the Orléans siege. Despite the consistency in artists' renderings of the saint, it seems the pageboy haircut and demure little face are part of the myth – there is no contemporary portrait of her, save for a clerk's doodle in the margin of the trial proceedings, kept in the Paris archives.

If you can read French, the **Centre Charles Péguy**, 11 rue Tabour (Mon–Fri 2–6pm; free), down the road from Joan's house in a Renaissance mansion, is worth a visit. It takes its themes from the life and work of Charles Péguy (1873–1914), a Christian Socialist writer from Orléans a great humanitarian and supporter of Dreyfus is well documented. Though there are cartoons and drawings, the main exhibits are texts. Among various books and pamphlets, there's Zola's front-page *J'accuse* letter to the president and explanations by both sides in the Dreyfus affair – Dreyfus, a Jewish army officer, was convicted of treason in 1894 on forged evidence; and documentation of the 1907 general strike call for the 40-hour week (which only became effective in 1936).

If you head back east, and down towards the river, you'll find the scattered vestiges of the old city. **Rue de Bourgogne** was the Gallo-Roman main street, and, in the basement of the modern Préfecture at no. 9, a spartan civic reception room provides odd surroundings for an excavated first-century dwelling – or bits of it – and the walls of a ninth-century church. It's not a site as such: ask the receptionist if you can have a look. Across the street is the facade of the **Salles des Thèses**, all that remains of the medieval university of Orléans where the Reformation theologian Calvin studied law.

Between the Préfecture and the river, the narrow streets of the old industrial area surround the former **Dessaux vinegar works**, a turn-of-the-century establishment whose buildings encircle the house Isabelle Romée moved to a few years after her daughter Joan was burnt at the stake in Rouen. Down the rue de Bourgogne, a plaque marks the house of Joan's brother and companion-in-arms on the corner of rue des Africains and rue de la Folie. At least two of the quarter's churches are on the list of precious monuments: the remains of **St-Aignan** and its eleventh-century crypt; and the Romanesque **St-Pierre-le-Puellier**, an old university church now used for concerts and exhibitions. St-Aignan was destroyed during the English siege, rebuilt by the Dauphin and extended into one of the greatest churches in France by Louis XII. During the Wars of Religion, more sieges of the city took their toll on the church, leaving just the choir and transepts standing. Visits to the crypt need to be arranged through the tourist office.

North of the city centre, next to the gare routière, is the **Muséum de Sciences Naturelles**, at 2 rue Marcel-Proust (daily 2–6pm; 21F), small, but well-organized and educational, with a large rooftop tropical greenhouse. A short distance to the east is the **parc Pasteur**, a pleasant and relaxing spot for a picnic.

Eating and drinking

Rue de Bourgogne is the main street for **restaurants** and **nightlife**. You can choose from among French, Spanish, North African, Middle Eastern, Indian and Asian cuisines, all of which can be sampled at very reasonable prices. For buying your own provisions there are the covered **market halls** on place du Châtelet, near the river.

Restaurants

Les Antiquaires, 2 & 4 rue au Lin (☎02.38.53.52.35). Run by one of the master chefs of France, this is Orléans's best restaurant and must be booked in advance. Seafood and ginger, Loire salmon, and a soup of summer fruits and honey are some of its delights, with menus starting at 200F. Closed Sun eve & Mon Oct–May & first three weeks of Aug.

L'Aviation, 473 bd du Faubourg-Bannier (☎02.38.73.91.88). Seasonal menus with plenty of game dishes in autumn and a wonderful crayfish omelette. From 100F; gastronomic menu around 200F. Closed Wed eve, Sun & Aug.

La Chancellerie, 95 rue Royale, cnr place Matroi (☎02.38.53.57.54). The most prominent brasserie in town for drinking wine, beer or cocktails till midnight, indulging in ice-cream concoctions, or eating good solid *plats du jour* from 50F; gastronomic menus around 150F. Closed Sun and 2 weeks in Feb.

Le Paris Dakar, 19 bd Jean-Jaurès, (☎02.38.53.76.66). Caribbean and African specialities from 100F in pleasant surroundings. Closed Sun, Feb & Aug.

Le Restaurant des Plantes, 44 rue Tudelle (☎02.38.56.65.55). On south side of the river serving traditional dishes such as *magret de canard* and snails. Menus from 106F. Closed Mon & first three weeks in Aug.

La Ripaille, 14 place du Châtelet (☎02.38.54.56.85). Simple grilled meat and fish with salads, served up in a convivial atmosphere; menus from 64F; closed Sun.

Bars and nightlife

Monté Cristo, 42 rue Etienne Dolet. A bar with billiards and games. Tues–Sat 3pm–3am.

Paxton's Head, 264–266 rue de Bourgogne. Funky jazz cellar with live music on Wed & Sat eve. Tues–Sat 3pm–3am.

Shannon Irish Pub, place du Châtelet. This popular Irish bar is worth a try, with a selection of beers and whiskies. May–Sept daily 5pm–3am.

Listings

Banks Several around place Martroi and on the rue de la Republique.

Bike rental Available from Kit Loisirs in Olivet, just outside Orléans (☎02.38.63.44.34), and from Véloland, 356 rue Cornaillère, St-Jean-Le-Blanc (02.38.56.69.79).

Car rental Avis, 13 rue Sansonnières (☎02.38.62.27.04); Budget, 5 rue Sansonnières (☎02.38.54.54.30); Europcar, 81 rue A-Dessaux (☎02.38.73.00.40); Hertz, 47 av de Paris (☎02.38.62.60.60).

Cinemas Select Studios, 45 rue Jeanne-d'Arc, often shows good art-house movies in the-original language (☎02.36.68.69.25); cheap tickets for midday and early evening performances.

Festivals Fête de Jeanne d'Arc: a period-piece parade on April 29, May 1 and May 7–8; Festival de Jazz d'Orléans in late June to early July held in the Campo Santo – 1998 line-up included Buddy Guy, Bootsy Collins, and Diane Reeves (tickets 130F, 300F for 3 nights; ☎02.38.79.23.77); Semaines Musicales Internationales d'Orléans, Nov & Dec; programme details and bookings from the tourist office.

Médiathèque 1 place Gambetta (☎02.38.65.45.45); new state-of-the-art media centre (library, video library, café, exhibition space).

Medical assistance SAMU (☎02.38.69.45.45); Centre Hospitalier, 1 rue Porte-Madeleine (☎02.38.51.44.44).

Police 63 rue du Faubourg-St-Jean (☎02.38.81.63.00).

Poste restante place de Gaulle, 45031 Orléans Cedex 1.

Public transport Bus information available from SEMTAO office (☎02.38.71.98.38) in the Centre d'Arc shopping mall, place Albert-1er.

Taxis ☎02.38.53.11.11.

Meung-sur-Loire

Little streams known as *les mauves* flow between the houses in the village of **MEUNG-SUR-LOIRE**, 14km southwest of Orléans on the Blois rail line. During the summer months they leave slimy green high-water marks, but the sound of water is always pleasant, and Meung is an agreeable place to spend an afternoon.

Meung has accumulated a number of literary associations over the years. Over seven hundred years ago one Jean de Meung added 18,000 lines to the already 4000-line-long *Roman de la Rose*, written half-a-century earlier in 1225 by Guillaume de Lorris. This extended tale of courtly love, all very formal and allegorical, inspired Chaucer, who wrote his own version before moving onto more material topics. More recently, the town featured in the works of Georges Simenon – his fictional hero, Maigret, takes his holidays here.

The town's most notable and imposing building is its grisly **château**, built for the Bishops of Orléans in the early Middle Ages (daily: April–June; Sept & Oct 10am–12.30pm & 2–5pm; July & Aug 9am–12.30pm & 1.30–6pm; Nov–March 10.30–noon & 2.30–4pm; 35F). The exterior of the château on the side facing the old drawbridge looks suitably spooky, retaining its thirteenth-century pepperpot towers, though much of the interior was remodelled in the nineteenth century. The highlight of the guided tour is the dreaded **dungeon**, where you're better off with minimal imagination: it was here that the poet François Villon (1431–85) – originator of the much-quoted line *Où sont les neiges d'antan?* ("Where are the snows of yesteryear?") – was imprisoned and supposedly wrote his famous *Grand Testament*. He is the only known survivor of this monstrous dungeon, where people were abandoned to die.

If you feel remotely inspired to pen a few poetic lines yourself while loitering over **lunch**, the *Café du Commerce*, on place de l'Église, provides the ideal atmosphere (Tues–Sun; menus from 73F).

Beaugency

Six kilometres southwest of Meung along the Loire, **BEAUGENCY** is a pretty little town which, in spite of its size and picturesque qualities, has played its part in the conniving games of early medieval politics. In 1152, the marriage of Louis VII of France and Eleanor of Aquitaine was annulled by the Council of Beaugency in the church of Notre-Dame, allowing Eleanor to marry Henry Plantagenet, the future Henry II of England. Her huge lands in southwest France thus passed to the English crown, which already controlled Normandy, Maine, Anjou and Touraine, and the struggles between the French and English kings over their claims to these territories – and to the French throne itself – lasted for centuries.

Liberated by the indefatigable Joan of Arc on her way to Orléans in 1429, Beaugency was a constant battleground in the Hundred Years' War due to its strategic significance as the only Loire bridge-crossing at that time between Orléans and Blois. Remarkably, the 26-arch **bridge** still stands and gives an excellent view of the once heavily fortified medieval heart of the town. The two central squares – **place St-Firmin**, with its statue of Joan and a tower of a church destroyed during the Revolution, and **place Dunois** – are atmospherically lit by flickering gaslights. Place Dunois is bordered by the massive eleventh-century **Tour de César**, which was formerly part of the rather plain fifteenth-century **Château Dunois** (daily except Tues: April–Sept 10–11am & 2–5pm; Oct–March closes 4pm; 20F). It now houses a small museum of traditional Orléanais life, whose guided tours can definitely be given a miss. The square is completed by the rather severe Romanesque **abbey church of Notre-Dame**, the venue for the Council's fatal matrimonial decision in 1152.

Today the town casts a much more romantic image of the medieval period, and wandering around the streets of the attractive old town and along the shaded river bank is probably the best way to pass the time peacefully here. But if the urge to sightsee is strong, go and look at the **embroidered wall hangings** in the council chamber of the **Hôtel de Ville** on place du Docteur-Hyvernaud, two blocks north of place Dunois (May–Sept

Mon–Fri 11am–4.30pm, Sat 11–3pm; rest of year Tues–Fri 3–4.30pm, Sat 11am–3pm; 8F).
One set illustrates the four continents as perceived in the seventeenth century, with the
rest dramatizing pagan rites such as gathering mistletoe and sacrificing animals.

Practicalities

If you want to stay in Beaugency, the cheapest **hotel** is the *Hôtel des Vieux Fossés*, 4 rue
des Vieux-Fossés (☎02.38.44.51.65. fax 02.38.46.45.05; ①). For somewhere special, try
the *Hôtel de l'Abbaye*, 2 quai de l'Abbaye (☎02.38.44.67.35, fax 02.38.44.87.92; ⑥), a
beautiful eighteenth-century abbey with painted ceilings and beds on raised platforms.
Much cheaper and less grand, though equally pleasant, is the *Hôtel de la Sologne*, 6
place St-Firmin (☎02.38.44.50.27, fax 02.38.44.90.19; ③; closed Dec 20–Jan 4). There's
also an HI **youth hostel** in the suburb of Vernon at 152 rte de Châteaudun, 2km north
off the main Orléans–Blois road from the east side of town (☎02.38.44.61.31;
March–Dec), and **camping** (☎02.38.44.50.39; April–Oct) in Beaugency.

There are no particularly special **restaurants** in Beaugency. *Le Relais du Château*, 8
rue du Pont (☎02.38.44.55.10), is plain and unpretentious with menus at 80F, 115F,
170F. A good place to **drink** is *Le Moulin Rouge*, 2 rue de la Bonde, east of rue du Pont
(daily except Mon 5pm–1am), which has good beers plus live blues, jazz and rock some
weekends.

Château de Chamerolles

Situated approximately 30km northeast of Orléans towards Pithiviers, **Chamerolles** is
a sixteenth-century chateau (April–Sept 10am–6pm; rest of year daily except Fri
10am–5pm; closed Jan; 25F), whose pristine condition might not be to everyone's taste.
Its history is not particularly exciting, but the south wing now houses the **Château-
Promenade des Parfums** (same hours and price), tracing the use of scents from the
sixteenth century to the present day. With its "press-and-smell" buttons and reconstructed "toilets" it's great fun, not least for its revelations about European lavatorial
habits over the last four hundred years. Behind the château is a reconstruction of a
Renaissance garden – interesting more for its construction than its beauty.

To **get there** using public transport, take the bus to Chielleurs-aux-Boix from
Orléans and walk the last 3km.

East to the Burgundy border

Upstream from Orléans, single-lane roads run along the top of the flood banks of the
Loire, ideal for cycling. To the north is the rambling **Forest of Orléans**, densely planted and crisscrossed with roads. Beyond it, a bland, treeless wheat plain stretches to
Paris, and the immediate countryside to the south is likewise drab: sticking to the Loire
itself is the best advice.

Along the river are plenty of lesser-known attractions, most notably **St Benoît's
abbey**, the **château of Sully**, the small town of **Gien**, the **aqueduct at Briare** and the
vines of **Sancerre** right on the Burgundy border, which make by far the most popular
dry whites of the region.

If you're out on or in the river, or even camping on the bank, beware that the Loire's
placid flow along these reaches is deceptive; it can swell within 24 hours and has been
known to break its banks.

Germigny-des-Près and St-Benoît

An afternoon's bike ride or a short drive east out of Orléans, crossing to the north bank
at **CHÂTEAUNEUF-SUR-LOIRE** (whose château has very pleasant gardens of

magnolias and rhododendrons), brings you to **GERMIGNY-DES-PRÈS**. The church here (daily 8am–7pm) was built in 806 in the form of a Greek cross. The eastern apse is original, with a rare early gold and silver mosaic on the dome, depicting angels and the Ark of the Covenant. Covered by distemper, this was only discovered by accident in the middle of last century when children were found playing with coloured glass cubes in the church.

A few kilometres further south along the D60, **ST-BENOÎT-SUR-LOIRE** offers an even more impressive ancient edifice: the **Abbaye de Fleury**, where a marble mosaic of Roman origin covers the chancel floor of one of the most awe-inspiring Romanesque churches in France, built in pale yellow and cream-coloured stone between 1020 and 1218 (daily 7am–10pm; guided tours 10.30am–3pm – available in English; 20F). The oldest part of the church, the porch, illustrates the Vision of the Apocalypse by the fantastically sculpted capitals and by the layout that follows the description of the New Jerusalem in Revelations – foursquare, with twelve foundations and three open gates on each side. The rest of the abbey was destroyed during the Revolution.

Sully-sur-Loire

SULLY-SUR-LOIRE lies on the south bank of the Loire, 7km east of St-Benoît and accessible by bus from Orléans. The grand **château** here is pure fantasy (daily: mid-June to mid-Sept 10am–6pm; March to mid-June & mid-Sept to Nov 10am–noon & 2–5/6pm; closed Dec–Feb; guided visits only; 25F), despite savage wartime bombing that twice destroyed the nearby Loire bridge and caused incidental damage to the château itself. The interior is not particularly interesting, apart from the immaculate fourteenth-century chestnut timberwork of the keep, but from the outside, rising massively out of its gigantic moat, the château has all the picture-book requirements of pointed towers, machicolations and drawbridge. Whether sunlit or floodlit, it is a real treat.

The castle originally belonged to one of Charles VII's favourites, La Trémoille, who infuriated Joan of Arc by encouraging the Dauphin to forget about the throne and loaf about in Sully eating nice dinners of deer and wild boar. After Joan's failure to liberate Paris in 1430, he attempted to ground her by virtually imprisoning her in the castle – to no avail. The castle changed hands in 1602, this time being snapped up by Henri IV's minister, the Duke of Sully, who added the moat and park, and pushed out the river bank to protect his glorious creation from the vagaries of the Loire. After Henri's death, the arrogant minister was forced into retirement, which he spent writing in his castle. In the eighteenth century young Voltaire, exiled from Paris for libellous political verse, also spent time at the château, sharpening his wit on the company of enlightened thinkers with whom the Duke of Sully of the time liked to surround himself.

From May 24 to July 15 the **International Music Festival** features concerts of contemporary, jazz and classical music in the château's Salle des Gardes and in a medieval-style pavilion in the park (details from the tourist office; see below).

Practicalities

More information on the attractions of Sully-sur-Loire are available from the **tourist office** on place du Général-de-Gaulle at the southern end of the old town (April–Sept Mon–Sat 9am–12.30pm & 2–7pm, Sun 10am–1pm; Oct–March 9am–noon & 2.30–6.30pm; closed Sun; ☎02.38.36.23.70, fax 02.38.36.32.21).

If you wish to **stay** in Sully, the *Hostellerie du Grand Sully*, 10 bd du Champ de Foire (☎02.38.36.27.56, fax 02.38.36.44.54; ③), has spacious rooms. Alternatively, there's a serene municipal **campsite** (☎02.38.36.23.93; April–Oct) in a great location by the river, practically in the grounds of the château.

Gien and around

The fifteenth-century red- and black-brick **château** at **GIEN** – where the young Louis XIV and his bride Anne d'Autriche hid during the revolts against taxation known as the *Frondes* – has been turned over to a **Musée International de la Chasse**, with weapons, stuffed and skeletal victims, horns and antlers, plus paintings, pottery and tapestries venerating the sport (daily: May–Oct 9.30am–6.30pm; Nov–April 9–noon & 2–5pm; 25F). The squat building itself is hardly worth the climb to reach it, though the interior is quite striking, with its combination of timbered ceilings and brick. Though the exhibits here are dominated by depictions of royal and aristocratic hunting as a sport, it's worth bearing in mind that one of the material gains of the French Revolution of great importance for rural people was the right to hunt.

The **town** of Gien is pretty enough, having been restored to its late fifteenth-century quaintness after extensive wartime bombing, and the sixteenth-century stone **bridge** spanning the river gives excellent views of its medieval mass as you approach from the south. Gien also has a history of fine china making, and there's the **Musée de la Faïencerie** in the cellars of the old workshops within the present-day factory on place de la Victoire, 1km west of the château and bridge (May–Sept Mon–Sat 9am–6.30pm, Sun 10am–6pm; Oct–April Mon–Sat 9am–noon & 2–6pm, Sun 10am–noon & 2–6pm; Jan & Feb daily 2–6pm; 20F). There are some beautiful nineteenth-century pieces and a video showing current fabrication techniques which you can see for real in the **factory** during the week (by appointment only; ☎02.38.67.00.05; 20F combined ticket with museum).

Practicalities

The **tourist office** on place Jean-Jaurès, between the château and the river (☎02.38.67.25.28, fax 02.38.38.23.16), is extremely helpful. Besides stocking a wealth of information on the region, they will make hotel reservations for you. Possible **hotels** in town are the *Relais Normand*, 64 place de la Victoire (☎02.38.67.28.56, fax 02.38.67.28.56; ③), or *Le Rivage*, 1 quai de Nice (☎02.38.37.79.00, fax 02.38.38.10.21; ④), very hospitable and well situated by the bridge. The *Camping Touristique de Gien*, 500m west of the bridge across the river on rue des Iris (☎02.38.67.12.50; Jan–Nov), has a quiet and well-equipped **campsite** with a good view of the town. As for **food**, *Le Rivage* does good menus from 155F, or you could try *Côté Jardin* south of the river, 14 rte de Bourges (☎02.38.38.24.67; closed Sat midday), with menus from 105F.

La Bussière and the Château de St-Brisson

Twelve kilometres northeast of Gien is another château dedicated to catching your own supper – this time by fishing. The **Château des Pêcheurs** at **LA BUSSIÈRE** is parked like a yacht on its lake, connected to a formal arrangement on its mainland of gardens and huge outbuildings (April to mid-Nov daily except Tues 10am–noon & 2–6pm; July & Aug daily; 35F). Initially a fortress, the château was turned into a luxurious residence at the end of the sixteenth century, but only the gateway and one pepperpot tower are recognizably medieval. Inside, tanks of freshwater fish and a coelacanth, one of the oldest fishes known, with paddle-like fins and a world-weary expression, are the key exhibits, but the seventeenth-century kitchens and old laundry are also quite fun.

On the south side of the Loire, halfway between Sully and Gien, medieval weaponry is the theme at the **Château de St-Brisson** (April–Nov daily except Wed 10am–noon & 2–6pm; 22F). Demonstrations are given at 3.30pm and 4.30pm every other Sunday during summer in the moat, using bows and arrows, battering rams and devices for lobbing stones. The château also has an **art gallery** with changing exhibitions of painting, sculpture and photography, which makes up for the rather unattractive mix of styles (twelfth- to seventeenth-century) of the building itself.

Briare

The small village of **BRIARE**, 10km from Gien on the Orléans–Nevers road and the Paris–Nevers rail line, centres on its Belle Époque iron aqueduct, the **Pont Canal**, linking the Canal de Briare to the north with the Canal Lateral à la Loire, which runs south to the Saône. The design of the Pont Canal came from the workshops of Gustav Eiffel of Eiffel Tower fame, but parts of the canal scheme date back to the early seventeenth century, when internal waterways linking the Mediterranean, Atlantic and Channel coasts were devised. You can walk along the aqueduct's extraordinary 625-metre span, with its wrought-iron crested lamps and railings, hopefully without a *bateau-mouche* spoiling the effect.

Practicalities

The **tourist office**, 1 Place Charles de Gaulle (daily 10am–noon & 2–5pm; ☎02.38.31.24.51, fax 02.38.37.15.16), can provide details of canal boats and canoe rental as well as maps of footpaths, towpaths and the locks (the one at Chatillon-sur-Loire, 4km upstream, is particularly appealing). For **accommodation**, there's the modern *Hôtel le Canal* at 19 rue du Pont-Canal (☎02.38.31.24.24, fax 02.38.31.92.12; ③), right next to the bridge.

Sancerre and around

Although you can buy its wines anywhere, and there's not much justification for making a detour to visit **SANCERRE**, a village huddled at the top of a steep, round hill with the vineyards below, there is something appealing about seeing the vineyards whose fruit you are drinking. Sancerre is an extremely dry wine made from the Sauvignon grape; the white is the most renowned, but there are good reds as well, and the rarer rosé is exquisite.

Around Sancerre are several **vignerons**, most of them small-scale traditional winemakers. Three you can visit are: M. Raimbault at the Caves de la Mignonne (☎02.48.54.07.06), on the D955 towards St-Satur on the left; M. Archambault at Caves du Clos de la Perrière, on the D134 in Verdigny-en-Sancerre (☎02.48.54.16.93), to the west of St-Satur; and M. Laporte at the Cave de la Cresle, on the D57 (☎02.48.54.04.07), to the northwest. Well suited to the wines is the local *crottin de Chavignol*, a hard goat's cheese named after Chavignol, the neighbouring village in which it's made; signs in Chavignol direct you to **fromageries** open to visitors, where you can sample the cheese.

Practicalities

If you're planning on **staying** in Sancerre, the *Panoramic*, Rempart des Augustins (☎02.48.54.22.44, fax 02.48.54.39.55; ③), is a lovely hotel with superb views to the north. There are also two excellent **restaurants**: *La Pomme d'Or*, 1 rue de la Panneterie (☎02.48.54.13.30; closed Mon & Wed eve), with menus from 80F; and *La Tour*, 31 place de la Halle (☎02.48.54.00.81), with menus from 80F.

La Sologne

Between the Loire and the Cher, from Gien in the east almost as far as Blois in the west, lies the area known as the **Sologne**, marked to the southeast by the low, abrupt **Collines du Sancerrois**, northwest of Sancerre. The autoroute and main road from Orléans to Bourges run almost together through the middle of the area.

Depending on the weather and the season it can be one of the most dismal areas in central France: damp, flat, featureless and foggy. But at other times its forests, lakes, ponds and marshes have a quiet magic – in summer when the heather is in bloom and the ponds are full of water lilies, or in early autumn when you can go hunting for wild mushrooms, egg-yolk orange *chanterelles* smelling of apricots, or *cèpes*, with caps like suede and bulging pure white stalks. Wild boar and deer roam here, not to mention ducks, geese, quails and pheasants; the human population is small.

Two *Grandes Randonnées* run through the Sologne, the **GR41** and **GR3C**, and there are numerous other paths, well-signposted and detailing the accessibility for bicycles. From Easter to the end of October, tourist offices in most of Sologne's towns and villages can provide maps, details of bike rental or horse riding, as well as accommodation details. Information about walks are also available from the tourist office at Orléans all year though you may have to pay for some of the maps. If you're exploring the Sologne after October 1, when the hunting season begins, don't stray from the marked paths.

Domaine du Ciran

Halfway between Ménestreau-en-Villette and Marcilly-en-Villette and 6km east of La Ferté-St-Aubin, just off the D108, is the little hamlet of **CIRAN**. Its tiny château has a **Musée de la Vie Traditionelle**, with photos showing such delights as dogs being used to pull carts, among other local revelations (daily 10am–noon & 2–5.30/6pm; winter closed Tues; 20F). But the main reason to come here is to explore the 300 hectares of the **Domaine de Ciran** and see its working farm, a typical Sologne set-up where the principal activities are deer breeding, keeping goats and making *chèvre*, as well as growing acres of asparagus. You may well catch a glimpse of wild deer in the forested parts of the *domaine*, herons and geese around the ponds, and sometimes even coypus. It's also possible to come across wild boar, so be careful, though they are not very threatening unless they're with their babies. The 6km signed walk – for which waterproof footwear is advisable – gives you an excellent taste of the different landscapes of the Sologne.

Argent-sur-Sauldre and around

In the grounds of the thirteenth-century château just outside the village of **ARGENT-SUR-SAULDRE**, on the D940 between Gien and Bourges, is the excellent **Musée Vassil Ivanoff** (May–Sept Mon–Fri 2–7pm, Sat & Sun 10am–noon & 2–6pm; closed Tues; 16F), which contains a small, fascinating collection of modern ceramics. The Bulgarian Ivanoff came to France in the 1920s and settled in La Borne, a small village in the Sancerre hills that has mutated into a highly commercialized pottery centre; there he produced a collection that has been described as a revolution in clay. The works on display in the museum – sensual forms expressing all the complexities of the human condition – demonstrate a range of his experimentation with different surface textures and glazes, the most successful of which is a unique, ox-blood red.

The other museum in the château is the **Musée des Métiers et Traditions de France** (mid-April to mid-Oct Mon–Thurs 2–5.45pm, Fri, Sat & Sun 10–11.30am & 2–6pm; 25F), a nostalgic meander through eighteenth- and nineteenth-century country crafts and trades, including bizarre machines for making brooms and clogs, looms, a windmill gear, and a display about the production of weathercocks. The exhibits continue into the roofspace, giving a good opportunity to view the rafters of the château.

For **accommodation** and good **food** in Argent, the comfortable *Relais de la Poste* (☎02.48.73.60.25, fax 02.48.73.30.62; ②) is directly opposite the château. Otherwise,

---

LA FÊTE ÉTRANGE

There is much dispute as to where the magical party in **Alain Fournier's novel** *Le Grand Meaulnes* was set, despite the fact that it was clearly an imaginary mixture of many places. Fournier was born in La Chapelle d'Angillon, 24km south of Argent-sur-Sauldre on the D940. He spent much of his childhood in the château there, but went to school in Epineuil-le-Fleurial (the Ste-Agathe of the novel) well beyond the Sologne and Bourges, some 25km south of St-Armand-Montrond (turn right off the Montluçon road from Bourges to cross the Cher at Meaulne). Albicoco's film of the book was shot around Epineuil, and the elementary school described in the book can be visited outside class hours. But the "domain with no name" where the *fête étrange* takes place is certainly in the Sologne: "In the whole of the Sologne," he wrote, "it would have been hard to find a more desolate spot." Nançay, between Salbris and La Chapelle d'Angillon on the D944, has a **Musée Imaginaire du Grand Meaulnes** dedicated to the novelist within the **Galaria Capazza**, an excellent gallery of contemporary art housed in one of the outbuildings of the château (Sat & Sun only 9.30am–12.30pm & 2.30–7.30pm; 20F).

---

there's a very pleasant hotel, *La Solognote*, Grande Rue, in the village of **BRINON-SUR-SAULDRE**, 16km west of Argent (☎02.48.58.50.29, fax 02.48.58.56.00; ④–⑤; closed Wed out of season, mid-Feb to mid-March, last week in May & three weeks in Sept; restaurant closed Wed & out of season Tues eve).

Close to Argent, 11km southeast on the D8 near Concressault, is a new witchcraft museum at La Jonchère, the **Musée de la Sorcellerie** (Easter–Oct daily 10am–6pm; 34F). It's a bit over the top with its animated reconstructions of witchcraft trials, but kids will probably enjoy it, and some of the prints and paintings of legendary witches are fun.

Romorantin-Lanthenay

ROMORANTIN-LANTHENAY, 67km due south of Orléans, is the biggest town in the Sologne and best visited in the last weekend in October for the **Journées Gastronomiques**, a major food festival when every restaurant and hundreds of street stalls tempt you with traditional and novel dishes centred on game, wild mushrooms, apples and pumpkins. Throughout the year, if you're feeling very rich and indulgent, you can **eat** and **stay**, at the *Grand Hôtel du Lion d'Or*, 69 rue G-Clemenceau (☎02.54.76.00.28; ⑥; meals well over 500F).

The **Musée de Sologne** in the old mills in the centre of Romorantin (Dec–March Mon & Wed–Sat 10–11am & 2–5pm, Sun 2–5pm; April–Nov Mon & Wed–Sat 10am–6pm, Sun 2–5pm; 25F) presents the history, ecology and traditions of the area. For more information about the Sologne, the **tourist office** is situated on place de la Paix (☎02.54.88.79.80).

Bourges

BOURGES, chief town of the rather dispiriting region of Berry, south of the Sologne, is some way from the Loire valley proper but historically linked to it. The miserable Dauphin Charles VII, mockingly dubbed "King of Bourges" by the English, retreated to the city after Henry V's victory at Agincourt had put all of northern France under English control. Today's handsome city has a substantial calendar of festivals and some good restaurants, but the main attraction is the glorious great Gothic **cathedral**, closely followed by the mansion belonging to the Dauphin's financial advisor, Jacques Cœur.

Arrival, information and accommodation

The **gare routière** is west of the city beyond boulevard Juranville on rue du Prado, while the **gare SNCF** lies 1km to the north of the centre, on avenue P-Sémard. The **tourist office**, which faces the south facade of the cathedral, is at 21 rue Victor-Hugo (Oct–June Mon–Fri 9am–6pm, Sun 10am–12.30pm; July–Sept 9am–7.30pm, Sun 10am–7.30pm; ☎02.48.23.02.60, fax 02.48.23.02.69). **Rue Moyenne** is the main street leading north from rue Victor-Hugo, with rue Porte-Jaune parallel to it from the cathedral parvis. If you feel like pedalling through the surrounding flat countryside, you can **rent bikes** from Loca Bourges, 118 rue Barbès, or from the youth hostel.

Hotels

de l'Agriculture, 15 rue du Prinal (☎02.48.70.40.84, fax 02.48.65.50.58). On the corner with bd Juranville, nondescript but a reasonable choice. ②.

d'Angleterre, place des Quatre-Piliers (☎02.48.24.68.51, fax 02.48.65.21.41). Right by the Palais de Jacques-Cœur in the centre. Pleasant service and a high level of comfort, as you'd expect from the price. ④.

Le Christina, 5 rue de la Halle (☎02.48.70.56.50, fax 02.48.70.58.13). A large, good hotel on the west of town. ③.

L'Étape, 4 rue Raphael-Casanova (☎02.48.70.59.47, fax 02.48.24.57.93). Very good value and on the edge of the old city centre. ①.

La Nation, 24 place de la Nation (☎02.48.24.11.96). Centrally placed modern hotel. Closed Sun & July. ①.

Olympia, 66 av d'Orléans (☎02.48.70.49.84, fax 02.48.65.29.06). Small but pleasant rooms. ②.

Youth hostels and campsite

HI youth hostel, 22 rue Henri-Sellier (☎02.48.24.58.09, fax 02.48.65.51.46). A short way southwest of the centre, overlooking the River Auron. Bus #1 to Maison de la Culture, stop Auberge de Jeunesse; only a 10min walk from the gare routière. Open mid-June to mid-Oct 7am–10pm; mid-March to mid-June & mid-Oct to mid-Nov 8.30am–noon & 3–8pm; closed Dec 13–Jan 5. HI membership needed.

Camping municipal, 29 bd de l'Industrie (☎02.48.20.16.85). South of the youth hostel by bus #6 from place Cujas, stop Joffre, or a 10-min walk from the gare routière. Open March 15 to Nov 15.

Centre International de Séjour, 17 rue Félix-Chédin (☎02.48.70.25.59, fax 02.48.69.01.21). A skateboard haven with every kind of ramp, plus plenty of cultural activities and meals for around 50F. For students under 25 only. A short walk north of the gare SNCF.

The city

The centre of Bourges sits on a hill rising from the River Yèvre, in the shadow of its main attraction, the magnificent early Gothic **Cathédrale St-Étienne** (daily 8am–6pm; 32F). The exterior of the twelfth-century building is characterized by the delicate, almost skeletal appearance of flying buttresses supporting an entire nave that has no transepts to break up its bulk. A much-vaunted example of Gothic architecture, it is modelled on Notre-Dame in Paris but incorporates improvements on the latter's design, such as the increased height of the inner aisles, which appear to ascend almost to vanishing point.

The **tympanum** above the main door of the west portal could engross you for hours with its tableau of the Last Judgment, featuring carved, naked figures whose faces are alive with expression and bodies full of movement. Thirteenth-century imagination has been given full rein in the depiction of the devils, complete with snakes' tails and winged bottoms and faces appearing from below the waist, symbolic of the soul in the service of sinful appetites. A cauldron filling with merry souls – one of whom appears to be wearing a bishop's mitre – contrasts sorely with the depiction of the gloomy-looking saved, while God, sitting in judgment, appears exceptionally sanctimonious.

The interior's best feature is its mostly twelfth- to thirteenth-century **stained glass**. There are geometric designs in lovely muted colours in the main body of the cathedral, but the most glorious and astonishingly bright windows are around the choir, all created between 1215 and 1225. You can follow the stories of the Prodigal Son, the Rich Man and Lazarus, the life of Mary, Joseph in Egypt, the Good Samaritan, Christ's crucifixion, the Last Judgment and the Apocalypse; binoculars come in handy for picking up the exquisite detail. But the most memorable way of seeing the cathedral is to come on a Sunday morning, when the powerful eighteenth-century organ is played, or to attend one of the concerts on Tuesday evenings.

In the **crypt**, you can see the design of the fourteenth-century rose window of the west front cut into the floor, suggesting that this was where it was assembled. Tickets for guided visits to the crypt (28F) also allow you to climb to the top of the north **tower**, rebuilt in Flamboyant style after the original collapsed in 1506.

The rest of Bourges

Having seen the cathedral, many people move straight on, but the rest of Bourges is worth at least a couple of hours of wandering. Bourges has its fair quota of ancient hôtels and burghers' houses, displaying the wealth of the city that was built to rival the ruling provincial city of Dijon.

The finest survivors from Bourges' heyday are contained within the loop of roads northwest of the cathedral to either side of rue Moyenne and rue Porte-Jaune, and although the town's museums are not particularly interesting, they are housed in some beautiful medieval buildings. Next to the cathedral in place E-Dolet, the recently opened **Musée des Meilleurs Ouvriers de France** (daily: Feb–Dec 2–6pm; free) has examples of what are considered to be the best works by French artisans; these are gathered under various categories such as pastry-making, musical instruments and glassware. Rue Bourbonnoux, parallel to rue Moyenne to the east of the cathedral, is worth a wander for the richly decorated **Hôtel Lallemant** (daily 10am–noon & 2–6pm; free), now a diverting enough museum of medieval artefacts, with displays of sculpture, tapestries and furniture; halfway along the road, you can take a narrow passage up to the remains of the Gallo-Roman town **ramparts**, lined with old houses and trees. Rue Gambon is noteworthy for the **Maison de la Reine Blanche** and the **Hôtel-Dieu**, and close by is the pleasant square of **place Notre-Dame**, with its eponymous church, clearly showing the shift from Gothic to Renaissance. The fifteenth-century **Hôtel des Échevins** on rue E-Branly (daily 10am–noon & 2–6pm; free) has a mellow courtyard that makes a contrasting entrance to the twentieth-century art collection within.

The continuation of rue E-Branly, **rue Jacques-Cœur**, was the site of the head office, stock exchange, dealing rooms, bank safes and home of Charles VII's finance minister, Jacques Cœur (1400–56), a medieval shipping magnate, moneylender and arms dealer who dominates Bourges as Joan of Arc does Orléans, while Charles VII just doesn't get a look-in. The **Palais de Jacques-Cœur** (guided tours daily May–Oct 9–11.15am & 2–5.10pm; Nov–April 9–11.10am & 2–4.10pm; 32F) is one of the most remarkable examples of fifteenth-century domestic architecture – the visit is memorable and especially fun for children, starting with the fake windows on the entrance front from which two realistically sculpted half-figures look down – possibly the man himself and his wife. There are hardly any furnishings inside, but the decorations on the stonework, including numerous hearts and scallop shells, clearly show the mark of the man who had it built. In the Salle du Trésor, there are carved scenes from the romance of Tristan and Iseult. The tour includes the kitchen, with its original water-heating system, and dining hall, with minstrels' gallery; it's also the only mansion where you are shown the original loos.

Eating and drinking

Bourges's main centre for **eating** is place Gordaine, at the end of rue Coursarlon, off rue Moyenne. The square is attractively medieval, a lovely place to sit and eat in the daytime, despite the continuous piped music: try *Lucky Luke*, a lively place serving hearty American hamburgers and salads from 45F; or *Le Comptoir de Paris* (☎02.48.24.17.16), a very popular and friendly restaurant with a terrace overlooking the square and *plats du jour* from 59F with wine, or menus from 98F. A short walk from here towards the cathedral, *D'Antan Sancerrois*, 50 rue Bourbonnoux (☎02.48.65.96.26; closed Mon & midday Tues), features local goodies cooked in wine and served in a medieval dining hall from 90F (no menus); just next to the food **market** (Wed–Sat am), at 28–30 rue des Cordeliers, is *Palais de la Bière* (☎02.48.70.32.22), which has menus for 70F and 85F and specializes in *fruits de la mer*.

Those with a sweet tooth should head for the excellent **pâtisserie** *Aux Trois Flûtes*, on the corner of rues Joyeuse and Bourbonnoux; for chocolates and the local sweet speciality of *fourrées au praliné* try the imposing *Maison Forestines*, on place Cujas.

Nightlife and festivals

For a small city, Bourges doesn't do too badly for **late-night venues**, which include: *Le Beau Bar*, 10bis rue des Beaux-Arts, a student hang-out open till 3am; *Le Must*, 50 rue Littré, with live music; *Le Guillotin*, place Gordaine, a bar and restaurant with café-théâtre; and *Le Bar des Remparts*, 53 rue Bourbonnoux – a good place to catch live rock and pop.

Bourges's **festival** programme is also impressive, with several major events in town. The Printemps de Bourges features every sort of music – including some big names – for one week between mid-April and the beginning of May (☎02.48.24.30.50; tickets from 100F). More esoteric is the Festival Synthèse, an electronic and acoustic music bash during the first week of June (☎02.48.20.41.87, fax 02.48.20.45.51); and Un Été à Bourges (mid-July to mid-Sept), a celebration of theatre, music and open-air and street performances.

St-Chartier, Nohant and La Châtre

If you're heading through the rather dismal **Berry** countryside for Limoges from Bourges, rather than taking the main road through Châteauroux, you could go via **La Châtre**, where George Sand and Chopin spent some time. If you're in the area around July 14, then a stop at the small village of **St-Chartier**, 9km north of La Châtre, should definitely be considered, to take part in the huge folk festival.

St-Chartier

ST-CHARTIER is the venue of one of the best **folk festivals** in Europe, the Rencontres Internationales de St-Chartier, an annual festival of folk and traditional music and dance that started as a hurdy-gurdy and pipe festival but has spread its horizons over the years. It takes place around the old château, the village church and in the surrounding parkland. Traditional-instrument makers set up their stalls, and there are dance workshops, competitions, concerts and a festive ball in the main square every night. To give some idea of the festival's range, past line-ups have included traditional music from Lombardy, folk bands from Moldavia, Spanish bagpipes, English and Irish folk, and a fifty-piece orchestra from Berry.

The festival takes place over four or five days around July 14, and inclusive tickets cost around 380F, or you can just go for the day for about 160F. There are free **campsites** all around the village for the duration. Details are available from the Comité George Sand, 141 rue Nationale, 36400 La Châtre (☎02.54.06.09.96).

On the route de Verneuil from St-Chartier there's the *Château de la Vallée Bleu*, a peaceful country park **hotel** (☎02.54.31.01.91; ④) with an excellent restaurant(menus from 130F).

Nohant and La Châtre

NOHANT, on the main Châteauroux–La Châtre road 5km from St-Chartier, is where nineteenth-century novelist **George Sand**, or Amandine Aurore Lucie Dupin as she was born, spent half her life. The **Château de Nohant** – not really a château but Sand's very pleasant eighteenth-century country house – is open for quick guided tours (daily: mid-Oct to Jan 2.30–3.30pm; July & Aug 9am–6.30pm; otherwise 9–11.15am & 2–5.30pm; 35F). You're shown the dining-room table where Flaubert, Turgenev, Dumas, Delacroix, Balzac and Liszt all dined on many occasions. The piano that George Sand gave Chopin, her guest for ten years, sits in the living room surrounded by the family portraits. There's also the puppet theatre made by Chopin and Sand's son Maurice, the pair no doubt trying to outdo each other in their well-documented rivalry for Sand's attentions.

Chopin's music is honoured in a week-long **piano festival**, Chopin chez George Sand, at Nohant and La Châtre towards the end of July. Tickets range from 30F to 200F; bookings and programme details from La Châtre's tourist office (see below).

There's more of Sand in nearby **LA CHÂTRE** about 10km from Nohant, where every other place name is connected with the novelist. The **Musée George Sand et de la Vallée Noire**, 71 rue Venose (daily: July & Aug 9am–7pm; Oct–April 9am–noon & 2–5pm; rest of year 9am–noon & 2–7pm; closed Jan; 20F), dedicates a floor to the writer, with plenty of pictures: George Sand's caricatures of her friends, a photo of Chopin, her son Maurice's illustrations for his mother's work and the doodles on her manuscripts. Apart from this, the town's most distinctive feature is the background noise of gentle tapping as competitors in the annual **stone sculpture competition** set to work each June. You can watch them at it and admire the results, which stay in the town.

Practicalities

The **tourist office** on square George-Sand in La Châtre (daily 10am–12.30pm & 2–6pm; ☎02.54.48.22.64, fax 02.54.06.09.15) can find you a room in the area. A good place to try is *Le Paradis Breton*, 4 rue Alphonse-Fleury (☎02.54.48.02.87; ①), pleasant

---

GEORGE SAND (1804–76)

After the publication of her novel *Valentine*, which was set locally and received considerable publicity, **George Sand** wrote: "This unknown Vallée Noire, this quiet and unpretentious landscape . . . all this had charms for me alone and did not deserve to be revealed to idle curiosity." What the critics jumped on in this novel, and in the rest of her writings, were "anti-matrimonial doctrines"; her view – reasonable enough – that ill-matched couples should be able to separate. Simone de Beauvoir described Sand as a "sentimental feminist", and, except for the brief period of the 1848 Revolution, she was certainly no activist. But her male contemporaries called her a man-eater, and she is still too often referred to simply as Chopin's mistress. Though her literary output was enormous and the French recognize her as one of their great writers, her lasting reputation is based on her – at the time – shocking lifestyle.

with just five very cheap rooms. *Le Lion d'Argent*, 2 av Lion d'Argent (☎02.54.48.11.69; ③), is well-equipped with a swimming pool and bikes for rental; its restaurant (closed Sun out of season; menus from 75F) serves generous helpings of traditional dishes and has a good wine selection. There's also a **youth hostel** by the River Indre on the east side of the town on rue du Moulin Borgnon (☎02.54.06.00.55; HI membership required), and a riverside **campsite**, the *Camping Solange Sand* (☎02.54.06.10.34; mid-March to mid-Nov), at Montgivray, 2.5km from La Châtre. The **restaurant** *Jardin de la Poste*, 10 rue Basse-Mouhet (☎02.54.48.05.62; closed Sun eve, Mon & mid-Sept to Oct 5), should leave you feeling well satisfied for little more than 100F.

Loches and around

Apart from Azay-le-Rideau near the confluence with the Loire (see p.479), **LOCHES** is the obvious place to head for on the River Indre. Its walled **citadel** is by far the most impressive of the Loire valley fortresses, with its unbreached ramparts and the Renaissance houses below still partly enclosed by the outer wall of the medieval town.

The **old town** is announced by the Tour St-Antoine belfry, close to place du Marché (Wednesday market), linking rue St-Antoine with Grande Rue. Two fifteenth-century gates to the old town still stand: the **Porte des Cordeliers** by the river at the end of Grande Rue, and the **Porte Picois** to the west, at the end of rue St-Antoine; rue du Château, lined with Renaissance buildings, leads to the twelfth-century towers of **Porte Royale**, the main entrance to the citadel.

The citadel

The Porte Royale contains the **Musée de Terroir**, a traditional museum of rural life and crafts (Thurs–Tues: 9–11.45am & 2–4/5/6pm; 20F). Beyond the gateway, down to the left is the **Musée Lansyer** with works by the local nineteenth-century painter Lansyer, overshadowed by a Japanese collection that includes a complete samurai suit of armour (daily except Tues: April–Sept 10am–7pm; rest of year 1.30–5pm; closed Dec & Jan; 20F). Straight ahead is the Romanesque church, the **Collégiale de St-Ours**, with its odd roofline of four turrets, two of which are supported by octagonal pyramids. The porch has some entertaining twelfth-century monster carvings and the stoup, or basin for holy water, is a Gallo-Roman altar.

The northern end of the citadel is taken up by the **Logis Royal**, or "Royal Lodgings" of Charles VII and his three successors (July–Sept 15 9am–7pm; mid-March to June & Sept 9am–noon & 2–6pm; rest of year daily 9am–noon & 2–5pm; 22F). The medieval half of the palace saw two women of some importance to Charles: Joan of Arc, victorious from Orléans, came here to give the defeatist Dauphin another pep talk about coronations, and later the less significant (but much sexier) Agnès Sorel, Charles's lover, resided here. Even the pope took a fancy to her, which allowed Charles to be the first French king to have an officially recognized mistress. She was buried at Loches and her tomb now lies in the fifteenth-century wing, her alabaster recumbent figure restored after anticlerical Revolutionary soldiers mistook her for a saint. Also in the same room there's a portrait of her in full regalia and a painting of the Virgin in her likeness; the semi-nudity in both was no artist's fantasy, but a courtly fashion trend set by Sorel.

While little remains today in the Logis Royal to give much impression of the highlife of kings' favourites, the nastiness of being out of favour is clear at the other end of the citadel. Here are the dungeons and two keeps, the larger one, the **donjon**, initiated by Foulques Nerra, the eleventh-century count of Anjou, with cells and a torture chamber added in the fifteenth century (daily July–Sept 15 9.30am–7pm; Oct to mid-March

9.30am–1pm & 2.30–6pm; rest of year 9.30am–12.30pm & 2.30–7pm; 22F). There is not much left of the fifteenth-century extension, thanks to the people of Loches, who destroyed most of the torture equipment during the Revolution, and although the very professional guides make up for the lack of exhibits with their spiel, they can't quite express the goriness – Louis XI's adviser, Cardinal La Balve, was supposed to have been locked up here in a wooden cage for eleven years. You can climb unescorted to the top of the keep, even if the surrounding countryside is unexciting.

Practicalities

From the gare SNCF on the east side of the Indre, avenue de la Gare leads to place de la Marne, with the **tourist office** on your left (☎02.47.59.07.98, fax 02.47.91.61.50) and the **gare routière** a short way down rue de Tours from the *place*. Loches is only an hour's train or coach journey away from Tours, but you may well want to stay, particularly if you're **camping** – the *Camping Municipal de la Citadelle* (☎02.47.59.05.91; mid-March to mid-Nov) is between two branches of the Indre by the swimming pool and stadium, looking up at the east side of the citadel. The *George Sand* **hotel**, 37 rue Quintefol (☎02.47.59.39.74, fax 02.47.91.55.75; ③), just below the eastern ramparts, has its best rooms at the back looking onto the river; its restaurant is not at all bad, with menus from 100F. The *Hôtel Tour Ste-Antoine*, 2 rue des Moulins (☎02.47.59.01.06, fax 02.47.59.13.80; ③), is the only hotel in the old town itself, but the *France*, 6 rue Picois, near the Porte Picois (☎02.47.59.00.32, fax 02.47.59.28.66; ④), is pleasanter, with an excellent restaurant, whose menus start at 85F. The best place for a **drink** is the *Café des Arts*, on place du Blé.

Around Loches

Just across the Indre from Loches is the village of **BEAULIEU-LES-LOCHES** – an extraordinary, little-known place, thoroughly medieval in appearance, with its parish church built into the spectacular ruins of an abbey contemporary with the Loches keep. Its other church, St-Pierre, holds the bones of Foulques Nerra, the eleventh-century count of Anjou responsible for Loches' grisly *donjon*. In Beaulieu-les-Loches, next to the ruined abbey, there's a charming low-budget **hotel**, the *Hôtel de Beaulieu*, 3 rue Foulques-Nerra (☎02.47.91.60.80; ②). The **bistrot** *L'Estaminet* (☎02.47.59.35.47; closed Mon) next door is run by the hotel owner's son and serves simple country cooking from around 80F.

If you follow the Indre upstream into the region of Berry, the river itself tends to be the only source of interest – other than the Romanesque church in the pretty town of **CHATILLON-SUR-INDRE**, on the Touraine–Berry border. **CHÂTEAUROUX**, the largest town on the banks of the Indre and a local route hub, is a grey and officious sort of place, but further south the river flows past George Sand's old haunt of Nohant and La Châtre (see p.459).

Blois and around

BLOIS is a handsome town, with much character and is certainly worth a visit. The biggest drawback of this former seat of the dukes of Orléans is the modern town around it, and particularly the broad, fast-moving boulevard that rings the château as if it were a mere traffic island rather than a sensational piece of architecture. There are, however, plenty of places around place Victor-Hugo that offer excellent views of the exterior of the building, Italian loggias and all, and it's worth braving the traffic for the pleasure of a non-guided visit around rooms steeped in power and intrigue.

If you want to get out into the countryside, there are several stretches of woodlands around Blois, including the **Forêt de Blois** to the west of the town on the north bank of the Loire, the **Parc de Chambord** and the **Forêt de Boulogne** around the Château de Blois, further upstream. And if you haven't yet slaked your thirst for châteaux, there are several other examples within easy reach of the town

Arrival, information and accommodation

Blois is easy to get around: av Jean-Laigret is the main street leading south from the **gare SNCF** (☎08.36.35.35.35) to place Victor-Hugo and the château, and past it to the town centre. The **gare routière** (☎02.54.58.55.75) is directly in front of the gare SNCF with **buses** leaving for Cheverny and Chambord (mid-June to mid-Sept; 65F). The **tourist office**, 3 avenue Jean-Laigret (April–Sept Mon–Sat 9am–12.30pm & 2–7pm, Sun 10.30am–12.30pm & 4.30–7pm; Oct–March Mon–Sat 9.15am–noon & 2–6pm; ☎02.54.90.41.41, fax ☎02.54.90.41.49), organizes hotel rooms for a small fee and changes money; during summer it has information desks open in the pedestrian precinct and place du Château (July & Aug daily 10am–7pm). **Bikes** can be rented from Cycles Leblond, 44 Levée des Tuileries.

Hotels worth trying are the inexpensive *St-Jacques*, 7 rue Ducoux (☎02.54.78.04.15; ①), near the gare SNCF; *À La Ville de Tours*, 2 place de la Grève (☎02.54.78.07.86; ②) overlooking the river, with a well-priced restaurant below serving traditional cuisine (75F& 99F menus); and the slightly more expensive *Hôtel du Bellay*, 12 rue des Minimes (☎02.54.78.23.62, fax 02.54.78.52.04; ②). *Le Savoie*, next to the *St-Jacques* at 6 rue Ducoux (☎02.54.74.32.21, fax 02.54.74.29.58; ③), is more appealing, but if you want somewhere classy, the best choice is the *Mercure*, 28 quai St-Jean (☎02.54.56.66.66, fax 02.54.56.67.00; ⑥), overlooking the river to the east of the town centre.

The HI **youth hostel**, 18 rue de l'Hôtel-Pasquier (☎02.54.78.27.21; March to mid-Nov), is further out at Les Grouets, 5km downstream, between the Forêt de Blois and the river. Take bus #4, direction "Les Grouets", stop Auberge. The Blois **campsite** is across the river 2km from the town centre on the Lac de Loire at Vineuil (☎02.54.74.22.78; bus #3c, stop "Mairie Vineuil"; bicycle rental).

Château de Blois

All six kings of the sixteenth century spent time at the **Château de Blois** (re-opening April 30 1999; daily: mid-March to Oct 9am–8pm; Nov to mid-March 9–6.30pm; 35F), and in the early nineteenth century it was given to Louis XVIII's brother to keep him away from Paris. Hence the courtiers' mansions that fill the town and, given its earlier non-royal ownerships, the château's architectural montage of distinct, unmatching wings – medieval, Gothic, Renaissance and classical. Much of the château can be visited, from its oldest part – the thirteenth-century manorial assembly hall of the Salle des États – to the Flamboyant Gothic east wing of Louis XII and the Italianate north wing of François I, with its double loggias and gallery, and the great staircase with the spiralling balconies and its windows not quite in alignment.

The Blois horror story is the murder by Henri III of the Duc de Guise and his brother the cardinal of Lorraine, the perpetrators of the execution of Huguenots at Amboise (see p.472). The king had summoned the States-General to a meeting in the Grande Salle, only to find an overwhelming majority supporting de Guise, along with the stringing up of Protestants, and aristocratic rather than royal power. He panicked and had de Guise ambushed and hacked to death in a corridor of the palace. The cardinal was murdered in prison the next day. Their deaths were avenged a year later when a monk assassinated the king himself.

The château was also home to Henri III's mother and manipulator, Catherine de Médicis, who died here a few days after the murders in 1589. The most famous of her suite of rooms is the study, where, according to Alexander Dumas, she kept poison hidden in secret caches in the skirting boards and behind some of the 237 narrow carved wooden panels. In the nineteenth century, revolutionaries were tried in the Grande Salle for conspiring to assassinate Napoléon III, a year before the Paris Commune of 1870.

Otherwise, the interior of the château is wonderfully colourful, or dreadfully garish if you're a purist, thanks to the mid-nineteenth-century restoration. The floors have intricate designs in tiling or parquet, walls are painted with repeating patterns, and the arches, pillars and fireplaces of the superb Salle des États are a riot of colour. Two ornamental regal emblems recur ostentatiously: the porcupine in Louis XII's wing and the salamander in that of François I.

In addition, the château houses three small museums: the **Beaux-Arts**, with plenty of regal portraits and a rather good collection of forged ironwork including locks and keys; a set of seventeenth-century **sculptures** in white Loire tufa, rescued from many of the neighbouring châteaux before their detail weathered away; and an **archeological collection**, with several fine examples of Merovingian and Carolingian glass and ceramics.

Finally, it's worth visiting the extraordinary **church of St-Nicholas**, just below the château on rue St-Laumen. Though altered greatly over the centuries, for the most part it is a stunning example of twelfth-century church architecture.

Eating and drinking

There are plenty of cheap **eating** places around Blois's town centre: rue St-Lubin, rue des Violettes and rue Foulérie are good streets to try. *La Garbure*, 36 rue St-Lubin (☎02.54.74.32.89; closed Sat & Wed midday), serves specialities from the southwest for under 100F, and the *garbure*, a filling duck soup, is excellent. *La Tocade*, 9–11 rue Chant-des-Oiseaux, is a popular brasserie with good-value set menus for as little as 65F. For straightforward meat grills, *La Forge*, 18 rue du Bourg-Neuf (☎02.54.74.43.45), is a friendly place (from 100F). A more upmarket restaurant is *Au Rendez-Vous des Pêcheurs*, 27 rue Foix (☎02.54.74.67.48; closed Sun midday & Mon), with delicious fish dishes, especially the salmon, and a menu for around 150F.

Around Blois

On the south bank of the river, within a twenty-kilometre radius south and east of Blois, are a handful of impressive and easily visited châteaux. By car you could call at all of them in a couple of days, but they also make ideal cycling or walking targets if you arm yourself with a map and strike out along minor roads and woodland rides. Of the two most imposing examples, Chaumont has frequent daily trains from Blois (Onzain gare SNCF on the other side of the river), and Chambord is a flat, beautiful ride – although to get there on public transport you have to use the expensive châteaux tour buses that leave from Blois, Tours or Amboise. The cheapest tour bus trips leave Blois from the gare SNCF (mid-June to mid-Sept), with two itineraries: Chaumont–Chenonceaux–Amboise 110F; Chambord–Cheverny 65F (tickets available from the tourist office in Blois; prices exclusive of entry fee).

Château de Chaumont

Catherine de Médicis forced Diane de Poitiers to hand over Chenonceau on the Cher (see p.475) in return for the **Château de Chaumont** (daily April–Sept 9.30am–6pm; Oct–March 10am–4.30pm; 32F), 16km downstream from Blois. Diane got a bad deal, but this is still one of the more fascinating châteaux.

Chaumont started life as a Gothic fortress – complete with towers, moat and draw-bridge – defending the river and valley below; during the Renaissance, the carcass of the building was dressed up with Renaissance frippery. The wings you see today form three sides of a square, the fourth side having been demolished in 1739 to improve views over the river, which are spectacular. Chaumont's interior, unlike those of many Loire châteaux, is furnished in an early nineteenth-century style which, combined with its unkempt air, gives it a surprising, homely feel. Look out for the tiled floor with its depictions of hunting scenes, and a copy of a sixteenth-century portrait of the young Catherine de Médicis in the Salles des Fêtes, on the first floor.

More interesting than anything inside the château, however, are the remarkable Belle Époque **stables**, with their porcelain troughs and elegant electric lamps for the benefit of the horses at a time before the château itself was wired – let alone the rest of the country. The best way to get a further feel of the château's equestrian character is to rent a horse or a pony and trap, available daily in the château grounds from May to October (☎02.54.20.90.60; winter daily except Tues).

Château de Cheverny

Seventeenth-century addicts are in for a treat 15km southeast of Blois with the **Château de Cheverny** (daily: April & May 9.15am–noon & 2.15–6.30pm; June to mid-Sept 9.15am–6.45pm; mid-Sept to March 9.30am–noon & 2.15–5/5.30/6.30pm; 35F). Built between 1604 and 1634 and never altered, it presents an immaculate picture of symmetry and harmony. The stone, from Bourré on the River Cher, from which it is built, lightens with age, so the château looks as if it were whitewashed yesterday. Its interior decoration has only been added to, never destroyed: the display of paintings, furniture, tapestries and armour against the gilded, sculpted and carved walls and ceilings is extremely impressive. Some highlights are the painted wall panels in the dining room telling stories from *Don Quixote*; the lily, daffodil and iris motifs in the Salles des Gardes; the bindings of the books in the library; and the embroidered Persian silk canopy on the king's bed.

The château is still lived in by a descendant of the original owner, whose **deer-hunting expeditions** every Tuesday and Saturday from October to March are something of a spectacle. Tourists are bused in to watch the local aristos tie their silk cravats while huntsmen sound their horns and the hounds mill around. There's a room full of deer-head trophies and even the feeding of the hounds is turned into a spectacle. The **son et lumière** every Saturday evening at 10pm from mid-July to August is also dedicated to the hunting theme.

Near Cheverny you can **stay** in the luxurious *Château du Breuil* (☎02.54.44.20.20, fax 02.54.44.30.40; ⑦; menus from 195F; half-board obligatory in season), on the road to Fougères-sur-Bièvre (see below); or, more reasonably, at the *Hôtel des Trois Marchands* (☎02.54.79.96.44, fax 02.54.79.25.60; ②), in **COUR CHEVERNY**, Cheverny's larger neighbour. The hotel's **restaurant** is not bad at all, with menus from 100F. Another good place to eat is *Le Pousse Rapière* in Cheverny (☎02.54.79.94.23). There's a **camp-site** on the D102 in Cheverny (☎02.54.79.90.01), and another on rue de Poussard in Cour Cheverny (☎02.54.79.95.63).

Château de Fougères

If you're on a château binge, the grim, medieval **Château de Fougères** provides a good contrast to Cheverny (April–Sept daily 9am–noon & 2–6pm; Oct–March daily except Tues 10am–noon & 2–4.30pm; 25F). It lies in the village of **FOUGÈRES-SUR-BIÈVRE**, 10km southwest of Cheverny, and was built in 1470 by Louis XI's chancellor, who was clearly sceptical about long-term peace. It is a veritable fortress, with spiky towers and the theme of war running through the building, with sculptured soldiers and battle scenes above arches and on door lintels and chimneys. Come the sixteenth century –

here as elsewhere – Italianate windows were fashioned onto former blank walls and steep roofs, but it still looks as if it expects an attack and is concealing its defences as a tactic. It could hardly be a more peaceful place now, and is rarely overrun with visitors.

Château de Beauregard

A cyclable ride from Blois, the relatively little-visited **Château de Beauregard**, 7km south of Blois on the D956 to Contres (July & Aug daily 9.30am–6.30pm; April–June, Sept & Oct daily 9.30–noon & 2–6.30pm; Nov–March daily except Wed 9.30–11.30am & 2–5pm; 45F) lies amid the Forêt de Russy. It was – like Chambord – one of François I's hunting lodges, but its transformation in the sixteenth century involved beautification rather than aggrandizement. It was added to in the seventeenth century; the result is a restrained – by Loire standards – and serene white building, very much at ease in its manicured geometric park.

The highlight of the château is a richly decorated **portrait gallery**, whose floor of Delft tiling depicts an army on the march. The 363 paintings of kings, queens and their cohorts are arranged by reign, beginning with Philippe VI at the start of the Hundred Years' War and ending with Louis XIII, who inherited the throne in 1610; also included are some characters, like Rabelais, who were not directly involved with the shifty-eyed monarchs and their power-brokers. The paintings are gradually being restored, often revealing other portraits beneath in the process.

Château de Chambord

The **Château de Chambord**, François I's little "hunting lodge", is the largest of the Loire châteaux (daily: April–June & Sept 9.30–6.15pm; July & Aug 9.30am–7.15pm; Oct–March 9.30am–5.15pm; 40F) and one of the most extravagant commissions of its age. Its patron's principal object – to outshine the Holy Roman Emperor Charles V – would, he claimed, leave him renowned as "one of the greatest builders in the universe", and the result is undoubtedly impressive. The palace has over 440 rooms and is surrounded by 34km of wall; its construction even involved diverting the Loire to accommodate the grand plan.

The Italian architect Domenico de Cortona was chosen to design the château in 1519 in an effort to introduce prestigious Italian Renaissance art forms to France; but the labour was supplied by French masons, hence the result is essentially French medieval: the massive round towers, with their conical tops, and the explosion of chimneys, pinnacles and turrets on the roof bring to mind Flamboyant Gothic. The details, however, are pure Italian: the Great Staircase (attributed by some to da Vinci), panels of coloured marble, niches decorated with shell-like domes, and free-standing columns. Wandering through, you can get a good feel for the contrasting architectural styles.

The building has its fans, though for many its mix of styles makes it the single ugliest building in the Loire – except perhaps for the nuclear power station at St-Laurent-des-Eaux, just to the north. Visits are unguided, and there's plenty of entertainment to be had from roaming around inside – up and down the double spiral staircase (devised so courtiers could ascend and descend without meeting up on the steps) around the spectacular chimneys and through endless rooms and corridors.

The **Parc de Chambord** around the château is an enormous walled game reserve, red deer being the main beast you're likely to spot. You can explore on foot, bike or on horseback, with mounts rented from the Centre Equestre near the château.

Accommodation in the village of Chambord itself can be found at the *Hôtel Le St-Michel* (☎02.54.20.31.31, fax 02.54.20.36.40; ④), which has direct views of the château. In **BRACIEUX**, a small village just beyond the southern wall of the Parc de Chambord, 8km from the château, there's the pleasant little *Hôtel de la Bonnheure*, 9bis rue R-Masson (☎02.54.46.41.57; ③), and the *Hôtel du Cygne*, 20 rue R-Brun (☎02.54.46.41.07, fax 02.54.46.04.87; ④). There's also a **campsite** in the village (☎02.54.46.41.84).

Tours and around

Chief town of the Loire valley and capital of the Touraine region, **TOURS** has long had a reputation as a staid, bourgeois city. An English travel writer wrote in 1913:

> *Tours has an immense air of good breeding . . . you have visions of portentously dull entertainments in lofty gilded saloons where everything is rather icily magnificent.*

The city is now only an hour's journey from Paris on the TGV line, and this, together with the building of a new conference centre, has meant an influx of business people and young commuters. With an increasing student population as well, a gradual, enlivening change is being effected. However, it has a prettified and fairly animated **old quarter**, some good **museums** – of wine, crafts, stained glass and an above-average Beaux-Arts museum – and a great many fine buildings, not least of which is **St-Gatien's cathedral**. And if you don't have your own transport, it's the obvious Touraine base, within striking distance of a snatch of notable châteaux – **Villandry**, **Langeais** and **Amboise** – as well as the celebrated wine-producing towns of **Vouvray** and **Bourgeuil**.

Arrival, information and accommodation

A short way southeast of the cathedral district, facing the mammoth "hypercentre" that shelters the Centre International de Congrès, there's the **gare routière** (☎02.47.05.30.49) and **gare SNCF** (☎08.36.67.68.69). Some trains, including most TGVs, stop at **St-Pierre-des-Corps**, an industrial estate outside the city. Frequent shuttles link the two stations (about 8min) or you can take bus #2 or #3 from St-Pierre-des-Corps to place Jean-Jaurès (15min). The huge and excellent **tourist office** is close by on the corner of rue Bernard-Palissy and boulevard Heuteloup (May–Sept Mon–Sat 8.30am–6.30pm, Sun 10am–1pm & 3–6pm; Oct–April Mon–Sat 9am–12.30pm & 1.30–6pm, Sun 10am–1pm; ☎02.47.70.37.37, fax 02.47.61.14.22). Unless there's a conference in town, **accommodation** shouldn't be a problem.

Hotels

au Chien Jaune, 74 rue B. Palissy, (☎02.47.05.10.17). A charming, friendly brasserie with basic clean rooms upstairs. ①.

Le Francillon, 9 rue des Bons-Enfants (☎02.47.66.44.66). A beautiful half-timbered house with rooms to match. ⑤.

du Manoir, 2 rue Traversière, cnr rue J-Simon (☎02.47.05.37.37, fax 02.47.05.16.00). A converted nineteenth-century town house offering exceptional service. ③.

Manoir du Grand Marigny, near Fondettes (☎02.47.42.29.87). A gorgeous sixteenth-century manor house 5km from the centre of Tours on the north bank of the river. ⑤

Mon Hôtel, 40 rue de la Préfecture (☎02.47.05.25.36, fax 02.47.66.08.72). Near the cathedral, this is a clean and comfortable cheapie with small rooms. ②.

du Musée, 2 place François-Sicard (☎02.47.66.63.81, fax 02.47.20.10.42). Right by the cathedral and museum, a quiet and unassuming hotel. ③.

Regina, 2 rue Pimbert (☎02.47.05.25.36, fax 02.47.61.12.72). Large, old hotel with good-sized rooms at a reasonable price. ②

St-Éloi, 79 bd Béranger (☎02.47.37.67.34, fax 02.47.39.34.67). Excellent value. An intimate hotel run by a friendly young couple. All rooms have TV. Booking advisable. 50F dinner available. ①.

Youth hostels and campsite

Le Foyer, 16 rue Bernard-Palissy (☎02.47.60.51.51). A workers' hostel that sometimes has free rooms for under-25s, recently redecorated. Closed Sat afternoon & Sun.

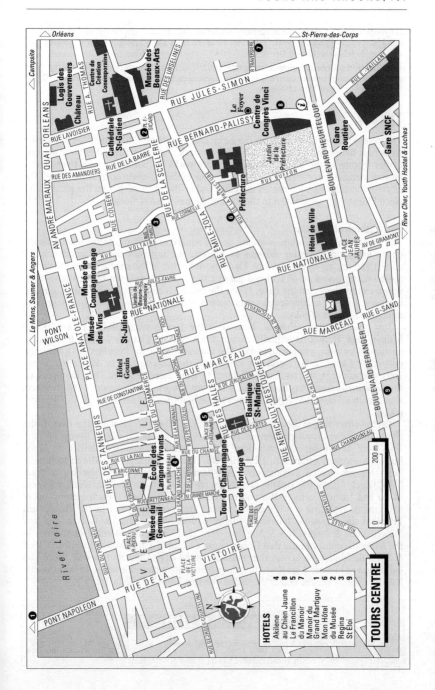

TOURS CENTRE

HOTELS
Akilene — 4
au Chien Jaune — 8
Le Francillon — 5
du Manoir — 7
Manoir du
Grand Martiguy — 1
Mon Hôtel
du Musée — 6
Regina — 2
St Éloi — 3
St Éloi — 9

HI youth hostel, av d'Arsonval in Parc de Grandmont (☎02.47.25.14.45). Reception 5–9/10pm; late-night key available with deposit. Take bus #6 or #2 from place Jean-Jaurès to Chambray, stop Auberge de Jeunesse. Closed Dec & Jan.

Les Bords du Cher municipal campsite (☎02.47.27.27.60). On the north bank of the Loire, about 1500m from the town centre, this is the closest municipal campsite to town. Take bus #7, stop Ste-Radegonde. Open May 11–Sept 8.

The city

The centre of Tours lies between the Loire and its tributary, the Cher, but has spread far across both banks, with industrial Tours north of the Loire. Neither river is a particular feature of the town, though there are parks on islands in both rivers and a newish footbridge across the Loire from the site of the old castle on quai d'Orléans. The city's old quarter focuses not on the cathedral or the château, but on the picturesque place Plumereau, some 600m to the west of the main rue Nationale.

The cathedral quartier

The **Cathédrale St-Gatien**, standing on the square of the same name, illustrates the entire evolution of Gothic designs in France, starting with the thirteenth-century chevet and ending in the glorious Flamboyant Gothic of the west front and towers, a mesmerizing overdose of sculpted pattern to which Renaissance belfries have been added as the cherry on the cake. When the sun is shining, the inside of the cathedral becomes a magic kaleidoscope experience of stained-glass windows projecting neat, multi-hued shards of colour.

Just south of the cathedral, housed in the former archbishop's palace, is the **Musée des Beaux-Arts** (daily except Tues 9am–12.45pm & 2–6pm; free), overshadowed by a huge Lebanon cedar. The museum has some beauties in its rambling collection: *Christ in the Garden of Olives* and the *Resurrection* by Mantegna; Frans Hals' portrait of Descartes; Balzac painted by Boulanger; prints of *The Five Senses* by the Tourainais Abraham Bosse; and a sombre Monet. The museum's top treasure, Rembrandt's *Flight into Egypt*, is unfortunately difficult to see through the security glass.

On the other side of the cathedral, between rue Albert-Thomas and the river, is the site of the ancient royal **château** of Tours, of which just two medieval towers remain. The **Tour de Guise**, now embedded in the seventeenth-century Pavillon de Mars, houses a waxworks museum, **Historial de Touraine** (daily: mid–March to June & Sept–Oct 9am–noon & 2–6pm; July & Aug 9am–6.30pm; Nov to mid-March 2–5.30pm; 35F), which makes the various courtly murders, marriages and machinations seem like a bad Disney cartoon. But you can push mock-medieval French history out of your mind, replacing it with gently waving multi-coloured fish in the **Aquarium Tropical** in the same buildings (daily: mid-March to June & Oct to mid-Nov 9.30am–noon & 2–6pm; July & Aug 9am–7pm; mid-Nov to mid-March 2–6pm; 30F). In the fifteenth-century **Logis des Gouverneurs** alongside (mid-March to mid-Dec Wed & Sat 3–6.30pm; free), across the remnants of the city's Gallo-Roman wall, there's an exhibition of historical artefacts that does give quite a plausible sense of how the city has developed over the centuries, called "Vivre à Tours" ("Life in Tours").

CARTE MULTI-VISITES

The tourist office offers a 50F ticket – **carte multi-visites** – that lets you into eight major sites, including the Musée des Beaux-Arts and the Musée du Gemmail.

Behind the cathedral, on rue Racine, is the **Centre de Création Contemporaine** (Wed–Sun 3–7pm; free), a contemporary art gallery, café and bookshop. There is no permanent display, but internationally renowned contemporary artists do get to show here.

The old quarter

The old part of Tours crowds around **place Plumereau**, over to the west of rue Nationale. Between the two, the **Hôtel Gouin**, 25 rue du Commerce, has a Renaissance facade to stop you in your tracks. Inside, it exhibits a surprising collection for an archeological museum, including a medicine chest belonging to Jean-Jacques Rousseau, and examples of early technical advances in physics, such as the Archimedes screw and a vacuum pump (mid-May to Sept 30 daily 10am–7pm; Oct to mid-March daily except Fri 10am–12.30pm & 2–5.30pm; rest of year daily 10am–12.30pm & 2–6.30pm; 20F).

But it's the old town's half-timbered houses and bulging stairway towers dating from the twelfth to fifteenth centuries that are the city's showpiece. Some of the earlier buildings look like cut-out models, but the Renaissance stone-and-brick constructions are sturdier – particularly the **Écoles des Langues Vivantes** on rue Briconnet, with its wonderful sculpted dogs, drunks, frogs and monsters. West of rue Bretonneau, around place Robert-Picou, modern artisans' workshops cluster between medieval dwellings.

Off rue Briconnet, at 7 rue du Mûrier, you'll find the **Musée du Gemmail** (mid-March to mid-Oct Tues–Sun 10am–noon & 2–6.30pm; 30F), a museum of non-leaded stained glass. Some of the works are displayed in an underground twelfth-century chapel, and artists include such leading lights as Picasso and Jean Cocteau. They shine with an extraordinary intensity and, through the use of layering, have a far greater colour range than traditional stained glass.

To the south, an enormous church once stood, with its nave stretching along rue des Halles from rue des Trois-Pavées-Ronds almost to place de Châteauneuf. Only the north tower, the Tour de Charlemagne, and the western clock tower remain of the ancient **Basilique de St-Martin**. The new church, a late nineteenth-century neo-Byzantine affair, guards the shrine of St-Martin, bishop of Tours in the fourth century and famous for giving half his cloak to a freezing beggar.

Around rue Nationale

At the head of **rue Nationale**, Tours' main street, statues of Descartes and Rabelais overlook the Loire. A short walk back from the river and you come to the **church of St-Julien**, whose old monastic buildings house two of the town's most compelling museums.

The **Musée de Compagnonnage** is in the eleventh-century guesthouse and sixteenth-century monks' dormitory at 8 rue Nationale (mid-Sept to mid-June daily except Tues 9am–noon & 2–5/6pm; otherwise daily 9am–6.30pm; 25F). Here, for once, the people who built – rather than ordered – the châteaux and cathedrals are celebrated. As well as documents of the origins and militant activity of the *compagnonnage* (the guilds), there are masterpieces (in the original sense of the term) of various crafts from cake-making and carpentry to locksmithery and bricklaying, with their relevant tools exhibited alongside.

The **Musée des Vins** in the twelfth-century cellars of the abbey at 16 rue Nationale (daily except Tues 9am–noon & 2–6pm; 15F) takes you through a comprehensive treatment of the history, mythology and production of wine, though there's nothing on recent technical innovations and no quaffing to look forward to. Behind the museum, a Gallo-Roman winepress from Cheillé sits in the former cloisters of the church.

If you take a left into rue Colbert and right into rue Jules-Favre, you can wander into the **Jardin de Beaune-Semblançay**, whose sixteenth-century fountain stands in front of the sad facade of the mansion that belonged to François I's finance minister. Back on rue Colbert, at no. 39, is the house where Joan of Arc is said to have had her suit of armour made.

Eating and drinking

Place Plumereau is set out with the tables of expensive **cafés** and **restaurants**; the bars in this area can be overpriced but many have a lot of character. The most promising restaurant streets are rue du Grand-Marché and rue de la Rôtisserie, on the periphery of old Tours, and rue du Commerce and rue Colbert. Sugar and chocolate freaks should make a detour to **pâtisseries** like La Marotte, 3 rue du Change and La Chocolatière, 6 rue de la Scellerie. The main **market** halls are to the west of St-Martin at the end of rue des Halles.

Académie de la Bière, 43 rue Lavoisier. A serious establishment near the cathedral for those dedicated to good ale; you can choose from among 150 types of beer while playing darts.

Atomic Café, off place Plumereau. Ultra-modern, with video screens everywhere, this hip bar is situated in a medieval courtyard just off the square.

Brasserie de l'Univers, 8 place Jean-Jaurès (☎02.47.05.50.92). Big and beautiful Belle Époque brasserie with its original painted glass. Grilled meat and fish, pizzas and menus from 85F. Service till midnight.

Brasserie de la Victoire, place de la Victoire. Simple brasserie in one of the less touristy squares. *Moules et frites* for 55F.

Au Chien Jaune, 74 rue B. Palissy (☎02.47.05.10.17). Simple good food. Menu 75F.

Le Franglais, 27 rue Colbert (☎02.47.61.62.44). This bar-cum-restaurant serves up enormous plates of meat with chips and salad for 60F, including wine. The owner and cook is English, which explains the name, but the cuisine is decidedly French.

Jean Bardet, 57 rue Groison (☎02.47.41.41.11). Tours's top restaurant and one of the best in France. Extremely sophisticated, health-conscious food with a minimum of butter and cream and a maximum of rare herbs and old varieties of vegetables. 500F à la carte, and fixed menus from 250F.

London Pub, rue du Commerce. Lively bar in the old town, popular with students of all nationalities.

Le Molière, cnr rue de la Scellerie & rue Corneille. Directly in front of the Grand Théâtre, this vast Belle Époque café has faded frescoes and a relaxed atmosphere.

La Rôtisserie Tourangelle, 23 rue du Commerce (☎02.47.05.71.21). Salmon pancakes, beef from Chinon, guinea fowl and other goodies, and excellent-value menus from 95F. Closed Sun eve & Mon.

Le Singe Vert, 5 rue Marceau (☎02.47.61.50.10). Another Belle Époque brasserie with lunchtime menus from 68F. Open till midnight.

Trois Caïmans, 91 rue Jules-Charpentier (☎02.47.37.71.26). Senegalese-African restaurant serving specialities such as *brochette d'antilope* and *chèvre yassa* (goat in onion and lime sauce). 65F and 95F menu. Closed Sun & Mon.

Les Trois Canards, 16 rue de la Rôtisserie (☎02.47.61.58.16). Traditional Tours dishes of veal and duck on very cheap menus from 50F. Closed 2 weeks in April & Oct.

Les Tuffeaux, 19 rue Lavoisier (☎02.47.47.19.89). An attractive setting for delicious classic cuisine, menus from 110F. Closed Sun & Mon midday.

Van Gogh, rue du Commerce. Fun student bar close to the place Plumereau.

Nightlife

Nightlife in the city is a lot more promising than in other Loire towns, with a fairly impressive selection of nightclubs, bars and cabaret-cafés: you can pick up a free copy of the **listings magazine** *Tours Spectacles*, which gives day-by-day details of musical and cultural events for the entire summer, from the Maison des Associations Culturelles, 5 place Plumereau (☎02.47.20.71.95).

L'Inox, 18 rue de la Longue-Échelle, off place du Grand-Marché (free admission, drink obligatory), is a **café/club** open from 6pm to 4am with disco music on Friday and a gay night on Sunday. *L'Excalibur*, in a vaulted cellar at 35 rue Briçonnet (daily 11pm–4am; Mon–Fri 60F, Sat & Sun 70F, free admission for women), caters for smart young clubbers. **Cafés with shows** include the popular *Petit Faucheaux*, 23 rue des Cerisiers, best known for jazz but also featuring comedians, and darts, cards and chess at any time; and *Le Vieux Mûrier* on place Plumereau has live music and an amazing decor of diverse objects. For **gigs**, try *Brind 'Zinc*, 72 rue Colbert, where you can see the latest in French rock; or *Le Bateau Ivre*, 146 rue Édouard-Vaillant, to the south of the gare SNCF, where top British and American rap/reggae/hip-hop bands play.

Listings

Bike rental Amster Cycles, cnr bd Heuteloup & rue de Buffon; Grammont Motocycles, 93 av de Grammont.

Books English books from 2 rue du Commerce and 20 rue Marceau.

Car rental Avis, gare de Tours (☎02.47.49.21.49); Budget, 2 place de la Gare (☎02.47.46.21.21); Europcar, 76 rue Bernard-Palissy (☎02.47.64.47.76); Hertz, 57 rue Marcel Tribune.

Change In the gare SNCF, or 24-hr automatic change machine on the wall of the Vinci centre on rue Bernard-Palissy. Most banks are on (or close to) place Jean-Jaurès.

Châteaux tours Service Touristiques de Touraine, gare SNCF (☎02.47.05.46.09); Tour Évasion, 19 rue Édouard-Vaillant (☎02.47.63.25.64). Tours from 100F (exclusive of entrance fees).

Cinema Studios, 2 rue des Urselines (☎02.47.05.22.80), shows the arty, obscure and old favourites in their original language.

City transport Bus tickets: flat fare of 6.50F for an hour's journey. Route map from SEMITRAT on place Jean-Jaurès.

Laundries 21–23 place Michelet; 56 rue du Grand-Marché; 45 rue Georges-Courteline.

Medical assistance SOS Médecins (☎02.47.38.33.33); SAMU (☎15); Hôpital Bretonneau, 2 bd Tonnelé (☎02.47.47.47.47); late-night pharmacy, phone police for address.

Police 70–72 rue Marceau (☎02.47.60.70.69).

Poste restante 1 bd Béranger.

Taxis (☎02.47.20.30.40).

Vouvray

The main reason to visit **VOUVRAY**, 10km east of Tours (bus #61) on the north bank, is for its wines, though it has its own charm in the villagey centre clustered around its thirteenth-century **church**. Vouvray's wonderful **Foire aux Vins** takes place from August 11 to 15. The **tourist office** at the Hôtel de Ville can provide addresses of **vignerons**, and information on guided tours, but all the roads leading up the steep valleys are lined with *caves*. The view of the vines from the top of the hill is almost intoxicating in itself.

If you choose to **stay** in Vouvray, there's the pleasant *Grand Veatel*, at 8 av Brulé (☎02.47.52.70.32, fax 02.47.52.74.52; ②; closed March 1–15) and a **campsite** between the Loire and the Cisse (☎02.47.52.68.81).

Amboise

Twenty kilometres upstream of Tours, **AMBOISE** is a prim little town trading on long-gone splendours, its one saving grace being Leonardo da Vinci's residence of Clos-Lucé and its mind-expanding exhibition on the great man's works. It is also one of Mick Jagger's favourite foreign residences – perhaps because few people recognize him here.

The one concession to twentieth-century art in Amboise is a **fountain** by Max Ernst of a turtle topped by a teddy bear (or ET figure), standing in front of the spot where the **market** takes place every Saturday and Sunday morning by the riverside. Behind, rising above the river, are the interesting remains of the **château** where Charles VIII was born and died (daily: April–June 9am–6.30pm; July & Aug 9am–7.30pm; Sept & Oct 9am–6pm; Nov–March 9am–noon & 2–5pm; 37F). It was in the late fifteenth century that Charles VIII decided to turn the old castle of his childhood days into a vast, extravagant and luxurious palace. Not long after the work was completed, he managed to hit his head, fatally, on a door lintel. The château continued to be enlarged under Louis XII and François I, but later wars and lack of finance have left less than half the total standing.

The **Tour des Minimes**, the original fifteenth-century entrance, is architecturally the most exciting part of the castle, designed for the maximum number of fully armoured men on horseback to get in and out as quickly as possible. From the top you step out onto the roof, with the Loire presenting one of its best panoramas. Before you've had time to orientate yourself, the guide launches into the story of how the hooks along the battlements were once smeared with the blood and guts of rebellious Huguenots. Caught plotting to get rid of the Catholic de Guise family, the power behind young François II, they were summarily tried in the Salle des Conseils and their corpses hung around the town.

The last French king, Louis-Philippe, stayed in this château, hence the abrupt switch from solid Gothic furnishings to 1830s post-First Empire style. People imprisoned in the castle include Louis XIV's finance minister, Fouquet, of Vaux-le-Vicomte fame, and, in the mid-nineteenth century, Abd el-Kader, an Algerian Resistance leader who spent fifteen years fighting against the French. A striking portrait of him hangs in the château.

A man of far greater renown today than any of the French kings was invited here by François I to bolster and encourage the French Renaissance. **Leonardo da Vinci** made his home at the **Clos-Lucé**, at the end of rue Victor-Hugo (daily: Feb–June & Sept–Dec 9am–6pm; July & Aug till 8pm; closed Jan; 38F), now a museum to him and his work, with some forty models of Leonardo's inventions, constructed according to his detailed plans. It's wonderful to see the mechanical manifestations of da Vinci's technological achievements, but even the best model – the wooden tank – does not have the same effect as Leonardo's sketch. Leonardo died here in 1519.

A contrast to Leonardo's output is the **Musée de la Poste** in the *Hôtel Joyeuse*, 6 rue Joyeuse (daily except Mon: June–Sept 9.30am–noon & 2–6.30pm; Oct–April 10am–noon & 2–5.30pm; 20F), whose exhibits trace the history of the postal delivery service, from the pony express to air and sea mail.

If you take the main road south out of Amboise and turn right just before the junction with the D31, you'll come to a very unlikely building in this land of châteaux. It's an eighteenth-century **pagoda** that once formed part of a château. You can climb to the top for fabulous views and also explore the park (daily: July & Aug 9.30 am–8pm; June & Sept 10am–7pm; April & Oct 10am–noon & 2–5 pm; closed Nov-Feb; March 10am–noon & 2–5pm; 28F).

Close to the château on rue Victor-Hugo, you'll find the **Caveau de Dégustation-Vente des Vins de Touraine Amboise** (daily June-Aug 10am–7.30pm), a good place to try some wines if you haven't got time to visit individual vineyards. Amboise celebrates its wines in a **Foire aux Vins** on August 15. And if you're heading towards Chenonceaux, you'll pass a farmhouse by a crossroads and a petrol station some 4.5km out from Amboise on the D81. Here, M. Delecheneau sells his *sec* and *demi-sec* white wine and sublime *demi-sec* rosé across the kitchen table. He'll show you his barrels named after cows (Dauphine, Jolie, Violette, etc), and the winepress his grandfather used.

WINE AND CHEESE OF TOURAINE

The food markets and vineyards of this fertile, affluent area of the Loire are famous. Chinon, Vouvray and Bourgueil have exceptional **wines**; the early ripening of fruits and vegetables, including asparagus, makes it clear that this is a different climate to northern France.

Vouvray is the *appellation* for one of the most delicious white wines of the Loire. A good vintage lives to be a hundred years old, can be *sec, demi-sec* or *pétillant* (lightly sparkling) and is best from the grape of a single vineyard. The other two famous Touraine *appellations* are **Chinon**, with mostly red wines and also a few very dry whites, and **Bourgueil**, renowned for its long-maturing red wine, but also producing a few dry rosés. Other *appellations* are **St-Nicholas de Bourgueil**, which – like its neighbour Bourgueil – is based exclusively on the Cabernet franc grape; **Montlouis**, with wines similar to Vouvray which it faces across the Loire; and, with fewer pretensions but still some excellent wines, **Touraine Amboise, Touraine** and **Touraine Azay-le-Rideau**.

To go with the wine, Touraine produces *chèvre* (**goat's cheese**); the best of those cylindrical and speckled miniature building blocks you see at market cheese stalls bear the name of Ste-Maure-de-Touraine, a small town 30km south of Tours.

The *appellation d'origine contrôlée* for Ste-Maure-de-Touraine *chèvre* covers a very wide area, stretching to the north bank of the Loire. The tourist offices of Tours, Amboise, Chinon, Bourgueil and Vouvray can provide addresses of farms. But if you want to visit Ste-Maure itself and you haven't got wheels, the Richelieu bus from Tours passes through. Ste-Maure's tourist office on rue du Château can provide addresses for *dégustations*, and the Friday market is well stocked. Cheese is celebrated on the first weekend in June with a **Foire aux Fromages**.

A group of **museums for children** have just opened to the east of Amboise on the D751: the Mini-Châteaux, Aquarium de Touraine and Le Fou de l'Âne (daily: May–Oct 9am–7pm; July &Aug 9am–midnight; 42F). Of the three, the first is the best, featuring two hectares of tiny châteaux.

Practicalities

Information on Amboise and its environs is available at the **tourist office** on quai du Général-de-Gaulle, on the riverfront (☎02.47.57.09.28, fax 02.47.57.14.35). Some of the town's **hotels** are overpriced, but worth trying are the central *Lion d'Or* (☎02.47.57.00.23, fax 47.23.22.49; ③); half-board compulsory in season), and *Belle Vue* (☎02.47.57.02.26, fax 02.47.30.51.23; ③), both on quai Charles-Guinot, just below the château. You can also try the pleasantly decorated, good value *Hôtel le Chaptal*, 13 rue Chaptal (☎02.47.57.14.46; ②). On the budget end of the scale, there's a good **campsite** on the island across from the castle, the *Île d'Or* (☎02.47.57.23.37), with a **hostel**, the *Centre Charles Péguy* (☎02.47.57.06.36; reception 3–8pm; closed Mon all year & Sun in winter) next door. **Bikes** can be rented from Cycles Richard, 2 rue Nazelles (☎02.47.57.01.79).

The **restaurants** in town don't stay open beyond 10pm, but try the dependable *Lion d'Or* (see above; menus from 66F), or the crêperies on the approach to the château eg. *Crêperie Anne de Bretagne* (closed Thurs) and at 7 rue Corneille (closed Sun & Mon during term-time). A cheap, hearty lunch can be had at 50 rue Rabelais, where a small working-man's cafe offers a 50F menu.

Villandry and around

Even if gardens aren't really your thing, those belonging to the château in the tiny, peaceful village of **VILLANDRY** (château daily 9am–6/7pm; château & gardens 45F; gardens only 32F) well worth a visit. Thirteen kilometres west of Tours along the Cher

– a superb cycle trip – this recreated Renaissance garden is no ordinary formal pattern of opposing primary colours, but more like a tapestry of that period, one that changes with the months and only fades in winter. Carrots, cabbages and aubergines are exalted to coloured threads woven beneath rose bowers; herbs and ornamental box hedges are part of the same artwork, divided by vine-shaded paths. From a terrace above, you can see the confluence of the Cher and the Loire and châteaux on the northern bank.

Just past the château, 1km down the D121 towards Druye, there's an upmarket farmhouse **restaurant**, the *Domaine de la Giraudière* (☎02.47.50.08.60; daily mid-March to Nov 12), which serves elaborate meals for 150–200F, with cheaper menus for 63F with some excellent specialities based on goat's cheese.

Alternatively, head back to **SAVONNIÈRES**, between Villandry and Tours, where *Le Faisan*, rte de Villandry (☎02.47.50.00.17, fax 02.47.50.14.90; ②), has rooms; and the *Ferme Auberge de la Tuilerie* (☎02.47.50.00.51; Easter–Oct; closed Tues), is a farm serving straightforward and very pleasant family meals, with a set menu from 110F; cross the Cher, follow the D288, take the first left along the bank of the Cher and the farm is on your left.

Langeais, St-Michel-sur-Loire, Bourgueil and Gizeux

On a high terrace on the river's north bank in the middle of **LANGEAIS** sits the town's **château**, looking sturdily severe (daily: April–Sept 9am–6.30pm; mid–July to Aug 9am–9pm; rest of year 9am–noon & 2–5/6.30pm; 35F). It is purely fifteenth century, with furnishings to match, and significant to the French because it was built to stop any incursions up the Loire by the Bretons. This threat ended with Charles VIII and Duchess Anne of Brittany's marriage in 1491, which was celebrated in this castle. A diptych of the couple portrays them looking less than joyous at their union – Anne had little choice in giving up her independence. There are fine tapestries on show, but this is a visit only for real château addicts. Langeais has a pleasant **hotel**, the *Hosten*, 2 rue Gambetta (☎02.47.96.82.12, fax 02.47.96.56.72; ③), with a good but expensive **restaurant**.

Five kilometres further west along the river bank, the little town **ST-MICHEL-SUR-LOIRE** has its **Musée Cadillac** located in the Château de Planchoury (daily: April–Sept 10am–6pm; 39F). This is the largest collection of Cadillacs outside the USA, comprising fifty different models of the American dream machine collected from all over the world, all in remarkable condition.

If you want to do some wine-buying, **BOURGUEIL** is just 13km west of St-Michel-sur-Loire. The Abbaye de Bourgueil has been making wine for nearly a thousand years and this is the best place to taste it. The Close de l'Abbaye (July–Aug Thurs–Mon 2–6pm; rest of year Sun only 2–6pm; 25F; ☎02.47.97.74.20), just east of the town centre, is open for visits. Bourgueil's **Foire aux Vins** is held the first weekend in March; on the third Tuesday in July they celebrate garlic; and on the third Tuesday in October, it's chestnuts that are honoured.

If you're heading north towards the Sarthe, an interesting stop is **GIZEUX**, 12km north of Bourgueil or 15km on a back-road route from St-Michel, whose fourteenth-to sixteenth-century **château** extends like a game of dominoes around its gardens (May–Sept Mon–Sat 10am–6.30pm, Sun 2–6pm; 35F). It contains some fine Renaissance paintings and beautiful seventeenth-century frescoes, but its speciality is the humble donkey: the **Musée Vivant de l'Ane** (daily April–Sept 9am–7pm; rest of year 10am–5pm; closed mid–Nov to Feb 4; 42F) has gathered together pack saddles and all the means of controlling and cajoling these stubborn beasts of burden, and has sixty different breeds for you to sympathize with in the park.

The Cher

Twenty kilometres southeast of Tours, spanning the slow-moving **River Cher**, the **Château de Chenonceaux** is perhaps the best of all the Loire châteaux for architecture, site, contents, organization and atmosphere. **Montrichard** and **St-Aignan** are two places to go to escape the endless stream of castle tours, but for still-unsatiated château buffs, there's **Valençay** on the way south towards the upper stretches of the Indre.

Château de Chenonceaux

Unlike the Loire, the gentle River Cher flows so slowly and passively between the exquisite arches of the **Château de Chenonceaux** that you are almost always assured of a perfect reflection (daily: Jan & Dec 9am–4.30pm; early Feb & Nov 9am–5pm; late Feb & Oct 9am–6pm; otherwise 9am–7pm; 45F).

The building of the château was always controlled by women. Catherine Briconnet, whose husband bought the site, hired the first architects in 1515 and had them begin building on the foundations of an old mill that stood on the granite bed of the Cher. The château's most characteristic feature, the set of arches spanning the River Cher, was begun later in the century by Diane de Poitiers (mistress of Henri II) and completed by the indomitable Catherine de Médicis (wife of Henri II), after she evicted Diane and forced her to hand over the château in return for the much more sober Chaumont (see p.463). Mary, Queen of Scots, child bride of François II, also spent time here until her husband's early death. Then, after a long period of disuse, one Mme Dupin brought eighteenth-century life to this gorgeous residence, along with her guests Voltaire, Montesquieu and Rousseau, whom she hired as tutor to her son. Restoration back to the sixteenth-century designs was completed by another woman in the late nineteenth century. It is now a profitable business, owned and run by the Menier chocolate family firm.

The best approach to the château is not straight up the path to the front door, but through the gardens laid out under Diane de Poitiers. After the pay-booths, cross the stream and follow signs to the maze. Walk along the stream through the woods, turn right to the Cher and, upriver, there's a magnificent view of the château.

During summer the place is teeming with people, but visits are unguided – a luxurious relief, for there's an endless number of arresting tapestries, paintings, ceilings, floors and furniture on show. On the ground floor the Chambre de François I features a portrait of Diane de Poitiers by Primaticcio and a case containing copies of her signatures. Another exceptional picture is Zurbaran's half-dressed *Archimedes*, his clothes inside out and his face full of fear and (justified) suspicion that his theories would be misunderstood. The Salle des Gardes on the same floor, its painted rafters emblazoned with the device of Catherine de Médicis, is used to exhibit Flemish tapestries. The elegant gallery across the Cher, despite the plastic potted plants, is worth spending time in if only to evoke the parties – all naked nymphs and Italian fireworks – held there by Catherine.

There's a **son et lumière** show, "Les Dames de Chenonceaux", tracing the history of the château from fortified mill to elegant residence, on June 3 and 4, then every evening from June 24 to Sept 3 (10.15pm; 40F). In July and August you can take **boats** out onto the Cher, and there's a crèche if you've got small children.

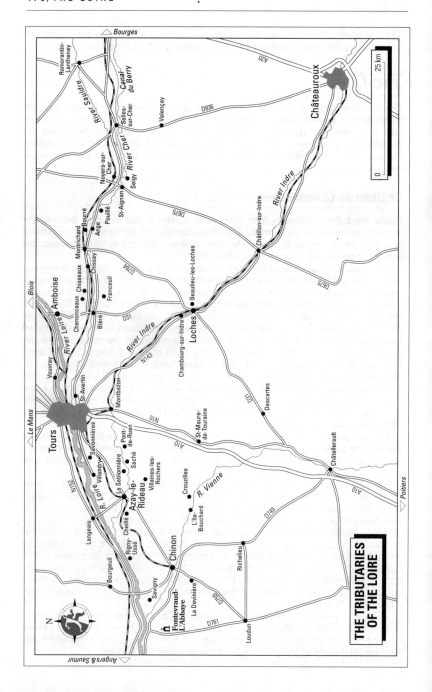

THE TRIBUTARIES
OF THE LOIRE

Practicalities

The **tourist office** for **Chenonceaux, Chisseaux** and **Franceuil**, three villages in close proximity, is at 13bis rue du Château in Chenonceaux (☎02.47.23.94.45).

If you wish to **stay** in the area, all the **hotels** in the village of Chenonceaux are on rue du Docteur-Bretonneau, within easy reach of the station and the château. The *Hôtel du Roy* at no. 9 (☎02.47.23.90.17, fax 02.47.23.89.81; ②) is comfortable and excellent value. At no. 6, the *Hôtel du Bon Laboureur et du Château* (☎02.47.23.90.02, fax 02.47.23.82.01; ④) is the most luxurious option. *Le Renaudière*, no. 24 (☎02.47.23.90.04, fax 02.47.23.90.51; ③), is very welcoming, with decent food on menus from 89F. If these are all booked up you could try *Le Cheval Blanc* at 5 place Charles-Bidault in **BLÉRÉ**, 5km downstream (☎02.47.30.30.14, fax 02.47.23.52.80; ④), a very pleasant place serving finely cooked meals, with menus from 100F, or the *Clair Cottage*, 27 rue de l'Europe at Chisseaux (☎02.47.23.90.69; ③), 2km east of Chenonceaux. For **camping**, there's *Le Moulin Fort* (☎02.47.23.86.22; April–Sept) in Franceuil, south of the river.

Montrichard and Bourré

If you're beginning to feel peeved that only dead royals had all the fun, take yourself to the Fraise-Or, 3km east of Chenonceaux, just beyond Chisseaux on the road to **MONTRICHARD**. It's an old-fashioned **distillery** (daily: Easter–Sept 9–11.30am & 2–6pm; 17F), complete with shiny copper stills, that specializes in fruit liqueurs. The visit includes a *dégustation* of three of their eighteen liqueurs and *eaux-de-vie*, based on various fruits, herbs, spices, nuts and, best of all, rose petals.

Montrichard itself is one of those laid-back market towns with its full complement of medieval and Renaissance buildings plus a ruined fortress, of which just the **keep** remains. Its Romanesque church was where the disabled 12-year-old princess, Jeanne de Valois, who would never be able to have children, married her cousin the Duc d'Orléans, who subsequently became King Louis XII after the unlikely death of Charles VIII at Amboise. Politics dictated that he marry Charles VIII's widow Anne of Brittany, so poor Jeanne was divorced and sent off to a nunnery in Bourges.

Three kilometres to the east of Montrichard, in **BOURRÉ**, are the quarries for the famous château-building stone that gets whiter as it weathers. Some of the caves are now used to cultivate mushrooms, a peculiar process that you can witness at the **Caves Champignonnières**, 40 rte des Roches (guided visits daily April–Oct at 10am, 11am, 2pm, 3pm, 4pm & 5pm; 28F).

Practicalities

Montrichard's **tourist office** is in the Maison Ave Maria (☎02.54.32.05.10, fax 02.54.23.75.29), an ancient house with saints and beasties sculpted down its beams, on rue du Pont. If the gentle pace of Montrichard takes your fancy, some **hotels** to try are *La Tête Noir*, 24 rue de Tours (☎02.54.32.05.55, fax 02.54.32.78.37; ③), by the river, or the cheaper *Hôtel de la Gare*, 20 av de la Gare (☎02.54.32.04.36, fax 02.54.32.78.17; ②). The **campsite** *L'Étourneau* (☎02.54.32.10.16; June to mid-Sept) is on the banks of the Cher, and you can rent **canoes** from the *Club Nautique* (☎02.54.71.49.49).

On the D17, the smaller of the two roads from Montrichard to St-Aignan (see below), between Angé and Pouillé, a good-value **restaurant**, *Le Bousquet*, serves simple meat dishes cooked over a charcoal grill and cheap jugs of local AOC wine in an old wine cellar (☎02.54.71.44.44; July & Aug Tues eve to Sun; otherwise Fri, weekends & holidays only; menus from 85F). There's also a pleasant gîte d'étape in the lock-keeper's house at Bourré, called the *Vallagon* (☎02.54.32.50.59; 60F). In **POUILLÉ**, on the N76, the *Auberge Le Bien-Allé* (☎02.54.71.47.45; closed Sun eve), in an attractive eighteenth-century country house overlooking the Cher, has similar fare, with menus starting at 88F.

St-Aignan

ST-AIGNAN, 15km upstream from Montrichard, is a small and charming town comprising a cluster of houses below a huge Romanesque collegiate church and sixteenth-century château.

La Collégiale de St-Aignan (Mon–Sat 9am–7pm, Sun 1–7pm) has some of the best ecclesiastical decoration in the region. Its capitals are adorned with mermaids, a multi-bodied snake biting its own necks, a man's head tunnelled by an eagle, doleful dragons and other wonders of the twelfth-century imagination, while in the crypt there are some very well-preserved, brightly coloured late-twelfth-century frescoes.

St-Aignan lends itself to aimless wandering, with the **château grounds** accessible to the public and some pleasant walks down by the river – or a swim if you feel inclined. On the road bridge above the long island facing the town is the Maison du Vin, open for tastings and sales of Côteaux du Cher wines (July & Aug). On the mainland east of the bridge, at 21 quai J-J-Delorme, Promenades sur le Cher runs boat trips (☎02.54.71.40.38; departures 3pm & 5pm April, June, Sept & Oct Sat, Sun & bank hols; July & Aug daily; 55F); or you can rent a **houseboat** (2100–2500F for four people for a weekend) and explore the Berry Canal, which joins the river at St-Aignan. At the Base Nautique Les Couflons, a couple of kilometres upstream in Seigy, you can windsurf, canoe and sail. **Bikes** can be rented in town from Le Tandem, 54 rue Constant-Ragot.

For a good break from ancient aristocratic artefacts, St-Aignan has the **Zoo Parc de Beauval** (daily 9am–dusk; 62F), 2km to the south of town on the D675. The space given to the animals is ample, and it's part of the European programme for breeding threatened species in captivity to reintroduce them to the wild. From a human viewpoint the park is very attractive, with sumptuous flower beds giving way to suitably wild areas of woods, little streams and lakes where the islands provide natural enclosures for some of the monkeys. Two hothouses with tropical flowers and greenery are home to an extraordinary collection of tropical birds and to a large group of chimpanzees and two families of orang-utans. But the creature most children will want to take home with them is the rare white tiger, in particular the ultimate fantasy cuddly pet, Katharina, the first cub to be bred in France.

Practicalities

The **tourist office** (☎02.54.75.22.85, fax 02.54.75.22.85) is on the island by the road bridge, opposite the Maison du Vin. If you're staying the night, **hotels** worth choosing from include *Le Moulin*, 7 rue Novilliers (☎02.54.75.15.54; ①; closed Sun), to the west of the bridge, with meals for only 55F, or *Le Grand Hôtel St-Aignan*, 7–9 quai J-J-Delorme (☎02.54.75.18.04; ④; Nov–March closed Sun eve; menus from 85F). Otherwise, you'll have to look for rooms in **NOYER-SUR-CHER** on the other side of the river. St-Aignan has an excellent **campsite**, near Seigy, the *Camping des Cochards* (☎02.54.75.15.59;April to mid-Sept).

St-Aignan has few **restaurants** and none of them is special. Besides the two hotels, you could try *Le Crepiot*, 36 rue Constant-Ragot (☎02.54.75.21.39; closed Mon & Tues midday), with a terrace where you can eat grills, crêpes and so forth.

Valençay

There is nothing medieval about the fittings and furnishings of the **Château de Valençay**, 20km southeast of St-Aignan on the main Blois–Châteauroux road (March 15–Nov 15 daily 10am–6pm; July & Aug daily 9am–7pm; rest of year weekends only 10am–12.30 & 1.30–5pm; 40F). This proud and overbearing castle was built to show off the wealth of a sixteenth-century financier. Two-hundred-and-fifty years later it was used to illustrate the power of Napoléon's France, as residence of the empire's foreign minister, the Prince de Talleyrand. The contrast of eras is one of the chief interests of Valençay.

Inside the château there hangs a portrait of the minister, a great political operator and survivor, by François Bonneau. A bishop before the Revolution, with a reputation for having the most desirable mistresses, he proposed the nationalization of church property, renounced his bishopric, escaped to America during the Terror, backed Napoléon and continued to serve the state under the restored Bourbons. One of his tasks for the emperor was keeping Ferdinand VII of Spain entertained for six years here after the king had been forced to abdicate in favour of Napoléon's brother Joseph. The Treaty of Valençay, signed in the château in 1813, put an end to Ferdinand's forced guest status, giving him back his throne.

The interior consequently is largely First Empire, with elaborately embroidered chairs on spindly legs, Chinese vases, ornate inlays and studdings to all the tables, finicky clocks and chandeliers: in short, the sort of furnishings dominated by strict rules of etiquette. Some of the Renaissance period rooms, in which it's easier to imagine more passionate and rougher lifestyles, are being opened.

The château **park** (same hours as above; 8F) keeps a collection of unhappy looking camels, zebras, llamas and kangaroos. There's also yet another **car museum** (same hours and ticket as the château) with pre-World War I Michelin maps and guides.

Azay-le-Rideau and around

Even without its **château** (daily April–Oct 9.30am–6pm; July & Aug 9am–7pm; winter 9.30am–12.30pm & 2–5.30pm; 32F), the quiet village of **AZAY-LE-RIDEAU** would bask in its serene setting complete with an old mill by the bridge and the Carolingian statues embedded in the facade of the church of St-Symphorien. The château exterior, however, on its little island in the Indre, is one of the loveliest in the Loire: pure turreted Renaissance, and required viewing. While the guided tours of the interior, furnished in period style, don't add much to the experience, the portrait gallery is worth seeing, since it has the whole sixteenth-century royal Loire crew – François I, Catherine de Médicis, the de Guises, and the rest – the highlight being a semi-nude painting of Gabrielle d'Estrée, Henri IV's lover.

Practicalities

The downside to Azay is that **hotels** don't come cheap, though *Le Balzac*, 4 & 6 rue A-Richer (☎02.47.45.42.08, fax 02.47.45.29.87; ③), and *Le Grand Monarque*, 3 place de la République (☎02.47.45.40.08, fax 02.47.45.46.25; ③; half-board compulsory in season), are both comfortable possibilities. Upstream from the château is a large **campsite**, the *Camping du Sabot*, near to the swimming pool and sports centre (☎02.47.45.42.72), signposted off the D84 to Saché. The **restaurant** of *Le Grand Monarque* is very acceptable, with a midday menu for around 100F, or try *L'Automate Gourmand*, 1 rue Parc (☎02.47.45.39.07; closed Tues & Mon eve out of season), with weekday menus from 120F. A rotating gourmet **night-time market** operates between Azay-le-Rideau, Bourgeuil and Langeais, from 5pm to midnight, June to September, and involves lots of drinking and delicious snacks – details are available from Azay's **tourist office**, on place de l'Europe (☎02.47.45.44.40, fax 02.47.45.31.46). You can rent **bikes** at the station or from Le Provost, 13 rue Carnot.

Rigny-Ussé

Fourteen kilometres west of Azay-le-Rideau, as the Indre approaches its confluence with the Loire, is the **Château d'Ussé** in **RIGNY-USSÉ** (daily: mid-July to Aug

9am–6.30pm; Sept 26 to Nov 11 10am–noon & 2–5.30pm; otherwise 9am–noon & 2–6pm; closed Nov 12 to mid-March; 57F). With its shimmering white towers and spires and idyllic wooded setting (best seen after dark when floodlit), this is the ultimate fairytale château, so much so that it's supposed to have inspired Charles Perrault's transcription of the Sleeping Beauty fairy story. Going inside for the visit – despite a display of models illustrating the Sleeping Beauty myth which might be of interest to children – isn't half as compelling, and perhaps not worth the rather excessive entrance fee.

Villaines-les-Rochers

Six kilometres south of Azay-le-Rideau is the troglodyte village of **VILLAINES-LES-ROCHERS**, famous for its wickerwork co-operative set up in 1849 by the local curate to keep the village economically sustainable; you can still visit the **Musée de l'Osier et de la Vannerie** (mid–May to Sept daily 2.30–6.30pm; free). Villaines now produces a third of all wickerwork articles in France. You can visit the **workshops** that are dug into the rock, providing perfect humid conditions for keeping the willow supple, and buy baskets, chairs and so forth from the *Maison d'Exposition*.

Upstream along the Indre

Following the D84 from Azay-le-Rideau eastwards along the north bank of the Indre you get glimpses of various privately owned châteaux. North of the hamlet of La Sablonnière, on the top of a hill surrounding the beautiful views of the Indre valley and the village of **SACHÉ**, is where Alexander Calder, sculptor of mobiles and stabiles, had his last *atelier*. He also worked at **LA CHEVRIÈRE** just down the slope to the east.

An Alexander Calder mobile decorates the main square of Saché, but it is Balzac who gets the honours here. The house where he often stayed and wrote several of his novels, notably the locally set *Le Lys dans la Vallée*, is inevitably a **Musée Balzac** (daily: Feb to mid-March 9.30am–noon & 2–5pm; mid-March to June & Sept 9am–noon & 2–6pm; July & Aug 9.30am–6.30pm; Oct & Nov 9am–noon & 2–5pm; closed Dec & Jan; 21F).

Chinon

CHINON lies on the north bank of the Vienne, 12km from its confluence with the Loire and surrounded by some of the best vineyards in the Loire valley. The spectacular line of towers and ramparts on the high ridge to the east of the town look as if they must enclose one of the best of this region's châteaux, but all is ruined within. In an attempt to make up for the loss, a medieval quarter below has been restored in over-sanitized fashion, and the town's total dedication to tourism has removed some of Chinon's charm.

Arrival, information and accommodation

The **gare SNCF** (☎02.47.93.11.04) lies to the east of the town with rue du Dr-P-Labussière and rue du 11-Novembre, leading to the **gare routière** on place Jeanne-d'Arc, where Joan is sculptured in mid-battle charge. Keep heading west, either along the river bank or across place Mirabeau into rue Rabelais, and you'll soon reach the medieval quarter. The **tourist office** is at 12 rue Voltaire (daily 10am–noon & 2–5.30pm; ☎02.47.93.17.85, fax 02.47.93.93.05), below the eastern end of the castle.

If you need a **room**, the two cheapest alternatives are the *Point du Jour*, 102 quai Jeanne-d'Arc (☎02.47.93.07.20; ①), and the *Jeanne d'Arc*, 11 rue Voltaire (☎02.47.93.02.85; ①). In a grand eighteenth-century house east of St-Mexme church, the *Hôtel Le Diderot*, 4 rue Buffon (☎02.47.93.18.87, fax 02.47.93.37.10; ③), is a more comfortable option. Dorm rooms and **bikes** for rental are available at the Location de Velos, close to the gare SNCF on rue Descartes (☎02.47.93.04.37); turn left out of the station onto avenue Gambetta, and first right into rue Descartes. The **campsite**, *Camping de l'Île Auger* (☎02.47.93.08.35; mid-March to Oct), overlooks the old town and château from the south bank of the Vienne; turn right from the bridge along quai Danton.

The town

A fortress of one kind or another existed at Chinon from the Stone Age until the time of Louis XIV, the age of the most recent of its ruins. It was a favourite residence of Henry Plantagenet, who held title to it long before he inherited the throne of England. He added a new castle to the first medieval fortress on the site, built by his ancestor Foulques Nerra, and died here. His son Richard the Lionheart is also said to have breathed his last in Chinon after being wounded in a battle against the French, though he was probably dead on arrival. Richard's son John, with no English inheritance, stayed in Chinon off and on but after a year's siege in 1204–05, Philippe Auguste finally took the castle and put an end to the Plantagenet rule over Touraine and Anjou.

Over two hundred years later, Chinon was one of the few places where Charles VII could safely stay while Henry V of England held Paris and the title to the French throne. Charles's situation changed with the arrival here in 1429 of a peasant girl from Domrémy in Lorraine, with a manic light in her eyes and a conviction so strong in her God-given mission that she was able to talk her way into the castle. Joan of Arc proposed, as proof of her divine guidance, that she would be able to recognize the Dauphin. The court officials agreed, no doubt thinking that humiliating this over-precocious 17-year-old would be an entertaining pastime for Charles. To their amazement, despite the Dauphin disguising himself in a crowd of courtiers, Joan instantly went down on her knees before him, begging him to allow her to lead his army against the English. And, to their horror, Charles said yes.

Today, all that remains in the **château** (daily: mid-March to June & Sept 9am–6pm; July & Aug 9am–7pm; Oct 9am–5pm; Nov–March 9am–noon & 2–5pm; 30F) is the scene of this encounter, the Grande Salle, with a wall and first-floor fireplace. Visits to this and to the restored Royal Lodgings – both guided – are not wildly exciting. More interesting is the Tour Coudray, over to the west, covered with intricate thirteenth-century graffiti carved by imprisoned and doomed Templar knights. Joan is said to have stayed here, too, and to have watered her horse at the pump and prayed in the church on rue Voltaire after her journey from eastern France.

Below, medieval streets vaunt olde-worldeness, overpriced cafés and brasseries, and a wine- and barrel-making museum with tacky, animated models and free tasting of the worst wine. On the first weekend in August there is a reconstruction of a medieval market. The **Marché à l'Ancienne** on the third Saturday of August is similar tourist fodder, the costumes this time of nineteenth-century peasants and the parades led by live pigs, geese and goats.

If you like boats, the models of barges and other vessels that used to carry goods along the Vienne and the Loire in the last century are likely to be the most appealing exhibits of the **Musée du Vieux Chinon** at 44 rue Haute St-Maurice (July–Sept daily 10am–12.30pm & 2.30–7pm; 20F).

Eating and drinking

The most reasonably priced of Chinon's decent **restaurants** is *Les Années 30*, 78 rue Voltaire (☎02.47.93.37.18; menus from 98F), although the best one is *Au Plaisir Gourmand*, 2 rue Parmentier (☎02.47.93.20.48; closed Sun eve & Mon), where you can try *filet de sandre* or wonderful langoustines on menus from 175F. These apart, you'll have to make do with indifferent pizzas and crêpes, or pay over the odds for "gargantuan" menus (see below for the Rabelais connection) in the restaurants of the medieval quarter.

Around Chinon

Although the town of Chinon has been affected by commercialism, it's a short distance to the open countryside, which you can explore on foot or by **boat**: Le Club Chinonais de Canoë-Kayak (☎02.47.93.39.59), on the south bank by Chinon's campsite, offers groups trips up to L'Île Bouchard or down to Candes (July & Aug 10am–6pm), or you can rent **canoes** and **kayaks** on Saturday afternoon and Sunday (around 80F for half a day).

Some of the region's **troglodyte dwellings** can be found just a short walk from Chinon. From St-Mexme's church at the eastern end of rue Jean-Jacques-Rousseau, the **Coteaux Ste-Radegonde** (GR3) forges a route lined with cave dwellings, some of which are still inhabited, and ends at the **Chapelle Ste-Radegonde**, a rock-cut church which is part of a complex of cave dwellings in which St Radegonde lived with her followers. The sixth-century German princess renounced the world and her husband – probably not a great sacrifice, since he eventually murdered her brother – in order to devote her life to God.

The other good excuse for getting out of Chinon is to discover the delights of the Chinon *appellation* ruby-red **wines**. The vineyards extend from **CROUZILLES**, just beyond L'Île Bouchard, 18km upstream, to **SAVIGNY-EN-VÉRON**, near the confluence of the Vienne and the Loire. *Vin de Pâques* (Easter wine) is the name given to the wine that should be drunk young, but most Chinon will age for thirty years, sometimes even longer. Though reds dominate, there are also a dry white and dry rosé. The Chinon tourist office can provide a list of wine-growers to visit.

The man who vies with Joan of Arc for shops and streets named in his honour in Chinon is François Rabelais (1494–1553), who wrote approvingly of wine, food and laughter in serious and rather difficult humanist texts, and whose most famous creations are the giant father and son Gargantua and Pantagruel. He was born at **LA DEVINIÈRE**, 6km southwest of Chinon, in a steep-roofed farmhouse that is now a **museum** to the great man (daily: May–Sept 10am–7pm; Oct, Nov & Jan–April 9am–noon & 2–5/6pm; 21F), completely furnished in the style of the time, right down to the stone kitchen sink.

Saumur and around

Unlike many small Loire towns, **SAUMUR** is not completely dominated by its château, nor by the military, though it's been the home of the French Cavalry Academy, and its successor the Armoured Corps Academy, since 1763. Even the local sparkling wines are based elsewhere. Saumur itself is simply peaceful and pretty. The Hôtel de Ville strives busily to attract festivals and conferences, and, when they're successful, finding a room can be a problem. Even at the best of times, reservations are essential.

From Chinon to Angers passing through Saumur you will find the loveliest stretch of the Loire, with the bizarre draw of **troglodyte dwellings** carved out of cliffs as early as the twelfth century. The land to the south, under grapes and sunflowers, gradually rises away from the river, with long-inactive windmills still standing. Across the water cows graze in wooded pastures. For transport you can either take the train or one of three buses: #5 along the south bank, #11 crossing halfway, or #10 staying north of the river.

Arrival, information and accommodation

Arriving at the **gare SNCF**, you'll find yourself on the north bank of the Loire: turn right onto avenue David-d'Angers and either take bus #A to the centre or cross the bridge to the island on foot. From the island the old **Pont Cessart** takes you to the main part of the town on the south bank. The **gare routière** is in the centre, a couple of blocks from the Pont Cessart on place St-Nicolas. Saumur's main street, rue d'Orléans, cuts back through the south bank sector: the **tourist office** is just across the river on the left, on place de la Bilange near the theatre (mid-May to mid-Oct Mon–Sat 9.15am–7pm; Sun 10.30am–12.30 & 3.30–6.30 pm; rest of the year Mon–Sat 9.15am–12.30 & 2–6pm; Sun 10am–noon. ☎02.41.40.20.60, fax 02.41.40.20.69). The **old quarter**, around St-Pierre and the castle, is reached along rue Dacier, also to the left of rue d'Orléans.

Hotels

Anne d'Anjou, 32 quai Mayaud (☎02.41.67.30.30, fax 02.41.67.51.00; closed Christmas). An eighteenth-century listed building with service and comfort to match. ④.

La Bouère-Salée, rue Grange-Couronne (☎02.41.67.38.85, fax 02.41.51.12.52). Delightful bed and breakfast situated 500m behind the train station. ③.

de Bretagne, 55 rue St-Nicolas (☎02.41.51.26.38). A few rooms above a bar. Not the quietest place, but central and clean. Closed Sun. ②.

Central, 23 rue Daillé (☎02.41.51.05.78, fax 02.41.67.82.35). Small, quiet and comfortable. ③.

Le Cristal, 10–12 place de la République (☎02.41.51.09.54, fax 02.41.51.12.14). One of the nicest hotels, with river views from most rooms and very friendly proprietors. ④.

du Roi René, 94 av du Général-de-Gaulle (☎02.41.67.45.30, fax 02.41.67.74.59). On the Île d'Offard with lovely river and château views. ③.

St-Pierre, 3 rue Haute-St-Pierre (☎02.41.50.33.00, fax 02.41.50.38.68). Large, well-equipped and very comfortable rooms in the old quarter. ⑥.

Youth hostel and campsites

Youth hostel, rue de Verden, Île d'Offard (☎02.41.40.30.00). From the station, take the second left off av du Général-de-Gaulle; it's at the east end of the island. Reception 8–10am & 5–10pm. Boat and bike rental available.

Camping municipal, rue de Verden, Île d'Offard (☎02.41.67.45.00). Next door to the youth hostel. You can even swim in the Loire from the north side of the island.

La Chantepie, on the D751, St-Hilaire-St-Florent (☎02.41.67.95.34). An alternative to the municipal campsite, a couple of kilometres west of Saumur. Open 1 May - 30 September.

The town

Saumur's **château** (daily except Tues Oct–May 9.30am–noon & 2–5pm; June–Sept 9.30am–6pm; closed Dec 25–Jan 1; 37F), a great, square building high above the town, is recognizable as the gleaming white, turreted subject of one of the scenes of *Les Très Riches Heures du Duc de Berry*. Its symmetry and witch-hat towers give it an air of fantasy, particularly on a misty morning or under night-time illumination. It was built in the fourteenth century and turned into a much more decorative and comfortable residence by Duke René of Anjou in the fifteenth. The star-shaped fortifications around it were added in 1590 during the Wars of Religion, when Saumur was a Protestant stronghold.

The dungeons and the watchtower can be visited on your own; for the two larger museums within the château, relaxed guides take over. The **Musée des Arts Décoratifs** in the former royal apartments has a huge and impressive collection of European china, plus several fifteenth-century tapestries, one of which portrays wonderfully snooty-looking medieval ladies out hunting. But it's the **Musée du Cheval**, in the attic of the château, that's the real treat. Progressing from a horse skeleton, through the evolution of bridles and stirrups over the centuries, you finally reach an amazing and diverse international saddlery collection. One of the best pieces is a Russian sleigh on which a fishy female figure looks up at a cherub wearing what seems to be a Roman helmet. The **Musée de la Figurine-Jouet**, located in an ancient powder magazine on the ramparts (mid-April to mid-Sept daily 2.30–6pm except Tues; rest of year reservations only; separate ticket from château entrance, 12F), offers a display of ancient toys: farm and zoo animals, circus and theatre figures, cowboys and Indians, and model soldiers.

Back down in the town, a real soldier will escort you around the **Musée de la Cavalerie** (Tues–Thurs & Sun 9am–noon & 2–5pm, Sat 2–5pm; 20F), if you knock at the guarded gate on avenue Maréchal-Foch, west of rue d'Orléans. Among the uniforms, weapons and battle scenes (including some very recent engagements), there's a particularly moving room, dedicated to the cavalry cadets who held the Loire bridges between Gennes and Montsoreau against the Germans for three days in 1940, after the French government had surrendered. The history of tank warfare is covered in the separate **Musée des Blindés**, at 1043 rue Fricotelle, to the southeast of the centre (daily mid-April to 30 Oct 9am–noon & 2–6pm; July–Aug 9am–6pm; Nov–14 April 9am–noon & 2–5pm; 20F).

The early medieval pointy-spired **church of St-Pierre** is most notable for its interesting selection of dragons; there are at least seven monsters carved in stone and wood or woven into the sixteenth-century tapestries that tell the legend of St Florent, an early scourge of the beautiful beasts that symbolize sin. Saumur's oldest church, **Notre-Dame de Nantilly**, by the public gardens south of the château, contains more sixteenth-century tapestries, with immensely crowded and detailed scenes.

Beyond the town centre

For a slightly less bellicose diversion you can visit the **École Nationale d'Équitation**, in St-Hilaire-St-Florent, a suburb to the east of the centre; take bus #B from the town centre. The Riding School provides guided tours in which you can watch training sessions (mornings only; closed Aug) and view the stables (Mon 2.30–4pm, Tues–Fri 9.30–11am & 2.30–4pm, Sat 9.30–11am; 32F morning visits, 20F afternoons; wheelchair access). Displays of dressage and anachronistic battle manœuvres by the crackshot Cadre Noir, the former cavalry trainers, are regular events (programme details from the tourist office or the school on ☎02.41.53.50.60).

Performances of a far greater diversity are celebrated in the **Musée du Masque**, a short walk back down towards Saumur from the Riding School, on rue de l'Abbaye (daily: mid-April to mid-Oct 10am–12.30pm & 2.30–6.30pm; mid-Oct to mid-April Sat & Sun 2–6pm; closed mid-Dec to mid-March; 25F). This is very much geared for children, with waxwork models of clowns and storybook characters wearing masks dating from the 1870s to the present day.

Another museum in St-Hilaire-St-Florent, of a very different nature, is the **Musée de Champignon** (daily mid-Feb to mid-Nov 10am–7pm; 38F; wheelchair access), which runs informative (if a bit dank and cold) tours through some of the region's 500km of underground *caves de champignons*, used to grow seventy percent of France's commonest cooking mushrooms, the *champignon de Paris*. The entrance is 1km downriver, along the D751 from the last bus stop in St-Hilaire-St-Florent.

SAUMUR WINES

The **Maison du Vin** at 25 rue Beaurepaire in Saumur has information on locally produced wines and addresses of wine-growers. The speciality here is sparkling – *méthode
champenoise* – wine, which can rival lesser-quality champagnes. Names to look out for are
Veuve Amiot and Gratien-Meyer. A good red is the Saumur Champigny from around the
village of the same name. The **Caves Coopératives** at St-Cyr-en-Bourg, a short train hop
south of Saumur and near the station, have kilometres of cellars, and you can taste different wines with no obligation to buy.

Eating and drinking

There are several cheap **eating places** around place St-Pierre: *Auberge St-Pierre*, 6
place St-Pierre (☎02.41.51.26.25; closed Mon out of season), has good 55F and 75F
menus; opposite, at no. 1, *Les Forges de St-Pierre* (☎02.41.38.21.79; closed Sun & Tues
eve; Oct) specializes in grilled meat, with an acceptable 55F menu; and *La Quichenotte*,
2 rue Haute-St-Pierre (☎02.41.51.31.98; closed Mon & Jan.), serves good crêpes at 55F.
Les Chandelles, 71 rue St-Nicolas (☎02.41.67.20.40; closed Wed, plus Thurs eve out of
season), offers more sophisticated food, with an excellent weekend lunch menu for 89F.
You can also eat in the château grounds at *L'Orangerie* (☎02.41.67.12.88; closed Sun
evening & Mon out of season), a restaurant and *salon de thé*, with 90F menu.

There are a couple of **bars** on place St-Pierre, like *Le Swing*, with its ancient
Wurlitzer jukebox and fruit cocktails, and *Le Richelieu*, with good music, Guinness and
pool. The *Café de la Poste*, opposite the post office on place du Petit-Thouars, is a student meeting place that serves cheap snacks. The hotel bar of *Le Cristal* (see p.483) is
also popular, along with the other bars along the riverfront on place de la République.

Troglodyte dwellings

The "falun" or soft shellstone found in the Loire valley lends itself to **troglodyte
dwellings**, homes carved out of rocky outcrops, of which there are more in this area –
between Saumur and Angers – than anywhere else in France. It's reckoned that in the
twelfth century half the local population here lived in semi-subsumed homes carved out
of the rock. Today, some of the rock dwellings have surprising uses, along with the
more predictable "Troglo" bars and restaurants.

Away from the Loire cliffs on the plains to the south, troglodyte villages were built
by digging holes like large craters and then carving out the walls. The best example is
at **ROCHEMENIER**, north of Doué-la-Fontaine, about 20km southwest of Saumur,
where an underground village housed a small farming community with its own underground chapel (daily: April–Nov 9.30am–7.30pm; rest of the year 2–6 pm; closed Dec &
Jan; 23F), and was only abandoned in the 1930s. The visit includes a typical troglodyte
dwelling, along with a museum of domestic items, including wine and oil presses.

Just 3km north, at **DÉNEZÉ-SOUS-DOUÉ**, there are underground carvings
thought to have been sculpted by a secret sixteenth-century sect of libertarians. The
cartoon-style figures mock religion, morality, the state and the ruling class, with scenes
of sex, strange deformities and perverted Christian imagery (July & Aug daily
9am–7pm; April–May Tues–Sun 2–6.30 pm; June & Sept 10am–7pm; 20F). There are
also concerts in the cave on Wednesday evenings (April–Oct).

Equally bizarre is the **Zoo de Doué** on the D960 to Cholet, 2km southwest of Doué-
la-Fontaine (daily: April–Sept 9am–7pm; Oct–March 10am–noon & 2–6pm; 60F), established in one of the region's complexes of quarried falun caverns. The natural setting

has been used to full advantage for a cave of fruit bats, a vivarium (formerly a cave dwelling but now home to pythons, anacondas and the like), and a lynx enclosure so spacious and overgrown it's hard to spot a cat.

At **PARNAY**, about 7km upstream from Saumur on the south bank of the Loire, you can taste and buy wines from a troglodyte mansion, the **Château du Marconnay**, 75 rte de Saumur (April–Sept Tues–Sun 10am–12.30pm & 2–6pm; 16F). Further on, just before Turquant, in **LE VAL-HULIN**, are the last producers of the once common Saumurois dried whole apples, known as *pommes tapées* – each apple, after drying, is given a little expert tap to make it a more amenable shape for bottle storage. You can tour one of the workshops at **Le Troglo des Pommes Tapées** (July & Aug Tues–Sun 10am–noon & 2.30–6.30pm; June & Sept Tues–Fri 2.30–6.30pm; Easter–May & Nov 1–11 Sat, Sun & hols 10am–noon & 2.30–6.30pm), where you are taken through the apple drying and tapping process and then top off the visit with a tasting.

About 10km south from Saumur towards Montreuil-Bellay is **La Magnanerie du Coudray** in **LE COUDRAY-MACOUARD** (Mon–Fri & Sun: April–Oct 2–7pm; July & Aug 10am–7pm; 25F; ☎02.41.67.91.24), a silkworm farm with small museum explaining the history of silk in the region and the various silk-reeling methods.

The Abbaye de Fontevraud

The **Abbaye de Fontevraud**, 13km southeast of Saumur on bus #16 (4 daily; 30min), is a key site in French and English history, because of its role as the burial place of both countries' monarchs (guided or independent visits June to mid-Sept daily 9am–7pm; mid-Sept to May 9.30am–12.30pm & 2–6pm/dusk; 32F). The community was established in 1099 as both a nunnery and a monastery with an abbess in charge – an unconventional move, even if the post was filled solely by queens and princesses. The remaining buildings date from the twelfth century and are immense, built as they were to house and separate not only the nuns and monks but also the sick, lepers and repentant prostitutes. There were originally five separate complexes, of which three still gracefully stand in Romanesque solidity. Used as a prison from the Revolution until 1963, its most famous inmate was the writer Jean Genet.

The **abbey church** is an awe-inspiring space, not least for its emptiness, though the restorers could be accused of being a little over-zealous in their cleaning work. This was the burial ground of the Plantagenet kings, and four tombstone effigies remain: Henry II, his wife Eleanor of Aquitaine who died here, their son Richard the Lionheart and daughter-in-law Isabelle of Angoulême, King John's queen. There's something a bit spooky about them, carved as they were at the time of their deaths – instead of being almost imaginary characters in the stories told at so many of the Loire châteaux, their deathly figures here come to life. The strange domed roof, the great cream-coloured columns of the choir and the graceful capitals of the nave add to the atmosphere.

Through the spacious **cloisters** adjoining the church, you pass through an exquisitely carved doorway to enter the **chapterhouse**, decorated with sixteenth-century murals, to which many of the abbesses had their portraits added. The **refectory**, on the opposite side of the cloisters to the church, is another vast impressive space with Gothic vaulting surmounting the Romanesque walls. All the cooking for the religious community, which would have numbered several hundred, was done in the perfectly restored Romanesque **kitchen**, an octagonal building as extraordinary from the outside (with its 21 spiky chimneys) as it is from within.

The abbey is now the Centre Culturel de l'Ouest (CCO), the cultural centre for western France, and one of Europe's most important centres of medieval archeology, and is used for a great many activities, from concerts to lectures, art exhibitions and theatre. Programme details are available at the abbey (☎02.41.51.73.52) or from the Saumur tourist office.

Angers

ANGERS, capital of the ancient county of Anjou, stands majestically on the banks of the Maine, which feeds the Loire just south of the city with the waters of the Mayenne, Sarthe and Loir rivers. Long known as "Black Angers" from the gloomy-coloured slate and stone quarried here since the ninth century, it is actually a very pretty town and a friendly place with a lively atmosphere. The overriding reason for coming here is to see its two prize **tapestry** series, more stirring and stunning than all the châteaux and their contents put together, the fourteenth-century *Apocalypse* and the twentieth-century *Chant du Monde*.

Arrival, information and accommodation

The **gare SNCF** is south of the centre (☎08.36.35.35.35), about a ten-minute walk from the château. Bus #2 makes the journey to the tourist office and château, bus #22 to place du Raillement, which is handy for cheap hotels. The **gare routière** is up past the Pont de Verdun on place de la Poissonnerie (☎02.41.88.59.25). **Local buses** operate on

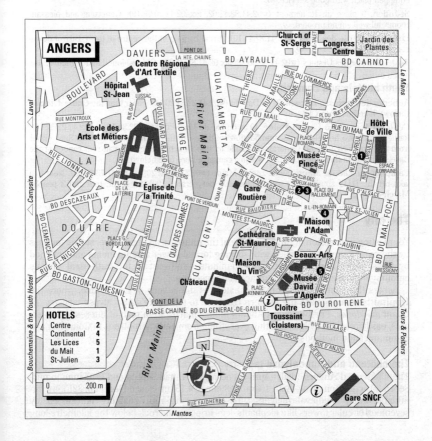

ANGERS

DAVIERS

Centre Régional d'Art Textile

Hôpital St-Jean

École des Arts et Métiers

Église de la Trinité

Church of St-Serge

Congress Centre

Jardin des Plantes

BD AYRAULT

BD CARNOT

RUE DU COMMERCE

Hôtel de Ville

RUE DU MAIL

Musée Pincé

Gare Routière

Maison d'Adam

Cathédrale St-Maurice

Maison Du Vin

Château

Beaux-Arts

Musée David d'Angers

Cloître Toussaint (cloisters)

BD DU GENERAL-DE-GAULLE

BD DU ROI RENE

PONT DE LA BASSE CHAINE

River Maine

Gare SNCF

HOTELS

Centre	2
Continental	4
Les Lices	5
du Mail	1
St-Julien	3

0   200 m

▽ Nantes

◁ Bouchemaine & the Youth Hostel

◁ Campsite

◁ Laval

▷ Le Mans

▷ Tours & Poitiers

ANGERS' MUSEUMS

A single 50F ticket allows access to the tapestries as well as the town museums and galleries.

a flat ticket rate of 6F; you can pick up a route **map** from Cotra, espace Lorraine. The main **tourist office**, which runs an accommodation service, is on place Kennedy, facing the château (mid-June to mid-Sept Mon–Sat 9am–7pm, Sun & public hols 10am–1pm & 2–6pm; mid-Sept to mid-June Mon–Sat 9am–6pm, Sun 10am–1pm; ☎02.41.23.51.11, fax 02.41.23.51.66).

As you'd expect from a large city, there's a wide range of **accommodation** on offer, and finding a room shouldn't present too many problems, though it's still wise to book ahead in summer.

Hotels

Centre, 12 rue St-Laud (☎02.41.87.45.07). Quiet, comfortable and central. ①

Continental, 12–14 rue Louis-de-Romain (☎02.41.86.94.94, fax 02.41.86.96.60). Central, well-equipped place with good service. ③.

St-Julien, 9 place du Ralliement (☎02.41.88.41.62, fax 02.41.20.95.19). Generous and pleasant rooms, all well sound-proofed. ③.

Les Lices, 25 rue des Lices (☎02.41.87.44.10). A real bargain in the centre of town. Bistrot downstairs; closed August 1–15. ②.

du Mail, 8 rue des Ursules (☎02.41.88.56.22, fax 02.41.86.91.20). Old-fashioned and attractive. ③.

Youth hostels and campsite

Auberge de Jeunesse Darwin, 3 rue Darwin (☎02.41.22.61.20). Cheaper than the *Centre d'Accueil* (below); take bus #8 to CFA.

Centre d'Accueil du Lac de Maine, 49 av du Lac de Maine (☎02.41.22.32.10, fax 02.41.22.32.11). Rather expensive hostel-style accommodation southwest of the town; bus #6 (#26 on Sun) either from the gare SNCF or bd Générale-de-Gaulle to stop Bouchemaine. You can rent canoes at the Base Nautique in the complex. There's also a campsite here (see below).

Camping du Lac de Maine, av du Lac de Maine (☎02.41.73.02.20, fax 02.41.73.05.03). Next to a lake off the D111 south of the city centre. 40F per person, 100F for a car, tent and 3 people. March–Nov.

The city

Your lasting impression of Angers will be of the **château**, an impressive, sturdy fortress by the river, its moat now filled with striking formal flower arrangements and softened by trees. From here, it's just a fifteen-minute stroll east to the **cathedral** and its entourage of several smaller churches and museums.

Across the pont Verdun from the château is the suburb of **La Doutre**, where the **Hôpital St-Jean** houses the modern response to the castle's Apocalypse tapestry, *Le Chant du Monde*. Further out of Angers in its suburbs are a rash of interesting museums, easily reached by bus, exalting everything from early aeroplanes to Cointreau and communication methods.

The château and Apocalypse tapestry

The **Château d'Angers** (daily: April 5–end May and mid-Sept to end Oct; June to mid-Sept 9.30am–6.15pm; Nov–April 10am–12.30pm & 4.15pm; closed Dec–Feb; 32F) is a formidable early medieval fortress whose sense of impregnability is created by seventeen circular towers like elephants' legs gripping the rock below the kilometre-long curtain wall. Inside there are a few miscellaneous remains of the counts' royal lodgings and chapels, but the immediate and obvious focus is the **Tapestry of the Apocalypse**, whose 100-metre length (of an original 140m) is well displayed in a modern gallery. Woven between 1375 and 1378 for Duke Réné of Anjou, it takes as its text St John's Vision of the Apocalypse, as described in the Book of Revelations. A bible would come in handy, since, though the French biblical quotations are given, the English "translation" is just explanation. The vision is of the lead-up to the Day of Judgment signalled by seven angels blowing their trumpets. After this...

hail and fire mingled with blood . . . were cast upon the earth and the third part of trees was burned up and all green grass . . . and as it were a great mountain burning with fire was cast into the sea and the third part of the sea became blood . . . (Rev. 8:7–8)

The battle of Armageddon rages, as Satan, "the great red dragon" (depicted with seven heads), and his minions of composite animals mark their earthly followers. The holy forces retaliate by breaking the seven vials of plagues. It all ends with heavenly Jerusalem, and Satan buried for a thousand years. The slightly flattened medieval perspective has a hallucinatory quality, extraordinarily beautiful and terrifying, evoking the end of the world either in accordance with the first-century text or as a secular holocaust.

If you can take in anything else after that, there are more tapestries, of a gentler nature, in the sporadically open Royal Lodgings and Governor's Lodge within the castle. Those feeling in need of a drink can head straight out of the castle and into the **Maison du Vin de l'Anjou** (daily 9am–1pm & 3–6.30pm; closed Mon & Sun in winter; Mon only in summer), where the very professional and helpful staff will offer you wine to taste before you buy, and provide lists of wine-growers to visit.

The cathedral and around

Ten minutes' walk along the quayside from the château to the right will bring you to a long flight of steps leading up to the **Cathédrale St-Maurice**. It's a dramatic approach, giving you the full benefit of the building's early medieval facade. Inside, the unusually wide, aisle-less nave with its dome-like Plantagenet vaulting is illuminated by twelfth-century stained glass. In the choir one window is dedicated to Thomas à Becket – it was made shortly after his death. The fifteenth-century rose windows in the transepts are particularly impressive, and there are modern examples of stained glass in the chapel of Notre-Dame de la Pitié, right of the entrance. The stone carving on the capitals and the supports for the gallery are beautiful, but the cathedral is overzealously furnished with a grandiose high altar and pulpit and a set of tapestries that can't compete with Angers's other woven treasures.

In front of the cathedral, on place Ste-Croix, is the town's favourite carpentry detail, the unlikely genitals of one of the carved characters on the medieval **Maison d'Adam**. The building is now used by crafts people for presenting their wares (daily 9.30am–7pm). There's a small **daily market** on the square.

Heading north from place Ste-Croix, you pass **place du Ralliement,** hub of modern Angers, which has just undergone a face-lift, the most impressive result being the facade of the nineteenth-century **Théâtre Municipal**. From here, proceed into rue Lenepveu, where a Renaissance mansion houses the **Musée Pincé** (mid-June to mid-Sept daily 9am–6.30pm; mid-Sept to mid-June daily except Mon 10am–noon & 2–6pm; 10F). It's a mixed bag of antiquities plus collections from China and Japan, the latter by far the more interesting, with a reconstruction of a tearoom and a gallery full of delicate prints, including the famous wave engulfing a boat with Mount Fuji in the background by Hokusaï.

Apart from its cathedral, the other great Gothic edifice in Angers is the chancel of the **church of St-Serge**, on avenue Mairie-Talet across boulevard Carnot, north of the centre near the congress centre. Though nothing much to look at from outside, the interior of the church has some of the most perfect vaulting rising from the slenderest of columns. Close by is the pleasant **Jardin des Plantes** (summer 7.30am–8pm; winter closes 5.30pm; free).

Arguably the greatest stoneworks in Angers, however, are the creations of the famous local sculptor David d'Angers (1788–1856), whose statue of St Cecilia adorns the cathedral chancel; his best works, some original, some copies and casts, are exhibited in a brilliant gallery built by glassing over the ruins of a thirteenth-century church, the **Église Toussaint**, 37bis rue Toussaint (mid-June to mid-Sept daily 9am–6.30pm; otherwise daily except Mon 10am–noon & 2–6pm; 10F). David d'Angers was a prime activist in the mid-nineteenth-century Republican struggles in Paris and was close friends with many of the great Romantic artists and thinkers of the time, some of them featuring here in busts or bronze medallions.

The **Musée des Beaux-Arts** next door, entered from 10 rue du Musée (mid-June to mid-Sept daily 9am–6.30pm, otherwise daily except Mon 10am–noon & 2–6pm; 10F), has delightfully purposeful babies as cupids in Boucher's *Génie des Arts*, Lorenzo Lippi's beautiful *La Femme au Masque*, the highly operatic *Paolo et Francesca* by Ingres, and other representative works from the thirteenth to the twentieth centuries.

La Doutre and Le Chant du Monde tapestry

The district facing the château from across the Maine is known as **La Doutre** (literally, "the other side"), and still has a few mansions and houses dating from the medieval period, despite redevelopment over the years.

In the north of the area, a short way from the Pont de la Haute-Chaine (about 15min walk from the château), the **Hôpital St-Jean**, at 4 bd Arago, was built by Henry Plantagenet in 1174 as a hospital for the poor, a function it continued to fulfil until 1854. Today it houses the **Musée Jean Lurçat et de la Tapisserie Contemporaine** (June to mid-Sept daily 9am–6.30pm; otherwise Tues–Sun 10am–noon & 2–6pm; 20F), which contains the city's great twentieth-century tapestry. The tapestry sequence, **Le Chant du Monde**, was designed by Jean Lurçat in 1957 in response to the Apocalypse tapestry, but he died nine years later, before its completion (the artist's own commentary is available in English). It hangs in a vast vaulted space, the original ward for the sick, or Salle des Malades. The first four tapestries deal with *La Grande Menace*, the threat of nuclear war: first the bomb itself; then Hiroshima Man, flayed and burnt with the broken symbols of belief dropping from him; then the collective massacre of the *Great Charnel House*; and the last dying rose falling with the post-Holocaust ash through black space – the *End of Everything*. From then on, the tapestries celebrate the joy of life and the interdependence of its myriad manifestations: fire, water, champagne, the conquest of space, poetry and symbolic language.

Modern tapestry is an unfamiliar art, and the colours and Lurçat's style are so unlike anything else that initially you may be overwhelmed. You can, however, take a rest by admiring the impressive old hospital building with its seventeenth-century pharmacy, the chapel's fine thirteenth-century stained-glass windows and soaring Gothic vaulting. Or you can just wander around the Romanesque cloisters that still preserve their original woodwork. There are more modern tapestries, too, in the building adjoining the Salle des Malades. Built up around the donation by Lurçat's widow of several of his paintings, ceramics, other tapestries and cartoons for *Le Chant du Monde*, this has become one of the best showcases for contemporary tapestry in a changing programme of exhibitions. If you want to see the different stages involved in carrying out a modern tapestry commission or restoring old tapestries, call in at the neighbouring **Centre Régional d'Art Textile**, 3 bd Daviers (*ateliers* Mon, Tues, Thurs & Fri

10.30am–noon & 2.30–4pm; *exposition* Tues–Sat 10–11.30am & 2.30–5.30pm; free), where you can watch artists at work.

South of the Hôpital St-Jean, on La Doutre's central square, place de la Laiterie, the ancient buildings of the **Abbaye de Ronceray** are used as an art and technology college, and when the school mounts exhibitions (or if you take one of the tourist office's guided tours of the town) you can visit the Romanesque galleries of the old abbey and admire their beautiful murals. Inside the adjacent twelfth-century **church of the Trinité** on the square, an exquisite Renaissance wooden spiral staircase fails to mask a great piece of medieval bodging used to fit the wall of the church around a part of the abbey that juts into it.

Suburban museums

The Château de Pignerolles, in the satellite village of **ST-BARTHELÉMY D'ANJOU**, to the east of Angers (signposted off the N147), is home to the **Musée Européen de la Communication** (daily 10am–12.30pm & 2.30–6.30pm; 50F), a typically histrionic French science and technology museum, which promises a complete history of communication "from the tom-tom to the satellite". It's quite good fun, with everything from Leonardo's helicopter drawings to German submarines brought into play, and fantastic scenes of the future, but don't expect to come out much the wiser. For something completely different, you could go on a guided tour around the **Distillerie Cointreau**, just off the ringroad between Angers and St-Barthelemy d'Anjou (mid-June to mid-Sept Mon–Fri 10 & 11am, 2pm, 3pm, 4pm & 5pm, Sat & Sun 4pm & 5.30pm; mid-Sept to mid-June Mon–Fri by appointment, Sun & bank hols 3pm & 4.30pm; 20F; ☎02.41.31.50.50), reached on bus #7, where the famous orange liqueur has been distilled since the mid-nineteenth century. You'll learn a lot about the Cointreau brothers and how marvellous the drink is, a little bit about distilling techniques, and nothing, of course, about the recipe. You get a little sip at the end, but the highlight is definitely the rows of gleaming copper stills.

Northwest of the city at the Angers-Avrillé aerodrome, one of the most romanticized twentieth-century means of transportation – early aeroplanes – are on show in the **Musée des Ailes Anciennes** (daily 2.30–6pm; free). There are around forty well-restored examples on display, starting with a classic 1935 Potez 60; take bus #6 from the centre.

Eating and drinking

The streets around place du Ralliement and place Romain have a wide variety of **bars** and **restaurants**, many of them very cheap.

Le Connétable, 13 rue des Deux-Haies (☎02.41.87.32.00). A good Breton crêperie, from 50F.

La Martinique, 75 rue du Mail (☎02.41.87.22.25). Ignore the tasteless decor and enjoy the Martinique cuisine that includes smoked chicken, lamb curry and coconut-milk crème caramel. Set menus start at 90F.

Papagayo, 50 bd Ayrault (☎02.41.87.03.35). Straightforward salad and meat dishes at this low-priced bistrot. Closed Sun & Mon eve.

Le Petit Mâchon, 43 rue Bressigny (☎02.41.86.01.13). Low-priced local wines to go with *andouilletes*, pigs' trotters and the like. Closed Sun eve & Mon.

La Rose d'Or, 21 rue Delâge (☎02.41.88.38.38). Delicious salmon and trout; menus from 105F. Closed Sun eve & Mon.

Le Soufflerie, 8 place Pilori. A café specializing in soufflés from 50F. Closed Sun, Mon & first half Aug.

Le Toussaint, 7 place Kennedy (☎02.41.87.46.20). High-class classic French cuisine with the best Anjou wines. Menus from 100F. Closed Sun eve & Mon.

Nightlife

Bars that stay open late congregate around rue St-Laud – *Bar du Centre*, below *Hôtel Centre*, and *Le Louisiane*, at no. 43, are the liveliest – and the other pedestrian streets around, and tend to have a young clientele. Over to the east of the city, the *Spirit Factory*, 14–16 rue Bressigny (open till 1am), is a cavernous bar with beer brewed on the premises, serving late-night *moules frites*. Over the river in La Doutre, *Le Rockmania*, 18 bd Arago, has live French rock/fusion/ska (Thurs–Sat 11.30pm–2am). To find out about gigs at *Chabada*, bd du Doyenné (in the northern suburbs – take bus #5), go to the FNAC record store on rue Lenepveu.

Listings

Bike rental Anjou Bike Centre, 2 square de la Penthière (☎02.41.73.83.77).

Boat rental Anjou Plaisance, rue de l'Écluse, Grez-Neuville (☎02.41.95.68.95), and Maine-Anjou-Rivières, Le Moulin, Chenillé-Changé (☎02.41.95.10.83), rent out boats of all kinds for exploring the Oudon, Mayenne and Sarthe rivers.

Car rental Anjou Location Auto, 32 rue Denis-Papin (☎02.41.88.07.53); Europcar, 26 bd du Général-de-Gaulle (☎02.41.87.87.10); Hertz, 14 rue Denis-Papin (☎02.41.88.15.16).

Emergencies ☎15; Centre Hospitalier, 1 av de l'Hôtel-Dieu (☎02.41.35.36.37); for late-night pharmacies, phone the police on ☎02.41.47.75.22.

Festivals During July and Aug, jazz and Latin-American music concerts are held in the Cloître Toussaint (programme details from tourist office). The Festival d'Anjou is a prestigious theatre festival using châteaux throughout the Maine-et-Loire *département* as venues in July (details on ☎02.41.88.14.14). There is also the World Folklore Festival (1–6 Sept) with acts from all over the globe; ☎02.41.87.28.28.

Laundries 17 rue Marceau; 25 place Grégoire-Bordillon; 15 rue Plantagênet; 5 place de la Visitation.

Market There are a number of markets Tues–Sat throughout the city including a large one held on place Grégoire-Bordillon on Sat.

Police 15 rue Dupetit-Thouars (☎02.41.47.75.22)

Poste restante 1 rue Franklin-Roosevelt, 49052 Angers(☎02.41.87.28.28).

Taxis ☎02.41.87.65.00.

Travel agencies Havas Voyages, 25 rue d'Alsace (☎02.41.88.41.45); Nouvelle Frontières, 77 rue Plantagênet (☎02.41.88.41.41).

Anjou vineyards, châteaux and churches

Lazing around the Loire and its tributaries between visits to vineyards can fill a good summer week around Angers, as long as you have your own transport. Otherwise it is a two-bus-a-day problem, or no buses at all. Worthy exceptions are the **Savennières vineyards**, which you can reach by train (see box); and you can rent rowing boats during the summer at **St-Aubin-de-Luigne**, 20km southwest of Angers and just south of Rochefort, at the tourist office, next to the campsite.

If you have your own car, there are a couple more châteaux in these parts: **Brissac-Quincé**, 20km south of the town (on the #9 bus), and **Le Plessis-Bourré** near Ecuillé (impossible to get to by public transport), 17km to the north. For a more accessible glimpse of a real monster of a mansion, try the **Château de Serrant**, just outside St-Georges-sur-Loire on bus route #18 from Angers. **Baugé**, north of the Loire and over to the east, is famous for a religious relic and is a pleasant little town for a short stopover, with four or five buses daily from Angers.

THE WINES OF ANJOU

A few kilometres west out of Angers, along the north bank of the Loire, Bouchemaine, Savennières and La Possonnière are the communes for the dry white **appellation Savennières** – one of the few white wines that can mature for a century. The most famous is Coulée de Serrant, which you can taste and buy at the **Château de la Roche-aux-Moines**, just upstream from Savennières. **Rochefort-sur-Loire**, on the south bank, is the first of the **appellations Côteaux du Layon-Villages**, a sweet golden wine. Following the trail of this wine along the River Layon, as the road winds below vineyard hills as far as **Faye-d'Anjou**, is a hedonist's dream. The road is free of *dégustation* signs, but the *vignerons* are not hard to find. In the fourth village upstream from Faye d'Anjou, the **Château of Tigné** produces a variety of good Anjou reds and whites, a Côteaux de Layon and a Cuvée Cyrano. Its owner is none other than the film actor Gérard Départieu who, it's said, thinks nothing of flying from any corner of the globe, mid-shoot, to inspect his grapes.

Château de Brissac

The **Château de Brissac**, at **BRISSAC-QUINCÉ** (April–June & mid-Sept to Oct daily except Tues 10am–noon & 2.15–5.15pm; July to mid-Sept daily 10am–5.45pm; closed Nov–March; 40F), has been owned since 1502 by the same line of dukes. Of the original fortress, only the fifteenth-century fortified towers remain, and they were long due to be pulled down in deference to the symmetry of the seventeenth-century additions.

The interior is a riot of bad taste, but it has some beautiful ceilings, as well as an interesting portrait in the Gallery of Ancestors of Mme Clicquot, the first woman to run a champagne business, and her granddaughter, the present duke's grandmother, apparently one of the first women to get a driving licence. The château has had a vineyard since 1515, with its own label; the current *vignerons* are the brothers Daviau at the Domaine de Bablut (visits by appointment only; ☎02.41.91.22.21).

Château du Plessis-Bourré

Five years' work at the end of the fifteenth century produced the fortress of **Le Plessis-Bourré** (March–June; Sept & Oct Mon, Tues, Fri–Sun 10am–noon & 2–6pm, Thurs 2–6pm; Feb & Nov daily except Wed 2–6pm; July & Aug daily 10am–6pm; closed Jan & Dec; 40F), 2km southeast of **ECUILLÉ** between the Sarthe and Mayenne rivers. It still looks as if it expects an attack any day from across its vast, full moat, spanned by an arched bridge with a still-functioning drawbridge. But inside, all is Renaissance elegance and comfort at its best. The treasurer of France at the time, Jean Bourré, built the château to receive important visitors, among them Louis XI and Charles VIII, and it is appropriately flamboyant. Everywhere is painted with secular and allegorical scenes interwoven with mottos, some enigmatic, some moralistic: a unicorn poses as Lust, a grisly operation is performed by a barber, people carouse and cook. In one of the turreted staircases, the ceiling supports are carved with symbols from alchemy. Less exotic but still impressive are the furnishings of the state rooms and the collection of fans displayed in the library. A visit to the château is capped by a tour of the attics with their ship's keel rafting, and a stroll out onto the roof to follow the sentry's walk.

Château de Serrant

At the **Château de Serrant**, 15km west of Angers beside the N23 near **ST-GEORGES-SUR-LOIRE**, the combination of dark-brown schist and creamy tufa give a rather pleasant biscuit-cake effect to the outside (guided tours April–June, Sept & Oct daily except Tues; July & Aug daily 10–11.20am & 2–5.20pm; closed Nov–March; 45F). But it has those heavy slate bell-shaped cupolas pressing down on massive towers, which ruin any impression of lightness and grace. The building was begun in the sixteenth century and was added to, discreetly for the most part, up until the eighteenth century. In 1755 it belonged to an Irishman, Francis Walsh, to whom Louis XV had given the title Count of Serrant as a reward for Walsh's help against the old enemy, the English. Walsh had provided the ship for Bonnie Prince Charlie to return to Scotland for the 1745 uprising.

Inside are endless tapestries, paintings and furniture; a Renaissance staircase and some richly carved ceilings; a bedroom prepared for Napoléon (who never came); and a library of well over ten thousand books. If you've already had your fill of château tours, then give this one a miss.

Baugé

In **BAUGÉ** – as easily reached by car from Saumur as Angers, 25km north of the river – the nuns at the **Chapelle des Incurables** claim to have a cross made from the True Cross. The wood is certainly Palestinian, though its history prior to its donation to an Angevin crusader is dubious. It is, anyhow, the double-armed cross that became the emblem of the dukes of Anjou and Lorraine and, in this century, of the Free French Forces. To see it, ring at 8 rue de la Girouardière (daily except Tues 2.30–4.15pm; free).

The **tourist office** in Baugé (mid–June to mid–Sept Mon–Sat 10am–12.30pm & 1.30–6.30pm; otherwise Mon–Sat 11.30–12.30pm & 1.30–6.30pm) is worth visiting merely for its location in a fifteenth-century **castle**, one of Duke Réné of Anjou's favourite residences and once home to his magnificent Apocalypse tapestry, now in Angers (see p.488). Take a look, too, at the Hôpital de Baugé, east of the château up rue Anne-de-Melun, for its seventeenth-century **apothecary**, to which the hospital receptionist will direct you (July & Aug Mon–Sat 10am–noon & 3–5pm, Sun 3–5pm; rest of year Mon & Wed–Sat 10am–noon & 3–5pm, Sun 3–5pm; free), with its beautiful woodwork shelves, parquetry floor and sculpted ceiling, and the vials, flacons and contents just as they were in 1874.

Staying in Baugé, there's a reasonably priced hotel-restaurant, the *Boule d'Or* 4 rue Cygne (☎02.41.89.82.12; ③; closed Mon & Sun out of season), as well as a pleasant **campsite** by a river just southeast of the town, *Le Pont des Fées* on chemin du Pont des Fées (☎02.41.89.14.79; mid-May to mid-Sept). Decent brasserie fare is available at *Le Commerce* **café** on place du Marché (☎02.41.89.14.15; closed Wed eve & Sun; menus around 65F).

Le Mans and around

LE MANS is 81km northwest of Tours in the *département* of Sarthe, some way from the Loire valley but included here as a good, relatively untouristy base between Normandy and the Loire valley, with swift transport connections down to Angers and Tours. The city is taken over by car fanatics in the middle of June for the famous 24-hour race, but for the rest of the year it's still lively enough, with some interesting museums and one of the most beautiful old quarters of any city in France. It was here, in 1129, that Geoffrey Plantagenet, Count of Maine and Anjou, married Matilda, daughter of Henry I of England, and where their son, the future Henry II, was born.

Arrival, information and accommodation

The hub of Le Mans today is the **place de la République**, with its assortment of Belle Époque facades, fountains and more modern office blocks. Beneath the square in the

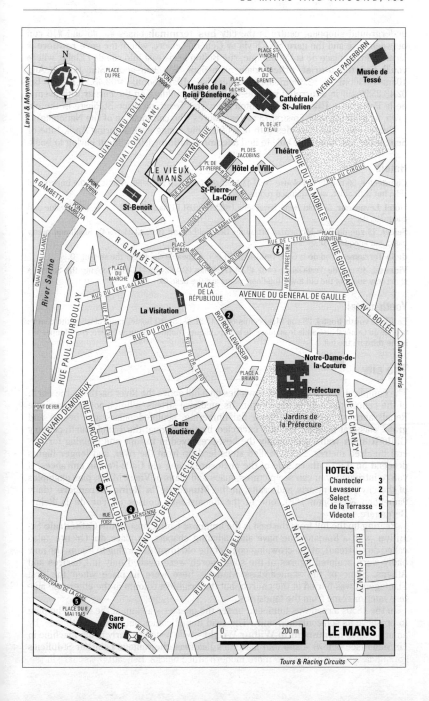

LE MANS

underground shopping centre is the city **bus terminal**; buses #3, #5 and #16 run between here and the **gare SNCF** via av Général-Leclerc, where the **gare routière** is located. From place de la République, rue Bolton leads east into rue de l'Étoile, where you'll find the **tourist office** (daily 9am–6pm, Sat 9am–noon; Sun July & Aug 10am–12.30pm & 2.30pm–5pm; otherwise 10am–noon; ☎02.43.28.17.22, fax 02.43.23.37.19) in a turreted seventeenth-century building on the corner with avenue de la Préfecture. **Bikes** can be rented from Top Team, on place St-Pierre in the old town, or from Métayer Loisirs, 73 av Jean-Jaurès (the continuation of rue Nationale).

Unless your visit coincides with one of the big racing events during April, June or September, you should be able to find **accommodation** easily without having to book.

Hotels

Chantecler, 50 rue de la Pelouse (☎02.43.14.40.00, fax 02.43.14.40.09). A little on the impersonal side, but with quiet, well-equipped rooms. ④.

Hotel Levasseur, 5–7 bld René Levasseur (☎02.43.39.61.61, fax 02.43.39.61.65). Good value and adequate. ①.

Select, 13 rue du Père-Mersenne, off av du Général-Leclerc (☎02.43.24.17.74). Small and pretty basic, but adequate. ①.

de la Terrasse, 15 bd de la Gare (☎02.43.24.91.00). A cheapie right near the station. ①.

Videotel, 40 rue du Vert-Galant (☎02.43.24.47.24, fax 02.43.24.58.41). Overlooking the Sarthe a short way south of the old town; top-floor rooms are the best. ③.

Youth hostel

Le Flore youth hostel, 23 rue Maupertuis (☎02.43.81.27.55). HI hostel, quite close to the centre: take av du Général-de-Gaulle from place de la République, continue along av Bollée; rue Maupertuis is the third on the left.

The city

The complicated web of the **old town** lies on a hill above the River Sarthe to the north of the central place de la République. Its medieval streets, a hotch-potch of intricate Renaissance stonework, medieval half-timbering, sculpted pillars and beams and grand classical facades, are still encircled by the original third- and fourth-century **Gallo-Roman walls**, supposedly the best-preserved in Europe and running for several hundred metres. Steep, walled steps lead up from the river, and longer flights descend on the southern side of the enclosure, using old Gallo-Roman entrances. If you're intrigued, you can see pictures, maps and plans of Vieux Mans, plus examples of the city's ancient arts and crafts, in the **Musée de la Reine Bérengère** (daily 9am–noon & 2–6pm; 16F), one of the Renaissance houses on rue de la Reine-Bérengère.

Rearing up the hill from the east is the immense Gothic apse of the **Cathédrale St-Julien**, with a Romanesque nave and radiating chapels, on place **du Grente** (also called du Château), at the crowning point of the old town. According to Rodin, the now badly worn sculpted figures of the south porch were rivalled only in Chartres and Athens. Some of the stained-glass windows here were in place when the first Plantagenet was buried in the church, but the brightest colours in the otherwise austere interior come from the tapestries.

In the 1850s a road was tunnelled under the quarter – a slum at the time – helping to preserve its self-contained unity. The road tunnel comes out on the south side, by an impressive **monument to Wilbur Wright** – who tested an early flying machine in Le Mans (see below) – and into place des Jacobins, the vantage point for St-Julien's double-tiered flying buttresses and apse. From here, you can walk east through the park to the **Musée de Tessé** (daily 9am–noon & 2–6pm; 16F), a mixed bunch of pictures and statues including Georges de la Tour's light at its most extraordinary in the *Extase de St-François*, along with copies of brilliant medieval populist murals in Sarthe churches. It also contains an enamel portrait of Geoffrey Plantagenet, which was originally part of his tomb in the cathedral.

The modern centre of Le Mans is **place de la République**, bordered by a mixture of Belle Époque buildings and more modern office blocks, with the Baroque bulk of the **church of the Visitation**, built in 1730 and with a balustrade inside designed by one of the sisters of the order. Just south of here is **Notre-Dame de la Couture**, a church with Plantagenet vaulting and a fine Last Judgment scene over the doorway on an otherwise rather ugly facade. The name has nothing to do with dressmaking but is a corruption of the word *culture* from the days when the church was surrounded by cultivated fields. Inside there are various treasures, including a shroud of the early seventh-century bishop of Le Mans, who founded the monastery to which this church belonged.

The racetrack and car museum

Stretching south from the outskirts of the city is the **car racing circuit** (daily 9am–5pm; free), where the world-renowned 24 Heures du Mans car race takes place each year in mid-June, continuing the city's associations with automobiles, begun when local bell-founder Amadée Bollée built his first car back in 1873 – Le Mans still has a huge Renault factory operating in its southwest suburbs.

The first big race at Le Mans was the Grand Prix de l'Automobile Club de l'Ouest in 1906, initiated by the newly formed automobile club. Two years later Wilbur Wright took off in his prototype aeroplane, alongside what is now the fastest stretch of the racetrack, remaining in the air for a record-breaking 1 hour and 31.5 minutes. The year 1923 saw the first 24-hour car race, run on the present 13.5km circuit. Thirty-three contestants took part, and the prize was taken by Lagache and Léonard in a Chenard and Walcker, covering over 2000km at an average speed of 92kph. The distance covered is now over 5000km, with average speeds in excess of 220kph.

Entrance to events at the racetrack is pricey today – around 310F for a seat at the 24 Heures du Mans – but practice sessions are much cheaper, at around 90F. Throughout the year motorcycles, go-karts and even trucks race on the 4.25Km Bugatti training circuit, so some practising vehicle is bound to provide you with the appropriate soundtrack for the scene.

The **Musée de l'Automobile** (daily June–Sept 10am–7pm; Oct–May till 6pm; 40F) is on the edge of the Bugatti and 24-hour circuits. It documents the early history of car racing, while the technical side examines research, automobile anatomy and automated assembly, with the emphasis on audience participation. The display includes a superb collection of 150 cars from as far back as 1885 to recent winners, almost all in working order, and the visit ends by examining the world of car racing through audiovisual displays, including a simulated high-speed track.

Eating, drinking and nightlife

In the centre of town, the **cafés** and **brasseries** on place de la République stay open till late and there's a very good, if pricey, **restaurant**, *Le Grenier à Sel* (☎02.43.23.26.30; closed Sat midday & Sun; menus from 135F), and a very cheap one, *La Brise* (☎02.43.28.20.52), on nearby place l'Éperon. Sophisticated fish dishes are served at *La Feuillantine*, 19bis rue Foisy (☎02.43.28.00.38), with menus under 100F during the week. The best restaurants, however, are located in the labyrinthine streets of the old town, particularly on and around Grande-Rue. Good value for a blowout is *Le Flambadou*, 14bis rue St-Flaceau (☎02.43.24.88.38), which offers a very meaty menu, including a fantastic *cassoulet landaise*, from around 200F; closed Sun. *Le Pantagruel* on place St-Pierre (☎02.43.24.87.63) is a good bet for fish and *fruits de mer*, with menus from 95F.

The **charcuterie** *À la Truie qui File*, 36 rue du Docteur-Leroy, near place de la République, provides excellent picnic fodder, including the Mans version of *rillettes* or potted pork. There's a daily **market** in the covered halls on place du Marché, plus a bric-a-brac market (with food on Fri) on Wednesday, Friday and Sunday mornings on place du Jet-d'Eau, below the cathedral on the new town side.

Le Mans has a lively **night-time scene**. There are a couple of good late-night **bars** on boulevard Émile-Zola, and a jazz bar, *Le Stan*, on place de l'Éperon (until 4am). **Nightclubs** are ubiquitous, but a couple worthy of mention are *Le City Bird*, on place d'Alger, and *Le Yani's Club*, on rue des Ponts-Neufs.

The Abbaye de L'Epau

If car racing holds no romance, there's another outing from Le Mans of a much quieter nature. The Cistercian **Abbaye de l'Epau** (daily: mid-April to mid-Sept 9.30–11.30am & 2–5pm; mid-Sept to mid-April; closed Thurs; opening hours may vary in summer to accommodate exhibitions; 15F; ☎02.43.84.22.29), 4km out of town off the Chartres–Paris road (bus #14 from place de la République in Le Mans, stop Pologne), was founded in 1229 by Queen Bérengère, consort of Richard the Lionheart. It stands, in a rural setting, on the outskirts of the Bois de Changé and is more or less unaltered since its fifteenth-century restoration after a fire. The visit includes the dormitory, with the remains of a fourteenth-century fresco, the abbey church and the scriptorium, or writing room. The church contains the recumbent figure of Queen Bérengère over her tomb.

travel details

Buses

Angers to: Baugé (5 daily; 1hr 15min); Brissac-Quincé (6 daily; 30min); Doué (6 daily; 55min); St-Georges-sur-Loire (3–4 daily; 35min); Saumur (3–4 daily; 1hr 30min).

Blois to: Cheverny (1 or 2 daily; 20min); Orléans (4 daily; 1hr 30min); St-Aignan (3 daily; 40min).

Bourges to: Cosne (4 daily; 1hr 50min); Sancerre (3 daily; 1hr).

Gien to: Argent-sur-Sauldre (3 daily; 35min); Bourges (2 daily; 1hr 50min).

Orléans to: Blois (4 daily; 1hr 30min); Chamerolle (2 daily; 1hr); Châteauneuf-sur-Loire (4 daily; 35min); Germigny (4 daily; 45min); Gien (3 daily; 1hr 40min); St-Benoit (3 daily; 50min); Sully (3 daily; 1hr 5min).

Saumur to: Chinon (daily; 45min); Doué (6 daily; 30min); Fontévraud (4 daily; 30min).

Bus tours to: Amboise (7 daily; 30min); Azay-le-Rideau (3 daily; 40min); Chenonceaux (3 daily; 1hr); Chinon (3 daily; 1hr); Loches (3 daily; 45min); Montrichard (3 daily; 1hr 15min); Ste-Maure (2 daily; 45min); Richelieu (2 daily; 1hr 30min).

Trains

Angers to: Le Mans (frequent, 1hr 30min; 11 TGVs daily, 35min); Nantes (frequent, 45min; 11 daily TGVs, 20min); Paris (frequent, 3hr

15min; 11 TGVs daily, 1hr 30min); Saumur (frequent; 45min); Savennières-Béhuard (4–5 daily; 15min); Tours (at least 10 daily; 1hr 30min).

Gien to: Briare (4 daily; 20min); La Charité (4 daily; 1hr); Cosne (5 daily; 20min); Nevers (5 daily; 1hr 5min); Paris (5 daily; 1hr 30min).

Le Mans to: Angers (frequent, 1hr 15min, or TGVs 30min); Nantes (frequent, 1hr 45min; 11 TGVs daily, 55min); Paris (frequent, 1hr 45min; 11 TGVs daily, 55min); Rennes (frequent; 2hr); Saumur (3 daily; 2hr).

Orléans (many trains require a change at Les Aubrais-Orléans 5min away) to: Beaugency (frequent; 25min); Blois (frequent; 1hr); Châteauroux (frequent; 1hr 10min); Meung-sur-Loire (frequent; 15min); Paris (2 hourly; 1hr 10min); Tours (several daily; 1hr 15min).

Train tours to: Angers (at least 10 daily; 1hr 30min); Azay-le-Rideau/Chinon (5 daily; 30min–1hr); Blois (at least hourly; 30min); Bourges (5 daily; 2hr); Chenonceaux-Chisseux/St-Aignan (4 daily; 30min–1hr); Langeais (several daily; 20min); Loches (6 daily; 1hr); Montrichard (7 daily; 35min); Orléans (at least hourly; 1hr 15min); Paris (at least hourly; 2hr 30min or TGVs 1hr); Saumur (at least 10 daily; 45min); Le Mans (at least 10 daily; 1hr 15min).

CHAPTER SEVEN

BURGUNDY

Peaceful, rural **Burgundy** is one of the most prosperous regions in modern France, but for centuries its powerful dukes remained independent of the French crown. During the Hundred Years' War, they even sided with the English, selling them the captured Joan of Arc. By the fifteenth century their power extended over all of Franche-Comté, Alsace and Lorraine, Belgium, Holland, Picardy and Flanders. Their state was the best organized and richest in Europe, its revenues equalled only by Venice. It only finally fell to the French kings when Duke Charles le Téméraire was killed besieging Nancy in 1477.

There is evidence everywhere of this former wealth and power, both secular and religious: in the dukes' capital of **Dijon**, in the great abbeys of **Vézelay** and **Fontenay**, in the ruins of the monastery of **Cluny** (whose abbots' influence was second only to the pope's), and in the châteaux of **Tanlay** and **Ancy**.

Because of its monastic foundations, Burgundy became – along with Poitou and Provence – one of the great church-building areas in the Middle Ages. Practically every village has its Romanesque church, especially in the country around Cluny and Paray-le-Monial. It is hard not to believe that this had something to do with the reminders of its own illustrious Roman past so visible in the substantial Roman remains at **Autun**. And the record goes back further. **Bibracte** on the atmospheric hill of Mont-Beuvray was an important Gallic capital, and **Alésia** was the scene of Julius Cæsar's epic victory over the Gauls in 52 BC, while in more modern times the rustic backwater of **Le Creusot** became a powerhouse of the Industrial Revolution, with the manufacture of railway engines, artillery pieces and nuclear boilers, using the ample forests and iron-ore deposits to fuel the forges.

For voluptuaries, **wine** is, of course, the region's most obvious attraction, and devotees head straight for the great **vineyards**, whose produce has played the key role in the local economy since Louis XIV's doctor prescribed wine as a palliative – perhaps an analgesic – for the royal dyspepsia. If you lack the funds to indulge your taste for expensive drink, go in September or October when the *vignerons* are recruiting harvesters.

Between bouts of gastronomic indulgence, you can engage in some moderate activity: for **walkers** there's a wide range of hikes, from the gentle to the relatively demanding, in the **Morvan Regional Park** and the Côte d'Or. There are also several long-distance canal paths, which make great **bike** trips. As for the waterways themselves, aficionados

---

ACCOMMODATION PRICE CATEGORIES

Each hotel in this chapter has a symbol which corresponds to one of eight price categories.

① Under 160F	④ 300–400F	⑦ 600–700F
② 160–220F	⑤ 400–500F	⑧ Over 700F
③ 220–300F	⑥ 500–600F	

The prices quoted are for the cheapest available double room in high season, though remember that many of the cheap places will have more expensive rooms with en-suite facilities.

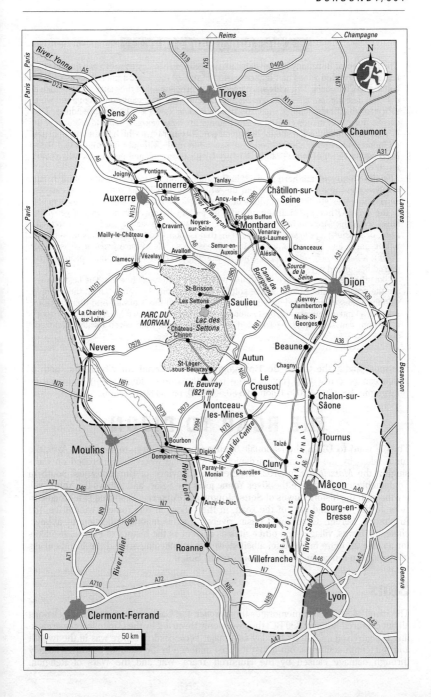

THE FOOD OF BURGUNDY

The **cuisine** of Burgundy is known for its richness, due in large part to two factors: the region's heavy red wines and its possession of one of the world's finest breeds of beef cattle, the Charollais. The **wines** are used in the preparation of the sauces which earn a dish the designation of *à la bourguignonne*. Essentially, this means cooked in a red wine sauce to which baby onions, mushrooms and *lardons* (pieces of bacon) are added. The classic Burgundy dishes cooked in this manner are *bœuf bourguignon* and *coq au vin*. It is important that the wine should be a good one. Another term which frequently appears on menus is *meurette,* another red wine sauce but made without mushrooms and flambéed with a touch of *marc* brandy. It is used with eggs, fish and poultry as well as red meat.

Snails (*escargots*) are hard to avoid in Burgundy, and the local style of cooking them involves stewing for several hours in the white wine of Chablis with shallots, carrots and onions, then stuffing them with a butter of garlic and parsley and finishing them off in the oven. **Other specialities** include the parsley-flavoured ham (*jambon persillé*); hams from the Morvan hills cooked in a cream *saupiquet* sauce; calf's head (*tête de veau,* or *sansiot*); a *pauchouse* of river fish, that is, poached in white wine with onions, butter, garlic and *lardons*; a *poussin* from Bresse; a saddle of hare (*rable de lièvre à la Piron*); a *potée bourguignonne,* or soup of vegetables cooked in the juices of long-simmered bacon and pork bits.

Like other regions of France, Burgundy produces a variety of **cheeses**. The best-known are the creamy white Chaource, the soft St-Florentin from the Yonne valley, the orange-skinned Époisses and the delicious goats' cheeses from the Morvan. And then there is *gougère,* a kind of cheesecake, best eaten warm with a glass of Chablis. A dinner in a good restaurant can sometimes be rounded off with no fewer than seven locally produced cheeses.

rate most highly the **Canal de Bourgogne** and the **Canal du Nivernais**, both of which can be cruised by rented barge (ring the Comité Régional du Tourisme de Bourgogne, BP 1602, 21035 Dijon ☎03.80.50.90.00, fax 03.80.30.59.45).

THE ROAD TO DIJON

The old **road to Dijon**, the Nationale 6, runs from Paris down to the Côte d'Azur, the route taken by the National Guardsmen of Marseille when they marched on Paris singing the *Marseillaise* in 1792. It enters the province of Burgundy just south of Fontainebleau, near where the River Yonne joins the Seine, and follows the Yonne valley through the historic towns of **Sens, Joigny** and **Auxerre**. Scattered in a broad corridor to the west and east of the road, in the valleys of the Yonne's tributaries, the Armançon, Serein, Cure and Cousin rivers, is a fascinating collection of abbeys, châteaux, towns, villages and other sites as ancient as the history of France. It makes for a route far more interesting, albeit slower, than speeding around the bland curves of its modern replacement, the **Autoroute du Soleil**.

Sens

The name of **SENS** commemorates the *Senones*, the Gallic tribe whose shaggy troops all but captured Rome in 390 BC; they were only thwarted by the Capitoline geese cackling the garrison awake. Its heyday as a major ecclesiastical centre was in the twelfth and thirteenth centuries, but it lost its pre-eminence in the ensuing centuries largely through damage caused by the Hundred Years' War and the Wars of Religion.

Nowadays, it is a quiet and unexciting place on the banks of the River Yonne, although the cathedral, its treasury and the adjacent museum make a stop worthwhile.

Contained within a ring of tree-lined boulevards where the city walls once stood, the town's ancient centre is still dominated by the **Cathédrale St-Étienne**, close to the intersection of Grande-Rue and rue de la République, which, together with their prolongations, neatly quarter the *centre ville*. Begun around 1130, this was the first of the great French Gothic cathedrals. Though an early example, the Gothic elements of airiness, space and weightlessness are fully realized in the height of the nave, the arcading of the aisles and the great rose window. The architect who completed it, William of Sens, was later to rebuild the choir of Canterbury Cathedral in England, the missing link being Thomas-à-Becket, who had previously spent several years in exile around Sens. The story of his murder is told in the twelfth-century windows in the north aisle of the choir, just part of the cathedral's outstanding collection of stained glass. The **treasury**, which can be entered either from the cathedral or the museum (see below for times), is also uncommonly rich, containing Islamic, Byzantine and French vestments, jewels and embroideries.

Next door is the thirteenth-century Palais Synodal, with its roof of Burgundian glazed tiles restored by the nineteenth-century "purist" Viollet-le-Duc, like so many other buildings in this region. Its vaulted halls, originally designed to accommodate the ecclesiastical courts, now houses the excellent **Musée de Sens** (July–Aug daily 10am–6pm; Sept–June Wed, Sat, Sun same hours, Mon, Thurs & Fri 2–6pm; 20F, free Wed), making all possible use of available space to display a prize collection of exhibits found in the region, including statuary from the cathedral and Gallo-Roman mosaics. Prize exhibits include the Villethierry treasure, which consists of 867 items of bronze jewellery in a jar, and thought to be a jeweller's hoard; a collection of bone combs; and the facade of Sens' second-century public baths. The vaults of the building – partly constituting the remains of a Gallo-Roman building, including baths heated through the pavement – have now been incorporated into the museum, along with displays of Gallo-Roman metalwork, jewellery and textile crafts, many of which were discovered when the basement was excavated.

Facing the cathedral across place de la République are fine wood and iron *halles*, where a **market** is held on Monday, Friday and Saturday mornings. The *place* stands right in the centre of town where the main streets, **rue de la République** and **Grande-Rue**, intersect. Lined with old houses now converted into shops, they are mainly reserved for pedestrians. There are two particularly finely carved and timbered houses on the corner of rue Jean-Cousin: the **Maison d'Abraham** and the **Maison du Pilier**, with **Maison Jean Cousin** on rue du Général-Alix.

Practicalities

At the far end of Grande-Rue, the road crosses two broad arms of the River Yonne and leads straight ahead to the **gare SNCF** (☎03.86.64.20.54), about fifteen minutes' walk from the cathedral. The **tourist office** is on place Jean-Jaurès (July–Aug Mon–Sat 9am–12.30pm & 2–7.30pm, Sun 10am–12.30pm & 2–5.30pm; Sept–June daily except Sun 9am–noon & 1.30–6.15pm; ☎03.86.65.19.49, fax 03.86.64.47.96), just north of the Hôtel de Ville, where rue de la République becomes rue Leclerc.

For places to **stay**, try the simple *Hôtel du Centre*, 4 place de la République, above a café opposite the cathedral (☎03.86.64.31.78; closed Wed eve & Thurs, March & Oct; ①), or the *Hôtel Esplanade*, 2 bd du Mail, (☎03.86.65.20.95, fax 03.86.65.95.75; ②; closed Aug). Also by the cathedral and a cut above the others is the old-time provincial *Hôtel de Paris et de la Poste*, 97 rue de la République (☎03.86.65.17.23, fax 03.86.64.48.45; ⑤), with an excellent restaurant specializing in traditional country cuisine; menu at 170F, *carte* considerably more. The **campsite**, *Entre-deux-Vannes*, is on avenue de Sénigallia (☎03.86.65.64.71; closed Nov–March), just out of town.

For **eating**, place de la République is where you'll find pizza, Mexican or French food and is the place for a coffee or drink. There's a good crêperie, *Aux P'tit Croux*, 3 rue de Brennus, almost on the doorstep of the cathedral, from 45F. There's also inexpensive, very good quality Vietnamese food at the *Saigon* on Grande-Rue near the bridge, where a delicious plate of beef and vermicelli is about 30F. For excellent seafood, try *Le Soleil Levant*, 51 rue Emile-Zola (☎03.86.65.71.82, closed Sun & Wed evenings & Aug; menus 93–155F).

Joigny

As you travel from Sens towards Auxerre, the next place of any size on the Yonne is the prosperous little town of **JOIGNY**, its elegant old houses ranged up the slope above the river. Its first fort was built here at the end of the tenth century, and the houses were built beneath it. It's not worth a prolonged visit, but makes a pleasant rest stop. Buildings worthy of attention are the **Château des Gondi**, built by Cardinal Gondi in the sixteenth century and borrowing Italian influences from the château at Ancy-le-Franc (see p.509); remains of the twelfth-century **ramparts** on Chemin de la Guimbard; and a number of half-timbered houses on **rue Montant-au-Palais**, the street leading up to the church of St-Jean, including the best-known **Maison du Pilori**, combining Gothic and Renaissance styles, with some carvings strangely reminiscent of crocodile heads.

The **tourist office** is at 4 quai Ragobert (summer Mon–Sat 9am–12.15pm & 2–6pm, Sun 10am–noon & 2–4pm; winter closed Mon; ☎03.86.62.11.05, fax 03.86.91.76.38), by the **gare routière**. Cheap **hotels** include the simple but adequate *Relais de L'Escargot*, 1 av Roger-Varrey (☎03.86.62.10.38; ①), and the *Relais Paris-Nice*, rond-point de la Résistance (☎03.86.62.06.72, fax 03.86.62.44.33; ②; restaurant from 75F, closed Sun eve & Mon). A much classier establishment is *Rive Gauche* on chemin du Port-au-Bois (☎03.86.91.46.66, fax 03.86.91.46.93; ④), with a very reasonable restaurant overlooking the river (menus 98–138F).

For reasonable **eating**, the *Marmite de Joigny* on rue Gabriel-Cortel (☎03.86.32.31.81; closed Wed) has a good 95F menu. There's a decent bar, the *Montmartre*, on place de Jean-de-Joigny. But the nicest place (both to stay and eat) is a little way out of town to the west, 6km along the D182 towards St-Julien-du-Sault – *Le P'tit Claridge*, in Thèmes (☎03.86.63.10.92, fax 03.86.63.01.34; ②; closed Jan & Feb), with a restaurant offering a very good-value menu at 90F (closed Sun eve, Mon & Jan & Feb).

An interesting sidetrip from Joigny is the village of **SAINT-SAUVEUR-EN-PUISAYE,** the birthplace, in 1873, of Colette. The **Musée Colette** is in the château (Jan–March & Nov–Dec Sat & Sun 2–6pm; April–Oct 10am–6pm, closed Tues; 25F) and includes a reconstruction of her apartment in Paris, as well as personal items and original manuscripts.

Auxerre

A pretty old town of narrow lanes and unexpected open squares, **AUXERRE** stands on a hill a further 50km up the Yonne. It looks its best seen from Pont Paul-Bert and the riverside **quays**, where houseboats and barges moor. Its churches soar dramatically and harmoniously above the surrounding rooftops, and the most interesting of them is the disused abbey church of **St-Germain**, now a museum (Wed–Mon: June–Oct 10am–6.30pm; Nov–May 10am–noon & 2–3.30pm; 20F), at the opposite end of rue Cauchois from the cathedral. Partial demolition has left its belfry detached from the body of the building, but what gives it special interest is the **crypt**, one of the few surviving examples of Carolingian architecture, with its plain barrel vaults still resting on their thousand-year-old oak beams. Deep inside, the faded ochre frescoes of St Stephen (St-Étienne) are among the most ancient in France, dating back to around 850 AD.

The **cathedral** itself (daily except Sun morning: July–Sept 9am–6pm; rest of year 9am–noon & 2–5/6pm) still remains unfinished, despite the fact that its construction was drawn out over more than three centuries from 1215 to 1560; the southernmost of the two west front towers has never been completed. Compensation for this lies in the richly detailed sculpture of the porches and the glorious colours of the original thirteenth-century glass that still fills the windows of the choir, despite the savagery of the Wars of Religion and the Revolution. There has been a church on the site since about 400 AD, though nothing visible survives earlier than the eleventh-century **crypt** (8F). Among its frescoes is a unique depiction of a warrior Christ mounted on a white charger, accompanied by four mounted angels.

From in front of the cathedral, rue Fourier leads to place du Marché and off left to the Hôtel de Ville and the old city gateway known as the **Tour de l'Horloge** with its fifteenth-century coloured clock face. The whole quarter, from place Surugue through rue Joubert and down to the river, is full of attractive old houses. Of somewhat recondite interest, the **Musée Leblanc-Duvernoy**, in an eighteenth-century *hôtel* at 9 rue Egleny, contains a collection of faïence and china of local provenance, furniture and tapestries (Wed–Mon 2–6pm; 20F, free Wed).

If you're finding the narrow streets a bit confining, then take a stroll to the **Clos de Chaînette**, off to the northeast, the only vineyard in Auxerre to be spared in the phylloxera disaster last century.

Practicalities

If you arrive by train at the **gare SNCF** in rue Paul-Doumer (☎03.86.46.04.68), you'll find yourself across the river from the town. Follow signs for the *centre ville* crossing Pont Paul-Bert. The **tourist office** is here by the river at 2 quai de la République (summer Mon–Sat 9am–1pm & 2–7pm, Sun 10am–1pm & 3–6.30pm; winter Mon–Sat 10am–12.30pm & 2–6pm; ☎03.86.52.06.91, fax 03.86.51.23.27), with an annexe in place des Cordeliers in summer. The **gare routière** lies in place des Migraines off the *boulevard périphérique* (☎03.86.46.90.66); the **market** happens in place de l'Arquebuse, also on the *périphérique* at the end of rue du Temple.

For somewhere to stay, the *Hôtel Normandie*, 41 bd Vauban, (☎03.86.52.57.80, fax 03.86.51.54.33; ③) is a wonderful, luxurious (providing a gym, sauna, room service and a 24-hour porter) but inexpensive hotel – with a current copy of the *Times* to read over breakfast. *Les Clairions* on av Worms in the Clairions district off the N6 to Paris (☎03.86.46.85.64, fax 03.86.48.16.38; ④; restaurant from 100F) is another good hotel. But if you are looking for something on the river, *Le Maxime* is the place at 2 quai de la Marine (☎03.86.52.04.41, fax 03.86.51.34.85; ⑤; closed mid–Dec to Jan). For a simple and inexpensive stay, try the central *Hôtel de la Renommée*, 27 rue d'Egleny (☎03.86.52.03.53, fax 03.86.51.47.83; ②; closed Sun, first week in March & 3 weeks in Aug), whose restaurant has menus from 50F to 145F. Cheapest of all are the **foyers**: there is one at 16 av de la Résistance, across the tracks by the footbridge at the train station (☎03.86.46.95.11; canteen 39F), and at 16 bd Vaulabelle (☎03.86.52.45.58), at the back of the courtyard of the Peugeot and Citroën garage. For campers, there's a pleasant **camping municipal**, 8 rte de Vaux, going south (☎03.86.52.11.15; April–Sept), next to the riverside football ground.

Finding somewhere to **eat** is easy, as there are numerous reasonably priced restaurants. *Le Bistrot de Palais*, 69 rue de Paris (☎03.86.51.47.02; closed Sun & Aug) is a lively place with a changing menu, from 65F. *La Primavera*, 37 rue du Pont, does good Greek, Italian and Mediterranean food (closed Wed eve, Sun & 3 weeks in Aug; menus 75–125F). *Le Quai*, in the very pretty place St-Nicholas, opening onto the river not far from the tourist office, does *plats du jour* at lunchtime for 59F – though it is really a place for a drink. For good traditional cuisine, there's *Le Saint Pélerin*, 56 rue St-Pélerin, near the Pont Paul-Bert (☎03.86.52.77.05; closed Sun, Mon & 3 weeks in Aug) with a menu at 100F. Finally, top of the range in culinary terms, the imaginative *Le Jardin Gourmand*, 56 bd Vauban, offers its cheapest menu at 140F (☎03.86.51.53.52; closed Tues & Wed, Feb–March & Sept).

Around Auxerre

On or close to the D965 and the Paris–Dijon railway line in the open, rolling country east of Auxerre lie several minor attractions, ranging from Greek treasures to Cistercian abbeys and Renaissance châteaux. The valley of the aptly named Serein River is the location of the villages of **Pontigny**, of monastic origin, **Chablis**, famed for its excellent vineyards, and the time-locked **Noyers-sur-Serein**; while to the south, a string of villages along the **upper valley of the Yonne** provide a glimpse of a gentler, more intimate countryside, with the possibility of a quiet night's rest for the long-distance traveller keen to get away from the main roads and towns.

Pontigny

The ravages of time – in particular, the 1789 Revolution – have destroyed most of the great monastic buildings of the Cistercian order of monks, whose rigorous insistence on simplicity and manual labour under their most influential twelfth-century leader, St Bernard, was a revolutionary response to the worldliness and luxury of the Benedictine abbeys of Cluny (see p.538). Cîteaux and Clairvaux, the first Cistercian foundations, are unrecognizable today: the only places in Burgundy you can get an idea of how Cistercian ideas translated into bricks and mortar are at Pontigny and Fontenay (p.510).

PONTIGNY lies 18km northeast of Auxerre, and its beautifully preserved twelfth-century **abbey church** stands on the edge of the village, where its functional mass rises from the meadows. There is no tower, no stained glass and no statuary to distract from its austere, harmonious lines, though the effect is marred by the seventeenth-century choir that occupies much of the nave. Begun in the early 1100s and finished in the late, it spans the transition between the old Romanesque and the new Gothic, and was much copied in the country round about – in Chablis, for example.

Three Englishmen played a major role in the abbey's early history, all of them archbishops of Canterbury: Thomas-à-Becket took refuge from Henry II in the abbey in 1164, Stephen Langton similarly lay low here during an argument over his eligibility for the primacy, and Edmund Rich died here – his tomb in the church is a goal of pilgrimages to this day. The abbey was also the origin of a tourist attraction with which a nearby village is more often associated: the famous **Chablis wine**. It was the monks of Pontigny who originally developed and refined the variety, and the village and its unassuming neighbouring hamlets are better places to sample the wine than in the expensive wine bars of Chablis itself.

There is a simple **hotel** in Pontigny: the *Relais de Pontigny* on the N77 (☎03.86.47.42.43; ①; restaurant from 75F), whose rooms have neither bath nor shower. With more cash, it's better to go for the *Relais St-Vincent*, 14 Grande-Rue in nearby Ligny-le-Chatel, 4km along the D91 (☎03.86.47.53.38, fax 03.86.47.54.16; ③; restaurant from 70F, closed Feb). Another hotel possibility is the *Soleil d'Or* at Montigny-la-Resle on the N77 (☎03.86.41.81.21, fax 03.86.41.86.88; ②; closed Jan; restaurant from 98F). Ligny also has a **campsite** by the Serein off the D8 Auxerre road (mid-May to Sept).

Chablis

Sixteen kilometres to the south, the pretty red-roofed town of **CHABLIS** is the home of the region's famous light dry white wines. It lies in the valley of the River Serein – brimful of fish waiting to be poached – between the wide and mainly treeless upland wheatfields typical of this corner of Burgundy. The **tourist office** (Maison de la Vigne et du Vin) is at 1 rue de Chichée (May–Nov daily 9.30am–12.30pm & 1.30–6pm; ☎03.86.42.80.80).

While wandering around you could take a look at the side door of the **church of St-Martin**, decorated with ancient horseshoes and other bits of rustic ironwork left as *ex votos* by visiting pilgrims. Legend has it that Joan of Arc was one of them.

Nearby, if you need to **stay** the night, *Hôtel de l'Étoile*, 4 rue des Moulins (☎03.86.42.10.50, fax 03.86.42.81.21; closed Sun eve, Mon in winter & Jan; ②; restaurant from 90F), is reasonable; and there's an attractive **campsite**, the *Camping du Serein*, beside the river just outside the village (mid-June to mid-Sept). If you're seeking **sustenance**, *Le Vieux Moulin*, 18 rue des Moulins (☎03.86.42.47.30; closed Mon eve & Tues) is good enough, with menus at 98F, 125F and 158F.

Noyers-sur-Serein

Twenty-three kilometres to the southeast – there's no choice but to hitch if you don't have your own transport – you come to the beautiful little town of **NOYERS-SUR-SEREIN**, sealed from the modern world in a medieval time warp. Its half-timbered and arcaded houses, ornamented with rustic carvings – particularly those on place de la Petite-Étape-aux-Vins and round place de l'Hôtel-de-Ville – are corralled inside a loop of the river and the town walls, and pleasant hours can be passed wandering the path between the river and the irregular walls with their robust towers. The Serein here is as pretty as in Chablis, but Noyers, being remarkably free of commercialism, has more authentic charm.

The town's main sight is the **Musée de l'Art Naïf** (June–Sept daily 11am–6.30pm; Oct–May Sat & Sun only, same hours; 15F), comprising the remarkable collection of art historian Jacques Yankel. The naive painters had no formal training and were often workers lacking academic education (one, Augustine Lesage, worked as a miner for sixty years before he started painting). Some star exhibits include Gérard Lattier's morbid comic-strip-style work and the excellent collages of Louis Quilici.

There's a **hotel** – also the best place to **eat** – in place du Grenier-à-Sel in the town centre: the creeper-covered seventeenth-century *Hôtel de la Vieille Tour* (☎03.86.82.87.69;

CHABLIS: THE WINE

The neatly staked **vineyards**, originally planted by the monks of Pontigny (see above), cover the sunny, well-drained, stony slopes on both sides of the valley. The grape is the *chardonnay*, which is to white wine what the *pinot noir* is to red: raw material of all the greatest Burgundies. But the town milks its product for all it's worth. Overpriced wine bars and stuffy restaurants abound. You don't get the opportunity to taste the cheaper varieties and there's haughty disapproval if you hope to spend less than 100F a bottle. Better to head for the co-operative, La Chablisienne, on bd Pasteur (Mon–Sat 8am–noon & 2–6pm, Sun 9.30am–noon & 2–6pm), or, better still, drink in one of the other villages like Pontigny or Maligny. If you want to buy a good wine, go for the ones with an *appellation*; the *grands crus*, from the northern slopes of the valley, are the best, with the *premiers crus* next in line. For information on the Chablis *appellation*, ask at the tourist office.

②),with ten beautifully furnished rooms (excellent *table d'hôte* meal for 75F) and views across the gardens to the river. At the entrance to the village the *Porte Peinte* restaurant (☎03.86.82.81.07; Easter–Oct closed Wed eve & Thurs) has menus at 120F and 180F.

South - the valley of the Yonne

If you're travelling south from Auxerre and want a break from the main roads, there's a twisting minor road that leaves Auxerre as the D163 and follows the course of the **River Yonne** through a score of peaceful rural villages. Several have places both to stay and eat, making for a much more restful overnight stop than the towns.

VAUX and **ESCOLIVES-STE-CAMILLE**, the first villages you come to, both have attractive Romanesque churches. **VINCELOTTES** and **IRANCY**, on the opposite bank of the river, are flower-decked and picturesque. Irancy produces the only red wine in this area, much loved by Louis XIV, while Vincelottes was the port for shipping it.

A nice place to stay, with a most attractive and attentive restaurant, is *Le Castel* in **MAILLY-LE-CHÂTEAU**, a further 10km along the river on place de l'Église (☎03.86.81.43.06, fax 03.86.81.49.26; ③; closed Wed & mid-Nov to mid-March), serving tasty snails, *coq au vin* and *magret de canard* at around 150F à la carte (menus 75–175F). The village is on high ground above the river, but don't miss the riverside quarter with its ancient houses huddling under the cliffs.

Half-a-dozen kilometres further upstream, more cliffs (the **Rochers du Saussois)** flank the east bank of the river: About 50m high, they are a series of broken rock walls, ideal for rock climbing, which is indeed what they are used for, with routes of all sorts of different grades. From here south to Clamecy, the river is at its most attractive, becoming more and more of a mountain stream.

The Canal de Bourgogne

From Migennes near Joigny on the N6, the River Armançon, in tandem with the **Canal de Bourgogne**, branches off to the north of the River Yonne. Along or close to its valley are several places of real interest: the Renaissance châteaux of **Ancy-le-Franc** and **Tanlay**, the eighteenth-century ironworks and **Fontenay monastery** near **Montbard**, and the site of Julius Cæsar's victory over the Gauls at **Alésia**. It is a route which is particularly worthwhile if you don't have your own transport, for all these places are served by trains on the Dijon–Migennes line (with connections to Sens and Auxerre).

Tonnerre and around

On the Paris–Sens–Dijon train route, **TONNERRE** is a useful starting point for exploring this corner of the region. A pleasant little town, its principal sight is the vast and well-conserved medieval hospital, the **Hôtel-Dieu** (guided tours June–Sept daily except Tues 10am–noon & 1–7pm; April, May & Oct Sat, Sun & hols only 1–6pm, tours on the hour; 23F), right on the main road in the middle of town. In the chapel is a super-expressive and realistic piece of Burgundian tableau statuary, an Entombment of Christ, in the style pioneered by Claus Sluter.

A couple of blocks from the hospital, the **Hôtel d'Uzès** saw the birth of Tonnerre's quirkiest claim to fame, an eighteenth-century gentleman with the impossible handle of Charles-Geneviève-Louis-Auguste-André-Timothé Déon de Beaumont (b.1728). He tickled his contemporaries' prurience by going about his important diplomatic missions for King Louis XV dressed in women's clothes. His act was so convincing that while he was in London bookmakers took bets on his real sex. Oddly enough, he was also a fearsome swordsman, though history does not relate what he wore to fight in. When he died, the results of the autopsy were eagerly awaited by the gossip columnists of the day. You can see the house where he lived from 1779–1785 at 22 rue du Pont.

The **tourist office** is at 12 rue François-Mitterrand (July–Aug Mon–Sat 9–12.30 and 2–6pm, Sun 10–12.30pm; Sept–June 9–noon & 2–5pm, closed Sun; ☎03.86.55.14.48). The cheapest **accommodation** is at the *Hôtel du Centre*, 65 rue de l'Hôpital (☎03.86.55.10.56, fax 03.86.51.10.63; ①), an old-fashioned provincial hotel with a reasonable little **restaurant** with menus from 60F. Slightly posher, there's *Hôtel de la Fosse Dionne*, 37 rue de l'Hôtel-de-Ville (☎03.86.55.11.92, fax 03.86.55.21.23; ③), near the beautiful old *lavoir* or public washing-place, also with restaurant and a menu from 90F. For luxury, try *L'Abbaye Saint Michel*, montée St-Michel (☎03.86.55.05.99, fax 03.86.55.00.10, ⑦) The **campsite,** *La Cascade,* (☎03.86.55.15.44; May–Sept) is between the River Armançon and the Canal de Bourgogne. For **drinking**, the wines of Tonnerre can be sampled at Les Vinées du Tonnerois, in the cellars of the *Hôtel-Dieu.*

The châteaux of Ancy-le-Franc and Tanlay

Close to Tonnerre are two of the finest, though least-known and least-visited, châteaux in France: Tanlay and Ancy-le-Franc. The former has the edge for romantic appeal, the latter for architectural purity.

The **Château of Ancy-le-Franc**, 8km from Tonnerre, was built in the mid-sixteenth century for the brother-in-law of the notorious Diane de Poitiers, mistress of Henri II (☎03.86.75.14.63; guided tours March 23–Nov 11 hourly at 10am, 11am & 2–6pm; Sept 15–Nov 11 last visit 5pm; 42F). More Italian than French, with its rather gloomy, austere classical countenance, it is the only accepted work of the Italian Sebastiano Serlio, one of the most important architectural theorists, who was brought to France in 1540 by François I to work on his palace at Fontainebleau. The inner courtyard is more elaborate, and some of the apartments are sumptuous, decorated by the Italian artists Primaticcio and Niccolò dell'Abbate, who also worked at Fontainebleau. The most impressive rooms are La Chambre des Arts with medallions by Primaticcio and La Galerie des Sacrifices with monumental battle scenes in monochrome by Abbate.

If you want to stay, Ancy has two small **hotels**, the *Hostellerie du Centre*, 34 Grande-Rue (☎03.86.75.15.11, fax 03.86.75.14.13; ③; closed Fri in winter & Dec 20–Jan 5; good restaurant from 76F), and *Hôtel de la Poste*, 79 Grande-Rue (☎03.86.75.11.08; ①; closed Wed & Oct 22–31; restaurant from 75F; closed in winter).

The **Château of Tanlay** (☎03.86.75.70.61; guided tours daily except Tues: April–Nov 15 9.30am, 10.30am & 11.30am, & every 45min from 2.15pm to 5.15pm; 40F), 15km along the canal from Tonnerre, is by contrast much more French and full of *fantaisie*. It is only slightly later in date, about 1559, but those extra few years were enough for the purer Italian influences visible in Ancy to have become Frenchified. It also feels much more feudal, the village crouching humbly at its gate and its approach road – a long straight tree-lined avenue – like a private drive, tying down the land on either side, proclaiming ownership.

Encircling the château are water-filled moats, and a wooded hill provides an effective backdrop. Standing guard over the entrance to the first grassy courtyard is the grand lodge, and it's here that you enter the château proper across a stone drawbridge. Domed and lanterned turrets terminate the wings of the *cour d'honneur*, urns line the ridge of the roof, from whose slates project carved and pedimented dormers. The white stone and round medieval towers, leftovers from the original fortress, add to the irregularity and charm. Inside, the most remarkable, if overpowering, room is the Grande Galerie, entirely covered by monochrome *trompe-l'œil* frescoes.

Montbard and around

The area around **MONTBARD** offers some insights into Burgundy's early industrial heritage. Blessed with iron-ore deposits, extensive forest for charcoal burning, and water for hydraulic power, this part of the country became the cradle of the French industrial revolution during the eighteenth century (see "Le Creusot", p.521). The earliest foundries were small-scale rural affairs, dependent on one man's knowledge, with minimal and costly production, despite the invention of the blast furnace (*haut fourneau*) and the use of water power to drive hammers and bellows.

The town itself is of no great interest, and its current predicament is typical of 1990s industrial Europe: a one-industry town – it makes steel tubes – so things are economically vulnerable. It was the family home of the celebrated botanist, the Comte de Buffon (see below), and the most interesting things are the pretty terraced gardens of the **Parc Buffon**, laid out by the great man, and the **museum** opposite, Cabinet de Travail de Buffon, devoted to his works (Wed–Mon: April–Sept 10am–noon & 2–5pm; Oct–March till 6pm; 10F), with a rather specialist display of books, manuscripts and drawings. There is also a **musée des Beaux Arts**, rue Piron (Wed–Mon: April & Sept–Oct 3–6pm; June–Aug 10am–noon & 3–6pm; 11F), with works by famous local artists, included the sculptor Pompon.

The **tourist office** is in rue Carnot (April–Oct daily 9am–noon & 2.30–6.30pm; Nov–March Mon–Sat 9.30am–12pm & 2–6pm, Sun 10am–noon; ☎03.80.92.03.75). There's **accommodation** opposite the train station at *Hôtel de la Gare*, 10 rue Maréchal-Foch (☎03.80.92.02.12, fax 03.80.92.41.72; closed Dec 22–Jan 31; ③), and a **campsite** near the swimming pool on rue Michel-Servet (☎03.80.92.21.60; Feb–Oct).

Forges de Buffon

Just outside Montbard, 6km north on D905, beside the River Armançon and the Canal de Bourgogne, are the remains of one of the most influential eighteenth-century foundries, the **Forges de Buffon** (April & Sept Wed–Fri 2.30–6.30pm; July–Aug Wed–Fri 10am–noon & 2.30–6pm, Sat & Sun 2.30–6pm; 25F) built in 1768 by Georges–Louis Buffon, distinguished scientist, landowner and lord of Montbard. Production was never more than 400 tonnes of iron a year, but Buffon's main interest was the experimental. The site, now owned by an Englishman and being restored as part of the growing French interest in industrial archeology, comprises model dwellings for workers (woodmen, ox-drivers and miners along with foundry workers) as well as the **foundry workshops**. These are situated on the banks of the river, designed in a most unindustrial classical style, with special viewing galleries for royal visitors and a grand staircase. There's not a great deal to see (some reproductions of machinery made by kids from the local school), but you get a unique insight into a pre-capitalist approach to industry. The foundry's most notable product was the railings, still in place, of the Jardin des Plantes in Paris.

The best approach to the Forges de Buffon is a pleasant hour's walk along the canal path. If that doesn't appeal, there are buses to St-Rémy, from where it's a mere two-kilometre hike to **BUFFON**. Here, on the main road if you're hungry, try the *Marronier* (☎03.80.92.33.65); meals from 60F.

Fontenay Abbey

Six kilometres east of Montbard and accessible from the GR213 footpath, the privately owned **Abbey of Fontenay** (Sept–June 45-min guided tours daily on the hour 9am–noon & 2–6pm; July–Aug every half hour 2–6pm; 40F), founded in 1118, is the only Burgundian monastery to survive intact, despite conversion to a paper mill in the early nineteenth century. It was restored earlier this century to its original form and is one of the most complete monastic complexes anywhere, comprising caretaker's lodge, guesthouse and chapel, dormitory, hospital, prison, bakery, kennels, dovecote, abbot's house, as well as church, cloister, chapterhouse and even a forge. There's not much to be seen in the forge, but it is interesting that there should have been such a large one here, where France's industrial ironmasters set up shop 500 years later.

On top of all this, the abbey's physical setting, at the head of a quiet stream-filled valley enclosed by woods of pine, fir, sycamore and beech trees, is superb. There is a bucolic calm about the place, but you still feel a *frisson* of unease at the spartan simplicity of Cistercian life. Not a scrap of decoration softens the church; not one carved capital – the motherly statue of the Virgin arrived after St Bernard's death; there's no direct lighting in the nave, just an other-worldly glow from the square-ended apse, beautiful but daunting, the perfect structural embodiment of St Bernard's ascetic principles.

Venarey-les-Laumes and around

One train stop south of Montbard (or 3hr on the footpath) brings you to **VENAREY-LES-LAUMES**, home to another ailing metal tube factory. It was here, or rather behind and above the town, on the flat-topped hill of Mont Auxois, that the Gauls, united for once under the leadership of Vercingétorix, made their last stand against the military might of Rome at the **Battle of Alésia** in 52 BC. Julius Cæsar himself commanded the Roman army, surrounding the hill with a huge double ditch and earthworks and starving the Gauls out, bloodily defeating all attempts at escape. Vercingétorix surrendered to save his people, was imprisoned in Rome for six years until Cæsar's formal triumph, and then strangled. The battle was a great turning point in the fortunes of the region. Thereafter, Gaul remained under Roman rule for 400 years. The site of **Alésia**, treeless and exposed, is back along the ridge 3km from the modern village of Alise-Ste-Reine (see below). While you can see little more than the layout today, it is extensive, and the interest of the whole area lies in imagined atmosphere rather than in anything concrete. There's a **tourist office** at place de Bingerbrûck (☎03.80.96.89.13) for information about the town and its surroundings.

Towards the top of Mont Auxois, the village of **ALISE-STE-REINE** has a small **museum** (daily April–June & mid-Sept to Nov 10am–6pm; July to mid-Sept 9am–7pm; 17F) displaying finds from the Gallic town of Alésia and Cæsar's earthworks (the line of them still clearly visible in aerial photographs). On the first weekend of September the martyrdom of Ste Reine is celebrated in a costume procession through the village, a custom that goes back to the year 866. Ste-Reine was a young Christian girl who was put to death in 262 for refusing to marry the proconsul of the Gauls, Olibrius. This martyrdom was the occasion for the conversion of Alésia.

Directly above the village, steps climb up to a great bronze **statue of Vercingétorix**. Erected by Napoléon III, whose influence popularized the rediscovery of France's pre-Roman roots, the statue represents Vercingétorix as a romantic Celt, half virginal Christ, half long-haired 1970s matinée idol. On the plinth is inscribed a quotation from Vercingétorix's address to the Gauls as imagined by Julius Cæsar: "United and forming a single nation inspired by a single ideal, Gaul can defy the world." Napoléon signs his dedication, "Emperor of the French", inspired by a vain desire to gain legitimacy by linking his own name to that of a "legendary" Celt.

Accommodation in Venarey-les-Laumes can be found at *Hôtel-Restaurant de la Gare,* 6 av de la Gare (☎03.80.96.00.46, fax 03.80.96.13.04; ③; restaurant from 85F; closed Fri & Sun eve). The **campsite** is off the D954.

The Château de Bussy-Rabutin

Six kilometres northeast of Alise on the D954, you can see the handsome **Château de Bussy-Rabutin** (guided tours April–Sept daily 9.30–11.30am & 2–5pm; July–Aug daily

9am–6pm; Oct–March Mon & Thurs–Sun 10am & 11am, 2pm & 3pm; 35F), built for Roger de Rabutin, member of the Academy in the reign of Louis XIV and a notorious womanizer. The scurrilous tales of life at the royal court told in his book, *Histoires Amoureuses des Gaules*, earned him a spell in the Bastille, followed by years of exile in this château, which contains some interesting portraits of great characters of the time, including the famous female beauties of the age, each underlined by a sharp little comment of this kind: "The most beautiful woman of her day, less renowned for her beauty than the uses she put it to."

Châtillon and the source of the Seine

If you're interested in pre-Roman France, there is one compelling reason for going to **CHÂTILLON-SUR-SEINE**: the so-called **Treasure of Vix**. Housed in the town's **museum** in the Maison Philandrier, 7 rue du Bourg, close to the centre (mid-June to mid-Sept daily 9am–noon & 1.30–6pm; mid-Sept to mid-Nov & mid-April to mid-June daily except Tues 9am–noon & 2–6pm; mid-Nov to mid-April daily except Tues 10am–noon & 2–5pm; 20F), it consists of the finds from the sixth-century BC tomb of a Celtic princess buried in a four-wheeled chariot. In addition to pieces of the chariot, these include staggeringly beautiful jewellery, Greek vases and Etruscan bowls. But the best on show is a gloriously simple gold tiara, actually found on the princess's head, and the largest bronze vase (*krater*) of Greek origin known from antiquity. It stands an incredible 1.64m high on triple tripod legs, and around its rim is a superbly modelled high-relief frieze depicting naked hoplites and horse-drawn chariots, with Gorgons' heads for handles. How these magnificent objects found their way to such a remote place is a mystery. One explanation lies in the fact that the village of **VIX**, 6km northwest of Châtillon, is the highest navigable point on the Seine, and it is thought that the Celtic chieftains who controlled it received such gifts, possibly from traders in Cornish tin shipped south from Britain via here on its way to the Adriatic, and perhaps to the bronze workers of Bibracte, the capital of the Aedui (see p.521).

The town of Châtillon has a few points of interest. On the rocky bluff overlooking the steep-pitched roofs of Châtillon's old quarter are the ruins of a **castle** and the early Romanesque **church of St-Vorles**. At its foot in a luxuriantly verdant spot, a **spring** swells out of the rock to join the infant Seine.

The **tourist office** is off place Marmont as you come into town from Chaumont (April–Oct daily 9am–noon & 2–6pm; Nov–March closed Wed & Sun; ☎03.80.91.13.19). There is a very welcoming **hotel**, the *Jura* on rue Docteur-Robert (☎03.80.91.26.96, fax 03.80.91.10.52; ②; closed Sun eve). Alternatives are the *Hôtel Sylvia*, standing in attractive grounds at 9 av de la Gare (☎03.80.91.02.44, fax 03.80.91.47.77; ②), and the *Hôtel de la Côte d'Or*, 2 rue Charles-Ronot (☎03.80.91.13.29, fax 03.80.91.29.15; ④; closed Dec 20–Jan 31), with its excellent restaurant from 95F.

The source of the Seine

To get to the **source of the Seine** you have to hitch 43km down N71 to the hamlet of **COURCEAU**, or take the GR2 footpath. From there, by road, take D103 through the upland hamlet of St-Germain, all crumbling stone farms and barns; or, better still, because rides are unlikely, pick up the GR2 at the bridge in Courceau for a two-hour walk.

The Seine, no more than a trickle here, rises in a tight little vale of beech woods. The spring is now covered by an artificial grotto complete with a languid nymph, Sequana, spirit of the Seine. In Celtic times it was a place of worship, as is clear from the numerous votive offerings discovered there, including a neat bronze of Sequana standing in a bird-shaped boat, now in the Dijon museum (see p.526). If you're here alone, it's a good place for rustic reverie, but if your arrival coincides with a coachload of Parisian day-trippers (the site belongs to the city of Paris), you'd be wise to retreat downstream. There's a **campsite** at **CHANCEAUX**, 5km away on the N71 (mid-April to Sept).

Semur-en-Auxois

Thirteen kilometres west of Alésia, the small fortress town of **SEMUR-EN-AUXOIS** sits on a rocky bluff, an extraordinarily beautiful little place of cobbled lanes, medieval gateways and ancient gardens cascading down to the River Armançon; only the patina of centuries could achieve such harmony of shape and colour. All roads here lead to place Notre-Dame, a handsome square dominated by the large thirteenth-century **church of Notre-Dame**, another Viollet-le-Duc restoration, characterized by its huge entrance porch and the narrowness of its nave. The twin-towered west front has had many of its statues removed and the niches left bare. The best view is from the east in place de l'Ancienne-Comédie, past the finely sculpted north transept door (the life of Doubting Thomas), with a couple of Burgundy snails, symbol of Burgundy's culinary traditions, carved on the flanking columns. Inside, the windows of the first chapel on the left commemorate American soldiers of World War I – a reminder that the battle-fields were not far away. Also on the left are further, fine fifteenth-century windows dedicated by the butchers' and drapers' guilds and illustrating their trades, and a masterly Sluteresque painted Entombment.

Down the street in front of the church and off to the left you come to the four sturdy towers of Semur's once powerful **castle**, dismantled in 1602 because of its utility to enemies of the French crown. There is a dramatic view of it from the **Pont Joly** on the river below. Less specifically, the whole town is full of interesting buildings: there is scarcely a street without something of note, and there's a pleasant shady walk around the **fortifications**. On rue J-J-Collenot, the **library** (Wed 2–6pm), which is part of the otherwise not very interesting **museum** (mid-June to mid-Sept daily except Tues 2–6pm; rest of year Wed & Fri only 2–5.30pm), has a fantastic collection of illuminated manuscripts and early printed books.

Practicalities

The **tourist office** is on the small place Gaveau (Jan–June & Sept–Dec Mon–Sat 8.30am–noon & 2–6.30pm; July & Aug daily same hours; ☎03.80.97.05.96), at the junction of rues de l'Ancienne-Comédie, de la Liberté and Buffon, where the medieval Porte Sauvigny and Porte Guillier combine to form a single long, covered gateway.

Hôtel des Gourmets, 4 rue de Varenne (☎03.80.97.09.41; ②), has the cheapest **hotel rooms** in town and an excellent, reasonably priced **restaurant** (closed Mon eve, Tues & Dec) with good home cooking from 90F; the *Hôtel de la Côte d'Or*, 3 place Gaveau (☎03.80.97.03.13, fax 03.80.97.29.83; ②) has a restaurant serving traditional Burgundy cuisine like *coq au vin, truite farcie* and *ris de veau aux morilles* from 90F (closed Wed & Dec 18–Feb 2). Alternatively, there's the modern and comfortable *Hôtel du Lac* down by the lake at Pont-et-Massène (☎03.80.97.11.11, fax 03.80.97.29.25; ③), also with a good restaurant (closed Sun eve, Mon & mid-Dec to Jan) featuring *coq au vin, jambon persillé* and *tête de veau* (menus 90–235F). There is a **youth hostel**, 1 rue du Champs-de-Foire, to the left off rue de la Liberté (☎03.80.97.10.22, fax 03.80.97.36.97), and a similar but more expensive establishment founded by a group of unemployed, the Centre CRAC, 10 rue du Couvent (☎03.80.97.03.81; ①). Both provide canteen meals for around 40F. The **campsite** is at Lac-de-Pont, 3km south of town.

Cheese connoisseurs might like to take a twelve-kilometre hop further west on the Avallon road to **ÉPOISSES**, not just for its village and **château** (July & Aug daily except Tues 10am–noon & 2–6pm), but for its distinctive soft orange-skinned cheeses washed in *marc de Bourgogne*.

THE MORVAN

The **Morvan** region lies smack in the middle of Burgundy between the valleys of the Loire and the Saône, stretching roughly from **Clamecy**, **Vézelay** and **Avallon** in the north to **Autun** and the **Charollais** in the south. It is a land of wooded hills, close and rounded rather than mountainous, although they rise to 900m above Autun. The villages and farms are few and far between, for the soil is poor and the pastures only good for a few cattle. In the old days timber was the main business: supplying firewood and charcoal to Paris; but in modern times, far from main roads and rail lines, the region's chief export has been its escaping young. It earned a reputation as one of the poorest and most backward regions in the country. In fine weather it is beautiful; in foul it is rather depressing.

The creation of a **parc naturel régional** in 1970 did something to promote the area as a place for outdoor activities and refuge from commuterdom. But more than anything it was the election of François Mitterrand, local politician and mayor of **Château-Chinon** for years, as president of the Republic that rescued the Morvan from oblivion. In addition to lending it some of the glamour of his office, he took concrete steps to beef up the local economy.

Avallon

Approaching **AVALLON** along the N6 from the north, you wouldn't give the place a second look. But the southern aspect is altogether more promising, as the town stands high on a ridge above the wooded valley of the River Cousin, looking out over the hilly, sparsely populated country of the Morvan regional park. Once a staging-post on the Romans' *Via Agrippa* from Lyon to Boulogne on the Channel coast, it is a small and ancient town of stone facades and comatose cobbled streets, bisected north to south by the narrow **Grande-Rue-Aristide-Briand**. Under the straddling arch of the fifteenth-century **Tour de l'Horloge**, whose spire dominates the town, this street brings you to the pilgrim **church of St-Lazare**, on whose battered Romanesque facade you can still decipher the graceful carvings of signs of the zodiac, labours of the months, and the old musicians of the Apocalypse. Almost opposite, in a fifteenth-century house, is the tourist office, with the municipal **museum** (daily Easter–Nov 10am–12.30pm & 2–6.30pm; 20F) behind it. Exhibits include a room of modern silverware designed by local boy Jean Despres, and a second-century mosaic from a Gallo-Roman villa. There is also a **musée du costume**, 6 rue de Belgrand (April–Nov 10am–6pm; 25F) with a collection of regional dress. Continuing down the street, now called rue Bocquillot, brings you to the lime-shaded **Promenade de la Petite Porte**, with precipitous views across the plunging valley of the Cousin. You can walk from here around the outside of the **walls**. From the **Parc des Chaumes**, on the east side of town, there is a great view back to the old quarter, snug within its walls, with garden terraces descending on the slope beneath. You can't miss the **statue of Vauban**, almost like a statue of Vercingétorix standing guard over the Place Vauban – the great military architect was born in the Morvan in 1633.

Practicalities

The **tourist office**, 4 rue Bocquillot (May, June & September daily 9.30am–noon & 2–6pm; July & Aug daily 9.30am–7pm; Oct–April Mon–Sat 9.30am–noon & 2–6pm ☎03.86.34.14.19). **Bike rental** is from Touvélo 26 rue de Paris (☎03.86.34.28.11) The main shopping centre is concentrated in the new town north of the city walls, but there's a Saturday **market** in place Vauban.

For cheap **accommodation**, the bargain-priced *Hôtel du Parc*, opposite the train station at 3 place de la Gare (☎03.86.34.17.00; ①), is a clean and friendly place with an inexpensive restaurant and locals' cafe. Modern, and more comfortable, there's the *Dak' Hôtel*, 119 rue de Lyon (☎03.86.31.63.20, fax 03.86.34.25.28; ③). *Auberge du Cheval Blanc*, 55 rue de Lyon (☎03.86.34.55.07; ①) also has a good restaurant. The road alongside the River Cousin is an attractive, though more roundabout, route to nearby Vézelay, and 5km from town you'll reach *Moulin de Ruats*, a more expensive hotel (☎03.86.34.97.00, fax 03.86.31.65.47; ④; closed mid-Jan to mid-Feb), with a very good restaurant (from 150F) and alfresco rural dining beside the river (closed all day Mon, Tues lunchtime, & all day Tues in low season).You'll find the attractive **camping municipal** de Sous-Roche (☎03.86.34.10.39; March–Oct), and the *Ferme-Auberge des Chatelaines* (☎03.86.34.16.37 Thurs–Sun only; closed Dec–Feb & June), a couple of kilometres out of town on the route de Corbigny/Us.

Reasonable **eating** is to be found on place Vauban at the *Hôtel du Centre* (☎03.85.34.03.53). *Grill des Madériens*, 22 rue de Paris (☎03.86.34.31.38) is another good restaurant, with meals from 50F. Most of the hotels in town have their own restaurants.

Vézelay

Cycling is a pleasant way of covering the distance to **VÉZELAY** (around 20km from Avallon). Alternatively, there are buses from Avallon (Cars de la Madeleine; 1 daily Mon–Fri) and trains to Sermizelles on the Auxerre–Avallon line with an SNCF bus link on to Vézelay.

A hundred years ago the village of Vézelay was abandoned, although its abbey church, **La Madeleine** (sunrise–sunset; closed during Sun Mass & daily 12.15–1.15pm; 10F), one of the seminal buildings of the Romanesque period, had already been saved from collapse by Viollet-le-Duc in 1840. Quintessentially picturesque and popular with the coach tours, it is undeniably an attractive place.

As you emerge puffing from the climb into the rather desolate square in front of the church, Viollet's reproduced west front looks disappointingly unauthentic. But veer to the right into the garden on the south side and you get an angle on the long buttressed nave and Romanesque tower that corrects the balance and sheds light on the nautical imagery of "nave" – *navis*, ship or hull.

The colossal narthex was added to the nave around 1150 to accommodate the swelling numbers of pilgrims attracted by the supposed presence of the bones of Mary Magdalen. Inside, your eye is first drawn to the superlative sculptures of the central doorway, on whose tympanum an ethereal Christ swathed in swirling drapery presides over a group of apostles and peoples going about their business with cows, fish, crossbows and so forth – among those featured are giants, pygmies (one mounting his horse with a ladder), a man with breasts and huge ears, and dog-headed heathens. Better preserved are the charmingly small-scale medallions of the zodiac signs and labours of the months in the outer arch. In the flanking portals are depicted nativity scenes on the right, and Christ on the road to Emmaus after the resurrection on the left.

From this great doorway you look down the long body of the church, vaulted by arches of alternating black and white stone, to a choir of pure early Gothic (completed in 1215), luminous with the delicacy of the inside of a shell by contrast with the heavier, more sombre Romanesque nave. Its arches and arcades are edged with fretted mouldings, and the supporting pillars are crowned with 99 finely cut capitals, depicting scenes from the Bible, classical mythology, allegories and morality stories. The finest of all is "The Mystic Mill" at the end of the fourth bay on the right, showing Moses pouring grain (Old Testament Law) through a mill (Christ), the flour (New Testament) being gathered by St Paul.

St Bernard preached the Second Crusade at Vézelay in 1146. Because the church was too small, he preached in the open, down the hill; a **commemorative cross** marks the spot. Richard the Lionheart and Philippe-Auguste, king of France, also made their rendezvous here before setting off on the Third Crusade in 1190. But the abbey's heyday came to an end in 1280 when it was discovered that the supposed Mary Magdalen bones belonged to someone else. Its decline was hastened by Protestant vandalism in the sixteenth century, and the whole establishment was disbanded during the Revolution.

Before moving on, be sure to take a look at the beautiful Gothic church in the village of **ST-PÈRE**, a half-hour walk from the abbey at the foot of the hill. The village is also home to one of the greatest restaurants in the land, *Marc Meneau* (☎03.86.33.33.33; upwards of 350F).

Practicalities

Vézelay's small **tourist office** (April–Oct 10am–1pm & 2–6pm daily except Wed & Sun; July & Aug same hours daily; ☎03.86.33.23.69) is on the right in rue St-Pierre as you go up towards the abbey, and SNCF **buses** for Sermizelles and buses for Avallon leave from Garage de la Madeleine on the main square.

For **accommodation**, reasonable-value hotels include the *Hôtel de la Terrasse*, right outside the church (☎03.86.33.25.50; ②), with only four rooms; and *Le Cheval Blanc* on place Champ-du-Foire (☎03.86.33.22.12, fax 03.86.33.34.29; ②; restaurant from 75F), although at weekends and in high season you'll find it best to avoid either eating or sleeping here. There are also two **youth hostels**: the *Centre de Rencontres Internationales* on rue des Écoles, run by the Amis de Pax Christi (☎03.86.33.26.73; July & Aug), and a hostel about 1km along the route de l'Étang (☎03.86.33.24.18; Easter–Sept), which also has **camping** space.

For a rather special and romantic stay, you could try the lovely creeper-covered *Moulin des Templiers* by the river near **PONTAUBERT**, back towards Avallon (☎03.86.34.10.80; ③; closed Nov to mid-March). Another possibility is Clamecy, or, for **campers**, a beautiful site in the little farming village of **BRÈVES** right beside the Yonne, midway between Vézelay and Clamecy (closed mid-Sept to mid-June).

Clamecy

A more workaday place to stay is **CLAMECY**, 23km to the west of Vézelay on the banks of the River Yonne. In sharp contrast to its rustic neighbours, it has a distinctly industrial feel as the centre of the Morvan's logging trade from the sixteenth century to the completion of the Canal du Nivernais in 1834. Individual woodcutting gangs working in the hills floated their logs down the Yonne and its tributaries as far as Clamecy, where they were made up into great rafts for shipment on to Paris. This contact with the capital – and cradle of new egalitarian political ideas – led to the early spread of revolutionary thoughts among the workers and peasantry of the Morvan, who staged a number of violent insurrections even before 1789. The history of the logging trade is documented in the **museum** on rue de la Mirandole (Easter–Oct daily 10am–noon & 2–6pm; closed Sun in winter; 20F).

There's nothing special to see in town, apart from the many fifteenth- to eighteenth-century buildings in the centre, but it does have an interesting history and a bizarre connection with Bethlehem. In 1168 William IV, crusading Count of Nevers, died in Palestine, bequeathing one of his properties in Clamecy to the bishopric of Bethlehem, to serve as a sanctuary in the case of Palestine falling into the hands of the infidel. When the Latin Kingdom of Jerusalem fell, the first bishop arrived to claim his legacy, and from 1225 until the Revolution fifty bishops of Bethlehem suceeded each other in

Clamecy, honouring the little town with the title of bishopric. A curious little **chapel** by the bridge, built in 1927 in reinforced concrete, commemorates the connection.

The **tourist office** is on rue du Grand-Marché, opposite the church of St-Martin (July–Aug Mon–Sat 9am–6.30pm, Sun–9am–noon; Sept–June Mon–Sat 9am–noon, 2–5.30pm; ☎03.86.27.02.51) For places to **stay**, try the lovely old-fashioned *Hostellerie de la Poste* on place Émile-Zola not far from the bridge (☎03.86.27.01.55, fax 03.86.27.05.99; ③; restaurant from 100F) or the good-value *La Boule d'Or*, 5 place Bethléem (☎03.86.27.11.55, fax 03.86.24.47.02; ②), with an attractive restaurant, located in a renovated thirteenth-century chapel just across the river, near the modern Chapel of Bethlehem on the road to Auxerre. For **campers**, there's a good riverside site on the edge of town on the route de Chevroches (May–Sept; ☎03.86.27.05.97). For places to **eat** outside the hotels, try *La Vieille Rome*, also by the church on place du 19-Août (closed Mon eve & Tues 70–120F). And if you're travelling south towards Nevers, the *Ferme-Auberge du Vieux Château*, near the village of Oulon just off the D977, makes an ideal place to treat yourself to a little luxury in beautiful surroundings (☎03.86.68.06.77; 250F half-board).

Saulieu and the Parc du Morvan

SAULIEU, having suffered something of a decline with the depopulation of the Morvan, then the construction of the A6 autoroute that took away the traffic from the old N6, is once more a relatively thriving market town, best known for its gastronomy. Halfway between Paris and Lyon, this may be a good place to stop for a meal – the D6 is lined with former coaching inns, and most of them have been turned into restaurants with very quiet rooms that face peaceful gardens at the back.

The old town – on the west side of the N6 – is pretty enough, perfect for an after-dinner stroll. Its main sight is the twelfth-century **Basilique St-Andoche**, noted for its lovely capitals, probably carved by a disciple of Gislebertus, the master sculptor of Autun. Next door, the **Musée François-Pompon** (Mon & Wed–Sat 10am–12.30pm & 2–6pm, Sun 10.30am–noon & 2–5pm; 22F) is also surprisingly interesting, with good local folklore displays and a large collection of the works of the local nineteenth-century animal sculptor, François Pompon.

The **tourist office** (July & Aug Mon–Sat 9.30am–6pm; otherwise Mon–Sat 9.30am–noon & 2–6pm, Sun 10am–noon; ☎03.80.64.00.21) is on the N6 near the hospital, in the direction of Paris. There is a Pompon statue of a bull in the little garden almost opposite. The **gare SNCF** (☎03.80.64.05.32) is straight up avenue de la Gare opposite the market place/car park.

Saulieu waits hungrily for the annual Charollais festival, on the third weekend of August every year. It's a super-gourmet festival featuring lots of meat and other local produce.

You may want to stay the night after you've seen the wine lists at some of the **restaurants**: *La Borne Imperiale,* 14–16 rue d'Argentine (☎03.80.64.19.76; ②; menus from 125F) is a roadside inn with a fantastic atmosphere, a lovely terrace, the rooms all with a view of the garden. Specialities here include *escargots* and, of course, *charollais*. Two other reasonable **hotels** to try are *La Vieille Auberge*, 15 rue Grillot (☎03.80.64.13.74; ③; restaurant from 70F; closed Tues eve, Wed & Jan) and *Le Lion d'Or*, by the hospital at 7 rue Courtépée (☎03.80.64.16.33, fax 03.80.64.01.75; ②), whose restaurant food starts at 90F (closed Sun eve, Mon & Jan 1–15). There are also a couple of gîtes d'étape (Easter–Nov) and a **camping municipal** (☎03.80.64.00.21; April–Oct 20), 1km out along the Paris road. *La Côte d'Or* at 2 rue d'Argentine in the middle of town (☎03.80.90.53.53, fax 03.80.64.08.92; ⑤), is run by a famous creative chef (Bernard L'Oiseau), menus 490–920F.

The Parc du Morvan

The **Parc Régional du Morvan** was only officially designated in 1970, when 170,000 hectares of hilly countryside were set aside in an attempt to protect the local cultural and natural heritage with a series of nature trails, animal reserves, museums and local craft shops. The **Maison du Parc,** its official information centre (Mon–Fri 8.45am–12.15pm & 1.30–5.30pm; ☎03.86.78.70.16), is at **ST-BRISSON**, 13km from Saulieu. There's no public transport to get you there, but if you're walking or cycling it's a good place to head for, as they have all available information on routes and facilities in the park, as well as a small **museum** (July to mid-Sept daily 2–6pm; 15F) devoted to the region's World War II Resistance movement, and a **herbarium** of regional plants. The *maison*, about a kilometre outside St-Brisson on the D6, is located in beautiful grounds, which include a deer park. At weekends the same service is provided by the exhibition centre next to the museum.

A map, *Saulieu Vélo Tout-Terrain en Morvan*, marks cycling and walking routes. For **walkers** the most challenging trip is the **GR13** footpath, which crosses the park from Vézelay to Mont-Beuvray, taking in the major lakes, which are among the park's most developed attractions. There are also less strenuous possibilities: for example, the four-kilometre walk to Lac Chamboux, leaving Saulieu by the D26 and taking a track to the left (blue and yellow markers) after about ten minutes. For a starting point deeper into the park, there is a bus to Moux.

Accommodation in the park includes a number of hotels and campsites. There are several campsites round the Lac des Settons, and municipal sites in St-Brisson (☎03.86.78.71.48; May–Oct) and in **MOUX** (☎03.86.76.18.81; June–Sept), 10km to the east of **SETTONS**, which also has a reasonable hotel, *Le Beau Site* (☎03.86.76.11.75, fax 03.86.76.15.84; ②; closed Dec 22–Feb 10, plus Sun & Mon eve out of season), whose good restaurant has meals from 64F. **MONTSAUCHE**, northwest of Settons, is a good bet for provisions, including camping gas, and also has a *camping municipal* (☎03.86.84.51.05). **Bikes** are available from a number of outlets, including Camping du Peron (☎03.80.64.16.19), Camping du Midi on Lac des Settons (☎03.86.84.51.97) and *La Margelle* pizzeria in Montsauche (☎03.06.84.54.55).

Château-Chinon

The most substantial community in the park itself is the rather ugly village of **CHÂTEAU-CHINON**, set in beautiful country (bus connection to Autun). President Mitterrand was a local council member here until 1983, and the town was the home base of his political life for half a century. Thanks largely to him, it boasts a major hosiery factory and military printing works.

In the **Musée du Septennat** (June–Sept daily 10am–6pm; Oct–May Sat & Sun only; 26F, 40F to include Musée du Costume) you can see the extraordinary variety of gifts Mitterrand received as head of state. The museum is light and airy, purpose-built to hold a collection of some of the finest handicrafts from their many countries of origin: carpets from the Middle East, ivory from Togo, Japanese puppets, beaded spears from Burundi and bizarre gifts, like a table decorated with butterfly wings. Another of the town's attractions is the **Musée du Costume**, 4 rue du Château; daily except Tues: Feb–April & Oct–Dec 10am–noon & 2–6pm; May–June & Sept 10am–1pm & 2–6pm; July–Aug daily 10am–1pm & 2–7pm; 26F, 40F to include Musée du Septennat) with a collection of over 5000 pieces, the biggest collection in France, and there are also interesting temporary exhibitions.

Mitterrand's preferred **hotel** was the *Vieux Morvan*, 8 place Gudin (☎03.86.85.05.01, fax 03.86.85.02.78; ③; closed Jan), with a nice bright restaurant with view, from 90F. If you're not budgeting at this level, you might be better off in the *Hostellerie l'Oustalet* on the route de Lormes (☎03.86.85.15.57; ①; closed Dec 20–Jan 1; restaurant from 60F), or in the comfortable *Lion d'Or*, rue des Fossés (☎03.86.85.13.56, fax 03.86.79.42.22; ②; restaurant from 70F; closed Sun eve & Mon). There's also a **campsite** here, *Le Petit L'Oiseau* (☎03.86.85.08.17; May–Sept).

Autun and around

With its Gothic spire rising against a backdrop of Morvan hills, **AUTUN**, even today, is scarcely bigger than the circumference of its medieval **walls**, and they in turn followed the line of earlier Roman fortifications. The emperor Augustus founded the town in about 10 BC as part of a massive and, in the long term, highly successful campaign to pacify and Romanize the brooding Celts of defeated Vercingétorix. Augustodunum, as it was called, was designed to eclipse by its splendour the memory of Bibracte (see p.521), the neighbouring capital of the powerful tribe of the Aedui. And it did indeed become one of the leading cities of Roman Gaul.

The town

Traces of the Roman period are still much in evidence. Two of the city's four Roman gates survive: **Porte St-André**, spanning rue de la Croix-Blanche in the northeast, and **Porte d'Arroux** in Faubourg d'Arroux in the northwest. In a field just across the River Arroux stands a lofty section of brick wall known as the **Temple of Janus**, which was probably part of the sanctuary of some Gallic deity, while on the east side of the town you can see the rather meagre remains of what was the largest **Roman theatre** in Gaul, with a capacity of 15,000 – in itself a measure of Autun's importance at that time. It's in avenue du 2ème-Dragon just off the Dijon road. It's not an evocative site – the remaining seats now overlook a football pitch – but in July and August its authenticity is enhanced by the performances of a play in which six hundred locals, dressed in period costume, reconstruct the Gallo-Roman past of the town.

The influence of the monuments of this Roman past is very much in evidence in Autun's great twelfth-century **Cathédrale St-Lazare**, built nearly a thousand years after the Romans had gone. It stands in the most southerly and best fortified corner of the town, and although its external appearance has been much altered by the addition of Gothic tower, spire and side chapels in the fifteenth century, and the twin towers flanking the front in the nineteenth, the Romanesque – and Roman – elements are very clear inside, and the church's greatest claim to artistic fame lies in its sculptures, the work of Gislebertus, generally accepted as one of the greatest Romanesque sculptors. The tympanum of the Last Judgment above the west door bears his signature – *Gislebertus hoc fecit* ("Gislebertus made this") – beneath the feet of Christ. To the left and right of Christ are depicted the elect entering heaven; the apostles; the Archangel Michael disputing souls with Satan, who tries to cheat by leaning on the scales; and the flames of hell licking at the damned. Luckily, during the eighteenth century the local clergy decided it was an inferior work and plastered it over, saving it from almost certain destruction during the Revolution. The interior, whose pilasters and arcading were modelled on the Roman architecture of the city's gates, was also decorated by Gislebertus, who himself carved most of the capitals. Conveniently for anyone wanting a close look, some of the finest are now exhibited in the old chapter library, up the stairs on the right of the choir, among them a beautiful *Flight into Egypt* and *Adoration of the Magi.*

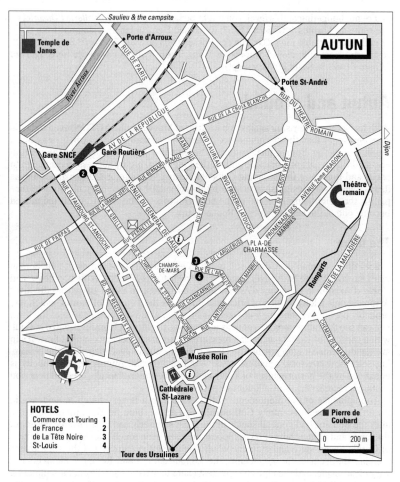

Just outside the cathedral on rue des Bancs, the **Musée Rolin** (Wed–Mon: April–Sept 9.30am–noon & 1.30–6pm; Oct–March 10am–noon & 2–4pm; 20F) occupies a Renaissance *hôtel* built by Nicolas Rolin, chancellor of Philippe le Bon, and is definitely worth a look. In addition to interesting Gallo-Roman pieces, the star attractions are Gislebertus's representation of Eve as an unashamedly sensual nude and the Maître de Moulins's brilliantly coloured *Nativity*.

The most enigmatic of the Gallo-Roman remains in the region, however, is the **Pierre de Couhard**, off Faubourg St-Pancrace to the southeast of the town. It's a 27-metre-tall stone pyramid situated on the site of one of the city's necropolises, thought to date from the first century, and most probably either a tomb or a cenotaph.

Practicalities

Whether you arrive at the **gare SNCF** (☎03.85.52.28.01) or **gare routière** next door, you'll find yourself on avenue de la République, which is bisected at right angles by avenue Charles-de-Gaulle, which in turn leads to the wide square of the Champs-de-Mars and into the old town. The **tourist office** is at 2 av de Charles-de-Gaulle (Easter–Sept Mon–Sat 9am–noon & 2–6pm, Sun 10am–noon & 3–6pm; Oct–Easter Mon–Fri 9am–noon & 2–7pm, Sat 9am–noon; ☎03.85.86.30.00, fax 03.85.86.10.17).

There is a good choice of **accommodation**. Opposite the station, the *Hôtel de France*, 18 av de la République (☎03.85.52.14.00, fax 03.85.86.14.52; ①), and *Hôtel Commerce et Touring* at 20 av de la République (☎03.85.52.17.90, fax 03.85.52.37.63; ①; closed Jan; reasonable restaurant from 65F) are both decent and inexpensive. For something a bit better, there are a couple of old coaching inns just off the Champs-de-Mars, both comfortable and with some character: *Hôtel St-Louis*, 6 rue de l'Arbalète (☎03.85.52.21.03, fax 03.85.86.32.54; ④), where the great Napoléon slept; and *Hôtel Moderne et de La Tête Noire* opposite at 3 rue de l'Arquebuse (☎03.85.86.59.99, fax 03.85.86.33.90; ②; restaurant from 85F). There's also a **campsite** just across the river, *Camping Pont d'Arroux* (☎03.85.52.10.82; April–Sept).

In addition to the hotel restaurants, the Champs-de-Mars has a couple of **brasseries**, but, best of all, in the bottom corner by the Hôtel de Ville, try the innovative cooking of the *Chalet Bleu*, 3 rue Jeannin (☎03.85.86.27.30; closed Mon eve, Tues & Feb 6–22) which, though expensive *à la carte*, has a weekday menu at 85F and a very good value one at 120F.

Mont-Beuvray and Bibracte

The base for the climb up Mont-Beuvray to the 2000-year-old site of the Gallic capital of Bibracte is **ST-LÉGER-SOUS-BEUVRAY**, about 26km southwest of Autun and reached along the N81 and D61 through typical Morvan countryside of wooded hills and scattered farms, coarse marshy pastures and brown streams. There's a morning and afternoon bus to St-Léger, or you can tackle the seven-hour walk on **GR131** from the Croix de la Libération outside Autun. If you need to spend the night, there's a **youth hostel** (☎03.85.82.55.46) and **camping municipal** in St-Léger (May–Oct).

From here, it's the best part of two hours further by the path, or 8km by the road, to **BIBRACTE** at the top of the hill, at an altitude of 800m. If you want to recapture a Celtic mood, it's worth doing this last stretch on foot along a path winding up through woods of conifer and beech. The settlement of Bibracte, the lines of which you can still follow through the trees, was inhabited from 5000 BC. In 52 BC it was the scene of an assembly of all the Gallic tribes, which resulted in the election of Vercingétorix as their commander-in-chief, in one last desperate attempt to fight off Roman imperialism. Although it is two millennia since Bibracte was abandoned – probably on Roman orders – vague memories of its significance were preserved in the folk tales of the Morvan and a fair was held on the summit every May until the beginning of World War I. Close to the fortified earthwork that surrounds the site, great ceremonial stones like the **Pierre de la Wivre** are still standing. The Bibracte **Musée de la Civilisation Celtique** mid-March to mid-June & mid-Sept to mid-Nov daily except Tues 10am–6pm; mid-June to mid-Sept Mon–Fri 10am–6pm, Sat & Sun 10am–7pm; 25F museum entry; 45F, with guided tour of archeological site 60F; ☎03.86.52.35 for bookings) is a fascinating state-of-the-art museum.

Le Creusot

LE CREUSOT means one thing to French ears: the **Schneider iron and steelworks**, maker of the first French railway engine in 1838, the first steamship in 1839, the 75mm field gun – mainstay of World War I artillery – the ironwork of the Pont Alexandre-III and the Gare d'Austerlitz in Paris. Its successor, Creusot-Loire, now manufactures specialized steels and boilers for the nuclear industry and, like many steel works in Britain, employs far fewer people.

As you travel south through the wooded hills from Autun, nothing prepares you for this former industrial powerhouse. You arrive to see, suddenly, over the brow of a hill, spilling down the bottom of a valley, abandoned factories and workers' housing. A small street of rustic-looking workers' dwellings survives in the **Combes des Mineurs**, while in place du 8-mai on the Montchanin road out of town a colossal 100-tonne Schneider **drop-hammer** has been set up as a monument to past glories. Climb to the rue des Pyrénées above the Combe des Mineurs, from where you can see Le Creusot spread before you, including the modern Creusot-Loire steelworks, the gleaming white Château de la Verrerie and the terraces of pastel-coloured houses, against a backdrop of hills which are the northeast border of the Massif Central.

The town's main attraction is the **Écomusée de la Communauté Urbaine du Creusot-Montceau-les-Mines** in the Château de la Verrerie on place Schneider (Mon–Fri 9am–noon & 2–6pm, Sat & Sun 2–6pm; 20F). Built as a glassworks in 1786–87 – Louis XVI was a shareholder before losing his head – the château was sold to the Schneider family in 1838 and transformed into their private home and the administrative centre of their business empire. The Schneiders were paternalistic but despotic employers, providing housing, schools and health care for their workers, even a theatre where Sarah Bernhardt once performed, but expecting "gratitude and obedience" in return. When a certain Dumay, one of their workers whose political interests and involvement in strikes they had been watching with disapproval, became mayor in 1870 and proclaimed adherence to the Paris Commune, he was sentenced to hard labour for life, while the army moved in to quell the unrest. They organized a private police force to keep an eye on workers' reading matter and church attendance, handed out building plots for "good behaviour", and rigged municipal elections in favour of "their" candidates. In the end they became so unpopular they had to turn the château into a kind of Fort Knox. But, by one of history's delightful ironies, the last Schneider married the granddaughter of Jules Guesde, father of the French Communist Party. The château remained in the family's possession until the widow of the last incumbent bequeathed it to the town in 1969. The peculiar cone-shaped constructions in the courtyard were the glass furnaces, recently transformed into a theatre and a chapel.

Today, the exhibits in the *écomusée* tell the story of heavy industry and agriculture in the area, with superb period photos, coin-slot push-button models of the works, steam cranes, reconstructed workshops, models of locomotives and a photo record of the great *Mistral* train's run from Paris to Marseille. Many examples of the glass produce are on display, with a video explaining methods of production.

Practicalities

The **tourist office** in the Château de la Verrerie (July & Aug daily 9am–noon & 2–7pm; Sept–June Tues–Fri 10am–noon & 2–6pm, Sat & Sun 10am–noon; ☎03.85.55.02.46) can provide information on tours of the town, the TGV industry workshops and some of the coal mines in the vicinity. Frequent buses connect Le Creusot with the TGV station 6km away in Montchanin, connecting with Paris. There are also good train connections for visiting other towns in the region, such as Cluny or Mâcon.

If you need to **stay** overnight, *Hôtel des Voyageurs*, 5 place Schneider (☎03.85.55.22.36, fax 03.85.77.48.21; ②), is acceptable and has a good restaurant from 65F (closed Fri & Sun eve). Vegetarians are catered for at *Les 4 Saisons*, at 37 rue du Président Wilson (☎03.85.56.01.26); closed Sun evenings, Mon & Aug).

DIJON AND THE CÔTE D'OR

If the much-touted image of "rural Burgundy" has conjured up an image of slightly backward and ramshackle rustic charm in your mind, you'll have to do some adjusting when you encounter the slick prosperity of **Dijon** and the wine-producing country to the south, known as the **Côte d'Or**. It may look peacefully pastoral, but there is nothing medieval about the methods or the profits made in today's wine business. For any trace of the older traditions you have to head into the southwestern corner of the region.

Dijon

DIJON owes its origins to its strategic position in Celtic times on the tin merchants' route from Britain up the Seine and across the Alps to the Adriatic. It became the capital of the dukes of Burgundy in around 1000 AD, but its golden age occurred in the fourteenth and fifteenth centuries under the auspices of dukes Philippe le Hardi (the Bold), who as a boy had fought the English at Poitiers and been taken prisoner, Jean sans Peur (the Fearless), Philippe le Bon (the Good), who sold Joan of Arc to the English, and Charles le Téméraire (the Bold). They used their tremendous wealth and power – especially their control of Flanders, the dominant manufacturing region of the age – to make Dijon one of the greatest centres of art, learning and science in Europe. It lost its capital status on incorporation into the kingdom of France in 1477, but has remained one of the country's pre-eminent provincial cities, especially since the rail and industrial booms of the mid-nineteenth century. Today, it is smart, modern and young, especially when the students are around.

Arrival, information and accommodation

Dijon is not an enormous city. The part you'll want to see is neatly confined in the centre and eminently walkable.Whether you arrive by road or rail from either Paris and the north or Lyon and the south, you will find yourself almost inevitably at the **gare SNCF** (☎03.80.41.50.50). The **gare routière** is next to the gare SNCF at the end of avenue Maréchal-Foch, five minutes from place Darcy. If you plan to use buses a lot it's worth getting a pass and bus map from STRD, in the middle of place Grangier.

From immediately outside the station, avenue Foch leads to place Darcy in five minutes on foot. You pass the **tourist office** (daily May–Oct 15 9am–9pm; Oct 16–April 9am–1pm & 2–7pm; ☎03.80.44.11.44, fax 03.80.42.18.83) on your left as you reach the square. There's another office at 34 rue des Forges (Mon–Fri 9am–noon & 1–6pm, May–Oct 15 open Sat also; closed Sun; ☎03.80.4411.44, fax 03.80.30.90.02), which also houses the Club Alpin, who produce a booklet, *Promenez-vous en Côte d'Or*, showing all the region's marked paths. Both offer services such as hotel booking, money changing, guided tours of the city, and – most worthwhile – a 30F museum card which allows access to all the museums listed below except the Musée Grevin. *Dijon Nuit et Jour* is a good guide to what's on, and has some good practical listings too.

Accommodation
There are some good, reasonably priced and very central **hotels**. Among the best bargains are *Hôtel Le Chambellan*, 92 rue Vannerie (☎03.80.67.12.67, fax 03.80.38.00.39; ②), with some cheaper attic rooms and a special deal with the traffic wardens, and *Hôtel Le Jacquemart*, 32 rue Verrerie (☎03.80.60.09.60, fax 03.80.60.09.69; ②). Both are in attractive old streets close to the dukes' palace. Only a little further away, at 3 rue du

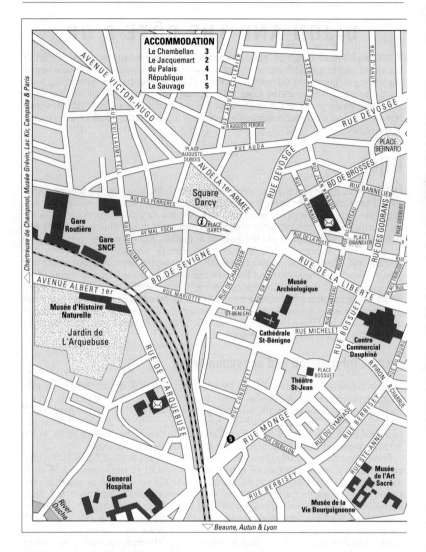

ACCOMMODATION
Le Chambellan 3
Le Jacquemart 2
du Palais 4
République 1
Le Sauvage 5

Beaune, Autun & Lyon

Nord near place de la République, the *Hôtel République* (☎03.80.73.36.76, fax 03.80.72.46.04; ②–③) offers good value for money with a fifty percent discount on Sunday if you stay two nights, as does the *Hôtel St-Bernard* at 7bis rue Courtépée midway between place de la République and square Darcy (☎03.80.30.74.07; ②). Two further possibilities are *Hostellerie Le Sauvage*, 64 rue Monge (☎03.80.41.31.21, fax 03.80.42.06.07; ③) in a former coaching inn with a lovely little courtyard for its restaurant tables, and the *Hôtel du Palais*, 23 rue du Palais (☎03.80.67.16.26, fax 03.80.65.12.16; ②), clean and modernized and close to the ducal palace.

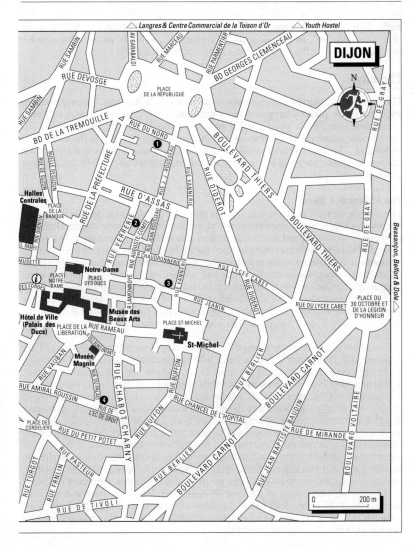

There are two **hostels**: the HI *Centre de Rencontres Internationales*, a proper youth hostel in a modern complex with a self-service canteen, 1 bd Champollion (☎03.80.72.95.20, fax 03.80.70.00.61; bus #5, direction "Épirey", from place Grangier, and the *Foyer International d'Étudiants* on rue Maréchal-Leclerc (☎03.80.71.51.01; bus #4, direction "St-Apollinaire", stop Billardon; also with canteen), which takes visitors when there is room, but don't rely on this option. Both are on the east side of the city, inconveniently located: it's better to go to one of the cheaper hotels which are in the centre of town. The last bus back to the hostel is at 9pm, so you can't really go out at night. The nearest **campsite**, *Camping du Lac* (☎03.80.43.54.72; bus #12, direction "Fontaine d'Ouche", or #18, direction "Plombières"), is off boulevard Chanoine-Kir near the lake: follow the signs for Paris and it's about 1km out of town.

The city

The **rue de la Liberté** forms the major east–west axis in the town, running from the wide, attractive **place Darcy** and the eighteenth-century triumphal arch of **Porte Guillaume**, once a city gate, past the **palace of the Dukes of Burgundy** on the semicircular **place de la Libération**, and moving still further east to the **church of St-Michel**. The street is pedestrianized and lined with smart shops and elegant old houses, and most places of interest are within fifteen minutes' walk to the north or south of it.

The Palais des Ducs

The geographical focus of a visit to Dijon is inevitably the seat of its former rulers, the **Palais des Ducs**, which stands precisely at the hub of the city overlooking Mansart's perfectly proportioned and deliciously mellow **place de la Libération**, built towards the end of the seventeenth century as place Royale to show off a statue of the Sun King. Though still functioning as the town hall, the palace's exterior has undergone so many alterations – especially in the sixteenth and seventeenth centuries when it became Burgundy's parliament – that the dukes themselves would scarcely recognize it. The only outward reminders of the older building that stood here are the fourteenth-century **Tour de Bar** above the east wing, which now houses the Musée des Beaux-Arts, and the fifteenth-century **Tour Philippe-le-Bon** which is unfortunately closed for an indefinite period.

The palace is now home to the excellent **Musée des Beaux-Arts** (daily except Tues & public hols 10am–6pm; 30F, Sun free), with a collection of paintings representing many different schools and periods, from Titian, Rubens and Schongauer to Manet, Monet and other Impressionists, with substantial numbers of Italian and Flemish works and quantities of religious artefacts, ivories and tapestries. One of the most interesting exhibits is a small room devoted to the intricate woodcarving of the sixteenth-century designer and architect Hugues Sambin, whose work appears throughout the old quarter of the city in the massive doors and facades of the aristocratic hôtels. Visiting the museum also provides the opportunity to see the surviving portions of the original ducal palace, including the vast **kitchens** needed to service the dukes' gargantuan appetites and the magnificent **Salle des Gardes**, richly appointed with panelling, tapestries and a minstrels' gallery. Here are displayed the **tombs** from the Chartreuse de Champmol (see below) of Philippe le Hardi and Jean sans Peur and his wife, Marguerite de Bavière. Both follow the same pattern: painted effigies of the dead, attended by angels holding their helmets and heraldic shields and accompanied by a cortege of brilliantly sculpted mourners.

The Quartier Notre-Dame

Architecturally more interesting than the palace, and much more suggestive of the city's former glories, are the lavish town houses of its rich burghers. These abound in the streets behind the palace: rue Verrerie, rue Vannerie, rue des Forges, rue Chaudronnière (look out for no. 28, Maison des Cariatides). Some are half-timbered, with storeys projecting over the street; others are in more formal and imposing Renaissance stone. Particularly fine are the **Hôtel de Vogüé**, 12 rue de la Chouette, and at no. 34, the **Hôtel Chambellan** (1490), housing one of Dijon's tourist offices and Club Alpin. There's a good view of the latter from the courtyard, with its open galleries reached by a spiral staircase, with a marvellous piece of stonemason's virtuosity at the top, where the vaulting of the roof springs from a basket held by the statue of a gardener. For a glimpse of what must be nearly genuine medieval character, take a look in the cobbled alleys by the **Tour St-Nicholas**, off rue Jean-Jacques-Rousseau.

Also in this quarter behind the dukes' palace, in the angle between rue de la Chouette and rue de la Préfecture, is the **church of Notre-Dame**, built in the early thirteenth century in the Burgundian Gothic style, with an unusual west front adorned with tiers of spectacularly leaning gargoyles. Inside, the north transept windows contain some beautiful fragments of the original stained glass, while in the south transept there is a twelfth-century black wooden Virgin that has long been an object of veneration to the citizens of Dijon. Outside on rue de la Chouette, in the north wall of the church, is a small sculpted owl – *chouette* – polished by the hands of passers-by who for centuries have touched it for luck and which gives the street its name. High on the south tower of the west front is a Jacquemard clock, liberated from Courtrai in Belgium in 1382, when Philippe le Hardi defeated the people of Ghent and took the clock as a present for Dijon.

From here rue de la Musette leads to the **market square**, the whole area full of sumptuous displays of food and always thronged with people. There are several good and attractive cafés and restaurants, too. The market operates from 6am on Tuesday, Friday and Saturday, spilling over into the surrounding streets, with bric-a-brac in rue de Soissons on the north side and clothes in the beautiful little **place François-Rude**, named after the sculptor and a favourite hang-out with its cafés and fountain graced by the bronze figure of a grape harvester.

South of the place de la Libération

On the south side of the axis place Darcy–church of St-Michel, and especially in the quartier behind place de la Libération, there is a concentration of magnificent hôtels from the seventeenth and eighteenth centuries, built for the most part by men who had bought themselves offices and privileges with the Parliament of Burgundy, established by Louis XIV in 1477 after the death of Duke Charles le Téméraire (the Bold) as a concession designed to win the compliance of this newly acquired frontier province. One of them, 4 rue des Bons-Enfants, houses the **Musée Magnin** (daily except Mon: summer 10am–6pm; winter 10am–noon & 2–6pm; free). The building, a seventeenth-century *hôtel particulier*, complete with its original furnishings, is more interesting than the exhibition of paintings by good but lesser-known artists, the personal collection of Maurice Magnin, donated to the state in 1938. Other noteworthy houses are to be found nearby in rue Vauban, some showing the marks of Hugues Sambin's influence in their decorative details (lions' heads, garlands of fruit, tendrils of ivy and his famous *chou bourguignon*, or "Burgundy cabbage"): notably, nos. 3, 12, 21 and 23. Also worth a look for its elaborate west front is the **church of St-Michel**, a ten-minute walk to the east behind place du Théâtre.

In the same area, in rue Ste-Anne near place des Cordeliers, are two museums. The **Musée de la Vie Bourguignonne**, 17 rue Ste-Anne (daily except Tues 9am–noon & 2–6pm; 10F, Sun free), housed in a stark, well-designed modern setting within a former convent, is all about nineteenth-century Burgundian life, with costumes, furniture, domestic industries like butter, cheese- and bread-making, along with a reconstructed kitchen. Practically next door at no. 15, the **Musée d'Art Sacré** (same hours as Vie Bourguignonne; 8F, Sun free) contains an important collection of church treasures, including a seventeenth-century statue of St Paul, the first in the world to be treated with gamma rays – carried out in Grenoble as part of the Nucle-art project. Formerly crumbling to dust, it is now solid. There's a free guided visit that really perks up these special-interest exhibits.

A little further to the west, at the end of rue du Dr-Maret in the direction of place Darcy, the **cathedral** – the once great abbey church of St-Bénigne – is no longer of very great interest, although its garish tiled roof and nineteenth-century spire dominate the skyline impressively enough. Its circular crypt is the original tenth-century Romanesque church. A little historical curiosity, however, is the fact that Raoul Glaber was a monk here: Glaber is famed as the historian who described the great burgeoning of Romanesque churches across France once the apocalyptic dangers of the first millennium were safely past and the earth began "clothing herself in a white garment of churches".

In the chestnut-shaded garden next to it, the **Musée Archéologique**, 5 rue du Docteur-Maret (daily except Tues: July–Sept 9.30am–6pm; Oct–June 9am–noon & 2–6pm; 12F, Sun free) has some extremely interesting finds from the Gallo-Roman period, especially funerary bas-reliefs depicting the perennial Gallic preoccupation with food and wine and a collection of *ex votos* from the source of the Seine, among them the little bronze of the goddess Sequana (Seine) upright in her bird-prowed boat. Also on show is Sluter's bust of Christ from the Chartreuse.

On a more profane level, the neighbouring streets – especially **rue Monge** and **rue Berbisey** – are very active at night with lots of bars and restaurants. The latter ends in a curious postmodern perspective joke: a sort of parody of a medieval housing estate. In place Bossuet at the start of rue Monge there is a theatre whose programmes are worth keeping an eye on, the Théâtre du Parvis St-Jean (Mon–Fri 9am–noon & 2–6pm; ☎03.80.30.63.53).

The Musée d'Histoire Naturelle and around

One of the greatest of Dijon's artistic monuments, however, lies some 1500m west of the city centre along avenue Albert-1er, beyond the gare SNCF. It is the **Chartreuse de Champmol** (daily 8am–6pm; free), founded by Duke Philippe le Hardi in 1383 to be the burial place of his dynasty – Dijon's equivalent of the cathedral of St-Denis in Paris. To adorn it, Philippe recruited a talented team of artists, foremost among them the Dutchman Claus Sluter, pioneer of realism in sculpture and founder of the Burgundian school. Although it was practically destroyed in the Revolution and most of the surviving works of art are in the city's museums, two of Sluter's finest – the so-called *Well of Moses* featuring six highly realistic portrayals of Old Testament prophets, and the portal of the chapel – remain *in situ*. The site is now part of a psychiatric hospital, and you enter at 1 bd Chanoine-Kir; bus #12, direction "Fontaine d'Ouche", from the station to stop *Hôpital des Chartreux*. On the way from the station to the Chartreuse de Champmol, you pass Dijon's waxworks, the **Musée Grevin** at 13b av Albert-1er (daily 9.30am–noon & 2–6pm; 30F), a not wildly interesting experience, consisting principally of scenes from Burgundy's history. You're better off strolling in the botanical garden, the **Jardin de l'Arquebuse** (daily 7.30am–6/7pm), site of the **Natural History Museum** (Mon & Wed–Sat 9am–noon & 2–6pm), with just about every stuffed bird and mammal you can think of, plus an exquisite collection of butterflies.

Eating, drinking and entertainment

Dijon has an inordinate number of **pâtisseries** in the town, full of high-quality, tempting confectionery in which marzipan and fruit feature prominently. The more exotic places also promote the Dijon specialities: *pain d'épices*, a gingerbread made with honey and spices and eaten with butter or jam (from Mulot et Petitjean, 13 place Bossuet & other branches all over town), and *cassissines* – blackcurrant candies. **Chocolate**, best made on the premises, is another speciality – try Au Parrain Généreux, 21 rue du Bourg.

And you can hardly forget that Dijon is also the high temple of **mustard**; there is the shop of leading producer **Maille** at 28 rue de la Liberté, selling a range from the mild to the cauterizing. Finally, a couple of ideas for buying good but affordable **wine**: first and foremost, there's Nicot, 48 rue Jean-Jacques-Rousseau, where you can taste, seek advice or take courses; alternatively, try La Cave du Clos, 3 rue Jeannin, or Nicolas, 6 rue François-Rude.

Restaurants

If you want to shell out to sample some of Dijon's cuisine – local and otherwise – in style, the listings that follow are just a small selection from a large number of excellent **restaurants** in town.

Bistrot des Halles, 10 rue Bannelier (☎03.80.49.94.15). Serious gourmet eating at a poor man's version of the top-rank Jean-Billoux establishment on place Darcy; around 160F, lunch menu at 92F. Closed Sun eve.

Chabrot, 36 rue Monge (☎03.80.30.69.61). Particularly good on salmon, with 75F menu at lunchtime, 98F in the evening, *carte* over 200F. Closed Sun & Mon lunch.

Le Clos des Capucines, 3 rue Jeannin, at the end of rue Jean-Jacques-Rousseau (☎03.80.65.83.03). In a beautiful medieval setting, this restaurant has very good traditional, rich Burgundy cuisine (*jambon persillé, escargots, bœuf bourguignon*) at very reasonable prices. Menus at 85F and up to 230F, *carte* around 200F. Closed Sun.

Côte St-Jean, 13 rue Monge (☎03.80.50.11.77). Rather chic restaurant offering such delights as a fricassee of lobster, duck tournedos, a gratin of pears and almonds. Menus 108–175F, *carte* over 200F. Closed Sat lunch & Tues.

Coum' Chez Eux, 68 rue Jean-Jacques-Rousseau (☎03.80.73.56.87). A restaurant that continues to provide genuine down-home regional cooking: *jambonneau* with lentils, leek pie, home-made terrines, rabbit sautéed Morvan-style. It also has an informal and agreeable atmosphere. A little to the south of République; *carte* around 130F. Closed Sat lunch & Sun.

Le Dôme, 16bis rue Quentin (☎03.80.30.58.92). Good for simple *plats*, this place has a good selection of interesting but lesser-known wines; menus 60–70F, *formule* at 83F in the evening. Closed Sun & Mon.

Le Germinal, 44 rue Monge (☎03.80.44.97.16). The best place in town for frogs' legs and inexpensive Burgundy specialities; 60F for an express lunch menu.

Grille Laure, 8 place St-Bénigne (☎03.80.41.86.76). Right by the cathedral, this restaurant is in a great location for eating pizzas, pasta, grills for around 100F. Closed Sun lunch.

Hostellerie de l'Étoile, 1 rue Marceau (☎03.80.73.20.72). Serves an excellent traditional meal in an attractive dining room just off place de la République; menus from 120F, *carte* around 200F. Closed Sun eve & Mon.

Hostellerie Le Sauvage, 64 rue Monge (see "Accommodation"). First-class grills in a great little courtyard. Lunch menu at 75F, *carte* around 130–150F. Closed Sat lunch & Sun.

Le Marrakech, 20 rue Monge (☎03.80.30.82.69). Serves excellent tajines and couscous, with a *carte* at 110–130F.

Le Potimarron, 4 av de l'Ouche (☎03.80.43.38.07). Vegetarian and macrobiotic dishes as well as organic meat and fish; menus at 75F and 85F, *carte* 70–90F. Closed Sun & Mon.

Le Simpatico, 30 rue Berbisey (☎03.80.30.53.53). Good Italian restaurant in lively street. Menus 65–185F. Closed Sun & Aug.

University restaurants, 3 rue du Dr-Maret in the town centre; 6 bd Mansart; 6 rue du Recteur-Bouchard, near the university to the southeast of the city. Students can eat for 12F (11.30am–1.15pm & 6.40–7.45pm).

Cafés, bars and nightclubs

Dijon is an important university city as well as one of France's main conference centres, so **nightspots** and cultural centres at both ends of the range are worth exploring. There's a good choice in rue Berbisey and many outdoor cafes in Place Emile Zola and

Rue Berbisey which are good places to start a night out. The English theme pubs seem to be the liveliest.

L'Acropole, 4 bd du Dr-Petitjean. Near the university on #9 bus route. Gay bar. Till 1am; closed Sun.

L'An-Fer, 8 rue Marceau. One of the livelier discos. Tues–Thurs 10.30pm–3am, Fri & Sat till 4am; admission weekdays 50F; weekends 60F.

Le Brighton, 33 rue Auguste-Comte. English pub with 200 different kinds of beer and dancing. 5pm–3am; summer 3pm–3am.

Café de la Cathédrale, 4 place St-Bénigne, next to the *Café au Carillon*. Two bars popular with students, in front of the cathedral. Daily 6.30pm–1am.

Le Café des Grands Ducs, 96 rue de la Liberté. Popular rendezvous for young people, with original decor and table jukeboxes. Pricey. Daily till 2am winter/3am summer.

Le Crocodil, rue Berbisey. Nice atmosphere, a good place for an afternoon coffee leading into an early evening drink. Open until 12am, sometimes later.

L'Escapade, Varois et Chaignot. Outdoor pool, and a huge dance floor. Young and popular. Admission 60F, women free on Fri. Thurs 10pm–3am, Fri & Sat till 4am.

Le Grand Café, rue du Château. A very pleasant bar/brasserie with an Art Deco interior.

Messire Bar, 3 rue Jules Mercier (☎03.80.30.16.40), tucked away in a side street in the old town, a very 70s bar. Open till late night every night.

Pub Kilkenny, 1 rue Auguste-Perdrix. Noisy, popular Irish bar: draught Guinness and week-night Irish bands. Daily till 3am.

Rhumerie la Jamaïque, 14 place de la République. Cocktails (38–70F) and ice-creams laced with alcohol in an exotic venue. Jazz bar in the basement. Daily except Sun 3pm–3am.

L'Univers, rue Berbisey. Check for rock concerts in the cellar. Open till midnight and later.

Listings

Cinemas L'Eldorado, 21 rue Alfred-de-Musset (☎03.80.66.12.34; closed July–Aug), is a three-screen arts cinema showing all films in original language with a concentration of foreign films. Devosge, 6 rue Devosge (☎03.80.30.74.79), shows some films in the original, and tries to deviate from the obvious classics. Other general release cinemas: ABC, 7 rue du Chapeau Rouge and Darcy Palace, 8 place Darcy (☎03.80.30.50.50 for both).

Festivals The city has a good summer music season, with classical concerts through June in its Été Musical programme. L'Estivade, June 20–Aug 15, puts on endless music, dance and street theatre performances. Fête de la Vigne at the beginning of Sept is a traditional costume/folklore jamboree, while the Foire gastronomique at the beginning of Nov celebrates all things edible.

Markets Tues, Fri & Sat mornings along the four streets surrounding the covered market – rue Bannelier, rue Quentin, rue C-Ramey, rue Odebert.

Swimming pool Oxygène-Parc Aquatique, (☎03.80.74.16.16) Centre Commercial de la Toison d'Or, bus #16; 10am–8pm, Sun till 7pm; adults 59F, kids 45F. Toboggans, jacuzzi & water slides.

The Côte d'Or

The attractive countryside of the **Côte d'Or** is characterized by the steep scarp of the *côte*, wooded along the top and cut by steep little valleys called *combes*, where local rock climbers hone their skills (**footpaths GR7 and GR76** run the whole length of the wine country as far south as Lyon). Spring is a good time to visit this region, when you avoid the crowds and the landscape is a dramatic symphony of browns – trees, earth, vines, with millions of bone-coloured vine stakes wheeling past as you travel through, like crosses in a vast war cemetery.

The villages, strung along the N74 through Beaune and beyond, have names – Gevrey-Chambertin, Vougeot, Vosne-Romanée, Nuits-St-Georges, Pommard, Volnay,

Meursault – that all sound like Pavlov's bell to the ears of wine buffs and are familiar to the most casually interested; but they turn out to be sleepy, dull and exceedingly prosperous places, full of houses inhabited by well-heeled *vignerons* in expensive suits and fat-cat cars. You make a very good living on a patch of four or five hectares, the average-sized plot, the proof being that none is ever up for sale.

There are numerous **caves** where you can taste (usually for a charge of 30–40F) and buy the local elixir, but remember that the former is meant to be a prelude to the latter. And there's no such thing as a cheap wine here, red or white, 100–120F being the minimum. The Hautes Côtes (Nuits and Beaune), wines from the top of the slope, are cheaper, but they lack the connoisseur cachet of the big names.

Beaune

BEAUNE, the principal town of the Côte d'Or, has many charms but is totally devoted to tourism. If you want a base for getting around in the area, it's cheaper and pleasanter to use Dijon or Chalon, as both are easily accessible by train and Transco buses, which service all the villages down the N74. Beaune is situated at a major autoroute junction (A6 from Paris/Lyon–A31 from Metz) and its hotels are pricey and likely to be full.

Beaune's town centre is a tightly clustered, rampart-enclosed *vieille ville*, and its chief attraction is the fifteenth-century hospital, the **Hôtel-Dieu** (daily Jan–March & Nov 20–Dec 31 9–11.30am & 2–5.30pm; April 18–Nov 19 9am–6.30pm; 32F), on the corner of place de la Halle. Once past the turnstile of the Hôtel-Dieu you find yourself in a cobbled courtyard surrounded by a wooden gallery overhung by a massive roof patterned with diamonds of gaudy tiles, green, burnt sienna, black and yellow – and similarly multi-coloured steep-pitched dormers and turrets. Inside is a vast paved hall with a painted timber roof, the Grande Salle des Malades, which until quite recently continued to serve its original purpose of accommodating the sick. The last item on the tour is a splendid fifteenth-century altarpiece of the Last Judgment by Rogier van der Weyden, commissioned by Nicolas Rolin, who also founded the hospital in 1443 (King Louis XI commented: "It was only fair that a man who had made so many people poor during his life should create an asylum for them before his death."). It is here that a major wine auction takes place during the annual Trois Glorieuses festival (see p.533), the prices paid setting the pattern for the season.

The private residence of the dukes of Burgundy on rue d'Enfer now contains the **Musée du Vin** (summer daily 9.30am–6pm; winter closed Tues; 25F, same ticket allows entry to the two fine arts museums listed below), with more giant winepresses and an interesting collection of tools of the trade. At the other end of rue d'Enfer the collegiate church of **Notre-Dame** which is about the only free thing in town (April–Nov 15; guided visit 15F). Inside are five very special Tournai tapestries from the fifteenth century, depicting the life of the Virgin and commissioned, once again, by the Rolin family.

There are two other museums, both in the former Ursuline convent that is now the Hôtel de Ville: the not-very-interesting **Musée des Beaux-Arts** and the **Musée Marey Etienne-Jules** (both daily April–Nov 21 2–6pm; 25F, same entry ticket as for the wine museum), devoted to early movie photography. On the outskirts of the town, by the autoroute A6 Beaune–Tailly–Merceuil rest area, there's an open-air park called the **Archéodrome**, illustrating the history of Burgundy with film and reconstructions of a Neolithic house, Cæsar's siege of Alésia (see p.511), a farm with ancient breeds of farm animals and so on. It costs 20–50F for adults, 15–40F for kids, depending on how many of the displays you wish to use.

THE WINES OF BURGUNDY

Burgundy farmers have been growing grapes since Roman times, and their rulers, the dukes, frequently put their **wines** to effective use as a tool of diplomacy. Today they have never had it so good, which is why they're reticent about the quirks of soil and climate and the tricks of pruning and spraying that make their wines so special. Vines are temperamental: frost on the wrong day, sun at the wrong time, too much water or poor drainage, and they won't come up with the goods. And they like a slope, which is why so many wines are called "Côte de" something. Burgundy's best wines come from a narrow strip of hillside called the **Côte d'Or** that runs southwest from Dijon to Santenay. It is divided into two regions, **Côte de Nuits** and **Côte de Beaune**. With few exceptions the reds of the Côte de Nuits are considered the best: they are richer, age better and cost more. Côte de Beaune is known particularly for its whites: Meursault, Montrachet and Puligny.

The single most important factor determining the "character" of wines is the **soil**. In the Côte d'Or, the relative mixture of chalk, flint and clay varies over very short distances, making for an enormous variety of taste. Chalky soil makes a wine *virile* or *corsé*, in other words "heady" – *il y a de la mâche*, they say, "something to bite on" – while clay makes it *féminin*, more *agréable*.

These and other more extravagant judgements are made after the hallowed procedure of **tasting**; in order to do it properly, by one account, you have to "introduce a draft of wine into your mouth, swill it across the tongue, roll it around the palate, churn it around, emitting the gargling sound so beloved of tasters, which is produced by slowly inhaling air through the centre of your mouth, and finally eject it". The ejection is what has to be learnt.

For an **apéritif** in Burgundy, you should try *kir*, named after the man who was both mayor and MP for Dijon for many years after World War II – two parts dry white wine, traditionally *aligoté*, and one part *cassis* or blackcurrant liqueur. To round the evening off there are many liqueurs to choose from, but Burgundy is particularly famous for its **marcs**, of which the best are matured for years in oak casks.

Practicalities

Beaune's **gare SNCF** is outside the old walls to the east of town in avenue du 8-septembre (☎03.80.22.13.13). If you arrive by bus, you're likely to be dropped at the main **gare routière** on the southwest side of town, just outside the walls at the end of rue Maufoux, a five-minute walk from the town's highlights. The **tourist office,** rue de l'Hôtel-Dieu (April to mid-Nov Mon 9am–6pm, Tues–Thurs 9am–8pm, Fri & Sat 9am–9pm, Sun 9am–7pm; mid-Nov to March daily 9am–6pm; ☎03.80.26.21.30, fax 03.80.26.21.39), and they are the best people to consult about all things to do with the region's wines. You can rent **bikes** from the tourist office and collect them from av du 8-Septembre.

If you're going to **stay** in Beaune, you'll have to be prepared to pay at least 200F a night. Be warned: the cheapest hotels may look good but you may encounter unhelpfulness (e.g. no showers after 9pm). The following are worth trying: the convenient *Hôtel Central*, 2 rue Victor-Millot (☎03.80.24.77.24, fax 03.80.22.30.40; ③), which also has a decent restaurant. *Hôtel Grillon*, 21 route de Seurre (☎03.80.22.44.25, fax 03.80.24.94.89; ③) is in an old family home. For a more comfortable stay, try *Le Home*, 138 rte de Dijon, on the way into Beaune (☎03.80.22.16.43, fax 80.24.90.74; ④). The pretty *Les Cent Vignes* **campsite**, 10 rue Dubois (☎03.80.22.03.91; mid-March to Oct), is about 1km out of town, off rue du Faubourg-St-Nicolas (the N74 to Dijon), before the bridge over the autoroute; booking is advisable, as it fills up through the day.

Eating can be an expensive business here. The best places to look for something cheap are rue Monge, place Carnot and rue Madeleine. *Le Carnot,* 18 rue Carnot, is a good cafeteria; and decent, reasonably priced restaurants include the *Brelinette*, 6 rue

Madeleine, where menus start at 60F. The *Restaurant de France* in rue du Faubourg-Bretonnière is good for a basic filling lunch. If you are looking for something more sophisticated, *Le Bénaton*, 25 rue du Faubourg-Bretonnière (☎03.80.22.00.26; closed Wed eve & Thurs), has a good-value 105F menu, with a choice of calf's head, *jambon persillé*, chocolate gâteau and *coq au vin*, although *à la carte* will set you back quite a bit more; there's also *Bernard Morillion*, 31 rue Mafoux (☎03.80.24.12.06; closed Mon & Tues lunch) and *Le Gourmandin*, 8 place Carnot (☎03.80.24.07.88; closed summer Tues & Wed lunch, winter Tues & Mon lunch) with a good menu at 90F. *Les Tontons*, 22 Faubourg Madeleine (☎03.80.24.19.64; closed Sun & Mon lunch) is stylish and unpretentious, with a more inspired way of interpreting the local specialities; menus 68–135F.

Château du Clos-de-Vougeot

If you find the French wine culture fascinating, it's worth visiting the **Château du Clos-de-Vougeot** to see the wine-making process (open April–Aug & Oct–Nov 9–11.30am & 2–5.30pm; Sept 9am–6.30pm; 20F), 15km north of Beaune between Gévry-Chambertin and Nuits-St-Georges, where you get to see the mammoth thirteenth-century winepresses installed by the Cistercian monks to whom these vineyards belonged for nearly 700 years until the Revolution. The château today is the home of a phoney chivalrous order founded in 1934, the Confrèrie des Chevaliers du Tastevin. Chivalrous or not, the "new" monks continue the good wine work. After you've seen how it's made, you can taste it nearby at La Grand Cave à Vougeot (9am–7pm). There is a three-day wine festival, Les Trois Glorieuses on the third Saturday in November, starting in Vougeot and continuing in Beaune, and Meursult.

FROM THE SAÔNE TO THE LOIRE

The **Saône valley** is prosperous and modern, nourished by the autoroute, tourism, industry and the wine trade. But turn your back on the river and head west and at once you enter a different Burgundy: close, hilly pasture and woodland, utterly rural and more populated by cattle than people. This is the hinterland – the Deep South – of Burgundy, where every village clusters under the tower of a Romanesque church, spawned by the influence of Cluny in the 1000s and 1100s. It is only when you reach the Loire and encounter the main traffic routes again that you re-enter the modern world.

It is beautiful country for cycling, though there are few places actually to rent a cycle. There are, however, plenty of bus and train connections, and all these are very conveniently listed in the *Guide des Transports Régionaux* available from any gare SNCF in Burgundy.

Chalon-sur-Saône

CHALON, is a sizeable port and industrial centre on a broad meander of the Saône, is not a place you'd want to stay very long, but its old riverside quarter does have an easy charm. Today it's a thriving business centre, and trade fairs frequently possess the town, but more festive occasions are also an important part of its appeal and good reasons to stop if you're around at the right time. Three major events are: a carnival in March, which features a parade of giant masks, confetti battle and "laughter evening"; a national festival of street artists in July; and a film festival in October.

The **old town** is just back from the river around Grande-Rue and rue du Châtelet. At the junction of these two streets you'll find a fifteenth-century timber-framed house, and there are a number of half-timbered jettied facades around the quarter. Nearby, 200m to the west on place de l'Hôtel-de-Ville, is the **Musée Denon** (daily except Tues and hols, 9.30am–noon & 2–5.30pm; 12F, Wed free), whose most vaunted exhibit is the 18,000-year-old Volgu flint, rated one of the finest stone tools yet discovered. Apart from the usual collection of bits and pieces excavated nearby, look out for the local furniture.

More interesting and unusual is the **Musée Niepce**, 28 quai des Messageries (daily except Tues: July & Aug 10am–6pm; Sept–June 9.30–11.30am & 2.30–5.30pm; 12F) just downstream from Pont St-Laurent. Niepce, who was born in Chalon, is credited with inventing photography in 1816, and the museum possesses a fascinating range of cameras from the first machine ever to the Apollo moon mission's equipment, plus a number of 007-type spy-camera devices, all attractively displayed under a set of glass domes. Upstairs is a library of works on the subject of photography, to be thumbed through at leisure, and a space for temporary exhibitions, with some big names in the history of the art.

The other interesting target in town is the **Maison des Vins** on Promenade Ste-Marie (daily 9am–7pm), where you can taste and buy Côte Chalonnaise wines, chosen from the wines of 44 local villages by a choice committee of professional wine tasters; even the cheaper ones are really good.

Practicalities

The **tourist office** is on bd de la République (Jan–June & Sept–Dec Mon–Sat 9am–12.30pm & 1.30pm–6.30pm, Sun 10am–12pm; July–Aug Mon–Sat 9am–12.30pm & 1.30–6.30pm, Sun 10.30am–12.30pm & 3–6pm; ☎03.85.48.37.97, fax 03.85.48.63.55), giving out excellent listings, a 5F map, and is just five minutes' walk from the **gare SNCF** at the end of av Jean-Jaurès (☎03.85.93.50.50).

The most attractive **hotel** in town is undoubtedly the *Hôtel St-Jean*, right on the river bank at 24 quai Gambetta (☎03.85.48.45.65, fax 03.85.93.62.69; ②). For something a little cheaper, there's *Hôtel au Vendanges de Bourgogne,* 21 rue du Général-Leclerc (☎03.85.48.01.90, ②) with charming rooms and a *crêperie* downstairs, and *Nouvel Hôtel*, 7 av Boucicaut (☎03.85.48.07.31, fax 03.85.48.86.42; ①) – from the station turn left at the end of av Jean-Jaurès and left again. Also in the centre on place Beaune, there's the *Hôtel Central*, 19 place de Beaune (☎03.85.48.35.00, fax 03.85.93.10.20; ②). The youth hostel has closed down, the building is still there, ignore it. *Camping de la Butte* (☎03.85.48.26.86), 3km east of town in St-Marcel, is accessible on bus #9, or, if you're walking, cross either Pont St-Laurent or Pont J-Richard and head east.

The nicest places to **eat** are in rue de Strasbourg on the island across Pont St-Laurent. Try the *Île Bleue*, whose speciality is seafood from a modest 89F, at no. 3 (☎03.85.48.39.83), *Le Bistrot* at no. 31 (☎03.85.93.22.01; closed July–Aug, from 79F) or *La Pierre Vive* at no. 7, one of the few vegetarian restaurants in the area (☎03.85.93.39.01; closed July–Aug; from 60F). *El Ranch* at no. 52 serves huge Mexican meals from 68F. There's also an Indian and a Chinese restaurant in the street, some places where you grill your own meat at the table such as *Le Braseiro,* plus some late-night bars, and the *Boogie Blues Bar* in the cross-street, rue d'Uxelles. In the centre, the place for cafés is Place St-Vincent with its lovely half-timbered houses, and not a single plastic chair in sight. *Cafe Meridien* is right by the bridge, one of the few cafes with a river view.

Tournus

TOURNUS is a beautiful small town on the banks of the Saône, just off the autoroute and N6, 27km south of Chalon and 30km north of Mâcon. Squeezed between the N6 and the river, the narrow huddled streets have the inward-looking, self-protecting feel of a Mediterranean town, belying a prosperous past when commercial traffic thronged the busy riverside quays. The quays are quiet today, and Tournus's modern prosperity is based on agriculture, light industry – domestic appliances in particular – and, increasingly, tourism. But the quays still make a delightful picnic spot, looking out over the broad sweep of the river and its wide flat valley beneath huge piling cloudscapes.

You enter the town from the N6 through a **gateway** flanked by medieval towers – once the entrance to a monastery compound – and are confronted by the old **abbey church of St-Philibert**, one of the earliest and most influential Romanesque buildings in Burgundy. The first construction dates back to around 900 AD and the foundation of the monastic community by monks fleeing Norman raids on their home community of Noirmoutier off the Atlantic coast. The facade of the church, with its powerful towers and simple decoration of Lombard arcading, has the massive qualities and clean, pared-down lines more associated with a fortress. It is equally sturdy inside, with its colossal round pillars and rough-looking masonry in the narthex, which is the oldest surviving part of the building along with the crypt. 'an ingenious idea, forced on the builders by the need to make good the damage caused by a disastrous fire around 1000 AD, and one which made possible the creation of windows in the ends of the vaults opening directly into the nave – very unusual given the state of the art.

Beside the church, the **Musée Perrin de Puycousin** (April–Oct daily except Tues 9am–noon & 2–6pm; 15F) is a moderately interesting exposition of local life and costumes. There is a new **Musée Greuze** under construction in the *Hôtel Dieu*, to display the interesting collection of portraits and domestic scenes by the local eighteenth-century painter, Jean-Baptiste Greuze. Check with the tourist office for opening dates.

Practicalities

The **gare SNCF** (☎03.85.51.07.30) is on av Gambetta, across the road from the old town and a ten-minute walk from the **tourist office**, 2 place Carnot (Mon–Sat 9am–noon & 2–6pm, Sun 10am–noon; ☎03.85.51.13.10).

If you're planning to **stay**, the nicest reasonably priced hotel is *Hôtel aux Terrasses*, 18 av du 23-Janvier (☎03.85.51.01.74, fax 03.85.51.09.99; ③; closed Jan; excellent restaurant from 90F; closed Jan, Sun eve & Mon), at the southern end of the old town where the continuation of rue de la République rejoins the N6. Alternatively, there's the *Hôtel-Restaurant de Saône*, Quai Georges-Bardin (☎03.85.51.20.65, fax 03.85.51.05.45; ③; closed mid-Oct to mid-March; restaurant from 95F) standing in splendid isolation on the east bank of the river. **Campers** should head for *Camping Municipal en Bagatelle* (☎03.85.51.16.58, fax 03.85.27.03.39, May–Sept), just south of the town; take av du 23-janvier out of town to the N6, direction "Lyon".

For further **eating** possibilities outside of the hotels, there are a number of cafés and brasseries in and around place de l'Hôtel-de-Ville.

Mâcon, the Mâconnais and the Beaujolais

MÂCON is a lively, prosperous place on the banks of the River Saône, 58km south of Châlon and 68km north of Lyon, with excellent transport connections between the two. It's a centre for the wine trade and numerous light industries, with a surprisingly sunny southern seaside feel, thanks to its long café-lined **river bank**. There are no great sights here, but it's worth finding the time for a riverside drink. If you're visiting in late July early August, look out for the free outdoor jazz concerts.

Lamartine, the nineteenth-century French Romantic poet (see box overleaf), was born here in 1790 and his name is much in evidence. He is remembered in the handsome eighteenth-century mansion, the Hôtel Senecé in rue Sigorgne, that houses the **Musée Lamartine** (Wed–Mon: 10am–noon & 2–6pm, Sun 2–6pm; 15F), part of which is dedicated to documents and other memorabilia to do with his personal, political and poetic lives. Nearby, on the corner of place des Herbes where a summertime fruit and veg market is held, stands the town's main tourist curiosity, an extraordinary wooden house built around 1500 and known as the **Maison du Bois Doré**, with a wonderful bar/café downstairs that serves cocktails until 2 or 3 am. The town's medieval art and Gallo-Roman archeological museum, **Musée des Ursulines**, is at 5 rue des Ursulines (Wed–Mon: 10am–noon & 2–6pm, Sun 2–6pm; 15F), housed in a seventeenth-century convent.

One tastebud-enlivening (and affordable) experience – and the quickest way to bone up on the Mâcon, Beaujolais and Châlonnais wines – is to visit the **Maison Mâconnaise des Vins**, 520 av Lattre-de-Tassigny (daily 8am–9pm; ☎03.85.38.62.22), where the N6 comes into town along the riverside from Châlon; you can taste and buy wines and eat regional dishes like *andouillette, petit salé* and goat's cheese from only 45F, wines from 12F by the glass. Food is available all day - a rare thing for a restaurant in France. It's a ten minute walk from the centre of town, and has a beautiful view over the river from its large shady balcony.

Practicalities

The **tourist office**, 187 rue Carnot (summer Mon–Sat 10am–7pm, Sun 2–6pm; winter Mon–Sat 10am–noon & 2–6pm; ☎03.85.39.71.37, fax 03.85.39.71.29). Around the corner in rue Dufour is the specialist tourist office for visiting the wine region, and it can provide information about the wine-growing villages of the region and how to get to them. The **gare SNCF** (**gare routière** adjacent) lies on rue Bigonnet at the southern end of rue Victor-Hugo, but note that TGV trains leave from Mâcon-Loché station 6km out of town.

There should be no difficulty finding places to **stay**. Across the Pont de Saint-Laurent is one of the nicest and cheapest hotels, *Hôtel de Beaujolais*, Saint-Laurent-sur-Saône (☎03.85.38.42.06, fax 03.85.38.78.02; ①) has very clean, simple rooms. The *Hôtel d'Europe et d'Angleterre* on the river at 92 quai Jean-Jaurès (☎03.85.38.27.94, fax 03.85.39.22.54; ②) has an air of former times – Queen Victoria once stayed here. The *Interhotel de Bourgogne* on the top side of place de la Barre at 6 rue Victor-Hugo (☎03.85.38.36.57, fax 03.85.38.65.92; ④; restaurant from 80F) also has character and an attractive atmosphere. Two other possibilities close to the gare SNCF, at the southern end of rue Victor-Hugo, are: the *Terminus* (☎03.85.39.17.11, fax 03.85.38.02.75; ④; restaurant from 90F), and *Hôtel de Genève*, 1 rue Bigonnet (☎03.85.38.18.10, fax 03.85.38.22.32; ③; restaurant from 70F).

If you want to **camp**, there's a site (☎03.86.38.16.22; closed Nov to mid-March) 3km north out of town on the N6.

For **food**, there are plenty of good restaurants to choose from. For cheap eats, head for the river. The *Lamartine*, 266 quai Lamartine, pulls in both diners and drinkers. There's the *Saint Laurent* on the other side of the river, with the best view and *plats* from 70F. For local meat, the place to go is *La Vigne et les Vins (Scoubidou)* 42 rue Joseph-Dufour (☎03.85.38.65.92), good prices and friendly service. *Chex Gilou*, 17 rue Joseph-Dufour (☎03.85.40.95.47; closed Sun lunch and Mon) does a good summer paella. *Le Rocher de Cancale,* 393 quai Jean-Jaurés (☎03.85.38.07.50; closed Sun evenings & Mon) is another superb restaurant – wonderful fish and some surprises; menus from 135F, *plats* from 65F.

Brou

BROU is an uninteresting suburban village outside Bourg-en-Bresse, 32km east of Mâcon, which happens to have an early sixteenth-century **church** (daily; 26F). If you're heading east to Geneva or the Alps, take a look, but don't lose a lift or miss a train for it. Aldous Huxley found it "a horrible little architectural nightmare", its monuments "positively and piercingly vulgar". Certainly, it was a very rich woman's expensive folly, crammed with virtuoso craftsmanship from the dying moments of the Gothic style; it was undertaken by Margaret of Austria after the death of her husband, Philibert, Duke of Savoy, as a mausoleum for the two of them and Philibert's mother. Interesting to see, but soulless, without a trace of vision or inspiration. It is no longer a place of worship.

Bourg-en-Bresse

BOURG-EN-BRESSE is the place to base yourself if you want to visit Brou's church, just a short bus (#1) ride away. The **tourist office** (Mon–Fri 9am–noon & 2–6.30pm; ☎04.74.22.49.40, fax 04.74.23.06.28) is in Centre Albert-Camus, 6 av Alsace-Lorraine, with an annexe by Brou church in summer. Wednesday is market day in place Carriat, and on the first and third Wednesdays of each month there's a livestock market as well. An attractive place to **stay** is the *Hôtel du Mail* near the station at 46 av du Mail (☎04.74.21.00.26, fax 04.74.21.29.55; ②; closed Dec 5–Jan 12 & July 12–Aug 7). The **camping municipal** (☎04.74.45.37.21; April to mid-Oct) is on av des Sports, the N83 northeast of town heading for Lons-le-Saunier.

The Mâconnais

The **Mâconnais** wine-producing country lies to the west of the valley of the Saône, a strip hardly 20km wide, stretching from Mâcon to Tournus. The land rises sharply into steep little hills and valleys, at its prettiest in the south, where the region's best white wines come from: the villages of **POUILLY, VINZELLES, PRISSÉ** and **FUISSÉ**, where, should you yearn for rustic rest, the *Hôtel La Vigne Blanche* will provide just the setting you're looking for (☎03.85.35.60.50, fax 03.85.35.67.13; ②; closed Dec 20–Jan 6), along with good regional cooking in its restaurant from 85F.

Directly above these villages rises the distinctive and precipitous 500-metre rock of **Solutré**, which in prehistoric times – around 20,000 BC – seems to have served as some kind of ambush site for hunters after migrating animals, with the bones of 100,000 horses found in the soil beneath the rock, along with mammoth, bison and reindeer carcasses. The history and results of the excavations are displayed in a museum at the foot of the rock: **Musée Départemental de Préhistoire** (daily except Tues June–Sept 10am–1pm & 2–7pm; Feb–April & Oct–Nov 10am–noon & 2–5pm; 20F). A steep path climbs to the top of the rock where you get a superb view, as far as Mont Blanc and the Matterhorn on a clear day, as well as your immediate surroundings. You look down on the huddled roofs of **SOLUTRÉ-POUILLY** and the slopes beneath you covered with the vines of the Chardonnay grape that makes the exquisite greenish Pouilly-Fuissé wine. It's at its most enchanting in early spring when the earth still shows its *terre-cuite* colours, punctuated by bursts of white cherry blossom and the blue drift of bonfire smoke from prunings amid the neatly staked rows of vines.

Aside from the sheer pleasure of wandering about in such reposeful landscapes – not so, however, if you are trying to tackle this very hilly country on a bike – there are some places to make for. One such is the sleepy hamlet of **ST-POINT**, where the poet Lamartine (see p.536) spent much of his life in the little medieval **château de St-Point**, now a museum dedicated to his memory (Thurs–Tues: March–Nov 15 10am–noon & 2–6pm, Sun 2–6pm; 23F), next to the Romanesque church where he is buried. If you continue up the road behind the château you come to an utterly rural farm where you can buy goat's cheese. There is a **campsite** by the Lac St-Point (☎03.85.50.52.31; April–Oct).

Cluny

The abbey of **CLUNY** is the major tourist destination of the region. The voice of its abbot once made monarchs tremble, as his power in the Christian world was second only to that of the Pope. The monastery was founded in 910 in response to the corruption of the existing church, and it took only a couple of vigorous early abbots to build the power of Cluny into a veritable empire. Gradually its spiritual influence declined, and Cluny became a royal gift. Both Richelieu and Mazarin did stints in the monastery as abbot.

Now, although the reputation of the place still pulls in the tourist coaches, little remains apart from the very attractive village. The Revolution suppressed the monastery, and Hugues de Semur's vast and influential eleventh-century **church**, the largest building in Christendom until the construction of St Peter's in Rome, was dismantled in 1810. Now all you can see of the former **abbey** (daily: April–June 9.30am–noon & 2–6pm; July–Sept 9am–7pm; Oct 9.30am–noon & 2–5pm; rest of year 10am–noon & 2–4/5pm; 26F or 32F abbey/museum pass) is an octagonal belfry, the south transept and, in the impressive granary, the surviving capitals from its immense column. From the top of the **Tour des Fromages** you can reconstruct it in your imagination; you enter the tower through the tourist office (see below). The **Musée d'Art et d'Archaeologie** (same hours as abbey; 14F), in the fifteenth-century palace of the last freely elected abbot, helps to flesh out the picture with reconstructions and fragments of sculpture, while the octagonal Romanesque belfry of the parish **church of St-Marcel** also recalls the belfries that once adorned the abbey.

There are some interesting old houses in rue Mercière/rue Lamartine and, in particular, rue de la République/rue d'Avril, where nos. 25 and 6 are nearly as old as the abbey itself. At the back of the abbey is one of France's national stud farms, **Haras National** (daily 9am–7pm; free), which can also be visited.

PRACTICALITIES

The **tourist office** is at 6 rue Mercière (daily May–Sept 10am–7pm, Nov–April 10am–noon & 2.30–6.30pm; ☎03.85.59.05.34, fax 03.85.59.06.95). For **accommodation** the *Hôtel de l'Abbaye* on av de la Gare (☎03.85.59.11.14, fax 03.85.59.09.76; ②; closed Jan to mid-Feb), which has reasonable rooms, as does the *Hôtel du Commerce*, 8 place du Commerce (☎03.85.59.03.09; ②). *Hôtel St-Odilon*, across the river on the left before the campsite (☎03.85.59.25.00, fax 03.85.59.06.18; ③; closed Dec 20–Jan 5), is quite new, but not to be shunned for that. There's a municipal **hostel**, *Cluny Séjour*, on rue Porte-de-Paris (☎03.85.59.08.83; closed Dec & Jan), and a **camping municipal**, *St-Vital* (☎03.85.59.08.34; May to mid-Sept), across Pont de la Levée in the direction of Tournus and on the right, where you can also hire **bicycles**.

For a **meal**, other than a crêpe or snack, try *Les Marronniers*, 20 av de Gaulle (closed Mon) or, for some good country cooking, *Le Potin Gourmand*, 4 place Champ-de-Foire (☎03.85.59.02.06; closed Mon & Jan 4–Feb 5; best value menus at 78F & 120F).

Taizé

Another powerful attraction for the converted might be the modern ecumenical community at **TAIZÉ**, 10km north of Cluny. It was founded in 1940 by the Swiss pastor Roger Schutz. There's a restored Romanesque church, and the new Church of Reconciliation. Hordes of youngsters come to take part in discussion groups and camp out. If you are seriously interested – and it is not likely to be to the taste of the merely curious – write to Communauté de Taizé, 71250 Cluny.

The Beaujolais

Imperceptibly, as you continue south, the Mâconnais becomes the **Beaujolais**, a larger area of terraced hills producing lighter, fruity red wines, which it is now fashionable to drink very early. The Beaujolais grape is the Gamay which, in contrast to other parts of Burgundy, thrives here on this granite soil. Of the four *appellations* of Beaujolais, the best are the *crus*, including Morgon and Fleurie, which come from the northern part of the region between St-Amour (the northernmost *cru*), and Brouilly in the south. If you have transport, you can follow the *cru* trail south from Mâcon by turning right at Crêches-sur-Saône up the D31 to St-Amour, and then south along the D68. Beaujolais Villages, which produces the best *nouveau*, comes from the middle of the Beaujolais region, south of the *cru* belt, while plain *Beaujolais* and *Beaujolais supérieur* are produced in the vineyards southwest of Villefranche.

The well-marked **route de Beaujolais** winds down through the wine villages to **VILLEFRANCHE**, not far from Lyon and a good base for the route. Here, the **tourist office** at 290 rue de Thizy (Mon–Sat 9am–noon & 1.30–6pm, Sun 9am–noon; ☎04.74.68.05.18) has all the information about *caves*, visits and wine tours. There are numerous cheap **hotels**, almost all near the **gare SNCF**. A good one to try is the friendly and clean *Hôtel la Colonne*, 6 place Carnot (☎04.74.65.06.42; ①), with a popular cheap **bar**, open every night – including Sunday, when everything else in the village is dead. Most of the cafés on rue Nationale are good for snacks or cheap menus, too.

Paray-le-Monial and the Charollais

Fifty kilometres west of Cluny, across countryside that becomes ever gentler and flatter as you approach the broad valley of the Loire, is **PARAY-LE-MONIAL**, whose major attraction is its **Basilique du Sacré-Cœur**. Not only is it a superb building in its own right, with a marvellously satisfying arrangement of apses and chapels stacking up in sturdy symmetry to its fine octagonal belfry, it's also the only place, albeit on a smaller scale, where you can get an idea of what the abbey of Cluny looked like (see above). Both churches are contemporary and the result of the same Hugues de Semur's influence.

The town itself is the archetypal country town, quiet and unpretentious, straddling the slow waters of the River Bourbince and the Canal du Centre. The only thing that disturbs its calm is the arrival of pilgrims of the Sacré-Coeur, or "Sacred Heart", a cult which originated here with Marguerite-Marie Alacoque, a local nun who received revelations advocating the worship of the sacred heart. The cult was later adopted by the entire Roman Catholic Church. The first pilgrimage took place in 1873, encouraged as a means of combatting the socialist ideas espoused by the Paris Commune, and it raised the money to construct the church of the Sacré-Cœur on the hill of Montmartre in Paris. Paray is now second only to Lourdes as a pilgrim centre.

The one secular building definitely worth a look, aside from just browsing down the main street – rue de la République/rue des Deux-Ponts/rue Victor-Hugo – is the highly ornamented **Maison Jayet**, now the Hôtel de Ville on place Guignaud, built in the 1520s.

Practicalities

The **tourist office** is in av Jean-Paul-II (Mon–Sat 9am–noon & 1–6.30pm; ☎03.85.81.10.92, fax 03.85.81.36.61). You can rent bikes from André Vaz, 24 rue de la République (☎03.85.81.08.51).

For **accommodation**, try the *Hostellerie des Trois Pigeons*, 2 rue Daugard, just beyond the Hôtel de Ville (☎03.85.81.03.77, fax 03.85.81.58.59; ③; closed Dec–Feb; restaurant from 70F), or, near the station, *Hôtel du Nord*, 1 av de la Gare (☎03.85.81.05.12, fax 03.85.81.58.93; ②; closed Dec 25–Jan 25; restaurant from 70F). Further possibilities are the *Hôtel aux Vendanges de Bourgogne*, 5 rue Denis-Papin (☎03.85.81.13.43, fax 03.85.88.87.59; ②; closed Nov 25–Dec 15; good-value restaurant from 68F), south of the Canal du Centre off the N79; or the *Grand Hôtel de la Basilique*, 18 rue de la Visitation (☎03.85.81.11.13, fax 03.85.88.83.70; ②; closed Nov to mid-March; restaurant from 75F), bang opposite the chapel that stands on the spot where Ste Marguerite had her revelations and consequently rather sought after by the pilgrims. The *Mambré* **campsite** is en route du Gué-Léger (☎03.85.88.89.20; April–Oct). If you want to explore the little villages throughout the Mâconnais (see below), there's no better base than the Merle family's organic farm at Vitry-en-Charollais (☎03.85.81.10.79; around 230F with breakfast for two and 80F a head for dinner), with delicious home cooking, about 6km southwest of Paray-le-Monial.

The Charollais

The **Charollais** is cattle country, taking its name from the pretty little water enclosed market town of **CHAROLLES**, with its 32 bridges, on the main N79 road, and in turn giving its name to one of the world's most illustrious breeds of cattle: the white, curly-haired and stocky Charollais, bred for its lean meat. The fields south of Paray are full of the beasts. Throughout this landscape, scattered across the rich farmland along the Arconce River, are dozens of small villages, all with more or less remarkable Romanesque churches, offspring of Cluny in its vigorous youth.

ANZY-LE-DUC, about 15km south off the main D982 to Roanne, boasts an exquisite complex of buildings: a perfect Romanesque church with jackdaw chatter echoing off the octagonal belfry, side by side with the remains of the old priory incorporated into a sort of fortified farm looking out over the Arconce valley, the whole built in a rich, warm stone. **MONTCEAUX-L'ÉTOILE**, a little nearer, has its special charm too: a quiet, worn church with beautiful sculptures adorning the porch, standing likewise above the Arconce valley, and, a little way down the village street, a curious tower-like house where a Marquis of Vichy is said to have practised alchemy with the notorious Italian wizard, Cagliostro. There is **camping à la ferme** (☎03.85.25.38.66; May–Sept) on the Paray side of the village.

Ten kilometres to the west, the Arconce flows into the Loire just upstream from **DIGOIN**. Although it's not a place you are likely to do more than pass through, the nineteenth-century **bridge** carrying the Canal du Centre over the Loire is worth a look and the riverside quays make a quiet, sunny picnic spot. The town is now France's chief centre of pottery manufacture, and has two very good **hotel-restaurants**: *Hôtel de la Gare*, 79 av de Gaulle (☎03.85.53.03.04, fax 03.85.53.14.70; ③; closed mid-Jan to mid-Feb; restaurant from 135F, closed Wed except in July & Aug), and *Hôtel Les Diligences*, 14 rue Nationale (☎03.85.53.06.31, fax 03.85.88.92.43; ③; closed Nov 20–Dec 10; restaurant from 95F; closed Mon eve & Tues except in July & Aug). There's **camping** *de la Chevrette* by the Loire on the Moulins road (☎03.85.53.11.49; April–Oct).

Nevers

At the western confines of Burgundy, **NEVERS** is a small provincial city on the confluence of the rivers Loire and Nièvre. In France it is known for its *nougatine* candies and fine porcelain, a hallmark since the seventeenth century, still produced in just three workshops and sold in a few elegant, expensive shops (*faïenceries*) around town. Parts of the **old town**, best viewed from the bridge over the Loire, date back to the twelfth century and make for a relaxed stroll away from the busier town centre. This, combined with an open-air concert programme in summer and a few lively bars and restaurants, makes Nevers an excellent stopover if you're travelling in the region.

The town

The town centres around **place Carnot**, close to the fifteenth-century **ducal palace**, former home of the dukes of Nevers, with octagonal turrets and an elegant central tower decorated with sculptures illustrating the family history of the first duke, François de Clèves, in the mid-seventeenth century. The building now houses an annexe of the law courts. Nearby, opposite the Hôtel de Ville, the **Cathédrale de St-Cyr** reveals a sort of wall display of French architectural styles from the tenth to the sixteenth centuries; it even manages to have two opposite apses, one Gothic, the other Romanesque. But more interesting and aesthetically satisfying is the late eleventh-century church of **St-Étienne** on the east side of the town centre. Behind its plain exterior lies one of the prototype pilgrim churches, with galleries above the aisles, ambulatory and three radiating chapels around the apse.

From the station, avenue de-Gaulle leads to place Carnot, where you take a left turn for the **Parc Roger-Salengro**, which has some unexpected sculptures – look out for *Les Sangliers* (wild boar). The north side of the park edges onto the **convent of St-Gildard**, where Bernadette of Lourdes ended her days. Her embalmed body is displayed in a glass-fronted **shrine** (daily summer 7am–7.30pm; winter 7am–noon & 2–7pm) in the convent chapel. A short walk away is the modern **église Sainte-Bernadette du Banlay**, built in 1966 in the style of *fonction oblique* by the architects Claude Parent and Paul Virilio.

Crossing to the other side of avenue de-Gaulle, five minutes' walk from the station by place Mossé and the bridge over the Loire, you pass a section of the old town walls and the **Tour Goguin**, partly dating back to the eleventh century. If you turn in here to the right you come to the **Porte de Croux,** a cream stone tower with intact machicolations and a steep tiled roof like those of its surrounding buildings; inside, the small local **archeology museum** (March–Nov Wed–Sun 2–6pm; 10F) displays mainly Greek and Roman statuary. Nearby in rue du 14-juillet, a seventeenth-century **faïencerie** sells antique pieces such as huge Nivernais plates. To your right again you get back to the oldest quarter of town around the cathedral – rue Morlon and rue de la Cathédrale – with its dilapidated half-timbered houses, alleys and stairs descending to the river.

To the north of the ducal palace on the way out of town towards Orléans, **Porte de Paris**, a triumphal arch, straddles rue des Ardilliers. It commemorates one of Europe's major conflicts, the battle of Fontenoy, fought out between Charlemagne's sons in 841

AD. The stakes were Charlemagne's empire, and the outcome the division of his lands east and west of the Rhine, which formed the basis of modern France and Germany.

Practicalities

The **tourist office**, in the foyer of the Palais Ducal (☎0386.68.46.00) provides maps and information on events in the summer music festival. The **gare SNCF** and **gare routière** are on rue du Chemin-de-Fer. **Bike rental** is available from Belair, 31bis rue de la Préfecture.

There are plenty of **hotels**: the best is the *Hôtel Beauséjour* at 5 rue St-Gildard (☎03.86.61.20.84, fax 03.86.59.15.37; ②), only ten minutes' walk from the station. *Hôtel Thermidor*, 14 rue Claude-Tillier (☎03.86.57.15.47; ②), reached by turning left out of the station and right after *Bar des Messages*, is good value and quiet. The **camping municipal** is on the other side of the Loire, just over the bridge, with the best view of the town. **IMPHY**, 10km from Nevers, has a **youth hostel**: *Foyer du Vignot*, 8 rue Jean-Sounié (☎03.86.90.95.20).

Avenue Charles de-Gaulle has a few inexpensive **restaurants** and **cafés**, like the superb *Gambrinus*, 37 av Général-de-Gaulle (closed midday Sat & Sun); *plats* from 50F. *Le Goemon*, 9 rue du 14-Juillet (closed Sun & Mon eve), is a crêperie with good salads, and live jazz on Saturday nights and *La Crêperie*, 24 av Général-de-Gaulle (☎03.86.57.28.61; closed Sun lunch and Mon) has good cheap meals. For fresh, tasty food in a friendly place, there's *La Grignote* at 7bis rue Ferdinand-Gambon near the market (☎03.86.36.24.99; closed Mon, Tues & Wed eve). *Donald's Pub* on rue François Mitterand near the river, is a good place for a drink.

travel details

Buses

Autun to: Beaune (1 daily; 1hr 10min); Chalon (2–3 daily; 1hr 20min); Château-Chinon (1 daily; 1hr); Le Creusot (several daily; 30min); Dijon (1 daily; 2hr 30min); Montchanin TGV station (several daily; 1hr); St-Léger-sous-Beuvray (2–3 daily; 1hr 15min).

Avallon to: Dijon (1 daily; 2hr 30min–3hr); Vézelay (1 daily; 30min).

Bourg-en-Bresse to: Lyon (1 daily; 1hr 40min).

Chablis to: Tonerre (2 daily; 1hr); to Auxerre (2 daily, 35min). No bus service in August.

Cluny to: Chalon (7 daily; 1hr 20min); Charolles (2–5 daily; 45min); Mâcon (7 daily; 45min); Paray-le-Monial (2–5 daily; 1hr).

Dijon to: Autun (1 daily; 2hr 30min); Avallon (daily; 2hr); Beaune (daily; 1hr); Châtillon-sur-Seine (4 daily; 1hr 30min); Chaumont (1 daily; 2hr 20min); Langres (1 daily; 1hr 40min); Nuits (daily; 35min); Saulieu (1 daily; 1hr 30min).

Mâcon to: Chalon (7 daily; 2hr 15min); Charolles (2–5 daily; 2hr); Cluny (7 daily; 45min); Paray-le-Monial (2–5 daily; 2hr 20min).

Semur to: Auxerre (1 daily; 2hr 50min); Les Laumes (1 daily; 40min); Montbard (1 daily; 1hr 10min); Saulieu (1 daily; 45min).

Sens to: Auxerre (4 daily; 2hr 5min); Joigny (4 daily; 1 hr 10min); Troyes (4–5 daily; 1hr 45min).

Trains

Autun to: Avallon (4–5 bus or train daily; 2hr); Le Creusot (2 daily; 1hr).

Auxerre to: Avallon (4–5 daily; 1hr 5min); Paris (7–8 daily; 2hr 15min–2hr 30min); Sens (2 daily; 55min).

Avallon to: Auxerre (4–5 daily; 1hr 5min); Dijon (4 daily; 2 hr); Paris (several daily via Laroche-Migennes; 3hr); Sens (2 daily; 55min).

Beaune to: Dijon (about 7 daily; 20min); Lyon (about 7 daily; 2hr); Paris (2 TGVs daily; 2hr).

Bourg-en-Bresse to: Dijon (2 daily direct trains; 1hr 45min–2hr 30min); Geneva (4 TGVs daily; 1hr 30min); Lyon (14 daily; about 1hr); Mâcon (12 daily; 20–30min); Paris (4 TGVs daily; 2hr).

Dijon to: Beaune (frequent; 25min); Chalon

(frequent; 40min); Laroche-Migennes (6 daily; 1hr 30min); Les Laumes (6 daily; 30min); Lyon (20 daily; 1hr 45min–2hr 30min); Mâcon (frequent; 1hr–1hr 20min); Montbard (6 daily; 35min); Nevers (4–5 daily; 2hr 30min–3hr); Nuits-St-Georges (frequent; 20min); Paris (15 daily; 1hr 40min–3hr); Tournus (frequent; 1hr); Sens (6 daily; 2hr 10min); Tonnerre via Ancy-le-Franc and Tanly (6 daily; 1hr 15min); Villefranche (frequent; around 1hr 40min).

Mâcon to: Bourg-en-Bresse (4 TGVs daily; 20min); Dijon (around 14 daily; 1hr 10min); Geneva (4 TGVs daily; 1hr 50min); Lyon (around 14 daily; 40min); Paris (5 direct TGVs daily; 1hr 40min).

Nevers to: Autun (3 daily; 1hr 30min); Clermont-Ferrand (5 daily; 1hr 50min); Le Creusot (5 daily;

1hr 30min); Dijon (5 daily; 2hr 30min); Étang (3 daily; 1hr–1hr 50min); Montchanin (6 daily; 1hr 30min); Paris (several daily; 2–3hr).

Paray-le-Monial to: Chagny (5 daily; 1–1hr 30min); Chalon (5 daily; 1hr 10min–1hr 40min); Dijon (2 daily; 1hr 45min); Montchanin (2 daily; 50min).

Sens to: Auxerre (3–5 daily changing at Laroche-Migennes; 45min); Autun (1 daily; 4hr); Avallon (3–5 daily; 2hr); Dijon (11 daily; 2hr 10min); Joigny (11 daily; 27min); Laroche-Migennes junction (11 daily; 30min); Montbard (11 daily; 1 hr 27min); Paris (frequent; 1hr–1hr 30min); Tonnerre (11 daily; 55min).

Tonnerre to: Dijon (6 daily; 1hr 15min); Paris (6 daily; 1hr 45min).

CHAPTER EIGHT

POITOU-CHARENTES AND THE ATLANTIC COAST

Newsstands selling *Sud-Ouest* remind you where you are: this is not the Mediterranean, certainly, but in summer the quality of the light, the warm air, the fields of sunflowers and the shuttered siesta-silence of the farmhouses give you the first exciting promises of the south.

The coast, on the other hand, remains unmistakably Atlantic – dunes, pine forest, reclaimed marshland and misty mud flats. While it has great charm in places, particularly out of season on the islands of **Noirmoutier**, **Ré** and **Oléron**, it's a family, camper-caravanner seaside, lacking the glamour and excitement of the Côte d'Azur. The principal port in the north, **La Rochelle**, is one of the prettiest and most distinctive towns in France. The sandy beaches are beautiful everywhere, though can occasionally be disappointing where the water is murky and shallow for a long way out: but this applies more to the northern stretches. On the dune-backed **Côte d'Argent**, south of Bordeaux, however, the sea can be lively, not to say dangerous.

Inland, the valley of the **Charente River**, slow and green, epitomizes blue-overalled, Gauloise-smoking, peasant France. The towpath is accessible for long stretches, on foot or mountain bike, and there are boat trips from **Saintes** and **Cognac**. The **Marais Poitevin**, too, with its groves of poplars and island fields reticulated by countless canals and ditches, is both unusual landscape and easy-going walking or cycling country.

But perhaps the most memorable aspect of the countryside – and indeed of towns like **Poitiers** – is the presence of exquisite Romanesque churches. This region formed a significant stretch of the medieval pilgrim routes across France and from Britain and northern Europe to the shrine of St Jacques (St James, or Santiago as the Spanish know him) at Compostela in northwest Spain, and was well endowed by its followers. The finest of the churches, among the best in all of France, are to be found in the countryside around Saintes and Poitiers: informal, highly individual and so integrated with their landscape they often seem as rooted as the trees.

ACCOMMODATION PRICE CATEGORIES

Each hotel in this chapter has a symbol which corresponds to one of eight price categories.

① Under 160F	④ 300–400F	⑦ 600–700F
② 160–220F	⑤ 400–500F	⑧ Over 700F
③ 220–300F	⑥ 500–600F	

The prices quoted are for the cheapest available double room in high season, though remember that many of the cheap places will have more expensive rooms with en-suite facilities.

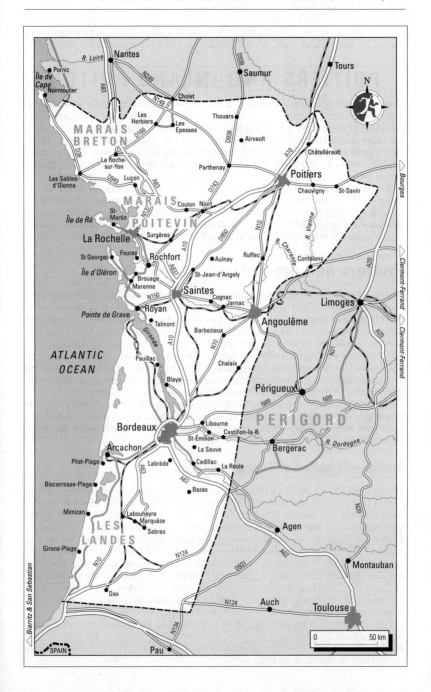

Lastly, of course, remember that this is a region of seafood – fresh and cheap in every market for miles inland – and, around **Bordeaux**, some of the world's top vineyards.

POITIERS AND INLAND POITOU

Most of the old province of **Poitou** is a huge expanse of rolling wheat land and sun-flower and maize plantations where the combines crawl and giant sprinklers shoot great arcs of white water over the fields in summertime. Villages are strung out along the valley floors. Heartland of the domains of Eleanor, Duchess of Aquitaine, whose marriage to King Henry II in 1152 brought the whole of southwest France under English control for 300 years, it is also the northern limit of the *langue d'oc*-speaking part of the country, whose Occitan dialect survives among old people even today.

West of **Poitiers** the open landscape of the Poitou plain gradually gives way to *bocages* – small fields enclosed by hedges and trees. The local farmers' co-operatives say that grubbing up woodland and creating vast windswept acreages in the name of efficiency and productivity is going out of fashion. And not just for aesthetic reasons: wind erosion has left scarcely 15cm of top soil.

Poitiers and around

Heading south from Tours on the Autoroute de l'Aquitaine, you'd hardly be tempted by the cluster of towers and office blocks rising from the plain, which is all you see of **POITIERS**. But approach more closely and things look very different. No seething metropolis, Poitiers is a country town with a unique charm that comes from a long and sometimes influential history – as the seat of the dukes of Aquitaine, for instance – discernible in the winding lines of the streets and the breadth of civic, domestic and ecclesiastical architectural fashions represented in its buildings. A hilltop town overlooking two rivers, with plenty of pedestrian precincts, restaurants and pavement cafés – and some wonderful central gardens – it makes for comfortable sightseeing.

For the dedicated, there are the two Romanesque churches not far from Poitiers at **Chauvigny** and **St-Savin** – both with some great sculpture and frescoes – as well as a huge postmodern cinema theme park, **Futuroscope**, to the north, that's become a huge attraction.

Arrival, information and accommodation

The **gare SNCF**(☎05.49.88.44.44) is on boulevard du Grand-Cerf, part of the ring-road system that encircles the base of the hill on which Poitiers is built. There is no gare routière: out of town **buses**, run by Rapides de Poitou (☎05.49.46.27.45), leave from the train station. The **tourist office**, fifteen minutes' walk away at 8 rue des Grandes-Écoles off place du Maréchal-Leclerc (July–Aug Mon–Fri 9am–7pm, Sat & Sun 9.45am–6.45pm; Sept–June Mon–Fri 9am–noon, Sat & Sun 1.30–6pm; ☎05.49.41.21.24, fax 05.49.88.65.84), won't actually reserve rooms but can give you hotel options in town, and also supplies walkers with a guide to the regional opportunities: the **GR364** sets out from here, reaching the Vendée coast via Parthenay. **Bikes** can be rented from Cyclamen, 49 rue Arsène-Orillard (☎05.49.88.13.25), **cars** from outlets near the train station on boulevard du Grand-Cerf, such as Citer at no. 48 (☎05.49.58.51.58).

There are plenty of **hotels** along bd du Grand-Cerf by the train station, but the area is not particularly salubrious; for more entertaining surroundings it's only a short uphill walk – boulevard Solférino, then to the right up the steep steps – to the town cen-tre on place du Maréchal-Leclerc.

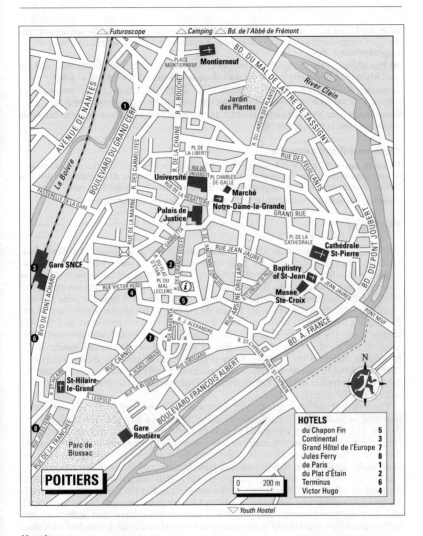

Montierneuf

PLACE
MONTIERNEUF

BD. DU MAL DE LATTRE DE TASSIGNY

River Clain

Jardin
des Plantes

AVENUE DE NANTES

BOULEVARD DU GRAND CERF

R. J. BOUCHET

R. DU JARDIN DES PLANTES

La Boivre

PASSERELLE DE LA GARE

RUE DES CARMELITES

R. DE LA CHAINE

PL DE
LA LIBERTE

RUE DES FEUILLANTS

RUE DE L'UNIVERSITÉ

Université

PL CHARLES
DE-GALLE

Marché

RUE DE LA REGATTERIE

RUE DE LA MARNE

Palais de
Justice

Notre-Dame-la-Grande

GRAND RUE

RUE GARIBALDI

RUE DE L'ANCIENNE COMEDIE

RUE DES GRANDES ECOLES

PL DE LA
CATHEDRALE

Cathédrale
St-Pierre

Gare SNCF

RUE VICTOR HUGO

DU PLAN
D'ÉTAIN

PL DU
MAL
LECLERC

RUE JEAN JAURES

Baptistry
of St-Jean

R. JEAN JAURES

BD. DU PONT JOUBERT

BVD DE PONT ACHARD

RUE ARSENE ORRILLARD

Musée
Ste-Croix

R. VINCENT AURIOL

PONT NEUF

RUE MAGENTA

R. J. ALEXANDRE

R. ST-CYPRIEN

PONT ST-CYPRIEN

BD. A. FRANCE

RUE CARNOT

R. ALSACE-LORRAINE

RUE GIROUARD

BOULEVARD FRANCOIS ALBERT

RUE ST-SAIRE

St-Hilaire-
le-Grand

RUE DE BLOSSAC

R. LEOPOLD

RUE JULES-FERRY

RUE DE LA TRANCHEE

Gare
Routière

Parc de
Blossac

POITIERS

N

HOTELS	
du Chapon Fin	5
Continental	3
Grand Hôtel de l'Europe	7
Jules Ferry	8
de Paris	1
du Plat d'Étain	2
Terminus	6
Victor Hugo	4

0   200 m

▽ *Youth Hostel*

Hotels

du Chapon Fin, 11 rue Lebasdes (☎05.49.88.02.97, fax 05.49.88.91.63). A substantial old two-star hotel in a great position right near the grand Hôtel de Ville; the spacious rooms all have showers. Closed mid-Dec to mid-Jan. ②.

Continental, 2 bd Solférino (☎05.49.37.93.93, fax 05.49.53.01.16). Comfortable two-star opposite the station, whose soundproofed rooms all have bath or shower and TV. ③.

Grand Hôtel de l'Europe, 39 rue Carnot (☎05.49.88.12.00, fax 05.49.88.97.30). Smart and very central, but its front courtyard set back from the street means it's very quiet. Covered parking 20F. ④.

Jules Ferry, 27 rue Jules-Ferry (☎05.49.37.80.14, fax 05.49.53.15.02). Friendly family-run establishment situated in a peaceful residential street near the church of St-Hilaire; clean and nicely decorated. ①.

de Paris, 123 bd du Grand-Cerf (☎05.49.58.39.37). A once superior hotel by the station, now run-down and inexpensive; suffers from traffic noise. If a little unfriendly, the simple, good-value restaurant compensates. ②.

du Plat d'Étain, 7 rue du Plat-d'Étain (☎05.49.41.04.80, fax 05.49.52.25.84). An attractive, well-run hotel in a central quiet street just off the main shopping precinct. ③. Closed Dec 17–Jan 8.

Terminus, 3 bd Pont-Achard (☎05.49.62.92.30, fax 05.49.62.92.40). A better class of station-located lodging, with an excellent brasserie. Rooms are very clean, modern and soundproofed. ③.

Victor Hugo, 5 rue Victor-Hugo (☎05.49.41.12.16). A central bargain above an agreeable bar – only five rooms, most of them simple. ②.

Youth hostel and campsite

HI youth hostel, 17 rue de la Jeunesse (☎05.49.58.03.05, fax 05.49.30.09.79). Large, modern hostel next to a swimming pool, often overrun with school groups. Take bus #3 from the gare SNCF to Bellejouanne, 3km away. Well-signposted, it's to the right off the N10 Angoulême road.

Camping municipal, rue du Porteau (☎05.49.41.44.88). 2km north of town; bus #7.

The town

The two poles of communal life in Poitiers are the tree-lined **place du Maréchal-Leclerc**, with its popular cafés and lively outdoor culture, and **place Charles-de-Gaulle** to the north, where a big and bustling food and clothes **market** takes place (Mon–Sat 7am–6pm, Sun 7.30am–1pm). Between the two is a warren of prosperous streets – as far along as the half-timbered medieval houses of **rue de la Chaine** – with the rue Gambetta cutting north past the old **Palais de Justice** with a nineteenth-century facade that hides a much older core. At the time of writing it could not be visited, and they are unsure about a re-opening date. Right behind you, you can look down upon one of the greatest and most idiosyncratic churches in France, **Notre-Dame-la-Grande** (daily 8am–7pm), begun in the twelfth-century reign of Eleanor and now freshly renovated; strangely enough, pigeon droppings and pollution weren't the major concern, but the salt from the market stalls of fishmongers and salt merchants seeping into the ground and up into the church's facade.

The weirdest and most spectacular thing about it is the west front. You can't call it beautiful, at least not in a conventional sense. It is squat and loaded with detail to a degree that the modern eye could regard as fussy. And yet it is this detail which is enthralling, ranging from the domestic to the disturbingly anarchic: in the blind arch to the right of the door, a woman sits in the keystone with her hair blowing out from her head; in the frieze above, Mary places her hand familiarly on Elizabeth's pregnant belly. You see the newborn Jesus admired by a couple of daft-looking sheep and gurgling in his bathtub. Higher still are images of the apostles, and at the apex, where the eye is carried deliberately and inevitably, Christ in Majesty in an almond-shaped inset. Such elaborate sculpted facades – and domes like pine cones on turret and belfry – are the hallmarks of the Poitou brand of Romanesque. The interior, crudely overlaid with nineteenth-century frescoes, is not nearly as interesting. But the stunning **Cathédrale St-Pierre** is definitely worth a visit (see below).

Another unusual church lies towards the southern tip of the old town, where the hump of the hill narrows to a point now occupied by the **Parc de Blossac**, a great spot to sit among the clipped limes and gravelled walks, to watch the boules and munch a baguette. The eleventh-century **church of St-Hilaire-le-Grand** on rue du Doyenné unbelievably was pruned of part of its nave in the last century, but the chevet from the outside is still a fine sight; the apse has a particularly beautiful group of chapels surrounding it. Inside, there is the usual ambulatory to accommodate the many pilgrims who flocked here, one of whom perhaps caused the fire around 1100 that destroyed the original wooden roof and necessitated the improvised arrangement that makes

St-Hilaire architecturally unique: eight heavy domes introduced for the reroofing had to be supported somehow, hence the forest of auxiliary columns that make three aisles either side of the nave.

While you are staying in Poitiers you will be surrounded by publicity advertising Futuroscope, a theme park entirely dedicated to cinema.

The cathedral and around

Poitiers' **Cathédrale St-Pierre**, at the east of the old town, is an enormous building on whose broad, pale facade pigeons roost and plants take root. Some of the stained glass dates from the twelfth century, notably the crucifixion in the centre window of the apse, in which the features of Henry II and Eleanor are supposedly discernible. The choir stalls, too, are full of characteristic medieval detail: a coquettish Mary and child, a peasant killing a boar, the architect at work with his dividers, a baker with a basket of loaves. But it's the grand eighteenth-century organ, the Orgue Clicquot, which is the cathedral's most striking feature, often playing deafening tunes, with organized concerts in the summer.

Opposite – literally in the middle of rue Jean-Jaurès – you come upon a chunky, square edifice with the air of a second-rate Roman temple. It is the mid-fourth-century **Baptistère St-Jean** (April–June & Sept–Oct Wed–Mon 10.30am–12.30pm & 3–6pm; July & Aug daily; Nov–March Wed–Mon 2.30–4.30pm; 4F), reputedly the oldest Christian building in France and, until the seventeenth century, the only place in town you could have had a proper baptism. The "font" was the octagonal pool sunk into the floor. The guide argues that the water pipes uncovered in the bottom show that the water could not have been more than 30–40cm deep, which casts doubt upon the popular belief that early Christian baptism was by total immersion. There are also some very ancient and faded frescoes on the walls, including one of the Emperor Constantine on horseback; and a collection of Merovingian sarcophagi. Striking a postmodern note between the cathedral and baptistry is the small domed shape of **Espace Mendès-France** (Tues–Fri 9.30am–6.30pm, Sat & Sun 2–6.30pm), containing a state-of-the-art planetarium (32F) and laserium (42F).

Next to the baptistry is Poitiers' museum, the **Musée Ste-Croix** (Tues–Fri 10am–noon & 1.15–5pm, Sat & Sun 10am–noon & 2–6pm; 15F, Tues free), featuring an interesting collection of farming implements like its *alambic ambulant* or itinerant still, of a kind in use until surprisingly recently. There is also a good Gallo-Roman section with some handsome glass, pottery and sculpture, notably a white marble Minerva of the first century. The same ticket is valid for the Hypogée (see below) and the **Musée de Chièvres** at 9 rue V-Hugo (same hours), a rather dusty old collection of not very exciting paintings, pottery, furniture and arms.

If you still have an appetite for buildings, there's a seventh-century subterranean chapel, the **Hypogée des Dunes** at 44 rue du Père de la Croix (June–Sept Mon–Fri 2–6pm, Sat 2–4pm; Oct–May by arrangement only (☎05.49.41.07.53), and the **Pierre Levée dolmen** itself, where Rabelais came with fellow students to talk, carouse and scratch his name. Descartes, Poitiers University's other most illustrious student, was rather more serious.

Alternatively, you could take a more relaxed walk along the **riverside path** – on the right across Pont Neuf – upstream to Pont St-Cyprien. On the far bank, you can see a characteristic feature of every French provincial town: neat, well-manured *potagers* – vegetable gardens – coming down to the water's edge with a little mud quay at the end and a moored punt.

Eating, drinking and nightlife

As for **eating**, there are good opportunities for fine food whatever your culinary persuasions. If you know where to head, the town offers everything from cheap fast food to high-priced restaurants with so many recommendations you can't see in the windows for stickers. There's a good range of ethnic options if you're bored with French cuisine. If you're really keen to make your money last, you can ask for any student/youth offers that may be available at CIJ, 64 rue Gambetta, or phone ☎05.49.60.68.68.

Alain Boutin, 65 rue Carnot (☎05.49.88.25.53). A good bet for regional dishes like *cailles au pineau* (quails cooked in a brandy liqueur), with a small, carefully chosen selection; menus from 90F. Closed Sat lunch, all Sun & first half of Aug.

Bleu Sel, 40 rue Moulin à Sel. A good range of salads and sandwiches at affordable prices. Mon–Sat noon–3pm & 7–11pm, Sun 6–10pm.

Les Bons Enfants, 11 bis rue Cloche-Perse (☎05.49.41.49.82). Good value for money; lunchtime menu at 67F on weekdays, evenings 111F and 145F. Closed Sun & Mon.

Le Cappuccino, 5 rue de l'Université (☎05.49.88.27.39) One of a number of Italian restaurants in this area with menus starting at 57F. Closed Sun eve & Mon.

Conforme Moderne, 185 Faubourg du Pont-Neuf (☎05.49.46.12.25) just over the Pont Neuf. French and Moroccan food in café connected to an exhibition centre and record store. Tues–Sat 2–7pm.

Le Poitevin, 76 rue Carnot (☎05.49.88.35.04). Regional food at decent prices, in an exaggeratedly "rustic" interior. Menus from 95F. Closed Sun.

Le St-Hilaire, 65 rue Théophraste-Renaudot (☎05.49.41.15.45). In a magnificent medieval cellar with stained glass and ancient columns – an extraordinary place to dine, and less expensive than it looks; a lunchtime menu at 95F, evening menus from 99F. Closed Sun.

Le St Nicholas, 7 rue Carnot (☎05.49.41.44.48). Actually in small traffic-free lane off rue Carnot, meaning you can eat outside peacefully. Traditional food served with a contemporary feel. Menus 89F and 119F. Closed Wed.

Futuroscope

Poitiers's best–known attraction is the giant high-tech film theme park called **Futuroscope: Le Parc Européen de l'Image**, 8km north of the city, a collection of virtual-reality rides which draw lookers-on into the action on screen, with the result that you feel you're flying, being flung around, rocketing down a ski slope or catapulting through the solar system in a vertigo-inducing 3-D nightmare. Not for those with fragile constitutions.

The futuristic **cinema pavilions** are set in several acres of greenery around a series of undulating lakes. The fifteen screens take some getting around, with plenty of walking between them, so arrive early to beat the huge queues. To see everything in the park in one day, with time off for lunch, takes about ten exhausting hours, and as well as seeing the screen entertainment, you've got to give yourself time to ride the oversized floating bicycles on the park's lakes. To orientate yourself, head first for **La Gyrotour** where a lift takes you to the top of the high rotating tower and you can get the full effect of the futuristic scenario.

All the films are in French, with English commentaries on headphones often available, but as these are not very effective, and as it's the visual impact that's most important anyway, it's better to do without; recommended screenings are listed below. Apart from the films, there's a **laser** show La Symphonie des Eaux, a display of music, colour and effects focused on the park's dancing fountains (April–Oct Sat 10.30pm, plus daily shows July to early Sept 10.30pm).

The park's opening hours vary with the seasons (daily: July & Aug 9am till end of laser show; Sept–June 9am–6pm; ☎05.49.49.30.80), and the only public **transport** to the park is the #17 bus from Poitiers' Hôtel de Ville, which runs twice a day during school term-time. A system of taxi shuttles from Poitiers' gare SNCF, with specific leaving and return times, is the best option (40F per person; you must book your return in advance). **Tickets** are valid for one or two days (one-day pass adult 185F, child aged

5–16 150F; two-day pass 335/275F); to avoid queues at the park, you can purchase tickets in advance from a booth at Poitiers' gare SNCF. **Food** is predictably expensive inside the park, with even a humble sandwich costing over the odds; a picnic lunch can cut costs substantially. There are various deals available that include admission plus a wide selection of accommodation on site, the cheapest of which costs 400F for an adult in a four-bed room.

The presentations – a selection

Le Cinéma 360°. Spain's contribution to Seville Expo '92 is now housed here permanently.

Le Cinéma Dynamique. You literally have to hang onto your seat for this one: a fast and thrilling ride as the seats move in sync with the images on the screen, among them a car chase through narrow streets and a host of unexpected traps in a haunted house.

Cyber Avenue. To keep the computer kids busy – 72 multi–media kiosks with virtual games and video games.

Imax Solido. The screen within a dome in conjunction with 3-D vision glasses gives a breathtaking view of life under the ocean, visions so engulfing and believable that you feel you could reach out and touch them.

Le Pavillon de Communication. A high-tech system of projection fires multiple images in rapid succession and attempts to tell the story of human communication. Dizzy-making.

Le Pavillon du Futuroscope. Using holographic images, a robot tells the story of the universe and its atoms.

Le Pavillon de Vienne. Moving seats parade before a huge wall of multiple images patchworking into a film on the region, which also tells the story of Futuroscope.

Paysages d'Europe. Very slow – for a change – and good for the faint-hearted and those in need of a rest, as a boat floats serenely past images of the continent.

Le Tapis Magique. Probably the most stunning presentation, with a vast screen in front of you, and another under your feet, creating the incredible feeling that you're flying to Mexico on a giant Monarch butterfly.

Chauvigny

Twenty-three kilometres east of Poitiers, **CHAUVIGNY** is a busy market town on the banks of the Vienne with half a dozen porcelain factories and lumber mills providing work for the area. Overlooking the bustling *ville basse*, the old town boasts five medieval castles whose imposing ruins stand atop a precipitous rock spur, but its pride and joy are the sculpted capitals in the Romanesque **church of St-Pierre**. Take rue du Château from the central **place de la Poste**, winding up the spur past the ruins of the **Château Baronnial**, which belonged to the bishops of Poitiers, and the better-preserved **Château d'Harcourt**, before you come to the attractive and unusual east end of St-Pierre.

Inside, the church is damp and in poor repair, but the choir capitals are a visual treat. Each one is different, evoking a terrifying, nightmarish world. Graphically illustrated monsters – bearded, moustached, winged, scaly, human-headed with manes of flame – grab hapless mortals – naked, upside down and puny – and rip their bowels and crunch their heads. The only escape offered is in the naively serene events of the nativity. On the second capital on the south side of the choir, for instance, the angel Gabriel announces Christ's birth to the shepherds, their flock represented by four sheep that look like Pooh's companion Eeyore, while just around the corner the archangel Michael weighs souls in hand-held scales and a devil tries to grab one for his dinner. The oddest scene is on the north side: a Siamese-twin dancer grips the hind legs of two horse-like monsters that are gnawing his upper arms. You get a strong feeling that here was an artist who came from the same peasant background as his audience, prey to the same fears of things that went bump in the night or lurked in the wet woods.

If you can manage it, making your visit coincide with the Saturday **market** gives an extra dimension to a day-trip here. Held between the church of Notre-Dame and the river, it offers a mouthwatering selection of food – oysters, prawns, crayfish, cheeses galore and pâtés in aspic. The cafés are fun, too, bursting with noisy wine-flushed farmers mixing business with pleasure.

If you want to **stay** overnight, *Le Lion d'Or*, 8 rue du Marché (☎05.49.46.30.28, fax 05.49.47.74.28; ③; closed mid-Dec to Feb; restaurant with menus from 85F), is comfortable enough. Chauvigny also has a **municipal campsite**, just east of the centre on rue de la Fontaine (☎05.49.46.31.94; fax 05.49.46.40.60).

St-Savin

You need to get an early start from Poitiers if you want to make a single day-trip by public transport to see both Chauvigny and **ST-SAVIN**, which is scarcely more than a hamlet in comparison with bustling Chauvigny.

The bus sets you down beside the abbey near the modern bridge over the poplar-lined River Gartempe; walk downstream a little way to the medieval bridge for a perfect view of the **abbey church**, now listed as a UNESCO monument of universal importance (Feb–Sept daily 9am–5pm; Oct & Nov daily 2–5pm; Dec & Jan Sat & Sun 9am–5pm). Built in the eleventh century, possibly on the site of a church founded by Charlemagne, it rises strong and severe above the gazebos, vegetable gardens and lichened tile roofs of the houses at its feet. Inside, steps descend to the narthex and from there to the floor of the nave, stretching out to the raised choir: high, narrow, barrel-vaulted and flanked by bare round columns, their capitals deeply carved with interlacing foliage. The whole of the vault is covered with paintings. The colours are few – red and yellow ochres, green mixed with white and black. Yet the paintings are full of light and grace, depicting scenes from the stories of Genesis and Exodus. Some are instantly recognizable: Noah's three-decked ark, Pharaoh's horses rearing at the engulfing waves of the Red Sea, graceful workers constructing the Tower of Babel.

If you do get caught in St-Savin, the *Hôtel du Midi* on the main road (☎05.49.48.00.40; ②; closed Jan) is a delightful place to stay, with a good restaurant serving menus from 70F (closed Jan, Sun eve & Mon except in July & Aug). There's a municipal **campsite** too (☎05.49.48.18.02, fax 05.49.48.28.56; closed Sept 16– May 19).

Parthenay and around

Directly west of Poitiers, and served by regular SNCF buses, stands the attractive small town of **PARTHENAY**, once an important staging point on the pilgrim routes to Compostela and now the site of a major **cattle market** every Wednesday. It's not a place to make a special detour for, but it's worth a stopover if you're heading north to Brittany or west to the sea.

Parthenay has nothing very remarkable to see, though its medieval heart is quite interesting. The main part of town – essentially the medieval core, and fairly restricted in area at that – lies to the west, towards the River Thouet. Rue Jean-Jaurès and rue de la Saunerie cut in through the largely pedestrian shopping precinct to the Gothic **Porte de l'Horloge**, the fortified gateway to the old citadel on a steep-sided neck of land above a loop of the Thouet.

Through the gateway, on rue de la Citadelle, the attractively simple Romanesque **church of Ste-Croix** faces the mairie across a small garden with a view over the ramparts and the **gully of St-Jacques**, with its medieval houses and vegetable plots climbing the opposite slope. Further along rue de la Citadelle is a house where Cardinal Richelieu used to visit his grandfather, and then a handsome but badly damaged Romanesque door, all that remains of the castle chapel of **Notre-Dame-de-la-Couldre**. Of the **castle** itself, practically nothing is left: from the tip of the spur where it once stood you look down on the twin-towered **gateway** and the **Pont St-Jacques**, a thirteenth-century bridge through which the nightly flocks of pilgrims poured into the town for shelter and security. To reach it, turn left under the Tour de l'Horloge and down the **Vaux St-Jacques**, as this medieval lane is called. It is highly evocative of that period, with its crooked half-timbered dwellings crowding up to the bridge. They are only now beginning to be restored. Some look as if they have received little attention since the last pilgrim shuffled up the street.

Practicalities

Finding your way around is easy. From the **gare SNCF**, avenue de Gaulle leads directly west to the central square, with the **tourist office** on the right-hand corner (Mon–Sat 9.30am–12.30pm & 2–6pm; ☎05.49.64.24.24, fax 05.49.94.61.94). If you're after shelter, a very reasonable **hotel** by the main square is *Grand Hôtel*, 85 bd Meilleraye (☎05.49.64.00.16; ③; restaurant from 50F, closed Sat eve & Sun out of season). Another possibility is the fancier two-star *Hôtel du Nord*, 86 av de Gaulle, opposite the station (☎05.49.94.29.11; ②; restaurant from 68F; closed Sat). There is a **youth hostel** at 35F some way from the centre at 16 rue Blaise-Pascal (☎05.49.94.00.71, fax 05.49.94.64.85), with a central annexe at 115 bd Meilleraye: phone first and they will let you into the annexe. **Campers** have to head to the three-star site at **LE TALLUD** (☎05.49.94.39.52; open all year), part of the huge Base de Loisirs river-bank recreation area, about 3km west of Parthenay on the D949.

As for **eating**, Parthenay has the usual provincial range of restaurants: Italian, Tunisian and Chinese, as well as traditional French. Best of the latter is *Le Fin Gourmet*, 28 rue Ganne (☎05.49.64.04.53; closed Sun eve & Mon), where high-quality cuisine combines well with a jovial atmosphere; affordable for all, with menus from 85F, or go the whole hog at 175F.

Around Parthenay

There are three more beautiful Romanesque churches you might like to see within easy reach of Parthenay. One – with a sculpted facade depicting a mounted knight hawking – is only a twenty-minute walk on the Niort road, at **PARTHENAY-LE-VIEUX**. The others are at **AIRVAULT**, 20km northeast of Parthenay and easily accessible on the Parthenay–Thouars SNCF bus route, and **ST-JOUIN-DE-MARNES**, 9km northeast of Airvault (you'll have to hitch or walk that). Or, you could go on north to **THOUARS** to see the abbey church of St-Laon, 21km from Airvault or 16km from St-Jouin (cheap hotels and *camping municipal*), and combine St-Jouin with a visit to the sixteenth-century **Château d'Oiron**, 8.5km northwest of St-Jouin.

Niort

NIORT is a stopover rather than a destination, particularly convenient if your goal is the Marais Poitevin, the so-called "Green Venice" (see p.554). In itself Niort is a pleasant morning's stroll and, if you're in a car, probably the best place to stay. If you're on foot, it's the last place before the marshes to get a really wide choice of provisions.

The most interesting part of the town is the mainly pedestrian area around **rue Victor-Hugo** and **rue St-Jean**, full of stone-fronted or half-timbered medieval houses. Coming from the gare SNCF, take rue de la Gare as far as avenue de Verdun with the tourist office and main post office on the corner, then turn right into place de la Brèche. Rue Ricard leaves the square on the left; rue Victor-Hugo is its continuation, following the line of the medieval market in a gully separating the two small hills on which Niort is built. Up to the right, opposite the end of rue St-Jean, is the old **town hall**, a triangular building of the early sixteenth century with lantern, belfry and ornamental machicolations, perhaps capable of repelling drunken revellers but no match for catapult or sledgehammer.

At the end of the street is the river, the **Sèvre Niortaise**, not to be confused with the Sèvre Nantaise which flows northwards to join the Loire at Nantes. There are gardens and trees along the bank and, over the bridge, the ruins of a glove factory, the last vestige of Niort's once thriving leather industry. At the time of the Revolution, it kept more than thirty cavalry regiments in breeches. Today Niort's biggest industry is insurance: the most bourgeois town in France, so it is said, because of the prosperity brought by the large number of major insurance firms making their headquarters here. Accordingly, restaurants are usually packed at lunchtime, and well-heeled shoppers throng the pedestrianized streets, giving a fairly lively – if affluent – feel.

Just downstream, opposite a riverside car park, is the **market hall** (with a café doing a good cheap lunch) and, beyond, vast and unmistakable on a slight rise, the keep of a **castle** begun by Henry II of England. Now housing a **museum** (daily except Tues 9am–noon & 2–5/6pm; 17F, free Wed), it displays mainly local furniture and an extraordinary variety of costumes that were still commonly worn in the villages until the beginning of the twentieth century.

If you want to see the surrounding Marais area, the most pleasurable way is by bike – it's completely flat and small enough to pretty well cover in three days.

Practicalities

The excellent **tourist office** on place de la Poste (July–Sept Mon–Fri 9.30am–7pm, Sat 10am–5pm, Sun 10am–1pm; Oct–June Mon–Fri 9.30–6pm, Sat 9.30am–noon; ☎05.49.24.18.79, fax 05.49.24.98.90) has plenty of information about walking itineraries around the Marais. It also offers a free room reservation service (☎05.49.24.98.92); for more rustic accommodation in the Marais itself, contact Relais des Gîtes Ruraux, at 15 rue Thiers (☎05.49.24.00.42). The **gare SNCF** is on rue Mazagran and has **bicycles** for rental. Beware that the gare has no *consigne automatique*, charging a hefty 30F for each piece of left luggage. **Buses** leave from the **gare routière**, just off place de la Brèche on rue Viala. If you need money, there's an **exchange facility** at Société Générale, rue Ricard (Mon–Fri 8.30am–5pm).

There's the usual crop of **hotels** close to the station including the *Terminus*, 82 rue de la Gare (☎05.49.24.00.38, fax 05.49.24.94.38; ①). The latter has an excellent restaurant, *La Poêle d'Or*, with menus from 55 to 180F. More centrally, the *St-Jean*, 21 av St-Jean-d'Angély (☎05.49.79.20.76; ②), is another good bet for cheap, comfortable rooms, while several more upmarket hotels cluster on avenue de Paris, including *Le Paris*, at no. 12 (☎05.49.24.93.78, fax 05.49.28.27.57; ③), and the three-star *Grand Hôtel*, at no. 32 (☎05.49.24.22.21, fax 05.49.24.42.41; ④). The three-star **campsite** *de Noron* (☎05.49.79.05.06; Feb–Sept) is on bd S-Allende next door to the stadium; bus #6 from place de la Brèche.

Two **restaurants** to head for are *Les Quatre Saisons* on 247 av de la Rochelle (☎05.49.79.41.06; closed Sun), for traditional Marais Poitevin specialities (menus from 59F), and, for lunches, *Sucrée Salée*, at 2 rue du Temple, which specializes in tarts and crumbles *à l'anglaise* (from 69F).

The Marais Poitevin

The **Marais Poitevin** is a strange, lazy landscape of fens and meadows, shielded by poplar trees and crisscrossed by an elaborate system of canals, dykes and slow-flowing rivers. Recently declared a National Park, the French know it as "La Venise Verte"

– Green Venice – and a tourist industry of sorts has been developing around the villages. But the marshes are not yet dead and the flat-bottomed punts remain the principal means of transport for many farmers – indeed there's no dry-land access to many of the fields. Be sure to avoid weekends, when evidence of the coming transformation is all too clear.

Access to the eastern edge of the marsh is easiest at the whitewashed village of **COULON**, on the River Sèvre, just 11km from Niort by bike or occasional bus. As you would expect in a marshland village, Coulon's houses are small, low and obviously poor. Punts, with or without a guide, can be rented here by the half-day at 6 rue de l'Église (☎05.49.35.02.29) – fun on a sunny day with a picnic.

There are two **hotels** in the village, both likely to be full in season: the family-run *Central*, 4 rue d'Autremont (☎05.49.35.90.20, fax 05.49.35.81.07; ③; closed mid-Jan to early Feb, plus Sun & Mon late-Sept to mid-Oct), and the pricey *au Marais*, 46–48 quai Louis Tardiy (☎05.49.25.90.43, fax 05.49.35.81.98; ④; closed late Dec to late Jan). If you're **camping**, there is the attractively sited *Camping Venise Verte* (☎05.49.35.90.36) in a meadow about 2km downstream (a 25min walk), or the *Camping Municipal la Niquière* (☎05.49.35.81.19; April to mid-Sept), north of Coulon on the road to Benet. The best **eating** option here is the regional cuisine of *Le Central*'s characterful restaurant; with generous servings, a well-deserved reputation and a menu from 96F, you would be wise to book.

For getting around the Marais by **bike**, La Bicyclette Verte, in rue du Coursault (☎05.49.35.42.56) in **ARÇAIS**, a village 10km west of Coulon, is an excellent place from which to rent one; they also have children's bikes and tandems. If you're walking the marshes, it's best to stick to the lanes since cross-country routes tend to end in fields surrounded by water and you have to backtrack continually. Once you're away from the riverside road from Coulon to Arçais, there's practically no traffic, just meadows and cows. At the seaward end of the marsh – the area south of **LUÇON** – the landscape changes, becoming all straight lines and open fields of wheat and sunflowers. The villages cap low mounds that were once islands.

LA ROCHELLE, THE COAST AND THE ISLANDS

The coast around **La Rochelle** – especially the islands – is great for young families, with miles of safe sandy beaches and shallow water. Beware, however, that in August, unless you're camping or have booked something in advance, accommodation is a near-insuperable problem. Out of season you can't rely on sunny weather, but that shouldn't deter you if you like the slightly melancholy romance of quiet misty seascapes and working fishing ports. La Rochelle and **Royan** in the south are the best bases, and are both served by train. Away from these centres – if you're not driving – you'll have to take potluck with the rather quirky bus routes.

Les Sables-d'Olonne and around

The area around **LES SABLES-D'OLONNE** and northwards has been heavily developed with Costa-style apartment blocks. If you're passing through, though, there's a surprisingly good modern art section in the **Musée de l'Abbaye Ste-Croix** on rue Verdun (☎02.51.32.01.16; mid-June to mid-Sept daily except Mon 10am–noon & 2–6.30pm; Oct–June guided visits by arrangement only; 30F, free Sun) and an **automobile museum**, 8km southeast of town on the road to Talmont (mid-March to June &

Sept daily 9.30am–noon & 2–6pm; July & Aug daily 9.30am–7pm;Oct to mid-March
Sat & Sun only 30am–noon & 2–6pm; 36F). The main reason to stay, though, is the
town's vast curve of clean, beautiful **beach**, which lures hordes in the summer.

Hotels get booked up well in advance for July and August, but a couple worth trying are *Le Merle Blanc*, near the beach at 59 av Aristide-Briand (☎02.51.32.00.35; ②),
and *Hôtel les Olonnes*, 25 rue de la Patrie (☎02.51.32.04.12, fax 02.51.23.72.63; ②; restaurant closed Sun eve & Mon). Budget options include a beachside HI **youth hostel**, 3km
from the centre at 92 rue du Sémaphore (☎02.51.95.76.21, fax 02.40.20.08.94;
April–Sept), a bus line #2 ride away in the direction of "Côte Sauvage" (stop
Armandèche); a municipal **campsite** (☎02.51.95.10.42, fax 02.51.33.94.04; April–Nov)
on rue des Roses, 400m from the beach; and several more campsites in the Pironnière
district, 3km south of town on the D949. For more accommodation options, ask at the
tourist office on rue du Maréchal Leclerc (daily Sept–June 9am–12.15 & 2–6.30pm,
Sun 10am–12.30pm; July & Aug 9am–7pm; ☎02.51.32.03.28, fax 02.51.32.84.49).

Les Épesses

Some 80km inland from Les Sables (on the N160 if you're driving), at the ruined **Château
du Puy du Fou** in the village of **LES ÉPESSES**, a remarkable lakeside extravaganza
happens during the summer months (June–Aug Fri & Sat 10pm; 1hr 45min; 120F;
☎02.54.64.11.11 – booking essential). This is a weird affair: the enactment of the life of a
local peasant from the Middle Ages to World War II, complete with fireworks, lasers,
dances on the lake and Comédie Française voice-overs. The story, summarized in a brief
English text, is interesting but incidental – the spectacle is the thing. The château also
houses a museum on life in the Vendée (Tues–Sun 10am–noon and 2–6/7pm).

To get to Les Épesses by public transport, you'll need to get to **CHOLET** (reasonably
connected by train) and take a bus south from there; Puy du Fou itself is 2.5km from Les
Épesses, on the D27 to **CHAMBRETAUD**. There is one reasonably priced hotel in Les
Épesses called *Le Lion d'Or*, 2 rue de la Libération (☎02.51.57.30.01;③) and a wider
choice (*Relais*, *Le Centre* or *Chez Camille;* all price bracket ②) 10km west at **LES HER-
BIERS**.

The Île de Noirmoutier

The twenty-kilometre-long **Île de Noirmoutier** was an early monastic settlement of the
seventh century; now it has bowed to pilgrims of a different type, serving as a relatively
plush tourist resort, though it has been spared the high-rise development of the adjoining coast. Although tourism is the island's main economy, it doesn't dominate everything. Salt marshes here are still worked, spring potatoes sown and fishes fished. The
island can be reached in three hours by bus from Les Sables, and is connected to the
shore by a toll bridge.

The island town, **NOIRMOUTIER-EN-L'ÎLE**, is a low-key type of place but still has
a twelfth-century **castle**, a **church** with a Romanesque crypt, an excellent **market**
(Tues & Fri) and most of the island's **nightlife** in the form of piano bars with longer-
than-usual café hours. There are **campsites** dotted around the island – maps from the
tourist office (☎02.51.39.80.71, fax 02.51.39.53.16) on the main road from the bridge at
MARMATRE. **Bike rental** is from Vel-hop, 55 av Joseph-Pineau in Noirmoutier, or
Charier, 23 av Joseph Pineau. Among hotels to try in the town are *Le Bois de la Chaize*,
23 av de la Victoire (☎02.51.39.04.62, fax 02.51.39.11.89; ②), *Hôtel Les Capucines*, 38 av
de la Victoire (☎02.51.39.06.82, fax 02.51.39.33.10; ②; closed mid-Nov to mid-Feb; nice
restaurant from 72F), and the *Hôtel Goéland*, 15 route du Gois in **BARBÂTRE**
(☎02.51.39.68.66; ②; closed mid-Nov to Jan; restaurant from 75F), in the south of the
island.

As for exploring the island, the western coast, with its great curves of sand, resembles the mainland, while the northern side dips in and out of little bays with rocky promontories between. Inland, were it not for the saltwater dykes, the horizon would suggest that you were far away from the sea. It is a strange place with only one hostile element apart from the storms in spring – a vicious mosquito population. The more southerly resorts, though built-up, have not been the main targets for the developers. In the village centres there are still the one-storey houses that you see throughout La Vendée and southern Brittany – whitewashed and ochre-tiled with decorative brickwork around the windows and S- or Z-shaped coloured bars on the shutters.

La Rochelle

LA ROCHELLE is the most attractive and unspoilt seaside town in France. Thanks to the foresight of 1970s mayor Michel Crépeau, its historic seventeenth- to eighteenth-century centre and waterfront were plucked from the clutches of the developers and its streets freed of traffic for the delectation of pedestrians. A real shock-horror outrage at the time, the policy has become standard practice for preserving old town centres across the country – more successful than Crépeau's picturesque yellow bicycle plan, designed to relieve the traffic problem (see p.558).

La Rochelle has a long history, as you would expect of such a sheltered Atlantic port, and the inevitable English connection. Eleanor of Aquitaine gave it a charter in 1199,

which released it from its feudal obligations, and it rapidly became a port of major importance, trading in salt and wine and skilfully exploiting the Anglo-French quarrels. The Wars of Religion, however, were particularly destructive for La Rochelle. It turned Protestant and, because of its strategic importance, drew the remorseless enmity of Cardinal Richelieu, who laid siege to it in 1627. To the dismay of the townspeople, who reasoned that no-one could effectively blockade seasoned mariners like themselves, he succeeded in sealing the harbour approaches with a dyke. The English dispatched the Duke of Buckingham to their aid, but he was caught napping on the Île de Ré and badly defeated. By the end of 1628 Richelieu had starved the city into submission. Out of the pre-siege population of 28,000, only 5000 survived. The walls were demolished and the city's privileges revoked. La Rochelle later became the principal port for trade with the French colonies in the Caribbean Antilles and Canada. Indeed, many of the settlers, especially in Canada, came from this part of France.

Arrival, information and transport

Finding your way around La Rochelle is straightforward. Arriving at the elaborate **gare SNCF** on bd Joffre, take av de Gaulle opposite to reach the town centre; on the left as you reach the waterfront you'll see the efficient **tourist office**, on quai de Gabut (June & Sept Mon–Sat 9am–7pm, Sun 11am–5pm; July & Aug Mon–Sat 9am–8pm, Sun 11am–5pm; Oct–May Mon–Sat 9am–12.30pm & 2–6pm, Sun 10.30am–12.30pm; ☎05.46.41.14.68, fax 05.46.41.99.85), which dispenses excellent **maps,** some of which you may have to pay for. Most things you'll want to see are in the area behind the waterfront; in effect, between the harbour and the place de Verdun, where the **gare routière** and the bus terminal for Autoplus, the town's efficient **public transport** system, are located. There is another local bus terminal at 44 cours des Dames. The town's other attractions, including an **aquarium** and an **alternative beach**, about 2km south of the centre at Les Minimes, reached by bus #10 from place Verdun or by the more entertaining **bus de mer**, a small boat which runs from the old port to Port des Minimes, stopping off at av Marillac en route (April–June & Sept Sat & Sun hourly 10am–7pm except 1pm; July & Aug half-hourly 10am–11pm except 1pm; Oct–March hourly 10am–6pm; 10F one-way). Interîles has guided day-trips from La Rochelle to the Île d'Oléron (July–Sept 9.30am–8.15pm; 175F – doesn't include lunch; ☎05.46.50.51.88); weather and tides may affect crossings). The **CDIJ Youth Centre**, 14 rue des Gentilshommes, (☎05.46.41.16.36) has an information service, including Allostop, for young people.

Getting around

Once you've stowed your luggage, you can use **bikes** to get around: on quai du Carénage, facing restaurant-lined cours des Dames across the Vieux Port, is the free municipal **bike park**, part of the Autoplus system and heir to Michel Crépeau's original no-identity-check, no-restrictions, pick-up-and-leave scheme. You get two hours of free bike time after handing over a piece of ID; after this it's a generous 6F per hour (office open May–Sept daily 9am–12.30pm & 1.30–7pm). You can also rent bikes from the gare SNCF and from Motive Location (opposite the Maritime Museum; ☎05.46.31.03.66) **Car rental** is available from Ada/Budget, 1 av de Gaulle or Tonic Car, 16 quai Georges-Simenon. Autoplus also have a nifty **taxi system** with flat rates between any two of 46 "*bornes*" – terminal posts with a card-activated calling system, operating 24 hours. You can buy the cards and find out the inexpensive going rate at Boutique Autoplus, 5 rue de l'Aimable-Nanette, near the tourist office (Mon–Fri 9am–noon & 2–6pm, Sat 9am–noon). **Boat trips** around La Rochelle and to neighbouring islands are organized by Océcars, on Place de Verdun (☎05.46.34.02.22).

M. HUGHES, TRAVEL INK

Chenonceau, Loire Valley

The château at Vitré, Brittany

M. HUGHES, TRAVEL INK

Côte de Granit Rose, Brittany

St-Cirq-Lapopie, in the Lot Valley

Troglodyte dwelling, Saumur, Loire Valley

Lescun and its cirque

Wine shop, Cahors, Lot region

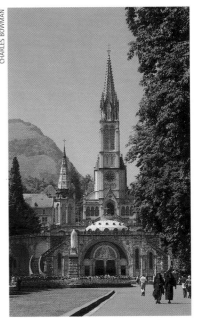

Lourdes

Cluny, Burgundy

Beynac, Dordogne

The Hôtel-Dieu, Beaune, Burgundy

Flea market, Bordeaux

Château de Hautefort, Dordogne

Accommodation

Accommodation in La Rochelle can be a bit of a problem in the summer season, so book ahead, even if you're camping. Expect to pay seaside-type prices in the hotels, especially in season. A possible alternative to hotels are self-catering apartments which abound, particularly around Les Minimes and its Village Informatique. The tourist office has a handy board of rented accommodation, and is able to reserve rooms for a 10F fee (see p.558). There's a handful of cheapies in the town centre, but be sure to book in advance from May until well into autumn.

Hotels and apartments

L'Atlantic, 23 rue Verdière, off cours des Dames (☎05.46.41.16.68, fax 05.46.21.25.69). Attractive eighteenth-century house with some studio apartments behind the waterfront. ②.

Le Bordeaux, 43 rue St-Nicolas (☎05.46.41.31.22, fax 05.46.41.24.43). Comfortable, friendly hotel in a characterful pedestrianized street between the train station and the port. ②.

Les Estuvales, Village Informatique, Les Minimes (☎05.46.45.12.34). A short walk along the seafront parkland to the beach of Les Minimes, these small modern self-catering apartments – normally occupied by university students during term-time – are good value, but a *"carte bleu"* (international student card) is required (available from the tourist office). Minimum one week rent (weekend to weekend); deposit (100F) and own bed linen required. From 1600F per week in summer.

Fasthotel, Village Informatique, Les Minimes (☎05.46.45.46.00, fax 05.46.44.72.71). Small, quiet hotel made up of modern bungalows, near the port des Minimes and the beach. ②.

de France-Angleterre et Champlain, 20 rue Rambaud (☎05.46.41.23.99, fax 05.46.41.15.19). The old, venerable half is *Le Champlain*; and the new Great Western addition is the *France-Angleterre*; both what you'd expect from a modern and an old-fashioned three-star; close to the extensive parklands. ④.

François I, 15 rue Bazoges (☎05.46.41.28.46, fax 05.46.41.35.01). Historic building with a walled courtyard. ②.

Frantour St-Nicolas, 13 rue Sardinerie (☎05.46.41.71.55, fax 05.46.41.70.46). A very attractive modernized hotel in a pretty street 2min from the harbour. ④.

Henri IV, 31 rue des Gentilshommes (☎05.46.41.25.79, fax 05.46.41.78.64). Excellent and very popular hotel right in the town centre on place de la Caille close to the harbourfront. ②.

de l'Océan, 36 cours des Dames (☎05.46.41.31.97, fax 05.46.41.51.12). Comfortable two-star air-conditioned rooms in an enviable position, many with views of the port. ②.

Le Printania, 9 rue Brave-Rondeau (☎05.46.41.22.86, fax 05.46.35.19.58). Pleasant, unpretentious and central place in a peaceful street. ②.

La Tour de Nesle, 2 quai Louis-Durand (☎05.46.41.05.86, fax 05.46.41.95.17). A large comfortable old hotel, right in the middle of things. ③.

Youth hostel and campsites

HI youth hostel, av des Minimes (☎05.46.44.43.11, fax 05.46.45.41.48). A big modern hostel overlooking the marina at Port des Minimes, 10min walk from the beach, shops and restaurants. Self-service restaurant and bar. Wise to book in summer, especially at weekends. Catch bus #10 from place de Verdun, or walk from the train station, following the signs to the left. When you get to the roundabout by the Musée Maritime, don't follow the sign to the left. Go straight ahead across the grass past a huge modern building with a distinctive sloping roof, then turn left on the Avenue Marillac and carry on until you meet the next crossroads where av des Minimes cuts through.

Camping Municipal de Port-Neuf, on the northwest side of town (☎05.46.43.81.20) Take bus #6 from Grosse Horloge, direction "Port-Neuf".

Camping Le Soleil, Port des Minimes (☎05.46.44.42.53). Near to the hostel. Take bus #10 from place Verdun to Les Minimes. Closed Sept–May.

The town

The **Vieux Port** is very much the focus of the town, with pleasure boats moored in serried ranks in front of the two impressive towers guarding the entrance to the port. Leading north from the **Porte de la Grosse Horloge**, the **rue du Palais** runs towards the cathedral and several of the museums on rue Thiers. Between the harbour and the **Port des Minimes**, a new marina development 2km south of the town centre, there are several excellent museums for children and a large frigate (permanently moored) providing some insight into the town's seagoing past.

The Vieux Port

Dominating the inner harbour, the heavy Gothic gateway of the **Porte de la Grosse Horloge** straddles the entrance to the old town. The quays in front are too full of traffic to encourage loitering; for that, it's best to head out along the tree-lined cours des Dames towards the fourteenth-century **Tour de la Chaine** (daily: April–Sept 10am–7pm; Oct–March 10am–12.30pm & 2–5.30pm; 25F June–Sept, otherwise free), so called because of the heavy chain that was slung from here across to the opposite tower, **Tour St-Nicolas**, to close the harbour at night. Today the only night-time intruders are likely to be yachties from across the Channel, whose craft far outnumber the working boats – mainly garishly painted trawlers. Beyond the tower, steps climb up to **rue Sur-les-Murs**, which follows the top of the old sea wall to a third tower, the **Tour de la Lanterne** or Tour des Quatre Sergents, named after four sergeants imprisoned and executed for defying the Restoration monarchy in 1822 (same times and prices as at Tour de la Chaine). There's a way up onto what's left of the **city walls**, planted with unkempt greenery. Beyond is the beach, backed by casino, hot-dog stands and amusement booths, along with an extensive, truly beautiful belt of park that continues up the western edge of the town centre and along the avenue du Mail behind the beach, where the first seaside village was built by the Rochelais rich.

The rue du Palais and around

The real charm of La Rochelle lies on the city's main shopping street, **rue du Palais**, leading up from the Vieux Port. Lining the street are eighteenth-century houses, some grey stone, some half-timbered, with distinctive Rochelais-style slates overlapped like fish scales, while the shop fronts are set back beneath the ground-floor arcades. Among the finest are the **Hôtel de la Bourse** – actually the Chamber of Commerce – and the **Palais de Justice** with its colonnaded facade, both on the left-hand side. A few metres further on, in **rue des Augustins**, there is another grandiose affair built for a wealthy Rochelais in 1555, the so-called **Maison Henri II**, complete with loggia, gallery and slated turrets, where the regional tourist board has its offices. Place de Verdun itself is dull and characterless, with an uninspiring, humpbacked eighteenth-century classical **cathedral** on the corner. Its only redeeming feature is the marvellously opulent Belle Époque **Café de la Paix**, all mirrors, gilt and plush, where La Rochelle's ladies of means come to sip lemon tea and nibble daintily at sticky cakes. And there is a tempting *charcuterie* and seafood shop next door.

To the west or left of rue du Palais, especially in **rue de l'Escale**, paved with granite setts brought back from Canada as ballast in the Rochelais cargo vessels, you get

---

LA ROCHELLE MUSEUMS

If you intend to get around a number of La Rochelle's excellent **museums**, a 39F ticket covers the Nouveau Monde, the Orbigny-Bernon and the Beaux-Arts, as well as two more not listed here – the Histoire Naturelle and the Musée Océanographique.

the discreet residences of the eighteenth-century shipowners and chandlers, veiling their wealth with high walls and classical restraint. A rather less modest gentleman had installed himself on the corner of **rue Fromentin**: a seventeenth-century doctor who adorned his house front with the statues of famous medical men – Hippocrates, Galen and others. In rue St-Côme closer to the town walls is the **Musée d'Orbigny-Bernon** (Mon & Wed–Sat 10am–noon & 2–6pm, Sun 2–6pm; 19F), with an extensive section on local history, important collections of local faïence, porcelain from China and Japan and some handsome furniture.

East of rue du Palais, and also starting out from place des Petits-Bancs, rue du Temple takes you up alongside the **Hôtel de Ville**, protected by a decorative but seriously fortified wall. It was begun around 1600 in the reign of Henri IV, whose initials, intertwined with those of Marie de Médicis, are carved on the ground-floor gallery. It's a beautiful specimen of Frenchified Italian taste, adorned with niches and statues and coffered ceilings, all done in a stone the colour of ripe barley. And if you feel like quiet contemplation of these seemingly more gracious times, there's no better place for it than the terrace of the *Café de la Poste*, right next to the post office, in the small, traffic-free square outside. For more relaxed vernacular architecture nearly as ancient, carry on up rue des Merciers, the other main shopping area, to the cramped and noisy **market square**, close to which you'll find the **Musée du Nouveau Monde** (Mon & Wed–Sat 10.30am–12.30pm & 1.30–6pm, Sun 3–6pm; 19F), whose entrance is in rue Fleuriau. Out of the ordinary, this museum occupies the former residence of the Fleuriau family, rich shipowners and traders who, like many of their fellow Rochelais, made fortunes out of the slave trade and Caribbean sugar, spices and coffee. There is a fine collection of prints, paintings and photos of the old West Indian plantations; seventeenth- and eighteenth-century maps of America; photogravures of Native Americans from around 1900, with incredible names like Piopio Maksmaks Wallawalla and Lawyer Nez Percé; and an interesting display of aquatint illustrations for Marmontel's novel *Les Incas* – an amazing mixture of sentimentality and coy salaciousness. Nearby in rue Gargoulleau is the **Musée des Beaux-Arts** (daily except Tues 2–5pm; 18F), whose works are centred around a few Rochelais artists and illustrate the history of art from the Primitives to the present day.

Back towards the port, from the maze of pedestrianized streets around the Hôtel de Ville, head down rue St-Sauveur, with its large gloomy church, across quai Maubec and quai Louis-Durand to **rue St-Nicolas** and adjoining **place de la Fourche** with its huge shady tree and outdoor café – both pedestrianized and boasting several antiques dealers, second-hand bookshops and a vintage clothes shop. The two streets share a Saturday flea/antiques **market**.

Towards Port des Minimes

On the east side of the old harbour behind the Tour St-Nicolas is the **quartier du Gabut**, the one-time fishermen's quarter of wooden cabins and sheds, now converted into bars, shops and eating places. Beyond it lies an extensive dock and the market and service buildings of the old fishing port. This is now the **Musée Maritime** (daily: April–Sept 10am–7pm; Oct–March 2–6pm; 45F), which includes an interesting collection of superannuated vessels as well as land-based exhibits. A further ten-minute walk brings you to the **Musée des Automates** (daily: June–Aug 9.30am–7pm; Sept–May 10am–noon & 2–6pm; 40F)on rue de la Désirée, a fascinating collection of three hundred automated puppets, drawing you into an irresistible fantasy world. Some of the puppets are interesting from a historical angle; others, like one that writes the name "Pierrot", are interesting from a mechanical viewpoint. Further down the same street is the **Musée des Modèles Réduits** (same hours & prices as the Automates, joint ticket for both museums 65F). The prices may be a bit prohibitive for families – especially considering the whole tour takes barely half-an-hour – but this does combine well with a visit to the neighbouring Musée des Automates. Scale models of every variety and era are on show, starting with cars and including models of a submerged shipwreck and La Rochelle train station.

The **Port des Minimes** is a large modern marina development with mooring for thousands of yachts, about 2km south of the old harbour or thirty minutes' walk along the waterside. There are shops, restaurants, bars and apartments. The young and beautiful flock out here at weekends and on summer evenings to sun and parade on the beautiful **plage des Minimes**. Right beside it are the high-tech **Aquarium** (daily: April–June 9am–7pm; July & Aug 9am–11pm; Sept–March 10am–noon & 2–7pm; 42F), with species from around the world.

Eating, drinking and nightlife

For **eating**, try the rue du Port/rue St-Sauveur area just off the waterfront, or the attractive rue St-Jean-du-Pérot, which has everything from crêperies and pizzerias to expensive gourmet restaurants and several ethnic eateries including Indian and Chinese places. Particularly worth seeking out are the town's many excellent **fish restaurants**.

Le Bistrot de l'Entr'acte, 22 rue St-Jean-du Pérot (☎05.46.50.62.60). A highly regarded place with turn-of-the-century decor, little table lamps and a mainly fish and seafood *carte* of some originality; people rave about the 155F menu. Closed Sun.

Café-Resto à la Villette, 4 rue de la Forme, behind the market. Tiny, authentic place popular with locals; good *plats du jour* from 50F. Closed Sun.

à Côté de Chez Fred, 30–32 rue St-Nicolas (☎05.46.41.65.76). A characterful corner restaurant with all sorts of charming fishing and seafaring paraphernalia. A blackboard *carte* changes depending on what's in at Fred the fishmonger next door. Guaranteed to be super-fresh and mouthwatering. Small and very popular, so best to book. Fish dishes from 40F, around 100F for a full meal. Closed Sun.

La Marie-Galante, 35 av des Minimes (☎05.46.44.05.54). Pretty yellow-and-white striped awnings over the outdoor seating overlooking the yacht basin at Les Minimes. Fish of the day 55F; generous menus from 80F. Its three neighbours are also good value.

Pub Lutèce, rue St-Sauveur. Reasonably priced brasserie with outdoor tables.

Les Pyramides, 59 rue St-Jean-du-Pérot. Serves a mixture of expensive Egyptian and Greek food in bright, pleasant surroundings.

Richard Coutanceau, plage de la Concurrence (☎05.46.41.48.19). Expensive certainly, but it is a veritable palace of gastronomic excellence, renowned for its fish and seafood and specialities. On the seafront just to the west of the old harbour. Menus at 220F and 410F.

Le St-Sauveur, 24 rue St-Sauveur (☎05.46.41.18.16). Opposite the old Protestant church, an unpretentious restaurant with good fish dishes (68–98F à la carte), particularly the fish soup entrée; good for families, with a fish tank filled with tropical types providing some entertainment for bored children. Menus 68F, 98F and 128F. Closed Sun, & Mon evening out of season.

La Solette, place de la Fourche, off rue St-Nicolas (☎05.40.41.74.45; closed Jan, Feb, & Sun off season). A pleasant little restaurant on a pretty square with menus from 59F and *plats* from 55F.

Teatro Bettini, 3 rue Thiers (☎05.46.41.07.03). Crowded noisy pizzeria (46–50F pizzas, many with delicious seafood toppings) with upbeat pink decor. Air-conditioning and *gelati* to beat the heat. Also pasta (35–48F) and fish. Closed Sun & Mon lunchtimes.

Bars and nightlife

Popular daytime **bars** to hang out at here include the dark and down-to-earth wine bar *Cave de la Guignette* at 8 rue St-Nicolas, the numerous brasseries round the old harbour, and the *Lou-Foc* next to the tourist office in quartier du Gabut.

To find out what's going on where **nightlife** is concerned, pick up the three-weekly *Sortir* from the tourist office, with theatre, cinema, and mainstream and classical music listings. Otherwise, head for the rue St-Nicolas for nightlife; many bars line the streets, some offering **live music** and most with a lively atmosphere. An older crowd heads for rue des Templiers, where you'll find the *Piano Pub*, the *Mayflower*, the *St-James* and the *Académie de la Bière*. **Nightclubs** worth checking out include *L'Oxford*, plage de la Concurrence, and *Le Triolet*, 8 rue des Carmes.

La Rochelle is also host to the major fesival of French-language music, Les Francofolies, in mid-July, which features musicians from overseas as well as France and attracts the best part of 100,000 fans to the city.

The Île de Ré

A half-hour drive from La Rochelle, the Île de Ré is a low, narrow island some 30km long, fringed by sandy beaches to the southwest and salt marshes and oyster beds to the northeast, with the interior a motley mix of small-scale vine, asparagus and wheat cultivation. All the buildings on Ré are restricted to two storeys and are required to incorporate the typical local features of whitewashed walls, curly orange tiles and green-painted shutters, which give the island villages a southerly holiday atmosphere.

Out of season the island has a slow, misty charm, and life in its little ports revolves exclusively around the cultivation of oysters and mussels. In season, though, it's extraordinarily crowded, with upwards of 400,000 visitors passing through. The crowds mainly head for the southern beaches; those to the northeast are covered in rocks and seaweed, and the sea is too shallow for bathing.

The island is connected to the mainland at **LA PALLICE**, a suburb of La Rochelle, by a three-kilometre-long toll bridge constructed in 1988 (110F round trip per car). La Pallice was once a big commercial port with important shipyards, and although it still serves as a naval base, times have changed. As you drive past, you'll notice some colossal weather-stained concrete sheds, submarine pens built by the Germans to service their Atlantic U-boat fleet during World War II. Too difficult to demolish, they are still in use. As an alternative to the toll-bridge connection, Interîles, 14 cours des Dames, La Rochelle, also run a bus and boat service to sablonceaux on Ré (110F return with a car), and combine trips to the Îles de Ré and Oléron (see p.568).

ST-MARTIN, the island's capital, is an atmospheric north-coast fishing port with whitewashed houses clustered around the stone quays of a well-protected harbour, from where trawlers and flat-bottomed oyster boats, piled high with cage-like devices used for "growing" oysters, slip out every morning on the muddy tide.

The quayside *Café Boucquingam* recalls the military adventures of the Duke of Buckingham, who attacked the island unsuccessfully in the mid-seventeenth century. To the east of the harbour, you can walk along the almost perfectly preserved **fortifications** – redesigned by Vauban in the late seventeenth century after Buckingham's attentions – to the citadel, long used as a prison. It was from here that the *bagnards* – prisoners sentenced to hard labour on Devil's Island in Guyana or New Caledonia in the Pacific – set out. Most did not return. One who eventually did was the notorious French General Papillon.

Practicalities

Rébus runs **bus services** all over the island from La Rochelle, leaving from place Verdun via the train station every hour; crossing to Sablonceaux just across the bridge costs 10F. For frequent travelling, ten trip cards are better value: La Rochelle–Sablonceaux costs 72F, La Rochelle–St-Martin 195F, anywhere on the island–La Rochelle 230F, but the timetable can be awkward if you want to tour the island.

The alternative is to **rent a bike** from the Sablonceaux bus depot or from Cyclo-Surf Location, 14 rue Henri-Lainé in seaside La Flotte between Sablonceaux and St-Martin;

Clos Vauban, av V-Bouthillier in St-Martin; and 2 route Joachim in La Couarde on the southern side of the island.

Hotels are plentiful in all the island's villages, though obviously packed very full through July and August. Most reasonably priced are the one-star *Le Sénéchal*, 6 rue Gambetta in Ars-en-Ré, on the other side of the island on a protected bay (☎05.46.29.40.42; ②; closed Oct–March); *L'Océan*, 4 rue St-Martin in Le-Bois-Plage (☎05.46.09.23.07, fax 05.46.09.05.40; ④; closed mid-Nov to Jan); and in La Flotte, the *L'Hippocampe*, 16 rue du Château-des-Mauléons (☎05.46.09.60.68; ①), and *Le Français*, 1 quai de Sénac (☎05.46.09.60.06, fax 05.40.09.58.77; ③; closed mid-Nov to March).

There are even more **campsites** on the island than there are hotels, and it shouldn't be difficult finding a place, except perhaps in desirable locations near the southern beaches at the height of the rush. A few names, if you want to book ahead, are the *Camping du Soleil* in Ars-en-Ré (☎05.46.29.40.62); *L'Île Blanche* in La Flotte (☎05.46.09.52.43; April–Oct); and *L'Océan*, La Passe in La Couarde (☎05.46.29.87.70; April–Sept).

Good-value **food** is available on the quayside in St-Martin at *Les Remparts*, 4 quai Daniel-Rivaille, which has a piano bar upstairs. *La Salicorne*, 16 rue de l'Olivette in La Couarde (☎05.46.29.82.37), has a high standard of cuisine starting at 130F for lunchtime menus, as does *Le Bistrot de Bernard*, 23 rue de l'Église in Le Bois-Plage.

Rochefort and around

ROCHEFORT dates from the seventeenth century. It was created by Colbert, Louis XIII's navy minister, to protect the coast from English raids and remained an important naval base until modern times with its shipyards, sail-makers, munitions factories and hospital. Built on a grid plan with regular ranks of identical houses, the town is a monument to the tidiness of the military mind, but is not without charm for all that. The central **place Colbert** is very pretty and the nearby **rue Courbet** is exactly as the seventeenth century left it, complete with lime trees and cobblestones brought from Canada as ships' ballast. The seventeenth-century warehouse buildings and old arsenal as yet are unrestored and cannot be visited, but there are still some sights worth making a special effort for.

Many of the towns along the pretty surrounding coastline are served by the Aunis and Saintonge buses, although you will find the simplest solution to travelling along this whole section of coast is renting a car or even cycling. Unless you have your own transport, Rochefort is a useless base for nearby Royan or the Île d'Oléron. Bus times are inconvenient and buses to Oléron generally involve a wait at Boucrefranc.

The town

If you have a taste for the bizarre, then there's one good reason for visiting Rochefort – the house of the novelist Julien Viaud, alias Pierre Loti. Forty years a naval officer, he wrote numerous best-selling romances with exotic oriental settings and characters. The **Maison Pierre Loti**, at 141 rue Pierre-Loti (guided tours every 20min July–Sept daily except Sun am 10–11am & 2–5pm; Oct–June daily except Tues & Sun 10–11am & 2–4pm; closed Dec 20–Jan 20 & public hols; 40F), is part of a row of modestly proportioned grey-stone houses, outwardly a model of petit-bourgeois conformity and respectability, inside an outrageous and fantastical series of rooms decorated to exotic themes. There's a medieval banqueting hall complete with Gothic fireplace and Gobelin tapestries, a monastery refectory with windows pinched from a ruined abbey, a Damascus mosque; a Turkish room, with kilim wall-hangings and a ceiling made from an Alhambra mould. To suit the mood of the place, Loti used to throw extravagant parties: a medieval banquet with swan's meat and hedgehog and a *fête chinoise* with the guests in costumes he had brought back from China, where he took part in the suppression of the Boxer rebellion.

A possible rainy hour's worth of museum is the **Centre International de la Mer** (daily 9am–6/8pm; 30F) situated in the Corderie Royale, or the royal ropeworks, off rue Toufaire. At 372m, the Corderie is the longest building in France and a rare and splendid example of seventeenth-century industrial architecture, substantially restored after damage in World War II. From 1660 until the Revolution, it furnished the entire French navy with rope, and the building now houses an appropriate exhibition on ropes and rope-making, including machinery from the nineteenth century. If you don't fancy visiting the museum, it's definitely worth a wander around the extensive building and its lawns along the River Charente, whose reed-fringed banks support a garden made up of plants brought back from long-forgotten expeditions overseas. One such, financed by Michel Bégon, quartermaster of Rochefort in 1688, brought back the flower we know as the begonia. The small harbour, the **Bassin Laperouse**, next to the Corderie, is also worth a stroll. If you're interested in finding out more about the town's history and naval importance, head for the **Musée d'Art et d'Histoire**, 63 av Charles-de-Gaulle (July & Aug daily 1.30–7pm, Sept–May Tues–Sat 1.30–5.30pm; 10F) and the **Musée de la Marine** (10am–noon & 2–6pm; closed Tues & Oct 15–Nov 15; 29F), in the seventeenth-century Hôtel de Cheusses on place de la Gallossinnière, which houses an excellent collection of model ships, figureheads, navigational instruments and other naval paraphernalia. One other attractive small museum is the **Musée des Métiers de Mercure** at 12 rue Lessan, which displays lovingly and authentically reconstructed shop interiors from the beginning of the century (July & Aug daily 10am–8pm; Sept–June daily except Tues 10am–noon & 2–7pm; 30F).

Practicalities

Should you want to stay, hotels need to be booked in advance to ensure reasonably priced accommodation. The efficient **tourist office** (daily: mid-June to mid-Sept 9am–8pm; mid-Sept to mid-June 9am–12.30pm & 2–6.30pm; ☎05.46.99.08.60, fax 05.46.99.52.64) is on avenue Sadi-Carnot off rue du Dr-Pelletier, two blocks north of the **gare routière**; the staff will reserve rooms for a charge of 15F.

The cheapest **hotel** rooms in town are at *Les Messageries* on place de la Gare opposite the handsome station buildings (☎05.46.99.00.90; ③). The *Hôtel de France*, 55 rue du Dr-Pelletier (☎05.46.99.34.00, fax 05.46.37.36.08; ①-③) also has some cheap but dingy rooms – much better is the extremely comfortable and friendly two-star *Caravelle*, at 34 rue Jaurès, off avenue C-de-Gaulle (☎05.46.99.02.53, fax 05.46.87.29.25; ③). Other choices include the two-star *Hôtel Roca Fortis*, 14 rue de la République (☎05.46.99.26.32, fax 05.46.87.49.48; ③), an old hotel with typical shuttered windows, with some rooms overlooking a garden. *Hôtel des Vermandois*, 33 rue Émile-Combes (☎05.46.99.62.75, fax 05.46.99.62.83; ④), next door to the Loti museum, is another oldie but with modern fittings: one room is accessible for the handicapped, and several are family studios. *La Corderie Royale* on rue Audebert (☎05.46.99.35.35, fax 05.46.99.78.72; ⑧; closed Feb 1–19) is the town's poshest place to stay within the seventeenth-century ropeworks.

For budget accommodation there's a new, modern **youth hostel**, centrally located for once at 97 rue de la République (☎05.46.82.10.40). The **camping municipal** (☎05.46.99.14.33; March–Nov) is a long haul if you've arrived at the gare SNCF: take avenue du Président-Wilson and keep going straight, until you reach the bottom of rue Toufaire, where you turn right, then left – about half an hour all the way.

For inexpensive **meals**, try *Le Galion*, a self-service restaurant by the arsenal on rue Toufaire, and there's a more than adequate Vietnamese/Chinese, *L'Asie*, at 45 rue Toufaire. Probably the best restaurant in Rochefort is *Le Tourne-Broche*, 56 av

Charles-de-Gaulle (☎05.46.99.20.19; closed Sun night & Mon, & 3 weeks in Jan), specializing in *grillades* but offering fish and seafood as well; menus from 110F. For an excellent morning café crème, try the local bar *La Givelte*. *Le Comptoir des Îles also* on place Colbert serves good **beer**, and you can finish the evening playing billiards, snooker or pool around the corner at *Le Roller*, 48 rue de la République.

Fouras and the Île d'Aix

FOURAS, some 30km south of La Rochelle, is the embarkation point for the tiny Île d'Aix (see below), where Napoléon spent his last days in Europe. It's an uninspiring town, redeemed only by a clutch of popular beaches and the *presqu'île*, the peninsula that extends 3km out to sea from the town centre, terminating at the ferry dock, **Pointe de la Fumée**. The peninsula is bordered by oyster beds, and off its westernmost tip at low tide can be seen the *bouchots à moules*, lines of mussel-encrusted stumps. At high tide this is a popular place to fish for *crevettes* – shrimp. The finger of land is hemmed by sea-dashed fortresses – originally intended to protect the Charente, and particularly La Rochelle, against Norman attack – which were later employed against Dutch invasions in the seventeenth century and English ones in the eighteenth. The seventeenth-century **Fort Vauban** (daily 3–5pm) now houses a small, uninspiring, local maritime museum, but its esplanade offers a magnificent panorama of neighbouring forts and islands.

Fouras's **tourist office**, which also serves the Île d'Aix, is situated in the Fort Vauban (mid-June to mid-Sept Mon–Sat 9am–7pm, Sun 10am–12.30pm & 1–6pm; mid-Sept to mid-June same days but Sun 9am–12.30pm & 2–6pm; ☎05.46.84.60.69, fax 05.46.84.28.04). As for places to **stay**, Fouras has a posse of overpriced **hotels**, but the *Roseraie* at 2 av du Port-Nord (☎05.46.84.64.89; ③) is fair value for money. There are also three **campsites** around the town: the *Fumée*, near the ferry port (☎05.46.84.26.77; May–Sept); the *L'Espérance* off avenue Philippe-Jannet (☎05.46.84.24.18; mid-April to Sept); and the *Cadoret* near to plage Nord, on avenue du Cadoret (☎05.46.84.02.84). The best-value **food** in town is probably from *Restaurant La Jetée* at Pointe de la Fumée (☎05.46.84.60.43; closed Jan, & Tues out of season), serving excellent seafood at affordable prices (menus 80–140F).

Île d'Aix

Less frequented than the bigger islands, the **Île d'Aix** is small enough – just 2km long – to be walked around in about three hours, giving a greater sense of its island status than is felt on the Île de Ré. Access is by frequent ferry (half-hourly in season) from Pointe de la Fumée (☎05.46.84.26.77), or with Interîles from La Rochelle (May–Sept 2–4 daily).

The crescent-shaped island is well defended, with a pair of forts and ramparts around its southern tip. The island, and particularly **Fort Liédot**, served as a prison for members of the Paris Commune and later held Russian prisoners in the Crimean and First World Wars. There's a **museum** (daily 10am–noon & 2–6pm; 25F) in the house constructed to Napoléon's orders and inhabited by him for a week in 1815 while he was planning his escape to America, only to find himself en route to St Helena and exile. Extensive displays fill ten rooms with the emperor's works of art, clothing, portraits and arms. The white dromedary from which he conducted his Egyptian campaign is lodged nearby in the **Musée Africain**, with its entire collection devoted to African wildlife (daily except Wed; same hours as above; 16F).

The only **hotel** on the island is the overpriced *Napoléon* on rue Gourgard (☎05.46.84.66.02; ②), and there's also a **campsite**, the *Fort de la Rade* (☎05.46.84.28.28; May–Sept).

OYSTERS

Marennes' speciality is fattening the **oysters** known as *creuses*. It's a lucrative but precarious business, extremely vulnerable to storm damage, changes of temperature or salinity in the water, the ravages of starfish and umpteen other improbable natural disasters.

Oysters begin life as minuscule larvae, which are "born" about three times a year. When a "birth" happens, the oystermen are alerted by a special radio service, and they all rush out to place their "collectors" – usually arrangements of roofing tiles – for the larvae to cling to. There the immature oysters remain for eight or nine months, after which they are scraped off and moved to *parcs* in the tidal waters of the sea: sometimes covered, sometimes uncovered. Their last move is to the *claires* – shallow rectangular pools where they are kept permanently covered by water less salty than normal sea water. Here they fatten up and acquire the greenish colour the market expects. With "improved" modern oysters, the whole cycle takes about two years, as opposed to four or five with the old varieties.

Brouage and Marennes

Eighteen kilometres southwest of Rochefort, **BROUAGE** is another seventeenth-century military base, this time created by Richelieu after the siege of La Rochelle. It is surrounded by salt marshes, now reclaimed and transformed into meadows grazed by white Charollais cattle and intersected by dozens of reed-filled drainage ditches, where herons watch and yellow flag blooms. It's a strangely beautiful landscape with huge skies specked with wheeling buzzards and kestrels and, being flat as a pancake, it's good cycling and walking country. To reach the town from Rochefort, you cross the Charente on the D733 near the disused **Pont Transbordeur**, a great iron gantry with a raft-like platform suspended on hawsers, on which a dozen cars were loaded and floated across the river – a technological wonder in its time. From there, either turn right for Soubise and Moëze or go on to St-Agnant.

The way into Brouage is through the **Porte Royale** in the north wall of the totally intact fortifications dating from the mid-seventeenth century. Locked within its 400-metre square, the town now seems abandoned and somnolent; even the sea has retreated, and all that's left of the harbour are the partly freshwater pools, or *claires*, where oysters are fattened in the last stage of their rearing.

Within the walls, the streets are laid out on a grid pattern, lined with low two-storey houses. On the second cross-street to the right is a **memorial** to Samuel de Champlain, the local boy who founded the French colony of Québec in 1608. In the same century, Brouage witnessed the last painful pangs of a royal romance: here, Cardinal Mazarin, successor to Richelieu, locked up his daughter, Marie Mancini, to keep her from her youthful sweetheart, Louis XIV. The politics of the time made the Infanta of Spain a more suitable consort for the King of France than his daughter – in his own judgement. Louis gave in, while Marie pined and sighed on the walls of Brouage. Returning from his marriage in St-Jean-de-Luz, Louis dodged his escort and stole away to see her. Finding her gone, he slept in her room and paced the walls in her footsteps.

Half-a-dozen kilometres south, on a narrow, drier spit of land, past the graceful eighteenth-century **Château de la Gataudière** with its unique interior and original furnishings (March–Nov Mon–Sat 10am–noon & 2–6.30pm, Sun 2–6.30pm; 35F) – built by the man who introduced rubber to France – you come to the village of **MARENNES**. This is the centre of oyster production for an area that supplies over sixty percent of France's requirements. If you want to visit the oyster beds and see how the business works, you can do so here; just ask at the **tourist office** on place Chasseloup-Laubat (☎05.46.85.04.36, fax 05.46.85.04.36) or out of season at the mairie, 6 rue Foch (☎05.46.85.25.55) – visits cost on average 50F for an adult, 20F for a child.

For **accommodation** in Marennes, there's the inexpensive *Hôtel du Commerce* at 9 rue de la République (☎05.46.85.00.09; ②), with a restaurant where you can eat generously and well from 65F. A good alternative for eating is *La Verte Ostréa* at the end of the pier at La Cayenne, where oysters and shellfish form the basis of every menu, from 65F.

The Île d'Oléron

The **Île d'Oléron** is France's largest island after Corsica and a favourite of day-trippers and families in the summer months for its beautiful sandy beaches. It's up the road from Marennes, joined to the mainland by a bridge. Buses from Rochefort are awkward, with irritating changes at Saintes or Boucrefranc, and it's easier to go direct from Saintes on one of the several daily Citram buses that stop at all the main towns on the island; alternatively, take one of Interîles' guided day-trips from La Rochelle (see p.558).

Flat and more wooded than the Île de Ré, Oléron has plenty of greenery, with the extensive pine-studded **Forêt des Saumonards** in the northeast of the island; here you can eyeball a dazzling panorama of the surrounding *parcs à huitres* and the mighty **Fort Boyard** stranded in the midst of sea between Oléron and the Île d'Aix to the northeast. At the island's southern tip, the larger **Forêt de St-Trojan** creeps up the western coast along **La Grande Plage**, a popular spot but far enough from the main towns. The island interior is pretty and distinctive. Waterways wind right into the land, their gleaming muddy banks overhung by round fishing nets suspended from ranks of piers. There are so many oyster *claires* that, from above, the island must look like an Afghan mirrored cushion, and the stretch from Boyardville to St-Pierre – with its pines, tamarisks and woods of evergreen oak – is the most attractive.

The island's most interesting attraction is off the D126 between St-Pierre and Dolus, right in the middle of the island. The bird park of **Le Marais aux Oiseaux** (daily: April, May & Sept 10am–noon & 2–7pm; June–Aug 10am–8pm; 25F) was originally established as a hospital for injured birds found in the wild, but is now a breeding centre with many examples of rare or endangered species. From 300 to 400 species of birds are given the freedom of twenty hectares of beautiful countryside, while sixty species are caged for observation alongside public walkways.

Most of the little towns on the island, inevitably, have been ruined by the development of hundreds of holiday homes – and it can be a real battle in the summer season to find a place to stay. There are a few places that still retain some amount of charm, not least of which is the main town in the south of the island, **LE CHÂTEAU**, named after the **citadel** that still stands, along with some seventeenth-century **fortifications**; the town thrives on its traditional oyster farming and boat-building, and there's a lively **market** in place de la République every morning. The chief town in the north – and most picturesque of the island's settlements – is **ST-PIERRE**, whose market square has an unusual thirteenth-century **monument**, or *lanterne aux morts*. A few kilometres to the northeast, **BOYARDVILLE** has no interest except for the ranks of *bouchots* – stakes for growing mussels – along the shore. It's tempting to help yourself, but these are private property and you'll be in trouble if someone sees you; instead, head to the major attraction around here: the superb stretch of sandy beach at **LA BRÉE-LES-BAINS**. Halfway down the west coast is the pretty fishing port of **LA COTINIÈRE**, with a daily morning fish market (except Sun), Criée aux Poissons, where the fishermen traditionally cry out their wares.

Practicalities

The main **tourist office** is on place de la République in Le Château (July–Sept daily 9.30am–12.30pm & 2.30–7pm; Oct–June same hours but closed Sun; ☎05.46.47.60.51, fax 05.46.47.73.65), also the location of a couple of affordable restaurants. St-Pierre's tourist office is on place Gambetta (June–Aug daily 9.15am–12.30pm & 2–7.30pm; Sept–May Tues–Sat 9.15am–12.30pm & 2–6pm; ☎05.46.47.11.39, fax 05.46.47.10.41); **bikes** are available in St-Pierre from Lespagnol, rue de la République, and from Lacellerie Michel, rue Maréchal-Foch.

Well-priced **accommodation** on the Île d'Oléron can be had at *Les Tamaris* in the port of St-Denis (☎05.46.47.86.04, fax 05.46.75.73.08; ②); at the *Hôtel de la Petite Plage à Domino*, rue de l'Océan, St-Georges (☎05.46.76.52.28; ③); and at *L'Albatross*, 11 bd du Dr-Pineau, St-Trojan-les-Bains (☎05.46.76.00.08, fax 05.46.76.03.58; ③; March–Sept). There are **campsites** all over the island: at La Brée, where the best beaches are, there's *Pertuis d'Antioche* (☎05.46.47.92.00), 150m from the beach off the D273. Further down the east coast, *Signol* at Boyardville (☎05.46.47.01.22) is pleasantly sited near pine forests. If you want to stay a week or so, you could rent a **holiday apartment**, easy enough outside of July and August; ask for a list at any of the tourist offices, or contact the *Agence Centrale Oléronaise* (☎05.46.75.32.53).

Places to **eat** abound on the island, and St-Pierre has the greatest choice of restaurants and brasseries. One place worth mentioning is in La Cotinière: *L'Écailler*, 65 rue du Port (☎05.46.47.10.31; mid-Nov to Jan closed Sun & Mon), for a slap-up, super-fresh seafood meal facing the port from 150F.

Royan and around

Before World War II, **ROYAN**, at the mouth of the Gironde, was a fashionable resort for the bourgeoisie. It is still popular – though no longer exclusive – and the modern town has lost its elegance to the dreary rationalism of 1950s town planning: broad boulevards, car parks, shopping centres, planned greenery. Ironically, the occasion for this planners' romp was provided by Allied bombing, an attempt to dislodge a large contingent of German troops who had withdrawn into the area after the D-Day landings. But the **beaches** – the most elegant and fashionable of which is in the suburb of **Pontaillac** to the northwest – are beautiful: fine pale sand, meticulously harrowed and raked near town and wild, pine-backed and pounded by the Atlantic to the north.

The town
One sight worth seeing in Royan is the 1950s **church of Notre-Dame**, designed by Gillet and Hébrard, in a tatty square behind the main waterfront. Though the concrete has weathered badly, the overall effect is dramatic and surprising. Tall V-sectioned columns give the outside the appearance of massive fluting, and a stepped roofline rises dramatically to culminate in a 65-metre bell tower, like the prow of a giant vessel. The interior is even more striking. Using uncompromisingly modern materials and designs, the architects have succeeded in out-Gothicking Gothic. The stained-glass panels, in each of which a different tone predominates, borrow their colours from the local seascapes – oyster, sea, mist and murk – before a sudden explosion of colour in the Christ figure above the altar.

The most attractive area in Royan is around **boulevard Garnier**, which leads southeast from Rond-Point-de-la-Poste along the beach and once housed Parisian high society in purpose-built, Belle Époque holiday villas. Some of these have survived, including **Le Rêve**, 58 bd Garnier, where Émile Zola lived and wrote; **Kosiki**, 100 av du Parc (running parallel to bd Garnier), a nineteenth-century folly of Japanese inspiration; and **Tanagra**, 34 av du Parc, whose facade is covered in sculptures and balconies.

Various **cruises** are organized from Royan in season, including one to the **Cordouan lighthouse**, erected by the Black Prince and commanding the mouth of the Gironde River. There's a twenty-minute **ferry** crossing (one-way pedestrians & cycles 17F, motorbikes 55F, cars 123F) to the headland on the other side of the Gironde, the

Pointe de Grave, from where a **bicycle trail** and the **GR8** head down the coast through the pines and dunes to the bay of Arcachon (see p.593).

Arrival, information and accommodation

The **tourist office** (June–Sept Mon–Sat 9am–7.30pm, Sun 10am–1pm & 3–6pm; Oct–March Mon–Sat 9am–12.30pm & 2–6pm; ☎05.46.05.04.71, fax 05.46.06.67.76; free accommodation booking service) and **PTT** are close to the Rond-Point-de-la-Poste at the east end of the seafront; the **gare routière** and **gare SNCF** are in the nearby cours de l'Europe. You can rent **bikes** from Cyclojet in the gare SNCF, or Cycl'Océan at 23 & 37 cours de l'Europe; **car rental** is available from either Europcar, 13 place du Dr-Gantier (☎05.46.05.20.88), or Avis, 75 av de Pontaillac (☎05.46.38.48.88).

Accommodation in Royan is expensive and in short supply in season, when your best bet is to camp up the coast to the north or visit for the day from Saintes or Rochefort. If you're booking ahead, try the *Nouvel Hôtel de la Plage*, 18 av de Cognac (☎05.46.39.00.18, fax 05.46.38.41.14; ①), a cheapie at Pontaillac beach to the west of town; frequent Aunis and Saintonge buses run from the train station via place Charles-de-Gaulle. The *Hôtel de l'Hôtel de Ville*, 1 bd Aristide-Briand (☎05.46.05.00.64; ①) is close to the beach, as is *Hôtel de la Plage*, right amidst the action at 26–28 Front de Mer (☎05.46.05.10.27, fax 05.46.38.37.79; ②). There's also the more comfortable and central two-star *Les Bleuets*, 21 facade de Foncillon (☎05.46.38.51.79, fax 05.46.23.82.00; ③), with sea or garden views. Finally, for those who want air-conditioning and beachfront balconies, the three-star *Family Golf Hotel*, 28 bd Frédéric-Garnier (☎05.46.05.14.66, fax 05.46.06.52.56; ③), fits the bill unless you're put off by its rather ugly 1950s exterior. Alternatively, 3km southeast of Royan, in **ST-GEORGES-DE-DIDONNE**, there's an excellent little hotel, the *Colinette*, 16 avenue de la Grande-Plage (☎05.46.05.15.75, fax 05.46.06.54.17; ①; half-board only mid-June to mid-Sept; ③), in pleasant surroundings 100m from the sea.

There are a number of **campsites** in the region and around Royan itself, including the *Clairefontaine* (☎05.46.39.08.11; June–Sept), a fairly pricey site at avenue Louise, allée des Peupliers in **PONTAILLAC**, and the municipal *La Triloterie* (☎05.46.05.26.91) off avenue d'Aquitaine – the road to Bordeaux.

Eating, drinking and nightlife

As for **food**, good-value menus are to be found at the huge, old-fashioned *Relais de la Mairie*, 1 rue du Chay, quite far from the centre off avenue de Pontaillac (☎05.46.39.03.15), and from *Les Filets Bleus*, near the cathedral at 14 rue Notre-Dame (☎05.46.05.74.00), specializing in seafood dishes and gourmet salads, with *plats du jour* from 55F and menus from 85F. The smart *Le Chalet*, 6 bd de la Grandière (☎05.46.05.04.90; closed Wed), serves imaginative seafood dishes reasonably cheaply and is crammed with French families on Sundays, when you'd be wise to book. Several **crêperies**, **pizzerias** and **snack bars** are situated on Front de Mer, the brassy strip leading from the tourist office to the beach and Port-de-Plaisance, with the *Crêperie de la Plage* at no. 40 recommended. The town's best-value bistrot, though, is packed-out *Le Tiki*, on the beachfront right by the tourist office: it dishes out an above-average variety of *plats du jour* from 37F as well as fish, pizza and grills. Self-caterers can head for the large covered **market**, the Marché Central, at the end of boulevard A-Briand, open every day (except Mon out of season) but particularly crowded and lively on Wednesday and Sunday mornings.

Nightlife is fairly restricted, considering the size of Royan: there's a disco, *Tropicana*, and a jazz bar at Plage de Pontaillac; and a piano bar, *Le Mylord*, and jazz bar, *Le Yachtman*, at Voûtes-de-Port.

Palmyre and Talmont

It's worth knowing about the **zoo park** in **PALMYRE** (daily: April–Sept 9am–7pm; Oct–March 9am–noon & 2–6pm; 55F), 10km northwest of Royan up the D25 coast road, especially if you're travelling with children, although its tacky advertising, with chimps dressed in human clothes, may put you off. Once you're inside, there are plenty of exotic species – from elephants and wild cats to gorillas and monkeys – housed in spacious enclosures covering fourteen hectares. To reach it, there are buses all day from Royan's gare routière and the place Charles-de-Gaulle.

An ideal bicycle or picnic excursion just over an hour's ride from Royan is to **TALMONT**, 16km up the Gironde on the GR360 and, apart from a few ups and downs through the woods outside Royan, it's all level terrain. The low-crouching village clusters about Talmont's twelfth-century **church of Ste-Radegonde**, standing at the edge of a cliff above the Gironde. With gabled transepts, a squat tower, an apse simply but elegantly decorated with blind arcading – all in weathered tawny stone and pocked like a sponge – it stands magnificently, in sun or cloud, against the forlorn browny-grey seascapes typical of the Gironde. The entrance is through the north transept, where the rings of carving in the arched doorway depict acrobats standing on each other's shoulders and, in the outer braid, two tug-of-war teams hauling roped lions up the arch. The inside is as unpretentiously beautiful as the exterior.

THE CHARENTE

It is hard to believe that the peaceful fertile valley of the **River Charente**, which has given its name to the two modern *départements* that cover much of this chapter, was once a busy industrial waterway, bringing armaments from **Angoulême** to the naval shipyards at Rochefort. Today peaceful, low ochre-coloured farms crown the valley slopes, with green swathes of vineyard sweeping up to the walls, and the graceful turrets of minor châteaux – properties of wealthy cognac-producers – poke up from out of the woods. The towns and villages may look old-fashioned, but the prosperous shops and classy new villas are proof that where the grape grows, money and modernity are not far behind.

The **valley** itself is easy to travel as the main road and train lines to Limoges run this way. North and south, Poitiers, Périgueux (for the Dordogne) and Bordeaux are also easily reached by train. Otherwise, for cross-country journeys, you are heavily reliant on your own transport.

Saintes and around

SAINTES was formerly much more important than its present size suggests. Today a busy market for the surrounding region, it was capital of the old province of Saintonge and a major administrative and cultural centre in Roman times. It still retains some impressive remains from that period, as well as two beautiful Romanesque pilgrim churches and an attractive centre of narrow lanes and medieval houses. It also has the doubtful distinction of being the birthplace of Dr Guillotin, whose instrument of decapitation came into its own during the Revolution.

PINEAU DES CHARENTES

Roadside signs throughout the Charente advertise **Pineau des Charentes**, a sweet liqueur that's a blending of grape juice stopped in its fermentation by adding cognac from the same vineyard. It's best drunk chilled as an apéritif; the locals also like it with oysters and love cooking with it. Favourite dishes include *moules au Pineau* (mussels cooked with tomatoes, Pineau, garlic and parsley) and *lapin à la saintongeaise* (rabbit casseroled with Pineau rosé, shallots, garlic, tomatoes, thyme and laurel).

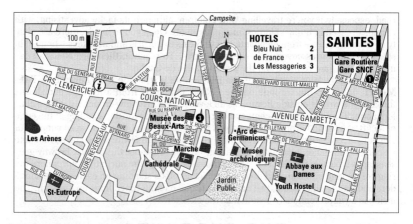

The town

The abbey church, the **Abbaye-aux-Dames** (daily: June–Sept 10am–12.30pm & 2–7pm; Oct–May 2–7 pm only; 15F), is as quirky as Notre-Dame in Poitiers. It stands back from the street on rue St-Pallais, in a sandy courtyard behind the smaller Romanesque church of St-Pallais. An elaborately sculpted doorway conceals the plain, domed interior. Its rarest feature is the eleventh-century tower, by turns square, octagonal and lantern-shaped, flanked with pinnacles and capped with the Poitou pine cone.

From here rue Arc-de-Triomphe brings you out on the river bank beside an imposing Roman arch – the **Arc de Germanicus** – which originally stood on the bridge until it was demolished in the mid-nineteenth century to make way for the modern crossing. The arch was dedicated to the emperor Tiberius, his son Drusus and nephew Germanicus in 19 AD. In a stone building next door is an **archeological museum** (summer Tues–Sun 10am–noon & 2–6pm, no midday break in July & Aug; winter Tues–Sat 10am–noon & 2–5.30pm, Sun 3–6pm; free) with a great many more Roman bits and pieces strewn about, mostly rescued from the fifth-century city walls into which they had been incorporated. This whole area comes alive on the first Monday of every month when a sprawling **market** extends from the abbey right through here and up most of avenue Gambetta.

A footbridge crosses from this point to the covered market on the west bank of the river and place du Marché at the foot of the rather uninspiring **Cathedral of St-Pierre**, which began life as a Romanesque church but was significantly altered in the aftermath of damage inflicted during the Wars of Religion, when Saintes was a Huguenot stronghold. Its enormous, heavily buttressed tower, capped by a hat-like dome instead of the intended spire, is the town's chief landmark. In front, the lime trees of place du Synode stretch away to the municipal buildings, with the old quarter up to the right and the Hôtel Martineau library in the rue des Jacobins with an exquisite central courtyard full of trees and shrubs. Back towards the bridge, a seventeenth-century mansion on rue Victor-Hugo houses the **Musée des Beaux-Arts** (Tues–Sun 10am–noon & 2–5/6pm; free), containing a collection of local pottery and some unexciting paintings.

Saintes's Roman heritage is best seen at **Les Arènes**, an amphitheatre whose ruins lie at the head of a leafy little valley reached by a footpath which begins by 54 cours Reversaux. The amphitheatre was dug into the end of the valley in the early first century, making it one of the oldest surviving. Although most of the seats are now grassed over, it is still an evocative spot.

On the way back from the amphitheatre, it's no extra trouble to take in the eleventh-century **church of St-Eutrope**. The upper church, which lost its nave in 1803, has some brilliant capital-carving in the old choir, best seen from the gallery. But it's the crypt – entered from the street – which is more atmospheric and primitive: here massive pillars carved with stylized vegetation support the vaulting in semi-darkness, and there is a huge old font and the third-century tomb of Saintes's first bishop, Eutropius himself.

Practicalities

Saintes' **tourist office** is housed in grand old Villa Musso, 62 cours National (Mon–Sat 9am–1pm & 2–6pm, no lunch break July & Aug; ☎05.46.74.23.82, fax 05.46.92.17.01), and organizes **boat trips** to Cognac during the summer.

The **gare SNCF** is on av de la Marne at the east end of the main road, av Gambetta, with several **hotels** in the vicinity. The now rather tatty old *Hôtel de France* (☎05.46.93.01.16, fax 05.46.74.37.30; ②) is the best of the bunch. Both more congenial and more central is *Les Messageries* in tiny rue des Messageries, off rue Victor-Hugo (☎05.46.93.64.99, fax 05.46.92.14.34; ③), with a laundry available. Another agreeable place is the *Bleu Nuit* at 1 rue Pasteur, the crossroads of cours National and cours Reversaux (☎05.46.93.01.72, fax 05.46.74.43.80; ③; locked garage 30F). The hotel has some character and is well insulated against the noise of the street. The **youth hostel**, 2 place Geoffroy-Martel (☎05.46.92.14.92, fax 05.46.92.97.82) is right behind the Abbaye aux Dames; it has been totally renovated and modernized. The **camping municipal** is to the right (if you are coming from the Arch of Germanicus) immediately after the bridge, along rue de Courbiac.

For **eating**, there's a good restaurant, the *Tartine,* by the river on place Blair, and a popular crêperie at 20 rue Victor-Hugo, off rue Alsace-Lorraine, the pedestrianized shopping street. *Le Jardin du Rempart,* 36 rue du Rempart, serves top-value menus from 89F, including salads, seafood and grills, while *Le Ciboulette*, 36 rue Pérat (☎05.46.74.07.36), serves lots of Charentais specialities at moderate prices. Out of town, the *Restaurant de la Charente* (☎05.46.11.00.73; closed Sun), 10km upstream at Chaniers, is the Sunday haunt of prosperous locals and makes a more expensive but fulfilling gastronomic experience.

Around Saintes

If you have a car, you could explore several of the marvellous Romanesque churches within easy reach of Saintes. In **FENIOUX** twenty-nine kilometres to the north towards St-Jean-d'Angély, there is the superb church of St-Eutrope with its mighty spire; and the church at **RIOUX**, 12km to the south, is well worth visiting for its detailed facade. There is also the fine **Château of Roche-Courbon**, 18km northwest off the Rochefort road – once described as the Sleeping Beauty's castle – with some stylish interiors and gardens.

One place worth any amount of trouble to get to is the twelfth-century pilgrim **church of St-Pierre** at **AULNAY**, 37km northeast of Saintes, and sadly not served by public transport. Aulnay church's finest sculpture is on the west front, the south transept and apse, with some more fine work inside. On the building's main facade, two blind arches flank the central portal. The tympanum of the right depicts Christ in Majesty; the left, St Peter, crucified upside down with two extraordinarily lithe and graceful soldiers balancing on the arms of his cross to get a better swing at the nails in his feet. On the south side, the doorway is decorated with four bands of even more intricate carving. The apse, too, is a beauty, framed by five slender columns and lit by three perfectly arched windows, the centre one enclosed by figures wrapped in the finest twining foliage. Inside, there is more extraordinary carving: capitals depicting Delilah cutting Samson's hair, devils pulling a man's beard, human-eared elephants, bearing the Latin inscription *Hi sunt elephantes*, "These are elephants" – presumably for the edification of ignorant locals.

You might also like to visit **NUAILLÉ-SUR-BOUTONNE**, 9km west of Aulnay, which boasts another remarkable church; and even nearer, just down the D129 east of Aulnay, you can walk to **SALLES-LES-AULNAY** (20min), or **ST-MANDÉ** (1hr), with humbler churches of the same period, each in its way as charming as that of Aulnay.

Cognac

Anyone who does not already know what **COGNAC** is about will quickly nose its quintessential air as they stroll about the medieval lanes of the town's riverside quarter. For here is the greatest concentration of *chais* (warehouses), where a high-quality brandy is matured, its fumes blackening the walls with tiny fungi. Cognac *is* cognac, from the tractor driver and pruning-knife wielder to the manufacturer of corks, bottles and cartons. Untouched by recession (80 percent of production is exported), it is likely to thrive as long as the world has sorrows to drown – a sunny, prosperous, respectable, self-satisfied little place.

The town

Cognac has a number of medieval stone and half-timbered buildings in the narrow streets of the old town – rue Saulnier and rue de l'Îsle-d'Or make atmospheric backdrops for a stroll, and picturesque **Grande-Rue** winds through the heart of the old quarter to the *chais*. On the right is all that remains of the **castle** where King François I was born in 1494.

To the left are the *chais* and offices of the **Hennessy Cognac Company** (Mon–Fri 10am–6pm; 30F), a seventh-generation family firm and widely thought the best of the houses to visit. The first Hennessy, an officer in the Irish brigade serving with the French army, hailed from Ballymacnoy in County Cork and gave up soldiering in 1765 to set up a little business here. The Hennessy visit begins with a film explaining what's what in the world of cognac. Only an *eau de vie* distilled from grapes grown in a strictly defined area can be called cognac, and this stretches from the coast at La Rochelle and Royan to Angoulême. It is all carefully graded according to soil properties: chalk essentially. The inner circle, from which the finest cognac comes – Grand Champagne and Petit Champagne (not to be confused with bubbly) – lies mainly south of the River Charente. Hennessy alone keep 180,000 barrels in stock. All are regularly checked and various *coupages* (blendings) made from barrel to barrel, of which only the best are kept – depending on the well-honed taste buds of the *maître du chais*.

Another important cog in the cognac mechanism is Europe's second biggest bottlemaker, the modern **St-Gobain glassworks**, which lies 2km south of town; guided tours of the trade can be arranged through the tourist office (see below).

Practicalities

From the **gare SNCF**, go down rue Mousnier, right on rue Bayard, past the **PTT**, up rue du 14-juillet to the central place François-I, dominated by an equestrian statue of the king rising from a bed of begonias. Close by is the **tourist office** at 16 rue 14-Juillet (daily 9am–12.30pm & 2–6.15pm; no lunch break July & Aug; ☎05.45.82.10.71, fax 05.45.82.34.47), where you can ask about visiting the various *chais*, the St-Gobain glassworks and river trips – upstream through the locks to Jarnac, where the late President

Mitterrand's modest grave has become a place of pilgrimage for elderly left-wingers, is a particularly beautiful excursion.

As for **rooms**, the tourist office can book hotels on its list; the cheapest are *Tourist Hôtel*, 166 av Victor-Hugo (☎05.45.82.09.61; ①), for no-frills lodgings above a boisterous bar on the noisy Angoulême road, and *Le Cheval Blanc*, 6–8 place Bayard (☎05.45.82.09.55, fax 05.45.82.14.82; ①), with a simple inexpensive restaurant downstairs. For something a bit more expensive and more comfortable, try: the characterful *Hôtel d'Orleans*, 25 rue d'Angoulême (☎05.45.82.01.26, fax 05.45.82.20.33; ②), in a calm pedestrianized street in the old part of town; *La Résidence*, 25 av Victor-Hugo (☎05.45.32.16.09, fax 05.45.36.62.49; ③), an attractive two-star with a clean modern interior; or *L'Étape*, a little further out on the N141 at 2 av d'Angoulême (☎05.45.32.16.15, fax 05.45.36.20.03; ③). Upstream from the bridge, the oak woods of the Parc François-I, where there's swimming in the river or a pool, stretch along the river bank to the Pont Chatenay and the town **campsite** (☎05.45.32.13.32).

Eating out shouldn't pose a problem. The relaxed and friendly *La Bonne Goule*, 42 allée de la Corderie (☎05.45.82.06.37; from 60F; closed Sun evening), serves up excellent Charentais specialities at inexpensive prices, and there's a good list of local wines. Those after a dining experience find it at *La Boîte-à-Sel*, 68 av Victor-Hugo (☎05.45.32.07.68; closed Mon), a seasoned restaurant with an emphasis on fresh natural produce; the good-value 75F menu gets you a *plat* from the 102F *menu de marché* and a dessert or entrée; the excellent *menu des gourmets* will set you back 195F. There is also good brasserie fare to be had at the *Coq d'Or* on the central place François-Ier.

Around Cognac

The area around Cognac is gentle enough for some restful walks taking in some pretty little Charentais villages. The best is the towpath or *chemin de hâlage* that follows the south bank of the Charente upstream to Pont de la Trâche, then on along a track to the village of **BOURG-CHARENTE**, with an excellent **restaurant** called *La Ribaudière* at the bridge, an interesting castle and a Romanesque church; the walk takes about three hours in all. A byroad leads back to **ST-BRICE** on the other bank, past sleepy farms and acres of shoulder-high vines. From there, another lane winds 3km up the hill and over to the ruined **abbey** of **LA CHÂTRE**, abandoned amid brambles and fields. Alternatively, at the hamlet of **RICHEMONT**, 5km northwest of Cognac, you can swim in the pools of the tiny River Antenne below an ancient church on a steep bluff lost in the woods.

Further afield, 18km northwest of Cognac between the villages of Migron and Authon, there's the fascinating **Écomusée du Cognac** (daily 9.30am–12.30pm & 2.30–6.30pm; free), which illustrates the history of the distillation process and the various tools involved, finishing off with a tasting of cognacs, liqueurs and cocktails. Follow the D731 to St-Jean-d'Angely for 13km as far as Burie, then turn right on the D131, 4km from Migron.

Angoulême

Today, the cathedral city of **ANGOULÊME** has a failing economy. The paper mills that dominated the town used to employ thousands of workers and bolstered the city's prosperity; now they are almost completely defunct. But in the past, the former capital of the Angoumois province was a much-coveted city, being heavily fought over in the fourteenth-century Anglo-French squabbles and again in the sixteenth century during the Wars of Religion, when it was a Protestant stronghold. After the revocation of the Edict of Nantes, a good proportion of its citizens – among them many of its skilled papermakers – emigrated to Holland, never to return.

The town

The **old town** occupies a high steep-sided plateau overlooking a bend in the Charente, a natural fortress. It has many charms, if few notable sights. The labyrinthine streets to the north of the delightful **place Louvel** and the massive Hôtel de Ville have been largely restored and pedestrianized. It is here that the restaurants and bars are concentrated, while the eastern section, down rue Marango and rue St-Martial, has become the main commercial centre. On the southern edge of the plateau stands the **Cathedral**, whose west front – like Notre-Dame at Poitiers – is a fascinating display board for some expressive and lively twelfth-century sculpture, culminating in a Risen Christ with angels and clouds about his head, framed in the usual blaze of a halo. The lively frieze beneath the tympanum to the right of the west door commemorates the recapture of Spanish Zaragoza from the Moors, showing a bishop transfixing a Moorish giant with his lance and Roland killing the Moorish king.

Next to the cathedral in the old bishop's palace, there's more art on show at the **Musée des Beaux-Arts** (Mon–Fri noon–6pm, Sat & Sun 2–6pm; 15F), with its emphasis on seventeenth- to nineteenth-century paintings, many by Charentais artists. From the front of the cathedral, you can walk all around the **ramparts** encircling the plateau, with long views over the surrounding country, now largely filled with urban sprawl. There are **public gardens** below the parapet at the far end of the fortifications, and a gravelly esplanade by the lycée where locals gather to play boules.

Angoulême's most fascinating museum lies just below the city walls on the north side close to the River Charente: the **Centre National de la Bande Dessinée**, 121 rue de Bordeaux (Tues–Fri 10am–6/7pm, Sat & Sun 2–6/7pm; open Mon during school hols; 30F; bus #3 or #5), devoted entirely to comic strips. Housed in a turn-of-the-century brewery, with contemporary high-rise and glass additions, the museum gets across the message that comics ("BD") – from politics to pornography – are regarded as a serious art form in France. The museum owns a collection of some 4000 original drawings which it displays in rotating exhibitions of about 300 at a time. They range from the earliest stories with pictures and captions, the nineteenth-century *images d'Épinal*, through the introduction of the speech bubble in the 1920s to some of the darker contemporary productions. Astérix, Peanuts, Tintin and many other characters and artists are represented. To make comic fiends further salivate, there's a vast library, much of it in English, and you're welcome to relax on cushions and devour.

Another riverfront museum close by is the **Atelier-Musée du Papier**, 134 rue de Bordeaux (Wed–Sun 2–6pm; free), located in a disused cigarette-paper factory – a fitting tribute to the declining Charentais paper industry. While exhibits get into the history and technicalities of paper-making, art isn't forgotten, with contemporary creations on show, utilizing paper, cardboard and pulp.

Practicalities

Angoulême is easily accessible by train from Cognac, Limoges and Poitiers. The main **tourist office**, 2 place St-Pierre (July & Aug Mon–Sat 9.30am–7pm, Sun 10am–noon & 2–5pm; Sept–June Mon–Fri 9am–12.30pm & 1.30–6pm, Sat 10am–noon & 2–5pm, Sun 10am–noon; ☎05.45.95.16,84, fax 05.45.92.27.57), is by the cathedral and can provide route details for walks in the area – *circuits pédèstres*; there's another branch office outside the **gare SNCF**, from which avenue Gambetta, with the **gare routière** and several cheap hotels, leads uphill to the town centre through place Pérot.

Both tourist offices can help with **accommodation**, although if you want to go it alone the cheapest rooms in town are at the peaceful family-run joint, *Le Crab*, 27 rue Kléber (☎05.45.95.51.80, fax 05.45.95.3852; ③; decent restaurant from 60F); and *Hôtel*

Gaste, 381 rte de Bordeaux (☎05.45.91.89.98; ①; closed first 3 weeks in Aug; restaurant from 60F), a long haul from the station on the opposite side of town. But far and away the nicest place to stay is the elegant old *Hôtel du Palais* overlooking the delightful shady place Louvel in the heart of the old town (☎05.45.92.54.11, fax 05.45.92.01.83; ③; garage 35F). Another place worth trying, especially for its excellent regional cuisine, is the *Hôtel La Palma*, 4 rampe d'Aguesseau, on the road leading up into the old town from the station (☎05.45.95.22.89, fax 05.45.94.26.66. ①; restaurant from 62F). Alternatively, there's a wonderfully positioned HI **youth hostel** (☎05.45.92.45.80, fax 05.45.95.90.71; with canteen) on an island in the Charente; take bus #7 from place du Champ-de-Mars. The **camping municipal** (☎05.45.92.83.22) is nearby, beyond the Pont de Bourgines.

Likely **restaurant** areas are rue de Genève, with a number of options including traditional French and international, and the narrow, pedestrianized rue Massilon; *Le Mektoub*, 28 rue des Trois-Notre-Dames, is good for inexpensive North-African cuisine, and just near the excellent daily covered **market** of Les Halles, *Le Chat Noir*, on rue du Chat, is crowded with lunchers after its cheap salads and snacks. One of the best restaurants in the region, with a number of interesting and inventive menus, starting at 170F, is *La Ruelle*, 6 rue Trois-Notre-Dames (☎05.45.95.15.19; closed Sat lunch, Sun, April 8–14 & Aug 5–18). A cheaper traditional option is *Le Gastro Cave*, located in a cellar in the same street at no. 3 (☎05.45.92.45.47; closed Wed & Thurs lunchtime), which serves regional specialities with menus from 62F, while *La Marine* on nearby rue Ludovic-Trarieux is its opposite – a modern and airy oyster/wine bar. Newly opened is *Chez Paul*, 1 place France Louval, (☎05.45.90.04.61) a friendly and very reasonable restaurant (and bar with live music) with a beautiful garden. The food is fantastic with menus starting at 59F and it is well worth a visit.

Around Angoulême

LA ROCHEFOUCAULD, 22km east of Angoulême, is the site of a huge Renaissance **château** on the banks of the River Tardoire, still belonging to the family that gave its name to the town a thousand years ago. The stately pile, although still lived in, opens its elaborate portals to the public (May–Sept daily 10am–7pm; Oct–May Mon–Sat same hours, Sun 2–7pm; 35F). In August it stages a massive *son et lumière* with a brigade-sized cast. If you want to stay, there is the lovely old *Auberge de la Carpe d'Or* at 13 Grande-Rue (☎05.45.62.02.72, fax 05.45.63.01.88; ②) and the **camping municipal** is on rue des Flots beneath the château.

Further east, the country becomes hillier and more wooded, with buttercup pastures grazed by liver-coloured Limousin cattle. A good way to see it is to drive up the back roads along the River Vienne to the beautiful, if now rather touristy, little town of **CONFOLENS**, about 40km northeast of La Rochefoucauld. Its ancient houses are stacked up a hillside above a broad brown sweep of the river, here crossed by a long narrow medieval bridge. The town's chief claim to fame today is the huge **International Folklore Festival**, held every year in the second week of August, when, of course, it is impossible to find anywhere to stay (festival information ☎05.45.84.00.77). The best place **to stay** is the *Hôtel de la Vienne* on the river bank beside the bridge at 4 rue de la Ferrandie (☎05.45.84.09.24, fax 05.45.84.11.60; ③; good restaurant with terrace overlooking the river, from 64F). There is also a **camping municipal** by the tributary River Goire.

Having come this far, it's worth continuing the extra 6km to the minuscule village of St-Germain-de-Confolens, huddled by the riverside beneath the romantic towers of its ruined castle, where you can eat good country fare at the *Auberge de la Tour* (closed Mon except in July and August) for as little as 75F.

AQUITAINE

In Roman times, **Bordeaux** was capital of the province of *Aquitania Secunda*. With the marriage of Eleanor of Aquitaine and King Henry II of England in 1152, it quickly became the principal English foothold for their three-hundred-year Aquitanian adventure, and it was to their presence, and particularly their taste for its red wines – imported back to England and termed "claret" – that the region owed its first great economic boom. The second boom, which financed the building of the gracious eighteenth-century centre of Bordeaux, came with the expansion of colonial trade in the eighteenth century.

The surrounding countryside is not the most enticing. The vineyards throughout the **Médoc** region north of the city are mainly flat and monotonous: you go for the wines, not the scenery. More interesting is the vast pine-covered expanse of **Les Landes** and the huge wild Atlantic beaches of the **Côte d'Argent** to the south. But it is not a landscape that charms. Its appeal, like desert, is more in its size and uniqueness – and you definitely need your own transport to explore it.

Bordeaux and around

The city of **BORDEAUX** is stunning when approached from the South along the river. It's big with a population of over half a million, and obviously rich – as it has been since

THE WINES OF BORDEAUX

With Burgundy and Champagne, the **wines of Bordeaux** form the "Holy Trinity" of French viticulture. Despite producing as many whites as reds, it is the latter – known as claret to the British – that have graced the tables of the discerning for centuries. The countryside that produces them encircles the city, enjoying near-perfect climatic conditions and soils ranging from limestone to sand and pebbles. It is the largest quality wine district in the world, turning out around 500 million bottles a year – over half the country's quality wine output.

The Gironde estuary, fed by the Garonne and the Dordogne, determines the lie of the land. The **Médoc** lies northwest of Bordeaux between the Atlantic coast and the River Gironde, with its vines deeply rooted in poor gravelly soil, producing good, full-bodied red wines; the region's eight *appellations* are Médoc, Haut Médoc, St-Estèphe, Pauillac, St-Julien, Moulis en Médoc, Listrac-Médoc and Margaux. Southwest of Bordeaux are the vast vineyards of **Graves**, producing the best of the region's dry white wines, along with some punchy reds, from some of the most prestigious communes in France – Pessac, Talence, Martillac and Villenave d'Ornon amongst them. They spread down to Langon and envelop the areas of **Sauternes** and **Barsac**, whose extremely sweet white dessert wines are considered among the world's best.

On the east side of the Gironde estuary and the Dordogne, the **Côtes de Blaye** feature some good quality white table wines, mostly dry, and a smaller quantity of reds. The **Côtes de Bourg** specialize in solid whites and reds, spreading down to the renowned **St-Émilion** area. Here, there are a dozen producers who have earned the accolade of *Premiers Grands Crus Classés*, and their output is a full, rich red wine that doesn't have to be kept as long as the Médoc wines. Lesser-known neighbouring areas include the vineyards of **Pomerol**, **Lalande** and **Côtes de Francs**, all producing reds similar to St-Émilion but at more affordable prices.

Between Garonne and Dordogne is **Entre-Deux-Mers**, an area which yields large quantities of inexpensive, drinkable table whites, mainly from the Sauvignon grape. The less important sweet whites of **Ste-Croix du Mont** come out of the area south of **Loupiac**, which itself produces sweet whites. Stretching along the north bank of the

the Romans set up a lively trading centre here. Especially attractive is the relatively small eighteenth-century centre, paid for by the expansion of colonial trade. The rest is scruffy and, even with its long history, contains few sights. But if you're just passing through – it's the main regional transport centre – there are a couple of sights worth checking out, and plenty of cheap places to sleep and eat. The atmosphere is inviting, and worth sticking around for.

Arrival, information and accommodation

Arriving by train, you'll find yourself at the **gare St-Jean** (☎05.56.35.35.35), with its own small tourist office (daily 9am–noon & 12.45–7pm; ☎05.56.91.64.70), right at the heart of a somewhat insalubrious area, half an hour's walk south of the city centre; buses #7 or #8 will save you the hike. They also rent out **bikes**. Tickets are available on the **buses** (7.50F), but it's cheaper if you buy a carnet of ten from a tabac (52F). You must punch your ticket on the bus; then it is valid for half an hour, even if you change bus. The **gare routière** (☎05.56.43.08.43) is just a short walk north of the centre on rue Fondaudège near place Tourny. The super-efficient main **tourist office**, 12 cours du 30-juillet (May–Oct daily 9am–8pm, Sun 9am–7pm; Nov–April Mon–Sat 9am–6/7pm, Sun 9.45am–4.30pm; ☎05.56.00.66.00, fax 05.56.00.66.01), can book accommodation free of charge; it also has useful information on the city and surrounding vineyards, to which it also books tours (see box below for details).

Garonne, the vineyards of the **Côtes de Bordeaux** feature fruity reds and a smaller number of dry and sweet whites.

The **classification** of Bordeaux wines is an extremely complex affair. Apart from the usual *appellation d'origine contrôlée* (AOC) labelling – guaranteeing origin but not quality – the wines of the Médoc châteaux are graded into five *crus*, or growths. These were established as long ago as 1855, based on the prices the wines had fetched over the previous hundred years. Four were voted the best or *Premiers Grands Crus Classés*: Margaux, Lafitte, Latour and Haut-Brion. With the exception of Château Mouton-Rothschild, which moved up a class in 1973 to become the fifth *Premier Grand Cru Classé*, there have been no official changes, so divisions between the *crus* should not be taken too seriously. Since then, additional categories have been devised, for instance *Crus Bourgeois*, which has three categories of its own. The wines of Sauternes were also classified in 1855.

If you are interested in **buying wines**, it is possible to find bargains at some of the châteaux. Advantages of buying at source include the opportunity to sample before purchasing and to receive expert advice about different vintages. In Bordeaux, the best place to go is *La Vinotèque* (Mon–Sat 9.15am–7.30pm), next to the tourist office. In recent years tales of machine oil and chemical additives have shaken many people's confidence in wine drinking; as a result, there's a growing fashion for organic methods and "green" wines, already available on many good labels.

To **visit the châteaux**, the Bordeaux tourist office has a leaflet detailing all the places that allow visits and wine tasting. For general **information** on the region's wines, the efficient *Maison du Vin* in Bordeaux (Mon–Fri 8.30am–6pm, Sat 9am–12.30pm & 1.30–5pm) has many leaflets in English detailing the types of Bordeaux wine. In addition, each wine-producing village has its own tourist office and *Maison du Vin*, which can provide the same service. Since getting to any of these places except St-Émilion without your own transport is hard work, the simplest thing is to take one of the Bordeaux tourist office's own half-day **guided tours**, with a different wine area for each day of the week (May–Oct daily 1.30pm; 160F). Generally interesting and informative, the guide translates into English the wine-maker's commentary and answers any questions. Tastings are generous and expert tuition on how to go about it is part of the deal.

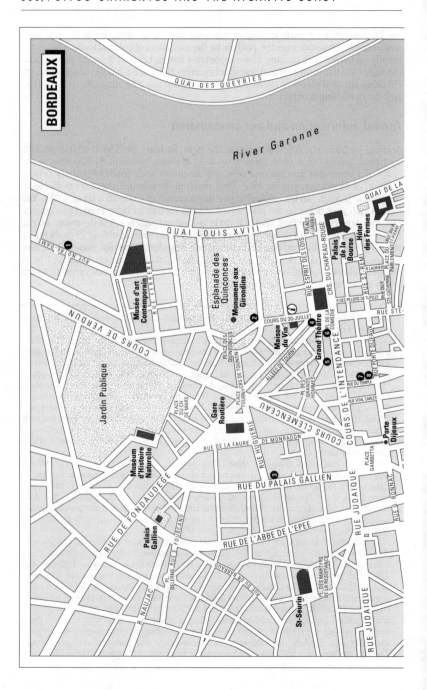

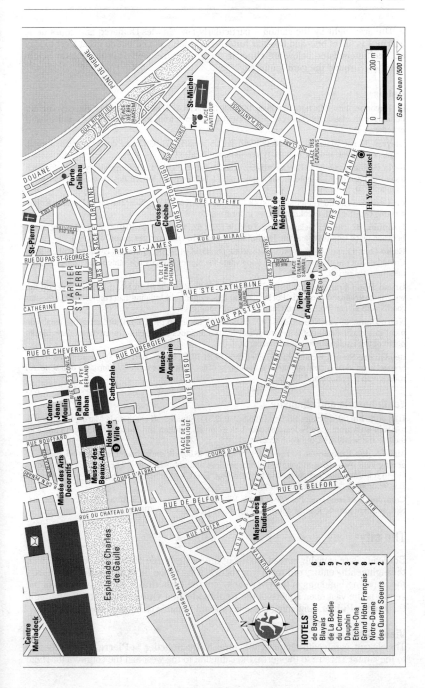

Gare St-Jean (500 m)

200 m

0

St-Michel

Tour

PLACE
CANTELOUP

PONT DE PIERRE

QUAI RICHELIEU

RUE DES FAURES

PLACE
DE BIR
HAKEIM

RUE DE PLANTEROSE

COURS DE LA MARNE

Hi Youth Hostel

PLACE DES
CAPUCINS

DOUANE

Porte
Calihau

QUAI DES SALINIERES

RUE ARNAUD MIQUEU

COURS VICTOR HUGO

RUE LEYTEIRE

Faculté de
Médecine

RUE DE LA CLAIRE

Grosse
Cloche

RUE DU CANCERA

RUE DU MIRAIL

COURS DE LA SOMME

St-Pierre

RUE DU PAS ST-GEORGES

RUE ST-JAMES

RUE COURS D'ALSACE ET LORRAINE

RUE DES AUGUSTINS

RUE DU CANAL

PLACE
GÉNÉRAL
SARRAIL

COURS DE LA VICTOIRE

CATHERINE

QUARTIER
ST-PIERRE

PL DE LA
FERME
RICHEMONT

RUE STE-CATHERINE

RUE ANDRÉE
DUMÉE

Porte
d'Aquitaine

PLACE DE LA VICTOIRE

RUE DE CHEVERUS

RUE DES 3 CONILS

RUE DUBERGIER

Musée
d'Aquitaine

COURS PASTEUR

RUE CURSOL

RUE HENRI IV

COURS D'ALBRET

COURS A. BRIAND

Centre
Jean-
Moulin

PL PEY
BERLAND

Cathédrale

Palais
Rohan

RUE BOUFFARD

CHN PENAULT

Musée des Arts
Décoratifs

Musée des
Beaux-Arts

Hôtel de
Ville

PLACE DE LA
RÉPUBLIQUE

COURS D'ALBRET

RUE DE BELFORT

RUE DE LA LIBERATION

Centre
Mériadeck

Esplanade Charles
de Gaulle

RUE DU CHATEAU D'EAU

RUE DE BELFORT

RUE LIGIER

Maison des
Etudiants

RUE DE TESSERE

COURS MAL JUIN

N

HOTELS

de Bayonne	6
Blayais	5
de La Boétie	9
du Centre	7
Dauphin	3
Etche-Ona	4
Grand Hôtel Français	8
Notre-Dame	1
des Quatre Soeurs	2

The area right by the station – particularly rue Charles-Domercq and cours de la Marne – is full of one- and two-star **hotels**, reasonably priced but no great treat to stay at. The hotels listed below are either in the city centre itself or in the quieter neighbourhood around the gare routière.

Hotels

de Bayonne, 4 rue Martignac (☎05.56.48.00.88, fax 05.56.48.41.60). Impressive eighteenth-century building with classic 1930s decor, just around the corner from the Grand Théâtre, and suitably expensive. ⑥.

Blayais, 17 rue Mautrec (☎05.56.48.17.87, fax 05.56.52.47.57). Off place de la Comédie, a good, clean, central bet, and one of the city's most economical. ②.

de la Boétie, 4 rue de la Boétie (☎05.56.44.38.51, fax 05.56.81.24.72). Surprisingly cheap for such a central location, this hotel is on a quiet street between the Musée des Beaux-Arts and place Gambetta. ①.

du Centre, 8 rue du Temple (☎05.56.48.13.29, fax 05.56.48.17.70). Near the Porte Dijeaux; a comfortable two-star with breakfast thrown in for free. ②.

Dauphin, 82 rue du Palais-Gallien (☎05.56.52.24.62, fax 05.56.01.10.91). Very pleasant place between place Gambetta and the Jardin Public, so not too far from the action. ①.

Etche-Ona, 11 rue Mautrec (☎05.56.44.36.49, fax 05.56.44.59.58). Quiet and central, off place de la Comédie. Not the cheapest, but very good value for money. Exactly the same standards as its partner, the *Bayonne*. ⑥.

Grand Hôtel Français, 12 rue du Temple (☎05.56.48.10.35; 56.81.76.18). In a quiet street off the busy pedestrianized rue de la Porte-Dijeaux, this elegant old building has comfortable three-star rooms with all conveniences, including air-conditioning. ⑤.

Notre-Dame, 36 rue Notre-Dame (☎05.56.52.88.24, fax 05.56.79.12.67). Quiet, attractive establishment in a small street at the centre of Bordeaux's antiques trade, close to the river a few blocks north of the Esplanade des Quinconces. ⑤

des Quatre Sœurs, 6 cours du 30-Juillet (☎05.57.81.19.20, fax 05.56.01.04.28). Pleasant and friendly hotel in an ideal central spot next to the tourist office above an excellent, affordable brasserie. All rooms with telephone and TV. ④.

Youth hostels and campsite

HI youth hostel, 22 cours Barbey (☎05.56.91.59.51). Situated off cours de la Marne, the hostel is a 10min walk from gare St-Jean, or take bus #7 or #8. Kitchen and laundry facilities. Drawbacks include the seedy area and poor security.

Maison des Étudiantes, 50 rue Ligier (☎05.56.96.48.30). Friendly hostel, with a good chance of getting your own room, although students pay less and get preference. The hostel is women-only Oct to June, and also accepts men in July and Aug. There's a kitchen, but you'll need your own pots. Bus #7 or #8 to cours de la Libération.

Camping les Gravières, Pont-de-la-Maye, Villeneuve-d'Ornon (☎05.56.87.00.36). A three-star site, 8km south of gare St-Jean, in a forest by the River Garonne. Bus #B from place de la Victoire.

The city

Bordeaux is reasonably spread out along the western side of the River Garonne, with the eighteenth-century **old town** lying between the **place de la Comédie** to the north, the imposing buildings of the river bank, and the **cathedral** to the west. North of the centre is the vast open square of the **Esplanade des Quinconces**, and further still, the **Jardin Public**, containing some very scant remains of Bordeaux's Roman past.

Vieux Bordeaux

The elegant, eighteenth-century city centres on the **quartier St-Pierre** and stretches up to the Grand Théâtre to the north, the cathedral to the west and the cours Victor-Hugo to the south. The narrow streets are lined with grand mansions from Bordeaux's glory days, and much of the area has been done up over the last ten years or so, though some of the streets remain seedy in anticipation of the restorer's touch.

The social hub of the eighteenth-century city was the impeccably classical **Grand Théâtre** on **place de la Comédie** at the northern end of rue Ste-Catherine. Built on the site of a Roman temple by the architect Victor Louis in 1780, this lofty building is faced with an immense colonnaded portico topped by twelve Muses and Graces. Inside, the interior is likewise opulently decorated in *trompe l'œil* paintings; the best way to see it is to attend one of the operas or ballets staged throughout the year, with seats in the gods from as little as 50F (☎05.56.48.30.30 for info & bookings), or ask at the tourist office about the guided tours they sometimes offer. Smart streets radiate from here: the city's main shopping street, **rue Ste-Catherine**, runs south and has been partially pedestrianized to ease the consumer flow; there's the ritzy cours de l'Intendance running west, and the sandy, tree-lined allées de Tourny leads to a **statue of Claude Boucher**, Marquis of Tourny – the eighteenth-century administrator who was prime mover of the city's "Golden Age" and supervised much of the rebuilding. Back in the narrow streets of the old town, the harmonious **place du Parlement** and **place St-Pierre** are both lined with typical Bordelais mansions and peppered with wrought-iron balconies and arcading, making impressive examples of town planning.

The riverfront was also given the once-over by early eighteenth-century planners, with the imposing **place de la Bourse** creating a focal point on the quayside. The impressive bulk of the old customs house of 1733 contains the **Musée des Douanes** (Tues–Sun 10am–noon & 1–5/6pm; 10F), giving a rundown on Bordeaux's port and seafaring history and retracing the history of the administration and work of French Customs. The square is balanced by the **stock exchange** looking out over the quayside and the broad River Garonne; further south down the river bank, the fifteenth-century **Porte Cailhau** takes its name from the stones (*cailloux* – *cailhaux* in dialect) unloaded on the neighbouring quay to be used as ballast for boats. Crossing the river just south of here, the only testimony to a nobler past is the impressive **Pont de Pierre** – "Stone Bridge", though in fact it's brick – built at Napoléon's command during the Spanish campaigns, with seventeen arches in honour of his victories. The views of the river and quays from here are memorable, although (apart from a few sleazy bars) the once-impressive quayside is little more than a noisy six-lane motorway now.

Place Gambetta, the cathedral and around

Cours de l'Intendance, a street lined with chic shops, links place de la Comédie with café-lined **place Gambetta**, a pivotal square for the city's museums, shops and the cathedral. Once a majestic space conceived as an architectural whole in the time of Louis XV, place Gambetta's house fronts are arcaded at street level and decorated with rows of carved masks. In the middle of the square a valiant attempt at an English garden adds some welcome relief, belying the fact that the guillotine lopped 300 heads here at the time of the Revolution. In one corner stands the eighteenth-century arch of the **Porte Dijeaux**, an old city gate.

By the esplanade Charles-de-Gaulle, to the west of the place Gambetta, is Bordeaux's acknowledgement of twentieth-century architectural fashions, the modern shopping centre called the **Centre Mériadeck**. Herald of a brighter future to some Bordelais – and a carbuncle to others – it delivers its streets to the automobile and elevates its humans to mid-air plazas and walkways.

South of place Gambetta is the **Cathédrale St-André** (daily 8am–noon & 2–6pm), whose most eye-catching feature is the great upward sweep of the twin steeples over the north transept, an effect heightened by the adjacent but separate bell tower, the fifteenth-century **Tour Pey-Berland**. The interior of the cathedral, begun in the twelfth century, is not particularly interesting, apart from the choir that provides one of the few complete examples of the florid late-Gothic style known as *Rayonnant*, and there's also some fine carving in the north transept door and the Porte Royale to the right that's worth closer examination.

The attractive **place Pey-Berland** surrounding the cathedral harbours an enticing array of pavement cafés, like the old-fashioned museum on the south side, and another on the west by the classical Hôtel de Ville, formerly Archbishop Rohan's palace. It's here – or at least close to it – that the cream of Bordeaux's museums lie. A handsome eighteenth-century house in rue Bouffard, the Hôtel de Lalande, houses the **Musée des Arts Décoratifs** (daily except Tues 2–6pm; 20F, free Wed), whose extensive collection includes some beautiful, mainly French, porcelain and faïence, period furniture, glass, miniatures, Barye animal sculptures and prints of the city in its maritime heyday. Just around the corner on cours d'Albret next to the Hôtel de Ville, the **Musée des Beaux-Arts** (daily except Tues 10.30am–6pm; 20F, free Wed) has a small but worthy selection of fine art, featuring works by Perugino, Veronese, Delacroix, Rubens, Matisse and Marquet (a native of the city), as well as Kokoschka's superb painting of the city's cathedral. Smaller still is the Resistance museum and archive, the **Centre Jean-Moulin** just off the square to the north (Mon–Fri 2–6pm; free).

A short walk past the Tour Pey-Berland down cours Pasteur, the imaginatively laid out **Musée d'Aquitaine** (Tues–Sun 10am–6pm; 20F, free Wed) is one of the best of the city's museums. A stimulating variety of objects and types of display emphasizes regional ethnography and covers the three main facets of the region's development: maritime, commercial and agricultural. Drawings and writings on the period enable you to see why eighteenth-century Bordeaux was so extolled by contemporary writers, who compared it to Paris. Take a look at the section on the wine trade before venturing off on a vineyard tour in the region (see p.578). Parallel rue Ste-Catherine is straddled by a heavy Gothic tower, the sixteenth-century **Grosse Cloche**, originally part of the medieval town hall.

North of the centre

North of the Grand Théâtre, cours du 30-Juillet leads into the bare, gravelly – and frankly unattractive – expanse of the **Esplanade des Quinconces**, said to be Europe's largest municipal square. At the quayside end are two tall columns, erected in 1829 and topped by allegorical statues of Commerce and Navigation; at the opposite end of the esplanade is the **Monument aux Girondins**, a glorious fin-de-siècle ensemble of statues and fountains built in honour of the influential local deputies to the 1789 Revolutionary Assembly, later purged by Robespierre as moderates and counter-revolutionaries. During the last war, in a fit of anti-French spite, the occupying Germans made plans to melt the monument down, only to be foiled by the local Resistance, who got there first and, under cover of darkness, dismantled it piece by piece and hid it in a barn in the Médoc for the duration of the war.

To the northwest is the beautiful formal park, the **Jardin Public** (daily summer 7am–9pm; winter 7am–6pm), containing the city's botanical gardens. Behind it, to west and north, lies a quiet, provincial quarter of two-storey stone houses. Concealed among the narrow streets, at the end of rue du Colisée, is a large chunk of brick and stone masonry, the so-called **Palais Gallien**, in fact a third-century arena that's all that remains of *Burdigala*, Aquitaine's Roman capital. Nearby, on place Delerme, the unusual round **market hall** makes a focus for a stroll through the quarter. To the east of the gardens, closer to the river, is the **Musée d'Art Contemporain** on rue Ferrère (Tues–Sun noon–7pm; 30F, free noon–2pm). There are no permanent collections, so it's hit-and-miss as to whether you'll like what's on display, although the building alone – a converted nineteenth-century warehouse for exotic goods – is worth the trek. It provides one of the best settings in Europe for the sculpture and installation-based work shown in four exhibitions annually, the vast space giving the work real power.

There's also a superb collection of glossy art books in the first-floor library and an elegant designer café-restaurant on the roof.

Further out, in an old German submarine base in Dock no. 2, off bd Alfred-Daney, a new museum called the **Conservatoire International de la Plaisance** is dedicated to yachts and pleasure boats (Wed–Fri 1–7pm; Sat & Sun 10am–7pm; 45F). Nearby, moored in the middle of the quai des Chartrons, is a postwar French cruiser, the *Colbert* (April–Sept daily 10am–6/7pm; Oct–March Tues–Sun 2–6/7pm; 42F).

Eating and drinking

Bordeaux is packed with numerous **restaurants**, many of them top-notch, and because of its position close to the Atlantic coast fresh seafood features prominently on many a Bordelais menu. Being a student town, there are also plenty of lively **cafés** and **bars**, with a reasonable choice of dance clubs and jazz spots.

For **picnic fodder**, there is the marvellous, round **market** near the church of Notre-Dame behind cours de l'Intendance. And on rue de Montesquieu, off place des Grands-Hommes, Jean d'Alos runs the city's best *fromagerie*, with over 150 farm-produced cheeses.

Cafés and restaurants

Salubrious place du Parlement has its fair share of fine **dining establishments**, while the quartier St-Pierre – particularly rue des Bahutiers – is full of enticing cafés and restaurants, not all of them pricey. There are numerous cheap eating places around the station, and ethnic restaurants in the area around the church of St-Michel and more centrally in rue des Augustins near the place Victoire, with everything from Greek, Indian, Vietnamese and African to Chinese.

Aero Bar, cours du Chapeau-Rouge. Popular lunchtime café with outdoor tables.

Le Bistrot d'Édouard, 16 place du Parlement (☎05.56.81.48.87). A premier spot to try Bordelais specialities under canopies in this lovely square. The express lunch menu (69F) is particularly good value, combining a *plat du jour*, a dessert, glass of Bordeaux and a coffee.

Le Bistro de Quinconces, 4 place des Quinconces (☎05.56.81.48.87). Fashionable, fun bistrot which doubles as a *salon de thé* in the daytime and a tapas bar in the evening; outdoor tables in a great spot facing the fountains. Modern, eclectic *carte* includes pasta from 70F, around 112F for full meal.

Le Blayais, 17 place Meynard, opposite the flea market in place St-Michel. A simple and nourishing four-course meal including wine for 38F. There are several other similar establishments on the square and in the surrounding streets.

Café des Arts, cnr rue Ste-Catherine and cours Victor-Hugo. A popular brasserie with a unique ambience created with relics of the 1940s.

Chez Gilles, 6 rue des Lauriers (☎05.56.81.17.38). Well-recommended, simple restaurant off place du Parlement, with a good-value 89F *menu du jour* that gives you the choice of two glasses of Bordeaux or dessert. Closed Sat lunch & Sun.

Chez Joël D, 13 rue des Pilliers-de-Tutelle (☎05.56.52.68.31). Airy, modern *bar à huîtres*, where the smart set quaffs oysters and Bordeaux. Daily noon to midnight.

Chez Philippe, 1 place du Parlement (☎05.56.81.83.15). An elegant restaurant specializing in shellfish and the freshest of fish. Lunchtime menu at 125F, otherwise 200F or more.

au Clair de la Lune, rue des Bahutiers (☎05.56.81.09.18). Plain, clean, spacious Berber restaurant, with couscous. From 49F. Closed Tues.

Le Dégustoir, 8 rue Andre-Dumercq (☎05.56.91.25.06). In a narrow street off rue Ste-Catherine. Good rich cuisine of the southwest: *magret, foie gras*, etc. Menu at 60F. Closed Sat eve, Sun, & Mon eve.

Didier Gélineau, 26 rue Pas-St-Georges (☎05.56.52.84.25). One of the high spots of Bordeaux eating: exquisitely cooked and presented food with something of the lightness of *nouvelle cuisine*, served in a cool, pastel decor. 200–350F. Closed Sat & Sun.

Jean Ramet, 7–8 place Jean-Jaurès (☎05.56.44.12.51). Simple, summery decor in an unstuffy – although predictably expensive – highly rated gourmet restaurant. Closed Sat lunch, Sun & Aug 4–25.

L'Ombrière, place du Parlement (☎05.56.44.82.69). Efficient service, lovely surroundings and good food for around 59–135F. Open daily except Dec 15–Jan.

Le Tire-Bouchon, 15 rue des Bahutiers (☎05.56.44.24.63). Congenial, friendly atmosphere for good French cooking; lunch is very popular. Menus 80–135F. Closed Sun & Sat lunch.

Aux Trois Arcades, 10 place du Parlement (☎05.56.81.21.68). Light lunches, salads at 40–90F, menu at 69F. Closed Feb.

Bars

Bordeaux's student population ensures a collection of young, lively **bars**, a host of which are found on place de la Victoire and down cours de la Somme running off it. There are also several happening bars on rue de Candale, between place de la Victoire and restaurant-crowded rue des Augustins. For drinking in the early hours, head for place des Capucins, south of St-Michel.

Le Bœuf sur le Toit Pub, 15 rue de Candale. Looking a bit like an American bar, with a rhythm-and-blues soundtrack for a happily rough-and-ready crowd. McEwans served.

Chez Auguste, place de la Victoire. A regular student hang-out.

Connemara, 18 cours d'Albret, next door to the Musée des Beaux-Arts. For the homesick pining for a pint of Guinness, this is Bordeaux's lively Irish pub, with a cheap fish-and-chip restaurant attached.

Le 18, 18 rue Louis-de-Foix. Gay bar and disco.

La Plana, 22 place de la Victoire. Slick contemporary decor, with cool young folk eyeing up the world from tables outside. Frequent live music, open Thurs after midnight.

Nightlife and entertainment

To find out the latest **events and happenings** in and around Bordeaux, it's best to get hold of a copy of the regional newspaper *Sud-Ouest*; or there's the bimonthly listings booklet *Confetti* for 2F. *Bordeaux 95*, a free monthly mag available from the tourist office, has a listings section with the highbrow culture events around town. To buy **tickets** for city and regional events, head for the box office in the nineteenth-century Galerie Bordelaise arcade (☎05.56.48.26.26), wedged between rue Ste-Catherine and rue Piliers-de-Tutelle.

For **jazz**, hit either *L'Alligator*, 3 place du Général-Sarrail (Mon–Sat 10pm–2am), or *Le Borie*, 43 rue Borie, both of which host jazz ensembles towards the end of the week. *The Cricketers*, 72 quai de Paludate (Tues–Sat 10pm–2am), the southward continuation of quai Richelieu, has a more regular live spot but of more variable quality. *Do Re Mi*, in the Galerie Bordelaise (☎05.56.81.43.73), hosts indie line-ups, including many grunge groups touring from the US. Since dance clubs come and go, *Drequez* (☎05.56.42.34.34), is a source of flyers and the latest club info; they also sometimes organize raves themselves.

Listings

Airlines Air France, 29 rue Esprit-des-Lois (☎05.56.00.40.40); British Airways, (☎08.02.80.29.02).

Airport Bordeaux-Mérignac, 10km west of the city (☎05.56.34.50.50), with its own tourist office (daily 8am–7pm; ☎05.56.34.39.39). It's connected on weekdays by half-hourly shuttle to and from the main tourist office (40min).

Bike rental Gare St-Jean (open 24hr).

Books Mollat, 83–91 rue Porte Dijeaux, the city's largest bookstore, has French and a few English titles, and a separate record store next door. Bradley's, 32 place Gambetta, a specialist English language bookshop has a large selection of English- and French-language textbooks, as well as a bulletin board for job adverts.

Car rental Numerous rental firms are located at the airport and near gare St-Jean. A selection of the latter include Citer, at 68 rue Tauzia (☎05.56.92.19.62); Leader Rent-a-Car at no. 46 Rue Peyronnet (☎05.56.92.60.40); Budget at 12 rue Charles-Domercq (☎05.56.91.41.70); and Europcar in the same street at no. 35 (☎05.56.31.20.30).

Cinema Head for the art-house cinema, Centre Jean Vigo, 6 rue Franklin, near the Marché des Grands-Hommes (☎05.56.44.35.17; 34F entry, 27F Mon), where you're more likely to find original-language (*v.o.*) screenings.

Consulates Britain, 15 cours de Verdun (Mon–Fri 9am–12.30pm & 2.30–5pm; ☎05.57.22.21.10); USA, 22 cours du Maréchal-Foch (Mon–Fri 9am–noon & 2–5pm; ☎01.43.12.23.47).

Hitching Allostop, 77 cours d'Argonne (☎05.57.95.91.11).

Laundries On cours de Marne and rue de la Boétie.

Money exchange American Express, 14 cours de l'Intendance (Mon–Fri 8.45am–noon & 1.30–6pm); the tourist office or Thomas Cook at the train station (daily).

Travel agents Council Travel, 9 place Charles-Gruet (☎05.52.92.70); USIT, 284 rue Ste-Catherine (☎05.56.33.89.90).

The Médoc

The landscape of **the Médoc**, a slice of land northwest of Bordeaux wedged between the forests bordering the Atlantic coast and the Gironde estuary, is itself rather monotonous. Its gravel plains occupying the west bank of the brown, island-spotted estuary rarely swell into anything resembling a hill, but, paradoxically, this poor soil is ideal for viticulture – vines root more deeply if they don't find the sustenance they need in the topsoil and, firmly rooted, they are less subject to drought and flooding. The region's eight *appellations* – Médoc, Haut Médoc, St-Estèphe, Pauillac, St-Julien, Moulis en Médoc, Listrac-Médoc and Margaux – produce only red wines, from the grape varieties of Cabernet Sauvignon, Cabernet Franc, Merlot and, to a lesser degree, Petit Verdot. Cabernet Sauvignon gives body, bouquet, colour and maturing potential to the wine, while Merlot gives it its "animal" quality, making it rounder and softer. The D2 wine road, heading off the N15 from Bordeaux, passes through Margaux, St-Julien, Pauillac and St-Estèphe and, while the scenery might not be stunning, the many famous – albeit mostly inaccessible – châteaux are.

The problem of accommodation is much worse in the Médoc than in the rest of the wine region, so it's a good idea to visit on a day-trip from Bordeaux. Considering it's one of the most prestigious wine-growing areas in Bordeaux, it's surprisingly unwelcoming for visitors, with places to eat, and particularly affordable ones, also in short supply. There are regular Citram buses to Pauillac, but it's worth considering car rental (see "Listings", above).

Château Margaux and Fort Médoc

Easily the prettiest of the Bordeaux châteaux, **Château Margaux** is an eighteenth-century villa in extensive, sculpture-dotted gardens close to the west bank of the Gironde, 27km north of Bordeaux. Its wine, a classified *Premier Grand Cru* and world-famous in the 1940s and 1950s, went through a rough patch in the two succeeding decades but improved in the 1980s after the estate was bought by a Greek family. The château (☎05.57.88.83.83; Mon–Fri 10am–noon & 2–4pm; otherwise by appointment only) is not included in any tours, and advance booking is essential.

In the small village of **MARGAUX** itself, there's an unusually friendly Maison du Vin (mid-May to Oct daily 9am–7pm; Nov to mid-May 9am–noon & 2–6pm; English spoken) that can book accommodation and reserve visits to the *appellation*'s châteaux. Nearby, the enterprising cellar L'Âme du Vin provides free tastings from lesser-known Margaux châteaux, giving you a chance to try and buy some very good wines. Besides the local bars, you can **eat** at the *Restaurant Le Savoie*

(☎05.56.88.31.76; closed Sun & second half of Feb), next to the *Maison du Vin*, with good traditional food and menus from 80F. The only place to **stay** is the wildly expensive four-star *Relais de Margaux* (☎05.57.88.38.30; ⑨), with a fine restaurant. Otherwise, try the chambre d'hôte *Domaine de Cerrat* (☎05.56.58.24.80; ②) at Castelnau-de-Médoc 10km to the west.

The seventeenth-century **Fort Médoc**, off the D2 road between Margaux and St-Julien by the banks of the estuary, is a good place to tuck into a few purchases between châteaux. It was designed by the prolific military architect Vauban to defend the Gironde estuary against the British. The remains of the fort are scant but scramble-able, and in summer its Toytown aspect has a leafy charm, marred only by a splendid view of the nuclear power station across the river just north of Blaye. Since 1990, the annual Fort Médoc **jazz festival**, with big-name international acts, has been held here in mid-July (☎05.56.58.91.30 for details).

A couple of kilometres south, **LAMARQUE** is a very pretty village, full of flowers and with a sweet church. It's a pleasant place to stop for lunch at a very agreeable restaurant/bistrot, *Relais du Médoc*. From here, seven or eight ferries (pedestrians & cycles 17F; motorbikes 41F, cars 77F; prices one-way) cross the Gironde daily to Blaye, another place fortified by Vauban and an important, although little-known, Bordeaux wine-growing centre (see p.592). If you've missed the boat-crossing, there are plenty of small *caves* in Lamarque to check out while you wait.

Pauillac and around

PAUILLAC is the largest town in the Médoc region and central to the most important vineyards of Bordeaux: no fewer than three of the top five *Grands Crus* come from around here. The town's rapid growth in recent years, however, is due not to its vineyards but to the giant oil refinery which now dominates the town and accounts for the bleak, industrial appearance of the place.

Pauillac tries to make amends for this with a huge Maison du Tourisme et du Vin along the waterfront (Mon–Sat 9.30am–12.30pm & 2–6pm; ☎05.56.59.03.08). They don't reserve rooms but can provide you with a list of gîtes, rent out bikes and make appointments for you to visit the surrounding châteaux. It's not a great place to **stay**, but should you wish or need to, try the *Hôtel Yachting*, Port de Plaisance (☎05.56.59.06.43; ③), or the well-recommended riverfront **campsite** on rte de la Rivière (☎05.56.59.10.03; April to mid-Sept). Campsites are rare in the Médoc: the only other alternative is the two-star *Camping Le Bled* at Bernos (☎05.56.59.41.33; mid-June to mid-Sept), over 8km southwest near **ST-LAURENT-DE-MÉDOC**, a peaceful, shady and clean option. Alternatively, there's an excellent chambre d'hôte about 8km northwest near the village of **CISSAC**: *Château Vieux Braneyre*, run by the Gugès family (☎05.56.59.54.03; ③; dinner 130F), in a large eighteenth-century house attached to a vineyard.

The most famous of the **Médoc châteaux** can be visited by appointment only, either direct or through the Maison du Vin: Château Lafite-Rothschild (☎05.56.73.18.18; English spoken), Château Latour (☎05.56.73.19.80; English spoken), and Château Mouton-Rothschild (☎05.56.73.21.29). Their vineyards occupy larger single tracts of land than elsewhere in the Médoc, and consequently the quality of the wines differs to a greater extent than other châteaux on neighbouring land: a good vintage Lafite is perfumed and refined, whereas a Mouton-Rothschild is strong and dark and should be kept for at least ten years. **Château Mouton-Rothschild** and its wine **museum** (April–Oct daily 9.30–11am and 2–4pm; Nov–March closed Sat & Sun; 20F) is the most absorbing of the big houses: as well as the viticultural stuff, you also get to see the Rothschilds' amazing collection of postwar art, which includes work by Picasso, Dali and Warhol.

St-Estèphe

North of Pauillac, the wine commune of **ST-ESTÈPHE** is Médoc's largest *appellation*, consisting predominantly of *crus bourgeois* properties and growers belonging to the local *cave coopérative*, **Marquis de St-Estèphe**, on the D2 towards Pauillac (tastings July to mid-Sept daily 9am–noon & 2–7pm; Oct–June Mon–Fri to 6pm, Sat to 5pm). One of the *appellation*'s five *crus classés* is the distinctive **Château Cos d'Estournel**, with its over-the-top eighteenth-century French version of a pagoda; the château can be visited by appointment (☎05.56.73.15.55; English spoken). The village of St-Estèphe itself is a sleepy affair dominated by its landmark, the eighteenth-century **church of St-Étienne**, with its highly decorative interior. The small, homespun Maison du Vin, presided over by a friendly old lady, is hidden in the church square.

For an elegant place to **stay**, back in the village, *Hôtel Château Pomys* (☎05.56.59.73.44, fax 05.56.59.35.24; ④) is a mansion set in its own park. There are also several good chambres d'hôte, including Jean-Pierre Fatin (☎05.56.59.35.28; ②) and Françoise Leeman (☎05.56.59.72.94; ④), both with table d'hôte. The other half of St-Estèphe is its port, where you'll find a typical roadside **restaurant**, *Le Peyrat*. In front of a grassy river stretch, it's casual and friendly, with simple, generous dishes; menus from 52F.

Sauternes

The **Sauternes** region, on the left bank of the River Garonne, 40km southeast of Bordeaux, is an ancient wine-making area, originally planted during the Roman occupation. The distinctive golden wine of the area is certainly sweet, but also round, full-bodied and spicy, with a long aftertaste. It's not necessarily a dessert wine, either: try it with some Roquefort cheese or with *foie gras*. Gravelly terraces with a limestone subsoil help create the delicious taste, but mostly it's due to a peculiar micro-climate of morning autumn mists and afternoons of sun and heat which causes *botrytis cinerea* fungus, or "noble rot", to flourish on the grapes, letting the sugar concentrate and introducing some intense flavours. When they're picked, they're not a pretty sight: carefully selected by hand, only the most shrivelled, rotting bunches are taken. The wines of Sauternes make up some of the most highly sought-after in the world, with bottles of Château d'Yquem, in particular, fetching thousands of francs.

SAUTERNES itself is a fairly quiet little village dominated by the rather intimidating **Maison du Sauternes** (daily summer 9.30am–7pm; winter 9.30am–12.30pm & 2–6pm) at one end of the village, and with a pretty church and a vineyard at the other. The *maison* is a room full of treasures, the golden bottles with white and gold labels being quite beautiful objects in themselves. Although they do tastings, they're unfortunately rather snooty about it, even if you buy. There are lots of other, smaller *caves* in the village, many offering tastings.

There are some good **eating** opportunities in Sauternes. Opposite the church is *Auberge Les Vignes* (☎05.56.76.60.06; closed Mon & Jan 15–Feb 15) a typical country restaurant with regional specialities like *lapin au Sauternes* (70F), and a lunch menu at 60F. You could also try nearby *Le Saprien*, combining regional-style elements with modern eclectic additions and featuring menus from 119F. For something refreshingly downmarket, there's a typical scruffy local **bar** across the road.

Entre-Deux-Mers

The landscape of **Entre-Deux-Mers** (literally "between two seas") – so called because it is sandwiched between the tidal waters of the Dordogne and Garonne – is much more attractive than the other wine regions, with its gentle hills and scattered

THE TRUTH ABOUT CADILLAC

According to the tourist office in the medieval town of **Cadillac**, 11km northwest of Langon on the Garonne, **Antoine Laumet**, the founder of Detroit, Michigan – home city of General Motors – originally came from Cadillac. Sadly, this is just too good to be true, and he was born in 1658 in St-Nicolas-de-la-Grave, halfway between Agen and Toulouse, and never set foot in Cadillac itself. On emigrating to Canada, he took the name of Lamothe-Cadillac, a family who had nothing whatsoever to do with the town of Cadillac. The story about General Motors naming their new limousines "Cadillacs" in honour of the 300th anniversary of Cadillac's birth seems also to be untrue. The totally independent Cadillac company was actually founded, on August 22, 1902, in Detroit, though it was later purchased by General Motors Ltd.

medieval villages. Its wines, including the Premières Côtes de Bordeaux, are mainly dry whites produced by over forty *caves coopératives*, and are regarded as good but inferior to the Médocs or super-dry Graves to the south. It's also a region which can be explored, at least in part, by public transport, should you feel like avoiding the tourist office tour.

La Sauve-Majeure

The one place you should really try to see is the ruined **abbey** 3km east of Créon at **LA SAUVE-MAJEURE**, an important stop for pilgrims en route to Santiago de Compostela in Spain (daily 10am–noon & 2–6pm; 25F). The bus from Bordeaux's tourist office drops you off in the middle of a tranquil valley of small vineyards and cornfields, but you can see the ruin as you approach. Once it was all forest here, the abbey's name being a corruption of the Latin *silva major* (big wood). It was founded in 1079, and the treasures of what remains are the twelfth-century Romanesque apse and apsidal chapels and the outstanding sculpted capitals in the chancel. The finest are the ones illustrating stories from the Old and New Testaments (Daniel in the lions' den, Delilah shearing Samson's hair and so on), while others show fabulous beasts and decorative motifs. There is a small **museum** at the entrance, with some excellent photos of the ruins, along with keystones from the fallen roofs. But what makes the visit so worthwhile is not just the capitals themselves, but the remote, undisturbed nature of the site. If you have the time, stroll over to the abbey's parish **church** along rue de l'Église, visible on the hill.

St-Macaire and around

If you're heading south through Entre-Deux-Mers, **LANGON** is the first town of any size you come to. But **ST-MACAIRE**, across the Garonne from Langon, is far better for a rest or food stop. St-Macaire still has its original **gates** and **battlements** and a beautiful medieval church, the **Église-Prieuré**. There's also the *Maison du Pays* at 8 rue Canton, which serves as an **écomusée** (☎05.56.63.32.14) and information centre for the region and its produce, with plenty of information for walkers, and free maps. In July and August, the museum runs a programme of visiting wine-makers hosting tastings of their products. Next door to the *maison* is an excellent **restaurant**, *Le Compostelle*, with 55F and 100F menus, often crowded with French families, particularly for Saturday lunch. Just below the ramparts is the small, well-run *Camping Les Remparts* (mid-June to mid-Sept).

   LA RÉOLE, on the north bank 18km further east, has a wealth of medieval architecture along a well-signposted walk through its narrow, hilly streets, and likewise makes an excellent stop for food or accommodation. France's oldest **town hall**, constructed for Richard the Lionheart in the twelfth century, and the well-preserved simple **Abbaye des Bénédictins** – with a fantastic view over the River Garonne and the surrounding countryside – reward a stroll through the town, although little remains of the fortified **castle**.

La Réole's **tourist office** on place de la Libération (Mon 3–6pm, Tues–Sat 9am–noon & 3–6pm; ☎05.56.61.13.55, fax 05.56.71.25.40) conducts tours of the city in July and August. For **accommodation**, the two-star *Hôtel de l'Abbaye*, 42 rue Armand-Caduc (☎05.56.61.02.64, fax 05.56.71.24.40; ③), is in the same street as the abbey. A good **restaurant** is *Les Fontaines* on rue André-Benac (closed Sun eve & Nov), with classic French cuisine in unstuffy surroundings and menus at 75F, 100F and 140F. A lively Saturday **market** on avenue Jean-Jaurès along the Garonne provides good picnic provisions if you're passing.

Thirteen kilometres south of Langon, the town of **BAZAS** has a laid-back, southern air. Its most attractive feature is the wide, arcaded place de la Cathédrale, overlooked by the lichenous grey **Cathédrale St-Jean-Baptiste** that displays a harmonious blend of Romanesque, Gothic and classical in its west front. A good place to **stay**, despite its kitschy decor, is the medium-priced *Hostellerie St-Sauveur*, 14 rue du Général-de-Gaulle (☎05.56.25.12.18; ②). To **eat**, head for the *Restaurant des Remparts*, espace Mauvezin, near the mairie (☎05.56.25.95.24; closed Mon), for delicious local specialities and menus from 110F.

Circling back east and north towards Sauternes, you could pass through **UZESTE**, a quiet little place where Pope Clément V – who caused a schism by moving the papacy to Avignon in the fourteenth century – erected the old **church** on the square. Beyond lies **VILLANDRAUT**, where Clément was born and built a colossal moated **castle**, whose ruinous curtain walls and corner towers still stand beside the road.

St-Émilion and around

ST-ÉMILION, 35km east of Bordeaux and a short trip by train or Citram bus from Bordeaux, is well worth a visit in its own right. The old grey houses of this fortified medieval village straggle down the south-hanging slope of a low hill with the green froth of the summer's vines crawling over its walls. Many of the growers still keep up the old tradition of planting roses at the ends of the rows, which in pre-pesticide days served as an early-warning system against infection, the idea being that the commonest bug, *oidium*, went for the roses first, giving three days' notice of its intentions.

The town

The town's **belfry** belongs to the rock-hewn subterranean **Église Monolithe** beneath it, which can be visited only on a **guided tour** (daily every 45min 10–11.30am & 2–5pm; 33F from the tourist office). The tour starts in a dark hole in someone's backyard, supposedly the cave where St Émilion lived a hermit's life in the eighth century. A rough-hewn ledge served as his bed and a carved seat as his chair, where infertile women reputedly still come to sit in the hope of getting pregnant.

Above is the half-ruined thirteenth-century **Trinity Chapel**, which was built in honour of St Émilion and converted into a barn during the Revolution; fragments of frescoes are still visible, including one of St Valérie, patron saint of wine-growers. On the other side of the yard, a passage tunnels beneath the belfry to the **catacombs**, where three chambers dug out of the soft limestone were used as ossuary and cemetery from the eighth to the eleventh centuries. In the innermost chamber – discovered by a neighbour enlarging his cellar some fifty years ago – a large tombstone bears the inscription: "Aulius is buried between saints Valérie, Emilion and Avic."

The ninth- and twelfth-century **church** itself is an incredible place. Simple and huge, the entire structure – barrel-vaulting, great square piers and all – has been hacked out of the rock. (The windows of Chartres Cathedral were stored here for safe-keeping during World War II.) The whole interior was painted once, but only faint traces survived the Revolution, when a gunpowder factory was installed in the church. These days, every June, the wine council – *La Jurade* – assembles here in distinctive red robes to evaluate the previous season's wine and decide whether each *viticulteur*'s produce deserves the *appellation contrôlée* rating.

Behind the tourist office, the town comes to an abrupt end with a grand view of the **moat** and old **walls**. To the right is the twelfth-century **collegiate church of the Cordeliers**, with a handsome but badly mutilated doorway and a lovely fourteenth-century **cloister** (daily 10am–noon & 2–7pm; free).

You should take advantage of the produce of this well-respected wine region, whose most famous wine originates at **Château Ausone**, south of St-Émilion. The cellars (which can be visited) have been dug out of limestone directly beneath the vineyards. If you are interested in seeing the vineyards, ask at the **Maison du Vin** (Mon–Sat 9.30am–12.30pm & 2–6.30pm, Sun 10am–12.30pm & 2.30–6.30pm; ☎05.57.55.50.55) at the top of the hill by the belfry.

Practicalities

The super-efficient **tourist office** on place des Créneaux by the belfry (daily: 9.30am–12.30pm & 2–6.30pm; July & Aug no lunchbreak; ☎05.57.55.28.28, fax 05.57.55.28.29) is a good source of information and organizes French or English tasting tours in various châteaux in the region (June–Sept 2pm & 4.15pm; 51F); they have a very detailed hand-out of châteaux open to the public for those who want to visit independently. If you haven't got a car, **bikes** can be rented from Loi Alouette, opposite the Collegiate Church (☎05.57.74.42.55).

If you're short of funds or without your own transport, St-Émilion is best left as a day-trip from Bordeaux, as there's a chronic shortage of budget **accommodation** within the town. However, the tourist office can furnish you with an extensive list of chambres d'hôte in the immediate area, and many of them are very reasonably priced. Within the town itself, the two-star *Auberge de la Commanderie* on rue des Cordeliers (☎05.57.24.70.19, fax 05.57.74.44.53; ③) is the only remotely affordable place to stay. Three kilometres northwest in the village of Montagne, there's a fantastic three-star campsite, *La Barbanne* (☎05.57.24.75.80), with its own swimming pool.

There's nowhere to buy groceries in town, but you should try the town's speciality once you're here: **macaroons** were devised here by the Ursuline sisters in 1620, and the one authentic place to buy them is at 1 rue Gaudet, where the tiny mouth-melting biscuits are baked to the original recipe. A good place to **eat**, though, is the relaxed contemporary-style bistrot *L'Envers du Decor* (closed Sun eve) on rue du Clocher, with *plats du jour* for 50F and wine by the glass, which you can accompany with gazpacho, cheese, salads and other light snacks.

Blaye

The green slopes behind the river, the **Côtes de Bourg** and **Côtes de Blaye**, were home to wine production long before the Médoc was planted. The wine is a rather heavier, plummier red, and cheaper than anything found on the opposite side of the river, and the **Maison du Vin des Côtes de Blaye** on cours Vauban, the main street of the pretty little town of **BLAYE**, serves up a representative selection of the local produce, with some ridiculously inexpensive wines, the priciest being around 40F.

The town was fortified yet again by Vauban, and the **citadelle** deserves a wander. People still live within it, and it's a strange combination of peaceful village and tourist attraction, typically with an old man sunning himself outside his tiny home, a revolving postcard rack only metres away. A beautiful spot, it has grass, trees, birds and a spectacular view over the Gironde estuary.

The riverfront **tourist office**, opposite the fort (June–Sept daily 9.30am–12.30pm & 2–7pm; Oct–May closed Sun & Mon; ☎05.57.42.12.09), is really helpful and can reserve rooms free of charge and give out details on wine-tasting. If you fancy **staying** here, the *Hôtel Bellevue* is a pleasant ivy-covered two-star on the main riverfront drag (☎05.57.42.00.36, fax 05.57.42.89.10; ②), or there's the expensive *Hôtel La Citadelle* on place d'Armes (☎05.57.42.17.10, fax 05.57.42.10.34; ④). Alternatively, the *Auberge du Porche* at 5 rue Ernest-Régnier, the street opposite the tourist office (☎05.57.42.22.69, fax 05.57.42.82.83; ③), has rooms that are pricey but serves food that's very good value, with local specialities as well as crêpes and grills, couscous and paella. Finally, there's a **camping municipal** within the *citadelle* (☎05.57.42.00.20).

The Côte d'Argent

The **Côte d'Argent** is the long stretch of coast from the mouth of the Gironde estuary to Biarritz, which – at over 200km – is the longest, straightest and sandiest in Europe. The endless beaches are backed by high sand dunes, while behind lies the largest forest in western Europe: **Les Landes**. Despite these attractions, the lack of conventional tourist sights means that the coast still gets comparatively few visitors, and away from the main resorts it is still possible to find deserted stretches of coastline.

Arcachon and around

On summer weekends, the Bordelais escape en masse to **ARCACHON**, the oldest resort on the Côte d'Argent and a forty-minute train ride across flat, sandy forest from Bordeaux. The beaches of white sand are magnificent but can be crowded, and its central jetties, Thiers and Eyrac, are busy with boats going off on an array of cruises to places like the Île aux Oiseaux and the **Dune de Pyla**.

The town itself is a sprawl of villas great and small, the most exclusive area being the **ville d'hiver** (winter town), whose wide shady streets are full of fanciful Second Empire mansions overlooking the seaside **ville d'été** (summer town). Well worth a wander, the area can be reached by following the lively pedestrianized and restaurant-filled rue de Maréchal-de-Lattre-de-Tassigny, running perpendicular to the seafront bd de la Plage; at the end of this mouthful of a street, a lift carries you up to the flower-filled, wooded **Parc Mauresque** (daily 9am–1pm & 2.15–7pm; 1F up & down), with the *ville d'hiver* beyond it. From the park, there are fine views over the seafront.

A well-stocked, modern **tourist office**, place Roosevelt (Mon–Sat 9am–12.30pm & 2–7pm, Sun 9am–1pm; July & Aug no lunchbreak; ☎05.56.83.01.69, fax 05.57.52.22.10), can be reached by following avenue Gambetta back from seafront place Thiers; it organizes excellent **guided visits** of the Médoc vineyards (Tues & Thurs 2–7pm; 120F). Boats leave the jetties of Thiers and Eyrac on **cruises** to the Île aux Oiseaux (2hr; 70F), an exploration of the Arcachon basin with a look at the Dune de Pyla (2hr 30min; 70F), and a visit to an oyster farm with tasting (1hr 15min; 55F). There's also a regular June to September boat service from here to Cap Ferret on the opposite peninsula (30min; 50F return).

The tourist office doesn't reserve rooms, and you'll be hard-pushed to find an inexpensive **hotel**; a couple of reasonable ones include *Le Provence*, 106 bd de la Plage (☎05.56.83.10.78; ②), and the small, friendly *St-Christaud*, 8 allée de la Chapelle

(☎05.56.83.38.53; ④; half-board only July & Aug). Pricier options include the modern two-star *Les Mimosas*, 77 av de la République (☎05.56.83.45.86, fax 05.56.22.53.40; ④), and in the *ville d'hiver*, the luxurious *Hôtel Sémiramis*, 4 allée Rebsomen (☎05.56.83.25.87, fax 05.57.52.22.41; ⑤). Alternatively, there are many **holiday apartments** to rent; ask for the booklet *Clévacances* from the tourist office. **Camping** is another option, with plenty of sites around the Arcachon basin, but only the three-star *Le Camping Club*, allée de la Galaxie (☎05.56.83.24.15; open all year), is actually within the town. Set in an expanse of bird-filled woodland, it's worth the high summer prices. Hostellers can take the boat to Cap Ferret, where there's an HI **youth hostel** at 87 av de Bordeaux (☎05.56.60.64.62; July & Aug only).

A great **restaurant** to sample some of the local seafood is the colourful, jam-packed *La Marée*, 21 rue de Lattre-de-Tassigny; not only is it inexpensive, but if you're lucky you can sit out on one of two tiny wrought-iron balconies.

The Dune du Pyla and Le Teich

The Côte d'Argent's chief curiosity is the **Dune du Pyla**. At 114m it is the highest sand dune in Europe – a veritable mountain of wind-carved sand, about 8km south of Arcachon. Buses leave from the gare SNCF (where you can also rent bikes) every thirty minutes in July and August – about five a day at other times. From the end of the line the road continues straight on uphill for about fifteen minutes and, if you're driving, it costs 15F to use the obligatory car park. There is the inevitable group of stands selling ice-cream, *galettes* and junk, but from the top you get a superb view over the bay of Arcachon and the forest of the Landes stretching away to the south. It's a great sandy slide down to the sea (the sides as steep as an Olympic ski–jump) and a long haul back up but well worth the effort. You can take a boat trip into the Arcachon basin and past the Dune du Pyla.

At **LE TEICH**, about 14km east of Arcachon in the southeast corner of the Bassin d'Arcachon, one of the most important expanses of wetlands remaining in France has been converted into a bird sanctuary, the **Parc Ornithologique du Teich** (daily 10am–6pm; 35F), one of only two in the country. The only **accommodation** in Le Teich is the **campsite** beside the sanctuary, but you can easily come here on a day-trip by train from Arcachon or Bordeaux.

Les Landes

Travelling south from Bordeaux by road or rail, you pass for half a day through an unremitting, flat, sandy pine forest known as **Les Landes**. Until the nineteenth century it was a vast, infertile swamp, badly drained because of the impermeable layer of grit deposited by the glaciers of the quaternary age and steadily encroached upon by the shifting sand dunes of the coast. Today it supports nearly 10,000 square kilometres of trees and since 1970 has been designated a *parc naturel régional*.

At **SABRES**, 18km east of Labouheyre on the Bordeaux–Bayonne road, you can take a restored steam train to the **Écomusée de Marquèze** (Easter–Nov daily 10.15am–5.40pm, Dec–Easter Sat & Sun only; 46F), set up by the park authorities to illustrate the traditional *landais* way of life, when shepherds used to clomp around the scrub on long stilts.

travel details

Buses

Bordeaux to: Blaye (at least 10 daily; 1hr 45min); Pauillac (daily but infrequent; 1hr); St-Émilion (5 daily; 1hr 15min).

Les Sables-d'Olonne to: Luçon (4 daily; 2hr); Nantes (4 daily; 5hr 30min).

Parthenay to: Airvault (several daily; 25min); Niort (8 daily; 50min); Thouars (at least 10 daily; 1hr).

Poitiers to: Châteauroux (3 daily; 3hr); Chauvigny (3 daily; 45min); Le Blanc (3 daily; 1hr 25min); Limoges (daily; 3hr); Parthenay (several daily; 1hr–1hr 30min); Ruffec (daily; 2hr 30min); St-Savin (3 daily; 1hr).

Rochefort to: Château d'Oléron (4–6 daily; 1hr); La Fumée-île d'Aix (4 daily; 30min).

Saintes to: Rochefort (2 daily; 1hr 20min); Royan (3 daily; 1hr); St-Pierre d'Oléron (2 daily; 2hr).

Trains

Angoulême to: Bordeaux (20 daily; 1hr); Limoges (4 daily; 1hr 30min–2hr); Poitiers (28 daily; 40min–1hr); Royan (12 daily; 2hr).

Bordeaux to: Angoulême (20 daily; 1hr); Arcachon (frequent; 45min); Bayonne-Biarritz (12 daily; 1hr 40min–2hr 30min); Bergerac (6 daily; 1hr 30min); Brive (5 daily; 2hr 30min); La Rochelle (several daily; 2hr 20min); Lourdes (4–5 daily; 2hr 30min–3hr); Marseille (5–6 daily; 6–7hr); Nice (4 daily; 9–10hr); Paris-Austerlitz (4 daily; 5hr 30min); Paris–Montparnasse (6 daily; 3hr); Périgueux (5 daily; 1hr 20 min); Poitiers (8 daily; 2hr); Saintes (7–11 daily; 1hr 20min); Sarlat (up to 4 daily; 2hr 35min); St-Jean-de-Luz (6 daily; 2hr 15min); Toulouse (frequent; 2hr 20min).

La Rochelle to: Bordeaux (12 daily daily; 2hr 20min); Nantes (10 daily; 1hr 50min); Rochefort (several daily; 20min); Saintes (several daily; 1hr).

Poitiers to: Angoulême (16 daily; 1hr); Bayonne (8 daily; 3hr 10min–4hr 30min); Biarritz (10 daily; 4hr 30min); Bordeaux (20 daily; 2hr 10min); Châtellérault (15 daily; 20min); Dax (2–3 daily; 2hr 45min–3hr 40min); Hendaye (3 daily; 4–5hr); Irun (2 daily; 4hr 5min–5hr 5min); La Rochelle (12 daily; 1hr 45min); Limoges (6 daily; 2hr); Niort (4–5 daily; 1hr); Paris-Austerlitz (7 daily; 2hr 50min); Paris-Montparnasse (20 daily; 1hr 45min); Surgères (frequent; 1hr 25min).

Royan to: Angoulême (3–4 daily; 2hr); Cognac (3 or 4 daily; 1hr); Saintes (3 or 4 daily; 40min).

Les Sables-d'Olonne to: Nantes (19 daily; 1hr 30min); Paris-Montparnasse (8 daily; 4hr 45min).

CHAPTER NINE

THE DORDOGNE, LIMOUSIN AND LOT

The land covered in this chapter forms a large westward-pointing triangle. Its base is the western edge of the uplands of the Massif Central and its apex almost exactly **Castillon-la-Bataille** on the River Dordogne, a little way downstream from **Bergerac**. It is the area which was most in dispute between the English and the French during the Hundred Years' War and most in demand among English visitors and second-home buyers in recent times.

Although it does not coincide exactly with either the modern French administrative boundaries or the old provinces of Périgord and Quercy, which constitute the core of the region, it has a physical and geographical homogeneity because of its great rivers: the **Dordogne**, the **Lot** and the **Aveyron**, all of which drain the waters of the western Massif Central into the mighty **Garonne**, which forms the southern limit covered by this chapter.

There are no great cities in the area: its charm lies in the landscapes and the dozens of harmonious small towns and villages, so it is impossible to establish a hierarchy of attractiveness. Some, like **Sarlat** and **Rocamadour**, are so well known that they are overrun with tourists. Others, like **Figeac**, **Villefranche-de-Rouergue**, **Gourdon**, **Montauban**, **Monflanquin** and the many *bastides* (fortified towns) that fill the area between the Lot and Dordogne, boast no single notable sight but are perfect organic ensembles.

The landscapes are surprisingly homogenous, too. From **Limoges** in the province of Limousin in the north to Montauban in the south towards Toulouse, the country is gently hilly, full of lush little valleys and miles of woodland, mainly oak. **Limousin**, at the north of this area, is slightly greener and wetter, the south more arid. But you can travel a long way without seeing a radical shift, except in the uplands of the **Plateau de Millevaches**, where the rivers plunge into gorges and the woods are beech, chestnut and conifer plantations. The other characteristic landscape is the *causses*, dry scrubby limestone plateaux like the **Causse de Gramat** between the Dordogne and the Lot and the **Causse de Limogne** between the Lot and Aveyron.

ACCOMMODATION PRICE CATEGORIES

Each hotel in this chapter has a symbol which corresponds to one of eight price categories.

① Under 160F	④ 300–400F	⑦ 600–700F
② 160–220F	⑤ 400–500F	⑧ Over 700F
③ 220–300F	⑥ 500–600F	

The prices quoted are for the cheapest available double room in high season, though remember that many of the cheap places will have more expensive rooms with en-suite facilities.

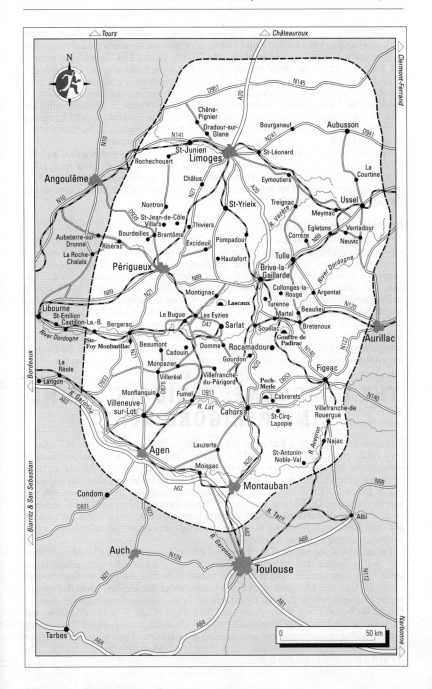

Where the rivers have cut their way through the limestone, the valleys are walled with overhanging cliffs riddled with fissures, underground stream-beds and caves. And in these caves – especially in the valley of the Vézère around **Les Eyzies** – are some of the most developed prehistoric paintings and reliefs to be found anywhere in the world. The other great artistic legacy of the area is the Romanesque sculpture, visible in its finest examples on the churches at **Souillac** and **Beaulieu-sur-Dordogne**, but all modelled on the supreme example of the cloister of St-Pierre in **Moissac**. And the dearth of luxurious châteaux is compensated for by the numerous splendid fortresses of purely military design: **Bonaguil**, **Najac**, **Excideuil**, **Beynac** and, for lovers of the romantic ruin, the untended remains of **Chalusset** and **Ventadour**.

The wartime Resistance was very active in these out-of-the-way regions, and the roadsides are dotted with tiny memorials to individuals or small groups of men, killed in ambushes or shot in reprisals. There is one monstrous monument to wartime atrocity: the ruined village of **Oradour-sur-Glane**, still as the Nazis left it after massacring the population and setting fire to the houses.

Dordogne – an identity crisis

To the French, the **Dordogne** is a river. To the British, it is a much looser term, covering a vast area roughly equivalent to what the French call Périgord. This starts south of Limoges and takes in the Vézère and Dordogne valleys and much in between. The Dordogne is also a *département*, with fixed boundaries that pay no heed to either definition. The central part of the *département*, around Périgueux and the River Isle, is known as **Périgord Blanc**, after the light, white colour of its rock outcrops; the southeastern half around Sarlat as **Périgord Noir**, said to be darker in aspect than the Blanc because of the preponderance of oak woods. To confuse matters further, the tourist authorities have added another two colours to the Périgord patchwork: **Périgord Vert**, the far north of the *département*, so called because of its woods and pastureland; and **Périgord Pourpre** in the southwest, purple because it includes the wine-growing area around Bergerac.

THE DORDOGNE: PÉRIGORD BLANC AND PÉRIGORD VERT

The close green valleys of **Périgord Vert** are like an Englishman's dream of England: very rural, with plenty of space and few people, large tracts of woodland and uncultivated land – and sunshine. Less-well known than the much-frequented Périgord Noir, its largely granite landscape bears a closer resemblance to the neighbouring Limousin that to the rest of the Périgord. It is partly for this reason that the most northerly tip, together with the southwestern part of the Haute-Vienne, has recently been designated as the **Parc Naturel Régional Périgord-Limousin** – to give it a sense of identity and draw attention to its natural assets, in an attempt to promote "green" tourism in this economically fragile and depopulated area.

Périgueux, in the centre of the **Périgord Blanc**, is interesting for its domed cathedral and its Roman remains, whose existence alone is a reminder of how long these parts have been civilized. But it is in the countryside that the region's finest monuments lie. One of the loveliest stretches is the **valley of the Dronne**, from **Aubeterre** on the Charente border through **Brantôme** to the marvellous Renaissance château of **Puyguilhem**, the abbey of **Boschaud** and the perfect village of **St-Jean-de-Côle**, and on to the great fortress of **Excideuil** and the Limousin border, where the country begins to change, becoming not mountainous but higher and less cosy. Truffle-lovers might like to take a look at **Sorges**, where there is a marked path through truffle country and a museum to explain it all.

Périgueux

PÉRIGUEUX, capital of the *département* of the Dordogne, is a small, busy and not particularly attractive market town for a province made rich by tourism and specialized farming. Its name derives from the Petrocorii, the local Gaullish tribe, but it was the Romans who transformed it into an important settlement. A few Roman remains, as well as a medieval *vieille ville*, survive to this day.

The city

The main hub of the city's contemporary life is the tree-shaded **boulevard Montaigne** with its cafés and brasseries, which marks the western edge of the *vieille ville*. At its southern end, a short walk along rue Taillefer brings you to the domed and coned **Cathédrale St-Front** (daily 8am–12.30pm & 2.30–6.30pm), its square, pineapple-capped belfry surging far above the roofs of the surrounding medieval houses. Unfortunately, it's no beauty, having suffered from the zealous attentions of the purist nineteenth-century restorer Abadie, best known for the white elephant of the Sacré-Cœur in Paris. The result is too white, too new, too regular, and the roof is spiked all over with ill-proportioned nipple-like projections serving no obvious purpose; "a supreme example of how not to restore", Freda White tartly observed in her classic travelogue, *Three Rivers of France*. It's a pity, for when it was rebuilt in 1173 following a fire, it was one of the most distinctive Byzantine churches undertaken in France, modelled on St Mark's in Venice and the Holy Apostles in Constantinople. Nevertheless, the Byzantine influence is still evident in the interior in the Greek-cross plan – unusual in France – and in the massive clean curves of the domes and

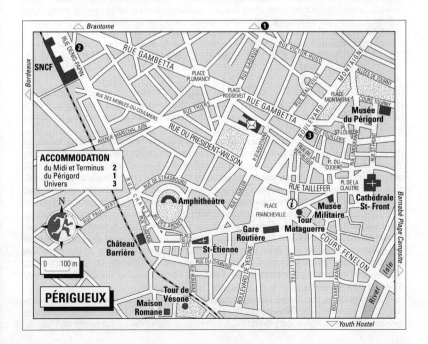

THE FOOD AND WINE OF PÉRIGORD

The two great stars of Périgord cuisine are **foie gras** and **truffles** (*truffes*). *Foie gras* is eaten on its own, in succulent slabs, often combined with truffles to accompany a huge variety of dishes from scrambled eggs to stuffed carp. In fact, you can be sure that this is what you are getting with any dish that has *sauce Périgueux* or *à la périgourdine* as part of its name. Truffles also come *à la cendre*, wrapped in bacon and cooked in hot ashes.

The other mainstay of Périgord cuisine is the grey Toulouse **goose**, whose fat is used in the cooking of everything, most commonly perhaps in the standard potato dish, *pommes sarladaises*. The goose fattens well: *gavé* or crammed with corn, it goes from six to ten kilos in weight in three weeks, with its liver alone weighing nearly a kilo. When the liver has been used for *foie gras*, the meat is cooked and preserved in its own thick yellow grease as *confits d'oie*, which you can either eat on its own or use in the preparation of other dishes, like *cassoulet*. **Duck** is used in the same way, both for *foie gras* and *confits*. *Magrets de canard*, or slices of duck breast, are one of the favourite ways of eating duck and appear on practically every restaurant menu.

Another common goose delicacy is *cou d'oie farci* – goose neck stuffed with sausage meat, duck liver and truffles, which you can also buy in pots; a favourite salad throughout the region is made with warm *gésiers* or goose gizzards. Try not to be put off by fare such as this, or your palate will miss out on some delicious experiences – like *tripoux* or sheep's stomach stuffed with tripe, trotters, pork and garlic, which is really an Auvergnat dish but is quite often served in neighbouring areas like the Rouergue. Other less challenging specialities include stuffed **cèpes** or wild mushrooms, **ballottines** or fillets of poultry stuffed, rolled and poached, the little flat discs of goat's cheese called *cabécou* and the sweet light bread called *fouasse*, rather like the Greek *tsoureki*.

The **wines** should not be scorned either. There are the fine dark, almost peppery reds from Cahors, and both reds and whites from the vineyards of Bergerac, of which the sweet, white Monbazillac is the most famous. Pecharmant is the fanciest of the reds, but there are some very drinkable Côtes de Bergerac, much like the neighbouring Bordeaux and far cheaper. The same goes for the wines of Duras, Marmande and Buzet. If you are thinking of taking a stock of wine home, you could do much worse than make some enquiries in Bergerac itself, Ste-Foy, or any of the villages in the vineyard area.

---

their supporting arches. The big Baroque altarpiece, carved in walnut wood, in the gloomy east bay, is worth a look, too, depicting the Assumption of the Virgin, with a humorous little detail in the illustrative scenes from her life of a puppy tugging the infant Jesus's sheets from his bed with its teeth.

At the west end of the cathedral in **place de la Clautre** beneath the blank facade of the original eleventh-century building, there is a twice-weekly fresh produce market on Wednesday and Saturday. From the terrace below you look across to the wooded hills beyond the River Isle, while north and south of the square crowd the renovated buildings of the medieval **old town**. The longest and finest street is the narrow **rue Limogeanne**, lined with Renaissance mansions, now turned into shops and pâtisseries. The surrounding streets are also scattered with fine Renaissance houses: particularly handsome are the **Hôtel de Gamançon**, 3 rue de la Constitution, now the seat of the *Conservation des Monuments Historiques*, and the more sedate **Hôtel de Crenoux** next door. Another curious one is at 17 rue de l'Éguillerie, on the corner of the attractive **place St-Louis**, where a turreted watchtower leans out over the street. There are other old houses down along the river by the Pont des Barris, notably the fifteenth-century **Maison des Consuls**.

At the northern end of rue Limogeanne, out on the broad tree-lined cours Tourny, is the city's museum, the **Musée du Périgord** (Mon, Wed–Fri noon–6pm; weekends 1–6pm; 15F), with some very beautiful Gallo-Roman mosaics, an extensive and important prehistoric collection, and some exquisite Limoges enamels near the exit, especially the portraits of the twelve Cæsars. Of less general interest is the **Musée Militaire**, near the cathedral at 32 rue des Farges (Jan–March Wed & Sat 2–6pm; April–Sept Mon–Sat 10am–noon and 2–6pm; Oct–Dec Mon–Sat 2–6pm; 20F), which nonetheless contains some unusual exhibits particularly relating to the French colonial wars in Vietnam.

La Cité

Roman Périgueux, known as **La Cité,** lies to the west of the town centre towards the gare SNCF. The main vestige is concealed in the Jardin des Arènes – the ruins of an enormous **amphitheatre**, dismantled in the third century and now an atmospheric ruin; while over by the train line in an attractive public garden at the end of rue Romaine is the high brick **Tour de Vésone**, the last remains of a temple to the city's guardian goddess. More bits and pieces – chiefly jumbled masonry – are visible (though only in guided visits - ask the tourist office for details) nearby in the so-called **Maison Romane** and also the **Porte Normande** off rue Turenne, essentially defensive works hastily cobbled together to keep the invading Visigoths at bay in the fourth century.

The rather mutilated church in this neighbourhood – the result of Huguenot anger in 1577 – is the former cathedral, the **church of St-Étienne**, condemned to life as a traffic island in place de la Cité.

Practicalities

The busiest and most interesting part of Périgueux is the square formed by the river, the allée de Tourny, boulevard Montaigne and cours Fénelon. At the junction of the two latter is the wide and unattractive place Francheville, with the **gare routière**, an underground car park and the **tourist office** at no. 26 (mid-June to mid-Sept Mon–Sat 9am–7pm, Sun 10am–6pm; rest of year Mon–Sat only; ☎05.53.53.10.63, fax 05.53.09.02.50), next to the Tour Mataguerre, the last surviving bit of the town's medieval defences. Périgueux's **gare SNCF** (☎05.53.06.21.00) lies to the west at the end of rue des Mobiles-du-Coulmiers, the continuation of rue Président-Wilson.

Opposite the train station, along rue Denis-Papin, you'll find a number of reasonable **hotels**, the most attractive of which is the old-fashioned *Hôtel du Midi et Terminus* at no. 18 (☎05.53.53.41.06; fax 05.53.08.19.32; ②), whose good regional restaurant has menus from 75F. An attractive option, close to the centre, is the *Hôtel Univers*, 18 cours de Montaigne (☎05.53.53.34.79; ②), with a pretty terrace and restaurant (menus from 85F). Best of all is the *Hôtel du Périgord* at 74 rue Victor-Hugo, the westward continuation of cours Tourny (☎05.53.53.33.63, fax 05.53.08.19.74; ②; closed Oct 18–Nov 4), in an attractive house with an exuberantly flowery garden behind; it has a good restaurant as well, with menus from 87F. There is also an HI **youth hostel** at the *Résidence Lakanal*, 32 bd Lakanal (☎05.53.09.22.77, fax 05.53.54.37.46) – follow the rail line south of the station to the far edge of town, or take rue Littré from place Francheville to rue Bertrand-de-Born.

Surprisingly, there is no great abundance of good **restaurants** in Périgueux. Apart from the brasseries around boulevard Montaigne and the hotel restaurants listed above, the best general area to look is around rue Limogeanne and the delightful place St-Louis. A couple of places to try are *Le Gourmandin*, 3 rue Aubergerie (lunch menus from 65F), and *Au Petit Chef*, 5 place du Coderc (from 60F; closed Sun eve). If you fancy a change from strictly French fare, *Le Canard Laqué*, 2 rue Lammary, is a good and popular Chinese place with menus from 65F, with the *Texas* in rue de la sagesse representing the US (closed Sun) – it even serves Californian wine.

Brantôme and the valley of the Dronne

Although **Brantôme** itself is very much on the tourist trail, the country both to the west and east of the town along the **River Dronne** remains largely undisturbed. It is tranquil, very beautiful and restoring, best savoured at a gentle pace, perhaps by bike or even by canoeing along the river.

Brantôme

BRANTÔME, 27km north of Périgueux on the Angoulême road and beloved of British tourists, sits in a bend of the River Dronne, whose still, water-lilied surface mirrors the limes and weeping willows of the riverside gardens. On the north bank of the river are the church and convent buildings of the **ancienne abbaye** that for centuries has been Brantôme's focus. Its stone facades, now masking the secular offices of the **Hôtel de Ville**, have that pallor and blank stare so characteristic of the self-denying institutional life. Not that self-denial was a virtue associated with this monastery's most notorious abbot, Pierre de Bourdeilles, the sixteenth-century author of scurrilous tales of life at the royal court.

Take a look inside the **église abbatiale** for the palm-frond vaulting of the chapter-house and the font made from a carved and grounded pillar capital; there is also a fine stone staircase at this end of the Hôtel de Ville. But Brantôme's best architectural feature is the Limousin-style Romanesque **belfry** standing behind the church against the wooded and cave-riddled scarp that forms the backdrop to the village.

Families with children may appreciate the **Musée de Rêve et Miniatures** in rue Puyjoli (July & Aug daily 10.30am–6pm; April–June & Sept Wed–Mon 10–12.30pm & 2–6pm; 28F), otherwise a walk through the nearby **gardens** and along the pleasant balustraded **river banks** is a must. There are also boat trips on the river in the summer.

Practicalities

The **tourist office** (Easter–June & Sept–Oct 10.30am–noon & 2–6pm; July & Aug 10am–noon & 2–7pm ☎05.53.05.80.52, fax 05.53.05.73.19) is in a lime-shaded Renaissance pavilion down on the river bank. There are three **buses** a day (Mon–Sat), connecting with the TGV in Angoulême.

The best cheap **accommodation** and **food** is to be had at the *Hôtel Versaveau*, 8 place de Gaulle, at the north end of the village (☎05.53.05.71.42; ②; restaurant from 60F; closed mid- to end Oct). Prettier and more comfortable accommodation is available at the *Hôtel Chabrol* (☎05.53.05.70.15, fax 05.53.05.71.85; ③; closed Feb & mid-Nov to mid-Dec), whose restaurant, *Les Frères Charbonnel*, is in the gourmet class, with its cheapest menu at 160F (closed Sun eve & Mon out of season). If you're feeling rich, you could treat yourself to a meal for 200F plus at the beautiful *Moulin de l'Abbaye* hotel by the tourist office (☎05.53.05.80.22; ⑧; restaurant closed Mon lunchtime). Outside the hotel restaurants, the café/brasserie *Au Fil de l'Eau*, on quai Bertin, with tables down by the river, is as cheap as Brantôme's restaurants come, as long as you don't go for the *omelette aux truffes*.

Those with a tent should head for the **campsite** north of the village on the D78 Thiviers road (☎05.53.05.75.24; May–Sept).

Bourdeilles

BOURDEILLES, 16km down the Dronne from Brantôme by a beautiful back road, is relatively hard to reach – perhaps the most appealing way is by canoe (boat rental from Brantome Canoe in Brantôme). It's a sleepy backwater, an ancient village clustering round its **château** on a rocky spur above the river (daily: Feb–March & Nov–Dec 10am–5.30pm; April–June & Sept–Oct Wed–Mon 10am–12.30pm & 1.30–7pm; July & Aug 10am–7pm; closed Jan; 28F). The château consists of two buildings: one a thirteenth-century fortress, the other an elegant Renaissance residence begun by the lady of the house as a piece of unsuccessful favour-currying with Catherine de Médicis – unsuccessful because Catherine never came to stay and the château remained unfinished. Climb the octagonal keep to look down on the town's clustered roofs, the weir and the boat-shaped mill parting the current, and along the Dronne to the cornfields and the manors hidden among the trees.

The château is now home to an exceptional collection of furniture bequeathed to the state by its former owners. Among the more notable pieces are some splendid Spanish dowry chests; a sixteenth-century Rhenish entombment with life-sized statues, embodying the very image of the serious, self-satisfied medieval burgher; and a fifteenth-century primitive Catalan triptych of an exorcism, with a bull-headed devil shooting skywards out of a kneeling princess.

For a **hotel**, *Les Tilleuls* (☎05.53.03.76.40; ①) right opposite the château makes a pleasant place to stay, with a restaurant from 60F.

Ribérac and around

Surrounded by an intimate, hilly countryside of woods and hay meadows and drowsy hilltop villages, **RIBÉRAC**, 30km downstream from Bourdeilles, is a pleasant if unremarkable town, whose greatest claim to fame is its major Friday **market**, bringing in producers and wholesalers from all around. With a couple of good **hotels**, it makes an agreeable base from which to explore the quiet, lush Dronne landscape. The cheapest of them is the *Hôtel L'Univers* at 2 av de Verdun on the corner of the wide central place de Gaulle (☎05.53.90.04.38, fax 05.53.90.98.39; ①), with a good restaurant from 55F. More attractive and very good value is the *Hôtel de France* on the opposite side of the square at 3 rue Marc-Dufraisse (☎05.53.90.00.61, fax 05.53.91.06.05; ②), with a terrace garden and a restaurant of some originality and local renown (menus 70F). For an even more rustic sojourn there's an old-fashioned country **hotel** in **VERTEILLAC**, 12km to the north: *Le Périgord* (☎05.53.91.62.79; ①; closed Feb; menu 75–120F, restaurant closed Mon), which would put you almost within walking distance of some delightful little villages. There's also a **camping municipal** on the Angoulême road outside Ribérac.

For further ideas about chambres d'hôte in the surrounding country Ribérac's **tourist office** on place de Gaulle, close to the *Univers*, is the place to ask (July to mid-Sept Mon–Sat 9am–noon & 1.30–7pm, Sun 10am–noon; rest of year Mon–Sat 9am–noon & 1.30–6pm; ☎05.53.90.03.10, fax 05.53.90.66.05); they can also provide information about the numerous Romanesque churches in outlying villages that could provide a focus for leisurely wandering. **Bikes** can be rented from the Peugeot bike shop at 19 rue Jean-Moulin.

Aubeterre-sur-Dronne and around

A little touristy, but very beautiful with its ancient galleried and turreted houses, **AUBETERRE-SUR-DRONNE** hangs on a steep hillside above the river. Its principal curiosity is the cavernous **Église Monolithe** (daily 9.30am–12.30pm & 2–6pm; May–Oct until 7pm; 20F), carved out of the soft rock of the cliff face in the twelfth century, with its rock-hewn tombs going back to the sixth. A tunnel connects with the **château** on the bluff overhead. There is also the extremely beautiful **church of St-Jacques**, with an eleventh-century facade sculpted and decorated in the richly carved Poitiers style on the street leading uphill from the square.

The **tourist office** is on the main square (Sept–June Mon 2–6pm, Tues–Sun 10am–noon & 2–6pm; July & Aug same days but afternoons 2.30–6.30pm; ☎05.45.98.57.18, fax 05.45.98.54.13), almost next door to the elderly *Hôtel de France*, now under Dutch ownership (☎05.45.98.50.43; ②). There is a **campsite** just below the village, and the delightful *Hôtellerie du Château* (☎05.45.98.50.11, fax 05.45.98.59.75; ②), where you can also eat for around 120F. There is a daily bus to Angoulême in term-time, and Chalais, which is on the Angoulême train line, is only 12km away.

South of Aubeterre, towards **LA ROCHE-CHALAIS**, the country gradually changes. Farmland gives way to extensive forest of oak and sweet chestnut, bracken and broom, interspersed with sour, marshy pasture, very sparsely populated. It's ideal cycling and picnicking country.

La Roche-Chalais has a couple of places to **eat** and **sleep**, along with a **campsite**. The *Hôtel Soleil d'Or*, 14 rue de l'Apre-Côte (☎05.53.90.86.71, fax 05.53.90.28.21; ④; restaurant from 70F lunchtime, 130F eve), has a magnificent view over the surrounding country and very comfortable rooms. There is also a small **restaurant** on the square by the church, *Au Petit Gourmet* (closed Sat eve & Sun; menu at 55F), opposite the **tourist office** (Tues–Sat 11am–noon & 3–6; ☎05.53.90.18.95), which provides local walking routes and information about visits to farms in the vicinity. There are **campsites** in Bonnes and St-Aulaye, and St-Aulaye also has a simple, old-fashioned **hotel** just off the village square, the *Champ de Foire* (☎05.53.90.82.29; ①), with a menu at 55F.

Villars and around

A dozen kilometres northeast of Brantôme lies the hamlet of **VILLARS**, a village with no particular sights but surrounded by beautiful countryside and making an excellent and not over-expensive base for visiting the **Château de Puyguilhem** and **St-Jean-de-Côle**. A short distance north of the hamlet are the **Grottes de Villars** (daily: mid-April to mid-June & mid-Sept to Oct 2–6.30pm; mid-June to mid-Sept 10am–noon & 2–6.30pm; July & Aug 10am–6.30pm; rest of year Sun only 2–6.30pm; 50F), where local cavers discovered impressive stalactites and stalagmites, together with a few prehistoric paintings – notably of horses and bison – in 1958.

Villars's one **hotel**, *Le Relais de l'Archerie*, is housed in a nineteenth-century mini-château with terrace and gardens (☎05.53.54.88.64, fax 05.53.54.21.92; ②; restaurant from 80F; closed Jan & Feb), or there is alternative accommodation and food only 6km away in Champagnac-de-Belair at the *Hôtel des Voyageurs* (☎05.53.54.21.29, fax 05.53.08.91.04; ②; restaurant from 70F).

Château de Puyguilhem

About a kilometre outside Villars, the appealing **Château de Puyguilhem** (Feb–March & Nov–Dec 10am–5.30pm; April–June & Sept–Oct Wed–Mon 10am–12.30pm & 1.30–7pm; July & Aug daily 10am–7pm; closed Jan; 28F) sits on the edge of a valley backed by oak woods. The building you see today was erected at the beginning of the sixteenth century on the site of an earlier and more military fortress. With its octagonal tower, broad spiral staircase, steep roofs, magnificent fireplaces and false dormer windows it is a perfect example of French Renaissance architecture. From the gallery at the top of the stairs you get a close-up of the roof and window decoration, as well as a view down the valley, which once was filled by a lake.

In the next valley, and very much worth a visit, the ruined Cistercian **Abbey of Boschaud** lies on the edge of the woods, reached by a lane not much bigger than a farm track. Its charm lies as much in the fact that it is – for once – unfenced, unpampered and uncharged for, as in the pure, stark lines of its twelfth-century architecture.

On the way, perched on the intervening hilltop overlooking Puyguilhem, is a farm called *Lafarge*, which does **B&B** for around 180F and delicious home-cooking from 75F.

St-Jean-de-Côle

Midway between Villars and Thiviers on the main Périgueux–Angoulême road, **ST-JEAN-DE-CÔLE** must rank as one of the loveliest villages in the Dordogne. Its ancient houses huddle together in typical medieval fashion around a wide sandy square dominated on one side by the huge **church of St-Jean-Baptiste**, built in the eleventh century, and the rugged-looking **Château de la Marthonie** (July & Aug daily 10am–noon & 2–7pm; 21F) on the other. The château, first erected in the fourteenth century, has acquired various additions in a pleasingly organic kind of growth.

The **tourist office** (April–Sept daily 10am–noon & 2–6pm; ☎05.53.62.14.15) is also on the square, as well as the most attractive *Coq Rouge* **restaurant** (☎05.53.62.32.71; closed Wed and Jan), whose excellent menus will set you back between 85F and 226F – it's wise to book. Equally, you can eat at the wisteria-covered *Hôtel St-Jean* on the main road through the village (☎05.53.52.23.20; ②; restaurant from 65F). There's a **campsite** at **LES VERGNES** on the Villars road.

Thiviers and Sorges

If you're heading along the main N21 Périgueux–Limoges road, stop off at **THIVIERS**, a village with some pretty old houses round the church; its **tourist office** is on the central square (July & Aug Mon–Sat 9am–6.15pm, Sun 10am–1pm; rest of year Tues–Fri 9am–12.15pm & 2–6.15pm, Sat 9am–12.15pm & 3–6pm; ☎05.53.55.12.50) and, for the non-squeamish, has a small *foie gras* **museum** (same hours; 10F), giving a thorough appraisal of the entire production process, past and present.

SORGES, closer to Périgueux, strung out along the road, has less to offer aesthetically than Thiviers. It does, however, have two reasonable **hotels**, now part of the same establishment: *Hôtel de la Mairie* by the church and *Auberge de la Truffe* on the main road (☎05.53.05.02.05, fax 05.53.05.39.27; ③; excellent restaurant from 80–330F). The **tourist office** (July & Aug daily 9.30am–12.30pm & 2.30–6.30pm; rest of year daily except Mon 10am–noon & 2–5pm) contains a fascinating **truffle museum** (same hours as tourist office, 20F), and can also direct you to a marked path that gives an idea of how and where truffles grow.

The Château de Hautefort

Forty kilometres northeast of Périgueux, the **Château de Hautefort** (Feb –March & mid-Oct to mid-Dec Sun 2–6pm; April to mid-July & Sept to mid-Oct daily 10am–noon & 2–6pm; mid-July to Aug daily 9.30am–7pm; 30F) enjoys a majestic position at the end of a wooded spur above its feudal village. A magnificent example of good living on a grand scale, the castle has an elegance that is out of step with the usual rough stone fortresses of Périgord. You approach across a wide esplanade flanked by formal gardens, cross the moat by a drawbridge through the oldest part of the building and enter a stylish Renaissance courtyard backed by an arcaded gallery and enclosed by slated towers. Once the property of well-known troubadour Bertrand de Born, it passed into the hands of the Hautefort family in the seventeenth century and was extensively remodelled. It was the childhood home of Marie de Hautefort, the young beauty who so captivated Louis XIII.

It is impossible to get from Périgueux to Hautefort and back in one day using public transport: although there is a morning **bus** from Périgueux via Cubjac (Wed & Sat), on other days there's only an evening service. You could get a Brive train as far as La Bachellerie from Périgueux, and hitch the final 15km. By car the most attractive route is along the River Auvézère via Cubjac and **TOURTOIRAC**, where Antoine-Orélie I, "King of Araucania", died in 1878. This bizarre character was a Périgueux lawyer who, deciding he was destined for higher things, borrowed money and set sail for Patagonia, where he proclaimed himself king of the Araucanian Indians.

Excideuil

EXCIDEUIL, connected by a bus service from Périgueux (Mon–Sat), is about 15km from Hautefort on the other side of the D704 Limoges road. In addition to its busy Thursday **market** and the tight streets of the old town, its real interest is the **castle,** splendidly impressive on its ridge overlooking the valley of the Loue and dominated by its skyscraping medieval keeps. You can enter the precinct but not the privately owned castle itself. It is, however, a classic and well worth seeing. An additional bonus is the typically French *Hostellerie du Fin Chapon* just below the castle at 3 place du Château (☎05.53.62.42.38, fax 05.53.52.39.60; ②; good restaurant with menus at 70–160F), with simple but agreeable rooms. The **tourist office** (☎05.53.62.95.56) is next door. There is also a simple but prettily sited **campsite** by the river on the Limoges side of town.

THE DORDOGNE: PÉRIGORD NOIR AND PÉRIGORD POURPRE

Périgord Noir covers the central part of the valley of the Dordogne, around its junction with the River Vézère. This is the distinctive Dordogne country: deep-cut valleys enclosed within the water-smooth cliffs their rivers have eroded, with fields of maize in the alluvial bottoms and dense oak woods on the heights, interspersed with patches of not-very-fertile farmland. Plantations of walnut trees (cultivated for their oil), flocks of low-slung grey geese (their livers enlarged for *foie gras*) and prehistoric-looking stone huts called *bories* are other hallmarks of the region, which for the purposes of this chapter we have extended to include Bergerac in the west and Argentat in the east.

The absolute highlight of the area must be the **prehistoric cave paintings** in the Vézère valley. But there are also the **bastides** – medieval military settlements – and some lovely villages in the Dordogne valley itself, as well as the breathtaking church of **St-Amand-de-Coly**, the sculptures in the porch of the church at **Beaulieu-sur-Dordogne**, and the wines of **Bergerac**, capital of the **Périgord Pourpre**.

Many of these places, especially round **Sarlat** and the caves, get very crowded in summer and yet the crowds stick very much to the beaten track. If you want to escape the masses, take the back roads and you will have them to yourself.

Bergerac and around

BERGERAC lies on the river bank in the wide plain of the Dordogne. Once a flourishing port for the wine trade, it is still the main market centre for the surrounding maize, vine and tobacco farms. Devastated in the Wars of Religion, when most of its Protestant population fled overseas, Bergerac is now essentially a modern town with some interesting and attractive reminders of the past.

From the gare SNCF, it's a ten-minute walk down cours Alsace-Lorraine and its continuation to the **vieille ville**, a calm and pleasant area to wander through, with drinking fountains on the street corners and numerous late medieval houses. In rue de l'Ancien-Pont, the splendid seventeenth-century Maison Peyrarède houses an informative **Musée du Tabac** (Tues–Sat 10am–noon & 2–6pm, Sun 2–6pm; 15F), detailing the history of the weed, with collections of pipes and tools of the trade.

Bergerac has a couple of other museums, the best of which is the small **Musée Éthnographique Régional** in rue des Conférences in the heart of the old town (mid-Nov to mid-March Tues–Fri 10am–noon & 2–5.30pm, Sat 10am–noon, Sun 2–5.30pm; mid-March to mid-Nov same hours except Sun 2.30–6.30pm; 15F), with displays on viticulture, barrel-making and the town's once-bustling river-trading past. Outside on the square is a statue in honour of **Cyrano de Bergerac**, the town's most famous association, in 1990 turned into the most expensive French film ever made, starring Gérard Départieu. The big-nosed lead character in Edmond Rostand's play, though fictional, was inspired by the seventeenth-century philosopher of the same name, who, sadly, had nothing to do with the town.

Practicalities

The **gare SNCF** is on cours Alsace-Lorraine, ten minutes' walk from the old town. The **tourist office** is at 97 rue Neuve-d'Argenson (summer daily 9am–7pm; winter Tues–Sat 9am–noon & 1.30–5.30pm; ☎05.53.57.03.11, fax 05.53.61.11.04). You can rent **bicycles** from 11 place Gambetta or 114 bd de l'Entrepôt. There is a vast **market** in the covered *halles* off the Grande-Rue in the old town on Wednesday and Saturday.

For **accommodation** in town, there are several small hotels in the backstreets. A cheap choice is the *Hôtel Pozzi*, 11 rue Pozzi (☎05.53.57.04.68; ①; restaurant from 55F), or the *Saint Louis* in rue Ste-Catherine (☎05.53.57.19.08; ②). For something more comfortable, try *Le Cyrano*, 2 bd Montaigne (☎05.53.57.02.76; ③), which has an excellent restaurant with menus in the range of 90–200F. There's also a **camping municipal**, *La Pelouse* (☎05.53.57.06.67; open all year), on the south bank of the river. For a brasserie-type **meal**, there's *Le Perroquet*, on place Malbee, or, for something more refined and regional, *Le Treille*, at 12 quai Salvette, down by the river in the old park (☎05.53.57.60.11; menus 65–165F).

If you should find yourself here in July, there is a magnificent **food festival** called La Table de Cyrano in the week of July 14, and the Récollets cloister hosts a week of chamber **music** at the beginning of July, plus jazz every Wednesday evening at 6.30pm throughout July and August.

Château de Monbazillac

Half-a-dozen kilometres south of Bergerac, looking out over the gently declining slopes of its long-favoured vineyards, stands the handsome Renaissance **château of Monbazillac** (mid-Feb to March & Nov to mid-Jan Tues–Sun 10am–noon & 2–5pm; April–Oct daily 10am–noon & 2–6/7.30pm; July & Aug 10am–6./7.30pm; closed mid-Jan to mid-Feb; 25F), part residence, but part fortress also, with its corners reinforced by four sturdy towers. Inside is an interesting museum of local traditions and crafts. The wine is white, velvety and sweet, best consumed with desserts or chilled as an apéritif. There is a good **restaurant** attached to the château (☎05.53.58.38.93; menus from 135F, closed Sun eve, Mon & Nov).

Ste-Foy-la-Grande and around

Driving west from Bergerac along the River Dordogne, the first place you come to of any size is the *bastide* town of **STE-FOY-LA-GRANDE,** whose narrow central streets still retain a number of ancient houses. One of these, at 102 rue de la République, now houses the exceptionally helpful **tourist office** (July & Aug Mon—Sat 10am–12.30pm &

3–7pm, Sun 10.30am–12.30pm; rest of year Mon 2.30–5.30pm, Tues–Sat 9.30am–12.30pm & 2.30–6pm; closed Sunday; ☎05.57.46.03.00, fax ☎05.57.46.18.15), which has a good list of chambres d'hôte and local wine-tasting sessions. Another draw is the town's mouthwatering Saturday **market**. In the absence of a car, the best means of visiting the sights in the surrounding countryside is by **bike**; rental outlets in Ste-Foy are Ets David, 29 rue Jean-Jacques-Rousseau, or Ets Vircoulon, 41 rue Victor-Hugo. The only other realistic option is to catch the 12.30pm **bus** to Lamothe-Montravel, which still leaves you with a three- or four-kilometre walk to either destination.

Thirteen kilometres from Ste-Foy lies **MONTCARET**, whose attraction is a third-century **Roman villa** (daily April–Sept 9am–noon & 2–6pm; rest of year 10am–noon & 2–4pm; 15F) with superb mosaics and baths plus an adjoining museum displaying the many objects exhumed on the site. It is another 3.5km to the **Château de Montaigne** (July & Aug daily 9.15am–noon & 2–7pm; Sept–June Wed–Sun same hours; closed Jan 6–Feb 17; 25F), built by Michel de Montaigne, whose chatty, digressive essays on the nature of life and humankind have influenced many writers since. All that remains of the original building is Montaigne's tower-study, its beams inscribed with his maxims; the rest of it was rebuilt in pseudo-Renaissance style after a fire in 1885.

The bastide country

During the long struggles of the thirteenth and fourteenth centuries for control of the southwest of France, both the English and the French combatants constructed dozens of new towns – principally in the disputed "frontier" areas between the Dordogne and Garonne rivers – in an attempt to consolidate their hold on their respective territories. These towns, known as **bastides**, were essentially fortified settlements, walled and gated and built on a rational grid-plan round a central arcaded market square, in marked contrast to the haphazard organic growth of the usual medieval town. As an incentive to local people, anyone who was prepared to build, inhabit and defend them was granted various perks and concessions, including a measure of self-government remarkable in feudal times.

There is a heavy concentration of these settlements in the country to the south of Bergerac between the rivers Dordogne and Lot. Many retain no more than vestiges of their original aspect, but two of the finest, which are almost entirely intact, lie within a fifty-kilometre radius of Bergerac: **Monpazier** and **Monflanquin**.

Monpazier and around

MONPAZIER, built in 1284 by King Edward I of England (who was also Duke of Aquitaine), is one of the most complete of the surviving *bastides*, and still relatively free of the commercialism that suffocates a place like Domme (see p.617). Picturesque and placid though it is today, the village has a hard and bitter history, being twice – in 1594 and 1637 – the centre of peasant rebellions provoked by the misery that followed the Wars of Religion. Both uprisings were brutally suppressed: the 1637 peasants' leader was broken on the wheel in the square. Sully, the Protestant general, describes a rare moment of light relief in the terrible wars, when the men of the Catholic *bastide* of Villefranche-de-Périgord planned to capture Monpazier on the same night as the men of Monpazier planned to capture Villefranche. By chance, both sides took different routes, met no resistance, looted to their hearts' content and returned home congratulating themselves on their luck and skill, only to find in the morning that things were rather different. The peace terms were that everyone should return everything to its proper place.

Monpazier is now severely depopulated. As the street ends the fields begin, and you look out over the surrounding country. There is an ancient *lavoir* where women used to wash clothes, a much-altered church and a gem of a central square – sunny, still and slightly menacing, like a Sicilian piazza at siesta time. Deep, shady arcades pass under all the houses, which are separated from each other by a small gap to reduce fire risk; at the corners the buttresses are cut away to allow the passage of laden pack animals.

The best place for an overnight **stay** in Monpazier is the *Hôtel de France*, 21 rue St-Jacques (☎05.53.22.60.06, fax 05.53.22.07.27; ③; closed Dec), with a fine regional restaurant from 70F. There are **campsites** in the direction of Bergerac (*Lac de Véronne*) and Villeréal (*Moulin de David*). Alternatively there is *camping à la ferme*, 5km along a country lane in a great spot at **LE BOUYSSOU** (☎05.53.22.66.58), signposted as you enter Monpazier.

Another possibility is to base yourself in one of the attractive villages within a twenty-kilometre radius. **BELVÈS** watches over the surrounding country from a ridge-top just 5km from Siorac on the Dordogne, and its *Hôtel Le Home*, on the through-road at the top of the hill, provides good cheap accommodation and food (☎05.53.29.01.65, fax 05.53.59.46.99; ②; restaurant from 60F). Make sure you take a look at the heart of the old village and place des Armes, with its old pillared **market** and the **tourist office** (☎05.53.29.10.20). The nearest **campsite** is at Les Nauves (☎05.53.29.12.64), 4.5km off the Monpazier road, or there's a *camping à la ferme* called *Le Bon Accueil* at the hamlet of Gratecap (☎05.53.29.09.11) near St-Amand-de-Belvès.

VILLEFRANCHE-DU-PÉRIGORD lies 20km further south in the midst of wooded country above the River Lemance. Built in 1261 in lovely warm-coloured stone, it retains much of its *bastide* layout. At the end of the main street, whose medieval **halle** is splendid, is the *Petite Auberge* (☎05.53.29.91.01, fax 05.53.28.88.10; ③; restaurant from 77F; closed Fri eve), on the way out of the village.

Biron, Villeréal and Monflanquin

Eight kilometres south of Monpazier, dominating the countryside for miles around, is the vast **Château de Biron** (Feb–March & Nov–Dec Tues–Sun 10am–12.30pm & 1.30–5.30pm; July & Aug daily 10am–7pm; rest of year Tues–Sun 10am–12.30pm & 1.30–7pm; 28F), begun in the eleventh century and added to piecemeal afterwards. You can only see the place on a guided tour – and that means everything, including the grassy courtyard within its walls, where there is a restored Renaissance chapel and guardhouse with tremendous views over the roofs of the feudal village below.

A single street runs through the village of **BIRON**, past a covered **market** on timber supports iron-hard with age, and out under an arched gateway. Well-manured vegetable plots interspersed with iris, lily and Iceland poppies lie under the tumbledown walls. At the bottom of the hill, another group of houses stands on a small *place* with a broken well in front of a half-ruined **church**, its Romanesque origins covered by motley alterations. The *Auberge du Château* serves a very good-value lunchtime menu at 50F (☎05.53.63.13.33).

West of Biron, the *bastide* of **VILLERÉAL** was founded a decade or so earlier than Monpazier by Alphonse de Poitiers in an attempt to check English expansion in the Dordogne. It failed to do so and was taken by the English during the Hundred Years' War. Its most outstanding feature is the oak-beamed *halles* in the central square, which dates from the fourteenth century. You can **stay** at the *Hôtel de l'Europe*, place Jean Moulin (☎05.53.36.00.35; ②; restaurant from 65F; closed Oct), or at one of the many nearby **campsites**, the closest of which is the *camping municipal* (☎05.53.36.05.63; mid-June to mid-Sept), off the D207 to Bergerac.

Some 25km further south in the direction of Villeneuve-sur-Lot, pretty **MONFLAN-QUIN,** founded by Alphonse de Poitiers in 1256, is just as perfectly preserved as

Monpazier, less touristy and even more impressively positioned on the top of a hill that rises sharply from the surrounding country and is visible for miles. It conforms to the regular pattern of right-angled streets leading from a central square to the four town gates. The square – place des Arcades – with its distinctly Gothic houses, derives a special charm from being on a slope and tree-shaded. Take a look at the fortified church too. The **tourist office** is on the place des Arcades (☎05.53.36.40.19, fax 05.53.36.42.91), and can furnish you with lists of chambres d'hôte. There's a **campsite** at **COULON** on the Cancon road.

Beaumont and the Abbaye de Cadouin

BEAUMONT, 17km north of Villeréal on the D676, is another thirteenth-century English *bastide*, founded by Edward I. Like many *bastides*, its church, **Église St-Front**, was built for military as well as religious reasons – a kind of final outpost of defence in times of attack, hence the bulky tower at each of the four corners and the well inside. There's the creeper-covered *Hôtel Beaumontois* in rue Romier, with very nice, inexpensive rooms and traditional Périgord cuisine (☎05.53.22.30.11; ②; fax 05.53.22.38.99; ③; restaurant from 65F), as well as a **campsite**, *Les Remparts* (☎05.53.22.40.86; May–Sept), to the southwest of town off the D676.

Around 15km northeast, and only 6km south of **LE BUISSON** on the Dordogne, is the twelfth-century Cistercian **Abbaye de Cadouin**. For 800 years until 1935 it drew flocks of pilgrims to wonder at a piece of cloth first mentioned by Simon de Montfort in 1214 and thought to be part of Christ's shroud. In 1935 the two bands of embroidery at either end of the cloth were shown to contain an Arabic text from around the eleventh century. Since then the main attraction has been the finely sculpted but badly damaged capitals of the flamboyant Gothic **cloister** (Feb–March & Nov–Dec Wed–Mon 10.30am–12.30pm & 1.30–5.30pm; July & Aug daily 10am–7pm; rest of year Wed–Mon 10am–12.30pm & 1.30–7pm; 28F). Beside it is a Romanesque **church** with a stark, bold front and wooden belfry roofed with chestnut shingles – chestnut trees abound around here, and the timber was used in furniture-making and the nuts ground for flour in the once-frequent famines. Inside the church, the nave is slightly out of alignment; this is thought to be deliberate and perhaps a vestige of pagan attachments, for the three windows are aligned so that at the winter and summer solstices the sun shines through all three in a single shaft. There's a **camping municipal** on the Montferrand road (Easter–Oct).

Sarlat and the valley of the Vézère

The valley of the **Vézère** is extraordinary beautiful country, hilly, wooded and close, fretted by other luxuriant valleys, some with streams, some without. Typically, the valley sides are smooth, with slightly overhanging cliffs worn away by the millennial action of water courses and riddled with caves that have been used as dwellings and sanctuaries for thousands of years.

It was here in the Vézère valley that the first skeletons of **Cro-Magnon people** – the first homo sapiens, tall and muscular with a large skull – were unearthed in 1868 by labourers digging out the Périgueux–Agen train line, and here, too, that an incredible wealth of archeological and artistic evidence of the life of late Stone Age people has since been found. The many **cave paintings** are remarkable not only for their great age, but also for their exquisite colouring and the skill with which they are drawn.

The international renown of these caves, combined with the well-preserved medieval architecture of **Sarlat,** has made this one of the most heavily touristed inland areas of France, with all the concomitant problems of crowds, high prices and tack. It is really

---

GÎTES D'ÉTAPE AROUND SARLAT

There are a number of **gîtes** in the vicinity of Sarlat, some on or near the GR6. For walkers, cyclists and campers they could provide much more enjoyable and hassle-free accommodation than anything in the towns.
Beynac: *La Grange* (☎05.53.49.40.93).
Le Breuil: *Lo Cobana* or *Les Cabanes du Breuil*, on the GR6, just north of the D6 midway between Les Eyzies and Sarlat – turn north at Benives (☎05.53.29.66.23). Camping and meals.
Cénac: M. et Mme Sardan (☎05.53.28.32.77).
Castelnaud-la-Chapelle: gîte municipal, below the château (☎05.53.29.51.21).
St-Vincent-le-Paluel: M. et Mme Saulière, at *Le Communal* on the GR6 7km east of Sarlat (☎05.53.31.00.21). Camping possible.

---

worth coming out of season, but if you can't, seek accommodation away from the main centres, and always drive along the back roads – the smaller the better – whenever there is a more direct route available.

Sarlat

SARLAT-LA-CANÉDA, capital of Périgord Noir, is held in a hollow between hills 10km or so back from the Dordogne valley. You hardly notice the modern town, as it is the mainly fifteenth- and sixteenth-century houses of the *vieille ville* in mellow, honey-coloured stone that draw the attention.

The **vieille ville** is an excellent example of medieval organic urban growth, violated only by the straight swath of the **rue de la République**, now thankfully pedestrianized, which cuts through its middle. The west side alone remains relatively un-chic; the east side is where most people wander. As you approach the old town from the station, turn right down rue Lakanal which leads to the large and unexciting **Cathédrale St-Sacerdos**, mostly dating from its seventeenth-century renovation. Opposite stands the town's finest house, the **Maison de La Boétie** once the home of Montaigne's friend Étienne de La Boétie, with its gabled tiers of windows and characteristic steep roof stacked with heavy limestone tiles (*lauzes*).

For a better sense of the medieval town, wander through the cool, shady lanes and courtyards around the back of the cathedral: **cours des Fontaines** and **cours des Chanoines**. To one side of the cours des Chanoines is the curious twelfth-century coned tower, the **Lanterne des Morts**, whose exact function has escaped historians, though the most popular theory is that it was built to commemorate Saint Bernard, who performed various miracles when he visited the town in 1147.

There are more wonderful old houses in the streets to the north, especially **rue des Consuls**, and up the slopes to the east. Eventually, though, Sarlat's labyrinthine lanes will lead you back to the central **place de la Liberté**, where the big Saturday **market** spreads its stands of geese, flowers, *foie gras*, truffles and mushrooms in season, and where various people trying to make a living from the hordes who hit Sarlat in the summer. Another development is the increasing number of museums that are cropping up in Sarlat as the town turns more and more to tourism, such as the **Musée Automobile** (April Wed–Sun 2.30–6.30pm; June & Sept daily same hours; July & Aug 10.30am–7pm; 35F), with its collection of some sixty cars, dating from as far back as 1890, or the **Aquarium** (daily: April–June & Sept to mid-Nov 10am–noon & 2–6pm; July & Aug 10am–7pm; 27F), which presents an interesting exhibition on the freshwater fish that live in the Dordogne river.

Practicalities

The **gare SNCF** (☎05.53.59.00.21) is just over 1km south of the old town, and there's a free bus shuttle into town. If you have no transport of your own, you can rent **bicycles** from Sarlat Sport on rue Jean-Leclaire, from the youth hostel, the train station or Cycles Cumenal, 52 av Gambetta. The **tourist office** lodges in the sixteenth-century Hôtel de Maleville on place de la Liberté (mid-June to mid-Sept Mon–Sat 9am–7pm, Sun 10am–noon & 4–6pm; rest of year Mon–Sat 9am–noon & 2–6pm; ☎05.53.31.45.45, fax 05.53.59.19.44). For a small fee, they'll find you a room in town or B&B accommodation in the surrounding area, though it's almost impossible to find cheap digs in season.

Hotels worth trying include: the *Marcel*, 50 av de Selves (☎05.53.59.21.98; fax 05.53.30.27.77; ③; March to mid-Nov); the very central *Hôtel de la Mairie* on place de la Liberté (☎05.53.59.05.71, fax 05.53.28.83.43; ③; restaurant from 65F); and *Les Récollets*, 4 rue J-J-Rousseau (☎05.53.59.00.49, fax 05.53.30.32.62; ③). There is a very pleasant HI **youth hostel** at 77 av de Selves (☎05.53.59.47.59; open all year), a ten-minute walk from the *vieille ville* along the Périgueux road. The nearest **campsite**, *Les Périères*, costs almost as much as a hotel; much better to try *Les Acacias*, about 2km beyond the railway viaduct in La Canéda (☎05.53.59.29.30; Easter–Sept).

Restaurants are generally overpriced in Sarlat. However, *Le Commerce* in rue Albert-Cahuet, just off rue de la République, with its menus at 50F and 70F and region-al specialities like *confits*, offers reasonable value for money, as does the fancier *Auberge de la Salamandre* in rue des Consuls, in spite of its touristy aspect (from 85F). For something a bit special, try *Criquettamus*, 5 rue des Armes (☎05.53.59.48.10; menus from 70–180F), which serves up *foie gras*, *magret* and *morilles* mushrooms. Otherwise, you could try the brasserie fare of the *Café de Paris* on place de la Grande-Rigaudie.

A very nice alternative to both staying and eating in Sarlat would be to put up in the little hilltop hamlet of **MARQUAY** about halfway to Les Eyzies, at the *Hôtel des Bories* (☎05.53.29.67.02, fax 05.53.29.64.15; ③; April–Oct), with a marvellous view, swimming pool and excellent restaurant (from 85F); it is vital to book several months in advance for July and August.

Les Jardins d'Eyrignac

The *manoir* of **Eyrignac** is a very lovely seventeenth-century example of what, in English, would be called a country house. It lies in the hilly country to the northeast of Sarlat, about 13km by road. Its great glory is its **garden**, which is remarkable for its spe-cial effects and atmosphere (daily: June–Sept 9.30am–7pm; rest of year 10am–12.30pm & 2–7pm, or dusk; 35F; house closed to the public). The original formal garden was the work of an eighteenth-century Italian architect, but all trace of it was destroyed as the owners – still the same family – adapted it to subsequent fashions. What you see today is the work of the last forty years, the creation of the present owner's father. There are practically no flowers: the garden consists of evergreens, mainly box, hornbeam, cypress and yew, clipped and arranged in formal patterns of alleys and parterres. A work of art in its own right, it's now classified as a national monument.

Les Eyzies

The main base for visiting many of the prehistoric painted caves of the Vézère valley is **LES EYZIES-DE-TAYAC**, an unattractive one-street village completely dedicated to tourism. But while you're here, visit the **Musée National de Préhistoire** (daily except Tues: July & Aug 9.30am–7pm, Fri until 10pm; mid-Nov to mid-March 9.30am–5pm; rest of year 9.30am–noon & 2–6pm; 22F), exhibiting numerous prehistoric artefacts and copies of one of the most beautiful pieces of Stone Age art, two clay bison from the

Tuc d'Audoubert cave in the Pyrenees, as well as the small bas-relief of an exaggerated female figure holding what looks like a slice of watermelon, found near Laussel (see p.615), known as the *Vénus à la Corne* (Venus with the Horn of Plenty): the original is in the Musée d'Aquitaine in Bordeaux (see p.584).

In April 1990, local farmer M. Pataud opened his own extensive private collection of prehistoric finds, next door in the **Musée de l'Abri Pataud** (July & Aug daily 10am–7pm; rest of year Wed–Mon 10am–12.30pm & 1.30–5.30/7pm; 28F). Much of the stuff was discovered during archeological digs in the 1950s and 1960s on Pataud's own farmland, which, it transpired, lay over an *abri* (shelter) used by reindeer hunters for more than 20,000 years.

Practicalities

The **tourist office** is on Les Eyzies's one street (July & Aug daily 9am–7pm; rest of year Mon–Sat 9am–noon & 2–6pm; ☎05.53.06.97.05). In addition to **bicycle rental**, they also give out information on private rooms in the area (roughly 150F per person). **Hotels** are pricey and likely to ask for *demi-pension*: the cheapest is *Les Falaises*, in the main street (☎05.53.06.97.35; ②), followed by the *Hôtel de France* on rue du Moulin (☎05.53.06.97.23, fax 05.53.06.90.97; ③; closed Oct–March; restaurant 80–193F). Alternatively, stay in Le Bugue, 10km downstream, where the *Hôtel de Paris*, 14 rue Paris (☎05.53.07.28.16, fax 05.53.04.20.89; ①), has much cheaper rooms.

There's a riverside **campsite**, *La Rivière* (☎05.53.06.97.14, fax 05.53.35.20.85; April–Sept), on the route de Périgueux, and a cheaper one in the direction of Le Bugue, *Le Pech Denissou*. There are hostel-priced beds at a very attractive self-catering **gîte d'étape**, *La Ferme Eymaries* (☎05.53.06.94.73; April–Oct), thirty minutes by foot from the village; to find it, cross the river bridge on the Périgueux road, turn sharp left and continue to the rail line, where there's a signpost to the right.

Eating out in Les Eyzies can be expensive unless you go for the no-nonsense brasserie-style food at *La Grignotière*, near the tourist office, or the hotels mentioned above.

The caves around Les Eyzies

There are more **prehistoric caves** around Les Eyzies than you could possibly hope to visit in one day. Besides, the compulsory guided tours are tiring, so it's best to select just a couple of the ones listed below.

No-one ever lived in these caves, and there are various theories as to why these inaccessible spots were chosen. Most agree that the caves were sanctuaries and, if not actually places of worship, they at least had religious significance. One theory is that making images of animals that were commonly hunted – like reindeer and bison – or feared – like bears and mammoths – was a kind of sympathetic magic intended to help men either catch or evade these animals. Another is that they were part of a fertility cult: sexual images of women with pendulous breasts and protuberant rumps are common, and it seems, too, that certain animals were associated with the feminine principle. Others argue that these cave paintings served educational purposes, making parallels with Australian aborigines who used similar images to teach their young vital survival information as well as the history and mythological origins of their people. But much remains unexplained – for instance, the abstract signs that appear in many caves and the arrows which clearly cannot be arrows, because Stone Age arrowheads looked different from these representations.

The size of the caves varies. **Font-de-Gaume** is only 130m long, but many caves, like **La Roque St-Christophe**, are far longer, with terrifyingly difficult access through twisting slippery passages, passable only on your belly. The artists had just the most primitive lamps to light their way and paint by.

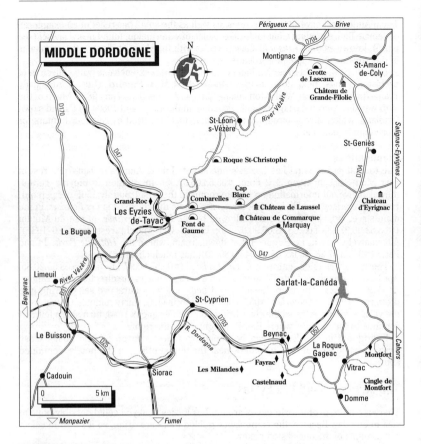

Grotte de Font-de-Gaume

Since its discovery in 1901, dozens of polychrome paintings have been found in the tunnel-like **Grotte de Font-de-Gaume** (daily except Wed: March & Oct 9.30am–noon & 2–5.30pm; April–Sept 9am–noon & 2–6pm; Nov–Feb 10am–noon & 2–5pm; 35F; maximum 20 per tour), 1.5km along the D47 to Sarlat. Be aware that tickets sell out fast and only two hundred people are allowed to tour the cave per day; advance booking, several days ahead in peak season, is essential (☎05.53.06.90.80, fax 05.53.35.26.18).

The cave mouth is no more than a fissure from which a resurgent stream once flowed. Concealed by rocks and trees, it now stands above a small lush valley, but when Stone Age people first settled here during the last Ice Age – about 25,000 BC – the Dordogne was the domain of roaming bison, reindeer and mammoths.

Inside, the cave is a narrow twisting passage of irregular height. There's no lighting, and you quickly lose your bearings in the dark. The first painting you see is a frieze of bison, at about eyelevel: reddish-brown in colour, massive, full of movement, and very far from the primitive representations you might expect. Further on, in a side passage, two horses stand one behind the other, forelegs outstretched as if to attempt – as the guide suggests with some relish – *un début d'accouplement* (the beginnings of copulation). But the most miraculous of all is a frieze of five bisons discovered in 1966 during cleaning operations. The colour, remarkably sharp and vivid, is preserved by a protective layer of calcite. Shading under the belly and down the thighs is used to give three-dimensionality with a sophistication that seems utterly modern. Another panel consists of superimposed drawings, a fairly common phenomenon in cave painting, sometimes the result of work by successive generations, but here an obviously deliberate technique. A reindeer in the foreground shares legs with a large bison behind to indicate perspective.

Stocks of artists' materials have also been found: kilos of prepared pigments; palettes – stones stained with ground-up earth pigments; and wooden painting sticks. Painting was clearly a specialized, perhaps professional, business, reproduced in dozens and dozens of caves located in the central Pyrenees and areas of northern Spain.

Grotte des Combarelles

The **Grotte des Combarelles** (hours as Font-de-Gaume; 35F), 2km along the D47 towards Sarlat, was discovered in 1910. The innermost part of the cave is covered with engravings from the Magdalenian period (about 12,000 years ago). Drawn over a period of 2000 years, many are superimposed one upon another. They include horses, reindeer, mammoths and crude human figures – among the finest are the heads of a horse and a lioness.

As with Font-de-Gaume, prebooking is essential, especially in peak season (same phone and fax); collect tickets from Font-de-Gaume.

Abri du Cap Blanc and the Château de Commarque

Not a cave but a natural rock shelter, the **Abri du Cap Blanc** (daily: April–June, Sept & Oct 10am–noon & 2–6pm; July & Aug 9.30am–7pm; 29F), lies on a steep wooded hillside about 7km east of Les Eyzies (turn left onto the D48 shortly after Les Combarelles). It contains a sculpted frieze of horses and bison dating from the Middle Magdalenian period, about 14,000 years ago. Of only ten surviving prehistoric sculptures in France, this is undoubtedly the best. The design is deliberate, with the sculptures polished and set off against a pock-marked background. But what makes this place extraordinary is not just the large scale, but the high relief of some of the sculptures. This was only possible in places where light reached in, which in turn brought the danger of destruction by exposure to the air. Cro-Magnon people actually lived in this shelter, and a female skeleton has been found that is some 2000 years younger than the frieze.

If you're looking for a non-cave detour, continue a little further up the primitive-looking and heavily wooded Beune valley from Cap Blanc, to the elegant sixteenth-century **Château de Laussel** (closed to the public). On the opposite side of the valley stand the romantically overgrown ruins of the **Château de Commarque**. Built in the thirteenth century, it was occupied by the English during the Hundred Years' War, and substantial sections of the fortifications still stand. You can reach it on foot via the GR6 footpath, which leaves the D47, past the Font-de-Gaume and just after *Pizzeria Girouteaux* or – much quicker – by a path that starts in the left-hand corner of the field below Cap-Blanc (flooded in wet weather).

Grotte du Grand Roc

As well as prehistoric cave paintings, you can see some truly spectacular stalactites and stalagmites in the area around Les Eyzies. Some of the best examples are off the D47 to Périgueux, 2km north of Les Eyzies, in the **Grotte du Grand Roc** (July & Aug daily 9.30am–7pm; rest of year except Jan 9.30am–6pm; closed Sat in Nov-Dec & Feb; 35F), whose entrance is high up in the cliffs that line much of the Vézère valley. There's a great view from the mouth of the cave and, inside, along some 50m of tunnel, a fantastic array of rock formations.

Roque St-Christophe

The enormous prehistoric dwelling site, **La Roque St-Christophe** (daily: March–Sept 10am–7pm; Oct to mid-Nov 10am–6.30pm; mid-Nov to Feb 11am–5pm; 31F), 9km northeast of Les Eyzies along the D706 to Montignac, is made up of about one hundred caves on five levels, hollowed out of the limestone cliffs. The caves are 700–800m long and lie 80m above the ground, where the River Vézère once flowed. The earliest traces of occupation go back over 50,000 years. The view is pretty good, and the guided tour instructive, but most of the finds are on display at the Musée National de Préhistoire in Les Eyzies (see p.612).

Montignac and the Lascaux caves

Some 26km up the Vézère valley, **MONTIGNAC** is the main base for visiting the **Lascaux caves**. It's a more attractive place than Les Eyzies, with several wooden-balconied houses leaning appealingly over the river, and a lively annual **arts festival** in mid-July, including international folklore. On place Bertrand-de-Born in the old hospital, the **Musée Eugène-Le-Roy** (July & Aug daily 9.30am–noon & 2–5.30pm; otherwise by arrangement; 15F) displays local crafts and trades, and includes a reconstruction of the household of Jacquou le Croquant, the peasant protagonist of the novel of the same name by Eugène le Roy, the Dordogne's native novelist, who lived and died here in Montignac. The novel describes the harshness of peasant life in the early nineteenth century and the depredations of the local squirearchy in spite of the reforms of the Revolution.

The **tourist office** shares the old hospital building with the museum on place Bertrand-de-Born (Mon–Sat: Feb–June & Sept–Dec 9am–12.30pm & 2–5.30pm; July & Aug 9am–7pm; ☎05.53.51.82.60, fax 05.53.50.49.72). Tickets for **Lascaux II** (see below) must be bought here, from the office on the ground floor.

Accommodation, as everywhere around here, is a problem. *Le Bon Accueil* (☎05.53.51.82.99; ①; menu from 60F) and *Hôtel de la Grotte* (☎05.53.51.80.48, fax 05.53.51.05.96; ②; restaurant from 60F), both on rue du 4-septembre, are reasonably priced. More expensive is the *Soleil d'Or*, also on the main rue du 4-septembre (☎05.53.51.80.22, fax 05.53.50.27.54; ④), whose restaurant has a menu at 70F. And there is a cheap **camping municipal** on the river bank 500m away (☎05.53.51.83.95; April to mid-Oct).

There are other worthwhile hotel options in the area. One of the most attractive, though not the cheapest, is *La Table du Terroir* at **LA CHAPELLE-AUBAREIL**, about 15km beyond the Lascaux caves (☎05.53.50.72.14, fax 05.53.51.16.23; ③; closed Dec–Jan), which has a swimming pool and an excellent restaurant (menus from 70F). Another, offering equally good food, is the *Hôtel Laborderie*, further to the south at **TAMNIES** on the Les Eyzies–St-Genies road (☎05.53.29.68.59, fax 05.53.29.65.31; ①–⑤; closed Nov–March; restaurant from 95F). For other possibilities, ask the tourist office in Montignac for their extensive list of B&B and farm **campsites**. A particularly good spot for campers with a taste for luxury is the site at the exquisite riverside village of **ST-LÉON-SUR-VÉZÈRE**.

Grotte de Lascaux and Lascaux II

The **Grotte de Lascaux** was discovered in 1940 by four boys who were, according to popular myth, looking for their dog and fell into a deep cavern decorated with marvellously preserved animal paintings. Executed by Cro-Magnon people 17,000 years ago, the paintings are among the finest examples of prehistoric art in existence. There are five or six identifiable styles, and subjects include the bison, mammoth and horse, plus the biggest known prehistoric drawing, of a 5.5-metre bull with astonishingly expressive head and face. In 1948, the cave was opened to the public, and over the course of the next fifteen years more than a million tourists came to Lascaux. Sadly, because of deterioration from the body heat and breath of visitors, the cave had to be closed in 1963; now you have to head 2km south of Montignac on the D704 to visit the replica known as **Lascaux II** (daily: Feb–March & Nov–Dec except Mon 10am–12.30pm & 1.30–5.30pm; April–Sept & Oct except Mon 9am–7pm; 48For 55F to include **Le Thot**; see below).

Opened in 1983, Lascaux II was the result of eleven years' painstaking work by twenty artists and sculptors, under the supervision of Monique Peytral, using the same methods and materials as the original cave painters. While the visit can't offer the excitement of a real cave, the reconstruction – which cost over 500 million francs – rarely disappoints the thousands who trek here every year. The guided tour lasts forty minutes (commentary in French or English). If you have bought the joint ticket to include entry into the **prehistoric theme park**, 5km down the Vézère at **LE THOT**, it's best to visit this first for an enhanced appreciation of the cave itself; particularly if you have kids. The video showing the construction of Lascaux II is particularly interesting, otherwise there are Disneyesque mock-ups of prehistoric scenes and live examples of some of the animals that feature in the paintings: European bison, long-horned cattle and Przewalski's horses, rare and beautiful animals from Mongolia believed to resemble the prehistoric wild horse: notice the erect mane.

Note that tickets must be bought from Montignac tourist office from 9am – there are 2000 on sale a day, but be warned: they go fast in peak season.

St-Amand-de-Coly

Nine kilometres east of Montignac, the village of **ST-AMAND-DE-COLY** boasts a superbly beautiful fortified Romanesque **church**, a magical venue for concerts in the summer. Despite its bristling military architecture, the twelfth-century church manages to combine great delicacy and spirituality. With its purity of line and simple decoration, it is at its most evocative in the low sun of late afternoon or early evening. Its defences left nothing to chance: the walls are 4m thick, a ditch runs all the way around, and a passage once skirted the eaves, with numerous positions for archers to rain down arrows, and blind stairways to mislead attackers.

There is a guard on hand to give guided tours, including an informative and evocative thirty-minute film. Although not officially sanctioned, he will usually agree to show you the roof and galleries if you make a special request. If you don't mind heights, you'll be rewarded with a magnificent view down into the church, and you can climb secret stairs for a bird's-eye view of the roof. Next to the church, the small *Hôtel la Gardette* (☎05.53.51.68.50; ②; restaurant from 60F, closed Nov–March) makes it possible to stay overnight in this tiny, idyllic place.

Villages and castles of the upper Dordogne

East of St-Cyprien the River Dordogne is at its most appealing, forming great loops between rich fields, wooded hills and craggy outcrops. The 10km between **Les Milandes** and **Domme** are particularly spectacular, with clifftop châteaux facing each other across the valley, mostly dating from the Hundred Years' War, when the river marked the frontier between French-held land to the north and English territory to the south.

Further upstream there are marvellous examples of Romanesque sculpture in the churches at **Souillac** and **Beaulieu**, and superbly preserved medieval villages at **Martel** and **Carennac**, both much less touristy than Sarlat or the *bastide* village of Domme.

Without a car, though, you can only reach Souillac, Vayrac and Beaulieu. One way to join them up might be to paddle downstream by canoe (see box on p.620 for details).

Châteaux: Les Milandes, Fayrac and Castelnaud

The first château you come to east of St-Cyprien is **Les Milandes** (daily April, May & Sept 10am–6pm; June—Aug 9am—7pm; Oct–March 10am–noon & 2–5pm; 43F), perched high on the south bank. Built in 1489, it was the property of the de Caumont family until the Revolution, but its most famous owner is the Folies Bergères star, **Josephine Baker** (see box below), who owned it in 1936–69. The stories surrounding the place are more intriguing than the château itself, which contains de Caumont treasures as well as Ms Baker's effects.

Further along on the same side of the river, the **Château de Fayrac** was an English forward position in the Hundred Years' War, built to watch over Beynac, on the opposite bank, where the French were holed up. All slated pepperpot towers, it is unfortunately closed to the public, but you can visit the ruins of the **Château de Castelnaud** (March–April & Oct–Nov 15 daily 10am–6pm; May–Sept daily 9/10am–7/8pm; Dec–Feb daily except Sat 2–5pm; 32F), a little to the south of Fayrac and the true rival to Beynac in terms of impregnability – although it was successfully captured by the bellicose Simon de Montfort as early as 1214. The English held it for much of the Hundred Years' War, and it wasn't until the Revolution that it was finally abandoned. Fairly heavily restored in the last two decades as it is, none of the architecture can match the views

---

JOSEPHINE BAKER AND THE RAINBOW TRIBE

Born on June 3, 1906, in the black ghetto of East St Louis, Illinois, **Josephine Baker** was one of the most bizarre women of this century. Her mother washed clothes for a living and her father was a drummer who soon deserted his family, yet by the late 1920s Josephine was the most celebrated cabaret star in France, primarily due to her role in the legendary Folies Bergères show in Paris. On her first night, de Gaulle, Hemingway, Piaf and Stravinsky were among the audience; her notoriety was further enhanced by her long line of illustrious husbands and lovers, which included the Crown Prince of Sweden and the crime novelist Georges Simenon; she mixed with the likes of Le Corbusier and Adolf Loos, and kept a pet cheetah called Mildred, with whom she used to walk around Paris. During the war, she was active in the Resistance, for which she won the Croix de Guerre. Later on, she became involved in the civil rights movement in North America, where she insisted on playing to non-segregated audiences, a stance which got her arrested in Canada and tailed by the FBI in the US.

By far her most bizarre project was the château of **Les Milandes**, which she bought in 1936, after her marriage to the French orchestra leader Jo Bouillon. Having equipped the place with two hotels, three restaurants, a minigolf course, tennis court and an autobiographical wax museum, she opened the château to the general public as a model multicultural community, popularly dubbed the "*village du monde*". In the course of the 1950s, she adopted babies (mostly orphans) of different ethnic and religious backgrounds from around the world. By the end of the decade, she had brought twelve children to Les Milandes, including a black Catholic Colombian and a Buddhist Korean, along with her mother, brother and sister from East St Louis.

Over 300,000 people a year visited the château in the 1950s, but the conservative local population were never very happy about Les Milandes and the "Rainbow Tribe". In the 1960s, Baker's financial problems, divorce and two heart attacks spelled the end for the project, and despite a sit-in protest by Baker herself (by then in her sixties), the château was sold off in 1969. Josephine died of a stroke while on stage, in 1975, and was given a grand state funeral at La Madeleine in Paris, mourned by thousands of her adopted countryfolk.

up and down the valley, though it does boast a Musée de la Guerre with an extenive collection of weaponry from the Middle Ages.

Beynac

Clearly visible on an impregnable cliff edge on the north bank of the river, the eye-catching village and castle of **BEYNAC-ET-CAZENAC** was built in the days when the river was the only route open to traders and invaders. By road, it is 3km to the **château** (daily: March–Oct 10am–noon & 2–6/6.30pm; Nov until 4.30pm; Dec–Feb noon to dusk; 30F), but a steep lane leads up through the village and takes only fifteen minutes by foot. It is protected on the landward side by a double wall; elsewhere the sheer drop of almost 200m does the job. The flat terrace at the base of the keep, which was added by the English, conceals the remains of the houses where the beleaguered villagers lived; one of the houses has been partly excavated. Richard the Lionheart held the place for a time, until a gangrenous wound received while besieging the castle of Châlus, north of Périgueux, ended his term of blood-letting.

Originally, to facilitate defence, the rooms inside the keep were only connected by a narrow spiral staircase – in stone, not wood as in the reconstruction, because of the danger of fire. The division of domestic space into dining rooms and so forth only came about when the advent of artillery made these old châteaux-forts militarily obsolete. From the roof, there is a stupendous – and vertiginous – view upriver to the **Château de Marqueyssac**, whose beautiful seventeenth-century gardens are open to the public in the summer.

In the main street below the castle is the *Hôtel Bonnet* (☎05.53.29.50.01, fax 05.53.29.83.7; ③; closed January; good restaurant from 80F), as well as a riverside **campsite**, *Le Capeyrou* (June–Sept; ☎05.53.29.54.95, fax 05.53.28.36.27).

La Roque-Gageac

The village of **LA ROQUE-GAGEAC** is almost too perfect, its ochre-coloured houses sheltering under dramatically overhanging cliffs. Regular winner of France's prettiest village contest, it inevitably pulls in the tourist buses, and since the main road separates the village from the river, the noise and fumes of the traffic can become oppressive. The best way to escape is to slip away through the lanes and alleyways that wind up through the terraced houses. The other option is to take the rowing-boat ferry service to the small island, where you can picnic and enjoy a much better view of La Roque than from among the crowds milling around beneath the village, at its best in the burnt-orange glow of the evening sun.

Most people just come here for the afternoon, so there's usually space if you want to **stay** the night, most pleasantly at *La Belle Étoile* (☎05.53.29.51.44, fax 05.53.29.45.63; ③; closed mid-Oct to March; good traditional cuisine from 110F). There are also four **campsites** in the vicinity, and there's a good **restaurant** serving Périgord food at **Les Veyssières**, *La Sanglière* (☎05.53.28.33.51; from 95F), 6km in the direction of Sarlat.

Domme

High on the scarp on the south bank of the river, **DOMME** is one of the best-preserved of the *bastides*, although now wholly given over to tourism. Its attractions, in addition to its position, include three original thirteenth-century **gateways** and a section of the old **walls**. From the northern edge of the village, known as the *barre*, marked by a drop so precipitous that fortifications were deemed unnecessary, you look out over a wide sweep of river country. Underneath the village are hundreds of metres of **caves**

CANOEING ON THE DORDOGNE

Canoeing is becoming increasingly popular on the Dordogne, with rental outlets at just about every twist on the Vézère and Dordogne rivers. In summer, both rivers are shallow and slow-flowing and ideal for beginners. Although it's possible to rent one-person kayaks or two-person canoes by the hour, it's best to take at least a half-day or longer, and simply cruise downstream. The company you book through will send a minibus to pick you up from your final destination and take you back to where you began. Prices vary according to what's on offer; expect to pay 60–110F per day. Most places function daily in July and August, on demand in May, June and September, and are closed the rest of the year. All companies are obliged to equip you with lifejackets (*gilets* or *ceintures*) and teach you basic safety procedures, most importantly how to capsize and get out without drowning. You must be able to swim. Below are just some of the choices on offer.

River Dordogne
Canoë Dordogne, Castelnaud-en-Périgord (☎05.53.29.58.50).
Copeyre (☎05.65.37.33.51). Based in Martel, this company has twelve outlets from Argentat to Beynac; choose your own route or longer accompanied trips of up to seven days (900F).
Kayak-Club, La Rogue-Gageac (☎05.53.29.40.07). Groléjac–Castelnaud (full day); Vitrac–Castelnaud (half-day); Castelnaud–Les Milandes (half-day).
Randonnée Dordogne, Le Port de Domme (☎05.53.28.22.01). Carsac–Beynac (full day); Carsac–Cénac or Cénac–Beynac (half-day); longer accompanied trips possible.
Safaraid (☎05.55.28.80.70). Seven outlets from Argentat to Beynac; choose your own route for the day or join longer trips of up to fifteen days.

River Vézère
L'Animation Vézère, Pont Routier, rte de Périgueux, Les Eyzies (☎05.53.06.92.92). Also with an outlet at Montignac; you can choose your distance, stopping anywhere between Montignac and Les Eyzies.
Randonnée Vézère, Condat-sur-Vézère (☎05.53.51.38.35). Choice of distance from Condat to Les Eyzies.

(April–Sept daily 10am–noon & 2–6pm; Oct daily 2–6pm; March Tues–Sun 2—5pm; 30F) in which the townspeople took refuge in times of danger. You enter the complex opposite the **tourist office** on the main square (same times as caves).

Lou Cardil, at the beginning of Grand'rue (☎05.53.28.38.92; ②; closed mid-Nov to March), is a nice and surprisingly reasonable **hotel**, while down by the river at **CÉNAC** there's a **camping municipal** (☎05.53.28.31.91; June to mid-Sept). If you come here, don't miss the round tile roof of the chapel or the beautifully proportioned twelfth-century **church** on rue St-Cybranet.

Souillac

The first place of any size east of Sarlat is **SOUILLAC**, at the confluence of the Borrèze and Dordogne rivers. Virginia Woolf stayed here in 1937, and was pleased to meet "no tourists . . . England seems like a chocolate box bursting with trippers afterward." There are still few tourists, since Souillac's only real point of interest is the twelfth-century **church of Ste-Marie**, just off the main road. Roofed with massive domes like the cathedrals of Périgueux and Cahors, its spacious interior creates just the atmosphere for cool reflection on a summer's day. On the back of the west door are some of the most wonderful Romanesque sculptures, including a seething mass of beasts devouring each other. The greatest piece of craftsmanship, though, is a bas-relief of

Isaiah, fluid and supple, thought to be by one of the artists who worked at Moissac (see p.652). Behind the church, a new museum has opened to try and draw a few more visitors to Souillac – the **Musée de l'Automate** (April–June & Aug–Oct daily 10am–noon & 3–6pm; July & Aug daily 10am–7pm; Nov–March Wed–Sun 2–5pm; 30F). Those under 12 are the ones most likely to enjoy the mostly nineteenth-century mechanical dolls, which dance, sing and perform magical tricks.

The **tourist office** (☎05.65.37.81.56, fax 05.65.27.11.45) is on the main boulevard Louis-Jean Malvy, next to the delightful *Grand Hôtel* (☎05.62.32.78.30, fax 05.65.32.66.34; ③; Nov–March), where you can sleep in the owner's former apartment, with its massive fireplace, for 500F; the hotel also has an excellent restaurant from 68F (closed Wed). But there is cheaper accommodation at the *Auberge du Puits*, in the pretty place du Puits in the old quarter (☎05.65.37.80.32, fax 05.65.37.07.16; ①–③; closed Sun eve, Nov & Dec), with good food from 75F. Alternatively, there's the large riverside **campsite**, *Les Ondines* (☎05.65.37.86.44, fax 05.65.27.11.45; May–Sept), and a gîte d'étape at Le Gachou on the Martel road (☎05.65.32.27.17). You can rent **bicycles** from the gare SNCF, 1.5km northwest of the centre, or from Évasion Sport, 36 bd L-J Malvy.

Martel

About 15km east of Souillac and set back even further from the river, **MARTEL** is a minor medieval masterpiece, built in a pale, almost white, stone, offset by the warm reddish-brown roofs, yet it suffers none of the crowds endured by the likes of Sarlat. Another Turenne-administered town (see p.633), its heyday came during the thirteenth and fourteenth centuries, when the viscounts established a court of appeal here.

The main square, **place des Consuls**, is mostly taken up by the large eighteenth-century covered *halles*, but on every side there are reminders of the town's illustrious past, most notably in the superb Gothic **Hôtel de la Raymondie**. Begun in 1280, it served as the Turenne law courts, though it doubled as the town's refuge, hence the distinctive corner turrets. Facing the hôtel is the **Tour des Pénitents**, one of the many medieval towers which gave the town its epithet, "*la ville aux sept tours*". Henry Short-Coat (see box on p.622) died in the striking building in the southeast corner of the square, the **Maison Fabri**. One block south, rue Droite leads east to the town's main church, the **church of St-Maur**, built in a fiercely defensive, mostly Gothic style, with a finely carved Romanesque tympanum depicting the Last Judgment above the west door.

If you'd rather **stay** here than in Souillac, head for the *Le Turenne* on av J-Lavayssière (☎05.65.37.30.30; ①; closed Dec–March), with traditional cuisine from 75F. There's also a **camping municipal**, *La Callopie* (05.65.37.30.03, fax 05.65.37.37.27; May–Oct), on the road to Quatre-Routes, and a little riverside campsite, 5km away in the village of **GLUGES**, where there are a couple of nice restaurants with menus from 60F, and canoe and kayak rental down by the water.

Carennac and Castelnau-Bretenoux

CARENNAC is without doubt one of the most beautiful villages along this part of the Dordogne river. Elevated just above the south bank of the river, 13km or so east of Martel, it's best known for its typical Quercy architecture, its Romanesque priory, where the French writer Fénelon spent the best years of his life, and for its greengages.

Carennac's feature, as so often in these parts, is the Romanesque tympanum above the west door, in the Moissac style. Christ sits in majesty with the Book of Judgment in his left hand, with the apostles and adoring angels below him. Inside the church, you can gain access to the old **cloisters and chapter house** (daily April—Oct 10am–1pm & 2–7pm; 7F), which contain an exceptionally expressive life-size entombment of Christ.

THE TALE OF HENRY SHORT-COAT

At the end of the twelfth century, Martel was the stage for one of the tragic events in the internecine conflicts of the Plantagenet family. When Henry Plantagenet (King Henry II of England) imprisoned his estranged wife Eleanor of Aquitaine, his sons took up arms against their father. The eldest son, **Henry Short-Coat** (Henri Court-Mantel), even went so far as to plunder the viscountcy of Turenne and Quercy. Furious, Henry II immediately stopped his allowance and handed over his lands to the third son, Richard the Lionheart. Financially insecure, and with a considerable army of soldiers to feed and clothe, Henry Short-Coat began looting the treasures of every abbey and shrine in the region. Finally, he decided to sack the shrine at Rocamadour, making off with various artefacts, including Roland's famous sword, Durandal. This last act was to be his downfall, for shortly afterwards he fled to Martel and fell ill with a fever. Guilt-ridden and afraid for his life, he confessed his crimes and asked his father for forgiveness. Henry II was busy besieging Limoges, but sent a messenger to pardon him. On the messenger's arrival in Martel, Henry Short-Coat died, and Richard the Lionheart became heir to the English throne.

There are two comfortable and reasonably priced **hotels** in the village, both with good restaurants specializing in traditional regional cuisine: the *Hôtel Fénelon* on the main street (☎05.65.10.96.46, fax 05.65.10.94.86; ③; closed Jan 10–March 10; good restaurant from 90F), and the *Auberge du Vieux Quercy* (☎05.65.10.96.59, fax 05.65.10.94.05; ③; closed mid-Nov to mid-March), whose restaurant has a particularly good value menu at 90F. There's also a **campsite**, *L'Eau Vive* in town (☎05.65.10.97.39, fax 05.65.28.12.12; May to mid-Oct).

Another 10km further upstream, the sturdy towers and machicolated red-brown walls of the eleventh-century **Château de Castelnau-Bretenoux** (April–Sept daily 9.30am–12.15pm & 2–6.15pm; July & Aug until 6.45pm with no lunchtime break; rest of year daily except Tues 10am–12.15pm & 2–5.15pm; 30F) dominate a sharp knoll above the Dordogne, making a harmonious whole with the village piled at its feet. Most of it has now been restored and refurnished. Below, on the banks of the River Cère, you come to the graceful little *bastide* of **BRETENOUX**, with two sides of its cobbled and arcaded square still intact.

Beaulieu-sur-Dordogne

Beautifully situated on the banks of the Dordogne, 8km upriver from Castelnau-Bretenoux, **BEAULIEU-SUR-DORDOGNE** boasts another of the great masterpieces of Romanesque sculpture on the porch of the **church of St-Pierre** in the centre of town. This doorway is unusually deep-set, with a tympanum presided over by an Oriental-looking Christ with one arm extended to welcome the chosen. All around him is a complicated pattern of angels and apostles, executed in characteristic "dancing" style, similar to that at Carennac. The dead raise the lids of their coffins hopefully, while underneath a frieze of monsters crunches heads. Take the opportunity also to wander through to the peaceful medieval **quartier de la Chapelle** to the north of the town centre, which boasts some handsome fourteenth-century houses with sculpted facades.

The *Hôtel Fournié* (☎05.55.91.01.34; fax 05.55.91.23.57; ③) has comfortable rooms and a restaurant from 100F. Equally appealing is the magnificent half-timbered and turreted HI **youth hostel**, in the Quartier de la Chapelle (☎05.55.91.13.82, fax 05.55.91.26.06; April–Sept). There are river-bathing and canoeing possibilities, and a riverside **campsite** close by.

Argentat

An SNCF bus can take you still further upstream to **ARGENTAT**, the last major town on the Dordogne and the last part of the river accessible by anything other than foot. Beyond Argentat, the Dordogne changes character entirely, due to the series of hydro-electric dams (*barrages*) that turn the river into a succession of grand reservoirs.

Argentat's whitewashed houses and rather sombre grey slate rooftops make a distinct change from the warm yellow stone of the rest of the Dordogne. It's easy enough to while away an hour or so sitting at one of the river-bank cafés or exploring the cobbled *petites ruelles* which slope down to the river. But there's nothing else to make you stay, except for the comfortable, reasonably priced **rooms** at the *Hôtel Fouillade*, 11 place Gambetta (☎05.55.28.10.17, fax 05.55.28.90.52; ②; closed Nov 4–Dec 10), with a **restaurant** from 70F.

THE LIMOUSIN

The **Limousin** – the country around Limoges – is hilly, wooded, wet and not particularly fertile: ideal pasture for the famous Limousin breed of cattle. This is herdsman's country, from where – presumably – the widespread use of the shepherd's cape known as a *limousine* gave its name to the big, wraparound, covered twentieth-century car.

The modern Limousin region stretches south to the Dordogne valley to include Brive and Tulle. But while these places, together with **Limoges** itself, are not without interest, the star of the show is the countryside, especially in the east on the **Plateau de Millevaches** round **Eymoutiers**, **Meymac** and **La Courtine**. Happily, there is a mountain rail line connecting Limoges and **Ussel**. Although it is remote and underpopulated, there are plenty of small hotels, gîtes and campsites to accommodate the wanderer.

Limoges

LIMOGES is not a city that calls for a long stay, but it is worth a look for a magnificent train station and the craft industries that made the city's name a household word: enamel in the Middle Ages and, since the eighteenth century, some of the finest china ever produced. If these appeal, then the city's unique museum collections – and its Gothic cathedral – will reward a visit. But it has to be said that the industry today seems a spent tradition, hard-hit by recession and changing tastes among the rich. The local *kaolin* (china clay) mines that gave Limoges china its special quality are exhausted, and the workshops survive mainly on the tourist trade.

Arrival, information and accommodation

The town is built on high ground overlooking the River Vienne, with a small city centre enclosed by modern boulevards. The cathedral stands directly above the river, with the main commercial streets behind it. The magnificent **Gare des Bénédictins** (☎05.55.77.58.11) lies slightly off to the northeast, connected to the chestnut-shaded **place Jourdan** by the av de Gaulle. The **bus station** is five minutes' walk away off av des Bénédictins (some buses leave from a second bus station on place des Charentes). The **tourist office** is on boulevard de Fleurus near place Wilson (daily: July & Aug 9am–7pm; rest of year 9am–noon & 2–6pm; ☎05.55.34.46.87, fax 05.53.34.19.12), and has a money-changing facility when the banks are closed.

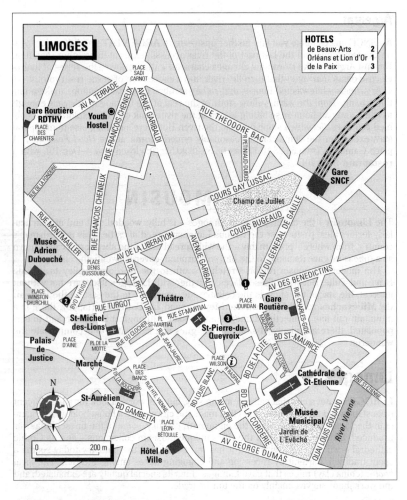

There are two conveniently central **hotels** on place Jourdan. The more comfortable of the two is the *Hôtel de la Paix* right in the quietest corner of the square (☎05.55.34.36.00, fax 05.55.32.37.06; ③). The other, *Hôtel Orléans et Lion d'Or*, is just round the corner at 11 cours Jourdan (☎05.55.77.49.71, fax 05.55.77.33.41; ③). Slightly cheaper and very nice, on the other side of the town centre at 28 bd Victor-Hugo between place d'Aine and place Dussoubs, is the *Beaux-Arts* (☎05.55.79.42.20, fax 05.55.79.29.13; ②). And, cheaper still, there's a **youth hostel** at 20 rue Encombe-Vineuse, off rue François-Chénieux close to place Carnot (☎05.55.77.63.97), or the *Foyer des Jeunes Travailleurs*, at 44 rue Emile-Montégut (☎05.55.79.64.41). The nearest **campsite** is *La Vallée de l'Aurence* (☎05.55.38.49.43, fax 05.55.37.32.78), 5km north of town on the N20 Paris road.

The city

The **Cathédrale St-Étienne** a landmark for miles around, was begun in 1273 and planned on the model of the cathedral of Amiens, though only the choir, completed in the early thirteenth century, is pure Gothic. The rest of the building was added piece-meal over the centuries, the western part of the nave not until 1876. The most striking external feature is the sixteenth-century facade of the north transept, built in full Flamboyant style with elongated arches, clusters of pinnacles and delicate tracery in window and gallery. At the west end of the nave, the tower, erected on a Romanesque base that had to be massively reinforced to bear the weight, has octagonal upper storeys, in common with most churches in the region. It once stood as a separate cam-panile and probably looked the better for it. Inside, the effects are much more pleasing, and the rose stone looks warmer than on the weathered exterior. The sense of soaring height is accentuated by all the upward-reaching lines of the pillars, the net of vaulting ribs, the curling, flame-like lines repeated in the arcading of the side chapels and the rose window and, above all, as you look down the nave, by the narrower and more pointed arches of the choir.

The best of the city's museums – with its showpiece collections of enamelware dat-ing back as far as the twelfth century – is the **Musée Municipal de l'Évêché** (June–Sept daily 10–11.45am & 2–6pm;Oct–May Wed–Mon till 5pm; free) in the old Bishop's Palace overlooking a classic eighteenth-century formal garden next to the cathedral. There's an interesting progression to be observed here, from the simple, sober, Byzantine-influenced *champlevé* (copper filled with enamel), to the later, espe-cially seventeenth- and eighteenth-century work that used a far greater range of colours and indulged in elaborate virtuoso portraiture. By the nineteenth century, however, the spirit and vigour had dissipated, and although there are contemporary artisans in the city using the medium, their work, too – judging from this display – is not much more successful. There is also an exhibition of the **wartime Resistance** housed in an out-building opposite the main entrance (same hours; free).

Outside, if the weather is good, the extremely well laid-out and interesting **botanical garden** is an inviting prospect (daily during daylight hours; free), descending grace-fully towards the River Vienne.

The old quarter

Over to the west of the cathedral is the partly renovated **old quarter** of the town. Make your way through to rue de la Boucherie, for a thousand years the domain of the Butchers' Guild, and today featuring several good but expensive restaurants. The dark, cluttered **chapel of St-Aurélien**, with a fourteenth-century cross outside, belongs to them. At the top of the street is the **market** in place de la Motte and, to the right, part-ly hidden by adjoining houses, the fourteenth- and fifteenth-century **church of St-Michel-des-Lions**, named after the two badly weathered Celtic lions guarding the south door and topped by one of the best towers and spires in the region. The inside is dark and atmospheric, with two beautiful, densely coloured fifteenth-century windows either side of the choir, one of which – in the south aisle – depicts the Tree of Jesse.

From place de la Motte, rue du Clocher leads to rue Jean-Jaurès, with the **post office** a couple of blocks up to the left. Straight across, **rue St-Martial** leads past place de la République – where the fourth-century crypt of the long-vanished **Abbey of St-Martial** (July–Sept daily 9.30am–noon & 2.30–7pm; 15F) was discovered during build-ing operations in 1960 – to the **church of St-Pierre-du-Queyroix**, whose belfry was the model for the cathedral and the church of St-Michel. The interior, partly twelfth-century (the exterior was remodelled in the sixteenth century), gains a sombre strength from the massive round pillars which still support the roof. Like the cathedral, it has a slightly pink granite glow. There is a fine window at the end of the south aisle depicting the Dormition of the Virgin, signed by the great enamel artist Jean Pénicault in 1510.

Limoges is renowned the world over for its porcelain, a craft well represented in the **Musée Adrien-Dubouché** (Wed–Mon: 10am–12.30pm & 2–5.45pm; July & Aug no lunch break; 20F), west of the old quarter off place Winston-Churchill and close to place Dussoubs. The collection includes samples of the local product and china displays from around the world, and various celebrity services ordered for the likes of Napoléon Bonaparte, Charles and Di, and sundry French royals. The exhibits are well laid out, with explanatory panels describing the processes for making the different wares, and form a much more interesting display than you might expect.

Eating, drinking and festivals

There is an abundance of good and not too expensive places to **eat**. Three places for a light lunch are the friendly *Le Croquembouche*, 14 rue de Haute-Cité, near the Cathedral (closed Sat & Sun), *La Louisiane*, place d'Aine (closed Mon & Sun), and *Le Khédive* at 39 bd Carnot. At night the rue Charles-Michels buzzes with life – there's a whole selection of ethnic restaurants here. If you'd prefer something more French, there's the rather posh *Brasserie Le Versailles*, also on place d'Aine, with menus from 65F; the business people's haunt of *Rive Gauche*, 3 av Garibaldi, close to place Jourdan, with a wide selection of seafood (closed Sun; menus at from 75F, *plats* around 45F); and for serious, first-class meat eating, the *Bœuf à la Mode*, 60 rue François-Chenieux (closed Sun; menus 80–170F). For a real treat of subtle and sophisticated cuisine (*foie gras* and a *tajine* of pigeon and dates, for example), there's no better place than *L'Amphitryon*, opposite the chapel of St-Aurélien at 26 rue de la Boucherie (☎05.55.33.36.39; closed Sun, Mon lunchtime & Aug 23–Oct 9); their menus start at 95F. In the same price-range and practically next door, at 20 rue de la Bouchiere, *Les Petits Ventres* will delight lovers of brain, brawn, tongue and other unmentionable cuts (☎05.55.33.34.02; closed Sun & Mon lunchtime).

For **drinks** at any time of the day, people sit out in the not-very-attractive place de la République. The *Lord John Pub* on avenue de-Gaulle near the train station – complete with darts – is a popular hang-out, whilst the *Blue Banana* at 16 rue Charles-Michels is frequented by the youthful members of Limoges's smart set.

Festivals

For French-speakers, there is an interesting gathering of writers, dramatists and musicians from other French-speaking countries at the **Festival International des Francophonies** in September and October. Gourmets should make sure their visit coincides with the third Friday in October, for the **Fête des Petits Ventres**, when the entire population turns out to gorge on everything from pig's trotters to sheep's testicles in the rue de la Boucherie. Otherwise there is the **Biennale de la Danse** every two years in January, the next one in 2000.

Around Limoges

There is a clutch of villages within a day's reach of Limoges. The Limoges tourist office has worked out a route linking places of interest on the south bank of the Vienne, like the **châteaux** of **Rochebrune**, **Rochechouart** and **Châlus**; they are detailed in the leaflet *Route Richard-Cœur-de-Lion*, so-called because of its associations with the English king. Visiting all of them really requires a car, but some at least are accessible by a combination of public transport and patient hitching.

Oradour-sur-Glane

Twenty-five kilometres northwest of Limoges and a few kilometres north of the N141 road to Angoulême, the village of **ORADOUR-SUR-GLANE** stands just as the soldiers of the SS left it on June 10, 1944, after killing all the inhabitants in reprisal for attacks by French *maquisards*. It seems irreverent to approach it as a "sight"; perhaps it should be treated more as a shrine.

A gate into the **old village** admonishes, "*Souviens-toi*" ("Remember"), and the main street leads past roofless houses gutted by fire. Telephone poles, tram cables and gutters are fixed in tormented attitudes where the fire's heat left them; prewar cars rust in the garages; a yucca, grown into an enormous clump, still blooms in the notary's garden; last year's grapes hang wizened on a vine whose trellis has long rotted away.

Behind the square is a **memorial garden**, a plain rectangle of lawn hedged with beech. A dolmen-like slab on a shallow plinth covers a crypt containing relics of the dead, and the awful list of names. Beyond, by the stream, stands the **church** where the women and children – five hundred of them – were burnt to death.

The **modern village** of Oradour has been constructed beside the old, with a 1950s concrete church trying to be impressive but struggling with the task of commemorating what happened here.

There are buses from place des Charentes in Limoges, although it might be more convenient to take the train to **ST-JUNIEN** and then bus back to Oradour. The *Hôtel au Rendez-vous des Chasseurs*, Pont-à-la-Planche (☎05.55.02.19.73, fax 05.55.02.06.98; ②; closed Aug 1–7 & Oct 15–31; good restaurant specializing in game from 72F) makes a good place to put up in St-Junien.

Rochechouart and Chassenon

ROCHECHOUART, a beautiful little walled town 11km southwest of St-Junien, has two claims to fame. Two hundred million years ago it was the site of impact of one of the largest meteorites ever to hit earth, a monster 1.5km in diameter and some 6000 million tonnes in weight. The traces of this cosmic pile-up still attract the curiosity of world's astronomers and moon-watchers. The only evidence that a layman might notice, however, is the unusual-looking breccia stone many of the region's older buildings are made of: the squashed, shattered, heat-transformed and reconstituted result of the collision.

One such building is Rochechouart's other source of pride: the handsome **château** that stands at the town's edge. It started life as a rough fortress before 1000 AD, was "modernized" in the thirteenth century (the sawn-off keep and entrance survive from this period) and civilized with Renaissance decoration and additions in the fifteenth. Until it was acquired as the mairie in 1832, it had belonged to the de Rochechouart family for 800 years. Today it is not only the town hall, but also the extremely well-regarded and adventurous **Musée Départemental d'Art Contemporain** (April, May & Oct–Dec Wed–Sun 2–6pm; June–Oct Mon & Wed–Sun 10am–12.30pm & 1.30–6.30pm; 15F) specializing in "land art" and the Arte Povera movement. For instance, in a room decorated with its original sixteenth-century frescoes of the Labours of Hercules, the British artist, Richard Long, has made a special installation of white stones, while in the garden strange bits of metal grapple with the trees. A collection of local archeological bits and bobs occupies other parts of the château.

Should you wish to **stay**, the *Hôtel de France*, just outside the old town centre on place Octave-Marquet, provides good board, comfortable lodgings and interesting food from 70F (☎05.55.03.77.40, fax 05.55.03.03.87; ③; restaurant closed Sun & Mon eve). The same proprietors run another good restaurant, *La Vallée de la Gorre* (☎05.55.00.01.27; from 70F), in nearby **ST-AUVENT**. For further information, the Rochechouart **tourist**

office is at 6 rue Victor-Hugo (mid-June to mid-Sept daily 9am–noon & 2–7pm; rest of year Mon–Sat 9am–noon & 2–6pm; ☎ and fax 05.55.03.72.73).

One side-trip worth making if you have come this far is to the **Roman baths** 5km along the Chabanais road at **CHASSENON** (guided tours only daily Easter–May & mid-Sept to mid-Nov 2–5.30pm; June to mid-Sept 10am–noon & 2–7pm; 25F). The site, known as Cassinomagus in Gallo-Roman times, stood at an important crossroads on the Via Agrippa, the Roman road that connected Lyon to Saintes via Clermont-Ferrand and Limoges. Only the baths survive: a grand temple and theatre were destroyed by use as quarries for their breccia stone. But the baths alone are ample testimony to the magnificence of the place. There are hot and cold pools with some of the original floor tiles in places, and waterproof plastering, boiler rooms and elaborate hypocaust piping systems; you can even see the marks of the shuttering used to make the vaults in some of the subterranean passages.

Châlus and Nexon

At **CHÂLUS**, 35km along the N21 from Limoges (1hr by bus), the principal point of interest is the ruined **château** (July to mid-Sept daily 10am–noon & 2–6pm; April–June Sun & hols only; free), where in 1199 Richard the Lionheart was mortally wounded by an archer shooting from the still-extant keep. Richard, son of Eleanor of Aquitaine and as much French as English, was campaigning to suppress a local rebellion against English rule. The archer was flayed to death for his marksmanship. For real enthusiasts, there are two further castles, both private homes: **Brie** has limited visiting days (April–Oct, Sunday and public holidays 2–7pm) and **Montbrun** (no visits), a short distance west of Châlus. For an overnight **stay** in Châlus, there's the friendly *Hôtel du Centre*, 8 place de la Fontaine (☎05.55.78.41.61; ①), with good-value menus from 60F in its restaurant; or a cheap and basic **campsite** in the grounds of the Hôtel de Ville.

Eighteen kilometres east, past another early medieval fortress at **RILHAC-LAS-TOURS**, the village of **NEXON**, also directly accessible by bus and train from Limoges, is of more general interest, with a fine, heavily restored late medieval **château** (only open to the public in summer), set in magnificent parklands with a **stud farm** (daily 9am–noon & 2–7pm), renowned for its Anglo-Arab breeds. You can **camp** in Nexon at the *Étang de la Lande* (☎05.55.58.35.44); for a **meal**, try the *Dexet* in avenue de la Gare.

Chalusset and Solignac

A dozen kilometres south of Limoges in the lovely wooded valley of the Briance, the Château de Chalusset and the abbey of Solignac make the most attractive day's outing from the city. There are daily buses to Le Vigen (on the St-Yrieix line), although the times do not allow for a return the same day.

It is a fifteen-minute walk from Le Vigen to Solignac. You can see the Romanesque **abbey of Solignac** ahead of you, with the tiled roofs of its octagonal apse and neat little brood of radiating chapels. The twelfth-century facade is plain with just a little sculpture, as the granite of which it is built does not permit the intricate carving of limestone. Inside it is beautiful, a flight of steps leading down into the nave with a dramatic view the length of the church. There are no aisles, just a single space roofed with two big domes, and no ambulatory either – an absolutely plain Latin cross in design. It is a simple, sturdy church, with the same feel of plain robust Christianity as the crypt of St-Eutrope in Saintes (see p.573).

There is a very pleasant, simple **hotel** in the village, *Les Sarrazins* (☎05.55.00.51.48; ①), which serves a generous meal for 50F, and another in **LE VIGEN**, *Les Touristes* (☎05.55.00.52.11; ②; restaurant from 55F).

The **Château de Chalusset** is a sixty- to ninety-minute walk up the valley of the Briance in the other direction – uphill quite a lot of the way. After about 45 minutes, at the highest point of the climb, there is a little ornamental belvedere in the trees on the right of the road, giving a dramatic view across the valley to the ruined keep of the castle rising above the woods. It is a further kilometre down to the bridge on the Briance, where a path follows the river bank for five minutes before winding up into the steep woods. You come first to a secondary keep, the **Tour Jeannette**, and then to the main bulk of the castle. Half-submerged in a jungle of oak and chestnut, hazel and broom, with wild flowers growing from its creviced walls, it is a splendidly dramatic and romantic ruin.

Built in the twelfth century, it was in English hands during the Hundred Years' War and, in the lawless aftermath, became the lair of a notorious local brigand, Perrot le Béarnais. Dismantled in 1593 for harbouring Protestants, it has recently been acquired by the local authorities who are in the process of making the ruins safe. It is still possible to visit, though some care is required.

St-Léonard-de-Noblat

ST-LÉONARD-DE-NOBLAT, 25 minutes by train from Limoges or 45 minutes by bus, is a beautiful little market town of narrow streets and medieval houses with jutting eaves and corbelled turrets. There's a very lovely eleventh- and twelfth-century **church**, whose six-storey tower looks out over the rising hills and woods where the River Vienne threads its course down from the heights of the Massif Central. The interior is strong and simple, with barrel vaults on big, square piles, a high dome on an octagonal drum and domed transepts – the whole in grey granite.

If you're in a car, St-Léonard can make a pleasant base for visiting Limoges. A good place to **stay** is the *Modern Hôtel* in the old town, 6 bd Pressemanne – not much to look at but very nice (☎05.55.56.00.25; ③; closed Feb; restaurant from 105F, closed Sun eve & Mon Oct–June). There is also a **camping municipal** beside the river below the town. The **tourist office** on place du Champs de Mars (July & Aug daily 10.30am–12.30pm; rest of year closed Sun & Mon; ☎05.55.56.25.06) publishes route maps for local walks and will point you to chambres d'hôte possibilities round about.

Aubusson

AUBUSSON is 90km east of Limoges and served by regular buses and trains. A neat grey-stone town in the bottom of a ravine formed by the River Creuse, it is of no great interest in itself. What makes it unique is its enormous reputation as a centre for weaving tapestries, second only to the Gobelins in Paris. If you're interested, the place to aim for is the **Musée Départemental de la Tapisserie** in avenue des Lissiers (daily except Tues am: July & Aug 10am–6pm; rest of year 9.30am–noon & 2–6pm; 20F). For information about further exhibits, ask at the **tourist office** at rue Vieille (July–Sept 15 daily 9.30am–6pm; rest of year Mon–Sat 9.30am–12.30pm & 1.30–6pm; ☎05.55.66.32.12, fax 05.55.83.84.51). If you want to stay, there are two inexpensive **hotels** in the main Grande-Rue: *Hôtel du Lissier*, at nos. 84–86 (☎/fax 05.55.66.14.18; ②; with restaurant), and *Hôtel du Chapître*, at nos. 53–55 (☎05.55.66.18.54; ①). The town's **campsite** is by the river on the Felletin road, or there is a youth hostel in the rue des Fusillées (June–Sept; ☎05.55.66.13.59).

Ussel and the Plateau de Millevaches

Millevaches, the plateau of a thousand springs, is undulating upland country 800–900m in altitude, a sort of step on the northern edge of the Massif Central. It is a wild and sparsely populated landscape, and the villages here are few and far between. The ones there are appear small, grey and sturdy, inured like their mainly elderly inhabitants to the buffeting of upland weather. It is a country of conifer plantations and natural woodland – of beech, birch and chestnut – interspersed with reed-fringed tarns, dam-created lakes and pasture grazed by sheep and cows, where you still find people haymaking with rake and pitchfork.

The small towns, like **Eymoutiers and Meymac**, have a primitive architectural beauty and an old-world charm largely untouched by modern development. It is an area to walk or cycle in, or at least savour at a gentle pace, and there are a surprisingly large number of attractive old-fashioned hotels.

Obviously, getting around by car is easiest, but there is access by public transport. **Ussel,** the main town, is on the main road and rail link between Brive and Clermont-Ferrand, and is also connected by a cross-country line through Meymac and Eymoutiers to Limoges.

Ussel

On the eastern edge of the plateau is **USSEL**, 90km west of Clermont-Ferrand and 60km northeast of Tulle, where the land begins its gradual descent to the uppermost reaches of the Dordogne valley, thickly wooded and cut by deep tributary valleys. The town is pleasant enough, with some attractive sixteenth- and seventeenth- century houses scattered about the central part. A giant battered granite eagle on the place Voltaire is all that remains of a Roman settlement hereabouts. It's not a place with much to see.

One building worth a look is the house of the local lords, the **Maison du Ducs de Ventadour**, who moved here from their draughty fortress in the hills to the south (see p.below). Just off place de la République behind the church, it has a very provincial and rather amateurish Renaissance grandeur, perhaps aping their rich metropolitan cousins. Also worth a quick look is the local **Musée du Pays d'Ussel**, one half of which is dedicated to traditional crafts and trades of the region and located in the eighteenth-century *Hôtel du Juge Choriol* on rue Michelet, parallel to avenue Thiers (July & Aug daily 10am–noon & 2–7pm; free).

The N89, the main Clermont road, passes through the town centre. The **tourist office** is on the wide place Voltaire (July & Aug Mon–Sat 9am–1pm & 3–7pm, Sun 10am–1pm & 3–6pm; Sept daily 9am–noon & 2–6pm; rest of year Mon–Sat 9.30am–noon & 2–5pm; ☎05.55.72.11.50, fax 05.55.72.54.44). At the top of the hill, the N89 becomes avenue Carnot and begins to descend towards the **gare SNCF**.

Perhaps the quietest place to **stay** is the *Hôtel L'Auberge* at 6 av Gambetta, opposite the **post office** (☎05.55.96.17.30; ②; restaurant from 75F; closed Sun & Mon). Alternatively, try the *Hôtel Le Midi*, 24 av Thiers (☎05.55.72.17.99, fax 05.55.72.90.04; ②; restaurant from 70F). There is a **camping municipal** (☎05.55.72.30.05, fax 05.55.72.95.19; March—Oct) just off the road to Tulle, and several brasserie-type **eating** places on avenue Carnot, and a cluster of hotel-restaurants in front of the station.

STEAM TRAINS ON MILLEVACHES

In July and August every year **steam-train trips** are run on the beautiful Limoges–Ussel mountain line. Prices are in the range of 160–200F (adults) and 80–100F (children), according to the length of the journey. You can do Limoges–Meymac, Limoges–Eymoutiers, Eymoutiers–Bujaleuf and Meymac–Ussel. For dates and times, consult the brochure *Trains Touristiques à Vapeur en Limousin* or the tourist offices in Limoges, St-Léonard-de-Noblat, Bujaleuf, Pyrat-le-Château, Île de Vassivière, Eymoutiers, Bugeat, Meymac or Treignac.

Meymac and around

Pepperpot turrets and steep slate roofs adorn the ancient grey houses of **MEYMAC**, 17km west of Ussel. The village is packed tightly around its Romanesque **church**, whose porch is flanked by striking pink capitals. Adjoining it are the remains of the original Benedictine **abbey**, whose foundation a thousand years ago brought the town into being.

Grande-Rue, the main street, ends in steps that climb past the round **bell tower**, the town's landmark, to the lime-shaded square in front of the town hall. The **tourist office** is opposite, the other side of a prettily jetting fountain (May–Sept Mon–Sat 10am–12.30pm & 3–7pm, Sun 10am–12.30pm; rest of year Mon–Sat 10—noon & 2.30–4.30pm; ☎05.55.95.18.43, fax 05.55.46.19.96), and can arrange **bike rental** and give out **hiking information**.

There are two simple but pleasant **hotels** on the main road, of which the more gracious is the *Hôtel Limousin*, 76 av Limousine (☎05.55.95.12.11, fax 05.55.95.25.61; ②; restaurant 65–145F). The other, close by, is *Les Voyageurs* (☎05.55.95.11.92; ①; restaurant from 65F). A municipal **campsite** is close at hand on the Sornac road.

One of the most touted sights in the area is the remains of a **Roman villa** and second-century **temple** at **CARS**. Although there is nothing very spectacular to see, the very presence of Roman influence here is interesting. And, if you want to stay, there is one of the loveliest, simple, old-fashioned country **hotels** just a few kilometres away at **PEROLS-SUR-VÉZÈRE**, Madame Gioux's *Hôtel des Touristes* (☎05.55.95.51.71; ①), with genuine home-cooking from 60F; another is the perfectly adequate *Hôtel des Touristes* in nearby **BUGEAT** (☎05.55.95.50.20; ①;), where there is also a **campsite**.

Five kilometres further, the six houses of **VIAM** perch prettily on the shores of an artificial lake. Its innocence has been slightly marred by watersporting, but it has an exquisite and proportionately minute, lopsided **church**, whose door is blocked by a small iron gate, like Bugeat's church – presumably a local device to keep wandering farm animals out. There is no accommodation in Viam except a **camping municipal** (☎05.55.95.52.05), but 6km on, towards Eymoutiers, there is a friendly **gîte d'étape** by the Étang de Goussolles (Mme Sarrazin; ☎05.55.95.54.99; June–Sept).

Eymoutiers

EYMOUTIERS, on the banks of the River Vienne, 45km from Limoges, is another attractive upland town of tall, narrow, stone houses crowding round a much-altered Romanesque **church**. Not interesting enough for a prolonged stay, it nonetheless makes another agreeable stopover, especially for campers, as it has a simple but magnificently sited **campsite,** the *St Pierre Château* (☎05.55.69.13.98) on top of a hill overlooking the town (access off the Meymac–Tulle road). If you prefer a **bed**, you can find a perfectly comfortable one, and food, in the rustic setting of the *Hôtel des Touristes* back on the St-Léonard road in the tiny village of **BUJALEUF** (☎05.55.69.50.01; ①; restaurant from 75F).

Château de Ventadour

The **Château de Ventadour**, like Chalusset, is a magnificent ruin, and all the more romantic for having no fence, no caretaker and no admission charge. It stands on the very tip of a high narrow spur way above the river valleys converging at its feet, with a lone tower rising above the trees and undergrowth, which someone has begun to clear. Built in the twelfth century, the château was abandoned in around 1600 by its owners, the dukes of Ventadour, in favour of a more comfortable house in Ussel. The celebrated troubadour Bernard de Ventadour was born here, child of a castle servant.

The castle is about 6km from Egletons on the Tulle–Ussel road. You take the dead-end turning to the farming hamlet of Moustier. But far the most dramatic approach is from below, up the winding road from **NEUVIC** – itself an ancient village, rather spoilt by the presence of an artificial lake which has elevated it to resort status. It does, however, have an interesting **Musée de la Résistance**, based on the life of Henri-Queuille, a former government minister and *résistant* (daily May to Oct 10am–noon & 3–6pm; 25F).

There are **hotels** in Egletons, but it is much nicer to stay in Clergoux or Gimel-les-Cascades (see p.634).

Brive-la-Gaillarde and around

BRIVE-LA-GAILLARDE is a major rail junction and the nearest thing to an industrial centre for miles around, but it makes an agreeable base for exploring the Corrèze *département* and its beautiful villages, as well as the upper reaches of the Vézère and Dordogne rivers.

Though it has no commanding sights, Brive-la-Gaillarde does have a few distractions. Right in the middle of town is the much-restored **church of St-Martin**, originally Romanesque in style, though now only the transept, apse and a few comically carved capitals survive from that era. Saint Martin himself, a Spanish aristocrat, arrived in pagan Brive in 407 AD on the feast of Saturnus, smashed various idols, and was promptly stoned to death by the outraged onlookers.

Numerous streets fan out from the surrounding square, **place du Général-de-Gaulle**, with a number of turreted and towered houses, some dating back to the thirteenth century. The most impressive is the sixteenth-century **Hôtel de Labenche** on boulevard Jules-Ferry, now housing the town's archeological finds as well as a collection of seventeenth-century tapestries (daily except Tues 10am–6/6.30pm; 27F). There is also the **Centre National d'Etude Edmond Michelet** at 4 rue Champanatier (Mon—Sat 10am—noon & 2—6pm; free), based in the former house of this minster of de Gaulle, and one of the town's leading *résistants*, with exhibitions portraying the occupation and resistance through photographs, posters and objects of the time.

From the **gare SNCF**, it's a ten-minute walk south along avenue Jean-Jaurès to the old town, south of which is the attractive square Auboiroux, with the **post office** and **gare routière** nearby. The **tourist office** is north of the ring road on place 14-juillet (July & Aug Mon–Sat 9am–7pm, Sun 10am–1pm; rest of year Mon–Sat 9am–noon & 2–6pm; ☎05.55.24.08.80, fax 05.55.24.58.24), alongside a modern timber-framed market.

There are numerous cheap **hotels** on avenue Jean-Jaurès towards the station, like the *Majestic et Voyageurs* (☎05.55.24.10.20; ①), the *Progress* (☎05.55.24.04.22; ①), or the *Hôtel de France* (☎05.55.74.08.13; ①). Alternatively, try the *Plaisance*, at 62 rue Emile Zola (☎05.55.24.04.06, fax 05.55.24.32.62; ②; menu from 55F). In addition, there's a clean modern HI **youth hostel** on the other side of town from the train station at 56 av Maréchal-Bugeaud (☎05.55.24.34.00, fax 05.55.74.82.80), 25 minutes by foot from the gare SNCF, with a **campsite**, *Les Îles*, just across the river.

For alternative places to **eat**, try the *Endroit Câfé* pizzeria, opposite the tourist office, *Le Boulevard* at 8 bd Jules-Ferry or, close to St-Martin in the centre, *Les Viviers St-Martin*, 4 rue Traversiens, with a 65F menu at lunchtime. There is also the *Corrèze* at 3 rue de Corrèze, off the main rue Toulzac, with a shop front that belongs to a bygone age and a menu at 40F.

Uzerche and Arnac-Pompadour

A half-hour train ride north of Brive along the course of the bubbling River Vézère, the town of **UZERCHE** is impressively located above a loop in the river's course. It's worth a passing visit as the town has several fine old buildings. From the **gare SNCF**, the old town is a five-minute walk south along the main road which tears through the town. The **tourist office** (☎05.55.73.15.71) – behind the main church – provides information on landmarks, but the place is so small you can easily find your own way around. For a grand view of Uzerche, and well worth the extra detour, turn left onto rue du Champ-de-Foire as you come down from the station; pass the church and keep on to rue Ste-Eulalie, turning right at the end to cross the river on rue du Pont. If you need a place to **stay**, the *Hôtel Ambroise* by the river (☎05.55.73.28.60, fax 05.55.98.45.73; ②; restaurant from 75F) is about all there is.

Roughly 20km west of Uzerche (40min by train, on a different line, from Brive), is **ARNAC-POMPADOUR**, a town dominated by its grey, turreted **château**, presented in 1745 by Louis XV to his mistress, Madame de Pompadour, though she never actually visited it. Set in the green countryside of southern Limousin – reminiscent of parts of Ireland – the château is home to one of France's best-known **stud farms** (*haras*), first created by Louis XV in 1761, although today only the terraces can be visited. For horse-lovers it's a must, and it's interesting even for the non-fanatic. Its forte is the Anglo-Arab breed, descendants of horses brought back from the Crusades; the stallions are kept at the Puy-Marmont stables west of the château (free guided tours every 40min mid-July to late Feb; closed Sat), the mares 4km away at La Jumenterie de la Rivière (afternoons only). From May to October there are frequent race meetings and open days. In spring the fields are full of mares and foals, the best being kept for breeding, the rest sold worldwide as two-year-olds.

The **gare SNCF** is southeast of the town, close to the racecourse and opposite the château. There's even a reasonable place to **stay**, and **eat**: the *Hôtel-Restaurant de l'Hippodrome* (☎05.55.73.35.03, fax 05.55.73.98.94; ②; restaurant from 90F, closed Oct–March).

Turenne

TURENNE, just 16km south of Brive, is the first of two very picturesque villages close to the town. Capital of the viscountcy of Turenne, whose most illustrious *seigneur* was Henri de la Tour d'Auvergne – the "Grand Turenne", whom Napoléon rated the finest tactician of modern times – the village today would still seem familiar to him. The same mellow stone houses still crowd in the lee of the sharp bluff whose summit sprouts the towers of their castle, one forming part of someone's house. The other, known as **La Tour de César**, can be visited (June–Sept daily 9–11.45am & 2–6.45pm; April, May & Oct 10—11.45am & 2—5.45pm; Nov–March Sun 2–5pm; 16F), and is worth climbing for the views away over the ridges and valleys to the mountains of Cantal.

Collonges-la-Rouge

COLLONGES-LA-ROUGE, 7km east of Turenne, is the epitome of rustic charm with its red-sandstone houses, pepper-pot towers and pink-candled chestnut trees, although you need to time your visit carefully, as the village is now very much on the tourist bus circuit. Though small-scale, there is a grandeur about the place, as if the resident Turenne administrators were aping, within their means, the grandiloquence of their superiors. On the main square a twelfth-century **church** testifies to the imbecility of shedding blood over religious differences: here, side by side, Protestant and Catholic conducted their services simultaneously. Outside, the covered **market hall** still retains its old-fashioned baker's oven.

If you want to **stay** somewhere nearby, it's best to head downhill a few minutes to **MEYSSAC**, a town built in the same red sandstone, though less grandly, for the cheaper

accommodation at the very pleasant *Relais du Quercy* (☎05.55.25.40.31, fax 05.55.25.36.22; ③), or the **campsite**, *Moulin de Valane* (☎05.55.25.41.59; April–Oct).

Getting to Collonges without your own wheels is difficult (bus July & Aug Tues only) but worth the effort. The prettiest route on foot from Turenne is along the back lanes through meadow and walnut orchards via **SAILLAC** (3hr), whose Romanesque **church** sports an elaborately carved tympanum upheld by a column of spiralling animal motifs.

Tulle

Seen from the distance, **TULLE**, 29km east of Brive, is a strange and unattractive-looking place. Strung out along the bottom of the narrow and deep valley of the Corrèze, it looks grey, run-down and industrial. But once you get down to the riverside and the area around the cathedral, it reveals itself to be full of fascinating winding lanes and stairways bordered by very handsome houses – many as old as the fourteenth century – with an imposing **hôtel de ville** at the end of rue du Trech, the main commercial street. If not worth a prolonged stay, Tulle certainly makes an interesting stopover.

The **Cathédrale Notre-Dame**, whose construction was drawn out from Romanesque to Gothic periods, stands on the riverside quays in place Émile-Zola. The cloister beside it has a small **museum** (daily except Wed & Sat 10am–noon & 2–5/6pm, Wed & Sat 2–5/6pm only; free), containing a mishmash of exhibits ranging from archeology to accordions, along with a large contingent of firearms, which once formed one of the town's major industries, along with lace. Next door is a collection of documents to do with the Resistance at the **Musée Départemental de la Résistance et de la Déportation**, 2 quai Edmond-Perrier (Mon–Fri 9am–noon & 2–6pm; free), particularly the terrible reprisals wreaked by the Germans when they recaptured the town from the Resistance on June 8, 1944 and hanged 99 people.

The **tourist office** is opposite the cathedral at 2 place Émile-Zola (July to mid-Sept Mon–Sat 9.30am–12.30pm & 2–7pm, Sun 10am–noon; rest of year Mon 2–6pm, Tues–Sat 9.30am–noon & 2–6pm; ☎05.55.26.59.61, fax 05.55.20.72.93), and you'll find the **bus and train stations** side by side on the southwest edge of the town on av Winston-Churchill. The **market** takes place every Wednesday and Saturday by the cathedral.

By far the most attractive place to **stay** is also the simplest: the *Hôtel au Bon Accueil*, 10 rue du Canton (☎05.55.26.70.57; ②; closed one week at Christmas; restaurant from 78F), in an old beamed house with stone mullion windows, across the river from the cathedral. Other places to stay include *Le Dunant* by the Pont Dunant bridge some way downstream from the centre (☎05.55.20.15.42, fax 05.55.26.70.50; ③; restaurant from 50F), and the *Toque Blanche* at 29 rue Jean-Jaurès (☎05.55.26.75.41, fax 05.55.20.93.95; ②), overlooking the car park by the very unattractive municipal offices, but only five minutes from the cathedral. The rooms at the *Toque Blanche* are acceptable but nothing special, whereas the **restaurant** is renowned, with an affordable weekday menu at 100F – otherwise, 148F and upwards. There is a **camping municipal** by the river on the Ussel side of town (☎05.55.26.75.97, fax 05.55.21.73.22; May–Sept).

Gimel and Clergoux

If you're travelling by car, you might consider staying in one of the villages in the hilly wooded country northeast of Tulle. **GIMEL-LES-CASCADES**, in particular, is very beautiful and, out of season at least, very quiet. It is a minute hamlet, about 10km away and clinging to the edge of a steep valley beside a spectacular waterfall, the **Montane**, which has sadly been turned into a paying "sight" (25F). There is also a superb twelfth-century reliquary, known as the *Chasse de St-Étienne*, in the treasury of the local **church**.

The attractive American-owned **hotel**, *Hostellerie de la Vallée* (☎05.55.21.40.60; ③; closed Jan) has a good restaurant from 95F. Two further possibilities for accommodation are the delightfully friendly and unpretentious *Hôtel Maurianges*, near the defunct Monteil train station, fifteen minutes up the road from Gimel, and serving delicious and copious home-cooked meals for 70F (☎05.55.21.28.88; ②; restaurant closed Sat & Sun eve out of season); and in **CLERGOUX**, another 15km east, the lovely creeper-covered *Hôtel Chammard* (☎05.55.27.76.04; ①; closed Nov–March; no restaurant). There is also a **campsite** by the beautiful lakelet, the Étang de Ruffaud (☎05.55.26.42.12), near Gimel, where you can swim and get a reasonable meal in the lakeside bar.

THE LOT

The core of this section is formed by the old provinces of Haut Quercy and Quercy: the land between the Dordogne and the Lot and between the Lot and the Garonne, Aveyron and Tarn. We have extended it slightly eastwards to include the gorges of the River **Aveyron** and Villefranche-de-Rouergue on the edge of the province of Rouergue.

It is hotter, drier, less well-known and, with few exceptions, less crowded here than the Dordogne, which does not mean that the area is less interesting. The cave paintings at **Pech-Merle** are quite the equal of those at Les Eyzies. **Najac, Penne** and **Peyrerusse** have ruined castles to rival those of the Dordogne. Towns like **Figeac** and **Villefranche-de-Rouergue** are without equal, as are villages like **Cardaillac** and **St-Antonin-Noble-Val**, and stretches of country like that below **Gourdon**, around **Les Arques** where Osip Zadkine had his studio, and the **Célé Valley**.

Again, without transport, many places are out of reach. Some consolation, however, is the existence of the Brive–Toulouse train line that makes Figeac, Villefranche-de-Rouergue and Najac accessible, while **Agen, Moissac** and **Montauban** are on the Bordeaux–Toulouse line.

Rocamadour and around

Tucked under a cliff in the deep and abrupt canyon of the Alzou stream, the spectacular setting of **ROCAMADOUR** is hard to beat; the village itself must have been beautiful once, too, but for centuries now it has been inundated by religious pilgrims (and latterly more secular-minded coach tours), whose constant stream has turned the place into something of a nightmare, with every house displaying mountains of unbelievable junk. The reason for its popularity since medieval times is the supposed miraculous ability of the cathedral's Black Madonna. Nowadays, pilgrims are outnumbered by tourists, who come here to wonder at the sheer audacity of its location, built almost vertically into its rocky backdrop.

Legend has it that the history of Rocamadour began with the arrival of Zacchaeus, husband of Ste-Veronica, who fled to France to escape religious persecution and lived out his last years here as a hermit. When in 1166 a perfectly preserved body was found in a grave high up on the rock, it was declared to be Zacchaeus, who thereafter became known as St-Amadour. Rocamadour soon became a major pilgrimage site and a staging post on the road to St-Jacques de Compostelle in Spain. St-Bernard, numerous kings of England and France and thousands of others crawled up the chapel steps on their knees to pay their respects and seek cures for their illnesses. Henry Short-Coat (see p.622) was the first to plunder the shrine, but he was easily outclassed by the Huguenots, who tried in vain to burn the saint's corpse and finally resigned themselves simply to hacking it to bits. What you see today, therefore, is not the real thing but a nineteenth-century reconstruction, carried out in the hope of reviving the flagging pilgrimage.

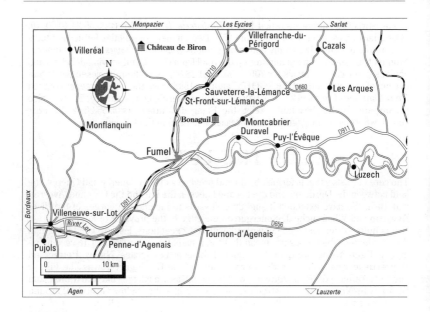

The town

Rocamadour is easy enough to find your way around. There's just one street, rue de la Couronnerie, strung out between two medieval gateways. Above it, the steep hillside supports no fewer than seven churches. The indolent take the lift dug into the rock-face (30F up & back), while the devout drag themselves on their knees up the 223 steps of the *Via Sancta* to the smoke-blackened and votive-packed **Chapelle Notre-Dame** where the miracle-working twelfth-century Black Madonna resides. The tiny, macabre statue of walnut wood is appropriately lit in the mysterious half-light of her protective black cage, but the rest of the chapel is unremarkable. High up in the rock above the entrance to the chapel is a sword, supposedly Roland's legendary blade, Durandal.

There's no relief for the non-religious in the **Musée Francis Poulenc** (daily: 10am–noon & 2–6pm; July & Aug 10am–7pm; 10F), which contains sacred art treasures, reliquaries and various historical documents. It's dedicated to the French composer Francis Poulenc (1899–1963) because he was one of the modern pilgrims who received miraculous inspiration from the shrine, though in his case the results were musical rather than medical.

You can climb still further to the ancient **ramparts** above the chapel, or take the winding shady path, *La Calvarie*, past the stations of the Cross: either way the views across the valley are stunning.

There are four different wildlife centres in Rocamadour: an **aquarium** (Easter–Nov 15 daily 10am–7pm; rest of year Sundays & school holidays 2–6pm; 22F); the **Rocher des Aigles** (April–Oct daily 10am–noon & 2–6pm; 35F), a breeding centre for birds of prey (falconry demonstrations 11am & hourly 3–5pm); the **Forêt des Singes**, off the D673, where 150 Barbary apes roam the relative freedom of a reserve in the plateau behind L'Hospitalet (daily April–June & Sept 10am–noon & 1–6pm; July & Aug 10am–7pm; Oct 10am–noon & 1–5pm; Nov 1–11 Wed, Sat & Sun 10am–noon & 1–5pm; 35F); and the Maison des Abeilles (July & Aug daily 10am–7pm; April–June &

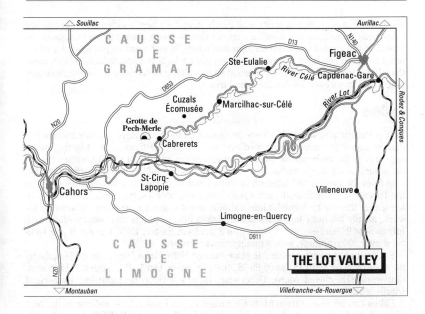

Sept–Nov Wed, Sun & daily in school hols 11am–5pm; 28F) where you can learn about apiculture.

Practicalities

Getting to Rocamadour without your own transport is awkward, unless you're prepared to walk or take a taxi the 3km from the Rocamadour-Padirac **gare SNCF** on the Brive–Capdenac line. If you arrive **by car**, you'll have to park in L'Hospitalet, 1.5km from Rocamadour (and with the best view of the town there is), where the **tourist office** (daily: April–June & Sept 10am–12.30pm & 2–6pm; July & Aug 9.30am–7pm;Oct–March 10am–noon & 2–6pm; ☎05.65.33.74.13, fax 05.65.33.74.14) or else in the car park, several hundred metres below the town. If you're carrying luggage, you can leave it at the seasonal tourist office in the Hôtel de Ville (April—Sept hours as above; ☎05.65.33.62.59), on the main street, rather than lug it up the chapel steps.

Rocamadour's **hotels** are not too expensive but they're completely booked out in the summer. If you ring ahead, you might get in at the *Lion d'Or*, Porte Figuier (☎05.65.33.62.04, fax 05.65.33.72.54; ③; restaurant from 59F), or the *Terminus*, on place de la Carretta (☎05.65.33.62.14, fax 05.65.33.72.10; ③; restaurant from 68F), both closed from November to Easter. There are also several **campsites** in L'Hospitalet, the nearest one being *Le Relais du Campeur* (☎05.65.33.63.28).

Gouffre de Padirac

The **Gouffre de Padirac** (daily guided tours April–June & Sept to mid-Oct 9am–noon & 2–6pm; July & Aug 8/8.30am–6.30/7pm; 43F) is about 20km east of Rocamadour on the other side of the main Brive–Figeac road. It is an enormous limestone sinkhole, about 100m deep and over 100m wide. There are some spectacular formations of stalactites and waterfalls created by the accumulation of lime, and beautiful underground lakes, but it is very, very touristy – so much so that it's best avoided at weekends and other peak periods, or you'll wait an age for tickets. Visits are partly on foot, partly by boat, and the guided tours last an hour and a half. In wet weather you'll need a waterproof jacket. If you have no car, the nearest **gare SNCF** is Rocamadour-Padirac, more than 10km to the west; the only alternative to walking or hitching is the summer-only bus, which costs over 50F for the round trip.

St-Céré

East of Padirac and about 9km from Bretenoux on the River Bave, a minor tributary of the Dordogne, you come to the medieval town of **ST-CÉRÉ**, dominated by the brooding ruins of the **château de St-Laurent-les-Tours** and full of ancient houses crowding around place du Mercadial. The two powerful keeps of St-Laurent, partially rebuilt, date from the twelfth and fifteenth centuries and were part of a fortress belonging to the Turennes. In wartime, the artist Jean Lurçat operated a secret Resistance radio post here; after the war he turned it into a studio, and it's now a marvellous museum of his work, mainly his huge tapestries but also sketches, paintings and pottery (daily mid-July to Sept 9.30am–noon & 2–6pm; also 2 weeks at Easter; 15F). The site is spectacular at over 200m altitude, with stunning views all round.

St-Céré has one very reasonable place to **stay**: *Hôtel Victor Hugo*, 7 av du Maquis, by the river (☎05.65.38.16.15, fax 05.65.38.39.91; ③; closed Oct 1–21 & March 1–15; restaurant from 87F, closed Mon). Otherwise, there's a riverside **camping municipal** (April–Sept).

Bikes can be rented from M. St-Charmant in rue Faidherbe – and one of the best trips you could pedal is to the hugely pretty little village of **AUTOURE**, in a tight side valley, about 10km to the west of St-Céré. Much hillier but glorious country lies to the east along the road to Aurillac via Sousceyrac and Laroquebrou.

Gourdon and around

GOURDON lies between Sarlat and Cahors, conveniently served by the Brive–Toulouse train line, and makes a quiet, pleasant base for visiting some of the major places in this part of the Dordogne and Lot. It's 17km south of the River Dordogne and pretty much at the eastern limit of the luxuriant woods and valleys of Périgord, which give way quite suddenly, at the line of the N20, to the arid limestone landscape of the **Causse de Gramat**. It is a beautiful town, its medieval centre of yellow-stone houses attached like a swarm of bees to a prominent hilltop, neatly ringed by modern boulevards containing all the shops.

In the Middle Ages, Gourdon was an important place, deriving wealth and influence from the presence of four monasteries. It was besieged and captured in 1189 by Richard the Lionheart, who promptly murdered its feudal lords. Legend has it that the archer who fired the fatal shot at him during the siege of Chalus was the last surviving member of this family. But more than anything it was the devastation of the Wars of Religion that dispatched Gourdon into centuries of oblivion.

From whichever direction you approach, all roads lead to place de la Libération in front of the fortified **gateway** over rue du Majou, the narrow main street of the old town. It is lined all the way up with splendid stone houses, some, like the **Maison d'Anglars** at no. 17, as old as thirteenth-century. At its uphill end, rue du Majou debouches into a lovely square in front of the massive but not particularly interesting fourteenth-century **church of St-Pierre**. **Market days** are Tuesday and Saturday in the *place*. There is a handsome **Hôtel de Ville** on one side and, in place des Marronniers behind the church, the family home of the Cavaignacs, who supplied the nation with numerous prominent public figures in the eighteenth and nineteenth centuries, including the notoriously brutal general who put down the Paris workers' attempts to defend the Second Republic in June 1848. From the square, steps climb to the top of the hill, where the castle once stood and where there is a superb view over the Dordogne valley and surroundings.

A couple of kilometres along the Sarlat road in the direction of Cougnac from Gourdon, there is a very interesting **cave**, the **Grottes de Cougnac**, discovered in 1949 (daily: April–June, Sept & Oct 10am–noon & 1–5/6pm; July & Aug 10am–7pm; 32F). It has beautiful rock formations as well as some fine prehistoric paintings rather similar to those at Pech-Merle (see p.647).

Practicalities

The **tourist office** is on the left at the beginning of rue du Majou (July & Aug daily 10am–7pm; June & Sept Mon–Sat 9.30am–noon & 2–6pm, Sun 10am–noon; rest of year Mon–Sat 10am–noon & 2–4pm; ☎05.65.27.52.50, fax 05.65.27.52.52), and has extensive lists of B&B options in the area. They also organize **day-trips** by bus to Rocamadour, Sarlat and other local sights (80–120F). **Bikes** can be rented from the **gare SNCF** or Gourdon Forme on rte de Salviac.

If you want to **stay** in the town itself, the *Hôtel Bissonnier*, 51 bd des Martyrs, on the eastern side of the ring road near the **post office** (☎05.65.41.02.48, fax 05.65.41.44.67; ③; closed Dec–Jan 15), is very agreeable and has a restaurant with such local specialities as *confits* and stuffed duck's neck (menu from 80F). Not so pleasant, but a little cheaper, is the *Terminus* in avenue de la Gare (☎05.65.41.03.29, fax 05.65.41.29.49; ③; restaurant from 70F), by the train station. There is an *Aire Naturelle* **campsite** (☎05.65.41.65.01).

For a pleasant independent **restaurant**, with a tiny outside terrace, try the *Croque-Note* on the corner of rue Jean-Jaurès and boulevard Gabanès on the south side of the old town (80–130F).

Les Arques

Twenty-five kilometres southwest of Gourdon on the Fumel road, you come to a pretty but not remarkable *bastide* called **CAZALS**; a left turn here takes you along the bottom of the valley of the Masse and up its left flank to the exquisite hamlet of **LES ARQUES**. This is quiet, remote, small-scale farming country, emptied of people by the slaughter of rustic sons in World War I and by migration to the towns in search of jobs and money.

Les Arques's main claim to fame is the Russian Cubist/Expressionist sculptor Ossip Zadkine, who bought the old house by the church here in 1934. Some of his sculptures adorn the space outside the church as well as its lovely interior, and his studio, which now belongs to the City of Paris, houses a **museum** with a number of his other works (June 15–Sept 15 daily 11am–7pm; rest of year Wed, Sun & daily in school hols 2–5pm; 15F). It is particularly interesting if you know the delightful secret garden of his house and studio in Paris.

The other reason to come here is the now superannuated village school, transformed into a most unusual **restaurant**, *La Récréation* (☎05.65.22.88.08), where you get a copious and delicious meal to eat beneath the wisterias and chestnut trees of the school yard for about 90–130F. On a summer night with the swifts screaming overhead, it is idyllic.

On the other side of the valley and well sign-posted, the tiny Romanesque **chapel of St-André-des-Arques** reputedly has some very lovely fifteenth-century frescoes discovered by Zadkine, but it is not easy to get the key from the house next door.

Cahors

CAHORS, on the River Lot, was the capital of the old province of Quercy. In its time, it has been a Gallic settlement; a Roman town; a briefly held Moorish possession; a town under English rule; a bastion of Catholicism in the Wars of Religion, sacked in consequence by Henri IV; a university town for four hundred years; and birthplace of

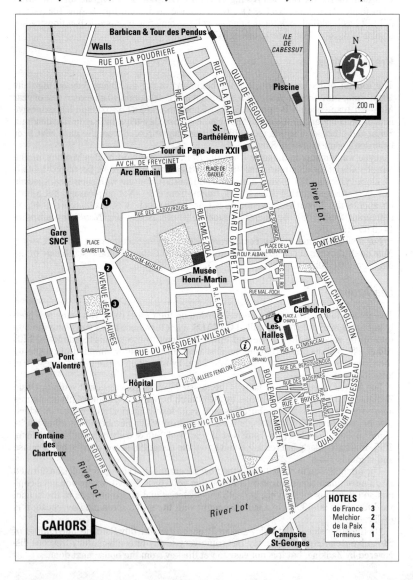

HOTELS	
de France	3
Melchior	2
de la Paix	4
Terminus	1

Gambetta, after whom so many French streets and squares are named. Modern Cahors is a sunny southern backwater, with two interesting sights in its **cathedral** and the remarkable fourteenth-century **Pont Valentré**.

While you're in the Cahors area, don't miss out on the local **wine**, heady and black but dry to the taste and not at all plummy like the Gironde wines from Blaye and Bourg, which use the same Malbec grape.

The town

Small and easily walkable, the town squats on a peninsula formed by a tight loop in the River Lot, and is protected on the northern side by a rank of fourteenth-century **fortifications**, with the **Barbacane de St-Jean** making a breach in the walls.

Right in the middle of the town is the **cathedral**. Consecrated in 1119, it is the oldest and simplest in plan of the Périgord-style churches. The exterior is not exciting: a heavy square tower dominates the plain west front, whose best feature is the elaborately decorated portal in the street on the north side, where a Christ in Majesty dominates the tympanum, surrounded by angels and apostles, while cherubim fly out of the clouds to relieve him of his halo. Side panels show scenes from the life of St Stephen. The outer ring of figures over the portal shows a line of naked figures being stabbed in the behind and hacked with axes.

Inside, the cathedral is much like St-Front at Périgueux, with a nave lacking aisles and transepts, roofed with two big domes; in the first are fourteenth-century frescoes of the stoning of St Stephen. The Gothic choir and apse are extensively but crudely painted. To their right a door opens into a delicate cloister in the Flamboyant style, still retaining some intricate, though damaged, carving. On the northwest corner pillar a graceful girl with broad brow and ringlets to her waist serves as a model for the Virgin. In the northeast corner, an arch opens onto a courtyard by the fine Renaissance **archdeacon's house**.

In the area between the cathedral and the river, there's a warren of narrow lanes and alleys, most of them handsomely restored during the last ten years. Many of the houses, turreted and built of flat, thin, southern brick, date from the fourteenth and fifteenth centuries. Rue Nationale, rue Bergougnoux and rue Lastié are particularly interesting, along with rue des Soubirons, rue St-Barthélémy and rue du Château-du-Roi to the north. Take a look at the impressive **Hôtel d'Issale** in rue Bergougnoux and the **Maison Roaldès** in place Henri-IV; also go out of your way to see the **Hôpital Grossia** in rue des Soubirous and the **Palais Duèze**, opposite the church of St-Barthélémy, built for the brothers of Pope John XXII in the fourteenth century.

Immediately south of the cathedral, the lime-bordered **place Jean-Jacques-Chapou** commemorates a local trade unionist and Resistance leader, killed in a German ambush on July 17, 1944. Next to it is the covered **market** and a shop still bearing the name Gambetta, which belonged to the family of the famous deputy of Belleville in Paris.

The reason most people venture to Cahors is the dramatic **Pont Valentré** (July & Aug daily 12.30pm & 2.30–6.30pm; 15F). Its three powerful towers, originally closed by portcullises and gates, made it effectively an independent fortress, guarding the river crossing on the west side of town. One of the finest surviving bridges of its time, it is, rightly, one of the most photographed monuments in France. Just upstream from the bridge is a resurgent river known as the **Fontaine des Chartreux**, flowing from the valleyside. The Roman town was named Divona Carducorum after it, and it still supplies Cahors with drinking water.

Practicalities

The **gare SNCF** and **gare routière** are at the end of avenue Jean-Jaurès off rue du Président-Wilson. For further information on the area, make for the **tourist office** on the corner of bd Gambetta and allée Fénelon close to the cathedral (July & Aug Mon–Sat 9am–6/6.30pm, Sun 10am–noon; rest of year Mon–Sat 9am–12.30pm & 1.30–6/6.30pm; ☎05.65.53.20.65, fax 05.65.53.20.74). **Bicycle rental** is possible either from Ets Combes, 117 bd Gambetta, or the gare SNCF.

A different and leisurely way to enjoy the spectacular views of the Lot valley between Cahors and Cajarc is to take the Quercyrail tourist train, which runs vintage diesel locomotives along this otherwise redundant line. Various round trips are available, including a boat trip at Cajarc, a walk along the towpath hewn into the rock at St-Cirq Lapopie, or a visit to the château of Cénevières. Prices range from 110–160F return, with departures from Cahors station or Capdenac. Reservation is advisable (☎05.63.40.11.93).

The central and characterful place to **stay** is the budget-priced *Hôtel de la Paix*, place de la Halle, opposite the covered market by the cathedral (☎05.65.35.03.40, fax 05.65.35.40.88; ①; closed Dec 15–Jan 15; restaurant from 65F, closed Sun). There are three good options in the area round the station: *Hôtel de France*, 252 av Jean-Jaurès (☎05.65.35.16.76, fax 05.65.22.01.08; ③; closed Christmas–New Year), *Hôtel Melchior*, opposite the station (☎05.65.35.03.38, fax 05.65.23.92.75; ②;③; closed Jan 15–31; restaurant from 68F; closed Sun); and the lovely old-time creeper-covered *Terminus*, 5 av Charles de Freycinet (☎05.65.35.24.50, fax 05.65.22.06.40; ⑤), just around the corner from the station and boasting the famous *Le Balandre* restaurant (closed Mon & Sun eves out of season; menu at 150F). There's an expensive **campsite** (☎05.65.30.06.30, fax 05.65.23.99.46) by the Pont Cabessut to supplement the grotty *camping municipal* (☎05.65.35.04.64) by Pont Louis-Philippe. In addition to the hotel-restaurants, there are several **brasseries** along bd Gambetta.

Villeneuve and around

VILLENEUVE-SUR-LOT, 75km west and downstream from Cahors, does not have a great deal to commend it: there are no very interesting sights, though the handful of attractive timbered houses in the old town go some way to compensate. If you're reliant on public transport note that there's no train station, and bus links are poor.

The town's most striking landmark is the red-brick tower of the church of **Ste-Catherine**, completed as late as 1937 in typically garish neo-Byzantine style, but rather unusually built on a north–south axis; inside, the church retains some attractive stained glass from the previous fourteenth-century building. In the streets around the main square, **place La Fayette**, a couple of towers alone survive from the fortifications of this originally *bastide* town; here is also thirteenth-century **Pont Vieux**, resembling the Pont Valentré in Cahors but devoid of towers.

The **tourist office** is in the theatre on boulevard de la République (July–Aug Mon–Sat 8.30am–7pm; rest of year Mon–Sat 9am–noon & 2–6pm; ☎05.53.36.17.30, fax 05.53.49.42.98). If you're looking for **accommodation** and don't fancy the **camping municipal** on the N21, try the cheap, cheerful and central *Remparts*, 1 rue Marcel (☎05.53.70.71.63, fax 05.53.40.52.25; ①), the *Hôtel Les Platanes*, 40 bd de la Marine (☎05.53.40.11.40, fax 05.53.70.71.95; ②), or La Résidence at 17 av Lazare Carnot (☎05.53.40.17.03, fax 05.53 01.57.34; ②), near the station. For a bit more luxury and a beautiful setting, there's the *Hôtel Les Chênes*, 3km to the south at Bel-Air, Pujols (☎05.53.49.04.55, fax 05.53.49.22.74; ③), with the very good and expensive **restaurant** *La Toque Blanche* nearby (☎05.53.49.00.30; closed June 26–July 7; from 145F). For something much simpler, *Chez Câline* in rue Notre-Dame offers menus from 75F.

Pujols and Penne d'Agenais

For a pleasant short walk – about half an hour from the Porte de Pujols – you can climb south to the tiny walled village of **PUJOLS** to see the faded Romanesque frescoes in the

church of Ste-Foy. The views over the surrounding country are great, but the village has caught a bad dose of "heritage-itis". The best place to forget it is over dinner on the terrace of *Lou Calel*, part of the same establishment as *La Toque Blanche*; for around 200F including wine you can sample some beautifully cooked traditional but light menus. Another side-trip could be to the beautiful but touristy old fortress town of **PENNE D'AGENAIS**, 8km upstream on a steep hill also on the south bank of the Lot, with remains of a thirteenth-century castle teetering on a cliff-edge; take the **bus** to St-Sylvestre on the north bank and walk. There are great views from the top. The **tourist office** in rue du 14-Juillet can supply comprehensive lists of B&Bs and gîtes in the area round about (daily 10am–noon & 2–5pm, ☎05.53.41.37.80, fax 05.53.49.38.37). There's a **campsite** by the river and a **gîte d'étape** near the **gare SNCF** on the Agen–Paris line.

The château de Bonaguil, Puy L'Évêque and Luzech

From Villeneuve as far as Fumel, the Lot valley is ugly and industrial, but upstream from here the vine-cloaked banks are dotted with small and ancient villages. An SNCF bus threads through them, and because there are six daily it's possible to get off, look around and pick up the next bus – not that any of the villages is worth more than a brief stay.

The first place worth heading for east of Fumel, the **Château de Bonaguil** (daily visits hourly June–Aug 10am–5.45pm; Feb–May & Sept–Nov at 10.30am, 2.30pm, 3.30pm & 4.30pm; 25F), is more difficult to get to. It's spectacularly perched at the end of a wooden spur commanding two valleys, about 8km northeast of Fumel. Built during the fifteenth and sixteenth centuries with a double ring of walls, five huge towers and a narrow boat-shaped keep designed to resist artillery, it was the last of the medieval castles to be constructed.

Back on the Lot, **PUY-L'ÉVÊQUE**, 15km east of Fumel, is probably the prettiest village in the entire valley, with many grand houses built in honey-coloured stone and overlooked by both a **church** and the **castle** of the bishops of Cahors. For the best view, stand on the suspension bridge which crosses the Lot. If you want to **stay** over, the *Hôtel Henry* has cheap and decent rooms (☎05.65.21.32.24, fax 05.65.30.85.18; ②), and there's a **campsite,** *Camping de la Plage* (May–Sept; ☎05.65.30.81.72, fax 05.65.30.85.89) by the river.

Several bends in the river later – 15km by road – you come to **LUZECH**, with scant Gaulish and Roman remains of the town of L'Impernal, and the **Chapelle de Notre-Dame-de-l'Île**, dedicated to the medieval boatmen who transported Cahors wines to Bordeaux. It stands in a huge river loop, overlooked by a thirteenth-century **keep**, with some picturesque alleys and dwellings in the quarter opposite place du Canal.

St-Cirq-Lapopie

If you have your own transport you could easily make a side-trip to the cliff-edge village of **ST-CIRQ-LAPOPIE**, perched high above the south bank of the Lot. The village was saved from ruin when poet André Breton came to live here earlier this century, and is now an irresistible draw for the tour buses with its cobbled lanes, half-timbered houses and gardens; but it's still worth the trouble, especially if you visit early or late in the day. **Public transport** in the form of an SNCF bus will get you from Cahors to Gare-St-Cirq in the valley bottom; thereafter, there's no alternative but to leg it up the steep hill. For **accommodation**, there is the very pretty *Auberge du Sombral* (☎05.65.31.26.08, fax 05.65.30.26.37; ③; closed Nov 11–March), whose excellent restaurant (closed Tues & Wed out of season) has a menu at 100F, and a **campsite**, *Camping de la Plage* (all year, ☎05.65.30.29.51, fax 05.65.30.26.48), down by the river – a slightly regimented site, but with access to the river and its swimming and canoeing possibilities. There's another campsite at **LA TRUFFIÈRE** (☎05.65.30.20.22; May–Sept), 3km to the southeast and over the rim of the valley; about 20km upstream, there is a **gîte** at **CAJARC** (Mme Mignot; ☎05.65.40.65.20). There is also a friendly and comfortable English-run chambres d'hôte at the hilltop village of Calvignac, 12km upstream (☎05.65.30.25.76).

Figeac and around

FIGEAC lies on the River Célé, 71km east of Cahors and some 8km north of the Lot. It's a beautiful little town with an unspoilt medieval centre, not too encumbered by tourism. Like many other provincial towns hereabouts, it owes its beginnings to the foundation of an abbey in the early days of Christianity in France, one which quickly became wealthy because of its position on the pilgrim routes to both Rocamadour and Compostella. In the Middle Ages it became a centre of tanning, which partly accounts for the many houses whose top floors have *soleilhos*, or open-sided wooden galleries used for drying skins. Again, as so often, it was the Wars of Religion that pushed it into eclipse, for Figeac threw in its lot with the nearby Protestant stronghold of Montauban and suffered the same punishing reprisals by the victorious royalists in 1662.

Both roads and train line funnel you automatically into the town centre, where the **Hôtel de la Monnaie** surveys place Vival (daily April–Oct 12 10am–12.30pm & 2.30–6pm; Nov–March 11am–noon & 2.30–5.30pm; 10F). It is a splendid building whose origins go back to the thirteenth century, when it served as a kind of depot for coins stamped out in the city's mint. The building now houses the tourist office, as well as a none-too-exciting museum of old coins and archeological bits and pieces found in the surrounding area. In the streets radiating off to the north of the square – Caviale, République, Gambetta and their cross-streets – there is a delightful range of houses of the medieval and classical periods, both stone and half-timbered with brick noggings, adorned with carvings and colonnettes, ogees, and interesting bits of ironwork. At the end of these streets are the two small squares of **place Carnot** and **place Champollion**, both of great charm. The former is the site of the old *halles*, under whose awning a restaurant now spreads its tables.

Jean-François Champollion, who cracked Egyptian hieroglyphics by deciphering the triple text of the Rosetta Stone, was born in the house at 4 impasse Champollion, off the square, and the building now houses a very interesting **museum** dedicated to his life and work (March–May Tues–Sun 10am–noon & 2.30–6.30pm; July & Aug daily same hours; Nov–Feb Tues–Sun 2–6pm; 20F). At the end of this alley, a larger-than-life reproduction of the Rosetta Stone forms the floor of the tiny **place des Écritures**, beside a little garden planted with tufts of papyrus.

On the other side of place Champollion, rue Boutaric leads up to the cedar-shaded **church of Notre-Dame-du-Puy**, most interesting for its views over the roofs of the town. More interesting is the **church of St-Sauveur** off place des Herbes near the tourist office, with its lovely Gothic chapterhouse decorated with heavily gilded but dramatically realistic seventeenth-century carved wood panels illustrating the life of Christ.

Practicalities

At the heart of the town on place Vival, you'll find the **tourist office** in the Hôtel de la Monnaie (April–Sept Mon–Sat 10am–1pm & 2–7pm, Sun 10am–12.30pm & 2.30–7pm; Oct–March same days 10am–noon & 2.30–6pm, Sun 10am–1pm; ☎05.65.34.06.25, fax 05.65.50.04.58). The **gare SNCF** (☎05.65.34.10.37) and **gare routière** are a few minutes' walk to the south across the river at the end of rue de la Gare and avenue des Poilus.

The nicest place to **stay** in the heart of Figeac is the *Hôtel Champollion* on place Champollion (☎05.65.34.04.37; ③), the only drawback being the absence of a restaurant. For a cheap alternative, there is the *Hôtel du Faubourg*, just to the east of the centre on the Rodez road (☎05.65.34.21.82, fax 05.65.34.24.19; ②). And there are two possibilities across the river: the great old *Hôtellerie de l'Europe* at 51 allées Victor-Hugo (☎05.65.34.10.16, fax 05.65.50.04.57; ③; closed mid-Jan to Feb 10), with a 1930s lounge and excellent regional menus at 88F and 195F (restaurant closed Sat & Sun eve out of season); and, opposite the station, the *Terminus St-Jacques*, 27 av Clemenceau (☎05.65.34.00.43, fax 05.65.50.00.94; ③; closed Oct 2–Nov 20), also with a good restaurant from 90F. A further possibility, and an attractive one, is to go on to **CAPDENAC-GARE**, 7km away, and stay at the riverside *Auberge la Diège* (☎05.65.64.70.54, fax 05.65.80.81.58; ③; closed Dec 24–Jan 3, where you can also eat from 58F (restaurant closed Fri out of season). The tourist office can recommend chambres d'hôte, and there's a well-equipped campsite, *les Rives du Célé* (April–Sept; ☎05.65.34.59.00, fax 05.65.34.83.83) by the river on avenue de Cahors, with a restaurant, shop and swimming pool, by the sports ground, where you can also rent **canoes**.

For **eating** somewhere other than a hotel restaurant, the *Puce à l'Oreille*, 5 rue St-Thomas, behind place Carnot, offers some rich Quercy dishes in menus that range from 85F to 240F (Sept–June closed Mon). For a light meal, there's the crêperie *La Chandeleur* (about 50F) in rue Boutaric, off place Champollion.

Cardaillac

Home of one of the great families of Quercy in the Middle Ages, the old part of the village of **CARDAILLAC**, about 10km to the north of Figeac off the N140, is gathered on the tip of a steep ridge above wild wooded valleys, an organic pile of houses, primitive machinery and crumbling fortifications of such antiquity you wonder that they are still there. The village has created what they call a **musée éclaté,** consisting of a tour of several old houses and giving an insight into the lifestyle and practices of yore, like bread-making, drying chestnuts and preparing prunes (July & Aug daily except Sat 3–6pm; otherwise by arrangement on ☎05.65.40.10.63; free). An additional plus point is the minute but delightful **hotel** *Chez Marcel*, on the through-road (☎05.65.40.11.16; ①), with a first-rate **restaurant** (closed Mon) offering such delights as a *gigot* of lamb from the *causse* and the regional offal speciality, *tripoux* (menus from 75F).

Foissac, Peyrerusse-le-Roc and Decazeville

Coming out of Figeac on the road to Villeneuve, you pass one of the so-called **aiguilles**, or stone needles, that used to ring Figeac. They are an incredible 8m high and date from the 1100s; no-one knows whether they were milestones, boundary markers for the abbey, or something completely different.

Some 20km further south, and west of the road to Villeneuve, is the village of **FOISSAC**, which has given its name to a local **cave** (daily: June & Sept 10–11.30am & 2–6pm, Sun 2–6pm; July & Aug 10am–6pm, Sun 2–6pm; 25F); in addition to the weird and wonderful geological formations here, there is an unusual prehistoric **potter's workshop** dating from about 4000 BC.

To the east of Foissac, about 20km by a beautiful lane across the *causse*, you happen upon one of the most remarkable old villages in this corner of France: **PEYRERUSSE-LE-ROC**. The "modern" village sits astride the head of a narrow wooded valley: a tiny patina-ed huddle of long-eaved, half-timbered houses abutting the ancient walls. In the valley below, hidden in the steep woods, lie the remains of a medieval stronghold, abandoned around 1700, that once stood guard over the silver-rich country round about. It is only now beginning to be excavated. A cobbled mule path leads to the gate towers and on into the woods, where the stones of a Gothic church, synagogue and hospital stand roofless beneath an unscalable pinnacle of rock crowned by twin towers. A path crosses the stream and climbs along the overgrown bank to an ancient packhorse bridge and ruined mill. From here you can scramble back up the valley side to a bridge of rock where a vertiginous ladder gives access to the towers. For the moment at least, it remains a moving and atmospheric place.

Somewhat surprising in such a quintessentially rural part of France, **DECAZEVILLE**, some 28km southeast of Figeac, owes its place in the annals of the nation's history to coal-mining and the role its well-organized Communist miners played in the local *maquis* and Resistance. It was the centre of the Rouergue – as this province of France is known – coalfield, and only came into being in the nineteenth century. The last mines ceased working in 1965 after prolonged industrial action by the miners, with the all-too-familiar economic and social consequences. The enormous crater of the last working mine, an opencast one known as **La Découverte,** is unmissable as you leave town on the Aubin road. The one curiosity in Decazeville is the presence in the **church of Notre-Dame** of a dozen early paintings by the Symbolist, Gustave Moreau, although you would need to be a committed devotee to come all this way for that reason alone.

Four kilometres south, neighbouring **AUBIN** has a mining museum, the **Musée de la Mine** (June to mid-Sept daily 10am–noon & 3–6pm; mid-Sept to May Sat & Sun 3–6pm; free), on the main square opposite the tourist office and a rather romantic bronze statue of a miner. Exhibits include an interesting collection of tools, clothing and equipment and documentary evidence about strikes, accidents and local history.

The valley of the Célé

For the last stretch of its course from Figeac to Conducé, where it joins the Lot, the **River Célé** flows through a luxuriant canyon-like valley cut into the limestone uplands of the Causse de Gramat. A twisting minor road follows the river here: a silent, backwater of a place, hot in summer, frequented mainly by canoeists (frequent opportunities to rent craft). The **GR651** follows the same route, sometimes close to the river, sometimes on the edge of the *causse* on the north bank.

Two villages, in particular, are worth a stop. The first is **ESPAGNAC-STE-EULALIE**, about 18km west of Figeac. It's a tiny and beautiful hamlet across an old stone bridge on the south bank of the river, under the limestone outcrops of the *causse*. A gorgeous hatted lantern crowns the belfry of the **church** (daily 10.30am–noon & 1.30–3.30pm), and under a weathered tower next door, an ancient gateway leads to the gîte d'étape (☎05.65.40.05.24). There are two **campsites** in **BRENGUES**, the next hamlet, as well as the *Hôtel de la Vallée* (☎05.65.40.02.50; ③; restaurant from 60F).

But the next place of real interest is **MARCILHAC**, 4km downstream, whose semi-ruinous **abbey**, with its gaping walls and broken columns, conjures a strongly romantic atmosphere. Very early and rather primitive ninth-century Carolingian sculpture decorates the lintel, and there are some handsome Romanesque capitals in the chapterhouse. In the damp interior are frescoes from around 1500 and old coats of arms of the local nobility, for Marcilhac was once mightily powerful, having even Rocamadour under its sway. During World War II, it was the scene of the one of the *maquis*'s first theatrical gestures of turning the tables on the occupier: on November 11, 1943 – Armistice Day – Jean-Jacques Chapou's group (see p.641) briefly occupied the village and laid a wreath at the war memorial.

There's a **gîte d'étape** in the abbey, as well as a **camping municipal** just outside the village and the small and attractive *Hôtel des Touristes* on the main street (☎05.65.40.65.61; ①; restaurant from 70F). You can also swim from the small village beach.

Musée de Plein Air du Quercy

Set back from the north side of the River Célé, about 13km from Marcilhac in Cuzals, the **Musée de Plein Air du Quercy** (daily except Sat: April–May & Sept –Oct 2–6pm; June–Aug 10am–7pm; 45F) is one of the better open-air museums, and was set up in the 1980s to preserve the distinctive rural architecture of France. Reconstructions that range from a half-timbered eighteenth-century farmhouse to a garage from the 1920s are scattered around the site, which is centred around a twentieth-century château burnt down by the Nazis in the last war. Many traditional activities like milling, hay-making and blacksmithing are illustrated. The information is dished out with an appealing blend of humour and didactics, and the whole place is less blatantly commercial than many other *écomusées*.

Grotte de Pech-Merle

Discovered in 1922, the **Grotte de Pech-Merle** (Easter–Oct daily 9.30am–noon & 1.30–5pm; rest of year phone ☎05.65.31.23.33; 44F) is bigger and less accessible than the caves at Les Eyzies, and doesn't suffer from the same problems of overcrowding and the consequent dangers of deterioration. It is well hidden on the scrubby hillsides above Cabrerets, which lies 15km from Marcilhac and 4km from Conduché, where the Célé flows into the Lot.

The cave itself is far more beautiful than those at Padirac or Les Eyzies, with galleries full of the most spectacular stalactites and stalagmites – structures tiered like wedding cakes, hanging like curtains, or shaped like whale baffles, discs or cave pearls. On the downside, the cave is wired for electric light and the guide, who talks like a recorded message, makes sure you're processed through in the scheduled time.

The first drawings you come to are in the so-called Chapelle des Mammouths, executed on a white calcite panel that looks as if it's been specially prepared for the purpose. There are horses, bison charging head down with tiny rumps and arched tails, and tusked, whiskery mammoths. You then pass into a vast chamber where the glorious horse panel is visible on a lower level; it's a remarkable example of the way in which the artist used the contour and relief of the rock to do the work, producing an utterly convincing mammoth by just two strokes of black. The cave ceiling is covered with finger marks, preserved in the soft clay. You pass the skeleton of a cave hyena that has been lying there for 20,000 years – wild animals used these caves for shelter and sometimes, unable to find their way out, starved to death in them. And finally, the most spine-tingling experience at Pech-Merle: the footprints of a Stone Age adult and child preserved in a muddy pool.

The admission charge includes a film and excellent **museum**, where prehistory is illustrated by colourful and intelligible charts, a selection of objects (rather than the usual 10,000 flints), skulls and beautiful slides displayed in wall panels.

There's a **gîte d'étape** and a **campsite** close by at **CABRERETS**, a tiny place that also has a pair of two-star **hotels**: the *Auberge de la Sagne*, 1km outside the village on the road to the caves (☎05.65.31.26.62, fax 05.65.30.27.43; ③; closed Oct–May 15), which has an excellent restaurant with a regional menu at 120F; and *Les Grottes* (☎05.65.31.27.02, fax 05.65.31.20.15; ③; closed Nov–March 29), also with a decent restaurant attached (closed Oct 6–May 5; menu from 83F).

Montauban

MONTAUBAN today is a prosperous middle-sized provincial city, capital of the largely agricultural *département* of Tarn-et-Garonne. It lies on the banks of the River Tarn, 53km from Toulouse, close to its junction with the Aveyron and their joint confluence with the Garonne, where the wide alluvial plain of the three rivers stretches boringly for miles around. But this is where the lines of communication run, and Montauban lies, conveniently, on the southwest Bordeaux–Toulouse autoroute and train line.

Its origins go back to 1144 when the count of Toulouse decided to create a *bastide* here as a bulwark against English and French royal power. In fact, it is generally regarded as the first *bastide*, the model for those rationally laid-out medieval new towns, and that plan is still clearly evident in the beautiful town centre.

Montauban has enjoyed various periods of great prosperity, as one can guess from the proliferation of fine town houses. The first followed the suppression of the Cathar heresy and the final submission of the counts of Toulouse in 1229 and was greatly enhanced by the building of the Pont-Vieux in 1335, making it the best crossing-point on the Tarn for miles around. The Hundred Years' War did its share of damage, as did Montauban's opting for the Protestant cause in the Wars of Religion, but by the time of the Revolution it had become once more one of the richest cities in the southwest, particularly successful in the manufacture of cloth.

Practicalities

The **tourist office** is on the northern corner of bd Midi-Pyrénées by the hideous market square, place Prax-Paris (July & Aug daily 9am–7pm; rest of year Mon–Sat 9am–noon & 2–5pm; ☎05.63.63.60.60, fax 05.63.63.65.12). At Montauban's centre lies the exquisite **place Nationale,** with the cathedral ten minutes' walk to the south on the unattractive **place Roosevelt,** with the most convenient underground parking. From here rue de l'Hôtel-de-Ville leads directly to the Pont-Vieux and across the river to av de Mayenne, at the end of which are both the **train** (☎05.63.63.50.50) and **bus station** (☎05.63.63.88.88).

If you are planning to **stay** the night, there are two perfectly adequate hotels right on the cathedral square. The cheaper of the two is the attractive, old-time *Hôtel du Commerce*, 9 place Roosevelt (☎05.63.66.31.32, fax 05.63.03.18.46; ②). The other, on the corner of rue de la Résistance, is the *Hôtel du Midi*, 12 rue Notre-Dame (☎05.63.63.17.23, fax 05.63.66.43.66; ③; restaurant from 79F). Alternatively, there is a comfortable hotel with an equally good restaurant just outside the train station: the *Hôtel d'Orsay*, 31 rue Roger-Salengro (☎05.63.66.06.66, fax 05.63.66.19.39; ③; closed second & third week of Aug & Dec 23–Jan 4; excellent restaurant from 100F, closed Sun).

The town

Montauban couldn't be easier to find your way around. The greatest delight is simply to wander the streets of the city centre, with their lovely pink brick houses; the town is only a ten- or fifteen-minute stroll from end to end. The visitable part is the small kernel of central streets based on the original *bastide*, and is enclosed within an inner ring of boulevards between boulevard Midi-Pyrénées on the east and the river on the west. The finest point of all is the **place Nationale**, rebuilt after a fire in the seventeenth century and surrounded on all sides by exquisite double-vaulted arcades with the octagonal belfry of St-Jacques showing above the western rooftops. It is the hub of the city's social life and the first place to head for coffee, drinks or food.

The adjacent **place du Coq** on rue de la République is also pretty, and if you follow the street down it brings you out by the **church of St-Jacques** (first built in the thirteenth century on the pilgrim route to Compostella) and the end of the **Pont-Vieux** with a wide view of the river. At the near end of the bridge, the former Bishop's residence is a massive half-palace, half-fortress, begun by the Black Prince in 1363 but never finished because the English lost control of the town. It is now the **Musée Ingres** (daily except Mon 9.30am–noon & 1.30–6pm; 15F), so called because it houses drawings and paintings that Jean-Auguste-Dominique Ingres, a native son of Montauban, left to the city on his death. It is a collection the city is very proud of, but unlikely to be of great interest to anyone but a definite Ingres fan. The same is true of the substantial collection of the works of Bourdelle, the ubiquitous monumental sculptor, also a native. There is a gruesome item in the middle of the basement room, known as a *banc de question*, used for extracting confessions by torture in the Montauban courts.

Across the road there is an interesting museum of local crafts, tools, costumes, furniture and the like, with a natural-history collection upstairs, under the name of the **Musée du Terroir et d'Histoire Naturelle** (Tues–Sat 9am–noon & 2–6pm; 25F).

The **Cathédrale Notre-Dame**, ten minutes' walk up rue de l'Hôtel-de-Ville, is a cold fish: an austere and unsympathetic building erected just before 1700 as part of the triumphalist campaign to reassert the glories of the Catholic faith after the cruel defeat and repression of the Protestants. But it is a bit of an architectural rarity in France, where there are few cathedrals built in the classical style.

Practicalities

In addition to the hotel-restaurants mentioned above, the simplest way of finding a place to **eat** is to go to the place Nationale, where you'll find *plats* under the arcades from around 35–45F at the *Agora* at no. 9, or *Brasserie des Arts* at no. 4, while on place de la Cathédrale the *Attrape-Cœur* does crêpes, and the *Bodega*, 40 rue de la République, tapas. For finer French fare, one of the top places is *Ambroisie*, 41 rue de la Comédie (closed Sun & July 12–31), with an interesting menu at 110F, or the *Ventadour*, 23 quai Villebourbon, magnificently sited in an old house on the river bank and specializing in regional cuisine (closed Mon eve, Sun & Aug 1–15; menus from 85F).

The place Nationale is also the obvious place to go for a **drink**, and you could add *Le Bouchon* wine bar to the list of places to try out. Other attractive options are the *Palais* on the neighbouring place du Coq and, for beers, *Le Flamand* at the corner of République and Soubirous-Bas, or *L'Irlandais* in rue Gillaque, just off place Nationale.

The valley of the Aveyron

About 25km east of Montauban, the flat alluvial plains break quite suddenly into abrupt hilliness, the tops rising between 300m and 400m in altitude. Through these hills, the **River Aveyron** and its main tributary, the Viaur, have cut deep, thickly wooded valleys peopled with numerous ancient villages.

One of the finest and most substantial is **ST-ANTONIN-NOBLE-VAL**, 50km east of Montauban. It sits on the bank of the Aveyron beneath the beetling cliffs of the **Roc d'Anglars**. It has endured all the vicissitudes of the old towns of the southwest: it went Cathar, then Protestant and each time was walloped by the alien power of the kings from the north. Yet, in spite of all, it recovered its prosperity, manufacturing cloth and leather goods, endowed by its wealthy merchants with a marvellous heritage of medieval houses in all the streets leading out from the lovely **place de la Halle** and its prolongation.

There's a café most conveniently and picturesquely placed at the end of the ancient *halle*, with a view of the town's finest building, the Maison des Consuls, whose origins go back to 1120. It now houses the town museum, **Musée du Vieux St-Antonin** (July–Sept daily except Tues 10am–1pm & 3–6.30pm; rest of year afternoons only; 15F), with collections of objects to do with the former life of the place, as well as a section on local prehistoric sites.

The **tourist office** is in the current town hall (July & Aug daily 9.30am–12.30pm & 2–6.30pm; rest of year Mon—Sat 10am—noon & 2—5.30pm; ☎05.63.30.63.47, fax 05.63.30.66.33), and will supply information about B&Bs, canoeing on the Aveyron and walks in the region round about. By the bridge as you cross from the Montauban road, there's a simple and attractive **hotel** immediately on the left, the *Hôtel Thermes* – so called because St-Antonin once tried to be a spa – with a terrace overlooking the water (☎05.63.30.61.08, fax 05.63.68.26.23; ②; restaurant from 59F). There are four local **campsites;** *Camping Anglars* is by the riverside (mid-April to mid-Oct; ☎05.63.30.69.76, fax 05.63.30.67.61).

Twenty kilometres downstream you come to the beautiful ridge-top village of **PENNE**, once a Cathar stronghold, with its ruined **castle** impossibly perched on an airy crag. Everything is old and leaning and bulging, but holding together nonetheless, with a harmony that would be impossible to create purposely.

Another hilltop **castle** commands its village at **BRUNIQUEL** (May–Oct daily 10am–12.30pm & 2–6/7pm; 15F), a few kilometres further on. You can also visit a handsome house in the village, the aristocratic **Maison des Comtes de Payrol** (mid-June to mid-Sept daily 10am–noon & 2–6pm, April to mid-June & mid- to end-Sept Sat & Sun only; 10F). There's also a small **hotel** called the *Étape du Château* (☎05.63.67.25.00; ①–②; restaurant from 75F), whose proprietor is a mountain-bike freak and will take you out on trips. *Le Payssel* campsite (May to mid-Sept, ☎05.63.67.25.95) is about 600m along the bottom road, and there's a **gîte** 3km along the GR46 towards Gaillac (☎05.63.67.27.21), which also serves meals to non-residents.

Najac

NAJAC occupies an extraordinary site on a conical hill isolated in a wide bend in the already deep valley of the Aveyron, 25km south of Villefranche-de-Rouergue and on the main Brive–Toulouse train line, with one direct train to Paris every day. Its photogenic castle, which graces many a travel poster, sits right on the peak of the hill, while the half-timbered and stone-tiled village houses tail out in a single street along the narrow back of the spur that joins the hill to the valleyside. It's all very attractive and consequently touristy, with the inevitable resident knick-knack shops and craftspeople.

The **castle** (daily April, May & Sept 10am–1pm & 3–5pm; June until 6pm; July & Aug until 7pm; 20F) is a model of medieval defensive architecture and was endlessly fought over because of its commanding and impregnable position in a region once rich in silver and copper mines. You can see clearly all the devices for restricting an attacker once he was inside the castle: the covered passages and stairs within the thickness of the walls, the multi-storey positions for archers and, of course, the most magnificent all-round view from the top of the keep. In one of the chambers of the keep you can see the stone portraits of Saint Louis, king of France, Alphonse de Poitiers, his brother, and Jeanne, the daughter of the count of Toulouse, the couple whose marriage was arranged in 1229 to end the Cathar wars by bringing the domains of Count Raymond and his allies under royal control. It was Alphonse de Poitiers who "modernized" the castle and made the place we see today. Signatures of the masons who worked on it are clearly visible on many stones.

Below the rather dull central *place* stretches the **faubourg**, a sort of elongated square bordered by houses raised on pillars as in the central square of a *bastide*, which reduces to a narrow waist of a street overlooked by more ancient houses and leading past a fountain to the castle gate. At the foot of the castle, in the centre of what was the medieval village, stands the very solid-looking **church of St-Jean**, which the villagers of Najac were forced by the Inquisition to build at their own expense in 1258 as a punishment for their conversion to Catharism. In addition to a lovely silver reliquary and an extraordinary iron cage for holding candles – both dating from the thirteenth century – the church has one architectural oddity: its windows are solid panels of stone from which the lights have been cut out in trefoil form. Below the church, by a derelict farm, a stretch of **Roman road** survives and, at the bottom of the hill, a thirteenth-century **bridge** spans the Aveyron.

The modern village balances on the shoulder of the spur round an open square with the *Oustal del Barry* **hotel** on the downhill side (☎05.65.29.74.32, fax 05.65.29.75.32; ③; April–Oct), whose rather expensive restaurant is renowned for its subtle and inventive cuisine (menus from 100F to 260F). The **tourist office** is on the *faubourg,* and there is a **gîte d'étape** at Le Païsserou (☎05.65.29.73.96).

Villefranche-de-Rouergue

No medieval junketing, not a craft shop in sight, **VILLEFRANCHE-DE-ROUERGUE** must be as close as you can get to what a French provincial town used to be like, and it's also where you are as likely to hear Occitan spoken as French. It's a small place, lying on a bend in the Aveyron, 35km due south of Figeac and 61km east of Cahors across the **Causse de Limogne**. Built as a *bastide* by Alphonse de Poitiers in 1252 as part of the royal policy of extending control over the recalcitrant lands of the south, the town became rich on copper from the surrounding mines and its privilege of minting coins. From the fifteenth to the eighteenth centuries, its wealthy men built the magnificent houses that grace the cobbled streets to this day.

Rue du Sergent-Bories and rue de la République, the main commercial street, are both very attractive, but they are no preparation for **place Notre-Dame**, the loveliest *bastide* central square in the region. It's built on a slope, so the uphill houses are much higher than the downhill, and you enter at the corners underneath the houses. All the houses are arcaded at ground-floor level, providing for a market where local merchants and farmers spread out their weekly produce. The houses are unusually tall and some are very elaborately decorated, notably the so-called **Maison du Président Raynal** on the lower side at the top of rue de la République, with its extraordinary spiral staircase leading out of a narrow medieval courtyard; you can push open the door and look in.

The east side of the square is dominated by the **church of Notre-Dame** with its colossal porch and bell tower, nearly 60m high. The interior has some fine late-fifteenth-century stained glass, carved choir stalls and misericords. Behind it is the marketplace. Thursday is market day, which, as the locals will tell you, is the quintessential Villefranche experience, and you won't hear any French spoken.

On the boulevard that forms the northern limit of the old town, the seventeenth-century **Chapelle des Pénitents-Noirs** (July–Sept daily 10am–noon & 2–6pm) boasts a splendidly Baroque painted ceiling and an enormous gilded retable. Another ecclesiastical building worth the slight detour is the **Chartreuse St-Sauveur** (same opening hours), about 1km out of town on the Gaillac road. It was completed in the space of ten years from 1450, giving it a singular architectural harmony, and has a very beautiful cloister and choir stalls by the same master as Notre-Dame in Villefranche, which, by contrast, took nearly 300 years to complete.

Aside from the pleasing details of many of the houses you notice as you explore the side streets, the town reserves one other most unexpected surprise. The **municipal library** in the seventeenth-century chapel of the order of the Pénitents-Bleus at 27 rue Sénéchal (☎05.65.45.59.45) includes an amazing collection of jazz records, books, papers, recordings and documents belonging to the late Hugues Panassié, famous French jazz critic and one of the founders of the *Hot Club de France*. Much of the material is unrecorded or unobtainable elsewhere and is open to perusal by researchers and enthusiasts. CD selections are on sale both here and at the tourist office.

Practicalities

The **tourist office** sits on place du Giraudet (daily 10am–noon & 2–5pm; ☎05.65.45.13.18), at the corner of the bridge. For those who want to stay overnight, there are two pleasant **hotels**: *Hôtel Lagarrigue* just behind the post office on place Bernard-Lehz in the old town (☎05.65.45.01.12, fax 05.65.81.22.89; ②–③; restaurant from 70F); and *L'Univers*, 2 place de la République at the end of the bridge opposite the tourist office (☎05.65.45.15.63, fax 05.65.45.02.21; ③; good traditional restaurant from 80F). For an even more sumptuous meal, as well as a comfortable sleep, there's *Le Relais de Farrou*, 3km out on the Figeac road (☎05.65.45.18.11, fax 05.65.45.32.59; ④; restaurant from 112F). For cheaper accommodation, there's the *Foyer des Jeunes Travailleurs* **hostel**, which has seen better days but has a lovely situation on the river bank behind the Hôtel de Ville and tourist office at 13 rue Émile-de-Rodat (☎05.65.45.09.68; meals 35F). There is also a **gîte d'étape** by the river at La Gasse, 1km out of town on the D269 back road to La Bastide-L'Evêque, at the start of **GR62b** (☎05.65.45.10.80; May–Oct), plus a **campsite**, 1.5km to the south on the D47 to Monteil (☎05.65.45.16.24; April–Sept). Finally, in the covered market is the workers' diner, *Café de la Halle*, where you can eat a substantial meal for 50F at shared tables, if you don't feel too self-conscious in such an ambience.

Moissac and around

There is nothing very memorable about the modern town of **MOISSAC**, 40km east of Agen, largely because of the terrible damage done by the flood of March 1930, when the Tarn, swollen by a sudden thaw in the Massif Central, burst its banks, destroying 617 houses and killing 120 people.

Luckily, the one thing that makes Moissac a household name in the history of art survived, and that is the cloister and porch of the **abbey church of St-Pierre**, a masterpiece of Romanesque sculpture and model for hundreds of churches and buildings elsewhere. Indeed, the fact that it has survived countless wars, including siege and sack by Simon de Montfort in 1212 during the crusade against the Cathars, is something of a miracle. During the Revolution it was used as a gunpowder factory and billet for soldiers, who damaged many of the sculptures. In the 1830s it only escaped demolition to make way for the Bordeaux–Toulouse train line by a whisker.

Legend has it that Clovis the Frank first founded a monastery here, though it seems more probable that its origins belong to the seventh century, which saw the foundation of so many monasteries throughout Aquitaine. The first Romanesque church on the site was consecrated in 1063 and enlarged in the following century. The famous **south porch**, with its magnificent tympanum and curious wavy door jambs and *trumeau*, dates from this second phase of building. It depicts Christ in Majesty, right hand raised in benediction, the Book in his hand, surrounded by the evangelists and the elders of the Apocalypse as described by Saint John in the Book of Revelations. It is a display whose influence, assimilated with varying degrees of success, can be seen in the work of artists who decorated the porches of countless churches across the south of France. There is more fine carving in the capitals inside the porch, and the interior of the church, which was remodelled in the fifteenth century, is interesting too, especially for some of the wood and stone statuary it contains.

The adjoining **cloister** (daily 9am–noon & 2–5/6/7pm) is now entered through the tourist office, and if you want to experience the silent contemplation for which it was originally built, you must get there first thing in the morning. The cloister surrounds a garden shaded by a majestic cedar, and its pantile roof is supported by 76 alternating single and double marble columns. Each column supports a single inverted wedge-shaped block of stone, on which are carved with extraordinary delicacy all manner of animals and plant motifs, as well as scenes from Bible stories and the lives of the saints: Daniel in the lions' den, the Evangelists, Saint Peter being crucified upside down, John the Baptist being decapitated, and many, many others. An inscription on the middle pillar on the west side explains that the cloister was made in the time of the Abbot Ansquitil in the year of Our Lord 1100.

Practicalities

The **tourist office** (☎05.63.04.01.85, fax 05.63.04.2.10) is outside the church cloister (same hours as cloister), with the **gare SNCF** and **gare routière** both on av Pierre-Chabrié. There's a weekly Saturday **market** in place des Récollets at the end of rue de la République, which leads away from the abbey, a marvel of colour and temptation.

Overlooking the south side of the square, the *Hôtel au Chapon Fin* makes a pleasant and reasonable place to **stay** (☎05.63.04.04.22, fax 05.63.04.58.44; ②; restaurant from 80F, closed Mon out of season). For **campers**, there's a shady site across the river and to the left by an old mill on a little island, the Île du Bidounet (April–Sept), where there is also a **gîte d'étape** (walkers only). For simple, quick **eating**, there's the *Salons du Cloître* (from 42F) right outside the church.

Agen

AGEN, capital of the Lot-et-Garonne *département*, is a pleasanter town than it first appears. It was quartered by modern boulevards in the nineteenth century in its own version of a Haussmann cleanup, and it is down these roads that you're funnelled into the town, with the result that you see nothing of interest.

The town lies on the broad, powerful River Garonne halfway between Bordeaux and Toulouse, and lived through the Middle Ages racked by war with England and internecine strife between Catholics and Protestants. But it was able to extract some advantage from disputes in possession, as it seesawed between the English and French, gaining more and more privileges of independence as the price of its loyalty – a tradition that it maintained during and after the Revolution by being staunchly republican (the churches still bear the legend: *Liberté, Fraternité, Égalité*).

Its pre-Revolutionary wealth derived from the manufacture of various kinds of cloth and its thriving port on the Garonne, which in those days was alive with river traffic. But the Industrial Revolution put paid to all of that. Agen's prosperity now is based on agriculture – in particular, its famous prunes and plums, said to have been brought back from Damascus during the Crusades.

The town

The interesting part of Agen centres on **place Goya**, where boulevard de la République, leading to the river, crosses boulevard du Président-Carnot. On the south side of boulevard de la République, the main shopping area is around place Wilson, rue Garonne and the partly arcaded place des Laitiers. A left turn at the end of rue Garonne brings you to the wide place du Dr-Esquirol and an exuberant turn-of-the-century municipal **theatre**; opposite this is the **Musée Municipal des Beaux-Arts** (daily except Tues 10am–noon & 2–6pm; free), magnificently housed in four adjacent sixteenth- and seventeeth-century mansions adorned with stair turrets, Renaissance window details, different roof angles. The collections include a rich variety of archeological finds, Roman and medieval, furniture and paintings – among the latter some Goyas. Not far from the museum, in place du Bourg at the end of rue des Droits-de-l'Homme, the cute little thirteenth-century **church of Notre-Dame** is worth a look.

Behind the theatre, rue Beauville, with heavily restored but beautiful medieval houses, leads through to rue Voltaire, which is full of ethnic restaurants, and rue Richard-Cœur-de-Lion, leading to the **Église des Jacobins**, a big brick Dominican church of the thirteenth century, its barn-like interior divided by a single centre row of pillars, very like its counterpart in Toulouse. Beyond lie the river and the public gardens of **Le Gravier**, where a market is held every Wednesday and Saturday; there's a footbridge across the Garonne, with a **canal bridge** dating from 1839 just downstream.

Opposite place Wilson on the north side of boulevard de la République, the arcaded rue Cornières leads through to the **Cathédrale St-Caprais**, somewhat misshapen but with a finely proportioned Romanesque apse and radiating chapels still surviving. There is a piece of the original fortifications still showing in rue des Augustins close by – the **Tour du Chapelet** – dating from around 1100. Again nearby, in rue du Puits-du-Saumon, is one of the finest houses in town, the fourteenth-century **Maison du Sénéchal**, with an elaborate open loggia on the first floor.

Practicalities

From the central place Goya, bd du Président-Carnot leads to the **gares SNCF** and **routière**. The **tourist office** is at 107 bd Carnot (July & Aug Mon–Sat 9am–7pm, Sun 10am–noon; rest of year Mon–Sat 9am–12.30/1pm & 2–6.30/7pm; ☎05.53.47.36.09, fax 05.53.47.29.98).

There are several reasonable **hotel** options in Agen. Right next to the tourist office, the *Stim'Otel*, 105 bd Carnot (☎05.53.47.31.23, fax 05.53.47.48.70; ③; restaurant from 65F), looks a bit dire but is actually comfortable and welcoming. Also very central and in a more attractive street is the *Hôtel des Ambans*, 59 rue des Ambans, near place Goya (☎05.53.66.28.60; ②), while the nice-looking *Périgord* overlooks a large traffic round-about at the eastern end of bd de la République at 42 cours du 14-juillet (☎05.53.66.10.01, fax 05.53.47.47.31; ②; restaurant from 74F). At the other end of the boulevard, close to the river, *Hôtel des Îles*, 25 rue Baudin (☎05.53.47.11.33, fax 05.53.66.19.25; ②), has slightly cheaper rooms. There is also an HI **youth hostel**, a bit of a trek at 17 rue Léo-Lagrange, not far from the canal bridge on the main D656 to Cahors (☎05.53.66.18.98; bus direction "Lalande"); it's possible to **camp** here as well.

The best places to **eat** well at reasonable prices are the *Bistrot Apicius*, 8 rue Sentini (☎05.53.66.07.81; menus from 48F), and *Le Petit Vatel*, 52 rue Richard-Cœur-de-Lion (☎05.53.47.66.00; closed Sat lunchtime & Mon; from 110F), which has a delicious variety of seafood. Alternatively, try *L'Étable* by the footbridge on the river at 41bis Péristyle du Gravier along Le Gravier (closed Sat & Sun lunchtime & Mon; from 60F), or the various places in Agen's rue Voltaire. If you like crêpes, there's no better place to eat them than the *Crêperie des Jacobins*, right opposite the Église des Jacobins.

Around Moissac

As you head north towards Cahors, leaving the wide flat valleys of the Tarn and Garonne behind you, the land rises gradually to gently undulating country, green and woody, cut obliquely by parallel valleys running down to meet the Garonne and planted with vines and sunflowers, maize, and apple and plum orchards. It's a very soft landscape, and villages are small and widely scattered. The pace of life seems about equal with that of a turning sunflower.

Should you find yourself taking this route, then the place to make a halt is **LAUZERTE**, one of Raymond of Toulouse's *bastides* and of great military importance as it commands the road to Cahors, the route down which the pilgrims of St-Jacques came pouring every spring, as they still do today, or at least the hardy who follow the GR65 on foot. The town is short on sights, but there are some old houses, a pretty arcaded central square and a good Baroque altarpiece in the church, as well as views of the countryside round about.

There's a very pleasant **hotel** at the entrance to the village for those who want to stay: *Hôtel du Quercy* (☎05.63.94.66.36; ②; closed Oct), which also serves excellent food, with menus from 80F (closed Sun & Mon eve out of season). There's a **campsite** and **gîte d'étape** for walkers on the GR65, plus the possibility of B&B at *Le Luzerta* at Vignals just below the village (③; closed Jan–March & Wed; restaurant).

travel details

Buses

Agen to: Barbaste (1–2 daily; 45min); Clairac (1 daily; 50min); Condom (3 daily except Sun; 50min); Nerac (4 daily; 30min); Tonneins (2 daily; 1hr); Villeneuve-sur-Lot (several daily; 45min).

Argentat to: Beaulieu-sur-Dordogne (July & Aug 3 daily; 40min); Souillac (1 daily; 2hr 15min).

Bergerac to: Bordeaux (1 daily; 1hr 15min); Castillon (1 daily; 1hr 15min); Marmande (1 daily; 1hr 55min); Montcaret (1 daily; 1hr 10min); Ste-Foy-la-Grande (1 daily; 45min).

Brive to: Argentat (1 daily; 1hr 20min); Arnac-Pompadour (1 daily; 1hr 45min); Collonges-le-Rouge (2 daily; 20–35min); Meyssac (2 daily; 40min); Sarlat (1 daily; 2hr 15min); Souillac (1–2 daily; 1hr 10min);Turenne (1–2 daily; 35min); Uzerche (2 daily; 1hr 30min); Vayrac (1–2 daily; 55min).

Cahors to: Cajarç (3–5 daily; 1hr); Conduché (3–5 daily; 30min); Figeac (3–5 daily; 1hr 45min); Fumel (6–8 daily; 1hr 10min); Limogne-en-Quercy (1—2 daily; 1hr); Luzech (6–8 daily; 30min); Montauban (1 daily ; 1hr 20min) ; Monsempron-Libos (6–8 daily; 1hr 20min); Puy-l'Évêque (6–8 daily; 45min); Rodez (1 daily; 2hr 40 min); Villefranche-de-Rouergue (1daily; 1hr 30min).

Limoges: Aubusson (2 daily; 2hr); Châlus (1 daily; 1hr); St-Léonard (3 daily; 35min).

Périgueux to: Angoulême (3 daily; 1hr 40min); Bergerac (3 daily; 1hr 30min); Brantôme (3 daily; 40min); Excideuil (3 daily; 1hr 15min); Montignac (1–2 daily; 1hr); Ribérac (3–4 daily; 1hr); Sarlat (1–2 daily; 1hr 30min).

Ribérac to: Angoulême (2 daily; 1hr 30min).

Tulle to: Argentat (4 daily; 50min–1hr 15min).

Trains

Agen to: Belvès (3–4 daily; 1hr 10min); Bordeaux (frequent; 1hr–1hr 50min); Le Buisson (3–4 daily; 1hr 10min); Les Eyzies (3–4 daily; 1hr 40min); Moissac (5 daily; 30min); Monsemprou-Libos (6 daily; 45min); Mont-de-Marsan (2 daily; 2hr 30min); Montauban (frequent; 40–50min); Périgueux (3–4 daily; 2hr 15min–2hr 50min); Toulouse (frequent; 1hr 20min); Villefranche-du-Périgord (3–4 daily; 1hr).

Bergerac to: Bordeaux (10–11 daily; 1hr–1hr 50min); Montcaret (3 daily; 25–30min); St-Émilion (3 daily; 50min); Ste-Foy-la-Grande (8 daily; 15min).

Brive to: Aurillac (5–6 daily; 1hr 45min); Bordeaux (6–7 daily; 2hr 30min–3hr); Cahors (11 daily; 1hr–1hr 15min); Clermont-Ferrand (3 daily; 3hr 40min); Figeac (6 daily; 1hr 20min); Gourdon (8 daily; 45min); Limoges (frequent; 1hr–1hr 10min); Montauban (6 daily; 2hr); Paris-Austerlitz (frequent; 4–5hr); Périgueux (3–4 daily; 1hr–1hr 30min); Rocamadour-Padirac (5–6 daily; 30–40min); Souillac (8 daily; 30min); Toulouse (6 daily; 2hr 30min); Uzerche (several daily; 30min); Villefranche-de-Rouergue (3 daily; 2hr–2hr 20min).

Cahors to: Brive (11 daily; 1hr–1hr 15min); Montauban (6 daily; 40min); Toulouse (6 daily; 1hr 10min).

Figeac to: Aubin (4–5 daily; 30min); Brive (6 daily; 1hr 20min); Decazeville (4–5 daily; 20min); Najac (4–5 daily; 40min); Rodez (4–5 daily; 1hr 45min); Toulouse (4–5 daily; 2hr 30min); Villefranche-de-Rouergue (4–5 daily; 40min).

Limoges to: Angoulême (4 daily; 2hr); Bordeaux (6–7 daily; 2hr 30 min); Brive (3 daily; 2hr 10min); Eymoutiers (4 daily; 50min); Meymac (3 daily; 1hr 40min); Nexon (3 daily; 25min); Paris-Austerlitz (frequent; 3hr 30min); Périgueux (10 daily; 1hr–1hr 30min); Poitiers (3 daily; 2hr); Pompadour (3 daily; 1hr 15min); St-Léonard (4 daily; 20min); St-Yrieix (3 daily; 45min); Thiviers (7 daily; 40min–1hr); Ussel (3 daily; 2hr).

Montauban to: Agen (frequent; 35–45min); Bordeaux (frequent; 1hr 40min–2hr 30min); Moissac (7 daily; 20min); Toulouse (frequent; 35min).

Périgueux to: Agen (3–4 daily; 2hr 20min); Belvès (3–4 daily; 1hr 10min); Bordeaux (10–12 daily; 1hr 20min–2hr); Brive (5–6 daily; 1hr–1hr 30min); Le Buisson (3–4 daily; 50min); Les Eyzies (3–4 daily; 35min); Limoges (11 daily; 1hr); Monsemprou-Libos (3–4 daily; 1hr 45min); Villefranche-du-Périgord (3–4 daily; 1hr 25min).

Sarlat to: Bergerac (6 daily; 1hr 20min); Beynac (2 daily; 20min); Bordeaux (5–6 daily; 2hr 30min–3hr 30min); Le Buisson (7 daily; 35–45min); Ste-Foy-la-Grande (5 daily; 1hr 30min–1hr 45min).

CHAPTER TEN

THE PYRENEES

Basque-speaking and wet in the west; craggy, snowy, patois-speaking in the middle; dry and Catalan in the east: the **Pyrenees** are physically beautiful, culturally varied and a great deal less developed than the Alps. The whole range is marvellous walkers' country, especially the central region around the **Parc National des Pyrénées**, with its 3000-metre peaks, streams, forests, flowers and wildlife. If you're a committed hiker, it's possible to go all the way across the mountains, from the Atlantic to the Mediterranean, along the **GR10** or the more difficult **Haute Randonnée Pyrénéenne** (HRP); and there are numerous local walking centres as well – **Cauterets**, **Luz-St-Sauveur**, **Barèges**, **Ax-les-Thermes** – with hikes to suit all temperaments and abilities. The hiking season is from mid-June through to September; earlier in the year, few refuges are open and you will run into snow even on parts of the GR10. Whatever you intend, bear in mind that these are big mountains and should be treated with respect: to cover any of the main walks you'll need hiking boots and, despite the southerly latitude, warm and windproof clothing.

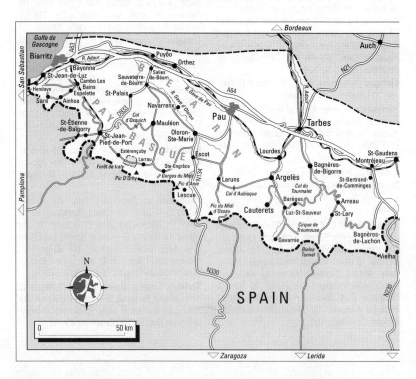

As for the more conventional of the tourist attractions, the **Basque coast** is lovely but very popular, suffering from seaside sprawl and a massive surfeit of campsites. **St-Jean-de-Luz** is by far the prettiest of the resorts, and once-smart **Biarritz** surely the most overrated; **Bayonne** is the most attractive town, with an excellent Basque museum, although, sadly, this is in abeyance right now due to local political wrangles. The foothill towns are on the whole rather dull, although **Pau** is worth at least a day or two, while **Lourdes** is such a monster of kitsch that it just has to be seen. The east – Catalan-speaking **Roussillon** – has beaches every bit as popular as those in the Basque country, but on the whole is less inviting. Its interior, however, is another matter: craggy landscapes split by spectacular canyons, a crop of fine Romanesque abbeys, of which **St-Martin-de-Canigou** and **Serrabonne** are the most dramatic, and a climate bathed in Mediterranean heat and light.

Hiking in the Pyrenees

If you're planning on doing even very basic walking or other outdoor activities – canoeing, riding, cycling, paragliding – in the Pyrenees, a good contact point for **ideas, information** and **publications** (in French) is Randonnées Pyrénéennes, 4 rue Maye-Lane, 65420, Ibos, near Tarbes (☎05.62.90.09.90; information centre ☎05.62.90.09.92).

There are plenty of walkers' **guidebooks** to the area, both in French and English (see p.1096), plus three small area guides produced by Arthur Battagel for West Col, which include the Spanish side of the range. The best **maps** are the *IGN* 1: 25,000 series; #1547, #1647 and #1748 cover the Parc National des Pyrénées.

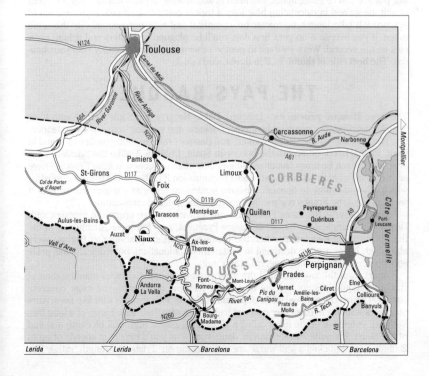

ACCOMMODATION PRICE CATEGORIES

Each hotel in this chapter has a symbol which corresponds to one of eight price categories.

① Under 160F	④ 300–400F	⑦ 600–700F
② 160–220F	⑤ 400–500F	⑧ Over 700F
③ 220–300F	⑥ 500–600F	

The prices quoted are for the cheapest available double room in high season, though remember that many of the cheap places will have more expensive rooms with en-suite facilities.

Wherever you plan to hike, **preparation** is crucial. Before taking to the hills, check the weather forecasts and be sure you are properly equipped with water, food, maps, bivvy bag, whistle and knife, as well as warm, wetproof and windproof clothing and suitable boots – not to mention ice axe and crampons if you are going anywhere near snow, which you shouldn't be doing unless you are already experienced. Above all, don't take any chances: mountain conditions can change very quickly, and sunny, warm weather in the valley doesn't necessarily mean it will be the same higher up. If you don't have any mountain-walking experience, it's probably best not to undertake anything more than a well-frequented path unless you're accompanied by someone who does.

Don't overdo things. One kilometre in twelve minutes (5kph) is a fairly average **walking pace**; if you're going uphill, you need to add at least an extra ten minutes per 100m of altitude gained in calculating how long a trek is going to take you. If you are out of practice it'll take longer, no matter how youthful and vigorous you are. By the same token, if you overdo it on your first day, you'll be plagued by blisters and aching muscles on the second. Work yourself in gently; otherwise you could easily ruin your holiday. The best rule of thumb is: if in doubt, don't do it.

THE PAYS BASQUE

The three **Basque provinces** – Labourd, Basse Navarre and Soule – share with their Spanish neighbours a common language, Euskara, and a strong sense of separate identity. The language is universally spoken, and Basques refer to their country as a land in itself, Euskal-herri, or, across the border in Spain, Euskadi. Unlike the Spanish, however, few French Basques favour an independent state or secession from France. There is no equivalent of the Basque nationalist organization ETA here, and the old sympathy, which allowed refuge to Spanish Basques wanted on terrorist charges, has waned. It was hatred of the Franco regime that provided the political momentum.

Administratively, the three French Basque provinces were organized together with Béarn in the single *département* of Basses-Pyrénées, now Pyrénées-Atlantiques, at the time of the 1789 Revolution, when the Basques' thousand-year-old *fors* (rights) were abolished. It was a move designed to curtail their nationalism, but ironically has probably been responsible for preserving their unity.

Apart from the language and the *beret basque*, the most obvious manifestation of Basque national identity are the ubiquitous *frontons* or *jaï alaï*, the huge concrete courts in which the national game of **pelota** is played. This game is a bit like fives: pairs of players wallop a hard leather-covered ball, either with their bare hands or a long basket-work extension of the hand called a *chistera*, against a high wall blocking one end of the court. It's quite extraordinarily dangerous – as you'd expect at speeds of up to 200kph – and knockouts and worse are not uncommon. Trials of strength, rather like

Scottish Highland Games, are also popular: tugs-of-war, lifting heavy weights, turning massive carts, sawing through giant tree trunks and the like.

The Côte Basque

Hardly more than 30km long and well served by bus and train, the **Basque coast** is easily accessible and, perhaps surprisingly, reasonably priced hotel accommodation is not that difficult to find – though space can be limited in summer. The most popular budget place is **Anglet**, which has a youth hostel and is within easy reach of the magnificent beaches and Biarritz hot spots. **Biarritz** itself is a rather exhausting place to stay in full season: families will certainly prefer **St-Jean-de-Luz** – in any case much the most attractive town.

Bayonne

BAYONNE stands back some 6km from the Atlantic, a position that has protected it from any real exploitation by tourism. It bestrides the confluence of the River Adour, which rises to the east in the region of the Pic du Midi de Bigorre, and the much smaller Nive, whose source is the Basque Pyrénées above St-Jean-Pied-de-Port. Although purists dispute whether it is truly a Basque rather than a Gascon city, it is the effective economic and political capital of the Pays Basque. To the lay person, at least, there seems no doubt about its Basque flavour, with its tall half-timbered houses and woodwork painted in the peculiarly Basque tones of green and red. Here, too, Basques in flight from Franco's Spain came without hesitation to seek refuge among their own. For many years the Petit Bayonne quarter was a hotbed of Basque nationalist ferment, until the French government clamped down on such dangerous tendencies.

The city's origins go back to Roman times, since when its Latin name of Lapurdum, corrupted to Labourd, has been extended to cover the whole of this westernmost of the

---

THE FOOD OF THE BASQUE COUNTRY

Although **Basque cooking** shares many of the dishes of the southwest, it does have some distinctive recipes of its own. One of the best known is the Basque omelette, **pipérade**, made with tomatoes, chillis and sautéed Bayonne ham (salt cured and resembling Parma ham), mixed into the eggs, so that it actually looks more like scrambled eggs. **Poulet basquaise** is also common, especially as takeaway food at the *traiteur*: pieces of chicken browned in pork fat and casseroled in a sauce of tomato, chilli, onions and a little white wine. And in season there is a chance of **palombe**, the wild doves netted or shot as they migrate north over the Pyrenees. A dish that is popular a bit further inland is the thick potato and cabbage soup, **garbure**, which is enlivened with a piece of pork or *confit* of goose or duck.

With the Atlantic close at hand, seafood is a speciality. The Basques inevitably have their version of fish soup, called **ttoro**. Another great delicacy are **elvers** or *piballes*, which are netted as they come up the Atlantic rivers from the Sargasso Sea. **Squid** are common, served here as *chiperons*, either in their own ink or stewed with onion, tomato, peppers and garlic. All the locally caught fish – cod (*morue*), tuna (*thon*), sardines (*sardine*) and anchovies (*anchois*) – are regular favourites, too.

Cheeses mainly comprise the delicious ewe's-milk *tommes* from the high pastures of the Pyrenees. Among sweets, one that is on show everywhere is the **gâteau basque**, a sweet flan pastry garnished with black cherries or filled with *crème pâtissière*.

As for liquid, the only Basque **wine** is the very drinkable red Irouléguy, with the potent green or yellow Izzara for liqueur.

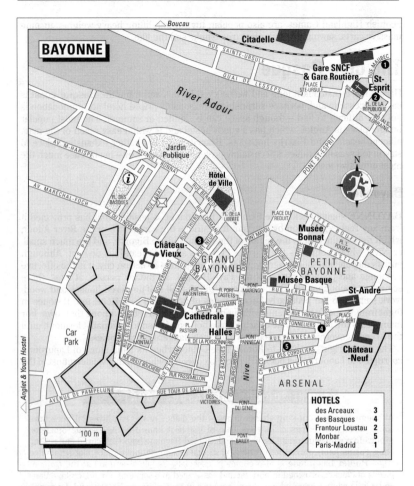

BAYONNE

Boucau

Citadelle

Gare SNCF & Gare Routière ①

St-Esprit ②

RUE SAINTE-URSULE

QUAI DE LESSEPS

RUE MAUBEC

PLACE STE-URSULE

PL. DE LA RÉPUBLIQUE

BD ALS-LORRAINE

River Adour

AV. M-HARISPE

AVENUE BONNAT

Jardin Publique

Hôtel de Ville

PONT ST-ESPRIT

N

AV. MARECHAL-FOCH

PL. DES BASQUES

RUE JACAT

RUE BERNEDE

RUE LORMAND

PL. DE LA LIBERTE

PLACE DU REDUIT

ALLÉES BOUFFLERS

AV. DU 11 NOVEMBRE

RUE THIERS

PONT MAYOU

Musée Bonnat

PL. POUZAC

RUE BASTIAT

ALLÉES PAULMY

Château-Vieux

RUE DES GOUVERNEURS

③ GRAND BAYONNE

QUAI DUBOURDIEU

QUAI DES CORSAIRES

RUE SECURTE

PETIT BAYONNE

RUE LAFFITE

RUE DE LA MONNAIE

RUE PORT-CASTETS

RUE ARGENTERIE

PONT-MARENGO

QUAI ROQUEBERT

RUE MERENGO

Musée Basque

RUE DES TONNELIERS

St-André

Car Park

RAMPART LACHEPAILLET

RUE DES FAURES

RUE PILORI GUILHAMIN

Cathédrale

PL. PASTEUR

Halles

RUE ESPAGNE

RUE LUC

RUE MONTAUT

R. DE LA POISSONNERIE

QUAI GALUPERIE

RUE TRINQUET

RUE DES TONNELIERS

PLACE PAUL-BERT

④

RUE DES CORDELIERS

RUE PANNECAU

⑤

Château-Neuf

Anglet & Youth Hostel

RUE VIELLE BOUCHERIE

RUE PASSEMILLON

RUE DES BASQUES

Nive

QUAI JAUREGUIBERRY

QUAI A. CHAO

PONT-PANNECAU

RUE PELLETIER

ARSENAL

AVENUE DE PAMPELUNE

RUE TOUR DE SAULT

PL. DES-VICTOIRES

PONT-DU GENIE

0   100 m

PONT-BAILEY

HOTELS

des Arceaux	3
des Basques	4
Frantour Loustau	2
Monbar	5
Paris-Madrid	1

three Basque provinces. For 300 years until 145 AD it enjoyed prosperity and security under English domination. Around 1500, Sephardic Jews fleeing the Spanish Inquisition arrived, bringing their chocolate manufacturing trade with them. The city reached the peak of its commercial success in the eighteenth century, when it was also a centre of the armaments industry (it gave its name to the bayonet). Later, its prestige suffered a blow in the 1789 Revolution when the anti-regionalist centralizing zealots of the Paris government subsumed the three Basque provinces under a single *département*, with its capital at Pau. More recently, there has been a renewal of economic activity based on the processing of by-products from the natural gas field at Lacq near Pau, but this, too, has been affected by the current hard times, leaving Bayonne with a higher-than-average level of unemployment.

These problems don't immediately impinge on the visitor, however, and first impressions are likely to be favourable. It's a small-scale, easily manageable city. Whether your intention is to head inland or down the coast, it may – as the hub of all major road and rail routes from the north and east – be your first encounter with the Pays Basque. Cheaper and quieter than neighbouring Biarritz, it could be worth considering as a base even for a seaside sojourn.

Arrival, information and accommodation

The **gare SNCF** (☎05.59.55.50.50) and **gare routière** are next door to each other, just off place de la République on the north bank of the river, across the wide Pont St-Esprit from the city centre. The **tourist office** is in place des Basques (July & Aug Mon–Sat 9am–7pm, Sun 10am–1pm; rest of year Mon–Fri 9am–6.30pm, Sat 10am–6pm; ☎05.59.46.01.46, fax 05.59.59.37.55), with a booth at the train station and the airport in summer only (July & Aug Mon–Sat 9.30am–12.30pm & 2–6.30pm). The tourist office organizes several good bus trips up into the mountains – ask for their list.

The best and most agreeable budget **hotel** is the old-fashioned *Hôtel des Arceaux*, 26 rue Port-Neuf (☎05.59.59.15.53; ①), below the cathedral; the cheapest is the basic but adequate *Hôtel des Basques*, on place Paul-Bert (☎05.59.59.08.02; ①), for sale at the time of writing but likely to continue as a hotel. A couple of good alternatives are the *Hôtel Monbar*, at 24 rue Pannecau in Petit Bayonne (☎05.59.59.26.80; ③), and *Hôtel Paris-Madrid* (☎05.59.55.13.98, fax 05.59.55.07.22; ①), outside the train station. For something a lot smarter, try the *Hôtel Frantour Loustau*, on place de la République (☎05.59.55.08.08, fax 05.59.55.69.36; ④), overlooking the river beside Pont St-Esprit.

Another possibility is the HI **youth hostel** at 19 rte des Vignes in Anglet (see p.664), between Bayonne and Biarritz; take the STAB bus #4 from the Hôtel de Ville, direction "Biarritz-Mairie", which stops right outside. The only **campsite** nearby is *La Chêneraie* (☎05.59.55.01.31; April–Oct), off the N117 Pau road close to the Bayonne-Nord exit from the autoroute, and also on the #4 bus route; take direction "Sainsontan" and get off at Navarre, from where the campsite is a 500-metre walk. Otherwise, try one of the sites at Anglet or Biarritz.

The city

Although there are no great sights in Bayonne, it's a pleasure to wander the deep narrow streets of the old town, bisected by the river Nive and still encircled by Vauban's defences. The cathedral is on the west bank in **Grand Bayonne**, and the museums east of the river in **Petit Bayonne**.

The **Cathédrale Ste-Marie** (Mon–Sat 10am–noon & 3–6pm, Sun 3.30–6pm) on the magnolia-shaded place Pasteur, with its twin towers and steeple rising with airy grace above the houses, is best seen from a distance. Up close, the yellowish stone reveals bad weathering, with most of the decorative detail lost. Inside, its most impressive features are the height of the nave and some sixteenth-century glass, set off by the prevailing gloom. Like other southern Gothic cathedrals of the period (about 1260), it was based on more famous northern models, in this case Soissons and Reims. On the south side is a quiet, secretive **cloister** (daily 9.30am–12.30pm & 2–5/6pm; 14F) with a lawn, cypress trees and beds of begonias.

The smartest streets in town are those radiating out from the cathedral: rue d'Espagne, the old commercial centre, and rue de la Monnaie, leading into rue Port-Neuf, with its aromatic pâtisseries and *confiseries*. Behind the cathedral, along rue des Faures and the streets above the old walls, there is a distinctly Spanish feel, with washing strung at the windows and strains of music drifting from dark interiors.

Below the cathedral, the riverside **quays** of the Nive are the city's most picturesque focus, with sixteenth-century arcaded houses on the Petit Bayonne side, one of which used to contain the excellent Basque ethnographic museum, the **Musée Basque**. When it re-opens after restoration, now scheduled for 2001, the exhibits will illustrate Basque life through the centuries, and include reconstructed farm buildings, house interiors, implements, tools and the *makhilas* – a kind of walking stick, often elaborately carved from medlar wood. There's also a section on Basque seagoing activities (Columbus's skipper was a Basque), and rooms on pelota – its history and stars, and famous Basques. For now, there are temporary exhibitions you can visit.

The city's second museum, the **Musée Bonnat**, close by at 5 rue Jacques-Lafitte (Mon, Wed, Thurs, Sat & Sun 10am–noon & 2.30–6.30pm, Fri till 8.30pm; 20F), is an unexpected treasury of art, with a well-displayed array of works that includes thirteenth- and fourteenth-century Italian pictures (notably a *Virgin and Child* by Matteo di Giovanni), Brussels tapestries, paintings by Goya, Constable, Rubens, Géricault and Delacroix, and some fine society portraits by Léon Bonnat, whose personal collection formed the basis of the museum.

Apart from savouring the wide river skies, there is little to draw you to the northern bank of the Adour. There is a **synagogue** in rue Maubec, a reminder that it was here that Bayonne's Jewish community settled first on arrival from Spain. The **church of St-Esprit**, opposite the station, is all that remains of a hostel that once ministered to the sore feet and other ailments of the St-Jacques pilgrims – worth a look for an interesting wood sculpture of the *Flight into Egypt*. Just behind the station is Vauban's massive **citadelle**; built in 1680 to defend the town against Spanish attack, it actually saw little action until the Napoleonic wars, when its garrison resisted a siege by Wellington for four months in 1813. Don't miss the **Jardin Botanique** inside the castle walls, with its beautiful garden and huge collection of plants labelled in French, Basque and Latin (daily: April 15–Oct 15 9am–noon & 2–6 pm; free).

If you have a car, it's worth making an evening trip northwest through the industrial suburb of **BOUCAU** and out to the breakwater that protects the mouth of the Adour. Sit at the bar and watch the leaden-backed Atlantic rollers come in; if you are tempted to bathe from the beautiful white beach that stretches from here to Bordeaux, remember that there are lethal currents close inshore, so be extremely careful.

Eating, drinking and entertainment

Apart from the much-frequented *Café du Théâtre*, on place de la Liberté, there are no obvious major gathering points in the city. The best area for **eating and drinking** places is along the banks of the Nive in the back streets of Petit Bayonne, especially rue Pannecau, rue des Cordeliers and rue des Tonneliers.

The *Xan Xan Gorri*, a friendly and popular wine bar at 9 rue des Cordeliers, serves tapas-style food in the evenings (menus from 60F; open until 2am); the nearby *Bar des Amis*, at no. 13 (from 60F; open until 9.30pm), is a cheap and cheery local restaurant. *La Pizzeria de la Nive* on quai Jauré Guiberry does *plats du jour* for 60F as well as pizzas. More sophisticated, and with greater choice, is *Le Chistera*, at 42 rue Port-Neuf,

---

VAUBAN

Sébastien Le Prestre, Seigneur de Vauban (1633–1707), was one of the most celebrated engineers in the history of France. He's best known for his military works, both fortified towns and strong points, erected during the reign of Louis XIV as part of a strategic plan to secure the frontiers of France, particularly in the north and east. Vauban's designs are in evidence all over France, though not all the structures were actually supervised by him. Good examples of his work are the walls of Bayonne, Gravelines, Sisteron and Concarneau, and the fortesses in Belfort, Lille, Besançon, Belle-Île and Mont-Louis.

He was also known as a progressive social thinker, the author of a scheme to tax farmers in proportion to the richness of their lands – an idea which did not find favour with the king – as well as a number of improvements in the irrigation and fertilization of agricultural land.

which serves Basque specialities (from 85F). Good for a midday meal or a dawn snifter (it opens at 5am) is the *Bar du Marché*, in rue des Basques, directly opposite the market, with *plats du jour* for less than 40F. For lunch or dinner, it's worth crossing the Adour to the welcoming *Le Bistrot Ste Cluque*, near the station at 9 rue Hugues, for its wide selection and affordable prices (menus from 65F). But for a real gastronomic treat, go to *Cheval Blanc*, at 69 rue Bourgneuf, whose cheapest menu is 105F.

As far as **festivals** go, Bayonne's biggest thrash of the year is the Fêtes Traditionelles, which starts on the first Wednesday in August and consists of five days and nights of continuous boozing and entertainment. This finishes up with a *corrida* on the following Sunday, and there are three or four more days of bullfighting beginning on August 15. The jazz festival held in mid-July has become a regular feature, and every October there is a Franco-Spanish theatre festival.

Biarritz

A few minutes by rail or road from Bayonne, **BIARRITZ**, until World War II, was the Monte Carlo of the Atlantic coast, transformed by Napoléon III in the mid-nineteenth century into a playground for monarchs, aristos and glitterati. Today, however, the town has something of a faded air, and the overriding impression is of a slightly sad combination of the chic and the shabby.

The focus of Biarritz is the **Casino Municipal**, on Grande-Plage, with the rest of the town an amorphous sprawl; the only part really worth a stroll is the streets between here and the Plage du Port-Vieux. On the **place Clemenceau**, the town's main square, you can nibble a cake or sip a lemon tea at *Dodin's pâtisserie* or *Miremont's salon de thé* – prissy and frightfully superior places. To the west, the faded old-time hotels of **place Ste-Eugénie**, and **place Attalaye**, down by the port, are worth a glance, as is the workaday **rue du Port-Vieux**, nearby.

The **shore**, however, is truly beautiful. White breakers crash on sandy strands, where beautiful people bronze their limbs cheek by jowl with suburban families and ageing Californian and Australian surf bums, against a backdrop of casinos and ocean-liner hotels, Gothic castles and unfinished apartment blocks. The **beaches** – served by STAB buses #4 and #9 from Biarritz centre – extend northwards from Plage de la Milady through Plage Marbella, Côte des Basques, Plage du Port-Vieux, Grande Plage and Plage Miramar to the Pointe St-Martin. Most of the action takes place between the Plage du Port-Vieux and the huge **Hôtel du Palais** overlooking the Plage Miramar, formerly the Villa Eugénie, built by Napoléon III in the mid-nineteenth century for his wife, whom he met and courted in Biarritz.

Just beside the **Plage du Port-Vieux**, the most sheltered and intimate of the beaches, a rocky promontory sticks out into the sea, ending in an iron catwalk anchoring the **Rocher de la Vierge**, an offshore rock adorned with a white statue of the Virgin, which has become Biarritz's trademark. Around it are scattered other rocky islets where the swell heaves and combs. It seems irresistible to lovers, for the seaward view is always obscured by pairs of backs and interlocking arms apparently in thrall to the ocean. On the bluff above the Virgin stands the **Musée de la Mer** (daily: mid-July to end Aug 9.30am–midnight; rest of year 9.30am–12.30pm & 2–6pm; 45F); hardly a must, but containing interesting exhibitions on the fishing industry and the region's birds, and an aquarium of North Atlantic fish.

Just below is the picturesque harbour of the **Port des Pêcheurs,** backed by tamarisks and pink and blue hydrangeas. The fishermen have now gone, but the waterfront tapas bars have affordable snacks, or you could indulge in some good if over-priced seafood at the doughty *Chez Albert* (menus from 170F). Beyond lies the **Grande Plage**, an immaculate sweep of sand that stretches past the casino, now restored to its 1930s grandeur, all the way to the lighthouse on the Pointe St-Martin.

Practicalities

The **tourist office** is on square d'Ixelles (daily: July & Aug 8am–8pm; rest of year 9am–6.45pm; ☎05.59.22.37.10, fax 05.59.24.14.19), in the vicinity of the casino. The **gare SNCF** (☎05.59.23.15.69) is 3km away at the end of av Foch/av Kennedy in the *quartier* known as La Négresse (bus #2 or #9 from the Hôtel de Ville).

Accommodation is heavily booked in July and August, but less expensive than you might expect. Try the family-run, friendly and clean *Hôtel de la Marine*, on the corner of rue des Goélands and rue du Port-Vieux (☎05.59.24.34.09; ②); or *Hôtel Palym*, 7 rue du Port-Vieux (☎05.59.24.16.56, fax 05.59.24.96.12; ③). Slightly more expensive but superbly placed overlooking the Plage du Port-Vieux, *Le Welcome* (☎05.59.24.10.42, fax 05.59.22.18.13; ③) has a charming, English-speaking *patronne* and a restaurant, pizzeria and bar. **Campers** should try *Biarritz-Camping*, at 28 route d'Harcet, the continuation of av de la Plage (☎05.59.23.00.12, fax 05.59.43.74.67; May–Sept), behind Plage de la Milady, to the south of town. The nearest HI **youth hostel** is in Anglet (see below).

Finding a reasonable place to **eat** is not easy, but there's always the friendly *Bistrot des Halles*, on rue du Centre, by the market (around 110F); or the nearby *Bar Jean*, at 5 rue des Halles, with dishes from 40 to 60F. Alternatively, try *Crêperie Bleue de Toi*, at 30 rue Mazagran (50–60F) in the old town.

Anglet

Immediately north of Biarritz, **ANGLET** sprawls up the coast from the Pointe St-Martin to the mouth of the Adour. There is nothing to see except for two superb beaches – the **Chambre d'Amour**, so named for two lovers trapped in their trysting place by the tide, and the **Sables d'Or**, much favoured by the surfers and with boards for rental. Here, too, the swimming is very dangerous, so do heed the warning signs.

You can catch a bus here from the Hôtel de Ville in Biarritz, or walk the distance in about thirty minutes, along av de l'Impératrice, av MacCroskey, then second left down to the seaside bd des Plages. Anglet is a good place to stay if you're hostelling, with an HI **youth hostel** at 19 rte des Vignes (☎05.59.58.70.00; STAB bus #4, direction "Bayonne-Sainsontran" from Biarritz). There is also a **campsite,** *Camping de Parme*, about 3km from the beach behind the airport, served by STAB bus #6 from Biarritz or Bayonne. For **eating**, you'll either have to bring a picnic or make do with overpriced snacks and pizzas from the seaside establishments.

St-Jean-de-Luz

With its fine sandy bay and magnificent harbourfront houses, **ST-JEAN-DE-LUZ** is far and away the most attractive resort on the Basque coast, but happily has not been submerged by tourism. As the only natural harbour on the coast between Arcachon and Spain, it has been a major port for centuries, with whaling and cod fishing the traditional preoccupations of its fleets. It remains one of the busiest fishing ports in France, and the principal one for landing anchovy and tuna.

The town

The wealth and vigour of St-Jean's seafaring past is evident in the town, most notably in the surviving seventeenth- and eighteenth-century houses of the merchants and shipowners. One of the finest, adjacent to the Hôtel de Ville on the plane-tree-lined **place Louis XIV**, is the turreted **Maison Louis XIV** (June–Sept Mon–Sat 10.30am–noon & 2.30–5.30/6.30pm, Sun 2.30–5.30/6.30pm; 25F), built for the shipowning Lohobiague family in 1635, but taking its name from the fact that the young King Louis stayed here in 1660 during the preparations for his marriage to Maria Teresa, Infanta of Castile; she lodged in the equally impressive pink Italianate villa known as the **Maison de l'Infante**

(June–Sept Tues–Sat 11am–12.30pm & 2.30–6.30pm, Sun & Mon 2.30–6.30pm; 15F) overlooking the harbour on the quay of the same name. It also houses the **Musée Grévin** waxworks museum (daily: April–Oct 10am–noon & 2–6.30/8pm; rest of year 2–6pm; 37F). The corner house on rue Mazarin, nearby, was the Duke of Wellington's HQ during the 1813–14 winter campaign against Marshal Soult.

In the school-book history of St-Jean-de-Luz, the wedding of King Louis and Maria Teresa was a major event. The couple were married in the **church of St-Jean-Baptiste** on **rue Gambetta**, the main shopping street today, though the door through which they left the church has been walled up ever since. The extravagance of the event defies belief. Cardinal Mazarin alone presented the queen with 12,000 pounds of pearls and diamonds, a gold dinner service and a pair of sumptuous carriages drawn by teams of six horses – all paid for by money made in the service of France. Plain and fortress-like on the outside, the church is the biggest of all Basque churches inside, with a barn-like nave roofed in wood and lined on three sides with tiers of dark oak galleries. These are a distinctive feature of Basque churches, and were reserved for the men, while the women sat at ground level in the nave. Equally Basque is the elaborate gilded retable of tiered angels, saints and prophets behind the altar. The walled-up door through which Louis and his bride passed is on the right of the main entrance. Hanging from the ceiling is an *ex voto* model of the Empress Eugénie's paddle-steamer, *Eagle*, which narrowly escaped wrecking on the rocks outside St-Jean in 1867.

On the other side of the harbour, **CIBOURE** looks like a continuation of St-Jean but is in fact a separate commune. Its streets are even prettier, especially opposite the end of the bridge from St-Jean, the waterfront **quai Maurice-Ravel** (the composer was born at no. 12) and the parallel **rue Pocolette** behind. Wide-fronted, half-timbered, gaily painted and sometimes balconied, the houses epitomize the local Labourdian Basque style. The octagonal tower protruding above the houses belongs to the sixteenth-century **church of St-Vincent**, where you'll find more characteristic Basque galleries and a Baroque altarpiece; the entrance is in rue Pocolette through a paved courtyard with gravestones embedded in it. It is also interesting to visit the **Château d'Urtubie** (April–Oct daily except Tues 11am–noon & 2–7pm; 30F) at Urrugne, just outside Ciboure, 3 km from St-Jean-de-Luz, which has belonged to the same family since its construction as a fortified château in 1341. It was enlarged and gentrified during the sixteenth and eighteenth centuries, and provided hospitality for the French King Louis XI, as well as for Soult and later Wellington during the Napoleonic Wars. If you fancy following in their footsteps, it is also a very up-market chambres d'hôtes (☎05.59.54.31.15, fax 05.59.54.62.51; ⑤—⑧) with a restaurant offering dinner, including wine and a visit of the château, for 200F.

From the bridge, the **fish dock** sticks out into the harbour, stacked with nets and blackened lobster traps, with grubby blue-painted tuna boats, redolent of diesel oil, tied up alongside. Upstream, smaller boats lie keeled over on the tidal mud flats of the little River Nivelle against a backdrop of green fields and the emerald flanks of La Rhune (900m); to ascend the peak, catch a bus from the gare SNCF to Col de St-Ignace and Sare (2–3 buses daily; see p.667).

Practicalities

The **gare SNCF** (☎08.36.25.25.35) is on the southern edge of the centre, 500m from the beach. The **tourist office** is close by on place Maréchal-Foch, behind the Hôtel de Ville (July & Aug 9am–8pm, Sun 10.30am–1pm & 3–7pm; rest of year Mon–Sat 9am–12.30pm & 2–7pm; ☎05.59.26.03.16, fax 05.59.26.21.47). On Friday and Tuesday there is a **market** in the adjacent boulevard Victor-Hugo. **Bikes** can be rented at Luz Evasion on place Maurice-Ravel or ADO on av Labrouche, as well as at the gare SNCF. **Pelota** matches take place throughout the summer in both St-Jean and Ciboure; ask in the tourist office for details.

Opposite the train station, on and around avenue Verdun, are several reasonable **hotels**: try *Hôtel de Verdun*, 13 av de Verdun (☎05.59.26.02.55; ②, restaurant from 70F), or *Hôtel de Paris*, 1 bd du Comandant-Passicot, on the corner of av Labrouche (☎05.59.26.00.62, fax 05.59.26.90.02; ③; May–Dec). A more expensive alternative is the English-run *Hôtel Agur*, 96 rue Gambetta (☎05.59.51.91.11, fax 05.59.51.91.21; ④; April–Oct). There are numerous **campsites**, all grouped in the so-called *zone des campings* to the left of the N10 between St-Jean and Guéthary.

Leading off place Louis-XIV – with its cafés and free summertime concerts in the bandstand (daily except Mon 10pm) – rue de la République has numerous touristy **restaurants**. *Le Kaiku*, in a handsome old house at no. 17, has an excellent reputation for fish and seafood but costs upward of 200F. A slightly cheaper alternative, at no. 5 on the same street, is *La Taverne Basque*, with menus from 98F. The next street east, rue Tourasse, also has a fair selection, notably the cheerful *La Vieille Auberge*, offering Basque menus from 69F; and *Le Tourasse*, another classic for seafood and dessert (menu at 110F). It's worth searching out popular *Chez Pablo*, behind the market hall at 5 rue Mademoiselle-Etcheto, for its excellent Basque home-cooking (dishes from around 60F). In summer, *La Sardinerie* sets up on the quayside near the tourist office; dishes of tuna, sardines or omelettes cost in the region of 40–50F, though portions are somewhat small. Also well worth a visit is the laid-back *Buvette de la Halle* on the corner of the market hall on bd Victor-Hugo, run by the same family for sixty years; dishes from 40F.

Hendaye and the Spanish frontier

HENDAYE, 16km south of St-Jean-de-Luz, is the last town in France before the Spanish frontier. Neither the town itself, **Hendaye-Ville**, nor the seaside quarter, **Hendaye-Plage**, is of any intrinsic interest, though the latter has a fine, safe beach and modern tourist amenities.

The town, served by the Paris–Bordeaux–Irun main rail line, lies on the estuary of the River Bidassoa, which forms the border with Spain at this point. Just upstream, a tiny wooded island known as the **Île des Faisans** was once used as a meeting place for the monarchs of the two countries. François I, taken prisoner at the battle of Pavia in 1525, was ransomed here. In 1659 it was the scene of the signature of the Treaty of the Pyrénées and in the following year of the marriage contract between Louis XIV and Maria Teresa, when the painter Velázquez, responsible for the nuptial decor, caught the cold which resulted in his death. Another interesting encounter was the meeting between Hitler and Franco at Hendaye station on October 23, 1940, when Hitler refused to commit himself to supporting Franco's colonial claims on Morocco. You might also like to see the house in rue des Pêcheurs, on the waterfront below bd de Gaulle, where the author Pierre Loti died in 1923 (no visit, as it's privately owned), and the château of the nineteenth-century Dublin-born explorer Antoine Abbadie, on the headland overlooking Hendaye Plage, just off the Route de la Corniche (June–Sept, Mon–Sat; visits at 11am, 3, 4 & 5pm; 35F). After expeditions in Ethiopia and Egypt, Abadie had the château built between 1860 and 1870; the architect was Viollet-le-Duc, and the result is a bizarrre Scottish gothic, flanked with palm trees, with Arabian boudoirs, Ethiopian frescoes, and inscriptions over the doors and lintels inside in Irish, Basque, Arabic and Ethiopian. It is also filled with objects collected by Abdie on his travels. He became president of the Académie des Sciences in 1891, to which he donated the château on his death in 1897.

If you are planning to **stay**, hotel prices are cheapest in Hendaye-Ville. The **campsites** are mainly grouped around Hendaye-Plage; *Le Moulin*, off the D658 (between the N10 and coastal D912), is one of the cheaper options. For further information, consult the **tourist office** at 12 rue des Aubépines in Hendaye-Plage (July & Aug Mon–Sat

9am–8pm, Sun 10am–1pm; rest of year Mon–Fri 9am–12.30pm & 2–6.30pm, Sat 9am–12.30pm & 2–6pm; ☎05.59.20.00.34, fax 05.59.20.79.17).

Around Hendaye: up the coast and inland

The best thing about Hendaye is in fact getting there, for the stretch of **coast** from St-Jean south has remained miraculously unspoilt, especially in the region of the **Pointe Ste-Anne** promontory, accessible from the **Chemin Piéton Littoral** footpath, which runs parallel to the coastal D912 Corniche Basque road. It is equally accessible from the beach at Hendaye-Plage.

Inland, both trans-Pyrenean walking routes – the **GR10 and HRP** – begin their course in Hendaye-Plage at the former casino on the front. The first stage is dull and gives no sense of the glories that lie ahead: along boulevard Général-Leclerc, through the town on rue des Citronniers, under the rail line, then 50m east on the N10 before following the waymarks to the right towards the A63 autoroute. A cattle track passes underneath and continues to the tiny hilltop village of **BIRIATOU**, where the walking starts to get interesting. If you are not concerned about the romance of starting at the very beginning, splash out on a taxi and start at Biriatou. A short steep section leads to a Basque **church** with a collection of weather-worn Celtic-type tombstones, next door to the pretty *Auberge Hirribarren*, a temporary haven for many escaping Allied soldiers during World War II. From here the main footpaths and a number of local variations rise rapidly above the coast to semi-isolation, where only the buzzing power lines (soon left behind) and the occasional walker or jogger disturb the peace.

Inland: Labourd and Basse Navarre

If you don't have your own transport, the simplest forays into the soft, seductive land-scapes of the Basque hinterland are along the St-Jean-de-Luz–Sare bus route and the Bayonne–St-Jean-Pied-de-Port train lines. Either gives a representative sample of places.

La Rhune, Ascain and Sare

The 900-metre cone of **La Rhune**, on the Spanish border, is the last skyward thrust of the Pyrenees before they decline into the Atlantic. It is *the* landmark of Labourd, in spite of its unsightly TV mast, and since it is also equipped with a rack-and-pinion rail service it is predictably popular as a viewing post, offering fine vistas way up the Basque coast and east to the rising Pyrenees. Two or three **buses** a day (July & Aug Mon–Sat; winter Mon–Fri) ply the thirty-minute route from the gare SNCF in St-Jean-de-Luz, stopping at Ascain, Col de St-Ignace and Sare.

ASCAIN, where Pierre Loti wrote *Ramuntcho*, is like so many Labourd villages – pretty as a picture and in danger of caricaturing itself, with its galleried church, *fronton* and half-timbered houses. To shake off this sweetness you could walk up La Rhune from here in about two and a half hours, or take the little train from **Col de St-Ignace** (daily: July–Sept about every 35min from 8.30/9am;April–June & Oct 10am–3pm, according to demand; 40F one-way, 50F return). The ascent takes thirty minutes, but you need to allow up to two hours for the round trip. Be warned: it's a popular spot in high season.

It is worth going on to **SARE**, even if you've missed the bus. You can either walk on the **GR10** from the station just below the summit of La Rhune in about an hour-and-a-quarter or follow the road from St-Ignace in about the same time. If you plan to continue further east, you can make an overnight stop at one of the village's **hotels**: the cheapest is the *Lastiry*, on place du Fronton (☎05.59.54.20.07; ②; restaurant from 85F), or the *Trinquet Pleka* (☎05.59.54.22.06; ②). Alternatively, try *La Petite Rhune* (☎05.59.54.23.97; April–Oct), or *Goyenetche* (☎05.59.54.21.71; June–Sept) which are **campsites** just south of the village.

Instead of going back to St-Jean-de-Luz, an easy three-to-four-hour stint on the GR10 would take you on to **AINHOA** to link up with the valley of the Nive (see below). Another gem of a village, once patronized by the Duke of Windsor and now touristy in season, it consists of scarcely more than a single street lined with substantial, mainly seventeenth-century houses, whose stone lintels are carved with the dates of their construction and details of their families' history. Take a look at the heavy-towered church with its rich altarpiece of prophets and apostles in niches, framed by Corinthian columns and capped with pediments. There is a **gîte d'étape** at the *Maison Elissaldia*, by the church (☎05.59.29.25.29), whilst the cheapest hotel is the *Ur-Egian* (☎05.59.29.91.16, fax 05.59.29.91.55; ②; menu from 60F), 3km away at **Dancheria** on the Spanish frontier. **Campers** should head for *Camping Xokoan* (☎05.59.29.90.26, fax 05.59.29.73.82) which is also found at Dancheria. For a **meal**, the *Hôtel Oppoca* on Ainhoa's main street (☎05.59.29.90.72, fax 05.59.29.81.03; ③), has a good restaurant (from 125F).

The valley of the Nive

The **River Nive** is the only public-transport artery east into the Basque interior, with four or five trains a day making the riverside journey from Bayonne to St-Jean-Pied-de-Port in about an hour. The luminous green landscape on the approach to the mountains is scattered with villages untouched by speculative development, and remains as peaceful and harmonious as in the lowlands.

Cambo-les-Bains

The first major stop is **CAMBO-LES-BAINS**, an old spa town whose favourable microclimate made it an ideal centre for the treatment of tuberculosis in the last century; the locals also claim that camellias flower a month earlier here than elsewhere in the region. It is an attractive town, green and open, but suffers from the usual genteel stuffiness of spas. The "new" town, with its ornate houses and hotels, radiates out from the baths over the heights above the River Nive, while the old quarter, typically Basque with its whitewashed houses and galleried church, lies beside the river.

The main thing to see here is the **Villa Arnaga**, just out of town on the Bayonne road (daily: April–Sept 10am–12.30pm & 2.30–7pm; mid-Feb to March & Oct to mid-Nov Sat & Sun 2.30–7pm; 30F), built for Edmond Rostand, author of *Cyrano de Bergerac*, who came here to cure his pleurisy in 1903. This larger-than-life Basque house overlooks an almost surreal formal garden with discs and rectangles of water and segments of grass punctuated by blobs, cubes and cones of box, lined by limes and blue cedars, with a distant view of green hills. Inside, it's very kitsch, with a minstrels' gallery, fake pilasters, allegorical frescoes, chandeliers, numerous portraits and various memorabilia.

The **tourist office** is in the Parc St-Joseph in the upper town centre (July & Aug Mon–Sat 8.30am–noon & 2–6.30pm, Sun 10am–12.30pm; rest of year Mon–Sat till 5.30pm, closed Sun; ☎05.59.29.70.25, fax 05.59.29.90.77). For an overnight **stay**, try the *Auberge de Tante Ursule* in Bas Cambo by the pelota court (☎05.59.29.78.23, fax 05.59.29.28.57; ③; good restaurant from 90F), or, for a cheaper alternative, the *Hôtel Trinquet* (☎05.59.29.73.38, fax 05.59.29.25.61; ②). The nearest year-round **campsite** is *Ur-Hégia* on route des Sept-Chênes (☎05.59.29.72.03), also in Bas Cambo; *Camping Bixta Eder* is on the other side of town along av d'Espagne (☎05.59.29.94.23; April to mid-Oct).

Espelette and Itxassou

Buses cover the five-kilometre distance southwest from Cambo to **ESPELETTE,** a village of wide-eaved houses, with a church notable for its heavy square tower, carved doors, painted ceiling and disc-shaped gravestones. The village's principal source of renown is its large red pimentoes, much used in Basque cuisine, and its *pottok* sales. Pottoks are a small stocky Basque breed of pony, once favoured for work in British coal mines but now reared mainly for meat and riding – herds of them are a common sight on the upland pastures. The annual sales take place on the last Tuesday and Wednesday in January; the pimento jamboree takes place on the last Sunday in October. There is a very good **hotel-restaurant** in the village, too, the *Euzkadi* on the main road (☎05.59.93.91.88, fax 05.59.93.90.19; ③; restaurant closed Mon), with menus (from 90F) specializing in Basque country cooking. The *Hôtel Chilar*, on the same road, has slightly cheaper rooms (☎05.59.93.90.01, fax 05.59.93.93.25; ②).

About the same distance from Cambo-les-Bains, next stop up the rail line (though there's only one train a day), is the delightful village of **ITXASSOU**, quieter than most of the others in the area, and surrounded by green wooded hills. Nearby, the River Nive cuts through a narrow looping defile by the so-called **Pas de Roland** – hardly more than a roadside boulder with a hole in it, supposedly struck by the hooves of the great knight's horse (see box on p.670). Somewhat more arresting is the little church of St Fructueux, about 1km out on the road to the Pas de Roland, its white-plastered walls set in a lush green bowl; inside, its typical wooden galleries are worth a quick look. Even without a car, Itxassou would be a great place for a gentle recharge of the batteries, especially if you were staying at the *Etchepare* (☎05.59.29.75.14, fax 05.59.29.80.59; ③; open April–Oct); restaurant from 65F); or the *Pas du Roland* (☎05.59.29.75.23; ②) on the route de Laïxa.

St-Étienne-de-Baïgorry

The next major stop is the station of Ossès-St-Martin-d'Arrossa, where SNCF **buses** meet the trains for the eight-kilometre journey south to **ST-ÉTIENNE-DE-BAÏGORRY**. Like other Basque villages, St-Étienne is divided into quite distinct quarters, more like separate hamlets than a unified village. A prosperous, sleek place, its business is still very much agriculture rather than tourism, with the Pays Basque's only vineyards centred here, producing a good, strong red wine named Irouléguy after a neighbouring village; a local shop, on the road north to St-Jean, offers **dégustation**.

There are no great sights here. There's a seventeenth-century **church** with a sumptuous Baroque retable, a picturesque bridge posing against a backdrop of romantic castle and distant hills, and the hills themselves. St-Étienne lies in the mouth of the **Vallée des Aldudes**, with the **GR10** running along the **Cresta de Iparla** ridge to the west, the classic ridge walk of the Basque country. The GR10 goes directly up from the village, or you could hitch a ride on the D949 to the Col d'Ispéguy. There are plenty of other gentler walks, too.

The **tourist office** is opposite the church (Mon–Sat 9am–12.30 & 2.30–6/7pm, Sun 10–12.30pm & 3–6pm; ☎05.59.37.47.28). There's a good restaurant in the *Hôtel Manechenea*, beyond Lespars (☎05.59.37.41.68, fax 05.59.37.46.03; ②; restaurant from 95F; Feb–Nov). As far as campsites are concerned, there is a **camping municipal**, *Camping Irouléguy* (☎05.59.37.43.96, fax 05.59.37.48.20), on the banks of the river, and another, *Camping à la Ferme Mendy*, in the Lespars quarter to the north, with a **gîte d'étape** (☎05.59.37.42.39).

St-Jean-Pied-de-Port

The old capital of Basse Navarre, **ST-JEAN-PIED-DE-PORT** lies in a circle of hills at the foot of the Roncevaux pass into Spain. It owes its name to its position "at the foot of the *port*" – a Pyrenean word for "pass". Only part of France since the Treaty of the Pyrénées in 1659, it was an important centre for the pilgrimage to St-Jacques-de-Compostelle in the Middle Ages. The routes from Paris, Vézelay and Le Puy converged here, and it was the pilgrims' last port of call before struggling over the pass

THE CHANSON DE ROLAND

Roland, with his sword Durandal, is the hero of the medieval **Chanson de Roland**. But he was also a historical character, warden of the Breton marches, who in 778 accompanied the Emperor Charlemagne on a campaign against the Moors in Spain, in the course of which the Navarrese capital of Pamplona was sacked. In revenge, the Basques ambushed and decimated Charlemagne's rearguard, commanded by Roland, as it withdrew through the gorges above Roncevaux. The *chanson* has it that infidel Saracens were the dastardly foe, but this was propaganda designed to make poor Roland's end more heroic.

to the Spanish monastery of Roncesvalles (Roncevaux in French), where Roland, Charlemagne's general celebrated in medieval romance, sounded his horn in vain (see above).

The town lies on the River Nive, enclosed by walls of pinky-red sandstone. Above it rises a wooded hill crowned by the inevitable Vauban **fortress**, while to the east a further defensive system guards the road to Spain. The more recent overspill, pleasant but unremarkable, spreads down across the main road onto lower ground.

The **old town** consists of a single cobbled street, **rue de la Citadelle**, running downhill from the fifteenth-century **Porte St-Jacques** – so named because it was the gate by which the pilgrims entered the town – to the **Porte d'Espagne**, commanding the bridge over the Nive, with a view of balconied houses overlooking the stream. Many of the painted houses bear inscriptions on their lintels from the sixteenth, seventeenth and eighteenth centuries. A fourteenth-century plain red church, **Notre-Dame-du-Bout-du-Pont**, stands beside the Porte d'Espagne and, opposite, a short street leads through the **Porte de Navarre** to place de-Gaulle and the modern road. Just to the north, beyond the dusky-pink Hôtel de Ville, is the *Jaï alaï* stadium where a bare-handed **pelota match** – the most macho kind – is held every Monday at 5pm (40–50F).

The **tourist office** is in place de-Gaulle (July & Aug Mon–Sat 9am–12.30pm & 2–7pm, Sun 10.30am–12.30pm & 3–6pm; rest of year Mon–Sat 9am–noon & 2–7pm; ☎05.59.37.03.57). The **gare SNCF** is at the end of av Renaud, on the northern edge of the centre. Among **hotels** in town, the *Remparts*, 16 place Floquet (☎05.59.37.13.79, fax 05.59.37.33.44; ②; restaurant from 85F), just before you cross the Nive coming into town on the Bayonne road, is the cheapest; more expensive are the *Ramuntcho*, just inside the city walls at 1 rue de France (☎05.59.37.03.91, fax 05.59.37.35.17; ③), with a good and reasonably priced restaurant from 80F; *Hôtel Itzalpea*, 5 place du Trinquet (☎05.59.37.03.66, fax 05.59.37.33.18; ②; restaurant from 60F); and *Hôtel Central* on place de Gaulle (☎05.59.37.00.22, fax 05.59.37.27.79; ④; restaurant from 98F; mid-Feb to mid-Dec). There is also a **gîte d'étape** at 9 rte d'Uhart, on the Bayonne road (M. Etchegoin; ☎05.59.37.12.08), and a **camping municipal** (☎05.59.37.11.19, fax 05.59.37.99.78; April to mid-Oct) on the south bank of the Nive, beside the *fronton*; as well as the *Arradoy* (☎05.59.37.11.75; March–Sept).

Walks around St-Jean

Numerous tracks lead south from St-Jean up into the mountains towards the Spanish border. It is sheep country, and if you are interested in getting an idea of what the old pastoral life was like, this is a good place to do it. If you are a walker, the last leg of the **GR65** pilgrim route starts from St-Jean and follows the line of the old Roman road across to Spanish Asturia.

Follow rue d'Espagne in St-Jean out through the city walls. The waymarks begin on the first telephone pole on the left. A little further on you turn up a lane to the right (called the Maréchal Harispe 1768-1855); the GR10 and GR65 run together here. Follow the lane, between grassy banks, past fields and isolated farms. The farmhouses have immensely broad roofs, one side short, the other long enough to cover space for stalls and tools; it's all very quiet and rural, with long views out across the valleys. The climb becomes steeper above a little group of houses known as **HOUNTO**. It is no good asking the way, even if you can find someone to ask, as the Basque names are impossible to pronounce if you don't know the language, and everyone speaks French. Above Hounto you come out on top of a grassy spur. The GR65 turns left up what looks like an old drove road to rejoin the tarmac higher up by two small sheds at the edge of beech woods. It is about two hours to these sheds. You get your first glimpse of the higher Pyrenean peaks to the east. Above the trees you come out on grassy uplands dotted with sheepfolds or *cayolars*.

The route continues along the track to a fork (3hr 30min) with a small white statue of the Virgin. Here, the GR65 turns right towards Spain (another 90min) and the GR10 turns left. For a while it follows the road before veering away to the right to Béhérobie (see below), while the road continues its twisting descent to the tiny hamlet of Esterençuby (see below), then down along the Nive and back to St-Jean-Pied-de-Port.

East of St-Jean

The **GR65** passes to the north of the espadrille-manufacturing town of **MAULÉON**, about 30km east of St-Jean, but if you are vaguely following the pilgrim route by car, then the road from St-Jean through Col d'Osquich and on towards Navarrenx is the most attractive to take.

There are two reasonable and agreeable **hotels** just west of Ordiarp at Musculdy: *Hôtel du Col d'Osquich* (☎05.59.37.81.23, fax 05.59.37.86.81; ②; restaurant from 80F; open June–Oct) and *Hôtel le Chistera* (☎05.59.28.06.74; ①; restaurant from 80F), where the rooms are peacefully situated in the old hotel in the village centre, but for the key and meals you have to go to the smart new restaurant of the same name just outside the village. There is also a riverside **campsite**, *Uhaitza Le Saison* (☎05.59..28.18.79; April–Sept), just outside Mauléon on the Tardets road, and another, *Le Landran* (Easter–Oct), at Ordiarp, back towards the Col d'Osquich.

Into the mountains

Le bout du monde – "the end of the earth" – is what they used to call the tiny settlement of **Ste-Engrâce**, locked in its cul-de-sac valley beneath the Spanish frontier at the easternmost extremity of the Basque country. And, although a new road has been built, the

---

TRANSHUMANCE

Like other shepherds in southern or Mediterranean climes, the Basques are forced to take their flocks to the high **mountain pastures** in summer in search of better grazing. They live out on the mountainside in stone huts with a couple of dogs, milking the ewes twice a day and making cheese, the *fromage de brebis*, whose soft and hard versions are a speciality throughout the pastoral Pyrenees. Most of the pastures today are accessible by car, at least at the gentler Basque end of the Pyrenees, so the shepherd's life is not as isolated as it used to be – though there are still areas in the higher mountains that are only accessible with mules or ponies. A measure of the pre-eminence of sheep in the Basque economy is the Basque word for "rich", *aberats* – whose literal meaning is "he who owns large flocks".

Much of the grazing is owned in common by various communes, who have over the centuries made elaborate agreements to ensure a fair share of the best pasture and avoid disputes. One of the oldest of these *faceries*, as they are called, concluded by the inhabitants of Roncal and Baretous in 1375, is still in force, renewed each year on payment of three white heifers.

place still feels very remote, especially if you've approached it over the hills from St-Jean-Pied-de-Port, either on foot by the GR10 or along the tortuous lane that accompanies it. There are no shops, no hotels, and no villages except **Larrau**. It's a land of open skies, where griffon vultures turn on the thermals without so much as a flick of their huge wings, of countless flocks of sheep and thousands of hectares of whispering beech woods. Although the overall distance is not very great, the slowness of the road and the grandeur of the scenery seem to magnify it. There is no public transport. Carrying a tent would give you the greatest flexibility: no-one objects if you pitch it discreetly, and to be on the safe side you can always ask the nearest shepherd. For the latest on **weather information** in the western Pyrenees, call ☎08.36.68.02.64.

Éstérençuby, Béhérobie and the Col d'Errozaté

From St-Jean-Pied-de-Port, the D301 follows the deepening valley of the Nive for 8km, past small red- and green-shuttered farms to the village of ÉSTÉRENÇUBY, and on a further 4 or 5km to **BÉHÉROBIE**. The river, now no more than a mountain stream, runs sparkling down between steep green slopes, whose only crops are hay and bracken. In late June and early July, entire families are out on the mountainside, scything the meadows or turning the sweet-smelling hay with wooden rakes. In the farmyards, stacks of bracken impaled on wooden stakes are dried for winter bedding.

At Béhérobie, the road climbs up to the right to the border and the **Col d'Arnostéguy**. In the valley bottom beside the infant Nive, the only building is the *Hôtel de la Nive* (☎05.59.37.10.57; ②; closed Jan; restaurant from 60F), invariably booked out in October for the wood-pigeon shooting season, but with a terrace overhanging the river, making a marvellous place for a quiet stay. There is an equally attractive hotel a little way back towards Estérençuby, the *Artzain-Etchea* (☎05.59.37.11.55, fax 05.59.37.20.16; ②; restaurant from 60F).

Just before the bridge at Béhérobie, a lane keeps up to the left, then drops down to cross a tributary stream of the Nive by an ancient barn and cottage with beautiful shady pools to bathe in: this is the **GR10**. To the right, a secondary path heads into the beech woods, bringing you to the bank of the Nive in about half an hour – a fantastic picnic spot – while the GR10 itself bears left over a bridge by the cottage, before climbing back to the right, contouring high along the sides of the valley until, after about an hour, you emerge above the tree line in a huge ravine of shining knee-deep grass. If you feel like continuing, it's another hour to the **Col d'Errozate** (1076m), or two hours to the summit of **Errozaté** (1345m).

The Iraty Forest

A kilometre or so on the Esterençuby side of Béhérobie, a lane turns up left towards the **Forêt d'Iraty**. It is very steep and full of tight hairpins, but, as you climb higher up the steep spurs and round the heads of labyrinthine gullies, ever more spectacular views open beneath you. You can see way back over the valley of the Nive, St-Jean and the hills beyond. Stands of beech fill the gullies, shadowing the lighter grass whose green is so intense it seems almost theatrical – an effect produced, apparently, by the juxtaposition of outcrops of rock whose purplish hue brings out the cadmium yellow in the grass.

Along the cols and ridges stand ranks of shooting butts, from which the well-heeled urban bourgeoisie open fire every October on the millions of migrating *palombes*, as they call wood pigeons in the southwest, heading north over the western Pyrenees from Spain. Many other species (not destined to be eaten) can be seen too; among them honey buzzards, black kites, red kites, cranes and storks. Herds of healthy-looking horses and ponies and big sleek caramel cows with bells at their throats on wooden collars marked with their owners' names wander across the road. Flocks of white sheep graze on the hillsides. There are superb places to camp, with views west to the orange and crimson striations of the sunset and the revolving beacon of the Biarritz lighthouse visible in the dark.

Over the col below **Occabé** (1456m) the road loops down past scattered sheepfolds to the **plateau d'Iraty**, where there is a small lake and a snack bar, and flat ground to camp on. A road leads south to Ochagavia in Spain via the **Chalet Pedro** (1km), where the GR10 swings right and up onto the flat-topped Occabé (90min), with its Iron Age **stone circle** and views across the forest and south to the Sierra de Abodi. Continuing east from the plateau, the road enters the densest part of the forest, climbing past a **campsite** half hidden in the magnificent beeches, to an unsightly collection of chalets at the **Col de Bargaguiac** (gîte d'étape: ☎05.59.28.51.29) and the **Col d'Orgambideska**, which is one of the prime viewing fields for the autumn bird migrations – it's now declared a protected area. As you come over the top, the ground drops sharply away into the **Vallée de Larrau**, 600m lower. To the right, the brilliant grassy swards of the **Pic d'Orhy** (2017m) culminate in swirling strata of rock below the summit, barring the way to Spain. And ahead, for the first breath-stopping time, you see the serrated horizon of peaks that dominate the **Cirque de Lescun**, a harbinger of the central Pyrenees.

Larrau, the gorges and Ste-Engrâce

The first thing you notice coming into **LARRAU** from the west is how different the architecture is. In contrast to the gaily painted facades and tiled roofs of Labourd and Basse Navarre, the houses here are grey and stuccoed, with slate roofs, the mood secretive and inward-looking. And, although it's the biggest place since St-Jean-Pied-de-Port, it is nonetheless very small and quiet – almost dead out of season.

There are two friendly and simple **hotels**: the *Hôtel Etchémaïté* (☎05.59.28.61.45, fax 05.59.28.72.71; ①; good restaurant from 75F; closed late Jan), and *Hôtel Despouey* (☎05.59.28.60.82; ①; open March–Oct). There are two **campsites** in Larrau, the *Iraty* (☎05.59.28.51.29, fax 05.59.28.72.38; June–Oct) and the *Ixtila* (☎05.59.28.63.09; April to mid-Nov) and a **gîte d'étape** 3km away at **LOGIBAR** (☎05.59.28.61.14), close to the mouth of the **Gorges d'Holzarte** – one of several in the region, cutting deep into northern slopes of the ridge that forms the frontier with Spain. A short track leads from Logibar across the turbulent and freezing stream to a car park, from where a steep path, part of the GR10, climbs through the beech woods to the junction of the Holzarte gorge with the Olhadybia in about one hour. Slung across the mouth of the latter is a spectacular Himalayan-style **suspension bridge**, which bounces and swings dizzily as you walk out over the 180-metre drop. The **GR10** continues to Ste-Engrâce in seven hours, or down to the beginning of the Gorges de Kakouetta in about six. But it is definitely worth coming this far; in June and July, the open spaces are full of flowers – columbines, cranesbills, orchids and vetches and, if you're lucky, you might see the beautiful, long-stemmed *bimbette des Pyrénées*.

The Gorges de Kakouetta and Gorges d'Ehujarré

Ten kilometres east of Larrau, you reach the **Gorges de Kakouetta** (Easter–Nov daily 8am–nightfall; 20F) by turning right off the D26 and down the D113. Just over halfway down, the minuscule hamlet of **LA CASERNE** is the site of the only **food shop** for kilometres around – opposite the mairie – and the *Ibarra* **campsite** (June–Sept). Kakouetta is on the tourist trail, but do not be put off: the gorge is truly dramatic and, outside peak season, is not crowded at all. It pays to be well-shod, for the path is precarious and very slippery in places; you are glad of the handrail. The walls of the gorge are very high – up to 300m and scarcely more than 5m apart – and are jungle-thick with luxuriant vegetation that thrives on the hothouse atmosphere produced by the myriad seepages and waterfalls that fill the air with a fine spray, refracting and filtering what sunlight gets in. There is a range of ferns that you wouldn't expect to see outside a houseplant nursery. The path continues for about an hour (2km) with a small cave at the end and just before it a full-blown waterfall spewing out of a hole in the rock.

There is a third gorge, the **Gorges d'Ehujarré**, a short distance southeast of La Caserne at Senta, the easternmost of the three hamlets that comprise Ste-Engrâce (see below). It's a straightforward walk – the route has been used for centuries for moving sheep up to the pastures of Pic Lakhoura – but requires about seven hours.

Ste-Engrâce and around

STE-ENGRÂCE remains a beautifully remote and peaceful little collection of houses spread in three little clusters along the main road, enclosed by hay meadows and green mountainsides. It is largely untroubled by the rhythms of the twentieth century, although the main road now continues east over the head of the valley, reducing its isolation. Life is not so simple for the locals: there is no work and the young won't stay, but for the outsider not caught in the rural poverty trap, it has great charm. Its hallmark is the eleventh-century Romanesque **church** in the hamlet of **SENTA**, which features in all the coffee-table books on the Pyrenees. It stands just as it should, with its heavily buttressed walls, belfry and penthouse roof, a sharply defined and angular assertion of humanity against the often mist-shrouded bulwarks of the mountains behind. Very simple inside, it has some good carved capitals, and the graveyard is full of traditional disc-shaped headstones.

There's a **gîte d'étape** (☎05.59.28.61.63) opposite the church, with an adjacent field to pitch a tent, and a **café-bar** that will serve meals. There's also the *Hôtel de la Pierre-St-Martin* (☎05.59.28.63.12, fax 05.59.28.71.71; ②; restaurant from 70F) at Calla.

Arette-la-Pierre-St-Martin and around

The new road up to the typically ugly modern ski resort of **ARETTE-LA-PIERRE-ST-MARTIN** gives fabulous views of the valley of Ste-Engrâce, through magnificent forests of pine and beech, though if the cloud is down, which it often is, you'll be lucky to see much at all. Just south of the resort is the **Col de la Pierre-St-Martin**, where every July 13 the mayors of Barétous and Roncal exchange heifers in renewal of an ancient grazing treaty (see box on p.671). Also nearby is the **Gouffre de la Pierre-St-Martin**, at 728m one of the deepest potholes in the world, but covered by a grill to prevent accidents. To the east begins the descent into the valley of the Aspe, which belongs to the ancient county of Béarn.

THE CENTRAL PYRENEES

The area immediately east of the Pays Basque – the **Central Pyrenees** – is home to the area's highest mountain peaks and is the most spectacular part of the region. The southernmost part is protected, contained within the **Parc National des Pyrénées Occidentales**. Getting to the area is simple enough, at least as far as the foothill towns, by train on the Bayonne–Toulouse line. But travelling around once there can be very slow. The few buses – and most other traffic – keep to the north–south valleys, which is frustrating when you want to switch from one valley system to the next without having to come all the way out of the mountains each time.

The **GR10** provides a good link if you are ready to walk all the way, and it's possible to hitch, at least up the valleys and across the main passes at **Col d'Aubisque** and **Col du Tourmalet**, though you will find you invariably get left on the top by drivers, who come up for the view and go back the same way.

Highlights – apart from the lakes, torrents, forests and 3000-metre peaks around **Cauterets** – are the *cirques* of **Lescun**, **Gavarnie** and **Troumouse**, each with its distinctive character. And for less hearty interests, there is many a flower-starred mountain meadow accessible by car, in which to quaff and gorge on a well-chosen picnic. The only real urban centres are **Pau**, which you may use as your entry point to the area, dull **Tarbes**, and the tacky pilgrimage target of **Lourdes**. Great monuments of the bricks-and-mortar kind – with the exception of the fortified church at **Luz-St-Sauveur** – are equally scarce.

The Parc National des Pyrénées Occidentales

The **Parc National des Pyrénées Occidentales** was created in 1968 to protect at least part of the high Pyrenees from the development brought about by modern tourism – ski resorts, roads, mountain-top restaurants, car parks and other amenities. It runs for more than 100km along the Spanish border, from the Pic de Labigouer, south of Lescun, in the west, to beyond the Pic de la Munia, east of Gavarnie. Varying in altitude between 1070m and 3298m at its highest point, Vignemale, south of Cauteret, the park takes in the spectacular cirques of Gavarnie and Troumouse, as well as over two hundred lakes, six valleys and more than 350km of marked walking routes.

Through the banning of hunting – apart from the traditional mountain peasants' pursuit of poaching or *braconnage* – it has also provided sanctuary for many rare and endangered species of birds and mammals. Among them are chamois, marmots, genets, griffon vultures, golden eagles, eagle owls and capercaillies, to say nothing of the rich and varied flora. The most celebrated animal – and the most depleted by hunting – is the Pyrenean brown bear, whose prewar numbers ran to as many two hundred, but now amount to barely a dozen individuals. Although largely herbivorous, bears will take the occasional sheep or cow, and the mountain shepherd communities are their remorseless enemies. To appease them, the park pays prompt and generous compensation for any losses, but this is not always enough to overcome the atavistic fear of the bear. In recent years the park has been embroiled in bitter controversy between environmentalists and partisans of the construction of the Zaragoza–Bordeaux autoroute along the Vallée d'Aspe. It has also been criticized for not doing enough to protect the bears – an accusation which angers the hard-pressed rangers, who complain that distant planners have no conception what it is really like trying to reconcile legitimate local economic needs with the protection of wild species and unsullied landscapes, to say nothing of coping with the litter, wear and tear on footpaths, illicit camping, and other problems caused by modern tourism.

The **GR10** runs through the entire park on its 700-kilometre journey from coast to coast, starting at Argelès-sur-Mer on the Mediterranean and ending up at Hendaye-Plage on the Atlantic shore; the tougher trail of the **Haute Randonnée Pyrénéenne** (HRP) also finishes its course in Hendaye-Plage and closely shadows the GR10, but takes in much more rugged terrain. Hikers are strongly advised to wear appropriate clothing, carry detailed maps and guides, and heed the words of warning on p.658. This terrain is not the place for an easy stroll.

There are **Maisons du Parc** in Cauterets, Gavarnie, Gabas and Etsaut, giving information about the park's wildlife and vegetation, lists of accommodation options and the best walks to do. There are over twenty refuges and plenty of hotels, campsites and hostels throughout the park, listed in the text of this chapter and highlighted on the map on p.676. For an update on weather conditions in the Hautes-Pyrénées, telephone ☎08.36.68.02.65.

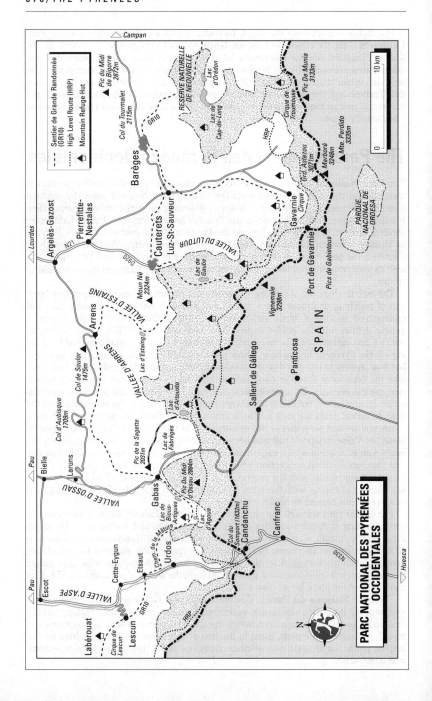

PARC NATIONAL DES PYRÉNÉES OCCIDENTALES

Sentier de Grande Randonnée (GR10)
High Level Route (HRP)
Mountain Refuge Hut

10 km
0

Campan

Pic du Midi de Bigorre 2872m
Col du Tourmalet 2115m
Lac d'Orédon
RESERVE NATURELLE DE NÉOUVIELLE
Lac de Cap-de-Long
Pic De Munia 3133m
Cirque de Troumouse
HRP
Marboré 3248m
Mte. Perdido 3335m
Grd. Astezou 3071m
Barèges
GR10
Cirque Cirque de Gavarnie
Gavarnie
PARQUE NACIONAL DE ORDESA
Port de Gavarnie
Pics de Gabietous
Cauterets
Luz-St-Sauveur
Pierrefitte-Nestalas
Argelès-Gazost
Lourdes
N21
D920
Moun Né 2324m
VALLÉE DU LUTOUR
Lac de Gaube
Vignemale 3298m
SPAIN
Arrens
VALLÉE D'ESTAING
Lac d'Estaing
Col de Soulor 1475m
VALLÉE D'ARRENS
Panticosa
Sallent de Gállego
Lac d'Artouste
Col d'Aubisque 1709m
Pic de la Sagette 2031m
Lac de Fabrèges
Pau
Bielle
Larnus
VALLÉE D'OSSAU
Gabas
Pic Du Midi d'Ossau 2884m
Lac de Bious-Artigues
Lac d'Ayous
Col du Somport (1632m)
Candanchu
Canfranc
N330
Huesca
Pau
Escot
Cette-Eygun
Etsaut
Urdos
chem. de la Mâture
VALLÉE D'ASPE
GR10
Labérouat
Lescun
Cirque de Lescun
HRP

N

Pau and around

From humble beginnings as a crossing on the Gave de Pau for flocks en route to and from the mountains, **PAU** became the capital of the ancient viscountcy of Béarn in 1464, and of the French part of the kingdom of Navarre in 1512. In 1567 its sovereign, Henri d'Albret, married the sister of the king of France, Marguerite d'Angoulême, friend and protector of artists and intellectuals and herself the author of a celebrated Boccaccio-like tale (the *Heptameron*), who transformed the town into a centre of the arts and nonconformist thinking.

Their daughter was Jeanne d'Albret, an ardent Protestant, whose zeal offended her own subjects as well as attracting the wrath of the Catholic king of France, Charles X, thus embroiling Béarn in the Wars of Religion – whose resolution, albeit only temporary, had to await the accession to the French throne of her own son, Henri IV, in 1589. An adroit politician, he renounced his faith to facilitate this transition, quipping that "Paris is worth a Mass" and then appeasing the regional sensibilities of his Béarnais subjects by announcing that he was giving France to Béarn rather than Béarn to France. He did not incorporate Béarn into the French state; that was left to his son and successor, Louis XIII, in 1620. As Pau's most famous son, Henri acquired a suitably colourful reputation. He was baptized in traditional Béarnais style with the local Juraçon wine and his infant lips were rubbed with garlic. In his adult life he was known as the *vert-galant* for his prowess as a lover. He also gave France one of its more famous recipes, *poule au pot* – chicken stuffed and boiled with vegetables: he is reputed to have said that he did not want anyone in his realm to be so poor as not to be able to afford a *poule* in the *pot* once a week.

The least-expected thing about Pau is its English connection, which dates from the arrival of Wellington and his troops after the defeat of Marshal Soult at Orthez in 1814. Seduced by its climate and persuaded of its curative powers by the Scottish doctor Alexander Taylor, the English flocked to Pau throughout the nineteenth century, bringing along their peculiar cultural obsessions – fox-hunting, horse racing, polo, croquet, cricket, golf (the first eighteen-hole course in continental Europe in 1860 and the first in the world to admit women), tearooms and parks. When the rail line opened in 1866, the French came, too: writers and artists like Victor Hugo, Stendhal and Lamartine, as well as the socialites. The first French rugby club opened here in 1902, after which the sport spread throughout the southwest. In the 1950s, natural gas was discovered at nearby Lacq, bringing new jobs and subsidiary industries, as well as massive production of acid pollution, now reduced by filtration but still substantial. In addition, there is a well-respected university.

Pau is within easy reach of numerous small, picturesque villages in **northwest Béarn**, as well as the FR65 footpath that runs some 60km down to the Spanish border.

Arrival, information and accommodation

Pau's international **airport** (information ☎05.59.33.33.00) has direct flights to London and Paris. The town lies on the A64 *Pyrénéenne* autoroute and on the main east–west rail route, with connections to Bayonne and Biarritz in the west, and Lourdes, Tarbes and Toulouse in the east, as well as to Bordeaux and Paris. The **gare SNCF** is on the southern edge of the city centre, across avenue Jean-Biray: SNCF buses leave from here, and private buses from the **gare routière** in rue Gachet, off place Clemenceau. **Buses** run south down the Vallée d'Ossau and to Oloron-Ste-Marie, with connections to the Vallée d'Aspe. A **free funicular** carries you up from the train station to the boulevard des Pyrénées, opposite place Royale, at the far end of which is the **tourist office** (July & Aug 9am–6pm; rest of year Mon–Sat 9am–12.30pm & 1.30–6pm;

☎05.59.27.27.08, fax 05.59.27.03.21). For information on walking and climbing try the local CAF, 5 rue Fournets (☎05.59.27.71.81), while *the Librairie des Pyrénées*, in rue St-Louis, stocks a wide range of books on the mountains.

For a very friendly, cheap and quiet **hotel**, try the *Hôtel d'Albret*, 11 rue Jeanne-d'Albret, close to the castle (☎05.59.27.81.58; ①). Two good alternatives that are equally central are the *Hôtel le Matisse*, 17 rue Mathieu-Lalanne, opposite the Musée des Beaux-Arts (☎05.59.27.73.80; ①), and the *Pomme d'Or* on rue Maréchal Foch (☎05.59.27.78.48; ①). A bit more comfort is available at the *Commerce* at 9 rue Maréchal-Joffre (☎05.59.27.24.40, fax 05.59.83.81.74; ③; restaurant 95–150F), or the *Colbert*, a few blocks north off rue Montpensier at 1 rue Manescau (☎05.59.32.52.78, fax 05.59.32.68.38; ②). For **youth hostels**, there's one at 30 rue Michel-Hounau (☎05.59.72.61.00), the HI *Logis des Jeunes* in the Base de Plein Air at Gelos (☎05.59.06.53.02), just over the river, and the *Maison Européenne de la Jeunesse*, 18 rue Bourbaki, at the end of rue Montpensier (☎05.59.62.50.50; canteen). The *Logis des Jeunes* also has a **campsite** (June–Sept), and there is a municipal one on bd du Cami-Salie, off av Sallenave towards the autoroute, on the northern edge of town (☎05.59.02.30.49; June–Sept).

The town

Pau has no great sights or museums, enabling you to enjoy its relaxed and friendly elegance without any sense of guilt. The parts to wander are the streets behind the **boulevard des Pyrénées**, especially the western end, which stretches along the rim of the scarp above the Gave de Pau, from the castle to the casino in the English-style **Parc Beaumont**. On a clear day, the view from the boulevard is out of this world, encompassing a ninety-kilometre sweep of the highest Pyrenean peaks, with the distinctive Pic du Midi d'Ossau slap in front of you.

In the narrow streets around the castle and down in the gully of the Chemin du Hédas are numerous cafés, restaurants, bars and boutiques, with the main **market** in the *halles* on place de la République each Saturday morning. The **château** itself (daily 9.30–11.45am & 2–5.15pm; guided tours only; 25F) is very much a landmark building. Not much remains of its original appearance beyond the brick keep built by Gaston Fébus in 1370. The handsome Renaissance windows and other details on the inner courtyard were added by Henri d'Albret. Louis-Philippe renovated it in the nineteenth century after it had stood empty for two hundred years, and Napoléon III and Eugénie titivated it further to make it suitable for weekend house parties. The visitable apartments are essentially theirs, with some fine tapestries and bits of Henri-IV memorabilia, like the turtle shell that allegedly served him for a cradle, while the ethnographic **Musée Béarnais** (same hours as the château; 10F) on the top floor has a good collection of costumes, Pyrenean animals, birds, butterflies and objects illustrating pastoral life.

A short distance northeast of the château, the mildly interesting **Musée Bernadotte**, 5 rue Tran (daily except Mon 10am–noon & 2–6pm; 10F), is the birthplace of the man who, having served as one of Napoléon's commanders, went on to become Charles XIV of Sweden. As well as fine pieces of traditional Béarnais furniture, the house contains some valuable works of art collected over his lifetime. Pau's other museum, the **Musée des Beaux-Arts** in rue Mathieu-Lalanne (daily except Tues 10am–noon & 2–6pm; 10F), has a splendidly eclectic collection of works, including Spanish, Italian, Dutch and French schools, and works by El Greco, Rubens and Degas.

Eating and drinking

Of the several **restaurants** in the area of the château, *La Brochetterie*, 7 rue Henri-IV, serves good grills and fish in a pleasant, family atmosphere for around 100F à la carte, or from 79F for a *menu fixe*. *La Taverne du Roy*, 7 rue de la Fontaine, on the north side of the Hédas gully (closed Sun & Mon), offers more interesting Spanish-influenced menus from 86F; or, if Chinese food takes your fancy, there's the excellent *Kim Lien* in rue de Foix, with menus from 68F, or the *Lotus d'Or*, 1 place Grammont, with menus from 85F. Other inexpensive possibilities include the lunchtime-only *Royalty*, 4 rue Serviez (menus from 40F), crêpes and salads at *Chez Maman*, 6 rue du Château (*plat du jour* from 35F), and decent pizzas at the *Taste-Croûte*, 16 rue Latapie (menus from 50F). For an Indian meal, the *Poppadum* by the château is cheap and good, while *l'Entracte* in rue St Louis has a good variety of original salads. For a bit of a splash without breaking the bank, try *La Gousse d'Ail*, 12 rue du Hédas (closed Sat noon & Sun), with traditional French menus from 96F, or near the station, *Au Fin Gourmet*, 24 av Gaston-Lacoste (menus from 85F). Brasseries include the *Belvedere* at 22 bd des Pyrénées, and the popular *Le Berry* on rue Gachet (☎05.59.27.42.95). Arrive early to be sure of a table or be prepared to queue, but it's worth the wait to sample their demi-Chateaubriand with *sauce béarnaise* (44F).

For drinking, *O'Gascon*, a small bar on the corner of rue Bordenave-d'Abère and rue du Château, is fun, as are *El Rio Loco*, at 23 rue Tran, and *Bar de la Poste*, in cours Bosquet.

Around Pau

One excursion worth making, particularly for families with children, is to the **Grottes de Bétharram** (March 25–Oct 25 daily 8.30am–noon & 1.30–5.30pm; 48F) at St-Pé-de-Bigorre, just off the D938/937 between Pau and Lourdes, 14km from the latter. Part of the eighty-minute tour to admire its spectacular stalactites and stalagmites takes place in a barge on an underground lake; the remaining kilometre is by miniature railway.

Thirty kilometres northwest of Pau, **ORTHEZ** was the original capital of Béarn, its wealth due in large part to its beautiful and still-surviving thirteenth-century **fortified bridge**, which controlled the most important commercial route across the Gave de Pau for English and Flemish textiles, Aragonese wool, olive oil and wine. It was also a major centre on the pilgrim routes to Compostella; the modern route, the **GR65**, crosses the river just 8km east of Orthez at Argagnon, and you can follow it 60km south to the Spanish frontier. The town also serves as a gateway to the hinterland of the Pays Basque: SNCF buses run from Puyôo, 12km west, to Salies-de-Béarn, Sauveterre and Mauléon.

The **tourist office** (July & Aug Mon–Sat 9am–12.30pm & 2–7pm, Sun 9.30am–12.30pm; rest of year Mon–Sat 9am–noon & 2–5/6pm; ☎05.59.69.02.75, fax 05.59.69.12.00) occupies the sixteenth-century **Maison Jeanne d'Albret**, and there are other fine old houses in the centre of town, especially in **rue Moncade**. The **church of St-Pierre**, close to the tourist office, still has some interesting Gothic sculptures, though it was badly damaged when the town was sacked by Jeanne d'Albret's Protestant general Montgomery in 1569. Should you need to **stay** overnight, there is the *Hôtel Terminus*, 14 rue St-Gilles (☎05.59.69.02.07; ①), and a **campsite**, *La Source* (☎05.59.67.04.81, fax 05.59.69.12.00; April–Oct), on the east side of the town.

Fifteen kilometres from Orthez (TPR bus from Pau), **SALIES-DE-BÉARN** is a typical Béarnais village of winding lanes and flower-decked houses with brightly painted woodwork. The River Saleys, hardly more than a stream, runs through the middle of it, separating the old village from the nineteenth-century development that sprang up to exploit the saline waters for which it has long been famous. It is a charming, if unremarkable place, good for an overnight stop, with a **camping municipal** (☎05.59.38.12.94; mid-March to mid-Oct), and a tiny HI **youth hostel** (☎05.59.38.29.66), both next to the rugby pitch.

Heading south again, the D933 winds over hilly farming country to **SAUVETERRE-DE-BÉARN**, another pretty country town beautifully sited on a scarp high above the Gave d'Oloron. From the terrace by the thirteenth-century **church** you look down over the river and the remains of another fortified bridge. At the end of the terrace a ruined **castle** dominates the steep slope, its empty joist sockets making perfect pigeon holes. For **accommodation**, there is the *Hostellerie du Château* in rue Léon-Bérard (☎05.59.38.52.10, fax 05.59.38.96.49; ②; closed mid-Jan to mid-Feb), and a **camping municipal** by the bridge (☎05.59.38.53.30; May–Sept).

Just across the river, the D936 bears left along the flat valley bottom to **NAVAR-RENX**, 18km away on the Pau–Mauléon bus route, an old-fashioned market town built as a *bastide* in 1316 and still surrounded by its ancient **walls**; you enter by the fortified **Porte St-Antoine**. The pleasure of the place is its sleepy rural atmosphere. The *Hôtel du Commerce* by the Porte St-Antoine (☎05.59.66.50.16, fax 05.59.66.52.67; ③; mid-Jan to mid-Oct; excellent restaurant from 60F), makes an agreeable place to **stay**, and there's also a **camping municipal** in allée des Marronniers (☎05.59.66.10.00, fax 05.59.66.11.01; April to mid-Sept).

The **GR65** passes through the town. You pick up the markers on the telephone poles in Susmiou at the western end of the bridge. Turn left over the bridge on the Mauléon road, then right on a back road shortly after. The path meanders west, following byroads, farm tracks and footpaths to the vicinity of St-Palais, where it turns southwest to follow the main St-Palais to St-Jean-Pied-de-Port road. To hitch to Mauléon, keep going to the intersection with the Sauveterre–Oloron road and go straight on. It is wooded, hilly country all the way.

Lourdes

LOURDES, about 30km southeast of Pau, has just one function. Over six million Catholic pilgrims arrive here each year, and the town is totally given over to looking after and exploiting them. Lourdes was hardly more than a village before 1858, when Bernadette Soubirous, the 14-year-old daughter of an ex-miller, had the first of eighteen visions of the Virgin Mary in the so-called Grotte de Massabielle by the Gave de Pau. Since then, Lourdes has grown a great deal, and it is now one of the biggest attractions in this part of France, many of its visitors hoping for a miraculous cure for scientifically intractable ailments.

The first large-scale **pilgrimage** took place in 1873, organized by a reactionary Catholic movement called the *Assomptionnistes*, whose avowed purpose was to stem the advancing tide of republicanism and rationalism. They took over the management of Lourdes, shoving aside the local priest who had wanted to organize the pilgrimages himself. Adroit propagandists and agitators, they sought to promote their cause by publishing a cheap mass-circulation paper called *La Croix*, aimed at the poor and uneducated, and by organizing these massive pilgrimages.

Practically every shop is given over to the sale of indescribable religious kitsch: Bernadette in every shape and size, adorning barometers, thermometers, plastic tree trunks, key rings, empty bottles that you can fill with holy Lourdes water, bellows, candles, sweets, and illuminated plastic grottoes. There's even a waxworks museum, the Musée Grévin (daily: April–Oct 9–11.30am & 1.30–6.30pm; July & Aug 8.30–10pm; 33F) with over a hundred lifesize figures illustrating the lives of Bernadette and Christ. Clustered around the miraculous grotto are the churches of the **Cité Réligieuse**, an annexe to the town proper that sprang up last century. The first to be built was the flamboyant **Basilique du Rosaire et de l'Immaculée Conception** (1871), swiftly followed by the massive subterranean **Basilique St-Pie-X**, which claims to be able to house 20,000 people at a time. The **Grotte de Massabielle** itself, where Bernadette had her visions, is the focus of the pilgrimages, but it's no more than a moisture-blackened overhang by the riverside with a statue of the Virgin in waxwork white and baby blue. Suspended in front are a row of rusting crutches, offered as *ex votos*.

Lourdes' only secular attraction is its **castle**, poised on a rocky bluff guarding the approaches to the valleys and passes of the central Pyrenees. Briefly an English stronghold in the late fourteenth century, it later became a state prison. Inside, it houses the surprisingly excellent **Musée Pyrénéen** (May to mid-Oct daily 9am–noon & 2–6/7pm; mid-Oct to April closed Tues 26F). Its collections include Pyrenean fauna, all sorts of fascinating pastoral and farming gear, and an interesting section on the history of Pyrenean mountaineering. In the rock garden outside are some beautiful models of various Pyrenean styles of house, as well as of the churches of St-Bertrand-de-Comminges and Luz-St-Sauveur.

Practicalities

Lourdes' **gare SNCF** is on the northeast edge of the town centre, at the end of avenue de la Gare; the **gare routière** is in the central place Capdevieille, and the **tourist office** is in place Peyramale (May to mid-Oct daily 9am–7pm, Sun 11am–6pm; mid-Oct to May Mon–Sat 9am–noon & 2–6/7pm; ☎05.62.42.77.40, fax 05.62.94.60.95).

Although it is very thin on good restaurants, Lourdes has more **hotels** than any city in France outside Paris. There's masses of cheap accommodation in the small central streets around the castle, while **hostel** accommodation can be had at the *Centre Pax Christi*, 4 rte de la Forêt (☎05.62.94.00.66, fax 05.62.42.94.44; April to mid-Oct), on the western edge of town. The nearest **campsite** (☎05.62.94.40.35; April to mid-Oct) is the *Poste*, 26 rue de Langelle, just south of the gare SNCF.

Tarbes

Twenty minutes away by train to the north, **TARBES** is useful as a base for visiting Lourdes or launching into the mountains to the south.There is an airport midway between Tarbes and Lourdes. The **Musée Massey**, in the very attractive **Jardin Massey** near the train station, which houses an extensive collection of cavalry uniforms, is closed for renovation until 2001. The Napoleonic stud farm, **Les Haras**, entered from Chemin de Mauhourat, is also worth seeing (July & Aug Mon–Fri 10am–noon & 2–5pm, plus occasional days; ☎05.62.56.30.80; 20F). The farm is best known for the *cheval Tarbais*, bred from English and Moorish stock as a cavalry horse, and you can watch them drilling during July and August at 3.15pm. A final sight is the house, at 2 rue de la Victoire, where **Marshal Foch**, supreme Allied commander in World War I, was born (10am–noon & 2–7pm; closed Tues & Wed; 15F), a missable repository of family and personal mementos.

The **gare SNCF** is on av Joffre, north of the centre (☎08.36.35.35.35), and the **gare routière** on the other side of town on place au Bois, off rue Larrey. The **tourist office** is near the central place de Verdun, at 3 cours Gambetta (Mon–Sat 9am–12.30pm & 2–7pm; ☎05.62.51.30.31, fax 05.62.44.17.63). Tarbes has some reasonable **hotels** in the vicinity of the station, like the *Hôtel Izard*, 70 av Maréchal Joffre (☎05.62.93.06.69, fax 05.62.93.99.35; ②; good restaurant from 68F), the *Victor Hugo*, 52 rue Victor-Hugo (☎05.62.93.36.71, fax 05.62.51.90.27; ①; restaurant from 65F), or the more comfortable *Hôtel de l'Avenue*, 80 av Barère (☎05.62.93.06.36; ①) as well as an HI **youth hostel** at 88 av Alsace-Lorraine (☎05.62.38.91.20).

The valleys of the Aspe and Ossau

The parallel north–south valleys of the **Aspe** and **Ossau** are the French Pyrenees at their most *sauvage*, and the region in which the Pyrenean brown bear most tenaciously resists extinction. About a dozen survive on the slopes of the valleys, in the **Cirque de Lescun** and in the adjoining parts of Spain.

Tourism is less developed here, especially in the Aspe valley, because of the unreliable snow conditions for skiing; but what tourism has failed to do, a major road-building scheme threatens to achieve twofold. To see the best of the region you should get out your map and walk, camping – with permission, of course – in the isolated farms along the way.

Along the Aspe

The **valley of the Aspe** begins at the grey town of **OLORON-STE-MARIE**, around 45km west of Lourdes, where the mountain streams of the Aspe and Ossau meet. It is served by train from Pau as well as by Citram buses, with five daily SNCF buses continuing down the valley to Urdos and three to Canfranc in Spain. The town's claim to fame is as the centre of the manufacture of the famous woollen pancake-shaped *beret basque*, once the standard titfer for all French men but now seldom seen on any but greybeards (though there's even a museum dedicated to it at Nay, to the southeast of Pau). However, the only real points of interest for the visitor are the town's two churches: **Ste-Croix**, one of the oldest Romanesque buildings in Béarn, with unusual interior vaulting copied from the Great Mosque at Cordoba, and the **Cathédrale Ste-Marie**, which boasts an unusually beautiful Romanesque portal in Pyrenean marble, supported by two chained slaves. In the upper arch, the elders of the Apocalypse play violins and rebecs, while in the second arch scenes from medieval life are represented – a cooper, the slaying of a wild boar, fishing for salmon. The gallant knight on horseback over the outer column on the right is Gaston IV, Count of Béarn, who commissioned the portal on his return from the first Crusade at the beginning of the twelfth century, hence the reference to Saracens in chains among the sculptures. The magnificent studded doors were a present from Henri IV. Inside, well away from the main area of worship, is a stoup reserved for the use of the Cagots, a stark reminder of the centuries-long persecution and segregation of this mysterious group of people, thought by some to have been lepers and by others to have been perhaps of Visigoth origin.

Oloron's **tourist office** is in place de la Résistance (mid-July to Aug Mon–Sat 9am–7pm, Sun 9am–1pm; rest of year Tues–Sat 9am–noon & 2–7pm; ☎05.59.39.98.00, fax 05.59.39.43.97). Should you find yourself stuck here, there are a couple of reasonable **hotels** – the *Hôtel de la Paix*, 24 av Sadi-Carnot near the train station (☎05.59.39.02.63, fax 05.59.39.98.20; ②), and the *Hôtel Bristol* at 9 rue Carréot (☎05.59.39.43.78, fax 05.59.39.08.19; ②; restaurant menus from 65F), as well as a **camping municipal** on the D919 Arrette road (☎05.59.39.11.26; April–Sept).

The Goutte d'Eau and Chemin de la Mâture

The narrow enclosed world of the valley proper begins south of Oloron at the village of **ESCOT**, where a beautiful side route, the D294, climbs through beech woods to the **Col de Marie-Blanque** and down to Bielle in the Vallée d'Ossau. It's a steep green world where the eye is perpetually carried upwards. South of Escot, the road follows the river through narrow defiles, past the attractive riverside village of **SARRANCE**, where there is **gîte** accommodation at *Accueil au Monastère* (☎05.59.34.54.78); there's also a youth hostel close by up the mountain at Lourdios (☎05.59.34.46.39); buses run as far as Asasp, from where it's a 3km walk.

Beyond Sarrance, **BEDOUS** has more accommodation – and food – at the cheap and very friendly *Le Choucas Blanc*, 4 rue Gambetta (☎05.59.34.53.71; ①), with other **gîtes d'étape** (☎05.59.34.73.23) in nearby **OSSE-EN-ASPE**, and a little further south at **L'ESTANGUET**, near the turning for Lescun (☎05.59.34.72.30).

Beyond here, **CETTE EYGUN** has an extremely alternative restaurant-bar-gîte, *La Goutte d'Eau* (☎05.59.34.78.83; food if you're lucky at negotiable prices) – occupying the old train station between the road and the river. It is run by the CSAVA (*Coordination pour la Sauvegarde de la Vallée d'Aspe*) whose protest activities against the building of a tunnel under the Col du Somport to link the Vallée d'Aspe with Spain take precedence over housekeeping concerns. There is accommodation of dubious quality (by their own admission) in an old train carriage parked on the tracks, and camping space on the banks of the river.

Beyond Eygun, the road continues up the valley to **ETSAUT**, where there's a food shop, a **gîte d'étape** (☎05.59.34.88.98), a **Maison du Parc** (☎05.59.34.88.30) for information on walks and accommodation in the Parc National des Pyrénées Occidentales (see p.675), and the *Hôtel des Pyrénées* (☎05.59.34.88.62, fax 05.59.34.86.96; ②). **BORCE**, an attractive medieval village on the west flank of the valley, is home to another gîte d'étape (☎05.59.34.86.40) and the squat, menacing **Fort du Portalet**, in which Léon Blum was imprisoned by Pétain's Vichy government, and then Pétain himself after the liberation of France. Just before the fort, at the Pont de Cebers, the GR10 to the left leads to the **Chemin de la Mâture**, an eighteenth-century mule path hacked out of the precipitous rock slabs that form the sides of a dizzy ravine, facilitating the transport of tree trunks felled for use as ships' masts. The path is broad enough, but if you don't like heights keep away from the edge. The GR10 reaches the **Lacs d'Ayous refuge** opposite the Pic du Midi d'Ossau (see p.684) in about five hours. Further on, at **URDOS**, you pass through French customs; you can stay at the *Hôtel Somport* (☎05.59.34.88.05, fax 05.59.34.86.74; ②; good restaurant from 70F). From here, three buses a day continue over the **Col de Somport** and the Spanish frontier post and on to Canfranc in Spain, the terminus for trains from Jaca.

Lescun

Six steep kilometres above the N134 at L'Estanguet, the ancient grey-stone houses of **LESCUN** huddle tightly together on the north slopes of a huge and magnificent green cirque. The bowl of the cirque and the lower slopes, dimpled with vales and hollows, have been gently and harmoniously shaped by generations of farming, while to the west it is overlooked by the great grey molars of **Le Billare** and **Le Petit Billare**, beyond whose shoulders bristle further leaning teeth of rock and the snow-slashed bulk of the **Pic d'Anie** (2504m). Below the village in the hollow of the cirque, the *Camping Le Lauzart* (☎05.59.34.51.77, fax 05.59.34.51.77; mid-April to Sept) must be one of the best sites anywhere, with an uninterrupted view of the peaks and no sound to disturb beyond the chiming of cow bells. If you're on foot, be sure to take provisions with you – it is some way from the village and the only food shop. Lescun also has a **hotel**, the *Pic d'Anie* (☎05.59.34.71.54, fax 05.59.34.53.22; ③; April–Sept), and a **gîte d'étape** (same phone number).

The obvious **walk** in the area is along the GR10 in the direction of La-Pierre-St-Martin. From Lescun, the path keeps close to the road as far as the refuge of *Labérouat* (☎05.59.34.50.43) – around a two-hour walk – then crosses meadows before entering beech forest beneath the organ-pipe crags of **Les Orgues de Camplong**, with fantastic views of the pine-stippled ridges of the Billares. It emerges above the tree line in a long, flower-strewn, hanging valley by the primitive **Cabane d'Ardinet**, reaching the shepherds' hut at **Cap de la Baitch** (1700m) in a further ninety minutes. From there you can either continue on the GR towards La-Pierre-St-Martin via the Pas d'Azuns, or swing south for the Col des Anies and the Pic d'Anie – a good two to three hours.

Along the Ossau

The **Ossau valley** is notable mainly for the distinctive Pic du Midi and some beautiful lakes. The valley is served by both Citram and SNCF **buses** as far as Laruns. At weekends in July and August, one SNCF bus goes on to Gabas and Artouste-Fabrèges, while Citram continues to Gourette every day from July to mid-September and again in the skiing season.

Between Pau and Laruns, the only place worth stopping at is **ARUDY**, principally to see the **Maison d'Ossau** (July & Aug 10am–noon & 3–6pm; Sept–June Mon 10am–noon, Tues, Thurs & Sat 2.30–5pm, Sun 3–6pm; 15F), which offers a comprehensive account of the prehistoric Pyrenees and an exhibition of the flora and fauna of the Parc National.

LARUNS, enclosed in the valley bottom by steep wooded heights, is of little interest in itself, though there are some fine old farms towards the river in the quarter known as Le Pon. If you **stay** here for the night, try the *Hôtel de France*, in rue de la Gare (☎05.59.05.33.71; ②; closed first two weeks of June & Dec), or the *Hôtel Le Lorry*, on rte des Cols (☎05.59.05.31.22; ②). There's also the refuge-auberge *L'Embaradère*, 13 av de la Gare (☎05.59.05.41.88; ①; meals from 60F), while the nearest **campsites** are *Le Gourzy* (☎05.59.05.31.12) and *Le Lauguère* (☎05.59.05.35.99) both on the west side of town near the old train station. The **tourist office** is in the main place de la Mairie (daily 9am–12.30pm & 2–6.30pm; ☎05.59.05.31.41, fax 05.59.05.35.49). If you are heading for the Pic du Midi d'Ossau, it is best to stock up with provisions in Laruns.

Gabas

The road to **GABAS**, 13km away, winds steeply into the upper reaches of the Gave d'Ossau valley, south of Laruns. On days when there is no bus, you should get a lift without much difficulty from other walkers or employees of the Parc National des Pyrénées Occidentales (see p.675), especially early in the morning. Primarily a base for climbers and walkers, there is nothing to it beyond a minuscule chapel, the **Maison du Parc** and its useful walking information (mid-June to mid-Sept daily 10am–1pm & 2–7pm; ☎05.59.05.32.13), a CAF **refuge** (☎05.59.05.33.14; meals from 70F), and a couple of **hotels** – *Le Biscau* (☎05.59.05.31.37, fax 05.59.05.43.23; ②) and *Le Vignau* (☎05.59.05.34.06; ①), both with restaurants from 50F.

Pic du Midi d'Ossau

The **Pic du Midi**, with its rocky twin-peaked summit (2884m), is a classic Pyrenean landmark, visible for kilometres around. From Gabas, it is a steep 4.5-kilometre climb up a wooded ravine to the artificial **Lac de Bious-Artigues**, so named because it flooded the *artigue* – a Pyrenean word for "mountain pasture" – that formerly existed beside the infant *gave*. Just below the dam are the stony terraces of *Camping Bious-Oumettes* (☎05.59.05.38.76; mid-June to mid-Sept), which also has a small provisions shop open around mid-June to September. Beside the lake, right under the *pic*, is the *Refuge Pyrénéa Sports* (☎05.59.05.32.12; June–Oct). The area within immediate reach of the road gets very crowded in summer and the refuges are likely to be full at weekends; it's worth phoning ahead.

A round trip of the peak, excluding the summit, takes about seven hours. It can be broken by a **stay** at the CAF *Refuge de Pombie* (☎05.59.05.31.78; June–Sept), below the vast southern walls of the mountain. From the lake, follow the GR10 up the left bank of the *gave* and past the turning to the Lacs d'Ayous (see below). Cross the Pont de Bious and continue upstream across an expanse of flat meadow until you come to a signpost indicating **Lac de Peyreget** to the left. There follows a steepish zigzagging climb to the timber line and a long traverse right to the junction with the HRP path (1hr from

Pyrénéa Sports). Keep left, with the ground falling away on your right. At the **Lac de Peyreget**, you can either follow the HRP steeply left towards the **Col de Peyreget**, or alternatively keep right – due south – to the **Col d'Iou**. From the latter, traverse left-wards, following the contour to the **Col de Soum**, where you turn northwards towards the *Refuge de Pombie* (about 4hr). The path continues north back to *Pyrénéa Sports* (about 3hr) via the **Col de Suzon**, where the standard ascent of the *pic* begins, the **Col de Moundelhs** and the **Col Long de Magnabaigt**.

There is a path off the mountain from the Col du Soum, and another from the *Refuge de Pombie*. The latter leads due east down the valley of the Pombie stream, through meadows full of daffodils, orchids, violets and fritillaries in June, where you might catch a glimpse of lizards. At the **Cabane de Puchéou**, a shepherd's hut, cross to the left bank of the stream and carry on down to the next bridge. The HRP continues on the left bank past the *Cabane d'Arrégatiou* and comes out at the southern end of the **Lac de Fabrèges**. The right-hand path crosses the bridge and descends through woods to the **Gave de Brousset** at Soques (about 2hr from Pombie), where you join the Col du Pourtalet road (which leads to the Spanish frontier) and can hitch back to Gabas.

Lac d'Artouste

A short distance out of Gabas, the Pourtalet road passes the **Lac de Fabrèges**, whence a *télécabine* swings up to the **Pic de la Sagette** (2032m) to connect with a **miniature rail line** that runs for 10km through the mountains to the **Lac d'Artouste**. Built in the 1920s to service a hydroelectric project, it was later convert-ed for tourist purposes. Weather permitting, the train normally starts operating in early June and keeps going until mid- or late September. It is a beautiful trip, lasting about four hours, including time to walk down to the lake (80F, including the *télécab-ine*; special 105F deal for walkers, allowing them to go out on the first train and return on the last). The first train leaves between 9 and 10am depending on the season, but allow a half-hour for the *télécabine*. Don't forget to take warm clothes, as you'll be at an altitude of 2000m.

The Lacs d'Ayous

In the opposite direction from Gabas, this is another classic walk, in some ways more impressive than doing the Pic itself, especially if you spend the night by the lakes to get the quintessential dawn view of the peak silhouetted against the rising sun and reflect-ed in the slaty waters of Lac Gentau.

It's a steady ninety-minute climb from *Pyrénéa Sports*. Instead of crossing the Pont de Bious, turn up the GR10 to the right through woods of pine and beech, with ever-widening views of the valley scattered with herds of horses and cows and flocks of sheep. The meadows are full of orchids and the stream banks thick with azalea-like alpenrose. You pass three small lakes. The third and largest is **Lac Gentau**, whose red-dish shallows are full of minnows that presumably turn into the trout so sought after by numerous fishermen. On its banks there's an expanse of flat, soft meadow for camping, while above it stands the *Refuge d'Ayous* at 1960m (☎05.59.05.37.00; mid-June to mid-Sept). Over the Col d'Ayous behind it, the GR10 continues west to the Chemin de la Mâture and the Aspe valley (see p.682).

The Col d'Aubisque and the road to Cauterets

The only way of reaching Cauterets by road without going back towards Pau is via the **Col d'Aubisque**, a grassy, rounded ridge 17km from (and nearly 1000m above) Laruns. There's a café on the top, served in July and August by a single afternoon bus from Laruns. It is also hitchable; if you're hitching on, remember that the next possible stopping place is 18km away, so it's best to stay close to the café.

The col is an important grazing ground, with tremendous views over the valleys below and the rocky precipices of the **Pic de Ger** (2613m) to the south. It is also a favourite place for slaughtering the migrating wood pigeons in autumn, as the numerous shooting butts along the ridge bear witness. The Tour de France often passes this way, making the col an irresistible challenge to any French cyclist worth his salt. You see swarms of them toiling up, making it a matter of pride to find the breath for a cheery "Bonjour".

Cauterets and the cirques of Gavarnie and Troumouse

Cauterets, 30km due south of Lourdes, and **Gavarnie**, a further 20km southeast, are established resorts on the edge of the Parc National des Pyrénées Occidentales, but the country they give access to is so spectacular that you should not miss it. Both towns are served by SNCF buses from Lourdes via the valley of the Gave de Pau. As ever, if you pick your season right or even the time of day, you can still enjoy the most popular sites in relative solitude. At Gavarnie, for instance, few people stay the night, so it is quiet in the early morning and evening, and **Troumouse**, which is just as impressive in its way (though much harder to get to without a car), has very few visitors. As for more conventional sights, there are interesting churches at **Luz-St-Sauveur** and **St-Savin**.

Aucun and St-Savin

Between Lourdes and Cauterets, 8km southwest of the dull town of Argelès-Gazost, **AUCUN** is worth a short detour for its small but fascinating private folk museum, the **Musée du Lavedan** (July & Aug guided visits daily at 5pm; otherwise by appointment ☎05.62.97.12.03; 20F), while, heading south from Argelès, it's worth taking a look at the twelfth-century **abbey church** at **ST-SAVIN**, to the right of the main road, with its fortifications and fine Romanesque doorway. Inside it boasts a magnificent Spanish wooden Christ, an interesting stoup, and amusing organ cabinet carved with grotesque faces that were designed to pull grimaces as the music played.

Cauterets and around

Thirty kilometres south of Lourdes, **CAUTERETS** is a pleasant if unexciting little town that owes its fame and its rather elegant Neoclassical architecture to its waters, much in demand now for the treatment of rheumatism and ear, nose and throat complaints. In modern times, it has also become one of the main Pyrenean ski and mountaineering centres.

Its origins as a spa began with Count Raymond de Bigorre's grant of land to the monks of St-Savin in 945 AD. In the seventeenth century, Marguerite d'Angoulême came to take the waters and wrote her *Heptameron* here. The eighteenth and nineteenth centuries were its heyday, especially the latter with its Romantic worship of mountains. Hugo visited, as did Chateaubriand, Baudelaire, Debussy, Edward VII and many other celebrities.

The modern town is so small that there is no difficulty in finding your way around. Most of it is still squeezed between the steep wooded heights that close the mouth of the Gave de Cauterets valley. Next door to the **gare routière** on the north edge of the centre, the **Maison du Parc** (daily 9.30am–noon & 1.30–7pm; ☎05.62.92.52.56) has a small museum of flora and fauna (10F), and film shows on Wednesday and Saturday in season (5.30pm; 20F). In the small centre of the town, two minutes' walk from here, you'll find the **tourist office** in place Clemenceau (daily: July to mid-Sept & school hols 9am–7pm; rest of year 9am–12.30pm & 2–6.30pm; ☎05.62.92.50.27, fax 05.62.92.59.12). In summer the tourist office has a mountain information centre, and there are two *bureaux des guides*: on place de la Mairie (☎05.62.92.62.02) and rue de Verdun (☎05.62.92.59.83).

Affordable **hotels** include *Le Béarn*, 4 av Leclerc (☎05.62.92.53.54; ①), *Le Centre-Poste*, 11 rue de Belfort (☎05.62.92.52.69, fax 05.62.92.05.73; ②), and *Le Bigorre*, 15 rue de Belfort (☎05.62.92.52.81; ①; restaurant from 75F; closed Nov to mid-Dec & May). For something a little more upmarket, try the *César*, 3 rue César (☎05.62.92.52.57, fax 05.62.92.08.19; ③; closed May & Oct). The cheapest accommodation is in the **gîtes** – *Le Beau Soleil*, on rue Maréchal-Joffre (☎05.62.92.53.52) and *Le Pas de l'Ours*, 1 rue Galliéni (☎05.62.92.58.07, fax 05.62.92.06.49); 2km away at **CONCÉ**, just outside town on the Lourdes road, there's also *Le GR Bienvenue à la Ferme*, with space for camping (☎05.62.92.54.02, fax 05.62.92.00.49). There are several proper **campsites** along the Lourdes road, one of the quietest being *Les Bergeronnettes* (☎05.62.92.50.69; June–Sept), across the river on the right before you reach the roadside *Les Glères* (☎05.62.92.55.34).

For **food**, the *Brasserie Le Paris*, in place de la Mairie, is a friendly and very reasonable establishment. Other places to try include the cafés *Le Béarn* and *Le Commerce*, in avenue Leclerc, and the pizzeria *Giovanni*, in rue de la Raillère.

Around Cauterets: some hikes

The classic excursion from Cauterets is up the Val de Jéret to the **Pont d'Espagne**, where the Gave de Gaube and Gave du Marcadau hurtle together in a boiling spume of spray, before rushing down to Cauterets over a series of spectacular waterfalls. For a beautiful and tourist-free route, take the **Parc National path** from **LA RAILLÈRE**, 3km from Cauterets (regular buses). It runs all the way beside the stream through woods of beech and pine to come out by the café-bar at Pont d'Espagne (about 2hr up, 90min down).

From Pont d'Espagne, you can fork right up the **Marcadau valley** to the *Refuge Wallon* (about 5hr round trip), or left up into the alpine valley of the Gave de Gaube, with the lovely little **Lac de Gaube** backed by the snowy wall and glaciers of **Vignemale** (3298m). There is even a *télésiège* (28F return) to save you the first part of the ascent. Beyond the lake, the path continues to the CAF *Refuge des Oulettes* below the north face of Vignemale (about 3hr from Pont d'Espagne), from where you can return to La Raillère via the *Refuge de Baysellance* and the beautiful and quieter **Lutour valley** (7hr round trip).

A less-frequented walk from Cauterets is to the **Lac d'Ilhéou** along the **GR10** (about 3hr). To avoid the initial steep climb you can take the *téléphérique du Lys* (37F return) to the **gare intermédiaire de Cambasque**, crossing the stream there and continuing up the right bank to the **Cabane de Courbet**, where you follow a track, first on the left bank, then on the right. After a short distance, the GR10 leaves the track and climbs up the slope to the left, steadily gaining height to cross a chute of boulders beside the long white thread of the **Cascade d'Ilhéou** waterfall. Over the rim of the chute, you come to a small lake, with the **Refuge d'Ilhéou** in sight ahead on the shore of the lake – it's very pretty in June, with snow still on the surrounding peaks and ice floes drifting on its still surface.

For other ideas for hiking, ask at the Cauterets tourist office (see above).

Luz-St-Sauveur and the road to Bagnères de Bigorre

The only approach to Gavarnie and Troumouse, best known of the Pyrenean cirques, is through **LUZ-ST-SAUVEUR**, on the GR10 and the daily bus route from Lourdes. It, too, was a nineteenth-century spa, patronized by Napoléon III and Eugénie, and it owes its elegant Neoclassical facades in the centre to this period.

Its principal sight is the **church of St-André**. Built in the late twelfth century and fortified in the fourteenth by the Knights of St John, it's a classic of its kind, with a crenellated outer wall and two stout towers. The entrance, beneath one of the towers, sports a handsome porch surmounted by a Christ in Majesty carved in fine-grained local stone. The lanes round about are crammed with **market stalls** every Monday.

The **tourist office**, with a *bureau des guides* (daily: July & Aug 9am–12.30pm & 1.30–7.30pm; rest of year 8.30/9am–noon & 2.30–6/7pm; ☎05.62.92.81.60, fax 05.62.92.87.19), is in the central place du 8-mai, by the crossroads for Gavarnie. Two **hotels** to try are *Les Templiers* (☎05.62.92.81.52; ②; closed May & Nov), by the church, and the *Londres* (☎05.62.92.80.09; ③; closed May & mid-Oct to mid-Dec), on the river bank in the town centre. There's a **campsite** and **gîte d'étape** at *Les Cascades* (☎05.62.92.94.14), uphill from the church, and also the *Camping Le Toy*, near the tourist office (☎05.62.92.86.85; closed May & Oct–Dec).

Twelve kilometres south in **GÈDRE**, where the road divides for the Cirque de Troumouse, there's another very pleasant **hotel** – *La Brèche de Roland* (☎05.62.92.48.54, fax 05.62.92.46.05; ③; mid-Dec to Sept; restaurant from 100F) – plus a couple of **campsites** nearby.

The road to Bagnères de Bigorre

From Luz-St-Sauveur begins the eighteen-kilometre pull up to the **Col du Tourmalet**, regularly one of the major torments of the Tour de France. The only village in between is **BARÈGES**, 7km away, linked with Lourdes by buses via Luz. It has been popular as a spa – its waters renowned for the treatment of gunshot wounds – since 1677, when it was visited by Madame de Maintenon with her infant charge, the 7-year-old Duc de Maine, son of Louis XIV; today it is a skiing and mountaineering centre. The **GR10** passes through and numerous other trails lead off into the **Néouvielle Massif**, full of lakes and highly recommended as a walking area.

Above Barèges, the road continues up a huge denuded valley, with clusters of stone *bergeries* dug into the slope. At its head, the **Pic du Midi de Bigorre** (2872m) comes into view, crossed by the Col du Tourmalet, which at 2115m is the highest road pass in the Pyrenees. It's a desolate, windy spot with a track – you have to pay – leading off left to the Pic and its observatory, still going strong and continuously staffed since its opening in 1882. The small **museum** inside, featuring an unprepossessing array of observatory bits and pieces, is temporarily closed for renovation.

Over the col, the road descends steeply past the monstrously ugly ski resort of **LA MONGIE** into lovely woods of spruce, pine and beech, continuing down to the gentle green **Vallée de Campan**, whose meadows are dotted with farms all turned south in ranks to face the sun. The architecture is quite distinct from the valleys to the west. The roofs are still slate, but house and barn are built in line as one building, with the balconied living quarters always to the right as you face the sun. In the village of **CAMPAN** there is an interesting sixteenth-century covered market, old houses and another curious-looking fortified church.

School buses cover the 6km from Campan to **BAGNÈRES DE BIGORRE**, another Pyrenean spa town trying to refurbish its somewhat faded image, but not a place to make a special stop. SNCF **buses** leave for Tarbes from the **gare SNCF** on avenue de Belgique just north of the town centre. Two buses daily continue south to Ste-Marie-de-Campan and, in summer, on to the Lac de Payolle, from where it is possible to hitch on over the pine-covered Col d'Aspin to Arreau in the Aure valley. The **tourist office** is in allées Tournefort (daily: July & Aug 9am–12.30pm & 2–7pm; rest of year Mon–Sat 9am–12.15pm & 2–6.30pm; ☎05.62.95.50.71, fax 05.62.95.33.13), close to the leafy allées des Coustous, the main drag, lined with **cafés**. If you need to stay, there are reasonable

rooms at the *Hôtel de Nice* (☎05.62.95.04.65; ③) in rue de l'Horloge, near the market, and the *Hôtel de la Paix* at 9 rue de la République (☎05.62.95.20.60, fax 05.62.91.09.88; ②). There are several **campsites** around the town, too.

The Cirque de Gavarnie

South of Luz-St-Sauveur, **GAVARNIE**, a further 8km up the ravine from Gèdre, is connected with Luz by two daily bus services (Mon, Thurs & Sat only outside the summer season), or, if you're really into hiking, you could walk it on the GR10. The village is a tacky and unpleasant mess of souvenir shops, car parks and snack bars. Poor and depopulated, it has found the attractions of mass tourism, much of it the excursion trade from Lourdes, too seductive to resist. It stinks, too, from the droppings of the dozens of mules, donkeys and horses used to ferry visitors up to the cirque. However, the **cirque** itself is magnificent – Victor Hugo called it "Nature's Colosseum" – a natural amphitheatre scoured out by a glacier, of which barely the roots of the tongue remain. Nearly 1700m high, it consists of three sheer bands of rock discoloured by the striations of seepage and waterfalls, and separated by sloping ledges covered with snow. To the east, it is dominated by the jagged peaks of **Astazou** and **Marboré**, both over 3000m. In the middle, a corniced ridge sweeps round to Le Taillon, hidden behind the Pic des Sarradets, which stands slightly forward of the rim of the cirque, obscuring the **Brèche de Roland**, a curious vertical slash, 100m deep and about 60m wide, said to have been hewn from the ridge by Roland's sword, Durandal (see p.670).

Practicalities

If you are carrying a **tent**, there's nothing to beat Gavarnie's *Camping La Bergerie* (☎05.62.92.48.41; mid-May to Oct; bar & breakfast) on the true right bank of the *gave*, on the cirque side of the village. The facilities leave something to be desired, but the site is away from the crowds and has a view right into the cirque. The other campsite, *Le Pain de Sucre* (☎/fax 05.62.92.47.55; June–Sept & mid-Dec to mid-April), is on the Luz side of the village.

As for **hotels**, much the nicest is the historic and unspoilt *Les Voyageurs*, at the entrance of the village (☎05.62.92.48.01, fax 05.62.92.40.89; ②), good restaurant from 60F), run by the same family since 1740, whose "Golden Book" contains the signatures of Count Henry Russell, the eccentric pioneer of Pyrenean mountaineering, George Sand, Flaubert and Hugo among others. The beds here, so the whisper goes, witnessed the conception of Napoléon III in an illicit encounter between Hortense de Beauharnais and a local *berger*. Otherwise, the best bets are the CAF **refuge**, *Les Granges de Holle* on the Port de Gavarnie road (☎05.62.92.48.77; closed Nov), which also does meals, or the **gîte d'étape** *Le Gypaëte*, (☎05.62.92.40.61) near *Les Voyageurs*. For a place to **eat**, *La Ruade* (June–Sept), also by *Les Voyageurs*, is the best.

For **weather information and snow conditions**, ask the CRS mountain rescue unit opposite *La Bergerie* (or ring ☎08.36.68.02.65); for **park information**, there's the *Maison du Parc* (daily 10am–noon & 1.30–4.30pm; ☎05.62.92.49.10) as you come into the village.

The cirque and around

It's an easy fifty-minute walk from Gavarnie to the cirque. Luckily, the scale of it is sufficient to dwarf the tourists, but it is still best to go up before 10am or after 5pm, when the grandeur and silence are almost alarming and the dung less overpowering. The track ends at the *Hôtellerie du Cirque*, once a famous meeting place for mountaineers and now a snack bar in summer. To get to the foot of the cirque walls, you have to clamber over slopes of frozen snow. Take care not to stand too close, especially in the afternoon, because of falling stones. To the left, the **Grande Cascade**, at 423m the highest water-fall in Europe, wavers and plumes down the rock faces – a fine sight in the morning, when it appears to pour right out of the eye of the sun. Scaling the cliffs is obviously a matter for climbers, but the relatively intrepid can get a powerful impression of the majesty of the place – and a superb vantage point for photography – by climbing the first stage of the **HRP path** to the CAF **Refuge des Sarradets**, which begins in the right-hand corner of the cirque at the edge of the first band of rock. The first 100m or so could be a little nerve-racking if you are not used to heights, but in dry weather they are perfectly safe.

If you do not want to retrace your steps, an enjoyable and not too demanding walk back to Gavarnie is via the path from the *Hôtellerie* up the east flank of the Gavarnie valley to the **Refuge des Espuguettes** (about 3hr). It is a beautiful path, cut into rocky pine-shaded slopes. At the top, you emerge into open meadows, with the *Cabane de Pailla* in a hollow and the *Refuge des Espuguettes* (Easter–Oct) on a grassy bluff about a 45-minute climb above you. The climb is well worth the effort for the views of the cirque and the Brêche de Roland. The committed may want to go from here on to **Piméné**, the bare peak above you. It's a couple of easy, if tedious, hours' climbing, but the view is fantastic: the Cirque d'Estaubé, Monte Perdido and away into Spain. To return to Gavarnie, turn right at the signpost below the refuge (allow 90min).

La Brêche de Roland

La Brêche de Roland is *the* walk to do in Gavarnie. It is high, and involves crossing a glacier, which means being properly equipped, preferably with ice axe and crampons. It is, however, extremely popular in summer, so there is a good chance of being able to team up with someone more experienced.

There are three approaches to the *Brêche*, all converging on the *Refuge des Sarradets* (☎05.62.92.40.41; May–Sept); contact the CRS in Gavarnie (☎05.62.92.48.24) for reservations at the refuge, which are always necessary in high season. The easiest route is up the road to the Port de Gavarnie/Col de Boucharo, where a clear path climbs under the north face of Le Taillon to join (1hr) the footpath coming directly from Gavarnie. This path starts beside the church, climbs steadily up the valley of Pouey Aspé, then zigzags steeply up to join the Port de Gavarnie path (4hr). From the junction of these two paths, it's less than an hour to the refuge. The third route (about 6hr in all from Gavarnie) is via the **Échelle des Sarradets** section of the HRP path (see above). The *Brêche* is about forty minutes above the refuge.

The Cirque de Troumouse

A vast, wild, desolate place, much bigger than Gavarnie and, in bad weather, rather frightening, the **Cirque de Troumouse** lies up an equally desolate valley, whose only habitations are the handful of farmsteads that make up the hamlet of **HÉAS** – until the construction of the road, one of the loneliest outposts in France. There is **camping à la ferme** on the road to Héas, and **chambres d'hôte** in the hamlet. As you reach the head of the valley there is a tollgate (22F per car), after which the road climbs in tight hairpins up treeless slopes to the *Auberge du Maillet* (☎05.62.92.48.97; ②; mid-May to mid-Oct) by the side of a small tarn. After this it climbs again, even more steeply, beneath bare shining crags, to a car park with a white statue of the Virgin Mary crowning a grassy knoll, enclosed by the wide sweeping walls of the cirque and enough pasture to feed thousands of sheep. The close moorland turf is channelled with streams and cut into dingles and hummocks, where gentians and saxifrage, sedums and houseleeks grow among the rock crevices. Beneath the walls of the cirque is a scatter of clear blue glacial lakelets, the **Lacs des Aires**. A Parc National path does the circuit from Héas.

The Comminges

Stretching from **Bagnères-de-Luchon** (Luchon for short) almost as far as Toulouse, the **Comminges** is an ancient feudal county that encompasses the upper valley of the River Garonne. It also boasts one of the finest buildings in the Pyrenees, the magnificent cathedral of **St-Bertrand-de-Comminges**, the product of three distinct periods of architecture. The mountainous southern part is what you will want to see, and access is via the unprepossessing little town of **St-Gaudens**, from where there are daily bus and train services to Luchon.

Valcabrère and St-Bertrand-de-Comminges

The village of **VALCABRÈRE** lies a short way south of Montréjeau on the main Bayonne–Toulouse rail line. It can be reached by SNCF bus (direction "Luchon") to the hamlet of Labroquère, by the Garonne, and a short stroll across the river. It's a little place of rough stone barns and open lofts for hay drying, with an exquisite Romanesque church in **St-Just-St-Pasteur** (daily: July–Sept 9am–7pm; April–June & Oct 10am–noon & 2–6/7pm; Nov 2–5pm; Dec–March weekends & school holidays only 2–5pm; 10F), whose square tower rises above a cemetery full of cypress trees. The porch is elegantly sculpted and the apse, decorated with a kind of inverted arcading, is quite remarkable. Both interior and exterior are full of recycled masonry from the old Roman settlement of **Lugdunum Convenarum**, whose remains are visible at the crossroads just beyond the village. Founded by Pompey in 72 BC, this was a town of some 60,000 inhabitants at its apogee, making it one of the most important in Roman Aquitaine. Josephus, the Jewish historian, says it was the place of exile of Herod Antipas and his wife Herodias, who had John the Baptist decapitated. It was destroyed by Vandals in the fifth century and again by the Burgundians in the sixth century, after which it remained deserted until Bishop Bertrand began to build his cathedral around 1120.

Further on is **ST-BERTRAND-DE-COMMINGES**, whose grey fortress-like **cathedral** (April–June & Sept daily 9am–noon & 2–7pm; no lunch break July & Aug; rest of year Mon–Sat 10am–noon & 2–6pm, Sun 9–10.30am & 2–6/7pm; 17F) commands the plain from the knoll ahead, the austere white-veined facade and heavily buttressed nave totally subduing the clutch of fifteenth- and sixteenth-century houses that gather at its feet. To the right of the west door a mainly Romanesque cloister looks out across a green valley to hills, where a local *maquis* unit had its lair during the war. In the aisleless interior, the small area at the west end reserved for the laity has a superbly carved sixteenth-century oak organ loft, pulpit and spiral stair, although the church's great attraction are its choir stalls, built by *toulousain* craftsmen and installed in 1535 in the great Gothic choir – an addition ordered by the future Pope Clement V. The elaborately carved stalls – 66 in all – are a feast of virtuosity, mingling piety, irony and malicious satire, each one the work of a different craftsman. It is in the misericords and partitions separating them that the ingenuity and humour of their creators is best seen: each of the gangways dividing the misericords has a representation of a cardinal sin on top of the end partition. In the middle gangway on the south side, for example, Envy is represented by two monks, faces contorted with hate, fighting over the abbot's baton of office, pushing against each other foot to foot in a furious tug of war. The armrest on the left of the rood-screen entrance depicts the abbot birching a monk, while the bishop's throne has a particularly lovely back panel in marquetry, depicting St Bertrand himself and St John. In the ambulatory a fifteenth-century shrine depicts scenes from St Bertrand's life, with the church and village visible in the background of the top right panel.

In July and August the cathedral and St-Just in Valcabrère play host to a **music festival;** details from the **tourist office** by the cathedral in St-Bertrand (daily: March–Nov 10am–noon & 2–7pm; no lunchbreak July & Aug; ☎05.61.95.44.44).

Across the small square in front of the cathedral, the *Hôtel du Comminges* (☎05.61.88.31.43, fax 05.61.94.98.22; ②; open April–Nov) makes a marvellous place to **stay**. You could eat at the friendly *Chez Simone*, in the rue du Musée just behind the hotel, with a spectacular view from its terrace (menu 65F), or try the *Hôtel Oppidum* (☎05.61.88.33.50, fax 05.61.95.94.04; ③) which has a restaurant with menus from 85F. The nearest **campsite** is *Es Pibous*, on the St-Just road (☎05.61.88.31.42; mid-May to Sept), with *La Vieille Auberge* nearby serving good basic food. Cars are no longer allowed in the village itself, but a minibus operates a shuttle service from the nearby car park. Fifteen kilometres northwest, the unprepossessing little town of **ST-GAUDENS** has an HI **youth hostel** at 3 rue de la Résidence (☎05.61.94.72.73), and a reasonable **hotel** – the *Esplanade*, 7 place Mas-St-Pierre, by the church in the town centre (☎05.61.89.15.90; ③).

The Grottes de Gargas

About 6km from St-Bertrand in the direction of Mazères-de-Neste, the **Grottes de Gargas** (July & Aug daily 10am–noon & 2–7pm; April–June & Sept–Oct 2–5pm; Nov–March Wed, Sat & Sun 2–4pm; 30F) are renowned for their 231 prehistoric painted hand prints. Outlined in black, red, yellow or white, they mostly seem mutilated or deformed – perhaps the result of disease or ritual sacrifice, though no-one really knows. There are representations of animals as well.

Bagnères-de-Luchon

There's none of the usual spa-town fustiness about **BAGNÈRES-DE-LUCHON**. It is small, but the main street, the **allées d'Étigny**, has a distinctly metropolitan elegance and bustle, lined with cafés and numerous places to eat. There is not, however, anything to see, apart from the slightly moth-eaten **Musée du Pays de Luchon** (daily 9am–noon & 2–6pm; 10F) by the tourist office, which has an extraordinarily eclectic collection of archeological finds, old skis, art and displays on the Pyrenees, and the nineteenth-century **baths** (guided tours Tues & Thurs 2pm; 30F) at the end of allées d'Étigny in the **Parc des Quinconces**.

Luchon is best as a comfortable base for exploring the surrounding mountains. The **gare SNCF**, which is also the **gare routière**, is in avenue de Toulouse across the River One in the northern part of the town. The **tourist office** is at 18 allées d'Étigny (July & Aug daily 9am–7pm; rest of year Mon–Fri 8am–12.30pm & 2–6/7pm; ☎05.61.79.21.21, fax 05.61.79.11.23) and includes a *bureau des guides* for walking information. **Bikes** can be hired at Luchon Mountain Bike (☎05.61.79.88.56) or Cycles Demiguel (☎05.61.79.12.87) – both on avenue Maréchal Foch – or Sun Park (☎05.61.79.81.41) in rue de Superbagnères.

An excellent-value **hotel** is the *Deux Nations* at 5 rue Victor-Hugo (☎05.61.79.01.71, fax 05.61.79.27.89; ①), with an equally good restaurant (menus from 59F). Alternatively, try the *Bon Accueil*, 1 place Maréchal-Joffre (☎05.61.79.02.20, fax 05.61.79.76.83; ③), also with a good restaurant. There are numerous **campsites** in and around the town. Less cramped than the in-town ones, *Camping La Lanette* is only 1500m away across the River Pique in Montauban-de-Luchon (down rue Lamartine from allées d'Étigny). However, the best deal of all for sleeping and eating is the romantically sited *Le Jardin des Cascades* (☎/fax 05.61.79.83.09; ②), in a wild steep garden uphill from the church in tiny **Montauban**, a kilometre to the east. In summer you can eat on a shaded terrace overlooking Luchon and the mountains to the west, where the hang-gliders and *parapentes* float hazily in the sunset. The food and service are excellent, the price around 200F per person, including wine. The four or five rooms are delightful, though not luxurious.

Around Luchon: some hikes

There are two classic hikes south of Luchon. To get to **Lac d'Oô**, you can either follow the **GR10** or drive up to Superbagnères (3hr on foot), then on west to the *Refuge d'Espingo* (☎05.61.79.20.01; mid-May to mid-Oct) and the lake (another 5hr), or take the road to **GRANGES D'ASTAU**, where there is a **gîte d'étape** (☎05.61.79.35.63) and **refuge** (☎05.61.79.14.92; July–Oct). From there it's an hour's walk to the lake, or two hours to the Espingo refuge. It's possible to continue into Spain via the Port d'Oô or the Lac du Portillon.

For the second hike to **Port de Venasque** on the Spanish frontier, follow the D125 up through the woods to its end by the **Hospice de France**, an ancient inn founded by the Knights of St John. From here a signposted path climbs the narrow valley to the frontier ridge past four small lakes where there is a small unstaffed CAF refuge. After that it's a steep climb up a scree (subject to avalanches in spring) to the narrow passage of the **Port de Venasque** (3hr), with superb views of the **Maladetta Massif** and the **Pico d'Aneto**, the highest summit of the Pyrenees (3404m).

THE EASTERN PYRENEES

The dominant climatic influence of the **Eastern Pyrenees** is the Mediterranean. The climate is hotter and drier here, and the landscape more arid. Mediterranean plants like the cistus, broom and thyme make their appearance here, and the lower slopes of the hills are planted with vines. The way of life is laid-back and outdoor-orientated. The proximity of Spain is evident, too, and much of the region is Catalan, incorporated into France a mere three hundred years ago. As with the rest of the Pyrenees, the countryside is spectacular, and densely networked with well-organized hiking trails. The historical sights, with the exception of the prehistoric caves at **Niaux** and the Cathar castle of **Montségur**, are most richly concentrated in the east towards the coast, in what is essentially French Catalonia.

Along the River Ariège

The first clear herald of the approaching Mediterranean, whether you're coming from the western Pyrenees or heading south from the major transport hub of Toulouse, is the **Valley of the Ariège**, thorny scrub and white eroded limestone cliffs beginning to make their appearance from **Tarascon** onwards. Transport is no problem as long as you stick to the valley, but for side-trips – into the Couserans and the hike to **Montségur** – you really need a car.

Foix and around

Administrative centre of the *département* of Ariège, **FOIX** lies 82km south of Toulouse on the main Paris–Barcelona train line and the N20 road to Ax-les-Thermes and the Spanish border. It is an agreeable country town of narrow alleys and half-timbered houses, with an attractive old quarter squeezed between the rivers Ariège and Arget, filled with houses from the sixteenth and seventeenth centuries.

Dominating all are the three distinctive hilltop towers of the **Château des Comtes de Foix**, which contains the eminently missable **Musée d'Ariège** (daily: May, June & Sept 9.45am–noon & 2–6pm; July & Aug 9.45am–6.30pm; Oct–April 10.30am–noon & 2–5.30pm; 25F) – though the views are worth the climb. Determined opponents of the territorial ambitions of the Capetian kings of France and stout defenders of Catharism, the counts drew upon themselves the wrath of Simon de Montfort, who four times laid unsuccessful siege to the castle, though he did capture the town in 1211. Their resistance was finally broken in 1229 when Roger-Bernard, the count of the time, was obliged to accept the feudal overlordship of the French king. Foix's age of glory came in 1290 when its counts married into the house of Béarn. Although they transferred their court to Orthez in the fourteenth century, this was the beginning of a powerful Pyrenean mini-state, whose influence lasted three centuries and came to include the kingdom of Navarre, leading finally to the throne of France with the accession of Henri III of Navarre as Henri IV of France in 1589.

The **gares SNCF and routière** are together in av de la Gare, off the N20 on the right bank of the Ariège; except on Sundays, there's a daily **bus** service east via Lavelanet to Quillan and four buses a day west to St-Girons. The **tourist office** is at 45 cours Gabriel-Fauré (July & Aug Mon–Sat 9am–7pm, Sun 10am–12.30pm & 2–6.30pm; rest of year Mon–Sat 9am–noon & 2–6pm; ☎05.61.65.12.12, fax 05.61.65.64.63).

For a place to **stay**, there's the rather superior *Hôtel Audoye-Lons*, on place Georges-Duthil, by the Pont-Vieux (☎05.61.65.52.44, fax 05.61.02.68.18; ③; restaurant from 70F), or the cheaper *La Barbacane*, at 1 av de Lérida, just west of the tourist office (☎05.61.65.50.44, fax 05.61.02.74.33; ②; April–Oct). Another possibility is the *Hôtel L'Echauguette*, on rue Senateur-P-Lafont by the post office (☎05.61.02.88.88, fax 05.61.65.29.49; ②); while the best budget accommodation is the **hostel** *Auberge Léo Lagrange*, in rue Noël-Peyrevidal (☎05.61.65.09.04), which has a wealth of information on the local area. There's also a **campsite**, the *camping du Lac,* on the N20 (☎05.61.65.11.58, fax 05.61.05.32.62; April–Oct).

One of the nicest places to **eat** in the old town is *Les 4 Saisons*, at 11 rue de la Faurie (menus from 64F), or try *Le Petit Creux*, nearby in rue Lazéma, where you can expect to pay around 70F. *Auberge Miranda*, rue Labistour, makes a good place for a **drink** and also offers simple meals (60F).

A site worth visiting in the region is the underground river at Labouiche, 6km northwest of Foix (July & Aug daily 9.30–6pm; May, June & Sept daily 10am–noon & 2–6pm; April & Oct to mid-Nov weekdays 2–5/6pm, Sun & school holidays 10am–noon & 2–6pm; 42F). Discovered in 1908 and since baptised the 'Venice of the Ariège', it's the longest navigable subterranean river in Europe. The visit consists of a barge trip lasting one and a quarter hours, along 1km of the river, 60m underground, to admire its stalactites and stalagmites.

Mas d'Azil

West of Foix, the **Mas d'Azil** was one of the first prehistoric caves to yield evidence of human habitation, but its most impressive feature is a magnificent natural tunnel, scoured by the River Arize, which now carries the main road (the D119). Without your own transport, however, it's not easy to get to as it lies 12km north of the Foix to St-Girons bus route: get off at Vic after La-Bastide-de-Sérou and take the D15. It's a pretty road, but without a lift it'll take a good two hours on foot. Failing that, four *Semvat* buses a day run from Toulouse.

Secondary caves leading off the river cavern are the focus of historical interest; they were inhabited in prehistoric times for more than 20,000 years and used as a refuge by Cathars and Protestants in more recent times. As usual, the most important galleries are sealed off, though this hasn't stopped damage from road pollution, and those caves you can visit are interesting mainly for their sheer size (guided tours daily: April & May 2–6pm; June–Sept 10am–noon & 2–6pm; Oct–March by appointment; ☎05.61.69.97.71; 40F joint ticket with museum).

A few tools, animal bones and other objects found during excavation have been left in the caves, but the best pieces are now on display in the village of **LE MAS-D'AZIL**, 1km to the north, in the **Musée de la Préhistoire** (daily: June–Sept 10am–noon & 2–6pm; rest of year 2–6pm; 30F). Among other engraved tools and weapons, the museum's most outstanding exhibit is the beautiful carved antler known as *le faon aux oiseaux*, perhaps used as a spear-thrower. If you wish to **stay**, there's a **camping municipal** (April–Sept), 1500m away on the Pamiers road, or the *Hôtel Gardel* on the main square (☎05.61.69.90.05, fax 05.61.69.70.27; ②; menus from 60F).

Tarascon and the Vicdessos valley

TARASCON-SUR-ARIÈGE lies 16km south of Foix, where the N20 crosses the Ariège (a new bypass diverts the worst of the traffic). Once a centre for the local iron-mining industry – there is still an aluminium plant in operation – it is a hot and unexciting little town enclosed by high wooded ridges. However, it is useful as a base for the Vicdessos valley and the prehistoric cave of Niaux (see below).

The **cafés** on the east bank of the river, dominated by the clock tower, are pleasant, sunny places to sit. Apart from that, it is worth taking a stroll up the narrow **rue de Barri** to the wide square by the church, a pleasant expanse with just one arcaded side and a single wooden house still standing, to the **Porte d'Espagne**, the only surviving piece of the town walls.

Quietest and most attractive of the **hotels** is the *Hôtel Confort*, on the riverside quai Sylvestre (☎05.61.05.61.90; ②). Otherwise try the *Bellevue*, also on the river at the head of the bridge on place Jean-Jaurès (☎05.61.05.60.45, fax 05.61.05.10.41; ①; restaurant from 53F), or the *Hostellerie de la Poste* (☎05.61.05.60.41, fax 05.61.05.70.59; ②; good restaurant from 65F). For **camping**, the *Pré Lombard* (☎05.61.05.61.94) site is on the left bank of the river, ten minutes' walk upstream from the bridge, while the **gare SNCF** is a few minutes' walk to the right. The **tourist office** is west of the bridge on av des Pyrénées in the smart new Centre Multimédia François Mitterrand (July & Aug daily 9am–1pm & 2–7pm; rest of year Mon–Sat 9am–noon & 2–6pm; ☎05.61.05.94.94, fax 05.61.05.57.79).

Niaux and the prehistoric caves

Just south of Tarascon, by the aluminium plant, the D8 cuts up right into the green valley of the Vicdessos past the riverside remains of a Catalan ironworks. The hamlet of **NIAUX** lies in the valley bottom, 5km further on. The tiny settlement has an interesting **Musée Pyrénéen** (daily: July & Aug 9am–8pm; rest of year 10am–noon & 2–6pm; 35F), with an unrivalled collection of tools, furnishings, old photos and odds and ends illustrating the vanished traditions of peasant Ariège.

But the real reason people descend on the little hamlet is for the **Grotte de Niaux**, a huge cave complex under an enormous rock overhang high on the south flank of the valley (guided visits daily: July–Sept every 45min 8.30–11.30am & 1.30–5.15pm; rest of year 11am, 2.30pm & 4pm; reservations essential, several days ahead in peak season; ☎05.61.05.88.37; 60F). There are about 4km of galleries in all, with paintings of the Magdalenian period (circa 11,000 BC) widely scattered throughout, although the twenty people allowed in the cave at any one time are led through just a fraction of the complex. The paintings you can see are in a vast chamber, a slippery 800-metre walk from the entrance of the cave along a subterranean river bed. The subjects are horses, ibex, stags and bison. No colour is used, just a dark outline and shading to give body to the drawings, which have been executed with a "crayon" made of bison fat and manganese oxide. They are an extraordinary mix of bold impressionistic strokes and delicate attention to detail: the nostrils, pupils and the tendons on the inner thighs of the bison are all drawn in.

The village of **ALLIAT**, right across the valley from Niaux, is home to **La Grotte de la Vache** (July & Aug daily 10am–5.30pm; April–June & Sept visits at 3 & 4.30pm; 40F), a relatively rare example of an inhabited cave where you can observe hearths, bones, tools and other remnants *in situ*. If you want to stay locally, there's a well-equipped but somewhat expensive **campsite**, *Les Grottes* (☎05.61.05.88.21; June to mid-Sept), in the village. Another cave in the vicinity, **Bedeilhac** (daily: July & Aug 10am–5.30pm; April–June & Sept 2.15–5pm; 40F), is in the side of the jagged Roc de Sédour ridge northwest of Tarascon on the D618 Massat road.

Although it can't compete with visiting the caves themselves, the **Parc Pyrénéen de l'Art Préhistorique** (April–Nov daily 10am–6/6.30pm; 55F) a few kilometres west of Tarascon on the road to Banat, provides a remarkable overview of cave art. Highlight is the "Grand Atelier", a compelling multi-media exploration including recreations of Niaux's inaccessible Clastres system, with its enigmatic footprints, and the famous "Salon Noir" as it would have looked to its creators 10,000 years ago. The surrounding landscaped park, complete with Magdalenian flower meadow, footprints stream and hunting panorama, continues the prehistoric theme.

Vicdessos and Auzat

From Niaux, the road continues deep in the valley bottom, beneath the romantically pinnacled ruins of the **Château of Miglos**, to **VICDESSOS** and **AUZAT**, the latter with an unsightly aluminium works. The villages themselves are not of much interest except as bases for exploring the magnificently wooded country round about. The **GR10** passes nearby on its way from Mérens, above Ax-les-Thermes, to Aulus-les-Bains (see below), and from the gîte d'étape at **Mounicou** (☎05.61.64.87.66), beyond Auzat, you can undertake the gruelling ascent of the **Pic de Montcalm**.

For **accommodation**, Auzat and Vicdessos have one hotel each, the *Hôtel Denjean* in Auzat (☎05.61.03.80.90; ③) and the *Hôtel Hivert* in Vicdessos (☎05.61.64.88.17; ①; restaurant from 65F). Both have a year-round campsite. **Goulier**, across the valley, has a gîte (☎05.61.64.81.84), and in **Capoulet**, back towards Niaux, a Dutch couple offer very comfortable, inexpensive chambres d'hôte (☎05.61.05.89.88). The **tourist office** in Auzat is also extremely helpful (July & Aug daily 8am–noon & 2–6pm; rest of year Mon–Fri 8am–noon & 2–6pm; ☎05.61.64.87.53, fax 05.61.03.82.05).

Into the Couserans

From Vicdessos, a really stunning route – the D18 – climbs the **valley of the Suc**, tunnelling through trees, past abandoned barns and occasional cottages in lush meadows, by waterfalls and streams, to the pass at the **Port de Lers** (1517m). On the far side, herds of grey cows graze the alpine meadows down to the Étang de Lers, where there is a snack bar. Then the road climbs again to another col overlooking the head of the valley of the little **River Garbet**. Below, the steep slopes are luxuriant with beech, while straight ahead you look into a high-walled crenellated cirque formed by the **Pic Rouge de Bassiès** and the **Pic des Trois Comtes** above the **Étang de Garbet**, where the heights are underlined by wedges of snow lying beneath the sheerest faces.

Aulus-les-Bains

Down in the Garbet valley, the road heads west to **AULUS-LES-BAINS**, a remote village lying among moist and fragrant meadows ringed by dramatic peaks. This is the beginning of the **Pays de Couserans**, one of the poorest, least-developed and most depopulated regions of the Pyrenees. Its villages, Aulus in particular, were once renowned for their bear-trainers, who, driven by poverty, toured the lowland towns with their performing beasts.

Aulus, like other spa towns, enjoyed its moment of glory and fell again into rustic somnolence, from which it is trying to resurrect itself once more. This is country for walking and enjoying the landscapes: there's nothing else, and, remote though it is, it is not inaccessible – there are two daily buses (Mon–Sat) to St-Girons. The classic walk here involves heading south along the GR10 to the **Cascade d'Ars** (round trip about 5hr).

For all information, consult the **tourist office** in the allée des Thermes (daily: July & Aug 10am–1pm & 2–7pm; rest of year 10am–noon & 2–6pm; ☎05.61.96.01.79). Among places to **stay**, try the *Hôtel La Terrasse* (☎05.61.96.00.98; ②; June–Sept; restaurant from 80F), or the *Hôtel de France* (☎05.61.96.00.90, fax 05.61.66.03.29; ②; Jan–Sept; restaurant from 65F). There's also a **gîte d'étape** in the village and **camping** at *Le Couledous* (☎05.61.96.02.26, fax 05.61.96.06.74), 500m to the north.

For routes on to St-Girons, both the Garbet and Ustou valleys are beautiful. For a brief stopover, there is a great little inn by the river, a little way beyond Ustou at **PONT DE LA TAULE**, called the *Auberge des Deux Rivières* (☎05.61.66.83.57; ①), with a restaurant.

St-Girons

With several SNCF buses a day from Boussens, on the main Tarbes–Toulouse rail line, and connections on to Aulus, Ustou, Massat and St-Lary, **ST-GIRONS** may be your first taste of this out-of-the-way region. Apart from its long association with making cigarette papers, the most striking thing about St-Girons is its pavements, made of a local dark-grey marble veined with white, and with finely chiselled gulleys to take the rainwater from down-pipes. And although there are no other memorable sights, it's a far from unpleasant town, with a folklore festival in mid-July as well as a theatre festival in early August.

The simplest centre for orientation is the **Pont-Vieux**. Straight ahead on the right bank of the River Salat, the bridge points you into the old commercial centre of the town, with some marvellously old-fashioned shops, their fronts and fittings unchanged for generations. To the right is the typically provincial **place des Poilus**, its cachet largely due to the faded elegance of the *Grand Hôtel de France* and the equally old-fashioned *Hôtel de l'Union*, opposite, where you can still stay (see below). The *Grand Café de l'Union* on the square is a splendid balconied period café that faces the mairie. Beside it, along the river bank, a wide gravelled *allée* of plane trees, the **Champ de Mars**, provides the site for a big general market on the second and fourth Mondays of every month, and for a regular produce market every Saturday morning.

The **tourist office** is down on the river bank (July & Aug Mon–Sat 9am–7pm, Sun 10am–1pm; rest of year Mon–Sat 9am–noon & 2–6pm; ☎05.61.96.26.60, fax 05.61.96.26.69). If you're **staying** over, the *Grand Hôtel de France* (☎05.61.66.00.23, fax 05.61.04.84.85; ②) has a good restaurant with menus from 90F. The *Hôtel de l'Union* is a little cheaper (☎05.61.66.09.12, fax 05.61.04.81.73; ①), or there's a **campsite** at the *Centre de Loisirs du Parc de Paletès* (☎05.61.66.06.79) – take av des Évadés from the church behind the mairie and keep going for about 2km – with a nice terrace restaurant overlooking the valley. On the left bank of the river, place des Capots is the terminus for **buses**, where there are also a couple of cheap **places to eat**. Otherwise, the *Grand Café de l'Union* does simple meals from 60F. There are two unusual English-run **chambres d'hôte** off the road between St-Girons and Foix: at Lescure, 8km from St-Girons, Pyrénéen Field Study Services (☎/fax 05.61.96.37.67) do accompanied walks and tours to discover the wildlife and flora of the mountain and forest, whilst at Rimont, 4km further on, there is – a rarity in France – excellent and reasonably priced **vegan** accommodation (☎05.61.96.37.03).

St-Lizier

ST-LIZIER, a five-minute ride by bus from the old gare SNCF on the St-Gaudens road, totally outclasses St-Girons in the tourism stakes. It sits on a hilltop, and is full of history; it's walled, arcaded, cobbled, cathedraled, half-timbered, pretty and lifeless.

Architecturally the most interesting building in town is the **Cathédrale de St-Lizier** (mid-June to mid-Sept Mon–Sat 10.30am–noon & 2.30–6.30pm, Sun afternoons only) with its distinctive octagonal Toulouse-style tower posing photogenically against the mountains to the south. Inside are some fine medieval frescoes, especially its representation of Christ in the apse, and a pretty little cloister with some lovely Romanesque basketwork carving on the supporting columns. A second cathedral, Notre-Dame-de-Sède, is closed for renovation, but you can still visit the neighbouring **bishop's palace** (daily: April, May, Sept & Oct 2–5.30pm; July & Aug 10am–12.30pm & 2–6.30pm; 25F), which now houses an excellent museum of rural life in the Bethmale valley. It's worth walking up to the palace anyway, for views over St-Lizier, and continuing on round the old **ramparts** (same hours; free). The **tourist office** is next door to the cathedral (May–Oct daily 10am–noon & 2–7pm; Nov–April Mon–Fri 2–6pm; ☎05.61.96.77.77, fax 05.61.96.08.01). For a place to **stay** there is the spectacularly sited *Hôtel de la Tour* (☎05.61.66.38.02, fax 05.61.66.38.0; ②; restaurant from 65F), overlooking the river Salat – though during the town's international music festival in the first half of August it is much in demand.

Ax-les-Thermes and around

Twenty kilometres south of Tarascon, and still on the river, the spa town of **AX-LES-THERMES** is completely walled in by mountains. Its principal value is as a base for exploring the surrounding mountains and as a staging post on the way to Andorra or on down the N20 to Font-Romeu and, ultimately, Perpignan and the Mediterranean.

The town itself is small and pleasant enough, but there's little to see once you've wandered a couple of streets in the quarter to the right of the N20, which forms the main street. Rue de l'École and rue de la Boucarie retain a few medieval buildings, and above place du Breilh, the **church of St-Vincent** is of architectural interest for its Romanesque tower. Just across the road you can dangle your feet for free in the **Bassin des Ladres**, a pool of hot sulphurous water which is all that remains of the hospital founded in 1260 by St Louis for soldiers wounded in the Crusades.

The **tourist office** on place du Breilh (daily 9am–noon & 2–6/7pm; ☎05.61.64.60.60, fax 05.61.64.41.08) has hiking information and lists of walks. A nice **place to stay** in Ax is the *Hôtel La Terrasse* at 7 rue Marcaillou (☎05.61.64.20.33, fax 05.61.64.66.89; ①), run by a jazz-loving couple and with a restaurant from 90F. Another possibility is *Hôtel Les Pyrénées*, on the main avenue Delcassé opposite the casino (☎05.61.64.21.01, fax 05.61.64.38.91; ②), with a restaurant from 80F. There is also a **campsite**, *Le Malazéou* (☎05.61.64.09.14), on the river bank just before the **gare SNCF** as you come into town from Tarascon.

The most atmospheric places to **eat** are the old *Grand Café*, next to *Hôtel Les Pyrénées*, and *Brasserie Le Club*, on place Roussel, which has jazz and food. Alternative places are the *Terminus Bar*, near the station (from 60–70F), or, for something smarter, the *Grillon*, on rue St-Udaut just south of the centre (☎05.61.64.31.64; menus from 95F).

Eight kilometres south along the N20 lies **Mérens-les-Vals**, on the GR10 which heads east to the Carlit Massif and Font-Romeu/Mont-Louis (see p.716). It has a **gîte d'étape** (☎05.61.64.32.50), and you could use it to link up with the GR7, making a tour of the **Réserve Nationale du Burrus** via the lakeside *Refuge d'En Beys* (☎05.61.64.24.24; June–Sept).

Montségur and around

The easiest approach to the village and castle of **MONTSÉGUR** is probably from Lavelanet, about 12km to the north (see p.700), or Villeneuve-d'Olmes, 6km closer. By far and away the most dramatic route, however, is the **walk** from Comus (see below), which takes about four hours.

Head west along the GR7B, following a lane beside the stream for about 3km until the lane doubles back hard to the left, leaving the stream to continue into the deep sunless

THE FALL OF MONTSÉGUR

In the early years of the thirteenth century, Montségur's castle was reconstructed by a local feudal lord as a strongpoint for the **Cathars** (see p.745) under attack by the Crusade. In 1232 it became the capital of the banned Cathar Church, with a population of some five hundred people, bishops and clergy as well as ordinary believers on the run from the persecution of the Inquisition, under the protection of a garrison commanded by Pierre-Roger de Mirepoix.

Provoked by a raid on Avignonet in May 1242, which successfully assassinated the Inquisitors, the forces of the Catholic Church and the king of France laid siege to the castle in the spring of 1243. By March 1244, Pierre-Roger, despairing of relief, agreed terms with them. At the end of a fortnight's truce, the 225 Cathars who still refused to recant were burnt on a communal pyre on March 16.

Four men who had made good their escape recovered the Cathar "treasure", which had been hidden in a cave for safekeeping since the preceding Christmas and vanished. Two of them later reappeared in Lombardy, where it seems probable these funds were used to support the refugee Cathar community established there. But numerous legends have grown up, especially in German writings, identifying this "treasure" with the Holy Grail, and the Cathars themselves with the Knights of the Round Table.

ravine of the **Gorges de la Frau**. The path descends steeply on the old mule road until you hit the dead end of the D5 from Bélesta. Continue along the tarmac to the first farm on the left, where the route turns up the lane between the buildings, becomes a track, then a narrow footpath beside a stream in a deep gully thickly wooded with beech, ash, wild cherry and fir. It crosses to the left flank of the gully (the true right bank of the stream) and the angle of ascent increases sharply, bringing you finally to an ancient quarry mule road that turns sharply and horizontally right back across the head of the valley to a signposted locality called Liam; from a patch of rough meadow here you get your first glimpse of the ruined walls of Montségur castle ringing the summit of a rocky pyramid. Turn left at the signpost, down a good path with open pastures in a shallow valley on your right with a tarmacked lane. When you hit the tarmacked lane, turn left for a short distance and then right on a clear path down through trees to a riverside campsite.

Cross the river to a road and make your way across allotment-like vegetable plots to the **village** of Montségur, whose houses are strung out in terraced lines, not the usual fetal huddle, at the foot of the castle rock. Silent and depopulated now, the place comes to life only with the influx of tourists, most of them day-trippers. It's worth having a glance at the one-room **museum** (daily 10am–1pm & 2–7pm; Oct–April ask at the mairie; 10F, or 25F combined ticket with the castle), with its collection of bits and pieces from the castle, before going up to the ruin itself.

A footpath from the top of the village shortens the way up to the saddle of the hill and the Prats des Cramats, the field where the Cathar martyrs were burnt (see above). From here it's a steep half-hour climb to the **castle** (daily: April–Sept 9am–7pm; March, Oct & Nov 10am–6pm; 20F, or 25F combined ticket with the museum), of which all that remain are the stout and now truncated curtain walls and keep. The space within is terribly cramped, and one can easily imagine the sufferings of the besieged. A somewhat precarious stairway leads to the top of the walls, whence you look out over kilometres of forested hills and snowy peaks, giving a sense of solitude and airy isolation that is in itself highly evocative.

There are a couple of **hotels**, the nicest of them the old-fashioned *Hôtel Couquet* (☎05.61.01.10.28; ①), fronted by pollarded lime trees and with a café and restaurant on the first floor (menus from 60F). The alternative is the more expensive *Hôtel Costes* (☎05.61.01.10.24, fax 05.61.03.06.28; ②; March to mid-Dec; restaurant from 79F), which also has a **gîte d'étape**, or there's the gîte d'étape in the village (☎05.61.01.20.97).

Another gîte lies in Comus, attached to the Centre École Pleine Nature (☎04.68.20.33.69), a 45-minute walk below Montaillou. In July and August there's a **tourist office** in Montségur (daily 10am–1pm & 2–7pm; ☎05.61.03.03.03); at other times you'll have to go to Lavelanet (see p.200).

Montaillou

About 11km southeast of Montségur as the crow flies, the almost deserted hamlet of **MONTAILLOU** lies above the road to the right just after Prades, over the steep Col de Chioula (1400m). There's little to see today, apart from the stump of a castle tower, once 45m high to facilitate visual communication with Montségur, but the pretty little settlement's interest lies in a fascinating study undertaken in the 1980s by French historian Le Roy Ladurie. Based on Inquisition records, his book covers the years around 1300, when the Inquisition was trying to extirpate the Cathar heresy from its last strongholds. What the poor victims revealed to their interrogators amounts to an extraordinarily detailed and intimate portrait of contemporary life. Much of the book reads like good gossip: who is sleeping with whom, where the sheep are being pastured this year and which paths are best for crossing into Spain.

Lavelanet and Mirepoix

LAVELANET has nothing to offer beyond its bus connections and a very clean and modern **camping municipal** (April–Sept), from which you can just see Montségur nudging over the brow of the intervening ridges. There is a **tourist office** (Mon–Sat 9am–noon & 2–7.30pm; ☎05.61.01.22.20, fax 05.61.03.06.39), and a couple of restaurants off the main square.

If you are heading north in the Carcassonne direction, it is definitely worth taking a look at **MIREPOIX**. It's a late thirteenth-century *bastide* built around one of the loveliest surviving arcaded market squares in the country, bordered by houses dating from between the thirteenth and the fifteenth centuries, with a relatively harmonious modern *halle* on one side and a not very exciting cathedral behind it. If you're feeling extravagant, you could **stay** in the *Maison des Consuls*, with its beautifully carved beams (☎05.61.68.81.81; ⑤) on the main square; otherwise the *Hôtel Le Commerce*, on the boulevard encircling the old town near the church (☎05.61.68.10.29; ②), is a safe place to stay, with a very agreeable restaurant in its lime-shaded courtyard (menus from 65F). There's a **camping municipal** on the Limoux road (☎05.61.01.55.44, fax 05.61.03.06.39; mid-June to mid-Sept). The **tourist office** is in the main square (July & Aug daily 9am–noon & 2–6/7pm; Sept–June same hours but closed Sun; ☎05.61.68.83.76, fax 05.61.68.89.48).

Along the Aude

South of Carcassonne, the road and the rail line both climb steadily up the twisting valley of the **River Aude**, between scrubby hills and vineyards and ever deeper and more forested ravines to **Quillan**. From there, the road squeezes through the **Gorges de l'Aude** in a sunless bottom before emerging once again towards the river's headwaters above Les Angles on the east side of the Carlit Massif in the high Pyrenees. It is a magnificent drive, and quite hitchable, as it is one of the main routes to Andorra, though buses do make the run through to **Quérigut** three times a week.

Limoux to Quillan

The first stop on the D118 road, 24km south of Carcassonne, **LIMOUX** is served several times daily by both the SNCF and the private Cars Teissier buses. It stands astride the Aude, which for much of the year is a powerful grey flood of snow melt. Life revolves around the pretty **place de la République** in the heart of the old town, with its Friday market, and the nineteenth-century **promenade du Tivoli**, in effect a bypass road. Known in the past for its woollens and the tanning of hides brought down from the mountains, the town's claim to fame today is the production of its excellent sparkling wine, Blanquette de Limoux, much cheaper than champagne. If you've got your own transport, the Romanesque abbeys of **St-Hilaire** (July & Aug daily 10am–noon & 3–7pm, or by appointment ☎04.68.69.45.42; 20F) and **St-Polycarpe** (key held by M. Laffont, in front of the under 10km away in the lovely green hills to the east, are worth the effort.

The **tourist office** is on promenade du Tivoli (July & Aug daily 9am–7pm; rest of year Mon–Sat 9am–noon & 2–6pm, Sun 10am–noon & 2–6pm; ☎04.68.31.11.82, fax 04.68.31.87.14). Right next door is the Musée Petiet (mid-June to mid-Sept daily 9am–7pm; rest of year 9am–noon & 2–6pm, closed Sat afternoons; 15F), displaying a collection of nineteenth-century paintings. For a central place to **stay**, cheapest are *Le Relais des Arts*, 47 rue de la Mairie (☎04.68.31.22.78; ①) and the superior *Hôtel des Arcades* at 96 rue St-Martin (☎04.68.31.02.57, fax 04.68.31.66.42; ②) from 75F). At the other end of the spectrum is the *Hôtel Moderne et Pigeon*, on place Général-Leclerc (☎04.68.31.00.25, fax 04.68.31.12.43; ⑤; mid-Jan to Dec), with its excellent restaurant (from 155F). Just upstream from the main part of town, on the right bank of the river, is a poplar-shaded **camping municipal** (June–Sept).

For an unusual and characterful place to **eat**, try the *Maison de la Blanquette*, on promenade du Tivoli, which promotes the local wines and serves excellent food (closed Wed; menus from 65F); otherwise there are plenty of cafés and brasseries on the main square, or try one of the hotels above. If you are interested in sampling or buying any **wine**, the best place to go is the co-operative, *Aimery-Sieur d'Arques*, in avenue du Mauzac (daily 9am–noon & 2.30–7pm).

South of Limoux, road and rail track the Aude valley, skirting the minuscule thermal resort of **ALET-LES-BAINS**, with its half-timbered houses and excellent **hotel**, the *Hostellerie de l'Évêché* (☎04.68.69.90.25, fax 04.68.69.91.94; ②; with a good restaurant from 68F; May–Sept), standing beside the ruined cathedral. If you've got your own transport it's worth taking a detour south of Alet, following the D52 as it climbs out of Couiza and spirals towards the mountain-top village of **RENNES-LE-CHÂTEAU**. The views alone repay the effort, but the primary reason for the jaunt is the mysterious **parish church** run by Abbé Saunière from 1885 until 1910, when he was suspended because of his inability to explain how he financed his comfortable lifestyle and the lavish restoration work on the church. The church is full of veiled symbols and secret codes, which, some say, indicate that he had discovered the lost treasure of Solomon, brought here by the Visigoths in the fifth century. This and a host of other theories are explored in a video shown in **Villa Bethania** (daily 10am–7pm; 25F), built by Saunière as a retirement home for priests, and in the small museum next to the church (daily 10am–noon & 2–6/7pm; 15F, including entry to the church). Strange events continue to surround the village, the latest being the discovery of aerial photos, dating back to 1967, which reveal the image of a virgin and child in a nearby field. More prosaically, the village has a good **restaurant**, *La Pomme Bleue*, with a pleasant summer terrace and menus from 78F (closed Wed & Thurs lunchtime except in July & Aug; ☎04.68.74.39.78).

Back on the main road, **QUILLAN**, 27km upstream from Limoux, is a pleasant little town, useful as a staging post on the way south into the mountains or east to the Cathar castles – it has daily bus connections with Perpignan via St-Paul-de-Fenouillet. The only monument of interest is the ruined **castle** that was burnt by the Huguenots in 1575 and partly dismantled in the eighteenth century.

The **gare SNCF**, **gare routière** and **tourist office** (mid-June to mid-Sept Mon–Sat 8am–noon & 2–7pm, Sun 9am–noon; rest of year Mon–Fri 8am–noon & 2–6pm, Sat 2–6pm; ☎04.68.20.07.87, fax 04.68.20.04.91) are all together on the main ring road, bd de-Gaulle. Opposite the station, the *Hôtel Terminus* (☎04.68.20.05.72, fax 04.68.20.13.71; ①; Feb–Nov), is a cheap place to **stay**. Other better but slightly more expensive alternatives on the same street are the *Canal*, 36 bd de-Gaulle, (☎04.68.20.08.62, fax 04.68.20.27.96; ③), and the *Cartier*, at no. 31 (☎04.68.20.05.14, fax 04.68.20.22.57; ③; mid-March to mid-Dec). All three have restaurants. The *Sapinette* **campsite** is at 21 rue René-Delpech (☎04.68.20.13.52; March–Oct), or there's another campsite by the river at **Pont d'Aliès** (☎04.68.20.53.27, fax 04.68.20.53.27; all-year canteen), a further 11km along the D117 by the junction for **Axat** and the Gorges de l'Aude (see below). At this junction you'll also find the *Maison des Pyrénées Cathares* for local **information** (July & Aug daily 8am–7pm; rest of year Mon–Fri 8am–noon & 2–6pm; ☎04.68.20.59.61, fax 04.68.20.64.50).

The Gorges du Rebenty and Gorges de l'Aude

From Pont d'Aliès there is a beautiful route west up the **valley of the Rebenty** on the tiny D107 through woods of beech, fir and oak, with a magnificent early summer display of orchids and other Pyrenean flowers. It's a marvellous cycling route, too, except for the agony of the climb out of the valley. The road continues to Ax-les-Thermes over the Col du Pradel, or you can escape onto the Plateau de Sault at **ESPEZEL**, some 20km west of Axat.

The narrowest and deepest stretch of the scenic **Gorges de l'Aude** is the eighteen or so kilometres between Axat and Usson. If you want to admire the scenery, don't drive: the road is much too dangerous to allow your eyes to wander. Towards the end there is a magnificent cave to investigate, the **Grotte de l'Aguzou**. It's expensive, but as near the real thing as you can get without being a pukka caver; you spend the entire day underground, accoutred like a professional (visits by arrangement with M. Moreno in Mijanès, ☎04.68.20.45.38; or the Quillan tourist office – see above; 200F), although the visits must be arranged a week in advance and there must be a minimum of four people. Camping *sauvage* is allowed by the river.

Upstream, the road divides just after Usson-les-Bains. On a shaggy bluff between the arms of the fork, dwarfed in turn by the heights either side, stand the forlorn ruins of the **Château d'Usson**, allegedly the hiding place for the "Cathar treasure" during the 1243 siege of Montségur (see p.699). Passing its foot, a road winds up through the attractive grey tiers of houses at **MIJANES** – where there's a good **hotel**, the *Relais de Pailhères* (☎04.68.20.46.97; ①; restaurant from 70F) – to the pass at the **Col de Pailhères**, which is at its loveliest in June when a cornice of snow still lines the crests above the small round lake.

From Mijanès another road branches up the valley to **QUERIGUT** passing through the village of **Le Pla**, where there is a primitive **campsite**. There's also a thrice-weekly bus (Mon, Wed & Fri afternoons) from Quillan to Quérigut, run by Petit Charles of Carcanières, that passes through the village. Quérigut, where there is another **campsite** and the *Hôtel du Donezan* (☎04.68.20.42.40, fax 04.68.20.47.06; ②; menus from 65F), stands at the head of a slope of neglected terraces, guarded by the ruin of its **castle**, last refuge of the Cathars who held out for eleven years after the fall of Montségur. Above, the forest begins: kilometres of beech and pine, interspersed with lush meadows, stretching to the windy plateau above Font-Romeu. This is the **Donezan** region, beautiful but the poorest, most neglected and depopulated corner of Ariège.

French Catalonia

The area that makes up the eastern fringe of the Pyrenees and the flatter stretch of land down to the Mediterranean coast is known as **Roussillon**, or **French Catalonia**. Catalan power first came into its own in the tenth century under the independent counts of Barcelona, who then became kings of Aragon as well in 1137. They attempted to create a joint power base with Occitan France under the counts of Toulouse, but that came to an unhappy end with the death of Pedro I at the battle of Muret in 1213, when he came to the aid of Raymond VI of Toulouse against Simon de Montfort in the anti-Cathar crusade. The height of Catalan power was reached in the thirteenth and fourteenth centuries, when the Franco-Catalan frontier was fixed along the base of the Corbières hills north of Perpignan. But Jaime I made the mistake of dividing his kingdom between his two sons at his death. What is now the French part became the kingdom of Majorca with its capital at Perpignan, but, coveted by the rival brother, the king of Aragon, it sought alliance with the kings of France, who saw this as a splendid opportunity to straighten out their southern border, thus ensuring continuous squabbling that was only finally ended by the Treaty of the Pyrénées, negotiated by Louis XIII in 1659.

After the Treaty, the French began a ruthless process of Frenchification, which was successful in Perpignan where the bourgeoisie tended to identify their commercial interest with a central power; the mountain hinterland, however, was left largely untouched until modern times, when the collapse of traditional agriculture, the introduction of compulsory education and the devastation of the vineyards by phylloxera combined to drive the peasantry off the land – a process which still continues today, albeit at a slower rate.

Although there is no real separatist impetus among French Catalans today, their sense of identity is still strong: the language is very much alive, and the national colours of yellow and red are much in evidence wherever you go. The **Pic du Canigou**, which completely dominates the French Catalan province of Roussillon, is much larger in presence than its actual 2784m, and it remains a powerful symbol of Catalan nationalism, attracting hordes of Catalans from Barcelona to celebrate the summer solstice. And in the little town of **Prades**, which, as the place of exile from Franquista Spain of the cellist Pablo Casals, became a symbol of Catalan resistance, the first Catalan-language primary school in France has recently opened its doors. Prades is also the seat of a Catalan summer university.

Most of the region's attractions are easily reached from the region's one major town, **Perpignan**. The coast and immediate hinterland above the Spanish frontier is beautiful, though predictably crowded, and the finest spots are in the **Tech** and **Têt valleys** which cut back west into the Pyrenees, where you can view the Romanesque monasteries of **Serrabonne**, **St-Michel-de-Cuxa** and **St-Martin-du-Canigou**, Vauban's fortress town of **Villefranche-de-Conflent**, the museum at **Céret** with its unique series of Picasso ceramics, and **Mont Canigou** itself and its foothill orchards of peaches and cherries.

Perpignan

This far south, climate and geography alone would ensure a palpable Spanish influence. But, in addition, a large part of **PERPIGNAN**'s population is of Spanish origin, refugees from the Civil War and their descendants. The southern influence is further augmented by a substantial admixture of North Africans, both Arabs and white French settlers repatriated after Algerian independence in 1962.

While there are no memorable monuments to visit, Perpignan is a lively, pleasant city that lives its life very much on the public street. Its heyday was in the thirteenth and fourteenth centuries, when the kings of Majorca held their court here, and it is from this period that most of its historical interest derives. Well placed on the main Mediterranean coast international lines of communication, it is much the best base for exploring the eastern end of the Pyrenees, and the Cathar castles of the Corbières, described in Chapter 11.

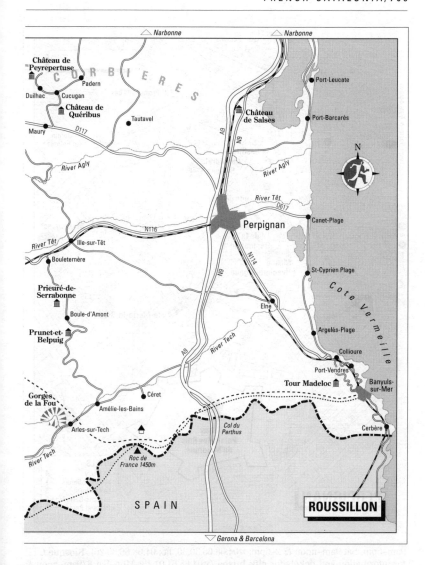

CORBIÈRES

△ Narbonne △ Narbonne

Château de Peyrepertuse

Padern

Duilhac Cucugan

Château de Quéribus

Tautavel

Maury D117

Port-Leucate

Château de Salses

Port-Barcarès

River Agly

River Agly

River Têt D617

Perpignan

Canet-Plage

N116

River Têt Ille-sur-Têt

Bouleternère

St-Cyprien Plage

Prieuré-de-Serrabonne

Boule-d'Amont

Elne

Côte Vermeille

Prunet-et-Belpuig

Argelés-Plage

River Tech

Collioure

A9

Port-Vendres

Tour Madeloc

Banyuls-sur-Mer

Gorges de la Fou

Céret

Amélie-les-Bains

Arles-sur-Tech

Col du Perthus

Cerbère

River Tech

Roc de France 1450m

SPAIN

ROUSSILLON

▽ Gerona & Barcelona

N

Arrival, information and accommodation

The **gare SNCF** (☎08.36.35.35.35) is on avenue Général-de-Gaulle, while long-distance **buses** pull in beside Pont Arago, on avenue Général-Leclerc. Both stations are a ten- to fifteen-minute walk from the **regional tourist office** on quai de Tassigny (daily 10am–12.30 & 2–6.30pm; ☎04.68.34.29.94, fax 04.68.34.71.01). Further along the River Basse is the **municipal tourist office** in the Palais des Congrès at the end of bd Wilson (June–Sept Mon–Sat 9am–7pm, Sun 10am–noon & 2–5pm; Oct–May Mon–Fri

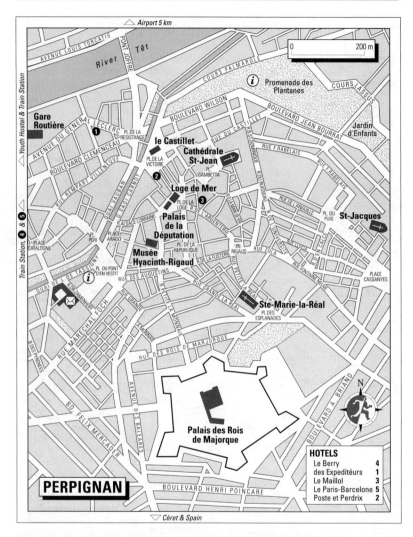

PERPIGNAN

HOTELS
Le Berry	4
des Expéditeurs	1
Le Maillol	3
Le Paris-Barcelone	5
Poste et Perdrix	2

9am–6pm, Sat 9am–noon & 2–6pm; ☎04.68.66.30.30, fax 04.68.66.30.26). Kiosque CTP, for information and tickets for **city buses** (☎04.68.61.01.13; Mon–Sat 8/9am–noon & 1.45–6.15pm) is on place Péri, near the regional tourist offfice.

There are some cheap **hotels** near the station, of which the best are *Le Berry*, 6 av de Gaulle (☎04.68.34.59.02; ①) and the *Paris-Barcelone* (☎04.68.34.42.60, fax 04.68.35.28.12; ②), right opposite the station. Another very cheap possibility, and convenient for the gare routière, is the *Expéditeurs*, on the rather desolate av Leclerc (☎04.68.35.15.80; ①), with a good cheap restaurant. More comfortable is the *Hôtel Poste et Perdrix*, 6 rue Fabriques-Nabot (☎04.68.34.42.53, fax 04.68.34.58.20; ②) whilst another attractive and reasonable alternative is *Le Maillol*, tucked away down impasse des Cardeurs off rue St-Jean (☎04.68.51.10.20, fax 04.68.51.20.29; ②), also nearby. In addition, there is a welcoming if somewhat noisy HI **youth hostel** (☎04.68.34.63.32), behind the public gardens of La Pépinière by Pont Arago (entrance around the back of the police HQ on av de Grande-Bretagne), and two **campsites**, *La Garrigole* (☎04.68.54.66.10) on rue Maurice-Lévy, and *Le Catalan* (☎04.68.63.16.92) on rte de Bompas, both signposted from the centre.

The city

The best place to begin your exploration of the city is at **Le Castillet**, built as a gateway in the fourteenth century and now home to the **Casa Pairal** (daily except Tues: mid-June to mid-Sept 9.30am–7pm; rest of year 9am–6pm; 25F), an interesting museum of Roussillon's Catalan folk culture, featuring religious art, agricultural and pastoral exposés and all sorts of local crafts. From the roof there is a great view of the dominant pile of Canigou, and, if you know where to look, you can see the **Château de Quéribus**, standing clear of its ridge to the northwest. A short distance down rue Louis-Blanc you come to the **place de la Loge**, focus of the renovated and pedestrianized heart of the old town. Dominating the cafés and brasseries of the narrow square is Perpignan's most interesting building, the Gothic **Loge de Mer**. Designed to hold the city's stock exchange and maritime court, and decorated with gargoyles and lacy balustrades, its ground floor has been taken over by an incongruous fast-food joint. Side by side next door are the **Hôtel de Ville**, with its magnificent wrought-iron gates and Maillol's statue of *La Méditerranée* in the courtyard, and the fifteenth-century **Palais de la Députation**, once the parliament of Roussillon.

From place de la Loge, rue St-Jean runs down to the fourteenth-century **Cathédrale St-Jean** on place Gambetta (daily 8–11.30am & 3–7pm), its external walls built of bands of river stones sandwiched by brick. The interior is most interesting for its elaborate Catalan altarpieces, shadowy in the gloom of the dimly lit nave, and for the tortured wooden crucifix known as the *Dévôt Christ* in a side chapel to the south. Dating from around 1400, it's of Rhenish origin and was probably brought back from the Low Countries by some travelling merchant.

From the cathedral, rue de la Révolution-Française and rue de l'Anguille lead into the close, dilapidated maze of the **Arab and gypsy quarter**, where women congregate on the secluded inner lanes but are seldom seen on the more public thoroughfares. There are North African shops and cafés, especially on rue Lucia, and a daily **market** on **place Cassanyes**. At the heart of the quarter, the wide and grimy **place du Puig** is overlooked by a Vauban **barracks** converted into public housing. Just past it, at the top of a shady uphill street, is the elegant Catalan **church of St-Jacques**, dating from around 1200, on the edge of the **La Miranda** gardens (daily 8am–noon & 2–6pm), laid out on a section of the old city walls. It is from this church that the Procession de la Sanch sets out on Good Friday.

A twenty-minute walk away through place des Esplanades, crowning the hill that dominates the southern part of the old town, is the **Palais des Rois de Majorque** (daily: June–Sept 10am–6pm; Oct–May 9am–5pm; 20F). Although Vauban's walls surround it now, the two-storey palace and its great arcaded courtyard date originally from the late thirteenth century. Thanks to the Spanish–Moorish influence, there's a sophistication and finesse about the architecture and detailing – for instance in the beautiful marble porch to the lower of the two chapels – that you don't often find in the heavier styles of the north.

Finally, at 16 rue de l'Ange near place Arago, there is Perpignan's museum of art, the **Musée Rigaud** (daily except Tues: mid-June to mid-Sept 9.30am–noon & 2.30–7pm; rest of year 9am–noon & 2–6pm; 25F), dedicated to the work of the locally born portraitist Hyacinthe Rigaud, who became official painter to the court of Versailles in the early eighteenth century. The collection also includes works by Dufy, Maillol, Picasso, Tapiès, Appel and others.

Eating, drinking and entertainment

For **eating**, there is nothing to beat the popular and reasonably priced *Perroquet*, near the station at 1 av de Gaulle, which has a good selection of very reasonably priced Catalan dishes (menus from 58F; closed Wed). Almost as recommendable is the *Expéditeurs* hotel-restaurant (see p.706; closed Sat eve & Sun), with a menu from 65F. For something smarter, there is the elegant brasserie *Le Vauban*, on quai Vauban near Le Castillet (menus from 100F; closed Sun). Other good places are *L'Arago* in place Arago for excellent pizzas and other dishes from 50F; *Le St-Jean*, in place Gambetta near the cathedral, with hearty Catalan home-cooking (from 95F); the *Casa Sansa*, 2 rue Fabriques-Nadel, with excellent food and a lively Spanish atmosphere (from 95F; closed Sun & lunchtime Mon); and, for the best food, *L'Opéra Bouffe*, in impasse de la Division, between place Argo and place de la Loge (menus from 125F; closed Sun).

There are plenty of places for a leisurely **drink** in Perpignan. The *Bodega du Castillet*, in the rue Fabriques-Couvertes, is a favourite bar with the locals (and also serves good-value tapas), and there are several cafés on place Arago. On place de Verdun, under the plane trees in front of Le Castille, the *Grand Café de la Poste* is a great place to watch the world go by, and it is here, too, that on summer evenings you will see the Catalan dance, the *sardana*, being performed by kids, grandparents – anyone whom the spirit moves. There is also **live street theatre and music** in the city centre every Thursday night during July and August (ask at the tourist office for details).

In midsummer, you can witness more music and general Catalan merrymaking at the festival of **Les Feux de St-Jean**, though Perpignan is better known for **La Procession de la Sanch**, the Good Friday procession of penitents that goes from the church of St-Jacques to the cathedral between 3pm and 5pm.

Around Perpignan

CANET-PLAGE is the best place near Perpignan to test the waters of the Mediterranean, although there is nothing to recommend the place, except that its beach is wide and sandy and the sea is wet; take a 25-minute bus ride east from place Catalogne in Perpignan (CTP bus #1; hourly). The same goes for the other resorts around here: Port Leucate, Port Bacarès (complete with weathered Greek ferry beached to make a casino and nightclub) and St-Cyprien.

Perhaps more interesting, 15km north and served by several trains a day, is the **Château de Salses** (daily: April, May & Oct 9.30am–12.30pm & 2–6pm; June–Sept 9.30am–6.30/7pm; Nov–March 10am–noon & 2–5pm; 32F), built for the king of Aragon in the early fifteenth century, and one of the first forts to be designed with a ground-hugging profile to protect it from artillery fire. Its superior design apparently put Vauban's nose so out of joint that he wanted it demolished, a task that proved impossible.

Another place, with not so much to see, but very moving because of its associations, is the vine-girt village of **TAUTAVEL**, 25km northwest off the St-Paul-de-Fenouillet road. In 1971 the remains of the oldest known European human being – dated to around 450,000 BC – were discovered near the village, and a reconstruction of the skull is on display in the village's **Musée de la Préhistoire** (daily: Jan–March & Oct–Dec 10am–12.30pm & 2–6pm; April–June & Sept 10am–6pm; July & Aug 9am–9pm; 35F; ☎04.68.29.07.76), along with various finds from the cave where he was unearthed, the **Caune d'Arago**, a few kilometres north, which can itself be visited in July and August (daily 10am–noon & 12.30–5.30pm) or by arrangement with the museum. The local wines are worth sampling, too, along with those of Estagel and Rivesaltes.

Thirteen kilometres to the south, on the way to the resorts of the Côte Vermeille (see below) and served by the same buses and trains, lies the town of **ELNE**. This small place once had the honour of seeing Hannibal camp at its walls en route for Rome, and used to be the capital of Roussillon. It was only overtaken by Perpignan when the latter became the seat of the kings of Majorca. Today, it's worth a stop for its fortified, partially Romanesque **cathedral** and extremely beautiful **cloister** (daily: June–Sept 9.30am–6.45pm; April & May 9.30am–5.45pm; Oct–March 10–11.45am & 2–4.45pm; 25F). Though only one side of the cloister is strictly Romanesque, immaculately carved with motifs such as foliage, lions, goats and biblical figures, the three fourteenth-century Gothic ones have been made to harmonize perfectly. It is the best introduction to Roussillon Romanesque you could want, especially if you're planning to visit places like Serrabonne and St-Michel-de-Cuxa further west. Below the cathedral there are still a few streets of the old town left, twisting back down to the drab and unremarkable modern development.

The Côte Vermeille

Known as the **Côte Vermeille**, the last few kilometres of shore before Spain, where the Pyrenees sweep down to the sea, once held a handful of attractive seaside villages. Tourism has put paid to that, though all are well served by buses and trains from Perpignan.

ARGELÈS, the first of the resorts with the last of the wide sandy beaches on this stretch of coast, is lively and friendly but packed out with foreign tourists. The **Musée Casa des Albères** in rue de l'Égalité (Mon–Fri 9am–noon & 3–6pm, Sat 9am–noon; 10F) has some interesting exhibits of local arts and traditions.

A few kilometres south, **COLLIOURE**, set on its bay and once by far the prettiest of these places, inspiring Matisse and Derain in 1905 to embark on their explosive Fauvist colour experiments, is now overly quaint, to the point where you can follow the *Chemin de Fauvisme* with reproductions of their works fixed to walls around the town. Palm trees line the curving beach, while behind the town, slopes of vines and olives rise to ridges crowned with ruined forts and watchtowers. The **Château des Templiers** (daily 10am–5/6pm; 20F), which dominates the town, was founded by the Templars in the twelfth century, and has undergone numerous alterations, especially at the hands of the kings of Majorca and Aragon in the fourteenth century and again after the Treaty of the Pyrenees gave Collioure to France. Today, it is largely given over to summertime exhibitions. Collioure's other landmark is the distinctive round belfry of the seventeenth-century **church of Notre-Dame-des-Anges** (daily 9am–noon & 2–6), formerly the harbour lighthouse; inside the nave are some exuberant Baroque altarpieces. Behind it two small **beaches** are divided by a causeway leading to the **chapel of St-Vincent**, built on what used to be a rocky islet, while to the left a concrete path follows the rocky shore to the bay of **Le Racou** back towards Argelès.

Behind the château lies the **old harbour**, where half a dozen brightly painted lateen-rigged fishing boats are often beached, all that remains of Collioure's traditional fleet. The attractive surrounding streets of pink- and beige-washed houses are the centre of tourist activity. The **tourist office** is here on place du 18-juin (July & Aug Mon–Sat 9am–8pm, Sun 10am–noon & 3–6pm; rest of year Mon–Sat 9am–noon & 2–6/7pm; ☎04.68.82.15.47, fax 04.68.82.46.29). Two pleasant places to **stay** are the *Triton* (☎04.68.98.39.39, fax 04.68.82.11.32; ②) and *Boramar* (☎04.68.82.07.06; ③; April–Oct), both on the main beach close to the through-road. Cheaper, though a little grim, is the *Majorque*, 16 av de-Gaulle (☎04.68.82.29.22; ①). The best **campsite** is the seaside *La Girelle* (☎04.68.81.25.56, fax 04.68.81.87.02; April–Sept), but there are numerous others in the area should it be full. Rue Camille-Pelletan, leading out to the harbour, has some moderate cafés and **restaurants**. Otherwise, try *El Capillo*, 22 rue St-Vincent (menus from 90F), or the smarter *La Marinade*, on place 18-juin (from 120F), both serving Catalan dishes.

PORT-VENDRES, 3km further down the coast, is a functional sort of place. Although the harbour has never been as busy as it was in the nineteenth century, with colonial trade and ferries from North Africa, it still lands more fish than any other place on this stretch of coast. The boats come in between about 4.30pm and 6pm every day except Sunday; you can watch them unload and auction the catch on the dock at the far end of the harbour. Otherwise, there is little to see here.

South towards **BANYULS**, 7km further on, where the **GR10** finally comes down to the sea, the road winds through attractive scenery with the Albères hills rising steeply on the right. The town, built round a broad sweep of pebble beach, is pleasant but lacks the charm of Collioure and the energy of more popular resorts. There are, however, several things to do before moving on. One is to visit the seafront **aquarium** of the Laboratoire Arago (daily summer 9am–noon & 2–10pm; winter closes 6.30pm; 24F), run by the Sorbonne's marine biology department, whose tanks contain a comprehensive collection of the region's fish and submarine life. Banyuls was also the birthplace of the sculptor Aristide **Maillol**, whose works can be seen in front of the Mairie and on the port, as well as at the museum at Mas Maillol, 4km outside the town, where he is buried (daily except Tues: May–Sept 10am–noon & 4–7pm; rest of year 10am–noon & 2–5pm; closed Dec; 20F). You could also sample the dark, full-bodied Banyuls **wine**, an *appellation* which, apart from Banyuls itself, applies only to the vineyards of Collioure, Port-Vendres and Cerbère. The best place to do this is the Cellier des Templiers, on rte du Mas-Reig, just under the rail line at the foot of the steep brown-stone terraces of Banyuls's own vineyards (April–Oct daily 9.30am–7pm; Nov–March Mon–Sat 9.30am–12.30pm & 2–6pm). For further information consult the **tourist office** opposite the Hôtel de Ville on the seafront (July & Aug Mon–Fri 9.30am–7.30pm, Sat & Sun 10am–7.30pm; rest of year Mon–Sat 9am–noon & 2.30–6.30pm). One of the cheaper **hotels** is *Le Manoir*, at 20 rue du Maréchal Joffre (☎04.68.88.32.98; ②), and there is a **camping municipal** on av Guy Malé (☎04.68.88.32.13; April to mid-Oct). For somewhere to **eat**, *Chez Rosa*, at 22 rue St-Pierre, serves hearty fare at reasonable prices (from 80F), while *La Pergola* (75F) and *Al Fanal* (95F), both on seafront avenue du Fontaulé, are more upmarket options.

A magnificent winding drive snakes up from Banyuls through the vineyards to the **Tour Madeloc**, a watchtower built by Jaime I of Majorca at the end of the thirteenth century on the crest of a ridge at about 650m. On a clear day, you can see down into Spain, along the coast, across to Montpellier and over the Corbières, with the castles of Quéribus and Peyrepertuse easily visible.

Vallespir and the valley of the Tech

The first stop on the D115, the main road which follows the **Tech valley** inland all the way up to the Spanish border at Prats-de-Mollo, is **CÉRET**, capital of the Vallespir region, and served like the rest of the valley by regular buses from Perpignan's gare routière. It is a delightful place, friendly and bustling, with a wonderfully shady old town overhung by huge plane trees. The streets are typically narrow and winding, opening onto small squares like the **place des Neuf-Jets**, so called because of its trickling fountain. There's a large and varied Saturday **market** spilling out of place Pablo-Picasso into the main street, av d'Espagne, where two remnants of the medieval walls, the **Porte de France** and **Porte d'Espagne**, are visible. In summer, Céret is also a big centre for corridas; the arena is on the other side of town from the market, out towards the Amélie-les-Bains road. Other high points include the Easter Sunday procession of the Resurrected Christ, at a time of year when Céret's famous cherry harvest is also getting under way. And there is an international *sardana* jamboree on the penultimate Sunday in August.

Céret's main sight, however, is the remarkable **Musée d'Art Moderne** (July–Sept daily 10am–7pm; rest of year daily except Tues 10am–6pm; 35F), just off bd Maréchal-Joffre. In the early years of this century, Céret's charms, coupled with the presence here of the Catalan artist and sculptor Manolo, drew a number of avant-garde artists to the town, including Matisse and Picasso, who personally dedicated a number of pictures to the museum; it also contains work by Chagall, Dali and Dufy, among others. Among the Picassos is a marvellous series of ceramic bowls illustrating bullfighting scenes, and a sketch of a *sardana*.

You can get more information on the corridas and other aspects of the town from the **tourist office** on av Clemenceau (July & Aug daily 9am–1pm & 3–7pm; rest of year Mon–Fri 10am–noon & 2–5pm, Sat 10am–noon; ☎04.68.87.00.53, fax 04.68.87.32.43). If you're **staying**, the *Hôtel Vidal* in the place du 4-septembre (☎04.68.87.00.85, fax 04.68.87.62.33; ②; restaurant from 78F) is a very attractive and reasonably priced place. The **camping municipal** is just out of town on the Maureillas road.

For **eating**, there is a good, cheap restaurant-crêperie, *Le Pied dans le Plat*, on place des Neuf-Jets, while gourmets with money to spare can try the best food for miles around at *Les Feuillants* (☎04.68.87.37.88; closed Sun eve & Mon; 260F upwards), whose sophisticated ambience features utterly delicious Catalan cuisine.

To the Spanish frontier

West of Céret, past the leaping single span of its fourteenth-century **Pont du Diable**, the view opens north towards the towering imminence of the Canigou Massif. **AMÉLIE-LES-BAINS**, the next place you come to, is a rather stodgy health spa for the elderly and rheumatic, and hardly worth a stop. If an **overnight stay** is necessary, *Hôtel La Chaumière* at 2 av du Vallespir (☎04.68.39.05.35; ②), right on the river in the middle of town, is an attractive place, and there are various **campsites**, including the *Hollywood* back towards Céret at La Forge (mid-March to mid-Nov).

ARLES-SUR-TECH, 4km up the valley, is a more interesting proposition. It has a beautiful Romanesque **abbey**, whose Carolingian origins in the ninth century are thought to account for its back-to-front alignment of altar at the west end and the entrance at the east. The massive interior is impressive, but the abbey's most renowned feature is the **cloister** (daily 10am–noon & 2–6pm; free), whose pointed white marble arches and twin columns prefigure the Gothic, showing its relative lateness compared to other examples of Romanesque in the region, like Serrabonne (see p.712). Twin towers flank the church, while against the wall outside the east front – whose plainness is beautifully relieved, as the sun turns, by the shadow of blind arcading – stands a very ancient (fourth- or fifth-century) sarcophagus, known as the **Ste Tombe**, which has the mysterious and scientifically inexplicable habit of slowly filling with very pure water. Every year, on 30 July, when Arles celebrates its fête dedicated to the saints Abdon and Sennen, the water is syphoned out and distributed after mass to the pilgrims who have come to worship. The town's other points of interest include the probably prehistoric **Fête de l'Ours**, a festival designed to exorcize human fear of the bear, traditionally held at the end of February when the bears woke from their winter hibernation. There is also a torchlight **Procession de la Sanch** at Easter. The **GR10** passes through Arles, climbing north towards the Cortalets refuge on Canigou and south towards the Roc de France.

The **tourist office** (Mon–Sat 2–6pm, July & Aug also 10am–noon; ☎/fax 04.68.39.11.99) is in rue Barjau, and you can **stay** at the attractive *Hôtel les Glycines* on rue du Jeu-de-Paume (☎04.68.39.10.09, fax 04.68.39.83.02; ②), with a good restaurant (from 85F) and wisteria-shaded terrace. The **campsite** is on the west side of town.

A couple of kilometres out of Arles, on the road to Prats-de-Mollo, is the entrance to the **Gorges de la Fou**, some 2km in length, very narrow and up to 250m deep (daily April–Oct 10am–6pm; closed in bad weather; 25F; ☎04.68.39.16.21). It's spectacular, but unfortunately something of a tourist trap, with a car park, admission charge, snacks, and a metal catwalk all along the bottom of the gorge.

After the gorge, the road climbs on towards the border, between valley sides thick with walnut, oak and sweet chestnut, to **PRATS-DE-MOLLO**. Prats is the last French town before the border with Spain, and has a very Spanish atmosphere. Most of the population seems to sit around or play pétanque in El Firal, the main square. It's surprisingly unspoilt for a border town, and its **ville haute** makes a wonderful wander, with steep cobbled streets and a weather-worn grey church with marvellous ironwork on the door under the porch. The encircling walls were rebuilt in the seventeenth century after the suppression of a local revolt against the taxation newly imposed by Louis XIV after the Treaty of the Pyrenees brought these lands under his sway. The **Fort Lagarde** (July & Aug daily 10am–7pm;April–June & Sept–Oct 2–5/6pm, closed Tues; 15F), on the heights above the town, also dates from this period, built to keep the local population in check as much as keeping the Spanish out. For **accommodation**, try *Hôtel des Touristes*, in av du Haut-Vallespir (☎04.68.39.72.12, fax 04.68.39.79.22; ②; June–Oct), or, if you're **camping**, there's a municipal site 1km along the road towards La Preste.

From here it is only 13km to the border on the **Col d'Ares**. The next place of any size on the other side is **Camprodon**, a village about 18km away. Alternatively, if you're feeling energetic, you can bus or hitch the 8km north to the spa town of La Preste, and then walk over the **Col Prégon**. It's about an hour's steep climb to the top, followed by another hour's more gentle descent down to the small village of **Espinavell** – leave the road at the first turning on the right before you get into La Preste, and then take the path from La Forge.

From the Tech to the Têt

The only practical route between the **valleys of the Tech and the Têt**, especially if you're hitching, is the D618 across the eastern spurs of Canigou from Amélie-les-Bains to Bouleternère. It's 43 slow kilometres of mountain road, twisting and climbing through magnificent woods of holm oak, cork oak, regular oak, chestnut, ash and cherry, with explosions of yellow broom and tangles of wild honeysuckle, past isolated half-derelict farms or *mas*, some still tenanted by survivors of the post-1968 migration from the towns. About halfway along, the three-house hamlet of **Belpuig** stands on the road. One of its buildings is the **Chapelle de la Trinité**, a tiny, dark Romanesque church in grey and yellow stone with elaborate doors and a particularly fine crucifix from the twelfth century. Past the cemetery and up the hill beside a pine plantation, a path climbs to the ruined **Château de Belpuig**, some fifteen minutes' walk from the road with long-range views over the surrounding country.

From here the road descends into the valley bottom, through the pretty hamlet of **Boule d'Amont**, before climbing again to the remarkable **Prieuré de Serrabonne** (daily 10am–5.30/6pm; 10F), some 4km up an asphalt lane above the road. Even without its carvings, Serrabonne (consecrated in 1151) would still be impressive purely by virtue of its location: high on the scrub-covered mountainside, with massive views over the rocky Boulès valley and into the valley of the Têt. Yet it is also one of the finest examples – perhaps the finest – of Roussillon Romanesque. The interior of the church is breathtakingly simple, making the beautiful carvings on the capitals of the pillars in the tribune even more striking: vividly carved lions, centaurs, griffins and human figures with Oriental faces and haircuts – motifs brought back from the Crusades – all in the local pink marble. The altar is made of the same stone, as are the pillars and equally elaborate capitals of the cloister, which is set to one side of the church on a high terrace. Despite the rigours of monastic life here – all abandoned now – the settlement was well developed, and the remains of terraced cultivation and irrigation systems are still visible.

When you reach the Têt at Bouleternère, a four-kilometre detour would take you to **Ile-sur-Têt**, where there is a very interesting museum of sacred art, the **Centre d'Art Sacré** (July & Aug daily 10am–noon & 2–7pm; rest of year Mon & Wed–Sat 10am–noon & 3–6pm, Sun 3–6pm; 15F), whose exhibits include both temporary and permanent shows. Two kilometres south, at St-Michel-de-Llotes, you'll find the **Musée de l'Agriculture Catalane**, (daily except Tues: June–Sept 10am–noon & 3–7pm; rest of year 10am–noon & 2–6pm; 15F), a well-presented collection of antique farming implements.

Canigou and the valley of the Têt

The upper part of the **Têt valley**, known as the **Pays de Conflent**, is utterly dominated by **Canigou**. The valley bottoms are lush with peach and apple orchards – with the possibility of work as a picker from June onwards – but the mountain presides over all, vast and uncompromising.

Prades

The valley capital is **PRADES**, easily accessible by train and bus on the Perpignan/Villefranche/La Tour-de-Carol route and, whether or not you stay, the obvious starting point for all excursions in the Canigou region. It is an attractive place, although there are no great sights beyond the **church of St-Pierre** in the town centre, but it enjoys a standing way out of proportion to its size or economic power. This is largely thanks to the Catalan cellist Pablo Casals, who set up home here as an exile and fierce opponent of the Franco regime in Spain. In 1950 he instituted the internationally renowned **music festival** now held every year in the abbey of St-Michel-de-Cuxa (see below) from late July to the middle of August. Prades is also a centre of ardent Catalan feeling. It hosts a Catalan university in August and boasts the first Catalan-language primary school in France.

The **tourist office** at 4 rue Victor-Hugo (July & Aug daily 9am–noon & 2–6.30pm; rest of year Mon–Fri 9am–noon & 2–5pm; ☎04.68.05.41.02, fax 04.68.05.21.79) is a mine of information about the area and can sort out advance bookings for the music festival. For **accommodation**, try the *Hostalrich* (☎04.68.96.05.38, fax 04.68.96.01.27; ②), or *Les Glycines* (☎04.68.96.51.65; b), both on avenue de-Gaulle, at the south end of rue Victor-Hugo. A slightly smarter alternative, though it's on the route nationale, is the *Hexagone* (☎04.68.05.31.31, fax 04.68.05.24.89; c). If you have a car, you could try the delightful *Hôtel St Joseph*, across the river in Molitg-les-Bains (☎04.68.05.02.11, fax 04.68.05.05.23; ②), which has an excellent restaurant (from 80F). Alternatively, head up towards Vernet-les-Bains on the flanks of Canigou (see below). The **camping municipal** (☎04.68.96.29.83; May–Oct) is by the river on the road to Molitg.

Close to Prades is one of the loveliest abbeys in the country. **St-Michel-de-Cuxa** (Mon–Sat 9.30–11.50am & 2–5/6pm, Sun 2–5/6pm; 20F), 3km from Prades, dates from around 1000, and although it was mutilated after the Revolution it is still beautiful, with its crenellated tower silhouetted against the wooded slopes of Canigou. The bare stone crypt and church – the altar slab was rediscovered doing duty as a balcony on a house in the village of Vinça – are impressive enough, but the glory of the place is the **cloister**. Although some of the capitals were shipped off to the Cloisters Museum in New York earlier this century, those that remain are a feast for the eyes. Carved in the twelfth century in rose-pink marble from Villefranche, they are decorated with exact and highly stylized human, animal and vegetable motifs. The monastery is still inhabited by a small community of Benedictines from Monserrat in Spain.

Eus to Comes

For an undemanding walk that will give you a sense of country life, at least as it used to be in these parts, head over to **EUS** on the far side of the valley from Prades. The upper, medieval, part of the village grouped round its **fortress church** has been largely taken over by Parisians and foreigners, to the displeasure of the farming inhabitants of the lower, more modern part – a common phenomenon in these picturesque but depopulated villages. To the left of the church, an old mule road climbs up through the scrubland to the derelict village of **Comes** – with a single shepherd and his family in residence – in about one hour.

Climbing the Pic

You can get at least part of the way up the **Pic du Canigou** by car or on foot. **Cars** – and you would be well advised not to try it in a much-loved saloon – can get as far as the *Chalet des Cortalets* refuge either by the track from Villerach or the even steeper and rougher mining road that begins by the *Al Pouncy* **campsite** near Fillols and passes the *Refuge de Balatg* and the now vandalized *Cabane des Cortalets*, where herds of cows and horses graze untended. (They are the best barometer of mountain weather, descending to lower altitudes when bad weather is imminent.) Both routes take about an hour. You can also **rent a jeep** and driver from Amalric (☎04.68.96.26.47), or Calas (☎60.46.05.27.08) in Prades, or Taurigna in Vernet-les-Bains (☎04.68.05.54.39) and Fillols (☎04.68.05.63.06). For **walkers**, the standard ascent is from Vernet on a path that begins about 1km along the road to Fillols, joining up with the **GR10** at the *Refuge de Bonaigua* (about 3hr) which you leave (about 90min) below the **Pic Joffre** to follow the HRP up the ridge to the summit (about 1hr). It is not for faint hearts, because the final ascent up a chimney is rather exposed. There is a five-hour alternative, starting from Casteil, passing the *Refuge Mariailles* (☎04.68.67.67.07; open all year; food served) on the GR10, then following the HRP for the last stretch via the *Cabane Arago*.

From the *Chalet des Cortalets* (☎04.68.96.36.19; May–Oct), which has a restaurant, or the smaller CAF refuge next door, it's an easy ninety-minute walk to the top. Strike west from the refuge through the last trees, past the little lake with a magnificent view into the cirque below the summit, round the back of the Pic Joffre, and up the long stony ridge to the cross and Catalan flag that crown the summit.

Although the **ascent** by this route is straightforward in good weather, you should be properly shod and clothed and have good large-scale maps. If you are not experienced and encounter frozen snow, turn back: a German couple slid to their deaths on the slopes between Pic Joffre and the summit in 1991. Midsummer is a great time to do the climb. On the night of June 23, which often coincides with the full moon, Catalans for kilometres around, including half the population of Barcelona, gather on the top to light the bonfire from which a flame is carried to kindle all the *feux de St-Jean* of the Catalan villages, though the scene around the refuge can be pretty horrendous, with tents, ghetto blasters and litter galore.

Vernet-les-Bains

A quiet and not unpleasant little spa, **VERNET-LES-BAINS** can make a useful base for picking up provisions and information. It has a **tourist office** in place de la Mairie (July & Aug daily 9am–12.30pm & 3–7pm, Sun 10am–noon; rest of year Mon–Fri 10am–noon & 2–5pm, Sat 10am–noon; ☎04.68.05.55.35, fax 04.68.05.60.33) and plenty of **eating and drinking** possibilities in the main square, place de la République. It's also a good place to **stay** the night, either at *Hôtel d'Angleterre*, 9 av de Burnay (☎04.68.05.50.58; ①), or *Hôtel des Deux Lions*, 18 bd Clémenceau (☎04.68.05.55.42; ②; good restaurant from 75F), both with information on climbing Canigou. For a meal, try the popular *Le Pommier* in placette du Cady, just off the main square (from 60F). There are several **campsites** around Vernet and a **gîte d'étape** (☎04.68.05.51.30) just up the road in Casteil. Returning to the valley bottom at Villefranche-de-Conflent, you might want to stop off and look at the magnificent Romanesque church in **Corneilla** (key from the caretaker next door).

The abbey near Vernet

St-Martin-du-Canigou is just 2km from Vernet-les-Bains, or a half-hour walk above the hamlet of Casteil – with restaurants under the apple orchards, and a **campsite**,

Camping St-Martin, with swimming pool. Resurrected from its ruins at the turn of the century, the monastery occupies a narrow promontory of rock at over 1000m altitude. Quiet and serene, it is surrounded by the deep shade of chestnut and oak woods, and above it rise the precipitous slopes and eroded pinnacles of Canigou. Below, the ground drops sheer into the ravine of the Cady stream that rushes down from the Col de Jou. The buildings are visitable, in silent groups (mid-June to mid-Sept daily 10am, noon, 2pm, 3pm, 4pm & 5pm; winter daily except Tues 10am, noon, 2.30pm, 3.30pm & 4.30pm; 20F). What you see is a beautiful little garden and cloister overlooking the ravine, a low dark atmospheric chapel beneath the church and the church itself. Founded in the tenth century, St-Martin was the inspiration for the Romanesque architecture of the region. The graves of the founder, Count Guifred of Cerdagne, and his wife lie in the rock by the church door.

From the reception building, a **path** leads up to a rocky viewpoint from which you can look down on the monastery and away across the valley to the surrounding mountains. As you go up, you pass a signpost to Moura on a path which leads first to the Col de Segalès on the GR10, then, on the HRP, to the *Cabane Arago* and finally to the summit of Canigou – the last stretch involving a rather steep hands-and-feet scramble which might alarm the inexperienced. For a different route back to Casteil, a path drops down into the Cady ravine just at the start of the monastery buildings.

Villefranche-de-Conflent and the Petit Train Jaune

A medieval garrison town suffering from arrested development, **VILLEFRANCHE-DE-CONFLENT** is a tourist classic and lives off it. But it is interesting: founded around 1100 by the counts of Cerdagne to bar the road to Moorish invaders, remodelled by Vauban in the seventeenth century after rebelling against annexation by France, its streets and fortifications have remained untouched by subsequent development. The **church of St-Jacques** is worth a look, and you can walk the **walls** for a fee (daily: July & Aug 10am–7pm; Sept–June 2–5pm; 20F). If you do so, you will see why Vauban constructed the **Libéria fortress** on the heights overlooking the town to protect it from "aerial" bombardment. The way up to the Libéria (daily 9am–8pm; 28F) is a stairway of a thousand steps beginning just across the old bridge and rail line at the end of rue St-Pierre. If you don't fancy the climb, ask at the **tourist office** (July & Aug daily 10am–noon & 2–6pm; rest of year Mon–Sat 2–5pm; ☎04.68.96.22.96, fax 04.68.96.07.24) by the church for the minibus (22F). For **accommodation**, it's better to try Vernet or Prades.

Villefranche is the terminus for trains from Perpignan (gare SNCF ☎04.68.96.56.62). From here up to **La Tour-de-Carol** on the Spanish frontier, transport is by SNCF bus, or, far nicer, the narrow-gauge **Petit Train Jaune**, which climbs to the valley head at a pace that allows you a walker's or cyclist's proximity to the scenery, especially in summer when some of the carriages are open-air.

On up the Têt

Just beyond Thuès-Entre-Valls, southwest of Villefranche on the left of the main N116, the wild wooded canyon of the **Gorges de la Carança** cuts south into the mountains towards Spain. A path follows the gorge to a junction with the GR10 at the refuge of the *Ras de la Carança* (3–4hr), while a further path continues on to meet the HRP on the frontier in another four hours.

At **Fontpédrouse**, 5km beyond Thuès, a road branches south across the river and up a grassy spur above the River Aigues towards the village of Prat-Balaguer. From the top of the rise directly opposite Fontpédrouse, a path leads down to the Aigues where water from **hot springs** forms three separate pools at different temperatures, where you can skinny-dip for free.

Another 10km up the main road brings you onto the wide **plateau of the Cerdagne**, whose once powerful counts controlled lands from Barcelona to Roussillon and endowed the monasteries of St-Michel-de-Cuxa, St-Martin-du-Canigou and Ripoll, now well inside Spain. It's an area that has never been sure whether it is Spanish or French. After the French annexation of Roussillon, it was partitioned, with Spain retaining – as it does today – the enclave of Lliva.

The first place you come to is the little garrison town of **MONT-LOUIS**, built by Vauban in 1679 and still used as a base for paratroops and marines. There isn't much to see, but it is a far pleasanter place to stay than the monstrous ski resort of **Font-Romeu**, just down the road. There's a **tourist office** (daily: mid-June to mid-Sept 10am–noon & 3–6pm; ☎04.68.04.21.97) and a delightful **hotel**, *Lou Roubaillou* (☎04.68.04.23.26, fax 04.68.04.14.09; ③), towards the back of the town near the barracks; its excellent restaurant has menus from 125F. **Campers** should head for the site at **Pla de Barres**, 3km away on the road to the Lac des Bouillousses (☎04.68.04.26.04, fax 04.68.04.21.18; June–Sept), and there's a **gîte d'étape** at La Cassagne farm (☎04.68.04.21.40), half an hour back down the main road.

Of things to do round about, there is a good four-hour walk from the pretty mountain village of **EYNE** up a valley renowned for its flowers and medicinal plants to the Col d'Eyne, and numerous walks in the **Carlit Massif** around the **Lac des Bouillousses** – where there's a CAF refuge (☎04.68.04.20.76), though the lake itself and parts accessible by car get very crowded in season. The region's curiosity is the **four solaire**, or solar power station (daily: June–Sept 10am–6/7.30pm; rest of year 10am–12.30pm & 2–6pm), at **ODEILLO** just below Font-Romeu, although the most impressive part of this, a screen composed of thousands of mirrors, can in fact be seen from the road.

travel details

Buses

Bayonne to: Biarritz (every 10/20 mins; 15–20min); Cambo-les-Bains (several daily; 40min); Capbreton (hourly; 30min); San Sebastian (2 daily; 1hr 45min); St-Jean-de-Luz (hourly; 45min).

Biarritz to: Bayonne (every 10/20 mins; 15–20min); Orthez (3 daily; 1hr 45min); Pau (3 daily; 2hr 30min); St-Jean-de-Luz (hourly; 30min); Salies-de-Béarn (4 daily; 1hr 20min).

Foix to: Ax-les-Thermes (7–8 daily except Sun; 1hr); Carcassonne (1 daily except Sun; 2hr 35min); Lavelanet (1 daily except Sun; 35min); Mirepoix (1 daily except Sun; 1hr 30min); Pamiers (4–6 daily; 25min); Quillan (1 daily; 3hr); Tarascon (7 daily except Sun; 20min); Toulouse (4–6 daily; 1hr 50min).

Lannemazan to: Arreau (4–5 daily; 30min); St-Lary (4–5 daily; 1hr).

Lourdes to: Argelès (8–9 daily; 20min); Bagnères-de-Bigorre (3 daily; 45min–1hr); Barèges (2–3 daily; 1hr); Cauterets (5 daily; 50min); Gavarnie (June to

mid-Sept 3 daily; 1hr 15min); Lannemazan (3 daily; 1hr); Luz-St-Sauveur (2–3 daily; 45min); Pau (4 daily; 1hr 15min); Pierrefitte-Nestalas (8–9 daily; 30min); Tarbes (hourly; 30min).

Pau to: Agen (1 daily; 3hr); Artouste and Gabas (summer Sat & Sun 1 daily; 1hr 45min); Bayonne (3–4 daily; 2hr 15min); Biarritz (3–4 daily; 2hr 30min); Eaux-Bonnes (2 daily; 1hr 15min); La Gourette (winter only 2 daily; 1hr 45min); Laruns (2 daily; 1hr 5min); Lembeye (2 daily; 1hr); Lourdes (4 daily; 1hr 15min); Mauléon (1 daily; 1hr 50min); Navarrenx (1 daily; 1hr 25min); Orthez (3–4 daily; 45min); Tarbes (6 daily; 1hr).

Perpignan to: Amélie-les-Bains (frequent; 1hr); Argelès (hourly; 30min); Arles-sur-Tech (frequent; 1hr 20min); Banyuls (5 daily; 1hr 10min); Céret (frequent; 55min); Collioure (5 daily; 45min); Font-Romeu (1 daily; 2hr 30min); Latour-de-Carol (3 daily; 3hr); Mont-Louis (3 daily; 2hr 15min); Port-Vendres (5 daily; 55min); Prades (3 daily; 1hr); Prats-de-Mollo (5 daily; 1hr 50min); La Preste (5 daily; 2hr 5min); Villefranche-de-Conflent (several daily; 1hr 15min).

Quillan to: Carcassonne (4 daily; 1hr 30min); Comus (2 daily; 1hr 5min); Limoux (4 daily; 40min); Perpignan (2 daily; 1hr 30min).

St-Girons to: Aulus-les-Bains (1–2 daily; 1hr 15min); Boussens (several daily; 40min); Foix (4 daily; 1hr); Sentein (1 daily; 1hr); Toulouse (2–3 daily; 2hr 30min).

St-Jean-de-Luz to: Cambo-les-Bains (2 daily; 50min); Espelette (2 daily; 40min); Hasparren (2 daily; 1hr 5min); Hendaye (half-hourly; 30min); Sare-la-Rhune (2–3 daily; 30min).

Tarascon to: Auzat (Mon & Fri 1 daily; 30min).

Tarbes to: Bagnères-de-Bigorre (hourly; 30min); Lourdes (hourly; 30min); St-Lary (1 daily; 2hr 10min); Tarbes-Ossun-Lourdes airport (1–2 daily; 30min–1hr).

Trains

Bayonne to: Biarritz (hourly; 10min); Bordeaux (8–9 daily; 1hr 50min); Boussens (4 daily; 3hr); Cambo-les-Bains (4 daily; 20min); Hendaye (hourly; 35min); Lannemazan (4 daily; 2hr 40min); Lourdes (6–7 daily; 1hr 40min); Montréjeau (4 daily; 2hr 50min); Orthez (4 daily; 50min); Pau (4 daily; 1hr 15min); San Sebastian (half-hourly; 1hr 40min); St-Gaudens (4 daily; 3hr); St-Jean-de-Luz (hourly; 30min); St-Jean-Pied-de-Port (4 daily; 1hr 10min); Tarbes (4 daily; 2hr); Toulouse (4 daily; 4hr).

Foix to: Ax-les-Thermes (5 daily; 45min); Barcelona (4 daily; 5hr 15min–6hr); Latour-de-Carol (5 daily; 1hr 40min–2hr); Tarascon (several daily; 20min); Toulouse (several daily; 40min–1hr).

Luchon to: Montréjeau (2 daily; 40min); Toulouse (2 daily; 2hr).

Montréjeau to: Boussens (4–5 daily; 25min); St-Gaudens (3–4 daily; 10min); Lourdes (7–8 daily; 50min); Luchon (2 daily; 40min); Pau (7–8 daily; 1hr 35min); Tarbes (7–8 daily; 35min); Toulouse (3–4 daily; 1hr 15min).

Pau to: Bordeaux (6–7 daily; 2hr); Dax (6–7 daily; 30min); Lourdes (8–9 daily; 30 min); Oloron-Ste-Marie (4 daily; 30min); Tarbes (8–9 daily; 40 min).

Perpignan to: Argelès (hourly; 20min); Banyuls (hourly; 40min); Barcelona (2–3 daily; 2hr 15min–5hr); Cerbère (hourly; 50min); Collioure (hourly; 23min); Elne (hourly; 10min); Leucate (hourly; 25min); Narbonne (hourly; 40min); Port-Bou (7–8 daily; 50min); Port-la-Nouvelle (hourly; 35min); Port-Vendres (hourly; 30min); Prades (7 daily; 40min); Rivesaltes (hourly; 10min); Salses (hourly; 15min); Villefranche-de-Conflent (7 daily; 40min).

Quillan to: Carcassonne (1–2 daily; 1hr); Limoux (1–2 daily; 30min).

Tarbes to: Bordeaux (6–7 daily; 3hr); Dax (6–7 daily; 1hr 30min); Lourdes (8–9 daily; 20min).

CHAPTER ELEVEN

LANGUEDOC

Languedoc is more an idea than a geographical entity. The modern region covers only a fraction of the lands where once **Occitan** or the *langue d'oc* – the language of *oc*, the southern Gallo-Latin word for *oui* – was spoken. These stretched south from Bordeaux and Lyon into Spain and northwest Italy.

The heartland today is the Bas Languedoc, the coastal plain and dry, stony, vine-growing hills between Carcassonne and Nîmes. It is here that the Occitan movement has its power base, demanding greater independence and recognition of its linguistic and cultural distinctiveness. Its appeal derives from widespread resentment against

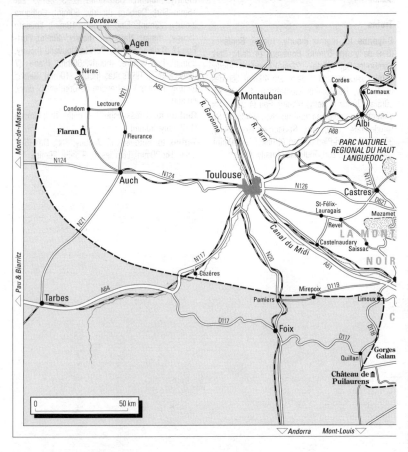

subservience to the bureaucrats of remote and alien Paris. In recent times this has been focused on Parisian determination to drag the province into the twentieth century, with massive tourist development on the coast and the drastic transformation of the cheap wine industry. But it is also mixed up in the collective folk-memory with the brutal repression of the Protestant Camisards around 1700, the thirteenth-century massacres of the Cathars, and the subsequent obliteration of the brilliant *langue d'oc* troubadour civilization. It is a hostility that has made an essentially rural and conservative population vote – paradoxically – for the Left.

It's a quirky, eccentric part of the world, and, although things are changing under the impact of a modernized economy, the Occitanian identity remains strong. Thousands of students take the language at school and follow courses at the universities of Montpellier and Toulouse, and a number of writers use Occitan as their normal medium of expression.

Toulouse, the cultural capital, though included in this chapter, lies outside the official region but is a deserved high spot among numerous and various other attractions. There are great stretches of dramatic landscape and river gorges, from the **Cévennes** foothills in the east to the **Montagne Noire** and the **Corbières** hills in the

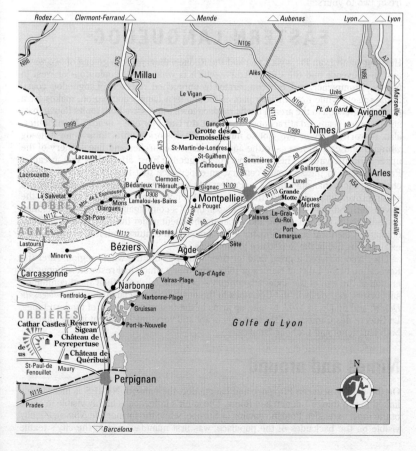

ACCOMMODATION PRICE CATEGORIES

Each hotel in this chapter has a symbol which corresponds to one of eight price categories.

① Under 160F   ④ 300–400F   ⑦ 600–700F
② 160–220F   ⑤ 400–500F   ⑧ Over 700F
③ 220–300F   ⑥ 500–600F

The prices quoted are for the cheapest available double room in high season, though remember that many of the cheap places will have more expensive rooms with en-suite facilities.

---

west There's superb ecclesiastical architecture in Albi and St-Guilhem-le-Désert, medieval towns in Cordes and Carcassonne, and the unforgettably romantic Cathar castles to the south. Nîmes has extensive Roman remains, and there are great swathes of beach where – away from the major resorts – you can still find a kilometre or two to yourself.

EASTERN LANGUEDOC

Heading south from Paris via Lyon and the Rhône valley, you can go one of two ways: east to Provence and the Côte d'Azur – which is what most people do – or west to Nîmes, Montpellier and the comparatively untouched northern Languedoc coast. **Nîmes** itself, while not officially part of the modern Languedoc region, makes for a good introduction to the area, a hectic modern town impressive both for its Roman past and for some scattered attractions – the **Pont du Gard** for one – nearby. **Montpellier**, also, is worth a day or two, not so much for any historical attractions as for a heady vibrancy and ease of access to the ancient villages, churches and fine scenery of the upper **Hérault valley**. This is the part of Languedoc most affected by the spread of Protestantism in the sixteenth century, an experience that has marked the region's character more than any other. The Protestants, with their attachment to rationality and self-improvement, espoused the cause of French over Occitan, supported the Revolution and the Republic, fought Napoléon III's coup against the 1848 Revolution and adhered to the anticlerical and socialist movement under the Third Republic. They dominated the local textile industry in the nineteenth century and, interestingly, were extremely active in the Resistance to the Nazis.

They also suffered a great deal for their cause, as did the whole region. After the Revocation of the Edict of Nantes in 1685 – the treaty which had restored religious toleration at the end of the sixteenth century – persecution drove their most committed supporters, especially in the Cévennes to the north, to form clandestine *assemblées du Désert*; and finally, in 1702, to take up arms in the first guerrilla war of modern times, La Guerre des Camisards. These conflicts are still very much present in the minds of both Huguenot and Catholic families.

Nîmes and around

On the border between Provence and Languedoc, the name of **NÎMES** is inescapably linked to two things – denim and Rome. The latter's influence is highly visible in some of the most extensive Roman remains in Europe, while the former (*de Nîmes*), equally visible on the backsides of the populace, was first manufactured in the city's textile mills, and exported to the southern USA in the nineteenth century to clothe slaves. It's worth a visit, in part for the ruins and, nowadays, for the city's new-found energy and direction, enlisting the services of a galaxy of architects and designers – including Norman Foster, Jean Nouvel and Philippe Starck – in its bid to wrest southern supremacy from neighbouring Montpellier.

Arrival, information and accommodation

The **gare SNCF** (☎04.66.23.50.50) is ten minutes' walk southeast of the city centre at the end of av Feuchères, which leads down from Esplanade Charles-de-Gaulle, with the **gare routière** (☎04.66.29.52.00) just behind in rue Ste-Félicité (access through the train station). There's a tourist office annexe in the station, which handles hotel bookings (daily 9.30am–12.30pm & 2–6pm), and a **main tourist office** at 6 rue Auguste, by the Maison Carrée (July & Aug Mon–Fri 8am–8pm, Sat 9am–7pm, Sun 10am–5pm; rest of year Mon–Fri 8.30am–7pm, Sat 9am–noon & 2–5pm, Sun 10am–noon; ☎04.66.67.29.11, fax 04.66.21.81.04).

Several recommended **hotels** are within easy walking distance of the station. The basic *Hôtel de la Couronne* is off to the right at 4 square de la Couronne (☎04.66.67.51.73; ①), but be warned that the streetside rooms can be very noisy. A little further away, at no. 3 on the quiet rue des Chapeliers, the friendly *Hôtel Concorde* (☎ & fax 04.66.67.91.03; ①) offers more acceptable accommodation, as do the nearby *Hôtel de la Mairie*, at 11 rue des Greffes (☎04.66.67.65.91; ①), and the old-fashioned but rather delightful *Hôtel Lisita* (☎04.66.67.66.20, fax 04.66.76.22.30; ②) at 2bis bd des Arènes – the visiting bullfighters' favourite. Another attractive alternative is the *Central*,

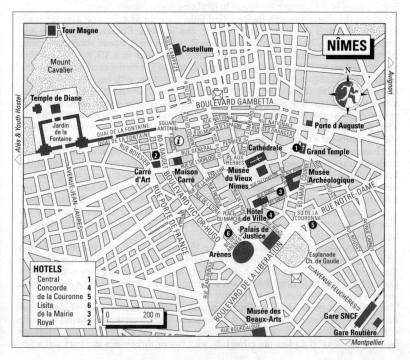

at 2 place du Château, close to the Protestant church (☎04.66.67.27.75, fax 04.66.21.77.79; ③), but best of all is the atmospheric *Royal*, near the Maison Carrée at 3 bd Alphonse-Daudet (☎04.66.58.28.27, fax 04.66.58.28.28; ③).

There's an attractive HI **youth hostel** with tent space on chemin de la Cigale, 2km northwest of the centre (☎04.66.23.25.04, fax 04.66.23.84.27); take bus #2 direction "Alès/Villeverte" from the gare SNCF to stop Stade. The last bus goes at 8pm. The **camping municipal** (☎04.66.38.09.21) is on rte de Générac, 5km south of the city centre, beyond the new Stade Costières and the autoroute.

The city

Most of what you'll want to see is contained within the boulevards de la Libération, Amiral-Courbet, Gambetta and Victor-Hugo, and there is much pleasure to be had from just wandering the narrow lanes that they enclose, discovering unexpected squares with their fountains and cafés. The focal point of the city, the first-century Roman arena, known as **Les Arènes** (daily: April–Oct 9am–6.30pm; Nov–March 9am–noon & 2–5pm; 28F), lies at the junction of boulevard de la Libération and boulevard Victor-Hugo. One of the best-preserved Roman arenas anywhere, its arcaded two-storey facade conceals massive interior vaulting, riddled with corridors and supporting raked tiers of seats with a capacity of more than 20,000 spectators, whose staple fare was the blood and guts of gladiatorial combat. When Rome's sway was broken by the barbarian invasions, the arena became a fortress and eventually a slum, home to an incredible 2000 people when it was cleared in the early 1800s. Today it has recovered something of its former role, with the passionate summer crowds still turning out for some real-life blood-letting – Nîmes is the premier European bullfighting scene outside Spain.

Behind the arena, through the beautiful little place du Marché, rue Fresque leads towards the city's other famous landmark, the **Maison Carrée** (daily: June–Aug 9am–noon & 2.30–7pm; Sept–May 9am–noon & 2–6pm; free), a neat, jewel-like temple, celebrated for its integrity and harmony of proportion. Built in 5 AD, it is dedicated to the adopted sons of the Emperor Augustus: all part of the business of blowing up the imperial personality cult. No surprise, then, that Napoléon, with his love of flummery and ennobling his cronies to boost his own legitimacy, should have taken it as the model for the church of the Madeleine in Paris. The temple stands in its own small square opposite rue Auguste, where the Roman forum used to be. Around it are scattered pieces of Roman masonry. On the north side of place de la Maison Carrée, there's a new example of French architectural boldness, the **Carrée d'Art**, by English architect Norman Foster. In spite of its size, this box of glass, aluminium and concrete sits modestly among the ancient roofs of Nîmes, its slender portico echoing that of the Roman temple opposite. Light pours in through walls and roof, giving it a grace and weightlessness that makes it not in the least incongruous. Housed within the Carrée d'Art is a state-of-the-art library of newspapers, periodicals, books, CDs and videos, plus a magnificent exhibition space that's generally used for shows of postwar art (Tues–Sun 10am–6pm; library free, exhibitions 28F). There is a roof-terrace café at the top, overlooking the Maison Carrée.

Though already a prosperous city on the Via Domitia, the main Roman road from Italy to Spain constructed in 118 BC, Nîmes did especially well by Augustus. He gave the city its walls, remnants of which surface here and there, and its gates, as the inscription on the surviving **Porte d'Auguste** at the end of rue Nationale – the Roman main street – records. He also, indirectly, gave it the chained crocodile of its coat of arms. The device was copied from an Augustan coin struck to commemorate his defeat of Antony and Cleopatra. And he settled his veterans on the surrounding land.

Running back east into the old quarter from the Maison Carrée, **rue de l'Horloge** leads to the delightful **place aux Herbes**, with two or three cafés and bars and a fine twelfth-century house on the corner of rue de la Madeleine. In the former bishop's palace, the **Musée du Vieux Nîmes** (Tues–Sun 11am–6pm; 28F) has displays of Renaissance furnishings and decor and documents to do with local history. Opposite, the **Cathédrale Notre-Dame-et-St-Castor** sports a handsome sculpted frieze on the west front illustrating the story of Adam and Eve, and a pediment inspired by the Maison Carrée. It is practically the only existing medieval building in town, as most were destroyed in the turmoil that followed the Michelade, the St Michael's Day massacre of Catholic clergy and notables by Protestants in 1567. Despite brutal repression in the wake of the Camisard insurrection of 1702, Nîmes was, and remains, a doggedly Protestant stronghold. Apart from that, the cathedral is of little interest, having been seriously mutilated in the Wars of Religion and significantly altered in the last century. The author, Alphonse Daudet, was born in its shadow, as was Jean Nicot – a doctor, no less – who introduced tobacco into France from Portugal in 1560 and gave his name to the world's most popular drug.

Banned from public office, the Protestants put their energy into making money. The results of their efforts can be seen in the seventeenth- and eighteenth-century hôtels they built themselves in the streets around the cathedral – rues de l'Aspic, Chapitre, Dorée and Grand-Rue, among others. Their church is the serious-looking **Grand Temple** on bd Amiral-Courbet. On the same street, **the Musée Archéologique** (Tues–Sun 11am–6pm; 28F), housed in a seventeenth-century Jesuit chapel at no. 13, is full of Roman bits and bobs. There's another museum, the **Musée des Beaux-Arts**, south of the Arènes in rue de la Cité-Foulc (Tues–Sun 11am–6pm; 28F), which prides itself on a huge Gallo-Roman mosaic showing the *Marriage of Admetus*, but is otherwise pretty ordinary.

The interior of the **Hôtel de Ville**, between rue Dorée and rue des Greffes, has been redesigned by the architect Jean-Michel Wilmotte, combining high-tech with classical stone. Most of the other major examples of revolutionary building are out on the southern edge of town: Jean Nouvel's pseudo-Mississippi-steamboat housing project off the Arles road behind the gare SNCF, named **Nemausus** after the deity of the local spring that gave Nîmes its name; and the magnificent sports stadium, the **Stades des Costières**, by Vittorio Gregotti, close to the autoroute along the continuation of avenue Jean-Jaurés. There's also a **bus depot** by Philippe Starck on avenue Carnot, just east of the centre.

Perhaps the most refreshing thing you can do while in Nîmes is head out to the **Jardin de la Fontaine**, northwest of the centre at the top end of avenue Jean-Jaurés, France's first public garden, created in 1750. At its foot flows the gloriously green and shady **Canal de la Fontaine**, built to supplement the rather unsteady supply of water from the *fontaine*, the Nemausus spring, whose presence in a dry, limestone landscape gave Nîmes its existence. Behind the formal entrance, where fountains, nymphs and formal trees enclose the so-called **Temple of Diana**, steps climb the steep wooded slope, adorned with grots and nooks and artful streams, to the **Tour Magne** (daily 9am–5/6.30pm; 12F), a 32-metre tower from Augustus's city walls, with a terrific view out over the surrounding country – as far, it is claimed, as the Pic du Canigou on the edge of the Pyrenees.

Eating and drinking

The best places to hang out for **coffees and drinks** are the numerous little squares scattered through the old town: place de la Maison-Carrée, place du Marché, place aux Herbes (breakfast here early at the *Café des Beaux-Arts*, as the sun is just climbing up behind the cathedral tower). Three classic Nîmes cafés are the *Napoléon*, in bd Victor-Hugo, and the *Grande* and *Petite Bourse*, side by side at the back of the Arènes on the corner of boulevard Victor-Hugo. For later in the evening, there's the very pretty *Carrée d'Art* piano bar on rue Gaston-Bossier, near the canal and the postmodern place d'Assas.

For **eating**, boulevard de la Libération and boulevard Amiral-Courbet harbour a stock of reasonably priced brasseries and pizzerias, and the squares too are full of possibilities. *La Truye qui Filhe*, 9 rue Fresque (lunchtimes only; closed Sun & Aug), is an attractive and not at all plastic self-service, where you can eat for around 50F. Also good for lunch is the *Flan Coco*, in an unbeatable courtyard setting in passage André-Malraux, 29 rue du Mérier-d'Espagne (Mon–Fri lunchtime only, Sat lunch & dinner; closed Sun & Aug; menus from 84F). Other possibilities include the popular and satisfying *Nicolas*, at 1 rue Poise, just off bd Amiral-Courbet (☎04.66.67.50.47; closed Mon & July 1–15; 70–140F), and the welcoming *Paradis du Couvent*, 21 rue du Grand Couvent (☎04.66.76.26.30; closed Mon; menus from 55–70F), while the *Zarzuela*, on pl du Marché, serves paella and other tasty Spanish fare (☎04.66.67.36.30; menus from 75F). For something a little more extravagant, try *La Belle Respire*, 12 rue de l'Étoile (☎04.66.21.27.21; closed Wed & Thurs noon; from 70F in summer or 130F, *carte* around 150F), which serves traditional home-cooked dishes; or *Ophélie*, 35 rue Fresque (☎04.66.21.00.19; closed Sun & Mon; dinner only, for around 200F), for something more imaginative.

The Pont du Gard and Uzès

Some twenty kilometres from Nîmes, the **Pont du Gard** is the greatest surviving stretch of a fifty-kilometre-long aqueduct built by the Romans in 19 AD to supply fresh water to the city. With just a seventeen-metre difference in altitude between start and finish, it was quite an achievement, running as it does up hill and down dale, through a tunnel, along the top of a wall, cut into trenches, and over rivers; the Pont du Gard carries it over the River Gard. Today the bridge is something of a tourist trap, but nonetheless a supreme piece of engineering, a brilliant combination of function and aesthetics. It made the impressionable Rousseau wish he'd been born Roman.

Three tiers of arches span the river, with the covered water conduit on the top, rendered with a special plaster waterproofed with a paint apparently based on fig juice. A visit here used to be a must for French journeymen masons on their traditional tour of the country, and many of them have left their names and home towns carved on the stonework. Markings made by the original builders are still visible on individual stones in the arches, such as "FR S III – frons sinistra", front side left no. 3. The Pont du Gard has recently undergone a massive restoration programme and work is now starting on improving the local amenities, including a historical museum planned for the summer of 1999.

THE BULLFIGHT

Nîmes's great passion is **bullfighting**, and its *ferias* are acknowledged and well-attended by both aficionados and fighters at the highest level. The wildest and most famous is the Feria de Pentecôte, which lasts five days over the Whitsun weekend. A couple of million people crowd into the town (hotel rooms need to be booked a year in advance), and every Tom, Dick and Harry opens a bodega at the bottom of the garden for dispensing booze. There are both *corridas*, which end with the killing of the bull, and semi-amateur *courses libres*, when a small posse of bulls are run through the streets and the daring try to snatch the *cocards* from their heads. In 1996, Nîmes witnessed the acclamation of the first ever woman matador, Cristina Sanchez, who won her spurs in the arena at Whitsun. Two other *ferias* take place: one at carnival time in February, when the inflatable roof of the Arènes is pulled over for protection from the weather; the other in the third week of September at grape-harvest time, the Feria des Vendanges. The **tourist office** can supply full details and advise you about accommodation if you want to visit at *feria* time.

Seventeen kilometres further on, near the start of the aqueduct and served by daily buses from Nîmes, **UZÈS** is a lovely old town perched on a hill above the River Alzon. Half-a-dozen medieval towers – the most fetching is the windowed Pisa-like **Tour Fenestrelle**, tacked onto the much later cathedral – rise above its tiled roofs and narrow lanes of Renaissance and Neoclassical houses, the residences of the seventeenth- and eighteenth-century local bourgeoisie, grown rich like their Protestant co-religionists in Nîmes on textiles. From the mansion of Le Portalet, with its view out over the valley, walk past the classical church of **St-Étienne** and into the medieval place aux Herbes, where there's a Sunday morning market, and up the arcaded rue de la République. The Gide family used to live off the square, the young André spending summer vacations with his granny there. To the right of rue de la République, the castle of **Le Duché** (daily: July–mid-Sept 10am–6.30pm; rest of year 10am–noon & 2–6pm; 50F), still inhabited by the same family a thousand years on, is dominated by its original keep, the **Tour Bermonde**. Today, there are guided tours around the castle building and exhibits of local history and vintage cars. Opposite, the courtyard of the eighteenth-century **Hôtel de Ville** holds summer concerts.

For details of these and other summer events, including more bull-running *corridas*, consult the **tourist office** in place Albert 1er on bd Gambetta (July & Aug Mon–Fri 9am–6pm, Sat 10am–noon & 2–5pm, Sun 10am–5pm; Sept–June Mon–Fri 9am–noon & 1.30–6pm, Sat 10am–noon; closed Sun; ☎04.66.22.68.88, fax 04.66.22.95.19), while the **bus station** (☎04.66.22.00.58) is further west on av de la Libération. Should you need a **bed**, the best bets are the *Hôtel La Taverne*, 4 rue Xavier-Sigalon (☎04.66.22.13.10, fax 04.66.22.45.90; ③), with a good restaurant up the road at no. 7 (from 78F); and the *Hôtel Provençale*, 1 rue Grande-Bourgade (☎ & fax 04.66.22.11.06; ②; restaurant from 79F). For luxurious surroundings and excellent food, head 4km west of town on the Arpaillargues road to the *Hôtel Marie d'Agoult* (☎04.66.22.14.48, fax 04.66.22.56.10; ⑦; restaurant from 145F; closed Nov–Easter). Alternatively, there is a **camping municipal** off av Maxime-Pascal (☎04.66.22.11.79; mid-June to mid-Sept), on the Bagnols-sur-Cèze road running northeast of town.

More Roman ruins ... and Sommières

About 25km west of Nîmes, off the Sommières road out of Lunel and close to the A9 autoroute, the Roman **Via Domitia** crosses the vineyards from the village of Gallargues to the bank of the River Vidourle, where one isolated arch of the original **Roman bridge** remains. On the west bank, a fine stretch of the old **cobbled way** is visible climbing the slopes of the former Roman settlement of **Ambrussum**, a fortified staging post on the road. From the top of the hill you look down on the modern international traffic still passing the same way, on the autoroute and parallel rail line. About 10km to the north, 28km from Nîmes, still on the Vidourle, the little medieval town of **SOMMIÈRES**, with a much-modified Roman bridge, is where Lawrence Durrell spent the last years of his life. There is nothing special to see: just wander the narrow old streets.

There are daily buses from Nîmes, while accommodation is available at *Le Commerce*, 15 quai Gaussorgues (☎04.66.80.97.22, fax 04.66.80.32.64; ②), a pleasant, inexpensive hotel with a restaurant; or the fancier *Auberge du Port Romain*, 2 av Émile-Jamais (☎04.66.80.00.58, fax 04.66.80.31.52; ③), set in an old château. There's also a **camping municipal** in rue Eugène-Rouch.

Montpellier

A thousand years of trade and intellect have made **MONTPELLIER** a teeming, energetic city. Benjamin of Tudela, the tireless twelfth-century Jewish traveller, reported its

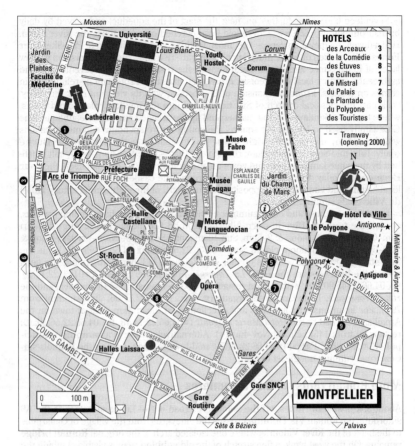

streets crowded with traders, Christian and Saracen, Arabs from the Maghreb, merchants from Lombardy, from the kingdom of Rome, from every corner of Egypt, Greece, Gaul, Spain, Genoa and Pisa. A few hiccups – like being sold to France in 1349, almost total destruction for its Protestantism in 1622, and depression in the wine trade in the early years of this century – have done little to dent this progress. Today it vies with Toulouse and Nîmes for the title of most dynamic city in the south. The reputation of its university especially, founded in the thirteenth century and most famous for its medical school, is a long-standing one: more than 60,000 students still set the intellectual and cultural tone of the city – the average age of whose residents is said to be just 25.

Arrival, information and accommodation

The **gare SNCF** (☎04.67.58.50.50) and **gare routière** (☎04.67.92.01.43) are next to each other at the opposite end of rue Maguelone from the central place de la Comédie. The **airport**, Montpellier-Méditerranée (☎04.67.20.85.00), is 8km to the southeast beside the Étang de Mauguio (buses 30F; 15min from the gare routière). The **tourist office** (Mon–Fri 9am–1pm & 2–6pm, Sat 10am–1pm & 2–6pm, Sun 10am–1pm &

2–5pm; ☎04.67.60.60.60, fax 04.67.60.60.61), which has money exchange facilities, lies at the east end of place de la Comédie, opposite the Polygone shopping centre. SMTU **city buses** ply between the stations and outer districts, while the Petibus traverses Montpellier's pedestrianized centre – tickets cost 7F and cover both services for one hour, including transfers. In mid-2000 a new **tramway** should also come into operation, running from the eastern suburbs via Antigone, the stations and place de la Comédie round the old city's northern extremity.

Most **hotel** accommodation is conveniently concentrated in the streets between the train station and place de la Comédie, or in the nearby centre of the old town. **Campers** should head towards the coast, to the semi-engulfed suburb of Lattes, on the D986 to Palavas (see p.731), where you'll find *Eden Camping* (☎04.67.15.11.05; April–Aug 31) and *L'Oasis Palavasienne* (☎04.67.15.11.61; April to mid-Oct), or to *Camping l'Estelle* (☎04.67.50.00.82) near Pérols, further east on the D21.

Hotels

des Arceaux, 33–35 bd des Arceaux (☎04.67.92.61.76, fax 04.67.92.05.09). A very pleasant, family-run hotel in a leafy spot under the aqueduct west of the Promenade du Peyrou. ③.

de la Comédie, 1bis rue Baudin (☎04.67.58.43.64, fax 04.67.58.58.43). Popular hotel offering good value for its central location. The recently renovated rooms are bright and comfortable, all with bath, TV and phone. ③–④.

des Étuves, 24 rue des Étuves (☎04.67.60.78.19, fax 04.67.60.31.29). Simple, spotless rooms in the old city, all with en-suite bathrooms. ①–②.

Le Guilhem, 18 rue J-J-Rousseau (☎04.67.52.90.90, fax 04.67.60.67.67). Beautifully restored sixteenth-century town-house whose cheerful rooms mostly overlook quiet gardens, with a sunny breakfast terrace. ④.

Le Mistral, 25 rue Boussairolles (☎04.67.58.45.25, fax 04.67.58.23.95). Comfortable and clean, a good option in the middle price range, offering satellite TV and garage parking. ③.

du Palais, 3 rue du Palais (☎04.67.60.47.38, fax 04.67.60.40.23). Pleasant establishment on the west side of the old town. ④.

Le Plantade, 10 rue Plantade (☎04.67.92.61.45). One of the cheapest options, just outside the city centre, off rue du Faubourg-du-Courreau. The rooms are all rather worn, but clean, and the welcome of the *patronne*, Chantal Gossel, is as warm as ever. ①.

du Polygone, 16 av du Pont-Juvénal (☎ & fax 04.67.65.81.41). A good, inexpensive option near Antigone for which you'd be wise to book ahead. ②.

des Touristes, 10 rue Baudin (☎04.67.58.42.37, fax 04.67.92.61.37). Friendly, inexpensive hotel with well-kept if somewhat spartan rooms. ②.

Youth hostel

Youth hostel, rue des Écoles-Laïques (☎04.67.60.32.22, fax 04.67.60.32.30). Pricey but popular hostel situated in the north of the old town, accessible by buses #2, #3, #5,# 6, #7, #9 and #16 from the station, stop Ursulines. Closed Dec 16–Jan 8.

The city

Montpellier's city centre – the **old town** – is small, compact, architecturally homogeneous, full of charm and teeming with life, except in July and August when the students are on holiday and everyone else is at the beach. And the whole place is now almost entirely pedestrianized, so you can walk the narrow streets without looking anxiously over your shoulder. Drivers, of course, have to find a place to park; the best areas are around Antigone, to the east, and boulevard des Arceaux, to the west.

At the hub of the city's life, joining the old part to its newer accretions, is **place de la Comédie**, "L'Oeuf" to the initiated. This colossal, oblong square, paved with cream-coloured marble, has a fountain at its centre and cafés either side. One end is closed by the Opéra, an ornate nineteenth-century **theatre**; the other opens onto the Esplanade, a beautiful tree-lined promenade which ends in the Corum **concert hall**, dug into the hillside and topped off in pink granite, with splendid views from the roof. The city's most trumpeted museum, the **Musée Fabre** (Tues–Fri 9am–5.30pm, Sat & Sun 9.30am–5pm; 20F), is close by on boulevard Sarrail and contains a large and historically important collection of seventeenth- to nineteenth-century French, Spanish, Italian, Dutch, Flemish and English painting, including works by Delacroix, Raphael, Jan van Steen and Veronese.

From the north side of L'Oeuf, rue de la Loge and rue Foch, opened in the 1880s in Montpellier's own Haussmann-izing spree, slice through the heart of the old city. Either side of them, a maze of narrow lanes slopes away to the encircling modern boulevards. Few buildings survive from before the 1622 siege, but the city's busy bourgeoisie quickly made up for the loss, proclaiming their financial power in lots of austere seventeenth- and eighteenth-century mansions. Known as "Lou Clapas" (rubble), the area is rapidly being restored and gentrified. It is a pleasure to wander through and come upon the secretive little squares like place St-Roch, place St-Ravy and place de la Canourgue.

First left off rue de la Loge is **Grand-Rue Jean-Moulin**, where Moulin, hero of the Resistance, lived at no. 21. To the left, at no. 32, the present-day Chamber of Commerce is located in one of the finest eighteenth-century hôtels, the Hôtel St-Côme, originally built as a demonstration operating theatre for medical students. On the opposite corner, rue de l'Argenterie forks up to place Jean-Jaurés. Through the Gothic doorway of no. 10, is the so-called palace of the kings of Aragon, who ruled Montpellier for a stretch in the thirteenth century. This square is a nodal point in the city's student life. On fine evenings between 6pm and 7pm you get the impression that the half of the population not in place de la Comédie is sitting here and in the adjacent place du Marché-aux-Fleurs. Close by is the **Halles Castellane**, a graceful, iron-framed market hall.

A short walk from place Jean-Jaurés, the Hôtel de Varenne, on place Pétrarque, houses two local-history museums of somewhat specialized interest, the Musée du Vieux Montpellier (Tues–Sat 9.30am–noon & 1.30–5pm; free), concentrating on the city's history, and the more interesting, private **Musée Fougau** on the top floor (Wed & Thurs 3–6pm; free), dealing with the folk history of Languedoc and things Occitan. Off to the right, the lively little rue des Trésoriers-de-France has one of the best seventeenth-century houses, the Hôtel Lunaret, at no. 5, while round the block on rue Jacques Coeur the **Musée Languedocien** (Mon–Sat: July & Aug 3–6pm, Sept–June 2–5pm; 20F), which houses a very mixed collection of Greek, Egyptian and other antiquities.

On the hill at the end of rue Foch, from which the royal artillery bombarded the Protestants in 1622, the formal gardens of the **Promenade du Peyrou** look out across the city and away to the Pic St-Loup, which dominates the hinterland behind Montpellier, with the distant smudge of the Cévennes beyond. At the farther end a swagged and pillared water tower marks the end of an eighteenth-century aqueduct modelled on the Pont du Gard. Beneath the grand sweep of its double tier of arches there is a pretty daily fruit and veg market and a huge Saturday **flea market**. At the city end of the promenade, a vainglorious **triumphal arch** shows Louis XIV-Hercules stomping on the Austrian eagle and the English lion, tactlessly reminding the locals of his victory over their Protestant "heresy".

Lower down the hill, on boulevard Henri-IV, the **Jardin des Plantes** (Tues–Sun: April–Sept 10am–7pm; Oct–March 10am–5pm; free), lovely but slightly run-down, with alleys of exotic trees, is France's oldest botanical garden. In the words of the poet Paul Valéry, this is where "the pensive, the careworn and talkers-to-themselves come towards evening". Across the road is the long-suffering **cathedral** with its massive porch, sporting a patchwork of styles from the fourteenth to the nineteenth centuries. Inside is a memorial to the bishop of Montpellier who sided with the half-million destitute vine-growers who came to demonstrate against their plight in 1907 and were fired on by government troops for their pains. Above it, on rue de l'École-de-Médecine in the university's prestigious medical school, the **Musée Atger** (Mon–Fri 1.30–4.30pm; free) has a distinguished academic collection of French and Italian drawings, and the macabre **Musée d'Anatomie** (Mon–Fri 2.15–5pm; free) displays all sorts of revolting things in bottles. Close by is the pretty little place de la Canourgue, and, beyond, down rue d'Aigrefeuille, the old university quarter, with some good bookshops on rue de l'Université.

Antigone

South of place de la Comédie stretches the controversial quarter of **Antigone**, a chain of postmodern squares and open spaces designed to provide a mix of fair-rent housing and offices, aligned along a monumental axis from the place du Nombre-d'Or, through place du Millénaire, to the glassed-in arch of the Hôtel de la Région. It's more interesting in scale and design than most attempts at urban renewal, but it has failed to attract the crowds away from the place de la Comédie and is often deserted. The enclosed spaces in particular work well, with their theatrical references to classical architecture, like oversized cornices and columns supporting only sky. The more open spaces are, however, disturbing, with something totalitarian and inhuman about their scale and blandness.

Eating, drinking and entertainment

Montpellier's year-round vitality supports some varied **restaurants** and **bars** to suit all budgets and tastes. **Cafés** line every square, large and small, while some of the more expensive restaurants use the city's ancient interiors to stunning effect. And Montpellier's youthful population ensures an energetic bar and nightclub scene right through to the early hours.

Restaurants and cafés

Arts et Buffet, place St-Roch. Tucked behind St Roch church, this delightful *salon de thé* is great for breakfast, a tea-break or light meals of salads, home-made pies and cakes. Magazines and books available, some in English. Closed Mon & Tues.

L'Aromate, 8 rue des Puits-des-Esquilles (☎04.67.66.06.27). Good Italian food for 80–120F, just west of the Préfecture building, off rue du Palais des Guilhem.

Chez Marceau, 7 place de la Chapelle-Neuve (☎04.67.66.08.09). A good, traditional bistrot on a pretty, crowded square; 60F at lunchtime, 90F or 110F in the evening. Closed Sun.

Crêperie des Deux Provinces, 7 rue Jacques-Cŀur. Huge choice of crêpes and salads at around 30F to 40F. Fast, friendly and open till late. Closed Sun.

La Diligence, 2 place Pétrarque (☎04.67.66.12.21). Atmospheric vaulted medieval setting for innovative French dishes. Lunch menus from 85F, or 145F in the evening, offering a good-value dip into the finest French cuisine. Closed Sat lunch & Sun.

L'Image, 6 rue du Puits-des-Esquilles (☎04.67.60.47.79). Imaginative, tasty food served in a small, vaulted room that fills up fast. Find it next door to *L'Aromate* (see above). Menus from 75F. Closed all day Sun & Mon eve.

Le Ménestrel, 2 impasse Perrier (☎04.67.60.62.51). A rather bourgeois establishment in a handsome old building at the east end of rue Foch, serving classic French dishes at very good prices; lunch menu from 90F, evening menu 150F. Closed Sun & Mon.

L'Olivier, 12 rue Aristide-Ollivier (☎04.67.92.86.28). Pretty little restaurant north of the station offering excellent-value traditional French cuisine. Menus at 160F and 200F. Closed Sun, Mon and in Aug.

La Posada, 20 rue du Petit-St-Jean (☎04.67.66.21.25). You'll need to book ahead for this popular restaurant with its well-priced Spanish and Mediterranean dishes, including paella and *moules à la crème de l'ail*. Menus from 50F.

Le Regency, 4 rue Cité-Benoît (☎04.67.64.42.69). Specialist in couscous and other dishes from the Maghreb, complete with traditional Moroccan decor and dances on Fri and Sat evenings. From around 120F. Closed Mon lunchtime.

Le Saleya, place du Marché aux Fleurs (☎04.67.60.53.92). In fine weather join the locals at the outdoor tables to feast on a daily selection of fish and regional fare for 70–100F. Open for lunch mid-March to Oct, and also evenings June–Sept, depending on the weather.

Salmon Shop, 5 rue de la Petite-Loge. Novel "mountain cabin" interior offering oak-smoked salmon main courses in half-a-dozen guises at around 70F. Just off place Jean-Jaurès. Closed Sun lunchtime.

La Tomate, 6 rue Four-des-Flammes (☎04.67.60.49.38). Friendly old standby: simple, copious and cheap food – 50F at lunchtime, 60–115F in the evening. Closed Sun & Mon.

Tripti Kulai, 20 rue Jacques-Cïur. Vegetarian dishes with flair, including a good choice of salads, from 50F. Closed Sun.

La Vie en Vert, 2 place St-Côme. On fine days tables spill out of this tiny, vegetarian restaurant onto a pretty square. Menus at 69F and 85F, or choose from a limited selection of nicely-presented platters. Open for lunch only Mon–Sat.

Le Vieux Four, 59 rue de l'Aiguillerie (☎04.67.60.55.95). Meat-eaters should head for this cosy, candlelit place specializing in *grillades au feu de bois*. Menu at 98F. Eve only.

Bars and nightlife

There's always plenty of **drinking** activity in the place de la Comédie, place du Marché-aux-Fleurs and place Jean-Jaurés, popular with Montpellier's students. Good options are *O'Carolans* Irish pub, south of rue Foch at 5 rue du Petit-Scel, or its sister-establishment, *Fitzpatrick's*, on place St-Côme. For something a little different, try *Pepe Carvalho*, a lively tapas bar at 2 rue Cauzit, just east of place St-Ravy. Still the old perennial for late-night **dancing** and live gigs is the *Rockstore* near the station on 20 rue de Verdun (☎04.67.58.70.10), with *Antirouille*, 12 rue Anatole-France (☎04.67.58.75.28), and *Le Fizz*, 4 rue Cauzit (☎04.67.66.22.89), offering other possibilities. *Mimi La Sardine*, 694 chemin des Cauquilloux (☎04.67.99.67.77), is a more spacious dance complex, but it's out of town on the road to Nîmes. For what's on at these and other venues, look for posters around town or check the free weekly listings magazine, *Le Sortir*.

Listings

Bikes Bike hire is available at Vill'à Vélo, in the gare routière, for 40F per day, but you have to leave a deposit of 1000F per bike. Daily 9am–6.30/7.30pm.

Books The Librairie Sauramps, at the entrance to the Polygone shopping centre, is the biggest bookshop in town with a full range of IGN maps and regional guides. For English-language books, head for rue de l'Université, where Bill's Book Company, at no. 44, specializes in second-hand books; and the Bookshop, at no. 4, in new volumes. As You Like It, at 8 rue du Bras-du-Fer, south of place Castellane, also offers home-made cakes and mugs of tea.

Doctors SAMU (☎15); SOS Médecins (☎04.67.45.62.45).

Festivals Montpellier is renowned for its cultural life, and hosts a number of annual festivals. Le Printemps des Comédiens (mid-June to mid-July) is a theatre festival; Montpellier Danse (end June to mid-July) is a festival of dance. There's also the music festival, Le Festival de Radio-France et de Montpellier, held in the second half of July, and the Festival du Cinéma Méditerranéen, in the second half of October. The tourist office will provide information about programmes and booking.

Hitching Allostop (☎04.67.04.28.88).

Markets The best central food markets are Halles Castellane, on rue de la Loge, and the open-air one on place de la Comédie. There's also a Sunday morning car boot fair at La Paillade on the city's western outskirts.

Post office The main office is on place Rondelet.

Shopping The most convenient place is the Polygone mall, containing a FNAC and Galeries Lafayette.

Swimming The nearest beaches for a dip are at Palavas (bus #17 from the train station), the best slightly to the west of the town.

Wine Try the Caves Notre-Dame wine cellar at 41 rue de l'Aiguillerie, or the Maison Régionale des Vins at 34 rue St-Guilhem, both with an excellent selection of local wines and other regional produce.

The coast: Aigues-Mortes to Agde

On the face of it the **Languedoc coast** isn't particularly enticing, the beaches bleak and treeless strands, often irritatingly windswept and cut off from their hinterland by marshy *étangs*. (ponds). But the area does have long hours of sunshine, 200km of sand still only sporadically populated, and relatively unpolluted water. This could change, as the French government has poured money into this area for the last couple of decades at an amazing rate, building seven new resorts in twice as many years. But, for the moment, as long as you steer well clear of the new towns – ugly, soulless places for the most part, anyway – deserted beaches are still there for the walking.

First-built of the new resorts, on the fringes of the Camargue, **LA GRANDE-MOTTE** is an extravagant futuristic vision of concrete and glass pyramids and cones ranged around a broad sandy beach. In summer, its seaside and streets are crowded with semi-naked bodies; in winter, it's a depressing, wind-battered place with few permanent residents. Both *Camping Louis Pibols* (☎04.67.56.50.08; April–Oct) and *Camping le Garden* (☎04.67.56.50.09; March–Oct) offer excellent facilities and are just a couple of minutes' walk from the beach.

A little way east are **PORT-CAMARGUE**, with a sparkling new marina, and **GRAU-DU-ROI**, which manages to retain something of its character as a working fishing port. Tourist traffic still has to give way every afternoon at 4.30pm when the swing bridge opens to let in the trawlers to unload the day's catch onto the quayside, whence it is whisked off to auction – *la criée* – conducted today largely by electronic means rather than the harsh-voiced shouting of former times. For a reasonable place to stay, try the *Hôtel Quai d'Azur*, on rue du Vidourle, near the harbour entrance (☎04.66.53.41.94; ②), or the well-shaded *Camping Abri de Camargue* (☎04.66.51.54.83; April–Oct), south of town.

Eight kilometres inland lies the appealingly named town of **AIGUES-MORTES**, built as a fortress port by Louis IX in the thirteenth century for his departure on the Seventh Crusade. Its massive walls and towers remain virtually intact. Outside the walls, amid drab modern development, flat salt pans lend a certain otherworldly appeal, but inside all is geared to the tourist. If you visit, consider a climb up the Tour de Constance on the northwest corner (daily: May–Sept 9.30am–6/7pm; Oct–April 10am–4pm; 32F), where Camisard women were imprisoned (Marie Durand was incarcerated for 38 years), and walk the wall, gazing out over the weird mist-shrouded flats of the Camargue.

Palavas and Maguelone

A dozen kilometres by road, **PALAVAS** is the bathing station for the citizens of Montpellier – a concrete sprawl with little to recommmend it apart from the presence of the sea, though there is plenty of summertime activity in the discos and the rip-off quayside bars and restaurants. The best place to swim and sunbathe is a little way to the west off the long flat strand that borders the marsh, where some of Europe's only flamingos feed, and herons, egrets and other sea birds squabble and dive. Here is the **Cathédrale de Maguelone** (daily 9am–7pm), dating mainly from the twelfth century, pale and grey and fortress-like on an island of vines and pines in the middle of the marsh, the only remains of a settlement largely destroyed by Louis XIII because of its

Protestant leanings. Cavernous and cool, the strong, simple church interior is the venue for a music festival in the second half of June. In the Dark Ages the island served as a base for Arab corsairs until Charles Martel drove them out in 737.

Sète

Some 28km southeast of Montpellier, twenty minutes away by train, **SÈTE** has been an important port for three hundred years. The upper part of the town straddles the slopes of the Mont St-Clair, which overlooks the vast Bassin de Thau, breeding ground of mussels and oysters, while the lower part is intersected by waterways lined with tall terraces and seafood restaurants. It has a lively workaday bustle in addition to its tourist activity, at its height during the summer *joutes nautiques*.

The pedestrian streets, crowded and vibrant, are scattered with café tables. Climb up from the harbour to the **cimetière marin**, the sailors' cemetery, where the poet Paul Valéry is buried. A native of the town, he called Sète his "singular island", and the **Musée Paul Valéry**, in rue Denoyer (July–Sept daily 10am–noon & 2–6pm; rest of year closed Tues; 30F), opposite the cemetery, has a room devoted to him, as well as a small but strong collection of modern French paintings. If you're feeling energetic, you should keep going up the hill, through the pines to the top, for a view that's fabulous when it's not engulfed in sea mist. Below the sailors' cemetery, and neatly above the water, is Vauban's **Fort St-Pierre**, now home to an open-air theatre. Over on the west side of the hill, George Brassens, associate of Sartre and the radical voice of a whole French generation, is buried in the Cimetière le Py, in spite of his song *Plea to be Buried on the Beach at Sète*. In **Éspace Brassens** (June–Sept daily 10am–noon & 2–6/7pm; Oct–May closed Mon; 30F), overlooking the cemetery, the locally born singer-songwriter lives again through his words and music, narrating his life-story on the museum's headsets.

Practicalities

The **tourist office**, at 60 Grand'Rue Mario-Roustan (July & Aug daily 9am–8pm, rest of year Mon–Sat 9am–noon & 2–6pm; ☎04.67.74.71.71, fax 04.67.46.17.54), has a good array of English-language information. The **gare routière** is awkwardly placed on quai de la République, and the **gare SNCF** further out still on quai Maréchal-Joffre – though it is on the main bus route, which circles Mont St-Clair (last bus about 7pm). **Ferries** for Morocco depart from quai d'Alger; tickets and information from SNCM, 4 quai d'Alger (☎04.67.46.68.00). Be warned that **hitching** out of Sète is horribly difficult; you're better off taking a train or bus to the nearest town and trying from there.

For **accommodation**, try *Hôtel Family*, right on the quayside at 28 quai de Lattre-de-Tassigny (☎04.67.74.05.03; ②), or the *Tramontane*, at 5 rue Frédéric-Mistral, between the canal and les Halles (☎04.67.74.37.92; ①). For somewhere more comfortable, there's the Belle Époque splendour of the *Grand Hôtel*, 17 quai de Lattre-de-Tassigny (☎04.67.74.71.77, fax 04.67.74.29.27; ④), or, if you want to be closer to the beaches, try *Hôtel P'tit Mousse*, along the Corniche on rue de Provence (☎04.67.53.10.66; May–Sept; ②). The HI **youth hostel** (☎04.67.53.46.68, fax 04.67.51.34.01) is high up in the town on rue Général-Revest. Campers should ask the tourist office for details of the numerous campsites in the area.

Seafood **restaurants** line the canal along quai Général-Durand, where both *La Marine* and *La Rascasse* serve reasonable-value menus from 85F. Alternatively, continue south towards the old port to find *L'Amphore* (85F), surrounded by fishing tackle and ice-packed fish, at 7 quai Maximin-Licciardi. One block inland, *La Trattoria*, 92 Grand'Rue Mario-Roustan (menus from 65F), is a workaday place, popular with the locals for its well-priced Sètoise specialities as well as pizzas and pastas, though service can be slow. Sardine fans will appreciate the *Musée Imaginaire de la Sardine*, 2 rue Alsace-Lorraine, where you can sample the delicacy in all its guises from 18F (Fri–Sun only). If you're staying out along the Corniche, the fairly pricey *Corniche*, on place Edouard-Herriot (☎04.67.53.03.30; 97F), is famed for its bouillabaisse, though you'll have to order a day in advance.

Agde

Midway between Béziers and Sète, at the western end of the Bassin de Thau, **AGDE** is historically the most interesting of the coastal towns. Originally Greek, and maintained by the Romans, it thrived for centuries on trade with the Levant. Outrun as a seaport by Sète, it later degenerated into a sleazy fishing harbour.

Today, it is a major tourist centre with a good deal of charm, notably in the narrow back lanes between rue de l'Amour and the riverside, where fishing boats tie up. The town's most distinctive and surprising feature is its colour – black – from the volcanic stone of the Mont St-Loup quarries. But it has few sights apart from its heavily battle-mented **cathedral**, though the **waterfront** is attractive, and by the bridge you can watch the Canal du Midi slip quietly and modestly into the River Hérault on the very last leg of its journey from Toulouse to the Bassin de Thau and Sète.

Hotel rooms aren't bargain-basement, but they're markedly cheaper here than on the coast. In the old town, *Les Arcades*, 16 rue Louis-Bages (☎04.67.94.21.64; ③), and *Le Donjon*, on place Jean-Jaurés (☎04.67.94.12.32, fax 04.67.94.34.54; ③), are comfortable and close to the river. Alternatively, try the welcoming *Hôtel Bon Repos*, just across the bridge at 15 rue Rabelais (☎04.67.94.16.26; ②). If you're **camping**, it's best to seek guidance from the **tourist office** in place Molière near the bridge (July & Aug Mon–Sat 9am–7pm, Sun 10–noon; rest of year Mon–Sat 9am–noon & 2–6pm; ☎04.67.94.29.68, fax 04.67.94.03.50). There are numerous places to **eat** around La Promenade; two restaurants worth trying are *La Belle Agathoise* and *Les Remparts*, both with menus from around the 60F mark. *Casa Pépé*, in the centre of the old town at 29 rue Jean-Roger (☎04.67.21.17.67), serves ultra-fresh fish dishes in an intimate, stone-walled room; menus from 80F.

An hourly bus service operates between the town and the sea at Cap d'Agde (see below); you can pick it up at the **gare SNCF** at the end of avenue Victor-Hugo, at the bridge and on La Promenade. To explore the **Canal du Midi**, take one of the boat trips organized by Bateaux du Soleil, 6 rue Chassefières (☎04.67.94.08.79).

Cap d'Agde

CAP D'AGDE, lies to the south of Mont St-Loup, 7km from Agde,. The largest (and by far the most successful) of the new resorts, it sprawls laterally from the volcanic mound of St-Loup in an excess of pseudo-traditional modern buildings that offer every type of facility and entertainment – all expensive. It is perhaps best known for its colossal **quartier naturiste**, one of the largest in France, with the best of the beaches, space for 20,000 visitors, and its own restaurants, banks, post offices and shops. Access is possible, though expensive, if you're not actually staying there (50F per car, plus 13F for each passenger).

If you have time to fill, the **Musée de l'Éphèbe** (July & Aug daily 9am–noon & 2–6pm; rest of year closed Tues; 15F) displays antiquities discovered locally, many of them from beneath the sea. It's worth a visit for the beautiful little Hellenistic bronze known as the Éphèbe d'Agde, until recently one of the treasures of the Louvre.

Inland from Montpellier

For getting out into the country of the Bas Languedoc, there are two good routes from Montpellier, both served by regular buses: the D986 **to Ganges** and the N109 **to Lodève**.

The Ganges route

The **Ganges road** weaves north across the plateau of the *garrigue*, a landscape of scrubby trees, thorns and fragrant herbs cut by torrent beds. The distance is dominated by the high limestone ridge of the **Pic St-Loup** until you reach the first worthwhile stopping place, **ST-MARTIN-DE-LONDRES**, 25km on, whose name derives from the Occitan word *loundres* ("otters").

It's a lovely little place of arcaded houses and cobbled passageways set around the roadside place de la Fontaine. Its pride is an exceptionally handsome early Romanesque **church**, reached through a vaulted passage just uphill from the square. The honey-coloured stone is simply decorated with Lombard arcading, the plain rounded porch with a worn relief of St-Martin on horseback, while the interior has an unusual clover-shaped ground plan. There's no hotel, only a **campsite** (☎04.67.55.00.53; April–Sept) just out on the Pic St-Loup road. A couple of outfits offer rafting and **canoeing** down the gorge from April to October; call Rapido (☎04.67.55.75.75) or Cano' St-Guilhem (☎04.67.57.44.99).

About 6km south, off the Gignac road near Viols-le-Fort (on the bus route) and the Château de Cambous, there is a marvellous **prehistoric village** (July & Aug daily except Mon & Thurs 3.30–7pm; Sept–June Sun & hols 2–4/6pm; 15F), dating from 2000 BC and only discovered in 1967. The site consists of a group of cabins, each about 20m long, their outlines clearly delineated, with the holes for the roof supports and the door slabs still in place. A reconstruction shows them to have been much like the sheep stalls in the old *bergeries* that dot the plateau.

Further north, almost as far as Ganges (see below), through dramatic river gorges, you reach the **Grotte des Demoiselles** (daily: April–June & Sept 9am–noon & 2–6pm; July & Aug 9am–7pm; rest of year 9.30am–noon & 2–5pm; 41F), the most spectacular of the region's many caves: a set of vast cathedral-like caverns hung with stalactites descending with millennial slowness to meet the limpid waters of eerily still pools. Deep inside the mountain, it is reached by funicular (hourly departures).

GANGES itself, 46km from Montpellier and also connected by regular buses (which continue to Le Vigan on the southern edge of the Cévennes), is an attractive and busy market town (Friday's the day) of small squares, tree-lined walks and vaulted alleys designed for defence in the Wars of Religion. This, too, was a Protestant town, peopled by refugees from the plains, who made it famous for its silk stockings. It was here that the last-ditch revolt of the Camisards earned its name; the rebels sacked and pillaged a shirt factory and went off wearing the shirts (*chemises/camises*).

The **tourist office** (July & Aug Mon–Sat 8.30am–noon & 2.30–6.30pm; rest of year Mon–Fri 8am–noon & 2–6pm, Sat 10am–noon; ☎04.67.73.00.56, fax 04.67.73.00.50) is on plan de l'Ormeau, in the centre of town near the church and market, where you'll also find an appealing place to **stay**, the *Hôtel de la Poste* (☎04.67.73.85.88, fax 04.67.73.83.79; closed Feb; ②). Alternatively, there's the *Relais du Pont Vieux*, 1km out of town on the road to Le Vigan (☎04.67.73.62.79; ②). For somewhere to **eat**, try *Au Bon Coin*, at 32 cours de la République, which offers Cévenol specialities and seafood (menus from 55F; closed Wed).

The Gignac route

The second inland route runs west via the small town of **GIGNAC**, 30km from Montpellier, amid vineyards where a fine eighteenth-century bridge spans the Hérault. There's just one **hotel**, the modern *Motel Vieux Moulin* (☎04.67.57.57.95, fax 04.67.57.69.19; ③), beside the river next door to *Camping du Pont* (☎04.67.57.52.40). For more upmarket accommodation, head 5km north to the town of **ANIANE**, home of the imposing classical **church of St-Sauveur** and the *Hostellerie St-Benoît* (☎04.67.57.71.63, fax 04.67.57.47.10; closed late Dec to mid-Feb; ③), with a pool and a good restaurant (from 100F). Three kilometres further on is the eleventh-century **Pont du Diable**, supposedly the earliest medieval bridge in the country; children used to dive into the pool beneath until it was banned. The narrowest part of the Hérault gorge begins here.

The glorious abbey and village of **ST-GUILHEM-LE-DÉSERT** lies in a side ravine, 6km further on. A ruined **castle** spikes the ridge above, and the ancient tiled houses of the village ramble down the banks of the rushing Verdus, everywhere channelled into carefully tended gardens. The grand focus is the tenth- to eleventh-century **abbey**, founded at the beginning of the ninth century by St Guilhem, comrade-in-arms of Charlemagne and scourge of the Saracens. It is a beautiful and atmospheric place, though architecturally impoverished by the dismantling and sale of its cloister – now in New York – in the nineteenth century. It stands on place de la Liberté, surrounded by honey-coloured houses and arcades with traces of Romanesque and Renaissance domestic styles in some of the windows. The interior of the church is plain and somewhat severe compared to the warm colours of the exterior, best seen from rue Cor-de-Nostra-Dama/Font-du-Portal, where you get the classic view of the perfect apse.

There are a couple of easy and worthwhile **walks** you can make from here – up the valley of the Verdus into the red-stained walls of the **Cirque du Bout-du-Monde** (from place de la Liberté, take rue du Bout-du-Monde out of the village and continue for about 30min), or up the zigzagging path of the **GR74**, through the sweet-scented shrubs and flowers towards the castle ridge (also about 30min). From the crest of the ridge the view down onto the village is magnificent. The path divides here: one branch leads back right to the ruins of the castle, while the other continues along the GR74 to the Ermitage Notre-Dame-de-Belle-Grâce (90min), and on to join the GR7 at St-Maurice-Navacelles on the Causse de Larzac.

In season the village is on every tour operator's route, making early mornings and late afternoons the best times for visiting. An overnight **stay** is possible at the charming *Taverne de l'Escuelle*, right beside the abbey (☎04.67.57.72.05, fax 04.67.57.74.02; ③), or at a gîte d'étape on the main street (☎04.67.57.34.00). The nearest campsite is *Le Moulin de Siau* (☎04.67.57.51.08; mid-June to mid-Sept), near Aniane on the road back down to Gignac. Nearby, cave enthusiasts will enjoy the **Grotte de Clamouse** (daily: Feb–May & Oct 10am–5pm; June–Sept 10am–6/7pm; Nov–Jan noon–5pm; 42F).

Clermont-l'Hérault

Eight kilometres west of Gignac, **CLERMONT-L'HÉRAULT** – accessible by bus from Montpellier – is the principal market town of the area and a major producer of table-grapes. The most interesting quarter to explore is between the huge Gothic **cathedral**, fortified in 1351 for protection against English raiders, and the ruined **château** on the hill above. From the plane-shaded **place de la République** outside the cathedral, follow the back streets, passage des Jacobins, rue de la Fontaine-de-la-Ville and rue Barbés, uphill to the steps that lead to the château. Tumbledown and overgrown, it affords a fantastic view of the surrounding country and makes a good place to picnic.

The **tourist office** (July & Aug Mon–Sat 9.15am–12.15pm & 2.30–6pm, Sun 10am–noon; rest of year Mon–Fri 9.15am–12.15pm & 2.30–7pm, Sat 9.15am–12.15pm; ☎04.67.96.23.86, fax 04.67.96.98.58) is at 9 rue René-Gosse, close to the cathedral. By far the best place to **stay** is *Le Terminus*, on allées Roger-Salengro, near the old station (☎ & fax 04.67.88.45.00; ③), with a good restaurant from 87F. Otherwise, there's the old *Grand Hotel*, at 2 rue Coutellerie (☎ & fax 04.67.96.00.04; ①–②), whose rooms on the back are not too bad. If you're **camping**, there's a year-round site, *Le Salagou* (☎04.67.96.13.13), northwest of Clermont near the lake. Reasonable **meals** can be had at the *Restaurant des Remparts*, on place de la République (menus from 65F; closed Tues), or try *l'Arlequin*, tucked under the south wall of the cathedral on place Saint-Paul (☎04.67.96.37.47; from 70F; closed Mon), for a more refined dining experience.

Around Clermont-l'Hérault

Three kilometres from Clermont-l'Hérault, on the main road to Bédarieux, lies **VIL-LENEUVETTE**, a model factory and workers' settlement created in the seventeenth century for the production of woollen cloth and subsidized by the royal government under Colbert's policy of trying to break the industrial supremacy of the Dutch and English. Although production ceased in 1954, the handsome buildings are still intact and partly inhabited. There is a very nice, if somewhat pricey, **hotel** adjoining – *La Source* (☎04.67.96.05.07, fax 04.67.96.90.09; ③), with a good restaurant (from 100F), pool and garden. Further west along the Bédarieux road, in the picturesque little village of **MOURÈZE**, there's the more modern *Hôtel Navas* (☎04.67.96.04.84, fax 04.67.96.25.85; ④; closed Nov–March; restaurant from 90F). If you're looking for something more simple, try the auberge *La Vallée du Salagou* (☎04.67.88.13.39, fax 04.67.96.15.62; ③; restaurant from 90F), high above the valley near Salasc, another village just off the main D908 to Bédarieux; they offer chambres d'hôte and camping from February to October.

Three other interesting and little-visited places east of Clermont are only feasible if you have a car. The first is a very fine **dolmen** on the end of a low ridge overlooking the D32 – best reached from the village of **LE POUGET**, where it is signposted. Continuing along the D139, you come within sight of the pale grey ruins of the keep and chapel of the **Château d'Aumelas**, romantically silhouetted on the edge of the plateau of the *causse*. To reach it by road – considerably further – you need to bear right onto the D114 and then take a dirt track opposite a farm. It's a beautiful and silent place, and the chapel is in near-perfect condition.

Two kilometres further along the D114, down an unsigned and bumpy track leading right onto the *causse*, there is a marvellous and remote silvery chapel, **St-Martin-de-Cardonnet**, built in the twelfth century – all that remains of an ancient priory.

On to Lodève

Heading north from Clermont to **LODÈVE,** 19km away, the new A75 autoroute brings heavy traffic down from Clermont-Ferrand. It passes through countryside further scarred by uranium mining – the area around the village of St-Martin-du-Bosc has some of the highest soil concentration of radioactivity in the world.

Lodève, entirely enclosed by vine-terraced hills at the confluence of the Lergues and Soulondres rivers, is almost in the shadow of the **Causse de Larzac**. There are really no sights here, but Lodève is a pleasant old-fashioned place to pause on your way up to Le Caylar or La Couvertoirade on the Causse. The **cathedral** – a stop on the route to St-Jacques-de-Compostelle – is worth a look, as is the unusual World War I **Monument aux Morts**, in the adjacent park, provided by local artist Paul Dardé; more of his work is on display in the unmemorable **town museum** in the **Hôtel Fleury** (daily except Mon 9am–noon & 2–6pm; 20F) and the **Halle Dardé** (daily 9am–6pm; free) in the place du Marché. With a bit of organizing it's also possible to visit the Annexe de la Savonnerie (by appointment only Tues–Thurs 2–5pm; 21F; ☎04.67.96.40.40), on the outskirts of Lodève, where priceless Gobelins carpets are woven.

A good place to stay is the *Hôtel de la Paix*, 11 bd Montalangue, by the bridge (☎04.67.44.07.46, fax 04.67.44.30.47; ③; closed Jan to mid-March), or *La Croix Blanche*, across the other bank of the river at 6 av de Fumel (☎04.67.44.10.87, fax 04.67.44.38.33; ②; closed Dec–March). There is a big Saturday **market**, where you can stock up on food. The **tourist office** is at 7 place de la République (July & Aug Mon–Fri 9am–12pm & 2–7pm, Sat 9am–5pm, Sun 9.30am–1.30pm; rest of year Mon–Fri 9am–noon & 2–6pm, Sat 9am–noon; ☎04.67.88.86.44, fax 04.67.44.01.84), next door to the **gare routière**, where you can catch buses to Montpellier, Béziers, Millau, Rodez and St-Afrique.

FROM BÉZIERS TO THE HILLS

The southern portion of Languedoc cuts a slender triangle west, its watery coastal flats rising to low undulating hills as you move inland. Though the coast is not generally noteworthy, **Narbonne** and **Béziers** are enjoyable diversions on the way to the more refreshing and spectacular upland delights of the **Monts de l'Espinouse** and the **Parc Naturel Régional du Haut Languedoc** (see p.742).

Béziers and around

Though no longer the rich city of its nineteenth-century heyday, **BÉZIERS** is still the capital of the Languedoc wine country and a focus for the Occitan movement, as well as being the birthplace of Resistance hero Jean Moulin. The fortunes of the movement and the vine have long been closely linked; Occitan activists have helped to organize the militant local vine-growers, and there were ugly events during the mid-1970s, when blood was shed in violent confrontations with the authorities over the importation of cheap foreign wines and the low prices paid for the essentially poor-grade local product. Things are calmer now, as the conservatism of Languedoc farmers has given way to more modern attitudes in the face of public demand for something better than the traditional table wine. As a result, some of the steam has also gone out of the movement; interest today is more in the culture than in anti-Paris separatist feelings.

The city

The finest view of the old town is from the west, as you come in from Carcassonne or the "Béziers-ouest" exit from the A9. Crossing the willow-lined River Orb by the Pont-Neuf, you can look upstream at the sturdy arches of the **Pont-Vieux**, above which rises a steep-banked hill crowned by the **Cathédrale St-Nazaire**, resembling a castle more than a church on account of its crenellated towers. The best approach is up the medieval lanes at the end of Pont-Vieux, rue Canterelles and passage Canterellettes. The cathedral is mainly Gothic, the original building having been burnt in 1209 during the sacking of Béziers, when Simon de Montfort's crusaders massacred some five thousand people at the church of the Madeleine for refusing to hand over about twenty Cathars.

From the top of the cathedral **tower**, there's a superb view out across the vine-dominated surrounding landscape. Next door, you can wander through the ancient cloister (daily: May–Sept 10am–7pm; Oct–April 10am–noon & 2–5pm; free) and out into the shady **bishop's garden** overlooking the river. In the adjacent **place de la Révolution**, a monument commemorates the people who died resisting Napoléon III's coup d'état in 1851 and their leader, Mayor Casimir Péret, who was shipped off to Cayenne where he drowned in a Papillon-style escape attempt. Also on the square, the Hôtel Fabrégat houses a **Musée des Beaux-Arts** (Tues–Sat 9am–noon & 2–6pm, Sun 2–6pm; 15F, or 20F joint ticket with the Musée du Biterrois), which, apart from an interesting collection of Greek Cycladic vases, won't keep you long. Nearby, **Hôtel Fayet**, at 9 rue Capus (Tues–Fri 9am–noon & 2–6pm; same ticket), has been pressed into service as an annexe to the museum, though it's as much of interest for its period interiors as its collection of nineteenth- and early twentieth-century art and works by local sculptor, Injalbert.

The city's other museum, the **Musée du Biterrois**, in the old St-Jacques barracks on avenue de la Marne near the train station (June 21–Sept 21 Tues–Sun 10am–7pm; rest of year Tues–Sun 9am–noon & 2–6pm; 15F), displays a variety of entertaining exhibits, ranging from Greek amphorae and nineteenth-century door knockers to distilling manuals, clogs and winepresses. Away from the medieval streets round the cathedral, the centre of life in Béziers are the **allées Paul-Riquet**, a broad, leafy esplanade lined with cafés, crêpes stalls, restaurants, banks and shops, named after the seventeenth-century tax collector who lost health and fortune in his obsession with building the Canal du Midi to join the Atlantic and the Mediterranean. Laid out in the last century, the *allées* run from an elaborate nineteenth-century theatre on place de la Victoire to the gorgeous little park of the **Plateau des Poètes**, whose ponds, palms and lime trees were laid out in the so-called English manner by the man who created the Bois de Boulogne in Paris.

Practicalities

If you arrive at the **gare SNCF** on bd Verdun, the best way into town is through the landscaped gardens of the Plateau des Poètes opposite the station entrance and up the allées Paul-Riquet. The **gare routière** is in place de Gaulle, at the northern end of the *allées*, while the **tourist office** is off to the east, at 29 av Saint-Saëns (July & Aug Mon–Sat 9am–7pm, Sun 10am–noon; rest of year Mon–Sat 9am–noon & 2–6pm; ☎04.67.76.47.00, fax 04.67.76.50.80).

For a central place to **stay**, one of the best options is the welcoming *Angleterre*, at 22 place Jean-Jaurés (☎04.67.28.48.42, fax 04.67.28.61.53; ①). Other good alternatives are *Hôtel Lux*, across the other side of allées Paul-Riquet at 3 rue Petits Champs (☎04.67.28.48.05, fax 04.67.49.97.73; ②), and *Hôtel des Poètes*, 80 allées Paul-Riquet (☎04.67.76.38.66, fax 04.67.76.25.88; ②), at the south end overlooking the gardens. Or there's the smarter *Hôtel du Théâtre*, at 13 rue Coquille (☎04.67.49.13.43, fax 04.67.49.31.58; ③), right beside the theatre. There's no **campsite** in town; the nearest is 9km south towards Valras-Plage.

For **food**, check out *Pizzeria da Patti* (from around 50F), on the north side of place Jean-Jaurés, or head up into the old quarter where rue Viennet has a good choice of restaurants. Two specific places to try here are the elegant *Le Cep d'Or*, at no. 7, serving mostly seafood (menus from 75F; closed Sun eve & Mon), and the *La Table Bretonne*, at no. 21, a homely crêperie in the shadow of the cathedral where you can eat well for around 60F (closed Sun & Mon). At the west end of rue Viennet, on place des Trois Six, *Le Vieux Siège* is a traditional brasserie with menus from 70F, while *Le Bistrot des Halles*, further north on place de la Madeleine behind the market square, is popular for its varied, well-priced menus (from 80F; closed Sun & Mon).

Béziers has one of the star **rugby** clubs in France, based at the Stade de la Méditerranée in the eastern suburbs (☎04.67.11.80.90). **Bullfighting** is also big in Béziers, with the main *feria* in mid-August. The principal cultural activity is a **music festival** in July. For more information on the Occitan movement, call in at the **Centre International de Documentation Occitane**, 44 bd Guesclin (☎04.67.49.98.98). If you fancy pottering along the Canal du Midi, you can hire bikes at La Maison du Canal (☎04.67.62.18.18) beside the Port Neuf, south of the gare SNCF, for 100F per day.

Pézenas and the Oppidum d'Ensérane

PÉZENAS lies 18km east of Béziers on the old N9. Market centre of the coastal plain, it looks across to rice fields and shallow lagoons, hazy with heat and dotted with pink flamingos. Despite its size, local tourist pamphlets have dubbed it the Versailles of Languedoc – a reference to its long-standing political importance as the seat of the provincial États-Généraux for Bas Languedoc. It has, however, retained the air of a gentrified resort, with its seventeenth-century centre, the **vieille ville**, carefully protected from development.

The town also plays up its association with Molière, who visited several times with his troupe in the mid-seventeenth century, when he enjoyed the protection of the local

Conti lords. He put on his own plays at the **Hôtel d'Alfonce** on rue Conti, including the first performance of *Le Médecin Volant*, according to local tradition. The building is now privately owned, but in summer you can visit the courtyard which served as Molière's theatre (July & Aug Mon–Fri 10am–noon & 2–6pm; 10F). When in town, he lodged at the *Maison du Barbier-Gély*, in the unspoiled **place Gambetta**, today occupied by the **tourist office** (July & Aug Mon–Sat 9am–7pm, Sun 10am–7pm; rest of year Mon–Fri 9am–noon & 2–6pm, Sun 2–5pm; ☎04.67.98.36.40, fax 04.67.98.96.80). Although Molière features in the eclectic Musée Vulliod St-Germain (July to mid-Sept daily 10am–noon & 3–7pm; rest of year Tues–Sat 10am–noon & 2–5pm, Sun 2–5pm; 10F), housed in a sixteenth-century palace just off the square, it's the grand salon, with its Aubusson tapestries and collection of seventeenth- and eighteenth-century furniture, that steals the show.

The tourist office sells a guide (10F) to all the town's eminent houses, taking in the former **Jewish ghetto** on rue des Litanies and rue Juiverie, but you can just as easily follow the explanatory plaques posted all over the centre, starting at the east end of rue Franéois-Outrin where it leaves the town's main square, place du 14-juillet. The **gare routière** is on the opposite side of the square on the river bank, with buses to Montpellier, Béziers and Agde, while an enormous market takes place each Saturday on cours Jean-Jaurés, a five-minute walk away.

Seven kilometres southwest of Béziers on the N9 Narbonne road, a sign points the way up a hill to **L'Oppidum d'Ensérune**, the site of a 2600-year-old Neolithic settlement, relics of which are displayed in a small **museum** (daily: July & Aug 9.30am–7pm; rest of year 10am–noon & 2–4pm; 25F). From the hill you can see the extraordinary, radial pattern of fields emanating from the now dry **Étang de Montady**, an egalitarian method of water management dating from pre-Roman times.

Pézenas has only two **hotels**: the rambling *Genieys*, on the main road at 9 av Aristide-Briand (☎04.67.98.13.99, fax 04.67.98.04.80; ②), and the more appealing *Grand Hôtel Molière*, on place du 14-juillet (☎04.67.98.14.00, fax 04.67.98.98.28; ③–④), with a good restaurant (from 90F). Other, cheaper places to **eat** on the main square include *Brasserie Molière* and *Pizzeria le Yacca*, or, for more atmosphere, head into the old streets to find *La Pomme d'Amour*, on place Gambetta (menus from 85F), and *Le Bateleur*, at the north end of cours Jean-Jaurés on place Ledru-Rollin (from 65F). For those with a sweet tooth, there are two local delicacies to sample: flavoured sugar-drops called *berlingots*, and *petits pâtés* – bobbin-shaped pastries related to mince pies, apparently introduced by Clive of India who stayed in Pézenas in 1768.

Narbonne and around

On the Toulouse–Nice main train line, 25km west of Béziers, is **NARBONNE**, once the capital of Rome's first colony in Gaul, Gallia Narbonensis, and a thriving port and communications centre in classical times and again in the Middle Ages. Plague, war with the English and the silting-up of its harbour finished it off in the fourteenth century. Today, despite the ominous presence of the Malvesi nuclear power plant just 5km out of town, it's a pleasant provincial city of tree-lined walks and esplanades converging on graceful squares.

In the summer of 1991 it acquired notoriety as a new flash point in France's continuing problems with its ethnic minorities, but with a difference. This time a long-suffering and long-forgotten minority forced itself on public attention. Among its mixed population of relative newcomers – fugitive Spanish Republicans, returning French settlers from Algeria and Algerian migrant workers – Narbonne has for thirty-odd years been home to a group of Harkis, Algerians who had enlisted in the French forces and fought with them against their own people in the Algerian war of independence in the late 1950s.

After the war they were settled in France for their own protection, and since then have received little or no help. The 1991 unrest was the protest of their children, angry at finding themselves still last in the pecking order in spite of their parents' sacrifice. Since then, the discontent has rumbled on, the most recent manifestation being a sit-in outside the mairie during the winter of 1997.

The only surviving legacy of Rome in Narbonne is the **Horreum**, at the north end of rue Rouget-de-l'Isle (May–Sept daily 9.30am–12.15pm & 2–6pm; rest of year Tues–Sun 10am–noon & 2–5pm; 20F, or 30F for all four museums), an unusual and interesting site consisting of two "streets" lined with small cubbyhole shops. Well preserved though now entirely underground, it was used to store grain and other produce. At the opposite end of the same street, close to the attractive tree-lined banks of the **Canal de la Robine**, which bisects the town, is Narbonne's other principal attraction, the enormous Gothic **Cathédrale St-Just-et-St-Pasteur**. With the Palais des Archévêques and its forty-metre keep, it forms a massive pile of masonry that completely dominates the restored lanes of the old town, and – like the cathedral of Béziers – can be seen for kilometres around. In spite of its size, it is actually only the choir of a much more ambitious church, whose construction was halted to avoid weakening the city walls. The immensely tall interior has some beautiful fourteenth-century stained glass in the chapels on the northeast side of the apse and imposing Aubusson tapestries. One of its most valuable tapestries is kept in the **Salle du Trésor** (May–Dec Mon–Sat 10–11.45am & 2.30–5.30pm; 10F) along with a small collection of ecclesiastical treasures, while in summer the high north tower is open for a panoramic view of the surrounding vineyards (June–Sept daily 10am–5pm; rest of year by appointment only ☎04.68.33.70.18; 15F).

The adjacent **place de l'Hôtel-de-Ville** is dominated by the great towers of St-Martial, the Madeleine and Bishop Aycelin's keep. From there the passage de l'Ancre leads through to the **archbishop's palace**, housing a fairly ordinary **museum of art** and a good **archeology museum** (both museums are the same hours and tarifs as the Horreum), whose interesting Roman remains include a milestone from the via Domitia bearing the name of Domitius Ahenobarbus – vital to the dating of the construction of the road.

If you're going across into the southern part of the town, beyond the bisecting Canal de la Robine and the built-over Pont des Marchands, the small early Christian crypt of the church of **St-Paul**, off rue de l'Hôtel-Dieu (daily 10am–noon & 2–6pm; free), is worth a quick look, as is the eerily empty deconsecrated church of **Notre-Dame-de-Lamourguié**, though the jumbled Roman stones of the **Musée Lapidaire** (July & Aug daily 9.30am–12.15pm & 2–6pm; same tarifs as Horreum) it houses are not very exciting.

Practicalities

The **gare routière** and the **gare SNCF** are next door to each other on av Carnot on the northwest side of town. The **tourist office** (mid-June to mid-Sept Mon–Sat 8am–7pm, Sun 9.30am–12.30pm; rest of year Mon–Sat 8.30am–noon & 2–6pm; ☎04.68.65.15.60, fax 04.68.65.59.12) is in place Salengro, next to the cathedral.

The best budget **accommodation** is the modern and friendly *MJC Centre International de Séjour*, in place Salengro (☎04.68.32.01.00; ①). A couple of reasonable hotels are *Will's Hotel*, 23 av Pierre-Sémard (☎04.68.90.44.50, fax 04.68.32.26.28; ②), near the station, and the spruce *Hôtel de France*, 6 rue Rossini (☎04.68.32.09.75, fax 04.68.65.50.30; ③), beside the attractive **market hall**. Fancier hotels include *La Dorade*, 44 rue Jean-Jaurés facing the canal (☎04.68.32.65.95, fax 04.68.65.81.62; ④), and the plush *La Résidence*, 6 rue du 1er-Mai (☎04.68.32.19.41, fax 04.68.65.51.82; ④). The nearest **campsite** is *Les Roches Grises*, on the rte de Perpignan to the southwest of town; at the end of bus #2 from the Hôtel-de-Ville.

As for **food**, you'll find a string of alfresco snackeries and brasseries, such as *Le Bistro*, along the terraces bordering the Canal de la Robine in the town centre. Otherwise, *L'Estagnol* (☎04.68.65.09.27; closed Sun; lunch menus 60F, or 98F in the evening), across the canal on Cours Mirabeau, attracts the crowds with its good-value, simple fare. For something a little fancier, there's *Le Chalutier*, on rue Limouzy near the market, offering seafood from 75F, and *Aux Trois Caves*, at 4 rue Benjamin-Crémieux (from 99F). The nicest place to eat in Narbonne, however, is the elegant *La Petite Cour*, north of the canal at 22 bd Gambetta (☎04.68.90.48.03), in a high-ceilinged room decked with seascape murals; again, seafood is the order of the day, with a good choice of lunchtime menus around 60F, or at 110F in the evening.

Fontfroide and the Étang de Bages

For a side-trip from Narbonne – only 15km, but nigh impossible without transport of your own – the lovely **abbey** of **FONTFROIDE** (daily: July & Aug 9.30am–6.30pm; rest of year 10am–noon & 2–4pm; 35F) enjoys a beautiful location, tucked into a fold in the dry cypress-clad hillsides. The extant buildings go back to the twelfth century, with some elegant seventeenth-century additions in the entrance and courtyards, and were in use from their foundation until 1900, first by Benedictines, then Cistercians. It was one of their monks, Pierre de Castelnau, whose murder as papal legate set off the Albigensian Crusade against the Cathars in 1208.

Visits to the recently restored abbey are only possible with a guide, and star features include the cloister with its marble pillars and giant wisteria, the church itself, some fine ironwork, and the rose garden. The stained glass in the windows of the lay brothers' dormitory are fragments from churches in north and eastern France damaged in World War I. Incidentally, if you do have transport the **D611**, a little further west, is a beautiful route south into the Corbières.

Just south of Narbonne, the **Étang de Bages et de Sigean** forms a large lagoon frequently visited by flamingos. A scenic drive leads out over the *étang* to Bages village. It is a notably arty community with some houses featuring unusually decorous ceramic drainpipes.

The road then continues south along the edge of the *étang* to **PEYRIAC-DE-MER**, and the **Réserve Africaine Sigean** (daily from 9am; last visit summer 6.30pm; winter 4pm; 98F), a better-than-average wildlife park with over 150 species from Africa and the rest of the world.

The coast: Valras to Gruissan

The coast close to Béziers and Narbonne enjoys the same attributes – and problems – as the rest of the Languedoc shoreline: fantastic sand but not a stitch of shade, and endless tacky development buffeted by a wind that would flay the shell off a tortoise.

For a quick escape from Béziers, you can take a thirty-minute bus ride across the flat vine-covered coastal plain to **VALRAS** at the mouth of the River Orb, whose old-fashioned family resort status is still just discernible. Further south, St-Pierre and Narbonne-Plage (reachable by bus from Narbonne) are uninspiring, modern resorts, and the only redeeming feature of this stretch of coast is the mini-landscape of the **Montagne de la Clape**, a former island, pine-covered and craggy, and not more than 200m above sea level, despite its name. At its further end the fishing village of **GRUISSAN**, 13km from Narbonne (there are buses), built in concentric rings around the hub of the Tour Barberousse, is the only real place of character left, and it, too, is under assault by the developers. Out along the beach, *plages des chalets,* is a section of houses originally built on stilts to keep them clear of the sea, but since the danger of flooding has receded many have now added ground floors.

The one really worthwhile thing to visit the **Chapelle Notre-Dame-des-Auzils**. It's about 4km up a winding lane into the Montagne and stands in a quiet and highly atmospheric spot in the pine woods. All along the road leading to it are moving **memorials** to the people of Gruissan lost at sea in merchant ships, trawlers and warships, from Haiti to the Greek island of Skiros. If the chapel's open, take a peak inside at the *ex votos* offered by grateful seamen and their families, many of them now painted onto the walls, the originals having been stolen in the 1960s.

Parc Naturel Régional du Haut Languedoc

Embracing Mont Caroux in the east and the Montagne Noire in the west, the **Parc Naturel Régional du Haut Languedoc** is the southernmost extension of the Massif Central. The west, above Castres and Mazamet, is Atlantic in feel and climate, with deciduous forests and lush valleys, while the east is dry, craggy and calcareous. Except in high summer you can have it almost to yourself. Buses serve the **Orb valley** and cross the centre of the park to **La Salvetat** and **Lacaune**, but you really need transport of your own to make the most of it.

Bédarieux to St-Pons: the valleys of the Orb and Jaur

Some 34km north of Béziers, the pleasant if unremarkable town of **BÉDARIEUX** lies right on the edge of the park. Served by buses from both Béziers and Montpellier, and by train from Béziers, it makes a good base for entering the park, especially as the service continues along the Orb and Jaur valleys to St-Pons beneath the southern slopes of the Monts de l'Espinouse.

The best part of town is to the east of the river, where the tall and crumbly old houses are redolent of a rural France long since vanished in more prosperous areas. *Hôtel Le Central*, on place aux Herbes (☎04.67.95.06.76; ①; closed 3wks in Oct), makes a cheap and atmospheric place to stay, and has a good, inexpensive restaurant. There's a **municipal campsite** on bd Jean-Moulin (☎04.67.23.30.19; mid-June to Sept;), and a **tourist office** on place aux Herbes (July & Aug Mon–Sat 9am–7pm, Sun 10am–noon & 3–6pm; rest of year Mon–Sat 9am–12.30pm & 2–6/7pm; ☎04.67.95.08.79, fax 04.67.95.39.69).

The Orb valley and Mons
Continuing **west**, the road is an easy hitch (if you don't want to wait for the bus) through spectacular scenery, with the peaks of the Monts de l'Espinouse rising up to 1000m on your right. The spa town of **LAMALOU-LES-BAINS**, 8km on, is notably livelier than neighbouring settlements lacking the attraction of recuperative springs where the likes of André Gide, Dumas *fils* and crowned heads of Spain and Morocco soothed their aches and pains. At the west end of the town by the main road, the **cemetery** is an untypically grand necropolis crowned with ornate mausoleums.

At the village of Colombières, 5km to the west, a path leaves the road to take you up into the **Gorges de Madale** where it joins the GR7, which crosses the southern part of the park to Labastide–Rouairoux beyond St-Pons.

Seven or eight kilometres further on is **MONS**, with a **gîte d'étape** (☎04.67.97.80.43) next to the church, and the small *Auberge des Gorges d'Héric* (☎04.67.97.72.98; ①; menus from 65F) by the suspension bridge at Tarassac, 2km away on the D14, near the **municipal campsite** (☎04.67.97.72.64). From Mons a road climbs 5km up the dramatic **Gorges d'Héric** to the hamlet of Héric, with the **Gorges de l'Orb** winding their way southwards back to Béziers along the D14.

Olargues and St-Pons-de-Thomières

Shortly after, you reach the medieval village of **OLARGUES** scrambling up the south bank of the Jaur above its thirteenth-century single-span bridge. The steep twisting streets, presumably almost unchanged since the bridge was built, lead up to a thousand-year-old belfry crowning the top of the hill. With the river and gardens below, the ancient and earth-brown farms on the infant slopes of Mont Caroux beyond, and swifts screaming round the tower in summer, you get a powerful sense of age and history. There's a tiny **tourist office** on rue de la Place near the church (July & Aug daily 10am–noon & 4–7pm; rest of year Wed & Sat 10am–noon & 2–6pm; ☎04.67.97.71.26). The old station is served only by SNCF **buses** now, but *Hôtel Laissac*, opposite (☎04.67.97.70.89; ①; closed Nov–Easter), still offers rooms in season and meals in its adjacent restaurant. Otherwise, there's a *Campotel* (☎04.67.97.77.25; ②; closed Jan–March), and *Camping Le Baous*, by the river (closed mid-Sept to mid-April; ☎04.67.97.71.50).

ST-PONS-DE-THOMIÈRES, 18km further west, is a little larger and noisier: it's on the Béziers–Castres and Béziers–La Salvetat bus routes, as well as the SNCF's Bédarieux–Mazamet bus route. This is the "capital" of the park, with the **Maison du Parc** at 13 rue du Cloître (☎04.67.97.38.22) by the **cathedral** – a strange mix of Romanesque and classical. It also boasts a small and reasonably interesting **Museum of Prehistory** (mid-June–Oct daily 10am–noon & 2.30–6pm; rest of year Wed, Sat & Sun 10am–noon & 2–5pm; 15F), across the river from the **tourist office** on place du Forail (July & Aug daily 9am–7.30pm; rest of year daily except Sun pm 10am–noon & 2.30–6pm; ☎04.67.97.06.65).

If you need to stay, there's the basic *Le Somail*, near the **tourist office** (☎04.67.97.00.12, fax 04.67.05.84; ①), or the much smarter *Les Bergeries de Ponderach*, 1km out of town on the Narbonne road (☎04.67.97.02.57, fax 04.67.97.29.75; ④; with a good restaurant). The municipal campsite (☎04.67.97.34.85) is on the main road east to Bédarieux. There's also a good *camping à la ferme*, *La Borio de Roque* (☎04.67.97.10.97; mid-June to Sept), 4km north of St-Pons on the D907, and chambres d'hôte 2km further on at *La Ferme de Tailhos* (☎04.67.97.27.62; ③). Continue along this road and you reach the Col du Cabaretou, with the stunningly situated *Auberge du Cabaretou* (☎04.67.97.02.31, fax 04.67.97.32.74; ③; closed mid-Jan to mid-Feb; restaurant from 95F). North of here the D907 leads to La Salvetat in the heart of the park.

The uplands of the park

There's no transport, but the prettiest route through the park to Mont Caroux and L'Espinouse is the D180 from Le Poujol-sur-Orb 2km west of Lamalou-les-Bains. The road winds up through cherry orchards to the village of **COMBES**, where the *Auberge de Combes* (☎04.67.95.66.55, fax 04.67.95.63.49; ①–②; Oct–May weekends only; restaurant from 85F) offers both a gîte d'étape and chambres d'hôte **accommodation**, and then through the **Forêt des Écrivains-Combattants**, named after the French writers who died in World War I. Just above the hamlet of Rosis, the road levels out in a small mountain valley, whose slopes are brilliant yellow with broom in June.

Douch and Héric

A left fork leads to the hamlet of **DOUCH**, beneath the summit of **Le Caroux** (1040m) – a perfect place where time seems really to have stood still. Half-a-dozen rough stone houses, inhabited by a handful of elderly residents, cluster tightly together for protection against the elements. There's a **gîte d'étape** (☎04.67.95.65.76) and a ferme auberge that provides meals in summer (by reservation only ☎04.67.95.21.41). In the meadows below nestles a jewel of a church with an ancient cemetery full of graves like iron cots.

The University of Toulouse maintains a research unit here to survey the largest *mouflon* population in France. If you go out early in the morning or just before dark in the evening, there is a good chance of seeing these short-fleeced sheep, and wild boar, too, as they come out to feed. The road provides some good vantage points a little further north round the **Col de l'Ourtigas** and the Pas de la Lauze.

The best short **walk** to do is down the GR7 to the hamlet of **HÉRIC** in the gorge of the same name. The path starts on the left at the end of the road in Douch and follows the telephone line. Once over the col and into the head of the gorge it becomes a beautiful paved mule track looping down through beech and chestnut woods. In the past people lived off the chestnuts, selling them, eating them and making flour from them. It takes about forty minutes to reach the two or three brown-stone houses of Héric, inhabited for several generations by the Clavel family, and 90 minutes to climb back up. They run a gîte d'étape and can provide **meals**, too, on reservation (☎04.67.97.77.29). Alternatively, make the popular three-kilometre ascent of Le Caroux, south of the village with fine views from the summit along L'Espinouse (see below), south to Béziers, the sea and even the Pyrenees, on a clear day.

Into the Agout valley

Continuing north from Douch, the road climbs another 12km above deep ravines and spectacular views to the summit of **L'Espinouse**. The Col de l'Ourtigas is a good place to stretch your legs and take in the grandeur surrounding you. Here the landscape changes from Mediterranean cragginess to marshy moor-like meadow and big conifer plantations, and the road begins to descend west into the valley of the River Agout. It runs through tiny Salvergues, with plain workers' cottages and a striking fortress-church; Cambon, where the natural woods begin; postcard-pretty **FRAISSE-SUR-AGOUT** – home to *Camping Le Pioch* (☎04.67.97.61.72), a gîte d'étape (☎04.67.97.52.26) beside the sports ground, and the pricier *Auberge de l'Espinouse* (☎04.67.97.56.14; ②; closed Nov–March); and thence to **LA SALVETAT-SUR-AGOUT**. Situated between the artificial lakes of La Raviège and Laouzas, this is another attractive mountain town built on a hill above the river, with car-wide streets and houses clad in huge slate tiles. It's usually half asleep except at holiday time, when it becomes a busy outdoor activities centre. With several **campsites** and the *Hôtel-Restaurant Cros* (☎04.67.97.60.21; ①; closed Nov–April), it's a convenient stopover for the centre of the park. There's a **camping municipal** (☎04.67.97.62.45; Easter–Sept) by the sports ground off the D907, and a **tourist office** in place des Archers at the top of the hill (July & Aug Mon–Sat 9am–7pm, Sun 10am–1pm; rest of year 9am–noon & 2–6pm; ☎04.67.97.64.44).

Lacaune

Twenty kilometres further north, **LACAUNE** makes another agreeable stop if you're heading for Castres. Surrounded by rounded wooded heights around the 1000m mark, it is very much a mountain town, one of the centres of Protestant Camisard resistance at the end of the seventeenth century, when its inaccessibility made the region ideal for clandestine worship. There are bus connections most days – not at very convenient times, usually afternoon or very early morning – to Castres, Albi and Bédarieux.

The air is fresh. The town, though somewhat grey in appearance because of the slates and greyish stucco common throughout the region, is cheerful enough. For a place to **stay**, the *Fusiés*, an erstwhile coaching inn opposite the church on rue de la République (☎05.63.37.02.03, fax 05.63.37.10.98; ③; closed first half of Jan), offers an old-fashioned classiness and has a restaurant (menus from 97F); while the *Hôtel Calas*, a little way up the hill (☎05.63.37.03.28, fax 05.63.37.09.19; ③; closed early Jan), is simpler and also has a good restaurant (from 80F).

From here to Castres the most agreeable route is along the wooded **Gijou valley**, following the now defunct train track, past minuscule Gijounet and **LACAZE**, where a nearly derelict **château** strikes a picturesque pose in a bend of the river.

CARCASSONNE AND THE CATHAR CASTLES

Right on the main Toulouse–Montpellier train link, **Carcassonne** couldn't be easier to reach; and for anyone travelling through this region it is a must – one of the most dramatic, if also most-visited, towns in the whole of Languedoc.

Carcassonne is a good historical introduction to the wild and ruinous **Cathar strongholds** to the north and south. These castles and fortified villages were the ultimate refuges of the **Cathars**, a sect strong in this part of France, who were proscribed as heretics by Pope Innocent III and hounded to death, first in the Albigensian Crusade, launched in 1208 under the leadership of the abbot of Cîteaux, then by the notoriously cruel Simon de Montfort, and finally by the king of France. The name of the sect derives from the Greek word for "clean, pure", *katharos*, and they abhorred the materialism and worldly power of the established Church, proclaiming the simple and humble Christianity of the Sermon on the Mount. Although their adherents probably never accounted for more than ten percent of the population, there were many members of the nobility and the influential classes among them, which alarmed the powers that be, as did the fact that their clergy or *parfaits* renounced the physical world as inherently evil, the creation of the Devil.

Cathars who were caught were burnt in communal conflagrations, 100 or 200 at a time. Their lands were laid waste or seized by northern barons, de Montfort himself grabbing the properties of the count of Toulouse. The effect of this brutality was to unite both the Cathars and their Catholic neighbours in southern solidarity against the barbarian north. Though military defeat became irreversible with the capitulation of Toulouse in 1229 and the fall of the castle of Montségur (seep.699) in 1244, it took the informers and torturers of the Holy Inquisition another seventy years to root out Cathars completely.

Carcassonne and around

CARCASSONNE owes its division into two separate "towns" – the **Cité** and the **Ville Basse** – to the wars against the Cathars. Following Simon de Montfort's capture of the town in 1209, its people tried in 1240 to restore their traditional ruling family, the Trencavels. In reprisal King Louis IX expelled them, only permitting their return on condition they built on the low ground by the River Aude.

Arrival, information and accommodation

Arriving by **train**, you'll find yourself in the *ville basse* on the north bank of the Canal du Midi at the northern limits of the town. To reach the **town centre** from the train station, cross the canal bridge by an oval lock, pass the Jardin Chénier and follow rue Clemenceau, which will take you through the central **place Carnot** and out to the exterior boulevard on the southern side of town (a 15min walk). **The gare routière** is on bd de Varsovie on the northwest side of town, south of the canal, while the airport (☎04.68.25.04.53) lies just west of the city, on the #7 bus route (15min; 7.50F).

The **tourist office** is at 15 bd Camille-Pelletan (July & Aug daily 9am–7pm; rest of year Mon–Sat 9am–noon & 2–6.30/7pm; ☎04.68.10.24.30, fax 04.68.10.24.38), at the end of square Gambetta, where the main road from Montpellier enters the town across the Pont-Neuf and the River Aude. There's also an annexe (daily 9am–6/7pm; ☎04.68.10.24.35, fax 04.68.10.24.37) just inside the main gate to the medieval Cité, Porte Narbonnaise. For information on the Cathars, consult the Centre National d'Études Cathares, 53 rue de Verdun (☎04.68.47.24.66), while local bookshops offer plenty of Cathar literature and souvenir picture books, some in English.

Accommodation

With the exception of the modern, clean, but frequently booked-up HI **youth hostel** on rue Trencavel (☎04.68.25.23.16, fax 04.68.71.14.84), the price of staying in the Cité can be high; if you don't mind paying, try the **hotels** *Le Donjon*, 2 rue Comte-Roger (☎04.68.71.08.80, fax 04.68.25.06.60; ④), or the more modest *des Remparts*, 3–5 place des Grand Puits (☎04.68.71.27.72, fax 04.68.72.73.26; ④). Just outside the walls, at 106 av Général Leclerc, the modern *Hôtel l'Octroi* (☎04.68.25.29.08, fax 04.68.25.38.71; ③) offers better value with its cheerful, spotless rooms.

There are, however, some very reasonably priced hotels in the *ville basse*. Pride of place goes to the newly decorated *Hôtel Astoria*, beside the station at 18 rue Tourtel (☎04.68.25.31.38, fax 04.68.71.34.14; ①), and the equally welcoming *Le Cathare*, 53 rue Jean-Bringer (☎04.68.25.65.92; ①), with a good restaurant from 65F. If these are full, try the *Hôtel Central*, 27 bd Jean-Jaurés (☎04.68.25.03.84, fax 04.68.72.46.41; ①). More upmarket, the *Bristol*, 7 av Foch (☎04.68.25.07.24, fax 04.68.25.71.89; ④; closed Dec–March), is situated on the canal bank opposite the gare SNCF, and the classy *Grand Hôtel Terminus* is nearby at 2 av Joffre (☎04.68.25.25.00, fax 04.68.72.53.09; ④; closed Dec–Feb).

The **campsite**, *Le Campéole* (☎04.68.25.11.77; March–Oct), is just west of the Cité off route de St-Hilaire and the D104, served by buses in season. There's also a rural campsite, *Le Martinet Rouge* (☎04.68.26.51.98; April–Oct), in the village of Brousses-et-Villaret, 14km north of town off the D118 Castres road.

The Cité

The attractions of the *ville basse* notwithstanding, what everybody comes for is the **Cité**, the double-walled and turreted fortress that crowns the hill above the River Aude. From a distance it's the epitome of the fairytale medieval town. Viollet-le-Duc rescued it from ruin in 1844, and his "too-perfect" restoration has been furiously debated ever since. It is, as you would expect, a real tourist trap. Yet, in spite of the chintzy cafés, arty-crafty shops and the crowds, you'd have to be a very stiff-necked purist not to be moved at all.

To reach the Cité from the *ville basse*, take bus #2 from outside the station, or a navette from square Gambetta. Alternatively, you can walk it in under thirty minutes, crossing the Pont-Vieux and climbing rue Barbacane, past the church of St-Gimer to the sturdy bastion of the **Porte d'Aude**. This is effectively the back entrance – the main gate is **Porte Narbonnaise**, round on the east side.

There is no charge for admission to the streets or the grassy *lices* – "lists" – between the walls, though cars are banned from 10am to 6pm. However, to see the inner fortress of the **Château Comtal** and to walk the walls, you have to join a guided tour (daily: Jan–March & Oct–Dec 10am–12.30pm & 2–5pm; April & May 9.30am–12.30pm & 2–6pm; June–Sept 9am–7pm; 32F). The tours – in English from June to September – assume some knowledge of French history, pointing out the various phases in the construction of the fortifications, from Roman to Visigothic to Romanesque and to the post-Cathar adaptations of the French kings.

In addition to wandering the narrow streets, don't miss the beautiful church of **St-Nazaire** (daily: April–Oct 9am–7pm; Nov–March 9am–noon & 2–5pm), towards the

CANAL DU MIDI

The **Canal du Midi** runs for 240km from the River Garonne at Toulouse, via Castelnaudary, Carcassonne and Béziers, to the Mediterranean at Agde or Sète. It was the brainchild of Pierre-Paul Riquet, a minor tax collector from Béziers, who succeeded in firing the imagination of Louis XIV with the idea of linking the Atlantic and the Mediterranean via the Garonne.

The work, begun in 1667, took fourteen years to complete. The crux of the problem from the engineering point of view was how to feed the canal with water when the Garonne at Toulouse was 132m above sea level, the Mediterranean obviously at 0m, and, in the middle, the Col de Naurouze at 190m. Riquet solved the problem by building a dam at St-Ferréol in the Montagne Noire and channelling water from there down to Naurouze, where a rather uninspiring obelisk commemorates his vision and determination. The poor man ruined himself financially in the course of realizing his great work and died before its inauguration in 1681, but for two hundred years the canal was a great success as a means of moving both goods and passengers. The final link-up with the Atlantic had to wait until the nineteenth century.

What survives today is a great architectural monument, marrying function and aesthetics in perfect classical style. The distinctive oval lock basins, the scale of the triple locks west of Carcassonne, the wide lake-like basin at Castelnaudary, and the Pont de Répudre, which carries the canal across a marshy stream near Paraza, are splendid examples.

Landscape and canal have changed little since Riquet's day. Commercial traffic has been superseded by holiday cruisers – between seventy and eighty a day in summertime, but the locks are still manned, many of them manually operated, and the keepers' cottages are beautifully kept. This is the way to see the canal today: hike it, bike it or rent a boat. It's a gentle, restful chug down a tunnel of greenery enhanced in spring by the bloom of yellow iris and wild gladioli, with occasional glimpses of a world beyond: a distant smudge of hills, the pinnacles of Carcassonne.

Several companies **rent boats**: among them, Crown Blue Line, Le Grand Bassin, 11400 Castelnaudary (☎04.68.94.52.72, fax 04.68.94.52.73), and Ad'Navis, 8 rue Péniches, Béziers (☎04.67.62.18.18, fax 04.67.35.05.12). Their boats, while well-appointed, are mostly in the gin palace class, though Ad'Navis also has several lovely old barges for hire – at a price. Another company whose boats at least look like the descendants of proper commercial craft is Locaboat, whose UK-based agent is French Country Cruises, 54 High Street East, Upingham, Rutland LE15 9PZ (☎01572/821 330, fax 01572/821 072).

southern corner of the Cité at the end of rue St-Louis. It's a serene combination of Romanesque nave with carved capitals and Gothic transepts and choir adorned with some of the loveliest stained glass. In the south transept is a tombstone believed to belong to Simon de Montfort senior. You can also climb the tower (same hours; 10F), for spectacular views over the Cité.

Eating, drinking and entertainment

With over fifty **restaurants** within its walls, the Cité is a good place to look for somewhere to eat, though it tends to be on the expensive side. If you want value for money, try the *Auberge de Dame Carcas*, 3 place du Château (☎04.68.71.23.23; menu at 85F), a traditional bistrot, offering cassoulet and other regional dishes. Other possibilities include the *Jardin de la Tour*, 11 rue Porte d'Aude (closed Mon), where you can eat outside, and the smarter *Brasserie du Donjon*, in the hotel (see above), both with menus around 90F. There's a much greater variety of affordable places in the *ville basse*. *La Rotonde*, on the corner of rue Clemenceau near the canal and station, serves straightforward brasserie fare, while the *Hippocampe*, at 38 rue du 4-Septembre (closed Sun; menus at 55F & 80F), is another simple, inexpensive option. Nearby, at 29 bd Jean-Jaurés, the *Divine Comédie* serves a more varied menu of pasta, pizzas and regional dishes in generous portions (closed Sun; about 120F). For something more sophisticated, try *Chez Fred*, beside Jardin Chénier at 31 bd Omer Sarraut (menus from 98F). For picnic provisions, the **market** is on place Carnot (Tues, Thurs & Sat mornings).

There is dance, theatre and music in the annual Festival de Carcassonne, throughout July, and at Les Médiévales, a medieval junket of lasers and special effects on themes like the Cathars and the Holy Grail, which takes place in the first fortnight of August.

Castelnaudary

Thirty-six kilometres west of Carcassonne, on the main road from Toulouse, **CASTELNAUDARY** is one of those innumerable French country towns that boast no particular sights but are nonetheless a real pleasure to spend a couple of hours in, having coffee or shopping for a picnic in the market. Today it serves as an important commercial centre for the rolling Lauragais farming country hereabouts, as it once was for the traffic on the Canal du Midi. In fact, the most flattering view of the town is still that from the canal's **Grand Bassin**, which makes it look remarkably like a Greek island town, with its ancient houses climbing the hillside from the water's edge.

The town's chief claim to fame, however, is as the world capital of **cassoulet**, which, according to tradition, must be made in an earthenware pot from Issel (a *cassolo*) with beans grown in Pamiers or Lavelanet, and cooked in a baker's oven fired with rushes from the Montagne Noire. For a taste of it, go to the *Grand-Hôtel Fourcade*, 14 rue des Carmes (☎04.68.23.02.08, fax 04.68.94.10.67; closed Sun eve & Mon in winter, plus 3 weeks in Jan) where you can gorge yourself for 100F, then sleep off the after-effects by taking a **room** upstairs (①). A more attractive alternative for spending the night is the modern *Hôtel du Canal*, 2 av Arnaut-Vidal (☎04.68.94.05.05, fax 04.68.94.05.06; ③), in a shady position beside the canal just west of the Grand Bassin, or there's the *Hostellerie Étienne* (☎04.68.60.10.08, fax 04.68.60.14.54; ①; closed mid-Nov to mid-Dec), 7km west of town at Labastide d'Anjou. Situated in lovely gardens, this is another restaurant with rooms – which locals swear serves the best cassoulet, for only 76F. For more information on the area, ask at the **tourist office** in Castelnaudary's central Halle aux Grains (Mon–Sat 9am–12.30pm & 2–6.30pm; ☎04.68.23.05.73, fax 04.68.23.61.40).

Minerve

The village of **MINERVE** lies a dozen kilometres north of the canal in the middle of the Minervois wine country, on a shelf-like terrain of rocky outcrops and magnificent views. Its location is extraordinary, isolated on an island of rock between the gorges of the Briant and Cesse rivers, the latter of which has cut its course through two enormous tunnels in the rock known as the *Ponts Naturels*.

The village turned Cathar at the beginning of the thirteenth century, which made it a target for Simon de Montfort's crusade. On July 22, 1210, after a seven-week siege, he took the castle and promptly burnt 180 *parfaits* (or clergy). There is a memorial to them by the **church** and, inside, one of the most ancient altars in Gaul, dated 456 – but you won't be allowed in for love or money. Nothing remains of the castle but the ruins of a tower.

If you want to stay, there's free camping in the valley bottom by the cemetry and a gîte d'étape (☎04.68.91.22.92) in the village itself. Here you'll also find the delightful *Hôtel Chantovent* (☎04.68.91.14.18, fax 04.68.91.81.99; ③; closed mid-Dec to mid-March, Sun eve & Mon out of season). The **tourist office** (Mon–Sat 9am–noon &

2.30–3.30/4.30pm; ☎04.68.91.81.43) has information about other accommodation possibilities in the area.

The Montagne Noire

There are two good routes from Carcassonne into the **Montagne Noire**, which forms the western extremity of the Parc Naturel Régional du Haut Languedoc (see p.742): Carcassonne–Revel and Carcassonne–Mazamet by the valley of the Orbiel. Neither is served by public transport, but both offer superlative scenery.

The Revel route: Saissac, Revel and around

The **Revel route** follows the N113 out of Carcassonne, then the D629 through Montolieu (17km) and Saissac. **MONTOLIEU**, semi-fortified and built on the edge of a ravine, has set itself the target of becoming France's second-hand book capital, with shops overflowing with dog-eared and antiquarian tomes. Drop in at the Librairie Booth, by the bridge over the ravine.

SAISSAC, 8km further on, is much more an upland village. Conifers and beech wood, interspersed with patches of rough pasture, surround it, and gardens are terraced down its steep slopes. Remains of towers and fortifications poke out among the ancient houses, and on a spur below the village stand the romantic ruins of its castle and the church of St-Michel.

If you wish to **stay** in the area, there's the rather aged *Hôtel de la Montagne Noire* (☎04.68.24.46.36, fax 04.68.24.46.20; ②; closed Oct–April) on the road through Saissac, with a good local restaurant open all year (from 70F). Farmhouse accommodation is available at *Domaine de l'Albejot* (☎04.68.24.44.03; chambres d'hôte ③, gîtes ①; meals at 70F), signed 3km northeast of town on the D408 La Galaube road. There are also two **campsites**. If you have your own transport, the best place for miles around and an experience in itself is the *Camping du Bout du Monde* (☎04.68.94.20.92; all year round), at a beautiful tumbledown farm near Verdun-en-Lauragais, to the west of Saissac. You camp among the broom at the edge of the woods. There is also a **gîte d'étape** at 55F, and a ferme auberge with meals at 80F on weekdays and 150–250F at weekends (open eves & Sun lunchtime; reservations required).

Some 14km west of Saissac on the D103 (or just a few kilometres southwest of the *Bout du Monde* campsite), the ancient village of **ST-PAPOUL**, with its walls and Benedictine abbey, makes a gentle side-trip. Though it's undergoing long-term restoration, but you can visit the church, and its pretty, fourteenth-century cloister, on a guided tour (April–Oct daily 10am–noon & 2–6/7pm; 20F).

Back on the "main" D629, the road winds down through the forest, past the Bassin de St-Férréol constructed by Riquet to supply water to the Canal du Midi, and on to **REVEL**. Revel is a *bastide* dating from 1342, with an attractive arcaded central square with a superb wooden-pillared *halle* in the middle. Now a prosperous market town (market day is Saturday), it makes an agreeably provincial stopover. The *Hôtel du Midi*, 34 bd Gambetta (☎05.61.83.50.50, fax 05.61.83.34.74; ③), has a restaurant, much appreciated by local gourmets, with menus from 90–180F (closed Nov 12 to Dec 6). A simpler place to stay and eat is the *Adelscott*, 19 bd de la République (☎05.61.83.51.39; ①); its restaurant has a 65F weekday lunch menu, otherwise it costs from 85F.

Lastours and the valley of the Orbiel

This is the region known as the **Cabardès**. Cut by the deep ravines of the Orbiel and its tributary streams, it's covered with Mediterranean scrub lower down and forests of chestnut and pine higher up. The area is extremely poor and depopulated, with rough stone villages and hamlets crouching in the valleys. Its people lived off beans and chestnut flour and the meat from their pigs, and worked from very ancient times in the region's copper, iron, lead, silver and gold mines. Nothing now remains of that tradition save for the gold mine at Salsigne (of which more below).

The most memorable site in the **Orbiel valley** is the **Châteaux de Lastours**, the most northerly of the Cathar castles, 16km north of Carcassonne. As the name suggests, there is more than one castle – four, in fact, their ruined keeps jutting superbly from a sharp ridge of scrub and cypress that plunges to rivers on both sides. The two oldest castles, Cabaret (mid-eleventh century) and Surdespine (1153), fell into de Montfort's hands in 1211, when their lords gave shelter to the Cathars. The other two, Tour Régine and Quertinheux, were added after 1240, when the site became royal property, and a garrison was maintained here as late as the Revolution. Today, despite their ruined state, they look as impregnable and beautiful as ever. A path winds up from the roadside, bright in early summer with iris, cistus, broom and numerous other flowers.

The **Salsigne gold mine**, atop a bleak windswept plateau over the hill to the west of Lastours, is a huge and unsightly opencast pit. Apparently the only material now going through the treatment plant comes from Greece – thousands of tonnes of rubble shipped through Port La-Nouvelle and Marseille, to be sifted for a few grammes of the stuff that glisters.

About 7km upriver from Lastours, the road and river divide. The left fork leads to the village of **Mas-Cabardès**, hunkered down defensively in the river bottom. The right goes to **Roquefère**, whose ancient château hosts summertime theatre. From here a steep, serpentine road winds up through magnificent scenery to the tiny hamlet of **Cupservies,** balanced on the edge of a sudden and deep ravine where the Rieutort stream drops some 90m into the bottom. A couple of kilometres further, by the crossroads at **Caninac**, there's a very early – tenth century – chapel of **St-Sernin** in the middle of the woods. To get here without transport, there's a marked footpath from Roquefère, which then returns via Labastide-Esparbairenque (a 4.5-hr round trip).

The Cathar castles

The best of the so-called **Cathar castles** – they sought refuge in them, but did not build them – are in the arid, herb-scented hills of the **Corbières** to the south of Carcassonne. **Walking** is undoubtedly the most direct way to experience them, and there are numerous paths, of which the **GR36**, crossing from Carcassonne to St-Paul-de-Fenouillet, and the Sentier Cathare, crossing east to west from Port La-Nouvelle to Foix, are the most exciting. The Sentier Cathare is divided into twelve stages with gîtes d'étape, described in *Sentier Cathare Topoguide* (Rando Ediitons), available in local bookstores.

Without transport or walking boots, the best way to tackle them is from the south, as the most spectacular ones are close to the **Perpignan–Quillan** road, which has a bus service. With transport it becomes possible to explore the wilder back roads and utterly ruinous castles like Durfort and Termes, and to cross the cols where orchids and cowslips shudder in the spring winds and the views southward all end in the snowy Pyrenean bulk of Canigou.

Although there are numerous gîtes, chambres d'hôte and basic campsites, hotel **accommodation** is rare in this region; there's a gîte d'étape at the *Moulin du Pont d'Aliès* campsite (☎ & fax 04.68.20.53.27), near **AXAT**, 11km southeast of Quillan, and another at the remote village of **BUGARACH**, 15km east of Quillan as the crow flies (☎04.68.69.83.88, fax 04.68.69.81.75; March–Dec).

Puilaurens

From Quillan, the road runs south through the incredibly narrow **défilé de Pierre-Lys** to the Pont d'Aliès before swinging 17km east to the village of Lapradelle and the first of the castles, the **Château de Puilaurens** (July & Aug daily 9am–8pm, April–June; Sept & Oct 10am–5/6pm; rest of year weekends only 10am–5pm; closed Jan; 20F).

You can either drive up or there's a shorter and fairly gentle path from the hamlet of **PUILAURENS**. The castle is perched on top of a high, wooded hill at 700m, its fine crenellated walls built around the very top of the rock outcrops. Although the existence of a castle here dates from the tenth century, it seems more likely that it was fortified to something like its present extent in the early thirteenth century, when it passed from the king of France to the count of Roussillon, and then to the king of Aragon. It sheltered many Cathars up to 1256, when Chabert de Barbera, effective controller of power in the region, was captured and forced to hand over his strongholds here and at Quéribus further east, to secure his release. The castle remained strategically important, being close to the Spanish border, until 1659, when France annexed Roussillon and the border was pushed away to the south. The view from the battlements, which you can climb up to at one point, is quite breathtaking.

Five kilometres south of the village is the *Hostellerie du Grand Duc* in **GINCLA** (☎04.68.20.55.02, fax 04.68.20.61.22; ④; closed mid-Nov to March; restaurant from 120F), or simpler accommodation in the next-door chambres d'hôte (☎ & fax 04.68.20.50.92; ③).

Quéribus, Cucugnan and Duilhac

The **Château de Quéribus** (April–June & Sept & Oct 10am–7/8pm; July & Aug daily 9am–8pm; rest of year weekends only 10am–5pm; closed Jan; 25F), 30km further east towards Perpignan, stands on the ridge above the vine-ringed village of Cucugnan (see below), a few kilometres north of the main Quillan-Perpignan road – with a good chance of a lift up to the castle. Again, it is spectacularly situated, balanced on a pillar of rock above a sheer cliff, whose crevices nourish a beautiful variety of wild flowers. Until 1659 this was the border with Spain.

Because of the extreme, cramped topography of the rock, the space within the walls is stepped in terraces, dominated by the polygonal keep and accessible by a single stairway. Inside, at the heart of the keep, is the remarkable **chapel** of St-Louis-de-Quéribus, surprisingly high and wide when you consider the keep's tortured position, and supported by a single pillar. The stairs to the roof are broken, but from the window halfway up there are fantastic views to Canigou and Perpignan, with other castles and watchtowers of the Spanish Marches dotting the peaks and ridges. To the northwest you're within easy eyeshot of Peyrepertuse.

The history of Quéribus is similar to that of Puilaurens, though the fortifications visible today are thirteenth-century. It was the last stronghold of Cathar resistance, holding out until 1255, eleven years beyond the fall of Montségur. Never reduced by siege, its role as a sanctuary for the Cathars ended with the capture of the luckless Chabert.

Entry to Quéribus also includes the *Théâtre Achille Mir* (same hours) in the small village of **CUCUGNAN**, in the valley to the north of the château. Through an imaginative slide-show the theatre retells the story of the Curé de Cucugnan, hero of Alphonse Daudet's book *Lettres de Mon Moulin*, whom locals claim is based on their own nineteenth-century abbot Ruffié. The village also has a rare statue of a pregnant Virgin Mary in its pretty little church. There's **accommodation** at the *Auberge du Vigneron*, opposite the theatre (☎04.68.45.03.00, fax 04.68.45.03.08; ③; closed mid-Dec to mid-Feb; good restaurant from 100F), while the *Auberge de Cucugnan* (☎04.68.45.40.84, fax

04.68.45.01.52; ③; closed Feb), near the church, is known for its hearty servings of game – from 100F including wine. The nearest other rooms are in **DUILHAC**, about 4km away below Peyrepertuse (see below), at the *Auberge du Vieux Moulin* (☎04.68.45.02.17, fax 04.68.45.02.18; ③; restaurant from 55–140F; closed late Dec–early Feb), or in the gîte d'étape (☎04.68.45.01.74). There is also an *alimentation* in the village, with bread, open even on Sunday morning.

Peyrepertuse

If you only have time to visit one of the Cathar castles, then your best bet is **Château de Peyrepertuse** (Feb–June & Sept–Nov 11 10am–6/7pm; July & Aug daily 9am–8.30pm; Nov 12 to end Dec Sat & Sun 10am–6pm; closed Jan; 20F), not only for its unbeatable site and stunning views, but also because the complex is unusually well-preserved. The access road starts in Duilhac (see above) or, alternatively, you can walk up from Rouffiac villlage, on the north side, by the GR36; in summer it's a tough, hot climb that takes the best part of an hour. But either way the effort is rewarded, for Peyrepertuse is one of the most awe-inspiring castles anywhere, clinging to the crest of a long, wickedly jagged spine of rock on the top of a mountain ridge, surrounded by sheer drops of hundreds of metres.

You enter on the north side through thickets of boxwood. The heaviest fortifications enclose the lower eastern end of the ridge, with a keep and barbican controlling the main gate. The castle is much larger than the others despite its precarious hold on the earth, with extensive buildings inside the outer wall, culminating in a keep and tower shutting off the highest point of the ridge, where such a pit of air opens at your feet that no artificial defence is necessary.

Surprisingly, the castle was taken by the French without much difficulty in 1240, and most of the existing fortifications were built after that. Whatever you do, don't go up in a thunderstorm; there can be some fierce ones in summer, and the ridge brings down the lightning as sure as a high-tension cable.

If you need to **stay** the night, head for **ROUFFIAC**. The hotel here, the *Auberge de Peyrepertuse* (☎ & fax 04.68.45.40.40; ②; closed late Dec to mid-Jan), also has dormitory accommodation (50F), plus a restaurant (from 95F), but there's no shop. There is, however, a bus on Wednesday and Saturday to St-Paul-de-Fenouillet on the main Perpignan D117 road, returning at 11am. Walkers can also call on the services of Balade Cathare (☎04.68.45.05.10), based in Rouffiac, which runs a minibus shuttling people and bags around the area; it helps if you can give them as much notice as possible.

Moving on from Peyrepertuse, by car or by the GR36, you can return to St-Paul-de-Fenouillet through the narrow **Gorges de Galamus**, and in many places you can get down to the river for a swim. On the way you pass the eagle's-nest **Hermitage St-Antoine**, built into the side of the ravine, where they plan to open a museum in the near future.

Alternatively, the drive eastwards offers more castles, including Padern and the especially fine **Aguilar**, near Tuchan, which overlooks the hills and vales of the Côtes de Roussillon-Villages wine area, with magnificent views from the twisty climbing roads. From here you have the possibility of heading either north towards Narbonne or south through Tautavel to Perpignan.

TOULOUSE AND THE WEST

With its own sunny, cosmopolitan charms, **Toulouse** is a very accessible kick-off point for any destination in the southwest of France. Of the immediately surrounding places, **Albi** is the number-one priority, with its highly original cathedral and comprehensive collection of Toulouse-Lautrec paintings. Once you've made it that far, it's worth the extra hop to the well-preserved medieval town of **Cordes**.

Toulouse

TOULOUSE, with its beautiful historic centre, is one of the most vibrant and metropolitan provincial cities in France. This is a transformation that has come about since the war, under the guidance of the French state, which has poured in money to make Toulouse the think-tank of high-tech industry and a sort of premier trans-national Euroville. Always an **aviation** centre – St-Exupéry and Mermoz flew out from here on their pioneering airmail flights over Africa and the Atlantic in the 1920s – Toulouse is now home to Aérospatiale, the driving force behind Concorde, Airbus and the Ariane space rocket. The national Space Centre, the European shuttle programme, the leading aeronautical schools, the frontier-pushing electronics industry . . . it's all happening in Toulouse, whose 110,000 students make it second only to Paris as a **university** centre. But it's not to the burgeoning suburbs of factories, labs, shopping and housing complexes that all these people go for their entertainment, but to the old **Ville Rose** – pink not only in its brickwork, but also in its politics.

This is not the first flush of pre-eminence for Toulouse. From the tenth to the thirteenth centuries the counts of Toulouse controlled most of southern France. They maintained the most resplendent court in the land, renowned especially for its troubadours, the poets of Courtly Love, whose work influenced Petrarch, Dante and Chaucer and thus the whole course of European poetry. Until, that is, the arrival of the papal thugs in the Albigensian Crusade; in 1271 Toulouse became crown property.

Arrival, information and accommodation

On the bank of the Canal du Midi, tree-lined and imaginatively planted, the train station, **gare Matabiau** (☎05.61.02.50.50 for information), and **gare routiere** (☎05.61.61.67.67), stand side by side in boulevard Pierre-Sémard. This is where you'll find yourself if you arrive by train, bus or air, for the **airport shuttle** (every 20–30min; 25F) puts you down at the bus station (with stops also in allées Jean-Jaurés and at place Jeanne-d'Arc). It is also the best spot to aim for if you are in a car: leave the **boulevard périphérique** at exit 15.

To reach the city centre from the train station takes just five minutes by métro (stop Capitole; 7.50F, covering one hour's transport by **métro** and Semvat city buses within the city centre), or twenty minutes on foot. Turn left out of the station, cross the canal and head straight down allées Jean-Jaurés, through place Wilson and on into place du Capitole, the city's main square. Just before it lie shady and much-frequented gardens of the square Charles-de-Gaulle, where the main **tourist office** (May–Sept Mon–Sat 9am–7pm, Sun 10am–1pm & 2–6.30pm; Oct–April Mon–Fri 9am–6pm, Sat 9am–12.30pm & 2–6pm, Sun 10am–12.30pm & 2–5pm; ☎05.61.11.02.22, fax 05.61.22.03.63) is housed in a sixteenth-century tower that has been restored to look like a castle keep; the Capitole métro stop is right outside.

The best guide to what's going on in and around the city – and usually there is a lot, from opera to cinema – is the weekly **listings** magazine, *Le Flash* (6F), which comes out on Wednesday. More highbrow interests are covered in the free monthly *Toulouse Culture*, available from the tourist office, among other places.

The best place to stay is in the city centre, where there are a number of excellent-value hotels, as well as many more up-market establishments. The area around the train station, though charmless and still retaining some of its red-light seediness, has a few acceptable options if you're stuck.

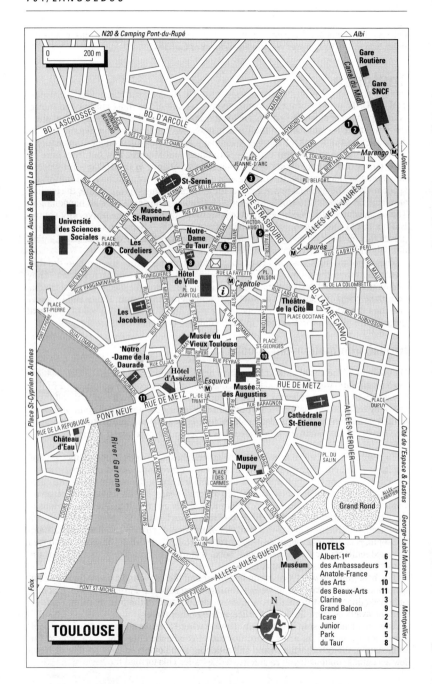

TOULOUSE

HOTELS

Albert-1er	6
des Ambassadeurs	1
Anatole-France	7
des Arts	10
des Beaux-Arts	11
Clarine	3
Grand Balcon	9
Icare	2
Junior	4
Park	5
du Taur	8

Hotels

Albert-1er, 8 rue Rivals (☎05.61.21.17.91, fax 61.21.09.64). Set in a quiet street near the Capitole and close to the central market in place Victor-Hugo. A small, comfortable and good-value establishment, with TV, air-con and en-suite bathroom as standard. ③.

des Ambassadeurs, 68 rue Bayard (☎05.61.62.65.84, fax 05.61.62.97.38). On the main road into from the station, so it's worth forking out a bit extra for rooms on the back. They're small but nicely decorated, with phone, TV and bathroom. ②.

Anatole-France, 46 place Anatole-France (☎05.61.23.19.96, fax 05.61.21.47.66). Quiet and rather functional place by the university, but still good value. ①.

des Arts, 1bis rue Cantegril (☎05.61.23.36.21, fax 05.61.12.22.37). Simple, friendly hotel in a nice area of backstreets off rue des Arts. Well used to backpacking foreigners. ①.

des Beaux-Arts, 1 place du Pont-Neuf (☎05.61.23.40.50, fax 05.61.22.02.27). Upmarket but intimate hotel whose modern, stylish rooms mostly overlook the river. ⑥.

Clarine (also known as *Clocher de Rodez*), 14 place Jeanne-d'Arc (☎05.61.62.42.92, fax 05.61.62.68.99). Decent, mid-range hotel just off bd de Strasbourg. Rooms are comfortable and quiet for the location. Secure parking available and a restaurant (closed Sat & Sun) with menus from 80F. ④.

Grand Balcon, 8 rue Romiguières (☎05.61.21.48.08, fax 05.61.21.59.98). A real classic, frequented by St-Exupéry and co in their pioneering days. It's now rather run-down, but definitely a good bargain, smack in the centre of things, on the northeast corner of place du Capitole. ①.

Icare, 11 bd de Bonrepos (☎05.61.63.66.55, fax 05.61.63.00.53). One of the better options near the station. The rooms are small but clean and surprisingly quiet, all with TV, phone, air-con and bathroom. ③.

Junior, 62 rue du Taur (☎05.61.21.69.67, fax 05.61.13.66.51). Nothing smart, but a perfectly decent and acceptable hotel in a great spot, practically in place St-Sernin. It also has an Italian restaurant where you can eat from around 85F. ②.

Park, 13 rue d'Austerlitz (☎05.61.21.25.97, fax 05.61.23.96.27). Just north of place Wilson, this new, imaginatively designed hotel offers sauna and jacuzzi (50F) as well as more traditional comforts. ③.

du Taur, 2 rue du Taur (☎05.61.21.17.54, fax 05.61.13.78.41). Cheerful place with well-appointed rooms at a reasonable price for the location, just north of the Capitole. ③.

Campsites

La Bouriette, 201 ch de Tournefeuille (☎05.61.49.64.46). The best of several campsites around the city, just 5km west of centre in the suburb of St-Martin du Touch. Take the métro to Arènes and then the #64 bus to the Bertier stop, from where the small campsite is a short walk south.

Pont du Rupé, 21 ch de Pont-du Rupé (☎05.61.70.07.35). On the north side of the city, its lakeside situation marred by a neighbouring factory. On the #59 bus route, then five minutes' walk from the Rupé stop.

The city

The part of the city you'll want to see is a rough hexagon clamped round a bend in the wide, brown River Garonne and contained within a ring of inner nineteenth-century boulevards – Strasbourg, Carnot, Jules-Guesde and others. An outer ring enclosing these is formed by the Canal du Midi, which here joins the Garonne on its way from the Mediterranean to the Atlantic.

Old Toulouse is effectively quartered by two nineteenth-century streets: the long shopping street, **rue d'Alsace-Lorraine/rue du Languedoc**, which runs north–south; and **rue de Metz**, which runs east–west onto the Pont-Neuf and across the Garonne. It is all very compact and easily walkable.

In addition to the general pleasure of wandering the streets, there are three very good museums and some real **architectural gems** in the churches of St-Sernin and Les Jacobins and in the magnificent Renaissance town houses – *hôtels particuliers* – of the merchants who grew rich on the woad-dye trade. This formed the basis of the city's economy from the mid-fifteenth to mid-sixteenth century, when the arrival of indigo from the Indian colonies wiped it out.

Place du Capitole is the centre of gravity for the city's social life. Its smart cafés throng with people at lunchtime and in the early evening when the dying sun flushes the pink facade of the big town hall opposite. This is the scene of a mammoth Wednesday **market** for food, clothes and junk, and of a smaller organic foods market on Tuesday and Saturday mornings. From place du Capitole, a labyrinth of narrow medieval streets radiate out to the town's several other squares, such as place Wilson, the more intimate place St-Georges, the delightful triangular place de la Trinité, and place St-Étienne, in front of the cathedral.

For green space, you have to head for the sunny banks of the Garonne or the lovely formal gardens of the **Grand-Rond** and **Jardin des Plantes** in the southeast corner of the centre. A less obvious but attractive alternative is the towpath of the Canal du Midi; the best place to join it is a short walk southeast of the Jardin des Plantes, by the neo-Moorish pavilion of the **Georges-Labit museum**, which houses a good collection of Egyptian and Oriental art.

The Capitole and the hôtels particuliers

Occupying the whole of the eastern side of the eponymous square, **the Capitole** has been the seat of Toulouse's city government since the twelfth century. In medieval times it housed the *capitouls*, who made up the relatively democratic and independent city council, from which its name derives. This institution, under the name of *consulat*, was common to other Languedoc towns and may have been the inspiration for England's first parliamentary essays, often attributed to Simon de Montfort, son of the general who became familiar with these parts in the course of his merciless campaigns against the Cathar heretics in the early 1200s. Today, these medieval origins are disguised by an elaborate pink and white classical facade (1750) of columns and pilasters, from which the flags of Languedoc, the Republic and the European Union are proudly flown. If there are no official functions taking place, you can have a peek inside (Mon–Fri 9am–5pm, Sat 9am–1pm; free) at the *Salle des Illustres* and a couple of other rooms covered in flowery, late-ninteenth-century murals and some more subdued impressionist works by Henri Martin.

Many of the old *capitouls* built their **hôtels** in the dense web of now mainly pedestrianized streets round about. The material they used was almost exclusively the flat Toulousain brick, whose rosy colour gives the city its nickname of *Ville Rose*. It is an attractive material, lending a small-scale, detailed finish to otherwise plain facades, and setting off admirably any wood- or stonework. Although many of the hôtels survive, they are rarely open to the public, so you have to do a lot of nonchalant sauntering into courtyards to get a look at them. The best known, now visitable thanks to its very handsome Bremberg collection of paintings, is the **Hôtel Assézat**, at the river end of rue de Metz (Tues–Sun 10am–6pm; 30F). Started in 1555 under the direction of Nicolas Bachelier, Toulouse's most renowned Renaissance artchitect, and never finished, it is a sumptuous palace of brick and stone, sporting columns of the three classical orders of Doric, Ionic and Corinthian, plus a lofty staircase tower surmounted by an octagonal lantern. The paintings within include works by Cranach, Tintoretto and Canaletto as well as moderns like Pissarro, Monet, Gauguin, Vlaminck, Dufy and a roomful of Bonnards. From April to October there's also a *salon de thé* in the covered entrance gallery.

Other fine houses exist just to the south: on rue Pharaon, in place des Carmes, on rue du Languedoc and on rue Dalbade, where the Hôtel Clary (also known as de Pierre), at no. 25, is unusual for being built of stone. To the north, it's worth wandering along rue St-Rome, rue des Changes, rue de la Bourse and rue du May, where the Hôtel du May at no. 7 houses the **Musée du Vieux-Toulouse** (June–Sept Mon–Sat 3–6pm; 12F), a rather uninspiring museum of the city's history.

The Musée des Augustins, the cathedral and the riverside

Right at the junction of rue de Metz and rue d'Alsace-Lorraine stands the **Musée des Augustins** (daily except Tues 10am–6pm; 12F). Outwardly unnattractive, the nine-teenth-century building incorporates two surviving cloisters of an Augustinian priory (one now restored as a monastery garden) and contains outstanding collections of Romanesque and medieval sculpture, much of it saved from the now-vanished church-es of Toulouse's golden age. Many of the pieces form a fascinating, highly naturalistic display of contemporary manners and fashions: merchants with forked beards touch-ing one another's arms in a gesture of familiarity, and the Virgin represented as a pret-ty, bored young mother looking away from the child who strains to escape her hold.

To the south of the museum, just past the Chambre de Commerce, the pretty **rue Croix-Baragon**, full of smart shops and galleries, opens at its eastern end onto the equally attractive **place St-Étienne**, which boasts the city's oldest fountain, the Griffoul (1546). Behind it stands the lopsided cathedral of St-Étienne, whose construc-tion was spread over so many centuries that it makes no architectural sense at all. But there is ample compensation in the quiet and elegant streets of the quarter immediate-ly to the south, and a few minutes' walk away along rue Tolosane and rue Mage in the **Musée Paul-Dupuy**, at 13 rue de la Pléau (daily except Tues 10am–5/6pm; 12F). It has a beautifully displayed and surprisingly interesting collection of clocks, watches, clothes, pottery and furniture from the Middle Ages to the present day, as well as a good display of religious art.

If you follow the rue de Metz westward from the cathedral, you come to **the Pont-Neuf** – begun in 1544, despite its name – and can cross over to the **St-Cyprien quar-ter** on the left bank of the Garonne. At the end of the bridge on the left, an old water tower, erected in 1822 to supply clean water to the city's drinking fountains, now hous-es the **Galerie Municipale du Château d'Eau** (daily except Tues 1–7pm; 15F), an influential photography exhibition space and information centre, with frequent changes of exhibition. The riverside is at its best on the right bank, where the grassy **waterside walk** is backed by the tree-lined quais in front of the art school and eighteenth-centu-ry church of La Daurade. Downstream you come to Pont St-Pierre, then the wildest and quietest stretch of quai, around the mouth of the lovely tree-lined Canal de Brienne and the Chaussée du Bazacle, formerly a ford across the Garonne.

The churches of Les Jacobins and St-Sernin

A short distance west of place du Capitole, on rue Lakanal, the church of **Les Jacobins** is an ecclesiastical building you can't miss. Started in 1230 by Dominicans who had set up here in the wake of their founding father, St Dominic (who himself had come to preach against the Cathars), the church is a huge fortress-like rectangle of unadorned brick, buttressed – like Albi – by plain brick piles, quite unlike the architecture you nor-mally associate with Gothic. The interior is a single space divided by a central row of ultra-slim pillars from whose minimal capitals spring an elegant splay of vaulting ribs – 22 from the last in line – like palm fronds. Beneath the altar lie the bones of the philoso-pher St Thomas Aquinas. On the north side, you step out into the calming hush of a **cloister** (daily 10am–7pm; 10F) with a formal array of box trees and cypress in the mid-dle and a superb view of the belfry. Nearby, at the corner of rue Gambetta and rue Lakanal, poke your nose in to the stone-galleried courtyard of the Hôtel de Bernuy, one of the city's most elaborate Renaissance houses.

From the north side of place du Capitole, **rue du Taur** leads past the belfry wall of **Notre-Dame-du-Taur**, whose diamond-pointed arches and decorative motifs repre-sent the acme of Toulousain bricklaying skills, to place St-Sernin. Here you're con-fronted with the largest Romanesque church in France, the basilica of **St-Sernin**, begun in 1080 to accommodate the passing hordes of St-Jacques pilgrims, and one of the loveliest examples of its genre. Its most striking external features are the octagonal brick belfry with rounded and pointed arches, diamond lozenges, colonnettes and mouldings picked out in stone, and the apse with nine radiating chapels. Entering from the south, you pass under the Porte Miégeville, whose twelfth-century carvings launched the influential Toulouse school of sculpture. Inside, the great high nave rests on brick piers, flanked by double aisles of diminishing height, surmounted by a gallery running right around the building. The small fee for the **ambulatory** (Mon–Sat 10–11.30am & 2.30–5pm; 10F) is well worth it for the exceptional eleventh-century marble reliefs on the end wall of the choir.

Right outside St-Sernin is the city's archeological museum, **Musée St-Raymond** (closed for renovation at time of writing; contact tourist office for latest info), housed in what remains of the poor students' block of the medieval university and containing a large collection of Roman objects, lamps, keys, bronze figurines, the Labours of Hercules in relief and similar items. On Sunday mornings the whole of place St-Sernin turns into a marvellous, teeming **flea market**.

The suburbs

To see something of the modern face of Toulouse, it's necessary to venture out into the suburbs, where you can visit a high-tech amusement park and a very specialized but surprisingly interesting aircraft assembly plant. The first of these is the **Cité de l'Espace** (June–Sept and school hols 9.30am–7pm; Oct–May Tues–Sun 9.30am–6/7pm; 60F; planetarium 35F), beside exit 17 of the A612 *périphérique* on the road to Castres, or take bus #19 from place Marengo. The theme is space and space-exploration, including satellite communications, space probes and, best of all, the opportunity to walk inside a mock-up of the MIR space station – fascinating, but absolutely chilling. Many of the exhibits are interactive and, though it's a bit on the pricey side, you could easily spend a half day here, especially if you've got children in tow.

In 1970 Toulouse became home to **Aérospatiale**, which, along with the aerospace industries of Germany, Britain and Spain, now manufactures Airbus passenger jets. The planes are assembled, painted and tested in a vast hanger, L'Usine Clément Ader, before taking their maiden flights from next-door Blagnac airport. Members of the public are allowed inside the plant on a highly informative guided tour (occasionally in English; 55F), but you need to apply at least two weeks before with your passport details, or a few days before for citizens of EU-member countries; contact Taxiway (☎05.61.15.44.00, fax 05.61.18.08.51) for further information. After a brief bus tour round the site and a short PR film, you climb high above the eerily quiet assembly bays where just one hundred people churn out five planes a week, ably assisted by scores of computerized robots.

Eating, drinking and entertainment

Regular daytime **café-lounging** can be pursued around the popular student/arty hangout of place Arnaud-Bernard, while place du Capitole is the early evening meeting-place. Place St-Georges remains popular, though its clientele is no longer convincingly Bohemian, and place Wilson also has its enthusiasts.

There are several good areas to look for a place to **eat**. One of the most attractive and fashionable, with a wide choice, is the rue de la Colombette, in the St-Aubin district just across boulevard Carnot, near the junction with allées Jean-Jaurés. Another is place Arnaud-Bernard and the tiny adjacent place des Tiercerettes, just north of St-Sernin. Rue du Taur has a number of Vietnamese places and sandwich bars, and the narrow rue du May has a crêperie, pasta place and restaurant. For lunch, however, there is no surpassing the row of five or six small restaurants jammed in line on the mezzanine floor above the gorgeous **food market** in place Victor-Hugo. They only function at lunchtime, are all closed on Monday, and cost as little as 58F. Both food and atmosphere are perfect.

Cafés

Bibent, 5 place du Capitole. On the south side of the square, this is Toulouse's most distinguised café, with exuberant plasterwork, marble tables and cascading chandeliers.

Le Café des Artistes, place de la Daurade. Lively, young café overlooking the Garonne. A perfect spot to watch the sun set on warm summer evenings, as floodlights pick out the brick buildings along the quais.

Le Florida, 12 place du Capitole. Relaxed café with a nicely retro air. One of the nicest places to hang out on the central square.

St-Sernin, place St-Sernin. An easy-going place to sit in the sun, on the east side of the basilica.

Restaurants

Asia Fast Food, 4 rue Bayard. If you want a quick bite on the way to the station, drop in this cheerful, self-service cafeteria at the south end of rue Bayard. Chinese, Vietnamese and Thai dishes at budget prices. Open daily till midnight.

Auberge Louis XIII, 1 rue Tripière (☎05.61.21.23.97). Good, uncomplicated home-cooking with local dishes in generous portions, and a nice courtyard for warm weather. Menus at 52F, 70F and 86F. Closed Sat & Sun.

La Bascule, 14 av Maurice-Hauriou (☎05.61.52.09.51). A Toulouse classic: well-cooked and well-presented regional dishes like cassoulet, *foie de canard* and oysters from the Bay of Arcachon. Menus from around 100F. Closed Sun eve & Mon eve.

Le Bistrot des Vins, place St-Étienne. Modern decor inside, plus tables on the pavement on the north side of the cathedral. An attractive, informal place with a huge selection of wines (from 8–40F per glass) and a *plat du jour* at around 50F. Closed Sun & Mon.

Le Chateaubriand, 42 rue Pargaminières. Named after the politician rather than the steak, this casual little restaurant serves an excellent cassoulet, made with flavourful *haricots Tarbais*, and scrumptious home-made desserts. Lunch menus from 65F, or 82F for dinner. Closed Sat lunch & Sun.

Chez Émile, 13 place St-Georges (☎05.61.21.05.56). One of Toulouse's best, and well situated on this pretty oblong square. Regional cuisine downstairs and seafood upstairs, at 110–240F on the menu. Closed Sun & Mon.

Chez Fazoul, 2 rue Tolosane (☎05.61.53.72.09). Welcoming restaurant serving local dishes in its pleasant, brick-walled dining room. Menus at 65–160F. Closed Sun.

Le Colombier, 14 rue Bayard (☎05.61.62.40.05). Cassoulet's the thing in this elegant restaurant, but there are other regional delights, such as *gésiers* (gizzards) and *foie gras*, as well as seafood and game. Menus from 100F. Closed Sat lunch & Sun.

au Gascon, 9 rue des Jacobins (☎05.61.21.67.16). Popular restaurant on the corner of rue Mirepoix serving hearty Gascon fare, with duck featuring strongly. Good portions and reasonable prices mean you need to get here early, or reserve. Menus from 45F at lunchtime, or 65F in the evenings. Oct–May closed Sun lunchtime.

Le May, 4 rue du May (☎05.61.23.98.76). Pretty little place serving good, uncomplicated food for 43–90F. Closed Sun lunch.

Mille et Une Pâtes, 1 rue Mirepoix (%05.61.21.97.83). Modern, unpretentious restaurant specializing in pasta (*pâtes*), with umpteen varieties on offer, even in the desserts. Count on around 100F for a full meal. Closed Sun.

La Tantina de Burgos, 27 ave de la Garonnette (☎05.61.55.59.29). Crowded, noisy, fun tapas bar, with a wide selection of tapas from 40F per plate, plus a lunchtime menu at 53F. Closed Sun & Mon.

à la Truffe du Quercy, 17 rue Croix-Baragnon (☎05.61.53.34.24). Good stand-by, offering traditional cooking at reasonable prices: 55–125F. Closed Sun & hols.

Le Verjus, 7 rue Tolosane (☎05.61.52.06.93). Good traditional cooking, served in a lovely little place close to the cathedral. Dinner only, for around 170F, but well worth it. Closed Sun & Mon.

Le Ver Luisant, 41 rue de la Colombette (☎05.61.63.06.73). A bar and simple restaurant frequented by the arty-alternative set. The food is good and copious and the atmosphere is fun. *Plat du jour* 35F at lunchtime, or 80–150F for an evening meal. Closed Sat lunch & Sun.

Bars and clubs

Le Bagamoyo, 27 rue des Couteliers. Friendly bar serving a wicked rhum punch (15F a glass), or beer, and a mix of Afro-Caribbean music. Daily 7pm–2am.

Bagdam Cafée, 4 rue Delacroix (☎05.61.99.03.62). Catering for women only, with readings, music and drama as well as coffee, drinks and food. Tues–Sat from 7pm. Closed mid-Aug to mid-Sept.

Bar du Matin, place des Carmes. Traditional, workaday bar that's popular with the literary/arty set. Closed Sun.

Le Bijou, 123 av de Muret (☎05.61.42.95.07). Café-théâtre with a varied programme of theatre, concerts and dancing. Tues–Sat from 9.30pm.

Le Bikini, 55 chemin des Ètroits, rte de Lacroix-Falgarde (☎05.61.55.00.29). On the city's southern outskirts, this is *the* hang-out of Toulouse rockers, and a prime venue for live gigs.

B Machine, 37 place des Carmes (505.61.55.57.59). Small, hip music bar with various theme nights, including women only on Tues. Open 11am till 2am, and all night on Sat.

Bodega-Bodega, 1 rue Gabriel-Péri. The old telegraph office makes a superb venue for this bar-restaurant, with its hugely popular disco after 10pm. Daily 7pm–2am, or 4am on Sat.

Café Classico, 37 rue des Filatiers. Trendy, designerish establishment that's a café by day and music bar by night. House, hip-hop and jungle. Daily 9am–1am, or 4am on Sat.

Erich Coffie, 9 rue Joseph-Vié (☎05.61.42.04.27). Just west of the river in the quartier St-Cyprien, this is one of the city's liveliest and most enjoyable music bars (food available), with an eclectic music policy. Live bands most evenings. Open Tues–Sat from 10pm.

The Frog & Rosbif, 14 rue de l'Industrie. Stop by this friendly British pub, just off bd Lazare-Carnot, for a pint of *Darktagnan* stout, or one of their other excellent home-brews. Quiz nights, football and fish and chips draws a surprisingly international crowd. Mon–Fri 5.30pm–2am, Sat & Sun 2pm–2/4am.

au Père Louis, 45 rue des Tourneurs (☎05.61.21.33.45). A lively, old-fashioned bar with chansons and music some nights. Open till 10pm. Closed Sun.

Puerta Habana, 12 port St-Étienne (☎05.61.54.45.61). Toulouse's hottest Latin-American venue, in a superb setting beside the Canal du Midi. Also has a recommended restaurant. Mon–Fri till 2am, Sat all night.

La Ragtime, 14 place Arnaud-Bernard (☎05.61.22.73.01). Good bar offering jazz, salsa and blues from 10pm until 2am, or 5am on Sat nights. Closed Sun & Mon.

La Strada, 4 rue Gabriel-Péri (☎05.61.62.56.31). Crowded dance club with a choice of retro on the ground floor or more recent sounds in the basement. Tues-Sat midnight till dawn.

L'Ubu, 16 rue St-Rome (☎05.61.23.26.75). Long-standing pillar of the city's dance scene, that remains as popular as ever. Mon–Sat 11pm till dawn.

Festivals, cinema and theatre

You may not think of it as the deep south, but you are only 100 or so kilometres from the Spanish border, and Toulouse ticks to the Spanish clock – siestas and late nights. Bars and clubs don't get going until after midnight.

Toulouse's own Orchestre National du Capitole, based in the Halle aux Grains in place Dupuy (☎05.61.62.02.70), features along with visiting ensembles in the Musique d'été **festival**, in July and August. September is the regular slot for the Festival International Piano, which takes place mainly in the beautiful cloister of the Église des Jacobins.

Major venues in town for **theatre**, as well as **music**, **dance** and **opera**, are the new Théâtre de la Cité, at 1 rue Pierre Baudis (☎05.34.45.05.05), and the splendid Théâtre du Capitole, in the main square (☎05.61.22.31.31). For **films**, the Cinémathèque at 69 rue du Taur (☎05.62.30.30.10), has a programme that changes daily, while the ABC, at 13 rue St-Bernard (☎05.61.29.81.00) and Utopia, 24 rue Montardy (☎05.61.23.66.20) often show English-language films. For relaxed, intimate shows – poetry, chansons, drama – keep an eye on the Cave Poésie (☎05.61.23.62.00), in a beautiful old building at 71 rue du Taur, close to St-Sernin.

Listings

Airlines Air France, 2 bd de Strasbourg (☎05.61.10.01.01); British Airways, at Toulouse airport (☎05.61.16.37.52); Continental Airlines, 7 bd Michelet (☎05.61.63.08.52); KLM, at Toulouse airport (☎05.61.71.10.00); Lufthansa, at Toulouse airport (☎05.61.71.10.00).

Airport 7km west at Blagnac; ☎05.61.42.44.00 for info.

Airport bus From the gare routière, allées Jean-Jaurés & place Jeanne-d'Arc every 20–30min Mon–Fri 5.20am–9pm, Sat & Sun 6am–8.20pm; from the airport, buses wait for the last flight at 11.20–11.50pm; 25F.

Ambulance ☎05.61.31.56.00.

Books The best general bookstores are Castéla, on place du Capitole, and FNAC, at 16 allées F-Roosevelt. Toulouse Presse, 60 rue Bayard, stocks a good range of IGN maps and guides. For English-language books, Books and Mermaides, 3 rue Mirepoix, specializes in second-hand tomes and will exchange, while The Bookshop, 17 rue Lakanal, stocks new titles. There are book markets on Thursday mornings in place Arnaud-Bernard, and all day Saturday in place St-Étienne.

Pharmacist 17 rue Rémusat (☎05.61.21.81.20). Open nightly 8pm–8am.

Police 23 bd de l'Embouchure (☎05.61.12.77.77).

Police/emergency ☎17.

Post office 9 rue Lafayette.

Taxis place Wilson (☎05.61.21.55.46); gare SNCF (☎05.61.62.37.34); place Jeanne-d'Arc (☎05.61.62.36.06). 24hr.

Albi and around

ALBI, 77km and an hour's train ride northeast of Toulouse, is a small industrial town with two unique sights: a museum containing the most comprehensive collection of Toulouse-Lautrec's work (Albi was his birthplace); and the most remarkable Gothic cathedral you'll ever see. Its other claim to fame comes from its association with Catharism; though not itself an important centre, it gave its name – Albigensian – to both the heresy and the crusade to suppress it.

The town hosts three good **festivals** over the course of the year: jazz in May, theatre at the end of June/beginning of July, and classical music at the end of July/beginning of August. During July and August there are also free organ recitals in the cathedral (Wed 5pm & Sun 4pm).

The city

The **Cathédrale Ste-Cécile** (daily June–Sept 8.30am–7pm; rest of year 8.30–11.45am & 2–5.45pm; entry to choir 5F), begun about 1280, is visible from miles around, dwarfing the town like some vast bulk carrier run aground, the belfry its massive superstructure. If the comparison sounds unflattering, perhaps it is not amiss, for this is not a conventionally beautiful building; it's all about size and boldness of conception. The sheer plainness of the exterior is impressive on this scale, and it is not without interest: arcading, buttressing, the contrast of stone against brick – every differentiation of detail becomes significant. Entrance is through the south portal, by contrast the most extravagant piece of flamboyant sixteenth-century frippery. The interior, a hall-like nave of colossal proportions, is dominated by a huge mural of the *Last Judgement*, believed to be the work of Flemish artists in the late-fifteenth century. Above, the vault is covered in richly colourful paintings of sixteenth-century Italian workmanship, while a rood screen, delicate as lace, shuts off the choir: Adam makes a show of covering himself, Eve strikes a flaunting model's pose beside the central doorway, and the rest of the screen is adorned with countless statuary.

Next to the cathedral, a powerful red-brick castle, the thirteenth-century **Palais de la Berbie**, houses the **Musée Toulouse-Lautrec** (April & May daily 10am–noon &

2–6pm;June–Sept daily 9am–noon & 2–6pm; Oct–March daily except Tues 10am–noon & 2–5pm; 24F), containing paintings, drawings, lithographs and posters from the earliest work to the very last – an absolute must for anyone interested in Belle Époque seediness and, given the predominant Impressionism of the time, the rather offbeat painting style of its subject. However, perhaps the most impressive thing about this museum is the building itself, its parapets, gardens and walkways giving stunning views over the river and its bridges.

Opposite the east end of the Cathedral, rue Mariés leads into the shopping streets of the old town, most of it impeccably renovated and restored. The little square and covered passages by the **church of St-Salvy** are worth a look as you go by.

Eventually you come to the broad **Lices Pompidou**, the main thoroughfare of modern Albi, which leads down to the river and the road to Cordes. Less touristy, this is the best place to look for somewhere to eat and drink.

Practicalities

From the **gare SNCF** on place Stalingrad it's a ten-minute walk into town along av Maréchal Joffre and av de-Gaulle; you'll see the **gare routière** on your right in place Jean-Jaurés as you reach the limits of the old town. The **tourist office** is in one corner of the Palais de la Berbie (July & Aug Mon–Sat 9am–7.30pm, Sun 10.30am–1pm & 3.30–6.30pm; rest of year Mon–Sat 9am–noon & 2–6pm, Sun 10.30am–12.30pm & 3.30–5.30pm; ☎05.63.49.48.80, fax 05.63.49.48.98). Ask for a copy of their English-language leaflet describing three walking-tours round Albi.

There are two attractive **hotels** near the station on av Maréchal-Joffre: *La Régence*, at no. 27 (☎05.63.54.01.42, fax 05.63.54.80.48; ①), and the slightly more expensive *Georges V*, at no. 29 (☎05.63.54.24.16, fax 05.63.49.90.78; ②.) On the opposite side of the town, just east of place du Bvigan, at.50 rue Séré de Rivières, the *Hôtel Chiffre* (☎05.63.54.04.60, fax 05.63.47.20.61; ⑤) is a more upmarket establishment with somewhat chintzy but comfortable rooms and a good restaurant (menus from 100F). In the heart of old Albi near the cathedral, both the *Hotel St-Clair*, 8 rue St-Clair (☎05.63.54.25.66, fax 05.63.47.27.58; ③), and *Le Vieil Alby*, 25 rue Toulouse-Lautrec (☎05.63.54.14.69, fax 05.63.54.96.75; ③; a recommended restaurant from 75F), are agreeable places to stay. Otherwise, there's a **youth hostel**, 13 rue de la République (☎05.63.54.53.65), and a **camping municipal** (☎05.63.60.37.06; April to mid-Oct) in the Parc de Caussels, about 2km east on the D999 Millau road.

The simplest and cheapest places for a **meal** are *Le Petit Bouchon*, 77 rue Croix-Verte, off place du Vigan (menus from 45F; closed Sun), and *Brasserie du Vigan* on the square itself, with useful supermarkets nearby. Vegetarian fare is served at *Le Tournesol*, in rue de l'Ort-en-Salvy, on the west side of place du Vigan (Tues–Sat noon–2pm, Fri also 7.15–9.30pm; dishes 47F). Good-value regional cuisine such as *lou tastou*, the local version of tapas, is available nearby at *Lou Sicret*, 1 rue Timbal, off the northwest corner of place du Vigan (☎05.63.38.26.40; closed Mon lunch & Sun; *plat du jour* 40F), and at the welcoming *Auberge St-Loup*, 26 rue Castelviel, just west of the cathedral (☎05.63.54.02.75; closed Mon lunch & Sun; menus from 62F). Real Spanish tapas are the order of the day at lively *Casa Loca*, 17 rue Puech Bérenguier (☎05.63.47.26.00; menus from 70F), or for something more upmarket, try *L'Occitan*, 11 rue de Piale (☎05.63.47.94.10; closed Sun lunch & Mon; from 100F), both in the lanes south of the cathedral.

Around Albi

The country between Albi and Carmaux, 16km to the north, has long been a coal-mining and industrial area, associated in particular with the political activity of Jean Jaurès, father figure of French socialism. Elected deputy for Albi in 1893, after defending the striking miners of Carmaux, he then championed the glassworkers in 1896 in a strike that led to the setting up of a pioneering workers' co-operative, La Verrerie Ouvrière, which still functions today. The **tourist offices** in Carmaux (place Gambetta) and Albi can provide a list of interesting industrial sites in the area, such as the pit at **CAGNAC-LES-MINES**, where visits include a trip down the shaft (visits Mon–Sat 10.30am, 11.30am, 2.30pm, 3.30pm & 4.30pm, Sun 3pm, 4pm & 5pm; 30F; ☎05.63.63.94.36).

Of more conventional tourist interest is the town of **CORDES**, perched on a conical hill 24km northwest of Albi, from which it's a brief trip by train (as far as Cordes-Vindrac, 5km away, with **bike rental** from the station) or bus (daily except Sun), or an easy hitch. Founded in 1222 by Raymond VII, Count of Toulouse, Cordes was a Cathar stronghold, and the ground beneath the town is riddled with tunnels for storage and refuge in time of trouble. As a perfect example of a medieval walled town, complete with thirteenth- and fourteenth-century houses climbing steep cobbled lanes, Cordes is inevitably a major tourist attraction: medieval banners flutter in the streets and artisans practise their crafts – unfortunately, the kiss of death. The **Musée d'Art et d'Histoire** (July & Aug daily 11am–noon & 3–6pm; April–June, Sept & Oct Sun & hols 3–6pm; 15F) depicts the history of one of the southwest's oldest and best-preserved *bastides*. Lovers of the bizarre should take a look at the **Musée de l'Art du Sucre** (daily 10am–noon & 2.30–6.30pm; closed Jan; 15F), containing outrageous sugar-sculptures created by famous local *pâtissier*, Yves Thuriès, and his underlings, The nicest **hotel** in town is the *Hôtel de la Cité* (☎05.63.56.03.53, fax 05.63.56.02.47; ③; closed mid-Oct to Easter), with some rooms looking out over the valley. Otherwise, there's the much more modest *Hôtel de la Bride* (☎05.63.56.04.02; ②–③; closed Jan), also in the old town, or the rather charming *Hostellerie du Parc* (☎05.63.56.02.59, fax 05.63.56.18.03; ③; recommended restaurant, from 90F), in the village of Les Cabannes, 2km west of Cordes on the D115. There's also a **campsite** (☎05.63.56.01.42; Easter–Oct) 1km southeast down the Gaillac road.

Castres and around

In spite of its industrial activities, **CASTRES**, 40km south of Albi, has kept a lot of its charm, in the streets on the right bank of the Agout and, in particular, the riverside quarter where the old tanners' and weavers' houses overhang the water. The centre is a bustling, businesslike sort of place, with a big morning **market** on Saturdays on place Jean-Jaurès. In marked contrast is the classical Mansart-designed **Hôtel de Ville**, just to the south, whose beautiful formal garden, of yew and clipped box and pristine avenues of limes, was designed by the celebrated seventeenth-century landscapist Le Nôtre.

The Hôtel de Ville makes a splendid home for the **Musée Goya** (July & Aug daily 9am–noon & 2–6pm; rest of year Tues–Sun 9am–noon & 2–5pm; 15F). That is something of a misnomer, for it's really a superb collection of sixteenth- and seventeenth-century Spanish painting, with Goya represented by just one self-portrait, the huge canvas of the *Philippines Junta* and a fair number of predictably macabre engravings.

Castres's other specialist museum is the **Musée Jean-Jaurès**, dedicated to its native son. It's located in place Pélisson (same hours as the Musée Goya; 10F), and getting to it takes you through the streets of the old town, past the splendid seventeenth-century **Hôtel Nayrac**, on rue Frédéric-Thomas. The museum was opened in 1988 by President Mitterrand – appropriately enough, because Mitterrand's Socialist Party is the direct descendant of Jaurès's SFIO, founded in 1905, which split at the Congress of Tours in 1920, when the "Bolshevik" element left to form the French Communist Party. The museum, though slightly hagiographic as you might expect, nonetheless pays well-deserved tribute to one of France's boldest and best political writers, thinkers and activists of modern times. Jaurès supported Dreyfus, founded the newspaper *L'Humanité*, campaigned against the death penalty and colonialism, and was murdered for his courageous pacifist stance at the outbreak of World War I – oddly enough, by a man called Villain. There could be no better epitaph than his own last article in *L'Humanité*, in which he wrote: "The most important thing is that we should continue to act and to keep our minds perpetually fresh and alive . . . That is the real safeguard, the guarantee of our future."

Practicalities

Arriving from Toulouse by train, you'll find the **gare SNCF** a kilometre southwest of the town centre on av Albert-1er. The **gare routière** is on place Soult, with bus services to Mazamet and Lacaune. The **tourist office** is beside the Pont Vieux at 3 rue Milhau-Ducommun (April–Oct Mon–Sat 8.30am–7/8pm, Sun 10am–noon & 2–6pm; rest of year Mon–Sat 8.30am–12.30pm & 1.30–6.30pm, Sun 2–6pm; ☎05.63.62.63.62, fax 05.63.62.63.60).

There are several reasonable hotels in Castres. Among the cheaper are *Le Périgord*, 22 rue Émile-Zola (☎05.3.59.04.74; ①; restarant from 75F), and *Hôtel Rivière*, 10 quai Tourcaudière (☎05.63.59.04.53, fax 05.63.59.61.97; ①–②). At the other end of the scale, there's the stylish *Hôtel l'Europe*, 5 rue Victor-Hugo (☎05.63.59.00.33, fax 05.63.59.21.38; ③), just off place Jean-Jaurès. The municipal camping (☎05.63.59.72.30; March–Sept) is in a riverside park 2km northeast of Castres on the road to Roquecourbe.

For simple, inexpensive meals, you can't beat the upstairs dining room in the *Brasserie des Jacobins*, on place Jean-Jaurès. Alternatively, take a stroll along rue Malpas, on the opposite side of the square, where *L'Eau à la Bouche*, at no. 6 (menus from 75F; closed Sun eve & Mon), is the best of a number of reasonable restaurants.

Le Sidobre

Just east of Castres rises the westernmost extremity of the Parc Naturel Régional du Haut Languedoc (see p.742), cut by deep river valleys and covered with marvellous woods. This is **Le Sidobre**, an area renowned for its granite: huge boulders litter the woods, often carved by the millennia into zoomorphic or other shapes – Les Trois Fromages and l'Oie, for example – that give them commercial value in the eyes of the tourist industry. Exploration is best done on foot: the **GR36** footpath passes this way.

LACROUZETTE, 15km from Castres, is the main town and the capital of the granite industry. The demand for tombstones being impervious to recession, the town continues to prosper, though it's not the most beautiful place. However, if you're on your way up the Agout and Gijou valleys (see pp.744 & 745) to Lacaze and Lacaune, the *Hôtel Relais du Sidobre*, 8 rte de Vabre (☎ & fax 05.63.50.60.06; ②–③; restaurant from 80F), makes a convenient and pleasant stopover. Further into the mountains and buried among beech forests, there's also the *Auberge de Crémaussel* (☎04.63.50.61.33; ②), with a good restaurant (menus from 90F); it's signed off the D30 to the northeast of Lacrouzette.

The Gers

West of Toulouse, the *département* of **Gers** lies at the heart of the historic region of Gascony. In the long struggle for supremacy between the English and the French in the Middle Ages it had the misfortune to form the frontier zone between the English base at Bordeaux and the French at Toulouse – hence the large number of fortified villages or *bastides* dominating the hilltops. It is attractive if unspectacular rolling agricultural land dotted with ancient, honey-stoned farms. Settlement is sparse and – with the exception of **Auch**, the capital – major monuments are largely lacking, which keeps it well off the beaten tourist trails.

The region's traditional sources of renown are its stout-hearted mercenary warriors – of whom Alexandre Dumas's d'Artagnan and Edmond Rostand's Cyrano de Bergerac are the supreme literary exemplars – its rich cuisine and Armagnac. The food and brandy still flourish: Gers is the biggest producer of *foie gras* in the country. Other traditional dishes are *magret de canard*, Henri IV's *poule au pot* (the chicken that he promised to provide for every peasant's Sunday dinner), *confit* of duck and goose, thick *garbure* soup and *daube de por*. Then there's *croustade*, a tart of apple and Armagnac, the speciality of Gascon *pâtissiers*. And to wash it all down the red wines of Madiran, Buzet and Saint-Mont, and the whites of Pacherenc du Vic-Bilh.

Auch

The sleepy provincial capital of Gers, **AUCH** is most easily accessible by rail from Toulouse, 78km to the east. The old town, which is the only part worth exploring, stands on a bluff overlooking the tree-lined River Gers with the cathedral prominent at its edge.

It is this building – the **Cathédrale Ste-Marie** – which makes a trip to Auch worthwhile. Although not finished until the latter part of the seventeenth century, it is built in basically late Gothic style, almost expiring Gothic in fact, with a classical facade. Of particular interest are the choir stalls (daily 8.30am–noon & 2–6pm; 6F) and the stained glass; both were begun in the early 1500s, though the windows are of clearly Renaissance inspiration, while the choir remains Gothic. The stalls are thought to have been carved by the same craftsmen who executed those at St-Bertrand-de-Comminges, and show the same extraordinary virtuosity and detail. The eighteen windows, unusual in being a complete set, parallel the scenes and personages depxicted in the stalls. They are the work of a Gascon painter, Arnauld de Moles, and are equally rich in detail. Immediately south of the cathedral, in the tree-filled place Salinis, is the forty-metre-high **Tour d'Armagnac**, which served as an ecclesiastical court and prison in the fourteenth-century. Descending

---

ARMAGNAC

Armagnac is a dry, golden brandy distilled in the district extending into the Landes and Lot and Garonne *départements*, divided into three distinct areas: Haut-Armagnac (around Auch), Ténarèze (Condom) and Bas-Armagnac (Éauze), in ascending order of output and quality. Growers of the grape like to compare brandy with whisky: equating malts with the individualistic, earthy Armagnac distilled by small producers, while the blended whiskies resemble the more consistent, standardized output of the large-scale Cognac houses. Armagnac grapes are grown on sandy soils and, importantly, the wine is distilled only once, giving the spirit a lower alcohol content but more flavour. Aged in local black oak, Armagnac matures quickly, so young Armagnacs are relatively smoother than corresponding Cognacs.

Armagnac was distilled originally for medicinal reasons, and many claims are made for its efficacy. Perhaps the most optimistic are those of the priest of Éauze de St-Mont, who held that the eau-de-vie cured gout and hepatitis. More reasonably, he also wrote that it "stimulates the spirit if taken in moderation, recalls the past, gives many joy above all else, conserves youth. If one retains it in the mouth, it unties the tongue and gives courage to the timid."

Many of the producers welcome visitors and offer tastings, whether you go to one of the bigger *chais* of Condom or Éauze, or follow a faded sign at the bottom of a farm track.

from here to the river is a **monumental stairway** of 234 steps, with a statue of d'Artagnan gracing one of the terraces. From place de la République, in front of the cathedral's main west door, rue d'Espagne connects with rue de la Convention and what is left of the narrow medieval stairways known as the **pousterles**, which give access to the lower town. On the north side of place de la République, the tourist office inhabits a splendid half-timbered fifteenth-century house on the corner with rue Dessoles, a pedestrianized street boasting an array of fine buildings. Just down the steps to the east of rue Dessoles, on place Louis-Blanc, the former Couvent des Jacobins houses one of the best collections of pre-Colombian and later South American art in France, left to the town by an adventurous son, M. Pujos, who had lived in Chile in the last years of the nineteenth century. Now known as the **Musée d'Auch** (daily except Mon; May–Sept 10am–noon & 2–6pm, rest of year closes 5pm; 10F), it also boasts a small collection of traditional Gascon furniture, religious artefacts and Gallo-Roman remains.

Practicalities
The **tourist office** (Mon 10am–noon & 2–6pm, Tues–Sat 9am–noon & 2–6pm; ☎05.62.05.22.89, fax 05.62.05.92.04) stands at the corner of place de la République and rue Dessoles. West of the tourist office, place de la Libération leads to the allées d'Étigny, with the **gare routière** off to the right.

For a very central place to stay, try the modest *Hôtel Sheherezade*, at 5 rue d'Espagne near the cathedral (☎05.62.05.13.25; ①; Moroccan restaurant downstairs). Slightly superior alternatives are the *Hôtel de Paris*, 38 av de la Marne (☎05.62.63.26.22, fax 05.62.60.04.27; ②; closed Nov), and *Le Relais de Gascogne*, 5 av de la Marne (☎05.62.05.26.81, fax 05.62.63.30.22; ③). To reach av de la Marne from the gare SNCF, turn right on av de la Gare, follow it to the end, then turn left.

There's also a rather drab HI **youth hostel**, *Foyer des Jeunes Travailleurs* (☎05.62.05.34.80), in the Le Garros housing development, about 25 minutes' walk from the station: turn left out of the station along av Pierre-Mendés-France, and left again at the T-junction; after crossing the railway tracks, take the first right and keep straight ahead to find the hostel at the far end of rue du Bourget. The **camping municipal** (☎05.62.05.00.22; mid-April to mid-Nov) is beside the river on the south side of town, and there's a GR653 **gîte d'étape**, 4km east at the Château St-Cricq (☎05.62.63.10.17).

Avenue d'Alsace, in the lower town, is the best place to look for inexpensive places to eat. Alternatively, up by the cathedral, place de la République and place de la Libération boast a fair selection of cafés and brasseries; try *Café Daroles*, by the fountain (menus from 70F). For something a bit more traditional, *La Table d'Hôtes*, off rue Dessolles at 7 rue Lamartine, offers good Gascon fare from 60F (closed Sun eve & Wed).

Fleurance, Lectoure and Condom

Outside Auch is a handful of quiet **country towns** with no great sights, but along with the surrounding countryside they make for a lazy taste of French provincial life. They are all connected by bus from Auch, but away from the main roads – the N21 for Fleurance and Lectoure, and the D930 for Condom – you'll be stymied without your own transport.

FLEURANCE, 24km north of Auch, has a typical *bastide* central square, **place de la République**, bordered by arcaded shops and houses, with the difference that its medieval *halle*, now the town hall, was successfully converted into mellow classical stone in the nineteenth century. The church is worth a look, too, for its octagonal Toulouse-style belfry and, more particularly, the three stained-glass windows executed by Arnaud de Moles, the artist of Auch cathedral. The **tourist office** is on the place de la République (July & Aug Mon–Sat 9/9.30am–6.30pm, Sun 9.30am–12.30pm; rest of year Tues–Sat 9am–6pm; ☎05.62.64.00.00, fax 05.62.06.27.80), and, if you wish to stay, the *Hôtel Capelli*, at 72 rue Gambetta (☎05.62.06.11.88; ①; restaurant from 55F), is a good option. For something a little smarter, try the *Hôtel de France*, 69 rue de la République (☎05.62.64.03.28, fax 05.62.06.07.13; ④; restaurant from 85F).

Eleven kilometres further north sits **LECTOURE**, the smallest and prettiest of these three towns, built astride a high ridge looking out over the surrounding farmland. Capital of the colony of Novempopulania in Roman times and of the counts of Armagnac until their demise at the hands of Louis XI in 1473, it is now renowned for its melons. In the middle of the main street, the **Cathédrale de St-Gervais-et-de-St-Protais** raises its enormous tower above the town, while down the rue Fontelié, among scarcely altered medieval houses, you come to **the Fontaine de Diane**. Apart from the handsome mairie, with its **Musée Lapidaire** (April–Sept daily 10am–noon & 2–5/6pm; Oct–March closed Tues; 15F), containing some interesting Roman bits and pieces, this pretty much exhausts the sights.

The **tourist office**, on place de la Cathédrale (Mon–Sat 8.30am–noon & 2–5/6pm, Sun 3–5pm; ☎05.62.68.76.98, fax 05.62.68.79.30), runs the GR65 **gîte d'étape** on nearby rue St-Gervais (same phone number). Just around the corner from the gîte is the superb but unfortunately named *Hôtel de Bastard* in rue Lagrange (☎05.62.68.82.44, fax 05.62.68.76.81; ③; closed Jan; menus from 88F). The *Auberge des Bouviers* (☎05.62.68.95.13; closed Sun eve & Mon; from around 80F), at 8 rue Montebello near the central market hall, makes an atmospheric place to eat.

Condom and around

Some 43km north of Auch and 21km west of Lectoure lies the town of **CONDOM**, whose road signs have predictably been interfered with by passing Brits: there's sadly no connection between the place and the device, though the mayor's considering opening a museum. Unremarkable in every other sphere, Condom is nonetheless good for a quick visit or an overnight stop, with an impressive cathedral and attractive old streets in the centre. Armagnac drinkers will be interested in the **Musée de l'Armagnac**, 2 rue Jules-Ferry (Wed–Mon: July & Aug 10am–noon & 3–6pm; rest of year 3–5pm; 13F), and the **Chais Ryst-Duperon**, where the liquor is aged (July & Aug daily 8am–noon & 2–6pm; rest of year closed Sat & Sun; free). For other places to taste and buy Armagnac, ask the **tourist office** in place Bossuet (July & Aug daily 10am–1pm & 2–7.30pm; rest of year Mon–Sat 9am–noon & 2–6pm; ☎05.62.28.00.80, fax 05.62.28.45.46).

The cheapest place to stay is the *Relais de la Ténaréze*, at 20 av d'Aquitaine (☎05.62.28.02.54, fax 05.62.28.46.96; ②). Two more appealing options, both with pools, are the *Hôtel Le Logis des Cordeliers*, in rue de la Paix (☎05.62.28.03.68, fax 05.62.68.29.03; ③; closed Jan), or, for a splurge, the *Hôtel des Trois Lys* (☎05.62.28.33.33, fax 05.62.28.41.85; ④; closed Feb; restaurant from 90F). There's another GR65 **gîte d'étape** at the *Centre Salvandy* (☎05.62.28.23.80), and a camping municipal (☎05.62.28.17.32; April–Oct) near the river on the road to Éauze. For a straightforward place to eat, try *Pizzéria l'Origan*, at 4 rue Cadéot in the town centre (closed Sun & Mon), or *Café des Sports*, on rue Charron by the cathedral, which does substantial salads and a *plat du jour* at 45F. Out of town, the **campsite**, *Le Moulin du Petit Gascon* (☎05.62.28.28.42; closed Dec–Feb, also Sun eve & Mon; menus from 95F) is attractively sited beside a canal lock.

Just 5km west of Condom, the tiny twelfth-century village of **LARRESSINGLE** is certainly very pretty, but is totally given over to the heritage industry as the "Carcassonne du Gers", with twee tearooms inside – and it only takes one coachload of visitors to swamp it.

More interesting is the very fine abbey of **FLARAN**, 8km along the road to Auch (daily 9.30am–noon & 2–6pm; July & Aug 9.30am–7pm; closed mid-Jan to mid-Feb; 25F). Built by the Cistercians in 1151 in pale white stone, it has the same scrubbed, ascetic appeal as Fontenay in Burgundy, with scarcely a hint of ornament – an effect totally destroyed by the decadent, incongruous plasterwork introduced into the monks' dormitory in the seventeenth century. Used as an Armagnac store until 1970, after undergoing many other vicissitudes in its long history, the monastery has only recovered its true identity in the last twenty years.

travel details

Buses

Auch to: Agen (6–11 daily; 1hr 30min); Bordeaux (1 daily; 3hr 40min); Condom (1–2 daily; 40min); Fleurance (6–11 daily; 20min); Lannemezan (1 daily; 1hr 45min); Lectoure (6–11 daily; 40min); Montauban (Mon–Sat 1–3 daily; 2hr); Tarbes (3–4 daily; 2hr); Toulouse (1–3 daily; 1hr 30min).

Bédarieux to: Olargues (4–5 daily; 40min); Pont-de-Tarassac (4–5 daily; 30min); St-Pons-de-Thomières (4–5 daily; 1hr).

Béziers to: Castres (2 daily; 2hr 30min); La Salvetat (1–2 daily; 2hr 10min); Mazamet (2 daily; 2hr); Montpellier (4–12 daily; 1hr 40min); Narbonne (2 daily; 1hr); Pézenas (4–12 daily; 40min); St-Pons-de-Thomières (1–2 daily; 1hr 20min).

Carcassonne to: Castelnaudary (1–3 daily; 1hr); Quillan (2–3 daily; 1hr 20min); Toulouse (1 daily; 2hr).

Montpellier to: Aigues-Mortes (2–4 daily; 1hr); Bédarieux (3–4 daily; 1hr 35min); Clermont-l'Hérault (3–4 daily; 1hr); Ganges (3–6 daily; 1hr 15min); Gignac (6–12 daily; 45min); Grau-du-Roi (4–11 daily; 1hr); La Cavalerie (daily; 1hr 50min); La Grande-Motte (5–12 daily; 45min); Le Vigan (3–5 daily; 1hr 40min); Lodève (3–8 daily; 1hr 15min); Millau (1–5 daily; 2hr); Nîmes (Mon–Sat 2 daily; 1hr 30min); Palavas (10–15 daily; 35min); Rodez (1–3 daily; 3hr 55min); St-Martin-de-Londres (3–9 daily; 1hr); Sète (3–11 daily; 1hr); Viols-le-Fort (3–9 daily; 40min).

Narbonne to: Béziers (2 daily; 1 hr); Carcassonne (1–4 daily; 1hr 30min); Gruissan (3–6 daily; 45min); Narbonne-Plage (2–3 daily; 45min); Perpignan (1 daily; 2hr).

Nîmes to Aigues-Mortes (6 daily; 1hr); Avignon (2–4 daily; 1hr 30min); Ganges (1–5 daily; 1hr 40min); Grau-du-Roi (6 daily; 1hr 10min); La Grande-Motte (5 daily; 1hr 20min); Le Vigan (1–5 daily; 2hr); Montpellier (Mon–Sat 2 daily; 1hr 30min); Pont-du-Gard (2–6 daily; 40min); Sommières (1–3 daily; 50min); Uzès (2–13 daily; 45min–1hr 20min).

Sète to: Montpellier (3–11 daily; 1hr).

Toulouse to: Albi (6 daily; 1hr 30min); Auch (1–3 daily; 1hr 30min); Ax-les-Thermes (3–5 daily; 2hr 30min–3hr); Castres (1 daily; 1hr 30min); Foix (3–5 daily; 2hr); Pamiers (3–5daily; 1hr 30min); Tarascon (3–5 daily; 2hr 20min).

Trains

Béziers to: Agde (1–2 hourly; 12min); Arles (8–12 daily; 2hr); Avignon (4–10 daily; 2hr); Bédarieux (6–9 daily; 40min); Carcassonne (10–14 daily; 1hr); Marseille (8–12 daily; 2hr 30min); Millau (3–6 daily; 2hr); Montpellier (4–6 hourly; 1hr); Nîmes (1–3 hourly; 1hr 20min); Paris (10 daily; 5–10hr); Narbonne (4–6 hourly; 20min); Perpignan (2–3 hourly; 1hr); Sète (4–6 hourly; 30min).

Carcassonne to: Arles (6–8 daily; 2hr 40min); Béziers (10–14 daily; 1hr); Bordeaux (5 daily; 3hr 20min); Marseille (3–4 daily; 3hr 20min); Montpellier (1–2 hourly; 1hr 30min); Narbonne (1–2 hourly; 30min); Nîmes (1–2 hourly; 2hr 10min); Quillan (1–2 daily; 1hr); Sète (1–2 hourly; 1hr 30min); Toulouse (2–3 hourly; 45min).

Montpellier to: Arles (1–2 hourly; 1hr); Avignon (2 hourly; 1hr); Béziers (4–6 hourly; 1hr); Carcassonne (1–2 hourly; 1hr 30min); Lyon (8 daily; 2hr 30min); Marseille (2–3 hourly; 1hr 40min); Mende (2–3 daily; 3hr 40min); Narbonne (1–2 hourly; 1hr); Paris (5–6 TGVs daily; 4hr 20min); Perpignan (3–4 hourly; 2hr); Sète (3–4 hourly; 20min); Toulouse (8–12 daily; 2hr 20min).

Narbonne to: Arles (6–8 daily; 2hr); Avignon (4–11 daily; 2hr 20min); Béziers (4–6 hourly; 20min); Bordeaux (3–4 daily; 2hr 25min); Carcassonne (10–14 daily; 30min); Cerbère (1–2 hourly; 1hr–1hr 30min); Marseille (7–8 daily; 2hr 40min); Montpellier (1–2 hourly; 1hr 20min); Nîmes (2–3 hourly; 1hr 50min); Perpignan (2–3 hourly; 30–40min); Port-Bou (1–2 hourly; 1hr 20min–1hr 40min); Sète (4–5 hourly; 40min); Toulouse (1–2 hourly; 1hr 20min–2hr).

Nîmes to: Arles (1–2 hourly; 30–40min); Avignon (1–2 hourly; 30min); Béziers (1–3 hourly; 1hr 20min); Carcassonne (1–2 hourly; 2hr 10min); Clermont-Ferrand (3 daily; 4–5hr); Génolhac (4–6 daily; 1hr 25min); La Bastide-St-Laurent (4–6 daily; 2hr 10min); Marseille (1–2 hourly; 1hr 20min); Montpellier (3–4 hourly; 30min); Narbonne (2–3 hourly; 1hr 50min); Paris via Alès (1–2 daily; 9hr); Paris (5–6 TGVs daily; 4hr 30min); Perpignan (6 daily; 2hr 30min); Sète (1–2 hourly; 40min); Vichy (1–2 daily; 6hr); Villefort (5–6 daily; 1hr 30min).

Sète to: Arles (6–8 daily; 1hr 15min); Avignon (8 daily; 1hr 30min); Béziers (4–6 hourly; 30min); Carcassonne (1–2 hourly; 1hr 30min); Marseille (7–10 daily; 2hr 10min); Montpellier (3–4 hourly; 20min); Narbonne (4–5 hourly; 40min); Nîmes (1–2 hourly; 40min); Perpignan (5–8 daily; 1hr 20min).

Toulouse to: Albi (9–19 daily; 1hr); Auch (4–7 daily; 1hr 30min); Ax-les-Thermes (5–7 daily; 1hr 45min); Barcelona (4 daily; 5hr–6hr 30min); Bayonne (5–6 daily; 4hr); Bordeaux (1–2 hourly; 2hr 45min); Brive (7–13 daily; 2hr 20min); Castres (5–10 daily; 1hr 20min); Foix (6–13 daily; 1hr 10min); La-Tour-de-Carol (4 daily; 2hr 35min); Lourdes (6–10 daily; 2hr 20min); Lyon (3 daily; 5hr); Marseille (8–9 daily; 3hr 30min–4hr 20min); Mazamet (5–10 daily; 1hr 40min); Pamiers (6–13 daily; 50min); Paris (1 hourly; 7–8hr); Pau (5–8 daily; 2hr–2hr 30min); Tarascon (5–7 daily; 1hr 20min); Tarbes (6–13 daily; 2hr).

CHAPTER TWELVE

THE MASSIF CENTRAL

One of the loveliest spots on earth . . . a country without roads, without guides, without any facilities for locomotion, where every discovery must be conquered at the price of danger or fatigue . . . a soil cut up with deep ravines, crossed in every way by lofty walls of lava, and furrowed by numerous torrents.

T
hus one of George Sand's characters described the Haute-Loire, the central *département* of **the Massif Central**, and it's a description that could still be applied to some of the region. Thickly forested and sliced by numerous rivers and lakes, these once volcanic uplands are geologically the oldest part of France and culturally one of the most firmly rooted in the past. Industry and tourism have made few inroads here, and the people remain rural and taciturn, with an enduring sense of regional identity. They also have a largely unfounded reputation for unfriendliness.

The Massif Central takes up a huge portion of the centre of France, but only a handful of towns have gained a foothold in its rugged terrain: **Le Puy**, spiked with theatrical pinnacles of lava, is the most compelling, with its steep streets and majestic cathedral; the spa of **Vichy** has an antiquated elegance and charm; even heavily industrial **Clermont-Ferrand**, the capital, has a certain cachet in the black volcanic stone of its historic centre and its stunning physical setting beneath the **Puy de Dôme**, a 1464-metre-high volcanic plug. There is pleasure, too, in the unpretentious provinciality of **Aurillac** and in the untouched medieval architecture of smaller places like **Murat**, **Besse**, **Salers**, **Orcival**, **Sauveterre-de-Rouergue**, **La Couvertoirade** and in the hugely influential abbey of **Conques**. But, above all, this is a country where the sights are landscapes rather than towns, churches and museums.

The heart of the region is the **Auvergne**, a wild and unexpected landscape of extinct volcanoes, stretching from the grassy domes and craters of the **Monts-Dôme** to the eroded skylines of the **Monts-Dore**, and deeply ravined **Cantal mountains** to the rash of darkly wooded pimples surrounding Le Puy. It is one of the poorest regions in France and has long remained outside the main national lines of communication. Much of it is above 1000 metres in height and snowbound in winter; it is only now that an autoroute is under construction through the middle. There is little arable land, just thousands of acres of upland pasture, traditionally grazed by sheep brought up from the southern

---

ACCOMMODATION PRICE CATEGORIES

Each hotel in this chapter has a symbol which corresponds to one of eight price categories.

① Under 160F	④ 300–400F	⑦ 600–700F
② 160–220F	⑤ 400–500F	⑧ Over 700F
③ 220–300F	⑥ 500–600F	

The prices quoted are for the cheapest available double room in high season, though remember that many of the cheap places will have more expensive rooms with en-suite facilities.

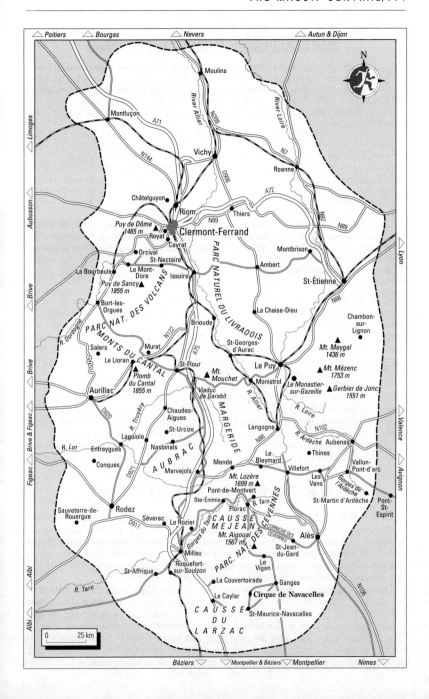

THE FOOD OF THE MASSIF CENTRAL

Don't expect anything very refined from the **cuisine of the Auvergne and Massif Central**: it is solid peasant fare as befits a poor and rugged region. The best-known dish is *potée auvergnate*, basically a **cabbage soup** to which other ingredients are added, often a piece of salt pork. It's easy to make and very nourishing. The ingredients – potatoes, pork or bacon, cabbage, beans, turnips – though added at different intervals, are all boiled up together.

Two potato dishes are very common – **la truffade** and **l'alicot**. For *truffade*, the potatoes are sliced and fried in lard, then fresh Cantal cheese is added; for an *alicot*, the potatoes are puréed and mixed with cheese. Less palatable for the squeamish, there's **tripoux**, usually a stuffing of either sheep's feet or calf's innards cooked in a casing of stomach lining. **Fricandeau**, a kind of pork pâté, is also wrapped in sheep's stomach.

By way of dessert, **clafoutis** is a popular fruit tart in which the fruit is baked with a batter of flour and egg simply poured over it. The classical fruit ingredient is black cherries, though pears, blackcurrants or apples can also be used.

The Ardèche in the east produces some wines, though these are not of any great renown. **Cheese** is a different story. In addition to the four great cow's milk cheeses – St-Nectaire (see p.784), Cantal, Fourme d'Ambert and Bleu d'Auvergne – this region also produces the prince of all cheeses, **Roquefort**, made from sheep's milk at the edge of the Causse du Larzac (see p.804).

lowlands for the summer. Nowadays, cows far outnumber the sheep, some raised for beef and some still for the production of Auvergne's four great cheeses (see box). The population has emigrated for generations, especially to Paris, where the café and restaurant trade has long been in the hands of Auvergnats. The same flight of population has affected the equally infertile but beautiful and more Mediterranean southern part of the region: the hills and valleys of the **Cévennes**, where Robert Louis Stevenson and his donkey made one of the more famous literary hikes in 1878.

Many of France's greatest rivers rise in the Massif Central: the **Dordogne** in the Monts-Dore, the **Loire** on the slopes of the Gerbier de Jonc in the east, and in the Cévennes the **Lot** and the **Tarn**. It is these last two rivers which create the distinctive character of the southern parts of the Massif Central, dividing and defining the special landscapes of the *causses*, or limestone plateaux, with their stupendous gorges.

This is territory, above all, for walkers and lovers of the **outdoors**, and everywhere you go tourist offices will supply ideas and routes for walks and bike rides, both long and short.

THE PARC DES VOLCANS

The **Parc Naturel Régional des Volcans d'Auvergne** encompasses the whole of the western edge of the Massif Central, from **Vichy** in the north to **Aurillac** in the south. It consists of three groups of extinct volcanoes – the **Monts-Dômes**, the **Monts-Dores** and the **Monts du Cantal** – with the high plateaux of Artense and the Cézallier which link them. It is big, wide-open country, sparsely populated and with largely treeless pasture for the cows whose milk produces Cantal and St-Nectaire cheese.

The park organization, whose headquarters are at the **Maison du Parc**, Château de Montlosier, 20km southwest of Clermont-Ferrand just off the Mont-Dore road (May–Oct daily 10am–noon & 2.30–7pm; ☎04.73.65.64.00), oversees the various subsidiary *maisons du parc*, each a kind of museum devoted to different themes or activities: fauna and flora, shepherd life, peat bogs and so on. While you can obviously just turn up at these places by car, you get a much closer understanding of what the park and its landscapes and activities are all about if you walk or bike around.

Four **GR footpaths** cross or make circuits within the park. The **GR40** runs from
north to south. The **GR441** makes a circuit round the Monts-Dômes, called the **Tour
de la Chaîne des Puys**. The **GR400** encircles the Cantal mountains, and the **GR30**
the lakes of the Artense plateau and Cézallier, under the title of the **Tour des Lacs
d'Auvergne**. There are also lots of shorter walks; ask at the local tourist office for more
information, and where to rent mountain bikes.

The towns in the area are few and of secondary interest, although **Orcival**, **Murat**
and **Salers** are unexpectedly attractive. **St-Nectaire** contains an exceptionally beautiful small church in the distinct Auvergne version of Romanesque; and **St-Flour** and
Aurillac have an agreeable provincial insularity.

Clermont-Ferrand and around

CLERMONT-FERRAND lies at the northern tip of the Massif Central. Although its
situation is magnificent, almost encircled by the wooded and grassy volcanoes of the

Monts-Dômes, it has for a century been a typical smokestack industrial centre, the home base of Michelin tyres, which makes it a rather incongruous capital for the rustic, even backward province of the Auvergne.

Its roots, both as a spa and a communications and trading centre, go back to Roman times. It was just outside the town, on the plateau of Gergovia to the south, that the Gauls under the leadership of Vercingétorix won their only, albeit indecisive, victory against Julius Cæsar's invading Romans. In the Middle Ages, the two towns of Clermont and Montferrand were divided by commercial and political rivalry and ruled respectively by a bishop and the Count of Auvergne. Louis XIII united them administratively in 1630, but it was not until the rapid industrial expansion of the late nineteenth century that the two really became indistinguishable. Indeed, it was Clermont that took the ascendancy, relegating Montferrand to a suburban backwater.

Michelin came into being thanks to the inventions of Charles Mackintosh, the Scotsman of raincoat fame. His niece married Édouard Daubrée, a Clermont sugar manufacturer, and brought with her some ideas about making rubber goods that she had learnt from her uncle. In 1889, the company became Michelin and Co, just in time to catch the development of the automobile and the World War I aircraft industry. The family ruled the town and employed 30,000 of its citizens until the early 1980s, when the industry went into decline. In the fifteen years since, the workforce has been halved, causing rippling unemployment throughout Clermont's economy. Many of those who have lost their jobs are Portuguese immigrants, imported over the last thirty years to fill the labour vacuum and well integrated with the local population.

As in many other traditional industrial towns hit by recession and changing global patterns of trade, Clermont has had to struggle to reorient itself, turning to service industries and the creation of a university of 34,000 students. Nonetheless, many people have moved elsewhere in search of work, reducing the population by nearly a tenth. The town has changed physically, too, as many of the old factories have been demolished.

Arrival, information and accommodation

The **gare SNCF** line (☎08.36.35.35.35; 7am–10pm) is on avenue de l'Union Sovietique, from where it is a ten-minute bus journey to place de Jaude, at the western edge of the cathedral hill. The **gare routière** (☎04.73.35.05.62) is on boulevard François-Mitterrand, with a city transport information kiosk called Boutique T2C on place de Jaude (☎04.73.28.56.56). If you're flying into town, the **airport** is at Aulnat, 7km east, with daily flights to and from Paris and other internal destinations, as well as to London during the summer (☎04.73.62.71.00).

The main **tourist office** is opposite the Cathedral in the place de la Victoire (June–Sept Mon–Sat 8.30am–7pm, Sun 9am–noon & 2–6pm; Oct–May Mon–Fri 8.45am–6.30pm, Sat 9am–noon & 2–6pm, Sun 9am–1pm; ☎04.73.98.65.00, fax 04.73.90.04.11), and there is another conveniently placed annexe immediately to the left outside the train station exit (Mon–Sat 9.15–11.30am & 12.15–5pm; Oct–May Mon–Fri only; ☎04.73.91.87.89). The **departmental office** is on the place de la Bourse (☎04.73.42.22.50), and the **regional office** at 43 av Julien (☎04.73.29.49.49). Specific hiking or mountain-bike information is available from Chamina, 5 rue Pierre-le-Vénérable (☎04.73.92.81.44).

Accommodation

The cheapest and friendliest **hotel**, conveniently placed, opposite the station, is the *Zurich*, 65 av de l'Union Sovietique (☎04.73.91.97.98; ②; arrive after 2pm); it looks rather old-fashioned from the outside but is perfectly comfortable. More upmarket options include the *Lyon*, 16 place de Jaude (☎04.73.93.32.55, fax 04.73.93.54.33; ④), with a lively bar and restaurant (☎04.73.34.36.34; menus from 50F), *Gallieni*, 51 rue

Bonnabaud (☎04.73.93.59.69, fax 04.73.34.89.29; ②), and *Regina*, close to place de Jaude at 14 rue Bonnabaud (☎04.73.93.44.76, fax 04.73.35.04.63; ③; menus at 90F). If these are full, choose between the *St-André*, opposite the station at 25 av de l'Union Sovietique (☎04.73.91.40.40, fax 04.73.90.72.19; ③; closed over Christmas), the *Albert Elisabeth*, a small walk away on av Albert-Elisabeth, at no. 37 (☎04.73.92.47.41, fax 04.73.90.78.32; ③), or the *Ravel*, nearby in rue Maringues opposite the old Marché St-Joseph (☎04.73.91.51.33, fax 04.73.92.28.48; ③; closed Jan).

The HI **hostel** is just across the street to the right from the train station at 55 av de l'Union de Sovietique (☎04.73.92.26.39, fax 04.73.92.99,96; closed Nov–Feb), and there's also the **Foyer St-Jean** just north of the cathedral at 17 rue Gaultier-de-Biauzat (☎04.73.31.57.00, fax 04.73.31.59.99; ①). For **campers**, there are *campings municipaux* at **Royat** (*L'Oclède*) to the west (☎04.73.35.97.05; April–Oct; bus #41), **Ceyrat** (*Le Chancet*) to the south (☎04.73.61.30.73; all year; bus #4C & #41, stop Preguille), and **Cournon** (*La Plage*) to the east (☎04.73.84.81.30; all year; bus #3, stop Plaine de jeux).

The city

The most dramatic and flattering approach to Clermont is from the Aubusson road or along the scenic railway line from Le Mont-Dore (see p.780), both of which cross the chain of the Monts-Dômes just north of the Puy de Dôme. This way you descend through the leafy western suburbs with marvellous views over the town, dominated by the black towers of the cathedral sitting atop the volcanic stump that forms the hub of the old town.

Clermont's reputation as a *ville noire* becomes immediately understandable when you enter the city's medieval quarter, clustered in characteristic medieval muddle around the cathedral, and the most appealing part of the city to wander through. It is due not to industrial pollution but to the black volcanic rock used in the construction of many of its buildings. The **Cathédrale Notre-Dame** stands at the centre and highest point of the old town; Freda White evocatively described its sombre grey-black-stone lava from the quarries at nearby Volvic (see p.779) as "like the darkest shade of a pigeon's wing". Begun in the mid-thirteenth century, it was not finished until the nineteenth, under the direction of Viollet-le-Duc, who was the architect of the west front and those typically Gothic crocketed spires, whose too methodically cut stonework at close range betrays the work of the machine rather than the mason's hand. The interior is swaddled in mysterious gloom, illuminated all the more startlingly by the brilliant colours of the medieval windows in the choir: look closely at the window in the second chapel on the left, where in the third panel on the right you can see woodmen and boatmen at work, and stone-cutters in the centre panel. If the day is fine, climb the **Tour de la Bayette** (Mon–Fri 8am–noon & 2–6pm, Sun 9.30am–noon & 3–7pm; 10F) by the north transept door: you look back over the rue des Gras to the Puy de Dôme (see p.777) looming dramatically over the city, white morning mist retreating down its sides like seaweed from a rock.

A short step northeast of the cathedral, down the elegant old rue du Port, stands Clermont's other great church, the Romanesque **Basilique Notre-Dame-du-Port** – a century older than the cathedral and in almost total contrast both in style and substance, built from softer stone in pre-lava-working days and consequently corroding badly from exposure to Clermont's polluted air. For all that, it's a beautiful building in pure Auvergnat Romanesque style, featuring a Madonna and Child over the south door in the strangely stylized local form, both figures stiff and upright, the child more like a dwarf than an infant. Inside, it exudes the broody mysteriousness so often generated by the Romanesque style. Put a coin in the slot and you can light up the intricately carved ensemble of leaves, knights and biblical figures on the church's pillars and capitals. It was here in all probability that Pope Urban II preached the First Crusade in 1095 to a vast crowd who received his speech with the Occitan cry of *Dios lo Volt* (God wills it) – a phrase adopted by the Crusaders in justification of all subsequent massacres.

For general animation, shopping, drinking and eating, the streets between the cathedral and place de Jaude are best, with the main morning market taking place in the conspicuously modern **place St-Pierre** just off rue des Gras. **Place de Jaude** remains another monument to planners' aberrations in spite of the shops, the cafés well placed to take in the morning sun and an attempt to make it more attractive with trees and a fountain. Smack in the middle of the traffic, a romantic equestrian statue of Vercingétorix lines up with the Puy de Dôme.

Away from these central streets, there is nothing to tempt the pedestrian, save perhaps **rue Ballainvilliers**, whose eighteenth-century facades recall the sober, sombre elegance of Edinburgh and lead to the city's most interesting museum, the **Musée Bargoin** (Tues–Sun 10am–6pm; 30F), with some remarkable archeological finds from round about. These include lots of fascinating domestic bits: Roman shoes, baskets, bits of dried fruit, glass and pottery, as well as a remarkable burial find from nearby Martres-de-Veyre dating back to the second century AD: a young girl's plaited blonde hair, her thigh-length boots, dress, belt and goatskin shoes. There is also an extraordinary collection of wooden limbs found during building operations, buried in a covered-over spring in the suburb of Chamalières: the gifts of people whose ailments had been cured thanks to these waters. Upstairs is a very handsome exhibition of Oriental carpets and kilims.

The two other museums are not of great interest. **Musée Lecoq**, directly behind the the Musée Bargoin (May–Sept 10 Tues–Sat noon & 2–6pm, Sun pm only; Oct–April 10am–noon & 2–5pm), is devoted mainly to natural history – and named after the gentleman who also founded the public garden full of beautiful trees and formal beds just across the street. **Musée du Ranquet**, 34 rue des Gras (Tues–Sun 10am–6pm; free), is housed in a noble sixteenth-century house, containing, at its most interesting, a collection of traditional tools and domestic objects and two versions of seventeenth-century philosopher and scientist Blaise Pascal's calculating machine.

Montferrand is today little more than a suburb of larger Clermont, standing out on a limb to the north, but it's good for a stroll if you're feeling active. Built on the *bastide* plan, its principal streets, rue de la Rodade and rue Jules-Guesde (the latter named for the founder of the French Communist Party, for Montferrand was home to many of the Michelin factory workers), are still lined with the fine town houses of its medieval merchants and magistrates.

Eating and drinking

If you are staying in the station area, there are a couple of reasonable places to **eat** without going further afield. The best is the *Auvergnat*, the restaurant of the *Hôtel St-André*, 27 av de l'Union Sovietique (from 73F), whose repertoire includes some standard Auvergne dishes like the *potée auvergnate*. Less expensive and very friendly, with a terrace at the back, is the *Hôtel des Commerçants*, opposite the station (from 62F).

In the centre of town, the best of the cheaper places is the ever-popular *Crêperie 1513*, 3 rue des Chaussetiers, opposite the cathedral, which occupies a superb Renaissance mansion built in 1513 (till 1am; lunchtime menu at 55F). In the same street, at no. 29, *Le Bougnat* offers local regional cuisine at affordable prices (closed Sun & Mon lunch; from 76F). Close by at 36 rue des Gras, there's good pizza and pasta at *Le Bistrot Vénitien* from about 55F (closed Sun). On the other side of the cathedral, there's good Vietnamese cooking at around 50F at the *Mai Lan*, 41 bd Trudaine (closed Sun & Mon lunch), and crêpes for 30–60F at the *Pescajoux* in the old rue du Port at no. 13.

For a more specialized gastronomic experience, there's nothing to beat the refined and inventive cooking of *Gérard Anglard* at 17 rue Lamartine, off place de Jaude, especially the lunchtime menu at 110F (☎04.73.93.52.25; closed Sun & Aug 1–15; 110F upwards). Also good value, especially at lunchtime, is the *Clos St-Pierre*, next to the St-Pierre market below the cathedral (closed Sun and Mon; 55F at lunchtime, otherwise 205F plus). And, if you don't mind the drive – barely 5km southeast off the old N9 Issoire road – the *Petit Bonneval* at **Pérignat-lès-Sarlière** makes an agreeable and delicious stop for dinner on a summer evening (☎04.73.79.11.11; closed Sun eve; menus from 110F).

For a daytime **drink** or coffee, *Le Suffren*, on the corner of place de Jaude, is one of the most popular and agreeable places to hang out. Also fashionable, especially at night, there's *Le Dérailleur*, 9 av Georges-Clemenceau, while young rockers head for the sub-urban village of **Orcines**, beneath the Puy de Dôme, to *Phidias* or *Boudu's*, still going strong on route de la Baraque (☎04.73.62.18.34; until 5am; closed Sun & Mon).

The Puy de Dôme

Visiting Clermont without going to the top of the **Puy de Dôme** (1464m) would be like visiting Athens without seeing the Acropolis. And if you choose your moment – early in the morning or late in the evening – you can easily avoid the worst of the crowds.

Clearly signposted from place de Jaude, it is about 15km from the city centre by the D941. The last 6.5km is a private road and costs 22F; when this is closed (July & Aug between 11am–6pm) there is a shuttle service (21F). If you are driving, make sure to pump your brakes on the descent; otherwise you may find yourself waiting for a long time before driving off, while your brakes cool down.. Alternatively, you can leave the car at the **Col de Ceyssat** and climb the Puy itself on foot in about an hour.

The result of a volcanic explosion about 10,000 years ago, the Puy is an abrupt 400m from base to summit. Although the weather station buildings and enormous television mast are pretty ugly close up, the staggering views and sense of airy elevation more than compensate. Even if Mont Blanc itself is not always visible way to the east – it can be if conditions are favourable – you can see huge distances, all down the Massif Central to the Cantal mountains. Above all, you get a bird's-eye view of the other volcanic summits to the north and south, both the rounded domes, largely forested since the nineteenth century, and the perfect 100-metre-deep grassy crater of the **Puy de Pariou**, just to the north.

Immediately below the summit are the scant remains of a substantial **Roman temple** dedicated to Mercury (free entry), some of the finds from which are displayed in the Musée Bargoin in Clermont-Ferrand (see opposite). Beside it is a memorial com-memorating the exploits of Eugène Renaux, who landed a plane here in 1911 in response to the offer of a 100,000 franc prize by the Michelin brothers. Today the avia-tors are hang-gliders and paragliding enthusiasts drifting like gaudy birds around the stern of a ship.

Riom

Just 15km north of Clermont-Ferrand, **RIOM** is sedate and provincial. One-time capi-tal of the entire Auvergne, its Renaissance architecture now secures the town's status as a highlight of the northern Massif. In 1942, just before the first trains of Jewish deportees were shipped to Nazi Germany, Léon Blum, Jewish Prime Minister and architect of the Socialist Popular Front government, was put on trial in Riom by Pétain, France's collaborationist ruler, in an attempt to blame the country's ills on the Left. Defending himself, Blum turned the trial into an indictment of collaboration and Nazism. Under pressure from Hitler, Pétain called it off, but nonetheless deported Blum to Germany, an experience which he survived, to give evidence against Pétain himself after the war.

You may only want to spend a morning here, but Riom does provide a worthwhile stopover for lunch if you're on the way up to Vichy. It's an aloof, old-world kind of place, still Auvergne's judicial capital, with a nineteenth-century **Palais de Justice** that stands on the site of a grand palace built when the dukes of Berry controlled this region in the fourteenth century. Only the **Sainte-Chapelle** survives of the original palace, with some fine stained glass and tapestries (guided visits only: May Wed 3–5pm; June & Sept Wed–Fri same hours; July & Aug daily 10am–noon & 2.30–5.30pm; 15F).

There is an interesting museum on the region's folk traditions nearby at 10bis rue Delille, the **Musée Régional d'Auvergne** (Wed–Mon: June–Sept 10am–noon & 2.30–6pm; Oct–May 10am–noon & 2–5.30pm; 25F; free on Wed), with the **Musée Mandet**'s displays of Roman finds and unexciting paintings not far away at 4 rue de l'Hôtel-de-Ville (daily except Tues: April–Sept 10am–noon & 2.30–6pm; Oct–March 10am–noon & 2–5.30pm; 25F; free on Wed). At 44 rue du Commerce, the **church of Notre-Dame-du-Marthuret** holds Riom's most-valued treasures, two statues of the Virgin and Child – one a Black Madonna, the other, the so-called *Vierge à l'Oiseau*, a touchingly realistic piece of carving that portrays the young Christ with a bird fluttering in his hands. A copy stands in the entrance hall of the church (its original site), where you can see it with the advantage of daylight.

Riom's **tourist office** is at 16 rue du Commerce in the town centre (July & Aug Sun 10am–noon & 2.30–4pm; Sept–June Mon–Sat 9am–12.30pm & 2–6/6.30pm; ☎04.73.38.59.45, fax 04.73.38.25.15). If you decide to **stay**, the *Grand Hôtel Desaix*, 1 place Martyrs-de-la-Résistance (☎04.73.38.20.36, fax 04.73.63.19.23; ①) is friendly and good value and has its own restaurant; menus from 49F.

Around Riom

SNCF buses run to **MOZAC**, on the edge of town, with a twelfth-century **abbey church** whose Romanesque sculpture is as beautiful as you'd expect, and continue to the bourgeois spa resort of **CHÂTEL-GUYON** in around twenty minutes. With thirty different **hot springs**, great views over the surrounding countryside and *puys*, and a couple of well-equipped **campsites**, this is as good a place as any if you want to rest up for a night. For an easy stroll from here, you can wander out along the leafy **valleys of the Sardon and Prades**.

The little town of **VOLVIC** is also close by, renowned for its spring water and the quarries that furnished the black rock for Clermont's cathedral, as well as so many other Auvergnat buildings. Its **Maison de la Pierre** (guided tours only: Wed–Mon: mid-March to April & Oct to mid-Nov 10am–5.15pm; May–Sept 9.15am–6pm; 20F) features a surprisingly engaging display about the use of lava rock, including a historical and geological explanation, as well as a tour of the disused quarries – a warm jacket is advised.

Vichy

VICHY is famous for two things: its World War II puppet government under Marshal Pétain; and its curative sulphurous springs, which attract thousands of ageing and ailing visitors, or *curistes*, every year. There's no mention of Pétain's government in town, but the fact that Vichy is one of France's foremost spa resorts colours everything you see here. The town is almost entirely devoted to catering for its largely elderly, genteel and rich population, which swells several-fold in summer; they come here to drink the water, wallow in it, inhale its steam or be sprayed with it. An attempt is now being made to rejuvenate the image of Vichy by appealing to a younger, more fitness-conscious generation.

The town

All of this makes Vichy seem unappealing and yet there is certain element of charm. There's a real *fin-de-siècle* atmosphere about the town and a curious fascination in its

VOLVIC TO LASCHAMP WALK

For a good day's walk and a thorough exploration of the *puys*, take the train from Clermont to Volvic-Gare. Follow the D90 road beside the train line for about 1km until you join up with the **GR441** path, where the road turns right under the train line. Keep along your side of the train track for a few minutes longer and follow the GR441 round to the left, almost doubling back southwest along the line of the wooded Puys Nugères, Jumes and Coquille to the northern foot of the Puy de Chopine (2–3hr). Here you join up with the **GR4** and follow the combined GR4–441 across the Orcines–Pontgibaud road to the summit of the Puy de Dôme (about 2hr 30min from the road). From the Puy, descend to the Col de Ceyssat in half an hour (good chance of a lift back to Clermont), or continue to **LASCHAMP** (50min), where there is a **gîte d'étape** (7–8hr, though a fit and experienced walker could do it in 6hr).

You should not set off without either the relevant section of the GR4 *Topoguide* or, preferably, the IGN 1:25,000 map, the *Chaîne des Puys*, which also marks the GR441 from Volvic-Gare. If you don't feel up to a walk, there is a really beautiful train ride from Clermont to the town of Le Mont-Dore (see p.781), all round the chain of the *puys*.

continuing function. The town revolves around the **Parc des Sources**, a stately tree-shaded park that takes up most of the centre. At its north end stands the **Hall des Sources**, an enormous iron-framed greenhouse in which people sit and chat or read newspapers, while from a large tiled stand in the middle the various waters emerge from their spouts, beside the just-visible remains of the Roman establishment. The *curistes* line up to get their prescribed cupful, and for a small fee you can join them. The Célestins is the only one of the springs that is bottled and widely drunk: if you're into a taste experience, try the remaining five. They are progressively more sulphurous and foul, with the Source de l'Hôpital, which has its own circular building at the far end of the park, an almost unbelievably nasty creation. Each of the springs is prescribed for a different ailment and the tradition is that – apart from the Célestins – they must all be drunk on the spot to be efficacious; a dubious but effective way of drawing in the crowds.

Although all the springs technically belong to the nation and treatment is partially funded by the state, they are in fact run privately for profit by the Compagnie Fermière, first created in the nineteenth century to prepare for a visit by the Emperor Napoléon III. The Compagnie not only has a monopoly on selling the waters but also runs the casino and numerous hotels. Even the chairs conveniently dotted around the Parc des Sources belong to the Compagnie.

Directly behind the Hall des Sources, along the leafy **Esplanade Napoléon III** (the emperor's interest in the waters brought Vichy to public notice in the mid-nineteenth century), is the enormous **Grand Établissement Thermal**, the thermal baths, decorated with Moorish arches and domes and blue ceramic panels of voluptuous mermaids. In the entrance hall, a massive third-century Roman milestone from the Vichy–Clermont road is displayed, with an expensive shopping arcade leading off. And behind this is the latest addition to the town's amenities: the startlingly modern **Bains Callou**.

To provide distraction for the *curistes*, a grand **casino** was built at the southern end of the Parc des Sources, which from May to September is the venue for regular concerts and opera productions, with lighter music oom-pah-ing out from the open-air bandstand in the park behind it.

After the waters, Vichy's curiosities are limited. There is pleasant, wooded riverside in **Parc de l'Allier**, created again for Napoléon III. And, not far from here, the old town boasts the strange **church of St-Blaise**, actually two churches in one, with a 1930s'

Baroque structure built onto the original Romanesque one – an effect that sounds hideous but is rather imaginative. Inside, another Auvergne Black Virgin, Notre-Dame-des-Malades, stands surrounded by plaques offered by the grateful healed who stacked their odds with both her and the sulphur.

Practicalities

Vichy's **gare SNCF** (☎04.70.46.50.50) is on the eastern edge of the city centre at the end of rue de Paris. The **gare routière** is on the corner of rue Doumier and rue Jardet, by the central place Charles-de-Gaulle, and there is a public transport information line (☎04.70.30.17.30). The building that used to house the wartime Vichy government at 19 rue du Parc is now home to the **tourist office** (June–Sept Mon–Sat 9am–7.30pm, Sun 9.30am–12.30pm & 3–7pm; Oct–April Mon–Sat 9am–12.30pm & 1.30–7pm; ☎04.70.98.71.94, fax 04.70.31.06.00).

There are so many **hotels** that finding a place to stay is not difficult. There are several around the station, but more agreeable are the freshly decorated and tranquilly bourgeois *Midland*, 2 rue de Paris (☎04.70.97.48.48, fax 04.70.31.31.89; ③; closed Oct 20–April 20; good restaurant from 85F), or the historic *Hôtel Londres*, 7 bd de Russie, behind the casino (☎04.70.98.28.27, fax 04.70.98.29.37;②; closed Oct 15–March 25). If you prefer something cheaper, there is a good choice in the old part of town: the *Hôtel du Bourbonnais Vieux Vichy*, near the church of St-Blaise, at 20 place d'Allier (☎04.70.32.16.10; ②; closed Oct–April), a simple, old-fashioned French hotel with home-cooking for 55F. But for real charm and a lovely view over the park, the best bargain must be the *Belle-Île*, 72 bd des États-Unis (☎04.70.98.20.61; ①; closed Jan). The **youth hostel** has moved to the *Le Villa Claudius Pendet*, 76 av des Celestins (☎04.70.96.01.10, fax 04.70.98.43.74), towards the station. There's a **camping municipal** (*La Graviere*), at the Centre Omnisports (☎04.70.59.21.00; March–Sept). However, if resting, solitude and recuperating is not your cup of tea, you may prefer to stay elsewhere.

For **eating**, apart from the hotel-restaurants listed above, the simplest solution is to head for the area around the junction of rue Clemenceau and rue de Paris, where there are several brasseries and cafés. For something rather more elegant, and not cheap, the beautiful *Brasserie du Casino*, 4 rue du Casino (☎04.70.98.23.06; closed Wed & Sun eve & Oct 18–Nov15; 85–145F), is an interesting experience: dressing smartly is advisable.

The Monts-Dore

The **Monts-Dore** lie about 50km southwest of Clermont. Also volcanic in origin – the main period of activity was around five million years ago – they are much more rugged and more obviously mountainous than their gentler, younger neighbours, the Monts-Dôme. Their centre is the precipitous, plunging valley of the River Dordogne, which rises on the slopes of the **Puy de Sancy**, at 1885m the highest point in the Massif Central, just above the little town of **Le Mont-Dore**.

In spite of their relative ruggedness, there are few crags and rock faces. Their upper slopes, albeit steep, are grassy and treeless for miles and miles. They are known as *montagnes à vaches* – mountains for cows, as they traditionally provided summer pasture land for herds of cows, raised above all for their milk and the production of **St-Nectaire** cheese. The herdsmen who milked them morning and evening and made the cheese set up their primitive summer homes in the dozens of (now mainly ruined) stone huts, or *burons*, that scatter the landscape.

Although these traditional activities still continue, many of the upland herds are now beef cattle being fattened for the autumn sales, often for export to Italy, Germany and Spain. And tourism has become an important part of the local economy, although mostly unobtrusive and low-key, with mainly walkers in summer and cross-country skiers in winter.

Le Mont-Dore and the Puy de Sancy

Squeezed out along the narrow wooded valley of the infant Dordogne, grey-slated **LE MONT-DORE** is a long-established spa resort, with Roman remnants testifying to just how old it is. Its popularity goes back to the eighteenth century when metalled roads replaced the old mule paths and made access possible, but reached its apogee with the opening of the railway around 1900. It is an altogether wholesome and civilized sort of place.

The **Établissement Thermal** – the baths, which give the place its *raison d'être* – are right in the middle of town and are certainly worth visiting (guided tours Mon–Sat: May 11 to Oct 10 2.30, 3.30, 4.30 & 5.30pm; 12F). Early every morning, the *curistes* stream into its neo-Byzantine halls – an extravaganza of tiles, striped columns and ornate ironwork – hoping for a remedy in this self-proclaimed "world centre for treatment of asthma". For many Parisians, of all ages and walks of life, this is their annual mecca; whiling away their days sniffing sulphur from bunsen burner tubes, and sitting in thick fog.

Walkers also frequent the town, the principal attraction being the **Puy de Sancy** (1885m), whose jagged skyline blocks the head of the Dordogne valley, 3km away (mid-May to Sept; 4 buses daily; 17F). Accessible by *téléférique* (36F return) since the 1930s, it's one of the busiest tourist sites in the country. As a result, the path from the *téléférique* station to the summit has had to be railed and paved with baulks of timber to prevent total erosion. Combined with the scars of access tracks for the ski installations, this has done little for its beauty.

However, with a little sweat and effort you can escape to wilder areas of the mountain. The **GR30** passes this way and on down to La Bourboule (see p.782), giving a good sense of the typical landscape: long views over meadows full of gentians and violets, grazed by sheep and cows. Start out along the summit path and at the first intermediate peak, take a right and go downhill. The GR30 is signposted. It follows the western ridge of the Dordogne valley for about an hour and a half, before turning ninety degrees left, away from the valley. Keep straight ahead at this point, go down a gravelly track, with the rocky dome of **le Capucin**, above Le Mont-Dore, directly in front of you. The track enters the woods to the left of this bump by a ruined house. Five minutes later, on the right, just past a concrete water-pipe junction, a path drops steeply down through beech trees to Le Capucin *téléférique* station and down again to Le Mont-Dore (3hr). Coming up, you need to allow four to five hours. The path starts behind the *Panorama Hotel*, near the tourist office.

A shorter, though steep, climb up from the town would take you directly to the summit of Le Capucin (2hr), with great views of the Puy de Sancy and across the Dordogne valley.

Practicalities

Without a car, Le Mont-Dore is most easily accessible by train from Clermont (see p.773). The **train** (☎04.73.65.00.02) and **bus stations** are at the entrance to the town. A ten-minute walk takes you to the centre, where the **tourist office** sits in the park on av de la Libération (Mon–Sat 9am–12.30pm & 2–6pm; July & Aug Mon–Sat same hours, Sun 10am–noon & 4–6.30pm; ☎04.73.65.20.21, fax 04.73.65.05.71); they will advise about other walking and cycling possibilities (VTT rental), as well as day bus excursions to some otherwise rather inaccessible places round about.

Accommodation is not hard to come by, as the town is brimming with hotels. Try the *Nouvel Hôtel* near the baths at 4 rue Jean-Moulin (☎04.73.65.11.34, fax

04.73.65.09.77; ②; closed Oct 10–Dec 20); or the *Russie*, also nearby at 3 rue Favart
(☎04.73.65.05.97, fax 04.73.65.22.10; ④; closed Nov & Dec). Turn onto rue Pasteur
and you'll immediately be drawn to simple and unique jazz bar, with an intriging proprietor. *La Chaumière*, a favourite with the locals and Parisians, has a few clean, basic
rooms upstairs (☎04.73.65.01.91;①). Also very comfortable, clean and very reasonably
priced is the *Piax* on rue Rigny (☎04.73.65.00.17, fax 04.73.65.00.31; ②). There's an
efficient modern **youth hostel** on the Puy de Sancy road, with a stunning view of the
mountains (☎04.73.65.03.53, fax 04.73.65.27.29; meals), and a gîte d'étape
(☎04.73.65.25.65), plus two municipal **campsites**, *Les Crouzets* (☎04.73.65.21.60)
opposite the station, and *L'Esquiladou* (☎04.73.65.23.74; Jan–Oct 15) off to the right on
the road to La Bourboule.

As far as **eating** is concerned, there are large numbers of brasseries and cafés in the
centre offering *plats* for 40–50F. A particularly pleasant place is *Le Bougnat* 23 av
Clemenceau, which offers various Auvergnat traditional dishes. (☎04.73.65.28.19;
closed Mon).

La Bourboule

LA BOURBOULE is just 7km down the road. Known as the sister to Le Mont-Dore, it
is another traditional spa – the "capital of allergies" – but with a more open feel and,
because of its lower altitude, temperatures a degree or two warmer. The big **casino**, the
domed **Grands Thermes baths** and several other turn-of-the-century buildings which
once housed privately run baths are ornate, gilded and wonderfully vulgar, with a
faded, permanently off-season look to them – much like the whole town. All in all, it's a
cool, tranquil place to unwind: as the tourist office's leaflet says, "You will be able to put
your vital node to rest in La Bourboule."

Behind the Hôtel de Ville, the large wooded **Parc Fenestre** has a *téléférique* taking
you right up to **Plateau de Charlannes** (1300m), where it's possible to stroll in the
woods or ski in winter; the **tourist office** in the Hôtel de Ville on place de la République
(☎04.73.65.57.71, fax 04.73.65.50.21) sells a booklet of local walks.

Hotels here are plentiful, three good bargains being the *Aviation Hôtel*, in rue de
Metz (☎04.73.81.32.32, fax 04.73.81.02.85;③; closed Oct–Dec 20; restaurant from 70F),
the newly renovated *Le Pavillon*, av d'Angleterre (☎04.73.65.50.18, fax 04.73.81.00.93;
③; closed Nov–March; restaurant from 80F), and *Des Fleurs* on av de Mussy
(☎04.73.81.09.44, fax 04.73.65.52.03; ①; closed Oct 10–Dec 20; restaurant from 90F).
There is also a good selection of **campsites**, with the *camping municipal*
(☎04.73.81.10.20) on av Maréchal Lattre-de-Tassigny, and another at **Murat-le-Quaire**,
4km away, along the Mont-Dore road.

WALKS AROUND LA BOURBOULE

Fit and serious walkers may want to conquer the **Puy de Sancy**, a six-hour hike south of
La Bourboule on the GR30-41, passing after about two hours the two fine waterfalls of the
Cascade de la Vernière and **Plat à Barbe** – themselves a satisfying destination. For
the summit of Puy de Sancy, see the account of Le Mont-Dore (p.781). An easier walk out
of La Bourboule is to the summit of the **Banne d'Ordanche** (1500m): pick up the GR
path to the east of the town where it crosses the D130 road and the train line, then take
the signposted GR41 where it diverges from GR30.

During winter months, both Le Mont-Dore and La Bourboule double as ski resorts –
centres of a **ski-de-fond** (cross-country) network of circular pistes, some over 20km
long. Skiable paths also connect La Bourboule to other ski centres in the locality – Sancy,
Besse, Chastreix and Picherande. Downhill skiing is possible, too, on the Puy de Sancy.

WALKS AROUND ORCIVAL

If you're keen on walking in the area, possibilities from Orcival include trips to **Lac de Servières** and **Lac de Guéry**. The first takes two-and-a-half hours, the second some five hours. For Lac de Servières, follow the **GR141–30** south through the woods above the valley of the Sioule. The lake is a beauty; it's 1200m up, with gently sloping shores surrounded by pasture and conifers. You can either head southeast to the **gîte d'étape** at Pessade (☎04.73.79.31.07), or continue to the larger Lac de Guéry, lent a slightly eerie air by the black basaltic boulders strewn across the surrounding meadows, where there is a romantically situated lakeside **hotel**, the *Lac de Guéry* (☎04.73.65.02.76, fax 04.73.65.08.78; ③; closed Oct 15–Jan 15; restaurant from 95F).

If you are driving to Le Mont-Dore, only 9km further on from here, just before the Lac de Guéry, the road takes you round the head of the **Fontsalade valley**, where two prominent rocks composed of banks of basalt organ-pipes rise spectacularly from the woods: the **Roche Tuilière** and the **Roche Sanadoire**. A *Chamina* footpath takes you on a two-hour walk round the valley, starting from the roadside belvedere overlooking Sanadoire. A little higher up, on the bare slopes of the **Puy de l'Aiguiller**, a roadside memorial commemorates some English airmen killed in an accident while making a parachute drop to the *maquis* in March 1944.

Orcival

Twenty-seven kilometres southwest of Clermont and about 20km north of Le Mont-Dore, lush pastures and green hills punctuated by the abrupt eruptions of the *puys* enclose the village of **ORCIVAL** (buses from Clermont), the home town of ex-President Valéry Giscard d'Estaing. A pretty, well-visited, little place, founded by the monks of La Chaise-Dieu in the twelfth century, it makes a suitable base for hiking in the region.

Orcival is dominated by the stunning Romanesque **church of Notre-Dame**, built of the same grey volcanic stone as the cathedral in Clermont and topped with a spired octagonal tower and fanned with tiny chapels. Inside, attention focuses on the choir, neatly and harmoniously contained by the semi-circle of pillars defining the ambulatory. Mounted on a stone column in the centre is the celebrated **Virgin of Orcival**, a gilded and enamelled statue of Mary enthroned, holding an adult-looking Child in her lap. The statue has been the object of a popular cult since the Middle Ages and is still carried through the streets on Ascension Day.

There's modest **accommodation** at the *Hôtel des Touristes* (☎04.73.65.82.55, fax 04.73.65.91.11; ③; closed Nov 15–Feb 15; restaurant 58–100F) and the *Hôtel Vieux Logis* (☎04.73.65.82.03, fax 04.73.65.88.07; ②; closed Oct to mid-Dec; restaurant from 68F). One kilometre away on GR30/GR441, the **gîte d'étape** *La Fontchartoux* (☎04.73.65.83.04; ①) has an adjoining restaurant run by the gîte proprietor. **Campers** are better off at **BONNET**, 5km away in the next valley.

St-Nectaire and around

ST-NECTAIRE lies some way to the south of Orcival, midway between Le Mont-Dore and Issoire. It comprises the tiny spa of **St-Nectaire-le-Bas**, whose main street is lined with grand but fading Belle Époque hotels, and the old village of **St-Nectaire-le-Haut**, overlooked by the magnificent Romanesque **church** that gives the place its renown. Like the church in Orcival and Notre-Dame-du-Port in Clermont, this is one of the jewels of the Auvergne's Romanesque architecture, with the same delightful features: patterned stonework, intricate arrangement of apse and radiating chapel, richly carved capitals within.

ST-NECTAIRE CHEESE

St-Nectaire is an *appellation contrôlée*, to which only cheeses made from herds grazing in a limited area to the south of the Monts-Dore are entitled. It is made in two stages. First, a white creamy cheese or *tomme* is produced. This is matured for two to three months in a cellar at a constant temperature, resulting in the growth of a mould on the skin of the cheese which produces the characteristic smell, taste and whitish or yellowy-grey colour.

There are two kinds: St-Nectaire **fermier** and St-Nectaire **laitier**. The *fermier* is the strongest and tastiest and some of it is still made entirely on the farm. Increasingly, however, individual farmers make the *tomme* stage, but then sell it on to wholesalers for the refining. The *laitier* is much more an "industrial" product, made from the milk of lots of different herds, sold onto a co-operative or cheese manufacturer for all its stages.

On the narrow valley floor, where the main street runs, two of the old **hotels** are being refurbished and provide a quiet and comfortable place to stay. One, in particular, the *Hôtel Régina* (☎04.73.88.54.55, fax 04.73.88.50.56; ③; closed Nov–March), has an excellent restaurant with menus at 82–160F. The *Thermalia* (☎04.73.88.30.28, fax 04.73.88.52.59; ③; closed Oct 15–March), next door, has more character and also provides a good meal from 85F. The best-value **campsite** is the *Clé des Champs* (☎04.73.88.52.33), and there is also a **gîte d'étape**, *Le Clos du Vallon* (☎04.73.88.50.92; April–Oct), for walkers on the GR30. This heads north from here to Lac Aydat in five hours, or west to the forest-girt **Lac Chambon** in three hours via Murol. There's another gîte on the way at **PHIALEIX** (☎04.73.79.32.43; April–Oct).

For shorter walks out of St-Nectaire, take the D150 past the church through the old village towards the **Puy de Mazeyres** (919m), and turn up a path to the right for the final climb to the summit (1hr), where you get a superb aerial view of the country round about. Alternatively, follow the D966 along the Couze de Chambon valley to **SAILLANT**, where the stream cascades down a high lava rock face in the middle of the village.

Murol

MUROL, 6km west of St-Nectaire by road (July & Aug twice-daily bus to Clermont), is an attractive, sleepy little place best known for its powerful medieval **château**, dramatically situated on top of a basalt cone commanding the approaches for kilometres around (May–Sept Mon–Sat 10am–noon & 1.30–6pm, Sun 2–5pm; Oct–April daily 2–5pm; 20F). In summer, a local organization re-enacts the medieval life of the castle in costume (45F).

There are several small family-run **hotels** here. Try the *Hôtel des Pins*, on rue de Levat (☎04.73.88.60.50, fax 04.73.88.60.29; ③; closed Oct 15–April; restaurant from 58F), or the *Hôtel de Paris*, on place de l'Hôtel-de-Ville (☎04.73.88.60.09, fax 04.73.88.69.62; ②; closed Sept 15–April). Of the **campsites**, the best value is the *Ribeyre*, a short distance away at **JASSAT** (☎04.73.88.64.29; May to mid-Sept).

Besse

Eleven kilometres due south of Murol, **BESSE** is one of the prettiest and oldest villages in the region. Its fascinating winding streets of noble lava-built houses – some as old as the fifteenth century – sit atop the valley of the Couze de Pavin, with one of the original fortified town **gates** still in place at the upper end of the village.

Its wealth was due to its role as the principal market for the farms on the eastern slopes of the Monts-Dore. Its co-operative is still one of the main producers of St-Nectaire cheese (see box), and the annual **festivals** of the Montée and Dévalade, marking the ascent of the herds to the high pastures in July and their descent in autumn, are still celebrated by the procession of the Black Virgin of Vassivière from the **church of St-André** in Besse to the chapel of **LA VASSIVIÈRE**, west of **Lac Pavin** (July 2 & the first Sun after Sept 21) and back again in autumn.

The lake lies 5km west of the village, on the way to the purpose-built ski resort of **SUPER-BESSE** (not very reliable because of snow conditions). It's a perfect volcanic lake, filling the now wooded crater. The **GR30** goes through, passing by the **Puy de Montchal**, whose summit (1407m) gives you a fine view over several other lakes and the rolling plateau south towards **ÉGLISENEUVE-D'ENTRAIGUES**, 13km by road, where the Parc des Volcans's **Maison du Fromage** gives a blow-by-blow account of the making of the different cheeses of Auvergne (daily: June 15–Sept 15 2–6pm; July & Aug 10am–12.30pm & 2.30–7pm; 18F).

Besse's **tourist office** is next to the church (Mon–Sat 9am–noon & 2–6/6.30pm, Sun 10am–noon & 3–6pm; ☎04.73.79.52.84, fax 04.73.79.52.08), and will provide information and advice about walking, mountain biking and skiing. For a place to **stay**, there is none better than the attractive old *Hostellerie du Beffroi*, 24 rue Abbé-Blot (☎04.73.79.50.08, fax 04.73.79.57.87; ③), whose good restaurant serves up a range of local specialities from 100F.

The Monts du Cantal

The **Cantal Massif** forms the most southerly extension of the Parc des Volcans. Still nearly 80km in diameter and once 3000m in height, it is one of the world's largest (albeit extinct) volcanoes, shaped like a wheel without a rim. The hub is formed by the three great conical peaks that survived the erosion of the original single cone: **Plomb du Cantal** (1885m), **Puy Mary** (1787m) and **Puy de Peyre-Arse** (1686m).

From this centre a series of deep-cut wooded valleys radiates out like spokes. The most notable are the **valley of Mandailles** and the **valleys of the Cère and Alagnon** in the southwest, where the road and railway line run, and in the north the **valleys of Falgoux and the Rhue**. Between the valleys, especially on the north side, are huge expanses of gently sloping grassland, most notably the **Plateau du Limon**, and it is these which for centuries have been the mainstay of life in the Cantal: summer pasture for the cows whose milk makes the firm yellow Cantal cheese, pressed in the form of great crusty drums. But this traditional activity has long been in serious decline; as elsewhere, many of the herds are now beef cattle. And tourism is on the increase, in particular walking, horse riding and skiing.

The main walking routes are the fairly arduous **GR400**, which does a circuit of the whole massif, and the **GR4**, which crosses it from the north to the southeast. There are also more than fifty shorter routes, details of which are obtainable through *Chamina* publications. The two main summits, Plomb du Cantal and Puy Mary, are – for better or worse – accessible to all: the former by *téléférique* from Super-Lioran, the latter by a veritable highway of a footpath from the road at Pas de Peyrol. The best section of the GR4–400 for an experienced hiker with limited time is the three-hour stretch between Super-Lioran and the Puy Mary, with the possibility of taking in a couple of extra summits on the way. For motorists, there's the long, sinuous **Route des Crêtes**, which does a rather wider circuit than the GR400. But, be warned, if you hit a period of bad weather, you'll drive a long way in low gear, seeing no more than white banks of mist illumined by your headlights.

The main centres within the massif lie on the N122 between Murat and Aurillac: **LE LIORAN**, where the road and rail tunnels begin, and **SUPER-LIORAN**, the downhill and cross-country ski centre, with the *Auberge du Tunnel* (☎04.71.49.50.02; ②; restaurant from 60F) and two gîtes d'étape, as well as a **tourist office** (Mon–Sat: July & Aug 9.30am–12.30pm & 2–6.30pm; Sept–Oct 8.30–12.30pm & 1.30–6pm; ☎04.71.49.50.08, fax 04.71.49.51.01). **THIEZAC**, 10km south, has a **tourist office** (Mon–Sat 9.30am–12.30pm & 3.30–7.30pm; ☎04.71.47.03.50, fax 04.71.47.02.23), as well as the *Hôtel La Belle Vallée* (☎04.71.47.00.22, fax 04.71.47.02.08; ③; closed Nov–Dec 22; restaurant from 88F), three gîtes d'étape and a **camping municipal**, *La Bedisse* (☎04.71.47.00.41; June to mid-Sept). Further south at **VIC-SUR-CÈRE** there's a **tourist office** (Mon–Sat 9.30am–noon & 2.30–6pm; ☎04.71.47.50.68, fax ☎04.71.49.60.63), and **accommodation** at the *Hôtel des Bains*, 9 av de la Promenade (☎04.71.47.50.16, fax 04.71.49.63.82; ②; closed Oct–April; restaurant from 85F), and the riverside **camping municipal** (☎04.71.47.51.04; April–Sept).

Aurillac

AURILLAC, the provincial capital of the Cantal, lies on the west side of the mountains, 98km east of Brive and 160km from Clermont-Ferrand. In spite of its good mainline train connections and the fact that its population has almost doubled in the last forty years, it remains one of the most out-the-way French provincial capitals. It was until recently a major manufacturer of umbrellas, though that seems doomed to eventual extinction, like its older traditional lace-making and tanning industries. It is now mainly an administrative and commercial centre, with important cattle markets in the suburb of Sistrières on Mondays. Although there are no important sights, it makes a very pleasant and unpretentious place to stop over on your way into the Massif Central from the west.

The most interesting part of town is the kernel of old streets, now largely pedestrianized and full of good shops, just to the north of the central **place du Square**. **Rue Duclaux** leads through to the attractive **place de l'Hôtel-de-Ville**, where the big Wednesday and Saturday markets are held in the shadow of the handsome grey-stone **Hôtel de Ville**, built in restrained Republican-classical style in 1801 in the aftermath of the Revolution. Beyond it, the continuation of **rue des Forgerons** leads to the beautiful little **place St-Géraud**, with a round twelfth-century fountain overlooked by a Romanesque house that was probably part of the original abbey guesthouse, and the externally rather unprepossessing **church of St-Géraud**, which nonetheless has a beautifully ribbed late Gothic ceiling.

At the back of the church, past a delightful small garden, **rue de la Fontaine** comes out on the river bank by the Pont du Buis, with a shady walk back along cours d'Angoulême on the other side to the Pont-Rouge and **place Gerbert**, where there is an ancient *lavoir*, or washing place, by the Birdland restaurant and disco. On a steep bluff overlooking this end of town is the eleventh-century keep of the Château St-Étienne, containing the town's only worthwhile museum, **le Muséum des Volcans** (July & Aug Mon–Sat 10.30am–6pm, Sun 2–6pm; rest of year Mon–Fri 2–6pm; closed Nov–Jan & March; 25F), with a good section on volcanoes and a splendid view over the mountains to the east.

Southeast of the town towards Aubrac, the road leads through **Carlat**, once an important feudal fiefdom, as well as the particularly attractive villages of **Mur-de-Barrez**, **Brommat** and **Albinhac**, with some lovely old houses and curious churches in the latter two villages.

Practicalities

The **tourist office** occupies a small kiosk on the downhill side of place du Square in the town centre (April–June & Sept Mon–Sat 9am–noon & 2–6.30pm, Sun 9am–noon & 2–6.30pm; July & Aug daily 9am–7pm; Oct–March Mon–Sat 9am–noon & 2–6.30pm; ☎04.71.48.46.58, fax 04.71.48.99.39), with a number of guidebooks and maps on sale, as well as a money-change facility when the banks are closed. The **gare SNCF** and **gare routière** are together on place Sémard, a ten-minute walk from the place du Square along av de la République and rue de la Gare.

For a place to stay in the centre of town, try the smart and comfortable*Le Square*, 15 place du Square (☎04.71.48.24.72, fax 04.71.48.47.57; ③; with a reasonable restaurant from 70F), or the comfortable *Renaissance*, just next door (☎04.71.48.09.80, fax 04.71.48.54.81;②). Also worth a try is the *Hôtel Delcher*, just off the square at 20 rue des Carmes (☎04.71.48.01.69, fax 04.71.48.86.66; ③; closed Dec & last two weeks of July; good food from 80F).

There is nowhere particularly exciting to **eat**, but the *Bistro-Cabaret Licence IV*, on the corner of av Gambetta and rue Paul-Doumer, is friendly and excellent value: despite looking like a fast-food joint, it serves well-cooked regional specialities and good desserts (50–100F; booking advisable). In the evening the lively atmosphere draws the locals until about 3am. Alternatively, there's the riverside *Birdland*, by the Pont-Rouge, done out in the French version of pub-style, with pizzas for around 40F and menus for about 110F (closed Sun); if you're looking for **nightlife**, the *Bateau-Lavoir* **disco** is part of the same establishment (daily 11pm–4/5am; 50F). Finally, Aurillac's most unexpected event is an annual international **street theatre festival** during the last full week in August, which attracts performers from all over Europe and fills the town with rather more exotic characters than are normally to be seen about its provincial streets.

Salers

SALERS lies 42km north of Aurillac, at the foot of the northwest slopes of the Cantal and within sight of the Puy Violent. Scarcely altered in size or aspect since its sixteenth-century heyday, it remains an extraordinarily homogeneous example of the architecture of that time. If it appears rather grand for a place so small, it's because the town became the administrative centre for the highlands of the Auvergne in 1564 and home of its magistrates. Exploiting this past is really all that is left to it but Salers still makes a very worthwhile visit, despite the large numbers of tourists.

If you arrive by the Puy Mary road, you'll enter town by the **church**, which is worth a look for the super-naturalistic statuary of the *Entombment of Christ* (1496) hidden in a side chapel. In front of you, the cobbled **rue du Beffroi** leads uphill, under the massive clock tower, and into the central **place Tyssandier-d'Escous**. It is a glorious little square, surrounded by the fifteenth-century mansions of the provincial aristocracy with pepper-pot turrets, mullioned windows and carved lintels, among them the sturdy **Maison du Bailliage**, and, nearby, the Maison de Salers with the small **Musée de Templiers** (April 1 to mid-Nov Mon–Sat 10.30am–12.30 & 2.30–6.30pm; 20F), with a

---

CATTLE RANCHING IN THE CANTAL: ALLANCHE

For an insider's view of the farming life of the Massif there's no better place to go than the age-old **cattle sales at Allanche**, little more than a straggling main street of ancient houses surrounded by windswept upland pastures, about 25km north of Murat (see p.788).

The September 7 sale, when the season's calves are sold off before winter, is typical. Activity starts at 1am or 2am with the clanging of cowbells, the cries of drivers and the thrumming of truck engines. By 4am two or three thousand cattle are tethered to the iron stanchions in the floodlit grassy marketplace, inspected and appraised by men in wellies and overalls and pancake-shaped berets. There is a great deal of bucking and bellowing and sudden uncontrollable charging as beasts are unloaded or loaded, some of them so big they'd have little trouble shifting a bulldozer. For information on other sales call the tourist office in Allanche (☎04.71.20.48.43).

If you are tempted to see the spectacle, there's a **campsite** at the south edge of the village (☎04.71.20.45.87; mid-June to mid-Sept) and, just beyond, the *Hôtel Le Foirail* (☎04.71.20.41.15; ①; restaurant from 60F).

collection of local interest. And, before you are done, be sure to make your way to the **Promenade de Barrouze** for the view out across the surrounding countryside and the Puy Violent.

The **tourist office** is in place Tyssandier-d'Escous (Feb–May, Oct–Nov 11 & Dec 21–Jan 4 Mon–Sat 10am–noon & 2.30–7pm, Sun 2.30–5.30pm; June–Sept same hours plus Sun 10am–noon & 3–7pm (☎04.71.40.70.68, fax 04.71.40.70.94). If you are planning to **stay**, try the *Hôtel des Remparts*, near the Promenade de Barrouze (☎04.71.40.70.33, fax 04.71.40.75.32; ③); closed Oct 20–Dec 19), whose good restaurant specializes in Auvergnat peasant cuisine (from 68F); or the small *Hôtel du Beffroi*, in rue du Beffroi (☎04.71.40.70.11, fax 04.71.40.70.16;③); closed mid-Nov to April), likewise with good solid regional food (from 65F). There's a **camping municipal** on the Puy Mary road (☎04.71.40.73.09; mid-May to mid-Oct).

Murat

MURAT, on the eastern edge of the Cantal, is the closest town to the high peaks. It is also the easiest to access, lying on the N122 road and main train line, about 12km north-east of Le Lioran. There is no one particular sight to see here. It's the ensemble of grey-stone houses that attracts, many dating from the fifteenth and sixteenth centuries. Crowded together on their medieval lanes, they make a magnificent sight, especially as you approach from the St-Flour road, with the backdrop of the steep basalt cliffs of the **Rocher Bonnevie**, once the site of the local castle and now surmounted by a huge white statue of the Virgin Mary. Facing the town, perched on the distinctive mound of the **Rocher Bredons**, on your left as you approach, there's a lovely little Romanesque **chapel of St-Pierre**. One of the finest of the old houses is now open to the public as the **Maison de la Faune** (July–Aug Mon–Sat 10am–noon & 3–7pm, Sun 3–7pm; rest of year Mon–Sat 10am–noon & 2–5pm; closed Nov–April; 22F), a modest museum illustrating the wildlife of the Parc des Volcans area.

The **monument** to deportees on place de l'Hôtel-de-Ville and the name of the **avenue des 12-et-24-Juin-1944**, opposite the tourist office, both commemorate one of the blackest days in Murat's recent history. On June 12, a local Resistance group interrupted a German raid on the town and killed a senior SS officer. In reprisal, the Germans burnt several houses down on June 24 and arrested 120 people, 80 of whom died in deportation.

The **tourist office** is on the place de l'Hôtel-de-Ville (July & Aug Mon–Sat 9.30am–noon & 2–7pm, Sun 10am–noon & 3–7pm; rest of year Mon–Sat 10am–noon & 2–6pm; ☎04.71.20.09.47), and you can rent **mountain bikes** from La Godille, opposite, or from Bernard Escure, in place Gandilhon-Gens-d'Armes. The **gare SNCF** is on the main road, av du Dr-Mallet (☎04.71.20.07.20), where there are also some good places to **stay**. The most comfortable is the *Hôtel des Breuils*, a handsome bourgeois house at 34 av du Dr-Mallet (☎04.71.20.01.25, fax 04.71.20.02.43; ④); closed Nov 3–Christmas & April). At no. 22 in the same street there is the equally friendly and simple *Les Globe-Trotters* (☎04.71.20.07.22, fax 04.71.20.16.88; ②); closed Oct 25–Nov 8; nice restaurant from 65F), and, at no. 18, *Les Messageries* (☎04.71.20.04.04, fax 04.71.20.02.81; ③); restaurant from 75F). The **campsite**, *Les Stalapos*, is open winter as well as summer (☎04.71.20.01.83; June–Sept).

St-Flour and the Margeride

Seat of a fourteenth-century bishopric, **ST-FLOUR** stands dramatically on a cliff-girt basalt promontory above the River Ander, 92km west of Le Puy and 92km south of Clermont-Ferrand, to which it has recently been joined by the new and toll-free autoroute A75. Prosperous in the Middle Ages because of its strategic position on the main road from northern France to Languedoc and the proximity of the grasslands of the Cantal whose herds provided the raw materials for its tanning and leather industries, it fell into somnolent decline in modern times, only partially reversed in the last thirty years.

While the lower town that has grown up around the station is of little interest, the wedge of old streets that occupies the point of the promontory surrounding the cathedral has considerable charm. If you are in a car, the best thing is to leave it in the park on the chestnut-shaded **Promenades**, which begin by the **memorial** to Dr Mallet, his two sons and other hostages and assorted citizens executed in reprisals by the Germans during World War II.

The narrow streets of the old town converge from here towards the **place d'Armes**, where the fourteenth-century **Cathédrale St-Pierre** stands, backing onto the edge of the cliff, with a terrace giving good views out over the countryside. From the outside, the plain grey volcanic rock of the cathedral makes for a rather severe and uninspiring appearance; it's an impression that is partly mitigated inside by the fine vaulting of the ceiling and the presence of a number of works of art, most notably by a carved, black-painted walnut figure of Christ of unknown origin, but dating from the thirteenth century.

Facing the cathedral on the place d'Armes are some attractive old buildings, housing a couple of cafés under their arcades, while at the north and south extremities of the square are the town's two museums. At the north end, the fine fourteenth-century building that was once the headquarters of the town's consuls contains the **Musée Alfred Douet's** somewhat ragbag collections of furniture, tapestries and paintings (mid–April to mid–Oct daily 9am–noon & 2–6/7pm; rest of year closed Sun; 20F, joint ticket with Haute-Auvergne museum 35F); the view from the cliffs behind the museum gives a sense of the impregnable position of the town. At the south end of the square, the current Hôtel de Ville, formerly the bishop's palace built in 1610, houses the much more interesting **Musée de la Haute-Auvergne** (June–Sept daily 10am–noon & 2–6pm; rest of year closed Sun; same prices as above), whose collections illustrate the trades, tools, costumes, traditions and activities of the region.

The **gare SNCF** is on av Charles de Gaulle in the lower town (☎04.71.60.03.37), but the **tourist office** is on the Promenades, opposite the memorial (July & Aug Mon–Sat 9am–8pm, Sun 10am–noon & 3–7pm; rest of year Mon–Sat 9–noon & 3–6/7pm; ☎04.71.60.22.50, fax 04.71.60.05.14). For a place to **stay**, try the attractive, modernized *Hôtel des Voyageurs*, at 25 rue du Collège on the north side of the old town (☎04.71.60.34.44, fax 04.71.60.00.21; ②; good restaurant from 88F; April–Oct); or the *Hôtel du Nord*, at 18 rue des Lacs on the south side (☎04.71.60.28.00, fax 04.71.60.07.33; ②), whose good, popular restaurant serves local specialities (from 65F). Another congenial place to eat is *Chez Geneviève*, 25 rue des Lacs, where menus start at 85F and you can eat a *pôtée auvergnate* for 55F.

The Margeride

South and west of St-Flour stretch the wild, rolling, sparsely populated wooded hills of the **Margeride**, one of the strongholds of the wartime Resistance groups. If you have your own transport, the D4 makes a slow but spectacular route east (92km) to Le Puy, crossing the forested heights of **Mont Mouchet**, at 1465m the highest point of the Margeride. A side turning, the D48 (signposted), takes you to the national Resistance **monument** by the woodman's hut that served as HQ to the local Resistance commander during the June 1944 battle to delay German reinforcements moving north to strengthen resistance to the D-day landings in Normandy. There is a **museum** (May–Sept 5 daily 9.30am–noon & 2–7pm; Sept 6 to mid-Oct same hours but Sat & Sun 10–noon & 2–6pm; 25F), sketching the progression of the Resistance movement in the area. The views back west from these heights to the Cantal are superb.

Further south, the new autoroute crosses the gorge of the River Truyère beside the delicate steel tracery of the **Viaduc de Garabit**, built by Gustave Eiffel (of Tower fame) in 1884 to carry the newly constructed rail line; experience he put to important use in the Tower. Not far away, about 20km south of St-Flour and perched above the waters of the lake created by the damming of the Truyère for hydroelectric power, are the romantic ruins of the keep of the **Château d'Alleuze**, stronghold in the 1380s of one Bernard de Garlan, a notorious leader of lawless mercenaries employed by the English in the Hundred Years' War to sow panic and destruction in French-held parts of the country.

THE SOUTHWEST: AUBRAC AND ROUERGUE

In the southwest corner of the Massif Central, the landscapes start to change and the mean altitude begins to drop. The wild, desolate moorland of the **Aubrac** is cut and contained by the savage gorges of the **Lot and Truyère rivers**. To the south of them, the arid but more southern-feeling plateaux of the *causses* form a sort of intermediate step to the lower hills and coastal plains of Languedoc. And they in turn are cut by the dramatic trenches formed by the **gorges of the Tarn**, **Jonte** and **Dourbie**, along with the spectacular caves of the **Aven Armand** and **Dargilan**. These are places best avoided at the height of the holiday season, when they turn into overcrowded outdoor playgrounds for amateur canoeists, parties of schoolchildren, motorists and campers.

The bigger towns, like **Rodez** and **Millau** in the old province of the **Rouergue**, also have much more of a southern feel. Both are worth a visit, although their attractions need not keep you for more than half a day. Rodez has a fine cathedral and Millau is worth considering as a base for exploring the *causses* and river gorges of the Tarn and Jonte.

The two great architectural draws of the area are **Conques**, with its medieval village and magnificent abbey, which owes its existence to the St-Jacques pilgrim route (now the GR65), and the perfect little *bastide* town of **Sauveterre-de-Rouergue**.

The mountains of Aubrac

The **Aubrac** lies to the south of St-Flour, east of the valley of the River Truyère and north of the valley of the Lot. It is a region of bleak, windswept uplands with long views and huge skies, dotted with glacial lakes and granite villages hunkered down out of the weather. The highest points are between 1200m and 1400m, and there are more cows up here than people; you see them grazing the boggy, peaty pastures, divided by dry-stone walls and turf-brown streams. There are few trees: a scatter of willow and ash along the streams and the occasional stand of hardy beeches on the tops, and only abandoned shepherds' huts testify to more populous times. It is an area which in bad weather is invisible, but which, in good climes, has a bleak beauty, little-disturbed by tourism or modernization.

Once this was sheep country, where shepherds from the dry summer lowlands of Quercy and Languedoc brought their flocks for the season. They were displaced in the nineteenth century by cows, raised for their more commercially exploitable production of milk and cheese, destined for the growing towns. And these in turn, as available labour shrank with the depopulation of the villages, ceded the pastures to beef cattle, as in the Cantal further north.

Aumont-Aubrac and Aubrac

The waymarked **Tour d'Aubrac footpath** does a complete circuit of the area in around ten days, starting from the town of **AUMONT-AUBRAC**, where you'll find the **hotel** *Prunières* (☎04.66.42.80.14, fax 04.66.42.92.20; ③; restaurant from 65F), the *Relais de Peyre* (☎04.66.42.85.88, fax 04.66.42.90.08; ②; closed Jan; restaurant from 60F) and a **camping municipal** (☎04.66.42.80.02). There is also a daily train connection on the Millau-St-Flour line.

The marathon **GR65** from Le Puy to Santiago de Compostela in Spain also crosses the area from northeast to southwest en route to Conques. In fact, the tiny village of **AUBRAC**, which gave its name to the region, owes its existence to this St-Jacques pilgrim route; around 1120, a way station was opened here for the express purpose of providing shelter for the pilgrims on these inhospitable heights. Little remains of it today, beyond the windy **Tour des Anglais**, which harbours the *Hôtel Moderne* (☎05.65.44.28.42, fax 05.65.44.21.47; ③; May–Oct; restaurant from 95F).

St-Urcize and Nasbinals

This is the wildest and most starkly beautiful part of the Aubrac. The close-huddled village of **ST-URCIZE**, 13km north of the town of Aubrac, hangs off the side of the valley of the River Lhère, with a lovely Romanesque church at its centre and a devastating World War I **memorial,** with so many names on it you wouldn't have thought it possible such a small place could furnish so much cannon fodder. It is ghostly out of season, for most of the unspoiled granite houses are owned by people who live elsewhere. Should you wish to **stay**, there is a campsite, a gîte d'étape (☎04.71.23.20.57), and the welcoming *Hôtel Remise* (☎04.71.23.20.02, fax 04.71.23.20.02; ①; excellent food from 75F); the *Relais de l'Aubrac* (☎04.66.32.52.06, fax 04.66.32.56.58; ③; closed Nov 11–Feb 10; restaurant from 95F) lies at the point where the road to Nasbinals crosses the River Bès at the Pont-du-Gournier, around 5km from St-Urcize.

NASBINALS, 8km to the southeast, is rather bigger and livelier, and something of a cross-country ski resort in winter. It, too, has a beautiful small-scale **church** of the twelfth century, joined onto the adjacent house with a round fortified tower incorporated in the transept wall by the entrance. Just below the building, the *Auberge Gourmande* (☎04.66.32.56.76; ①) has dormitory beds, while above it the *Hôtel La Route d'Argent* (☎04.66.32.56.03, fax 04.66.32.56.77; ②) provides comfortable accommodation and good food (from 60F). The village **tourist office** is on the other side of the road (May–Sept Mon–Sat 9am–noon & 2–6.30pm, Sun 9am–noon; Oct–April Tues–Sat 9am–noon & 1.30–4.30pm; ☎04.66.32.55.73) and can rent out mountain bikes. There is also a **campsite** and **gîte d'étape** (☎04.66.32.50.65; meals available), both on the St-Urcize road.

Laguiole

Seventeen kilometres west of St-Urcize and 24km north of Espalion, **LAGUIOLE** passes for a substantial town in these parts. It is a name which means but one thing in France: knives, and specifically ones with a long, pointed, stiletto-like blade and bone handle that fits the palm; the genuine article should bear the effigy of a bull stamped on the clasp that holds the blade open. It is an industry that started in the last century, then moved to industrial Thiers, outside Clermont-Ferrand, before returning to Laguiole in 1987, when the Société Laguiole opened a factory designed by Philippe Starck on the St-Urcize road, with a giant knife projecting from the roof of the windowless all-aluminium building. Of all the numerous outlets selling knives in the village, only the Société's are made entirely in Laguiole. They have a shop on the main through-road, on the corner of the central marketplace opposite the **tourist office kiosk** (Mon–Sat 9am–12.30pm & 3–7pm, Sun 10.30am–noon & 2–7pm; ☎05.65.44.35.94, fax 05.65.54.10.29); their wares include pricey knives designed by Starck himself.

There is nothing of great moment to see in the village, though the **Musée du Haut-Rouergue** (July & Aug daily 3.30–6.30pm; 15F), with its collection of objects illustrative of the pastoral life, might be of interest. Nonetheless, it is a relatively metropolitan base for exploring round about, with several **hotels** on the main street. Try the *Aubrac* (☎05.65.44.32.13, fax 05.65.48.48.74; ②; restaurant from 58F) opposite the marketplace, the *Régis* (☎05.65.44.30.05, fax 05.65.48.46.44; ③; restaurant from 87F), or the *Grand Hôtel Auguy* (☎05.65.44.31.11, fax 05.65.51.50.81; ③), with a good restaurant from 130F.

Alternatively, there's a sort of chambre d'hôte at **Le Combaire**, in a quiet rural setting 3km west on the D42 (☎05.65.44.33.26; *demi-pension* 16F); gîtes d'étape at **Le Vayssaire** (☎05.65.48.44.69) and **Soulanges-Bonneval** (☎05.65.44.42.18; meals available), 5km away on the D54; and a **camping municipal** (☎05.65.44.39.72; mid–June to mid–Sept) on the St-Urcize road. Communications, however, are not good, and if you don't have a car your only chance of getting in or out is the daily bus to Rodez.

Marvejols

MARVEJOLS lies at the southeast extremity of the Aubrac, on the main N9 road (the autoroute has not yet arrived) and the Paris–Béziers train line. The country changes drastically as you approach. The bare, granite-strewn plateau opens into a wide deep basin, wooded with pines and punctuated by the erosion-formed table-topped pinnacles known hereabouts as *trucs*. It is a small, undeveloped and unpretentious country town, whose ancient streets are contained within surviving medieval gates. There is little to do beyond savouring the atmosphere.

The **tourist office** is in the main gateway on the main road (June–Sept Mon–Sat 9am–noon & 2–7pm, Sun 10am–noon; Oct–May Mon–Sat 9am–noon & 2–6pm; ☎04.66.32.02.14), and **accommodation** comes in the form of the pleasant *Hôtel de la Gare et des Rochers* (☎04.66.32.10.58, fax 04.66.32.30.63; ②; good restaurant from 75F), opposite the **gare SNCF** (☎04.66.32.00.10), which is 800m uphill to the right off the N9 in the direction of Chirac. There's also a **camping municipal** beside a tributary stream on the other side of the River Colagne from the town.

WOLVES AND THE BÊTE DU GÉVAUDAN

In Marvejols, at the junction of the bridge across the Colagne and the N9, there stands a hideous, flattened-out bronze statue of a semi-wolf, which represents the terrible legendary **Bête du Gévaudan**, supposedly the culprit of a series of horrific attacks in the eighteenth century. Between 1764 and 1767, the whole area between here and Le Puy was terrorized, and 25 women, 68 children and 6 men were slain. The king sent his dragoons, then his best huntsman, who eventually found and killed an enormous wolf, but the mysterious deaths continued until one Jean Chastel shot another wolf near Saugues.

It has never been established if a wolf was really guilty of these deaths – a wolf that attacked women and children almost exclusively, that moved about so rapidly, that never touched a sheep. Was it perhaps a human psychopath?

If you would like reassurance about the temperament of real wolves, visit the **Parc Zoologique du Gévaudan** in the hamlet of Ste-Lucie just off the N9, 9km north of Marvejols, where about eighty wolves live in semi-liberty (daily 10am–5.30pm; closed Jan; 33F), the first to do so in France since the beginning of the century.

Rodez and the upper valley of the Lot

A particularly beautiful and out-of-the-way stretch of country lies on the southwestern periphery of the Massif Central, bordered roughly by the valley of the **River Lot** in the north and the **Viaur** in the south. The upland areas are open and wide, with views east to the mountains of the Cévennes and south to the Monts de Lacaune and the Monts de l'Espinouse. **Rodez**, capital of the Rouergue, with a fine cathedral, is the only place of any size, accessible on the main train and bus routes. But the most dramatic places are in the river valleys, in particular the great abbey of **Conques** and the towns of **Entraygues** and **Espalion**.

Rodez

Until the 1960s, **RODEZ** and the Rouergue were synonymous with back-country poverty and underdevelopment. Today it is an active and prosperous provincial town with a charming, renovated centre, even though the approach, through spreading commercial districts, is uninspiring.

Built on high ground above the River Aveyron, the **old town**, dominated by the massive red-sandstone **Cathédrale Notre-Dame**, is visible for kilometres around. No matter from what direction you approach, you will find yourself in the **place d'Armes**, where the cathedral's plain, fortress-like west front and the seventeenth-century bishop's palace sit side by side – both buildings were incorporated into the town's defences. The cathedral was begun in 1277 and was one of the first Gothic buildings in southern France, its plain facade relieved only by an elaborately flowery rose window. Towering over the square is the cathedral's 88-metre **belfry**, decorated with pinnacles, balustrades and statuary almost as fantastical as that of Strasbourg cathedral. The impressively spacious interior, architecturally as plain as the facade, is adorned with a magnificently extravagant seventeenth-century walnut organ loft and choir stalls by André Sulpice, who crafted it in 1468.

If you leave by the splendid south porch, you find yourself in the tiny place Rozier in front of the fifteenth-century **Maison Cannoniale**, whose courtyard is guarded by jutting turrets. From the back of the cathedral to the north and the south, a network of well-restored medieval streets connects place de-Gaulle, place de la Préfecture and the attractive place du Bourg, with its fine sixteenth-century houses. In place Foch, just south of the cathedral, the Baroque chapel of the old **lycée** is worth a look for its amazing painted ceiling, while in place Raynaldy, the new **Hôtel de Ville** and the **médiathèque** are interesting examples of attempts to graft modern styles onto old buildings.

Practicalities

The **tourist office** is situated on place Foch, just off bd Gambetta and the place d'Armes, near the cathedral (July & Aug Mon–Sat 9am–1pm & 2–7pm, Sun 10am–noon; rest of year Mon–Fri 9am–noon & 2–6pm, Sat 10am–12.30pm & 3–5pm; ☎05.65.68.02.27, fax 05.65.68.78.15). The **gare routière** is on av V-Hugo (☎05.65.68.11.13), and the **gare SNCF** on bd Joffre (☎08.36.35.35.35.), on the northern edge of town.

For reasonable if somewhat charmless hotel **accommodation**, try the *Hôtel Victor-Hugo* at 19 av V-Hugo (☎05.65.68.14.59; ③), or the better *Hôtel du Clocher* to the left off the east end of the cathedral at 4 rue Séguy (☎05.65.68.10.16, fax 05.65.68.64.27; ②). Equally central but more upmarket is *La Tour Maje*, in bd Gally, behind the tourist office (☎05.65.68.34.68, fax 05.65.68.27.56; ④), a modern building tacked onto a medieval tower. Budget accommodation is available at the *Foyer*

Ste-Thérèse, 21 rue Bonald, parallel to rue Séguy (☎05.65.77.14.00, fax 05.65.77.14.10;①), and at the new HI **youth hostel** in **ONET-LE-CHÂTEAU**, 3km to the north, at 26 bd des Capucines, Quatre-Saisons (☎05.65.42.35.45, fax 05.65.67.37.97; ①; good canteen for around 50F), which you can reach by taking bus #1 or #3, direction Quatre Saisons, stop Marché d'Oc/Les Rosiers/Capucine. Rodez' **camping municipal** (☎05.65.67.09.52; June–Sept) is on the river bank in the quartier Layoule, about 1km from the centre.

As for **eating**, there are no outstanding restaurants in Rodez. *Le Bistroquet*, 17 rue du Bal, off place d'Olmet (closed Sun & Mon), does good salads and grills for around 80F, and the prettily situated brasserie *Le Kiosque*, in the garden on av V-Hugo (closed Sun eve in Oct–April), does seafood and some good regional dishes with menus from 60F. Otherwise, try the *Éspace Embergue* at the end of rue Bonald, and the area behind the cathedral. For a **drink**, a good place to go is the *Café de la Paix*, on place Jean-Jaurès, or the *Majesté* bar, in the Tour Maje, if you want some gentle music to accompany it.

Sauveterre-de-Rouergue and the gorges of the Viaur

Forty kilometres southwest of Rodez and 6.5km northwest of Naucelle, **SAUVET-ERRE-DE-ROUERGUE** makes the most rewarding side-trip in this part of the Rouergue. It is a perfect, otherworldly *bastide*, founded in 1281, with a wide central square, part cobbled, part gravelled, and surrounded by stone and half-timbered houses built over arcaded ground floors. Narrow streets lead off to the outer road, lined with stone-built houses the colour of rusty iron. On summer evenings, pétanque players come out to roll their bowls beneath chestnut and plane trees, while swallows and swifts swoop and dive overhead.

There are several agreeable **hotels**, including the cheap and charming *Hôtel La Grappe d'Or*, on the outer road (☎05.65.72.00.62; ②), whose restaurant (Oct–April) offers an excellent menu at 70F, with dishes like *gésiers chauds*, *tripoux*, cheese, ice-cream and *fouace* (a kind of sweet cake). More expensive is the *Sénéchal*, at the entrance to the village (☎05.65.71.29.00, fax 05.65.71.29.09; ⑥; closed Jan–Feb), also with an excellent restaurant closed Mon plus Tues lunch; from 130F. There's also a **campsite** (☎05.65.47.05.32).

The country round about, known as the **Ségala**, is high (around 500m) and wide, cut by sudden and deep river valleys full of lush greenery. The most spectacular of these is the valley of the **River Viaur** to the south and west of Sauveterre. A car is essential. If you are heading west towards Najac (see p.650), there is a marvellous back-country route through **La Salvetat**, crossing the Viaur at **Bellecombe** and again at **Moulin-de-Bar**, where there is a riverside **campsite**, *Le Gomvassou*. The wartime Resistance was very active hereabouts and there are numerous memorials to the Resistance fighters who lost their lives in the aftermath of the D-day landings. There is a particularly interesting one beside the tiny church in **Jouqueviel**, further downstream, dedicated to a unit of Polish volunteers and 161 escaped Soviet POWs.

Conques

CONQUES, 37km north of Rodez, is one of the great villages of southwest France. It occupies a spectacular position on the flanks of the steep wooded gorge of the little **River Dourdou**, a tributary of the Lot. The only public transport to the village is a daily service to Rodez, leaving there in the afternoon and returning the following morning; in July and August, there are also bus connections two or three times a week with Villefranche-de-Rouergue and Entraygues/Espalion, as well as Rodez, allowing you to visit Conques and return the same day.

It is the abbey which brought the village into existence. Its origins go back to a hermit called Dadon who settled here around 800 AD and founded a community of Benedictine monks, one of whom pilfered the relics of the martyred girl, Ste-Foy, from the monastery at Agen. Known for her ability to cure blindness and liberate captives, Ste-Foy's presence brought the pilgrims flocking to Conques in ever-increasing numbers, which earned the abbey a prime place on the pilgrim route to Compostela.

The abbey church

At the village's centre, dominating the landscape, stands the renowned Romanesque **church of Ste-Foy**, whose giant pointed towers are echoed in those of the medieval houses that cluster tightly about it. Begun in the eleventh century, its plain fortress-like facade rises on a small cobbled square beside the tourist office (see below) and pilgrims' fountain, the slightly shiny silvery-grey schist prettily offset by the greenery and flowers of the terraced gardens.

In startling contrast to this plainness, the elaborately sculpted *Last Judgement* in the tympanum above the door admonishes all who see it to espouse virtue and eschew vice. Christ sits in judgement in the centre. On his right hand are the chosen, among them Dadon the hermit and the emperor Charlemagne, while his left hand directs the damned to Hell, as usual so much more graphically and interestingly portrayed with all its gory tortures than the boring bliss of Paradise, depicted in the bottom left panel. This was not, however, the message that would have been received by the swarming masses of illiterate pilgrims.

The inside of the church is designed to accommodate the pilgrims and channel them down the aisles and round the ambulatory, where they could gawp at Ste-Foy's relics displayed in the choir, which was shut off from them by a lovely wrought-iron screen, still in place. There is some fine carving on the capitals, especially in the triforium arches: too high up to see from the nave, you need to climb to the organ loft, which gives you a superb perspective on the whole interior.

The other unrivalled asset of this church is the survival of its medieval treasure of extraordinarily rich, bejewelled **reliquaries**, including that of Ste-Foy, bits of which are as old as the fifth century, and one known as the *A of Charlemagne*, because it is thought to have been the first in a series given as presents by the emperor to monasteries he founded. Writing in 1010, a cleric named Bernard d'Angers gave an idea of the effect of these wonders on the medieval pilgrim: "The crowd of people prostrating themselves on the ground was so dense it was impossible to kneel down . . . . When they saw it for the first time [Ste-Foy], all in gold and sparkling with precious stones and looking like a human face, the majority of the peasants thought that the statue was really looking at them and answering their prayers with her eyes." The treasure is kept in a room adjoining the now ruined cloister (same hours as tourist office, see below; 25F); the second part of the Conques museum, displayed on three floors of the house containing the tourist office, consists of a miscellany of tapestries, furnishings and architectural relics.

The village

The **village** of Conques is very small, largely depopulated and mainly contained within the medieval **walls**, parts of which still survive, along with three of its **gates**. The houses date mainly from the late Middle Ages. The whole ensemble of cobbled lanes and stairways is a pleasure to stroll through. There are two main streets, the old **rue Haute**, or "upper street", which was the route for the pilgrims coming from Estaing and Le Puy and passing onto Figeac and Cahors through the **Porte de la Vinzelle**; and the lane, now **rue Charlemagne**, which leads steeply downhill through the **Porte de Barry** to the river and the ancient **Pont Romain**, with the little **chapel of St-Roch** off to the left, whence you get a fine view of the village and church. Better still: climb the road on the far side of the valley. The new and rather grandiose **European centre for medieval art and civilization**, hidden in a bunker right at the top of the hill (9am–noon & 2–6pm), has a constant programme of exhibitions and displays.

Walkers can use sections of the **GR65** and **GR62**, both of which pass through the village, and the tourist office will provide information about shorter local walks.

Practicalities

The **tourist office** is on the square beside the church (July & Aug daily 9am–7pm; rest of year Mon–Sat 9am–noon & 2–6pm; ☎05.65.72.85.00, fax 05.65.72.87.03). There is hostel-type **accommodation** at the *Résidence Dadon* (☎05.65.72.82.98; ①) directly above the abbey, and a gîte d'étape next door (Mme Guibert; ☎05.65.72.82.98), as well as various hotel possibilities, both here and in the surrounding country. In the village, try the *Auberge St-Jacques* (☎05.65.72.86.36, fax 05.65.72.82.47; ②), with restaurant menus from 72F and *plats du jour* at 50–60F. The best alternative is the *Auberge du Pont Romain* (☎05.65.69.84.07; ②; closed Nov 2–15; menus from 75F), on the main road below the hill on which Conques stands – it's a twenty-minute walk from here to the church. If both of these are full, head 7km up the Dourdou to **St-Cyprien**, where the *Auberge du Dourdou* (☎05.65.69.83.20; ②; closed Oct–March) has a restaurant featuring good, simple country cooking from 80F. There are several **campsites** in Conques: try Beau Rivage (☎05.65.69.82.23; April–Sept), St–Cyprien–sur–Dourdou (☎05.65.72.80.52) and Grand-Vabre (☎05.65.72.87.28; April–Oct), 5km downstream.

The upper valley: Grand-Vabre to Entraygues and Espalion

The most beautiful stretch of the **Lot valley** are the 21.5km between the bridge of Coursavy, below **Grand-Vabre**, and **Entraygues**: deep, narrow and wild, with the river running full and strong, as yet unaffected by the dams higher up, with scattered farms and houses high on the hillsides among long-abandoned terracing.

There is a *Logis de France* **hotel**, the *Hôtel du Pont* (☎04.71.49.94.21, fax 04.71.49.96.10; ②; restaurant from 68F), in the old stone hamlet of **ST-PROJET** (2.5km), and two more 4km further east in **VIEILLEVIE**, where canoe rental is also available. Try the *Hôtel de la Terrasse* (☎04.71.49.94.00, fax 04.71.49.99.81;②; restaurant from 58F), or the simpler *Le Canton au Relais des Pêcheurs* (☎04.71.49.98.82; ②; restaurant from 65F). A further possibility is the delightful *Auberge du Fel*, some 10km further on, high on the north slopes of the valley in the hamlet of **LE FEL** (☎05.65.44.52.30, fax 05.65.48.64.96; ③; closed mid-Nov to March; excellent restaurant with menus from 70F), which by an unexpected quirk of climate produces a little local wine. There is also a beautifully sited **camping municipal** high on the hillside (☎05.65.44.51.86; June–Sept).

Entraygues and around

ENTRAYGUES, with its narrow riverside streets and attractive grey houses, has the feel of a sleepy mountain town. It lies right in the angle of the junction of the Lot with the equally beautiful River Truyère. The brown towers of a thirteenth-century **château** overlook the meeting of the waters. A magnificent four-arched **bridge** of the same date crosses the Truyère a little way upstream.

The **tourist office** is on the main street (July & Aug daily except Sun pm 9.30am–7pm; June & Sept 9.30am–12.30pm & 2–6pm, closed Mon pm & Sun; Oct–May 9.30am–12.30pm & 1.30pm–5.30pm, closed Sun, Sat pm & Mon am; ☎05.65.44.56.10) and will provide information about walking, mountain biking and canoeing in the area. The *Hôtel de la Truyère*, on the river bank at the end of the bridge, makes a splendid place to stay (☎05.65.44.51.10, fax 05.65.44.57.78; ②; closed mid-Nov to March; restaurant from 68F; closed Mon). Alternatively, try the *Hôtel du Centre* (☎05.65.44.51.19, fax 05.65.48.63.09; ②; restaurant from 70F). There are also two **campsites**: *Le Val-de-Saures* (☎05.65.44.56.92; July & Aug) and *Le Roquepailhol* (☎05.65.44.56.92; July & Aug), and two **gîtes d'étape** – Mme Galan (☎05.65.44.50.73) and *Le Battedou* (☎05.65.48.61.62) – on the GR65 at **GOLINHAC**, about 7km south of Entraygues on the other side of the Lot. There is one bus per weekday to Aurillac in the north and Rodez to the south.

There are further accommodation options at **ESTAING**, another beautiful village grouped round a rocky bluff and castle in a bend of the Lot about 10km beyond Golinhac. The *Hôtel aux Armes d'Estaing*, named for the family who occupied the castle for five hundred years, offers attractive rooms and very good food in the centre of the village (☎05.65.44.70.02, fax 05.65.44.74.65; ②; closed Nov 15 to Feb; restaurant from 65F). There is also a **camping municipal** (☎05.65.44.72.77; May–Sept) and **gîte d'étape** on the GR65 (☎05.65.44.71.74). A date to watch out for, however, is the first Sunday in July when the place fills up with people, many in medieval dress, who come to honour the relics of St Fleuret, bishop of Clermont, who died here in 621 AD and was buried in the fifteenth-century church by the castle.

Espalion

The substantial little town of **ESPALION** lies in a mild, fertile opening in the valley of the Lot, 10km from Estaing and 32km northeast of Rodez. It was the "first smile of the south" to the muleteers, pilgrims and other travellers coming down from the rude heights of the Massif Central and places north. Home town of the composer Francis Poulenc, as well as Benoit Rouqayrol and Louis Denayrouze, inventors of diving suits, Espalion is best known in France for its exiles, in particular its countless sons and daughters who set up in the café business in Paris from the 1850s onwards.

The only interesting part of town is the **riverside quarter**, with its galleried and balconied old houses, once used as tanneries, hanging over the water. The finest view of the area is from the Pont Neuf, where the main road to Rodez crosses the Lot, for just upstream there is a lovely red sandstone packhorse **bridge** with a domed and turreted **château** dating from 1572 right behind it.

Surprisingly, there is an interesting museum dedicated principally to the life of the region: **Musée Joseph Vaylet**, on the main road, boulevard Poulenc (daily July–Sept 10am–noon & 2–7pm; rest of the year 2–6pm; closed Tues;15F), which contains mainly furniture and domestic objects plus an exhibition of diving gear (thanks to the two Espalionnais mentioned above).

Don't miss the glorious little **church of St-Hilarion**, built in the eleventh and twelfth centuries on the spot, so the story goes, where, in the reign of Charlemagne, the Saracens lopped off the head of St Hilarion. It sits on the edge of the cemetery, about fifteen minutes' walk to the left of the bridge on the château side of the river, past the campsite. Very small and built in the red sandstone, with a wall belfry and wide porch with sculpted tympanum and dozens of figures adorning the corbel ends of the apse and a beautiful Virgin and Child above the south transept door, it's a delight.

Also well worth a visit is the **Château de Calmont d'Olt** (June–Sept daily 9am–7pm; rest of year 10–noon & 2–6pm, closed Thurs & Fri; 30F) for its unbeatable views of the town and the country beyond. It's a rough and atmospheric old fortress dating from the eleventh century, on the very peak of an abrupt bluff, 535m high and directly above the town on the south bank. There are reconstructions of medieval siege works and a catapult in the grounds.

For **accommodation**, there's no better place to stay than the *Hôtel Moderne* on the crossroads in the middle of town at 27 bd Guizard (☎05.65.44.05.11, fax 05.65.48.06.94; ③; closed Nov). Its rooms are comfortable, but, more importantly, its restaurant is first-rate, especially for its river fish (menus from 80F).

For uncomplicated **eating**, there are several brasseries on the main through-street. But, for something special, Espalion has a second first-rate restaurant in the *Méjan*, by the old bridge (☎05.65.48.22.37; closed Sun eve & Mon, plus Feb, March & July), specializing in regional cuisine with a post-*nouvelle* influence: from 150F. There is a riverside **campsite**, Roc de l'Arche, behind the château (☎05.65.44.06.79) but it's unnecessarily fancy and expensive and gets very crowded in season; better, if you have the time and the means, to go to the prettier, simpler and cheaper riverside *Belle Rive* in the attractive village of **ST-CÔME**, another 4km upstream, where there is also a **gîte d'étape** in a beautiful old house (☎05.65.44.07.24; March–Oct) lying on the GR65, GR6 and GR620.

Millau, Roquefort and the Gorges du Tarn

MILLAU, subprefecture of the Aveyron *département* and second town after Rodez in the old province of Rouergue, occupies a beautiful site in a bend of the River Tarn at its junction with the Dourbie. It is enclosed on all sides by impressive white cliffs formed where the rivers have worn away the edges of the *causses*, especially on the north side, where the spectacular table-top hill of the **Puech d'Andan** stands sentinel over the town. From medieval until modern times, thanks to its proximity to the sheep pastures of the *causses*, it was a major manufacturer of leather goods, especially gloves. Although outclassed by cheaper producers in the mass market and suffering serious unemployment as a result, Millau still leads in top-of-the-range goods.

Arrival, information and accommodation

The **tourist office** (July & Aug daily 9am–7pm; Mon–Sat 9am–12.30pm & 2–6.30pm; ☎05.65.60.02.42, fax 05.65.61.36.08) is on the corner of av Alfred-Merles, at the end of which you'll find both bus and train stations. **Bikes and outdoor equipment** can be rented from *Roc et Canyon*, 55 av Jean-Jaurès.

For an overnight **stay**, there's the *Grand Hôtel Moderne*, 11 av Jean-Jaurès (☎05.65.60.59.23, fax 05.65.59.29.01; ②; closed Oct–March), or the *Hôtel Le Commerce*, 8 place du Mandarous (☎05.65.60.00.56, fax 05.65.60.96.50;①–②), where it's best to take a room at the back to avoid any noise from the square, though all are clean and proper. A bit more expensive is *Les Causses*, in an attractive building at 56 av Jean-Jaurès, the N9 (☎05.65.60.03.19, fax 05.65.60.86.90; ③), with a reasonable restaurant (from 60F). There's a good **youth hostel** about 1km down av Jean-Jaurès at 26 rue Lucien-Costes (☎05.65.61.27.74; ①), and there are also several **campsites**: the municipal *Millau-Plage* is on the left bank of the Tarn, north of the confluence with the Dourbie – take the bridge at the end of av Gambetta (☎05.65.60.10.97; April–Sept).

The town

There are no remarkable sights in Millau; it is simply a very pleasant, smallish provincial town whose clean and well-preserved old streets have a summery, southern charm. It owes its original prosperity to its position on the ford where the Roman road from Languedoc to the north crossed the Tarn, marked today by the truncated remains of a medieval **bridge** surmounted by a watermill jutting out into the river beside the modern bridge.

Whether you arrive from north or south, you will find yourself sooner or later in **place du Mandarous**, the main square, where avenue de la République, the road to Rodez, begins. South of here, the **old town** is built a little way back from the river to avoid the floods and contained within an almost circular ring of shady boulevards. The rue Droite cuts through the centre, linking the three squares: place Emma-Calve, place des Halles and place Foch. The prettiest by far is **place Foch**, with its cafés, shaded by two big plane trees and bordered by houses supported on stone pillars; some are as old as the twelfth century. In one corner, the **church of Notre-Dame** is worth a look, for its octagonal Toulouse-style belfry, originally Romanesque. In the other, there's the very interesting **Musée de Millau** (April–Sept daily 10am–noon & 2–6pm; rest of year closed Sun; 26F), whose collections revolve around the bizarre combination of arche-ology and gloves, but include France's one and only complete 180-million-year-old ple-siosaurus and the magnificent red pottery of the Graufesenque works (see below). The other two squares have been the subject of some rather questionable attempts at rec-onciling old stones and Richard Rogers-inspired contemporary urban design, but the **clock tower** off place Emma-Calve (June & Sept Mon–Sat 10–11.30am & 3–5.30pm; July & Aug daily 10–11.30am & 3.30–6.30pm, Sun 4–6.30pm; 15F) is worth a climb for the great all-round view. Take a look also in the streets off the square – rue du Voultre, rue de la Peyrollerie and their tributaries – for a sense of the old working-class and bourgeois districts.

Clear evidence of the town's importance in Roman times is to be seen in the **Graufesenque pottery works**, just upstream on the south bank (daily 9am–noon & 2–6.30pm; 35F), whose renowned sigillated ware was distributed throughout the Roman world. It was a huge production line in its day, involving four hundred potters and a hundred kilns; today, there is an archeology museum with a permanent exhibi-tion of the bowls, vases and cups that were produced.

Eating and drinking

If you are just looking for a quick **meal**, go to place du Mandarous, where there are numerous brasseries and cafés. For light meals and music – in summer – you could try the *Locomotive* at 33 av Gambetta (till 2am; around 50F). For more substantial, tradi-tional restaurant fare, try the *Auberge Occitane*, at 15 rue Peyrollerie (menus from 70F), or the more upmarket *La Braconne*, on place Foch (from 98F; ☎05.65.60.30.93; closed Sun eve & Mon). Alternatively, head for boulevard de la Capelle on the northeast side of the old town, where three good establishments spread their tables under the trees: *La Mangeoire*, at no. 8 (from 90F), which serves good grilled fish, meat and game dish-es; *La Marmite du Pêcheur*, featuring menus from 60F, including the local potato and cheese dish, *aligot*; and *Le Cyrano*, at no. 2 (from 65F).

Roquefort-sur-Soulzon

Twenty-one kilometres south of Millau, the little village of **ROQUEFORT-SUR-SOULZON** has nothing to say for itself except cheese, and almost every building is devoted to the cheese-making process.

What gives the cheese its special flavour is the fungus, *penicillium roqueforti*, that grows exclusively in the fissures in the rocks created by the collapse of the sides of the valley on which Roquefort now stands. Legend has it that once upon a time a local shep-herd one day forgot his lunch of bread and cheese, and found it some months later, cov-ered with mould. He bit tentatively and discovered to his surprise that instead of ruining the cheese, the mould had much improved its taste.

While the sheep's milk used in the making of the cheese comes from different flocks and dairies as far afield as the Pyrenees, the crucial fungus is grown here, on bread. Just 2g of powdered fungus are enough for 4000 litres of milk, which in turn makes 330 Roquefort cheeses; they are matured in Roquefort's many-layered cellars, first unwrapped for three weeks and then wrapped up again. It takes three to six months for the full flavour to develop.

Two of the cheese manufacturers have organized **visits**: Société (daily July & Aug 9.30am–noon & 2–6pm; rest of year 9.30–11.30am & 2–5pm; 15F) and Papillon (April–June daily 9.30–11.30am & 1.30–5.30pm; July–Sept daily 10am–6pm, rest of year

Mon–Fri 9–11.30am & 1.30–5pm; free). Each visit consists of a short film, followed by a tour of the cellars – not, in fact, very interesting.

The Gorges du Tarn

Jam-packed with tourists in July and August, but absolutely spectacular nonetheless, the **Gorges du Tarn** cut through the limestone plateaux of the Causse de Sauveterre and the Causse Méjean in a precipitous trench 400–500m deep and 1000–1500m wide. Its sides, cloaked with woods of feathery pine and spiked with pinnacles of eroded rock, are often sheer and always very steep, creating within them a microclimate in sharp distinction to the inhospitable plateaux above. The permanent population is tiny, though there is plenty of evidence of more populous times in abandoned houses and once-cultivated terraces. Because of the press of people and the subsequent over-pricing of **accommodation**, the best bet, if you want to stay along the gorge, is to head up onto the Causse Méjean, where there are several small family-run hotels and chambres d'hôte.

The most attractive section of the gorge runs for 53km from pretty **LE ROZIER**, 21km northeast of Millau, to **ISPAGNAC**. If you want to **stay** in Le Rozier, try the *Hôtel Arnal* (☎05.65.62.66.00; ③; closed Oct and Easter) or *Hôtel Doussière* (☎05.65.62.60.25; ②; closed mid-Nov to Easter), or for budgeters there's a **camping municipal** (☎05.65.62.63.98, fax 05.65.62.60.83; closed Oct–April). **ST-CHÉLY-DU-TARN** has the very prettily sited *Auberge de la Cascade* (☎04.66.48.52.82, fax 04.66.48.52.45; ②; restaurant from 70F; closed mid-Oct to mid-March).

A narrow and very twisty road follows the right bank of the river from Le Rozier, but it's not the best way to see the scenery. For the car-borne, the best views are from the road to St-Rome-de-Dolan above Les Vignes, and from the roads out of La Malène and the attractive **STE-ÉNIMIE**, where you'll find a well-informed **tourist office** (July & Aug daily 10am–12.30pm & 2.30–7pm; rest of year Mon–Sat 9.30am–noon & 1.30–4.30pm; ☎04.66.48.53.44). La Malène has a **camping municipal** (☎04.66.48.58.55; April to mid-Oct) and the nearby *La Blanquière* site (☎04.66.48.54.93; May to mid-Sept), which is beautifully sited on the main road towards Les Vignes.

But it's best to walk if possible, or follow the river's course by boat or canoe, and there are literally dozens of places to rent canoes. For walkers, the **GR6a**, a variant of the GR6 which crosses the *causses*, climbs steeply out of Le Rozier between the junction of the Tarn with the equally spectacular gorges of the River Jonte onto the Causse Méjéan, then follows the rim of the Tarn gorge for a while before descending to rejoin the GR6 at Les Vignes (4–5hr).

Also eminently worth seeing are two beautiful **caves** about 25km up the Jonte from Le Rozier: the **Aven Armand** (daily mid-March to Nov 9.30am–noon & 1.30–5/6pm; July & Aug 9.30am–7pm; 45F) on the edge of the Causse Méjean, and the **Grotte de Dargilan** (daily March–June & Sept 9am–noon & 1.30–6pm; July & Aug 9am–7pm; Oct 10am–noon & 1.30–5pm; 39F) on the south side of the river on the edge of the Causse Noir. **HYELZAS**, near the Armand-Aven cave, has a gîte d'étape (M. Pratlong; ☎04.66.45.65.22), and **LA VIALE** a chambre d'hôte (M. Poquet; ☎04.66.48.82.39: from 250F for two, including breakfast; closed Nov–April).

THE CÉVENNES AND ARDÈCHE

The **Cévennes** mountains and River **Ardèche** have given their names to a *département*.. Mountains and *département* overlap, but together they form the southeastern defences of the Massif Central, overlooking the Rhône valley to the east and the Mediterranean littoral to the south. The bare upland landscapes of the inner or western edges are those of the central Massif. The outer edges, Mont Aigoual and its radiating valleys and the tributary valleys of the Ardèche, are distinctly Mediterranean: deep, dry, close and clothed in forests of sweet chestnut, oak and pine.

Remote and inaccessible country until well into the twentieth century, it has bred rugged and independent inhabitants. For centuries it was the most resolute stronghold of Protestantism in France, and it was in these valleys that the persecuted Protestants put up their fiercest resistance to the tyranny of Louis XIV and Louis XV. In World War II, it was heavily committed to Resistance. In the aftermath of 1968, it became the promised land of the hippies – *zippies*, as the locals called them; they moved into the countless abandoned farms and hamlets, whose native inhabitants had been driven away by hardship and poverty. The odd hippy has stuck it out, true to the last to the alternative life. In more recent times, it has been colonized by Dutch and Germans.

The author Robert Louis Stevenson crossed it in 1878 with Modestine, a donkey he bought in miserable Le Monastier-sur-Gazeille near the astounding town of **Le Puy** and sold at journey's end in the former Protestant stronghold of **St-Jean-du-Gard**, a now-famous route described in *Travels with a Donkey* (see p.1091).

The Parc National des Cévennes

The **Parc National des Cévennes** was created in 1970 to protect and preserve the life, landscape, flora, fauna and architectural heritage of the most typical parts of the Cévennes. North to south, it stretches from **Mende** on the Lot to **Le Vigan** and includes both **Mont Lozère** and **Mont Aigoual**, which exemplify both types of upland landscape. Access, to the periphery at least, is surprisingly easy, thanks to the Paris–Clermont–Alès–Nîmes train line and the Montpellier–Mende link.

The quickest way of getting around the park is by car since a bike would be very tough going due to the relentlessly hilly terrain. **Walking** is best for real contact with the land and its flavours. There are numerous **GRs: the 7, 6 and 60** cross all or part of the range, and other paths complete various circuits. The **GR66** does the tour of Mont Aigoual in 78.5km, the **GR68** of Mont Lozère in 110km. Another good route is the 130-kilometre **Tour des Cévennes** on the GR67.

If you do go off hiking, remember that these are proper mountains for all their southerly latitude. You need good hiking boots, warm and weatherproof clothing, emergency shelter, adequate food, maps and guidebooks. The current weather situation is obtainable on: ☎07.08.36.68.02 (Ardèche); ☎08.36.68.02.30 (Gard); ☎08.36.68.02.48 (Lozère).

The **main information office** for the park is at Florac (see p.803). It publishes numerous leaflets on the flora, fauna and traditions of the park, plus activities and routes for walkers, cyclists, canoeists and horse riders. They also provide a list of **gîtes d'étape** in the park and can provide information for those following Stevenson's route, including where to hire a donkey. In July and August, it is wise to book ahead for accommodation; otherwise you could find yourself sleeping out.

Mende and Mont Lozère

Capital of the Lozère *département*, **MENDE** lies well down in the deep valley of the Lot at the northern tip of the Parc des Cévennes, 28km east of Marvejols and 40km north of Florac, with train and bus links to the Paris–Nîmes and Clermont–Millau lines. It's a very attractive, unspoilt southern town, well worth a visit and a nice place to make an overnight stay.

In front of the **cathedral** stands a statue of Pope Urban IV, who was born locally and used his office to the benefit of his natal soil. It was he who launched the construction of the cathedral in 1369, although it took several centuries to complete; its two unequal towers standing against the haze of the mountain background are the town's landmarks. There's a fine view back along the pine-clad Lot valley from the porch, and inside is a handsome choir and eight great Aubusson tapestries suspended from the clerestory.

But most pleasure resides in a quiet wander in the narrow medieval streets and minuscule squares behind the cathedral. In **rue Notre-Dame**, which separated the Christian from Jewish quarters in medieval times, the thirteenth-century house at no. 17 was once a synagogue. The municipal Musée Ignon-Fabre is closed for major renovations, so carry on down to the river to see the medieval packhorse bridge, the **Pont Notre-Dame**, with its worn cobbles arching over the water.

The **tourist office** is at 14 bd Henri-Bourillon, to the right as you reach the centre of town from the N88 (July & Aug Mon–Sat 8.30am–12.30pm & 2–8pm, Sun 2.30–6.30pm; rest of year Mon–Fri 8.30am–12.30pm & 2–6pm, Sat 8.30am–12.30pm; ☎04.66.65.02.69, fax 04.66.65.02.69). The departmental tourist office is in the same building, with all the information you could want on the Lozère. The **gare SNCF** (☎04.66.49.00.39) is across the river, north of the centre. **Buses** depart from either the station or place du Foirail, at the southern end of rue Bourillon.

For a place to **stay,** there's the *Hôtel du Palais*, right in front of the cathedral on place Urbain-V (☎04.66.49.04.04, fax 04.66.65.24.43;③). Just the other side of the square, in rue d'Aigues-Passes, the *Hôtel du Gevaudan* (☎04.66.65.14.74; ①; restaurant from 58F) is pleasant inside. For more comfort, try the much prettier *Hôtel de France* on bd Lucien-Arnault, the northern part of the inner ring road (☎04.66.65.00.04, fax 04.66.49.30.47; ③; closed Dec 1–15; restaurant from 92F). Apart from the hotel **restaurants,** *La Gogaille* at 5 rue Notre-Dame serves up wholesome, traditional fare (from 78F); *Les Voutes*, 13 rue d'Aigues-Passes, is also worth a try (menus from 55F).

Mont Lozère

Mont Lozère is a long, high, windswept desolate barrier of granite and yellow grassland, rising to 1699m at the summit of **Finiels**, still grazed by herds of cows, but in nothing like the numbers of bygone years when half the cattle in Languedoc came up here for their summer feed. Snowbound in winter and wild and dangerous in bad weather, it has claimed many a victim among lost travellers. In some of the squat granite hamlets on the northern slopes, like Servies, Auriac and Les Sagnes, you can still hear the bells known as *clochers de tourmente* that tolled in the wind to give travellers some sense of direction when the cloud was low.

If you're travelling by car from Mende, the way to the summit is via the village of **LE BLEYMARD**, about 30km to the east on the bank of the infant River Lot, with accommodation in the form of *Hôtel La Remise* (☎04.66.48.65.80, fax 04.66.48.63.70; ③; closed Dec & Jan; restaurant from 68F). From here, the D20 winds 7km up through the conifers to **LE CHALET**, with its gîte d'étape (☎04.68.48.62.84; food available), where it is joined by the GR7, which has taken a more direct route from Le Bleymard. This is the route that Stevenson took, waymarked as the "Tracé Historique de Stevenson". Road and footpaths run together as far as the **Col de Finiels,** where the GR7 strikes off on its own to the southeast. The source of the River Tarn is about 3km east of the col, the summit of Lozère 2km to the west. From the col, the road and Stevenson's route drop down in tandem, through the lonely hamlet of **FINIELS** to the pretty but touristy village of **LE PONT-DE-MONTVERT**.

At Le Pont, a seventeenth-century **bridge** crosses the Tarn by a stone **tower** that once served as a tollhouse. In this building in 1702, the Abbé du Chayla, a priest appointed by the crown to reconvert the rebellious Protestants enraged by the revocation of the Edict of Nantes, set up a torture chamber to coerce the recalcitrant. Incensed by his brutality, a group of them under the leadership of one Esprit Séguier attacked and killed him on July 23. Reprisals were extreme; nearly 12,000 were executed, so precipitating the Camisards' guerrilla war against the state.

At the edge of the village, there is also an *écomusée* on the life and character of the region, the **Maison du Mont Lozère** (mid-April to Sept daily 10.30am–12.30pm & 2.30–6.30pm; 20F). If you are tempted to **stay**, there's the small *Auberge des Cévennes* (☎04.66.45.80.01; ③; closed Nov–March; restaurant from 90F), overlooking the bridge. There's also a gîte d'étape in the Maison du Mont Lozère (☎04.66.45.80.10; closed Jan & Feb; reservations obligatory).

Florac and Mont Aigoual

Situated 39km south of Mende, **FLORAC** lies in the bottom of the trench-like valley of the Tarnon just short of its junction with the Tarn. Behind it rises the steep wall that marks the edge of the Causse Méjean. When you get here, you will have already passed the frontier between the northern and Mediterranean landscapes; the dividing line seems to be the **Col de Montmirat** at the western end of Mont Lozère. Once you begin the descent, the scrub and steep gullies and the tiny abandoned hamlets, with their eyeless houses oriented towards the sun, speak clearly of the south.

The village, with some 2000 inhabitants, is strung out along the left bank of the Tarnon and the main street, **avenue Jean-Monestier**. There is little specific to see, though the close lanes of the village up towards the valley side have their charms, especially the plane-shaded **place du Souvenir**. A red-schist castle stands above the village, housing the **Centre d'Information du Parc National des Cévennes** (June to mid-Sept daily 9am–7pm, rest of year Mon–Fri 9am–noon & 2–7pm; ☎04.66.49.53.01). The helpful **tourist office** is on the av Jean-Monestier (July & Aug Mon–Sat 9am–12.30pm & 2–7pm, Sun 9am–12.30pm; rest of year Mon–Sat 9am–12.30pm & 2–7pm; ☎04.66.45.01.14, fax 04.66.45.25.80). **Mountain bike rental** is available from Cévennes Evasion, in place Boyer (☎04.66.45.18.31).

The **accommodation** on offer is not fantastic. The best and cheapest place is *Chez Bruno*, on the tree-lined **Esplanade** (☎04.66.45.11.19, fax 04.66.45.06.65; ①; restaurant from 55F). More expensive, there's the *Hôtel du Parc* on av Jean-Monestier (☎04.66.45.03.05, fax 04.66.45.11.81; ②; closed Dec to mid–March; restaurant from 88F). The *Central Hôtel et de la Poste* has a lovely terrace over the stream, but the rooms are a bit dowdy (☎04.66.45.00.01, fax 04.66.45.14.04; ②; closed mid-Jan to Feb; restaurant from 70F). Better perhaps to try the *Lozérette*, in **COCURÈS**, 5km back towards Mont Lozère, on the Pont-de-Montvert road (☎04.66.45.06.04, fax 04.66.45.12.93; ④; closed Nov–April; restaurant from 90F).

Three **gîtes d'etape** in and around Florac include M. Martinez, 18 rue du Pêcher (☎04.66.45.24.54); Mme Rives, rue de l'Église (☎04.66.45.14.93; closed Dec), and M. Serrano in Le Pont-du-Tarn, 1km north (☎04.66.45.20.89). The best-value **campsites** are the municipal one at Pont-du-Tarn out on the road towards Ispagnac (☎04.66.45.18.26; Dec–Feb), and two more on the other side of town on the Corniche de Cévennes road, beside the River Tarnon.

Florac's Esplanade is a good place to look for somewhere to **eat**, or try *Le Chapeau Rouge*, on the corner of rue Théophile Roussel and Jean-Monestier, offering *cévenoles* specialities (☎04.66.45.23.40; menus from 58F). For something a bit more upmarket, there's *La Source du Pêcher* at 1 rue du Rémuret, in the old town beside the stream (menus from 189F; ☎04.66.45.03.01).

Mont Aigoual

By road it's 24km up the beautiful valley of the Tarnon to the **Col de Perjuret**, where a right turn will take you on to the **Causse Méjean** to the strange rock formations of **Nîmes-le-Vieux**, and a left turn takes you along a rising ridge a further 15km to the

1565-metre summit of **Mont Aigoual** (GR6, GR7, GR66), from where, they say, you can see a third of France, from the Alps to the Pyrenees, with the Mediterranean coast from Marseille to Sète at your feet. It is not a craggy summit, although the ground drops away pretty steeply into the valley of the River Hérault on the south side, but the view and the sense of exposure to the elements is dramatic enough. There is a **CAF refuge** and **gîte d'etape** in the observatory (☎04.67.82.62.78; May–Sept).

The descent to Le Vigan (see below) by the valley of the Hérault is superb; a magnificent twisty road follows the deepening ravine through dense beech woods, to come out at the bottom in rather Italianate scenery, with tall, close-built villages and vineyards beside the stream. If you have to stay the night there's the *Hôtel du Touring et de l'Observatoire* (☎04.67.82.60.04, fax 04.67.82.60.04; ③; restaurant from 70F), at **L'ESPÉROU**, a rather soulless mountain resort just below the summit. Better to go down to **VALLERAUGUE** and stay at *Le Petit Luxembourg* (☎04.67.82.20.44, fax 04.67.82.24.66; ③; good restaurant from 80F).

The Causse du Larzac

In the 1970s, the **Causse du Larzac** was continually in the headlines over sustained political resistance to the high-profile presence of the French military. Originally there was a small military camp outside the village of **LA CAVALERIE** on the N9, long tolerated for the cash its soldiers brought in. But in the early 1970s the army decided to expand the place and use it as a permanent strategic base, expropriating a hundred or so farms. The result was explosive. A federation was formed – Paysans du Larzac – which attracted the support of numerous ecological, left-wing and regionalist groups in a protracted campaign of resistance under the slogan "Gardarem lo Larzac". Successful acts of sabotage were committed, and three huge peace festivals were held here, in 1973, 1974 and again in 1977. The army's plans were scotched by Mitterrand when he came to power in 1981, but you still find Larzac graffiti from here to Lyon, shorthand for opposition to the army, the state and the Parisian central government, and in favour of self-determination and independence for the south.

The best way to immerse yourself in the empty, sometimes eerie atmosphere of Larzac is to walk: **GRs 7**, **71** and **74** cross the plateau, though you shouldn't attempt them without a *Topoguide*. If you have no time for anything else, the area between La Couvertoirade, Le Caylar and Ganges in the foothills of the Cévennes will give you a real sense of life on the *causse*.

LA COUVERTOIRADE lies 5km off the main road, a perfect Templar village, still completely enclosed by its towers and walls and almost untouched by renovation. Its forty remaining inhabitants live by tourism, and you have to pay to walk around the ramparts (daily: mid-March to June & Sept to mid-Nov 10am–noon & 2–5pm; July & Aug 10am–6.30pm; 20F including video presentation). Just outside the walls on the south side is a *lavogne*, a paved water hole of a kind seen all over the *causse* for watering the flocks, whose milk is used for Roquefort cheese (see p.799). If you want to stay, there's the GR71 **gîte d'étape** (☎05.65.62.28.06) in the far corner from the entrance. Half-a-dozen kilometres south, the village of **LE CAYLAR** clusters in similar fashion at the foot of a rocky outcrop, the top of which has been fashioned into a fortress – worth clambering up for the aerial view of the surrounding *causse*, where mean little patches of cultivated ground have been stolen from among the merciless upthrusts of rock.

If you've got your own transport and a good map, the back road from here, via St-Michel to St-Maurice-Navacelles, is strongly recommended. Wild box grows along the lanes, often meticulously clipped into hedges. Here and there among the scrubby oak and thorn or driving home along the road at milking time, you pass flocks of sheep. Occasional farmhouses materialize, like *Les Besses* – one of the few still in use – huge, self-contained and fortress-like, with the living quarters upstairs and the sheep stalls down below. **ST-MAURICE** itself, on the GR7 and GR74, is small and sleepy, with a shop in summer only and the *Hôtel des Tilleuls* (☎04.67.44.61.60; ②; closed Dec–Easter; meals from 55F) opposite a fine World War I memorial by Paul Dardé. There is no official **campsite**, but if you ask you are directed to a grassy place by the cemetery, where a traditional *glacière* – a stone-lined pit for storing snow for use as ice before the days of refrigerators – has been restored. Its chief advantage is as a base for visiting the **Cirque de Navacelles**, 10km north on the D130 past the beautiful ruined seventeenth-century sheep farm of La Prunarède. The cirque is a widening in the 150-metre deep trench of the Vis gorges, formed by a now dry loop in the river that has left a neat pyramid of rock sticking up in the middle like a wheel hub. An ancient and scarcely inhabited hamlet survives in the bottom – a bizarre phenomenon in an extraordinary location, and you get literally a bird's-eye view of it from the edge of the cliff above. Both road and GR7 go through. Continuing to Le Vigan or Ganges via Montdardier, you pass a prehistoric **stone circle** on the left of the road, a silent and evocative place, especially in a close *causse* mist. There are other stones and dolmens in the vicinity.

Le Vigan and the Huguenot strongholds

Only 64km from Montpellier and 18km from Ganges, **LE VIGAN** makes a good starting point for exploring the southern part of the Cévennes. It's a leafy, cool and thoroughly agreeable place, at its liveliest during the **Fête d'Isis** at the beginning of August and the colossal fair that takes over the Parc des Châtaigniers on September 9 and 22.

The prettiest part of the town is around the central place du Quai by the **Protestant church**, where there is a concentration of cafés and brasseries. From there it's only a two-minute walk south, down rue Pierre-Gorlier, to reach the gracefully arched **Pont Vieux**, with beside it the **Musée Cévenol** (July–Aug daily 10am–noon & 2–6pm; Sept–June ring before to arrange a visit; 15F; ☎04.66.44.71.02), a well-presented look at traditional rural occupations in the area, including the woodcutter, butcher, shepherd and wolf-hunters. Interestingly, Coco Chanel also features: she had local family connections and it seems found inspiration for her designs in the *cévenol* silks (see below).

The **tourist office**, and *maison de pays*, occupies a modern block in the centre of the place du Marché, just north of the church (July & Aug Mon–Sat 8.30am–12.30pm & 1.30–7pm, Sun 10am–12.30pm; rest of year Mon–Fri 8.30am–12.30pm & 1.30–6.30pm, Sat 9am–12.30pm & 2–5pm; ☎04.67.81.01.72, fax 04.67.81.86.79).

For somewhere to **stay**, try the simple but very nice *Hôtel du Commerce*, 26 rue des Barris (☎04.67.81.03.28; ②). The best alternative is a couple of kilometres out of town, south towards Montdardier on the D48: the handsome old *Auberge Cocagne* in **AVÈZE** (☎04.67.81.02.70, fax 04.67.81.07.67; ③; closed Dec 21–Feb; restaurant from 69F). There are **campsites** in Avèze (☎04.67.81.95.01; June-Sept), or a little way upriver from Le Vigan, on the opposite bank, is the well-shaded riverside *Val de l'Arre* (☎04.67.81.02.77; April–Sept). There's a **gîte d'étape** at 1 rue de la Carrierrasse (☎04.67.81.01.71). On place d'Assas, the northern extent of place du Quai, the *Brasserie d'Assas* is as good a place to **eat** as any, or try *Le Vieux Pont*, 3 rue Pierre-Gorlier, for pizzas as well as more traditional dishes.

From Le Vigan, or more particularly from the Pont de l'Hérault bridge, a beautiful lane (D153) winds northeast through typical south Cévennes landscape – deep valleys thick with sweet chestnut and thinly peopled with isolated farms half-buried in greenery – from Sumène to St-Jean-du-Gard, a distance of around 45km, but very slow. **SUMÈNE** is a run-down but lovely old place, the entrance to its close, narrow streets still blocked by its medieval **gates**. It was once a centre for silk spinning, which for a couple of centuries until the 1900s was the mainstay of economic life in the Cévennes

– that and the cultivation of the sweet chestnut, which provided the staple diet for the entire population.

There is a **gîte d'étape** (☎04.66.85.28.84) at **COLOGNAC** and another in the valley bottom outside the big village of **LASALLE** (☎04.66.85.27.29), where there is also the *Hôtel des Camisards* in the main street (☎04.66.85.20.50; ②; restaurant from 70F; closed Nov to April).

St-Jean-du-Gard and around

Thirty-two kilometres west of Alès, **ST-JEAN-DU-GARD** was the centre of Protestant resistance during the Camisard war during 1702–04 (see below). It straggles along the bank of the River Gardon, crossed by a magnificent eighteenth-century bridge, with a number of picturesque old houses still surviving in the main street, **Grand-Rue**. One of them contains a splendid **Musée des Vallées Cévenoles**, a museum of local life, with displays of tools, trades, furniture, clothes, domestic articles and a fascinating collection of pieces related to the silk industry (May–Sept daily10am–7pm; 21F).

The **tourist office** is just off the main street by the post office (mid–June to mid-Sept Mon–Sat 9.30am–7pm, Sun 9.30am–1pm; rest of year Mon–Sat 9.30am–5pm; ☎04.66.85.32.11, fax 04.66.85.16.28). They can advise you about the times of the steam train that operates between St-Jean and Anduze (March–Sept; 55F return). There is a big **market** all along Grand-Rue on Tuesday mornings.

The finest place to **stay** is the *Hôtel l'Orange*, in Grand-Rue (☎04.66.85.30.34, fax 04.66.85.39.73; ③; closed Jan & Feb; good restaurant from 63F). **LE MOULINET** has a **camping municipal** by the river at Mas de la Cam, 3km north along the D907 (☎04.66.85.12.02; April–Sept).

The Musée du Désert

Signposts at St-Jean direct you to the museum at **MAS SOUBEYRAN**, a minuscule hamlet of beautiful rough-stone houses in a gully above the village of Mialet, about 12km east. The **Musée du Désert** (March–Nov Mon–Sat 9.30–noon & 2.30–6pm; July–Sept Sun 9.30–noon & 2.30–6pm; 22F), is in the house of Roland, one of the Camisards' self-taught but most successful military leaders, and it is pretty much the same as it would have been in 1704, the year of his death. It catalogues the appalling sufferings and sheer dogged heroism of the Protestant Huguenots in defence of their freedom of conscience: the "desert" they had to traverse between the Revocation of the Edict of Nantes in 1685 and the promulgation of the Edict of Tolerance in 1787, which restored the rights enshrined in the Edict – a process which was not completed until the Declaration of the Rights of Man in the first heady months of the Revolution in 1789. During this period they had no civil rights, unless they abjured their faith. They could not bury their dead, baptize their children, or marry. Their priests were forced into exile on pain of death. Troops were dispatched to put pressure on the recalcitrant, the infamous *dragonnades*, which involved the forcible billeting of troops in private homes, at the expense of the occupants. As if this were not enough, the soldiers would beat their drums continuously for days and nights in people's bedrooms in order to deprive them of sleep. People were put to death and sent to the galleys for life; their houses were destroyed.

Not surprisingly, such brutality led to armed rebellion, inspired by the prophesying of the lay preachers who had replaced the banished priests, calling for a holy war. On display are documents, private letters and lists of those who died for their beliefs, including the names of 5000 who died as galley slaves and the women who were immured in the Tour de Constance prison in Aigues-Mortes. There are also the chains and rough uniform of a *galérien* (galley slave).

Prafrance and the Mine Témoin

Twelve kilometres from St-Jean in the direction of Anduze, **PRAFRANCE** has an extraordinary and very appealing garden consisting exclusively of bamboos of all shapes and sizes: **La Bambouseraie** (daily 9.30am–7pm; 30F), the result of its creator's pet passion.

If you want to leave the area by train, the place to head for is **ALÈS** on the Nîmes–Paris line. This was a major coal-mining centre, though 25,000 jobs have been lost and all but two opencast pits closed in the last thirty years. Today, it has a superb museum on the history and techniques of coal-mining, known as the **Mine Témoin**, in the underground workings of a disused mine on chemin de la Cité Ste-Marie in the Rochebelle district (tours daily: April, May & Sept–Nov 11 9am–12.30pm & 2–5.30pm; June–Aug 9.30am–7pm; 36F; last visit one-and-a-half hours before closing).

Aubenas and the northern Cévennes

A small but prosperous and surprisingly industrial town of around 14,000 people, **AUBENAS** sits in the middle of the southern part of the Ardèche *département* overlooking the middle valley of the River Ardèche. It is 91km southeast of Le Puy and 42km west of Montelimar on the Rhône. With a character and non-tourist-dependent economy of its own, it makes a much better base than places further downstream around Vallon-Pont-d'Arc, with their nightmarish crowds.

The central knot of streets with their cobbles and bridges, occupying the highest point of town around **place de l'Hôtel-de-Ville**, have great charm, particularly towards place Grenette and place 14-Juillet. The hôtel itself is the old feudal **château**, from which the local seigneurs ruled the area right up until the Revolution (guided tours July & Aug daily at 11am, 2pm & 3pm; June & Sept Tues–Sat 11am, 3pm & 4pm; Oct–May Tues–Sat 3pm & 4pm; 25F). There's a magnificent view of the Ardèche snaking up the valley below from under an arch beside the castle, as there is from the end of **bd Gambetta** 200m downhill, where the **tourist office** is located on the corner (July & Aug daily 9am–12.30pm & 1.30–7pm; rest of year Mon–Sat 9am–noon & 2–6pm; ☎04.75.89.02.03, fax 04.75.89.02.04).

There are two inexpensive and old-fashioned provincial **hotels** right by the castle: *Hôtel des Négociants* on place de l'Hôtel-de-Ville (☎04.75.35.18.74; ①; closed Oct), with good, nourishing meals from 50F, and *Chez Jacques*, 9 rue Béranger-de-la-Tour, in the opposite corner of the tree-lined *place* (☎04.75.93.88.74, fax 04.75.35.37.54; ②; good food from 50F). There are several **campsites**, the cheapest being *Le Trou d'Oo* down by the river at **VILLE**, off the N102 (☎04.75.35.04.39; July–Sept). Cafés and brasseries line boulevard de Vernon on the south side of town; for fancier and more expensive places to **eat**, try *Le Fournil*, 34 rue du 4-septembre, at the end of Béranger-de-la-Tour (from 98F; closed Sun eve & Mon), or *Le Chat Qui Pêche*, nearby on place de la Grenette (from 98F; closed Tues eve & Wed lunch).

The Gorges de l'Ardèche

The **Gorges de l'Ardèche** begin at the **Pont d'Arc**, an extraordinary and very beautiful arch that the river has cut for itself through the limestone, just downstream from Vallon, itself 39km south of Aubenas. And they continue for about 35km to **ST-MARTIN-D'ARDÈCHE** in the valley of the Rhône.

The gorges are fantastic. They wind back and forth with reptilian sinuosity, much of the time dropping 300m straight down like a knife cut in the almost dead-flat scrubby Plateau des Gras. But they are also an appalling tourist trap; the road which follows the rim, with spectacular viewpoints marked out at regular intervals, is jammed with traffic, and anyway you don't really see very much. The river, down in the bottom, which is where you really want to be to appreciate the grandeur of the canyon, is likewise packed with canoes in high season. But it is walkable, depending on the water level, but you would need to bivouac midway at either Gaud or Gournier. Generally speaking, if you can't go out of season, give it a miss.

The plateau itself is riddled with caves. **Aven Marzal**, a stalactite cavern north of the gorge (11am–5.30pm; 40F, joint ticket with zoo 65F) has a prehistoric **zoo**, which consists of reconstructions of dinosaurs and friends (April–Oct daily 10am–7.30pm; 40F, joint ticket 65F), but the frequency of visits to the cave depends on the number of visitors waiting – they are approximately every twenty minutes in July and August, falling to four per day in other months.

Best of the area's caves is the **Aven Orgnac**, to the south of the gorge (March, Oct & Nov 9.30am–noon & 2–5pm; April–June & Sept 9.30am–noon & 2–6pm; July & Aug 9.30am–6pm; 45F), one of France's most spectacular and colourful stalactite formations. There's also a very good prehistory **museum** (same hours except it opens at 10am; 30F, joint ticket 55F). Further upstream near **VALLON-PONT-D'ARC**, a complex series of cave paintings was discovered in December 1994, after being left untouched for 30,000 years, making the **Chauvet-Pont d'Arc cave** the oldest-known decorated cave in the world. Adorned with an elaborate sequence of Stone Age paintings depicting woolly rhinos, bison, lions and bears, the cave system is currently being investigated by archeologists, and causing a major rethink about the history of art. It's unlikely that Chauvet-Pont d'Arc will ever be open to the public but there are plans afoot to construct a replica nearby. For the moment, you can get a glimpse of the most important discoveries at a small but rewarding **exhibition** in Vallon, behind the mairie, highlight of which is a video taken inside the cave (Tues–Sun 2–5.30pm; 25F).

Accommodation in the area can be a problem during the high season. The cheapest place in Vallon itself is the *Hôtel du Parc*, on bd Alizon (☎04.75.88.02.17; ②), but by far the best is *Le Manoir du Raveyron*, rue Henri-Barbusse (☎04.75.88.03.59, fax 04.75.37.11.12; ③; closed mid-Oct to mid-March), with a good restaurant from 98F. The river is lined with **campsites**, the cheapest being the municipal one (☎04.75.88.04.73; April–Sept). There's a **gîte d'étape** on place de la Mairie (☎04.75.88.07.87), and a **tourist office** (July & Aug Mon–Sat 9am–1pm & 3–7pm, Sun 10am–noon; rest of year Mon–Fri 9am–noon & 2–6pm, Sat 9am–noon; ☎04.75.88.04.01, fax 04.75.37.19.79) on the south side of town. Eight kilometres upstream, there is a well-priced **camping municipal** at RUOMS (☎04.75.93.99.16; May 15–Sept).

The valley of the Chassezac and the Corniche du Vivarais

Between Aubenas and Les Vans, 27km to the southwest, several wild mountain streams flow out of the northern part of the Cévennes to join the Ardèche. One of the most beautiful is the **Chassezac**, which rises north of Villefort and carves a dry, twisting ravine covered with pine, bracken and sweet chestnut down to **LES VANS**.

The centre of the town is occupied by the wide and cheerful **place Léopold-Ollier**, on one side of which is the eccentrically decorated *Hôtel des Cévennes* (☎04.75.37.23.09; ③), whose decor, friendly welcome and good cooking (from 75F) make a stop here worthwhile. Other attractions are the remains of the old town and, just outside, the bizarre rock formations of the **Bois de Paiolive**. There is a **gîte d'étape** across the river at **Chambonas** (☎04.75.37.24.99).

Thines to the Col de Meyrand

THINES is a dozen twisting kilometres up the Chassezac from Les Vans, past isolated farms, abandoned terracing and numerous tumbling streams, then a further 5km or so up a side valley. The lane that leads to it is no wider than a car, and nature encroaches on either side. Traces remain of the old mule road, and in the torrent bed are the stumps of packhorse bridges long since carried away. Among the scrubby oaks are beehives made from old tree trunks.

The village itself is at the end of the road high on a spur, looking back down the valley: just a handful of squat, grey-stone houses tightly grouped around a very lovely twelfth-century **church**, decorated with bands of red and white stone, the faces of its sculptures smashed during the Wars of Religion. At the top of the village, where the **GR4** and the local **GRP** enter from the scrubby heights behind, there is a strange **rock-cut relief** commemorating Resistance people killed here in August 1943. There's also a **gîte d'étape** (Mme Bacconnier; ☎04.75.36.94.33) and ferme auberge (Mme Archambault; ☎04.75.36.94.47; Easter–11 Nov).

If your car is reasonably robust, you can get up onto the D4 on the 1000m ridge above Thines by a track that starts just above the bridge over the stream below the village. This is the so-called **Corniche du Vivarais Cévenol**, which you would otherwise have to make a long detour to reach. **SABLIÈRES**, another desolate Cévennes village, lies in the valley of the Drobie down to your right.

The landscape changes completely up here. The Mediterranean influence is left behind; it's windswept moorland, with natural beechwoods and mountain ash around the few bleak farms and plantations of conifers on the tops. The land rises steadily to over 1400m above the **Col de Meyrand**, itself at 1370m, whence it is possible to escape back down to the main road and train line at **LUC**, which is 18km to the west.

Le Puy-en-Velay and the northeast

Right in the middle of the Massif Central, 78km from St-Étienne and 132km from Clermont, **LE PUY** is one of the most remarkable towns in the whole of France. Both landscape and architecture are totally theatrical. Slung between the higher mountains to east and west, the landscape erupts in a chaos of volcanic acne: everywhere a confusion of abrupt conical hills, scarred with dark outcrops of rock and topknotted with woods. Even in the centre of the town, these volcanic thrusts burst through.

In the past, Le Puy enjoyed influence and prosperity because of its ecclesiastical institutions. It was – and in a limited way, still is – a centre for pilgrims embarking on the 1600-kilometre trek to Santiago-de-Compostella. The starting point is place du Plot (also the scene of a lively Saturday market) and rue St-Jacques. History has it that Le Puy's Bishop Godescalk, in the tenth century, was the first pilgrim to make the journey. And in the Wars of Religion it managed to resist the Protestant fervour of much of the Massif Central. Today, however, it has fallen somewhat on hard times, and its traditional industries – tanning and lace – have essentially gone bust.

Even today Le Puy is somewhat inaccessible for the capital of a *département*: the three main roads out all cross passes more than 1000m high, which causes problems in winter. But it is far from run-down. And it still produces its famous green lentils.

Arrival, information and accommodation

If you arrive at the **gare SNCF** (☎08.36.35.35.35) or **gare routière** (☎04.71.09.25.60), facing each other in place Maréchal-Leclerc, you'll find yourself barely a ten- minute walk from the central place du Breuil and the **tourist office** (Mon–Sat 8.30am–noon & 1.45–6.30pm, Sun 10am–noon; June–Aug daily 8.30am–7.30pm; ☎04.71.09.38.41, fax 04.71.05.22.62), with the **Comité Départemental du Tourisme** at 12 bd Philippe-Jourde (Mon–Sat 8.30am–noon & 2–6pm; June–Aug Mon–Sat 8.30am–7.30pm, Sun 9am–noon & 2–6pm; ☎04.71.09.38.41).

Le Puy doesn't have a superabundance of **hotels**, but it has enough to deal with the town's tourists except in peak season. Three to try on bd Maréchal-Fayolle, the main boulevard connecting the station and place Breuil, are the odd-looking *Dyke Hôtel*, at no. 37 (☎04.71.09.05.☎03, fax 04.71.02.58.66;③), the *Régional*, at no. 36 (☎04.71.09.37.34; ①), and the rather handsome old *Régina*, at no. 34, (☎04.71.09.14.71, fax 04.71.09.18.57; ③; restaurant 78–160F) with a tempting terrace. Alternatively, there's the *Bristol*, at 7 av Foch (☎04.71.09.13.38, fax 04.71.09.51.70; ③) with a tempting terrace; some of the rooms have been modernized in soulless style, but its restaurant does an excellent regional set menu from 89F. For those watching the pennies, there's a good official **youth hostel** at the *Centre Pierre-Cardinal*, 9 rue Jules-Vallès (☎04.71.05.52.40, fax 04.71.05.61.80), just off rue Lafayette. **Campers** should head for the municipal *Camping de Bouthézard*, off av d'Aiguilhe in the northwest corner of town.

The old town

It would be hard to lose your bearings in Le Puy, for the town centre is marked by the **Rocher Corneille**, 755m above sea level and 130 abrupt metres above the lower town. On its summit is a colossal, brick-red statue of the Virgin and Child, cast from 213 guns captured at Sebastopol and coloured like this to match the tiled roofs below. You can climb to the base of the statue (20F) for stunning views of the city, the church of St-Michel atop its needle-pointed pinnacle a few hundred metres northwest, and the surrounding volcanic countryside.

In the maze of steep cobbled streets and steps that terrace the Rocher, lace-makers – a traditional, though now commercialized industry – do a fine trade, with doilies and lace shawls hanging enticingly outside souvenir shops. The main focus here, in the **old town**, is the Byzantine-looking **Cathédrale Notre-Dame-de-France**, begun in the eleventh century and decorated with parti-coloured layers of stone and mosaic patterns and roofed with a line of six domes. It is best approached up the rue des Tables, where you get the full theatrical force of its five-storeyed west front towering above you. In the rather exotic eastern gloom of the interior, a black-faced Virgin in spreading golden robes stands upon the main altar, the copy of a revered original destroyed during the Revolution; the copy is still paraded through the town every August 15. Other lesser treasures are displayed at the back of the church in the sacristy, beyond which is the entrance to the exceptionally beautiful twelfth-century **cloister** (daily: April–June 9.30am–12.30pm & 2–6pm; July–Sept 9.30am–6.30pm; rest of year 9.30am–noon & 2–6.30pm; 25F), with its carved capitals, cornices and magnificent views of the cathedral and the towering Virgin and Child overhead. The passageway to the cloisters takes you past the so-called **Fever Stone**, whose origins may have been as a prehistoric dolmen and which was reputed to have the power of curing fevers. The surrounding ecclesiastical buildings and the **place du For**, on the south side of the cathedral, all date from the same period and form a remarkable ensemble.

It's a ten-minute walk from the cathedral to the **church of St-Michel** (signposts lead the way), perched atop the 82-metre needle-pointed lava pinnacle of the **Rocher d'Aiguilhe**. The little Romanesque church, built on Bishop Godescalk's return from his pilgrimage (see above) and consecrated in 962, is a beauty in its own right, and its improbable situation atop this ridiculous needle of rock is quite extraordinary – it's a long haul up 265 steps to the entrance (daily: mid-March to mid-June 10am–noon & 2–5/7pm; mid-June to mid-Sept 9am–7pm; mid-Sept to mid-Nov 9.30am–5/6pm; mid-Nov to mid-March 2–4pm; 12F).

In the new part of town, beyond the squat **Tour Pannessac**, which is all that remains of the city walls, **place de Breuil** joins **place Michelet** and forms a social hub backed by the spacious Henri Vinay public gardens, where the **Musée Crozatier** (May–Sept Mon & Wed–Sat 10am–noon & 2–6pm, Sun 2–6pm; Oct–April Mon & Wed–Sat

10am–noon & 2–4pm, Sun 2–4pm; 20F) is best known for its collections relating to the region's traditional lace-making activities. Busy bd Maréchal-Fayolle converges with place Cadelade, where there's another of Le Puy's craziest aspects: the extraordinary bulbous tower of the **Pagès Verveine distillery**. The *verveine* (verbena) plant is normally used to make *tisane* (herb tea), but in this region provides a powerful digestive liqueur instead.

Eating and drinking

Apart from the hotel restaurants and the brasseries on the main street opposite the tourist office, there are several good and not too expensive places to **eat**. The best is the *Tournayre*, at 12 rue Chênebouterie (☎04.71.09.58.94; closed Sun eve, Mon, & Jan), specializing in the region's cuisine – menus from 110F. Two cheaper establishments, both in rue Raphael, which begins at the bottom of rue des Tables, are the *Nom de la Rose*, at no. 48 (closed Tues), specializing in Mexican food from 69F, and the Middle Eastern *La Felouque*, at no. 49 (from 50F, closed Tues, Nov & Feb). One other, offering regional cuisine, is *Le Parentaine*, 8 av de la Cathédrale (from 80F; closed Sat & Sun).

For a drink or light snack, the terrace of *Le Miramande*, at the bottom of rue des Tables, makes a pleasant stop in summer (menus from 55F; closed Jan). For an evening drink, you can always try *Harry's Bar*, on rue Raphael (Mon–Sat till 1am), near the corner with rue des Tables.

North of Le Puy

North of Le Puy, the D906 crosses a vast and terminally depopulated area of pine-clad uplands – now a national regional park – and continues all the way to Vichy. After 42km you come to the little town of **LA CHAISE-DIEU**, renowned for the **abbey church of St-Robert** (daily: June–Sept 9am–noon & 2–7pm, rest of year 10am–noon & 2–5pm; 15F), whose square towers dominate the town. Founded in 1044 and restored in the fourteenth century at the expense of Pope Clement VI, who had served as a monk here, the church was destroyed by the Huguenots in 1562, burnt down in 1692, and remained unfinished when the Revolution brought a wave of anticlericalism. It was only really finished in this century. Its interior contains the tomb of Clement VI, some magnificent Flemish tapestries of Old and New Testament scenes hanging in the choir, which also boasts some fine Gothic stalls, and a celebrated fresco of the **Danse Macabre**, depicting Death plucking at the coarse plump bodies of 23 living figures, representing the different classes of society. "It is yourself", says the fifteenth-century text below, as indeed it might easily have been in an age when plague and war were rife.

Nearby on the place de l'Echo, the **Salle de l'Echo** (same times except closed Sun am; free) is another product of the risk of contagion; if not from plague, then from leprosy. For in this room, once used for hearing confession from the sick and dying, two people can turn their backs on each other and stand in opposite corners and have a perfectly audible conversation just by whispering.

A **classical music festival** takes place here in late August and early September, details of which are available from the **tourist office**, on place de la Mairie (April to mid-Sept daily except Mon 10am–noon & 2–6pm; rest of year also closed Sun; ☎04.71.00.01.16, fax 04.71.00.03.45). The *Hôtel Monastère et Terminus*, on av de la Gare (☎04.71.00.00.73, fax 04.71.00.09.18; ③; closed Feb; restaurant from 68F), and *Hôtel au Tremblant*, on the D906 (☎04.71.00.01.85, fax 04.71.00.08.59; ③; restaurant from 75F), offer reasonable comfort for a night's stay. There's also a **camping municipal** on the Vichy side of the D906 (☎04.71.00.07.88; June–Sept).

Ambert and Thiers

Twenty-five kilometres north of La Chaise-Dieu, the little town of **AMBERT** was an important centre of cottage industry in the Middle Ages. From the fourteenth to eighteenth centuries it was the centre of papermaking in France, supplying in particular the printers of Lyon, a connection which brought the region into contact with new ideas, in particular the revolutionary teachings of the Reformed church. Although those small-scale operations have long since been sidelined, there is a still a **paper mill** in operation at Richard-de-Bas just east of the town, with its **Musée Historique du Papier** (daily 9am–noon & 2–6pm, no lunch break July & Aug; 23F), featuring exhibits and explanations from papyrus to handmade samples from medieval days. In the town itself, there's a small **museum** (July & Aug daily 10am–noon & 2–5pm; rest of year closed Mon; 25F) devoted to the manufacture of the soft blue Fourme d'Ambert cheese, the region's speciality.

THIERS, another 49km to the north, has an illustrious industrial history: it is the country's great manufacturer of knives. In spite of serious decline, especially since decolonization and the loss of such huge captive markets, it still accounts for some seventy percent of French production. It is an interesting little town, built over the steep slopes of the valley of the Durolle, whose water power drove the forges and blade-makers' wheels for centuries. There's the **Maison des Couteliers**, devoted to the knife, at 58 rue de la Coutellerie in the centre (daily 10am–noon & 2–6/6.30pm; Jan closed Mon; 21F), while all along the deep valley bottom you can see where the old workshops were. You probably wouldn't want to stay overnight – there are frequent trains from Clermont Ferrand (30min).

East of Le Puy

East of Le Puy lies the barrier of the mountains of the Vivarais, rounded and wooded with beech, pine and fir, interspersed with open cow pastures. The highest points are the **Gerbier de Jonc** (1551m) and **Mont Mezenc** (1753m), with long views west across the whole of the Massif Central.

The Gerbier is a curious mound rising out of the otherwise flattish surrounding uplands, about 50km southeast of Le Puy, with the River Loire rising on its upper slopes. To get out there you take the D535 through **MONASTIER-SUR-GAZEILLE**, where R. L. Stevenson bought his donkey and started his famous journey. Although the village is pretty, with a particularly lovely church, there is something forlorn and unfriendly about it. The rather bleak *Hôtel de Provence* above the village would do for a night's stay (☎04.71.03.82.37; ②; restaurant from 65F). The riverside **camping municipal** (☎04.71.03.82.24; June–Sept) and **gîte d'étape** (☎04.71.03.82.24) are more welcoming.

Fifty kilometres further north, and about 40km east of Le Puy, behind the gentle bulk of **Mont Meygal** (1436m), lies the area known as the *Montagne Protestante*, because its people converted very early and have remained staunch Protestants ever since, albeit with some fairly far-out tendencies among them. Black-stone farmhouses stand in isolation among the pastures strewn with autumn crocus and the dark woods of fir. At the centre of the region lies **CHAMBON-SUR-LIGNON**, a rambling, rather unattractive village with a somewhat faded air, made famous, however, for its extraordinary wartime record as a haven for several thousand Jewish children. Everyone knew of their presence, everyone was involved in protecting them, and no-one ever betrayed them, bound together in their obdurate resolve by religious conviction. Their story is told in *Les Armes de l'Esprit* , a documentary film made by one of the surviving children who emigrated to the USA available from the Mairie. Albert Camus also stayed nearby in 1942 and wrote part of *La Peste* here. The **tourist office** is on the central square (Mon–Sat 9am–noon & 2/3–6/6.30pm, Sun 11am–noon; ☎04.71.59.71.56, fax 04.71.65.88.78).

More local information can be had from the tourist office in **TENCE**, a rather more aesthetic village, 8km down the road (Tues–Sat 9am–noon & 2–6pm, Sun 10.30am–12.30pm; ☎04.71.59.81.99, fax 04.71.65.47.13).

St-Étienne

ST-ÉTIENNE, 78km northeast of Le Puy, is not an appealing town. Almost unrelievedly industrial, it was a major armaments manufacturer, enclosed for kilometres around by mineworkings, warehouses and factory chimneys. But, like so many other industrial centres, it has fallen on hard times and the demolition gangs have moved in to raze its archaic industrial past, which does not add to its charms.

The centre is bland, and the mood is that of decline since the closure of the coalfields, but its **Musée d'Art Moderne** at La Terrasse (daily except Tues 10am–6pm; 28F) justifies a detour for anyone interested in twentieth-century art – a quite unexpected treasure house of contemporary work, both pre- and post-World War II, with a good modern American section, in which Andy Warhol and Frank Stella figure prominently, along with work by Rodin, Matisse, Léger and Ernst, and rooms filled entirely with French art, imaginatively laid out to exciting effect. The **Musée d'Art et d'Industrie**, 2 place Louis-Comte, is also good on St-Étienne's industrial background, including the development of the revolutionary Jacquard loom, but it is closed for renovation until 2000.

Buses #10 & #7 runs from the **train station** into the centre of town, and the **tourist office** is on ☎16 Ave de la Liberation (Mon–Sat 9am–7pm, Sun 10am–1pm; ☎04.77.49.39.00, fax 04.77.49.39.03). If you are forced to **stay**, try *Hôtel de la Tour*, 1 rue Mercière (☎04.77.32.28.48, fax 04.77.21.27.90; ①), *Le Cheval Noir*, 11 rue François-Gillet (☎04.77.33.41.72, fax 04.77.37.79.19; ②; closed 1–15 Aug), or *Hôtel Terminus du Force*, 29 av D-Rochereau, leading to the station (☎04.77.32.48.47, fax 04.77.34.03.30; ③; closed Aug 8–23).

travel details

Buses

Ambert to: St-Étienne (1 daily; 2hr).

Aubenas to: Alès (2–3 daily; 2hr 10min); Joyeuse (several daily; 25–40min); Les Vans (4 daily; 1hr 10min); Privas (7 daily; 1hr); Valence (7 daily; 2hr); Vallon-Pont-d'Arc (1–2 daily; 45min).

Aurillac to: Brommat (change at Mut-de-Barrez, 3 weekly; 2hr); Carlat (3–4 daily; 30min); Décazeville (1 daily; 2hr); Entraygues (1 daily; 1hr 30min); Mandailles (1 daily; 1hr 20min); Murat (1 daily; 1hr 40min); St-Flour (1 daily; 2hr 10min); Ste-Géneviève-sur-Argence (change at Mur-de-Barrez, 3 weekly; 2hr 30min); Super-Lioran (1 daily; 1hr 20min); Thiézac (2 daily; 55min); Vic-sur-Cère (2–3 daily; 40min).

Chambon-sur-Lignon to: St-Agrève (4 daily; 20min); Valence (2 daily; 2hr 30min).

Clermont-Ferrand to: Ambert (1–2 daily; 1hr 45min); Aydat (1–2 daily; 40min); Besse (July & Aug 2 daily; 1hr 35min); Bort-les-Orgues (1–2

daily; 2hr 15min); Chaubon (July & Aug 2 daily; 1hr 35min); La Chaise-Dieu (1 Mon; 2hr); Le Puy (1 daily; 2hr 15min); Mauriac (1–2 daily; 2hr 45min); Moulins (4 daily; 2hr 30min); Murol (July & Aug 2 daily; 1hr 10min); St-Flour (2 weekly; 2hr); St-Nectaire (July & Aug 2 daily; 1hr); Superbesse (July & Aug 2 daily; 1hr 45min); Thiers (several daily; 1hr); Vichy (5 daily; 2hr).

Conques to: Entraygues (July & Aug Tues, Thurs & Sat 1 daily; 35min); Espalion (July & Aug Tues, Thurs & Sat 1 daily; 1hr 20min); Najac (July & Aug Tues & Fri 1 daily; 2hr 30min); Rodez (July & Aug Tues, Thurs & Sat 1 daily; 1hr); St-Geniez-d'Olt (July & Aug & Tues, Thurs & Sat 1 daily; 2hr 15min); Villefranche-de-Rouergue (July & Aug Tues & Fri 1 daily; 2hr).

Florac to: Alès (1–2 daily; 1hr 30min).

Mende to: Langogne (2 daily; 1hr); Le Puy (2 daily; 2hr); Marvejols (3 daily; 50min); St-Chély-d'Apcher (1 daily; 1hr 10min); St-Étienne (1 daily; 3hr).

Millau to: Aven Armand (July & Aug 2 daily; 1hr 45min); Meyrueis (1–4 daily; 1hr 15min); Rodez (4 daily; 1hr 30min); Rozier (1–4 daily; 45min); Ste-Énimie (July & Aug 2 daily; 2hr 25min); Toulouse (2 daily; 4hr).

Neussargues to: Allanche (2–3 daily; 20min); Bort-les-Orgues (2–3 daily; 1hr 45min); Condat (2–3 daily; 30min); Riom-ès-Montagnes (2–3 daily; 1hr 15min); St-Flour (2–3 daily; 30min).

Le Puy to: Aubenas (2 weekly; 3hr 15min); Clermont-Ferrand (1 daily; 3hr); La Chaise-Dieu (2 daily; 1hr); Monistrol d'Allier (3 weekly; 45min); St-Étienne (4 daily; 2hr 10min); Saugues (3 weekly; 1hr 10min).

Rodez to: Albi (3 daily; 2hr); Conques (July & Aug Tues, Thurs & Sat 1 daily; 1hr); Entraygues (1 daily; 2hr); Espalion (3–4 daily; 45min); Laguiole (1 daily; 1hr 45min); Mende (1 daily; 3hr 30min); Millau (4–5 daily; 1hr 30min); Montauban (1 daily; 3hr 15min); Montpellier (3 daily; 3hr 20min); Mur-de-Barrez (1 daily; 2hr 45min); Séverac-le-Château (several daily; 45min); Toulouse (2–4 daily; 3hr 30min); Villefranche-de-Rouergue (1–2 daily; 1hr 30min).

St-Affrique to: Le Caylar (1 daily; 1hr 40min); Lodève (1 daily; 2hr 10min); Millau (2 daily; 50min); Montpellier (1 daily; 3hr 25min); Rodez (1 daily; 2hr 15min).

St-Agrève to: Chambon-sur-Lignon (4 daily; 20min); St-Étienne (4 daily; 2hr); Tence (4 daily; 35min).

St-Chély-d'Aubrac to: Espalion (1 daily; 30min).

St-Flour to: Chaudes-Aigues (2 daily; 1hr); Laguiole (Tues, Thurs & Sat 1 daily; 3hr); Massiac (3 daily; 35min).

St-Martin-d'Ardèche to: Avignon (1 daily; 1hr 40min); Pont St-Esprit (2 daily; 15min); Vallon-Pont d'Arc (2 daily; 1hr 10min).

Vichy to: Ambert (5 daily; 2hr 10min); Thiers (several daily; 40min).

Le Vigan to: Ganges (4 daily; 25min); Montpellier (3 daily; 2hr); Nîmes (4 daily; 2hr).

Villefranche-de-Rouergue to: Conques (July & Aug Tues & Fri 1 daily; 2hr); Décazeville (July & Aug Tues & Fri 1 daily; 30min); Najac (July & Aug Tues & Fri 1 daily; 30min).

Trains

Alès to: Genolhac (3–4 daily; 40min); Langogne (3–4 daily; 1hr 30min); Nîmes (6–7 daily; 35min); Villefort ((3–4 daily; 1hr).

Aurillac to: Brive: (4 daily; 1hr 40min).

Clermont-Ferrand to: Aurillac (6 daily; 2hr 30min); Béziers (1 daily; 6hr); Brive (3 daily; 3hr 40min); Le Lioran (6 daily; 2hr); Le Mont Dore (6 daily; Limoges (2 daily; 3hr 30min); Lyon (6 daily; 2hr 45min–3hr); 1hr 30min); Millau (3 daily; 4hr 20min); Murat (6 daily; 1hr 20min); Neussargues (6 daily; 1hr 30min); Paris (5 daily; 5hr); Le Puy (3 daily; 2hr 10min); Riom (10 daily; 10min); St-Flour-Chaudes-Aigues (5 daily; 2hr); Thiers (6 daily; 35min); Vic-sur-Cère (6 daily; 2hr 15min); Vichy (10 daily; 35min); Volvic (5 daily; 24min).

Le Puy to: St-Étienne (8 daily; 1hr 20min).

Mende to: La Bastide-Puylaurens (2–3 daily; 1hr); Langogne (2 daily; 1hr 30min); Marvejols (3 daily; 40min); Montpellier (several daily; 3hr); Nîmes (several daily; 2hr 30min–4hr).

Millau to: Aumont-Aubrac (5 daily; 1hr 30min); Béziers (4–5 daily; 2hr); Marvejols (5 daily; 1hr 10min); Paris (2 daily direct; 8hr–9hr 30min).

Rodez to: Millau (bus & train, 2 daily; 1hr 20min).

St-Étienne to: Clermont-Ferrand (3–6 daily; 2hr 40min); Lyon (3 daily TGVs; 45min); Paris (3 daily TGVs; 2hr 50min); St-Germain-des-Fosses (2 daily; 3hr).

St-Flour to: Neussargues (2–3 daily; 25 min).

Vichy to: Clermont-Ferrand (frequent; 38min); Nîmes (1–2 daily; 7hr); Paris (4 daily; 3hr 30min).

CHAPTER THIRTEEN

THE ALPS

Rousseau wrote in his *Confessions*, "I need torrents, rocks, pine trees, dark forests, mountains, rugged paths to go up and down, precipices at my elbow to give me a good fright." Formed by the collision of two continental plates two hundred million years ago, **the Alps** contain some of France's most dramatic landscapes, with roads, railways and population confined to the deep valley floors. To get the best out of this region you have to walk – or in winter, ski (a short roundup of the resorts is on p.832). There are four national or **regional parks** in the area covered by this chapter – Vanoise, Écrins, Queyras and Vercors – all with round-the-park trails, requiring one to two weeks' walking. The **Tour of Mont Blanc** path is of similar length. Then there are two transalpine routes: the **Grande Traversée des Alpes**, which crosses all the major massifs from St-Gingolph on Lake Geneva to Nice, and **Le Balcon des Alpes**, a gentler, village-to-village itinerary through the western foothills.

All these routes are clearly marked, equipped with refuge huts and gîtes d'étape, and described in *Topoguides*. The CIMES office in Grenoble (see p.817) will provide information on all GR paths. In addition, local tourist offices often produce detailed maps of walks in their own areas. You should not undertake any high-level **long-distance hikes**, however, unless you are an experienced hillwalker; if you aren't, but nonetheless like the sound of some of these trails, read a specialized hiking book before making any plans, or simply limit your sights to more local targets. You can find plenty of day walks from bases in or close to the parks; and there are some satisfying road routes, too. The **Vercors**, **Chartreuse**, **Aravis**, **Faucigny** and **Chablais** areas are the gentlest and quietest introductions.

As for **accommodation**, you can **camp** freely on the fringes of the parks, but once inside you are supposed to pitch only in an emergency and move on after one night. **Hotels** are often seasonal (closed in late spring and late autumn), overbooked and overpriced – if you're on a budget but don't want to carry camping equipment, using **gîtes** and **refuges** is the better solution. The Alps are as crowded in midsummer as they are in winter (the **Chamonix-Mont Blanc** area is the worst black spot), but you are more or less obliged to go in high season if you want to walk; unreliable weather aside, anywhere above 2000m will be snowbound until the beginning of July. Drivers should remember that some high passes such as the **Col du Galibier** and the **Col de l'Iseran** in the east of the region can remain closed well into June, requiring long detours or excursions into Italy via Alpine tunnels.

ACCOMMODATION PRICE CATEGORIES

Each hotel in this chapter has a symbol which corresponds to one of eight price categories.

① Under 160F	④ 300–400F	⑦ 600–700F
② 160–220F	⑤ 400–500F	⑧ Over 700F
③ 220–300F	⑥ 500–600F	

The prices quoted are for the cheapest available double room in high season, though remember that many of the cheap places will have more expensive rooms with en-suite facilities.

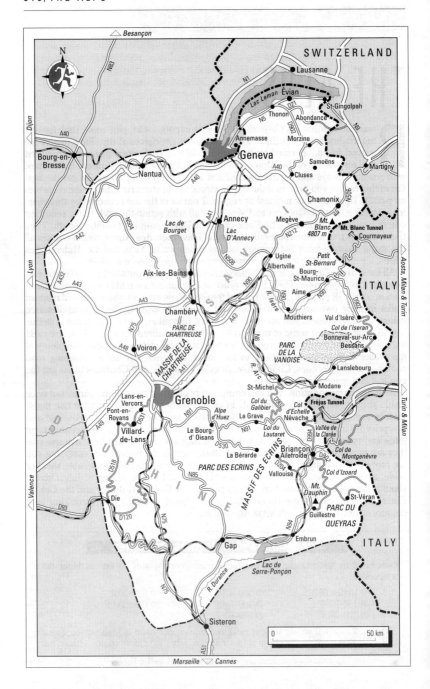

The handful of towns in the Alps offer good facilities for campers and hikers, and often provide attractions of their own. **Grenoble**, an ancient town in a stunning setting, is the economic and intellectual capital of the region, with a lively student population and plenty of nightlife; **Chambéry** and **Annecy** make the most of their spectacular positions; and **Briançon**, the highest town in Europe, is close to three of the parks.

Grenoble

The economic and intellectual capital of the French Alps, **GRENOBLE** is a lively, thriving, modern city, beautifully situated on the Drac and Isère rivers, surrounded by mountains and home to a university of more than 35,000 students. The city's prosperity was originally founded on glove-making, but in the nineteenth century its economy diversified to include mining, cement, paper mills, hydroelectric power (white coal, as they called it) and metallurgy. Today, it is a centre of chemical and electronics industries and nuclear research, with the big, new laboratories of the Atomic Energy Commission on the banks of the Drac.

Grenoble has also been at the forefront of social, environmental and cultural innovation, particularly during the twenty-year mayoralty of Hubert Dubedout, who was killed in a climbing accident in 1986. His Villeneuve housing project (between av Jean-Jaurès and cours de la Libération), though tatty and of ill repute today, started out as an idealistic attempt to provide integrated living space for a complete mix of social classes, including Arab and other immigrant workers, together with open schooling and other community-based programmes. The current mayor, previously Chirac's environment minister, has revived one of Dubedout's ideas in the construction of the city's pride and joy, its pollution-free tram network.

Arrival, information and accommodation

The most interesting sections of the city are easily accessible on foot, just ten minutes from the **gare SNCF** (☎08.36.36.35.35) and **gare routière** down av Félix-Viallet, mainly on the left bank of the Isère, where, not far from place Grenette at 14 rue de la République, you will find the **tourist office** (Mon–Sat 9am–12.30pm & 1.30–6/7pm, Sun 10am–noon; ☎04.76.42.41.41, fax 04.76.51.28.69). Here you can buy copies of the *Guide DAHU*, (25F) a restaurant and nightlife guide compiled by local students and available in English translation, and you'll also find the local SNCF and **public transport** information offices next door: the splendid new trams and the buses each operate on a fixed fare of 7.80F – more economical to buy a carnet of ten or a day pass if you're going to use them regularly. Walkers and climbers should check out the CIMES office, also known as the Bureau Info Montagne (Mon–Fri 9am–noon & 2–6pm, Sat 10am–noon & 2–6pm; ☎04.76.42.45.90), and maybe also the Club Alpin Français at 32 av Félix-Viallet (☎04.76.87.03.73). Good-value **car hire** is available from Self Car, opposite the station at 24 rue Émile Gueymard (☎04.76.50.96.96, fax 04.76.87.37.54), with a ten percent discount if you have the voucher from the tourist office.

For **hotels**, there is the friendly *Hôtel des Patinoires*, 12 rue Marie-Chamoux (☎04.76.44.43.65, fax 04.76.44.44.77; ③), very close to the Palais des Sports. There are plenty of hotels near the train station: *Hôtel Terminus*, 10 Place de la Gare, right opposite the station (☎04.76.87.24.33, fax 04.76.50.38.28; ③) and the nearby *Hôtel des Alpes*, 45 av Félix-Viallet (☎04.76.87.00.71, fax 04.76.56.95.45; ③), both offering comfortable, spacious rooms. The *Bellevue* (☎04.76.46.69.34, fax 04.76.85.20.12; ③) has a better location, as its name suggests, on the corner of quai Stéphane-Jay and rue Belgrade near the *téléférique*. Still in the town centre, the *Grand Hôtel*, 5 rue de la République (☎04.76.44.49.36, fax 04.76.63.14.06; ④), offers comfort in the three-star category. Less

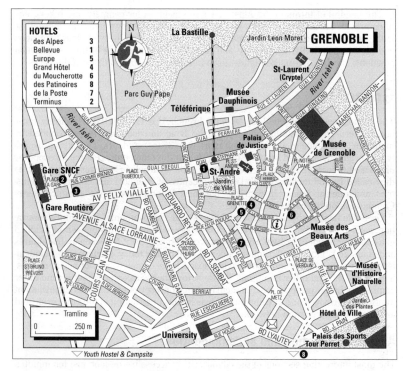

HOTELS

des Alpes	3
Bellevue	1
Europe	5
Grand Hôtel	4
du Moucherotte	6
des Patinoires	8
de la Poste	7
Terminus	2

expensive establishments include the *Hôtel de l'Europe*, 22 place Grenette (☎/fax 04.76.46.16.94, ②) in the city centre, the *Hôtel du Moucherotte*, 1 rue Auguste-Gaché, near place Ste-Claire (☎04.76.54.61.40, fax 04.76.44.62.52; ③); and *Hôtel de la Poste* at 25 rue de la Poste (☎04.76.46.67.25; ①), off place Vaucanson, whose English-speaking *patronne* keeps a friendly but rather old-fashioned establishment.

There's also an HI **youth hostel** at 18 av du Grésivaudan, Échirolles (☎04.76.09.33.52; open year-round), a four-kilometre bus ride south (#8 from cours Jean-Jaurès to La Quinzaine stop). **Campers** should make for the left bank of the Drac, west of town, where there's the campsite *Les Trois Pucelles* 58 rue des Allobroges, in **SEYSSINS** (☎04.76.96.45.73) – about fifteen minutes on the bus.

The city

The best way to start your stay is to take the **téléférique** (9/10/11am–6/7.30pm/midnight; 33F return) from the riverside quai Stéphane-Jay to **Fort de la Bastille** on the steep slopes above the north bank of the Isère. It may be a touristy thing to do, but if you eschew all *téléfériques* in the Alps – and there are hundreds of them – you'll miss out on a lot of spectacular views. The ride is hair-raising, for you are whisked steeply and swiftly into the air in a sort of transparent egg, which allows you to see very clearly how far you would fall in the event of an accident.

Although the fort is of little interest, the **view** is fantastic. At your feet the Isère, milky-grey and swollen with snow-melt, tears at the piles of the old bridges which join the St-Laurent quarter, colonized by Italian immigrants in the nineteenth century, to the nucleus of the medieval town, whose red roofs cluster tightly around the church of St-André. To the east, snowfields gleam in the gullies of the Belledonne massif (2978m). Southeast is Taillefer and south-southeast the dip where the *Route Napoléon* passes over the mountains to Sisteron and the Mediterranean – this is the road Napoléon took after his escape from Elba in March 1815 on his way to rally his forces for the campaign that led to his final defeat at Waterloo. To the west are the steep white cliffs of the Vercors massif; the highest peak, dominating the city, is Moucherotte (1901m). The jagged peaks at your back are the outworks of the Chartreuse massif. Northeast on a clear day you can see the white peaks of Mont Blanc up the deep glacial valley of the Isère, known as La Grésivaudan. It was in this valley that the first French hydroelectric project went into action in 1869. Heading back, you can walk down through the public gardens.

Upstream from the *téléférique* station is the sixteenth-century **Palais de Justice** (open to the public), with **place St-André** and the church of St-André behind. Built in the thirteenth century and heavily restored, the church is of little architectural interest, but the narrow streets leading back towards places Grenette, Vaucanson and Verdun take you through the liveliest and most colourful quarter of the city. Life focuses on a chain of little squares – aux Herbes, Claveyson, de Gordes, Grenette and Notre-Dame – where people congregate at the numerous cafés and restaurants.

Close to place St-André, in the former town hall at 1 rue Hector-Berlioz, in the corner of the Jardin de Ville gardens, is the **Musée Stendhal** (Easter–Oct daily except Mon 2–6pm; Nov–Easter Sat & Sun only; free), with one dusty room of objects associated with the author, who, as Henri Beyle, was born in Grenoble. He spent his childhood in his grandfather's house at 20 Grand-Rue (daily except Mon: 10am–noon & 2–6pm; closed Sept 1–20; free).

Two far more interesting museums are the **Musée de Grenoble,** 5 place de Lavalette by the river (Mon & Thurs–Sun 11am–7pm, Wed 11am–10pm; 25F) and the **Musée Dauphinois,** 30 rue Maurice-Gignoux (daily except Tues: May–Oct 10am–7pm; Nov–Apr 10am–6pm; 20F). The former is an enormous new gallery of mainly contemporary art. The building itself is impressive, and the collection is both stunning and very large for a provincial museum, including some weird and wonderful installations. The latter is across the river and up a cobbled path opposite the St-Laurent footbridge. Housed in the former convent of Ste-Marie-d'en-Haut, it is largely devoted to the history, arts and crafts of the province of Dauphiné – unlike neighbouring Savoie, which was only relinquished by the Italians in 1860, Dauphiné has been French since the fourteenth century. There are exhibits on the life of the mountain people, *les gens de là-haut* ("the people from up there"), who (like most poor mountaineers) were obliged to travel the world as pedlars and knife-grinders. Many, too, were involved in smuggling, and there is a fascinating collection of body-hugging flasks used for contraband liquor. The most unusual section is the *Roman des Grenoblois*, the story of the people of Grenoble told in an excellent audiovisual presentation through the lives of various members of a representative selection of families, ranging from immigrant workers to wealthy industrialists. France's first trade union was established in Grenoble in 1803 by the glove-makers.

If you are interested in early Christian art, it's worth taking a look at the crypt in the church of **Musée Archéologique Église St-Laurent** place St-Laurent (daily except Tues 9am–noon & 2–6pm; 20F), which dates from the Merovingian period and features some beautiful sculpted capitals.

To the south of the old town lies the **Parc Paul-Mistral**, to one side of which is the Hôtel de Ville (1967), one of the earliest of France's now numerous and bold architectural experiments with its public buildings. In the park behind is an earlier and more frivolous structure, an 87-metre concrete tower designed in 1925 by Perret, one of the pioneers of avant-garde French architecture. The concrete looks shabby now and you could hardly call it attractive, but it is bold and unapologetically modern.

Across the road from the town hall, standing among the fine trees of the Jardin des Plantes is the **Muséum d'Histoire Naturelle** (Mon & Wed–Sat 9.30am–noon & 1.30–5.30pm, Sun 2–6pm; 15F). It has a marvellous collection but is very badly displayed: in this case, it includes all the Alpine birds of prey. Reasonably nearby, at 19 rue Hébert, there is the **Musée des Troupes de Montagne**, a small museum devoted to the French mountain regiment, the Chasseurs Alpins (Mon & Wed–Fri 2–5pm; free); at no. 14 you'll find the **Musée de la Résistance et de la Déportation** (daily except Tues 9am–noon & 2–6pm; 20F).

Eating and drinking

Interesting, atmospheric places to drink are easy to find in Grenoble. Places Grenette, St-André and Notre-Dame are full of **café-bars**. *Le Bagatel, Le Perroquet* and the *Café de la Table Ronde* (the second oldest café in France) on place St-André, are particularly popular, especially on sunny evenings. Another good spot is the *Café du Nord*, in nearby place Claveyson. And, if you're feeling nostalgic for a pub and English voices, seek refuge at *Bukana*, on the riverside at 1 quai Créqui. There's a cyber café on rue Bayard just off place Notre-Dame, and *Le Bibliothèque* near the place aux-Herbes is a good late-night bar.

As for **eating**, *Le Tonneau de Diogène*, on place Notre-Dame, is a cheap standby. *Le Couscous*, 19 rue de la Poste (from 38F), has excellent couscous and a wonderful atmosphere created by the enthusiastic owner. The north bank of the river is a continuous line of pizzerias. If you can't decide which one to go for, try the *Notte e Di*, 64 quai Perrière. For a more sophisticated meal, there is no better restaurant than *Le Mal Assis*, 9 rue Bayard (☎04.76.54.75.93; lunch 55F, dinner 120F; closed Sun & Mon), which serves traditional French dishes in simple but elegant surroundings. A good place for classic French dishes is *Le Bistrot Lyonnais*, 168 cours Berriat (☎04.76.21.95.33; menus 110F and 140F; closed Sun eve & Mon). And the *Restaurant de l'Arche*, 4 rue Pierre-Duclot (☎04.76.44.22.62; menu 90–195F; closed Mon & Tues lunch), excels at fish and has some delightful desserts. There's a vegetarian restaurant, *La Mandragore*, 11 rue Marx-Dormoy, on the corner of place St-Bruno (☎04.76.96.18.95, closed Sun & Mon).

The Vercors and Chartreuse massifs

The **Vercors Massif** and **Chartreuse Massif** are very close to Grenoble, particularly the Vercors, which stretches out to the southwest, parallel to the River Drac on the west side of the N75. Chartreuse is northwest of the city, running up the west bank of the River Isère towards Chambéry.

Both ranges are relatively gentle and not too high, so if you're starting your Alpine ventures here, you can use them to break your feet in. The Grenoble CIMES office publishes route descriptions. Neither massif is heavily populated, and the lack of industry – apart from age-old pastoralism – makes them authentic and unspoilt Alpine destinations, popular with all types of energetic outdoor enthusiasts from cavers to mountain bikers.

The Vercors Massif

The **Vercors Massif**, a limestone plateau featuring ridges, valleys and a variety of wildlife, is very pretty and undeveloped, but the only way to get around is to drive or hitch, unless you're walking. CIMES leaflets detail a number of walks of varying difficulty around the area from the simplest and most accessible to St-Nizier, detailed below, to other good but more strenuous walks such as Villard-de-Lans to Claix, near Grenoble (1700m descent; 7hr) and the circuit of Mont Aiguille, starting from Clelles (1hr by train south of Grenoble; 6hr 30min/9hr).

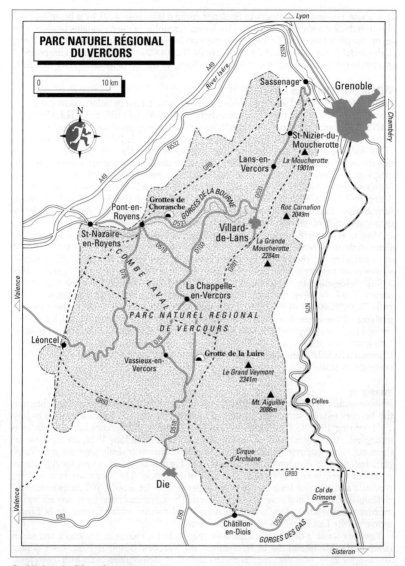

St-Nizier-du-Moucherotte

The easiest of the CIMES walks is a four-hour circular walk to **ST-NIZIER**, just over the rim of the Vercors Massif, with a fantastic view of the whole area. Start by taking bus #5 from place Victor-Hugo in Grenoble and get off in Seyssinet village by the school. For most of the way you follow **GR9** with its red and white waymarks. The path starts about 200m uphill from the school on the right. It is not difficult, but the path crosses the D106 a few times, and the continuation is not always obvious, so it is worth getting the leaflet.

It is about two-and-a-half hours to St-Nizier (return the same way) by a beautiful path through thick woods with long views back over Grenoble to the mountains beyond. The lovely purplish Martagon lily blooms in the woods in early July. For a place to stay, there is the *Hôtel Concorde* (☎04.76.53.42.61, fax 04.76.53.43.28; ③) and a small **campsite**. It is a further three-and-a-half hours (there and back) to the top of **Moucherotte** on GR91.

Villard-de-Lans to La Chapelle

From St-Nizier the road winds up through a steep wooded gorge before coming out into a wide valley full of hay meadows towards **LANS-EN-VERCORS** and **VILLARD-DE-LANS**, 18km southwest of Grenoble. Villard makes a very good base for exploring the Vercors further. There is a **tourist office** (9am–12.30pm & 2–7pm) with information about walks and skiing. **Accommodation** in town includes the *Villa Primerose,* 147 ave des Bains (☎04.76.95.13.17, closed Nov; ③) with a particularly warm welcome and self-catering facilities in a communal kitchen; the inexpensive *Hôtel du Centre,* rue Gambetta (☎04.76.95.14.12; ②; closed Oct), and the smart *Hôtel Le Pré Fleuri,* 509 rue Albert Piétri (☎04.76.95.10.96, fax 04.76.95.56.23; ④; closed May & Oct–Nov). For **food**, *Jack Burger,* 45 rue de la République (☎03.76.95.94.97, open every day) has an interesting selection of gourmet burgers from 40F.

Moving on from Villard, turn right at Villard on the Pont-en-Royans road into the **Gorges de la Bourne**. The gorge becomes rapidly deeper and narrower with the road cut right in under the rocks, the river running far below, and tree-hung cliffs almost shutting out the sky above. Take a left fork here and climb up to a lovely green valley before descending to St-Martin and **LA CHAPELLE**, where there's the reasonably priced *Hôtel du Nord* (☎04.75.48.22.13; ①), and the *Maison de l'Aventure* hostel (☎04.75.48.22.38, fax 04.75.48.21.79; ①); thence the road climbs again to the wide dry **plateau of Vassieux**, bordered to the east by a rocky ridge rising from thick pine forest and to the west by low hills covered with scrubby vegetation. Underground is interesting too: stay on the road to Pont-en-Royans and you will come to the **Grottes de Choranche** (daily 10am–6pm), the most famous, beautiful and tourist-congested of the many caves in the area.

Vassieux

It was around the village of **VASSIEUX**, 10km south of La Chapelle, that the fighters of the Vercors *maquis* suffered a bloody and bitter defeat at the hands of the SS in July 1944. During 1942–43 they had been gradually turning the Vercors into a Resistance stronghold, to the annoyance of the Germans who finally, in June 1944, decided to wipe them out. They encircled and attacked the *maquisards* with vastly superior forces and parachuted an SS division on to Vassieux. The French appealed in vain for Allied support and were very bitter about the lack of response. The Germans took vicious reprisals and, despite their attempts to disperse into the woods, 700 *maquisards* and civilians were killed and several villages razed. The Germans' most ferocious act was to murder the wounded, along with their nurses and doctors, in the **Grotte de la Liure**, a cave off the La Chapelle–Col de Rousset road.

Vassieux itself, a dull little village now rebuilt, has a memorial cemetery and small musum, the **Memorial de la Résistance du Vercors** (summer 10am–6pm; winter 10am–5pm; 25F), with documents, photos and other memorabilia to do with the *maquis* and the battle. In the field outside are the remains of two gliders used by the German paratroops. If you want to **stay,** there's the simple and comfortable *Hôtel La Cornefine* by the roundabout (☎04.75.48.28.57, fax 04.75.48.28.86; ①; restaurant from 75F).

Die to Grimone

From Vassieux, the **Col de Rousset** road winds south through 8km of woods of pine and fir before taking the final steep twisting descent of 10km to **DIE**, with terrific views of the white crags and pinnacles of the southeast end of the massif. Although an attractive little place, Die is worth no more than a brief stop - to sample the local *crémant,* Clairette de Die, which can be tasted and bought in the *caves* surrounding the town. There's a **tourist office** in place St-Pierre (Mon–Sat 9am–12.30pm & 2.30–7pm, Sun 9.30am–12.30pm; ☎04.75.22.03.03). If you do plan to **stay** the night here, there are five **campsites,** the cheapest being the *camping municipal,* or the *Hôtel St-Domingue,* rue Camille Buffardel (☎04.75.22.03.08, fax 04.75.22.24.48; ②; restaurant from 90F).

Six kilometres south along the River Drôme at the **Pont de Quart** the road forks left for **CHÂTILLON,** 6km away – not a bad place to wait on a hot day, for you can swim in the river below the bridge. Châtillon village is lovely, lying in a narrowing valley bottom surrounded by apple and peach orchards, vineyards, walnut trees and fields of lavender; it also has a couple of good **hotels** and a three **campsites.**

From here on, the road enters the sunless trench of the **Gorges des Gats,** winding up between sheer rock walls to **GRIMONE,** a mountain hamlet on the flanks of a grassy valley with fir trees darkening the higher slopes. The **Col de Grimone** is visible above the village. A path cuts across the valley directly to the col from which it's about 7km down to the main Grenoble road, a tarmac trudge alleviated by the view eastwards to the mountains.

The Chartreuse Massif and Grande Chartreuse monastery

The **Chartreuse Massif** stretches north from Grenoble towards Chambéry and, like Vercors, it is not easy to visit without your own vehicle. The landscape, however, is spectacular, and very different to that of the Vercours: precipitous limestone peaks, mountain pastures and thick forest. The **Grande Chartreuse monastery**, the main local landmark, lies up the narrow Gorges des Guiers Mort, southeast of St-Laurent-du-Port. It is not open to visitors, but near **VOIRON** and the village **ST-PIERRE-EN-CHARTREUSE,** there is the **Musée de la Grande Chartreuse,** formerly **La Correrie** monastery, which illustrates the life of the Carthusian order (April–Oct daily 9.30am–noon & 2–6pm; 15F). Every year in July, St-Pierre has a festival devoted to Jacques Brel. **Voiron** is the main town in the area, the **tourist office** is at 58 cours Becquart-Castelban (☎04.76.05.00.38, for more information about the Jacques Brel festival & accommodation). You can also visit the Caves de Chartreuse (Easter to Oct daily 8.30–11.30am & 2–6pm; July–Aug 8.30am–6.30pm; Nov–March Mon–Fri 8.30–11.30am & 2–5.30pm) for a free visit and tasting of the sticky yellow or green liqueur.

Just south of St-Pierre, at the gorge's eastern end, a narrow road leads a couple of kilometres south to the village of **ST-HUGUES.** Its otherwise ordinary-looking **church of St-Hugues** (daily except Tues 9am–noon & 2–7pm; free) has been transformed inside by local artist Jean-Marie Pirot (aka Arcabas), who was originally commissioned to redecorate the interior in 1953 and ended up making it his life's work. His paintings, tapestries, statues and, most notably, the stained glass make an unusual and striking impression and have earned Arcabas and the church a worldwide reputation.

Chambéry

CHAMBÉRY, 55km north of Grenoble, lies just south of the Lac du Bourget in a valley separating the Chartreuse Massif from the Bauges mountains: historically, an important strategic position commanding the entrance to the big Alpine valleys leading to the passes into Italy. The earliest settlement was on the rock of Lemenc, behind the train station; and the church of St-Pierre-de-Lemenc, off boulevard de Lemenc, hides a sixth-century baptistry in its crypt.

The present town grew up around the château built by Count Thomas of Savoie in 1232, when Chambéry became capital of the ancient province, and flourished particularly in the fourteenth century. Although superseded as capital by Turin in 1563, it remained an important commercial and cultural centre and the emotional focus of all French Savoyards: "the winter residence of almost all the nobility of Savoy", Arthur Young reported in 1789, before its mid-nineteenth-century incorporation into France.

The town

Halfway down the broad, leafy boulevard de la Colonne is the splendidly extravagant **Fontaine des Éléphants**, with the heads and shoulders of four large bronze elephants projecting from a stone pediment supporting a tall column, on top of which stands a statue of Comte de Boigne, a native son who made a fortune in the French East India Company in the eighteenth century and spent some of it on his home town. Past this, on the right, and you're at the **Musée Savoisien**, square de Lannoy-de-Bissy (daily except Tues 10am–noon & 2–6pm; 20F), which records the lost rural life of the Savoyard mountain communities. On the first floor are some very lovely paintings by Savoyard primitives and painted wood statues from various churches in the region; up above are tools, carts, hay-sledges, old photos, and some very fine furniture from a house in Bessans, including a fascinating kitchen range made of wood and lined with *lauzes* (slabs of schist).

Next to the museum, in the enclosed little place Métropole, the **cathedral** has a handsome, though much restored, Flamboyant facade. The inside is painted in elaborate nineteenth-century *trompe l'œil*, imitating the twisting shapes and whorls of the Flamboyant style. During the Revolution it became the seat of the National Assembly of the Allobroges in a Revolutionary attempt to revive pre-Roman tribal identity.

A passage leads from the square to **rue de la Croix-d'Or**, with numerous restaurants and the Italianate **Théâtre Charles Dullin**, named after the avant-garde director who was born in the region. To the right, there's the long, rectangular **place St-Léger**, with a fountain and more cafés, where street musicians and players perform on summer evenings. Rousseau and Mme de Warens lived here in 1735, and also had a country cottage, Les Charmettes, just 2km south of the town on the rustic chemin des Charmettes. It's now the **Musée Jean-Jacques Rousseau** (daily except Tues: April–Sept 10am–noon & 2–6pm; Oct–March until 4.30pm; 20F), containing personal possessions of the famous couple.

Towards the further end of the square, the town's smartest street, **rue de Boigne**, leads back to the Elephant Fountain. Past this intersection, on the left, a narrow medieval lane, rue Basse-du-Château, brings you out beneath the elegant apse of the **Ste-Chapelle**, the castle chapel, whose lancet windows and star vaulting are the building's best feature. It was built to house the Holy Shroud, that much-venerated and today highly controversial piece of linen brought back from the Crusades and reputed to bear the image of the dead Christ. The dukes took it with them to Turin, where it still lies in the cathedral. The entrance to the **Château des Ducs de Savoie** (guided tours March–May, Oct & Nov Sat 2.15pm, Sun 3.30pm; June & Sept 2 daily; July & Aug 5 daily; 20F) is on the left. A massive and imposing structure, it was the home of the dukes of Savoie until they transferred to Turin, and is now occupied by the *préfecture*, although you can still visit the fine chapel.

Practicalities

The **gare SNCF** is on rue Sommeiller, 500m north of the old town, with the **gare routière** just outside in place de la Gare. Five minutes' walk away at no. 24 on the tree-lined boulevard de la Colonne, where all the **city buses** stop, is the **tourist office** (June 15–Sept 15 Mon–Sat 9am–12.30pm & 1.30–6.30pm, Sun 10am–12.30pm; Sept 16–June 14 Mon–Sat 9am–noon & 2–6pm; ☎04.79.33.42.47, fax 04.79.85.71.39).

Inexpensive **accommodation** is not hard to find. Try the *Hôtel du Château*, 37 rue Jean-Pierre Veyrat (☎04.79.69.48.78; ①); the *Home Savoyard*, 15 place St-Léger (☎04.79.33.47.80; ②); or *des Voyageurs*, 3 rue Doppet (☎04.79.33.57.00; ①). More expensive are the *Revard*, 41 av de la Boisse (☎03.79.62.04.64, fax 04.79.96.37.26; ④; restaurant from 62F), and the *Hôtel les Princes*, 4 rue de Boigne (☎04.79.33.45.36, fax 04.79.70.31.47; ④). But for rural peace and a lovely view there's no better than the *Hôtel aux Pervenches* (☎04.79.33.34.26, fax 04.79.60.02.52; ①; good restaurant from 95F), in the village of **LES CHARMETTES**, where Rousseau used to live, 2km south of the centre. The nearest **campsite** is *Le Nivolet* (☎04.79.85.47.79) at **BASSENS**, reached on bus #C, direction "Albertville", from the tourist office.

You'll find good **food** at restaurants and cheap pizzerias around the rue de la Croix-d'Or. The *Café chez Chabert* (closed Sun, Mon & Aug), 41 rue Basse-du-Château, has wonderful meals at amazingly cheap prices, from 38F, and the *Restaurant La Vanoise*, 44 rue Pierre-Lanfrey, offering as fine a meal as you'll find in town, with menus between 90F and 170F, and a terrace during summertime.

Annecy

At the edge of the turquoise Lac d'Annecy, bounded to the east by the turreted peaks of La Tournette and to the west by the long wooded ridge of Le Semnoz, **ANNECY** is one of the most popular resort towns of the French Alps. Historically, it enjoyed a brief flurry of importance in the early sixteenth century, when Geneva opted for the Reformation and the fugitive Catholic bishop decamped here with a train of ecclesiastics and a prosperous, cultivated elite.

Arrival, information and accommodation

The **gare SNCF** is northwest of the centre, five minutes' walk north of the rue Royale. The road's continuation is the arcaded **rue Paquier**, which contains the modern shopping precinct of **Centre Bonlieu**, housing the **tourist office** (July & Aug Mon–Sat

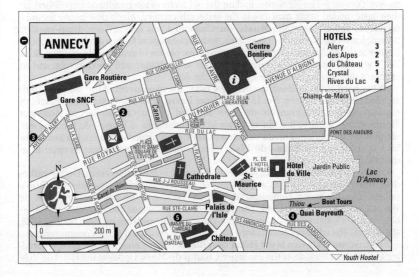

9am–6.30pm, Sun 9am–noon & 1.45–6.30pm; rest of year Mon–Sat 9am–noon & 1.45–6.30pm, Sun 9am–noon & 3–6pm; ☎04.50.45.00.33), which can help you find accommodation and will supply an excellent 1:25,000 map (57F) of the Annecy area, showing walking trails. There's **bike rental** from Sports Passion, 3 av de Parmelan (there are many places to rent bikes around the lake - the tourist office has a complete list), and round-the-lake **boat trips** stopping off at various points along the lake – expect to pay around 15F per hour – from Compagnie des Bateaux or Bateaux Dupraz by the mouth of the Thiou canal.

The best inexpensive **hotels** are the *Rive du Lac*, 6 rue des Marquisats (☎04.50.51.32.85, fax 04.50.45.77.40; ①), and the *Crystal Hôtel*, 20 rue Louis-Chaumontet (☎04.50.57.33.90, fax 04.50.67.86.43; ②). More upmarket options include the *Hôtel Alery*, 5 av d'Alery (☎04.50.45.24.75, fax 04.50.51.26.90; ③), the *Hôtel des Alpes*, 12 rue de la Poste (☎04.50.45.04.56, fax 04.50.45.12.38; ③), and, close to the old château, the charming *Hôtel du Château*, 16 rampe du Château (☎04.50.45.27.66, fax 04.50.52.75.26; ③), whose terrace overlooks the town. There is a modern **youth hostel** a short distance from the centre, just uphill past the Centre Hospitalier at 4 rte du Semnoz, overlooking the lake (☎04.50.45.33.19, fax 04.50.52.77.52), follow the signs to Semnoz. The **camping municipal**, *Le Belvedere* (☎04.50.45.48.30) is situated off bd de la Corniche – turn right up the lane opposite Chemin du Tillier; it's on the left past the *Hôtel du Belvédère*. Other sites exist all around the shore of the lake.

The town

The most interesting part of Annecy lies at the foot of the castle mound, a warren of lanes, passages and arcaded houses, below and between which flow branches of the **Canal du Thiou**, draining the lake into the River Fier. The houses, canalside railings and numerous restaurants and cafés are stacked with displays of geraniums and petunias – picture-book pretty and inevitably full of tourists.

From rue de l'Isle on the canal's south bank, the narrow Rampe du Château leads up to the **château**, former home of the counts of Genevois and the dukes of Nemours, a junior branch of the house of Savoy. There has been a castle on this site from the eleventh century. The Nemours, finding the old fortress too rough and unpolished for their taste, added living quarters in the sixteenth century, which now house the miscellaneous collections of the **Musée du Château** (daily except Tues: 10am–noon & 2–6pm; June–Sept no lunch break; 30F), with archeological finds from Roman Boutae, Bronze and Iron Age metalwork with comparative photos of similar still-surviving skills like scythe- and axe-making, Savoyard popular art, furniture and woodcarving, and an excellent display illustrating the geology of the Alps.

At the base of the château is **rue Ste-Claire**, the main street of the old town, with arcaded shops and houses. No. 18 is the **Hôtel Favre**, where in 1606 Antoine Favre, an eminent lawyer, and François de Sales founded the literary-intellectual *Académie Florimontane* "because the Muses thrive in the mountains of Savoie". At the west end of the street is its original medieval gateway. Down at the canalside, there is a good view back to the grand old **Palais de l'Isle** (prison, mint and courtroom in its time) from the bridge.

On rue J-J-Rousseau, running parallel to the canal, is the uninteresting Gothic **cathedral**, where Rousseau sang as a chorister; just past it is an eighteenth-century **bishop's palace**, now the police commissariat, built on the site of the house where Mme de Warens, Rousseau's lover, lived. The 16-year-old Rousseau, on the run from his miserable engraver's apprenticeship in Geneva, came to lodge with her on Palm Sunday 1728; she was 28. His admirers have placed his bust in the courtyard of the commissariat.

Five minutes' walk east is the **Hôtel de Ville**, backed by shady public gardens, leading to the lakeside lawns of the extensive **Champ de Mars**. Opposite the Hôtel de Ville is the fifteenth-century **church of St-Maurice**, originally built for a Dominican convent and dedicated to the commander of a Theban legion sent to put down a rebellion in the late third century. Converted to Christianity, he and his soldiers refused to sacrifice to the pagan gods of Rome and were put to death for their scruples. Inside the church, the apse, with attractive Flamboyant windows, is badly distorted, the walls leaning outwards to an alarming degree; on the left of the choir is a fine fresco dated 1438, all in tones of grey.

Eating and drinking

Among Annecy's many **restaurants**, the *Restaurant La Cave*, 10 faubourg des Annonciades (closed Nov, Tues & Wed lunch out of season), and the *Café des Arts*, 4 passage de l'Isle, are both pleasantly situated in the heart of the old town and feature menus from 62F. Also nearby is the *Taverne du Fréti*, 12 rue Ste-Claire (closed Mon & lunchtimes except in school hols), which specializes in the region's cheeses and includes *raclettes*, a rather complicated method of grilling and melting half-rounds of cheese to mouthwatering effect. For a drink or classic brasserie fare, there is no better than the *Taverne de Maître Kanter*, overlooking the most touristy stretch of the canal close to the lake. Or for good and unpretentious homely cooking, with some regional specialities, try *Le Faucigny*, 17 rue Filaterie, behind the cathedral (closed Sat eve & Sun lunch). *Le Belvédère*, on rte du Semnoz, is much more expensive (upwards of 200F) but the food is classic and the view over the lake unbeatable (☎04.50.45.04.90; closed Sun lunch, Mon & Nov). There's also a cluster of good Italian restaurants in rue du Pâquier, and down a little alleyway is *Le Phenx Imperial*, which serves inexpensive traditional Vietnamese food.

Around Annecy

While Annecy's high-season crowds may be bearable for only a day or two, the town's hinterland offers a number of agreeable ways to stretch your eyes and legs. As well as the **boat tours** mentioned (see above), cycling is an enjoyable means of appreciating Lac Annecy. The forty-kilometre road circuit of the lake is a very popular Sunday morning activity among sporty Annéciens and a traffic-free **cycle route** follows the west bank of the lake. The surrounding hills offer walking and mountain-biking excursions (as well as more specialized pursuits) to suit all. The ascent of **La Tournette** (2351m) is one of the less demanding walks to be found in the forested **Semnoz mountains** on the lake's west side.

Ten kilometres west of Annecy, the **Gorges du Fier** and nearby Château Montrottier combine both natural and historical spectacle within a short distance of each other; and, if you're leaving Annecy to the north, the **Ponts de la Caille** are also worthy of a passing inspection.

Around the lake

Although a road rings Lake Annecy, a far more tranquil way of appreciating the lakeside is aboard one of the frequent boats that depart from Annecy's canalside port, with the possibility of stopovers or returning later in the day. The lakeside village of **MENTHON-ST-BERNARD** sits on the east shore. Signposted just out of Menthon-St-Bernard is the striking edifice of **Château de Menthon** (May, June & Sept Thurs, Sat & Sun 2–6pm; July & Aug daily noon–6pm; 28F). Inhabited since the twelfth century and birthplace of St Bernard (the patron saint of mountaineers for having established hospices on the Franco-Swiss mountain pass that now bears his name), the fortress was extensively renovated in the last century in the romantic Gothic-revival style and possesses a fine collection of period furniture and views across the lake back to Annecy. By the lakeside, the *Buvette du Port* offers *plats du jour* for around 50F.

TALLOIRES, also a couple of kilometres down the road, is a lovely lakeside village. Its ninth-century Benedictine abbey is now the luxurious *Hotel de l'Abbaye* (☎04.50.60.77.33, fax 04.50.60.78.81; ⑦; closed Nov–April 14), one of the many comfortable and pricey seasonal hotels the village sports.

On the west side of the lake, the village of **DUINGT** occupies a peninsula where there are two more 1000-year-old **châteaux**, one in ruins and the other partly rebuilt. Like Menthon-St-Bernard and Talloires, it boasts a lakeside beach and gives the opportunity to rent pleasure craft. The town has a few good-value hotels such as the *Hôtel Le Chalet* (☎04.50.68.66.51; ②; restaurant from 90F); or for a pricier and more tranquil overnight stay, head 7km south to the village of **DOUSSARD**, where the *Hôtel Marceau*, 115 rue de la Chappelière (☎04.50.44.30.11, fax 04.50.44.39.44; ⑤), offers very comfortable accommodation in attractive surroundings.

La Tournette and the Semnoz mountains

Experienced hill-walkers wanting a stiff but straightforward mountain ascent could tackle **La Tournette** (2351m), which dominates the east side of the lake with its patchy snowfields and crenellated summits. A road just north of Talloires crosses the **Col de la Forclaz**, doubles back to the left before the hamlet of **MONTMIN**, and ends in a steep but drivable track up to the **Col de l'Aulp**, less than 1000m from the summit. From the col, the climb is immediate, steep and clear, leading to the **refuge**, where late snow and increasing exposure demand extra care. Some scrambling (with fixed chains and handrails) is required to take you up to a broad, exposed shoulder. You cross some scree slopes and after a little more scrambling, arrive at the summit. To the east, the **Chaîne des Aravis** stretches before the snowbound massif of Mont Blanc on the horizon, just 50km away, while in the other direction the turquoise lake and Annecy itself lie at your feet.

Facing La Tournette on the lake's opposite shore, the wooded ridges of the **Semnoz mountains** offer less radical hiking. From the village of Duingt, a four-hour walk leads southwards up the Taillefer ridge, involving just over 300m of ascent to the 765-metre summit of **Taillefer** itself. From the town church follow the signs for **Grotte de Notre Dame du Lac**, a steep walk up the ridge, and follow the red and yellow markers thereafter. Towards the summit of Taillefer, there is some scrambling, but nothing too difficult, and 1500m after the peak the path turns round and returns north via the hamlet of **LES MAISONS**.

The highest peak in the Semnoz is the **Crêt de Châtillon**, 16km directly south of Annecy along the D41. At 1699m it offers panoramic views, most impressively east past La Tournette towards Mont Blanc. A twenty-minute walk across meadows from the road's highest point leads to the cross on the summit and an orientation table pointing out the surrounding features.

The Gorges du Fier and Pont de la Caille

The River Fier, which trickles out of the lake through Annecy's picturesque canals, has cut a narrow crevice through the limestone rock at the **Gorges du Fier** (daily mid-March to mid-Oct 9am–noon & 2–6pm; mid-June to mid-Sept 9am–7pm; 28F). Signposted off the D14 at Lovagny, a footpath leads down into the 300-metre-long gorge which is traversed along a high-level walkway pinned to the gorgeside. As you pass by the gorge, you'll catch glimpses of the **Château de Montrottier** (guided visits late March to mid-Oct 9–11.30am & 2–5.30pm; 28F), which can be reached by continuing along the path for another 3km or by road from the car park. The castle, which dates from the thirteenth century, possesses an eclectic collection of furniture, earthenware and lace as well as exotic objects from former French colonies in West Africa and the Far East, amassed during the last century by one Léon Mares.

Sixteen kilometres north of Annecy, just after the N201 Geneva road parts from the autoroute, the highway spectacularly bridges the gorge of the River Usses, 140m below. Known as the **Pont de la Caille**, the present bridge was built in 1925, at which time it possessed one of the longest single spans in Europe. Next to it is the stunning spectacle of the original bridge, built under the orders of the King of Sardinia, Charles Albert, in 1839, and now disused. Its castellated towers, supported by two dozen cables, are an impressive example of bold, mid-nineteenth-century engineering.

Briançon and the Écrins region

BRIANÇON, an imposing fortified town on a rocky height above the valleys of the Durance and Guisane, some 10km from the Italian border, guards the road to the desolate and windswept **Col de Montgenèvre**, one of the oldest and most important passes into Italy. Originally a Gallic settlement, the town was fortified by the Romans to guard their *Mons Matrona* road from Milan to Vienne. During the Middle Ages, it was the capital of the *république des escartons*, a federation of mountain communities grouped together for mutual defence and the preservation of their liberties and privileges. But, in marked contrast to the relatively untouristy Queyras, Briançon and the other towns and villages on this side of the **Parc National des Écrins** are crawling with people in summer.

The **old town**, mainly eighteenth-century, is enclosed within another set of Vauban's walls. If you come in a car the best thing is to stop at the **Champ de Mars** at the top of the hill and look around from there. You enter the walls by the **Porte Pignerol**. In front of you the narrow main street, bordered by ancient houses, tips steeply downhill. It is known as the *grande gargouille* because of the stream running down the middle. To your right is the sturdy, plain **collegiate church**, designed under the supervision of Vauban, again with an eye to defence. Beyond it there is a fantastic **view** from the walls, especially on a clear starry night, when the snows on the surrounding barrier of mountains give off a silvery glow. Vauban's **citadel** above the Porte Pignerol, the highest point of the fortifications, can be visited (guided tours Jul–Aug daily 3pm).

Practicalities

Briançon's **tourist office** is in the place du Temple close to the Porte Pignerol gateway onto the Champ de Mars (Mon–Sat 9am–noon & 1.30–6.30pm, Sun 9am–noon & 2–6pm; ☎04.92.21.08.50, fax 04.92.20.56.45). The **mountain guides office** is in Parc Chancel (☎04.92.20.15.73). The Maison du Parc National des Écrins is in Place Médecin-Général-Blanchard (☎04.92.21.42.15). For places to **stay**, try the *Hôtel aux Trois Chamois* in the Champ de Mars (☎04.92.21.02.29, fax 04.92.23.45.89; ②; *demi-pension* available). Alternatively, there's the modern *Hôtel de Paris* (☎04.92.20.15.30, fax 04.92.20.30.82; ②; good restaurant from 45F) near the station or, better, the *Edelweiss* at 32 av de la République (☎04.92.21.02.94, fax 04.92.21.22.55; ②), on the main road down to the new town. There's a very nice **youth hostel** at Le Bez (Serre-Chevalier) (☎04.92.24.74.54, fax 04.92.24.83.39; ①), 8km north on the main Grenoble road – hitchable and also served by local buses. The nearest **campsite** is *Camping des 5 Vallées* (☎04.92.21.06.27) at St Blaise, 2km from town. There is also a gîte d'étape at **Le Fontenil**, *Le Petit Phoque*, (☎03.92.20.07.27) 2km along the Montgenèvre road.

As for **eating**, the old town is full of wonderful Italian cafés, with delicious cakes and pizzas and there are plenty of reasonably priced restaurants such as *Le Pied de la*

Gargouille, 64 Grande-Rue, opposite the library (closed Wed), or the *Restaurant Le Passé Simple*, 3 rue Porte-Méane (closed Sun eve & Mon), both with menus for around 68F.

The Clarée valley

For a really beautiful day excursion from Briançon, head for the valley of the **River Clarée**. Without your own transport, you'll have to hitch or walk, but that should be no hardship because the scenery is truly magnificent.

Leave Briançon by the Montgenèvre road and take the left fork after 2km. A lane follows the wooded river bank in the bottom of a narrow ravine parallel to the Italian frontier. On foot you could follow the **GR5**, which passes through the main villages. If you want to spend a night up here, the depopulated and half-ruined hamlet of **PLAMPINET** has both hotel and hostel-type **accommodation** in a vast renovated farm, *La Cleida* (☎04.92.21.32.48; ①; June 15–Sept 15; Christmas & Feb school hols) as well as rooms at the *Auberge de la Clarée* by the bridge (☎04.92.21.37.71; ②). And there is more at **NÉVACHE**, where the valley widens. There's already been a good deal of holiday development here, though the old village nucleus of wide-roofed houses still huddles protectively around the **church** – this is worth a look for its carving, Baroque altarpiece, and a few items in the treasury, including some eleventh-century doors. In addition to the hotels, there are plenty of **gîtes** including *Le Creux des Souches* (☎04.92.21.16.34).

The finest country is beyond Névache towards the head of the valley, where in May the meadows are running with snow melt and carpeted with crocuses, and fat marmots whistle from the rocks. Six kilometres past the village, there are more **refuges,** including two by the first bridge – *Fontcouverte* and *La Fruitière* – another at the end of the road, as well as the CAF *Refuge des Drayères* on the slopes of Mont Thabor (☎04.92.21.36.01), none of which are open for much more than the summer season. A full list of refuges and gîtes with a map of their locations is available from the tourist office at Briançon.

The Parc National des Écrins

The **Parc National des Écrins** covers 93,000 hectares (230,000 acres) of Alpine terrain, some 50km southeast of Grenoble and 20km west of Briançon, its highest peaks rising to around 4100m in the **Massif de Pelvoux** in the north of the park. The easiest route into the park is from Argentières-la-Bessée, a scruffy, depressed little place, 16km south of Briançon. From here a small road cuts west into the valley towards Vallouise, with the ice-capped monster of **Mont Pelvoux** itself (3946m) rearing in front of you all the way. It's terrain for serious climbers and walkers.

The Vaudois and Les Vigneaux

The first place you come to on the road into the park from Argentières is **LA BÂTIE**, where there are remains of the so-called **Mur des Vaudois**. The origins of the wall are uncertain: it was probably built either to keep out companies of marauding soldiers-turned-bandits, or to control the spread of plague in the fourteenth century. The wall has nothing to do with the Vaudois ("Waldensians" in English), a religious sect founded in the late twelfth century by Pierre Valdo, a merchant from Lyon, who preached against worldly wealth and the corruption of the clergy. Practising as he preached, he gave his wealth to the poor. Excommunicated in 1186, the Vaudois came more and more to deny the authority of the Church, and they sought refuge from persecution in the remote mountain valleys of Pelvoux, especially in the area around Vallouise and Argentières. Their numbers were also probably augmented by refugees from the Inquisition's persecutions of the Cathars in Languedoc.

There was a crop of executions for sorcery in the early fifteenth century, and many of the victims were probably Vaudois, burnt to death in wooden cabins built for this purpose. In 1488, Charles VIII launched a full-scale crusade against them. There is a spot west of Ailefroide (see below), known as **Baume Chapelue**, where they were smoked out by the military and butchered. After the Revocation of the Edict of Nantes, they were finally exterminated in the eighteenth century, when 8000 troops went on the rampage, creating total desolation and "leaving neither people nor animals".

On the right, a couple of kilometres beyond La Bâtie, the village of **LES VIGNEAUX** shrugs off such a past: a lovely place, surrounded by apple orchards and backed by the fierce crags of Montbrison. The **church** has a fine old door and lock under a vaulted porch. Beside it on the exterior wall of the church are two bands of paintings depicting the Seven Deadly Sins. In the upper band, the sins are representations of men and women riding various beasts (a lion, hound and a monkey) and chained by the neck. A man carrying a leg of mutton and drinking wine from a flask represents Gluttony; a woman with rouged cheeks, green stockings and displaying an enticing expanse of thigh represents Lust. In the lower band they are all getting their comeuppance, writhing in the agonies of hellfire.

Vallouise

VALLOUISE lies under a steep wooded spur at the junction of two valleys, the Gyrond (or Gyr, as it is called upstream of Vallouise) and the Gérendoine, about 10km from Argentière. The great glaciered peaks visible up the latter valley are Les Bans; up in front is Mont Pelvoux. The nucleus of the old village – narrow lanes between sombre stone chalets – is again its **church**, fifteenth-century with a characteristic tower and steeple and a sixteenth-century porch on pink marble pillars. A fresco of the Adoration of the Magi adorns the tympanum above the door, itself a magnificent object, with carved Gothic panels along the top and an ancient lock-and-bolt with a chimera's head. Remains of an enormously long-legged figure, partially painted over, cover the end wall of the apse. Inside are some more frescoes, and at the back of the church six naive statues of painted wood.

The **GR54,** which does the circuit of the Écrins park, passes through Vallouise: the stage on from here to Le Monetier via **Lac de l'Eychauda** is one of the best. Another good walk is to the hamlet of **PUY AILLAUD**, high on the west flank of the Gyr valley. The path starts just to the right of the church and zigzags up the steep slope behind it with almost aerial views of the valley beneath.

Vallouise has a **campsite** and some **gîtes**, and several **hotels**: the *Edelweiss* is the least expensive (☎04.92.23.38.58; ②; Dec 20–May 15 & June–Sept), but all rooms in the village are likely to be full in July and August. The Vallouise Maison du Parc des Écrins provides **hiking information** and there is a **tourist office** in place de l'Eglise (☎04.92.23.36.12). There is a minibus service as far as Ailefroide in summer, starting from the bar next to the *Edelweiss* hotel; to walk takes two hours or so.

Ailefroide

The lane that continues another 6km up to **AILEFROIDE** is absolutely spectacular, as is the site of Ailefroide itself, overwhelmed by the daunting ridges, peaks and glaciers of Pelvoux and the **Barre des Écrins**, at 4102m the highest summit in the massif. The place is really no more than a huge campsite with a couple of shops and a climbing centre and is, for that reason, not a particularly pleasant place to stay. In July and August it is overrun with climbers and walkers, but it is easy to understand why they are attracted by this magnificent scenery. And it becomes even more magnificent as you climb beyond Ailefroide towards the end of the road at the Pré du Madame Carle and the old Refuge Cézanne.

SKIING THE ALPS: THE RESORTS

Skiing in the French Alps is based on resorts that are either purpose-built or have been ruthlessly modernized. It's a highly organized industry, and you can ski away from your front door in the morning and ski straight back at night, rarely having to queue much along the way. The disadvantage is that these resorts offer little else. Many are astonishingly ugly functionalist brutes isolated in the middle of open snowfields – even worse if you see them in summer – which offer nothing in the way of après-ski and often little entertainment at all. There's certainly none of the alpine atmosphere here that you might associate with Austria, for example.

What you get instead at the best of the resorts is a series of vast linked territories with some of the best high-altitude skiing in Europe. At **Val d'Isère** or **Chamonix**, you can at least get some of the atmosphere of older-established resorts as well, though both are too large to be at all picturesque. Val d'Isère is very British-oriented in the ski season and one of the liveliest resorts in France, with a magnificent ski terrain linked to **Tignes** (among the ugliest of the resorts), and endless challenges and off-piste possibilities, plus impressive new facilities built for the Olympics – the downhill and other blue riband events were held here. Chamonix is bigger still, with even more going on, but as a place to ski is definitely less attractive; the local pass covers a wide area, but it's very un-French in the lack of links between ski areas and relatively awkward transport. The other obvious choice is **Les Trois Vallées** – Courchevel, Méribel and Val Thorens/Les Menuires – which claims to be *le plus grand domaine skiable du monde*. ("the biggest skiing area in the world"). This may be true, but it often seems less exciting than the Val d'Isère area. Of the resorts, **Courchevel** (actually four separate villages at different heights) is the most glamorous; **Méribel**, in the central valley, is the best placed but full of British yuppies in season; **Val Thorens** and **Les Menuires** are the ugly ducklings in terms of both architecture and cachet. Of the smaller resorts, the pick are probably **Les Arcs**, cleverly designed with varied terrain but no walking at all; **Flaine**, especially good for beginners; **La Plagne**, one of the less ugly modern places with a vast area, though no great challenges; and **L'Alpe d'Huez** and **Valmorel**, among the newest and prettiest developments.

At any of these places you can simply turn up, buy a pass (90–200F a day, 450–800F a week) and rent equipment for a day. If you want to stay longer you'll almost certainly get a better deal by arranging a package before you leave – and accommodation can often be very hard to arrange on the spot.

The classic walk to do is the steep climb to the CAF Refuge du Glacier Blanc (☎04.92.23.50.24) right beside the beetling glacier, but it can be a real circus on a summer's day. Quieter, and a good deal longer, is the approach to the CAF Refuge du Sélé (04.92.23.39.49) and the Pointe du Sélé due west of Ailefroide. But it cannot be overemphasized that this is not afternoon-strollers' territory. The best guide is: if you haven't done it before, don't do it.

La Bérarde

To reach **LA BÉRARDE**, right in the midst of the park's mightiest peaks at the end of the Vénéon valley, you leave the road from Grenoble some 6km after Le Bourg-d'Oisans (see below). A tiny hamlet and mountaineering centre 38km up a very narrow lane, La Bérarde has a CAF refuge (☎04.76.79.53.83; April–Sept), mountain rescue base and the small *Hôtel Tairraz* with rooms and dormitories (☎04.76.79.53.46; ①; late May to late Sept; restaurant from 90F). There are plenty of accessible valley walks without the need to risk your neck, including the approach to the back of the magnificent, near-4000-metre bulk of **La Meije**, with its dazzling glacier, the **Glacier Carré**.

North of the Écrins: Alpe d'Huez, the Col du Lautaret, the Galibier and beyond

Connecting Grenoble to Briançon, the **N91** twists through the precipitous valley of the Romanche and over the **Col du Lautaret** (2058m), which is kept open all year round and served regularly by the Grenoble–Briançon bus.

The first major settlement on the route, **LE BOURG-D'OISANS**, 20km southeast of Grenoble, is of no great interest in itself, but it's a good place to catch your breath and pick up information from the **tourist office** on quai Girard, by the river in the middle of town (Mon–Sat 9am–noon & 2–6pm; ☎04.76.80.03.25, fax 04.76.80.10.38) and the **park information centre** on avenue Gambetta (June–Aug Mon–Fri 10am–noon & 2–5pm). There are also numerous places to **stay**, with a **camping municipal** on rue Humbert near the town centre and a concentration of sites across the river on the Alpe d'Huez road. Among the better-value **hotels** are *Beau Rivage* (☎04.76.80.03.19, fax 04.76.80.00.77; ③; good restaurant from 75F), the *Hôtel des Alpes* on the main road (☎04.76.80.00.16, fax 04.76.79.15.13; ②; restaurant from 68F), and the *Hôtel Le Florentin* on rue Thiers (☎04.76.80.01.61, fax 04.76.80.05.49; ③; restaurant from 98F). If you like the idea of cycling in sharp mountain air, **bikes** can be rented from Cycles d'Oisans on rue Viennois – not such a crazy undertaking as you might think, for if you keep to the valley bottoms the gradients aren't too fearsome.

L'Alpe d'Huez

One place you're unlikely to be cycling to is the ski resort of **L'ALPE D'HUEZ**, signposted just outside Le Bourg. It is situated more than a vertical kilometre above the valley floor, and the eleven-kilometre road which crawls up the valley side has often been a stage in the Tour de France. As you ascend through the 21 hairpins, you get a fine view of the acutely crumpled strata of rock exposed by passing glaciers on the south side of the Romanche valley. Undoubtedly a skier's paradise in winter, the purpose-built resort itself has little character in July and August, when it's only partially open. The extensive network of *télécabines*, extending as far as the 3327-metre **Pic du Lac Blanc**, at the bottom of the Chaîne des Rousses ridge north of the resort, does support some summertime skiing, but they can also be used to undertake some superb **high mountain walks**. Two recommended ones, detailed in the map *L'Oisans au bout des pieds* (15F from the tourist office), are the eight-kilometre Lac Blanc and Refuge de la Fare walk, which winds through the bleak wilderness past the lakes encircling the Dôme des Petites Rousses to the east of the glacier-clad *chaîne*, or the less exposed ten-kilometre hike to the gorges of the Sarennes valley to the east of the resort along the GR54. Both walks will require the *IGN 3335 Est 1: 50,000* map. A narrow and impressively scenic road through the Sarennes valley also offers an alternative descent back to the Romanche valley floor when the Col de Sarennes is free of snow. There is a **tourist office** in the Maison de l'Alpe (☎04.76.11.44.44), for information about accommodation and walks.

La Grave and the Col du Lautaret

A few kilometres out of Le Bourg, the ascent into the **Gorges de l'Infernet** commences as the slate-black valley walls close around you, broadening out again as you cross the Barrage du Lac du Chambon, where roads diverge to the resort of Les Deux-Alpes and the Col de Sarennes to the north. Continuing towards La Grave you'll pass two waterfalls issuing from the north side of the valley: early summer runoff will enhance the slender, 300-metre plume of the **Cascade de la Pisse** and, 6km further on, a near-vertical fall of churning white water, the **Saut de la Pucelle**, gives practitioners of the new waterfall-abseiling craze something to think about.

LA GRAVE, 26km from Le Bourg at the foot of the Col du Lautaret, faces the majestic glaciers of the north side of **La Meije**. It's a good base for walking: the **GR54** climbs up to Le Chazelet on the slopes northwest of the village and continues to the **Plateau de Paris** and the **Lac Noir**, which numerous walkers recommend for its breathtaking views of La Meije. A similar and less energetic appreciation of these stunning vistas can be made by taking the **cable car** close to the 3200-metre summit of Le Rateau, just west of La Meije (late June to early Sept; 105F return), a 35-minute ride that's very good value for money when you consider the view of the barely accessible interior of the Écrins is normally seen by only the most intrepid mountain-walkers.

From La Grave it's only 11km to the top of the **Col du Lautaret**, a pass that's been in use for centuries. The Roman road from Milan to Vienne crossed it, and its name comes from the small temple (*altaretum*) the Romans built to placate the deity of the mountains. They called it *collis de altareto*. Around the col is a huge expanse of meadow long known to botanists for its glorious variety of alpine flowers, seen at their best in mid-July. There is the **Jardin Alpin** right on the col, maintained by the University of Grenoble (daily: June 25–Sept 5 8am–noon & 2–6pm; 25F), which includes plants from mountain ranges throughout the world. This is a great spot for picnicking or lounging while waiting for a ride, for the view into the glaciers hanging off La Meije is intoxicating. Indeed, on a clear sunny day the dazzling luminosity of the ice and the burning intensity of the sky above are such that you can hardly bear to look.

The Galibier and Valloire

Turn north at Lauteret and you're on your way to the even higher **Col du Galibier** (no public transport), which is closed by snow from mid-October to mid-June – sometimes the snow lingers longer, making life for riders in the Tour de France yet more hellish. The road to the **Galibier** is a tremendous haul up to 2556m, utterly bare and wild, with the huge red-veined peak of the Grand Galibier rearing up on the right and a fearsome spiny ridge blocking the horizon beyond. The pass used to mark the frontier between France and Savoie, and you can see fine views of Mont Blanc to the north. A monument on the south side of the col commemorates Henri Desgranges, founder of the Tour de France. Crossing the col is one of the most gruelling stages in the race, with a long, brutal ascent and terrifying descent at breakneck speed. The road loops down in hairpin after hairpin, through **VALLOIRE**, a sizeable ski resort, whose church is one of the most richly decorated in Savoie, then over the **Col du Télégraphe** at 1570m and down into the deep wooded valley of the Arc, known as **La Maurienne**, with the Massif de la Vanoise rising abruptly behind. Valloire has pleasant, reasonably priced **hotels** in *Les Gentianes* (☎04.79.59.03.66, fax 04.79.83.36.55; ③; closed Oct, Nov & April to mid-June), and the *Hôtel Christiania* (☎04.79.59.00.57, fax 04.79.59.00.06; ②; restaurant from 88F). There are gîtes nearby.

Le Casset

LE CASSET, back on the Briançon road about 12km beyond the Col du Lautaret, is a hamlet of dilapidated old houses clustered around a church with a bulbous dome. The site is superb: streams and meadows everywhere, reaching to the foot of the larch-covered mountainsides, the Glacier du Casset dazzling above the green of the larches. The **GR54** goes through the village. A good day's walk is to follow it as far as the **Col d'Arsine** (about 3hr), from which point you can either turn back or go on down to La Grave on the north side of the park, making an overnight stop at the CAF *Refuge de l'Alpe du Villar* (☎04.76.79.94.66), below the col.

The path crosses the Guisane and follows a track through the woods, first on the left and later on the right bank of the Petit Tabuc stream. From the end of the track you cross some grassy clearings before entering the trees again and climbing up to a milky-looking lakelet, the **Lac de la Douche**, at the foot of the Glacier du Casset. From here a clear path zigzags up a very steep slope, coming out in a long valley and eventually leading to the Col d'Arsine. Masses of ground-hugging red rhododendrons grow along the banks of the stream. About halfway up are some tumbledown huts, the **Chalets d'Arsine**, by a series of blue-grey tarns. Up on the left are a whole series of glaciers. The biggest is the **Glacier d'Arsine**, hanging from the walls of the long jagged ridge suspended between the Montagne des Agneaux and the Pic de Neige Cordier to the west. Early in the morning there are colonies of marmots playing above the banks of the stream.

There are a **campsite** and **gîte d'étape**, *Le Casset* (☎04.92.24.45.74) near the church, with another (☎04.92.24.76.42) at neighbouring **LES BOUSSARDES**. But provided you choose a spot where the hay has already been mown it seems you can camp anywhere. There are a café and grocery store in the village, which in season is overcrowded. Other budget accommodation nearby includes a **gîte d'étape**, *Chef Lieu* (☎04.92.24.41.13) in **Monetier-Les-Bains**, and the HI **youth hostel** at **LE BEZ** in the ski resort of Serre-Chevalier (☎04.92.24.74.54), (see p.829).

Parc Régional du Queyras

The **Parc Régional du Queyras**, spreading southeast of Briançon to the Italian border, becomes increasingly Mediterranean in appearance, with low scrub covering the mountainsides, poor shallow soil, white friable rock, and a huge variety of flora. The park has some good walking opportunities, with the **GR58** path making a circuit of the park, running through **St-Véran** and L'Échalp, and the **GR5** crossing through **Arvieux** and Ceillac on its way towards **Briançon**.

Embrun and Mont-Dauphin

EMBRUN, 49km south of Briançon, is a quiet and beautiful little town of narrow, rather Italianate streets on a rocky bluff above the River Durance on the edge of both the Parc du Queyras and the Parc des Écrins. It has been a fortress town for centuries. Hadrian made it the capital of the Maritime Alps, and from the third century to the Revolution it was the seat of an important archbishopric. Its chief sight is its twelfth-century **cathedral** (concerts in summertime), with a porch in alternating courses of black and white marble in the Italian Lombard style, its roof supported on columns of pink marble resting on lions' backs – an arrangement that inspired numerous imitators throughout the region. The **tourist office**, in a former chapel of the Cordeliers (April–Sept daily 10am–noon & 2–5pm; ☎04.92.43.01.80, fax 04.92.43.54.06), is next door to the bureau for **mountain guides**, which organises a daily programme of walks in the surrounding mountains.

There are two very agreeable hotels by the central place de la Mairie. The *Hôtel du Commerce* in particular, ten paces from the square in rue St-Pierre, is a delight: it is simple, comfortable and run by charming people (☎04.92.43.54.54; ②; excellent restaurant from 90F; demi-pension 220F per person). The other is the flower-decked *Hôtel de la Mairie* on the square itself (☎04.92.43.20.65, fax 04.92.43.47.02; ③; closed Oct–Nov & first half of May; good restaurant from 90F; closed Mon & Sun eve in winter). A third possibility is the more modern *Hôtel Notre-Dame* a little further out on av Genéral-Nicolas (☎04.92.43.08.36, fax 04.92.43.58.41; ③; restaurant from 80F). There are also several campsites; two reasonably priced ones are *Le Moulin* (June 8–Sept 15), on the left after the bridge on the Gap road (N94), and *La Tour*, close to the Durance off the D994 (June 15–Sept 15). There is also a **youth hostel** 10km away at **SAVINES-LE-LAC** (☎04.92.44.20.16, fax 04.92.44.24.54; May–Sept),

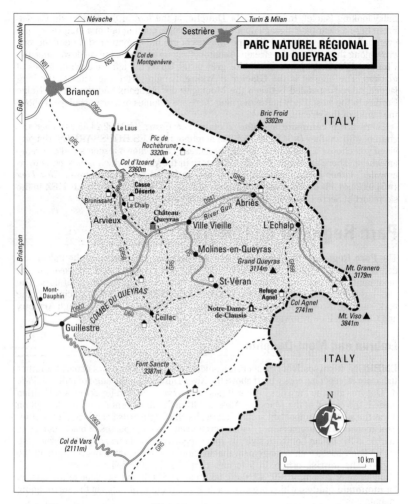

Sestrière

PARC NATUREL RÉGIONAL DU QUEYRAS

Col de Montgenèvre

Briançon

Bric Froid
3302m

ITALY

Le Laus

Pic de Rochebrune
3320m

Col d'Izoard
2360m

Casse Déserte

Brunissard

La Chalp

Château-Queyras

Arvieux

River Guil   Abriès

Ville Vieille

L'Echalp

Molines-en-Queyras

Grand Queyras
3114m

Mt. Granero
3179m

Mont-Dauphin

COMBE DU QUEYRAS

St-Véran

Refuge Agnel

Col Agnel
2741m

Ceillac

Notre-Dame-de-Clausis

Mt. Viso
3841m

Guillestre

ITALY

Font Sancte
3387m

N

Col de Vars
(2111m)

0   10 km

overlooking the enormous artificial Lac de Serre-Ponçon created by damming and taming the wild Durance.

Eighteen kilometres up the road you come to **MONT-DAUPHIN**, where **buses** leave for Ville-Vieille and St-Véran within the Queyras park. They meet the Paris–Briançon trains; the 7.40am bus going all the way to St-Véran (arriving 9.10am every day except Sun throughout the year), others only as far as Ville-Vieille (the 4.55pm operates only in the summer season). It is, however, easy to get a lift in these parts; there are always climbers and hikers with transport. Mont-Dauphin itself is just a station, with – opposite – an abandoned but formidably bastioned village, one of the many Alpine fortifications designed by Vauban in the seventeenth century, commanding the entrance to the valley of the Guil.

Guillestre

The road into the Queyras park follows the River Guil from Mont-Dauphin. First stop is **GUILLESTRE**, a pretty mountain village which only really comes to life in summer. Its houses, in typical Queyras style, have open granaries on the upper floors and its church has a lion-porch in emulation of the cathedral at Embrun. Head for the **tourist office** on the modern square at the top of the main street for information about the surrounding area (daily: July & Aug 9am–7pm, Sun 9am–noon & 2–7pm; Sept–June 9am–noon & 2–6pm; ☎04.92.45.04.37, fax 04.92.45.29.09).

The village lies at the foot of the long climb southwards to the **Col de Vars** (2108m), which gives access to the remote and beautiful walking country of the upper Ubaye valley; it's six hours, via Lac Miroir, Lac Sainte-Anne and the Col Girardin, to the CAF *Refuge de Maljasset* (☎04.92.84.34.04, fax 04.92.84.35.28).

If you want to stay in Guillestre, there is a primitive **youth hostel,** *Les Quatre Vents* (☎04.92.45.04.32, fax 04.92.45.04.32; Dec–Sept) in the same grounds as the **camping municipal**. For more comfortable accommodation, try the *Hôtel Martinet* (☎04.92.45.00.28, fax 04.92.45.29.79; ③; restaurant from 70F) or the better-appointed *Hôtel Barnières* (☎04.92.45.04.87, fax 04.92.45.28.74; ④; restaurant from 110F; mid-Dec to mid-Oct).

Château-Ville-Vieille and around

The road route into the park from Guillestre strikes northeast through the narrow gorge of the **Combe du Queyras**, scarcely more than a claustrophobic crack with walls up to 400m high. Far below the road, the clear stream boils down over red and green rocks. It was only in this century that road-building techniques became sufficiently sophisticated to cope with these narrows – previously they had to be circumvented by a detour over the adjacent heights.

At the upper end of the Combe, the valley broadens briefly, and ahead you see the ruinous fort of **Château-Queyras** barring the way so completely that there is scarcely room for the road to squeeze around its base – Vauban at work again, though the original fortress was medieval. Just beyond is **CHÂTEAU-VILLE-VIEILLE**, where the road for St-Véran branches right over the Guil and up the ravine of the Aigue Blanche torrent. A smaller place than Guillestre, it has only a few old houses still intact and a **church** with its square tower and octagonal steeple flanked by four short triangular pinnacles – a style characteristic of this corner of the Alps. A Latin inscription in the porch says the church was destroyed in 1574 by the "impiety of the Calvinists" and restored by the "piety" of the Catholics. There is a painted sundial on the tower, which is also characteristic of the region.

Straight on, the road follows the Guil through the villages of Aiguilles, Abriès and La Monta (all with gîtes d'étape), to the **Belvédère du Viso**, close to the Italian border and **Monte Viso**, at 3841m the highest peak in the area. Above the Belvédère is the **Col de la Traversette**, where in 1480 the Marquis of Saluces drove a seventy-metre tunnel through the mountain. It has been re-opened at various times through history, but is finally closed now.

East of L'Échalp, a variant of the **GR58**, which does the circuit of the park, climbs up to the **Col de la Croix**, used in former times by Italian peasants bringing their produce to market in Abriès. South of the village, the path climbs to the pastures of **Alpe de Médille**, where you can see across to Monte Viso, then on past the lakes of **Egourgéou, Bariche** and **Foréant** to **Col Vieux** and west to the **Refuge Agnel**; from here you can continue onto St-Véran.

St-Véran

At 2040m, **ST-VÉRAN** claims to be the highest permanently inhabited village in Europe. It lies on the east side of the valley of the Aigue Blanche, backed by hectares of steep lush mountain pasture, 7km south of Ville-Vieille. Opposite, rock walls and slopes of scree rise to snowy ridges. In the valley bottom and on any treeless patch of ground, no matter how steep, you can see the remains of abandoned terraces. They were in use up until World War II, though, as with most high Alpine villages, tradition-al farming activity has now practically died out. Today the principal economic activity is entertaining tourists. The route up from Ville-Vieille takes you through **Molines**, which – like its neighbours **La Rua** and **Fontgillarde** – seems to have preserved their tradi-tional rural character better than St-Véran, with well-kept houses and hay meadows still mown – there is nothing prettier than these little patches of Alpine meadow, always steep and irregular in shape, full of wild flowers and neatly scythed by hand.

St-Veran's houses are part stone and part timber, and there are several refurbished old drinking fountains, made entirely of wood. The stone **church** stands prettily on the higher of the two "streets", its white tower silhouetted against the bare crags across the valley. The columns of its porch rest on crudely carved lions, one holding a man in its paws. The interior is surprisingly rich, with Baroque altars and retables.

Just south of the village, past a triple cross adorned with the instruments of Christ's passion and an inscription urging the passer-by to choose between the devout or rebel-lious life ("l'homme révolté qui n'est jamais content"), the **GR58**, waymarked and easy to follow, turns right down to the river, beside which there are some good spots to **camp**. The path continues up the left bank through woods of pine and larch as far as the chapel of Notre-Dame-de-Clausis. There, above the timber-line, it crosses to the right bank of the stream and winds up damp grassy slopes to the **Col de Chamoussière**, about three-and-a-half hours from St-Véran. The ridge to the right of the col marks the frontier with Italy. In the valley below, you can see the *Refuge Agnel*, about an hour away, with the **Pain de Sucre** (3208m) behind it. From there you can continue to L'Échalp (see above). In early July, there are glorious flowers in the mead-ows leading up to the col: violets, Black Vanilla orchids, pinks and gentians.

Practicalities

It is hard to get good-value **accommodation** around here. The best deal is the *Auberge Monchu* (☎04.92.45.83.96, fax 04.92.45.80.09; 235F half-board per person; closed April 21–June 5 & Oct–Dec 19), which also provides gîte d'étape facilities (160F half-board). Otherwise, there's a couple of **hotels** – *Le Grand Tétras* (☎04.92.45.82.42, fax 04.92.45.85.98; ③; June–Sept) and the *Coste Belle* (☎04.92.45.82.17, fax 04.92.45.86.62; ③; Dec–Sept) – and the *Les Gabelous* gîte d'étape (☎04.92.45.81.39). There are only two small shops, and they have a tendency to run out of bread, fruit and vegetables.

Queyras to Briançon

The direct route from Queyras to Briançon, crossing the 2360m **Col d'Izoard**, is a beautiful trip, but you need a car do do it – there are no buses.

The road turns up right just west of Château-Queyras along a wooded ravine to the village of **AVRIEUX**, lying in a high valley surrounded by fields and meadows, just 16km from Briançon. A **church** with the characteristic tower and steeple stands guard at the entrance to the village. The **GR5** passes through; but, if you want to **stay**, try *La Casse Déserte* (☎04.92.46.72.91, fax 04.92.46.85.88; ②). Further up the valley there are more gîtes: in **LA CHALP** there is *La Teppio* (☎04.92.46.73.90) and in **BRUNISSARD** there is *Les Bons Enfants* (☎04.92.46.73.85). The **tourist office** in Arvieux (☎04.92.46.75.76) can make further suggestions.

Going up to the col, above the timber-line, you cross the **Casse Déserte**, a wild, desolate region with huge screes running down off the peaks and weirdly eroded orangey rocks. From the top the view extends over many kilometres of mountain landscape. On the other side, the road loops down through thick forest to **LE LAUS**, a cluster of old stone houses with long, sloping, wooden roofs set in meadows beside the stream, before swinging west into the deep valley of the Durance at Briançon, dominated by the vast **Massif des Écrins**.

Parc National de la Vanoise

The **Parc National de la Vanoise** occupies the eastern end of the **Vanoise Massif**, the area contained between the upper valleys of the Isère and Arc rivers. It is extremely popular, with over 500km of marked paths, including the **GR5**, **GR55** and **GTA** (*Grande Traversée des Alpes*), with numerous refuges along the trails. For information on the spot, the tourist offices in **Modane**, **Val d'Isère** and **Bourg-St-Maurice** are helpful. The Maison du Parc at 135 rue Docteur-Juilland in Chambéry also gives advice and sells maps.

Access to the **Vanoise** park is easiest from Chambéry, with frequent trains to Modane.

Modane and the Arc valley

MODANE, 32km due north of Briançon, is a dreary little place, destroyed by Allied bombing in 1943 and now little more than a rail junction. Nonetheless, it's a good kicking-off point for walkers on the south side of the park – easily accessible by train and with a well-sited grassy **camping municipal** just up the road to the Fréjus tunnel (which leads to Bardonecchia in Italy). If you're road-weary, try the *Hôtel Bellevue*, 15 rue Replat (☎04.79.05.20.64, fax 04.79.05.37.42; ②; restaurant from 70F).

The **GR5** sets out from the northern edge of the transpontine section of Modane and leads up to the **Refuge de l'Orgère**, where a path joins up with the **GR55** leading north to Pralognan, over the **Col de la Vanoise** and right across the park to Val Claret on the Lac de Tignes – a tremendous walk. The **GR5** itself keeps east of La Dent Parrachée mountain, describing a great loop through the **Refuge d'Entre-Deux-Eaux** before continuing up the north flank of the Arc valley and over the Col de l'Iseran to Val d'Isère. Southwest of Modane, you can continue along the GR5 to include the **Tour de Mont Thabor**, a six- to eight-day walk encircling the 3181-metre heights of Mont Thabor – ask for details at the **tourist office** in Modane, at the exit of the Fréjus tunnel (April–Aug Mon–Fri 9am–6pm, Sat & Sun 10am–5pm; Sept–March Mon–Sat 10am–6pm, Sun 10am–noon & 2–5pm; ☎04.79.05.22.35).

The Arc valley

The **Arc valley**, dark and enclosed below Modane, widens and lightens above it, with meadows and patches of cultivation in the valley bottom and the lighter foliage of larches gracing the mountainsides. It is hardly a joyous landscape, especially under a stormy sky. Bare crags hang above the steep meadows on the north flanks, glaciers threaten to the south and east. The villages, though attractive, are poor and humble places, the houses squat and built of rough grey stone, the homes of people who have had to struggle to wring a living from harsh weather and unyielding soil. It is surprising at first to find such a wealth of exuberant **Baroque art** in the outwardly simple **churches** in small villages like Avrieux, Bramans, Termignon, Lanslevillard and Bessans. But probably it is precisely because of the harshness and poverty of their lives that the mountain people sought to express their piety with such colourful vitality. Schools of local artists flourished, particularly in the seventeenth and eighteenth centuries, inspired and influenced by itinerant Italian artists who came and went across the adjacent frontier.

In **LANSLEBOURG**, 20km upstream of Modane, **Haute Maurienne Information** organize tours of the churches in Avrieux, Bramans, Termignon, Lanslevillard and Bessans, all within a twenty-kilometre radius of each other along the Arc valley. Lanslebourg is also the start of the climb to the **Mont Cenis pass** over to Susa in Italy, another ancient transalpine route. Last stop before the perils of the trek, it was once a prosperous and thriving town. Relief at finishing the climb from the French side was tempered by an alarming descent *en ramasse*, a sort of crude sledge, which shot downhill at breakneck speed much to the alarm of travellers. "So fast you lose all sense and understanding", a terrified merchant from Douai recounted in 1518. Lanslebourg has a **camping municipal** and a **youth hostel** with a fantastic view (☎04.79.05.90.96; closed Oct–Dec 14); alternatively, try the *Hôtel de la Vieille Poste* (☎04.79.05.93.47, fax 04.79.05.86.85; ③; restaurant from 68F; closed Nov and weekends out of season).

BESSANS, further up the valley, retains its village character better than most. Its squat dwellings are built of rough stone with tiny window openings, and roofed with heavy slabs to withstand the long hard winters. Most have south-facing balconies to make the most of the sun and galleries under deep eaves for drying *grebons*, the bricks of cow dung and straw used locally for fuel. The **church** has a collection of seventeenth-century painted wooden statues and a retable, signed by Jean Clappier. The Clappiers were a local family who produced several generations of artists. On the other side of the small cemetery, the **chapel of St-Antoine** has exterior murals of the Virtues and Deadly Sins and fine sixteenth-century frescoes; ask the priest to unlock the chapel – his house is on the right of the road leading east from the village square. Two kilometres up the road you pass the **chapel of Notre-Dame-des-Grâces** on the right, with another *ex-voto* by Clappier. For **accommodation**, try the *Hôtel Le Mont Iseran* (☎04.79.05.95.97, fax 04.79.05.84.07; ③; closed April 15–June 20 & Oct–Dec 15); alternatively, on the opposite side of the river, the hamlet of **LE VILLARON** has a gîte d'étape in a handsome old farm (☎04.79.05.95.84; meals available).

BONNEVAL-SUR-ARC, 10km upstream and 1835m above sea level, lies at the foot of the **Col de l'Iseran** in a rather bleaker setting close to the timber-line. At the head of the Arc valley to the east, you can see the huge glaciers of the **Sources de l'Arc**. Better preserved and more obviously picturesque than Bessans, Bonneval stops a lot of tourists on their way to and from the col. It is in danger of becoming twee, with its houses clustered tightly around the church, with only the narrowest of lanes between them. You sense how very isolated these places were until only a few years ago, cut off for months by heavy snow, forced in upon their own resources. Several graves in the churchyard record deaths by avalanche.

Col de l'Iseran and Haute Tarentaise

As with all the other high Alpine passes, the **Col de l'Iseran** has been used for centuries by local people. Despite the dangers of weather and the arduous climb, it was by far the quickest route between the remote upper valleys of the Arc and Isère. The volume of traffic was too small to disturb the nature of the tiny communities that eked out an existence on the approaches, but twentieth-century roads and the development of winter sports have changed all that. Small mountain communities have metamorphosed into monster modern developments, catering to an upmarket ski crowd.

From October to June, the pass is usually blocked by snow. But in summer, being the highest pass in the Alps (2770m), it is one of the sights that tourists with cars feel they must see; consequently it's relatively easy to hitch. A word of warning, though: if you do try, don't do it in light summer clothing, especially on a cool cloudy day, as temperatures can still hover around freezing point and blizzards are not unknown.

The climb begins above Bonneval (see above), with splendid views of the glaciers at the head of the Arc, and then follows the rocky gully of the Lenta stream through a narrow defile and out into a desolate cirque, where the Lenta rises and masses of anemones bloom in the stony ground. Behind the chalet on the col, a path climbs west to the **Pointe des Lessières** (round trip 2hr 30min), where on a clear day you have views of the Italian side of Mont Blanc and the whole of the frontier chain of peaks.

Val d'Isère and Tignes

VAL D'ISÈRE, at the foot of the col on the north side, can be reached by buses from Bourg-St-Maurice, 23km northwest. Once a tiny mountain village, Val d'Isère has become a hideous agglomeration of cafés, supermarkets, apartments and chalets for skiers – with some of the finest skiing in Europe. It also makes a convenient centre for walking (details from the tourist office ☎04.79.06.06.50, fax 04.79.06.04.56), but is no place to stay unless you're feeling extremely rich. There's a **campsite** on the edge of the resort at **LE LAISINANT** and a **youth hostel,** *Les Clarines* (☎04.79.06.35.07, fax 04.79.41.03.36; Jan–April, July–Dec) about 12km away at **TIGNES**, an unattractive, purpose-built resort on the artificial Lac de Chevril. But thereafter the valley is lovely, deep and wooded, with villages perched on grassy shoulders high on either flank.

The Isère valley

If you're interested in exploring the valley, make for the village of **LES BREVIÈRES**, huddled below an enormous dam. Seven kilometres beyond, a lane turns left into the valley bottom to **LA SAVINAZ** and **LA GURRAZ**, whose creamy church tower is a landmark for miles around. High above, though looking dangerously close, the green ice cliffs that terminate the Glacier de la Gurraz hang off the edge of **Mont Pourri** (3779m). From the turn, the lane veers steeply down through trees and hay meadows full of flowers, past ruined houses, to the river. The climb up the opposite bank is hard going, past impossibly steep fields. You take a right fork for La Gurraz across a rickety plank bridge in the jaws of a defile. It's about an hour's walk, once you're on the lane.

The village is tiny and untouched by tourism. Its dozen old houses have wide eaves and weathered balconies spread with sweet drying hay, and firewood stacked outside. The houses are all sited in the lee of a knoll for protection against the avalanches that come thundering off the glacier above, thousands of tonnes of snow and rock, almost sheer down into a cirque behind. If you are unlucky enough to be out of doors when an avalanche occurs, the blast knocks you off your feet and can even suffocate you. There are no provisions available, so bring your own. Other hamlets on the opposite flank of the valley are just as interesting, the prettiest being **LE MONAL**, in the mouth of a small hanging valley, also accessible by car from **LA THUILE**, further along the Bourg-St-Maurice road.

From La Gurraz, a signposted path climbs to **Refuge de la Martin** in an hour and a half. It zigzags up the slope behind the village of La Savinaz, onto a spur by a ruined chalet, where a right-hand path goes up the rocks overhead to the edge of the glacier. The refuge path continues left along the side of a deep gully, whose flanks are thick with the white St Bruno's lily. It crosses a ferocious torrent by a plank bridge and follows a mule track up to the mountain pastures by the refuge, where cows and sheep graze. The **Mont Pourri glaciers** are directly above. Opposite is the big **Glacier de la Sassière** and up to your right Val d'Isère, with the Col de l'Iseran behind.

Bourg-St-Maurice

If you continue down the valley, **BOURG-ST-MAURICE** is the midpoint of the Tarentaise and, although of little interest itself, it can be a useful place to stop. The big purpose-built ski resorts of **LES ARCS** and **LA PLAGNE** are nearby and the classic pass into the Italian Val d'Aosta, the **Col du Petit St-Bernard**, right behind. With its Swiss twin, the Grand St-Bernard, it was the only route around the Mont Blanc massif until the tunnel was opened in 1965. It's a rather spooky crossing, reaching a height of 2188m, with a couple of barrack-like buildings and a row of statues of St Bernard. It's at its most dramatic when you're coming over from the Italian side in the early evening, right into the eye of the setting sun. (There is one daily bus crossing in July and August.)

There are no very appealing **places to stay** in the town. One place to try is *La Petite Auberge* just off the N90 on the Moûtiers side of town (☎04.79.07.05.86; ②; restaurant from 75F). There is also a **youth hostel**, *La Verdache*, just beyond **SEEZ** (☎04.79.41.01.93, fax 04.79.41.03.36; Jan–Sept), 4km away on the dreary main road, av Leclerc, where you'll also find the **train and bus stations**, with the **tourist office** almost opposite (Mon–Sat 10am–noon & 2–5.30pm; ☎04.79.07.04.92, fax 04.79.07.24.90). The town's **campsite**, *Camping le Versoyen*, is on route des Arcs (☎04.79.07.03.45), on the right past the sports ground on the Val d'Isère road.

Towards Chambéry

There are a couple of places worth a brief stop as you head west towards Chambéry. The first is the village of **AIME**, 6km from Bourg-St-Maurice, whose main Grande-Rue presents a pretty and little-spoilt succession of buildings. Its principal sight is the rough-stone **church of St-Martin**, whose origins go back to a first-century Roman temple, swept away by the Isère in the third century – an indication of how dangerous these mountain rivers could be in the days before flood control. What survives today is basically early Romanesque.

The other place that rewards a brief detour is **CONFLANS**, a small medieval town on a spur overlooking grim, modern **ALBERTVILLE** (centre of the 1992 winter Olympics), and rather too cutely revived for its own good. From the public garden by the Tour Sarrazine, you can contemplate the contrast in town-planning styles: spreading below are gaunt, rectangular blocks of apartments separated by rushing highways, against a steep backdrop of verdant slopes, vineyard terraces and hay meadows.

Mont Blanc

First climbed in 1786, **Mont Blanc**, right on the Italian border, is the biggest tourist draw in the Alps, but so spectacular that it's worth seeing in spite of the crowds. If you're going to walk in the area, you soon get away from most of the visitors. Annecy is the easiest place to approach the mountain from, and, of the two road routes, the one via the old ski resort of Megève is the more interesting.

The two main approach roads to Mont Blanc come together at Le Fayet, where the **tramway du Mont Blanc** begins its 75-minute haul to the **Nid d'Aigle**, a vantage point on the northwest slope (128F return). **Chamonix-Mont Blanc**, the base camp for all Mont Blanc activities, is just 30km further on.

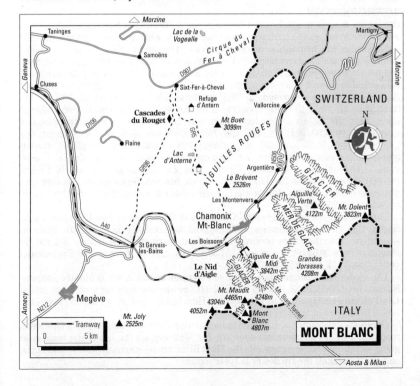

Chamonix-Mont Blanc

Expensive, tourist-choked **CHAMONIX** may have long since had its village identity submerged in a sprawl of tourist development, but the glaring snowfields, eerie green glaciers and ridges of shark-toothed *aiguilles* surrounding Mont Blanc are more than ample compensation. The town itself is of little interest while being extremely expensive, and it crawls with tourists in the high summer season. The **Musée Alpin**, off av Michel-Croz in the town centre (daily: June–Sept 2–7pm; Christmas–Easter 3–7pm; 20F) will interest mountaineers, but is not as exciting as you would expect; among various bits of equipment, documents and letters is Jacques Balmat's account of his first ascent of Mont Blanc in 1786, written in almost phonetically spelt French.

Practicalities

The **tourist office**, at 45 place du Triangle-de-l'Amitié (daily: summer 8.30am–7.30pm; winter 8.30am–12.30pm & 2–7pm; ☎04.50.53.00.24, fax 04.50.53.58.90), can help with accommodation. For up-to-the minute **walking and climbing information**, consult the tourist office or the nearby Maison de la Montagne (☎04.50.53.03.40), which also houses the Compagnie des Guides (☎04.50.53.00.88, fax 04.50.53.48.44), the Office de Haute Montagne (☎04.50.53.22.08) and a meteorological service. The tourist office also publishes a **map of summer walks** (25F) in the area, while the guides run rock- and ice-climbing schools and will, if you wish, accompany you on any expedition they reckon is within your capabilities.

ACCOMMODATION

One of the biggest headaches in Chamonix can be **finding a bed**, especially if, as a walker or climber, you're having to sit out bad weather while waiting to get into the hills – the weather in Chamonix is notoriously fickle. The tourist office keeps lists of dormitories and hotels and can help with reservations – all hotels need booking in advance and tend to be expensive. There is, however, a fair supply of **hostel or gîte** accommodation, and the tourist office can supply a full list. The closest to the centre of Chamonix is the English-run *Vagabond*, at 365 av Ravanel-le-Rouge (☎04.50.53.15.43, fax 04.50.53.68.21; ①), with music concerts in the bar some nights. On the Swiss side of town, near the Bois du Bouchet, you'll find *La Montagne*, 789 promenade des Crèmeries (☎04.50.53.11.60; ①), and *Hôtel Crèmerie Balmat*, 749 chemin des Crèmeries (☎04.50.53.24.44; ③). Not far away, in rte de la Frasse, two places offering gîte-type accommodation are *Le Chamoniard Volant*, 45 rte de la Frasse (☎04.50.53.14.09, fax 04.50.53.23.25; ①), and *La Tapia*, 152 rte de la Frasse (☎04.50.53.18.19, fax 04.50.53.67.01; ①), which has wonderful views. Another gîte d'etape is the *Ski Station*, close to the Brévent cable car station at 6 rte des Moussoux (☎04.50.53.20.25; ①).

Three kilometres north of central Chamonix in the suburb of **Les Praz**, there's *La Bagna*, 337 rte des Gaudenays (☎04.50.53.62.90, fax 04.50.53.04.88; ①); while in Argentière, a further 5km towards Switzerland there is *Le Belvédere*, 501 rte du Plagnolet (☎04.50.54.02.59, fax 04.50.54.02.59; ①), and *La Boerne*, 288 Trelechamp (☎04.50.54.05.14, fax 04.50.54.05.14; ①).

The modernized, comfortable and friendly **youth hostel** is at 103 Montée Jacques-Balmat (☎04.50.53.14.52, fax 04.50.55.92.34), in the western part of town called **Les-Pèlerins-en-Haut;** take the bus to Les Houches and get off at *Pèlerins École* – the hostel is signposted from there.

Campsites are numerous, though in high season there may only be room for a small mountain tent. Two convenient sites are *Les Molliases*, on the left of the main road going west from Chamonix towards the Mont Blanc tunnel entrance (June to mid-Sept), and *Les Rosières* off the rte des Praz (year round).

EATING AND DRINKING

Getting a cheap **meal** is another of Chamonix's problems. Take advantage of hostel canteens where you can. *La Poêle*, 79 av de l'Aiguille-du-Midi, specializes in omelettes (60–70F), but like its competitors tends to become very crowded. There are hearty sandwiches and paninis at *La Belouga*, 56 rue Paccard - the vegetarian sandwich with lots of avocado and chilli sauce is very good. *Bistrot des Sports*, in rue Joseph-Vallot is a nice café with simple *plats,*. Rue Joseph-Vallot has plenty of gourmet food shops with local cheeses and other alpine delicacies. It's worth taking a look at *Le Choucas*, rue Paccard, right in the centre of town – it's the hang-out of climbers when they're not celebrating their successes at the *Wild Wallabies* bar in rue de la Tour, with pool tables, swimming pool, and Australian beers for a hard-earned thirst (summer 11.30am–2am; winter 4pm–2am).

Around Chamonix – the rack railway and cable car

There are two touristy but exhilarating excursions around Chamonix which you might want to experience. Take your student card or youth hostel card for reduced rates on some of the *téléfériques*. One is to take the **rack railway** from the Gare du Montenvers through the pine woods up to the vast glacier known as the **Mer de Glace** (trains every 20min 8am–6pm in July & Aug, otherwise hourly 9am–5pm; closed mid-Nov to mid-Dec; return 90F), a favourite with Victorian travellers. Once you get there you have the option of taking a short cable-car ride down into the **ice cave** carved out of the Mer de Glace every year.

The other is to ride the very expensive *téléférique* (summer daily from 7am; return 194F) to the **Aiguille du Midi** (3842m), one of the longest cable-car ascents in the world, rising no less than 3000m above the valley floor in two impossibly steep stages. Penny-pinching by buying a ticket only as far as the Plan du Midi, which is used principally by climbers heading up to the routes on the Aiguilles du Chamonix, is a waste of money: go all the way or not at all. If you do go up, make the effort to go before 9am, as the summits tend to cloud over towards midday and huge crowds may force you to wait for hours if you go up later. Take warm clothes, for even on a summer day it will be well below zero on the top. You need a steady head, too: the drop beneath the little bubble of steel and glass is appalling.

The Aiguille is a terrifyingly exposed granite pinnacle on which the *téléférique* dock and a restaurant are precariously balanced. The view is incredible. At your feet is the snowy plateau of the **Col du Midi**, with the glaciers of the Vallée Blanche and Géant crawling off left at their millennial pace. To the right a steep snowfield leads to the easy ridge route to the summit with its cap of ice (4807m). Away to the front, rank upon rank of snow-and-ice-capped monsters recede into the distance. Most impressive of all, closing the horizon to your left, from the east to south, is a mind-blowing cirque of needle-sharp **peaks and precipitous cliffs**: the Aiguille Verte, Triollet, the Jorasses, with the Matterhorn and Monte Rosa visible in the far distance across a glorious landscape of rock, snow and cloud-filled valleys – the lethal testing ground of all truly crazed climbers.

Chamonix valley: some hikes

Opposite Mont Blanc, the north side of Chamonix valley is enclosed by the lower but nonetheless impressive **Aiguilles Rouges**, with another *téléférique* to **Le Brévent** (15min; return 80F), the 2525-metre peak directly above the town. Classic walks this side of the valley include the **Lac Blanc**, starting from Les Praz and the Flégère *téléférique* (20min; return 55F), and the **Grand** and **Petit Balcon Sud** trails, giving spectacular views of Mont Blanc. A highly recommended **two-day hike** is the **GR5** stage north from Le Brévent to the village of **Sixt** (see below) via **Lac d'Anterne**, with a night at the **Refuge d'Anterne**. The classic long-distance route is the two-week **Tour**

du Mont Blanc (TMB), described in a *Topoguide*, Andrew Harvey's *Tour of Mont Blanc* and *Chamonix-Mont Blanc: A Walker's Guide* .

Northern pre-Alps: Samoëns and around

The **Northern pre-Alps**, climbing back from the shore of Lake Geneva, are softer, greener and a lot less crowded than the mighty ranges further south. A fine place to absorb the region's atmosphere is the gentle and attractive village of **SAMOËNS**, 21km from Cluses on the main Geneva–Chamonix road, lying at the foot of the Aiguille de Criou, with the tall peak of Le Buet in the distance. Its principal architectural claim to fame is its sixteenth-century Gothic **church** on a Romanesque base, with a doorway of crouching lions like those in the Queyras.

The village is chiefly known for its stonemasons and for Marie-Louise Cognacq-Jay, who left to seek her fortune in Paris at the age of 15 in 1853, and found it – as the founder of the famous French department store, La Samaritaine. There is a beautiful botanical garden on the slope above the old village centre, created by Madame Jay and planted with specimens of mountain flora from all over the world. Hers was an exceptional success but migration was part of the pattern of local life. Up to World War I the men of the village would set out every spring with their tools on their backs to seek work in the cities of France and Switzerland. Their guild, *les frahans*, evolved its own peculiar dialect, *le mourne*, so they could communicate secretly among themselves.

There is a **camping muncipal** by the Giffre and some **gîtes d'étape** – *Les Couadzous*, in the centre (☎04.50.34.41.62), and *Les Moulins*, 1km away on the road up to **LES ALLAMANDS** (☎04.50.34.95.69). For a **hotel**, try *Les Drugères* (☎04.50.34.43.84, fax 04.50.34.19.06; ③; restaurant from 75F, closed May & Nov) or the *Gai Soleil* (☎04.50.34.40.74, fax 04.50.34.10.78; c) at the north end of town.

Sixt and the Cirque du Fer-à-Cheval

East of Samoëns, the valley narrows into the **Gorge des Tines** before opening out again at **SIXT**, 7km away, another pretty village on the confluence of two branches of the Giffre: the Giffre-Haut, which comes down from Salvagny; and the Giffre-Bas, which rises in the **Cirque du Fer-à-Cheval**.

The cirque begins about 6km from Sixt – there is a footpath along the left bank of the Giffre-Bas. It is a vast semi-circle of rock walls, up to 700m in height and 4–5km long, blue with haze on a summer's day and striated with the long chains of white water from the waterfalls. The left-hand end of the cirque is dominated by a huge spike of rock known as *La Corne du Chamois* (The Goat's Horn). At its foot the valley of the Giffre bends sharply north to its source in the glaciers above the Fond de la Combe. The bowl of the cirque is thickly wooded except for a circular meadow in the middle where the road ends.

There is a **tourist office** and a **park office** in **SIXT** (both Mon–Sat 9am–noon & 2–7pm; ☎04.50.34.40.28, fax 04.50.34.95.82). The park office produces a useful and well-illustrated folder of walks in the region; they recommend, in particular, the walk to the **Refuge du Lac de la Vogeale** (3hr 30min); the **Chalets de Sales** via the spectacular **Cascade du Rouget** waterfalls on the GR5 and GR96 (2.5hr from the end of the road); and the GR5 stage to the **Lac d'Anterne**, and on to Le Brévent (about 4hr from the Anterne refuge) and Chamonix. Sixt also has three **gîtes d'étape** and the *Hôtel Beau Site* (☎04.50.34.44.05; ②).

Abondance

A drive across country by the back roads from Samoëns to Évian will reward you with some lovely scenery. If you need a port of call, **ABONDANCE**, in the middle of the Chablais region, is the place to make for. Remote and beautiful, it is renowned for its abbey and cloisters. There is a gîte d'étape (☎04.50.73.12.93) here, and several hotels, the cheapest of which are the *Voyageurs* (☎04.50.73.10.02; ②) and the *Hôtel L'Abbaye* (☎04.50.73.02.03, fax 04.50.81.60.46; ②).

Évian and Lake Geneva

Some 60km north of Mont Blanc lies the dolphin-shaped volume of **Lake Geneva** ("Lac Léman" to the French), forming a natural border with Switzerland. Around 70km long, 13km wide and an amazing 310m deep, the lake is fed and drained by the Rhône. It is a real inland sea, subject to violent storms, as Byron and Shelley discovered to their discomfort in 1816. On a calm day, though, sailing slowly across its silky-smooth surface is a serene experience.

There probably isn't any point in visiting **ÉVIAN** unless you are a well-heeled invalid or gambler, but it's actually a very peaceful town, not destroyed by tourism, and it is pleasant to take a leisurely trip on the lake. The famous water is now bottled at Amphion, 3km along the lakeside, but the **Source Cachat** still bubbles away behind the Évian company's beautiful nineteenth-century offices in rue Nationale, all wood, coloured glass, cupolas and patterned tiles. Anyone can go along and help themselves to spring water. The **waterfront** is elegantly laid out with squares of billiard-table grass, brilliant flowerbeds and trees, mini golf, water slides, and other peaceful ways of amusing oneself. In summer, the Centre Nautique swimming pool complex also has outdoor film screenings by the lake. There are **ferries** to explore other towns around the lake, including Lausanne in Switzerland (10–15 daily; 120F return) and the medieval town of **YVOIRE** on the French side towards Thonon-les-Bains (120F return).

The **tourist office** is in place d'Allinges (Oct–May Mon–Fri 8.30am–noon & 2–6.30pm; June–Sept Sat & Sun 10am–noon & 3–6pm; ☎04.50.75.04.26, fax 04.50.75.61.08). There is a **youth hostel** on av de Neuvecelle (☎04.50.75.35.87, fax 04.50.75.45.67) – the D21 towards Abondance – as well as several **hotels** that would make a somewhat larger hole in your budget, and one or two that may wipe it out completely. Ignore these, as there is a wonderful hotel in the centre of town, *Hôtel Continental*, 65 rue Nationale (☎04.50.75.37.54, fax 04.50.75.31.11; ③), it's run by a friendly French-American couple, and rooms on the top floor have a view of the lake. Two cheap options are the *Régina*, 25 rue Nationale, near the port, at the east end of the street (☎04.50.75.21.09, fax 04.50.74.61.71; ①; restaurant from 65F), and the *Hostellerie du Lac*, on the lakeside av Grande-Rive (☎04.50.75.02.92, fax 04.50.75.57.63; ②). The nearest **campsite** is the *Grande Rive* off av Grande-Rive (April–Sept).

travel details

Buses

Bourg-St-Maurice to: Aosta (1 daily July & Aug; 2hr 30min); Val d'Isère (1–2 daily; 50min–1hr 20min).

Chambéry to: Aix-les-Bains (several daily; 20min); Annecy (several daily; 1hr); Grenoble (several daily; 1hr).

Chamonix to: Annecy via La-Roche-sur-Foron (3 daily; 3hr); Annecy via Megève (1 daily; 3hr); Geneva (1 daily; 2hr 30min); Grenoble (1 daily; 3hr 30min).

Cluses to: Samoëns (3 daily; 35mins); Sixt (3 daily; 45min).

Grenoble to: Alpe-d'Huez (2 daily; 45min); Bourg-d'Oisans (5 daily; 1hr 20min); Briançon (several daily; 2hr); Chambéry (several daily; 1hr); Col du Lautaret (1 daily; 2hr); Gap (1 daily; 2hr 45min); La Grave (1 daily; 1hr 40min); Monetier-les-Bains (1 daily; 2hr 25min); Villard-de-Lans (at least 1 daily; 45min).

Mont-Dauphin to (summer only): Ceillac (2 daily; 35min); Guillestre (2–3 daily; 5min); St-Véran (2–3 daily; 1hr 30min); Vars (2 daily; 50min); Ville-

Vieille (2–3 daily; 1hr 5min).

Valloire (summer only) to: St-Michel-de-Maurienne (2 daily; 45min).

Trains

Annecy to: Chambéry (several daily; 45min); Grenoble (several daily; 2hr); Lyon (several daily; 2hr); Paris (frequent; 4hr 30min); St-Gervais (10 daily; 1hr 15min–2hr).

Annemasse to: Annecy, changing at La-Roche-sur-Foron (4–5 daily; 1hr 30min); Évian (frequent; 35min); Paris (1 daily; 8hr).

Briançon to: Marseille (3 daily; 4hr 30min).

Chambéry to: Aix-les-Bains (frequent; 10min); Annecy (frequent; 45min); Bourg-St-Maurice (5 daily; 2hr); Geneva (several daily; 1hr 30min); Grenoble (several daily; 1hr); Lyon (frequent; 1hr 30min–2hr 30min); Modane (frequent; 40min–1hr 20min); Paris (frequent; 5hr 30min).

Evian to Geneva (7 daily, 1 hr).

Grenoble to: Annecy (several daily; 2hr); Briançon, changing at Veynes-Dévoluy (2 daily; 4hr); Chambéry (several daily; 1hr); Gap (2 daily; 2hr 30min); Lyon (frequent; 1hr 30min–1hr 45min); Paris-Lyon (several daily; 3hr 12min–7hr 15min).

St-Gervais to: Chamonix (7 daily; 35min).

CHAPTER FOURTEEN

THE RHÔNE VALLEY AND PROVENCE

O f all the areas of France, **Provence** is the most irresistible. Geographically it ranges from the snow-capped mountains of the **southern Alps** to the delta plains of the **Camargue** and has the greatest European canyon, the **Gorges du Verdon**. Fortified towns guard its old borders; countless villages perch defensively on hilltops; its great cities – **Aix-en-Provence** and **Avignon** – are full of cultural glories. The sensual inducements of Provence include warmth, food and wine, and the perfumes of Mediterranean vegetation. Along with its coast – which we've covered in the following chapter – it has attracted the rich and famous, the artistic and reclusive, and countless arrivals who have found themselves unable to conceive of life elsewhere.

In appearance, despite the throngs of foreigners and French from other regions, **inland Provence** remains remarkably unscathed. The history of its earliest known natives, of the Greeks, then Romans, raiding Saracens, schismatic popes, and shifting allegiances to different counts and princes, is still in evidence. Provence's complete integration into France dates only from the nineteenth century and, though the Provençal language is only spoken by a small minority, the accent is distinctive even to a foreign ear. In the east the rhythms of speech become clearly Italian.

Unless you're intending to stay for months, the main problem with Provence is choosing where to go. In the west along the **Rhône valley** are the Roman cities of **Orange**, **Vaison-la-Romaine**, **Carpentras** and **Arles**, and the papal city of Avignon, with its brilliant summer festival. Aix-en-Provence is the mini-Paris of the region and home to Cézanne, for whom the **Mont Ste-Victoire** was an enduring subject; Van Gogh's links are with **St-Rémy** and Arles. The Gorges du Verdon, the **Parc National du Mercantour** along the Italian border, **Mont Ventoux** northeast of Carpentras, and the flamingo-filled lagoons of the **Camargue** are just a selection of the diverse and stunning landscapes of this region.

ACCOMMODATION PRICE CATEGORIES

Each hotel in this chapter has a symbol which corresponds to one of eight price categories.

① Under 160F	④ 300–400F	⑦ 600–700F
② 160–220F	⑤ 400–500F	⑧ Over 700F
③ 220–300F	⑥ 500–600F	

The prices quoted are for the cheapest available double room in high season, though remember that many of the cheap places will have more expensive rooms with en-suite facilities.

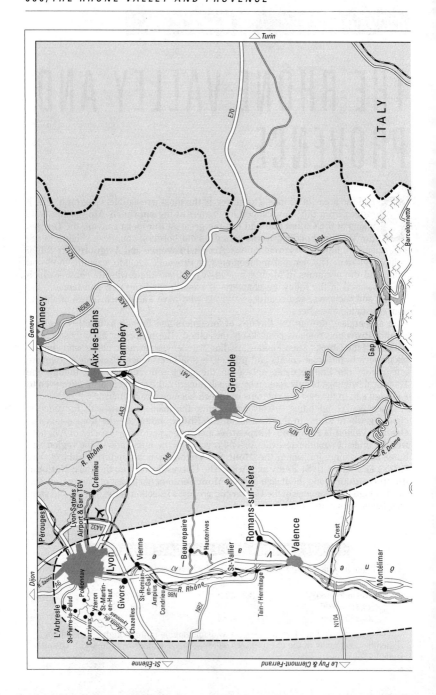

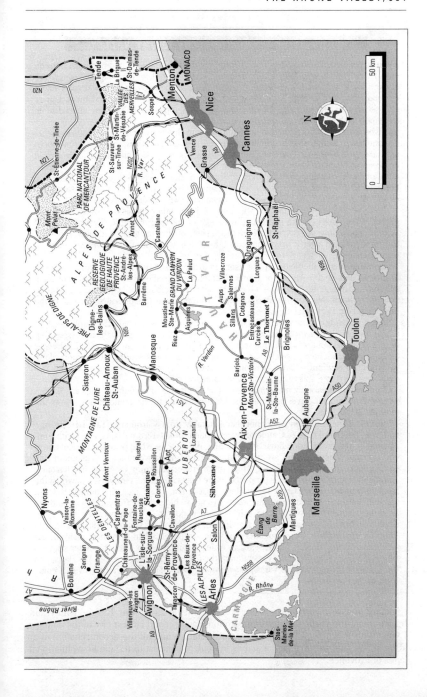

FOOD OF PROVENCE AND THE RHÔNE VALLEY

Lyon is renowned as a gastronomic centre, combining southern and northern ingredients. Its rich and hearty food is very meat and offal oriented, with sausages of every variety and a fine selection of cheeses. A Lyonnais salad includes bacon and a soft-cooked egg; potatoes also tend to be cooked with egg, cheeses and cream; and meat, fish or cheese are turned into fat, filling *quenelles*, or dumplings. Pâtisseries specialize in extremely rich chocolate gâteaux.

Olives were introduced to Provence by the ancient Greeks two-and-a-half thousand years ago and today accompany the traditional Provençal apéritif of *pastis*; they appear in sauces and salads, on tarts and pizzas, and mixed with capers in a paste called *tapenade* to spread on bread or biscuits. They are also used in traditional meat stews, like *daube Provençale*. Olive oil is the starting point for most Provençal dishes; spiced with chillis or Provençal herbs (wild thyme, basil, rosemary and tarragon), it is also poured over pizzas, sandwiches and, of course, used in vinaigrette and mayonnaise with all the varieties of salad.

The ingredient most often mixed with olive oil is the other classic of Provençal cuisine: **garlic**. Whole markets are dedicated to strings of pale purple garlic. Two of the most famous concoctions of Provence are **pistou**, a paste of olive oil, garlic and basil, and **aïoli**, the name for both a garlic mayonnaise and the dish in which it's served with salt cod and vegetables.

Vegetables have double or triple seasons in Provence, often beginning while northern France is still in the depths of winter. Ratatouille ingredients – tomatoes, capsicum, aubergines, courgettes and onions – are the favourites, along with asparagus. Courgette flowers, or *fleurs de courgettes farcies*, stuffed with *pistou* or tomato sauce, are one of the most exquisite Provençal delicacies.

Sheep, taken up to the mountains in the summer months, provide the staple meat, of which the best is *agneau de Sisteron*, often roasted with Provençal herbs as a *gigot d'agneau aux herbes*. But it is **fish** that features most on traditional menus, with freshwater trout, salt cod, anchovies, sea bream, monkfish, sea bass and whiting all common, along with brilliant **seafood**: clams, periwinkles, sea urchins, oysters, spider crabs and langoustines piled into spiky sculptural *plateaux de fruits de mer*.

Cheeses are invariably made from goat's or ewe's milk. Two famous ones are Banon, wrapped in chestnut leaves and marinated in brandy, and the aromatic Picadon, from the foothills of the Alps.

Sweets of the region include chocolates, notably from Valrhona in Tain L'Hermitage and from Puyricard near Aix, almond sweets called *calissons* from Aix, candied fruit from Apt and nougat from Montélimar. As for **fruits**, the melons, white peaches, apricots, figs, cherries and Muscat grapes are unbeatable. Almond trees grow on the plateaux of central Provence, along with lavender, which gives Provençal **honey** its distinctive flavour.

Some of France's best wine is produced in the Côtes du Rhône **vineyards**, of which the most celebrated is the Crozes-Hermitage *appellation*. Once past the nougat town of Montélimar and into Provence, the best wines are to be found in the villages around the Dentelles, notably Gigondas, and at Châteauneuf-du-Pape. To the west are the light, drinkable, but not particularly special wines of the Côtes du Ventoux and the Côtes du Lubéron *appellations*. Huge quantities of wine are produced in Provence, many of the vineyards planted during World War I in order to supply every French soldier with his ration of a litre a day. With the exception of the Côteaux des Baux around Les Baux, and the Côtes de Provence in the Var *département*, the best wines of southern Provence come from along the coast.

Before you reach Provence there are the **vineyards of the Rhône valley** and, before them, the French centre of gastronomy and second largest city of the country, **Lyon**. With its choice of restaurants, clubs, culture and all the accoutrements of an affluent and vital western city, it stands in opulent contrast to the medieval hilltop villages of Provence.

THE RHÔNE VALLEY

The **Rhône valley**, the north–south route of ancient armies, medieval traders and modern rail and road, is now as industrialized as the least attractive parts of the north. Though the river is still a means of transport, its waters now also cool the reactors of the Marcoule and Tricastin nuclear power station between **Montélimar** and Avignon and act as a dumping ground for the heavy industries along its banks. Following the River Rhône holds few attractions, with the exceptions of the stretch of **vineyards** and fruit orchards between the Roman city of **Vienne** and the distinctly southern city of **Valence**. But the big magnet is, of course, the gastronomic paradise of **Lyon**, with hundreds of sophisticated bars, restaurants and movies.

Lyon

LYON is physically the second biggest city in France, a result of its uncontrolled urban sprawl. Viewed at high speed from the Autoroute du Soleil, the impression it gives is of a major confluence of rivers and roads, around which only petrochemical industries thrive. In fact, silk was the city's main industry from the sixteenth century right up until the postwar dominance of metalworks, chemicals and transport. But what has stamped its character most on Lyon is the commerce and banking that grew up with its industrial expansion. It is this that gives the town its staid, stolid and somewhat austere air.

The city is now busy forging a role for itself within a new Europe. International schools and colleges, the new HQ for Interpol, a second TGV station with links to the north that bypass Paris, high-tech industrial parks for international companies, research institutes at the cutting edge of medicine and biology – Lyon, more so than any other French city, has embraced the monetarist vision of the European Union and is acting, with some success, as a postmodern city-state within it.

Most French people would find themselves in Lyon for business rather than for recreation: it's a get-up-and-go place, not a lie-back-and-rest one. You probably wouldn't plan a two-week stay – as you might in Provence's cities – but Lyon certainly has its charms. Foremost among these is **gastronomy**; there are more restaurants per Gothic and Renaissance square metre of the old town than anywhere else on earth, and the city could form a football team with its superstars of the international chef circuit. While the **textile museum** is the second famous reason for stopping here, Lyon's nightlife, cinema and theatre (including the famous Lyonnais puppets), its antique markets, music and other cultural festivities might tempt you to stay at least a few days.

Lyon is organised into arrondissements, of which there are nine. A visit to Lyon will necessarily take you into the Presqu'île (1^e and 2^e arrondissements), the area between the Rivers Saone and Rhône, and you are more than likely to spend some time in Vieux-Lyon (5^e) on the west bank of the Saône, as well as the east bank of the Rhône (3^e) including the modern development known as la Part-Dieu.

Arrival, information and accommodation

The **Lyon-Satolas international airport** (information ☎04.72.22.72.21) and its new TGV station are off the Grenoble autoroute, 20km to the southeast of the city, with a 45-minute Satobus bus link to the town centre (50F). The Paris to Lyon trip is actually quicker by TGV, but it's only from the air that you can appreciate architect Santiago Calatrava's design of a huge bird alighting or taking flight from the station roof.

Central Lyon has two train stations: the **Gare de Perrache** on the Presqu'île is used mainly for ordinary trains rather than TGVs, with the **gare routière** alongside. **La**

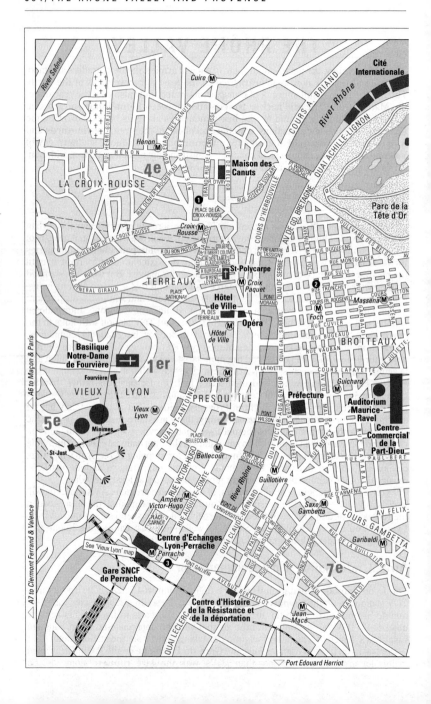

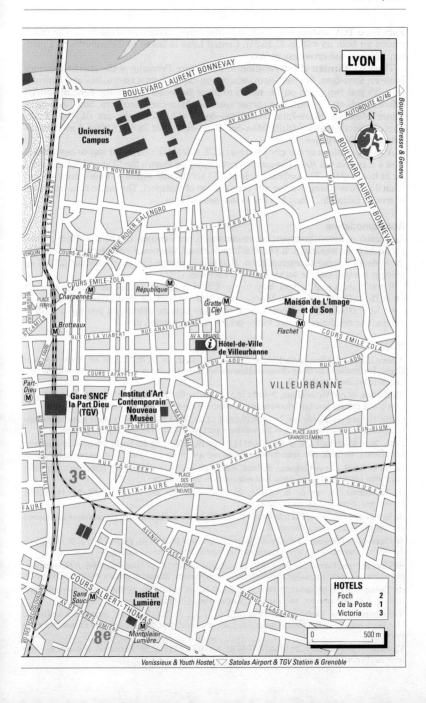

LYON

BOULEVARD LAURENT BONNEVAY

AUTOROUTE 42/46

Bourg-en-Bresse & Geneva

N

AV. ALBERT EINSTEIN

RUE DU 8 MAI 1945

BOULEVARD LAURENT BONNEVAY

University Campus

BD DU 11 NOVEMBRE

DE STALINGRAD

AVENUE ROGER SALENGRO

RUE ALEXIS-PERRONCEL

VERGUIN

COURS A. PHILIP

RUE FRANCIS-DE-PRESSENSE

COURS ÉMILE-ZOLA

Charpennes (M)

PLACE J. FERRY

BD DES BROTTEAUX

RECAMIER

République (M)

Gratte (M) Ciel

Maison de L'Image et du Son

Brotteaux (M)

BD J. FAVRE

RUE DE LA VIABERT

RUE ANATOLE-FRANCE

Flachet

COURS ÉMILE ZOLA

AV. A. BRIAND

(i) Hôtel-de-Ville de Villeurbanne

Part-Dieu (M)

COURS LAFAYETTE

RUE DU 4-AOÛT

RUE DU 4-AOÛT

VILLEURBANNE

Gare SNCF la Part Dieu (TGV)

Institut d'Art Contemporain Nouveau Musée

COURS TOLSTOÏ

ALMAS-SANBLER

BD MARIUS VIVIER MERLE

AVENUE GEROGES-POMPIDOU

RUE LÉON-BLUM

PLACE JULES GRANDECLEMENT

RUE PAUL-BERT

RUE JEAN-JAURÈS

3e

PLACE DES MAISONS NEUVES

AV. FÉLIX-FAURE

AVENUE PAUL-KRUGER

FAURE

AVENUE LACASSAGNE

AVENUE LACASSAGNE

COURS ALBERT-THOMAS

Sans Souci

AV. DE FRÈRES LUMIÈRE

Institut Lumière

BD DES TCHECOSLOVAQUES

8e

Montplaisir Lumière (M)

HOTELS
Foch	2
de la Poste	1
Victoria	3

0   500 m

Venissieux & Youth Hostel, ▽ Satolas Airport & TGV Station & Grenoble

Part-Dieu TGV station is in the 3e arrondissement to the east of the Presqu'île (information for both on ☎08.36.35.35.35). Central Lyon is linked to the suburbs by a modern, efficient and driverless **métro**.

There's a **Bureau d'Information** in the Centre Perrache at the station (summer Mon–Fri 9am–6pm, Sat 9am–5pm) where you can pick up a métro, bus and funicular map; it's just two stops on the métro to place Bellecour, where the **central tourist office** stands on the southeast corner (summer Mon–Sat 10am–8pm, Sun 10am–6pm; winter Mon–Sat 10am–7pm, Sun 10am–6pm; ☎04.72.77.69.69, fax 04.78.42.04.32). There is another office (daily Mon–Sat 10am–6pm; ☎04.78.68.13.20)at 3 av Aristide-Briand in Villeurbanne.

At métro stations or the city transport TCL offices, the cheapest way to buy **tickets** is in a carnet of ten (68F, discounts for students), or there's the "Ticket Liberté", valid for 24 hours (24F). The ordinary tickets (8F) are flat-rate within an hour's duration and limited to three changes using any combination of transport. The métro runs from 5am to around midnight. Many bus lines close around 8pm.

Accommodation

As a result of Lyon's commercial pre-eminence, hotel **rooms** can be a problem to find, particularly on weekdays. If you don't book ahead, you could end up paying well over the odds for inferior accommodation. Hotels in Perrache (2e) and Bellecour (2e) fill up quickly, but you may be luckier around Terreaux (1er).

If you're on a real budget, stop by the **CROUS** offices, 59 rue de la Madeleine, 7e (☎04.78.80.13.13; M° Jean-Macé), or **CRIJ** offices, 9 quai des Celestins, 2e (☎04.72.77.00.66; M° Bellecour), both of whom may be able to fix you up in student lodgings or residences closer to the centre during vacation time.

HOTELS

d'Ainay, 14 rue des Remparts d'Ainay, 2e (☎04.78.42.43.42, fax 04.72.77.51.90; M° Ampère–Victor-Hugo). Preferable to its many cheap neighbours because of its decent-sized rooms, but does fill fast. In a pleasant, lively quarter. ②.

Alexandra, 49 rue Victor-Hugo, 2e (☎04.78.37.75.79, fax 04.72.40.94.34; M° Ampère–Victor-Hugo). Large, well-run old hotel overlooking place Ampère – a lively pedestrian zone. ③.

Celtic, 10 rue François-Vernay, 1er (☎04.78.28.01.12, fax 04.78.28.01.34; M° Vieux-Lyon). Large, fairly comfortable and cheap place in the northern part of Vieux-Lyon close to place St-Paul. ②.

Foch, 59 av Maréchal-Foch, 6e (☎04.78.89.14.01, fax 04.78.93.71.69; M° Foch). Pleasant and superior hotel close to the park, with soundproofed rooms and a video library. Closed first two weeks in Aug. ⑤.

Globe et Cécil, 21 rue Gasparin, 2e (☎04.78.42.58.95, fax 04.72.41.99.06; M° Bellecour). Attractive place with good service and a touch of originality in the decor. ⑤.

de la Marne, 78 rue de la Charité, 2e (☎04.78.37.07.46, fax 04.72.41.70.64; M° Perrache). Convenient, clean and excellent value. ②.

de la Poste, 1 rue Victor-Fort, 4e (☎04.78.28.62.67; M° Croix-Rousse). An acceptable old-fashioned cheapie near place Croix-Rousse. ②.

St-Pierre-des-Terreaux, 8 rue Paul-Chenavard, 1er (☎04.78.28.24.61, fax 04.72.00.21.07; M° Hôtel-de-Ville). A convenient if rather charmless establishment in a good location. ③.

St-Vincent, 9 rue Pareille, 1er (☎04.78.27.22.56, fax 04.78.30.92.87; M° Hôtel-de-Ville). A pleasant, old-fashioned hotel near the Saône and the St-Vincent footbridge. Marble fireplaces still in the rooms. ③.

du Théâtre, 10 rue de Savoie, 2e (☎04.78.42.33.32, fax 04.72.40.00.61; M° Bellecour). A comfortable hotel with some character, well run by a pleasant young couple. ④.

Vaubecour, 28 rue Vaubecour, 2e (☎04.78.37.44.91, fax 04.78.42.90.17; M° Ampère-Victor-Hugo). One block back from the Saône quays, this place is comfortable, friendly and well-furnished for the price. ①.

Victoria, 3 rue Delandine, 2e (☎04.78.37.57.61, fax 04.78.42.91.07; M° Perrache). A decent two-star near the Perrache station. ③.

YOUTH HOSTELS AND CAMPSITE

HI youth hostel (Vieux Lyon), 41–45 Montée du Chemin Neuf, 5e (☎04.78.15.05.50, fax 04.78.15.05.51; M⁰ Vieux-Lyon-St-Jean/Minimes). A brand new and highly modern hostel. Brilliant views over Lyon and access to an Internet terminal. Set in a steep part of the old town, the nearest métro station is Vieux-Lyon-St-Jean, but if you want to avoid the climb, get the funicular to Minimes and walk down the Montée du Chemin Neuf.

HI youth hostel, 51 rue Roger-Salengro, Vénissieux (☎04.78.76.39.23). The other official hostel of Lyon is 4km southeast of the centre and only worth the trip if the central hostel is full. Take bus #53 from Perrache, stop États-Unis-Viviani, or bus #36 from Part-Dieu to stop Joliot-Curie then follow the footpath round to the right beside the autoroute. Alternatively, take bus #35 from Bellecour to G-Lévy-Auberge-de-Jeunesse stop, then head towards the flyover, turning left just before it, the hostel is indicated and is just on the other side of the car park.

Centre International de Séjour de Lyon, 48 rue Commandant-Pégoud, 8e (☎04.78.01.23.45). Not far from the Vénissiux youth hostel, but a lot more expensive; the advantage is that it's out of earshot of the main ring road. Take bus #53 from Perrache or #36 from Part-Dieu, stop États-Unis-Beauvisage. Open 24hr.

Porte de Lyon campsite, Dardilly (☎04.78.35.64.55). East along the N6 from Lyon or by bus #89 (direction "Ecully-Dardilly") from the Hôtel de Ville. Pleasant though expensive, and has a tourist information bureau (daily June to mid-Sept 8am–11pm; rest of the year 8am–8.30pm; ☎04.78.35.64.55).

The city

The centre of Lyon is the **Presqu'île**, or "peninsula", the tongue of land between the rivers Saône and Rhône, just north of their confluence. Most of it lies within the 2e arrondissement, but it's known by its quartiers, which include **Bellecour**, around the central square, and **Perrache** around the station. At the top end of the Presqu'île, as the Saône veers west, is the 1er arrondissement, known as **Terreaux**, centred on place des Terreaux and the Hôtel de Ville. On the west bank of the Saône is the old town, or **Vieux Lyon**, at the foot of Fourvière, on which the Romans built their capital of Gaul, Lugdunum. Vieux Lyon is made up of three villages: St-Paul, St-Jean and St-Georges, and forms the eastern end of the 5e arrondissement. The 9e lies to its north.

To the north of the Presqu'île is the old silk-weavers' district of **La Croix Rousse**, the 4e arrondissement. **Modern Lyon** lies east of the Rhône, with the 7e and 8e arrondissements to the south; the 3e arrondissement in the middle, with **La Part-Dieu TGV station** amidst an assertive cultural and commercial centre; and to the north the 6e arrondissement, known as **Brotteaux**. North of Brotteaux is Lyon's main open space, the **Parc de la Tête d'Or**. The district of **Villeurbanne**, home to the university and the Théâtre National Populaire, lies east of the 6e and the park.

The Presqu'île

The pink gravelly acres of **place Bellecour** were first laid out in 1617, and today form a focus on the peninsula, with views up to the looming bulk of Notre-Dame-de-Fourvière. The square is vast, dwarfing even the central statue of Louis XIV in the guise of Roman emperor. Running south, **rue Auguste-Comte** is full of antique shops selling heavily framed eighteenth-century art works, and **rue Victor-Hugo** is a pedestrian precinct that continues north of place Bellecour on rue de la République all the way up to the back of the Hôtel de Ville below the area of La Croix Rousse (see p.859).

South of place Bellecour on rue de la Charité, running parallel to rue Auguste-Comte on the Rhône side, is Lyon's best museum, the **Musée des Tissus** (Tues–Sun 10am–5.30pm; 28F). It doesn't quite live up to its claim to cover the history of decorative cloth through the ages, but it does have brilliant collections from certain periods, most notably third-century Greek-influenced and sixth-century Coptic tapestries, woven silk and painted linen from Egypt. The fragment of woven wool *aux poissons* ("with fish") (second to third century AD) has an artistry unmatched in European work

THE SILK STRIKE OF 1831

The modern silk-weaving machines are no different in principle from the Jacquard loom of 1804, although they made it possible for one person to produce 25cm in a day instead of taking four people four days. But silk workers, or *canuts* – whether masters and apprentices, or especially women and child workers – were badly paid whatever their output. Over the three decades following the introduction of the Jacquard, the price paid for a length of silk was reduced by over fifty percent. Attempts to regulate the price were ignored by the dealers, even though hundreds of skilled workers were languishing in debtors' jails. On November 21, 1831, the *canuts* called an all-out strike. As they processed down the Montée de la Grande Côte with their black flags and the slogan "Live working or die fighting", they were shot at and three people died. After a rapid retreat uphill they built barricades, assisted by half the National Guard, who refused to fire canon at their "comrades of Croix-Rousse". For three days, until the reinforcements were brought in, the battle raged on all four banks, the silk workers using sticks, stones and knives to defend themselves. Some 600 people were killed or wounded, and in the end the silk industrialists were free to pay whatever pitiful fee they chose. But the uprising was one of the first instances of organized labour taking to the streets during the most revolutionary fifty years of French history.

until at least the eighteenth century. There are silks from Baghdad contemporary with the *Thousand and One Nights*, and carpets from Iran, Turkey, India and China. The most boring stuff is that produced in Lyon itself, with seventeenth- to eighteenth-century hangings and chair covers. Sadly, there's almost nothing from the period of the Revolution, but there are some lovely twentieth-century pieces – Sonia Delaunay's *Tissus Simultanés*, Michel Dubost's *L'Oiseau Bleu* and Raoul Dufy's *Les Coquillages*. The dull **Musée des Arts Décoratifs** next door (daily except Mon 10am–noon & 2–5.30pm; same ticket as Musée des Tessus) has seventeenth- and eighteenth-century tapestries, furniture and ceramics.

To the south, the station area around Perrache is of little interest, but across the adjacent pont Gallieni, at 14 av Berthelot, is the **Centre d'Histoire de la Résistance et de la Déportation** (Wed–Sun 9am–5.30pm; 25F; Mº Perrache/Jean-Macé). In addition to a library of books, videos, memoirs and other documents recording experiences of Resistance, Occupation and Deportation to the camps, there's an exhibition space housed in the very cellars and cells in which Klaus Barbie, the Gestapo boss of Lyon, tortured and murdered his victims. Barbie was brought back from Uruguay a few years ago and tried in Lyon for crimes against humanity; the principal "exhibit" is a 45-minute video of the trial in which some of his victims recount their terrible ordeal at his hands – very moving and upsetting.

To the right at the top of quai St-Antoine is the **quartier Mercière**, the old commercial centre of the town, with sixteenth- and seventeenth-century houses lining rue Mercière, and the **church of St-Nizier**, whose bells used to announce the closing of the city's gates. In the silk weavers' uprising of 1831 (see box), workers fleeing the soldiers took refuge in St-Nizier only to be massacred. The bourgeoisie had certainly been running scared, with only the area between the rivers, place des Terreaux and just north of St-Nizier still under their control. Unfortunately for the *canuts* (the silk workers), their bosses could call on outside aid – which they did, to the tune of 30,000 extra troops. Traces of this working-class life are rapidly disappearing. The district is now full of fashionable bars and restaurants that come alive at night, and full, also, of smart shops all down the long pedestrian rue de la République. Close to St-Nizier, at 13 rue de la Poulaillerie, is the **Musée de l'Imprimerie et de la Banque** (Wed–Sun 9.30am–noon & 2–6pm; 25F). Its collection is unattractively displayed, which is a pity, for Lyon was both a leading publishing and banking centre in Renaissance times.

The monumental nineteenth-century **fountain** in front of the even more monumental **Hôtel de Ville** on place des Terreaux symbolizes rivers straining to reach the ocean. It was designed by Bartholdi, of Statue of Liberty fame. The rows of watery leaks, however, that sprout up unexpectedly across the rest of the square, are a modern addition. Opposite is the large bulk of the **Musée des Beaux-Arts** (Wed–Sun 10.30am–6pm; 25F), housed in a former Benedictine abbey and whose collections are second in France only to those in the Louvre. The museum is organised roughly by genre with nineteenth and twentieth century sculpture, represented by Canova, Barye and Rodin's *Temptation of St Anthony* in the ex-chapel on the ground floor. Medieval sculpture is on the first floor along with antiquities and *objets d'art*, including a particularly fine collection of sixth- to nineteenth-century Japanese, Korean and Chinese ceramics used in the tea ceremony, and an elegant Guimard bedroom recreated with the furniture from the Hôtel Guimard in Paris. At the top of the stairway leading to the second floor, turn around for the best view of Puvis de Chavannes' murals depicting his ideas of artistic inspiration, *Vision Antique, Inspiration Chrétienne* and *Le Bois Sacré*. In the painting collection, the twentieth century is particularly well represented: Gino Severini's *La Famille du Peintre* of 1939; spring and summer light in Bonnard's canvases beside wintry port scenes by Marquet; Van Dongens and de la Fresnayes throwing amused looks at their women friends; one of Monet's Thames series; *La Petite Niçoise* by Berthe Morisot; and Degas' almost luminous pastel of the *Café-Concert at Les Ambassadeurs*. Of the early nineteenth-century collection, *La Maraichère*, attributed to David, is outstanding, and you can work your way back through Rubens, Zurbarán, El Greco, Tintoretto, and a hundred others.

Behind the Hôtel de Ville, on the edge of several linked squares, stands Lyon's Neoclassical **opera house**, slightly uncertain of itself having just been redesigned by the architect Jean Nouvel. The Neoclassical exterior now supports a huge glass Swiss roll by way of a roof, and the interior – at least the only part accessible without a ticket – is now entirely black with silver stairways climbing into the darkness.

La Croix-Rousse

La Croix-Rousse is the old silk-weavers' district spreading up the steep slopes of the hill above the northern end of the Presqu'île. It's still a working-class area, but barely a couple of dozen people operate the modern high-speed computerized looms that are kept in business by the restoration and maintenance of France's palaces and châteaux. You can watch traditional looms in mesmerizing action at **La Maison des Canuts** at 10–12 rue d'Ivry, north of place de la Croix-Rousse (Mon–Sat 8.30am–noon & 2–6.30pm; Aug closed Mon; 15F; M° Croix-Rousse), and see some rare and beautiful cloths, including silk, damask and brocade, produced by this ancient home-weavers' co-operative.

The streets running down from **boulevard de la Croix-Rousse** – as well as many across the river in Vieux Lyon – are intersected by alleyways and tunnelled passages known as **traboules**. The original purpose of these was to provide shelter from the weather for the silk-weavers as they moved their delicate pieces of work from one part of the manufacturing process to another. Of course they also provided a secret and impenetrable warren for the Lyon underworld and, in time of war, for the local Resistance fighters. Some *traboules* have visible exits and entrances; others have doors like any street door that often lead to an upstairs apartment and the passage itself. Try going up past the right of St-Polycarpe on **rue Réné-Leynaud** above place Terreaux, then take the *traboule* opposite 36 rue Burdeau, go right around **place Chardonnet**, through 55 rue des Tables-Claudiennes, opposite 29 rue Imbert-Colomès and up the stairs into 14bis, across three more courtyards, and you should come out at **place Colbert**.

Quite a number of *traboules* have been closed today for security reasons, and the area is gradually being gentrified. The long climb up the **Montée de la Grande Côte**, however, still gives an idea of what the quartier was like. Take a look at the pretty **place**

Sathonay at the bottom, where the Croix-Rousse mairie overlooks that public garden and a lively local café and, if you have enough energy left, come down by the **rue Joséphin-Soulary**, which looks more like a lane in a country village and will bring you down a long flight of steps to the pont Winston-Churchill.

Vieux-Lyon

Reached by one of the three *passerelles* (footbridges) crossing the Saône from Terreaux and the Presqu'île, **Vieux Lyon** is made up of the three villages of St-Jean, St-Georges and St-Paul at the base of the hill overlooking the Presqu'île.

South of place St-Paul, the streets of Vieux Lyon, pressed close together beneath the hill of **Fourvière**, form a backdrop of Renaissance facades, bright night-time illumination and a swelling chorus of well-dressed Lyonnais in search of supper or a midday splurge. One of the most impressive buildings at the northern end is the sixteenth-century **Hôtel Paterin** at 4–6 rue Juiverie, a galleried mansion best viewed from the bottom of Montée St-Barthélémy, just up from place St-Paul.

A short way south, the **Musée Historique de Lyon**, on place du Petit-Collège (Wed–Mon 10.45am–6pm; 25F), has a good collection of Nevers ceramics, but the **Musée de la Marionnette**, on the first floor of this fifteenth-century mansion (same hours and ticket), is a lot more entertaining. As well as the eighteenth-century Lyonnais creations, *Guignol* and *Madelon* (the French equivalents of Punch and Judy), there are glove puppets, shadow puppets and rod-and-string toy actors from all over Europe and the Far East. If you want to see them in action, check out the times of performances at the **Théâtre de Guignol**, in the conservatory on rue Louis-Carrand by quai de Bondy (Oct–May Weds, Sat & Sun 3pm; for tickets and other shows, ring ☎04.78.28.92.57).

The central pedestrianized **rue St-Jean** ends at the twelfth- to fifteenth-century **Cathédrale St-Jean**. The west facade, the most recent part, lacks much of its statuary as a result of various religious wars and revolutions, but the thirteenth-century stained glass above the altar and in the rose windows of the transepts is in perfect condition. In the northern transept is a fourteenth-century clock, rivalling modern digital watches for function: you can compute religious feast days till the year 2019, and most days on the strike of noon, 2pm and 3pm, the figures of the Annunciation go through an automated set piece.

Just beyond the cathedral, opposite avenue Adolphe-Max and pont Bonaparte, is the **funicular station** and the Vieux Lyon métro, from which you can ascend to the town's Roman remains (direction "St-Just", stop Minimes). The antiquities consist of two ruined **theatres** dug into the hillside (entrance at 6 rue de l'Antiquaille; daily: summer 7am–9pm; winter 7am–7pm; free) – the larger of which was built by Augustus and extended in the second century by Hadrian to seat 10,000 spectators – and an underground museum of Lyonnais life from prehistoric times to 7 AD, the **Musée de la Civilisation Gallo-Romain**, 17 rue Cléberg (Wed–Sun 9.30am–noon & 2–6pm; 20F). Here, a mosaic illustrates various Roman games; bronze inscriptions detail economic, legal and administrative matters; there's a Gaulish lunar calendar and models aid the imagination in reconstructing the theatres outside.

From the museum, it's just a moment's walk to the **Basilique de Fourvière**, an awful wedding cake of a church built like the Sacré-Cœur in Paris in the aftermath of the 1871 Commune to emphasize the defeat of the godless socialists. And like the Sacré-Cœur, its hilltop position has become an almost defining element in the city's skyline. What makes a visit worthwhile, however, is the magnificient **view** of the city; you can distinguish the different quarters and see how they have grown and been shaped by the Saône and Rhone over the centuries. The Basilique is also accessible direct from the Vieux-Lyon funicular station: if you arrive by this route, take the trouble to walk down, by (for

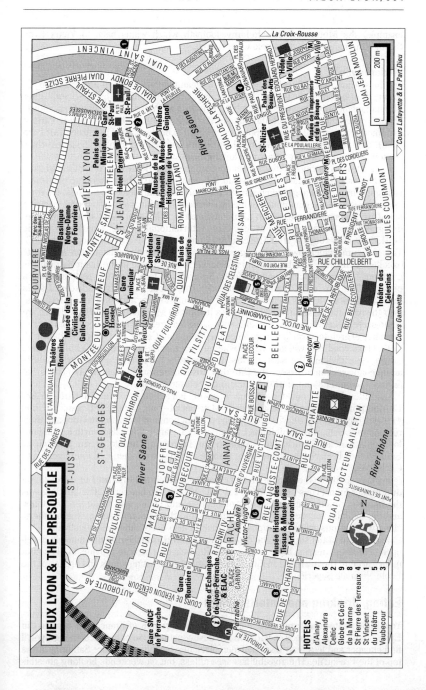

VIEUX LYON & THE PRESQU'ÎLE

△ La Croix-Rousse

▷ Cours Lafayette & La Part Dieu

▷ Cours Gambetta

200 m

HOTELS

d'Ainay	7
Alexandra	6
Celtic	2
Globe et Cécil	8
de la Marne	9
St Pierre des Terreaux	4
St Vincent	1
du Théâtre	5
Vaubecour	3

example) the **Montée St-Barthélemy** footpath which winds back to Vieux Lyon through the hanging gardens below the church.

Modern Lyon

On the skyline from Fourvière, you'll see a gleaming cylinder with a pointed top – a tower that belongs to Lyon's home-grown Crédit Lyonnais bank – and other Manhattanish protuberances around it. This is **La Part-Dieu**, a business-culture-commerce conglomerate including one of the biggest public libraries outside Paris, a mammoth concert hall and a shopping centre said to be the largest in Europe (M° Part-Dieu). On the corner of rue Garibaldi and cours Lafayette in front of these less-than-homely structures are the **main market halls** of Lyon.

For a break from city buildings head north to the **Parc de la Tête d'Or** (bus #4 from Part-Dieu or métro to Masséna, then walk up rue Masséna), where there are ponds and rose gardens, botanical gardens, a small zoo and lots of amusements for kids. It's over-looked by the bristling antennae of the international headquarters of Interpol, part of a new **Cité Internationale**, which also includes a new **Musée d'Art Contemporain**, designed by Renzo Piano, at 81 Cité Internationale, quai Charles-de-Gaulle (☎04.72.69.17.17; bus #4, stop Musée d'Art Contemporain; Wed–Sun noon–7pm; 25F). The museum, which owns the largest museum collection of installation art, hosts excellent temporary exhibitions and is also the regular home of the Lyon Biennale, is a curious-looking structure with a 1930s' Neoclassical facade on the park side and a pink concrete box tacked onto the riverside. The colour echoes the adjacent **Palais des Congrès** conference centre, whose front is masked by a glass screen curving up over the roof, reminiscent of Jean Nouvel's Institut du Monde Arabe in Paris. There are some screens, catwalks and companionways: the features that have become part of the currency of architectural language since the Pompidou Centre first shocked the world. But it looks good, and will look better when the area ceases to resemble a building site. To the east, dividing the park and the university, is boulevard de Stalingrad, where antique-fanciers can browse in the **Cité des Antiquaires** arcades at no. 117 (Thurs, Sat & Sun 9.30am–12.30pm & 2.30–7pm; summer closed Sun pm).

In Villeurbanne, not far to the east of Part-Dieu, is the **Institut d'Art Contemporain**, 11 rue Dr-Dolard (daily May–Sept 1–7pm; Oct–April 1–6pm; 20F; bus #1 stop Nouveau Musée), which questions the function of art and architecture and their relation to society, with exhibitions by contemporary artists. It's also worth looking out for exhibitions at Villeurbanne's **Maison du Livre de l'Image et du Son**, on av Émile-Zola (M° Flachet), which might feature anything from medieval illuminations to CD-ROMs.

Further south, on the edge of the 8e arrondissement, is the **Institut Lumière**, 25 rue du Premier-Film (Tues–Sun 2–7pm; 25F; M° Monplaisir/Lumière). The building was the home of Antoine Lumière, father of Auguste and Louis, who made the first films, and the exhibits feature early magic lanterns and the cameras used by the brothers, along with various art photographs. The Institut also hosts various film festivals.

Right down in the south of the city, in the **Gerland quartier** (7e), is a newly devel-oped area with a marina and a park on the Rhône's east bank to provide an illusion of nature around the mirrored Institut Pasteur and the thrusting wings and arches of the École Normale Supérieure.

Eating, drinking and entertainment

You'll find **restaurants** offering dishes from every region of France and overseas in Lyon. Vieux Lyon is the area with the greatest concentration of eateries, though you'll find cheaper and less busy ones between place des Jacobins and place Sathonay at the top of the Presqu'île. The possibilities are endless, but on weekends booking ahead is always a good idea. The most affordable type of Lyonnais eating establishment, the **bouchon** (cork), derived its name from the vast quantities of Lyonnais wine consumed there. Tradition has it that wine bottles were lined up as the evening progressed, and at the end of the night the bill was determined by measuring from the first cork to the last. There are several *bouchons* located in the streets between Cordeliers and Terreaux, particularly in rue Mercière.

Lyon is almost as good a place for **nightlife** as it is for eating, with a good range of clubs, cinema, opera, jazz, classical music concerts and theatre. The tourist office brings out a bimonthly brochure, *Le Progrèscope,* with broad mainstream listings. Or there's the weekly *Lyon Poche* available from newsagents (every Tues; 7F).

Restaurants

Alain Chapel, Mionnay (☎04.78.91.82.02). This restaurant, 19km north of Lyon, is almost as good as *Paul Bocuse* (see below) and in the same price bracket. Superb fish dishes, spicy pigeon stuffed with wild mushrooms, lime soufflé – every dish is a work of art.

L'Amphitryon, 33 rue St-Jean, 5ᵉ (☎04.78.37.23.68). Usually packed restaurant featuring Lyonnais specialities; menu for under 100F. Service till midnight.

Café des Fédérations, 8 rue du Major-Martin, 1ᵉʳ (☎04.78.28.26.00). Typical *bouchon* serving the earthiest of Lyonnais specialities (marinated tripe, black pudding and fish *quenelles*) in an atmosphere to match: there's even sawdust on the floor. Menu at 118F lunchtimes, 148F dinner. Closed Sat, Sun & Aug.

Chez Léa "La Voûte", 11 place Antoine-Gourju, 2ᵉ (☎04.78.42.01.33). Excellent traditional Lyonnais cooking and especially good salads. From 120F. Closed Sun.

Chez Léon, Halles de la Part-Dieu, 102 cours Lafayette, 3ᵉ (☎04.78.62.30.28). Bar and resto in the market halls for seafood and snails. Around 150F for full whack. Closed May–Aug.

Léon de Lyon, 1 rue Pléney, 1ᵉʳ (☎04.78.28.11.33). Sophisticated dishes and many traditional Lyonnais recipes in an upmarket brasserie setting. From 450F but with a lunch menu for 290F.

La Mère Brazier, 12 rue Royale, 1ᵉʳ (☎04.78.28.15.49). A beautiful setting complements the excellent food, like Bresse chicken, artichoke hearts on *foie gras*, truffle crêpes – but it's very expensive. From 350F. Closed Sun, Sat lunch & Aug.

La Meunière, 11 rue Neuve, 1ᵉʳ (☎04.78.28.62.91). Booking is essential in this excellent *bouchon*, but it's worth it for the 150F menu of course after course of Lyonnais specialities. Other menus start at 90F. Closed Sun, Mon, July & Aug.

Paul Bocuse, 40 rue de la Plage, Collonges-au-Mont-d'Or (☎04.72.42.90.90). Lyon's most famous restaurant, named after its celebrity chef-owner, is 9km north of the city, on the west bank of the Saône. Traditional French gluttony is the bill of fare, with stunning *crème brûlée* and *baba au rhum*. 500F upwards.

La Tour Rose, 22 rue Bœuf, 5ᵉ (☎04.78.37.25.90). Gastronomic palace with concoctions like asparagus with an oyster mousse or salad of lobster and spinach with a creamed truffle sauce. From 320F. Closed Sun.

Bars and clubs

The best places to wander if you are looking for a **bar** are rue Mercière and rue de la Monnaie and, most particularly, the streets of Vieux Lyon, especially the southern part around the place Bertras. And make a point of crossing the river by the *passerelles*; the whole district looks magnificent at night.

66 Road Café, 9 place des Terreaux, 1ᵉʳ. American decor. Rock, R&B, blues, etc, plus billiards. Daily 2pm–3am.

Albion Public House, 12 rue Ste-Catherine, 1ᵉʳ. English pub with draught beer where you can play darts and listen to jazz, R&B and soul on Sat and Sun nights. Mon–Thurs 5pm–2am, Fri–Sat 5pm–3am, Sun 6pm–1am.

Antidote, 108 rue St-Georges, 5ᵉ. Irish pub with free concerts of rock, folk, blues and jazz in the basement. Daily 5pm–1am.

B52 Club, 67 rue des Rancy, Part-Dieu, 3ᵉ. Rock concerts. Wed–Sat 10pm–4am.

Le Chicanos, 2 rue Octavio-Mey, 5ᵉ. Mexican bar with cheap drinks; popular with the young. Daily 7.30pm–3am.

Country Rock, 1 quai des Célestins, 1ᵉʳ. 1950s country music, cocktails and American food – drinks are pricey. Mon–Fri noon–1am, weekends till 4am.

Écossais, 7 rue Charles-Dullin, 2ᵉ. Scots-style piano bar serving 100 different whiskies. Mon–Sat 6pm–5am.

Éspace Gerson, 1 place Gerson, 5ᵉ. Has café-théâtre some nights, otherwise jazz or performance art, plus darts and billiards. Mon–Sat 5pm–2am.

Fish, opposite 21 quai Augagneur, 3ᵉ. Lyon's newest, hippest night club. Admission 60F, drinks 20–30F. Open 10pm–5am, Thurs student night, Fri theme night and Sat house and garage.

Hot Club, 26 rue du Lanterne, 1ᵉʳ. Jazz of all varieties in a vaulted cellar. Tues–Sat 8pm–2am. Closed July & Aug.

Mylord, 112 quai Pierre-Scize, 5ᵉ. Gay disco with drag shows and an interesting decor of statues and a sculpted stone bar. Mon–Sat 10.30pm–4am.

Paradiso Club, 24 rue Pizay, 1ᵉʳ. Funky music and transvestite or burlesque cabaret. Daily 10pm–dawn.

Le Village, 8 rue St-Georges, 5ᵉ. Lesbian club with a friendly atmosphere. Shows, songs and cabaret acts, plus mixed night Thurs – men must be accompanied. Tues–Fri from 6pm, Sat from 8pm.

Theatre, music and film

Look out for **stage productions** by the Théâtre National Populaire (TNP), 8 place Lazare-Goujon (☎04.78.03.30.40), based across the street from Villeurbanne's town hall. Less radical stuff will be shown at the city's gilded Théâtre des Célestins, in place des Célestins, 2ᵉ (☎04.72.77.40.00). The **opera house**, one of the best in France, is on place de la Comédie, 1ᵉʳ (☎04.72.00.45.45), with cheap tickets sold just before performances begin. For avant-garde, classic and obscure **films**, usually in their original language, check the listings for the cinemas CNP Terreaux, Ambiance, Opéra and Le Cinéma.

Listings

Boat trips Bateaux-Mouches Lui, Société Naviginter, 13bis quai Rambaud, 2ᵉ (☎04.78.42.96.81) from quai des Célestins; up the Saône or down to the confluence to the Île Barbe (daily April–Nov). The Société Naviginter also run a boat, *Elle*, down the Rhône to Vienne.

Books English bookshop, Eton, 1 rue du Plat, near Bellecour.

Car rental Europcar, 40 rue de la Villette, 3ᵉ (☎04.72.68.84.60); Hertz, 102 av Jean-Jaurès, 3ᵉ (☎04.72.80.76.76); Avis 8 rte de Vienne (☎04.78.58.32.69); all the above have offices at the airport and at the Perrache centre.

Changing money AOC, 20 rue Gasparin (Mon–Sat 9.30am–6.30pm, Sun 10am–5pm); AOC Opéra, 3 rue de la République (Mon–Fri 9am–6pm); Thomas Cook, Gare de la Part-Dieu (Mon–Sat 8am–7pm, Sun & holidays 10.30am–7pm); the tourist office on Bellecour has a money-changing machine (open hours of tourist office, see above).

Consulates Ireland, 4 rue Jean-Desparmet, 8ᵉ (☎04.78.76.44.85); UK, 24 rue Childebert, 2ᵉ (☎04.72.77.81.70).

Emergencies SOS Médecins (☎04.78.83.51.51). Hospitals: Hôtel-Dieu, 1 place de l'Hôtel-Dieu, 2ᵉ (☎04.72.41.30.00); Hôpital Édouard-Herriot on place d'Arsonval, 3ᵉ (☎04.72.11.73.11). Pharmacy open till midnight: Blanchet, 5 place des Cordeliers, 2ᵉ.

Police The main commissariat is on rue de la Charité, 2ᵉ (☎04.78.42.26.56).

Post office PTT, place Antonin-Poncet, Lyon 69002.

Taxis ☎04.78.28.23.23 or 04.78.26.81.81.

Around Lyon

Within easy reach of the city, the **Monts du Lyonnais** to the south and west of Lyon may not reach spectacular heights, but they offer quiet and solitude among steep, forested hills and unassuming villages surrounded by cherry orchards, the region's main source of income. Tourism is low-key, but food and accommodation in the hostels of the mountain villages are rarely a problem for visitors to the area's parks and museums. **Bus** services from Lyon to the larger villages are reasonably frequent, and to the east of Lyon, the small medieval cities of **Pérouges** and **Crémieu** can easily be reached by train. The mountains can be visited every Sunday from June until the middle of September by steam train, leaving from **L'Arbresle**, just west of Lyon (frequent trains from Lyon-Perrache); it's a scenic service but not very useful for getting anywhere.

Worth a visit if you're not returning straight to Lyon, the **Musée de la Mine** at **ST-PIERRE-LA-PALUD**, 15km west of the city (March–Nov Sat, Sun & hols 2–6pm; 25F), is guaranteed to instil admiration for the endurance of the miners who put up with working conditions like those simulated in the reconstructed mine shaft which forms the main exhibit. Going down into the copper sulphate mine shaft while an ex-miner explains its workings in meticulous detail (2hr; in French) is not recommended if you're claustrophobic. Back on the surface, you move onto an exhibition on the former mining village and pit.

Most of the villages in the Lyonnais mountains have some form of auberge serving food and providing a bed for the night. A typical, attractive example is the tiny village of **YZERON**, 12km south of the wildlife park at Courzieu, on whose main square are a crêperie and the excellent *Auberge de Tonton* (☎04.78.81.01.42; ③), which serves duck and salmon as part of a 125F menu. There are a couple of hotels and restaurants in the village of **ST-MARTIN-EN-HAUT**, eight winding kilometres south of Yzeron, as well as a **tourist office** (Mon 2–4pm, Tues–Sat 9am–noon & 2–6pm, Sun 10am–noon; ☎04.78.48.64.32), and a **camping municipal** just outside the village on the D122 (☎04.78.48.62.16; all year).

Pérouges and Crémieu

Twenty-nine kilometres northeast of Lyon on the N84, **PÉROUGES** is a pretty little town of cobbled alleyways, whose charm has not gone unnoticed by the French film industry – historical dramas like *The Three Musketeers* and *Monsieur Vincent* were filmed within the town walls – nor by some of the residents, who have fought long and hard for preservation orders on its most interesting buildings.

Local traditional life is also thriving in the hands of a hundred or so workers who still weave locally grown hemp. No particular monument stands out, but the central square, the **place du Halle**, and its main street, the **rue du Prince**, have some of the best-preserved French medieval remains. The **lime tree** on place du Halle is a symbol of liberty, planted in 1792. *The* place both to **stay** and eat in Pérouges, if you can afford it, is the *Ostellerie du Vieux Pérouges* (☎04.74.61.00.88, fax 04.74.34.77.90; ⑤–⑧), in a medieval town house on place Tilleul; its **restaurant** serves traditional mountain dishes of rabbit and carp, with menus from 190F.

CRÉMIEU, to the south on the D517, is less compelling, despite its local sausages (*sabodet*), monumental architecture and early origins – the city can be traced back to 835 AD. It was once an important commercial centre, signified by the fourteenth-century **market buildings** on rue du Lt-Col-Bel, and a border-post of the kingdom of Dauphiné, a number of imposing doorways being all that remain of the medieval fortifications.

Vienne and around

On leaving Lyon, it's tempting to head straight for the Med, and the first stretch of motorway between Lyon and Vienne is unlikely to distract you from that goal. There is nothing here but oil refineries, steel, chemical and paper works, cement, fertilizer and textile factories, all spewing plumes of grey and orange pollution into the air and water.

VIENNE'S MUSEUMS

The Théâtre Antique, Église and Cloître de St-André-le-Bas, Musée des Beaux-Arts et d'Archéologie and Église-Musée St-Pierre can be visited on a single ticket (24F or 29F if there is a temporary exhibition in any of the sites).

VIENNE is still a bit too close to all this for comfort. Taking a reluctant exit off the Autoroute du Soleil en route to Provence is well worth the trouble, however, as the town contains extensive remnants of its ancient history as a major seat of Roman power in Gaul. Every street corner seems to sprout some monument: a Roman temple, a medieval church or cloister. The old quarter is crisscrossed with pedestrian precincts which make for enjoyable menu-browsing around **rue des Clercs** and **place Charles-de-Gaulle**. And there's a feeling that despite the distant rumble of the autoroute calling you to sunnier climes, the town has maintained a character and sense of purpose.

The town

Roman monuments are scattered liberally around the streets of Vienne, and it requires little effort to take in the magnificently restored **Temple d'Auguste** on place du Palais, a scaled-down version of Nîmes's Maison Carrée, or the scanty remains of the **Théâtre de Cybèle**, off place de Miremont. The **Théâtre Antique** (April–Aug daily 9.30am–1pm & 2–6pm; Sept–mid-Oct daily except Mon, same hours; mid-Oct–March Tues–Sat 9.30am–noon & 2–5pm, Sun 1.30–5.30pm; 11F) is more of a haul, off rue du Cirque at the base of Mont Pipet to the north, but it's worth making the trip for the view of the town and river from the very top seats. The theatre is the venue of an **international jazz festival** for the first two weeks of July, when it plays host to some of the biggest names on the jazz circuit.

The **Église-Musée St-Pierre** (same hours and price as Théâtre Antique, except mid-Oct to March Sun 2–5pm) was possibly the first cathedral ever built in France. Since its origins in the fifth century, the building has suffered much destruction and rebuilding, but despite a short period when it was used as a factory in the nineteenth century, it is still one of Vienne's most graceful and attractive buildings. The museum itself is predictably dominated by finds from Vienne's Roman past, though many of the exhibits have now been moved to the new museum at St-Romain-en-Gal (see below). Close by is the most prominent – and vaunted – of Vienne's monuments, the **Cathédrale St-Maurice**, whose unwieldy facade, a combination of Romanesque and Gothic, appears as if its upper half has been dumped on top of a completely alien building. The interior, with its ninety-metre-long vaulted nave, is impressive though, and there are some superb stained-glass windows.

The **Église** and **Cloître de St-André-le-Bas** on rue des Clercs (same hours and price as St-Pierre) date from the ninth and twelfth centuries, though much of the stone had already been used by the Romans. The cloister, where temporary exhibitions are staged, is particularly pretty with small delicate pillars with capitals diversely decorated with mythological and biblical figures.

The major museum in Vienne is the **Musée des Beaux-Arts et d'Archéologie** on place de Miremont (same hours and price as St-Pierre), with a preponderance of eighteenth-century French pottery, but also some attractive pieces of third-century Roman silverware. More enlightening is the small textile museum, the **Musée de la Draperie** (April–Sept Tues–Sun 2.30–6.30pm; 20F) in the Espace St-Germain to the south of the centre off rue Vimaine which, with the aid of videos, working looms and weavers, illustrates the complete process of cloth-making as it was practised in the city for over two hundred years.

Practicalities

The cours Brillier runs at right angles to the river, with the **tourist office** at no. 3, near quai Jean-Jaurès (mid-June to mid-Sept Mon–Sat 9am–12.30pm & 1.30–7pm, Sun 10am–noon & 2.30–6pm; rest of year Mon–Sat 8.30am–noon & 2–6pm; ☎04.74.53.80.30, fax 04.74.31.75.98), and the **gare SNCF** at the other end. Halfway up the *cours*, rue Boson leads up to the west front of the cathedral.

If you plan to **stay** over, the *Poste*, 47 cours Romestang (☎04.74.85.02.04, fax 04.74.85.16.17; ③), between the station and place de Miremont, has an excellent restaurant and good rooms overlooking the *cours*. For small budgets try the *Pile ou Face*, 35 cours Brillier (☎04.74.85.05.84; ②), just down from the tourist office. *Le Grand Hôtel du Nord* (☎04.74.85.77.11, fax 04.74.53.23.62; ④) is a more upmarket central option at 9 place de Miremont. If you have your own transport, you could stay at the *Château des Sept Fontaines*, 5km northwest on the N7 at **Seyssuel** (☎04.74.85.25.70, fax 04.74.31.74.47; ④; closed Nov–March), with a large garden, sauna and gym, and comfortable rooms. There's also an HI **youth hostel** on the other side of the park from the tourist office at 11 quai Riondet (☎04.74.53.21.97, fax 04.74.31.98.93).

The old town has a number of promising places to **eat**, including a good selection of cheapies in rue de la Table Ronde (near St-André-le-Bas). There is *L'Estancot* at no. 4 (☎04.74.85.12.09; closed Mon & Sun), and *Au Petit Chez Soi* at no. 6 (☎04.74.85.19.77; closed Sun) with *moules frites* and menus under 100F. *Le Bec Fin*, 7 place St-Maurice (☎04.74.85.76.72; closed Sun eve & Mon), offers filling menus of Lyonnais dishes from 125F. Vienne's superlative restaurant is *La Pyramide*, 14 bd Fernand-Point (☎04.74.53.01.96; Oct–Dec closed Wed & Thurs lunch) with weekday menus at 120F and 280F; going à la carte will cost you at least 500F. For good beer, head for *La Brasserie de Maître Kanter* at 61 cours Romestang.

St-Romain-en-Gal

Across the Rhône from Vienne, several hectares of Roman ruins constitute the site of **ST-ROMAIN-EN-GAL**, also the name of the town which faces Vienne from the other bank of the Rhône. The excavations, to the right of the N86 as you head away from Vienne towards Lyon, are immaculately restored and well preserved, particularly the frescoes. They attest to a significant community dating from the first century BC to the third AD, and give a vivid picture of the daily life and domestic architecture of Roman France. Particularly evocative is the **House of the Sea Gods** with a beautiful mosaic floor featuring bearded Neptune and other marine images. More mosaics, including the spectacular *mosaïque d'Orphée*, depicting birds and animals in subtle colouring, are on show in the beautiful new **Musée Archéologique de St-Romain-en-Gal** (site & museum Tues–Sun 9.30am–6.30pm; 30F).

Between Vienne and Valence

Between Vienne and Valence are some of the oldest, most celebrated **vineyards** in France: the renowned Côte Rotie, Hermitage and Crozes-Hermitage *appellations*. If you've got any spare luggage space, it's well worth stopping to pick up a bottle from the local co-op; even their *vin ordinaire* is superlative and unbelievably cheap, considering its quality. Just south of Ampuis on the west bank, 8km south of Vienne, is the tiny area producing one of the most exquisite French white wines – *Condrieu* – and close by one of the most exclusive – Château-Grillet – an *appellation* covering just this single château (shop open Mon–Fri 8am–5pm; ☎04.74.59.51.56).

Between **St-Vallier** and **Tain l'Hermitage**, the Rhône becomes quite scenic, and after Tain you can see the Alps. You may even conclude that it's worth slowing down.

In spring you're more likely to be conscious of orchards everywhere rather than vines. Cherries, pears, apples, peaches and apricots, as well as bilberries and strawberries, are cultivated in abundance.

Tain-l'Hermitage and around

TAIN-L'HERMITAGE, accessible from both the N7 and the A7, is unpretentious and uneventful. The only reason to stay here is to drink wine and eat chocolate. You can sample a good selection of the renowned *Hermitage* and *Crozes-Hermitage* wines at the Cave de Tain-l'Hermitage, 22 rte de Larnage (Mon–Sat 8am–noon & 2–6pm, Sun opens 9am; ☎04.75.08.20.87), and if your visit happens to fall on the last weekend in February you can try out wines from 78 vineyards in the Foire aux Vins des Côtes du Rhône Septentrionales. The celebrated chocolates in question are made by Valrhona and available at their shop (Mon–Fri 9am–7pm, Sat 9am–6pm) on av du Président-Roosevelt (the RN7), past the junction with the RN95 as you're heading south. The **tourist office** at 70 av Jean-Jaurès (Mon–Sat 9am–noon & 2–6pm; ☎04.75.08.06.81, fax 04.75.08.34.59), on the RN7 further north, can provide you with lists of vineyard addresses.

If you need to **stay**, there's a low-price hotel at 9 place Taurobole, off av Jean-Jaurès in the centre of town, *L'Escale* (☎04.75.08.31.67; ①; closed Nov) and the bit more upmarket *Les 2 Côteaux*, 18 rue Joseph-Péala, running off Jean-Jaurès south of place Taurobole (☎04.75.08.33.01, fax 04.75.08.44.20; ②).

For a cheap **meal** in Tain try the crêperie *La Récré*, 8 place Taurobole (☎04.75.08.19.00), as an alternative to the stuffier establishments on av Jean-Jaurès. Tain's best restaurant, *Reynaud*, 82 av du Président-Roosevelt (☎04.75.07.22.10; closed Sun eve & Mon), has an excellent-value 160F menu, with à la carte upwards of 300F.

On the third weekend of September, the different wine-producing villages celebrate their cellars in the Fête des Vendanges. But at any time of the year you can go bottle-hunting along the N86 for some 30km north of Tain along the right bank, following the *dégustation* signs and then crossing back over between Serrières and Chanas.

Hauterives

HAUTERIVES, 25km northeast of Tain, is a small village with a remarkable creation – a manic, surreal **Palais Idéal** built by a local postman by the name of Ferdinand Cheval (1836–1912). The eccentric building took him thirty years to carve, and he designed a likewise bizarre tombstone. Various Surrealists have paid homage to the building; psychoanalysts have given it their all, but it defies all classification (daily April 15 to Sept 15 9am–7pm; Dec & Jan 10am–4.30pm; rest of year 9.30am–5.30pm; 26F). If you want to stay here, there's the *Camping du Château* on the N538 (☎04.75.68.80.19, fax 04.75.68.90.94; April to mid-Oct) and one **hotel**, *Le Relais* (☎04.75.68.81.12, fax 04.75.68.92.42; ②).

Romans-sur-Isère

South of Hauterives and 15km east of the Rhône at Tain is **ROMANS-SUR-ISÈRE**. It's not the most exciting of towns but it does have a fascinating museum of shoemaking – the industry that has kept Romans going for the last five centuries. The extensive **Musée Internationale de la Chaussure** is in the former Convent of the Visitation at 2 rue Ste-Marthe (July & Aug Mon–Sat 10am–6.30pm, Sun 2.30–6pm; Sept–June Tues–Sat 9–11.45am & 2–5.45pm, Sun 2.30–6pm; 25F) and also includes a permanent exhibition on the Resistance. Your toes will curl in horror at the extent to which women have been immobilized by their footwear from ancient times to the present on every continent, while at the same time you can't help but admire the craziness of some of the creations. Romans is also a good place to buy shoes, with several factory shops in the town.

If you need information, there's a **tourist office** on place Jean-Jaurès (April–Oct Mon–Fri 9am–7pm, Sat 9am–6pm, Sun 9.30am–12.30pm; Nov–March Mon–Fri 9am–6pm, Sat 9am–6pm, Sun 9.30am–12.30pm; ☎04.75.02.28.72). Romans has plenty of beautiful old streets and buildings to admire, and its region has two gastronomic specialities: a ringed spongy bread flavoured with orange water, known as a *pogne*, and *ravioles*, cornflour-based ravioli with an eggy, cheesy, buttery filling. You can sample these at the restaurant *La Cassolette*, 16 rue Rebatte (☎04.75.02.55.71; closed Sun & Mon throughout the year & 3 weeks from last week in July; menus under 100F).

Romans' **hotels** include *Les Balmes*, northwest of the town centre in the quartier Les Balmes (☎04.75.02.29.52, fax 04.75.02.75.47; ③), with a reputed and inexpensive **restaurant** (closed Sun eve out of season). A cheaper option for **rooms** is the *Magdeleine*, 31 av Pierre-Sémard (☎04.75.02.33.53; ②; closed Sun eve out of season), or the *Terminus*, 48 rue Pierre-Sémard (☎04.75.02.46.88, fax 04.75.05.13.04; ②). The municipal **campsite**, *Les Chasses* (☎04.75.72.35.27; May–Sept), is 1km off the N92 northeast of the city, near the aerodrome.

Valence

At an indefinable point along the Rhône, there's an invisible sensual border. By the time you reach **VALENCE**, you know you've crossed it. The quality of light is different and the temperature higher, bringing with it the scent of eucalyptus and pine. The colours and contours have suddenly become worlds apart from the cold lands of Lyon and the north. Valence is the obvious place to celebrate your arrival in the Midi (as the French call the south), with plenty of good bars and restaurants in the old town.

Arrival, information and accommodation

If you come in on the autoroute, running along the Rhône's left bank, you exit onto avenue Gambetta, with the old town, its ramparts replaced by boulevards, to your left. To the southeast of the old town you'll find the **gare routière**, the **gare SNCF** and the **tourist office** on Parvis de la Gare (June–Aug Mon–Sat 9am–7pm, Sun 9am–noon; Sept–May Mon 2–6.30pm, Tues–Sat 9am–12.30pm & 2–6.30pm; ☎04.75.44.90.40, fax 04.75.44.90.41).

For mid-range hotel **rooms**, try *California*, 174 av Maurice-Faure (☎04.75.44.36.05, fax 04.75.41.20.25; ③) or *Europe*, 15 av Félix-Faure (☎04.75.43.02.16, fax 04.75.43.61.75; ③). If you want to splash out, *Yan's Hotel* has spacious rooms in a stylish modern building with park and pool south of the city on the rte de Montéléger (☎04.75.55.52.52, fax 04.75.42.27.37; ④). Budget options include the *Angleterre*, 11 av Félix-Faure (☎04.75.43.00.35, fax 04.75.43.75.17; ②) or the HI **youth hostel** *L'Epervière*, on chemin de l'Epervière (☎04.75.42.32.00, fax 04.75.56.20.67), by the Rhône, 2km south of the city. The **hostel** is quite expensive but has good sports facilities – swimming pool, sailing – and bike rental. The **camping municipal** is in the youth hostel grounds (same number; all year).

The town

The focus of Vieux Valence, the **Cathédrale St-Apollinaire**, was founded in 1095 and largely reconstructed in the seventeenth century after a local baron went on the rampage, avenging the execution of three Protestants during the Wars of Religion. More work was carried out later, including the horribly mismatched nineteenth-century tower, but the interior still preserves its original Romanesque grace.

Between the cathedral and **Église de St-Jean** at the northern end of Grande Rue, which has preserved its Romanesque tower and porch capitals, are some of the oldest and narrowest streets of Vieux Valence. They are known as **côtes**: côte St-Estève just northwest of the cathedral; côte St-Martin off rue du Petit-Paradis; and côte Sylvante off rue du Petit-Paradis's continuation, rue A-Paré. Diverse characters who would have walked these steep and crooked streets include Rabelais, a student at the university founded here in 1452 and suppressed during the Revolution, and the teenage Napoléon Bonaparte, who began his military training as a cadet at the artillery school.

Though Valence lacks the cohesion of the medieval towns and villages further south, it does have several vestiges of the sixteenth-century city, most notably the Renaissance **Maison des Têtes** at 57 Grande Rue, with its eroded but still discernibly bizarre statuary, and the **Maison Dupré-Latour** on rue Pérollerie, with a superbly sculptured porch and spiral staircase. Valence's **Musée des Beaux-Arts** near the cathedral on place des Ormeaux (Mon, Tues, Thurs & Fri 2–6pm; Wed, Sat & Sun 9am–noon & 2–6pm; 15F, free Sun) is hard work. The tedium is only relieved by the Roman mosaic of the labours of Hercules, some modern sculpture and abstract art, and a collection of drawings by Hubert Robert, a reminder of the days when the Rhône valley was an essential part of the Grand Tour.

A good place if you need to fill in time is the **Parc Jouvet** overlooking the river (and the motorway) south of avenue Gambetta. At evening time around sunset, or even better at dawn, this is definitely the best place to be in the city – with a bottle of Cornas or sparkling St-Peray from the vineyards across the water.

Eating and drinking

For **restaurants**, *L'Épicerie*, 18 place Belat (☎04.75.42.74.46; closed Sat lunch & Sun), is one of the most congenial places to eat, with art exhibitions on the fifteenth-century walls, jazz some nights, and imaginative food on menus from 99F to 300F. *Père Joseph*, 9 place des Clercs (☎04.75.42.57.80) serves excellent-value traditional food with menus starting from 65F. Valence also has several good old-fashioned brasseries with a wide range of dishes and prices, including *Café Victor-Hugo*, 30 av Victor-Hugo and *Le Bistrot des Clercs*, 48 Grande Rue; plus an excellent *salon de thé*, *One Two Tea* at 37 Grande Rue. If you want to eat very well and are prepared to pay over 600F for the pleasure (or 280F for a lunch weekday menu), *Restaurant Pic*, 285 av Victor-Hugo (☎04.75.44.15.32; closed Sun eve & 3 weeks in Aug), is the city's top-notch eating house. Roast lobster with truffles, asparagus with hollandaise sauce and caviar, and frozen nougat are some of the delights.

Montélimar

In **MONTÉLIMAR**, 40km south of Valence, every street proclaims the glory of the nougat that has been made here for centuries and is the town's chief raison d'être. It's a lively enough place with a pleasant *vieille ville* and a fascinating museum dedicated to miniaturization.

The main street of the old town, **rue Pierre-Julien**, runs from the one remaining medieval **gateway** on the nineteenth-century ring of boulevards at place St-Martin, south past the **church of Ste-Croix** with its well-populated square, and onto place Marx-Dormoy. At no. 19, opposite the *Poste*, is the **Musée de la Miniature** (June to mid-Sept daily 10am–6pm; mid-Sept to May Wed–Sun 2–6pm; 30F) whose tiny exhibits, some so small you have to use a microscope, have been created by leading contemporary artists. A grain of rice bears a portrait of Pushkin and one of his poems; a table laid with a chess game is no bigger than a ten franc coin.

Leading off rue Pierre-Julien are plenty of medieval lanes with sixteenth- and seventeenth-century town houses, and around the pastel facades and old arcades of **place du Marché** you'll find *Le Métro* bar, done up as an old Paris métro station with a young clientele playing chess and backgammon. Above the old town to the east is the impressive fourteenth-century fortress, the **Château des Adhémar** on rue du Château (April–Oct daily 9.30–11.30am & 2–5.30pm; July & Aug same days but closes at 6pm; Nov–March closed Tues; 12F), with an interesting medieval chapel and relics from the castle's history. If you just want to sample and buy some of the town's moreish nougat, try Chabert et Guillot, 9 rue Charles-Chabert, just south of the gare SNCF (Mon–Thurs 8am–3pm).

Practicalities

The **gare SNCF** is a short way west of the old town, with the **tourist office** in the adjacent park on the allée Champs-de-Mars (July & Aug daily 8.30am–7.30pm; rest of year Mon–Fri 8.30am–6.30pm, Sat 9am–6.30pm; ☎04.75.01.00.20, fax 04.75.52.33.69); they can fix up visits to a nougat factory. There are plenty of **hotels** around the boulevards, including the very pleasant *Le Sphinx* in a seventeenth-century town house at 19 bd Marre-Desmarais (☎04.75.01.86.64, fax 04.75.52.34.21; ③) and the *Traget*, 25 av Kennedy (☎04.75.53.02.07, fax 04.75.01.83.78; ②), overlooking the river south of the centre. Within the old town you could try *Pierre*, 7 place des Clercs (☎04.75.01.33.16; ②) – peaceful, apart from the nearby bell of Ste-Croix tolling the hours. The **campsite**, *International Deux Saisons* (☎04.75.01.88.99; March–Nov) is 500m east on the D540, then right towards Alexis.

Enticing smells emanate from *La Papillote* **restaurant** on place du Temple (☎04.75.01.99.28; closed Sun & Mon; menus under 100F). For a greater outlay, you can feast on good traditional food at the *Relais de l'Empereur*, 1 place Max-Dormoy (☎04.75.01.29.00; menus from 139F; closed mid-Nov to mid-Dec).

WESTERN PROVENCE

The richest area of Provence, the Côte d'Azur apart, is the **west**. Most of the large-scale production of fruit, vegetables and wine is based here in the low-lying plains beside the Rhône and the Durance rivers. The only heights are the rocky outbreaks of the **Dentelles** and the **Alpilles**, and the narrow east–west ridges of **Mont Ventoux**, the **Luberon** and the **Mont Ste-Victoire**. The two dominant cities of inland Provence, **Avignon** and **Aix**, both have rich histories and contemporary fame in their festivals of art; **Arles**, **Orange** and **Vaison-la-Romaine** have impressive Roman remains. Around the Rhône delta, the **Camargue** is a unique self-contained region, as different from the rest of Provence as it is from anywhere else in France.

Orange and around

ORANGE was the former seat of the counts of Orange, a title created by Charlemagne in the eighth century, and passed to the Dutch crown in the sixteenth century. Its most memorable member was Prince William, who ascended the English throne with his consort Mary, but the town is today best known for its spectacular **Roman theatre**, which hosts the important summer Chorégies **music festival**. While the rest of the town is attractive enough, there's not a lot to detain you once you've visited the theatre and adjacent museum and taken a quick look at the Roman triumphal arch at the northern approach to the town centre. Unfortunately, the victory of Le Pen's Front National in the municipal elections of 1995 has forced the May strip-cartoon festival, which brought in all kinds of weird and wonderful entertainment, to be abandoned, and led many artists to boycott Orange's festivals, creating strong and unpleasant divisions.

Arrival, information and accommodation

The **gare SNCF** is about 1500m east of the centre, at the end of avenue Frédéric-Mistral. The nearest bus stop is at the bottom of rue Jean-Reboul, the first left as you

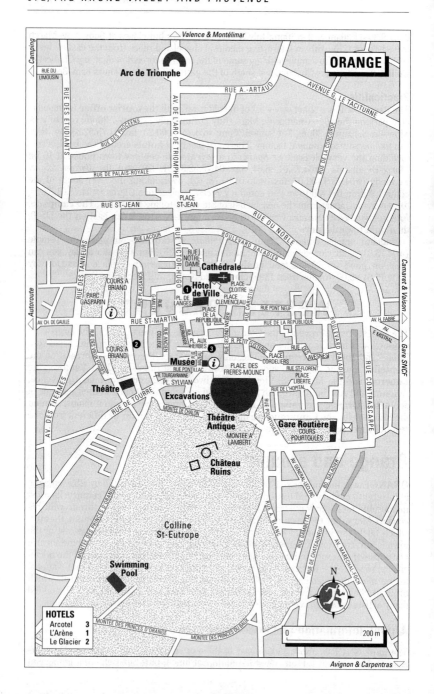

walk away from the station. Bus #2, direction "Nogent", takes you to the Théâtre Antique, opposite which there's a seasonal tourist office (April–Sept Mon–Sat 10am–1pm & 2–6pm, Sun 10am–6pm) and the next stop, Gasparin, to the main **tourist office** on cours Aristide-Briand (April–Sept Mon–Sat 9am–7pm, Sun 10am–6pm; Oct–March Mon–Sat 9am–5pm; ☎04.90.34.70.88). The **gare routière** is close to the centre on place Pourtoules.

Of the **hotels**, the *Arcotel*, 8 place aux Herbes (☎04.90.34.09.23; ②), is small, appealing and good-value. Others to try are *L'Arène* on place de Langes (☎04.90.11.40.40, fax 04.90.11.40.45; ④), with spacious rooms and all mod cons, and the very comfortable *Le Glacier*, 46 cours Aristide-Briand (☎04.90.34.02.01, fax 04.90.51.13.80; ③). Orange's **campsite**, *Le Jonquier*, rue Alexis-Carrel (☎04.90.34.19.83, fax 04.90.34.86.54; mid-March to Oct), to the northwest, is equipped with tennis courts and a pool.

The town

Days off in Orange circa 5 BC were most entertainingly spent from dawn to dusk at the huge Roman **theatre** (daily: April–Sept 9am–6.30pm; Oct–March 9am–noon & 1.30–5pm; 30F joint ticket with museum), watching farce, clownish improvisations, song and dance, and occasionally, for the sake of a visiting dignitary, a bit of Greek tragedy in Latin. The acoustics allowed a full audience of 9000 to hear every word. The hill of St-Eutrope, into which the seats were built, plus a vast awning strung from the top of the stage wall, protected the spectators from the weather. It is the best-preserved example in existence, and the only one with the stage wall still standing – 103m across and 36m high, and completely plain like some monstrous prison wall when you see it from outside. The interior, although missing much of its original decoration, has its central, larger-than-life-size statue of Augustus, and niches for lesser statues.

The best view of the theatre in its entirety is from St-Eutrope hill. You can follow a path up the hill either from the top of cours Aristide-Briand (montée P. de Chalons) or from cours Pourtoules (montée Albert Lambert) until you are looking directly down onto the stage. The ruins around your feet are those of the short-lived seventeenth-century castle of the princes of Orange. Louis XIV had it destroyed and the principality of Orange annexed to France – a small price to pay for the ruler of the Netherlands who was also to become king of England.

The **municipal museum**, across the road from the theatre entrance (daily: April–Sept 9.30am–7pm; Oct–March 9.30am–noon & 1.30–5pm; 30F joint ticket with theatre), has documents concerning the Orange dynasty, including a suitably austere portrait of the very first Orangeman, Guillaume "the Taciturn". It also has Roman bits and pieces and a collection rotated on a yearly basis containing diverse items such as the contents of a seventeenth century apothecary and an unlikely selection of works by Frank Brangwyn, a Welsh painter who had no connections with Orange. The pictures here are stark portrayals of British workers early this century.

If you've arrived by road from the north you will have passed the town's second major Roman monument, the **Arc de Triomphe**, whose intricate frieze and relief celebrates imperial victories against the Gauls. It was built around 20 BC outside the town walls to proclaim the importance of the Roman settlement.

Orange's old town is very small, hemmed in between the theatre and the River Meyne, featuring some pretty fountained squares and houses with ancient porticos and courtyards.

Eating, drinking and entertainment

For **food**, cheap *frites* with *plats du jour* to eat in or take away can be had at *La Fringale*, 10 rue de Tourre (till 11pm; closed Weds & Sat lunch, plus Sun lunch out of season).

Le Yaca, 24 place Silvain (☎04.90.34.70.03; closed Tues & Wed eve & Nov), gives a generous choice of dishes for 100F in an old vaulted chamber. The best food you're likely to get in Orange is at *Le Parvis*, 3 cours des Pourtoules (☎04.90.34.82.00; closed Weds & Tues eve out of season) with a weekday lunch menu around 100F. For **drinking**, head for place de la République in the centre, where there's *Les Négociants* and the less expensive *Café de l'Univers* painted in Provençal yellow. On the other side of cours Aristide-Briand, the *Café des Thermes*, 29 rue des Vieux-Fossés, has pool, a good selection of beers, and a youngish clientele.

Orange's main festival is the **Chorégies**, a programme of opera, oratorios and orchestral concerts in July (details and tickets from the Bureau des Chorégies, 18 place Silvain, ☎04.90.34.24.24).The theatre is also used throughout the year for jazz, film, folk and rock concerts. Prices range from 90F to 150F, and some performances are free; details from the Service Culturel de la Ville, 14 place Silvain (☎04.90.51.57.57). Tickets for all events can be bought from FNAC shops in all big French cities.

Sérignan-du-Comtat

The village of **SÉRIGNAN-DU-COMTAT**, 8km northeast of Orange (three buses daily from Orange and Avignon), was the final home of **Jean-Henri Fabre**, a remarkable self-taught scientist, famous for his insect studies, who composed poetry, wrote songs and painted his specimens with artistic brilliance as well as scientific accuracy. In the 1860s he had to resign from his teaching post at Avignon because parents and priests thought his lectures on the fertilization of flowering plants were licentious, if not downright pornographic. In his **house**, which he named the *Harmas* (daily except Tues 9–noon & 2–4/6pm; 15F), you can see his jungly garden, the study with his complete classification of the herbs of France and, on the ground floor, a selection from his extraordinary watercolour series of the fungi of the Vaucluse. At the crossroads in the centre of the town (the *Harmas* is on the N976 towards Orange) there's a statue of Fabre in front of the red-shuttered buildings of the church and mairie.

Châteauneuf-du-Pape

If you're heading down to Avignon, the slower route through **CHÂTEAUNEUF-DU-PAPE** (four buses daily) exerts a strong pull. The village takes its name from the summer palace of the Avignon popes. But neither the miserable ruins of the fourteenth-century **château** (freely acccessible) nor the medieval streets around **place du Portail** – the hub of the village – give Châteauneuf its special appeal. The wines produced by the local vineyards, warmed at night by the large pebbles that cover the ground and soak up the sun's heat during the day, are its real attraction. The rich ruby red is one of France's most renowned, but the white, too, is exquisite.

The *appellation Châteauneuf-du-Pape* does not, alas, come cheap, nor is there a centre where you can taste a good selection from the scores of *domaines*. For a casual introduction, the Cave Père-Anselme on av Bienheureux-Pierre-de-Luxembourg has a **Musée des Outils de Vigneron** (daily 9am–noon & 2–6pm; free) plus free tastings of its wines. Otherwise, the **tourist office** on place du Portail (July & Aug Mon–Sat 9am–7pm, Sun 10am–5pm; rest of year Mon–Sat 9am–12.30pm & 2–6pm; ☎04.90.83.71.08, fax 04.90.83.50.34), or the Fédération des Syndicats de Producteurs, 12 av Louis-Pasteur (☎04.90.83.72.21), can provide a complete list of producers, or you can visit an Association de Vignerons such as Prestige et Tradition at 3 rue de la République (Mon–Sat 8am–noon & 2–6pm; open Sun same hours Aug & Sept), who bottle the wine of ten producers.

If you can make your visit coincide with the first weekend of August you'll find free *dégustation* stalls throughout the village as well as parades, dances, equestrian contests, folkloric floats and so forth, all to celebrate the reddening of the grapes in the **Fête de la Véraison**. As well as wine, a good deal of grape liqueur – *marc* – gets consumed.

Accommodation is confined to four very pleasant but small **hotels**: *La Garbure*, 3 rue Joseph-Ducos (☎04.90.83.75.08, fax 04.90.83.52.34; ④; closed last 2 weeks in Oct and first 2 weeks in Nov); the four-star *Hostellerie du Château des Fines Roches* on rte d'Avignon (☎04.90.83.70.23, fax 04.90.83.78.42; ⑧; closed Sun evening and Mon out of season); *La Mère Germaine* on av Cdt-Lemaitre (☎04.90.83.54.37, fax 04.90.83.50.27; ④; closed Weds); and *La Sommellerie* on rte de Roquemaure (☎04.90.83.50.00, fax 04.90.83.51.85; ⑤; closed Feb).

You can **eat** well for under 100F at the brasserie *La Mule du Pape*, 2 rue de la République (restaurant closed Mon), or pay a bit more at *La Mère Germaine* (see above; closed Weds), and much more at *La Sommellerie* (see above; menus between 160F and 390F; closed Sun eve & Mon out of season), where the cook is one of France's master chefs.

Vaison-la-Romaine and around

VAISON-LA-ROMAINE lies 27km northeast of Orange and hit the headlines in 1992 when the River Ouvèze which divides the medieval and eighteenth-century towns burst its banks, destroying riverside houses, the modern road bridge, and an entire industrial quarter. Though the town has recovered remarkably, its character has changed. It seems much more commercialized and less friendly – perhaps because of the mass of ghoulish tourists who flocked to the town to see the damage.

It still, however, has the strong attractions of its medieval *haute ville*, with a ruined clifftop castle, a **Roman bridge** that held out against the floods, a cloistered former cathedral and the exceptional excavated remains of two **Roman districts**. Just south of Vaison there are sculptures in natural settings to be discovered at the **Crestet Centre d'Art**.

Arrival, information and accommodation

Buses to and from Carpentras, Orange and Avignon stop at the **gare routière** on av des Choralies near the junction with av Victor-Hugo, east of the town centre on the north side of the river. The **tourist office** is on place du Chanoine-Sautel (July & Aug daily 9am–12.30pm & 2–6.45pm; Sept–June Mon–Sat 9am–noon & 2–5.45pm; ☎04.90.36.02.11, fax 04.90.28.76.04), between the two archeological sites in the north of the modern town.

There's not a great choice of **hotels** and few bargains. The best deal is at *Le Burrhus* on place Montfort (☎04.90.36.00.11, fax 04.90.36.39.05; ③), above all the terraced cafés. Vaison's best hotel and restaurant is *Le Beffroi*, a sixteenth-century residence on rue de l'Évêché in the *haute ville* (☎04.90.36.04.71, fax 04.90.36.24.78; ⑤– ⑦). On rte de St-Marcellin, 1km east of town down av Geoffroy from the Pont Romain, you'll find the *Centre Culturel à Cœur Joie*, with simple rooms (☎04.90.36.00.78; ①). For **campers**, there's the central *Camping du Théâtre Romain* on chemin du Brusquet, off av des Choralies, Quartier des Arts (☎04.90.28.78.66; mid-March to Oct).

The town

The *haute ville* lies on the south side of the river, with **rue du Pont** climbing up towards place des Poids and the fourteenth-century **gateway** to the town. More steep zigzags take you past the Gothic gate and overhanging portcullis of the **belfry** and into the heart of this sedately quiet, uncommercialized and rich quartier.

On the north bank from the **Pont Romain**, a Roman bridge that has been patched up over the years but survived the 1992 floods, Grande-Rue leads up to the central streets of rue de la République and cours Henri-Fabre, after which it becomes avenue Général-de-Gaulle. The two excavated **Roman residential districts** lie to either side of this avenue: Puymin to the east and La Villasse to the west (March–May daily 10am–12.30pm & 2–6pm; June–Sept daily 9.30am–12.30pm & 2.00–7pm; Nov–Feb Wed–Mon 10am–noon & 2–4.30pm; ticket for both plus Puymin museum and cathedral cloisters 40F).

The Puymin excavations contain the theatre, several mansions and houses, a colonnade known as the *portique de Pompée* and the museum for all the items discovered. The excavations of La Villasse reveal a street with pavements and gutters with the layout of a row of arcaded shops running parallel, more patrician houses (some with mosaics still intact), a basilica and the baths. The houses require a certain amount of imagination, but the street plan of La Villasse, the colonnade with its statues in every niche, and the theatre, which still seats 7000 people during the July festival, make it easy to visualize a comfortable, well-serviced town of the Roman ruling class.

Most of the detail and decoration of the buildings are displayed in the **museum** (March–May & Oct daily 10am–12.30pm & 2.30–6pm; June–Sept daily 10am–1pm & 2–7.30pm; Nov–Feb Wed–Mon 10–11.30am & 2–4pm) in the Puymin district. Tiny fragments of painted plaster have been jigsawed together with convincing reconstructions of how whole painted walls would have looked. There are mirrors of silvered bronze, lead water pipes, taps shaped as griffins' feet, dolphin door knobs, weights and measures, plus impressive busts and statues.

Tickets can be bought at the Puymin entrance just by the tourist office or in the cloisters of the former **Cathédrale Notre-Dame**, west down chemin Couradou, which runs along the south side of La Villasse. The apse of the cathedral is a confusing overlay of sixth-, tenth- and thirteenth-century construction, using pieces quarried from the Roman ruins. The **cloisters** are fairly typical of early medieval workmanship – pretty enough but not wildly exciting. The only surprising feature is the large inscription visible on the north wall of the cathedral, a convoluted precept for the monks.

Eating and drinking

The **restaurant** to head for is *Le Bateleur*, 1 place Théodore-Aubanel, downstream from the Pont Romain on the north bank (☎04.90.36.28.04; closed Sun eve, Mon & mid-Nov to mid-Dec; weekday lunch menu 98F, à la carte around 200F). The lamb stuffed with almonds and the *rascasse soufflé* are highly recommended. *L'Auberge de la Bartavelle*, 12 place Sus-Auze (☎04.90.36.02.16; closed Mon), has specialities from southwest France for between 100F and 200F. Imaginative salads and savoury tarts are to be had at *Laure y Est*, 5 rue Buffaven (closed Sun, & Mon–Weds eve; ☎04.90.28.81.11) as well as traditional *plats* for around 60F. You can get crêpes and pizzas in the old town and brasserie fare on place de Montfort, the obvious drinking place to gravitate towards. For a more local atmosphere, try *Vasio Bar* on cours Taulignan.

Le Crestet and the Centre d'Art

South of Vaison, 3.5km down the Malaucène road, a turning to the right leads up to the tiny hilltop village of **LE CRESTET** from where signs direct you the short distance to the **Crestet Centre d'Art** (permanent and free access), where modern sculptures have been placed, almost hidden, in an expanse of oak and pine woods. There is a map on the wall at the Centre but the idea is to wander freely: to start off, go behind the building and then turn sharp left within 20m. Some of the sculptures are formed from the trees themselves, others are startling metal structures such as a mobile and a Meccano cage.

Mont Ventoux

Mont Ventoux, whose outline repeatedly appears upon the horizon from the Rhône and Durance valleys, rises some 20km east of Vaison. White with snow, black with storm-cloud shadow or reflecting myriad shades of blue, the barren pebbles of the uppermost 300m are like a weather vane for all of western Provence. Winds can accelerate to 250km per hour around the meteorological, TV and military masts and dishes on the summit, but if you can stand still for a moment the view in all directions is unbelievable. A road, the D974, climbs all the way to the top, though no buses take it.

If you want to make the ascent on foot, the best path is from Les Colombets or Les Fébriers, two hamlets off the D974, east of **BEDOIN** – whose **tourist office** on the Espace M-L-Gravier (July–Aug Mon–Fri 9am–1pm & 2–6pm, Sat 9am–noon & 2–6pm, Sun 9am–noon; Sept–June Mon–Fri 9am–12.30pm & 2–6pm, Sat 9am–noon; ☎04.90.65.63.95) can give details (including a once a week night-time ascent in July & Aug), plus addresses of campsites and gîtes *ruraux*.

Mont Ventoux is one of the challenges of the Tour de France, hence its appeal in summer for committed cyclists. Around the treeline is a **memorial** to the British cyclist Tommy Simpson, who died here from heart failure on one of the hottest days ever recorded in the race; according to race folklore his last words were "Put me back on the bloody bike."

The Dentelles and around

The **Dentelles**, a row of jagged limestone pinnacles, run across an arid, windswept and near-deserted upland area, the **Massif Montmirail-St-Amand**, just south of Vaison-la-Romaine. Their name refers to lace – the limestone protrusions were thought to resemble the contorted pins on a lace-making board – though the word's alternative connection with teeth (*dents* means "teeth") is equally appropriate.

The area is best known for its wines. On the western and southern slopes lie the wine-producing villages of **Gigondas, Beaumes-de-Venise, Sablet, Séguret, Vacqueyras** and, across the River Ouveze, **Rasteau**. Each one carries the distinction of having its own individual *appellation contrôlée* within the Côtes du Rhône or Côtes du Rhône Villages areas: in other words, their wines are exceptional. In addition, some of the villages are alluringly picturesque, with Séguret super-conscious of its Provençal beauty.

The most reputed red **wine** in the Dentelles is made at Gigondas – it's strong with an aftertaste of spice and nuts. You can taste the produce from forty different *domaines* at the Caveau des Vignerons on place de la Mairie in the village (daily 10am–noon & 2–5.30pm). The most distinctive wine, and elixir for those who like it sweet, is the pale amber-coloured *Beaumes-de-Venise* muscat which you can buy from the Cave des Vignerons (Mon–Sat 8.30am–noon & 2–6pm, Sun 9am–12.30pm & 2–6pm) on the D7 just outside Beaumes.

Besides *dégustation* and bottle-buying, you can go for long walks in the Dentelles, stumbling upon mysterious ruins or photogenic panoramas of Mont Ventoux and the Rhône valley. The pinnacles are favourite scaling faces for apprentice rock-climbers – though their wind-eroded patterns can be appreciated just as well without risking your neck on an ascent. Information on walking and climbing is available from the Gigondas **tourist office** on place du Portail (Easter–Sept Mon–Fri 10am–noon & 2–6pm, Sat & Sun 10am–noon; Oct–Easter Mon–Fri 10am–noon & 2–5pm, Sat 10am–noon; ☎04.90.65.85.46, fax 04.90.65.88.42) who sell a local footpath map for 20F, and from *Le Gîte* (see below).

Although it's possible to get to the villages by public transport from Vaison or Carpentras, your own vehicle is definitely an advantage. You can **hire bikes** at *Café du Court*, in the centre of Vacqueyras. **Hotel** possibilities include, in Beaumes, the old-fashioned and quiet *Auberge St-Roch* on av Jules-Ferry (☎04.90.65.08.21; ②; closed Tues eve & Wed) and *Le Relais des Dentelles* (☎04.90.62.95.27; ②; closed Mon), past the old village and over the river. Gigondas has *Les Florets*, 2km from the village along the rte des Dentelles (☎04.90.65.85.01, fax 04.90.65.83,80; ④–⑤; half-board obligatory in season), and the more upmarket *Hôtellerie de Montmirail*, which you reach via Vacqueyras (☎04.90.65.84.01, fax 04.90.65.81.50; ⑤–⑦). There are **campsites** in Sablet (☎04.90.46.96.27), Beaumes (☎04.90.62.95.07) and Vacqueyras (☎04.90.65.84.24, fax 04.90.65.83.28), a **gîte d'étape** on the rte de Sablet 500m out of Séguret (☎04.90.65.93.31; ①; closed mid-Nov to March) and *Le Gîte* at the entrance to Gigondas (☎04.90.65.80.85; ①), with double rooms and dormitory accommodation.

Besides the restaurants of the hotels mentioned above, places to stop for a **drink or eat** are few and far between once you leave the villages. In Séguret *Le Mesclun*, rue des Poternes (☎04.90.46.93.43; closed Mon & Nov–Easter; 155F menu) is renowned for the fresh local ingredients in its dishes. *L'Oustalet*, place du Portail, in Gigondas (☎04.90.65.85.30; closed Mon & Sun eve; menus 100F lunch, 140F eve) has a pleasant shaded terrace; cheaper eats can be had at the *Café de la Poste* on rue Principale.

Carpentras

With a population of around 30,000, **CARPENTRAS** is a substantial city for this part of the world. It is also a very old city, its known history commencing in 5 BC as the capital of a Celtic tribe. The Greeks who founded Marseille came to Carpentras to buy honey, wheat, goats and skins, and the Romans had a base here. For a brief period in the fourteenth century, it became the papal headquarters and gave protection to Jews expelled from France.

For all its ancient remains, Carpentras seems incapable of working up an atmosphere to imbue the present with its past. The local history museum – the **Musée Comtadin** on bd Albin-Durand (Wed–Mon 10am–noon & 2–4/6pm; 2F) – is dark and dour. The erotic fantasies of a seventeenth-century cardinal frescoed by Nicolas Mignard in the **Palais de Justice**, formerly the episcopal palace, were effaced by a later incumbent. The *palais* is attached to the dull **Cathédrale St-Siffrein** behind which, almost hidden in the corner, stands a **Roman arch** inscribed with scenes of prisoners in chains. Fifteen hundred years after its erection, Jews – coerced, bribed or otherwise persuaded – entered the cathedral in chains to be unshackled as converted Christians. The door they passed through, the **Porte Juif**, is on the southern side and bears strange symbolism of rats encircling and devouring a globe. The **synagogue** (Mon–Thurs 10am–noon & 3–5pm, closes 4pm Fri, closed Jewish feast days; free), near the Hôtel de Ville, is a seventeenth-century construction on the foundations of what was the oldest place of Jewish worship in France.

Carpentras cheers up, however, every Friday for the **market**, which from mid-November to March specializes in truffles, and during **festival** time in the second half of July. It also makes a useful base for excursions into the Dentelles, Mont Ventoux and the towns and villages south towards Apt. **Buses** (trains are freight only) arrive either on av Victor-Hugo or place Terradou, a short walk away from place Aristide-Briand. The **tourist office** (July & Aug daily 9am–7pm; rest of year Mon–Fri 9am–12.30pm & 2–6.30pm, closes 6pm on Sat; ☎04.90.63.00.78, fax 04.90.60.41.02) is at 170 allée Jean-Jaurès, which runs northeast from place Aristide-Briand. If you want to **stay**, *Le Théâtre*, 7 bd Albin-Durand (☎04.90.63.02.90; ②) and *La Lavande*, 282 bd A-Rogier (☎04.90.63.13.49; ②) are both rock-bottom options. For something much more pleasant, try *Le Fiacre*, 153 rue Vigne (☎04.90.63.03.15, fax 04.90.60.49.73; ③), an old town house with a garden, or *Safari Hotel,* 1 av J-H-Fabre (☎04.90.63.35.35, fax 04.90.60.49.99; ③–⑤), which is a bit characterless but has a pool and tennis courts.

As far as **eating** goes, *Le Marijo* at 73 rue Raspail (☎04.90.60.42.65; closed Sun) is excellent, with menus under 130F. *Le Vert Galant*, 12 rue Clapies (☎04.90.67.15.50; closed Sat lunch & Sun), serves more sophisticated fare, with a lunch menu for around

100F, otherwise from 170F. Takeaway Thai, Chinese and Vietnamese food is available from *La Perle d'Asie* on place du Théâtre. Café-crawling is best done on place Aristide-Briand or around the cathedral.

Avignon

AVIGNON, great city of the popes, and for centuries one of the major artistic centres of France, can be very daunting. The monuments and museums are huge; it's always crowded in summer and it can be stiflingly hot. But it is an immaculately preserved medieval town with endless impressively decorated buildings, ancient churches, chapels and convents, and more places to eat and drink than you could cover in a month. During the **Festival d'Avignon** in July and the beginning of August, it is *the* place to be.

Central Avignon is enclosed by medieval walls, built by one of the nine popes who based themselves here throughout most of the fourteenth century, away from the anarchic feuding or, in the case of the last two, away from the rival popes in Rome. Avignon was a lively place while the papacy had its headquarters here. According to Petrarch, the overcrowded, plague-ridden papal entourage was "a sewer where all the filth of the universe has gathered". In 1403 the Anti-Pope Benoît, who had built the walls in a fit of justified paranoia during the shifting alliances of the Great Schism, was ousted and the city had to content itself with mere cardinals.

THE FESTIVAL

Unlike most provincial festivals of international renown, the **Festival d'Avignon** is dominated by theatre rather than classical music, though there is also plenty of that, as well as lectures, exhibitions and dance. It uses the city's great buildings as backdrops to performances, and takes place every year for three weeks from the second week in July. During festival time everything stays open late and everything gets booked up; there can be up to 200,000 visitors, and getting around or doing anything normal becomes virtually impossible.

The 1998 festival saw theatrical interpretations of Sophocles, Corneille, Shakespeare and Chekhov, with directors and companies as diverse as Jacques Lassalle and Cheek by Jowl, plus a new circus act with the Centre National des Arts du Cirque, as well as a whole host of events paying homage to Brecht. Each year a non-European country or region is invited to bring the best of its performing arts, traditional, modern and avant-garde, to the festival. In 1998 it was South-East Asia, with an adaptation of Shakespeare's *Macbeth* in the style of the Peking Opera – contemporary dance, traditional dance and shadow theatre among the offerings. As well as the mainstream festival, there's a fringe contingent known as the **Festival Off**, using a hundred different venues and the streets for a programme of innovative, obscure or bizarre performances.

The **main festival programme**, with details of how to book, is available from the second week in May from the Bureau du Festival d'Avignon, 8bis rue de Mons, 84000 Avignon (☎04.90.27.66.50) or from the tourist office. Ticket prices are reasonable (between 130F and 200F) and go on sale from the second week in June. As well as phone sales (11am–7pm; ☎04.90.14.14.14), they can be bought from FNAC shops in all major French cities. During the festival, tickets are available until 4pm for the same day's performances. The **Festival Off programme** is available from the end of June from Avignon Public Off BP5, 75521 Paris Cedex 11 (☎01.48.05.01.19). During the festival, the office is in the Conservatoire de Musique on place du Palais. Tickets prices range from 50F to 90F and a *Carte Public Adhérent* for 75F (50F during the festival) gives you thirty percent off all shows.

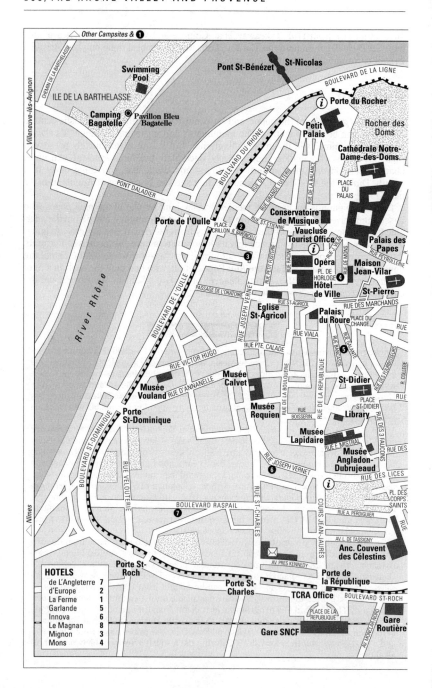

△ Other Campsites & ❶

Villeneuve-lès-Avignon

CHEMIN DE LA BARTHELASSE

ILE DE LA BARTHELASSE

Swimming Pool

Camping Bagatelle

Pavillon Bleu Bagatelle

PONT DALADIER

River Rhône

BOULEVARD DU RHONE

Pont St-Bénézet

St-Nicolas

BOULEVARD DE LA LIGNE

Porte du Rocher

Rocher des Doms

Petit Palais

Cathédrale Notre-Dame-des-Doms

PLACE DU PALAIS

RUE GRANDE FUSTERIE

RUE DE LA BALANCE

RUE DU MAS

Porte de l'Oulle

PLACE CRILLON

R. BARONCELLI

RUE ST-ETIENNE

Conservatoire de Musique

Vaucluse Tourist Office

Palais des Papes

RUE PETROLLERIE

BOULEVARD DE L'OULLE

RUE PETIT FUSTERIE

RUE RACINE

RUE DE MONS

RUE J. VILAR

Opéra

PL. DE HORLOGE

Maison Jean-Vilar

Hôtel de Ville

St-Pierre

PASSAGE DE L'ORATOIRE

RUE JOSEPH VERNET

Eglise St-Agricol

RUE ST-AGRICOL

RUE DES MARCHANDS

Palais du Roure

PLACE DU CHANGE

RUE

RUE VIALA

RUE BALANCE

RUE PTE. CALADE

RUE B. RASCASSE

RUE VICTOR HUGO

RUE DES FOURBISSEURS

R. COLLEGE

Musée Vouland

RUE D'ANNANELLE

Musée Calvet

RUE DE LA BOULOUERIE

RUE DE LA REPUBLIQUE

St-Didier

RUE

Porte St-Dominique

BOULEVARD ST-DOMINIQUE

Musée Requien

RUE BOISSERIN

PLACE ST-DIDIER

Library

RUE DES 3 FAUCONS

Musée Lapidaire

RUE VELOUTERIE

RUE F. MISTRAL

Musée Angladon-Dubrujeaud

RUE DES

RUE JOSEPH VERNET

RUE DES LICES

PL. DES CORPS SAINTS

BOULEVARD RASPAIL

RUE ST-CHARLES

COURS JEAN-JAURES

RUE A. PERDIGUIER

RUE

Nîmes

AV. L. DE TASSIGNY

Anc. Couvent des Célestins

Porte St-Roch

AV. PRES KENNEDY

Porte de la République

Porte St-Charles

TCRA Office

BOULEVARD ST-ROCH

PLACE DE LA REPUBLIQUE

Gare Routière

Gare SNCF

AV. MONCLAR NORD

HOTELS

de L'Angleterre	7
d'Europe	2
La Ferme	1
Garlande	5
Innova	6
Le Magnan	8
Mignon	3
Mons	4

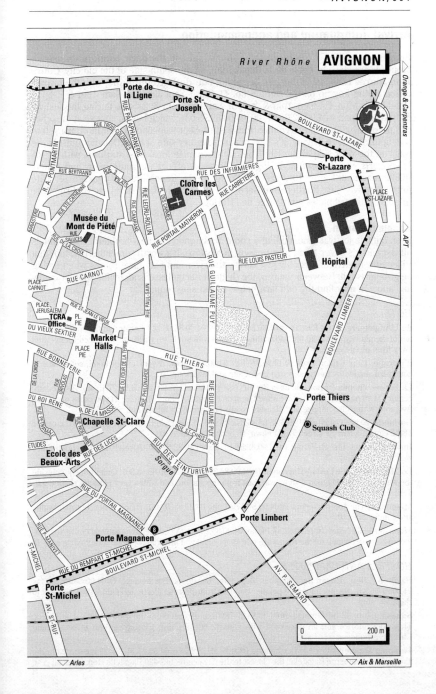

Arrival, information and accommodation

Both the **gare SNCF** on boulevard St-Roch and and the **gare routière** on avenue Montclar are close to Porte de la République, on the south side of the old city. **Cours Jean-Jaurès** runs inside the gate becoming **rue de la République**, with the **tourist office** a little way up on the right at no. 41 (April–Sept also Sun 9am–1pm & 2–5pm; Oct–March Mon–Fri 9am–1pm & 2–6pm, Sat 9am–1pm & 2–5pm; during the festival daily 10am–7pm; ☎04.90.82.65.11, fax 04.90.82.95.03), which has an annexe at the other end of town by the Pont d'Avignon (daily April–Sept 9am–6pm; Oct–March 9am–1pm & 2–5pm). If you're driving, it's best to park to either side of Pont Daladier outside the walls on the west side of the city. The city's two main local **bus stations**, with TCRA (*Transports en Commun de la Région d'Avignon*) offices for route maps and tickets (6.50F each; 48F for 10), are by Porte de la République (stops Poste, Cité Administrative, Gare Routière and Gare) and place Pie, in the centre of town. From Cité Administrative all buses go to place de l'Horloge.

Accommodation

Even outside festival time, finding a **room** in Avignon can be a problem: cheap hotels fill fast and it's never a bad idea to book in advance. It's worth remembering, too, that Villeneuve-lès-Avignon is only just across the river and may have rooms when its big neighbour is full. Between the two, the Île de la Barthelasse is an idyllic spot for camping, and you may find the odd farmhouse advertising rooms.

HOTELS

de L'Angleterre, 29 bd Raspail (☎04.90.86.34.31, fax 04.90.86.86.74). Located in the southeast corner of the old city, this is an old and traditional hotel with some very reasonably priced rooms, well away from night-time noise. ③.

d'Europe, 12 pl Crillon (☎04.90.14.76.76, Fax 04.90.85.43.66). A very classy hotel, set back in a courtyard shaded by the canopy of a tree. Calm and luxurious. ⑧.

La Ferme, chemin du Bois, Île de la Barthelasse (☎04.90.82.57.53, fax 04.90.27.15.47). A sixteenth-century farm on the island in the Rhône (signposted right off Pont Daladier as you cross over from Avignon) with well-equipped and pleasant rooms and greenery all around. ④.

Garlande, 20 rue Galante (☎04.90.85.08.85, fax 04.927.16.58). Delightful address right in the centre of the city on a narrow street. Well-known, so book in advance. ④.

Innova, 100 rue Joseph-Vernet (☎04.90.82.54.10, fax 04.90.82.52.39). A small, friendly hotel that's well worth booking. ②.

Le Magnan, 63 rue Portail-Magnanen (☎04.90.86.36.51, fax 04.90.85.48.90). Quiet hotel just inside the walls by Porte Magnan a short way east from the station, and with a very pleasant shaded garden. ④.

Mignon, 12 rue Joseph-Vernet (☎04.90.82.17.30, fax 04.90.85.78.46). Dated decor, but good-value and comfortable. ③.

Mons, 5 rue de Mons (☎04.90.82.57.16, fax 04.90.85.19.15). A central, imaginatively converted thirteenth-century chapel. All the rooms are odd shapes and you breakfast beneath a vaulted ceiling. ③.

HOSTELS AND CAMPSITES

Pavillon Bleu Bagatelle, camping Bagatelle, Île de la Barthelasse (☎04.90.86.30.39, fax 04.90.27.16.23). Rooms for 4 to 8 people. Bus #10 from Poste to Porte de l'Oulle, then bus #20 to Bagatelle stop.

Squash Club, 32 bd Limbert (☎04.90.85.27.78) Bus #2 east from the gare SNCF; stop Thiers. Three dormitories and an obsession with squash; 60F a night. Closed Sun out of season and Christmas holidays.

Camping Bagatelle, Île de la Barthelasse (☎04.90.85.78.45, fax 04.90.27.16.23). Three-star campsite alongside the Auberge Bagatelle; the closest to the city centre; bus #20 Bagatelle stop. Open all year.

Camping Municipal St-Bénézet, Île de la Barthelasse (☎04.90.82.63.50, fax 04.90.85.22.12). Four-star, about 3km from the centre overlooking Pont St-Bénézet. Bus #20 to stop Bénézet. March–Oct.

The city

Avignon's walls still form a complete loop around the city. They appear far too low to be a serious defence, but half the full height is buried since it was impossible to excavate the moat during the nineteenth-century restoration work. All the gates and towers, however, were successfully repaired and there's a strong sense of being in an enclosed space quite separate from the modern spread of the city.

Rue de la République, the extension of cours Jean-Jaurès and the main axis of the old town, ends at **place de l'Horloge**, the city's main square. Beyond that is **place du Palais**, with the city's most imposing monument, the **Palais des Papes**, the **Rocher des Doms** park and the Porte du Rocher overlooking the Rhône by the **pont d'Avignon**, or pont St-Bénézet as it's officially known.

The Palais des Papes and around

Rising high above place du Palais on the east side is the **Palais des Papes** (April–July daily 9am–7pm; during the festival closes at 9pm; post-festival–Oct 9am–8pm; Nov–March 9am–5.45pm; throughout June & Aug occasional late openings 9–11pm; last ticket 1hr before closure; 40F, price of ticket includes either an audio-guide or a guided tour, 11.30am & 4.45pm in English. It is a monster of a building, doing to the vertical what Versailles does to the horizontal. If you want to get a dramatic neck-cricking view of the whole towering pile, follow rue Peyrolerie around the south end of the Palais. Inside the palace, so little remains of the original decoration and furnishings that you can be deceived into thinking that all the popes and their retinues were as pious and austere as the last official occupant, Benoît XII. The denuded interior certainly gives sparse indication of the corruption and decadence of fat, feuding cardinals and their mistresses, the thronging purveyors of jewels, velvet and furs, musicians, chefs and painters competing for patronage, the riotous banquets and corridor schemings.

The visit begins in the **Pope's Tower**, otherwise known as the Tower of Angels. You enter the **Treasury** where the serious business of the church's deeds and finances went on. Four large holes found in the floor (covered over) of the smaller downstairs room served as safes. The same cunning storage device was used for the Chamberlain who lived upstairs in the **Chambre du Camérier** (just off the Jesus Hall), where the safes have been revealed. As the Pope's right-hand man, the quarters would have been lavishly decorated, but successive occupants have left their mark, most recently military whitewash, and what is now visible is a confusion of layers. The other door in this room leads into the **Papal Vestiary**, where the Pope would dress before sessions in the consistory. He also had a small library here and could look out onto the gardens below.

A door on the North side of the Jesus Hall leads to the **Consistoire** of the **Vieux Palais**, where sovereigns and ambassadors were received and the cardinals' council held. The only decoration that remains are fragments of frescoes moved from the cathedral and a nineteenth-century line-up of the popes, in which all nine look remarkably similar thanks to the artist using the same model for each portrait. Some medieval artistry is in evidence, however, in the **Chapelle St-Jean**, off the Consistoire, and in the **Chapelle St-Martial** on the floor above. Both were decorated by a Sienese artist, Matteo Giovanetti, and commissioned by Clement VI who demanded the maximum amount of blue – the most expensive pigment, derived from lapis lazuli. The **kitchen** on this floor also gives a hint of the scale of papal gluttony with its square walls becoming an octagonal chimneypiece for a vast central cooking fire. In the **Palais Neuf**, Clement VI's bedroom and study are further evidence of this pope's secular concerns, with wonderful food-orientated murals and painted ceilings. But austerity resumes in the cathedral-like proportions of the **Grande Chapelle** or Chapelle Clementine and in the **Grande Audience**, its twin in terms of volume on the floor below.

When you've completed the circuit, which includes a heady walk along the roof terraces, you can watch a glossy but informative film on the history of the palace (English headphones available). There are also concerts: programmes are available from the ticket office.

The **Cathédrale Notre-Dame-des-Doms**, next to the Palais des Papes, might once have been a luminous Romanesque structure, but the interior has had a bad attack of Baroque. In addition, nineteenth-century maniacs mounted an enormous gilded Virgin on the belfry, which would look silly enough anywhere, but when dwarfed by the fifty-metre towers of the popes' palace is absurd. There's greater reward behind, in the **Rocher des Doms** park. As well as ducks and swans and views over the river to Villeneuve and beyond, it has a sundial in which your own shadow tells the time.

The **Petit Palais** (Wed–Mon: July & Aug 10.30am–6pm; rest of year 9.30am–noon & 2–6pm; 20F; Oct–March free Sun), just below the Dom rock, also has treats, though the size of the collection (predominantly of thirteenth- to fifteenth-century Italian painting and sculpture), is daunting. It's worth seeking out the works of Simone Martini and Gentile da Fabriano, both masters of colour and facial expression, and, amongst the surfeit of Madonna and child portraits, that of Louis Bréa, as well as the sublime Botticellis.

Behind the Petit Palais, and well signposted, is the half-span of Pont St-Bénézet, or the **Pont d'Avignon** of the famous song (April–Sept daily 9am–6.30pm; rest of year Tues–Sun 9am–1pm & 2–5pm; 15F, 31F combined ticket with Musée en Images). One theory has it that the lyrics say "*Sous le pont*" (under the bridge) rather than "*Sur le pont*" (on the bridge), and refer to the thief and trickster clientele of a tavern on the Île de la Barthelasse (which the bridge once crossed) dancing with glee at the arrival of more potential victims. Repairing the bridge from the ravages of the Rhône was finally abandoned in 1660, three-and-a-half centuries after it was built, and only four of the original 22 arches remain. It can be walked, danced or sat upon, but beware the precipitous, barely protected drops on either side.

To the right of the entrance to the bridge is the **Musée en Images** (April–Sept daily 9am–7pm; Oct to mid-Nov & Feb 10–March Tues–Sun 10am–5pm; 26F, 31F combined ticket with bridge), a twenty-minute slide show telling the history of the city (English headphones available). It's a bit pricey and predictable, but a pleasantly lazy way of seeing some of the glories of the city's art and architecture.

Around place de l'Horloge

The café-lined **place de l'Horloge**, frenetically busy most of the time, is the site of the city's imposing **Hôtel de Ville** and **clock tower**, and the **Opéra**. Around the square, on rues de Mons, Molière and Corneille, famous faces appear in windows painted on the buildings. Many of these figures from the past were visitors to Avignon, and of those who recorded their impressions of the city it was the sound of over a hundred bells ringing that stirred them most. On a Sunday morning, traffic lulls permitting, you can still hear a myriad different peals from churches, convents and chapels in close proximity. The fourteenth-century **church of St-Agricole**, just behind the Hôtel de Ville (Wed 10am–noon, Sat 4–6pm, Sun 8–10pm), is one of Avignon's best Gothic edifices, with a beautifully carved fifteenth-century facade.

To the south, just behind rue St-Agricole on rue Collège du Roure, is the beautiful fifteenth-century **Palais du Roure**, a centre of Provençal culture. The gateway and the courtyard are definitely worth a look; there may well be temporary art exhibitions, and if you want a rambling tour through the attics to see Provençal costumes, publications and presses, photographs of the Carmargue in the 1900s and an old stagecoach, you need to turn up at 3pm on Tuesday (20F).

To the west of place de l'Horloge are the most desirable Avignon addresses – both now and three hundred years ago. High, heavy facades dripping with cupids, eagles, dragons, fruit and foliage range along **rue Joseph-Vernet** and **rue Petite-Fusterie** with expensive shops and restaurants to match.

The Banasterie and Carmes quartiers

The **quartier de la Banasterie** behind the Palais des Papes is almost solid seventeenth- and eighteenth-century, and the heavy wooden doors, with their highly sculptured lintels, today bear the nameplates of lawyers, psychiatrists and doctors.

Between Banasterie and **place des Carmes** are a tangle of tiny streets guaranteed to get you lost. Pedestrians have priority over cars on many of them, and there are plenty of tempting café or restaurant stops. At 24 rue Saluces, you'll find the peculiar **Musée du Mont de Piété**, an ex-pawnbroker's shop and now the town's archives (Mon–Fri 8.30–11.30am & 1.30–5.30pm; free). It has a small display of papal bulls and painted silk desiccators for determining the dry weight of what was the city's chief commodity.

Rue de la République to place Pie

Between rue de la République and the hideous **market hall** on **place Pie** (every morning except Mon) is the main pedestrian precinct centring around **place du Change**. **Rue des Marchands** and **rue du Vieux-Sextier** have their complement of chapels and late-medieval mansions, in particular the **Hôtel des Rascas** on the corner of rue des Marchands and rue Fourbisseurs, and the **Hôtel de Belli** on the corner of rue Fourbisseurs and rue du Vieux-Sextier. The Renaissance **church of St-Pierre** on place St-Pierre has superb doors sculpted in 1551; in the Annunciation scene on the right-hand door, Mary looks as if she's saying "Who the hell are you?" to Gabriel, who points to the dove as his credentials.

More Renaissance art is on show in the fourteenth-century **church of St-Didier** (Mon–Sat 9am–noon & 2–7pm, Sun 10am–noon), chiefly *The Carrying of the Cross* by Francesco Laurana, commissioned by King René of Provence in 1478. There are also fourteenth-century frescoes in the left-hand chapel.

Musée Calvet and around

The excellent **Musée Calvet**, 65 rue Joseph-Vernet (Wed–Mon 10am–1pm & 2–6pm; 30F), and the impressive eighteenth-century palace housing it, are undergoing gradual restoration and transformation. Some of the collection will therefore be reshuffled. However, the **Galerie des Sculptures**, the first room, is completed and set to stay where it is. A better introduction to a museum couldn't be wished for, the handful of languorous nineteenth century marble sculptures, including Bosio's *Young Indian*, are perfectly suited to this elegant space, lit from either side. The end of the gallery houses the Puech collection with a large selection of silverware, Italian and Dutch paintings, but more unusually a Flemish curiosities cabinet, painted with scenes from the story of Daniel. Upstairs, the Provençal dynasties of the Mignards and the Vernets are well represented. Nicolas Mignard sets off with a fine set of seasons in the Joseph Vernet room, whilst Joseph Vernet himself sticks to representing the different times of the day. Further down Horace Vernet donated the subtle *Death of Young Barra* by Jacques-Louis David as well as Géricault's *Battle of Nazareth*. On the way out don't miss the Victor Martin collection, including Vlaminck's *At the Bar,* Bonnard's *Winter Day*, and the haunting *Downfall* by Chaïm Soutine. The rest of the eclectic collection – from an Egyptian mummy of a five-year-old boy to intricate wrought-iron work, taking in along the way Gallo-Roman pots and Gothic clocks – is due to be on show again by 2002.

The remaining museums are considerably less compelling. Next door to the Musée Calvet is the **Musée Requien** (Tues–Sat 9am–noon & 2–6pm; free). Its subject is natural history and its sole advantage is in being free and having clean loos. With little more to recommend it is the **Musée Lapidaire**, a museum of Roman and Gallo-Roman stones housed in the Baroque chapel at 27 rue de la République (Wed–Mon 10am–1pm & 2–6pm; free Nov–March, summer 10F). Finally, at the **Musée Vouland** at the end of rue Victor-Hugo near Porte St-Dominique (June–Sept Tues–Sat 9am–noon & 2–6pm, Oct–May 2–6pm only; 20F) you feast your eyes on the fittings, fixtures and furnishings that French aristocrats indulged in both before and after the Revolution. There's some brilliant Moustiers faïence, exquisite marquetry and Louis XV ink-pots with silver rats holding the lids – but little that you can't see better *in situ* elsewhere.

Southeast: to rue des Teinturiers

Between the noisy rue de la République and place St-Didier, on rue Labourer is the **Musée Angladon-Dubrujeaud** (Weds–Sun April–Sept 1–6pm; Oct–March closes at 7pm; 30F), displays the remains of the private collection of Jacques Doucet. Once a mighty cutting-edge collection, containing such treasures as Picasso's *Demoiselles d'Avignon* and Douanier-Rousseau's *The Snakecharmer* (now in the Musée d'Orsay), much of the collection was either given away or sold. Testimony to grander days is in the first room, where photographs of Jacques Doucet's house, with rooms decorated according to the style of the paintings therein, reveal a man ahead of his time. The rest of the downstairs room shows what is left of what was his contemporary collection; *Portrait of Mme Foujita* and a *Self-Portrait* by Foujita, Modigliani's *The Pink Blouse*, various Picassos, and Van Gogh's *The Railroad Cars*, the only painting from Van Gogh's stay in Provence to be on display in Provence. The theme of decorating rooms around a style has been taken up in the rest of the museum with a room dedicated to the medieval and Renaissance periods, three dedicated to the eighteenth century (Doucet's first passion) and a Far East room.

Through the park by the tourist office (where there's an old British red phone box) you come to **place des Corps-Saints**, a lively area of cafés and restaurants whose tables fill the square. Just to the north, rue des Lices runs eastwards, past the École des Beaux-Arts, to **rue des Teinturiers**, the city's most atmospheric street. Its name refers to the eighteenth- and nineteenth-century business of calico printing. The cloth was washed in the Sorgue which still runs alongside the street, turning the wheels of long-gone mills and, although the water is fairly murky and sometimes smelly, this is still a great street for evening strolls, with a large number of cheap restaurants.

Eating, drinking and nightlife

Good-value midday **meals** are two a penny in Avignon and eating well in the evening needn't break the bank. The large terraced café-brasseries on place de l'Horloge, rue de la République, place du Change and place des Corps-Saints all serve quick basic meals. Rue des Teinturiers is good for menu-browsing if you're budgeting, and the streets between place de Crillon and place du Palais are full of temptation if you're not.

Restaurants

Le Belgocargo, 10 place des Châtaignes (☎04.90.85.72.99). Belgian restaurant specializing in *moules frites* and beer; lunch menu with drink for under 50F. Closed Sun out of season.

Brunel, 46 rue Balance (☎04.90.85.24.83). Superb regional dishes, with menus from 200F. Closed Sun & Mon, and mid-July to mid-Aug.

L'Entrée des Artistes, 1 place des Carmes (☎04.90.82.46.90). Small, friendly bistrot serving traditional French dishes; 120F weekday menu. Closed lunch Sat, Sun & first 2 weeks of Sept.

La Ferme, chemin du Bois, Île de la Barthelasse (☎04.90.82.57.53). A traditional farmhouse with well-prepared simple dishes. From 100F. Closed Sat lunch, & Mon out of season.

Hiély-Lucullus, 5 rue de la République (☎04.90.86.17.07). This is one of Avignon's top gastronomic palaces, serving beautiful Provençal cuisine. The Rhône wines are the very best, and will add a good whack to an already groaning bill if you order à la carte. 220F menu or else 320F menu *gourmand*. Closed Mon, & Tues lunch out of season, and last 2 weeks of June.

Le Petit Bedon, 70 rue Joseph-Vernet (☎04.90.82.33.98). The *"Potbelly"* does the best meal for under 250F to be had anywhere in the city. Closed Mon eve & Sun, and the last two weeks in Aug.

La Tache d'Encre, 22 rue des Teinturiers (☎04.90.85.46.03). The food isn't brilliant but the musicians – jazz, rock, chansons, African or salsa – usually are; there's live music on Fri and Sat nights, occasionally weekdays, too; booking advisable. Congenial atmosphere; menus under 100F. Closed Mon & Tues eve & Sun lunch.

Le Venaissin, 16 place de l'Horloge (☎04.90.86.20.99). In the height of summer, you'd be lucky to get a table here – it's the only cheap brasserie on place de l'Horloge that serves more than *steak frites*; two menus under 100F.

Cafés, bars and salons de thé

Les Célestins, pl des Corps-Saints. 7am–1am. Café-bar with a young, fairly trendy clientele. Closed Sun.

Grand Café du Commerce, 21 rue St-Jean-de-Vieux. Pleasant café for all tastes.

Pub Z, cnr rue Bonneterie & rue Artaud. Rock bar with black and white decor in honour of the zebra. Open till 1.30am; closed Sun & first 3 weeks of Aug.

Shakespeare, 155 rue Carreterie. English bookshop and *salon de thé*. Closed Sun, Mon & evenings.

Le Red Zone, 25 rue Carnot (☎04.90.27.02.44). Thurs–Sat 7pm–1.30am. Bar with DJs and weekly concerts.

Tapalocas, 10 rue Galante (☎04.90.82.56.84). Daily 11.45am–1.30am. Tapas at 12F each; Spanish music, sometimes live.

Nightlife

There's a fair amount of **nightlife** and cultural events in Avignon: the **Opéra**, on place de l'Horloge (☎04.90.82.23.44), mounts a good range of productions; Le Chêne Noir, 8bis rue Ste-Catherine (☎04.90.86.58.11), is a theatre company worth seeing, with mime, musicals or Molière on offer; and plenty of **classical concerts** are performed in churches, usually for free.

For **live music**, *AJMI Jazz Club*, La Manutention, rue Escalier-Ste-Anne (☎04.90.86.08.61), hosts live jazz every Thursday night and features major acts and some adventurous new groups. *Le Bistroquet*, Quartier du Mouton on Île de la Berthelasse, is a rock bar with live gigs except in June, and the restaurant *La Tache d'Encre* (see above) has some good live sounds on Friday and Saturday nights. *L'Esclave Bar*, 12 rue du Limas is a **gay** bar and disco (10pm–5am; shows Wed & Sun). The tourist office hands out a free bi-monthly calendar called *Rendez-Vous*, They may also have the weekly arts, events and music free magazine *César* which is otherwise found in arts centres.

Listings

Bike rental Aymard, 80 rue Guillaume-Puy; Masson Richard, place Pie; Transhumance Voyages, at the main tourist office.

Boat trips Le Mireio, allée de l'Oulle (☎04.90.85.62.25). All year round, 2-week advance booking recommended. Upstream towards Châteauneuf-du-Pape and downstream to Arles.

Car rental On bd St-Ruf are AAC at no. 15 (☎04.90.85.69.11), Europcar at no. 27 (☎04.90.14.40.80), and ASL at no. 3 (☎04.90.86.06.61).

Changing money Chaix Conseil, 43 cours Jean-Jaurès and place Carnot; automatic exchange at CIC, 13 rue République and Caixa Bank, 64 rue Joseph-Vernet.

Emergencies Doctor/ambulance ☎15 or Médecins de Garde (☎04.90.87.75.00); hospital, Centre Hospitalier H-Duffaut, 305 rue Raoul-Follereau (☎04.90.80.33.33); night chemist, call police at bd St-Roch (☎04.90.16.81.00) for addresses.

Police 10 place Pie (☎08.00.00.84.00).

Post office Poste, cours Président-Kennedy, Avignon 84000.

Swimming pool Piscine de la Barthelasse on the Île de la Barthelasse; May–Aug 10am–7pm.

Taxis place Pie (☎04.90.82.20.20).

Villeneuve-lès-Avignon

VILLENEUVE-LÈS-AVIGNON rises up a rocky escarpment above the west bank of the Rhône, looking down upon its older neighbour from behind far more convincing fortifications. Historically, Villeneuve operated largely as a suburb to Avignon, with palatial residences constructed by the cardinals and a great monastery founded by Pope Innocent VI.

To this day, Villeneuve is technically a part of Languedoc and not Provence, and would score better in the hierarchy of towns to visit were it further from Avignon, whose monuments it can almost match for colossal scale and impressiveness. In summer, at least, it benefits, providing venues for the Avignon Festival as well as alternatives for accommodation overspill; and it's certainly worth a day, whatever time of year you visit.

Arrival, information and accommodation

From Avignon's **gare SNCF** (see p.882) the half-hourly Villeneuve–Les Angles #10 bus (rather than the Les Angles–Villeneuve bus #10) runs direct to place Charles-David (Bellevue stop) taking less than ten minutes, or five if you catch it from Porte d'Oulle. After 7pm you'll have to take a taxi or walk; it's only 3km. On place Charles-David you'll find the **tourist office** (July & Aug daily 8.45am–12.30pm & 2.30–6.30pm; Sept–July Mon–Sat 8.45am–12.30pm & 2–6pm; ☎04.90.25.61.55, fax 04.90.25.91.55) and a food **market** on Thursday morning and bric-a-brac on Saturday morning. Rue Gabriel-Péri leads west off the place past the mairie to place St-Marc. From here, the main street, rue de la République, runs due north.

For reasonably priced **accommodation**, try the *Beauséjour*, 61 av Gabriel-Péri (☎04.90.25.20.56; ③), overlooking the river near the Pont du Royaume. If money is no object, *Le Prieuré*, 7 place du Chapitre (☎04.90.15.90.15, fax 04.90.25.45.39; ⑧), is indisputably the first choice, both for the rooms and for its restaurant. For half the price, you could stay in equally ancient surroundings at *L'Atelier*, 5 rue de la Foire (☎04.90.25.01.84, fax 04.90.25.80.06; ③), a sixteenth-century house with huge open fireplaces and a walled garden. Alternatively there's a Louis XIV mansion, *Les Cèdres*, 39 bd Pasteur (☎04.90.25.43.92, fax 04.90.25.14.66; ④), with pool and restaurant.

The **YMCA hostel**, 7bis chemin de la Justice (☎04.90.25.46.20, fax 04.90.25.30.64; half-board compulsory for stays of more than one night), is an attractive alternative, beautifully situated overlooking the river by Pont du Royaume, with balconied rooms for two to six people and an open-air swimming pool (stop Pont d'Avignon on Les Angles–Villeneuve bus or Général-Leclerc on the Villeneuve-Les Angles bus). For **campers**, the three-star Camping Municipal de la Laune is in chemin St-Honoré (☎04.90.25.76.06; April–Sept) off the D980, near the sports stadium and swimming pools.

The town

For a good overview of Villeneuve – and Avignon – make your way to the **Tour Philippe-le-Bel** at the bottom of montée de la Tour (bus stop Philippe-le-Bel). This tower was built to guard the French end of Avignon's Pont St-Bénézet (or Pont d'Avignon; see p.884), and a climb to the top (Tues–Sun: April–Sept 10am–12.30pm &

MUSEUMS AND MONUMENTS

A **Passeport pour l'Art** (45F) gives you entry to the Fort St-André, Tour Philippe-le-Bel, La Chartreuse du Val de Bénédiction, the Collègiale Notre-Dame and its cloister and the Musée Pierre-de-Luxembourg. The ticket is available from each of the monuments and from the tourist office.

3–7pm; Oct–March 10am–noon & 2–5.30pm; closed Feb; 10F) will be rewarded with stunning views.

Even more indicative of French distrust of its neighbours is the enormous **Fort St-André** (visit to the towers daily April–Sept 10am–noon & 2–5pm; Oct–March 10am–noon & 2–6pm; 25F), whose bulbous double-towered gateway and vast white walls loom over the town. Inside, refreshingly, there's not a hint of a postcard stall or souvenir shop – just tumbledown houses and the former **abbey**, with its gardens of olive trees, ruined chapels, lily ponds and dovecotes (Tues–Sun same hours as the Fort towers; 20F). Its cliff-face terrace is the classic spot for artists to aim their brushes, or photographers their cameras, over Avignon. You can reach the approach to the fortress, montée du Fort, from place Jean-Jaurès on rue de la République, or by the "rapid slope" of **rue Pente-Rapide**, a cobbled street of tiny houses leading off rue des Recollets on the north side of place Charles-David.

Almost at the top of rue de la République, on the right, allée des Muriers leads from place des Chartreux to the entrance of **La Chartreuse du Val de Bénédiction** (daily 9am–6.30pm; Oct–March closes 5.30pm; 32F). This Charterhouse, one of the largest in France, was founded by the sixth of the Avignon popes, Innocent VI, whose sharp profile is outlined on his tomb in the church. The buildings, which were sold off after the Revolution and gradually restored this century, are totally unembellished. With the exception of the Giovanetti frescoes in the chapel beside the refectory, all the paintings and treasures of the monastery have been dispersed, leaving you with a strong impression of the austerity of the Carthusian order. You're free to wander around unguided, through the three cloisters, the church, chapels, cells and communal spaces, which have little to see but plenty of atmosphere to absorb. It is one of the best venues in the Festival d'Avignon.

Another festival venue is the fourteenth-century **Église Collègiale Notre-Dame** and its cloister (7F) on place St-Marc close to the mairie (April–Sept Tues–Sun 10am–12.30pm & 3–7pm; Oct–March Tues–Sun 10am–noon & 2–5.30pm; June 15–Sept 15 daily; closed Feb). Notre-Dame's most important treasure is a rare fourteenth-century smiling Madonna and Child made from a single tusk of ivory, now housed, along with many of the paintings from the Chartreuse, in the **Musée Pierre-de-Luxembourg**, just to the north along rue de la République (same hours as Eglise Collègiale Notre-Dame; 20F). The spacious layout includes a single room, with comfortable settees and ample documentation, given over to the most stunning painting in the collection – *The Coronation of the Virgin*, painted in 1453 by Enguerrand Quarton as the altarpiece for the church in the Chartreuse.

Eating and drinking

Villeneuve's centre has a good choice of **eating** places. Try *La Calèche*, 35 rue de la République (☎04.90.25.02.54; closed Sun out of season; menus around 100F), or the Italian *La Mamma Lucia* on place V-Basch (☎04.90.25.00.71; closed Sun out of season; around 80F). For a blowout meal, *La Magnanerie*, 37 rue Camp de Bataille (☎04.90.25.11.11), off rue de la Magnanerie, is the posh and perfect answer, with a menu for 170F (à la carte over 400F). Alternatively, *Aubertin*, 1 rue de l'Hôpital

(☎04.90.25.94.84; closed Mon out of season), serves a 120F lunch menu in the shade of the old arcades by the Collègiale Notre-Dame (à la carte from 300F).

St-Rémy-de-Provence and the Alpilles

The watery and intensely cultivated scenery of the Petite Crau plain south of Avignon changes abruptly with the eruption of the **Chaîne des Alpilles**, whose peaks look like the surf of a wave about to engulf the plain. At their northen foot nestles **ST-RÉMY**, a dreamy place whose old town is contained within a circle of boulevards no more than half a kilometre in diameter. Outside this ring, the modern town is sparingly laid out, so for once you don't have to plug your way through dense developments to reach the centre. It is a beautiful place, as unspoilt as the villages around it.

Arrival, information and accommodation

There's no train station in St-Rémy; **buses** from Avignon, Aix and Arles drop you in place de la République, the main square abutting the old town on the east. The **tourist office** on place Jean-Jaurès (June–Sept Mon–Sat 9am–noon & 2–7pm, Sun 9am–noon; rest of year Mon–Sat 9am–noon & 2–6pm; ☎04.90.92.05.22, fax 04.90.92.38.52) is just south of the centre, reached by following bd Marceau/av Durand-Maillane. They have excellent free guides to **cycling and walking routes** in and around the Alpilles and can provide addresses for renting **horses**. If you want to rent a **bike** or **car**, go to Ferri, 35 av de la Libération, the road to Cavaillon (☎04.90.92.10.88). It's difficult to get to Glanum or Les Baux (see p.892) except by foot or taxi (taxis ☎04.90.92.48.20, ☎04.90.92.25.71 & ☎04.90.92.46.92).

The town has a fairly wide choice of **accommodation**, though real bargains are hard to come by. In the old town, pleasant hotels with some cheap rooms are *Les Arts-La Palette*, above the *Café des Arts* at 30 bd Victor-Hugo (☎04.90.92.08.50, fax 04.90.92.55.09; ③; closed Tues & Feb) and *Mexican Café*, 4 rue du 8-Mai 1945 (☎04.90.92.17.66; ③). *Nostradamus*, 3 av Taillandier (☎04.90.92.13.23, fax 04.90.92.49.54; ③) to the north of the old town, offers studios for two. The *Ville Verte* on the corner of place de la République and av Fauconnet (☎04.90.92.06.14, fax 04.90.92.56.54; ③), is central and has some rooms with facilities for the disabled, a garden and pool, and also organizes walking, climbing and cycling trips. *Le Castellet des Alpilles*, 6 place Mireille (☎04.90.92.07.21, fax 04.90.92.52.03; ⑤; closed Nov–Feb), south of the old town past the tourist office, is small and friendly, with some rooms with great views. Close by the tourist office, the *Antiques*, 15 av Pasteur (☎04.90.92.03.02, fax 04.90.92.50.40; ⑤; closed Nov–March), is a nineteenth-century mansion with huge grounds, pools and wonderfully aristocratic furnishings in the dining room and salons.

There are three **campsites** near St-Rémy: the municipal *Le Mas de Nicolas*, 2km along rte de Mollèges (☎04.90.92.27.05; closed Nov to mid-March); *Monplaisir*, 1km along rte de Maillane (☎04.90.92.22.70, fax 04.90.92.18.57; closed Nov–Feb); and *Pegomas*, 1km along rte de Noves (☎04.90.92.01.21, fax 04.90.92.56.17; closed Nov–Feb).

The town

To reach the old town from place de la République, take avenue de la Résistance, which runs alongside the town's main church, the **Collégiale St-Martin** (organ recitals July–Sept Sat 5pm), and start wandering up the alleyways into immaculate, leafy squares. For an introduction to the region, a good first visit is to the **Musée des Alpilles** on place Favier, housed in the Hôtel Mistral de Mondragon (daily: April–June

& Sept–Oct 10am–noon & 2–6pm; July & Aug closes 7pm; Nov–Dec closes 5pm; 18F). The museum features interesting displays on folklore, festivities and traditional crafts, plus some intriguing local landscapes, some creepy portraits by Marshal Pétain's first wife, and souvenirs of local boy Nostradamus.

You can buy a combined 40F ticket for the Musée des Alpilles and the neighbouring **Musée Archéologique** in the Hôtel de Sade (guided visits several times daily 10am–5pm/6pm; closed Jan; 15F), displaying finds from the archeological digs at the Greco-Roman town of Glanum (see overleaf), for which the combined ticket is also valid. The hour's tour may be a bit much for the non-committed, but there are some stunning pieces, in particular the temple decorations.

In addition to the two fifteenth- to sixteenth-century hôtels that house the museums, you'll find more ancient stately residences as you wander through the old town, particularly along **rue Parage**. On rue Hoche is the birthplace of **Nostradamus**, though only the facade is contemporary with the savant, and the house is not open for visits. The Hôtel d'Estrine, 8 rue Estrine, houses the **Centre d'Art Présence Van Gogh** (April–Dec Tues–Sun 10.30am–12.30pm & 2.30–6.30pm; 20F), which hosts contemporary art exhibitions and has a permanent exhibition of Van Gogh reproductions and extracts from letters, as well as audiovisual presentations on the painter.

Eating, drinking and festivals

You'll find plenty of **brasseries** and **restaurants** in and around old St-Rémy. *Le Jardin de Frédéric*, 8 bd Gambetta (☎04.90.92.27.76; closed Wed), has a 130F lunch menu, and usually some interesting dishes on offer. There are a few good options on rue Carnot (leading from boulevard Victor-Hugo east through the old town to boulevard Marceau), including *La Gousée d'Ail* at no. 25 (04.90.92.16.87; closed Wed) with live jazz on Thursday nights, and *La Maison Jaune* at no. 15 (☎04.90.92.56.14; closed Mon & Sun eve) with a 100F weekday lunch menu and a fabulous *menu dégustation provençal* for 245F. *Xa*, 24 bd Mirabeau (☎04.90.92.41.23; closed Wed & Nov–March; 140F menu) is a new modish restaurant with excellent food. For a scenic spot to dine on crêpes, try *Lou Planet*, 7 place Favier, by the Musée des Alpilles, and for brasserie fare there's *Le Bistrot des Alpilles*, 15 bd Mirabeau (open till midnight; closed Sun). For café-lounging, head for the *Café des Arts*, 30 bd Victor-Hugo (open till 12.30am; closed Tues & Feb), where the works of local painters are exhibited.

The best time to visit St-Rémy is during the **Fête de Transhumance** on Whit Monday, when a 2000-strong flock of sheep, accompanied by goats and donkeys, does a tour of the town before being packed off to the Alps for the summer. Or come for the **Carreto Ramado**, on August 15, a harvest thanksgiving procession in which the religious or secular symbolism of the floats reveals the political colour of the various village councils. A pagan rather than workers' **May Day** is celebrated with donkey-drawn floral floats on which people play fifes and tambourines.

South of St-Rémy: Les Antiques, St-Paul-de-Mausole and Glanum

About 1.5km south of the old town, following avenue Vincent-Van-Gogh past the tourist office, you'll come to **Les Antiques** (free access), a triumphal arch celebrating the Roman conquest of Marseille, and a mausoleum thought to commemorate two grandsons of Augustus. Save for a certain amount of weather erosion, the mausoleum is perfectly intact; the arch less so, but both display intricate patterning and the unaesthetic proportional sense of the Romans.

The arch would have been a familiar sight to **Vincent Van Gogh**, who in 1889 requested that he be put under medical care for several months. He was living in Arles at the time, and the hospital chosen by his friends was in the old monastery

St-Paul-de-Mausole, a hundred metres or so east of the Antiques; it remains a psychiatric clinic today. Although the regime was more prison than hospital, Van Gogh was allowed to wander out around the Alpilles and painted prolifically during his twelve-month stay. The *Oliviers' Fields, The Reaper, The Enclosed Field* and *The Evening Stroll* are among the 150 canvases of this period. The church and cloisters can be visited (9am–6pm): take avenue Edgar-Leroy or allée St-Paul from avenue Vincent-Van-Gogh, go past the main entrance of the clinic and into the gateway on the left at the end of the wall.

Not very far beyond the hospital is a signposted farm called **Mas de la Pyramide** (daily 9am–noon & 2–5/7pm; wait by the gate if there's no immediate answer to the bell; 20F). It's an old troglodyte farm in the Roman quarries for Glanum with a lavender and cherry orchard surrounded by cavernous openings into the rock filled with ancient farm equipment and rusting bicycles. The farmhouse is part medieval and part Gallo-Roman, with pictures of the owner's family who have lived there for generations.

One of the most impressive ancient settlements in France, **Glanum**, 500m south of Les Antiques (daily: April–Sept 9am–7pm; Oct–March 9.30am–noon & 2–5pm; 32F, 40F combined ticket with Musée des Alpilles and Musée Archéologique), was dug out from alluvial deposits at the very foot of the Alpilles. The site was originally a Neolithic homestead; then, between the second and first centuries BC, the Gallo-Greeks, probably from Massalia (Marseille), built a city here, on which the Gallo-Romans, from the end of the first century BC to the third century AD, constructed yet another town.

Though Glanum is one of the most important archeological sites in France, it can be very difficult to get to grips with. Not only were the later buildings moulded onto the earlier, but the fashion at the time of Christ was for a Hellenistic style. You can distinguish the Greek levels from the Roman most easily by the stones: the earlier civilization used massive hewn rocks while the Romans preferred smaller and more accurately shaped stones. The leaflet at the admission desk is helpful, as are the attendants if your French is good enough.

The site is bisected by a road running from north to south, with several **Hellenic houses** to the northwest. East of here are the **Thermes**, a complex of furnaces, bathing chambers and pools, and beyond this the **Maison du Capricorne** with some fine mosaics. A **forum** dating from Roman times is south of here, near a restored **theatre** and the superb sculptures on the Roman **Temples Geminées** (Twin Temples). The temples also have fragments of mosaics, fountains of both Greek and Roman periods, and first-storey walls and columns. As the site narrows in the ravine at the southern end, you find a Grecian edifice around a **sacred spring** – the feature that made this location so desirable. Steps lead down to a pool, with a slab above for the libations of those too disabled to descend. An inscription records that Agrippa was responsible for restoring it in 27 BC and dedicating it to Valetudo, the Roman goddess of health.

Les Baux and the Val d'Enfer

At the top of the Alpilles ridge, 7km southwest of St-Rémy, lies the distinctly unreal fortified village of **LES BAUX**, where the ruined eleventh-century citadel is hard to distinguish from the edge of the plateau, whose rock is both foundation and part of the structure.

Once Les Baux lived off the power and widespread possessions in Provence of its medieval lords, who owed allegiance to no-one. When the dynasty died out at the end of the fourteenth century, however, the town, which had once numbered 6000 inhabitants, passed to the counts of Provence and then to the kings of France, who eventually, in 1632, razed the feudal citadel to the ground and fined the population into penury. From that date until the nineteenth century, both citadel and village were inhabited almost exclusively by bats and crows. The discovery in the neighbouring hills of the mineral bauxite (whose name derives from "Les Baux") brought back some life to the village, and tourism has more recently transformed the place. Today the population stays steady at around 400, while the number of visitors exceeds 1.5 million each year.

The lived-in village has many very beautiful buildings. There are half-a-dozen museums, one of the best being the **Musée Yves Brayer** in the Hôtel des Porcelets (April–Sept daily 10am–12.30pm & 2–6.30pm; Oct–March Wed–Mon 10am–12.30pm & 2–5.30pm; closed Jan–mid-Feb; 25F) showing the paintings of the twentieth-century figurative artist whose work also adorns the seventeenth-century **Chapelle des Pénitents Blancs**. Changing exhibitions of contemporary Provençal artists' works are displayed in the Hôtel de Manville (hours vary, check with the tourist office; free). The museum of the **Fondation Louis Jou** in the fifteenth-century Hôtel Jean de Brion contains the presses, wood lettering blocks and hand-printed books of a master typographer (visit by reservation only ☎04.90.54.34.17; 20F). The **Musée des Santons** in the old Hôtel de Ville (daily 8am–7pm; free) displays traditional Provençal Christmas crib figures.

Following the signs to the Château, will bring you to the entrance to the **Citadelle de la Ville Morte**, the main reason for coming to Les Baux (March–Nov 9am–7.30/8.30pm; Nov–Feb 9am–5/6pm; 35F), and where you can find ruins and several more museums. Pick of the bunch is the **Musée de l'Olivier** in the Romaneque Chapelle St-Blaise, featuring slide shows of paintings of olive trees and their artistic treatment by Van Gogh, Gauguin and Cézanne. The **Musée d'Histoire des Baux** in the vaulted space of Tour de Brau has a collection of archeological remains and models to illustrate the history from medieval splendour to Bauxite works. The most impressive ruins are those of the feudal castle demolished on Richelieu's orders; there's also the partially restored **Chapelle Castrale** and the **Tour Sarrasine**, the cemetery, ruined houses half carved out of the rocky escarpment, and some spectacular views, the best of which is out across the Grande Crau from beside the statue of Provençal poet Charloun Riev at the southern edge of the plateau.

The **tourist office** is at the beginning of Grand-Rue (March–Sept daily 9am–7pm; Oct–April 9am–6pm; ☎04.90.54.34.39, fax 04.90.54.51.15). You have to park – and pay – before entering the village. Nothing in Les Baux comes cheap, least of all **accommodation**. There is just one cheapish option, the *Hostellerie de la Reine Jeanne* (☎04.90.54.32.06, fax 04.90.54.32.33; ④) by the entrance to the village, with a good restaurant (menus from 100F). If you're feeling rich and want to treat yourself, just below Les Baux to the west on the road leading down to the Val d'Enfer is the luxurious hotel-restaurant *Oustau de Baumanière* (☎04.90.54.33.07; ⑧).

The Val d'Enfer

Within walking distance of Les Baux, along the D27 leading northwards, is the valley of quarried and eroded rocks named the **Val d'Enfer** – the Valley of Hell. One quarry has been turned into an audiovisual experience under the title of the **Cathédrale des Images** (daily mid-Feb to mid-Nov 10am–6/7pm; 43F), signposted to the right downhill from Les Baux's car park. The projection is continuous, so you don't have to wait to go in. You're surrounded by images projected all over the floor, ceilings and walls of these vast rectangular caverns, and by music that resonates strangely in the captured space. The content of the show, which changes yearly, does not really matter. It just is an extraordinary sensation, wandering on and through these changing shapes and colours. As an erstwhile work site put to good use, it couldn't be bettered.

Arles

ARLES is a major town on the tourist circuit, its fame sealed by the extraordinarily well-preserved Roman arena, **Les Arènes**, at the city's heart, and backed by an impressive

variety of other stones and monuments, both Roman and medieval. It was the key city of
the region in Roman times, then, with Aix, main base of the counts of Provence before
unification with France. For centuries it was Marseille's only rival, profiting from the
inland trade route up the Rhône whenever the enemies of France were blocking
Marseille's port. Arles declined when the railway put an end to this advantage, and it was
an inward-looking depressed town that **Van Gogh** came to in the late nineteenth century. Today it is a staid and conservative place, but comes to life for the **Saturday market**
that brings everyone from the surrounding countryside into town.

Arrival, information and accommodation

Arriving by train eases you gently into the city, with the **gare SNCF** conveniently located a few blocks to the north of the Arènes. Most buses also arrive here at the adjacent
gare routière, though some, including all local buses, stop on the north side of bd
Georges-Clemenceau just east of rue Gambetta. Rue Jean-Jaurès, with its continuation
rue Hôtel-de-Ville, is the main axis of old Arles. At the southern end it meets bd
Georges-Clemenceau and bd des Lices, with the **tourist office** directly opposite
(April–Sept daily 9am–7pm; Oct–March Mon–Sat 9am–6pm, Sun 10am–noon;
☎04.90.18.41.20); there's also an annexe in the gare SNCF. You can rent **bikes** from
Peugeot, 15 rue du Pont or or Europbike at the newspaper kiosk on esplanade Charles-
de-Gaulle, and **cars** from Europcar (☎04.90.93.23.24), Eurorent (☎04.90.93.50.14), or
Hertz (☎04.90.96.75.23), all on bd Victor-Hugo.

There's little shortage of **hotel** rooms at either end of the scale. The best place to
look for cheap rooms is in the area around Porte de la Cavalerie near the station. If you
get stuck, the tourist office will find you accommodation for a small fee.

Hotels

de l'Amphithéatre, 5 rue Diderot (☎04.90.96.10.30, fax 04.90.93.98.69). Recently redecorated
with plenty of warm colours, tiles and wrought ironwork. Close to les Arènes. Closed mid-Jan to
end Feb. ④.

Calendal, 22 place Pomme (☎04.90.96.11.89, fax 04.90.96.05.84). Generous rooms overlooking a
garden. ③.

Le Cloître, 16 rue du Cloître (☎04.90.96.29.50,Fax 04.90.96.02.88). A cosy hotel with some rooms
giving views of St-Trophime. Closed mid-Nov to Feb. ③.

Constantin, 59 bd de Craponne, off bd Clemenceau (☎04.90.96.04.05, fax 04.90.96.84.07). Pleasant,
well-kept and comfortable, with prices kept down by the proximity of the Nîmes highway (some traffic noise) and its location some distance from the centre. Closed mid-Nov to mid-March. ③.

Le Forum, 10 place du Forum (☎04.90.93.48.95, fax 04.90.93.90.00). Spacious rooms in an old
house at the ancient heart of the city, with a swimming pool in the garden. A bit noisy but very welcoming. Closed Nov–March. ⑥.

Galoubet, 18 rue du Dr-Fanton (☎04.90.93.18.11). Lovingly restored old building in the old part of
town. Simply furnished and decorated rooms in rustic Provençal style. ③.

Gauguin, 5 place Voltaire (☎04.90.96.14.35, fax 04.90.18.98.87). Comfortable, cheap and well run.
Advisable to book. ②.

Grand Hôtel Nord Pinus, 14 place du Forum (☎04.90.93.44.44, fax 04.90.93.34.00). Favoured by
the *vedettes* of the bullring and decorated with their trophies, but one of the most luxurious and elegant options. ⑧.

Musée, 11 rue du Grand-Prieuré (☎04.90.93.88.88, fax 04.90.49.98.15). Quiet location opposite
Musée Réattu. Closed Jan. ③.

Terminus & Van Gogh, 5 place Lamartine (☎04.90.96.12.32). The Van Gogh theme is rather over-
played but at least colourful. A cheap option just outside one of the city gates, close to the train and
bus stations. ①.

Youth hostel and campsites

HI youth hostel, 20 av Maréchal-Foch (☎04.90.96.18.25). The hostel is open all year; reception 7.30–10am and 5–11pm; 11pm curfew; take bus #5 from pl Lamartine, direction "Fourchon", stop Fournier. Closed Jan.

La Bienheureuse, 7km out on the N453 at Raphèles-les-Arles (☎04.90.98.35.64). Best of Arles' half-dozen campsites; the restaurant here is furnished with pieces similar to those displayed in the Museon Arlaten, and full of pictures of popular Arlesian traditions. Open all year; regular buses from Arles.

Camping City, 67 rte de Crau (☎04.90.93.08.86, fax 04.90.93.91.07). The closest campsite to town on the Crau bus route. March–Oct.

The city

The centre of Arles fits into a neat triangle between boulevard E-Combes to the east, boulevards Clemenceau and des Lices to the south, and the Rhône to the west. The **Musée de l'Arles Antiques** is south of the expressway by the river, not far from the end of boulevard Clemenceau; **Les Alyscamps** is down across the train lines to the southeast. But these apart, all the **Roman and medieval monuments** are within easy walking distance in this very compact city centre.

Roman Arles

Roman Arles provided grain for most of the western empire and was one of the major ports for trade and shipbuilding. Under Constantine it became the capital of Gaul and reached its height as a world trading centre in the fifth century. Once the empire crumbled, however, Arles found itself isolated between the Rhône, the Alpilles and the marsh-lands of the Camargue – an isolation that allowed its Roman heritage to be preserved.

A good place to start any tour of Roman Arles is the **Musée de l'Arles Antique** (daily April to mid Sept 9am–7pm; mid Sept–March 9.30am–noon & 1.30–6pm; 35F), west of the town centre on the spit of land between the Rhône and the Canal de Rhône. It is housed in a resolutely contemporary building positioned on the axis of the second-century **Cirque Romaine**, an enormous chariot racetrack (currently being excavated) that stretches 450m from the museum to the town side of the expressway. The museum is a

---

THE BULLFIGHT

Bullfighting in Arles and the Camargue is not usually the Spanish-style *mise-à-mort*. Though the bulls probably don't enjoy their appearances very much, it is the bullfighters, or *razeteurs*, who get hurt, not the beast. Bulls are fêted and adored, and before retirement are given a final tour around the arena while people weep and throw flowers.

It's a passion with the populace, who treat the champion *razeteurs* like football stars. The shows involve various feats of daring, but the most common form is where the bull has a cockade at the base of its horns and ribbons tied between them. Using blunt razor-combs the *razeteurs* have to cut the ribbons and get the cockades. There's no betting, but people add to the prize money as the game progresses. The drama and grace of the spectacle is the stylish way the men leap over the barrier away from the bull. You are much closer to the scene than with other dangerous sports and there are occasional casualties. For some shows involving horsemen, arrows are shot at the bull, though these don't go in deep enough to make the animal bleed.

All this may leave you feeling cold, or sick, but it's your best way of taking part in local life and of experiencing the Roman arena in Arles. The tourist office, local papers and publicity around the arena will give you the details – be sure to check shows are not *mise-à-mort*.

ARLES' MONUMENTS AND MUSEUMS

A **global ticket** (55F available for all the museums and monuments covered) is available, covering the Arènes, Théâtre Antique, Museon Arlaten, Musée de l'Arles Antique, Cloître St-Trophime, Cryptoportiques, Les Alyscamps, Thermes de Constantin and the Musée Réattu. All, except the Museon Arlaten and the Musée d'Arles Antique, have the same opening hours (daily Jan & Dec 10am–noon & 2–4.30pm; Feb & Nov 10am–noon & 2–5pm; March & Oct 10am–12.30pm & 2–5.30pm; April–June & Sept 9am–12.30pm & 2–7pm; July–Aug 9am–7pm; the ticket offices close 30min before) and the same individual price (15F).

---

treat, open-plan, flooded with natural light and immensely spacious. It covers the pre-history of the area, then takes you through the five centuries of Roman rule from Julius Cæsar's legionary base through Christianization to the period when spices and gems from Africa and Arabia were being traded here. Fabulous mosaics are laid out with walkways above; and there are numerous sarcophagi with intricate sculpting depicting everything from music and lovers, to gladiators and Christian miracles.

Back in the centre of Arles, the most impressive Roman monument is the amphithe-atre, known as the **Arènes** (see box for hours and price), dating from the end of the first century. To give an idea of its size, it used to shelter over two hundred dwellings and three churches built into the two tiers of arches that form its oval surround. This medieval quarter was cleared in 1830 and the Arènes was once more used for enter-tainment. Today, though missing its third storey and most of the internal stairways and galleries, it is a very dramatic structure and a stunning venue for performances. It can still seat 20,000 spectators.

The **Théâtre Antique** (see box for hours and price), just south of the Arènes, comes to life during July, with the Fête du Costume in which local folk groups parade in tra-ditional dress, and the Mosaïque Gitane gypsy festival. The theatre is nowhere near as well preserved as the arena, with only one pair of columns standing, all the statuary removed and the sides of the stage littered with broken bits of stone.

At the river end of rue Hôtel-de-Ville, the **Thermes de Constantine** (see box for hours and price), which may well have been the biggest Roman baths in Provence, are all that remain of the Emperor's palace that extended along the waterfront. The Roman forum was up the hill on the site of **place du Forum**, still the centre of life in Arles. You can see the pillars of an ancient temple embedded in the corner of the *Nord-Pinus* hotel.

The Romans had their burial ground southwest of the centre, and it was used by well-to-do Arlesians well into the Middle Ages. Now only one alleyway, foreshortened by a train line, is preserved. To reach **Les Alyscamps** (see box for hours and price), follow avenue des Alyscamps from boulevard des Lices. Sarcophagi still line the shaded walk, whose tree trunks are azure blue in Van Gogh's rendering. There are numerous tragedy masks, too, though any with special decoration have long since been moved to serve as municipal gifts, as happened often in the seventeenth century, or to reside in the museums. But there is still magic to this walk, which ends at the ruins of a Romanesque church.

The cathedral, museums and medieval Arles

The doorway of the **Cathédrale St-Trophime** on Arles's central **place de la République** is one of the most famous examples of twelfth-century Provençal stonecarving in existence. It depicts the Last Judgment, trumpeted by angels playing with the enthusiasm of jazz musicians while the damned are led naked in chains down to hell and the blessed, all draped in long robes, process upwards. The cathedral itself was started in the ninth century on the spot where, in 597 AD, St Augustine was con-secrated as the first bishop of the English. It was largely completed by the twelfth century. A font in the north aisle and an altar illustrating the crossing of the Red Sea in the north transept were both originally Gallo-Roman sarcophagi. The nave is decorated with d'Aubusson tapestries, in which the one depicting Mary Magdalene bathing Christ's feet has a cat jumping from one oil container to another chased by a dog being ridden by a child. There is more superlative Romanesque and Gothic stonecarving in the extraordinarily beautiful **cloisters**, accessible from place de la République to the right of the cathedral (see box for hours and price).

Across place de la République from the cathedral stands the palatial seventeenth-century **Hôtel de Ville**, inspired by Versailles. You can walk through its vast entrance hall with a flattened vaulted roof, designed to avoid putting extra stress on the **Cryptoporticus du Forum** below. This is a huge, dark, dank and wonderfully spooky three-sided underground gallery, built by the Romans, possible as a food store, possibly as a barracks for public slaves, but certainly to provide sturdy foundations for the forum above. Access is from rue Balze (see box for hours and price) though it may be switched to the Museon Arlaten.

In case you feel that life stopped in Arles – if not after the Romans, then at least after the Middle Ages – head for the **Museon Arlaten** on rue de la République (April–May & Sept Tues–Sun 9.30am–12.30pm & 2–6pm; June–Aug 9.30am–1pm & 2–6.30pm; Oct–March 9.30am–12.30pm & 2–5pm; closed Mon except July–Sept; 20F). The museum was set up in 1896 by Frédéric Mistral, the Nobel Prize-winning novelist who was responsible for the turn-of-the-century revival of interest in all things Provençal and whose statue stands in place du Forum. The collections of costumes, documents, tools, pictures and paraphernalia of Provençal life is alternately tedious and intriguing. The evolution of Arlesian dress is charted in great detail for all social classes from the eighteenth century to World War I and there's a mouthwatering life-size scene of a bourgeois Christmas dinner.

The main collection of the **Musée Réattu** (see box for hours and price), opposite the Roman baths, comprises tedious and rigid eighteenth-century works by the museum's founder and his contemporaries. But dotted round this beautiful fifteenth-century priory are some good modern works: Zadkine's study in bronze for the two Van Gogh brothers, Mario Prassinos' monochrome studies of the Alpilles, Cesar's *Compression 1973*, and, best of all, Picasso's *Woman with Violin* sculpture and 57 ink-and-crayon sketches made in Arles between December 1970 and February 1971. Amongst the split faces and clowns is a beautifully simple portrait of his mother.

Van Gogh in Arles

At the back of the Réattu museum, lanterns line the river wall where **Van Gogh** used to wander, wearing candles on his hat, watching the night-time light: *The Starry Night* is the Rhône at Arles. Much of the riverfront and its bars and bistrots were destroyed during the war. Another casualty of the bombing was the "Yellow House" on place Lamartine, where the artist lived before entering the hospital at St-Rémy. However, the café painted in *Café de Nuit* still stands in place du Forum. Van Gogh had arrived by train in February 1888 to be greeted by snow and a bitter Mistral wind. But he started painting straight away, and in this period produced such celebrated canvases as *The Sunflowers, Van Gogh's Chair, The Red Vines* and *The Sower*. Van Gogh found few kindred souls in Arles and finally managed to persuade Gauguin to join him. No-one knows what provoked the frenzied attack on his friend and the self-mutilation. He was packed off to the Hôtel-Dieu hospital on rue du Président-Wilson down from the Museon Arlaten, now the **Espace Van Gogh**, an academic and cultural centre with arty shops in its arcades and courtyard flower beds recreated according to Van Gogh's painting and descriptions of the hospital garden.

Arles has none of the artist's works but the **Fondation Vincent Van Gogh** (daily: mid-March to Nov 10am–7pm; Nov to mid-March 9.30–noon & 2–5.30pm; 30F), facing the

Arènes at 26 Rond-Point des Arènes, exhibits works by contemporary artists inspired by van Gogh, including Francis Bacon, Jasper Johns, Hockney and Lichtenstein.

Eating and drinking

Arles has a good number of excellent-quality and cheap restaurants. If you're looking for quick meals, or just want to watch the world go by, there's a wide choice of brasseries on the main boulevards. Place du Forum is the centre of café life; here you'll find *Le Café La Nuit*, immaculately recreated à la Van Gogh and open late, and the young and noisy *Bistrot Arlésien*.

L'Affenage, 4 rue Molière (☎04.90.96.07.67). Provençal specialities in generous portions. Menus from 100F; closed Sun.

Boitel, 4 rue de la Liberté. A *salon de thé* with a whole pâtisserie full of goodies to go with the Earl Grey. Open daily except Sun.

Le Galoubet, 18 rue du Dr-Fanton (☎04.90.93.18.11). Pleasant vine-covered terrace on which to taste the modern Provençal cuisine on a good value 105F menu. Closed Sun.

La Gueule du Loup, 39 rue des Arènes (☎04.90.96.96.69). Cosy restaurant serving traditional dishes, with one menu under 120F. Closed Sun & Mon lunch.

Hostellerie des Arènes, 62 rue du Réfuge (☎04.90.96.13.05). The service may be a bit abrupt but the food is real French family cooking. Good pizzas and menus under 100F. Closed Tues.

Lou Marquès, *Hôtel Jules-César*, bd des Lices (☎04.90.93.43.20). The top gourmet palace in the top grand hotel. The specialities, which include *baudroie* (monkfish), langoustine salad and Camargue rice cake, are all served with the utmost pomposity. Menus from 210F. The other restaurant in the hotel, *Le Cloître*, has a lunch menu at around 100F. Closed Nov & Dec.

La Paillote, 28 rue Dr-Fanton (☎04.90.96.33.15). Very friendly place with a good 95F menu. Closed Thurs & Sat out of season.

Le Vaccarès, 9 rue Favorin (☎04.90.96.06.77). Overlooks place du Forum and serves both new and traditional dishes in a light, inventive fashion. The lamb with *tapenade* and the fish *à la poutargue* are exceptional. Menus from 135F, otherwise á la carte from 300F. Closed Mon & Sun eve.

The Camargue

The boundaries of **the CAMARGUE** are not apparent until you come upon them. Its horizons are infinite because land, lagoon and sea share the same horizontal plain. Both wild and human life have traits peculiar to this drained, ditched and now protected delta land. Today, the whole of the Camargue is a Parc Naturel Régional, with great efforts made to keep an equilibrium between tourism, agriculture, industry and hunting on the one hand, and the indigenous ecosystems on the other.

The region is home to the **bulls** and the **white horses** that the Camargue *gardiens* or herdsmen ride. Neither beast is truly wild, though both run in semi-liberty. The Camargue horse, whose origin is unknown, remains a distinct breed, born dark brown or black and turning white around its fourth year. It is never stabled, surviving the humid heat of summer and the wind-racked winter cold outdoors. The *gardiens* likewise are a hardy community. Their traditional homes, or *cabanes*, are thatched and windowless one-storey structures, with bulls' horns over the door to ward off evil spirits. They still conform, to some extent, to the popular cowboy myth, and play a major role in guarding Camarguais traditions. Throughout the summer, with spectacles involving bulls and horses in every village arena, they're kept busy and the work carries local glamour. Winter is a good deal harder, and fewer and fewer Camarguais property owners can afford the extravagant use of land that bull-rearing requires.

The Camargue bulls and horses are just one element in the area's exceptionally rich **wildlife**, which includes flamingos, marsh and sea birds, waterfowl and birds of prey; wild boars, beavers and badgers; tree frogs, water snakes and pond turtles; and a rich flora of reeds, wild irises, tamaris, wild rosemary and juniper trees. These last, which grow to a height of 6m, form the **Bois des Rièges** on the islands between the **Étang du Vaccarès** and the sea, part of the central national reserve to which access is restricted to those with professional credentials.

After World War II, the northern marshes were drained and re-irrigated with fresh water. The main crop planted was rice, and so successful was it that by the 1960s the Camargue was providing three-quarters of all French consumption of the grain. Vines were also reintroduced – in the nineteenth century they had survived the disease that devastated every other wine-producing region because their stems were under water. There are other crops – wheat, rapeseed and fruit orchards – as well as trees in isolated clumps. To the east, along the last stretch of the Grand Rhône, the chief business is the production of salt, which was first organized in the Camargue by the Romans in the first century AD. It's one of the biggest saltworks in the world, with salt pans and pyramids adding a somehow extraterrestrial aspect to the Camargue landscape.

Though the Étang du Vaccarès and the central islands are out of bounds, there are paths and sea dykes from which their inhabitants can be watched, and special nature trails (see below). The ideal months for bird-watching are the mating period of April to June, with the greatest number of flamingos present between April and September.

The only town, or rather overgrown village, and the main resort, is Stes-Maries-de-la-Mer on the sea close to the mouth of the Petit Rhône.

Getting round the Camargue

Fairly frequent **buses** run between Arles and Stes-Maries, where you can rent **bikes** at Le Vélociste on place des Remparts (☎04.90.97.83.26), and Le Vélo Sanitois on avenue de la République (☎04.90.97.74.56). The other means of transport to consider is riding, as there are around thirty farms that rent out **horses** by the hour, half-day or day. The tourist office in Stes-Maries (see below) has a complete list.

For transport as an end in itself, there's the **paddle steamer** *Le Tiki III*, which leaves for river trips from the mouth of the Petit Rhône, off the route d'Aigues-Mortes, 2.5km west of Stes-Maries (mid-March to mid-Nov☎04.90.97.81.68), and the *Soleil*, which leaves from the port in Stes-Maries (April–Sept ☎04.90.97.85.89).

Be wary of taking your car or bike along the **dykes**: although maps and road signs show which routes are closed to vehicles and which are accessible only at low tide, they don't warn you about the road surface. The other problem is **theft** from cars. There are well-organized gangs of thieves with a particular penchant for foreign licence plates.

If you stay in the area, be warned that **mosquitoes** are rife from March through to November; staying right beside the sea will be OK, but otherwise you'll need serious chemical weaponry. Biting flies are also prevalent and can take away much of the pleasure of this hill-less land for bicycling. The other problem is the **winds**, which in autumn and winter can be strong enough to knock you off your bike (though fortunately you won't have to cope simultaneously with biting insects and high winds). Conversely, in summer the weather can be so hot and humid that the slightest movement is an effort. There's really no ideal time for visiting the area.

There are three main **trails** around the protected central area of the Carmargue. You can skirt the Réserve des Impériaux along a drovers' path, the *draille de Méjanes*, between Cacharel, 4km north of Ste-Maries, and the D37 just north of Méjanes. Another trail, with one of the best observation points for **flamingos**, follows the dyke between the Étangs du Fangassier and Galabert, starting 5km west of Salin-de-Giraud. Between these two is the *Digue à la Mer* running just back from the beach of Stes-Maries's bay.

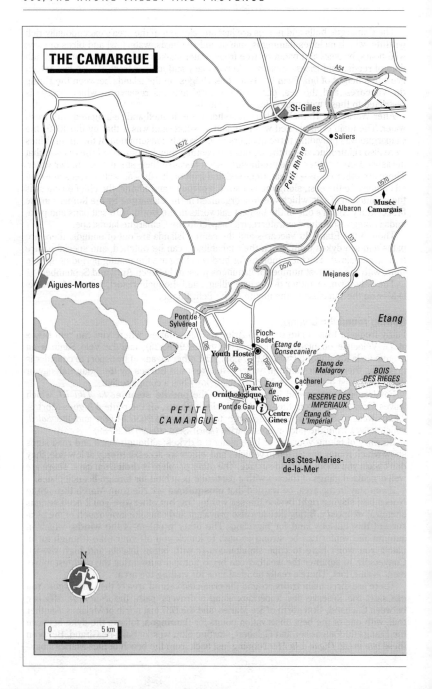

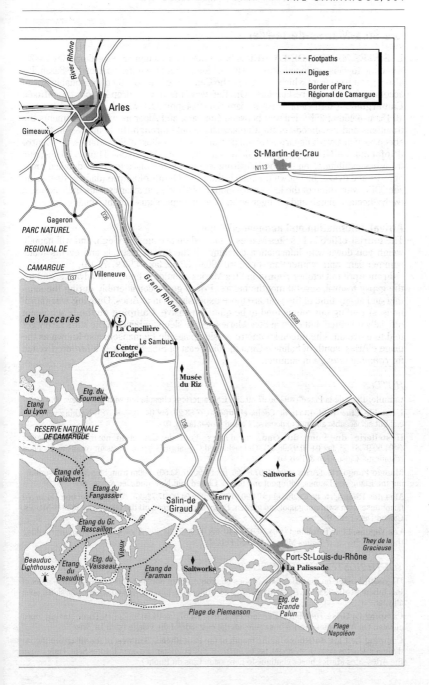

Les Stes-Maries-de-la-Mer

LES STES-MARIES-DE-LA-MER is best known for its annual festival on May 24–25, when the town is swamped with gypsies asking favours from their patron Ste-Sarah. It's also a good base from which to explore the Camargue, with plenty of reasonably priced accommodation and restaurants. On the way there you drop in on the **Musée Camarguais** (April–Sept daily 9.15am–5.45/6.45pm; Oct–March Mon & Wed–Sun 10.15am–4.45pm; 25F), halfway between Gimeaux and Albaron, which documents the traditions and livelihoods of the Camarguais people through the centuries, in the old sheep barn of a working farm. At Pont de Gau, just 4km short of Stes-Maries, the **Centre d'Information Ginès** (April–Sept daily 9am–6pm; Oct–March Sat–Thurs 9.30am–5pm; free) has exhibitions on the local environment and is the place to go for detailed maps of paths and dykes. Just down the road is the **Parc Ornithologique** (daily 9/10am–sunset; 33F), with some of the less easily spotted birds kept in aviaries, plus trails across a twelve-hectare marsh and a longer walk, all with ample signs and information.

Arrival, information and accommodation

The **tourist office** in Les Stes-Maries is located on avenue Van-Gogh, and will happily weigh you down with information detailing all the town's festivals and events (daily summer 9am–8pm; winter 9am–6pm; ☎04.90.97.82.55, fax 04.90.97.71.15).

From April to October **rooms** in Stes-Maries should be booked in advance, and for the gypsy festival, several months before. Prices go up considerably during the summer and at any time of the year are more expensive than at Arles. Outlying *mas* (farmhouses) renting out rooms tend to be quite expensive. **Camping** on the beach is not officially tolerated, but even at Stes-Maries people sleeping beneath the stars rarely get told to move on. The fifteen-kilometre seaside plage de Piemanson, also known as the plage d'Arles, south of Salin-de-Giraud, 10km east of Stes-Maries, is a favoured venue for *camping sauvage* in summer.

HOTELS

Camille, 13 av de la Plage (☎04.90.97.80.26). Characterless cheapie but with a sea view. ②.

L'Estable Chez Kiki, 13 rte de Cacharel (☎04.90.97.83.27, fax 04.90.97.87.78). Nothing very special but serviceable and not expensive. Closed Nov–March. ③.

Hostellerie du Pont du Gau, rte d'Arles, Pont de Gau, 4km north of Stes-Maries (☎04.90.97.81.53, fax 04.90.97.98.54). Old-fashioned Camarguais decor, pleasant rooms and a good restaurant. Closed Jan & Feb. ③.

Mangio Fango, rte d'Arles (☎04.90.97.80.56, fax 04.90.97.83.60). 600m from Stes-Maries, overlooking the Étang des Launes, with pool and patios. Closed mid Nov–mid Dec & Jan. ⑥.

Mas des Rièges, rte de Cacharel (☎04.90.97.85.07, fax 04.90.97.72.26). An upmarket hotel in an old farmhouse, with swimming pool and garden. Down a track signed off the D85a close to Stes-Maries. Closed Dec–Feb. ⑤.

Les Vagues, 12 av T-Aubunal (☎04.90.97.84.40, fax 04.90.97.84.40). A low-priced option overlooking the sea on the rte d'Aigues-Mortes. Closed Feb. ②.

YOUTH HOSTEL AND CAMPSITES

HI youth hostel, on the Arles–Stes-Maries bus route, 10km north of Stes-Maries in the hamlet of Pioch-Badet (☎04.90.97.51.72, fax 04.90.97.54.88). Bike hire, horse rides and other excursions; open all year.

Camping La Brise, rue Marcel-Carrière (☎04.90.97.84.67, fax 04.90.97.72.01). Three-star site, open all year. On Arles–Stes-Maries bus route, on the east side of the village (stop La Brise).

Camping Le Clos du Rhône, at the mouth of the Petit Rhône, 2km west of the village on the rte d'Aigues-Mortes (☎04.90.97.85.99, fax 04.90.97.78.85). Four-star site open Easter–Sept. Only two of the Arles–Stes-Maries buses continue to here (stop Clos du Rhône).

THE LEGEND OF SARAH

Sarah was the servant of Mary Jacobé, Jesus' aunt, and Mary Salomé, mother of two of the apostles, who, along with Mary Magdalene and various other New Testament characters, are said to have been driven out of Palestine by the Jews and put on a boat without sails or oars.

The boat apparently drifted to an island in the mouth of the Rhône, where the Egyptian god Ra was worshipped. Here Mary Jacobé, Mary Salomé and Sarah, who was herself Egyptian, settled to carry out conversion work while the others headed off for other parts of Provence. In 1448 their relics were "discovered" in the fortress church of Stes-Maries on the erstwhile island, around the time that the Romanies were migrating to western Europe from the Balkans and from Spain.

The gypsies have been making their **pilgrimage** to Stes-Maries since at least the sixteenth century. It's a time for weddings and baptisms, as well as music, dancing and fervent religious observation. After Mass on May 24, the shrines of the saints are lowered from the high chapel to an altar where the faithful stretch out their arms to touch them. Then the statue of Black Sarah is carried by the gypsies to the sea. On the following day the statues of Mary Jacobé and Mary Salomé, sitting in a wooden boat, follow the same route, accompanied by the mounted *gardiens* in full Camargue cowboy dress, Arlesians in traditional costume, and all present. The sea, the Camargue, the pilgrims and the gypsies are blessed by the bishop from a fishing boat, before the procession returns to the church with much bell-ringing, guitar playing, tambourines and singing. Another ceremony in the afternoon sees the shrines lifted back up to their chapel.

The town

Stes-Maries is an extremely pretty, if excessively commercialized town. Its streets of white houses and the grey-gold Romanesque church, with its strange outline of battlements and watchtower, have been turned into one long picture-postcard pose. It exploits its monopoly as the only Camargue resort and every leisure activity is catered for, to excess. Apart from peace and quiet you're not going to want for anything. There are kilometres of **beach**; a pleasure port with boat trips to the lagoons; horses – or bikes – to ride; watersports; and the *arènes* for bullfights, cavalcades and other entertainment (events are posted on a board outside). Flamenco guitarists play on the restaurant and café terraces – it can be very good fun.

As for sights, the fortified **church of Stes-Maries** allows a look at Sarah's tinselled and sequined statue which is carried into the sea each year (see box). It's at the back of the crypt on the right, and always surrounded by candles and abandoned crutches and calipers from the miraculously cured. The church itself has beautifully pure lines and fabulous acoustics. During the time of the Saracen raids it provided shelter for all the villagers and even has its own fresh-water well. Between March and Oct the church tower is open (10am–12.30pm & 2–sunset; 10F), affording the best possible view over the Camargue.

On rue Victor-Hugo, the **Musée Baroncelli** (April to mid-Nov daily 10am–noon & 2–6pm; mid-Nov to March Thurs–Tues same hours; 10F) is named after the man who, in 1935, was responsible for initiating the gypsies' procession down to the sea with Sarah. This was motivated by a desire to give a special place in the pilgrimage to the Romanies. The museum covers this event, other Camarguais traditions and the region's fauna and flora.

Eating and drinking

Few of the restaurants in Stes-Maries are bargains, though there are any number to choose from, and out of season the quality improves and prices come down. Right in the centre of town on place des Impériaux, *L'Impérial* (☎04.90.97.81.84; closed Nov–March & Tues except July & Aug) serves pleasant fish dishes on a 130F menu. Or try the tapas and bargain wine at *Kahlua Bodéga*, 1 rue Jean Roche (☎04.90.97.98.41; closed Jan & Feb, Weds out of season; around 100F). The best places to try local fish specialities are at the beach hut restaurants *Chez Juju* and *Chez Marc et Mireille* in **BEAUDUC**, over the dykes on the spit of sand on the opposite side of the bay from Stes-Maries.

From Avignon to Gordes

If you're heading east from Avignon towards Apt and the Luberon, two worthwhile stops are the exquisitely romantic **Fontaine-de-Vaucluse** and the picturesque **Gordes**, close to the **Abbaye de Sénanque**. Between Gordes and Apt are the old ochre-quarrying villages of **Roussillon** and **Rustrel**. Visiting all these places without your own transport is not that easy; Fontaine is accessible by bus from Avignon or from L'Isle-sur-la-Sorgue's gare SNCF 6km away; Gordes from **Cavaillon**, 24km southwest of Avignon, and Roussillon only infrequently from Apt.

Fontaine-de-Vaucluse

The source of the Sorgue, the stream that runs alongside rue des Teinturiers in Avignon, is at **FONTAINE-DE-VAUCLUSE**, 29km southwest of Avignon, and one of the most powerful natural springs in the world. At the top of the gorge above the village is a mysterious tapering fissure deeper than the sheer 230-metre cliffs that barricade its opening. This is where the waters of the Sorgue appear, sometimes in spectacular fashion, bursting down the gorge (in March and April normally), other times seeping stealthily through subterranean channels to meet the river bed further down. The best time to admire it is in the early morning before the crowds arrive.

Fontaine-de-Vaucluse was once a rustic backwater where the fourteenth-century poet Petrarch pined for his Laura. It remains a supremely romantic place despite its hordes of visitors. If you're intrigued by the source of the river and speak French, visit the **Le Monde Souterrain** (April–Aug daily 10am–noon & 2–6pm; Feb–March & Sept–Nov Weds–Sun visits at 11am & hourly 2–5pm; closed Dec–Jan; 30F) in the underground commercial centre alongside the chemin de la Fontaine, the path to the source. At the upper end of the centre, you'll find a re-creation of the medieval method of pulping rags to paper – using river power – with a vast array of printed matter on the product for sale.

On chemin de la Fontaine, there's also the impressive **Musée d'Histoire 1939–1945** (April 15 to Oct 15 & school holidays Wed–Mon 10am–noon & 2–6pm; Oct 16 –Dec & March–April 14 same hours Sat & Sun only; 20F) portraying life under the Vichy regime and commemorating the Resistance. A few doors down, the **Musée de la Justice et des Chatiments** (daily: July & Aug 10am–8pm; Sept–June 10am–7pm; 10F), with a horrible collection of torture and execution equipment, is one to avoid. Across the river, through an alleyway just past the bridge, is the much more comforting **Musée de Pétrarque** (mid-April to mid-Oct Wed–Sun 9.30am–noon & 2–6.30pm; winter weekends only; 15F), with beautiful books dating back to the fifteenth century and pictures of Petrarch, his beloved Laura and of Fontaine, where he passed sixteen years of his unrequited passion.

The cheapest and most characterful **hotel** is the *Grand Hôtel des Sources* (☎04.90.20.31.84; ②) with a whole variety of *vieille France* rooms. On the road out, 3km from the village, are two hotels worth trying: *L'Ermitage* (☎04.90.20.32.20; ②) and *Font de Lauro* (☎04.90.20.31.49; ②). There's also a **youth hostel** on chemin de la Vignasse,

1km south on the road to Lagnes (☎04.90.20.31.65; reception 8–10am & 5–11pm; closed Dec & Jan), and a **campsite**, *Les Pres* (☎04.90.20.32.38; all year), 500m downstream from the village, with tennis courts and swimming pool. The **tourist office** (summer Mon–Sat 9am–6/7.30pm, winter same days 10am–6pm; ☎04.90.20.32.22, fax 04.90.20.21.37) is on chemin de la Fontaine.

Gordes and around

GORDES, just 5km east of Fontaine as the crow flies, but 18km by road, is a picturesque Provençal village much favoured by Parisian media personalities, film directors, artists and the like. This might prompt you to give it a miss – and it is an expensive place – but there are good reasons for its popularity with the rich and famous, for it's a spectacular sight. You climb winding roads past buildings of ancient stone before arriving at the summit, where church and houses surround a mighty twelfth- to sixteenth-century **château**, housing the contemporary paintings of the Flemish artist Pol Mara (July–Aug daily 10am–noon & 2–6pm; Sept–June Wed–Mon; 25F).

The **tourist office** is in the château (daily 9am–noon & 2–6pm; Oct–March open at 10am; ☎04.90.72.02.75, 04.90.72.04.39). If you're looking for somewhere to **stay**, the most reasonably priced hotel within the village is *Le Provençal* (☎04.90.72.10.01; ③). *Les Romarins* (☎04.90.72.12.13; ⑦), overlooking the village on the route de Sénaque, is an old country house with comfortable, traditionally styled rooms. The best eating place in town is the *Comptoir du Victuailler* on place du Château (☎04.90.72.01.31; closed Tues eve & Wed out of season), always full of Parisians in summer; menus from 175F. *Tante Yvonne* (☎04.90.72.02.54; closed Sun eve & Wed) on place du Château is a bit less expensive.

Four kilometres north of Gordes, amidst fields of lavender in a hollow of the hills, stands the twelfth-century Cistercian **Abbaye de Sénanque** (March–Oct Mon–Sat 10am–noon & 2–6pm, Sun 2–6pm; Nov–Feb Mon–Fri 2–5pm, Sat & Sun 2–6pm; 25F). It is still in use as a Cistercian monastery and you can visit the church, cloisters and all the main rooms of this huge and austere building; a shop sells the monks' produce, including liqueur, as well as honey and lavender essence.

The other stone construction of note near Gordes is the **Village des Bories** (daily 9am–sunset; 30F), 3.5km east off the D2 to Cavaillon, a strange collection of dry-stone dwellings with peculiar geometric shapes that suggest prehistoric pedigree. In fact most were built in the eighteenth century and inhabited up until a hundred years ago.

The best and most surreal detour in the vicinity is to the old **ochre mines** between Gordes and Apt. The houses in the village of **ROUSSILLON** radiate all the different shades of the seventeen ochre tints once quarried here; a well-signed footpath leads from the car park on place de la Poste to the old workings. More dramatic quarries, known as the **Colorado Provençal**, are signed off the D22 towards Gignac, just before you reach **RUSTREL** from Apt. Various paths lead you to an amphitheatre of coffee, vanilla and strawberry ice-cream whipped into pinnacles and curving walls.

The Luberon

After its descent from the Alps, the River Durance makes a wide southern curve before joining the Rhône, skirting the massive rock-fold known as the **Luberon** that runs for 50km between Cavaillon and Manosque. The Luberon has long been escape country for well-heeled Parisians, Dutch and British, but has also attracted a good number of artists; the artists' organization Artifices currently organizes summer exhibitions and visits to studios in Apt and the surrounding villages (details on ☎04.90.74.01.26). But the main attraction is the countryside itself and the tiny, immaculately preserved villages.

The Luberon's northern face is damper, more alpine in character, extremely cold in winter, and dotted with tiny villages clinging stubbornly to the foothills. The southern slopes, by contrast, are Mediterranean in scent and feel. It's almost all wooded, except for the summer sheep pastures at the top, and there's just one main route across it, through the Combe de Lourmarin.

Apt

The sole town base for exploring the Luberon is **APT**, though in itself it's not much of a town for sightseeing, nor is it renowned for the charm and friendliness of its people. Its large confectionery factory spews mucky froth into a concrete-channelled River Coulon and, as late as early spring, when mimosa is blossoming down on the coast, the temperature around Apt can drop to well below freezing. It cheers up, however, every Saturday for the weekly **market** when cars are barred from the town centre to allow artisans and cultivators from all the surrounding countryside to set up stalls. As well as featuring every imaginable Provençal edible, the market is accompanied by barrel organs, jazz musicians, stand-up comics, aged hippies and assorted freaks.

Arriving by **bus** – Apt's gare SNCF is freight-only – you'll be dropped at **place de la Bouquerie**, the main square lined with cafés and restaurants, or at the **gare routière** on av de la Libération at the eastern end of the town (☎04.90.74.20.21). The **tourist office** is at 20 av Philippe-de-Girard (July & Aug Mon–Sat 9am–1pm & 3–7pm, Sun 9am–noon; rest of year Mon–Sat 9am–noon & 2–6pm; ☎04.90.74.03.18, fax 04.90.04.64.30), just up to your left from place de la Bouquerie as you face the river. There's a good choice of **accommodation** in Apt, unlike the more scenic hilltop villages, where all rooms are reserved months before the summer season. On the south-eastern edge of the town centre is *L'Aptois*, 289 cours Lauze de Perret (☎04.90.74.02.02, fax 04.90.74.64.79; ③); *Le Palais*, 24 place Gabriel-Péri (☎04.90.04.89.32; closed mid-Oct to March; ②) is right in the centre; and there are very pleasant rooms across the river at the *Auberge du Luberon*, 8 place du Faubourg du Ballet (☎04.90.74.12.50, fax 04.90.04.79.49; ⑤). **Campers**, for once, are treated to a municipal ground within easy walking distance of the town: *Les Cèdres* on av de Viton (☎04.90.74.14.61; all March–Nov), across the bridge from place St-Pierre.

Outside Apt, you could try: the *Auberge du Presbytère* on place de la Fontaine in **SAIGNON**, a perched village 4km southeast of Apt (☎04.90.74.11.50; ③); the *Auberge des Seguins*, quartier de la Combe in **BUOUX**, a village 10km south of Apt (☎04.90.74.16.37, fax 04.90.74.16.37; ③), which is popular with climbers and walkers, and with some cheaper dormitory rooms available; or the *Relais de Roquefure* (☎04.90.04.88.88, fax 04.90.74.14.86; ③) in **LE CHÊNE**, 6km from Apt on the N100 towards Avignon, which organizes horse and cycle outings.

If you haven't stuffed yourself with chocolates and candied fruit (Apt's speciality), you can get cheap and decent **meals** at *Le Chat qui Pêche*, 237 cours Lauze-de-Perrez or the *Grand Café Grégoire* on place Bouquerie (open till midnight). More entertainingly *Pub 66*, in the industrial zone on the Avignon road opposite the turning to Gargas, is a Tex-Mex restaurant which doubles up as a disco with theme nights (☎04.90.74.22.18; menus around 120F). Further out on the Avignon road, at Le Chêne, there's real gourmandise to be had at *Bernard Mathys* (☎04.90.04.84.64; closed Tues & Wed; menus from 160F).

The Parc Naturel Régional du Luberon

A large area of the Luberon has been designated the **Parc Naturel Régional du Luberon**, with the aim of conserving the natural fauna and flora and limiting development. The park is administered by the **Maison du Parc**, 60 place Jean-Jaurès in Apt (Mon–Sat 8.30am–noon & 1.30–6/7pm; ☎04.90.04.42.00), which is the place to go for information about every aspect of the Luberon: the fauna and flora, footpaths, cycle routes, pony trekking, and gîtes and campsites. You can watch a video about plant and animal life and buy recordings of Luberon birdsong. The centre also houses a small **Musée de la Paléontologie** (10F) which is specifically designed to amuse children and is fun. A submarine-type "time capsule" door leads down to push-button displays that include magnified views of insect fossils and their modern descendants.

Given the region's general dearth of public transport, the only practical and pleasurable way to explore is by hiking or cycling. In Apt, **bikes** can be hired from Cucles Ricaud, 44 quai de la Liberté, Guy Agnel, 86 quai Général-Leclerc, or Cycles Peugeot a few doors down.

The Abbaye de Silvacane

If you're heading for Aix-en-Provence from Apt, you'll pass close to another ancient Cistercian abbey contemporary with Sénanque (see p.905), 29km south of Apt, just across the Durance. After a long history of abandonment and evictions, the **Abbaye de Silvacane** (March–Oct Mon–Sat 10am–noon & 2–6pm, Sun 2–6pm; Nov–Feb Mon–Fri2–5pm, Sat & Sun 2–6pm; 25F) is once again a monastic institution. It is isolated from the surrounding villages on the bank of the Durance and its architecture has hardly changed over the last 700 years; you can visit the stark, pale-stoned splendour of the church, its cloisters and surrounding buildings.

Aix-en-Provence

AIX-EN-PROVENCE would be the dominant city of central Provence were it not for the great metropolis of Marseille, just 25km away. Historically, culturally and socially, the two cities are moons apart and the tendency is to love one and hate the other. Aix is complacently conservative and a stunningly beautiful place, its riches based on landowning and the liberal professions. The youth of Aix are immaculately dressed; hundreds of foreign students, particularly Americans, come to study here; and there's a certain snobbishness, almost of Parisian proportions.

From the twelfth century until the Revolution, Aix was the capital of Provence. In its days as an independent fiefdom, its most mythically beloved ruler, King Réné of Anjou, held a brilliant court renowned for its popular festivities and patronage of the arts. Réné also introduced the muscat grape to the region, and today he stands in stone in picture-book medieval fashion, a bunch of grapes in his left hand, looking down the majestic seventeenth-century replacement to the old southern fortifications, the cours Mirabeau.

Arrival, information and accommodation

Cours Mirabeau is the main thoroughfare of the town, with the multi-fountained place Général-de-Gaulle, or La Rotonde, at its west end, the main point of arrival. The **gare SNCF** (☎08.36.35.35.35) is on rue Gustavo-Desplace at the end of av Victor-Hugo, the avenue leading south from the square; the **gare routière** is between the two western avenues, av des Belges and av Bonaparte, on rue Lapierre (☎04.42.27.17.91). The **tourist office** is at 2 place Général-de-Gaulle (daily: July & Aug 8.30am–10pm; Sept 8.30am–8pm; Oct–June 8.30am–7pm; ☎04.42.16.11.61, fax 04.42.16.11.62), between av des Belges and av Victor-Hugo.

From mid-June to the end of July (festival time) your chances of getting a hotel **room** are pretty slim unless you've reserved a couple of months in advance at least. Outside this time, there is a decent range of accommodation to choose from.

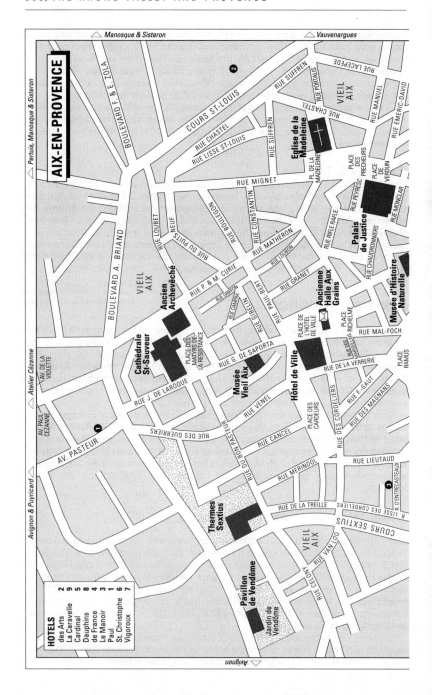

AIX-EN-PROVENCE

△ Manosque & Sisteron
△ Vauvenargues

△ Pertuis, Manosque & Sisteron
△ Atelier Cézanne
△ Avignon & Puyricard

▽ Avignon

HOTELS

des Arts	2
La Caravelle	9
Cardinal	5
Dauphins	8
de France	4
Le Manoir	3
Paul	1
St. Christophe	6
Vigoroux	7

BOULEVARD F. & E. ZOLA
COURS ST-LOUIS
RUE CHASTEL
RUE LISSE ST-LOUIS
RUE SUFFREN
RUE PORTALIS
RUE LACÉPÈDE
RUE MANUEL
RUE ÉMÉRIC-DAVID
VIEIL AIX
RUE MIGNET
Église de la Madeleine
PL DE LA MADELEINE
RUE PEYRESC
PLACE DES PRÊCHEURS
PLACE DU VERDUN
RUE MONCLAR
RUE LOUBET
RUE DU PUITS NEUF
RUE BOULÉGON
RUE CONSTANTIN
RUE MATHERON
RUE RIFLE RAFLE
Palais de Justice
RUE CHAUDRONNIERS
BOULEVARD A. BRIAND
VIEIL AIX
Ancien Archevêché
RUE P. & M. CURIE
RUE GRIFFON
RUE CAMPRA
RUE GIBELIN
RUE PAUL-BERT
RUE LOUBON
RUE GRANET
Ancienne Halle Aux Grains
Musée d'Histoire Naturelle
Cathédrale St-Sauveur
PLACE DES MATYRS DE LA RÉSISTANCE
RUE G. DE SAPORTA
PLACE DE L'HOTEL DE VILLE
RUE MASSILLON RICHELME
PLACE RAMUS
RUE MAL-FOCH
AV. DE LA VIOLETTE
RUE J. DE LAROQUE
Musée Vieil Aix
Hôtel de Ville
RUE DE LA VERRERIE
AV. PAUL CÉZANNE
RUE DES GUERRIERS
RUE VENEL
RUE F.-GAUT
RUE DES CORDELIERS
RUE DES MAGNANS
AV. PASTEUR
RUE DU BON PASTEUR
RUE CANCEL
PLACE DES CARDEURS
RUE LIEUTAUD
RUE MÉRINDOL
R D'ENTRECASTEAUX
RUE DE LA TREILLE
LISSE DES CORDELIERS
Thermes Sextius
VIEIL AIX
RUE VAN LOO
COURS SEXTIUS
Pavillon de Vendôme
Jardin de Vendôme
RUE CELONY

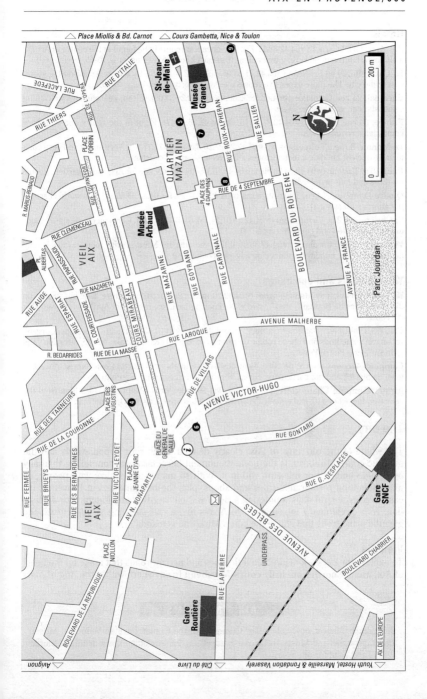

Hotels

des Arts, 69 bd Carnot (☎04.42.38.11.77). The cheapest rooms to be found in the centre of Aix are a bit noisy, but the hotel is very welcoming. You can't book, so turn up early. ①–②.

La Caravelle, 29 bd Roi-Réné (☎04.42.21.53.05, fax 04.42.96.55.46). By the boulevards to the southeast of the city. The more expensive rooms overlook courtyard gardens. ③–⑤.

Cardinal, 24 rue Cardinale (☎04.42.38.32.30, fax 04.42.26.39.05). Clean, peaceful and welcoming establishment, great value. ③–⑤.

France, 63 rue Espariat (☎04.42.27.90.15, fax 04.42.26.11.47). Right in the centre and with very comfortable rooms. ③–④.

Le Manoir, 8 rue d'Entrecasteaux (☎04.42.26.27.20, fax 04.42.27.17.97). Very smart and very comfortable ancient building which includes a fourteenth-century cloister. ⑤.

Paul, 10 av Pasteur (☎04.42.23.23.89, fax 04.42.63.17.80). Good value for Aix, with a garden. Rooms for three and four people. ②.

Quatre-Dauphins, 54 rue Roux-Alphéran (☎04.42.38.16.39, fax 04.42.38.60.19). Old-world charm in the quartier Mazarin. ④.

St-Christophe, 2 av Victor-Hugo (☎04.42.26.01.24, fax 04.42.38.53.17). Convenient and classy, close to both the station and cours Mirabeau. ④.

Vigoroux, 27 rue Cardinale (☎04.42.38.26.42). In the quartier Mazarin with rooms available only during university holidays and needing advance booking. ③.

Youth hostels and campsites

HI youth hostel, 3 av Marcel-Pagnol (☎04.42.20.15.99). 2km from the centre; take bus #8 or #12, direction "Òjas de Bouffan", stop Vasarely. No cooking facilities; restaurant April–Oct. Closed Dec 20–Feb 1.

CROUS, Cité Universitaire des Gazelles, 38 av Jules-Ferry (☎04.42.26.47.00). This student organization can sometimes find cheap rooms on campus during July & Aug. Take bus #5, direction "Bel Ormeau", stop Pierre-Puget.

Camping Arc-en-Ciel, rte de Nice, Pont des Trois Sautets (☎04.42.26.14.28). 3km southeast of town on bus #3, and not particularly cheap. Very good facilities. Mid-March to Sept.

Airotel Camping Chanteclerc, rte de Nice, Val St-André (☎04.42.26.12.98). Also 3km from the centre on bus #3 or #10, and equally expensive. Facilities are excellent. Open all year.

The city

The whole of the **old city of Aix**, clearly defined by its ring of boulevards and the majestic cours Mirabeau, is the great monument here, far more compelling than any one single building or museum within it. With so many streets alive with people, so many tempting restaurants, cafés and shops, plus the best markets in Provence, it's easy to pass several days wandering around without needing any itinerary or destination. As a preliminary introduction to Aixois life, a café-stopping stroll beneath the gigantic plane trees that shade the cours Mirabeau is mandatory.

Vieil Aix

To explore the network of jumbled little lanes and narrow roads that make up the heart of Aix, wander north from leafy **cours Mirabeau** to anywhere within the ring of *cours*

AIX'S MUSEUMS

A *Passeport Musées*, covers L'Atelier Cézanne, Musée Granet, Pavillon Vendôme, Musée des Tapisseries and Musée d'Histoire Naturelle and is available for 40F from the tourist office, and valid for one year.

and boulevards. The layout of **Vieil Aix** is not designed to assist your sense of direction, but it hardly matters when there's a fountained square to rest at every 50m and a continuous architectural backdrop of treats from the sixteenth and seventeenth centuries. On Saturdays, and to a lesser extent on Tuesdays and Thursdays, the centre is taken up with **markets**: fruit and veg on place Richelme; fish on rue des Marseillais; flowers on place de l'Hôtel-de-Ville; clothes on rues Peyresc, Rifle-Rafle, Bouteilles, Chaudronniers and Monclar; a flea market on place de Verdun; and food on place des Prêcheurs and place de la Madeleine.

The **church of the Madeleine** (closed Sun pm), on the central place des Prêcheurs, is decorated with paintings by Rubens and Van Loo (who was born in Aix in 1684), and a three-panel medieval *Annunciation*. On place Richelme, a delicate though fairly massive foot hangs over the architrave of the old corn exchange, now the **post office**. It belongs to the goddess Cybele, dallying with the masculine River Rhône. Just to the north, the **Hôtel de Ville** displays perfect classical proportions and embroidery in wrought iron above the door.

Rue Gaston-de-Saporta takes you up from place Hôtel-de-Ville to the **Cathédrale St-Sauveur**, a conglomerate of fifteenth- to sixteenth-century building, full of medieval art treasures. The best of these is a triptych commissioned by King Réné in 1475, *Le Buisson Ardent*, whose side panels are regularly opened up by the sacristan (daily except Tues & Sun), revealing an elaborately depicted Mary and Child in a burning bush, a scene loaded with symbolic references.

A short way down from the cathedral, through place des Martyrs-de-la-Résistance, is the former bishop's palace, the **Ancien Archevêché**, housing the **Musée des Tapisseries** (daily except Tues 10am–noon & 2–5.45pm; 10F), a superb collection including a contemporary section, for which the definition of tapestry is broadened to include textiles made of rope, raffia or feathers. The **Musée du Vieil Aix** at 17 rue Gaston-de-Saporta (Tues–Sun: summer 10am–noon & 2.30–6pm; winter 10am–noon & 2–5pm; closed Oct; 15F) could be worth a glance while you're in this part of town. It has a set of religious marionettes and a huge collection of *santons* (Provençal crib figures).

Quartier Mazarin

Aix's other central museums are in the **quartier Mazarin**, south of cours Mirabeau. On place St-Jean-de-Malte the most substantial of the lot, the **Musée Granet** (Wed–Mon 10am–noon & 2–6pm; 10F), covers art and archeology. It exhibits the finds from the Oppidum d'Entremont, a Celtic-Ligurian township 3km north of Aix, which flourished for about a hundred years, along with the remains of the Romans who routed them in 124 BC and established their city of Aquae Sextiae, the future Aix. The museum's paintings are a mixed bag: Italian, Dutch, French, mostly seventeenth- to nineteenth-century, not very well hung or lit. The portraits of Diane de Poiters by Jean Capassin and Marie Mancini by Nicolas Mignard are an interesting contrast, and there is also a self-portrait by Rembrandt. The rows upon rows of eighteenth- and early nineteenth-century French paintings, including Ingres's revolting *Jupiter and Thetis*, are mostly abysmal, though Ingres's portrait of Granet is certainly worth a look. You finally reach one wall dedicated to the most famous Aixois painter, **Paul Cézanne**, who studied on the ground floor of the building, at that date the art school. Two of his student drawings are here as well as a handful of minor canvases such as *Bathsheba*, *The Bathers* and *Portrait of Madame*.

Beyond the centre

Cézanne used many studios in and around Aix but he finally had a house built for the purpose in 1902 at what is now 9 av Paul-Cézanne, overlooking Aix from the north. It was here that he painted the *Grandes Baigneuses*, the *Jardinier Vallier* and some of his greatest still lifes. The **Atelier Cézanne** (daily 10am–noon & 2/2.30–5/6pm; 25F; bus

#1 or #21, stop P. Cézanne) is exactly as it was at the time of his death in 1906; coat, hat, wineglass and easel, the objects he liked to paint, his pipe, a few letters and drawings . . . . everything save the pictures he was working on.

Collective cultural life is the basis of the **Cité du Livre** in the old matchmaking factory at 8–10 rue des Allumettes, a short way southwest from the tourist office (Tues, Thurs & Fri noon–6pm, Wed & Sat 10am–6pm; free). Entered by doorways in the form of giant books leaning together as if on a shelf, it includes libraries, a cinema, theatre space, a *videothèque d'art lyrique* (where you can watch just about any French opera performance) and all manner of exhibitions.

For a totally different experience, both visually and conceptually, you can escape the sometimes cloying grandeur of seventeenth-century Aix by visiting the **Fondation Vasarely** on av Marcel-Pagnol in Jas-de-Bouffan, 4km west of the city centre (daily: Mon—Fri 10am–1pm & 2–7pm, Sat & Sun 10am–7pm; 35F; bus #12, stop V. Vasarely). There are innumerable sliding showcases, showing images related to all the themes of architect/artist Vasarely's work, including his "plastic alphabet" and designs for apartment buildings. But the seven high hexagonal spaces on the ground floor, each hung with six huge colour-wonder dimension-doubling designs, is where you'll get the immediate impact of this extraordinary man's work.

Eating, drinking and entertainment

Aix is stuffed full of **restaurants** of every price and ethnic origin. Place des Cardeurs, just northwest of the Hôtel de Ville, is nothing but restaurant, brasserie and café tables, while rue de la Verrerie running south from Hôtel de Ville and place Ramus has an immense variety of Indian, Chinese and North African restaurants. Rue des Tanneurs is a good street for low budgets. The café-brasseries on cours Mirabeau are also tempting, and in between them you'll find cheaper snackeries and pedlars of delicious fresh fruit juice.

Cafés and restaurants

L'Aixquis, 22 rue Victor-Leydet (☎04.42.27.76.16). Classy restaurant, serving Provençal specialities; lunch menus at 100F and 140F (not Sun); otherwise from 190F. Closed Mon lunch & first 3 weeks of Aug.

L'Aligote, 6 place des Cardeurs (☎04.42.63.00.26). Specialities from southwest France from 150F. Closed Sun & Mon out of season.

de l'Archevêché, (☎04.42.21.43.57) place des Martyrs-de-la-Résistance. Good midday pasta, tapas and salads for under 100F. Closed Sun.

Le Basilic Gourmand, 6 rue du Griffon (☎04.42.96.08.58). Classic Provençal food on a 90F lunch menu, accompanied by exhibitions of paintings. Closed Sun.

Le Bistrot Latin, 18 rue Couronne (☎04.42.38.22.88). Escargot and black olive sauce profiteroles and honey and garlic rabbit are two of the top dishes here. Lunch menu 75F, evening from 100F. Closed Sun eve & Mon lunch.

La Bodèga, 1 rue des Muletiers (☎04.42.96.54.00). Spanish resto serving *paella Valenciennes* for around 165F on Fri & Sat. Closed Sun.

Le Clos de la Violette, 10 rue de la Violette (☎04.42.23.30.71). Aix's most renowned restaurant with dishes that might not sound very seductive, like stuffed lamb's feet and *pieds et pâquets* (tripe and salt pork), but are in fact gastronomic delights. More obviously alluring are the puddings: a *clafoutis* of greengages and pistachios with peach sauce and a tart of melting dark chocolate. 200F lunch menu, otherwise menus start at 350F and à la carte from 450F. Closed Mon lunch & Sun.

Les Deux Garçons, 53 cours Mirabeau. The erstwhile haunt of Camus is done up in faded 1900s style and still attracts a motley assortment of literati. Good brasserie food, but not cheap. Service daily till midnight.

L'Hacienda, cnr rue Mérindol & place des Cardeurs (☎04.42.27.00.35). Outdoor tables and a cheap lunch menu including wine, with delicious hacienda beef à la carte. Closed Sun.

Le Jasmin, 6 rue de la Fonderie (☎04.42.38.05.89). Iranian food for around 120F. Closed Sat & Sun eve.

Khéops, 28 rue de la Verrerie (☎04.42.96.59.05). Egyptian cuisine featuring *falafel*, stuffed pigeon and gorgeous milk-based desserts. From 120F. Closed Mon.

Pizza Chez Jo/Bar des Augustins, place des Augustins (☎04.42.26.12.47). Cheap pizzas and traditional *plats du jour*, usually packed. Closed Sun.

Le Platanos, 13 rue Rifle-Rafle (☎04.42.21.33.19). Very cheap and popular Greek resto with menus under 100F. Closed Sun & Mon.

Nightlife and festivals

For **jazz**, the best club is *Hot Brass*, chemin de la Plaine-des-Verguetiers, rte d'Éguilles-Célony (☎04.42.21.05.57; 10.30pm onwards), or there's *Le Scat*, 11 rue de la Verrerie (☎04.42.23.00.23) with jazz, rock and funk. *Le Richelme*, 24 rue de la Verrerie (☎04.42.23.49.29; from 9pm) is a mainstream **disco**. For **pubs** with live music try *Key Largo* and *Bugsy* at 34 and 25 rue de la Verrerie, respectively; *Pub Solferino*, place d'Armenie; or *Le Festival*, 67bis rue Espariat.

During the annual **music festivals**, Aix en Musique (rock, jazz, experimental and classical; mid-June to first week in July; ☎04.42.21.69.69) and the Festival International d'Art Lyrique (opera and classical concerts; last 2 weeks of July), the alternative scene - of street theatre, rock concerts and impromptu gatherings – turns the whole of Vieil Aix into one long party. Tickets for events range from 80F to 800F and can be obtained, along with programmes, from the Comité Officiel des Fêtes at Espace Forbin, 3 place John-Rewald off cours Gambetta (☎04.42.63.06.75). Details of the Festival International Danse (2 weeks in mid-July) are available from the same address.

Listings

Bike rental Cycles Naddeo, 54 av de Lattre-de-Tassigny (☎04.42.21.06.93); or Cycles Zammit, 27 rue Mignet (☎04.42.23.19.53).

Books Paradox Bookstore, 15 rue du 4-Septembre, for English books; Vents du Sud, place du Petit-Marché, is the best French bookshop.

Car rental ADA Discount, av Henri Mouret (☎04.42.52.36.36); Avis, 11 rue Gambetta (☎04.42.21.64.16); Budget, 16 av des Belges (☎04.42.38.37.36); Europcar, 55 bd de la République (☎04.42.27.83.00); National Citer, 724 av du Club Hippique (☎04.42.17.22.50).

Changing money American Express, 15 cours Mirabeau; Change d'Or, 22 rue Thiers; automatic machine outside Crédit Lyonnais, place Jeanne-d'Arc.

Emergencies Hospital Centre Hospitalier, av de Tamaris (☎04.42.33.90.28); SOS Médecins (☎04.42.26.24.00); for a late-night chemist, ring the gendarmerie on (☎04.42.26.31.96).

Laundry 3 av St-Jérôme; 5 rue de la Fontaine; 60 rue Boulegon; 36 cours Sextius.

Police av de l'Europe (☎04.42.93.97.00).

Post office 2 rue Lapierre, 13100 Aix.

Taxis ☎04.42.26.29.30; ☎04.42.27.62.12 or ☎04.42.27.71.11 (24 hrs).

Travel agents Nouvelles Frontières, 52 cours Sextius (☎04.42.26.47.22).

Mont Ste-Victoire

Mont Ste-Victoire, a rough pyramid whose apex has been pulled off-centre, lies 10km east of Aix. Ringed at its base by the dark green and orange-brown of pine woods and cultivated soil, the limestone rock reflects light, turning blue, grey, pink or orange. In the last years of his life **Cézanne** painted and drew Ste-Victoire more than fifty times, and, as part of his childhood landscape, it came to embody the incarnation of life within nature.

You may, however, be more interested in climbing Mont Ste-Victoire and in the view from it. The southern face has a sheer 500-metre drop, but from the north the two-hour walk requires nothing more than determination. The **GR9**, also called the Chemin des Venturiers, leaves from a small car park on the D10 just before **VAUVENARGUES**, 14km east of Aix. Having reached the 945-metre ridge, marked by a monumental nineteenth-century cross that doesn't figure in any of Cézanne's pictures, you can follow the path east along the ridge to the summit of the massif and then descend south to **PUYLOUBIER** (about 15km from the cross). Bring plenty of water and protection against the fierce sun if walking during summer.

At Vauvenargues, a perfect weather-beaten, red-shuttered fourteenth-century **château** (definitely not open to the public) stands just outside the village, with nothing between it and the slopes of Ste-Victoire. **Picasso** bought the château in 1958, lived there until his death and now lies buried in the gardens, his grave adorned with his sculpture *Woman with a Vase*. There is a friendly, good-value hotel in the village, *Au Moulin de Provence*, 33 rue de Maquisards (☎04.42.66.02.22, fax 04.42.66.01.21; ②) whose owners speak English.

EASTERN PROVENCE

In **eastern Provence**, it is the landscapes not the towns that dominate. The gentle hills and villages of the **Haut-Var**, the northern half of the Var *département*, make for happy exploration by car or bike, before the foothills of the Alps gradually close in, eventually reaching heights of over 3000m in the far northeastern corner, around **Barcelonnette**. Winter visitors are almost exclusively skiers, while the summer brings a variety of dedicated hikers, bird-watchers, botanists and climbers. The **Parc National du Mercantour** is a conservation area in this mountainous terrain, but the most exceptional geographical feature is the **Gorges du Verdon** – Europe's answer to the Grand Canyon – in the heart of Provence.

Between Valence and Montélimar, the River Drôme joins the Rhône at **Livron-sur-Drôme**. Following the river upstream by train to **Sisteron**, or by road to Sisteron or Barcelonette, is one of the most dramatic ways of entering eastern Provence.

Haut-Var villages

Between **ST-MAXIMIN-DE-LA-STE-BAUME**, 35km east of Aix and famous for its supposed possession of the relics of Mary Magdalene, and **DRAGUIGNAN**, an eminently avoidable military town, a network of small roads links a dozen villages, all of which are ideal for Provençal-style loafing. The roads wind through farmland, vineyards and woods, alongside streams and lakes.

East of the **Lac de Carcès**, between Cabasse and Carcès, off the D19, lies the last of the three great Cistercian monasteries of Provence. Even more so than Silvacane and Sénanque, the **Abbaye du Thoronet** (April–Sept Mon–Sat 9am–7pm, Sun 9am–noon & 2–7pm; Oct–March 9am–noon & 2–5pm; 35F) has been unscathed by the vicissitudes of time, and during the Revolution was kept intact as a remarkable monument of history and art; today it is occasionally used for concerts. It was first restored in the 1850s; a more recent campaign has brought it to clear-cut perfection. As with the other two abbeys, its interior spaces, delineated by walls of pale rose-coloured stone, are inspiring.

LORGUES, further east, has a serious gourmet stop in the **restaurant** *Chez Bruno* on rte de Vidauban (☎04.94.73.92.19; closed Mon & Sun eve out of season; menu at 280F, à la carte around 400F), where the truffle reigns supreme, appearing in myriad forms, even in desserts.

Heading 13km northwest, **ENTRECASTEAUX** has an ancient stone **laundry** by the river that's still used, and a very beautiful **château** (April–Sept Thurs–Tues 11am–12.30pm

& 2.30–6pm; July & Aug daily; Oct–March Thurs–Tues 11am–noon & 2.30–5pm; 30F). The interior of the castle is spacious, light and charmingly rustic, typified by the terracotta tiles, a style that was all the rage when the Count and Countess of Grignan used the château as their summer residence. The minimal furnishings add to the general effect, but the reception room and the countess's bedroom (adjoined by a horrid 1970s' marble bathroom) give some idea of the status of the one-time inhabitants. Exhibitions on the first floor relate to later occupants, firstly Raymond Bruny, who charted part of the coast of western Australia and Tasmania; and secondly, photos of the sorry state in which Ian McGarvie-Munn found the château before beginning his extensive restoration.

COTIGNAC, 9km west of Entrecasteaux, is the Haut-Var village *par excellence*, with a shaded main square for pétanque and passages and stairways bursting with begonias, jasmine and geraniums leading through a cluster of medieval houses. More gardens sprawl at the foot of the bubbly rock cliff that forms the back wall of the village. Places to **stay** in the village include the over-unctuous but good-value *Lou Calen* at the bottom of cours Gambetta (☎04.94.79.60.40, fax 04.94.04.76.64; ④) and *Du Cours*, 18 cours Gambetta (☎04.94.04.78.50; closed mid-Nov to Jan; ⑤).

North of Cotignac, **SILLANS-LA-CASCADE** has a beautiful walk, signposted off the main road, to an immense waterfall and aquamarine pool (about 20min). **SALERNES**, 6km east of Sillans, makes tiles and pottery and has the good, old-fashioned *Grand Hôtel Allègre*, on rte de Sillans (☎04.94.70.60.30; ③). **VILLECROZE** and **TOURTOUR** to the northeast are both suitably picturesque. The *Auberge des Lavandes* on place du Général-de-Gaulle in Villecroze (☎04.94.70.76.00; ③) is one of the best-value hotels in the region, while in Tourtour, on rte de Flayosc, you can shelter in total luxury at *La Bastide de Tourtour* (☎04.94.70.57.30, fax 04.94.70.54.90; ⑦). Between the two villages is a much-reputed **restaurant**, *Les Chênes Verts* (☎04.94.70.55.06; closed Tues eve & Wed) with menus from 250F.

Aups

As a base for visiting the villages of Haut-Var or the Gorges du Verdon, the small town of **AUPS** is ideal, as long as you have your own transport. It has a lot of charm and still depends to a large extent on agriculture rather than tourism. Its speciality is truffles and, if you're here on a Thursday between November and mid-March, you can witness the **truffle market**.

On **place Martin-Bidauré**, which, along with **place Frédéric-Mistral** (Wed & Sat market), makes up the leafy open space before the start of the old town, a rare monument commemorates the town's citizens who died in 1851 defending the republic and its laws. The year was that of Louis Napoléon's coup d'état. Peasant and artisan resistance was strongest in Provence, and the defeat of the insurgents was followed by a bloody massacre of men and women. This might explain the enormous *République Française, Liberté, Egalité, Fraternité* sign on the **church of St-Pancrace**, proclaiming it as state property. The church was designed by an English architect 400 years ago, and has recently had its doors restored by two local British carpenters.

Surprisingly for such a small place, Aups has a museum of modern art, the **Musée Simon Segal** in the former chapel of a convent on avenue Albert-1er (mid-June to mid-Sept daily 10.30am–noon & 4–7pm; 15F). The best works are those by the Russian-born painter Simon Segal, but there are interesting local scenes in the other paintings, such as the Roman bridge at Aiguines, now drowned beneath the artificial lake of Ste-Croix. Just outside Aups, 3.5km along the Tourtour road, is a **sculpture park** by local artist Maria de Faykod (daily: June–Sept 10am–noon & 3–7pm; Oct–May 2–6pm; 10F) with dramatic human forms in marble.

The **tourist office** is on place Frédéric-Mistral (April–June & Sept Mon 3–6pm, Tues–Sat 10am–noon & 3–6pm; July & Aug Mon–Sat 9am–12.30pm & 3–7pm, Sun

9.30am–12.30pm; Oct–March Mon 2–4pm, Tues–Sat 10am–noon & 2–4pm; ☎04.94.70.00.80). All the **hotels** are good value: *Le Provençal* on place Martin-Bidauré (☎04.94.70.00.24; ④) is the most expensive; the *Grand Hôtel* on place Duchâtel (☎04.94.70.10.82; ②; closed Jan–March) is the cheapest. More comfort is to be had at *L'Escale du Verdon*, 1km out on the rte de Sillans-la-Cascade (☎04.94.84.00.04, fax 04.94.84.00.05; ④; closed Oct to mid-June). There are two **campsites** close to town: the two-star *Camping Les Prés*, to the right off allée Charles-Boyer towards Tourtour (☎04.94.70.00.93, fax 04.94.70.14.14; all year), which has **bikes** for hire, and the three-star *Saint Lazare* 2km along the Moissac road (April–Sept; ☎04.94.70.12.86), which has a pool.

For **meals**, your first choice should be the hotel-restaurant *St-Marc* (☎04.94.70.06.08; ③; closed second & third week of June), a nineteenth-century mill on rue Aloisi. Serving local dishes, truffles and boar in season, it offers a very cheap lunch menu and evening menus from 100F (closed Tues eve & Wed). For standard, reliable food try the *Yucca* (closed Mon evening and Tues) at 3 rue Mal-Foch, and for snacks, the boulan-gerie-pâtisserie at no. 20 av Albert 1er (May–Nov).

The Gorges du Verdon and around

From Aups, the road north leads to the western end of the **Gorges du Verdon**. A more dramatic approach crosses the vast military terrain of the Camp de Canjuers from Comps-sur-Artuby. The road runs west through 16km of deserted heath and hills with each successive horizon higher than the last. When you reach the canyon, it is as if a silent earthquake had taken place during your journey.

From this vantage point, known as the **Balcons de la Mescla**, you are looking down 250m to the base of the V-shaped, 21-kilometre-long gorge incised by the River Verdon through piled strata of limestone. Ever changing in its volume and energy, the river falls from Rougon at the top of the gorge, disappearing into tunnels, decelerating for shal-low, languid moments and finally exiting in full, steady flow at the **Pont de Galetas**. The huge artificial **Lac de Ste-Croix**, filled by the Verdon as it leaves the gorge, is great for swimming when the water levels are high; otherwise the beach becomes a bit sludgy. West from the Balcons runs the **Corniche sublime**, the D71, built expressly to give the most breathtaking and hair-raising views. On the north side, the **Route des Crêtes**, the D952, does the same, at some points looking down a sheer 800-metre drop to the sliver of water below.

The entire circuit around the gorge is 130km long and it's cycling country solely for the preternaturally fit. Even for drivers it's hard work, as the hidden bends and hairpins in the road are perilous and, in July and August, so is the traffic.

Public transport around the canyon is less than comprehensive. There's just one bus between Aix, Moustiers, La Palud, Rougon and Castellane on Monday, Wednesday and Saturday from July to mid-September; and one other bus daily except Sunday between La Palud, Rougon and Castellane in July and August.

The north side of the gorge: La Palud-sur-Verdon and Rougon

The loop of the Route des Crêtes joins at **LA PALUD-SUR-VERDON**, the tiny village on the northern face of the gorge and the best base from which to explore it. Life in the village revolves around the *Lou Cafetier* bar-restaurant. There are one or two other places to eat and a market on Wednesday morning around the church.

The **tourist office** is on the main road in La Palud (Easter to mid-Dec Thurs & Fri 10am–noon & 4–6pm Sat 10am–noon; June–Aug daily 10am–noon & 4–6pm; closed mid-Dec to Easter; ☎04.92.77.32.02), with a nearby **Bureau des Guides** (Mon–Sat 10am–12.30pm & 2–5.30pm; ☎04.92.77.30.50) where you can find out about guided walks. UCPA (☎04.92.77.30.29) has information on all Verdon activities, and is another contact point for guides, as is the climbing shop, Le Perroquet Vert (☎04.92.77.33.39). If you want to **stay**, there's *Le Provence* on the rte de la Maline (☎04.92.77.36.50, fax 04.92.77.31.05; ④), and the slightly cheaper *Auberge des Crêtes*, 1km east towards Castellane (☎04.92.77.38.47, fax 04.92.77.30.40; ③). The *Auberge du Point Sublime* in **ROUGON** (☎04.92.77.60.35, fax 04.92.83.74.31; ③) is stunningly situated and not wildly expensive. The **youth hostel**, *Le Trait d'Union*, with camping in its grounds, is 500m below La Palud (☎04.92.77.38.72; April–Oct), and there's a municipal **campsite** 800m to the west of the village (☎04.92.77.38.13). Two **gîtes** to try are *L'Étable*, on route des Crêtes (☎04.92.77.30.63; ①) and *Le Wapiti* just outside the village on the Moustiers road (☎04.92.77.30.02; ②; April to mid-Nov). The *Chalet de la Maline*, on route des Crêtes to the south of La Palud (☎04.92.77.38.05; April to mid-Nov), is a mountain **refuge** run by the Club Alpin Français.

The south side of the gorge: Aiguines and the Falaise des Cavaliers

AIGUINES, perched high above the **Lac de Ste-Croix** on its eastern side, has a turreted château (not open to the public) and a history of wood-turning – the boules for pétanque made from ancient boxwood roots used to be its speciality. There's the tiny **Musée des Tourneurs sur Bois** (mid-June to mid-Sept daily except Tues 10am–noon & 2–6pm; 10F), a museum devoted to the intricate art of wood-turning, and some very expensive and beautiful woodwork, as well as pottery and faïence, to be viewed at the **Galerie d'Art** opposite the **tourist office** (Sept–June Mon–Fri 10am–noon & 2–5pm; July–Aug daily 10am–1pm & 3–7pm; ☎04.94.70.21.64).

For **rooms**, there's the hotel-restaurant *du Vieux Château* (☎04.94.70.22.95; ②; breakfast included), or the rather characterless *Altitude 823* (☎04.94.70.21.09; ③; half-board compulsory; April–Oct). Of the seven **campsites**, *Le Galetas* (☎04.94.70.20.48; April–Oct) is almost within diving distance of the lake, a long way down from the village.

The best place to stay on the south side – as long as you don't suffer from vertigo – is the *Hôtel du Grand Canyon du Verdon* by the **Falaise des Cavaliers** (☎04.94.76.91.31, fax 04.94.76.92.29; ④) on the Corniche Sublime, a good 20km from Aiguines and with stunning views. The restaurant serves reasonable food.

West of the gorge: Moustiers-Ste-Marie and Riez

MOUSTIERS-STE-MARIE is one place to avoid, particularly during the high season, when the road west out of the gorge through the town is one long traffic jam and the village a tourist trap. There's a glut of hotels, restaurants, souvenir stands and a veritable surfeit of *ateliers* making glazed pottery – Moustiers's traditional speciality. The pottery, like the village itself, is pastel-coloured and pretty and on sale in Liberty or Bloomingdales, but if you want to lug plates home with you, here's your chance.

A more pleasant option is low-key **RIEZ**, 15km west of Moustiers, where the main business is derived from the lavender fields that cover this corner of Provence. Just over the river on the road south is a lavender distillery making essence for the perfume industry. At the other end of the town, 1km along the road to Digne, is the **Maison de l'Abeille** (House of the Bee), a research and visitors' centre (daily 10am–12.30pm & 2.30–7pm; free). Visitors can buy various honeys (including the local speciality, lavender honey) and hydromel – the honey alcohol of antiquity made from nectar – and, if you show interest, you'll get an enthusiastic tour.

In size, Riez is more village than town, but it soon becomes clear that it was once more influential than it is now. Some of the houses on **Grande-Rue** and **rue du**

Marché – the two streets above the main allées Louis-Gardiol – have rich Renaissance facades, and the **Hôtel de Ville** on place Quinquonces is a former episcopal palace. The sixth-century **cathedral**, which was abandoned 400 years ago, has been excavated just across the river from allées Louis-Gardiol. Beside it is a **baptistry**, restored in the nineteenth century but originally constructed, like the cathedral, around 600 AD (visitable between Easter and mid-Sept, check with the tourist office for times). If you recross the river and follow it downstream, you'll find the even older and much more startling relics of four **Roman columns** standing in a field.

A rather more strenuous walk, heading first for the clock tower above Grande-Rue and then taking the path past the cemetery and on uphill (leaving the cemetery to your left), brings you to a cedar-shaded platform on the hilltop where the pre-Roman Riezians lived. The only building now occupying the site is the eighteenth-century **Chapelle Ste-Maxime**, with a gaudily patterned interior.

The **tourist office** is at 4 cours allées Louis-Gardiol (daily: March & Oct 11am–noon & 2–5pm; April–June & Sept 10.30am–12.30 & 2–6pm; July & Aug 10am–12.30pm & 2–7.30pm; Nov–Feb 2–5pm; ☎04.92.77.99.09). For accommodation there's an executive-style hotel on the other side of the river, the *Hôtel Carina* (☎04.92.77.85.43, fax 04.92.77.74.93; April to mid-Nov; ④) with views and comfort to make up for its lack of character. Alternatively head out of town on the route de Valensole to the *Château de Pontfrac*(☎04.92.77.78.77; ③). The **restaurant** *Les Abeilles* on allées Louis-Gardiol (☎04.92.77.89.29; open daily for lunch; summer open evenings also) is a real treat with imaginative cooking, specialities like *aïoli* and menus including wine for under 100F.

Castellane

In the other direction from the gorge, 12km upstream from La Palud on the Route Napoléon (see below), **CASTELLANE**'s only distinguishing feature is the abrupt, massive rock to the east of the town. Since there's little else to do you might as well climb up to it – thirty minutes' worth from behind the modern church. The gorge itself is out of sight, but the view is still worth the trouble.

The **tourist office**, at the top of rue Nationale (April–June & Sept–Oct Mon–Sat 9am–noon & 2–6pm; July–Aug Mon–Sat 9am–noon & 1.30–7pm, Sun 10am–12.30pm; Nov–Jan Mon–Fri 9am–noon & 2–6pm; ☎04.92.83.61.14, fax 04.92.83.76.89), can provide a full list of the many hotels and campsites in the village and its environs. The *Auberge Bon Accueil* on place Marcel-Sauvaire (April–Sept ☎04.92.83.62.01; ③) is one of the cheapest; the *Hôtel du Commerce* on place de l'Église (☎04.92.83.61.00, fax 04.92.83.72.82; ④) is the swanky option, and has an amazing 120F menu with dishes such as artichoke hearts and ravioli stuffed with wild mushrooms and goat's cheese. The closest **campsite** to town, off the D952 or rte de Moustiers, is the *Frédéric-Mistral* (☎04.93.82.62.27; all year). For **canoeing** and **rafting** on the Lac de Castellane and the Gorges de Verdon, *Aqua-Verdon* at 9 rue Nationale (☎04.92.83.72.75) is the place for information; it also rents out **bikes**.

The Route Napoléon to Sisteron

North of Castellane, the **Route Napoléon** passes through the barren scrubby rocklands of some of the most obscure and empty parts of Provence. The road was built in the 1930s to commemorate the great leader's journey north through Haute Provence on return from exile on Elba in 1815, in the most audacious recapture of power in French history. Using mule paths still deep with winter snow, Napoléon and his 700 soldiers forged ahead towards **Digne-les-Bains** and **Sisteron** on their way to Grenoble – a total of 350km – in just six days. One hundred days later, he lost the battle of Waterloo and was permanently incarcerated on the island of St-Helena.

At Barrème, the road is joined by the narrow-gauge Chemin de Fer de Provence, also known as the Train des Pignes, which runs between Nice and Digne-les-Bains. Other stations on the line are Annot and St-André-les-Alpes, both with bus connections to Castellane. Local tourist offices will have timetables.

Digne-les-Bains

DIGNE-LES-BAINS is the chief town of the Alpes-de-Haute-Provence *département*, and lies in a superb position between the Durance valley and the start of the real mountains. Though a somewhat dispiriting place, it has particular attractions for geologists and admirers of Tibet. Covering over 150,000 hectares to the north and east of Dignes, the **Réserve Naturelle Géologique de Haute Provence** is the largest geological reserve in Europe, with fossils dating back 300 million years. Guided day-trips are organized by the tourist office during July and August (not every day, so phone first), and just north of the city, down to the left after the bridge across the Barles road, is the **Centre de Géologie** (April–Oct daily 9am–noon & 2–5.30pm, closes Fri 4.30pm; Nov–March Mon–Fri only; 25F) with extremely good videos, workshops and exhibitions on the Reserve. A couple of kilometres further along the Barles road you can see, on a bank to your left, a wall of ammonites.

The town's connection with Tibet is through the explorer Alexandra David Neel, who managed to spend two months in the forbidden city of Lhasa disguised as a beggar in 1924. She spent the last years of her long life in Digne, dying there at the age of 101, and her house, Samten Dzong at 27 av du Maréchal-Juin, is now the **Fondation Alexandra David Neel** (guided visits daily: July–Sept 10.30am, 2pm, 3.30pm & 5pm; Oct–June 10.30am, 2pm & 4pm; free), devoted to her memory. The Dalai Lama himself has visited the place twice. Also a cut above the normal is the town's **municipal museum** at 64 bd Gassendi (closed for restoration work in 1998 but should be open in 1999, check with the tourist office for hours), with some great sixteenth- to nineteenth-century paintings and homages to local seventeenth-century mathematician and savant Pierre Gassendi.

The **tourist office** is on the Rond-Point du 11-novembre-1918 (May–June & Sept–Oct Mon–Sat 8.45am–noon & 2–6.30pm, Sun 9.30am–12.30pm; July–Aug Mon–Sat 8.45am–12.30pm & 2–7pm, Sun 9am–noon & 3–7pm; Nov–April Mon–Sat 8.45am–noon & 2–6pm, Sun 10am–noon; ☎04.92.31.42.73, fax 04.92.32.27.24) with the **gare routière** just to the north. The **gare SNCF** and the **Chemin de Fer de Provence** are both to the west over the river on av Pierre-Sémard. A very cheap **hotel** option is the *Origan*, 6 rue Pied-de-Ville (☎04.92.31.62.13; ②), with an excellent and inexpensive **restaurant** (closed Mon & Sun). *Le Grand Paris*, 19 bd Thiers (☎04.92.31.11.15, fax 04.92.32.32.82; ⑤), is considerably more luxurious and also has a good, though expensive, restaurant (closed Sun evening & Mon out of season; 100F midday menu Mon–Sat, otherwise from around 200F).

Sisteron

The Route Napoléon leads eventually to **SISTERON**, 25km west of Digne, and the most important mountain gateway to Provence. The site has been fortified since time immemorial and even now, half destroyed by the Anglo-American bombardment of 1944, its citadel stands as a fearsome sentinel over the city and the solitary bridge across the River Durance.

A visit to the **citadel** (mid-March to June & Sept to mid-Nov 9am–5pm; July & Aug daily 9am–6pm; 22F) can easily take up half a day. There are no guides, just recordings in French attempting to recreate historic moments, such as Napoléon's march, of course, and the imprisonment in 1639 of Jan Kazimierz, the future king of Poland. Most of the extant defences were constructed after the Wars of Religion, and added to a century later by Vauban when Sisteron was a front-line fort against neighbouring Savoy. The eleventh-century castle was destroyed in the mid-thirteenth century during a pogrom against the local Jewish population.

The best view is from the Guérite du Diable lookout post. The outcrop on which the citadel sits abruptly stops here, 500m above the narrow passage of the Durance. In July and August, the festival known as Nuits de la Citadelle has open-air performances of music, drama and dance in the citadel grounds. There is also a **historical museum** with a room dedicated to Napoléon, and temporary art exhibitions in the vertiginous late medieval chapel, **Notre-Dame-du-Château**, restored to its Gothic glory and given very beautiful subdued stained-glass windows in the 1970s.

Back in Sisteron's old town, you'll see three huge **towers** which belonged to the ramparts built in 1370. Beside them is the much older **Cathédrale Notre-Dame-des-Pommiers**. From the cathedral, rue Deleuze leads to **place de l'Horloge**, where the Wednesday and Saturday **market** is held and which, on the second Saturday of every month, hosts a fair.

Arriving by train at Sisteron, turn right out of the **gare SNCF** along avenue de la Libération until you reach place de la République, where you'll find the **tourist office** (Feb–June Mon–Sat 9am–noon & 2–6pm; July & Aug Mon–Sat 9am–7pm, Sun 10am–noon & 2–5pm; Sept–Oct & Nov–Jan same days & hours as Sept only closing at 5pm; ☎04.92.61.12.03, fax 04.92.61.19.57) and the **gare routière**. Rooms come very cheap in the *Select'Hôtel* on place de la République (☎04.92.61.12.50; ①) and nearby *Andrônes* on av J-Moulin, just up from place de la République (☎04.92.61.01.68; ①). The genteel and old-fashioned *Grand Hôtel du Cours* on allée de Verdon (☎04.92.61.04.51, fax 04.92.61.41.73; ④) is the best hotel in town. Sisteron's four-star **campsite** is across the river and 3km along the D951 (March–Oct; ☎04.92.61.19.69).

The food in Sisteron's **restaurants** is nothing special, though the view down the valley from the terrace of the *Hôtel-Restaurant de la Citadelle*, 126 rue Saunerie, certainly is. *Le Cours*, on the allée de Verdon (☎04.92.61.00.50), serves copious meals with the renowned *gigot d'agneau de Sisteron* included on a 120F menu, and you'll find plenty of eating places along rue Saunerie and on the squares around the clock tower. *Le Mondial* bar at the top of rue Droite stays open late, as does *L'Horloge* on place de l'Horloge. Finally, if you fancy a **swim**, there's a large artificial lake between the allée de Verdon and the river.

Northeast Provence

Depending on the season, the **northeastern corner of Provence** is two different worlds. In winter, the sheep and shepherds find warmer pastures, leaving the snowy heights to horned mouflons, chamois and the perfectly camouflaged ermine. The villages, where shepherds came to summer markets, are battened down for the long, cold haul, while modern conglomerations of Swiss-style chalet houses, sports shops and discotheques come to life around the ski lifts. From November to April many of the mountain road passes are closed, cutting off the dreamy northern town of **Barcelonnette** from its lower neighbours.

In spring, the fruit trees in the narrow valley orchards blossom, and melting waters swell the Vésubie, the Tinée and the Roya, sometimes flooding villages and carrying whole streets away. In summer and early autumn you move from the valleys to the snow-capped peaks through groves of chestnut and olive trees, then pine forests edged with wild raspberries and bilberries, up to moors and grassy slopes covered with Alpine flowers.

An uninhabited area of 68,500 hectares along the Italian border has been designated the **Parc National du Mercantour** (see box). It can be explored from the small towns

THE PARC NATIONAL DU MERCANTOUR

The **Parc National du Mercantour** is a long, narrow band of mountainland running for 75km close to the Italian border, from south of the town of Barcelonnette almost as far as Sospel, 16km north of the Mediterranean. The area is a haven for wildlife, with colonies of chamois, mouflon, ibex and marmots, breeding pairs of golden eagles and other rare birds of prey, great spotted woodpeckers and hoopoes, blackcocks and ptarmigan. The fauna too is very special, with many unique species of lilies, orchids and Alpine plants, including the rare multi-flowering saxifrage.

It's crossed by numerous paths, including the G5 and G52, with refuge huts providing basic food and bedding for hikers. For more detailed information, contact the **Maison du Parc** in Barcelonnette or St-Martin-Vésubie (see p.923), which provide maps and accommodation details as well as advice on footpaths and weather conditions. Camping, lighting fires, picking flowers, playing radios or doing anything that might disturb the delicate environment is strictly outlawed.

of **St-Étienne-de-Tinée**, **St-Martin-Vésubie**, **St-Sauveur-sur-Tinée** and from the **upper Roya valley**, but all the countryside in this mountainous region is breathtaking. To the south, the Italianate town of **Sospel** is a real delight.

Transport other than by foot or vehicle is a problem. Apart from the Turin–Nice train line down the Roya valley, there are regular bus connections going out from Barcelonnette or from Sospel but they don't meet, and there are only infrequent buses between villages on market days.

Barcelonnette

BARCELONNETTE is a place of immaculate charm with snow-capped mountains visible at every turn. It is not very big, and a more ideal spot for doing nothing would be hard to find. The central square, **place Manuel**, has café tables from which to gaze at the blue sky or at the white clock tower commemorating the centenary of the 1848 Revolution. It's close to several ski resorts and to the northern edge of the Parc de Mercantour.

The Maison du Parc for the Mercantour (summer only; ☎04.92.81.21.31) shares premises at 10 av de la Libération with the **Musée de la Vallée** (daily during school hols, otherwise Wed, Thurs & Sat 3–6pm; July & Aug daily 10am–noon & 3–7pm; 20F) which details the popular emigration to Mexico during the nineteenth-century. Barcelonnette is full of Mexican connections (many came back with fortunes); in summer the Maison du Mexique, opposite the Musée de la Vallée, puts on films and exhibitions.

Barcelonnette's **tourist office** is on place Frédéric-Mistral (May–June & Sept–Nov Mon–Sat 9am–noon & 2–6pm; July–Aug daily 9am–8pm; Dec–April daily 9am–noon & 2–7pm; ☎04.92.81.04.71, fax 04.92.81.22.67). The best place to **stay** is the Mexican style *Azteca* on rue François-Arnaud (☎04.92.81.46.36, fax 04.92.81.43.92; ④), closely followed by the *Grande Épervière*, 18 rue des Trois-Fréres-Arnaud (☎04.92.81.00.70, fax 04.92.81.29.50; ④). The *Grand Hôtel* overlooking place Manuel (June to mid-Oct & Jan to mid-May ☎04.92.81.03.14; ②), is one of the cheaper options. There are three local **campsites**, the closest being the three-star *Du Plan* at 52 av E-Aubert (☎04.92.81.08.11; mid-May to Sept).

Excellent **food** can be had at *La Mangeoire*, in an old sheep barn on place des Quatre-Vents (☎04.92.81.01.61; closed Mon, Tues, second half May & Nov; 100F menu, à la carte 250F upwards). Less sophisticated but still very good dishes are served at *Le Troubadour* on place Frédéric-Mistral (☎04.92.81.24.24; closed Tues evening & Wed; menus from under 100F).

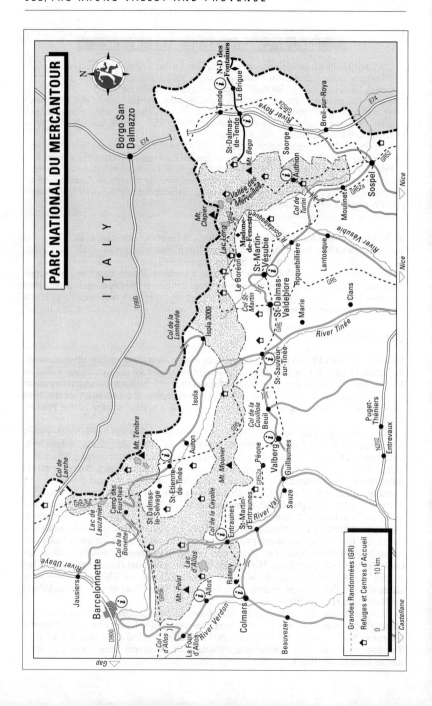

PARC NATIONAL DU MERCANTOUR

N

ITALY

Borgo San Dalmazzo

N-D des Fontaines

Tende

La Brigue

Breil-sur-Roya

St-Dalmas-de-Tende

Mt. Bego

Saorge

Authion

Vallée des Merveilles

Sospel

Nice

Mt. Clapier

Madone-de-Fenestre

Col de Turini

Moulinet

Lac Long

St-Martin-Vésubie

Roquebillière

Lantosque

River Vésubie

Nice

Le Boréon

Col St-Martin

St-Dalmas-Valdeblore

Isola 2000

Marie

Clans

Col de la Lombarde

River Tinée

St-Sauveur-sur-Tinée

Isola

Col de la Couillole

Beuil

Puget-Théniers

Mt. Ténibre

Col de Larche

Auron

Mt. Mounier

Valberg

Entrevaux

St-Etienne-de-Tinée

Péone

Guillaumes

Camp des Fourches

St-Dalmas-le-Selvage

Col de la Cavolle

St-Martin-d'Entraunes

Sauze

GR5/56

Lac de Lauzanier

Col de la Bonette

Entraunes

River Var

River Ubaye

Jausiers

Barcelonnette

Mt. Pelat

Allos

Lac d'Allos

Ratery

Col d'Allos

La Foux d'Allos

River Verdon

Colmars

Beauvezer

Gap

Castellane

Grandes Randonnées (GR)
Refuges et Centres d'Accueil

0   10 km

The road from Barcelonnette to Sospel

The road across the Cime de la Bonette pass (the D2205 from Barcelonnette) claimed to be the highest in Europe, reaches over 2800m and gives a feast of high-altitude views. You may have to brake for a seventy-centimetre-long furry marmot or for an army truck (as the military are rather fond of this deserted spot), but the green and silent spaces of the approach to the summit, circled by barren peaks, are magical.

Once over the pass, you descend into the Tinée valley and its highest town, **ST-ÉTIENNE-DE-TINÉE**, which comes to life only during its sheep fairs, held twice every summer, and the Fête de la Transhumance at the end of June. On the west side of the town off boulevard d'Auron, a cable car ascends to the summit of La Pinatelle, a good starting point for walks. The two **hotel-restaurants** on offer are the *Regalivou*, bd d'Auron (☎04.93.02.49.00; ③), and *Des Amis*, 1 rue Val-Gélé (☎04.93.02.40.30; ②).

The next stretch downstream from St-Étienne has nothing but white quartz and heather, with only the silvery sound of crickets competing with the water's roar. After Isola, the road and river turn south through the **Gorges de Valabre** to **ST-SAUVEUR-SUR-TINÉE**, a pleasantly sleepy place, with a useful boulangerie on place de la Mairie selling general provisions (Wed–Mon 1–4pm).

Shifting east to the Vésubie valley, you come to the lovely little town of **ST-MARTIN-VÉSUBIE** where a cobbled, narrow street of Gothic houses with a channelled stream runs through the old quarter beneath the overhanging roofs and balconies of Gothic houses. Of the five **hotels**, try *La Bonne Auberge*, 27 rue du Dr-Cagnoli (☎04.93.03.20.49; ②; closed mid-Nov to Jan), or *La Châtaigneraie* (☎04.93.03.21.22; ⑤; closed Oct–May), both on the allées de Verdon. The closest **campsite** is the *Ferme St-Joseph* (☎04.93.03.20.14; all year) on the rte de Nice by the lower bridge over La Madone. The pleasantest **restaurant** in St-Martin is *La Trappa* on place du Marché (closed Mon in term-time; around 100F). The **tourist office** on place Félix-Faure (June–Aug daily 9am–12.30pm & 3–7pm; Sept–May Mon–Sat 10am–noon & 2.30–5.30pm, Sun 10am–noon; ☎04.93.03.21.28, fax 04.93.03.20.01) provides details on walks and gîtes/refuges in the vicinity, and the **Maison du Parc** at 8 rue Kellerman provides practical information for exploring the Mercantour park (☎04.93.03.23.15).

Sospel and the Roya valley

The road from the Vésubie valley joins the **Roya valley** at **SOSPEL**, a dreamy Italianate town spanning the gentle River Bévéra. You may find it over-tranquil after the excitements of the high mountains or the flashy speed of the Côte d'Azur, but it can make a pleasant break.

The main street, **avenue Jean-Médecin**, follows the river on its southern bank. The central bridge, the **Vieux Pont**, was built in the eleventh century to link the town centre on the south bank with its suburb across the river. The best approach to the old town is from the eastern place St-Pierre, along the gloomy, deeply shadowed rue St-Pierre. Suddenly it opens up into **place St-Michel**, one of the most beautiful series of peaches-and-cream Baroque facades in all Provence, made up of the **Église St-Michel**, two chapels and several arcaded houses. The road behind the church, rue de l'Abbaye, reached by steps between the chapels, leads up to an ivy-covered **castle** ruin, from which you get a good view of the town. An even better view can be had from the **Fort St-Roch**, part of the ignominious interwar Maginot Line, along chemin de St-Roch, which houses the **Musée de la Résistance**, illustrating the courageous local Resistance movement during the last war (June–Sept Tues–Sun 2–6pm; April–May & Oct Sat & Sun 2–6pm; 25F).

The **gare** SNCF is southeast of the town on avenue A-Borriglione, which becomes avenue des Martyrs-de-la-Résistance, before leading down to the park on place des Platanes opposite place St-Pierre. The **tourist office** is housed in the Vieux Pont (Easter–Sept daily 10am–noon & 2–6pm; Oct–Easter daily 10am–noon & 2–5pm; ☎04.93.04.18.44). If you want to **stay**, the *Auberge du Pont-Vieux*, 3 av J-Médecin (☎04.93.04.00.73; ②), is Sospel's cheapest hotel. The *Auberge Provençale*, on rte du Col de Castillon 1500m uphill from the town (☎04.93.04.00.31; closed mid-Nov to mid-Dec; ④), is much nicer, with a pleasant garden and terrace from which to admire Sospel. There are five **campsites** around the town, the closest of which is *Le Mas Fleuri* in quartier La Vasta (☎04.93.04.03.48; all year), with its own pool, 2km along the D2566 to Moulinet following the river upstream.

There are various **eating** places along av J-Médecin. At *L'Escargot d'Or*, 3 rue de Verdun (☎04.93.04.00.43; closed Fri out of season), just across the eastern bridge, you can eat for between 100F and 150F on a terrace above the river.

The upper Roya valley

One of the strangest sights in the Provençal Alps is best approached from **ST-DALMAS-DE-TENDE** in the upper Roya valley, three stops on the train from Sospel. The first person to stumble upon the lakes and tumbled rocks of the **Vallée des Merveilles**, on the western flank of Mount Bego, was a fifteenth-century traveller who had lost his way. He described it as "an infernal place with figures of the devil and thousands of demons scratched on the rocks": a pretty accurate description, except that some of the carvings are of animals, tools, people working and mysterious symbols, dated to some time in the second millennium BC, and that is about all that's known about them.

The easiest route into the valley is the ten-kilometre hike (5–7hr there and back) that starts at *Les Mesces Refuge*, about 8km west of St-Dalmas-de-Tende, on the D91. The engravings are beyond the *Refuge des Merveilles* (where you can get sustenance and shelter); certain areas are out of bounds unless accompanied by an official guide; and remember that blue skies and sun can always turn into violent hailstorms and lightning. You can join a guided walk organized by the Bureau des Guides du Val des Merveilles in Tende (☎04.93.04.77.73; 35F).

St-Dalmas is the nearest town to the Vallée des Merveilles and has a reasonably priced **hotel** on rue Martyres-de-la-Résistance, the *Terminus* (closed Dec–April ☎04.93.04.96.96, fax 04.93.04.96.97; ③).

LA BRIGUE, one stop up the line from St-Dalmas-de-Tende, is a better place to stay in the upper Roya valley, with some good-value hotels. While you're here, make the trip 4km east of town to the sanctuary of **Notre-Dame-des-Fontaines**, whose frescoes were executed by one Jean Canavéso at around the same time the anonymous fifteenth-century traveller was freaking out about the demons of the Vallée des Merveilles. The frescoes, which cover the entire building, are akin to an arcade of video nasties. The goriest detail is a devil extracting Judas's soul from his disembowelled innards. The chapel is open in the summer (May–Sept daily 9.30am–7pm) and in the winter you can let yourself in with a key obtained from the mairie or the *Auberge St Martin*. The three **hotels** in La Brigue are: *Le Mirval*, rue Vincent-Ferrier (☎04.93.04.63.71, fax 04.93.04.79.81; ④; April–Oct); and, on place St-Martin, the *Auberge St-Martin* (☎04.93.04.62.17; ②; closed Tues out of season & Dec–Feb) and the *Fleurs des Alpes* (☎04.93.04.61.05; ②; closed Wed out of season & Dec to mid-Feb).

One more stop north on the train line brings you to **TENDE**, where the French spoken has a distinctly Italian accent. If you've missed the Vallée des Merveilles engravings you can see them reproduced outside the beautifully designed **Musée des Merveilles** (May–Oct 15 daily 10.30am–6.30pm; 16 Oct–April Wed–Mon 10.30am–5pm; 30F) on av du 16-septembre-1947, a very contemporary museum covering the wildlife, prehistory and geology of the region. That apart, the old town is fun to wander through, looking at the symbols of old trades on the door lintels, the overhanging roofs and multiple balconies. Tende is a busy place with plenty of shops and restaurants, though nothing very special on the gourmet front. To **stay**, there's *Le*

Centre on place de la République (☎04.93.04.62.19; ②; closed Nov) or *Le Cheval Blanc*, 18 rue Maurice-Sassi (☎04.93.04.62.22; ③). The **tourist office** is on av du 16-septembre-1947 (May–Sept Mon–Wed & Fri–Sat 9am–noon & 2–6pm; Oct–April Mon–Wed & Fri–Sat 9am–noon & 1–5pm; ☎04.93.04.73.71).

travel details

Buses

Aix-en-Provence to: Apt (2 daily; 1hr 45min); Arles (3 daily; 2hr); Avignon (6 daily; 1hr–1hr 15min); Barcelonnette (2 daily; 4hr); Draguignan (2 daily; 2hr 25min); Marseille (4 daily; 25min); Sisteron (3 daily; 2hr).

Arles to: Aix (3 daily; 1hr 55min–2hr); Avignon (6–10 daily; 20min–1hr 5min); Les Baux (1–4 daily; 30–40min); Marseille (5 daily; 2hr 5min–2hr 30min); Stes-Maries-de-la-Mer (7 daily; 55min); St-Rémy (1 daily; 35min).

Aups to: Aiguines (1 daily; 1hr 10min); Cotignac (2 daily; 20min); Draguignan (1–2 daily; 1hr–1hr 20min); Tourtour (1–2 daily; 20min); Sillans (1–2 daily; 10min).

Avignon to: Aix (4 daily; 1hr–1hr 15min); Apt (4 daily; 1hr–1hr 55min); Arles (frequent; 20min–1hr 5min); Carpentras (frequent; 45 min); Cavaillon (frequent; 45min); Châteauneuf-du-Pape (4 daily; 15min); Digne (2 daily; 3hr 30min); Les Baux (2 daily; 55min); L'Isle-sur-la-Sorgue (40min); Orange (4–6 daily; 45min); St-Rémy (8 daily; 40min); Vaison (1 daily; 1hr 15min).

Barcelonnette to: Digne (1 daily; 1hr 45min); Gap (3 daily; 1hr 20min); Marseille (2 daily; 3hr 55min).

Carpentras to: Aix (3 daily; 1hr 50min); Apt (3 weekly during school time; 1hr 5min); Beaumes (2 daily; 15min); Cavaillon (4 daily; 45min); Gigondas (2 daily; 40min); L'Isle-sur-la-Sorgue (3 daily; 20min); Orange (4 daily; 40min); Sablet (2 daily; 45min); Vacqueyras (2 daily; 25min); Vaison (2 daily; 45min).

Digne to: Avignon (2 daily; 3hr 30min); Barcelonnette (1 daily; 1hr 55min); Castellane (1 daily; 1hr 15min); Grenoble (1 daily; 4hr 30min); Marseille (4 daily; 2hr–2hr 40min); Nice (2 daily; 2hr 55min–3hr 15min).

Draguignan to: Aups (1–2 daily; 1hr 10min); Moustiers-Ste-Marie (1–2 daily; 2hr); Nice airport (2 daily; 1hr).

Gordes to: Cavaillon (2 daily; 45min).

Orange to: Avignon (hourly; 45min); Carpentras (4 daily; 40min); Châteauneuf-du-Pape (4 daily; 25min); Sablet (3 daily; 50min); Seguret (3 daily; 55min); Sérignan (5 daily; 20min); Vaison-la-Romaine (4 daily; 1hr 10min).

St-Rémy to: Les Baux (2 daily; 15min).

Sospel to: Menton (3 daily; 50min).

Trains

Aix-en-Provence to: Briançon (1–2 daily; 3hr 30min); Marseille (every 30min; 30–35min); Sisteron (3–4 daily; 1hr 15min–1hr 40min).

Arles to: Aix (6 daily; 1hr 15min); Avignon (9–13 daily; 20–45min); Marseille (10–12 daily; 45min).

Avignon to: Arles (hourly; 20–45min); Cavaillon (5–9 daily; 25min); L'Isle-sur-la-Sorgue (6–9 daily; 15–25min); Lyon (15–20 daily; 2hr 40min); Marseille (hourly; 50min–1hr); Orange (9–13 daily; 20–25min); Paris (8 daily; 4hr–7hr 30min).

Digne to: Nice (4–5 daily; 3hr 20min).

Lyon (La Part-Dieu or Perrache) to: Arles (frequent; 2hr 45min); Avignon (15–20 daily; 2hr 10min); Bordeaux (3 daily; 7–9hr); Bourg-en-Bresse (8–10 daily; 1hr 50min); Dijon (8–10 daily; 2hr); Grenoble (8–10 daily; 1hr 15min); Marseille (frequent; 3hr 40min); Montélimar (10–15 daily; 1hr 35min); Orange (7–9 daily; 2hr 30min); Paris (frequent; 2hr 10min–5hr); Roane (hourly; 1hr 30min); St-Étienne (8–10 daily; 47min); Strasbourg (5 daily; 5hr); Tain l'Hermitage (5 daily; 1hr 5min); Valence (8–10 daily; 55min); Vienne (7 daily; 20 min).

Lyon (Satolas or La Part-Dieu) to: Lille Europe (7 daily; 2hr 55min); Valence (5 daily; 40min).

Sospel to: La Brigue (4–5 daily; 45min–1hr); Nice (4–5 daily; 50min); St-Dalmas-de-Tende (4–5 daily; 40–55min); Tende (4–5 daily; 1hr 20min).

CHAPTER FIFTEEN

THE CÔTE D'AZUR

The **Côte d'Azur** polarizes opinions like few other places in France. For some, it is the quintessential Mediterranean playground – the glamour queen of the coast – for others, it has become almost a parody of its image, an overdeveloped expensive victim of its own hype.

But in the gaps between the uncontrolled and often eclectic developments, and on the offshore islands, the remarkable beauty of the hills and land's edge, the scent of the plant life, the mimosa blossom in February and the strange synthesis of the Mediterranean pollutants that make the water so translucent, still devastate the senses. The chance to see the works of innumerable artists seduced by the land and light also justifies the trip: Cocteau in **Menton** and **Villefranche**, Matisse, Dufy and Chagall in **Nice** and **Vence**, Léger in **Biot**, Picasso in **Antibes** and **Vallauris**, and collections of Fauvists and Impressionists at **St-Tropez** and Hauts-de-Cagnes. And it must be said that **Monaco** and **Cannes**, places you either love or hate, certainly have an entertainment value, while the two great cities of **Marseille** and Nice have their own special magnetism.

The months to try to avoid are July and August, when hotels are booked up, overflowing campsites become health hazards, the locals get short-tempered, and the vegetation is at its most barren.

FROM MARSEILLE TO TOULON

From the vast and wonderful scruffiness of **Marseille** to the squalid naval base of **Toulon**, this stretch of the Mediterranean is definitely not what most people think of as the Côte d'Azur. There is no continuous corniche, few villas in the grand style, and work is geared to an annual rather than summer cycle. **Cassis** is the exception, but the overriding attraction here is Marseille – a city that couldn't be confused with any other, no matter where you are dropped in it.

Marseille

The most renowned and populated city in France after Paris, **MARSEILLE** has – like the capital – prospered and been ransacked over the centuries. It has lost its privileges

---

ACCOMMODATION PRICE CATEGORIES

Each hotel in this chapter has a symbol which corresponds to one of eight price categories.

① Under 160F	④ 300–400F	⑦ 600–700F
② 160–220F	⑤ 400–500F	⑧ Over 700F
③ 220–300F	⑥ 500–600F	

The prices quoted are for the cheapest available double room in high season, though remember that many of the cheap places will have more expensive rooms with en-suite facilities.

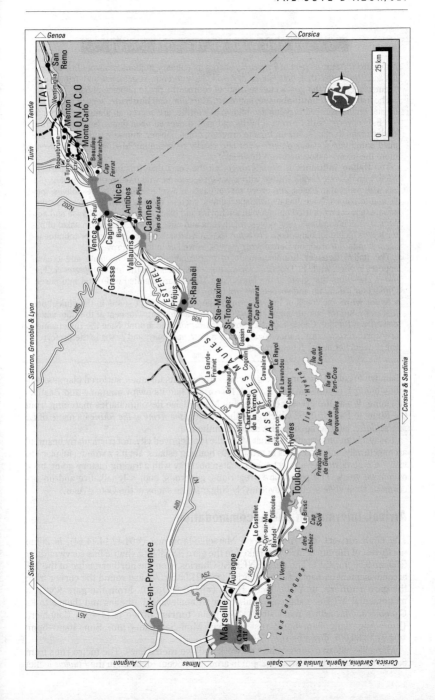

FOOD AND WINE OF THE CÔTE D'AZUR

The **Côte d'Azur**, as part of Provence, shares its culinary fundamentals of olive oil, garlic and the herbs that flourish in dry soil, its gorgeous vegetables and fruits, plus Menton's lemons, the goat's cheeses and, of course, the predominance of fish.

The fish soups of **bouillabaisse**, famous in Marseille, and **bourride**, served with a garlic and chilli-flavoured mayonnaise known as **rouille**, are served all along the coast, as are **fish** covered with Provençal herbs and grilled over an open flame. **Seafood** – from spider crabs to clams, sea urchins to crayfish, crabs, lobster, mussels and oysters – are piled onto huge *plateaux de mer* – not necessarily representing Mediterranean harvest, more the luxury associated with this coast.

The **Italian influence** is even stronger on the coast than it is inland, particularly in Nice, with delicate ravioli stuffed with asparagus, prawns, wild mushrooms or *pestou*, pizzas with wafer-thin bases, and every sort of pasta as a vehicle for anchovies, olives, garlic and tomatoes. **Nice** has its own specialities, such as *socca*, a chickpea flour pancake, *pissaladière*, a tart of fried onions with anchovies and black olives, salade niçoise and *pan bagnat*, which combines egg, olives, salad, tuna and olive oil, and *mesclum*, a salad of bitter leaves including dandelion. *Petits farcies* – stuffed aubergines, peppers or tomatoes – are a standard feature on Côte d'Azur menus, as well as in inland Provence.

The Italian **dessert** tiramisu, made of marscapone cheese, chocolate and cream, appears in Nice, while St-Tropez has its own sweet speciality in the *tarte Tropezienne*. The sweet chestnuts that grow in the Massif des Maures are candied or turned into purée. Outlets for ice-cream and sorbets are ubiquitous.

As for **wine**, the rosés of Provence might not have the great status in the viniculture hierarchy, but for baking summer days they are hard to beat. The best of the Côte wines come from Bandol: Cassis too has its own *appellation*, and around Nice the Bellet wines are worth discovering. Fancy cocktails are a Côte speciality, and *pastis* is the preferred thirst quencher at any time of the day.

to sundry French kings and foreign armies, refound its fortunes, suffered plagues, religious bigotry, republican and royalist Terror and had its own Commune and Bastille-storming. It was the presence of so many Marseillaise Revolutionaries marching from the Rhine to Paris in 1792 which gave the *Hymn of the Army of the Rhine* its name of *La Marseillaise*, later to become the national anthem.

Today, it's an undeniable fact that Marseille is a deprived city, not particularly beautiful architecturally, and with acres of grim 1960s housing estates. Yet it's a wonderful place to visit – a real, down-to-earth yet cosmopolitan port city with a trading history going back over 2500 years. The people are gregarious, generous, endlessly talkative and unconcerned if their style seems provocatively vulgar to the snobs of the Côte d'Azur.

Arrival, information and accommodation

The city's **airport**, the Aéroport de Marseille-Provence (☎04.42.14.14.14), is 20km northwest of the city centre, and linked to the gare SNCF by a shuttle bus service (daily 5.50am–9.50pm; 45F). The **gare SNCF St-Charles** is on the northern edge of the 1er arrondissement on esplanade St-Charles (☎04.91.08.50.50), just round the corner from the **gare routière**, on place Victor-Hugo (☎04.91.08.16.40). From the gare SNCF, a monumental Art Deco staircase leads down to boulevard d'Athènes and thence to La Canebière, Marseille's main street. The main **tourist office** is at 4 La Canebière (June–Aug daily 9am–8pm; rest of year Mon–Sat 9am–7pm, Sun 10am–5pm; ☎04.91.13.89.00), down by the Vieux Port.

Marseille has an extensive **bus** network and two **métro** lines. The métro runs from 5am to 9pm, night buses from 9.25pm to around 12.30am (detailed in the *Fluobus* leaflet available from L'Espace Infos, 6 rue des Fabres, 1er; or Métro sales points). Single **tickets**, known as *cartes solo* (9F), are valid for any journeys made within an hour; a day pass (*carte journée*) costs 25F; *cartes liberté*, for either 50F or 100F, give you seven or fourteen hours' worth of journeys and can be shared among up to four people. Better value is the *Maestro* option on a *carte mistral* (52F), which offers seven days' travel up to a maximum of 52 hours' worth of journeys, for which you'll need a passport photo. Métro stations, L'Espace Infos and many tabacs and bookshops sell tickets; *cartes solo* can also be bought on buses. All tickets must be punched in the machines at the start of your journey.

Since Marseille is not a great tourist city, **finding a room** in July or August is no more difficult than during the rest of the year. Hotels are plentiful, though if you get stuck the tourist office on La Canebière (see above) offers a free **accommodation service**. The most inexpensive options are the city's **youth hostels**, both quite a way from the centre. **Camping** is only possible at the Bois-Luzy hostel, for twenty tents only.

Hotels

Alizé, 35 quai des Belges, 1er (☎04.91.33.66.97, fax 04.91.54.80.06). Comfortable, soundproofed rooms, the more expensive looking out onto the Vieux Port. ④.

Le Béarn, 63 rue Sylvabelle, 6e (☎04.91.37.75.83, fax 04.91.81.54.98). Very good bargain for a pleasant, quiet hotel close to the centre. ①.

Le Corbusier, Cité Radieuse, 280 bd Michelet, 8e (☎04.91.77.18.15, fax 04.91.16.78.28). Simple rooms with great views on the third floor of the architect's prototype tower block (see p.938); book in advance. ③.

Edmond-Rostand, 31 rue Dragon, 6e (☎04.91.37.74.95, fax 04.91.57.19.04). Helpful management and good atmosphere. ③.

Esterel, 124 rue Paradis, 6^{e} (☎ 04.91.37.13.90, fax 04.91.81.47.01). In a good, animated location with all mod cons. ③.

Frantour-Tonic Hotel, 42 quai des Belges, 1er (☎04.91.55.67.46, fax 04.91.55.67.56). The smartest of the Vieux Port hotels; jacuzzi and steam bath in many rooms; for port view ⑥, otherwise ⑤.

POWER AND POLITICS

Marseille has all the social, economic and political ills of France writ large. In addition, it has to contend with its notoriety for protection rackets and shoot-outs, corruption, drug-money laundering and prostitution. But the city's dangerous reputation is unfair – not because it's unfounded but because underworld activities flourish just as much, if not more, elsewhere on the Côte d'Azur.

The career of Marseille's most famous politician has been more spectacular than any gangster activities. Millionaire businessman **Bernard Tapie** entered politics in the 1980s with the express intention of seeing off the neo-fascist Le Pen. He became a *député* and MEP, and even held a cabinet post. He bought the city's football team, delighting the Marseillais with its success, but a match-rigging scandal in 1993 led to Olympique de Marseille's relegation from the First Division and investigations into not just the team's finances but the whole of Tapie's financial empire. The subsequent lifting of his parliamentary immunity and charges of fraud and tax evasion did nothing to dent his appeal, however, and in 1994 seventy percent of the Bouches-du-Rhône electorate voted for him. He then survived bankruptcy proceedings, and was convicted of bribery, embezzlement and misuse of funds, but got off with suspended sentences and a brief spell in jail. While defending his last case he entered a new career, starring in a film by Claude Lelouch, and finally resigned from parliament in 1996, faced with lengthy appeals against ongoing litigation. OM is now back again at the top of the French football league, and returned to compete in Europe in the 1998-99 season.

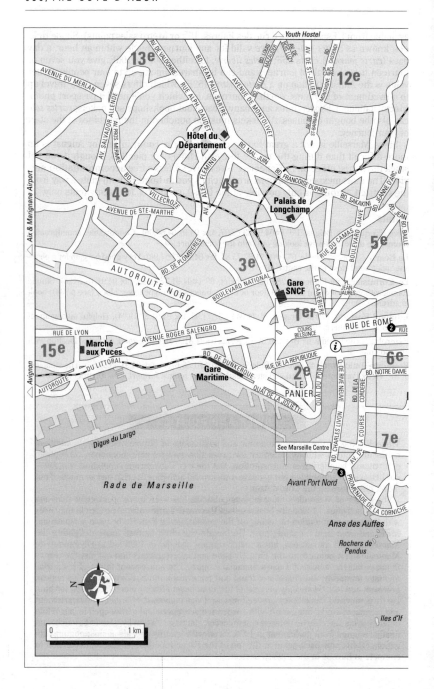

Youth Hostel

13e

12e

AVENUE DU MERLAN

AV DE VALDONNE

BD JEAN PAUL SARTRE

RUE ALPH DAUDET

AVENUE DE MONTOLIVET

BD LOUIS MAZARGUES

AV DE ROCH LUCY

AV DE ST-JULIEN

PLACE CAIRE

AV BD GILET

AV PROS MÉRIMÉE

AV SALVADOR ALLENDE

Hôtel du Département

BD MAL JUIN

AV BARNABÉ

BD FRANÇOISE DUPARC

14e

BD DE VILLECROZE

AVENUE DE STE-MARTHE

AV ALEX FLEMING

4e

Palais de Longchamp

BD SAKAKINI

BD JEANNE D'ARC

5e

Aix & Marignane Airport

BD DE PLOMBIÈRES

3e

BOULEVARD NATIONAL

RUE DU CAMAS

BOULEVARD CHAVE

BD JEAN BD BAILLE

AUTOROUTE NORD

Gare SNCF

LA CANEBIÈRE

PL JEAN-JAURES

Avignon

RUE DE LYON

AVENUE ROGER SALENGRO

1er

COURS BELSUNCE

RUE DE ROME

2

RUE

15e

Marché aux Puces

DU LITTORAL

BD DE DUNKERQUE

Gare Maritime

RUE DE LA RÉPUBLIQUE

2e

LE PANIER

QUAI DU PORT

BD DE RIVE NEUVE

BD DE LA CORDERIE

BD NOTRE DAME

6e

AUTOROUTE

QUAI DE LA JOLIETTE

BD CHARLES LIVON

AV DE LA COURSE

7e

Digue du Largo

See Marseille Centre

3

Avant Port Nord

Rade de Marseille

PROMENADE DE LA CORNICHE

Anse des Auffes

Rochers de Pendus

N

Iles d'If

0   1 km

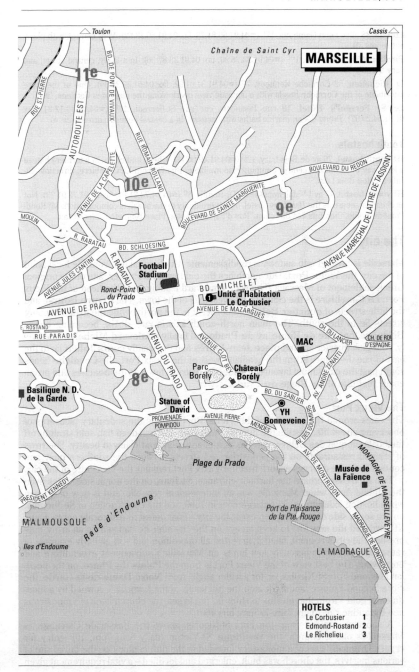

△ Toulon

Cassis △

Chaîne de Saint Cyr

MARSEILLE

11e

RUE ST-PIERRE

BD. DE PONT DE VIVAUX

AUTOROUTE EST

RUE FLOMAIN ROLLAND

AVENUE DE LA CAPELETTE

10e

BOULEVARD DU REDON

BOULEVARD DE SAINTE MARGUERITE

9e

AVENUE MARÉCHAL DE LATTRE DE TASSIGNY

MOULIN

R. RABATAU

BD. SCHLOESING

AVENUE JULES CANTINI

R. RABATAU

Football
Stadium

Rond-Point
du Prado M

BD. MICHELET

Unité d'Habitation
Le Corbusier

AVENUE DE PRADO

AVENUE DE MAZARGUES

CH. DU LANCIER

CH. DE ROU
D'ESPAGNE

E. ROSTAND

RUE PARADIS

AVENUE DU PRADO

AVENUE CLOT BEY

MAC

AV. ANDRE ZENATTI

8e

Parc
Borély

Château
Borély

**Basilique N. D.
de la Garde**

Statue of
David

PROMENADE
POMPIDOU

AVENUE PIERRE

MENDES

BD. DU SABLIER

YH
Bonneveine

AV. DES DOUANIERS

PRÉSIDENT KENNEDY

Plage du Prado

AV. DE MONTREDON

Musée de
la Faïence

MONTAGNE DE MARSEILLEVEYRE

MALMOUSQUE

Rade d'Endoume

Iles d'Endoume

*Port de Plaisance
de la Pte. Rouge*

MADRAGUE DE MONTREDON

LA MADRAGUE

HOTELS
Le Corbusier   1
Edmond-Rostand   2
Le Richelieu   3

Lutétia, 38 allée Léon-Gambetta, 1er (π04.91.50.81.78, fax 04.91.50.23.52). Very central, with pleasant rooms. ③.

Pavillon, 27 rue Pavillon, 1er (π04.91.33.76.90, fax 04.91.33.87.56). In a lively, central street, and very friendly. ②.

Le Richelieu, 52 Corniche Kennedy, 7e (π04.91.31.01.92, fax 04.91.59.38.09). One of the more affordable of the Corniche hotels with a fantastic view overlooking the plage des Catalans. ③.

Le St Ferréol's Hôtel, 19 rue Pisançon, cnr rue St-Ferréol, 1er (π04.91.33.12.21, fax 04.91.54.29.97). Pretty decor, marble baths with jacuzzis, in a central pedestrianized area. ④.

Youth hostels

HI youth hostel, 76 av de Bois-Luzy, 12e (π04.91.49.06.18). Cheap and clean, in a former château a long way out from the centre. Camping also available. Bus #8 from La Canebière, direction "St-Julien", stop Bois Luzy.

HI youth hostel, 47 av J-Vidal, impasse du Dr-Bonfils, 8e (π04.91.73.21.81, fax 04.91.73.91.23). Not as cheap or secure as the *Bois Luzy* hostel, but its proximity to the beach is compensation. M° Rond-Point-du-Prado, then bus #44 direction "Roy d'Espagne", stop Place Bonnefon. Closed Jan.

The city

Marseille is divided into sixteen arrondissements which spiral out from the focal point of the city, the **Vieux Port**. Due north lies the old town, **Le Panier**, site of the original Greek settlement of Massalia. The wide boulevard leading from the head of the Vieux Port, **La Canebière** is the central east–west axis of the town. The **Centre Bourse** and the little streets of **quartier Belsunce** border it to the north, while the main shopping streets lie to the south. The main north–south axis is **rue d'Aix**, becoming **cours Belsunce** then **rue de Rome, av du Prado** and finally **boulevard Michelet**. The lively, youngish quarter around **place Jean-Jaurès** and the trendy **cours Julien** lie to the east of rue de Rome. From the headland west of the Vieux Port, the **Corniche** heads south past the city's most favoured residential districts towards the **beaches** and promenade nightlife of the **Plage du Prado**.

The Vieux Port

The cafés around the east end of the **Vieux Port** indulge the sedentary pleasures of observing street life, despite the fumes of exhausts and half-dead fish sold straight off the boats on quai des Belges, and the lack of any quayfront claim to beauty. The rows of seafood restaurants on the pedestrianized streets between the southern quay and cours d'Estienne-d'Orves ensure that the Vieux Port remains the life centre of the city.

Two **fortresses** guard the harbour entrance. **St-Jean**, on the north side, dates from the Middle Ages when Marseille was an independent republic, and is now only open when hosting exhibitions. Its enlargement in 1660, and the construction of **St-Nicolas**, on the south side of the port, represent the city's final defeat as a separate entity. Louis XIV ordered the new fort to keep an eye on the city after he had sent in an army, suppressed the city's council, fined it, arrested all opposition and – in an early example of rate-capping – set ludicrously low limits on Marseille's subsequent expenditure and borrowing. The best view of the Vieux Port is from the **Palais du Pharo**, on the headland beyond Fort St-Nicolas, or, for a wider angle, from **Notre-Dame-de-la-Garde**, the city's Second Empire landmark atop the hill south of the harbour. Crowned by a monumental gold Virgin that gleams to ships far out to sea, the church itself is a monstrous neo-Byzantine riot (daily 7am–7/8pm; bus #60).

A short way inland from the Fort St-Nicolas, above the Bassin de Carénage, is Marseille's oldest church, the **Basilique St-Victor** (daily 8am–7pm; 10F entry for crypt). Originally part of a monastery founded in the fifth century on the burial site of various martyrs, the church was built, enlarged and fortified – a vital requirement given its position outside the city walls – over a period of 200 years from the middle of the tenth century. It looks and feels like a fortress, with some of the walls almost 3m thick, and it's no ecclesiastical beauty. You can descend to the **crypt** and **catacombs**, a warren of chapels and passages where the weight of stone and age – not to mention the photographs of skeletons exhumed – create an appropriate atmosphere in which to recall the horrors of early Christianity; St Victor himself, a Roman soldier, was slowly ground to death between two millstones.

Le Panier

To the north of the Vieux Port is the oldest part of Marseille, **Le Panier**, where, up until the last war, tiny streets, steep steps and houses of every era formed a *vieille ville* typical of the Côte. In 1943, however, with Marseille under German occupation, the quarter became an unofficial ghetto for *Untermensche* of every sort, including Resistance fighters, Communists and Jews. The Nazis gave the 20,000 inhabitants one day's notice to quit; many were deported to the camps. Dynamite was carefully laid, and everything from the waterside to rue Caisserie was blown sky-high, except for three old buildings that appealed to the fascist aesthetic: the seventeenth-century **Hôtel de Ville**, on the quay; the **Hôtel de Cabre**, on the corner of rue Bonneterie and Grande-Rue; and the **Maison Diamantée**, on rue de la Prison. After the war, archeologists reaped some benefits from this destruction when they discovered the remains of a Roman dockside warehouse, equipped with vast food-storage jars, which can be seen *in situ* at the **Musée des Docks Romains**, on place de Vivaux (Tues–Sun 10/11am–5/6pm; 12F).

At the junction of rue de la Prison and rue Caisserie, the steps of Montée des Accoules lead up and across to **place de Lenche**, site of the Greek *agora* and a good café stop. At 29 Montée des Accoules, the **Préau des Accoules**, a former Jesuit college, puts on wonderful exhibitions specially designed for children (Wed & Sat only: summer 1.30–5.30pm; winter 1–5pm; free). What's left of old Le Panier is above here, though many of the tenements have recently been demolished. At the top of rue du Réfuge stands the restored **Hospice de la Vieille Charité**, a seventeenth-century workhouse with a gorgeous Baroque chapel surrounded by columned arcades in pink stone; only the tiny grilled exterior windows recall its original use. Local people say it was "beaucoup plus jolie" when it was lived in by a hundred families, all with ten children each. It's now a cultural centre, and alarmingly empty except during its major temporary exhibitions – usually brilliant – and evening concerts. It houses two museums (Tues–Sun 10/11am–5/6pm; 12F, 18F during exhibitions, or 25F for both and the chapel): the **Musée d'Archéologie Méditerranéenne** with some very beautiful pottery and glass, and an Egyptian collection with a mummified crocodile, and the dark and spooky **Musée des Arts Africains, Océaniens et Amérindiens**.

The expansion of Marseille's **Joliette docks** started in the first half of the nineteenth century. Like the new cathedral, wide boulevards and Marseille's own Arc de Triomphe – the **Porte d'Aix** at the top of **Cours Belsunce**/rue d'Aix – the docks were paid for with the profits of military enterprise, most significantly the conquest of Algeria in 1830. Anyone fascinated by industrial architecture should join a tour of the docks run by the tourist office.

La Canebière

La Canebière, the broad boulevard that runs for about a kilometre down to the port, is the undisputed hub of the town, its name taken from the hemp (*canabé*) that once grew here and provided the raw materials for the town's thriving rope-making trade. Fashioned originally with the Champs-Élysées in mind, La Canebière is a more patchwork affair of hotels, cafés and shops, neatly providing a division between the monied

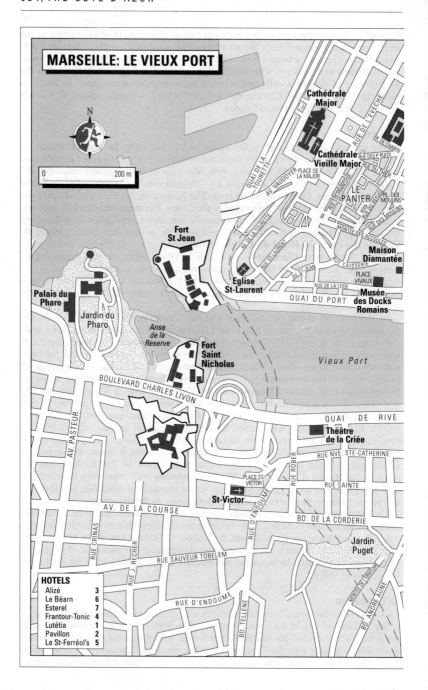

MARSEILLE: LE VIEUX PORT

N

0   200 m

Cathédrale
Major

RUE DE L'EVECHE

R. DE CHARITE

Cathédrale
Vieille Major

RUE DES P. PUITS

RUE DU THER

PLACE DE
LA MAJOR

LE
PANIER

PL. DES
MOULINS

AV. VAUDOYER

RUE FRANÇAISE

RUE DU REFUGE

RUE DES MOULINS

QUAI DE LA TOURETTE

AV. DE LA TOURETTE

RUE ST-LAURENT

MONTÉE DES ACCOULES

RUE CAISSERIE

Maison
Diamantée

Fort
St Jean

Eglise
St-Laurent

AV. ST-JEAN

PLACE
VIVAUX

RUE DE LA LOGE

QUAI DU PORT

Musée
des Docks
Romains

Palais du
Pharo

Jardin du
Pharo

Anse
de la
Reserve

Fort
Saint
Nicholas

Vieux Port

BOULEVARD CHARLES LIVON

AV. PASTEUR

QUAI   DE   RIVE

Théâtre
de la Criée

RUE NVE. STE-CATHERINE

RUE ROBER

RUE SAINTE

PLACE ST-
VICTOR

RUE D'ENDOUME

St-Victor

BD. DE LA CORDERIE

AV. DE LA COURSE

Jardin
Puget

RUE CRINAS

RUE J. RECHER

RUE SAUVEUR TOBELEM

MONTÉE DE L'ORATOIRE

BD. ANDRE AUNE

RUE D'ENDOUME

BD. TELLENE

HOTELS
Alizé	3
Le Béarn	6
Esterel	7
Frantour-Tonic	4
Lutétia	1
Pavillon	2
Le St-Ferréol's	5

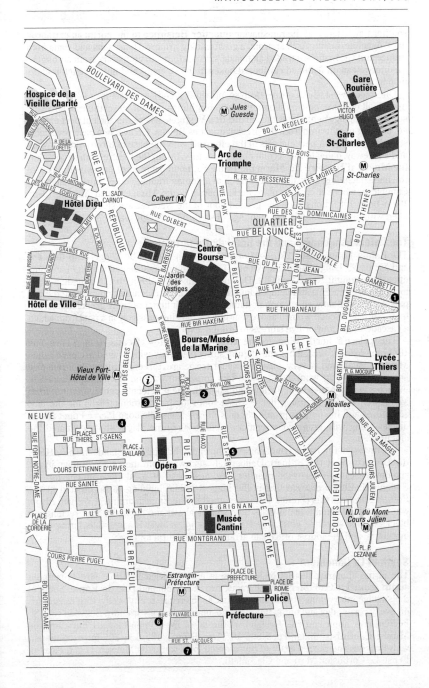

southern quartiers and the ramshackle **quartier Belsunce** to the north: an extraordinary, dynamic, mainly Arab area and a great trading ground. Hi-fis, suits and jeans from France and Germany are traded alongside spices, cloth and metalware from across the Mediterranean on flattened cardboard boxes in the streets – and not a French middleman in sight.

One block west, the **Centre Bourse** provides a stark contrast in a fiendish giant hypermall of noise, air-conditioning and over-lighting – useful, nevertheless, for mainstream shopping. Behind it is the **Jardin des Vestiges**, where the ancient port extended, curving northwards from the present quai des Belges. Excavations have revealed a stretch of the Greek port and bits of the **city wall** with the base of three square towers and a gateway, dated to the second or third century BC. In the Centre Bourse complex, the **Musée d'Histoire de Marseille** (Mon–Sat noon–7pm; free) presents the rest of the finds, including a third-century wreck of a Roman trading vessel. Further along La Canebière, where it crosses place de la Bourse, is the **Musée de la Marine** (daily 10am–6pm; 10F), housed on the ground floor of the Neoclassical stock exchange and filled with intricate models and paintings of ships on the high seas.

The Palais Longchamp and the Hôtel du Département

The **Palais Longchamp**, 2km east of the port at the end of bd Longchamp (bus #80 and #41 or Mº Longchamp-Cinq-Avenues), forms the grandiose conclusion of an aqueduct that brought water from the Durance to the city. Although the aqueduct is no longer in use, water is still pumped into the centre of the colonnade connecting the two palatial wings. Below, an enormous statue looks as if it honours some great feminist victory – three muscular women above four bulls wallowing passively in a pool from which a cascade drops four or five storeys to ground level.

The palace's north wing is the city's **Musée des Beaux-Arts** (Tues–Sun 10/11am–5/6pm; 12F), a hot and slightly stuffy place, but with a fair share of delights. Most unusual, and a very pleasant visual treat, are three paintings by Françoise Duparc (1726–76), whose first name has consistently found itself masculinized to François in catalogues both French and English. The nineteenth-century satirist from Marseille, Honoré Daumier, has a whole room for his cartoons. Plans for the city, sculptures and the famous profile of Louis XIV by Marseille-born Pierre Puget are on display along with graphic contemporary canvases of the plague that decimated the city in 1720.

Northwest of the Palais Longchamp, at the end of bd Mal-Juin, stands the new **Hôtel du Département** (Mº St-Just). Deliberately set away from the centre of town in the run-down St-Just–Chartreux quartier, the new seat of local government for the Bouches-du-Rhône *département* is the biggest public building to be erected in the French provinces this century. It was designed by the English architect William Alsop, who used his hallmark ovoid glass tube shapes above and alongside vast rectangular blocks of blue steel and glass. The Hôtel's great glass foyer is accessible during working hours, and the tourist office can arrange architectural tours.

South of La Canebière

The prime shopping district of Marseille is encompassed by three streets running **south from La Canebière**: rue Paradis, rue St-Ferréol and **rue de Rome**. Some of the smaller, intervening streets close to La Canebière are pretty seedy, with prostitutes on every corner day and night, but the atmosphere is usually friendly. Between rues St-Ferréol and Rome, on rue Grignan, is the city's most important art museum, the **Musée Cantini** (summer Tues–Sun 10/11am–5/6pm; 12F, 15—20F for exhibitions), with Fauvists and Surrealists well represented, plus works by Matisse, Léger, Picasso, Ernst, Le Corbusier, Miró and Giacometti.

A few blocks west of rue de Rome is one of the most pleasant places to idle in the city, the **cours Julien** (M° N-D-du-Mont Cours Julien), with pools, fountains, pavement restaurant tables and enticing boutiques. Streets full of bars and music shops lead west to **place Jean-Jaurès**, where the daily market is a treat, particularly on Saturdays.

The corniche, beaches and Parc Borély

The most popular stretch of sand close to the city centre is the **plage des Catalans**, a few blocks south of the Palais du Pharo. This marks the beginning of Marseille's **corniche**, av J-F-Kennedy, which follows the cliffs past the dramatic statue and arch that frames the setting sun of the **Monument aux Morts des Orients**. South of the monument, steps lead down to an inlet, **Anse des Auffes**, which is the nearest Marseille gets to being picturesque. Small fishing boats are beached on the rocks, the dominant sound is the sea, and narrow stairways and lanes lead nowhere. The corniche then turns inland, bypassing the **Malmousque peninsula**, whose coastal path gives access to tiny bays and beaches – perfect for swimming when the Mistral wind is not inciting the waves. You can see along the coast as far as Cap Croisette and, out to sea, the abandoned monastery on the Îles d'Endoume and the Château d'If (see below).

The corniche ends at the **Plage du Prado**, the city's main sand beach, where the water is remarkably clean. A short way up **av du Prado**, av du Park-Borély leads into the city's best green space, the **Parc Borély**, with a boating lake, rose gardens, palm trees and a botanical garden (daily 8am–9pm; free). The quickest way to the park and the beaches is by bus #19, #72 or #83 from M° Rd-Pt-du-Prado; for the corniche, take bus #83 from the Vieux Port.

The Château d'If

The **Château d'If**, on the tiny island of If, is best known as the penal setting for Alexandre Dumas's *The Count of Monte Cristo*. Having made his watery escape after five years of incarceration as the innocent victim of treachery, the hero of the piece, Edmond Dantès, describes the island thus: "Blacker than the sea, blacker than the sky, rose like a phantom the giant of granite, whose projecting crags seemed like arms extended to seize their prey." The reality, for most prisoners, was worse: they went insane or died (and sometimes both) before reaching the end of their sentences. Only the nobles living in the less fetid upper-storey cells had much chance of survival, like de Niozelles, who was given six years for failing to take his hat off in the presence of Louis XIV, and Mirabeau, who was doing time for debt. The sixteenth-century castle and its cells are horribly well-preserved, and the views back towards Marseille are brilliant. **Boats** for If leave regularly from the quai des Belges on the Vieux Port (at 6.45am, hourly 9am–noon, 2–5pm & 7pm, with slight seasonal variations; 50F; journey time 15–20min). The château's opening hours (admission 25F) fit the boat timetable, and the last boat back during the summer leaves at 6.40pm.

The Musée de la Faïence, the MAC and the Cité Radieuse

From the plage du Prado the promenade continues, with a glittering array of restaurants, clubs and cafés, all the way to the suburb of **Montredon** where the nineteenth-century Château Pastré, set in a huge park, contains the **Musée de la Faïence** (Tues–Sun 10/11am–5/6pm; 12F). The eighteenth- and nineteenth-century ceramics, most produced in Marseille, are of an extremely high quality, and a small collection of novel modern and contemporary pieces is housed on the top floor. The entrance to the park (free) is at 157 av de Montredon (bus #19 from M° Rd-Pt-du-Prado, stop Montredon-Chancel). Along the coast from here are easily accessible *calanques* (rocky inlets), ideal for evening swims and supper picnics as the sun sets.

Between Montredon and **bd Michelet**, the main road out of the city, is the contemporary art museum, **MAC** (daily except Mon 11/10am–5/6pm; 12F) at 69 av d'Haïfa (bus

#23 or #45 from M° Rd-Pt-du-Prado, stop Haïfa or Marie-Louise). The permanent collection, in perfect pure-white surrounds, includes works from the 1960s to the present day by Buren, Christo, Klein, Niki de Saint-Phalle, Tinguely and Warhol, as well as Marseillais artists César and Ben. There's also a cinema, the **Cinémac** (☎04.91.25.01.07), showing feature films, shorts and videos on different themes each month.

Set back just west of boulevard Michelet stands a building that broke the mould, Le Corbusier's seventeen-storey block of flats, the **Cité Radieuse**, designed in 1946 and completed in 1952. The Cité only fails to amaze now because so many architects the world over have tried to imitate Le Corbusier's revolutionary model. Each apartment has two levels and balconies on both sides of the building, with unhindered views of mountains and sea. On different floors there are shops, offices and a gymnasium; the third floor is now a hotel (see p.929); and the top floor features sculptural and ceramic roof decoration as well as a pool and a running track. To reach the Cité, take bus #21 from M° Rd-Pt-du-Prado to Le Corbusier.

Eating and drinking

The Marseillais **eat** just as well, if not better, than the ageing aristos and skin-stretched celebrities of the Riviera. Fish and seafood are the main ingredients, and the superstar of dishes is the city's own expensive invention, bouillabaisse, a saffron- and garlic-flavoured fish soup with bits of fish, croutons and *rouille* to throw in; theories conflict as to which fish should be included and where and how they must be caught, but one essential fish is the *rascasse* or scorpion fish. The other city speciality is the less exotic *pieds et paquets*, mutton or lamb belly and trotters.

Good **restaurant** hunting grounds to head for include cours Julien (international options), the pedestrian precinct behind the Vieux Port's southern quay (a bit more upmarket and fishy), rue Pavillon (cheap lunches), the plage du Prado (glitzy and pricey) or Le Panier (snacks and old-time bistrots). Gourmet palaces lurk close to the corniche, while stalls on cours Belsunce sell chips and sandwiches with meaty fillings for under 20F. Note that many Marseille restaurants take long summer breaks.

Cafés and bars

Bar de la Marine, 15 quai Rive Neuve, 1er A favourite bar for Vieux Port lounging and the inspiration for Pagnol's celebrated Marseille trilogy. Closed Sun.

Boulangerie, bd Baille. Open 24 hours, so ideal for late-night snacks.

Le Cadratin, 17 rue St-Saëns, 1er. Friendly and cheap bar with 1960s music playing on the jukebox and a great mix of people, both foreign and local.

Café Parisien, 1 place Sadi-Carnot, 2e. Very beautiful old-fashioned café, where people play cards and chess. Occasional painting exhibitions.

Le Petit Nice, 26 place Jean-Jaurès, 1er. Cosy, local bar overlooking the market.

La Samaritaine, 2 quai du Port, 2e. Sunny café, with the best panorama of the Vieux Port.

Restaurants

Les Arcenaulx, 25 cours d'Estienne-d'Orves, 1er (☎04.91.54.77.06). Superb food with menus from 135F in an intellectual haunt which is also a bookshop. Closed Sun.

L'Assiette Marine, 142 av Mendez-France, 8e (☎04.91.71.04.04). Serves fresh pasta in lobster sauce, aubergine and lamb with truffles, and other exquisite dishes, just north of the plage du Prado. Menus at 135F and 200F.

L'Atelier du Chocolat, 18 place aux Huiles, 1er (☎04.91.33.55.00). Georgeous chocolate puds to finish off an excellent meal; 100F menu including wine. Closed Sun, Mon & Tues eve.

Auberge "In", 25 rue du Chevalier-Roze, 2e (☎04.91.90.51.59). In a health-food shop on the edge of Le Panier. Vegetarian *menu fixe* served lunchtimes and early evenings. Closed Sun.

Le Carré d'Honoré, 34 place aux Huiles, 1er (04.91.33.16.80). Fish and seafood dishes; two week-day, lunchtime menus under 100F, otherwise from 120F. Closed Sat lunch, Sun & Aug.

Chez Angèle, 50 rue Caisserie, 2e (☎04.91.90.63.35). Packed Le Panier local, with a bargain *menu fixe* for basic French food. Closed Sat eve, Sun & Aug.

Chez Étienne, 43 rue Lorette, 2e. Old-fashioned Le Panier bistrot; hectic, cramped and crowded. Full meal 150–250F but you can just have a pizza. No bookings. Closed Sun & Mon.

Chez Michel, 6 rue des Catalans, 7e (☎04.91.52.30.63). There's no debate about the bouillabaisse ingredients here. A basket of five fishes, including the elusive and most expensive one, the *rascasse*, is presented to the customer before the soup is made. Quite simply *the* place to eat this dish. Expect to pay 250F for the bouillabaisse alone. Open daily.

La Coupole, 5 rue Haxo, 1er (☎04.91.54.88.57). Elegant brasserie serving a midday *plat du jour* with a glass of wine for around 100F.

Dar Djerba, 15 cours Julien, 6e (☎04.91.48.55.36). Excellent Tunisian restaurant with beautiful tiling – ignore the stuffed camel's head. Around 150F.

La Kahena, 2 rue de la République, 1er. Popular Moroccan with grills and couscous from 60F. Closed Sun & Mon lunch.

Maurice Brun, 18 quai Rive-Neuve, 7e (☎04.91.33.35.38). A Marseille institution serving authentic Provençal food; lunch menu 230F, evening 250F. Closed Sun, & Mon lunch.

Nightlife

Marseille's **nightlife** has something for everyone, with plenty of live rock and jazz, as well as more choice pastimes of theatre-, opera- and concert-going. Virgin Megastore, at 75 rue St-Ferréol (Mon–Thurs 9am–9pm, Fri & Sat till midnight, Sun till 7pm), and the ticket bureau in the tourist office are the best places to go for **tickets and information** on gigs, concerts, theatre, free films and whatever cultural events are going on. Virgin also stocks a wide selection of English books and runs a café on the top floor. Other places with info are the book and record shop FNAC, on the top floor of the Centre Bourse (Mon–Sat 10am–7pm), the café, travel agency and comic shop La Passerelle, 26 rue des Trois-Mages (noon–midnight), and the New Age music shop *Tripsichord*, next door. At any of these places, you can pick up a copy of *Taktik*, Marseille's independent free weekly listings paper, which comes out on a Wednesday.

The **clubs** around cours d'Estienne-d'Orves – mainly jazz, some Caribbean – are for trendy kids from the upper-crust arrondissements, with prices to match.

Live music and clubs

Cité de la Musique, 4 rue Bernard du Bois, 1er (☎04.91.39.28.28). Jazz cellar and auditorium.

Maison de l'Étranger, 9 av Général-Leclerc, 3e (☎04.91.28.24.01). A club not far from the gare SNCF St-Charles, which puts on regular world music gigs, especially Raï. On an insecure financial footing however, so check it still exists before turning up.

La Maison Hantée, 10 rue Vian, 6e (☎04.91.92.09.40). Café-théâtre and cinema alternates with country music, R&B and rock. Closed Mon.

May Be Blues, rue Poggioli, 6e (☎04.91.42.41.00). Relaxed blues/jazz club. No entry charge, though drinks go up once the music starts. Closed Mon & Tues.

au Moulin, 47 bd Perrin (☎04.91.06.33.94). An obscure venue in the northwest of the city specializing in weird and wonderful European bands.

New Cancan, 20 rue Sénac (☎04.91.47.50.18). Gay club with high camp and transvestite shows.

Palacio de la Salsa, 19 rue Neuve Ste-Catherine (☎ 04.91.33.92.57). Dance venue playing mainly Latin vibes. Closed Mon–Wed.

Pelle Mêle, 8 place aux Huiles, 1er (☎04.91.54.85.26). Jazz bistrot and piano bar. Closed Sun.

Le Pourquoi Pas, 1 rue Fortia, 1er (☎04.91.33.50.54), has Caribbean music and punch to get drunk on.

Le Stendhal, 92 rue Jean-de-Bernady, 1er (☎04.91.84.74.80). Wide selection of malt whiskies and beers, including Courage, and live music Tues & Thurs. Red and black interior, naturally enough.

Film, theatre and concerts

Ballet National de Marseille, 20 bd Gabès, 8e (☎04.91.71.03.03). The home base of Roland Petit's famous dance company.

Bastide de la Magalone, 245 bd Michelet, 9e (☎04.91.39.28.28). Classical music concerts.

Chocolat Théâtre, 59 cours Julien, 6e (☎04.91.42.19.29). Theatre-restaurant-exhibition-space with shows ranging from male striptease to avant-garde improvisations.

Cinéma Paris, 31 rue Pavillon, 1er (☎04.91.33.15.59). The only cinema in Marseille which regularly shows *v.o.* films.

Théâtre Nationale de Marseille "La Criée", 30 quai Rive Neuve, 7e (☎04.91.54.70.54). The top theatre.

Listings

Airlines Air France (☎04.91.39.39.39); British Airways (☎04.42.14.21.24).

Bike rental Green Bike, 135 av Clot Bey, 8e (☎04.91.72.42.63). Touring and mountain bikes at around 90F a day.

Car hire Budget 232 av du Prado, 8e (☎04.91.71.75.00); Citer, 96 bd Rabatau, 8e (☎04.91.83.05.05); Europcar, 7 bd Maurice-Bourdet, 1er (☎04.91.90.11.00); Thrifty, 6 bd Voltaire, 1er (☎04.91.05.92.18).

Consulates UK, 24 av du Prado, 6e (☎04.91.15.72.10); USA, 12 bd Peytral, 6e (☎04.91.54.92.00).

Disabled Office Municipal pour Handicapés, 128 av du Prado, 8e (☎04.91.81.58.80). Information on disabled access and facilities. Also operates a transport service (call ☎04.91.78.21.67 a day ahead).

Emergencies Ambulance ☎15; Doctor: ☎15, or SOS Médecins (☎04.91.52.91.52); 24hr casualty: La Conception, 144, rue St-Pierre, 5e (☎04.91.38.36.52).

Ferries SNCM, 61 bd des Dames (☎04.91.56.32.00) runs ferries to Corsica and Tunisia.

Lost property 10 rue de la Cathédrale, 2e (☎04.91.90.99.37).

Money exchange Comptoir de Change Méditerranéen, gare St-Charles, daily 8am–6pm; Comptoir Marseillais de Bourse, 22 La Canebière, Mon–Sat 8.30am–7pm.

Pharmacy Brachat Bel, 29 rue Longue des Campucins; 24hr.

Police Commissariat Centrale, 2 rue Antoine Becke, 2e (☎04.91.39.80.00). Daily 8am–noon & 2–6pm.

Post office 1 place de l'Hôtel-des-Postes, 13001, Marseille.

Taxis ☎04.91.02.20.20, ☎04.91.49.91.00, English-speaking ☎04.91.97.12.12.

Youth information Centre d'Information Jeunesse, 4 rue de la Visitation, 4^e (☎04.91.49.91.55).

Cassis, La Ciotat and Bandol

Hard as it is to picture now, chic little **Cassis** once had a busy industrial harbour, while at **La Ciotat** ships were built right up until 1989. La Ciotat is probably the friendliest of all the resorts between Marseille and Toulon, and has the distinction of being at the origin of film-making.

Cassis

A lot of people rate **CASSIS** the best resort this side of St-Tropez – its inhabitants most of all. Hemmed in by high white cliffs, its modern development has been limited to a model toytown on the steep inclines above the port. Portside posing and drinking aside, there's not much to do except sunbathe and look up at the ruins of the town's medieval

THE COSQUER CAVE

In 1991, diver **Henri Cosquer** found paintings and engravings of animals, painted hand-prints and finger tracings in a cave between Marseille and Cassis, whose sole entrance has been underwater since the end of the last ice age. Carbon dating has shown that the oldest work of art here was created around 27,000 years ago. Over a hundred animals have been identified, including seals, auks, horses, ibex, bisons, chamois, red deer and a giant deer only known from fossils. Fish are also featured along with sea creatures that might be jellyfish. Most of the finger tracings are done in charcoal and have fingertips missing, possibly a sign language. Since the entrance is 37m below sea level, it's unlikely that the cave will ever be made accessible to the public.

castle, built in 1381 and refurbished by Monsieur Michelin, the authoritarian boss of the family tyres and guides firm.

The favoured lazy pastime, though, is to take a boat trip to the **calanques** – long, narrow, deep fjord-like inlets that have cut into the limestone cliffs. Several companies operate from the port, but check if they let you off or just tour in and out, and be prepared for rough seas. If you're feeling energetic, you can take the well-marked footpath from the route des Calanques behind the western beach; it's about ninety minutes' walk to the furthest and best *calanque*, **En Vau**, where you can climb down rocks to the shore. Intrepid pine trees find root-holds, and sunbathers find ledges on the chaotic white cliffs. The water is deep blue and swimming between the vertical cliffs is an experience not to be missed.

Les Sports Loisirs Nautiques (☎04.42.01.80.01) rents out windsurfing and watersports equipment by the beach next to the port, and will offer a ten percent discount if you show your *Rough Guide* to the guy who runs it.

Practicalities

Buses from Marseille arrive at rond-point du Pressoir between the port and the beach. The **gare SNCF** is 3km out of town, with only two bus connections daily.

Cheap **rooms** in high season don't exist in Cassis. The least expensive are *Le Provençal*, rue Victor-Hugo (☎01.42.01.72.13; ③), and *Le Laurence*, 8 rue de l'Arène (☎04.42.01.88.78; ③), both close to the port. For a little more, and a view over the port, try *Le Golfe*, on quai Calendal (☎04.42.01.00.21, fax 04.42.01.92.08; ④). Further out, there's also *Le Joli Bois*, rte de la Gineste (☎04.42.01.02.68; half-board obligatory in season; ②), just off the main road to Marseille, 3km from Cassis. Far more isolated is the gorgeously scenic but rather inaccessible **youth hostel** *La Fontasse*, in the hills above the *calanques* west of Cassis (☎04.42.01.02.72; all year); from the D559 (stop Les Calanques), a road leads down towards the Col de la Gardiole, and when it becomes a track, take the left fork, and after another 2km you'll find the hostel. Rainwater, beds and electricity are the only mod cons, but if you want to explore this wild uninhabited stretch of limestone heights, the people running it are happy to give advice. To get to Cassis you can descend to the *calanques* and walk along the coast (about 1hr). If you're **camping**, don't bother going into town – the campsite, *Les Cigales* (☎04.42.01.07.34; mid-March to mid-Nov), is just off the D559 from Marseille before av de la Marne turns down into Cassis, a gruelling one-kilometre walk from the port.

Restaurant tables are in abundance along the portside quai des Baux; prices vary greatly, but if you can afford it your best bet has to be to follow your nose, and seek out the most enticing fish smells. The authentic Provençal ratatouille and freshly caught fish at *Chez Gilbert*, 19 quai Baux (☎04.42.01.71.36; closed Tues eve & Wed), are hard to beat, with a 120F menu. *El Sol*, at no. 23 (☎04.42.01.76.10; closed Wed), costs a bit less, as do restaurants on the back streets, such as the family-run *La*

Boulangerie, 19 rue Michel Arnaud (☎04.42.01.38.31). Cassis white **wines** are very special: the **tourist office** on place Baragnon (summer daily 9am–7.30pm; winter Mon–Sat 10am–1pm & 2–6pm; ☎04.42.01.71.17, fax 04.42.01.28.31) can provide addresses of the vineyards.

La Ciotat

You might not associate the building of 300,000-tonne oil and gas tankers with the pleasures of a Mediterranean resort. But it is one of the surprising charms of **LA CIOTAT** that the **Vieux Port**, below a golden stone old town, shelters the dramatic massive cranes and derricks of the former shipyards as well as the fishing fleet and the odd yacht or two. La Ciotat is not a town for keyed-up museum or monument motivation. It's a relaxing place with excellent **beaches** to loaf on and little glamour glitter.

In 1895, **August and Louis Lumière** filmed the first ever moving pictures here, including the arrival of a train at the gare SNCF, which had people jumping out of their seats in fright. The town celebrates its relatively unknown status as the cradle of cinema with an annual **film festival** (in mid-June) using the world's oldest movie house, the **Eden Cinema**, on the corner of boulevard A-France and boulevard Jean-Jaurès. The brothers are commemorated by a solid 1950s monument on plage Lumière and in a mural on the covered market halls that house the modern cinema, visible as you walk up rue Regnier from boulevard Guérin north of the port.

The streets of the old town, apart from rue Poilus, are uneventful and a bit run-down. If you feel the need to do something constructive you can take a boat trip out to the tiny offshore **Île Verte** from the quai de Gaulle (15min; ☎04.42.83.11.44 or 04.42.71.53.32), and to a number of nearby *calanques* from quai Ganteaume (☎04.42.83.54.50). Alternatively, take a walk through the **Parc du Mugel** (daily: June–Sept 8am–8pm; Oct–May 9am–6pm; free; bus #3 to La Garde, stop Mugel) with its strange cluster of rock formations on the promontory beyond the shipyards. A path leads up through overgrown vegetation to a narrow terrace overlooking the sea. Here, the cliff face looks like the habitat of some gravity-defying, burrowing beast rather than the erosions of wind and sea. If you continue on bus #3 to Figuerolles you can reach the **Anse de Figuerolles** *calanque* down the avenue of the same name, and its neighbour, the **Gameau**.

Practicalities

The **gare SNCF** is 5km from the Vieux Port, but a bus meets every train. The old town and port look out across the Baie de la Ciotat, whose inner curve provides the beaches and resort lifestyle of La Ciotat's modern extension, **La Ciotat Plage**. The **gare routière** (☎08.36.35.35.35 for train information) is at the end of boulevard Anatole-France by the Vieux Port right beside the **tourist office** (June–Sept Mon–Sat 9am–8pm, Sun 10am–1pm; rest of year Mon–Sat 9am–noon & 2.30–6pm; ☎04.42.08.61.32, fax 04.42.08.17.88).

For **hotels**, the cheapies are *Bellevue*, 3 bd Guérin (☎04.42.71.86.01; ②), and *La Rotonde*, 44 bd de la République (☎04.42.08.67.50, fax 04.42.08.45.21; ③), both in the old town. In La Ciotat Plage, *Miramar*, 3 bd Beaurivage (☎ & fax 04.42.83.09.54; e; half-board compulsory in summer) is set amidst pines by the sea, while across the bay, on Corniche du Liouquet, you can stay in little villas in a park at *Ciotel Le Cap* (☎04.42.83.90.30, fax 04.42.83.04.17; ⑤). La Ciotat has nine **campsites**, three of them by the sea, of which *St-Jean*, 30 av St-Jean (☎04.42.83.13.01 fax 04.42.71.46.41; end March–Sept; bus #4, stop St-Jean Village), is the closest to the centre.

La Ciotat's best **restaurant** is *La Fresque*, 18 rue des Combattants (☎04.42.08.00.60), with exquisite seafood dishes and menus from 150F. Otherwise, *Coquillages Franquin,*

Mont Ste-Victoire, nr Aix-en-Provence

The cloisters of St-Trophime, Arles

Villefranche-sur-Mer, on the Côte d'Azur

An alpine Ibex

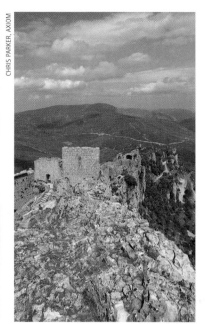

Château de Peyrepertuse, Languedoc

View from Salers, Auvergne

ies

NCF, on place de l'Europe, and **gare routière**, on place Albert-1er, lie north-
own centre. There's a **tourist office** (July & Aug Mon–Sat 9am–7pm, Sun
Sept–June Mon–Sat 9am–6pm, Sun 10am–noon; ☎04.94.18.53.00) on place
e **old town**: head down rue Vauban, turn left at place d'Armes, follow the busy
runs parallel to the coast, and turn left into rue Letuaire. Around place Victor-
find any number of cheap shops and places to eat, and a market (Tues–Sun).
get stuck here, there's plenty of cheap **accommodation**: the *Foyer de la*
stel, 12 place d'Armes (☎04.94.22.62.00), just west of the old town; the *Hôtel*
18 allées Amiral-Courbet (☎04.94.91.10.02; ①); or *Little Palace*, 6–8 rue
☎04.94.92.26.62, fax 04.94.89.13.77; ②) – all very central.

THE CENTRAL RESORTS AND ISLANDS

son, the stretch of coastline between **Hyères** and the **St-Raphael–Fréjus**
n and its backdrop of wooded hills hold their own against the cynicism
d by tourist brochure overkill. The magic lies in the scented Mediterranean
silver beaches glimpsed between purple cliffs, secluded islands and
lltop villages.
which preserves a certain air of gentility, flashy St-Raphael and historic
he only significant towns, though the urban sprawl around the erstwhile fish-
s of **Le Lavandou**, **Cavalaire-sur-Mer** and **Ste-Maxime** keeps any sense of
at bay. But there are moments when it's almost possible to imagine the coast-
near the **Cap de Bregançon** south of **Bormes**, between **Le Rayol** and
n the **Domaine de Rayol gardens**, and around the southern tip of the **St-**
ninsula. And out to sea, on the **Îles d'Hyères** (often called the Îles d'Or) you
ence untrammelled landscapes with some of the best fauna and flora in
La Croix-Valmer is probably the most pleasant of the resorts, and **St-Tropez**
for a day's visit at least. Inland, amidst the dense wooded hills of the **Massif**
es, are the gorgeous ancient villages of **Collobrières** and **La Garde Freinet**.
xpense aside, **transport** is the one big problem. There are no trains, traffic
ly slow in high season, and cycling doesn't get you very far unless you're
rance material.

S

is the oldest resort on the Côte, listing Queen Victoria and Tolstoy among its
rers, but the lack of a central seafront meant the town lost out when the for-
switched from winter convalescents to quayside strutters. It is, nevertheless,
ular resort, but has the rare distinction, for this part of the world, of not being
pendent on the summer influx. The town exports cut flowers and exotic
most important being the date palm, which graces every street in the city –
rous desert palaces in Arabia. The orchards, nursery gardens and vineyards,
land which elsewhere would have become a rash of holiday shelving units,
l to its economy. Hyères is consequently rather appealing.

information and accommodation

SNCF is on place de l'Europe (☎08.36.35.35.35), 1500m south of the town
th frequent buses to **place Clemenceau**, at the entrance to the old town, and

Lavender fields in Provence

Olive market, Aix-en-Provence

The old town, Nice

The old port of Marseille

Calvi, Corsica

13 bd Anatole-France (☎04.42.83.59.50), serves perfe⋯ there are plenty of cafés and brasseries around the Vie⋯ in La Ciotat Plage.

Bandol

Across La Ciotat bay are the fine sand beaches and unr⋯ **LECQUES**, an offshoot of the old town of **St-Cyr-Sur-**⋯ is in St-Cyr, but the **tourist office** (June to mid-⋯ 10am–1pm & 3–7pm; rest of year Mon–Sat 9am–noon⋯ l'Appel du 18 Juin, on the seafront in Les Lecques. St-C⋯ **dation**, such as the *Auberge Le Clos Fleurie* (☎ 04.94.2⋯ av Général-de-Gaulle, but there's a greater choice in⋯ **coastal path** (signposted in yellow) runs from the ea⋯ through a rare villa-free stretch of secluded beaches and⋯ resort of **BANDOL**, while inland are **vineyards** produc⋯ the Côte, the *appellation* Bandol. The *appellation* covers⋯ Cyr to Le Castellet up in the hills to the edge of Ollioule⋯ *dégustation* signs along the route. The reds are the most⋯ years on a good harvest, with bouquets sliding between⋯ black cherries.

In Bandol, one of the cheapest places to stay is conven⋯ **train station** at the top end of town: *Le Provence* (☎04.⋯ plenty of other middle-range hotels such as the *Hôtel Bri*⋯ the beach (☎04.94.29.41.70; ③). The **tourist office**, on⋯ (July & Aug daily 9am–1pm & 2–7pm; Sept–June M⋯ ☎04.94.29.41.35) will help if you are stuck during the bus⋯

The other stretch of **coastal path** this side of Toulon⋯ the **Sicié peninsula** from Le Brusc. The path climbs up⋯ Notre-Dame-du-Mai, once a primitive lighthouse, which⋯ coast and hinterland. The chapel itself is only open in May⋯ (Easter Monday, August 15, and for the pilgrimage on Se⋯

Toulon

TOULON was half destroyed in the last war, and its rebu⋯ military and associated industries. The arsenal that Louis⋯ the major employers of southeast France, and the port is⋯ Mediterranean fleet. The shipbuilding yards of La Seyne⋯ closing the book on a centuries-old and at times notorious⋯ teenth century, slaves and convicts were still powering the⋯ the Revolution, convicts were sent to Toulon with iron colla⋯ tences of hard labour. After 1854 convicts were deported t⋯ quest ships from Toulon played a major part.

Today, French nationals of non-European origin receive⋯ the Town Hall, controlled since May 1995 by the Front Nat⋯ significant electoral gain for the extreme-right party to da⋯ France.

Toulon has never been a particularly pleasant city, and⋯ new masters. The museums are dull, motorway traffic craw⋯ all the paranoia of a big city with few of the charms, and is c⋯ short, a place to avoid.

Practicali⋯
The **gare** ⋯
east of the ⋯
10am–noo⋯
Raimu, in t⋯
avenue tha⋯
Hugo you'⋯
If you d⋯
Jeunesse h⋯
des Allées⋯
Berthelot ⋯

Out of se⋯
conurbati⋯
engender⋯
vegetation⋯
medieval ⋯
Hyères⋯
Fréjus are⋯
ing village⋯
wilderness⋯
line of ol⋯
Cavalaire⋯
Tropez p⋯
can expe⋯
Provence⋯
is a must ⋯
des Mau⋯
Sheer ⋯
is extrem⋯
Tour de ⋯

Hyèr⋯

HYÈRES⋯
early adm⋯
eign rich⋯
a very po⋯
totally d⋯
plants, th⋯
and num⋯
taking u⋯
are cruc⋯

Arriva⋯

The **gar**⋯
centre, v⋯

Lavender fields in Provence

Olive market, Aix-en-Provence

The old town, Nice

M. HUGHES, TRAVEL INK

The old port of Marseille

A. SWAINE, TRIP

Calvi, Corsica

13 bd Anatole-France (☎04.42.83.59.50), serves perfectly respectable fish dishes and there are plenty of cafés and brasseries around the Vieux Port and along bd Beaurivage in La Ciotat Plage.

Bandol

Across La Ciotat bay are the fine sand beaches and unremarkable family resort of **LES LECQUES,** an offshoot of the old town of **St-Cyr-Sur-Mer**, behind. The **train station** is in St-Cyr, but the **tourist office** (June to mid-Sept Mon–Sat 9am–7pm, Sun 10am–1pm & 3–7pm; rest of time Mon–Sat 9am–noon & 2–6pm) is on the place de l'Appel du 18 Juin, on the seafront in Les Lecques. St-Cyr has the cheapest **accommodation**, such as the *Auberge Le Clos Fleurie* (☎ 04.94.26.27.46; ②), near the station on av Général-de-Gaulle, but there's a greater choice in Les Lecques. A ten-kilometre **coastal path** (signposted in yellow) runs from the east end of Les Lecques' beach through a rare villa-free stretch of secluded beaches and *calanques* to the unpretentious resort of **BANDOL**, while inland are **vineyards** producing some of the best wines on the Côte, the *appellation* Bandol. The *appellation* covers a large area stretching from St-Cyr to Le Castellet up in the hills to the edge of Ollioules, just east of Toulon; you'll see *dégustation* signs along the route. The reds are the most reputed, maturing for over ten years on a good harvest, with bouquets sliding between pepper, cinnamon, vanilla and black cherries.

In Bandol, one of the cheapest places to stay is conveniently located just beneath the **train station** at the top end of town: *Le Provence* (☎04.94.32.32.25; ②), but there are plenty of other middle-range hotels such as the *Hôtel Brise*, 12 bd Victor Hugo, close to the beach (☎04.94.29.41.70; ③). The **tourist office**, on allée Vivien by the quayside (July & Aug daily 9am–1pm & 2–7pm; Sept–June Mon–Sat 9am–noon & 2–6pm; ☎04.94.29.41.35) will help if you are stuck during the busy high season.

The other stretch of **coastal path** this side of Toulon is along the southern edge of the **Sicié peninsula** from Le Brusc. The path climbs up to the sturdy clifftop chapel of Notre-Dame-du-Mai, once a primitive lighthouse, which affords fantastic views of the coast and hinterland. The chapel itself is only open in May and on certain special dates (Easter Monday, August 15, and for the pilgrimage on September 14).

Toulon

TOULON was half destroyed in the last war, and its rebuilt whole is dominated by the military and associated industries. The arsenal that Louis XIV created is today one of the major employers of southeast France, and the port is home to the French Navy's Mediterranean fleet. The shipbuilding yards of La Seyne have, however, been axed, closing the book on a centuries-old and at times notorious industry. Up until the eighteenth century, slaves and convicts were still powering the king's galleys, and following the Revolution, convicts were sent to Toulon with iron collars round their necks for sentences of hard labour. After 1854 convicts were deported to the colonies in whose conquest ships from Toulon played a major part.

Today, French nationals of non-European origin receive second-class treatment from the Town Hall, controlled since May 1995 by the Front National. Its victory – the most significant electoral gain for the extreme-right party to date – shocked the whole of France.

Toulon has never been a particularly pleasant city, and it isn't improving under its new masters. The museums are dull, motorway traffic crawls through the centre, it has all the paranoia of a big city with few of the charms, and is claustrophobic and ugly – in short, a place to avoid.

Practicalities

The **gare SNCF**, on place de l'Europe, and **gare routière**, on place Albert-1er, lie northeast of the town centre. There's a **tourist office** (July & Aug Mon–Sat 9am–7pm, Sun 10am–noon; Sept–June Mon–Sat 9am–6pm, Sun 10am–noon; ☎04.94.18.53.00) on place Raimu, in the **old town**: head down rue Vauban, turn left at place d'Armes, follow the busy avenue that runs parallel to the coast, and turn left into rue Letuaire. Around place Victor-Hugo you'll find any number of cheap shops and places to eat, and a market (Tues–Sun).

If you do get stuck here, there's plenty of cheap **accommodation**: the *Foyer de la Jeunesse* hostel, 12 place d'Armes (☎04.94.22.62.00), just west of the old town; the *Hôtel des Allées*, 18 allées Amiral-Courbet (☎04.94.91.10.02; ①); or *Little Palace*, 6–8 rue Berthelot (☎04.94.92.26.62, fax 04.94.89.13.77; ②) – all very central.

THE CENTRAL RESORTS
AND ISLANDS

Out of season, the stretch of coastline between **Hyères** and the **St-Raphael–Fréjus** conurbation and its backdrop of wooded hills hold their own against the cynicism engendered by tourist brochure overkill. The magic lies in the scented Mediterranean vegetation, silver beaches glimpsed between purple cliffs, secluded islands and medieval hilltop villages.

Hyères, which preserves a certain air of gentility, flashy St-Raphael and historic Fréjus are the only significant towns, though the urban sprawl around the erstwhile fishing villages of **Le Lavandou**, **Cavalaire-sur-Mer** and **Ste-Maxime** keeps any sense of wilderness at bay. But there are moments when it's almost possible to imagine the coastline of old: near the **Cap de Bregançon** south of **Bormes**, between **Le Rayol** and Cavalaire, in the **Domaine de Rayol gardens**, and around the southern tip of the **St-Tropez peninsula**. And out to sea, on the **Îles d'Hyères** (often called the Îles d'Or) you can experience untrammelled landscapes with some of the best fauna and flora in Provence. **La Croix-Valmer** is probably the most pleasant of the resorts, and **St-Tropez** is a must – for a day's visit at least. Inland, amidst the dense wooded hills of the **Massif des Maures**, are the gorgeous ancient villages of **Collobrières** and **La Garde Freinet**.

Sheer expense aside, **transport** is the one big problem. There are no trains, traffic is extremely slow in high season, and cycling doesn't get you very far unless you're Tour de France material.

Hyères

HYÈRES is the oldest resort on the Côte, listing Queen Victoria and Tolstoy among its early admirers, but the lack of a central seafront meant the town lost out when the foreign rich switched from winter convalescents to quayside strutters. It is, nevertheless, a very popular resort, but has the rare distinction, for this part of the world, of not being totally dependent on the summer influx. The town exports cut flowers and exotic plants, the most important being the date palm, which graces every street in the city – and numerous desert palaces in Arabia. The orchards, nursery gardens and vineyards, taking up land which elsewhere would have become a rash of holiday shelving units, are crucial to its economy. Hyères is consequently rather appealing.

Arrival, information and accommodation

The **gare SNCF** is on place de l'Europe (☎08.36.35.35.35), 1500m south of the town centre, with frequent buses to **place Clemenceau**, at the entrance to the old town, and to the **gare routière** on place Mal-Joffret, two blocks south (☎04.94.12.55.12). The modern Hyères–Toulon **airport** is between Hyères and Hyères-Plage, 3km from the centre (☎04.94.00.83.83), to which it's connected by a regular shuttle. The **tourist office** is next door to place Mal-Joffre in the Rotunde Jean-Salusse, on av de Belgique (daily 10am–noon & 2–5.30pm; ☎04.94.65.18.55, fax 04.94.35.85.05). **Bikes** and **mopeds** can be rented from Holiday Bikes, on chemin du Palyestre, between the airport and the gare SNCF (☎04.94.38.79.45), or from the Mistral Centre, on rte de Giens (☎04.94.58.26.87).

Hotels in the old town include the *Hôtel le Soleil*, on rue du Rempart (☎04.94.65.16.26, fax 04.94.35.44.00; ③), in a renovated house at the foot of the parc St-Bernard, and the smaller *Hôtel du Portalet*, 4 rue de Limans (☎04.94.65.39.40, fax 35.86.33; ②). Right in the centre of the modern town, the *Hôtel de la Poste*, 7 av Lyautey (☎04.94.65.02.00; ②), is an inexpensive reliable option. One kilometre from L'Almanarre beach, *La Québécoise*, on av Amiral (☎04.94.57.69.24, fax 04.94.38.78.27; ④; half-board obligatory in July & Aug), is a quiet and very pleasant hotel on the wooded slopes of Costabelle, with a pool and sea views.

There are any number of **campsites** on the coast. Two smaller ones are *Camping-Bernard*, a two-star in Le Ceinturon (☎04.94.66.30.54; open Easter–Sept), and *Clair de Lune*, av du Clair de Lune (☎04.94.58.20.19; open all year), a three-star one on the Presqu'Île de Giens.

The town

Walled and medieval **old Hyères** perches on the slopes of Casteou hill, 5km from the sea; below it lies the **modern town**, with avenue Gambetta the main north–south axis. At the coast, the **Presqu'Île de Giens** is leashed to the mainland by an isthmus, known as **La Capte**, and a parallel sand bar enclosing the salt marshes and a lake. Le Ceinturon, Ayguade and Les Salins d'Hyères are the village-cum-resorts along the coast north-east from Hyères-Plages; L'Almanarre is to the west where the sand bar starts.

From place Clemenceau, a medieval gatehouse, the **Porte Massillon**, opens onto rue Massillon and the **old town**. At **place Massillon**, you encounter a perfect Provençal square, with terraced cafés overlooking the twelfth-century **Tour St-Blaise**, the remnant of a Knights Templar lodge now elegantly converted into exhibition space for contemporary art (10am–noon & 4–7pm; closed Tues; free). To the right of the tower, a street leads uphill to **place St-Paul**, from which you have a panoramic view over a section of medieval town wall to Costabelle hill and the Golfe de Giens.

Wide steps fan out from the Renaissance door of the former collegiate **church of St-Paul** (daily: summer 3–6pm; winter 2.30–5pm), whose distinctive belfry is pure Romanesque, as is the choir, though the simplicity of the design is masked by the collection of votive offerings hung inside. The decoration also includes some splendid wrought-iron candelabras, and a Christmas crib with over-life-size *santons* (traditional crib figures). Today, the church is only used for special services – the main place of worship is the mid-thirteenth-century former monastery **church of St-Louis**, on place de la République.

To the right of St-Paul, a Renaissance house bridges rue St-Paul, its turret supported by a pillar rising beside the steps. Through this arch you can head up rue Ste-Claire to the entrance of **parc Ste-Claire** (daily 8am–dusk; free), the exotic gardens around **Castel Ste-Claire**, once home to the American writer and interior designer Edith Wharton and now the offices of the Parc National de Port-Cros. Cobbled paths lead up the hill towards the **parc St-Bernard** (daily 8am–dusk; free), full of almost every Mediterranean flower known. At the top of the park, above montée des Noailles (which by car you reach from cours Strasbourg and avenue Long), is the **Villa Noailles**, a

Cubist mansion enclosed within part of the old citadel walls, designed by Mallet-Stevens in the 1920s and a home to all the luminaries of Dada and Surrealism. Restoration work should finish by the year 2000 and until then it is only open between the end of June and beginning of September when it's the setting for a major art exhibition (10am–noon & 3–7pm; free). To the west of the park and further up the hill you come to the remains of the **castle**, whose keep and ivy-clad towers outreach the oak and lotus trees and give stunning views out to the Îles d'Hyères and east to the Massif des Maures.

The switch from medieval to eighteenth- and nineteenth-century Hyères at **av des Îles-d'Or** and its continuation, **av Général-de-Gaulle**, is as abrupt as it is as radical, with wide boulevards and open spaces, opulent villas and waving palm fronds. If you're keen on the ancient history of this coast, the **Musée d'Art et d'Archéologie**, on the top floor of the city's administrative building on place Lefèbvre (Mon & Wed–Fri 10am–noon & 2.30–5.30pm; free), should appeal. It displays Roman and Greek finds from L'Almanarre as well as local paintings and natural history exhibits. An alternative pastime is to wander around the spectacular array of cacti and palms in the **Jardins Olbius-Riquier**, just to the south east of the bottom of avenue Gambetta (daily 8am–5.30/7pm; free).

Eating and drinking

For **eating and drinking**, there are the terraced café-brasseries in place Massillon; and, all around this corner of the old town, a good choice of crêperies, pizzerias and little bistrots which serve *plats du jour* for around 80F. *La Bergerie*, 16 rue de Limans (closed Sat lunch & Sun), is a friendly and down-to-earth pizzeria-crêperie. On the edge of the new town, *Les Jardins de Bacchus*, 32 av Gambetta (☎04.94.65.77.63; menus from 145F) serves novel concoctions with panache, while a little way out of town, at 15 av du Toulon, *La Crèche Provençale* (☎04.94.65.30.28; closed Sat lunchtime; menus from 125F) is excellent value for sophisticated food.

Around Hyères

Hyères's coastal suburbs have plenty of beaches for you to choose from, but can be subject to mosquito plagues. **L'Almanarre**, about 5km south of town, hosts French sailing championships at the end of April and has a narrow crescent of sand from which you can swim. **La Capte** is rather built-up, but offers warmer, shallow water and a long sandy beach. Alternatively, take the route du Sel to the **Presqu'Île de Giens** for a glimpse of the saltworks and the flamingos on the adjoining lake. Besides the peculiarity of its attachment to the mainland (last broken by storms in 1811), **Giens** is a fairly nondescript and overpopulated resort. There are, however, some fine cliffs facing the sea, and in rough weather you can understand why so many wrecks have been discovered here. **La Tour Fondue**, a Richelieu construction on the eastern side of Giens, overlooks the small port that serves the Îles d'Hyères.

Traffic fumes and the proximity to the airport make the beaches between Hyères-Plage and Le Centurion/Ayguade rather undesirable despite the pines and ubiquitous palms. Best to head further up the coast to the little fishing port of **Les Salins d'Hyères**. East of Les Salins, where the coastal road finally turns inland, you can follow a path between abandoned saltflats and the sea to a naturist beach.

The Îles d'Hyères

A haven from tempests in ancient times, then the peaceful home of monks and farmers, the **Îles d'Hyères** became, from the Middle Ages onwards, the target of piracy and

FERRIES TO THE ÎLES D'HYÈRES

Departures from

La Tour Fondue on the Presqu'Île de Giens (☎04.94.58.21.81). The closest port to Porquerolles; summer services to all three islands, all year round to Porquerolles.

Toulon, quai Stalingrad (☎04.94.62.41.14). June–Sept services to all three islands.

Le Lavandou, 15 quai Gabriel-Péri (☎04.94.71.01.02). The closest port to Port-Cros and Levant; year-round daily services to Levant and Port-Cros, three-weekly service to Porquerolles (daily from mid-July to Aug).

Port d'Hyères in Hyères-Plage (☎04.94.57.44.07). Services to Port-Cros and Levant all year and to all three islands in July & Aug.

coastal attacks by an endless succession of assorted aggressors. The three main islands, **Porquerolles**, **Port-Cros** and **Levant**, are covered in half-destroyed, rebuilt or abandoned forts, dating from the sixteenth century, when François I started a trend of underfunded fort building, up to the twentieth century, when the German gun positions on Port-Cros and Levant were put out of action by the Americans. Porquerolles and Levant are not yet free of garrisons, thanks to the knack of the French armed forces for securing prime beauty sites for their bases. But their presence has prevented the otherwise inevitable Côte build-up and, in the non-military areas, the islands' very fragile environment is protected by the Parc National de Port-Cros and the Conservatoire Botanique de Porquerolles.

The islands' wild, scented greenery and fine sand beaches constitute the essence of what makes this part of the planet so desirable – and are a reminder of what so much of the mainland coast was like forty years ago. To **stay** on them, the only reasonable option is Levant, as long as you book months in advance. Accommodation on Porquerolles is limited, expensive, and again needs reserving in advance; on Port-Cros it is almost non-existent. All visitors should take note of the signs forbidding smoking (away from the ports), flower-picking and littering.

Île de Porquerolles

The most easily accessible of the Îles d'Hyères is **Porquerolles**, whose permanent village, also called **PORQUEROLLES**, has a few hotels and restaurants, plenty of cafés, a market and interminable games of boules. It dates from a nineteenth-century military settlement, and the village still focuses around the central **place d'Armes**, the erstwhile military exercise ground. In summer its population explodes to over 10,000, but there is some activity all year round. This is the only cultivated island of the three and has its own wine, *appellation* Côtes des Îles.

Porquerolles is big enough to find yourself alone – get lost on – amid its stunning landscapes. The **lighthouse** due south of the village and the **calanques** to its east make good destinations for an hour's walk, though don't even think of swimming on this side of the island. The southern shoreline is all cliffs, with scary paths meandering close to the edge through heather and exuberant *maquis* scrub. The longest beach is the **plage de Notre-Dame**, 3km northeast of the village just before the *terrain militaire* on the northern tip. The nearest beach to the village is the **plage d'Argent**, 1km away (continue west from the port past the Arche de Noë and take the first, well-signed right). This 500-metre strip of white sand fringes a curving bay backed by pine forests, and has a pleasant **restaurant**, *La Plage d'Argent* (☎04.94.58.32.48; April to Sept; midday menu under 100F).

Practicalities

There's a small **information centre** by the harbour (daily June–Sept 9am–12.30pm & 2.30–6pm) where you can get basic maps of the island. You can rent **bikes** from several outlets in the village or pay for one with your ferry ticket at La Tour Fondue. All the **hotels** in Porquerolles have obligatory half-board in season except for the *Relais de la Poste*, place d'Armes (☎04.94.58.30.26, fax 04.94.58.33.57; ⑥; April–Oct) and *Les Mèdes*, rue de la Douane (☎04.94.12.41.24, fax 04.94.58.32.49; ⑦; April–Dec). *Sainte-Anne*, on place d'Armes (☎04.94.58.30.04, fax 04.94.58.32.26; ⑧; mid-Feb to Dec), has the most character. There's no campsite on Porquerolles and *camping sauvage* is strictly forbidden, so it's inadvisable to miss the last ferry to the mainland. Most of the cafés and **restaurants** in the village are pure tourist fodder, with the exception of the *Auberge des Glycines*, on place d'Armes (☎04.94.58.30.36; menu around 120F), but if you arrive in the morning you will be able to buy picnic provisions.

Île de Port-Cros

The dense vegetation and mini-mountains of **Port-Cros** make its exploration much tougher than Porquerolles, even though it is less than half the size. Aside from ruined forts and the handful of buildings around the port, the only intervention on the island's wildlife are the classification labels on some of the plants and the extensive network of paths; you're not supposed to stray from these signposted routes and it would be very difficult to do so given the thickness of the undergrowth. The entire island is a protected zone, and has the richest fauna and flora. Kestrels, eagles and sparrowhawks nest here; there are shrubs that flower and bear fruit at the same time, and more common species like broom, lavender, rosemary and heather flourish in abundance. It takes a couple of hours to walk from the port to the nearest beach, **plage de la Palu**; a similar time to cross the island via the **Vallon de la Solitude** or **Vallon de la Fausse Monnaie**. You can also follow a ten-kilometre **circuit of the island**.

The only **hotel**, *Le Manoir* (☎04.94.05.90.52, fax 04.94.05.90.89; mid-May to mid-Sept; half-board from 700F per head; menus from 255F), is probably booked up till the year 2001. Almost as expensive is dining in the few **restaurants** around the port, though you can get a sandwich or a slice of pizza. Again, **camping** is forbidden.

Île du Levant

The **Île du Levant** – ninety percent military reserve – is almost always humid and sunny. Cultivated plant life goes wild, with the result that giant geraniums and nasturtiums climb three-metre hedges, overhung by gigantic eucalyptus trees and yucca plants. The tiny bit of the island spared by the military is a **nudist colony**, set up in the village of **HELIOPO-LIS** in the early 1930s. About sixty people live here all the year round, joined by thousands who come just for the summer, and by tens of thousands of day-trippers.

Visitors who come to the colony for just a couple of hours tend to be treated as voyeurs. If you **stay**, even for one night, you'll generally receive a much friendlier reception. The three most reasonable **hotels** are *Le Gaëtan* (☎04.94.05.91.78, fax 04.94.36.77.17; April–Oct; ③; half-board obligatory in season), *La Source* (☎04.94.05.91.36, fax 04.94.05.93.47; ③; April to mid-Oct) and *La Brise Marine* (☎04.94.05.91.15, fax 04.94.05.93.21; ③; April–Oct). There are three **campsites**: *Le Colombero* (☎04.94.05.90.29; Easter–Sept), *La Joie de Vivre* (☎04.94.05.90.49; June–Sept) and *La Pinède* (☎04.94.05.90.47; April–Oct).

Levant has a better choice of **restaurants** than the other islands, though prices and quality still don't match, even taking into account the cost of transporting supplies. The restaurant of *La Source* (see above) is reasonable, with a good 130F menu and one around 100F.

The Corniche des Maures

The Côte really gets going with the resorts of the **Corniche des Maures**, as multi-million-dollar residences lurk increasingly in the hills, even more luxurious yachts moor in the bays, and seafront prices become alarming. You can sip the divinest cocktail under the warmest moon, purchase leopard-skin swimwear, or have your car stereo nicked while you're waiting at the lights. This is the place where the rich and famous go to seed: Douglas Fairbanks Jr, the late Grand Duke of Luxembourg, and a host of sundry titled names who have pushed this coastline into legend.

The Corniche des Maures has beaches that shine silver (from the mica crystals in the sand), tall dark pines, oaks and eucalyptus to shade them, glittering rocks of purple, green and reddish hue; and chestnut-forested hills keeping winds away.

Bormes-les-Mimosas and around

Seventeen kilometres east of Hyères, **BORMES-LES-MIMOSAS**, like all good Provençal villages, is indisputably medieval, with a ruined but restored **castle** at the summit of its hill, protected by spiralling lines of pantiled houses backing onto shortcut flights of steps. The mimosas here, and all along the Côte d'Azur, are no more indigenous than the people passing in their Porsches: the tree was introduced from Mexico in the 1860s, but the town still has some of the most luscious climbing flowers of any Côte town.

To the southwest of Bormes is one of those rare unbuilt-up stretches of coast around **BREGANÇON** and **CABASSON**, good wine-growing terrain, harbouring a presidential residence in the castle at **Cap de Bregançon**. Unfortunately, access to the sea is heavily controlled, with three **beaches** charging hefty parking fees (and a small charge for pedestrians and cyclists). The beach by the castle past Cabasson is the best.

Practicalities

Two reasonable **hotels** in old Bormes are *La Terrasse*, 19 place Gambetta (☎04.94.71.15.22; ②), with simple rooms; and the rather plain and old-fashioned *Bellevue*, on place Gambetta (☎04.94.71.15.15; ② per person half-board). In Cabasson, there's also the very attractive and peaceful *Les Palmiers*, 240 chemin du Petit-Fort (☎04.94.64.81.94, fax 04.94.64.04.93.61; ⑥; half-board compulsory in summer) with its own path to the beach. All **campsites** are just below the main road or in La Favière by the mindlessly ugly pleasure port, closer to Le Lavandou than to Bormes. One of the best options is the four-star *Clos-Mar-Jo* at 895 ch de Bénat (☎04.94.71.53.39; April–Sept). For more information, the **tourist office** in Bormes is on place Gambetta (June & Sept daily 9am–12.30pm & 2.30–7pm; July & Aug daily 9am–12.30pm & 3–8pm; Oct–May Mon–Sat 9am–12.30pm & 2–6pm; ☎04.94.71.15.17, fax 04.94.64.79.57).

Good **restaurants** include *La Tonnelle des Délices*, on place Gambetta (☎04.94.71.34.84; closed Wed; menus from around 100F); *L'Escoundudo*, 2 ruelle du Moulin (☎04.94.71.15.53; closed Mon & Tues midday out of season; 100F midday menu, otherwise 160F); and *Pâtes . . . et Pâtes*, on place du Bazar (☎04.94.64.85.75; closed Tues), which serves the best pasta for 100–150F. More ordinary dinners can be had at the less expensive hotels listed above.

Le Lavandou to La Croix-Valmer

One of many Mediterranean fishing villages turned pleasure port, **LE LAVANDOU**, a few kilometres east of Bormes, has nothing wildly special to recommend it, apart from the seduction of its name (which comes from *lavoir* or "wash-house" rather than "lavender"), some tempting shops and a general Azur atmosphere. From the central promenade of quai Gabriel-Péri the sea is hardly visible for pleasure boats moored at the three harbours and it's only upmarket restaurant demand that keeps the dozen or so fishing vessels from a fleet, that once numbered fifty, still in business. If you want to indulge in watersports or nightlife, the **tourist office** on quai Gabriel-Péri (May–Sept Mon–Sat 9am–12.30pm & 2.30–7.30pm, Sun 10am–noon & 3.30–6.30pm; Oct–April Mon–Sat 9am–noon &2.30–6pm; ☎04.94.71.00.61, fax 04.94.64.73.79) will happily advise.

But if you're after the fabled silver beaches you need to head out of town and east along the classic Côte d'Azur corniche lined with pink oleander bushes and purple bougainvillea, to **CAVALIÈRE, PRAMOUSQUIER, LE CANADEL** and **LE RAYOL**. It's hardly countryside, but you can explore the **Pointe du Layet** headland just east of Cavalière, follow the sinuous D27 up to the **Col du Canadel** for breathtaking views and beautiful cork-oak woodland, and, in Le Rayol, visit a superb garden, the **Domaine de Rayol** (daily: Jan–June & Sept–mid Nov 9.30am–12.30pm & 2.30–6.30pm; July & Aug 9.30am–12.30pm & 4.30–8pm; 40F) with plants from different parts of the world that share the Mediterranean climate.

Beyond Le Rayol the corniche climbs away from the coast through 3km of open countryside, scarred almost every year by fires. As abruptly as this wilderness commences, it ends with the choking, hideous sprawl of **Cavalaire-sur-Mer**. From here another exceptional sight of coastline, dressed only in its natural covering of rock and woodlands, is visible across the Baie de Cavalaire. This is the **Domaine de Cap Lardier**, a wonderful coastal conservation area around the southern tip of the St-Tropez peninsula, easily accessible from **La Croix-Valmer**. The resort's centre is some 2.5km from the sea, but this only adds to its charm, since some of the land in between is taken up by vineyards which produce a very decent *Côte de Provence*.

La Croix-Valmer's **tourist office** is in Les Jardins de la Gare (mid-June to mid-Sept Mon–Sat 9am–7pm, Sun 9am–1pm; mid-Sept to mid-June 9am–noon & 2–6pm, closed Sun pm; ☎04.94.55.12.12, fax 04.94.55.12.10) just up from the junction of the D559 and D93. A good-value **hotel** for this part of the world is *La Bienvenue* on rue L-Martin (☎04.94.79.60.23, fax 04.94.79.70.08; ③) in the centre of the village. One of the least expensive options near the beach is the family-run *Hostellerie La Ricarde*, quartier de la Plage (☎04.94.79.64.07, fax 04.94.54.30.14; ③), whilst at the other end of the scale is *Le Château de Valmer*, on rte de Gigaro (☎04.94.79.60.10, fax 04.94.54.22.68; ⑧), a seriously luxurious old Provençal manor house in walking distance of the sea. You can **camp** at the four-star *Sélection*, on bd de la Mer (☎04.94.55.10.30, fax 04.94.55.10.39; mid-March to mid-Oct; booking advisable), 400m from the sea and with excellent facilities. Good, inexpensive pizzas are guaranteed at *L'Italien* (☎04.94.79.67.16) on plage de Gigaro, at almost the last commercial outlet before the conservation area. Two other good but expensive **restaurants** on this beach are *La Brigantine* and *Souleïas*.

The Massif des Maures

The secret of the Côte d'Azur is that however grossly vulgar the conglomeration of the coast, Provence is still just behind – old, sparsely populated, village-orientated and dependent on the land for produce, not real estate. Between Marseille and Menton, the most bewitching hinterland is the **Massif des Maures**, stretching from Hyères to Fréjus. The highest point of these hills stops short of 800m, but the quick succession of ridges, the sudden drops and views and then closure again, and the curling, looping roads, are pervasively mountainous. Where the lie of the land gives a wide bowl of sunlit slopes, vines are grown. Elsewhere the hills are thickly forested, with aleppo and umbrella pines, holly, cork oaks and sweet chestnut trees.

Much of the Massif is inaccessible even to walkers. However, the **GR9 footpath** follows the highest and most northerly ridge from Pignans on the N97 past Notre-Dame-des-Anges, La Sauvette, **La Garde-Freinet** and down to the head of the Golfe de St-Tropez. If you're **cycling**, the **D14** that runs for 42km through the middle, parallel to the coast, from Pierrefeu-du-Var, north of Hyères, to **Cogolin** near St-Tropez, is manageable and stunning, climbing from 150m to 411m above sea level.

Collobrières and La Chartreuse de la Verne

At the heart of the Massif is the ancient village of **COLLOBRIÈRES**, reputed to have been the first place in France to learn from the Spanish that a certain tree plugged into bottles allows a wine industry to grow. From the Middle Ages until very recent times, cork production has been the major business of the village and Collobrières is still the best place in the region to buy items roughly fashioned from raw cork. However, the sweet chestnut tree is the mainstay of the local economy nowadays. The church, the mairie and the houses don't seem to have been modernized this century, but the **Confiserie Azurienne**, bd Koenig (9am–noon & 2–6pm), exudes efficiency and modern business skill in the manufacture of all things chestnut: ice-cream, jam, nougat, purée and *marrons glacés*.

Collobrières' **tourist office** on bd Charles-Caminat (July & Aug Mon–Sat 10am12.30pm & 3.30–6.30pm; Sept–June Tues–Sat 10am–12.30pm & 2.30–6pm; ☎04.94.48.08.00) can supply details of **walks** in the fantastic surrounding hills for 10F. If you're too overdosed on sticky chestnut to move, or you've fallen in love with the place, there are two **hotels**: *Notre-Dame*, 15 av de la Libération (☎04.94.48.07.13, fax 04.94.4805.93; ④), and the excellent-value *Auberge des Maures*, 19 bd Lazare Carnot (☎04.94.48.07.10, fax 02.73; ①, and ② per person full board). There are also two great **chambres d'hôte**: *L'Atelier*, Colette Brésis's ceramic studio at Les Bonnaux, two kilometres west of the village along the D14 (☎04.94.48.05.92; April–Oct; ③); and Andrée Cécile's *La Bastide de La Cabrière*, six kilometres in the direction of Gonfaron on the D39 (☎04.94.48.04.31, fax 04.94.48.09.90; ⑤ breakfast included). A municipal **campsite**, the *St-Roch* south of the village near place Charles-de-Gaulle is open from July to August (bookings through the tourist office on ☎04.94.48.08.00). *Camping sauvage* is forbidden: one stray spark and you could be responsible for a thousand acres of burnt forest.

For **food** other than chestnuts, the **restaurant** *La Petite Fontaine*, 6 place de la République (☎ 04.94.48.00.12; closed Sun eve & Mon), is congenial and affordable, but books up fast. If you want to buy some local **wines**, visit *Les Vignerons de Collobrières* close to the *Hôtel Notre-Dame*. Local **market** days are Thursday and Sunday.

Hidden in the forest, 12km from Collobrières off the D14 towards Grimaud, is the ruin of a huge twelfth-century monastery, **La Chartreuse de la Verne** (WedMon: June–Sept 11am–6pm, Oct & Dec–May 11am–5pm; closed all Nov; 30F), abandoned at the time of the Revolution. Though now much restored, it still retains its desolate atmosphere.

La Garde-Freinet

LA GARDE-FREINET, 8km northwest of La Croix-Valmer, was the Saracens' tenth-century base for their occupation of the Maures. The foundations of their fortress are still visible above the village beside the ruins of a fifteenth-century castle (take the path from La Planette car park at the eastern end of the village). Today the occupiers of the village include Oxbridge professors and other leisured Brits, but it still feels that it belongs to the locals (thanks in part to the regeneration of forestry business around cork and chestnut). It also has top-notch medieval charm; easy walks to stunning panoramas; markets twice a week (Wed & Sun); a chestnut co-operative on the northern approach to the village; tempting food shops like La Voute, selling organic produce and good local wines; and very reasonable accommodation possibilities. The enthusiastic and helpful **tourist office** operates from 1 place Neuve (July & Aug Mon–Sun am 10am–12.30pm & 3–6pm; Sept–June Mon–Sat same hours; ☎04.94.43.67.41), and will provide details for all of the Maures region, including suggested walks and hikes such as the spectacular 21-kilometre GR9 **route des Crêtes** to the west of the village.

For **rooms**, *La Sarrazine* (☎04.94.43.67.16; ②), on the main road after it turns west at the top of the village and *La Claire Fontaine*, on place Vieille (☎04.94.43.60.36, fax 04.94.43.63.76; ②), and *Le Fraxinois*, on rue François-Pelletier (☎04.94.43.62.84, fax 04.94.43.69.65; ③), are incredibly good value for this part of the world. The two three-star **campsites** are the municipal *St-Eloi*, opposite the municipal pool (☎04.94.43.62.40; June–Sept), and *La Ferme de Bérard*, five kilometres along the D558 towards Grimaud (☎04.94.43.21.23, fax 04.94.43.32.33; Easter–Oct).

The place to be of an evening is *Le Lézard* bar, art gallery and **restaurant**, on the exquisite place du Marché (☎04.94.43.62.73; closed Sun; menu under 100F; jazz concerts held every second Sat). *La Colombe Joyeuse* on place Vieille (lunchtime menu at 95F; closed Mon; ☎04.94.43.65.24) has pigeon as its à la carte speciality, whilst *La Faucado*, on the main road to the south (☎04.94.43.60.41; closed Tues and Jan–Feb; 110F midday menu, otherwise à la carte from 300F), is overpriced, but serves some beautiful dishes from local produce.

Grimaud

GRIMAUD, halfway between la Garde-Freinet and the Golfe de St-Tropez, is a film set of a *village perché*. The cone of houses enclosing the eleventh-century church and culminating in the ruins of a medieval castle appears as a single, perfectly unified entity, decorated by its trees and flowers. The most vaunted street in this ensemble is the arcaded **rue des Templiers**, which leads up to the pure Romanesque **Église de St-Michel** and a house of the Knights Templar. The view from the **castle** ruins is superb. There is a small **tourist office** at 1 bld des Aliziers just off the main road passing the village (Mon–Sat: July & Aug 9am–12.30pm & 3–7pm; Sept–June 9am–12.30pm & 2.30–6.30pm; ☎04.94.43.26.98). If you're stopping to **eat**, prime-value midday menus from 120F are offered at *Le Coteau Fleuri*, place des Pénitents (☎04.94.43.20.17, fax 04.94.43.33.42; d; closed Tues except in July & Aug), which also has a few **rooms**.

Cogolin

COGOLIN, the town just south of Grimaud, is remarkable for its combination of tourism with traditional craft manufacturing – of reeds for wind instruments, pipes for smoking, wrought-iron furniture, silk yarn and knotted wool carpets. These are all serious businesses for the one-off, made-to-order, high-quality and high-cost Côte d'Azur market. As a consequence Cogolin is fairly animated all year round.

Visits to some of the **craft factories** can be arranged and are free. The helpful **tourist office** on place de la République (July & Aug Mon–Sat 9am–12.30pm & 2.30–7pm, Sun 9.30am–12.30pm; rest of year Mon–Fri 9am–noon & 2.30–6.30pm, Sat 9am–noon; ☎04.94.55.01.10, fax 04.94.55.01.11) will provide you with a complete list of addresses and times, and help with making appointments. Or you can just wander down **avenue Georges-Clemenceau** and pop into the retail outlets. Pipes made from briar wood are on show in Courrieu, at no. 58; the Manufacture de Tapis, just off the avenue on boulevard Louis-Blanc, recreates designs by famous artists such as Léger and Mondrian (exhibition room open Mon–Fri 9am–noon & 2–6pm); and world-famous musicians get their reeds from Rigotti, on rue Barbusse.

From place Bellevue, at the top of the town away from the bustling centre, you can see across the St-Tropez peninsula, to Gassin, Ramatuelle and St-Tropez itself. Having taken in that view and seen enough of Cogolin's manufacturing businesses, the one thing left to do is try the local **wines**: the *Cave des Vignerons* is on rue Marceau, just before the junction with the N98 heading westwards (closed Sun out of season). There are several reasonably inexpensive **hotels** in Cogolin clustered close together that make viable bases for trips into congested St-Tropez: the amiable, comfortable *Coq Hôtel*, pl de la Mairie (☎04.94.54.13.71, fax 04.94.54.03.06; ③); the *Clemenceau* (☎04.94.54.15.17, fax 04.94.54.42.78; ③) next door at 1 rue Carnot; and the *du Golfe* (☎04.94.54.30.34, fax 04.94.54.14.48; ③) at 13 av Clemenceau.

St-Tropez and its peninsula

The origins of **ST-TROPEZ** are unremarkable: a little fishing village that grew up around a port founded by the Greeks of Marseille, which was destroyed by the Saracens in 739 and finally fortified in the late Middle Ages. Its sole distinction from the myriad other fishing villages along this coast was its inaccessibility. Stuck out on the southern shores of the Golfe de St-Tropez, away from the main coastal routes on a wide peninsula that never warranted real roads, St-Tropez could only easily be reached by boat. This held true as late as the 1880s, when the novelist Guy de Maupassant sailed his yacht into the port during his final high-living binge before the onset of syphilitic insanity.

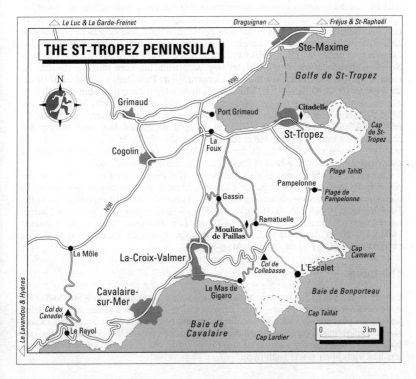

Soon after de Maupassant's fleeting visit, the painter and leader of the neo-Impressionists, Paul Signac, was sailing down the coast when bad weather forced him to moor in St-Tropez. He instantly decided to build a house there, to which he invited his friends. Matisse was one of the first to accept, with Bonnard, Marquet, Dufy, Dérain, Vlaminck, Seurat and Van Dongen following suit, and by the eve of World War I St-Tropez was pretty well established as a hang-out for bohemians. The 1930s saw a new influx of artists, this time more as much as painters: Cocteau, Colette and Anaïs Nin, whose journal records "girls riding bare-breasted in the back of open cars". In 1956 Roger Vadim arrived to film Brigitte Bardot in *Et Dieu Créa la Femme*. The international cult of Tropezian sun, sex and celebrities took off – even the 1960s hippies who flocked to the revamped Mediterranean Mecca of liberation managed to look glamorous – and the resort has been big-money mainstream ever since.

Arrival, information and accommodation

Buses run between the main coast road at **La Foux** and St-Tropez, 5.5km away, every two hours or so (in summer), dropping you at the **gare routière** on av Général-de-Gaulle. From here it's a short walk, along av du 8-Mai-1945, to the **Vieux Port** where you'll find the **tourist office** opposite, on quai Jean-Jaurès (summer daily 9.30am–1pm & 3–10.30pm; winter Mon–Sat 9am–1pm & 2–7pm; ☎04.94.97.45.21, fax 04.94.97.79.08). **Bikes** can be rented at MAS (☎04.94.97.00.60; April to mid-Oct) at 3 rue Joseph Quaranta.

With more and more people wanting to pay homage to St-Trop, **accommodation** is a problem; indeed, between April and September you won't find a room unless you've booked months in advance or are prepared to pay exorbitant prices. The tourist office can help with reservations, but, transport permitting, you might be better off staying in La Croix-Valmer or La Garde-Freinet (see pp.950 and 951). Out of season you may be luckier, though in winter few **hotels** stay open. One of the cheaper options is *Les Chimères*, Quartier du Pilon (☎04.94.97.02.90, fax 04.94.97.63.57; ④; mid-Feb to mid-Nov & Christmas/New Year), a short way back from the gare routière towards La Foux; if they're booked up, try the *Lou Cagnard*, 18 av Paul Roussel (☎04.94.97.04.24, fax 04.94.97.09.44; ④; Jan—Oct), which looks dreary from the outside but has a decent garden, or the rather scruffy *La Méditerranée*, 21 bd Louis-Blanc (☎04.94.97.00.44, fax 04.94.97.47.83; ③; open all year). If you're prepared to blow more cash, *Le Baron*, 23 rue de l'Aïïoli (☎04.94.97.06.57, fax 04.94.97.58.72; ⑥; closed Jan), overlooking the citadel, is a bit quieter than those in the centre, or there's the luxurious *La Ponche*, on place du Révelin (☎04.94.97.02.53, fax 04.94.97.78.61; ⑧; April—Oct), an old block of fishermen's houses with a host of famous arty names in its guest book.

Camping near St-Tropez is also a problem. The nearest are the two sites on the plage du Pampelonne, which charge extortionate rates and are massively crowded in high summer. Otherwise, 6km away on the N559 near Gassin is the three-star *Camping Parc Montana* (☎04.94.55.20.20, fax 04.94.56.34.77; April–Sept). Within a three-kilometre radius of Ramatuelle (see p.956) are *Les Tournels*, on rte de Camarat (☎04.94.55.90.90, fax ☎04.94.55.90.99), and *La Croix du Sud*, rte des Plages (☎04.94.79.80.84, fax 04.94.79.89.21; May–Sept).

The town

Beware of coming to St-Tropez in high summer, unless by yacht and with limitless credit. The road from Le Foux has traffic jams as bad as Nice or Marseille; the pedestrian jams to the port are not much better; the hotels and restaurants are full and very expensive; overnighting in vehicles is prohibited; the beaches are not the cleanest . . . So save your visit, if you can, for a spring or autumn day, and you'll understand why this place has had such history and such hype.

The **Vieux Port**, with the old town rising above the eastern quay, is where you'll get the classic St-Tropez experience: the quayside café clientele *face-à-face* with the yacht-deck martini sippers, and the latest fashions parading in between, defining the French word *frimer*, which means to stroll ostentatiously in places like St-Tropez. It's surprising just how entertaining this spectacle can be.

Up from the port, at the end of quai Jean-Jaurès, you enter place de l'Hôtel-de-Ville, with the **Château Suffren**, originally built in 980 by Count Guillaume 1er of Provence (occasionally hosting art exhibitions), and the very pretty mairie. A street to the left leads down to the rocky **baie de la Glaye**; while, straight ahead, rue de la Ponche passes through an ancient gateway to place du Revelin above the **fishing port** and its tiny beach. Turning inland and upwards, struggling past continuous shop fronts, stalls and café tables, you finally reach the open space around the sixteenth-century **citadel**. Its maritime museum is not much fun, but the walk round the ramparts on an overgrown path has the best views of the gulf and the back of the town – views that have not changed since their translations in oil onto canvas before the war.

Some of these paintings you can see at the marvellous **Musée de l'Annonciade**, in the deconsecrated sixteenth-century chapel on place Georges-Grammont, just west of the port (Wed–Mon: June–Sept 10am–noon & 3–7pm; Oct–May 10am–noon & 2–6pm; closed Nov; 25F). It was originally Signac's idea to have a permanent exhibition space for the neo-Impressionists and Fauvists who painted here, though it was not until 1955 that the collections of various individuals were put together. The Annonciade features works by Signac, Matisse and most of the other artists who worked here: grey, grim, northern views of Paris, Boulogne and Westminster, and then local, brilliantly sunlit scenes by the same brush – a real delight and unrivalled outside Paris for the 1890–1940 period of French art.

The other pole of St-Trop's life, south of the Vieux Port, is **place des Lices**. The café-brasseries have become a bit too Champs-Elysées in style, and a new commercial block has been added near the northern corner, but you can still sit on benches in the shade of sad but surviving plane trees and watch the boules games.

The beaches

The beach within easy walking distance is **Les Graniers**, below the citadel just beyond the port des Pêcheurs along rue Cavaillon. From there, a path follows the coast around the **baie des Canoubiers**, with its small beach, to Cap St-Pierre, Cap St-Tropez, the very crowded **Les Salins** beach and right round to **Tahiti-Plage**, about 11km away.

Tahiti-Plage is the start of the almost straight, five-kilometre north–south **Pampelonne** beach, famous bronzing belt of St-Tropez and world initiator of the topless bathing cult. The water is shallow for 50m or so, and the beach is exposed to the wind, and sometimes scourged by dried sea vegetation, not to mention more distasteful garbage. But spotless glitter comes from the unending line of beach bars and restaurants, all with patios and sofas, serving cocktails and gluttonous ice-creams (as well as full-blown meals).Though you'll stumble across people in the nude on all stretches of the beach, only some of the bars welcome people carrying wallets and nothing else.

Transport from St-Tropez to the beaches is provided by a frequent **minibus** service from place des Lices to Salins and Pampelonne, or a bus from the gare routière to Tahiti, Pampelonne and L'Escalet. If you're driving, you'll be forced to pay high parking charges at all the beaches, or to leave your car or motorbike some distance from the sea and easy prey to thieves.

Eating and drinking

There are **restaurants** to cover every budget in St-Tropez, as well as plenty of snack bars and takeaway outfits, particularly on rue Georges-Clemenceau and place des Lices.

Auberge des Maures, rue du Dr Boutin, off rue Aillard (☎04.94.97.01.50). Roast lamb, stuffed peppers and gooey chocolate cake at reasonable prices; menus from 130F.

Bistrot des Lices, 3 place des Lices (☎04.94.97.29.00). Turn-of-the-century decor for traditional preening and overpriced eats; midday menu 185F, otherwise from 280F; closed Thurs mid-Oct to Dec & Jan–March.

Café des Arts, place des Lices (☎04.94.97.02.25). The number-one brasserie on the square. Old-timers still gather in the bar at the back. Menus from 200F.

Café Sénéquier, on the port. The top quayside café, horribly expensive, but selling sensational nougat (also on sale from the shop at the back).

Glaces Alfred, rue Sibille. Ice-creams made on the premises.

Le Gorille, quai Suffren (☎04.94.97.03.93). Straightforward quayside fare of *plats du jour, moules-frites*, hamburgers, etc. Under 100F. Open 24hr in July & Aug.

Joseph, 5 rue Cepoun-San-Martin and 6 rue Sibille (☎04.94.97.03.90). Good bouillabaisse and *bour-ride*, and great desserts; 160F menu, à la carte 250F upwards.

La Patate, rue Clemenceau. Snack bar with omelettes, pasta, *pain beignets* and so forth.

Le Petit Charron, 6 rue des Charrons (☎04.94.97.73.78). Tiny terrace and dining room serving beautifully cooked Provençal specialities. Midday menu under 80F, otherwise from 130F; closed Wed out of season.

Regis et Lolo, montée de la Citadelle (☎04.94.97.15.53). Small, friendly bistrot, usually full of exuberant youth; around 140F.

La Tarte Tropezienne, 1 rue G-Clemenceau. Pâtisserie claiming to have invented this sponge and cream custard cake.

Nightlife

In season St-Tropez stays up late, as you'd expect. You can spend the evening trying on fancy clothes in the amazing array of couturier shops; the boules games on place des Lices continue till well after dusk; and the portside spectacle doesn't falter till the early hours. If you're mad enough to want to pay to see – and be seen with – the **nightlife** creatures of St-Trop, clubs include *Les Caves du Roy*, in the flashy *Hôtel Byblos* on rue Paul-Signac (the most expensive and exclusive); *L'Esquinade*, on rue du Four, which has been going strong since Bardot was young; and the **gay** disco *Le Pigeonnier*, 13 rue de la Ponche. All are open every night in summer, and usually Saturday only in winter.

Gassin and Ramatuelle

Though the coast of the **St-Tropez peninsula** sprouts second residences like a cabbage patch gone to seed, the interior is almost uninhabited, thanks to government intervention, complex ownerships and the value of some local wines. The best view of this richly green and flowering countryside is from the hilltop village of Gassin, its lower neighbour Ramatuelle, or the tiny road between them, the dramatic route des Moulins de Paillas, where three ruined windmills could once catch every wind.

GASSIN is the shape and size of a small ship perched on a summit; once a Moorish stronghold, it is now, of course, highly chic. It's an excellent place for a blowout dinner, sitting outside by the village wall with a spectacular panorama east over the peninsula. Of the handful of **restaurants**, *Bello Visto*, 9 place des Barrys (☎04.94.56.17.30, fax 04.94.43.45.36; closed Tues), has very acceptable Provençal specialities on a 120F menu, plus nine **rooms** at excellent prices for this brilliant setting (④).

RAMATUELLE is bigger than its neighbour, though just as old, and is surrounded by some of the best Côte de Provence vineyards. The twisting, arcaded streets are full of arts and crafts of dubious talent, but it's all very pleasant nonetheless. The most beautiful French actor ever to have appeared on screen, Gérard Philippe (1922–59), is buried in Ramatuelle's **cemetery**. His ivy-covered tomb, shaded by a rose bush, is set against the wall on the right as you look down. **Hotels** worth trying are *Chez Tony*, 31 rue Clemenceau (☎04.94.79.20.46; ②), and *Lou Castellas*, rte des Moulins (☎ & fax 04.94.79.20.67; ③); great pasta dishes are to be had at *Au Fil à la Pâte*, 27 rue Victor-Léon (☎04.94.79.27.81; closed Wed; good *plat du jours* at 85F).

Port Grimaud

At the head of the Golfe de St-Tropez, just north of La Foux on the main coast road, the ultimate Côte d'Azur property development half stands and half floats. **PORT GRI-MAUD** was created in the 1960s as a private lagoon pleasure city, with waterways for roads and yachts parked at the bottom of every garden. All the houses are in exquis-itely tasteful old Provençal style and their owners, Joan Collins for example, more than just a little well-heeled. In a way it's surprising that the whole enclave isn't wired off and patrolled by Alsatian dogs.

The main visitors' entrance is 800m up the well-signed road off the N98. You don't have to pay to get in, but you can't explore all the islands without hiring a boat or join-ing a crowded boat tour (around 18F). Even access to the church tower for views is con-trolled by an automatic paying barrier (5F). However, if you want to **eat and drink**, there are rows upon rows of brasseries, restaurants and cafés, clearly designed for the visiting public rather than the residents, and not particularly good value (though afford-able enough).

Ste-Maxime and around

Facing St-Tropez across its gulf, **STE-MAXIME** is the perfect Côte stereotype: palmed corniche and enormous pleasure-boat harbour, beaches crowded with confident bronzed windsurfers and waterskiers, and an outnumbering of estate agents to any other businesses by something like ten to one. It sprawls a little too much – like many of its neighbours – but the magnetic appeal of the water's edge is hard to deny.

To enjoy the resort, however, requires money. If your budget denies you the pleasures of promenade cocktail sipping and seafood-platter picking (not to mention waterskiing, wet-biking and windsurfing), you might as well choose somewhere rather prettier to swim, lie on the beach and walk along the shore.

For the spenders, **Cherry Beach** (or its five neighbours on the east-facing plage de la Nartelle, 2km west from the centre towards Les Issambres), is the strip of sand to head for. As well as paying for shaded cushioned comfort, you can enter the water on a variety of different vehicles, eat grilled fish, have drinks brought to your mattress, and listen to a piano player as dusk falls. A further 4km on, **plage des Eléphants** has much the same facilities but is slightly cheaper.

Ste-Maxime's *vieille ville* has several good **markets**: a covered flower and food mar-ket on rue Fernand-Bessy (winter Tues–Sun 6am–1pm & 4.30–8pm); a fish market every morning on quai des Plaisanciers; a Thursday morning food market on and around place du Marché; bric-a-brac every second and third Saturday of the month on place Jean-Mermoz; and arts and crafts in the pedestrian streets (summer daily 10am–11pm).

High up in the Massif des Maures on the road to Le Muy, some 10km north of Ste-Maxime, the marvellous **Musée du Phonographe et de la Musique Mécanique**, in the parc St-Donat (Easter to mid-Oct Wed–Sun 10am–noon & 3–6pm; 15F), is the result of one amazing woman's forty-year obsession with collecting audio equipment. She has amassed a wide selection of automata, musical boxes and pianolas, as well as various outstanding pieces: one of Thomas Edison's "talking machines" of 1878, the first recording machines of the 1890s, and an amplified lyre (1903). Almost half the exhibits still work. If you get a tour from Madame herself, you'll find it hard to resist her enthusiasm for the history of this branch of twentieth-century technology. You can get the Le Muy bus to here from Ste-Maxime's place J-Mermoz.

Practicalities

Buses into town stop outside the **tourist office** on the promenade Simon-Lorière (July & Aug Mon–Sat 9am–8pm, Sun 10am–noon & 4–7pm; rest of year Mon–Sat 9am–12.30pm & 2–6/7pm; ☎04.94.96.19.24, fax 04.94.49.17.97), which can give you all the relevant information on trips and pleasures and will advise on hotel vacancies – once again, rare in summer. If you're heading for St-Tropez from Ste-Maxime, an alternative to the bus, at not much greater cost, is to go by **boat**; the twenty-minute service from Ste-Maxime's gare maritime on the port runs daily from April to October, with more frequent crossings in July and August. **Bikes** can be rented at Holiday Bikes, 8 av St-Exupéry (☎04.94.43.90.19).

The best of the cheaper hotels is the good-value and welcoming *Auberge Provençale*, 49 rue Aristide Briand (☎04.94.55.76.90, fax 04.94.55.76.91; ③), with its own restaurant; or there's the small *Castellamar*, 21 av G-Pompidou (☎04.94.96.19.97; closed mid-Nov to Dec; ③), on the west side of the river but still close to the centre and the sea. For more expensive surroundings, the *Hôtel de la Poste*, 11 bd Frédéric-Mistral (☎04.94.96.18.33, fax 04.94.96.41.68; ⑤), is an ugly modern construction but with very nice rooms and is right in the centre; or the Marie-Louise, 2km west in the Hameau de Guerre-Vieille (☎04.94.96.06.05; ④), tucked away in greenery but in sight of the sea. For camping, *Les Cigalons*, in quartier de la Nartelle, is the three-star seaside option (June to mid-Sept; ☎04.94.96.05.51, fax 79.62.

For non-beach eating, the *Hostellerie de la Belle Aurore*, 4 bd Jean-Moulin (closed Wed lunctime & Oct–March; ☎04.94.96.02.45; weekday menu 180F), offers gourmet food on a sea-view terrace; or, less expensively, there are good fish dishes at Le Sarrazin, 7 place Colbert (☎04.94.96.10.84; closed Tues out of season & Jan; menus from 110F).

Fréjus and St-Raphaël

The major conurbation of **St-Raphaël** on the coast and **Fréjus**, centre 3km inland, has a history dating back to the Romans. Fréjus was established as a naval base under Julius Cæsar and Augustus, St-Raphaël as a resort for its veterans. The ancient port at Fréjus, or Forum Julii, had 2km of quays and was connected by a walled canal to the sea, which was considerably closer then. After the battle of Actium in 31 AD, the ships of Antony and Cleopatra's defeated fleet were brought here.

The area between Fréjus and the sea is now the suburb of **Fréjus-Plage** with a hideous 1980s development of a marina, **Port-Fréjus**. Both Fréjus and Fréjus-Plage merge with St-Raphaël, which in turn merges with **Boulouris** to the east.

Despite the obsession with facilities for the seaborne rich – there were already two pleasure ports at St-Raphaël before Port-Fréjus was built – this is no bad place for a stopover. There's a wide price range of hotels and restaurants in St-Raphaël, good transport links, and some interesting sightseeing to be done in Fréjus.

Fréjus

The population of **FRÉJUS**, remarkably, was greater in the first century BC than it is today if you just count the residents of the town centre, which lies well within the Roman perimeter. But very little remains of the original Roman walls that once circled the city; and the harbour that made Fréjus an important Mediterranean port silted up early on and was finally filled in after the Revolution. It is the **medieval centre**, much more than the classical remnants, that evokes a feel for this ancient town.

Arrival, information and accommodation

About four trains a day stop at Fréjus's **gare SNCF**, just three to four minutes away from St-Raphaël. Buses between the two towns are much more frequent and take ten minutes on the St-Raphaël–Draguignan route. The **gare routière** is on the east side of the town centre on place Paul-Vernet (☎04.94.53.78.46), opposite which is the **tourist office**, at 325 rue Jean-Jaurès (Mon–Sat 9am–noon & 2–6pm, Sun 10am–noon & 2.30–5.30pm; ☎04.94.17.19.19, fax 04.94.51.00.26). Holiday Bikes, 943 av de Provence (☎04.94.52.30.65), has **bikes** for rent.

If you're looking to stay the night in Fréjus, three central **hotels** worth trying are the plush *Aréna*, 139 rue de Général-de-Gaulle (☎04.94.17.09.40, fax 04.94.52.01.52; ⑤), with pretty, if rather small rooms and a pool; *La Bellevue*, place Paul-Vernet (☎04.94.51.39.04, fax 04.94.51.35.20; ②), in a convenient though not particularly quiet location; and *La Riviera*, 90 rue Grisolle (☎04.94.51.31.46; ②), very small and not very modern, but clean and perfectly acceptable. There's an HI **hostel** 2km northeast from the centre of Fréjus at chemin du Counillier (☎04.94.53.18.75, fax 04.94.53.25.86); bus #7 leaves quai 7 of St-Raphaël gare routière at 6pm, or take a regular bus #4, #8 or #9 from St-Raphaël or Fréjus, direction "L'Hôpital" to stop Les Chênes and walk up av du Gal-d'Armée Jean-Calies – the chemin du Counillier is the first left. There is also a large **campsite** in the grounds. An alternative campsite is *Les Acacias*, 370 rue Henri-Giraud (☎04.94.53.21.22), 2.5km from the centre and open all year.

The Roman town

A tour of the Roman remains will give you a good idea of the extent of Forum Julii, but they are scattered throughout and beyond the town centre and take a full day to get around. Turning right out of the gare SNCF and then right down boulevard Severin-Decuers brings you to the **Butte St-Antoine**, against whose east wall the waters of the port would have lapped, and which once was capped by a fort. It was one of the port's defences, and one of the ruined **towers** may have been a lighthouse. A path around the southern wall follows the quayside (odd stretches are visible) to the medieval **Lanterne d'Auguste**, built on the Roman foundations of a structure marking the entrance of the canal into the ancient harbour.

In the other direction from the station, past the Roman **Porte des Gaules** and along rue Henri-Vadon, you come to the **amphitheatre** (Wed–Mon 9/9.30am–noon & 2–4.30/6.30pm; free), smaller than those at Arles and Nimes, but still able to seat around 10,000. Today it's used for bullfights and concerts. Its upper tiers have been reconstructed in the same greenish local stone used by the Romans, but the vaulted galleries on the ground floor are largely original. The Roman **theatre** (Wed–Mon 9.30am–5/6pm; free) is north of the town, along avenue du Théâtre-Romain, its original seats long gone, though again it is still used for shows in summer. Northeast of it, at the end of avenue du XVème-Corps-d'Armée, a few arches are visible of the forty-kilo-metre **aqueduct**, once as high as the ramparts. Closer to the centre, on rue des Moulins, are the arcades of the **Porte d'Orée**, positioned on the former harbour's edge alongside what was probably a **bath complex**.

The medieval town

The **Cité Episcopale**, or cathedral close, takes up two sides of **place Formigé**, the marketplace and heart of both contemporary and medieval Fréjus. It comprises the cathedral flanked by the fourteenth-century bishop's palace, now the Hôtel de Ville, the baptistry, chapterhouse, cloisters and archeological museum. Visits to the cloisters and baptistry are guided (April–Sept daily 9am–7pm; Oct–March Tues–Sun 9am–noon & 2–5pm; 25F including entrance to museum); access to the main body of the cathedral is free (9am–noon & 4–6pm).

The oldest part of the complex is the **baptistry**, built in the fourth or fifth century and so contemporary with the decline and fall of the city's Roman founders. Its two doorways are of different heights, signifying the enlarged spiritual stature of the baptized. Bits of the early Gothic **cathedral** may belong to a tenth-century church, but its best features, apart from the bright diamond-shaped tiles on the spire, are Renaissance: the choir stalls, a wooden crucifix on the left of the entrance, and the intricately carved doors with scenes of a Saracen massacre, protected by a wooden cover and only opened for the guided tours. Far the most beautiful and engaging component of the whole ensemble, however, are the **cloisters**. In a small garden of scented bushes around a well, slender marble columns, carved in the twelfth century, support a fourteenth-century ceiling of wooden panels painted with apocalyptic creatures. Out of the original 1200 pictures, 400 remain, each about the size of this page. The subjects include multi-headed monsters, mermaids, satyrs and scenes of bacchanalian debauchery. The **Musée Archéologique** on the upper storey of the cloisters is an archeological museum, whose star pieces are a complete Roman mosaic of a leopard and a copy of a double-headed bust of Hermes.

Eating and drinking

One of the best **restaurants** in the old town is the tiny *Les Potiers*, 135 rue des Potiers (☎04.94.51.33.74), with menus of fresh seasonal ingredients from 165F. The similarly priced restaurant at *L'Aréna* hotel (see p.959) is excellent for fish and seafood (closed Sat & Mon midday in season, plus Sun eve out of season). Cheaper eats can be found on place Agricola, place de la Liberté and the main shopping streets. *L'Arcosolium*, rue V-Paulin, offers a vegetarian menu at 90F, as well as *moules* and seafood. At Fréjus-Plage there's a string of eating houses to choose from, with more upmarket *plateau des fruits de mer* outlets at Port-Fréjus. The *Bar du Marché*, on the place de la Liberté, is a good establishment for a bit of café lounging. The main **market days** are Wednesday and Saturday, plus Monday in summer.

Around Fréjus

Unlikely remnants of the more recent past come in the shape of a **Vietnamese pagoda** and an abandoned **mosque**, both built by French colonial troops. The pagoda (daily 9am–noon & 3–6.30pm), still maintained as a Buddhist temple, is on the crossroads of the RN7 to Cannes and the D100, about 2km out of Fréjus. The Mosquée Missiri de Djenné is on the left off the D4 to Bagnols, in the middle of an army camp 2km from the RN7 junction. A strange, guava-coloured, fort-like building, it is a replica of a Sudanese mosque in Mali, decorated inside with fading murals of desert journeys gracefully sketched in white on the dark-pink walls.

Fréjus has a **modern art gallery** (Tues–Sun 2–6/7pm; winter Tues–Sat; free), bizarrely located in the *Zone Industrielle du Capitou* just by turnoff 38 from the motorway; from place Paul-Vernet, take bus #2 to Z.I. Capitou. It has no permanent collection but some quite interesting temporary exhibitions.

If you like **zoos** there's one just across the motorway from Capitou (May–Sept 9.30am–6pm, Oct–April 10am–5pm; 57F, children 33F; bus #2). A kinder habitat, for the human young at least, is the **water amusement park**, Aquatica (daily: July & Aug 10am–7pm; June & Sept 10am–6pm; 98F, children 55F; bus #19 or #29), off the RN98 to St-Aygulf. Toboggans and pedal boats; chutes into an enchanted river; lakes, a huge swimming pool with artificial waves, a beach for the less energetic and a Black Hole are some of its main attractions. In the same entertainment zone there's a **funfair**, a **go-cart track** Azur Karting (mid-June to mid-Sept daily 11am–midnight, rest of year daily except Tues 11am–9pm; 80F, children 45F) and a one-kilometre motorbike and quad circuit (daily 11am–9pm/midnight; 80F).

St-Raphaël

A large resort and now one of the richest towns on the Côte, **ST-RAPHAËL** became fashionable at the turn of the century. Its seafront Belle Époque mansions and hotels, flattened by bombardments in World War II, have mostly been rebuilt, while the **old town** beyond place Carnot on the other side of the railway line has suffered years of neglect. On rue des Templiers a crumbling fortified Romanesque church, the **Église St-Pierre**, has fragments of the Roman aqueduct that brought water from Fréjus in its courtyard along with a local history and underwater archeology **museum** (church and museum Mon–Sat 10am–noon & 2–5pm; winter Wed–Mon 10am–noon & 3–6pm; free).

The **beaches** stretch between the old port in the centre and the newer **Port Santa Lucia**, with opportunities for every kind of water sport. You can also take boat trips to St-Tropez, the Iles d'Hyères and the much closer *calanques* of the Esterel coast from the gare maritime on the south side of the Vieux Port. When you're tired of sea and sand you can lose whatever money you have left on slot machines or blackjack at the **Grand Casino** on Square de Gand overlooking the Vieux Port (daily 11am–4am), or there's **bowling** at the Bowling Raphaëlois, on promenade René-Coty, and plenty of snooty discotheques.

Arrival, information and accommodation

St-Raphaël's **gare SNCF**, in the centre of town, is the main station for the Marseille–Ventigmilia line; the **gare routière** is on avenue Victor-Hugo (☎04.94.95.16.71), across the railway line behind the gare SNCF. A poor accommodation service and information on the surrounding region are available from the unhelpful **tourist office**, just to the left out of the gare SNCF on rue W-Rousseau (daily 8.30am–7pm; ☎04.94.19.52.52, fax 04.94.83.85.40). **Bikes** can be hired from Patrick Moto, 280 av Général-Leclerc (☎04.94.53.87.11).

Seafront **accommodation** in St-Raphaël is available on promenade René-Coty at the *Beau Séjour*, (☎04.94.95.03.75, fax 04.94.83.89.99; ④), one of the cheaper hotels along here, with a pleasant terrace; or at the *Excelsior* (☎04.94.95.02.42, fax 04.94.95.33.82; ⑦), whose rooms are luxurious and well-equipped. *Bellevue*, 22 bd Félix-Martin (☎04.94.19.90.10, fax 04.94.19.90.11; ③), is good value for its central location; and *La Bonne Auberge*, 54 rue de la Garonne (☎04.94.95.69.72; ③), is a cheapie close to the old port. East of the centre, the *Hôtel du Soleil*, 47 bd du Domaine de Soleil, off bd Christian-Lafon (☎04.94.83.10.00, fax 04.94.83.84.70; ③), is a small, pretty villa with its own garden. There's **hostel** accommodation and double rooms in Boulouris, 5km east of St-Raphaël, at the *Centre International Le Manoir*, impasse Raoul Blanchard, chemin de l'Escale (☎04.94.95.20.58, fax 04.94.83.85.06; ③). The *Centre* has friendly, helpful staff and is close to the beach right by the Boulouris gare SNCF (trains or buses every 30 min from St-Raphaël). A four-star **campsite** close to the beach, *Le Val Fleury*, on the N98 in Boulouris (☎04.94.95.21.52, fax 19.09.47), is open all year.

Eating and drinking

Food markets are held every day on place Victor-Hugo and place de la République. You'll find reasonably priced cafés and brasseries around these, and plenty of pizzerias, crêperies and restaurants of varying quality around Port Santa Lucia and along the promenades. Of the more expensive establishments, two of the best are *Le Sirocco*, 35 quai Albert-1er (☎04.94.95.39.99), a smart restaurant specializing in fish, with a menu for around 125F plus a view of the sea; and *Pastorel*, 54 rue de la Liberté (☎04.94.95.02.36; closed Sun & Mon), with menus from around 160F, which has decently priced Provençal wines, *aïoli* on Fridays and wonderful hors d'œuvres.

For **drinking**, try the selection of beers at the *Blue Bar*, on bd de la Libération on plage du Veillat (open till 4am in summer); for expensive cocktails with piano accompaniment, there's the *Madison Club* at the Casino (7pm–4am) or the *Coco-Club* at Port Santa Lucia (till dawn); or there are a series of beachfront discos open in the summer along the promenade to the west of town. If you're staying outside the centre though, beware that late-night **taxis** are almost impossible to come by in this part of the world.

THE RIVIERA

The **Riviera**, the seventy-odd kilometres of coast between **Cannes** and **Menton** by the Italian border, was once an inhospitable shore with few natural harbours, its tiny local communities preferring to cluster round feudal castles high above the sea. It wasn't until the nineteenth century that the first foreign aristocrats began to choose to winter in the region's mild climate. But the real transformation came with the onslaught of 1950s mass tourism. Nowadays, it's an almost uninterrupted promenade, lined by palms and megabuck hotels, with speeding sports cars on the corniche roads and yachts like ocean liners moored at each resort.

Attractions, however, still remain, most notably in the legacies of the artists who stayed here: Picasso, Léger, Matisse, Renoir and Chagall. **Nice**, too, has real substance as a major city.

Cannes and around

The film industry and all other manner of business junketing represent **CANNES's** main source of income in an ever-multiplying calendar of festivals, conferences, tournaments and trade shows. The spin-offs from servicing the day and night needs of the jetloads of agents, reps, dealers, buyers and celebrities are even more profitable than providing the strictly business facilities. Cannes may be more than its film festival, but it's still a grotesquely overhyped urban blight on this once exquisite coast – a contrast reinforced by the sublime **Îles de Lérins**, a short boat ride offshore and the best reason for coming here.

The old town, known as **Le Suquet** after the hill on which it stands, provides a great panorama of the twelve-kilometre beach, and has, on its summit, the remains of the fortified priory lived in by Cannes' eleventh-century monks and the beautiful twelfth-century chapelle Ste-Anne. These house the **Musée de la Castre** (Wed–Mon: July–Sept 10am–noon & 3–7pm; Oct–June 10am–noon & 2–5/6pm; 12F), which has an extraordinary collection of musical instruments from all over the world, along with pictures and prints of old Cannes and an ethnology and archeology section.

MUSEUMS PASSPORT

An **Art'Pass** (price 140F for seven days; 70F for three days), gives free entry to over 60 of the region's most important art and history museums, monuments and gardens. The pass is available from participating museums, major tourist offices, branches of Thomas Cook exchange, and several FNAC department stores.

You'll find non-paying **beaches** to the west of Le Suquet, along the plages du Midi and just east of the Palais des Festivals. But the sight to see is **La Croisette**, the long boulevard along the seafront, with its palace hotels on one side and private beaches on the other. It is possible to find your way down to the beach without paying, but not easy (you can of course walk along it below the rows of sunbeds). The beaches, owned by the deluxe palais-hôtels – the *Majestic*, the *Carlton* and the *Noga Hilton* – is where you're most likely to spot a face familiar in celluloid or a topless hopeful, especially during the film festival, though you'll be lucky to see further than the sweating backs of the paparazzi. At the quays at the end of La Croisette and the Vieux Port, you'll find millionaires eating their meals served by white-frocked crew on their yacht decks, feigning oblivion of landborne spectators a crumb's flick away. As an alternative to the dubious entertainment of watching langoustines disappear down overfed mouths, you can buy your own food in the **Forville covered market** two blocks behind the mairie, or wander through the day's flower shipments on the allées de la Liberté, just back from the Vieux Port.

Strolling on and off the main streets of Cannes – **rue d'Antibes, rue Meynardier** and the **promenade de la Croisette** – is like wading through a hundred current issues of *Vogue*. If you thought the people on the beach were wearing next to nothing, now you can see where they bought the sunglasses and swimming suits, the moisturizers and creams, the watch, the perfume, and the collar and leash for little Fou-Fou.

Practicalities

The **gare SNCF** is on rue Jean-Jaurès, five blocks north of the orange, concrete **Palais des Festivals** on the seafront – the main venue for Cannes' big events, of which the premier celeb-puller is the International Film Festival in May. There are **tourist offices** at the train station (July & Aug Mon–Fri 9am–1pm & 3–7pm; Sept–June 9am–12.30pm & 2–6pm; ☎04.93.99.19.77) and in the Palais des Festivals (July & Aug daily 9am—8pm; Sept Mon–Sat 9am–7pm; Oct–June Mon–Sat 9am–6.30pm; ☎04.93.39.24.53, fax 04.92.99.84.23). There are two **gare routières**: one on place B-Cornut-Gentille between the mairie and Le Suquet, serving coastal destinations; and the other next to the gare SNCF for buses inland to places such as Grasse. The Midnight Bus service runs from the mairie and the Hôtel de Ville along four routes, from 8pm until about 1am (Bus Azur, ☎04.93.39.18.71).

You'll find the best concentration of **hotels** in the centre, between the gare SNCF on rue Jean-Jaurès and La Croisette, around the central axis of rues Antibes and Félix-Faure. The *Alnea*, 20 rue Jean de Riouffe (☎04.93.39.39.90, fax 04.92.98.07.05; ⑤) is central and has high standards of service; the *Cybelle*, 14 rue du 24 Août (☎04.93.38.31.33, fax 04.93.38.43.47; ②), is good-value if fairly basic and has a popular restaurant; and another above-average option is *Chanteclair*, 12 rue Forville (☎ & fax 04.93.39.68.88; ③), right next to the old town. *Beau Séjour*, 5 rue des Fauvettes (☎04.93.39.63.00, fax 04.92.98.64.66; ⑤), just to the northwest of Le Suquet, is quiet and has good facilities. There's also a **youth hostel**, 35 av de Vallauris (☎ & fax 04.93.99.26.79), ten minutes' walk from the train station; whilst more cramped and slightly more expensive hostel-style accommodation can be found at the *Auberge Le Chalit*, 27 av Galliéni (☎ & fax 04.93.99.22.11; ①), five minutes' walk north of the gare SNCF. A three-star campsite, *Le Grand Saule*, 24 bd Jean-Moulin (☎04.93.90.55.10; April–Sept), lies 2km out of town, off the D9 towards Pégomas (bus #9 from gare SNCF, direction "Lamartine", stop Le Grande Saule). **Bikes** and **mopeds** can be rented from Holiday Bikes, 16 rue du 14 Juillet (☎04.97.06.30.30).

Cannes has hundreds of **eateries** catering for every budget. Rue Meynadier, Le Suquet and quai St-Pierre are good places to look. For menus under 100F, try *au Bec Fin*, in the *Hôtel Cybele*, 12 rue du 24-Août (☎04.93.38.35.86; closed Sat eve & Sun), or *Le Bouchon*

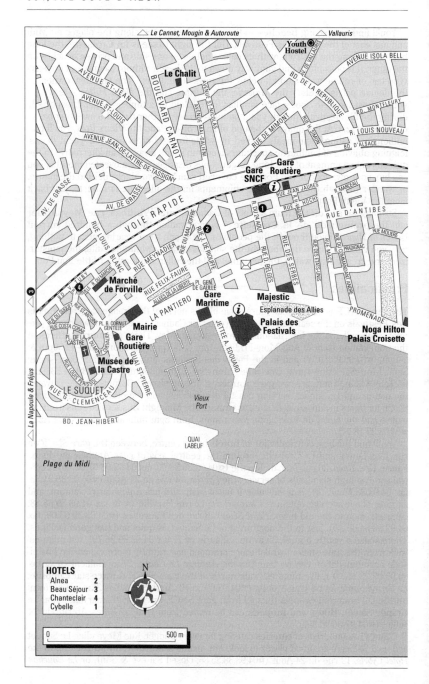

△ *Le Cannet, Mougin & Autoroute*   △ *Vallauris*

Youth Hostel
Le Chalit
AVENUE ST-JEAN
AVENUE ST-LOUIS
AVENUE JEAN-DE-LATTRE-DE-TASSIGNY
BOULEVARD CARNOT
AVENUE ST-NICOLAS
AVENUE MAL-GALIENI
AVENUE ISOLA BELL
BD. DE LA REPUBLIQUE
BD. MONTFLEURI
RUE DE MIMONT
RUE J. SIMON
R. LOUIS NOUVEAU
BD. D'ALSACE
Gare Routière
Gare SNCF
AV. DE GRASSE
AV. DE GRASSE
VOIE RAPIDE
RUE LOUIS BLANC
RUE MEYNADIER
RUE DU MAL JOFFRE
RUE DE ROUFFE
RUE DU 24 AOUT
RUE JEAN JAURES
RUE HOCHE
RUE B. PAGLIANO
RUE MARCEAU
R. MARCEAU
RUE D'ANTIBES
RUE MOLIERE
RUE DES BELGES
RUE DES SERBES
RUE MACE
RUE DES ETATS-UNIS
RUE PRADIGNAC
R. COMMANDANT ANDRE
Marché de Forville
RUE FELIX-FAURE
RUE JEAN DE RIOUFFE
ALLEES DE LA LIBERTE
PL. GEN. DE GAULLE
LA PANTIERO
Gare Maritime
Majestic
Esplanade des Allies
Palais des Festivals
PROMENADE
Noga Hilton Palais Croisette
BD. TUBBY
RUE ST ANTOINE
PL. DUMARCHE
PL. B. CORNUT-GENTILLE
RUE DU SUQUET
RUE ST ANTOINE
PL. DE LA CASTRE
Mairie
Gare Routière
RUE ST. DIZIER
RUE PERISSOL
RUE LOUIS PERISSOL
RUE CHEVALIER
Musée de la Castre
LE SUQUET
RUE G. CLEMENCEAU
QUAI ST-PIERRE
JETTEE A. EDOUARD
QUAI ST-PIERRE
Vieux Port
BD. JEAN-HIBERT
QUAI LABEUF
Plage du Midi
La Napoule & Fréjus

HOTELS
Alnea	2
Beau Séjour	3
Chanteclair	4
Cybelle	1

N

0   500 m

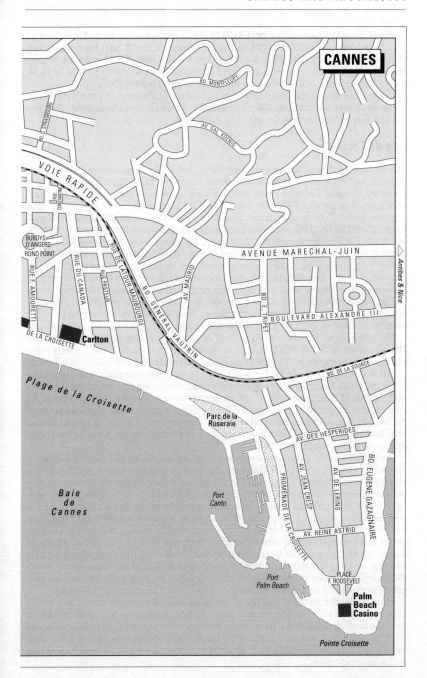

d'Objectif, 10 rue de Constantine (☎04.93.99.21.76; closed Sun eve & Mon). *La Brouette de Chez Grand-Mère*, 9 rue d'Oran (☎04.93.39.12.10; closed midday & Sun) has a single very filling 200F menu including wine. If you'd just won a film festival prize the place to celebrate would be *La Palme d'Or* in the Hôtel Martinez, 73 La Croisette (☎04.92.98.74.14; closed Mon & Tues; 295F lunch menu except Sun; à la carte from 500F).

Cannes has one of the oldest **gay** bars in France, *Le Zanzibar*, 85 rue Félix-Faure (6pm–6am), and a lesbian bar *Exterieur Nuit*, 16 rue du Duquet (4pm–2am). 1996 saw the first Gay Pride march in the city.

Îles de Lérins

The **Îles de Lérins** would be lovely anywhere, but at fifteen minutes' ferry ride from Cannes, they're not far short of paradise facing purgatory. **Boats** leave from the old port (summer frequent 7.30am–5.15pm; winter 5 daily 7.30am–2.45pm), with the last boats back from St-Honorat at 4.45pm or 5.45pm, and Ste-Marguerite at 5 or 6pm (winter and summer times). The best company to use is Trans Côte d'Azur, leaving from quai Laubeuf (☎04.92.98.71.30) as it stops at both islands. Tickets cost 60F return to visit the two islands; 40F return for just Ste-Marguerite; 45F return for just St-Honorat. Taking a picnic is a good idea, as the handful of restaurants on the islands are overpriced.

Ste-Marguerite is far more commercial and touristy than its peaceful neighbour, St-Honorat. It is still beautiful, though, and large enough for visitors to find seclusion by following the trails that lead away from the congested port, through the aleppo pines and woods of evergreen oak that are so thick they cast a sepulchral gloom. The western end is the most accessible, but the lagoon here is brackish, so the best points to swim are the rocky inlets across the island from the port.

The dominating structure of the island is the **Fort Ste-Marguerite** (Wed–Mon 10.30am–noon & 2–4.30/6.30pm; 10F), a Richelieu commission that failed to prevent the Spanish occupying both of the Lérin islands between 1635 and 1637. Later, Vauban rounded it off, presumably for Louis XIV's *gloire* – since the strategic value of greatly enlarging a fort facing your own mainland without upgrading the one facing the sea is pretty minimal. There are cells to see, including the one in which Dumas' *Man in the Iron Mask* is supposed to have been held, a small aquarium hosting specimens of local marine life, and a **Musée de la Mer** (same times as fort), containing mostly Roman local finds but also remnants of a tenth-century Arab ship. Access is free to the grassy ramparts of this vast construction.

Owned by monks almost continuously since its namesake and patron founded a monastery here in 410 AD, **St-Honorat**, the smaller southern island, was home to a famous bishops' seminary, where St Patrick trained before setting out for Ireland. The present **abbey** buildings date mostly from the nineteenth century, though some vestiges of the medieval and earlier constructions remain in the austere church (free to visit) and the cloisters. A shop sells the benevolent white wine, spirits and honey produced by the 28 Cistercian brothers of the monastic community. Behind the cloisters on the sea's edge stands an eleventh-century **fortress**, used by the monks in times of danger. Of all the protective forts against invaders built along this coast, this is the only one that looks as if it still might serve its original function. At the same time it shows its age without heavy-handed cosmetic reconstruction or being a picture-postcard ruin (monastery and fortress 10am–12.30pm & 2.30—5pm; 15F entrance June–Sept).

These days, the forces of this island are peace and silence, with pine leaves gently stirring and the sea mapping out its minuscule tide. Apart from one small restaurant near the landing stage, there are no bars, hotels or cars: just vines, lavender, herbs and olive trees mingled with wild poppies and daisies, and pine and eucalyptus trees shading the paths beside the white rock shore mixing with the scents of rosemary, thyme and wild honeysuckle.

Vallauris

Picasso spent ten years just northeast of Cannes in **VALLAURIS**, set in the hills above the Golfe Juan. It was here that he first began to use clay, thereby reviving one of the traditional crafts of this little town. Today the main street, **av Georges-Clemenceau**, sells nothing but pottery, much of it the garishly glazed bowls and figurines that could feature in souvenir shops anywhere. Picasso used to work in the **Madoura workshop**, on av des Ancien-Combattants-d'AFN, to the right as you come down avenue Georges-Clemenceau; it still has sole rights on reproducing Picasso's designs, which it sells, at a price, in the shop (Mon–Fri only).

The bronze statue of **Man with a Sheep**, Picasso's gift to the town, stands in the main square and marketplace, place de la Libération, beside the church and castle. The local authorities also suggested he should decorate the early medieval deconsecrated **chapel** in the castle courtyard (Wed–Mon 10am–noon/12.30pm & 2–5/6.30pm; 17F), which he finally did in 1952: his subject was war and peace. The space is tiny and has the architectural simplicity of an air-raid shelter, and at first glance it's easy to be unimpressed by the painted panels covering the vault – as many critics still are – since the work looks mucky and slapdash, with paint-runs on the plywood panel surface. But stay a while and the passion of this violently drawn pacifism slowly emerges. On the "War" panel, a music score is trampled by hooves and about to be engulfed in flames; a fighter's lance tenuously holds the scales of justice and a shield that bears the outline of a dove. "Peace" is represented by Pegasus, the winged horse of poetry; people dancing and suckling babies; trees bearing fruit; owls; books; and the freedom of the spirit to mix up images and concepts with unmalicious mischief. The ticket for the chapel also gives admission to the **Musée de Céramique** (same hours) in the castle, which exhibits Picasso's and other ceramics.

There are regular buses from Cannes and from Golfe-Juan SNCF to place de la Libération. The **tourist office** is at the bottom of av Georges-Clemenceau on square du 8-Mai-1945 (Mon–Sat: July–Sept 9am–7pm; Oct–June 9am–noon & 2–6pm; ☎04.93.63.18.38).

Grasse

GRASSE, 16km inland from Cannes and with some stunning views over the Côte, is the world capital of *parfumiers* and has been for almost 300 years. These days it likes to flaunt itself, promoting its perfumed image as a chic eighteenth-century village with a medieval heart surrounded by hectares of scented flowers. Making perfumes is presented as a mysterious process, an alchemy, turning the soul of the flower into a liquid of luxury and desire, and the industry is at pains to keep quiet about modern innovations and techniques.

Grasse is the official starting point of the Route Napoléon (see p.918) but is equally easy to visit as a day-trip from the coast.

The town

Vieux Grasse, despite its touristy shops and full range of restaurants, is surprisingly humble, a working-class enclave where lines of washing festoon the high, narrow streets – rates of pay for the pickers of raw ingredients for perfume essences are notoriously low. Inhabitants say it's like a village where everyone knows each other, and out of season that's certainly the atmosphere that prevails.

Place aux Aires, at the top of the old town, is the main meeting point for all and sundry and the venue for the daily flower and vegetable **market**. It is ringed by arcades of different heights and the elegant wrought-iron balcony of the *Hôtel Isnard* at no. 33, and at one time was the exclusive preserve of the tanning industry. At the opposite end of Vieux Grasse lie the **cathedral** – containing various paintings, including three by Rubens and a wondrous triptych by the sixteenth-century Niçois painter Louis Bréa – and the **bishop's palace**, now the Hôtel de Ville, both built in the twelfth century.

A museum you might like to take a quick flit through is the **Musée d'Art et d'Histoire de Provence**, 2 rue Mirabeau, (June–Sept daily 10am–7pm; Oct & Dec–May Wed–Sun 10am–noon & 2–5pm; 20F, or 40F with Musée International de la Parfumerie and Villa Fragonard) housed in a luxurious town house commissioned by Mirabeau's sister for her social entertainment duties. As well as all the gorgeous fittings and the original eighteenth-century kitchen, the historical collection adds a nice eclectic touch. It includes wonderful eighteenth- to nineteenth-century faïence from Apt and Le Castellet, Mirabeau's death mask, a tin bidet and six prehistoric bronze leg bracelets. The fascinating **Musée International de la Parfumerie**, 8 place du Cours (June–Sept daily 10am–7pm; Oct & Jan–May Wed–Sun 10am–noon & 2–5pm; 25F, or 40F with Musée d'Art et d'Histoire and Villa Fragonard), displays perfume bottles from the ancient Greeks to the present via Marie-Antoinette and has a reconstruction of a perfume factory with a little test you can do on identifying fragrances. The guided tours are highly recommended.

The perfume factories

There are thirty major **parfumeries** in and around Grasse, most of them making not perfume but essences-plus-formulas which are then sold to Dior, Lancôme, Estée Lauder and the like, who make up their own brand-name perfumes. One litre of pure rose essence can cost as much as 125,000F; perfume contains twenty percent essence (eau de toilette and eau de Cologne considerably less). The major cost in this multi-billion-dollar business is marketing. The grand Parisian couturiers, whose clothes, on strictly cost-accounting grounds, serve simply to promote the perfume, go to inordinate lengths to sell their latest fragrance, spending hundreds of millions of francs a year on advertising alone.

The ingredients that the "nose" – as the creator of the perfume's formula is known – has to play with include resins, roots, moss, beans, bark, civet (extract of cat genitals), ambergris (intestinal goo from whales), bits of beaver and musk from Tibetan goats. If that hasn't put you off, you can visit the various **showrooms**, with overpoweringly fragrant shops and free guided tours, in English, of the traditional perfume factory set-up (the actual working industrial complexes are strictly out of bounds). These visits are free and usually open daily without interruption in summer; a few to choose from are **Fragonard**, 20 bd Fragonard; **Galimard**, 73 rte de Cannes; and **Molinard** at 60 bd Victor-Hugo.

Practicalities

Grasse's **gare routière** is to the north of the old town at the Parking Notre-Dame-des-Fleurs. Head downhill on avenue Thiers becoming boulevard du Jeu de Ballon (where there's an annexe of the tourist office) and you'll find the museums and the main **tourist office** on cours Honoré-Cresp (July & Aug daily 9am–7pm; rest of year Mon–Sat 9am–noon & 2–6pm; ☎04.93.36.66.66, fax 04.93.36.86.36).

Two possible **hotels** at the cheaper end of the market are: *Napoléon,* 6 av Thiers (☎04.93.36.05.87; ②), right next to the gare routière, and *Les Palmiers,* 17 av Y-Baudoin (☎04.93.36.07.24; ②), with a pleasant garden and good views, if not particularly friendly. More expensively, the *Panorama,* on place du Cours (☎04.93.36.80.80, fax 04.93.36.92.04; ④), offers rooms with views and all mod cons.

Restaurants in the old town are good value with several menus to choose from on rue de la Fontette. *Pierre Baltus* at no. 15 (☎04.93.36.32.90; closed Wed eve and Sat lunchtime, mid-Feb to mid-March; menus from 100F) does very fine cooking based on dependably fresh ingredients. At the *Maison Venturini*, 1 rue Marcel Journet (closed Sun & Mon), you can buy fabulous sweet *fougassettes*, flavoured with the Grasse speciality of orange blossom. Tasty pizzas and *socca* (chickpea pancakes) won't break the bank at the relaxed *La Socca*, 17 rue Paul-Goby, and the **bars** on place aux Aires are friendly.

Antibes and around

ANTIBES, or rather its promontory the **Cap d'Antibes**, is one of the select places on the Côte d'Azur where the *really* rich and the very, *very* successful still live, or at least have residences. Yet it's not immediately obvious why this area should be so desirable: it's just as built-up as the rest of the Riviera, with no open countryside separating Golfe Juan, **Juan-les-Pins** and Antibes. Long-time resident Graham Greene said it was the only town on the Côte that hadn't lost its soul; perhaps he was right, though he also gave his reason for living there as simply to be with the woman he loved. Be that as it may, Antibes is extremely animated, has one of the finest **markets** on the coast, and the best **Picasso collection** in its ancient seafront castle; and the southern end of the Cap still has its woods of pine, in which the most exclusive mansions hide.

The sixteenth-century **Château Grimaldi** is a beautifully cool, light space, with hexagonal terracotta floor tiles, windows over the sea and a terrace garden with sculptures by Germaine Richier, Miró, César and others. In 1946, Picasso was offered the dusty building – by then already a museum – as a studio. Several extremely prolific months followed before he moved to Vallauris, leaving all his Antibes output to what is now the **Musée Picasso** (Tues–Sun: June to Sept 10am–6pm; rest of year 10am–noon & 2–6pm; 30F). Although Picasso donated other works later on, the bulk of the collection belongs to this one period. There's an uncomplicated exuberance in the numerous still lifes of sea urchins, the goats and fauns in Cubist non-disguise, and the wonderful *Ulysses and his Sirens* – a great round head against a mast around which the ship, sea and sirens swirl. Picasso himself is the subject of works here by other painters and photographers, including Man Ray and Bill Brandt; there are several anguished canvases by Nicholas de Staël, who stayed in Antibes for a few months from 1954 to 1955; and works by other contemporaries and more recent artists. Alongside the castle is the **cathedral**, built on the site of an ancient temple. The choir and apse survive from the Romanesque building that served the city in the Middle Ages while the nave and stunning ochre facade are Baroque. Inside, in the south transept, is a medieval sumptious altarpiece surrounded by immaculate panels of tiny detailed scenes.

One block inland, the **covered market** on cours Masséna overflows with Provençal goodies and a profusion of cut **flowers**, the traditional and still-flourishing Antibes business (daily am: June–Aug; rest of year Tues–Sun). On Friday and Sunday (plus Easter–Sept Tues & Thurs) a craft market takes over in the afternoon. When the stalls are all packed up, café tables take their place.

Cap d'Antibes

Plage de la Salis, the longest Antibes beach, runs along the eastern neck of Cap d'Antibes with no big hotels owning mattress exploitation rights – an amazing rarity on the Riviera. To the south, at the top of chemin du Calvaire, you can get superb views from the **Église de la Garoupe** (9.30/10am–noon & 2.30–5/6pm) which contains Russian spoils from the Crimean War and hundreds of *ex votos*. To the west, on boulevard du Cap between chemins du Tamisier and G-Raymond, you can wander around the **Jardin Thuret** (Mon–Fri 8.30am–noon & 2.30–5.30pm; free), botanical gardens belonging to a national research institute. Back on the east shore, further south, a second beach, **plage de la Garoupe**, again public and untrammelled, is linked by a **footpath** to the peninsula's southern tip. There are more sandy coves and little harbours along the western shore, where you'll also find the **Musée Naval et Napoléonien** (Mon–Fri 9.30am–noon & 2.15–6pm, Sat 9.30am–noon; closed Oct; 30F), at the end of av J-F-Kennedy. This documents the great return from Elba along with the usual Bonaparte paraphernalia of hats, cockades, and signed commands.

Juan-les-Pins

JUAN-LES-PINS, less than 2km from the centre of Antibes, is another of those overloaded Côte d'Azur names: the summer St-Moritz, the night-time playground for the extravagantly outfitted front-page myths who retreat at dawn, like supernatural creatures, to their well-screened cages on Cap d'Antibes. Until this century it was nothing more than a pine grove on the western neck of Cap d'Antibes. A casino was built in 1908 and by the late 1920s Juan-les-Pins had taken off as the original summer resort of the Côte d'Azur. Revealing swimsuits, as opposed to swimming "dresses", were reputedly first worn here in the 1930s. Now, like so much of the Côte, it's so overcrowded and overbuilt that it's impossible to see what all the fuss is about – or to imagine it as a pine forest.

But its **international jazz festival** in the last two weeks of July is the best in the region and takes place in what's left of the pine forest, the **Jardin de La Pinède** (known simply as La Pinède), and **Square Gould** above the beach by the casino. This urban park and the 2km of sheltered sand beach are all that Juan-les-Pins has to offer for free, apart from the dizzying array of architectural styles along its streets.

Practicalities

Antibes's **gare SNCF** lies to the north of the old town at the top of av Robert-Soleau. Turn right out of the station and three minutes' walk along av R-Soleau will bring you to the place de Gaulle. The **tourist office** is on this square, at no.11 (July & Aug Mon–Sat 8.30am–7.30pm, Sun 10am–1pm; Sept–June Mon–Fri 9am–12.30pm & 2–6.30pm, Sat 9am–noon & 2–6pm; ☎04.92.90.53.00; fax 04.92.90.53.01). The **gare routière** is off the adjoining place Guynemer (☎04.93.34.37.60) with frequent buses to and from the gare SNCF (Mon–Sat); otherwise it's a five-minute walk from the train station. Bus #2A goes to Cap d'Antibes; bus #1A and #3A to Juan-les-Pins, #10A to Biot. **Bikes** can be hired from three outlets on bd Wilson, at nos. 43, 93 and 122. Rue de la République leads into the heart of Vieux Antibes around place Nationale, from where rue Sade leads to cours Masséna, beyond which lie the cathedral, the castle and the sea.

The most economical **hotels** are both close to the gare routière: the *Brasserie Nouvelle*, 1 av Niquet (☎04.93.34.10.07; ②), with just five rooms, and *Le Nouvel Hôtel*, 1 av du 24-Août (☎04.93.34.44.07, fax 04.93.34.06.66; ③). For greater comfort, try the *Mas Djoliba*, 29 av de Provence (☎04.93.34.02.48, fax 04.93.34.05.81; closed Nov–Jan; ⑤), between the old town and the beach, or *Le Ponteil*, 11 impasse Jean-Mensier (☎04.93.34.67.92. fax 04.93.34.49.47; ④), in a quiet location at the end of a cul-de-sac close to the sea.

There's a **youth hostel** on Cap d'Antibes, the *Relais International de la Jeunesse* on bd de la Garoupe (☎04.93.61.34.40, fax 04.93.34.89.88; June–Sept; bus #2A to *La Bouée* and head north along bd de la Garoupe) which needs booking well in advance. All of Antibes's **campsites** are 3–5km north of the city in the quartier of La Brague (bus #10A or one train stop to Gare de Biot). The three-star *Logis de La Brague* (☎04.93.33.54.72;

May–Sept) is closest to the station, while the two-star *Idéal-Camping* (☎04.93.74.27.07; March–Oct) is south of the station; both are on the route de Nice and close to the sea.

Place Nationale and cours Masséna are lined with **cafés**; rue James Close is nothing but **restaurants** and rue Thuret and its side streets also offer numerous menus to browse through. For pizzas, there's *Il Giardino*, 21 rue Thuret, though you may have a long wait to be served, and *La Famiglia*, a cheap family-run outfit at 34 av Thiers (closed Sun lunch & Wed). *Le Romantic*, 5 rue Rostan (☎04.93.34.59.39; closed Wed lunch & Tues; menus from 125F), lives up to its name; *Le Relais du Postillon*, 8 rue Championnet (☎04.93.34.20.77; menus from 95F), is another good possibility. For something really special, *Les Vieux Murs*, near the castle at avenue Amiral-de-Grasse (☎04.93.34.06.73; closed Mon & Oct–March), does a superb meal for 200F.

Juan-les-Pins has one of the **star restaurants** of the Côte, *La Terrasse*, on avenue Gallice (☎04.93.61.20.37; lunch menu 275F, otherwise 420F minimum), with original 1930s decor, exquisite fish and seafood dishes and mouth-melting desserts. At the other end of the scale you can get brasserie food, crêpes, pizzas and similar snacks from **street stalls** till the early hours, and many shops and bars also keep going in summer till 3am or 4am. Juan-les-Pins is also one of the liveliest places along the coast for nightlife, with a whole host of **nightclubs** and bars for you to spend any dollars that are surplus to your budget. Entrance is typically 100F with a "complimentary" drink. You might like to try *Le Village / Voom Voom* at 1 bd de la Pinède, which attracts a young crowd and goes on till dawn; or *Le Pam-Pam*, 137 bd Président Wilson, with frequent live Brazilian bands.

Finally, if you've run out of reading material, Heidi's English Bookshop at 24 rue Aubernon in Antibes (daily 10am–7pm) is the cheapest English **bookshop** on the coast.

Biot

Frequent buses connect Antibes with the village of **BIOT**, 8km to the north, where Fernand Léger lived for a few years at the end of his life. A stunning collection of his intensely life-affirming works, created between 1905 and 1955, can be seen at the **Musée Fernand Léger**, built especially to display them (Wed–Mon: July–Sept 11am–6pm; Oct–June 10am–noon & 2–5pm; 38F, 28F on Sun). The museum is just southeast of the village on the chemin du Val de Pome, stop Fernand Léger on the Antibes bus, or a 30-min walk from Biot's gare SNCF.

Few artists have had such consistency and power in their use of space and colour and the ability to change the relations between objects or figures without ever descending to surrealism. Léger's art has the capacity to inflict instant pleasure – the pattern of the shapes and the colours, particularly in his ceramic works – or harsh horror as in the charcoal black to brown on off-white paper in *Stalingrad*. It's interesting to compare his life and work with Picasso, fellow pioneer of Cubism and long-time comrade in the Communist Party. While Léger's commitment to collective working-class life never wavered, Picasso only nodded at it when he needed it. Picasso wanted to embrace the whole world and be embraced in return. He chose a complex, dominating, sometimes perverted persona in which to do it, while Léger stuck within the reality of himself and the world, an outlook captured by Alexander Calder's wire sculpture portrait of Léger in the museum. He was vocal on the politics of culture, arguing for museums to be open after working hours; for public spaces to be adorned with art; and for making all the arts more accessible to ordinary people.

The village of Biot is extremely beautiful and oozes with art in every form – architectural, sculpted, ceramic, jewelled, painted and culinary. The **tourist office**, on place de la Chapelle, at the far end of the main street, rue St-Sébastien (daily except Sat am & Sun am: summer 10am–noon & 2.30–7pm; winter 9am–noon & 2–6pm;

☎04.93.65.05.85, fax 04.93.65.70.96), can provide copious lists of art galleries and glass-works (the traditional industry that brought Léger here, and which produces the famous hand-blown **bubble glass**). If you book well in advance you could **stay** at the very reasonable *Hôtel des Arcades*, 16 place des Arcades (☎04.93.65.01.04, fax 04.93.65.01.05; ③), full of old-fashioned charm and with huge rooms in the medieval centre of the village. Its **café-restaurant**, which also doubles as an art gallery, serves delicious traditional Provençal food (closed Sun eve & Mon; 160F menu).

Above the Baie des Anges

Between Antibes and Nice, the **Baie des Anges** laps at twentieth-century resorts with two fine examples of concrete corpulence: the giant petrified sails with viciously point-ed corners of the Villeneuve-Loubet-Plage marina, and an apartment complex, 1km long and sixteen storeys high, barricading the stony beach.

The old towns and softer visual stimulation lie inland. **Cagnes** is another artists' town – associated in particular with Renoir – as is **St-Paul-de-Vence**, which houses the won-derful modern art collection of the Fondation Maeght. **Vence** has a small chapel deco-rated by Matisse, and is a relaxing place to stay, if quiet in the evenings.

Cagnes

CAGNES is made up of a nondescript coastal district known as Cros-de-Cagnes, Haut-de-Cagnes, the original medieval village overlooking the town from the northwest heights, and Cagnes-sur-Mer, the town centre situated inland between the two.

At the top of place de Gaulle, the main square in **Cagnes-sur-Mer**, avenue Auguste-Renoir runs right and crosses the road to La Gaude. A short way further on, chemin des Collettes leads off to the left up to **Les Collettes**, the house that Renoir had built in 1908 and where he spent the last twelve years of his life (bus #4 from square Bourdet, or stop Béat-Les Collettes on the Antibes or Nice bus). It's now a memorial **museum** (Wed–Mon 10am–noon & 2–5/6pm; closed first three weeks of Nov; 20F; free entry to garden), and you're free to wander around the house and through the olive and rare orange groves that surround it. One of the two studios in the house – north-facing to catch the late afternoon light – is arranged as if Renoir had just popped out. Albert André's painting, *A Renoir Painting*, shows the ageing artist hunched over his canvas; plus there's a bust of him by Aristide Maillol, and a crayon sketch by Richard Guido. Bonnard and Dufy were also visitors to Les Collettes; Dufy's *Hommage à Renoir*, transposing a detail of *Moulin de la Galette*, hangs here. Renoir's own work is represented by several sculptures, including *La Maternité*, and a medallion of his son Coco, some beautiful, tiny watercolours in the studio, and ten paintings from his Cagnes period.

Haut-de-Cagnes is a favourite haunt of successes in the contemporary art world, as well as those of decades past, and it lives up to everything dreamed of in a Riviera *vil-lage perché*. The ancient village backs up to a crenellated feudal **château** (daily except Tues summer 10am–noon & 2.30–7pm, winter 10am–noon & 2–5/6pm; closed Nov; 20F; bus #9 from square Bourdet to Le Château or the steep ascent along rue Général-Bérenger and montée de la Bourgade), with a stunning Renaissance interior. It houses museums of local history, fishing and olive cultivation, along with the **Musée d'Art Moderne Méditerranéen**, with changing exhibitions of the painters who have worked on the coast in the last hundred years, and the **Donation Suzy Solidor**, which consists of wonderfully diverse portraits by all the great twentieth-century painters of the les-bian cabaret star who inspired the music-hall song *If You Knew Suzy, Like I Know Suzy*. In addition, if you're here between the end of November and January, you can see the entries from forty-odd countries for Haut-de-Cagnes' big event of the year, the **Festival International de la Peinture** (when the château is open daily).

Practicalities

The **gare SNCF** Cagnes-sur-Mer (one stop from the gare SNCF Cros-de-Cagnes) is southwest of the centre alongside the autoroute; turn right on the northern side of the autoroute along avenue de la Gare to head into town. If you want to rent a **bike**, take the second right, rue Pasqualini, where you'll find Cycles Marcel at no. 5 (☎04.93.20.64.07). The sixth turning on your right, rue des Palmiers, leads to the **tourist office** at 6 bd Maréchal-Juin (Mon–Sat: June–Sept 9am–12.45pm & 3–7pm; Oct–May 8.30am–12.15pm & 2–6pm; ☎04.93.20.61.64, fax 04.93.20.52.63). Bus #2 runs from the gare SNCF to the **gare routière** on square Bourdet.

Economical **hotels** include *La Caravelle*, 42 bd de la Plage (☎04.93.20.10.09; ①) on the seafront, and *Le Saratoga*, 111 av de Nice (☎04.93.31.05.70; ②), on the busy N7, both in Cros-de-Cagnes (bus #2 from square Bourdet or Cagnes-sur-Mer gare SNCF). *Le Grimaldi*, at 6 place du Château (☎04.93.20.60.24, fax ☎04.92.02.19.47; ③), has very pleasant rooms with views of the sea. **Campsites** are not marvellous, though there are plenty of them. The four-star *Panoramer*, chemin des Gros-Buaux (☎04.93.31.16.15; April–Oct), about 1km northeast of Cagnes-sur-Mer, is the closest, though not the cheapest.

The best places to **eat** are in Haut-de-Cagnes, and for café lounging, place du Château or place Grimaldi, to either side of the castle, are the obvious spots. The *Restaurant des Peintres*, 71 montée de la Bourgade (☎04.93.20.83.08; closed Wed), serves light Provençal delicacies and has menus from 200F. *Le Clap*, despite the unfortunate name, at 4 rue Hippolyte-Guis, off montée de la Bourgade (☎04.92.02.06.28; closed Wed), has reasonable menus starting from 95F. If you're feeling extremely flush, *Le Cagnard*, rue Pontis-Long (☎04.93.20.73.21; closed Nov–Easter; menus from 300F) is the top-notch hotel-restaurant in the ancient guard room of the château.

In mid-July there are free **jazz concerts** on place du Château and, at the end of August, a bizarre **square boules** competition takes place down montée de la Bourgade.

St-Paul-de-Vence: the Fondation Maeght

Further into the hills, the fortified village of **ST-PAUL-DE-VENCE** is home to yet another artistic treat, and one of the best in the whole region: the remarkable **Fondation Maeght** created in the 1950s by Aimé and Marguerite Maeght, art collectors and dealers who knew all the great artists who worked in Provence (daily July–Sept 10am–7pm, Oct–June 10am–12.30pm & 2.30–6pm; 40F, or 50F during exhibitions). The Nice–Vence **bus** has two stops in St-Paul: the Fondation is signposted from the second, and is approximately 1km from the old town. By **car or bike**, follow the signs just before you reach the village, off the D7 from La-Colle-sur-Loup or the D2 from Villeneuve. Admission includes the permanent collections, temporary exhibitions, bookshop, library and cinema, and it's worth every last centime.

Once through the gates, any idea of dutifully seeing the catalogue of priceless museum pieces crumbles. Alberto Giacometti's *Cat* is sometimes stalking along the edge of the grass; Miró's *Egg* smiles above a pond and his totemed *Fork* is outlined against the sky. It's hard not to be bewitched by the Calder mobile swinging over watery tiles, by Léger's *Flowers, Birds and a Bench* on a sunlit rough stone wall, by Zadkine's and Arp's metallic forms hovering between the pine trunks, or by the clanking tubular fountain by Pol Bury. The building itself is a superb piece of architecture: multi-levelled and flooded with daylight, making inside and outside hard to distinguish, and the collection it houses of works by Braque, Miro, Chagall, Léger and Matisse, along with more recent artists and the young up-and-comings, is fabulous. Not all the works are exhibited at any one time, and during the summer, when the main annual exhibition is mounted, none are on show, apart from those that make up the decoration of the building.

The other famous sight in this extremely busy tourist village is the hotel-restaurant **La Colombe d'Or** on place du Général-de-Gaulle (☎04.93.32.80.02, fax 04.93.32.77.78; closed Nov–Christmas; ⑨), where if you are prepared to splash out 400F for a mediocre meal or more than 1300F for a room, you can enjoy the Braques, Picassos, Matisses and Bonnards that hang from the walls, most of which were acquired by the establishment in the lean post-World War I years in lieu of the artists' unpaid bills.

Vence

A few kilometres north, with abundant water and the sheltering pre-Alps behind, **VENCE** has always been a significant city. The old town is blessed with numerous ancient houses, gateways, fountains, chapels and a **cathedral** (daily 9am–6pm) containing Roman funeral inscriptions and a Chagall mosaic. In the 1920s it became yet another haven for painters and writers: André Gide, Raoul Dufy, D.H. Lawrence (who died here in 1930 whilst being treated for tuberculosis contracted in England) and Marc Chagall were all long-term visitors, along with **Matisse** whose work is the reason most people come to Vence.

Towards the end of World War II, Matisse moved to Vence to escape the Allied bombing of the coast, and his legacy is the town's most famous and exciting building, the **Chapelle du Rosaire**, at 466 av Henri-Matisse, on the road to St-Jeannet from carrefour Jean-Moulin at the top of av des Poilus (Tues & Thurs 10–11.30am & 2.30–5.30pm, more regularly during school holidays but check with tourist office; closed Nov; free). The chapel was his last work – consciously so – and not, as some have tried to explain, a religious conversion. "My only religion is the love of the work to be created, the love of creation, and great sincerity," he said in 1952 when the five-year project was completed.

The drawings on the chapel walls – black outline figures on white tiles – were executed by Matisse with a paintbrush fixed to a two-metre long bamboo stick specifically to remove his own stylistic signature from the lines. He succeeded in this to the extent that many people are bitterly disappointed, not finding the "Matisse" they expect. The only source of colour in the chapel comes from the light diffused through green, blue and yellow stained-glass windows, which changes according to the time of day. Yet it is a total work – every part of the chapel is Matisse's design – and one that the artist was content with. It was his "ultimate goal, the culmination of an intense, sincere and difficult endeavour".

Vieux Vence has all the the chic boutiques and arty restaurants worthy of an *haut-lieu* of the Côte aristocracy, but it also has an everyday feel about it, with ordinary people and run-of-the-mill cafés. On place du Frêne, by the western gateway, the fifteenth-century **Château de Villeneuve** (June to mid-Oct daily 10am–6pm, rest of year daily except Mon 10am–12.30pm & 2–6pm; 25F) provides a beautiful temporary exhibition space for the works of artists such as Matisse, Dufy, Dubuffet and Chagall.

Current artistic creation has a home at the **Centre d'Art VAAS**, 14 traverse des Moulins, just north of the old city (Tues–Sat 9.30am–noon & 2.30–6pm; Oct–March by appointment only; free). A garden of sculptures leads to what was, from 1955 to 1970, Jean Dubuffet's studio. As well as a gallery of figurative art, this is a space for artists to meet and work, and the high-quality courses of art and sculpture it runs are open to anyone who wishes to pay the fees. It also gives the best view of the blue-tiled rooftop of the Chapelle du Rosaire.

Yet more art, this time by the likes of César, Klein, Arman, Ben, Tinguely and Warhol, are shown in changing temporary exhibitions at the **Galerie Beaubourg** in the Château Notre-Dame des Fleurs, halfway along the road from Vence to Tourettes-sur-Loup (April–Sept Mon–Sat 11am–7pm; Oct–March Tues–Sat 11am–5.30pm; 30F).

Practicalities

Arriving by bus, you'll be dropped near place du Frêne at the **gare routière** on place du Grand-Jardin, where you'll find the **tourist office** (Mon–Sat summer 9am–12.30pm & 2–7pm, winter 9am–noon & 2–6pm; Sun all year 10am–noon; ☎04.93.58.06.38, fax 04.93.58.91.81) and **bike rental** at Vence Motocycles.

Vence is a real town, with affordable places to stay. For **hotels**, good budget options are the rather down-at-heel *Les Alpes*, 2 av Général-Leclerc, on the eastern edge of the old town (☎04.93.58.13.30; ①), the welcoming, peaceful *La Closerie des Genêts*, 4 impasse Maurel, off av M-Maurel to the south of the old town (☎04.93.58.33.25☎, fax 04.93.58.78.50; ③), and *Le Provence*, 9 av Marcellin Maurel (☎04.93.58.04.21, fax 04.93.58.35.62; ③), with a good garden. A little more luxury, including a pool, is available at *La Roseraie*, 14 av Henri-Giraud (☎04.93.58.02.20, fax 04.93.58.99.31; ⑤). There's a **campsite**, *La Bergerie*, 3km west off the road to Tourette-sur-Loup (☎04.93.58.09.36; mid-March to mid-Oct).

For a special **meal**, try *La Farigoule*, 15 av Henri-Isnard (☎04.93.58.01.27; closed Fri & Sat lunch out of season; menus from 115F). Also good, and with menus from 130F (only 95F for residents), is the restaurant at *La Closerie des Genêts* hotel (see above; closed Sun eve). The fabled chef Jacques Maximin has opened a gourmet palace in Vence: imaginatively titled the *Maximin Restaurant*, 689 chemin de la Gaude (☎04.93.58.90.75), it prepares exquisite fare, with the cheapest menu starting at 250F and rising rapidly in price and indulgence. For more run-of-the-mill fare, try the astounding choice of pizzas at *Le Pêcheur du Soleil*, 1 place Godeau. You'll find plenty of **cafés** in the squares of Vieux Vence. *La Clemenceau*, on place Clemenceau, is the big café-brasserie-glacier, but you might find *Henry's Bar*, on place de Peyra, more congenial. *La Régence*, on place du Grand-Jardin, serves excellent coffee to sip beneath its stylish parasols.

Nice

The capital of the Riviera and fifth largest town of France, **NICE** scarcely deserves its glittering reputation. Living off inflated property values and fat business accounts, its ruling class has hardly evolved from the eighteenth-century Russian and English aristocrats who first built their mansions here; today it's the *rentiers* and retired people of various nationalities whose dividends and pensions give the city its startlingly high ratio of per capita income to economic activity.

Their votes ensured the monopoly of municipal power held for decades by the right-wing dynasty, whose corruption was finally exposed in 1990 when mayor Jacques Médecin fled to Uruguay. He was finally extradited and jailed. Despite the disappearance of 400 million francs of taxpayers' money, public opinion remained in his favour. From his Grenoble prison cell, Médecin, who had twinned Nice with Cape Town during the height of South Africa's apartheid regime, backed the former Front National member and close friend of Jean-Marie Le Pen, Jacques Peyrat, in the 1995 local elections. Peyrat won with ease.

Politics apart, Nice has other reasons to qualify it as one of the more dubious destinations on the Riviera: it's a pickpocket's paradise; the traffic is a nightmare, miniature poodles appear to be mandatory, phones are always vandalized, and the beach isn't even sand. And yet Nice still manages to be delightful. The sun and the sea and the laid-back, affable Niçois cover a multitude of sins. The medieval rabbit warren of the old town, the Italianate facades of modern Nice and the rich, exuberant, turn-of-the-century residences that made

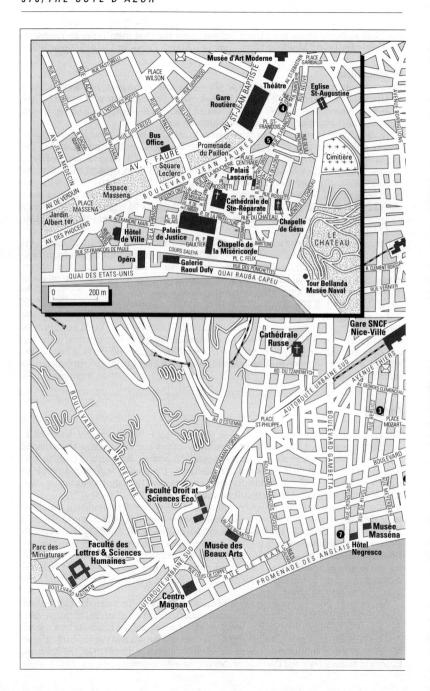

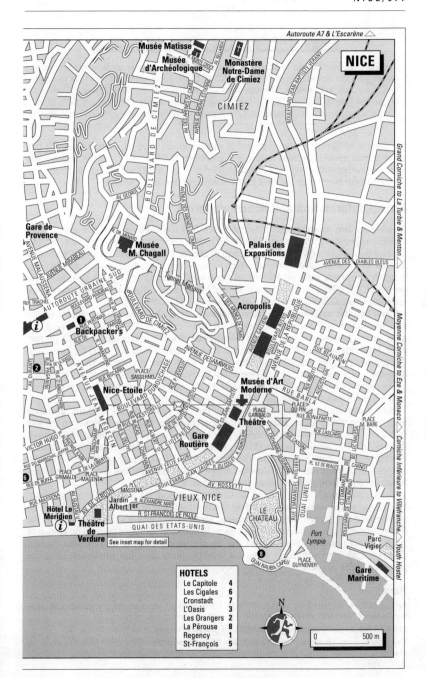

NICE

Autoroute A7 & L'Escarène

Musée Matisse
Musée d'Archéologique
Monastère Notre-Dame de Cimiez

CIMIEZ

Grand Corniche to La Turbie & Menton

AV GEORGE

Gare de Provence

Musée M. Chagall

Palais des Expositions

AVENUE DES DIABLES BLEUS

Moyenne Corniche to Eze & Monaco

Tunnel Malaux

Acropolis

BOULEVARD DE CIMIEZ

Backpackers

AVENUE DESAMBROIS

Corniche Inférieure to Villefranche

Musée d'Art Moderne

Nice-Etoile

Théâtre

Gare Routière

Youth Hostel

VICTOR HUGO

VIEUX NICE

Hôtel Le Méridien

Théâtre de Verdure

Jardin Albert 1er

QUAI DES ETATS-UNIS

LE CHÂTEAU

Port Lympia

Parc Vigier

See inset map for detail

Gare Maritime

HOTELS

Le Capitole	4
Les Cigales	6
Cronstadt	7
L'Oasis	3
Les Orangers	2
La Pérouse	8
Regency	1
St-François	5

N

0   500 m

CHEMINS DE FER DE LA PROVENCE

The **Chemins de Fer de la Provence** runs one of France's most scenic and fun railway routes from the new station on Nice's rue Alfred Binet, 10 minutes' walk north of the gare SNCF (or buses #4 or #5). The line runs up the valley of the Var between **Nice** and **Digne-les-Bains** (see p.919), climbing through some spectacular scenery as it goes. Four trains run daily, year-round, and the whole, inexpensive, journey takes 3hr 15min.

the city one of Europe's most fashionable winter retreats have all survived intact. It has also retained mementos from its ancient past, when the Romans ruled the region from here, and earlier still, when the Greeks founded the city. In addition, its bus and train connections make Nice by far the best base for visiting the rest of the Riviera.

Arrival, information and accommodation

Arriving by **air**, you can get different buses into town: bus #23 to the gare SNCF (8.50F); a speedy *navette* (taking 15min; 26F); or a bus (every 20min, 22F) from outside the end door of Aérogare I to the junction of avenue Gustav V and the promenade des Anglais, or onto the **gare routière**, which for once is very central, close to the old town beneath the promenade du Paillon on boulevard Jean-Jaurès (☎04.93.85.61.81). The **gare SNCF** is a little further out, a couple of blocks west of the top end of avenue Jean-Médecin (☎08.36.35.35.35; bus #12 or #15 to place Masséna).

You'll find the main **tourist office** beside the gare SNCF on avenue Thiers (daily: mid June–mid Sept 7.30am–8pm; rest of year 8am–7pm; ☎04.93.87.07.07). It's one of the most useful, helpful and generous of Côte tourist offices and has **annexes** at 5 promenade des Anglais (☎04.92.14.48.00) and at Nice-Ferber (☎04.93.83.32.64) further along the promenade des Anglais near the airport (both mid-June to mid-Sept Mon–Sat 8am–8pm, Sun 9am–1pm; rest of year Mon–Sat 9am–6pm), and another at Terminal 1 of the airport (daily 8am–10pm; ☎04.93.21.44.11). Any of these offices can supply you with a free listings magazine, *Le Mois à Nice*.

Buses operate frequent services around the city, running until 12.15am, with four lines running until 1.10am. Fares are flat-rate and you can buy a single ticket on the bus (8.50F) or a carnet of ten tickets (68F). There are also one-day (22F; available on bus), five-day (85F) or weekly passes (110F), all of which can be bought at tabacs, kiosks, newsagents and from Sunbus, the transport office at 10 av Félix-Faure, where you can also pick up a free route map. **Bicycles**, **mopeds** and **motorbikes** can be rented from Nicea Location Rent at 9 av Thiers, just by the gare SNCF.

Before you start hunting around for **accommodation**, it's well worth taking advantage of the **reservation service** offered by the tourist office at the train station. The area around the station teems with cheap, seedy hotels, but it's perfectly possible to find reasonably priced rooms in Vieux Nice. In summer, there's a fairly good choice of youth accommodation. Sleeping on the beach, which used to be common though always illegal, is now difficult since it's brightly illuminated the whole length of the promenade des Anglais.

Hotels

Le Capitole, 4 rue de la Tour (☎04.93.80.08.15, fax 04.93.85.10.58). A good if potentially noisy location in Vieux Nice, with a warm atmosphere though not over-generous rooms. ④.

Les Cigales, 16 rue Dalpozzo (☎04.93.88.33.75). Clean, quiet and close to the beach. ②.

Cronstadt, 3 rue Cronstadt (☎04.93.82.00.30). Hidden away one block away from the seafront; charming *patronne*; free parking on street; old-fashioned clean and comfortable rooms; amazingly good value. ③.

L'Oasis, 23 rue Gournod (☎04.93.88.12.29, fax 04.93.16.14.40). In a quiet part of town not far from the station. Small rooms, but comfortable. ④.

Les Orangers, 10bis av Durante (☎04.93.87.51.41, fax 04.93.82.57.82). A cheapie that all American students head for and unfailingly recommend. ②.

La Pérouse, 11 quai Rauba-Capeu (☎04.93.62.34.63, fax 04.93.62.59.41). A wonderful location at the foot of Le Château, with views across the bay. Very luxurious. ⑦.

Regency, 2 rue St-Siagre (☎04.93.62.17.44, fax 04.93.92.23.26). Good-value self-contained studio apartments for 2–4 people run by a friendly, helpful manager. Near station, but quiet. ②.

St-François, 3 rue St-François (☎04.93.85.88.69). On a busy pedestrian thoroughfare in the old town, above a restaurant hosting live jazz on Friday nights. An ideal base if you're not bothered by noise. ②.

Hostels and campsite

HI youth hostel, rte Forestière du Mont-Alban (☎04.93.89.23.64, fax 04.93.04.03.10). Nice's hostel is 4km out of town and, for two people, not a lot cheaper than sharing a hotel room. The last bus from the centre leaves at 7.30pm; bus #14 from place Masséna, direction "Place du Mont-Boron", stop L'Auberge.

Backpacker's Hotel, 32 rue Pertinax (☎04.93.80.30.72). Close to gare SNCF; dorms with kitchen facilities and no curfew. ①.

Clairvallon Relais International de la Jeunesse, 26 av Scudéri (☎04.93.81.27.63, fax 04.93.53.35.88). 10km north of the centre, but it's slightly cheaper than the youth hostel, pleasantly informal and has a pool; take bus #15 or #25, stop Scudéri.

MJC Magnan, 31 rue Louis-de-Coppet (☎04.93.86.28.75, fax 04.93.44.93.22). The least expensive of the hostel options: not too far from the centre and close to the beach. Take buses #3, #9, #10, #12, #22 or #23, stop Magnan. Mid-June to mid-Sept. ①.

Camping Terry, 768 rte de Grenoble, St-Isidore (☎04.93.08.11.58). The only campsite anywhere near Nice, 6.5km north of the airport on the N202: take the #700 bus from the gare routière to La Manda stop, or the Chemins de Fer de la Provence railway to Bellet-Tennis des Combes.

The city

It doesn't take long to get a feel for the layout of Nice. Shadowed by mountains that curve down to the Mediterranean east of its port, it still breaks up more or less into old and new. **Vieux Nice**, the old town, groups about the hill of **Le Château**, its limits signalled by **boulevard Jean-Jaurès**, built along the course of the River Paillon. Along the seafront, the celebrated **promenade des Anglais** runs a cool 5km until forced to curve inland by the sea-projecting runways of the airport. The central square, **place Masséna**, is at the bottom of the modern city's main street, **avenue Jean-Médecin**, while off to the north is the exclusive hillside suburb of **Cimiez**.

The château and Vieux Nice

For initial orientation, with brilliant sea and city views, fresh air and the scent of Mediterranean vegetation, the best place to make for is the **Château park** (daily: April, May & Sept 9am–7pm; June–Aug 9am–8pm; Oct–Mar 10am–5.30pm). It's where Nice

NICE'S MUSEUMS

Entrance is free to all Nice's municipal **museums** on the first Sunday of each month. A **seven-day pass** allowing a single entrance to all museums except the Chagall Museum costs 40F. A museum pass, valid for fifteen visits of your choice within one year, is available from all the museums, price 120F (reduced rate 60F).

began as the ancient Greek city of Nikea, hence the mosaics and stone vases in mock Grecian style. There's no château as such, but the real pleasure lies in looking down on the scrambled rooftops and gleaming mosaic tiles of Vieux Nice and along the sweep of the promenade des Anglais. To reach the park, you can either take the lift by the Tour Bellanda, at the eastern end of quai des États-Unis, or climb the steps from rue de la Providence or rue du Château in the old town.

Vieux Nice has been greatly gentrified over the last decade, but the expensive shops, smart restaurants and art galleries still coexist with little hardware stores selling brooms and bottled gas; tiny cafés are full of men in blue overalls; and washing strung between the tenements. The streets are too narrow for buses and are best explored on foot.

The central square is **place Rossetti**, where the soft-coloured Baroque **Cathédrale de St-Réparate** (daily 8am–7pm) just manages to be visible in the concatenation of eight narrow streets. There are two cafés to relax in, with the choice of sun or shade, and a magical ice-cream parlour, *Fenocchio*, with an extraordinary choice of flavours. The real magnet of the old town, though, is **cours Saleya** and the adjacent place Pierre-Gautier and place Charles-Félix. These are wide-open, sunlit spaces alongside grandiloquent municipal buildings and Italianate chapels and the site of the city's main **market**. Every day except Monday from 6am to 1pm there are gorgeous displays of fruit, vegetables, cheeses and sausages, plus cut flowers and potted roses, mimosa and other scented plants displayed till 5.30pm; on Monday the stalls sell bric-a-brac and secondhand clothes. Café and restaurant tables fill the *cours* on summer nights, when literally thousands of people are enjoying the warmth and extraordinary animation.

To feast your eyes on Baroque splendour, pop into the **chapels** and **churches** of Vieux Nice: La Chapelle de la Miséricorde, on cours Saleya (open for Sunday Mass 10.30am or through the Palais Lascaris, see below); L'Église du Gesu, on rue Droite (9am–6pm); or L'Église St-Augustine, on place St-Augustine (open for Mass Sat 4pm & Sun 9am), which also contains a fine *Pietà* by Louis Bréa. For contemporary graphic and photographic art, some of the best **art galleries** in Vieux Nice include Galerie Espace Ste-Réparate, 4 rue Ste-Réparate; *Galerie Municipale Renoir*, 8 rue de la Loge and Galerie du Château, 14 rue Droite.

Also on rue Droite is the **Palais Lascaris** (Tues–Sun 10am–noon & 2–6pm; closed Nov; 25F), a seventeenth-century palace built by a family whose arms, engraved on the ceiling of the entrance hall, bear the motto "Not even lightning strikes us". It's all very noble, with frescoes, tapestries and chandeliers, along with a collection of porcelain vases from an eighteenth-century pharmacy.

In contrast, the light and joyous art of Raoul Dufy can be seen at the **Musée Dufy/Galerie des Ponchettes**, between cours Saleya and the sea at 77 quai des États-Unis (Tues–Sat 10am–noon & 2–6pm, Sun 2–6pm; 15F, or 25F with Musée Mossa). It exhibits the town's considerable collection of Dufy's works, including many painted in Nice, in temporary exhibitions. Nearby, at 59 quai des États-Unis, is the less appealing collection of the **Musée Alexis et Gustav Adolf Mossa** (same hours and prices): vapid watercolours by the father, lurid symbolist paintings reeking of misogyny by the son.

Place Masséna and around

The stately **place Masséna** is the hub of the new town, built in 1835 across the path of the River Paillon, with good views north past fountains and palm trees to the mountains. A balustraded terrace and steps on the south of the square lead to Vieux Nice; the new town lies to the north. It's a pretty and spacious expanse, without being very significant – in fact the only things of interest here are the sundry ice-cream vendors who shelter their goods under the arcades during summer. A short walk to the west lie the **Jardins Albert 1er**, on the promenade des Anglais, where the Théâtre de Verdune occasionally hosts concerts.

The covered course of the Paillon to the north of place Masséna has provided the sites for the city's more recent municipal prestige projects. At their worst, up beyond traverse Barla, they take the form of giant packing crates for high-tech goods, in the multi-media, mega-buck conference centre grotesquely called the **Acropolis**. Though theoretically a public building, with exhibition space, a cinema and bowling alley (11am–2am), international business often limits casual entry. There are, however, various modern sculptures outside the building on which to vent your critical frustration.

Downstream from the Acropolis is the vast marble **Musée d'Art Moderne et d'Art Contemporain**, or MAMAC (Wed–Mon 10am–6pm; 25F), with rotating exhibitions of avant-garde French and American movements from the 1960s to the present. New Realism (smashing, burning, squashing, wrapping, etc, the detritus or mundane objects of everyday life) and Pop Art feature strongly with works by, among others, Warhol, Klein, Lichtenstein, César, Arman and Christo. It's good fun, and the huge, light galleries are a delight to walk around.

Running north from place Masséna, **avenue Jean-Médecin** is the city's main shopping street, with nothing much to distinguish it from any other big French city high street. You'll find all the mainstream clothes and household accessory chains, plus FNAC for books and records, at the Nice-Étoile **shopping complex** between rue Biscarra and bd Dubouchage. **Couturier** shops are to be found west of place Masséna on rue du Paradis and av de Suède. Both these streets lead to the pedestrianized **rue Masséna** and the end of **rue de France** – all hotels, bars, restaurants, ice-cream and fast-food outlets, with no regard for quality or style.

Skirting this, the chief interest in western Nice is in the older architecture: eighteenth and nineteenth-century Italian Baroque and Neoclassical, florid Belle Époque, and unclassifiable exotic aristo-fantasy. The trophy for the most gilded, exotic and elaborate edifice goes to the **Russian Orthodox Cathedral**, off boulevard Tsaréwitch at the end of av Nicolas-II (daily except Sun am summer 9am–noon & 2.30–6pm, winter 9.30am–noon & 2.30–5pm; 15F; bus #14 or #17, stop Tsaréwitch).

The promenade des Anglais and the beaches

The point where the Paillon flows into the sea marks the beginning of the world-famous palm-fringed **promenade des Anglais**, created by nineteenth-century English residents for their afternoon's sea-breeze stroll along the Mediterranean sea coast. Today it's the city's unofficial high-speed racetrack, bordered by some of the most fanciful turn-of-the-century architecture on the Côte d'Azur.

Most celebrated of all is the opulent **Negresco Hotel** at no. 37, built in 1906, and filling up the block between rues de Rivoli and Cronstadt. Though they will try to stop you if you are not deemed to be wearing *tenue correcte* (especially in the evenings), you can try wandering in to take a look at the Salon Louis XIV and the Salon Royale. The first, on the left of the foyer, has a seventeenth-century painted oak ceiling and mammoth fireplace, plus royal portraits, all from various French châteaux. The Salon Royale, in the centre of the hotel, is a vast domed oval room, decorated with 24-carat gold leaf and the biggest carpet ever to have come out of the Savonnerie workshops. The chandelier is one of a pair commissioned from Baccarat by Tsar Nicholas II – the other hangs in the Kremlin.

Just before the *Negresco*, with its entrance at 65 rue de France, the **Musée Masséna** (Tues–Sun 10am–noon & 2–5/6pm; 25F) is one of those dire historical museums committed to making its subjects – in this case the history of Nice, Garibaldi and Napoleonic times – as inaccessible and uninteresting as possible.

A kilometre or so down the promenade and a couple of blocks inland at 33 av des Baumettes is the **Musée des Beaux-Arts** (Tues–Sun 10am–noon & 2–6pm; 25F; bus #38, stop Chéret). It has too many whimsical canvases by Jules Chéret, who died in Nice in 1932, a great many Belle Époque paintings to go with the building, a room dedicated to the Van Loos, plus modern works that come as unexpected delights: a Rodin bust of Victor Hugo and some very amusing Van Dongens, such as the *Archangel's Tango*. Monet, Sisley – one of his famous poplar alleys – and Degas also grace the walls.

The **beach** below the promenade des Anglais is all pebbles and mostly public, with showers provided. It's not particularly clean and you need to watch out for broken glass. There are, of course, the mattress, food and drinks concessionaries, but nothing like to the extent of Cannes. There's a small, more secluded beach on the west side of Le Château, below the sea wall of the port. But the best, and cleanest, place to swim, if you don't mind rocks, is the string of coves beyond the port that starts with the **plage de la Reserve** opposite parc Vigier (bus #32 or #3). From the water you can look up at the nineteenth-century fantasy palaces built onto the steep slopes of the **Cap du Nice**. Further up, past **Coco Beach** (bus #3 only, stop Villa La Côte), rather smelly steps lead down to a coastal path which continues around the headland. Towards dusk this becomes a gay pick-up place.

The **port**, flanked by gorgeous red to ochre eighteenth-century buildings and headed by the Neoclassical Notre-Dame du Port, is full of bulbous yachts but has little quayside life despite the restaurants along quai Lunel. On the hill to the east, prehistoric life in the region has been reconstructed on the site of an excavated fossil beach in the **Musée de Terra Amata**, 25 bd Carnot (closed, possibly for good, 1998 – enquire at the tourist office ☎04.93.88.11.34; if open, bus #32 from the port).

Cimiez

The northern suburb of **Cimiez** has always been a posh place. Its principal streets, avenue des Arènes-de-Cimiez and boulevard de Cimiez, rise between plush, high-walled villas to what was the social centre of the town's elite some 1700 years ago, when the city was capital of the Roman province of Alpes-Maritimae. Part of a small amphitheatre still stands, and excavations of the **Roman baths** have revealed enough detail to distinguish the sumptuous and elaborate facilities for the top tax official and his cronies, the plainer public baths and a separate complex for women. All the finds, plus an illustration of the city's history up to the Middle Ages, are displayed in the impressive, modern **Musée d'Archéologie**, rue Monte-Croce (Tues–Sun: April–Sept 10am–noon & 2–6pm; Oct–March 10am–1pm & 2–5pm; 25F; bus #15, #17, #20 or #22, stop Arènes).

The seventeenth-century villa between the excavations and the arena is the **Musée Matisse** (daily except Tues 10am–5/6pm; 25F). Matisse spent his winters in Nice from 1916 onwards, staying in hotels on the promenade – from where *A Tempest at Nice* was painted – and then from 1921 to 1938 renting an apartment overlooking place Charles-Félix. It was here that he painted his most sensual, colour-flooded canvases of odalisques posed against exotic draperies. As well as the Mediterranean light, Matisse loved the cosmopolitan aspect of Nice, the rococo salons of the hotels and the presence of fellow artists Renoir, Bonnard and Picasso in neighbouring towns. He died in Cimiez in November 1954, aged 85. Almost all his last works in Nice were cut-out compositions, with an artistry of line showing how he could wield a pair of scissors with just as much strength and delicacy as a paintbrush.

The museum's collection, with work from every period, includes a great number of drawings and an almost complete set of his bronze sculptures. There are sketches for one of the *Dance* murals; models for the Vence chapel plus the priests' robes he designed; book illustrations; and excellent examples of his cut-out technique, of which the most delightful are *The Bees* and *The Créole Dancer*. Among the paintings are the 1905 portrait of Madame Matisse; *The Storm at Nice* (1919–20), which seems to get wetter and darker the further you step back from it; *Odalisk*; the 1947 *Still Life with Pomegranates*; and one of his two earliest attempts at oil painting, *Still Life with Books*, painted in 1890.

The Roman remains and the Musée Matisse back onto an old olive grove, one of the best open spaces in Nice and venue for the July **jazz festival**. At its eastern end are the sixteenth-century buildings and exquisite gardens of the **Monastère Notre-Dame de Cimiez** (Mon–Sat 10am–12.30pm & 3–7pm; free); the oratory has brilliant murals illustrating alchemy, while the church houses three masterpieces of medieval painting by Louis Bréa and Antoine Bréa.

At the foot of Cimiez hill, just off boulevard-Cimiez on avenue du Docteur-Menard, **Chagall's Biblical Message** is housed in a museum built specially for the work and opened by the artist in 1972 (daily except Tues 10am–5/6pm; 30F, or 38F for summer exhibitions; bus #15 stop Musée Chagall). The rooms are light, white and cool, with windows allowing you to see the greenery of the garden beyond the indescribable shades between pink and red of the *Song of Songs* canvases. The seventeen paintings are all based on the Old Testament and complemented with etchings and engravings. To the building itself, Chagall contributed a mosaic and stained-glass window.

Theme and leisure parks

Right out by the airport is a vast tourist attraction, the **Phoenix Parc Floral de Nice**, 405 promenade des Anglais (Tues–Sun: Feb & March & Oct–Dec 9am–5pm; April–Sept 9am–7pm; 45F; exit St-Augustin from the motorway or bus #9, #10, or #23 from Nice). It's a cross between botanical gardens, a bird and insect zoo, and a tacky theme park: automated dinosaurs and mock Mayan temples along with alpine streams, ginkgo trees, butterflies and cockatoos. The greenhouse full of butterflies fluttering around is the star attraction, but the assumption that the world's fauna and flora is yours to admire may make you feel a bit uneasy.

More manageable in size is the **Musée des Trains Miniatures**, in the park on boulevard Impératrice-Eugénie (daily 9.30am–5.30/7pm; 30F; bus #22), which displays model train sets with all the scenery and rolling stock from steam to TGV.

Eating, nightlife and festivals

Nice is a great place for **food** indulgence, whether you're picnicking on market fare, snacking on Niçois specialities or dining in the palace hotels. The Italian influence is strong in all restaurants, with pasta on every menu; seafood is also a staple. For **snacks**, many of the cafés sell sandwiches with typically Provençal fillings such as fresh basil, olive oil, goat's cheese and *mesclum*, the unique green salad mix of the region. If you want to buy the best bread or croissants in town, seek out *Espuno*, 22 rue Vernier, in the old town.

Excellent restaurants can be found throughout most of Nice. Vieux Nice has a dozen on every street catering for a wide variety of budgets; the port quaysides have very good, but pricey, fish restaurants. In summer it's wise to book tables or turn up before 8pm, especially in Vieux Nice.

Given the city's staid, affluent population, the late-night scene tends to be dominated by luxury hotel **bars**. But **pubs** are popular with the young, and Vieux Nice has a wide choice of venues for drinking and dancing, though the music tends not to be very novel. As for Niçois **nightclubs**, bouncers judging your wallet or exclusive membership lists are the rule.

Cafés and bars

Bar des Oiseaux, 9 rue St-Vincent. Named for the birds that fly down from their nests in the loft and the pet parrot and screeching myna bird that perch by the door. Serves delicious and copious baguette sandwiches. Erratic opening hours, sometimes closed all afternoon.

Caves Ricord, 2 rue Neuve. An old-fashioned wine bar with faded peeling posters and drinkers to match. A wide selection of wine by the glass, plus pizzas and other snacks. Closed Wed & mid-June to mid-July.

La Douche à l'Etage, 34 cours Saleya. A cyber café with four terminals linked up to the Internet while upstairs there really is a shower, plus comfy settees, billiards and music. Open till 12.30am.

Les Ponchettes and **La Civette du Cours**, cours Saleya. At Le Château end of the marketplace, neighbouring cafés with cane seats fanning out a good 50m from the doors. Open late in summer.

Scarlet O'Hara, 22 rue Droite. Tiny Irish folk bar on the corner of rue Rosetti serving the creamiest, priciest Guinness this side of the Irish Sea. Daily 6pm–12.30am; closed Mon & first half of July.

Restaurants

L'Auberge de Théo, 52 av Cap-de-Croix (☎04.93.81.26.19). Pleasant Italian food up in Cimiez. 130F menu (except Sat & Sun eve). Closed Mon & third week Aug–second week Sept.

Le Bateleur, 12–14 cours Saleya (☎04.93.85.77.15). Generous and delicious pizzas for around 50F, plus live bands of dubious talent. Open till 2.30am.

Chantecler and **La Rotonde**, *Hôtel Negresco*, 37 promenade des Anglais (☎04.93.16.64.00). *Chantecler* is the best restaurant in Nice and over 400F à la carte, but chef Dominique Le Stanc provides a lunchtime menu, wine and coffee included, for 250F, which will give you a good idea of how sublime Niçoise food at its best can be. At *La Rotonde* you can taste less fancy but still mouthwatering dishes on 110F and 150F menus. Closed mid-Nov to mid-Dec.

Chez Flo, 4 rue Sacha-Guitry (☎04.93.13.33.38). A big brasserie behind Galeries Lafayette, serving *choucroute*, *confit de canard*, seafood and great *crème brûlée*. 95F menu with wine after 10pm. Open till 1am.

Chez René Socca, 2 rue Miralhéti, off rue Pairolière. The cheapest meal in town: you can buy helpings of *socca*, *pissaladière*, stuffed peppers, pasta or *calamares* at the counter and eat with your fingers on stools ranged haphazardly across the street; the bar opposite serves the drinks. Closed Mon & Nov.

L'Estrilla, 13 rue de l'Abbaye (☎04.93.62.62.00). Very popular restaurant serving ace *petites fritures* and paella in huge earthenware pots. From 150F; menu around 100F before 8pm. Closed Mon lunch & Sun.

du Gesú, 1 place du Jésus (☎04.93.62.26.46). Extremely popular restaurant with a great atmosphere, serving no-nonsense Niçoise/Provençal food, including good *daube* and pizzas. In an attractive church square in the heart of Vieux Nice. Closed Sun.

Nissa La Bella, 6 rue Ste-Réparate (☎04.93.62.10.20). *Socca*, pizzas and other real Niçois specialities. From 80F. Closed Wed & Sun lunchtime.

La Noisetine, cours Saleya, near rue Gassin. One of the cheapest places to eat on the cours Saleya with generous and tasty crêpes, huge salads, nice desserts and fresh fruit juices. Open till midnight.

Virginie, 2 place A-Blanqui (☎04.93.55.10.07). Excellent *plateau des fruits de mer*. From 80F.

Clubs

B52, 8 Descente Crotti. Small dance floor, young clientele and good value. Daily 11pm–4am, free entry until 1am.

Le Baby Doll, 227 bd de la Madeleine. Lesbian disco, not exclusively female. Daily from 10pm.

Le Blue Boy, 9 rue Jean-Baptiste-Spinétta. Lesbians and heteros are welcome at this, Nice's best gay venue off bd François-Grosso. Two bars, two dance floors, DJs who know what's what, and a floorshow every Wed night. Daily 11pm–dawn; entrance charge Wed & weekends.

Blue Whales, 1 rue Mascoïnat (☎04.93.85.00.57). Intimate venue with friendly atmosphere, and live music after 10pm ranging from Latin to rock. Open till 2.30am.

Chez Wayne, 15 rue de la Préfecture. Popular bar on the edge of the old town run by an expat who shares the French penchant for good old rock'n'roll. Live bands – of greatly varying quality – Fri and Sat nights. Daily 10am–midnight.

L'Iguane, 5 quai des Deux-Emmanuel. Very stylish night bar with dance floor for the poseurs. Daily till 6am.

Subway, 19 rue Droite. Reggae, soul and rock; reasonably priced. Tues–Sat from 11.30pm.

Festivals

Details of Nice's lively **festival** calendar are available from the pamphlet *Nice: vos rendez-vous* or the main tourist office. The **Mardi Gras Carnival** opens the year's events in February, with the second and third week of July taken up by the **Nice Jazz Festival** in the Parc de Cimiez (☎04.93.87.19.18 for info; or fax the main tourist office in May/June time).

Listings

Airlines Air France ☎08.02.80.28.02; British Airways ☎08.02.80.29.02; Debonair ☎08.00.90.16.16; Delta ☎08.00.35.40.80; EasyJet ☎04.93.21.48.33; Virgin Express ☎08.00.52.85.28.

Airport information ☎04.93.21.30.30.

Books English bookshop: The Cat's Whiskers, 26 rue Lamartine.

Car rental Major firms represented at the airport. Otherwise try: ADA, 24 av Clemenceau (☎04.93.82.27.00); Avis, 2 av Phocéens (☎04.93.80.63.52); Budget, quai Papacino (☎04.93.56.45.50); Europcar, 89 rue de France (☎04.93.88.64.04); Hertz, 12 av de Suède (☎04.93.87.11.87).

Consulate Canada, 64 av Jean Médecin (☎04.93.92.93.22); UK, 8 rue Alphonse Karr (☎04.93.82.32.04); USA, 31 rue Maréchal Joffre (☎04.93.88.89.55).

Cyber café La Douche, 34 cours Saleya (☎04.93.92.34.34); Internet Self-Service, 2 rue St-Siagre (☎04.93.97.92.33).

Disabled Access Transport for people with reduced mobility ☎04.93.86.39.87 or 04.93.96.09.99

Emergencies Doctor: SOS. Médecins ☎04.93.85.01.01; Casualty: Hôpital St-Roch, 5 rue Pierre-Dévoluy (☎04.92.03.33.75); Ambulance: ☎15 or ☎04.93.92.55.55.

Ferries to Corsica SNCM gare Maritime, quai du Commerce (☎04.93.13.66.66) or Corsica Ferries (☎04.92.00.42.93).

Lost property 10 cours Saleya (☎04.93.80.65.50). SOS Voyageurs for help with lost or stolen luggage at gare SNCF (Mon–Fri 9am–noon & 3–6pm; ☎04.93.16.02.61).

Money exchange Change Halévy, 1 rue Halévy, daily 8am–7pm; Change d'Or Charrière, 10 rue de France, daily winter 8am–8pm, summer 8am–midnight.

Police Commissariat Central de Police, 1 av Maréchal Foch (☎04.92.17.22.22).

Post office place Wilson, 06000 Nice.

Pharmacy 7 rue Masséna 7.30pm–8am (☎04.93.87.78.94); 66 av J-Médecin (☎04.93.62.54.44).

Taxis ☎04.93.80.70.70 or ☎04.93.13.78.78.

Trains Information and reservations ☎08.36.35.35.35. For the scenic line to Digne: Chemins de Fer de la Provence, 4 bis rue Alfred Binet (☎04.93.82.10.17).

Youth information Centre Information Jeunesse, 19 rue Gioffredo (☎04.93.80.93.93).

The Corniches

Three **corniche roads** run east from Nice to the independent principality of Monaco and to Menton, the last town of the French Riviera. Napoléon built the **Grande Corniche** on the route of the Romans' Via Julia Augusta; and the **Moyenne Corniche** dates from the first quarter of the twentieth century, when aristocratic tourism on the Riviera was already causing congestion on the lower, coastal road, the **Corniche Inférieure**. The upper two are the classic location for executive car commercials, and for fatal car crashes in films. Real deaths occur too – most notoriously Princess Grace of Monaco, who died on the Moyenne Corniche.

Buses take all three routes; the **train** follows the lower corniche, and all three are superb means of seeing the most mountainous stretch of the Côte d'Azur. Staying in a **hotel** anywhere between Nice and Menton is expensive; it makes more sense to base yourself in Nice and treat these routes as pleasure rides.

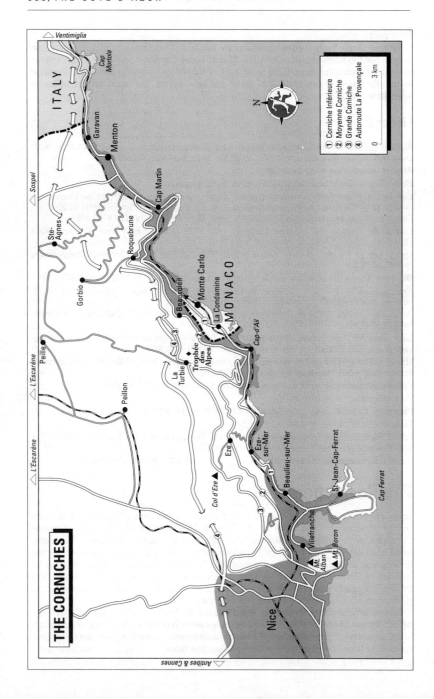

THE CORNICHES

Ventimiglia

Cap Mortola

ITALY

Garavan

Menton

Sospel

Cap Martin

Ste-Agnès

Roquebrune

Gorbio

Monte Carlo

Beausoleil

MONACO

La Condamine

Cap-d'Ail

L'Escarène

Peille

Trophée des Alpes

La Turbie

Peillon

L'Escarène

Eze-sur-Mer

Eze

Beaulieu-sur-Mer

Col d'Eze

St-Jean-Cap-Ferrat

Cap Ferrat

Villefranche

Mt. Alban

Mt. Baron

Nice

Antibes & Cannes

N

① Corniche Inférieure
② Moyenne Corniche
③ Grande Corniche
④ Autoroute La Provençale

0   3 km

The Corniche Inférieure

The characteristic Côte d'Azur mansions that represent the stylistically incompatible fantasies of their original owners parade along the **Corniche Inférieure**. Or they lurk screened from view on the promontories of **Cap Ferrat**, their gardens infested with killer cacti and piranha ponds if the plethora of "Défense d'entrer – Danger de Mort" signs is anything to go by.

VILLEFRANCHE-SUR-MER is just over the other side of Mont Alban from Nice, and has been spared architectural eyesores only to be marred by lurking US and French warships attracted by the deep waters of the bay. But as long as your visit doesn't coincide with shore leave, the old town on the waterfront, with its active fleet of fishing boats, sixteenth-century citadel and its rue Obscure running beneath the houses, feels almost like the genuine article – an illusion which the quayside restaurants' prices quickly dispel.

The tiny fishing harbour is overlooked by the medieval **Chapelle de St-Pierre**, (Tues–Sun: spring 9.30am–noon & 3–7pm; summer 10am–noon & 4–8.30pm, winter 9.30am–noon & 2—6pm; closed mid-Nov to mid-Dec; 12F), decorated by Jean Cocteau in 1957 in shades he described as "ghosts of colours". The colours fill drawings in strong and simple lines portraying scenes from the life of St Peter and homages to the women of Villefranche and to the gypsies. Above the altar, Peter walks on water supported by an angel to the outrage of the fish and to the amusement of Christ. The fishermen's eyes are drawn as fish; the ceramic eyes on either side of the door are the flames of the apocalypse; and the altar candelabras of night-time fishing forks rise above single eyes. The chapel is used just once a year, on June 29, when local fishermen celebrate the feast day of St Peter and St Paul with a mass.

On the main road along the neck of the **Cap Ferrat peninsula**, between Villefranche and Beaulieu, stands the **Villa Ephrussi** (mid-Feb to Oct daily 10am–6/7pm; rest of year Mon–Fri 2–6pm, Sat & Sun 10am–6pm; 46F). Built in 1912 for a Rothschild heiress, it overflows with decorative art, paintings, sculpture and artefacts ranging from the fourteenth to the nineteenth centuries, and from European to Far Eastern origins. In addition, the villa is surrounded by huge, elaborate gardens.

BEAULIEU, overlooking the pretty Baie des Fourmis, is sheltered by a ring of hills that ensure some of the highest temperatures on the Côte. Its main point of interest is the **Villa Kerylos** (mid-Feb to mid-Nov daily 10.30am–6pm; July & Aug daily till 7pm; mid-Dec to mid-Feb Mon–Fri 2–6pm, Sat & Sun 10.30am–6pm; 40F), a near-perfect reproduction of an ancient Greek villa, just east of the casino on avenue Gustav-Eiffel. Théodore Reinach, the archeologist who had it built, lived here for twenty years, eating, dressing and acting like an Athenian citizen, taking baths with his male friends and assigning separate suites to women. However perverse the concept, it's a visual knockout, with faithfully reproduced mosaics and vases and lavish use of marble and alabaster. The Villa is only five minutes walk from the **gare SNCF**. For those tempted to **stay** overnight, two economical options are the family-run *Hôtel Riviera*, at 6 rue Paul Doumer right in the centre near the sea (☎04.93.01.04.92, fax 19.31; ③), and the *Select*, 1 place Gén-de-Gaulle (☎04.93.01.05.42, fax 34.30; ③), which is basic but clean, comfortable and excellent value for this part of the world.

The Moyenne Corniche

Of the three roads, the **Moyenne Corniche** is the most photogenic, a real cliff-hanging, car-chase highway. Eleven kilometres from Nice, the medieval village of **EZE** winds round its conical rock just below the corniche. No other *village perché* is more infested with antique dealers, pseudo-artisans and other caterers to the touristic rich, and it requires a major mental feat to recall that the labyrinth of tiny vaulted passages and stairways was designed not for charm but from fear of attack. At the summit, a cacti garden, the **Jardin Exotique** (daily: summer 9am–8pm;winter 9am–noon & 2–7pm; 15F) covers the site of the former castle.

From place du Centenaire, just outside the old village, you can reach the shore through open countryside via the **sentier Frédéric-Nietzsche**. The philosopher is said to have conceived part of *Thus Spake Zarathustra*, his shaggy dog story against believing answers to ultimate questions, on this path – which isn't quite as hard going as the book. You arrive at the Corniche Inférieure at the eastern limit of Eze-sur-Mer (coming upwards, it's signposted to *La Village*).

The Grande Corniche

At every other turn on the **Grande Corniche**, you're invited to park your car and enjoy a *belvédère*. At certain points, such as **Col d'Eze**, you can turn off upwards for even higher views. Eighteen stunning kilometres from Nice, you reach the village of **LA TURBIE** and its **Trophée des Alpes**, a 6 BC monument to the power of Rome and the total subjugation of the local peoples. Originally a statue of Augustus Cæsar stood on the 45-metre plinth, which was pillaged, ransacked for building materials and blown up over the centuries. Painstakingly restored in the 1930s, it now stands statueless, 35m high, and, viewed from a distance, still looks imperious. If you want a closer inspection, you'll have to buy a ticket (April–June daily 9.30am–6pm; July to mid-Sept daily 9.30am–7pm; mid-Sept to March Tues–Sun 10am–5pm; 25F). Several buses a day run from here to Monaco and Nice, from Monday to Saturday.

As the corniche descends towards Cap Martin, it passes the eleventh-century castle of **ROQUEBRUNE**, its village nestling round the base of the rock. The **castle** (Feb–May Sat–Thurs 10am–12.30pm & 2–6pm; June–Sept daily 10am–12.30pm & 3–7.30pm; Oct—Jan Sat–Thurs 10am–12.30pm & 2–5pm; 20F) has been kitted out enthusiastically in medieval fashion, while the tiny vaulted passages and stairways of the village are almost too good to be true. One thing that hasn't been restored is the vast millenial **olive tree** that lies just to the east of the village on the chemin de Menton. To get to the *vieux village* from the **gare SNCF**, turn east and then right up avenue de la Côte d'Azur, then first left up escalier Corinthille, across the Grande Corniche and up escalier Chanoine-J-B-Grana. The only hotel worth trying in the old village is *Les Deux Frères*, place des Deux-Frères (☎04.93.28.99.00, fax 04.93.28.99.10; ⑤), which is worth booking in advance to try to get one of the rooms with the awesome view (rooms #1 or #2).

Southeast of the old town and the station is the peninsula of **Cap Martin**, with a **coastal path**, giving you access to a wonderful shoreline of white rocks and wind-bent pines. The path is named after **Le Corbusier**, who spent several summers in Roquebrune and died by drowning off Cap Martin in 1965. His grave – designed by himself – is in the **cemetery** (square J near the flagpole), high above the old village on promenade 1er-DFL.

A gourmet treat here is the panoramic **restaurant** *Le Vistaero*, on the Grande Corniche (☎04.92.10.40.20), with a brilliant lunchtime menu for 190F (Mon–Sat; closed mid-Jan to Feb).

Monaco

Monstrosities are common on the Côte d'Azur, but nowhere – not even Cannes – can outdo **MONACO**. This tiny independent principality, no bigger than London's Hyde Park, has lived off gambling and catering for the desires of the idle international rich for the last hundred years. Meanwhile, it has become one of the greatest property speculation sites

---

Monaco phone numbers have only eight digits and no -04 French area code. If you are phoning from France you must dial Monaco's international code 00377-, then the number.

---

in the world – a sort of Manhattan-on-Sea without the saving aesthetic grace of the skyscrapers rising from a single level.

The principality has been in the hands of the ruling Grimaldi family since the thirteenth century, and legally Monaco would once again become part of France were the royal line to die out. The current ruler, Prince Rainier, is the one constitutionally autocratic ruler left in Europe, under whose nose every French law is passed for approval prior to being applied to Monaco. There is a parliament, but with limited functions and elected only by Monegasque nationals – about sixteen percent of the population. But there is no opposition to the ruling family. The citizens and non-French residents pay no income tax and their riches are protected by rigorous security forces; Monaco has more police per square metre than any other country in the world.

One time to avoid Monaco – unless you're a motor-racing enthusiast – is the second week in May, when racing cars burn around the port and casino for the Formula 1 **Monaco Grand Prix**. Every space in sight of the circuit is inaccessible without a ticket, making casual sightseeing out of the question.

The Principality

The oldest part of the two-kilometre-long state is **Monaco-Ville**, around the palace on the high rocky promontory, with the new suburb and marina of **Fontvieille** in its western shadow. **La Condamine** is the old port quarter on the other side of the promontory; **Larvotto**, the bathing resort with artificial beaches of imported sand, reaches to the eastern border; and **Monte-Carlo** is in the middle.

Monte-Carlo

Monte-Carlo is the area of Monaco where the real money is flung about, and its famous **casino** (bus #1 or #2) demands to be seen. Entrance is restricted to over-21s and you may have to show your passport; dress code is rigid, with shorts and T-shirts frowned upon, and skirts, jackets, ties and so forth more or less obligatory for the more interesting sections. Any coats or large bags involve hefty cloakroom fees.

In the first gambling hall, the **Salons Européens** (open from noon; 50F), slot machines surround the American roulette, craps and blackjack tables, the managers are Vegas-trained, the lights low and the air oppressively smoky. Above this slice of Nevada, however, the decor is turn-of-the-century Rococo extravagance, while the ceilings in the adjoining Pink Salon Bar are adorned with female nudes smoking cigarettes. The heart of the place is the **Salons Privés** (from 3pm), through the Salles Touzet. To get in, you have to look like a gambler, not a tourist (no cameras), and dispense with 100F at the door. Much larger and more richly decorated than the European Rooms, the early-afternoon or out-of-season atmosphere is that of a cathedral. No clinking coins, just sliding chips and softly spoken croupiers. Elderly gamblers pace silently, fingering 500F notes (the maximum unnegotiated stake here is 500,000F), closed-circuit TV cameras above the chandeliers watch the gamblers watching the tables, and no-one drinks. On midsummer evenings the place is packed out and the vice loses its sacred and exclusive touch.

Adjoining the casino is the gaudy **opera house**, and around the palm-tree-lined place du Casino are more casinos plus the city's palace-hotels and *grands cafés*. The *American Bar* of the **Hôtel de Paris** is, according to its publicity, the place where "the world's

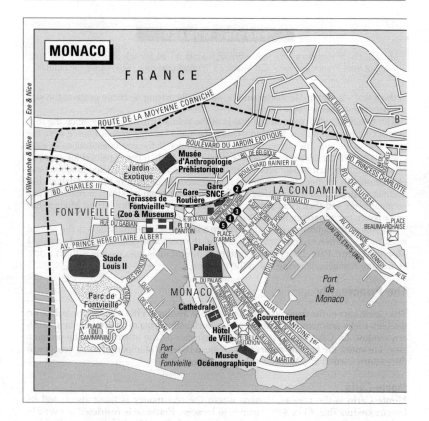

most elite society" meets. As long as you dress up and are prepared to be challenged if you haven't ordered a 200F drink, you can entertain yourself free of charge against the background of Belle Époque decadence by watching humans whose bank accounts are possibly the most interesting thing about them.

Monaco-Ville and Fontvieille

After the casino, the amusements of the glacé-iced **Monaco-Ville** (bus #1 or #2) where every other shop sells Prince Rainier mugs and assorted junk, are less rewarding. You can trail gasping round the state apartments of the **Palace** (daily: June–Sept 9.30am–6.30pm; Oct 10am–5pm; closed Nov–May; 30F); look at waxwork princes in **L'Historial des Princes de Monaco**, 27 rue Basse (daily: April—Sept 9.30am–6pm; rest of year 11am–4pm; 26F); watch a dreadful slide show on different aspects of the place in the **Monte Carlo Story** (daily March–Oct hourly 11am–5/6pm, Nov–Feb hourly 2–5pm; 38F); or traipse around the tombs of the former princes and Princess Grace in the neo-Romanesque-Byzantine **cathedral**, whose right-hand transept features a reredos by Louis Bréa.

One point of real interest in the old town, however, is to be found on the place de la Visitation: the **Musée de la Chapelle de la Visitation** (Tues–Sun 10am–4pm; 20F),

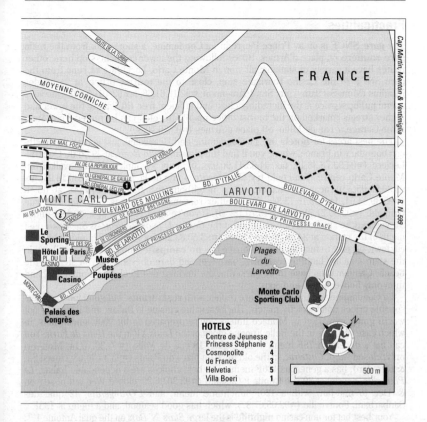

displaying a part of the collection of religious art of Barbara Piasecka Johnson. This small but exquisite collection includes works by Zurbarán, Rivera, Rubens, and even an extremely rare, early religious work by Vermeer.

Perhaps the best site to visit in the whole of Monaco is the **aquarium** in the basement of the imposing **Musée Océanographique** (daily: April–Sept 9am–7/8pm; rest of year 9.30/10am–7/6pm; 60F), where the fishy beings outdo the weirdest Kandinsky or Hieronymus Bosch creations. Less exceptional, but still peculiar, cactus equivalents can be viewed in the **Jardin Exotique**, on boulevard du Jardin Exotique high above Fontvieille (daily 9am–6/7pm; 39F; bus #2).

There are yet more museums in **Fontvieille**, of His Serene Highness's cars (daily 10am–6pm; closed Nov; 30F), his coins and stamps (daily 10am–5pm; 20F), his model ships (daily 10am–6pm; 25F), plus a zoo of his rare wild animals (daily June–Sept 9am–noon & 2–7pm, rest of year 10am–noon & 2–5/6pm; 20F), at the **Terrasses de Fontvieille** (bus #6) by the port.

Near the Larvotto beach, the **Musée National**, 17 av Princesse Grace (Easter–Sept daily 10am–6.30pm; Oct–Easter daily 10am–12.15pm & 2.30–6.30pm; 26F), is dedicated to the history of **dolls and automata**, and is better than skeptics would think: some of the dolls' house scenes and the creepy automata are quite surreal and fun.

Practicalities

The **gare SNCF** is on av Prince-Pierre in La Condamine, a short walk from the main **gare routière** on place d'Armes. Buses following the lower corniche stop here; other routes have a variety of stations; all stop in Monte Carlo. Local bus #4 runs from the gare SNCF to the Casino-Tourisme stop, close to the **tourist office** at 2a bd des Moulins (Mon–Sat 9am–7pm, Sun 10am–noon; ☎92.16.61.66, fax 92.16.60.00). One very useful public service is the incredibly clean and efficient **free lift** linking the lower and higher streets (marked on the tourist office map). **Bicycles** can be rented from Auto-Moto-Garage, 7 rue de Millo, off place d'Armes (☎93.50.10.80).

The best areas for **hotels** are La Condamine and Beausoleil, just across the northern boundary in France, where you'll find the pleasant *Villa Boeri*, at 29 bd du Général-Leclerc (☎04.93.78.38.10, fax 04.93.41.90.95; ③), only a couple minutes' walk from Monte Carlo centre. You could try *Cosmopolite*, 4 rue de la Turbie (☎93.30.16.95, fax 93.30.23.05; ③) near the station, or its neighbour the *Hôtel de France*, at no. 6 (☎93.30.24.64, fax 92.16.13.34; ④). Another reasonable option is *Helvetia*, 1bis rue Grimaldi (☎93.30.21.71, fax 92.16.70.15; ⑥). If you're aged 16 to 26 or a student under 31, you may be able to get a **hostel** bed at the *Centre de Jeunesse Princess Stéphanie*, just north of the station at 24 av Prince-Pierre (☎93.50.83.20, fax 93.25.29.82; midnight/1am curfew); be sure to turn up early. Monaco has **no campsite**, and caravans are illegal in the state – as are bathing costumes, bare feet and bare chests once you step off the beach. Camper vans have to be parked at the Parking des Écoles, in Fontvieille, and then only between 8am and 8pm.

La Condamine and the old town are replete with **restaurants**, but good food and reasonable prices don't exactly match. The best-value cuisine is Italian, and it's really not worth going upmarket in Monaco unless you're prepared to hit 900F-a-head bills, in which case you dine in the Belle Époque glory of the *Louis XV* in the *Hôtel de Paris*. You can eat a decentish 75F menu at *La Cigale*, 18 rue de Millo (☎93.30.16.14; Mon–Fri only; closed Aug). *Castelroc*, in the old town on place du Palais (☎93.30.36.68; closed Sat & Dec–Jan), has a generous 120F menu. The best choices are a dependable Italian, *Le Pinocchio*, nearby at 30 rue Comte-F-Gastaldi (☎93.30.96.20; closed Wed out of season & Dec to mid-Jan) with a 120F lunchtime menu; and *L'Orangeraie*, 42 quai des Sanbarbani, Fontvieille (☎92.05.67.37), which has good seafood, and a menu at 135F.

Your best bet for non-casino **nightlife** is the large *Stars 'N' Bars* on the quai Antoine 1er: packed out on Fridays and Saturdays, with a lively club upstairs where drinks will cost you 60F. Otherwise you might like to try out *Chérie's Café*, right near Monte Carlo's Casino, at 9 av des Spélugues, which serves food throughout the night and has regular live bands.

Menton

Of all the Côte d'Azur resorts, **MENTON** – the warmest and most Italianate, being within a couple of kilometres of the border – is the one that retains an atmosphere of aristocratic tourism, being even more of a rich retirement haven than Nice. It doesn't go in for the ostentatious wealth of Monaco nor the creativity cachet of Cannes and some hilltop towns, but glories chiefly in its climate and year-round lemon crops. Ringed by protective mountains, hardly a whisper of wind disturbs this suntrap of a city; you'll notice the difference in winter, when you'll need a change of clothes between here and the exposed central resorts.

Arrival, information and accommodation

Roquebrune and Cap Martin merge into Menton along the three-kilometre shore of the **Baie du Soleil**. The modern town is arranged around three main streets parallel to the promenade du Soleil. The **gare SNCF** is on the top one, bd Albert-1er, from which a short walk to the left as you come out brings you to the north–south av de Verdun and av de Boyer divided by the Jardins Biovès – central location for citrus sculptures during February's **Fête du Citron**. The **tourist office** is at 8 av Boyer (Mon–Sat 10am–noon & 2–5.30pm, Sun 10am–noon; closed Sun out of season; ☎04.93.57.57.00), in the Palais de l'Europe; the building was once a casino, but now hosts various cultural activities and contemporary art exhibitions.

The **gare routière** and the **urban bus station** are between the continuation of the two avenues north of the train line on the esplanade de Carei. All the local bus lines (flat rates) pass through the gare routière. The district of **Garavan**, further east again, is the most exclusive residential area and overlooks the modern marina.

Accommodation is, as ever, a problem. Menton is no less popular than the other major resorts, so in summer you should definitely book ahead. The tourist office won't make reservations for you, though they will tell you where there are rooms free.

Hotels

L'Aiglon, 7 av de la Madonne (☎04.93.57.55.55, fax 04.93.35.92.39). Spacious rooms in a nineteenth-century residence surrounded by a large garden. ⑤.

Beauregard, 10 rue Albert-1er (☎04.93.28.63.63, fax 04.93.28.63.79). Classically furnished rooms and no attempt to foist breakfast on you. Closed Oct–Dec. ③.

Belgique, 1 av de la Gare (☎04.93.35.72.66, fax 04.93.41.44.77). More mundane option than the above, but no less clean, and conveniently close to the station. Closed Dec. ③.

M. Paul Gazzano, 151 rte de Castellar (☎04.93.57.39.73). Chambres d'hôte 2km from Menton; a delightful house with a terrace looking down over the wooded slopes to the sea. ③.

Napoléon, 29 porte de France, Garavan (☎04.93.35.89.50, fax 04.93.35.49.22). Wonderful views from the rooms. ⑤.

Hostel and campsite

HI youth hostel, plateau St-Michel (☎04.93.35.93.14, fax 04.93.35.93.07). This well-run hostel is up a gruelling flight of steps signposted "Camping St-Michel", from the north side of the railway tracks, or take bus #6 from the gare routière, direction "Ciappes de Castellar", stop Camping St-Michel. No advance booking or card needed.

Camping St-Michel, plateau St-Michel (☎ & fax 04.93.35.81.23). Reasonably priced campsite in the hills above the town, with plenty of shade and good views out to sea. March–Nov.

The town

The **promenade du Soleil** runs along the pebbly beachfront of Menton's aptly named Baie du Soleil, stretching from the quai Napoléon-III past the casino towards Roquebrune. The most diverting building on the front is a seventeenth-century fort by the quai Napoléon-III south of the old port, now the **Musée Jean Cocteau** (Wed–Mon 10am–noon & 2–6pm; 20F), set up by the artist himself. It contains pictures of his Mentonaise lovers in the *Inamorati* series, a collection of delightful *Fantastic Animals* and the powerful tapestry of *Judith and Holofernes* simultaneously telling the sequence of seduction, assassination and escape. There are also photographs, poems, ceramics, and a portrait by his friend Picasso.

As the quai bends around the western end of the Baie de Garavan from the Cocteau museum, a long flight of black-and-white pebbled steps leads up into the **vieille ville** to the **Parvis St-Michel**, an attractive Italianate square hosting concerts during the summer and giving a good view out over the bay. The frontage of the **Église St-Michel** proclaims its Baroque supremacy in perfect pink and yellow proportions, and a few more steps up to another square will reward you with the beautiful facade of the **chapel of the**

Pénitents-Noirs in apricot-and-white marble, with pastel campaniles and disappearing stairways between long-lived houses. The **cemetery**, at the very top of the old town on the site once occupied by the town's château, is low on gloom and high on panoramic views, and is a good place to find yourself at sunset.

In the middle of the modern town, the **Salles des Mariages** (Mon–Fri 8.30am–12.30pm & 1.30–5pm; 10F), or registry office, forms part of the **Hôtel de Ville** on place Ardoiono and was decorated in inimitable style by Jean Cocteau in 1957. It can be visited without matrimonial intentions by asking the receptionist by the main door. On the wall above the official's desk, a couple face each other with strange topological connections between the sun, her headdress and his fisherman's cap. A *Saracen Wedding Party* on the right-hand wall reveals a disapproving mother of the bride, the spurned girlfriend of the groom and her armed, revengeful brother among the cheerful guests. On the left-hand wall is the story of *Orpheus and Eurydice* at the moment when Orpheus has just looked back. Meanwhile, on the ceiling are *Poetry Rides Pegasus* and tattered *Science Juggles with the Planets*, and *Love*, open-eyed, waiting with bow and arrow at the ready. Adding a little extra confusion, the carpet is mock panther-skin.

On avenue de la Madone, at the other end of the modern town, an impressive collection of paintings from the Middle Ages to the twentieth century can be seen in the **Palais Carnolès** (daily except Tues 10am–noon & 2–6pm; bus #3; free), the old summer residence of the princes of Monaco. Of the early works, the *Madonna and Child with St Francis* by Louis Bréa is exceptional. The most recent include canvases by Graham Sutherland, who spent some of his last years in Menton.

If it's cool enough to be walking outside, the public parks up in the hills and the gardens of **Garavan**'s once elegant villas make a change from shingle beaches. The best of all the Garavan gardens used to be **Les Colombières**, just north of boulevard de Garavan (closed 1998, but enquire in tourist office for present status; bus #8, direction "Bd de Garavan", stop Colombières). Designed by the artist Ferdinand Bac, they lead you through every Mediterranean style of garden. There are staircases screened by cypresses; balustrades to lean against for the soaring views through pines and olive trees out to sea; fountains, statues and a frescoed swimming pool. Otherwise, nearer to the *vieille ville* on the same bus route, there's the public **Parc du Pian**, shaded by olive trees, and the **Jardin Exotique** (Wed–Mon: June–Sept 10am–12.30pm & 3–6pm; Oct–May 10am–12.30pm & 2–5pm; 20F), both below boulevard de Garavan.

Eating and drinking

Surprisingly, Menton is not blessed with streets of gorgeous Provençal **restaurants**. If you're not bothered about what you eat as long as it's cheap, the pedestrianized rue St-Michel is promising ground. For a proper **restaurant** meal in very elegant surroundings, there's *La Veranda* in *Hôtel Les Ambassadeurs*, 2 rue du Louvre (☎04.93.28.75.75; closed Sun eve), with an evening bistrot menu for 160F. Menton also has two excellent Moroccan restaurants, both around the 200F mark: *Le Darkoum*, 23 rue St-Michel (☎04.93.35.44.88), and *La Mamounia*, 51 porte de France, Garavan (☎04.93.57.95.39).

travel details

Buses

Cannes to: Aéroport Nice-Côte-d'Azur (hourly; 45min–1hr 30min); Antibes (frequent; 30min); Cagnes-sur-Mer (every 20mins; 50min); Grasse (frequent; 45min); Nice (frequent; 1hr 30min); St-Raphaël (3–7 daily; 1hr 10min); Vallauris (frequent; 15min).

Hyères to: Bormes (frequent; 25min); La Croix-Valmer (8 daily; 1hr 15min); Le Lavandou (frequent; 35min); Le Rayol (8 daily; 55min); St-Tropez (8 daily; 1hr 35min–1hr 45min); Toulon (every 30min; 35–50min).

Le Lavandou to: Bormes (6 daily; 30min); Cogolin (2 daily; 40min); Grimaud (2 daily; 45 min); Hyères (frequent; 35min); La Croix-Valmer (8–9 daily; 40min); La Garde Freinet (2 daily; 1hr); Le Rayol (8–9 daily; 20min); St-Tropez (8 daily; 55min–1hr 5min); Toulon (frequent; 1hr 10min).

Marseille to: Aix (frequent; 25–30min); Arles (4 daily; 2hr 10min–2hr 30min); Aubagne (frequent; 20–30min); Barcelonnette (2 daily; 3hr 55min); Cassis (7 daily; 50min); Digne (4 daily; 2hr–2hr 50min); Grenoble (1 daily; 3hr 55min); La Ciotat (8 daily; 1hr 5min); Sisteron (5–6 daily; 2hr 25min).

Menton to: Monaco (frequent; 25min); Nice (frequent; 1hr); Sospel (3 daily; 35–55min).

Monaco to: Eze Village (7 daily; 35min); Menton (frequent; 25min); Nice (frequent; 30–40min); La Turbie (5–6 daily; 30min).

Nice to: Aix (3–5 daily; 2hr 20min–4hr 25min); Beaulieu (frequent; 15–20min); Cagnes-sur-Mer (frequent; 25–50min); Digne (1–2 daily; 2hr 55min–3hr 25min); Draguignan (3 weekly; 1hr 15min); Eze-sur-Mer (frequent; 20min); Eze-Village (3–7 daily; 20min); Grasse (frequent; 1hr 5min–1hr 15min); La Turbie (4 daily; 40min); Menton (frequent; 1hr 15min); Monaco (frequent; 30–40min); Roquebrune (frequent; 40–55min); St-Paul (frequent; 40–45min); Sisteron (1–2 daily; 3hr 45min–4hr 10min); Toulon (2 daily from place Masséna; 2hr 30min); Vence (frequent; 55min); Villefranche (14 daily; 10–15min).

St-Raphaël to: Cannes (10—13 daily; 1hr 10min); Cogolin (7 daily; 1hr–1hr 25min); Draguignan (10–12 daily; 1hr 15min–1hr 25min); La Foux (8 daily; 1hr 15min); Fréjus (frequent; 10min); Grimaud (8 daily; 1hr); Nice Airport (3 daily; 1hr 5min)); Ste-Maxime (10 daily; 30–40min); St-Tropez (8–10 daily; 1hr–1hr 25min).

St-Tropez to: Bormes (8 daily; 1hr 5min–1hr 15min); Cogolin (8 daily; 15min); Gassin (1 daily; 25min); Grimaud (8 daily; 20–35min); Hyères (8 daily; 1hr 30min–1hr 40min); La Croix-Valmer (8 daily; 20min); La Garde Freinet (1 daily; 45min); Le Lavandou (8 daily; 55min–1hr 5min); Le Rayol (8 daily; 40–55min); Ramatuelle (1 daily; 25min); Ste-Maxime (8 daily; 45min); St-Raphaël (8–10 daily; 1hr–1hr 25min); Toulon (8 daily; 2hr–2hr 15min).

Toulon to: Aix (4 daily; 1hr 15min); Draguignan (5 daily; 2hr 10min); Hyères (every 30min; 35–50min); La Croix-Valmer (7 daily; 1hr 50min); Le Lavandou (7 daily; 1hr 10min); Nice (2 daily; 2hr 30min); St-Raphaël (4 daily; 2hr); St-Tropez (8 daily; 2hr 15min).

Trains

Cannes to: Antibes (frequent; 13min); Biot (frequent; 17min); Cagnes-sur-Mer (frequent; 24min); Juan-les-Pins (frequent; 10min); Marseille (frequent; 1hr 5min); Nice (frequent; 25–40min); St-Raphaël (frequent; 25–35min).

Marseille to: Aix (frequent; 30–35min); Arles (frequent; 45min); Avignon (frequent; 55min–1hr 15min); Cannes (frequent; 1hr 5min); Cassis (every 30min; 20–25min); Hyères (2 daily; 1hr 25min); La Ciotat (every 30min; 25–30min); Les Arcs-Draguignan (every hour; 1hr 20min–2hr 15min); Lyon (8 daily; 2hr 35min); Menton (8 daily; 3hr 25min–4hr); Nice (frequent; 2hr 20min–3hr 30min); Paris (10 daily; 4hr 20min–8 hr 35min; estimated 3hr 30min when TGV link completed c.2001); St-Raphaël (frequent; 1hr 45min); Toulon (frequent; 40min–1hr 5min).

Nice to: Beaulieu-sur-Mer (frequent; 13min); Cagnes-sur-Mer (frequent; 15min); Cap d'Ail (frequent; 18min); Cap Martin-Roquebrune (frequent; 37min); Digne (4 daily; 3hr 10min); Eze-sur-Mer (frequent; 18min); Marseille (frequent; 2hr 45min–3hr 15min); Menton (frequent; 35min); Paris Gare de Lyon (7 daily; 10hr 40min–12hr); St-Raphaël (frequent; 1hr–1hr 20min); Sospel (4 daily; 50min); Tende (4 daily, 2 changing at Breil-sur-Roya; 2hr 5min–2hr 10min); Villefranche-sur-Mer (frequent; 9min).

St-Raphaël to: Boulouris (9 daily; 4min); Cannes (frequent; 35min); Marseille (frequent; 1hr 45min); Nice (frequent; 1hr–1hr 20min).

Toulon to: Hyères (4 daily; 20min); Marseille (frequent; 1hr 5min).

Flights

Hyères to: Corsica (2 daily; 50min); Lille (April–Sept 1 weekly; 1hr 25min); Paris (10 daily; 1hr 25 min.

Marseille to: London (4 daily; 1hr 30min); Lyon (3–5 daily; 40min); New York (4–6 daily; 8hr 30min); Paris (21 daily; 1hr 5min).

Nice to: Lille (1 daily; 1hr 30min); London (9 daily; 2hr 5min); Lyon (4 daily; 50min); New York (4 daily; 9hr); Ottawa (2 weekly; 8hr 30min); Paris (frequent; 1hr 20min).

Ferries

For Îles d'Hyères and Îles de Lérins services, see p.947 & p.966.

Marseille to: Corsica (4–10 weekly; 8–12 hr).

Nice to: Corsica (April–Sept daily; Oct–May 1 daily–3 weekly; 2hr 30min–11hr 30min).

Toulon to: Corsica (2–5 weekly; 7–11hr).

CHAPTER SIXTEEN

CORSICA

Around one-and-a-half million people visit Corsica each year, drawn by a climate that's mild even in winter and by some of the most astonishingly diverse landscapes in all Europe. Nowhere in the Mediterranean has beaches finer than Corsica's perfect half-moon bays of white sand and transparent water, or seascapes more inspiring than the granite cliffs of the west coast. Even though the annual influx of tourists now exceeds the island's population sixfold, tourism hasn't spoilt the place: there are a few resorts, but overdevelopment is rare and high-rise blocks are confined to the main towns.

The island has always been of strategic and commercial appeal, set on the western Mediterranean trade routes. Greeks, Carthaginians and Romans came in successive waves, driving native Corsicans into the interior. The Romans were ousted by Vandals, and for the following thirteen centuries the island was attacked, abandoned, settled and sold as a nation-state, with generations of islanders fighting against foreign government. Two hundred years of French rule have had a limited effect on Corsica, and the island's Baroque churches, Genoese fortresses, fervent Catholic rituals and a Tuscan-influenced indigenous language and cuisine show a more profound affinity with neighbouring Italy.

Corsica's uneasy relationship with its motherland has worsened in recent decades. Economic neglect and the French government's reluctance to encourage Corsican language and culture spawned a nationalist movement in the early 1970s, whose clandestine armed wing – the FLNC (Fronte di Liberazione Nazionale di a Corsica) – is currently engaged in a bloody conflict with the central government. The violence seldom affects tourists but signs of the "troubles" are everywhere, from the black "Corsica Nazione" graffiti sprayed over roadsigns, to the bullet holes plastering public buildings.

The late 1990s have also seen a marked upsurge in political assassinations, most of them episodes in long-standing vendetta-style feuds between rival separatist factions and their Mafia partners. Attempts by Alain Juppé's Gaullist government to diffuse the crisis, however, became embroiled in controversy when the prime minister himself was accused of conducting secret negotiations with the FLNC while outwardly insisting he "never talked to terrorists". Lionel Jospin's new socialist government has fared little better. It kept alive an eight-month ceasefire, but this ended violently in February

---

ACCOMMODATION PRICE CATEGORIES

Each hotel in this chapter has a symbol which corresponds to one of eight price categories.

① Under 160F	④ 300–400F	⑦ 600–700F
② 160–220F	⑤ 400–500F	⑧ Over 700F
③ 220–300F	⑥ 500–600F	

The prices quoted are for the cheapest available double room in high season, though remember that many of the cheap places will have more expensive rooms with en-suite facilities.

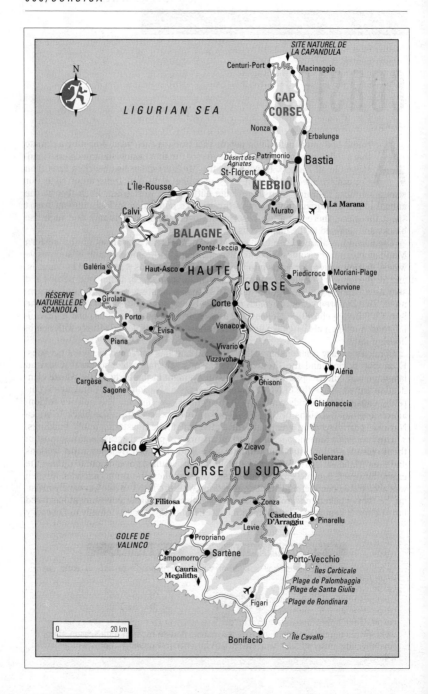

1998 when the island's popular prefect (the de facto governor of Corsica) was shot dead on the streets of Ajaccio. Although none of the mutually-loathing terrorist groups admitted responsibility, the killing provoked widespread public outrage and a definite erosion of support for the armed struggle. The arrests of several high-profile FLNC activists has further weakened the movement, and Corsica is now in the midst of an uneasy peace.

Where to go

Capital of the north, Bastia was the principal Genoese stronghold, and its fifteenth-century old town has survived almost intact. Of the island's two large towns, this is the more purely Corsican, and commerce rather than tourism is its main concern. Also relatively undisturbed, the northern Cap Corse harbours inviting sandy coves and fishing villages such as Erbalunga and Centuri-Port. Within a short distance of Bastia, the fertile region of the Nebbio contains a plethora of churches built by Pisan stoneworkers, the prime example being the cathedral of Santa Maria Assunta at the appealingly chic little port of St-Florent.

To the west of here, **L'Île-Rousse** and **Calvi**, the latter graced with an impressive citadel and fabulous sandy beach, are major targets for holiday-makers. The spectacular **Scandola** nature reserve can be visited by boat from the tiny resort of **Porto**, from where walkers can also strike into the wild **Gorges de la Spelunca** and **Fôret d'Aitone**. **Corte**, at the heart of Corsica, is the best base for exploring the stupendous mountains and gorges of the interior which form part of the **Parc Naturel Régional** that runs almost the entire length of the island.

Sandy beaches and rocky coves punctuate the west coast all the way down to **Ajaccio**, Napoléon's birthplace and the island's capital. Its pavement cafés and

---

THE FOOD OF CORSICA

It is the herbs – thyme, marjoram, basil, fennel and rosemary– of the *maquis* (the dense, scented scrub that covers lowland Corsica) – enhanced by olive oil and spices – that lend the island's cuisine its distinctive flavour, especially in the south, where flavours are less subtle than in the north.

You'll find the best **charcuterie** in the north, where pork is smoked and cured in the cold cellars of village houses – it's particularly tasty in the Castagniccia, where wild pigs feed on the chestnuts which were once the staple diet of the locals. Here you can also taste chestnut fritters (*fritelli a gaju frescu*) and chestnut cake (*pulenta*) sprinkled with sugar or eau de vie. **Brocciu**, a soft fromage frais made with ewe's milk, is found everywhere on the island, forming the basis for many dishes, including omelettes stuffed with *brocciu* and mint, and *cannelloni al brocciu*. *Fromage Corse* is also very good – a unique hard **cheese** made in the sheep- and goat-rearing central regions, where *cabrettu a l'istrettu* (kid stew) is a speciality.

Game – mainly stews of hare and wild boar but also roast woodcock, partridge and wood pigeon – features throughout the island's mountain and forested regions. Here blackbirds (*merles*) are made into a fragrant pâté, and eel and trout are fished from the unpolluted rivers. **Fish** like red mullet (*rouget*), sea bream (*loup de mer*) and a great variety of shellfish is eaten along the coast – the best crayfish (*langouste*) comes from around the Golfe de St-Florent, whereas oysters (*huitres*) are a speciality of the eastern plain.

Of the local **wine**, you should be sure to try the Santa Barba or Fiumicicoli wines of the Sartène area, which come in both rosé and red, and the Patrimonio, a robust white wine from Cap Corse. The favoured apéritifs are the sweet muscat produced on Cap Corse and the drink known as *Cap Corse*, a fortified wine flavoured with quinine and herbs. Note that **tap water** is particularly good-quality in Corsica, coming from the fresh mountain streams.

palm-lined boulevards are thronged with tourists in summer. Slightly fewer make it to nearby **Filitosa**, greatest of the many prehistoric sites scattered across the south. Brash **Propriano**, the spot that has perhaps been transformed most from the tourist boom, lies close to stern **Sartène**, seat of the wild feudal lords who once ruled this region and still the quintessential Corsican town.

More megalithic sites are to be found south of Sartène on the way to **Bonifacio**, a comb of ancient buildings perched atop furrowed white cliffs at the southern tip of the island. Equally popular **Porto-Vecchio** provides a springboard for excursions to the amazing beaches of the south. The eastern plain has less to boast of, but the Roman site at **Aléria** is worth a visit for its excellent museum.

Getting to Corsica

Two French companies – SNCM Ferryteranée and CMN – dominate **ferry** services to Corsica from the mainland ports of Marseille, Toulon and Nice, although a third, smaller firm, Euro-Mer, also offer crossings from the Cote d'Azur. In addition an Italian operator, Corsica Ferries, has recently entered the fray with superfast services from Nice to Calvi and Bastia. Crossings takes between seven and twelve hours on a regular ferry, and from two-and-a-half to three-and-a-half hours on the hydrofoil. The cost of tickets varies according to the season, with the lowest between October and May; during July and August fares triple. On average, a one-way crossing will set you back between 280F and 320F per person (depending on when you travel), plus 220F to 660F per vehicle.

From Marseille a maximum of four ferries a week run to Ajaccio and Bastia, with one weekly service to L'Île Rousse and Propriano. There are up to four ferries a week from Toulon to Ajaccio, Bastia and Propriano, and more frequent services sail from Nice to Ajaccio (up to six weekly) and Bastia (up to twelve weekly). Up to three ferries a week run from Nice to Calvi or L'Île Rousse - with a faster service to Bastia (except Wednesday) and Calvi (except Saturday). (See p.1051 for details.)

You can **book** through SNCM Ferryteranée in France at 61 bd des Dames, Marseille 13002 (☎04.91.56.30.10); at the gare maritime, quai du Commerce, Nice 06303 (☎04.93.13.66.66); or 21 and 49 av de l'Infanterie de Marine, Toulon 83000 (☎04.94.16.66.66). CMN's main office is in Marseille at 4 quai d'Arenc (☎04.01.99.45.00). To reserve tickets for Corsica Ferries' superfast navette, contact them in Paris at 25 rue de l'Arbre Sec (☎01.47.03.96.30). Finally, Euro-Mer, 5 quai de sauvage, Montpellier (☎04.67.65.67.30), also offers competitive tariffs for crossings from southeast. Note that advance reservation is essential for all ferry journeys in July and August, for which berths and car space can be completely booked up by early February.

THE CORSICAN LANGUAGE

Corsican, originally a Latin-based language with similarities to Romanian, developed an Italianate vocabulary and syntax during Pisan and Genoese occupation. Arabic and French influences have added to the complexity of Corsican, which was predominantly an oral tongue until around two hundred years ago – hence the confusing variety of spellings for place names, despite attempts at standardization. The commonest variants come about through the transposition of ll and dd – as in "casteddu" and "castellu". Buildings and monuments are often labelled in different languages (San Pietro/San Pietru), and on maps you'll find mountain passes, rivers and regions marked in a mixture of Italian, French and Corsican. Deep in the country, many old people are still easier with Corsican than French. Pronunciation is generally as for Italian, but look out for two tricky clusters of consonants – chj/chi and ghj/ghi, pronounced *ty* or *dy*.

Direct **flights** to Corsica depart from most major French cities, including Paris, Lyon, Bordeaux, Nantes, Strasbourg, Toulouse, Marseille, Toulon and Nice. Fares on holiday season charters tend to be cheaper than on scheduled flights, but even the latter can still work out good value when you consider the time and expense involved in travelling over land and sea from the mainland. The largest operator is Air France (☎08.02.80.28.02), whose 14-day advance fares from Paris start at 1200F return in July and August, dropping to 1000F out of season. Corse Méditerranée (☎08.36.67.95.20) offer routes from a range of mainland airports, via Marseille and Nice. Their fares from these cities on the Côte d'Azur vary little according to the season: roughly 650F/350F return/one-way. The other carrier with scheduled flights to Corsica are TAT European Airlines (☎08.03.80.58.05). For information on charter deals, call at any Ollandini travel agent in France (there's one in the high street of nearly every major town and city).

Getting around

With public transport woefully inadequate even at the height of the tourist season, much the most convenient way of **getting around** Corsica is by rental car. The big three companies, Hertz, Avis, and Europcar all have offices at airports and towns across the island, allowing you to collect and return vehicles in different places Even if your budget won't stretch to a week or more, it's well worth renting a car for at least a couple of days to explore the dramatic back roads of the interior. Rely solely on **buses**, and you'll have to stick to the main arteries. Services are fairly frequent between Bastia, Corte and Ajaccio, and along the east coast from Bastia to Porto Vecchio and Bonifacio, but some of the most scenic stretches of the west coast (between Porto and Calvi, for example), and large chunks of the interior, are off-limits for much of the year without your own vehicle. Getting accurate timetable information for bus services can also be difficult, as different routes are operated by different companies, and timings change from year to year. The best way to check bus information is to call a tourist office

Corsica's diminutive **train**, the *Micheline* or *Trinighellu* (little train), rattles through the mountains from Ajaccio to Bastia via Corte, with a branch line running northwest as far as Calvi. Following a precarious route through the heart of the island, it's far slower than the bus, but takes you through some stupendous scenery, much of which remains inaccessible by road. Try, at least, to make time for the memorable stretch between Ajaccio and Corte; the trip from Ponte Leccia, in northern Corsica, to Calvi along the Balagne coast, is equally stunning.

Motorcycles and **scooters** can be rented at several towns and resorts, but cost almost as much as cars. A 125cc machine, for example, will set you back around 250–280F per day, plus a deposit of 4000F or more. If you do decide to splash out on a bike, check your insurance policy to make sure you have adequate cover: Corsican roads are among the most lethal in Europe.

Bastia and around

The dominant tone of Corsica's most successful commercial town, **BASTIA**, is one of charismatic dereliction, as the city's industrial zone is spread onto the lowlands to the south, leaving the centre of town with plenty of aged charm. The old quarter known as the Terra Vecchia makes a tightly packed network of haphazard streets, flamboyant Baroque churches and lofty tenements, their crumbling golden-grey walls set against a backdrop of *maquis*-covered hills. Terra Nova, the historic district on the opposite side of the old port, is a tidier area that's now Bastia's yuppie quarter.

The city dates from Roman times, when a base was set up at Biguglia to the south, although Bastia began to thrive under the Genoese, when wine was exported to the Italian mainland from Porto Cardo, forerunner of Bastia's Vieux Port, or Terra Vecchia.

Despite the fact that in 1811 Napoléon appointed Ajaccio capital of the island, initiating a rivalry between the two towns which exists to this day, Bastia soon established a stronger trading position with mainland France. The Nouveau Port, created in 1862 to cope with the increasing traffic with France and Italy, became the mainstay of the local economy, exporting chiefly agricultural products from Cap Corse, Balagne and the eastern plain.

Arrival, information and accommodation

Bastia's **Poretta airport** is 16km south of town off the Route Nationale (☎04.95.54.54.54); shuttle buses into the centre coincide with flights, dropping passengers opposite the train station for a fare of 48F; the journey takes thirty minutes. **Ferries** arrive at the Nouveau Port, just a five-minute walk to the centre of town; the SNCM office is at 15 bd de Gaulle (☎04.95.54.66.88). **Buses** pull in to several different stops. Arriving from Ajaccio, Corte, Cap Corse and St-Florent, you'll be dropped at the station, just north of av Maréchal-Sebastiani (see map), whereas services from Bonifacio and Porto-Vecchio work from the Rapides Bleus office opposite the post office. Beaux Voyages, who operate buses to Calvi, stop outside the train station. A summary of bus times and departure points for most local and long-distance services is available at the **tourist office**, at the north end of place St-Nicolas (June–Sept 15 daily 8am–8pm; Sept 16–May Mon–Sat 8am–6pm, Sun 8am–noon & 2–5pm; ☎04.95.31.81.34).

You can rent **cars** from Avis/Ollandini, 40 bd Paoli (☎04.95.32.57.30; or airport ☎04.95.36.03.56), or Europcar, 1 rue du Nouveau Port (☎04.95.31.59.26; or airport ☎04.95.30.09.50). **Bikes** can be rented from Locacycles, behind the Palais de Justice (☎04.95.32.30.64), and **scooters** and **motorcycles** from Plaisance Service Location, in the marina (☎04.95.31.49.01). **Luggage** may be left at the Nouveau Port's gare maritime (daily 8–11.30am & 2–7.30pm; 12F per article per day); there's another *consigne* at the train station, but it's a lot more expensive

Although you are usually guaranteed to find somewhere to **stay** in Bastia, the choice of hotels is not great. Apart from the *Posta-Vecchia*, the classier places line the road to Cap Corse north of the port; the more basic ones are found in the centre of town, and there are a few even cheaper small *pensions* around the Nouveau Port.

Hotels

Central, 3 rue Miot (☎04.95.31.71.12). Clean and spacious rooms close to the south edge of place St-Nicolas. By far the best deal at the bottom of the range, although not the cheapest. ③.

Forum, 20 bd Paoli (☎04.95.31.02.53, fax 04.95.31.26.41). Attractively chic, with spacious rooms and a relaxing enclosed terrace. ④.

Posta-Vecchia, quai des Martyrs de la Libération (☎04.95.32.32.38, fax 04.95.32.14.05). The only hotel close to the Vieux Port, with rooms looking onto a narrow alley or out to sea. Smart, comfortable and central. ③.

Riviera, 1 rue du Nouveau Port (☎04.95.31.07.16, fax 04.95.34.17.39). Efficient budget hotel that's handy for the ferry port, with quiet and comfortable rooms. Advance booking essential. ③.

Sud Hôtel, av de la Libération, Lupino (☎04.95.30.20.61, fax 04.95.30.53.85). Charming place with a car park and friendly owners. About 1km south of town. ③.

L'Univers, 3 av du Maréchal-Sebastiani (☎04.95.31.03.38, fax 04.95.31.19.91). A no-frills option opposite the post office whose cheapest rooms are a bit pokey, but clean enough for a night. Single occupancy rates available. ②.

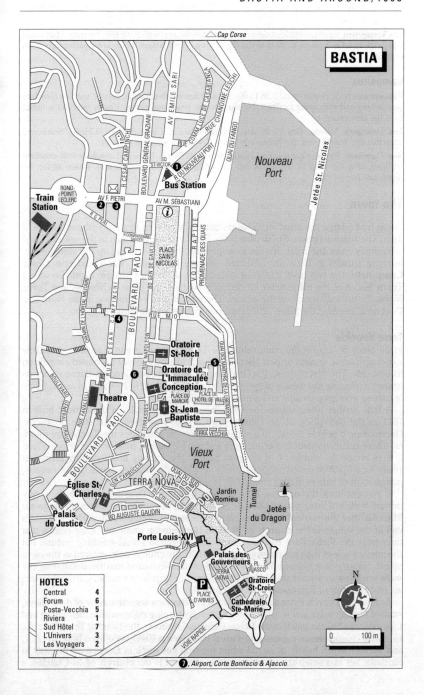

△ *Cap Corse*

BASTIA

Nouveau Port

Jetée St. Nicolas

AV. EMILE SARI

RUE COMM. LUC DE CASABIANCA

RUE CHANOINE LESCHI

RUE

R DU NOUVEAU PORT

QUAI DU FANGO

BOULEVARD GÉNÉRAL GRAZIANI

R. CÉSAR CAMPINCHI

SQ ST-VICTOR

Bus Station ❶

ROND POINT LECLERC

AV. F. PIETRI ❷ ❸

R.G. PERI

Train Station

AV. M. SÉBASTIANI

(i)

R CONVENTIONNEL SALICETI

VOIE RAPIDE

PROMENADE DES QUAIS

PLACE SAINT-NICOLAS

BD GÉN DE GAULLE

BOULEVARD PAOLI

R. CÉSAR CAMPINCHI

CHEMIN DE L'HÔPITAL MILITAIRE

❹

RUE MIOT

RUE NAPOLÉON

Oratoire St-Roch ✝

❺

QUAIS DES MARTYRS DE LA LIBÉRATION

VOIE RAPIDE

Oratoire de L'Immaculée Conception ✝

❻

PLACE DU MARCHÉ

PLACE DE L'HÔTEL DE VILLE

PLACE DE VILLABRÉTON

Theatre

R. DES TERRASSES

St-Jean Baptiste ✝

BOULEVARD PAOLI

RUE TAVALELLI

TERRA VECCHIA

Vieux Port

BOULEVARD GÉNÉRAL GIRAUD

R. EN CARBUCCIA

QUAI DU SUD

QUAI DU NORD

Église St-Charles ✝

TERRA NOVA

Jardin Romieu

Tunnel

☀

Palais de Justice

BD AUGUSTE GAUDIN

Jetée du Dragon

Porte Louis-XVI ▲

Palais des Gouverneurs

PL GUASCO

TERRA NOVA

P

Oratoire St-Croix ✝

Cathédrale Ste-Marie ✝

PLACE D'ARMES

N

VOIE RAPIDE

0   100 m

HOTELS	
Central	4
Forum	6
Posta-Vecchia	5
Riviera	1
Sud Hôtel	7
L'Univers	3
Les Voyagers	2

▽ ❼, Airport, Corte Bonifacio & Ajaccio

Les Voyageurs, 9 av Maréchal-Sebastiani (☎04.95.34.90.80, fax 04.95.30.00.65). Recently refurbished mid-range hotel in a prime location at the top of town. Their budget rooms are a particularly good deal. ③.

Campsites

Esperenza, rte de Pineto (☎04.95.36.15.09). About 20km south of Bastia, beyond the *San Damiano* (see below) and with fewer facilities, but close to the beach and cheap. Hourly buses in summer from the gare routière.

Les Orangers, Miomo, 4km north along the route to Cap Corse (☎04.95.33.24.09). Shady and attractive site near the sea; the half-hourly bus to Erbalunga will drop you here.

San Damiano, Pineto, 6km south of Bastia (☎04.95.33.68.02). Huge and spacious with excellent facilities; take the road to the left across the bridge at Furiani roundabout. Buses as for the *Esperenza*. April–Oct.

The town

Bastia isn't a large town and all its sights can easily be seen in a day without the use of a car. The spacious **place St-Nicolas** is the focus of town life: open to the sea and lined with shady trees and cafés, it's the most pleasant spot for soaking up the atmosphere. Running parallel to it on the landward side are **boulevard Paoli** and **rue César Campinchi**, the two main shopping streets, but all Bastia's historic sights lie within **Terra Vecchia**, the old quarter immediately south of the place St-Nicolas, and **Terra Nova**, the area surrounding the citadel. There's not much of interest in the **Nouveau Port** area, north of the *place*, other than restaurants and downmarket bars.

Terra Vecchia

From place St-Nicolas the main route into Terra Vecchia is rue Napoléon, a narrow street with some ancient offbeat shops and a pair of sumptuously decorated chapels on its east side. The first of these, the **Oratoire de St-Roch**, is a Genoese Baroque extravagance, reflecting the wealth of the rising bourgeoisie. Built in 1604, it has walls of finely carved wooden panelling and a magnificent gilt organ.

A little further along stands the **Oratoire de L'Immaculée Conception**, built in 1611 as the showplace of the Genoese in Corsica, who used it for state occasions. Overlooking a pebble mosaic of a sun, the austere facade belies the flamboyant interior, where crimson velvet draperies, a gilt and marble ceiling, frescoes and crystal chandeliers create the ambience of an opera house. The sacristy houses a tiny **museum** (daily 9am–6pm) of minor religious works, of which the wooden statue of St Erasmus, patron saint of fishers, dating from 1788, is most arresting.

If you cut back through the narrow steps beside the Oratoire de St-Roch, a two-minute walk will bring you to place de l'Hôtel-de-Ville, commonly known as **place du Marché** after the market that takes place here each morning. Shouldering the south end of the square is the **church of St-Jean-Baptiste**, an immense ochre edifice that dominates the Vieux Port. Its twin campaniles are Bastia's distinguishing feature, but the interior is less than impressive – built in 1636, the church was restored in the eighteenth century in a hideous Rococo overkill of multi-coloured marble. decorating the walls are a few unremarkable Italian paintings from Napoléon's uncle, Cardinal Fesch, an avid collector of Renaissance art (see p.1030).

Around the church extends the oldest part of Bastia, a secretive zone of dark alleys, vaulted passageways and seven-storey houses. By turning right outside the church and following rue St-Jean you'll come to rue General-Carbuccia, the heart of Terra Vecchia. Corsican independence campaigner Pascal Paoli (see p.1046) once lived here, at no. 7, and Balzac stayed briefly at no. 23 when his ship got stuck in Corsica on the way to Sardinia. Set in a small square at the end of the road is the **church of St-Charles**, a

Jesuit chapel whose wide steps provide an evening meeting place for the locals; opposite stands the **Maison de Caraffa**, an elegant house with a strikingly graceful balcony.

The **Vieux Port** is easily the most photogenic part of town: soaring houses seem to bend inwards towards the water, peeling plaster and boat hulls glint in the sun, while the south side remains in the shadow of the great rock that supports the citadel. Site of the original Roman settlement of *Porto Cardo*, the Vieux Port later bustled with Genoese traders, but since the building of the ferry terminal and commercial docks it has become a backwater. The most atmospheric time to come here is early evening, when huge flocks of swifts swirl in noisy clouds above the harbour. Things liven up after sunset, with the glow and noise from the waterside bars and restaurants, which continue round the north end of the port along the wide **quai des Martyrs de la Libération**, where live bands clank out pop covers for the tourists in summer.

A small 'Cuncolta' sign above a door on the north side of the Vieux Port marks the spot where a car bomb exploded in July 1996, killing a prominent nationalist, and seriously injuring Charles Pieri, national secretary of A Cuncolta, the political front of the FLNC. Fourteen other people were hurt in the blast, which was the first time a bomb had been planted in a public place, in broad daylight, since the begining of the troubles in Corsica.

Terra Nova

The military and administrative core of old Bastia, Terra Nova (or the citadel) has a distinct air of affluence, its lofty apartments now colonized by Bastia's yuppies. The area is focused on **place du Donjon**, which gets its name from the squat round tower that formed the nucleus of Bastia's fortifications and was used by the Genoese to incarcerate Corsican patriots – Sampiero Corso was held in the dungeon for four years in the early sixteenth century. Next to the tower, the strategically placed *Bar de la Citadelle* commands a magnificent view that extends to Elba on a clear day.

Facing the bar is the impressive fourteenth-century **Palais des Gouverneurs**. With its great round tower, arcaded courtyard and pristine peach-coloured paintwork, this building has a distinctly Moorish feel and was built for the governor and local bishop during the town's Genoese heyday. When the French transferred the capital to Ajaccio it became a prison, then was destroyed during Nelson's attack of 1794. The subsequent rebuilding was not the last, as parts of it were blown up by the Americans in 1943, and today the restorers are trying to regain something of the building's former grandeur. Part of the palace is given over to the **Musée d'Éthnographie** (daily: June–Aug 9am–6.30pm; Sept–May 9am–noon & 2–6pm; 18F), which presents the history of Corsica from prehistoric times to the present day. Its dusty, vaulted chambers contain some fascinating historical titbits, like a diminutive Roman sarcophagus decorated with hunting scenes, busts of famous Corsicans and an original 1755 Flag of Independence, with its distinctive Moorish emblem.

On the terrace of the museum stands the conning tower of the **submarine Casabianca**, which played a major part in the liberation of Corsica in World War II by ferrying weapons and ammunitions from Algeria. The sub was named after 12-year-old Giocante de Casabianca, who died at Aboukir in 1798 when he refused to leave his father's ship after it had been attacked by Nelson's fleet – giving Felicia Hemans her inspiration for the poem beginning "The boy stood on the burning deck".

Back in place du Donjon, if you cross the square and follow rue Notre-Dame you come out at the **church of Ste-Marie**. Built in 1458 and overhauled in the seventeenth century, it was the cathedral of Bastia until 1801, when the bishopric was transferred to Ajaccio. The over-restored facade is an ugly shade of peach, and there's nothing of interest inside except a small silver statue of the Virgin. Virtually next door, in rue de l'Evêché, stands the **Oratoire Ste-Croix**, a sixteenth-century church decorated in Louis XV style, all rich blue paint and gilt scrollwork. It houses another holy item, the

Christ des Miracles, a blackened oak crucifix which in 1428 was discovered floating in the sea surrounded by a luminous haze. Beyond the church, the narrow streets open out to the tiny **place Guasco**, a delightful square at the heart of the citadel that typifies the exclusivity of Terra Nova. A few benches offer the chance of a rest before descending into the fray.

The beaches

Crowded with schoolchildren in the summer, the pebbly town **beach** in Bastia is only worth visiting if you're desperate for a swim. To reach it, go left at the flower shop on the main road south out of town, just beyond the citadel. A better alternative is the long beach of **L'Arinella** at Montesoro, a further 1km along the same road, the beginning of a sandy shore that extends along the whole east coast. A bus to L'Arinella leaves from outside *Café Riche* on bd Paoli every twenty minutes; just get off at the last stop and cross the train line to the sea. There are a couple of sailing and windsurfing clubs here, and a bar.

Eating and drinking

Numerous pizza vans are scattered about town, evidence of a strong Italian influence that's also apparent in the predominance of **pizzerias** and pasta places in the Nouveau Port area. The town also boasts some excellent inexpensive **restaurants** serving Corsican specialities: the posh places on the quai des Martyrs do the best *aziminu*, a Corsican version of bouillabaisse. Most of the good restaurants are to be found around the Vieux Port and on the quai des Martyrs, with a sprinkling in the citadel.

Drinking is serious business in Bastia, with the Casanis *pastis* factory on the outskirts of town in Lupino making the town's favourite drink. There are many bars and cafés all over town, varying from the stark and brightly lit bars of Terra Vecchia that are the haunt of old men, to the elegant, dimly lit cafés on place St-Nicolas. For a more sedate atmosphere, bd Paoli and rue Campinchi are lined with chi-chi *salons de thé* offering elaborate creamy confections, local chestnut cake and doughnuts.

Bars and cafés

Bar de la Citadelle, opposite the palais des gouveneurs in Terra Nova. This unpretentious bar is the perfect postcard-writing location, with fine views over the old port and out to sea, and they serve passable sandwiches. Not to be confused with the (posh) restaurant of the same name up the alley on rue du Dragon.

Bar Corsica, 2 rue Spinola. Tucked away behind the Vieux Port and the place to hear traditional Corsican singing.

Café Napoléon, 16 bd Général-de-Gaulle. Recently refurbished, elegant café, famous for its surly waiter, a character straight out of *Asterix*.

Café Riche, 29 bd Paoli. Large and busy café that's a centre for gambling, next door to the first betting shop in Corsica.

Cybercafé de Bastia, 2 rue Castagna, Vieux Port (Web site: *le.cyber.cafe.de.bastia@wanadoo.fr*). Tiny but sociable cyber café that serves sandwiches and burgers while you surf. Internet access 50F per hour, or 10F for email.

Le Pub Assunta, 5 place Fontaine-Neuve. Lively café-bar with a snooker table on its mezzanine floor, and a shady terrace opening onto the old quarter. A good choice of draught beers, with live music on Thurs evening. Recommended for kids.

Restaurants

L'Ambada, Vieux Port. An old-established pizzeria on the harbourfront. Great pizzas and fresh pasta served in various seafood sauces. Closed, surprisingly, Sat lunchtime and Sun in July–Aug.

La Braise, 7 bd Hyacinte-de-Montera. Situated close to the theatre, this is among Bastia's most popular restaurants. It's particularly renowned for its definitive Corsican pizzas and flame-grilled meat dishes. Inexpensive.

U Cantarettu, Vieux Port. Corsican lasagne and sublime pizzas, along with a nightly concert of popular Corsican ballads courtesy of the owner.

Chez Vincent, rue du Dragon, Citadelle. A small, inexpensive café-restaurant occupying a prime site directly above the Vieux Port. Set menus from 50–90F, and a choice of run-of-the-mill pizzas

Le Caveau du Marin, 4 quai des Martyrs. Welcoming little place decked out like a fishing hut, sharks' teeth and all. Seafood pasta's a speciality.

La Citadelle, 6 rue du Dragon (☎04.95.31.44.70). This gourmet Corsican restaurant, in a tastefully restored period building at the heart of the citadel, ranks among the top places to eat on the island. Set menus start at 180F (without wine).

A Scaletta, Vieux Port. Entrance on the steps leading from the port to the church of St-Jean-Baptiste. Fresh fish, served on a precarious balcony overlooking the boats. Generous Corsican speciality menu at 75F. Eau-de-vie on the house if you're lucky.

U Tianu, 4 rue Monsigneur Rigo. Sparse, trendy nationalist hang-out in a narrow alley off quai des Martyrs. Excellent charcuterie and a different fixed menu everyday for 120F, featuring local dishes such as blackbird pâté and hare and olive stew. Not to be missed.

Le Zagora, Vieux Port. An attractively decorated Moroccan restaurant with great views over the harbour. Try their delicious veal with plums and almonds, washed down with mint tea. Most main dishes around 75–110F.

La Marana, Mariana and the Étang de Biguglia

Traditionally the summer haunt of prosperous Bastia families, the sixteen-kilometre littoral known as **LA MARANA** lies a few kilometres south of Bastia. The beach here offers shady pine woods, restaurants and bars, though the sea is quite polluted. All this part of the coast is divided into holiday residences or sections of beach attached to bars, the latter freely open to the public. Try **A Pagoda**, about 5km along the road – popular with the young crowd, it has a disco and a large open-air bar. Another good spot is **Pineto**, the furthest beach along the road and therefore the least crowded in the summer, where the bus terminates.

Fed by the rivers Bevinco and Golo, the **Étang de Biguglia** is the largest lagoon in Corsica, with reed, moustached and cetti warblers during summer. In winter, Biguglia is a stop-off point for migrating grey herons, kingfishers, great crested grebes, little grebes, water rails and various species of duck, such as the spectacular red-crested pochard, immediately identifiable by its red bill, red feet and a bright-red head.

The Roman town of **MARIANA**, just south of Étang de Biguglia, can be approached by taking the turning for Bastia's Poretta airport, 16km along the N193, or the more scenic coastal route through La Marana. It was founded in 93 BC as a military colony, but today's houses, baths and basilica are too ruined to be of great interest. It's only the square baptistry, with its remarkable mosaic floor decorated with dancing dolphins and fish looped around a bearded Neptune, that is worth seeking out.

Adjacent to Mariana stands the **church of Santa Maria Assunta**, known as La Canonica. Built in 1119 close to the old capital of Biguglia, it is the finest of around three hundred churches built by the Pisans in their effort to evangelize the island. Modelled on a Roman basilica, the perfectly proportioned edifice is decorated outside with Corinthian capitals plundered from the main Mariana site and with plates of Cap Corse marble, their delicate pink and yellow ochre hues fusing to stunning effect.

About 300m to the south of La Canonica stands **San Parteo**, built in the eleventh and twelfth centuries over the site of a pagan burial ground. A smaller edifice than La Canonica, the church also displays some elegant arcading and fine sculpture – on the south side, the door lintel is supported by two writhing beasts reaching to a central tree, a motif of Oriental origins.

Cap Corse

Until Napoléon III had a coach road built around **Cap Corse** in the nineteenth century, the promontory was effectively cut off from the rest of the island, relying on Italian maritime traffic for its income – hence its distinctive Tuscan dialect. Many *Capicursini* later left to seek their fortunes in the colonies of the Caribbean, which explain the distinctly ostentatious mansions, or *palazzus*, built by the successful emigrés (nicknamed "les Américains"), on their return. For all the changes brought by the modern world, Cap Corse still feels like a separate country, with wild flowers in profusion, vineyards and quiet, traditional fishing villages.

Forty kilometres long and only fifteen across, the peninsula is divided by a spine of mountains called the Serra, which peaks at Monte Stello, 1037m above sea level. The coast on the east side of this divide is characterized by tiny ports, or *marines*, tucked into gently sloping river-mouths, alongside coves which become sandier as you go further north. The villages of the western coast are sited on rugged cliffs, high above the rough sea and tiny rocky inlets that can be glimpsed from the corniche road.

For those without transport, a circular tour bus operates daily from Bastia during the summer. There are also buses throughout the year to **Erbalunga**, a placid fishing village on the east of Cap Corse where the buildings, ending in one of the ruined lookout towers for which the cape is famous, rise directly from the sea. In addition, sporadic services run from Bastia's gare routière to **Macinaggio** (Mon, Weds & Fri), on the far north tip of the cape, and to **Canari** (Mon & Wed), on the northwest side.

Erbalunga

Built along a rocky promontory 10km north of Bastia, the small port of **ERBALUNGA** is the highlight of the east coast, with aged, pale buildings stacked like crooked boxes behind a small harbour and ruined Genoese watchtower. A little colony of French artists lived here in the 1920s, and the village has drawn a steady stream of admirers ever since. It attracts a fair number of tourists throughout the year, and come summer it's transformed into something of a cultural enclave, with concerts and art events adding a spark to local nightlife. The town is most famous, however, for its Good Friday procession, known as the *Cerca* (Search), which evolved from an ancient fertility rite. Hooded penitents, recruited from the ranks of a local religious brotherhood, form a spiral known as a *Granitola*, or snail, which unwinds as the candlelit procession moves into the village square.

A port since the time of the Phoenicians, Erbalunga was once a more important trading centre than Bastia or Ajaccio. With the increasing exportation of wine and olive oil, in the eleventh century it became the capital of an independent village state, ruled by the da Gentile family, who lived in the **palazzo** that dominates place de-Gaulle.

In the harbour, a few **bars** shaded by an enormous chestnut tree look out across the water to the tower. The one **hotel**, the stylish *Castel'Brando*, is sited at the entrance to the square (☎04.95.30.10.30, fax 04.95.33.98.18; ⑨; closed Nov–March). A beautifully restored Latin-American-style *palazzu*, it has plenty of period charm, but is closed in winter and doesn't have a restaurant. For a meal you have the choice of *Le Pirate*, right on the sea some 30m from place de-Gaulle, which has been here for years and serves mainly fish and fresh ravioli, and *U Frangu*, along the alley leading north of the marina, which serves classy Corsican cuisine in a converted olive mill whose rear terrace is lapped by the waves. The latter has more character and is less expensive, with set menus starting at 100F.

Macinaggio and around

A port since Roman times, well-sheltered **MACINAGGIO**, 20km north of Erbalunga, was developed by the Genoese in 1620 for the export of olive oil and wine to the Italian peninsula. Pascal Paoli landed here in 1790 after his exile in England, whereupon he kissed the ground and uttered the words "O ma patrie, je t'ai quitté esclave, je te retrouve libre" (Oh my country, I left you as a slave, I rediscover you a free man) – a plaque commemorating the event adorns the wall above the ship chandlers. There's not much of a historic patina to the place nowadays, but with its boat-jammed **marina** and its line of colourful seafront awnings, Macinaggio has a certain appeal in itself. In addition, its proximity to some of the best beaches on Corsica make it irresistible.

The best hotel is *Les Îles*, opposite the marina (☎04.95.35.43.02, fax 04.95.35.47.05; ③; closed Nov–Feb), which has cosy rooms overlooking the port and a good restaurant. Otherwise your best bet is *U Libecciu*, behind the marina on the road that leads north off the D80 road to Rogliano (☎04.95.35.43.22; ③; closed mid-Oct to Feb), with spacious rooms and an excellent restaurant. *U Ricordu*, on the south side of the road to Rogliano (☎04.95.35.40.20, fax 04.95.31.41.88; ⑤; includes breakfast), is along the same lines, and has a swimming pool. Macinaggio has one **campsite**, *U Stazzu* (☎04.95.35.43.76), 1km north and with good access to the nearby town beach. As for **restaurants**, the *Pizzeria San Columbu*, at the end of the port facing out to sea, does a passable seafood pizza, or you can have a Corsican feast at *Les Îles*, which specializes in imaginative seafood dishes.

North of the town lie some stunning stretches of white sand and clear sea. A marked footpath, known as **Le Sentier des Douaniers** because it used to be patrolled by customs officials, threads its way across the hills and caves along the coast, giving access to an area that cannot by reached by road. The **Baie de Tamarone**, 2km along this path, has deep clear waters, making it a good place for diving and snorkelling. Just behind the beach the road forks, and if you follow the left-hand track for twenty minutes you'll come to the isolated Romanesque **Chapelle Santa-Maria**. Raised on the foundations of a sixth-century church, the building comprises a tenth-century chapel and a twelfth-century chapel merged into one, hence the two discrepant apses.

Three kilometres north of the chapel you come to **plage Santa Maria**, a perfect arc of white sand overlooked by the huge Tour Chiapelle. Dramatically cleft in half and entirely surrounded by water, the ruined three-storeyed building was one of three built on the northern tip of the cape by the Genoese in the sixteenth century (the others are at Tollare and Barcaggio) as lookout posts against the increasingly troublesome Moorish pirates. As Macinaggio grew in importance, the towers began to be used also by health and customs officers, who controlled the maritime traffic with Genoa. Pascal Paoli established his garrison here in 1761, having been unsuccessful in his attempt to take Macinaggio, and contemplated building a rival port.

Centuri

From Macinaggio you can drive west across the promontory along an eight-kilometre hairpin road over the **Col St-Nicolas** (303m) and the **Col de Serra** (365m). Once over the second col you soon come to **CAMERA**, the first hamlet of the commune of **CENTURI**, where the bizarre cylindrical turrets of the **Château de Général Cipriani** (not open to the public) peer from the woods beneath the road. The smaller hamlet of **CANELLE**, overlooking Centuri-Port and accessible from Camera along the road heading north or on foot from the port, is known for its enormous fig trees, whose drooping branches overhang the houses and shadow the road.

When Boswell arrived here from England in 1765, the former Roman settlement of **CENTURI-PORT** was a tiny fishing village, recommended to him for its peaceful detachment from the dangerous turmoil of the rest of Corsica. Not much has changed since Boswell's time: Centuri-Port exudes tranquillity despite a serious influx of summer residents, many of them artists who come to paint the fishing boats in the slightly prettified harbour, where the grey-stone wall is highlighted by the green serpentine roofs of the encircling cottages, restaurants and bars. The only drawback is that you'll find the small beach disappointingly muddy and not ideal for sunbathing (although it is an excellent spot for snorkelling).

Centuri-Port has more **hotels** than anywhere else on Cap Corse. Best of the bunch is *Hôtel-Restaurant du Pêcheur* (☎04.95.35.60.14; ③; closed Nov–March), the pink building in the harbour, is among the most pleasant and fills up quickly in the high season; its rooms are agreeably cool, with thick stone walls, and it has a popular restaurant. A slightly less expensive option is the *Vieux Moulin* (☎04.95.35.60.15, fax 04.95.60.24; ③; closed Oct–March), a restored *palazzu* that occupies a prime location behind the harbour (on the right as you enter the village), but the rooms can be stuffy in summer and the obligatory 150F menu is a poor deal. Otherwise you have *Hôtel U Marinara* (☎04.95.35.62.95; ②; closed Oct–March), behind *du Pêcheur*, also with a restaurant. For **campers** there's *Camping l'Isolettu*, 400m south (☎04.95.35.62.81; open all year), an uninviting option but the only choice in the vicinity.

Nonza

Eighteen kilometres south of Centuri and set high on a black rocky pinnacle dropping vertically into the sea, the village of **NONZA** is one of the highlights of the Cap Corse shoreline. It was formerly the main stronghold of the da Gentile family, and the remains of the **fortress** are still standing on the furthest rocks on the overhanging cliff.

Nonza is also famous for **Ste-Julia**, patron saint of Corsica, who was martyred here in the fifth century. The story goes that she had been sold into slavery at Carthage and was being taken by ship to Gaul when the slavers docked here. A pagan festival was in progress, and when Julia refused to participate she was crucified; the gruesome legend relates that her breasts were then cut off and thrown onto a stone, from which sprang two springs, now enshrined in a chapel by the beach. To get there, follow the sign on the right-hand side of the road before you enter the square, which points to **La Fontaine de Ste-Julia**, down by the rocks. Reached by a flight of six-hundred steps, Nonza's long grey **beach** is discoloured as a result of pollution from the now disused asbestos mine up the coast. This may not inspire confidence, but the locals insist it's safe (they take their own kids there in summer), and from the bottom you do get the best view of the tower, which looks as if it's about to topple in to the sea.

You can **stay** in Nonza at *Auberge Patrizi* (☎04.95.37.82.16; ④ including breakfast; closed mid-Oct to March), run from the big peach-coloured restaurant in the square. Made up of two village houses, the *Patrizi* is an old-fashioned place where half-board is obligatory, but the food is good and plentiful. The nearest campsite is *A Stella*, 9km south on the St-Florent Road (☎04.95.37.14.37; April–Oct), which is cheap and right next to a great beach.

The Nebbio

Taking its name from the thick mists that sweep over the region in winter, the **Nebbio** has for centuries been one of the most fertile parts of the island, producing honey, chestnuts and some of the island's finest wine. Tourism, however, has so far made little impact on this depopulated area, which comprises the amphitheatre of rippled hills, vineyards and cultivated valleys that converge on **St-Florent**, a handful of kilometres due west of Bastia. Aside from EU subsidies, the major money earner here is **viticulture**: some of the wines produced around the commune of **Patrimonio** rival those of Sartène, and *caves* offering wine tastings are a feature of the whole region.

A bishopric until 1790, St-Florent is a chic coastal resort at the base of Cap Corse. It remains the Nebbio's chief town, and is the obvious base for daytrips to the beautifully preserved Pisan church of **Santa Maria Assunta**, just outside the town, and the **Désert des Agriates**, a wilderness of parched *maquis*-covered hills whose rugged coastline harbours one of Corsica's least accessible, but most beautiful, beaches.

The only **public transport** serving Nebbio is the twice-daily bus from Bastia to St-Florent, which leaves the gare routière at 11am (or noon on Weds) and 5.30pm on Mon–Sat.

St-Florent and around

Viewed from across the bay, **ST-FLORENT** (San Fiurenzu) appears as a bright line against the black tidal wave of the Tenda hills, the pale ancient houses seeming to rise straight out of the sea, overlooked by a squat circular **citadel**. It's a relaxing town, blessed with a decent beach and a good number of restaurants, but the key to its success is the **marina**, which has made St-Florent something of a low-key St-Tropez.

In Roman times, a town called Cersunam existed a kilometre east of the present village. Few traces remain of the settlement that grew up there, which in the fifteenth century was eclipsed by the port that developed around the new Genoese citadel. St-Florent prospered as one of Genoa's strongholds, and it was from here that Paoli set off for London in 1796, never to return.

Place des Portes, the centre of town life, has café tables facing the sea in the shade of plane trees, and in the evening fills with strollers and nonchalant boules players. In rue du Centre, which runs west off the square, parallel to the seafront and marina, you'll find some restaurants, a few shops and a couple of wine-tasting places – be sure to sample the sweet, *maquis*-scented muscat made around here. To reach the fifteenth-century circular **citadel** you climb to the end of rue du Centre and pass through the large wire gate. It's filled with pigeons, but does give a beautiful view of the hills of the Nebbio and the mountains of Cap Corse.

Just a kilometre to the east of the town off a small road running off place des Portes, on the original site of the Roman settlement of Nebbium, the **church of Santa Maria Assunta** – the so-called cathedral of the Nebbio – is a fine example of Pisan Romanesque architecture. Built of warm yellow limestone, the cathedral has a distinctly barn-like appearance – albeit a superlatively elegant one. Gracefully symmetrical blind arcades decorate the western facade, and at the entrance twisting serpents and wild animals adorn the pilasters on each side of the door. The interior, too, appears deceptively simple. Carved shells, foliage and animals adorn the capitals of the pillars dividing the nave where, immediately to the right, you'll see a glass case containing the mummified figure of St-Flor, a Roman soldier martyred in the third century.

Practicalities

Buses run from Bastia to St-Florent twice daily (except Sun), and arrive in the village car park. The journey takes one hour. The **tourist office** (May–Oct daily 8.30am–12.30pm & 2–7pm; Nov–April Mon–Fri 9am–noon & 2–5pm, Sat 9am–noon) is in the same building as the **post office**, about five minutes' walk from place des Portes.

St-Florent is a popular resort and **hotels** fill up quickly, especially at the height of summer when prior booking is essential. The elegant *Hôtel Europe* in place des Portes (☎04.95.37.00.03; ③) is the most attractive option in town – and it's the only one open in winter. *Hôtel du Centre*, just up the road from the *Europe* (☎04.95.37.00.68; ③), has tiny rooms but is the cheapest place in town. Otherwise, try the excellent value *Chez*

Gisèle et Pierre, 9 route de la Plage d'Oro (☎04.95.37.13.14; ②). Offering a cosy bed and breakfast close to the beach, it's a friendly, comfortable place, and thus often booked up, so phone ahead. A fair number of **campsites** are dotted about the coast, but are packed in August and closed out of season. *Camping U Pezzu*, rte de la Plage (☎04.95.37.01.65), is closest to town, 1km west on the small road which backs the beach. *Camping Kalliste*, 2km further on the same road (☎04.95.37.03.08), is clean and large, with its own beachside bar and restaurant.

St-Florent is renowned for its crayfish and red mullet, and a reasonably priced **restaurant** for excellent fish and Corsican specialities is *Le Cabistan* in the rue du Centre. More expensive is *La Marinuccia* at the far end of the same street, which serves the best fish in St-Florent and has a terrace jutting out into the sea. Otherwise *Pizzeria Citadel*, the fortress-shaped place just over the bridge south of the square, does very good pizzas and salads. Another cheap and cheerful option (at least by St-Florent standards) is *Ind'e Lucia*, on the place Doria, whose inexpensive set menus feature plenty of local specialities; their house wine is top value, too.

Patrimonio

Leaving St-Florent by the Bastia road, the first village you come to, after 6km, is **PATRIMONIO**, centre of the first Corsican wine region to gain *appellation controlée* status. Apart from the local, which can be sampled in the village or at one of the *caves* along the route from St-Florent, Patrimonio's chief asset is the sixteenth-century **church of St-Martin**, occupying its own little hillock and visible for kilometres around. The colour of burnt sienna, it stands out vividly against the rich green vineyards. In a garden 200m south of the church stands a limestone statue-menhir known as **U Nativu**, a late megalithic piece dating from 800–900 BC. A carved T-shape on its front represents a breastbone, and two eyebrows and a chin can also be made out.

The Désert des Agriates

Extending westwards from the Golfe de St-Florent to the mouth of the Ostriconi River, the **Désert des Agriates** is a vast area of uninhabited land, dotted with clumps of cacti and scrub-shrouded hills. It may appear inhospitable now, but during the time of the Genoese this rocky moonscape was, as its name implies, a veritable bread basket (*agriates* means "cultivated fields"). In fact, so much wheat was grown here that the Italian overlords levied a special tax on grain to prevent any build-up of funds that might have financed an insurrection. Fires and soil erosion eventually took their toll, however, and by the 1970s the area had become a total wilderness.

Numerous crackpot schemes to redevelop the Désert have been mooted over the years – from atomic weapon test zones to concrete Club-Med-style resorts – but during the past two decades the government has gradually bought up the land from its various owners (among them the Rothschild family) and designated it as a protected nature reserve. Nevertheless, species such as the Agriate's rare wild boar remain under threat, mainly from trigger-happy hunters and bush fires.

Marked footpaths are being established around the coast of the desert, but it remains a difficult area to penetrate by motor vehicle. Only one of its beautiful beaches is accessible by 4WD car. A glistening stretch of silver sand and translucent green water, **Plage de Saleccia**, 10km west along the coast from St-Florent by the Punta di Curza, is among the most exquisite beaches in Corsica. To get there, head west of St-Florent as far as the hamlet of **CASTA**, a short way beyond which a dirt track drops downhill from the *Hôtel Le Relais* (if you're driving, check at the hotel to make sure the track is passable). After 11km of relentless ruts, the *piste* passes the island's most

Crowning rocky promontories and clifftops from Cap Corse to Bonifacio, the 91 crumbling Genoese watchtowers that punctuate the Corsican coast have become emblematic of the island's picture-postcard tranquillity. Yet they date from an era when these shores were among the most troubled in Europe. During the fifteenth century, Saracen **pirates** from North Africa began to menace the coastal villages and became so common that many Corsicans fled the coast altogether, retreating to villages in the hills. To protect those that remained, as well as their threatened maritime trade, the Genoese erected a chain of watchtowers, or **torri**, at strategic points on the island. They were paid for by local villagers and staffed by watchmen whose job it was to signal the approach of any unexpected ships by lighting a fire on the crenellated rampart at the top of the tower. In this way, it was possible to alert the entire island in single hour.

Piracy more or less died out by the end of Genoese rule, but the *torri* remained in use long after, proving particularly effective during the Anglo-Corsican invasions of the late eighteenth century. The British were so impressed with the system that they erected similar structures along the south coast of England and Ireland to warn of attacks by the French. Named after the first Genoese watchtower ever built in Corsica – on the Pointe de Martella, protecting the port of St-Florent and the Nebbio – these **Martello towers** were later used as lookout towers in World War II. The one overlooking the mouth of the River Liffey in Dublin has even become a world-famous landmark, immortalized as the setting for the first chapter of James Joyce's *Ulysses*.

remote **campsite**, *U Paradisu* (☎04.95.37.82.51; May–Oct), and ends at a car park, a great base from which to explore the desert on foot.

The Balagne

The Balagne, the region stretching west from the Ostriconi Valley as far as the red-cliffed wilderness of Scandola, has been renowned since Roman times as "Le Pays de l'Huile et Froment" (Land of Oil and Wheat). Backed by a wall of imposing, pale-grey mountains, the characteristic outcrops of orange granite punctuating its spectacular coastline shelter a string of idyllic beaches, many of them sporting ritzy marinas and holiday complexes. These, along with the region's two honeypot towns, **L'Île Rousse** and **Calvi**, get swamped in summer, but the scenery more than compensates. In any case, Calvi, with its cream-coloured citadel, stunning white-sand bay and mountainous backdrop, should not be missed.

Year-round **transport** in the Balagne is limited to the Micheline train, which descends the Ostriconi Valley and runs west along the coast as far as Calvi, and a bus connection with Bastia, via Ponte Leccia. In July and August, you can also travel to Calvi from Porto by bus.

L'Île Rousse

Developed by Pascal Paoli in the 1760s as a "gallows to hang Calvi", the port of **L'ÎLE ROUSSE** (Isula Rossa) simply doesn't convince as a Corsican town, its palm trees, smart shops, neat flower gardens and colossal pink seafront hotel creating an atmosphere that has more in common with the French Riviera. Pascal Paoli had great plans for his new town on the Haute-Balagne coast, which was laid out from scratch in 1758 as a port to export the olive oil produced in the Balagne region. A large part of the new port was built on a grid system, featuring lines of straight parallel streets quite at odds with the higgledy-piggledy nature of most Corsican villages and towns. Thanks to the busy trading of wine and oil, it soon began to prosper and, two- and-a-half centuries later, still thrives as a successful port. These days, however, the main traffic consists of holiday-makers, lured here by brochure shots of the nearby beaches. This is officially the hottest corner of the island, and the town is thus deluged by German and Italian sunworshippers in July and August. Given the proximity of Calvi, and so much unspoilt countryside, it's hard to see why you should want to stop here for more than a couple of hours.

L'Île Rousse is easily accessible by **bus** from Bastia and Calvi, and the **train** pauses here on the Calvi–Ponte-Leccia line.

Arrival, information and accommodation

The **train station** (☎04.95.60.00.50) is on rte du Port, 500m south of where the ferries arrive. The Bastia–Calvi **bus** stops just south of place Paoli in the town's main thoroughfare, av Piccioni. The SNCM office is on av J-Calizi (☎04.95.60.09.56), and the **tourist office** on the south side of place Paoli (May–June & Sept–Oct Mon–Fri 9.30am–noon & 3–6pm; July & Aug daily 9am–1pm & 2.30–7.30pm; ☎04.95.60.04.35).

L'Île Rousse fills up early in the year and it can be difficult to find a **hotel** at any time from May to October. Most places are modern buildings, more functional than personable. L'Île Rousse has two main **campsites**: *Les Oliviers*, 1km east (☎04.95.60.19.92) and *L'Orniccio*, 2km south on the rte de Montincello (☎04.95.60.17.32). The latter is cheaper and has better views.

HOTELS

Le Grillon, 10 av Paul Doumer (☎04.95.60.00.49, fax 04.95.60.43.69). L'Île Rousse's best budget option is very ordinary-looking outside (no sea views), but is neat and clean, and with a good-value restaurant downstairs. Double rooms under 200F outside July and August. ③.

Napoléon Bonaparte, 3 place Paoli (☎04.95.60.06.09). Garish, converted *palazzu* which for years was the only luxury hotel on the island; although downgraded, it still has a certain old-fashioned appeal. Closed Nov–March. ④.

Santa Maria, in the port (☎04.95.60.13.49, fax 04.95.60.32.48). A good value three-star, in a great location, with views of Cap Corse, immaculate air-conditioned rooms, pool and garden. ③.

Splendid, bd Valéry-François (☎04.95.60.00.24, fax 04.95.60.04.57). Palatial 1930s-style building with a new swimming pool. Price includes breakfast, and their 70F half-board supplement deal is good value. ④.

The town

All roads in L'Île Rousse lead to **place Paoli**, a shady square that's open to the sea and has as its focal point a fountain surmounted by a bust of "U Babbu di u Patria" (Grandfather of the Nation), one of many local tributes to Pascal Paoli. There's a Frenchified covered **market** at the entrance to the square, which hosts a popular artisan-cum-antiques sale on Saturday mornings, while on the west side rises the grim facade of the **church of the Immaculate Conception**.

To reach the **Île de la Pietra**, the islet that gives the town its name, continue north, passing the station on your left. Once over the causeway connecting the islet to the mainland, you can walk through the crumbling mass of red granite as far as the lighthouse at the far end, from where the view of the town is spectacular, especially at sundown, when you get the full effect of the red glow of the rocks. Heading back along **A Marinella**, which follows the seafront behind the town beach, a ten-minute walk will bring you to the aquarium, the main sight in the town. The overpriced **Musée Océanographique** (May–Sept Mon–Fri 10.30am–1pm & 2–7pm; 45F), situated at the north end of the beach, publicizes itself as the "Grotte aux Requins", but the only members of the shark family on display here are some timid dogfish. If the stiff entry charges don't put you off, then the decidedly cramped tanks housing the larger creatures probably will.

Although L'Île Rousse has a decent beach, the most popular one hereabouts is **plage de Rindara**, a fantastic duned strand with pale-green translucent water, 4km southwest of the town. Equally spectacular, **plage de Lozari**, a long semi-circular sweep of white sand, lies 7km northeast. A decent road signposted "Lozari" leads down to the shore and a discreet holiday village.

Eating and drinking

Tourism has taken its toll here, hence the abundance of mediocre **eating** places crammed into the narrow alleys of the old town. A few restaurants do stand out, however, some with classic gourmet menus and other Corsican places serving superb fresh seafood. The best cafés are found in place Paoli along the southern side.

Chez Paco, rue Paoli. Arguably the best inexpensive restaurant in town, serving copious portions of fresh seafood, Spanish-style calamari and paëlla under awnings in the street.

Le Grand Bleu, rue Napoléon. Brash decor but excellent and expensive food, mainly French fish dishes such as sea bass with fennel.

Le Grillon, 10 av Paul Doumer. Inexpensive French-style bistrot, whose *steak au Roquefort* is a dream. Set menus under 100F. Good value.

L'Île d'Or, place Paoli. Basic terrace bistrot pitched squarely at foreign tourists, but in a prime location for watching the boules players.

La Jonque, rue Paoli. A tiny Vietnamese restaurant in the old quarter. Tacky formula decor, but the food is fine and makes a pleasant change. Menus from 90F.

L'Ostéria, place Santilli (☎04.95.60.09.39). The most traditional restaurant in town, specializing in fresh, simple Corsican cooking. Exposed stone arches and old peasant tools add to the ambience. 115F menu.

Calvi

Seen from the water, **CALVI** is a beautiful spectacle, with its three immense bastions topped by a crest of ochre buildings, sharply defined against a hazy backdrop of snow-capped mountains. Twenty kilometres west along the coast from L'Île Rousse, the town began as a fishing port on the site of the present-day *ville basse* below the citadel, and remained just a cluster of houses and fishing shacks until the Pisans conquered the island in the tenth century. Not until the arrival of the Genoese did the town become a stronghold when, in 1268, Giovaninello de Loreto, a Corsican nobleman, built a huge citadel on the windswept rock overlooking the port and named it Calvi. A fleet commanded by Nelson launched a brutal two-month attack on the town in the 1750s, when Nelson lost his eye; he left saying he hoped never to see the place again.

The French concentrated on developing Ajaccio and Bastia during the nineteenth century, and the town became primarily a military base, used as a point for smuggling arms to the mainland in World War II. A hang-out for European glitterati in the 1950s, Calvi these days has the ambience of a slightly kitsch Côte d'Azur resort, whose glamorous marina, souvenir shops and fussy boutiques jar with the down-to-earth villages of its rural hinterland. It's also an important base for the French Foreign Legion, and immaculately uniformed legionnaires are a common sight around the bars lining avenue de la République.

Arrival, information and accommodation

Ste-Catherine airport lies 7km south of Calvi (☎04.95.65.88.68); the only public transport into town is by taxi, which shouldn't cost more than 70F (or 100F at night). The **train station** is on av de la République, close to the marina (☎04.95.65.00.61), where you'll find the **tourist office** on quai Landry (May–Oct daily 9am–1pm & 2.30–7.30pm; Nov–April Mon–Fri 9am–noon & 2–5.30pm; ☎04.95.65.16.67). **Buses** from Bastia stop

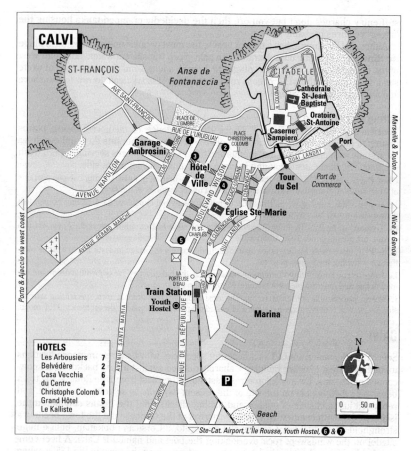

CALVI

ST-FRANÇOIS

Anse de
Fontanaccia

CITADELLE

Cathédrale
St-Jean
Baptiste

Oratoire
St-Antoine

Caserne
Sampiero

Port

Garage
Ambrosini

Hôtel
de
Ville

Tour
du Sel

Port de
Commerce

Eglise Ste-Marie

Train Station

Youth
Hostel

Marina

HOTELS
Les Arbousiers	7
Belvédère	2
Casa Vecchia	6
du Centre	4
Christophe Colomb	1
Grand Hôtel	5
Le Kalliste	3

Ste-Cat. Airport, L'Île Rousse, Youth Hostel, **6** & **7**

outside the station but those from Porto use place Christophe-Colomb. You can find bus information at the tourist office and at Agence des Beaux Voyages on place de la Porteuse d'Eau (☎04.95.65.11.35). **Ferries**, including NGV hydrofoils, dock at the Port de Commerce at the foot of the citadel, and the SNCM office is at quai Landry (☎04.95.65.01.38). You can rent **bikes** from Ambrosini on place Bel-Ombra, heading out of town towards Porto (☎04.95.65.02.13), and **cars** from Hertz, 2 rue Maréchal-Joffre (☎04.95.65.06.64), or Budget at the airport (☎04.95.65.88.34).

Accommodation is easy to find in Calvi except during the jazz festival (third week of June). There are some excellent hotels, ranging from cheap *pensions* to more upmarket and extremely pricey places, as well as a wide choice of mid-range hotels. Those on a tight budget can choose between two youth hostels and several campsites within walking distance of the town.

HOTELS

Les Arbousiers, route de la Pietra-Maggiore (☎04.95.65.04.47, fax 04.95.65.26.14). Large, fading pink place set back from the main road, 1km south of town, with rooms ranged around a quiet court-yard. Good value (200F for doubles) outside July and Aug. ④.

Belvédère, av de l'Uruguay (☎04.95.65.01.25). Large, simple rooms, in a good location in between the citadel and *ville basse*. Generous off-season discounts. ③.

Casa Vecchia, route de Santore (☎04.95.65.09.33, fax 04.95.65.37.95). Small chalets set in leafy garden, 500m east of town, and a stone's throw from the beach. May, June and Sept doubles at 170F. A safe budget option. ②.

du Centre, 14 rue Alsace-Lorraine (☎04.95.65.02.01). Converted nineteenth-century *gendarmerie* slap in the middle of the old quarter, with lower tariffs and more character than most. Doubles at 180F outside July and Aug. ③.

Christophe Colomb, place Christophe-Colomb (☎04.95.65.06.04, fax 04.95.65.29.65). Spacious rooms and expansive views across the bay. Closed Nov–March. ④.

Grand Hotel, 3 bd Wilson (☎04.95.65.09.74, fax 04.95.65.25.18). Old-fashioned luxury hotel in centre of town. Swish cocktail bar and restaurant. Closed mid-Oct to mid-March. ④.

Le Kalliste, 1 av du Commandant-Marche (☎04.95.65.09.81, fax 04.95.65.35.65). Small dark rooms close to the citadel, but with its own restaurant and shady garden. Closed Nov–April. ④.

YOUTH HOSTELS AND CAMPSITES

Corsotel BVJ, 43 av de la République (☎04.95.65.14.15, fax 04.95.65.33.72). Huge youth hostel in a prime position opposite the station and facing the sea. Very clean rooms for up to six people, some with balconies. Enormous breakfast included in 120F tariff. Book ahead (the staff speak English).

Relais International de la Jeunesse, 4km from the centre of town on rte de Pietra-Maggiore (☎04.95.65.14.16, fax 04.95.80.65.30). Follow the N197 for 2km, turn right at the sign for Pietra-Maggiore, and the hostel – two little houses with dormitories looking out over the gulf – is another 2km further on. Breakfast included in excellent-value-80F tariff, but obligatory half-board (140F) in July and August. Open June–Sept.

International Camping, opposite the *Balagne* hotel on rte de L'Île Rousse (☎04.95.65.01.75). Small and fairly central site (500m from centre), popular with bikers and backpackers. The bar is lively and stays open late, with live rock bands on weekends.

Camping-Caravanning Bella Vista, 2km along the N197 from Calvi (☎04.95.65.11.76). A quiet and friendly site, 20min walk from the centre; to get to it, turn right at the sign to Pietra-Maggiore, and the campsite's another 1km along on the right-hand side. April–Oct.

The town and citadel

Social life in Calvi focuses on the restaurants and cafés of the **quai Landry**, a spacious seafront walkway linking the marina and the port. This is the best place to get the feel of the town, but as far as sights go there's not a lot to the *ville basse*. At the far end of the quay, under the shadow of the citadel, stands the sturdy **Tour du Sel**, a medieval lookout post once used to store imported salt. If you strike up through the narrow passageways off quai Landry, you'll come to **rue Clemenceau**, where restaurants and souvenir shops are packed into every available space. In a small square giving onto the street stands the pink-painted **Ste-Marie-Majeure**, built in 1774, whose spindly bell tower rises elegantly above the cafés on the quay but whose interior contains nothing of interest. From the church's flank, a flight of steps connects with **boulevard Wilson**, a wide modern high street which rises to **place Christophe-Colomb**, point of entry for the **ville haute**, or citadel.

Beyond the ancient **gateway** to the citadel, with its inscription of the town's motto, you come immediately to the enormous **Caserne Sampiero**, formerly the governor's palace. Built in the thirteenth century, when the great round tower was used as a dungeon, the **castle** was recently restored and is currently used for military purposes, and therefore closed to the public. The best way of seeing the rest of the citadel is to follow the ramparts, which connect three immense bastions. From each bastion the views across the sea, the Balagne and the Cinto Massif are magnificent.

Within the walls the houses are tightly packed along tortuous stairways and narrow passages that converge on the diminutive place d'Armes. Dominating the square is the

Cathédrale St-Jean-Baptiste, set at the highest point of the promontory and sitting uncomfortably amid the ramshackle buildings. This chunky ochre edifice was founded in the thirteenth century, but was partly destroyed during the Turkish siege of 1553 and then suffered extensive damage twelve years later, when the powder magazine in the governor's palace exploded. It was rebuilt in the form of a Greek cross, as you see today. The church's great treasure is the **Christ des Miracles**, housed in the chapel on the right of the choir; this crucifix was brandished at marauding Turks during a siege of 1553, an act which reputedly saved the day.

To the north of place d'Armes in rue de Fil stands the shell of the building that Calvi believes was **Christopher Columbus's birthplace**, as the plaque on the wall states, but the claim rides on pretty tenuous, circumstantial evidence. The house itself was destroyed by Nelson's army during the siege of 1794, but as recompense a statue was erected on May 20, 1992, the 500th anniversary of his "discovery" of America; his alleged birthday, October 12, is now a public holiday in Calvi.

Calvi's outstanding **beach** sweeps right round the bay from the end of quai Landry, but most of the first kilometre or so is owned by bars which rent out sun loungers for a hefty price. To avoid these, follow the track behind the sand which will bring you to the start of a more secluded stretch. The sea might not be as sparklingly clear as at many other Corsican beaches, but it's warm, shallow and free of rocks. You can also sunbathe, and swim off the rocks, at the foot of the citadel, which have the added attraction of fine views across the bay.

Eating and drinking

Eating is a major pastime in Calvi, where you'll find a wide selection of restaurants and snack bars catering for all tastes. Fish restaurants predominate in the marina, where – at a price – you can eat excellent seafood fresh from the bay. It's cheaper to eat in the inland streets of the *ville basse* whose stairways and cramped forecourts hide a host of buzzing pizzerias and Corsican restaurants. **Cafés**, complete with raffia parasols, line the marina, becoming more expensive the nearer they are to the Tour du Sel.

CAFÉS AND BARS

Café des Marins, quai Landry. Looks like a huge boat inside, with portholes and a curvy bar. The best place for breakfast.

Café Rex, at the top of bd Wilson, on the corner of place Christophe-Colomb. The most down-to-earth and animated bar in central Calvi, with a small but sunny terrace and a mixed clientele. A good breakfast venue for crowd-watching.

International Bar, *Camping International*, rte de l'Île Rousse. A campsite bar, but the most consistently fun spot on weekends, when local bands play thumping rock covers through the small hours. Drinks at regular prices, and an internationally mixed crowd.

RESTAURANTS

Auberge Ajgha, 5km out of Calvi, south along the D251, next to *Hôtel La Signoria*. Beautifully situated hillside auberge, with wicker tables in a picturesque garden. The food ranges from sophisticated Corsican cuisine to simple pizzas.

Chez Fifi, place du Marché. Inexpensive and deservedly popular for its copious four-course menus, from 80F. Mostly local produce and dishes, and the house wine is *AOC*. During the summer, live folk guitar music, too.

Chez Tao, rue St-Antoine, in the citadel. Expensive, legendary nightclub in a sixteenth-century vaulted room, now turned into a piano bar that serves excellent nouvelle cuisine and local fish dishes. Outstanding view of the bay.

A Funtana, place Maréchal (☎04.95.15.29). Unpretentious terrace restaurant overlooking the main street A simple 60F menu features delicious fish soup and filling bean stew, with chestnut flan for pudding; and the *pichet* is palatable *AOC*, too.

U Minellu, 3 bd Wilson. A friendly and renowned pizzeria that serves Corsican specialities and paëlla on traditional hot stone plates. Menus from 100F.

Le Santa-Maria, rue Clemenceau. Good-value four-course tourist menus. One of the few places you can eat *stifatu*, a local dish combining different meats rolled up. Popular with tour groups of British hikers.

The Réserve Naturel de Scandola and Girolata

The **Réserve Naturel de Scandola** takes up the promontory west of Girolata, its name derived from the wooden tiles (*scandules*) that cover many of the island's mountain houses, but the area's roof-like rock formations are only part of its amazing geological repertoire. Its stacked slabs, towering pinnacles and gnarled claw-like outcrops were formed by Monte Cinto's volcanic eruptions 250 million years ago, and subsequent erosion has fashioned shadowy caves, grottoes and gashes in the rock. Scandola's colours are as remarkable as the shapes, the hues varying from the charcoal grey of granite to the incandescent rusty purple of porphyry.

The headland and its surrounding water were declared a nature reserve in 1975 and now support significant colonies of seabirds, dolphins and seals, as well as 450 types of seaweed and some remarkable fish such as the grouper, a species more commonly found in the Caribbean. In addition, nests belonging to a rare kind of giant gull are visible on the cliffs, and you might see the odd osprey – there used to be only seven pairs here, but careful conservation has increased this number to twenty- four.

Scandola is off-limits to hikers and can be viewed only by **boat**, which means taking one of the daily excursions from Calvi and Porto. These leave from Calvi at 9.15am and 2pm, and from Porto at 9.30am and 2.30pm (April–Oct), the first two stopping for two hours at Girolata (see below) and returning in the late afternoon. The later boat from Porto only stops for 45 minutes, but is a fascinating journey and well worth the 250F, although it's a good idea to take a picnic, as the restaurants in Girolata are very pricey.

Girolata
Connected by a mere mule track to the rest of the island (90min on foot from the nearest road), the tiny fishing haven of **GIROLATA**, immediately west of Scandola, has a dreamlike quality that's highlighted by the vivid red of the surrounding rocks. A short stretch of stony beach and a few houses are dominated by a stately watchtower, built by the Genoese later in the seventeenth century in the form of a small castle on a bluff overlooking the cove. For most of the year, this is one of the most idyllic spots on the island, with only the odd yacht and party of hikers to threaten the settlement's tranquillity. From June through September, though, daily boat trips from Porto and Calvi ensure the village is packed during the middle of the day, so if you want to make the most of the grandiose scenery, and peace and quiet, walk here and stay a night in one of the gîtes.

The head of the Girolata trail is at **Bocca â Crocce** (Col de la Croix), on the Calvi–Porto road, from where a clear path plunges downhill through dense *maquis* and forest to a flotsam-covered cove known as **Cala di Tuara** (30min). The more rewarding of the two tracks that wind onwards to Girolata is the more gentle one running left around the headland, but if you feel like stretching your legs, follow the second, more direct route uphill to a pass.

In Girolata, *La Cabane du Berger*, behind the beach, offers inexpensive **gîte d'étape accommodation** in eucalyptus-shaded cabins (☎04.95.20.16.98; ① dorm bed or ② with half-board). Meals are served in their quirky beachside restaurant, but the food isn't up to much so make the most of the self-catering kitchen. If this place is full, try the equally pleasant *Le Cormorant* gîte at the north end of the cove (☎04.95.20.20.15; ①), whose beds are in four- to six-person dormitories.

Winding some 200km from Calenzana (12km from Calvi) to Conça (22km from Porto-Vecchio), the **GR20** (pronounced "jay-air-*van*") is Corsica's most demanding long-distance footpath. Only one-third of the hikers who start it complete all sixteen stages (*étapes*), which can be covered in ten to twelve days if you're in good physical shape – if you're not, don't even think about attempting this route. Marked with red-and-white splashes of paint, it comprises a back-to-back series of harsh ascents and descents, sections of which exceed 2000m and become more of a climb than a walk, with stanchions, cables and ladders driven into the rock as essential aids. The going is made tougher by the necessity of carrying a sleeping bag, all-weather kit, and two or three days' food with you. That said, the rewards more than compensate. The GR20 takes in the most spectacular mountain terrain in Corsica, from the shattered granite peaks of the central watershed to the fragrant pine forests and flower-spotted slopes of the island's highest valleys. Along the way you can expect to spot the elusive *mouflon* mountain goat, glimpse eagles wheeling around the crags, and swim in ice-cold torrents and waterfalls.

The first thing you need to do before setting off is get hold of the Parc Naturel Régional's indispensable **Topoguide**, published by the Fédération Française de la Randonnée Pédestre, which gives a detailed description of the route, along with relevant sections of IGN contour maps, lists of refuges and other essential information. Most good bookshops in Corsica stock them, or you can call in at the office of the Parc Naturel Régional de Corse in Ajaccio.

The route can be undertaken in either **direction**, but most hikers start in the north at Calenzana, tackling the most demanding *étapes* early on. These first few days are relentlessly tough, but the hardship is alleviated by extraordinary mountain-scapes as you round the Cinto massif, skirt the Asco, Niolo, Tavignano and Restonica valleys, and scale the sides of Monte d'Oro and Rotondo. At Vizzavona on the main Bastia–Corte–Ajaccio road, roughly the halfway mark, you can call it a day and catch a bus or train back to the coast, or press on south across two more ranges to the needle peaks of Bavella. With much of

Porto and around

The overwhelming proximity of the mountains, combined with the pervasive eucalyptus and spicy scent of the *maquis,* give **PORTO**, 30km south of Calvi, a uniquely intense, loaded atmosphere that makes it one of the most interesting places to stay on the west coast. Except for a watchtower built here by the Genoese in the second half of the sixteenth century, the site was only built upon with the onset of tourism since the 1950s; today the village is still so small that it can become claustrophobic in July and August, when overcrowding – thanks to predominantly German tourists – is no joke. Off-season, the place becomes eerily deserted, so you'd do well to choose your times carefully; the best months are May, June and September.

The crowds and traffic jams tend to be most oppressive passing the famous **Calanche**, a huge mass of weirdly eroded pink rock just southwest of Porto, but you can easily sidestep the tourist deluge in picturesque **Piana**, which overlooks the gulf from its southern shore, or by heading inland from Porto through the **Gorges de Spelunca**. Forming a ravine running from the sea to the watershed of the island, this spectacular gorge gives access to the equally grandiose **Forêt d'Aitone**, site of Corsica's most ancient Laricio pine trees and a deservedly popular hiking area. Throughout the forest, the river and its tributories are punctuated by strings of *piscines naturelles* (natural swimming pools) - a refreshing, tranquil alternative to the beaches hereabouts, which tend to be cramped in peak season. If you're travelling between Porto and Ajaccio, a worthwhile place to break the journey is the clifftop village of Cargèse where the two main attractions are the Greek church and spectacular beach.

the forest east of here blackened by fire, hikers in recent years have been leaving the GR20 at Zonza, below the Col de Bavella (served by daily buses to Ajaccio and Porto-Vecchio), and walking to the coast along the less arduous Mare a Mare Sud trail.

Accommodation along the route is provided by **refuges**, where, for around 50F, you can take a hot shower, use an equipped kitchen and bunk down on mattresses. Usually converted *bergeries* located hours away from the nearest road, these places are staffed by wardens during the peak period (July & Aug), when up to one thousand people per day may be using the GR20 at any one time. Advance reservation is not possible; beds are allocated on a first-come-first-served basis, so be prepared to bivouac if you arrive late. Better still, set off as early as possible to arrive before everyone else. Another reason to be on the trail soon after dawn is that it allows you to break the back of the *étape* before 2pm, when clouds tend to bubble over the mountains and obscure the views.

The **weather** in the high mountains is notoriously fickle, with extreme and sudden changes. A sunny morning doesn't necessarily mean a sunny day, and during July and August violent storms can rip across the route without warning, confining hikers to the refuges or sheltered rock crevices for hours or even days. It is therefore essential to take good wet weather gear with you, as well as a hat, sunblock and shades for the baking heat that is the norm in summer. In addition, make sure you set off on each stage with adequate **food** and **water**. At the height of the season, many refuges sell basic supplies (*alimentation*), but you shouldn't rely on this service; ask hikers coming from the opposite direction where their last supply stop was and plan accordingly (basic provisions are always available at the main passes of Col de Vergio, Col de Vizzavona, Col de Bavella and Col de Verde). The refuge wardens (*gardiens*) will be able to advise you on how much water to carry at each stage.

Finally a word of **warning**: each year, injured hikers have to be air-lifted to safety off remote sections of the GR20, normally because they strayed from the marked route and got lost. Occasionally, fatal accidents also occur for the same reason, so always keep the paint splashes in sight, especially if the weather closes in – don't rely purely on the many cairns that punctuate the route, as these sometimes mark more hazardous paths to high peaks.

The town

Eucalyptus-bordered **route de la Marine** links the two parts of the resort. The village proper comprises a strip of supermarkets, shops and hotels 1km from the sea, but the main focus of activity is the small **marina**, located at the avenue's end. Overlooking the entrance to the harbour is the much photographed **Genoese Tower**, a square chimney-shaped structure that was cracked by an explosion in the seventeenth century, when it was used as an arsenal. An awe-inspiring view of the crashing sea and *maquis*—shrouded mountains makes it worth the short climb. The **beach** consists of a pebbly cove south beyond the shoulder of the massive rock supporting the tower. To reach it from the marina, follow the little road that skirts the rock, cross the wooden bridge which spans the River Porto on your left, then walk through the car park under the trees. Although it's rather rocky and exposed, and the sea very deep, the great crags overshadowing the shore give the place a vivid edge.

Practicalities

Buses from Calvi, via Galéria, and from Ajaccio, via Cargèse, pull into the junction at the end of route de la Marine, opposite the Banco supermarket, en route to the marina. Timetables are posted at the stops themselves, and at the **tourist office**, down in the marina (May & Oct Mon–Fri 2.30–6.30pm, June–Sept Mon–Sat 9am–noon & 2.30–6pm; 04.95.26.10.55), where you can buy *Topoguides* and brochures for hikes in the area. Tickets for the **boat excursions** to Scandola, the Calanche and Girolata (depart 9.30am & 2.30pm) are available in advance from the operator at their office in the marina.

Mountain **bikes** and **scooters**, ideal for daytrips up the Spelunca gorge, can be rented from the café opposite Timy supermarket, at the top of the village, though the cost is well over the odds (90F/330F per day per bicycle/80cc step-through). There are no automatic cash machines in the village, but several places change money; the bureau de change at Timy offers encashments on major credit cards.

Porto has plenty of **hotels**, and stiff competition between them means that tariffs are surprisingly low outside peak season. The best all-round budget option is *Le Maquis*, above the village on the rte d'Ota (☎04.95.26.12.19; ②), which has plain but comfortable rooms with and without en-suite bathrooms. If it's full, try the *Bella Vista*, on the Calvi road a short way further up the hill (☎04.95.26.11.08, fax 04.95.26.15.18; ②), whose well-furnished rooms have balconies and superb views of the mountains. The *Panorama*, down in the marina (☎04.95.26.11.05; ②), is another good choice, with a wonderful little terrace restaurant on its ground floor, as is the *Brise de Mer* next door (☎04.95.26.10.28, fax 04.95.26.13.02; ③), which looks over the eucalyptus trees in the valley to the sea. Apart from the dismal *camping municipal* behind the beach, Porto's **campsites** are all grouped in the village near the supermarkets. Pick of the bunch is the *Sol e Vista* (☎04.95.26.15.71), which has lots of shady terraces stacked up the hillside; *Le Porto* (☎04.95.26.13.67), on the opposite side of the road bridge, is almost as pleasant, and within easy reach of natural swimming pools in the river.

Pizzerias and standard hotel-restaurants make up the bulk of **eating places** in Porto, with prices generally increasing the nearer you get to the tower. Try the moderately priced *Le Maquis*, in the hotel of the same name at the top of the village, which serves honest, affordable home cooking in a warm bar or on a tiny terrace overlooking the valley. On the northside of the bay beneath the tower, the expensive *La Mer* is the place to sample top-notch fresh seafood straight from the gulf. Another place to eat that's well worth considering if you have transport, or are happy to walk 4km, is *Chez Felix* in Ota, whose sunny terrace offers a stunning view across the valley to Capo d'Orto, with delicious local specialities such as *sanglier en daube*, a rich wild-boar stew.

The Calanche

The UNESCO-protected site of **the Calanche**, 5km southeast of Porto, takes its name from *calanca*, the Corsican word for creek or inlet, but the outstanding characteristics here are the vivid orange and pink rock masses and pinnacles which crumble into the dark blue sea. Liable to unusual patterns of erosion, these tormented rock formations and porphyry needles, some of which reach 300m above the sea, have long been associated with different animals and figures, of which the most famous is the *Tête de Chien* at the north end of the stretch of cliffs. Other figures and creatures conjured up include a Moor's head, a monocled bishop, a bear and a tortoise.

One way to see the fantastic cliffs of the Calanche is by boat from Porto; excursions leave daily in summer, cost 120F and last about an hour. Alternatively, you could drive along the corniche road which weaves through the granite archways on its way to Piana. Eight kilometres along the road from Porto, the *Roches Bleues* café is a convenient landmark for walkers.

Piana

Picturesque **PIANA** occupies a prime location overlooking the Calanche, but for some reason does not suffer the deluge of tourists that Porto endures. Retaining a sleepy feel, the village comprises a cluster of pink houses ranged around an eighteenth-century church and square, from the edge of which the panoramic views over the Golfe de Porto are sublime.

If you want to **stay**, head straight for the *Hôtel les Roches Rouges*, at the entrance to the village on the Porto side (☎04.95.27.81.81; ④). Built in the 1930s, this wonderfully dated place lay empty for nearly twenty years, but was recently reopened with most of its original fittings and furniture. The tariffs are exceptionally low, too, considering the hotel's situation and character. Even if your budget won't stretch to a room, drop in for coffee and a game of chess on the magnificent terrace. A cheaper alternative is the *Hôtel Continental*, an old house with high wooden ceilings and a leafy garden, on the right as you leave Piana for Porto (☎04.95.27.82.02; ②). There's also an excellent new **gîte d'étape** (☎04.95.27.82.05; ②), where double rooms cost a mere 120F per night, and the friendly *patronne* offers good value half-board for 160F.

The Gorges de Spelunca

Spanning the 2km between the villages of Ota and Évisa, a few kilometres east of Porto, the **Gorges de Spelunca** are a formidable sight, with bare orange granite walls, 1km deep in places, plunging into the foaming green torrent created by the confluence of the rivers Porto, Tavulella, Onca, Campi and Aitone. The sunlight, ricocheting across the rock walls, creates a sinister effect that's heightened by the dark jagged needles of the encircling peaks. The most dramatic part of the gorge can be seen from the road, which hugs the edge for much of its length.

ÉVISA's bright orange roofs emerge against a lush background of chestnut forests about 10km from Ota, on the eastern edge of the gorge, and the village makes the best base for hiking in the area. Situated 830m above sea level, it caters well for hikers and makes a pleasant stop for a taste of mountain life – the air is invariably crisp and clear, and the food particularly good.

The best place to **stay** is *La Chataigneraire*, on the west side of the village towards Porto (☎04.95.26.24.27, fax 04.95.26.33.11; ③); it's a rambling schist and granite building with rooms set amid chestnut trees. The cosy, rambling *Hôtel du Centre* (☎04.95.26.20.92; ③; closed Oct–June), opposite the statue in the centre of the village, is another good choice, with friendly proprietors and an excellent little restaurant serving wholesome Corsican specialities. *Hôtel l'Aitone*, at the north exit to the village (☎04.95.26.20.04, fax 04.95.20.24.18; ③; closed mid-Nov to Dec), is a large country hotel with comfortable rooms, a swimming pool and a reputation for gastronomic prowess. *Camping Paisolu d'Aitone* 1km east of the village (☎04.95.26.20.39), is a smart all-year **campsite**.

Forêt d'Aitone

Thousands of soaring Laricio pines, some of them as much as 50m tall, make up the **Forêt d'Aitone**, just a few kilometres east of Évisa, the most beautiful forest in Corsica. It reaches 1391m at its highest point – the **Col de Salto** – and extends over ten square kilometres between Évisa and the **Col de Verghio** (1477m), the highest point in Corsica that's traversable by road. Well-worn tourist paths cross the forest at various points, but local wildlife still thrives here.

You can park 7km along the road from Évisa by the **Maison Forestière d'Aitone**, the forest headquarters and information centre (June–Sept 9am–noon & 2–6pm) and a starting-off point for walks in the area. One of the most popular short walks goes to the **Belvédère**, a great projecting rock 5km north of Évisa. To reach it, follow the signposted track leading into the forest, from beside a wide lay-by on the left-hand side of the road. The magnificent view across the valley takes in the rivers Aitone and Porto, rushing between high walls of copper-tinted rocks down to the Gorges de Spelunca. Another well-trekked route leads to the multiple **Cascades de la Valla Scarpa**, where the crystalline waters of the Aitone crash into a pool hollowed out by the falls. It's just fifteen minutes' walk from the *maison forestière*, signposted "Piscines/les Cascades", and it does become overcrowded in summer – though you don't have to walk much farther along the river to find more tranquil spots for a picnic and a swim.

If you want to reach the higher slopes, an hour's walk from the *maison forestière* will bring you to the Col de Salto, and a further three hours' heavy climbing along the same rocky track will bring you to **Col de Felce**, for a fantastic vista of the Golfe de Porto. For the more ambitious, the **Col de Cuccavera** – above the tree line at 1500m – can be attained by cutting north before the Col de Felce, striking right up the mountainside. Once you're this far up, you can make out hazy distant views of the Gorges d'Asco.

Just 4km beyond the *maison forestière*, the Col de Verghio borders the remote district of the Niolo and marks the limit of the **Fôret de Valdo-Niello**. The ugly concrete *Castellacciu* hotel (☎04.95.26.20.09; ④), situated at the point where the GR20 (see p.1020) makes one of its rare descents to road level, doubles as a refuge and basic ski station, but these days there's rarely enough snow to keep it in use.

Cargèse

Sitting high above a deep blue bay on a cliff scattered with olive trees, **CARGÈSE** (Carghjese), 20km southwest of Porto, oozes a lazy charm that attracts hundreds of well-heeled summer residents to its pretty white houses and hotels. The full-time locals, half of whom are descendants of Greek refugees who fled the Turkish occupation of the Peloponnese in the seventeenth century, seem to accept with nonchalance this inundation, and the proximity of a large Club Med complex, but the best times to visit are May and late September, when Cargèse empties.

Two churches stand on separate hummocks at the heart of the village, a reminder of the old antagonism between the two cultures (resentful Corsican patriots ransacked the Greeks' original settlement in 1715 because of the newcomers' refusal to take up arms against their Genoese benefactors). The **Roman Catholic church** was built for the minority Corsican families in 1828 and is one of the latest examples of Baroque with a *trompe l'œil* ceiling that can't really compete with the view from the church's terrace. The **Greek church**, however, is the more interesting of the two: a large granite neo-Gothic edifice built in 1852 to replace a building that had become too small for its congregation. Inside, the outstanding feature is an unusual iconostasis, a gift from a monastery in Rome, decorated with uncannily modern-looking portraits. Behind it hang icons brought over from Greece with the original settlers – the graceful Virgin and Child, to the right-hand side of the altar, is thought to date as far back as the twelfth century.

The best beach in the area, **plage de Pero**, is 2km north of Cargèse – walk up to the junction with the Piana road and take the left fork down to the sea. Overlooked by a Genoese tower, this white stretch of sand has a couple of bars and easily absorbs the crowds that descend on it in August. **Plage du Chiuni**, a further 2km along the same road, is much busier thanks to its windsurfing facilities and the presence of Club Med. A more secluded spot lies 1km south of the village at **plage du Monachi**; this small, sandy cove is reached by climbing down the track at the side of the road past the little chapel on the cliff side.

Practicalities

There's a **tourist office** on rue Dr-Dragacci (daily: June–Sept 9am–noon & 4–7pm; Oct–May 3–5pm; ☎04.95.26.41.31), which can help find accommodation and sells tickets for summer boat trips to the Calanche (see p.1022), costing about 170F. **Buses** for Ajaccio and Porto stop outside the **post office**, set back from the road in the main square.

All the best **hotels** are located within minutes of the centre, with the budget places at the top end of the village. The least expensive is the *Continental*, on the left as you descend into the main square from Porto (☎04.95.26.42.24; ②), which is a bit dingy but clean and comfortable enough. If you can afford to splash out a little more, head for the *Bel'Mare*, 400m out of the village towards Ajaccio (☎04.95.26.40.13; ③); all the rooms have superb sea views from balconies, and it offers good low-season discounts. An equally comfortable option is *Thalassa* on plage de Pero (☎04.95.26.40.08; ④; closed winter; meal included), an intimate little place with friendly owners. The nearest **campsite**, *Camping Torraccia* (☎04.95.26.42.34), is 4km north of Cargèse on the main road.

A fair number of **restaurants** are scattered about the village, as well as the standard crop of basic pizzerias. *A Volta*, behind the Catholic church on place Mattei, offers a good-value 100F menu, featuring seafood, game and pasta served on a spectacular terrace that juts out over the sea. Cargèse's most reputed, and expensive, restaurant is located down in the marina. Don't be fooled by *Chez Antoine*'s rustic fishing shack appearance; their *bouillabaisse* is legendary, and draws yachties from the nearby moorings, and well-heeled Ajacciens in equal number. For a **drink**, go no further than the main square, where you can watch all the action from *Bar Chantilly*, whose breakfast customers munch take-away croissants and *pains au chocolat* from the bakery opposite. Another equally atmospheric spot is the rear terrace of the *Bar Au Bon Accueil*, on the main street, which affords optimum views over the old quarter and gulf.

Ajaccio and around

Edward Lear claimed that on a wet day it would be hard to find so dull a place as **AJACCIO** (Aiacciu), a harsh judgement with an element of justice. The town has none of Bastia's sense of purpose and can seem to lack a definitive identity of its own, but it is a relaxed and good-looking place, with an exceptionally mild climate, a wealth of cafés, restaurants and shops, and a more welcoming attitude to tourists than you might find elsewhere in Corsica.

Although it's an attractive idea that Ajax once stopped here, the name of Ajaccio derives from the Roman *Adjaccium* (place of rest), a winter stop-off point for shepherds descending from the mountains to stock up on goods and sell their produce. This first settlement, to the north of the present town in the area called Castelvecchio, was destroyed by the Saracens in the tenth century, and modern Ajaccio grew up around the citadel that was founded in 1492. Napoléon gave Ajaccio international fame, but though the self-designated *Cité Impériale* is littered with statues and street names related to the Bonaparte family, you'll find the Napoleonic cult has a less dedicated following in his home town than you might imagine. The emperor is still considered by many Ajacciens as a self-serving Frenchman rather than as a Corsican, and his impact on the townscape of his birthplace isn't enormous. Ajaccio remains memorable for the things that have long made it attractive – its battered old town, chic cafés and the encompassing view of its glorious bay.

Arrival, information and accommodation

Ajaccio's Campo dell'Oro **airport** (☎04.95.21.07.07) is 6km south of town; hourly buses provide a shuttle service into the centre, stopping on cours Napoléon, the main street; tickets cost 20F, and the journey takes around fifteen minutes. Heading in the other direction, the best place to pick up buses to the airport is the parking lot adjacent to the main bus station (**terminal routière**), a five-minute walk north of the centre (☎04.95.21.28.01). **Ferries** also dock nearby, and the SNCM office is directly opposite at quai L'Herminier (☎04.95.29.66.88). The **gare SNCF** lies almost a kilometre north along bd Sampiero (☎04.95.23.11.03), a continuation of the quai l'Herminier. The **tourist office** is on the ground floor of the Hôtel de Ville (May–Oct Mon–Sat 8.30am–8.30pm, Sun

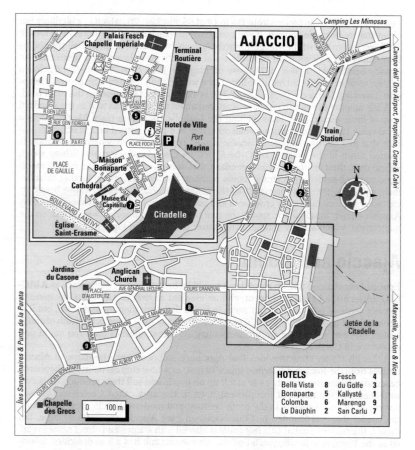

AJACCIO

Camping Les Mimosas

Campo dell' Oro Airport, Propriano, Corte & Calvi

Palais Fesch
Chapelle Impériale

Terminal
Routière

Hotel de Ville
*Port
Marina*

Train
Station

Maison
Bonaparte

Cathedral

Musée du
Capitellu

Citadelle

PLACE
DE GAULLE

Église
Saint-Erasme

Jardins
du Casone

Anglican
Church

PLACE
D'AUSTERLITZ

Marseille, Toulon & Nice

Jetée de la
Citadelle

Îles Sanguinaires & Punta de la Parata

Chapelle
des Grecs

0   100 m

HOTELS			
		Fesch	4
Bella Vista	8	du Golfe	3
Bonaparte	5	Kallysté	1
Colomba	6	Marengo	9
Le Dauphin	2	San Carlu	7

8.30am–1.30pm; Nov–April Mon–Fri 8.30am–6pm, Sat 8.30am–1pm; ☎04.95.51.53.03).
You can rent **cars** from Aloha at the airport (☎04.95.20.52.00), Avis, 3 place de Gaulle
(☎04.95.21.01.86), or Hertz, 8 cours Grandval (☎04.95.23.24.17, or at the airport
☎04.95.22.14.82), and **scooters and motorbikes** from BMS, jetée de la Citadelle, at the
far end of the marina (☎04.95.21.37.75 or ☎04.95.24.36.43), *Hôtel Kalliste*, 51 cours
Napoléon (☎04.95.51.34.45), or Locacorse, 10 av Bévérini (☎04.95.20.71.20).

For **accommodation** you'll find a dearth of cheap hotels, but a fair number of moderate to upmarket places. The town's only **campsite**, *Les Mimosas*, lies 4km northeast
of the centre (☎04.95.20.99.85). To get there, catch a #4 bus from cours Napoléon to
Brasilia, walk 100m to the roundabout at the bottom of the hill, and follow the signs
from there.

Hotels

Bella Vista, 20 bd Lantivy (☎04.95.21.07.97, fax 04.95.21.81.88). Large, imposing place on the
seafront offering views of the gulf. ③.

Bonaparte, 1 rue Étienne-Conti (☎04.95.21.44.19). The rooms are a little overpriced, but immaculately clean; ask for one on the upper storey. Closed Nov–March. ③.

Colomba, 8 av de Paris (☎04.95.21.12.66). Cheap, pension-style hotel run by an elderly couple on the third floor of an old tenement, opposite place de Gaulle. A good budget fallback if the *Dauphin* is booked up, but dingy and airless. Closed winter. ②.

Le Dauphin, 11 bd Sampiero (☎04.95.21.12.94, fax 04.95.21.88.69). Directly opposite the ferry port, and easily Ajaccio's best budget hotel, with simple double rooms from 140F. The bar downstairs (see p.1030) serves inexpensive breakfasts, and it's well-placed for the airport bus. They also store luggage for no extra charge. Book in advance. ①.

Fesch, 7 rue Cardinal-Fesch (☎04.95.51.62.62, fax 04.95.21.83.36). Among the most appealing mid-range hotels in Ajaccio, with sheepskin furnishings and medieval-style decor designed by Corsicada, a group of local artisans. Closed mid-Dec to mid-Jan. ④.

du Golfe, 6 bd du Roi-Jérôme (☎04.95.21.47.64, fax 04.95.21.71.05). Balconies overlooking the bay; televisions in every room; modern decor. Closed Feb. ⑤.

Kallysté, 51 cours Napoléon (☎04.95.51.34.45, fax 04.95.21.79.00). Slap in the centre of town, and very comfortable; most of this popular hotel's rooms can accommodate four people. Proprietor speaks English. ③.

Marengo, off bd Mme-Mère (☎04.95.21.43.66, fax 04.95.21.51.26). Pleasant, small hotel in quiet suburban backstreet, with rooms overlooking a flowery courtyard. Closed mid-December to mid-March. ③.

San Carlu, 8 bd Danielle-Casanova (☎04.95.21.13.84, fax 04.95.21.09.99). Spruce, upmarket hotel opposite the citadel, close to the beach, with its own parking facilities. Recommended for disabled travellers. Closed mid-Dec to mid-Jan. ⑤.

The town

The core of the **old town** holds the most interest in Ajaccio: a cluster of ancient streets spreading north and south of **place Foch**, which opens out to the seafront by the port and the marina. Nearby **place de Gaulle** forms the town centre and is the source of the main thoroughfare, **cours Napoléon**, which extends parallel to the sea almost 2km to the northeast. West of place de Gaulle stretches the modern part of town fronted by the **beach**, overlooked at its northern end by the citadel.

Around place de Gaulle and the new town.

Place de Gaulle – otherwise known as place du Diamant, after the Diamanti family who once owned much of the property in Ajaccio – is the most useful point of orientation, even if it's not much to look at – just a windy concrete platform surrounded by a shopping complex. The only noteworthy thing on the square is the huge, bronze equestrian statue, a pompous lump commissioned by Napoléon III in 1865 showing the first Napoléon in Roman attire, surrounded by his four brothers.

Devotees of Napoléon should take a stroll 1km up cours Grandval, the wide street rising west of place de Gaulle and ending in a square, the **Jardins du Casone**, where gaudily spectacular son et lumière shows take place in summer. An impressive **monument to Napoléon** dominates the square, standing atop an appropriately huge, proto-Fascist pedestal inscribed with the names of his battles. Behind the monument lies a graffiti-bedaubed cave where Napoléon is supposed to have frolicked as a child.

Place Foch

Once the site of the town's medieval gate, **place Foch** lies at the heart of old Ajaccio. A delightfully shady square sloping down to the sea and lined with cafés and restaurants, it gets its local name – place des Palmiers – from the row of palms bordering the central strip. Dominating the top end, a fountain of four marble lions provides a mount for the inevitable **statue of Napoléon**, this one by Ajaccien sculptor Maglioli. A humbler effigy occupies a niche high on the nearest wall – a figurine of Ajaccio's patron saint, **La Madonnuccia**, dating from 1656, a year in which Ajaccio's local council, fearful of infection from plague-struck Genoa, placed the town under the guardianship of the Madonna in a ceremony which took place on this spot.

NAPOLÉON AND CORSICA

Napoléon Bonaparte was born in Ajaccio in 1769, a crucial date in the history of Corsica as it was during this year that the French took over the island from the Genoese. They made a thorough job of it, crushing Paoli's troops at Ponte Nuovo and driving the Corsican leader into exile (see p.1046). Napoléon's father Carlo, a close associate of Paoli, fled the scene of the battle with his pregnant wife in order to escape the victorious French army. But Carlo's subsequent behaviour was quite different from that of his former leader – he came to terms with the French, becoming a representative of the newly styled Corsican nobility in the National Assembly, and using his contacts with the French governor to get a free education for his children.

At the age of nine, Napoléon was awarded a scholarship to the Brienne military academy, an institution specially founded to teach the sons of the French nobility the responsibilities of their status, and the young son of a Corsican Italian-speaking household used his time well, leaving Brienne to enter the exclusive École Militaire in Paris. At the age of sixteen he was commissioned into the artillery. When he was twenty the Revolution broke out in Paris and the scene was set for a remarkable career.

Always an ambitious opportunist, he obtained leave from his regiment, returned to Ajaccio, joined the local Jacobin club and – with his eye on a colonelship in the Corsican militia – promoted enthusiastically the interests of the Revolution. However, things did not quite work out as he had planned, for Pascal Paoli had also returned to Corsica.

Carlo Bonaparte had died some years before, and Napoléon was head of a family that had formerly given Paoli strong support. Having spent the last twenty years in London, Paoli was pro-English and had developed a profound distaste of revolutionary excesses. Napoléon's French allegiance and his Jacobin views antagonized the older man, and his military conduct didn't enhance his standing at all. Elected second-in-command of the volunteer militia, Napoléon was involved in an unsuccessful attempt to wrest control of the citadel from Royalist sympathizers. He thus took much of the blame when, in reprisal for the killing of one of the militiamen, several people were gunned down in Ajaccio, an incident which engendered eight days of civil war. In June 1793, Napoléon and his family were chased back to the mainland by the Paolists.

Napoléon promptly renounced any special allegiance he had ever felt for Corsica. He Gallicized the spelling of his name, preferring Napoléon to his baptismal Napoleone. And, although he was later to speak with nostalgia about the scents of the Corsican countryside, he put the city of his birth fourth on the list of places he would like to be buried.

At the northern end of place Foch is the **Hôtel de Ville** of 1826, with its prison-like wooden doors. The first-floor **Salon Napoléonien** (Mon–Sat 9am–noon & 2–5pm; 7F) contains a replica of the ex-emperor's death mask in pride of place, along with a solemn array of Bonaparte family portraits and busts. A smaller medal room has a fragment from Napoléon's coffin and part of his dressing case, plus a model of the ship that brought him back from St-Helena, and a picture of the house where he died.

South of place Foch

The south side of place Foch, standing on the former dividing line between the poor district around the port and the bourgeoisie's territory, gives access to **rue Bonaparte**, the main route through the latter quarter. Built on the promontory rising to the citadel, the secluded streets in this part of town – with their dusty buildings and hole-in-the-wall restaurants lit by flashes of sea or sky at the end of the alleys – retain more of a sense of the old Ajaccio than anywhere else.

Napoléon was born in what's now the colossal **Maison Bonaparte**, on place Letizia (May–Sept Mon 2–6pm, Tues–Sat 9am–noon & 2–6pm, Sun 9am–noon; Oct–April Tues–Sat 10am–noon & 2–5pm, Sun 10am–noon; 22F), off the west side of rue Napoléon. The house passed to Napoléon's father in the 1760s and here he lived, with his wife and family, until his death. But in May 1793, the Bonapartes were driven from the house by Paoli's partisans, who stripped the place down to the floorboards. Requisitioned by the English in 1794, Maison Bonaparte became an arsenal and a lodging house for English officers until Napoléon's mother Letizia herself funded its restoration. Owned by the state since 1923, the house now bears few traces of the Bonaparte family's existence.

One of the few original pieces of furniture left in the house is the wooden sedan chair in the hallway – the pregnant Letizia was carried back from church on it when her contractions started. Upstairs, there's an endless display of portraits, miniatures, weapons, letters and documents. Amongst the highlights of the first room are a few maps of Corsica dating from the eighteenth century, some deadly "vendetta" daggers and two handsome pairs of pistols belonging to Napoléon's father. The next-door Alcove Room was, according to tradition, occupied by Napoléon in 1799 when he stayed here for the last time, while in the third room you can see the sofa upon which the future emperor first saw the light of day on August 15, 1769. Adjoining the heavily restored long gallery is a tiny room known as the Trapdoor Room, whence Letizia and her children made their getaway from the marauding Paolists.

Napoléon was baptized in 1771 in the **cathedral** (no tourist visits on Sun), around the corner in rue Forcioli-Conti. Modelled on St Peter's in Rome, it was built in 1587–1593 on a much smaller scale than intended, owing to lack of funds – an apology for its diminutive size is inscribed in a plaque inside, on the wall to the left as you enter. Inside, to the right of the door, stands the font where he was dipped at the age of 23 months; his sister, Elisa Baciochi, donated the great marble altar in 1811. Before you go, take a look in the chapel to the left of the altar, which houses a gloomy Delacroix painting of the Virgin.

Musée Capitellu and the citadel

A left turn at the eastern end of rue Forcioli-Conti brings you onto bd Danielle-Casanova. Here, opposite the citadel, an elaborately carved capital marks the entrance to **Musée Capitellu** (April–Oct Mon–Sat 10am–noon & 2–6pm, Sun 10am–noon; 22F), a tiny museum mainly given over to offering a picture of domestic life in nineteenth-century Ajaccio. The house belonged to a wealthy Ajaccien family, the Baciochi, who were related to Napoléon through his sister's marriage. Amid the watercolour landscapes and marble busts, the glass display cases hold the most fascinating exhibits, including a rare edition of the first history of Corsica, written by Agostino Giustiniani, a bishop of the Nebbio who drowned in 1536, and the 1796 Code Corse, a list of laws set out by Louis XV for the newly occupied Corsica.

Opposite the museum, the restored **citadel**, a hexagonal fortress and tower stuck out on a wide promontory into the sea, is occupied by the military and usually closed to the public. Founded in the 1490s, the fort wasn't completed until the occupation of Ajaccio by Sampiero Corso and the powerful Marshall Thermes in 1553–58. The building overlooks the town beach, plage St-François, a short curve of yellow sand which faces the expansive mountain-ringed bay. Several flights of steps lead down to the beach from bd Danielle-Casanova.

North of place Foch

The dark narrow streets backing onto the port to the **north of place Foch** are Ajaccio's traditional trading ground. Each weekday and Saturday morning (and on Sundays during the summer), the square directly behind the Hôtel de Ville hosts a small **artisans' market**, a rarity in Corsica, where you can browse and buy top-quality fresh produce from around the island, including myrtle liqueur, wild-boar sauces, ewe's cheese from the Niolo valley and a spread of fresh vegetables, fruit and flowers.

Behind here, the principal road leading north is rue Cardinal-Fesch, a delightful meandering street lined with boutiques, cafés and restaurants. Halfway along the street, set back from the road behind iron gates, stands Ajaccio's best gallery, the **Musée Fesch** (June 15–Sept 15 Wed–Mon 10am–5.30pm; Sept 16–June 14 Tues–Sat 9.30am–noon & 2.30–6pm; 30F). Cardinal Joseph Fesch was Napoléon's step-uncle and Bishop of Lyons, using his lucrative position to invest in large numbers of paintings, many of them looted by the French armies in Holland, Italy and Germany. His bequest to the town includes seventeenth-century French and Spanish masters, but it's the Italian paintings that are the chief attraction: Raphael, Titian, Bellini, Veronese and Botticelli all have a place here.

You'll need a separate ticket for the **Chapelle Impériale** (same hours; 12F), which stands across the courtyard from the museum. With its gloomy monochrome interior the chapel itself is unremarkable, and its interest lies in the crypt where various members of the Bonaparte family are buried. It was the cardinal's dying wish that all the Bonaparte family be brought together under one roof, so the chapel was built in 1857 and the bodies subsequently ferried in.

Eating, drinking and nightlife

Restaurants in Ajaccio vary from basic bistrots to trendy pizzerias and pricey fish restaurants, the majority of which are found in the old town. **Bars** and **cafés** jostle for pavement space along cours Napoléon, generally lined with young people checking out the promenaders, and on place de Gaulle, where old-fashioned cafés and *salons de thé* offer a more sedate scene. If you fancy a view of the bay, check out one of the flashy cocktail bars that line the seafront on boulevard Lantivy, which, aside from the casino, two cinemas and a handful of euro-trashy clubs whose only outstanding feature are their extortionate entrance charges, comprise the sum total of Ajaccio's **nightlife**.

Bars and cafés

Le Dauphin, 11 bd Sampiero. An eccentric bar straight out of a 1950s French *policier*, complete with pinball machine, camp barman and sundry dodgy characters sipping *pastis* under a haze of Gauloise smoke.

L'Empereur, 12 place de Gaulle. Brassy, ersatz Art Nouveau *salon du thé*, overlooking the main square.

Le Menestrel, 5 rue Fesch. Dubbed "le rendez-vous des artistes" because local musicians play here most evenings after 7pm – mostly traditional mandolin and guitar tunes, with the odd popular singalong number "in the club style".

La Rade, 1 place Foch. The most congenial of the cafés fronting the *port de plaisance* and an ideal spot for crowd-watching over a chilled *pastis*.

Safari, 18 bd Lantivy. One of a row of lookalike cocktail bars next to the casino, overlooking the promenade. Good for a breezy coffee, and for watching Ajaccio's *beau monde* strut their stuff on Saturday nights.

Snack La Serre, 91 cours Napoléon. Popular budget-travellers' place, serving good-value bistrot dishes and inexpensive snacks.

Restaurants

L'Aquarium, rue des Halles. One of the best places in town for seafood. Unpretentious cooking that relies on freshness – everything comes straight from the fish market across the square. Set menus 80–125F.

Chez Coco, Strada di u Peveru. Cavernous Italian restaurant, with kitsch, shell decor and tables along a narrow alley, that serves filling, homely cooking at affordable prices; and there are plenty of *tagliatelle* options for vegetarians.

Les Halles, rue des Halles. Open since 1920, and the favourite lunch venue for market stall-holders and local office workers. They do a great-value 80F menu with wild boar, fresh fish of the day and a choice of omelettes.

Da Mamma, passage Guinghetta. Tucked away down a narrow passageway connecting cours Napoléon and the rue Fesch. Authentic but affordable Corsican cuisine, such as *cannelloni al brocciu*, roast kid and seafood, or good-value set menus starting at 65F. Slick service and a lively atmosphere. Reserve one of the tables under the rubber tree.

A Pignata, 15 bd du Roi-Jérôme. The classiest of a clutch of small restaurants around rue des Halles and the market. House specialities include *marcassin* (baby wild boar) and unusual fresh pasta dishes. Menus from 80F.

Point U, 30 rue Fesch. One of the town's top restaurants. Strictly traditional Corsican cooking – artisanal charcuterie, rabbit cooked in myrtle wine, veal with olives, etc – served in cosy surroundings. Pricey, but not prohibitively so.

Rong Vang, rue Maréchal d'Ornano. The Golden Dragon is one of Corsica's few Chinese restaurants, serving French-influenced Cantonese cuisine (frogs' legs *à la pékinoise* or with lemon curry); no set menus, but à la carte dishes are a reasonable 45–60F. Closed Sun.

Le Golfe de Valinco: Filitosa, Propriano and Campomorro

From Ajaccio, the vista of white-washed villas and sandy beaches lining the side of the gulf opposite may tempt you out of town when you first arrive. On closer inspection, however, **Porticcio** turns out to be a faceless string of leisure settlement for Ajaccio's smart set, complete with tennis courts, malls and flotillas of jetskis. Better to skip this stretch and press on south along the route nationale (RN194) which, after scaling the **Col de Celaccia**, winds down to the stunning **Golfe de Valinco**. A vast blue inlet bounded by rolling, scrub-covered hills, the gulf presents the first dramatic scenery along the coastal highway. It also marks the start of militant and Mafia-ridden south Corsica, more closely associated with vendetta, banditry and separatism than any other part of the island. Many of the mountain villages glimpsed from the roads hereabouts are riven with age-old divisions, exacerbated in recent years by the spread of organized crime and nationalist violence. But this seamier side of island life is rarely discernible to the hundreds of thousands of visitors who pass through each summer, most of whom stay around the small port of **Propriano**, at the eastern end of the gulf. In addition to offering most of the area's tourist amenities, this busy resort town lies within easy reach of the menhirs at **Filitosa**, one of the western Mediterranean's most important prehistoric sites, and the secluded fishing village of **Campomorro**, on the opposite shore of the gulf, from where you can strike out south on foot to explore one of Corsica's wildest stretches of coast.

The Golfe de Valinco region is reasonably well served by **public transport**, with buses running four times per day between Ajaccio and Bonifacio, via Propriano and Sartène. Note, however, that outside July and August there are no services along this route on Sundays.

Propriano

Tucked into the narrowest part of the Golfe de Valinco, the small port of **PROPRIANO** (Prupria), 8km northwest of Sartène, centres on a fine natural harbour that was exploited by the ancient Greeks, Carthaginians and Romans, but became a prime target for Saracen pirate raids in the eighteenth century, when it was largely destroyed. Redeveloped in the 1900s, it now boasts a thriving marina, and handles ferries to Toulon, Marseille and Sardinia. The town around the port has also grown in importance, largely under the direction of a powerful coalition consisting of the mayor, a second-generation Italian immigrant named Émile Mocchi; his nephew, one of the leaders of a prominent nationalist group; and southern Corsica's most renowned godfather, Jean-Jérôme (aka "Jean-Jé") Colonna, veteran of the infamous "French Connection". Together, this alliance has somewhat held in check power struggles between the area's political and mafia organizations, allowing Propriano to prosper as a tourist resort, although reports of mob and nationalist violence still crop up from time to time in the local press.

The occasional eruption of violence, however, doesn't deter the tourists, who come here in droves for the area's **beaches**. The nearest of these, **plage de Lido**, lies 1km west, just beyond the Port de Commerce; it's patrolled by lifeguards during the summer and is much safer and more appealing than the grubby **plage de Baracci**, 1km north of town, where the undertow is precariously strong. Just 3km beyond the Baracci beach, the D157 branches off to the left and continues along the coast, which is built up with hotels and package-tour holiday blocks until **Olmeto plage**, 10km west, where an abundance of campsites are on offer (see below). You can reach Olmeto on the three daily buses from Propriano to Porto.

Practicalities

Ferries from the mainland and Sardinia dock in the Port de Commerce, ten minutes' walk from where the **buses** stop at the top of rue du Général-de-Gaulle, the town's main street; the SNCM office is on quai Commandant-L'Herminier (☎04.95.76.04.36), while the **tourist office** is down in the harbour master's office in the marina (June–Sept Mon–Sat 8am–1pm & 3–6pm, Sun 8am–1pm; Oct–May Mon–Fri 8.30am–noon & 1.30–6pm; ☎04.95.76.01.49).

For **accommodation** there's a reasonable choice of hotels in the centre of town, like the high-tech *Loft Hotel*, 3 rue Camille-Pietri (☎04.95.76.17.48, fax 04.95.76.22.04; ④; closed Feb), directly behind the port; the *Bellevue* on av Napoléon (☎04.95.76.01.86, fax 04.95.76.27.77; ③) overlooks the marina and has the cheapest central rooms. If you have a car, two other places worth trying are the *Arcu di Sole*, 3km northeast on the route de Baracci (☎04.95.76.05.10, fax 04.95.76.13.36; ④) which has a pool and gourmet restaurant, or the more modest *Centre Équestre Baracci*, an excellent gîte d'étape just down the road from the *Arc di Sole*, which offers beds in four-person dorms for 85F, or double rooms for 210F (☎04.95.76.19.48). **Campers** are well provided for, although the best sites are well out of town: for the best facilities go to *Camping Colomba* (☎04.95.76.06.42), 3km north along rte de Baracci and with a swimming pool. At Olmeta plage, the best site is *U Libecciu* (☎04.95.74.01.28), the first place on the beach coming from Propriano, or you could try *Chez Antoine* (☎04.95.76.06.06) in Marina d'Olmeto, north of the beach.

Cafés and **restaurants** are concentrated along the marina's avenue Napoléon, with *Resto Nicoli* just about the cheapest place to eat, with excellent omelettes and Italian specialities. For fresh seafood, though, you can't beat *L'Hippocampe*, tucked away behind the port on rue Pandolphi, which serves a superb-value 100F menu on a pretty rear terrace.

Filitosa

Set deep in the countryside of the fertile Vallée du Taravo, the extraordinary **Station Préhistorique de Filitosa** (March–Oct daily 8am–7.30pm; 25F; out-of-season visits are possible by arrangement; ☎04.95.74.00.91), 17km north of Propriano, comprises a wonderful array of statue-menhirs and prehistoric structures encapsulating some eight thousand years of history. There's no public transport to this site, but organized trips leave once a day from both Ajaccio (May–Sept; 120F for full day) and Propriano (June–Sept; 65F for half-day; services depend on demand, so check at Propriano tourist office or telephone Proservices ☎05.95.76.00.02). Vehicles can be left in the small car park in the hamlet of Filitosa, where you pay the entrance fee; from here it's a fifteen-minute walk to the site, which includes a café, a small museum and a workshop producing reproduction prehistoric ceramics.

The site was settled by Neolithic farming people who lived here in rock shelters until the arrival of megalithic navigators from the East in about 3500 BC. These invaders were the creators of the menhirs, the earliest of which were possibly phallic symbols worshipped by an ancient fertility cult. When the seafaring people known as the Torréens (after the towers they built on Corsica) conquered Filitosa around 1300 BC, they destroyed most of the menhirs, incorporating the broken stones into the area of dry-stone walling surrounding the site's two *torri* or towers, examples of which can be found all over the south of Corsica. The site remained undiscovered until a farmer stumbled across the ruins on his land in the late 1940s.

Filitosa V looms up on the right shortly after the main entrance to the site. The largest statue-menhir on the island, it's an imposing sight, with clearly defined facial features and a sword and dagger outlined on the body. Beyond a sharp left turn lies the oppidum or central monument, its entrance marked by the **eastern platform**, thought to have been a lookout post. The cave-like structure sculpted out of the rock is the only evidence of Neolithic occupation and is generally agreed to have been a burial mound. Straight ahead, the Torréen **central monument** comprises a scattered group of menhirs on a circular walled mound, surmounted by a dome and entered by a corridor of stone slabs and lintels. Nobody is sure of its exact function.

Nearby **Filitosa XIII** and **Filitosa IX**, implacable lumps of granite with long noses and round chins, are the most impressive of the menhirs. Filitosa XIII is typical of the figures carved just before the Torréen invasion, with its vertical dagger carved in relief – **Filitosa VII** also has a clearly sculpted sword and shield. **Filitosa VI**, from the same period, is remarkable for its facial detail. On the eastern side of the central monument stand some vestigial Torréen houses, where fragments of ceramics dating from 5500 BC were discovered; they represent the most ancient finds on the site, and some of them are displayed in the museum.

The western monument, a two-roomed structure built underneath another walled mound, is thought to have been some form of Torréen religious building. A flight of steps leads to the foot of this mound, where a footbridge opens onto a meadow that's dominated by five statue-menhirs arranged in a semi-circle beneath a thousand-year-old olive tree. A bank separates them from the **quarry** from which the megalithic sculptors hewed the stone for the menhirs – a granite block is marked ready for cutting.

The **museum** is a shoddy affair, with poorly labelled exhibits and very little contextual information (the owners have even put the light on a timer switch so that you're plunged into darkness every two or three minutes), but the artefacts themselves are fascinating. The major item here is the formidable Scalsa Murta, a huge menhir dating from around 1400 BC and discovered at Olmeto. Like other statue-menhirs of this period, this one has two indents in the back of its head, which are thought to indicate that these figures would have been adorned with headdresses. Other notable exhibits are **Filitosa XII**, which has a hand and a foot carved into the stone, and **Trappa II**, a strikingly archaic face.

Campomorro

A cluster of sturdy old buildings and a tiny chapel make up **CAMPOMORRO**, a picturesque fishing village 17km southwest of Propriano. The main attraction here is a two-kilometre-long **beach**, overlooked by an immense, and well-preserved, Genoese watchtower. In late July and August, it's swamped by Italian families from the adjacent campsites, but for the rest of the year Campomorro remains a tranquil enough place, with barely enough permanent residents to support a post office.

Another incentive to venture out here is the wild and windswept stretch of coast **south of Campomorro**, which is punctuated by outlandish rock formations and a string of empty pebble beaches. The absence of a road into the area, recently designated a regional nature reserve, means the only way to explore it is by boat or on foot, via the waymarked **coastal path** that begins below Campomorro's watchtower. From here, the path is easy to follow for the first eighty minute or so as it threads through a series of dramatic granite outcrops, eroded into phantasmagorical shapes. But once you hit the **anse d'Eccia**, and its sandy bottle-necked cove, the going gets tougher. Determined, well-equipped hikers can walk all the way to Tizzano, 20km down the coast, via the much photographed **Senetosa Tower**, but to do so it's essential to take along a detailed map, plenty of fresh water, and camping equipment in case you get lost. For additional route advice, contact the owner of Grand Bleu boat trips at his caravan near the tourist office in Propriano (☎04.95.76.04.26). He takes customers to anse d'Eccia by catamaran, and provides photographs to help you follow the trail back to Campomorro; the cost of this half-day trip is 140F.

Practicalities

There are no bus services to Campomorro, but hitching is fairly reliable once you've turned off the main Propriano–Bonifacio road. The village possesses only two **hotels**, plus a couple of campsites: *Le Ressac*, about 100m behind the chapel (☎04.95.74.22.25; ③ closed Oct–May), is a friendly family-run place with excellent views across the bay, and generally a better option than the more expensive, but less welcoming, *Le Campomorro*, overlooking the beach at the tower end of the village (☎04.95.74.20.89; ④). Of the two **campsites**, *Camping Peretto Les Roseaux*, 300m from the post office towards the tower (☎04.95.74.20.52; May–Oct) is the more peaceful. For food, try the popular *La Mouette* café opposite the church, which serves a selection of filling salads for under 50F on its beachside terrace. Alternatively, *Le Ressac*'s pricier restaurant is renowned for its *bouillabaisse*, which contains six or more kinds of fresh local fish, including lobster.

Sartène and around

Prosper Mérimée famously dubbed **SARTÈNE** (Sartè) "La plus corses des villes corse" (The most Corsican of Corsican towns), but the nineteenth-century German chronicler Gregorovius put a less complimentary spin on it when he described it as a "town peopled by demons". Sartène hasn't shaken off its hostile image, due in large part to a heavy presence of wealthy-looking Godfather types. On the other hand it's a smart, clean place, noticeably better-groomed than many small Corsican towns, its principal income coming from Sartène wine – the best on the island. The main square doesn't offer many diversions once you've explored the enclosed old town and prehistory museum, and the only time of year Sartène teems with tourists is at Easter for **U Catenacciu**, a Good Friday procession that packs the main square with onlookers.

Close to Sartène are some of the island's best-known prehistoric sites, most notably **Filitosa** (see above), the megaliths of **Cauria** and the **Alignement de Palaggiu** –Corsica's largest array of prehistoric standing stones.

The town

Place Porta – its official name, place de la Libération, has never caught on – forms Sartène's nucleus. Once the arena for bloody vendettas, it's now a well-kept square opening onto a wide terrace that overlooks the rippling green valley of the Rizzanese. Flanking the south side of place Porta is the **church of Ste-Marie**, built in the 1760s but completely restored to a smooth granitic appearance. Inside the church, the most notable feature is the weighty wooden cross and chair carried through the town by hooded penitents during the Catenacciu procession.

A flight of steps to the left of the **Hôtel de Ville**, formerly the governor's palace, leads past the post office to a ruined **lookout tower**, which is all that remains of the town's twelfth-century ramparts. This apart, the best of the old town is to be found behind the Hôtel de Ville in the **Santa Anna district**, a labyrinth of constricted passageways and ancient fortress-like houses that rarely give any signs of life. Featuring few windows and often linked to their neighbours by balconies, these houses are entered by first-floor doors which would have been approached by ladders – dilapidated staircases have replaced these necessary measures against unwelcome intruders. To the left of rue Frère-Bartoli are the strangest of all the vaulted passageways, where outcrops of rock block the paths between the ancient buildings. Just to the west of the Hôtel de Ville, signposted off the tiny place Maggiore, you'll find the **impasse Carababa**, a remarkable architectural puzzle of a passageway cut through the awkwardly stacked houses. A few steps away, at the western edge of the town, **place Angelo-Maria-Chiappe** offers a magnificent view of the Golfe du Valinco.

Set in a shady garden a short distance east of place Porta is the uninspiring **Musée de la Préhistoire Corse** (June 15–Sept 15 Mon–Fri 10am–noon & 2–5pm, Sat 2–6pm; 15F), Corsica's centre for archeological research. Its rather dry collection comprises findings from digs throughout the island, mostly Neolithic and Torréen pottery fragments, with some bracelets from the Iron Age, and painted ceramics from the thirteenth to sixteenth centuries.

Practicalities

Buses from Ajaccio, Propriano, Bonifacio and Porto Vecchio stop outside the travel agent's at the top of av Gabriel-Péri. A short distance northeast of here at 6 rue Borgo, one of the narrow lanes running south off the Place Porta, lies Sartène's tiny **tourist office** (May–Sept Mon–Fri 9am–noon & 3–7pm; ☎04.95.77.15.40).

The only **hotel** in Sartène itself is *Les Roches* on rue Jean-Jaurès, a large family-run place just below the old town (☎04.95.77.07.61, fax 04.95.77.19.93; ④); it commands panoramic views of the Vallée du Rizzanese and has a restaurant that serves hearty Corsican food. At the delightful *Le Jardin des Orangers*, 1km west of town along the road to Propriano (☎04.95.77.01.80; ③; April–Oct), you can rent studios and rooms set amid orange orchards. Otherwise try the *Villa Piana*, 1km out of town on the Propriano road (☎04.95.77.07.04; ③; May–Oct), an upmarket place overlooking the Golfe de Valinco – or simply stay in Propriano (see p.1031), which has a wider choice of accommodation. The nearest **campsite**, *Camping Olva* (*Les Eucalyptus*), lies 5km along the D69 to Castagna (☎04.95.77.11.58) – it offers a free bus service to and from Sartène.

As for **restaurants**, try the cheap and cheerful *Aux Gourmets*, on the cours Sœur-Amélie, whose good-value 75F set menu includes wild-boar steak and chips. Marginally upmarket is the ersatz rustic *La Chaumière*, south of the square on the rue Capitaine-Benedetti, where you can eat local specialities such as *tripettes sartènaises*, fresh trout and charcoal grilled pork. For a quick snack, *Pizza Porta* on the square is your best bet, serving toasted sandwiches, fresh salads, crêpes and pizzas. **Bars** cluster around place Porta, and are great places for crowd-watching.

The megalithic sites

Sparsely populated today, the rolling hills of the southwestern corner of Corsica are rich in prehistoric sites. The megaliths of **Cauria**, standing in ghostly isolation 10km southwest from Sartène, comprise the Dolmen de Fontanaccia, the best-preserved monument of its kind on Corsica, and the nearby alignments of **Stantari** and **Renaggiu** have an impressive congregation of statue-menhirs.

More than 250 menhirs can be seen northwest of Cauria at **Palaggiu**, another rewardingly remote site. Equally wild is the coast hereabouts, with deep clefts and coves providing some excellent spots for diving and secluded swimming.

The only public transport in this region is the twice-daily Ajaccio–Bonifacio **bus**.

Cauria

To reach the **Cauria megalithic site**, you need to turn off the N196 about 2km outside Sartène, at the Col de l'Albitrina (291m), taking the D48 towards Tizzano. Four kilometres along this road a left turning brings you onto a winding road through *maquis*, until eventually the **Dolmen de Fontanaccia** comes into view on the horizon, isolated in a clearing amidst a sea of scrubland.

Known to the locals as the **Stazzona del Diavolu** (Devil's Forge), a name that does justice to its enigmatic power, the Dolmen de Fontanaccia is in fact a burial chamber from around 2000 BC. This period was marked by a change in burial customs – whereas bodies had previously been buried in stone coffins in the ground, they were now placed above, in a mound of earth enclosed in a stone chamber. What you see today is the great stone table, comprising six huge granite blocks nearly 2m high, topped by a stone slab that remained after the earth rotted away.

The twenty "standing men" of the **Alignement de Stantari**, 200m to the east of the dolmen, date from the same period. All are featureless, except two which have roughly sculpted eyes and noses, with diagonal swords on their backs and sockets in their heads where horns would probably have been attached.

Across a couple of fields to the south is the **Alignement de Renaggiu**, a gathering of forty menhirs standing in rows amid a small shadowy copse, set against the enormous granite outcrop of Punta di Cauria. Some of the menhirs have fallen, but all face north to south, a fact that seems to rule out any connection with a sun-related cult.

Palaggiu

For the **Alignement de Palaggiu**, the largest single concentration of menhirs in Corsica, you regain the D48 and continue 3km south of the Cauria turning until you reach the Domaine La Mosconi wine warehouse, where you should park your car. From here, head along the dirt track marked "Proprieté privé" which leads 1.5km to the archeological site. The 258 menhirs, stretching in straight lines across the countryside like a battleground of soldiers, include three statue-menhirs with carved weapons and facial features – they are amidst the first line you come to. Dating from around 1800 BC, the statues give few clues as to their function, but it's a reasonable supposition that proximity to the sea was important – one persuasive theory is that the statues were some sort of magical deterrent to invaders.

Bonifacio

BONIFACIO (Bonifaziu) enjoys a superbly isolated situation at Corsica's southernmost point, a narrow peninsula of dazzling white limestone creating a town site unlike any other on the island. Separated from the rest of the island by an expanse of *maquis*, Bonifacio has maintained a certain temperamental detachment from Corsica, and is distinctly more Italian than French in atmosphere. The old town, a maze of tortuous streets, retains Renaissance features found only here, and with Sardinia just a stone's throw away, much of the property in the area is owned by upper-echelon Italians. A haven for boats for centuries, the town's perfect natural harbour is nowadays a marina that attracts yachts from all around the Med, with a plethora of hotels and restaurants to cater for the thousands of summer visitors.

Such a place has its drawbacks: exorbitant prices, stifling crowds from late June to mid-September, and a commercial cynicism that's atypical of Corsica. But Bonifacio is perhaps the island's best-looking maritime town, and boasts a lively nightlife, centred on the cafés and bars lining the quayside.

Arrival, information and accommodation

The nearest airport to Bonifacio is **Figari** (☎04.95.71.00.22), 17km north. There's no bus service from here so you'll have to take a taxi into town – around 230F. **Buses** pull in to the car park at the far eastern end of the marina, close to most of the hotels. The **tourist office** is up in the *ville haute* just off place de l'Europe next to the mairie (July–Sept daily 9am–8pm; Oct–June Mon–Fri 8.30am–12.30pm & 1.45–6pm; ☎04.95.73.11.88). You can rent a **car** from Avis (☎04.95.73.02.47) or Hertz (☎04.95.73.06.41), both quai Banda del Ferro, Citer, quai Noël Beretti (☎04.95.73.13.16), or Europcar, by the Esso garage on the way into town coming from Sartène (☎04.95.73.10.99). If you need to change money, note that Bonifacio's only **cash distributor**, at the Société Générale on the quai J Comparetti, frequently runs out of money, so get there early in the day or you'll be at the mercy of the rip-off bureaux de change dotted around the town.

Finding a place to **stay** can be a chore, as Bonifacio's hotels are quickly booked up in high season; if you want to stay centrally, make sure you ring in advance. Better still, save yourself the trouble, and a considerable amount of money, by finding a room somewhere else and travelling here for the day; tariffs in this town are the highest on the island. The same applies to the large **campsites** dotted along the road to Porto-Vecchio, which can get very crowded.

Hotels

La Caravelle, 37 quai Comparetti (☎04.95.73.00.03, fax 04.95.73.00.41). Stylish olde-worlde place with an excellent restaurant in a prime location. Closed mid-Oct to Easter. ⑨.

Centre Nautique, on the marina (☎04.95.73.02.11, fax 04.95.73.17.47). Relaxed, chic hotel on the harbourside. Popular with yachters. All rooms have two storeys, spiral staircases and air-conditioning. Good off-peak discounts. ⑧.

des Étrangers, 4 av Sylvère-Bohn (☎04.95.73.01.09). On the road to Ajaccio, 300m past the port, this is the least expensive place in town – its only outstanding feature. Closed Nov–March. ④.

Le Genovese, Quartier de la Citadelle (☎04.95.73.12.34, fax 04.95.73.09.03). Modern luxury hotel overlooking the port; sea views cost extra. ⑥.

Le Royal, 8 rue Fred-Scamaroni (☎04.95.73.00.51, fax 04.95.73.04.68). Above a modern bar in the *ville haute*. Bright, clean place with views of the citadel and the sea. All rooms air-conditioned. Good value by Bonifacio standards. ⑨.

Campsites

L'Araguina, av Sylvère-Bohn, opposite the Total service station near *Hotel des Étrangers* (☎04.95.73.02.96). Closest site to town, but overcrowded, with stony ground and less than pleasant toilet blocks. Only worth considering if you can't get anywhere else.

Camping Asciaghju, route de Palombaggia (☎04.95.70.37.87). Roughly mid-way between Bonifacio and Porto-Vecchio, on the road to Palombaggia beach. Nothing flash, but correct prices and access to a private beach – a godsend in summer. June–Sept.

Campo di Liccia, opposite *U Farniente* (☎04.95.73.03.09). Well-shaded and large, so you're guaranteed a place. They also run a free shuttle bus to the nearest beach in summer. June–Sept.

Camping Rondinara, Rondinara beach, signposted east off N198, 10km north of Bonifacio (☎04.95.70.43.15). One of the best value, and best situated, sites in the area, although quite a drive north. Pool, and close to an exquisite shell-shaped beach (see p.1040). June–Sept.

The town

Apart from the cafés, hotels and restaurants of quai Comparetti, the only attraction in the **ville basse** is the marina's **aquarium** (daily 10am–8pm; 22F), where the octopuses, flying crabs and blue lobsters are the star attractions. At the far end lies the port where ferries leave for Sardinia and, in between, a cluster of restaurants and shops lies at the foot of montée Rastello, the steps up to the **ville haute**, where many of the houses are bordered by enormous battlements which, like the houses themselves, have been rebuilt many times – the most significant modifications were made by the French during their brief period of occupation following the 1554 siege, after they had reduced the town walls to rubble.

From the top of the montée Rastello steps you can cross avenue Général-de-Gaulle to **montée St-Roch**, which gives a stunning view of the white limestone cliffs and the huge lump of fallen rock-face called the **Grain de Sable**. At the **Chapelle St-Roch**, built on the spot where the last plague victim died in 1528, more steps lead down to the tiny beach of **Sutta Rocca**.

At the top of the montée St-Roch steps stands the drawbridge of the great **Porte des Gênes**, once the only entrance to the *ville haute*. Through the gate, in place d'Armes, you can see the **Bastion de l'Étendard** (April, May & Sept Mon–Sat 11am–5.20pm; July & Aug 10am–9pm; 10F, kids under 12 free), sole remnant of the fortifications destroyed during the siege of 1554. A few paces further lies **rue des deux Empereurs**, where no. 4 features the flamboyant marble escutcheon of the Cattacciolo family, one of many such adornments on the houses of this quarter. Opposite stands the house in which Napoléon resided for three months in 1793.

Cutting across to rue Palais-du-Garde brings you to the **church of Ste-Marie-Majeure**, originally Romanesque but restored in the eighteenth century, though the richly sculpted belfry dates from the fourteenth century. The facade is hidden by a loggia where the Genoese municipal officers used to dispense justice in the days of the republic. This church's treasure, a relic of the True Cross, was saved from a shipwreck in the Straits of Bonifacio; for centuries after, the citizens would take the relic to the edge of the cliff and pray for calm seas whenever storms raged. The relic is kept in the sacristy, along with an ivory cask containing relics of St Boniface, and you'll only be able to get a glimpse if you can find someone to open the room for you.

Nearby **rue du Palais de Garde** is one of the handsomest streets in Bonifacio, with its closed arcades and double-arched windows separated by curiously stunted columns. The oldest houses along here did not originally have doors; the inhabitants used to climb up a ladder which they would pull up behind them to prevent a surprise attack, while the ground floor was used as a stable and grain store.

South of here, rue Doria leads towards the Bosco (see below); at the end of this road a left down rue des Pachas will bring you to the **Torrione**, a 35-metre-high lookout post built in 1195 on the site of Count Bonifacio's castle. Descending the cliff from here, the **Escalier du Roi d'Aragon**'s 187 steps were said to have been built in one night by the Aragonese in an attempt to gain the town in 1420, but in fact they had already been in existence for some time and were used by the people to fetch water from a well.

The Bosco

To the west of the tower lies the **Bosco**, a quarter named after the wood that used to stand here in the tenth century. In those days a community of hermits dwelt here, but nowadays the limestone plateau is open and desolate. The only sign of life comes from the military training camp where young Corsicans sweat out their national service. The entrance to the Bosco is marked by the **church of St-Dominique**, a rare example of Corsican Gothic architecture – it was built in 1270, most probably by the Templars, and later handed over to the Dominicans.

Beyond the church, rue des Moulins leads onto the ruins of three **mills** dating from 1283, two of them decrepit, the third restored. Behind them stands a memorial to the 750 people who died when a troopship named *Sémillante* ran aground here in 1855, on its way to the Crimea, one of the many disasters wreaked by the notoriously windy straits.

The tip of the plateau is occupied by the **Cimetière Marin**, its white crosses standing out sharply against the deep blue of the sea. Open until sundown, the cemetery is a fascinating place to explore, with its flamboyant mausoleums displaying a jumble of architectural ornamentations: stuccoed facades, Gothic arches and classical columns. Next to the cemetery stands the **Couvent St-François**, allegedly founded after St Francis sought shelter in a nearby cave – the story goes that the convent was the town's apology to the holy man, over whom a local maid had nearly poured a bucket of slops. Immediately to the south, the **Esplanade St-François** commands breathtaking views across the bay to Sardinia.

Eating, drinking and nightlife

Eating possibilities in Bonifacio might seem unlimited, but it's best to avoid the chintzy restaurants in the marina, few of which merit their exorbitant prices – the places in the *ville haute* are less pretentious. The bars and cafés on quai Comparetti are the social focus for much of the day and in the evening.

Restaurants

Archivolto, rue Archivolto. Antiques and Bonifacio (☎04.95.73.17.58). Bric-à-brac set the tone of this cosy, olde worlde bistrot next to the church in the *ville haute*. The menu's classy, too, and changes daily. Main dishes 70–80F. Reserve a table on the candlelit terrace.

La Main à la Pâtes, 1 place Bonaparte (☎04.95.73.04.50). Fresh homemade pasta with imaginative sauces – mint, cocoa, seaweed, and around thirty more to choose from. Quite pricey (most main dishes 70–100F), but worth it.

de la Poste, 6 rue Fred-Scamaroni (☎04.95.73.13.31). Among the best-value places in the citadel, serving standard Corsican dishes like *spaghetti au brocciu*, fish, seafood and plenty of inexpensive pizzas. Open daily year round, except Sun during the winter.

Le Rustic, 7 rue Fred-Scamaroni. Basic and inexpensive Corsican dishes, including delicious stuffed aubergine – a local speciality. Menus from 95F.

Stella d'Oro, 23 rue Doria, near Église St-Jean-Baptiste (☎04.95.73.03.63). Quality local cuisine including *ravioli au brocciu*, stuffed aubergines and dozens of delicious pizzas served in a cosy rustic-style interior. No set menus, but plenty of choice. Most dishes around 60–70F. Open daily April–Oct.

Le Tiki, 3 rue de Palais du Garde, opposite the church. The cheapest place in the *ville haute* for snacks, salads and pasta. 55F menus.

Bars and clubs

Amnésia, 9km north on the Porto-Vecchio road. During the summer this is the place to party, with three open-air dance floors, visiting DJs and occasional live acts. Entrance costs vary from 50–120F according to what's on (alcoholic drinks 60F each); you can get there on a free shuttle bus from the marina.

Bar du Quai, at the foot of montée Rastello. This quayside café catches the morning sun, and is less expensive than those further down the marina. A good breakfast venue.

Central, 4 rue Fred-Scamaroni. Bonifacio's party set come to this little *ville haute* bar for a night-cap, so it's often livelier for later than most places down in the marina.

Nearby beaches

Some beautiful **beaches** lie northeast of Bonifacio, along a stretch of coast that has become the preserve of the Côte d'Azur jet set. The nearest accessible ones are the small and picturesque **plage de la Catena** and **plage de l'Arinella**, 1km to the west on the north side of Bonifacio's harbour – a track just before *Camping L'Araguina* (see p.1037) leads down to them. For the best local bathing places head northeast along the D58, where about 3km along there's a junction for a trio of beaches: the popular **plage de Pianterella**, the dullest of the three but a favourite with watersports enthusiasts; the adjacent **plage de Sperone**, a large, sheltered cove with pearl-white sand and calm turquoise water; and **Cala Lunga**, a small yellow-sand cove with great views of Cavallo and Sardinia in the distance.

Further along the D58, a second right-hand turn leads to the hamlet of Gurgazu, on the southern edge of the Golfe de Santa Manza. Stretching to the right is the **plage de Santa Manza**, a narrow silver strip backed by a rough road. A better proposition is **plage de Maora**, a wider beach with cleaner sand and a makeshift bar – reached by taking a left at the junction of the D60 and D58. The third beach of the gulf, **plage de Balistra**, situated by a marshy lagoon, is less pleasant and not accessible from here; to get to it you need to follow the N198 north of Bonifacio for 12km, then take a right down a dirt track for 4km to the sea.

To reach the **plage de la Rondinara**, one of the most photographed beaches in Corsica, take the N198 north for about 10km, until a turning signposted "Camping Rondinara" (see p.1037) appears suddenly to the right – the track to the sea is strewn with boulders in places, but motorable if you take your time. Sheltered by the Punta di Rondinara and backed by dunes, the small shell-shaped beach looks like a Pacific lagoon, with turquoise water and a perfect curve of soft white sand; it's also very popular, so be prepared to walk north around the bay to less-frequented coves if you want to avoid the crowds.

Porto-Vecchio and around

Set on a hillock overlooking a beautiful deep blue bay, **PORTO-VECCHIO**, 25km north of Bonifacio, was rated by James Boswell as one of "the most distinguished harbours in Europe". It was founded in 1539 as a second Genoese stronghold on the east coast, Bastia being well-established in the north. The site was perfect; close to the unexploited and fertile plain, it benefited from secure high land and a sheltered harbour, although the mosquito population spread malaria and wiped out the first Ligurian settlers within months. Things began to take off mainly thanks to the cork industry, which still thrived well into this century. Today a third of Corsica's wine is exported from here, but most revenue comes from tourists, the vast majority of them well-heeled Italians who flock here for the fine outlying **beaches**: spectacular stretches of shoreline lie to the south, with Palombaggia the most popular and Golfe de Santa Giulia coming a close second, while to the north, the deep inlet of the Golfe de Porto-Vecchio boasts some fine pine-backed strands. To the northwest, the little town of **Zonza** makes a good base for exploring the dramatic forestry that surrounds the **route de Bavella**.

Around the centre of town there's not much to see, apart from the well-preserved **fortress** and the small grid of **ancient streets** backing onto the main place de la République. East of the square you can't miss the **Porte Génoise**, which frames a delightful expanse of sea and saltpans and through which you'll find the quickest route down to the modern marina, lined with cafés and hotels.

Practicalities

Buses from Bastia stop outside the Corsicatours travel agent's on rue Jean Jaurès, southwest of the old town; coming from Bonifacio, Propriano, Sartène and Ajaccio, you'll be dropped at Trinitours' shop on rue Pasteur. From here it's a five- minute walk southwest to the main square, place de l'Hôtel-de-Ville, site of the efficient **tourist office** (July–mid-Sept Mon–Sat 9am–8pm, Sun 9am–1pm; mid-Sept–June Mon–Fri 9am–noon & 2–6pm, Sat 9am–noon; ☎04.95.70.09.58), where you can consult timetables for local buses.

Accommodation is easy to come by except in high summer. One of the least expensive places in town is the noisy but central *Le Modern*, 10 cours Napoléon (☎04.95.70.06.36; ④; closed Oct–April), followed by the simple, family-run *Panorama*, 12 rue Jean-Nicoli, just above the old town (☎04.95.70.07.96; ④). It's worth spending a bit extra for a place in the marina, like the pleasant *Goéland*, port de Plaisance (☎04.95.70.14.15; ⑤), or the *Roches Blanches*, port de Plaisance (☎04.95.70.06.96; ⑤; closed Nov–April). If you're **camping** and don't have a vehicle, your best bet is the *Matonara* site, just north of the centre at the Quatre-Chemins intersection – it's large, with lots of cork trees for shade. Otherwise, try the well-equipped *Arutoli* on rte de l'Ospédale, 2km northwest of town along the D368 (☎04.95.70.12.73), which has an enormous pool. *Les Amis de la Nature* is a basic site in a pine wood, 4km north of town (☎04.95.70.21.57).

For **eating**, try the moderately priced *Chez Mimi*, 5 rue du Général-Abbatucci (☎04.95.70.28.54), whose Corsican set menu (70–80F) is one of the best deals in town, or splash out on a meal at pricier *L'Antigu*, 51 rue Borgu (☎04.95.70.39.33), which offers the best views of the gulf and most-renowned Corsican cuisine in town, with set menus from 100–140F. Pizzerias are found all over the centre: *U Borgu*, also on rue Borgu, does a fair selection, and the views from its terrace are on a par with those at *L'Antigu*. If you're on a really tight budget, though, head for *Sur le Pouce*, a hole-in-the-wall joint on the rue Porte Génoise, which does toasted sandwiches and *paninis* made with quality local cheeses for around 25F.

Nightlife in Porto-Vecchio centres on the main square in the old town where, in the summer, hordes of suntanned Italians strut their stuff. A lively bar to head for, and a must for Tintinophiles, is *Objectif Lune*, 3 rue Jérôme-Léandri (on the left as you leave the old town on cours Napoléon), which hosts regular live music sessions in its Tintin-memorabilia-filled-bar. The best club in the area, however, is *Amnésia*, midway between Porto-Vecchio and Bonifacio, which is only open from late-June through August.

Golfe de Porto-Vecchio

Much of the coast of the **Golfe de Porto-Vecchio** and its environs is characterized by ugly development, bombed-out building sites and hectares of dismal swampland, yet some of the clearest, bluest sea and whitest beaches on Corsica are also found around here. The most frequented of these, Palombaggia and Santa Giulia, can be reached by **bus** from the town in summer, timetables for which are posted in the tourist office (see above); at other times you'll need your own transport, or be prepared to hitch. The same applies to the **Casteddu d'Araggiu**, one of the island's best-preserved Bronze Age sites, which stands on a ledge overlooking the gulf to the north of town.

Heading **south of Porto-Vecchio** along the main N198, take the turning signposted for **PALOMBAGGIA**, a golden semicircle of sand edged by short twisted umbrella pines that are punctuated by fantastically shaped red rocks. This might be the most beautiful beach on the island were it not for the crowds, which pour on to it in such numbers that a wattle fence has had to be erected to protect the dunes. A few kilometres further along the same road takes you to **SANTA GIULIA**, a sweeping sandy bay backed by a lagoon. Despite the presence of several holiday villages and facilities for windsurfing and other noisier watersports, crowds are less of a problem here, and the shallow bay is an extraordinary turquoise colour.

North of Porto-Vecchio, the first beach worth a visit is **SAN CIPRIANU**, a half-moon bay of white sand, reached by turning left off the main road at the Elf garage.

Carry on for another 7km, and you'll come to the even more picturesque beach at **PINARELLU**, a uncrowded, long sweep of soft white sand with a Genoese watchtower and, like the less inspiring beaches immediately north of here, benefiting from the spectacular backdrop of the Massif de l'Ospédale.

The coast between Porto-Vecchio and Solenzara is also strewn with **prehistoric monuments**. The most impressive of these, **Casteddu d'Araggiu**, lies 12km north along the D759. From the site's car park (signposted off the main road), it's a twenty-minute stiff climb through *maquis* and scrubby woodland to the ruins. Built in 2000 BC and inhabited by a community that lived by farming and hunting, the *casteddu* consists of a complex of chambers built into a massive circular wall of pink granite, splashed with vivid green patches of lichen, from the top of which the views over the gulf are superb.

The route de Bavella

The D268 – the **route de Bavella** – is perhaps the most dramatic road in all Corsica, starting from the unassuming **ZONZA**, 20km northwest of Porto-Vecchio, and running northeast towards the coast. It penetrates the **Forêt de Zonza**, a dense expanse of pine and chestnut trees as it rises steadily to the **Col de Bavella** (1218m). A towering statue of **Notre-Dame-des-Neiges** marks the pass itself, which has a bleak and blasted look, the flattened pines crouched from the wind, their jagged branches sharply black against the green-hued granite peaks. An amazing panorama of peaks and forests surrounds the col: to the northwest the serrated granite ridge of the **Cirque de Gio Agostino** is dwarfed by the pink pinnacles of the **Aiguilles de Bavella**; behind soars Monte Incudine; and the east is dominated by the ruddy shades of **Paglia Orba** and the distant sea.

From this point it's a steep descent through what's left of the **Forêt de Bavella**, which was devastated by fire in 1960 but still features some huge Laricio pines. The winding road offers numerous breathtaking glimpses of the Aiguilles de Bavella and plenty of places to pull over for a swim in the river. About 10km from the pass you'll come to the **Col de l'Arone** (608m), which offers stunning vistas of the mountains and the Forêt de Tova in the north.

The best place to **stay** locally is Zonza, which has a cluster of hotels, all with more than decent restaurants, such as *Le Tourisme*, set back on the west side of the Quenza road north of the village (☎04.95.78.67.72, fax 04.95.78.72.23; ④; closed Nov–March), or *L'Aiglon* in the village centre (☎04.95.78.67.79, fax 04.95.78.63.62; ④; closed Jan–March), whose 540F half-board is obligatory between June and September. The **Parc Naturel Régional office** is 500m north of the village (June–Sept daily 9am–noon & 3–5pm; ☎04.95.78.66.58). Regular buses run to Zonza from Ajaccio, Propriano, Sartène and Porto-Vecchio; for the current timetables ask at a tourist office.

Aléria

Built on the estuary at the mouth of the River Tavignano on the island's east coast, 40km southeast of Corte along the N200, **ALÉRIA** was first settled in 564 BC by a colony of Greek Phocaeans as a trading port for the copper and lead they mined from the land and the wheat, olives and grapes they farmed. After an interlude of Carthaginian rule, the Romans arrived in 259 BC, built a naval base and re-established its importance in the Mediterranean. Aléria remained the east coast's principal port right up until the eighteenth century. Little is left of the historic town except Roman ruins and a thirteenth-century Genoese fortress, which stands high against a background of chequered fields and green vineyards. To the south, a strip of modern buildings straddling the main road makes up the modern town, but it's the village set on the hilltop just west of here which holds most interest.

The best plan is to begin with the **Musée Jerôme Carcopino** (May 16–Sept 8am–noon & 2–7pm; Oct–May 15 Mon–Fri 8am–noon & 2–5pm; 10F), housed in the Fort Matra and crammed with remarkable finds from the Roman site, including Hellenic and Punic coins, rings, belt links, elaborate oil lamps decorated with Christian symbols, Attic plates, and a second-century marble bust of Jupiter Ammon. Etruscan bronzes fill another room, with jewellery and armour from the fourth to the second century BC.

It's a stone's throw from here to the **Roman site** (closes 30min before museum), where most of the excavation was done as recently as the 1950s, despite the fact that French novelist Prosper Merimée noticed signs of the Roman settlement during his survey of the island in 1830. Most of the site still lies beneath ground and is undergoing continuous excavation, but the *balneum* (bathhouse), the base of Augustus's triumphal arch, the foundations of the forum and traces of shops have already been unearthed.

First discovered was the arch, which formed the entrance to the governor's residence – the *praetorium* – on the western edge of the forum. In the adjacent *balneum*, a network of reservoirs and cisterns, the *caldarium* bears traces of the underground pipes that would have heated the room, and a patterned mosaic floor is visible inside the neighbouring chamber. To the north of the site lie the foundation walls of a large house, while at the eastern end of the forum the foundations of the temple can be seen, and at its northern edge, over a row of column stumps, are the foundations of the apse of an early Christian church.

Some traces of the **Greek settlement**, comprising the remains of an acropolis, have been discovered further to the east. It's believed that the main part of the town would have extended from the present site over to this acropolis and down to the Tavignano estuary. The port was located to the east of the main road, where the remnants of a second-century bathhouse have been found.

Practicalities

Of Aléria's few **hotels**, *Les Orangers* (☎04.95.57.00.31; ②), situated 50m north of the Cateraggio crossroads in the centre of the modern part, is the cheapest. *L'Atrachjata* (☎04.95.57.03.93, fax 04.95.57.08.03; ③), a little further north, does good meals; *L'Empereur*, a big motel-style building a little further up from *Les Orangers* (☎04.95.57.02.13; ②), is clean and comfortable, with large chalet rooms opening onto a central garden. For campers, there's a pleasant and well-equipped site, the *Marina d'Aléria*, 3km east at the beach in a eucalyptus wood (☎04.95.57.01.42; Easter–Oct).

Corte

Situated amidst mountains and gorges near the centre of the island, **CORTE** (Corti), 40km east of Porto and 50km southwest of Bastia, has been the home of Corsican nationalism since the first National Constitution was drawn up here in 1731. It is also where Pascal Paoli, *U Babbu di u Patria* (Father of the Nation), formed the island's first democratic government later in the eighteenth century and set up the first Corsican printing press and the **Università di Corsica**, the first university to be established here. Reopened in 1981 as a response to the rise in nationalism in the 1970s, the university offers courses in Corsican studies in addition to the usual subjects, and boasts 2500 students – far fewer than the nationalists would like (a common subject for political graffiti in the town is that the number of students hasn't increased since the university was reopened). For the outsider, Corte's charm is concentrated in the tranquil *ville haute* where a network of narrow cobbled lanes wind via a couple of picturesque squares to the foot of the citadel, perched atop a craggy outcrop like a vision from a Gothic novel. The town is also well-situated for **hikes** into the mountains of the nearby watershed.

Arrival, information and accommodation

Buses from Ajaccio and Bastia stop in the centre of town on av Xavier-Luciani, but the **gare SNCF** is at the foot of the hill near the university (☎04.95.46.00.97), a ten-minute walk from the centre and campsites. If you're driving, the best place to park is at the top of av Jean-Nicoli, the road which leads into town from Ajaccio. Corte's **tourist office** (July to mid-Sept Mon–Sat 9am–8pm; mid-Sept to June Mon–Fri 9am–noon & 2–5pm; ☎04.95.46.24.20) is tucked away in a tiny square, Fontaine des Quatre Canons, just off cours Paoli, which runs through the middle of town to Corte's main square, place Paoli. **Cars** can be rented from Europcar, 9 cours Paoli (☎04.95.31.03.79), or Hertz, c/o Cyrnea Tourisme, 9 av Xavier-Luciani (☎04.95.46.24.62).

Finding a place to **stay** can be a problem from mid-June until early September, when it's advisable to book in advance. With three **campsites** in the town, and a couple a short drive away, tent space is at less of a premium, although the sites 1km south of town, across the river, get crowded in high season.

Hotels

L'Auberge de la Restonica, Vallée de la Restonica (☎04.95.46.09.58, fax 04.95.61.03.91). Comfortable hotel by the river, with a restaurant, medium-sized garden and pool, 1.5km southwest of town. Pricey half-board (⑧) obligatory April–Sept. Closed Nov–Feb. ③.

Cyrnos, 1–3 av Xavier-Luciani (☎04.95.46.01.09). Basic but comfortable rooms above a local-oldies-only bar, slap in the centre of town. ②.

HR, allé du 9 Septembre (☎04.95.45.11.11, fax 04.95.61.02.85). A stone's throw from the train station, this ugly converted *gendarmerie* houses dozens of rooms, some of them costing as little as 150F off-peak. Worth a try if there are no vacancies elsewhere. Fitness room and sauna included. Closed Nov–May. ②.

du Nord et de l'Europe, 22 cours Paoli (☎04.95.46.00.68). Pleasant, clean place right in the centre, with huge old-fashioned rooms and rock-bottom rates. Closed Oct–May. ②.

de la Paix, 1 av Général-de-Gaulle (☎04.95.46.06.72, fax 04.95.46.23.84). Large and central hotel set in an elegant part of town. The outside's in dire need of renovation, but the rooms are immaculate. ③.

de la Poste, 2 place Padoue (☎04.95.46.01.37). Huge, shabby old place, but central and with lots of character. The cheapest place in town. ②.

Le Refuge, gorges de Restonica, 2km from centre (☎04.95.46.09.13, fax 04.95.46.22.38). Upscale but unpretentious hotel-restaurant on the roadside overlooking the stream, with a sunny terrace for meals. Half-board obligatory (⑦) in August. Closed Nov–Easter. ④.

Campsites

Le Restonica, rte de la Restonica (☎04.95.46.09.07). Closest to the main town, at the foot of the valley beside the river, this is the best of the sites. Has a view of the citadel, plenty of shade and a recently opened restaurant. 10min walk from the centre.

Santa Barbara, 2.5km east on the N200 (☎04.95.46.20.22). An attractive, small site well out of town, with its own pool and restaurant. May–Sept.

U Tavignanu, behind the citadel (☎04.95.46.16.85). The hikers' choice. There's no road access, so it's a peaceful site, located on a terraced garden with views. The adjacent gîte d'étape offers cheap dorm beds, too. Follow the road around the back of the citadel, cross over the river bridge and bear right; the site lies another 10min up the path.

The town

Corte is a very small town whose centre effectively consists of one street: **cours Paoli**, which runs from **place Paoli**, at the southern end, a tourist-friendly zone packed with cafés, restaurants and market stalls, to **place du Duc-de-Padoue**, an elegant square of turn-of-the-century buildings. Its statue, a grim bronze lump by Bartholdi, designer of the Statue of Liberty, is of **Arrighi di Casanova**, a general whose service under Napoléon earned him the title of Duke of Padua; his ancestral home can be seen in place Poilu in the *ville haute*.

The old **ville haute** is next to the cours Paoli, reached by climbing one of the cobbled ramps on the west side of the cours or by taking the steep rue Scoliscia from place Paoli. **Place Gaffori**, the centre of the *ville haute*, is dominated by a statue of General Gian' Pietru Gaffori pointing vigorously towards the church in the midst of the square's restaurant tables. On the base of the statue a bas-relief depicts the siege of the Gaffori house by the Genoese, who attacked in 1750 when Gaffori was out of town and his wife Faustina was left holding the fort. Their house stands right behind, and you can clearly make out the bullet marks made by the besiegers.

Opposite the house is the **church of the Annunciation**, built in 1450 but restored in the seventeenth century. Inside, there's a delicately carved pulpit and a hideous wax statue of St-Theophilus, patron of the town, on his deathbed. The saint's birthplace – behind the church in place Théophile – is marked by the **Oratoire St-Théophile**, a large arcaded building which commands a magnificent view across the gorges of Tavignano and Restonica.

For the best view of the citadel, follow the signs uphill to the viewing platform, aptly named the **Belvédère**, which faces the medieval tower, suspended high above the town on its pinnacle of rock and dwarfed by the immense crags behind. The platform also gives a wonderful view of the converging rivers and encircling forest – a summer bar adds to the attraction. In **place du Poilu**, the forecourt to the citadel, stands the house of the di Casanova family, where Napoléon's father – a friend of the Casanovas – lived in 1768 when he was Pascal Paoli's secretary.

At the gates to the citadel stands the **Palais National**, a great, solid block of a mansion that's the sole example of Genoese civic architecture in Corte. Having served as the seat of Paoli's government for a while, it became the Università di Corsica in 1765, offering free education to all (Napoléon's father studied here). In the spirit of the Enlightenment, Franciscan monks taught the contemporary social thought of philosophers such as Rousseau and Montesquieu as well as traditional subjects like theology, mathematics and law. The university closed in 1769 when the French took over the island after the Treaty of Versailles, not to be resurrected until 1981. Today several modern buildings have been added, among them the Institut Universitaire d'Études Corses, dedicated to the study of Corsican history and culture.

The Museu di a Corsica (Musée de la Corse) and citadel

At the far north end of the university complex, Corte's new **Museu di a Corsica** (April–June 20 & Sept 20–Oct Tues–Sun 10am–5.45pm; June 21–Sept 19 daily 10am–7.45pm; Nov–March Tues–Sat 10am–5.45pm; 20F, or 35F if temporary exhibition) occupies a prime site overlooking the town and valley – a feature the architects have exploited to maximum effect. Unfortunately, the exhibits – largely run-of-the-mill geological and ethnographic material such as farming implements, traditional costumes and craft tools – fail to measure up to the state-of-the-art design and decor. Attractive though all the white walls, curved glass and sensitive lighting are, you come away wondering why such expense has been lavished on such objects. The answer is that the subject matter, traditional Corsican culture, lends enormous symbolic importance to the museum, which Corsicans have been demanding for decades. This also explains why you won't find sections on less palatable, but equally significant, aspects of island life, such as vendetta, banditry and separatism. That said, amateur geologists will enjoy the wonderful rock specimens, and the display on Corsica's enigmatic religious brotherhoods is engaging.

The museum's entrance charge also admits you to Corte's principal landmark, the **citadel**. The only such fortress in the interior of the island, the Genoese structure served as a base for the Foreign Legion from 1962 until 1984, but now houses a pretty feeble exhibition of nineteenth-century photographs. It is reached by a huge staircase of Restonica marble, which leads to the medieval tower known as the **Nid d'Aigle** (Eagle's Nest). The fortress, of which the tower is the only original part, was built by Vincentello d'Istria in 1420, and the barracks were added during the reign of Louis-Philippe. These were later converted into a prison, in use as recently as World War II, when the Italian occupiers incarcerated Corsican resistance fighters in tiny cells.

PASCAL PAOLI

Pascal Paoli was born in Morosaglia into a family of campaigners for Corsican independence. At the age of 14 Pascal accompanied his father into exile in Naples, where the boy became a keen student of political enlightenment. At the time of Corsican leader Gaffori's assassination, Pascal was a 29-year-old sublieutenant in a Neapolitan regiment, but his brother Clemente was in the thick of the rebellion. Appointed one of four regents after Gaffori's death, Clemente invited his younger brother to take over the position of General of the Nation, a title he accepted in 1755 and was to hold for the next fourteen years.

Paoli's intention was to drive out the Genoese by force, but he wasn't an experienced soldier and was always short of the necessary supplies. He proved to be adept at the art of government, giving the island a democratic constitution which anticipated that of the United States of America, founding the university at Corte, building a navy strong enough to break the Genoese blockade, and establishing a mint, a printing press and an arms factory.

Then in 1768 the French moved in once more, this time intending to stay after having bought out the Genoese under the terms of the Treaty of Versailles. Determined to crush the rebels for good, the French overwhelmed the Corsican troops at Ponte Nuovo, whereupon Paoli went into exile in London.

In 1789, at the start of the French Revolution, the people of Corsica were declared to be subject to the same laws as the revolutionary state, and it was in this changed political climate that Paoli returned triumphantly to the island in the following year. Initially he sympathized with the new republicanism, but the Corsican Jacobites – the Bonaparte family amongst them – owed too much to France to have much sympathy with separatist politics. Disagreements came to a head with Paoli's arraignment in June 1793. His response was dramatic – setting up an independent government in Corte, he approached the British government for help. The British, driven out of Toulon by the French, were in search of a naval base in the area, and sent Sir Gilbert Elliot to evaluate the situation. English troops and naval forces quickly moved in, and after some fighting – during which the future Admiral Nelson lost the sight in one eye – the French moved out. A new constitution was drawn up that gave Corsica an attachment to the English crown, but with a large degree of autonomy. It's questionable whether Paoli was ever entirely happy with the course of events, but he was in a difficult situation, as the guillotine was waiting for him if France ever regained control. There seems no doubt that he expected to be appointed viceroy of the island, and when Elliot was given the job things began to turn sour.

The parliament of 1795 elected Paoli as president, but Elliot objected; soon after, rioting was provoked by a rumour that Paoli's bust had been deliberately smashed at a ball given in the viceroy's honour. When the English began talking again to the republican French the game was over. In 1796 Paoli was persuaded to return to London, shortly before Elliot withdrew as Napoléon's army landed to secure the island for France.

Given a state pension, Paoli died in London in 1807 at the age of 82, a revered figure. He was initially buried in his place of exile – there's a bust of him in Westminster Abbey – but his body now lies in his birthplace.

Adjacent to the cells is a former **watchtower** which at the time of Paoli's government was inhabited by the hangman.

Eating and drinking

Corte has a fair number of **restaurants** and more casual eating places, with the usual sprinkling of pizzerias and crêperies, nearly all of them on cours Paoli – place Gaffori is the only place in the *ville haute* with restaurants. The **bars** of cours Paoli are strictly for posing; place Paoli is more touristy, but at least you can sit and drink in comfort.

Cafés and bars

Bip's, overlooking the car park behind cours Paoli. A low-ceilinged bar that hosts live music most nights 10.30pm–1.30am. Drinks cost a hefty 30F, but this is about as lively as Corte gets.

Pâtisserie Bagh, mid-way along the west side of cours Paoli. A delightfully old-fashioned pâtisserie-cum-*salon de thé*, where you can stock up on savoury Corsican specialities, such as *bastelles brocciu*, as well as the usual fussy French pastries.

de la Place, place Paoli. The most down-to-earth café-bar on the shady side of the square. A popular spot for crowd-watching, with locals and tourists alike, and they serve good sandwiches.

Restaurants

A Cantina, 20m south of place Gaffori, towards the Belvédère. Artisanal cheeses and charcuterie served in an attractive stone cellar, wih a tasting counter and shop upstairs. Pricey, but quality guaranteed.

Le Gaffory, place Gaffori. Among least expensive terrace restaurants in town, with a 60F menus and loads of omelettes, salads and spaghetti.

U Museu, rampe Ribanelle, at the foot of the, 30m down rue Colonel-Feracci. Attractively situated restaurant, with stone terrace and garden. Their Corsican set menu (80F) is a particularly good deal, offering lasagne with wild-boar sauce, trout from the river and delicious *fiadone*. They also do superb salads that are filling enough for a main meal (try the delicious *chèvre chaud*).

Osteria San Teofatu, off rue Colonel-Feracci. Cosy little budget bistrot in the *ville haute*, with four differently priced set menus, served in a cavernous room with a vaulted stone ceiling.

Central Corsica

Central Corsica is a non-stop parade of stupendous scenery, and the best way to immerse yourself in it is to get onto the region's ever-expanding network of trails and forest tracks. The ridge of granite mountains forming the spine of the island is closely followed by the epic **GR20** footpath (see p.1020) which can be picked up from various villages and is scattered with refuge huts, most of them offering no facilities except shelter. For the less active there also are plenty of roads penetrating deep into the forests of **Vizzavona**, **la Restonica** and **Rospa Sorba**, crossing lofty passes that provide exceptional views across the island.

The most popular attractions in the centre, though, are the magnificent **gorges of la Restonica** and **Tavignano**, both within easy reach of Corte.

Gorges du Tavignano

A deep cleft of ruddy granite beginning 5km to the west of Corte, the **Gorges du Tavignano** offer one of central Corsica's great walks, marked in yellow paint flashes alongside the broad cascading River Tavignano, and is only accessible on foot. You can pick up the trail from opposite the Chapelle Ste-Croix in Corte's *ville haute* and follow it as far as the **Lac de Nino**, 30km west of the town, where it joins the **GR20**. There's a refuge, *A Sega*, 15km along the route, but check at the Corte tourist office to make sure it's open (it was firebombed a few years back).

Gorges de la Restonica

The glacier-moulded rocks and deep pools of the **Gorges de la Restonica** make the D936 running southwest from Corte the busiest mountain road in Corsica – if you come in high summer, expect to encounter traffic jams all the way up to the car park at the **Bergeries de Grotelle**, 15km from Corte. **Minibuses** run from Corte to the Bergeries, costing 85F, but hitching is usually reliable. The gorges begin after 6km, just beyond where the route penetrates the **Forêt de la Restonica**, a glorious forest of chestnut, Laricio pine and the tough maritime pine endemic to Corte. Not surprisingly, it's a popular place to walk, picnic and bathe in the many pools fed by the cascading torrent of the River Restonica, easily reached by scrambling down the rocky banks.

From the *bergeries,* a well-worn path winds along the valley floor to a pair of beautiful glacial lakes. The first and larger, **Lac de Melo**, is reached after an easy hour's hike through the rocks. One particularly steep part of the path has been fitted with security chains, but the scramble around the side of the passage is perfectly straightforward, and much quicker. Once past Lac de Melo, press on for another forty minutes along the steeper marked trail over a moraine to the second lake, **Lac de Capitello**, the more spectacular of the pair. Hemmed in by vertical cliffs, the deep turquoise-blue pool affords fine views of the Rotondo massif on the far side of the valley, and in clear weather you can spend an hour or two exploring the surrounding crags, scoured by rock pipits. Beyond here, the trail climbs higher to meet the GR20, and should only be attempted by well-equipped mountain walkers.

Venaco and Vivario

Immediately south of Corte you ascend into a landscape of lush chestnut forests that lasts as far as the **Col de Bellagranjo** (723m), before the road sweeps through **VENACO**, an elegant village of rusty buildings emerging from deep green verdure on the slopes of Monte Padro. You might want to halt here to admire the vistas – from the terrace of the Baroque church there's a spectacular view of the lower Vallée du Tavignano in the east.

About 5km from Venaco the road passes the **Pont de Vecchiu**, an arched stone bridge that flies over the River Vecchiu and under the iron bridge designed by Gustave Eiffel in 1888, putting the final touches to the Bastia–Ajaccio train line. The river's gorge is dominated by **VIVARIO**, a large innocuous village located at the junction of the routes to the **Forêt de Rospa Sorba** and the **Col de Verde**, and thus a good base for walkers, who stay here at the basic *Macchje Monte* (☎04.95.47.22.00; ②; obligatory 250F half-board July & Aug; closed Jan & Feb). Vivario's attraction lies in its forest setting, a savage environment that once supported its own wild man. In 1800 a 10-year-old boy went missing here after arguing with his parents, and stayed on the run for twenty years until ensnared by a group of hunters down by the river. The only traversable spot across the **Gorge du Vecchiu**, a three-hour walk west of Vivario, is a three-metre jump still known as the **Saut du Sauvage**, or "wild man's leap".

A shorter walk from Vivario takes you to the **Fort de Pasciolo**, an evocative ruin 1km south of the village beside the N193. Set in a wild site facing a great circle of peaks and overlooking the deep Gorge du Vecchiu, the fort was built around 1770 by the French, and was transformed into a prison to incarcerate the rebels of Fiumorbo.

Vizzavona and its forest

Monte d'Oro dominates the route south of Vivario to **VIZZAVONA**, about 10km away. Shielded by trees, the village is invisible from the main road, so keep your eyes peeled for a couple of tracks on the right, one of them signposted for the train station – the place where the legendary bandit Bellacoscia surrendered to the police at the age of 75 (see **below**). With its handful of auberges and restaurants, Vizzavona is an ideal place to spend a few days walking in the forest, although it gets crowded in summer when it fills with hikers taking a break from the GR20, which passes nearby.

If you want to **stay**, try the *I Laricci* (☎/fax 04.95.47.21.12; ③) opposite the station, which offers a good 360F half-board deal; better still, the *Relais de Monte d'Oro* (☎04.95.47.25.27; ②; Nov–April), a huge place in the hamlet of **LA FOCE**, deep in the forest 3km south along the main road, with *fin-de-siècle* furniture and a magnificent terrace looking out onto the mountain. A stopover on the GR20, it has a choice of very basic, refuge-style dorms (60F per bed), communal gîte accommodation (75F per bed), or more comfortable double rooms. If you're **camping**, head for the *Savaggio* campsite, 4km north of the village (☎04.95.47.22.14); note that the train will make a special request stop at the site if you give the conductor plenty of warning.

The Forêt de Vizzavona

A glorious forest of beech and Laricio pine, the **Forêt de Vizzavona** is the most popular walking area in Corsica, thanks to the easy access by main road or train. A lot of people come here to tackle the ascent of 2389-metre-high **Monte d'Oro**, but there are many less demanding trails to follow, one of the most frequented of these being the walk to the **Cascade des Anglais**, connected to Vizzavona by a marked trail.

Less than a kilometre west of the hamlet of La Foce lies the highest pass on the Ajaccio–Bastia road, the **Col de Vizzavona** (1163m), usually jammed with picnickers. Fifteen minutes south of the col along the forest trail you come to a magnificent viewpoint over the forested peaks, with the ruins of the Genoese **Fort de Vizzavona** prominent on a rise in the valley below. You can reach the fort itself in just fifteen minutes along a wide path north of the picnic tables. A walk to **La Madonuccia** – a mound of scrambled rocks that's supposed to look like the Virgin – takes about thirty minutes from the col, following the trail signposted "Bergeries des Pozzi", which branches off southeast. Another marked path from the col takes you to the **Fontaine de Vitulo**, the source of the Foce stream, which joins the River Gravona further down the mountain.

To get the best out of the forest, though, you should walk to **Col de Palmente** (1460m), a relatively strenuous four-hour there-and-back hike along the GR20 from the *maison forestière* just south of Vizzavona on the main road. The path winds through magnificent woodland before rising to the col, which affords fantastic views of Monte Renoso and the Forêt de Vizzavona.

Bocognano

From the Col de Vizzavona, the route winds southwards for 6km before reaching the appealing ochre cottages of **BOCOGNANO** (Bucugnanu). Set on a plateau amidst a chestnut forest, the village gives a perfect panorama of Monte d'Oro's pale grey domes, and is well-placed for walks to the **Cascade du Voile de la Mariée**, where the River Gravona crashes from a height of 150m in a series of cascades. The best approach to the falls is a thirty-minute walk south from the main road 3km south of Bocognano.

Bocognano is indissolubly associated with Antoine and Jacques Bellacoscia, born here in 1817 and 1832 respectively. Antoine, the elder son, took to the *maquis* in 1848, having killed the mayor of the village after an argument over some land. With his brother he went on to commit several more murders in full view of the hapless gendarmes, yet remained at liberty thanks to the support of the local population. In 1871, Jacques and Antoine managed to gain a safe pass into Ajaccio to organize an expedition to fight for the French in the war with Prussia. They returned from the war with their reputations restored, and took up residence in the family home, from where they continued to flout the law. In 1888, the police finally succeeded in ousting them from their house, which was converted into a prison. Antoine eventually surrendered at Vizzavona station on June 25, 1892, whereupon he was acquitted and exiled to Marseille in true Corsican tradition. The fate of Jacques is unknown.

travel details

Note that the details apply to June–Sept only; during the winter both train and bus services are considerably scaled down.

Buses

Ajaccio to: Bastia (2 daily; 3hr); Bonifacio (2 daily; 3–4hr); Cargèse (2–3 daily; 1hr 10min); Corte (2 daily; 1hr 45min); Évisa (2 daily; 2hr); Porto (2–3 daily; 2hr 15min); Porto-Vecchio (2 daily; 3hr–3hr 30min); Propriano (4 daily; 1hr 30min); Sartène (5 daily; 1hr 50min); Vizzavona (2 daily; 1hr); Zonza (3 daily; 2hr 15min).

Aléria to: Bastia (2 daily; 1hr 30min); Porto-Vecchio (2 daily; 1hr 30min).

Bastia to: Ajaccio (2 daily; 3hr); Bonifacio (2–4 daily; 3hr 35min); Calvi (1 daily; 3hr); Centuri (3 weekly in summer; 2hr); Corte (2 daily; 2hr); Erbalunga (hourly; 20min); L'Île Rousse (1 daily; 2hr); La Marana (2 daily; 30min); Porto-Vecchio (2 daily; 3hr); St-Florent (2 daily; 1hr).

Bonifacio to: Ajaccio (2 daily; 3hr 30min–4hr); Bastia (2–4 daily; 3hr 35min); Porto-Vecchio (2 daily; 30min); Propriano (2 daily; 1hr 40min–2hr 15min); Sartène (2 daily; 1hr 25min–2hr).

Calvi to: Bastia (1 daily; 3hr); Porto (1 daily; 2hr 30min); St-Florent (1 daily; 3hr).

Cargèse to: Ajaccio (2–3 daily; 1hr 10min); Porto (2–3 daily; 30min).

Corte to: Ajaccio (2 daily; 2hr); Bastia (2 daily; 2hr).

Évisa to: Ajaccio (2 daily; 2hr).

Porto to: Ajaccio (2–3 daily; 2hr 15min); Calvi (1 daily; 2hr 30min); Cargèse (2–3 daily; 1hr).

Porto-Vecchio to: Ajaccio (2 daily; 3hr–3hr 30min); Bastia (2 daily; 3hr); Bonifacio (2 daily; 30min); Propriano (2 daily; 1hr 45min); Sartène (2 daily; 1hr 30min).

Propriano to: Ajaccio (4 daily; 1hr 15min); Bonifacio (2 daily; 1hr); Porto-Vecchio (2 daily; 2hr 10min); Sartène (2 daily; 20min).

Trains

Ajaccio to: Bastia (4 daily; 4hr); Bocognano (4 daily; 1hr); Calvi (2 daily; 5hr 15min); Corte (4 daily; 2hr 15min); L'Île Rousse (2 daily; 4hr 45min); Venaco (4 daily; 2hr); Vizzavona (4 daily; 1hr 15min).

Bastia to: Ajaccio (4 daily; 3hr); Bocognano (4 daily; 2hr 50min); Calvi (2 daily; 3hr 15min); Corte (4 daily; 1hr 35min); L'Île Rousse (2 daily; 2hr 45min); Venaco (4 daily; 2hr 10min); Vivario (4 daily; 2hr 10min); Vizzavona (4 daily; 2hr 40min).

Calvi to: Ajaccio (2 daily; 4hr 40min); Bastia (2 daily; 3hr 10min); Corte (2 daily; 2hr 40min); L'Île Rousse (2 daily; 40min).

Corte to: Ajaccio (4 daily; 2hr); Bastia (4 daily; 2hr 15min); Bocognano (4 daily; 1hr 10min); Venaco (4 daily; 15min); Vivario (4 daily; 30min); Vizzavona (4 daily; 1hr).

L'Île Rousse to: Ajaccio (2 daily; 3hr 25min); Bastia (2 daily; 2hr 30min); Corte (2 daily; 2hr).

Venaco to: Ajaccio (4 daily; 1hr 45min); Bastia (2hr); Bocognano (4 daily; 40min); Corte (4 daily; 15min); Vivario (4 daily; 15min); Vizzavona (4 daily; 25min).

Vizzavona to: Ajaccio (4 daily; 1hr); Bastia (4 daily; 2hr 45min); Bocognano (4 daily; 10min); Corte (4 daily; 1hr); Ponte Leccia (4 daily; 1hr 15min); Venaco (4 daily; 45min); Vivario (4 daily; 20min).

Ferries

Marseille to: Ajaccio (2–4 weekly; 10hr overnight); Bastia (1–3 weekly; 10hr); L'Île Rousse

(Aug 1 weekly; 8hr); Propriano (1 weekly; 12hr overnight).

Nice to: Ajaccio (1–6 weekly; 11hr 30min overnight); Bastia (1–12 weekly, 6hr; fast 1 daily except Wed, 4hr 30min), Calvi (1–3 weekly, 5hr; fast 1 daily except Sat, 2hr 30min) and L'Île Rousse (1–3 weekly; 5hr).

Toulon to: Ajaccio (1–4 weekly; 10hr overnight), Bastia (1–3 weekly; 12hr overnight) or Propriano (1–4 weekly; 8hr).

PART THREE

THE

CONTEXTS

HISTORICAL FRAMEWORK

EARLY CIVILIZATIONS

Traces of human existence are rare in France until about 50,000 BC. Thereafter, beginning with the "Mousterian civilization", they become ever more numerous, with an especially heavy concentration of sites in the Périgord region of the Dordogne. It was here, near the village of Les Eyzies, that remains were discovered of a late Stone Age people, subsequently dubbed "Cro-Magnon". Flourishing from around 25,000 BC, these cave-dwelling hunters seem to have developed quite a sophisticated culture, the evidence of which is preserved in the beautiful paintings and engravings on the walls of the region's caves.

By 10,000 BC human communities had spread out widely across the whole of France. The ice cap receded, the climate became warmer and wetter, and by about 7000 BC **farming and pastoral communities** had begun to develop. By 4500 BC, the first **dolmens** (megalithic stone tombs) showed up in Brittany; around 2000 BC copper made its appearance; and by 1800 BC the **Bronze Age** had arrived in the east and southeast of the country, and trade links had begun with Spain, central Europe and Wessex in Britain.

Significant population shifts occurred, too, at this time. Around 1200 BC the **Champs d'Urnes people**, who buried their dead in sunken urns, began to make incursions from the east. By 900 BC, they had been joined by the

Halstatt **people** who worked with iron and settled in Burgundy, Alsace and Franche-Comté near the principal ore **deposits**. At some point around 450 BC, the first Celts made an appearance in the region.

PRE-ROMAN GAUL

There were about fifteen million people living in **Gaul**, as the Romans called what we know as France (and parts of Belgium), when Julius Cæsar arrived in 58 BC to complete the Roman conquest.

The southern part of this territory – more or less equivalent to modern **Provence** – had been a colony since 118 BC and exposed to the civilizing influences of Italy and Greece for much longer. **Greek colonists** had founded Massalia (Marseille) as far back as 600 BC. But even the inhabitants of the rest of the country, what the Romans called "long-haired Gaul", were far from shaggy barbarians. Though the economy was basically rural, the **Gauls** had established large **hilltop towns** by 100 BC, notably at Bibracte near Autun, where archeologists have identified separate merchants' quarters.

The Gauls had also invented the barrel and soap and were skilful manufacturers. By 500 BC they were capable of making metal-wheeled carts, as was proved by the "chariot tombs" of **Vix**, where a young woman was found buried seated in a cart with its wheels pushed against the wall. She was wearing rich gold jewellery and lying next to Greek vases and Black Figure pottery, dating the burial at around 500 BC and revealing the extent of commercial relations. Interestingly, too, the Gauls' money was based on the gold *staters*, minted by Philip of Macedon.

ROMANIZATION

Gallic **tribal rivalries** made the Romans' job very much easier. And when at last they were able to unite under **Vercingétorix** in 52 BC, the occasion was their total and final defeat by **Julius Cæsar** at the battle of **Alésia**.

This event was one of the major turning points in the history of France. **Roman victory** fixed the frontier between Gaul and the Germanic peoples at the Rhine. It saved Gaul from disintegrating because of internal dissension and made it a Roman province. During the five centuries of peace that followed, the Gauls farmed, manufactured and traded, became urbanized, and educated – and learnt Latin. Roman victory at Alésia laid the foundations of modern French culture and established them firmly enough to survive the centuries of chaos and destruction that followed the collapse of Roman power.

Augustus and **Claudius** were the emperors who set the process of **Romanization** going. Lugdunum (Lyon) was founded as the capital of Roman Gaul as early as 43 BC. Augustus founded numerous other cities – such as Autun, Limoges and Bayeux – built roads, settled Roman colonists on the land and reorganized the entire administration. Gauls were incorporated into the Roman army and given citizenship; Claudius made it possible for them to hold high office and become members of the Roman Senate, blurring the distinction and resentment between colonizer and colonized. Vespasian secured the frontiers beyond the Rhine, thus ensuring a couple of hundred years of peace and economic expansion.

Serious **disruptions** of the Pax Romana only began in the third century AD. Oppressive aristocratic rule and an economic crisis turned the destitute peasantry into gangs of marauding brigands – precursors of the medieval *jacquerie*. But most devastating of all, there began a series of incursions across the Rhine frontier by various restless **Germanic tribes**, the Alemanni and Franks first, who pushed down as far as Spain, ravaging farmland and destroying towns.

In the fourth century the reforms of the emperor **Diocletian** secured some decades of respite from both internal and external pressures. Towns were rebuilt and fortified, an interesting development that foreshadowed feudalism and the independent power of the nobles since, due to the uncertainty of the times, big landed estates or *villae* tended to become more and more self-sufficient – economically, administratively and militarily.

By the fifth century, however, the Germanic invaders were back: **Alans**, **Vandals** and **Suevi**, with **Franks** and **Burgundians** in their wake. While the Roman administration assimilated them as far as possible, granting them land in return for military duties, they gradually achieved independence from the empire. Many Gauls, by now thoroughly Latinized, entered the service of the **Burgundian court of Lyon** or of the **Visigoth kings of Toulouse** as skilled administrators and advisers.

THE FRANKS AND CHARLEMAGNE

By 500 AD, the **Franks**, who gave their name to modern France, had become the dominant invading power. Their most celebrated king, **Clovis**, consolidated his hold on northern France and drove the Visigoths out of the southwest into Spain. In 507 he made the until-then insignificant little trading town of Paris his capital and became a Christian, which inevitably hastened the **Christianization** of Frankish society.

Under the succeeding **Merovingian** – as the dynasty was called – rulers, the kingdom began to disintegrate until in the eighth century the Pepin family, who were the Merovingians' chancellors, began to take effective control. In 732, one of their most dynamic scions, **Charles Martel**, reunited the kingdom and saved western Christendom from the northward expansion of Islam by defeating the Spanish Moors at the **Battle of Poitiers**.

In 754 Charles's son, Pepin, had himself crowned king by the pope, thus inaugurating the **Carolingian dynasty** and establishing for the first time the principle of the divine right of kings. His son was **Charlemagne**, who extended Frankish control over the whole of what had been Roman Gaul, and far beyond. On Christmas Day in 800, he was crowned emperor of the **Holy Roman Empire**, though again, following his death, the kingdom fell apart in squabbles over who was to inherit various parts of his empire. At the Treaty of Verdun in 843, his grandsons agreed on a division of territory that corresponded roughly with the extent of contemporary France and Germany.

Charlemagne's administrative system had involved the royal appointment of counts and bishops to govern the various provinces of the empire. Under the destabilizing attacks of Normans/Norsemen/Vikings during the ninth century, Carolingian kings were obliged to delegate more power and autonomy to these **provincial governors**, whose lands, like **Aquitaine** and **Burgundy**, already had separate regional identities as a result of earlier invasions – the Visigoths in Aquitaine, the Burgundians in Burgundy, for example.

Gradually the power of these governors overshadowed that of the king, whose lands were confined to the Île-de-France. When the last Carolingian died in 987, it was only natural that they should elect one of their own number to take his place. This was Hugues Capet, founder of a dynasty that lasted until 1328.

THE RISE OF THE FRENCH KINGS

The years 1000 to 1500 saw the gradual extension and consolidation of the power of the **French kings**, accompanied by the growth of a centralized administrative system and bureaucracy. These factors also determined their foreign policy, which was chiefly concerned with restricting papal interference in French affairs and checking the English kings' continuing involvement in French territory. While progress towards these goals was remarkably steady and single-minded, there were setbacks, principally in the seesawing fortunes of the conflict with the English.

Surrounded by vassals much stronger than themselves, **Hugues Capet** and his successors remained weak throughout the eleventh century, though they made the most of their feudal rights. As dukes of the French, counts of Paris and anointed kings, they enjoyed a prestige their vassals dared not offend – not least because that would have set a precedent of disobedience for their own lesser vassals.

At the beginning of the twelfth century, having successfully tamed his own vassals in the Île-de-France, Louis VI had a stroke of luck. **Eleanor**, daughter of the powerful Duke of Aquitaine, was left in his care on her father's death, so he promptly married her off to his son, the future Louis VII.

Unfortunately, the marriage ended in divorce and immediately, in 1152, Eleanor married Henry of Normandy, shortly to become **Henry II** of England. Thus the **English** gained control of a huge chunk of French territory, stretching from the Channel to the Pyrenees. Though their fortunes fluctuated over the ensuing three hundred years, the English rulers remained a perpetual thorn in the side of the French kings and a dangerous source of alliance with any rebellious French vassals.

Philippe Auguste (1180–1223) made considerable headway in undermining English rule by exploiting the bitter relations between Henry II and his three sons, one of whom was Richard the Lion-Heart. But he fell out with Richard when they took part in the **Third Crusade**

together. Luckily, Richard died before he was able to claw back Philippe's gains, and by the end of his reign Philippe had recovered all of Normandy and the English possessions north of the Loire.

For the first time, the royal lands were greater than those of any other French lord. The foundations of a systematic administration and civil service had been established in **Paris**, and Philippe had firmly and quietly marked his independence from the papacy by refusing to take any interest in the crusade against the heretic Cathars of Languedoc. When Languedoc and Poitou came under royal control in the reign of his son Louis VIII, France was by far the greatest power in western Europe.

THE HUNDRED YEARS' WAR

In 1328 the Capetian monarchy had its first succession crisis, which led directly to the ruinous **Hundred Years' War** with the English. Charles IV, last of the line, had only daughters as heirs, and when it was decided that France could not be ruled by a queen, the English king, **Edward III**, whose mother was Charles's sister, claimed the throne of France for himself.

The French chose **Philippe, Count of Valois**, instead, and Edward acquiesced for a time. But when Philippe began whittling away at his possessions in Aquitaine, Edward renewed his claim and embarked on war. Though, with its population of about twelve million, France was a far richer and more powerful country, its army was no match for the superior organization and tactics of the English. Edward won an outright victory at **Crécy** in 1346 and seized the port of Calais as a permanent bridgehead. Ten years later, his son, the Black Prince, actually took the French king, Jean le Bon, prisoner at the **Battle of Poitiers**.

Although by 1375 French military fortunes had improved to the point where the English had been forced back to Calais and the Gascon coast, the strains of war and administrative abuses, as well as the madness of Charles VI, caused other kinds of damage. In 1358 there were **insurrections** among the Picardy peasantry (the *Jacquerie*) and among the townspeople of Paris under the leadership of Étienne Marcel. Both were brutally repressed, as were subsequent risings in Paris in 1382 and 1412.

The king's madness led to the formation of two rival factions, after the murder of his brother, the Duke of Orléans, by the Duke of Burgundy. The **Armagnacs** gathered round the young Orléans, and the other faction round the **Burgundians**. Both factions called in the English to help them, and in 1415 Henry V of England inflicted another crushing defeat on the French army at **Agincourt**. The Burgundians seized Paris, took the royal family prisoner and recognized Henry as heir to the French throne. When Charles VI died in 1422, Henry's brother, the Duke of Bedford, took over the government of France north of the Loire, while the young king Charles VII ineffectually governed the south from his refugee capital at Bourges.

At this point **Jeanne d'Arc** arrived on the scene. In 1429 she raised the English siege of the crucial town of Orléans and had Charles crowned at Reims. Joan fell into the hands of the Burgundians, who sold her to the English, resulting in her being tried and burnt as a heretic. But her dynamism and martyrdom raised French morale and tipped the scales against the English: except for a toehold at Calais, they were finally driven from France altogether in 1453.

By the end of the century, **Dauphiné**, **Burgundy**, **Franche-Comté** and **Provence** were under royal control, and an effective standing army had been created. The taxation system had been overhauled, and France had emerged from the Middle Ages a rich, powerful state, firmly under the centralized authority of an absolute monarch.

THE WARS OF RELIGION

After half a century of self-confident but inconclusive pursuit of military glory in Italy, brought to an end by the **Treaty of Cateau-Cambrésis** in 1559, France was plunged into another period of devastating internal conflict. The **Protestant** ideas of Luther and Calvin had gained widespread adherence among all classes of society, despite sporadic brutal attempts by François I and Henri II to stamp them out.

When **Catherine de Médicis**, acting as regent for Henri III, implemented a more tolerant policy, she provoked violent reaction from the ultra-Catholic faction led by the **Guise** family. Their massacre of a Protestant congregation coming out of church in March 1562 began a civil **war of religions** that, interspersed with ineffective truces and accords, lasted for the next thirty years.

Well-organized and well-led by the Prince de Condé and Admiral Coligny, the **Huguenots** – French Protestants – kept their end up very successfully, until Condé was killed at the Battle of Jarnac in 1569. Three years later came one of the blackest events in the memory of French Protestants, even today: the **massacre of St Bartholomew's Day**. Coligny and three thousand Protestants who had gathered in Paris for the wedding of Marguerite, the king's sister, to the Protestant Henri of Navarre were slaughtered at the instigation of the Guises – a bloodbath was repeated across France, especially in the south and west where the Protestants were strongest.

In 1584 the king's son died, leaving his brother-in-law, **Henri of Navarre**, heir to the throne, to the fury of the Guises and their Catholic league, who seized Paris and drove out the king. In retaliation, Henri III murdered the Duc de Guise, and found himself forced into alliance with Henri of Navarre, whom the pope had excommunicated. In 1589 Henri III was himself assassinated, leaving Henri of Navarre to become Henri IV of France. It took another four years of fighting and the abjuration of his faith for the new king to be recognized. "Paris is worth a mass," he is reputed to have said.

Once on the throne Henri IV set about reconstructing and reconciling the nation. By the **Edict of Nantes** of 1598 the Huguenots were accorded freedom of conscience, freedom of worship in certain places, the right to attend the same schools and hold the same offices as Catholics, their own courts and the possession of a number of fortresses as a guarantee against renewed attack, the most important being La Rochelle and Montpellier.

KINGS, CARDINALS AND ABSOLUTE POWER

The main themes of the seventeenth century, when France was ruled by just two kings, **Louis XIII** (1610–43) and **Louis XIV** (1643–1715), were, on the domestic front, the strengthening of the centralized state embodied in the person of the king; and in external affairs, the securing of frontiers in the Pyrenees, on the Rhine and in the north, coupled with the attempt to prevent the unification of the territories of the Habsburg kings of Spain and Austria. Both kings had the good fortune to be served by capable, hardworking ministers dedicated to these objectives.

Louis XIII had **Cardinal Richelieu** and Louis XIV had cardinals **Mazarin** and **Colbert**. Both reigns were disturbed in their early years by the inevitable aristocratic attempts at a coup d'état.

Having crushed revolts by Louis XIII's brother Gaston, Duke of Orléans, **Richelieu**'s commitment to extending royal absolutism brought him into renewed conflict with the Protestants. Believing that their retention of separate fortresses within the kingdom was a threat to security, he attacked and took La Rochelle in 1627. Although he was unable to extirpate their religion altogether, Protestants were never again to present a military threat.

The other important facet of his domestic policy was the promotion of economic self-sufficiency – **mercantilism**. To this end, he encouraged the growth of the luxury craft industries, especially textiles, in which France was to excel right up to the Revolution. He built up the navy and granted privileges to companies involved in establishing **colonies** in North America, Africa and the West Indies.

In pursuing his foreign policy objectives, Richelieu adroitly kept France out of actual military involvement by paying substantial sums to the great Swedish king and general, Gustavus Adolphus, helping him to fund war against the Habsburgs in Germany. When in 1635, the French were finally obliged to commit their own troops, they made significant gains against the Spanish in the Netherlands, Alsace and Lorraine, and won Roussillon for France.

Richelieu died just a few months before Louis XIII in 1642. As Louis XIV was still an infant, his mother, Anne of Austria, acted as regent, served by Richelieu's protégé, **Cardinal Mazarin**, who was hated just as much as his predecessor by the traditional aristocracy and the *parlements*. These unelected bodies, which had the function of high courts and administrative councils, were protective of their privileges and angry that an upstart should receive such preferment. Spurred by these grievances, which were in any case exacerbated by the ruinous cost of the Spanish wars, various groups in French society combined in a series of revolts, known as the **Frondes**.

The first Fronde, in 1648, was led by the *parlement* of Paris, which took up the cause of the hereditary provincial tax-collecting officials – a group that resented the supervisory role of the *intendants*, who had been appointed by the central royal bureaucracy to keep an eye on them. Paris rose in revolt but capitulated at the advance of royal troops. This was quickly followed by an aristocratic Fronde, supported by various peasant risings round the country. These revolts were suppressed easily enough. They were not really revolutionary movements but, rather, the attempts of various groups to preserve their privileges in the face of growing state power.

The economic pressures that contributed to their support were relieved when in 1659 Mazarin successfully brought the Spanish wars to an end with the **Treaty of the Pyrenees**, cemented by the marriage of Louis XIV and the daughter of Philip IV of Spain. On reaching the age of majority in 1661, **Louis XIV** declared that he was going to be his own man and do without a first minister. He proceeded to appoint a number of able ministers, with whose aid he embarked on a long struggle to modernize the administration.

The war ministers, Le Tellier and his son Louvois, provided Louis with a well-equipped and well-trained professional army that could muster some 400,000 men by 1670. But the principal reforms were carried out by **Colbert**, who set about streamlining the state's finances and tackling bureaucratic corruption. Although he was never able to overcome the opposition completely, he did manage to produce a surplus in state revenue. Attempting to compensate for deficiencies in the taxation system by stimulating trade, he set up a free-trade area in northern and central France, continued Richelieu's mercantilist economic policies, established the French East India Company, and built up the navy and merchant fleets with a view to challenging the world commercial supremacy of the Dutch.

These were all policies that the hard-working king was involved in and approved of. But in addition to his love of an extravagant court life at Versailles, which earned him the title of the **Sun King**, he had another obsession, ruinous to the state: the love of a prestigious military victory. There were sound political reasons for the **campaigns** he embarked on, but they did not help balance the budget.

Using his wife's Spanish connection, Louis demanded the cession of certain Spanish provinces in the Low Countries, and then embarked on a war against the Dutch in 1672.

Forced to make peace at the **Treaty of Nijmegen** in 1678 by his arch-enemy, the Protestant William of Orange (later king of England), he nonetheless came out of the war with the annexation to French territory of **Franche-Comté**, plus a number of northern towns. In 1681 he simply grabbed Strasbourg, and got away with it.

In 1685, under the influence of his very Catholic mistress, Madame de Maintenon, the king removed all privileges from the **Huguenots** by revoking the Edict of Nantes. This incensed the Protestant powers, who combined under the auspices of the League of Augsburg. Another long and exhausting war followed, ending, most unfavourably to the French, in the **Peace of Rijswik** (1697).

No sooner was this concluded than Louis became embroiled in the question of who was to succeed the moribund Charles II of Spain. Both Louis and Leopold Habsburg, the Holy Roman Emperor, had married sisters of Charles. The prospect of Leopold acquiring the Spanish Habsburgs' possessions in addition to his own vast lands was not welcome to Louis or any other European power. However, when Charles died and it was discovered that he'd named Louis's grandson, Philippe, as his heir, that was a shift in the balance of power the English, Dutch and Austrians were not prepared to tolerate.

William of Orange, now king of England as well as ruler of the Dutch United Provinces, organized a Grand Alliance against Louis. The so-called **War of Spanish Succession** broke out and it went badly for the French, thanks largely to the brilliant generalship of the Duke of Marlborough. A severe winter in 1709 compounded the hardships with famine and bread riots at home, causing Louis to seek negotiations. The terms were too harsh for him and the war dragged on until 1713, leaving the country totally impoverished. The Sun King went out with scarcely a whimper.

LOUIS XV AND THE PARLEMENTS

While France remained in many ways a prosperous and powerful state, largely because of colonial trade, the tensions between central government and traditional vested interests proved too great to be reconciled.

The *parlement* of Paris became more and more the focus of opposition to the royal will,

eventually bringing the country to a state of virtual ungovernability in the reign of Louis XVI. Meanwhile, the diversity of mutually irreconcilable interests sheltering behind that parliamentary umbrella came more and more to the fore, bringing the country to a climax of tension which would only be resolved in the turmoil of **Revolution**.

The next king, **Louis XV**, was two when his great-grandfather died. During the **Regency**, the traditional aristocracy and the *parlements*, who for different reasons hated Louis XIV's advisors, scrabbled – successfully – to recover a lot of their lost power and prestige. An experiment with government by aristocratic councils failed, and attempts to absorb the immense national debt by selling shares in an overseas trading company ended in a huge collapse. When the prudent and reasonable **Cardinal Fleury** came to prominence upon the regent's death in 1726, the nation's lot began to improve. The Atlantic seaboard towns grew rich on trade with the American and Caribbean colonies, though industrial production did not improve much and the disparity in wealth between the countryside and the growing towns continued to grow.

In the mid-century there followed more disastrous military ventures, including the **War of Austrian Succession** and the **Seven Years' War**, both of which were in effect contests with England for control of the colonial territories in America and India, contests that France lost. The need to finance the wars led to the introduction of a new tax, the Twentieth, which was to be levied on everyone. The *parlement*, which had successfully opposed earlier taxation and fought the crown over its religious policies, dug its heels in again. This led to renewed conflict over Louis' pro-Jesuit religious policy. The Paris *parlement* staged a strike, was exiled from Paris, then inevitably reinstated. Disputes about its role continued until the *parlement* of Paris was actually abolished in 1771, to the outrage of the privileged groups in society, which considered it the defender of their special interests.

The division between the *parlements* and the king and his ministers continued to sharpen during the reign of **Louis XVI**, which began in 1774. Attempts by the enlightened finance minister Turgot to co-operate with the *parlements* and introduce reforms to alleviate the tax burden on the poor produced only short-term results. The national debt trebled between 1774 and 1787. Ironically, the one radical attempt to introduce an effective and equitable tax system led directly to the Revolution. Calonne, finance minister in 1786, tried to get his proposed tax approved by an **Assembly of Notables**, a device that had not been employed for more than a hundred years. His purpose was to bypass the *parlement*, which could be relied on to oppose any radical proposal. The attempt backfired. He lost his position, and the *parlement* ended up demanding a meeting of the **Estates-General**, representing the nobles, the clergy and the bourgeoisie, as being the only body competent to discuss such matters. The town responded by exiling and then recalling the *parlement* of Paris several times. As law and order began to break down, it gave in and agreed to summon the Estates-General on May 17, 1789.

REVOLUTION

Against a background of deepening economic crisis and general misery, exacerbated by the catastrophic harvest of 1788, controversy focused on how the **Estates-General** should be constituted. Should they meet separately as on the last occasion – in 1614? This was the solution favoured by the *parlement* of Paris, a measure of its reactionary nature: separate meetings would make it easy for the privileged, namely the clergy and nobility, to outvote the **Third Estate**, the bourgeoisie. The king ruled that they should hold a joint meeting, with the Third Estate represented by as many deputies as the other two Estates combined, but no decisions were made about the order of voting.

On June 17, 1789, the Third Estate seized the initiative and declared itself the National Assembly. Some of the lower clergy and liberal nobility joined them. Louis XVI appeared to accept the situation, and on July 9 the Assembly declared itself the National Constituent Assembly. However, the king then tried to intimidate it by calling in troops, which unleashed the anger of the people of Paris, the *sans-culottes* (literally, "without trousers").

On July 14 the *sans-culottes* stormed the fortress of the **Bastille**, symbol of the oppressive nature of the *ancien régime*. Similar insurrections occurred throughout the country, accompanied by widespread peasant attacks on landowners' châteaux and the destruction of records of debt and other symbols of their oppression. On the night of August 4, the Assembly abolished the feudal rights and privileges of the nobility – a momentous shift of gear in the Revolutionary process, although in reality it did little to alter the situation. Later that month they adopted the **Declaration of the Rights of Man**. In December church lands were nationalized, and the pope retaliated by declaring the Revolutionary principles impious.

Bourgeois elements in the Assembly tried to bring about a compromise with the nobility, with a view to establishing a constitutional monarchy, but these overtures were rebuffed. Émigré aristocrats were already working to bring about foreign invasion to overthrow the Revolution. In June 1791 the king was arrested trying to escape from Paris. The Assembly, following an initiative of the wealthier bourgeois **Girondin** faction, decided to go to war to protect the Revolution.

On August 10, 1792, the *sans-culottes* set up a **revolutionary Commune** in Paris and imprisoned the king. The Revolution was taking a radical turn. A new National Convention was elected and met on the day the ill-prepared Revolutionary armies finally halted the Prussian invasion at Valmy. A major rift swiftly developed between the **Girondins** and the **Jacobins** and *sans-culottes* over the abolition of the monarchy. The radicals carried the day. In January 1793, Louis XVI was executed. By June the Girondins had been ousted.

Counter-revolutionary forces were gathering in the provinces and abroad. A Committee of Public Safety was set up as chief organ of the government. Left-wing popular pressure brought laws on general conscription and price controls and a deliberate policy of de-Christianization. **Robespierre** was pressed onto the Committee as the best man to contain the pressure from the streets.

The **Terror** began. As well as ordering the death of the hated Marie-Antoinette, Robespierre felt strong enough to guillotine his opponents on both Right and Left. But the effect of so many rolling heads was to cool people's faith in the Revolution; by mid-1794, Robespierre himself was arrested and executed, and his fall marked the end of radicalism. More conservative forces gained control of the government, decontrolled the economy, repressed popular risings, limited the suffrage, and established a five-man executive Directory (1795).

THE RISE OF NAPOLÉON

In 1799, one **General Napoléon Bonaparte**, who had made a name for himself as commander of the Revolutionary armies in Italy and Egypt, returned to France and took power in a coup d'état. He was appointed First Consul, with power to choose officials and initiate legislation. He redesigned the tax system and created the Bank of France, replaced the power of local institutions by a corps of *préfets* answerable to himself, made judges into state functionaries – in short, laid the foundations of the modern French administrative system.

Though Napoléon upheld the fundamental reforms of the Revolution, the retrograde nature of his regime became more and more apparent with the proscription of the Jacobins, granting of amnesty to the émigrés and restoration of their unsold property, reintroduction of slavery in the colonies, recognition of the Church and so on. Although alarmingly revolutionary in the eyes of the rest of Europe, his Civil Code worked essentially to the advantage of the bourgeoisie. In 1804 he crowned himself **emperor** in the presence of the pope.

Decline, however, came only with military failure. After 1808, Spain – under the rule of Napoléon's brother – rose in revolt, aided by the British. This signalled a turning of the tide in the long series of dazzling military successes. The nation began to grow weary of the burden of unceasing war.

In 1812, Napoléon threw himself into the **Russian campaign**, hoping to complete his European conquests. He reached Moscow, but the long retreat in terrible winter conditions annihilated his veteran Grande Armée. By 1814, he was forced to abdicate by a coalition of European powers, who installed **Louis XVIII**, brother of the decapitated Louis XVI, as monarch. In a last effort to recapture power, Napoléon escaped from exile in Elba and reorganized his armies, only to meet final defeat at **Waterloo** on June 18, 1815. Louis XVIII was restored to power.

THE RESTORATION AND 1830 REVOLUTION

The years following Napoléon's downfall were marked by a determined campaign, including the **White Terror**, on the part of those reactionary elements who wanted to wipe out all trace of the Revolution and restore the *ancien*

régime. **Louis XVIII** resisted these moves and was able to appoint a moderate royalist minister, Decazes, under whose leadership the liberal faction that wished to preserve the Revolutionary reforms made steady gains. This process, however, was wrecked by the assassination of the Duc de Berry in an attempt to wipe out the Bourbon family. In response to reactionary outrage, the king dismissed Decazes. An attempted liberal insurrection was crushed and the four Sergeants of La Rochelle were shot by firing squad. Censorship became more rigid and education was once more subjected to the authority of the Church.

In 1824, Louis was succeeded by the thoroughly reactionary **Charles X**, who pushed through a law indemnifying émigré aristocrats for property lost during the Revolution. When the opposition won a majority in the elections of 1830, the king dissolved the Chamber and restricted the already narrow suffrage.

Barricades went up in the streets of Paris. Charles X abdicated and parliament was persuaded to accept **Louis-Philippe**, Duc d'Orléans, as king. On the face of it, divine right had been superseded by popular sovereignty as the basis of political legitimacy. The **1814 Charter**, which upheld Revolutionary and Napoleonic reforms, was retained, censorship abolished, the tricolour restored as the national flag, and suffrage widened.

However, the **Citizen King**, as he was called, had somewhat more absolutist notions about being a monarch. In the 1830s his regime survived repeated challenges from both attempted coups by reactionaries and some serious labour unrest in Lyon and Paris. The 1840s were calmer under the ministry of Guizot, the first Protestant to hold high office. It was at this time that **Algeria** was colonized.

Guizot, however, was not popular. He resisted attempts to extend the vote to enfranchise the middle ranks of the bourgeoisie. In 1846, economic crisis brought bankruptcies, unemployment and food shortages. Conditions were appalling for the growing urban working class, whose hopes of a more just future received a theoretical basis in the **socialist writings** and activities of Blanqui, Fourier, Louis Blanc and Proudhon, among others.

When the government banned an opposition *banquet*, the only permissible form of political meeting, in February 1848, workers and students took to the streets. When the army fired on a demonstration and killed forty people, civil war appeared imminent. The Citizen King fled to England.

THE SECOND REPUBLIC

A provisional government was set up and a **republic** proclaimed. The government issued a right-to-work declaration and set up national workshops to relieve unemployment. The vote was extended to all adult males – an unprecedented move for its time.

All was not plain sailing, though. By the time elections were held in April, a new tax designed to ameliorate the financial crisis had antagonized the countryside. A massive conservative majority was re-elected, to the dismay of the radicals. Three days of bloody street fighting at the barricades followed, when General Cavaignac, who had distinguished himself in the suppression of Algerian resistance, turned the artillery on the workers. More than 1500 were killed and 12,000 arrested and exiled.

A reasonably democratic constitution was drawn up and elections called to choose a president. To everyone's surprise, Louis-Napoléon, nephew of the emperor, romped home. In spite of his liberal reputation, he restricted the vote again, censored the press and pandered to the Catholic Church. In 1852, following a coup and further street fighting, he had himself proclaimed Emperor Napoléon III.

NAPOLÉON III AND THE COMMUNE

Through the 1850s, **Napoléon III** ran an authoritarian regime whose most notable achievement was a rapid growth in industrial and economic power. Foreign trade trebled, the rail system grew enormously, and the first investment banks were established. In 1858, in the aftermath of an attempt on his life by an Italian patriot, the emperor suddenly embarked on a policy of **liberalization**, initially of the economy, which alienated much of the business class. Reforms included the right to form trade unions and to strike, an extension of public education, lifting of censorship, and the granting of ministerial "responsibility" under a government headed by the liberal opposition.

Disaster, however, was approaching in the shape of the **Franco-Prussian** war. Involved in

a conflict with Bismarck and the rising power of Germany, Napoléon III declared war. The French army was quickly defeated and the emperor himself taken prisoner in 1870. The result at home was a universal demand for the proclamation of a **third republic**. The German armistice agreement insisted on the election of a national assembly to negotiate a proper peace treaty. France lost Alsace and Lorraine and was obliged to pay hefty war reparations.

Outraged by the monarchist majority re-elected to the new Assembly and by the attempt of its chief minister, Thiers, to disarm the National Guard, the people of Paris created their own municipal government known as the **Commune** (see "Paris" chapter).

THE THIRD REPUBLIC

In 1889, the collapse of a company set up to build the Panama Canal involved several members of the government in a corruption scandal, which was one factor in the dramatic **Socialist gains** in the elections of 1893. More importantly, the urban working class was becoming more class-conscious under the influence of the ideas of Karl Marx. The strength of the movement, however, was undermined by divisions, the chief one being Jules Guesde's Marxian Party. Among the independent Socialists was **Jean Jaurès**, who joined with Guesde in 1905 to found the **Parti Socialiste**. The trade union movement, unified in 1895 as the **Confédération Générale du Travail** (CGT), remained aloof in its anarcho-syndicalist preference for direct action.

In 1894, **Captain Dreyfus**, a Jewish army officer, was convicted by court martial of spying for the Germans and shipped off to the penal colony of Devil's Island for life. It soon became clear that he had been framed – by the army itself – yet they refused to reconsider his case. The affair immediately became an issue between the Catholic Right and the Republican Left, with Jaurès, Émile Zola and Clemenceau coming out in favour of Dreyfus. Charles Maurras, founder of the fascist Action Française – precursor of Europe's Blackshirts – took the part of the army.

Dreyfus was officially rehabilitated in 1904, his health ruined by penal servitude in the tropics. But in the wake of the affair the more radical element in the Republican movement had begun to dominate the administration, bringing the army under closer civilian control and dissolving most of the religious orders.

The country enjoyed a period of renewed prosperity in the years preceding World War I, yet there remained serious unresolved conflicts in the political fabric of French society. On the Right was Maurras's lunatic fringe with its strong-arm Camelots du Roi, and on the Left, the far bigger constituency of the working class – unrepresented in government. Although most workers now voted for it, the Socialist Party was not permitted to participate in bourgeois governments under the constitution of the Second International, to which it belonged. Several major strikes were brutally suppressed.

WORLD WAR I

With the outbreak of **World War I** in 1914, France found itself swiftly overrun by Germany and its allies, and defended by its old enemy, Britain. At home, the hitherto anti-militarist trade union and Socialist leaders (Jaurès was assassinated in 1914) rallied to the flag and to the forces.

The cost of the war was even greater for France than for the other participants because it was fought largely on French soil. Over a quarter of the eight million men called up were either killed or crippled; industrial production fell to sixty percent of the prewar level. This – along with memories of the Franco-Prussian war of 1870 – was the reason that the French were more aggressive than either the British or the Americans in seeking war reparations from the Germans.

In the **postwar struggle for recovery** the interests of the urban working class were again passed over, save for Clemenceau's eight-hour-day legislation in 1919. An attempted general strike in 1920 came to nothing, and the workers' strength was again undermined by the formation of new Catholic and Communist unions, and most of all by the irreversible split in the Socialist Party at the 1920 Congress of Tours. The pro-Lenin majority formed the **French Communist Party**, while the minority faction, under the leadership of Léon Blum, retained the old SFIO title. The bitterness caused by this split has bedevilled the French Left ever since. Both parties resolutely stayed away from government.

As the **Depression** deepened in the 1930s and Nazi power across the Rhine became more menacing, fascist thuggery and anti-parliamen-

tary activity increased in France, culminating in a pitched battle outside the Chamber of Deputies in February 1934. The effect of this fascist activism was to unite the Left, including the Communists led by the Stalinist Maurice Thorez, in the **Front Populaire**. When they won the 1936 elections with a handsome majority in the Chamber, there followed a wave of strikes and factory sit-ins – a spontaneous expression of working-class determination to get their just deserts after a century and a half of frustration.

Frightened by the apparently revolutionary situation, the major employers signed the **Matignon Agreement** with Blum, which provided for wage increases, nationalization of the armaments industry and partial nationalization of the Bank of France, a forty-hour week, paid annual leave, and collective bargaining on wages. These **reforms** were pushed through parliament, but when Blum tried to introduce exchange controls to check the flight of capital, the Senate threw the proposal out and he resigned. The Left remained out of power, with the exception of coalition governments, until 1981. Most of the Front Populaire's reforms were promptly undone.

WORLD WAR II

The agonies of **World War II** were compounded for France by the additional traumas of **occupation, collaboration and Resistance** – in effect, a civil war.

After the 1940 defeat of the Anglo-French forces in France, **Maréchal Pétain**, a cautious and conservative veteran of World War I, emerged from retirement to sign an armistice with Hitler and head the collaborationist **Vichy government**, which ostensibly governed the southern part of the country, while the Germans occupied the strategic north and the Atlantic coast. Pétain's prime minister, Laval, believed it his duty to adapt France to the new authoritarian age heralded by the Nazi conquest of Europe.

There has been endless controversy over who collaborated, how much and how far it was necessary in order to save France from even worse sufferings. One thing at least is clear: Nazi occupation provided a good opportunity for the Maurras breed of out-and-out French fascist to go on the rampage, tracking down Communists, Jews, Resistance fighters, freemasons – indeed all those who, in their demonology, were considered "alien" bodies in French society.

While some Communists were involved in the **Resistance** right from the start, Hitler's attack on the Soviet Union in 1941 freed the remainder from ideological inhibitions and brought them into the movement on a large scale. Resistance numbers were further increased by young men taking to the hills to escape conscription as labour in Nazi industry. Général de Gaulle's radio appeal from London on June 18, 1940, rallied the French opposed to right-wing defeatism and resulted in the Conseil National de la Résistance, unifying the different Resistance groups in May 1943. The man to whom this task had been entrusted was Jean Moulin, shortly to be captured by the Gestapo and tortured to death by Klaus Barbie, who was convicted as recently as 1987 for his war crimes.

Although British and American governments found him irksome, **de Gaulle** was able to impose himself as the unchallenged spokesman of the Free French, leader of a government in exile, and to insist that the voice of France be heard as an equal in the Allied councils of war. Even the Communists accepted his leadership, though he was far from representing the kind of political interests with which they could sympathize.

Thanks, however, to his persistence, representatives of his provisional government moved into liberated areas of France behind the Allied advance after D-day, thereby saving the country from what would certainly have been at least localized outbreaks of civil war. It was also thanks to his insistence that Free French units, notably General Leclerc's Second Armoured Division, were allowed to perform the psychologically vital role of being the first Allied troops to enter Paris, Strasbourg and other emotionally significant towns in France.

THE AFTERMATH OF WAR

France emerged from the war demoralized, bankrupt and bomb-wrecked. The only possible provisional government in the circumstances was de Gaulle's **Free French** and the Conseil National de la Résistance, which meant a coalition of Left and Right. As an opening move to deal with the shambles, coal-mines, air transport and Renault cars were nationalized. But a new constitution was required and **elections**,

in which French women voted for the first time, resulted in a large Left majority in the new Constituent Assembly – which, however, soon fell to squabbling over the form of the new constitution. De Gaulle resigned in disgust. If he was hoping for a wave of popular sympathy, he didn't get it.

The constitution finally agreed on, with little enthusiasm in the country, was not much different from the discredited Third Republic. And the new **Fourth Republic** appropriately began its life with a series of short-lived coalitions. In the early days the foundations for welfare were laid, banks nationalized and trade union rights extended. With the exclusion of the Communists from the government in 1947, however, thanks to the Cold War and the carrot of American aid under the Marshall Plan, France found itself once more dominated by the Right.

If the post-Liberation desire for political reform was quickly frustrated, the spirit that inspired it did bear fruit in other spheres. From being a rather backward and largely agricultural economy prewar, France in the 1950s achieved enormous industrial **modernization and expansion**, its growth rate even rivalling that of West Germany at times. In foreign policy France opted to remain in the US fold, but at the same time took the initiative in promoting closer **European integration**, first through the European Coal and Steel community and then, in 1957, through the creation of the European Economic Community.

COLONIAL WARS

In its **colonial policy**, on the other hand, the Fourth Republic seemed firmly committed to nineteenth-century imperialism, despite the cosmetic reform of renaming the Empire the French Union.

On the surrender of Japan to the Allies in 1945, **Vietnam**, the north half of the French Indochina colony, came under the control of Ho Chi Minh and his Communist organization Vietminh. Attempts to negotiate were bungled and there began an eight-year armed struggle which ended with French defeat at Dien Bien Phu and partition of the country at the Geneva Conference in 1954 – at which point the Americans took over in the south, with well-known consequences.

In that year the government decided to create an **independent nuclear arsenal** and got embroiled in the **Algerian war of liberation**. If you want to take a charitable view, you can say that the situation was complicated from the French viewpoint by the legal fiction that Algeria was a *département*, an integral part of France, and by the fact that there were a million or so settlers or *pieds noirs* claiming to be French, plus there was oil in the south. But by 1958, half a million troops, most of them conscripts, had been committed to the war, with all the attendant horrors of torture, massacre of civilian populations and so forth.

When it began to seem in 1958 that the government would take a more liberal line towards Algeria, the hard-line Rightists among the settlers and in the army staged a putsch and threatened to declare war on France. Général de Gaulle, waiting in the wings to resume his mission to save France, let it be known that in its hour of need and with certain conditions – ie stronger powers for the president – the country might call upon his help. Thus, on June 1, 1958, the National Assembly voted him full powers for six months and the Fourth Republic came to an end.

DE GAULLE'S PRESIDENCY

As prime minister, then president of the **Fifth Republic** – with powers as much strengthened as he had wished – **de Gaulle** wheeled and dealed with the *pieds noirs* and Algerian rebels, while the war continued. In 1961, a General Salan staged a military revolt and set up the OAS (secret army) organization to prevent a settlement. When his coup failed, his organization made several attempts on de Gaulle's life – thereby strengthening the feeling on the mainland that it was time to be done with Algeria.

An episode in the same year – covered up and censored until the 1990s – when between seventy and two hundred French Algerians were killed by the police in Paris, reinforced this feeling. This "secret massacre" began with a peaceful demonstration in protest against police powers to impose a curfew on any place in France frequented by North Africans. The police, it seems, went mad – shooting at crowds, batoning protesters and then throwing their bodies into the Seine. For weeks corpses were recovered, but the French media remained silent.

Eventually in 1962, a referendum gave an overwhelming yes to **Algerian independence**,

and *pieds noirs* refugees flooded into France. Most of the rest of the French colonial empire had achieved independence by this time also, and the succeeding years were to see a resurgence of fascist and racist activity, both among the French "returnees" and the usual insular, anti-immigrant sectors. From the mid-1950s to the mid-1970s a French labour shortage led to massive recruitment campaigns for workers in North Africa, Portugal, Spain, Italy and Greece. People were promised housing, free medical care, trips home and well-paid jobs. When they arrived in France, however, these **immigrants** found themselves paid half as much as their French co-workers, accommodated in prison-style hostels, and sometimes poorer than they had been at home. They had no vote, no automatic permit renewal, were subject to frequent racial abuse and assault and were forbidden to form their own organizations.

De Gaulle's leadership was haughty and autocratic in style, more concerned with *gloire* and grandeur than the everyday problems of ordinary lives. His quirky strutting on the world stage greatly irritated France's partners. He blocked British entry to the EC, cultivated the friendship of the Germans, rebuked the US for its imperialist policies in Vietnam, withdrew from NATO, refused to sign a nuclear test ban treaty, and called for a "free Québec". If this projection of French influence pleased some, the very narrowly won presidential election of 1965 (in which Mitterrand was his opponent) showed that a good half of French voters would not be sorry to see the last of the general.

MAY 1968

Notwithstanding a certain domestic discontent, the sudden explosion of **May 1968** took everyone by surprise. Beginning with protests against the paternalistic nature of the education system by students at the University of Nanterre, the movement of revolt rapidly spread to the Sorbonne and out into factories and offices.

On the night of May 10, barricades went up in the streets of the Quartier Latin in Paris, and the CRS (riot police) responded by wading into everyone, including bystanders and Red Cross volunteers, with unbelievable ferocity. A **general strike** followed, and within a week more than a million people were out, with many factory occupations and professionals joining in with journalists striking for freedom of expression, doctors setting up new radically organized practices and so forth.

Autogestion – workers' participation – was the dominant slogan. More than specific demands for reform, there was a general feeling that all French institutions needed overhauling: they were too rigid, too hierarchical and too elitist.

De Gaulle seemed to lose his nerve and on May 27 he vanished from the scene. It turned out he had gone to assure himself of the support of the commander of the French army of the Rhine. On his return he appealed to the nation to elect him as the only effective barrier against left-wing dictatorship, and dissolved parliament. The frightened silent majority voted massively in his favour.

Although there were few short-term radical changes (except in education), the shock waves of May 1968 continued to be felt over the next two decades. Women's liberation, ecology groups, a relaxing of the formality of French society, a lessening of authoritarianism – all these can be traced to the heady days of May.

POMPIDOU AND GISCARD D'ESTAING

Having petulantly staked his presidency on the outcome of yet another referendum (on a couple of constitutional amendments) and lost, de Gaulle once more took himself off to his country estate and retirement. He was succeeded as president by his business-orientated former prime minister, **Georges Pompidou**.

The new regime was devotedly capitalist. Pompidou hoped to eradicate the memory of 1968 in the creation of wealth, property and competition. His visions, however, had little time to reach reality. Having survived an election in 1972, Pompidou died, suddenly. His successor – and the 1974 presidential election winner by a narrow margin over the socialist François Mitterrand – was the former finance minister **Valéry Giscard d'Estaing**.

Having announced that his aim was to make France "an advanced liberal society", Giscard opened his term of office with some spectacular media coups, inviting Parisian trash collectors to breakfast, visiting prisons in Lyon, and addressing the nation on television from his living-room every evening. But, aside from reducing the voting age to 18 and liberalizing divorce laws, the advanced liberal society did not make

a lot of progress. In the wake of the 1974 oil crisis the government introduced economic austerity measures. Giscard fell out with his ambitious prime minister, **Jacques Chirac**, who set out to challenge the leadership with his own RPR Gaullist party. And in addition to his superior, monarchical style, Giscard further compromised his popularity by accepting diamonds from the (literally) child-eating emperor of the Central African Republic, Bokassa, and by involvement in various other scandals.

The Left seemed well placed to win the coming 1978 elections, when the fragile union between the Socialists and Communists cracked, the latter fearing their roles as the coalition's junior partners. The result was another right-wing victory, with Giscard able to form a new government, with the grudging support of the RPR. Law and order and immigrant controls were the dominant features of Giscard's second term.

THE MITTERRAND ERA, 1981–95

When **François Mitterrand** won the presidential elections over Giscard in 1981, he embodied all the hopes of a generation of Socialists who had never seen their party in power. Headed by **Pierre Mauroy** as prime minister and including four Communist ministers, the **Socialists'** first government after 23 years in opposition started off bright, popular and optimistic. It was committed to an increase in state control over industry, high taxation for the rich, more power to local government, a public spending programme to raise the living standards of the least well-off, and support for liberation struggles around the world. For Mitterrand, European integration was of great importance - France was after all, one of the founder members of the EEC - but was a primarily political rather than economic project, to ensure peace and security and to create a counterweight to American hegemony. By 1984, however, the flight of capital, inflation and budget deficits had forced a complete volte-face. The new prime minister, **Laurent Fabius**, presided over a cabinet of centrist to conservative "socialist" ministers, clinging desperately to power. Their 1986 election slogan was "Help – the Right is coming back", a bizarrely self-fulfilling message.

The Socialist government had lifted the ban on immigrants forming their own organizations, given a ten-year automatic renewal of permits and even promised voting rights. Able to organize for the first time, immigrant workers staged protests at the racist basis of lay-offs in the major industries. The Front National responded with the age-old bogey of foreigners taking jobs from the French; the Gaullists joined in with the spectre of falling birth rates (a French obsession since 1945); and both benefited in the 1986 elections. With a clear right-wing majority in parliament, Mitterrand appointed **Jacques Chirac** as prime minister, so beginning **cohabitation** – the head of state

and head of government belonging to opposite sides of the political fence.

Although throughout 1987 the chances of Mitterrand's winning the presidential election in 1988 seemed very slim, Chirac's economic policies of **privatization** and monetary control failed to deliver the goods. He not only reversed the preceding Socialists' nationalizations, but also sold off banks and industries that de Gaulle had taken into the public sector after 1945. Unemployment rose steadily, and Chirac made the fatal mistake of flirting with the extreme Right.

PARTIES AND POLITICIANS

ON THE LEFT

PS (Parti Socialiste). The Socialist Party to which **François Mitterrand** belonged but whose difficulties he chose to ignore during the *cohabitation* years. After an all-time electoral low in 1993 the party's fortunes were restored by **Lionel Jospin**'s creditable vote in the 1995 presidentials, several by-election successes and victory in the 1997 parliamentary elections. Key figures include **Michel Rocard** (prime minister 1988–91 and party leader until forced to resign in 1994), a libertarian social democrat, strong on individual rights and responsibilities, decentralization and workers' participation in management; **Laurent Fabius** (prime minister 1984–86), leader of the parliamentary group; and **Martine Aubry** (currently Minister of Employment), daughter of **Jacques Delors**, who is seen as a possible future first woman president. The current Socialist government is characterized by a strong female presence, with other important ministers being **Elisabeth Guigou** (Minister of Justice) and **Catherine Trautmann** (Minister of Culture). The left wing of the party has favoured a coalition with the Greens, Communists and small left-wing groupings like the Mouvement des Radicaux de Gauche (MRG) and the Mouvement des Citoyens (MDC) led by former Socialist **Jean-Pierre Chevènement**, who resigned as defence minister in protest at the Gulf War. With the two right-wing parties always operating a parliamentary coalition, a majority for the PS alone is almost impossible.

PCF (Parti Communiste Français). The veteran Stalinist leader **Georges Marchais** was succeeded by **Robert Hue** as party leader in 1994. Hue has proposed a new broad coalition

with progressive Greens, Socialists, community groups, churches, etc, which constitutes a big break from the old line, but has come too late to get very far. The PCF remains influential within the trade union movement and in local government. It is now also in the left-wing coalition government and is softening its anti-Europe stance.

Lutte Ouvrière. Trotskyist party whose presidential candidate **Arlette Laguillier** has stood in every contest since 1974 (with an identical workers' revolutionary programme). In 1995 she was credited with being the only honest candidate and won five percent of the vote in the first round, her highest ever score.

ON THE RIGHT

UDF (Union pour la Démocratie Française). Confederation of centre-right parties in alliance with the RPR (see below) created by aloof, aristocratic **Valéry Giscard d'Estaing**, French president 1974–1981. In 1995, members split their support between Balladur and Chirac and were then embroiled in a bitter leadership battle after Giscard stepped down in 1996. **François Léotard**, culture minister under Chirac and defence minister under Balladur (despite charges of corruption), is now the leader. **Raymond Barre**, mayor of Lyon and prime minister under Giscard, is an old stalwart who may yet return to high office. However, in the 1997 elections, they only got one of their lowest scores of 108 seats.

PR (Parti Républicain). Part of the UDF, though some members want to form their own independent group. Key figures are Léotard (see above), who supported Balladur in the presidentials, and his rival for the UDF leadership, **Alain Madelin**,

As prime minister, Chirac instituted a series of **anti-immigration laws** that were jointly condemned by the Archbishop of Lyon and the head of the Muslim Institute in Paris. Several leading politicians in the government's coalition partners, among them **Simone Weil**, a concentration-camp survivor, denounced Chirac's concessions to Le Pen and human rights groups. Churches and trade unions joined immigrants' groups in saying that France was on its way to becoming a police state. Mitterrand, the grand old man of politics, with decades of experience, played off all the group-

ings of the Right in an all-but-flawless campaign, and won another mandate.

Mitterrand's party, however, failed to win an absolute majority in the parliamentary elections soon afterwards. The austerity measures of his new prime minister, **Michel Rocard**, upset traditional Socialist supporters in the public-service sector. He ruled out renationalization and allowed partial privatizations. Subsidies to large state-owned firms continued, but there was no coherent industrial strategy. Though Chirac's programmes were halted, they were not reversed. Strikes failed to halt

the finance minister sacked by Juppé, who headed the pro-Chirac camp.

RPR (Rassemblement pour la République). Gaullist, conservative party headed by **Jacques Chirac**, mayor of Paris 1977–95, prime minister 1974–76 and 1986–88, and now president. **Edouard Balladur**, prime minister 1993–95, stood against Chirac in the presidentials. Chirac then appointed **Alain Juppé** as prime minister. Two key rivals to Juppé, both right-wing Eurosceptics, are **Phillipe Séguin**, Speaker of the French Parliament, and **Charles Pasqua**, home affairs minister under Chirac and Balladur. Nicolas **Sarkozy**, former spokesman and current secretary-general of the party is the most influential of the up-and-coming younger generation.

Philippe de Villiers A Catholic aristocrat and former Gaullist who campaigned against Europe with industrialist James Goldsmith and won 12 percent of the vote in the 1994 Euro elections.

FN (Front National). Extreme Right party led by nationalist and racist **Jean-Marie Le Pen**. Policies include: "Preference for the French" (meaning the ethnically French); expulsion of immigrants; greater police powers and resources; tougher sentences and the restoration of the death penalty; outlawing of abortion (for ethnically French women); higher defence spending; no European integration, lower taxation, a higher minimum wage and less state interference in family and business life; and proportional representation for parliamentary elections (the electoral system was changed after the 1986 elections to rid parliament of the 35 FN deputés). With strong working-class support, it has eleven MEPs, several hundred local councillors and can count on 13–15 percent of the vote and up to 45 percent or more support for its anti-immigration pronouncements. Key figures include Le Pen's deputy **Bruno Mégret**, and **Jean-Pierre**

Stirbois, chief racist ideologue. Le Pen has been stripped of his civic rights for two years following his assault of a female Socialist candidate.

GREEN PARTIES

The environmental movement in France is patchy and divided, with the strongest support in Alsace, Brittany and Corsica. Though represented at, and good at campaigning on, a local level – against roads, protecting national parks, pollution control in cities, etc – they tend not to take on national issues such as **nuclear power**. With 70 percent of its energy produced by nuclear power (and 15 percent from hydro-power), France scores very well on global-warming pollutants, yet there is very little opposition to the nuclear industry, and a strong belief that French farming is clean and the French countryside unthreatened. The Greens did succeed in obtaining seven seats in the 1997 elections, and Green thinking has made some inroads into public consciousness, but ecology is not a national preoccupation. There are five splintered Green parties, of which the following are the main players:

GE (Génération Écologie). Aims to get environmental issues on the main political parties' agendas and is led by **Brice Lalonde**, who served in the Socialist government of 1988–91 as environment minister but switched allegiance in 1993 and supported Chirac for president in 1995.

Les Verts. A more purist Green party with no leader as such. Put up shared candidates with GE in the 1993 parliamentary elections but with very disappointing results. Despite this, the separatist line of 1988 presidential candidate and MEP **André Waechter** was subsequently overturned. **Dominique Voynet** was the Greens' 1995 presidential candidate, scoring an unspectacular 3.3 percent.

lay-offs in the mines, shipyards, transport and the denationalized industries.

On returning to power, the Socialists also played electoral games with the immigration issue, reneged on the vote promise, and failed to tackle the social and economic deprivation of France's immigrant ghettos. Polls showed over two-thirds of the adult French population to be in favour of deporting legal immigrants for any criminal offence or for being unemployed for over a year. Le Pen's proposals that immigrants should have second-class citizenship, segregated education and separate social security also received widespread support.

The 1980s ended with the most absurd blow-out of public funds ever – the **Bicentennial celebrations of the French Revolution**. They symbolized a culture industry spinning mindlessly around the vacuum at the centre of the French vision for the future. And they highlighted the contrast between the unemployed and homeless begging on the streets and the limitless cash available for prestige projects.

In 1991, Mitterrand sacked Michel Rocard and appointed **Édith Cresson** as France's first woman prime minister. Her brand of left-wing nationalist rhetoric combined with centrist pragmatism made her highly unpopular at home and abroad. Furthermore, she jumped on the rampant racism bandwagon, and said special planes should be chartered to deport illegal immigrants. Kofi Yamgname, the minister for integration and only black member of the Socialist cabinet, suggested that immigrants who maintained traditional habits should go home. In 1992 the International Federation of Human Rights published a highly critical report on racism in the **French police** force and said France "was not the home of human rights".

Ironically, throughout the postwar years, France has maintained an independent and nationalist-orientated **foreign policy**, presenting its stance as a combination of French prestige and promotion of *liberté*, *égalité* and *fraternité*. In **major conflicts** France always tries to play a key role (and, as one of the five permanent members of the UN Security Council, it gets a say). However, high-profile diplomacy has given way to unprestigious military action, as in the **Gulf War** when the small French force was under American command. Mitterrand's visit, under gunfire, to Sarajevo in July 1992 was universally applauded, yet at the same time the French were reluctant to commit troops for UN actions in **former Yugoslavia**.

The important **Maastricht referendum,** held in 1992, split the Right and widened the gulf between the Socialists and Communists. Only the extreme end of the political spectrum, the Communists and the Front National remained determinedly anti-Europe. The voters divided along the lines of the poorer rural areas voting "No" and the rich urbanites voting "Yes". The very narrow margin in favour was a considerable disappointment to Mitterrand, but all the parties suffered.

Scandals over cover-ups and corruption that had erupted under Fabius continued to dog the Socialists, and in 1992 Cresson was replaced with **Pierre Bérégovoy**. He survived a wave of strikes by farmers, dockers, car workers and nurses, but then news broke of a private loan from a friend of Mitterrand accused of insider dealing. Mitterrand distanced himself from his prime minister, the Socialists were routed in the 1993 parliamentary elections, and Bérégovoy shot himself two months later, on May Day, leaving no note of explanation.

The new prime minister, **Edouard Balladur**, a fresh and fatherly face from the Right, soon lost the respect of his natural supporters after a series of U-turns following demonstrations by Air France workers, teachers, farmers, fishermen and school pupils, and the state's rescue of the Crédit Lyonnais bank after spectacular losses. Now popularly known as the Débit Lyonnais, the bank had to be bailed out to the tune of 100 billion FF (or £1000 per taxpayer), having run up colossal debts through dodgy speculative investments. Blame could also be laid at the Socialist administrations' door – for failing to appoint competent management at Crédit Lyonnais.

The change in government in 1993 heralded a new privatization programme and ever greater reliance on **market forces**. The central French Bank was made independent in 1993; many now say it takes instructions straight from the Bundesbank. As in Britain, French banks, whether private or public, prefer short-term speculation in money and property markets rather than long-term investment in industry.

Mitterrand tottered on to the end of his presidential term, looking less and less like the nation's favourite uncle. Two months after Bérégovoy's suicide, Réné Bousquet, head of police in the Vichy government and responsible for the rounding up of Jews in 1942, was murdered. A personal friend of Mitterrand's, he was thought to have carried shady secrets about the president to his grave. On the twentieth anniversary of President Pompidou's death in April 1994, there was a wave of nostalgia for a time when "things were right and proper". Allegations of **corruption** against mayors, members of parliament, ministers and leading figures in industry were becoming an almost weekly occurrence. In 1994 a member of parliament leading a crusade against drugs and corruption on the Côte d'Azur was assassinated. Instead of increasing democracy, decentralization appeared to have licensed fraud and nepotism on an alarming scale. Several mayors ended up in jail, but it seemed as if the Paris establishment was above the law.

Meanwhile, France continued to stay outside NATO and sustain its own **nuclear arsenal**, for which there has long been cross-party consensus, and indeed national pride. In 1994 both sides in parliament approved huge increases in defence spending.

In 1994 a group of intellectuals, including the philosophers Bernard-Henri Lévy and André Glucksmann, ran a "Sarajevo" campaign to put **Bosnia** at the centre of the European debate, and received considerable support. By 1995 France was annoying its allies by taking unilateral action and accusing Britain and the US of Munich-style appeasement. In 1994, France sent troops into **Rwanda**, whose previous murderous government they had supported and armed. French troops were accused of giving protection to French-speaking Hutus responsible for the genocide, and of acting too late to save any of the English-speaking Tutsis. The policy backfired with the new regime in Rwanda taking an anti-French line and the unresolved conflicts spreading to the neighbouring former French colony, **Zaire**.

The fragmentation of the parties in the 1994 **European elections** saw the RPR/UDF lose votes to the anti-Europeans whilst the maverick left-wing crook **Bernard Tapie** took votes from the PS, which seemed to be in terminal decline.

In 1995, with Mitterrand dying from cancer but refusing to step down before the end of his term, revelations surfaced about his war record as an official in the Vichy regime before he joined the Resistance. A biography of

Mitterrand, *Le Grand Secret*, detailing a whole host of scandals, was banned in France but avidly read on the Internet.

The Socialist Party was desperate for the popular **Jacques Delors**, who, as chair of the European Commission, saw Europe as having a strong social dimension, tackling unemployment, raising living standards, regulating the free play of global market forces and strengthening human rights to stand as their presidential candidate and do the same on a national level. Instead they had to make do with **Lionel Jospin**, the rather uncharismatic former education minister, who performed remarkably well, topping the poll in the first round in which right-wing votes were split between Balladur, Chirac, the extremist Le Pen (who scored 15.5 percent) and the anti-European Philippe de Villiers. Chirac stole the Left's clothes by placing **unemployment and social exclusion** at the centre of his manifesto, and heaped promises of better times on every section of the electorate. He won, by a small margin, and was inaugurated as the new president of France in May 1995.

By the time Mitterrand finally stepped down, he had been the French head of state for fourteen years, presiding over two Socialist and two Gaullist governments. During the period of his presidency, official unemployment figures passed three million, crime and insecurity rose, and increasing numbers of people found themselves excluded from society by racism, poverty and homelessness. Corruption scandals touched the president, politicians of all parties and business chiefs; terrorist bombs went off in Paris; and, as faith in old left-wing certainties foundered, support for extreme Right policies propelled the Front National from a minority faction to a serious electoral force. Despite this, when he died in January 1996, Mitterrand was genuinely mourned as a man of culture and vision, a supreme political operator, and for his unwavering commitment to the vision of a united Europe – a certainty that has not been wholly shared by the succeeding generation of French politicians or by the French people.

CHIRAC'S PRESIDENCY

An immediate dramatic change wrought by Chirac was the **abolition of conscription**, to give France more efficient and effective armed forces. The move provoked impassioned responses by the PCF and other left-wingers for whom conscription represents social levelling, the useful acquisition of skills and the revolutionary spirit expressed in the words of the national anthem – "Aux Armes, Citoyens . . ." Another early decision taken by President Chirac was to delay signing the Nuclear Non-Proliferation Treaty until France had carried out a new series of **nuclear tests** in the South Pacific. This provoked almost universal condemnation (Britain and China being the exceptions), boycotts of French goods, attacks on French Embassy buildings in Australia and New Zealand, plus all-out riots in Tahiti. Chirac and most of the French press gloried in Gallic isolation, with no qualms at the French navy capturing Greenpeace's Rainbow Warrior II, almost ten years to the day after the bombing of Rainbow Warrior I in Auckland harbour by French secret service agents.

Chirac's new prime minister was **Alain Juppé**, a clever and clinical technocrat. It was down to him to square the circle of Chirac's election pledges of job creation, maintaining the value of pensions and welfare benefits, reducing the number of homeless, tax cuts, a continuing strong franc and a reduction in the budget deficit to stay on course for European monetary union. However, the Banque de France's control over interest rates and its commitment to the overvalued franc have made Chirac's election promises to reduce unemployment impossible. Not only are the French workforce terrified about job security and living standards, but French businesses were also up in arms at the cost of borrowing and the uncompetitiveness of their exports; in 1996, bankruptcies were running at an average of 6000 a month. Even the indebted state-owned defence and electronics giant Thomson was put up for sale and its multimedia arm offered to the Korean company Daewoo for a symbolic 1F. People were scandalized and the deal was retracted, though Thomson was still sold, raising doubts about the government's commitment to retaining control over strategic industries.

In a television broadcast in October 1995, Chirac announced that rigorous economic measures to meet the criteria for European monetary union would have to take priority over social issues. Juppé then announced dramatic changes in social security provision and a "downsizing" of the state-owned railways, sparking off the **strikes** of November and December 1995. Students, teachers and nurses, workers in the transport, energy, post and telecommunications industries, bank clerks and civil servants took to the streets with the strong support of private sector employees struggling to get to work. With five million people out over a period of 24 days, it was the strongest show of protest in France since May 1968. Though the slogan was "*Tous ensembles*" ("Everyone together"), and people were united in their opposition to arrogant, elitist politicians, their false election promises and the austerity measures emanating from the free market philosophy, there were no united positive demands from the protesters, who ranged from working-class Front National supporters to middle-class Gaullists to Communist trade unionists.

The idea was propagated that Germany was responsible for imposing the currency. As the government imposed increasingly severe austerity measures to meet the convergence criteria for a European single currency, views on Europe felt the wind of change. In the 1995 winter strikes, many protesters said that a repeat Maastricht referendum would show a clear majority against, and by 1996 even senior UDF politicians were beginning to question the commitment to monetary union at any price.

Juppé promised to clean up **corruption** and was almost immediately embroiled in a scandal involving his subsidized luxury flat in Paris. Accusations of cover-ups and perversion of the course of justice followed, punctuated by revelations of illegal funding of election campaigns, politicians taking bribes, and dirty money changing hands during privatizations. In the past, politicians feathering their own nests never roused much public anger. But ordinary people, faced with job insecurity and falling living standards, were now becoming disgusted by the behaviour of the "elites". Even the normally obsequious right-wing press asked questions about the judiciary's independence, something Chirac had promised to uphold in his election manifesto. The consequences have been twofold: a widening of the gulf between the governors and the governed, which was one of the key themes of the 1995 strikes; and a further boost to the **Front National**.

Municipal elections in June 1995 gave the Front National control of three towns, including the major port of Toulon. In 1996, a rare pact between Gaullists and Socialists prevented

Jean-Pierre Stirbois from becoming the fourth FN mayor. The French constitution has prevented FN town halls from fully carrying out their promised racial discrimination in housing, social services, etc, but local organizations, particularly those dealing with social integration, gay rights, AIDS support, feminism, contemporary art or the Jewish or Muslim communities – have lost all their funding.

The **Algerian bomb attacks** fuelled racism, added to the general feelings of insecurity, and diminished public confidence in the government as guardians of law and order. On the Right, Giscard used the potent word "invasion" and said that citizenship should be based on blood ties, not on place of birth. Chirac talked of the "noise and smell" of immigrants, and a UDF senator compared the four million immigrants in France to the German occupation. All of which boosted the confidence of Jean-Marie Le Pen and of the home affairs minister, **Charles Pasqua**, who reintroduced random identity checks, took away the automatic entitlement to French citizenship of those born in France, and made it far harder for legal immigrants' families, asylum seekers and students to enter France. Around 250,000 people living and working in France had their legal status removed. In March 1996 three hundred Malian immigrants, many of them failed asylum seekers, sought refuge in a Paris church, and became known as the "*sans-papiers*". On the eve of the International Day Against Racism, they were forcibly evicted by truncheon-wielding riot police with the complicity of the local bishop and the curé of the church. In August ten immigrants from African countries, who had all legally worked and paid taxes in France, went on hunger strike in another Paris church (this time with the priest's support) against their **deportation**. Similar protests took place in other times and cities. In each case police action was swift and brutal. Trade unions, intellectuals and human rights groups denounced the government, which responded by announcing that three planes a month would be chartered to expel illegal immigrants. The Loi Debré was proposed so that all visiting foreign nationals' arrival and departure dates be notified, a law based on one passed during the Vichy Regime. A wave of protest marches ensued. An amended version was still passed in March 1997, which the entire majority right-wing

assembly voted for, and the left-wing minority voted against.

The fate of immigrants and their French descendants was never so precarious. Fury and frustration at discrimination, assault, abuse and economic deprivation has erupted into battles on the street. Several young blacks died at the hands of the police, while the right-wing media has revelled in images of violent Arab youths. Two hundred French Muslims arrested on suspicion of involvement with the Algerian bomb attacks went on hunger strike to protest their innocence. Racist assaults have increased dramatically, and xenophobic opinions have become accepted platitudes. On a larger scale, it seems again ironic that in 1996 the French called for military intervention in Zaire. However, it was again motivated less out of humanitarian concern than for fear that Americans were taking over a traditional French sphere of influence, with the concomitant threat of English gradually replacing French across Central Africa.

But the overriding **opposition to the government**, and to the political elite in general, came from the daily impact of economic policies on people's lives. Wages in former state-owned industries now in the hands of multinationals have plummeted, deregulation led to deteriorating working conditions, and **unemployment** soared from 2.4 million in 1986 to 3.4 million (over 12 percent of the workforce) in 1996. Taking into account young people palmed off with training schemes and older people forced into early retirement, the true figure was close to 5 million. Six million people were living on or below the poverty line with at least another six million teetering on the edge of **poverty**. Jobs that used to be secure, in the defence industries, banking and teaching, are disappearing. In the dispossessed housing estates of city suburbs violence and drug addiction have become endemic. The plight of the *exclus* (excluded), whether begging on the streets, sleeping rough or rioting, is a major public concern and one for which the government is blamed. While **inflation and interest rates** have long been lower than in the UK, France experienced **negative growth** in 1996, prompting serious fears that France was about to enter a deflationary spiral. Some politicians, for the first time, called into question the strong franc policy, while the French public lost faith in any politician's ability to manage the economy, and showed considerable sympathy for the strikes. Even the bully boys in Chirac and Juppé's own party, Séguin and Pasqua, started stirring trouble.

Amazingly, Juppé survived this "winter of discontent", abandoning some proposals and putting others on hold. A new tax to pay off the social security deficit was imposed, and cuts in the health service went ahead. More strikes and protests were held in 1996, but the three main trade unions (which in France are organized around political allegiance rather than occupation) returned to bickering amongst themselves, and Juppé was careful not to provoke public sector workers.

In April 1997, Chirac unexpectedly dissolved the parliament and called early elections for May of that year, which had been due the following March. Even though Juppé announced his resignation whatever the outcome, Chirac spectacularly lost his gamble when the Socialists were elected. The Left was back in force with a strong majority, and the right-wing parties got their lowest score since 1958. There was a new cohabitation. Lionel Jospin took over as France's Prime Minister with election promises of job creation and economic growth. He pursues a strong pro-European policy despite members of the Communist party being in the coalition. Indeed, France is, with Germany, the only country to reach the **European Monetary Union** near-target deficit. Mainly because of the strong economic recovery, he is still popular in the opinion polls and is regarded as a prudent wise owl figure. Unemployment remains a worrying problem, with twelve percent of the population unemployed. However, the government promised that 300,000 jobs would be created in addition to 100,000 youth jobs in 1998. The 1999 Budget has just been announced and has a clear left-wing slant, aiming to cut taxes, raise spending and penalise the rich.

Meanwhile, the right-wing parties have suffered from a series of **debacles**. The main scandal concerns Jean **Tiberi**, current mayor of Paris, involving subsidised real-estate and salaries for fake jobs. This reflected badly on Chirac as all the scandals in the Mairie de Paris took place whilst he was mayor. However, the revelation that Tiberi's wife earned money for a fake job led to a similar revelation about Jospin. President and Prime Minister united to impress upon the nation that the real problems did not lie with these tabloid issues.

Le Pen managed to alienate himself from the political scene by assaulting and punching a female socialist candidate who was running against his daughter in the April 1998 National Assembly elections, whilst the cameras were rolling. Consequently, he was stripped of his civic rights, and thus cannot vote, nor be a candidate in any election. As the Front National likes to keep their political ideology a family affair, his wife is now standing in his place. Similarly, his then buddy Mégret got his completely politically inexperienced wife to stand in 1997, and she was elected to the town of Vitrolles, beating the left-wing candidate who, in turn, was implicated in a shady deal. Members of the RPR-UDF parties caused a massive uproar in March 1998 by standing on joint tickets with FN candidates in an attempt to win local elections. There is now widespread disillusion with the right-wing parties. Even the bastion of fascism that was the port of Toulon was freed from National Front domination when the left-wing candidate won the municipal elections in April 1998. This time, Le Chevallier, the National Front former mayor, was involved in yet another legal embroglio and had put forward his wife in his place. The left-wing former Foreign Minister Roland Dumas is also alleged to be involved in a corruption scandal. The Thomson saga continues, this time with the addition of the Elf Aquitaine group.

The World Cup held in France in June and July 1998 finally (but only temporarily) united the nation. Even Le Pen couldn't think of anything to say for a few days when the French team won with a largely immigrant team. "Une France tricolore et multicolore" was celebrated with festivities all over the country, and the July 14 weekend was a multi-ethnic event. Fears that it remains superficial are entirely grounded and the prominence of the fanatically nationalist Front National is still a dangerous problem. With the advent of the single European currency on January 1, 1999, France has taken a leap forward, adding more European credentials to its name.

ART

From the Middle Ages to the twentieth century, France has held – with occasional gaps – a leading position in the history of European painting, with Paris, above all, attracting artists from the whole continent. The story of French painting is one of richness and complexity, partly due to this influx of foreign painters and partly due to the capital's stability as an artistic centre.

BEGINNINGS

In the late Middle Ages, the itinerant life of the nobles led them to prefer small and transportable works of art; splendidly **illuminated manuscripts** were much praised and the best painters, usually trained in Paris, continued to work on a small scale until the fifteenth century. In spite of the size of the illuminated image, painters made startling steps towards a realistic interpretation of the world and in the exploration of new subject matters.

Many of these illuminators were also panel painters, foremost of whom was **Jean Fouquet** (c1420–1481), born in Tours in the Loire valley and the central artistic personality of fifteenth-century France. Court painter to Charles VIII, Fouquet drew from both Flemish and Italian sources, utilizing the new fluid oil technique that had been perfected in Flanders, and concerning himself with the problem of representing space convincingly, much like his Italian contemporaries. Through this he moulded a distinct personal style, combining richness of surface with broad, generalized forms and, in his

feeling for volume and ordered geometric shapes, laying down principles that became intrinsic to French art for centuries to come, from Poussin to Seurat and Cézanne.

Two other fifteenth-century French artists deserve brief mention here, principally for the broad range of artistic expression they embody. **Enguerrand Quarton** (c1410–c1466) was the most famous Provençal painter of the time; his art, profoundly religious in subject as well as feeling, already shows the impact of the Mediterranean sun in the strong light that pervades his paintings. His *Pietà* in the Louvre is both stark and intensely poignant, while the *Coronation of the Virgin* that hangs at Villeneuve-lès-Avignon is a vast panoramic vision not only of heaven but also of a very real earth, in what ranks as one of the first city/landscapes in the history of French painting: Avignon itself is faithfully depicted and the Mont Ste-Victoire, later to be made famous by Cézanne, is recognizable in the distance.

The **Master of Moulins**, active in the 1480s and 1490s, was noticeably more northern in temperament, painting both religious altarpieces and portraits commissioned by members of the royal family or the fast-increasing bourgeoisie.

MANNERISM AND ITALIAN INFLUENCE

At the end of the fifteenth and the beginning of the sixteenth centuries, the French invasion of Italy brought both artists and patrons into closer contact with the Italian Renaissance.

The most famous of the artists who were lured to France was **Leonardo da Vinci**, spending the last three years of his life (1516–19) at the court of François I. From the Loire valley, which until then had been his favourite residence, the French king moved nearer to Paris, where he had several palaces decorated. Italian artists were once again called upon, and two of them, **Rosso** and **Primaticcio**, who arrived in France in 1530 and 1532 respectively, were to shape the artistic scene in France for the rest of the sixteenth century.

Both artists introduced to France the latest Italian style, **Mannerism**, a sometimes anarchic derivation of the High Renaissance of Michelangelo and Raphael. Mannerism, with its emphasis on the fantastic, the luxurious and the large-scale decorative, was eminently compatible with the taste of the court, and it was first put to the test in the revamping of the old Château de Fontainebleau.

There, a horde of French painters headed by the two Italians came to form what was subsequently called the **School of Fontainebleau**. Most French artists worked at Fontainebleau at some point in their career, or were influenced by its homogeneous style, but none stands out as a personality of any stature, and for the most part the painting of the time was dull and fanciful in the extreme.

Antoine Caron (c1520–c1600), who often worked for Catherine de Médicis, the widow of Henry II, contrived complicated allegorical paintings in which elongated figures are arranged within wide, theatre-like scenery packed with ancient monuments and Roman statues. Even the Wars of Religion, raging in the 1550s and 1560s, failed to rouse French artists' sense of drama, and representations of the many massacres then going on were detached and fussy in tone.

Portraiture tended to be more inventive. The portraits of **Jean Clouet** (c1485–1541) and his son **François** (c1510–72), both official painters to François I, combined sensitivity in the rendering of the sitter's features with a keen sense of abstract design in the arrangement of the figure, conveying with great clarity social status and giving clues to the sitter's profession. Though influenced by sixteenth-century Italian and Flemish portraits, their work remains, nonetheless, very French in its general sobriety.

THE SEVENTEENTH CENTURY

In the **seventeenth century**, Italy continued to be a source of inspiration for French artists, most of whom were drawn to Rome – at that time the most exciting artistic centre in Europe. There, two Italian artists, especially, dominated the scene in the first decade of the century: Michelangelo Merisi da Caravaggio and Annibale Carracci.

Caravaggio (1571–1610) often chose lowlife subjects and treated them with remarkable realism, a realism that he extended to traditional religious subject matter and that he enhanced by using a strong, harsh lighting technique. Although he had to flee Rome in great haste under sentence of murder in 1606, Caravaggio had already had a profound effect on the art of the age, both in terms of subjects and in his uncompromising use of realism.

Some French painters like **Moise Valentin** (c1594–1632) worked in Rome and were directly influenced by Caravaggio; others, such as the great painter from Lorraine, **Georges de la Tour** (1593–1652), benefited from his innovations at one remove, gaining inspiration from the Utrecht Caravaggisti who were active at the time in Holland. Starting with a descriptive realism in which naturalistic detail made for a varied painted surface, La Tour gradually simplified both forms and surfaces, producing deeply felt religious paintings in which figures appear to be carved out of the surrounding gloom by the magical light of a candle. Sadly, his output was very small – just some forty or so works in all.

Lowlife subjects and attention to naturalistic detail were also important aspects of the work of the **Le Nain Brothers**, especially **Louis** (1593–1648), who depicted with great sympathy, but never with sentimentality, the condition of the peasantry. He chose moments of inactivity or repose within the lives of the peasants, and his paintings achieve timelessness and monumentality by their very stillness. The other Italian artist of influence, the Bolognese **Annibale Carracci** (d. 1609), impressed French painters not only with his skill as a decorator but, more tellingly, with his ordered, balanced landscapes, which were to prove of prime importance for the development of the classical landscape in general, and in particular for those painted by **Claude Lorrain** (1604/5–82).

Claude, who started work as a pastry cook, was born in Lorraine, near Nancy. He left France for Italy to practise his trade, and worked in the household of a landscape painter in Rome, somehow persuading his master, who painted landscapes in the classical manner of Carracci, to let him abandon pastry for painting. Later he travelled to Naples, where the beauty of the harbour and bay made a lasting impression on him, the golden light of the southern port, and of Rome and its surrounding countryside, providing him with endless subjects of study which he drew, sketched and painted for the rest of his life. Claude's landscapes are airy compositions in which religious or mythological figures are lost within an idealized, Arcadian nature, bathed in a luminous, transparent light which, golden or silvery, lends a tranquil mood.

Landscapes, harsher and even more ordered, but also recalling the Arcadian mood of antiquity, were painted by the other French painter who elected to make Rome his home, **Nicolas Poussin** (1594–1665). Like Claude, Poussin selected his themes from the rich sources of Greek, Roman and Christian myths and stories; unlike Claude, however, his figures are not subdued by nature but rather dominate it, in the tradition of the masters of the High Renaissance, such as Raphael and Titian, whom he greatly admired. During the working out of a painting Poussin would make small models, arrange them on an improvised stage and then sketch the puppet scene – which may explain why his figures often have a still, frozen quality. Poussin only briefly returned to Paris, called by the king, Louis XIII, to undertake some large decorative works quite unsuited to his style or character. Back in Rome he refined a style that became increasingly classical and severe.

Many other artists visited Italy, but most returned to France, the luckiest to be employed at the court to boost the royal images of Louis XIII and XIV and the egos of their respective ministers, Richelieu and Colbert. **Simon Vouet** (1590–1649), **Charles Le Brun** (1619–90) and **Pierre Mignard** (1612–95) all performed that task with skill, often using ancient history and mythology to suggest flattering comparisons with the reigning monarch.

The official aspect of their works was paralleled by the creation of the new **Academy of Painting and Sculpture** in 1648, an institution that dominated the arts in France for the next few hundred years, if only by the way artists reacted against it. **Philippe de Champaigne** (1602–74), a painter of Flemish origin, alone stands out at the time as remotely different, removed from the intrigues and pleasures of the court and instead strongly influenced by the teaching and moral code of Jansenism, a purist and severe form of the Catholic faith. The apparent simplicity and starkness of his portraits hides an unusually perceptive understanding of his sitters' personalities. But it was the more courtly, fun-loving portraits and paintings by such artists as Mignard that were to influence most of the art of the following century.

THE EARLY EIGHTEENTH CENTURY

The semi-official art encouraged by the foundation of the Academy became more frivolous and light-hearted in the **eighteenth century**. The court at Versailles lost its attractions, and many patrons now were to be found among the hedonistic bourgeoisie and aristocracy living in Paris. History painting, as opposed to genre scenes or portraiture, retained its position of prestige, but at the same time the various categories began to merge and many artists tried their hands at landscape, genre, history or decorative works, bringing aspects of one type into another. **Salons**, at which painters exhibited their works, were held with increasing frequency and bred a new phenomenon in the art world – the art critic. The philosopher **Diderot** was one of the first of these arbiters of taste, doers and undoers of reputations.

Possibly the most complex personality of the eighteenth century was **Jean-Antoine Watteau** (1684–1721). Primarily a superb draughtsman, Watteau's use of soft and yet rich, light colours reveals how much he was struck by the great seventeenth-century Flemish painter Rubens. The open-air scenes of flirtatious love painted by Rubens and by the fifteenth/sixteenth-century Venetian Giorgione provided Watteau with precedents for his own subtle depictions of dreamy couples (sometimes depictions of characters from the Italian Comedy) strolling in delicate, mythical landscapes. In some of these *Fêtes Galantes* and in pictures of solitary musicians or actors (*Gilles*), Watteau conveyed a mood of melancholy, loneliness and poignancy that was largely lacking in the works of his many imitators and followers (Nicolas Lancret, JB Pater).

The work of **François Boucher** (1703–70) was probably more representative of the eighteenth century: the pleasure-seeking court of Louis XV found the lightness of morals and colours in his paintings immensely congenial. Boucher's virtuosity is seen at its best in his paintings of women, always rosy, young and fantasy-erotic.

Jean-Honoré Fragonard (1732–1806) continued this exploration of licentious themes but with an exuberance, a richness of colour and a vitality (*The Swing*) that was a feast for the eyes and raised the subject to a glorification of love. Far more restrained were the paintings of **Jean-Baptiste-Siméon Chardin** (1699–1779), who specialized in homely genre scenes and still lifes, painted with a simplicity that belied a complex use of colours, shapes and space to promote a mood of stillness and tranquillity. **Jean-Baptiste Greuze** (1725–1805) chose stories that anticipated reaction against the laxity of the times; the moral, at times sentimental, character of his paintings was all-pervasive, reinforced by a stage-like composition well suited to cautionary tales.

NEOCLASSICISM

This new seriousness became more severe with the rise of **Neoclassicism**, a movement for which purity and simplicity were essential components of the systematic depiction of edifying stories from the classical authors. Roman history and legends were the most popular subjects, and though **Jacques-Louis David** (1748–1825), a pupil of an earlier exponent of Neoclassicism, JM Vien, conformed to that to a certain extent, he was different in that he was also keenly sensitive to the changing mood and philosophies of his time and to the reaction against frivolity and self-indulgence. Many of his paintings are reflections of Republican ideals and of contemporary history, from the *Death of Marat* to events from the life of Napoléon, who was his patron. For the emperor and his family, David painted some of his most successful portraits – *Madame Recamier* is not only an exquisite example of David's controlled use of shapes and space and his debt to antique Rome, but can also be seen as a paradigm of Neoclassicism.

Two painters, **Jean-Antoine Gros** (1771–1835) and **Baron Gérard** (1770–1837), followed David closely in style and in themes (portraits, Napoleonic history and legend), but often with a touch of softness and heroic poetry that pointed the way to Romanticism.

Jean-Auguste-Dominique Ingres (1780–1867) was a pupil of David; he also studied in Rome before coming back to Paris to develop the purity of line that was the essential and characteristic element of his art. His effective use of it to build up forms and bind compositions can be admired in conjunction with his recurrent theme of female nudes bathing, or in his magnificent and stately portraits that depict the nuances of social status.

ROMANTICISM

Completely opposed to the stress on drawing advocated by Ingres, two artists created, through their emphasis on colour, form and composition, pictures that look forward to the later part of the nineteenth century and the Impressionists. **Théodore Géricault** (1791–1824), whose short life was still dominated by the heroic vision of the Napoleonic era, explored dramatic themes of human suffering in such paintings as *The Raft of Medusa*, while his close contemporary, **Eugène Delacroix** (1798–1863), epitomized the **Romantic movement** – its search for emotions and its love of nature, power and change.

Delacroix was deeply aware of tradition, and his art was influenced, visually and conceptually, by the great masters of the Renaissance and the seventeenth and eighteenth centuries. In many ways he may be regarded as the last great religious and decorative French painter, but through his technical virtuosity, freedom of brushwork and richness of colours, he can also be seen as the essential forerunner of the Impressionists. For Delacroix there was no conflict between colour and design: David and Ingres saw these elements as separate aspects of creation, but Delacroix used colours as the basis and structure of his designs. His technical freedom was partly due to his admiration for two English painters, John Constable and his close friend, Richard Parkes Bonington, with whom he shared a studio for a few months. Bonington especially had a freshness of approach to colour and a free handling of paint, both of which had a strong impact on Delacroix. His numerous themes ranged from intimate female nudes, often with mysterious and erotic Middle Eastern overtones, to studies of animals and hunting scenes. Ancient and contemporary history supplied him with some of his most harrowing and dramatic paintings: The *Massacre at Chios* was based on an event that took place during the Greek War of Independence from the Turks, and *Liberty Guiding the People* was painted to commemorate the Revolution of 1830. Both paintings were his personal response to contemporary events and the human tragedies they entailed.

Other painters working in the Romantic tradition were still haunted by the Napoleonic legends, as well as by North Africa (Algeria) and the Middle East, which had become better known to artists and patrons alike during the Napoleonic Wars. These were the subjects of paintings by **Horace Vernet** (1789–1863), **Jean-Louis-Ernest Meissonier** (1815–91) and **Théodore Chassériau** (1819–56).

Among their contemporaries was **Honoré Daumier** (1808–79): very much an isolated figure, influenced by the boldness of approach of caricaturists, he was content to depict everyday subjects such as a laundress or a third-class rail car – caustic commentaries on professions and politics that work as brilliant observations of the times.

THE NINETEENTH CENTURY

Some painters of the first part of the **nineteenth century** were fascinated by other themes. Nature, in its true state, unadorned by conventions, became a subject for study, and running parallel to this was the realization that painting could be the visual externalization of the artist's own emotions and feelings. These two aspects, which until this time had only been very tentatively touched upon, were now more fully explored and led directly to the innovations of the Impressionists and later painters.

Jean-Baptiste-Camille Corot (1796–1875) started to paint landscapes that were fresh, direct and influenced as much by the unpretentious and realistic country scenes of seventeenth-century Holland as by the balanced compositions of Claude. His loving and attentive studies of nature were much admired by later artists, including Monet.

At the same time a whole group of painters developed similar attitudes to landscape and nature. Helped greatly by the practical improvement of being able to buy oil paint in tubes rather than as unmixed pigments, they – known as the **Barbizon School** after the village on the outskirts of Paris round which they painted – soon discovered the joy and excitement of *plein-air* (open-air) painting.

Théodore Rousseau (1812–67) was their nominal leader, his paintings of forest undergrowth and forest clearings displaying an intimacy that came from the immediacy of the image. **Charles-François Daubigny** (1817–78), like Rousseau, often infused a sense of drama into his landscapes.

Jean-François Millet (1814–75) is perhaps the best-known associate of the Barbizon group, though he was more interested in the human figure than simple nature. Landscapes, however, were essential settings for his figures; indeed, his most famous pictures are those exploring the place of people in nature and their struggle to survive. *The Sower*, for instance, was a typical Millet theme, suggesting the heroic working life of the peasant. As is so often the case for painters touching on new themes or on ideas that are uncomfortable to the rich and powerful, Millet enjoyed little success during his lifetime, and his art was only widely recognized after his death.

The moralistic and romantic undertone in Millet's work was something that **Gustave Courbet** (1819–77) strove to avoid. Courbet was a socialist and his frank, outspoken attitude led to his being accused of taking part in the destruction of the column in Paris's place Vendôme after the outbreak of the Commune and, eventually, to his exile. After an initial resounding success in the Salon exhibition of 1849, he endured constant criticism from the academic world and patrons alike: scenes of ordinary life, such as the *Funeral at Orléans*, which he often chose to depict, were regarded as unsavoury and deliberately ugly.

But Courbet had a deep admiration for the old masters, especially for Rembrandt and the Spanish painters of the seventeenth and eighteenth centuries. This link with tradition was probably one of the underlying themes of his large masterpiece, The *Studio*, which was emphatically rejected by the jury of the 1855 Exposition Universelle, and in which Courbet portrayed himself, surrounded by his model, his friends, colleagues and admirers, among them the poet Baudelaire. Courbet subsequently decided to hold a private exhibition of some forty of his works, writing at the same time a manifesto explaining his intentions of being true to his vision of the world and of creating "living art". Writing the word **Realism** in large letters on the door leading to the exhibition, he stated his intentions and gave a label to his art.

IMPRESSIONISM

Like Courbet, **Edouard Manet** (1832–83) was strongly influenced by Spanish painters, whose works had become more easily accessible to artists when a large collection belonging to the Orléans family was confiscated by the state in 1848. Unlike Courbet, though, he never saw himself as a socialist or indeed as a rebel or avant-garde painter, yet his technique and interpretation of themes was quite new and shocked as many people as it inspired. Manet used bold contrasts of light and very dark colours, giving his paintings a forcefulness that critics often took for a lack of sophistication. And his detractors saw much to decry in his reworking of an old subject originally treated by the sixteenth-century Venetian painter, Giorgione, *Le Déjeuner sur l'Herbe*. Manet's version was shocking because he placed naked and dressed figures together, and because the men were dressed in the costume of the day, implying a pleasure party too specifically contemporary to be "respectable".

Manet was not interested in painting moral lessons, however, and some of his most successful pictures are reflections of ordinary life in bars and public places, where respectability, as understood by the late-nineteenth-century bourgeoisie, was certainly lacking. To Manet, painting was to be enjoyed for its own sake and not as a tool for moral instruction – in itself an outlook on the role of art that was quite new, not to say revolutionary, and marked a definite break with the paintings of the past. With Manet, the basis of our present expectations and understanding of modern art was established.

From the 1870s, Manet began to adopt the **Impressionist** techniques of painting out-of-doors, and his work became lighter and freer. Although it is doubtful whether Manet either wanted or expected to assume the role of leader, he found himself a much-admired member of that group of painters, one of whom was **Claude Monet** (1840–1926). Born in Le Havre, Monet came in contact with **Eugène Boudin** (1824–98), whose colourful beach scenes anticipated the way the Impressionists approached colour. He then went to Paris to study under Charles Gleyre, a respected teacher in whose studio he met many of the people with whom he formulated his ideas. Monet soon discovered that, for him, light and the way in which it builds up forms and creates an infinity of colours was the element that governed all representations. Under the impact of Manet's bright hues and his unconventional attitude, ("art for art's sake"), Monet soon began using pure colours side by side, blended together to create areas of brightness and shade.

In 1874, a group of some thirty artists exhibited together for the first time. Among them were some of the best-known names of this period of French art: Dégas, Monet, Renoir, Pissarro. One of Monet's paintings was entitled *Impression: Sun Rising*, a title that was singled out by the critics to ridicule the colourful, loose and unacademic style of these young artists.

Overnight they became, derisively, the "Impressionists".

Camille Pissarro (1830–1903) was slightly older than most of them and seems to have played the part of an encouraging father-figure, always keenly aware of any new development or new talent. Not a great innovator himself, Pissarro was a very gifted artist whose use of Impressionist technique was supplemented by a lyrical feeling for nature and its seasonal changes. But it was really with **Monet** that Impressionist theory ran its full course: he studied endlessly the impact of light on objects and the way in which it reveals colours. To understand this phenomenon better, Monet painted the same motif again and again under different conditions of light, at different times of the day, and in different seasons, producing whole series of paintings such as *Grain Stacks*, *Poplars* and, much later, his *Waterlilies*. In the late 1870s and the early 1880s many other artists helped formulate the new style, though few remained true to its principles for very long.

Auguste Renoir (1841–1919), who started life as a painter of porcelain, was swept up by Monet's ideas for a while, but soon felt the need to look again at the old masters and to emphasize the importance of drawing to the detriment of colour. Renoir regarded the representation of the female nude as the most taxing and rewarding subject that an artist could tackle. Like Boucher in the eighteenth century, Renoir's nudes are luscious, but rarely, if ever, erotic. They have a healthy, uncomplicated quality that was, in his later paintings, to become cloyingly, almost overpoweringly, sickly and sweet. Better were his portraits of women fully clothed, both for their obvious and innate sympathy and for their keen sense of design.

Edgar Degas (1834–1917) was yet another artist who, although he exhibited with the Impressionists, did not follow their precepts very closely. The son of a rich banker, he was trained in the tradition of Ingres: design and drawing were an integral part of his art, and, whereas Monet was fascinated mainly by light, Degas wanted to express movement in all its forms. His pictures are vivid expressions of the body in action, usually straining under fairly exacting circumstances – dancers and circus artistes were among his favourite subjects, as well as more mundane depictions of laundresses and other working women.

Like so many artists of the day, Degas had his imagination fired by the discovery of **Japanese prints**, which could for the first time be seen in quantity. These provided him with new ideas of composition, not least in their asymmetry of design and the use of large areas of unbroken colour. **Photography**, too, had an impact, if only because it finally liberated artists from the task of producing accurate, exacting descriptions of the world.

Degas's extraordinary gift as a draughtsman was matched only by that of the Provençal aristocrat **Henri de Toulouse-Lautrec** (1864–1901). Toulouse-Lautrec, who had broken both his legs as a child, was unusually small, a physical deformity that made him particularly sensitive to free and vivacious movements. A great admirer of Degas, he chose similar themes: people in cafés and theatres, working women and variety dancers all figured large in his work. But, unlike Degas, Toulouse-Lautrec looked beyond the body, and his work is scattered with social comment, sometimes sardonic and bitter. In his portrayal of Paris prostitutes, there is sympathy and kindness; to study them better he lived in a brothel, revealing in his paintings the weariness and sometimes gentleness of these women.

POST-IMPRESSIONISM

Though a rather vague term, as it's difficult to date exactly when the backlash against Impressionism took place, **Post-Impressionism** represents in many ways a return to more formal concepts of painting – in composition, in attitudes to subject and in drawing.

Paul Cézanne (1839–1906), for one, associated only very briefly with the Impressionists and spent most of his working life in relative isolation, obsessed with rendering, as objectively as possible, the essence of form. He saw objects as basic shapes – cylinders, cones, etc – and tried to give the painting a unity of texture that would force the spectator to view it not so much as representation of the world but rather as an entity in its own right, as an object as real and dense as the objects surrounding it. It was this striving for pictorial unity that led him to cover the entire surface of the picture with small, equal brush strokes which made no distinction between the textures of a tree, a house or the sky.

The detached, unemotional way in which Cézanne painted was not unlike that of the seventeenth-century artist Poussin, and he found a contemporary parallel in the work of **Georges Seurat** (1859–91). Seurat was fascinated by current theories of light and colour, and he attempted to apply them in a systematic way, creating different shades and tones by placing tiny spots of pure colour side by side, which the eye could in turn fuse together to see the colours mixed out of their various components. This **pointillist** technique also had the effect of giving monumentality to everyday scenes of contemporary life.

While Cézanne, Seurat and, for that matter, the Impressionists, sought to represent the outside world objectively, several other artists – the **Symbolists** – were seeking a different kind of truth, through the subjective experience of fantasy and dreams. **Gustave Moreau** (1840–98) represented, in complex paintings, the intricate worlds of the romantic fairy tale, his visions expressed in a wealth of naturalistic details. The style of **Puvis de Chavannes** (1824–98) was more restrained and more obviously concerned with design and the decorative. And a third artist, **Odilon Redon** (1840–1916), produced some weird and visionary graphic work that especially intrigued Symbolist writers; his less frequent works in colour belong to the later part of his life.

The subjectivity of the Symbolists was of great importance to the art of **Paul Gauguin** (1848–1903). He started life as a stockbroker who collected Impressionist paintings, a Sunday artist who gave up his job in 1883 to dedicate himself to painting.

During his stay in Pont-Aven in Brittany, Gauguin worked with a number of artists who called themselves the **Nabis**, among them **Paul Serusier** and **Émile Bernard**. He began exploring ways of expressing concepts and emotions by means of large areas of colour and powerful forms, and developed a unique style that was heavily indebted to his knowledge of Japanese prints and of the tapestries and stained glass of medieval art. His search for the primitive expression of primitive emotions took him eventually to the South Sea Islands and Tahiti, where he found some of his most inspiring subjects and painted some of his best-known canvases.

A similar derivation from Symbolist art and a wish to exteriorize emotions and ideas by means of strong colours, lines and shapes underlies the work of **Vincent Van Gogh** (1853–90), a Dutch painter who came to live in France. Like Gauguin, with whom he had an admiring but stormy friendship, Van Gogh started painting relatively late in life, lightening his palette in Paris under the influence of the Impressionists, and then heading south to Arles where, struck by the harshness of the Mediterranean light, he turned out such frantic expressionistic pieces as *The Reaper* and *Wheatfield with Crows*. In all his later pictures the paint is thickly laid on in increasingly abstract patterns that follow the shapes and tortuous paths of his deep inner melancholy.

Both Gauguin and Van Gogh saw objects and colours as means of representing ideas and subjective feelings. **Édouard Vuillard** (1868–1940) and **Pierre Bonnard** (1867–1947) combined this with Cézanne's insistence on unifying the surface and texture of the picture. The result was, in both cases, paintings of often intimate scenes in which figures and objects are blended together in a series of complicated patterns. In some of Vuillard's works, people dressed in checked material, for example, merge into the flowered wallpaper behind them, and in the paintings of Bonnard, the glowing design of the canvas itself is as important as what it's trying to represent.

THE TWENTIETH CENTURY

The **twentieth century** kicked off to a colourful start with the **Fauvist** exhibition of 1905, an appropriately anarchic beginning to a century which, in France above all, was to see radical changes in attitudes towards painting.

The painters who took part in the exhibition included, most influentially, **Henri Matisse** (1869–1954), **André Derain** (1880–1954), **Georges Rouault** (1871–1958) and **Albert Marquet** (1875–1947), and they were quickly nicknamed the Fauves (Wild Beasts) for their use of bright, wild colours that often bore no relation whatsoever to the reality of the object depicted. Skies were just as likely to be green as blue since, for the Fauves, colour was a way of composing, of structuring a picture, and not necessarily a reflection of real life.

Fauvism was just the beginning: the first decades of the twentieth century were times of intense excitement and artistic activity in Paris, and painters and sculptors from all over Europe

flocked to the capital to take part in the liberation from conventional art that individuals and groups were gradually instigating. **Raoul Dufy** (1877-1953) used Fauvist colours in combination with theories of abstraction to paint an effervescent industrial age.

Pablo Picasso (1881–1973) was one of the first, arriving in Paris in 1900 from Spain and soon thereafter starting work on his first Blue Period paintings, which describe the sad and squalid life of intinerant actors in tones of blue. Later, while Matisse was experimenting with colours and their decorative potential, Picasso came under the sway of Cézanne and his organization of forms into geometrical shapes. He also learned from "primitive", and especially African, sculpture, and out of these studies came a painting that heralded a definite new direction, not only for Picasso's own style but for the whole of modern art – *Les Demoiselles d'Avignon*. Executed in 1907, this painting combined Cézanne's analysis of forms with the visual impact of African masks.

It was from this semi-abstract picture that Picasso went on to develop the theory of **Cubism**, inspiring artists such as **Georges Braque** (1882–1963) and **Juan Gris** (1887–1927), another Spaniard, and formulating a whole new movement. The Cubists' aim was to depict objects not so much as they saw them but rather as they knew them to be: a bottle and a guitar were shown from the front, from the side and from the back as if the eye could take in all at once every facet and plane of the object. Braque and Picasso first analysed forms into these facets (analytical Cubism), then gradually reduced them to series of colours and shapes (synthetic Cubism), among which a few recognizable symbols such as letters, fragments of newspaper and numbers appeared. The complexity of different planes overlapping one another made the deciphering of Cubist paintings sometimes difficult, and the very last phase of Cubism tended increasingly towards abstraction.

Spin-offs of Cubism were many: such movements as **Orphism**, headed by **Robert Delaunay** (1885–1941), and **Francis Picabia** (1879-1953) who experimented not with objects but with the colours of the spectrum, and **Futurism**, which evolved first in Italy, then in Paris, and explored movement and the bright new technology of the industrial age. **Fernand**

Léger (1881–1955), one of the main exponents of the so-called School of Paris, had also become acquainted with modern machinery during **World War I**, and he exploited his fascination with its smoothness and power to create geometric and monumental compositions of technical imagery that were indebted to both Cézanne and Cubism.

The war, meanwhile, had affected many artists: in Switzerland, **Dada** was born out of the scorn artists felt for the petty bourgeois and nationalistic values that had led to the bloodshed, a nihilistic movement that sought to knock down all traditionally accepted ideas. It was best exemplified in the work of the Frenchman **Marcel Duchamp** (1887–1968), who selected ready-made, everyday objects and elevated them, without modification, to the rank of works of art by pulling them out of their ordinary context, or defaced such sacred cows as the *Mona Lisa* by decorating her with a moustache and an obscene caption.

Dada was also a literary movement, and through one of its main poets, André Breton, it led to the inception of **Surrealism**. It was the unconscious and its dark unchartered territories that interested the Surrealists: they derived much of their imagery from Freud and even experimented in words and images with free-association techniques.

Strangely enough, most of the "French" Surrealists were foreigners, primarily the German **Max Ernst** (1891–1976) and the Spaniard **Salvador Dali** (1904–89), though Frenchman **Yves Tanguy** (1900–55) also achieved international recognition. Mournful landscapes of weird, often terrifying images evoked the landscape of nightmares in often very precise details and with an anguish that went on to influence artists for years to come. Picasso, for instance, shocked by the massacre of the Spanish town of Guernica in 1936, drew greatly from Surrealism to produce the disquieting figures of his painting of the same name.

World War II interrupted Paris's position as the artistic melting pot of Europe. Artists had rushed there at the beginning of the twentieth century and after World War I, contributing by their individuality, originality and different nationalities to the richness and constant renewal of artistic endeavour. Although at the outbreak of World War II many artists emigrated to the United States, where the economic climate was more favourable, Paris remained full of vibrant new work. Sculptors like Romanian **Brancusi** (1876–1957) or the Swiss **Giacometti** (1886–1966) lived most of their lives in Paris, for example.

The last coherent French art movement of the century, largely of the 50s and 60s, was **Nouveau Réalisme**, which concentrated on the distortion of the objects and signs of contemporary culture, and loosely encompassed artists and sculptors such as Dubuffet, Arman, César, Jean Tinguely and Niki de Saint-Phalle.

Jean Dubuffet (1901–85) pioneered the depreciation of traditional artistic materials and methods, fashioning junk, tar, sand and glass into the shape of human beings. His work (which provoked much outrage) influenced both the French-born American, **Arman** (1928–) and **César** (1921–), both of whom made use of scrap metals – their output ranging from presentations of household debris to towers of crushed cars. Even more controversially, the Swiss **Daniel Spoerri** (1930–) used the remnants – including the crockery – of his dinners and glued them onto a canvas.

Nouveau Réaliste sculpture is best represented by the works of another Swiss, **Jean Tinguely** (1925–91) whose work was concerned mainly with movement and the machine, satirizing technological civilization. His most famous work, done in collaboration with **Niki de Saint-Phalle** (1926–) is the exuberant fountain outside the Pompidou Centre, featuring fantastical birds and beasts shooting water in all directions.

Later artists wanted to reassert their position as individuals and, though influenced by their cultural context, were not attached to any clear manifesto. Perhaps the most important post-World War II French artist is **Yves Klein** (1928–1962). He redefined the void and the immaterial as having a pure energy. He also patented his own colour, International Klein Blue, which he used on his monochromes, also signalling painting simply as pure colour. Klein and Duchamp laid the foundations for several currents in contemporary art.

Orlan, an eccentric body-artist, was associated with the Flexus performance art movement in the 60s and 70s, when she sold artist's kisses (her own) to passers-by. She has now progressed to making her body into a cybernetic art-object through cosmetic surgery, modelling herself on representations of Venus, Diana, Psyche and the

Mona Lisa, with the operations being broadcast worldwide via satellite.

Other artists explore their relationship with the environment. **Christian Boltanski** (1944–) explores the individual's position in society. His installations use technology to take emotion from objects, rather than investing the objects with emotions. **Christo** (1935–) who is Bulgarian but whose wife and collaborator **Jeanne-Claude** (1935–) is French, covers buildings using different materials, and wrapped Paris's Pont-Neuf in woven polyamide fabric in 1985, in order to focus attention on the structure itself rather

than its function. Jean-Marc Bustamante (1952–) constructs in situ installations, using building materials in his art. Philippe Meste is part of a trend in guerrilla-action art, holding Toulon's port under siege with a balaclaved group in 1993.

The works of **Louise Bourgeois** (1911–), still a prolific sculptress despite her age, are often oddly erotic and remarkable combinations of wrought iron, old clothes and huge spiders. They assemble the diverse themes which have permeated her later work: memory, the family and the affirmation and negation of the self as fiction and simulacrum.

ARCHITECTURE

France's architectural legacy is rich and important, reflecting the power and personality of subsequent kings, the Church and the state, vying to outdo their peers with bold, lavish statements in brick and stone. Many architectural trends filtered into France from Italy – Romanesque, Renaissance and Baroque – but they have been refined and developed by the French. Rococo grew from Baroque, Neoclassicism came from the Renaissance, and Art Nouveau was a brilliant, confused jumble of Baroque features combined with the newly developed cast-iron industry. Architecture this century has produced two great names – Auguste Perret and Le Corbusier – but France's contemporary scene is still thriving, with a host of new developments throughout the country.

THE ROMANS

The south of France was colonized by the **Romans** by around 120 BC in order to expand their trading operations, and they set up substantial settlements at Marseille, Narbonne, Orange, Arles, Fréjus, Glanum near St-Rémy, and Nice, with a network of roads linking them.

The Romans were fine town planners, linking complexes of buildings with straight roads punctuated by decorative fountains, arches and colonnades. They built essentially in the Greek style, and their large, functional buildings were concerned more with strength and solidity than design. A number of substantial Roman building

works survive: in **Nîmes** you can see the Maison Carrée, the best-preserved Roman temple still standing, and the Temple of Diana, one of just four vaulted Roman temples in Europe. Gateways remain at **Autun, Orange, Saintes** and **Reims**, and largely intact amphitheatres can be seen at Nîmes and **Arles**. The **Pont du Gard** aqueduct outside of Nîmes is still a magnificent and ageless monument of civil engineering, built to carry the town's fresh water over the gorge, and Orange has its massive theatre, with Europe's only intact Roman façade. There are excavated archeological sites at **Glanum** near St-Rémy, **Vaison-la-Romaine** and **Lyon**.

CAROLINGIAN AND ROMANESQUE

The **Carolingian dynasty** of Charlemagne attempted a revival of the symbols of civilized authority by recourse to Roman or "**Romanesque**" models. Of this era, practically nothing remains visible, though the motifs of arch and vault are carried on in their simplest forms; and the semi-circular apse and the basilican plan of nave and aisles persists as the basis of the succeeding phases of Christian architecture. An interesting anomaly is the plan of the **church of St-Front** at Périgueux, a copy of St Mark's in Venice, brought by trading influence west along the Garonne in the early twelfth century.

Elsewhere development may be divided roughly north–south of the Loire. Southern Romanesque is naturally more Roman, with stone barrel vaults, aisleless naves and domes. **St-Trophime** at Arles (1150) has a porch directly derived from Roman models and, with the church at St-Gilles nearby, exhibits a delight in carved ornament peculiar to the south at this time. The cathedral at **Angoulême** typifies the use of all these elements.

The south, too, was the readiest route for the introduction of new cultural developments, and it is here that the pointed arch and vault first appear – from Saracen sources – in churches such as **Notre-Dame** at Avignon, the cathedral at **Autun**, and **Ste-Madeleine** at Vézelay (1089–1206), which contains the earliest pointed cross vault in France.

In the north of the country, the nave with aisles is more usual, together with the development of twin western towers to mask the end of the aisles. The **Abbaye-aux-Hommes** at Caen (1066–77) is typical. It contains the elements later developed as "Gothic", in piers, pillars, buttresses, arcades, ribbed vaults and spires. The best examples may be found in Normandy, and it is from here, with the introduction of the pointed arch from the south, that the Gothic style developed.

GOTHIC

The reasons behind the development of the **Gothic style** lie in the pursuit of sensations of the sublime; to achieve great height without apparent great weight would seem to imitate religious ambition. Its development in the north is partly due to the availability of good building stone and soft stone for carving, but perhaps more to the growth of royal aspiration and power based in the Île de France, which, allied with the papacy, stimulated the building of the great **cathedrals** of Paris, Bourges, Chartres, Laon, Le Mans, Reims and Amiens in the twelfth and thirteenth centuries.

The Gothic phase began with the building of the choir of the **abbey of St-Denis** near Paris in 1140, and ran through to the end of the fifteenth century. Architecturally, it encompasses the development of wider, traceried windows of coloured glass, filling the wall spaces liberated by the refinement of vertical structure; the "rose" or wheel is an early and especially French feature in window tracery. The glass at Chartres shows better than anywhere the concerted architectural effect of these developments. Another distinctive element is the flying buttress outside the walls to resist the outward push of the vaulting.

In the south, as at Albi and Angers, the great churches are generally broader and simpler in plan and external appearance, with aisles often almost as high as the nave. Many secular buildings survive – some of the most notable the work of Viollet-le-Duc, the pre-eminent nineteenth-century restorer – and even whole towns, for example **Carcassonne** and **Aigues Mortes**; **Avignon** has the bridge and the papal palace.

Castles, of necessity, lent themselves less to the disappearing walls of the Gothic style. The **Château de Pierrefonds**, as restored by Viollet, may be taken as typical. The walls of many others disappeared by force, not whim, as gunpowder made them obsolete and a more

settled and subjugated order led to the development of château-palaces, such as **Châteaudun** (1441) and **Blois**. The **Château de Josselin** in Brittany is a marvellous example of the smaller fortresses that became common towards the end of the Gothic period. A series of colonial settlements, the **bastides**, or fortified towns, of the English occupation, remain in the Dordogne region and are a refreshing antidote to triumphal French bombast.

RENAISSANCE

Quite early in the sixteenth century the influence of the new style of the Italian **Renaissance** began to appear. Coupled with the persistence of Gothic traditions and the necessity of steep roofs and tall chimneys in a French climate, it appears immediately "Frenchified" rather than in its pure imported form. The châteaux of kings and courtiers round Paris and in the Loire valley, such as **Blois, Chambord, Chenonceau and Fontainebleau**, exemplify this style, with their wholly un-Italian concentration of interest on the skyline and an elaboration of detail in the facades at the expense of the clear modelling of form. With the passing of time, however, the style became more purely classical. The Louvre in Paris and the Château de Blois are notable examples of the developing **classicism**. The wing of the **Château de Blois** containing the famous staircase designed for François I in 1515 shows the beginning of an emphasis on horizontal lines and an overlay of Italian motifs on a basically Gothic form. The elevations, designed by **Mansart** in 1635, though distinctively French, are just as typically classical.

The **Louvre** even more embodies the whole history of the classical style in France, having been worked over by all the grand names of French architecture from Lescot in the early sixteenth century, via François Mansart and Claude Perrault in the seventeenth, to the later years of the nineteenth century. A recent turning point is the work of **IM Pei**, whose pyramid addition has proved a controversial departure from the Louvre's sober style.

It is unfortunate that the Renaissance style in France is chiefly seen in such structures as the Louvre and Versailles, which because of their scale can scarcely be experienced as buildings. That this is the case is largely due to the developing despotism and concentration of power under Louis XIII and XIV. But there was a lighter side to this. François Mansart, at Blois and **Maisons Lafitte** (1640), shows a certain suavity and elegance, which appears again in the eighteenth century in the town houses of the Rococo period, the generally reticent exteriors of which belie the vivacity and charm of the private life within.

On the other hand, **Claude Perrault** (1613–88), who designed the great colonnaded east front of the Louvre, gives an austere face to the official architecture of despotism, magnificent but far too imperial to be much enjoyed by common mortals. The high-pitched roofs, which had been almost universal until then, are replaced here by the classical balustrade and pediment, the style grand but cold and supremely secular. Art and architecture were at the time organized by boards and academies, and in the latter style and employment were strictly controlled by royal direction. Between 1643 and 1774 France was governed by two monarchs who both ruled by the same maxim – absolute power. With such a limitation of ideas at the source of patronage, it is hardly surprising that there was a certain dullness to the era, at least in the acknowledged monuments of French architecture.

BAROQUE AND ROCOCO

In a similar way to the preceding century, the churches of the **seventeenth and eighteenth centuries** have a coldness quite different from the German and Flemish Baroque or the Italian. When the Renaissance style first appeared in the early sixteenth century, there was no great need for new church building, the country being so well endowed from the Gothic centuries. **St-Étienne-du-Mont** (1517–1620) and **St-Eustache** (1532–89), both in Paris, show how old forms persisted with only an overlay of the new style.

It is with the Jesuits in the seventeenth century that the Church embraced the new style to combat the forces of rational disbelief. In Paris the churches of the **Sorbonne** (1653) and **Val-de-Grâce** (1645) exemplify this, as do a good number of other grandiose churches in the **Baroque** style, through **Les Invalides** at the end of the seventeenth century to the **Panthéon** of the late eighteenth century. Here is the Church triumphant rather than the state, but no more beguiling.

The architect of Les Invalides was **Jules Hardouin Mansart**, a product of the academy, who also greatly extended the palace of **Versailles** and so created the Cinemascope view of France with that seemingly endless horizon of royalty. As an antidote to this pomposity, the **Petit Trianon** at Versailles is as refreshing now as it was to Louis XV, who had it built in 1762 as a place of escape for his mistress. And even more so is this true of that other pearl formed of the grit of boredom in the enclosed world of Versailles – **La Petite Ferme,** where Marie-Antoinette played at being a milkmaid, which epitomizes the Arcadian and "picturesque" fantasy of the painters Boucher and Fragonard.

The lightness and charm that was undermining official grandeur with Arcadian fancies and **Rococo** decoration was, however, snuffed out by the Revolution. There is no real Revolutionary architecture, as the necessity of order and authority soon asserted itself and an autocracy every bit as absolute returned with Napoléon, drawing on the old grand manner but with a stronger trace of the stern old Roman. One architect, **Claude Ledoux**, was highly original and influential, both in England and Germany. And the visionary millennialist **Boullée** could also be said to be a child of Revolutionary times, though it is likely that such men were inspired as much by the rediscovered plainness of the Greek Doric order as by radical politics.

In Paris it was not the democratic Doric but the imperial Corinthian order that re-emerged triumphant in the church of the **Madeleine** (1806) and, with the **Arc de Triomphe** like some colossal paperweight, reimposed the authority of academic architecture, in contrast to the fancy-dress architecture of contemporary Regency England.

THE NINETEENTH CENTURY

The restoration of legitimate monarchy after the **fall of Napoléon** stimulated a revival of interest in older Gothic and early Renaissance styles, which offered a symbol of dynastic reassurance not only to the state but also to the newly rich. So in the private and commercial architecture of the nineteenth century these earlier styles predominate – in mine-owners' villas and bankers' headquarters.

By the mid-**nineteenth century**, a neo-Baroque strain had established itself, a style exemplified by Charles Garnier's **Opéra** in Paris (1861–74), which, under the heading of Second Empire and with its associations of voluptuous good living, seductive painting and general "ooh-la-la", provides probably the most persistent image of France among the non-French – though you should avoid being blinded by Puritan distaste to the splendid spatial and decorative sensations that the style can arouse.

In addition to the correct, official classicism and the robust, exuberant and commercial Baroque, there is a third strand running through the nineteenth century that was ultimately more fruitful. The rational engineering approach, embodied in the official **School of Roads and Bridges** and invigorated by the teaching of Viollet-le-Duc, who reinterpreted Gothic style as pure structure, led to the development of new structural techniques out of which "modern" architectural style was born. Iron was the first significant new material, often used in imitation of Gothic forms and destined to be developed as an individual architectural style in America. In the **Eiffel Tower** (1889), France set up a potent symbol of things to come.

A more significantly French development was in the use of reinforced concrete towards the end of the century, most notably by **Auguste Perret**, whose 1903 apartment house at 25 rue Franklin, Paris 16ᵉ, turns the concrete structure into a visible virtue and breaks with conventional façades. Changes in the patterns of work and travel were making the need for new urban planning very acute in such cities as Paris. Perret and other **modernists** were all for the high-rise buildings that were going to better the haphazard layouts in America by a rational integration to new street systems. Some of their designs for gigantic skyscraper avenues and suburban rings now look like totalitarian horror-movie sets. But it was tradition, not charity, that blocked their projects at the time.

THE TWENTIETH CENTURY

The greatest proponent of the super New York scale, who also had genuine if mistaken concern for how people lived, was **Le Corbusier**, the most famous **twentieth-century** French architect. His stature may now appear diminished by the ascendancy of a blander style in concrete boxing, as well as by the significant technical and social failures of his buildings and his total disregard for historic streets and monuments.

But while his manifesto, *Vers une architecture moderne*, sounds like a call to arms for a new and revolutionary movement, Le Corbusier should perhaps be more fairly assessed as the original, inimitable and highly individual artist he undoubtedly was. You should try to see some of his work – there's the **Cité Radieuse** in Marseille and plenty of examples in Paris – to make up your own mind about the man largely responsible for changing the face and form of buildings throughout the world.

One respect in which Paris at the turn of the century lagged behind London, Glasgow, Chicago and New York was in **underground transport**. First proposed in the 1870s, it took twenty years of furious debate before the Paris métro was finally realized in 1900. The design of the entrances was as controversial as every other aspect of the system, but the first commission went to **Hector Guimard**, renowned for his variations on the then-current fashion in style. The whirling metal railings, Art Nouveau lettering and bizarre antennae-like orange lamps were his creation. Conservatives were less amused when it came to sites such as the Opéra: **Charles Garnier**, architect of that edifice, demanded classical marble and bronze porticoes for every station, and his line was followed, on a less grandiose scale, wherever the métro steps surfaced by a major monument. Thus Guimard was out of a job. Some of the early ones remain (**Place des Abbesses**, 18ᵉ, is one), as do some of the white-tiled interiors, replaced after World War II in central stations by bright paint with matching seats and display cases.

Art Nouveau designs also found their way on to buildings – the early department stores in Paris are the best example – but the new materials and simple geometry of the modern or International Style favoured the **Art Deco** look; again, you're most likely to come across them in the capital.

Skipping the miserable 1950s and 1960s buildings everywhere, France again becomes one of the most exciting patrons of international **contemporary architecture**. The **Centre Beaubourg**, by **Renzo Piano** and **Richard Rogers**, derided, adored and visited by millions, maximizes space by putting the service elements usually concealed in walls and floors on the outside. The visible ducts, cables and pipes are painted in accordance with the colour code of architectural plans. You might think the whole thing is a professional in joke, but Beaubourg is one of the great contemporary buildings in western Europe – for its originality, popularity and practicality. The structure is currently being renovated and is due to re-open on January 1, 2000.

In **housing**, new styles and forms are to be seen in city suburbs and vacation resorts, many of them disastrous and visually unappealing, but interesting to look at when you don't have to live there. The latest state-funded projects confirm French seriousness about innovative design: just outside Poitiers is the postmodern **Futuroscope** cinema and virtual reality complex, and in Marseilles, William Alsop's mammoth seat of regional government. Regional projects include Nîmes's **Carré d'Art** Modern Art museum by Sir Norman Foster, characterized by its simple transparent design. The **Cathédrale d'Evry**, masterminded by Swiss Mario Botta and finished in 1995, is a huge cylindrical red-brick tower which houses an art centre, concert-hall and cinema screen, besides the religious accoutrements that befit its function. Its roof is slanted at 45 degrees to receive more light, and is crowned by 24 trees emulating the laurel wreaths of Roman Emperors Hadrian and Augustus. Its stained glass window is at the foot of the building and symbolises the roots of a tree.

President Mitterrand's "*grands travaux*" project foregrounded a new architectural era for Paris in the 1980s. He commissioned the **Cité de la Musique** from Christian de Fartzamparc as a finishing touch to the **Parc de la Villette** complex which was built under Giscard d'Estaing on the site of an old abbatoir, and which also houses the Cité de la Science and Bernard Tschemi's 21 "*folies*" of urban life. The **Institut du Monde Arabe**, by Jean Nouvel - who also did the Fondation Cartier building and the 426 metre high, 100-storey Tour Sans Fins in the Défense area - is made up of metal and glass facades mathematically positioned according to traditional Islamic geometrical proportions, with light-sensitive shutters best admired in action on a sunny March day with racing clouds. The "**Grand Louvre**" project displaced the **Ministry of Finance** into a huge new building in Bercy, thus clearing the Richelieu wing of the Louvre for museum use, increasing exhibition space by 83

percent. Ieoh Ming Pei's glass **pyramid** in the Cour Napoléon is now loved by Parisians and this new entrance to the museum takes visitors through the underground Carrousel du Louvre and its boutiques. The **Grande Arche de la Défense**, designed by Von Spreckelsen is a square arch aligned on the map and in mathematical proportions with the Arc de Triomphe - except that the former also has a fibreglass cloud hung in the space under the arch. Situated at the west of Paris, it is emblematic of the new business district – not quite the centre of communation that Mitterrand had wanted – housing 87,000 square metres of office space. The **Opéra Bastille** by Carlos Ott was designed to be a "modern and popular" alternative to the Opéra Garnier. Although the sound unfortunately resonates, the crowds still flock to see the performances. The new **National Library** in the 13th arrondissment fits in extraordinarily well with the surrounding tower blocks. Designed by Dominique Perrault, it's a complex made up of four corners, which represent four open books. This apparently facile design is made up for by the complexity (and expense) of the detail. The aluminium shutters are covered in rare *oukoumé* reddish wood, which contrasts with the grey *ipé* and yellow *doussié* wood, to give the impression from a distance that the towers are bookshelves containing different bound volumes. By the year 2001, it will house more than 350, 000 books stored under the four and is divided into separate sections for academics and the general public. The interior design is metallic and wood-based, and the library is a shrine to multimedia with excellent audiovisual research capacities.

The country's ever-advancing transport network has provided sites for some of the most high-tech office buildings with state-of-the-art engineering in Europe, as at **Eurolille**, the complex around Lille's TGV station, and in **Roissy**, around the Charles-de-Gaulle airport. The TGV **Lyon-Satolas** station is another typical 1990s creation, both elegant and thrustingly optimistic.

The new **European Parliament** building in Strasbourg, designed by the Architecture Studio group, was finished in 1997, and is a huge boomerang-shaped structure with a glass dome and metal tower. Most recently, the **Stade de France** in Saint-Denis, near Paris, was built to host many of the World Cup 98 matches, including, as it happened, the French victory in the final.

But the French are also very good at preserving the past. Throughout the country you'll see far older period streets – medieval and Renaissance – that look as though they've never been touched. More often than not, the restoration has been carried out by the **Maisons de Compagnonage**, the old craft guilds, which have maintained traditional building skills, handing them down as of old from master to apprentice (and never to women), while also taking on new industrial skills.

Above all, though, bear in mind the extent and variety of architecture in France and don't feel intimidated by the established sights. If the empty grandeur of the Loire châteaux is oppressive, there are numerous smaller country houses open to the public, and such municipal buildings as the **Hôtels de Ville** tend to offer some charm or amusement, even in the smallest towns.

It is also possible in France to experience whole towns as consistent places of architecture, not only Carcassonne and Aigues-Mortes, Dinan and Nancy, but villages off the main roads in which time seems to have stopped long ago. And, besides, from any hotel bedroom you can simply delight in what Le Corbusier called "the magnificent play of forms seen in light", in the movement of morning sunlight over ordinary provincial tiles and chimneys.

BOOKS

Publishers are detailed below in the form of British publisher; American publisher, where both exist. Where books are published in one country only, UK or US follows the publisher's name.

Abbreviations: o/p (out of print); UP (University Press).

TRAVEL

James Boswell *An Account of Corsica*, current edition published as *The Journal of a Tour to Corsica* (In Print Publishing, UK). Typically robust and witty account of encounters with the Corsican people. Excerpts published in *Journals of James Boswell* (Mandarin/Yale UP).

Dorothy Carrington *Granite Island* (Penguin, UK). A fascinating and immensely comprehensive book, combining the writer's personal experiences with an evocative portrayal of historical figures and events. By far the best study of Corsica ever written in English.

Julien Green *Paris* (Marion Boyars). A collection of very personal sketches and impressions of the city, by an American who has lived all his life in Paris, writes in French, and is considered one of the great French writers of the century. Bilingual text.

Richard Holmes *Fatal Avenue* (Pimlico; Trafalgar Square). The phrase is de Gaulle's, used to describe France's northeast frontier whose notorious topographical vulnerability has made it the natural route for invaders since time began. From the Channel to Alsace, Holmes relates the wars and the personalities to the places as they are today, from the Hundred Years' War to World War II. An exciting and informative read.

Richard Holmes *Footsteps* (Flamingo;Vintage). A marvellous mix of objective history and personal account, such as the tale of the author's own excitement at the events of May 1968 in Paris, which led him to investigate and reconstruct the experiences of the British in Paris during the 1789 Revolution.

Laurence Sterne *A Sentimental Journey Through France and Italy* (Penguin/Viking). Rambling tale by the eccentric eighteenth-century author of *Tristram Shandy* who, despite the title, never gets further than Versailles.

Robert Louis Stevenson *Travels with a Donkey* (OUP; Koneman). Mile-by-mile account of Stevenson's twelve-day trek in the Haute Loire and Cévennes uplands with the donkey Modestine. Devotees of Stevenson's footpaths – and there's a surprising number of both in France – might be interested in his first book, *Inland Voyage*, on the waterways of the north.

Freda White *Three Rivers of France* (Pavilion;Faber, o/p), *West of the Rhone* (Faber, US, o/p), *Ways of Aquitaine* (o/p). Freda White spent a great deal of time in France in the 1950s before tourism came along to the backwater communities that were her interest. These are all evocative books, slipping in the history and culture painlessly, if not always too accurately.

HISTORY

GENERAL

Alfred Cobban *A History of Modern France* (3 vols: 1715–99, 1799–1871 and 1871–1962, Penguin; Viking). Complete and very readable account of the main political, social and economic strands in French history from the death of Louis XIV to mid-de Gaulle.

Colin Jones *The Cambridge Illustrated History of France* (CUP, o/p). A political and social history of France from prehistoric times to the mid-1990s, concentrating on issues of regionalism, gender, race and class. Good illustrations and a friendly, non-academic writing style.

Theodore Zeldin *France 1845–1945* (OUP). Five thematic volumes on diverse French matters – all good reads.

Theodore Zeldin *The French* (Harvill; Kodansha). Urbane and witty survey of the French worldview – chapter titles include "How to be chic" and "How to appreciate a grandmother".

THE MIDDLE AGES

Natalie Zemon Davis *The Return of Martin Guerre* (Harvard UP). A vivid account of peasant life in the sixteenth century and a perplexing and titillating hoax in the Pyrenean village of Artigat. Better than the movie or the musical.

JH Huizinga *The Waning of the Middle Ages* (Penguin; Dover). Primarily a study of the culture of the Burgundian and French courts – but a masterpiece that goes far beyond this, building up meticulous detail to recreate the whole life and mentality of the fourteenth and fifteenth centuries.

Emmanuel Le Roy Ladurie *Montaillou* (Penguin; Random House). Village gossip of who's sleeping with whom, tales of trips to Spain and details of work, all extracted by the Inquisition from Cathar peasants of the eastern Pyrenees in the fourteenth century, and stored away until recently in the Vatican archives. Though academic and heavy going in places, most of this book reads like a novel.

Barbara Tuchman *A Distant Mirror* (Papermac; Ballantine). The history of the fourteenth century – plagues, wars, peasant uprisings and crusades – told through the life of a sympathetic French nobleman whose career takes him through England, Italy and Byzantium and finally ends in a Turkish prison.

EIGHTEENTH AND NINETEENTH CENTURIES

Dorothy Carrington *Napoleon and his Parents on the Threshold of History* (NAL-Dutton, US, o/p). Lucid study of Napoléon's early years.

Rupert Christiansen *Tales of the New Babylon, Paris 1869–1875* (Minerva; published in US as *Paris Babylon* by Penguin). The compulsive and irresistible story of Paris in the last years of the Second Empire and the physical and social upheavals of the Prussian siege and the Commune. It combines a serious historical overview with tabloid-style detail.

Richard Cobb & Colin Jones (eds) *The French Revolution* (Simon & Schuster, o/p). One of the best 1989 offerings on 1789 with lots of pictures, texts of the time and clear explanations by a host of historians.

Vincent Cronin *Napoleon* (Fontana; Harper Collins). Enthusiastic and accessible biography.

Norman Hampson *A Social History of the French Revolution* (Routledge, UK, o/p). An analysis that concentrates on the personalities involved. Its particular interest lies in the attention it gives to the *sans-culottes*, the ordinary poor of Paris.

Christopher Hibbert *The French Revolution* (Penguin; Morrow, o/p). Good, concise popular history of the period and events.

Alistair Horne *The Fall of Paris* (Papermac; Penguin, o/p). A very readable and humane account of the extraordinary period of the Prussian siege of Paris in 1870 and the ensuing struggles of the Commune.

Lissagaray *History of the Paris Commune* (New Park, UK, o/p). A highly personal and partisan account of the politics and fighting by a participant. Although Lissagaray is reticent about it, history has it that the last solitary Communard on the last barricade – in rue Ramponneau in Belleville – was in fact himself.

Karl Marx *On the Paris Commune* (Lawrence & Wishart in the collected works; Pathfinder). Rousing prose from Karl, along with a history of the Commune by Engels.

Peter McPhee *A Social History of France 1780–1880* (Routledge, o/p). A scholarly work arguing that historians have underestimated the fundamental differences between how people lived and thought in 1880 compared with the time of the 1789 Revolution. He goes into such subjects as relations between men and women, education and reading material, the loss of diversity in rural France of languages and culture, and changes in the physical environment.

Thomas Paine *The Rights of Man* (Penguin). Written in 1791 in response to English conservatives' views on the situation in France, this reasoned and passionate tract expresses the ideas of both the American and French revolutions. It was immediately banned on publication, and its author charged with treason, but enough copies had crossed the Channel and been translated for Paine to be elected to the Convention by the people of Calais.

Simon Schama *Citizens* (Penguin; Random House). Best-selling and highly tendentious revisionist history of the Revolution, which pretty well takes the line that the ideologues of the Revolution were a gang of fanatics who simply failed to see how good the *ancien régime* was.

It reveals as much about the intellectual climate of conservative America in the 1980s as it does about 1789, but it's a well-written, racy and provocative book.

JM Thompson *The French Revolution* (Blackwell). A detailed and passionate account, first published in 1943, but still the classic account in English.

TWENTIETH CENTURY

Marc Bloch *Strange Defeat* (Norton). Moving personal study of the reasons for France's defeat and subsequent caving-in to fascism. Found among the papers of this Sorbonne historian after his death at the hands of the Gestapo in 1942.

Geoff Dyer *The Missing of the Somme* (Penguin, UK, o/p). Structured round the author's visits to the war graves of northern France, this is a highly moving meditation on the trauma of World War I and the way its memory has been perpetuated.

HR Kedward *In Search of the Maquis: Rural Resistance in South France 1942–44* (OUP). Slightly dry style, but full of fascinating detail about the brave and often mortal struggle of the countless ordinary people across France who fought to drive the Germans from their country.

François Maspero *Cat's Grin* (New Amsterdam Books, US). Semi-autobiographical novel about a young teenager in Paris during the war with his brother in the Resistance, his parents taken to concentration camps as Paris is liberated, and everyone else busily collaborating. An intensely moving and revealing account of the war period.

Barbara Tuchman *The Proud Tower* (Papermac; Ballantine). A portrait of England, France, the US, Germany and Russia in the years 1890–1914. Written in Tuchman's inimitable and readable style, it includes a superb chapter on the extraordinary passions and enmities of the Dreyfus Affair which rocked French society between 1894 and 1899 and on the different currents in the rising socialist movement in the run-up to World War I, centring on the life of Jean Jaurès.

Paul Webster *Pétain's Crime: The Full Story of French Collaboration in the Holocaust* (Papermac; IR Dee). The fascinating and alarming story of the Vichy regime's more than willing collaboration with the Holocaust and the bravery of those, especially the Communist resistance in occupied France, who attempted to prevent it.

Alexander Worth *France 1940–55* (Beacon Press, US, o/p). Extremely good and emotionally engaged portrayal of the taboo Occupation period in French history, followed by the Cold War and colonial struggle years in which the same political tensions and heart-searchings were at play.

SOCIETY AND POLITICS

NA Addinall (ed) *French Political Parties: A Documentary Guide* (Uni of Wales Press, UK). Clear and concise textbook introduction to the constitution and political parties of the Fifth Republic; quotations and source materials are not translated but this need not deter non-French speakers.

John Ardagh *France Today* (Penguin). A journalistic overview of contemporary France (up to the 1980s), covering food, film, education and holidays as well as politics and economics.

Roland Barthes *Mythologies* (Vintage; Noonday) and *The Eiffel Tower* (California UP, US). *Mythologies* is an immensely readable structuralist critique on the socio-historical importance of myth and its signs in France today, accompanied by a series of quirky examples. The short text, *The Eiffel Tower*, demystifies the Eiffel tower as synecdoche of Paris – he accepts Maupassant's solution of eliminating it from the vista by going to have dinner in the Eiffel Tower restaurant.

Jean Baudrillard *Selected Writings* (Stanford UP) Essential reading to get an overview of the most interesting contemporary French philosopher and artist. His notion of the simulacrum (the image of the essence of an object) and the role of the object as sign within the consumer system is complex but revelatory.

Simone de Beauvoir *The Second Sex* (Vintage). One of the prime texts of western feminism, written in 1949, covering women's inferior status in history, literature, mythology, psychoanalysis, philosophy and everyday life. The style is dry and intellectual, but the subject matter easily compensates.

Denis Belloc *Slow Death in Paris* (Quartet, UK). A harrowing account of a heroin addict in

Paris. Not recommended holiday reading but if you want to know about the seedy underbelly of the city this is the book.

Émilie Carles *Wild Herb Soup* (Indigo, UK). A moving and inspiring autobiography of a girl born and raised in the remote Alpine valley of the Névache near Briançon in the early years of the twentieth century. As well as giving an interesting account of peasant life, it records the development of social conscience and an extraordinary moral toughness as Émilie becomes aware of the brutality and harshness of peasant life, sees her brothers die in World War I, experiences Resistance in World War II, and finally finds herself, as an old lady, leading the campaign to stop the desecration of her beautiful natal valley by the construction of an autoroute.

Claire Duchen *Feminism in France: From May '68 to Mitterrand* (Routledge). Charts the evolution of the women's movement through to its mid-1980s crisis, clarifying the divergent political stances and feminist theory that informs the various groups, and placing them in the wider French political context.

Gisèle Halimi *Milk for the Orange Tree* (Quartet, UK). Born in Tunisia, daughter of an Orthodox Jewish family; ran away to Paris to become a lawyer; defender of women's rights, Algerian FLN fighters and all unpopular causes. A gutsy autobiographical story.

Bernard Henri-Lévy *Adventures on the Freedom Road: The French Intellectuals in the 20th Century* (Harvill). Huge, clever and complex essays by contemporary philosopher-celebrity, mercilessly analysing the response of all the great French thinkers, of Left and Right, to the key events of the century. Easy to dip into, surprisingly readable, and very provocative.

Patrick Marnham *Crime and the Académie Française* (Penguin, UK, o/p). A very entertaining collection of essays and newspaper articles on some of the most bizarre, as well as mainstream, aspects of French life. Irreverent and sometimes very funny.

David Thomson *Democracy in France Since 1870* (Cassell, UK, o/p). An inquiry into why a country with such a strong socialist tradition should have had so many reactionary governments.

Gillian Tindall *Célestine: Voices from a French Village* (Minerva; Holt). Intrigued by some nineteenth century love letters left behind in the house she has bought in Chassignolles, Berry, Tindall researches the history of the village back to the 1840s. She produces a meticulous, thoughtful and moving portrait of rural French life and its slow but dramatic transformation. A brilliant piece of social history.

Eugen Weber *My France* (Harvard UP). A collection of essays, fascinating and offbeat, about numerous aspects of French culture and politics. Some prior knowledge of mainstream French history is needed to make the most of them.

ARTS

John Berger *The Success and Failure of Picasso* (Penguin, o/p Vintage). The success is self-explanatory; the failure (and the tragedy) lies in Picasso's poverty of subject matter – or so Berger argues in this brief and highly persuasive book. Perhaps the best one-volume study of Picasso in English.

Brassaï *The Secret Paris of the Thirties* (Thames & Hudson, UK). Extraordinary photos of the capital's nightlife in the 1930s – brothels, music halls, street cleaners, transvestites and the underworld – each one a work of art and a familiar world (now long since gone) to Brassaï and his mate, Henry Miller, who accompanied him on his nocturnal expeditions.

David J Brown *Bridges Across Time* (Mitchell Beazley, UK). A very beautiful book about both the technical and aesthetic aspects of bridge building; not exclusively about France, but includes many French bridges from the Roman Pont-du-Gard to the Pont d'Avignon, Eiffel's constructions and the state-of-the-art Pont de Normandie across the Seine estuary.

André Chastel *French Art: The Ancien Régime 1620–1775* (Flammarion). This sumptuous volume by a renowned art historian combines exquisite pictures with political, cultural and artistic detail to illustrate the painting, sculpture and architecture that emerged during the reigns of Louis XIII, XIV and XV.

Kenneth J Comant *Carolingian and Romanesque Architecture, 800–1200* (Yale UP). Good European study with a focus on Cluny and the St-Jacques pilgrim route.

FRANCE IN LITERATURE

Listed below is a highly selective recommendation of works – mostly novels – that are rooted in the various French regions, and which would make good holiday reading.

PARIS AND AROUND
Steven Barclay (ed) *A Place in the World Called Paris*
Julian Barnes *Metroland*
Baudelaire *Baudelaire's Paris*, trans Laurence Kitchen.
André Breton *Nadja*
Blaise Cendrars *To the End of the World*
Didier Daeninckx *Murder in Memoriam*
Charles Dickens *A Tale of Two Cities*
Gustave Flaubert *A Sentimental Education*
Ernest Hemingway *A Moveable Feast*
Victor Hugo *Les Misérables*
Jack Kerouac *Satori in Paris*
Henry Miller *Quiet Days in Clichy, Tropic of Cancer, Tropic of Capricorn*
Anaïs Nin *Journals 1917–1974*
George Orwell *Down and Out in Paris and London*
Georges Perec *Life: A User's Manual*
Raymond Queneau *Zazie dans le Métro*
Paul Rambali *French Blues*
Jean Rhys *Quartet, Good Morning Midnight*
Jean-Paul Sartre *Roads to Freedom Trilogy*
Georges Simenon *Any Maigret thriller*
Patrick Süsskind *Perfume*
Michel Tournier *The Golden Droplet*
Émile Zola *Nana, L'Assommoir, La Bête Humaine, La Curée, Le Ventre de Paris*.

CALAIS TO CHAMPAGNE
Julien Gracq *A Balcony in the Forest, The Opposing Shore*
Émile Zola *Germinal, La Débâcle*

ALSACE, FRANCHE-COMTÉ AND JURA
John Berger *Pig Earth*
Bernard Clavel *The Spaniard*
Colette *My Mother's House*
Pierre Gascar *Women and the Sun*
Stendhal *Scarlet and Black*

NORMANDY AND BRITTANY
Honoré de Balzac *Les Chouans*
Colette *Ripening Seed*

Sebastian Faulks *Birdsong*
Gustave Flaubert *Madame Bovary*
André Gide *Strait is the Gate*
Pierre Loti *Pêcheur d'Islande*
Guy de Maupassant *Selected Short Stories*
Marcel Proust *Remembrance of Things Past*
Jean Rouard *Fields of Glory, Of Illustrious Men*
Jean-Paul Sartre *La Nausée*

THE LOIRE
Alain Fournier *Le Grand Meaulnes*
Rabelais *Gargantua and Pantagruel*
Georges Sand *The Devil's Pool*
Émile Zola *The Earth*

BURGUNDY
Gabriel Chevallier *Clochemerle*

ATLANTIC COAST
François Mauriac *Thérèse*

THE PYRENEES
Pierre Loti *Ramuntcho*

LANGUEDOC
Hannah Closs *High Are the Mountains*

RHÔNE VALLEY AND PROVENCE
Lawrence Durrell *The Avignon Quintet*
Jean Giono *The Horseman on the Roof, The Man Who Planted Trees, Joy of Man's Desiring*
Marcel Pagnol *Jean de Florette, Manon des Sources*
Émile Zola *Fortune of the Rougons*

CÔTE D'AZUR
Colette *Collected Stories*
Alexandre Dumas *The Count of Monte Cristo*
F Scott Fitzgerald *Tender is the Night*
Graham Greene *Loser Takes All, May We Borrow Your Husband?*
Katherine Mansfield *Selected Short Stories*
Françoise Sagan *Bonjour Tristesse*

Norma Evenson *Paris: A Century of Change, 1878–1978* (Yale UP). A large, illustrated volume that makes the development of urban planning and the fabric of Paris an enthralling subject –

mainly because the author's ultimate concern is always with people, not panoramas.
Edward Lucie-Smith *A Concise History of French Painting* (Thames & Hudson, US, o/p). If

you're after an art reference book, this will do as well as any . . . though there are of course hundreds of books on particular French art movements.

John Richardson, *The Life of Picasso: Vol 1 1881–1906* (Pimlico; Random House) and *Vol 2 1907–17* (Cape; Random House). No twentieth-century artist has ever been subjected to scrutiny as close as Picasso receives in Richardson's exhaustive and brilliantly illustrated biography. The author has taken many years to complete the first two volumes, and there's a risk that he'll never reach the end, but the mould-breaking years have now been covered, and it's impossible to imagine how anyone could surpass Richardson's treatment of them. Volumes 3 and 4 are to be pubished by Cape, UK, in December 1999.

Vivian Russell, *Monet's Garden* (Frances Lincoln; Stewart Tabori & Chang). Sumptuous colour photographs by the author, old photographs of the artist and reproductions of his paintings. Superb opening chapter on Monet as "poet of nature" and a detailed description of the garden's evolution, seasonal cycle and its current maintenance which will delight serious gardeners.

Gertrude Stein *The Autobiography of Alice B Toklas* (Penguin; Vintage). The goings-on at Stein's famous salon in Paris. The most accessible of her works, written from the point of view of Stein's long-time lover, gives an amusing account of the Paris art and literary scene of the 1910s and 1920s.

GUIDES

100 Walks in the French Alps (Hodder & Staughton). A very good guide to hiking in the Alps, detailing which walks are appropriate for different abilities.

James Bromwich *The Roman Remains of Southern France* (Routledge). The only comprehensive guide to the subject – detailed, well illustrated and approachable. In addition to accounts of the famous sites, it will lead you off the map to little-known discoveries.

Glynn Christian *Edible France* (Grub Street; Interlink). A guide to food rather than restaurants: regional produce, local specialities, markets and best shops for buying goodies to bring back home.

Cicerone Walking Guides (Cicerone, UK). Neat, durable guides, with detailed route descriptions. Titles include *Tour of Mont Blanc*; *Chamonix-Mont Blanc*; *Tour of the Oisans* (GR54); *French Alps* (GR5); *The Way of Saint James* (GR65); *Tour of the Queyras*; *The Pyrenean Trail* (GR10); *Walks and Climbs in the Pyrenees*.

Robin G Collomb *Corsica Mountains* (West Col, UK). Covers all the principal mountain peaks, with information on different approaches and ascents backed up with diagrams.

Elizabeth David *French Provincial Cooking* (Penguin, UK). A classic cookery book, written in 1960 by the English expert on French food. The recipes are in fine prose rather than manual speak, with excellent detail and warnings about tricky processes or the need for particular skills; and they work, even with non-French ingredients. She makes the subject of kitchen equipment fascinating and beautifully describes the different regional cuisines.

Mary Davis *The Green Guide to France* (Green Print, UK). Definitely not the Michelin, this is a resource guide to French national parks and wildlife reserves, veggie restaurants, communes and the like.

Emplois d'Été en France (published in France, distributed by Vacation Work, UK). Annual listings (in French) of thousands of summer jobs available in France.

Footpaths of Europe Series (16 titles; Robertson McCarta, UK). Route guides to most areas of France including Corsica, covering the system of GR footpaths, illustrated with 1:50,000 colour survey maps. These are English versions of the *Topoguides des Sentiers de Grande Randonnée* (CNSGR, Paris), which are widely available in France and not hard to follow with a working knowledge of French.

Mark Hampshell *Live and Work in France* (Vacation Work, UK). An invaluable guide for anyone considering residence or work in France; packed with ideas and advice on job hunting, bureaucracy, tax, health, etc.

Haute-Savoie & Mont Blanc (Two Wheels, UK). The only English-language guide to mountain biking, detailing fifty off-road routes of varying difficulty in that region.

Louisa Jones *Gardens of the French Riviera* (Flammarion). The history and traditions of Riviera gardens accompanied by gorgeous photographs.

W Lippert *Fleurs des Montagnes, Alpages et Forêts* (Miniguide Nathan Tout Terrain, Paris). Best palm-sized colour guide if you want something to pack away with your gear in the mountains.

Carol Pineau & Maureen Kelly *Working in France* (AL Books, US, o/p). A practical guide, aimed at American readers, on how to get jobs in France, highlighting the cultural differences that affect job interviews and business practice generally.

Kev Reynolds *Walks and Climbs in the Pyrenees* (Cicerone Press, UK). The classic English guide for walking in the Pyrenees.

Georges Véron *Haute Randonnée Pyrénées* (Randonnées Pyrénéennes, Paris;Gastons-West Col, o/p). East-to-west description of the High Level route across the Pyrenees.

LANGUAGE

French can be a deceptively familiar language because of the number of words and structures it shares with English. Despite this, it's far from easy, though the bare essentials are not difficult to master and can make all the difference. Even just saying "Bonjour Madame/Monsieur" and then gesticulating will usually get you a smile and helpful service. People working in tourist offices, hotels and so on, almost always speak English and tend to use it when you're struggling to speak French – be grateful, not insulted.

FRENCH PRONUNCIATION

One easy rule to remember is that **consonants** at the ends of words are usually silent. *Pas plus tard* (not later) is thus pronounced "pa-plu-tarr". But when the following word begins with a vowel, you run the two together: *pas après* (not after) becomes "pazaprey".

Vowels are the hardest sounds to get right. Roughly:

a	as in h**a**t	*i*	as in mach**i**ne
e	as in g**e**t	*o*	as in h**o**t
é	between g**e**t and g**a**te	*o, au*	as in **o**ver
è	between g**e**t and g**u**t	*ou*	as in f**oo**d
eu	like the **u** in h**u**rt	*u*	as in a pursed-lip version of **u**se

More awkward are the **combinations** *in/im, en/em, an/am, on/om, un/um* at the ends of words, or followed by consonants other than n or m. Again, roughly:

in/im	like the **an** in **an**xious	*on/om*	like the **don** in **Don**caster said
an/am, en/em	like the **don** in **Don**caster when said with a nasal accent		by someone with a heavy cold
		un/um	like the **u** in **u**nderstand

Consonants are much as in English, except that: "*ch*" is always sh, "*c*" is s, "*h*" is silent, "*th*" is the same as t, "*ll*" is like the y in "yes", "*w*" is v, and "*r*" is growled (or rolled).

LEARNING MATERIALS

Rough Guide French Phrasebook (Rough Guides). Mini dictionary-style phrasebook with both English–French and French–English sections, along with cultural tips for tricky situations and a menu reader.

Mini French Dictionary (Harrap/Prentice Hall). French–English and English–French, plus a brief grammar and pronunciation guide.

Breakthrough French (Pan; book and 2 cassettes). Excellent teach-yourself course.

French and English Slang Dictionary (Harrap/Prentice Hall); **Dictionary of Modern**

Colloquial French (Routledge). Both volumes are a bit large to carry, but they are the key to all you ever wanted to understand.

Verbaid (Verbaid, Hawk House, Heath Lane, Farnham, Surrey GU9 0PR). CD-size laminated paper "verb wheel" giving you the tense endings for the regular verbs.

A Vous La France; Franc Extra; Franc-Parler (BBC Publications/EMC Publishing; each has a book and 2 cassettes). BBC radio courses, running from beginners' level to fairly advanced language.

A BRIEF GUIDE TO SPEAKING FRENCH

BASIC WORDS AND PHRASES

French nouns are divided into masculine and feminine. This causes difficulties with adjectives, whose endings have to change to suit the gender of the nouns they qualify. If you know some grammar, you will know what to do. If not, stick to the masculine form, which is the simplest – it's what we have done in this glossary.

today	*aujourd'hui*	that one	*celà*
yesterday	*hier*	open	*ouvert*
tomorrow	*demain*	closed	*fermé*
in the morning	*le matin*	big	*grand*
in the afternoon	*l'après-midi*	small	*petit*
in the evening	*le soir*	more	*plus*
now	*maintenant*	less	*moins*
later	*plus tard*	a little	*un peu*
at one o'clock	*à une heure*	a lot	*beaucoup*
at three o'clock	*à trois heures*	cheap	*bon marché*
at ten-thirty	*à dix heures et demie*	expensive	*cher*
at midday	*à midi*	good	*bon*
man	*un homme*	bad	*mauvais*
woman	*une femme*	hot	*chaud*
here	*ici*	cold	*froid*
there	*là*	with	*avec*
this one	*ceci*	without	*sans*

NUMBERS

1	*un*	11	*onze*	21	*vingt-et-un*	95	*quatre-vingt-quinze*
2	*deux*	12	*douze*	22	*vingt-deux*	100	*cent*
3	*trois*	13	*treize*	30	*trente*	101	*cent-et-un*
4	*quatre*	14	*quatorze*	40	*quarante*	200	*deux cents*
5	*cinq*	15	*quinze*	50	*cinquante*	300	*trois cents*
6	*six*	16	*seize*	60	*soixante*	500	*cinq cents*
7	*sept*	17	*dix-sept*	70	*soixante-dix*	1000	*mille*
8	*huit*	18	*dix-huit*	75	*soixante-quinze*	2000	*deux milles*
9	*neuf*	19	*dix-neuf*	80	*quatre-vingts*	5000	*cinq milles*
10	*dix*	20	*vingt*	90	*quatre-vingt-dix*	1,000,000	*un million*

DAYS AND DATES

January	*janvier*	November	*novembre*	August 1	*le premier août*
February	*février*	December	*décembre*	March 2	*le deux mars*
March	*mars*			July 14	*le quatorze juillet*
April	*avril*	Sunday	*dimanche*	November 23	*le vingt-trois novem-*
May	*mai*	Monday	*lundi*		*bre*
June	*juin*	Tuesday	*mardi*		
July	*juillet*	Wednesday	*mercredi*	1999	*dix-neuf-cent-quatre-*
August	*août*	Thursday	*jeudi*		*vingt-dix-neuf*
September	*septembre*	Friday	*vendredi*		
October	*octobre*	Saturday	*samedi*		*continued overleaf...*

continued from previous page

TALKING TO PEOPLE

When addressing people you should always use *Monsieur* for a man, *Madame* for a woman, *Mademoiselle* for a girl. Plain *bonjour* by itself is not enough. This isn't as formal as it seems, and it has its uses when you've forgotten someone's name or want to attract someone's attention.

Excuse me	*Pardon*	please	*s'il vous plaît*
Do you speak English?	*Vous parlez anglais?*	thank you	*merci*
		hello	*bonjour*
How do you say it in French?	*Comment ça se dit en Français?*	goodbye	*au revoir*
What's your name?	*Comment vous appelez-vous?*	good morning/ afternoon	*bonjour*
My name is . . .	*Je m'appelle . . .*	good evening	*bonsoir*
I'm English/	*Je suis anglais[e]/*	good night	*bonne nuit*
Irish/Scottish	*irlandais[e]/écossais[e]/*	How are you?	*Comment allez-vous?/ Ça va?*
Welsh/American/	*gallois[e]/américain[e]/*		
Australian/	*australien[ne]/*	Fine, thanks	*Très bien, merci*
Canadian/	*canadien[ne]/*	I don't know	*Je ne sais pas*
a New Zealander	*néo-zélandais[e]*	Let's go	*Allons-y*
yes	*oui*	See you tomorrow	*A demain*
no	*non*	See you soon	*A bientôt*
I understand	*Je comprends*	Sorry	*Pardon, Madame./Je m'excuse*
I don't understand	*Je ne comprends pas*		
Can you speak slower?	*S'il vous plaît, parlez moins vite*	Leave me alone (aggressive)	*Fichez-moi la paix!*
OK/agreed	*d'accord*	Please help me	*Aidez-moi, s'il vous plaît*

FINDING THE WAY

bus	*autobus/bus/car*	hitchhiking	*autostop*
bus station	*gare routière*	on foot	*à pied*
bus stop	*arrêt*	Where are you going?	*Vous allez où?*
car	*voiture*		
train/taxi/ferry	*train/taxi/ferry*	I'm going to . . .	*Je vais à . . .*
boat	*bâteau*	I want to get off at . . .	*Je voudrais descendre à . . .*
plane	*avion*		
train station	*gare (SNCF)*	the road to . . .	*la route pour . . .*
platform	*quai*	near	*près/pas loin*
What time does it leave?	*Il part à quelle heure?*	far	*loin*
		left	*à gauche*
What time does it arrive?	*Il arrive à quelle heure?*	right	*à droite*
		straight on	*tout droit*
a ticket to . . .	*un billet pour . . .*	on the other side of	*à l'autre côté de*
single ticket	*aller simple*	on the corner of	*à l'angle de*
return ticket	*aller retour*	next to	*à côté de*
validate your ticket	*compostez votre billet*	behind	*derrière*
		in front of	*devant*
valid for	*valable pour*	before	*avant*
ticket office	*vente de billets*	after	*après*
how many kilometres?	*combien de kilomètres?*	under	*sous*
		to cross	*traverser*
how many hours?	*combien d'heures?*	bridge	*pont*

QUESTIONS AND REQUESTS

The simplest way of asking a question is to start with *s'il vous plaît* (please), then name the thing you want in an interrogative tone of voice. For example:

Where is there a bakery?	*S'il vous plaît, la boulangerie?*
Which way is it to the Eiffel Tower?	*S'il vous plaît, la route pour la tour Eiffel?*

Similarly with requests:

We'd like a room for two.	*S'il vous plaît, une chambre pour deux.*
Can I have a kilo of oranges?	*S'il vous plaît, un kilo d'oranges?*

Question words

where?	*où?*	when?	*quand?*
how?	*comment?*	why?	*pourquoi?*
how many/how much?	*combien?*	at what time?	*à quelle heure?*
		what is/which is?	*quel est?*

ACCOMMODATION

a room for one/two people	*une chambre pour une/deux personnes*	do laundry	*faire la lessive*
a double bed	*un lit double*	sheets	*draps*
a room with a shower	*une chambre avec douche*	blankets	*couvertures*
		quiet	*calme*
a room with a bath	*une chambre avec salle de bain*	noisy	*bruyant*
		hot water	*eau chaude*
for one/two/three nights	*pour une/deux/trois nuits*	cold water	*eau froide*
		Is breakfast included?	*Est-ce que le petit déjeuner est compris?*
Can I see it?	*Je peux la voir?*	I would like breakfast	*Je voudrais prendre le petit déjeuner*
a room on the courtyard	*une chambre sur la cour*		
a room over the street	*une chambre sur la rue*	I don't want breakfast	*Je ne veux pas de petit déjeuner*
first floor	*premier étage*	Can we camp here?	*On peut camper ici?*
second floor	*deuxième étage*	campsite	*un camping/terrain de camping*
with a view	*avec vue*	tent	*une tente*
key	*clef*	tent space	*un emplacement*
to iron	*repasser*	youth hostel	*auberge de jeunesse*

CARS

service station	*garage*	put air in the tyres	*gonfler les pneus*
service	*service*	battery	*batterie*
to park the car	*garer la voiture*	the battery is dead	*la batterie est morte*
car park	*un parking*	plugs	*bougies*
no parking	*défense de stationner/ stationnement interdit*	to break down	*tomber en panne*
		gas can	*bidon*
gas station	*poste d'essence*	insurance	*assurance*
fuel	*essence*	green card	*carte verte*
(to) fill it up	*faire le plein*	traffic lights	*feux*
oil	*huile*	red light	*feu rouge*
air line	*ligne à air*	green light	*feu vert*

continued overleaf . . .

continued from previous page

HEALTH MATTERS

doctor	*médecin*	stomach ache	*mal à l'estomac*
I don't feel well	*Je ne me sens pas bien*	period	*règles*
medicines	*médicaments*	pain	*douleur*
prescription	*ordonnance*	it hurts	*ça fait mal*
I feel sick	*Je suis malade*	chemist	*pharmacie*
I have a headache	*J'ai mal à la tête*	hospital	*hôpital*

OTHER NEEDS

bakery	*boulangerie*	bank	*banque*
food shop	*alimentation*	money	*argent*
supermarket	*supermarché*	toilets	*toilettes*
to eat	*manger*	police	*police*
to drink	*boire*	telephone	*téléphone*
camping gas	*camping gaz*	cinema	*cinéma*
tobacconist	*tabac*	theatre	*théâtre*
stamps	*timbres*	to reserve/book	*réserver*

ARCHITECTURAL TERMS: A GLOSSARY

These are either terms you'll come across in the *Guide*, or come up against while travelling around.

ABBAYE abbey

AMBULATORY passage round the outer edge of the choir of a church

APSE semi-circular termination at the east end of a church

BAROQUE High Renaissance period of art and architecture, distinguished by extreme ornateness

CAROLINGIAN dynasty (and art, sculpture, etc) named after Charlemagne; mid-eighth to early tenth centuries

CHÂTEAU mansion, country house, castle

CHÂTEAU FORT castle

CHEVET east end of a church

CLASSICAL architectural style incorporating Greek and Roman elements: pillars, domes, colonnades, etc, at its height in France in the seventeenth century and revived, as **Neoclassical**, in the nineteenth century

CLERESTORY upper storey of a church, incorporating the windows

DONJON castle keep

ÉGLISE church

FLAMBOYANT florid form of Gothic

MEROVINGIAN dynasty (and art, etc), ruling France and parts of Germany from sixth to mid-eighth centuries

NARTHEX entrance hall of church

NAVE main body of a church

PORTE gateway

RENAISSANCE art/architectural style developed in fifteenth-century Italy and imported to France in the sixteenth century by François I

RETABLE altarpiece

ROMAN Romanesque (easily confused with Romain – Roman)

ROMANESQUE early medieval architecture distinguished by squat, rounded forms and naive sculpture, called Norman in Britain.

STUCCO plaster used to embellish ceilings, etc

TOUR tower

TRANSEPT transverse arms of a church

TYMPANUM sculpted panel above a church door

VOUSSOIR sculpted rings in arch over church door

INDEX

Stay in touch with us!

ROUGH*NEWS* is Rough Guides' free newsletter.
In three issues a year we give you news, travel
issues, music reviews, readers' letters and the
latest dispatches from authors on the road.

I would like to receive ROUGH*NEWS*: please put me on your free mailing list.

NAME . . . .

ADDRESS . . . .

Please clip or photocopy and send to: Rough Guides, 62–70 Shorts Gardens, London WC2H 9AB,
England or Rough Guides, 375 Hudson Street, New York, NY 10014, USA.

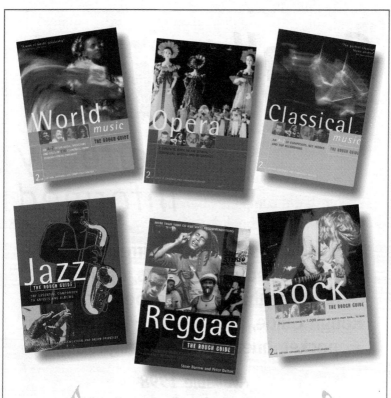